Dutch

Dictionary

Dutch

Dictionary

Dutch–English
English–Dutch

Fernand G. Renier

Routledge

London and New York

Reprinted in 1989 by
Routledge
11 New Fetter Lane, London EC4P 4EE
29 West 35th Street, New York, NY 10001

First published in 1949
by Routledge & Kegan Paul plc
Reprinted 1955, 1961, 1966, 1972, 1976 and 1978
Reprinted and First published as a Paperback in 1982
Paperback reprinted 1985

Printed in Great Britain by
Cox & Wyman Ltd, Reading

ISBN 0415-04610-6

CONTENTS

v

PREFACE

The task I have set myself in compiling this dictionary has been to use the space given me to the fullest. I have aimed at giving as many words, meanings, and idioms as possible, at avoiding the superfluous and at affording clues that may guide the user to the translation most suitable to his particular need. Where possible formal words and expressions in the one language have been translated by words and expressions used formally in the other. Idioms and colloquialisms have, wherever possible, been translated by idioms and colloquialisms. In this way the user can assess the value of words and expressions in the other language. As the two halves have been independently compiled, reference from one half to the other will be found helpful.

ARRANGEMENT AND SPELLING

To make the fullest use of the space at our disposal and thereby to increase the number of words and expressions included, we have, as far as possible, entered words in groups, under the first word of the group.

Plural of Nouns : Dutch nouns generally add -*en*. Whenever there is any deviation from this rule the ending of the plural is given, starting from the last letter that has remained unchanged. The indication -*ven* shows that the final -*f* has become a *v*, the indication -*zen* that the final -*s* has become a *z*.

Present Tense of Verbs : The general rule is that the 1st person singular is formed from the infinitive by removing the final -*en*. Whenever this is not the case the syllable in which the deviation occurs is given.

The spelling used in this dictionary is that made official on 1st May, 1947. It had already been used for a number of years by the more educated section of the Dutch people, although, before its official acceptance, with a number of variations, such as the ending -*lik* instead of the now accepted -*lijk*, or the ending -*ies* instead of the now accepted -*isch*.

Many Dutch books, documents, and papers will, however, still be found in the old spelling. Users of this Dictionary are advised to familiarize themselves with the salient points of the old spelling, so that they may be able to look up words in the old spelling in the present handbook.

1*a.* Old Spelling had in many cases nouns ending in -*sch*, where Modern Spelling has -*s*, e.g. *mensch* and *flesch* for modern *mens* and *fles* ;

1*b.* the plurals of such nouns in Old Spelling ended in (*s*)*schen* ; in Modern Spelling this has become (*s*)*sen : flesschen—flessen, menschen—mensen ;*

1*c.* similarly Old Spelling had a number of verbal forms ending in -*sschen, -sch, -scht, -schte, -schten,* which, in Modern Spelling have respectively become : -*ssen, -s, -st, -ste, -sten* as e.g. *wasschen, wasch, wascht, waschte, waschten,* which have respectively become *wassen, was, wast, waste, wasten ;*

1*d.* adjectives which in Old Spelling ended in -*sch* have in Modern Spelling lost the -*ch : frisch—fris* ; in the declensional form -*ssche* has become -*sse : frissche—frisse* ; this does not apply to the ending -*isch* which has been retained in Modern Spelling, e.g. *electrisch.*

2. in a number of open syllables Old Spelling had *ee* or *oo*, where Modern Spelling has but *e* or *o*, e.g. : *teere—tere, roode—rode ;*

3. *c* has in many cases been replaced by *k*, and *ph* by *f*.

LIST OF ABBREVIATIONS USED IN THIS DICTIONARY

LIJST VAN DE IN DIT WOORDENBOEK GEBRUIKTE AFKORTINGEN

a.	adjective	bijvoeglijk naamwoord
adv.	adverb	bijwoord
aux. v.	auxiliary verb	hulpwerkwoord
c.	conjunction	voegwoord
excl.	exclamation	uitroeping
imp.	impersonal	onpersoonlijk
int.	interjection	tussenwerpsel
inv.	invariable	onveranderlijk
irr.	irregular	onregelmatig
n.	noun of common gender, i.e. either the old masculine or the old feminine	zelfstandig naamwoord, mannelijk en/of vrouwelijk
N	proper noun of common gender, i.e. either the old masculine or the old feminine	naamwoord, mannelijk en/of vrouwelijk
n.n.	neuter noun	onzijdig zelfstandig naamwoord
n.N.	proper noun of neuter gender	onzijdig naamwoord
no pl.	no plural	zonder meervoud
num.	numeral	telwoord
num. card.	cardinal numeral	hoofdtelwoord
num. ord.	ordinal numeral	rangtelwoord
prep.	preposition	voorzetsel
pron.	pronoun	voornaamwoord
pron. dem.	demonstrative pronoun	aanwijzend voornaamwoord
pron. poss.	possessive pronoun	bezittelijk voornaamwoord
str.	strong	sterk
v.i.	intransitive verb	ònovergankelijk werkwoord
v.i.s.	separable intransitive verb	scheidbaar ònovergankelijk werkwoord
v.r.	(intransitive) reflexive verb	(ònovergankelijk) wederkerig werkwoord
v.r.s.	separable reflexive verb	scheidbaar wederkerig werkwoord
v.r.t.	transitive reflexive verb	overgankelijk wederkerig werkwoord
v.t.	transitive verb	overgankelijk werkwoord
v.t.s.	separable transitive verb	scheidbaar overgankelijk werkwoord

LIST OF STRONG AND IRREGULAR
DUTCH VERBS

N.B.—The less common forms are given between brackets. The numbers indicate the grammatical persons. Compound verbs, both separable and inseparable, are conjugated like their root-verbs. The form of the 1st person sg. of the Present Tense is given in the Dutch–English half of the Dictionary whenever it differs from the infinitive without -*en*. The plural of the Past Tense adds -*en* to the form given below, or -*n* should this form end in an -*e*; where there are other changes, these are included in the list below.

Infinitive.	Imperfect.	Past Participle.
bakken	bakte	gebakken
bannen	bande	gebannen
barsten	barstte	gebarsten
bederven	bedierf, *pl.* bedierven	bedorven
bedriegen	bedroog, *pl.* bedrogen	bedrogen
beginnen	begon, *pl.* begonnen	begonnen
begrijpen	begreep, *pl.* begrepen	begrepen
belijden	beleed, *pl.* beleden	beleden
bergen	borg	geborgen
bevelen	beval, *pl.* bevalen	bevolen
bewegen	bewoog, *pl.* bewogen	bewogen
bezwijken	bezweek, *pl.* bezweken	bezweken
bidden	bad, *pl.* baden	gebeden
bieden	bood, *pl.* boden	geboden
bijten	beet, *pl.* beten	gebeten
binden	bond	gebonden
blazen	blies, *pl.* bliezen	geblazen
blijken	bleek, *pl.* bleken	gebleken
blijven	bleef, *pl.* bleven	gebleven
blinken	blonk	geblonken
braden	braadde	gebraden
breken	brak, *pl.* braken	gebroken
brengen	bracht	gebracht
brouwen	brouwde	gebrouwen
buigen	boog, *pl.* bogen	gebogen
delven	dolf, *pl.* dolven	gedolven
denken	dacht	gedacht
dingen	dong	gedongen
doen	dee(d), *pl.* deden	gedaan
1. doe		
2 & 3. doet		
dragen	droeg	gedragen
drijven	dreef, *pl.* dreven	gedreven
dringen	drong	gedrongen
drinken	dronk	gedronken
druipen	droop, *pl.* dropen	gedropen
duiken	dook, *pl.* doken	gedoken
dunken	docht	gedocht
durven	durfde, dorst	gedurfd
dwingen	dwong	gedwongen
eten	at, *pl.* aten	gegeten
fluiten	floot, *pl.* floten	gefloten
gaan	ging	gegaan
1. ga		
2 & 3. gaat		
gelden	gold	gegolden

Infinitive.	Imperfect.	Past Participle.
genezen	genas, *pl.* genazen	genezen
genieten	genoot, *pl.* genoten	genoten
geven	gaf, *pl.* gaven	gegeven
gieten	goot, *pl.* goten	gegoten
glijden	gleed, *pl.* gleden	gegleden
glimmen	glom, *pl.* glommen	geglommen
graven	groef, *pl.* groeven	gegraven
grijpen	greep, *pl.* grepen	gegrepen
hangen	hing	gehangen
hebben	had, *pl.* hadden	gehad
1. heb		
2. hebt		
3. heeft		
heffen	hief, *pl.* hieven	geheven
helpen	hielp	geholpen
heten	heette	geheten
hijsen	hees, *pl.* hesen	gehesen
houden	hield	gehouden
houwen	hieuw	gehouwen
jagen	jaagde, joeg	gejaagd
kerven	kerfde, (korf, *pl.* korven)	gekorven
kiezen	koos, *pl.* kozen	gekozen
kijken	keek, *pl.* keken	gekeken
kijven	keef, *pl.* keven	gekeven
klimmen	klom, *pl.* klommen	geklommen
klinken	klonk	geklonken
kluiven	kloof, *pl.* kloven (kluifde)	gekloven (gekluifd)
knijpen	kneep, *pl.* knepen	geknepen
komen	kwam, *pl.* kwamen	gekomen
kopen	kocht	gekocht
krijgen	kreeg, *pl.* kregen	gekregen
krijten	kreet, *pl.* kreten	gekreten
krimpen	kromp	gekrompen
kruipen	kroop, *pl.* kropen	gekropen
kunnen	kon, *pl.* konnen, konden	gekund
1 & 3. kan		
2. kan, kunt		
kwijten	kweet, *pl.* kweten	gekweten
lachen	lachte	gelachen
laden	laadde	geladen
laten	liet	gelaten
leggen	legde (lei)	gelegd
lezen	las, *pl.* lazen	gelezen
liegen	loog, *pl.* logen	gelogen
liggen	lag, *pl.* lagen	gelegen
lijden	leed, *pl.* leden	geleden
lijken	leek, *pl.* leken	geleken
lopen	liep	gelopen
luiken	look, *pl.* loken	geloken
malen	maalde	gemalen
melken	melkte, molk	gemolken
meten	mat, *pl.* maten	gemeten
mijden	meed, *pl.* meden	gemeden
moeten	moest	gemoeten
mogen	mocht	gemoogd
1 & 3. mag		
2. mag, moogt		
nemen	nam, *pl.* namen	genomen
nijgen	neeg, *pl.* negen	genegen
nijpen	neep, *pl.* nepen	genepen
ontginnen	ontgon, *pl.* ontgonnen	ontgonnen
plegen	placht	———
pluizen	ploos, *pl.* plozen	geplozen
prijzen	prees, *pl.* prezen	geprezen

Infinitive.	Imperfect.	Past Participle.
raden	raadde (ried)	geraden
rijden	reed, *pl.* reden	gereden
rijgen	reeg, *pl.* regen	geregen
rijten	reet, *pl.* reten	gereten
rijzen	rees, *pl.* rezen	gerezen
roepen	riep	geroepen
ruiken	rook, *pl.* roken	geroken
scheiden	scheidde	gescheiden
schelden	schold	gescholden
schenden	schond	geschonden
schenken	schonk	geschonken
scheppen	schiep	geschapen
scheren	schoor, *pl.* schoren	geschoren
schieten	schoot, *pl.* schoten	geschoten
schijnen	scheen, *pl.* schenen	geschenen
schrijden	schreed, *pl.* schreden	geschreden
schrijven	schreef, *pl.* schreven	geschreven
schrikken	schrok, *pl.* schrokken	geschrokken
schuilen	school, *pl.* scholen	gescholen
schuiven	schoof, *pl.* schoven	geschoven
slaan	sloeg	geslagen
1. sla		
2. & 3. slaat		
slapen	sliep	geslapen
slijpen	sleep, *pl.* slepen	geslepen
slijten	sleet, *pl.* sleten	gesleten
slinken	slonk	geslonken
sluiken	slook, *pl.* sloken	gesloken
sluipen	sloop, *pl.* slopen	geslopen
sluiten	sloot, *pl.* sloten	gesloten
smelten	smolt	gesmolten
smijten	smeet, *pl.* smeten	gesmeten
snijden	sneed, *pl.* sneden	gesneden
snuiten	snoot, *pl.* snoten	gesnoten
snuiven	snoof, *pl.* snoven	gesnoven
spannen	spande	gespannen
spijten	speet, *pl.* speten	gespeten
spinnen	spon, *pl.* sponnen	gesponnen
splijten	spleet, *pl.* spleten	gespleten
spouwen	spouwde	gespouwen
spreken	sprak, *pl.* spraken	gesproken
springen	sprong	gesprongen
spruiten	sproot, *pl.* sproten	gesproten
spuiten	spoot, *pl.* spoten	gespoten
staan	stond	gestaan
1. sta		
2 & 3. staat		
steken	stak, *pl.* staken	gestoken
stelen	stal, *pl.* stalen	gestolen
sterven	stierf, *pl.* stierven	gestorven
stijgen	steeg, *pl.* stegen	gestegen
stijven	steef, *pl.* steven	gesteven
stinken	stonk	gestonken
stoten	stootte, stiet	gestoten
strijden	streed, *pl.* streden	gestreden
strijken	streek, *pl.* streken	gestreken
stuiven	stoof, *pl.* stoven	gestoven
tijgen	toog, *pl.* togen	getogen
treden	trad, *pl.* traden	getreden
treffen	trof, *pl.* troffen	getroffen
trekken	trok, *pl.* trokken	getrokken
vallen	viel	gevallen
vangen	ving	gevangen
varen	voer	gevaren

Infinitive.	Imperfect.	Past Participle.
vechten	vocht	gevochten
verdrieten	verdroot, *pl.* verdroten	verdroten
verdwijnen	verdween, *pl.* verdwenen	verdwenen
vergeten	vergat, *pl.* vergaten	vergeten
verliezen	verloor, *pl.* verloren	verloren
verschuilen	verschool, *pl.* verscholen	verscholen
verslinden	verslond	verslonden
verzwinden	verzwond	verzwonden
vinden	vond	gevonden
vlechten	vlocht	gevlochten
vlieden	vlood, *pl.* vleden	gevloden
vliegen	vloog, *pl.* vlogen	gevlogen
vlieten	vloot, *pl.* vloten	gevloten
vouwen	vouwde	gevouwen
vragen	vroeg, vraagde	gevraagd
vreten	vrat, *pl.* vraten	gevreten
vriezen	vroor, *pl.* vroren	gevroren
waaien	waaide, woei	gewaaid
wassen	waste (wies)	gewassen
wegen	woog, *pl.* wogen	gewogen
werpen	wierp	geworpen
werven	wierf, *pl.* wierven	geworven
weten	wist	geweten
weven	weefde	geweven
wijken	week, *pl.* weken	geweken
wijten	weet, *pl.* weten	geweten
wijzen	wees, *pl.* wezen	gewezen
willen	wilde, wou	gewild
1 & 3. wil		
2. wilt		
winden	wond	gewonden
winnen	won, *pl.* wonnen	gewonnen
worden	werd	geworden
wreken	wreekte	gewroken
wrijven	wreef, *pl.* wreven	gewreven
wringen	wrong	gewrongen
zeggen	zei, zeide	gezegd
zenden	zond	gezonden
zien	zag, *pl.* zagen	gezien
1. zie		
2 & 3. ziet		
zijgen	zeeg, *pl.* zegen	gezegen
zijn	was, *pl.* waren	geweest
1. ben		
2. bent		
3. is		
zingen	zong	gezongen
zinken	zonk	gezonken
zinnen	zon, *pl.* zonnen	gezonnen
zitten	zat, *pl.* zaten	gezeten
zoeken	zocht	gezocht
zouten	zoutte	gezouten
zuigen	zoog, *pl.* zogen	gezogen
zuipen	zoop, *pl.* zopen	gezopen
zullen	zou, *pl.* zou(d)en	——
1 & 3. zal		
2. zult		
zwelgen	zwolg	gezwolgen
zwellen	zwol, *pl.* zwollen	gezwollen
zwemmen	zwom, *pl.* zwommen	gezwommen
zweren (1: *swear*)	zwoer	gezworen
zweren (2: *fester*)	zwoor, *pl.* zworen	gezworen
zwerven	zwierf, *pl.* zwierven	gezworven
zwijgen	zweeg, *pl.* zwegen	gezwegen

LIST OF STRONG AND IRREGULAR ENGLISH VERBS

LIJST VAN STERKE EN ONREGELMATIGE ENGELSE WERKWOORDEN

N.B.—Minder gebruikelijke vormen worden tussen haakjes gegeven.

Onbepaalde Wijs en 1ste p. enkelvoud Tegenwoordige Tijd	Onvoltooid Verleden Tijd	Verleden Deelwoord
abide	abode (abided)	abode
arise	arose	arisen
awake	awoke	awoke (awaked)
be	was, *pl.* were	been
1. am		
2 & *Pl.* are		
3. is		
bear	bore	born (borne)
beat	beat	beaten
become	became	become
befall	befell	befallen
beget	begot	begotten
begin	began	begun
bend	bent	bent (bended)
bereave	bereft (bereaved)	bereft (bereaved)
beseech	besought	besought
3. -es		
bespeak	bespoke	bespoken
bestride	bestrode ·	bestridden, bestrid, bestrode
bid	bad, bade, bid	bid, bidden
bind	bound	bound
bite	bit	bitten (bit)
bleed	bled	bled
blend	blended (blent)	blended (blent)
blow	blew	blown
break	broke	broken (broke)
breed	bred	bred
bring	brought	brought
build	built	built
burn	burned (burnt)	burned (burnt)
burst	burst	burst
buy	bought	bought
can	could	——
3. can		
cast	cast	cast
catch	caught	caught
3. -es		
chide	chid	chid(den)
choose	chose	chosen
cleave	clove, cleft	cloven, cleft

N.B.—Er is ook een zwak ww. *cleave.*

Onbepaalde Wijs en 1ste p. enkelvoud Tegenwoordige Tijd	Onvoltooid Verleden Tijd	Verleden Deelwoord
cling	clung	clung
clothe	clothed, clad	clothed, clad
come'	came	come
cost	cost	cost
creep	crept	crept
crow	crowed, crew	crowed
cut	cut	cut
dare	durst, dared	dared
3. dare(s)		
deal	dealt	dealt
dig	dug	dug
do	did	done
3. does		
draw	drew	drawn
dream	dreamt, dreamed	dreamt, dreame
drink	drank	drunk
drive	drove	driven
dwell	dwelt	dwelt
eat	ate (eat)	eaten
fall	fell	fallen
feed	fed	fed
feel	felt	felt
fight	fought	fought
find	found	found
flee	fled	fled
fling	flung	flung
fly	flew	flown
3. flies		
forbear	forbore	forborne
forbid	forbade	forbidden
forego	forewent	foregone
3. foregoes		
foretell	foretold	foretold
forget	forgot	forgotten
forsake	forsook	forsaken
forswear	forswore	forsworne
freeze	froze	frozen
get	got	got (gotten)
gild	gilded (gilt)	gilded (gilt)
gird	girded (girt)	girded (girt)
give	gave	given
go	went	gone
3. goes		
grind	ground	ground
grow	grew	grown
hang	hung	hung

N.B.—Er is ook een zwak ww. *hang.*

have	had	had
3. has		
hear	heard	heard
heave	heaved, hove	heaved, hove
hew	hewed	hewn, hewed
hide	hid	hidden
hit	hit	hit
hold	held	held
hurt	hurt	hurt
keep	kept	kept
kneel	knelt	knelt
knit	knitted, knit	knitted, knit
know	knew	known
lade	laded	laden

xvi

Onbepaalde Wijs en 1ste p. enkelvoud Tegenwoordige Tijd	Onvoltooid Verleden Tijd	Verleden Deelwoord
lay	laid	laid
lead	led	led
lean	leaned, leant	leaned, leant
leap	leapt, leaped	leapt, leaped
learn	learnt, learned	learnt, learned
leave	left	left
lend	lent	lent
let	let	let
lie	lay	lain
light	lit, lighted	lit (lighted)
lose	lost	lost
make	made	made
may 3. may	might	——
mean	meant	meant
meet	met	met
melt	melted	melted, molten
mow	mowed	mown
must 3. must	(must)	——
ought 3. ought	——	——
outbid	outbid, outbade	outbid(den)
pay	paid	paid
pen	pent	pent
put	put	put
read	read	read
rend	rent	rent
rid	ridded, rid	rid
ride	rode	ridden
ring	rang	rung
rise	rose	risen
run	ran	run
saw	sawed	sawn
say	said	said
see	saw	seen
seek	sought	sought
sell	sold	sold
send	sent	sent
set	set	set
sew	sewed	sewn, sewed
shake	shook	shaken
shall 3. shall	should	——
shear	sheared	shorn
shed	shed	shed
shew	shewed	shewn
shine	shone	shone
shoe	shod	shod
shoot	shot	shot
show	showed	shown
shrink	shrank	shrunk
shut	shut	shut
sing	sang	sung
sink	sank	sunk
sit	sat	sat
slay	slew	slain
sleep	slept	slept
slide	slid	slid
sling	slung	slung
slink	slunk	slunk
slit	slit	slit

Onbepaalde Wijs en 1ste p. enkelvoud Tegenwoordige Tijd	Onvoltooid Verleden Tijd	Verleden Deelwoord
smell	smelt	smelt
smite	smote	smitten
sow	sowed	sown, sowed
speak	spoke	spoken
speed	sped	sped
spell	spelt, spelled	spelt, spelled
spend	spent	spent
spill	spilt, spilled	spilt, spilled
spin	spun, span	spun
spit	spat	spat
split	split	split
spread	spread	spread
spring	sprang	sprung
stand	stood	stood
stave	staved, stove	staved, stove
steal	stole	stolen
stick	stuck	stuck
sting	stung	stung
stink	stank, stunk	stunk
strew	strewed	strewn, strewed
stride	strode	stridden
strike	struck	stricken, struck ·
string	strung	strung
strive	strove	striven
swear	swore	sworn
sweep	swept	swept
swell	swelled	swollen
swim	swam	swum
swing	swung	swung
take	took	taken
teach 3. teaches	taught	taught
tear	tore	torn
tell	told	told
think	thought	thought
thrive	throve	thriven
throw	threw	thrown
thrust	thrust	thrust
tread	trod	trodden
wake	woke, waked	waked, woken, woke
wear	wore	worn
weave	wove	woven
weep	wept	wept
will 3. will	would	——
win	won	won
wind	wound	wound
wrap	wrapped, wrapt	wrapped, wrapt
wring	wrung	wrung
write	wrote	written

DUTCH DICTIONARY

A

à, *pr.* at.
aaien, *v.t.* to stroke, caress.
aak, **aken**, *n.* barge, flat-bottomed lighter.
aal, **alen**, *n.* eel. **aalachtig**, *a.* eel-like, eely.
aalfuik, *n.* eel-net. **aalgeer**, **-geren**, *n.*
eel-spear. **aalkaar**, **-karen**, *n.* eel-buck.
eel-pot. **aalkorf**, **-ven**, *n.* eel-basket.
aalpuit, *n.* eel-pout, burbot, blenny.
aalschoiver, **-s**, *n.* cormorant. **aalsteker**,
-s, *n.* eel-fork. **aalsvel**, **-llen**, *n.n.* eel-skin.
aalvijver, **-s**, *n.* eel-bed.
aalbes, **-ssen**. *See* **bes**.
aalmoes, **-zen**, *n.* alms. **aalmoeze·nier**, **-s**,
n. almoner, chaplain.
aambeeld. *See* **aanbeeld**.
aambei, *n.* pile, haemorrhoids.
aam·borstig, *a.* short-winded, wheezy.
aan, *pr.* at, on, upon, near by; to. ~ *het
eten*, eating, at a meal; ~ *het werk*, at
work. ¶ *adv.* on. *zijn jas is* ~ , his coat
is on; *de kerk is* ~, church (*service*) has
begun; *de lamp is* ~, the lamp is lit;
de moer is ~, the bolt is (screwed) tight;
er is niets van ~, there is no truth in it.
¶ *prefix to* (*usually separable*) *verbs.*
aanbeeld, *n.n.* anvil.
aanbelanden, *v.i.s.* to arrive at (*by chance*).
aanbellen, **bel aan**, *v.i.s.* to ring the bell.
aanbesteden, **besteed aan**, *v.t.s.* to invite
tenders for. **aanbesteding**, *n.* tender;
putting out to contract. *bij* ~, by contract.
aanbevelen, **beveel aan**, *v.t.s.*, *str.* to recommend. **aanbevelens·waardig**, *a.* [re]com-
mendable. **aanbeveling**, *n.* recommendation. *op* ~ *van*, on the recommendation
of; *ter* ~ *van*, in recommendation of.
aanbevelingsbrief, **-ven**, *n.* letter of
recommendation.
aan·biddelijk, *a.* adorable. ¶ *adv.* adorably.
aan·bidden, **aanbid**, *v.t.*, *str.* to adore,
worship. **aan·bidder**, **-s**, *n.* worshipper.
aanbieden, *v.t.s.*, *str.* to offer, present, proffer,
tender. **aanbieding**, *n.* presentation,
tender.
aanbinden, *v.t.s.*, *str.* to fight, close with.
de strijd ~ *met*, to begin the struggle
against.
aanblaffen, **blaf aan**, *v.t.s.* to bark at.
aanblazen, **blaas aan**, *v.t.s.*, *str.* to fan
(*flames*, *passions*). **aanblazing**, *n.* inspiration.
aanblijven, **blijf aan**, *v.i.s.*, *str.* to remain
ajar (*door*); to keep on (*coat*, *light*).

aanblik, no pl., *n.* aspect; sight, look, view.
bij de eerste ~, at first sight. **aanblikken**,
blik aan, *v.t.s.* to glance at.
aanbod, **-biedingen**, *n.n.* offer; supply. *een*
~ *doen*, to make an offer.
aanbonzen, **bons aan**, *v.i.s.* ~ *tegen*, **to**
bump against, bump into.
aanboren, **boor aan**, *v.t.s.* to strike (*oil*); **to**
broach.
aanbotsen, *v.i.s.* ~ *tegen*, to bump against,
bump into.
aanbouw, no pl., *n.* (*process of*) construction;
cultivation. *in* ~, in process of construction, in cultivation. **aanbouwen**, *v.t.s.*
~ *tegen*, to build (*against*); to grow (*crops*).
aanbranden, *v.t.s.*, to burn (*in cooking*).
aanbrandsel, **-s**, *n.n.* burnt food adhering
to pan.
aanbrassen, **bras aan**, *v.t.s.* to brace (*sail*).
aanbreien, *v.t.s.* to foot (*sock*).
aanbreken, **breek aan**, *v.t.s.*, *str.* to break
into (*capital*), start (*loaf*), broach (*cask*,
subject), tap. ¶ *v.i.s.*, *str.* to dawn, to
break (*day*).
aanbrengen, *v.t.s.*, *str.* to bring (*to a place*);
to construct, fix up; to make (*changes*); to
introduce (*economies*); to inform (*against*).
aanbrommen, **brom aan**, *v.t.s.* to growl at.
aanbrullen, **brul aan**, *v.t.s.* to roar at.
aandacht, no pl., *n.* attention, interest.
de ~ *afwenden van*, to turn one's attention
away from; *de* ~ *boeien*, to fascinate;
~ *schenken aan*, to pay attention to; *de*
~ *trekken*, to attract attention; *de* ~
vestigen op, to draw attention to; *de* ~
vragen, to ask for attention. **aan·dachtig**,
a. attentive. ¶ *adv.* attentively. **aan-
dachtstreep**, **-strepen**, *n.* dash (—).
aandeel, **-delen**, *n.n.* share; portion. *gewone,
preferente, en uitgestelde aandelen*, ordinary,
preferred, and deferred shares; ~ *aan
toonder*, share to bearer; ~ *op naam*,
registered share; ~*bewijs*, voucher (*for
share*); ~ *aan*, part in (*crime*); ~ *hebben
in*, to participate in, share in. **aandelen-
kapitaal**, **-talen**, *n.n.* share capital, capital stock. **aandeelhouder**, **-s**, *n.n.* shareholder.
aandenken, no pl., *n.n.* remembrance,
memory, keepsake.
aandichten, *v.t.s.* to impute. **aandichting**,
n. imputation.
aandienen, *v.t.s.* to announce; to usher in
~ *bij*, to announce (*person*). ¶ *v.r.*
zich ~; to announce oneself.
aandijken, *v.t.s.* to connect by means of
dyke.

1

·aandikken, dik aan, *v.t.s.* to thicken; to become stouter; to emphasize.

·aandoen, doe aan, *v.t.s.*, *irr.* to put on (*clothes*); to cause (*sadness*); to call at (*of ship at port*). See ·aangedaan. ·aandoening, *n.* affection (*disease*). ¶ no pl., *n.* emotion. aan·doenlijk, *a.* touching, moving. ¶ *adv.* touchingly, movingly. aan·doenlijkheid, -heden, *n.* pathos.

·aandraaien, *v.t.s.* to tighten (*by turning*); to turn on (*gas*), switch on (*electricity*).

·aandragen, draag aan, *v.t.s.*, *str.* to carry (*towards*). komen ~ met, to bring.

·aandrang, no pl., *n.* urge, insistence.

·aandraven, draaf aan, *v.i.s.* komen ~, to approach at a trot.

·aandrentelen, *v.i.s.* komen ~, to come sauntering along.

·aandribbelen, *v.i.s.* komen ~, to come tripping along.

·aandrift, *n.* strong impulse, instinct.

·aandrijven, drijf aan, *v.i.s.*, *str.* komen ~, to come floating along. ¶ *v.t.s.*, *str.* to urge on, instigate; to set and keep (*machinery*) going. ·aandrijver, -s, *n.* instigator. ·aandrijving, no pl., *n.* instigation.

·aandringen, *v.i.s.*, *str.* to insist. ~ bij, to be insistent with (*person*); ~ op, to insist on. ¶ no pl., *n.n.* op ~ van, at the instance of.

·aandrukken, druk aan, *v.t.s.* to press (down). ~ tegen, to press up against.

·aanduiden, *v.t.s.* to indicate, mark; to denote, mean. nader ~, to specify; terloops ~, to hint at. ·aanduiding, *n.* indication, sign.

aan·een, *adv.* together, consecutively. ¶ *prefix*, together. aan·eenblijven, blijf aaneen, *v.i.s.*, *str.* to remain together, keep together. aan·eenflansen, *v.t.s.* to join haphazardly. aan·eensluiten, *v.t.s.* *str.* to fit together; to close (*ranks*). aan·eenvriezen, vriest aaneen, *v.i.s.*, *irr.*, *imp.* to freeze together, congeal.

aan·eenge-, *prefix.* See verbs in aaneen-.

·aanfluiting, *n.* taunt, reproach. ~ van, object of mockery to.

·aanfokken, fok aan, *v.t.s.* to breed, rear, raise.

·aangaan, ga aan, *v.i.s.*, *irr.* to catch alight. ~ bij, to call in on; ~ op, to go towards. ¶ *v.t.s.*, *irr.* to concern; to conclude (*contract*). aan·gaande, *pr.* concerning.

·aangaలopperen, galoppeer aan, *v.i.s.* komen ~, to come galloping along.

·aangapen, gaap aan, *v.t.s.* to gape at, stare at.

·aange-. See verbs in aan-.

·aangeboren, *a.* innate, inborn. ~ recht, native right.

·aangedaan, -dane, *a.* moved.

·aangeklaagde, -n, *n.* accused, defendant.

·aangelegen, *a.* adjacent. aange·legenheid, -heden, *n.* matter, concern.

·aangenaam, -name, *a.* agreeable, pleasant, pleasing, comfortable. ¶ *adv.* agreeably, pleasantly, pleasingly, comfortably. ~!, Pleased to meet you!, How do you do! ·aangenaamheid, -heden, *n.* agreeableness, pleasantness. ·aangenomen, *c.* supposing, granted (that). See aannemen.

·aangeschoten, *a.* slightly intoxicated, tipsy.

·aangespen, *v.t.s.* to buckle on.

·aangeven, geef aan, *v.t.s.*, *str.* to give, hand, pass; to record (*on instrument*); to register (*luggage, birth*); to declare (*at customs*). ·aangever, -s, *n.* declarant.

·aangezetenen, pl. only, *n.* the guests (*at table*).

·aangezicht, *n.n.* visage, countenance.

·aangezien, *c.* since, as.

·aangieren, *v.i.s.* komen ~, to come roaring along (*storm wind*).

·aangifte, -n, *n.* declaration (*of value; of particulars on form*). ~ doen, to enter, declare, inform; formulier van ~, (application) form, declaration.

·aangluren, gluur aan, *v.t.s.* to stare at, goggle at.

·aangonzen, gons aan, *v.i.s.* komen ~, to come buzzing along (*insects*), come whizzing along (*bullet*).

·aangooien, *v.t.s.* ~ tegen, to throw against.

·aangorden, *v.t.s.* to gird on. de wapens ~ to gird up one's loins.

aan·grenzend, *a.* adjacent.

·aangrijnzen, grijns aan, *v.t.s.* to grin, grimace.

·aangrijpen, *v.t.s.*, *str.* to seize (on); attack; to move (*emotions*). aan·grijpend, *a.* touching, moving. ¶ *adv.* touchingly, movingly. ·aangrijpingspunt, *n.n.* point of attack.

·aangroei, no pl., *n.* growth, increase, accretion, increment. ·aangroeien, *v.i.s.* to grow, increase, augment. doen ~, to swell (*numbers*).

·aanhaken, haak aan, *v.t.s.* to hook on.

·aanhalen, haal aan, *v.t.s.* to tighten (*knot*); to fondle, caress; to quote (*words*); to place between quotation-marks; to seize (*goods*). aan·halig, *a.* over-affectionate, fond. ·aanhaling, *n.* quotation; seizure (*of goods*). ·aanhalingsteken, -s, *n.n.* inverted comma[s] , quotation-mark[s] .

·aanhang, no pl., *n.* adherents, followers, following, hangers-on. ·aanhangen, *v.t.s.*, *str.* to hang on to; to adhere to. ·aanhanger, -s, *n.* follower, partisan, supporter. aan·hangig, *a.* pending. ~ maken, to introduce (*bill*); to bring an action. ·aanhangmotor, *n.* detachable auxiliary motor (*of boat*). ·aanhangsel, -s, *n.n.* appendix (pl. appendices), rider, codicil, addendum (pl. addenda); appendage. ·aanhangwagen, -s, *n.* trailer (*of car*). aan·hankelijk, *a.* affectionate, attached, devoted.

aan·hankelijkheid, -heden, *n.* affection, attachment, devotion.

·**aanharden,** *v.i.s.* to harden.

·**aanharken,** *v.t.s.* to rake (over).

·**aanhebben,** *v.t.s., irr.* to have on, wear; to have on (*light*).

·**aanhechten,** *v.t.s.* to affix, attach. ·**aan**·**hechting,** *n.* fastening. ·**aanhechtingspunt,** *n.n.* point of contact.

·**aanhef,** no pl., *n.* opening words (*of letter, song*), exordium. ·**aanheffen, hef aan,** *v.t.s., str.* to begin, strike up.

·**aanhelpen,** *v.t.s., str.* to help on with (*garment*).

·**aanhijgen,** *v.i.s. komen* ∼, to come panting along.

·**aanhinken,** *v.i.s. komen* ∼, to come limping along.

·**aanhitsen,** *v.t.s.* to set on (*dog on man*). ∼ *op,* to set against.

·**aanhoeven, hoef aan,** *v.t.s. niet* ∼, not having to be put on.

·**aanhollen, hol aan,** *v.i.s. komen* ∼, to come tearing (*running*) along.

·**aanhoorder, -s,** *n.* listener. ·**aanhoren, hoor aan,** *v.t.s.* to listen to. *ten* ∼ *van,* in the hearing of. **aan**·**horen, aanhoor,** *v.t.* to listen to. **aan**·**horig,** *a.* appertaining to, belonging to. **aan**·**horigheid, -heden,** *n.* appurtenance.

·**aanhouden,** *v.i.s., irr.* to stop (*at a place*); to insist, persist, continue. ∼ *op.* to make for (*port*). ¶ *v.t.s., irr.* to' arrest. ∼ *wegens,* to arrest for; *betrekkingen* ∼, to keep up relations; *een kachel* ∼, to keep a stove burning; *goederen* ∼, to seize goods. **aan**·**houdend,** *a.* constant, incessant, continual, continuous. ¶ *adv.* constantly, incessantly, continually, continuously. **aan**·**houdendheid,** no pl., *n.* perseverance, persistence. ·**aanhouder,** *n.* one who perseveres. *de* ∼ *wint,* dogged does it. ·**aanhouding,** *n.* seizure, detention (*of goods*); arrest, detention (*of persons*).

·**aanhuppelen,** *v.i.s. komen* ∼, to come hopping along, come frisking along.

·**aanhuwen,** *v.t.s.* to obtain by marriage.

·**aanijlen,** *v.i.s. komen* ∼, to come rushing along.

·**aanjagen, jaag aan,** *v.t.s. & v.t.s., str.* to drive on (*at greater speed*). ·**aanjager, -s,** *n.* feeder, suction hose (*of fire-engine*).

·**aankalken,** *v.t.s.* to chalk up, score.

·**aankanten.** *See* ·**tegenkanten.** ·**aankanting.** *See* ·**tegenkanting.**

·**aankap,** no pl., *n.* felling of timber. ·**aan**·**kappen, kap aan,** *v.t.s.* to begin felling.

·**aankeffen, kef aan,** *v.t.s.* to yap at.

·**aankijken,** *v.t.s., str.* to look at. *de zaak nog eens* ∼, to put off decision.

·**aanklacht,** *n.* accusation, charge, indictment. *een* ∼ *afwijzen,* to nonsuit (*plea*); *een* ∼ *gegrond vinden,* to find a (true) bill; *een* ∼ *indienen tegen,* to lodge a complaint against. ·**aanklagen, klaag aan,** *v.t.s.* to accuse of, charge with. ·**aanklager. -s,** *n.* accuser, plaintiff.

·**aanklampen,** *v.t.s.* to board (*ship*); to accost, button-hole.

·**aankleden, kleed aan,** *v.t.s.* to dress; to cover.

·**aankleve,** no pl., *n. met* (*den*) ∼ *van* . . ., with the inclusion of . . . ·**aankleven kleef aan,** *v.t.s.* to stick to, adhere to.

·**aankloppen, klop aan,** *v.i.s.* to knock (*at door*). *bij iemand* ∼ *om geld,* to apply to someone for money.

·**aanklotsen,** *v.t.s.* ∼ *tegen,* to lap against (*of waves*).

·**aanknopen, knoop aan,** *v.t.s.* to button on to; to knot together. *onderhandelingen* ∼, to enter into negotiations; *weer* ∼, to resume (*relations, negotiations*). ·**aan**·**knopingspunt,** *n.n.* point of contact; point in common, common ground.

·**aankomeling,** *n.* beginner, newcomer. ·**aan**·**komen,** *v.i.s., irr.* to arrive; to improve in health. ∼ *bij,* to arrive at (*place*), to call on; ∼ *om,* to arrive at (*time*); *hard* ∼, to make itself felt (*blow*); *ergens* ∼, to touch something; *er is geen* ∼ *aan,* it is unobtainable, unprocurable; *het komt er* (*weinig*) *op aan,* it (hardly) matters; *het komt aan op* . . ., it depends on . . . ·**aankomend,** *a.* adolescent; coming, next. ·**aankomst,** no pl., *n.* arrival. *bij* ∼, on arrival.

·**aankondigen,** *v.t.s.* to announce, notify, proclaim; to foretell (*of barometer*). ·**aan**·**kondiging,** *n.* announcement, notice, notification; review (*of book*).

·**aankoop, -kopen,** *n.* purchase, acquisition. *door* ∼, by purchase. ·**aankoopsom, -mmen,** *n.* purchasing price. ·**aankopen, koop aan,** *v.t.s., irr.* to buy, purchase.

·**aankoppelen,** *v.t.s.* to couple (*wagons*).

·**aankrijgen,** *v.t.s., str.* to succeed in getting (*coat*) on; to succeed in getting (*fire*) to burn.

·**aankruien,** *v.t.s.* to bring along in wheelbarrow. ¶ *v.i.s. komen* ∼, to come piling up (*of ice-floes*).

·**aankruipen,** *v.i.s., str. komen* ∼, to come creeping along.

·**aankuieren,** *v.i.s. komen* ∼, to come strolling along.

·**aankunnen,** *v.t.s., irr.* to be able to tackle, be a match for. ¶ *v.i.s., irr.* as used in: *het kan aan,* it can be put on (*clothes*); it can be lit (*light*). ∼ *op,* to be able to rely on.

·**aankwakken, kwak aan,** *v.t.s.* ∼ *tegen,* to fling against, dash against.

·**aankweek,** no pl., *n.* cultivation. ·**aan**·**kweken, kweek aan,** *v.t.s.* to cultivate, grow (*plants*); to foster, cultivate (*friendship, morals*); to train (*teachers*).

·**aankwispelen,** *v.i.s. komen* ∼, to come along wagging tail.

·aanlachen, v.t.s., irr. to smile upon.
·aanlanden, v.i.s. to land, land oneself.
aan·landig, a. landward.
·aanlappen, lap aan, v.t.s. to pass off on.
·aanlaten, laat aan, v.t.s., str. to leave on (light).
·aanleg, no pl., n. aptitude, talent, ability, turn, bent; construction, installation; plan. ~ voor, talent for. in ~, in course of construction. ·aanleggen, leg aan, v.i.s. to stop at (a place). ~ op, to take aim at. ¶ v.t.s. to apply (bandage); to construct, instal, lay down, lay out; to follow a plan. iets handig ~, to manage something cleverly. ·aanleghaven, -s, n. port of call. ·aanlegplaats, n. landing-place. ·aanlegsteiger, -s, n. landing-stage.
·aanlegger, -s, n. originator, prime mover.
·aanleidend, a. aanleidende oorzaak, primary cause. ·aanleiding, n. occasion, trigger-cause. ~ tot, immediate cause of; ~, geven tot, to give rise to; bij de geringste ~ on the slightest provocation; naar ~ van, with reference to, on account of, in connection with; zonder enige ~, without any apparent reason.
·aanlengen, v.t.s. to dilute.
·aanleren, leer aan, v.t.s. to learn, acquire (knowledge).
·aanleunen, v.i.s. to lean. ~ tegen, to lean against; zich iets laten ~, to put up with (insult), stomach, pocket (affront). ·aan-leuningspunt, n.n. point of support (of army).
·aanliggend, a. adjacent, contiguous, adjoining.
·aanloeven, loef aan, v.i.s. to luff, sail to windward.
aan·lokkelijk, a. alluring, attractive, inviting. aan·lokkelijkheid, -heden, n. attractive-ness. ·aanlokken, lok aan, v.t.s. to tempt, decoy. ·aanlokking, n. enticement. ·aanloksel, -s, n.n. bait, decoy.
·aanlonken, v.t.s. to ogle.
·aanloop, -lopen, n. run (before jump). een ~ nemen, to take a run; preliminaries; ~ hebben, to have many visitors or customers. ·aanloophaven, -s, n. port of call. ·aanlopen, loop aan, v.i.s., str. komen ~, to come walking along; bij iemand ~, to drop in on someone; op iets ~, to run towards something; tegen iets ~, to run up against something.
·aanmaak, no pl., n. manufacture. ·aan-maken, maak aan, v.t.s. to manufacture; to dress (salad); to kindle. ¶ v.i.s. to hurry.
·aanmanen, maan aan, v.t.s. to admonish. ~ tot, to exhort, urge on; iemand tot spoed ~, to urge someone on to greater speed; iemand tot betaling ~, to press someone for payment. ·aanmaning, n. demand-note; reminder.
·aanmatigen, zich, v.r.s. to presume, arrogate

to oneself. aan·matigend, a. arrogant, presumptuous. ¶ adv. arrogantly, presumptuously. ·aanmatiging, n. arrogance, presumption.
·aanmelden, v.t.s. to announce. ¶ zich ~, v.r.s. to announce oneself; to present oneself (for examination). zich laten ~, to send in one's name. ·aanmelding, n. announcement; application.
·aanmengen, v.t.s. to dilute.
aan·merkelijk, a. considerable, notable. ¶ adv. considerably, notably. ·aanmerken, v.t.s. to comment (unfavourably). is er iets op aan te merken?, is there anything to find fault with? ·aanmerking, n. (un-favourable) comment, criticism; considera-tion; comparison. ~ op, comment on; uit ~ van, in consideration of; in ~ komen voor, to be considered for; in ~ nemen, to take into consideration, make allowance for; in ~ komen bij, to compare with.
·aanmeten, meet aan, v.t.s., str. to measure for (clothes).
aan·minnig, a. amiable, charming. ¶ adv. amiably, charmingly.
·aanmoedigen, v.t.s. to encourage. iemand tot iets ~, to encourage a person to do something. ·aanmoediging, n. encourage-ment.
·aanmoeten, v.i.s., irr. to have to be put on (clothes); to have to be lit.
·aanmogen, mag aan, v.i.s., irr. to be allowed to be put on; to be allowed to be lit.
·aanmonsteren, v.t.s. to sign on (crew). ¶ v.i.s. to sign on. ¶v.r.s. zich laten ~ op een schip, to sign on (of crew). ·aan-monstering, n. signing on.
·aanmunten, v.t.s. to coin. ·aanmunting, n. coinage (process).
·aannaaien, v.t.s. to sew on.
aan·nemelijk, a. acceptable; plausible, likely. aan·nemelijkheid, -heden, n. acceptability; plausibility, likelihood. ·aannemen, neem aan, v.t.s., str. to accept, take; to pass, carry (by vote); to recognize (truth); to suppose; to take on (contract); to embrace (religion); to confirm, receive (into church); to engage (staff); to assume (colour). goed van ~, intelligent; aangenomen dat, assuming that; ~! Waiter! ·aannemer, -s, n. builder, contractor. ·aanneming, n, acceptance (of bill). bij ~, as per con-tract (tender having been accepted); con-firmation (in Protestant church). ·aan-nemingssom, -mmen, n. amount of tender.
·aanpakken, pak aan, v.t.s. to take hold of; to tackle (problem). flink ~, to make an effort.
·aanpalend, a. adjacent.
·aanpappen, pap aan, v.i.s. ~ met, to become familiar with (person).
·aanpassen, pas aan, v.t.s. to try on (clothes). iets ~ (bij), to make something agree (with). ¶ v.r.s. zich ~ (aan), to adapt

oneself (to). ·**aanpassing,** n. adaptation: adaptability. ·**aanpassingsvermogen.** no pl., n.n. power of adaptation.

·**aanplakbiljet, -tten,** n.n. poster. ·**aanplakbord,** n.n. notice-board. ·**aanplakken,** plak aan, v.t.s. to put up (poster, notice). ·**aanplakzuil,** n. advertising pillar.

·**aanplant,** no pl., n. (process of) planting: plantation. ·**aanplanten,** v.t.s. to plant (more land).

·**aanplempen,** v.t.s. to fill up (ditch).

·**aanporren, por aan,** v.t.s. to spur on, shake up.

·**aanpraten, praat aan,** v.t.s. to talk (person) into (doing, buying something).

·**aanprijzen, prijs aan,** v.t.s., str. to praise highly.

·**aanpunten,** v.t.s. to sharpen (point).

·**aanraden, raad aan,** v.t.s., irr. to advise, recommend. ¶ no pl., n.n. op ~ van, on the advice of.

·**aanraken, raak aan,** v.t.s. to touch. ·**aanraking,** n. touch, contact. in ~ met, in touch with. ·**aanrakingspunt,** n.n. point of contact.

·**aanranden,** v.t.s. to assault, attack. iemands eer ~, to attack a person's honour. ·**aanrander, -s,** n. assailant. ·**aanranding,** n. assault (on honour).

·**aanrecht,** n., ·**aanrechtbank,** n. (fixed) kitchen dresser.

·**aanreiken,** v.t.s. to hand, pass.

·**aanrekenen,** v.t.s. to account against, to blame for. ¶ v.r.t.s. het zich als een eer ~, to count as an honour.

·**aanrennen, ren aan,** v.i.s. komen ~, to come running along.

·**aanrichten,** v.t.s. to cause (damage).

·**aanrijden,** v.i.s., str. to drive or ride faster. op iemand ~, to drive or ride towards someone; tegen iets ~, to run (i.e. drive or ride) into something. komen ~, to come riding along. ¶ v.t.s., str. to bring in carts; to knock down (by vehicle). ·**aanrijding,** n. collision.

·**aanristen,** v.t.s. to string (onions).

·**aanroeien,** v.i.s. to row faster. komen ~, to come rowing along.

·**aanroepen,** v.t.s., str. to call, hail (ship); to invoke. ·**aanroeping,** n. invocation.

·**aanroeren,** v.t.s. to touch (lightly), een onderwerp ~, to touch upon a subject.

·**aanrollen, rol aan,** v.t.s. to roll along. ¶ v.i.s. ~ tegen, to roll up against; komen ~, to come rolling along.

·**aanruisen,** v.i.s. komen ~, to come rustling along, come rippling along (breeze, stream).

·**aanrukken, ruk aan** v.i.s. to approach (of troops). laten ~, to bring forward (troops), to order (bottle).

·**aanschaffen, schaf aan,** v.t.s. to buy. ¶ v.r.t.s. zich iets ~, to buy oneself something.

·**aanscharrelen,** v.i.s. to come along (busily and awkwardly).

·**aanschieten,** v.t.s., str. to wound, wing; throw on, put on hurriedly (clothes). ¶ v.i.s., str. ~ op, to rush up to.

·**aanschijn,** no pl. n.n. appearance; countenance.

·**aanschikken, schik aan,** v.i.s. to draw up (chair to table).

·**aanschoffelen,** v.i.s. komen ~, to come shuffling along. ¶ v.t.s. to hoe.

·**aanschouw,** no pl., n. in ~ nemen, to examine. **aan·schouwelijk,** a. clear. ~ maken, to demonstrate (by ocular proof); ~ onderwijs, visual education, object teaching; ~ voorstellen, to represent graphically. **aan·schouwelijkheid,** no pl., n. graphical clearness. **aan·schouwen,** v.t. to behold. ¶ n.n. ten ~ van, before the eyes of. **aan·schouwer, -s,** n. spectator. **aan·schouwing,** n. contemplation. **aanschouwingsvermogen,** no pl., n.n. intuitive faculty.

·**aanschrappen, schrap aan,** v.t.s. to tick (mark).

·**aanschrijven, schrijf aan,** v.t.s., str. to score (write down); to circularize. goed aangeschreven staan bij iemand, to be in somebody's favour; iemand iets ~, to credit a person with (action). ¶ no pl., n.n. circular. op ~ van, upon notification by. ·**aanschrijving,** n. circular, notification.

·**aanschroeven, schroef aan,** v.t.s. to screw on. vast ~, to screw (tight).

·**aansjokken, sjok aan,** v.i.s. komen ~, to joggle along.

·**aansjorren, sjor aan,** v.t.s. to tighten (rope).

·**aansjouwen,** v.t.s. to drag along. ¶ v.i.s. komen ~ met, to come along with (object).

·**aanslaan, sla aan,** v.t.s., irr. to strike (note); to give tongue; to confiscate; to affix (bail, poster); to put up (property) for sale; to assess (for income-tax). een hoge toon ~, to be overbearing. ¶ v.i.s., irr. to salute; to tarnish; to become covered (with moisture). ~ tegen, to strike against. ·**aanslag,** n. attempt (on life); assessment (for income-tax). een ~ doen op, to make an attempt on. ¶ no pl., n. fur (in kettle), sediment; touch (music). **aanslagbiljet, -tten,** n.n. income-tax demand.

·**aanslepen, sleep aan,** v.t.s. to drag along. met iets komen ~, to use far-fetched argument.

·**aanslibben, slib aan,** v.i.s. to silt up. ·**aanslibbing,** n. alluvial soil. ·**aanslibsel, -s,** n.n. alluvial soil.

·**aanslijken,** v.i.s. to silt up.

·**aanslijpen,** v.t.s., str. to whet (tool).

·**aanslingeren,** v.i.s. komen ~. to come swaying along.

·**aansloffen, slof aan,** v.i.s. komen ~, to come shuffling along.

·**aansluipen,** v.i.s., str. komen ~, to come sneaking along, come stealing along.

·aansluiten, *v.t.s.*, *str.* to join, connect (*objects*); ~ *met*, to connect with (*by telephone-operator*). ¶ *v.i.s.*, *str.* to join. ¶ *v.r.s.*, *str.* zich ~ *bij*, to join (*party*); to agree with (*statement*). ·aansluiting, *n.* connection. ~ *krijgen*, to be put through (*telephone*). ·aansluitingspunt, *n.n.* junction.

·aansmeren, smeer aan, *v.t.s.* to smear on (*plaster*); to palm off on.

·aansmijten, *v.t.s.*, *str.* to throw on (*clothes*). ~ *tegen*, to fling against.

·aansnauwen, *v.t.s.* to snap at (*talking*).

·aansnellen, snel aan, *v.i.s.* komen ~, to come rushing along; ~ *op*, to rush towards.

·aansnijden, *v.t.s.*, *str.* to cut (into).

·aansnoeren, *v.i.s.* to lace tightly.

·aansnorren, snor aan, *v.i.s.* komen ~, to come whizzing along.

·aanspannen, span aan, *v.t.s.*, *irr.* to put (*horse*) to (*cart*); to tighten (*string*).

·aanspelden, *v.t.s.* to pin on.

·aanspijkeren, *v.t.s.* to nail on.

·aanspoeden, *v.i.s.* to approach speedily.

·aanspoelen, *v.t.s.* to wash ashore. ¶ *v.i.s.* to be washed ashore.

·aansporen, spoor aan, *v.t.s.* to spur on. ~ *tot*, to incite, urge on. ·aansporing, *n.* incitement. *op* ~ *van*, at the instigation of.

·aanspraak, -spraken, *n.* address, speech; claim. *een* ~ *houden*, to deliver an address; ~ *hebben*, to know people to talk to; ~ *hebben op*, to have a claim to; ~ *maken op*, to lay claim to; *geen* ~ *maken op*, to have no claim to. aan·sprakelijk, *a.* responsible; liable. *zich* ~ *stellen*, to answer for. aan·sprakelijkheid, no pl., *n.* responsibility; liability.

·aanspreken, spreek aan, *v.t.s.*, *str.* to address, speak to. ~ *met*, to address by (*title*); *de fles* ~, to partake freely (*drink*); *zijn kapitaal* ~, to break into one's capital; ~ *om*, to approach (*for help*); *in rechten* ~, to institute proceedings against. ·aan·spreker, -s, *n.* undertaker's man.

·aanspringen, *v.i.s.*, *str.* komen ~, to come jumping along.

·aanstaan, sta aan, *v.t.s.*, *irr.* to please; to be ajar (*door*). *het staat me* (*niet*) *aan*, it pleases (does not please) me. aan·staande, *a.* next, coming; future. ¶ -n, *n.* fiancé(e).

·aanstalte, -n, *n.* preparation(s). ~n *maken tot* or *voor*, to make preparations for; ~n *maken om*, to prepare to.

·aanstampen, *v.t.s.* to ram down, tamp. ¶ *v.i.s.* komen ~, to come stamping along.

·aanstappen, stap aan, *v.i.s.* to step out. komen ~, to come marching up.

·aanstaren, staar aan, *v.t.s.*, to stare at.

aan·stekelijk, *a.* contagious (*disease*); infectious (*laughter*). aan·stekelijkheid, no pl., *n.* contagiousness. ·aansteken, steek aan, *v.t.s.*, *str.* to light; to broach, to contamin-

ate. *aangestoken*, worm-eaten, carious. ·aansteker, -s, *n.* lighter.

·aanstellen, stel aan, *v.t.s.* to appoint. ~ *tot*, to appoint as. ¶ *v.r.s.* zich ~, to pose, to make a fool of oneself. ·aansteller, -s, *n.* poseur. aan·stellerig, *a.* affected. ¶ *adv.* affectedly. aanstelle·rij, no pl., *n.* affectation. ·aanstelling, *n.* appointment; commission (*army*).

·aansterken, *v.i.s.* to get stronger (*after illness*), convalesce, get better.

·aanstevenen, *v.i.s.* komen ~, to come sailing along; ~ *op*, to bear down on.

·aanstichten, *v.t.s.* to contrive, instigate. ·aanstichter, -s, *n.* instigator. ·aan·stichting, *n.* *op* ~ *van*, at the instigation of.

·aanstippen, stip aan, *v.t.s.* to tick off (*on list*); to mention in passing.

·aanstoken, stook aan, *v.t.s.* to poke (*fire*), ~ *tot*, to incite to (*quarrel, rebellion*). ·aanstoker, -s, *n.* instigator.

·aanstomen, stoom aan, *v.i.s.* komen ~, to come steaming along (*ship*).

·aanstommelen, *v.i.s.* komen ~, to come bumping along.

·aanstonds, *adv.* presently.

·aanstoot, no pl., *n.* offence, scandal. ~ *geven*, to give offence, scandalize; ~ *nemen* (*aan*), to take offence (at); *steen des* ~ *s*, stumbling-block. aan·stotelijk, *a.* offensive. ¶ *adv.* offensively aan·stotelijk·heid, no pl., *n.* offensiveness. ·aanstoten, stoot aan, *v.t.s.*, *str.* to nudge. ¶ *v.i.s.*, *str.* ~ *tegen*, to knock up against.

·aanstormen, *v.i.s.* komen ~, to come tearing along; ~ *op*, to rush up to.

·aanstrepen, streep aan, *v.t.s.* to mark (*on list*).

·aanstrijken, *v.t.s.*, *str.* to strike (match).

·aanstromen, stroom aan, *v.i.s.* komen ~, to come streaming along.

·aanstrompelen, *v.i.s.* komen ~, to come hobbling along.

·aanstuiven, stuif aan, *v.i.s.*, *str.* to grow (*sand-dunes*). ~ *op*, to rush upon; komen ~, to come rushing along. ·aan·stuiving, *n.* sand-drift.

·aansturen, stuur aan, *v.i.s.* ~ *op*, to make for (*harbour; changes*).

·aansukkelen, *v.i.s.* komen ~, to come along with difficulty.

·aantal, no pl., *n.n.* number (of), quantity (of).

·aantasten, *v.t.s.* to touch; to affect (*health*); to attack (*enemy*). *zijn kapitaal* ~, to encroach upon one's capital, break into one's capital; *iemand in zijn eer* ~, to injure a person's honour.

·aantekenen, *v.t.s.* to note (down), mark; to register (*letter*). *protest* ~ *tegen*, to enter a protest against; *hoger beroep* ~, to appeal to a higher tribunal. ·aantekenboekje, -s, *n.n.* small note-book, scribbling-block. ·aantekening, *n.* note, memo. ~ *houden van*, keep notes of.

·aantijgen, *v.t.s.*, *str.* to impute. ·aantijging, *n.* imputation.

·aantikken, tik aan, *v.i.s.* ~ *tegen*, to tap against.

·aantocht, no pl., *n.* approach. *in* ~ *zijn*, to approach (*army, storm*).

·aantonen, toon aan, *v.t.s.* to show, demonstrate. *aantonende wijs*, indicative mood.

·aantrappen, trap aan, *v.t.s.* to stamp down. ¶ *v.i.s.* komen ~, to come pedalling along.

·aantreden, treed aan, *v.i.s.*, *str.* to fall in (*for roll-call*). ~ *op*, to march up to.

·aantreffen, tref aan, *v.t.s.*, *str.* to come across, meet with.

aan·trekkelijk, *a.* attractive. ¶ *adv.* attractively. aan·trekkelijkheid, -heden, *n.* attractiveness, attraction. ·aantrekken, trek aan, *v.t.s.*, *str.* to draw (*magnet*); to attract; to draw on (*clothes*); to draw (*of stove*). *vaster* ~, to tauten; *aangetrokken door*, attracted by. ¶ *v.r.t.s.*, *str.* zich *iets* ~, to care about something, take something to heart. ·aantrekking, no pl., *n.* attraction. ·aantrekkingskracht, *n.* (power of) attraction.

·aantrippelen, *v.i.s.* komen ~, to come tripping along.

·aantrouwen, *v.t.s.* to obtain by marriage.

aan·vaardbaar, *a.* acceptable. aan·vaarden, *v.t.* to undertake; to set out on (*journey*), begin (*tenancy*); to accept (*bill of exchange, present*); to assume (*office*). aan·vaarding, no pl., *n.* acceptance; commencement; assumption (*of office*).

·aanval, -llen, *n.* attack. *een* ~ *afslaan, afweren, keren,* to beat off, repel, repulse an attack; *een* ~ *doen op,* to attack; *tot den* ~ *overgaan,* to launch an attack. ·aanvallen, val aan, *v.t.s.*, *str.* to attack. ¶ *v.i.s.*, *str.* ~ *op,* to tackle (*food*). ·aanvallend, *a.* offensive. ~ *optreden,* to assume the offensive. ·aanvallenderwijs, *adv.* offensively. ·aanvaller, -s, *n.* attacker.

aan·vallig, *a.* sweet, charming. aan·valligheid, -heden, *n.* grace, charm.

·aanvalsfront, *n.n.* front line of offensive. ·aanvalskolonne, -s, *n.* offensive column. ·aanvalspatrouille, -s, *n.* offensive patrol. ·aanvalsplan, -nnen, *n.n.* plan of attack. ·aanvalspunt, *n.n.* point of attack. ·aanvalswapen, -en, *n.n.* offensive arm.

·aanvang, no pl., *n.* commencement, beginning. *in den* ~, *bij den* ~, at the beginning; *vanaf den* ~, from the beginning; *een* ~ *nemen,* to commence; *een* ~ *maken met,* to make a start. ·aanvangen, *v.t.s.*, *str.* & *v.i.s.*, *str.* to commence. *men kan er niets mee* ~, one can do nothing with it. ·aanvanger, -s, *n.* beginner. ·aanvangsletter, -s, *n.* first letter, initial letter. ·aanvangspu··, *n.n.* starting point. ·aanvangssalaris, -ssen, *n.n.* initial salary. ·aanvangssnelheid, -heden, *n.* initial

velocity. aan·vankelijk, *a.* initial. ¶ *adv.* at first.

·aanvaren, vaar aan, *v.i.s.*, *str.* ~ *op,* to sail towards; ~ *tegen,* to sail into; *komen* ~, to come sailing along. ¶ *v.t.s.*, *str.* to bring by ship (*goods*). ·aanvaring, *n.* collision (*of ships*).

·aanvatten, vat aan, *v.t.s.* to seize, lay hold of; to tackle.

·aanvechten, *v.t.s.*, *str.* to tempt, assail. aan·vechtbaar, *a.* assailable, debatable. ·aanvechting, *n.* temptation; sudden impulse.

·aanvegen, veeg aan, *v.t.s.* to sweep.

·aanverwant, *n.* relation (by marriage). ¶ *a.* related (*subjects*). ·aanverwantschap, no pl., *n.* relationship.

·aanvetten, vet aan, *v.t.s.*, to grease; to fatten (up).

·aanvijlen, *v.t.s.* to sharpen (*with file*).

·aanvliegen, *v.t.s.*, *str.* to go for (*person*). ¶ *v.i.s.*, *str.* komen ~, to come flying along. ·aanvlijen, *v.r.s.* zich ~ *tegen,* to nestle (up) against.

·aanvoegen, *v.t.s.* to add. ~ *aan,* to join to; ~*de wijs,* subjunctive mood. ·aanvoegsel, -s, *n.n.* addition.

·aanvoelen, *v.t.s.* to feel. *zacht* ~, to be soft to the touch.

·aanvoer, *n.* supply; arrival (*of goods*). ·aanvoerbuis, -buizen, *n.* supply-pipe, feeder. ·aanvoerpijp, *n.* supply-pipe, feeder. ·aanvoerder, -s, *n.* leader, commander; ·aanvoeren, *v.t.s.* to lead; to supply, convey (*goods*); to put forward (*argument*). ·aanvoering, *n.* command. *onder* ~ *van,* under the leadership of.

·aanvraag, -vragen, *n.* official request, application. ~ *doen,* to make a request; *op* ~, on application; ~ *om,* request for. ·aanvraagformulier, *n.n.* request-form. ·aanvragen, vraag aan, *v.t.s.*, *irr.* to apply for. ·aanvrager, -s, *n.* applicant.

·aanvullen vul aan, *v.t.s.* to fill up; to replenish; to supplement. ·aanvulling, *n.* replenishment; supplement. ·aanvullingsbegroting, *n.* supplementary estimates. ·aanvullingsexamen, -s, *n.n.* supplementary examination. ·aanvullingskleur, *n.* complementary colour. ·aanvullingstroepen, pl. only, *n.* reserves (*of army*). ·aanvulsel, -s, *n.n.* supplement; padding.

·aanvuren, vuur aan, *v.t.s.* to stimulate, spur on. ·aanvuring, *n.* stimulation.

·aanwaaien, *v.t.s.* & *v.t.s.*, *an.* to be carried (*by wind*). ¶ *v.i.s.*, *irr.* komen ~, to come blowing along (*on wind*).

·aanwaggelen, *v.i.s.* komen ~, to come waddling along.

·aanwakkeren, *v.t.s.* to fan (*flames*); to stir up (*emotions*). ¶ *v.i.s.* to freshen, increase (*of wind*). ·aanwakkering, *n.* stirring up.

·aanwas, -ssen, *n.* growth, increase. ·aanwassen, was aan, *v.i.s.* to grow, increase.

·aanwellen, wel aan, *v.t.s.* to weld on.

·aanwenden, *v.t.s.* to apply, use. *een poging* ~, to make an attempt. ·aan·wendbaar, *a.* applicable. ·aanwending, *n.* application, use.

·aanwennen, wen aan, *v.i.s., imp.* to become bearable. *het went wel aan,* one gets used to it. ¶ *v.t.r.s.* *zich iets* ~, to get used to something. ·aanwensel, -s, *n.n.* acquired habit. *een eigenaardig* ~, a mannerism.

·aanwerven, werf aan, *v.t.s., str.* to recruit. ·aanwerving, *n.* recruitment.

£an·wezend, *a.* present (*not used of time*). aan·wezig, *a.* present (*not used of time*). aan·wezigheid, no pl., *n.* presence.

·aanwijzen, wijs aan, *v.t.s., str.* to point out. *de aangewezen persoon,* the indicated person; *aanwijzend voornaamwoord,* demonstrative pronoun. ·aanwijzer, -s, *n.* indicator. ·aanwijzing, *n.* indication; allocation.

·aanwillen, wil aan, *v.i.s., irr. het wil niet aan,* it will not go on (*of clothes*).

·aanwinnen, win aan, *v.t.s., str.* to gain. *in kracht* ~, to gain in strength. ·aanwinst, *n.* gain, acquisition.

·aanwippen, wip aan, *v.i.s.* ~ *bij,* to drop in on.

·aanwrijven, wrijf aan, *v.t.s., str.* to impute, *iets* ~ *tegen . . .,* to rub something against . . . ¶ *v.i.s., str.* ~ *tegen,* to rub against.

·aanzanden, *v.i.s.* to slit up.

·aanzeggen, zeg aan, *v.t.s., irr.* to announce, notify. *men zou het hem niet* ~, one would not think it of him. ·aanzegger, -s, *n.* undertaker's man. ·aanzegging, *n.* notification.

·aanzeilen, *v.i.s.* ~ *op,* to sail towards; ~ *tegen,* to sail into; *komen* ~, to come sailing along (*of sailing ship*).

·aanzetriem, *n.* (razor-) strop. ·aanzetsel, -s, *n.n.* crust, fur (*adhering to vessel*). ·aanzetstaal, -stalen, *n.n.* steel (*for sharpening*). ·aanzetstuk, -kken, *n.n.* extension. ·aanzetten, zet aan, *v.t.s.* to place (against); to tighten; to sew on (*buttons*); to set ajar; to sharpen, whet; to start (*engine*). ~ *tot,* to urge on to. ¶ *v.i.s.* to adhere (*to vessel*). *komen* ~, to approach; *komen* ~ *met,* to come and bring. ·aanzetwiel, *n.n.* starting-wheel.

·aanzeulen, *v.t.s.* to drag along. ¶ *v.i.s. met iets komen* ~, to come dragging something along.

·aanzicht, *n.n.* aspect. ·aanzien, zie aan, *v.t.s., irr.* to look at; to consider. ~ *voor* or *als,* to take for, to mistake for. ¶ no pl., *n.n. van* ~ *kennen,* to know by sight; *ten* ~ *van,* with regard to; *uit* ~ *van,* in consideration of; *zonder* ~ *des persoons,* irrespective of persons; *een man van* ~, a man of good social position. ·aan-zienlijk, *a.* considerable; prominent. ¶ *adv.* considerably. aan·zienlijkheid, no pl., *n.* importance; distinction.

·aanzijn, no pl., *n.n.* being. *in het* ~ *roepen,* to call into being; *in mijn* ~, in my (*divine*) presence.

·aanzitten, zit aan, *v.i.s., str.* to sit down (*at table*).

·aanzoek, *n.n.* request; offer (*of marriage*), proposal. *op* ~ *van,* at the request of; *een* ~ *afwijzen* or *afslaan,* to turn down a proposal; *een* ~ *ontvangen,* to receive a proposal. ·aanzoeken, *v.t.s., irr.* to request; to propose (*marriage*). ·aanzoeker, -s, *n.* applicant; suitor.

·aanzuiveren, *v.t.s.* to settle (*debt*). ·aanzuivering, *n.* settlement (*of debt*).

·aanzwaaien, *v.i.s. komen* ~, to come swinging along.

·aanzwellen, zwel aan, *v.t.s.* to swell out, belly (*sails*); to increase (*in volume*).

·aanzwemmen, zwem aan, *v.i.s., str. komen* ~, to come swimming along; ~ *op,* to swim towards.

·aanzwepen, zweep aan, *v.t.s.* to urge on.

·aanzweven, zweef aan, *v.i.s. komen* ~, to come floating along.

aap, ·apen, *n.* monkey, ape. *een* ~ *van een jongen,* a young rascal; *de* ~ *kwam uit de mouw,* the truth came out, he let the cat out of the bag; *in den* ~ *gelogeerd zijn,* to be caught. ·aapachtig, *a.* ape-like, apish. ·aapje, -s, *n.n.* (horse-) cab.

aar, ·aren, *n.* ear (*of corn, etc.*).

aard, no pl., *n.* nature, disposition. *vrolijk van* ~, of a jolly disposition; *naar den* ~, of a kind; *van dien* ~ *dat,* such that; *uit den* ~ *der zaak,* by the nature of the thing. ·aarden, *v.i.s.* to thrive; to take to (*dwelling-place*). ~ *naar,* to take after. ·aardig, *a.* nice, pleasant. ~ *vinden,* to appreciate, like. ¶ *adv.* pretty, fairly, nicely. ~ *wat,* quite a lot. ·aardigheid, -heden, *n.* pleasantness; fun, pleasantry. *uit de* ~, *voor de* ~, for fun; *er is geen* ~ *aan,* there is no fun in it; *de* ~ *is er af,* it has lost its attraction; ~ *krijgen in,* to become interested in. ·aardigjes, *adv.* nicely.

·aardappel, -s, *n.* potato. ·aardappelboer, *n.* potato-seller (*greengrocer*). ·aardappelcampagne, -s, *n.* potato-season. ·aardappelkever, -s, *n.* potato-beetle. ·aardappelmeel, no. pl., *n.n.* potato-flour. ·aardappeloogst, *n.* potato-crop. ·aardappelschil, -llen, *n.* potato-peel. ·aardappelstijfsel, no pl., *n.* potato-starch. ·aardappelstroop, no pl., *n.* potato-syrup, potato-treacle. ·aardappelziekte, -n, *n.* potato-blight. ·aardas, no pl., *n.* axis of the earth. ·aardbei, *n.* strawberry. ·aardbeving, *n.* earthquake. ·aardbezie, -ziën, *n.* *See* ·aardbei. ·aardbodem, no pl., *n.* earth's surface; earth. ·aardbol, no pl., *n.* globe (*earth*). ·aardboor, -boren, *n.* auger. ·aarde, no pl., *n.* (the) earth; earth, mould. *ter* ~ *bestellen,* to inter; *ter* ~, on earth, to earth; *in goede* ~ *vallen,* to fall on

good soil. ·aardegoed, no pl., *n.n.* earthenware. ·aarden, *a.* earthen. *een ~ pijp*,
a clay pipe. ·aardewerk, no pl., *n.n,*
earthenware. ·aardewerker, -s, *n.* potter.
·aardewerkfabriek, *n.* pottery (works).
·aardgas, no pl., *n.n.* marsh-gas, fire-
damp. ·aardgoed, no pl., *n.n.* tobacco
leaves (*inferior quality*). ·aardgordel, -s,
n. zone (*of earth*). ·aardhars, *n.n.* bitumen.
·aardhommel, -s, *n.* bumble-bee. aard-
klomp, *n.* clod of earth. ·aardkluit, *n.*
lump of earth. ·aardkorst, no pl., *n.* crust
of the earth. ·aardlaag, -lagen, *n.* layer
(*of earth*). ·aardmagnetisme, no pl., *n.n.*
terrestrial magnetism. ·aardmannetje, *n.n.*
gnome. ·aardmolm, no pl., *n.* & *n.n.*
mould (*earth*). ·aardnoot, -noten, *n.* pignut, peanut. ·aardnootolie, -liën, *n.*
peanut oil. ·aardolie, -liën, *n.* mineral
oil. ·aardoppervlakte, no pl., *n.* surface of
the earth. ·aardpeer, -peren, *n.* Jerusalem
artichoke. ·aardpek, no pl., *n.n.* bitumen.
·aardrijk, no pl., *n.n.* earth, world.
·aardrijkskunde, no pl., *n.* geography.
·aardrijkskundig, *a.* geographical. ·aard-
rijkskundige, -n, *n.* geographer. ·aardrol,
-llen, *n.* (garden) roller. ·aards, *a.* worldly.
·aardsgezind, *a.* worldly-minded. ·aard-
schok, -kken, *n.* earth-tremor. ·aardschors,
no pl., *n.* crust of the earth. ·aardslak,
-kken, *n.* slug. ·aardsoort, *n.* type of soil.
·aardstorting, *n.* land-fall. ·aardvarken,
-s, *n.n.* aardvark ·aardverschuiving, *n.*
land-slide. ·aardwerker, -s, *n.* navvy.
aars, ·aarzen, *n.* arse.
aarts-, *prefix.* arch- (*extreme-ly*). *as in:*
aartsvijand, *n.* arch-enemy; *aartsdom, a.*
excessively stupid. ·aartsbisdom, -mmen,
n.n. archbishopric. ·aartsbisschop, -ppen,
n. archbishop. ·aartsbisschoppelijk, *a.*
archiepiscopal. ·aartsdeken, -en, *n.* arch-
deacon. ·aartsengel, -s, *n.* archangel.
·aartshertog, *n.* archduke. ·aartshertogdom,
-mmen, *n.n.* archduchy. ·aartshertogin,
-nnen, *n.* archduchess. ·aartskanselier, -s,
n. archchancellor (*of Papal Court*).
·aartspriester, -s, *n.* archpriest. ·aarts-
vader, -s, *n.* patriarch.
·aarzelen, *v.i.* to waver, hesitate. ·aarzeling,
n. hesitation.
aas, ·azen, *n.* ace (*playing-cards*). ¶ no pl.,
n.n. bait; carrion. ·aasgier, *n.* vulture.
·aaskever, -s, *n.* carrion-beetle. ·aasvlieg,
n. bluebottle.
ab·ces, -ssen, *n.n.* abscess.
ab·dij, *n.* abbey. **ab·dis**, -ssen, *n.* abbess.
a·beel, -belen, *n.* (*type of*) poplar.
abnor·maal, *a.* abnormal. ¶ *adv.* abnormally.
·abnormali·teit, *n.* abnormality.
abon·né, -'s, *n.* subscriber; ticket-holder.
·abonne·ment, *n.n.* subscription; season-
ticket. *een ~ nemen op* or *voor*, to take
out a season-ticket for. ·abon·neren,
-nneer, *v.r. zich ~ op*, to subscribe to.

·**Abraham**, *proper name. in ~s schoot*, in
Abraham's bosom.
abri·koos, -kozen, *n.* apricot. ·abri·kozeboom,
-bomen, *n.* apricot-tree. ·abri·kozepit,
-tten, *n.* apricot-stone. ·abri·kozengelei,
no pl., *n.* apricot jam.
·**Absalon**, *proper name.* Absalom.
ab·sent, *a.* absent. ·absen·teren, zich, -teer,
v.r. to absent oneself. ·ab·sentie, -s, *n,*
absence. ·ab·sentielijst, *n.* attendance
register.
abso·lutie, -tiën, *n.* absolution.
absolu·tisme, no pl., *n.n.* absolutism.
abso·luut, -lute, *a.* absolute. ¶ *adv.*
absolutely. *~ niet*, not at all: by no
means; *~ niets*, nothing at all.
absor·beren, -beer, *v.t.* to absorb. ·ab·sorptie,
n. absorption. ·ab·sorptievermogen, no
pl., *n.n.* absorptive power.
ab·stract, *a.* abstract; distrait. ·ab·stractie.
n. abstraction. ·abstra·heren. -heer, *v.t.*
to abstract.
abt, *n.* abbot.
a·buis, -uizen, *n.n.* error. *per* or *bij ~*, by
mistake; *~ hebben*, to be mistaken.
abu·sief, -ieve, *a.* erroneous. ·abu·sievelijk,
adv. erroneously.
a·cacia, -'s, *n.* acacia.
aca·demie, -miën or -mies, *n.* academy;
university. *op de ~*, at college. ·aca-
·demici, pl. only, *n.* university people.
·aca·demiestad, -steden, *n.* university town.
·aca·demisch, *a.* academical. *~e graad,*
academic degree. ¶ *adv.* academically.
~ gevormd, academically trained.
ac·cent, *n.n.* accent. ·accentu·atie, -s, *n.*
accentuation. ·accentu·eren. -tueer, *v.t.*
to accent.
ac·cept, *n.n.* acceptance (*of bill*). ·accep·tant,
n. acceptor. ·accep·tatie, -s, *n.* acceptation
(*of bill*). ·accep·teren, -teer, *v.t.* to accept,
put up with; to accept (*of bill*). *niet ~*.
to refuse, dishonour (*bill*).
ac·cijns, -nzen, *n.* excise. ·ac·cijnsplichtig.
a. excisable.
accla·matie, -s, *n.* acclamation. *bij ~*. with
acclamation.
acclimati·satie, no pl., *n.* acclimatization.
·acclimati·seren, -seer, *v.t.* & *v.i.* to
acclimatize. ¶ *v.r. zich ~*. to acclimatize
(oneself).
acco·lade, -s, *n.* accolade; bracket ({or}).
accomo·datie, no pl., *n.* accommodation (*to
circumstances*). ·accomo·datievermogen. no
pl., *n.n.* power of accommodation.
accompag·neren, -gneer, *v.t.* to accompany
(*on musical instrument*). ·accompagne·ment.
n. accompaniment.
ac·countant, *n.* accountant.
accredi·teren, -teer, *v.t.* to accredit (*ambassador*); to credit (*account*).
·**accu**, -'s, *n.* accumulator. ·accumu·lator, -s
or -toren, *n.* accumulator.
accu·raat, -rate, *a.* accurate. ¶ *adv.*

accurately. **accura·tesse,** no pl., *n.* accuracy.

acety·leen, no pl., *n.n.* acetylene.

ach!, *int.* Oh! (*surprise* or *commiseration*).

A·chilleshiel, *n.* the heel of Achilles. **A·chillespees, -pezen,** *n.* the tendon of Achilles.

acht, *num.* eight. *in een dag of ~,* in seven or eight days' time; *vandaag over ~ dagen,* to-day week. ¶ *n.* eight. **·achtdaags,** *a.* eightfold. **·achtdubbel,** *a.* eightfold. **·achten,** *num.* met ons ~, the eight of us; *met zijn ~,* with seven others; *met hun ~,* the eight of them; *de trein van ~,* the eight o'clock train; *bij ~,* just on eight; *in ~,* into eight. **·achtentwintig,** *num.* twenty-eight. **·achtendertig,** *num.* thirty-eight.

acht, no pl., *n.* attention, care. *~ geven* or *slaan op,* to pay attention to; *Geef ~!,* Attention!; *in ~ nemen,* to observe (*rules*); *zich in ~ nemen,* to take care of oneself; *zich in ~ nemen voor,* to beware of. **·achtbaar, -bare,** *a.* estimable; honourable. **·achtbaarheid,** no pl., *n.* respectability. **·achteloos, -loze,** *a.* careless, negligent. ¶ *adv.* carelessly, negligently. **·achteloosheid, -heden,** *n.* carelessness, negligence. **·achten,** *v.t.* to esteem; to pay attention to; to deem. ¶ *v.r. zich gelukkig ~,* to consider oneself fortunate. **achtens·waard,** *a.* estimable. **achtens·waardig,** *a.* estimable. **·achter,** *pr.* behind; at the back; after. *naar ~,* to the back, backward; *naar ~ gaan,* to go to the lavatory; *ten ~,* behindhand; *van ~,* at the back; *ik ben er ~,* I have found out about it; *~ op,* at or on the back. ¶ *adv.* behind, behindhand. *de klok is* or *loopt ~,* the clock is slow; *ten ~ zijn bij* or *met,* to be behindhand with.

achter·aan, *adv.* at the back. **achter·aanblijven, blijf achteraan,** *v.i.s., str.* to remain at the back. **achter·aankomen, kom achteraan,** *v.i.s., irr.* to lag behind.

achter·af, *adv.* towards the back; later. *~ bekeken,* looked at now; *~ ben ik blij,* now it is over, I am glad about it.

achter·baks, *a.* clandestine. ¶ *adv.* hidden. *iets ~ houden,* to keep something back; *zich ~ houden,* to keep oneself out of sight.

·achterbalkon, -s, *n.n.* rear-platform (*train, tram*); rear-balcony. **·achterband,** *n.* back-tyre. **·achterblijven, blijf achter,** *v.i.s., str.* to stay behind. *de achtergeblevenen,* the survivors. **·achterblijver, -s,** *n.* straggler. **·achterbout,** *n.* hind-quarter (*beef*). **·achterbuur, -buren,** *n.* neighbour at the back. **·achterbuurman, -buren,** *n.* neighbour at the back. **·achterbuurt,** *n.* slum. **·achterdek, -kken,** *n.n.* after-deck. **·achterdeur,** *n.* back door. *een ~tje openhouden,* to leave a loophole. **·achterdocht,** no pl., *n.* suspicion. *~ hebben* or *koesteren,* to nurse

suspicions; *~ krijgen* or *opvatten,* to become suspicious; *~ (op)wekken,* to rouse suspicion. **achter·dochtig,** *a.* suspicious. **achter·dochtigheid,** no pl., *n.* suspiciousness.

achter·een, *adv.* consecutively; at a stretch. *driemaal ~,* three times running. **achtereen·volgend,** *a.* successive. **achtereen·volgens,** *adv.* successively.

·achtereind(e), -(e)n, *n.n.* back part.

achterel·kaar, *adv.* one after another.

·achteren, *pr.* naar ~, backward; *ten ~,* behindhand; *van ~,* at the back. *also see* **·achter.**

·achtererf, -rven, *n.n.* back yard (*of farm*). **·achtergaan, ga achter,** *v.i.s., irr.* to lose, be slow (*clock*). **·achtergalerij.** *n.* back verandah. **·achtergevel, -s,** *n.* back (*of house*). **·achtergrond,** *n.* background. *op de ~ raken,* to fall into the background. **achter·halen, -haal,** *v.t.* to overtake. **·achterhand,** *n.* hind quarters (*horse*). **achter·heen,** *adv.* behind. *ergens ~ zitten,* to hurry something up. **·achterhoede, -n.** *n.* rear, rearguard. **·achterhoofd,** *n.n.* back of the head, occiput. **·achterhouden,** *v.t.s., irr.* to keep back. **achter·houdend,** *a.* secretive. **achter·houdendheid,** no pl., *n.* secretiveness. **·achterhouding,** no pl., *n.* keeping back, withholding. **·achterhuis, -uizen,** *n.n.* back premises. **achter·in,** *adv.* at the back, in the back.

·achterkamer, -s, *n.* back room. **·achterkant,** *n.* back. **·achterklap,** no pl., *n.* slander, backbiting. **·achterkleindochter, -s,** *n.* great-granddaughter. **·achterkleinkind, -deren,** *n.n.* great-grandchild. **·achterkleinzoon, -s,** *n.* great-grandson. **·achterlaadgeweer, -weren,** *n.n.* breech-loader. **·achterland,** *n.n.* hinterland; interior. **·achterlap, -ppen,** *n.* heel-piece. **·achterlaten, laat achter,** *v.t.s., str.* to leave behind. **·achterlating,** no pl., *n. met ~ van,* with loss of, leaving behind. **·achterlicht,** *n.n.* rear-light. **·achterliggen, lig achter,** *v.i.s., str. ~ bij,* to lie behind, follow after. **·achterlijf, -ven,** *n.n.* hind part; abdomen (*insect*). **·achterlijk,** *a.* backward. *school voor ~en,* school for mental defectives; *~ met,* in arrears with. **achter·middag, -en,** *n.* afternoon.

achter·na, *adv.* afterwards; behind. ¶ *prefix.* after. **achter·nalopen, loop achterna,** *v.t.s., str.* to run after. **achter·nazitten, zit achterna,** *v.t.s., str.* to pursue.

·achterneef, -neven, *n.* second cousin, distant cousin (*male*). **·achternicht,** *n.* second cousin, distant cousin (*female*).

achter·om, *adv.* round the back.

achter·op, *adv.* at or on the back; in arrears. **achter·opkomen, kom achterop,** *v.i.s., irr.* to catch up with. **achter·oplopen,** loop **achterop,** *v.t.s., str.* to catch up with.

achter·over, *adv.* backward. **achter·overdrukken, druk achterover,** *v.t.s.* to press backward; to knock off, steal. achter·overleunen, *v.i.s.* to lean back. achter·overvallen, val achterover, *v.i.s., str.* to fall backwards. achter·overwippen, wip achterover, *v.t.s.* to tilt back (*chair*). ·achterplaats, *n.* back yard. ·achterplecht, *n.* stern (*of small craft*). ·achterpoort, *n.* back gate. ·achterpoot, -poten, *n.* hind leg. ·achterruim, *n.n.* after-hold. ·achter·schip, -schepen, *n.n.* stern (*ship*). ·achterst, *a.* hindmost. ·achterstaan, sta achter, *v.i.s., irr.* ~ *bij,* to lag behind; to be inferior to. ·achterstaand, *a.* following; below. ·achterstal, -llen, *n.n.* arrears. achter·stallig, *a.* outstanding, overdue. ·achterstand, *n.* arrears. ·achterste, *n.n.* back part; backside, posterior. ·achter·stellen, stel achter, *v.t.s.* to neglect. ~ *bij,* to neglect for. ·achterstelling, no pl., *n.* met ~ *van,* to the neglect of. ·achtersteven, -s, *n.* stern (*ship*). achterste·voren, *adv.* back to front. ·achterstraat, -straten, *n.* back street.

achter·uit, *adv.* backward(s); retrograde; astern. ~!, stand back! ¶ *n.n.* back yard. ¶ *prefix* backward. achter·uitboeren, *v.i.s.* to go downhill (*business, etc.*). achter·uitdeinzen, deins achteruit, *v.i.s.* to stagger back. achter·uitgaan, ga achteruit, *v.i.s., irr.* to go backwards; to become worse. achter·uitgang, no pl., *n.* deterioration. achter·uitkrabbelen, *v.i.s.* to back out (of).

·achtervoegen, *v.t.s.* to affix, add. ·achter·voeging, *n.* addition. ·achtervoegsel, -s, *n.n.* suffix. achter·volgen, *v.t.* to pursue. achter·volgens, *adv.* successively. achter·volging, *n.* pursuit. ·achterwaarts, *a.* backward. ¶ *adv.* backward(s). achter·wege, *adv.* ~ *blijven,* to fail to appear; ~ *houden,* to keep back; ~ *laten,* to leave out. ·achterwerk, *n.n.* posterior. ·achterwiel, *n.n.* back wheel. ·achterzak, -kken, *n.* stern pocket. ·achterzetten, zet achter, *v.t.s.* to put back (*clock*). ·achthoek, *n.* octagon. ·achthoekig, *a.* octagonal.

·achting, no pl., *n.* esteem. ~ *hebben voor iemand,* to esteem someone; *iemand* ~ *toedragen,* to esteem someone; *de* ~ *genieten van,* to enjoy the esteem of; *in iemands* ~ *stijgen (dalen),* to rise (to sink) in someone's esteem.

achtjarig, *a.* eight years old. ·achtkantig, *a.* octagonal. ·achtpotig, *a.* eight-legged. ·achtpuntig, *a.* eight-pointed. ·achtregelig, *a.* of eight lines. ·achtste, *a.* eighth. ¶ -n, *n.* the eighth. ¶ -n, *n.n.* eighth part. ·achttal, -llen, *n.n.* about eight. ·achttien, *num.* eighteen. acht·urendag, -en, *n.* eight hour day. ·achturig, *a.* of eight hours. ·achtvlak, -kken, *n.n.* octahedron. ·achtvlakkig, *a.* octahedral. ·achtvoetig, *a.* of eight feet. ·achtvoud, *n.n.* eightfold.

·achtzaam, -zame, *a.* careful. ¶ *adv.* carefully. ·achtzaamheid, no pl., *n.* attention. ·achtzijdig, *a.* eight-sided.

acous·tiek, no pl., *n.* acoustics. ac·quit, no pl., *n.n.* spot (*billiards*); receipt. ~ *geven,* to start off (*in billiards*). acquit·teren, -tteer, *v.t.* to receipt.

acro·baat, -baten, *n.* acrobat. acroba·tiek, no pl., *n.* acrobatics. acro·batisch, *a.* acrobatic.

·acte. See akte.

ac·teren, -teer, *v.i. & v.t.* to act. ac·teur, -s, *n.* actor.

·actie, -s, or -tiën, *n.* share (*security*); lawsuit; campaign. *een* ~ *instellen tegen,* to bring an action against; ~ *voeren voor,* to agitate for. ac·tief, -ve, *a.* active. *in actieve dienst,* on active service; *op non-*~ *stellen,* to place on the retired list. ¶ *actieven* or *activa, n.n.* assets.

acti·vist, *n.* pro-German Flemish nationalist (*1st World War*). activi·teit, *n.* activity.

actio·naris, -ssen, *n.* shareholder.

ac·trice, -s, *n.* actress.

actu·aris, -ssen, *n.* actuary. actuali·teit, *n.* topicality. actu·eel, -ele, *a.* topical; real.

a·cuut, -cute, *a.* acute (*illness*).

·Adamsappel, -s, *n.* Adam's apple. ·Adams·kostuum, no pl., *n.n. in* ~, in (one's) birthday suit.

·adat, no pl., *n.* native customary law (*East Indies*).

·adder, -s, *n.* viper, adder. *een* ~ *aan zijn borst* (or *in den boezem*) *koesteren,* to cherish a viper in one's bosom; *er schuilt een* ~ *in* (or *onder*) *het gras,* there is a snake lurking in the grass. ·adderbeet, -beten, *n.* sting of a viper. ·adderengebroed, no pl., *n.n.* brood of vipers. ·addergif, no pl., *n.n.* adder's venom. ·adderwortel, -s, *n.* adder's wort.

additio·neel, -nele, *a.* additional.

·adel, no pl., *n.* nobility (*aristocracy*); nobility. *van* ~ *zijn,* to belong to the nobility. ·adelborst, *n.* midshipman. ·adelbrief, -ven, *n.* patent of nobility. ·adelen, *v.t.* to ennoble. ·adellijk, *a.* noble. ·adelstand, no pl., *n.* nobility. *tot de* ~ *verheffen,* to raise to the nobility.

·adelaar, -s, *n.* eagle. ·adelaarsblik, -kken, *n.* eagle eye. ·adelaarsvaren, -s, *n.* bracken.

·adem, no pl., *n.* breath. ~ *scheppen,* to take a breath; *de* ~ *inhouden,* to hold one's breath; *de* ~ *uitblazen,* to expire (*die*); *buiten* ~, out of breath; *in één* ~, in the same breath; *met ingehouden* ~, with bated breath; *naar* ~ *snakken,* to gasp for breath; *op* ~ *komen,* to recover one's breath; *van langen* ~, long-winded. ·ademen, *v.i. & v.t.* to breathe. ·adem·halen, haal adem, *v.i.s.* to breathe, draw breath. ·ademhaling, *n.* breathing.

·ademhalingswerktuigen, pl. only, *n.n.* respiratory organs. ·ademloos, -loze, *a.* breathless. ¶ *adv.* breathlessly. ·ademtocht, no pl., *n.* breath (*poetical*). *tot den laatsten* ~, unto death.

·ader, -s & -en, *n.* vein; seam (*ore*); grain (*marble*). ·aderbreuk, *n.* rupture (*bloodvessel*). ·aderlaten, laat ader, *v.t.s.*, *str.* to bleed, let blood. ·aderlating, *n.* bleeding, blood-letting. ·aderlijk, *n.* venous. ·aderspat, -tten, *n.* varix. ·aderverkalking, no pl., *n.* arterio-sclerosis.

ad·hesie, *n.* adhesion. ~ *betuigen met.* to give in one's adhesion.

adi·pati, *n.* (*East Indian native title*).

adju·dant, *n.* adjutant. adju·dant-·onderofficier, *n.* warrant officer.

ad·junct, *n.* adjunct, assistant.

administra·teur, -s & -en, *n.* administrator, manager; director. adminis·tratie, -s, *n.* administration. administra·tief, -ve, *a.* administrative. ¶ *adv.* administratively. adminis·tratiekantoor, -toren, *n.n.* offices of the administration. adminis·tratiekosten, pl. only, *n.* administrative costs. adminis·treren, -treer, *v.t.* to administer; to manage.

admi·raal, -s or -ralen, *n.* admiral. admi·raalschap, no pl., *n.n.* admiralship. admi·raalsschip, -schepen, *n.n.* flag-ship. admi·raalsvlag, -ggen, *n.* admiral's flag. admi·raalvlinder, -s, *n.* red or white admiral (*butterfly*). admirali·teit, *n.* admiralty.

ad·missie, no pl., *n.* admission. ad·missieexamen, -s, *n.n.* entrance examination.

a·dres, -ssen, *n.n.* address (*postal*); memorial, petition. *een* ~ *richten tot*, to petition, memorialize; *per* ~, care of; *dat is aan zijn* ~, that is meant for him; *U bent aan het verkeerde* ~, it is no good asking me. a·dresboek, *n.n.* directory; a·dreskaart, *n.* business card. a·dreskantoor, -toren, *n.n.* inquiry office. adres·sant, *n.* petitioner, applicant. adres·seermachine, -s, *n.* addressograph. adres·seren, -seer, *v.t.* to address (*letter*). ¶ *v.r.* zich ~ *aan*, to apply to.

adspi·rant. See aspi·rant.

ad·vent, *n.* advent (*season before the Nativity*). adver·teren, -teer, *v.t.* to advertise. adver·tentie, -s, *n.* advertisement. *een* ~ *plaatsen*, to insert an advertisement; *op een* ~ *schrijven*, to answer an advertisement. adver·tentieblad, -bladen, *n.n.* advertiser (*newspaper*). adver·tentiebureau, -'s, *n.n.* advertising office. adver·tentiekosten, pl. only, *n.* cost of advertising.

ad·vies, -zen, *n.n.* advice. *van* ~ *dienen*, to advise; ~ *geven*, to give advice; ~ *inwinnen*, to consult; *van* ~ *zijn*, to be of the opinion; *per* or *volgens* ~, as per advice. ad·viesbrief, -ven, *n.* letter of advice. advi·seren, -seer, *v.t.* to advise.

advi·serend, *a.* advisory. *een* ~*e* ㅅ *m*, a consultative power. advi·seur, -s, *n.* adviser; counsel.

advo·caat, -caten, *n.* barrister, lawyer; egg and brandy. *een* ~ *van kwade zaken*, a shady lawyer. advo·caat-gene·raal, advocaten-generaal, *n.* solicitor-general. advo·catenkantoor, -toren, *n.n.* solicitor's office. advo·catenstreek, -streken. *n.* lawyer's trick.

·aether. See ·ether.

af, *adv.* off; down. ~ *en aan* or ~ *en toe*, off and on; *op de minuut* ~, to the minute. ¶ *a.* off; finished. ¶ *prefix* off. ¶ *suffix* on, onward. See vanaf.

·afbakenen, *v.t.s.* to beacon; to mark out.
·afbedelen, *v.t.s.* to obtain by begging.
·afbeelden, *v.t.s.* to depict, portray. ·afbeelding, *n.* image, representation.
·afbellen, bel af, *v.i.s.* to ring off.
·afbestellen, bestel af, *v.t.s.* to call off, countermand.
·afbetalen, betaal af, *v.t.s.* to pay off. ·afbetaling, *n.* payment. *op* ~ *kopen*, to buy on the instalment plan, buy on hire purchase; ~ *bij termijnen*, payment in instalments.
·afbeulen, *v.t.s.* to work to death. ¶ *v.r.s.* zich ~, to work oneself to death.
·afbidden, bid af, *v.t.s.*, *str.* to obtain by prayer. ·afbijten, *v.t.s.*, *str.* to bite off.
·afbikken, bik af, *v.t.s.* to chisel off.
·afbinden, *v.t.s.*, *str.* to untie; to ligature.
·afbladderen, *v.i.s.* to peel (off) (*paint*).
·afblazen, blaas af, *v.t.s.*, *str.* to blow off.
·afblijven, blijf af, *v.i.s.*, *str.* ~ *van.* to keep off.
·afborstelen, *v.t.s.* to brush off.
·afbraak, no pl., *n.* rubbish, rubble (*demolition*). *voor* ~ *verkopen*, to sell for demolition.
·afbranden, *v.t.s.* to burn off, burn down. ¶ *v.i.s.* to be burnt down.
·afbreken, breek af, *v.t.s.*, *str.* to break off; to interrupt; to pull down (*house*); to demolish (*argument*). ¶ *v.i.s.*, *str.* to break off. ·afbreker, -s, *n.* housebreaker. ·afbreking, *n.* breaking off. ·afbrekingsteken, -s, *n.n.* dash (—).
·afbrengen, *v.t.s.*, *str.* to get off, float (*ship*); to manage. *het er goed* ~, to manage all right; *hij is er niet van af te brengen*, he will not give up his idea; *van de goede weg* ~, to lead astray.
·afbreuk, no pl., *n.* ~ *doen aan*, to damage, be detrimental to.
·afbrokkelen, *v.i.s.* to crumble off. ·afbrokkeling, *n.* crumbling off; erosion.
·afdak, -daken, *n.n.* shed, lean-to. ·afdalen, daal af, *v.i.s.* to descend. ~ *tot*, to descend to; *in bizonderheden* ~, to go into particulars; *een afdalende reeks*, a descending progression. ¶ *v.t.s.* to descend, go down.

·afdammen, dam af, *v.t.s.* to dam up. ·afdamming, *n.* damming up.

·afdanken, *v.t.s.* to dismiss; to cast off (*clothes*).

·afdeinzen, deins af, *v.i.s.* to fall back, withdraw. ·afdekken, dek af, *v.t.s.* to uncover; to cope (*wall*). ¶ *v.i.s.* to clear the table.

·afdelen, deel af, *v.t.s.* to divide, classify. ·afdeling, *n.* part, section; division, unit (*army*); department. ·afdelingschef, -s, *n.* departmental head.

·afdingen, *v.t.s.*, *str.* to beat down, haggle, bargain. ~ *op de prijs*, to beat down the price; ~ *op iemands verdiensten*, to disparage a person's merits. ¶ *v.t.s.* to beat down, reduce (*price*).

·afdoen, doe af, *v.t.s.*, *irr.* to take off (*clothes*); to remove; to dust; to dispatch (*business*); to settle (*debt*). *afgedaan hebben*, to be finished with, to be out of favour, *or* out of date. af·doend, *a.* conclusive; effective. ·afdoening, *n.* payment. *ter* or *tot* ~ *van*, in settlement of.

·afdokken, dok af, *v.t.s.* to dock (*money*). ·afdonderen, *v.t.s.* to chuck down. ¶ *v.i.s.* to fall down.

·afdraaien, *v.t.s.* to turn off; to twist off; to play (*record*); to show, run through (*film*); to rattle off. ·afdragen, draag af, *v.t.s.*, *str.* to carry down; to wear out; to hand over (*money*). ·afdraven, droaf af, *v.t.s.* to trot down (*road*).

·afdreggen, dreg af, *v.t.s.* to drag (*river, canal*).

·afdreigen, *v.t.s.* to extort. ·afdreiging, *n.* extortion.

·afdrijven, drijf af, *v.i.s.*, *str.* to drift (off), drift down. ¶ *v.t.s.*, *str.* to expel, abort; to refine.

·afdrogen, droog af, *v.t.s.* to dry, wipe.

·afdruipen, *v.i.s.*, *str.* to drip down; to slink off.

·afdruk, -kken, *n.* print; imprint. ·afdrukken, druk af, *v.t.s.* to print. ·afdruksel, -s, *n.n.* impression (*on surface*).

·afdruppelen, *v.i.s.* to trickle down.

·afduwen, *v.t.s.* to push off.

·afdwalen, dwaal af, *v.i.s.* to wander. ~ *van*, to stray ·rom. ·afdwaling, *n.* digression.

·afdwingen, *v.t.s.*, *str.* to extort; to command (*respect*).

·afexerceren, exerceer af, *v.t.s.* to train (*soldiers*).

af·faire, -s, *n.* affair; business.

affec·tatie, -s, *n.* affectation.

·affletsen, *v.i.s.* to cycle down.

affi·neren, -neer, *v.t.s.* to refine (*precious metals*). affini·teit, *n.* affinity.

af·freus, -ze, *a.* awful. ¶ *adv.* awfully.

af·front, *n.n.* affront. affron·teren, -teer, *v.t.s.* to affront.

af·fuit, *n.n.* gun carriage.

·afgaan, ga af, *v.t.s.*, *irr.* to go down to

ebb. *het afgaand getij*, the ebb. ¶ *v.i.s.*, *irr.* to go off (*firearms*); to defecate; to remit (*fever*). ~ *van*, to go away from; ~ *op*, to go towards, to rely on; *afgaand op*, relying on.

·afge-. *See verbs in af-*.

·afgeknot, -tte, *a.* truncated.

·afgelasten, *v.t.s.* to countermand.

·afgeleefd, *a.* decrepit.

·afgelegen, *a.* remote. afge·legenheid, no pl., *n.* remoteness.

·afgelopen, *a.* past. ¶ *int.* ~!, all over!

·afgemat, -tte, *a.* exhausted.

·afgemeten, *a.* measured. *op* ~ *toon*, in formal tones. ¶ *adv.* formally. afge·metenheid, no pl., *n.* ~ *van toon*, formality.

·afgepast, *a.* exact, precise. ~ *geld*, the exact amount. afge·pastheid, no pl., *n.* precision.

·afgeplat, -tte, *a.* flattened (*at top*).

·afgericht, *a.* trained. ·afgerond, *a.* rounded off.

·afgescheiden, *a.* separate. ¶ *adv.* separately. ~ *van*, apart from. afge·scheidene, -n, *n.* member of a special Dutch Protestant community.

·afgesloofd, *a.* worn out (*of person*).

·afgesloten, *a.* shut off, closed. *een* ~ *geheel*, an entity. afge·slotenheid, no pl., *n.* inaccessibility.

·afgestorven, *a.* dead. afge·storvene, -n, *n.* deceased.

·afgetobd, *a.* careworn.

·afgetrokken, *a.* absent-minded, distrait; abstract. ¶ *adv.* absent-mindedly. afge·trokkenheid, no pl., *n.* abstracted look.

afge·vaardigde, -n, *n.* delegate; representative. *Huis van Afgevaardigden*, Parliament.

·afgeven, geef af, *v.t.s.*, *str.* to give off; to deliver (*message*); to hand over. *een wissel* ~ *op*, to draw a bill on. ¶ *v.i.s.*, *str.* to run (*colour*). ~ *op*, to run down. ¶ *v.r.*, *str. zich* ~ *met*, to become connected with (*unfavourably*).

·afgezaagd, *a.* hackneyed, stale. afgezant, *n.* ambassador; messenger. afgezien, *adv.* ~ *van*, apart from. ·afgezonderd, *a.* secluded. ¶ *adv.* in seclusion. ~ *van*, separate from.

·afgieten, *v.t.s.*, *str.* to pour off; to drain; to cast (*in mould*). ·afgietsel, -s, *n.n.* cast (*in mould*). ·afgietseldiertje, -s, *n.n.* infusoria (*pl. only*).

·afgifte, no pl., *n.* delivery. *dag van* ~, day of issue.

·afglijden, *v.i.s.*, *str.* to glide off. afglippen, glip af, *v.i.s.* to slip off.

·afgod, -goden, *n.* false god (*idol*). afgodendienaar, -s *or* -en, *n.* idolater. afgodendienares, -ssen, *n.* idolatress. afgodentempel, -s, *n.* heathen temple. afgode·rij,

-en, *n.* idolatry. **af·godisch**, *a.* idolatrous. ·**afgodsbeeld**, *n.n.* idol (*image*).
·**afgooien**, *v.t.s.* to throw off.
·**afgraven**, **graaf af**, *v.t.s.*, *str.* to dig away; to level. ·**afgrazen**, **graas af**, *v.t.s.* to graze, crop.
af·grijselijk, *a.* horrible. ¶ *adv.* horribly. ·**afgrijzen**, no pl., *n.n.* horror. *met ~,* with horror; *met ~ vervuld,* horror-struck; *een ~ hebben van,* to abhor.
·**afgrissen**, **gris af**, *v.t.s.* to snatch away from.
·**afgrond**, *n.* abyss, precipice; gulf (*figurative*). *in de ~ storten,* to ruin.
·**afgunst**, no pl., *n.* envy. **af·gunstig**, *a.* envious. *~ op,* envious of. ¶ *adv.* enviously.
·**afhaken**, **haak af**, *v.t.s.* to unhook. ·**afhakken**, **hak af**, *v.t.s.* to hack off; to cut up (*carcase*). ·**afhalen**, **haal af**, *v.t.s.* to collect; to meet (*train, etc.*); to take down; to take away from; to string (*beans*). *iemand van de trein ~,* to meet someone at the station; *het bed ~,* to strip the bed.
·**afhandelen**, *v.t.s.* to dispatch (*business*). ·**afhandeling**, *n.* dispatch (*of business*).
af·handig, *a. iemand iets ~ maken,* to trick a person out of something.
·**afhangen**, *v.i.s.*, *str.* to hang down. *~ van,* to depend on. ¶ *v.t.s.* to take down, unsling.
af·hankelijk, *a.* dependent. *~ van,* dependent on. **af·hankelijkheid**, no pl., *n.* dependence. *~ van,* dependence on.
·**afhaspelen**, *v.t.s.* to reel off, wind off.
·**afhebben**, **heb af**, *v.t.s.*, *irr.* to have finished.
·**afhechten**, *v.t.s.* to cast off (*knitting*).
·**afhellen**, **hel af**, *v.i.s.* to slope. ·**afhelling**, *n.* slope.
·**afhelpen**, *v.t.s.*, *str.* to help off. *iemand ~ van,* to rid someone of.
·**afhoeven**, **hoef af**, *v.t.s. niet ~,* not having to be taken off; *hoeft het deksel af?* need the lid be taken off? ·**afhollen**, **hol af**, *v.t.s.* to rush down. ·**afhoren**, **hoor af**, *v.t.s.* to overhear; to hear (*lesson*). ·**afhouden**, *v.t.s.*, *irr.* to keep off; to deduct. *de handen van iets ~,* to keep one's hands. off something; *een hond van zich ~,* to keep a dog at bay; *van het werk ~,* to keep from work. ¶ *v.i.s.*, *irr. ~ van,* to stand off (*shore*), to keep clear of; *rechts ~,* to turn to the right. ·**afhouwen**, *v.t.s.*, *str.* to hew off.
·**afhuren**, **huur af**, *v.t.s.* to hire.
·**afjagen**, **jaag af**, *v.t.s.*, *irr.* to over-tire (*horse*); to cover (*field during shoot*). *~ van,* to chase away from. ·**afjakkeren**, *v.t.s.* to over-tire (*horse*); to overwork. ¶ *v.r.s. zich ~,* to exhaust oneself (*by working in haste*).
·**afkalven**, **kalf af**, *v.i.s.* to crumble away (*bank, glacier*). ·**afkalving**, *n.* crumbling off.
·**afkammen**, **kam af**, *v.t.s.* to comb (*off*); to run down.

·**afkantelen**, *v.t.s., ~ van,* to ease off (*over edge*). ¶ *v.i.s.* to topple off. ·**afkanten**, *v.t.s.* to bevel off.
·**afkapen**, **kaap af**, *v.t.s., ~ van,* to pinch (from).
·**afkappen**, **kap af**, *v.t.s.* to cut off (*with chopper*). ·**afkapping**, *n.* cutting off. ·**afkappingsteken**, -s, *n.n.* apostrophe.
·**afkeer**, no pl., *n.* aversion, dislike. *~ hebben van,* to dislike; *~ inboezemen,* to inspire dislike; *~ krijgen van,* to get to dislike; *~ verwekken,* to cause aversion. ·**afkeren**, **keer af**, *v.t.s.* to turn away; to avert. ¶ *v.r.s. zich ~ van,* to turn away from. **af·kerig** *a.* averse. *~ van,* averse to. **af·kerigheid**, no pl., *n.* aversion.
·**afketsen**, *v.i.s.* to glance off. ¶ *v.t.s.* to reject (*plan*).
·**afkeuren**, *v.t.s.* to reject (*as unfit*); to disapprove of. *voor den dienst ~,* to reject for military service. ·**afkeurenswaardig**, *a.* reprehensible. ·**afkeuring**, *n.* rejection; disapprobation.
·**afkijken**, *v.i.s.*, *str.* to copy (*cheat*). ¶ *v.t.s.*, *str.* to look down (*street*). *iemand de kunst ~,* to learn by watching someone else work.
·**afklaren**, **klaar af**, *v.t.s.* to clarify (*liquid*). ·**afklauteren**, *v.t.s.* to clamber down. ·**afklemmen**, **klem af**, *v.t.s.* to pinch off. ·**afklimmen**, **klim af**, *v.t.s.*, *str.* to climb down. *~ langs,* to climb down by way of; *~ van,* to climb down from; *een berg ~,* to climb down a mountain. ·**afkloppen**, **klop af**, *v.t.s.* to beat (*for dust*); to touch wood (*superstition*). ·**afkluiven**, **kluif af**, *v.t.s.* to gnaw, pick.
·**afknabbelen**, *v.t.s.,irr.* to nibble off. ·**afknagen**, **knaag af**, *v.t.s.* to gnaw off. ·**afknappen**, **knap af**, *v.i.s.* to snap off. ·**afknellen**, **knel af**, *v.t.s.* to pinch off. ·**afknevelen**, *v.t.s.* to extort (from). ·**afknijpen**, *v.t.s.*, *str.* to pinch off.
·**afknippen**, *v.t.s.* to cut off (*with scissors*). ·**afknipsel**, -s, *n.n.* cuttings (*waste*), parings.
·**afknotten**, **knot af**, *v.t.s.* to poll (*tree*); to truncate.
·**afkoelen**, *v.i.s. & v.t.s.* to cool (down, off). ·**afkoeling**, no pl., *n.* cooling off.
·**afkoken**, **kook af**, *v.t.s.* to decoct; to boil thoroughly, boil to mash.
·**afkomen**, *v.t.s.*, *irr.* to come down (*stairs*). ¶ *v.i.s.*, *irr.* to go down (*stairs, road*); to get rid of. *er goed ~,* to come off well; *~ van,* to get away from, to originate from; *~ op,* to make for. ·**afkomst**, no pl., *n.* origin. *van goede ~,* of good family. **af·komstig**, *a. ~ uit* or *van,* originating from.
·**afkondigen**, *v.t.s.* to proclaim. ·**afkondiging**, *n.* proclamation, publication.
·**afkooksel**, -s, *n.n.* decoction.
·**afkoop**, -**kopen**, *n.* buying off; ransom. **af·koopbaar**, -**bare**, *a.* redeemable.

·afkoopgeld, *n.n.* ransom (*sum of money*). ·afkoopsom, -mmen, *n.* ransom (*sum of money*). ·afkoopwaarde, no pl., *n.* surrender value. ·afkopen, koop af, *v.t.s., irr.* to buy off, redeem. *iemand iets ~*, to buy something from someone. ¶ *v.r.s., irr. zich ~ van*, to buy oneself out of (*army*).

·afkoppelen, *v.t.s.* to uncouple; to disconnect. ·afkorten, *v.t.s.* to shorten. *~ tot*, to abridge to. ·afkorting, *n.* abbreviation. ·afkortingsteken, -s, *n.n.* sign of abbreviation.

·afkrabben, krab af, *v.t.s.* to scratch off. ·afkrabsel, -s, *n.n.* scraping(s).

·afkrijgen, *v.t.s., str.* to get off; to finish. *iets ~ van*, to get something away from. ·afkruimelen, *v.i.s.* to crumble off. ·afkruipen, *v.t.s., str.* to creep down.

·afkunnen, *v.t.s., irr.* to be able to finish; to be able to tackle. *hij kan het werk best af*, he can easily finish the work. ¶ *v.i.s., irr.* to be able to get finished. *het werk kan niet af*, the work will not get finished; *~ van*, to get rid of; *ik kan niet van hem af*, I cannot get rid of him; *het kan er af*, it can be deducted; *het kan er best af*, he can well afford it.

·afkussen, kus af, *v.t.s.* to kiss away (*tears, quarrel*). *het ~*, to make it up.

·aflaat, -laten, *n.* indulgence (*religious*). *met ~ van zonden*, with remission of sins; *volle ~*, plenary indulgence. ·aflaatbrief, -ven, *n.* letter of indulgence. ·aflaatgeld, *n.n.* indulgence money. ·aflaathandel, no pl., *n.* traffic in indulgences.

af·landig, *a.* seaward. ·aflaten, laat af, *v.t.s., str.* to let down; to leave off.

·afleggen, leg af, *v.t.s.* to put down (*arms, etc.*); to cast off, discard (*clothes*); to cover (*distance*); to lay out (*corpse*). *een bezoek ~*, to pay a visit; *een examen ~*, to take an examination; *een eed ~*, to take an oath; *het ~*, to have the worst of it. ·afleggertje, -s, *n.n.* cast-off garment.

·afleiden, *v.t.s.* to lead away or down; to divert (*liquid; attention*); to conduct (*lightning*); to entertain; to deduce. *iemand ~ van zijn werk*, to distract a person's attention from his work. ·afleiding, *n.* diversion; entertainment; distraction; derivation. *tot ~ van*, for diverting; *~ bezorgen*, to provide a distraction. ·afleidsel, -s, *n.n.* derivative.

·aflekken, lek af, *v.i.s. ~ van*, to trickle down.

·afleren, leer af, *v.t.s.* to unlearn; to learn (*by imitation*). *iemand iets ~*, to teach a person not to do something.

·afleveren, *v.t.s.* to deliver (*goods*). *~ aan*, to deliver to. ·aflevering, *n.* delivery (*of goods*); issue (*of periodical*). *in ~en*, in parts.

·aflezen, lees af, *v.t.s., str.* to read (*list to the end; thermometer*).

·aflikken, lik af, *v.t.s.* to lick (off).

·afloden, lood af, *v.t.s.* to sound (*for charting*). ·afloeren, *v.t.s. iemand iets ~*, to spy out someone's method.

·aflokken, lok af, *v.t.s.* to entice away.

·afloop, no pl., *n.* end; result. *na ~ van*, after. ·aflopen, loop af, *v.i.s., str.* to run down (*alarum-clock*); to come to an end. *~ op*, to walk towards; *alles zal goed ~*, everything will come right. ¶ *v.t.s., str.* to wear down (*shoes; paint*); to canvass, importune; to run down (*liquid; person*).

af·losbaar, -bare, *a.* redeemable (*loan*). ·aflossen, los af, *v.t.s.* to redeem (*loan*); to relieve (*guard*). *elkaar ~*, to take turns. ·aflossing, *n.* redemption (*of loan*). ·aflossingstermijn, *n.* term (*of redemption*).

·afluisteren, *v.t.s.* to overhear.

·afmaaien, *v.t.s.* to mow, cut, reap. ·afmaken, maak af, *v.t.s.* to finish, complete; to slaughter, dispatch; to run down (*book*). ¶ *v.r.s. zich ergens van ~*, to dismiss a subject (*in a few words*).

·afmarcheren, marcheer af, *v.i.s.* to march off. ·afmars, *n.* homeward march, retreat.

·afmartelen, *v.t.s.* to cudgel (*brain*).

·afmatten, mat af, *v.t.s.* to exhaust. af·mattend, *a.* exhausting. ·afmatting, *n.* weariness; lassitude.

·afmeten, meet af, *v.t.s., str.* to measure (off). *anderen naar zichzelf ~*, to judge others by oneself. ·afmeting, *n.* dimension(s).

·afmijnen, *v.t.s.* to sell by Dutch auction. *~ op*, to sell (at auction) for.

·afmoeten, *v.i.s., irr.* to have to be taken off (*hat*); to have to be finished.

·afmonsteren, *v.t.s.* to pay off (*crew*). ¶ *v.i.s.* to sign off (*from crew*). ·afmonstering, *n.* paying off.

af·neembaar, -bare, *a.* removable. ·afnemen, neem af, *v.t.s., str.* to take off or down; to take away from; to raise (*hat*). *stof ~*, to dust. ¶ *v.i.s., str.* to decrease, wane. ·afnemer, -s, *n.* purchaser. ·afneming, *n.* diminution. *~ van het Kruis*, descent from the Cross.

·afpakken, pak af, *v.t.s.* to snatch away. ·afpalen, paal af, *v.t.s.* to fence in. ·afpassen, pas af, *v.t.s.* to measure (*in paces*). *geld ~*, to give exact amount (*money*).

·afpeilen, *v.t.s.* to sound (*for charting*). ·afpellen, pel af, *v.t.s.* to shell (*eggs*), peel (*shrimps*). ·afpennen, pen af, *v.t.s.* to write (much and quickly). ·afperken, *v.t.s.* to peg out (*field*).

·afpersen, *v.t.s.* to extort. ·afpersing, *n.* extortion.

·afpingelen, *v.t.s.* to haggle.

·afplatten, plat af, *v.t.s.* to flatten. ·afplatting, *n.* flattening.

afpluizen, pluis af, *v.t.s.* to pluck off (*fluff*). **afplukken, pluk af,** *v.t.s.* to pluck, pick, gather. **afpoeieren,** *v.t.s.* to get rid of, send packing. **afpoetsen,** *v.t.s.* to clean off. **afpraten, praat af,** *v.t.s.* to talk a great deal; to talk out of. **afraden, raad af,** *v.t.s.* to dissuade (from). **afraken, raak af,** *v.i.s.* to be broken off; to near completion. *de aardigheid raakt er af,* it has lost its first attraction; ~ *van,* to get away from, to get rid of. **aframmelen,** *v.t.s.* to trounce; to rattle off. **aframmeling,** *n.* trouncing. **afranselen,** *v.t.s.* to trounce. **afraspen,** *v.t.s.* to rasp off. **afrasteren,** *v.t.s.* to rail off. **afrastering,** *n.* railing, fence. **afreis, no pl.,** *n.* departure. **afreizen, reis af,** *v.i.s.* to depart, set off. ¶ *v.t.s.* to travel (through), tour. **afrekenen,** *v.i.s.* to reckon. ~ *met,* to settle with (*money, quarrel*). ¶ *v.t.s.* to deduct. **afrekening,** *n.* settlement. ~ *houden,* to settle; *op* ~, on account. **afrepelen,** *v.t.s.* to ripple (*flax*). **africhten,** *v.t.s.* to train. **afrij,** *n.* start (*race*). **afrijden,** *v.i.s., str.* to ride off. ¶ *v.t.s., str.* to ride down. **afrijten,** *v.t.s., str.* to rip off. **Afri-kaans,** *a.* African. ¶ **-kanen,** *n.* African. **Afri-kaander, -s,** *n.* South African. **afristen,** *v.t.s.* to stalk (*currants*). **afrit, -tten,** *n.* sloping road *or* drive; start (*race*). **afritsen,** *v.t.s.* to scoot down. **afroeien,** *v.t.s.* to row down. **afroepen,** *v.t.s., str.* to call down; to call over; to announce. **afroffelen,** *v.t.s.* to rough-plane; to scamp. **afrollen, rol af,** *v.t.s.* to roll off. ~ *van,* to roll off from. **afronden,** *v.t.s.* to round off. *naar boven* (*beneden*) ~, to round off upwards (downwards). **afronding,** *n.* rounding off; approximation. **afrossen, ros af,** *v.t.s.* to trounce. **afrossing,** *n.* trouncing. **afrotten, rot af,** *v.i.s.* to rot off. **afrukken, ruk af,** *v.t.s.* to tear away. ¶ *v.i.s.* ~ *op,* to march towards. **afschaduwen,** *v.t.s.* to shade; to adumbrate. **afschaduwing,** *n.* adumbration. **afschaffen, schaf af,** *v.t.s.* to abolish. **af-schaffer, -s,** *n.* teetotaller. **afschaffing, no pl.,** *n.* abolition. **afschampen,** *v.i.s.* to glance off. ~ *langs,* to glance off from. **afschaven, schaaf af,** *v.t.s.* to plane; to graze (*skin*). **afscheid, no pl.,** *n.n.* parting; farewell. *bij het* ~, on parting; *tot* ~, as a last farewell. **af-scheidbaar, -bare,** *a.* separable. **af-scheiden,** *v.t.s.* to separate, segregate; to secrete. ¶ *v.r.s. zich* ~ (*van*), to secede (from). **afscheiding,** *n.* separation; partition; excretion. **afscheidingslijn,** *n.* line of

demarcation. **afscheidingsmuur, -muren.** *n.* partition wall. **afscheidingsorgaan. -ganen,** *n.n.* excretory organ. **afscheid-nemen, neem afscheid,** *v.i.s.* to take leave. ~ *van,* to take leave of. **afscheidsbezoek.** *n.n.* farewell visit. **afscheidsdronk,** *n.* stirrup cup. **afscheidsgroet,** *n.* farewell (*salutation*). **afscheidsrede, -denen,** *n.* valedictory address. **afschenken,** *v.t.s., str.* to decant. **afschepen, scheep af,** *v.t.s.* to ship; to fob off. **af-scheppen, schep af,** *v.t.s.* to skim (off). **afscheren, scheer af,** *v.t.s., str.* to shave (off). **afscheuren,** *v.t.s.* to tear off. **afschieten,** *v.t.s., str.* to fire (*arms*); to shoot off; to partition off. ~ *op,* to dash towards. **afschijn, no pl.,** *n.* reflection. **afschijnen,** *v.i.s., str.* ~ *op,* to cast a glow on; ~ *van.* to shine from. **afschijnsel, -s,** *n.n.* reflection. **afschilderen,** *v.t.s.* to depict. **afschildering,** *n.* portrayal. **afschilferen,** *v.i.s. & v.t.s.* to flake off. **afschilfering,** *n.* peeling off. **afschoppen, schop af,** *v.t.s.* to kick off or down. **afschraapsel, afschrapsel, no pl.,** *n.n.* scrapings. **afschrabben, schrab af,** *v.t.s.* to scrape off. **afschrapen, schraap af,** *v.t.s.* to scrape off. **afschrappen, schrap af,** *v.t.s.* to scrape off. **afschrift, n.n.** copy. *een* ~ *maken,* to make a copy. **afschrijven, schrijf af,** *v.t.s., str.* to finish (*writing*); to copy (*writing*); to write off (*amount*); to remove (*from a list*). **afschrijving,** *n.* copying; depreciation. **afschrik,** *n.* horror (*dislike*). *een* ~ *hebben van,* to abhor. **afschrikken, schrik af,** *v.t.s., str.* to deter, frighten away. *zich laten* ~ *door,* to be intimidated by. **afschrik-wekkend,** *a.* horrible, terrifying; prohibitive. **afschroeien,** *v.t.s.* to singe. **afschroeven, schroef af,** *v.t.s.* to unscrew, screw off. **afschudden, schud af,** *v.t.s.* to shake off. **afschuimen,** *v.t.s.* to skim; to scour (*seas*). **afschuiven, schuif af,** *v.t.s., str.* to push off. ¶ *v.i.s., str.* to slide down. **afschuren, schuur af,** *v.t.s.* to scour off. **afschutten, schut af,** *v.t.s.* to board off. **afschuw, no pl.,** *n.* horror (*loathing*). *een* ~ *hebben van,* to abhor. **afschuwelijk,** *a.* horrible, loathsome. **af-schuwelijkheid, -heden,** *n.* horribleness. **afseinen,** *v.t.s.* to countermand (*by wire*). **afsijpelen,** *v.i.s.* to trickle down. **afsjouwen,** *v.t.s.* to slave. **afslaan, sla af,** *v.t.s., irr.* to beat off; to turn down; to separate. *hij slaat niets af dan vliegen,* he never refuses an offer. ¶ *v.i.s., irr.* to turn (*in another direction*). *van zich* ~, to hit out. **afslag, -slagen,** *n.* erosion; reduction; sale by Dutch auction; market (*for sale by Dutch auction*). *bij* ~

verkopen or *veilen*, to sell by Dutch auction.
afslager, -s, *n.* auctioneer.
afslepen, sleep af, *v.t.s.* to drag down; to tow down.
afslijpen, *v.t.s.*, *str.* to grind off. **afslijten**, *v.t.s.*, *str.* to wear off; to wear down.
afslingeren, *v.t.s.* to hurl off.
afsloven, zich, sloof af, *v.r.s.* to drudge.
afsluitboom, -bomen, *n.* barrier; boom. **afsluitdam, -mmen**, *n.* enclosing dam.
afsluitdijk, *n.* enclosing dyke. **afsluiten**, *v.t.s.*, *str.* to lock; to cut off (*gas, water, electricity*); to shut out (*light*); to close (*account*); to balance (*account-books*); to conclude (*transaction*). ¶ *v.r.s.. str. zich ~ van*, to cut oneself from. **afsluiting**, *n.* turning off, closing. **afsluitkraan, -kranen**, *n.* stop-cock.
afsmeken, smeek af, *v.t.s.* to implore.
afsmelten, *v.t.s.* to melt off.
afsnauwen, *v.t.s.* to snap (*somebody's*) head off.
afsnijden, *v.t.s.*, *str.* to cut (off). *iemand de pas ~*, to bar a person's way.
afsnoepen, *v.t.s.* to snatch (from). *iemand iets ~*, to get something before someone else gets it.
afspannen, span af, *v.t.s.*, *irr.* to unyoke.
afspatten, spat af, *v.i.s. ~ van*, to splash (off).
afspelen, speel af, *v.t.s.* to finish (*game*). ¶ *v.r.s. zich ~*, to occur, to be enacted.
afspiegelen, *v.t.s.* to reflect (*image; times*). ¶ *v.r.s. zich ~*, to be mirrored. **afspiegeling**, *n.* reflection.
afsplijten, *v.t.s.*, *str.* to split off.
afspoelen, *v.t.s.* to rinse off, wash away.
afspraak, -spraken, *n.* (verbal) agreement; date, appointment. *zich aan een ~ houden*, to stand by an agreement; *volgens ~*, according to the agreement. **afspreken, spreek af**, *v.t.s.*, *str.* to agree upon (verbally).
afspringen, *v.i.s.*, *str.* to jump off; to fly off, chip off. *~ op*, to jump towards.
afstaan, sta af, *v.t.s.*, *irr.* to cede; to let (*person*) have. ¶ *v.i.s.*, *irr.* to stand away from.
afstammeling, *n.* descendant. **afstammen, stam af**, *v.i.s. ~ van*, to be descended from. **afstamming**, no pl., *n.* descent. **afstammingsleer**, no pl., *n.* theory of heredity.
afstand, *n.* distance. *een ~ afleggen*, to cover a distance; *~ doen van*, to give up; *op een ~ houden*, to keep at a distance; *van een ~*, from a distance; *van ~ tot ~*, at intervals. **afstandsmars**, *n.* long-distance march. **afstandsmeter, -s**, *n.* taximeter; range-finder. **afstandsrit, -tten**, *n.* long-distance race.
afstappen, stap af, *v.i.s.* to step down, step off. *~ in*, to put up at; *~ van*, to step down from.

afsteken, steek af, *v.t.s.*, *str.* to cut (*turf*); to cut (*throat*); to let off (*firework*); to make (*speech*). ¶ *v.i.s.*, *str. ~ tegen*, to contrast with (*surroundings*); *~ bij*, to contrast with, differ from.
afstel, no pl., *n.n.* delay. **afstelen, steel af**, *v.t.s.*, *str.* to steal (from). **afstemmen, stem af**, *v.t.s.* to reject (*by vote*). **afstempelen**, *v.t.s.* to cancel (*with stamp*).
afsterven, sterf af, *v.i.s.*, *str.* to die off.
afstijgen, *v.i.s.*, *str.* to get off, dismount. ¶ *v.i.s.*, *str.* to go down.
afstoffen, stof af, *v.t.s.* to dust (*room*).
afstomen, stoom af, *v.i.s.* to steam down.
afstompen, *v.t.s.* to blunt. **afstomping, n.** blunting.
afstormen, *v.t.s.* to rush down. ¶ *v.i.s. ~ op*, to rush down upon.
afstoten, stoot af, *v.t.s.*, *str.* to push off; to repel, rebuff. **afstotend**. *a.* repellent, forbidding.
afstorten, *v.t.s.* to hurl down. ¶ *v.r.s. zich ~ van*, to hurl oneself down from.
afstraffen, straf af, *v.t.s.* to punish. **afstraffing**, *n.* punishment.
afstralen, straal af, *v.t.s.* to radiate.
afstrijken, *v.t.s.*, *str.* to wipe off; to strike (*match*).
afstremen, stroom af, *v.t.s.* to stream down.
afstropen, stroop af, *v.t.s.* to skin.
afstuderen, studeer af, *v.i.s.* to complete one's studies.
afstuiten, *v.i.s.* to rebound. *~ op*, **to** rebound off.
afstuiven, stuif af, *v.i.s.*, *str.* to blow off (*dust*). *~ op*, to rush towards.
afsturen, stuur af, *v.t.s.* to steer off. ¶ *v.i.s. & v.t.s.* to steer off. *~ op*, to steer for; to send to.
aftakelen, *v.t.s.* to unrig, dismantle; to go downhill, be on the decline.
aftands, *a.* elderly, long in the tooth. *~ worden*, to have passed one's prime.
aftappen, tap af, *v.t.s.* to draw off, tap, bottle.
aftekenen, *v.t.s.* to delineate; to sign, endorse.
aftelefoneren, -neer, *v.t.s.* to countermand by telephone. **aftelegraferen, -feer**, *v.t.s.* to countermand by telegram.
aftobben, zich, tob af, *v.r.s.* to weary oneself (*with worry*).
aftocht, *n.* retreat. *de ~ slaan* or *blazen*, to sound the retreat.
aftonnen, ton af, *v.t.s.* to buoy (*channel*).
aftornen. *v.t.s.* to unrip; to run down (*merits*).
aftrap, no pl., *n.* kick-off (*football*). *de ~ doen*, to kick off. **aftrappen, trap af**, *v.i.s.* to kick off (*in football*). *van zich ~*, to kick out. ¶ *v.t.s.* to kick down *or* off. *~ van*, to kick off *or* out of.
aftreden, treed af, *v.i.s.*, *str.* to stand down; to resign. **aftreden**, *n.n.* resignation. **aftreding**, *n.* resignation.

aftrek, no pl., *n.* deduction; demand (*for goods*). *na* or *onder* ~ *van*, after deducting; ~ *vinden*, to find a ready sale. **aftrekken, trek af**, *v.t.s.*, *str.* to pull off; to distract; to deduct; to retreat; to infuse. **aftrekker, -s**, *n.* subtrahend. **aftrekking**, *n.* deduction. **aftreksel, -s**, *n.n.* infusion. **aftreksom, -mmen**, *n.* substraction (*sum*). **aftrektal, -llen**, *n.n.* minuend.

aftroeven, troef af, *v.t.s.* to trump. **aftroggelen**, *v.t.s.* to trick out of. **aftronen, troon af**, *v.t.s.* to wheedle out of.

aftuigen, *v.t.s.* to unharness; to unrig.

aftuimelen, *v.t.s.* to tumble down.

afturen, tuur af, *v.t.s.* to gaze down.

afvaardigen, *v.t.s.* to delegate. ~ *naar*, to delegate to. **afvaardiging**, *n.* delegation.

afvaart, *n.* sailing, departure.

afval, no pl., *n.* waste (matter), scraps; windfall (*fruit*); apostasy. **afvallen, val af**, *v.i.s.*, *str.* to fall down; to fall away (*from party, religion*); to lose weight. ~ *van*, to fall from. ¶ *v.t.s.*, *str.* to fall away from (*party, religion*). **af·vallig**, *a.* disloyal; apostate. **af·vallige, -n**, *n.* renegade, apostate. **af·valligheid**, no pl., *n.* apostasy. **afvalproduct**, *n.n.* waste product.

afvaren, vaar af, *v.i.s.*, *irr.* to sail (*leave*). ¶ *v.t.s.*, *irr.* to sail down (*river*).

afvegen, veeg af, *v.t.s.* to wipe (off).

afvijlen, *v.t.s.* to file off. **afvijlsel**, no pl., *n.n.* filings.

afvissen, vis af, *v.t.s.* to drag.

afvliegen, *v.i.s.*, *str.* to fly off; ~ *op*, to fly at; *komen* ~ *op*, to come flying towards.

afvloeien, *v.i.s.* to flow down.

afvoer, no pl., *n.* removal. **afvoerbuis, -zen**, *n.* outlet (*pipe*). **afvoeren**, *v.t.s.* to carry off (*liquid*). **afvoerkanaal, -nalen**, *n.n.* drainage canal; excretory duct. **afvoerpijp**, *n.* outlet (*pipe*).

afvragen, vraag af, *v.t.s.*, *str.* to demand. ¶ *v.r.s.*, *str. zich iets* ~, to wonder.

afvreten, vreet af, *v.t.s.*, *str.* to eat (*bare*); eat (*leaves*) off.

afvriezen, vries af, *v.t.s.*, *irr.* to freeze off.

afvuren, vuur af, *v.t.s.* to fire (off).

afwaaien, *v.i.s.*, *irr.* to be blown off (*by wind*). ¶ *v.t.s.*, *irr.* to blow off (*by wind*).

afwaarts, *a.* downward; aside. ¶ *adv.* downwards; away.

afwachten, *v.t.s.* to wait. ¶ *v.i.s.* to await (*developments*). *een afwachtende houding aannemen*, to assume an expectant attitude. **afwachting**, *n.* expectation. *in* ~ *van*, in expectation of, awaiting.

afwasbakje, *n.n.* washing-up bowl. **afwaswater**, *n.n.* water (*for washing-up*), dishwater. **afwassen**, *v.t.s.*, *irr.* to wash up.

afwateren, *v.i.s.*, & *v.t.s.* to drain (into). **afwatering**, no pl., *n.* drainage. **afwateringskanaal, -nalen**, *n.n.* drainage canal.

afweer, no pl., *n.* defence. **afweergeschut**, no pl., *n.n.* anti-aircraft artillery.

afwegen, weeg af, *v.t.s.*, *str.* to weigh (out).

afweiden, *v.t.s.* to graze.

afweken, week af, *v.t.s.* to soak off.

afwenden, *v.t.s.* to avert; to deflect. ¶ *v.r.s. zich* ~, to turn away.

afwennen, wen af, *v.t.s.* to unlearn (*habit*), get out of the habit.

afwentelen, *v.t.s.* to roll off.

afweren, weer af, *v.t.s.* to repel; to parry.

afwerken, *v.t.s.* to finish, put the last touches to; to cover (*programme*). **afwerking**, no pl., *n.* finish (*workmanship*).

afwerpen, *v.t.s.*, *str.* to cast (down).

af·wezig, *a.* absent. **af·wezige, -n**, *n.* absentee, the person absent, pl. those absent. **af·wezigheid**, no pl., *n.* absence. *bij* ~ *van*, in the absence of.

afwijken, *v.i.s.*, *str.* to deviate, deflect. ~ *van*, to deviate from. **afwijking**, *n.* deviation.

afwijzen, wijs af, *v.t.s.*, *str.* to decline; to turn away, refuse admittance. **af·wijzend**, *a.* unfavourable (*decision*). **afwijzing**, *n.* refusal.

afwikkelen, *v.t.s.* to unroll; to wind up (*business*).

afwinden, *v.t.s.*, *str.* to unreel.

afwisselen, *v.i.s.* to alternate. ¶ *v.t.s. elkaar* ~, to relieve one another. **afwisselend**, *a.* varied; alternating. ¶ *adv.* alternately. **afwisseling**, *n.* variation. *bij* ~, in turns; *tot* ~, or *voor de* ~, for a change.

afwissen, wis af, *v.t.s.* to wipe off.

afzagen, zaag af, *v.t.s.* to saw off. *see* **afgezaagd**.

afzakken, zak af, *v.i.s.* to come down. ¶ *v.t.s.* to go down (*river*).

afzeggen, zeg af, *v.t.s.*, *irr.* to countermand. **afzegging**, *n.* counter-order.

afzeilen, *v.i.s.* to sail away.

afzenden, *v.t.s.*, *str.* to send off, dispatch. **afzender, -s**, *n.* sender. **afzending**, *n.* shipment, dispatch (*goods*).

afzengen, *v.t.s.* to scorch off.

afzet, no pl., *n.* sale. **afzetgebied**, *n.n.* market; outlet. **afzetsel, -s**, *n.n.* trimming (*ornament*).

afzetten, zet af, *v.t.s.* to take off (*clothes*); to dismiss; to amputate; to trim (*ornament*); to rope off; to put down, put at a distance; to cheat. ¶ *v.i.s.* to push off (*from shore*). **afzetter, -s**, *n.* cheat. **afzette·rij**, *n.* swindle; daylight robbery (*facetious*).

af·zichtelijk, *a.* hideous. ¶ *adv.* hideously.

afzien, zie af, *v.i.s.*, *irr.* to look away from; to copy (*cheat*). ~ *van*, to give up. ¶ *v.t.s.*, *irr.* to look down (*road*); to learn by watching someone else. **af·zienbaar, -bare**, *a.* measurable. *binnen* α· *in afzienbare tijd*, shortly.

af·zijdig, *a.* impartial. ¶ *adv. zich* ~ *houden*, to keep oneself aloof.

·afzoeken, *v.t.s.*, *irr.* to search, scour.
·afzoenen, *v.t.s.* to kiss away (*quarrel*).
·afzonderen, *v.t.s.* to segregate. ·afzondering, *n.* seclusion. af·zonderlijk, *a.* separate. ¶ *adv.* separately.
·afzwaaien, *v.i.s.* to be demobilized.
·afzweren, zweer af, *v.t.s.*, *str.* to abjure, forswear. ·afzwering, *n* abjuration.
a·gaat, -gaten, *n.* agate. a·gaten, *a.* (*made of*) agate.
a·geren, -geer, *v.i.* to act; to agitate.
a·genda, -'s, *n.* agenda; note-book. op de ∼, on the agenda.
a·gent, *n.* agent. ∼ (*van politie*), policeman. a·gentschap, -ppen, *n.* agency; branch. agen·tuur, -turen, *n.* agency.
aggre·gatietoestand, *n.* state of aggregation.
·agio, no pl., *n.* agio, premium. agio·tage, no pl., *n.* stock-jobbing. agio·teur, -s, *n.* stock-jobber.
agi·tatie, -s, *n.* agitation.
a·grariër, -s, *n.* agrarian. a·grarisch, *a.* agrarian. ∼*e Bank*, Farmers' Bank.
agres·sief, *a.* aggressive.
agro·noom, -nomen, *n.* agronomist, agricultural expert. agro·nomisch, *a.* agronomic.
a·gurk. *See* augurk.
·ahorn, *n.* maple.
ai!, *exclamation of pain.*
ai, -'s, *n.* (*three-toed*) sloth.
air, -s, *n.n.* air, appearance, mien. *zich een* ∼ *geven,* to swagger; *zich* ∼*s geven,* to give oneself airs; *het* ∼ *aannemen van,* to take on the air of.
a·jakkes!, a·jasses!, *exclamation of disgust.*
a·jour, *a. & adv.* openwork(ed).
a·juin, *n.* onion. a·juinachtig, *a.* onion-like.
a·kant, *n.* acanthus.
ake·lei, -en, *n.* columbine.
·akelig, *a.* nasty, boring. ¶ *adv.* awfully. *ik ben* or *word er* ∼ *van,* it makes me sick.
·aker, -s, *n.* acorn; bucket.
akke·fietje, -s, *n.n.* small (*unpleasant*) job; trifle.
·akker, -s, *n.* field (*under cultivation*). *Gods* ∼, the churchyard; *Gods water over Gods* ∼ *laten lopen,* to let things take their course, be lazy. ·akker-, *in compounds often* field-. ·akkerbouw, *n.* tillage. ·ak·kerklokje, *n.n.* bluebell. ·akkerland, *n.n.* arable land. ·akkermaalshout, *n.n.* copse. ·akkerwetten, pl. only, *n.* agrarian law. ·akkerwinde, -n, *n.* bindweed, convolvulus.
ak·koord, *n.n.* chord; agreement. *het op een* ∼*je gooien,* to make a compromise; *tot* ∼ *komen* or *geraken,* to come to terms; *een* ∼ *aangaan, maken, sluiten, treffen,* to come to an agreement. ¶ *a.* correct. ∼ *zijn,* to be correct; ∼ *gaan met,* to agree with. ¶ *exclamation.* ∼ !, O.K.!
ako·lei. *See* ake·lei.
ako·niet, *n.* aconite.
·akte, -n *or* -s, *n.* deed, document; act

(*drama*); certificate (*teaching*); act (*of faith,* Roman Catholic prayer*). ·akte-examen, -s, *n.n.* teachers' examination. ·aktentas, -ssen, *n.* brief-case. ·aktentrommel, -s, *n.* deed-box.
al, -lle, *a.* all, every. ¶ *pron. alle drie,* all three of them (us, you). ¶ no pl., *n.n.* all; everything; the universe. *met kleren en* ∼, with clothes and all; ∼ *wat,* all (that), everything (which). ¶ *uninfl., adv.* already, yet; whether. ∼ *te duur,* far too expensive; *niet* ∼ *te duur,* not too expensive; ∼ *dan niet,* whether or not; ∼ *doende leert men,* one learns by practice. ¶ *uninfl., c.* (al)though; even. ∼ *pratende,* whilst talking.
·alang-·alang, no pl., *n.* East Indian grass.
·alant, no pl., *n.* flea-wort.
a·larm, no pl., *n.n.* alarm, alarum. ∼ *blazen,* to sound the alarm (*with bugle*); ∼ *maken,* to give the alarm; ∼ *luiden,* to sound the alarm (*with bells*); ∼ *slaan,* to beat the alarm (*with drum*); *loos* ∼, false alarm. alar·meren, -meer, *v.t.* to alarm. a·larmfluit, *n.* alarm-whistle, siren. a·larmgeklep, no pl., *n.n.* tolling. alar·mist, *n.* alarmist. alar·mistisch, *a.* alarmist. a·larmklok, -kken, *n.* tocsin. a·larmpeil, no pl., *n.n.* danger level. a·larmsignaal, -nalen, *n.n.* danger signal. a·larmtoestel, -llen, *n.n.* alarum (*apparatus*).
alba·nees, -nezen, *n.* Albanian. ¶ -nese, *a.* Albanian.
al·bast, no pl., *n.n.* alabaster. al·basten, *a.* (*made of*) alabaster.
·albatros, -ssen, *n.* albatross.
·al·bino, -'s, *n.* albino.
·album, -s, *n.n.* album.
al·cali. *See* al·kali.
alche·mie, alchi·mie, no pl., *n.* alchemy. alchi·mist, *n.* alchemist.
·alcohol, no pl., *n.* alcohol. ·alcoholhoudend, *a.* alcoholic. alco·holica, pl. only, *n.n.* spirituous liquors. alcoholi·satie, alcoholi·sering, no pl., *n.* alcoholization. alco·holisch, *a.* alcoholic. alcoho·lisme, no pl., *n.n.* alcoholism. ·alcoholvergiftiging, *n.* alcoholic poisoning, alcoholism. ·alcoholvrij, *a.* non-alcoholic.
al·daar, *adv.* there; of that place.
·aldoor, *adv.* continuously.
al·dra, *adv.* shortly.
al·dus, *adv.* thus; therefore.
al·eer, *adv.* before.
alexan·drijn, *a.* alexandrine (*metre*).
alge, -n, *n.* alga (*pl.* algae).
·algebra, no pl., *n.* algebra. alge·braïsch, *a.* algebraic.
·algeheel, *a.* entire. ¶ *adv.* entirely.
alge·meen, -mene, *a.* general, universal, common. *de Algemene Staten,* the States General. ¶ *adv.* generally, universally, commonly. ¶ no pl., *n.n. in* or *over het* ∼, in general; *Maatschappij tot Nut van het*

Algemeen (*Dutch cultural league*). **alge-**
·meenheid, -heden, *n.* generality, universality.
alge·rijn, *n.* Algerian. **alge·rijns,** *a.* Algerian.
al·hier, *adv.* here; of this place.
alhoe·wel, *c.* (al)though.
·alias, *adv.* alias. ¶ **-ssen,** *n.* alias.
·alibi, -'s, *n.n.* alibi.
·alikruik, *n.* (peri)winkle.
a·linea, -'s, *n.* paragraph.
alk, *n.* auk.
al·kali, -liën, *n.n.* alkali. **al·kalisch,** *a.*
alkaline.
·alkohol. *See* **·alcohol.**
al·koof, -koven, *n.* alcove.
alle·bei(de), *num.* both.
alle·daags, *a.* daily, everyday; commonplace.
alle·daagsheid, -heden, *n.* commonness.
al·leen, *a.* alone. *adv.* only. **al·leenhandel,**
no pl., *n.* monopoly. **al·leenheerschappij,**
no pl., *n.* absolute rule. **al·leenheerser,**
-s, *n.* absolute ruler. **al·leenspraak,**
-spraken, *n.* monologue, soliloquy. **al-**
·leenstaand, *a.* isolated. **al·leenverkoop,**
no pl., *n.* exclusive sale. **al·leenvertegen-**
woordiger, *n.* sole representative.
alle·gaartje, -s, *n.n.* medley, hodge-podge.
allego·rie, -rieën, *n.* allegory. **alle·gorisch,**
a. allegorical. ¶ *adv.* allegorically.
al·leluja, alle·luja, -'s, *n.n.* halleluja.
·allehens, *indef. pron.* all hands (*on ship*).
~ *aan dek,* all hands on deck.
·allemaal, *indef. pron.* altogether.
alle·machtig!, *exclam.* Good Lord! ¶ *adv.*
mighty, extremely.
·alleman, no pl., *n.* everybody. *Jan en* ~,
all and sundry. **·allemansgeheim,** *n.n.*
open secret. **·allemansvriend,** *n.* hail
fellow well met.
·allen, *pron.* all.
al·lengs, *adv.* gradually.
·aller, *pron.* of all. **aller-,** *prefix denoting*
superlative quality, e.g., alleraardigst, most
charming; *allerbest,* the very best; *aller-*
dolst, screamingly funny. **aller·eerst,** *a.*
& *adv.* first of all. **aller·hande,** *a.* all
sorts of. **Aller·heiligen,** *n.,* **Aller·heili-**
gendag, *n.* **Aller·heiligenfeest,** *n.n.* All
Hallows, All Saints' Day. **Aller·heiligste,**
no pl., *n.n.* the Holy of Holies. **Aller·**
·hoogste, no pl., *n.* the Most High. **aller·**
·ijl, *n. in* ~, post haste. **Aller·kinderen,**
no pl., *n.n.* **Aller·kinderendag,** *n.* Innocents'
Day. **·allerlaatst,** *a.* the very last; recent.
¶ *n.n.* the very last. **·allermeest,** *a.* &
adv. at the most. **·allerminst,** *a.* the very
least; lowliest. ¶ *adv.* at the very least.
¶ no pl., *n. in het* ~ *e,* the very least.
·alleruiterst, *a.* utmost. **·allerwegen,** *adv.*
everywhere. **Aller·zielen,** *n.,* **Aller·zie-**
lendag, *n.* **Aller·zielenfeest,** *n.n.* All Souls,
All Souls' Day. **allerzijds,** *adv.* everywhere.
·alles, *pron.* all, everything. ¶ no pl., *n.n.,*

everything. ~ *en* ~, all in all; *boven* ~
above all; *van* ~, all sorts of things; *vóór*
~, above all. **·allesbehalve,** *adv.* anything
but; far from. **·allesbeheersend,** *a.* pre-
dominating. **·allesetend,** *a.* omnivorous.
·alleseter, -s, *n.* omnivorous creature.
·alleszins, *adv.* in every respect.
alli·age, -s, *n.* alloy.
alli·antie, -s, *n.* alliance.
a!·licht, *adv.* probably, possibly.
allite·ratie, -s, *n.* alliteration. **allite·reren,**
-reer, *v.i.* to alliterate.
al·looi, no pl., *n.n.* alloy. *van verdacht* ~,
of suspicious character. *van het zuiverste*
~, of the purest water.
allo·paath, -pathen, *n.* allopath. **allopa·thie,**
no pl., *n.* allopathy. **allo·pathisch,** *a.*
allopathic.
al·lure, -s, *n.* air(s).
alluvi·aal, -iale, *a.* alluvial.
·almacht, no pl., *n.* omnipotence. **al-**
·machtig, *a.* omnipotent. *de* ~*e God,*
Almighty God.
·almanak, -kken, *n.* almanac.
al·mede, *adv.* also.
·aloë, -'s, *n.* aloe(s).
al·om, *adv.* everywhere. **alomtegen·woordig,**
a. omnipresent. **alomtegen·woordigheid,**
no pl., *n.* omnipresence, ubiquity. **·alom-**
vattend, *a.* comprehensive.
al·oud, *a.* ancient, time-honoured.
al·paca, no pl., *n.* alpaca (*wool*); German
silver.
·alpen-, *in compounds:* Alpine. **·alpen-**
beklimmer, -s, *n.* Alpinist, Alpine climber.
·alpenclub, *n.* Alpine Club. **·alpengids,** *n.*
Alpine guide. **·alpengloeien,** no pl., *n.n.*
Alpine glow. **·alpenhoorn, -s,** *n.* Alpine
horn. **·alpenjager, -s,** *n.* Alpine hunter.
pl. mountain troops. **·alpenroos, -rozen,**
n. (*kind of*) rhododendron. **·alpenstok,**
-kken, *n.* alpenstock. **·alpenviooltje, -s,**
n.n. (*kind of*) cyclamen.
·alphabet, -tten, *n.n.* alphabet. **·alpha-**
·betisch, *a.* alphabetical. ¶ *adv.* alpha-
betically.
al·reeds, *adv.* already.
al·ruin, *n.* mandrake. **al·ruinmannetje, -s,**
n.n. (*man-shaped*) mandrake root.
als, *c.* if, when; like, as, by way of.
als·dan, *adv.* then.
·alsem, -s, *n.* wormwood.
alsje·blieft, *int.* if you please.
als·mede, *c.* as well as. **als·nog,** *adv.* as yet.
als·nu, *adv.* now. **als·of,** *adv.* as if.
alt, *n.* alto; contralto.
·altaar, -taren, *n.n.* altar. **·altaardienaar,**
-naren, *n.* acolyte. **·altaardoek,** *n.n.* altar
cloth. **·altaargeheim,** *n.n.* the holy
mystery of the Eucharist. **·altaargereed-**
schap, no pl., *n.n.* altar vessels. **·altaar-**
scherm, *n.n.* reredos, altar piece. **·altaar-**
schilderij, *n.* reredos, altar piece. **·altaar-**
stuk, -kken, *n.n.* reredos, altar piece.

·altaarspijs, no pl., *n.* consecrated bread and wine.
altc·rna·tief, -ven, *n.n.* alternative. ¶ -ve, *a.* alternative. ¶ *adv.* alternatively.
al·thans, *c.* in any case, at least.
·altijd, *adv.* always. ·altijddurend, *a.* everlasting. ·altoos, *adv.* always.
altru·isme, no pl., *n.n.* altruism. altru·istisch, *a.* altruistic. ¶ *adv.* altruistically.
·altsleutel, -s, *n.* tenor clef. ·altstem, -mmen, *n.* (contr)alto voice. ·altviool, -violen, *n.* viola. ·altzanger, -s, *n.* alto singer. ·altzangeres, -ssen, *n.* contralto singer.
a·luin, no pl., *n.* alum. a·luinaarde, no pl., *n.* alumina. a·luinachtig, *a.* aluminous.
alu·minium, no pl., *n.n.* aluminium. ¶ *a.* (*made of*) aluminium.
al·vast, *adv.* for the time being; in the meantime.
·alvleesklier, *n.* pancreas.
al·vorens, *adv. & c.* before(hand).
al·waar, *c.* whereas. al·weer, *adv.* again.
al·wetend, *a.* omniscient. al·wetendheid, no pl., *n.* omniscience.
·alziend, *a.* all-seeing.
al·zijdig, *a.* many-sided, versatile. ¶ *adv.* universally. al·zijdigheid, no pl., *n.* versatility.
al·zo, *adv.* thus.
amal·gaam, -gamen, *n.n.* amalgam. amalga·matie, -s, *n.* amalgamation. amalga·meren, -meer, *v.t.* to amalgamate.
a·mandel, -s, *n.* almond-tree. a·mandel, -s *or* -en, *n.* almond; *pl.* tonsils. a·mandelachtig, *a.* almond (*flavour, smell*). a·mandelbloesem, -s, *n.* almond blossom. a·mandelboom, -bomen, *n.* almond tree. a·mandelgebak, no pl., *n.n.* almond cake. a·mandelmelk, milk of almonds. a·mandelolie, no pl., *n.* almond oil. a·mandelontsteking, *n.* tonsillitis. a·mandelpas, no pl., *n.*, a·mandelpers, no pl., *n.* almond paste. a·mandelvormig, *a.* almond-shaped.
amanu·ensis, -ssen, *n.* laboratory assistant, lab. boy.
ama·ril, no pl., *n.* emery.
ama·teur, -s, *n.* amateur.
·ambacht, *n.n.* trade (handi)craft; domain, district. *hij is timmerman van zijn ~*, he is a carpenter by trade; *op een ~ doen*, to apprentice to a trade; *op een ~ gaan*, to be apprenticed; *twaalf ~en, dertien ongelukken!*, he is a Jack of all trades and master of none. ·ambachtschool, -scholen, *n.* trade-school, technical school. ·ambachtsgilde, -n, *n.n.* trade guild. ·ambachtsman, ambachtslieden *or* ambachtslui, *n.* artisan, mechanic. ·ambachtsonderwijs, no pl., *n.n.* trade schooling, technical instruction.
ambas·sade, -s, *n.* embassy. ambassa·deur, -s, *n.* ambassador. ambassa·deursvrouw, *n.* ambassador's wife.

·amber, no pl., *n.* amber. ·ambergrijs, no pl., *n.n.* ambergris.
ambi·ëren, -ieer, *v.t.* to aspire to. am·bitie, no pl., *n.* ambition. ambiti·eus, -ze, *a.* ambitious.
ambo·nees, -nezen, *n.* Amboynese. ¶ -nese, *a.* Amboynese.
ambro·zijn, no pl., *n.n.* ambrosia.
ambt, *n.n.* (small) domain; office, post, dignity, function. ·ambtelijk, *a.* official. ¶ *adv.* officially. ·ambteloos, -loze, *a.* out of office; retired. ·ambtenaar, -s *or* -naren, *n.* official (*government*). *~ van het Openbaar Ministerie*, public prosecutor; *~ van de Burgerlijke Stand*, registrar (*of births, deaths, and marriages*). ·ambtenaars-, *in compounds*; official, of official(s). ·ambtenaarswereld, no pl., *n.* officialdom. ambtena·res, -ssen, *n.* official (*female*). ambtena·rij, no pl., *n.* officialdom. ·ambtgenoot, -noten, *n.* colleague. ambts-, *in compounds:* of office, official. ·ambtsbejag, no pl., *n.n.* place-hunting. ·ambtsvervulling, no pl., *n.* discharge of (one's) duties. ·ambtsbeslommeringen, pl. only, *n.* cares of office. ·ambtseed, -seden, *n.* oath of office. *de ~ afleggen*, to be sworn in. ·ambtsgeheim, *n.n.* official secret. ambts·halve, *adv.* ex officio, in virtue of one's office. ·ambtsijver, no pl., *n.* professional zeal. ·ambtsmisbruik, *n.n.* abuse of power. ·ambtsplicht, *n.* professional duty. ·ambtsvervulling, no pl., *n.* discharge of (one's) duties. ambts·wege, *adv.* ex officio, in virtue of one's office. ·ambtswoning, *n.* official residence.
ambu·lance, *n.* ambulance; mobile surgical unit. ambu·lancetrein, *n.* hospital-train.
ambu·lant, *a.* ambulatory, ambulant.
a·mechtig, *a.* breathless. ¶ *adv.* breathlessly. a·mechtigheid, no pl., *n.* breathlessness.
·amen, *int.* amen.
amen·deren, -deer, *v.t.* to amend. amende·ment, *n.n.* amendment. *~ op*, amendment to.
Ameri·kaans, *a.* American. ¶ *n.* American (*man*). Ameri·kaanse, -n, *n.* American (*woman*).
ame·thist, *n.* amethyst.
ameuble·ment, *n.n.* (*suite of*) furniture.
ami·caal, -cale, *a.* amicable. ¶ *adv.* amicably. *~ omgaan met*, be on friendly terms with. a·mice, -s, *n.* friend.
am·monia, no pl., *n.* ammonia. ammoni·ak, no pl., *n.* liquid ammonia.
ammu·nitie, no pl., *n.* ammunition; munition. ammu·nitiewagen, -s, *n.* caisson.
amne·sie, no pl., *n.* amnesia.
amnes·tie, -tieën, *n.* amnesty. *algemene ~*, general pardon; *~ verlenen*, to grant an amnesty.
·amok, no pl., *n.n.* amuck, amok. *~ maken*,

to run amuck. **·amokmaker, -s,** *n.* one who runs amuck.

a·morph, *a.* amorphous.

amorti·satie, -tiën *or* **-ties,** *n.* amortisation. **amorti·satiefonds,** *n.n.* sinking fund. **amorti·seren, -seer,** *v.t.* to redeem, amortise.

·ampel, *a.* ample. ¶ *adv.* amply.

·amper, *adv.* scarcely, barely, hardly.

am·père, -s, *n.* ampere. **am·pèremeter, -s,** *n.* ammeter.

amphi·bie, -bieën, *n.* amphibian. **amphi·bietank, -s,** *n.n.* amphibian-tank. **amphi·bievliegtuig,** *n.n.* amphibian-aeroplane. **am·phibisch,** *n.* amphibious, amphibian.

amphithe·ater, -s, *n.n.* amphitheatre. **amphithe·aterswijze,** *adv.* amphitheatrically.

amplifi·catie, -s, *n.* amplification.

ampli·tudo, no pl., *n.* amplitude (*vibratory*).

ampu·tatie, -s, *n.* amputation. **ampu·teren, -teer,** *v.t.* to amputate.

amu·let, -tten, *n.* amulet, charm, talisman.

amu·sant, *a.* amusing. **amu·seren, -seer,** *v.t.* to amuse. ¶ *v.r.* **zich ~,** to amuse oneself, enjoy oneself. **amuse·ment.** *n.n.* amusement, entertainment.

anae·mie, no pl., *n.* anaemia.

anaesthe·sie, no pl., *n.* anaesthesia.

analo·gie, -gieën, *n.* analogy. **ana·logisch,** *a.* analogical. ¶ *adv.* analogically. **ana·loog,** *a.* analogous.

ana·lyse, -n, *n.* analysis. **ana·lytisch,** *a.* analytical, analytic. ¶ *adv.* analytically. **analy·seren, -seer,** *v.t.* to analyse.

ana·nas, -ssen, *n.* pineapple.

anar·chie, no pl., *n.* anarchy. **ana·logisch,** no pl., *n.n.* anarchism. **anar·chist,** *n.* anarchist. **anar·chistisch,** *a.* anarchist, anarchical.

anato·mie, no pl., *n.* anatomy. **ana·tomisch,** *a.* anatomic.

anciënni·teit, no pl., *n.* seniority.

·ander, *a.* other (*second*); other (*different*). **om de ~e dag,** every other day; **om den ~,** in turns. ¶ pl. **-en,** *pron.* other. **een ~,** another; **de een doen dit, de ~ dat,** one does this, another does that; **bij een ~,** at someone else's place, from someone else.

·anderdaags, *a.* tertian. **·anderdeels,** *adv.* on the other hand. **·anderhalf, -ve,** *num.* one and a half. **~ maal zoveel,** half as much again. **·andermaal,** *adv.* repeatedly. **·anderman,** *pron.* someone else.

·anders, *a.* different. ¶ *pron. preceded by pronoun:* else. **iemand ~,** someone else; **iets ~,** something else; **niets ~ dan,** nothing but; **niets ~,** nothing else. ¶ *adv.* differently; formerly; otherwise. **anders·denkend,** *a.* of another opinion (*esp. in religion*). **anders·denkende, -n,** *n.* dissentient. **·andersgezind,** *a.* of another opinion (*esp. in religion*). **anders·om,** *adv.* the other way round. **·anderszins,** *adv.* otherwise.

an·dijvie, no pl., *n.* endive, chicory.

ane·mie. *See* **anaemie.**

ane·moon, -monen, *n.* anemone, windflower.

·angel, -s, *n.* sting; (fish-)hook; barb.

·angelus, no pl., *n.* angelus. **·angelusklokje, -s,** *n.n.* angelus bell.

An·gorageit, *n.* Angora goat. **An·gorakat, -tten,** *n.* Angora cat. **An·gorawol,** no pl., *n.* Angora wool.

angst, *n.* fear, terror. **uit ~ voor,** for fear of; **~ doorstaan** *or* **uitstaan,** to experience fear. **·angstgeroep,** no pl., *n.n.* shriek of terror, distress. **·angstgeschrei,** no pl., *n.n.* cry *or* cries of terror, distress. **·angstig,** *a.* fearful, afraid, anxious. ¶ *adv.* fearfully, anxiously. **·angstkreet, -kreten,** *n.* cry of distress. **angst·vallig,** *a.* anxious; painstaking. ¶ *adv.* anxiously; painstakingly. **angst·valligheid,** no pl., *n.* anxiety, timidity; conscientiousness. **angst·wekkend,** *a.* alarming. **·angstzweet,** no pl., *n.n.* cold sweat.

a·nijs, no pl., *n.* anise. **a·nijsolie,** no pl., *n.* aniseed oil. **a·nijszaad, -zaden,** *n.n.* aniseed.

ani·line, no pl., *n.* aniline.

ani·meren, -meer, *v.t.* to encourage, liven up. **·animo,** no pl., *n.* or *n.n.* zest, gusto. **animosi·teit,** no pl., *n.* animosity.

anje·lier, *n.* pink, carnation.

·anker, -s, *n.n.* anchor (*of ship*; *leverage of watch*); brace (*in wall*); armature (*of magnet*); anker. **het ~ laten vallen,** to drop anchor; **het ~ lichten,** to weigh anchor; **ten ~,** anchored; **het ~ werpen,** to cast anchor; **voor ~ liggen,** to ride at anchor. **·ankerboei,** *n.* anchor-buoy. **·ankeren,** *v.t.* to anchor. **·ankergeld,** *n.n.* anchorage (*dues*). **·ankergrond,** *n.* anchorage-ground. **·ankerhand,** *n.* fluke. **·ankerhorloge, -s,** *n.n.* lever-watch. **·ankerkluis, -zen,** *n.* hawse. **·ankerlicht,** *n.n.* riding light. **·ankerplaats,** *n.* anchorage. **·ankertros, -ssen,** *n.* anchor chain.

an·nalen, pl. only, *n.* annals.

an·nex, *n.* & *n.n.* annexe. ¶ *a.* enclosed, attached. **anne·xatie, -s,** *n.* annexation. **anne·xeren, -xeer,** *v.t.* to annex. **annexio·nist,** *n.* annexationist. **annexio·nisme,** no pl., *n.n.* annexationism. **annexio·nistisch,** *a.* annexationist.

an·nonce, -s, *n.* advertisement.

annui·teit, *n.* annuity.

ano·niem, *a.* anonymous. ¶ *adv.* anonymously. **anonimi·teit,** *n.* anonymity.

·anorganisch, *a.* inorganic.

an·sjovis, -ssen, *n.* anchovy.

an·tenne, -s, *n.* antenna; aerial.

anthropolo·gie, no pl., *n.* anthropology. **anthropo·loog, -logen,** *n.* anthropologist.

anticham·breren, -breer, *v.i.* to wait in antechamber; to lobby.

an·tiek, *a.* antique.

anti·lope, -n, *n.* antelope.
anti·monium, no pl., *n.n.* antimony.
antipa·thie, -thieën, *n.* antipathy; dislike.
antipa·thiek, *a.* antipathetic.
anti·quaar, -quaren, *n.* antiquary, antiquarian. antiquari·aat, -iaten, *n.n.*
second-hand bookshop; antique shop.
anti·quarisch, *a.* second-hand. antiqui-
·teit, *n.* antiquity (*period*); antique (*object*).
antirevolution·nair, *n.* member of Dutch
Calvinist Conservative Party. ¶ *a.* per-
*taining to the Dutch Calvinist Conservative
Party.*
·Antwerps, *a.* (from *or* of) Antwerp. ·Antwer-
penaar, -naren, *n.* person from Antwerp.
·antwoord, *n.n.* answer, reply. *als* ~, by
way of answer; *in* ~ *op,* in answer to;
op ~ *wachten,* to wait for an answer;
ten ~ *geven,* to reply. ·antwoordcoupon,
-s, *n.* (postal) reply coupon. ·antwoorden,
v.t. to answer, reply. ~ *op,* to reply to.
a·part, *a.* separate; apart. ¶ *adv.* separately;
apart. ¶ *n.n. iets* ~s, something special.
a·partje, -s, *n.n.* aside.
apa·thie, no pl., *n.* apathy. a·pathisch, *a.*
apathetic. ¶ *adv.* apathetically.
·apegapen, no pl., *n.n. op* ~ *liggen,* to be at
one's last gasp.
·apenbroodboom, -bomen, *n.* baobab.
·ap- en depen·denties, pl. only, *n.* appurtenances.
·apenkooi, *n.* monkey cage. ·apenkool,
no pl., *n.* rubbish, nonsense. ·apenkop,
-ppen, *n.* jackanapes, monkey (*term of
playful contempt to* or *of child*). ·apenkuur,
-kuren, *n.* monkey-trick(s). ·apenliefde,
no pl., *n.* foolish fondness. ·apennootje,
-s, *n.n.* monkey nut. ·apenspel, -llen, *n.n.*
monkey show. ·apentuin, *n.* Zoo. a·pin,
-nnen, *n.* ape, monkey (*female*).
a·plomb, no pl., *n.n.* assurance.
apolo·geet, *n.* apologist. apolo·getisch, *a.*
apologetic. apolo·gie, -ën, *n.* apology.
a·postel, -s, *n.* apostle. a·postellepel, -s, *n.*
apostle spoon. aposto·laat, -laten, *n.n.*
apostolate. apos·tolisch, *a.* apostolic.
apo·theek, -theken, *n.* chemist's (*shop*).
apo·theker, -s, *n.* (pharmaceutical) chemist.
apo·thekersbediende, -n, *n.* chemist's
assistant. apo·thekersflesje, -s, *n.n.*
medicine bottle. apo·thekersrekening,
n. chemist's bill.
appa·raat, -raten, *n.n.* apparatus.
apparte·ment, *n.n.* apartment.
ap·pel, (1) -s, *n.n.* appeal; roll-call; signal for
roll-call. ~ *aantekenen,* to appeal (*to
higher court*); *in* ~ *gaan,* to lodge an appeal;
~ *blazen,* to sound the roll-call (*on
bugle*); ~ *houden,* to call the roll; ~ *slaan,*
to sound the roll-call (*on drum*); *op het* ~
ontbreken, to be absent.
·appel, (2) -s, *n.* apple (*fruit*); apple (*pupil of
the eye*); pommel (*sword*). *voor een* ~
en een ei, for next to nothing, for a song;

de ~ *valt niet ver van de boom,* like father
like son, (he is) a chip of the old block.
See appeltje. ·appelaar, -s, *n.* apple-tree.
·appelbeignet, -tten, *n.* apple-fritter.
·appelblauw, *a.* blue-green. ·appelbloesem,
-s, *n.* apple-blossom. ·appelbol, -llen, *n.*
apple-dumpling. ·appelboom, -bomen, *n.*
apple-tree. ·appelboomgaard, *n.* apple-
orchard. ·appelboor, -boren, *n.* apple-
corer. ·appelflauwte, -s, *n.* fainting fit
(*usu. sham*). ·appellijster, -s, *n.* misselthrush. ·appelmoes, no pl., *n.* or *n.n.*
apple-sauce. ·appelmotje, -s, *n.n.* codling-
moth, leaf-roller. ·appelschil, -llen,
n. apple peel. ·appelschimmel, -s, *n.*
dapple-grey (*horse*). appel·sien, *n.* orange.
·appelstroop, no pl., *n.* apple-treacle.
·appeltaart, *n.* apple pie. ·appeltje, -s,
n.n. little apple. *een* ~ *voor de dorst
bewaren,* to keep something by for a
rainy day; *ik moet nog een* ~ *met hem
schillen,* I have a bone to pick with him.
·appelvink, *n.* hawfinch, common gros-
beak. ·appelwijn, no pl., *n.* cider.
appel·lant, *n.* appellant. appel·leren, -lleer,
v.i. to appeal (*to higher court*).
applaudis·seren, -sseer, *v.i.* to applaud.
applaudisse·ment, no pl., *n.n.* applause.
ap·plaus, no pl., *n.n.* applause.
ap·port!, *word of command to dog:* fetch it!
appreci·ëren, -cieer, *v.t.* to appreciate.
approvian·deren, -deer, *v.t.* to provision.
approxima·tief, -ve, *a.* approximate. ¶ *adv.*
approximately.
a·pril, *n.* April. *de eerste* ~ *zendt men de
gekken waar men wil,* (a jingle meaning
that) practical jokes are played on April
fool day; *de eerste* ~ *verloor Alva zijn
bril,* (a jingle referring to) the loss of the
town of Briel by the Duke of Alva.
a·prilgrap, -ppen, *n.* April joke (*on April
fool day*).
apro·pos, *adv.* timely. ¶ *int:* by the way!
¶ no pl., *n.n.* subject. *hij laat zich niet
van zijn* ~ *afbregen,* you cannot easily
put him off (*distract*).
a·quarium, -s *or* -ia, *n.n.* aquarium.
ar, ·arren, *n.* sleigh.
ar, *a.* used only in: *in arren moede,* angry.
ara·besk, *n.* arabesque.
a·rak, no pl., *n.* arrack.
·arbeid, no pl., *n.* labour, work, toil. *aan
de* ~, at work; *aan de* ~ *gaan,* to set to
work. ·arbeiden, *v.i.* to labour, work, toil.
de ~*de klasse,* the working class. ·arbeider,
-s, *n.* workman, labourer. ·arbeidersbevol-
king, *n.* working class population. ·arbei-
dersbeweging, *n.* Labour movement.
·arbeiders·jeugdcentrale, -s, *n.* Labour
League of Youth. ·arbeidersklasse, no pl.,
n. working class. ·arbeiderspartij, *n.*
Labour Party. ·arbeidersraden, pl. only,
n. workers' councils. ~*en soldatenraden,*
(*revolutionary*) workers' and soldiers'

councils. **arbeidersregering**, *n.* Labour government. **arbeidersstand**, no pl., *n.* working class. **arbeiderstrein**, *n.* workmen's train. **arbeidersvereniging**, *n.* workmen's association. **arbeidersverzekering**, *n.* workers' insurance. **arbeiderswoning**, *n.* workman's dwelling, working class house. **arbeidster**, **-s**, *n.* worker (*female*). **arbeidsbeurs**, **-zen**, *n.* Labour Exchange. **arbeidsbureau**, **-'s**, *n.n.* Labour Office. **arbeidscontract**, *n.n.* labour contract. **arbeidsdag**, **-dagen**, *n.* working day. **arbeidsduur**, no pl., *n.* length of working day. **arbeidsenquête**, **-s**, *n.* labour investigation. **arbeidsgeschil**, **-llen**, *n.n.* labour dispute. **arbeidskosten**, pl. only *n.* labour costs. **arbeidsloon**, **-lonen**, *n.n.* wages. **arbeidsraad**, **-raden**, *n.* (advisory) labour board. **arbeidsveld**, *n.* field of action. **arbeidsvermogen**, **-s**, *n.n.* energy, working power. ~ *van beweging*, kinetic *or* actual energy; ~ *van plaats*, potential energy. **arbeidsverzekering**, *n.* labour insurance. **arbeidswet**, **-tten**, *n.* labour law. **arbeids·willige**, **-n**, *n.* non-striker. **ar·beidzaam**, **-zame**, *a.* laborious, diligent. **ar·beidzaamheid**, no pl., *n.* industry, laboriousness.

arbi·trair, *a.* arbitrary. ¶ *adv.* arbitrarily. **arbi·treren**, **-treer**, *v.i.* to arbitrate.

ar·ceren, **-ceer**, *v.t.* to hatch, shade. **ar·cering**, *n.* hatching, shading.

ar·chief, **-ven**, *n.n.* archives.

·archipel, **-s**, *n.* archipelago.

archi·valia, pl. only, *n.n.* documents, records (*in archives*). **archi·varis**, **-ssen**, *n.* keeper of (the) records.

archi·tect, *n.* architect. **architec·tonisch**, *a.* architectonical. **architec·tuur**, no pl., *n.* architecture.

ar·duin, no pl., *n.n.* freestone. **ar·duinen**, *a.* (*made of*) freestone.

·are, **-s**, *n.* are, one hundred square metres.

a·rena, **-'s**, *n.* arena.

·arend, *n.* eagle. **arendbuizerd**, *n.* (*kind of*) buzzard. **arendsblik**, **-kken**, *n.* eagle-eye. **·arendsjong**, *n.n.* eaglet. **·arendsklauw**, *n.* eagle's talon. **·arendsnest**, *n.n.* eyrie. **·arendsneus**, **-zen**, *n.* aquiline nose. **·arendsoog**, **-sogen**, *n.n.* eagle-eye.

·argeloos, **-loze**, *a.* unsuspecting, harmless. ¶ *adv.* unsuspectingly. **arge·loosheid**, no pl., *n.* unsuspectingness.

·arglist, *n.* guile, cunning. **arg·listig**, *a.* cunning. ¶ *adv.* cunningly.

argu·ment, *n.n.* argument. **argumen·tatie**, *n.* argumentation. **argumen·teren**, **-teer**, *v.t. & v.i.* to argue, reason.

·Argusoog, **-sogen**, *n.n.* Argus-eye. *met* ~, Argus-eyed.

·argwaan, no pl., *n.* suspicion. ~ *hebben or koesteren t·gen*, to harbour suspicion against. **arg·wanend**, *a.* suspicious. ¶ *adv.* suspiciously (*feeling suspicion*).

·Ariër, **-s'** *n.* Aryan. **·Arisch**, *a.* Aryan.

aristo·craat, **-raten**, *n.* aristocrat. **aristocra·tie**, no pl., *n.* aristocracy. **aristo·cratisch**, *a.* aristocratic. ¶ *adv.* aristocratically.

ark, *n.* ark. *de Ark des Verbonds*, the Ark of the Covenant. **·Arke**, **-n**, *n.* (*biblical form*) *de* ~*e Noachs*, Noah's Ark.

arm, *n.* arm; bracket; handle. *iemand·de* ~*en binden*, to tie a person's hands (*figurative*); *een sterke or lange* ~ *hebben*, to be influential; *iemand in de* ~ *nemen*, to have a word with (*influence*); *met de* ~*en over elkaar*, arms crossed; *een slag om de* ~ *houden*, to keep a trick *or* two up one's sleeve; *hij loopt met zijn ziel onder zijn* ~, he wanders about like a lost soul. **·armband**, *n.* bracelet, bangle. **·armbandhorloge**, **-s**, *n.n.* wrist-watch. **armsgat**, **-gaten**, *n.n.* arm-hole. **·armslengte**, no pl., *n. op* ~, at arm's length. **armstoel**, *n.* arm-chair. **armvol**, pl. armen vol, *n.* armful.

arm, *a.* poor; needy, indigent. ¶ *adv.* poorly, meanly. **armbestuur**, **-sturen**, *n.n.* Board of Guardians, Public Assistance Committee. **armbezoek**, no pl., *n.n.* visitation of the poor. **arme**, **-n**, *n.* poor (*person*). *de* ~*n*, the poor; *de* ~*n van geest*, the poor of spirit; *van den* ~, wretched; *van den* ~ *begraven worden*, to be buried by the parish; *van den* ~ *trekken*, to receive poor relief. **armeiijk**, *a.* poor, shabby. **arme·lui**, pl. only, *n.* poor people. **arme·luiskind**, **-deren**, *n.n.* poor man's child. **armendoktor**, **-s**, *n.* poor man's doctor. **armenfonds**, *n.n.* poor relief fund. **armengeld**, *n.* poorrate. **armenhuis**, **-zen**, *n.n.* workhouse. **armenhuisjongen**, **-s**, *n.* charity boy, parish boy. **armenkas**, **-ssen**, poor relief fund. **armenpraktijk**, *n.* doctor's practice among the poor. **armenschool**, **-scholen**, *n.* charity school. **armenvoogd**, *n.* parish guardian. **armenwet**, **-tten**, *n.* Poor Law. **armenzakje**, **-s**, *n.n.* poor-box. **armenzorg**, no pl., *n.* poor relief. **arme·zondaarsbankje**, **-s**, *n.n.* penitents' form. **arme·zondaarsgezicht**, *n.* hang-dog look. **armhuis**, **-zen**, *n.n.* workhouse. **arm·lastig**, *a.* (dependent) on the parish. **arm·lastige**, **-n**, *n.* person receiving outdoor relief. **arm·lastigheid**, no pl., *n.* pauperism. **armmeester**, **-s**, *n.* relieving officer. **armoede**, no pl., *n.* poverty. ~ *is troef*, poverty reigns; *tot* ~ *geraken*, to be reduced to poverty; *uit* ~, from poverty; *van* ~, from sheer misery. **ar·moedig**, *a.* miserable. **armoedzaaier**, **-s**, *n.* (*person*) down and out. **armwezen**, no pl., *n.n.* pauperism; poor relief. **arm·zalig**, *a.* pitiful, miserable. **arm·zaligheid**, no pl., *n.* misery.

Ar·mada, *n.* Armada (*Spanish fleet of 1588*).

a·roma, **-'s**, *n.n.* aroma. **aro·matisch**, *a.* aromatic.

·aronskelk, *n.* arum. *witte* ~, arum lily; *gevlekte* ~, wild arum-lily, cuckoo-pint.
arran·geren, -geer, *v.t.* to arrange; to orchestrate.
·arre, -n, *n.*, ·arreslee, ·:eeën, *n.*, ·arreslede, -n, *n.* sleigh. ·arren, ar, *v.i.* to sleigh.
arren. *See* ar.
ar·rest, *n.n.* arrest, custody; seizure; judgement (*of High Court*). *in* ~, under arrest; *in* ~ *nemen,* to arrest; *in* ~ *stellen,* to place under arrest; *bij* ~ *van,* in accordance with the decision of. arres·tant, *n.* arrested person, prisoner. arres·tantenlokaal, -kalen, *n.n.* detention-room. arres·tatie, -s, *n.* arrest, apprehension. arres·teren, -teer, *v.t.* to arrest; to confirm (*minutes*).
arri·veren, -veer, *v.i.* to arrive; to happen.
arro·gant, *a.* arrogant. ¶ *adv.* arrogantly. arro·gantie, no pl., *n.* arrogance.
arrondisse·ment, *n.n.* district. arrondisse·mentsrechtbank, *n.* county court.
arse·naal, -nalen, *n.n.* arsenal.
ar·senicum, no pl., *n.n.* arsenic.
ar·tesisch, *a.* artesian.
articu·latie, -iën, *n.* articulation (*speech; bones*). articu·leren, -leer, *v.t.* to articulate (*speech; bones*).
ar·tikel, -s, *or* -en, *n.n.* section (*of act*), clause; article (*in periodical*); article, commodity. *de 12* ~*en des geloofs,* the Apostles' Creed. ar·tikelsgewijs, -ze, *a.* point by point. ¶ *adv.* ~ *behandelen,* to discuss section by section.
artille·rie, no pl., *n.* artillery. artille·rist, *n.* artillery-man.
·Artis, no pl., *n. name of the Amsterdam Zoo.*
arti·sjok, -kken, *n.* artichoke.
ar·tist, *n.* artist (*male*); artiste (*male*). ar·tistenkamer, -s, *n.* green-room. artis·tiek, *a.* artistic. ¶ *adv.* artistically. ar·tiste, -n, *n.* artist (*male*); artiste (*female*).
arts, *n.* physician. artse·nij, *n.* physic, medicine. artse·nijkunde, no pl., *n.* pharmacology.
as, (1) -ssen, *n.* axle; axis. *per* ~ *vervoeren,* to transport by vehicle.
as, (2) -ssen, *n.* ash, ashes; (mortal) remains. *in zak en* ~ *zitten,* to wear sackcloth and ashes. *uit de* ~ *verrijzen,* to rise from one's ashes. ·asachtig, *a.* ashy. ·asbak, -kken, *n.* ash pan. ·asbakje, -s, *n.n.* ash tray. ·asbelt, *n.* ash-dump.
as·best, no pl., *n.n.* asbestos.
a·sceet, -sceten, *n.* ascetic. a·scetisch, *a.* ascetic. ¶ *adv.* ascetically. asce·tisme, no pl., *n.n.* asceticism.
·asgrauw, *a.* ashen. ·ashoop, -hopen, *n.* ash-heap. ·askar, -rren, *n.* dust cart. ·askruik, *n.* funeral urn. ·asman, -nnen, *n.* dustman. ·asregen, -s, *n.* rain of ashes. ·asvaalt, *n.* refuse dump. As·woensdag, -dagen, *n.* Ash Wednesday.

·asem, -s, *n.* breath. *geen* ~ *geven op,* not to answer, not to react to.
asje·blief(t), *int.* if you please; here you are.
as·perge, -s, *n.* asparagus. as·pergebed, -dden, *n.n.* asparagus bed.
as·phalt, *n.n.* asphalt, bitumen. as·phaltbestrating, *n.* asphalt paving. asphal·teren, -teer, *v.t.* to asphalt.
aspi·rant, *n.* candidate, aspirant. aspi·rant-contro·leur, -s, *n.* assistant joint magistrate and collector. aspi·ratie, -s, *n.* aspiration. aspi·reren, -reer, *v.t.* to aspire; to aspirate. ~ *naar,* to aspire to.
·aspunt, *n.n.* pole (axle).
assai·neren, -neer, *v.t.* to sanitate, sanify. assai·nering, no pl., *n.* improvement of sanitary conditions.
·Assepoester, *proper name.* Cinderella.
assig·natie, -s, *n.* assignment; money order.
assimi·latie, -s, *n.* assimilation.
assis·tent, *n.* assistant; demonstrator (*university*). assis·tent-apo·theker, -s, *n.* chemist's qualified assistant. assis·tentie, no pl., *n.* assistance.
associ·atie, -s, *n.* association.
assor·teren, -teer, *v.t.* to assort. assorti·ment, *n.n.* assortment.
assura·deur, -s, *n.* insurer; underwriter. assu·rantie, -s, *n.* insurance, assurance. assu·rantiekantoor, -toren, *n.n.* insurance office. assu·rantiepolis, -ssen, *n.* insurance policy. assu·rantiepremie, -s, *or* -iën, *n.* insurance premium.
·aster, -s, *n.* aster.
as·trant, *a.* rude, cheeky. ¶ *adv.* rudely, cheekily.
astro·noom, -nomen, *n.* astronomer.
·aswenteling, *n.* rotation (*round axis*).
a·syl, *n.n.* asylum (*shelter*). a·sylrecht, *n.n.* right of asylum *or* sanctuary.
·atap, no pl., *n.* nipah.
ate·lier, -s, *n.n.* workshop, studio (*of artist, photographer, dressmaker*).
ath·leet, -leten, *n.* athlete. athle·tiek, no pl., *n.* athletics. ath·letisch, *a.* athletic.
·atlas, -ssen, *n.* atlas. ·atlasvlinder, -s, *n.* atlas-moth.
a·tol, -llen, *n.* atoll.
a·toom, -tomen, *n.n.* atom.
at·tent, *a.* attentive. *iemand* ~ *maken op,* to draw a person's attention to. ¶ *adv.* attentively. at·tentie, -s, *n.* attention.
at·test, *n.n.* certificate, testimonial. attes·tatie, -iën, *n.* attestation. attes·teren, -teer, *v.t.* to attest, certify.
·attisch, *a.* Attic. ~ *zout,* Attic salt, Attic wit.
at·tractie, -s, *n.* attraction.
attra·peren, -peer, *v.t.* to catch (*in act*).
au! *int. denoting pain.*
a.u.b., *abbrev.* if you please.
audi·ëntie, -s, *n.* audience. ~ *aanvragen,* to seek an audience; ~ *geven* or *verlenen,*

to grant an audience; *op* ~ *gaan bij,* to have an audience with. **audi·ëntiezaal, -zalen,** *n.* audience-chamber.

audi·teur, -s, *n.* auditor.

au·ditie, -s, *n.* audition.

audi·torium, no pl., *n.n.* audience; auditorium.

·auerhaan, -hanen, *n.* capercailye, cock of the woods. **·auerhoen, -ders,** *n.n.* capercailye, woodgrouse.

·aueros, -ssen, *n.* aurochs.

au·gurk, *n.* gherkin.

Augus·tijn, *n.* Augustine. **Augus·tijner,** *a.* Augustine. ~ *monnik,* Austin friar. **·au·gustus,** *n.* August (*month*).

aure·ool, -reolen, *n.* aureole.

au·rikel, -s, *n.* auricula.

au·teur, -s, *n.* author. **au·teurschap,** no pl., *n.n.* authorship. **au·teursrecht,** *n.n.* copyright; royalty. **au·teurswet, -tten,** *n.* copyright act, law of copyright.

·auto, -'s, *n.* motor-car. **autoband,** *n.* car-tyre. **·autobandiet,** *n.* motor-bandit. **·autobril, -llen,** *n.* motor-goggles. **autobus, -ssen,** *n.* motor-bus. **autocar, -s,** *n.* motor-coach. **·autoën, auto,** *v.i.* to motor. **automo·biel,** *n.* automobile. **automobi·list,** *n.* motorist. **·auto-ongeluk, -kken,** *n.n.* car accident. **·autotocht,** *n.* car trip. **·autoval, -llen,** *n.* police trap. **autowiel,** *n.n.* car-wheel.

autodi·dact, *n.* self-taught person. **autodi·dactisch,** *a.* self-taught. **auto·giro, -'s,** *n.* autogyro, helicopter.

auto·maat, -maten, *n.* automaton. **auto·matisch,** *a.* automatic.

·autoped, -s, *n.* scooter.

autori·seren, -seer, *v.t.* to authorize. **autori·tair,** *a.* arbitrary, high-handed. **autori·teit,** *n.* authority.

autoty·pie, ieën, n. autotype.

a·val, no pl., *n.n.* guarantee (*of bill*). **avali·seren, -seer,** *v.t.* to guarantee (*bill*). **ava·list,** *n.* guarantor (*of bill*).

a·vance, -s, *n.* advance. ~*s doen* or *maken,* to make overtures. **avan·ceren, -ceer,** *v.i.* to advance, make headway; to be promoted. ¶ *v.t.* to advance (*money*). **avance·ment,** *n.* promotion.

ave·gaar, -s, *n.* auger.

ave·nant, *naar* ~, in proportion.

·averechts, *a.* inverted; wrong (*cock-eyed*). ¶ *adv.* backwards; wrongly; ¶ *n.* purl (*knitting*).

ave·rij, *n.* average, damage. ~ *grosse,* general average; ~ *particulier,* particular average; ~ *belopen,* to sustain damage (*at sea*).

·avond, *n.* evening, night; eve (*evening before*). *de* ~ *te voren,* the previous night; *goeden* ~! Good evening!, Good night!; *des* ~*s* or *'s* ~*s,* in the evening, at night, of an evening; *in den* ~, at night, in the evening; *tegen den* ~, towards nightfall; *op de* ~ *van zijn leven,* in the evening of his life;

van ~, to-night, this evening. **·avond-bede, -n,** *n.* evening prayer. **·avondblad, -bladen,** *n.n.* evening paper. **·avonddienst,** *n.* evening service, Evening Prayer, Evensong. **·avondduister,** no pl., *n.n.* gloaming. **·avondeten,** no pl., *n.n.* supper. **·avondje, -s,** *n.n.* party, social evening. **·avondkerk,** *n.* (*Protestant*) Evensong. **·avondklok, -kken,** *n.* Angelus (*bells*). **·avondkoelte,** no pl., *n.* cool of the evening. **·avondland,** no pl., *n.n.* Occident. **·avondlied,** no pl., *n.n.* evensong. **·avondlucht,** no pl., *n.* evening air. **·avondmaal, -malen,** *n.n.* evening meal. *het Heilig* ~, the Lord's Supper. **·avondrood,** no pl., *n.n.* red sunset. **·avondschemering,** *n.* twilight. **·avondschool, -scholen,** *n.* night school. **·avondster,** no pl., *n.* Evening Star. **·avondstond,** *n.* evening, evening hour. **·avondtoilet, -tten,** *n.n.* evening dress, evening clothes. **·avondvlinder, -s,** *n.* moth. **·avondwandeling,** *n.* evening walk. **·avondwind,** *n.* evening breeze.

avon·turen, -tuur, *v.t.* to risk, venture. **avontu·rier, -s,** *n.* adventurer. **avon·tuur, -turen,** *n.n.* adventure. *op* ~ *uitgaan,* to go in search of adventure. **avon·tuurlijk,** *a.* adventurous. ¶ *adv.* adventurously.

·azen, aas, *v.i.* ~ *op,* to feed upon, prey upon.

a·zijn, no pl., *n.* vinegar. **a·zijnachtig,** *a.* vinegary. **a·zijnfles, -ssen,** *n.* vinegar bottle, vinegar cruet. **a·zijnlucht,** no pl., *n.* vinegary smell. **a·zijnsmaak,** no pl., *n.* vinegary taste. **a·zijnstel, -llen,** *n.n. het olie- en* ~, the cruet stand. **a·zijnzuur,** no pl., *n.n.* acetic acid.

a·zuren, uninfl., *a.* azure. **a·zuur,** no pl., *n.n.* azure. **a·zuursteen,** no pl., *n.* lapis lazuli.

B

ba!, *int. exclamation of disgust.*

·baadje, -s, *n.n.* Oriental jacket, sailor's jacket. *iemand op zijn* ~ *geven* or *komen,* to give someone a hiding; *op zijn* ~ *krijgen,* to be given a hiding.

baai, *n.* bay, bight; (*kind of*) Maryland tobacco; (red) flannel. **·baaien,** *a.* made of (red) flannel.

baak, *n. See* **·baken.**

baal, ·balen, *n.* bale; 10 reams (*paper*).

baan, ·banen, *n.* road, track; path, trajectory; length (*of material*). ~ *breken,* to do pioneer work; *in andere banen leiden,* to lead into different channels; *op de lange* ~ *schuiven* or *van de* ~ *schuiven,* to put off ad infinitum; *iemand van de* ~ *knikkeren,* to put a person out of the running; *van de* ~ *zijn,* to be shelved. **baan·brekend,**

a. epoch-making, pioneering. ·**baan-breker, -s,** *n.* (*fig.*) pioneer. ·**baanschuiver, -s,** *n.* cow-catcher. ·**baantje, -s,** *n.n.* job. ·**baantjesjager, -s,** *n.* job-hunter. ·**baanvak, -kken,** *n.n.* section (*of railway line*). ·**baanveger, -s,** *n.* sweeper (*on ice-track*). ·**baanwachter, -s,** *n.* signalman; man who keeps a crossing. ·**baanwerker,** *n.* lineman.

baar, ·baren, *n.* billow, wave; bar, ingot; bier; greenhorn, freshman. ¶ ·**-bare,** *a.* ready (*money*); unadorned. *de bare duivel,* the very devil; *de bare zee,* the stormy sea; *bare onzin,* utter nonsense.

baard, *n.* beard; barb; baleen; whiskers (*cat*); bit (*of key*); vane (*of feather*). *hij heeft de* ∼ *in de keel,* his voice is breaking; *zijn* ∼ *laten staan,* to let one's beard grow; *om de keizer zijn* ∼ *spelen,* to play for love. ·**baardaap, -apen,** *n.* lion-tailed monkey. ·**baardeloos, -loze,** *a.* beardless. ·**baardgier,** *n.* bearded vulture. ·**baardmannetje, -s,** *n.n. or* ·**baardmees, -mezen,** *n.* bearded tit(mouse). ·**baardvogel, -s,** *n.* barbet.

·**baarlijk,** *a. de* ∼*e duivel,* the devil incarnate.

·**baarmoeder, -s,** *n.* womb, uterus.

baars, -zen, *n.* perch, bass.

baas, ·bazen, *n.* master; boss; overseer; fellow, chap; governor! boss! ∼ *boven* ∼, Greek meets Greek; *hij is er de* ∼, he is the chief man there; iemand (niet) ∼ kunnen, (not) to be able to get the best of someone; *de* ∼ *spelen,* to lord it; *de* ∼ *worden,* to get the better; *de* ∼ *zijn,* to be master; *hij is me de* ∼ (*af*), he is cleverer than I am. ·**baasje, -s,** *n.n.* little chap.

baat, ·baten, *n.* benefit; relief. *baten,* assets; *iets te* ∼ *nemen,* to avail oneself of something; *ten bate van,* for the benefit of; *alle baten helpen,* every little helps; ∼ *geven,* to cause relief; ∼ *vinden bij,* to derive benefit from; *zonder* ∼, without avail. ·**baatzucht,** no pl., *n.* selfishness. **baat·zuchtig,** *a.* selfish. ¶ *adv.* selfishly.

baat-zuchtig, *a.* selfish. ¶ *adv.* selfishly.
·**babbel, -s,** *n.* chatterbox. ·**babbelaar, -s,** *n.* chatterbox; butterscotch. ·**babbelen,** *v.i.* to chatter, to babble. ·**babbelkous, -n.** chatterbox. ·**babbelziek,** *a.* over-talkative. ·**babbelzucht,** no pl., *n.* loquacity.

·**baboe, -'s,** *n.* native nurse (*East Indies*).

ba·cil, -llen, *n.* bacillus.

bac·terie, -iën, *n.* bacterium, pl. bacteria.

bad, ·baden, *n.n.* bath, bathe; baths; bath(tub). *een koud* ∼, a cold shower *or* discouragement; *het* ∼ *loopt,* the bath is (turned) on; *een* ∼ *geven,* to bath(e); *een* ∼ *nemen,* to have a bath(e); *de baden gebruiken,* to take the waters. ·**baden, baad,** *v.i.irr.,* & *v.t.irr.* to bath, bathe; to bathe (*in tears*), wallow (*in riches*). ·**bader, -s,** *n.* bather. ·**badgast,** *n.* visitor

at seaside *or* watering-place. ·**badgoed,** no pl., *n.n.* bathing gear. ·**badhanddoek,** *n.* bathing-towel. ·**badhandschoen,** *n.* washing-glove. ·**badhotel, -s,** *n.n.* seaside hotel. ·**badhuis, -zen,** *n.n. or* ·**badinrichting,** *n.* public baths. ·**badkamer, -s,** *n.* bathroom. ·**badknecht,** *n.* bath attendant. ·**badkoetsje, -s,** *n.n.* bathing machine. ·**badkostuum, -s,** *n.n.* bathing costume. ·**badkuip,** *n.* bath-tub. ·**badkuur, -kuren,** *n.* course of (*spa*) waters. ·**badmantel, -s,** *n.* bath-wrap. ·**badmeester, -s,** *n.* bath superintendent. ·**badmuts,** *n.* bathing-cap. ·**badplaats,** *n.* seaside resort, watering-place. ·**badschoen,** *n.* bathing slipper. ·**badseizoen,** *n.n.* bathing season. ·**badstoel,** *n.* beach-chair. ·**badvrouw,** *n.* bath attendant (*female*).

ba·gage, no pl., *n.* luggage. **ba·gagebureau, -'s,** *n.n.* luggage-office, parcels office. **ba·gagedepot, -s,** *n.n. or* **ba·gagekamer, -s,** *n.* cloakroom. **ba·gagedrager, -s,** *n.* carrier (*on bicycle*). **ba·gagereçu, -'s,** *n.n.* luggage receipt. **ba·gagetrein,** *n.* regimental train. **ba·gageverzekering,** *n.* luggage insurance. **ba·gagewagen, -s,** *n.* luggage van.

·**bagger,** no pl., *n.* mud, slush. ∼ *ophalen,* to dredge mud. ·**baggeren,** *v.i.* to dredge; to wade (*through mud*). ·**baggerlaarzen,** pl. only, *n.* waders. ·**baggermolen, -s,** *n.* dredger (*machine*). ·**baggerman, -lui** *or* **-lieden,** *n.* dredger (*man*). ·**baggernet, -tten,** *n.n.* dredge-net. ·**baggerschuit,** *n.* mud-hopper. ·**baggerturf,** no pl., *n.* bog peat.

·**baisse,** no pl., *n.* fall (*of prices*). *à la* ∼ *speculeren,* to engage in bear speculations. **bais·sier, -s,** *n.* bear (*stock exchange*).

bajo·net, -tten, *n.* bayonet. *met gevelde* ∼, *de* ∼ *op het geweer,* bayonet(s) drawn; *met de* ∼ *aanvallen,* to make a bayonet attack; *met de* ∼ *nemen,* to take by a bayonet attack. **bajo·netaanval, -llen,** *n.* bayonet attack. **bajo·netschermen,** no pl., *n.n.* bayonet practice. **bajo·netsluiting,** *n.* bayonet-joint.

bak, ·bakken, *n.* box; bin; cistern; trough; bucket (*of dredger*); frame (*in garden*); body (*of carriage*); mess (*on board ship*); fo'c's'le head; pit (*theatre*); clink, quod; joke. ·**bakbarometer, -s,** *n.* cistern barometer. ·**bakbeest,** *n.n.* huge object. *een* ∼ *van een . . .,* a huge . . . ·**bakboord,** no pl., *n.n.* port, larboard. *van* ∼ *naar stuurboord,* from pillar to post; *aan* ∼, on the port side. ·**bakboordzijde,** no pl., *n.* port side. ·**baken, -s,** *n.n.* beacon. *de* ∼*s zijn verzet,* times have changed; *als het tij verloopt verzet men de* ∼*s,* one must follow the times. ·**bakengeld,** *n.n.* beaconage. ·**bakenen,** *v.t.* to beacon.

baker, -s, *n.* dry nurse. ·**bakeren,** *v.t.* to

nurse (*dry-nurse*). ¶ *v.i.* to go out nursing (*dry-nurse*). *heet* or *haastig gebakerd zijn*, to be excitable, hasty. ·**bakerkleren**, pl. only, *n.n.* swaddling clothes. ·**bakermat**, -**tten**, *n.* cradle; birth-place. *van de* ~, from early youth. ·**bakerpraat**, no pl., *n.* or ·**bakerpraatje**, -**s**, *n.n.* old wives' tale(s). ·**bakerrijmpje**, -**s**, *n.n.* nursery rhyme. ·**bakerspeld**, *n.* large safety pin. ·**bakersprookje**, -**s**, *n.n.* nursery tale.
·**bakhuis**, -**zen**, *n.n.* bakehouse.
·**bakje**, -**s**, *n.n.* small dish.
·**bakkebaard**, *n.* whisker(s).
bakke·leien, *v.i.* to scrap, quarrel.
·**bakken**, *v.t.irr.* to bake (*bread*); to fry (*pancakes, etc.*). *iemand een poets* ~, to play a trick on someone. ¶ *v.i.irr.* to bake; to fail (*in examination*). ·**bakker**, -**s**, *n.* baker. **bakke·rij**, *n.* bakery, baker's shop, bakehouse. **bakke·rin**, -**nnen**, *n.* baker's wife. ·**bakkersbedrijf**, no pl., *n.n.* baker's trade. ·**bakkersbond**, *n.* bakers' union. ·**bakkersgezel**, -**llen**, *n.* journeyman baker. ·**bakkersknecht**, *n.* baker's man. ·**bakkersoven**, -**s**, *n.* baking oven. ·**bakkerswagen**, -**s**, *n.* baker's cart. ·**bakkerswinkel**, -**s**, *n.* baker's (shop).
·**bakkes**, *n.n.* (*slang*) mug, dial. *iemand op zijn* ~ *geven*, to give someone a beating; *hou je* ~!, shut up!
·**bakmeel**, no pl., *n.n.* self-raising flour. ·**bakpan**, -**nnen**, *n.* frying pan. ·**bakpoeder**, no pl., *n.* baking powder. ·**baksel**, -**s**, *n.n.* batch (*from the oven*).
·**baksmaat**, -**s**, *n.* mess-mate.
·**bakstag**, *n.* backstay.
·**baksteen**, -**stenen**, *n.* brick. *zinken als een* ~, to sink like a stone; *zakken als een* ~, to fail badly (*in examination*). ·**bakstenen**, *a.* (made of) brick. ·**bakvis**, -**ssen**, *n.* frying-fish; flapper.
·**bakzeilhalen**, **haal bakzeil**, *v.i.s.* to back the sails; to back down.
bal, ·**ballen**, *n.* ball, bowl. *de* ~ *misslaan*, to miss the bus (*fig.*); *elkaar de* ~ *toeslaan*, to play into each other's hands; *wie kaatst moet de* ~ *verwachten*, you can't play with fire without getting burnt; *geen* ~, not a hang. **bal**, -**s**, *n.n.* ball, dance. ~ *champêtre*, open air ball, lawn dance; ~ *masqué*, masked ball.
balan·ceerstok, -**kken**, *n.* balancing-pole. **ba·lans**, *n.* balance, pair of scales; beam (*of engine*); balance-sheet. *in* ~ *houden*, to keep balanced; *de* ~ *opmaken*, to draw up a balance-sheet, to strike a balance; *de* ~ *sluit*, the balance agrees; *een geflatteerde* ~, fake balance-sheet. **ba·lansopruiming**, *n.* stock-taking sale. **ba·lansrekening**, *n.* balance-account. **ba·lanswaarde**, -**n**, *n.* balance-sheet value, inventory value.
ba·lata, no pl., *n.* balata.
·**balboekje**, -**s**, *n.n.* (dance) programme.

bal·dadig, *a.* wanton, rowdy. **bal·dadigheid**, -**heden**, *n.* rowdiness, hooliganism.
balda·kijn, -**s** or -**en**, *n.* canopy.
·**baleh**- **baleh**, -**s**, or ·**balé**- **balé**, -**'s**, *n.* (*East Indian*) bench.
ba·lein, *n.* whalebone; busk; rib (*of umbrella*). **ba·leinen**, *a.* (made of) whalebone.
balg, *n.* skin; skin bag; bellows.
·**balie**, -**s**, *or* -**iën**, *n.* tub; rail(ing); bar (*in court of law*). *tot de* ~ *toelaten*, to call to the bar. **baliekluiver**, -**s**, *n.* loafer.
·**baljapon**, -**nnen**, *n.* dance-frock. **baljurk**, *n.* dance-frock (*of child*).
baljuw, -**s**, *or* -**en**, *n.* bailiff (*king's*). **baljuwschap**, -**ppen**, *n.n.* bailiwick.
balk, *n.* beam, joist, rafter; girder; bar (*on shield*); staff, stave (*in musical notation*). *balken onder de ogen*, pouches under the eyes; *je kunt het* (*met een krijtje*) *aan de* ~ *schrijven*, it is a noteworthy occurrence, a red-letter day; *het geld over de* ~ *gooien*, to be wasteful; *een* ~ *in het wapen hebben*, to be born on the wrong side of the blanket.
·**balken**, *v.i.* to bray; to bawl.
bal·kon, -**s**, *n.n.* balcony. **bal·kondeur**, *n.* french window.
·**balkostuum**, -**s**, *n.n.* ball-room dress.
bal·lade, -**s**, *n.* ballad.
·**ballast**, *n.* ballast. ~ *innemen*, to take in ballast; ~ *inhebben*, to be in ballast. ·**ballastbed**, -**dden**, *n.n.* ballast-way. ·**ballasten**, *v.t.* to ballast. ·**ballastschuit**, *n.* ballast lighter.
·**ballen**, **bal**, *v.t.* to ball; to clench (*fists*).
bal·let, -**tten**, *n.n.* ballet. **bal·letdanser**, -**s**, *n.* ballet dancer (*male*). **bal·letdanseres**, -**ssen**, *n.* ballet dancer (*female*). **bal·letmeester**, -**s**, *n.* ballet master. **bal·letmuziek**, no pl., *n.* ballet music.
·**balletje**, -**s**, *n.n.* little ball. ~ *gehakt*, forcemeat ball; *een* ~ *opgooien*, to put out a feeler.
·**balling**, *n.* exile (*person*). ·**ballingschap**, no pl., *n.* exile, banishment.
ballis·tiek, no pl., *n.* ballistics.
bal·lon, -**s**, *n.* balloon. **bal·lonband**, *n.* balloon-tyre.
ballo·tage, -**s**, *n.* ballot. **ballo·teren**, -**teer**, *v.i. & v.t.* to vote by ballot. *over iemand* ~, to ballot for someone.
ba·lorig, *a.* cross, petulant. *je wordt er* ~ *van*, it is enough to make one lose all patience. **ba·lorigheid**, no pl., *n.* contrariness.
·**balroos**, -**rozen**, *n.* guelder rose.
·**balsem**, -**s**, *n.* balm, balsam. ·**balsemen**, *v.t.* to embalm. ·**balsemer**, -**s**, *n.* embalmer. **balse·mien**, *n. or* **balse·mijn**, *n.* balsamine, garden balsam. ·**balseming**, *n.* embalming. ·**balsemkruid**, no pl., *n.n.* basil.
·**balspel**, -**spelen**, *n.n.* ball game.
bal·sturig, *a.* obstinate, refractory. **bal·sturigheid**, no pl., *n.* obstinacy.

·bamboe, no pl., *n.n.* bamboo. ¶ -s, *n.*
bamboo-cane. ¶ *a.* bamboo. ~ *rotting*,
bamboo-cane. bam·boezen, *a.* (*made of*)
bamboo.
ban, -nnen, *n.* ban, excommunication.
in den ~ *doen*, to excommunicate, put
under a ban.
ba·naal, -nale, *a.* banal. banali·teit, *n.*
platitude.
ba·naan, -nanen, *n.* banana.
band, *n.* band, belt (*on machine*); string
(*apron*), tape, etc.; bond, tie, link; hoop,
rim, tyre; kerb; cushion (*billiards*); cover
(*book*). *aan de* ~ *leggen*, to tie up; *aan de* ~
liggen, to be tied up; *aan* ~*en leggen*, to
put under restraint, to muzzle (*fig.*);
iemand in de ~ *houden*, to keep a person
within bounds; *uit de* ~ *springen*, to kick
over the traces; *door de* ~, on an average.
bande·lier, -s, *n.* bandoleer. ·bandeloos,
-loze, *a.* lawless, unrestrained, riotous.
¶ *adv.* unrestrainedly. bande·loosheid,
no pl., *n.* lawlessness. ·bandenpech, no
pl., *n.* tyre trouble. bande·rol, -llen, *n.*
banner, streamer; banderole; cigar-band.
banderol·leren, -leer, *v.t.* to band (*cigars*).
·bandje, -s, *n.n.* small band; cigar-band.
ban·diet, *n.* bandit.
·bandijzer, no pl., *n.n.* hoop iron.
·bandjer, -s, *n.* or ·bandjir, -s, *n.* spate
(*East Indian*).
·bandrekel, -s, *n.* bandog.
·banen, baan, *v.t.* to clear (*way, path*). *de
weg* ~ *voor*, to prepare the way for;
zich een weg ~ *door*, to force one's way
through; *de gebaande weg*, the beaten
track.
bang, *a.* afraid, scared; terrifying; anxious
(*times*). ~ *voor*, afraid of *or* for; ~ *maken*,
to scare; ~ *zijn*, to be afraid; ~ *zijn
om* . . ., to be afraid to (*perform action*);
~ *zijn dat*, to be afraid lest. ¶ *adv.* timidly.
·bangerd, -s, *n.* or ·bangerik, *n.* muff, scare-
cat. ·bangheid, no pl., *n.* or ·bangig-
heid, no pl., *n.* fear, anxiety. ·bangmaker,
-s, *n.* intimidator. bangmake·rij, *n.*
intimidation.
ba·nier, *n.* banner. *een* ~ *ontplooien*, to
unfurl a banner; *een* ~ *opsteken*, to raise a
banner; *een* ~ *planten*, to plant a banner.
ba·nierdrager, -s, *n.* standard bearer.
·banjir, -s, *n. See* bandjer.
bank, *n.* bench; desk, form; bank; bank
(*sand, cloud*). ~ *van lening*, pawnshop;
iets niet onder stoelen of ~*en steken*,
not to make a secret of something; *aan
een* ~ *zijn* or *op een* ~ *werken*, to work
in a bank; *achter de* ~ *gooien*, to discard;
geld op de ~ *hebben*, to have money in
the bank; *geld op de* ~ *plaatsen*, to put
money in the bank; *de* ~ *hebben* or
houden, to keep the bank; *de* ~ *doen*
or *laten springen*, to break the bank.
·bankaanwijzing, *n.* cheque; bank post

bill; bank-bill. ·bankbedrijf, no pl.,
n. banking. ·bankbiljet, -tten, *n.n.* bank-
note. ·bankbreuk, *n.* bankruptcy. ·bank-
briefje, -s, *n.n.* banknote; pawn ticket.
·bankdisconto, no pl., *n.n.* bank rate.
·banken, *v.i.* to play vingt-et-un. ban·ket,
-tten, *n.n.* banquet; fancy cakes, pastries.
ban·ketbakker, -s, *n.* pastry cook, confectioner. banke·teren, -teer, *v.i.* to
banquet. ban·ketletter, -s, *n.* kind of
pastry made in letter shapes. ·bankgeld,
n.n. bank money. ·bankhouder, -s, *n.*
banker (*of gaming bank*); pawnbroker.
ban·kier, -s, *n.* banker. ban·kiershuis,
-zen, *n.n.* banking house. ban·kierskan-
toor, -s *or* -toren, *n.n.* bank. ban·kierszaak,
-zaken, *n.* banking business. ban·kiers-
zaken, pl. only, *n.* banking. ·bankin-
stelling, *n.* bank, banking establishment.
·bankje, -s, *n.n.* small bench; footstool.
·bankkonto, -'s, *n.n.* bank(ing) account.
·bankloper, -s, *n.* bank messenger. ·bank-
noot, -noten, *n.* banknote. ·bankoctrooi,
n.n. bank charter. ·bankoverval, -llen, *n.*
hold-up. ·bankpapier, no pl., *n.n.* bank-
notes. ·bankrekening, *n.* bank(ing)
account. ·bankreserve, -s, *n.* banking
reserve. ban·kroet, *n.n.* bankruptcy.
~ *gaan*, to fail, to go bankrupt; *iemand* ~
verklaren, to declare someone a bankrupt;
frauduleus ~, fraudulent bankruptcy.
¶ *a.* bankrupt. bankroe·tier, -s, *n.* bankrupt. ·banksaldo, -'s, *n.n.* bank balance.
·bankschroef, -ven, *n.* bench vice. ·bank-
schuld, *n.* overdraft. ·bankstaat, -staten,
n. bank return. ·bankvereniging, *n.*
banking company, joint-stock bank.
·bankwerker, -s, *n.* fitter. bankwerke·rij,
n. fitting shop. ·bankwet, -tten, *n.* banking
law. ·bankwezen, pl. only, *n.n.* banking.
·bankzaken, pl. only, *n.* banking.
·banneling, *n.* exile (*person*). ·bannen, ban,
v.t.irr. to banish, exorcise. ·banvloek, *n.*
anathema, ban. ·banvonnis, -ssen, *n.n.*
excommunication, sentence of exile.
bar, ·barre, *a.* naked, barren; inclement
(*weather*). ¶ *adv.* awfully, very.
ba·rak, -kken, *n.* shed. ba·rakkenkamp, *n.n.*
hutment, encampment.
bar·baar, -baren, *n.* barbarian. bar·baars, *a.*
barbarous, barbaric. ¶ *adv.* barbarously.
bar·baarsheid, -heden, *n.n.* barbarousness,
barbarity. barba·risme, -n, *n.n.* barbarism
(*in language*).
bar·beel, -belen, *n.* barbel.
bar·bier, -s, *n.* barber. bar·biersjongen, -s,
n. barber's apprentice. bar·bierswinkel,
-s, *n.* barber's (shop).
·baren, baar, *v.t.* to bear, give birth to; to
cause. *angst* ~, to cause fear; *onrust* ~,
to cause uneasiness; *opzien* ~, to create
a stir; *de tijd baart rozen*, time heals
everything; *geld baart zorgen*, money
brings cares. ·barensnood, no pl., *n.* or

·barensweeën, pl. only, n. labour, birth-pangs, travail. *in barensnood verkeren*, to be in labour.

ba·ret, -tten, n. biretta.

bar·goens, no pl., n.n. gibberish; thieves' cant.

·barheid, no pl., n. barrenness, infertility.

bark, n. bark, barque.

bar·kas, -ssen, n. launch.

barm·hartig, a. merciful, charitable. ¶ *adv.* mercifully. barm·hartigheid, -heden, n. mercy, charity. *uit ~,* out of charity.

·barmsijsje, -s, n.n. whin-chat.

·barnsteen, n. amber. ·barnstenen, a. (*made of*) amber.

·barometer, -s, n. barometer. ·barometerstand, n. barometer reading.

ba·ron, -s, or -nnen, n. baron. baro·nes, -ssen, or baro·nesse, -n, n. baroness. baro·nie, -ieën, n. barony.

barre·biesjes, pl. only, n.n. *naar de ~ gaan,* to go to Davy Jones's locker.

·barrevoets, adv. barefooted.

barri·ère, -s, n. barrier. *~ tractaat,* Barrier Treaty.

bars, a. stern, gruff. ¶ *adv.* sternly. ·barsheid, no pl., n. sternness.

barst, n. crack, burst. ·barsten, v.i., irr. to burst, crack; to explode; to chap. *~de hoofdpijn,* splitting headache; *tot ~s toe,* to bursting point.

·bartjens. *volgens ~,* according to Cocker.

bas, -ssen, n. bass.

ba·salt, n.n. See bazalt.

bas·cule, -s, n. bascule; platform weighing machine. bas·culebrug, -ggen, n. bascule bridge.

ba·seren, -seer, v.t. to base. *~ op,* to base on. ¶ *v.r. zich ~ op,* to base oneself on.

basi·liek, n. basilica.

·basis, bases, n. basis; base. ·basisch, a. basic.

·bassen, bas, v.i. to bay.

bas·sin, -s, n.n. basin (*harbour; swimming*).

·bassleutel, -s, n. bass clef. ·basstem, -mmen, n. bass(-voice).

bast, n. bark (*of tree*). *iemand op zijn ~ geven (vulg.),* to thrash a person.

·basta! int. enough! stop! hold! *en daarmee ~,* but that's enough.

·bastaard, n. bastard; mongrel; hybrid. ·bastaard· or ·basterd· *in compounds.* hybrid. bastaar·dij, no pl., n. bastardy. ·bastaardvloek, n. mild oath, imprecation. ·bastaardvorm, n. hybrid, hybrid form. ·bastaardwoord, n. hybrid word. ·basterd-aap, -dapen, n. half-ape. ·basterdnach·tegaal, -galen, n. hedge-sparrow. ·basterdspin, -nnen, n. harvest spider. ·basterd-suiker, no pl., n. moist sugar.

baston·nade, -s, n. bastinado.

·basviool, -violen, n. violoncello.

batal·jon, -s, n.n. battalion. batal·jons-commandant, n. battalion commander.

bate, n.n. See baat.

·baten, baat, v.t. to avail.

·batig, a. *~ slot* or *saldo,* credit balance, surplus.

·batik, -s, n. batik(-work). ·batikken, batik, v.i. to batik.

ba·tist, no pl., n.n. batiste, cambric. ba·tisten, a. (*made of*) cambric.

batte·rij, n. battery (*number of guns; men of battery*); battery (*electric*). *droge ~,* dry battery.

bavi·aan, -ianen, n. baboon.

ba·zalt, no pl., n.n. basalt. ba·zalten, a. (*made of*) basalt.

·bazelen, v.i. to drivel.

·bazig, a. domineering, bossy. ¶ *adv.* domineeringly.

ba·zin, -nnen, n. farmer's or countryman's wife.

ba·zuin, n. trombone; trump (*angel's*). *de ~ steken,* to make a song about; *de ~ van het Laatste Oordeel,* the Last Trump, the Trump of Doom. ba·zuingeschal, no pl., n.n. flourish of trumpets.

be·aarden, v.t. to inter. be·aarding, n. interment.

be·ademen, v.t. to breathe on.

be·ambte, -n, n. official (*not of government*).

be·amen, beaam, v.t. to assent to. *hij beaamt het,* he agrees to it.

be·angst, a. scared. ¶ *adv.* with fear, fearfully. be·angstheid, no pl., n. alarm. be·angstigen, v.t. to alarm. ¶ *zich ~, v.r.* to be alarmed.

be·antwoorden, v.t. and v.i. to answer, reply to; to return (*feelings*); to fulfil (*requirements*); to come up to (*expectation*). *~ aan,* to answer to, correspond with; *aan het doel ~,* to answer the purpose. be·antwoording, n. (*act of*) answering. *ter ~ van,* in reply to.

be·arbeiden, v.t. See bewerken.

be·bakenen, v.t. to beacon. be·bakening, no pl., n. beaconage.

be·bladerd, a. leafy.

be·bloed, a. bloody.

be·boeten, v.t. to fine. *iemand ~ met een bedrag van . . .,* to fine someone a sum of . . .

be·bossen, bebos, v.t. to afforest. be·bossing, n. afforestation.

be·bouwen, v.t. to build on; to cultivate. be·bouwbaar, -bare, a. arable; suitable (for building).

be·broeden, v.t. to incubate, hatch. be·broed, a. hardset.

be·cijferen, v.t. to figure out. be·cijfering, n. calculation.

becriti·seren, -seer, v.t. to criticize.

bed, -dden, n.n. bed (*for sleeping; of river; of plants*); bed-side. *aan or bij het ~,* at the bed-side; *op or in or te ~ liggen,* to lie in bed; *naar ~,* to bed; *uit (het) ~,* out of bed; *het ~ houden,* to keep one's bed; *het ~ van eer,* the field of honour; *kinderen van het eerste ~,* children of the first marriage; *kamer met twee ~den,* double bedroom; *t ʋfel en* ~, bed and board.

be·daagd, *a.* aged.

be·daard, *a.* calm, sedate, composed. ¶ *adv.* sedately, composedly. **be·daardheid**, no pl., *n.* composure.

be·dacht, *a.* ~ *op*, mindful, thoughtful of, prepared for. **be·dachtzaam**, *a.* circumspect, cautious. ¶ *adv.* circumspectly. **be·dachtzaamheid**, no pl., *n.* circumspection.

be·daken, **bedak**, *v.t.* to roof (in).

be·dammen, **-dam**, *v.t.* to dam.

be·dankbrief, **-ven**, *n.* letter of thanks. **be·dankbriefje**, **-s**, *n.n.* note of thanks. **be·danken**, *v.t.* to thank; to dismiss. ¶ *v.i.* to thank; to decline; to resign. *ergens voor* ~, to decline something. ¶ no pl., *n.n.* resignation. *wegens het* ~ *van*, on account of the resignation of. **be·dankje**, **-s**, *n.n.* note of thanks; acknowledgement. *'t is geen* ~ *waard*, don't mention it.

be·daren, **-daar**, *v.i.* & *v.t.* to calm (down), compose. *doen* ~, to calm (down). ¶ no pl., *n.n. tot* ~ *komen*, to quiet down.

be·dauwen, *v.t.* to bedew.

·beddedeken, **-s**, *n.* blanket. **·beddegoed**, no pl., *n.n.* bed-clothes. **·beddekruik**, *n.* hot-water bottle. **·beddelaken**, **-s**, *n.n.* sheet. **·beddenwinkel**, **-s**, *n.* bedroom-furniture shop. **·beddesprei**, *n.* bedspread, counterpane. **·beddetijk**, *n.* bed-tick. **·beddezak**, **-kken**, *n.* bed cover. **·bedding**, *n.* bed (*of river*); platform (*gun*).

·bede, **-n**, *n.* prayer; supplication. *op zijn* ~, at his entreaty. **·bededag**, *n.* day of prayer.

be·deeld, *a.* endowed. *ruim* ~ *met*, richly blessed with; ~ *worden*, to receive parish relief. **be·deelde**, **-n**, *n.* recipient of poor-law relief.

be·deesd, *a.* bashful. ¶ *adv.* bashfully. **be·deesdheid**, no pl., *n.* bashfulness.

·bedehuis, **-zen**, *n.n.* house of worship.

be·dekken, **bedek**, *v.t.* to cover. **be·dekking**, *n.* cover; (*act of*) covering. **be·dekt**, *a.* covered, covert, veiled. *op* ~*e wijze*, covertly. ¶ *adv.* covertly. **be·dektbloeiend**, *a.* cryptogamous. **be·dektbloeiende**, **-n**, *n.* cryptogam. **be·dektzadig**, *a.* angiospermous. **be·dektzadige**, **-n**, *n.* angiosperm.

·bedeklokje, **-s**, *n.n.* angelus (*bell*).

·bedelaar, **-s**, *n.* beggar (*male*). **·bedelaarsgebed**, no pl., *n.n. een* ~ *doen*, to count one's money. **·bedelaarskolonie**, **-iën**, *n.* beggars' reclamation settlement. **·bedelachtig**, *a.* beggarly. **bedela·res**, **-ssen**, *n.* beggar (*female*). **bedela·rij**, no pl., *n.* begging. **·bedelbrief**, **-ven**, *n.* begging letter. **·bedelᵇbroeder**, **-s**, *n.* mendicant friar. **·bedelen**, **bedel**, *v.t.* & *v.i.* to beg. *om geld* ~, to beg for money. **·bedelmonnik**, *n.* mendicant friar. **·bedelorde**,

-n, *n.* mendicant order. **·bedelpartij**, *n.* persistent begging; begging-stunt. **·bedelstaf**, no pl., *n.* beggar's staff; beggary. *tot de* ~ *brengen*, to reduce to beggary. **·bedelvolk**, no pl., *n.n.* beggars. **·bedelzak**, **-kken**, *n. getrouw tot de* ~, faithful to the last.

be·delen, **bedeel**, *v.t.* to endow. *de armen* ~, to give alms to the poor. **be·deling**, *n.* poor relief. *van de* ~ *krijgen*, to receive out-door relief; *van de* ~, ludicrous (*of clothing*).

be·delven, **-delf**, *v.t.*, *str.* to bury, cover. *bedolven onder de sneeuw*, snowed under.

be·denkelijk, *a.* uncertain, doubtful; questionable, suspicious. ¶ *adv.* seriously (*ill*); doubtfully; suspiciously. **be·denkelijkheid**, **-heden**, *n.* riskiness. **be·denken**, *v.t.*, *irr.* to bear in mind, to consider; to think out, devise; to remember (*in will*, *etc.*). *als men bedenkt dat*, considering (that); *iemand* ~ *met*, to present someone with. ¶ *zich* ~, *v.r.*, *irr.* to reflect; to change one's mind. *zonder zich te* ~, without a thought. **be·denking**, *n.* consideration; objection. **be·denktijd**, no pl., *n.* time to think it over.

·bedeplaats, *n.* place of pilgrimage.

be·derf, no pl., *n.n.* decay, corruption, deterioration. *aan* ~ *onderhevig*, perishable; *tot* ~ *overgaan*, to go bad. **be·derfelijk**, *a.* perishable. **bederf·werend**, *a.* preservative. *een* ~ *middel*, a preservative. **be·derven**, **-derf**, *v.t.*, *str.* to spoil (*object; child*); to corrupt (*manners*). *het bij iemand* ~, to spoil one's chances with someone; *alles* ~, to spoil it all. ¶ *v.i.*, *str.* to decay, go bad. **be·derver**, **-s**, *n.* corrupter.

·bedevaart, *n.* pilgrimage. **·bedevaartganger**, **-s**, *n.* pilgrim.

·bedgenoot, **-noten**, *n.* bedfellow.

be·dienaar, **-s** *or* **-naren**, *n.* minister (*of gospel*). **be·diende**, **-n**, *n.* servant, domestic (*male*); (*shop*) assistant; employee. *jongste* ~, junior clerk, office boy. **be·diendenkamer**, **-s**, *n.* servants' hall. **be·diendenpersoneel**, no pl., *n.n.* domestic staff. **be·dienen**, *v.t.* to serve (*customers; mass; gun*); to attend to; to administer the last sacraments. *iemand op zijn wenken* ~, to wait on a person hand and foot. ¶ *v.i.* to wait (*at table*). ¶ *zich* ~, *v.r.* to help oneself (*at table*). *zich* ~ *van*, to help oneself to, to avail oneself of (*opportunity*); *zich goed* ~, to take a large helping. **be·diening**, *n.* attendance, service; administration of the last sacraments. **be·dieningsmanschappen**, pl. only, *n.* or **be·dieningspersoneel**, no pl., *n.n.* gun crew(s).

be·dijken, *v.t.* to embank. **be·dijking**, *n.* embankment; damming in.

be·dilal, -llen, *n.* caviller. **be·dillen, -dil,** *v.t.* to cavil, carp. **be·dilziek,** *a.* censorious. **be·dilzucht,** no pl., *n.* censoriousness.

be·ding, *n.n.* condition. *onder één ~,* on one condition; *onder ~ van* or *dat,* on condition (that). **be·dingen,** *v.t., str.* to stipulate; to obtain (*conditions*).

be·disselen, *v.t.* to arrange, make arrangement.

bed·legerig, *a.* bedridden. *~ zijn,* to be confined to bed, laid up.

be·doeld, *a.* in question. **be·doelen,** *v.t.* to mean, signify; to mean, intend. *~ met,* to mean by; *goed bedoeld,* well meant. **be·doeling,** *n.* meaning; intention; purpose. *het ligt in onze ~,* it is our intention to; *het ligt niet in onze ~,* we have no intention of; *met de ~,* with a view to.

be·dompt, *a.* close, stuffy.

be·donderen, *v.t.* (*vulg.*) to fool. **be·donderd,** *a.* (*vulg.*) mad.

be·dorven, *a.* spoilt, bad.

be·dotten, bedot, *v.t.* to trick, cheat; to take in.

be·drag, -dragen, *n.n.* amount. *ten ~e van, tot een ~ van,* to the amount of. **be·dragen, -draag,** *v.t., str.* to amount to.

be·dreigen, *v.t.* to threaten. **be·dreiging,** *n.* threat.

be·dremmeld, *a.* confused. ¶ *adv.* confusedly.

be·dreven, *a.* expert. **be·drevenheid,** no pl., *n.* skill.

be·driegen, *v.t., str.* to deceive; to victimize. *schijn bedriegt,* appearances are deceptive; *bedrogen uitkomen,* to be disappointed. ¶ **zich** *~, v.r., str.,* to delude oneself. *zich in iemand ~,* to find oneself mistaken in someone. **be·drieger, -s,** *n.* cheat; impostor (*male*). *de ~ bedrogen,* the biter bit. **bedriege·rij,** *n.* deceit, fraud. **be·drieglijk,** *a.* deceitful; deceptive. ¶ *adv.* deceitfully; deceptively. **be·drieglijkheid,** no pl., *n.* deceitfulness. **be·driegster, -s,** *n.* cheat; impostor (*female*).

be·drijf, -ven, *n.n.* trade, profession; business; deed, action; act (*of play*). *onder de bedrijven door,* meanwhile. **be·drijfsbelasting,** *n.* tax on trade profits. **be·drijfsinstallatie, -s,** *n.* plant (*works*). **be·drijfskapitaal, -talen,** *n.n.* working capital. **be·drijfskosten,** pl. only, *n.* working expenses. **be·drijfsleider, -s,** *n.* works manager. **be·drijfsmateriaal, -ialen,** *n.n.* working stock. **be·drijfsorganisatie, -s,** *n.* industrial organization. **be·drijfsraad, -raden,** *n.* industrial council. **be·drijfsstoring,** *n.* stoppage of work (*in factory*). **be·drijfsverzekering,** *n.* consequential loss insurance. **be·drijfswinst,** *n.* trade profits. **be·drijven, -drijf,** *v.t., str.* to commit, perpetrate. **be·drijvend,** *a.* active (*grammar*). **be·drijvig,** *a.* active, industrious. **be·drijvigheid,** no pl., *n.* activity; bustle.

be·drinken, zich, *v.r., str.* to get drunk.

be·droefd, *a.* sad, sorrowful; pitiful. *~ over* or *om,* sad about or at. ¶ *adv.* painfully, awfully. *~ weinig,* precious little. **be·droefdheid,** no pl., *n.* sadness. **be·droeven, -droef,** *v.t.* to grieve, distress. *het bedroeft me,* it grieves me . . . . **be·droevend,** *a.* deplorable.

be·drog, no pl., *n.n.* deceit; fraud. *~ plegen,* to practise deceit, cheat; *optisch ~* optical illusion. **be·drogene, -n,** *n.* person cheated, dupe.

be·druipen, *v.t., str.* to baste; to drip on. ¶ **zich** *~, v.r., str.* to manage for oneself.

be·drukken, -druk, *v.t.* to print on or over. **be·drukt,** *a.* depressed, dejected. **be·druktheid,** no pl., *n.* depression, dejection.

·bedsermoen, *n.n.* curtain lecture. **·bedstede, -n,** *n.* or **·bedstee, -steeën,** *n.* bed built inside a cupboard. **·bedstijl,** *n.* bedpost. **·bedtijd,** no pl., *n.* bedtime.

be·ducht, *a.* apprehensive. *~ voor,* apprehensive of. **be·duchtheid,** no pl., *n.* apprehension.

be·duiden, *v.t.* to signify; to indicate, mean; to portend. *het heeft niets te ~,* there's nothing in it.

be·duimelen, *v.t.* to thumb.

be·duvelen, *v.t.* to trick.

be·duusd, *a.* taken aback, flabbergasted. ¶ *adv.* in a flabbergasted way.

be·dwang, no pl., *n.n. in ~,* under control; *in ~ hebben,* to keep in order; *in ~ houden,* to restrain, control; *zich in ~ houden,* to control oneself.

be·dwelmen, *v.t.* to stupefy, drug. **be·dwelming,** *n.* stupor, narcosis.

be·dwingen, *v.t., str.* to conquer, subdue, restrain. ¶ **zich** *~, v.r., str.* to contain oneself, restrain oneself.

be·ëdigd, *a.* sworn (in). **be·ëdigen,** *v.t.* to swear in, administer the oath to. **be·ëdiging,** *n.* swearing in.

·beefaal, -falen, *n.* electric eel.

be·ëindigen, *v.t.* to conclude, terminate. **be·ëindiging,** *n.* conclusion, termination.

beek, beken, *n. and* **beekje, -s,** *n.n.* brook, stream. **·beekbezinking,** *n.* silt (*along stream*). **·beekpunge, -n,** *n.* brooklime.

beeld, *n.n.* statue; image; representation; emblem; figure of speech. *een ~ van een kind,* a beautiful child; *zich een ~ vormen van,* to visualize. **·beeldend,** *a.* plastic (*of art*). **·beeldenaar, -s,** *n.* head (*on coin*). **·beeldenstorm,** no pl., *n.* iconoclasm; iconoclastic riot. **·beeldenstormer, -s,** *n.* iconoclast. **·beelderig,** *a.* delightful charming. ¶ *adv.* delightfully. **·beeldgieter, -s,** *n.* caster (*of statues*). **·beeldhouwen,** *v.i.* to carve (*stone or wood*). **·beeldhouwer, -s,** *n.* sculptor. **·beeldhouwkunst,** no pl., *n.* sculpture. **·beeldhouwwerk,** *n.n.* piece of sculpture. ¶ no pl. statue(s), carving. **·beeldig,** *a.* charming.

¶ *adv.* charmingly. ·**beeldje, -s,** *n.n.*
statuette. ·**beeldjeskoop,** no pl., *n.* itinerant
(*Italian*) figurine-vendor. ·**beeldrijk,** *a.*
imaginative, rich. ·**beeldschoon,** *a.* extremely beautiful. ·**beeldschrift,** no pl.,
n.n. picture-writing. ·**beeldspraak,** no pl.,
n. metaphor. ·**beeldwerk,** *n.n.* carving(s).
·**beeltenis, -ssen,** *n.* image, effigy.
beemd, *n.n.* lush meadow. ·**beemdgras,** no
pl., *n.n.* meadow grass.
been, (1) -deren, *n.n.* bone. *van de ~deren
ontdoen,* to bone; *door merg en ~
dringen,* to pierce the marrow; *in merg
en ~,* right through; *ergens geen ~ in
zien,* to make no bones about something;
steen en ~ klagen, to complain bitterly.
been, (2) ·benen, *n.n.* leg (*usu: human*);
leg (*of stocking*); arm(s) (*of compasses, of
angle*); side (*of angle*); loop (*of letter*).
op de ~ blijven, to keep one's feet; *op
de ~ brengen,* to raise, levy (*army*); *op de
~ helpen,* to help up; *op de ~ houden,*
to keep going; *op de ~ komen,* to recover
one's feet; *vlug ter ~,* fleet-footed, quick
on one's feet; *met één ~ in het graf staan,*
to have one foot in the grave; *met het
verkeerde ~ uit bed stappen,* to get out of
bed on the wrong side, *i.e.,* to get up in
a bad temper; *op eigen benen staan,* to
stand on one's own feet, be independent;
op zijn laatste benen lopen, to be on one's
last legs; *het zijn sterke benen die de
weelde kunnen dragen,* set a beggar on
horseback and he will ride to the devil.
·**beenachtig,** *a.* bony, osseous. ·**beenbreuk,**
n. fracture of or in bone. ·**beenderas,** no
pl., *n.* bone-ash. ·**beendergestel, -llen,** *n.*
bony structure, skeleton. ·**beenderhuis,
-zen,** *n.n.* charnel-house. ·**beenderkool,**
no pl., *n.* bone charcoal. ·**beenderlijm,** no
pl., *n.* bone glue. ·**beendermeel,** no pl., *n.n.,*
bone-meal. ·**beendermest,** no pl., *n.*
bone-manure. ·**beenderstelsel, -s,** *n.n.*
bony structure, skeleton. ·**beendroog,** *a.*
bone-dry. ·**beenkap, -ppen,** *n.* leggings.
·**beenontsteking,** *n.* inflammation of the
bone. ·**beentje, -s,** *n.n.* little bone *or* leg.
zijn beste ~ voor zetten, to put one's best
foot forward; *iemand ~ lichten,* to trip
someone up; *~-over rijden,* to skate (left
over right and *vice versa*). ·**beenvlies, -zen,**
n.n. periosteum. ·**beenvliesontsteking,** *n.*
periostitis. ·**beenwindsels,** pl. only, *n.n.*
puttees.
beer, ·beren, *n.* bear; debt; bill; boar;
buttress. *de grote ~,* the Great Bear;
de kleine ~, the Little Bear; *een ongelikte
~,* an uncouth person. ¶ no pl., *n.*
nightsoil. ·**beerput, -tten,** *n.* cess-pool.
be·erven, beërf, *v.t.* to inherit.
beest, *n.n.* beast. animal; brute. ·**beestachtig,**
a. beastly; bestial. ¶ *adv.* bestially;
horribly. ·**beestachtigheid, -heden,** *n.*
beastliness; brutality. ·**beesten-** *in*

compounds see **vee-.** ·**beestenboel,** no pl.,
n. pig-sty (*fig. only*). ·**beestenspel, -llen,**
n.n. menagerie. ·**beestenwagen, -s,** *n.*
cattle-truck. **beesti·aal,** no pl., *n.n.* cattle.
·**beestig,** *a.* beastly; bestial.
beet, ·beten, *n.* bite, sting; bite, mouthful.
in één ~, at one bite. ·**beethebben, heb
beet,** *v.t.s., irr. iets ~,* to keep hold of
something; *iemand ~,* to keep hold of
someone, to trick someone; *het ~,* to
have caught it (*illness*). ¶ *v.i.s., irr.* to
have a bite (*fishing*). ·**beetje, -s,** *n.n.*
little bit. *een ~,* a little bit, a little,
somewhat; *~ bij ~,* bit by bit; *een ~
(beter),* a little (better); *lekkere ~s,* titbits;
alle ~s helpen, every little helps. ·**beet-
krijgen, krijg beet,** *v.t.s., str.* to get hold
of. ¶ *v.i.s., str.* to get a bite (*fishing*).
·**beetnemen, neem beet,** *v.t.s., str.* to get
hold of; to trick, make fun of. *zich laten
~,* to allow oneself to be caught. **beet-
neme·rij,** *n.* leg-pull. ·**beetpakken, pak
beet,** *v.t.s.* to lay hold of. ·**beetwortel, -s,**
n. beetroot. sugar-beet. ·**beetwortelstroop,**
no pl., *n.* black treacle (from sugar-beet).
·**beetwortelsuiker,** no pl., *n.* beet sugar.
bef, -ffen, *n.* bands.
be·faamd, *a.* renowned, noted.
be·fietsen, *v.t.* to cycle on *or* over.
·**beflijster, -s,** *n.* ring ouzel.
be·floersen, *v.t.* to muffle (*drum*).
be·gaafd, *a.* gifted. **be·gaafdheid, -heden,** *n.*
ability, talent.
be·gaan, -ga, *v.t., irr.* to walk upon; to
commit (*crime; error*). *iemand laten ~,*
to let someone carry on. ¶ **-gane,** *a.*
trodden, beaten. *op de begane grond,* on
ground level; *begane paden,* the beaten
track; *~ zijn met,* to feel sorry for.
be·gaanbaar, -bare, *a.* practicable, passable.
be·geerlijk, *a.* desirable; avid. ¶ *adv.* desir-
ably; avidly. **be·geerlijkheid, -heden,** *n.*
desirability; greed. **be·geerte, -n,** *n.* desire,
craving; lust.
bege·leiden, *v.t.* to accompany; to escort.
bege·leidend, *a.* accompanying; covering
(*letter*); attendant (*circumstances*). **bege-
·leider, -s,** *n.* escort; accompanyist (*male*).
bege·leiding, *n.* accompaniment; escort.
bege·leidster, -s, *n.* escort; accompanyist
(*female*).
bege·nadigen, *v.t.* to pardon, reprieve.
bege·nadiging, *n.* pardon, reprieve.
be·geren, -geer, *v.t.* to desire, covet. ¶ no
pl., *n.n. wat is er van uw ~?* what can I do
for you? **be·gerig,** *a.* desirable. *~ naar,*
avid for; *~ om te,* desirous to. **be·gerig-
heid,** no pl., *n.* desirability, cupidity.
be·geven, -geef, *v.t., str.* to bestow, confer;
to break down, give way (*of health*); to
forsake. *zijn benen begaven hem,* his legs
gave way, failed him; *zijn kracht begaf
hem,* his strength gave way. ¶ *zich ~.*

v.r., *str.* to proceed; to embark (on). *zich ~ naar*, to proceed to; *zich naar huis ~*, to go home; *zich ter ruste ~*, to retire (*to bed*); *zich in het huwelijk ~*, to enter the married state; *zich in gevaar ~*, to go int̩o danger; *zich op weg ~ (naar)*, to set out (to).

be·gieten, *v.t.*, *str.* to water (*plants*).

be·giftigen, *v.t.* to endow (*with qualities*).

be·gijn, *n.n.* beguine. **be·gijnhof, -hoven,** *n.n.* beguinage.

be·gin, no pl., *n.n.* beginning, start. *aan het ~*, at the beginning; *bij het ~*, at or in the beginning; *in het ~*, in the beginning, at first; *heel in het ~*, in the very beginning; *van 't ~ af aan*, from the very beginning; *in den beginne*, in the beginning; *van den beginne aan*, from the beginning. **be·ginkoers,** *n.* opening price. **be·ginletter, -s,** *n.* initial letter. **be·ginne,** *n. See* **be·gin.** **be·ginneling,** *n.* beginner. **be·ginnen, -gin,** *v.t.*, *str.*, & *v.i.*, *str.* to begin, start; to open (*new shop, business, school*). *~ te . . .*, to begin to (+ *verb*); *aan iets ~*, to make a beginning at something, to begin on something; *met iets ~*, to begin with something, to begin by; *er is niets mee te ~ or er is geen ~ aan*, the task is hopeless or endless; *er is niets met hem te ~*, you cannot do anything with him; *~ om . . .*, to start at (*time*); *~ over . . .*, to begin about (*subject*); *opnieuw ~*, to begin again. **be·ginsel, -s** *or* **-en,** *n.n.* element(s), rudiment(s), first principles; origin, beginning. *in ~*, in principle; *uit ~*, on principle. **be·ginselloos, -loze,** *a.* unprincipled. **beginsel·loosheid,** no pl., *n.* lack of principle(s). **be·ginsnelheid, -heden,** *n.* initial velocity. **be·ginstadium, -ia,** *n.* initial stage. **be·gintraktement,** *n.n.* commencing salary.

be·gluren, -gluur, *v.t.* to peep at, spy on.

be·goochelen, *v.t.* to bewitch, fascinate; to delude. **be·goocheling,** *n.* bewitchment, fascination; delusion.

be·graasd, *a.* grassy.

be·graafplaats, *n.* cemetery. **be·grafenis, -ssen,** *n.* funeral, burial. **be·grafenisfonds,** *n.n.* burial club. **be·grafeniskosten,** pl. only, *n.* funeral expenses. **be·grafenisonderneming,** *n.* undertaker's business. **be·grafenisplechtigheid, -heden,** *n.* obsequies. **be·grafenisstoet,** *n.* funeral procession. **be·graven, -graaf,** *v.t.*, *str.* to bury.

be·grensd, *a.* limited, circumscribed. **be·grensdheid, -heden,** *n.* limitation, circumscription. **be·grenzen, -grens,** *v.t.* to limit, border; to circumscribe. *~ door*, to limit by. **be·grenzing,** *n.* limitation.

be·grijpelijk, *a.* understandable, intelligible, comprehensible, conceivable. **be·grijpelijkheid,** no pl., *n.* comprehensibility, intelligibility. **be·grijpen,** *v.t.*, *str.* to

understand; to conceive, grasp (*mentally*); to contain, include. *het (niet) begrepen hebben op,* (not) to be keen on; *(dat) kun je ~!* by no means! *begrepen?* do you get me?

be·grinten, *v.t.* to gravel.

be·grip, -ppen, *n.n.* concept, idea, notion; comprehension; judgment. *kort ~,* short survey; *vlug van ~,* quick on the uptake; *niet het flauwste ~,* not the slightest idea; *zich een ~ vormen van,* to form an idea of, to get the hang of; *het gaat mijn ~ te boven,* it is beyond me; *volgens mijn ~,*, in my opinion. **be·gripsverwarring,** *n.* confusion of ideas.

be·groeien, *v.t.* to grow over.

be·groeten, *v.t.* to greet, welcome. **be·groeting,** *n.* salutation.

be·groten, -groot, *v.t.* to estimate (*cost*). **be·groting,** *n.* estimate; budget. **be·grotingsdebat, -tten,** *n.n.* debate on the Budget. **be·grotingsjaar, -jaren,** *n.n.* financial year. **be·grotingsrede, -voeringen,** *n.* Budget speech.

be·gunstigen, *v.t.* to favour; to patronize. **be·gunstiger, -s,** *n.* patron, supporter. **be·gunstiging,** no pl., *n.* favour; favouritism. *onder ~ van de duisternis,* under cover of darkness.

be·haaglijk, *a.* pleasant, comfortable. ¶ *adv.* comfortably. **be·haaglijkheid,** no pl., *n.* comfort. **be·haagziek,** *a.* over-anxious to please; coquettish. **be·haagzucht,** no pl., *n.* coquetry.

be·haard, *a.* hairy, hirsute.

be·hagen, -haag, *v.t.* to please. ¶ no pl., *n.n.* pleasure. *~ scheppen in,* to take pleasure in.

be·halen, -haal, *v.t.* to obtain; to gain, conquer, score. *een overwinning ~ op,* to gain a victory over; *eer ~ met,* to gain credit by.

be·halve, *c.* except, apart from, save, but for, besides.

be·handelen, *v.t.* to treat; to give treatment to; to discuss; to deal with. *iemand uit de hoogte ~,* to behave haughtily towards someone. **be·handeling,** *n.* treatment. *in ~,* under discussion; *in ~ komen,* to come up for trial; *onder ~,* receiving medical treatment.

be·hang, no pl., *n.n.* wall-paper; wall-coverings. **be·hangen,** *v.t.*, *str.* to paper (*room*); to festoon, drape. **be·hanger, -s,** *n.* paper-hanger. **be·hangsel, -s,** *n.n. See* **be·hang.** **be·hangselpapier,** no pl., *n.n.* wall-paper.

be·hartigen, *v.t.* to have at heart; to look after (*interest*); to take to heart. **be·hartiging,** no pl., *n.* care.

be·heer, no pl., *n.n.* administration, control, management. *in eigen ~,* under direct management; *onder zijn ~ hebben,* to have under one's control; *het ~ voeren* *over*, to superintend, control. **be·heerder**, **-s**, *n*. administrator, manager. **be·heersen**, *v.t.* to command (*nation; circumstances*); to control (*passions; situation*); to dominate (*field of operations*); to be master of (*knowledge*). ¶ **zich** ~, *v.r.* to govern oneself, control oneself. **be·heerser**, **-s**, *n*. master, ruler. **be·heersing**, *n*. domination, command.

be·heksen, *v.t.* to bewitch.

be·helpen, **zich**, *v.r.*, *str*. to made do. *zich* ~ *met*, to make shift with.

be·helzen, **-hels**, *v.t.* to contain, cover (*subject matter*).

be·hendig, *a*. dexterous, skilful. ¶ *adv*. dexterously, skilfully. **be·hendigheid**, **-heden**, *n*. dexterity, skill.

be·hept, *a*. ~ *met*. afflicted with (*illness; unpleasant habit*).

be·heren, **-heer**, *v.t.* to rule, administer.

be·hoeden, *v.t.* to guard. ~ *voor*, to protect from. **be·hoeder**, **-s**, *n*. protector, defender. **be·hoedmiddel**, *n*. preventative. **be·hoedzaam**, *a*. circumspect, cautious, wary. ¶ *adv*. circumspectly. **be·hoedzaamheid**, no pl., *n*. circumspection. *met* ~ *te werk gaan*, to set about a task with circumspection.

be·hoefte, **-n**, *n*. need, want. ~ *hebben aan*, to be in need of; *in een* ~ *voorzien*, to supply a want; *een* ~ *doen*, to relieve nature; *een kleine* ~, number one (*micturation*); *een grote* ~, number two (*defecation*). **be·hoeftig**, *a*. necessitous. **be·hoeftigheid**, no pl., *n*. destitution. **be·hoeve**, no pl., *n. ten* ~ *van*, for the benefit of, on behalf of; *te zijnen* ~, on his behalf. **be·hoeven**, **-hoef**, *v.t.* to need, want, require. *het behoeft niet*, it need not be done.

be·hoorlijk, *a*. proper, due; decent; fair-sized. ¶ *adv*. properly; decently. **be·horen**, **-hoor**, *v.i.* to belong. ~ *aan*, to belong to (someone); ~ *bij*, to belong to, go with; *bij elkaar* ~, to belong together; ~ *tot*, to belong to, be part of. ¶ *v. imp*. to be fitting, be proper. ¶ no pl., *n.n. naar* ~, as it should be, proper.

be·houd, no pl., *n.n. met* ~ *van*, with the aid of; *tot* ~ *van*, as a help to. **be·hulpzaam**, **-zame**, *a*. helpful. *de behulpzame hand bieden*, to lend a helping hand.

be·houden, no pl., *n.n. met* ~ *van*, for the preservation of; *met* ~ *van salaris*, on full pay. **be·houden**, *v.t.*, *irr*. to keep, to retain; to save. ¶ *a*. safe. **be·houdend**, *a*. conservative. **be·houdenis**, no pl., *n*. conservation. **be·houdens**, *prep*. except, but for, bar.

be·houwen, *v.t.*, *irr*. to rough-hew, dress.

be·huisd, *a*. domiciled. *goed* ~ *zijn*, to live in a good house; *klein* ~ *zijn*, to live in cramped quarters. **be·huizing**, no pl., *n*. housing.

be·huwd-, *in compounds:* in-law, related by marriage. **be·huwdbroeder**, **-s**, *n*. brother-in-law. **be·huwddochter**, **-s**, *n*. daughter-in-law. **be·huwdmoeder**, **-s**, *n*. mother-in-law. **be·huwdvader**, **-s**, *n*. father-in-law. **be·huwdzoon**, **-s**, *or* **-zonen**, *n*. son-in-law. **be·huwdzuster**, **-s**, *n*. sister-in-law. **be·huwen**, *v.t.* to acquire by marriage.

bei, **-s**, *n*. bey.

beiaard, *or* **beierd**, **-s**, *n*. carillon. **beiaar·dier**, **-s**, *n*. carillon player.

beide, *a*. & *pron*. both. *mijn* ~ *handen*, both my hands. ¶ no pl., *pron*. (*things*), **-n**, *pron*., (*persons*). *één van* ~, one of the two; *geen van* ~, neither (of them). *met ons* ~*n* or *wij* ~*n*, both of us, between us; *met jullie* ~, *jullie* ~*n*, you two, between you; *met hun* ~*n*, both of them, between them; *met z'n* ~*n*, between them, both of them.

beiden, *v.i.* to tarry. ¶ *v.t.* to bide.

beiderhande, *a*. of both sorts. **beiderlei**, *a*. of both sorts. *op* ~ *wijs*, both ways, either way; *van* ~ *kunne*, of both sexes, either sex. **beiderzijds**, *adv*. on both sides.

beieren, *v.t.* to ring, chime; to dangle.

beiers, *a*. Bavarian.

beig·net, **-tten**, *n*. fritter.

be·ijveren, *v.r. zich* ~ *om te*, to do one's utmost in order to.

be·ijzeld, *a*. white with frost; covered with hoar-frost.

be·invloeden, *v.t.* to influence.

beitel, **-s**, *n*. chisel. *holle* ~, gouge **beitelen** *v.t.* to chisel.

beits, *n.n.* (wood)-stain. **beitsen**, *v.t.* to stain (*wood*).

be·jaard, *a*. aged, elderly. **be·jaardheid**, no pl., *n*. old age.

be·jag, *n.n.* pursuit (*fig.*). ~ *naar*, pursuit of. **be·jagen**, **-jaag**, *v.t.*, *irr*. to pursue, strive after; to hunt (*cover estate or shoot*).

be·jammeren, *v.t.* to deplore, lament. **be·jammerens·waardig**, *a*. deplorable.

be·jegenen, *v.t.* to treat (*manner*). *iemand met vriendelijkheid* ~, to be friendly towards; *wat is U bejegend?*, what has happened to you? **be·jegening**, *n*. treatment.

bek, **-kken**, *n*. beak, bill; mouth (*of animal; of man: vulgar*); jaw, bit; spout, nozzle, burner. *hou je* ~!, hold your jaw! *hij heeft een grote* ~, he has too much to say for himself.

be·kaaid, *adv. er* ~ *afkomen*, to come off badly.

bek·af, *a*. dead-beat, dog-tired.

be·kalken, *v.t.* to plaster.

be·kappen, **-kap**, *v.t.* to roof in. **be·kapping**, *n*. roofing.

be·keerde, **-n**, *n*. convert, proselyte. **be·keerder**, **-s**, *n*. proselytizer. **be·keerling**,

n. convert, proselyte (*male*). **be·keerlinge, -n,** *n.* convert, proselyte (*female*).
be·kend, *a.* well-known; known; familiar. *goed* ~, familiar; ~ *in,* known in *or* at; ~ *met,* acquainted with; *ergens* ~ *zijn,* to be known somewhere, to be familiar *or* acquainted with some place; *voor zover mij* ~ *is,* so far as I know; ~ *maken,* to announce; *zich* ~ *maken,* to disclose one's identity; *iemand* ~ *maken met,* to acquaint a person with; ~ *staan als,* to be known as; ~ *staan wegens,* to be known on account of; *het komt me* ~ *voor,* it strikes me as familiar. **be·kende, -n,** *n.* acquaintance (*person*). *een oude* ~, an old friend. **be·kendheid,** no pl., *n.* acquaintance, familiarity; ~ *met,* familiarity with (*knowledge*); *de* ~ *van,* the fame of. **be·kendmaken, maak bekend,** *v.t.s.* to announce. **be·kendmaking,** *n.* announcement, notice; publication (*of result, etc.*). **be·kennen,** *v.t.* to admit, confess; to know (carnally); to see. *kleur* ~, to follow suit (*cards*); *er valt niets te* ~, there is no trace of anything. **be·kentenis, -ssen,** *n.* admission, confession. *een* ~ *afleggen,* to make a full confession.
·beker, -s, *n.* beaker, goblet; chalice. **·bekermos, -ssen,** *n.n.* cup-moss. **·bekerplant,** *n.* pitcher-plant. **·bekervormig,** *a.* cup-shaped. ~ *kraakbeen,* arytenoid (cartilage) **·bekerwedstrijd,** *n.* cup-match, cup-tie, cup-final.
be·keren, -keer, *v.t.* to convert. ¶ **zich** ~, *v.r.* to repent. *zich* ~ *tot,* to be converted to. **be·kering,** *n.* conversion; repentance.
be·keurde, -n, *n.* person summoned. **be·keuren,** *v.t.* to summon, take a person's name (*for offence*). **be·keuring,** *n.* summons, fine.
be·kijk, no pl., *n.n. veel* ~*s hebben,* to be much looked at. **be·kijken,** *v.t., str.* to look at; to consider. *alles goed bekeken,* after due consideration.
be·kijven, -kijf, *v.t., str.* to scold.
be·kisting, *n.* mould, casing; coffer-dam.
·bekje, -s, *n.n.* small beak; face (*of child* or *girl: affectionate*).
·bekken, -s, *n.n.* basin; cymbal; pelvis; catchment area. **bekke·neel, nelen,** *n.n.* skull. **·bekkenholte,** *n.* pelvic cavity. **bekke·nist,** *n.* cymbal-player.
·bekkesnijden, *v.i., str.* to cut about the face. **·bekkesnijder, -s,** *n.* member of razor-gang; duelling German student.
be·klaagde, -n, *n.* person accused; defendant; prisoner (*at the bar*).
be·kladden, -klad, *v.t.* to besmirch; to bespatter.
be·klag, no pl., *n.n.* complaint. *recht van* ~, right to lodge complaint; *reden van* ~, cause for complaint; *zijn* ~ *indienen* (*bij*), to lodge a complaint about something (with somebody). **be·klagen, -klaag,**

v.t. to deplore; to pity ¶ **zich** ~, *v.r.* to complain. *zich* ~ *over iets bij iemand,* to complain about something to somebody; *hij zal het zich* ~, he will be sorry for it. **beklagens·waardig,** *a.* pitiable, lamentable.
be·klant, *a.* well-patronized (*shop*).
be·klauteren, *v.t.* to clamber up.
be·kleden, -kleed, *v.t.* to cover, line, upholster; to fill, occupy (*post*). ~ *met,* clothed with. **be·kleder, -s,** *n.* holder (*of post*). **be·kleding,** *n.* covering, lining; tenure. **be·kleedsel, -s,** *n.n.* cover, lining (*material only*).
be·klemd, *a.* oppressed (*physical feeling*); stressed, accented. *met een* ~ *hart,* with a heavy heart; *een* ~*e breuk,* a strangulated hernia. **be·klemdheid,** no pl., *n.* oppressiveness. **be·klemmen, -klem,** *v.t.* to oppress (*feeling*); to catch (*between two objects*). **be·klemming,** *n.* oppressiveness.
be·klimmen, -klim, *v.t., str.* to climb, ascend. **be·klimming,** *n.* climbing, ascent.
be·klinken, *v.t., str.* to rivet; to clinch, settle; to drink to.
be·kloppen, -klop, *v.t.* to tap, percuss.
be·kneld, *a. See* **beklemd. be·kneldheid,** no pl., *n. See* **beklemdheid. be·knellen, -knel,** *v.t. See* **beklemmen.**
be·knibbelen, *v.t.* to stint, whittle down.
be·knopt, *a.* concise, succinct. ¶ *adv.* concisely, succinctly. **be·knoptheid,** no pl., *n.* conciseness, brevity.
be·knorren, -knor, *v.t.* to reprove, chide.
be·knotten, -knot, *v.t.* to curtail. **be·knotting,** *n.* curtailment.
be·kocht, *a.* cheated, done. *hij is eraan* ~, he has paid too much for it.
be·koelen, *v.t. & v.i.* to cool down *or* off. *doen* ~, to damp down (*ardour*).
be·kokstoven, -stoof, *v.t.* to concoct (*mischief*).
be·komen, -kom, *v.t., irr.* to obtain; to agree with. *het zal je slecht* ~, you'll regret it; *wel bekome het U,* may it do you good. ¶ *v.i., irr.* to recover. ~ *van,* to recover from.
be·kommerd, *a.* worried, anxious. ~ *over,* worried about. **be·kommeren,** *v.r. zich* ~ *om* or *over,* to worry, be anxious about. *zonder zich te* ~ *om,* without a thought about. **be·kommering,** *n.* anxiety, care. **be·kommernis, -ssen,** *n.* anxiety, care.
be·komst, no pl., *n. zijn* ~ *eten,* to eat one's fill; *zijn* ~ *hebben van,* to be fed up with.
be·konkelen, *v.t.* to scheme, plot.
be·koorder, -s, *n.* charmer; tempter. **be·koorlijk,** *a.* charming. ¶ *adv.* charmingly. **be·koorlijkheid, -heden,** *n.* charm. **be·koorster, -s,** *n.* charmer, temptress.
be·kopen, -koop, *v.t., irr.* to pay for. *hij moest het met de dood* ~, he paid for it with his life. ¶ **zich** ~, *v.r., irr.* to make a bad bargain.

be·koren, -koor, *v.t.* to charm; to tempt. be·koring, *n.* charm; temptation.

be·korten, *v.t.* to shorten, abbreviate. ¶ zich ~, *v.r.* to be brief. be·korting, *n.* shortening, abridgment.

be·kostigen, *v.t.* to defray (*expenses*); to afford. be·kostiging, *n.* defrayment.

be·krachtigen, *v.t.* to confirm; to ratify. be·krachtiging, *n.* ratification, sanction.

be·krammen, *v.t.* to strengthen (*outside of dyke*).

be·kransen, *v.t.* to wreathe.

be·krassen, -kras, *v.t.* to cover with scratches.

be·kreten, *a.* tear-stained.

be·kreunen, *v.r.* zich ~ *over*, to care about, worry about.

be·krimpen, zich, *v.r.*, *str.* to retrench, stint oneself. be·krimping, *n.* retrenchment.

be·krompen, *a.* restricted; narrow-minded. ¶ *adv.* narrow-mindedly. ~ *wonen*, to live in cramped quarters. be·krompenheid, no pl., *n.* narrow-mindedness.

be·kronen, ·kroon, *v.t.* to crown. be·kroning, *n.* coronation; award. be·kroond, *a.* prize-(*animal or commodity*).

be·kruipen, *v.t.*, *str.* to steal upon. *de lust bekroop hem om*, he was tempted to.

be·kwaam, -kwame, *a.* able, capable. *te bekwamer tijd*, in due time; *met bekwame spoed*, with all speed. be·kwaamheid, -heden, *n.* ability, capability. be·kwamen -kwaam, *v.t.* to fit, train. *iemand ~ voor*, to prepare a person for (*exam, task*). ¶ *v.r.* zich ~ *voor*, to qualify for (*post*); *zich tot iets ~*, to prepare oneself for (*job*).

be·kwijlen, *v.t.* to beslobber.

bel, -llen, *n.* bell; bubble; ear-ring.

be·labberd, *a.* foul, rotten (*slang*); awful (*feeling*). ¶ *adv.* awfully.

be·lachelijk, *a.* ridiculous, laughable. *iemand ~ maken*, to hold someone up to ridicule. ¶ *adv.* ridiculously. be·lachelijkheid, -heden, *n.* ridiculousness.

be·laden, -laad, *v.t.*, *irr.* to load, burden. ¶ *a.* laden.

be·lagen, -laag, *v.t.* to waylay, lay in wait for, ambush. be·lager, -s, *n.* waylayer.

be·landen, *v.i.* to arrive at, get to.

be·lang, *n.n.* interest (*desire to know*); importance; advantage, interest. ~ *stellen in*, to take an interest in; ~ *gaan stellen in*, to become interested in; *van ~ zijn*, to be important; to matter; *van groot or weinig ~*, of great or little importance; *in iemands ~*, to someone's advantage; *eigen ~*, self interest; ~ *hebben bij*, to be interested in, to have an interest in; *in het ~ van*, in the interest(s) of, for the sake of. be·langeloos, -loze, *a.* disinterested. ¶ *adv.* disinterestedly. be·langloosheid, no pl., *n.* disinterestedness. be·langen, *v.t.* to concern. be·langende, *prep.* concerning. belang·hebbend, *a.* interested, concerned. belang·hebbende, -n, *n.*

person or party interested or concerned. be·langrijk, *a.* important; considerable, ¶ *adv.* considerably. be·langrijkheid, no pl., *n.* importance. belang·stellend, *a.* interested, sympathetic. ¶ *adv.* interestedly. belang·stellenden, pl. only, *n.* persons interested. be·langstelling, no pl., *n.* interest, sympathy. ~ *inboezemen* or *wekken voor*, to rouse interest in; *zijn ~ verliezen*, to lose interest; *een blijk* or *bewijs van ~*, a sign of interest. belang·wekkend, *a.* interesting.

be·last, *a.* laden. *erfelijk ~*, congenitally tainted. be·lastbaar, -bare, *a.* taxable, rateable, assessable. be·lasten, *v.t.* to load, burden; to entrust (*task to*); to tax; to debit (*account*). *iemand ~ met*, to charge a person with (*task*). ¶ *v.r.* zich ~ *met*, to take (*task*) upon oneself.

be·lasteren, *v.t.* to slander. be·lastering, *n.* defamation.

be·lasting, *n.* burdening; weight, load; taxation; tax(es), rates. ~ *op openbare vermakelijkheden*, entertainment tax; ~ *heffen op*, to levy a tax on. be·lasting-aangifte, -n, *n.* (tax-) return. be·lasting-aanslag, -slagen, *n.* (tax-) assessment. be·lastingambtenaar, -naren, *n.* (tax) official. be·lastingbetaler, -s, *n.* taxpayer, ratepayer. be·lastingbiljet, -tten, *n.n.* demand note (*tax*). be·lastingjaar, -jaren. *n.n.* year of assessment. be·lastingkantoor, -toren, *n.n.* tax-collector's office. be·lastingkohier, *n.n.* assessment list. be·lasting-ontduiking, *n.* tax evasion. belasting-plichtig, *a.* taxable, rateable. belasting-schuldig, *a.* taxable, rateable. be·lasting-vrij, *a.* tax-free. be·lastingwet, -tten, *n.* fiscal law.

be·lazeren, *v.t.* to diddle (*vulgar*). *ben je belazerd?* you're up the pole! (*vulgar*); don't you believe it!

belboei, *n.* bell-buoy.

beldeurtje, no pl., *n.n.* ~ *spelen*, to ring a bell and run away.

be·ledigen, *v.t.* to offend, insult. *zich beledigd gevoelen*, to feel injured; *zich laten ~*, to put up with insults. be·ledigend, *a.* insulting. be·lediger, -s, *n.* one who insults. be·lediging, *n.* insult. *iemand een ~ aandoen*, to offend someone; *een ~ voor*, an insult to.

be·leefd, *a.* polite, civil. ¶ *adv.* politely. ~ *maar dringend*, gently but firmly. be·leefdelijk, *adv.* politely. be·leefdheid, -heden, *n.* politeness, civility. *een ~*, an act of courtesy; *ik laat het aan uw ~ over*, I leave it to you; *de ~ vordert*, politeness demands; *beleefdheden bewijzen*, to perform small courtesies; *beleefdheden in acht nemen*, to observe common politeness. be·leefdheidshalve, *adv.* out of politeness. be·leefdheidsvorm, *n.* convention(s), etiquette.

be·leenbaar, -bare, *a.* pawnable.   be·leen-briefje, -s. *n.n.* pawnticket.

be·leg, no pl., *n.n.* siege. *het ~ slaan voor,* to lay siege to; *het ~ opbreken,* to raise the siege; *de staat van ~,* a state of siege. be·legeraar, -s, *n.* besieger. be·legeren, *v.t.* to besiege. be·legering, *n.* siege. be·legeringsgeschut, no pl., *n.n.* siege-artillery. be·legeringsoorlog, *n.* siege warfare.

be·legen, *a.* matured, seasoned.

be·leggen, -leg, *v.t.* to cover, carpet; to spread (*bread with meat, cheese, etc.*); to invest (*money*); to convene. *~ met,* to cover with. be·legger, -s, *n.* investor. be·legging, *n.* cover; investment. be·legsel, -s, *n.n.* trimming(s), facing(s) (*on clothes*). be·legstuk, -kken, *n.n.* trimming.

be·leid, no pl., *n.n.* government, statesmanship; prudence, wisdom, discretion. *met ~ handelen,* to act wisely. be·leidvol, -lle, *a.* prudent, tactful. ¶ *adv.* prudently, tactfully.

be·lemmeren, *v.t.* to hinder, obstruct. *in de groei ~,* to stunt. be·lemmering, *n.* hindrance, impediment.

be·lenden, *v.i.* to abut. be·lendend, *a.* adjacent, contiguous.

be·lenen, -leen, *v.t.* to pawn. be·lener, -s, *n.* pawnbroker. be·lening, *n.* pawn(ing).

be·let, no pl., *n.n.* ~ ! you can't come in! *iemand ~ geven,* not to be at home to someone; *~ hebben,* to be engaged; *~ krijgen,* to be told that someone is not at home to visitors; *~ vragen,* to inquire whether someone is at home to visitors.

bel-é·tage, -s, *n.* first floor.

be·letsel, -s, *n.n.* hindrance, obstacle, impediment. *een ~ uit de weg ruimen,* to remove an obstacle. be·letten, -let, *v.t.* to prevent, make impossible. *iemand iets ~,* to prevent a person from doing something.

be·leven, -leef, *v.t.* to experience, witness; to live through. *vreugde ~ aan,* to experience joy from.

be·lezen, *a.* well-read. be·lezeneid, no pl., *n.* (wide) reading. *een man van grote ~,* a man of wide reading.

Belg, *n.* Belgian. België, *n.N.* Belgium. ·Belgisch, *a.* Belgian. ·Belgische, -n *n.* Belgian (*woman*).

·belgen, *v.r. zich ~ over,* to be angered at; *zich gebelgd tonen over,* to show anger at; *gebelgd zijn over,* to be angered by.

·belhamel, -s, *n.* bell-wether; ringleader; young rascal.

be·lichamen, -chaam, *v.t.* to embody, represent. be·lichaming, no pl., *n.* embodiment, incarnation.

be·lichten, *v.t.* to illuminate; to throw light upon. *te lang ~,* to over-expose (*photography*); *te kort ~,* to under-expose (*photography*). be·lichting, no pl., *n.* lighting, illumination; elucidation.

be·liegen, *v.t., str.* to tell lies to.

be·lieven, -lief, *v.t.* to please. *wat blieft U?* what can I do for you? *or* I beg your pardon; *als 't U belieft,* if you please *or: polite phrase used on handing objects.* ¶ no pl., *n.n.* pleasure, discretion. *naar ~,* at (your, etc.) pleasure; *naar ~ handelen,* to use one's discretion.

be·lijden, *v.t., str.* to confess (*sins*); to avow; to profess (*religion*). be·lijdenis, -ssen. *n.* confession, avowal; confession (*of faith*); confirmation; denomination. *zijn ~ doen,* to be confirmed. be·lijder, -s, *n.* confessor; adherent (*of creed*).

bella·donna, no pl., *n.* deadly nightshade; belladonna.

belle·fleur, -s, *n.* (kind of) eating apple.

·bellen, bel, *v.i.* to ring (*bell*). *er wordt gebeld,* there is a ring at the door. ¶ *v.t.* to ring for.

·bellenbaan, -banen, *n.* wake (*of torpedo*).

bellet·trie, no pl., *n.* belles-lettres. bellet·trist, *n.* belletrist. bellet·tristisch, *a.* belletristic.

be·loeren, *v.t.* to spy on; to pry.

be·lofte, -n, *n.* promise. *een ~ afleggen,* to make a (solemn) promise; *iemand aan een ~ houden,* to hold a person to his word; *~ maakt schuld,* a promise is a promise.

be·loken, *a.* ~ *Pasen,* Low Sunday.

be·lommeren, *v.t.* to give shade.

be·lonen, -loon, *v.t.* to reward; to remunerate. be·loning, *n.* reward. *ter ~ van,* as a reward for; *een ~ uitloven,* to offer a reward.

be·lonken, *v.t.* to ogle.

be·loop, -lopen, *n.n.* amount (*of bill, account*). ¶ no pl., *n.n.* course. *'s werelds ~,* the way of the world; *iets op zijn ~ laten,* to let something take its course; *naar ~ van zaken,* as things turn out. be·lopen, -loop, *v.i., str.* to walk (on). ¶ *v.t., str,* to amount (to), run into. ¶ *a. met bloed ~,* bloodshot.

be·loven, -loof, *v.t.* to promise; to be promising. *het belooft veel goeds voor,* it promises well for.

·belroos, no pl., *n.* St. Anthony's fire, erysipelas.

belt, *n.* refuse-heap.

be·luisteren, *v.t.* to eavesdrop; to auscult.

be·lust, *a.* desirous. *~ op* or *naar,* eager for; *iemand ~ maken op,* to make someone's mouth water for.

be·machtigen, *v.t.* to seize, secure. be·machtiging, *n.* seizure, capture.

be·malen, -maal, *v.t.* to drain (*by pumping*). be·maling, *n.* draining, drainage (*by pumping*).

be·mannen, -man, *v.t.* to man. be·manning, *n.* crew, ship's company; garrison.

be·mantelen, *v.t.* to veil, cloak.

be·masten, *v.t.* to mast. *opnieuw ~,* to remast.

be·merkbaar, -bare, *a.* noticeable, perceptible. be·merkbaarheid, no pl., *n.* perceptibility. be·merken, *v.t.* to notice, perceive.

be·mesten, *v.t.* to manure. be·mesting, *n.*
manuring.

be·middelaar, -s, *n.* mediator, intermediary
(*male*). be·middelaarster, -s, *n.* mediator,
intermediary (*female*). be·middeld, *a.*
well-to-do. be·middeldheid, no pl., *n.*
financial ease. be·middelen, *v.t.* to mediate.
be·middelend, *a.* conciliatory. ¶ *adv.*
conciliatory. ~ *optreden*, to mediate.
be·middeling, no pl., *n.* mediation. *door*
~ *van*, through the intermediary of.
be·middelingspoging, *n.* attempt at mediation. be·middelingsvoorstel, -llen, *n.n.*
offer of mediation.

be·mind, *a.* beloved. *zich* ~ *maken*, to
endear oneself. be·minde, -n, *n.* sweetheart. be·minnaar, -s, *n.* ~ *van*, lover of,
amateur of. be·minnelijk, *a.* lovable,
amiable. ¶ *adv.* amiably. be·minnelijk-
heid, -heden, *n.* charm, amiability;
charming habit (*sarcastic*). be·minnen,
-min, *v.t.* to love. beminnens·waardig, *a.*
lovable, amiable. beminnens·waardigheid,
-heden, *n.* amiability, lovableness.

be·modderen, *v.t.* to cover with mud.

be·moedigen, *v.t.* to encourage, hearten.
be·moedigend, *a.* encouraging, hearten-
ing. be·moediging, *n.* encouragement.

be·moeial, -llen, *n.* busybody. be·moeien,
v.r. zich ~ met, to deal with *or* to meddle
with; *bemoei je met je eigen zaken*, mind
your own business; *zich met iets gaan* ~,
to take a matter in hand. be·moeienis,
-ssen, *n.*, be·moeiing, *n.* exertion, trouble;
interference. be·moeiziek, *a.* meddlesome, interfering. be·moeizucht, no pl.,
n. love of interfering.

be·moeilijken, *v.t.* to hamper, hinder.
iemand in iets ~, to make something
difficult for someone. be·moeilijking, *n.*
difficulty (*put in someone's way*).

be·monsteren, *v.t.* to provide with sample.
een bemonsterde offerte, an offer accom-
panied by sample.

be·morsen, *v.t.* to soil (*with liquid*).

be·most, *a.* moss-grown, mossy.

be·muren, -muur, *v.t.* to wall (in).

ben, -nnen, *n.* basket, hamper.

be·nadelen, -deel, *v.t.* to prejudice, harm.
iemand in zijn zaken or eer ~, to injure a
person's business *or* honour; ~ *bij iemand*,
to injure in someone's eyes. be·nadeling,
no pl., *n.* injury, damage. ~ *van*, injury
to.

be·naderen, *v.t.* to approximate; to compute;
to confiscate. *tot in zes decimalen* ~, to
carry through to six decimal places.
be·nadering, *n.* seizure, confiscation;
approximation. *bij* ~, approximately;
bij ~ *bepalen*, to approximate.

be·naming, *n.* name. *onder* ~ *van*, under
the title of.

be·nard, *a.* critical, difficult. *in* ~*e omstandigheden verkeren*, to be in desperate straits;

~*e tijden*, hard times. be·nardheid,
no pl., *n.* distress.

be·nauwd, *a.* close, stifling; oppressed,
stifled; bad, anxious (*dream*); afraid. *het* ~
krijgen, to get a choking feeling, to
become anxious; *het* ~ *hebben*, to have
difficulty in breathing, to feel anxious;
~ *zijn over*, to be anxious about. ¶ *adv.*
een ~ *klein beetje*, very, very little.
be·nauwdheid, -heden, *n.* oppression,
choking fit; fear, anxiety. *in de* ~ *zitten*,
to be scared. be·nauwen, *v.t.* to oppress,
stifle. be·nauwend, *a.* oppressive. ¶ *adv.*
oppressively. be·nauwing, *n.* oppression,
anguish.

·bende, -n, *n.* band, gang (*thieves; irregulars*);
untidy mess; heap, lot (*of*). *de hele* ~,
the whole lot. ·bendehoofd, *n.n.* gang-
leader, chief of a band.

be·neden, *prep.* below, beneath, underneath, under. *iets niet* ~ *zich achten*,
not to be above doing something. ¶ *adv.*
downstairs, down, below. ~ *wonen*,
to live downstairs; *naar* ~ *gaan*, to go
downstairs; ~ *aan*, *at or* near the bottom;
van ~, from the bottom. be·nedenarm,
n. forearm. be·nedenbuur, -buren, *n.*
downstairs neighbour. be·nedendek,
-kken, *n.n.* lower deck. be·nedendijks,
adv. at the foot of the dyke. be·neden-
eind(e), -(e)n, *n.n.* lower end, bottom.
be·nedenhuis, -zen, *n.n.* lower floor(s).
be·nedenkamer, -s, *n.* downstairs room.
be·nedenloop, -lopen, *n.* lower course
(*river*). be·nedenstad, -steden, *n.* lower
town. be·nedenste, *a.* lowest, nether-
most. be·nedenverdieping, *n.* ground-
floor. be·nedenwaarts, *a.* downward.
¶ *adv.* downward(s). be·nedenwoning, *n.*
See benedenhuis.

bene·fice, -s, *n.n. ter* ~ *van*, for the benefit
of. bene·ficie, -ciën, *n.n.* benefit. ·bene·fiet,
n.n. benefit (*performance*).

be·nemen, -neem, *v.t.*, str. to take away
(from), rob (of). *iemand iets* ~, to take
away something from somebody; *het
uitzicht* ~, to obstruct the view; *de
moed* ~, to dishearten. ¶ *v.r.t. zich het
leven* ~, to take one's life.

·benen, been, *v.t.* to bone. ¶ *v.i.* to walk.
¶ *a.* (*made of*) bone.

be·nepen, *a.* petty, mean; small, timid
(*voice*); faint (*courage*); drawn (*features*);
cramped. be·nepenheid, no pl., *n.* meanness, smallness (*mental*).

be·neveld, *a.* hazy, misty; clouded (*intelligence*). be·nevelen, *v.t.* to cloud (*mist*);
to obscure (*intelligence*).

be·nevens, *prep.* besides, in addition to,
along with.

Ben·gaals, *a.* Bengali. ~ *vuur*, Bengal light.
Ben·galen, *n.N.* Bengal. Benga·lees, -lezen,
n. Bengali.

·bengel, -s, *n.* clapper (*bell*); scamp. ·bengelen,

v.i. to dangle. ¶ *v.t. laten* ~, to dangle, swing.

be·nieuwd, *a.* curious, anxious to know. ~ *naar,* curious about; *ik ben* ~ *of,* I wonder whether. **be·nieuwen,** *infin. only. het zal me* ~ *of,* I am anxious to know whether; *het zal me* ~ *!* I wonder!

be·nijdbaar, -bare, *a.* enviable. **be·nijden,** *v.t.* to envy. **benijdens·waardig,** *a.* enviable.

·**benig,** *a.* bony.

be·nodigd, *a.* required, necessary. **be·nodigd-heden,** pl. only, *n.* requisites.

be·noembaar, -bare, *a.* eligible. ~ *voor,* eligible for *or* to. **be·noemd,** *a.* concrete (*number*). **be·noemde, -n,** *n.* person appointed. **be·noemen,** *v.t.* to appoint; to nominate. ~ *tot,* to appoint to *or* as. **be·noeming,** *n.* appointment.

be·noorden, *adv.* (to the) north. ¶ *prep.* northward, north of.

bent, *n.* clique. ·**bentgenoot, -noten,** *n.* member of clique.

·**benting,** *n.* native fortification (*East Indies*).

be·nul, no pl., *n.n.* notion. *ergens geen* ~ *van hebben,* not to have the faintest idea of something.

be·nutten, -nut, *v.t.* **be·nuttigen,** *v.t.* to utilize.

ben·zine, no pl., *n.* petrol.

·**benzoë,** no pl., *n.* benzoin, gum benjamin.

ben·zol, no pl., *n.n.* benzol, benzene.

be·oefenaar, -s, *n.* votary, student (*of art, etc.*). **be·oefenen,** *v.t.* to practise, study, cultivate. **be·oefening,** *n.* practice, study. *tot* ~ *van,* for the study of; *in* ~ *brengen,* to put into practice.

be·ogen, -oog, *v.t.* to eye. *ergens iets mee* ~, to aim at something by doing something.

be·oliën, -lie, *v.t.* to oil.

be·oordelen, -deel, *v.t.* to judge, criticize. ~ *naar,* to judge by. **be·oordeling,** *n.* judgment. *ter* ~ *van,* for the judgment of.

be·oorlogen, -log, *v.t.* to wage war upon.

be·oosten, *adv.* (to the) east. ¶ *prep.* eastward, east of.

be·paalbaar, -bare, *a.* determinable, definable. **be·paald,** *a.* fixed; specified; definite; certain, definite. *in een* ~ *geval,* in a certain case; ~ *tot,* restricted to; *boete bij de wet* ~, fine in accordance with the law; *niets* ~*s,* nothing definite. ¶ *adv.* decidedly; emphatically. *niet* ~ *goed,* not exactly *or* particularly good. **be·paaldelijk,** *adv.* expressly, specifically. **be·paaldheid,** no pl., *n.* exactness, certainty.

be·pakken, -pak, *v.t.* to pack, load. **be·pak-king,** *n.* pack (*military*). *met volle* ~, in full marching order. **be·pakt,** *a.* ~ *en gezakt,* booted and spurred, all ready to go.

be·palen, -paal, *v.t.* to limit; to determine, fix; to stipulate, prescribe (*law*); to define.

zijn gedachten ~ *tot,* to concentrate (*thought*) upon. ¶ *v.r. zich* ~ *tot,* to limit oneself to. **be·palend,** *a.* ~ *lidwoord,* definite article (*grammar*). **be·paling,** *n.* definition; fixing; stipulation, provision; ascertainment; adjunct (*grammar*).

be·pantseren, *v.t.* to armour-plate. **be·pant-sering,** *n.* armour-plating.

be·parelen, *v.t.* to adorn with pearls; to bedew.

be·peinzen, -peins, *v.t.* to ponder (on, over). **be·peinzing,** *n.* meditation.

be·pekken, -pek, *v.t.* to (coat with) pitch.

be·perken, *v.t.* to limit; to qualify; to restrict; to retrench, narrow down. ¶ *v.r. zich* ~ *tot,* to confine oneself to. **be·perking,** *n.* restriction; limitation; restraint; retrench-ment. **be·perkt,** *a.* restricted, limited. **be·perktheid,** no pl., *n.* restriction.

be·plakken, -plak, *v.t.* to paste over. ~ *met,* to plaster with.

be·planten, *v.t.* to plant (with). **be·planting,** *n.* planting; plantation (*garden*).

be·pleisteren, *v.t.* to plaster (over) (*wall*); to put (sticking-)plaster on.

be·pleiten, *v.t.* to plead, argue for, advocate.

be·ploegen, *v.t.* to plough.

be·poeieren, *v.t.* to powder (over).

be·poten, -poot, *v.t.* to plant (with potatoes).

be·praten, -praat, *v.t.* to talk over; to per-suade. *bepraat worden,* to be talked about; *iemand tot iets* ~, to talk a person into something.

be·proefd, *a.* well-tried; trusty. *zwaar* ~, bereaved, afflicted. **be·proeven, -proef,** *v.t.* to try, endeavour; to try, visit; to test. **be·proeving,** *n.* trial, ordeal.

be·raad, no pl., *n.n.* deliberation, considera-tion. *na rijp* ~, after mature considera-tion; *iets in* ~ *houden,* to think something over; *iets in* ~ *nemen,* to take something into consideration; *in* ~ *staan of,* to be in two minds whether; *recht van* ~, right of deliberation; *tijd van* ~, time for reflec-tion. **be·raadslagen, -slaag,** *v.i.* to deliber-ate. ~ *met,* to consult with; ~ *over,* to deliberate upon. **be·raadslaging,** *n.* deliberation, discussion. **be·raden, zich, -raad,** *v.r., str.* to consider; to change one's mind. ¶ *a.* (well-)considered, de-liberate.

be·ramen, -raam, *v.t.* to estimate; to devise; to plot. **be·raming,** *n.* estimate; plotting.

be·rapen, -raap, *v.t.* to plaster (*wall*).

·**berberis, -ssen,** *n.* barberry.

ber·ceau, -'s, *n.n.* pergola; pleached walk.

·**berde,** no pl., *n.n. te* ~ *brengen,* to broach, bring on the carpet.

be·rechten, *v.t.* to administer last sacraments to; to adjudicate. **be·rechting,** *n.* admini-stration of last sacraments; adjudication.

be·redderen, *v.t.* to arrange, put in order. **be·reddering,** *n.* putting in order; fuss.

be·reden, *a.* broken in (*horse*); mounted (*on horse*). ~ *politie*, mounted police; ~ *artillerie*, field artillery.

berede·neerd, *a.* reasoned (out). *een* ~ *man*, a man of sound judgment. **berede·neren, -neer**, *v.t.* to reason out, discuss.

be·reid, *a.* ready; prepared; willing. *zich* ~ *verklaren tot*, to express oneself willing to. **be·reiden**, *v.t.* to prepare; to dress (*leather*). ¶ *zich* ~, *v.r.* to prepare oneself. **be·reiding**, *n.* preparation. **be·reids**, *adv.* already. **bereid·vaardig**, *a.*, **bereid·willig**, *a.* ready, willing. **bereid·vaardigheid**, no pl., *n.*, **bereid·willigheid**, no pl., *n.* readiness, willingness.

be·reik, no pl., *n.n.* reach, range. *binnen het* ~ *van*, within reach *or* range of; *boven mijn* ~, beyond my strength; *onder het* ~ *van het geschut*, within artillery range. **be·reikbaar, -bare**, *a.* attainable, within reach. **be·reikbaarheid**, *n.* attainability, accessibility. **be·reiken**, *v.t.* to reach (*be able to touch*); to reach, arrive at; to achieve, attain (*purpose*). **be·reiking**, no pl., *n.* reaching, achieving. *tot or ter* ~ *van*, in order to achieve.

be·reisd, *a.* (widely) travelled; much frequented. **be·reizen, -reis**, *v.t.* to travel about.

be·rekend, *a.* calculated. ~ *naar*, calculated on the basis of; (*niet*) ~ *op*, (not) calculated for; (*niet*) ~ *voor*, (not) equal to (*task*). **be·rekenen**, *v.t.* to calculate, compute; to charge. ~ *op*, to compute at. **be·rekening**, *n.* calculation.

·beren, beer, *v.t.* to clear cess-pool; to run up debts. **berenjacht**, *n.* bear hunt. **beren·jong**, *n.n.* bear-cub. **berenklauw**, *n.* brank-ursine, acanthus. **berenkuil**, *n.* bear-pit, bear-garden. **berenleider, -s**, *n.* bear-leader. **berenmuts**, *n.* bear-skin, busby. **berenoor, -noren**, *n.n.* auricula.

berg, *n.* mountain, mount; (high) hill; large quantity, piles of. *vuurspuwende* ~, volcano; *gouden* ~*en beloven*, to promise wealth untold; ~*en hoog*, mountain high; ~*op* ~*af*, over ~*en dal*, up hill and down dale; *zijn haar te* ~*e doen rijzen*, to make his hair stand on end. **·bergachtig**, *a.* mountainous. **berg·af**, *adv.* downhill. **bergop**, ~, up hill and down dale. **berg·afwaarts**, *adv.* downhill. **bergbeklimmer, -s**, *n.* mountaineer (*climber*). **·bergbewoner, -s**, *n.* mountaineer (*dweller*). **bergcultuur, -turen**, *n.* cultivation on mountain estates. **bergeend**, *n.* sheldrake. **·bergen**, *v.t.*, *str.* to put away, store; to hold, contain; to salvage (*ship, cargo*); to take in (*sail*). *geborgen zijn*, to be safe (*personal safety*) *or* to be safe, to have made one's money. ¶ *zich* ~, *v.r.*, *str.* to hide oneself. **·bergengte, -n**, *n.* (mountain-)pass, defile. **·berger, -s**, *n.* salvor; wrecker. **·bergforel, -llen**, *n.*

char, hill-trout. **·berggeest**, *n.* mountain spirit. **·berggeld**, *n.n.* salvage money. **·berggeschut**, no pl., *n.n.* mountain artillery. **·berghelling**, *n.* mountain slope. **·berghout**, *n.n.* wale. **·berging**, *n.* salvage (*of ship, cargo*). **bergingsauto, -'s**, *n.* breakdown lorry. **·bergingsmaatschappij**, *n.* salvage company. **berging·materiaal, -ialen**, *n.n.* salvage plant. **bergings·vaartuig**, *n.n.* salvage vessel. **·bergings·werk**, no pl., *n.n.* salvage operations. **·bergkam, -mmen**, *n.* mountain ridge. **·bergketen, -s**, *n.* mountain range. **·bergkloof, -kloven**, *n.* ravine, gully. **·bergkristal, -llen**, *n.n.* rock crystal. **·bergkruin**, *n.* mountain top. **·bergland**, no pl., *n.n.* mountainous country; highlands. **·berglandschap**, no pl., *n.n.* mountain scenery. **·berglelie, -s**, *or* **-iën**, *n.* martagon. **·bergloon, -lonen**, *n.n.* salvage money. **·bergmuis, -zen**, *n.* lemming. **berg·op**, *adv.*, **berg·opwaarts**, *adv.* uphill. *cf.* **bergaf**. **·bergpas, -ssen**, *n.* mountain pass. **·bergpek**, no pl., *n.n.* asphalt. **·bergplaats**, *n.* store, depository. **·bergrat, -tten**, *n.* marmot. **·bergrede**, no pl., *n.* Sermon on the Mount. **·bergrug, -ggen**, *n.* mountain ridge. **·bergruimte, -n**, *n.* storage room or space. **·bergspits**, *n.* (mountain) peak. **·bergstelling**, *n.* mountain position (*fortified*). **·bergstorting**, *n.* landslide. **·bergstreek, -streken**, *n.* mountainous region. **·bergvesting**, *n.* mountain fortress *or* stronghold. **·bergvink**, *n.* brambling, mountain finch. **·bergvlas**, no pl., *n.n.* amianthus. **·bergwand**, *n.* steep mountain-side. **·bergzolder, -s**, *n.* storage loft. **·bergzout**, no pl., *n.n.* rock salt.

be·richt, *n.n.* news, news-item; notice, advice, information. ~ *van ontvangst*, acknowledgement of receipt; ~ *van verscheping*, advice of shipment; *er is* ~ *gekomen van or dat*, news was received from *or* that; ~ *krijgen van*, to be informed by *or* of; *gemengde* ~*en*, miscellaneous news; *nader* ~, further information. **be·richten**, *v.t.* to inform, report, advise. *men bericht uit*, it is reported from. **be·richt·geefster, -s**, *n.* correspondent, informant (*female*). **be·richtgever, -s**, *n.* informant, correspondent, reporter.

be·rijdbaar, -bare, *a.* passable, practicable (*road*); ridable. **be·rijden**, *v.t.*, *str.* to ride (*animal*); to ride, drive (*on or over road*). *druk bereden*, much used by traffic. **be·rijder, -s**, *n.* rider (*male*). **be·rijdster, -s**, *n.* rider (*female*).

be·rijmen, *v.t.* to put into verse.

be·rijpt, *a.* covered with hoar frost.

be·rin, -nnen, *n.* she-bear.

be·rispelijk, *a.* reprehensible. ¶ *adv.* reprehensibly. **be·rispen**, *v.t.* to rebuke, reprimand. ~ *wegens*, to censure for. **be·risping**, *n.* rebuke, reproof, reprimand.

berk, *n.,* **berkeboom, -bomen,** *n.* birch (*tree*). **berken,** *a.* birchen. **berkenbos, -ssen,** *n.n.* birch forest. **berkenhout,** no pl., *n.n.* birch wood. **berkenloof,** no pl., *n.n.* foliage of birch. **berkenrijs, -zen,** *n.n.* birch (rod).

berm, *n.* (grass) verge (*of road*).

berm·pje, -s, *n.n.* groundling (*fish*).

ber·nagie, no pl., *n.* borage.

be·roemd, *a.* famous. ~ *worden,* to achieve fame. **be·roemdheid, -heden,** *n.* fame, celebrity; celebrity (*person*). **be·roemen,** *v.r. zich* ~ *op,* to pride oneself on.

be·roep, *n.n.* profession; call (*ecclesiastical*); appeal (*to higher tribunal*); appeal (*to emotions*). *van* ~, by profession; *zonder* ~, of no occupation, of independent means; *een* ~ *naar een zekere gemeente krijgen,* to be called to a certain parish; *voor een* ~ *bedanken,* to refuse a call; *hoger* ~ *aantekenen* or *in hoger* ~ *gaan,* to appeal to a higher court; *in hoger* ~ *behandelen,* to be heard in a higher court; *een* ~ *doen op,* to appeal to. **be·roepbaar, -bare,** *a.* eligible (*for new parish*). **be·roepen,** *v.t., str.* to call (*invite clergyman to new parish*); to reach (*by hailing*). ~ *worden naar,* to receive a call from (*new parish*); *iemand tot* or *als predikant* ~, to nominate someone to become clergyman *of parish; wel te* ~, within hail, within earshot. ¶ *v.r., str.* ~ *op,* to appeal to, refer to. **be·roeps-,** *in compound words often meaning:* professional. **be·roepsbezigheid, -heden,** *n.* professional duty. **beroeps·halve,** *adv.* by virtue of one's profession. **be·roepskeuze, -n,** *n.* choice of career. **be·roepsmisdadiger, -s,** *n.* habitual criminal. **be·roepssoldaat, -daten,** *n.* regular (soldier). **be·roepsziekte, -n,** *n.* occupational disease.

be·roerd, *a.* miserable, wretched, rotten. ¶ *adv.* wretchedly. **be·roeren,** *v.t.* to stir, disturb, trouble. **be·roering,** *n.* commotion, disturbance, turmoil. *in* ~ *brengen,* to stir up. **be·roerling,** *n.* unpleasant person, rotter (*coll.*). **be·roerte, -n,** *n.* fit, stroke. *pl.* troubles (*in country*). *een (aanval van)* ~ *krijgen,* to have an apoplectic fit.

be·rokkenen, *v.t.* to cause, bring (upon) (*sorrow, pain, anxiety*).

be·rooid, *a.* poor, shabby. *een* ~*e schatkist,* an empty treasury.

be·roken, -rook, *v.t.* to fumigate. **be·rookt,** *a.* smoke-stained.

be·rouw, *n.n.* remorse, repentance. *zonder* ~, unrepentant; ~ *hebben over* or *van,* to repent of, regret. **be·rouwen,** *v.t.* to repent (of), regret. ¶ *v.imp. het berouwt mij,* I repent (of) it; *het zal je* ~, you will be sorry for it. ¶ *zich* ~, *v.r.t.* to regret, rue. *hij zal het zich* ~, he will rue the day. **be·rouwhebbend,** *a.,* **be·rouwvol, -lle,** *a.* repentant, contrite, penitent.

be·roven, -roof, *v.t.* ~ *van,* to rob (of), deprive (of). ¶ *v.r. zich van het leven* ~, to take one's life. **be·roving,** *n.* robbery, deprivation.

berrie, -s, *n.* stretcher; bier.

bersten. *See* **barsten.**

be·rucht, *a.* notorious; disreputable, ill-famed. *zich* ~ *maken,* to become notorious; ~ *om* or *wegens,* notorious for. **be·ruchtheid,** no pl., *n.* notoriety.

be·ruiken, *v.t., str.* to smell (at), sniff (at).

be·rusten, *v.i.* ~ *bij,* to be deposited with or to be vested in or to rest with (*decision*); *laat het daarbij* ~, leave it at that; ~ *in,* to resign oneself to, put up with, acquiesce in; *in het onvermijdelijke* ~, to resign oneself to fate; ~ *op,* to depend on or to be based on or to rely on. **be·rusting,** no pl., *n.* acquiescence, resignation. *onder* ~ *van,* in the care of, in the custody of.

bes, -ssen, *n.* berry; currant. *rode* ~, red currant; *witte* ~, white currant; *zwarte* ~, black currant. ¶ no pl., *n.* B flat.

be·schaafd, *a.* civilized; cultured; well-bred. ¶ *adv.* in a civilized or cultured or well-bred way. ¶ no pl., *n.n. het algemeen* ~, the standard speech. **be·schaafdheid,** no pl., *n.* good manners; culture, civilization.

be·schaamd, *a.* ashamed; bashful. *met* ~*e kaken,* shamefaced; *iemand* ~ *maken, iemand* ~ *doen staan,* to make a person feel ashamed, put a person to shame; ~ *zijn over,* to be ashamed of.

be·schadigen, *v.t.* to damage. **be·schadigdheid,** no pl., *n. vrij van* ~, free of particular average. **be·schadiging,** *n.* damage, hurt.

be·schaduwen, *v.t.* to shade, overshadow.

be·schamen, -schaam, *v.t.* to put to shame, embarrass; to disappoint. *iemand in zijn verwachtingen* ~, to dash a person's hopes, let a person down. **be·schamend,** *a.* humiliating, mortifying. **be·schaming,** *n.* confusion; disappointment. *tot* ~ *van,* to the shame of.

be·schaven, -schaaf, *v.t.* to plane; to civilize. **be·schaving,** *n.* civilization, culture.

be·scheid, *n.n.* information; answer; document. ~ *geven,* to send word; ~ *krijgen,* to be told; ~ *vragen,* to ask for information; *iemand* ~ *doen,* to answer a toast; *iemand* ~ *zenden,* to inform a person; *om* ~ *komen,* to come for the answer; *het* ~ *is,* the decision is; ~ *weten,* to know what to do; *officiële* ~*en,* official documents. **be·scheiden,** *v.t.* to summon, send for; to apportion. *de hem* ~ *taak,* his allotted task. ¶ *a.* modest, unassuming. ¶ *adv.* modestly. **be·scheidenheid,** no pl., *n.* modesty, unobtrusiveness.

be·schenken, *v.t., str.* ~ *met,* to present, endow with.

be·scheren, *v.t., str.* to allot (*fate, happiness*). *dat lot is mij beschoren,* such is my allotted fate.

be·schermeling, *n.* protégé. **be·schermelinge, -n,** *n.* protégée. **be·schermen,** *v.t.* to protect, screen. ~ *voor,* to protect from; ~ *tegen,* to protect against. **be·schermend,** *a.* protective. ~*e rechten,* protective duties. ¶ *adv.* protectingly. **be·schermengel, -s,** *n.* guardian angel. **be·schermer, -s,** *n.* protector, patron. **be·schermgeest,** *n.* tutelary spirit. **be·schermheer, -heren,** *n.* patron. **be·schermheilige, -n,** *n.* patron saint. **be·scherming,** no pl., *n.* protection; patronage. *in* ~ *nemen,* to take under (one's) protection; *onder* ~ *van,* under cover of *or* under the auspices of; *tot* ~ *van,* for the protection of. **be·schermster, -s,** *n.* patroness; protectress. **be·schermvrouw,** *n.* patroness.

be·schieten, *v.t., str.* to fire on; to wainscoat, panel. **be·schieting,** *n.* bombardment, shelling.

be·schijnen, *v.t., str.* to shine on, illuminate.

be·schikbaar, -bare, *a.* available. ~ *stellen,* to place at (someone's) disposal. **be·schikbaarheid,** no pl., *n.* availabi ity. **be·schikken, -schik,** *v.t.* to decree, arrange. *de mens wikt, God beschikt,* man proposes, God disposes; *God beschikt ons lot,* God rules our destiny. ¶ *v.i.* ~ *over,* to dispose (of), to have at (one's) disposal, to have the disposal of. *afwijzend* ~ (*op*), to make an adverse decision (about). **be·schikking,** *n.* arrangement; decision. *de vrije* ~ *hebben over,* to have the free disposal of; *de* ~ *der voorzienigheid,* the dispensation of Providence; *bij* ~ *van,* by order of; *ter* ~ *staan van,* to be at the disposal of; *ter* ~ *stellen,* to place at (someone's) disposal; *ter* ~ *zijn,* to be available.

be·schilderen, *v.t.* to paint (over). *beschilderde ramen,* stained glass windows. **be·schildering,** *n.* painting.

be·schimmeld, *a.* mouldy. **be·schimmelen,** *v.i.* to go mouldy.

be·schimpen, *v.t.* to jeer at, abuse. **be·schimper, -s,** *n.* jeerer, scoffer. **be·schimping,** *n.* jeering, scoffing.

be·schoeien, *v.t.* to campshed. **be·schoeiing,** *n.* campshot, campshedding, campsheeting.

be·schonken, *a.* intoxicated. **be·schonkenheid,** no pl., *n.* intoxication.

be·scheren, *a.* See **bescheren.**

be·schot, -tten, *n.n.* wainscoting; partition; yield, crop. *een ruim* ~ *opleveren,* to yield a plentiful crop.

be·schouwen, *v.t.* to view, contemplate; to consider. ~ *als,* to look upon as; *als verloren* ~, to give up as lost; *op zichzelf beschouwd,* on its own merits. **be·schouwer, -s,** *n.* spectator, contemplator. **be·schouwing,** *n.* contemplation;

dissertation. *bij nadere* ~, on closer examination; *buiten* ~ *laten,* to leave out of consideration. **be·schouwend,** *a.* contemplative.

be·schreid, *a.* tear-stained.

be·schrijven, -schrijf, *v.t., str.* to describe; to describe, draw (*circle, curve*); to write upon; to convoke, convene. **be·schrijvend,** *a.* descriptive (*geometry; prose*). **be·schrijving,** *n.* description. **be·schrijvingsbiljet, -tten,** *n.n.* income tax return.

be·schroomd, *a.* timid, diffident. ¶ *adv.* timidly. **be·schroomdheid,** no pl., *n.* timidity.

be·schuit, *n.n.* rusk. **be·schuitje, -s,** *n.n.* biscuit. **be·schuitbakker, -s,** *n.* baker and confectioner. **be·schuitbakkerij,** *n.* baker's and confectionery shop. **be·schuitbus, -ssen,** *n.* biscuit-tin.

be·schuldigde, -n, *n.* (person) accused. **be·schuldigen,** *v.t.* to accuse; to indict. *iemand* ~ *van,* to accuse someone of. **be·schuldiger, -s,** *n.* accuser. **be·schuldiging,** *n.* accusation, charge.

be·schutten, -schut, *v.t.* to protect, screen, shelter. ~ *voor or tegen,* to protect from *or* against. **be·schutting,** *n.* protection, shelter. ~ *geven or verlenen,* to give shelter; ~ *zoeken,* to take *or* seek shelter.

be·sef, no pl., *n.n.* realization, awareness, notion, comprehension. *zijn* ~ *kwijt raken or zijn,* to lose *or* have lost consciousness; *iemand tot het* ~ *brengen van,* to make a person aware of; *tot het* ~ *komen van,* to realize; *geen* ~ *hebben van or niet het flauwste* ~ *hebben dat,* not to have the faintest notion of. **be·seffen, -sef,** *v.t.* to realize.

·besje, -s, *n.n.* old woman, crone. **·besjeshuis, -zen,** *n.n.* almshouse (*for women*).

be·slaan, -sla, *v.t., irr.* to cover (*with metal*), shoe, stud; to beat, stir (*dough, batter*); to take up, fill, occupy (*room, space*). ¶ *v.i., irr.* to be covered with condensed moisture, to dim. **be·slag,** no pl., *n.n.* added metal ornamentation *or* protection: mount, band(s), ferrule, fittings; seizure, distraint; dough, batter. ~ *leggen op or in* ~ *nemen,* to seize, confiscate (*property*) *or* to engross (*time*) *or* to occupy (*space*); *het* ~ *opheffen,* to remove distraint; *iets zijn* ~ *geven,* to clinch matter; *zijn* ~ *krijgen,* to be settled. **be·slagen,** *a.* shod (*horse*); steamed over; dull, tarnished; furred (*tongue*). *goed* ~, well equipped *or* well versed. **be·slaglegging,** *n.* seizure, distraint, distress.

be·slapen, -slaap, *v.t., str.* to sleep on. ¶ *v.r., str. zich* ~ *op,* to sleep on, think over.

be·slechten, *v.t.* to settle (*dispute*). **be·slechting,** *n.* settlement (*dispute*).

be·slijkt, *a.* mudstained.

be·slissen, -slis, *v.t.* to decide. ~ *over,* to decide on; ~ *ten gunste van,* to decide for:

~ *ten nadele van*, to decide against.
be·slissend, *a.* decisive. ~*e stem*, casting
vote. ¶ *adv.* decisively. **be·slissing**, *n.*
decision, resolution. *een ~ nemen*, to
come to a decision. **be·slissingswedstrijd**,
n. final match. **be·slist**, *a.* decided, certain;
firm, resolute. ¶ *adv.* resolutely, firmly;
decidedly. **be·slistheid**, no pl., *n.* peremptoriness, decision.
be·slommering, *n.* care, trouble.
be·sloten, *a.* resolved, determined; private;
intimate. ~ *jachttijd*, close season.
be·sluipen, *v.t.*, *str.* to stalk, steal upon;
to creep over (*fear, despondency*).
be·sluit, *n.n.* end, termination; conclusion;
decision; decree. *tot ~*, in conclusion;
tot een ~ komen, to make up one's mind;
een ~ trekken, ·to draw a conclusion;
Koninklijk ~, Order in Council. **be·sluite-
loos, -loze**, *a.* undecided, irresolute.
¶ *adv.* undecidedly, irresolutely. **besluite-
·loosheid**, no pl., *n.* indecision. **be·sluiten**,
v.t., *str.* to close; to conclude; to decide;
to contain. ~ *met*, to close (wind up)
with; ~ *uit*, to infer from; ~ *tot*, to
resolve upon; *hij kan er niet toe besluiten,*
he can't decide on it, he can't make up
his mind about it.
be·smeren, -smeer, *v.t.* to smear, besmear,
spread. ~ *met*, to spread with.
be·smettelijk, *a.* contagious, infectious
(*disease*), catching; infectious (*laughter*).
be·smettelijkheid, no pl., *n.* contagiousness,
infectiousness. **be·smetten, -smet**, *v.t.*
to infect, contaminate; to pollute, taint.
be·smetting, *n.* infection, contagion;
contamination. **be·smettingshaard**, *n.*
seat of infection.
be·smeuren, *v.t.* to soil, besmirch.
be·snaren, -snaar, *v.t.* to string (*instrument*).
fijn besnaard, highly-strung.
be·sneeuwd, *a.* snowy, snow-clad.
be·snijden, *v.t.*, *str.* to cut down; to carve;
to circumcise. *fijn besneden trekken*, finely
cut features. **be·snijdenis**, no pl., *n.*
circumcision.
be·snoeien, *v.t.* to lop, prune; to curtail;
to retrench. **be·snoeiing**, *n.* pruning;
curtailment.
be·snuffelen, *v.t.* to sniff at (*dog*).
be·sogne, -s, *n.* occupation, work on
hand.
be·sommen, -som, *v.t.* to amount to.
be·spannen, -span, *v.t.*, *irr.* to span; to string
(*instrument; racquet*); to harness to (*horse*).
~ *met vier paarden*, drawn by four horses.
be·spanning, *n.* team (*of horses*).
be·sparen, -spaar, *v.t.* to save, economize.
aan krachten ~, to save in strength.
¶ *v.r.t. zich moeite ~*, to save oneself
trouble. **be·sparing**, *n.* economy, saving.
ter ~ van, in order to save.
be·spatten, -spat, *v.t.* to bespatter.
be·speelbaar, -bare, *a.* playable. **be·spelen**,

-speel, *v.t.* to play (on). *niet te ~*, not
playable.
be·speuren, *v.t.* to perceive, spot.
be·spieden, *v.t.* to spy on, watch. **be·spieding**,
n. spying.
be·spiegelend, *a.* contemplative; speculative
(*philosophy*). **be·spiegeling**, *n.* contemplation; speculation.
be·spijkeren, *v.t.* to stud (*with nails*).
be·spikkelen, *v.t.* to speckle.
bespion·neren, -neer, *v.t.* to spy (on).
be·spoedigen, *v.t.* to hasten, expedite.
be·spoediging, *n.* acceleration. *ter ~ van*,
in order to hasten.
be·spoelen, *v.t.* to wash (*shore*).
be·spottelijk, *a.* ridiculous, ludicrous. *zich ~
aanstellen*, to make a fool of oneself;
iets ~ maken, to ridicule something;
zich ~ maken, to make oneself ridiculous;
zich ~ voordoen, to make a foolish impression. ¶ *adv.* ridiculously. **be·spotten**,
-spot, *v.t.* to mock, ridicule. **be·spotting**,
n. ridicule, derision. *iets aan de ~ prijsgeven*, to hold something up to ridicule.
be·spraakt, *a.* fluent. **be·sprek**, no pl., *n.*
negotiation. *in ~ zijn met iemand over
iets*, to negotiate with someone about
something. **be·spreken, -spreek**, *v.t.*,
str. to discuss; to review; to book, order,
bespeak. *te ~*, bookable. **be·spreking**, *n.*
discussion; review; booking.
be·sprenkelen, *v.t.* to sprinkle; to besprinkle,
asperse. **be·sprenkeling**, *n.* sprinkling;
aspersion.
be·springen, *v.t.*, *str.* to spring, leap, pounce
upon. **be·springer, -s**, *n.* assailant.
be·sproeien, *v.t.* to spray; to irrigate. **be-
·sproeiing**, *n.* spraying; irrigation.
be·spuiten, *v.t.*, *str.* to spout; to squirt;
to play upon (*with hosepipe*).
be·spuwen, *v.t.* to spit upon or at.
·bessengelei, *n.* currant jam. **·bessensap**,
no pl., *n.n.* currant juice.
best, *a.* best. ¶ *adv.* best; certainly;
quite. *het is mij ~*, that is all right by
me, I don't mind; *niet al te ~*, not too
well; *ik wil het ~ doen*, I am quite prepared
to do it. ¶ *n.n.* advantage, welfare, good.
het gemene ~, the common good; *op zijn ~*,
at its best, at the utmost; *zijn ~ doen*,
to do one's best; *zijn uiterste ~ doen*, to
do one's very best. ¶ -*e*, *n.* or *n.n. de ~e*,
the best (one); *het ~e*, the best (thing), *or*
all the best!; *als de ~e*, as well as anybody;
ten ~e geven, to render (*song*), to give
(*opinion*): (stilted); *ten ~e keren* or *wenden*,
to turn out for the best; *ten ~e raden*,
to advise for the best.
be·staan, -sta, *v.i.*, *irr.* to exist; to subsist;
to consist (*in* or *of*). ~ *van*, to subsist on;
~ *in*, to consist in; ~ *uit*, to consist of.
¶ *v.t.*, *irr.* to be related to; to undertake; to risk. *iemand in den bloede ~*,
to be a blood-relation of. ¶ no pl., *n.n.*

existence, being; subsistence, livelihood. reden van ~, reason of existence; middelen van ~, means of support. be·staanbaar, -bare, a. possible. ~ met, compatible with. be·staanbaarheid, no pl., n. possibility; compatibility. be·staansmiddel, n.n. means of existence or subsistence. be·stand, a. ~ tegen, proof against. ¶ no pl., n.n. truce. be·standdeel, -delen, n.n. component, part, ingredient.

be·stedeling, n. charity boy, charity girl. be·steden, -steed, v.t. to spend (money; time; energy). ~ aan, to spend, expend on; ~ bij, to put out to board with.

be·stek, -kken, n.n. compass, space; scope; specification, estimate; reckoning (of position at sea). in klein or kort ~, in a small compass, in a nutshell; binnen het ~ vallen, to come within the scope; buiten het ~ vallen, to fall outside the scope; een ~ maken, to make an estimate; een ~ opmaken, to calculate the ship's position.

·bestekamer, -s, n. lavatory.

be·steken, -steek, v.t., str. ~ met, to stick with.

be·stel, no pl., n.n. ordinance; fuss. Gods ~, the dispensation of Providence; wat een ~, what a fuss. be·stelauto, -'s, n. (motor) delivery van. be·stelbrief, -ven, n. order (letter). be·stelbriefje, -s, n.n. order-form. be·steldienst, n. delivery service.

be·stelen, -steel, v.t., str. to rob, defraud.

be·stelformulier, n.n. order-form. be·stelgoed, -eren, n.n. parcels. be·stelkantoor, -toren n.n. parcels office. be·stelkaart, n. order-form. be·stelkosten, pl. only, n.n. cost of delivery. be·stelkring, n. delivery area. be·stellen, -stel, v.t. to deliver (parcels, letters and written messages, groceries); to order. ~ bij, to order from. be·steller, -s, n. postman; carrier; carman. be·stelling, n. order (for goods); delivery (of parcels, letters, etc.). op ~, to order; volgens ~, as per order. be·stelloon, -lonen, n.n. carriage (fee). be·stelwagen, -s, n. carrier's van, delivery van.

be·stelpen, v.t. to snow under (fig.); to bury.

be·stemmen, -stem, v.t. to destine, intend. ~ voor, to set apart for, intend for; bestemd naar, bound for. be·stemming, n. destination; destiny. met ~ naar, bound for.

be·stempelen, v.t. to stamp, cancel; to label, designate. ~ als or ~ met de naam van, to designate as.

be·stendig, a. constant; continuous, steady; fair (of barometer). ¶ adv. constantly; continuously be·stendigen, v.t. to make permanent, perpetuate. be·stendigheid, no pl., n. permanence, durability. be·stendiging, n. perpetuation.

D.E.D.

be·sterven, -sterf, v.t., str. to die (fig.); to hang (freshly killed meat). ik zal het (nog) ~, it will be the death of me; ik bestierf van schrik, I nearly died of fright; het woord bestierf op zijn lippen, the words died on his lips. cf. bestorven.

·bestevaar, -s, n. gaffer.

be·stier, no pl., n.n. guidance (divine).

be·stijgen, v.t., str. to ascend; to mount. be·stijging, n. ascent.

be·stikken, -stik, v.t. to stitch, embroider.

be·stoken, -stook, v.t. to shell, keep under fire. iemand met vragen ~, to fire questions at someone.

be·stormen, v.t. to storm, assault. iemand met vragen ~, to bombard someone with questions. be·storming, n. assault; rush.

be·storven, a. livid, ashen; hung, tender (meat).

be·stoven, a. covered with dust; pollinated.

be·straffen, -straf, v.t. to punish. iemand voor or over or wegens iets ~, to punish someone for something; een ~de blik, a reproving glance, dirty look. be·straffing, n. punishment.

be·stralen, -straal, v.t. to shine or beam upon; to irradiate. be·straling, n. irradiation.

be·straten, -straat, v.t. to pave. be·strating, n. paving.

be·strijden, v.t., str. to fight (against), combat; to meet (expenses). be·strijder, -s, n. antagonist, opponent. be·strijding, n. fighting (action of); defrayal. ~ van, fight against; ter ~ van . . ., to fight . . .

be·strijken, v.t., str. to pass (hand) over; to cover, besmear; to sweep, cover, command (of artillery or strategic position).

be·strooien, v.t. to strew (with), besprinkle.

bestu·deren, -deer, v.t. to study.

be·stuiven, -stuif, v.t., str. to cover with dust; to pollinate. be·stuiving, n. pollination.

be·sturen, -stuur, v.t. to steer; to pilot (plane); to drive (car); to guide, direct; to rule, govern. be·sturing, n. steering; direction, management. be·stuur, -sturen, n.n. government, rule; guidance; management, control; committee, governing body. plaatselijk ~, local government, local authorities; het dagelijks ~, executive committee, mayor and aldermen. be·stuurbaar, -bare, a. dirigible; manageable. be·stuurder, -s, n. governor, director, administrator; pilot (of plane); driver (of car). be·stuursambtenaar, -s, or -naren, n. government official, civil servant. be·stuurskamer, -s, n. board room. be·stuurslid, -leden, n.n. member of the board, committee member. be·stuurster, -s, n. governess. be·stuursvergadering, n. board or committee meeting. be·stuurszetel, -s, n. seat on board or committee.

·bestwil, no pl., n. een leugen om ~, a white

c

lie; *om Uw ~*, for your good; *uit ~ (handelen) voor*, (to act) for the good of.

be·taalbaar, -bare, *a.* payable. *~ aan toonder*, payable to bearer; *~ op zicht*, payable at sight; *~ stellen*, to make payable, domicile (*bill*). **be·taalbaarstelling,** *n.* domiciliation (*of bill*). **be·taalbriefje, -s,** *n.n.* pay-chit. **be·taaldag,** *n.* pay-day. **be·taalkantoor, -toren,** *n.n.* pay-office. **be·taalmeester, -s,** *n.* paymaster. **be·taalmiddel,** *n.n.* means of payment. *wettig ~*, legal tender. **be·taalsrol, -llen,** *n.* pay-roll. **be·talen, -taal,** *v.t.* *goed ~*, to pay well *or* promptly; *slecht ~*, to pay badly, not punctually; *ten volle ~*, to pay in full; *vooruit ~*, to pay in advance; *iemand iets betaald zetten*, to make someone pay for what he has done; *betaald logé*, paying guest. ¶ no pl., *n.n. slecht van ~*, slow in paying. **be·taler, -s,** *n.* payer. **be·taling,** *n.* payment. *~en doen*, to make payments; *~en staken*, to cease payment; *bij gebrek van ~*, in the absence of payment; *tegen ~ van*, on payment of; *tegen contante ~*, on payment of, cash down; *ter ~ van*, in payment of. **be·talings-,** *in compounds:* of payment(s).

be·tamelijk, *a.* proper, decent, seemly. **be·tamelijkheid,** no pl., *n.* propriety. **be·tamen, -taam,** *v.t.* to be becoming, be seemly; to behove. *het betaamt U niet*, it is not for you to . . .

be·tasten, *v.t.* to finger; to feel, palpate.

·bete, -n, *n.* mouthful. *een ~ broods*, a morsel of bread. See **beet.**

be·tekenen, *v.t.* to mean, signify; to stand for; to serve (*writ*). *niet veel te ~ hebben*, not to be very important, not to amount to much; *het heeft niets te ~*, it doesn't matter at all; *wat moet dat ~?*, what's all this? **be·tekenis, -ssen,** *n.* meaning, significance. *een man van ~*, a man of importance; *niet van ~*, of no importance.

·betel, no pl., *n.* betel. **·betelnoot, -noten,** *n.* betel-nut. **·betelpalm,** *n.* areca palm.

·beter, *a. & adv.* better. *~ af zijn*, to be better off; *er ~ aan toe zijn* or *het ~ hebben*, to be in better circumstances; *het ~ maken*, to be better; *~ worden*, to get better; *je doet* or *deed ~ . . .*, you had better . . .; *het staat ~*, it looks better; *des te ~*, all the better; *aan de ~e hand zijn*, to be improving (*in health*). ¶ no pl., *n.n. niets ~s dan*, nothing better than; *iets ~s* or *wat ~s*, something better. **·beteren, -v.i.** to get better, recover. ¶ *v.t.* to mend, improve. *ik kan het niet ~*, I cannot help it. ¶ **zich ~, -v.r.** to mend one's ways, reform. **be·teren, -teer,** *v.t.* to tar. **·beterhand.** See **beter.** **·betering,** *n.* improvement (*moral or physical*). **·beterkoop,** *a.* cheaper. ¶ *adv.* more cheaply. **·beters.**

See **beter.** **·beterschap,** no pl., *n.* convalescence, recovery. *~!*, I hope you'll soon be better; *~ beloven*, to promise to be good; *hopen op ~*, to hope for recovery.

be·teugelen, *v.t.* to check, restrain. **be·teugeling,** *n.* check, restraint, curb.

be·tuniebloem, *n.* petunia.

be·teuterd, *a.* taken aback, confused. ¶ *adv. ~ kijken*, to show confusion.

be·tichten, *v.t.* to accuse. *iemand van iets ~*, to charge someone with something. **be·tichting,** *n.* accusation, imputation.

be·tijen, *v.t. iemand laten ~*, to let a person go his own way.

be·timmeren, *v.t.* to board, wainscot. *iemands licht ~*, to obstruct a person's lights. **be·timmering,** *n.* panelling, wainscoting.

be·titelen, *v.t.* to style, address. **be·titeling.** *n.* title of address.

be·togen, -toog, *v.t.* to demonstrate, argue; to urge. **be·toger, -s,** *n.* demonstrator (*in public gathering*). **be·toging,** *n.* demonstration (*public meeting*).

be·tomen, -toom, *v.t.* See **beteugelen.**

be·ton, no pl., *n.n.* concrete. *gewapend ~*, reinforced concrete, ferro-concrete. **be·tonbouw,** no pl., *n.* ferro-concrete architecture. **be·tonmolen. -s,** *n.* concrete mixer. **be·tonnen,** *a.* (made of) concrete. ¶ **-ton,** *v.t.* to buoy (*channel*). **be·tonning,** *n.* buoying; buoys.

be·tonen, -toon, *v.t.* to show, manifest; to accent. *hulde ~*, to pay homage, pay a tribute. ¶ **zich ~,** *v.r.* to prove oneself.

be·toog, -togen, *n.n.* argument, argumentation, demonstration. *het behoeft geen ~*, it is self-evident. **be·tooggrond,** *n.* argument (*thesis*). **be·toogkracht,** no pl., *n.* argumentative power. **be·toogtrant,** no pl., *n.* method of arguing.

be·toon, no pl., *n.n.* show, proof, demonstration.

be·toveren, *v.t.* to bewitch, enchant; to charm, fascinate. **be·toverend,** *a.* bewitching. **be·tovering,** *n.* spell, fascination.

·betovergrootmoeder, -s, *n.* great greatgrandmother.

be·traand, *a.* tear-stained, tearful.

be·trachten, *v.t.* to practise (*virtues*); to exercise (*care*); to perform (*duty*). **be·trachting,** *n.* practice, exercise, performance.

be·traliën, -lie, *v.t.* to cover with grating *or* trellis.

be·trappen, *v.t.* to catch, detect, find out. *iemand op een fout* or *leugen ~*, to catch someone out in a mistake *or* lie; *op heter daad ~*, to catch redhanded.

be·treden, -treed, *v.t.*, *str.* to tread (on), set foot on. *de kansel ~*, to mount the pulpit; *de planken ~*, to tread the boards.

be·treffen, -tref, *v.t.*, *str.* to concern. *wat mij betreft* . . ., as regards me . . ., as for me . . . be·treffende, *prep.* concerning, regarding, respecting; with respect *or* regard to; in respect of. ¶ *a.* in question.

be·trekkelijk, *a.* relative; comparative. *dat is* ~, that depends. ¶ *adv.* relatively; comparatively. be·trekklijkheid, no pl., *n.* relativity. be·trekken, -trek, *v.t.*, *str.* to occupy, move into (*premises, quarters*); to mount (*guard*). ~ *in or bij*, to implicate in, drag into; ~ *uit*, to obtain *or* order from. ¶ *v.i.*, *str.* to become overcast, cloud over (*sky; face*). be·trekking, *n.* relation; situation. *pl.* relations, relatives. *met* ~ *tot*, in relation to ; ~ *hebben op*, to refer to, relate to; *in* ~ *staan met*, to have relations with; *zich in* ~ *stellen met*, to open up relations with; *diplomatieke* ~*en*, diplomatic relations; *in een* ~, in a job; *buiten* ~, out of a job; *een* ~ *bekleden*, to fill a post.

be·treuren, *v.t.* to regret, deplore, mourn. *het is te* ~, it is to be regretted. betreurens·waardig, *a.* regrettable, deplorable.

be·trokken, *a.* overcast; concerned. be·trok·kene, -n, *n.* person concerned.

be·trouwbaar, -bare, *a.* trustworthy. *van or uit betrouwbare bron*, from a reliable source. be·trouwbaarheid, no pl., *n.* reliability. be·trouwbaarheidsrit, -tten, *n.* reliability trial. be·trouwen, *v.t.* ~ *op*, to depend on, rely on.

·betten, bet, *v.t.* to bathe (*wound, eyes*).

be·tuigen, *v.t.* to testify (*faith*); to express (*thanks*). be·tuiging, *n.* declaration; expression, protestation.

be·twijfelen, *v.t.* to doubt, call in question.

be·twistbaar, -bare, *a.* debatable; contestable. be·twistbaarheid, no pl., *n.* disputability. be·twisten, *v.t.* to dispute, contest (*ground*); to deny. *iemand iets* ~, to dispute something with someone.

beu, *a.* fed-up. *ik ben het* ~ *or ik ben er* ~ *van*, I am fed up with it.

beug, *n.* codline, long line, trot. ·beuglijn, *n.* long line, trot. ·beugvisser, -s, *n.* long line fisherman. ·beugvisserij, no pl., *n.* long line fishing.

·beugel, -s, *n.* (*curved metal mechanical device:*) stirrup; leg-iron; guard (*of sword*); trigger-guard; clasp (*of bag*); trawl-head; gimbal; trolley-pole. *dat kan niet door de* ~, that will not do, that goes too far. ·beugeltas, -ssen, *n.* (clasp) handbag.

beuk, *n.* beech; nave. ·beukeblad, -eren, *n.n.* beech leaf. ·beukeboom, -bomen, *n.* beech tree. ·beuken, *v.t.* to batter, pound, pommel. *er op los* ~, to batter away. ¶ *a.* (*made of*) beech wood. ·beukenbos,

-ssen, *n.n.* beech wood (*forest*). ·beukenhout, no pl., *n.n.* beechwood (*substance*). ·beukenlaan, -lanen, *n.* avenue of beeches. ·beukenoot, -noten, *n.* beech nut.

beul, *n.* executioner, hangman; brute. ·beulen, *v.i.* to slave. ·beulshanden, pl. only, *n.* *sterven door or onder* ~, to be executed. ·beulsknecht, *n.* hangman's assistant.

·beuling, *n.* gut; sausage.

beun, *n.* fish-pot; attic. ·beunhaas, -hazen, *n.* blackleg; pettifogger; dabbler. ·beunhazen, -haas, *v.i.* to dabble; to blackleg. beunhaze·rij, *n.* undercutting; dabbling.

·beuren, *v.t.* to lift; to receive, collect (*money*).

beurs, -zen, *n.* purse; Exchange; scholarship. *in de* ~ *tasten*, to put one's hand in one's pocket; *met zijn* ~ *te rade gaan*, to consult one's purse; *het gaat uit een ruime* ~, it is being done lavishly; *met gesloten beurzen*, without having to pay one another; *op de* ~ *or ter beurze*, on the Exchange; *uit een* ~ *studeren*, to have a scholarship. ¶ *a.* sleepy. ·beursaffaire, -s, *n.* exchange business. ·beursbelasting, no pl., *n.* tax on Stock Exchange dealings. ·beursbericht, *n.n.* stock list, list of quotations. ·beursbezoeker, -s, *n.* member of the Exchange. ·beursfondsen, pl. only, *n.n.* marketable securities. ·beursgebouw, *n.n.* Exchange. ·beursnotering, *n.* Stock Exchange quotation. ·beursspeculant, *n.* stock jobber. ·beursspel, no pl., *n.n.* gambling on the Exchange, speculation. ·beursusantie, -s, *n.* custom(s) of the Stock Exchange. ·beursvacantie, -s, *n.* bank holiday. ·beurswaarde, -n, *n.* market value; pl. stocks and shares. ·beurzaken, pl. only, *n.* (Stock) Exchange transactions.

·beursjeskruid, no pl., *n.n.* shepherd's purse.

beurt, *n.* turn (*in succession*). *een* ~ *geven*, to give a turn (*in class*), or to do *or* clean a room; *een* ~ *krijgen*, to be given a turn; *aan de* ~ *komen*, to be the next one; *op zijn* ~, in his turn, in turn; *om de* ~ *or om* ~*en*, in turn; ~ *om* ~, in turn; *vóór zijn* ~, too soon, out of turn; *te* ~ *vallen*, to fall to one's lot, to happen to one. ·beurtelings, *adv.* in turn. ·beurtschip, -schepen, *n.n.* carrier barge (*regular service*). ·beurtschipper, -s, *n.* skipper of carrier barge. ·beurtvaart, no pl., *n.* carrier service (*by barge*).

·beuzelaar, -s, *n.* dawdler. ·beuzelachtig, *a.* trifling, footling. beuzela·rij, *n.* trifle. ·beuzelen, *v.i.* to dawdle; to fib. ·beuzeling *n.* trifle. ·beuzelpraat, no pl., *n.* twaddle, piffle.

be·vaarbaar, -bare, *a.* navigable. be·vaarbaar·heid, no pl., *n.* navigability.

be·vallen, -val, *v.i.*, *str.* to be confined. ~ *zijn van*, to be delivered of (*child*); *ze moet* ~, she is expecting (*baby*); ¶ *v.t.*

to please, suit. *het bevalt me*, it pleases me; *het bevalt me niet*, it does not please me, I do not like it; *het bevalt me hier*, I like it here. **be·vallig**, *a.* graceful, charming. ¶ *adv.* gracefully. **be·valligheid, -heden,** *n.* grace, charm. **be·valling,** *n.* confinement, delivery (*child-birth*).

be·vangen, *v.t., str.* to seize, overcome (*fear, heat*). ∼ *door vrees*, seized by fear; ∼ *door de hitte*, overcome by the heat. **be·vangenheid,** no pl., *n.* embarrassment, constraint; heat-stroke.

be·varen, -vaar, *v.t., str.* to sail, navigate (on). ¶ *a.* experienced (*at sea*). ∼ *matroos*, old salt.

be·vattelijk, *a.* comprehensible, lucid; quick, intelligent. ¶ *adv.* comprehensibly. **be·vattelijkheid,** no pl.; *n.* intelligibility, lucidity. **be·vatten, -vat,** *v.t.* to comprehend, grasp; to contain. *kunnen* ∼, to hold. **be·vatting,** no pl., *n.* comprehension. *vlug van* ∼, quick on the uptake; *boven zijn* ∼, beyond his grasp. **be·vattingsvermogen,** no pl., *n.n.* comprehension, grasp; comprehensive ability.

be·vechten, *v.t., str.* to fight combat; to gain (*by fight*).

be·vederd, *a.* feathered.

be·veiligen, *v.t.* to protect, safeguard. ∼ *tegen* or *voor*, to protect against or from. ¶ *zich* ∼, *v.r.* to safeguard oneself. **be·veiliging,** *n.* protection, safeguard. *tot* ∼ *van*, for the protection of; *onder* ∼ *van*, under cover of.

be·vel, *n.n.* order; command. ∼ *tot aanhouding*, warrant (*of arrest*); ∼ *tot beslaglegging*, distress warrant; ∼ *tot huiszoeking*, search warrant; ∼ *geven*, to issue an order; (*het*) ∼ *voeren* or *hebben over*, to be in command of; *het* ∼ *overnemen*, to take over a command; *onder* ∼ *staan van*, to be under the orders of; *op* ∼ *van*, by order of; *op hoog* ∼, by royal command. **be·velen, -veel,** *v.t.* to order, command; to be in command; to commend (*to care*). **be·velhebber, -s,** *n.* commander, leader. **be·velhebberschap,** no pl., *n.n.* command, leadership. **be·velschrift,** *n.n.* mandate; warrant. **be·velvoerder, -s,** *n.* commander, leader. **be·velvoerend,** *a.* in command, commanding. **be·velvoering,** no pl., *n.* command, leadership.

·**beven, beef,** *v.i.* to tremble, shake, shiver, quiver. ∼ *bij de gedachte*, to shudder at the thought; ∼ *van schrik*, to tremble with fear.

·**bever, -s,** *n.* beaver. ¶ no pl., *n.n.* beaver (*fur*). ·**beverbont,** no pl., *n.n.* beaver (*fur*).

·**beverig,** *a.* shaky, shivery, tremulous.

bever·nel, no pl., *n.* burnet.

be·vestigen, *v.t.* to fix, fasten, attach; to confirm (*report*); to consolidate (*authority*); to induct (*clergyman*); to confirm (*new*

member of *Church*). ∼ *aan*, to secure to; ∼ *.met*, to secure with. **be·vestigend,** *a.* affirmative. ¶ *adv.* affirmatively, in the affirmative. **be·vestiging,** *n.* confirmation, corroboration; induction (*of clergyman*); confirmation (*Church members*).

be·vind, no pl., *n.n. naar* ∼ *van zaken*, as circumstances demand. **be·vinden,** *v.t., str.* to find (*opinion*); to realize, decide that. ¶ *zich* ∼, *v.r., str.* to be, find oneself. *zich in gevaar* ∼, to be in danger; *zich* ∼ *onder*, to be among; *zich ergens wel bij* ∼, to do well out of something. **be·vinding,** *n.* finding(s); experience.

·**beving,** *n.* trembling, trepidation.

be·vitten, -vit, *v.t.* to cavil at.

be·vlekken, -vlek, *v.t.* to stain, pollute. **be·vlekking,** *n.* defilement.

be·vliegen, *v.t., str.* to come over (*impulse*). **be·vlieging,** *n.* whim, fancy. *een* ∼ *van*, a fit of.

be·vlijtigen, zich, *v.r.* to exert oneself.

be·vloeien, *v.t.* to irrigate. **be·vloeiing,** *n.* irrigation.

be·vloeren, *v.t.* to floor. **be·vloering,** *n.* flooring.

be·vochtigen, *v.t.* to moisten, humidify. **be·vochtiging,** *n.* moistening.

be·voegd, *a.* competent, qualified; authorized; entitled. *van* ∼*e zijde*, on good authority. **be·voegdheid, -heden,** *n.* qualification; power, authority. *met de* ∼ *om*, with power(s) to, qualified to.

be·voelen, *v.t.* to finger, feel.

be·volken, *v.t.* to people, populate. **be·volking,** *n.* people, population. **be·volkingsbureau, -'s,** *n.n.* registry office. **be·volkingscijfer, -s,** *n.n.* number of inhabitants. **be·volkingsleer,** no pl., *n.* theory of population. **be·volkingsregister, -s,** *n.n.* parish register. **be·volkingsrubber,** no pl., *n.* native rubber. **be·volkingsstatistiek,** *n.* vital statistics. **be·volkt,** *a.* populated. *dicht* ∼, densely populated, populous.

be·voordelen, -deel, *v.t.* favour, benefit.

bevoor·oordeeld, *a.* prejudiced, biased.

be·voorrechten, *v.t.* to favour, privilege. **be·voorrechting,** *n.* favouritism.

be·vorderaar, -s, *n.* promoter, patron (*of art, sport*). **be·vorderen,** *v.t.* to promote, encourage (*art, sport*); to be conducive to (*good health*); to promote, prefer (*to higher office*); to move (*to higher class*). ∼ *tot*, to promote to the rank of. **be·vordering,** *n.* furtherance; benefit; promotion; preferment. *ter* ∼ *van*, for the improvement of. **be·vorderlijk,** *a.* beneficial. ∼ *aan* or *voor*, conducive to.

be·vrachten, *v.t.* to load, freight; to charter (*ship*). **be·vrachter, -s,** *n.* charterer; shipper. **be·vrachting,** *n.* freighting, chartering.

be·vragen, -vraag, *v.t., str. te* ∼ *bij*, for further

particulars apply to; *alhier te* ~, enquire within; *te* ~ *bureau van dit blad*, further particulars on enquiry.

be·vredigen, *v.t.* to satisfy, gratify; to pacify. *moeilijk te* ~, hard to please. **be·vredigend**, *a.* satisfactory, gratifying. **be·vrediging**, *n.* satisfaction; gratification; pacification.

be·vreemden, *v.t.* (*usu. imp.*) to surprise. *het bevreemdt me*, it surprises me, I wonder. **be·vreemdend**, *a.* curious, strange. **be·vreemding**, *n.* wonderment. *met* ~, with surprise; *zijn* ~ *te kennen geven*, to express one's surprise.

be·vreesd, *a.* afraid, apprehensive. ~ *voor*, afraid of *or* for. **be·vreesdheid**, no pl., *n.* fear, apprehension.

be·vriend, *a.* friendly, on friendly terms.

be·vriezen, -**vries**, *v.i.*, *irr.* to freeze (over), congeal; to be frostbitten. ¶ *v.t.*, *irr.* to freeze.

be·vrijden, *v.t.* to free, deliver, liberate. ~ *van*, to free from *or* of. ¶ *v.r. zich* ~ *van*, to get rid of. **be·vrijder**, -**s**, *n.* liberator, deliverer. **be·vrijding**, *n.* liberation, deliverance.

be·vroeden, *v.t.* to realize; to suspect.

be·vroren, *a.* frozen; frostbitten. ~ *credieten*, frozen credits.

be·vruchten, *v.t.* to fertilize, impregnate. **be·vruchting**, *n.* fecundation, fructification.

be·vuilen, *v.t.* to dirty, (be)foul.

be·waakster, -**s**, *n.* watcher, guardian (*female*).

be·waarder, -**s**, *n.* keeper, custodian. **be·waargeld**, *n.n.* storage fee. **be·waargever**, -**s**, *n.* depositor. **be·waargeving**, *n.* depositing.

be·waarheiden, *v.t.* to corroborate, bear out, confirm, to come true.

be·waarkluis, -**zen**, *n.* safe-deposit. **be·waarloon**, -**lonen**, *n.n.* deposit fee. **be·waarplaats**, *n.* storehouse, repository. **be·waarschool**, -**scholen**, *n.* kindergarten. **be·waarschooljuffrouw**, *n.* kindergarten mistress.

be·waasd, *a.* steamed over (*window*).

be·waken, -**waak**, *v.t.* to watch, keep watch over, guard. **be·waker**, -**s**, *n.* guardian; keeper, warder. **be·waking**, *n.* guard, watch (*act*). *onder* ~ *van*, guarded by, in the charge of.

be·wandelen, *v.t.* to walk (on). *het pad der deugd* ~, to tread the path of virtue.

be·wapenen, *v.t.* to arm. **be·wapening**, no pl., *n.* arming; armament.

be·waren, -**waar**, *v.t.* to keep; to preserve; to maintain; to guard, defend. ~ *tegen*, to guard against; ~ *voor*, to guard from; *God beware!, God bewaar me!*, God forbid!, good gracious. **be·waring**, *n.* keeping; preservation; custody. *in* ~ *geven*, to deposit; *in* ~ *hebben*, to have in one's keeping; *in* ~ *nemen*, to take charge of; *in verzekerde* ~ *nemen*, to take (*person*) into custody; *ter* ~, in trust.

be·wasemen, *v.t.* to steam over (*with moisture*). **be·wassen**, -**was**, *v.t.* to cover (*with vegetation*).

be·wateren, *v.t.* to water, irrigate. **be·watering**, *n.* irrigation.

be·weegbaar, -**bare**, *a.* movable. **be·weegbaarheid**, no pl., *n.* mobility, movability. **be·weegkracht**, *n.* motive power *or* force. **be·weeglijk**, *a.* mobile; movable; lively. **be·weeglijkheid**, no pl., *n.* mobility, liveliness. **be·weegreden**, *n.* motive, ground. **be·wegen**, -**weeg**, *v.i.*, *str.* to move (*objects*); to move (*feelings*); to induce (*to action*). ¶ *zich* ~, *v.r.*, *str.* to move, stir. *zich in hoge kringen* ~, to move in the best circles. **be·weging**, *n.* movement (*physical or social*); exercise; commotion. *in* ~ *brengen*, to set going; *in* ~ *houden*, to keep going; *in* ~ *komen*, to begin to move; *uit eigen* ~, of one's own accord. **be·wegingloos**, -**loze**, *a.* motionless. **be·wegingsleer**, no pl., *n.* kinetics. **be·wegingsoorlog**, *n.* mobile warfare. **be·wegingsorganen**, pl. only, *n.n.* organs of locomotion. **be·wegingsverschijnsel**, *n.n.* motor phenomenon. **be·wegingszenuw**, *n.* motor nerve.

be·wenen, -**ween**, *v.t.* to mourn, deplore.

be·weren, -**weer**, *v.t.* to assert, contend, claim; to pretend, allege. *hij heeft teveel te* ~, he has too much to say for himself; *hij heeft hier niets te* ~, he has no authority here. **be·wering**, *n.* assertion, allegation.

be·werkelijk, *a.* laborious; inefficient. **be·werken**, *v.t.* to prepare for use; to dress (*material*); to hammer (*metal*); to fashion (*ivory*); to till; to edit, revise, adapt (*book*); to achieve, bring about; to influence. ~ *tot*, to fashion into; *bewerkt naar . . .*, after . . . (*book, story*); ~ *voor*, to arrange, adapt for (*orchestra; school use*). **be·werker**, -**s**, *n.* originator, engineer (*of happening*); compiler, adapter. **be·werking**, *n.* process, manipulation; tillage; revision, adaptation, version; operation (*mathematical*). *in* ~, in preparation (*book*). **be·werkstelligen**, *v.t.* to achieve, compass. **be·werktuigd**, *a.* organized. **be·werktuiging**, no pl., *n.* organization.

be·westen, *adv.* (to the) west ¶ *prep.* westward, west of.

be·wieroken, -**rook**, *v.t.* to incense (*fumigate*); to praise (*in flattery*). **be·wieroking**, no pl., *n.* incensation; adulation.

be·wijs, -**zen**, *n.n.* proof, demonstration; mark (*of esteem*); certificate. ~ *leveren*, to demonstrate, prove; *ten bewijze waarvan*, in proof whereof; ~ *van herkomst* or *oorsprong*, certificate of origin; ~ *van goed gedrag*, testimonial of good conduct; ~ *van lidmaatschap*, certificate of membership, member's card; ~ *van onvermogen*, proofs of poverty; ~ *van ontvangst*,

receipt; ~ *van toegang*, ticket of admission.
be·wijsbaar, -bare, *a.* provable. **be·wijs-
baarheid,** no pl., *n.* demonstrability.
be·wijsgrond, *n.* argument. **be·wijskracht,**
no pl., *n.* conclusive force. **be·wijslast,**
no pl., *n.* burden *or* onus of proof. **be-
·wijsmateriaal,** no pl., *n.n.* evidence.
be·wijsmiddel, *n.* proof, means of proving.
be·wijsstuk, -kken, *n.n.* document; documentary evidence. **be·wijsvoering,** *n.*
argumentation. **be·wijzen, -wijs,** *v.t.,*
str. to prove, demonstrate; to substantiate,
make good (*claim*); to show (*kindness*);
to render (*service*).
be·willigen, *v.t.* ~ *in,* to grant, concede.
be·williging, *n.* consent.
be·wimpelen, *v.t.* to disguise, cloak, gloss
over.
be·wind, no pl., *n.n.* government, rule,
administration. *het ~ voeren,* to rule;
aan het ~ komen, to come into power, be
called to the throne; *aan het ~ geplaatst
or geroepen worden,* to be put into office or
on the throne; *aan het ~ zijn,* to be in
power, in office, on the throne; *onder het ~
zijn van,* to be ruled by. **be·windhebber, -s,**
n. ruler; director. **be·windsman, -slieden,**
n. ruler; statesman. **be·windvoerder, -s,** *n.*
ruler; director; trustee.
be·wogen, *a.* moved, affected.
be·wolken, *v.i.* to cloud over. **be·wolkt,** *a.*
clouded, cloudy, overcast.
be·wonderaar, -s, *n.* admirer (*male*). **be-
·wonderaarster, -s,** *n.* admirer (*female*).
be·wonderen, *v.t.* to admire. **bewonderens-
·waardig,** *a.* admirable. ¶ *adv.* admirably.
be·wondering, *n.* admiration. ~ *voor,*
admiration of *or* for; *uit ~ voor,* out of
admiration for, in admiration of.
be·wonen, -woon, *v.t.* to inhabit, occupy,
live in. *de bewoonde wereld,* civilization.
be·woner, -s, *n.* inhabitant. . **be·woonbaar,
-bare,** *a.* habitable. **be·woonbaarheid,** no
pl., *n.* habitability. **be·woonster, -s,** *n.*
inhabitant (*female*).
be·woording, *n.* wording. *in algemene ~en,*
in general terms.
be·wust, *a.* conscious; in question. *ik ben het
me niet ~ or ik ben er me niet van ~,*
I am not aware of it; *van geen kwaad
~,* not conscious of having done wrong;
het zich ~ worden, to become conscious
of something; *ik werd het me ~,* it dawned
on me. **be·wusteloos, -loze,** *a.* unconscious,
senseless. **be·wusteloosheid,** no pl., *n.*
unconsciousness, faint. **be·wustheid,** no
pl., *n.* consciousness. **be·wustzijn,** no pl.,
n.n. consciousness, realization. *het ~
verliezen,* to lose consciousness; *bij zijn
volle ~,* in full consciousness; *buiten ~,*
unconscious; *in de ~,* in the consciousness of; *met ~,* consciously; *tot ~ komen,*
to recover consciousness.
be·zaaien, *v.t.* to sow; to strew, litter.

be·zaan, -zanen, *n.* mizzen. **be·zaansboom,
-bomen,** *n.* spanker boom. **be·zaansmast,**
n. mizzenmast. **be·zaansschoot,** no pl.,
n. de ~ aanhalen, to split the main-
brace. **be·zaanswant,** no pl., *n.n.* mizzen
rigging.
be·zadigd, *a.* level-headed, sedate, staid.
¶ *adv.* sedately, level-headedly. **be·zadigd-
heid,** no pl., *n.* sedateness.
be·zakken, -zak, *v.i.* to settle (*of sediment*).
be·zegelen, *v.t.* to seal.
be·zeild, *a.* able to sail, fast. *een ~ vaartuig,*
a fine sailing ship. **be·zeilen,** *v.t.* to sail
(on *or* over). *er is geen land met hem te ~,*
he is of no use, intractable.
·bezem, -s, *n.* broom, besom. **·bezembinder,
-s,** *n.* broom-maker. **·bezemkruid,** *n.n.*
broom (*plant*). **·bezemschoon, -schone,** *a.*
swept. **·bezemsteel, -stelen,** *n.,* **·bezemstok,
-kken,** *n.* broom-stick.
be·zending, *n.* consignment. *de hele ~,* the
whole shoot.
be·zeren, -zeer, *v.t.* to hurt, injure. ¶ *zich ~,*
v.r., to hurt oneself.
be·zet, -tte, *a.* taken (*seat*); occupied (*seat;
country; time*); filled (*theatrical part*).
~ *met,* set with (*jewels*).
be·zeten, *a.* possessed. **be·zetene, -n,** *n.*
one possessed. *als een ~,* like one
possessed.
be·zetsel, -s, *n.n.* trimming (*on clothes*).
be·zetten, -zet, *v.t.* to occupy (*seat; country;
time*); to man *or* fill (*post*); to set (*with
jewels*); to cast (*play*); to plaster (*wall*).
~ *met,* to trim with. **be·zetting,** *n.* occupation (*by troops*); garrison; casting (*of play*).
een ~ leggen in, to garrison (*town*).
be·zettingsleger, -s, *n.n.* army of occupation. **be·zettingstroepen,** pl., *n.* troops of
occupation.
be·zichtigen, *v.t.* to view, inspect. *te ~,* on
view. **be·zichtiging,** no pl., *n.* view.
ter ~, on view.
·bezie, -ziën, *n.* See **bes.**
be·zield, *a.* inspired; animated. ~ *met,*
actuated by. **be·zielen,** *v.t.* to inspire.
wat bezielt hem?, what has come over him?
be·zieling, no pl., *n.* inspiration; animation.
be·zien, -zie, *v.t., irr.* to look at, consider.
iets van nabij ~, to have a close look at;
het staat te ~, it remains to be seen.
beziens·waardig, *a.* worth looking at.
beziens·waardigheid, -heden, *n.* place of
interest, object of curiosity.
·bezig, *a.* busy, working. *druk ~,* very busy,
busily occupied; ~ *zijn aan,* to be at work
or engaged on; ~ *zijn met,* to be engaged
on, busy doing (something); *iemand ~
houden,* to keep someone busy; *zich ~
houden met,* to keep oneself busy with,
to interest oneself in. ¶ *adv.* busily, busy.
·bezigen, *v.t.* to use, make use of. **·bezig-
heid, -heden,** *n.* occupation, business.
dagelijkse bezigheden, daily pursuits.

·bezighouden, *v.t.s.*, *irr.* to keep busy; to engage, exercise (*thoughts*, *mind*).

be·zijden, *prep.* beside. ~ *de waarheid*, away from the truth. ¶ *adv. van* ~, sidelong.

be·zingen, *v.t.*, *str.* to sing of.

be·zinken, *v.i.*, *str.* to settle (*of sediment*); to sink in (*idea*). be·zinksel, -s, *n.n.* dregs, sediment, lees.

be·zinnen, -zin, *v.t.*, *str.* to reflect, consider. ¶ *zich* ~, *v.r.*, *str.* to consider; to change one's mind. be·zinning, no pl., *n.* consciousness; senses. *zijn* ~ *verliezen*, to lose consciousness *or* one's senses; *tot* ~ *komen*, to come to one's senses.

be·zit, no pl., *n.n.* possession, ownership; possession(s). *in* (*het*) ~ *komen* or *geraken van*, to come into possession of; *iets in* ~ *nemen*, to take possession of something; *zich in* (*het*) ~ *stellen van*, to possess oneself of; *in* (*het*) ~ *zijn van*, to own, possess; *uit het* ~ *stoten van*, to dispossess of, oust from. be·zitnemer, -s, *n.* occupant. be·zitneming, *n.* occupancy, possession. be·zitrecht, no pl., *n.n.* right of property. be·zitster, -s, *n.* owner, proprietress. be·zittelijk, *a.* possessive (*grammar*). be·zitten, -zit, *v.t.*, *str.* to own, possess. be·zitter, -s, *n.* owner, proprietor. be·zitting, *n.* possession, property. ~*en*, assets *or* belongings.

be·zocht, *a.* frequented. *druk* ~, much frequented.

be·zoden, -zood, *v.t.* to turf.

be·zoedelen, *v.t.* to soil, sully, pollute. be·zoedeling, *n.* defilement, contamination.

be·zoek, *n.n.* visit; visitor(s), company. *herderlijk* ~, pastoral visitation; *een* ~ *afleggen* or *brengen aan*, to pay a visit to; *een* ~ *beantwoorden*, to return a call; *er is* ~, there are visitors; *geen* ~, not at home to visitors; *op* ~, on a visit. be·zoekdag, *n.* visiting day. be·zoeken, *v.t.*, *irr.* to visit; to call on; to attend (*school*). be·zoeker, -s, *n.* visitor; frequenter. be·zoeking, *n.* visitation, trial. be·zoekster, -s, *n.* visitor (*female*).

be·zoldigen, *v.t.* to pay (*wages*, *salary*). be·zoldiging, *n.* pay, salary.

be·zondigen, zich, *v.r.* to sin. *zich* ~ *jegens* or *tegen* or *aan*, to sin against; *zich* ~ *aan*, to go in for, to be keen on.

be·zonken, *a.* well-considered, mature.

be·zonnen, *a.* level-headed, steady. be·zonnenheid, no pl., *n.* level-headedness.

be·zopen, *a.* (*vulg.*) boozed. ¶ *adv.* (*vulg.*) drunkenly.

be·zorgd, *a.* anxious; provided for. ~ *over*, concerned at; *zich* ~ *maken over*, to worry about; ~ *voor*, solicitous for *or* apprehensive for; *goed* ~, well provided for. be·zorgdheid, -heden, *n.* anxiety, concern. be·zorgen, *v.t.* to procure, help to; to deliver (*parcel*); to cause

(*trouble*); to edit. *iets* ~ *bij*, to deliver something at. be·zorging, *n.* delivery (*of parcel*).

be·zuiden, *prep.* (to the) south of. ¶ *adv.* south of, southward. ~ *om gaan*, to go round the south of.

be·zuinigen, *v.t.* to economize; to retrench. ~ *op*, to economize on. be·zuiniging, *n.* economy. ~*en maken*, to make cuts, economize. be·zuinigingsmaatregel, *n.* measure of economy.

be·zuipen, zich, *v.r.*, *str.* (*vulg.*) to get boozed.

be·zuren, -zuur, *v.t.* to rue, regret, pay for. *hij zal het moeten* ~, he will rue it; *het zal je* ~, you will be sorry for it.

be·zwaar, -zwaren, *n.n.* objection, scruple. ~ *hebben tegen*, to object to; *bezwaren indienen*, to raise objections; *bezwaren maken* or *hebben*, to object, make objections; ~ *opleveren*, to give rise to difficulties; *buiten* ~ *van de Schatkist*, at private expense; *op bezwaren stoten*, to encounter difficulties. be·zwaard, *a.* weighted; burdened, oppressed. *een* ~ *geweten*, a troubled conscience; ~ *met*, encumbered with (*mortgage*). ¶ *adv. zich* ~ *gevoelen*, to feel troubled (*in mind*, *conscience*). be·zwaarlijk, *a.* difficult, hard. ¶ *adv.* with difficulty. be·zwaarschrift, *n.n.* petition, remonstrance. *een* ~ *indienen*, to present a petition.

be·zwachtelen, *v.t.* to swathe, bandage.

bezwangeren, *v.t.* to impregnate; to imbue. be·zwangerd, *a.* laden. ~ *met*, heavy with (*fumes*, *odour*).

be·zwaren, -zwaar, *v.t.* to weight; to burden; to encumber. ¶ *v.r. zich* ~ *over iets bij iemand*, to complain of something to someone. be·zwarend, *a.* burdensome; onerous. ~*e omstandigheden*, damaging facts.

be·zweet, -zwete, *a.* perspiring, sweaty.

be·zweren, -zweer, *v.t.*, *str.* to swear to; to conjure, adjure; to raise, conjure up (*spirits*); to lay, exorcise (*spirits*). be·zwering, *n.* swearing (*on oath*); adjuration; conjuration; exorcism. be·zweringsformulier, *n.n.* incantation, spell.

be·zwijken, *v.i.*, *str.* to succumb; to yield. ~ *aan*, to succumb to; ~ *onder*, to give way beneath; ~ *voor*, to yield to, to give way before.

be·zwijmen, *v.i.* to swoon. be·zwijming, *n.* swoon.

·bibberen, *v.i.* to shiver.

biblio·graaf, -grafen, *n.* bibliographer. bibliogra·fie, -fieën, *n.* bibliography. bibliografisch, *a.* bibliographic(al). biblio·maan, -manen, *n.* book-lover. biblio·fiel, *n.* bibliophile. bibliothe·caris, -ssen, *n.* librarian. biblio·theek, -theken, *n.* library.

·biddag, *n.* day of prayer. ·bidden, bid, *v.i.*, *str.* to pray; to say grace (*before meal*). ~ *tot* . . . *om* or *voor* . . ., to pray to . . .

for . . .; ~ en smeken, to beg and pray. ¶ vt., str. to beseech, implore; to pray to; to recite (prayer). wat ik U ~ mag, pray! (please!). **·bidder, -s,** n. undertaker's man. **·bidplaats,** n. oratory, chapel. **·bidprentje, -s,** n.n. in memoriam card. **·bidstoel,** n. prie-dieu, praying chair. **·bidstond,** n. prayer meeting.

biecht, n. confession. iemand de ~ afnemen or horen, to hear a person's confession; te ~(e) gaan, to go to confession; bij de duivel te ~ gaan, to confide in one's enemy. **·biechteling,** n. confessant, penitent. **·biechtelinge, -n,** n. confessant, penitent (female). **·biechten,** v.t. to confess. gaan ~, to go to confession. **·biechtgeheim,** n.n. secret of the confessional. **·biechtstoel,** n. confessional. **·biechtvader, -s,** n. father confessor.

·bieden, v.t., str. to offer, tender; to make a bid. ~ op, to bid for; iemand de hand ~, to hold out one's hand to someone; het hoofd ~ aan, to resist; weerstand ~, to offer resistance. **·bieder, -s,** n. bidder.

·biefstuk, -kken, n. beefsteak, piece of steak.

biel, -s, n. sleeper (railway).

bier, n.n. beer, ale. boven zijn ~ zijn, to be half-seas over. **·bierbottelaar, -s,** n. beer bottler. **·bierbottelarij,** n. brewery stores. **·bierbrouwer, -s,** n. brewer. **·bierbrouwerij,** n. brewery. **·bierbuik,** n. pot-belly. **·bierkaai,** no pl., n. vechten tegen de ~, to fight against hopeless odds. **·bierton, -nnen,** n. beer barrel. **·bierwagen, -s,** n. brewer's dray.

bies, -zen, n. rush, bullrush; piping (on clothes), (coloured) line. zijn biezen pakken, to clear out. **·bieslook,** no pl., n.n. chive.

biet, n. beet. rode ~, beetroot.

·bietebauw, n. bugbear.

·biezen, a. rush. ~ stoel, rush-bottomed chair.

big, -ggen, n. piglet, porker. **·biggelen,** v.i. to trickle down (of tears). **·biggen,** big, v.i. to farrow, cast (pigs). **·biggenkruid,** no pl., n.n. cat's ear.

bij,(1) n. bee.

bij, (2) prep. near, by, with; at; to; during, in the course of; on, in. ¶ adv. approximately. ~ zijn, to be bright; er ~ zijn, to be caught. ¶ prefix. extra, additional, subsidiary. **bijal·dien,** c. if, in case. **·bijbaantje, -s,** n.n. extra job. **·bijbank,** n. branch of bank. **·bijbedoeling,** n. ulterior motive. **·bijbehorend,** a. appertaining. met ~e . . ., with . . . to match.

·bijbel, -s, n. bible; Bible, Scripture(s). **·bijbelkennis,** no pl., n. scriptural knowledge. **·bijbelkundig,** a. versed in the Scriptures. **·bijbels,** a. biblical. **·bijbelspreuk,** n. biblical text. **·bijbelvast,** a. well versed in the Scriptures.

·bijbestellen, bestel bij, v.t.s., to order extra. **·bijbetalen, betaal bij,** v.t.s., to pay extra. **·bijbetaling,** n. extra payment.

·bijbetekenis, -ssen, n. additional meaning; connotation.

·bijbetrekking, n. See bijbaantje.

·bijblad, n.n. supplement, extra sheet (newspaper).

·bijblijven, blijf bij, v.t.s., str. to keep up (with); to stick (to one or in one's mind). de woorden bleven hem bij, he never forgot those words.

·bijboek, n.n. subsidiary book (book-keeping). **·bijboeken,** v.t.s. to enter, book up to date.

·bijbrengen, v.t.s., irr. to bring forward, adduce; to bring round (from faint); to impart, inculcate.

bijde·hand, -nte, a. sharp, smart, bright. **bijde·handje, -s,** n.n. sharp-witted child or girl. **bijde·hands,** a. near (horse in team).

·bijdoen, doe bij, v.t.s., irr. to add, throw in.

·bijdraaien, v.i.s. to heave to.

·bijdrage, -n, n. contribution. **·bijdragen, draag bij,** v.t.s., str. to contribute. ~ tot, to contribute to.

bij·een, adv. together. ¶ prefix to nouns and sep. verbs: together. **bij·eendoen, doe bijeen,** v.t.s., irr. to put together. **bij·eenge-** See verbs in **bijeen-**. **bij·eenkomen,** v.i.s., irr. to meet. **bij·eenkomst,** n. meeting, assembly, gathering. **bij·eenleggen, leg bijeen,** v.t.s., irr. to put together. **bij·eenliggen, lig bijeen,** v.i.s., str. to lie close together. **bij·eennemen, neem bijeen,** v.t.s., str. to gather; to put together. **bij·eenroepen,** v.t.s., str. to call, convene, summon. **bij·eenroeping,** no pl., n. convocation, summons. **bij·eenscholen, school bijeen,** v.i.s. to crowd or flock together. **bij·eentrommelen,** v.t.s. to rake up. **bij·eenvoegen,** v.t.s. to combine, put together. **bij·eenvoeging,** n. combination, joining. **bij·eenzijn, zijn bijeen,** v.i.s., irr. to be together; to be in session. ¶ n.n. gathering, meeting.

·bijenangel, -s, n. bee-sting. **·bijeneter, -s,** n. bee-eater. **·bijenhouder, -s,** n. beemaster, apiarist. **·bijenkoningin, -nnen,** n. queen bee. **·bijenkorf, -ven,** n. beehive. **·bijenstal, -llen,** n. apiary. **·bijenteelt,** no pl., n. apiculture. **·bijenzwerm,** n. swarm of bees.

·bijfiguur, -guren, n. subsidiary figure. **·bijgaand,** a. enclosed. **·bijgebouw,** n.n. annexe, outhouse. **·bijgedachte, -n,** n. ulterior motive. **·bijgelegen,** a. adjacent.

·bijgeloof, no pl., n.n. superstition. **bijge·lovig,** a. superstitious. **bijge·lovigheid, -heden,** n. superstitiousness.

·bijgeluid, n.n. extraneous sound. **·bijge-naamd,** a. nicknamed, named. **bijge·val,**

c. in case. ¶ *adv.* by chance. **als je** ~ **...**, if you happen to ... **bijge·volg**, *adv.* hence, consequently. **·bijhalen, haal bij,** *v.t.s.* to draw near. *iets er met de haren* ~, to drag something into it. **·bijharken,** *v.t.s.* to rake up, tidy up.

·bij·horig, *a.* appertaining. **bij·horigheden,** pl. only, *n.* appurtenances.

·bijhouden, *v.t.s., irr.* to keep up with; to keep up to date (*accounts, diary; knowledge*). **·bijkaart,** *n.* inset-map. **·bijkantoor, -toren,** *n.n.* branch-office. **·bijker, -s,** *n.* apiarist. **·bijkeuken, -s,** *n.* scullery. **·bijknippen, knip bij,** *v.t.s.* to trim (*with scissors*).

·bijkomen, *v.i.s., irr.* to recover (*from faint*); to be added; to put on weight. **·bijkomend,** *a.* additional. ~*e onkosten,* incidental expenses; ~*e omstandigheden,* attendant circumstances. **bij·komstig,** *a.* accidental; incidental. **bij·komstigheid, -heden,** *n.* attendant *or* accidental circumstances.

bijl, *n.* axe, hatchet, adze. **·bijlage, -n,** *n.* enclosure; appendix, supplement. **·bij·lappen, lap bij,** *v.t.s.* to patch up.

·bijleggen, leg bij, *v.t.s., irr.* to add; to add, contribute (*money*); to settle, compose (*differences*). *ergens geld op* ~, to lose money on something; *het* ~, to make it up (*quarrel*). **·bijlegging,** *n.* settlement (*of dispute*).

·bijlichten, *v.t.s.* to light (*way*). ¶ *v.i.s. also:* to heave to, to lie to. *iemand* ~, to tell a person straight out. **·bijloper, -s,** *n.* hanger-on. **·bijltje, -s,** *n.n.* little axe. *het* ~ *er bij neerleggen,* to throw one's hand in; *hij heeft al lang met dat* ~ *gehakt,* he is an old hand at it.

·bijmengen, *v.t.s.* to mix. **·bijmenging,** *n.,* **·bijmengsel, -s,** *n.n.* admixture.

·bijna, *adv.* almost, nearly; all but. ~ *niemand,* hardly anybody; ~ *nooit,* hardly ever.

·bijnaam, -namen, *n.* surname; nickname.

·bijpad, *n.n.* by-path.

·bijpassen, pas, *v.t.s.* to pay extra; to make up the price. **·bijpassend,** *a.* to match.

·bijrivier, *n.* tributary (*river*). **·bijschaduw,** *n.* penumbra. **·bijschenken,** *v.t.s., str.* to add (*liquid*). **·bijschilderen,** *v.t.s.* to paint in; to touch up. **·bijschrift,** *n.n.* caption, letterpress. **·bijschrijven, schrijf bij,** *v.t.s., str.* to add (*in writing*). **·bijschuiven, schuif bij,** *v.t.s., str.* to draw up (*chair*). **·bijslaap, -slapen,** *n.* cohabitation; copulation; mistress. **·bijslag,** *n.* bonus. **·bijsmaak, -smaken,** *n.* funny taste, tang. **·bijspijkeren,** *v.t.s.* to nail on; to make up arrears. **·bijspringen,** *v.t.s., str.* to help.

·bijstaan, sta bij, *v.t.s., irr.* to assist, succour. **·bijstand,** no pl., *n.* assistance. ~ *verlenen,* to render assistance; **gewapende** ~,

armed assistance (*military* or *police*); *rechtskundige* ~, legal aid. **·bijstander, -s,** *n.* helper.

·bijstelling, *n.* apposition (*grammar*).

·bijster, *adv.* extremely. *niet* ~ *knap,* not particularly bright. ¶ *a.* lost. *het spoor* ~ *maken,* to throw off the scent; *het spoor* ~ *raken,* to lose the scent; *het spoor* ~ *zijn,* to have lost the scent *or* the way.

·bijstorten, *v.t.s.* to make additional payment.

bijt, *n.* hole (*cut in ice*).

·bijtekenen, *v.i.s.* to re-enlist.

·bijten, *v.t., str., & v.i., str.* to bite; to bite, burn, corrode. *willen* ~, to take the bait; *van zich af* ~, to answer back; *in het zand or stof* ~, to be killed, bite the dust; *iemand iets in het oor* ~, to make an angry retort; ~ *naar,* to snap at; *zich op de lippen or de tong* ~, to clench one's teeth. **·bijtend,** *a.* corrosive; biting, caustic. ~*e spot,* sarcasm.

bij·tijds, *adv.* in good time, betimes.

·bijtmiddel, *n.n.* corrosive substance.

·bijtoon, -tonen, *n.* overtone; secondary stress.

·bijtrekken, trek bij, *v.t.s., str.* to pull up (*chair*). ¶ *v.i.s., str.* to disappear (*of stain*).

·bijvak, -kken, *n.n.* subsidiary subject.

·bijval, no pl., *n.* approbation; applause. ~ *vinden,* to meet with approval. **·bijvallen, val bij,** *v.t.s., str.* to back up; to concur with. **·bijvalsbetuiging,** *n.* mark *or* show of approval; applause.

·bijverdienste, -n, *n.* extra earnings.

·bijvoegen, *v.t.s.* to add. **·bijvoeging,** *n.* *onder* ~ *van,* with the addition of. **bij·voeglijk,** *a.* adjectival. ~ *naamwoord,* adjective. ¶ *adv.* adjectivally. **·bijvoegsel, -s,** *n.n.* addition; supplement.

·bijvoet, no pl., *n.* mugwort.

bij·voorbeeld, *adv.* for instance.

·bijvorm, *n.* variant.

·bijvullen, vul bij, *v.t.s.* to fill up, replenish.

·bijwagen, -s, *n.* trailer (*tramway*). **·bijweg,** *n.* by-pass. **·bijwerken,** *v.t.s.* to touch up; to bring up to date. **·bijwezen,** no pl., *n.n.* See **bijzijn. bij·wijlen,** *adv.* once in a while. **·bijwonen, woon bij,** *v.t.s.* to be present at, attend, witness.

·bijwoord, *n.n.* adverb. **bij·woordelijk,** *a.* adverbially. ¶ *adv.* adverbially.

·bijzaak, -zaken, *n.* matter of secondary importance. *dat is maar* ~, that doesn't matter so much; *geld is* ~, money is no object.

·bijzetten, zet bij, *v.t.s.* to place by *or* near; to lay (*in burial vault*); to apply (*strength*); to set (*sail*). *alle zeilen* ~, to set all sails, to make every effort. **·bijzetting,** *n.* burial, interment (*in vault*).

·bijziend, *a.* shortsighted, myopic. **bij·ziendheid,** no pl., *n.* shortsightedness, myopia.

·**bijzijn**, no pl., *n.n. in het* ~ *van*, in the presence of.
·**bijzin**, -**nnen**, *n.* subordinate clause.
·**bijzit**, -**tten**, *n.* concubine. ·**bijzitter**, -**s**, *n.* assessor; assistant examiner.
bij·zonder, *a.* particular, special; private; peculiar. *in het* ~, in particular, particularly; ~*e school*, non-provided school; *niets* ~*s*, nothing special. ¶ *adv.* particularly, especially. **bij·zonderheid**, -**heden**, *n.* particularity, detail; peculiarity. *bijzonderheden*, particulars; *geen bijzonderheden*, nothing particular; *in de kleinste bijzonderheden*, down to the smallest detail.
·**bikhamer**, -**s**, *n.* pick hammer.
·**bikkel**, -**s**, *n.* knuckle-bone, fivestone. *zo hard als een* ~, as hard as flint. ·**bikkelen**, *v.i.* to play at fivestones. ·**bikkelspel**, no pl., *n.n.* game of fivestones.
·**bikken**, **bik**, *v.t.* to chip, scale, scrape; to tuck in (*eat*).
bil, -**llen**, *n.* buttock; *billen*, rump (*of beef*); *wie zijn billen brandt moet op de blaren zitten*, as he makes his bed so must he lie on it; *een pak op or voor de billen*, a trouncing.
bil·jart, *n.n.* billiard table; billiards (*game*). ~ *spelen*, to play billiards; *een partij* ~, a game of billiards. **bil·jartbal**, -**llen**, *n.* billiard ball. **bil·jartband**, *n.* cushion (*billiards*). **bil·jartbok**, -**kken**, *n.* cue-rest. **bil·jarten**, *v.i.* to play billiards. **bil·jartkeu**, -**s**, *n.* billiard cue. **bil·jartlaken**, no pl., *n.n.* billiard cloth. **bil·jartspel**, no pl., *n.n.* billiards. **bil·jartspeler**, -**s**, *n.* billiard player. **bil·jartzaal**, -**zalen**, *n.* billiard room. **bil·jartzak**, -**kken**, *n.* pocket (*billiards*).
bil·jet, -**tten**, *n.n.* ticket; note; handbill.
·**billijk**, *a.* fair, equitable. ~ *tegenover*, fair towards. ·**billijken**, *v.t.* to justify; to approve of. **billijker·wijze**, *adv.* in fairness, in justice. ·**billijkheid**, no pl., *n.* fairness, justice. ·**billijkheidshalve**, *adv.* for the sake of fairness.
bil·lioen, *n.n.* billion (*million millions*).
·**bilnaad**, -**naden**, *n.* perineum. ·**bilstuk**, -**kken**, *n.n.* rump (*of beef*).
·**bilzenkruid**, no pl., *n.n.* henbane.
·**binden**, *v.t.*, *str.* to bind (*prisoner; book; sheaf*); to tie (*rope*); to tie up (*parcel*); to bind, thicken (*sauce*); to make (*broom*). *iemand de handen* ~, to tie a person's hands; *aan handen en voeten* ~, to bind hand and foot; *iemand iets op het hart* ~, to enjoin something on someone; *gebonden zijn*, to be tied; ~ *aan*, to bind, tie to; ~ *tot*, to tie into. ¶ *zich* ~, *v.r.*, *str.* to commit oneself. ·**bindend**, *a.* binding. ·**binder**, -**s**, *n.* binder. **binde·rij**, *n.* binder's shop. ·**bindgaren**, -**s**, *n.n.* string, packthread. ·**bindmiddel**, *n.n.* agglutinant. ·**bindrijs**, no pl., *n.n.* osier. ·**bindsel**, -**s**,

n.n. band; bandage. ·**bindtouw**, *n.n.* string, twine. ·**bindvlies**, -**zen**, *n.n.* conjunction. ·**bindweefsel**, -**s**, *n.n.* (cellular connective) tissue.
·**binnen**, *prep.* within, in. ¶ *adv.* in. *naar* ~ *gaan*, to go in(side); *te* ~ *schieten*, to think of suddenly; *van* ~, inside, on the inside; *van* ~ *naar buiten*, from inside; ~ *zijn*, to have made one's money. ¶ *prefix to nouns and sep. verbs:* in-, inner-, inside-. ·**binnenband**, *n.* inner tube (*bicycle tyre*). ·**binnenblijven**, **blijf binnen**, *v.i.s.*, *str.* to stay inside. **binnen·boord**, *adv.* inboard. ·**binnenbrand**, *n.* small conflagration. ·**binnenbrengen**, *v.t.s.*, *irr.* to carry *or* bring in. ·**binnendeur**, *n.* inner door. ·**binnendijk**, *n.* inner dyke. **binnendijks**, *a.* & *adv.* on the landside of the dyke(s). **binnen·door**, *adv.* ~ *gaan*, to take a short cut. ·**binnendringen**, *v.t.s.*, *str.*, & *v.i.s.*, *str.* to force one's way in, penetrate into. ·**binnengaan**, **ga binnen**, *v.t.s.*, *irr.* & *v.i.s.*, *irr.* to enter. **binnengaats**, *a.* & *adv.* inside the harbour; on inland waters. **binnengalerij**, *n.* inner gallery, hall (*East Indies*). ·**binnengedeelte**, -**n**, *n.n.* inner part. ·**binnengoed**, no pl., *n.n.* filling(s) (*cigar*). ·**binnenhalen**, **haal binnen**, *v.t.s.* to fetch, gather in. ·**binnenhaven**, -**s**, *n.* inner harbour; inland harbour. ·**binnenhof**, -**ven**, *n.n.* inner court. ·**binnenhouden**, *v.t.s.*, *irr.* to keep in, retain, ·**binnenhuis**, -**zen**, *n.n.* interior (*domestic*). **binnen·in**, *adv.* inside. ·**binnenkamer**, -**s**, *n.* closet. ·**binnenkant**, *n.* inside. ·**binnenkomen**, *v.i.s.*, *irr.* to come in, enter. ·**binnenkomst**, *n.* entry, coming in. **binnen·kort**, *adv.* shortly, before long. ·**binnenkrijgen**, *v.t.s.*, *str.* to get inside. ·**binnenkruipen**, *v.t.s.*, *str.* to creep in(to). ·**binnenland**, *n.n.* interior (*land*). *in het* ~, at home (*opposite of abroad*). ·**binnenlands**, *a.* inland, interior, internal; home, home-made. ~ *Bestuur*, Civil Service (*East Indies*); ~ *nieuws*, home news; ~ *verlof*, home leave; *het Ministerie van* ~*e Zaken*, the Home Office. ·**binnenlaten**, **laat binnen**, *v.t.s.*, *str.* to let in. ·**binnenleiden**, *v.t.s.* to lead in. ·**binnenloodsen**, *v.t.s.* to pilot in. ·**binnenlopen**, **loop binnen**, *v.t.s.*, *str.* to walk in; to put into (*harbour*). ·**binnenmeid**, *n.* parlourmaid. ·**binnenmoeder**, -**s**, *n.* matron (*in institution*). ·**binnenmuur**, -**muren**, *n.* inner wall. ·**binnenplaats**, *n.* courtyard. ·**binnenrijden**, *v.t.s.*, *str.* to drive into (*town*, *street*). ·**binnenroepen**, *v.t.s.*, *str.* to call in(side). ·**binnenrukken**, **ruk binnen**, *v.t.s.* to enter (*of army*). ·**binnenscheepvaart**, *n.* inland navigation. ·**binnenschip**, -**schepen**, *n.* barge, inland craft. ·**binnenschipper**, -**s**, *n.* master of barge. **binnens·huis**, *adv.* indoors, within doors. **binnens·lands**, *adv.* in the country,

at home. ·binnenslepen, **sleep binnen**, *v.t.s.* to drag inside. ·binnensmokkelen, *v.t.s.* to smuggle in. **binnens·monds**, *adv.* under one's breath. ·binnenst(e), *a.* inmost. ¶ *n.n.* inside. ~ *buiten*, inside out; *in het* ~ *van zijn hart*, in his heart of hearts. ·binnenstad, -steden, *n.* inner town, old town. ·binnenstappen, **stap binnen**, *v.t.s.* to step in. **binnens·tijds**, *adv.* before the set date. ·binnenstomen, **stoom binnen**, *v.t.s.* to steam into. ·binnenstormen, *v.t.s.* to rush into. ·binnenstromen, **stroom binnen**, *v.t.s.* to stream *or* surge into. ·binnenstuiven, **stuif binnen**, *v.t.s. str.* to rush into. ·binnentreden, **treed binnen**, *v.t.s., str.* to enter (*room*). ·binnenvaart, no pl., *n.* inland navigation. ·binnenvader, -s, *n.* master (*of workhouse*). ·binnenvallen, **val binnen**, *v.t.s., str.* to drop in; to put into (*port*). ·binnenvragen, **vraag binnen**, *v.t.s., irr.* to ask in. ·binnenwaaien, *v.t.s., irr.* to blow in. ¶ *v.i.s., irr.* to blow in. ~ *bij*, to drop in on. ·binnenwaard, *n.* polder (*by river*). ·binnenwaarts, *a. & adv.* inward. ·binnenwater, *n.* inland waterway. ·binnenweg, *n.* lane, bypath. ·binnenwerk, no pl., *n.n.* indoor work; inner works. ·binnenwerks, *adv.* inside (*measurement*). ·binnenzak, -kken, *n.* inside pocket. ·binnenzee, -zeeën, *n.* inland sea. ·binnenzeilen, *v.t.s.* to sail into. ·binnenzijde, -n, *n.* inside, inner side.

bint, *n.n.* tie-beam.

bio·graaf, -grafen, *n.* biographer. **biegra·fie**, **-iëen**, *n.* biography. **bio·grafisch**, *a.* biographic(al). ¶ *adv.* biographically.

bio·loog, -logen, *n.* biologist.

bio·scoop, -scopen, *n.* cinema, picture-theatre. **bio·scoopvoorstelling**, *n.* cinema show.

bis, *adv.* encore! ¶ ño pl., *n.* B sharp.

bis·cuitje, -s, *n.n.* biscuit.

·**bisdom**, **-mmen**, *n.n.* bishopric, diocese. ·bisschop, -ppen, *n.* bishop; mulled wine. **bis·schoppelijk**, *a.* episcopal. ·bisschopsambt, *n.n.* episcopacy. ·bisschopsstaf, -staven, *n.* crozier. ·bisschopszetel, -s, *n.* episcopal see.

bissec·trice, -s, *n.* bisector.

bis·seren, -seer, *v.t.* to encore.

bit, -tten, *n.n.* bit (*of horse*).

bits, *a.* sharp, tart, cutting. ¶ *adv.* bitingly. ·bitsheid, no pl., *n.* tartness.

·**bitter**, *a.* bitter. ~ *maken*, to embitter. ¶ *adv.* bitterly. ~ *slecht*, atrocious; ~ *weinig*, next to nothing. ¶ *n.n. een glaasje* ~, a glass of gin and bitters. ·bitterachtig, *a.* bitterish. ·bitterappel, -s, *n.* bitter-apple, colocynth. ·bitteren, *v.t.* to drink gin and bitters *or* apéritifs. ·bitterheid, -heden, *n.* bitterness, acrimony. ·bitterkers, no pl., *n.* bitter cress. **bitter·koekje, -s**, *n.n.* (small) macaroon (*biscuit*). ·bittertafel, -s, *n.* table *or* place where one has one's apéritif. **aan de** ~,

at the club (*source of rumour*). ·bitterje, -s, *n.n.* glass of gin and bitters. ·bitteruur, -uren, *n.n.* bitteruurtje, -s, *n.n.* apéritif time. ·bitterwortel, -s, *n.* bitterwort. ·bitterzoet, *a.* bittersweet.

bi·vak, -kken, *n.n.* bivouac. *zijn* ~ *opslaan*, to bivouac, pitch one's tents. **bivak·keren, -keer**, *v.i.* to bivouac. **bi·vakmuts**, *n.* balaclava helmet. **bi·vakvuur, -vuren**, *n.n.* camp-fire.

·**bizon, -s**, *n.* bison.

·**blaadje, -s**, *n.n.* small leaf; leaflet; small tray. *het* ~ *is gekeerd*, the tables are turned; *bij iemand in een goed* ~ *staan*, to be in a person's good books.

blaag, blagen, *n.* troublesome child.

blaam, no pl., *n.* blame, censure, reproach; blemish. *iemand een* ~ *aanwrijven*, to cast a slur on someone's character; *er kleeft een* ~ *op hem*, a stigma is attached to his name; *op hem rust geen* ~ *or hem treft geen* ~, no blame is attached to him; ~ *verdienen*, to deserve censure; ~ *werpen op*, to cast blame on; *zich van alle* ~ *zuiveren*, to clear one's reputation.

blaar, blaren, *n.* blister; white spot. *blaren trekken*, to raise blisters. ·blaartrekkend, *a.* vesicatory. ~ *middel*, vesicant.

blaas, blazen, *n.* bladder; bubble. ·blaasbalg, *n.* bellows. ·blaasinstrument, *n.n.* wind instrument. ·blaasje, -s, *n.* vesicle; bubble. ·blaasjeskruid, no pl., *n.n.* bladderwort. ·blaaskaak, -kaken, *n.* windbag, gasbag. ·blaasorkest, *n.n.* brass band, wind ensemble. ·blaaspijp, *n.* blow-pipe; pea-shooter. ·blaasroer, *n.n.* blow-pipe (*dart tube*). ·blaaswier, no pl., *n.n.* bladderwrack, kelp. ·blaasworm, *n.* bladder worm.

blad, *n.n.* leaf (*of book*); sheet (*of paper, metal*); (news)paper; flap (*of table*); tray; blade (*of oar, propeller, etc.*). ¶ -eren, *n.n.* leaf (*of plant, tree*). ·bladaarde, no pl., *n.* leafmould. ·bladader, -s, *or* -en, *n.* vein of leaf. ·bladerdeeg, no pl., *n.n.* puff paste. ·bladerdos, no pl., *n.* foliage. ·bladeren, *v.i.* ~ *in een boek*, to turn over the leaves of a book. ·bladerloos, -loze, *a.* leafless. ·bladerrijk, *a.* leafy. ·bladgoud, no pl., *n.n.* gold-leaf. ·bladgroen, no pl., *n.n.* chorophyll. ·bladgroente, -n, *n.* green vegetables. ·bladkoper, no pl., *n.n.* sheet copper. ·bladluis, -zen, *n.* green fly. ·bladstil, -lle, *a.* dead calm, windless. *het was* ~, not a leaf stirred. ·bladvulling, *n.* fill up(s) (*in printing*). ·bladwijzer, -s, *n.* table of contents; index; book-mark. ·bladzij, -zijden, *n.*, ·bladzijde, -n, *n.* page (*one side*).

·**blaffen, blaf**, *v.i.* to bark. *tegen de maan* ~, to bay at the moon.

·**blaken, blaak**, *v.i.* to blaze (*of sun*); to glow (*with emotion*). ~ *van vaderlandsliefde*, to burn *or* glow with patriotism.

¶ *v.t.* to scorch. ·**blakend**, *a.* blazing, scorching; ardent. *in ~e gezondheid* or *welstand*, in the pink of health. ·**blaker**, **-s**, *n.* candlestick (*with handle*). ·**blakeren**, *v.i.* & *v.t.* to burn, parch, scorch (*of fire, sun*).

bla·meren, -meer, *v.t.* to blame.

·**blanco**, *adv.* blank. *~ cheque*, blank cheque; *~ crediet*, open credit; *~ laten*, to leave blank; *~ stem*, blank vote; *in ~ opmaken*, to draw in blank; *in ~ tekenen*, to sign a blank. . . .

blank, *a.* white; clear; fair (*complexion*); naked (*sword*); blank (*verse*). *~ staan*, to be awash, stand under water. ¶ *adv.* brightly. *~ schuren*, to polish, sandpaper. ·**blanke, -n**, *n.* white (*man* or *woman*). ·**blankheid**, no pl., *n.* whiteness. ·**blankvoorn, -s**, *n.* roach.

·**blaten, blaat**, *v.i.* to bleat.

blauw, *a.* blue. *~e boon* (*facetious*), bullet; *van de ~e knoop*, teetotal; *~e kruis*, teetotal league; *een ~e Maandag*, a very short time; *~ oog*, black eye; *~e plek*, bruise; *~e regen*, wistaria; *iets ~ ~ laten*, to let a matter rest; *~ van*, blue with. ¶ *n.n.* blue. ·**blauwachtig**, *a.* bluish. ·**blauwbekken**, *v.i. staan ~*, to stand and freeze. ·**blauwbes, -ssen**, *n.* bilberry. ·**blauwborstje, -s**, *n.n.*, ·**blauwkeeltje, -s**, *n.n.* blue-throat. ·**blauwgeruit**, *a.* blue-check. ·**blauwgrijs, -ze**, *a.* bluish grey. ·**blauwheid**, no pl., *n.* blueness. ·**blauwhout**, no pl., *n.n.* logwood. ·**blauwkopmees, -mezen**, *n.* blue-tit. ·**blauwkous**, *n.* blue-stocking. ·**blauwogig**, *a.* blue-eyed. ·**blauwsel**, no pl., *n.n.* (laundress's) blue. ·**blauwspecht**, *n.* nut-hatch. ·**blauwtje, -s**, *n.n. een ~ lopen*, to be turned down (*of suitor*). ·**blauwvoet**, *n.* gerfalcon. ·**blauwzucht**, no pl., *n.* cyanosis. ·**blauwzuur**, no pl., *n.* prussic acid.

·**blazen, blaas**, *v.i.*, *str.* to blow; to spit (*of cat*); to sound (*siren*). *beter hard geblazen dan de mond gebrand*, prevention is better than cure; *~ op*, to blow, sound (*instrument; alarm*). ¶ *v.t.*, *str.* to blow. *iemand iets in het oor ~*, to whisper something to someone.

bla·zoen, *n.n.* blazon. **blazoe·neren, -neer**, *v.t.* to emblazon.

bleek, bleke, bleke, *a.* pale, wan. *~ worden*, to pale; *~ zien*, to look pale; *zo ~ als de dood*, as white as death; *~ van schrik*, pale with fright. ¶ *n.* bleaching lawn; linen out on lawn. *op de ~ leggen*, to put (*linen*) out on lawn. ·**bleekachtig**, *a.* palish. ·**bleekgezicht**, *n.n.* pale-face. ·**bleekgroen**, *a.* pale green. ·**bleekheid**, no pl., *n.* pallor. ·**bleekjes**, *adv.* palish. ·**bleekmiddel**, *n.n.* bleaching agent. ·**bleekneus, -zen**, *n.* pale person (*after illness*). ·**bleekpoeder**, no pl., *n.n.* bleaching powder. ·**bleekrood, -rode**, *a.* pale red. ·**bleekveld**,

n.n. bleaching lawn. ·**bleekvos, -ssen**, *n.* light bay (*horse*). ·**bleekwater**, no pl., *n.n.* bleaching fluid. ·**bleekzucht**, no pl., *n.* chlorosis. ·**bleekzuchtig**, *a.* chlorotic. ·**bleken, bleek**, *v.t.* to bleach, whiten. **bleke·rij**, *n.* bleaching works.

blei, *n.* white bream.

blein, *n.* blister.

·**blende, -n**, *n.* blende.

·**blèren**, *v.i.* (*coll.*) to bawl, cry.

bles, -ssen, *n.* blaze (on horse's face); horse with blaze.

bles·seren, -seer, *v.t.* to wound.

bleu, *a.* timid, bashful. ·**bleuheid**, no pl., *n.* bashfulness.

bliek, *n.* See **blei**.

blieven, *v.t.* See **believen**.

blij, or **blijde**, *a.* glad, happy, joyous. *~ om*, glad of; *~ mee*, happy with; *in blijde verwachting*, expecting a happy event; *de blijde Boodschap*, the gospel; *~ maken*, to gladden; *zich ~ maken met een dode mus*, to be easily pleased. ¶ *adv.* gladly. ·**blijdschap**, no pl., *n.* gladness. ·**blijeindend**, *a.* with happy ending. *~ treurspel*, tragi-comedy. **blij·geestig**, *a.* cheerful. ¶ *adv.* cheerfully. **blij·geestigheid**, no pl., *n.* cheerfulness. ·**blijheid**, no pl., *n.* gladness. *vrijheid ~*, live and let live.

blijk, *n.n.* token, mark. *~ geven van*, to give evidence of, show; *ten ~e waarvan*, in witness thereof. ·**blijkbaar, -bare**, *a.* apparent, evident, obvious. ¶ *adv.* apparently, evidently, obviously. ·**blijken**, *v.i.*, *str.*, & *v.t.*, *str.*, to be evident; to appear. *~ te zijn*, to turn out to be, prove to be; *doen ~ van*, to give proof of; *laten ~*, to betray, show (*emotions*); *het moet nog ~*, it remains to be seen; *~ uit*, to appear, show from. ·**blijkens**, *adv.* as appears from.

blij·moedig, *a.* joyful, cheerful. ¶ *adv.* joyfully. **blij·moedigheid**, no pl., *n.* cheerfulness. ·**blijspel**, *n.n.* comedy. ·**blijspeldichter, -s**, *n.* writer of comedies.

·**blijven, blijft**, *v.i.*, *str.* to remain, stay; to perish (*in war* or *accident*); to keep. *waar zijn we gebleven?*, where have we got to?; *waar blijft . . .?*, where is . . .?; *waar blijft het geld?*, where does the money go?; *~ eten*, to stay to a meal; *~ steken*, to get stuck; *~ bij*, to abide by, adhere to. ·**blijvend**, *a.* lasting.

blik, -kken, *n.* look, glance; expression. *een ~ werpen* or *slaan op*, to cast a glance at; *zijn blikken richten naar*, to let one's eye rest on; *een brede ~*, a wide outlook; *een goede ~ hebben op*, to have sound views on; *bij de eerste ~*, at first glance; *in één ~*, at a glance. ¶ no pl., *n.n.* tin(plate); dustpan; tin, can. ·**blikgroenten**, pl. only, *n.* tinned vegetables. ·**blikje, -s**, *n.n.* tin, can (*of preserves*). ·**blikjesvlees**, no pl., *n.n.* tinned meat(s).

·blikken, blik, *v.i.* to glance. *zonder ~ of blozen*, without a blush. ¶ *a.* tin. ·blikkeren, *v.i.* to sparkle. ·blikopener, -s, *n.* tin-opener. ·blikschaar, -scharen, *n.* plate shears. ·blikslager, -s, *n.* tinsmith. ·blikwerk, no pl., *n.n.* tinware.

·bliksem, -s, *n.* lightning; (*vulg.*) blazes; (*slang*) person (*derogatory* or *pitying*). *als de ~*, like blazes; *als door de ~ getroffen*, thunder-struck (*fig.*); *loop naar de ~*, go to blazes; *naar de ~*, spoilt, lost; *wat ~!*, what the dickens!; *geen ~*, not a hang; *hete ~*, (sort of) stew; *een arme ~*, a poor fellow; *een gemene ~*, a low scoundrel; *een vervelende ~*, an unpleasant person. ·bliksemafleider, -s, *n.* lightning-conductor. ·bliksemen, *v.i.* to lighten (*lightning*), to flash; to fulminate; (*vulg.*) to chuck. ·bliksemflits, *n.* flash of lightning. ·bliksemlicht, no pl., *n.n.* flash-light. ·bliksems, *a.* (*coll.*) devilish, damned. ¶ *adv* damnably. ¶ *int. See* bliksem. ·bliksemschicht, *n.* flash of lightning, thunderbolt. ·bliksemsnel, -lle, *a.* quick as lightning. ¶ *adv.* with lightning speed. ·bliksemsnelheid, no pl., *n.* lightning speed. ·bliksemstraal, -stralen, *n.* flash or streak of lightning. *een ~ uit heldere hemel*, a bolt from the blue. ·bliksemtrein, *n.* non-stop train.

blind, *a.* blind; invisible; blank. *ziende ~*, blind to the obvious; *~ worden*, to go blind; *zich ~ staren op*, to stare one's eyes out at; *~ aan één oog*, blind in one eye; *~ voor*, blind to; *~e darm*, appendix; *~e darmontsteking*, appendicitis; *~e passagier*, stowaway; *~e klip*, submerged rock; *~e muur*, blank wall. ¶ *adv.* blindly. ¶ *n.n.* shutter. blin·dage, no pl., *n.* armour(-plating). ·blinddoek, *n.* bandage. *een ~ voorbinden*, to blindfold. ·blinddoeken, *v.t.* to blindfold; to hoodwink. ·blinde, -n, *n.* blind man *or* woman; dummy (*at cards*). *in den ~*, at random. ·blindelings, *adv.* blindly; implicitly. ·blindeman, -nnen. *n.* blind man. *blindemannetje spelen*, to play blind man's buff. ·blindeninstituut, -tuten, *n.n.* institution for the blind. blin·deren, -deer, *v.t.* to armour-plate. blin·dering, *n.* armour-plating. ·blindgeboren, *a.* blind from birth. ·blindheid, no pl., *n.* blindness. *met ~ geslagen*, struck with blindness. ·blindslang, *n.*, ·blindworm, *n.* blind-worm, slow-worm.

·blinken, *v.i.*, *str.* to shine, beam, glisten. ·blinkerd, -s, *n.* high sand dune.

bloc, no pl., *n.n. en ~*, in the lump (*buying and selling*). ·bloc-notes, pl. only, *n.* (writing) pad, block (*for scribbling*).

bloed, no pl., *n.n.* blood. *het ~ kruipt waar het niet gaan kan*, blood is thicker than water; *het ~ in de aderen doen stollen*, to freeze one's blood; *er uitzien als melk en ~*, to look apple-cheeked, rosy; *kwaad ~ zetten*, to create bad blood; *nieuw ~*, fresh blood; *in koelen ~e*, in cold blood; *het zit in het ~*, it runs in the blood; *met ~ belopen*, bloodshot; *naar ~ dorsten*, to thirst for blood; *van koninklijken ~e*, of royal blood; *van den ~e*, of the blood (*royal*). ¶ *-en*, *n.* simpleton. ·bloedaandrang, no pl., *n.* congestion, rush of blood to the head. ·bloedarmoede, no pl., *n.* anaemia. ·bloedbad, no pl., *n.n.* slaughter, carnage. *een ~ aanrichten onder*, to cause havoc among, to slaughter. ·bloedbeuling, *n.* black-pudding. ·bloeddorst, no pl., *n.* thirst for blood. bloed·dorstig, *a.* bloodthirsty. bloed·dorstigheid, no pl., *n. See* bloeddorst. ·bloedeigen, *a.* (very) own. ·bloedeloos, -loze, *a.* bloodless. ·bloeden, *v.i.* to bleed. *hij zal er voor moeten ~*, he will have to pay for it. ¶ no pl., *n.n. tot ~s toe*, until it bleeds. ·bloeder, -s, *n.* bleeder (*haemophilic*). ·bloederig, *a.* bloody (*meat*). ·bloedgeld, no pl., *n.n.* blood-money. ·bloedgever, -s, *n.* blood donor. ·bloedig, *a.* bloody, gory; bitter. *~e tranen*, tears of blood. ¶ *adv.* hard. ·bloedkoraal, ralen, *n.* red coral. ·bloedlichaampje, -s, *n.n.* corpuscle. ·bloedloop, no pl., *n.* dysentry. ·bloedluis, -zen, *n.* species of aphis. ·bloedneus, -zen, *n.* bloody nose. ·bloedonderzoek, no pl., *n.n.* blood test. ·bloedoverbrenging, *n.* blood transfusion. ·bloedplakkaat, -katen, *n.n.* Bloody Edict. ·bloedplas, -ssen, *n.* pool of blood. ·bloedraad, no pl., *n.* Council of Blood (Holland, 1567). ·bloedrijk, *a.* sanguineous. ·bloedschande, no pl., *n.* incest. ·bloedschender, *n.* incestuous person. ·bloedschuld, *n.* blood-guilt. ·bloedsomloop, no pl., *n.* circulation (*of the blood*). ·bloedspuwing, *n.* spitting of blood. ·bloedstelpend, *a.* styptic. ·bloedstroom, no pl., *n.* blood stream. ·bloedvat, *n.n.* blood-vessel. ·bloedvergieten, no pl., *n.n.* bloodshed. ·bloedvergiftiging, *n.* blood poisoning. ·bloedverlies, no pl., *n.n.* loss of blood. ·bloedverwant, *n.* (blood-)relation, relative, kins(wo)man. ·bloedverwantschap, no pl., *n.* (blood-)relationship. ·bloedvete, -n, *n.* blood-feud. ·bloedvink, *n.* bullfinch. ·bloedworst, *n.* blackpudding. ·bloedwraak, no pl., *n.* vendetta, blood-feud. ·bloedzuiger, -s, *n.* bloodsucker, leech. ·bloedzweer, -zweren, *n.* boil, running sore.

bloei, no pl., *n.* flowering; bloom, flower (*fig.*); prosperity. *in de ~ des levens*, in the prime of life; *in (volle) ~ staan*, to be in (full) bloom *or* blossom; *tot ~ komen*, to become prosperous. ·bloeien, *v.i.* to flower, bloom; to prosper, flourish. ·bloeiend, *a.* in bloom; prosperous. ·bloeimaand, *n.* May. ·bloeitijd, no pl.,

n. flowering time; blossom time; flourishing period. ·bloeiwijze, -n, *n.* inflorescence.
bloem, *n.* flower; flour. *de ~en staan op de ramen,* the windows are frosted over; *~ van zwavel,* flowers of sulphur. ·bloembed, -dden, *n.n.* flower-bed. ·bloemblad, *n.n.* petal. ·bloembol, -llen, *n.* bulb *(of tulip, etc.).* ·bloembollenkweker, -s, *n.* bulb grower. ·bloembollenveld, *n.n.* bulb-field. ·bloemen, *v.i.* to be floury *(of boiled potato).* ·bloemencorso, -'s, *n.n.* floral procession. ·bloemenhandelaar, -s, *n.* florist. ·bloementeelt, no pl., *n.* flower growing. ·bloemetje, -s, *n.n.* little flower. *de ~s buiten zetten,* to paint the town red, have a good time. ·bloemig, *a.* flowery; blooming; floury *(of potato).* bloe·mist, *n.* florist. bloemiste·rij, *n.* florist's shop. ·bloemkelk, *n.* calyx. ·bloemknop, -ppen, *n.* flower bud. ·bloemkool, -kolen, *n.* cauliflower. ·bloemkrans, *n.* wreath. ·bloemkroon, -kronen, *n.* corolla. ·bloemkweker, -s, *n.* flower grower. ·bloemkwekerij, *n.* flower farm. ·bloemlezing, *n.* anthology. ·bloemperk, *n.n.* flower-bed. ·bloempje, -s, *n.n.* little flower. ·bloemrijk, *a.* flowery; florid. ·bloemstuk, -kken, *n.n.* flower-piece. ·bloemtuil, *n.* bouquet. ·bloesem, -s, *n.* blossom, bloom. ·bloesemen, *v.i.* to blossom, bloom.
bloes, -zen, *n.* blouse.
blok, -kken, *n.n.* block *(wood, stone, metal);* log; pulley; stocks *(torture);* block *(houses);* section *(railway);* bloc *(political). een ~ aan het been,* a hindrance, handicap. ·blokhuis, -zen, *n.n.* blockhouse, log-cabin. ·blokje, -s, *n.n.* cube. blok·kade, -s, *n.* blockade. *door de ~ heensluipen,* to run the blockade. blok·kadebreker, -s, *n.* blockade-runner. blok·keren, -keer, *v.t.* to blockade; to block up. ·blokken, **blok,** *v.i.* to swot, grind *(for exam.), ~ op,* to swot at. ·blokkendoos, -dozen, *n.* box of cubes, box of bricks *(toys).* ·blokker, -s, *n.* swot; one who swots. ·bloklood, no pl., *n.n.* pig-lead. ·blokschaaf, -schaven, *n.* plane *(tool).* ·bloksein, *n.n.* block-signal. ·blokwachter, -s, *n.* signalman.
blom, *n. See* bloem. ·blommig, *a. See* bloemig.
blond, *a.* blond, fair. ·blondharig, *a.* fair-haired. blon·dine, -s, *n.* blonde *(girl, woman).*
blood, blode, *a.* bashful; cowardly. *beter blode Jan dan dode Jan,* discretion is the better part of valour. ·bloodaard, -s, *n.* coward.
bloot, blote, *a.* bare, naked. *de blote feiten,* the bald facts; *een ~ toeval,* a mere chance; *onder de blote hemel,* in the open *(air);* ¶ *adv.* barely, merely. *See* blote. ·blootgeven, zich, geef bloot, *v.t.s.* to (lay) bare, expose. ·blootleggen, leg bloot, *v.i.s.,* *irr.* to lie bare *or* open. ·blootshoofds, *adv.*

bareheaded. ·blootstaan, sta bloot, *v.i.s., irr. ~ aan,* to be exposed to. ·blootstellen, stel bloot, *v.t.s.* to expose. ¶ *v.r.s. zich ~ aan,* to expose oneself to. ·blootstelling, *n.* exposure. ·blootsvoets, *adv.* barefooted.
blos, no pl., *n.* blush, flush; bloom. ·blote, no pl., *n. in de ~ (coll.),* bare; *voor de ~ geve,* to spank *(child's)* bare bottom.
·**blouse,** -s, *n.* blouse.
·**blozen, bloos,** *v.i.* to blush. *iemand doen ~,* to make someone blush; *~ om,* to blush at; *~ tot over de oren,* to blush to the roots of one's hair. ·blozend, *a.* blushing; rosy, ruddy.
bluf, no pl., *n.* boasting; swank. ·bluffen, bluf, *v.i.* to brag. *~ op,* to swank about. ·bluffer, -s, *n.* braggart, boaster. ·blufferig, *a.* boastful. bluffe·rij, *n.* boastfulness.
·**blusapparaat, -raten,** *n.n.* fire-extinguishing apparatus. ·blusgereedschap, -ppen, *n.n.* fire-extinguishing appliances. ·blusmiddel, *n.n.* fire-extinguisher *(substance; apparatus).* ·blussen, blus, *v.t.* to extinguish; to slake *(lime).*
blut, bluts, *a. (slang)* broke *(without money).* **bluts,** *n.* bruise; dent. ·blutsen, *v.t.* to bruise; to dent.
·**bobbel, -s,** *n.* bubble; lump. ·bobbelen, *v.i.* to bubble. ·bobbelig, *a.* lumpy.
bo·bijn, *n.* bobbin. bo·bijnen, *v.i.* to wind *(on bobbin);* to make lace.
·**bobslee, -leeën,** *n.* bob-sleigh.
·**bochel, -s,** *n.* hump; hunchback. *zich een ~ lachen,* to split one's sides with laughter.
bocht, *n.* bend, curve; bight, bay, gulf; bight, loop *(of rope);* contortion; paddock. *in de ~ springen,* to skip *(with rope); voor iemand in de ~ springen,* to take up the cudgels for someone; *zich in allerlei ~en wringen,* to make contortions *or* to try and wriggle out of it. ¶ no pl., *n.n.* rubbish, trash. ·bochtig, *a.* tortuous, winding.
bod, pl. **aanbiedingen,** *n.n.* bid, offer. *een ~ doen naar,* to make a bid for; *aan ~,* about to be bid for.
·**bode, -n,** *n.* messenger; beadle, usher; carrier; letter-carrier. *boden,* servants. ·bodeloon, no pl., *n.n.* porterage.
·**bodem, -s,** *n.* bottom *(of receptacle);* soil; territory; floor; vessel. *de ~ inslaan,* to stave in *or* to frustrate; *op de ~ van de zee,* at the bottom of the sea; *op eigen ~,* at home *(not abroad); op vreemde ~,* on foreign soil; *tot de ~ leegdrinken,* to drain to the last drop. ·bodemen, *v.t.* to bottom. bodeme·rij, *n.* bottomry. ·bodeme·rijbrief, -ven, *n.* bottomry-bond. ·bodemgesteldheid, no pl., *n.* nature of the soil. ·bodemloos, -loze, *a.* bottomless.
boe, *int. ~ noch ba zeggen,* not to open one's mouth; *zonder ~ of ba te zeggen,* without saying a word.

·boedel, -s, n. personal estate; goods and chattels. een ~ beheren, to administer an estate. ·boedelafstand, no pl., n. cession. ·boedelbeschrijving, n. inventory. ·boedelbezorger, -s, n. executor. ·boedelscheiding, n. division of an estate.

boef, -ven, n. rogue, villain; convict. ·boefachtig, a. scoundrelly. ·boefje, -s, n.n. urchin, street-arab.

boeg, n. bow(s) (of ship); counter (of horse). het over een andere ~ gooien or wenden, to change one's tack; iets voor de ~ hebben, to have something ahead of or before one. ·boeganker, -s, n.n. boweranchor. ·boeglijn, n. bowline. boeg·seren, -seer, v.t. to tow; to pilot, guide skilfully. ·boegspriet, n. bowsprit.

boei, n. fetter, shackle, manacle; buoy; life-buoy. iemand de ~en aandoen, to manacle a person; in ~en klinken or slaan, to put in irons, fetter; zijn ~en verbreken, to break one's bonds; een kleur als een ~, as red as a lobster. ·boeien, v.t. to fetter, shackle; to captivate, grip. de aandacht ~, to hold the attention. ·boeiend, a. fascinating. ¶ adv. captivatingly. ·boeienkoning, n. handcuff-king. ·boeier, -s, n. boyer.

boek, n.n. book; quire. een gesloten ~, a sealed book; te ~ staan als or voor, to be known as; te ~ stellen, to put down in book-form. ·boekaankondiging, n. announcement (of book). ·boekachtig, a. bookish.

boeka·nier, -s, n. buccaneer.

·boekbeoordeling, n., ·boekbeschouwing, n. book review. boekbinde·rij, n. bookbinder's shop. ·boekdeel, -delen, n.n. volume. ·boekdrukken, no pl., n.n. printing (art, trade). ·boekdrukker, -s, n. printer. boekdrukke·rij, n. printing-house. ·boekdrukkunst, no pl., n. art of printing. ·boeken, v.t. to book, enter; to record. geboekt staan, to be down in the books. ·boekenhanger, -s, n. hanging bookshelves. ·boekenkast, n. bookcase, bookshelves. ·boekenkraam, -kramen, n.n. bookstall (stall, barrow). ·boekenlegger, -s, n. bookmark. ·boekenliefhebber, -s, n. booklover. ·boekenmolen, -s, n. revolving bookcase. ·boekenplank, n. bookshelf. ·boekenstalletje, -s, n.n. bookstall. ·boekentaal, no pl., n. bookish speech. ·boekentas, -ssen, n. satchel. ·boekformaat, -maten, n.n. format. ·boekhandel, no pl., n. book trade; bookselling. ¶ -s, n. bookshop. ·boekhandelaar, -s, or -laren, n. bookseller. ·boekhouden, v.i.s., irr. to keep the books, keep accounts. ¶ no pl., n.n. book-keeping. dubbel or enkel ~, book-keeping by double or single entry. ·boekhouder, -s, n. book-keeper. ·boekhouding, n. book-keeping, accountancy. ·boekhoudster, -s, n. book-keeper (female).

·boekjaar, -jaren, n.n. financial year. ·boekje, -s, n.n. booklet. een ~ van or over iemand opendoen, to give the lowdown about someone; buiten zijn ~ gaan, to exceed one's authority; in een slecht ~ staan bij iemand, to be in someone's bad books. ·boekmaag, -magen, n., ·boekpens, n. third stomach (of ruminant). ·boekstaven, -staaf, v.t. to record, commit to paper. ·boekverkoping, n. book auction. ·boekwerk, n.n. book, tome, volume. ·boekwinkel, -s, n. bookshop. ·boekvink, n. finch, chaffinch. ·boekweit, no pl., n.n. buckwheat. ·boekweitemeel, no pl., n.n. buckwheat flour. ·boekweiten, a. buckwheat.

boel, no pl., n. lot(s). een ~, a lot, lots of, heaps of; een hele ~, a great deal of; een mooie ~, a fine pickle, pretty pickle; een saaie or dooie ~, a dull show; een vuile ~, a mess; de ~ kort en klein slaan, to smash up everything; de ~ verraden, to give the show away. ·boeldag, n. auction day. ·boelgoed, -eren, n.n. effects (at public sale). ·boelhuis, -zen, n.n. auction rooms; house in which public sale takes place. ·boelijn, n. bowline. ·boeltje, no pl., n.n. zijn ~, his belongings; zijn ~ pakken, to pack one's traps.

boem! exclam. bang!

·boeman, no pl., n. bugbear, bogey.

·boemel, no pl., n. spree. aan de ~ (coll.), on the spree, on the razzle. ·boemelaar, -s, n. reveller; loose liver. ·boemelen, v.i. (coll.) to be on the razzle. ·boemeltrein, n. slow train.

·boender, -s, n. scrubbing-brush; polisher. ·boenen, v.t. to scrub; to polish. ·boenlap, -ppen, n. polishing-rag. ·boenwas, no pl., n. furniture polish, floor polish.

boer, n. peasant, farmer; boor, rustic; jack, knave (cards); belch. Boer, Boer (South Africa); de ~ opgaan, to peddle round the countryside; lachen als een ~ die kiespijn heeft, to laugh on the wrong side of one's face; een ~ laten, to belch. boerde·rij, n. farm. ·boeren, v.i. to farm; to belch. goed or slecht ~, to do well or badly. boeren·arbeider, -s, n. farmlabourer, farm-hand. ·boerenbedrieger, -s, n. trickster. ·boerenbedrijf, -ven, n.n. farming, husbandry. ·boerenbedrog, no pl., n.n. humbug. ·boerenbond, n. farmers' league. ·boerenboon, -bonen, n. broad bean. boeren·bruiloft, n. country wedding; noisy show, flamboyant show. ·boerenboter, no pl., n. farmhouse butter. boeren·deern, -s, n. country lass. boerendochter, -s, n. farmer's daughter, country girl. ·boeren·dracht, n. country dress. boeren·erf, -ven, n.n. farmyard. boerenhoeve, -n, n., boeren·hofstede, -n, n., boeren·hoefstee, -steën, n. farm, homestead. boerenjas·mijn, no pl., n. mock

orange, syringa. **boeren·jongen, -s,** *n.*
country lad. ¶ *pl.* only, *n.* raisins in
brandy. **boeren·kermis, -ssen** *n.* country
fair. **boeren·kinkel, -s,** *n.,* **boeren·kaffer, -s,**
n. (*terms of abuse*) yokel, clodhopper.
boeren·knecht, -s, *n.* farm-hand. **boeren·**
kool, -kolen, *n.* curly kale. **boeren·kost,**
no pl., *n.* country fare. **boeren·leenbank,**
n. rural bank. **boeren·meid,** *n.* peasant girl.
boeren·meisjes, pl. only, *n.n.* apricots in
gin. **boeren·mens,** *n.n.* country person,
countryman. **boeren·paard,** *n.n.* farm
horse. **boeren·plaats,** *n.* farmstead. **boeren·**
pummel, -s, *n.* lout, yokel. **boeren·sjees,**
-sjezen, *n.* (type ot) farmer's carriage.
boerenstand, no pl., *n.* peasant class.
boeren·vrouw, *n.* peasant woman. **boeren·**
wagen, -s, *n.* farm cart, farm wagon.
boeren·woning, *n.* farmhouse. **boeren·**
wormkruid, no pl., *n.n.* tansy. **boeren·**
zoon, -s, *n.* farmer's son. **boerenzwaluw,**
n. barn swallow. **boe·rin, -nnen,** *n.*
farmer's wife; peasant woman. **boers,**
a. boorish, rustic, countrified. **·boers·**
heid, -heden, *n.* boorishness, rusticity.
boert, *n.* jest. **·boertig,** *a.* jocular.
boete, -n, *n.* fine; penance. ~ *betalen,*
to pay a fine; ~ *doen,* to do penance;
~ *krijgen,* to be fined; *iemand een* ~
opleggen van . . . to fine someone (*so much*);
~ *oplopen,* to incur a fine; *er staat* ~ *op,*
there is a fine attached to it; *op* ~ *van,*
under penalty of. **·boetedoening,** *n.*
penance. **·boetekleed, -klederen,** *n.*
penitent's garb. **·boeteling,** *n.* penitent
(*male*). **·boetelinge, -n,** *n.* penitent (*female*).
·boeten, *v.t.* to mend (*nets*); to expiate.
iets met het leven ~, to pay for something
with one's life. ¶ *v.i.* ~ *voor,* to atone
for, expiate, pay for. **·boetpredikatie,**
-tiën, *n.* penitential sermon. **·boetprediker,**
-s, *n.* preacher of penitential sermon.
·boetpsalm, *n.* penitential psalm. **boet·**
vaardig, *a.* penitent. **boet·vaardigheid,** no
pl., *n.* penitence.
boet·seerder, -s, *n.* modeller. **boet·seerklei,**
no pl., *n.* modelling clay. **boet·seerkunst,**
no pl., *n.* art of modelling. **boet·seerwerk,**
no pl., *n.n.* modelling work. **boet·seren,**
-seer, *v.i.* to model.
·boevenbende, -n, *n.* pack of rogues.
·boevenpak, -kken, *n.n.* pack of rogues;
prison-garb; rough's get-up. **·boeventaal,**
no pl., *n.* criminal slang. **·boeventstreek,**
-streken, *n.* knavery. **·boeventronie, -s,** *n.*
murderous face. **·boeventuig,** no pl., *n.n.*
criminal, rogues (*in general*).
·boezelaar, -s, *n.* pinafore, apron.
·boezem, -s, *n.* bosom, breast; auricle (*of*
heart); catchment basin (*of polder*);
bay (*of sea*). *de hand in eigen* ~ *steken,* to
search one's own heart; *verdeeldheid in*
eigen ~, dissension in the camp; *in*
or *uit* or *buiten de* ~ *der vergadering,* in

or from *or* outside the meeting. **·boezem·**
vriend, *n.* bosom-friend (*male*). **·boezem·**
vriendin, -nnen, *n.* bosom-friend (*female*).
·boezemwater, no pl., *n.n.* water in catchment basin (*of polder*).
boeze·roen, *n. & n.n.* blouse, smock.
bof, no pl., *n.* piece of luck, fluke; mumps.
wat een ~, how lucky; *op de* ~, at random;
de ~ *hebben,* to have mumps. **·boffen,**
bof, *v.i.* to be lucky. *daar bof je bij,* you are
in luck. **·boffer, -s,** *n.* lucky dog; piece of
luck.
·bogen, -boog, *v.i.* ~ *op,* to boast of, glory
in.
·bogerd, -s, *n.* orchard.
Bo·heems, *a.* Bohemian. **Bo·hemen,** *n.N.*
Bohemia.
bok, -kken, *n.* he-goat, billy-goat; buck;
surly person; vaulting-horse; derrick;
howler, blunder; box (*coachman's seat*).
de bokken van de schapen scheiden, to
separate the sheep from the goats.
bo·kaal, -kalen, *n.n.* cup, gobiet; bowl (*glass*);
bottle, (large) jar.
·bokje, -s, *n.n.* little goat, kid. ~ *springen,*
to play leapfrog. **·bokkebaard,** *n.* goat's
beard. **·bokkeleer,** no pl., *n.n.* kid, buckskin. **·bokkeleren,** *a.* (made of) kid,
buckskin. **·bokken, bok,** *v.i.* to buck.
·bokkepruik, no pl., *n. de* ~ *op hebben,*
to be in a bad temper. **·bokkesprong,** *n.*
caper. ~*en maken,* to cut capers. **·bokkig,**
a. surly. ¶ *adv.* sulkily. **·bokking,** *n.*
bloater. **·bokkinghang,** *n.,* **·bokkingro·**
kerij, *n.* smoke house. **·boksbaard,** no pl.,
n. See **bokkebaard. ·boksbeugel, -s,** *n.*
knuckle-duster. **·boksen,** *v.i.* to box
(*sport*). **·bokser, -s,** *n.* boxer. **·boksijzer, -s,**
n.n. See **boksbeugel. ·bokspartij,** *n.* fisticuffs. **·bokspoot, -poten,** *n.* goat's foot
(*of satyr*). **·bokspringen,** no pl., *n.n.*
vaulting. **·bokstavast,** *exclam.* hicockA-
lorum. **·bokswedstrijd,** *n.* boxing match.
·boktor, -rren, *n.* capricorn beetle.
bol, -llen, *n.* ball, sphere, globe; bulb (*plant;*
thermometer); crown (*of hat*); head (*face-*
tious); bright boy; bun; (kind of) sweet.
¶ **-lle,** *a.* convex; rounded (*cheeks*); bulging (*sail*); gusty (*wind*). ¶ *adv·* gusty
(*of wind*).
·bolder, -s, *n.* mooring post. **·bolderen,** *v.i.*
to swell, bulge (*of sail*); to rumble (*of*
cart). **·bolderik, -kken,** *n.* cornrose.
·bolderwagen, -s, *n.* rumbling cart.
·boldriehoek, *n.* spherical triangle. **·bolge·**
was, -ssen, *n.n.* bulbous plant. **·bolheid,**
no pl., *n.* convexity; roundness. **bolle·boos,**
-bozen, *n.* dab. ~ *in,* dab at. **·bollen, bol,**
v.i. to swell, belly (*of sail*). **·bollen-** in
compounds: **bulb-. ·bollenkweker, -s,**
n. bulb-grower. **·bollenteelt,** no pl., *n.*
bulb-growing. **·bollenveld,** *n.n.* bulb-
field. **·bolrond,** *a.* spherical, bulbous.
·bolstaand, *a.* bulging (*sail*). **·bolster, -s,**

n. shell, husk; bolster. ·**bolsteren**, *v.t.* to shell, shuck. ·**bolus, -ssen**, *n.* (kind of) bun. ·**bolvorm,** *n.* spherical shape. **bol**·**vormig,** *a.* spherical. ·**bolwerk.** *n.n.* bulwark, rampart, bastion, stronghold. ·**bolwerken,** *v.t. het* ~, to manage (*job, task*). ·**bolworm,** *n.* maggot.

bom, -mmen, *n.* bomb; bung; (type of) fishing smack. *de* ~ *is gebarsten,* the secret is out *or* the fat is in the fire; *de* ~ *is verkeerd gesprongen,* the plot has miscarried; *als een* ~ *uit de lucht vallen,* to appear unexpectedly. ·**bomaanslag,** *n.* bomb outrage. **bombar**·**deerdienst,** no pl., *n.* bomber command. **bombarde**·**ment,** *n.n.* bombardment. **bombar**·**deren, -deer,** *v.t.* to bomb; shell; to bombard. **bombar**·**dier, -s,** *n.* bombardier. **bom**·**barie,** no pl., *n.* noise, fuss. ~ *maken,* to kick up a row. **bom**·**barieschopper, -s,** *n.* maker of row.

bomba·**zijn,** no pl., *n.n.* bombasine. **bomba**·**zijnen,** *a.* (*made of*) bombasine. ·**bomen, boom,** *v.t.* to punt, pole (*barge*); to talk, yarn.

·**bomgat,** *n.n.* bung-hole; sound-hole (*in belfry*). ·**bomijs,** no pl., *n.n.* cat-ice. ·**bommen,** *v.t. het kan me niet* ~, I don't care a hang. ·**bommenwerper, -s,** *n.* bomber. ·**bomvrij,** *a.* bomb-proof. ~*e kazerne,* casemate.

bon, -nnen, *n.* ticket, coupon; voucher. ·**bonboekje, -s,** *n.n.* coupon-book, rationbook.

bon·**bon, -s,** *n.* (a) chocolate. **bon**·**bondoosje, -s,** *n.n.* chocolate box. **bon**·**bonschaaltje, -s,** *n.n.* dish for sweets.

bond, *n.* league; alliance; association; federation; (trade-)union. ·**bondgenoot, -noten,** *n.* ally. ·**bondgenootschap, -ppen,** *n.n.* alliance. **bondgenoot**·**schappelijk,** *a.* pertaining to alliance. ·**bondig,** *a.* terse, succinct. ¶ *adv.* tersely, succinctly. ·**bondigheid,** no pl., *n.* conciseness, succinctness. ·**bondshotel, -s,** *n.n.* hotel recommended by Dutch touring club (A.N.W.B.). ·**bondskas, -ssen,** *n.* union funds. ·**bondskist,** *n.* repair and tool box (*of Dutch touring club*). ¶ no pl., *n.* Ark of the Covenant. ·**bondslid, -leden,** *n.n.* member of league (*especially of Dutch touring club*). ·**bondsraad, -raden,** *n.* federal diet. ·**bondsregering,** *n.* federal government. ·**bondstaat, -staten,** *n.* federal state.

·**bongerd, -s,** *n.* orchard.

bon·**jour!** *exclam.* good morning, *etc.*; goodbye. **bon**·**jouren,** *v.i.* to wave (*greeting*). *iemand er uit* ~, to throw someone out.

bonk, *n.* bone; old horse; lump, chunk; thump. *een* ~ *van een vent,* a hulking great fellow; *hij is één* ~ *zenuwen,* he is a mass of nerves. ·**bonken,** *v.i.* ~ *op,* to thump on. ·**bonkig,** *a.* bony, chunky.

bonne·**fooi,** no pl., *n. op de* ~, on the offchance, haphazardly.

bons, *exclam.* thump! ¶ **-nzen.** *n.* thump, thud; (*coll.*) sack, push. *iemand de* ~ *geven,* to give someone the push; *de* ~ *krijgen,* to get the sack.

bont, *n.n.* fur; print (*cotton fabric*). ¶ *a.* multi-coloured, parti-coloured; variegated; motly; spotted (*cow*), piebald (*horse*). ~*e kraai,* hooded crow; *het te* ~ *maken,* to go too far; ~ *en blauw slaan,* to beat black and blue. ·**bonten,** *a.* (*made of*) fur. ·**bontheid,** no pl., *n.* variegation. ·**bontgekleurd,** *a.* gaily coloured. ·**bontgevlekt,** *a.* spotted, variegated. ·**bontjas, -ssen,** *n.* fur coat (*man's*). ·**bontje, -s,** *n.n.* fur collar. ·**bontkleurig,** *a. See* bontgekleurd. ·**bontmantel, -s,** *n.* fur coat (*woman's*). ·**bontmuts,** *a.* fur cap. ·**bontwerk,** no pl., *n.n.* furriery, peltry. ·**bontwerker, -s,** *n.* furrier. ·**bontwerkerswinkel, -s,** *n.* furrier's (shop).

·**bonze, -n,** *n.* bonze; bigwig.

·**bonzen, bons,** *v.i.* to bump, thump; to throb, pound (*heart*). ~ *op or tegen,* to thump on; *met het hoofd* ~ *tegen,* to bump one's head into.

·**boodschap, -ppen,** *n.* message; errand; commission. *boodschappen doen,* to run errands *or* go shopping; *boodschappen verrichten,* to carry out commissions; *een* ~ *sturen,* to send word; *om een* ~ *sturen,* to send out on an errand; *de blijde* ~, the glad tidings, the gospel; *een blijde* ~, good news; *een kleine* ~ *doen,* to do number one; *een grote* ~ *doen,* to do number two; *oppassen is de* ~, you must be careful. ·**boodschapjongen, -s,** *n.* errand-boy. ·**boodschappen, -schap,** *v.t.* to bring word. ·**boodschapper, -s,** *n.* messenger; harbinger.

boog, bogen, *n.* bow (*weapon*); arch; arc (*of circle*), curve. ·**booggewelf, -ven,** *n.n.* arched vault. ·**booggraad, -graden,** *n.* degree. ·**booglamp,** *n.* arc-lamp. ·**boogscheut,** *n.* bowshot (*measurement*). ·**boogschutter, -s,** *n.* archer. ·**boogsgewijze,** *adv.* archwise. ·**boogvenster, -s,** *n.n.* arched window. ·**boogvormig,** *a.* arched.

boom, bomen, *n.* tree; pole, shaft (*cart, carriage*); beam, spindle (*loom*); boom (*harbour*). *een vent als een* ~, a man as tall as a tree; stalwart fellow; *een* ~ *opzetten,* to have a long talk; *hoge bomen vangen veel wind,* great position brings cares; *van de hoge* ~ *teren,* to live at a high rate. ·**boomgaard,** *n.* orchard. ·**boomkikvors,** *n.* tree-frog. ·**boomklever, -s,** *n.* nuthatch. ·**boomkruiper, -s,** *n.* treecreeper (*bird*). ·**boomkweker, -s,** *n.* nursery-man. **boomkweke**·**rij,** *n.* (tree-) nursery. ·**boomleeuwerik, -kken,** *n.* woodlark. ·**boomloos, -loze,** *a.* treeless.

·boommarter, -s, *n.* pine-marten. ·boom-pieper, -s, *n.* pipit. ·boomschors, no pl., *n.* bark (*of tree*). ·boomspecht, *n.* woodpecker. ·boomstam, -mmen, *n.* tree-trunk. ·boomstronk, *n.* tree-stump. ·boomtak, -kken, *n.* branch (*of tree*). ·boomvalk, *n.* hobby (*falcon*). ·boomvaren, -s, *n.* tree-fern. ·boomzwam, -mmen, *n.* agaric.

boon, bonen, *n.* bean. *blauwe* ∼ (*fac.*), bullet; *bruine* ∼, brown haricot bean; *grote* or *platte* ∼, broad bean; *witte* ∼, white haricot bean; *in de bonen zijn* (*coll.*), to be up the pole; *honger maakt rauwe bonen zoet,* hunger is the best sauce; *voor spek en bonen,* all for nothing. ·boontje, -s, *n.n.* little bean. ∼ *komt om zijn loontje,* be sure your sin will find you out; *een heilig* ∼, a plaster saint. ·bonenschil, -llen, *n.* bean-pod. ·bonenstaak, -staken, *n.* bean-pole, bean-stick. ·bonenstengel, -s, *n.* bean-stalk.

boor, boren, *n.* drill; brace and bit; gimlet, auger; borer.

boord, *n.* border (*of carpet*); edge, bank (*of river,* etc.); brim (*of cup*). ¶ *n.n.* collar (*of shirt*); board (*ship*). *aan* ∼, on board (*ship*); *aan* ∼ *van de* . . ., on board the . . .; *aan* ∼ *gaan,* to embark, go on board; *binnen* ∼, inboard; *buiten* ∼, outboard; *buiten* ∼ *steken,* to stick overboard; *over* ∼ *gooien,* to throw overboard; *over* ∼ *zetten,* to make (*prisoners*) walk the plank; *van* ∼ *gaan,* to go ashore, disembark. ·boordeknoopje, -s, *n.n.* collar-stud. ·boorden, *v.t.* to border, edge, hem. ·boordevol, -lle, *a.* brim-full. ·boordje, -s, *n.n.* collar (*of shirt*). ·boordmecanicien, -s, *n.* flight engineer. ·boordschutter, -s. *n.* gunner (*in aircraft*). ·boordsel, -s, *n.n.* edging.

·boorgat, *n.n.* bore-hole. ·boorijzer, -s, *n.n.* bit (*of drill*). ·boorinstallatie, -s, *n.* drilling plant. ·boorkever, -s, *n.* wood-beetle. ·boormachine, -s, *n.* boring-machine. ·boormossel, -s, *n.* stone-borer (*mollusc*). ·boortoren, -s, *n.* (drilling-)derrick.

·boorwater, no pl., *n.n.* boracic lotion. ·boorzalf, no pl., *n.* boracic ointment. ·boorzuur, no pl., *n.n.* boracic or boric acid.

boos, boze, *a.* cross, angry; wicked, evil, malign. ∼ *maken,* to anger; *zich* ∼ *maken,* to lose one's temper; *zo* ∼ *als wat,* very angry; ∼ *om* or *over,* angry at or about. ¶ *adv.* crossly, angrily; wickedly. ∼ *kijken,* to give black looks. boos·aardig, *a.* malicious; malignant. ¶ *adv.* maliciously; malignantly. ·boosdoener, -s, *n.* malefactor, evil-doer. ·boosdoenster, -s, *n.* malefactor (*female*). ·boosheid, -heden, *n.* anger, wickedness. ·booswicht, *n.* criminal; wretch, villain.

boot, boten, *n.* boat. *met de* ∼, by steamer. ·bootje, -s, *n.n.* little boat. ∼ *varen,* to go rowing or sailing (*for pleasure*). ·boots-gezel, -llen, *n.* seaman, sailor. ·bootshaak, -haken, *n.* boat-hook. ·bootsman, -lieden or -lui, *n.* boatswain, bo's'n. ·bootsvolk, no pl., *n.n.* (ship's) crew. ·boottocht, *n.* boating-trip. ·bootwerker, -s, *n.* docker, dock-labourer, stevedore.

bord, *n.n.* plate (*crockery*); (name-)plate; sign- or notice-board; blackboard; board (*games*).

bor·deel, -delen, *n.n.* brothel.

·bordenkwast, *n.* dish-mop. ·bordenwasser, -s, *n.* dish-washer (*person*). ·bordenwater, no pl., *n.n.* dish-water. ·bordenwisser, -s, *n.* wiper, duster (*for blackboard*).

borde·rel, -llen, *n.n.* statement, list; docket.

bor·des, -ssen, *n.n.* (flight of) steps (*outside house*).

·bordje, -s, *n.n.* small plate; notice (*cardboard* or *small board*). *de* ∼*s zijn verhangen,* the tables are turned. ·bordpapier, no pl., *n.n.* cardboard, pasteboard. ·bord-papieren, *a.* (*made of*) cardboard.

bor·duren, -duur, *v.t.* to embroider. bor·duurder, -s, *n.* embroiderer (*male*). bor-duurgaas, no pl., *n.n.* canvas. bor·duur-garen, -s, *n.n.* embroidery cotton. bor-duurpatroon, -tronen, *n.n.* embroidery pattern. bor·duurraam, -ramen, *n.n.* embroidery frame. bor·duursel, -s, *n.n.* embroidery. bor·duurster, -s, *n.* embroiderer (*female*). bor·duurwerk, no pl., *n.n.* embroidery.

·boren, boor, *v.t.* to bore, drill. *een schip in de grond* ∼, to sink a ship (*by gunfire or torpedo*); ∼ *naar,* to drill for (*oil*).

borg, *n.* surety, guarantee; pledge, bail. ∼ *blijven* or ∼ *staan* or *zich* ∼ *stellen* or ∼ *spreken* or ∼ *worden,* to become or stand surety, go bail; *een* ∼ *stellen van,* to stand surety for; ∼ *staan voor,* to go bail for or to answer for, guarantee. ·borgen, *v.t.* to give credit; to buy on credit; to borrow. ∼ *baart zorgen,* he that goes aborrowing goes asorrowing. ·borgspreking, *n.* suretyship. ·borgsteller, -s, *n.* surety (*person*). ·borgstelling, *n.*, ·borgtocht, *n.* security, surety, bail.

·boring, *n.* boring, drilling (*operation*).

·borrel, -s, *n.* glass of (*usually*) gin. *hij is aan de* ∼, he has taken to drink. ·borrelaar, -s, *n.* gin-drinker. ·borrelen, *v.i.* to bubble, drink gin. *See* bitteren. ·borrelfles, -ssen, *n.* gin-bottle. ·borreling, *n.* bubbling. ·borrelpraat, no pl., *n.* gossip, pub-talk.

borst, *n.* chest; breast, bosom; lad. *de* ∼ *hoog dragen* or *een hoge* ∼ *zetten,* to thrust out one's chest; *met onbeklemde* ∼ or *uit volle* ∼, lustily (*sing*); *aan de* ∼, breast-fed; *iemand aan zijn* ∼ *drukken,* to press someone to one's bosom; *het op de* ∼ *hebben,* to be short of breath; *zich op de* ∼ *slaan,* to strike one's breast; *het stuit me tegen de* ∼, it goes against the grain.

·**borstaandoening**, *n.* chest affection. ·**borstbeeld**, bust; effigy (*on coin*). ·**borstbeen**, -**deren**, *n.n.* breastbone.
·**borstel**, -**s**, *n.* brush; bristle. ·**borstelen**, *v.t.* to brush. ·**borstelig**, *a.* bristly. ·**borstelmaker**, -**s**, *n.* brush-maker. ·**borstelmakerij**, *n.* brush-factory. ·**borstelwerk**, no pl., *n.n.* brushwork.
·**borstholte**, -**n**, *n.* chest cavity. ·**borstkas**, -**ssen**, *n.* chest, thorax. ·**borstklier**, *n.* pectoral gland. ·**borstkwaal**, -**kwalen**, *n.* chest-complaint. ·**borstlijder**, -**s**, *n.* sufferer from tuberculosis. ·**borstplaat**, -**platen**, *n.* breastplate. ¶ no pl., *n.* fondant (*traditional sweet*). ·**borstrok**, -**kken**, *n.* vest. ·**borstslag**, *n.* breast stroke. ·**borstvin**, -**nnen**, *n.* pectoral fin. ·**borstvlies**, -**zen**, *n.n.* pleura. ·**borstvliesontsteking**, *n.* pleurisy. ·**borstwering**, *n.* rampart, parapet. ·**borstzak**, -**kken**, *n.* breast-pocket.
bos, -**ssen**, *n.* bunch (*keys, flowers*); bundle (*sticks, straw*); shock (*of hair*). ¶ *n.n.* wood, forest. ·**bosaanplant**, no pl., *n.* afforestation. ·**bosachtig**, *a.* woody, wooded. ·**bosanemoon**, -**monen**, *n.* wood anemone, windflower. ·**bosbeheer**, no pl., *n.n.* forest administration. ·**bosbes**, -**ssen**, *n.* bilberry, whortleberry. ·**bosbouw**, no pl., *n.* forestry, silviculture. ·**bosbrand**, *n.* forest fire. ·**boscultuur**, no pl., *n. See* **bosbouw**. ·**bosduif**, -**ven**, *n.* wood-pigeon. ·**bosduivel**, -**s**, *n.* mandrill. ·**bosgeus**, -**zen**, *n.* Beggar of the Forest (*Eighty Years' War guerillas*). ·**bosgod**, *n.* sylvan deity. ·**bosgrond**, no pl., *n.* woodland. ·**boshaan**, -**hanen**, *n.* woodcock. ·**boshoen**, -**ders**, *n.n.* woodhen. ·**bosje**, -**s**, *n.n.* little wood; bundle, bunch. *een* ~ *cigaren*, a bundle of cigars; *bij* ~*s*, in quantities. ·**bosjesman**, -**nnen**, *n.* Bushman. ·**boskant**, no pl., *n.* outskirts of wood. ·**boskat**, -**tten**, *n.* wild cat. ·**bosland**, no pl., *n.n.* woodland. ·**boslandschap**, -**ppen**, *n.n.* woodland scenery. ·**bosmens**, *n.* orang-utan. ·**bosmier**, *n.* red ant. ·**bosneger**, -**s**, *n.* maroon (*West Indian negro*). ·**bosnimf**, *n.* wood nymph. ·**bosopzichter**, -**s**, *n.* forester. ·**bospartij**, *n.* woodland scenery; ornamentally wooded estate. ·**bosproducten**, pl. only, *n.n.* forest produce. ·**bosrank**, *n.* wild creeper. ·**bosrecht**, *n.n.* forest law; ¶ *rl.* forest rights. ·**bosrijk**, *a.* woody, wooded. ·**bosrubber**, no pl., *n.* wild rubber. ·**bosschage**, -**s**, *n.n.* grove. ·**bossen**, **bos**, *v.t.* to tie up in bundles. ·**bosuil**, *n.* tawny owl. ·**bosviooltje**, -**s**, *n.n.* violet. ·**boswachter**, -**s**, *n.* gamekeeper, forester. ·**bosweg**, *n.* forest track. ·**boswet**, -**tten**, *n.* forest law. ·**boswezen**, no pl., *n.n.* forestry; forest services (*official*).
bot, -**tte**, *a.* blunt, dull. ¶ *adv.* bluntly. ¶ -**tten**, *n.* flounder; bud; bone; length of rope. ~ *vangen*, to draw a blank;

---

het in de botten hebben, to be troubled by gout; *een stuk in de botten hebben*, to be drunk. ·**botaf**, *adv.* bluntly, flatly, point-blank.
bo·tanicus, -**ci**, *n.* botanist. **bo·tanisch**, *a.* botanical. **botani·seertrommel**, -**s**, *n.* specimen-box.
·**botenhuis**, -**zen**, *n.n.* boat-house.
·**boter**, no pl., *n.* butter. *sterke* ~, rancid butter; *met zijn neus in de* ~ *vallen*, to come at the right time, hit on a good thing; *het is* ~ *aan de galg (gesmeerd)*, it is all no use; ~ *bij de vis (fac.)*, cash down *or* no credit. ·**boterachtig**, *a.* buttery. ·**boterbanket**, no pl., *n.n.* (kind of) biscuit. ·**boterbiesje**, -**s**, *n.n.* (kind of) biscuit. ·**boterbloem**, *n.* buttercup. ·**boterboer**, *n.* butter-seller (*farmer-hawker*). ·**boterbriefje**, -**s**, *n.n.* (*fac.*), bill, official document. ·**boteren**, *v.t.* to butter. ¶ *v.i.* to make butter, churn. *de melk wil niet* ~, the butter will not come; *het wil niet* ~ *tussen die twee*, those two can't hit it off. ·**boterfabriek**, *n.* butter factory, creamery. ·**boterham**, -**mmen**, *n.* slice of bread and butter. ·**boterhamspek**, no pl., *n.n.* bacon (*raw slice on bread*). ·**boterhamworst**, no pl., *n.* breakfast sausage. ·**boterkoek**, no pl., *n.* butter-cake. ·**boterkoekje**, -**s**, *n.n.* (kind of) biscuit. ·**boterletter**, -**s**, *n.* almond-paste cake (*letter-shaped*). ·**botermelk**, no pl., *n.* buttermilk. ·**botermijn**, *n.* butter-auction. ·**boterpeer**, -**peren**, *n.* (kind of juicy) pear. ·**boterpot**, -**tten**, *n*, butter crock. ·**boterspaan**, -**spanen**, *n.* butter-pat, butter-scoop. ·**botersprits**, no pl., *n.* (kind of) biscuit. ·**botertje**, *n.n. het is* ~ *tot den boom*, everything in the garden is lovely. ·**boterton**, -**nnen**, *n.* butter cask. ·**botervis**, -**ssen**, *n.* gunnel, butter-fish. ·**botervlootje**, -**s**, *n.n.* butter-dish. ·**boterwaag**, -**wagen**, *n.* butter weigh-house. ·**boterzuur**, no pl., *n.n.* butyric acid.
·**botheid**, no pl., *n.* bluntness, dullness. ·**botje**, no pl., *n.n.* ~ *bij* ~ *leggen*, to club together, go shares (*in paying*).
bots, *exclam.* bang, thump (*of clash*). ·**botsen**, *v.i.* to clash. *tegen elkaar* ~, to bump into one another. ·**botsing**, *n.* clash ; collision; impact. *in* ~ *komen met*, to clash with, collide with.
·**bottel**, -**s**, *n.* hip (*rose*).
·**bottelaar**, -**s**, *n.* bottler. **bottela·rij**, *n.* bottling works. **botte·lier**, -**s**, *n.* butler, steward.
·**botten**, **bot**, *v.i.* to bud.
·**botter**, -**s**, *n.* (type of) fishing boat.
·**botterik**, -**kken**, *n.* blockhead.
·**botvieren**, *v.t.s. zijn hartstochten* ~, to give full rein to one's passions. ·**botweg**, *adv.* bluntly, flatly. ~ *weigeren*, to refuse point-blank.
boud, *a.* bold. ¶ *adv.* boldly. ·**boudweg**, *adv.* boldly, brazenly.

bou·gie, -s, *n.* sparking plug.
bouil·lon, no pl., *n.* (clear) broth, beef-tea.
bou·quet, -tten, *n.n.* bouquet, nosegay, posy.
Bour·gogne, -s, *n.* Burgundy (*wine*). Bour-·gondië, *n.N.* Burgundy (*country*). Bour-·gondisch, *a.* Burgundian.
bout, *n.* bolt; pin (*wooden*); quarter (*of meat*); leg (*of fowl or mutton*). ·boutje, -s, *n.n.* leg (*of fowl*), drumstick.
bouw, no pl., *n.* construction, building (*act*); frame, build (*of person*). *krachtig van* ~, of powerful build. ·bouwbedrijf, no pl., *n.n.* building trade. ·bouwdoos, -dozen, *n.* box of bricks (*toy*). ·bouwen, *v.t.* to build, construct, erect; to cultivate (*field*); to grow (*produce*). *op iemand* ~, to rely on someone; *ergens op* ~, to be certain of something; *hooi* ~, to make hay; *zee* ~, to plough the sea *or* to be seaworthy. ·bouwer, -s, *n.* builder. ·bouwgrond, *n.* building site; arable land. ·bouwkunde, no pl., *n.* architecture. bouw·kundig, *a.* architectural. ~ *ingenieur*, constructional engineer. ¶ *adv.* architecturally. bouw-·kundige, -n, *n.* architect. ·bouwkunst, no pl., *n.* architectural ability. ·bouwland, *n.n.* arable land. ·bouwmaatschappij, *n.* building company, building society. ·bouwmeester, -s, *n.* architect, builder. ·bouworde, -n, *n.* style, order (*architectural*). ·bouwplan, -nnen, *n.n.* building scheme *or* project; plan(s) (*of house*); blueprint. ·bouwval, -llen, *n.* ruin(s). bouw-·vallig, *a.* dilapidated, rickety. bouw-·valligheid, no pl., *n.* dilapidation. ·bouwvergunning, *n.* building license. ·bouwverordening, *n.* building regulations *or* by-laws. ·bouwwerk, *n.n.* edifice; building.
·boven, *prep.* above; over; beyond. ~ *de wind*, to windward; ~ *en behalve*, over and above. ¶ *adv.* upstairs; above; aloft. *naar* ~, upstairs *or* upward; *van* ~, from above *or* at the top; *te* ~ *gaan*, to exceed; *te* ~ *komen*, to surmount, overcome. ·bovenaan, *adv.* at *or* near the top. ·bovenaards, *a.* supernatural. ·bovenaf, *adv. van* ~, from the top. ·bovenal, *adv.* above all. ·bovenarm, *n.* upper arm. ·bovenarms, *adv.* overarm. ·bovenbedoeld, *a.* (referred to) above. ·bovenbouw, no pl., *n.* superstructure. boven·bramra, -raaa, *n.* royal yard. boven·bramsteng, *n.* royal mast. boven·bramzeil, *n.n.* royal sail. ·bovenbuur, -buren, *n.* upstairs neighbour. ·bovendek, -kken, *n.n.* upper deck. boven·dien, *adv.* moreover. ·bovendrijven, drijf boven, *v.i.s., str.* to float at the top. ·boveneind(e), -(e)n, *n.n.* upper end, head. ·bovengemeld, *a.,* ·bovengenoemd, *a.* above-mentioned, aforesaid. ·bovengronds, *a.* overground, overhead. ·bovenhand, *n. de* ~ *hebben or krijgen*, to have *or* get the upper hand. ·bovenhelft, *n.* top half.

·bovenhoek, *n.* top corner. ·bovenhouden, *v.t.s., irr.* to keep above the surface. ·bovenhuis, -zen, *n.n.* upper maisonette; upper part of the house. ·bovenin, *adv.* at the top (*inside*). ·bovenkaak, -kaken, *n.* upper jaw. ·bovenkant, *n.* upper side. ·bovenkleren, pl. only, *n.n.* outer clothes. ·bovenkomen, *v.i.s., irr.* to come upstairs *or* to come up; to rise. ·bovenlaag, -lagen, *n.* top layer. ·bovenlaken, -s, *n.n.* top sheet. ·bovenland, *n.n.* upland. ·bovenlast, *n.* deck cargo. ·bovenlicht, *n.n.* skylight, top light. ·bovenlijf, -ven, *n.n.* upper part of body, trunk. ·bovenloop, -lopen, *n.* upper course *or* reaches. ·bovenmate, *adv.* extremely, exceedingly. boven·matig, *a.* excessive. ¶ *adv.* excessively. ·bovenmeester, -s, *n.* headmaster (*village school*). boven·menselijk, *a.* superhuman. ¶ *adv.* superhumanly. boven·om, *adv.* round the top. boven·op, *adv.* on top. *er* ~ *komen*, to pull through, pick up, recover. ·bovenst, *a.* upper(most), topmost. *een* ~ *e beste*, one of the very best (*person*); ¶ -e, *n.* or *n.n.* top one; the upper part. ·bovenstaand, *a. See* bovengemeld. ·boventoon, -tonen, *n.* overtone. *de* ~ *voeren*, to predominate. boven·uit, *adv.* above (everything) (*usu.: sticking out*). ·bovenverdieping, *n.* upper floor. ·bovenvermeld, *a. See* bovengemeld. ·bovenvlak, -kken, *n.n.* upper surface. ·bovenwaarts, *a. & adv.* upward(s). boven·winds, *adv.* to windward. ·bovenwoning, *n. See* bovenhuis. boven·zinnelijk, *a.* transcendental, supersensual. ¶ *adv.* transcendentally.
·boycotten, -cot, *v.t.* to boycott.
·braadpan, -nnen, *n.* frying-pan. ·braadspit, -tten, *n.n.* spit, broach (*for roasting*). ·braadvet, -tten, *n.n.* cooking fat. ·braadworst, *n.* (kind of) sausage.
braaf, brave, *a.* good, honest, upright; good, well-behaved. *een brave Hendrik*, a prig. ¶ *adv.* honestly; hard, heavily (*of drinking or lying*). ·braafheid, no pl., *n.* goodness, honesty.
braak, *a.* fallow. ~ *liggen*, to lie fallow. ·braakjaar, -jaren, *n.n.* year that land lies fallow. ·braakland, no pl., *n.n.* fallow (ground). ·braakloop, no pl., *n. Aziatische* ~, cholera. ·braakmiddel, *n.n.* emetic. ·braaknoot, -noten, *n.* nux vomica. ·braakwortel, -s, *n.* ipecacuanha.
braam, bramen, *n.* sea-bream; burr (*of knife*); blackberry (*fruit*), bramble. ·braambes, -ssen, *n. See* braam. ·braambos, -ssen, *n.* blackberry, bramble. *het brandende* ~, the Burning Bush. ·braamstruik, *n.* blackberry, bramble.
·Brabander, -s, *N.* person from Brabant. ·Brabants, *a.* from *or* of Brabant.
·brabbelaar, -s, *n.* jabberer. ·brabbelen, *v.i.* to jabber, talk gibberish. ·brabbeltaal, no pl., *n.* gibberish.

·**braden, braad,** *v.t., irr. & v.i., irr.* to bake, broil, fry, grill, roast. *in de zon liggen* ~, to lie baking in the sun.

brah·maan, -manen, *n.* brahmin.

brak, -kke, *a.* brackish. ¶ **-kken,** *n.* beagle.

·**braken, braak,** *v.t. & v.i.* to vomit; to belch (*flames, smoke*); to break (*flax, hemp*). ·**braking,** *n.* vomiting.

·**brallen, bral,** *v.i.* to boast; **to** shout drunkenly.

tram, -mmen, *n.* topgallant-sail. ·**bramsteng,** *n.* topgallant·mast. ·**bramzeil,** *n.n.* topgallant-sail.

bran·card, -s, *n.* stretcher.

·**branche, -s,** *n.* branch (*of business*).

brand, *n.* fire, conflagration; fuel; (*prickly*) heat, rash; blight (*in corn*). **brand!,** fire!; *er is* ~, house on fire; *een uitslaande* ~, a big fire (*leaping flames*); ~ *stichten,* to set on fire; *in* ~ *staan,* to be on fire; *in* ~ *raken* or *schieten* or *vliegen,* to catch alight; *in* ~ *steken,* to set on fire; *in de* ~ *zitten,* to be in trouble; *iemand uit de* ~ *helpen,* to help someone out; *moord en* ~ *schreeuwen,* to shout blue murder. ·**brandalarm,** *n.n.* fire-alarm, fire call. ·**brandbaar, -bare,** *a.* combustible, inflammable. ·**brandbaarheid,** no pl., *n.* combustibility. ·**brandblaar, -blaren,** *n.* blister (*from burn*). ·**brandbom, -mmen,** *n.* incendiary bomb. ·**branden,** *v.i.* to burn, be on fire. ~ *van verlangen,* to burn with desire. ¶ *v.t.* to burn; to brand; to roast (*coffee*); to stain (*glass*). ·**brandend,** *a.* burning; ardent. ~ *heet,* burning hot, scalding hot. ·**brander, -s,** *n.* burner (*of lamp*); distiller; fire-ship. ·**branderig,** *a.* burnt (*flavour*); feverish; covered with rash. **brande·rij,** *n.* distillery. ·**brandewijn,** no pl., *n.* brandy. ·**brandgevaar,** no pl., *n.n.* risk of fire. ·**brandgierig,** *a.* extremely avaricious. ·**brandglas, -zen,** *n.n.* burning glass. ·**brandhelder,** *a.* spotless, bright. ·**brandhout,** no pl., *n.n.* firewood. ·**brand·ijzer, -s,** *n.n.* branding iron. ·**branding,** *n.* surge, surf. ·**brandkast,** *n.* (*fire-proof*) safe. ·**brandkraan, -kranen,** *n.* fire-plug. ·**brandladder, -s,** *n.* fire-escape. ·**brand·lucht,** no pl., *n.* smell of burning. ·**brand·meester, -s,** *n.* officer of fire-brigade. ·**brandmerk,** *n.n.* brand (*on cattle or goods*); stigma. ·**brandmerken,** *v.t.* to brand; to stigmatize. ·**brandnetel, -s,** *n.* stinging nettle. ·**brandoffer, -s,** *n.n.* burnt offering. ·**brandpolis, -ssen,** *n.* fire policy. ·**brand·punt,** *n.n.* focus. ·**brandpuntsafstand,** *n.* focal distance. ·**brandschade,** no pl., *n.* damage by fire. ·**brandschatten, -schat,** *v.t.* to put to ransom. ·**brandschatting,** *n.* levy (*of ransom*). ·**brandschel, -llen,** *n.* fire-alarm. ·**brandscherm,** *n.n.* fire-curtain. ·**brandschoon, -schone,** *a. See* **brandhelder.** ·**brandspiritus,** no pl., *n.* methylated spirits. ·**brandspuit,** *n.* fire-engine. ·**brandstapel,**

·**-s,** *n.* funeral pile. *op de* ~, at the stake. ·**brandstichter, -s,** *n.* incendiary. ·**brand·stichting,** *n.* arson, incendiarism. ·**brand·stof, -ffen,** *n.* fuel, combustibles ·**brand·verf, -ven,** *n.* enamel paint. ·**brand·verzekering,** *n.* fire insurance. ·**brandvos, -ssen,** *n.* (kind of) sorrel (*horse*). ·**brandvrij,** *a.* fire-proof. ·**brandwacht,** *n.* fire-watch, fire guard. ·**brandweer,** no pl., *n.* fire-brigade, fire-service. ·**brandweerkazerne, -s,** *n.* fire-station. ·**brandweerman, -nnen,** *n.* fireman. ·**brandwond,** *n.* burn, scald. ·**brandzalf, -ven,** *n.* ointment for burns.

·**brani,** no pl., *n.* daring; swank, swagger. ·**braniachtig,** *a.* swanky. ¶ *adv.* swankily. ·**branikraag, -kragen,** *n.* sailor collar.

bras, -ssen, *n.* brace (*nautical*). ·**brasem, -s,** *n.* bream.

·**braspartij,** *n.* orgy, drinking party. ·**brassen, bras,** *v.i.* to carouse; to brace (*sails*).

bra·vade, -s, *n.* bravado, swagger. **bra·vo!** *exclam.* bravo! hear, hear! ¶ **-s,** *n.n.* applause. **bra·vogeroep,** no pl., *n.n.* shouts of applause. **bra·vour,** no pl., *n.* bravura.

breed, brede, *a.* broad, wide. *een brede blik,* a large or generous view; *hij heeft het niet* ~, he is not very well off; *iets in den brede behandelen,* to deal with something at great length. ¶ *adv.* broadly, generously. ·**breedgebouwd,** *a.* square-built. ·**breed·gerand,** *a.* broad-brimmed. ·**breed·geschouderd,** *a.* broad-shouldered. **breed·sprakig,** *a.* verbose, long-winded. ¶ *adv.* long-windedly. **breed·sprakigheid,** no pl., *n.* prolixity. ·**breedte, -n** or **-s,** *n.* breadth, width; latitude (*geographical*). ·**breed·tecirkel, -s,** *n.* parallel (of latitude). ·**breedtegraad, -graden,** *n.* degree of latitude. **breed·voerig,** *a.* detailed. ¶ *adv.* in detail. **breed·voerigheid,** no pl., *n.* fullness (of detail).

·**breekbaar, -bare,** *a.* breakable, fragile. ·**breekbaarheid,** no pl., *n.* fragility. ·**breekijzer, -s,** *n.n.* crow-bar, jemmy.

·**breeuwen,** *v.t.* to caulk. ·**breeuwer, -s,** *n.* caulker.

·**breidel, -s,** *n.* bridle; check, curb. ·**breidelen,** *v.t.* to check, curb. ·**breidelloos, -loze,** *a.* unbridled.

·**breien,** *v.t. & v.i.* to knit. ·**breier, -s,** *n.* knitter (*male*). ·**breigaren, -s,** *n.n.* knitting yarn. ·**breikous,** *n.* knitting (*stocking*). ·**breimachine, -s,** *n.* knitting-frame. ·**breinaald,** *n.* knitting-needle. ·**breister, -s,** *n.* knitter (*female*). ·**breiwerk,** no pl., *n.n.* knitting.

brein, *n.n.* brain(s).

bre·kage, -s, *n.* breakage. ·**brekebeen, -benen,** *n.* bungler. ·**breken, breek,** *v.t., str.* to break; to fracture; to refract. ¶ *v.i., str.* to break; to part, snap (*rope*); to be refracted. ~ *door,* to break or burst through (*enemy, clouds*). ·**breker.**

-s, n. breaker (wave). ·**breking**, no pl., n. refraction.

brem, no pl., n. broom (plant). ·**bremstruik**, n. broom (plant).

·**bremraap**, **-rapen**, n. chokeweed.

brems, n. gadfly.

·**bremzout**, a. briny, very salt.

·**brengen**, v.t., irr. to bring, take, carry. aan het licht ~, to bring to light, reveal; naar de post ~, to take to the post; tot stand ~, to bring about; iemand iets aan het verstand ~, to make someone understand something; laten ~, to send; het ver ~, to go far, be successful; zich iets te binnen ~, to recall something; het ~ op, to bring (subject) round to or to make (amount) up to; iemand ertoe ~, to induce a person to; het ~ tot, to get as far as (position, office).

bres, **-ssen**, n. breach; gap. een ~ schieten in, to breach; in de ~ springen or zich op de ~ stellen, to step into the breach.

Bre·tagne, n.N. Brittany.

bre·tels, pl. only, n. braces.

breuk, n. break, burst; breakage; fracture; rupture, hernia; fraction. ·**breukband**, n. truss.

bre·vet, **-tten**, n.n. certificate, patent, brevet.

bre·vier, n.n. breviary.

brief, **-ven**, n. letter; epistle. een ~ spelden, a paper of pins; per ~, by letter. ·**briefgeheim**, no pl., n.n. secrecy of the post. ·**briefkaart**, n. postcard. ·**briefport**, n.n., ·**briefporto**, **-ti**, n.n. postage. ·**briefwisseling**, n. correspondence. ~ houden met, to keep up a correspondence with.

bries, no pl., n. breeze. een flinke ~, a stiff breeze.

·**briesen**, v.i. to roar (lion); to snort (horse). ~ van woede, to roar with anger.

·**brievenbesteller**, **-s**, n. postman. ·**brievenbus**, **-ssen**, n. letter-box; pillar-box. ·**brievenweger**, **-s**, n. letter scales.

briga·dier, **-s**, n. brigadier; police-sergeant.

brij, n. mash, porridge.

brijn, no pl., n.n. brine.

brik, **-kken**, n. brig; break (carriage).

bri·ket, **-tten**, n. briquet(te).

bril, **-llen**, n. (pair of) spectacles; lavatory seat.

bril·jant, n. brilliant (diamond).

·**brilledoos**, **-dozen**, n., ·**brillehuisje**, **-s**, n.n., ·**brillekoker**, **-s**, n. spectacle case. ·**brillen**, bril, v.i. to wear glasses. ·**brilslang**, n. cobra.

brink, n. (kind of) village green.

bri·santbom, **-mmen**, n. high explosive bomb. **bri·santgranaat**, **-naten**, n. high explosive shell.

brits, n. sleeping bench. voor de ~ geven, to spank. ·**britsen**, v.t. to flog.

bro·caat, no pl., n.n. See bro·kaat.

broche, **-s**, n. brooch. **bro·cheren**, **-cheer**,

v.t. to sew, stitch (books). **bro·chure**, **-s**, n. pamphlet, brochure.

·**broddelaar**, **-s**, n. botcher. **broddela·rij**, n. botched work. ·**broddelen**, v.i. to bungle, botch.

·**brodeloos**, **-loze**, a. without employment or source of income.

broed, no pl., n.n. brood, hatch; fry (of fish). ·**broedei**, **-eren**, n.n. egg for hatching. ·**broeden**, v.i. to brood, hatch, sit on eggs. ~ op, to brood over (revenge). ¶ v.t. to brood, hatch.

·**broeder**, **-s**, n. brother; friar. onze bruine ~s, our black brethren; een vrolijke ~, a jolly companion; hij is de ware ~ niet, he is not the genuine article. See broer. ·**broederdienst**, no pl., n. vrijstelling wegens ~, (military) exemption on account of brother in the services. ·**broederhand**, no pl., n. de ~ reiken, to hold out the hand of fellowship to. ·**broederlijk**, a. brotherly. ¶ adv. fraternally. ·**broedermoord**, n. fratricide. ·**broederschap**, **-ppen**, n. fraternity; brotherhood. ·**broedertrouw**, no pl., n. fraternal loyalty. ·**broedertwist**, no pl., n. quarrel between brothers.

·**broedhen**, n. brood-hen. ·**broedmachine**, **-s**, n. incubator. ·**broedplaats**, n. breeding place or ground. ·**broeds**, a. broody. ·**broedsel**, **-s**, n.n. brood. ·**broedtijd**, n. brooding time; nesting season.

·**broeibak**, **-kken**, n. hot-bed, forcing-frame. ·**broeien**, v.t. See broeden. ¶ v.t. to be sultry, thundery; to brew (mischief, trouble); to burn (spontaneous combustion). ·**broeierig**, a. sultry. ·**broeiing**, n. spontaneous combustion (of hay). ·**broeikas**, **-ssen**, n. glass-house, hothouse. ·**broeinest**, n.n. (fac.) hotbed.

broek, n. (pair of) trousers; marsh. korte ~, shorts, knickerbockers; een proces aan zijn ~ krijgen, to be involved in a law suit; iemand achter de ~ zitten, to keep someone up to the mark; voor de ~ geven, to spank; voor de ~ krijgen, to be spanked. ·**broekje**, **-s**, n.n. short trousers; whippersnapper. ·**broekspijp**, n. trouser-leg.

broer, **-s**, n. brother (relative). mijn oudste ~, my oldest or elder brother; mijn jongste ~, my youngest or younger brother. **broertje**, **-s**, n.n. little brother. ik heb er een ~ aan dood, I cannot stand it.

brok, **-kken**, n. lump, fragment.

bro·kaat, no pl., n.n. brocade. ·**brokkelen**, v.t. & v.i. to crumble. ·**brokkelig**, a. crumbly. ·**brokken**, brok, v.i. to break (into lumps). hij heeft niets in de melk te ~, he is not very important. ·**broksgewijze**, adv. piecemeal. ·**brokstuk**, **-kken**, n.n. fragment.

brom, n. een ~ in hebben, to be tipsy. ·**brombeer**, **-beren**, n. grouser, grumbler. ·**brommen**, brom, v.i. to grumble; to mutter; to growl; to buzz (insect); (fac.) to

be in quod. ·**brommer, -s,** *n.* grumbler.
·**brompot, -tten,** *n.* grouser, grumbler.
·**bromtol, -llen,** *n.* humming-top. ·**bromvlieg,** *n.* bluebottle.
·**bromium,** no pl., *n.n.* bromine.
bron, -nnen, *n.* source, well, spring; fountainhead. *uit goede ~ vernemen,* to hear from
a reliable source. ·**bronnenstudie,** no pl.,
n. original research.
brons, *n.n.* bronze. ·**bronskleurig,** *a.* bronze-
coloured. ·**bronstijd,** no pl., *n.* bronze age.
bronst, *n.* rut, heat. ·**bronsttijd,** no pl., *n.*
rutting season.
·**bronwater,** no pl., *n.n.* spring water; mineral
water.
·**bronzen,** *a.* (*made of*) bronze. ¶ *v.t.* to
bronze.
brood, broden, *n.n.* bread; loaf. *wiens ~ men
eet, diens woord men spreekt,* one doesn't
quarrel with one's bread and butter; *zich
de kaas niet van het ~ laten eten,* not to be
put upon, to be sharp; *de een zijn dood
is de ander zijn ~,* it's an ill wind that
blows nobody any good; *zijn ~ verdienen,*
to earn one's living; *om den brode,* for the
sake of one's job. ·**broodbakker,** *n. See*
bakker. broodbakke·rij, *n. See* **bakkerij.**
brood·dronken, *a.* wanton. **brood·dronken-
heid,** no pl., *n.* wantonness. ·**broodboom,
-bomen,** *n.* bread-tree. ·**broodje, -s,** *n.n.*
small loaf; roll. *zoete ~s bakken,* to make
up to someone. ·**broodkar, -rren,** *n.* bread
cart. ·**broodkruim,** no pl., *n.n.* bread
crumb (*inside part of loaf*). ·**broodkruimel,
-s,** *n.* (a) breadcrumb. ·**broodmager,** *a.*
scraggy. ·**broodmes, -ssen,** *n.n.* bread-
knife. ·**broodnijd,** no pl., *n.* professional
jealousy. ·**broodnodig,** *a.* essential.
·**broodsuiker,** no pl., *n.* loaf-sugar. ·**brood-
trommel, -s,** *n.* bread-bin, bread-tin.
·**broodwinner, -s,** *n.* bread-winner. ·**brood-
winning,** *n.* livelihood. ·**broodwortel, -s,**
n. yam; manioc; cassava.
broom, no pl., *n.n.* bromine. **broom·kali,**
no pl., *n.* bromide of potassium.
broos, broze, *a.* brittle, frail. **bros, -sse,** *a.*
crisp; brittle, fragile. ·**brosheid,** no pl., *n.*
crispness, brittleness.
·**brouwen,** *v.t., irr.* to brew; to concoct, plot.
¶*v.i., irr.* to mispronounce the letter r (*in
Dutch*). ·**brouwer, -s,** *n.* brewer. **brouwe-
·rij,** *n.* brewery. *er komt leven in de ~,*
things are livening up. **brouwers·knecht,**
n. brewer's man, drayman. **brouwers-
·wagen, -s,** *n.* brewer's dray. ·**brouwketel,
-s,** *n.* brewing-copper. ·**brouwkuip,** *n.*
brewing-vat. ·**brouwsel, -s,** *n.n.* brew;
concoction.
brug, -ggen, *n.* bridge; parallel bars. *over
de ~ komen,* to pay, put down the money.
·**Brugge,** *n.N.* Bruges. **brugge(n)hoofd,** *n.n.*
bridgehead. ·**bruggewachter, -s,** *n.* bridge
keeper. ·**brugleuning,** *n.* railing *or* parapet
of bridge. ·**Brugman,** *N. praten als ~,* to

have the gift of the gab, talk the hind
leg off a donkey.
brui, no pl., *n. de hele ~,* the whole show,
hij geeft er de ~ van (*coll.*); he is giving
it the chuck.
bruid, *n.* bride-to-be; bride (*on wedding day*).
·**bruidegom, -mmen,** *n.* bridegroom. ·**bruidschat, -tten,** *n.* marriage portion, dowry.
·**bruidsjapon, -nnen,** *n.* bridal gown.
·**bruidsjonker, -s,** *n.* bridal page; best man.
·**bruidsjuffer, -s,** *n.* bridesmaid. ·**bruids-
tranen,** pl. only, *n.* hippocras.
·**bruien,** *v.t. wat bruit het mij,* what do I care!
·**bruikbaar, -bare,** *a.* usable, serviceable.
·**bruikbaarheid,** no pl., *n.* usefulness, utility.
·**bruikleen, -lenen,** *n.n.* loan (*of object*),
lease-lend. *in ~ afstaan,* to lend, grant
use of. ·**bruikleenovereenkomst,** *n.* lease-
lend agreement.
·**bruiloft,** *n.* wedding(-feast). *een ~ houden,*
to celebrate a wedding. ·**bruiloftsdag,** *n.*
wedding day. ·**bruiloftsmaal, -malen,** *n.n.*
wedding dinner, wedding breakfast.
bruin, *a.* brown. *~e beuk,* copper-beech.
bruin(e), -(e)n, *n.* brown one; brown (*paint*).
dat kan de ~ niet trekken, we cannot afford
it. ·**bruinachtig,** *a.* brownish. ·**bruinen,**
v.t. to brown; to tan (*by sun*). *door de zon
gebruind,* sun-tanned, sunburnt. **brui-
·neren, -neer,** *v.t.* to brown; to burnish.
·**bruinharig,** *a.* brown-haired. ·**bruin-
kleurig,** *a.* brown-coloured. ·**bruinkool,
-kolen,** *n.* browncoal, lignite. ·**bruinogig,**
a. brown-eyed. ·**bruinvis, -ssen,** *n.* porpoise.
·**bruisen,** *v.i.* to fizz, effervesce; to foam,
seethe (*of sea, river*). *~ van woede,* to
seethe with rage. ·**bruispoeder, -s,** *n.n.*
effervescent powder, Seidlitz powder.
·**brulaap, -lapen,** *n.* howler (*monkey*). ·**brul-
boei,** *n.* siren-buoy. ·**brullen, brul,** *n.* to
roar. *het op een ~ zetten,* to set up a
roar; *~ van lachen,* to roar with
laughter.
·**Brunswijk,** *n.N.* Brunswick.
·**Brussel,** *n.N.* Brussels.
bru·taal, -tale, *a.* impudent, insolent, rude;
daring; brutal (*of violence*). *~ als de beul,*
bold as brass; *een ~ mens heeft de halve
wereld,* fortune favours the bold; *~ zijn
tegen,* to be rude to. ¶ *adv.* impudently.
bru·taaltje, -s, *n.n.* saucy girl. **bru·taalweg,**
adv. coolly, boldly. **brutali·seren, -seer,**
v.t. to be rude to. **brutali·teit,** *n.* effrontery;
sauce, cheek.
·**bruto,** *a.* gross (*weight, profits*). *door ~ geweld,* by
sheer violence. ¶ **bruten,** *n.* brute. ·**bruut-
heid,** no pl., *n.* brutishness.
·**buffel, -s,** *n.* buffalo. ·**buffelachtig,** *a.*
churlish.
·**buffer, -s,** *n.* buffer (*railway*). ·**bufferstaat,
-staten,** *n.* buffer state.
buf·fet, -tten, *n.n.* sideboard; buffet, bar.
buf·fetbediende, -s *or* **-n,** *n.* barman.

buf·fethouder, -s, n. barkeeper. **buf·fetjuffrouw,** n. barmaid.

bui, n. shower; squall; whim, humour. *Maartse bui,* April shower; *in een kwade ~,* in a bad temper; *een goede ~ hebben,* to be in a good temper *or* humour; *bij ~en,* by fits and starts, now and then. **buiig,** a. showery, squally.

·**buidel, -s,** n. bag, pouch; purse; pouch (*of animal*). ·**buidelbeer, -beren,** n. koala. ·**buideldas, -ssen,** n. bandicoot. ·**buideldier,** n.n. marsupial (animal). ·**buidelrat, -tten,** n. opossum. **buidelwolf, -ven,** n. Tasmanian wolf.

·**buigbaar, -bare,** a. flexible, pliant. ·**buigbaarheid,** no pl., n. flexibility. ·**buigen,** v.i., str. to bend, bow, curve. *~ of barsten,* bend or break; *~ voor iemands wil,* to bend before a person's will. ¶ v.t., str. to bend, bow. *het hoofd ~,* to give way; to stoop. ¶ *zich ~, v.r., str.* to bend down, stoop; to curve. *zich ~ voor,* to submit to. ·**buiger, -s,** n. flexor. ·**buiging,** n. bend, curve; curtsey; inflexion; declension. *een ~ maken,* to bow, to curtsey. ·**buigingsleer,** no pl., n. accidence. ·**buigingsuitgang,** n. inflexional ending. ·**buigtang,** n. (pair of) pliers. ·**buigzaam, -zame,** a. flexible, supple.

buik, n. belly, stomach; loop, sine curve. *hij heeft er de ~ vol van,* he is fed up with it; *twee handen op één ~,* they are hand in glove; *zijn ~ vasthouden van het lachen,* to hold one's sides with laughter. ·**buik·ademhaling,** no pl., n. abdominal respiration. ·**buikband,** n. belly band. ·**buikholte, -n,** n. abdominal cavity. ·**buikloop,** no pl., n. diarrhœa. ·**buikpijn,** n. belly-ache, pain in the stomach. ·**buikpotig,** a. gasteropodous. ·**buikriem,** n. girth (*of horse*). ·**buikspreken,** infin. only, v.i. to ventriloquize. ¶ no pl., n.n. ventriloquy. ·**buikspreker, -s,** n. ventriloquist. ·**buiktyphus,** no pl., n. enteric fever. ·**buikvin, -nnen,** n. ventral fin. ·**buikvlies, -zen,** n.n. peritoneum. ·**buikvliesontsteking,** n. peritonitis. ·**buikziek,** a. sleepy (*pear*).

buil, n. lump, bruise; paper bag; bolter, boulter (*flour sieve*). ·**builen,** v.t. to bolt, boult (*flour*). ·**builenpest,** no pl., n. bubonic plague. ·**builmolen, -s,** n. bolting-mill.

buis, -zen, n. tube, pipe; herring-boat. ¶ n.n. jerkin. ·**buisleiding,** n. pipe-line(s).

buit, no pl., n. loot, booty, spoil(s). *iets ~ maken,* to capture something.

·**buitelaar, -s,** n. tumbler, acrobat. ·**buitelen,** v.i. to tumble. ·**buiteling,** n. tumble, somersault. *een ~ maken,* to turn a somersault.

·**buiten,** prep. outside, out of; without; beyond, apart from. *~ zichzelf van woede,* beside oneself with anger; *~ iemand om,* behind someone's back, over someone's head; *zich ergens ~ houden,* to keep out of something; *ergens ~ kunnen,* to be able to do without; *iemand er ~ laten,* to leave someone out of it. ¶ adv. outside, without, out of doors, in the country; except, beyond, besides. *zich te ~ gaan,* to exceed all bounds (*decency, authority*); *van ~,* on the outside, from without; *van ~ kennen* or *leren,* to know *or* learn by heart. ¶ -s, n.n. country house, country-seat. ·**buitenaf,** adv. on *or* from the outside. ·**buitenband,** n. outer tyre. ·**buitenbeentje, -s,** n.n. by-blow. ·**Buitenbezittingen,** pl. only, n. Outer Possessions, Dependencies (*in East Indies*). ·**buitenboord(s),** a. & adv. outboard. **buiten·dien,** adv. *See* **bovendien.** **buiten·dijks,** a. & adv. outside the dyke(s). **buiten·echtelijk,** a. extra-marital, out of wedlock. **buiten·gaats,** adv. out of port (*at sea*). **buitenge·meen, -mene,** a. **buitenge·woon, -wone,** a. extraordinary. *niets ~s,* nothing unusual. ¶ adv. extraordinarily, uncommonly. ·**buitengoed, -eren,** n.n. country-seat. ·**buitenhaven, -s,** n. outer harbour. **buiten·issig,** a. out of the way. **buiten·issigheid, -heden,** n. oddity. ·**buitenkans,** n. windfall, stroke of luck. ·**buitenkant,** n. outside, exterior. ·**buitenland,** no pl., n.n. abroad; foreign countries. *in het ~,* abroad. ·**buitenlander, -s,** n. foreigner, alien. ·**buitenlands,** a. foreign, from abroad. *ministerie van ~e Zaken,* Foreign Office. ·**buitenlucht,** no pl., n. open air. *in de ~,* in the open. ·**buitenlui,** n. *See* **buitenman.** ·**buitenman, buitenlui,** n. countryman. ·**buitenmate,** adv. extremely, beyond measure. **buiten·matig,** a. excessive. ¶ adv. excessively. **buitenmo·del,** a. non-regulation (*in army*). **buiten·om,** adv. round the outside. **buiten·op,** adv. on the outside. ·**buitenplaats,** n. country-seat. **buitens·huis,** adv. out of doors. **buitens·lands,** adv. abroad. ·**buiten·sluiten, v.t.s., str.** to exclude, shut out. **buiten·sporig,** a. extravagant, excessive. ¶ adv. extravagantly, exorbitantly. **buiten·sporigheid, -heden,** n. extravagance. ·**buitenstaander, -s,** n. outsider. ·**buitenste,** a. outmost. **buiten(s)·tijds,** adv. out of season. ·**buitenverblijf, -ven,** n.n. country-seat. ·**buitenwaarts,** a. & adv. outward(s). ·**buitenwacht,** n. outpost. *ik heb het van de ~,* I have outside information, a little bird told me. ·**buitenwereld,** no pl., n. outside world. ·**buitenwerk, n.n.** outdoor work; outwork. ·**buitenwerks,** adv. on the outside (*measurement*). ·**buitenwijk, n.** outskirt. ·**buitenzijde, -n.** n. outside, exterior.

·**buitmaken,** v.t.s. *See* **buit.**
·**buizerd, -s,** n. buzzard.
·**bukken, buk,** v.i. to bend, duck. *~ voor,* to bow to; *gebukt gaan onder,* to be bowed down by. ¶ v.t. to bend (*head*).

buks, *n.* (small-bore) rifle; box (*shrub*).

bul, -llen, *n.* bull (*papal*). ¶ pl. only, *n.* things, possessions.

·bulderen, *v.i.* to roar (*gun, wind*); to roar, bluster (*person*). ~ van het lachen, to roar with laughter.

·bullebak, -kken, *n.* bully, bugbear. **·bullebijter, -s,** *n.* bulldog; bully. **·bullepees, -pezen,** *n.* bull's pizzle.

bult, *n.* hump; hunch. **·bultenaar, -s,** *n.* hunchback. **·bultig,** *a.* humpy; hunchbacked. **·bultos, -ssen,** *n.* zebu. **·bultzak, -kken,** *n.* straw mattress.

·bundel, -s, *n.* bundle; sheaf (*papers; arrows*), wad. **·bundelen,** *v.t.* to put in a bundle. **·bunder, -s,** *n.* hectare.

·bungelen, *v.i.* to dangle. ~ aan, to dangle from.

·bunker, -s, *n.* bunker (*coal*). **·bunkeren,** *v.t.* to bunker (*coal*). **·bunkerhaven, -s,** *n.* coaling-station.

·bunzing, *n.* polecat.

burcht, *n.* (fortified) castle. **·burchtheer, -heren,** *n.* lord of the manor. **·burchtvrouw,** *n.* chatelaine, lady of the manor.

bu·reau, -'s, *n.n.* desk; office, department. **bureau·list,** *n.* booking clerk. **bu·reel, relen,** *n.n.* office.

·buren, buur, *v.i.* to visit one's neighbours. **·burengerucht,** *n.n.* disturbance.

burge·meester, -s, *n.* burgomaster, mayor. **burge·meestersbuik,** *n.* pot-belly, corporation. **burge·meesterschap,** no pl., *n.n.* burgomaster's office, mayoralty. **·burger, -s,** *n.* town-dweller; citizen; commoner, bourgeois; civilian. **·burgerbestaan,** no pl., *n.n.* decent living. **·burgerdeugd,** *n.* civic virtue. **burge·rij,** *n.* the bourgeoisie, middle classes; the citizens (*as a whole*). **·burgerjongen, -s,** *n.* boy from the middle classes. **burger·juffrouw,** *n.* middle class woman. **·burgerkleding,** no pl., *n.* civilian clothes; town clothes. **burger·lieden,** pl. only, *n.* middle class people. **·burgerlijk,** *a.* civic, civil; middle class, bourgeois; civilian. ~*e beleefdheid*, common politeness; *de* ~*e stand*, register of births, deaths, and marriages; *het bureau van de* ~ *atand*, registrar's office. **·burgerlui,** pl. *n.* See **burgerlieden. burger·luitjes,** pl. only, *n.* lower middle class people. **·burgermanskind, -eren,** *n.n.* middle class child. **burger·mens,** *n.n.* plain middle class person. **·burgeroorlog,** *n.* civil war. **·burgerrecht,** *n.n.* civic rights, citizens' rights. ~ *verkrijgen*, to become current; *het* ~ *verlenen aan*, to enfranchize, give citizens' rights to; *het* ~ *verliezen*, to forfeit one's civic rights. **·burgerschap,** no pl., *n.n.* citizenship. **·burgerschool, -scholen,** *n.* hogere ~, secondary school. **·burgerstand,** no pl., *n.* the middle classes. **·burgervader, -s,** *n.* burgomaster, city father. **·burgerwacht,** *n.* civic guard.

·burggraaf, -graven, *n.* burgrave, viscount. **·burggraafschap, -ppen,** *n.n.* viscountcy. **·burggravin, -nnen,** *n.* viscountess.

bus, -ssen, *n.* tin, canister; drum, barrel; pillar box; (sick-)fund. *het sluit als een* ~, it fits beautifully; *een brief op de* ~ *doen*, to post a letter. **·busdokter, -s,** *n.* panel doctor. **·busgroente, -n,** *n.* tinned vegetable(s). **·buskruit,** no pl., *n.n.* gunpowder. **·buslichting,** *n.* collection (postal). **·buspatient,** *n.* panel patient.

·buur, buren, *usu. pl., n.* neighbour. **·buurkind, -eren,** *n.n.* neighbour's child. **·buurman, buurlui or -lieden,** *n.* neighbour. **·buurmeisje, -s,** *n.n.* neighbour's daughter. **·buurpraatje, -s,** *n.n.* gossip, neighbourly talk. **buurt,** *n.* neighbourhood; vicinity. *in de* ~, nearby; *in de* ~ *blijven*, to remain near at hand; *ver uit de* ~, a long way away. **·buurtbezoek,** *n.n.* district visiting. **·buurtschap, -ppen,** *n.n.* hamlet. **·buurtspoor, -sporen,** *n.n.* local railway. **·buurtverkeer,** no pl., *n.n.* local service. **·buurvrouw,** *n.* neighbour (*female*).

C

See K

ca·cao, no pl., *n.* cocoa. **ca·caoboon, -bonen,** *n.* cocoa bean. **ca·caoboter,** no pl., *n.* cocoa butter.

ca·chet, -tten, *n.n.* seal; cachet.

ca·deau, -'s, *n.n.* present. *iets* ~ *geven*, to make a present of something, give away free; *iets* ~ *krijgen*, to receive something as a present. **ca·deaustelsel, -s,** *n.n.* free-gift scheme.

ca·det, -tten, *n.* cadet (*army*). **ca·dettenschool, -scholen,** *n.* military academy.

ca·fé, -'s, *n.n.* café; public house. **caféchan·tant, -s,** *n.n.* cabaret. **ca·féhouder, -s,** *n.* publican, proprietor of café. **cafe·ïne,** no pl., *n.* caffeine. **café-restau·rant, -s,** *n.n.* café and restaurant.

calami·teus, -ze, *a.* calamitous; not self-supporting (*of polder*).

calli·graaf, -grafen. *n.* calligrapher.

calo·rie, -rieën, *n.* calorie.

cal·queerpapier, no pl., *n.n.* tracing-paper. **cal·queerplaatje, -s,** *n.n.* transfer (*picture*). **cal·queren, -queer,** *v.t.* to trace.

Cal·vijn, *N.* Calvin.

ca·mee, -meeën, *n.* cameo.

ca·melia, -'s, *n.* camellia.

camou·fleren, -fleer, *v.t.* to camouflage.

cam·pagne, -s, *n.* campaign (*army; election; publicity*); season (*industrial crops such as sugar-beets, coffee, etc.*).

cana·pé, -'s. *n.* settee, sofa.

ca·nard, -s, *n.* newspaper hoax.

cande·laber, -s, *n.* candelabrum.

candi·daat, -daten, *n.* candidate, applicant; person holding one of the lower academic degrees. *iemand ~ stellen*, to nominate a person; *zich ~ stellen*, to stand (*for parliament*), put up for election. **candi·daatno·taris**, -ssen, *n.* qualified but not practising notary. **candi·daatsexamen**, -s, *n.n.* examination for one of the lower academic degrees. **candida·tuur**, -turen, *n.* candidature, nomination.

cano·niek, *a.* canonical. **canoni·satie**, -s, *n.* canonization. **canoni·seren**, -seer, *v.t.* to canonize.

can·tate, -s, *n.* cantata.

can·tine, -s, *n.* canteen.

ca·outchouc, no pl., *n.* rubber.

ca·pabel, *a.* able, capable. *tot iets ~*, quite likely to (*do something*); *niet ~*, drunk and incapable. **capaci·teit**, *n.* ability; capacity; capacity (*volume, carrying power, power*).

capil·lair, *a.* capillary. **capillari·teit**, no pl., *n.* capillarity.

capiton·neren, -neer, *v.t.* to pad.

capitu·latie, -s, *n.* capitulation. **capitu·leren**, -leer, *v.i.* to capitulate.

·captain, -s, *n.* captain (*of team*).

·captie, -s, *n.* quibble, objection. *~s maken*, to raise objections, find fault.

carambo·lage, no pl., *n.* cannon (*billiards*). **caram·bole**, -s, *n.* cannon (*billiards*). **carambo·leren**, -leer, *v.i.* to make a cannon (*billiards*).

car·bid, no pl., *n.n.* carbide.

car·bol, no pl., *n.n.* carbolic (acid).

carbu·rator, -s, *n.* carburettor.

carga·door, -s, *n.* ship-broker.

Ca·ribisch, *a.* Caribbean. *~e Eilanden*, Caribbees.

caril·lon, -s, *n.n.* carillon, chimes.

carna·val, -s, *n.n.* carnival.

carosse·rie, -s, *n.* coachwork, (body of) car.

carous·sel, -s, *n.* merry-go-round.

car·ré, -'s, *n.n.* square (*military*).

carri·ère, -s, *n.* career.

·casco, no pl., *n.* hull (*of ship in insurance*).

·cassa, -'s, *n.* cash desk, till; box-office.

cas·satie, no pl., *n.* cassation. *Hof van C~*, Court of Appeal; *~ aantekenen*, to give notice of appeal.

cas·save, -n, *n.* cassava, manioc.

cas·seren, -sseer, *v.t.* to reverse (*judgment*); to cashier.

castag·netten, pl. only, *n.* castanets.

cas·traat, -traten, *n.* eunuch.

casu·eel, -uele, *a.* casual, accidental. ¶ *adv.* casually.

catalogi·seren, -seer, *v.t.* to catalogue. **ca·talogus**, -gi, *n.* catalogue.

catas·trofe, -n, *n.* catastrophe. **catastro·faal**, -fale, *a.* catastrophic.

catechi·sant, *n.* candidate for confirmation (*Protestant*). **catechi·satie**, *n.* catechism

class (*Protestant*). **catechi·seren**, -seer, *v.t.* to catechize. **cate·chismus**, -ssen, *n.* catechism (*Roman Catholic*). **catechi·seermeester**, -s, *n.* catechizer (*Protestant*).

catego·rie, -rieën, *n.* category. **cate·gorisch**, *a.* categorical. ¶ *adv.* categorically.

cau·saal, -sale, *a.* causal. **causali·teit**, no pl., *n.* causality.

cause·rie, -rieën, *n.* talk. *een ~ houden*, to give a talk. **cau·seur**, -s, *n.* conversationalist.

cavale·rie, no pl., *n.* cavalry. **cavale·rieaanval**, -llen, *n.* cavalry charge. **cavale·rist**, *n.* cavalry-man, trooper. **cava·lier**, -s, *n.* partner (*at ball*).

·ceder, -s, *n.* cedar. **·cederhout**, no pl., *n.n.* cedar(-wood). **·cederhouten**, *a.* (*made of*) cedar.

ceel, celen, *n.* document, certificate; lease.

ce·dille, -s, *n.* cedilla.

cein·tuurbaan, -banen, *n.* circular railway.

cel, -llen, *n.* cell; call-box.

celi·baat, no pl., *n.n.* celibacy. **celiba·tair**, -s, *n.* bachelor.

celkern, *n.* nucleus (*biology*).

cel·list, *n.* violoncellist. **·cello**, -'s, *n.* violoncello.

celstof, no pl., *n.* cellulose. **·celstraf**, no pl., *n.* solitary confinement. **·celvormig**, *a.* cellular. **·celwagen**, -s, *n.* prison van.

ce·ment, no pl., *n.n.* cement. **ce·menten**, *a.* (*made of*) cement. ¶ *v.t.* to cement. **cemen·teren**, -teer, *v.t.* See **cementen**.

·censor, -s *or* -en, *n.* censor. **censu·reren**, -reer, *v.t.* to censure; to censor. **cen·suur**, no pl., *n.* censorship; censure. *een ~ instellen*, to impose a censorship; *onder ~ staan*, to be subject to censorship; *onder ~ stellen*, to censor.

cent, -s *or* -en, *n.* coin worth $\frac{1}{100}$ of a guilder; farthing (*i.e.*, worthless coin). *~en hebben*, to have cash; *om de ~en*, for the money; *het kan me geen ~ schelen*, I do not care in the least; *ik heb geen ~*, I haven't a bean; *een aardig ~je*, a tidy sum. **·centenaar**, -s, *n.* weight of 100 kilograms. **·centenbakje**, -s, *n.n.* collecting box. **·centi-**, *prefix.* $\frac{1}{100}$ part of —.

cen·traal, -trale, *a.* central. **cen·trale**, -s, *n.* power station; telephone exchange. **centrali·satie**, no pl., *n.* centralization. **centrali·seren**, -seer, *v.t.* to centralize. **centri·fuge**, -s, *n.* centrifugal machine. **·centrum**, -s, *or* -tra, *n.n.* centre.

cere·monie, -niën, *n.* ceremony. **ceremo·nieel**, no pl., *n.n.* ceremonial. ¶ *a.* ceremonial. ¶ *adv.* ceremonially. **cere·moniemeester**, -s, *n.* M.C., master of ceremonies. **ceremo·nieus**, -ze, *a.* ceremonious, formal.

certifi·caat, -caten, *n.n.* certificate. **certifi·ceren**, -ceer, *v.t.* to certify.

cerve·laatworst, *n.* saveloy.

cessie, -s *or* -ssiën, *n.* cession.

cha·grijn, no pl., *n.n.* chagrin, vexation.
cha·grijnig, *a.* cantankerous.
chaise, -n, *n. See* sjees.
chalce·doon, -donen, *n.* chalcedony.
Cham, *N.* Ham.
·champie no pl., *n.* fizz (*vulg. for champagne*).
champig·non, -s, *n.* mushroom.
chan·tage, no pl., *n.* blackmail. ~ *plegen
jegens,* to levy blackmail upon.
·chaotisch, *a.* chaotic. ¶ *adv.* chaotically.
chaperon·neren, -neer, *v.t.* to chaperon.
cha·piter, -s, *n.n.* subject of conversation.
·charge, -s, *n.* charge (*military*); burlesque.
getuige à ~, witness for the prosecution.
char·geren, -geer, *v.t.* to charge (*military*);
to exaggerate.
char·mant, *a.* charming. ¶ *adv.* charmingly.
·charme, -s, *n.* charm. char·meren, -meer,
v.t. to charm. char·meur, -s, *n.* charmer.
·chartepartij, *n.* charter party. ·charteren,
v.t. to charter.
·chassis, inv., *n.n.* chassis.
chauf·feren, -ffeer, *v.i.* to drive (*car*). chauf-
·feur, -s, *n.* chauffeur.
chef, -s, *n.* chief, principal, head. ~ *de
bureau,* head clerk; ~ *boekhouder,* chief
accountant.
chemi·caliën, pl. only, *n.* chemicals. ·chemi-
cus, -mici, *n.* (*analytical or research*)
chemist. ·chemisch, *a.* chemical.
cheru·bijn, *n.* cherub.
chic, *a.* smart, fashionable, chic. ¶ *adv.*
smartly.
chijl, no pl., *n.* chyle.
chijm, no pl., *n.* chyme.
·chimpansé, -'s, *n.* chimpanzee.
Chi·nees, -nezen, *N.* Chinese, Chinaman.
¶ -nese, *a.* Chinese.
chi·rurg, *n.* surgeon. chirur·gie, no pl., *n.*
surgery (*art*). chi·rurgisch, *a.* surgical.
chloor, no pl., *n.n.* chlorine. ·chloorkalk,
no pl., *n.* chloride of lime. ·chloro·form,
no pl., *n.* chloroform. chlorofor·meren,
-meer, *v.t.* to chloroform.
choco·laadje, -s, *n.n.* chocolate drop. choco-
·la(de), no pl., *n.* chocolate (*substance*).
·christelijk, *a.* christian. ¶ *adv.* in a christian
way. ·Christelijkheid, no pl., *n.* Christianity. ·Christelijk-his·torisch, *a. de* ~*e
partij,* a Dutch political party. ·Christen, *n.*
Christian. ·Christendom, no pl., *n.n.*
Christianity. ·Christenheid, no pl., *n.*
Christendom. ·Christenziel, *n. geen* ~,
not a soul. ·Christus, *N.* Christ.
chro·matisch, *a.* chromatic.
·chronisch, *a.* chronic. ¶ *adv.* chronically.
chroom, no pl., *n.n.* chromium. ·chroomgeel,
no pl., *n.n.* chrome yellow. ·chroomzuur,
no pl., *n.n.* chromic acid.
chry·sant, *n.* chrysanthemum.
ci·borie, - riën *or* -s, *n.* ciborium.
cicho·rei, *n.* chicory.
ciga·rette, *n. See* sigaret.
·cijfer, -s, *n.n.* figure, digit; mark (*at school*).

·cijferaar, -s, *n.* cipherer. ·cijferen, *v.t.*
to cipher. ·cijferkunst, no pl., *n.* arithmetic.
·cijferschrift, *n.n.* cipher, code.
cijns, -zen, *n.* tribute (*money*); tax. ~
heffen van, to levy a toll on. ·cijnsbaar,
-bare, *a.,* cijns·plichtig, *a.* tributary;
taxable.
ci·linder, -s, *n.* cylinder. ci·lindrisch, *a.*
cylindrical.
cim·baal, -balen, *n.* cymbal.
·cinema, -'s, *n. See* bioscoop.
ci·pier, -s, *n.* gaoler, warder.
·cipres, -ssen, *n.* cypress.
circu·laire, -s, *n.* circular (letter). circu·latie,
no pl., *n.* circulation. *in* ~ *brengen,* to
put into circulation. circu·leren, -leer,
v.i. to circulation. ·circus, -ssen, *n.n.*
circus (*performing*). ·cirkel, -s, *n.* circle.
·cirkelen, *v.i.* to circle. ·cirkelvormig, *a.*
circular. ·cirkelzaag, -zagen, *n.* circular
saw.
cis, no pl., *n.* C sharp.
cise·leren, -leer, *v.t.* to chisel, chase. cise·
·leerwerk, no pl., *n.n.* chasing, chased
work.
ci·taat, -taten, *n.n.* quotation. ci·tatie, -s,
n. summons. ci·teren, -teer, *v.t.* to quote;
to summons.
ci·troen, *n.* lemon. ci·troenboom, -bomen, *n.*
lemon-tree. ci·troengeel, -gele, *a.* citrine.
ci·troenolie, no pl., *n.* oil of citron. ci·troen-
pers, *n.* lemon squeezer. ci·troenzuur,
no pl., *n.n.* citric acid.
ci·viel, *a.* civil; moderate, reasonable (*price*).
~*e partij,* party in a civil suit. ¶ *adv.*
civilly; reasonably. ci·viel-ingeni·eur, -s,
n. civil engineer. ci·viel-recht, no pl., *n.n.*
civil law.
clas·siek, *a.* classic(al). *de* ~*e letteren,* the
classics. ¶ pl. only, *n.* the classics. classifi-
·catie, -s, *n.* classification. classifi·ceren,
-ceer, *v.t.* to classify, class.
clau·sule, -s, *n.* clause, proviso.
cle·mentie, no pl., *n.* clemency; indulgence.
cleri·caal, -cale, *a.* clerical.
cli·ché, - 's, *n.n.* block (*printing*); cliché.
·clubfauteuil, -s, *n.,* ·clubzetel, -s, *n.* leather
armchair.
coa·litie, -s, *n.* coalition.
coche·nille, -s, *n.* cochineal.
co·con, -s, *n.* cocoon.
·cocosmat, -tten, *n.* door-mat. ·cocosnoot,
-noten, *n.* cocoanut. ·cocospalm, *n.*
cocoanut tree.
cognosse·ment, *n.n.* bill of lading.
co·hesie, no pl., *n.* cohesion.
coif·feren, -ffeer, *v.t.* to dress (person's)
hair. coif·feur, -s, *n.* hairdresser. coif·fure,
-s, *n.* hairdressing.
·cokes, no pl., *n.* coke.
col·bertcostuum, -s, *n.n.* lounge suit.
collec·tant, *n.* collector (*for charities*).
col·lecte, -s, *n.* collection. *een* ~ *houden,*
to make a collection. *een* ~ *langs de*

huizen, a door to door collection. **col·lectebus, -ssen**, *n.* collection box. **collec·teren, -teer**, *v.t.* to collect (*money*); to take up collection (*in church*). **col·lecteschaal, -schalen**, *n.* collection plate. **col·lectezakje, -s**, *n.n.* offertory bag. **col·lectie, -s**, *n.* collection. **collec·tief, -ve**, *a.* collective. ¶ *adv.* collectively.

col·lega, -'s, *n.* colleague. **col·lege, -s**, *n.n.* board (*of guardians*), college (*of cardinals*); (university) lecture. ~ *van burgemeester en wethouders*, mayor and aldermen in council; ~ *geven*, to give lectures; ~ *lopen* or ~*s volgen*, to go to lectures. **col·legegeld**, *n.n.* college fees. **col·legezaal, -zalen**, *n.* lecture room, lecture theatre. **collegi·aal, -iale**, *a.* of a good colleague. ¶ *adv.* as a good colleague should.

·colli, -'s, *n.n. See* collo.
col·lier, -s, *n.n.* necklace.
·collo, -lli, *n.n.* parcel, package.
col·lodium, no pl., *n.n.* collodion.
co·lonne, -s, *n.* column.
Colo·radokever, -s, *n.* Colorado beetle.
colpor·teren, -teer, *v.t.* to peddle (*printed matter*). **colpor·teur, -s**, *n.* peddler (*of printed matter*), canvasser.
combi·natie, -s, *n.* combination. **combi·neren, -neer**, *v.t.* to combine.
com·fort, -s, *n.n.* personal comfort, convenience. **comfor·tabel**, *a.* comfortable, commodious.
comi·té, -'s, *n.n.* committee.
comman·dant, *n.* commander, captain. **comman·deren, -deer**, *v.t.* to command. *ik laat me niet* ~, I will not be ordered about; ~*de officier*, commanding officer, officer in command. **comman·deur, -s**, *n.* knight commander. **commandi·tair**, *a.* ~*e rennoot*, sleeping partner; ~*e vennootschap*, limited partnership; ~ *kapitaal*, capital of limited partnership. **comman·dite, -s**, *n.* limited partnership. **com·mando. -'s**, *n.n.* (word of) command; commando. **com·mandobrug, -ggen**, *n.* navigating bridge. **com·mandotoren, -s**, *n.* conning tower.
commen·saal, -salen, *n.* boarder.
commen·taar, -taren, *n.n.* commentary, comment.
commerci·eel, -iele, *a.* commercial. ¶ *adv.* commercially.
commissari·aat, -iaten, *n.n.* police-station; directorate. **commis·saris, -ssen**, *n.* commissioner; (company) director; (chief-) inspector (*of police*). ~ *der Koningin*, Royal provincial governor. **com·missie, -s**, *or* -ssiën, *n.* commission, task; committee, commission; commission, percentage. ~ *van advies*, advisory committee; ~ *van onderzoek*, board of enquiry; *in een* ~ *zitten*, to be on a committee. **com·missieloon**, no pl. *n.n.* commission (*percentage*). **com·missiehandel**, no pl., *n.*

commission business. **commissio·nair, -s**, *n.* commission agent; commissionaire.
communi·ceren, -ceer, *v.t.* to communicate to. ¶ *v.i.* to communicate. **com·munie, -s**, *n.* communion (*Roman Catholic*). *zijn* ~ *doen*, to make one's first communion; *te* ~ *gaan*, to go to communion; *de* ~ *ontvangen*, to receive communion.
com·pact, *a.* compact. ¶ *adv.* compactly.
compag·nie, -nieën, *n.* company (*financial; military*). **compag·niescommandant**, *n.* company commander. **compag·non, -s**, *n.* partner.
compa·rant, *n.* partner (*to a suit*). **compa·reren, -reer**, *v.i.* to appear (*in court*). **compa·ritie, -s**, *n.* appearance (*in court*).
comparti·ment, *n.n.* compartment (*railway*).
compen·satie, -s, *n.* compensation. **compen·satieslinger, -s**, *n.* compensation pendulum.
compe·tent, *a.* competent; cognizant. **compe·tentie, -s** *or* -tiën, *n.* competency; cognizance.
compi·lator, -s *or* -toren, *n.* compiler. **compi·leren, -leer**, *v.t.* to compile.
com·pleet, -plete, *a.* complete. ¶ *adv.* completely. **comple·teren, -teer**, *v.t.* to complete.
compli·ceren, -ceer, *v.t.* to complicate.
compli·ment, *n.n.* compliment. ~*en doen* or *maken*, to give or make compliments; *iemand een* ~ *maken*, to compliment somebody; *een* ~ *afstelen*, to turn a compliment; *veel* ~*en maken*, to have a lot to say for oneself; *geen* ~*en*, no ceremony; *zonder* ~*en*, without more ado; *naar een* ~ *vissen*, to angle for compliments; *de* ~*en thuis*, remember (*me*) at home; *de* ~*en aan allemaal*, remember (*me*) to all; *de* ~*en van mij en zeg hem dat* . . ., just tell him from me that. . . . **compliment·teren, -teer**, *v.t.* to compliment. **complimen·teus, -ze**, *a.* complimentary.
compo·neren, -neer, *v.t.* to compose (*music*). **compo·nist**, *n.* composer (*of music*).
compromit·teren, -tteer, *v.t.* to compromise. ¶ *zich* ~, *v.r.* to compromise oneself.
comptabili·teit, *n.* accountancy; accounts.
concen·treren, -treer, *v.t.* to concentrate. **con·centrisch**, *a.* concentric.
con·cept, *n.n.* draft. ~ *overeenkomst*, draft agreement.
con·cert, *n.n.* concert (*orchestral*). **con·certgebouw**, *n.n.* concert hall (*building*). **con·certmeester, -s**, *n.* leader (*of orchestra*). **con·certzaal, -zalen**, *n.* concert hall (*room*).
con·cessie, -s, *n.* concession. *een* ~ *aanvragen*, to apply for a concession; *een* ~ *doen*, to make a concession; *een* ~ *verlenen*, to grant a concession. **conces·sio·naris, -ssen**, *n.* concessionary.
con·ciërge, -s, *n.* caretaker; hall-porter.
con·cilie, -s, *n.n.* council (*ecclesiastical*).

conclu·deren, -deer, v.t. to conclude, infer. con·clusie, -s, n. conclusion. tot een ~ komen, to arrive at a conclusion; een ~ trekken uit, to draw a conclusion from.

con·cours, n.n. match, competition.

con·creet, -crete, a. concrete. ¶ adv. concretely.

concur·reren, -rreer, v.i. to compete. ~ met, to compete with; ~ tegen, to compete against. concur·rent, a. competitive, competing. ¶ n. competitor. concur·rentie, no pl., n. competition, rivalry.

conden·sator, -s or -en, n. condenser. conden·seren, -seer, v.t. to condense.

con·ditie, -s, n. condition; form (in sport). op ~ dat, on condition. ¶ pl. terms.

condo·leren, -leer, v.t. to condole. iemand ~ met, to condole with a person on.

conduc·teur, -s, n. conductor (bus, tram); guard (train).

con·duitelijst, no pl., n., con·duitestaat, -staten, n. conduct sheet(s).

con·fectie, no pl., n. ready-made clothes. con·fectiepak, -kken, n.n. ready-made suit. con·fectiemagazijn, n.n., con·fectiezaak, -zaken, n. ready-made shop.

confe·rentie, -s, n. conference. confe·reren, -reer, v.i. to confer, hold a conference.

confi·seur, -s, n. confectioner.

confis·queren, -queer, v.t. to confiscate.

confi·tuur-, prefix jam-. confituren, pl. n. preserves, jam(s).

con·flict, n.n. conflict. in ~ komen met, to come into conflict with.

con·form, a. exact, true (copy). ¶ adv. in conformity with.

con·fuus, -fuse, a. confused, abashed. ¶ adv. confusedly.

con·gé, no pl., n.n. iemand zijn ~ geven, to dismiss or sack a person; zijn ~ krijgen, to get the sack.

con·gres, -ssen, n.n. congress (meeting).

congru·ent, a. congruent. congru·entie, no pl., n. congruity.

·conisch, a. conic(al).

·conjunctief, -ven, n. subjunctive.

con·nectie, -s, n. connection. in ~ staan met, to be connected with.

conse·quent, a. consistent. ¶ adv. consistently. conse·quentie, -s, n. consistency (logical); conclusion (logical).

conser·vator, n. curator (of museum).

con·serven, pl. only, n. tinned goods. con·servenfabriek, n. tinned goods factory.

conside·rans, n. preamble (of law).

con·signe, -s, n.n. password; instructions (military).

concis·torie, -s, n. consistory; vestry.

consoli·deren, -deer, v.t. to consolidate.

con·sorten, pl. only, n. (unfavourable) associates. con·sortium, -s, n.n. combine, syndicate.

·con·stant, a. constant. ¶ adv. constantly.

consta·teren, -teer, v.t. to state; to establish (fact).

conster·natie, n. consternation, dismay.

constitu·eren, -tueer, v.t. to constitute. ¶ v.r. zich ~ tot, to constitute oneself into. consti·tutie, -s, n. constitution.

con·structie, -s, n. construction. con·structiefout, n. structural error, flaw. con·structietekening, n. blueprint, plan. con·structiewinkel, -s, n. machine-shop. constru·eren, -ueer, v.t. to construct.

·consul, -s, n. consul. consu·laat, -laten, n.n. consulate. consu·lair, a. consular. con·su·lent, n. adviser, expert.

con·sult, n.n. consultation. consul·teren, -teer, v.t. to consult. consul·terend, a. consulting; advisory.

consu·ment, n. consumer. con·sumptie, -s, n. consumption; food and drink (in restaurant). con·sumptieartikel, n.n. food-stuff.

con·tact, n.n. contact, touch. in ~ staan met, to be in contact with.

con·tant, a. cash. ~e betaling, cash payment; de ~e waarde, the cash value. ¶ adv. cash (down). ~ betalen, to pay cash. con·tanten, pl. only, n.n. ready money, cash.

contin·gent, n.n. contingent; quota. contingen·teren, -teer, v.t. to regulate (imports, exports). contingen·tering, n. quota-system; regulation (of imports, exports).

continuï·teit, no pl., n. continuity.

·contrabande, no pl., n. contraband.

con·tract, n.n. contract. contrac·tant, ·. contracting party. con·tractbreuk, n. breach of contract. contrac·teren, -teer, v.i. & v.t. to contract. contractu·eel, -uele, a. contractual. ¶ adv. contractually.

·contradans, n. country dance. ·contramerk, n.n. countermark, door-check. ·contra·mijn, n. countermine. contra·mine, no pl., n. in de ~ zijn, to be contrary, be difficult. ·contramoer, n. check-nut. ·contrapunt, no pl., n.n. counterpoint. con·trarie, a. contrary. ¶ adv. contrari-wise. contrari·ëren, -rieer. v.t. to thwart.

con·trast, n.n. contrast.

contri·butie, -s, n. contribution.

con·trôle, -s, n. check, control; supervision; inspection. ~ uitoefenen over or op, to check, supervise, inspect, keep control over. contro·leren, -leer, v.t. to check, verify. contro·leur, -s, n. controller, inspector; guard, conductor; ticket-collector; assistant-collector (East Indian government official).

conveni·ëren, -nieert, v.t., imp. het convenieert me niet, it is not convenient just now.

con·ventie, -s, n. convention.

conver·satie, -s, n. conversation; (social) intercourse. hij heeft geen ~, he has no small talk *or* he knows few people. **con·ver·seren, -seer,** *v.i.* to converse. ~ *met*, to associate with. **con·versie, -s,** *n.* conversion. **con·versielening,** *n.* conversion loan. **conver·teerbaar, -bare,** *a.* convertible. **conver·teren, -teer,** *v.t.* to convert.

coöpe·ratie, no pl., *n.* co-operation. **coöpera·tief, -ve,** *a.* co-operative. *de coöperatieve* (*coll.*), the co-op.

co·pie, -pieën, *n.* copy (*replica, carbon-copy*). *voor* ~ *conform*, a true copy; *in 5 copieën*, with 4 carbon-copies. **co·pieboek,** *n.n.* letter-book. **copi·eerinkt,** *n.* copying ink. **copi·ëren, -eer,** *v.t.* to copy.

·Cornwallis, *n.N.* Cornwall. *van* ~, Cornish.

corps, *n.n.* corps; student union.

cor·rect, *a.* correct. ¶ *adv.* correctly. **cor·rectheid,** no pl., *n.* correctness. **cor·rector, -s,** *n.* proof-reader. **cor·rectie, -s,** *n.* correction, punishment.

correspon·deren, -deer, *v.i.* to correspond. **correspon·dentie, -s,** *n.* correspondence.

corri·geren, -geer, *v.t.* to correct.

cor·ruptie, -s, *n.* corruption.

cor·vée, -véeën, *n.n.* fatigue (*military*); tiresome job. *hij heeft* ~, he is on fatigue.

cosinus, -ssen, *n.* cosine.

costu·meren, -meer, *v.t.* to dress up. **cos·tume, -s,** *n.* costume, suit.

·cotangens, *n.* cotangent.

cou·lant, *a.* pleasantly businesslike. **cou·lisse, -n,** *n.* wing (*on stage*), coulisse. *achter de* ~n, behind the scenes, in the wings. **cou·loir, -s,** *n.* corridor, passage; lobby (*parliamentary*).

cou·pé, -'s, *n.* compartment. **cou·peren, -peer,** *v.t.* to cut (*cards*). **cou·peur, -s,** *n.* (tailor's) cutter (*male*). **cou·peuse, -s,** *n.* (tailor's) cutter (*female*). **cou·pon, -s,** *n.* coupon (*finance*); length of material. **cou·pure, -s,** *n.* denomination (*of shares, notes*).

cour, no pl., *n.* lavatory.

cou·rant, *a.* current. ¶ *n.* newspaper (*in title only*). *See* **krant.**

cour·tage, -s, *n.* brokerage.

cou·vert, -s *or* **-en,** *n.n.* envelope; cover (*at table*).

cou·veuse, -s, *n.* incubator.

cra·paud, -s, *n.* low easy-chair.

cre·atie, -s, *n.* creation. **crea·tuur, -turen,** *n.n.* creature.

cre·diet, *n.n. See* **krediet. ·credit,** no pl., *n.n.* credit (*in accountancy*). **credi·teren, -teer,** *v.t.* to credit. **credi·teur,** *n.* creditor. **·creditzijde,** no pl., *n.* credit side.

cre·peren, -peer, *v.i.* (*vulg., with dislike*) to die.

cri·ant, *a.* atrocious. ¶ *adv.* atrociously.

crimi·neel, -nele, *a.* criminal; outrageous. ¶ *adv.* criminally; outrageously.

·crisis, crises, *n.* crisis. *een* ~ *bereiken*, to come to a crisis; *een* ~ *doormaken*, to pass through a crisis.

·criticus, -ci, *n.* critic. **cri·tiek,** *n.* criticism. *beneden* ~, below par, beneath contempt; ~ *uitoefenen op*, to criticize. **·critisch,** *a.* critical (*attitude*). ¶ *adv.* critically (*of attitude*). **criti·seren, -seer,** *v.t.* to criticize.

culmi·natie, -s, *n.* culmination. **culmi·neren, -neer,** *v.i.* to culminate.

cul·tuur, -tures, *n.* culture (*civilization, etc.*); culture (*of bacilli*); cultivation. **cul·tuurgeschiedenis,** no pl., *n.* history of civilization. **cul·tuurgewas, -ssen,** *n.n.* economic crop. **cul·tuurhistorisch,** *a.* socio-historical. **cul·tuurmaatschappij,** *n.* company for cultivation of (*certain crops*). **cul·tuurstelsel,** no pl., *n.n.* culture-system (*East Indies*).

cura·tele, -n, *n.* guardianship; tutelage. *onder* ~ *staan*, to be under guardianship; *onder* ~ *stellen*, to place under legal control, appoint a guardian over; ~ *uitoefenen*, to exercise guardianship. **cu·rator, -s** *or* **-en,** *n.* curator; guardian; official receiver (*bankruptcy*).

curi·eus, -ze, *a.* curious, odd. **curi·osum, -sa,** *n.n.* remarkable fact, remarkable object.

cur·sief, -ve, *a.* italicized. *cursieve druk*, italics. ¶ *adv.* in italics. **cursi·veren, -veer,** *v.t.* to italicize.

·cursus, -ssen, *n.* course (of studies); curriculum.

cyaan·kali, no pl., *n.n.* cyanide of potassium. **cy·aanzuur,** no pl., *n.n.* cyanic acid.

cy·clopisch, *a.* cyclopean.

·cyclus, -ssen, *n.* cycle.

·cynicus, -ci, *n.* cynic. **·cynisch,** *a.* cynical. **cy·nisme,** no pl., *n.n.* cynicism.

·Cypers, *a.* Cyprian. *~e kat*, tabby.

·cypres, -ssen, *n.* cypress.

D

daad, daden, *n.* action, deed, act. *de* ~ *bij het woord voegen*, to suit the action to the word; *iemand op heter* ~ *betrappen*, to catch a person in the act; *een man van de* ~, a man of action. **daad·werkelijk,** *a.* actual, real. ¶ *adv.* actually.

da·ag! *See* **dag! daags,** *a.* week-day, every-day. ¶ *adv.* a day, per diem; in the day-time. ¶ *n.* (*old genitive*) day, day-time. *des* ~, during the day; ~ *te voren*, the previous day; *des anderen* ~, the other day; ~ *daarna*, the following day.

·daalder, -s, *n.* one and a half guilder (*value*).

daar, *adv.* there. ¶ *c.* as. ¶ *prefix. replacing pronouns:* dit, dat, die, hem, haar, *etc.* **daar·aan,** *adv.* = aan + dit, dat, die, hem, haar, *etc.* *wat heb ik* ~, what use is that to me; *het zit* ~ *vast*, it is attached to that. **·daaraantoe,** *adv. dat is tot* ~, never mind that *or* that is all right as far as it goes. **daaraan·volgend,** *adv.* next. **daar·achter,** *adv.,* **daarbe·neden,** *adv.,* **daar·binnen,** *adv.,* **daar·boven,** *adv.,* **daar·buiten,** *adv.* See **daar,** *prefix.* **daar·bij,** *adv.* near it; including. ～ *bleef het,* that is all that happened *or* was done. **daar·door,** *adv.* through it; through there; because of it. **daaren·boven,** *adv.* besides, moreover. **daaren·tegen,** *adv.* on the contrary, on the other hand. **daar·even,** *adv.* just now; a moment ago. **·daargelaten,** *past part.* See **daarlaten. daar·ginder,** *adv.,* **daar·ginds,** *adv.* over there. **daar·in,** *adv.,* **daar·langs,** *adv.* See **daar,** *prefix.* **·daarlaten, laat daar,** *v.t.s., str.* to pass over in silence. *dit daargelaten,* not to mention this. **daar·mede,** *adv.,* **daar·mee,** *adv.,* **daar·na,** *adv.,* **daar·naast,** *adv.* See **daar,** *prefix.* **daar·naar,** *adv.* accordingly, by that. **daar·net,** *adv.* just now, a moment ago. **daar·nevens,** *adv.* besides. **daar·om,** *adv.* hence. ～*!,* because! **daarom·heen,** *adv.* See **daar,** *prefix.* **daarom·streeks,** *adv.,* **daarom·trent,** *adv.* thereabouts. **daar·onder,** *adv.* See **daar,** *prefix.* **daar·op,** *adv.* (up)on it, *etc.*; thereupon. **daarop·volgend,** *adv.* next, following. **daar·over,** *adv.,* **daar·tegen,** *adv.* See **daar,** *prefix.* **daartegen·over,** *adv.* opposite. **daar·toe,** *adv.* for that purpose. **daar·tussen,** *adv.,* **daar·uit,** *adv.,* **daar·van,** *adv.* See **daar,** *prefix.* **·daarvandaan,** *adv.* from there; therefore, hence. **daar·voor,** *adv.* in front of it; before that; for it; for that purpose.

daas, dazen, *n.* horse-fly.

·dadel, -s, *n.* date (*fruit*); date-palm.

·dadelijk, *a.* immediate. ¶ *adv.* immediately. **·dadelijkheden,** *pl.* only, *n. tot.* ～ *komen,* to come to blows.

·dader, -s, *n.* perpetrator, author. *de* ～ *ligt op het kerkhof,* no one knows who has done it.

dag, *n.* day, daylight, day-time. ～*!* or *da-ag!,* goodbye; ～*!,* good day!; *goeden* ～ *zeggen,* to greet *or* to say goodbye to; *de jongste* ～, Judgment Day; *de laatste* ～*en,* these last few days; *een dezer* ～*en,* one of these days *or* recently, lately; *de* ～ *des Heren,* the Lord's Day; *de oude* ～, old age; ～ *en nacht,* night and day; *het wordt* ～, day is breaking; *alle* ～*en,* every day; *aan den* ～ *komen* or *brengen,* to come *or* to bring to light, *aan den* ～ *leggen,* to evince, display; ～ *aan* ～, day by day; *morgen aan de* ～, to-morrow first thing; *in vroeger* ～*en,* in days gone by; *met de* ～ *erger worden,* to get worse every day; *om de andere* ～, every other day; *op de* ～ *af,* to the very day; *later op de* ～, later in the day; *midden op de* ～, in the middle of the day; *op een goeie* ～, one (*fine*) day; *op zekeren* ～, one day; *over* ～, during the day-time; *Maandag over acht* ～*en,* Monday week;

over een ～ *of acht,* in about a week's time; *voor* ～ *en dauw,* before daybreak, excessively early; *voor den* ～ *halen,* to produce; *voor den* ～ *komen,* to appear, show oneself. **·dagblad,** *n.n.* daily (newspaper). **·dagbladschrijver, -s,** *n.* journalist. **·dagboek,** *n.n.* diary; day-book. **·dagdief, -ven,** *n.* idler. **·dagdieven, -dief,** *v.i.* to idle. **dagdieve·rij,** *n.* idling. **·dagelijks,** *a.* daily. ¶ *adv.* daily; from day to day. **·dagen, daag,** *v.t.* to summon, summons. **·dag-en-nachtevening,** *n.* equinox. **·dageraad, -raden,** *n.* dawn, day-break. **·dageld,** *n.n.* day's pay, daily wage. **·daggelder, -s,** *n.* day-labourer. **·dagje, -s,** *n.n.* day (*usu. of enjoyment*). **·dagjesmens,** *n.n.* day-tripper. **·dagkaart,** *n.* day-ticket. **·daglicht,** no pl., *n.n.* daylight. *in het volle* ～, in broad daylight; *iets in een ander* ～ *stellen,* to put a different complexion on something. **·dagloon, -lonen,** *n.n.* day's pay. **·dagloner, -s,** *n.* day-labourer. **·dagmars,** *n.* day's march. **·dagmeisje, -s,** *n.n.* daily help. **·dagorde,** no pl., *n.* order of the day. *op de* ～ *staan,* to be on the agenda. **·dagorder, -s,** *n.* order of the day (*army*). **·dagpauwoog, -wogen,** *n.* peacock butterfly. **·dagregister, -s,** *n.n.* day-book, journal. **·dagreis, -zen,** *n.* day's journey. **·dagtaak,** no pl., *n.* day's work. **·dagtekenen,** *v.t.* to date. ～ *uit,* to date from. **·dagtekening,** *n.* date. **·dagvaarden,** *v.t.* to summon, summons. **·dagvaarding,** *n.* summon(s), subpoena, writ. **·dagvlinder, -s,** *n.* butterfly. **·dagwerk,** no pl., *n.n.* day-work. ～ *hebben,* to work without end.

·Dajakker, -s, *N.* Dyak. **·Dajaks,** *a.* Dyak.

dak, *n.n.* roof. *een* ～ *boven zijn hoofd hebben,* to have a roof over one's head; *onder* ～ *brengen,* to give shelter to; *onder* ～ *zijn,* to be under cover; *onder één* ～ *wonen met,* to live under the same roof as; *op zijn* ～ *krijgen,* to get it in the neck; *iemand op zijn* ～ *komen,* to go for someone; *iets van de* ～*en prediken,* to proclaim something from the housetops; *het gaat van een leien* ～*je,* it goes very smoothly; *een zilveren* or *papieren* **dak** (*fac.*), a mortgage. **·dakgoot, -goten,** gutter (*of roof*). **·dakhaas, -hazen,** *n.* (*fac.*) cat. **·dakkamertje, -s,** *n.n.* attic, garret. **·daklicht,** *n.n.* skylight. **·daklook,** no pl., *n.n.* houseleek. **·dakloos, -loze,** *a.* homeless; roofless. **·dakpan, -nnen,** *n.* tile, pantile. **·dakpijp,** *n.* drain-pipe; gutter-spout. **·dakvenster, -s,** *n.n.* attic-window. **·dakvorst,** *n.* ridge of roof.

dal, *n.n.* valley. **·dalen, daal,** *v.i.* to descend, go down, drop, sink. *laten* ～, to lower. **·dalgrond,** *n.* sandy subsoil (*of peat*). **·daling,** *n.* descent, fall, drop, decline.

dam, -mmen, *n.* dam; (raised) causeway; weir; king (*in draughts*). *een* ～ *leggen,* to build a dam; *een ~ opwerpen tegen*, to throw up a dam against.

damas·ceren, -ceer, *v.t.* to damascene. **da·mast**, *n.n.* damask **da·masten**, *a.* (*made of*) damask.

·dambord, *n.n.* draughts-board.

·dame, -s, *n.* lady. *~s*, ladies (only). **·dames-**, *prefix.* ladies'.

·damhert, *n.n.* fallow deer.

·dammen, dam, *v.i.* to play draughts. **·dammer, -s**, *n.* draughts-player.

damp, *n.* vapour; smoke, fumes. **·dampen**, *v.i.* to steam, smoke; to puff away (*at pipe or cigar*). **·dampig**, *a.* vapoury. **·dampkring**, no pl., *n.* atmosphere (*round earth, etc.*). **·dampvormig**, *a.* vaporiform.

·damschijf, -ven, *n.* draughtsman (*in game*). **·damspel**, *n.n.* (game of) draughts.

dan, *adv.* then. *~ ook*, consequently, therefore; *~ toch*, yet; *spreek ~ toch*, do say something. ¶ *c.* except, but for; than.

·danig, *a.* exceeding, tremendous. *hij heeft een ~e honger*, he is exceedingly hungry. ¶ *adv.* exceedingly. *zich ~ vergissen*, to be badly mistaken.

dank, no pl., *n.* thanks. *geen ~*, don't mention it; *~ zij*, thanks to; *God zij ~*, thank God; *in ~*, with thanks, gratefully; *~ betuigen*, to express one's thanks; *ergens geen ~ van hebben*, to get little thanks for something; *iemand ~ verschuldigd zijn*, to owe a debt of gratitude to someone; *iemand ~ weten voor*, to be grateful to someone for; *iemand ~ zeggen voor*, to thank someone for. **·dankbaar, -bare**, *a.* grateful, thankful. ¶ *adv.* gratefully. **·dankbaarheid**, no pl., *n.* gratitude, thankfulness. **·dankbetuiging**, *n.* expression *or* vote of thanks. **·dankdag**, *n.* Thanksgiving Day. **·danken**, *v.t.* to thank. *dank U*, thank you (*on receiving something*) *or* no thank you (*on being offered something*); *iets danken aan*, to owe something to; *ik zou je ~* or *daar dank ik voor*, certainly not. ¶ *v.i.* to say grace (*after food*). **·dankzeggen, zeg dank**, *v.i.s.*, *irr.* to thank. **·dankzegging**, *n.* thanks.

dans, *n.* dance (*action; music*). *de ~ ontspringen*, to escape by the skin of one's teeth. **·dansclub, -s**, *n.* dancing-club. **·dansen**, *v.t. & v.i.* to dance. *~ op muziek*, to dance to music; *naar iemands pijpen ~*, to run round after a person, dance attendance. **·danser, -s**, *n.* dancer (*male*). **·danseres, -ssen**, *n.* dancer (*female*). **dan·seuse, -s**, *n.* ballet dancer. **·danspas, -ssen**, *n.* dance step. **·danswoede**, no pl., *n.* dancing craze. **·danszaal, -zalen**, *n.* dance hall.

·dapper, *a.* brave, gallant. ¶ *adv.* bravely; wholeheartedly, lustily. **·dapperheid**, no pl., *n.* bravery, gallantry, valour.

dar, -rren, *n.* drone.

darm, *n.* intestine, gut, bowel. *dikke ~*, large intestine; *dunne ~*, small intestine; *blinde ~*, appendix; *twaalfvingerige ~*, duodenum. **·darmkanaal, -nalen**, *n.n.* intestinal canal. **·darmontsteking**, *n.* enteritis. **·darmvlies, -zen**, *n.n.* peritoneum. **·darmvliesontsteking**, *n.* peritonitis.

·dartel, *a.* playful, frisky. **·dartelen**, *v.i.* to frisk, gambol.

das, -ssen, *n.* (neck-)tie; scarf, muffler; badger. **·dashond**, *n.* dachshund. **·dassenhol**, *n.n.* badger's burrow. **·dassenjacht**, *n.* badger drawing. **·dasspeld**, *n.* tie-pin.

dat, *dem. pron.* that; those. ¶ *rel. pron.* that; which. ¶ *c.* that; when. **·datgene**, *pron.* that. *~ wat*, that which. **·datje, -s**, *n.n.* over *ditjes en ~s spreken*, to talk about this and that; *ditjes en ~s*, small-talk, quibbles.

da·teren, -teer, *v.t.* to date. *~ van*, to date from. **·dato**, no pl., *n.* date. *na ~*, after date. **·datum, -s**, *n.* date.

dauw, no pl., *n.* dew. **·dauwachtig**, *a.* dewy. **·dauwdroppel, -s**, *n.* dew-drop. **·dauwen**, *v.i., imp.* to dew. **·dauwtrappen**, *infin. only*, *v.i.* early morning walk on Whit Sunday *or* Whit Monday. **·dauwworm**, *n.* dew-worm. ¶ no pl., *n.* ringworm.

daveren, *v.i.* to boom, thunder, reverberate. **·daverend**, *a.* thunderous.

·davits, pl. only, *n.* davits.

·dazen, daas, *v.i.* to buzz; to talk nonsense.

de, *def. art.* the.

de·bat, -tten, *n.n.* debate, discussion. *in ~ treden met*, to enter into a debate with. **debat·teren, -tteer**, *v.i.* to debate, discuss. *~ over*, to debate on.

·debet, no pl., *n.n.* debit; debt. ¶ *a. iemand ~ zijn*, to be in someone's debt. **·debetsaldo, -'s**, *n.n.* debit-balance. **·debetzijde**, no pl., *n.* debit-side. **de·biet**, no pl., *n.n.* sale(s); retail sales. *een groot ~ hebben*, to command a ready sale. **debi·tant**, *n.* retailer. **debi·teren, -teer**, *v.t.* to debit; to retail (*goods; stories*). **debi·teur, -s** *or* **-en**, *n.* debtor.

de·buut, no pl., *n.n.* début, first appearance.

·Decagram, -mmen, *n.* decagram(me) (*10 grammes*). **·Decaliter, -s**, *n.* decalitre (*10 litres*). **·Decameter, -s**, *n.* decametre (*10 metres*). **·Decastère, -s**, *or* **-n**, *n.* decastère (10 *cubic metres*).

de·cent, *a.* decent. ¶ *adv.* decently.

decentrali·satie, -s, *n.* decentralization. **decentrali·seren, -seer**, *v.t.* to decentralize.

de·ceptie, -s, *n.* disappointment, disillusionment.

dé·charge, no pl., *n.* discharge. *~ verlenen*, to grant a discharge; *getuige à ~*, witness for the defence. **dechar·geren, -geer**, *v.t.* to discharge.

·decigram, -mmen, *n.* decigram(me) ($\frac{1}{10}$ *gramme*). **·deciliter, -s**, *n.* decilitre ($\frac{1}{10}$ *litre*). **deci·maal, -male**, *a.* decimal.

¶ -malen, *n.* decimal, decimal place.
deci·maalteken, -s, *n.n.* decimal point
(*comma, in Dutch*). ·decimeter, -s, *n.*
decimetre ($\frac{1}{10}$ *metre*). deci·stère, -s *or*
-n, *n.* decistere ($\frac{1}{10}$ *cubic metre*).
decla·meren, -meer, *v.t.* to recite, declaim.
decli·natie, -s, *n.* declination (*of star*);
declension (*grammar*). decli·neren, -neer,
v.t. to decline (*grammar*).
dé·cor, -s, *n.n.* scenery (*stage*). décora·teur, -s,
n. decorator. deco·ratie, -s, *n.* decoration
(*medal*). decora·tief, -ve, *a.* decorative.
deco·reren, -reer, *v.t.* to decorate.
de·creet, -creten, *n.n.* decree. decre·teren,
-teer, *v.t.* to decree.
dedu·ceren, -ceer, *v.t.* to deduce, infer.
deeg, degen, *n.n.* dough, paste. ·deegachtig,
a. doughy.
deel, delen, *n.n.* part, portion; share; volume.
~ *hebben aan,* to be a party to; *part noch*
~ *hebben aan,* to have no share in; ~
hebben in, to have a share in; *zijn* ~ *hebben*
van, to have one's share of; ~ *nemen*
aan, to participate in, be present at;
~ *nemen in,* to participate in, share in;
~ *uitmaken van,* to form part of; *ten* ~
vallen, to fall to one's share *or* lot; *ten*
dele or *voor een* ~, partly, in part; *voor*
een groot ~, to a large extent. ¶ *n.*
board, deal; threshing floor. ·deelachtig,
a. iemand iets ~ *maken,* to impart something to someone; ~ *worden* or *zijn,*
to participate in *or* to obtain. ·deelbaar,
-bare, *a.* ~ *door,* divisible by. ·deelbaarheid, no pl., *n.* divisibility. ·deelgenoot,
-noten, *n.* partner, sharer (*male*). ·deelgenootschap, -ppen, *n.n.* partnership. ·deelgenote, -n, *n.* partner; sharer (*female*).
deelge·rechtigd, *a.* entitled to a share.
deelge·rechtigdheid, no pl., *n.* title to a
share. ·deelhebber, -s, *n.* partner. ·deelneemster, -s, *n.* participant, participator
(*female*). ·deelnemen, neem deel, *v.i.s.,* str.
See deel. ·deelnemend, *a.* sympathetic. ·deelnemer, -s, *n.* participant; participator
(*in match, etc.*). ·deelneming, *n.* sympathy,
condolence; participation. ~ *aan* or
in. See deel. *zijn* ~ *betuigen,* to condole
(*with person*). deels, *adv.* partly. ·deelsom,
-mmen, *n.* division sum. ·deelstreepje,
-s, *n.n.* hyphen. ·deeltal, -llen, *n.n.*
dividend (*maths.*). ·deelteken, -s, *n.n.*
diaeresis; division sign. ·deelwoord, *n.n.*
participle.
·deemoed, *n.* humility, meekness. dea·moedig,
a. humble, meek. ¶ *adv.* humbly, meekly.
dee·moedigen, *v.t.* to humble, humiliate.
¶ *zich* ~, *v.r.* to humble oneself.
Deen, Denen, *n.* Dane. Deens, *a.* Danish.
·deerlijk, *a.* sad, pitiful. ¶ *adv.* grievously,
badly. *zich* ~ *vergissen,* to make a bad
mistake.
deern, *n.* lass, wench, girl.
·deernis, no pl., *n.* commiseration, com-
D.E.D.

passion. ~ *hebben met,* to have pity on.
deernis·waardig, *a.* pitiable.
de·fect, *a.* defective; out of order. *de motor*
is ~, there is engine trouble. ¶ *n.n.* fault;
trouble (*with engine*).
de·fensie, no pl., *n.* defence (*military*).
defen·sief, *a.* defensive. ¶ *adv.* defensively.
de·filé, -·s, *n.n.* defile; march past. defi·leren,
-leer, *v.i.* to march past, defile.
defini·ëren, -ieer, *v.t.* to define. defi·nitie,
-s, *n.* definition. defini·tief, -ve, *a.* definite.
¶ *adv.* definitely. ~ *benoemd worden,*
to have one's appointment confirmed.
·deftig, *a.* respectable, stately, dignified,
distinguished-looking, well-to-do, bourgeois. ¶ *adv.* stately; solemnly. ~ *doen,*
to give oneself airs. ·deftigheid, no pl.,
n. dignity, respectability.
·degel, -s, *n.* platen.
·degelijk, *a.* of good quality; sound, substantial; thorough; upright (*character*).
¶ *adv.* thoroughly. *wel* ~, without
a doubt. ·degelijkheid, no pl., *n.* good
quality; thoroughness; reliability.
·degen, -s, *n.* sword; foil. ·degenslikker, -s,
n. sword-swallower. ·degenstok, -kken, *n.*
sword-stick. ·degenstoot, -stoten, *n.*
sword-thrust.
de·gene, -n, *pron.* he, she. *pl.* they. ~ *die,*
he *or* she who;. ~*n die,* they who.
degra·deren, -deer, *v.t.* to degrade; to reduce
in rank, reduce to the ranks.
·deinen, *v.i.* to heave, to rise and fall (*of*
swell). ·deining, *n.* swell (*at sea*).
·deinzen, deins, *v.i.* to shrink back, give way.
dek, -kken, *n.n.* cover; horse-blanket;
bed-clothes; deck (*of ship*). ·dekblad, *n.n.*
bract; outer leaf, wrapper (*of cigar*).
·deken, -s, *n.* dean; doyen; blanket,
·dekgeld, *n.n.* stud-fee. ·dekglaasje, *n.n.*
(microscope) slide. ·dekhengst, *n.* stallion.
stud-horse. ·dekken, dek, *v.t.* to cover;
to shield; to serve (*mare*); to defray;
to lay (*table*). ¶ *zich* ~, *v.r.* to cover
oneself (*against loss*); to put on one's
hat; to take cover. ·dekking, *n.* cover;
shelter;· defrayment. ·dokkingstroepen,
pl. only, *n.* covering force(s). ·dekkleed,
-kleden, *n.n.* tarpaulin; cover. ·dekknecht,
n. deck-hand. ·deklaag, -lagen, *n.* top
layer. ·deklading, *n.,* ·deklast, *n.* deck-cargo. ·dekmantel, *n.* (*fig.*) cloak. ·dek·officier, -s *or* -en, *n.* petty-officer. ·dekriet,
no pl., *n.n.* thatch. ·dekschaal, -schalen, *n.*
vegetable dish. ·dekschild, *n.n.* wing-case.
·deksel, -s, *n.n.* lid, cover. *wat* ~!, what
the dickens! ·deksels, *a.* confounded.
·deksteen, -stenen, *n.* coping-stone. ·dek·verf, -ven, *n.* body-colour, scumble.
·dekzeil, *n.n.* tarpaulin.
·delen, deel, *v.t.* to divide, share; to split
(*difference*). ~ *in,* to participate in; ~ *met,*
to share with. ·deler, -s, *n.* divider;
divisor. ·deling, *n.* division.

                                                  D

·delfstof, -ffen, n. mineral. ·delfstoffenrijk, no pl., n.n. mineral kingdom.
·delgen, v.t. to wipe out, clear, pay off (debt). ·delging, n. discharge, payment (of debt). ·delgingsfonds, n.n. sinking-fund.
·delven, delf, v.t., irr. to dig; scoop; to delve. ·delver, -s, n. digger.
demi-fi·nale, -s, n. semi-final. demi-sai·son, -s, n. spring-coat, autumn-coat.
demobili·seren, -seer, v.t. to demobilize.
demons·treren, -treer, v.t. to demonstrate.
demon·teren, -teer, v.t. to dismount, dismantle.
·dempen, v.t. to fill up (ditch, pond, etc.); to muffle, deaden, dim, subdue (sound, light, fire); to quell, crush (revolt). als het kalf verdronken is, dempt men de put, to lock the stable door after the horse has been stolen; de vuren ~, to damp down a fire; met gedempte stem, in a hushed voice. ·demper, -s, n. damper; mute (on violin).
den, -nnen, n. fir. ·denappel, -s, n. fir-cone.
·denderen, v.t. to rumble, thunder (of vehicle).
·Denemarken, n.N. Denmark.
·denkbaar, -bare, a. imaginable, conceivable, thinkable. ·denkbeeld, n.n. idea, concept; notion. zich ergens een ~ van maken, to form an idea of something. ·denk·beeldig, a. imaginary, hypothetical. ·denkelijk, adv. probably, likely. ·denken, v.i., irr. & v.t., irr. to think. ~ aan, to think of; bij zichzelf ~, to think to oneself; ~ om, to remember, mind; ~ van, to think of, say to; kun je ~! I don't think! ·denkend, a. thinking, rational. ·denker, -s, n. thinker. ·denkvermogen, no pl., n.n. intellectual power. ·denkwijze, -n, n. way of thinking, habit of thought.
·denneboom, -bomen, n. fir tree. ·dennehout, no pl., n.n. fir-wood (substance). ·dennebos, -ssen, n.n. fir-wood (forest).
departe·ment, n.n. department; ministerial department. See ministerie.
depen·dentie, -s, n. See ap- en dependentie.
depo·neren, -neer, v.t. to deposit; to pay in (into bank); to register (trade-mark).
depor·teren, -teer, v.t. to deport.
de·posito, -'s, n.n. deposit.
de·pot, -s, n.n. depot; branch (of firm). de·pothouder, -s, n. branch-manager.
depreci·ëren, -cieer, v.t. to depreciate.
de·pressie, -s, n. depression.
depri·meren, -meer, v.t. to depress.
derail·leren, -lleer, v.t. & v.i. to leave the track, run off the rails. deraille·ment, n.n. derailment.
deran·geren, -geer, v.t. to put to inconvenience. ¶ zich ~, v.r. to put oneself to inconvenience.
·derde, a. third. ¶ -n, n.n. third (part or person). ·derdedaags, a. tertian (of fever). derde·machtsvergelijking, n. cubic equation. derde·machtswortel, -s, n. cube root.

·derdenmale, n. ten ~, for the third time.
·derderangs, a. third-rate.
·deren, deer, v.t. to harm, hurt.
·dergelijk, pron. similar. iets ~s, something similar; en ~e, and things like that.
der·halve, adv. hence. ·dermate, adv. in such a manner, to such a degree.
·derrie, no pl., n. muck; salty peat.
·dertien, num. thirteen. ·dertiende, num. thirteenth. ¶ n.n. thirteenth (part, person). ·dertig, num. thirty. ·dertiger, -s, n. person aged thirty. ·dertigste, num. thirtieth.
·derven, derf, v.t. to lack, go without. ·derving, n. lack, loss.
·derwaarts, adv. thither. ·derwijze, adv. in such a manner.
des, no pl., n. D flat. ¶ def. art., genitive. of the; of an. ~ avonds, in the evening. ¶ adv. ~ te beter, all the better; ~ te meer, the more or all the more. desalniette·min, adv. nevertheless. desbe·treffend, a. in question; pertinent to.
·desem, no pl., n. leaven. ·desemen, v.t. to leaven.
deser·teren, -teer, v.i. to desert. deser·teur, -s, n. deserter. de·sertie, -s, n. desertion.
·desgelijks, adv. likewise. desge·vraagd, adv. if required, if asked for. desge·wenst, adv. if required.
desil·lusie, -s, n. disillusion(ment). desillusion·neren, -neer, v.t. to disillusion.
desinfec·teren, -teer, v.t. to disinfect. desin·fectiemiddel, n.n. disinfectant.
des·kundig, a. expert. des·kundige, -n, n. expert.
desniettegen·staande, adv., desniette·min, adv., ·desondanks, adv. See desalniettemin. des·noods, adv. if necessary, if need be.
despe·ratie, no pl., n. despair.
·dessa, -'s, n. East Indian village.
des·sert, n.n. dessert.
·destijds, adv. at the time, in the past. desver·kiezend, adv., desver·langend, adv. if desired. ·deswege, adv. therefore, on that account.
deta·cheren, -cheer, v.t. to detail, draft (soldiers, officials). detache·ment, n.n. detachment, party (of soldiers). deta·che·ring, n. detachment, detailing (action).
de·tail, -s, n.n. detail, particular. en ~, (by) retail; in ~s treden, to enter into particulars. de·tailhandel, no pl., n. retail trade.
de·tentie, no pl., n. detention. deti·neren, -neer, v.t. to detain.
deto·neren, -neer, v.t. to detonate.
·deugd, n. virtue; (good) quality. lieve ~! good gracious. ·deugdelijk, a. sound, durable, reliable; valid (of argument). ¶ adv. reliably, thoroughly. ·deugdelijkheid, no pl., n. reliability, soundness; validity. ·deugdzaam, -zame, a. virtuous. ¶ adv.

virtuously. ·deugdzaamheid, no pl., *n.*
virtue, durability. ·deugen, *v.i.* ~ *niet*
or *nooit. niet* ~, to be no good *or* to be a
good-for-nothing; *niet* ~ *voor*, to be no
good for *or* as *or* at. ·deugniet, *n.* rascal
(*child*); ne'er-do-well. deugniete·rij, *n.*
roguish tricks.
deuk, *n.* dent. ·deuken, *v.t.* to dent. ·deuk-
hoed, *n.* felt hat, trilby.
deun, *n.*, ·deuntje, -s, *n.n.* tune, air, song.
deur, *n.* door; gate. *in de* ~, in the doorway; *met gesloten* ~*en*, behind closed
doors; *dat doet de* ~ *toe*, that has torn it
or that has put the lid on it; *de* ~ (*niet*)
uitgaan, (never) to go out of doors; *iemand
de* ~ *uitzetten*, to throw someone out;
met de ~ *in huis vallen*, to waste no time
on preliminaries; *voor de* ~ *staan*, to
be at hand. ·deurplaat, -platen, *n.* finger-
plate. ·deurwaarder. -s, *n.* bailiff; usher.
·deurwaardersexploit, *n.n.* writ (of execution).
devalu·atie, no pl., *n.* depreciation (*of
coinage*).
de·veine, no pl., *n.* run of bad luck.
de·vies, -zen, *n.n.* device, motto. *pl.* foreign
bills.
de·votie, -s, *n.* devotion.
de·welke, *pron.* (*stilted*) who, which, that.
de·wijl, *adv.* since, as.
dex·trine, no pl., *n.* dextrin.
·deze, *pron.* this, these. ~ *en gene*, this one
and the other; ~ *of gene*, one person or
another; *bij* ~*n*, herewith; *in* ~*n*, in
this (*matter*); *na* ~*n*, after this (*date*);
voor ~*n*, before this (*date*); *de 15de* ~*r*,
the 15th inst.; *de schrijver* ~*s*, the present
writer. de·zelfde, *pron.* the same. de·zelve,
pron. he, she, same. ·dezer, *pron. See*
deze. ·dezerzijds, *a. & adv.* on this side.
·dezes, *pron. See* deze. de·zulke(n), *pron.*
such. ~ *die*, such as.
di·aken, -s or -en, *n.* deacon. di·akenhuis-
mannetje, -s, *n.n.* inmate of almshouse.
diako·nes, -ssen, *n.* sick-nurse (*Protestant*).
diako·nessenhuis, -zen, *n.n.* institutional
nursing home (*Protestant*). diako·nie, *n.*
poor-relief board. diako·niehuis, -zen, *n.n.*
almshouse.
dia·mant, *n.* diamond. dia·manten, *a.* (*made
of*) diamond. dia·mantslijper, -s, *n.* diamond-cutter. dia·mantslijperij, *n.* dia-
mond-cutting establishment. dia·mant-
werker, -s, *n.* diamond-cutter.
dicht, *a.* shut, closed (*door*); dense, thick
(*forest*); close (*writing*); *zo* ~ *als een pot*,
as close as an oyster. ¶ *adv.* densely;
closely. ~ *bij*, near to or close upon.
·dichtbij, *adv.* close by, near, near at
hand. ·dichtbinden, *v.t.s.*, *str.* to tie up.
·dichtdoen, doe dicht, *v.t.s.*, *irr.* to close,
shut; to draw (*curtains*) ·dichtdraaien,
v.t.s. to turn off (*tap*). ·dichtduwen,
v.t.s. to push to. ·dichten, *v.t.* to stop

(up). ¶ *v.i.* to write poetry *or* verse.
·dichter, -s, *n.* poet. dichte·res, -ssen, *n.*
poetess. ·dichterlijk, *a.* poetical. ¶ *adv.*
poetically. ·dichtgaan, ga dicht, *v.i.s.*, *irr.* to
shut, close; to heal up. ·dichtgooien, *v.t.s.* to
slam; to fill up (*hole*). ·dichtgroeien, *v.i.s.*
to heal up. ·dichtheid, no pl., *n.* closeness, density. ·dichtklappen, klap dicht,
v.t.s. to slam (*book*) shut. ·dichtknijpen,
v.t.s. *str.* to squeeze shut. ·dichtknopen,
knoop dicht, *v.t.s.*, *str.* to button up.
·dichtkunst, no pl., *n.* art of poetry, poetic
art. ·dichtmaat, -maten, *n.* metre. *in* ~,
in verse. ·dichtmaken, maak dicht, *v.t.s.*
to close, shut, fasten. ·dichtmetselen,
v.t.s. to brick up, wall up. ·dichtnaaien,
v.t.s. to sew up. ·dichtplakken, plak
dicht, *v.t.s.* to stick down, seal (*envelope*).
·dichtregel, -s, *n.* line (of verse). ·dicht-
schroeven, schroef dicht, *v.t.s.* to screw
down. ·dichtschuiven, schuif dicht, *v.t.s.*,
str. to draw to (*curtains*). ·dichtslaan,
sla dicht, *v.t.s.*, *irr.* to slam to. ·dicht-
slibben, slib dicht, *v.i.s.* to silt up. ·dicht-
smijten, *v.t.s.*, *str.* (*coll.*) to slam to.
·dichtsoort, -n. type of poetic form. ·dicht-
spijkeren, *v.t.s.* to nail down. ·dicht-
stoppen, stop dicht, *v.t.s.* to stop up,
plug. ·dichtstuk, -kken, *n.n.* poem, piece
of poetry. ·dichttrappen, trap dicht,
v.t.s., *str.* to kick to (*door*). ·dichttrekken,
trek dicht, *v.t.s.*, *str.* to pull to (*door*).
·dichtvouwen, *v.t.s.*, *irr.* to fold up. ·dicht-
vriezen, vriest dicht, *v.imp.* *s.*, *irr.* to
freeze over. ·dichtwaaien, *v.i.s.*, *irr.* to
blow shut (*door*).· ·dichtwerk, *n.n.* poem,
poetical work.
dic·taat, -taten, *n.n.* dictation. dicta·tuur,
no pl., *n.* dictatorship. dic·tee, -s, *n.n.*
dictation.
die, *dem. pron.* that, those; this, these;
the one(s); he, she, they. ¶ *rel. pron.*
who, which, that.
·Diederik, *N.* Theodor...
di·eet, no pl., *n.n.* diet. *een* ~ *houden* or
volgen, to be on a diet; *op* ~ *zetten*, to
put on a diet.
dief, -ven, *n.* thief. *houdt de* ~! stop thief!;
een ~ *aan de kaars*, a thief in the candle-
wick. ·diefachtig, *a.* thievish. ¶ *adv.*
thievishly. ·diefachtigheid, no pl., *n.*
thievishness. ·diefjesmaat, no pl., *n.*
het is dief en ~, they are all rogues together. ·diefstal, -llen, *n.* theft, robbery.
·diegene, *pron.* he, she. *pl.* those. ~ *die*,
he who.
·Diemensland, *n.N. Van* ~, Tasmania.
dien, *pron. See* die. dienaan·gaande, *adv.*
as to that, with respect to that.
·dienaar, -s *or* -naren, *n.* (*fig.*) servant (*male*).
Uw dienstwillige ~, your obedient servant.
diena·res, -ssen, *n.* (*fig.*) servant (*female*).
·dienbak, -kken, *n.* serving-tray. ·diender,
-s, *n.* (*slang*) copper (*policeman*). ·dienen,

v.t. to serve, be of use to. *om U te* ~, at your service; *iemand van antwoord* ~, to let a person have it; *iemand van raad* ~, to advise a person. ¶ *v.i.* to serve (*in army; as excuse*); to wait (*at table*); to be of use, serve; to permit (*of weather*); to behove; should, ought. *gaan* ~, to go out to service; ~ *als*, to serve as *or* for; ~ *bij*, to take service with; *hij is er niet mee gediend*, it is of no use to him; *tot niets* ~ *or nergens toe* ~, to be of no use; *waartoe dient het?*, what use is it?; *tot waarschuwing* ~, to be a warning; *ik ben er niet van gediend*, I will not have it, will not put up with it.

dienovereen·komstig, *adv.* accordingly.

dienst, *n.* service. *een* ~ *bewijzen*, to render a service; ~ *doen* (*als*), to serve, be useful (as); ~ *hebben*, to be on duty; *geen* ~ *hebben*, to be off duty; ~ *nemen*, to enlist; *de* ~ *opzeggen*, to give notice; *buiten* ~, off duty *or* laid up; *buiten* ~ *stellen*, to lay up; *in* ~ *gaan*, to go out to service *or* to enlist; *in* ~ *nemen*, to engage; *in* ~ *stellen*, to put into service; *in* ~ *zijn*, to be in the army; *onder* ~ *gaan*, to enlist, be called up; *ten* ~*e van*, for the use *or* service of; *tot Uw* ~, at your service; *van* ~ *zijn*, to be of use; *de ene* ~ *is de andere waard*, one good turn deserves another. ·**dienstbaar, -bare,** *a.* ~ *maken*, to subjugate; ~ *maken aan*, to make subservient to. ·**dienstbaarheid**, no pl., *n.* servitude, bondage. ·**dienstbe·toon**, no pl., *n.n.* service(s) rendered. ·**dienstbode, -n,** *n.* servant (*female*). ·**dienstdoend,** *a.,* ·**diensthebbend,** *a.* on duty; in charge. ·**dienstig,** *a.* serviceable, useful. ·**dienstjaar, -jaren,** *n.n.* year of service. ·**dienstklopper, -s,** *n.* martinet. ·**dienstknecht,** *n.* (*biblical*) servant (*male*). ·**dienstmaagd,** *n.* (*biblical*) handmaid. ·**dienstmeid,** *n.* maid, servant girl. ·**dienstmeisje, -s,** *n.n.* servant (*female*). ·**dienstpersoneel,** no pl., *n.n. het* ~, the servants. ·**dienstplicht,** no pl., *n.* conscription. **dienst·plichtig,** *a.* liable to conscription. *van* ~*e leeftijd*, of military age. **dienst·plichtige, -n,** *n.* conscript. ·**dienstregeling,** *n.* time-table. ·**dienstreis, -zen,** *n.* official journey, tour. **dienst·vaardig,** *a.* eager to serve. **dienst·vaardigheid**, no pl., *n.* eagerness to serve. ·**dienstvrij,** *a.* exempt from conscription. ·**dienstweigeraar, -s,** *n.* conscientious objector. ·**dienstweigering,** *n.* refusal to obey orders. **dienst·willig,** *a.* willing to serve. ·**dienstzaak, -zaken,** *n.* official business.

dientenge·volge, *adv.* hence, in consequence.

diep, *a.* deep, profound. *een* ~ *geheim*, a dead secret; *in* ~*e gedachten*, deep in thought; *uit het* ~*st van mijn hart*, from the bottom of my heart. ¶ *adv.* deep(ly). ¶ *n.n.* canal, channel. ·**diepbedroefd,** *a.*

grief-stricken, deeply afflicted. ·**diepden·kend,** *a.* profound (*philosopher, etc.*). ·**diepgaand,** *a.* searching, profound; radical (*change*), with considerable draught (*ship*). ·**diepgang,** no pl., *n.* draught (*of ship*). *10 voet* ~ *hebben*, to draw 10 ft. of water. ·**diepliggend,** *a.* deep-set, sunken. ·**dieplood, -loden,** *n.n.* lead, plummet. ·**diepte, -n,** *n.* depth. ·**dieptebom, -mmen,** *n.* depth charge. ·**dieptestuur, -sturen,** *n.n.* diving rudder. **diep·zeeonderzoek, -ingen,** *n.n.* deep sea research. diep·**zinnig,** *a.* profound, abstruse. ¶ *adv.* profoundly, abstrusely. **diep·zinnigheid, -heden,** *n.* profoundness, profundity, abstruseness.

dier, *n.n.* animal, living creature. *redeloos* ~, brute beast. ¶ *a.* (*stilted*) dear. ·**dierbaar, -bare,** *a.* dearly beloved. ·**dieren-,** *prefix meaning:* of *or* pertaining to animals. ·**dierenarts,** *n.* veterinary surgeon. ·**dierenbeul,** *n.,* ·**dierenkweller, -s,** *n.* tormentor of animals. ·**dierenriem,** no pl., *n.* zodiac. ·**dierenrijk,** no pl., *n.n.* animal kingdom. ·**dierentuin,** *n.* zoological gardens, zoo. ·**diergaarde, -n,** *n.* zoological gardens, zoo. ·**dierkunde,** no pl., *n.* zoology. ·**dierkundig,** *a.* zoological. ·**dierlijk,** *a.* animal; bestial. ·**dierlijkheid, -heden,** *n.* brutality, bestiality.

dier·voege, no pl., *n. in* ~, in such a manner.

dies, *adv.* consequently. *wat* ~ *meer zij*, and so on and so forth.

diets, *a. iemand iets* ~ *maken*, to make someone believe something. **Diets,** *a.* (*stilted*) Dutch. ¶ *n.n.* Old Dutch (*language*).

die·vegge, -n, *n.* thief (*female*). ·**dievenbende, -n,** *n.* band of thieves. ·**dievenlantaarn, -s,** *n.,* ·**dievenlantaren, -s,** *n.* dark lantern, bull's-eye. ·**dieventaal,** no pl., *n.* (thieves') cant. **dieve·rij,** *n.* thieving.

differenti·aal-rekening, no pl., *n.* differential calculus.

digni·taris, -ssen, *n.* dignitary.

dij, *n.* thigh.

·**dijen,** *v.i.* to thrive.

dijk, *n.* dike, dyke, embankment. *iemand aan de* ~ *zetten*, to give someone the sack. ·**dijkbaas, -bazen,** *n.* dyke-reeve. ·**dijkbestuur, -sturen,** *n.n.* board of dyke-inspectors. ·**dijkbreuk,** *n.* dyke-burst. ·**dijkgeld,** *n.n.* dyke-rates. ·**dijkgraaf, -graven,** *n.* dyke-reeve. ·**dijkheemraad, -raden,** *n.* member of polder-board. **dijk·heemraadschap, -ppen,** *n.n.* polder *or* dyke-board. ·**dijkraad,** *n.* dyke-reeve; dyke-board; member of dyke-board. ·**dijkrechten,** pl. only, *n.n.* dyke-law; dyke-dues. ·**dijkschot,** no pl., *n.n.* dyke-rates. ·**dijkschouw,** *n.* dyke-inspection. ·**dijkslag,** *n.* (*administrative*) section of dyke. ·**dijkwerker, -s,** *n.* navvy (*on dyke*). ·**dijkwezen,** no pl., *n.n.* dyke-maintenance service.

dijn, *n.n. mijn en* ~, mine and thine (*of property*).
dik, -kke, *a.* thick; dense; fat; pregnant. *dikke vrienden,* close friends; *een dikke 20 gulden,* 20 odd guilders; *een* ~ *uur,* a good hour; *zich* ~ *maken,* to get angry. ¶ *adv.* thickly; densely. *het er* ~ *opleggen,* to lay it on thick; *er* ~ *op liggen,* to be laid on thick. ¶ *n.* thick; thick part. *door* ~ *en dun,* through thick and thin. **dik-bloedig,** *a.* thick-blooded. **dik·buikig,** *a.* pot-bellied. **dik·huidig,** *a.* thick-skinned; pachidermatous. **dikke·darmontsteking,** *n.* colitis. **dikkerd, -s,** *n.* (*coll.*) fatty. **dikkop, -ppen,** *n.* fathead; tadpole. **dikte, -n,** *n.* thickness. **dikwerf,** *adv.* (*stilted*). *See* **dikwijls. dikwijls,** *adv.* often, frequently. **dikzak, -kken,** *n.* fat person.
dili·gence, -s, *n.* stage-coach.
di·né, -'s, *n.n. See* diner. **di·nertje, -s,** *n.n.* dinner party. **di·ner,** *n.n.* dinner. **di·neren, -neer,** *v.i.* to dine. ~ *bij iemand,* to dine at a person's house.
ding, *n.n.* thing. *een lief or aardig* ~, a pretty girl. **dingen,** *v.i., str.* to haggle, bargain; ~ *naar,* to compete for *or* to sue for (*hand of*). **dinges,** no pl., *n.* what's-his- (*her-, its-*) name. **dingsigheidje, -s,** *n.n.* gadget, trifle.
dinsdag, *n.* Tuesday. **dinsdags,** *a.* (of) Tuesday(s). ¶ *adv.* on Tuesdays.
diphte·rie, no pl., *n.,* **diphte·ritis,** no pl., *n.* diphtheria.
diplo·maat, -maten, *n.* diplomat. **diploma·tie,** no pl., *n.* diplomacy. **diploma·tiek,** *a.,* **diplo·matisch,** *a.* diplomatic. *lang* ~*e weg,* by diplomatic channels. ¶ *adv.* diplomatically. **diplo·meren, -meer,** *v.t.* to certificate.
dip·tiek, *n.* diptych.
di·rect, *a.* direct. ¶ *adv.* directly; at once. **direc·teur, -s** *or* **-en,** *n.* director; manager; managing director; postmaster; principal, headmaster. **direc·teur-gene·raal, -s generaal,** *n.* director-general; Postmaster-General. **di·rectie, -s,** *n.* management; board of directors. **direc·trice, -s,** *n.* manageress; headmistress; matron.
diri·geerstok, -kken, *n.* baton (*of conductor*). **diri·gent,** *n.* conductor (*of orchestra*). **diri·geren, -geer,** *v.t.* to conduct (*orchestra*).
dirkjespeer, -peren, *n.* jargonelle.
dis, no pl., *n.* D sharp; table, board.
disagio, no pl., *n.* discount (*financial*). **dis·cant,** *n.* descant, treble.
disgenoot, -noten, *n.* person with whom one shares a meal; fellow guest.
discipli·nair, *a.* disciplinary. **disci·pline,** no pl., *n.* discipline. **discipli·neren, -neer,** *v.t.* to discipline.
discon·teren, -teer, *v.t.* to discount (*financial*). **dis·conto,** no pl., *n.n.* (rate of) discount, bank-rate. *in* ~ *nemen,* to discount

(*financial*). **dis·contovoet,** no pl., *n.* rate of discount.
dis·cours, *n.n.* conversation. **discrediet,** no pl., *n.n.* discredit. *in* ~ *brengen,* to discredit, throw discredit upon. **dis·creet, -crete,** *a.* discreet, modest, tactful. ¶ *adv.* discreetly. **dis·cretie,** no pl., *n.* tact, discretion. **discussi·ëren, -ssieer,** *v.t.,* discu·teren, -teer, *v.t.* to discuss, debate. ~ *over iets met iemand,* to discuss a subject with someone. **dis·pache, -s,** *n.* average adjustment. **dispa·cheur, -s,** *n.* average adjuster. **dispen·seren, -seer,** *v.i.* ~ *van,* to dispense from. **dispo·neren, -neer,** *v.i.* to arrange; to collect (*sum*). ~ *over,* to have at one's disposal. **dispo·nibel,** *a.* available. **disputeren, -teer,** *v.i.* to dispute, argue. **dis·puut, -puten,** *n.n.* dispute, debate, argument. **disqualifi·ceren, -ceer,** *v.t.* to disqualify.
dissel, -s, *n.* adze; pole, shaft (*of cart, carriage*). **disselboom, -bomen,** *n.* pole, shaft (*of cart, carriage*).
disser·tatie, -s, *n.* dissertation; thesis (*for degree*).
distel, -s, *n.* thistle. **distelig,** *a.* thistly. **distelvink,** *n.* goldfinch, thistle-finch. **distelvlinder, -s,** *n.* painted lady (*butterfly*). **distilla·teur, -s,** *n.* distiller. **distil·latie, -iën,** *n.* distillation. **distilleerde·rij, -en,** *n.* distillery. **distil·leertoestel, -llen,** *n.n.* still. **distil·leren, -leer,** *v.t.* to distil.
distinc·tief, -ven, *n.n.* badge, insignia. **distribu·eren, -ueer,** *v.t.* to distribute. **distri·butie, -s,** *n.* distribution; rationing scheme; (postman's) delivery.
dit, *prcn.* this. **ditje, -s,** *n.n. over* ~*s en datjes praten,* to talk of one thing and another. **ditmaal,** *adv.* this time, this once.
dito, no pl., *n.* ditto. ¶ *adv.* ditto, likewise.
divan, -s, *n.* divan.
di·vers, *a.* various. **di·versen,** pl. only, *n.* sundries.
divi·dend, *n.n.* dividend. **divi·dendbewijs, -zen,** *n.n.* dividend coupon, dividend-warrant.
di·visie, -s, *n.* division (*military*). **di·visie-commandant,** *n.* divisional commander.
djatiboom, -bomen, *n.* teak (*tree*). **djatihout,** *n.n.* teak (*wood*).
dobbelaar, -s, *n.* dicer; gambler. **dobbelbeker, -s,** *n.* dice-box. **dobbelen,** *v.i.* to play dice; to gamble. **dobbelspel, -llen,** *n.n.* game of dice. **dobbelsteen, -stenen,** *n.* die (*pl.* dice). **dobbelzucht,** no pl., *n.* gambling fever.
dobber, -s, *n.* float (*of fishing-line*); buoy. *een harde* ~ *hebben om . . .,* to have great trouble to. . . . **dobberen,** *v.i.* to bob; to pitch and toss. *tussen hoop en vrees* ~, to hover between hope and fear.
do·cent, *n.* teacher, lecturer (*in university*). **do·ceren, -ceer,** *v.i. & v.t.* to teach (*in university*).

doch, c. but, however.
docht, n. thwart.
·dochter, -s, n. daughter. *een jonge ~,* a young woman.
·doctor, -en or **-s,** doctor (*physician with doctor's degree*); doctor (*in any subject*). **docto·raat, -raten,** n.n. doctorate. **docto·randus, -dussen,** n. person preparing doctor's thesis. **docto·reren, -reer,** v.i. to' take one's doctor's degree.
docu·ment, n.n. document. **documen·teren, -teer,** v.t. to document.
·dodaars, -zen, n. little grebe; dodo.
·doddegras, no pl., n.n. timothy-grass.
·dode, -n, n. *de ~,* the dead (*person*), deceased; *de ~n,* the dead; *aan ~n en gewonden,* in killed and wounded. **·dodelijk,** a. deadly, mortal; lethal. ¶ *adv.* mortally.
·doden, dood, v.t. to kill, slay. **·dodenakker, -s,** n. God's acre; cemetery. **·dodend,** a. deadly. **·dodenmars,** n. funeral march. **·dodenrijk,** n.n. realm of the dead. **·dodenstad, -steden,** n. city of the dead. **·doder, -s,** n. killer.
·doedelen, v.t. to play the bagpipe. **·doedelzak, -kken,** n. bagpipe(s).
doek, no pl., n.n. woven material, cloth. ¶ n.n. (painting) canvas; flag; sail; (projection) screen. ¶ n. cloth, rag. *zo wit als een ~,* as white as a sheet; *een ~je voor het bloeden,* eyewash (*fig.*); *ergens geen ~jes om winden,* not to mince matters. **·doekspeld,** n. brooch.
doel, n.n. target, goal. ¶ **·einden,** n.n. aim, purpose, object. *het ~ treffen,* to hit the target; *zijn ~ bereiken,* to achieve one's end; *zijn ~ missen,* to miss one's mark; *zijn ~ voorbijstreven.* to overshoot the mark; *het ~ heiligt de middelen,* the end ji stifies the means; *met het ~ om,* with a view to; *recht op het ~ afgaan,* to keep the end in view or to go straight to' the point; *zich iets ten ~ stellen* or *iets ten ~ hebben,* to set out to (*do something*). **·doelbewust,** a. purposeful. **·doelbe·wustheid,** no pl., n. singleness of purpose. **·doeleinde, -n,** n.n. purpose. **·doelen,** v.i. *~ op,* to aim at *or* to allude to. **·doelloos, -lloze,** a. aimless. **·doelloosheid,** no pl., n. aimlessness. **doel·matig,** a. appropriate, suitable. **·doelpaal, -palen,** n. goal-post. **·doelpunt,** n.n. goal. **doel·treffend,** a. effective. **doel·treffendheid,** no pl., n. effectiveness. **·doelwit, -tten,** n.n. (*stilted*) target; aim.
·doemen, v.t. to doom. *ten ondergang gedoemd,* doomed.
doen, doe, v.t., irr. to do; to make; to take; to put; to ask. *het er om ~,* to do it on purpose; *hij kan het goed ~,* he can well afford it; *dat doet het hem!,* that's the reason!; *wat doet het buiten?,* how is the weather out?; *er is niets aan te ~,* it cannot be helped; *hij kan er niets aan ~,*

he cannot help it; *het doet er niets toe,* it makes no difference; *wat ~ . . . ?,* how much do . . . fetch?; *wat doet dat huis?,* what is the rent of that house? ¶ v.i., irr. to do. *te ~ hebben met,* to have dealings or trouble with *or* to be sorry for; *te ~ krijgen met,* to come up against; *het is hem te ~ om . . . ,* he is after . . . ; *~ aan,* to go in for; *~ alsof,* to pretend; *je deed beter,* you had better; *~ in,* to deal in; *lang ~ over,* to take a long time over; *vreemd ~,* to behave strangely. ¶ no pl., n.n. doings. *iemands ~ en laten,* a person's doings; *er is geen ~ aan,* it is no use; *in goeden ~,* well-to-do, well-off; *in zijn gewone ~,* his usual self; *voor zijn ~,* for him. **·doende,** a. busy. ¶ *adv.* by doing. *al ~ leert men,* practice makes perfect. **·doeniet,** n. idle, good-for-nothing. **·doenlijk,** a. feasible, practicable.
·doerian, -s, n. durian.
does, -zen, n. poodle.
·doezel, -s, n., **·doezelaar, -s,** n. stump (*art material*). **·doezelen,** v.t. to stump (*art*); to drowse. **·doezelig,** a. blurred; drowsy.
dof, -ffe, a. dull (*colour, sound*); lack-lustre.
·doffer, -s, n. pigeon (*male*).
·dofheid, no pl., n. dullness.
dog, -ggen, n. mastiff, bulldog.
·dogger, -s, n. cod-fisher. **·doggerboot, -boten,** n. dogger.
dok, -kken, n.n. dock (*for ships*). **·dokken, dok,** v.t. & v.i. to dock (*of ships*); to fork out (*money*).
·dokkeblaren, pl. only, n.n. dock-leaves.
·dokter, -s, n. doctor, physician. *onder ~s handen,* under medical treatment. **·dokteren,** v.i. to doctor.
·dokwerker, -s, n. docker, dock-labourer, stevedore.
dol, -llen, n. thole, rowlock. ¶ **-lle,** a. mad, frantic; stripped (*of screw*). *een dolle streek,* a mad prank; *~ zijn op,* to be crazy about; *be very fond of; ~ van vreugde,* mad with joy; *om ~ te worden,* enough to drive one mad. *See* **dolle.** ¶ *adv.* frantically. *~ verliefd,* madly in love.
·dolappel, -s, n. thorn-apple.
·dolblij, a. mad with joy.
·dolboord, n.n. gunwale.
·doldriest, a. foolhardy, dare-devil. **dol·driestheid,** no pl., n. dare-devilry. **·doldriftig,** a. hot-headed. **dol·driftigheid,** no pl., n. hot-headedness; frenzy.
·dolen, dool, v.i. to wander; to err.
do·lerend, a. dissenting, Noncomformist (*Dutch Protestant sect*).
dol·fijn, n. dolphin.
·dolgraag, adv. with the greatest pleasure.
·dolheid, -heden, n. madness, frenzy; wildness; prank.
dolk, n. dagger. **·dolkmes, -ssen,** n.n. (kind of) bowie-knife.

·dolkop, -ppen, *n.* hothead, madcap.
·dolksteek, -steken, *n.*, ·dolkstoot, -stoten, *n.* stab, dagger-thrust.
·dollarprinses, -ssen, *n.* American heiress.
·dolle, no pl., *n.n.* *door het* ~ *heen*, overexcited *or* like mad. ·dolle·kervel, no pl., *n.* hemlock. ·dolleman, no pl., *n.* (*fig.*) madman. ·dollemanspraat, no pl., *n.* mad *or* wild talk. ·dollemanswerk, no pl., *n.n.* sheer madness. ·dolprettig, *a.* very pleasant. ·dolveel, *adv.* ever so much. ~ *houden van*, to be extremely fond of.
dol·zinnig, *a.* mad, frantic. dol·zinnigheid, -heden, *n.* madness.
dom, -mme, *a.* stupid, dull, foolish. *hij is niet zo* ~, he is no fool; *dat is nog zo* ~ *niet*, that is not a bad idea. *See* domme. ¶*adv.* stupidly. *zich* ~ *houden*, to pretend ignorance. ¶-mmen, *n.* cathedral; dome (*of church; of engine*). do·mein, *n.n.* domain; crown land. ·domheer, -heren, *n.* canon, prebendary. ·domheid, -heden, *n.* stupidity.
domi·cilie, -s *or* -liën, *n.n.* domicile. domicili·ëren, -lieer, *v.t.* to domicile.
·dominee, -s, *n.* rector, vicar, parson (*Protestant clergyman*). ·domineesvrouw, *n.* clergyman's wife.
·domino, -'s, *n.* domino. ·dominoën, -no, *v.i.* to play dominoes. ·domino-spel, -llen, *n.n.* (game of) dominoes. ·domino-steen, -stenen, *n.* domino.
·domkapittel, -s, *n.n.* chapter (*of cathedral*). ·domkerk, *n.* cathedral; minster.
·domme, no pl., *n.* *zich van den* ~ *houden*, to sham ignorance. ·dommekracht, *n.* jack, jack-screw.
·dommel, no pl., *n.* *in de* ~, in a doze. ·dommelen, *v.i.* to doze. ·dommelig, *a.* drowsy. ·dommerik, -kken, *n.*, ·domoor, -moren, *n.* stupid person.
dompelaar, -s, *n.* diver (*bird*); plunger. ·dompelen, *v.t.* to plunge, immerse. ·dompeling, *n.* plunge, immersion. ·domper, -s, *n.* extinguisher. ·dompig, *a.* close, stuffy.
·domproost, *n.* dean (*of chapter*). ·domtoren, -s, *n.* cathedral tower.
·Donau, *N.* Danube. ¶*prefix.* Danubian.
·donder, -s, *n.* thunder. *door de* ~ *getroffen*, thunder-struck; *een arme* ~ (*coll.*), a poor fellow; *geen* ~ (*vulg.*), not a damn; *iemand op zijn* ~ *geven* (*vulg.*), to beat *or* go for a person. ·donderbui, *n.* thunderstorm. ·donderbus, -ssen, *n.* blunderbuss. ·donderdag, *n.* Thursday. ·donderdags, | *a.* (of) Thursday(s). ·donderen, *v.i.* to thunder; to fling; to fall. *het kan niet* ~ (*vulg.*), it doesn't matter; *hij keek of hij het in Keulen hoorde* ~, he looked thunderstruck; *van de trap* ~, to fall *or* be thrown downstairs. ·donderend, *a.* thunderous, roaring. ·donderjagen, -jaag, *v.i.* (*coll.*) to make a fuss, badger. ·donderkop, -ppen,

n. thunder cloud. ·donderpad, -dden, *n.* miller's thumb (*fish*). ·donders, *a.* (*coll.*) damn, thundering. ¶*adv.* ~ *goed*, damn well. ·donderslag, *n.* thunderclap.
·donker, *a.* dark; gloomy. ¶no pl., *n.n.* *tussen licht en* ~, at *or* by twilight; *bij* ~, during the hours of darkness; *vóór* ~, before dark; *in het* ~, in darkness; *na* ~, after dark; *in het* ~ *tasten* (*fig.*), to grope in the darkness; *tegen* ~, about dusk.
dons, no pl., *n.n.* down, fluff. ·donsachtig, *a.* downy, fluffy. ·donzen, *a.* (made with) down. ·donzig, *a.* downy.
dood, dode, *a.* dead. *zo* ~ *als een pier*, as dead as a doornail; *op sterven na* ~, all but dead; ~ *getij* *or* ~ *tij*, neaptide; *de dode hand*, mortmain; *op het dode puntkomen*, to reach a deadlock; ~ *verklaren*, to ostracise; *zich* ~ *houden*, to sham death; *zich* ~ *lachen*, to die with laughing; *zich* ~ *schrikken*, to be scared to death. ¶no pl., *n.* death. *een kind des* ~*s*, a dead man; *zo bang als de* ~, mortally afraid; *de* ~ *voor ogen hebben*, to face death; *de* ~ *sterven (stilted)*, to die; *de* ~ *vinden*, to meet one's death; *in* or *na de* ~, after death; *met de* ~ *straffen*, to punish by death; *om de* ~ *niet!*, not on your life!; *ten dode opgeschreven*, doomed *or* doomed to failure; *ter* ~ *brengen*, to execute; *ter* ~ *veroordelen*, to condemn to death; *tot in den* ~ *getrouw*, faithful unto death; *uit den* ~ *opstaan*, to rise from the dead. ·doodaf, *a.* dead-beat. ·doodakte, -n, *n.* certificate of death. ·doodarm, *a.* poor as a church-mouse. ·doodbedaard, *a.* perfectly composed, cool as cucumber. ·doodbidder, -s, *n.* mute, undertaker's man. ·doodbijten, *v.t.s.*, *str.* to bite to death. ·doodblijven, blijf dood, *v.i.s.*, *str.* to be killed. ·doodbloeden, *v.i.s.* to bleed to death. ·dooddoener, -s, *n.* knock-down argument, stumper. ·dooddrukken, druk dood, *v.t.s.* to crush to death. ·doodeenvoudig, *a.* dead easy, very simple. ·doodeter, -s, *n.* idler. ·doodfamiliaar, -iare, *a.* very familiar. ·doodgaan, ga dood, *v.i.s.*, *irr.* to die. ·doodgeboren, *a.* stillborn. ·doodgemakkelijk, *a.* dead easy. ·doodgemoedereerd, *a.* entirely unconcerned. ·doodgewoon, -wone, *a.* quite ordinary. ·doodgoed, *a.* extremely kind. ·doodgooien, *v.t.s.* to stone to death. ·doodgraver, -s, *n.* grave-digger; gravedigger (*beetle*). ·doodhongeren, *v.i.s.* to starve to death. ·doodjammer, *a.* *het is* ~, it is a great pity. ·doodkist, *n.* coffin. ·doodkloppertje, -s, *n.n.* deathwatch beetle. ·doodleuk, *a.* quite coolly, quietly humorous. ·doodliggen, *v.t.s.*, *str.* to overlay (*child*). ·doodlopen, *v.i.s.*, *str.* to come to dead end. ·doodmoe, *a.* tired to death. ·doodnuchter, *a.* quite sober. ·doodonschuldig, *a.* perfectly innocent.

·doodop, *a.* dead-beat. **doods,** *a.* deathly, deathlike. ·doodsangst, *n.* mortal fear, terror. ~ *uitslaan,* to be in a state of terror. ·doodsbang, *a.* mortally afraid. ·doodsbeenderen, pl. only, *n.n.* bones (*human skeleton*). ·doodsbenauwd, *a.* scared to death. ·doodsbericht, *n.n.* obituary notice. ·doodsbleek, -bleke, *a.* deathly pale. ·doodschamen, zich, schaam dood, *v.r.s.* to be desperately ashamed. ·doodschieten, *v.t.s.,* str. to shoot (dead). ·doodsengel, -s *or* -en, *n.* angel of death. ·doodshoofd, *n.n.* skull, death's head. ·doodshoofdvlinder, -s, *n.* death's head moth. ·doodskleur, *n.* livid colour. ·doodsklok, -kken, *n.* death-knell, passing-bell. ·doodslaan, sla dood, *v.t.s.,* irr. to kill, beat to death; swat. ·doodslag, no pl., *n.* manslaughter, homicide. ·doodschrik, no pl., *n.* mortal fright. *iemand de* ~ *op het lijf jagen,* to frighten a person to death. ·doodsteek, -steken, *n.* deathblow. ·doodstil, -lle, *a.* stock-still. ·doodstraf, no pl., *n.* capital punishment, death penalty. ·doodstrijd, no pl., *n.* agony; death struggle. ·doodsverachtig, no pl., *n.* contempt for death. ·doodtrappen, trap dood, *v.t.s.* to kick to death. ·doodvallen, val dood, *v.t.s.,* str. to drop (down) dead. ·doodvijand, *n.* mortal enemy. ·doodvonnis, -ssen, *n.n.* sentence of death. ·doodvriezen, vries dood, *v.i.s.,* irr. to freeze to death. ·doodwerken, zich, *v.r.s.* to work oneself to death. ·doodziek, *a.* dangerously ill. ·doodzonde, -n, *n.* deadly sin. ·doodzwak, -kke, *a.* extremely weak. ·doodzwijgen, *v.t.s.,* str. to ignore, take no notice of. **doof, dove,** *a.* deaf. *dove kool,* dead coal; *zo* ~ *als een kwartel,* as deaf as a post; ~ *aan zijn rechter oor,* deaf in his right ear; ~ *zijn voor,* to be deaf to; *Oostindisch* ~ *zijn* or *zich* ~ *houden,* to turn a deaf ear. ·doofachtig, *a.* slightly deaf. ·doofheid, no pl., *n.* deafness. ·doofpot, -tten, *n.* extinguisher of burning coals. *iets in de* ~ *stoppen,* to hush something up. doof·stom, -mme, *a.* deaf and dumb. doof·stomheid, no pl., *n.* deaf-and-dumbness. doof·stomme, -n, *n.* deaf-mute.

dooi, no pl., *n.* thaw. ·dooien, *v.i.,* imp. to thaw. ·dooiweer, no pl., *n.n.* thaw.

·dooie, *a.* *een* ~ *boel,* a dull show. *See* **dood.** ·dooier, -s, *n.* yolk.

·doolhof, -ven, *n.* labyrinth, maze. ·doolweg, *n.* wrong way. *op een* ~ *geraken,* to go astray.

doop, no pl., *n.* baptism, christening. *ten* ~ *houden,* to present at the font. ·doopjurk, *n.* christening-gown. ·doopmaal, -malen, *n.n.* christening feast. ·doopnaam, -namen, *n.* baptismal name. ·doopsel, -s, *n.n.* baptism. **Doopsge·zind,** *a.* of the Baptist faith. **Doopsge·zinde,** -n, *n.* Baptist. ·doopvont, *n.* (baptismal) font.

door, *prep.* through; throughout; by; on account of. ¶*adv.* through; on. *het hele jaar* ~, all through the year; *de hele wereld* ~, all the world over; *het kan er* ~, it can pass; *er* ~ *zijn,* to have got through; ~ *en* ~, thoroughly, through and through. ¶*prefix. meaning:* through *or* on. door·aderd, *a.* veined. door·bakken, *a.* well baked, baked right through. ·doorboren, **boor door,** *v.i.s.* to pierce, perforate; to bore through. door·boren, -boor, *v.t.* to run through, transfix (*with sword; glance*); to riddle (*with bullets*); to tunnel. ·doorbraak, -braken, *n.* burst, breaking (*of dike*); breach (*of front line*). ·doorbranden, *v.i.s.* to burn on. ¶*v.t.s.* to burn through. ·doorbreken, **breek door,** *v.t.s.,* str. to break; to burst. ·doorbrengen, *v.t.s.,* irr. to spend, pass (*time*). ·doorbuigen, *v.i.s.,* str. to bend; to sag. door·dacht, *a.* well thought-out. door·dat, *c.* because. door·dien, *c.* (*stilted*) as, since. ·doordraaier, -s, *n.* profligate. ·doordraven, **draaf door,** *v.i.s.* to trot on; to run on; to rattle on (*talking*). ·doordraver, -s, *n.* person who talks at length without reflection. ·doordrijven, **drijf door,** *v.t.s.,* str. *zijn wil* ~, to have one's own way, carry one's point. ·doordrijver, -s, *n.* persistent person. doordrijve·rij, *n.* persistence. door·dringbaar, -bare, *a.* permeable, pervious. door·dringbaarheid, no pl., *n.* permeability, perviousness. ·doordringen, *v.i.s.,* str. to penetrate; ~ *in,* to penetrate into; ~ *tot,* to reach *or* to dawn on. door·dringen, *v.t.,* str. to penetrate, permeate, pervade. ~ *van,* to make fully conscious of. door·dringend, *a.* penetrating, piercing. ·doordringingsvermogen, no pl., *n.n.* penetrative power. ·doordrukken, **druk door,** *v.t.s.* to push through. ¶*v.i.s.* to·print on. door·een, *adv.* all mixed; pell-mell, higgledy-piggledy. ~ *genomen,* on an average. door·eenhalen, **haal dooreen,** *v.t.s.,* door·eenhaspelen, *v.t.s.* to muddle. door·eenschudden, **schud dooreen,** *v.t.s.* to jolt, shake up. door·eenvlechten, *v.t.s.* to interlace. door·eenweven, **weef dooreen,** *v.t.s.,* irr. to interweave. ·doorgaan, **ga door,** *v.i.s.,* irr. to go on. *niet* ~, to be called off; ~ *met,* to carry on with; ~ *op* or *over,* to pursue (*subject*); *er van* ~, to run away, make oneself scarce; ~ *voor,* to pass for. ·doorgaand, *a.* through (*of traffic*). ·doorgaans, *adv.* generally, usually. ·doorgang, *n.* passage. *geen* ~, no thoroughfare. ·doorgestoken, *a.* *een* ~ *kaart,* a put-up job. ·doorgeven, **geef door,** *v.t.s.,* str. to pass (on). ·doorgoed, *a.* thoroughly kind(-hearted). ·doorgraven, **graaf door,** *v.t.s.,* str. to dig through; to cut through (*digging*). ·doorgraving, *n.* cutting (*digging, e.g. through isthmus*). ·doorhakken, **hak door,** *v.t.s.* to cut through (with axe, sword). ·doorhalen, haal door, v.t.s. to pull through; to cross out. iemand duchtig ∼, to haul someone over the coals. door·heen, adv. through. door·heenslaan, sla doorheen, v.i.s.r., irr. zich er ∼, to fight one's way through, pull through. ·doorheet, -hete, a. boiling hot. ·doorjager, -s, n. thin person who eats a lot. door·kneed, a. ∼ zijn in, to be well versed in. ·doorkomen, v.i.s., irr. to get through. er is geen ∼ aan, it is impossible to get through. ¶v.t.s., irr. to pass. door·kruisen, v.t. to cross; to range (over). ·doorlaten, laat door, v.t.s., str. to let through; to transmit (light). ·doorlopen, loop door, v.i.s., str. to walk on; to mend one's pace, walk more quickly. ¶v.t.s., str. to walk or wear through (soles), become footsore. door·lopen, -loop, v.t., str. to go or run through. door·lopend, a. continuous. ¶adv. continuously, consecutively. door·luchtig, a. illustrious; serene (in title). door·luchtigheid. -heden, n. illustriousness; Serene Highness. ·doormaken, maak door, v.t.s. to go or live through. ·doormars, n. march-through. door·midden, adv. in two, in half.

doorn, n. thorn. een ∼ in het oog, a thorn in the flesh. ·doornachtig, a. thorny; spinous. ·doornappel, -s, n. thorn-apple. ·doornbos, -ssen, n.n. bramble-bush. ·doornen, a. thorny. ·doornenkroon, -kronen, n. crown of thorns. ·doornhaai, n. dogfish (shark). ·doornig, a. thorny. ·Doornik n.N. Tournai. ·Doornroosje, n.N. The Sleeping Beauty. ·doornstruik, n. thorn-bush.

·doornat, -tte, a. wet through. ·doorploegen, v.i.s. to keep on ploughing. door·ploegen, v.t.s. to plough (sea). door·regen, a. streaky (bacon). ·doorreis, -zen, n. journey (through). ·doorrijden, v.i.s., str. to ride or drive on. ¶v.t.s., str. to ride or drive through. ·doorroker, -s, n. (kind of) pipe (which colours on smoking). ·doorschemeren, v.i. to glimmer through. iets laten ∼, to intimate something. ·doorschieten, v.i.s., str. to continue shooting. door·schieten, v.t.s., str. to interleave. door·schijnend, a. translucent, diaphanous. ·doorschrappen, schrap door, v.t.s. to cross out. ·doorslaan, sla door, v.t.s., irr. to beat, drive through. ¶v.i.s., irr. to go on beating; to tip the beam (of scales); to race (propeller); to blether. ¶v.r.s. zich er ∼, to fight one's way through. ·doorslaand, a. conclusive. ·doorslag, n. punch (tool); (carbon) copy; makeweight. de ∼ geven, to turn the scale. ·doorsnede, -n, n. section. dwarse ∼, transverse section; overlangse ∼, longitudinal section. ·doorsnee, no pl., n. in ∼, on an average. door·spekken, -spek, v.t. to lard, interlard. door·staan, -sta, v.t., irr. to stand, sustain; to bear, endure, de proef ∼, to stand the test. ·doorsteken,

steek door, v.t.s., str. to pierce; cut (dyke). ·doorsteker, -s, n. pipe-cleaner. ·doortasten, v.i.s. to go ahead, act energetically. door·tastend, a. energetic; sweeping. door·tastendheid, no pl., n. energy. door·timmerd, a. goed ∼, well built (house). ·doortocht, n. passage, march through. de ∼ versperren, to bar the way; zich een ∼ banen, to force one's way through. door·trapt, a. consummate, out-and-out. door·traptheid, no pl., n. cunning. ·doortrekken, trek door, v.t.s., str. to pull through; to produce (line); to extend, push on (railway, road). door·trekken, -trek, v.t., str. to permeate, pervade. doortrokken van or met, soaked or permeated with. ·doorvaart, n. passage (by water). door·voed, a. well-fed. ·doorvoer, n. transit. ·doorvoeren, v.t.s. to convey in transit; to carry through (plan); to sustain (part). door·waadbaar, -bare, a. fordable. doorwaadbare plaats, ford. door·weekt, a. sodden. door·wrocht, a. elaborate. ·doorzetten, zet door, v.t.s. to carry through; to persist; to press (attack); to persevere. ·doorzettingsvermogen, no pl., n.n. perseverance, doggedness. ·doorzicht. n.n. penetration, perspicacity, insight. door·zichtig, a. transparent; obvious. ·doorzien, zie door, v.t.s., irr. (lit.) to see through. door·zien, -zie, v.t., irr. (fig.) to see through, penetrate, read. door·zoeken, v.t., irr. to search, ransack, comb.

doos, ·dozen, n. box; (small) case; quod, jug (slang for prison). een blikken ∼, a tin; uit de oude ∼, old-fashioned; iemand in de ∼ stoppen (slang), to shove someone in quod. ·doosvrucht, n. capsule (of seed).

dop, ·ppen, n. shell (egg, nut); pod, shuck (pea, bean); cup (acorn); husk (seeds in general); cap, top (bottle); (fac.) top-hat, bowler; (fac.) pl. eyes. ·doperwt, n. green pea. ·dopheide, no pl., n. heather. ·doppen, dop, v.t. to shell, shuck (peas). ·dopper, -s, n., ·doppertje, -s, n.n. See doperwt.

·dopeling, n. child or person being baptized. ·dopen, doop, v.t. to baptize, christen; to name (ship). de melk ∼, to water the milk. ·doper, -s, n. baptizer. Johannes de D∼, John the Baptist.

dor, -rre, a. dry, withered; arid, barren. ·dorheid, no pl., n. dryness, aridity.

Dordt, n.N. Dordrecht. Dordts, a. from or of Dordrecht.

·doren, -s, n. See doorn.

·Dorisch, a. Doric.

dorp, n.n. village. op een ∼ wonen, to live in a village. ·dorpachtig, a. village-like. ·dorpeling, n. villager. ·dorper, -s, n. villain, villein; boor. dorps, a. countrified, rustic. ¶adv. in rustic fashion. ¶prefix. (of a) village. ·dorpshoofd, n.n. village headman (East Indies).

·dorpel, -s, n. threshold.

·dorren, dor, *v.t.* & *v.i.* to wither.
dors, *n.* torsk.
·dorsen, *v.t.* & *v.i.* to thresh. ·dorser, -s, *n.* thresher. ·dorsmachine, -s, *n.* threshing machine. ·dorsvlegel, -s, *n.* flail. ·dorsvloer, *n.* threshing floor.
dorst, no pl., *n.* thirst. ~ *hebben*, to be thirsty; ~ *krijgen*, to become thirsty; *de* ~ *lessen*, to slake one's thirst; *van* ~ *versmachten*, to be parched with thirst; *een* ~ *naar*, a thirst for *or* after. ·dorsten, *v.i.* ~ *naar*, to thirst for *or* after. ·dorstig, *a.* thirsty. ·dorstlessend, *a.* thirst-quenching.
dos, no pl., *n.* attire; (*poetic*) raiment. ·dossen, dos, *v.t.* to attire.
·dosis, -issen, *n.* dose. *te grote* ~, overdose.
dot, -tten, *n.* knot, tuft; pet (*term of endearment*). *een* ~ *van een kind*, a little angel.
·dotterbloem, *n.* kingcup, marsh marigold.
dou·ane, no pl., *n.* Customs, custom house. *ambtenaar van de* ~, customs officer. dou·anerechten, *pl.* only, *n.n.* customs duties, customs. doua·nier, -s, *n.* customs officer.
douai·rière, -s, *n.* dowager.
dou·blé, no pl., *n.n.* plated gold *or* silver. dou·bleren, -bleer, *v.t.* to double. dou·blure, -s, *n.* understudy.
dou·ceurtje, -s, *n.n.* (*fig.*) windfall; tip.
·douw(en), *v.t.* See duw(en).
·dove, -n, *n.* deaf person. *voor* ~*n preken*, to preach to deaf ears. ·doveman, no pl., *n. aan* ~*s deur kloppen*, to talk to the wind. ·doven, doof, *v.t.* to extinguish; to dim; to damp down, cover (*fire*). dove·netel, -s, *n.* dead-nettle. ·dovig, *a.* hard of hearing.
·dozenmaker, -s, *n.* box-maker.
do·zijn, *n.n.* dozen. ~*en* . . . , dozens of . . .
draad, draden, *n.* thread; (screw-)thread; filament; string, fibre; wire. *er loopt een rode* ~ *door*, they have the same failing; *een* ~*je alle dagen maakt een hemdsmouw in het jaar*, every little helps; *de* ~ *in handen hebben*, to hold the clues; *ergens mee voor de* ~ *komen*, to come out with something; *met or tegen de* ~, with *or* against the grain; *tot op de* ~ *versleten*, threadbare, worn to a thread. ·draadloos, -loze, *a.* wireless. ¶*adv.* by wireless. ·draadnagel, -s, *n.* wire-nail. ·draadschaar, -scharen, *n.* wire-cutter. ·draadtang, *n.* (pair of) pliers. ·draadtrekken, no pl., *n.n.* wiredrawing. draadtrekke·rij, *n.* wire-drawing mill. ·draadvormig, *a.* threadlike. ·draadworm, *n.* threadworm.
·draagbaar, -bare, *a.* portable; wearable. ¶-baren, *n.* stretcher. ·draagbalk, *n.* girder. ·draagkracht, no pl., *n.* capacity (*for loads; taxation*); range (*of gun; voice*). ·draaglijk, *a.* tolerable; passable. · ·draagloon, -lonen, *n.n.* porterage. ·draagvermogen, no pl., *n.n.* (*carrying*) capacity. ·draagvlak,

-kken, *n.n.* carrying plane. ·draagwijdte, no pl., *n.* range (*of gun*).
draai, *n.* turn, twist; turning, bend. *een* ~ *om de oren*, a box on the ears. ·draaibaar, -bare, *a.* revolving. ·draaiband, *n.* lathe. ·draaibord, *n.n.* turn-table (*for games, etc.*). ·draaibrug, -ggen, *n.* swivel bridge. ·draaien, *v.i.* to turn, spin, revolve; to equivocate, twist. *mijn hoofd draait*, my head is swimming; *met alle winden* ~, to agree with everybody; ~ *om*, to revolve on; *er omheen* ~, to beat about the bush. ¶*v.t.* to turn; to wind. ¶*v.r. zich eruit* ~, to wriggle out of it. ·draaiend, *a.* rotatory. ·draaier, -s, *n.* turner; twister. ·draaierig, *a.* dizzy, giddy. ·draaierigheid, no pl., *n.* giddiness. draaie·rij, *n.* turnery; prevarication; (*slang*) funny business. *met* ~*en omgaan*, to be unreliable. ·draaigewricht, *n.n.* pivot joint. ·draaihals, -zen, *n.* wryneck. ·draaiing, *n.* turn, rotation. ·draaikever, -s, *n.* whirligig (*beetle*). ·draaikolk, *n.* whirlpool, eddy. ·draaikrukje, -s, *n.n.* revolving stool. ·draaimolen, -s, *n.* merry-go-round. ·draaiorgel, -s, *n.n.* barrel-organ. ·draaipunt, *n.n.* centre of rotation. ·draaischijf, -ven, *n.* turn-table (*for locomotives, etc.*); potter's wheel. ·draaispil, -llen, *n.* capstan. ·draaispit, -tten, *n.n.* spit (*roasting*). ·draaistroom, -stromen, *n.* whirlpool; rotatory current. ·draaitrap, -ppen, *n.* spiral staircase. ·draaiziekte, no pl., *n.* staggers.
draak, draken, *n.* dragon. *de* ~ *steken met*, to poke fun at, ridicule; *gevleugelde* ~, winged dragon, wyvern.
drab, drabbe, no pl., *n.* dregs, lees. ·drabbig, *a.* murky, thick.
dracht, *n.* dress, costume, wear (*in general*); litter (*of animals*). ·drachtig, *a.* with young, pregnant (*of animals*).
·draderig, *a.* thready, stringy; ropy.
draf, no pl., *n.* trot; swill, hogwash. *in snelle* ~, at a brisk trot; *in gestrekte or volle* ~, at full trot; *op een* ~, at a trot; *het op een* ~*je zetten*, to break into a trot (*of person*).
·dragelijk, *a.* bearable. ·dragen, draag, *v.t.*, *str.* to bear, carry; to wear. *iemand op de handen* ~, to worship a person. ¶*v.i.*, *str.* to bear (fruit); to be strong enough (*of ice*); to carry, be pregnant (*of animals*). ·drager, -s, *n.* bearer; carrier, porter.
dra·gon, no pl., *n.* tarragon.
dra·gonder, -s, *n.* dragoon.
drai·neren, -neer, *v.t.* to drain.
·drakenbloed, no pl., *n.n.* blood-wort, bloody dock.
·dralen, draal, *v.i.* to linger, tarry; to hesitate. ·draler, -s, *n.* dawdler; laggard. ·dralend, *a.* hesitating.
·drama, -'s, *n.n.* drama; tragedy. dra·matisch, *a.* dramatic. drama·turg, *n.* dramatist.

drang, no pl., *n.* urge, impulse; pressure. ~ *naar,* urge to; *onder de* ~ *der omstandigheden,* under the stress of circumstances. **drank,** *n.* drink, beverage; alcoholic liquor. *See* **drankje.** *aan de* ~ *raken,* to take to drink; *aan de* ~ *zijn,* to be given to drinking. **·drankbestrijding,** *n.* temperance movement. **·drankfles, -ssen,** *n.* spirits-flask. **·drankflesje, -s,** *n.n.* medicine bottle. **·drankgelegenheid, -heden,** *n.* place for sale of drink. **·drankje, -s,** *n.n.* draught, potion. **·drankoffer, -s,** *n.n.* libation, drink-offering. **·drankorgel, -s,** *n.n.* drunken sot. **·drankverbod,** no pl., *n.n.* prohibition. **·drankvergunning,** *n.* licence (*for sale of alcoholic liquors*). **·drankwet, -tten,** *n.* licensing act. **·drankzucht,** no pl., *n.* dipsomania. **drank·zuchtige, -n,** *n.* dipsomaniac.

dra·peren, -peer, *v.t.* to drape.

dras, -sse, *a.* soggy, marshy. **·drasland,** *n.n.* marshy ground, marshland. **·drassig,** *a.* marshy, swampy. **·drassigheid,** no pl., *n.* marshiness.

·drastisch, *a.* drastic.

·draven, draaf, *v.i.* to trot.

dreef, dreven, *n.* avenue, lane. *op* ~, in form; *iemand op* ~ *helpen,* to give someone a start; *op* ~ *komen,* to get into one's stride; *op* ~ *zijn,* to be in good vein.

dreg, -ggen, *n.* drag, grapnel, grappling iron. **·dreganker, -s,** *n.n.* grapnel. **·dreggen, dreg,** *v.i.* to drag (*water for body or for fish*). ~ *naar* . . . to drag for . . . **·dreghaak, -haken,** *n.* grapple. **·dregnet, -tten,** *n.n.* trawl, drag-net.

·dreigbrief, -ven, *n.* threatening letter. **dreige·ment,** *n.n.* threat. **·dreigen,** *v.t.* & *v.i.* to threaten, menace; to threaten, be about to. **·dreigend,** *a.* menacing; lowering; imminent.

·dreinen, *v.i.* to whimper, whine.

drek, no pl., *n.* filth, ordure; (*animal*) excrement. **·drekkig,** *a.* mucky.

·drempel, -s, *n.* threshold, doorstep; bar (*of harbour*). *ergens de* ~ *platlopen,* to call frequently somewhere; *hij zal mijn* ~ *niet meer overschrijden,* he shall not darken my door again.

·drenkeling, *n.* drowning person; person drowned. **·drenken,** *v.t.* to water (*cattle*); to drench. **·drenkplaats,** *n.* watering place (*for cattle*). **drenktrog, -ggen,** *n.* drinking trough.

·drentelaar, -s, *n.* saunterer. **·drentelen,** *v.i.* to saunter, stroll.

dres·seren, -sseer, *v.t.* to train (*animals*). **dres·seur, -s,** *n.* (animal) trainer. **·dressuur,** no pl., *n.* training (*of animals*).

·dreumes, -ssen, *n.* toddler.

dreun, *n.* rumble, roar; drone (*monotonous voice*). *op een* ~, droning along (*in reading aloud*). **·dreunen,** *v.i.* to rumble, roar; to shake, vibrate; to drone.

·dreutel, -s, *n.* toddler. **·dreutelen,** *v.i.* to dawdle.

·drevel, -s, *n.* punch (*tool*). **·drevelen,** *v.t.* to punch (*holes*).

·dribbelaar, -s, *n.* toddler. **·dribbelen,** *v.i.* to toddle; to trip; to dribble.

drie, *num.* three. ~ *aan* ~, three by three. ¶-**ieën,** *n.* three. **drie·armig,** *a.* three-armed. **·driebladig,** *a.* trifoliate. **·driedaags,** *a.* three-day. **·driedekker, -s,** *n.* three-decker; triplane. **·driedelig,** *a.* tripartite. **·driedik, -kke,** *a.* three times as thick. **·driedistel, -s,** *n.* carline. **·driedubbel,** *a.* treble, threefold. **Drie·eenheid,** no pl., *n.* Trinity. **·drieën,** *num. met ons* ~, the three of us; *alle goeie dingen bestaan in* ~, third time lucky; *de trein van* ~, the three o'clock train; *bij* ~, just on three; *in* ~, into three; *met hun* ~, the three of them; *met z'n* ~, with two others. **drieërhande,** *a.*, **·drieërlei,** *a.* of three sorts. **·driehoek,** *n.* triangle; set square. **drie·hoekig,** *a.* triangular. **·driehoeksmeting,** *n.* trigonometry; triangulation. **·driehoofdig,** *a.* three-headed. **·driejaarlijks,** *a.* triennial. **·driekaart,** *n.* sequence of three (*cards*). **·driekantig,** *a.* triangular; trilateral; three-cornered (*hat*). **·drieklank,** *n.* triphthong. **·driekleur,** *n.* tricolour. **·driekleurendruk, -kken,** *n.* three-colour process. **·driekleurig,** *a.* three-coloured. **Drie·koningen,** no pl., *n.,* **Drie·koningenfeest,** *n.n.* Twelfth Night, Epiphany. **Drie·koningenavond,** *n.* eve of Twelfth Night. **·driekwart,** *num.* three-quarters. **·driekwartsmaat,** no pl., *n.* three-four measure. **·drieledig,** *a.* tripartite. **·drielettergrepig,** *a.* trisyllabic. **·drieling,** *n.* triplet(s). **·drieluik,** *n.n.* triptych. **·driemaal,** *a.* & *adv.* thrice, three times. **·driemaandelijks,** *a.* & *adv.* three-monthly, quarterly. **·driemanschap, -ppen,** *n.n.* triumvirate. **·driemaster, -s,** *n.* three-master. **·drieponder, -s,** *n.* three-pounder. **·driepoot, -poten,** *n.* tripod. **·drieslagstelsel,** no pl., *n.n.* rotation of crops. **·driesnarig,** *a.* three-stringed. **·driespan, -nnen,** *n.n.* team of three horses (*etc.*). **·driesprong,** *n.* three-forked road. *op de* ~, at the parting of the ways.

driest, *a.* bold, audacious. **·driestheid,** no pl., *n.* boldness.

·driestal, -llen, *n.* three-legged stool. **·driestemmig,** *a.* for three voices. **·drietal, -llen,** *n.n.* two or three. *het* ~, the three of them. **·drietand,** *n.* trident. **·drievoet,** *n.* tripod. **·drievoud,** *n.n.* treble. *in* ~, in triplicate. **drie·voudig,** *a.,* **drie·vuldig,** *a.* threefold; triple; tripartite. ¶ *adv.* three-fold. **Drie·vuldigheid,** no pl., *n.* Trinity. **Drie·vuldigheidsdag,** no pl., *n.* Trinity (*feast*). **·driewerf,** *adv.* three times, thrice. **·driewieler, -s,** *n.* tricycle. **·driezijdig,** *a.* three-sided, trilateral.

drift, *n.* passion (*usu: evil*); anger; precipitation; drove (*of oxen*); drift (*current*). *in ~*, in a fit of passion; *op ~ gaan*, to go adrift. ·**driftig**, *a.* hot-tempered, choleric; in a passion, angry; adrift. *~ worden* or *zich ~ maken*, to fly into a passion, lose one's temper. ¶*adv.* angrily. ·**driftigheid**, no pl., *n.* quickness of temper. ·**driftkop, -ppen,** *n.* hothead, spitfire.

·**drijfanker, -s,** *n.n.* drag-anchor, sea-anchor. ·**drijfas, -ssen,** *n.* driving shaft. ·**drijfhout,** no pl., *n.n.* drift-wood. ·**drijfijs, -s,** *n.n.* drift-ice. *tussen het ~ beklemd raken,* to be caught in the ice-floes. ·**drijfijzer, -s,** *n.n.* driving bolt. ·**drijfjacht,** *n.* drive, beat (*hunting, shooting*). *een ~ houden,* to beat up game. ·**drijfkracht,** no pl., *n.* motive power; driving force; moving spirit. ·**drijfnat, -tte,** *a.* soaking *or* sopping wet. ·**drijfnet, -tten,** *n.n.* drift-net. ·**drijfrad, -eren,** *n.n.* fly-wheel. ·**drijfriem,** *n.* conveyor (belt). ·**drijfstang,** *n.* connecting-rod. ·**drijftol, -llen,** *n.* whipping-top. ·**drijfveer, -veren,** *n.* mainspring; motive, incentive. ·**drijfwerk,** no pl., *n.n.* chased work. ·**drijfwiel,** *n.n.* fly-wheel. ·**drijfzand,** no pl., *n.n.* quicksand. ·**drijven, drijf,** *v.i.,* *str.* to float, be afloat; to swim (*of substance*); to waft; to drift, be adrift; to be soaking wet; to be fanatic. *het dreef van het bloed,* it was soaked with blood. ¶*v.t.,* *str.* to drive, propel; to urge on, impel; to carry on (*business*); to chase, emboss. *het te ver ~,* to carry matters too far; *in de hoogte ~,* to force up. ·**drijver, -s,** *n.* drover; float; fanatic. ·**drijve·rij,** *n.* zealotry.

dril, -llen, *n.* drill; jelly. ·**drilboor, -boren,** *n.* drill. ·**drillen, dril,** *v.t.* to drill, bore; to drill (*soldiers*).

·**dringen,** *v.t.,* *str.* & *v.i.,* *str.* to push, crowd, jostle; to press (*of time*). *~ door . . . ,* to force one's way through. . . . ¶*v.r.,* *str.* *zich ~ in,* to worm one's way into. ·**dringend,** *a.* urgent, pressing. ¶*adv.* urgently, earnestly.

·**drinkbaar, -bare, a.** drinkable, potable. ·**drinkbak, -kken,** *n.* drinking trough; water bowl. ·**drinkbakje, -s,** *n.n.* birdcage fountain. ·**drinkbeker, -s,** *n.* goblet. ·**drinkebroer, -s,** *n.* toper. ·**drinken,** *v.t.,* *str.* & *v.i.,* *str.* to drink; to absorb. *op iemands gezondheid ~,* to drink a person's health. ¶no pl., *n.n.* beverage. *eten en ~,* food and drink. ·**drinker, -s,** *n.* drinker. ·**drinkgelag,** *n.n.* drinking bout. ·**drinkgeld,** *n.n.* tip, gratuity. ·**drinkwater,** no pl., *n.n.* drinking water.

droef, -ve, *a.* sad. ·**droefenis,** no pl., *n.* grief, sorrow. ·**droef·geestig,** *a.* mournful, melancholy, gloomy. ·**droef·geestigheid,** no pl., *n.* melancholy, mournfulness. ·**droefheid,** no pl., *n.* sadness.

droes, no pl., *n.* glanders; devil. ·**droezig,** *a.* glandered.

·**droesem,** no pl., *n.* dregs, sediment. ·**droesemig,** *a.* grouty, dreggy.

·**droevig,** *a.* sad, sorrowful; pitiful.

·**drogbeeld,** *n.n.* illusion (*visual*).

·**droge,** no pl., *n.n.* *op het ~,* on dry land; *op het ~ brengen,* to land; *op het ~ zitten,* to be stranded; *hij heeft zijn schaapjes op het ~,* he has made his pile. ·**drogen,** *v.t.* & *v.i.* to dry. ·**droge·rij,** *n.* drying plant. ¶pl. only, *n.* drugs, druggist's stock. ·**dro·gist,** *n.* druggist. ·**drogiste·rij,** *n.* druggist's (shop).

·**drogrede, -nen,** *n.* sophism, fallacy. ·**drogredenaar, -s** *or* **-naren,** *n.* sophist.

drom, -mmen, *n.* throng. *dichte ~,* dense crowd.

drome·daris, -ssen, *n.* dromedary.

·**dromen, droom,** *v.t.* & *v.i.,* to dream. ·**dromer, -s,** *n.* dreamer, visionary. ·**dromerig,** *a.* dreamy. **drome·rij,** *n.* daydream, reverie.

·**drommel, -s,** *n.* devil, deuce. *wat ~!,* what the dickens; *om de ~ niet (slang),* by no means; *een arme ~,* a poor devil. ·**drommels,** *a.* confounded. ¶*adv.* devilish, exceedingly; (*coll.*) darned. ¶*int.* by Jove!

dronk, *n.* toast, drink, draught. *een ~ instellen,* to propose a toast. ·**dronkaard, -s,** *n.* drunkard. ·**dronkelap, -ppen,** *n.* (*coll.*) drunk. ·**dronkemansgebed,** no pl., *n.n.* *een ~ doen,* to count one's money. ·**dronkemanspraat,** no pl., *n.* maudlin talk. ·**dronken,** *a.* drunk. *~ van vreugde,* drunk with joy. ·**dronkenschap,** no pl., *n.* drunkenness, inebriation.

droog, droge, *a.* dry; arid, parched. *~ weer,* fine weather. See **droge.** ·**droogdok, -kken,** *n.n.* dry-dock. *drijvend ~,* floating dry-dock. ·**droogheid,** no pl., *n.* dryness. ·**droogje,** no pl., *n.n.* *op een ~ zitten,* to be drinking nothing. ·**droogjes,** *adv.* drily, with dry humour. ·**droogkamer, -s,** *n.* drying room. ·**droogkomiek,** *n.* dry humorist. ¶*a.* & *adv.* dryly humorous. ·**droogleggen,** leg droog, *v.t.s.* to drain, reclaim; to introduce prohibition. ·**drooglegging,** *n.* draining, reclamation; introduction of prohibition. ·**drooglijn,** *n.* clothesline. ·**drooglopen,** loop droog, *v.i.s.,* *str.* to run dry. ·**droogmaken,** maak droog, *v.t.s.* to dry; to reclaim (*by pumping*). ·**droogmake·rij,** *n.* reclaimed lake *or* swamp. ·**droogmalen,** maal droog, *v.t.s.* to reclaim (*pump dry*). ·**droogoven, -s,** *n.* dessicator, drying kiln. ·**droogpruimer, -s,** *n.* (*coll.*) dry old stick. ·**droograam, -ramen,** *n.n.* ·**droogrek, -kken,** *n.n.* drying frame *or* rack; clothes-horse. ·**droogscheren, -scheer,** *v.i.* to shear cloth. ·**droogstoppel, -s,** *n.* See **droogpruimer.** ·**droogte, -n,** *n.* dryness, drought; sandbank, shoal. ·**droogvoets,** *adv.* dry-shod. ·**droogweg,** *adv.* See **droogjes.** ·**droogzolder, -s.** *n.* drying loft.

droom, dromen, n. dream. *in dromen verzonken,* lost in dreams; *iemand uit de ～ helpen,* to undeceive someone. ·**droombeeld,** *n.n.* vision, illusion.

drop, -ppen, n. drop; drip. ¶no pl., n. *een pijp ～,* a stick of licorice. ·**dropje, -s,** *n.n.* Pontefract cake, *etc.* ·**droppel, -s,** n. See **druppel. drops,** no pl., n. licorice. ·**dropwater,** no pl., *n.n.* licorice water.

·**drossen, dros,** *v.i.* to run away, desert.

dru·ïde, -n, n. druid.

druif, -ven, n. grape. ·**druifluis, -zen,** n. phylloxera.

·**druilen,** *v.i.* to mope. ·**druilerig, -e** a. mopish; drizzling. ·**druiloor, -oren,** n. person who mopes. **druil·orig,** a. moping, mopish.

druipen, *v.i., str.* to drip; to run, gutter (*of candle*); to be sopping wet; to be ploughed (*exam.*) ～ *van,* to drip with. ·**druipnat, -tte,** n. dripping wet. ·**druipneus, -zen,** n. wet nose; sniveller. ·**druipstaartend,** a. with (his) tail between (his) legs. ·**druipsteen,** no pl., n. calcareous deposit. ¶**-stenen,** n. stalactite, stalagmite. ·**druipsteengrot, -tten** n. cave with stalactites.

·**druisen,** *v.i.* to roar, rush (*of water*).

·**druiveblad, -eren** *or* **-blaren,** *n.n.* vine-leaf. ·**druivennat,** no pl., *n.n.* (*stilled*) wine. ·**druivenpit, -tten,** n. grape-stone. ·**druivenplukken,** no pl., *n.n.* vintage. ·**druivensap,** no pl., *n.n.* grape-juice. ·**druivenschil, -llen,** n. grape-skin. ·**druiventros, -ssen,** n. bunch of grapes.

druk, -kke, a. busy; brisk; lively, restless. *het ～ hebben,* to be busy; *zich ～ maken over,* to get excited about. ¶*adv.* busily. ～ *bezig,* very busy; ～ *gebruik maken van,* to make great *or* frequent use of. ¶no pl., n. pressure; print, type; printing, edition. ～ *uitoefenen op,* to exert pressure, put pressure on, bring pressure to bear on; *onder hoge ～,* at high pressure. ·**drukfout,** n. printer's error, misprint. ·**drukken, druk,** *v.t.* to press; to squash, squeeze; to weigh upon; to force down; to print. *iemand aan zijn hart ～,* to press someone to one's heart; *iemand iets op het hart ～,* to impress something on a person. ¶*v.i.* to press. ～ *op,* to press (*button*). ·**drukkend,** a. oppressive; burdensome; sultry, close. ·**drukker, -s,** n. printer. **drukke·rij,** n. printing office. **drukkers·knecht, -s** *or* **-en,** n. journeyman printer. **drukkers·jongen, -s,** n. printer's devil. **drukkerspa·troon, -tronen,** n. master-printer. ·**drukknoopje, -s,** n. press-stud; popper. ·**drukkunst,** no pl., n. art of printing, typography. ·**drukletter, -s,** n. type; block letter. ·**drukpers,** n. (printing-)press. *vrijheid van ～,* freedom of the press. ·**drukproef, -ven,** n. printing proof. ·**drukte**, no pl., n. great deal of work, rush; excitement, to-do; bustle (*of crowd*); swank. *kouwe ～*, swank; ～ *maken,* to make a fuss

or to swank. ·**druktemaker, -s,** n. braggart, pretentious person. ·**drukwerk,** *n.n.* printed matter.

drup, n. See **drop.** ·**druppel,** n. drop; drip. *op elkaar lijken als twee ～s water,* to be as like as two peas. ·**druppelen,** *v.i.* to drop, drip, trickle. ·**druppelfiesje, -s,** *n.n.* dropping bottle. ·**druppelsgewijs,** *adv.* drop by drop; by driblets.

d-trein, n. corridor train.

·**dubbel,** a. double; dual. ～*e bodem,* false bottom; ～*e deur,* folding doors; *de ～e prijs,* double the price. ¶*adv.* doubly. *hij heeft het ～ en dwars verdiend,* he has more than deserved it; ～ *zo groot,* twice as large. ¶*n.n.* double. *het ～e van de waarde,* double the value. ·**dubbelen,** *v.t.* to double. ·**dubbelganger, -s,** n. double twin (*in appearance*). ·**dubbel·hartig,** a. double-faced. **dubbel·koolzuur, -zure,** a. bicarbonate of. ·**dubbelkruis,** *n.n.* double sharp (*music*). ·**dubbelmol, -llen,** n. double flat (*music*). ·**dubbelspoor,** no pl., *n.n.* double track (*railway*). ·**dubbeltje, -s,** *n.n.* silver coin of 10 Dutch cents. *het is een ～ op zijn kant,* the outcome is very uncertain; *het is vreemd, hoe een ～ rollen kan,* life contains many surprises. ·**dubbeltjeskwestie, -s,** n. a matter of £.s.d. **dubbel·zinnig,** a. ambiguous; equivocal; with double meaning (*joke*). **dubbel·zinnigheid, -heden,** n. ambiguity; double entendre.

dubi·eus, -ze, a. dubious, doubtful.

duc·dalf, -ven, n. See **dukdalf.**

·**duchten,** *v.t.* to dread, apprehend. ·**duchtig,** a. strong, terrible. ¶*adv.* fearfully, terribly. *iemand ～ afranselen* or *iemand er ～ van langs geven,* to give someone a good hiding.

du·el, -llen, *n.n.* duel. **duel·leren, -lleer,** *v.i.* to fight a duel.

duf, -ffe, a. musty, stuffy. ¶*adv.* with a musty smell *or* taste. ·**dufheid,** no pl., n. mustiness.

·**duffel,** no pl., *n.n.* duffel, duffle. ·**duffels,** a. (*made of*) duffle.

·**duidelijk,** a. clear, plain, distinct. ·**duidelijkheid,** no pl., n. clearness. **duidelijkheidshalve,** *adv.* for the sake of clearness. ·**duiden,** *v.i.* ～ *op,* to point to, hint at. ¶*v.t. iemand iets ten kwade ～,* to take offence at something someone does.

duif, -ven, n. pigeon, dove.

duig, n. stave (*of barrel*). *in ～en vallen,* to collapse, fall through.

·**duikboot, -boten,** n. submarine, U-boat. ·**duikbootjager, -s,** n. submarine destroyer. ·**duikbootoorlog,** n. U-boat campaign. ·**duikeend,** n. diver (*duck*). ·**duikelaar, -s,** n. tumbler (*acrobat*); lead-bottomed toy. ·**duikelen,** *v.i.* to turn somersaults; to tumble. ·**duikeling,** n. somersault. *een ～ maken,* to turn a somersault. ·**duiken,** *v.i.*..

str. to dive, plunge; to duck. ·duiker, -s, *n.* diver; culvert. ·duikerklok, -kken, *n.* diving-bell. ·duikvogel, -s, *n.* diving-bird.
duim, *n.* thumb; inch. *op zijn ~ fluiten,* to whistle for it; *iets uit zijn ~ zuigen,* to invent it all, make it all up. *See* duimpje. ·duimbreed, no pl., *n.n. geen ~ wijken,* not to yield an inch. ·duimeling, *n.* thumb-stall. ·duimelot, -tten, *n.n.* thumb-stall; thumb (*nursery word*). ·duimpje, -s, *n.n.* little thumb. *Klein D~,* Tom Thumb; *iets op zijn ~ kennen,* to know something inside out. ·duimpjezuigen, *n.n.* thumb-sucking. ·duimschroef, -ven, *n.* thumb-screw. *de duimschroeven aanleggen,* to put on the screw. ·duimstok, -kken, *n.* folding-rule.
duin, *n.n.* (sand-)dune. *in het ~,* in the dunes. ·duindoorn, *n.* sea buckthorn. ·duinenrij, *n.* range of dunes. ·duingrond, *n.* dune-soil, dune-land. ·Duinkerken, *n.N.* Dunkirk. Duins, *N.* The Downs.
·duister, *a.* obscure, dark; mysterious. ¶*n.n.* (the) dark. *in het ~ tasten,* to grope in the dark; *in het ~ zitten,* to be in darkness. ·duisterheid, -heden, *n.* obscurity, darkness. ·duisternis, -ssen, *n.* darkness, dark. *de macht der ~,* the powers of darkness.
duit, *n.* doit (*formerly a coin*). *geen ~* or *geen rooie ~,* not a sou; *een flinke duit kosten* or *verdienen,* to cost *or* earn a pretty penny; *een ~ in het zakje doen,* to put in a word; *~en hebben,* to have lots of money; *erg op de ~en,* keen on the dibs; *om de ~en,* for (the sake of) the money. ·duitblad, no pl., *n.n.* frogbit.
Duits, *a.* German. *een ~e,* a German woman. ¶no pl., *n.n.* the German language. ·Duitser, -s, *n.* German. ·Duitse-zind, *a.* pro-German. ·Duitsland, *n.N.* Germany.
·duivel, -s, *n.* devil, fiend. *daar mag de ~ wijs uit worden,* I can't make head or tail of it; *loop naar de ~,* go to blazes; *om de ~ niet,* not on your life; *te dom om voor de ~ te dansen,* too stupid to live. ·duivelachtig, *a.* devilish. ·duivela-rij, *n.* devilry. ·duivelbezweerder, -s, *n.* exorcist. ·duivelbezwering, *n.* exorcism. ·duive-lin, -nnen, *n.* she-devil. ·duivels, *a.* devilish, fiendish, diabolical; furious. ¶*adv.* devilish, extremely. ·duivelsadvocaat, -caten, *n.* devil's advocate. ·duivelsbrood, no pl., *n.n.* toadstool. ·duivelsdrek, no pl., *n.* asafoetida. ·duivelskind, -eren, *n.n.* limb of Satan. ·duivelstoejager, -s, *n.* factotum, odd-job-man. ·duiveltje, -s, *n.n.* little devil. *een ~ in een doosje,* a jack-in-the-box.
·duivenboon, -bonen, *n.* broad bean. ·duiven-hok, -kken, *n.n.* pigeon-house, dovecote. ·duivenmelker, -s, *n.* pigeon-fancier. ·duivenslag, *n.* pigeon-loft. ·duiventil, -llen, *n.* pigeon-house.
·duizelen, *v.i.* to grow dizzy. *het duizelt me,*

my brain reels, my head swims. ·duizelig, *a.* giddy, dizzy, ·duizeligheid, -heden, *n.* giddiness. ·duizeling, *n.* fit of giddiness. ·duizeling-wekkend, *a.* vertiginous, giddy.
·duizend, *num.* thousand. *D~ en een Nacht,* the Arabian Nights' Entertainment. ·duizendblad, no pl., *n.n.* milfoil. ·duizen-derlei, *a.* of a thousand kinds. duizend-guldenkruid, no pl., *n.n.* centaury. ·duizendhoofdig, *a* many-headed. ·duizend-jarig, *a. het ~ Rijk,* the Millennium. ·duizendmaal, *adv.* a thousand times. ·duizendpoot, -poten, *n.* centipede, milli-pede. ·duizendschoon, -schonen, *n.* sweet-william. ·duizendste, *num.* thousandth. ·duizendtal, -llen, *n.n.* (a) thousand. ·duizendvoud, *n.n.* multiple of thousand; thousandfold. ·duizendwerf, *adv.* a thousand times.
du-kaat, -katen, *n.* ducat.
duk-dalf, -ven, *n.* dolphin (*mooring post*). ·duldbaar, -bare, *a.* bearable. ·duldeloos, -loze, *a.* unbearable. ·dulden, *v.t.* to bear, endure; to stand, tolerate, put up with. *geen uitstel ~,* to brook no delay.
dun, -nne, *a.* thin; slender. *het is ~,* it is poor stuff. ¶*adv.* thinly, sparsely. *het zit er ~ op,* it is very superficial. ¶no pl., *n.n. door dik en ~,* through thick and thin. ·dunbier, no pl., *n.n.* small beer. ·dundoek, no pl., *n.n.* (stilted) flag. ·dunheid, no pl., *n.* thinness. ·dunnen, dun, *v.t. & v.i.* to thin (out). ·dunnetjes, *adv.* thinly, poorly. *het ~ overdoen,* to make another half-hearted effort. ·dunsel, -s, *n.n.* thinnings.
dunk, no pl., *n.* opinion. *een hoge ~ hebben van,* to have a high opinion of; *geen hoge ~* or *een slechte ~ hebben van,* to think little of. ·dunken, *v.i., imp. irr. mij dunkt,* I think, methinks; *wat dunkt U?,* what do you think?
·duo, -'s, *n.n.* duo, duet. *~ rijden,* to ride pillion. ·duorijder, -s, *n.* pillion-rider. ·duozitting, *n.* pillion(-seat).
·dupe, -s, *n.* dupe, victim. du-peren, -peer, *v.t.* to dupe, victimize.
·duplo, no pl., *n.n. in ~ opmaken,* to draw up in duplicate.
·duren, duur, *v.i.* to last, continue; to endure; to keep (*not go bad*). *het duurde niet lang of . . .,* it was not long before . . .
durf, no pl., *n.* daring, pluck. ·durfal, -llen, *n.* dare-devil. ·durfniet, *n.* coward. ·durven, durf, *v.t., irr.* to have the courage, dare. *ik durf beweren,* I venture to say; *jij durft!,* you have a nerve!; *als je durft!,* I dare you to.
dus, *adv.* thus, in that way. ¶*c.* therefore, consequently. ·dusdanig, *pron.* such. ¶*adv.* in such a way. ·dusver(re), *adv. tot ~,* so far, hitherto.
dut, no pl., *n.* doze. *in de ~,* in a doze; *in de ~ raken,* to doze off; *iemand uit*

de ~ *helpen*, to undeceive a person. ·**dutje, -s,** *n.n.* snooze. *een* ~ *doen*, to have a snooze. ·**dutten, dut,** *v.i.* to doze, snooze.

duur, no pl., *n.* duration. *op den* ~, in the long run; *kort van* ~ or *van korte* ~, of short duration; *hij heeft rust noch* ~, he is restless. ¶**dure,** *a.* expensive, dear. *hoe* ~ *is dat?*, how much is that; *een dure plicht*, one's bounden duty; *een dure eed zweren*, to swear a solemn oath. ¶*adv.* dear(ly). ~ *bevochten*, dearly won. ·**duurkoop,** *a.* dear at the price. ·**duurte,** no pl., *n.* dearness. ·**duurtetoeslag,** *n.* cost of living bonus. ·**duurzaam, -zame,** *a.* lasting, durable. ·**duurzaamheid,** no pl., *n.* durability.

duw, *n.* push, shove. *iemand een* ~ *geven*, to push someone. ·**duwen,** *v.t.* to push; to shove, jolt; to nudge. ·**duwtje, -s,** *n.n.* nudge, touch. *iemand een* ~ *geven*, to nudge someone.

·**dwaalbegrip, -ppen,** *n.n.* fallacy, misconception. ·**dwaalleer, -lleren,** *n.* heresy, false doctrine. ·**dwaallicht,** *n.n.* will-o'-the-wisp. ·**dwaalspoor, -sporen,** *n.n.* wrong track. *op een* ~ *brengen*, to lead astray, put off the scent; *op een* ~ *geraken* or *zijn*, to go astray. ·**dwalen, dwaal,** *v.i.* to roam, wander; to err. ·**dwaling,** *n.* error. *gerechtelijke* ~, miscarriage of justice.

dwaas, dwaze, *a.* foolish, silly. ¶**dwazen,** *n.* fool. ·**dwaasheid, -heden,** *n.* folly, foolishness.

dwang, *n.* compulsion, coercion. ·**dwangarbeid,** no pl., *n.* hard labour, penal servitude. ·**dwangarbeider, -s,** *n.* convict. ·**dwangbevel,** *n.n.* warrant, writ. ·**dwangbuis, -zen,** *n.n.* strait waistcoat. ·**dwangmiddel,** *n.n.* means of coercion. ~*en gebruiken*, to use forcible means.

·**dwarrelen,** *v.i.* to whirl (*of leaves, snowflakes*). ·**dwarreling,** *n.* whirl; reeling. ·**dwarrelwind,** *n.* whirlwind.

dwars, *a.* transverse, diagonal; pigheaded, contrary. *dubbel en* ~, more than, over and again. ¶*adv.* transversely, diagonally; pigheadedly. *iemand* ~ *zitten*, to obstruct someone, put obstacles in someone's way; *het zit hem* ~, he can't stomach it; ~ *door* (*heen*), right through; ~ *over*, right across; ~ *tegenover*, straight opposite; ~ *voor de boeg*, across (her) bows. ·**dwarsbalk,** *n.* crossbeam. ·**dwarsbomen, -boom,** *v.t.* to cross, thwart. ·**dwarsdraads,** *a.* cross-grained. ·**dwarsdrijven, -drijf,** *v.t.*, *str.* to cross, thwart. ·**dwarsdrijver, -s,** *n.* obstructionist. **dwarsdrijve·rij,** *n.* cussedness, contrariness. ·**dwarsfluit,** *n.* flute, Boehm flute. ·**dwarshout,** *n.n.* cross-beam. ·**dwarskijker, -s,** *n.* spy; boss's man. ·**dwarskop, -ppen,** *n.* cussed *or* obstinate person. ·**dwarsligger, -s,** *n.* (railway) sleeper. ·**dwarsscheeps,** *adv.*

abeam. ·**dwarsstraat, -raten,** *n.* side street. ·**dwarste,** no pl., *n. in de* ~, across. ·**dwarspachtig,** *a.* gushing, romantic; fanatic. ·**dweepster, -s,** *n.* woman who raves about something. ·**dweepziek,** *a.* extravagantly enthusiastic, intense. ·**dweepzucht,** no pl., *n.* romantic enthusiasm. ·**dwepen, dweep,** *v.i.* to be extremely enthusiastic about, gush. ~ *met*, to have a passion for, rave about. ·**dweper, -s,** *n.* enthusiast, person who raves about something. **dwepe·rij,** *n.* fanaticism.

dweil, *n.* floor-cloth, mop. ·**dweilen,** *v.i.* & *v.t.* to mop, swab. *langs de straat* ~, to hang about the streets.

dwerg, *n.* dwarf. ·**dwerggachtig,** *a.* dwarfish, stunted. ·**dwergmuis, -zen,** *n.* harvest mouse.

·**dwingeland,** *n.* tyrant. **dwingelan·dij,** *n.* tyranny. ·**dwingen,** *v.t.*, *str.* to force, compel, coerce. *iemand* ~ *tot*, to force a person to *or* into; *hij laat zich niet* ~, he won't be driven; *het laat zich niet* ~, you can't force it. ¶*v.i.*, *str.* ~ *om*, to insist on, cry for. ·**dwingerig,** *a.* troublesome, insistent (*of child*).

dyna·miet, no pl., *n.n.* dynamite. **dy·namo, -'s,** *n.* dynamo.

E

eb, ebbe, no pl., *n.* ebb(-tide). *het is* ~, the tide is out; ~ *en vloed*, low tide and high tide. ·**ebbeboom, -bomen,** *n.* ebony (*tree*). ·**ebben, eb,** *v.i.* to ebb. *het tij is aan het* ~, the tide is going out. ¶*a.* (made of) ebony. ·**ebbenhout,** *n.n.* ebony (*wood*). ·**ebbenhouten,** *a.* (made of) ebony. **ebo·niet,** no pl., *n.n.* ebonite, vulcanite.

é·**chec, -s,** *n.n.* check, set-back, failure. ~ *lijden*, to meet with failure; *in* ~ *houden*, to keep in check.

echt, *a.* real, genuine, true; legitimate. ¶*adv.* truly, really. ~ *waar*, really true. ¶no pl., *n.* wedlock. ·**echtbreekster, -s,** *n.* adulteress. ·**echtbreken,** *v.i.*, *infin.* to commit adultery. ·**echtbreker, -s,** *n.* adulterer. ·**echtbreuk,** no pl., *n.* adultery. ·**echtelieden,** pl. only, *n.* married people. *de* ~, the married couple. ·**echtelijk,** *a.* conjugal. *de* ~*e staat*, the married state. ·**echten,** *v.t.* to legitimize (*child*). ·**echter,** *adv.* however. ·**echtgenoot, -noten,** *n.* husband; spouse. ·**echtgenote, -n,** *n.* wife; spouse. ·**echtheid,** no pl., *n.* genuineness, authenticity. ·**echtpaar, -paren,** *n.n.* (*stilted*) married couple. ·**echtscheiding,** *n.* divorce.

eco·**nomisch,** *a.* economic.

·**edel,** *a.* noble; precious (metal, stone). ¶pl. only, *n. de* ~*en*, the nobility. **edel·achtbaar, -bare,** *a.* honourable, worshipful (*title of burgomaster, judge, magistrate*). **edelge·boren,** *a.* of noble birth. **·edelgesteente, -n,** *n.n.* precious stone, gem. **·edelheid,** no pl., *n.* nobleness, nobility. **·edelhert,** *n.n.* red deer. **·edelknaap, -knapen,** *n.* page, squire. **·edellieden,** *pl. of* **edelman,** *n.* nobleman. **·edelmarter, -s,** *n.* pine-marten. **edel·moedig,** *a.* magnanimous, generous. **edel·moedigheid,** no pl., *n.* magnanimity. **·edelvrouw,** *n.* noblewoman.

e·ditie, -s, *n.* edition.

e·doch, *c.* (*stilted*) however.

eed, eden, *n.* oath. *een ~ afleggen,* to take an oath; *iemand de ~ afnemen,* to swear someone (in); *een ~ doen op,* to swear an oath to; *onder ede staan,* to be on oath; *onder ede verklaren,* to declare on oath. **·eedaflegging, -en,** *n.* taking an oath. **·eed-afneming,** *n.* swearing-in. **·eedbreker, -s,** *n.* perjurer. **·eedbreuk,** *n.* perjury. **·eed-formulier,** *n.n.* prescribed oath. **·eedgenoot, -noten,** *n.* confederate. **·eedgenootschap, -ppen.** *n.n.* confederacy.

·eega, -gaas, *n.* spouse.

·eekhoorn, -s, *n.* squirrel.

eelt, no pl., *n.* horny skin, callosity. **·eeltachtig,** *a.* callous, horny. **·eelterig,** *a.* horny. **·eeltknobbel, -s,** *n.* callosity; callus.

een, 'n, *indef. art.* a, an. ¶ *~,* **één,** *num.* one. *~ zijn,* to be united; *~ en al,* all or a mass of; *~ en ander,* one thing and another *or* the points mentioned; *het ~ en ander,* a few things; *de ~ na de ander,* one after another; *het ~ of ander,* something *or* other; *het ~ of het ander,* one thing or the other; *op ~ na,* but one *or* but for one; *~ voor ~,* one at a time. ¶*n.* one. *See* **eentje, enen.** **·eenakter, -s,** *n.* one-act play. **·eenarmig,** *a.* one-armed. **·eencellig,** *a.* unicellular. **·eendagsvlieg,** *n.* ephemera, ephemeron, May-fly. **·eendekker, -s,** *n.* monoplane.

eend, *n.* duck. *een vreemde ~ in de bijt,* an outsider. **·eendachtig,** *a.* stupid. **·eendebout,** *n.* leg of duck (*cooked*). **·eendenéi, -eieren,** *n.n.* duck egg. **·eendenkom, -mmen,** *n.* duck-pond. **·eendenkroos,** no pl., *n.n.* duck-weed. **·eendenmossel, -s,** *n.* barnacle.

·eender, *a.* similar. *het is mij ~,* it is all the same to me; *net ~,* (very much) alike. ¶*adv.* equally, in the same way. **eendracht,** no pl., *n.* union, concord. *~ maakt macht,* union is strength. **een·drachtig,** *a.* united, unanimous.

·eendvogel, -s, *n.* duck.

·eenheid, -heden, *n.* unity; unit. **·eenheidsfront,** *n.n.* united front. **·eenheidsprijs, -zen,** *n.* standard price. **een·hoevig,** *a.* one-hoofed. **·eenhoofdig,** *a.* monarchical. *~e regering,* monarchy. **·eenhoorn, -s,** *n.* unicorn. **een·huizig,** *a.* monoecious. **·eenjarig,** *a.* one year old; of one year.

~e plant, annual plant. **een·kennig,** *a.* shy, timid (*of small child*). **·eenkleurig,** *a.* of one colour, unicoloured. **·eenlettergrepig,** *a.* monosyllabic. *~ woord,* monosyllable. **·eenling,** *n.* individual. **·eenmaal,** *adv.* once; one day. *~ is geenmaal,* once doesn't count; *~, andermaal, ten derden male,* going, going, gone; *het is nu ~ gebeurd,* it can't be helped now; *het moet nu ~ gedaan worden,* it has got to be done. **·eenmanswagen, -s,** *n.* tramcar with driver-conductor. **·eenoog, -nogen,** *n.* one-eyed person. **·eenogig,** *a.* one-eyed. **een·parig,** *a.* unanimous; uniform. *~e beweging,* uniform motion. ¶*adv.* unanimously; with one accord. **een·parigheid,** no pl., *n.* unanimity; uniformity. **·eenpersoons,** *a.* one-man, single.

eens, *adv.* once; one day; once upon a time; just; in agreement. *kom ~ hier,* come here; *hoor ~,* I say; *niet ~,* not even; *het ~ zijn met,* to agree with; *het ~ worden over,* to agree upon. *See* **ineens, opeens. ·eensdeels,** *adv.* partly. *~ . . ., anderdeels,* partly . . ., partly. **·eensge·zind,** *a.* unanimous. **·eensge·zindheid,** no pl., *n.* unanimity. **·eensklaps,** *adv.* suddenly. **eens·luidend,** *a.* identical (*wording*). *~ afschrift,* true copy. **een·stemmig,** *a.* unanimous; for one voice. **een·stemmigheid,** no pl., *n.* unanimity.

·eentje, -s, *n.n.* single one. *op zijn or mijn ~,* on one's or my own; *jij bent er ook ~,* you are a one; *er ~ pakken,* to have one (*drink*). **een·tonig,** *a.* monotonous. **·eenvoud,** no pl., *n.* simplicity, innocence. **een·voudig,** *a.* simple, plain, homely. ¶*adv.* simply. *het is ~ idioot,* it is downright foolish. **een·voudigheid,** no pl., *n.* simplicity, plainness. **eenvoudigheidshalve,** *adv.* for the sake of simplicity. **·eenzaam, -zame,** *a.* lonely, solitary; isolated; desolate. ¶*adv.* in solitude. **·eenzaamheid,** no pl., *n.* loneliness, solitude. *in de ~,* in solitude. **een·zelvig,** *a.* solitary; introvert. **een·zelvigheid,** no pl., *n.* solitariness; introversion. **een·zijdig,** *a.* one-sided; unilateral. **een·zijdigheid,** no pl., *n.* one-sidedness.

eer, no pl., *n.* honour, credit. *~ aandoen,* to honour; *de laatste ~ bewijzen,* to render the last honours; *de ~ hebben van,* to have the honour to; *de ~ aan zich houden,* to save one's face; *in ere brengen,* to bring into recognition; *in ere komen,* to come into favour; *in alle ~ en deugd,* with honourable motives; *te zijner ~,* in his honour *or* to his credit; *ter ere van,* in honour of; *tot iemands ~,* to someone's credit (*fig.*); *ere wie ere toekomt,* honour where honour is due. ¶*adv.* before; sooner, rather. *hoe ~ hoe liever,* the sooner the better. ¶*c.* before; ere. **·eerbaar, -bare,** *a.* virtuous, honourable. **·eerbaarheid,** no

pl., *n.* modesty, virtue. ·eerbetoon, no pl., *n.n.* ·eerbewijs, -zen, *n.n.* mark of honour, homage. ·eerbied, no pl., *n.* respect, awe. eer·biedig, *a.* respectful, deferential. eer·biedigen, *v.t.* to respect. eer·biediglijk, *adv.* respectfully. eerbieds·halve, *adv.* out of regard, as a mark of esteem. eerbied·waardig, *a.* venerable, respectable. eerbied·wekkend, *a.* imposing. ·eergevoel, no pl., *n.n.* sense of honour. eer·gierig, *a.* ambitious.
·eerder, *adv.* sooner. See eer, *adv.*
·eergisteren, *adv.* the day before yesterday. ·eergisternacht, *adv.* the night before last.
·eerlang, *adv.* before long, shortly.
·eerlijk, *a.* honest; fair; honourable. ~ *duurt het langst*, honesty is the best policy; ~ *is* ~, fair is fair. ¶*adv.* honestly; fairly. ~ *gezegd*, honestly!; ~ *waar*, really true. ·eerlijkheid, no pl., *n.* honesty. ·eerloos, -loze, *a.* infamous. ·eerloosheid, no pl., *n.* infamy. ·eerroof, no pl., *n.* defamation of character. ·eershalve, *adv.* for honour's sake.
eerst, *a.* first; chief, principal. *E~e Minister*, Prime Minister; ~*e redevoering*, maiden speech; ~*e steen*, foundation stone; *de* ~*e de beste*, the first (*who comes along*), anyone; *niet de* ~*e de beste*, not just anyone; *ten* ~*e*, in the first place; *voor het* ~, for the first time. ¶*adv.* first; firstly; at first; only. ~ *gisteren*, not before *or* until yesterday; *nu* ~, only now. ·eerst·aanwezend, *a.* senior, chief. ·eerstdaags, *adv.* one of these days. ·eersteling, *n.* first(-born). ·eerstens, *adv.* in the first place. ·eersterangs, *a.* first-rate. ·eerst·geboorte, no pl., *n.* primogeniture. ·eerstgenoemd, *a.* first-mentioned. eerst·komend, *a.*, eerst·volgend, *a.* next, following. *de* ~*e dagen*, the next few days.
·eertijds, *adv.* formerly, in former times.
·eervol, -lle, *a.* honourable. eer·waarde, *a.* (*title of lower clergy*). *de* ~ *heer* . . ., the Reverend. . . . eer·waardig, *a.* venerable. ·eerzaam, -zame, *a.* respectable. ·eerzucht, no pl., *n.* ambition. eer·zuchtig, *a.* ambitious.
eest, *n.* oast(-house); kiln. ·eesten, *v.t.* to kiln-dry.
·eetbaar, -bare, *a.* eatable, edible. ·eetbaarheid, no pl., *n.* edibility. ·eetgerei, no pl., *n.n.* table-appointments. ·eetkamer, -s, *n.* dining room. ·eetlepel, -s, *n.* table-spoon. ·eetlust, *n.* appetite. *geen* ~ *hebben*, to be off one's food. ·eetservies, -zen, *n.n.* dinner-set. ·eetstokje, -s, *n.n.* chopstick. ·eetwaar, -waren, *n.* victuals. ·eetzaal, -zalen, *n.* dining hall.
eeuw, *n.* century; age (*long period*). *in de vorige* ~, in the last century; *in geen* ~*en*, not for ages. ·eeuwenlang, *a.* age-

long. ·eeuwenoud, *a.* centuries old. ·eeuwfeest, *n.n.* centenary. ·eeuwig, *a.* eternal; perpetual, everlasting. *ten* ~*en dage*, for ever and ever. ¶*adv.* eternally; awfully. *het is* ~ *jammer*, it is an awful pity. ·eeuwigdurend, *a.* everlasting. ·eeuwigheid, -heden, *n.* eternity; ages (*long time*). *de* ~ *ingaan*, to depart from this life; *nooit in der* ~ *or in der* ~ *niet*, never; *tot in der* ~, to all eternity; *van* ~ *tot* ~, for ever and ever.
ef·fect, *n.n.* effect; side (*billiards*). ~ *hebben*, to take effect; ~ *najagen*, to be out after effect; *op* ~ *berekend*, calculated for effect. ¶*pl.* only, *n.n.* securities; stocks and shares. ef·fectenbeurs, -zen, *n.* stock exchange. ef·fectenhandel, no pl., *n.* broking. ef·fectenhandelaar, -s, *n.*, ef·fectenmakelaar, -s, *n.* stockbroker. effec·tief, -ve, *a.* effective, real. *in effectieve dienst*, on active service. ¶-ven, *n.n.* effective (*military*).
·effen, *a.* smooth, even; plain (*without pattern*); settled (*account*). *een* ~ *gezicht*, a straight face. ·effenen, *v.t.* to smooth, level. ·effenheid, no pl., *n.* smoothness.
eg, -ggen, *n.* harrow. ·eggen, eg, *v.t.* & *v.i.* to harrow.
e·gaal, -gale, *a.* even, equal. *het is mij* ~, it is all the same to me.
E·geïsch, *a.* Aegean. ~*e Zee*, Aegean Sea.
·egel, -s, *n.* hedgehog.
egelan·tier, -s *or* -en, *n.* eglantine, sweetbriar.
·egelvis, -ssen, *n.* globe-fish.
ego·isme, no pl., *n.n.* egoism, egotism, selfishness. ego·ïst, *n.* egoist, egotist. ego·istisch, *a.* selfish.
E·gyptenaar, -naren, *n.* Egyptian. E·gyptisch, *a.* Egyptian.
ei, *int.* ah! ¶-eren, *n.n.* egg; embryo. *het* ~ *van Columbus*, a simple but overlooked explanation; *voor een appel en een* ~, for a mere song; *koek en* ~, love and friendship; *beter een half* ~ *dan een lege dop*, half a loaf is better than none; ~*eren voor zijn geld kiezen*, to make the best of a bad bargain.
·eiber, -s, *n.* stork.
·eiderdons, no pl., *n.n.* eiderdown (*feathers*). ·eidergans, -zen, *n.* eider(-duck).
·eierbriket, -tten, *n.* egg-shaped block of compressed coal-dust. ·eierdop, -ppen, *n.* egg-shell. ·eierdopje, -s, *n.n.* egg-cup. ·eierkolen, no pl., *n.* See eierbriket. ·eiermijn, *n.* egg market. ·eierschaal, -schalen, *n.* egg-shell. ·eierstok, -kken, *n.* ovary. ·eierstruif, -ven, *n.* omelet(te).
·eigen, *a.* own, of one's own; intimate. *voor* ~ *gebruik*, for one's own use, for private use; *op zijn* ~ *houtje*, off his own bat; ~ *zijn met*, to be on terms of intimacy with; *zich iets* ~ *maken*, to acquire

something. **eigenaar**, **-s** *or* **-naren**, *n.* owner. **eigen·aardig**, *a.* peculiar, singular, curious. **eigen·aardigheid**, **-heden**, *n.* peculiarity. **eigena·res**, **-ssen**, *n.* owner (*female*). **eigenbaat**, no pl., *n.n.* selfishness. **eigenbelang**, no pl., *n.n.* self-interest. **eigendom**, **-mmen**, *n.n.* property, possession. ¶no pl., *n.* ownership. **eigendoms·bewijs**, **-zen**, *n.n.* title-deed. **eigendoms·recht**, *n.n.* ownership, title; proprietary rights; copyright. **eigendunk**, no pl., *n.* self-conceit. **eigen·dunkelijk**, *a.* arbitrary. **eigengebakken**, *a.* home-made (*bread*, *cakes*). **eigengerechtig**, *a.* self-righteous. **eigen·handig**, *a.* with one's own hand(s). **eigenliefde**, no pl., *n.* self-love. **eigenlijk**, *a.* real, proper. ¶*adv.* strictly speaking. really. *wat doet hij* ~, what does he do?; *wat wil je* ~?, what do you want? **eigenlof**, no pl., *n.* ~ *stinkt*, don't blow your trumpet. **eigen·machtig**, *a.* arbitrary. **eigennaam**, **-namen**, *n.* proper name. **eigenschap**, **-ppen**, *n.* property, attribute; quality. **eigenwaan**, no pl., *n.* self-conceit. **eigenwaarde**, no pl., *n. een gevoel van* ~, self-respect. **eigen·wijs**, **-ze**, *a.* opinionated; pig-headed. **eigen·wijsheid**, no pl., *n.* opinionatedness. **eigen·zinnig**, *a.* headstrong, obstinate. **eigen·zinnigheid**, no pl., *n.* obstinacy, wilfulness.

eik, *n.* oak. **eikeblad**, **-eren**, *n.n.* oak-leaf. **eikeboom**, **-bomen**, *n.* oak-tree. **eikel**, **-s**, *n.* acorn. **eikeloof**, no pl., *n.n.* oak-leaves. **eikenbos**, **-ssen**, *n.* oak-wood (*forest*). **eikenhout**, no pl., *n.n.* oak-wood (*substance*). **eikenhouten**, *a.* oak, oaken.

eiland, *n.n.* island, isle. **eilandbewoner**, **-s**, *n.* islander. **eilandengroep**, *n.* archipelago. **eilandenrijk**, *n.n.* island kingdom.

eind(e), **-(e)n**, *n.n.* end, ending, conclusion; piece, length; distance. *een* ~ *weegs*, some way, part of the way; *een heel* ~, a long way; *het bij het rechte* ~ *hebben*, to have got hold of the right idea; *het bij het verkeerde* ~ *hebben*, to have got hold of the wrong end of the stick; *daar is het* ~ *van weg*, *er komt geen* ~ *aan*, there is no end to it; *een* ~ *maken aan*, to put a stop to; *aan het kortste* ~ *trekken*, to be handicapped; *in het* ~, in the end; *op het* ~, at the end; *te dien einde*, for that reason; *ten einde*, in order that *or* in order to *or* at an end; *ten einde raad*, at one's wit's end; *tegen het* ~, towards the end; *tot het* ~ *toe*, until the end. **einddoel**, no pl., *n.n.* ultimate object. **eindelijk**, *adv.* at last, at length, finally. **eindeloos**, **-loze**, *a.* endless. **eindeloosheid**, no pl., *n.* endlessness, infinity. **eindig**, *a.* finite. **eindigen**, *v.i.* to finish, end. ~ *met*, to end in *or* with *or* by; ~ *op*, to end in (*of words*). ¶*v.t.* to end, terminate, finish. **eindje**, **-s**, *n.n.*

short length of; stub, stump. ~ *touw*, piece of string; *een* ~, a short way. **eindpunt**, *n.n.* farthest point. **eindwed·strijd**, *n.* final match, cup final.

eirond, *a.* egg-shaped, oval.

eis, no pl., *n.* E sharp. **eis**, *n.* demand, claim; requirement(s), exigencies. *naar den* ~, as required; *een* ~ *stellen*, to make a demand; *aan een* ~ *voldoen*, to meet a demand; *een* ~ *afwijzen*, to reject a claim; *van een* ~ *afzien*, to waive a claim. **eisen**, *v.t.* to demand, claim, require. **eiser**, **-s**, *n.* plaintiff; claimant (*male*). **eise·res**, **-ssen**, *n.* plaintiff; claimant (*female*).

eivol, **-lle**, *a.* chock-full. **eiwit**, **-tten**, *n.n.* white of egg; albumen. **eiwithoudend**, *a.* albuminous.

ekster, **-s**, *n.* magpie. **eksteroog**, **-rogen**, *n.n.* corn (*on foot*). *iemand op zijn eksterogen trappen*, to tread on a person's corns.

el, **-llen**, *n.* ell (*Dutch = about 69cm.*).

eland, *n.* elk.

elas·tiek, no pl., *n.n.* elastic. **elas·tiekje**, **-s**, *n.n.* rubber band. **e·lastisch**, *a.* elastic.

elders, *adv.* elsewhere. *overal* ~, everywhere else.

electri·cien, **-s**, *n.* electrician. **electrici·teit**, no pl., *n.* electricity. **electrifi·ceren**, **-ceer**, *v.t.* to electrify. **e·lectrisch**, *a.* electric, electrical. ~*e centrale*, power station. **electro·technicus**, **-ci**, *n.* electrical engineer. **electrotech·niek**, no pl., *n.* electrical engineering. **electrothera·pie**, no pl., *n.* electro-therapeutics. **electroty·pie**, no pl., *n.* electrotype.

ele·ment, *n.n.* element; cell (*electric*). **elemen·tair**, *a.* elementary.

ele·vatie, **-s** *or* **-tiën**, *n.* elevation.

elf, *num.* eleven. *op zijn* ~*en-dertigst*, slowly and clumsily. ¶**-ven**, *n.* elf; eleven. See **elven**. **elfde**, *a.* eleventh. *ten* ~, in the eleventh place; *ter* ~*r ure*, at the eleventh hour. ¶**-n**, *n.n.* eleventh part. **elftal**, **-llen**, *n.n.* eleven (*team*). **elfvoud**, *n.n.* multiple of eleven.

elft, *n.* shad.

elimi·natie, **-s**, *n.* elimination. **elimi·neren**, **-neer**, *v.t.* to eliminate.

elk, *pron.* every, each. **el·kaar**, *pron.* each other, one another. *aan* ~, together *or* to one another; *achter* ~, one behind the other, in succession; *bij* ~, together; *door* ~, mixed; *in* ~, together; *in* ~ *zakken*, to collapse; *met* ~, together; *na* ~, one after the other; *naast* ~, side by side; *onder* ~, among one another *or* one under the other; *op* ~, on top of one another; *over* ~, crossed; *uit* ~ *jagen*, to scatter, disperse; *uit* ~ *kennen*, to know apart; *van* ~, from one another; *van* ~ *gaan*, to separate; *het is voor* ~, it is all settled. **elk·een**, *pron.* (*stilted*) everyone, everybody.

·elleboog, -bogen, *n.* elbow. *met de ~ aanstoten,* to nudge. ·ellegoed, -eren, *n.n.* soft goods.

el·lende, no pl., *n.* misery, distress. el·lende-ling, *n.* wretch (*despicable*). el·lendig, *a.* miserable, wretched. el·lendige, -n, *n.* wretch (*unfortunate*).

·ellenlang, *a.* yards long; endless. ·ellepijp, *n.* ulna. ·ellestok, -kken, *n.* yard-stick.

els, -zen, *n.* awl (*needle*); alder.

·elven, *n.* eleven. *de trein van ~,* the eleven o'clock train; *bij ~,* just on eleven; *in ~,* into eleven; *met hun ~,* the eleven of them; *met ons ~,* the eleven of us; *met z'n ~,* with ten others. *See* elf.

·Elzas, *N. de ~,* Alsace; *~ -Lotharingen,* Alsace-Lorraine. ·Elzasser, -s, *n.* Alsatian (*person*).

·elzeboom, -bomen, *n.* alder. ·elzenhout, no pl., *n.n.* alder wood.

é·mail, no pl., *n.n.* enamel. émail·leren, -lleer, *v.t.* to enamel.

embal·lage, -s, *n.* packing. embal·leren, -lleer, *v.t.* to pack (*parcel*).

em·bargo, no pl., *n.n.* embargo. *onder ~ leggen,* to lay an embargo on; *het ~ opheffen,* to remove the embargo.

embryo·naal, -nale, *a.* embryonic.

emeri·taat, -taten, *n.n.* superannuation, pension (*clerical and academic*).

emi·greren, -greer, *v.i.* to emigrate.

emi·nentie, -s, *n.* eminence.

e·missie, -s, *n.* issue (*of stocks and shares*).

emmer, -s, *n.* bucket, pail.

e·motie, -s, *n.* emotion.

emplace·ment, *n.n.* railway yard, goods yard; gun-site.

em·plooi, *n.n.* employ; use. emplo·yé, -'s, *n.* employee.

e·mulsie, -s, *n.* emulsion.

en, *c.* and. *~ ... ~ ...,* both ... and ....

enca·dreren, -dreer, *v.t.* to frame.

end, *n.n. See* eind. ·endeldarm, *n.* rectum.

endos·seren, -sseer, *v.t.* to endorse (*cheque*). endosse·ment, *n.n.* endorsement.

·enen, *num. de trein van ~,* the one o'clock train; *bij ~,* just on one. *See* een.

·enenmale, *adv. ten ~,* altogether, absolutely.

ener·gie, no pl., *n.* energy. ener·giek, *a.* energetic.

·enerlei, *a.* of the same kind. ¶*adv.* in the same way, identically. ·enerzijds, *adv.* on the one side.

en·fin, *adv.* in short; to proceed.

eng, *a.* narrow, tight; creepy, weird. ¶*adv.* in a narrow way.

engage·ment, *n.n.* engagement. enga·geren, zich, -geer, *v.r.* to become engaged.

·engel, -s, *n.* angel. ·engelachtig, *a.* angelic. engelbe·waarder, -s, *n.* guardian angel. ·engelenbak, -kken, *n.* gallery, the gods. ·engelengeduld, no pl., *n.n.* angelic patience.

·Engeland, *n.N.* England. ·Engels, *a.*

English, British. *~e sleutel,* monkey-wrench; *~e vlag,* British flag, Union Jack; *~e ziekte,* rickets; *~ zout,* Epsom salts. ·Engelse, *n.* Englishwoman. ·Engels-gezind, *a.* Anglophile. ·Engelsman, Engelsen, *n.* Englishman.

·engerd, -s, *n.* horrible, frightening person. ·engerling, *n.* grub of the cockchafer. ·engheid, no pl., *n.* narrowness. ·engte, -n, *n.* narrow(s), strait(s); narrow-ness.

en-·gros, *a.* & *adv.* wholesale.

·enig, *a.* sole, only, unique; delightful, funny. ¶*adv.* solely, wonderfully. ¶*pron.* some, any. eniger·hande, *a.,* eniger·lei, *a.* of some kind. eniger·mate, *adv.* somewhat, to some extent. eniger·wijs, *adv.,* eniger·wijze, *adv.* in some way (or other).

·eniglijk, *adv.* solely. ·enigszins, *adv.* somewhat; slightly. *ook maar ~,* at all.

·enkel, -s, *n.* ankle. *tot aan de ~s,* up *or* down to the ankles. ¶*a.* & *pron.* single; rare. *pl.* a few. ¶*adv.* only, merely. *~ en alleen,* merely, solely. ·enkeling, *n.* individual. ·enkelvoud, *n.n.* singular. enkel·voudig, *a.* singular (*not plural*); simple.

e·norm, *a.* enormous. enormi·teit, *n.* enormity.

en·quête, -s, *n.* (official) enquiry, investiga-tion. *een ~ instellen naar,* to set up an enquiry into. en·quêtecommissie, -s, *n.* board of enquiry.

ensce·neren, -neer, *v.t.* to stage, produce.

en·semble, -s, *n.n.* combination.

ent, *n.* graft. ·enten, *v.t.* to graft; to inocu-late. ·enter, -s, *n.* grafter; yearling. ·enterbijl, *n.* boarding axe. ·enterdreg, -ggen, *n.* grapnel. ·enteren, *v.t.* to board. ·enterhaak, -haken, *n.* grappling-iron. ·entering, *n.* boarding.

·enting, *n.* grafting; inoculation. ·entmes, -ssen, *n.n.* grafting knife.

entre·pot, -s, *n.n.* bonded warehouse. *in ~,* in bond; *goederen in ~,* bonded goods.

enve·loppe, -s, *n.* envelope.

enzo·voort, no pl., *n.n.* and so on, etcetera.

epau·let, -tten, *n.* epaulette.

epi·centrum, -tra, *n.n.* epicentre. epi·curisch, *a.* epicurean. epide·mie, -ieën, *n.* epidemic. epi·demisch, *a.* epidemic.

·episch, *a.* epic. ·epos, epen, *n.n.* epic.

er, *adv.* there; *often untranslated.* er·af, *adv.* off it.

er·barmelijk, *a.* pitiful, lamentable, poor. er·barmen, *v.r. zich ~ over,* to have mercy on; *erbarm U onzer,* have pity on us. er·barming, *n.* pity, compassion.

er·bij, *adv.* in addition.

·ere, *n. See* eer. ·erebaantje, -s, *n.n.* post of honour. ·ereboog, -bogen, *n.* triumphal arch. ·ereburger, -s, *n.* freeman (*of city*) ·eredegen, -s, *n.* presentation sword.

·eredienst, *n.* worship. ·erediploma, -'s, *n.n.* award of honour. ·ereschot, *n.n.* salute (*of guns*). ·erewoord, *n.n.* word of honour; parole. ·eren, eer, *v.t.* to honour, revere. er·eis, *adv.* once. *er was* ~, once upon a time there was.

erf, -ven, *n.n.* (farm-)yard; compound (*East Indies*). ·erfbezit, -tten, *n.n.* hereditary property. ·erfcijns, -zen, *n.* ground rent on hereditary tenure. ·erfdeel, -delen, *n.n.* portion, heritage. ·erfelijk, *a.* hereditary. ~e belasting, hereditary taint. ·erfelijkheid, no pl., *n.* heredity. ·erfenis, -ssen, *n.* heritage, inheritance. ·erfgenaam, -namen, *n.* heir (*male*). ·erfgename, -n, *n.* heir (*female*). ·erfgoed, -eren, *n.n.* inheritance, estate. ·erfhuis, -zen, *n.n.* house where dead person's effects are sold; sale of dead person's effects. ·erflaatster, -s, *n.* testatrix. ·erflater, -s, *n.* testator. ·erflating, *n.* bequest, legacy. ·erfleen, -lenen, *n.n.* hereditary fief. ·erfoom, -s, *n.* uncle from whom one hopes to inherit. ·erfopvolging, *n.* succession. ·erfpacht, *n.* hereditary tenure; ground rent on hereditary tenure. *in* ~, on long lease. ·erfpachter, -s, *n.* long lease holder. ·erfrecht, *n.n.* law or right of succession. ·erfstelling, *n.* testamentary disposition. ·erfstuk, -kken, *n.n.* heirloom. ·erftante, -s, *n.* aunt from whom one hopes to inherit. ·erfvijand, *n.* hereditary enemy. ·erfzonde, -n, *n.* original sin.

erg, *a.* bad, serious. *heel* ~, very bad, deplorable. ¶*adv.* badly; very. *iets* ~ *nodig hebben*, to need something badly; ~ *lelijk*, very ugly; *er* ~ *aan toe zijn*, to be in a bad state. ¶*n.n. ergens (geen)* ~ *in hebben*, (not) to notice something; *zonder* ~, unintentionally. erg·denkend, *a.* suspicious. erg·denkendheid, no pl., *n.* suspiciousness.

·ergens, *adv.* somewhere, anywhere. ¶ + *prep.* something. ~ *aan werken*, to work at something; ~ *mee bezig zijn*, to be at work on something.

·erger, *a.* worse. *des te* ~, so much the worse *or* worse luck. ·ergeren, *v.t.* to annoy; to give offence. ¶*v.r. zich* ~ *over*, to be offended at, be indignant at. ·ergerlijk, *a.* annoying, scandalous. ¶*adv.* offensively. ·ergernis, -ssen, *n.* offence; umbrage, annoyance. ~ *geven* or *kosten*, to cause offence; *tot grote* ~ *van*, to the great annoyance of. ·ergst, *a.* worst.

·erica, no pl., *n.* heather.

er·kennen, -ken, *v.t.* to acknowledge, recognize; to admit, own. *niet* ~, to repudiate; *iets openlijk* or *ronduit* ~, to admit something freely. er·kenning, no pl., *n.* recognition (*of fact*); acknowledgement. er·kentelijk, *a.* grateful, thankful. er·kentelijkheid, no pl., *n.* gratitude. er·kentenis, no pl., *n.* recognition (*of fact*).

·erker, -s, *n.* bay-window, bow-window, oriel.

ernst, no pl., *n.* earnest(ness), seriousness; gravity. *het is hem geen* ~, he is not serious (about it); *het wordt nu* ~, things are getting serious now; *iets in* ~ *opvatten*, to take something seriously; *in* ~, in earnest. ·ernstig, *a.* serious, solemn, earnest.

er·onder, *adv.* under (it *or* them). er·op, *adv.* on (it *or* them). ~ *of eronder*, kill or cure.

e·rotisch, *a.* erotic.

erts, *n.n.* ore. ·ertsader, -s, *n.* mineral vein, lode. erts·houdend, *a.* ore-bearing. ·ertslaag, -lagen, *n.* mineral deposit.

er·uit, *adv.* out, out of it.

er·varen, *v.t.* to experience. ¶*a.* experienced. er·varenheid, no pl., *n.* experience, skill. er·varing, *n.* experience.

·erven, pl. only, *n.* heirs. ¶erf, *v.t.* & *v.i.* to inherit.

erwt, *n.* pea. *pl.* peas, pease. ·erwtedop, -ppen, *n.* pea-pod, peasecod. erwtensoep, no pl., *n.* pea-soup.

es, no pl., *n.* E flat. ¶-ssen, *n.* ash, ash-tree.

esca·drille, -s, *n.* squadron (*air force*).

·esdoorn, -s, *n.* maple.

es·corte, -s, *n.n.* escort. escor·teren, -teer, *v.t.* to escort.

es·kader, -s, *n.n.* squadron (*naval*).

esp, *n.* asp, aspen. ·espeblad, -eren, *n.n.* aspen leaf. ·espeboom, -bomen, *n.* asp, aspen. ·espen, *a.* (*made of*) asp, aspen.

essai·ëren, -ieer, *v.t.* to assay. essai·eur, -s, *n.* assayer.

·esseblad, -eren, *n.n.* ash leaf. ·esseboom, -bomen, *n.* ash(-tree). ·essehout, *n.n.* ash wood. ·essehouten, *a.* (*made of*) ash.

essenti·eel, -iële, *a.* essential.

es·thetisch, *a.* æsthetic.

·Estland, *n.N.* Esthonia.

etablisse·ment, *n.n.* establishment.

é·tage, -s, *n.* storey, floor. *bel* ~, first floor. é·tagebewoner, -s, *n.* flat-dweller. éta·gère, -s, *n.* whatnot. é·tagewoning, *n.* flat, apartment.

éta·lage, -s, *n.* shop-window. éta·lagekast, *n.* show-case. éta·lageverpakking, *n.* dummy (*package*). éta·leren, -leer, *v.t.* to display.

é·tappe, -s, *n.* stage, halting place; stage, lap; supply base.

·eten, eet, *v.t.*, *irr.* to eat. *wat* ~ *we vandaag?*, what are we having for dinner? ¶*v.i.*, *irr.* to eat; to have a meal, have (*one's*) food. *hoe laat* ~ *we?*, what time is dinner?; ~ *wat de pot schaft*, to take pot-luck; *bij iemand* ~, to dine at somebody's place; *uit* ~ *gaan*, to dine out. ¶no pl., *n.n.:* food; meal, dinner, supper. ~ *en drinken*, food and drink; *het* ~ *staat*

op tafel, dinner is on the table; *iemand te ~ vragen,* to invite someone to dinner; *na den ~,* after the meal; *onder den ~,* during the meal; *voor den ~,* before the meal. ·**etensbakje, -s,** *n.n.* feeding bowl. ·**etenslucht,** no pl., *n.* smell of cooking. ·**etenstijd,** no pl., *n.* meal-time, dinner-time, supper-time. ·**etensuur, -suren,** *n.n.* dinner hour. ·**eter, -s,** *n.* eater.
·**ether, -s,** *n.* ether. **e·therisch,** *a.* etherial. **etheri·seren, -seer,** *v.t.* to etherize.
·**ethisch,** *a.* ethical.
eti·ket, -tten, *n.n.* (stick-on) label.
·**etmaal, -malen,** *n.n.* space of 24 hours.
ets, *n.* etching. *droge ~,* dry-point etching. ·**etsen,** *v.t.* & *v.i.* to etch. ·**etser, -s,** *n.* etcher. ·**etsnaald,** *n.* etching-needle.
·**ettelijk,** *a.* & *pron.* several, some.
·**etter,** no pl., *n.* pus, matter. ·**etterachtig,** *a.* purulent. ·**etterbuil,** *n.* abscess. ·**etteren,** *v.i.* to fester, suppurate. ·**ettergezwel, -llen,** *n.n.* ulcer. ·**ettervorming,** *n.* suppuration.
Euro·pees, -pese, *a.* European.
·**euvel, -s,** *n.n.* evil, fault. ¶*adv. iemand iets ~ duiden (stilted),* to take offence at something someone does. ·**euveldaad, -daden,** *n.* evil deed, crime.
evan·gelie, -iën, *n.n.* gospel. *het ~ naar,* the gospel according to; *tot het ~ bekeren,* to convert, evangelize; *het is geen ~,* it is not all gospel truth. **evan·geliedienaar, -s** *or* **-naren,** *n.* minister of the gospel. **evan·gelieprediker, -s** *or* **-s,** *n.* preacher of the gospel. **evan·geliewoord,** *n.n.* gospel *(doctrine).*
·**even,** *a.* even. *een ~ getal,* an even number; *~ of oneven,* odd or even. ¶no pl., *n.n. het is mij om het ~,* it is all the same to me. ¶*adv.* equally; a moment, just. *hoor eens ~,* yes but . . ., *or* look here; *kijk eens ~,* just have a look; *wacht ~,* wait a moment; *zo ~,* just now; *~ voor tienen,* just before 10 o'clock. ·**evenaar, -s,** *n.* equator. ·**evenals,** *c.* (just) as or like. **even·aren, -aar,** *v.t.* to equal, approximate. ·**evenbeeld,** *n.n.* image, likeness *(fig.).* **even·eens,** *adv.* also, likewise. ·**evengoed,** *adv.* just as well. ·**evenknie, -ieën,** *n.* equal, compeer. **even·matig,** *a.* proportional. *~ deel,* aliquot part. ·**evenmens,** *n.* fellow man. **even·min,** *adv.* no more; nor . . . neither. *hij is ~ geslaagd als,* he succeeded no more than . . .; *en hij ~,* nor he either. **even·naaste, -n,** *n.* fellow man. **even·nachtslijn,** *n.* equinoctial line. **even·redig,** *a.* proportional *(representation);* proportionate. *omgekeerd or recht ~ met,* inversely *or* directly proportionate to. ¶*adv.* proportionally; proportionately. *~ met or aan,* in proportion to. **even·redigheid, -heden,** *n.* proportion. ·**eventjes,** *adv.* just; a moment. *See* **even,** *adv.*
eventuali·teit, *n.* conti~gency, eventuality.

eventu·eel, -uele, *a.* possible. *eventuele onkosten,* expenses if any, expenses that may occur; *eventuele klachten,* complaints if any. ¶*adv.* by any chance.
·**evenveel,** *adv.* & *pron.* as much, as many. **even·wel,** *adv.* however. ·**evenwicht,** no pl., *n.n.* balance, equilibrium. *het ~ bewaren,* to keep one's balance; *uit het ~ brengen,* to throw out of balance; *het ~ herstellen,* to redress the balance; *iets in ~ houden,* to keep something balanced; *het ~ verbreken,* to upset the balance; *het ~ verliezen,* to lose one's balance; *in ~ zijn,* to be well balanced. **even·wichtig,** *a.* well balanced. ·**evenwichtstoestand,** *n.* state of equilibrium. **even·wijdig,** *a.* & *adv.* parallel. *~ met,* parallel to. **even·wijdigheid,** no pl., *n.* parallelism. **even·zeer,** *adv. (stilted)* as much. *~ als,* as much as. ·**evenzo,** *adv.* just as.
·**ever, -s,** *n.,* ·**everzwijn,** *n.n.* wild boar.
evo·lutie, -s, *n.* evolution.
e·xact, *a.* exact, precise.
e·xamen, -s, *n.n.* examination, exam. *een ~ afleggen,* to undergo an examination; *een ~ afnemen,* to examine *(candidate);* *~ doen,* to take an examination; *voor een ~ ingaan,* to enter for an examination; *voor een ~ slagen,* to pass an examination. **e·xamencommissie, -s,** *n.* examining board, board of examination. **e·xamenopgaaf, -gaven,** *n.* examination paper. **exami·nandus, -di,** *n.* examinee. **exami·nator, -s** *or* **-en,** *n.* examiner. **exami·neren, -neer,** *v.t.* to examine *(candidate).*
excel·lentie, -s, *n.* Excellency.
excu·seren, -seer, *v.t.* to excuse. ¶*zich ~,* *v.r.* to excuse oneself *or* to beg to be excused. **ex·cuus, -cuses,** *n.n.* excuse. *zijn ~ maken,* to offer one's apologies; *~ vragen,* to beg *(someone's)* pardon.
execu·teren, -teer, *v.t.* to execute. *iemand ~,* to sell a person's goods. **execu·teur, -s** *or* **-en,** *n.* executor. **exe·cutie, -s,** *n.* execution. **execu·toir,** *a.* executory.
e·xempel, -s *or* **-en,** *n.n.* medieval didactic tale. **exem·plaar, -plaren,** *n.n.* copy, specimen. **exem·plair,** *a.* exemplary.
exer·ceren, -ceer, *v.t.* & *v.i.* to drill. **exer·citie, -s,** *n.* drill *(military).*
expedi·ëren, -ieer, *v.t.* to dispatch, forward, ship. **expedi·teur, -s** *cr* **-en,** *n.* sender; forwarding agent, shipping agent. **expe·ditie, -s,** *n.* expedition; dispatch, forwarding, shipping. **expe·ditiekantoor, -toren,** *n.n.* shipping- *or* forwarding office. **expe·ditieleger, -s,** *n.n.* expeditionary force.
experi·ment, *n.n.* experiment. **experimen·teel, -tele,** *a.* experimental. **experimen·teren, -teer,** *v.i.* to experiment.
ex·pert, *n.* expert. **exper·tise,** *n.* survey; report.

ex·ploit, *n.n. See* exploot. exploi·tatie, -s, *n.* working, exploitation. *in* ~, in operation, under development; *in* ~ *brengen,* to open up. exploi·tatieka·pitaal, -talen, *n.n.* working capital. exploi·tatiekosten, pl. only, *n.* working expenses. exploi·tatiemaatschappij, *n.* company for the exploitation of. exploi·teren, -teer, *v.t.* to work, exploit; to exploit, selfishly utilize. ex·ploot, -ploten, *n.n.* writ. *iemand een* ~ *betekenen,* to serve a writ on someone.

ex·port, *n.* export. expor·teren, -teer, *v.t.* to export. expor·teur, -s, *n.* exporter.

ex·pres, -sse, *a.* express. *expresse bestelling* or *brief,* express delivery *or* letter. ¶*adv.* on purpose. ex·presse, -n, *n.* express. *per* ~, per express. ex·presselijk, *adv.* on purpose. ex·prestrein, *n.* express (train).

ex·tase, no pl., *n.* ecstasy. *in* ~ *geraken,* to go into ecstasies. ex·tatisch, *a.* ecstatic, enraptured. ¶*adv.* ecstatically.

·extra, *a.* extra, special. ¶*adv.* extra. extra·heren, -heer, *v.t.* to extract. ex·traneüs, -nei, *n.* external student. extraparlemen·tair, *a.* non-party (*cabinet*). ·extratje, -s, *n.n.* little extra, windfall.

·ezel, -s, *n.* ass, jackass, donkey; dunce; easel. *een* ~ *stoot zich geen tweemaal aan dezelfde steen,* once bitten twice shy. ·ezelachtig, *a.* stupid, asinine. ¶*adv.* stupidly. *zich* ~ *aanstellen,* to make a fool of oneself. ·ezelachtigheid, -heden, *n.* (a) stupidity. eze·lin, -nnen, *n.* she-ass, jenny (-ass). eze·linnenmelk, no pl., *n.* ass's milk. ·ezelsbrug, -ggen, *n.* mnemonic. ·ezelshuid, *n.* ass's skin. ·ezelsoor, -soren, *n.n.* dog's-ear, dog-ear (*of book*). *vol ezelsoren,* dog-eared.

F

faam, no pl., *n.* fame, reputation.
·fabel, -s, *n.* fable. ·fabelachtig, *a.* fabulous.
fabri·cage, no pl., *n.* manufacture (*process*). fabri·ceren, -ceer, *v.t.* to manufacture. fa·briek, *n.* factory. fa·brieksarbeider, -c, *n.* factory hand. fa·brieksarbeidster, -s, *n.* factory hand (*female*). fa·brieksbaas, -bazen, *n.* foreman, overseer. fa·briekseigenaar, -s, *n.* mill-owner. fa·brieksgebouw, *n.n.* factory building. fa·brieksinstallatie, -s, *n.* factory plant. fa·brieksmerk, *n.n.* trade mark. fa·brieksstad, -steden, *n.* manufacturing town. fa·brieksterrein, *n.n.* factory site. fa·briekswezen, no pl., *n.n.* factory system; manufacturing industry. fabri·kaat, -katen, *n.n.* manufacture, make. fabri·kant, *n.* manufacturer; mill-owner.
face-à-main, -s, *n.* lorgnette.

facili·teit, *n.* facility.
·factie, -s, *n.* faction.
facto·rij, *n.* trading-post, factory. fac·tuur, -turen, *n.* invoice.
faculta·tief, -ve, *a.* facultative. *iets* ~ *stellen,* to make something optional. facul·teit, *n.* faculty.
fae·caliën, pl. only, *n.* faeces.
fa·got, -tten, *n.* bassoon.
fail·liet, *n.n.* bankruptcy, failure. ¶*a.* bankrupt, insolvent. ~*e boedel,* insolvent estate; ~ *gaan,* to go bankrupt, fail; ~ *verklaard worden,* to be declared bankrupt. fail·lietverklaring, *n.* adjudication in bankruptcy. faillisse·ment, *n.n.* bankruptcy, failure. ~ *aanvragen,* to file one's petition in bankruptcy; *in staat van* ~ *verkeren,* to be a bankrupt. faillisse·mentsaanvrage, -n, *n.* petition of bankruptcy.
·fakkel, -s, *n.* torch. ·fakkeldrager, -s, *n.* torch-bearer, link-boy.
·falen, faal, *v.i.* to fail; to miss; to lack.
·faliekant, *a.* ~ *uitkomen,* to go wrong (*of plan*).
fal·saris, -ssen, *n.* forger, falsifier.
fa·meus, -ze, *a.* famous; wonderful. ¶*adv.* wonderfully, enormously.
famili·aar, -liare, *a.* familiar, informal; over-familiar. ~ *omgaan met,* to be on friendly terms with; *al te* ~, far too familiar. familiari·teit, *n.* familiarity. *zich* ~*en veroorloven,* to take liberties. fa·milie, -s, *n.* family; relations, relatives. *de* ~ *X,* the X's; *ze zijn* ~ *van elkaar,* they are related; *van goede* ~ *zijn,* to come of a good family; *het zit in de* ~, it runs in the family. fa·milieberichten, pl. only, *n.n.* births, deaths and marriages (*in newspaper*). fa·miliebescheiden, pl. only, *n.n.* family documents. fa·miliebetrekking, *n.* relationship. fa·miliekring, *n.* family *or* domestic circle. fa·milielid, -leden, *n.n.* member of the family; relative, relation. fa·milietrek, -kken, *n.* family trait *or* characteristic. fa·miliezwak, no pl., *n.n.* indulgence towards member(s) of the family.
fana·tiek, *a.* fanatic(al).
fan·fare, -s, *n.* flourish, fanfare. fan·farecorps, *n.n.* brass band.
fanta·seren, -seer, *v.t.* to invent (*stories, etc.*). ¶*v.i.* to indulge in fancies. fanta·sie, -ieën, *n.* fantasy, fancy. fanta·sieartikelen, pl. only, *n.* fancy goods. fanta·siestof, -ffen, *n.* material in fancy colours. fan·tast, *n.* person with fantastic ideas. fan·tastisch, *a.* fantastic.
Fari·zeeër, -s, *n.* Pharisee.
fat, -tten, *n.* dandy.
fa·taal, -tale, *a.* fatal. fata·listisch, *a.* fatalistic.
fat·soen, *n.n.* good manners; decency, respectability; shape, form. *geen* ~

kennen, to have no manners; *zijn* ~ *houden*, to behave decently; *met* ~, decently; *voor zijn* ~, for decency's sake; *zijn* ~ *ophouden*, to keep up appearances; *uit zijn* ~ *zijn*, to be out of shape. **fatsoe·neren, -neer,** *v.t.* to shape. **fat·soenlijk,** *a.* respectable, reputable, decent. **fat·soenlijkheid,** no pl., *n.* respectability, decency. **fat·soenshalve,** *adv.* for decency's sake.

·fatterig, *a.* dandyish. ¶*adv.* like a dandy.

fa·veur, -s, *n.* favour. **fa·veurtje, -s,** *n.n.* windfall.

fa·zant, *n.* pheasant. **fazanten·haan, -hanen,** *n.* cock-pheasant. **fazanten·hen, -nnen,** *n.* hen-pheasant.

febru·ari, *N.* February.

fee, feeën, *n.* fairy. **·feeachtig,** *a.* fairylike. **feeks,** *n.* shrew, virago. **feeë·riek,** *a.* fairylike.

feest, *n.n.* feast, festivity, fête. *een waar* ~, a proper treat. **·feestavond,** *n.* festive evening. **·feestbanket,** *n.n.* banquet. **·feestcommissie, -s,** *n.* entertainment committee. **·feestdag,** *n.* holy day, festive day. **·feestdos,** no pl., *n.* festive garb. **·feestdronk,** *n.* toast (*drink*). **·feestdrukte,** no pl., *n.* bustle, excitement (*of feast*). **·feestelijk,** *a.* festive. *dank je* ~!, no thanks! (*ironic refusal*). **·feestelijkheid, -heden,** *n.* festivity. **·feesten,** *v.i.* to celebrate. **·feestgenoot, -noten,** *n.* fellow guest at feast. **·feestgelag,** *n.n.* revel, drinking bout. **·feestje, -s,** *n.n.* party, celebration. **·feestmaal, -malen,** *n.n.* banquet. **·feeststemming,** *n.* festive mood. **·feestvieren,** *v.i.s.* to celebrate; make merry.

feil, *n.* (*stilted*) fault, error. **·feilbaar, -bare,** *a.* fallible. **·feilbaarheid,** no pl., *n.* fallibility. **·feilen,** *v.i.* to err. **·feilloos, -lloze,** *a.* faultless.

feit, *n.n.* fact. *voor het* ~ *staan*, to be faced by the fact. **·feitelijk,** *a.* actual, de facto. ¶*adv.* in point of fact, virtually, practically. **·feitelijkheden,** pl. only, *n.* acts of violence.

fel, -lle, *a.* fierce, keen. ~ *zijn op*, to be (dead) keen on.

felici·tatie, -s, *n.* congratulation. **felici·teren, -teer,** *v.t.* to congratulate. ~ *met*, to congratulate on; *wel gefeliciteerd!*, my very best congratulations! *or* many happy returns!

·femelaar, -s, *n.* hypocrite, sanctimonious person. **femela·rij,** *n.* hypocrisy, sanctimony. **femelen,** *v.i.* to be sanctimonious.

·feniks, *n.* phœnix.

feo·daal, -dale, *a.* feudal.

ferm, *a.* firm, steady.

fes, no pl., *n.* F flat.

fes·tijn, *n.n.* feast, banquet. **festivi·teit,** *n.* festivity.

fes·toen, *n.n.* festoon. **feston·neren, -nneer,** *v.t.* to festoon.

fê·teren, -teer, *v.t.* to fête.

feu·daal, -dale, *a. See* **feodaal.**

feuille·ton, -s, *n.* serial story (*in newspaper*). *als* ~ *verschijnen*, to run as a serial.

fez, -zzen, *n.* fez.

fi·asco, -'s, *n.n.* fiasco.

·fiat, *n.n.* fiat. *van* ~ *voorzien*, to attach one's fiat to.

·fiche, -s, *n.* counter (*in games*); slip (*in card index*).

·fictie, -s, *n.* fiction (*of imagination*). **fic·tief, -ve,** *a.* fictitious, imaginary.

fi·deel, -dele, *a.* jovial.

fiduci·air, *a.* fiduciary. **fi·ducie,** no pl., *n.* faith, confidence.

·fiedel, -s, *n.* fiddle. **·fiedelen,** *v.i.* to fiddle.

fielt, *n.* rogue, knave. **·fieltenstreek, -streken,** *n.* knavish *or* dirty trick. **·fielterig,** *a.* knavish.

fier, *a.* proud. **·fierheid,** no pl., *n.* pride.

fiets, *n.* bike. **·fietsband,** *n.* bicycle tyre. **·fietsen,** *v.i.* to cycle. **·fietser, -s,** *n.* cyclist. **·fietstocht,** *n.* cycling tour. **·fietstochtje, -s,** *n.n.* cycling trip.

figu·rant, *n.* super (*stage, film*). **fi·guur, -guren,** *n.* figure. *een gek* ~ *slaan* or *maken*, to look foolish; *een goed* ~ *maken*, to make a good showing. **fi·guurlijk,** *a.* figurative. **fi·guurzaag, -zagen,** *n.* fretsaw. **fi·guurzagen, -zaag,** *v.i.* to do fretwork. ¶no pl., *n.n.* fretwork.

fijn, *a.* fine; pure; shrewd; delicate; delicious, exquisite; narrowly orthodox (*calvinist*). ~*e gereedschappen*, instruments of precision, precision tools; *een* ~*e neus voor iets hebben*, to be good at spotting something; *een* ~ *heer*, a nice customer; ~!, lovely!. ¶*adv.* finely; nicely; *iets* ~ *malen*, to grind something to powder. **·fijne, -n,** *n.n.* narrowly orthodox godly person (*mocking*); essence, fine part. *het* ~ *van de grap*, the cream of the jest; *het* ~ *van de zaak*, the essence of the matter. **fijne·voelig,** *a.* sensitive, delicate. **fijnge·voeligheid, -heden,** *n.* sensitiveness. **·fijnhakken, hak fijn,** *v.t.s.* to chop up. **·fijnheid, -heden,** *n.* fineness; nicety. **·fijnigheid, -heden,** *n.* trick, subtlety. **·fijnkauwen,** *v.t.* to masticate. **·fijnmaken, maak fijn,** *v.t.s.* to pulverize, break up. **·fijnproever, -s,** *n.* connoisseur (*of food and drink*). **·fijnstampen,** *v.t.s.* to pound up. **·fijntjes,** *adv.* cleverly, nicely; smartly. **·fijnwrijven, wrijf fijn,** *v.t.s., str.* to rub down, pulverize.

fijt, *n.* whitlow.

·fikken, pl. only, *n.* (*coll.*) fingers.

fiks, *a.* good, sound, hard.

·file, -s, *n.* file, row.

fili·aal, -ialen, *n.n.* branch, branch office.

fili·graan, -granen, *n.n.* filigree; watermark.

film, -s, *n.* film (*cinema*). *een* ~ *afdraaien*, to show a film; *bij de* ~ *zijn*, to be on the films. ·filmopname, -n, *n.* shot (*by film-camera*). ·filmen, *v.t.* to film.

·filter, -s, *n.* filter, percolator; screen. fil·traat, -traten, *n.n.* filtrate. fil·treer-machine, -s, *n.* filtering apparatus. fil·treerpapier, no pl., *n.n.* filter-paper. fil·treren, -treer, *v.t.* to filter.

Fin, *n.* Finn. Fins, *a.* Finnish.

fi·naal, -nale, *a.* final; total. ¶*adv.* finally, completely. fi·nale, -s, *n.* finale; final (*match, event*).

financi·eel, -iele, *a.* financial. fi·nanciën, pl. only, *n.* finance(s). finan·cieren, *v.t.* to finance. fi·nanciewezen, no pl., *n.n.* finance; financial system.

fi·neren, -neer, *v.t.* to refine (*gold, silver*); to veneer. fi·nesse, -s, *n.* finesse, subtlety.

fin·geren, -geer, *v.t.* to pretend, feign.

fi·ool, fiolen, *n.* phial. *de fiolen des toorns uitstorten over*, to pour forth the vials of wrath upon.

·firma, -'s, *n.* firm, company. fir·mant, *n.* partner.

·fiscus, no pl., *n.* treasury, revenue. fis·kaal, -kale, *a.* fiscal. ~ *recht*, revenue tax.

·fistel, -s, *n.* fistula.

·fitis, -ssen, *n.* willow-warbler.

·fitter, -s, *n.* fitter.

fi·xeerbad, *n.n.* fixing bath. fi·xeren, -xeer, *v.t.* to fix (*photography*). *iemand* ~, to stare fixedly at a person.

fla·con, -s, *n.* bottle (*small*), scent bottle.

·fladderen, *v.i.* to flutter, flit.

·flakkeren, *v.i.* to flicker.

·fam·bouw, *n.* torch.

Flamin·gant, *N.* Flemish nationalist.

fla·neren, -neer, *v.i.* to saunter, stroll. fla·neur, -s, *n.* person who saunters *or* strolls.

fla·nel, no pl., *n.n.* flannel. fla·nellen, *a.* (*made of*) flannel. fla·nelletje, -s, *n.n.* flannel vest.

flank, *n.* flank. *links* or *rechts uit de* ~ *mars!*, left *or* right about turn! ·flankaan-val, -llen, *n.* flank attack. ·flankbeweging, *n.* flanking movement. flan·keren, -keer, *v.t.* to flank.

·flansen, *v.t. in elkaar* ~, to throw together carelessly.

flap, *excl.* slap, bang. ·flaphoed, *n.* slouch hat. ·flappen, flap, *v.t.* to flap; to blab. *iets eruit* ~, to blurt something out. ·flapuit, *n.* blabber.

·flarden, pl. only, *n.* rags, tatters. *aan* ~, in tatters *or* shreds.

·flater, -s, *n.* blunder.

flat·teren, -tteer, *v.t.* to flatter. *de balans* ~, to cook the balance sheet. flat·teus, -ze, *a.* flattering.

flauw, *a.* weak; insipid, flat; faint; vague, dim; silly. *hij had er geen* ~ *idee van*, he had not the faintest idea of it; ~ *vallen*, to faint. ·flauwerd, -s, *n.*, ·flauwerik, -kken, *n.* silly person; milksop. flauw·hartig,

a. fainthearted. ·flauwheid, -heden, *n.* weakness, silliness. flauwi·teit, *n.* silly joke. ·flauwte, -s, *n.* faint. *een* ~ *krijgen*, to faint. ·flauwtjes, *adv.* faintly.

·flegma, no pl., *n.n.* phlegm, stolidity. fleg·matisch, *a.* phlegmatic, stolid.

·flemen, fleem, *v.i.* to coax, cajole. ·flemer, -s, *n.* coaxer. fleme·rij, *n.* coaxing.

flens, -zen, *n.* flange. ·flensje, -s, *n.n.* (thin) pancake.

fles, -ssen, *n.* bottle. *op flessen doen*, to bottle; *op de* ~ *gaan* (*coll.*), to go bankrupt. ·flessenbier, no pl., *n.n.* bottled beer. ·flessenmelk, no pl., *n.* milk in bottles. ·flessentrekker, -s, *n.* swindler. flessentrekke·rij, *n.* swindling.

flets, *a.* pallid; faded. ~ *worden*, to wilt. ¶*adv.* dimly. ·fletsheid, no pl., *n.* fadedness, paleness.

fleur, no pl., *n.* prime, flower, hey-day. *in volle* ~, in full bloom. ·fleurig, *a.* blooming.

·flikflooien, *v.i.* & *v.t.* to fawn (on), flatter, cajole. ·flikflooier, -s, *n.* flatterer, sycophant, toady. flikflooie·rij, *n.* flattery, fawning.

·flikje, -s, *n.n.* chocolate drop.

·flikken, flik, *v.t.* to cobble; to manage. *ik zal het hem wel* ~, I shall manage all right. ·flikker, -s, *n.* caper. *een* ~ *slaan*, to cut a caper. ·flikkeren, *v.i.* to flicker (*of lamp*); to twinkle (*star*); (*v. coll.*) to fall; to chuck. ·flikkering, *n.* flicker(ing), twinkling. ·flikkerlicht, *n.n.*, ·flikkervuur, *n.n.* intermittent flashes, flashing light (*heliograph, lighthouse*).

flink, *a.* fine, stout, lusty; plucky; energetic, smart; thorough; considerable; substantial. ¶*adv.* vigorously; thoroughly. ~ *afranselen*, to give a sound thrashing; ~ *eten*, to eat heartily; ~ *optreden*, to be firm; ~ *regenen*, to rain hard; ~ *vooruitgaan*, to get on well. ·flinkheid, no pl., *n.* spirit; energy. ·flinkweg, *adv.* boldly.

flits, *n.* flash. ·flitsen, *v.i.* to flash.

·flodder. -s, *n.* mud. *losse* ~, blank cartridge. ·flodderbroek, *n.* baggy trousers. ·flodderen, *v.i.* to flounder (*in mud*); to flap, flop. ·flodderig, *a.* floppy, baggy. ·floddermadam, -s, *n.* dowdy woman, frump. ·floddermuts, *n.* voluminous lace cap.

floers, *n.n.* crape.

·flonkeren, *v.i.* to twinkle, sparkle. ·flonkerlicht, no pl., *n.n.* sparkling light.

flo·reren, -reer, *v.i.* to flourish, thrive. floris·sant, *a.* flourishing. flo·ret, -tten, *n.n.* foil (*fencing*).

flo·tielje, -s, *n.*, flo·tille, -s, *n.* flotilla.

fluim, *n.n.* phlegm. ~*en opgeven*, to expectorate.

·fluisteraar, -s, *n.* whisperer. ·fluisteren, *v.t.* & *v.i.* to whisper. *iemand iets in het oor* ~, to whisper something into a person's ear. ·fluisterend, *adv.* in a whisper.

fluit, *n.* flute. ·fluiteend, *n.* widgeon. ·fluiten,
v.t., *str.* & *v.i.*, *str.* to whistle; to warble,
pipe. *je kunt er naar* ∼, you can whistle
for it; *tweemaal* ∼, to give two blasts on the
siren. ·fluiter, -s, *n.* whistler; garden-
warbler. ·fluitglas, -zen, *n.n.* flute (*wine-
glass*). flui·tist, *n.* flautist. ·fluitje, -s, *n.n.*
whistle. ·fluitketel, -s, *n.* whistling-
kettle. ·fluitregister, -s, *n.n.* flute-stop.
fluks, *a.* quick. ¶*adv.* speedily.
flu·weel, no pl., *n.n.* velvet. flu·weelachtig,
a. velvety. flu·welen, *a.* (made of) velvet.
met ∼ *handschoenen aanpakken*, to handle
with kid gloves; ∼ *tong*, honeyed tongue.
flu·welig, *a.* velvety.
·fnuiken, *v.t.* to break, cripple. ·fnuikend,
a. fatal.
foe·draal, -dralen, *n.n.* cover, sheath.
·foefje, -s, *n.n.* dodge, trick; excuse. *het
ouwe* ∼, the same old dodge.
foei, *excl.* shame! ·foeilelijk, *a.* & *adv.* as
ugly as sin.
·foelie, no pl., *n.* mace (*spice*); foil, tain.
·foeliesel, no pl., *n.n.* tain.
foe·rier, -s, *n. See* fourier.
·foeteren, *v.i.* to grumble, curse under one's
breath.
fok, -kken, *n.* foresail; spectacles (*fac.*).
·fokkemast, *n.* foremast. ·fokkera, -raas,
n. foreyard.
·fokhengst, *n.* stallion, stud-horse. ·fokken,
fok, *v.t.* to breed (*cattle*). ·fokker, -s, *n.*
(cattle-)breeder.   fokke·rij, *n.* cattle-
breeding; stock-farm.   ·fokvee, no pl.,
n.n. breeding-cattle.
foli·ant, *n.* folio (*volume*). ·foliopapier, no pl.,
n.n. foolscap.
·folteraar, -s, *n.* torturer, tormentor. ·folter-
bank, *n.* rack (*torture*). ·folteren, *v.t.* to
torture, torment. ·folterend, *a.* excruciating. ·foltering, *n.* torture. ·folterkamer,
-s, *n.* torture chamber.
fond, *n.* background; bottom. ·fonda·ment,
n.n. See fundament. fonds, *n.n.* fund;
(publisher's) stock; (*fig.*) stock. ¶pl. only,
n.n. funds; securities, stocks and shares.
·fondscatalogus, -gi, *n.* publisher's catalogue. ·fondsdokter, -s, *n.* panel doctor.
·fondspatiënt, *n.* panel patient. ·fonds-
restanten, pl. only, *n.n.* publisher's
remainders.
·fonkelen, *v.i.* to sparkle, scintillate. ·fonkel-
nieuw, *a.* brand new.
fon·tein, *n.* fountain. fon·teinkruid, no pl.,
n.n. pond weed. fon·teintje, -s, *n.n.* wash-
basin (*with tap*); drinking bowl (*in
birdcage*).
fooi, *n.* tip, gratuity. *een* ∼ *geven*, to
tip.
·foppen, fop, *v.t.* to fool, hoax. ·fopper, -s,
n. hoaxer. foppe·rij, *n.* hoax(ing).
·fopspeen, -spenen, *n.* (baby's) comforter,
dummy.
for·ceren, -ceer, *v.t.* to force; to strain.

fo·rel, -llen, *n.* trout. fo·relkwekerij, *n.*
trout-farm.
fo·rens, *n.* non-resident. fo·rensenbelasting,
n. tax on non-residents.
for·maat, -maten, *n.n.* format, size. formali-
·teit, *n.* formality. *zekere* ∼*en vervullen*,
to carry out certain formalities. forma-
·teur, -s, *n.* person who forms a cabinet.
for·matie, -s, *n.* formation; establishment (*military*).   for·meel, -mele, *a.*
formal. ¶*adv.* formally; absolutely. for-
·meren, -meer, *v.t.* to form, create. for-
·mering, *n.* formation (*of new cabinet*).
for·mule, -s, *n.* formula.   formu·leren,
-leer, *v.t.* to formulate. formu·lering, *n.*
wording. formu·lier, *n.n.* form, blank.
∼ *van aangifte*, application form.
for·nuis, -zen, *n.n.* kitchen range.
fors, *a.* stalwart, robust. ¶*adv.* vigorously.
·forsgebouwd, *a.* robust, strongly built.
·forsheid, no pl., *n.* robustness, vigour.
fort, *n.n.* fort. fortifi·catie, -s, *n.* fortification.
for·tuin, *n.n.* fortune. ¶no pl., *n.* Fortune,
fate. for·tuinlijk, *a.* fortunate, lucky.
for·tuinzoeker, -s, *n.* fortune-hunter.
fos·siel, *n.n.* fossil. ¶*a.* fossil.
·foto, -'s, *n.* photo. foto·graaf, -grafen, *n.*
photographer. fotogra·feren, -feer, *v.t.*
to photograph. *zich laten* ∼, to have one's
photo taken.   fotogra·fie, -fieën, *n.* photograph.   fotogra·fietoestel, -llen, *n.n.*
camera.   foto·grafisch, *a.* photographic.
∼ *atelier*, photographic studio. fotogra-
·vure, -s, *n.* photogravure.   fototy·pie, no
pl., *n.* phototype.
fouil·leren, -lleer, *v.t.* to search (*person*).
fou·rage, no pl., *n.* stores, forage. fou·rier,
-s, *n.* quartermaster.
four·neren, -neer, *v.t.* to furnish, provide.
fout, *n.* mistake, error; fault. *een grove* ∼
maken, to blunder; *zonder* ∼, without
fail. ¶*a.* wrong. fou·tief, -ve, *a.* wrong,
erroneous.
fraai, *a.* handsome, fine, pretty. ·fraaiheid,
no pl., *n.* prettiness. ·fraaiigheid, -heden,
n. fine sayings, pretty speeches (*ironical*).
en dergelijke fraaiigheden, and suchlike
rubbish. ·fraaitjes, *adv.* nicely.
·fractie, -s, *n.* fraction; grouping (*within
political party*); group, bloc (*of political
party en representative body*). frac·tuur,
-turen, *n.* fracture.
fram·boos, -bozen, *n.* raspberry.   fram-
·bozeboom, -bomen, *n.*, fram·bozestruik,
∼n.   raspberry bush, raspberry cane.
fram·bozengelei, no pl., *n.* raspberry jam.
·franco, *a.* & *adv.* post-paid; carriage-paid.
∼ *boord*, free on board, f.o.b.; ∼ *lichter*,
free alongside ship, f.a.s.; ∼ *spoor*, free
on rail, f.o.r.; ∼ *wagon*. free on truck;
∼ *wal*, free on quay.
·franje, -s, *n.* fringe, frills.
frank, *a.* frank. fran·keren, -keer, *v.t.* to
stamp, prepay (*letters*). fran·kering, *n.*

postage, prepayment. **fran·keerkosten,** pl. only, *n.* postage, carriage. **fran·keerwaarde, -n,** *n.* postal value. **fran·keerzegel, -s,** *n.n.* postage stamp. **·Frankrijk,** *n.N.* France. **Frans,** *a.* French. *een* ~*e,* a Frenchwoman; *zich met een* ~*e slag van iets afmaken,* to scamp a job; *er is geen woord* ~ *bij,* that is plain speaking. **·Fransgezind,** *a.* pro-French. **·Fransman, Fransen,** *N.* Frenchman. **Fran·soos, -sozen,** *N.* Froggy (*Frenchman*).

frap·pant, *a.* striking. **frap·peren, -ppeer,** *v.t.* to strike (*thought*); to ice (*drink*).

·frater, -s, *n.* lay brother.

·fratsen, pl. only, *n.* pranks; grimaces; nonsense. **·fratsenmaker, -s,** *n.* clown (*not circus*).

·fraude, -s, *n.* fraud. ~ *plegen,* to practise fraud. **frau·deren, -deer,** *v.i.* to practise fraud. **fraudu·leus, -ze,** *a.* fraudulent.

frees, frezen, *n.* fraise.

fre·gat, -tten, *n.n.* frigate. **fre·gatvogel, -s,** *n.* frigate bird.

fret, -tten, *n.n.* ferret; gimlet. **·fretten, fret,** *v.i.* to ferret. **·fretzaag, -zagen,** *n.* fretsaw.

·freule, -s, *n.* the Hon. Miss. . . .

·frezen, freies, *v.t.* to enlarge hole with fraise.

·frictie, -s, *n.* friction.

·friemelen, *v.i.* to fiddle, fumble.

fries, -zen, *n.* frieze.

Fries, *a.* Frisian. ¶ **-zen.** *N.* Frisian (*man*). ~*e ruiter,* chevaux de frise. **·Friesland,** *n.N.* Frisia. **Frie·zin, -nnen,** *N.* Frisian woman.

frikka·del, -llen, *n.* minced meat, forcemeat ball.

fris, -sse, *a.* fresh; fit. *zo* ~ *als een hoen,* as fresh as a daisy. **·frisheid,** no pl., *n.* freshness. **·frisjes,** *a.* & *adv.* fresh.

fri·seertang, *n.* curling tongs. **fri·seren, -seer,** *v.t.* to curl, frizz.

·fröbelschool, -scholen, *n.* kindergarten. **·fröbeljuffrouw,** *n.* kindergarten mistress.

·frommelen, *v.t.* to crumple.

frons, -zen, *n.* frown. **·fronsen,** *v.t. de wenkbrauwen* or *het voorhoofd* ~, to frown.

front, *n.n.* front. **·frontaanval, -llen,** *n.* frontal attack. **fron·taal, -tale,** *a.* frontal. **·frontje, -s,** *n.n.* dickey (*false shirt front*). **fron·ton, -s,** *n.n.* pediment.

fruit, no pl., *n.n.* fruit. **·fruithandelaar, -s,** *n.* fruiterer. **·fruitwinkel, -s,** *n.* fruiterer's (shop).

fuif, -ven, *n.* party, beano, binge. *een* ~ *geven,* to throw a party. **·fuifnummer, -s,** *n.n.* dissipated person.

fuik, *n.* fish-trap, eel-pot. *in de* ~ *lopen,* to be caught.

·fuiven, fuif, *v.i.* & *v.t.* to celebrate, revel.

·functie, -s, *n.* function. *in* ~ *treden,* to enter upon one's duties; *in zijn* ~ *van,* in his capacity of. **functio·naris, -ssen,** *n.*

functionary. **function·neren, -nneer,** *v.i.* to function.

funda·ment, *n.n.* foundation; fundament.

fu·nest, *a.* fatal, tragic.

fu·reur, no pl., *n.* furore. ~ *maken,* to create a furore.

fuse·lier, -s, *n.* fusilier.

·fusie, -s, *n.* fusion.

fusil·leren, -lleer, *v.t.* to shoot, execute.

fust, *n.n.* cask, barrel. *op* ~ *liggen,* to be stored in barrel.

fut, no pl., *n.* spirit, spunk. *de* ~ *is eruit* (*coll.*), it has lost its vigour.

·futselaar, -s, *n.* trifler, fiddler. **futsela·rij,** *n.,* **·futselwerk,** no pl., *n.n.* trifling, fiddling. **·futselen,** *v.i.* to trifle, fiddle.

fuut, futen, *n.* grebe.

G

gaaf, gave, *a.* whole, entire, sound. **·gaafheid,** no pl., *n.* soundness.

gaai, *n.* jay; popinjay (*archery*).

gaan, ga, *v.i., irr.* to go; to sell, be popular. *hoe gaat het?,* how are you?; *hoe gaat het met . . .?,* how is . . .?; *het gaat niet,* it is impossible; *eraan* ~, to be lost; *erin* ~, to go down, become popular; *er vandoor,* to run away; *het gaat om . . .,* it concerns . . . *or . . . is* at stake; *het gaat niet op,* it does not follow. **·gaande,** *a.* going; afoot, on foot. *iets* ~ *houden,* to keep something going; ~ *maken,* to set in motion; *de* ~ *en komende man,* those coming and going. **gaande·rij,** *n.* gallery. **·gaandeweg,** *adv.* gradually. **gaans,** *n.n. een uur* ~, an hour's walk.

gaap, gapen, *n.* yawn.

gaar, gare, *a.* cooked, done. *niet* ~, underdone; *te* ~, overdone; *half* ~, half-baked, not all there; *een halve gare,* a halfwit.

·gaarde, -n, *n.* (*poetic*) garden.

·gaarkeuken, -s, *n.* eating house; communal kitchen.

·gaarne, *adv.* (*stilted*) readily, gladly.

gaas, no pl., *n.* gauze; wire netting. **·gaasachtig,** *a.* gauzy.

·gaatje, -s, *n.n.* small hole.

gade, -n, *n.* spouse.

·gadeslaan, sla gade, *v.t.s., irr.* to behold, observe. **·gading,** *n.* taste, liking. *van mijn* ~. to my liking; *zijn* ~ *vinden,* to find something to one's taste.

gaffel, -s, *n.* pitch-fork; gaff. **gaffelzeil,** *n.n.* trysail.

gage, -s, *n.* pay (*of crew*).

gagel, -s, *n.* gale, bog-myrtle.

·gaggelen, *v.i.* to gaggle.

gal, no pl., *n.* gall, bile. *de* ~ *loopt hem over,* he has reached the end of his patience; *zijn·* ~ *uitbraken,* to vent one's spleen. ¶ **-llen,** *n.* gall (*of horses*). **·galachtig,** *a.*

bilious; choleric. **·galappel, -s**, *n.* gall-nut. **·galblaas, -blazen**, *n.* gall-bladder.
ga·lant, *a.* gallant, courteous. **¶***n.* (*stilted*) fiancé. **galante·rie, -rieën**, *n.* gallantry, courtesy. **¶**pl. only, *n.* fancy goods. **galante·riewinkel, -s**, *n.* fancy goods shop.
ga·lei, *n.* galley. **ga·leiboef, -ven**, *n.*, **ga·lei-slaaf, -slaven**, *n.* galley slave.
gale·rij, *n.* gallery; verandah (*East Indies*).
galg, *n.* gallows, gibbet. *voor* ∼ *en rad opgroeien*, to be born to be hanged. **·galgebrok, -kken**, *n.* gallows-bird. **·galge-maal, -malen**, *n.n.* last *or* parting meal. **·galgenaas, -nazen**, *n.n.* gallows-bird. **·galgehumor**, no pl., *n.* grim humour. **·galgestrop, -ppen**, *n.* gallows-bird. **·galge-tronie, -s**, *n.* villainous face.
gal·joen, *n.n.* galleon.
·Gallië, *n.N.* Gaul.
galm, *n.* reverberation, resounding noise. **·galmbord**, *n.n.* sounding board. **gal·mei**, no pl., *n.n.* calamine. **·galmen**, *v.i.* to resound, boom. **·galmgat**, *n.n.* sound-hole.
·galnoot, -noten, *n.* gall-nut.
ga·lon, -s, *n.* braid, lace. **galon·neren, -nneer**, *v.t.* to (trim with) braid.
ga·lop, -s, *n.* gallop. *korte* ∼, canter; *in* ∼, at a gallop; *in volle* ∼, at full gallop. **galop·peren, -ppeer**, *v.i.* to gallop.
·galsteen, -stenen, *n.* gall-stone. **·galwesp**, *n.* gall-fly.
·gammel, *a.* ramshackle, dilapidated.
gang, *n.* passage, corridor (*in house*); gallery (*in mine*); alley; walk, gait; pace; rate of progress; speed. **¶**pl. movements. *zijn* ∼ *gaan*, to carry on; *zijn eigen* ∼ *gaan*, to go one's own way; *alles gaat zijn* ∼, everything goes on as usual; ∼ *maken*, to make the pace (*on racing track*); ∼ *hebben*, to have way on (*of ship*); *aan de* ∼ *blijven*, to keep working; *aan de* ∼ *zijn*, to be at work or to be at it (*quarrel*); *de* ∼ *van zaken*, the course of events; *iemands* ∼*en nagaan*, to watch a person's movements. **·gangbaar, -bare**, *a.* current. **·gangbaarheid**, no pl., *n.* currency (*time*). **·gangboord**, *n.n.* gang-way (*on ship*). **·gangetje**, no pl., *n.n. het gewone* ∼ *gaan*, to jog along as usual. **·gangloper, -s**, *n.* hall-carpet. **·gangmaker, -s**, *n.* pace-maker. **·gangmat, -tten**, *n.* hall-mat. **·gangspil, -llen**, *n.n.* capstan. **·gangwerk**, no pl., *n.* mechanism (*of clock*).
·gannef, -ven, *n.* (*slang*) thief, rascal.
gans, -zen, *n.* goose. *Moeder de G*∼, Mother Goose. **¶***a.* entire, whole. **¶***adv.* wholly, entirely. **·ganselijk**, *adv.* (*stilted*) wholly.
·ganzekuiken, -s, *n.n.* gosling. **·ganzelever, -s**, *n.* goose-liver. **·ganzenbloem**, *n.* margue-rite. **·ganzenhoedster, -s**, *n.* goosegirl. **·ganzenroer**, *n.n.* fowling piece. **·ganzepen, -nnen**, *n.* goose-quill. **·ganzerik, -kken**,

n. gander; goose-grass, silverweed. **·ganze-voet**, *n.* goose-foot.
·gapen, gaap, *v.i.* to yawn; to gape. **·gaper, -s**, *n.* gaper. **·gaperig**, *a.* yawny. **·gaping**, *n.* gap, hiatus, lacuna. *een* ∼ *aanvullen*, to fill a gap.
·gappen, gap, *v.t.* to pinch (*steal*). **·gapper, -s**, *n.* sneak-thief.
garan·deren, -deer, *v.t.* to guarantee. **ga·rant**. *n.* guarantor. **ga·rantie, -s**, *n.* guarantee, security. **ga·rantiebewijs, -zen**, *n.n.* warranty.
gard, *n.* rod, birch.
·garde, -s, *n.* guard. **garde·robe, -s**, *n.* wardrobe; cloakroom.
ga·reel, -relen, *n.n.* harness, collar. *in het* ∼, in harness, in the traces; *in het* ∼ *slaan* or *spannen*, to harness, put to *or* set to work; *in het* ∼ *lopen*, to toil.
·garen, -s, *n.n.* thread, yarn. ∼ *en band*, haberdashery. **¶***a:* yarn, string (*gloves*).
garf, -ven, *n.* sheaf.
gar·naal, -nalen, *n.* shrimp. *garnalen vangen*, to shrimp. **gar·nalenvisser, -s**, *n.* shrimper.
gar·neersel, -s, *n.* trimming. **gar·neren, -neer**, *v.t.* to trim; to garnish. **garni·tuur, -turen**, *n.* trimming(s); (*mantelpiece*) ornaments; set of jewels.
garni·zoen, *n.n.* garrison. *in* ∼ *liggen*, to be garrisoned; *een* ∼ *leggen in*, to garrison (*a town*).
·garstig, *a. & adv.* rancid. **·garstigheid**, no pl., *n.* rancidity.
·garven, garf, *v.t.* to sheave.
gas, -ssen, *n.n.* gas. **·gasachtig**, *a.* gaseous. **·gasarm**, *n.* gas-bracket. **·gasbek, -kken**, *n.* gas-jet. **·gasfabriek**, *n.* gas-works. **·gasfornuis, -zen**, *n.n.* gas-cooker, gas-stove. **·gashouder, -s**, *n.* gasometer. **·gaskachel, -s**, *n.* gas-fire. **·gaskomfoor, -foreu**, *n.n.* gas-ring. **·gaskousje, -s**, *n.n.* gas-mantle. **·gaslantaarn, -s**, *n.* gas-lamp (*in street*). **·gasleiding**, *n.* gas-main(s); gas-pipe(s).
·gaspeldoorn, -s, *n.* gorse, furze.
·gaspijp, *n.* gas-pipe. **·gaspit. -tten**, *n.* gas-jet. **·gasstel, -llen**, *n.n.* gas-cooker. **·gastoestel, -llen**, *n.n.* gas-cooker.
gast. *n.* guest; visitor; fellow. *bij iemand te* ∼ *zijn*, to be someone's guest. **·gastheer, -heren**, *n.* host. **·gasthuis, -zen**, *n.n.* hospital, hospice. **·gastmaal, -malen**, *n.n.* banquet.
·gastrisch, *a.* gastric.
·gastrol, -llen, *n.* star part; guest performance. **·gastvrij**, *a.* hospitable. **gast·vrijheid**, no pl., *n.* hospitality. ∼ *bewijzen* or *verlenen*, to render hospitality; ∼ *genieten*, to enjoy hospitality. **·gastvrouw**, *n.* hostess.
·gasvormig, *a.* gasiform, gaseous. **·gas-vorming**, *n.* gasification.
gat, *n.n.* hole, gap; channel; hamlet; dead-and-alive place; bum. *een* ∼ *in de dag slapen*, to sleep far into the day; *iets in*

de ~*en hebben* or *krijgen*, to spot *or* get wind of something; *iemand in de* ~*en houden*, to keep an eye on a person.
gauw, *a.* quick. *iemand te* ~ *af zijn*, to be too quick for someone. ¶*adv.* quickly; soon. *dat is* ~*er gezegd dan gedaan*, that is easier said than done; *dat gaat zo* ~ *niet*, that is not easily done. ·**gauwdief**, **-ven**, *n.* sneak-thief. **gauwdieve·rij**, *n.* pickpocketing. ·**gauwigheid**, **-heden**, *n.* quickness. *in de* ~, in passing *or* hurriedly.
·**gave**, **-n**, *n.* gift.
ga·zel, **-llen**, *n.* gazelle.
·**gazen**, *a.* (made of) gauze.
ga·zon, **-s**, *n.n.* lawn (*grass*).
ge, *pron.* you. **ge-**, *prefix of past participle.*
ge·aard, *a.* disposed. *goed* ~, good-natured. **ge·aardheid**, **-heden**, *n.* disposition, nature.
geacciden·teerd, *a.* accidented. **ge·acht**, *a.* esteemed. **geadres·seerde**, **-n**, *n.* addressee. **geaffec·teerd**, *a.* affected.
gealli·eerd, *a.* allied. **Gealli·eerden**, pl. only, *N. de* ~, the Allies.
ge·appeld, *a.* dappled. **ge·armd**, *a.* arm in arm.
ge·baar, **-baren**, *n.n.* gesture. *gebaren maken*, to gesticulate. **ge·baard**, *a.* bearded. **ge·babbel**, no pl., *n.n.* chatter.
ge·bak, no pl., *n.n.* pastry (*in general*). **ge·bakje**, **-s**, *n.n.* pastry, (small) cake.
gebakke·lei, *n.n.* fisticuffs. **ge·balk**, no pl., *n.n.* braying.
ge·barenspel, *n.n.* mime; gesticulation. **ge·barentaal**, no pl., *n.* language of gestures.
ge·bazel, no pl., *n.n.* twaddle. **ge·bed**, *n.n.* prayer. *een* ~ *doen*, to say a prayer; *zijn* ~*en doen*, to say one's prayers.
ge·bedel, no pl., *n.n.* begging. **ge·bedenboek**, *n.n.* prayer-book.
ge·beente, **-n**, *n.n.* bones (*of skeleton*). **ge·beft**, *a.* with bands (*of academic gown*). **ge·beier**, no pl., *n.n.* ringing (*of bells*). **ge·bekt**, *a.* beaked. **ge·bel**, no pl., *n.n.* ringing (*of doorbell*). **ge·belgdheid**, no pl., *n.* resentment, anger. **gebene·dijd**, *a.* blessed. **ge·bergte**, **-n**, *n.n.* mountain range. **ge·beten**, *a.* ~ *zijn op*, to be dead set against. **ge·beuk**, no pl., *n.n.* banging, battering.
ge·beuren, *v.imp.* to happen, take place. *het moet* ~, it must be done. **ge·beurlijk**, *a.* possible. **ge·beurtenis**, **-ssen**, *n.* event, happening.
ge·beuzel, no pl., *n.n.* twaddle; trifling.
ge·bied, *n.n.* territory; domain; jurisdiction; field, sphere. **ge·bieden**, *v.t.*, *str.* to order, command. **ge·biedend**, *a.* imperative. **ge·bieder**, **-s**, *n.* ruler, lord.
ge·binte, **-n**, *n.n.* cross-beams. **ge·bit**, **-tten**, *n.n.* (set of) teeth; bit (*of horse*). *vals* ~, artificial (*set of*) teeth, denture. **ge·blaas**, no pl., *n.n.* blowing. **ge·blaat**, no pl., *n.n.* bleating. **ge·bladerte**, no pl., *n.n.* foliage. **ge·blaf**, no pl., *n.n.* barking. **ge·blèr**, no pl., *n.n.* (coll.) crying (*of child*). **ge·bloemd**,

a. flowered. **ge·blok**, no pl., *n.n.* swotting. **ge·bluf**, no pl., *n.n.* boasting. **ge·blust**, *a.* slaked (*of lime*). **ge·bocheld**, *a.* hunchbacked. **ge·bod**, *n.n.* command; commandment. *de* ~*en aflezen*, to publish the banns; *de* ~*en sluiten*, to forbid the banns. **ge·boefte**, no pl., *n.n.* rabble, riff-raff. **ge·bogen**, *a.* bent, curved.
ge·bonden, *a.* tied; bound; thick (*of sauce*). *aan handen en voeten* ~, bound hand and foot. **ge·bondenheid**, no pl., *n.* lack of freedom.
ge·bons, no pl., *n.n.* banging. **ge·boomte**, no pl., *n.n.* trees, timber.
ge·boorte, **-n**, *n.* birth. *bij de* ~, at (the) birth; *van de* ~, by birth. **ge·boorteakte**, **-n**, *n.* birth-certificate. **ge·boortecijfer**, **-s**, *n.n.* birth-rate. **ge·boortegrond**, no pl., *n.n.* native soil. **ge·boortejaar**, **-jaren**, *n.n.* year of birth. **ge·boorterecht**, no pl., *n.n.* birthright. **ge·boortig**, *a.* ~ *uit* . . . a native of . . . **ge·boren**, *a.* born; by birth; née. ~ *uit*, born of; ~ *en getogen*, born and bred.
ge·borrel, no pl., *n.n.* bubbling; tippling. **ge·bouw**, *n.n.* building, edifice. **ge·braad**, no pl., *n.n.* roast meat (*game*).
ge·brek, *n.n.* fault, flaw; failing, infirmity; defect. ¶no pl., *n.n.* want, poverty; deficiency; lack, shortage, dearth. ~ *hebben* or *lijden*, to suffer want; ~ *hebben aan*, to be short of; ~ *aan*, shortage of; *bij* or *door* or *uit* ~ *aan*, for lack of. **ge·breke**, no pl., *n.n.* in ~ *blijven*, to default, to fail; *in* ~ *stellen*, to hold liable; *bij* ~ *van*, in the absence of. **ge·brekkelijk**, *a.* infirm, crippled. ¶*adv.* lamely. **ge·brekkig**, *a.* defective, poor, imperfect. ¶*adv.* haltingly, badly.
ge·broddel, no pl., *n.n.* bungling.
ge·broed, no pl., *n.n.* brood; spawn. **ge·broeders**, pl. only, *n.* brothers. *de* ~ *R.*, the R. brothers, R. Bros.
ge·broken, *a.* broken; fractional. ~ *weide*, a ploughed-up meadow.
ge·brom, no pl., *n.n.* growling; grumbling; murmur.
ge·bruik, *n.n.* use, custom, habit. ~ *maken van*, to make use of, avail oneself of; *buiten* ~, out of use, in disuse; *ten* ~*e van*, for the use of. **ge·bruikelijk**, *a.* customary. *op de* ~*e wijze*, in the customary way. **ge·bruiken**, *v.t.* to use; to take, partake of (*food*). **ge·bruiker**, **-s**, *n.* user. **ge·bruiksaanwijzing**, *n.* directions (*for use*). **ge·bruikswaarde**, no pl., *n.* utility value. **ge·bruikt**, *a.* used, secondhand. *niet meer* ~, no longer used, disused.
ge·bruind, *a.* browned; tanned. **ge·bruis**, no pl., *n.n.* effervescence; roaring (*of waves*). **ge·brul**, no pl., *n.n.* roar(ing) (*of lion*). **ge·bulder**, no pl., *n.n.* roar (*of cannon*). **ge·bulk**, no pl., *n.n.* lowing (*of cattle*).

gecommit·teerde, -n, *n.* delegate. **ge··daagde, -n,** *n.* defendant. **ge·daan, -dane,** *a.* done, finished. *gedane zaken nemen geen keer,* it's no use crying over spilt milk; ~ *geven,* to sack; ~ *krijgen,* to be sacked.

ge·daante, -n, *n.* shape, figure. *in zijn ware* ~, in his true colours; *van* ~ *veranderen,* to change shape. **ge·daanteverwisseling,** *n.* metamorphosis.

ge·daas, no pl., *n.n.* hot air (*talk*).

ge·dachte, -n, *n.* thought, idea. *de* ~ *aan,* the memory of; *bij de* ~ *aan,* when thinking of *op de* ~ *komen,* to hit upon the idea; *iemand op de* ~ *brengen,* to suggest to someone; *geen* ~ *hebben op,* to have no thought of; *op twee gedachten hinken,* to halt between two opinions; *van* ~ *veranderen,* to change one's mind; *zich een* ~ *maken van,* to form an idea of; *iemands* ~(*n*) *aangaande* or *omtrent* or *over* or *van,* someone's opinion concerning. **ge·dachteloos, -loze,** *a.* thoughtless. **ge·dachte·loosheid,** no pl., *n.* thoughtlessness. **ge·dachtengang,** no pl., *n.* train of thought. **ge·dachtenis, -ssen,** *n.* memory; memento. *ter* ~ *van,* in memory of; *zaliger* ~, of blessed memory. **ge·dachtenstreep, -strepen,** *n.* dash (*typographical*). **ge··dachtig,** *a.* mindful. ~ *aan,* mindful of.

ge·dans, no pl., *n.n.* dancing. **ge·dartel,** no pl., *n.n.* frolicking. **ge·daver,** no pl., *n.n.* booming, trepidation.

ge·deelte, -n, *n.n.* part; instalment. *voor het grootste* ~, for the major part. **ge··deeltelijk,** *a.* partial. *ter* ~*e betaling,* in part payment. ¶*adv.* partly, in part.

ge·degen, *a.* native (*gold, silver*).

ge·denkboek, *n.n.* memorial volume; annals. **ge·denkdag,** *n.* anniversary. **ge·denken,** *v.t.* to commemorate; (*stilted*) to remember. **ge·denkjaar, -jaren,** *n.n.* jubilee year. **ge·denknaald,** *n.* obelisk. **ge·denkschrift,** *n.n.* memoirs.

gedepo·neerd, *a.* deposited (*trade-mark*).

gedepu·teerd, *a.* deputed. *G~e Staten,* executive committee of Dutch Provincial Parliament. **gedepu·teerde, -n,** *n.* deputy.

gedetail·leerd, *a.* detailed. ¶*adv.* in detail.

gedeti·neerde, -n, *n.* prisoner (*before trial*).

ge·dicht, *n.n.* poem.

ge·dienstig, *a.* obliging. *de* ~*e geest,* attendant spirit *or* (*fac.*) servant. **ge·dienstigheid, -heden,** *n.* obligingness.

ge·dierte, no pl., *n.n.* living creatures (*in general*). *het* ~ *des wouds,* the beasts of the forest.

ge·dijen, *v.i.* to thrive, prosper; to tend, develop. *ten kwade* ~, to come to evil.

ge·ding, *n.n.* lawsuit, action.

gediplo·meerd, *a.* certificated, qualified.

gedispo·neerd, *a.* disposed, inclined.

gedistil·leerd, *a.* distilled.

gedistin·geerd, *a.* distinguished.

gedocumen·teerd, *a.* documented.

ge·doe, no pl., *n.n.* fuss, bother, goings-on. *het hele* ~, *al dat* ~, the whole business.

ge·dogen, -doog, *v.t.* to tolerate, suffer.

ge·donder, no pl., *n.n.* thunder; (*coll.*) unpleasant business. **ge·donderjaag,** no pl., *n.n.* fuss and bother, palaver.

ge·draaf, no pl., *n.n.* trotting (around).

ge·draai, no pl., *n.n.* turning (*act*).

ge·drag, no pl., *n.n.* conduct, behaviour. **ge·dragen, zich, -draag,** *v.r., str.* to behave, conduct oneself. *zich goed* ~, to behave (*well*); *zich slecht* ~, to misbehave. **ge··dragingen,** pl. only, *n.* conduct, behaviour. **ge·dragslijn,** *n.* line of conduct; policy.

ge·drang, no pl., *n.n.* throng, crush. *in het* ~ *komen,* to be hard-pressed.

ge·drentel, no pl., *n.n.* sauntering.

ge·dreun, no pl., *n.n.* shaking, trepidation.

ge·drocht, *n.n.* monster. **ge·drochtelijk,** *a.* monstrous. **ge·drochtelijkheid, -heden,** *n.* monstrosity.

ge·drongen, *a.* squat. **ge·drongenheid,** no pl., *n.* compactness.

ge·druis, no pl., *n.n.* roar; clash.

ge·drukt, *a.* printed; depressed; low; depressed, weak (*prices*). **ge·druktheid,** no pl., *n.* depression.

ge·ducht, *a.* fearful, formidable. ¶*adv.* tremendously.

ge·duld, no pl., *n.n.* patience. **ge·duldig,** *a.* patient.

ge·durende, *adv.* during. ~ *een aantal jaren,* for a number of years.

ge·durfd, *a.* daring.

ge·durig, *a.* continual. ¶*adv.* continuously.

ge·duw, no pl., *n.n.* pushing.

ge·dwarrel, no pl., *n.n.* whirling.

ge·dwee, -weeë, *a.* meek. **ge·dweeheid,** no pl., *n.* meekness.

ge·dweep, no pl., *n.n.* schwärmerei; tiresome enthusiasm, fanaticism.

ge·dwongen, *a.* enforced, compulsory; forced, constrained. **ge·dwongenheid.** no pl., *n.* forcedness.

ge·ëerd, *a.* honoured.

geef, no pl., *n. het is te* ~, it is dirt cheap. **geefster, -s,** *n.* giver (*female*).

geel, gele, *a.* yellow. ¶no pl., *n.n.* yellow; yolk. **geelachtig,** *a.* yellowish. **geelbek, -kken,** *n.* fledgling. **geelgieter, -s,** *n.* brass-founder. **geelgieterij,** *n.* brass-foundry. **geelgors,** *n.* yellow-hammer. **geelheid,** no pl., *n.* yellowness. **geelkoper,** no pl., *n.n.* brass. **geelkoperen,** *a.* (made of) brass. **geelsel,** no pl., *n.n.* yellow dye. **geelvink,** *n.* greenfinch. **geelzucht,** no pl., *n.* jaundice. **geelzuchtig,** *a.* jaundiced.

geen, *pron.* no, none, not a, not any, not one. ~ *één* or ~ *enkel,* not (a single) one; ~ *van hen* or ~ *van beiden,* neither (of them); ~ *mens,* no one, not a soul; ~ *zier,* nothing at all; *hij kent* ~ *Engels,* he knows no English; *hij keet* ~ *Jan,* he is not called John; ~ *10 gulden*, less than 10 guilders. **geen·eens**, *adv.* not even. ·**geenszins**, *adv.* by no means, not at all.

geep, gepen, *n.* garfish; sea-needle.

geer, geren, *n.* gore, gusset.

·**geervalk**, *n.* gerfalcon.

geest, *n.* spirit, mind, intellect; wit; ghost, spectre. ~ *van zout*, spirits of salt; *de ~ des tijds*, the spirit of the age; *de Heilige G~*, the Holy Ghost; *zijn goede* or *boze ~*, his good or evil genius; *de armen van ~*, the poor in spirit; *in dezelfde ~*, in the same strain; *in die ~*, along those lines; *voor de ~*, before the mind's eye. **geest-·dodend**, *a.* soul-destroying, monotonous. ·**geestdrift**, no pl., *n.* enthusiasm. **geest-·driftig**, *a.* enthusiastic. ·**geestelijk**, *a.* spiritual; mental, intellectual; ecclesiastical, clerical. ·**geestelijke, -n,** *n.* clergyman, priest, minister. ·**geestelijkheid**, no pl., *n.* clergy. **geeste·loos, -loze,** *a.* spiritless, dull. ·**geestenbezweerder, -s,** *n.* exorcist. ·**geestenrijk**, no pl., *n.n.* spirit world. ·**geestesarbeid**, no pl., *n.n.* brain-work. ·**geestesgave, -n,** *n.* intellectual gift. ·**geestesrichting**, *n.* attitude of mind. ·**geestestoestand**, *n.* state of mind. ·**geestgrond**, *n.* ·**geestland**, *n.* sandy soil behind sand dunes.

·**geestig**, *a.* witty, ·**geestigheid, -heden,** *n.* wit; witticism. ·**geestkracht**, *n.* strength of mind. ·**geestrijk**, *a.* witty; spirituous. ·**geestverheffend**, *a.* elevating, sublime. ·**geestvermogen, -s,** *n.n.* intellectual faculties. ·**geestverschijning**, *n.* apparition. ·**geestverwant**, *a.* congenial, kindred.

geeuw, *n.* yawn. ·**geeuwen**, *v.i.* to yawn. ·**geeuwerig**, *a.* yawny. ·**geeuwhonger**, no pl., *n.* bulimia.

geëven·redigd, *a.* ~ *aan*, proportionate to.

ge·femel, no pl., *n.n.* cant, canting.

gefin·geerd, *a.* fictitious.

ge·fladder, no pl., *n.n.* fluttering, flitting.

ge·fleem, no pl., *n.n.* coaxing.

ge·flikflooi, no pl., *n.n.* wheedling.

ge·flikker, no pl., *n.n.* twinkling, flashing; messing about.

ge·fluister, no pl., *n.n.* whispering.

ge·fluit, no pl., *n.n.* whistling.

ge·foeter, no pl., *n.n.* cursing, grumbling.

gefor·ceerd, *a.* forced.

ge·fronst, *a.* *met ~e wenkbrauwen*, with a frown.

ge·futsel, no pl., *n.n.* fiddling about.

ge·gadigde, -n, *n.* person interested, prospective buyer; candidate.

gege·neerd, *a.* embarrassed.

ge·geven, *a.* given. ¶**-s**, *n.n.* datum, *pl.* data.

ge·gichel, no pl., *n.n.* giggling.

ge·gil, no pl., *n.n.* screaming.

gegla·ceerd, *a.* glazed; iced (*with sugar*).

ge·gleufd, *a.* slotted.

ge·goed, *a.* well-to-do. ~*e stand*, the propertied classes; *de meer ~en*, the better

situated; *de minder ~en*, the less well-off. **ge·goedheid**, no pl., *n.* wealth.

ge·golfd, *a.* wavy, undulating; corrugated.

ge·gomd, *a.* gummed.

ge·gons, no pl., *n.n.* buzzing.

ge·goochel, no pl., *n.n.* juggling.

ge·goten, *a.* cast (*iron*).

ge·grinnik, no pl., *n.n.* grinning.

ge·groefd, *a.* grooved.

ge·grom, no pl., *n.n.* growling.

ge·grond, *a.* well-founded; sound, reasonable. **ge·grondheid**, no pl., *n.* soundness (*of argument*).

ge·haast, *a.* hurried. ~ *zijn*, to be in a hurry.

ge·haat, **-hate**, *a.* hated.

ge·hakkel, no pl., *n.n.* stammering.

ge·hakt, no pl., *n.n.* minced meat, sausage meat.

ge·halte, -n, *n.n.* percentage (of purity) (*of metal*); proof (*of alcohol*), gravity (*of beer*); content; grade; value, worth. *van laag ~*, low-grade; *van twijfelachtig ~*, questionable.

ge·hamer, no pl., *n.n.* hammering.

ge·hard, *a.* hardened; hardy; tempered. ~ *tegen*, inured to. **ge·hardheid**, no pl., *n.* hardiness. ~ *tegen*, inurement to.

ge·harnast, *a.* in armour.

ge·harrewar, no pl., *n.n.* bickering.

ge·haspel, no pl., *n.n.* bungling.

ge·havend, *a.* damaged, battered.

ge·hecht, *a.* ~ *aan*, attached or devoted to; *aan elkaar ~*, devoted (*couple*). **ge·hechtheid**, no pl., *n.* attachment, devotion.

ge·heel, -hele. See **heel.** ¶*a.* whole, entire, complete. *de gehele dag*, the whole day, all day. ¶*adv.* wholly, entirely, completely. ~ *en al*, altogether, quite; ~ *anders*, altogether different; *ik ben ~ aandacht*, I am all attention. ¶no pl., *n.n.* whole. *een ~ uitmaken*, to form a whole; *in het ~*, in all; *in het ~ niet*, not at all; *in het ~ niets*, nothing at all; *over het ~*, on the whole. **ge·heelonthouder, -s,** *n.* teetotaller. **ge·heelonthouding**, no pl., *n.* teetotalism.

ge·heiligd, *a.* sacred.

ge·heim, *n.n.* secret. *een diep ~*, a dead secret; *publiek ~*, open secret; *in het ~*, in secret. ¶*a.* secret; occult. *G~e Raad*, Privy Council. **ge·heimenis, -ssen,** *n.* mystery. **ge·heimenisvol, -lle-** *a.* mysterious. **ge·heimhouden**, *v.t.s.*, *irr.* to keep secret. **geheim·houdend**, *a.* secretive, close. **ge·heimhouding**, *n.* secrecy. *iemand ~ opleggen*, to enjoin secrecy upon a person. **ge·heimschrift**, *n.n.* cypher, cryptogram. **geheim·zinnig**, *a.* mysterious. **ge·heim·doenerij**, *n.* secretiveness.

ge·hekel, no pl., *n.n.* heckling.

ge·helmd, *a.* helmeted.

ge·hemelte, -n, *n.n.* palate; canopy.

ge·heugen, *v.t.*, *imp.* to remember. ¶no pl., *n.n.* memory, remembrance. *iets in het ~*

prenten, to impress something on one's memory; *iets in het ~ roepen*, to recall something to mind.

ge·hijg, no pl., *n.n.* panting.

ge·hik, no pl., *n.n.* hiccoughing.

ge·hinnik, no pl., *n.n.* neighing.

ge·hoest, no pl., *n.n.* coughing.

ge·hol, no pl., *n.n.* running.

ge·hoor, no pl., *n.n.* hearing; audience, auditory; audience (*interview*). *muzikaal ~ hebben*, to have an ear for music; *op het ~ af*, by ear, from hearing; *een talrijk ~*, a large audience; *~ krijgen*, to be given a hearing; *om een ~ verzoeken*, to ask for an audience; *een ~ schenken* or *weigeren*, to grant or refuse an audience. **ge·hoorbeen, -deren**, *n.n.* tympanic bone. **ge·hoorbuis, -zen**, *n.* acoustic duct.

ge·hoornd, *a.* horned.

ge·hoorsafstand, no pl., *n.* hearing distance. **ge·hoorzaal, -zalen**, *n.* auditory, auditorium.

ge·hoorzaam, -zame, *a.* obedient. **ge·hoorzaamheid**, no pl., *n.* obedience. **ge·hoorzamen, -zaam**, *v.t.* & *v.i.* to obey.

ge·hoorzenuw, *n.* auditory nerve. **ge·hore**, *n.n.* ten *~ van*, in the hearing of.

ge·hos, no pl., *n.n.* dancing and jumping.

ge·houden, *a.* bound to. **ge·houdenheid**, no pl., *n.* obligation.

ge·hucht, *n.n.* hamlet.

ge·huichel, no pl., *n.n.* hypocrisy.

ge·huil, no pl., *n.n.* howling.

ge·huisvest, *a.* domiciled.

gehu·meurd, *a. goed ~*, good-tempered; *slecht ~*, bad-tempered.

ge·hunker, no pl., *n.n.* craving.

ge·huwd, *a.* wedded.

ge·ijkt, *a.* officially checked (*of weights and measures*). *~e termen*, standing phrase(s).

geil, *a.* lascivious, randy, lewd.

geïllus·treerd, *a.* illustrated.

·geintje, -s, *n.n.* joke.

geit, *n.* she-goat, nanny-goat. **·geitebok, -kken**, *n.* billy-goat. **·geitenmelk**, no pl., *n.* goat's milk. **·geitenmelker, -s**, *n.* nightjar.

ge·jaagd, *a.* hurried, agitated, flustered. **ge·jaagdheid**, no pl., *n.* agitation, flurry.

ge·jakker, no pl., *n.n.* restless hurry.

ge·jammer, no pl., *n.n.* wailing.

ge·jank, no pl., *n.n.* yapping, whining.

ge·joel, no pl., *n.n.* cheering, shouting.

ge·jouw, no pl., *n.n.* jeering, booing.

ge·jubel, no pl., *n.n.* cheering, jubilation.

ge·juich, no pl., *n.n.* cheering.

gek, -kke, *a.* mad, crazy; odd, curious, funny. *~ worden*, to go mad; *~ zijn op*, to be mad on. ¶*n.* madman, fool; cowl (*on chimney*). *iets ~s*, something queer; *als een ~*, like mad; *de ~ scheren met*, to make fun of; *voor de ~ houden*, to make a fool of; *voor ~ laten lopen*, to send a person out for nothing. *See* **gekke**.

ge·kabbel, no pl., *n.n.* babbling, lapping.

ge·kakel, no pl., *n.n.* cackling.

ge·kanker, no pl., *n.n.* grousing.

ge·kant, *a. ~ zijn tegen*, to be set against.

ge·karteld, *a.* crenate(d) (*leaf*); milled (*coin*).

ge·kef, no pl., *n.n.* yapping.

ge·kerm, no pl., *n.n.* moaning.

ge·keuvel, no pl., *n.n.* chatting.

·gekheid, -heden, *n.* folly, madness; joke, prank. *~ uithalen*, to play pranks; *uit ~*, for a joke; *zonder ~* or *alle ~ op een stokje*, joking apart.

ge·kibbel, no pl., *n.n.* bickering.

ge·kijf, no pl., *n.n.* scolding.

ge·kir, no pl., *n.n.* cooing.

·gekke, no pl., *n.n. het ~ van het geval*, the curious thing about it. **·gekken, gek**, *v.i.* to joke, jest. *met iemand ~*, to make fun of someone. **·gekkenhuis, -zen**, *n.n.* madhouse. **·gekkennummer**, no pl., *n.n.* number eleven. **·gekkenpraat**, no pl., *n.* foolish talk. **gekker·nij**, *n.* joke, prank.

·gekko, -'s, *n.* gecko.

ge·klaag, no pl., *n.n.* complaining.

ge·klad, no pl., *n.n.* daubing.

ge·klap, no pl., *n.n.* clapping.

ge·klater, no pl., *n.n.* clatter, splashing.

ge·kleed, -klede, *a.* dressed. *geklede jas*, frock-coat.

ge·klep, no pl., *n.n.* tolling; clatter (*of hooves*).

ge·klets, no pl., *n.n.* talking, gossiping.

ge·kletter, no pl., *n.n.* clatter.

ge·kleurd, *a.* coloured.

ge·klok, no pl., *n.n.* clucking.

ge·klop, no pl., *n.n.* knocking.

ge·knabbel, no pl., *n.n.* nibbling, gnawing.

ge·knars, no pl., *n.n.* gnashing; grating.

ge·knetter, no pl., *n.n.* crackling (*of fire*).

ge·knoei, no pl., *n.n.* bungling; shady transactions.

ge·knor, no pl., *n.n.* grunting.

ge·knutsel, no pl., *n.n.* pottering.

ge·konkel, no pl., *n.n.* underhand dealings.

ge·kraai, no pl., *n.n.* crowing.

ge·kraak, no pl., *n.n.* creaking.

ge·krabbel, no pl., *n.n.* scratching; scribbling.

ge·kreun, no pl., *n.n.* groaning.

ge·kriebel, no pl., *n.n.* tickling.

ge·krioel, no pl., *n.n.* swarming.

ge·kruist, *a.* crossed, cross-bred.

ge·kruld, *a.* curled, curly.

·gekscheren, -scheer, *v.t.* to jest, banter.

ge·kuch, no pl., *n.n.* coughing, hawking.

ge·kuip, no pl., *n.n.* intriguing.

ge·kunsteld, *a.* artificial, affected.

ge·kwaak, no pl., *n.n.* quacking; croaking (*of frog*).

ge·kwebbel, no pl., *n.n.* chattering.

ge·kwispel, no pl., *n.n.* wagging.

ge·laarsd, *a.* booted. *de ~e Kat*, Puss in Boots.

ge·laat, -laten, *n.n.* visage. **ge·laatstrek, -kken**, *n.* feature (*of face*). **ge·laatsuitdrukking**, *n.* facial expression.

ge·lach, no pl., *n.n.* laughter.
ge·lag, *n.n.* score (*payment*). het ~ betalen, to pay the score, pay the piper; *een hard* ~, a sad case. ge·lagkamer, -s, *n.* taproom.
ge·lang, *adv.* naar ~, according to, as; *alles was naar* ~, everything was in keeping.
ge·lasten, *v.t.* to order, direct. ge·lastigde, -n, *n.* deputy, proxy.
ge·laten, *a.* resigned. ge·latenheid, no pl., *n.* resignation.
geld, *n.n.* money. *vals* ~, false coins; *militairen half* ~, soldiers half price; *het ~ groeit me niet op de rug,* I am not made of money; *aan or in* ~, in money; *het is met geen ~ te betalen,* it is worth its weight in gold; ~ *munten,* to coin money; ~ *kloppen or slaan uit,* to make money out of; *zijn ~ ergens in steken,* to put one's money into something. ·geldadel, no pl., *n.* moneyed aristocracy. ·geldbelegging, *n.* investment. ·geldboete, -n, *n.* fine. ·gelddorst, no pl., *n.* lust for money. ·geldelijk, *a.* monetary; pecuniary, financial. ·geldeloos, -loze, *a.* penniless. ·gelden, *v.i., str.* to apply (to); to refer to. *het geldt niet,* it does not count; *het geldt hier niet,* it does not apply here; *doen* ~, to assert; *zich doen or laten* ~, to assert oneself. ·geldend, *a.* prevailing, generally received; ruling. ·geldgebrek, no pl., *n.n.* shortage of money. ·geldig, *a.* valid. *niet meer* ~, invalid, out of date. ·geldigheid, no pl., *n.* validity. *onderlinge* ~, interavailability. ·geldkist, *n.* money chest. ·geldkoers, *n.* rate of exchange. ·geldlening, *n.* loan. ·geldmiddelen, pl. only, *n.n.* finances. ·geldnemer, -s, *n.* borrower (*of money*). ·geldschieter, -s, *n.* money-lender. ·geldstuk, -kken, *n.n.* coin. ·geldstraf, -ffen, *n.* fine. ·geldswaarde, no pl., *n.* monetary value. ·geldverlegenheid, no pl., *n.* pecuniary embarrassment. *in* ~ *verkeren,* to be hard pressed. ·geldverspilling, *n.* waste of money. ·geldwezen, no pl., *n.n.* world of finance. ·geldzaak, -zaken, *n.* money matter. ·geldzorgen, pl. only, *n.* financial worries. ·geldzucht, no pl., *n.* greed for money.
ge·leden, *a.* past; ago. *het is lang* ~ *dat . . .,* it is long since . . .; *kort* ~, recently.
ge·lederen, *pl. of* gelid. ge·leding, *n.* articulation, joint. ge·leed, -lede, *a.* articulated, sectional; indented (*coast*).
ge·leerd, *a.* learned, scholarly. *dat is mij te* ~, that is too deep for me; ~ *doen,* to put on an air of wisdom. ge·leerde, -n, *n.* scholar; scientist. ge·leerdheid, no pl., *n.* erudition.
ge·legen, *a.* situate(d); convenient. ~ *aan,* situated on; *er is me veel aan* ~, it means a great deal to me; *het komt me niet* ~, it is not convenient to me now; *als het U ~ valt,* if it is convenient to you; *te* ~*er tijd or ure,* in due time; *net* ~,

opportune. ge·legenheid, -heden, *n.* occasion; opportunity; place. *iemand de ~ geven,* to give someone an opportunity; *de ~ krijgen,* to get a chance; *bij* ~, some time; *bij de ~ van,* on the occasion of; *in de ~ stellen,* to enable; *op eigen* ~, separately; *per eerste* ~, at the first opportunity; *ter ~ van,* on the occasion of. ge·legenheidsgedicht, *n.n.* occasional poem. ge·legenheidsgezicht, *n.n.* an expression (*facial*) to suit the occasion.
ge·lei, *n.* jam, marmalade, jelly. ge·leiachtig, *a.* jelly-like.
ge·leibiljet, -tten, *n.n.* way-bill. ge·leibrief, -ven, *n.* safe-conduct. ge·leide, no pl., *n.n.* guidance; escort. *onder* ~ *van,* escorted by. ge·leidelijk, *a.* gradual. ge·leidelijkheid, no pl., *n.* gradualness. ge·leiden, *v.t.* to lead; to conduct (*heat, light*); to escort. ge·leider, -s, *n.* leader, guide; conductor (*of heat, light*). ge·leiding, *n.* conduction; wiring (*of electricity*); pipes (*gas, water*). ge·leidraad, -draden, *n.* conducting wire.
·gelen, geel, *v.i.* to turn yellow.
ge·letterd, *a.* literary.
ge·leuter, no pl., *n.n.* twaddle.
ge·lid, -lederen, *n.n.* joint (*of limb*); rank (*of column*). *gesloten gelederen,* serried ranks; *in het* ~ *staan,* to be lined up; *uit het* ~ *vallen,* to fall out, leave the ranks; *de gelederen opstellen,* to draw up; *de gelederen sluiten,* to close the ranks.
ge·liefd, *a.* dear, beloved. ge·liefkoosd, *a.* favourite. ge·lieven, -lief, *v.t.* to please.
·gelig, *a.* yellowish.
ge·lijk, *a.* equal; identical; similar; even, level. *de klok is* ~, the clock is right; *het is mij* ~, it is all the same to me; *te* ~*er tijd or te* ~, at the same time; *met de grond* ~ *maken,* to raze to the ground; ~ *maken,* to equalize; ~ *en gelijkvormig,* congruent. ¶*adv.* equally; evenly; simultaneously. ¶*c.* as, like. ¶no pl., *n.n.* ~ *hebben in iets,* to be right about something; *groot* ~ *hebben,* to be very wise *or* quite right; *iemand in het* ~ *stellen* or *iemand* ~ *geven,* to agree with a person; *van 's gelijke!*, the same to you! gelijk·benig, *a.* isosceles. ge·lijke, -n, *n.* equal. ge·lijkelijk, *adv.* equally. ge·lijken, *v.i., str.* ~ *op,* to look like, resemble. ge·lijkenis, -ssen, *n.* likeness; parable. ge·lijkerwijs, *adv.* likewise. ge·lijkgaan, *v.i.s., irr.* to keep time. gelijkge·rechtigd, *a.* equal (*of partners*). ge·lijkheid, no pl., *n.* equality; similarity. gelijk·luidend, *a.* true (*of copy*). gelijk·matig, *a.* uniform; equable. gelijk·matigheid, no pl., *n.* uniformity; equability. gelijk·moedig, *a.* equable. gelijk·namig, *a.* of the same name; with the same denominator; similar, analogous. gelijk·slachtig, *a.* homogenous. gelijk·soortig, *a.* similar. gelijk·soortigheid.

n. similarity. **ge·lijkstaan, sta gelijk,** *v.i.s., irr.* to be equal. ~ *met,* to be equal to, on a level with. **ge·lijkstroom, -stromen,** *n.* direct current. **gelijk·tijdig,** *a.* simultaneous. ¶ *adv.* simultaneously, at the same time. **gelijk·vloers,** *a.* on the ground floor; on the same floor. **gelijk··vormig,** *a.* of the same form, similar. **gelijk·vormigheid, -heden,** *n.* conformity, similarity. **gelijk·waardig,** *a.* equivalent. **gelijk·waardigheid, -heden,** *n.* equivalence. **ge·lijkzetten, zet gelijk,** *v.t.s. zijn horloge* ~, to set one's watch. **gelijk·zijdig,** *a.* equilateral. **gelijk·zijdigheid, no pl.,** *n.* state of being equilateral.
ge·likt, *a.* polished.
gelini·eerd, *a.* ruled.
ge·lispel, no pl., *n.n.* lisping.
ge·loei, no pl., *n.n.* lowing, bellowing.
ge·loer, no pl., *n.n.* spying, peering.
ge·lofte, -n, *n.* vow. *de* ~ *afleggen,* to take the vow; *een* ~ *doen* or *afleggen* to take a vow.
ge·loken, *a.* closed.
ge·lonk, no pl., *n.n.* ogling.
ge·loof, -loven, *n.n.* belief, faith; religion. *blind* ~, implicit faith; ~ *hechten aan,* to give credit to; ~ *stellen in,* to put faith in; ~ *aan,* belief in; *in het* ~ *verkeren,* to be under the impression. **ge·loofbaar, -bare,** *a.* believable. **ge·loofbaarheid, no pl.,** *n.* credibility. **ge·loofsartikel,** *n.n.* article of faith. **ge·loofsbelijdenis, -ssen,** *n.* profession of faith. **ge·loofsbezwaren, pl.** only, *n.n.* religious scruples. **ge·loofsbrieven, pl.** only, *n.* credentials (*of ambassador*). **geloofs·halve,** *adv.* for the sake of one's religion. **ge·loofsvrijheid, no pl.,** *n.* religious liberty. **ge·loofszaak, -zaken,** *n.* matter of faith. **geloof·waardig,** *a.* credible, reliable. **geloof·waardigheid, no** pl., *n.* credibility, veracity.
ge·loop, no pl., *n.n.* running about.
ge·loven, -loof, *v.t.* & *v.i.* to believe; to think, believe. ~ *aan* or *in,* to believe in; *niet* ~, to disbelieve; *niet te* ~, unbelievable. **ge·lovig,** *a.* believing, faithful.
ge·lui, no pl., *n.n.* ringing, tolling.
ge·luid, *n.n.* sound, noise. **ge·luidloos, -loze,** *a.* soundless. **ge·luidsgolf, -ven,** *n.* soundwave.
ge·luier, no pl., *n.n.* idling.
ge·luimd, *a.* -humoured. *goed* ~, in a good temper; *slecht* ~, in a bad temper.
ge·luk, no pl., *n.n.* happiness; luck, good luck, chance, fortune. *op goed* ~ (*af*), on the off-chance, at random; *zijn* ~ *beproeven,* to try one's luck; ~ *hebben,* to be lucky *or* fortunate; *van* ~ (*mogen*) *spreken,* to consider oneself lucky; *iemand* ~ *wensen,* to congratulate a person. **ge·lukken, geluk,** *v.i.* to succeed. *het is hem niet gelukt,* he did not succeed, was unsuccessful. **ge·lukkig,** *a.* happy; lucky;

fortunate; felicitous. ¶ *adv.* happily. ~ *zijn,* to be in luck. **ge·lukkigerwijze,** *adv.* fortunately. **ge·lukskind, -eren,** *n.n.* child of fortune. **ge·lukspenning,** *n.* lucky token, charm. **ge·luksspinnetje, -s,** *n.n.* money spider. **ge·luksvogel, -s,** *n.* lucky person. **ge·lukwens,** *n.* congratulation. **ge·lukwensen,** *v.t.s.* to congratulate. ~ *met,* to congratulate on. **geluk·zalig,** *a.* blessed, blissful. **geluk·zaligheid, -heden,** *n.* bliss, beatitude. **ge·lukzoeker, -s,** *n.* adventurer, fortune-hunter.
ge·maakt, *a.* ready-made, made-up; affected. **ge·maaktheid, no pl.,** *n.* affectation.
ge·maal, -s or **-malen,** *n.* consort; (*stilted*) husband. ¶no pl., *n.n.* grinding; endless bother. ¶-**malen,** *n.n.* pumping-station (*of polder* or *catchment board*).
ge·machtigde, -n, *n.* proxy, deputy.
ge·mak, no pl., *n.n.* ease, comfort. *hou je* ~!, don't get excited; *met* ~, easily, with ease; *op zijn* ~, comfortable, comfortably; *voor het* ~, for convenience sake. ¶-**kken,** *n.n.* privy; convenience. **ge·makkelijk,** *a.* easy; comfortable. **ge·makkelijkheid, no pl.,** *n.* facility, easiness. **gemaks·halve,** *adv.* for the sake of convenience. **ge·makzucht, no pl.,** *n.* love of ease. *uit* ~, from love of ease. **gemak·zuchtig,** *a.* easy-going.
gema·lin, -nnen, *n.* consort, spouse.
gema·nierd, *a.* mannered.
gemari·neerd, *a.* pickled.
ge·marmerd, *a.* marbled, mottled.
ge·matigd, *a.* moderate; measured. **ge·matigdheid, no pl.,** *n.* moderation.
gember, no pl., *n.* ginger. **gemberkoek, n.** gingerbread.
ge·meen, -mene, *a.* common, public; common, general; ordinary; mean; low, obscene. *gemene deler,* common factor; *gemene veelvoud,* common multiple; *niets* ~ *hebben met,* to have nothing in common with. ¶ *adv.* meanly. **ge·meengoed, -eren,** *n.n.* common property. **ge·meenheid, no** pl., *n.* meanness; dirty trick. **ge·meenlijk,** *adv.* commonly. **ge·meenplaats, n.** platitude. **ge·meenschap, -ppen,** *n.* community; intercourse. *in* ~ *staan met,* to be in communication with. **gemeen·schappelijk,** *a.* common; joint; communal. ¶ *adv.* jointly; in common. **ge·meente, -n, n.** municipality; parish; congregation. **ge··meente-,** *prefix.* municipal . . . , local . . . , town-. *e.g.* **ge·meentebestuur, -sturen,** *n.n.* town council. **ge·meenteraadslid, -leden,** *n.n.* town-councillor. **ge·meenzaam, -zame,** *a.* familiar. **ge·meenzaamheid, -heden,** *n.* familiarity, intimacy.
ge·meld, *a.* above-mentioned.
gemelijk, *a.* peevish. **gemelijkheid, no pl.,** *n.* peevishness.
gemene·best, no pl., n.n. commonwealth; republic.

ge·mengd, *a.* mixed; miscellaneous.
gemeubi·leerd, *a.* furnished.
ge·middeld, *a.* average, mean. ¶*adv.* on an average. **ge·middelde, -n,** *n.n.* average.
ge·mier, no pl., *n.n.* fiddling.
ge·mijmer, no pl., *n.n.* musing.
ge·mijterd, *a.* mitred.
ge·mis, no pl., *n.n.* lack, want. ∼ *aan,* lack of.
ge·modder, no pl., *n.n.* muddling.
gemode·reerd, *a.* moderate.
ge·moed, -eren, *n.n.* mind, heart. *in* ∼*e,* in all conscience; *de* ∼*eren,* the minds or feelings (*of the people*). **ge·moedelijk,** *a.* kindhearted, jovial. *een* ∼ *praatje,* a heart-to-heart talk. **ge·moedelijkheid,** no pl., *n.* kind-heartedness. **ge·moedsaandoening,** *n.* emotion. **ge·moedsaard,** no pl., *n.* nature, disposition. **ge·moedsbezwaar, -zwaren,** *n.n.* conscientious objection. **ge·moedsleven,** no pl., *n.n.* inner or emotional life. **ge·moedsrust,** no pl., *n.* peace of mind. **ge·moedstoestand,** no pl., *n.* state of mind.
ge·mor, no pl., *n.n.* grumbling.
ge·morrel, no pl., *n.n.* fumbling, fiddling.
ge·mors, no pl., *n.n.* spilling, being messy.
gems, -zen, *n.* chamois.
ge·murmel, no pl., *n.n.* mumbling; babbling (*brook*).
ge·mutst, *a.* tempered (*emotion*).
ge·naakbaar, -bare, *a.* accessible. **ge·naakbaarheid,** no pl., *n.* accessibility.
ge·naamd, *a.* named, called.
ge·nade, no pl., *n.* mercy; grace. *goeie* ∼!, good gracious! *door Gods* ∼, by the grace of God; *iemand weer in* ∼ *aannemen,* to restore a person to favour; *iemand* ∼ *betonen* or *schenken,* to pardon a person; *geen* ∼ *geven,* to give no quarter; *aan de* ∼ *overgeleverd zijn van,* to be at the mercy of; *om* ∼ *smeken,* to pray for mercy. **ge·nadebrief, -ven,** *n.* letter of pardon. **ge·nadebrood,** no pl., *n.n.* bread of charity. **ge·nadeslag,** no pl., *n.,* **ge·nadestoot,** no pl., *n.* death-blow. **ge·nadig,** *a.* merciful; gracious. *God zij ons* ∼, God have mercy on us. ¶*adv. er* ∼ *afkomen,* to get off lightly.
ge·naken, -naak, *v.t.* (*stilted*) to approach. *niet te* ∼, unapproachable.
·gene, *pron.* that; the former; yonder. *deze en* ∼, a number of people.
ge·neesheer, -heren, *n.* doctor, physician. **ge·neeskunde,** no pl., *n.* medicine (*science*). **genees·kundig,** *a.* medical. **ge·neeslijk,** *a.* curable. **ge·neesmiddel,** *n.n.* remedy, medicine.
ge·negen, *a.* inclined, disposed. *iemand* ∼ *zijn,* to be favourably disposed towards someone. **ge·negenheid,** no pl., *n.* affection; inclination. **ge·neigd,** *a.* inclined. ∼ *tot,* prone to.
gene·raal, -s, *n.* general. ¶ **-rale,** *a.* general.

generale repetitie, dress rehearsal. **gene·raal-majoor, -s,** *n.* major-general **generali·seren, -seer,** *v.i.* to generalize. **generali·satie, -s,** *n.* generalization.
gene·ratie, -s, *n.* generation.
ge·neren, -neer, *v.t.* to inconvenience. ¶**zich** ∼, *v.r.* to feel embarrassed. *zich niet* ∼, not to stand on ceremony.
ge·nerfd, *a.* nervate.
gene·reren, -nereer, *v.t.* to generate.
·generhande, *pron.,* **·generlei,** *pron.* of no kind. ∼ *middel,* no manner of means.
ge·neugte, -n, *n.n.* delight, enjoyment.
ge·neurie, no pl., *n.n.* humming.
ge·nezen, -nees, *v.t., str.* to cure; to heal. ¶*v.i., str.* to get better, recover. **ge·nezing,** *n.* cure, recovery.
geni·aal, -iale, *a.* ingenious; brilliant. **geniali·teit,** no pl., *n.* genius (*quality*). **ge·nie, -nieën,** *n.n.* genius (*person and quality*). ¶no pl., *n.* engineers (*military*). *de G* ∼, the Royal Engineers.
ge·niep, no pl., *n.n. in 't* ∼, on the sly. **ge·niepig,** *a.* underhand, mean. ¶*adv.* sneakingly. **ge·niepigerd, -s,** *n.* sneak. **ge·niepigheid, -heden,** *n.* meanness, underhand trick.
ge·niesoldaat, -daten, *n.* soldier in the Royal Engineers.
ge·nieten, *v.t., str.* to enjoy. *een goede opvoeding* ∼, to receive a good education. ¶*v.i., str.* to enjoy oneself. ∼ *van,* to enjoy. **ge·nieting.** *See* genot.
ge·nietroepen, pl. only, *n.* engineers, Royal Engineers.
ge·nodigde, -n, *n.* person invited, guest.
ge·noeg, *adv.* enough. *ik heb er* ∼ *van,* I have had enough of it; *mans* ∼ *zijn,* to be strong enough. **ge·noegdoening,** no pl., *n.* satisfaction, reparation. **ge·noege,** no pl., *n.n. ten* ∼ *van,* to the satisfaction of. **ge·noegen, -s,** *n.n.* pleasure, enjoyment. ∼ *beleven van,* to get pleasure out of; *iemand een* ∼ *doen,* to please someone (*by doing something*); *het doet me* ∼, I am pleased to hear it; ∼ *scheppen in,* to find pleasure in; *voor zijn* ∼, for pleasure. ¶no pl., *n.n.* satisfaction. ∼ *nemen met,* to be satisfied with, put up with; *naar* ∼, to (*one's*) satisfaction; *zijn* ∼ *eten,* to eat one's fill. **ge·noeglijk,** *a.* pleasant, enjoyable. **ge·noeglijkheid, -heden,** *n.* pleasurableness. **ge·noegzaam -zame,** *a.* sufficient. **ge·noegzaamheid,** no pl., *n.* sufficiency.
ge·noemd, *a.* named; above-mentioned.
ge·noopt. *See* nopen.
ge·noot, -noten, *n.* companion; partner. **ge·nootschap, -ppen,** *n.n.* society, association.
ge·not, genietingen, *n.n.* enjoyment, delight. ∼ *verschaffen,* to afford pleasure; *in het volle* ∼ *van,* in full possession of; *onder het* ∼ *van,* while enjoying. **ge·notmiddel,** *n.n.* luxury (*eating, drinking, smoking*).

ge·notziek, *a.* pleasure-loving. ge·notzucht, no pl., *n.* love of pleasure; sensuality. genot·zuchtig, *a.* sensual.

Gent, *n.N.* Ghent.

gent, *n.* gander.

genti·aan, -ianen, *n.* gentian.

·Genua, *n.N.* Genoa. Genu·ees, -uezen, *n.* Genoese. ¶-uese, *a.* Genoese.

ge·oefend, *a.* practised, trained.

geo·graphisch, *a.* geographic(al).

geolo·gie, no pl., *n.* geology. geo·logisch, *a.* geological. geo·loog, -logen, *n.* geologist.

ge·oorloofd, *a.* permitted, admissible, lawful.

georgani·seerd, *a.* organized.

ge·paard, *a.* in pairs *or* couples. ~ *gaan met,* to be coupled with.

ge·pakt, *a.* ~ *en gezakt,* with bag and baggage *or* booted and spurred.

ge·pantserd, *a.* armoured. *de ~e vuist,* the mailed fist.

ge·pareld, *a.* ~*e gerst,* pearl barley.

ge·past, *a.* proper, becoming, fit, fitting. ~ *geld,* exact money. ge·pastheid, no pl., *n.* fitness, suitability, propriety.

ge·peins, no pl., *n.n.* meditation, pondering. *in ~ verzonken,* rapt in thought.

ge·peld, *a.* peeled.

ge·peperd, *a.* peppered, peppery; steep (*charges*).

ge·peupel, no pl., *n.n.* populace, mob.

ge·peuter, no pl., *n.n.* fiddling.

ge·pieker, no pl., *n.n.* worrying, brooding.

ge·piep, no pl., *n.n.* squeaking, chirping.

gepi·queerd, *a.* piqued.

ge·pimpel, no pl., *n.n.* tippling.

ge·plaag, no pl., *n.n.* teasing.

ge·plas, no pl., *n.n.* splashing.

ge·ploeter, no pl., *n.n.* splashing (*in mud*); toiling.

ge·poch, no pl., *n.n.* boasting.

ge·praat, no pl., *n.n.* talk(ing); scandal.

ge·prevel, no pl., *n.n.* muttering.

ge·pruttel, no pl., *n.n.* bubbling, simmering.

ge·pruts, no pl., *n.n.* toying.

ge·punt, *a.* pointed.

ge·raakt, *a.* touched, offended. *licht ~,* touchy. ge·raaktheid, no pl., *n.* touchiness.

ge·raamte, -n, *n.n.* skeleton; frame.

ge·raas, no pl., *n.n.* din, noise. ge·raaskal, no pl., *n.n.* nonsense, nonsensical talk.

ge·raden, *a.* advisable. *het is je ~,* you had better; *iets ~ achten,* to think something advisable.

geraffi·neerd, *a.* refined (*lit. & fig.*). *een ~e schurk,* a thorough-going scoundrel.

ge·raken, -raak, *v.i.* to get (to), arrive. *in gesprek ~,* to fall into conversation; *onder dieven ~,* to fall among thieves; *te water ~,* to fall into the water; *tot bloei ~,* to attain prosperity.

ge·rammel, no pl., *n.n.* rattling.

ge·rand, *a.* edged, trimmed.

ge·raspt, *a.* grated.

ge·ratel, no pl., *n.n.* rattling.

gera·vot, no pl., *n.n.* romping.

ge·recht, *n.n.* course; dish; tribunal; court of justice. *voor het ~ dagen,* to summon; *zich aan het ~ overleveren,* to give oneself up to justice; *voor het ~ verschijnen,* to appear in court. ¶*a.* just, righteous. ge·rechtelijk, *a.* judicial; legal. ¶*adv.* in law; judicially, legally. *iemand ~ vervolgen,* to take legal proceedings against a person. ge·rechtigd, *a.* entitled, justified. ge·rechtigheid, no pl., *n.* justice. ge·rechts·dienaar, -naren, *n.* officer of the law. ge·rechtshof, -ven, *n.n.* court of justice. ge·rechtszaak, -zaken, *n.* lawsuit. ge·rechtszitting, *n.* session.

ge·redelijk, *adv.* readily.

gerede·neer, no pl., *n.n.* arguing.

ge·reed, -rede, *a.* ready; prepared; finished. ge·reedheid, no pl., *n.* readiness. *in ~ brengen,* to put in readiness. ge·reed·houden, *v.t.s., irr.* to keep ready. ¶*zich ~, v.r., irr.* to keep oneself in readiness. ge·reedkomen, *v.i.s., irr.* to get finished. ~ *met iets,* to finish something. ge·reedleggen, leg gereed, *v.t.s., irr.* to lay ready. ge·reedliggen, lig gereed, *v.i.s., str.* to lie ready. ge·reedmaken, maak gereed, *v.t.s.* to prepare. ¶*zich ~, v.r.s.* to prepare oneself. ge·reedschap, -ppen, *n.n.* tools, instruments. ge·reedschapskist, *n.* tool box, tool chest. ge·reedstaan, sta gereed, *v.i.s., irr.* to stand ready. ge·reedzetten, zet gereed, *v.t.s.* to put ready.

gerefor·meerd, *a.* Reformed (*Calvinist sect*).

ge·regeld, *a.* regular, orderly; regular, fixed. ge·regeldheid, no pl., *n.* regularity.

ge·rei, no pl., *n.n.* tackle; utensils.

ge·rekt, *a.* protracted, long-drawn (out). ge·rektheid, no pl., *n.* protractedness.

gereser·veerd, *a.* reserved; guarded. gereser·veerdheid, no pl., *n.* reserve, restraint.

ge·reutel, no pl., *n.n.* death-rattle.

ge·ribd, *a.* ribbed, grooved.

ge·richt, no pl., *n.n. het jongste ~,* Judgment Day.

ge·rief, no pl., *n.n.* convenience, comfort. ge·riefelijk, *a.* convenient, commodious. ge·riefelijkheid, -heden, *n.* convenience. ge·rieve, no pl., *n.n. ten ~ van,* for the use of. ge·rieven, -rief, *v.t.* to accommodate, oblige.

ge·rijmel, no pl., *n.n.* rhyming.

ge·rimpeld, *a.* wrinkled.

ge·ring, *a.* inconsiderable, small, trifling, mean, scanty. ge·ringschatten, schat gering, *v.t.s.* to deprecate. ge·ringschatting, *n.* deprecation; disdain.

ge·rinkel, no pl., *n.n.* clanking, rattle.

ge·ritsel, no pl., *n.n.* rustling, rustle.

ge·rochel, no pl., *n.n.* death-rattle; expectoration.

ge·roep, no pl., *n.n.* calling. ge·roepen, *a. zich ~ voelen,* to feel called upon.

ge·roezemoes, no pl., *n.n.* bustle.

ge·roffel, no pl., *n.n.* roll (*of drum*).
ge·rokt, *a.* wearing frock-coat *or* skirt.
ge·rol, no pl., *n.n.* rolling.
ge·rommel, no pl., *n.n.* rumble.
ge·ronk, no pl., *n.n.* whir(r); snoring.
ge·ronnen, *a.* clotted, coagulated.
gerst, no pl., *n.* barley. **·gerstebier**, no pl., *n.n.* barley beer. **·gerstekorrel**, -s, *n.* barley-corn. **·gerstemeel**, no pl., *n.n.* barley-meal.
ge·rucht, *n.n.* rumour; noise. *een los* ∼, a wild rumour; *in kwaad* ∼ *staan*, to be in bad odour. **ge·ruchtmakend**, *a.* sensational.
ge·ruim, *a.* considerable, ample.
ge·ruis, no pl., *n.n.* rushing (*noise*), rustling. **ge·ruisloos, -loze**, *a.* noiseless.
ge·ruit, *a.* checked, chequered. *een* ∼*e stof*, a check.
ge·rust, *a.* easy; quiet. *iemand* ∼ *laten*, to leave someone in peace. ¶*adv.* quietly, peacefully; safely. *je kunt het* ∼ *doen*, you can do it without having to worry about it; *hij kan* ∼ *wegblijven*, for all I care he may stay away. **ge·rustheid**, no pl., *n.* peace of mind. *met* ∼, confidently. **ge·ruststellen, stel gerust**, *v.t.s.*, to reassure. **ge·ruststelling**, *a.* relief, assurance.
ge·schacher, no pl., *n.n.* haggling, bartering.
ge·schal, no pl., *n.n.* flourish (*of trumpets*).
ge·scharrel, no pl., *n.n.* rummaging; bungling.
ge·schater, no pl., *n.n.* peals of laughter.
ge·scheiden, *a.* divorced.
ge·schenk, *n.n.* present, gift.
ge·schept, *a.* ∼ *papier*, hand-made paper.
gescher·mutsel, no pl., *n.n.* skirmishing.
ge·scherts, no pl., *n.n.* jesting.
ge·schetter, no pl., *n.n.* blare, flourish.
ge·schieden, *v.i.* to happen, occur. *Uw wil geschiede*, Thy will be done. **ge·schiedenis, -ssen**, *n.* history; story. *een lastige* ∼, an awkward affair; *een mooie* ∼*!*, a pretty business!; *nieuwe* ∼, modern history; *oude* ∼, ancient history. **geschied·kundig**, *a.* historical. **ge·schiedschrijver**, -s, *n.* historian, historiographer.
ge·schikt, *a.* suitable, fit, proper. *slecht* ∼ *voor*, ill adapted for. **ge·schiktheid**, no pl., *n.* suitability.
ge·schil, -llen, *n.n.* dispute, difference. **ge·schilpunt**, *n.n.* point at issue.
ge·schimp, no pl., *n.n.* scoffing.
ge·schipper, no pl., *n.n.* temporizing.
ge·schitter, no pl., *n.n.* glittering.
ge·schommel, no pl., *n.n.* swinging.
ge·schoold, *a.* trained. ∼*e arbeider*, skilled workman.
ge·schreeuw, no pl., *n.n.* shouting. *veel* ∼ *en weinig wol*, much ado about nothing.
ge·schrei, no pl., *n.n.* crying, weeping.
ge·schrift, *n.n.* writing (*document, publication*). **ge·schrijf**, no pl., *n.n.* (*action of*) writing.
ge·schubd, *a.* scaly.

ge·schuifel, no pl., *n.n.* shuffling.
ge·schut, no pl., *n.n.* ordnance, gunnery, artillery. *zwaar* ∼, big guns. **ge·schut-bedding**, *n.* gun platform. **ge·schutkoepel**, -s, *n.* gun cupola. **ge·schuttoren**, -s, *n.* gun turret. **ge·schutvuur**, no pl., *n.n.* gunfire. **ge·schutwerf**, -ven, *n.* artillery park.
·gesel, -s, *n.* scourge. **·geselen**, *v.t.* to flog, flagellate. **·geseling**, *n.* scourging, flagellation. **·geselmonnik**, -kken, *n.* flagellant (*monk*). **·geselpaal, -palen**, *n.* whipping-post. **·geselstraf**, no pl., *n.* flogging.
ge·sis, no pl., *n.n.* hissing.
ge·sjochten, *a.* done, had, diddled.
ge·slacht, *n.n.* family, lineage; genus; sex; gender. *het menselijk* ∼, the human race. ¶no pl., *n.n.* slaughtering. **ge·slachtelijk**, *a.* sexual. **ge·slachtloos, -loze**, *a.* sexless. **ge·slachtsboom, -bomen**, *n.* family tree, pedigree. **ge·slachtsdelen**, pl. only, *n.n.* genitals. **ge·slachtsnaam, -namen**, *n.* family name. **ge·slachtsziekte**, -n, *n.* venereal disease.
ge·slagen, *a.* beaten (*gold, etc.*). ∼ *vijanden*, sworn enemies.
ge·slepen, *a.* sharpened; cut (*stone*); cunning. **ge·slepenheid**, no pl., *n.n.* cunning.
ge·sloten, *a.* shut; close. ∼ *gelederen*, serried ranks.
ge·sluierd, *a.* veiled.
ge·smeek, no pl., *n.n.* supplications.
ge·smul, no pl., *n.n.* eating (*with gusto*).
ge·snaater, *a.* stringed.
ge·snater, no pl., *n.n.* quacking; chatter.
ge·snauw, no pl., *n.n.* snarling, snapping.
ge·snik, no pl., *n.n.* sobbing.
ge·snoef, no pl., *n.n.* boasting.
ge·snor, no pl., *n.n.* whir(r).
ge·snuffel, no pl., *n.n.* sniffing.
ge·snuif, no pl., *n.n.* snorting.
gesp, *n.* buckle, clasp. **·gespen**, *v.t.* to buckle, clasp.
ge·spannen, *a.* tense; bent (*bow*).
ge·spartel, no pl., *n.n.* floundering, sprawling.
ge·speel, no pl., *n.n.* playing.
ge·spekt, *a.* well-lined (*purse*).
ge·spierd, *a.* muscular.
ge·spikkeld, *a.* speckled.
ge·spot, no pl., *n.n.* mocking.
ge·sprek, -kken, *n.n.* conversation, talk. *een* ∼ *aanknopen met*, to get into conversation with; *een* ∼ *voeren*, to hold a conversation; *het* ∼ *brengen op*, to bring the conversation round to; *in* ∼, number engaged (*telephone*).
ge·spuis, no pl., *n.n.* rabble, mob.
ge·stadig, *a.* constant, steady. ¶*adv.* constantly. ∼ *vooruitgaan*, to make steady progress.
ge·stalte, -n, *n.* figure, stature.
ge·stamel, no pl., *n.n.* stammering.
ge·stand, no pl., *n.n.* zijn woord *or* belofte ∼ doen, to keep one's word *or* promise.

ge·steente, no pl., *n.n.* (precious) stone(s); rock.

ge·stel, -llen, *n.n.* system, structure; constitution (*physical*). ge·steld, *a.* arranged, placed; drawn-up, written; keen. *de ~e voorwaarden*, the conditions made; *het is er treurig mee ~*, it is in a sad state; *~ zijn op*, to be keen on. ¶*c.* supposing. gestelde, no pl., *n.n.* data; given that (*in problem*). ge·steldheid, -heden, *n.*, ge-·steltenis, no pl., *n.* state, condition.

ge·stemd, *a.* tuned; disposed. *gunstig ~ zijn jegens*, to be favourably disposed towards.

ge·sternte, -n, *n.n.* constellation.

ge·sticht, *n.n.* institution, establishment. ¶*a.* founded; edified.

gesti·leerd, *a.* stylized.

ge·stoelte, -n, *n.n.* pulpit.

ge·stotter, no pl., *n.n.* stuttering.

ge·streept, *a.* striped.

ge·strekt, *a.* stretched. *in ~e galop*, at full gallop.

ge·streng, *a.* strict, severe. ge·strengheid, no pl., *n.* strictness.

gestu·deerd, *a. een ~ man*, a university man.

ge·suis, no pl., *n.n.* buzzing.

ge·sukkel, no pl., *n.n.* ailing; bungling.

ge·takt, *a.* branching.

ge·tal, -llen, *n.n.* number. ge·tale, *n.n. in groten ~*, in large numbers, in force; *in vollen ~*, in full force; *ten ~ van*, to the number of. ge·talsterkte, no pl., *n.* numerical strength.

ge·tand, *a.* toothed; cogged.

ge·tapt, *a.* draught (*beer*); skimmed (*milk*); popular.

ge·tegeld, *a.* tiled.

ge·tekend, *a.* marked; branded.

ge·tier, no pl., *n.n.* clamour, shouting.

ge·tij, -den, *n.n.* tide. *dood ~*, neap tide; *het ~ verloopt*, the tide turns. ge·tijde, -n, *n.n.* hours (*in Roman Catholic liturgy*); tide. *See* getij. ge·tijdenboek, *n.n.* breviary. ge·tijhaven, -s, *n.* tidal harbour. ge·tij-tafel, -s, *n.* tide table.

ge·tik, no pl., *n.n.* ticking.

ge·timmer, no pl., *n.n.* hammering, carpentering.

ge·tintel, no pl., *n.n.* sparkling; tingling.

ge·tjangel, no pl., *n.n.*, ge·tingel, no pl., *n.n.*, ge·tjingel, no pl., *n.n.* tinkling (*poor music*).

ge·tjilp, no pl., *n.n.* chirping.

ge·tob, no pl., *n.n.* worrying.

ge·togen, *a. geboren en ~*, born and bred.

ge·tokkel, no pl., *n.n.* strumming.

ge·touw, *n.n.* loom.

ge·trapt, *a.* indirect. *~e verkiezingen*, elections by indirect vote.

ge·treuzel, no pl., *n.n.* dawdling.

ge·trokken, *a.* rifled (*of gun-barrel*).

ge·trommel, no pl., *n.n.* drumming.

ge·troost, *a.* comforted. *hij is zijn lot ~*, he is resigned to his fate. ge·troosten, zich, *v.t.r.* to put up with.

ge·trouw, *a.* faithful, loyal; true to. *~ tot in den dood*, faithful unto death. ¶*adv.* faithfully, truly. ge·trouwe, -n, *n.* follower. ge·trouwelijk, *adv.* faithfully, truly. ge··trouwheid, no pl., *n.* fidelity.

ge·tuigd, *a.* rigged.

ge·tuige, -n, *n.* witness; reference, testimonial. *~ à charge*, witness for the prosecution; *~ à décharge*, witness for the defence; *van goede ~n voorzien*, with good references. ge·tuigen, *v.t.* & *v.i.* to witness, testify. *hij weet er van te ~*, he has had experience of it; *~ van*, to bear witness to, speak for; *~ voor*, to speak in favour of. ge·tuigenis, -ssen, *n.* evidence, testimony, witness. *~ afleggen van*, to bear witness to. ge·tuigenverhoor, -horen, *n.n.* examination of witnesses. ge·tuigenverklaring, *n.* testimony, evidence. ge·tuigschrift, *n.n.* testimonial.

geul, *n.* gully; channel.

geur, *n.* fragrance, smell. *iets in ~en en kleuren vertellen*, to tell something in full detail. ·geuren, *v.i.* to smell (*pleasant*); to swank, show off. ·geurig, *a.* fragrant. ·geurigheid, no pl., *n.* fragrance, perfume. ·geurtje, -s, *n.n. er is een ~ aan*, there is something fishy about it.

Geus, -zen, *N.* Beggar (*16th century Dutch guerilla fighter*).

ge·vaar, -varen, *n.n.* danger; peril. *~ lopen*, to run the risk; *er is geen ~ bij*, there is no danger attached to it; *er is geen ~ voor*, there is no danger of it; *buiten ~*, out of danger; *in ~ brengen*, to endanger; *in ~ verkeren*, to be in danger; *met ~ van*, at the risk of; *op ~ af U te vervelen*, at the risk of boring you. ge·vaarlijk, *a.* dangerous. ge·vaarloos, -loze, *a.* without danger. ge·vaarte, -n, *n.n.* colossus; large shape *or* object.

ge·val, -llen, *n.n.* case (*occurrence*). *bij ~*, by chance; *als je bij ~ . . .*, should you happen to . . .; *in geen ~*, on no account; *in alle or elk ~*, in any case; *voor het ~*, in case; *het ~ wilde . . .*, it so happened . . . ge·vallen, *v. imp.*, *str.* to happen to. *zich alles laten ~*, to put up with anything. ge·vallig, *a.* pleasing.

ge·vangen, *a.* captive. *zich ~ geven*, to surrender; *~ nemen*, to take prisoner. ge·vangenbewaarder, -s, *n.* gaoler. ge·van-gene, -n, *n.* prisoner. ge·vangenis, -ssen, *n.* prison; imprisonment. ge·vangenisstraf, -ffen, *n.* imprisonment. ge·vangenschap, no pl., *n.* captivity, imprisonment. ge·vangenzetten, zet gevangen, *v.t.s.* to put in prison. ge·vankelijk, *adv.* as a prisoner.

ge·vat, -tte, *a.* quick-witted, ready. ¶*adv.* wittily. ge·vatheid, no pl., *n.* quick-wittedness.

ge·vecht, *n.n.* fight. *buiten ~ stellen*, to put out of action. ge·vechtsklaar, -klare *a.* ready for battle. **ge·vechtskruiser, -s,** *n.* battle cruiser. **ge·vechtslinie, -s,** *n.* fighting line. **ge·vechtsvliegtuig,** *n.n.* fighter(-plane). **ge·vechtswaarde,** no pl., *n.* military value.

ge·vederte, -n, *n.n.* plumage.

ge·veins, no pl., *n.n.* dissimulation. **ge·veinsd,** *a.* feigned.

·gevel, -s, *n.* facade. **·geveltop, -ppen,** *n.* gable.

·geven, geef, *v.t., str.* to give; to give out; to yield; to deal (*at cards*). *het geeft niets, it does not matter or it is of no use; wat geeft het?,* what does it matter?; ~ *om,* to care for; *zijn betrekking eraan* ~, to throw up one's job; *zijn tijd eraan* ~, to devote all one's time to; *iemand ervan langs* ~, to blame *or* go for someone; *acht* ~ *aan,* to pay attention to; *gehoor* ~ *aan,* to respond to; *zich gewonnen* ~, to give in; *een teken* ~, to make a sign. **·gever, -s,** *n.* giver, donor.

ge·vest, *n.n.* hilt. **ge·vestigd,** *a.* established.

ge·vierd, *a.* fêted.

ge·vit, no pl., *n.n.* fault-finding.

ge·vlamd, *a.* grained.

ge·vlei, no pl., *n.n.* flattering.

ge·vlekt, *a.* spotted.

ge·vleugeld, *a.* winged.

ge·vlij, no pl., *n.n. bij iemand in het* ~ *zien te komen,* to make up to a person.

ge·vloek, no pl., *n.n.* cursing.

ge·voeg, no pl., *n.n. zijn* ~ *doen,* to relieve oneself (*defecate*). **ge·voeglijk,** *adv.* decently, well.

ge·voel, no pl., *n.n.* feeling; touch; sensation; feel. *op het* ~ *af,* by touch. **ge·voelen, -s,** *n.n.* feeling, sentiment; opinion. *naar mijn* ~, in my opinion. ¶*v.t.* to feel; to realize. **ge·voelig,** *a.* sensitive; susceptible, impressionable; touchy; smart, sharp (*blow*). ~ *voor,* sensitive to; ~ *maken,* to sensitize. ¶*adv.* feelingly. **ge·voeligheid, -heden,** *n.* sensitiveness. **ge·voelloos, -lloze,** *a.* unfeeling, callous; numb. ~ *voor,* insensible to. **ge·voelloosheid,** no pl., *n.* insensibility. **ge·voelsleven,** no pl., *n.n.* emotional life.

ge·voerd, *a.* lined.

ge·vogelte, no pl., *n.n.* birds (*in general*).

ge·volg, *n.n.* outcome, result; effect; train, retinue. ~ *geven aan,* to carry into effect, to respond to. **ge·volge,** *n.n. ten* ~ *hebben,* to result in *or* to be the cause of; *ten* ~ *van,* in consequence of. **ge·volgtrekking,** *n.* deduction, inference. *een* ~ *maken,* to draw a conclusion.

gevol·machtigde, -n, *n.* plenipotentiary.

ge·vorderd, *a.* advanced.

ge·vorkt, *a.* forked, bifurcated.

ge·vrij, no pl., *n.n.* courting.

ge·vuld, *a.* full, well-filled.

ge·waad, -waden, *n.n.* robe, attire.

ge·waagd, *a.* risky, hazardous. *ze zijn aan elkaar* ~, they are well matched.

ge·waand, *a.* supposed.

ge·waarworden, *v.t.s.* to perceive, become aware of. **ge·waarwording,** *n.* perception; sensation.

ge·wag, no pl., *n.n.* ~ *maken van,* to make mention of. **ge·wagen, -waag,** *v.i.* ~ *van,* to make mention of.

ge·wapend, *a.* armed. ~*e macht,* armed forces. **ge·wapenderhand,** *adv.* by force of arms.

ge·wapper, no pl., *n.n.* fluttering (*flag*).

ge·warrel, no pl., *n.n.* whirl.

ge·was, -ssen, *n.n.* vegetation; crop.

ge·wast, *a.* waxed.

ge·wauwel, no pl., *n.n.* chattering.

ge·weeklaag, no pl., *n.n.* lamentation(s).

ge·weer, -weren, *n.n.* gun, rifle. *in 't* ~, up in arms. **ge·weerkogel, -s,** *n.* bullet. **ge·weerkolf, -ven,** *n.* butt-end (*of rifle*).

ge·wei, no pl., *n.n.* antlers.

ge·weld, no pl., *n.n.* violence; disturbance. ~ *aandoen,* to do violence to; *zichzelf* ~ *aandoen,* to restrain oneself; *in iemands* ~ *zijn,* to be in someone's power; *met* ~ *van wapenen,* by force of arms; *met* ~, by main force; *hij wou het met alle* ~, he insisted on it. **geweld·dadig,** *a.* violent. **ge·weldenaar, -s** *or* **-naren,** *n.* oppressor, usurper. **geweldena·rij,** *n.* tyranny. **ge·weldig,** *a.* mighty, terrific; enormous; awful. ¶*adv.* terrifically, dreadfully. ~ *veel,* an awful lot. **ge·weldpleging,** *n.* violence.

ge·welf, -ven, *n.n.* vault, arch. **ge·welfd** *a.* domed, arched.

ge·wemel, no pl., *n.n.* teeming, swarming.

ge·wend, *a.* accustomed. ~ *zijn om . . .,* to be used to . . . **ge·wennen, -wen,** *v.t.* to accustom. ¶*v.i.* ~ *aan,* to become accustomed to. ¶*v.r. zich* ~ *aan,* to accustom oneself to, to get used to.

ge·wenst, *a.* desired; advisable. **ge·wenstheid,** no pl., *n.* desirability.

ge·werveld, *a.* vertebrate.

ge·west, *n.n.* district, province. *betere* ~*en,* a better land (*heaven*). **ge·westelijk,** *a.* regional.

ge·weten, no pl., *n.n.* conscience. **ge·wetenloos, -loze,** *a.* unprincipled. ¶*adv.* unscrupulously. **geweten·loosheid,** no pl., *n.* unscrupulousness. **ge·wetensbezwaar, -zwaren,** *n.n.* scruple, conscientious objection. **ge·wetensvrijheid,** no pl., *n.* liberty of conscience. **ge·wetenszaak, -zaken,** *n.* matter of conscience.

ge·wettigd, *a.* justified, legitimate (*hope*).

ge·weven, *a.* woven.

ge·wezen, *a.* former, late.

ge·wicht, *n.n.* weight; importance. *soortelijk* ~, specific gravity; *bij het* ~, by weight; *van* ~, of consequence *or* importance; ~ *in de schaal leggen,* to carry weight; ~ *hechten aan,* to attach importance to. **ge·wichtig,** *a.* important; weighty, ponderous. ¶*adv.* ~ *doen,* to assume a look of importance. **ge·wichtsverlies,** no pl., *n.n.* loss of weight.

ge·wiebel, no pl., *n.n.* wobbling.

ge·wiekst, *a.* clever, sharp. **ge·wiekstheid,** no pl., *n.* cunning.

ge·wijd, *a.* sacred, consecrated.

ge·wild, *a.* in demand, popular; laboured.

ge·willig, *a.* willing. **ge·willigheid,** no pl., *n.* willingness.

ge·win, no pl., *n.n.* gain. *'t eerste* ~ *is kattegespin,* that's beginner's luck.

ge·wis, -sse, *a.* certain. ¶*adv.* surely.

ge·woel, no pl., *n.n.* bustle, turmoil.

ge·wonnen, *a.* won. ~ *en geboren,* born and bred; *zo* ~ *zo geronnen,* easy come, easy go; *zich* ~ *geven,* to give up.

ge·woon, -wone, *a.* ordinary; customary, usual. ~ *worden* or *raken,* to get accustomed to; ~ *zijn,* to be used to. ¶*adv.* commonly; simply. **ge·woonlijk,** *adv.* usually. *als* ~, as usual. **ge·woonte, -n,** *n.* habit, custom, practice. (*als*) *naar* ~ or *ouder* ~, as usual; *uit* ~, by force of habit. **ge·woonterecht,** *n.n.* customary *or* common law. **ge·woonweg,** *adv.* simply, just.

ge·worden, *v.t.* to reach. *iemand iets doen* ~, to have something sent to someone.

ge·worstel, no pl., *n.n.* struggling, wrestling.

ge·wricht, *n.n.* joint, articulation. **ge·wrichtsontsteking,** *n.* arthritis.

ge·wriemel, no pl., *n.n.* wriggling.

ge·wrocht, *n.n.* (*stilted*) creation, work.

ge·wrongen, *a.* distorted, twisted. **ge·wrongenheid, -heden,** *n.* distortion.

ge·zaag, no pl., *n.n.* sawing; boring talk.

ge·zag, no pl., *n.n.* authority; prestige. *op eigen* ~, on one's own authority, off one's own bat; *het openbaar* ~, the public authorities; *het wettig* ~, the lawful authority; *misbruik van* ~, abuse of power; ~ *voeren* or *uitoefenen,* to be in command; ~ *voeren over,* to be in command of. **ge·zaghebbend,** *a.* authoritative. *op* ~*e toon,* authoritatively. **ge·zaghebber, -s,** *n.* person in authority; captain, master (*of merchantship, warship*).

ge·zakt, *a.* failed, ploughed (*in examination*). See **gepakt.**

ge·zalfde, -n, *n.* anointed.

ge·zamenlijk, *a.* joint; concerted. ~*e werken,* complete works; *voor* ~*e rekening,* on joint account. ¶*adv.* jointly, together.

ge·zang, no pl., *n.n.* singing. ¶*n.n.* song, hymn. **ge·zangboek,** *n.n.* hymnal.

ge·zanik, no pl., *n.n.* bothering.

ge·zant, *n.* ambassador, minister. **ge·zantschap, ppen,** *n.n.* embassy, legation.

ge·zegd, *a.* (above-)said, (above-)mentioned. **ge·zegde, -n,** *n.n.* saying; predicate.

ge·zegeld, *a.* sealed.

ge·zegend, *a.* blessed.

ge·zeggelijk, *a.* amenable. **ge·zeggen,** infin.

only, *v.t.* *zich laten* ~, to be amenable; *zich niet laten* ~, not to be open to reason.

ge·zel, -llen, *n.* companion, fellow; journeyman (*carpenter, etc.*). **ge·zellig,** *a.* sociable; pleasant, cosy; gregarious. **ge·zelligheid,** no pl., *n.* sociability, pleasantness. **gezel·lin, -nnen,** *n.* companion (*female*). **ge·zelschap, -ppen,** *n.n.* company, party; troupe. **ge·zelschapsdame, -s,** *n.* lady companion. **Ge·zelschapseilanden,** *pl. n.N.* Society Islands. **ge·zelschapsreis, -zen,** *n.* conducted tour.

ge·zet, -tte, *a.* corpulent, stout; set, regular (*times*). **ge·zeten,** *a.* settled; well-to-do. ~ *burger,* substantial citizen. **ge·zetheid,** no pl., *n.* corpulence.

ge·zicht, *n.n.* eye-sight; sight; face; view. ~*en trekken,* to pull faces; *een ernstig* ~ *zetten,* to put on a serious air; *hou je* ~!, shut up!; *bij het* ~ *van,* at the sight of; *in het* ~ *komen,* to heave in sight; *iets in het* ~ *krijgen,* to catch sight of *or* to sight something; *op het* ~, at sight; *op het eerste* ~, at first sight; *iemand op zijn* ~ *geven,* to beat a person; *uit het* ~ *verliezen,* to lose sight of; *iemand van* ~ *kennen,* to know a person by sight. **ge·zichtsas, -ssen,** *n.* visual axis. **ge·zichtsbedrog,** no pl., *n.n.* optical illusion. **ge·zichtseinder,** no pl., *n.* horizon. **ge·zichtskring,** no pl., *n.* horizon (*mental*). **ge·zichtspunt,** *n.n.* point of view, viewpoint.

ge·zien, *a.* esteemed, respected; read and approved of. ¶*c. as.*

ge·zin, -nnen, *n.n.* family, household.

ge·zind, *a.* inclined, disposed. *Engels* ~, pro-English. **ge·zindheid, -heden,** *n.* disposition; persuasion (*religious*). **ge·zindte, -n,** *n.* denomination.

ge·zinshoofd, *n.n.* head of the family (*i.e., household*). **ge·zinsleden,** pl. only, *n.n.* members of the family (*i.e., household*).

ge·zocht, *a.* in demand; laboured, forced. ¶*adv.* affectedly. **ge·zochtheid,** no pl., *n.* affectation.

ge·zoem, no pl., *n.n.* buzzing.

ge·zond, *a.* healthy, sound; sane; wholesome. ~ *en wel,* safe and sound; ~ *verstand,* commonsense; ~ *naar geest en lichaam,* sound in body and mind; ~ *van geest,* healthy-minded; ~ *blijven,* to keep well; ~ *worden,* to get well (*again*). ¶*adv.* healthily, soundly. **ge·zondheid,** no pl., *n.* health; sanity. *op uw* ~!, your very good health! **ge·zondheidscommissie, -s,** *n.* board of health, public health committee. **ge·zondheidshalve,** *adv.* for the sake of one's health. **ge·zondheidsoord,** *n.n.* health resort. **ge·zondheidsredenen,** pl. only, *n. om* ~, for reasons of health.

ge·zouten, *a.* salt(ed).

ge·zusters, pl. only, *n.* sisters. *de* ~ *A,* the A. sisters.

ge·zwam, no pl., *n.n.* rot (*talk*).

ge·zwel, -llen, *n.n.* tumour, growth.
ge·zwendel, no pl., *n.n.* swindling.
ge·zwets, no pl., *n.n.* boasting.
ge·zwind, *a.* swift.
ge·zwoeg, no pl., *n.n.* toiling.
ge·zwollen, *a.* swollen.
ge·zworen, *a.* sworn.
gids, *n.* guide.
giechelen, *v.i.* to giggle, titter.
giek, *n.* gig (*boat*).
gier, *n.* vulture; liquid manure. **·gierbrug,**
-ggen, *n.* flying bridge. **·gieren,** *v.i.* to
howl (*of wind*); to sheer; to dress (*with
liquid manure*). ~ *van 't lachen,* to scream
with laughter. **·gierpont,** *n.* ferry-punt
(*attached to wire*).
·gierig, *a.* avaricious, miserly. **·gierigaard,**
-s, *n.* miser. **·gierigheid,** no pl., *n.* avarice,
miserliness.
gierst, *n.* millet.
·giervalk, *n.* gerfalcon. **·gierzwaluw,** *n.*
swift, martin.
·gietcokes, no pl., *n.* foundry coke. **·gieteling,**
n. pig (*of iron*). **·gieten,** *v.t.,* *str.* to pour;
to cast, mould. *het regent dat het giet,*
it is pouring with rain. **·gieter, -s,** *n.*
watering can; founder (*of metals*). **giete·rij,**
n. foundry. **·gietijzer,** no pl., *n.n.*
cast iron. **·gietkroes, -zen,** *n.* crucible.
·gietsel, -s, *n.n.,* **·gietstuk, -kken,** *n.n.*
casting. **·gietvorm,** *n.* casting-mould.
·gietwerk, no pl., *n.n.* cast work.
gift, (1) *n.* gift, present. **·giftbrief, -ven,** *n.*
deed of gift.
gift, (2) *n.n.* **gif, -ten,** *n.n.,* poison, venom.
·giftbeker, -s, *n.* poison cup. **·giftblaas,
-blazen,** *n.* poison-bag. **·giftgas, -ssen,**
n.n. poison gas. **·giftig,** *a.* poisonous,
venomous. **·giftigheid,** no pl., *n.* venomous-
ness, virulence. **·giftklier,** *n.* poison-gland.
·giftmenger, -s, *n.* poisoner (*male*). **·gift-
mengster, -s,** *n.* poisoner (*female*). **·gift-
slang,** *n.* poisonous snake. **·gifttand,** *n.*
poison-fang. **·giftvrij,** *a.* non-poisonous.
gift·werend, *a.* antidotal.
gij, *pron.* you, thou, ye (*sing., pl., bibl.,
and poet.*). **gij·lieden,** *pron.* (*stilted*) you
(*plural*).
·gijzelaar, -s, *n.* hostage. **·gijzelen,** *v.t.* to
take as hostage. **·gijzeling,** *n.* hostageship.
in ~ *verkeren,* to be a hostage; *in* ~
worden genomen, to be made a hostage.
gil, -llen, *n.* yell, scream, shriek. **·gillen,**
gil, *v.i.* to yell, scream, shriek.
·gilde, -n, *n.n.* guild. **·gildehuis, -zen,** *n.n.*
guildhall. **·gildewezen,** no pl., *n.n.* system
of guilds.
·ginder, *adv.,* **ginds,** *adv.* yonder, over there.
daar ~, over there, out there. **ginds,** *a.*
yonder.
·ginnegappen, -gap, *v.i.* to giggle.
gips, no pl., *n.n.* gypsum, plaster of Paris.
·gipsen, *a.* (made of) plaster of Paris.
¶*v.t.* to plaster. **·gipsornament,** *n.n.* stucco
ornament. **·gipsverband,** *n.n.* plaster of
Paris dressing.
gi·reren, -reer, *v.t.* to transfer, endorse (*bills*).
·giro, no pl., *n.* clearing, transfer. **·giro-
bank,** *n.* clearing *or* transfer bank. **·giro-
biljet, -tten,** *n.n.* transfer form. **·giro-
rekening,** *n.* transfer account.
gis, -ssen, *n.* guess. *op de* ~, at random.
·gispen, *v.t.* to censure. **·gisping,** *n.* censure.
·gissen, gis, *v.t.* to guess. **·gissing,** *n.* guess.
naar ~, at a guess.
gist, no pl., *n.* yeast, barm. **·gisten,** *v.i.* to
ferment. *laten* ~, to (*cause to*) ferment.
¶no pl., *n.n.* *aan het* ~, in a ferment.
·gister(en), *adv.* yesterday. *hij is niet van* ~,
he was not born yesterday; ~ *voor* or
over een week, yesterday week. **gister-
·avond,** *adv.* last night (*evening*). **gister-
·middag,** *adv.* yesterday afternoon. **gister-
·morgen,** *adv.* yesterday morning. **gister-
·nacht,** *adv.* last night (*not evening*).
gister·ochtend, *adv.* (*stilted & poet.*)
yesterday morning.
·gisting, *n.* fermentation. ferment. **·gistkuip,**
n. fermenting vat.
git, no pl., *n.n.* jet (*stone*). **·gitten,** *a.* (made
of) jet. **·gitzwart,** *a.* jet-black.
gi·taar, -taren, *n.* guitar.
·glaasje, -s, *n.n.* (small) glass; (microscope)
slide. *een* ~ *teveel hebben,* to have a glass
too many; *een* ~ *pakken,* to have one
(*drink*).
gla·ceren, -ceer, *v.t.* to ice (*cakes*); to glaze
(*pottery*).
glad, -dde, *a.* slippery; smooth; cunning.
~ *van tong,* glib; *zich op* ~ *ijs wagen,*
to skate on thin ice; *dat is nogal* ~, that
is obvious. ¶*adv.* smoothly; absolutely,
altogether. *het gaat hem* ~ *af,* it comes
easy to him; *ik ben het* ~ *vergeten,* I have
clean forgotten it; ~ *verkeerd* or *mis,*
absolutely *or* altogether wrong. **·gladaf,**
adv. straight out.
·gladakker, -s, *n.* pariah dog; clever rascal.
·gladboenen, *v.t.s.* to polish. **·gladdigheid,**
no pl., *n.* slipperiness. **·gladgeschoren,** *a.*
cleanshaven. **glad·harig,** *a.* smooth-
haired. **·gladheid, -heden,** *n.* smoothness,
slipperiness. **·gladstrijken,** *v.t.s.,* *str.* to
smooth out *or* down. **gladweg,** *adv.*
flatly. **·gladwrijven, wrijf glad,** *v.t.s.,* *str.*
to polish.
glans, -zen, *n.* shine, sheen; gloss, lustre,
glitter; glory. *met* ~, brilliantly. **·glans-
loos, -loze,** *a.* lacklustre. **·glansperiode, -s,**
n. heyday, great period. **·glanspunt,** *n.n.*
crowning feature, high spot. **·glansrijk,** *a.*
glorious, brilliant. **·glansrijkheid,** no pl.,
n. brilliance, splendour. **·glansverf, -ven,** *n.*
glossy *or* enamel paint. **·glanzen, glans,** *v.i.*
to shine, gleam. **·glanzig,** *a.* shiny, glossy.
glas, no pl., *n.n.* glass (*substance*). ¶**-zen,**
n.n. glass (*receptacle* or *cover*); window-
pane; lens (*of spectacles*); bell (*time signal*);

glass (*barometer*). *een stevig* ~ *drinken*, to be a steady drinker; *zijn eigen glazen ingooien*, to cut off one's nose to spite one's face. ·**glasachtig**, *a.* glassy, vitreous. ·**glasblazen, blaas glas,** *v.i.s., str.* to blow glass. ·**glasblazer, -s,** *n.* glass-blower. ·**glasblazerij,** *n.* glassworks. ·**glasdicht,** *a.* glazed. ·**glashelder,** *a.* clear as glass, crystal-clear. ·**glasruit,** *n.* window-pane. ·**glazen,** *a.* (*made of*) glass. ·**glazendoek,** *n.* glass-cloth. ·**glazenmaker, -s,** *n.* glazier; dragon-fly. ·**glazenspuit,** *n.* window-spray. ·**glazenwasser, -s,** *n.* window-cleaner. ·**glazig,** *a.* glassy. **gla·zuren, -zuur,** *v.t.* to glaze. **gla·zuur,** no pl., *n.n.*, **gla·zuursel,** no pl., *n.n.* glaze (*of pottery*); enamel (*of teeth*).
·**gletscher, -s,** *n.* glacier.
gleuf, -ven, *n.* groove; slot. ·**gleufhoed,** *n.* trilby (hat).
·**glibberen,** *v.i.* to slither. ·**glibberig,** *a.* slippery.
·**glijbaan, -banen,** *n.* slide. ·**glijbank,** *n.* sliding-seat. ·**glijden,** *v.i., str.* to glide, slide. *door de vingers* ~, to slip through one's fingers. ·**glijvliegtuig,** *n.n.* glider.
·**glimhout,** no pl., *n.n.* touchwood. ·**glimlach,** *n.* smile. ·**glimlachen,** *v.i.* to smile. ~ *tegen*, to smile at, smile on (*person*); ~ *over*, to smile at (*something*). ·**glimlachje, -s,** *n.n.* half-smile. ·**glimmen, glim,** *v.i., str.* to shine, be shiny; to gleam; to glow (*of embers*). ·**glimmend,** *a.* shining, shiny. ·**glimworm,** *n.* glow-worm, firefly.
glimp, *n.* glimpse, gleam.
·**glinsteren,** *v.i.* to glitter, sparkle. ·**glinstering,** *n.* glitter, glint.
·**glippen, glip,** *v.i.* to slip. *er door* ~, to slip through.
glo·baal, -bale, *a.* rough. ¶*adv.* roughly. ~ *genomen*, broadly speaking.
gloed, no pl., *n.* glow, blaze; ardour, verve. ·**gloednieuw,** *a.* brand-new. ·**gloeidraad, -draden,** *n.* filament (*of lamp*). ·**gloeien,** *v.i.* to glow; to be aglow. ~ *van*, to glow with. ¶*v.t.* to make red-hot; to anneal. ·**gloeiend,** *a.* glowing; red-hot. ~*e kolen*, live coals; ~ *van*, ablaze with. ¶*adv.* ~ *heet*, burning hot, red-hot. ·**gloeihitte,** no pl., *n.* glowing heat. ·**gloeikousje, -s,** *n.n.* incandescent mantle. ·**gloeilamp,** *n.* (electric) bulb, incandescent lamp. ·**gloeioven, -s,** *n.* annealing furnace.
·**glooien,** *v.i.* to slope, shelve. ·**glooiend,** *a.* sloping. ·**glooiing,** *n.* slope. ·**glooiingshoek,** *n.* gradient.
·**gloren, gloor,** *v.i.* (*lit.*) to gleam, glimmer. *bij het* ~ *van de dag*, at break of day. ·**glorie,** no pl., *n.* glory. ·**glorierijk,** *a.*, **glori·eus, -ze,** *a.* glorious.
·**gluipen,** *v.i.* to sneak. ·**gluiper, -s,** *n.*, ·**gluiperd, -s,** *n.* sneak. ·**gluiperig,** *a.* sneaking, furtive.

·**glunder,** *a.* cheerful, bonny. ·**glunderen,** *v.i.* to beam.
·**gluren, gluur,** *v.i.* to peer; to peep. ~ *naar*, to peer at. ·**gluurogen, -oog,** *v.i.* to peer.
gnoe, -s, *n.* gnu.
·**gnuiven, gnuif,** *v.i.* to snigger.
God, no pl., *n.* God (N.B. *in many English expressions the words Heaven or Goodness are preferred.*) ~ *noch gebod vrezen*, to be utterly fearless; ~ *noch gebod weten*, to be ruthlessly lawless; ~*s water over* ~*s akker laten lopen*, to let things take their own course; ~ *zij dank!*, thank God!; ~ *beware!*, God forbid!; ~ *betere het!*, can you beat it? **god,** *n.* god. **god·dank,** *int.* thank God. ·**goddelijk,** *a.* divine, heavenly. ·**goddelijkheid, -heden,** *n.* divinity, divineness. **godde·loos, -loze,** *a.* godless, ungodly, unholy. **godde·loosheid, -heden,** *n.* godlessness, impiety. **god·dorie,** *int.* (*v. coll.*) dammit. ·**godendienst,** *n.* idolatry. ·**godenleer,** no pl., *n.* mythology. ·**godenschemering,** *n.* twilight of the gods. ·**godgans,** *a. de* ~*e dag*, the livelong day. ·**godgeklaagd,** *a. het is* ~, it cries to Heaven. ·**godgeleerd,** *a.* theological. **godge·leerde, -n,** *n.* theologian, divine. **godge·leerdheid,** no pl., *n.* theology. **godge·vallig,** *a.* pleasing to God. ·**godheid,** no pl., *n.* deity, godhead. ¶**-heden,** *n.* divinity. **go·din, -nnen,** *n.* goddess. ·**godloochenaar, -s,** *n.* atheist. ·**godloochenend,** *a.* atheistic. ·**godloochening,** no pl., *n.* atheism. ·**godsakker, -s,** *n.* God's acre. ·**godsdienst,** *n.* religion; worship. **gods·dienstig,** *a.* religious. ·**godsdienstijver,** no pl., *n.* religious zeal. ·**godsdienstleraar, -s,** *n.* minister of religion. ·**godsdienstoefening,** *n.* divine service, worship. ·**godsdienstoorlog,** *n.* religious war. ·**godsdienstwaanzin,** no pl., *n.* religious mania. ·**godsdienstzin,** no pl., *n.* piety. ·**godsgericht,** *n.n.* (trial by) ordeal. **gods·jammerlijk,** *a.* wretched. ·**godslasteraar, -s,** *n.* blasphemer. **gods·lasterend,** *a.*, **gods·lasterlijk,** *a.* blasphemous. **gods·lastering,** *n.* blasphemy. ·**godsnaam,** *int. in* ~, for God's sake; *één, twee, drie, in* ~*!*, one, two, three, there she goes! ·**godsoordeel, -delen,** *n.n.* See **godsgericht.** ·**godspenning,** *n.* earnest-money. ·**godsrijk,** no pl., *n.n.* kingdom of God. ·**godsvrede,** no pl., *n.* truce of God, political truce. ·**godsvrucht,** no pl., *n.* devotion, piety. ·**godswege,** *int. van* ~, in the name of God. ·**godswil,** *int. om* ~, for God's sake. ·**godvergeten,** *a.* godforsaken. **god·vrezend,** *a.*, **god·vruchtig,** *a.* devout, pious. **god·vruchtigheid,** no pl., *n.* devotion, piety.
goed, *a.* good; kind; goodly; well (*in health*). *een* ~ *eind*, a goodly distance; *een* ~ *uur*, a full hour; ~ *volk*, honest people; *de Goede Week*, Holy Week; ~ *en wel*, safe and sound *or* well and good; *mij* ~ *or*

ook ~, very well, I don't mind; *dat is alles* ~ *en wel*, that is all very well; *het is maar* ~ *ook*, a good thing, too; ~ *zo!*, well done!; ~ *in . . .*, good at . . .; *op een* ~*e dag*, one (fine) day; *voor* ~, forever; *zo* ~ *als*, practically; *zo* ~ *als dood*, as good as dead; *zo* ~ *als niets*, hardly anything; *net zo* ~, just as good. ¶*adv.* well; properly. *hij kan* ~ *lezen*, he is good at reading; *het is* ~ *te zien*, it is easy to see; *hij heeft* ~ *praten*, it is easy for him to talk *or* however much he talks; *er* ~ *in zitten*, to be well-off; ~ *bij*, quick at learning; *zo* ~ *en zo kwaad als het kan*, as well as can be expected; *net zo* ~, just as well. ¶no pl., *n.n.* stuff, material; ware; stuff, rubbish; clothes, things; luggage. *schoon* ~, clean linen. ¶*-eren*, *n.n.* property, goods, wares; estate. *gestolen* ~ *gedijt niet*, cheats never prosper; ~ *en bloed*, life and property; *onroerend* ~, real property; *roerend* ~, movables, personal property. **goed**(e), no pl., *n.n.* good. ~ *en kwaad*, good and evil; ~ *doen*, to do good; *zich te* ~ *doen aan*, to feast upon; *iets te* ~ *hebben*, to have something owing to one; *iemand iets te* (or *ten*) *goede houden*, to excuse a person *or* to credit a person with something; *ten goede komen*, to benefit; *iets goeds*, something good *or* nice; *niets dan goeds*, nothing but good; *teveel van het goede*, too much of a good thing. **goed·aardig**, *a.* good-natured, kindhearted; mild (*of illness*). **goed·aardigheid**, no pl., *n.* kindheartedness; mildness (*of illness*). **·goeddeels**, *adv.* for the greater part. **·goeddoen**, doe goed, *v.i.s.*, *irr.* to do good. **·goeddunken**, *v.i.s.*, *irr.* to think fit, please. ¶no pl., *n.n.* pleasure, discretion. *naar* ~, at will; *naar* ~ *van*, at the discretion of. **goeden·avond**, *int.* good evening. **goeden-dagzeggen**, zeg go**e**ndag, *v.t.s.*, *irr.* to greet; to say goodbye to. **·goederen**, *pl.* of **goed. ·goederenhandel**, no pl., *n.* goods trade. **·goederenkantoor, -toren**, *n.n.* goods office, luggage office, parcels office. **·goederenloods**, *n.* goods shed. **·goederenverkeer**, no pl., *n.n.* goods traffic. **·goederenvliegtuig**, *n.n.* cargo-plane. **·goederenvoorraad, -raden**, *n.* stock. **·goederenwagen, -s**, *n.* goods-van, truck. **·goederhand**, no pl., *n. van* ~, from a good source, on good authority. **·goedertieren**, *a.* merciful. **goeder·tierenheid**, no pl., *n.* mercy. **goed·geefs**, *a.* open-handed, liberal. **goed-geefsheid**, no pl., *n.* liberality. **goedge-lovig**, *a.* credulous; orthodox. **·goedge-lovigheid**, no pl., *n.* credulity. **·goedgezind**, *a.* well-disposed. **goed·gunstig**, *a.* (*stilted*) kind, obliging. ¶*adv.* (*stilted*) favourably. **goed·hartig**, *a.* kindhearted. **goed·hartigheid**, no pl., *n.* kindness of heart. **·goedheid, -heden**, *n.* goodness, kindness. **goed·heilig**, *a.* kindly. **·goedig**,

a. good-natured. **·goedje**, no pl., *n.n.* stuff. **·goedkeuren**, *v.t.s.* to approve of; to adopt (*report*); to pass (*for military service*). **·goedkeurend**, *a.* approving. **·goedkeuring**, *n.* approval, approbation; assent. *zijn* ~ *hechten aan*, to approve of; *zijn* ~ *onthouden*, to withhold one's consent; *ter* ~ *voorleggen*, to submit for approval; *iemands* ~ *wegdragen*, to meet with someone's approval. **goed·koop, -kope**, *a.* cheap. ~ *duurkoop*, cheap goods are dearest in the long run. **goed·lachs**, *a.* laughing readily. **goed·leers**, *a.* teachable, quick. **·goedmaken**, maak goed, *v.t.s.* to repair, mend; to make good, make up for. *het weer* ~, to make it up again. **goed·moedig**, *a.* kindhearted. **·goedpraten**, **praat goed**, *v.t.s.* to explain away. **goed·rond**, *a.* straightforward. **·goedschiks**, *adv.* with a good grace, willingly. ~ *kwaadschiks*, willy-nilly. **·goedsmoeds**, *adv.* cheerfully. **·goedvinden**, *v.t.s.*, *str.* to think fit; to approve (of). ¶no pl., *n.n.* consent, approval. *naar* ~ *handelen*, to use one's discretion. **goed·willig**, *a.* willing. **goed·willigheid**, no pl., *n.* willingness. **·goedzak, -kken**, *n.*, **·goeierd, -s**, *n.* kind soul; simpleton.

·gokken, gok, *v.i.* to gamble. **·gokker, -s**, *n.* gambler. **gokke·rij**, *n.* gambling. **·gokspel**, *n.n.* gamble.

golf, -ven, *n.* wave, billow; wave (*vibration*); gulf, bay. ¶no pl., *n.n.* golf. **·golfbaan, -banen**, *n.* golf links. **·golfbreker, -s**, *n.* breakwater. **·golfslag**, no pl., *n.* beating of waves. **·Golfstroom**, no pl., *N.* Gulf Stream. **·golven, golf**, *v.t.* & *v.i.* to wave, undulate. **·golvend**, *a.* wavy, undulating, rolling. **·golving**, *n.* waving; undulation.

gom, no pl., *n.* gum. *Arabische* ~, gum Arabic. ¶*-mmen*, *n.* rubber, eraser. **·gomachtig**, *a.* gummy. **·gomboom, -bomen**, *n.* gum-tree. **·gomelastiek**, no pl., *n.n.* indiarubber. ¶*n.n.* rubber, eraser. **·gomelastieken**, *a.* (*made of*) rubber. **·gomhars**, *n.n.* gum-resin. **·gommen**, gom, *v.t.* to gum. **·gommetje, -s**, *n.n.* rubber, eraser.

·gondel, -s, *n.* gondola; car (*of aircraft*). **gonde·lier, -s**, *n.* gondolier. **·gondellied, -eren**, *n.n.* barcarole.

gonio·metrisch, *a.* goniometric(al).

·gonzen, gons, *v.i.* to buzz, drone.

·goochelaar, -s, *n.* conjurer, juggler. **goochela-rij**, *n.* jugglery. **·goochelbeker, -s**, *n.* juggler's vase. **·goochelen**, *v.i.* to juggle, perform conjuring tricks. **·goochelkunst**, no pl., *n.* prestidigitation. **·goochelkunstje, -s**, *n.n.* conjuring trick. **·goocheltoer**, *n.* conjuring trick. **·goochem**, *a.* knowing, clever. **·goochemerd, -s**, *n.* wide awake individual.

gooi, *n.* throw, fling, toss. *een* ~ *doen naar*, to have a shot at. **·gooien**, *v.i.* to throw, fling; to cast, pitch; to pelt. *door elkaar* ~,

119 ·gokken — gra·deerwerk

to muddle; *het* ~ *op*, to switch over to (*in conversation*).
goor, gore, *a.* sallow; nasty, dirty.
goot, goten, *n.* gutter, drain. ·**gootpijp,** *n.* drain-pipe. ·**gootsteen, -stenen,** *n.* sink. *in de* ~, down the sink.
·**gordel, -s,** *n.* belt, girdle; belt, zone. ·**gordeldier,** *n.n.* armadillo. ·**gordelriem,** *n.* belt, girdle. ·**gordelroos,** no pl., *n.* shingles. ·**gorden,** *v.t.,* to gird. ¶*v.r. zich tot de strijd* ~, to gird oneself for battle.
gor·dijn, *n.n.* curtain.
·**gorgeldrank,** *n.* gargle. ·**gorgelen,** *v.i.* to gargle; to warble.
gors, -zen, *n.* yellow-hammer; mud flat, salting. ·**gorsland,** *n.n.* salting (*pasture*).
gort, no pl., *n.* groats; barley. *iemand kennen van haver tot* ~, to know a person very intimately. ·**gortebrij,** no pl., *n.,* ·**gortepap,** no pl., *n.* (barley-)gruel.
·**gortig,** *a.* measly (*of swine*).
·**gossie(mijne),** *int.* golly!
goud, no pl., *n.n.* gold. *het is niet alles* ~ *wat er blinkt,* all that glitters is not gold; *het is* ~ *waard,* it is worth its weight in gold. ¶*a.* golden. *See* **gouden.** ·**goudachtig,** *a.* golden, aureous. ·**goudagio,** no pl., *n.* premium on gold. ·**goudblond,** *a.* golden (*of hair*), blonde. ·**goudbrasem, -s,** *n.* gilthead. ·**gouddelver, -s,** *n.* gold-digger. ·**gouddraad, -draden,** *n.* gold-wire. ·**gouden,** *a.* (*made of*) gold, golden. ~ *bergen beloven,* to promise heaps of gold; *de* ~ *eeuw,* the golden age; *de* ~ *koets,* the gilt coach (*of the Queen*); *de* ~ *standaard,* the gold standard; *een* ~ *tientje* or *vijfje,* a gold ten or five guilder piece. ·**gouden-regen, -s,** *n.* laburnum. ·**goudenaar, -s,** *n.* church-warden (*pipe*). ·**goudfazant,** *n.* golden pheasant. ·**goudgeel, -gele,** *a.* golden (*yellow*). ·**goudgerand,** *a.* gilt-edged. ·**goudhaantje, -s,** *n.n.* gold-crest; gold beetle. ·**goudhoudend,** *a.* auriferous. ·**goudkever, -s,** *n.* goldsmith beetle. ·**goudkleurig,** *a.* gold-coloured. ·**goud-korrel, -s,** *n.* grain of gold. ·**goudlaken,** no pl., *n.n.* gold cloth, gold brocade. ·**goudlakens,** *a.* (*made of*) gold cloth. ~*e fazant,* golden pheasant. ·**goudleer**, no pl., *n.n.* gilt leather. ·**goudleren,** *a.* (*made of*) gilt leather. ·**goudmerel, -s,** *n.* oriole. ·**goudpletter, -s,** *n.* gold-beater. ·**goudrenet, -tten,** *n.* golden rennet, russet (apple).
Gouds, *a.* from or of Gouda. ~*e pijp,* churchwarden.
·**goudsbloem,** *n.* marigold. ·**goudschaal, -schalen,** *n.* gold scales. *zijn woorden op een* ~ *wegen,* to weigh one's every word. ·**goudslager, -s,** *n.* gold-beater. ·**goud-smederij,** no pl., *n.* goldsmith's craft. ¶*n.* goldsmith's workshop. ·**goudsmid, -smeden,** *n.* goldsmith. ·**goudstuk, -kken,** *n.n.* gold coin. ·**goudvink,** *n.* bullfinch. ·**goudvis,**

-ssen, *n.* goldfish. ·**goudviskom, -mmen,** *n.* goldfish bowl. ·**goudvlies, -zen,** *n.n.* gold-beater's skin. ·**goudvos, -ssen,** *n.* bay (*horse*). ·**goudwerk,** no pl., *n.n.* goldware.
gouver·nante, -s, *n.* governess. **gouverne-ment,** *n.* government. **gouverne·ments-dienst,** *n.* government service. **gouver·neur, -s,** *n.* governor; tutor. **gouver·neur-generaal, gouverneurs-generaal,** *n.* governor general. **gouver·neurschap, -ppen,** *n.n.* governorship. **gouver·neurse, -n,** *n.* wife of governor general.
gouw, *n.* district.
·**gouwe, -n,** *n. stinkende* ~, swallow-wort, celandine.
·**gouwenaar, -s,** *n.* churchwarden (*pipe*).
·**govie, -s,** *n.* gudgeon, bogy.
graad, graden, *n.* degree (*of measurement*); degree, grade, rank. *bij 80 graden,* at 80 degrees; *in hoge* ~, to a high degree; *in zekere* ~, to a certain degree; *op 45 graden noorderbreedte,* at 45 degrees latitude; *een* ~ *behalen,* to take a degree. ·**graadboog, -bogen,** *n.* graduated arc. ·**graadmeter, -s,** *n.* graduator. ·**graad-verdeling,** *n.* graduation (*on instrument*).
graaf, graven, *n.* count; earl. ·**graafschap, -ppen,** *n.n.* county.
·**graafmachine, -s,** *n.* excavator. ·**graafwerk,** *n.n.* excavation, diggings. ·**graafwesp,** *n.* digger-wasp.
graag, grage, *a.* eager. ¶*adv.* gladly, with pleasure. *heel* ~, with great pleasure; *hij doet het* ~, he likes doing it. ·**graagte,** no pl., *n.* eagerness.
·**graaien,** *v.t.* to rummage. ~ *naar,* to grab at.
Graal, *N.* Grail.
graan, granen, *n.n.* corn, grain; cereals. ·**graanbeurs, -zen,** *n.* corn exchange. ·**graanbouw,** no pl., *n.* corn growing. ·**graangewas,** no pl., *n.n.* corn crop. ·**graangewassen,** cereals. ·**graanhandelaar, -s,** *n.* corn-chandler. ·**graankorrel, -s,** *n.* grain of corn. ·**graanpakhuis, -zen,** *n.n.,* ·**graanschuur, -schuren,** *n.* granary. ·**graan-vruchten,** pl. only, *n.* cereals. ·**graanzolder, -s,** *n.* corn-loft ·**graanzuiger, -s,** *n.* corn elevator.
graat, graten, *n.* fish-bone. *het is niet zuiver op de* ~, there is something fishy about it; *van de* ~ *vallen,* to faint or to lose flesh.
·**grabbel,** no pl., *n. te* ~ *gooien,* to throw to be scrambled for or to throw away recklessly. ·**grabbelen,** *v.i.* to scramble. ~ *naar,* to scramble for. ·**grabbelaar, -s,** *n.* one who scrambles. ·**grabbelton, -nnen,** *n.* bran-tub (*lucky dip*).
gracht, *n.* town canal; moat.
gra·deerwerk, *n.n.* graduation works. **gra-deren, -deer,** *v.t.* to graduate (*solution*). **gradu·eel, -uele,** *a.* in degree. ¶*adv.* gradually. **gradu·eren, -ueer,** *v.t.* to graduate.

graf, -ven, *n.n.* grave, tomb. *het heilige ~,* the holy sepulchre; *tot aan het ~,* till death. **grafdelver, -s,** *n.* gravedigger. **grafelijk,** *a.* of *or* like a count. **grafkelder, -s,** *n.* family vault. **grafkuil,** *n.* grave. **grafrede, -nen,** *n.* funeral oration. **grafschennis,** no pl., *n.* violation of tombs. **grafschrift,** *n.n.* epitaph. **grafsteen, -stenen,** *n.* tombstone. **grafstem, -mmen,** *n.* sepulchral voice. **graftombe, -s** *or* **-n,** *n.* tomb. **grafwaarts,** *adv.* graveward.
gram, -mmen, *n.* gramme.
grammatica, -'s, *n.* grammar.
gramofoon, -s, *n.* gramophone. **gramofoonplaat, -platen,** *n.* gramophone record.
gramschap, no pl., *n.* wrath, ire.
granaat, -naten, *n.* shell (*cannon*); grenade; garnet. **granaatappel, -s,** *n.* pomegranate (*fruit*). **granaatboom, -bomen,** *n.* pomegranate(-tree). **granaatkartets,** *n.* shrapnel. **granaatscherf, -ven,** *n.* shell splinter. **granaatsteen, -stenen,** *n.* garnet. **granaattrechter, -s,** *n.* shell-hole, crater. **granaatvuur,** no pl., *n.n.* shell-fire. **granaten,** *a.* (*made of*) garnet.
graniet, no pl., *n.n.* granite. **granieten,** *a.* (*male of*) granite.
grap, -ppen, *n.* joke, jest. *~ maken,* to be troublesome; *~ vertellen,* to tell jokes; *daar zul je grappen van beleven,* you will have some trouble with that; *voor or uit de ~,* for fun. **grapjas, -ssen,** *n.,* **grappenmaker, -s,** *n.* joker; buffoon. **grappenmakerij,** *n.* funny business. **grapje, -s,** *n.n.* joke; fun. *hij maakt er een ~ van,* he is turning it into a joke; *~ uithalen,* to play jokes *or* tricks. **grappig,** *a.* funny, comic. ¶*adv.* funnily.
gras, -ssen, *n.n.* grass. *hem het ~ voor de voeten wegmaaien,* to cut the ground from under his feet. **grasachtig,** *a.* grassy; grasslike, graminaceous. **grasboer,** *n.* dairy-farmer. **grasboter,** no pl., *n.* fresh butter (*from grass-fed cows*). **grasduinen,** *v.i. ergens in ~,* to browse somewhere (*fig.*). **grashalm,** *n.* grass-blade. **grasland,** *n.n.* pasture land. **grasmaand,** *n.* April. **grasmus, -ssen,** *n.* hedge-sparrow. **grasperk,** *n.n.* grass-plot, lawn. **graspieper, -s,** *n.* meadow-pipit. **grasrijk,** *a.* grassy. **graspriet,** *n.* blade of grass. **grasveld,** *n.n.* greensward. **graszode, -n,** *n.* sod.
gratie, no pl., *n.* grace; free pardon. *in de ~ komen or zijn,* to come into *or* to be in favour; *uit de ~ geraken,* to fall from grace; *uit de ~ zijn,* to be out of favour.
grauw, *a.* grey. ¶no pl., *n.n.* grey; rabble. **grauwachtig,** *a.* greyish.
grauwen, *v.i.* to snarl. *~ en snauwen,* to snap and snarl.
grauwgors, *n.* corn-bunting. **grauwtje, -s,** *n.n.* (*coll.*) donkey. **grauwvuur,** no pl., *n.n.* fire-damp.

grave, *n.n. ten ~ dalen,* to sink into the grave; *ten ~ dragen,* to bear to the grave. *See* **graf.**
graveel, no pl., *n.n.* gravel, calculus.
graveerder, -s, *n.* engraver. **graveernaald,** *n.* **graveerstift,** *n.* burin. **graven, graaf,** *v.t., str.* to dig, burrow; to sink (*well*). ¶*v.i., str.* to dig. **graver, -s,** *n.* digger. **graveren, -veer,** *v.t. & v.i.* to engrave. **graveur, -s,** *n.* engraver. **gravure, -s,** *n.* engraving.
gravin, -nnen, *n.* countess.
grazen, graas, *v.i.* to graze. *het vee laten ~,* to graze the cattle; *iemand te ~ nemen,* to pull a person's leg. **grazig,** *a.* grassy, lush.
greep, grepen, *n.* grip, grasp; pinch, handful; grip, handle, pull, hilt, haft, fork. *een stoute ~,* a bold stroke; *een ~ doen in,* to dip into.
grein, *n.* grain (*seed*); grain (*weight*). **greineren, -neer,** *v.t.* to granulate. **greintje, -s,** *n.n.* particle. *geen ~,* not a grain, not an atom.
greling, *n.* hawser.
grendel, -s, *n.* bolt. *de ~ op de deur doen,* to bolt the door; *achter slot en ~,* behind lock and key. **grendelen,** *v.t.* to bolt (*door*).
greneboom, -bomen, *n.* fir-tree. **grenen,** *a.* deal. **grenenhout,** no pl., *n.n.* deal, pinewood.
grens, -zen, *n.* frontier, border; limit. *er zijn grenzen,* there are limits; *een vaste ~,* a hard and fast line; *geen grenzen kennen,* to know no bounds; *de ~ trekken,* to draw the line; *aan de ~,* on the frontier; *binnen de grenzen der mogelijkheid,* within the bounds of possibility; *alle grenzen te buiten gaan,* to exceed all bounds; *op de ~,* on the border-line; *op de ~ van,* on the verge of; *over de ~ zetten,* to put across the frontier. **grensgebied,** *n.n.* borderland. **grensgeval, -llen,** *n.n.* border-line case. **grenslijn,** *n.* line of demarcation. **grensrechter, -s,** *n.* linesman (*football*). **grenswaarde, -n,** *n.* limit. **grenswacht,** *n.* frontier guard. **grenzen, grens,** *v.i. ~ aan,* to border on, be bounded by. **grenzenloos, -loze,** *a.* boundless, unlimited. **grenzenloosheid,** no pl., *n.* boundlessness.
greppel, -s, *n.* ditch; furrow.
gretig, *a.* eager, desirous. **gretigheid,** no pl., *n.* avidity, eagerness.
Grevelingen, *n.N.* Gravelines.
grief, -ven, *n.* grievance. *een ~ hebben tegen,* to nurse a grievance against.
Griek, *n.* Greek. **Griekenland,** *n.N.* Greece. **Grieks,** *a.* Greek. *een ~e,* a Greek woman.
griel, *n.* stone-curlew.
griend, *n.,* **griendland,** *n.n.* holm; osier bed. **griendhout,** *n.n.* osiers.
grienen, *v.i.* to cry, blubber.
griep, *n.* 'flu.
griesmeel, no pl., *n.n.* semolina.
griet, *n.* brill; godwit.

·**grieven, grief,** *v.t.* to offend, hurt. ·**grievend,** *a.* grievous; offensive.
·**griezelen,** *v.i.* to shudder. ·**griezelig,** *a.* gruesome, creepy.
grif, -ffe, *a.* quick, ready. ·**griffel, -s,** *n.* slate pencil. ·**griffeldoos, -dozen,** *n.,* ·**griffelkoker, -s,** *n.* pencil-case. ·**griffelen,** *v.t.* to write (*with slate pencil*). ·**griffen, grif,** *v.t.* in het geheugen ~, to engrave on one's memory. ·**griffie, -s,** *n.* record office. ter ~ deponeren, to file at record office. **grif·fier, -s,** *n.* clerk (of the court). **grift,** *n. See* griffel. ·**grifweg,** *adv.* readily.
grijns, -zen, *n.* grin. ·**grijnslach,** *n.* sneer, sardonic smile. ·**grijnslachen,** *v.i.* to sneer. ·**grijnzen,** *v.i.* to grin, sneer.
grijp, *n.* griffin.
·**grijpen,** *v.t., str. & v.i., str.* to seize, grasp, grip. in elkaar ~, to gear into each other (*wheels*); ~ naar, to clutch at; naar de wapens or de pen ~, to take up arms or the pen; snel om zich heen ~, to spread rapidly (*fire, disease*); voor het ~, plentiful. ·**grijpstaart,** *n.* prehensile tail. ·**grijpvogel, -s,** *n.* griffin.
grijs, -ze, *a.* grey. het ~ verleden, the dim past. ·**grijsaard, -s,** *n.* greybeard. ·**grijsachtig,** *a.* greyish. ·**grijzen, grijs,** *v.i.* to grow grey. ·**grijzig,** *a.* greyish.
gril, -llen, *n.* whim; freak; vagary. ·**grillig,** *a.* capricious, whimsical; fitful. ·**grilligheid, -heden,** *n.* whimsicality.
gri·mas, -ssen, *n.* grimace.
·**grime, -s,** *n.* make-up. **gri·meren, -meer,** *v.t.* to make up. ¶ zich ~, *v.r.* to make up (*oneself*).
·**grimlach,** no pl., *n.* grin, sneer. ·**grimlachen,** *v.i.* to grin, sneer. ·**grimmig,** *a.* grim. ·**grimmigheid,** no pl., *n.* grimness.
·**grinniken,** *v.i.* to grin, snigger.
grint, no pl., *n.n.* gravel. ·**grintweg,** *n.* gravelled road.
·**grissen, gris,** *v.t.* to snatch.
groef, -ven, *n.* groove; furrow.
groei, no pl., *n.* (*act of*) growth. in de ~ zijn, to be growing; op de ~ maken, to make (*clothes*) allowing for growth. ·**groeien,** *v.i.* to grow (*become bigger*). iemand boven or over het hoofd ~, to outgrow a person; in iets ~, to revel in something. ·**groeikoorts,** *n.* growing pains. ·**groeikracht,** no pl., *n.* vigour, vitality. ·**groeizaam, -zame,** *a.* favourable (*to crops*).
groen, *a.* green. ~e zeep, soft soap; het werd me ~ en geel voor de ogen, my head was swimming. ¶no pl., *n.n.* green; verdure; freshman, fresher; greenhorn. ·**groenachtig,** *a.* greenish. ·**groenen,** *v.i.* to grow green. ·**groengrond,** *n.* fertile deposits along rivers and brooks. ·**groenharing,** *n.* fresh herring. ·**groenheid,** no pl., *n.* greenness. ·**Groenland,** *n.N.* Greenland.

·**groenmarkt,** *n.* vegetable market. ·**groente, -n,** *n.* vegetable(s), greens. ·**groenteboer,** *n.* greengrocer. ·**groentemarkt,** *n.* vegetable market. ·**groentetuin,** *n.* kitchen garden. ·**groentewinkel, -s,** *n.* greengrocer's (shop). ·**groentijd,** *n.* first days at college (*ragging time*). ·**groenvink,** *n.* greenfinch.
groep, *n.* group. **groe·peren, -peer,** *v.t.* to group. **groe·pering,** *n.* grouping. ·**groepsgewijs,** *adv.* in groups.
groet, *n.* greeting, salute. de ~en aan . . ., remember me to . . . or my compliments to . . .; met vriendelijke ~en, with kind regards. ·**groeten,** *v.t.* to greet, salute, say goodbye to. hij laat U ~, he wishes to be remembered to you; gegroet!, goodbye. ·**groetenis, -ssen,** *n.* salutation.
·**groeve, -n,** *n.* pit, quarry. ·**groeven, groef,** *v.t.* to groove.
·**groezelig,** *a.* grubby. ·**groezeligheid,** no pl., *n.* dinginess.
grof, grove, *a.* coarse, rough; rude, crude; crass, rank. ~ geschut, heavy guns. ¶ *adv.* coarsely. ~ spelen, to play high; het te ~ maken, to go too far. **grof·dradig,** *a.* coarse-threaded. ·**grofgebouwd,** *a.* large-limbed, big-boned. ·**grofgrein,** no pl., *n.n.* grogram. ·**grofheid, -heden,** *n.* coarseness, coarse act. ·**grofsmid, -smeden,** *n.* blacksmith. ·**grofte,** no pl., *n.* coarseness, thickness. ·**grofwild,** no pl., *n.n.* big game.
grol, -llen, *n.* antic. ·**grollen, grol,** *v.i.* to growl, grumble.
·**grommen, grom,** *v.i.* to growl. ·**grommig,** *a.* grumpy. ·**grompot, -tten,** *n.* grumbler.
grond, *n.* ground, earth; soil, ground, earth; bottom; ground(s), basis, reason. de begane ~, ground level; aan de ~ raken or zitten, to run or be aground; boven de ~, above ground; in de ~, at bottom; in de ~ boren, to sink or to torpedo; met ~, with good reason, on good grounds; met de ~ gelijkmaken, to level to the ground; onder de ~, underground; op de ~ vallen, to fall to the ground; op goede ~en rusten, to be based on good grounds; te ~e gaan, to go to rack and ruin; van de ~ van mijn hart, from the bottom of my heart; van alle ~ ontbloot, devoid of all foundation; van de koude ~, outdoor (*crop*). ·**grondachtig,** *a.* earthy (*taste*). ·**grondbeginsel,** *n.n.* basic principle. ~en, rudiments. ·**grondbegrip, -ppen,** *n.n.* basic concept. ·**grondbelasting,** *n.* land tax. ·**grondbezit,** no pl., *n.n.* landownership. ·**grondbezitter, -s,** *n.,* ·**grondeigenaar, -s,** *n.* landowner. ·**grondeigendom,** no pl., *n.n.* landownership. ¶ -mmen, *n.n.* landed property. ·**grondeigenschap, -ppen,** *n.* axiom. ·**grondel, -s,** *n.* gudgeon. ·**grondeloos, -loze,** *a.* groundless, bottomless; unfathomable. ·**gronde·loosheid, -heden,** *n.* abysmal depth. ·**gronden,** *v.t.* to found.

base. ·**gronderig**, *a.* earthy (*with earth*). ·**grondgebied**, *n.n.* territory, soil. ·**grondgedachte**, -**n**, *n.* underlying idea. ·**grondgesteldheid**, no pl., *n.* nature of the soil. ·**grondig**, *a.* earthy; thorough, searching, exhaustive. ·**grondigheid**, no pl., *n.* thoroughness. ·**grondijs**, no pl., *n.n.* ground ice. ·**grondkleur**, *n.* ground colour; primary colour. ·**grondlaag**, -**lagen**, *n.* bottom layer. ·**grondlasten**, pl. only, *n.* land tax. ·**grondlegger**, -**s**, *n.* founder. ·**grondloon**, -**lonen**, *n.n.* basic wages. ·**grondlucht**, no pl., *n.* earthy smell. ·**grondoorzaak**, -**zaken**, *n.* prime cause. ·**grondpacht**, *n.* ground-lease. ·**grondrente**, no pl., *n.* ground rent. ·**grondslag**, *n.* foundation(s); basis. *de ~ leggen tot* or *van* or *voor*, to lay the foundation(s) of; *op hechte ~ plaatsen*, to place on a firm footing; *ten ~ liggen aan*, to underlie. ·**grondsoort**, *n.* (type of) soil. ·**grondstelling**, *n.* axiom. ·**grondtoon**, -**tonen**, *n.* key note. ·**grondtrek**, -**kken**, *n.* characteristic feature. ·**grondverf**, -**verven**, *n.* first coat (*paint*). ·**grondverzakking**, *n.* subsidence. ·**grondvesten**, pl. only, *n.* foundations. *op zijn ~ schudden*, to shake to its foundations. ¶ *v.t.* to found. ·**grondvester**, -**s**, *n.* founder. ·**grondvorm**, *n.* primitive form. ·**grondwaarheid**, -**heden**, *n.* fundamental truth. ·**grondwater**, no pl., *n.n.* water in subsoil. ·**grondwerk**, *n.n.* groundwork. ·**grondwerker**, -**s**, *n.* navvy. ·**grondwet**, -**tten**, *n.* constitution (*law*). ·**grondwetsherziening**, *n.* revision of the Constitution. **grond·wettelijk**, *a.* constitutional (*belonging to Constitution*). **grond·wettig**, *a.* constitutional (*in accordance with the Constitution*). **grond·wettigheid**, no pl., *n.* constitutionality. ·**grondzee**, -**zeeën**, *n.* ground swell.

groot, **grote**, *a.* large, big; great; tall; grown-up. *10 H.A. ~*, 10 hectares in size; *~ worden*, to grow up; *~ met elkaar*, thick as thieves; *zo dom als hij ~ is*, as stupid as they make them; *een ~ man*, a great man; *een grote man*, a big man; *de grote mars*, the maintop; *de grote mast*, the mainmast; *grote mensen*, grown-ups; *de Grote Oceaan*, the Pacific Ocean; *grote ogen opzetten*, to be surprised; *het grote publiek*, the general public; *de grote ra*, the mainyard; *een ~ uur*, a good hour; *op grote voet leven*, to live at a high rate; *het ~ want*, the main rigging; *de grote weg*, the high road; *de grote wereld*, Society. ¶ *adv.* greatly. *het niet ~ hebben op . . .*, not to be keen on . . .; *~ gelijk hebben*, to be perfectly right; *~ leven*, to live in style. ¶ no pl., *n.n. in het ~*, on a grand scale *or* wholesale; *iets ~s*, something great. ¶ **groten**, *n.* groat (*coin*). ·**grootbedrijf**, no pl., *n.n.* big industry. ·**grootboek**, *n.n.* ledger. ·**grootbrengen**, *v.t.s.*, irr.,

to bring up, rear, raise. ·**grootdoen**, **doe groot**, *v.i.s.*, irr. to swagger, swank. ·**grootdoener**, -**s**, *n.* swanker. ·**grootdoenerij**, no pl., *n.* swank. **groot·grondbezit**, no pl., *n.n.* large landownership. **groot·grondbezitter**, -**s**, *n.* big landowner. ·**groothandel**, no pl., *n.* wholesale trade. ·**groothandelaar**, -**s**, *n.* wholesale dealer, wholesaler. **groot·hartig**, *a.* magnanimous. **groot·hartigheid** no pl., *n.* magnanimity. ·**grootheid**, -**heden**, *n.* greatness; magnitude; quantity, magnitude. **groot·heidswaanzin**, no pl., *n.* megalomania. *lijder aan ~*, megalomaniac. ·**groothertog**, *n.* grand duke. ·**groothertogdom**, -**mmen**, *n.n.* grand duchy. ·**groothertogelijk**, *a.* grand ducal. ·**groothertogin**, -**nnen**, *n.* grand duchess. ·**groothouden**, **zich**, *v.r.s.*, irr. to be brave, not show sorrow. ·**grootindustrie**, no pl., *n.* big industry. ·**grootindustrieel**, -**iëlen**, *n.* captain of industry. ·**grootje**, -**s**, *n.n.*, granny, very old woman. ·**grootkapitaal**, no pl., *n.n.* big business. ·**Grootkruis**, *n.n.* Grand Cross. ·**grootmarszeil**, *n.n.* maintopsail. ·**grootmeester**, -**s**, *n.* grand master. ·**grootmoeder**, -**s**, *n.* grandmother. **groot·moedig**, *a.* magnanimous. **groot·mogend**, *a.* puissant. **Groot-Nederland**, *N.* Greater Holland. **Groot-Nederlands**, *a.* Pan-Dutch. ·**grootouders**, pl. only, *n.* grandparents. ·**groots**, *a.* grand, grandiose, noble. *~ op*, proud of. ·**grootscheeps**, *a.* grand, ambitious. ¶ *adv.* in grand style. ·**grootspant**, *n.n.* beam (*of ship*). ·**grootspraak**, no pl., *n.* boast(ing). **groot·sprakig**, *a.* grandiloquent, bombastic. ·**grootspreken**, **spreek groot**, *v.i.s.*, str. to boast. ·**grootspreker**, -**s**, *n.* braggart. ·**grootsprekerij**, *n.* boast(s), bragging. ·**grootsteeds**, *a.* of a city. ¶ *adv.* as in a city. ·**grootte**, -**n** *or* -**s**, *n.* size, magnitude. *in deze ~*, of this size; *op ware ~*, life-size, full-sized; *ter ~ van . . .*, the size of . . . ·**grootvader**, -**s**, *n.* grandfather. ·**grootvorst**, *n. See* **groothertog**. **groot·waardigheidsbekleder**, -**s**, *n.* high dignitary. ·**grootzeil**, *n.n.* mainsail.

gros, -**ssen**, *n.n.* gross (*twelve dozen*). ¶ no pl., *n.n.* gross, mass, main body. **gros·sier**, *n.* wholesale dealer. ·**grossierderij**, *n.* wholesale business.

grot, -**tten**, *n.* cave, grotto.

·**grote**, -**n**, *n.* grandee; big one; grown-up. *de ~n der aarde*, the great of this earth. ·**grotelijks**, *adv.* greatly, to a great extent. **grote·lui**, pl. only, *n.* the great folk. **grote·luiskind**, -**eren**, *n.n.* rich man's child; pl. children of the rich. **groten·deels**, *adv.* largely, for the greater part.

gro·tesk, *a.* grotesque.

·**grovelijk**, *adv.* grossly, badly.

gruis, no pl., *n.n.* grit; (coal-)dust. *aan* or *in ~ vallen*, to disintegrate. **gruizele·menten**, pl. only, *n.n.* *aan* ~, in smithereens. ·**gruizelen,** *v.t.* to pulverize.

grut, no pl., *n.n.* *het kleine* ~, the small fry. ¶ **-tten,** *n.n.* groats. ·**grutmolen, -s,** *n.* hulling-mill, pearling-mill. ·**gruttenbrij,** no pl., *n.* gruel. ·**gruttenmeel,** no pl., *n.n.* buckwheat meal. ·**grutter, -s,** *n.* corn-chandler. **grutte·rij,** *n.* corn-chandler's (shop).

·**grutto, -'s,** *n.* godwit.

·**gruwel,** *n.n.* atrocity, horror. ·**gruweldaad, -daden,** *n.* atrocity. ·**gruwelijk,** *a.* horrible, atrocious, abominable. ·**gruwelkamer, -s,** *n.* chamber of horrors. ·**gruwelstuk, -kken,** *n.n.* atrocity. ·**gruwen,** *v.i.* to shudder. ·**gruwzaam, -zame,** *a.* horrible, gruesome. ¶ *adv.* horribly.

guit, *n.* (little) rogue, scamp. ·**guitenstreek, -streken,** *n.* trick (*playful*). ·**guitig,** *a.* roguish. ¶ *adv.* roguishly, archly.

gul, *-lle,* *a.* generous, liberal; open, frank. ·**gulden, -s,** *n.* guilder, florin. ¶ *a.* golden. *de* ~ *middelmaat,* the golden mean. ·**guldenroede,** no pl., *n.* golden-rod.

gul·hartig, *a.* open, frank. ·**gulheid,** no pl., *n.* open-handedness, generosity.

gulp, *n.* fly (*of trousers*). ·**gulpen,** *v.t.* to pour forth.

·**gulweg,** *adv.* openly.

·**gulzig,** *a.* greedy. ¶ *adv.* greedily. ·**gulzigaard,** *n.* glutton. ·**gulzigheid,** no pl., *n.* greed, gluttony.

·**gummi,** no pl., *n.* or *n.n.* (india-)rubber. ·**gummiband,** *n.* (rubber) tyre. ·**gummilaarzen,** pl. only, *n.* gum-boots. ·**gummioverschoenen,** pl. only, *n.* goloshes. ·**gummislang,** *n.* rubber tube. ·**gummistok, -kken,** *n.* (rubber) truncheon.

·**gunnen, gun,** *v.t.* to grant, allow; not to begrudge. *het is je gegund,* you're welcome to it; *niet* ~, to begrudge; *het* ~ *aan,* to grant (*an order*) to. ¶ *v.r. zich de tijd* ~, to allow oneself the time. ·**gunning,** *n.* allocation, award. **gunst,** *n.* favour. ~ *nog toe!,* goodness gracious!; *een* ~ *bewijzen,* to do a favour; *in de* ~ *komen bij* . . ., to find favour with . . .; *in de* ~ *staan bij iemand,* to be in someone's good books; *uit de* ~ *zijn,* to be in disfavour; *ten* ~*e van,* in favour of. ·**gunstbejag,** no pl., *n.n.* favour-seeking. ·**gunstbetoon,** no pl., *n.n.* favouritism. ·**gunstbewijs, -zen,** *n.n.* mark of favour. ·**gunsteling,** *n.* favourite. ·**gunstig,** *a.* favourable. *het geluk was hem* ~, luck favoured him; *bij* ~ *weer,* weather permitting; *een* ~ *oog werpen op,* to consider something favourably. ¶ *adv.* favourably. ~ *bekend staan,* to have a good reputation; ~ *stemmen,* to propitiate; *zich* ~ *voordoen,* to present a favourable appearance.

guts, *n.* gouge. ·**gutsen,** *v.t.* to gouge. ¶ *v.i.* (*lit.*) to gush, spout. *het zweet gutste hem langs het gezicht,* sweat poured down his face.

guur, gure, *a.* cold and stormy, bleak, inclement. ¶ *adv.* cold and bitter. *het waait* ~, there is a cold and bitter wind blowing. ·**guurheid,** no pl., *n.* bleakness, bitterness (*of winter weather*).

gymnasi·aal, -iale, *a.* belonging to a grammar school. **gymnasi·ast,** *n.* pupil of grammar school. **gym·nasium, -ia,** *n.n.* grammar school. **gymnas·tiek,** no pl., *n.* gymnastics. **gymnas·tiekleraar, -s,** *n.* physical training instructor. **gymnas·tiekschoenen,** pl. only, *n.* gym shoes. **gymnas·tiekzaal, -zalen,** *n.* drill hall. **gym·nastisch,** *a.* gymnastic.

H

haag, hagen, *n.* hedge, hedgerow. *achter de* ~ *lopen,* to play truant. **Haag,** *N. den* ~, The Hague. ·**haagappel, -s,** *n.* hawberry. ·**haagbeuk,** *n.* hornbeam. ·**haagdoorn, -s,** *n.* hawthorn. ·**haageik,** *n.* holm-oak. **Haags,** *a.* from *or* of The Hague. ·**haagwinde, -n,** *n.* bindweed.

haai, *n.* shark. *naar de* ~*en gaan,* to go to the bottom (*ship*); *voor de* ~*en zijn,* to be lost, gone to the dogs; *er zijn* ~*en op de kust,* there is danger of interference. ·**haairog, -ggen,** *n.* shark-ray.

haak, haken, *n.* hook. *haken en ogen,* hooks and eyes; *iets aan de* ~ *slaan,* to hook something; *dat is niet in de* ~, that is not as it should be. ·**haakbus, -ssen,** *n.* harquebus. ·**haakgaren,** no pl., *n.n.* crochet cotton. ·**haakje, -s,** *n.n.* parenthesis, bracket. *tussen* (*twee*) ~*s,* between brackets *or* by the way. ·**haakkruis,** *n.n.* swastika. ·**haaknaald,** *n.,* ·**haakpen, -nnen,** *n.* crochet hook. **haaks,** *a.* square. *niet* ~, out of square. ·**haakster, -s,** *n.* crochet worker. ·**haakwerk,** no pl., *n.n.* crochet work.

haal, halen, *n.* stroke (*of pen*); pull (*at pipe, cigar*). *aan de* ~ *gaan,* to take to one's heels. ·**haalmes, -ssen,** *n.n.* spoke-shave.

haam, hamen, *n.* drag-net. ¶ *n.n.* hames.

haan, hanen, *n.* cock (*bird*); cock, hammer (*of gun*). *zijn* ~ *kraait koning,* he is cock of the walk; *er zal geen* ~ *naar kraaien,* no one will be any the wiser; *de gebraden* ~ *uithangen,* to celebrate (*feast*); *de rode* ~ *laten kraaien,* to set fire to a house; *de* ~ *van een geweer overhalen,* to cock a gun. ·**haantje, -s,** *n.n.* young cock, cockerel. *het* ~ *van de toren,* the weather-cock; ~ *de voorste,* ringleader.

haar, *pers. pron.* her. ¶ *poss. a.* her. ¶ **haren,** *n.n.* hair. *het is geen* ~ *beter,* it has not improved it; *ik ben geen* ~ *wijzer,* I don't know any more now; *de haren rijzen hem te berge,* his hair stood on end; *geen* ~ *van mijn hoofd dat er aan denkt,* I would not dream of it; *ze heeft* ~ *op 'r tanden,* she knows how to hold her own; *iemand geen ~ krenken*, not to touch a hair of a person's head; *hij zal er geen grijs ~ van krijgen*, he won't lose any sleep over it; *iets met de haren erbij slepen*, to drag something into the conversation; *het scheelde geen ~*, it was touch and go; *elkaar in het ~ vliegen* or *zitten*, to be at each other's throats; *zijn wilde haren verliezen*, to sow one's wild oats; *alles op haren en snaren zetten*, to leave no stone unturned; *met de handen in het ~ zitten*, to be at one's wit's end. ¶ *int.* left! (*to horse*). *See* **hot.** ·**haarborstel, -s,** *n.* hair-brush. ·**haarbos, -sen,** *n.* shock *or* mop of hair. ·**haarbreed,** no pl., *n.* hair's breadth. ·**haarbuis, -zen,** *n.* capillary vessel.

baard, *n.* hearth, fireplace, fireside; hearth, centre, focus. *eigen ~ is goud waard*, there's no place like home.
·**haardos,** no pl., *n.* head of hair. ·**haardot, -tten,** *n.* bun, knot of hair.
·**haardscherm,** *n.n.* fire-screen. ·**haardstede, -n,** *n.* hearth; homestead. ·**haardstel, -llen,** *n.n.* (set of) fire-irons.
·**haarfijn,** *a.* minute, delicate. ¶ *adv.* in detail, minutely. ·**haargroei,** no pl., *n.* growth of hair. ·**haarkloven, -kloof,** *v.i.* to split hairs. ·**haarklover, -s,** *n.* hair-splitter. ·**haarklove·rij,** no pl., *n.* hair-splitting. ·**haarknippen,** no pl., *n.n.* hair-cut.

Haarlemmer·olie, no pl., *n.* castor oil.
·**haarlint,** *n.n.* hair-ribbon. ·**haarloos, -loze,** *a.* hairless. ·**haarpijn,** no pl., *n.* the morning-after feeling. ·**haarrook,** no pl., *n.* peat smoke. ·**haarvat,** *n.n.* capillary vessel. ·**haarwater, -s,** *n.n.* hair lotion. ·**haarworm,** *n.* threadworm. ·**haarzakje, -s,** *n.n.* hair sac, hair follicle.

haas, hazen, *n.* hare. **haasje-·over,** no pl., *n.n.* leap-frog.

haast, no pl., *n.* haste. *~ hebben*, to be in a hurry; *er is ~ bij*, it is urgent; *in ~* or *in der ~*, in a hurry, in haste; *in vliegende ~*, in a tearing hurry. ¶ *adv.* almost, nearly. ·**haasten,** *v.t.* to hasten, hurry. *zijn gehaast*, to be in a hurry. ¶ *zich ~*, *v.r.* to hurry, make haste. *haast U langzaam*, hasten slowly; *haast je rep je!*, helter-skelter. ·**haastig,** *a.* hasty, hurried. *~e spoed is zelden goed*, more haste less speed. ¶ *adv.* hastily, in a hurry. ·**haastigheid,** no pl., *n.* hastiness.

haat, no pl., *n.* hatred, hate. *iemand ~ toedragen*, to harbour feelings of hatred towards a person. **haat·dragend,** *a.* vindictive, resentful. **haat·dragendheid,** no pl., *n.* resentment, rancour.

ha·bijt, *n.* frock (*of monk*).
ha·chée, no pl., *n.n.* hash (*meat*).
·**hachelijk,** *a.* perilous, critical. ·**hachelijkheid, -heden,** *n.* perilousness. ·**hachje,** no

pl., *n.n.* life, skin. *bang zijn voor zijn ~*, to be anxious to save one's skin; *er zijn ~ bij inschieten*, to lose one's life; *zijn ~ redden*, to save (his) bacon; *zijn ~ wagen*, to risk one's life.
haft, *n.n.* day-fly, ephemera.
·**hagebeuk,** *n.* hornbeam. **hage·dis, -ssen,** *n.* lizard. ·**hagedoorn, -s,** *n.* hawthorn.
·**hagel,** no pl., *n.* hail; (*small*) shot. ·**hagelbui,** *n.* hail-storm. ·**hagelen,** *v.imp.* to hail. *het hagelde bakstenen*, it hailed brickbats, there was a hail of brickbats. ·**hagelkorrel, -s,** *n.* hail-stone; grain of shot, pellet. ·**hagelnieuw,** *a.* brand-new. ·**hagelschade,** no pl., *n.* damage (*caused by hail*). ·**hagel-slag,** no pl., *n.* hail-storm; damage (*caused by hail-storm*); minute sweets (*scattered on bread and butter*). ·**hageltas, -ssen,** *n.* shot-bag. ·**hagelwit, -tte,** *a.* white as snow.
·**Hagenaar, -s,** *n.* person from *or* of The Hague.
·**hageprediker, -s,** *n.* hedge-priest. ·**hagepreek, -preken,** *n.* hedge-sermon. ·**hageroos, -rozen,** *n.* briar-rose.
·**hak, -kken,** *n.* cut, blow; hoe, mattock; heel. *iemand een ~ zetten*, to put a spoke in someone's wheel; *de ~ op iemand hebben*, to be gunning for someone; *van de ~ op de tak springen*, to jump from one subject to another. ·**hakbeitel, -s,** *n.* mortise chisel. ·**hakbijl,** *n.* chopper, hatchet. ·**hakblok, -kken,** *n.n.* chopping-block. ·**hakbord,** *n.n.* chopping-board.
·**haken, haak,** *v.t.* to hook; to crochet. *iets ~ aan*, to hook or hitch something on to. ¶ *v.i. blijven ~*, to catch in; *~ naar*, to long *or* hanker for. ·**hakig,** *a.* hooked.
·**hakhout,** no pl., *n.n.* copse, coppice. ·**hakkebord,** *n.n.* dulcimer. ·**hakkelaar, -s,** *n.* stammerer. ·**hakkelen,** *v.i.* to stammer, stutter. ·**hakkelig,** *a.* faltering, stammered. ·**hakken, hak,** *v.t.* to hack, chop; to hoe. *in de pan ~*, to cut to pieces, destroy (*enemy*); *op iemand ~*, to have one's knife in someone; *erop in ~*, to lay about one.
hakke·nei, *n.* ambler.
·**hakmes, -ssen,** *n.n.* chopping knife, cleaver. ·**hakpees, -pezen,** *n.* hough tendon. *de ~ doorsnijden*, to hamstring, hough. ·**haksel,** no pl., *n.n.* chopped straw, chaff. ·**hakstro,** no pl., *n.n.* straw for fodder.
hal, -llen, *n.* (market-)hall.
ha·lali, *int.* tally ho.
·**halen, haal,** *v.t.* to pull, draw; to fetch; to meet; to catch, make; to fetch (*price*). *laten ~*, to send for; *adem ~*, to breathe; *er is niets te ~*, there is nothing to be got out of it; *het haalt daar niet bij*, it does not come up to it; *door elkaar ~*, to mix up, confuse; *waar haal je 't vandaan?* what on earth makes you think that?
half, -ve, *a.* half; semi-; demi-. *~ April*, mid-April. ¶ *adv.* half, partly. *er ~ aan denken om . . .*, to have half a mind to . . .

¶ **-ven,** *n.n.* half. *het slaat* ~, it strikes the half hour; ~ *om* ~, half-and-half (*drink*). **half·acht,** *num.* half-past seven. **·half·bakken,** *a.* half-baked. **·halfbloed,** *n.* half-caste. **·halfdek, -kken,** *n.n.* quarter-deck. **·halfdonker,** no pl., *n.n.* semi-darkness. **half·drie,** *num.* half-past two. **·half·een,** *num.* half-past twelve. **half·elf,** *num.* half-past ten. **half·gaar, -gare,** *a.* half-baked. **·halfgod,** *n.* demigod. **·half·heid,** no pl., *n.* irresolution. **half·jaarlijks,** *a. & adv.* half-yearly. **·halfje, -s,** *n.n.* half cent (*coin*). **·halfluid,** *a.* soft, subdued. ¶ *adv.* half aloud. **half·maandelijks,** *a. & adv.* fortnightly. **half·negen,** *num.* half-past eight. **·halfrond,** *n.n.* hemisphere. **·halfschaduw,** *n.* penumbra. **·halfslachtig,** *a.* amphibious; half-hearted. **half·slachtigheid,** no pl., *n.* half-heartedness. **half·stok,** *adv.* at half-mast. **half·tien,** *num.* half-past nine. **·halfttj,** no pl., *n.n.* half tide. **half·twaalf,** *num.* half-past eleven. **half·twee,** *num,* half-past one. **half·uur, halve uren,** *n.n.* half-hour. **·half·vasten,** no pl., *n.* mid-Lent. **half·vier,** *num.* half-past three. **half·vijf,** *num.* half-past four. **·halfwas, -ssen,** *n.* (half-grown) apprentice. **·halfwassen,** *a.* half-grown. **·halfweg,** *adv.* half-way. **·halfwijs, -ze,** *a.* half-witted. **half·zes,** *num.* half-past five. **half·zeven,** *num.* half-past six.

halm, *n.* stalk, straw, blade.

hals, -zen, *n.* neck; simpleton. ~ *over kop,* precipitately, helter-skelter; *om de* ~ *brengen,* to kill a person; *zich iets op de* ~ *halen,* to bring something on oneself; *iemand iets op de* ~ *jagen,* to land someone in for something; *zich iets van de* ~ *schuiven,* to get rid of a responsibility. **·halsband,** *n.* (dog-)collar. **·halsbrekend,** *a.* breakneck. **·halsdoek,** *n.* neckcloth, neckerchief. **·halskraag, -kragen,** *n.* ruff. **·halssieraad, -raden,** *n.n.* necklace. **·hals·slagader, -s,** *n.n.* carotid (*artery*). **·halssnoer** *n.n.* necklace. **hals·starrig,** *a.* stubborn, obstinate. **hals·starrigheid,** no pl., *n.* stubbornness, obstinacy. **·halswervel, -s,** *n.* cervical vertebra.

·halster, -s, *n.* halter (*of horse*). **·halsteren,** *v.t.* to halter (*horse*).

halt, *int.* halt! ¶no pl., *n.* halt. ~ *houden* or *maken,* to halt; ~ *laten maken,* to call a halt. **·halte, -s** or **-n,** *n.* stopping place (*along route*).

·halter, -s, *n.* dumb-bell.

·halve, no pl., *n.* ter or ten ~, by halves. *See* **half. halve·maan,** no pl., *n.* half moon. **hal·veren, -veer,** *v.t.* to halve. **·halver·hoogte,** *adv.* ter ~, half-way up. **·halver·wege,** *adv.* half-way.

·halzen, hals, *v.i.* to veer.

·halzerig, *a.* miserable.

·hamel, -s, *n.* wether.

·hamer, -s, *n.* hammer; mallet. *onder de* ~

brengen, to put up for auction; *onder de* ~ *komen,* to be sold by auction; *de* ~ *passeren,* to be auctioned. **·hameren,** *v.t. & v.i.* to hammer. *op iets* ~, to keep on coming back to something. **·hamerhaai,** *n.* hammer-head. **·hamerslag,** *n.* hammer blow.

·hammebeen, -benen, *n.n.* hambone.

·hamster, -s, *n.* hamster. **·hamsteraar, -s,** *n.* hoarder (*of food*). **·hamsteren,** *v.t. & v.i.* to hoard (*food*).

hand, *n.* hand. *iemand de* ~ *geven* or *drukken,* to shake hands with a person; *iemand de* ~ *boven 't hoofd houden,* to protect a person; *de* ~ *houden aan,* to enforce; *de* ~ *leggen op,* to lay hands on; *de* ~*en in de schoot leggen,* to become resigned; *hij wil geen* ~ *omdraaien* or *uitsteken,* he will not lift a finger; *de* ~*en aan het werk slaan,* to set to work; *de* ~*en uit de mouw steken,* to put one's shoulder to the wheel; *hij kon geen* ~ *voor ogen zien,* he could not see a thing; *de laatste* ~ *leggen aan,* to put the finishing touch to; *met de vlakke* ~, with the flat of one's hand; *twee* ~*en op één buik,* in cahoots; *aan de* ~ *van,* on the basis of; *aan de betere* ~, improving; *iemand iets aan de* ~ *doen,* to procure something for someone; *bij de* ~, quick, forward; *iets bij de* ~ *hebben,* to have something handy; *iemand iets in de* ~ *spelen,* to make something fall purposely into someone's hands; *in de* ~ *werken,* to assist; *met* ~ *en tand,* tooth and nail; *met de* ~ *over 't hart strijken,* to stretch a point; *met de* ~*en in 't haar zitten,* to be at one's wits' end; *onder* ~*en nemen,* to take in hand; *op* ~*en,* at hand; *op eigen* ~, off one's own bat; *op de* ~*en dragen,* to venerate; *op iemands* ~ *zijn,* to be on a person's side; *iets ter* ~ *nemen,* to take something in hand; *uit de* ~ *verkopen,* to sell privately; *iets van de* ~ *doen,* to dispose of something; *van de* ~ *in de tand leven,* to live from hand to mouth. **·handappel, -s,** *n.* eating apple. **·handboeien,** pl. only, *n.* handcuffs, manacles. **·handboor, -boren,** *n.* gimlet. **·handbreed,** no pl., *n.n.* hand's breadth. **·handbreedte, -n,** *n.* hand's breadth. **·handdoek,** *n.* towel. **·handdruk, -kken,** *n.* handshake. *een* ~ *wisselen,* to shake hands. **·handel, -s,** *n.* handle. ¶no pl., *n.* trade, commerce, traffic. ~ *drijven,* to do business; *in de* ~ *brengen,* to put on the market; *in de* ~ *zijn,* to be in business; *niet in de* ~, not supplied to the trade; *zijn* ~ *en wandel,* his mode of life. **·handelaar, -s** or **-laren,** *n.* merchant, dealer. **·handelbaar, -bare,** *a.* tractable. **·handel·drijvend,** *a.* trading. **·handelen,** *v.i.* to act; to trade. ~ *in,* to deal in; ~ *naar* or *volgens,* to act in accordance with; ~ *over,* to deal with, treat of. **·handeling,** *n.* action. ~*en,* proceedings (*of learned* *society* or *parliament*). ·handelmaatschappij, *n.* trading company. ·handelsartikel, -s *or* -en, *n.n.* commodity, article of commerce. ·handelsattaché, -'s, *n.* commercial attaché. ·handelsbalans, *n.* balance of trade. ·handelsbediende, -n, *n.* clerk. ·handelsbrief, -ven, *n.* business letter. ·handelscorrespondentie, no pl., *n.* commercial correspondence. ·handelsfirma, -'s, *n.*, ·handelshuis, -zen, *n.n.* (trading) firm. ·handelshaven, -s, *n.* shipping port. ·handelsmerk, *n.n.* trade mark. ·handelsonderneming, *n.* trading concern. ·handelsoorlog, *n.* trade war. ·handelsreiziger, -s, *n.* commercial traveller. ·handelsusance, -s, *n.* trade custom. ·handelsvennootschap, -ppen, *n.* trading company; ltd. ·handelsvloot, -vloten, *n.* merchant fleet. ·handelsvrijheid, no pl., *n.* freedom of trade. ·handelsweg, *n.* trade route. ·handelszaak, -zaken, *n.* firm, business. ·handelwijze, -n, *n.* proceeding, way of acting. ·handenarbeid, no pl., *n.* manual labour. ·handgalop, no pl., *n.* canter. ·handgebaar, -baren, *n.n.* gesture. ·handgeklap, no pl., *n.n.* clapping, applause. ·handgeld, no pl., *n.n.* earnest-money; first takings. ·handgemeen, *a.* ~ *worden*, to come to blows *or* grips. ¶no pl., *n.n.* hand-to-hand fighting. ·handgetouw, *n.n.* handloom. ·handgreep, -grepen, *n.* grip; knack. ·handhaven, -haaf, *v.t.* to maintain. ·handhaving, *n.* preservation, maintenance. ·handig, *a.* handy, clever; skilful. ¶*adv.* skilfully, cleverly; neatly. ·handigheid, -heden, *n.* handiness. ·handigheidje, -s, *n.n.* trick, knack. ·handje, -s, *n.n.* little hand. ¶no pl., *n.n.* knack, habit; hand. *een* ~ *helpen*, to lend *or* bear a hand; *ergens een* ~ *van hebben*, to have a (bad) habit of doing something. ·handkar, -rren, *n.* hand-cart. ·handkoffer, -s, *n.* attaché case. ·handlanger, -s, *n.* accomplice; henchman. ·handlangster, -s, *n.* accomplice (*female*). ·handleiding, *n.* manual. ·handomdraai, no pl., *n. in een* ~ in the twinkling of an eye. ·handoplegging, *n.* laying on of (hands). ·handpeer, -peren, *n.* eating pear. ·handpenning, *n.* earnest-money. ·handreiking, *n.* assistance. ·handschoen, *n.* glove. *de* ~ *opnemen*, to take up the gauntlet; *iemand de* ~ *toewerpen*, to throw down the gauntlet; *met de* ~ *trouwen*, to marry by proxy. ·handschrift, *n.n.* handwriting; manuscript. ·handslag, *n.* slap with the hand. *iets met* or *onder* ~ *beloven*, to give one's hand upon it. ·handspaak, -spaken, *n.* hand-spike. ·handspuit, *n.* hand syringe; stirrup pump. ·handtasje, -s, *n.n.* handbag. ·hand·tastelijk, *a.* palpable, obvious. ~ *worden*, to come to blows. ·hand·tastelijkheden, pl. only, *n.* physical violence. *tot* ~ *komen*, to come to blows. ·handtekening, *n.* signature. ·handvat,

-tten, *n.n.*, ·handvatsel, -s, *n.n.* handle. ·handvest, *n.n.* charter. ·handvol, handenvol, *n.* handful. ·handvormig, *a.* hand-shaped. ·handwagen, -s, *n.* hand-cart. ·handwerk, *n.n.* trade, (handi)craft; work by hand; needlework. *fraaie* ~*en*, fancy needlework; *nuttige* ~*en*, plain needlework. ·handwerken, *v.i.* to do needlework. ·handwerkje, -s, *n.n.* piece of needlework. ·handwerksman, -werkslieden *or* -werkslui, *n.* artisan. ·handwijzer, -s, *n.* signpost. ·handwoordenboek, *n.n.* pocket dictionary. ·handzaag, -zagen, *n.* hand-saw. ·hanebalk, *n.* purlin. *onder* or *in de* ~*en*, under the tiles. ·hanekam, -mmen, *n.* cockscomb. ·hanengekraai, no pl., *n.n.* cockcrow(ing). ·hanengevecht, *n.n.* cockfight(ing). ·hanepoot, -poten, *n.* pot-hook; scrawl. ·hanevoet, *n.* crowfoot. ·hangbrug, -ggen, *n.* suspension bridge. ·hangen, *v.t.*, *str.* to hang. ¶*v.i.*, *str.* to hang; to droop. *tussen* ~ *en wurgen*, uncertain, a narrow squeeze; ~ *aan*, to cling to; *blijven* ~ *aan*, to be caught on; *zijn hart aan iets* ~, to set one's heart on something; *als droog zand aan elkaar* ~, to be disconnected, to be disjointed. ·hangend, *a.* hanging; pending. *met* ~*e pootjes*, crestfallen. ·hanger, -s, *n.* hanger; pendant. ·hangerig, *a.* heavy, listless. ·hangijzer, -s, *n.n.* pot hanger. ·hangkast, *n.* wardrobe. ·hangklok, -kken, *n.* wall-clock. ·hanglip, -ppen, *n.* hanging lip; drooler. ·hangmat, -tten, *n.* hammock. ·hangoor, -goren, *n.* lop-ear. ·hangop, no pl., *n.* cheese made from sour milk. ·hangslot, *n.n.* padlock. han·sop, -ppen, *n.* sleeping suit (*child's, one-piece*). hans·worst, *n.* buffoon, Jack Pudding. han·teren, -teer, *v.t.* to handle, wield, operate. han·tering, *n.* handling, manipulation. ·Hanze, no pl., *n.* Hansa. Hanze·aten, pl. only, *n.* members of the Hansa. ·Hanzestad, -steden, *n.* Hanseatic town. hap, -ppen, *n.* bite, mouthful. ·haperen, *v.i.* to falter, fluff. *er hapert iets aan*, there is something wrong with it; *het hapert hem aan geduld*, he lacks patience; *zonder* ~, without a hitch. ·hapje, -s, *n.n.* bit, morsel. ·happ.., hap, *v.i.* to bite. ~ *naar*, to snap at. ·happig, *a.* keen. ·happigheid, no pl., *n.* keenness. hard, *a.* hard; loud, harsh. *een* ~ *ei*, a hard-boiled egg; ~*e woorden*, hard *or* harsh words; ~ *voor iemand*, hard on someone; ~ *worden*, to solidify, set. ¶*adv.* hard; harshly. ~ *nodig*, badly needed; *het gaat* ~ *tegen* ~, pull devil pull baker. ·hard·draven, *v.i.* to run (*in trotting match*). ·harddraver, -s, *n.* (fast) trotter. hard·drave·rij, *n.* trotting match. ·harden, *v.t.* to harden, temper. *ik kan het niet langer* ~, I cannot stand it any longer. hard·handig, *a.* hard-handed, rough. **hard·handigheid,** no pl., *n.* hard-handedness. ·**hardheid, -heden,** *n.* hardness. **hard·hoofdig,** *a.* obstinate, headstrong. **hard·horig,** *a.* hard of hearing. **hard·horigheid,** no pl., *n.* hardness of hearing. **hard·huidig,** *a.* thick-skinned. **hard·leers,** *a.* dull, slow (to learn). **hard·lijvig,** *a.* costive. **hard·lijvigheid,** no pl., *n.* costiveness, constipation. ·**hard·lopen,** no pl., *n.n.* running. ~ *met hindernissen,* obstacle race. ·**hardloper, -s,** *n.* runner, sprinter. **hard·nekkig,** *a.* obstinate, stubborn; persistent. **hard·nekkigheid,** no pl., *n.* obstinacy, persistence. **hard·op,** *adv.* aloud, loudly; out loud. ·**hardrijden,** no pl., *n.n.* racing; skating match. ·**hardrijder, -s,** *n.* racer (*usu. in skating match*). **hardrijde·rij,** *n.* race; skating match. ·**hardsteen,** no pl., *n.* freestone. ·**hardstenen,** *a.* (made of) free-stone. ·**hardvallen, val hard,** *v.t.s., str. iemand* ~ *over,* to be hard on a person about. **hard·vochtig,** *a.* hard-hearted, heartless. **hard·vochtigheid,** no pl., *n.* hard-heartedness.

·**haren,** *a.* (*made of*) hair.

·**harent,** *pron. te* ~, at her place. ·**harentwege,** *adv.* on her behalf; in her name; for her sake. ·**harentwil,** *adv. om* ~, for her sake. ·**harerzijds,** *adv.* on her part.

·**harig,** *a.* hairy; hirsute.

·**haring,** *n.* herring. *ik wil er* ~ *of kuit van hebben,* I want to get to the bottom of it; *als* ~*en in een ton,* like sardines in a tin. ·**haringbuis, -zen,** *n.* herring boat. ·**haring-haai,** *n.* porbeagle, mackerel shark. ·**haringkaken, kaak haring,** *v.i.s.* to cure (and gut) herring. ·**haringkaker, -s,** *n.* herring curer. ·**haringlogger, -s,** *n.* herring drifter. ·**haringsla,** no pl., *n.* salmagundi. ·**haringtijd,** no pl., *n.* herring season. ·**harington, -nnen,** *n.* herring tub. ·**haring-vangst,** *n.* herring catch; herring fishery.

hark, *n.* rake; stiff, clumsy person. *zo stijf als een* ~, as stiff as a rod. ·**harken,** *v.t.* to rake. ·**harkerig,** *a.* stiff, wooden.

harle·kijn, *n.* harlequin. **harleki·nade, -s,** *n.* harlequinade.

har·monica, -'s, *n.* concertina, accordion. **har·monicatrein,** *n.* corridor train. **harmo·nie, -ieën,** *n.* harmony. **harmoni·ëren, -ieer,** *v.i.* to harmonize. **harmo·nieleer,** no pl., *n.* theory of harmony. **harmo·nieorkest,** *n.n.* band (*wind instruments*). **harmoni·eus, -ze,** *a.* harmonious. **har·monisch,** *a.* harmonious; harmonic.

·**harnas, -ssen,** *n.n.* armour, cuirass. *iemand in het* ~ *jagen,* to put a person's back up. ·**harnassen, -nas,** *v.t.* to armour. ¶*zich* ~, *v.r.* to put on one's armour.

harp, *n.* harp. **harpe·nist,** *n.* harpist.

har·pij, *n.* harpy.

har·poen, *n.* harpoon. **har·poenen,** *v.t.,*

harpoe·neren, -neer, *v.t.* to harpoon. **harpoe·nier, -s,** *n.* harpooner.

·**harpspel,** no pl., *n.n.* harp-playing.

har·puis, no pl., *n.n.* mixture of pitch, tar, and rosin. **har·puizen, -puis,** *v.t.* to pay.

·**harrewarren, -war,** *v.i.* to bicker.

hars, *n.* resin; rosin. ·**harsachtig,** *a.* resinous.

hart, *n.n.* heart. *een goed* ~ *hebben,* to be kindhearted; *het heilige* ~, the sacred heart; *zijn* ~ *klopte in de keel,* his heart was in his mouth; *het* ~ *hoog dragen,* to be proud; *het* ~ *op de tong hebben,* to wear one's heart on one's sleeve; *zijn* ~ *ophalen aan,* to (*e.g. eat*) to one's heart's content; *waar het* ~ *van vol is loopt de mond van over,* (he spoke) from the fullness of his heart; *in zijn* ~, in his heart of hearts; *in* ~ *en nieren,* to the backbone; *na aan het* ~, near to one's heart; *naar mijn* ~, after my own heart; *iemand een* ~ *onder de riem* (or *een riem onder het*) ~ *steken,* to give someone new courage; *iets op het* ~ *hebben,* to have something on one's mind; *ik kan het niet over mijn* ~ *krijgen,* I have not the heart to do it; *dat is een steen van mijn* ~, that is a load off my mind; *van zijn* ~ *een moordkuil maken,* to suppress one's feelings; *van zijn* ~ *een steen maken,* to harden one's heart. ·**harte,** no pl., *n.n. ter* ~ *nemen,* to take to heart; *van* ~, with conviction; *van ganser* ~, with all (one's) heart. ·**hartader, -s,** *n.* aorta. ·**hartbrekend,** *a.* heartbreaking. ·**hartebloed,** no pl., *n.n.* heart's blood, life blood. ·**hartedief,** no pl., *n.* darling. ·**hartelijk,** *a.* hearty, cordial. *met* ~*e groeten,* with kind regards. ¶*adv.* heartily. ·**hartelijkheid,** no pl., *n.* heartiness. ·**harteloos, -loze,** *a.* heartless. ·**hartelust,** no pl., *n. naar* ~, to one's heart's content. ·**harten,** pl. only, *n.n.* hearts (*cards*). **harten·aas, -nazen,** *n.n.* ace of hearts. **harten·boer,** *n.* jack of hearts. **harten·heer, -heren,** *n.* king of hearts. **harten·vrouw,** *n.* queen of hearts. ·**hartewens,** *n.* heart's desire. *naar* ~, as desired. **hart·grondig,** *a.* heartfelt. ¶*adv.* wholeheartedly. ·**hartig,** *a.* salt, well seasoned; hearty. *een* ~ *woord,* plain speaking. ·**hartigheid,** no pl., *n.* saltness; heartiness. ·**hartje, -s,** *n.n.* little heart; heart. *in 't* ~ *van,* in the heart of (*country*) *or* in the dead of (*winter*) *or* in the height of (*summer*). ·**hartklop,** no pl., *n.* heart-beat. ·**hartklopping,** *n.* palpitation. ·**hartkwaal, -kwalen,** *n.* disease of the heart, heart trouble. **hart·roerend,** *a.* pathetic, touching. ·**harts·geheim,** *n.n.* secret of the heart. ·**hart·stikkedood,** *a.* stone-dead. ·**hartstikkedoof,** *a.* stone-deaf. ·**hartstocht,** *n.* passion. **harts·tochtelijk,** *a.* passionate; impassioned; ardent. **harts·tochtelijkheid, -heden,** *n.* passionate words *or* action.

·**hartsvanger, -s,** *n.* hanger, cutlass.

hartver·heffend, *a.* exalting, sublime. ·**hartverlamming,** *n.* heart failure. **hartver·scheurend,** *a.* heartrending. ·**hartvervetting,** *n.* fatty degeneration of the heart. ·**hartvlies, -zen,** *n.n.* pericardium. ·**hartvormig,** *a.* heart-shaped. ·**hartzeer,** no pl., *n.n.* heartache.

·**haspel, -s,** *n.* reel. **haspela·rij,** *n.* bungling. ·**haspelen,** *v.t.* to wind; to bungle.

·**hatelijk,** *a.* hateful; spiteful, malicious. ·**hatelijkheid, -heden,** *n.* spitefulness; nasty dig. ·**haten, haat,** *v.t.* to hate. ·**hater, -s,** *n.* hater.

·**hausse,** no pl., *n.* rise. *à la ~ speculeren,* to engage in bull speculations. **haus·sier, -s,** *n.* bull (on *Stock Exchange*).

·**have,** no pl., *n.* property; stock (*cattle*). *~ en goed,* goods and chattels; *levende ~,* livestock. ·**haveloos, -loze,** *a.* ragged. ¶*adv.* shabbily. ·**haveloosheid,** no pl., *n.* raggedness, shabbiness.

·**haven, -s,** *n.* harbour, port; haven. *een ~ binnenlopen* or *binnenvallen,* to drop into a port; *in behouden ~ zijn,* to be safe in port. ·**havenarbeider, -s,** *n.* dock labourer, stevedore. ·**havendam, -mmen,** *n.* jetty, pier, mole.

·**havenen,** *v.t.* to damage.

·**havengeld,** *n.n.* harbour dues. ·**havenhoofd,** *n.n.* pier, jetty. ·**havenplaats.** *n.,* ·**havenstad, -steden,** *n.* harbour(-town), port. ·**havenwerken,** pl. only, *n.n.* harbour works.

·**haver,** no pl., *n.* oats. *iemand van ~ tot gort kennen,* to know a person's family history. ·**haverdegort,** no pl., *n.* groats.

have·rij, *n. See* **averij.**

·**haverklap,** no pl., *n. om de ~,* on the slightest provocation. ·**havermeel,** no pl., *n.n.* oatmeal. ·**havermout,** no pl., *n.* oatmeal (*porridge*). ·**haverzak, -kken,** *n.* oatbag, nosebag.

·**havik,** *n.* hawk. ·**haviksneus, -zen,** *n.* hawknose, aquiline nose.

·**hazardspal,** *n.n.* gambling game.

·**hazelaar, -s,** *n.* hazel(-tree). ·**hazelaarshout,** no pl., *n.n.* hazelwood. ·**hazelhoen, -ders,** *n.n.* hazel grouse. ·**hazelkatjes,** pl. only, *n.n.* hazel catkins. ·**hazelmuis, -zen,** *n.* dormouse. ·**hazelnoot, -noten,** *n.* hazelnut. ·**hazelworm,** *n.* blindworm, slowworm.

·**hazendistel, -s,** *n.* milk-thistle. ·**hazenjacht,** *n.* hare shooting *or* hunting. ·**hazenlip, -ppen,** *n.* hare lip. ·**hazenpad,** no pl., *n.n. het ~ kiezen,* to take to one's heels. ·**hazenslaap,** no pl., *n.* dogsleep. **hazenwind(hond),** *n.* greyhound. ·**hazepeper,** no pl., *n.* jugged hare.

·**hebbeding,** *n.n.* thing, object (*contempt*). ·**hebbelijkheid, -heden,** *n.* habit (*unpleasant*). *de ~ hebben om,* to have a way of. ·**hebben, heb,** *v.t., irr.* to have. *wat heb je eraan?,* what is the use of it?; *je weet niet wat je aan hem hebt,* you cannot

rely on him; *iets bij zich ~,* to have something on *or* about one; *het ~ over,* to be talking about; *het ~ tegen,* to be talking to; *ik moet er niets van ~,* I won't have any of it *or* I don't like it *or* I don't hold with it. ¶*aux.v.* to have. ¶no pl., *n.n. ~ is ~ maar krijgen is de kunst,* possession is nine points of the law; *zijn hele ~ en houden,* all his worldly goods. ·**hebberig,** *a.* acquisitive. ·**hebzucht,** no pl., *n.* greed, cupidity. **heb·zuchtig,** *a.* greedy, grasping.

He·breeër, -s, *n.* Hebrew (*person*). **He·breeuws,** *a.* Hebrew.

hecht, *n.n.* haft, handle. ¶*a.* firm, solid. ·**hechtdraad, -draden,** *n.* ligature thread. ·**hechten,** *v.t.* to attach, fix; to suture, sew up. ¶*v.i. ~ aan,* to be keen on, attached to. ¶*v.r. zich ~ aan,* to attach oneself to. ·**hechtenis,** no pl., *n.* custody, detention. *in ~ nemen,* to arrest, take into custody; *in ~ zijn,* to be under arrest. ·**hechtheid,** no pl., *n.* firmness. ·**hechting,** *n.* suture. ·**hechtpleister, -s,** *n.n.* adhesive plaster. ·**hechtrank,** *n.* tendril. ·**hechtwortel, -s,** *n.* aerial root.

·**hectoliter, -s,** *n.* hectolitre. ·**hectometer, -s,** *n.* hectometre.

·**heden,** *adv.* (*stilted*) to-day. *~ ten dage,* nowadays; *over 8 dagen,* to-day week; *tot ~ toe* or *tot op ~,* up to the present; *vanaf ~* or *van ~ aan* or *van ~ af aan,* (as) from to-day. ¶no pl., *n.n. het ~,* the present. **heden·avond,** *adv.* (*stilted*) tonight. **heden·daags,** *a.* (*stilted*) modern, present-day. ¶*adv.* nowadays. **heden·middag,** *adv.* (*stilted*) this afternoon. **heden·ochtend,** *adv.* (*v.stilted*) this morning. **heden·nacht,** *adv.* (*stilted*) to-night; last night (*not evening*).

·**hederik, -kken,** *n.* charlock.

heel, hele, *a.* entire, whole. *een ~ aantal,* a considerable number; *een hele geschiedenis,* a long story; *een hele meneer,* quite a gentleman; *hele sommen,* large sums of money; *een hele tijd,* a long time; *door heel . . .,* throughout . . . ¶*adv.* very, quite. *~ veel,* a great many *or* a great deal; *~ wat,* quite a lot; *~ iets anders,* something entirely different; *~ in de verte,* in the far distance; *~ en al,* entirely. **heel·al,** no pl., *n.n.* universe. ·**heelhuids,** *adv.* unscathed, scotfree.

·**heelbaar, -bare,** *a.* healable, curable. ·**heelkracht,** no pl., *n.* healing power. ·**heelkunde,** no pl., *n.* surgery (*art*). ·**heelkundig,** *a.* surgical. **heel·kundige, -n,** *n.,* ·**heelmeester, -s,** *n.* surgeon.

·**heemraad, -raden,** *n.* dyke-reeve; board of dyke-reeves. ·**heemraadschap, -ppen,** *n.n.* office of dyke-reeve; polder.

heen, *adv.* away. *~ en terug,* there and back; *~ en weer,* to and fro; *waar ga je ~?,* where are you going?; *waar wil je ~?,* where do you want to go? *or* what are you driving at? ¶*prefix* away. ·heenkomen, no pl., *n.n.* een goed ~ zoeken, to make good one's escape. ·heenreis, -zen, *n.* outward journey, outward bound voyage. ·heenreizen, reis heen, *v.i.* to set out.

heer, heren, *n.n.* host (*army*). ¶*n.* gentleman, man; lord; Lord; king (*cards*). *de* ~ *A,* Mr. A; *de heren A,* Messrs. A; *de* ~ *des huizes,* the master of the house; ~ *en meester zijn,* to be absolute master; *zo* ~ *zo knecht,* like master like man; *twee heren dienen,* to serve two masters; *langs 's heren wegen lopen,* to wander about; *onze Lieve Heer,* our Lord; *in het jaar onzes Heren,* in the year of our Lord; *met grote heren is het kwaad kersen eten,* the weakest go to the wall; *de grote* ~ *uithangen,* to give oneself airs; *nieuwe heren nieuwe wetten,* new lords new laws; *de oude* ~, the old man, the governor.

·heerbaan, -banen, *n.* military road. ·heerleger, -s, *n.n.* host (*army*).

·heerlijk, *a.* manorial; delicious, lovely. ·heerlijkheid, -heden, *n.* manor; splendour, magnificence. heer·oom, -s, *n.* your reverence (*to uncle who is also priest*).

·beerschaar, -scharen, *n.* host. *de Heer der heerscharen,* the Lord of hosts.

beerschap, -ppen, *n.n.* master; gent (*ironical*). heerschap·pij, no pl., *n.* mastery, power; dominion, rule. *de* ~ *uitoefenen over,* to hold sway over. ·heersen, *v.i.* to rule; to prevail, obtain. ~ *over,* to rule (over). ·heersend, *a.* ruling; prevalent, prevailing. ·heerser, -s, *n.* ruler. heerse·res, -ssen, *n.* ruler (*female*). ·heerszucht, no pl., *n.* ambition, lust for power. heers·zuchtig, *a.* domineering, imperious. ·heertje, -s, *n.n.* young gentleman. *het* ~ *zijn,* to be as pleased as Punch.

bees, hese, *a.* hoarse. ·heesheid, no pl., *n.* hoarseness.

·heester, -s, *n.* shrub. ·heesterachtig, *a.* shrubby.

heet, hete, *a.* hot. ¶*adv.* hotly. *het zal er* ~ *toegaan,* things are going to hum. ·heetgebakerd, *a.* quick-tempered. ·heethoofd, *n.* hot-head. heet·hoofdig, *a.* hot-headed. heet·hoofdigheid, no pl., *n.* hot-headedness.

·hefboom, -bomen, *n.* lever. ·heffen, hef, *v.t.*, *str.* to raise, lift; to levy. ·heffing, *n.* levying, raising (*of taxes, etc.*).

heft, *n.n.* haft, handle. *het* ~ *in handen houden,* to remain in control.

·heftig, *a.* violent, vehement. ·heftigheid, -heden, *n.* violence, vehemence.

beg, -ggen, *n.* hedge. ~ *noch steg weten,* not to know one's way; *over* ~ *en steg,* up hill and down dale. ·heggerank, *n.* bryony.

bei, *int.* hey! ¶*n.* rammer (*instrument*). ¶-den, *n.* heath; heather. ·heibaas, -bazen, *n.* foreman (*ramming or pile-driving*).

·heibel, no pl., *n.* row, racket.

·heibezem, -s, *n.* heather-brown. ·heiblok, -kken, *n.* rammer, pile-driver. ·heide, -n, *n.* heath; heather. ·heideachtig, *a.* heathery ·heidebrand, *n.* heath-fire. ·heidegrond, *n.* heath. ·heidekruid, no pl., *n.n.* heather.

·heiden, *n.* heather, pagan. ·heidendom, no pl., *n.n.* heathendom; paganism. ·heidens, *a.* heathenish. ~ *lawaai,* unholy row.

·heideplant, *n.*, ·heidestruik, *n.* heather.

hei·din, -nnen, *n.* heathen, pagan; gipsy (*female*).

·heien, *v.t.* & *v.i.* to ram, drive (*pile*). ·heier, -s, *n.* pile-driver.

·heiig, *a.* hazy.

heil, no pl., *n.n.* salvation; welfare, good, *tot* ~ *van,* for the good of; *tot* ~ *strekken,* to be beneficial; *geen* ~ *zien in,* to see no good in; *zijn* ~ *zoeken in,* to have recourse to. ·Heiland, no pl., *n.* Saviour.

·heilbot, -tten, *n.* halibut.

·heildronk, *n.* toast (*drink*). *een* ~ *instellen,* to propose a toast. ·heilig, *a.* holy; sacred, saint, solemn. *een* ~*e overtuiging* or *eerbied,* a deep, earnest, conviction or respect; *de* ~*e waarheid,* gospel truth; ~ *verklaren,* to canonize. ¶*adv.* solemnly. *zich* ~ *voornemen om . . .,* to make a firm resolution to . . . ·heiligbeen, no pl., *n.n.* os sacrum. ·heiligdom, -mmen, *n.n.* sanctuary; sanctum. ·heilige, -n, *n.* saint. ·heiligen, *v.t.* to sanctify, hallow; to keep holy. ·heiligenbeeld, *n.n.* image of saint. ·heiligendag, *n.* saint's day. ·heiligheid, no pl., *n.* holiness. *Zijne H~,* His Holiness. ·heiliging, *n.* sanctification. ·heilmakend, *a.* sanctifying. ·heiligschender, -s, *n.* sacrilegious person. ·heiligschennend, *a.* sacrilegious. ·heiligschennis, -ssen, *n.* sacrilege. ·heiligverklaring, *n.* canonization. ·heilloos, -lloze, *a.* impious; fatal. ·heilsleger, no pl., *n.n.* salvation army. ·heilsoldaat, -daten, *n.* salvationist. ·heilstaat, -staten, *n.* Utopia, ideal state. ·heilwens, *n.* congratulation. ·heilzaam, -zame, *a.* salutary; wholesome. ·heilzaamheid, no pl., *n.* beneficial influence.

·heimachine, -s, *n.* pile-driver.

·heimelijk, *a.* secret, clandestine. ·heimelijkheid. -heden, *n.* secrecy, secretiveness.

·heimwee, no pl., *n.n.* homesickness, nostalgia. ·heinde, *adv.* ~ *en ver,* far and wide.

·heining, *n.* hoarding, fence.

·heipaal, -palen, *n.* pile (*for foundation*).

heir, *n.n.* host (*army*). *See* heer.

·heirook, no pl., *n.* peat-smoke.

·heitoestel, -llen, *n. See* heimachine.

hek, -kken, *n.n.* railing(s), fence; gate. *het* ~ *is van de dam,* all restraint has gone; *de hekken zijn verhangen,* the tables are turned.

·hekel, -s, *n.* heckle. *over de* ~ *halen,* to criticize (*unkindly*). ¶no pl., *n.* dislike. *een* ~ *hebben aan,* to dislike. ·hekelaar,

-s, n. heckler. ·hekelachtig, a. censorious. ·hekeldicht, n.n. satire (poem). ·hekeldichter, -s, n. satirist. ·hekelen, v.t. to hackle; to heckle; to satirize. ·hekelmachine, -s, n. decorticator. ·hekelschrift, n.n. satire. ·hekelvers, -zen, n.n. satire (verse).

heks, n. witch. oude ~, old hag. ·heksen, v.i. to practise witchcraft. ·heksenbezem, -s, n. witch's broom. ·heksenketel, -s, n. witch's cauldron. ·heksenkring, n. fairy ring. ·heksentoer, n. impossible task, amazing performance. ·heksenwerk, no pl., n. sorcery; difficult task. hekse·rij, no pl., n. sorcery, witchcraft.

·heksluiter, -s, n. last-comer. ·hekwerk, no pl., n.n. railing(s), trellis-work.

hel, no pl., n. hell. ¶-lle, a. bright.

he·laas, excl. alas, alack. ¶adv. unfortunately.

held, n. hero. ·heldendaad, -daden, n. heroic action, act of heroism. ·heldendicht, n.n. epic. ·heldendood, no pl., n. de ~ sterven, to die in action. ·heldenmoed, no pl., n. heroism. ·heldentijd, n. heroic period. ·heldenverering, no pl., n. hero-worship. ·heldenzang, n. epic song.

·helder, a. clear, bright; lucid; clean. ¶adv. clearly, brightly. ~ wakker, wide awake. ·helderblauw, a. bright blue. ·helderheid, no pl., n. brightness clearness; lucidity, clarity. helder·ziend, a. clearsighted; clairvoyant. helder·ziende, -n, n. clairvoyant. helder·ziendheid, no pl., n. clearsightedness; clairvoyance.

held·haftig, a. heroic. ¶adv. heroically. held·haftigheid, no pl., n. heroism. hel·din, -nnen, n. heroine.

·helemaal, adv. entirely, altogether, wholly; quite, clean. ~ alleen, all by (him)self; ~ niet, not at all.

·helen, heel, v.t. to receive (stolen goods); to heal, cure. ¶v.i. to heal (up). ·heler, -s, n. receiver (of stolen goods), fence.

helft, n. half; moiety. de ~ van het werk, half the work; op de ~, half-way; tegen de ~ van de prijs, at half-price; tot op de ~ terugbrengen, to reduce by half; voor de ~, half; voor de ~ van . . ., for half . . .

·heling, no pl., n. receiving (of stolen goods).

helio·troop, -tropen, n. heliotrope.

·helium, no pl., n.n. helium.

·hellebaard, n. halberd. hellebaar·dier, -s, n. halberdier.

·hellen, hel, v.i. to slope, slant; to dip, shelve. ·hellend, a. inclined. ~ vlak, inclined plane, slippery slope.

·hellevaart, no pl., n. harrowing of hell. ·helleveeg, -vegen, n. shrew, virago, termagant.

·helling, n. slope, incline; gradient; inclination. ·hellingshoek, n. angle of inclination.

helm, n. helmet, tin hat. met de ~ geboren, born with a caul. ¶no pl., n. beach-grass.

·helmhoed, n. sun-helmet. ·helmkruid, no pl., n.n. figwort.

·helmstok, -kken, n. tiller, helm.

·helpen, v.t., str. to help, aid, assist; to avail, be of use; to attend to (customers). wat helpt het?, what's the use of it?; ~ aan, to help to; er is geen ~ aan, it cannot be helped; ~ bij, to assist in. ¶v.i., str. to avail, help. het helpt, it is being useful. ·helper, -s, n. helper. ·helpster, -s, n. helper (female).

hels, a. devilish, hellish. een ~e machine, an infernal machine; ~e steen, lapis infernalis; ~ zijn, to be furious. ¶adv. infernally.

hem, pron. him. van ~, his.

hemd, n.n. shirt. het ~ is nader dan de rok, charity begins at home; tot het ~ toe uitkleden, to fleece a person; iemand het ~ van het lijf vragen, to question a person closely. ·hemdsknoop, -knopen, n. shirt button. ·hemdsmouw, n. shirtsleeve.

·hemel, n. heaven; sky, firmament. de ~ weet, goodness knows; de ~ beware ons, heaven forbid; de vogelen des ~s, the birds of the air; aan de ~, in the sky; in de ~, in heaven; onder de blote ~, in the open; het schreit ten ~, it cries to heaven; ten ~ varen, to ascend to heaven; tussen ~ en aarde, in mid-air. ¶-s, n. canopy. ·hemeldragonder, -s, n. sky-pilot. ·hemelgewelf, no pl., n.n. vault of heaven. ·hemelhoog, -hoge, a. sky-high. ¶adv. sky-high, to the skies. ·hemelkaart, n. astronomical map. ·hemelkoor, -koren, n.n. heavenly choir. ·hemellichaam, -chamen, n.n. heavenly body. ·hemelrijk, no pl., n.n. kingdom of heaven. ·hemels, a. heavenly, celestial; divine. ¶adv. heavenly, celestially; divinely. ·hemelsblauw, a. sky-blue. ·hemelsbreed, -brede, a. enormous. een ~ verschil, an enormous difference, all the difference. ·hemelsbreedte, no pl., n. astronomical latitude. ·hemelstreek, -streken, n. point of the compass. hemeltergend, a. & adv. crying to heaven. ·hemeltrans, n. vault of heaven. ·Hemelvaart, no pl., n. Ascension. Maria H~, Assumption of the Holy Virgin. ·Hemelvaartsdag, n. Ascension Day. ·Hemelvaartsweek, n. Rogation week. ·hemelvuur, no pl., n.n. (poet.) lightning. ·hemelwaarts, a. & adv. heavenward.

·hemmen, hem, v.i. to hem (and haw).

hen, pron. them. ¶-nnen, n. hen.

·Henegouwen, n.N. Hainault.

·henen, adv. See heen.

·hengel, -s, n. fishing rod. ·hengelaar, -s, n. angler. ·hengelen, v.i. to angle. ~ naar, to fish or angle for. ·hengelroede, -n, n. See hengel. ·hengelsnoer, n.n. fishing line.

·hengsel, -s, n.n. handle (movable); hinge. uit de ~s, off its hinges ·hengselmand, n. shopping basket.

hengst, *n.* stallion. **·hengsten**, *v.i.* to swot. **·hengstveulen, -s,** *n.n.* colt.

·hennep, no pl., *n.* hemp. **·hennepen,** *a.* hemp(en). **·hennepgaren,** no pl., *n.n.* hemp yarn. **·hennepolie,** no pl., *n.* hemp seed oil. **·hennepzaad, -zaden,** *n.n.* hemp seed.

hens, pl. only, *n. alle ~ aan dek,* all hands on deck.

her, *prefix.* re-, again. ¶*adv. ~ en der,* here and there; *van eeuwen ~,* going back for centuries; *van ouds ~,* of old. **her·ademen,** *v.i.* to breathe again. **her·ademing,** no pl., *n.* relief.

heral·diek, *n.* heraldry. **he·raldisch,** *a.* heraldic. **he·raut,** *n.* herald.

·herbenoemen, *v.t.* to reappoint. **·herbenoeming,** *n.* reappointment.

·herberg, *n.* inn; public house. **·herbergen,** *v.t.* to put up, lodge; to harbour. **herber·gier, -s,** *n.* innkeeper, landlord. **herber·gierster,** *n.* landlady *(of public house).* **her·bergzaam, -zame,** *a.* hospitable. **her·bergzaamheid,** no pl., *n.* hospitableness.

·herbesteden, *v.t.* to invite new tenders. **·herbesteding,** *n.* further invitation for tenders. **her·boren,** *a.* born again, regenerate.

herbori·seren, -seer, *v.i.* to herborize, botanize.

·herbouw, *n.* rebuilding, reconstruction. **·herbouwen,** *v.t.* to rebuild. **her·denken,** *v.t., irr.* to commemorate; to recall to mind. **her·denking,** *n.* commemoration, remembrance. *ter ~ van,* in memory of *or* in commemoration of. **her·denkingsdienst,** *n.* memorial service.

·herder, -s, *n.* shepherd; shepherd, pastor. **herde·rin, -nnen,** *n.* shepherdess. **·herderlijk,** *a.* pastoral. *~ schrijven,* pastoral letter. **·herdersambt,** *n.n.* pastoral office. **·herdersdicht,** *n.n.* pastoral poem, bucolic. **·herdersfluit,** *n.* shepherd's reed. **·herdershond,** *n.* sheepdog. **·herdersstaf, -taven,** *n.* shepherd's crook. **·herderstasje, -s,** *n.n.* shepherd's purse.

·herdoop, no pl., *n.* rebaptism. **·herdopen, -doop,** *v.t.* to rebaptize. **·herdoper, -s.** *n.* anabaptist.

·herdruk, -kken, *n.* reprint. **·herdrukken, -druk,** *v.t.* to reprint.

·hereboer, *n.* gentleman farmer.

here·miet, *n.* hermit, recluse.

·herendiensten, pl. only, *n.* corvée, statute labour. **·herenfiets,** *n.* (gentle)man's bicycle.

her·enigen, *v.t.* to re-unite. **·herexamen, -s,** *n.n.* re-examination.

herfst, no pl., *n.* autumn. **herfstachtig,** *a.* autumnal. **·herfstkleuren,** pl. only, *n.* autumn colours. **·herfstnachtevening,** *n.* autumnal equinox. **·herfstsering,** *n.* phlox. **·herfsttijloos, -lozen,** *n.* meadow saffron.

·hergeven, -geef, *v.i., str.* to deal again *(cards).* **her·haald,** *a.* repeated. *~e malen,*

repeatedly. **her·haaldelijk,** *adv.* repeatedly. **her·halen, -haal,** *v.t.* to repeat. ¶**zich ~,** *v.r.* to repeat oneself. **her·haling,** *n.* repetition; recapitulation. **her·halingsonderwijs,** no pl., *n.n.* continuation classes. **her·halingsteken, -s,** *n.n.* repeat *(music).*

·herig, *a.* like a gentleman. ¶*adv. ~ doen,* to put on airs.

·herijk, *n.* regauging *(weights and measures).* **·herik,** no pl., *n.* charlock.

her·inneren, *v.t.* to remind. *iemand ~ aan,* to remind a person of; *~ aan,* to recall the fact that. ¶*zich ~, v.r.* to remember, recollect. **her·innering,** *n.* memory, recollection; souvenir, keepsake; reminder. *iemand iets in ~ brengen* to remind a person of something; *ter ~ aan,* in memory of. **·herkauwen,** *v.t. & v.i.* to ruminate, chew the cud. **·herkauwend,** *a.* ruminant. **·herkauwer, -s,** *n.* ruminant. **her·kenbaar, -bare,** *a.* recognizable. ¶*adv.* recognizably. **her·kennen, -ken,** *v.t.* to recognize; to identify. *~ aan,* to recognize by. **her·kenning,** *n.* recognition. **her·kenningsteken, -s,** *n.n.* mark of recognition. **·herkeuren,** *v.t.* to re-examine. **·herkeuring,** *n.* re-examination. **her·kiesbaar, -bare,** *a.* re-eligible. **her·kiesbaarheid,** no pl., *n.* re-eligibility. **her·kiezen, -kies,** *v.t., str.* to re-elect. **her·kiezing,** *n.* re-election. **·herkomst.** no pl., *n.* origin, provenance. **her·komstig,** *a. ~ uit or van,* originating from. **·herkoop,** no pl., *n.* re-purchase. **her·krijgen,** *v.t., str.* to get back, recover. **her·krijging,** *n.* recovery. **her·leidbaar, -bare,** *a.* reducible. **her·leiden,** *v.t.* to reduce. **her·leiding,** *n.* reduction, conversion. **her·leidingstabel, -llen,** *n.* conversion table. **her·leven, -leef,** *v.t.* to revive. *doen ~,* to revive *(something or someone).* **her·leving,** *n.* revival. **her·lezen, -lees,** *v.t., str.* to re-read.

herme·lijn, *n.* ermine *(animal).* ¶no pl., *n.n.* ermine *(fur).* **herme·lijnen,** *a. (made of)* ermine.

her·metisch, *a.* hermetic, air-tight. ¶*adv.* hermetically. *~ gesloten,* hermetically sealed.

her·nemen, -neem, *v.t., str.* to resume *(seat);* to retake. **her·neming,** *n.* recapture.

·Hernhutter, -s, *N.* Moravian (brother).

her·nieuwbaar, -bare, *a.* renewable. **her·nieuwen,** *v.t.* to renew. **her·nieuwing,** *n.* renewal.

he·roïsch, *a.* heroic.

her·openen, *v.t.* to re-open. **her·overaar, -s,** *n.* reconqueror. **her·overen,** *v.t.* to re-conquer. *~ op,* to reconquer from. **her·overing,** *n.* reconquest.

·herrie, no pl., *n.* noise, din, shindy. *~ krijgen,* to get into a row; *~ maken or schoppen,* to kick up a row. **herrieschopper, -s,** *n.* quarrelsome *or* noisy fellow.

her·rijzen, -rrijs, *v.i.*, *str.* to rise (*from dead*). her·roepbaar, -bare, *a.* revocable. her·roepbaarheid, no pl., *n.* revocability. her·roepen, *v.t.*, *str.* to revoke, repeal; to recall, retract, recant; to reverse, countermand. her·roeping, *n.* revocation, recantation, reversal. her·schapen, *a.* transformed. her·scheppen, -schep, *v.t.*, *str.* to recreate, regenerate. her·schepping, *n.* recreation, transformation.

·hersenarbeid, no pl., *n.* brain-work. ·hersenen, pl. only, *n.*, ·hersens, pl. only, *n.* brain(s). *grote* ~, cerebrum; *kleine* ~, cerebellum; *iets uit zijn* ~ *laten*, to give up all thought of something. ·hersengezwel, -llen, *n.n.* tumour on the brain. ·hersenkas, -ssen, *n.* skull, cranium. ·hersenloos, -loze, *a.* brainless. ·hersenontsteking, *n.* encephalitis. ·hersenpan, -nnen, *n.* skull, cranium. ·hersenschim, -mmen, *n.* chimera, phantasm; figment of the imagination. ·hersenschudding, *n.* concussion. ·hersenvlies, -zen, *n.n.* meninx (*pl.* meninges), cerebral membrane. ·hersenvliesontsteking, *n.* meningitis. ·hersenverweking, *n.* softening of the brain. ·hersenwerk, no pl., *n.n.* brain-work.

her·stel, no pl., *n.n.* repair; restoration; recuperation; redress, rehabilitation. her·stelbaar, -bare, *a.* reparable. her·stellen, -stel, *v.t.* to repair; to redress, restore, rectify; to re-instate. *in zijn eer* ~, to rehabilitate. ¶*v.i.* to recover (*from illness*). ¶zich ~, *v.r.* to recover (*from shock*). her·stelling, *n.* repair, restoration; re-instatement. her·stellingsoord, *n.n.* health resort. her·stellingswerk, no pl., *n.n.* repair-work. ·herstemmen, -stem, *v.i.* to vote again. ·herstemming, *n.* second ballot.

hert, *n.n.* deer, stag. *vliegend* ~, stag beetle. ·hertebok, -kken, *n.* stag, buck. ·hertebout, *n.* haunch of venison. ·hertenjacht, *n.* stag-hunting, deerstalking. ·hertenkamp, *n.n.* deer park. ·hertevlees, no pl., *n.n.* venison.

·hertog, *n.* duke. ·hertogdom, -mmen, *n.n.* duchy. her·togelijk, *a.* ducal. 's Hertogen-bos, *n.N.* Bois-le-Duc. herto·gin, -nnen, *n.* duchess.

her·trouwen, *v.i.* to marry again.

·hertshoorn, no pl., *n.n.* hartshorn. ·hertzwijn, *n.n.* hog-deer.

·heruitzenden, *v.t.s.*, *str.* to re-transmit; to relay. ·heruitzending, *n.* retransmission; relay. her·vatten, -vat, *v.t.* to resume. her·vatting, no pl., *n.* resumption. ·herverzekeren, *v.t.* to re-insure. ·herverzekering, *n.* re-insurance. her·vormd, *a.* reformed. her·vormde, -n, *n.* member of Dutch Reformed Church. her·vormen, *v.t.* to reform. her·vormer, -s, *n.* reformer. her·vorming, *n.* reformation, reform.

·herwaarts, *adv.* hither.

her·winnen, -win, *v.t.*, *str.* to regain, win back. her·zien, -zie, *v.t.*, *irr.* to revise, review. her·ziening, *n.* revision.

hèt, *art*, the. ¶*pron.* it. *ik ben* ~, it is me, it is I.

·heten, heet, *v.t.*, *irr.* to heat; to name, call. ¶*v.i.*, *irr.* to be called. *hoe heet dat?*, what is its name?; *zoals het heet*, supposedly; ~ *naar*, to be called after.

het·geen, *pron.* that which, what; which. het·welk, *pron.* which. het·zelfde, *pron.* the same. het·zelve, *pron.* (the) same, it. het·zij, *c.* either, or; whether, or.

heug, no pl., *n. tegen* ~ *en meug*, reluctantly. ·heugel, -s, *n.* pot-hook; rack.

·heugen, *v.t.*, *imp. het heugt me*, I remember; *dat zal je* ~, you won't forget that one. ·heugenis, no pl., *n.* memory, remembrance. ·heuglijk, *a.* joyful, glad.

heul, no pl., *n.* poppy. ·heulbol, -llen, *n.* poppy-head. ·heulen, *v.i.* ~ *met*, to be in collusion with. ·heulsap, no pl., *n.n.* opium. ·heulzaad, no pl., *n.n.* poppy-seed, mawseed.

heup, *n.* hip. *het op de* ~*en hebben* or *krijgen*, to be in a bad temper. ·heupdoek, *n.* loin-cloth.

heur, *pron.* (*poet.*) her.

heus, *a.* courteous, obliging. ¶*adv.* really; truly. *het is* ~ *waar*, it is really true, *ik meen het* ~, I do mean it. ·heusheid, no pl., *n.* courtesy.

·heuvel, -s, *n.* hill. ·heuvelachtig, *a.*, ·heuvelig *a.* hilly. ·heuvelland, no pl., *n.n.* hilly country. ·heuvelreeks, *n.* chain of hills.

·hevel, -s, *n.* syphon. ·hevelen, *v.t.* to syphon, draw off.

·hevig, *a.* violent; vehement; fierce, heavy (*fighting*). ·hevigheid, no pl., *n.* fierceness, violence, intensity.

hi·aat, hiaten, *n.n.* hiatus, gap.

hiel, *n.* heel. *de* ~*en lichten*, to take to one's heels; *iemand op de* ~*en zitten*, to pursue someone. ·hielen, *v.t.* to heel.

hier, *adv.* here. ~ *te lande*, in this country. hier·aan, *adv.* at this, by this, on this, *etc.* hier·achter, *adv.* behind this; hereinafter. hierbe·neden, *adv.* down here. hier·bij, *adv.* herewith, enclosed; hereby. hier·binnen, *adv.* within. hier·boven, *adv.* up here; up above. hier·buiten, *adv.* outside (this). hier·door, *adv.* in consequence, owing to this; through here. ·hierheen, *adv.* this way, here. ·hierin, *adv.* in here, in this. hier·langs, *adv.* this way, past here. ·hierme(d)e, *adv.* with this. hier·na, *adv.* after this. ·hiernaar, *adv.* according to this, from this. hier·naast, *adv.* next door; alongside. hier·namaals, *adv.* hereafter. ¶no pl., *n.n. het* ~, the hereafter. hier·nevens, *adv.* (*stilted*) enclosed. ·hierom, *adv.* for this reason; round this. hierom·heen, *adv.* round here. hierom·streeks, *adv.* roundabout here, hereabout(s).

·hieromtrent, *adv.* concerning this; hereabout(s). hier·onder, *adv.* below; among these. hier·op, *adv.* upon this, hereupon. hier·over, *adv.* opposite; on this subject. hier·tegen, *adv.* against this. hiertoe, *adv.* for this purpose, to this end. *tot* ~, thus far so far. hier·tussen, *adv.* in between. hier·uit, *adv.* hence; from this. ·hiervan, *adv.* of this. ·hiervoor, *adv.* for *or* before this.

·hieuwen, *v.t.* to heave (*anchor*).

·hijgen, *v.i.* to pant. *naar adem* ~, to gasp for breath.

·hijsblok, -kken, *n.n.* pulley-block. ·hijsen, *v.t., str.* to hoist. *de vlag* ~, to hoist *or* run up the flag. ·hijskraan, -kranen, *n.* crane, elevator. ·hijstouw, *n.n.* hoisting rope.

hik, no pl., *n.* hiccough. ·hikken, hik, *v.i.* to hiccough.

·hinde, -n, *n.* hind, doe. ·hindekalf, -kalveren, *n.n.* fawn.

·hinder, no pl., *n.* hindrance; inconvenience. ~ *hebben van*, to be hindered by. ·hinderen, *v.t.* to hinder, impede; to annoy. ¶*v.i.* to be a hindrance. *het hindert niet*, it doesn't matter. ·hinderlaag, -lagen, *n.* ambush. *in* ~ *leggen*, to ambush. ·hinderlijk, *a.* troublesome, annoying. ·hindernis, -ssen, *n.* hindrance, obstacle. *wedren met hindernissen*, obstacle race. ·hinderpaal, -palen, *n.* obstacle. *hinderpalen in de weg leggen*, to lay obstacles in someone's path; *hinderpalen uit de weg ruimen*, to remove all obstacles. ·hinderwet, no pl., *n.* nuisances act.

·hinkelen, *v.i.* to play hopscotch. ·hinken, *v.i.* to limp; to play hopscotch. *op twee gedachten* ~, to hesitate between two opinions.

·hinniken, *v.i.* to neigh, whinny.

his·torie, -s *or* -riën, *n.* history; story. his·torisch, *a.* historic; historical.

hit, -tten, *n.* pony; skivvy.

·hitte, no pl., *n.* heat. ·hittegolf, -ven, *n.* heat wave.

·hittenwagen, -s, *n.* pony cart.

·hobbel, -s, *n.* knob, bump. ·hobbelde·bobbel, *adv.* bumpity-bumpity. ·hobbelen, *v.i.* to jolt, toss. ·hobbelig, *a.* bumpy. ·hobbelpaard, *n.n.* rocking-horse.

·hobo, -'s, *n.* oboe, hautboy. hobo·ïst, *n.* oboe-player.

hoe, *adv.* how. ~ *vraag je dat?*, why do you ask?; ~ *dan ook*, anyhow, anyway; ~ *zo?*, how is that?; ~ *dom hij ook zij*, however stupid he may be; ~ *gauwer* ~ *beter*, the sooner the better; ~ *langer* ~ *beter*, better and better; ~ *langer* ~ *erger*, worse and worse; *ik wil weten* ~ *of wat*, I want a definite answer. ¶*excl.* what! ¶*n.n. het* ~ *en wat*, the ins and outs.

hoed, *n.* hat. *hoge* ~, top hat, silk hat; *de* ~ *afnemen voor*, to raise one's hat to; *met de* ~ *in de hand*, hat in hand.

hoe·danig, *pron.* what (sort of). hoe·danigheid, -heden, *n.* quality, nature. *in zijn* ~ *van*, in his quality of.

·hoede, no pl., *n.* care; guard. *aan iemands* ~ *toevertrouwd*, placed in someone's care; *in veilige* ~, in safe custody *or* keeping; *op zijn* ~ *zijn voor*, to be on one's guard *or* on the alert against.

·hoededoos, -dozen, *n.* hatbox, bandbox. ·hoedelint, *n,n.* hatband.

·hoeden, *v.t.* to guard; to tend, look after (*flocks*). ¶*v.r. zich* ~ *voor*, to guard against.

·hoedenmaakster, -s, *n.* milliner. ·hoedenmaker, -s, *n.* hatter, hat-maker. ·hoedenwinkel, -s, *n.* hat shop. ·hoedepen, -nnen, *n.* hat pin.

·hoeder, -s, *n.* keeper.

·hoedje, -s, *n.n.* little hat. *onder één* ~ *spelen*, to be hand in glove; *onder een* ~ *te vangen*, very much humbled.

hoef, (1) -ven, *n.*, ·hoeve, -n, *n.* farm.

hoef, (2) -ven, *n.* hoof. ·hoefbeslag, no pl., *n.n.* horseshoes. ·hoefblad, *n.n.* coltsfoot. ·hoefgetrappel, no pl., *n.n.* clatter of hoofs. ·hoefijzer, -s, *n.n.* horseshoe. ·hoefnagel, -s, *n.* horseshoe nail. ·hoefslag, *n.* hoofbeat. hoefsmede·rij, *n.* farriery. ·hoefsmid, -smeden, *n.* farrier. ·hoefstal, -llen, *n.* shoeing frame.

hoege·naamd, *adv.* ~ *geen* . . ., no . . . whatever; ~ *niet*, not at all; ~ *niets*, absolutely nothing, nothing whatever.

hoek, *n.* corner; angle; hook. *in alle* ~*en en gaten*, in every nook and corner; *met een* ~ *van 45 graden*, at an angle of 45 degrees; *om de* ~, round the corner; *op de* ~, at the corner; *aardig uit de* ~ *komen*, to be unexpectedly witty. ·hoeker, -s, *n.* hooker. ·hoekig, *a.* angular. ·hoekje, -s, *n.n.* small corner. *het* ~ *om zijn*, to have turned the corner. ·hoeklijn, *n.* diagonal. ·hoekmeter, -s, *n.* goniometer; graphometer. ·hoekmeting, *n.* goniometry. ·hoekplaats, *n.* corner seat. ·hoekpunt, *n.n.* angular point. ·hoekswijs, *adv.* diagonally. ·hoeksteen, -stenen, *n.* cornerstone, keystone. ·hoektand, *n.* eyetooth, canine tooth.

hoen, -ders, *n.n.* hen, fowl. ·hoenderachtig, *a.* gallinaceous. ·hoenderei, -eren, *n.n.* chicken's egg. ·hoenderhof, -ven, *n.* poultry yard. ·hoenderhok, -kken, *n.n.* chicken house. ·hoenderpark, *n.n.* chicken farm. ·hoenderrek, -kken, *n n.*, ·hoenderstok, -kken, *n.* hen roost. ·hoenderteelt, no pl., *n.* chicken farming. ·hoentje, -s, *n.n.* pullet.

·hoepel, -s, *n.* hoop. *de* ~*s om een vat leggen*, to hoop a barrel; *met ijzeren* ~*s*, cross-hooped. ·hoepelbenen, pl. only, *n.n.* bandy-legs. *met* ~, bandy. ·hoepelen, *v.i.* to trundle *or* play with hoop. ·hoepelrok, -kken, *n.* crinoline.

hoer, *n.* whore, harlot. **hoe·reren, -reer,** *v.i.* to whore.

hoes, -zen, *n.* cover, dust sheet.

hoest, no pl., *n.* cough. **·hoestbonbon, -s,** *n.* coughdrop. **·hoestbui,** *n.* coughing fit. **·hoestdrank,** *n.* cough mixture. **·hoesten,** *v.i.* to cough. **·hoestmiddel,** *n.n.* cough medicine. **hoest·stillend,** *a.* pectoral.

·hoeve, -n, *n. See* **hoef** (1).

hoe·veel, *num.* how much, how many. **~ ook,** however much *or* many. **hoe·veel·heid, -heden,** *n.* quantity, amount. *in gelijke hoeveelheden,* in equal proportions; *in grote hoeveelheden,* in quantities. **hoe·veelste,** *num. de ~ zijn we vandaag?,* what is the date?; *de ~ keer is het?,* how many times is that?

·hoeven, hoef, *v.t.* to need.

hoe·ver(re), *adv. in ~,* how far, as to how far. **hoe·wel,** *c.* though, although.

hoe·zeer, *c.* however much.

hof, -ven, *n.* garden. ¶*n.n.* court. *aan het ~;* at court; *het ~ maken aan,* to court (*someone*). **·hofarts,** *n.* court physician. **·hof·beambte, -n,** *n.* court official. **·hofdame, -s,** *n.* lady-in-waiting, maid of honour. **·hofdichter, -s,** *n.* poet laureate. **·hofdienst,** *n.* duty at court. **·hoffelijk,** *a.* courteous; courtly. **·hoffelijkheid, -heden,** *n.* courtesy; courteousness. **·hofhouding,** *n.* royal household. **·hofje, -s,** *n.n.* almshouse. **·hofjonker, -s,** *n.* page (*at court*). **·hofkapel, -llen,** *n.* royal band. **·hofkapelaan, -s,** *n.* royal chaplain. **·hoflakei,** *n.* royal footman. **·hofleverancier, -s,** *n.* purveyor to royalty; by appointment. **·hofmaarschalk,** *n.* Lord Chancellor. **·hofmakerij,** *n.* courting. **·hofmeester, -s,** *n.* steward. **hofmeeste·res, -ssen,** *n.* stewardess. **·hofprediker, -s,** *n.* royal chaplain. **·hofstede, -n,** *n.* farm.

hoge, no pl., *n. God in den ~,* God on high; *uit den ~,* from on high. *See* **hoog.** **·hogelijk,** *adv.* highly, greatly. **·hogen, hoog,** *v.t.* to heighten. **·hogepriester, -s,** *n.* high priest. **·hogere,** *a. H~ Burgerschool,* secondary school. *See* **hoog. hoger·hand,** no pl., *n. van ~,* on high authority. **hoger·op,** *adv.* higher up. **hoger·wal,** no pl., *n.* wind-side. **hoge·school, -scholen,** *n.* university. *aan de ~,* in the university; *op de ~,* at college.

hok, -kken, *n.n.* kennel, sty, pen, hutch; shed. **·hokduif, -ven,** *n.* domestic pigeon. **·hokje, -s,** *n.n.* small shed; pigeonhole. **·hokken, hok,** *v.i.* to go wrong (*of machinery*). *er hokt iets aan,* there is a hitch somewhere; *het gesprek hokte,* conversation flagged; *bij elkaar ~,* to huddle together; *altijd thuis ~,* to remain cooped up at home. **·hokkerig,** *a.* poky. **·hokvast,** *a.* stay-at-home.

hol, *n.n.* cave, cavern; den, lair; haunt, den. ¶no pl., *n. op ~ slaan* or *raken* or *gaan,* to run away, bolt (*of horse*); *iemand het hoofd op ~ brengen,* to turn a person's head. ¶*-lle a.* hollow, empty; concave. *holle ogen,* sunken eyes; *holle stempel,* female die; *holle weg,* sunken road; *in het holle* or *~st van de nacht,* at dead of night. **·holbewoner, -s,** *n.* cave-dweller, troglodyte. **·holderde·bolder,** *adv.* helterskelter, head over heels. **·holheid,** no pl., *n.* hollowness. **·holklinkend,** *a.* hollow-sounding.

·Holland, *n.N.* Holland, the Netherlands. **·Hollander, -s,** *N.* Hollander, Dutchman. **·Hollands,** *a.* Dutch. **·Hollandse, -n,** *n.* Dutchwoman.

·hollen, hol, *v.i.* to run, scamper. *het is met hem ~ of stilstaan,* he always goes to extremes. **·hollend,** *a.* runaway (*horse*). **·holletje,** no pl., *n.n. het op een ~ zetten,* to break into a run. **hol·ogig,** *a.* hollow-eyed. **·holrond,** *a.* concave. **hol·rondheid,** no pl., *n.* concavity.

·holster, -s, *n.* holster.

·holte, -n, *n.* hollow, cavity; socket (*of eye*). **hol·wangig,** *a.* hollow-cheeked.

hom, -mmen, *n.* milt, soft roe. *met ~ en kuit,* hair and hide.

·hommel, -s, *n.* bumble-bee; drone.

·hommeles, no pl., *n.n. het is ~,* there are ructions; *'t wordt weer ~,* there is unpleasantness ahead.

homo·geen, -gene, *a.* homogenous. **homo·geni·teit,** no pl., *n.* homogeny. **homo·niem,** *n.n.* homonym.

homp, *n.* hunk, lump, chunk.

·hompelen, *v.i.* to hobble.

hond, *n.* dog; hound, cur. *jonge ~,* pup, puppy; *vliegende ~,* flying fox; *men moet geen slapende ~en wakker maken,* let sleeping dogs lie; *twee ~en vechten om een been, een derde loopt er ras mee heen,* when rogues fall out honest men gain; *de ~ in de pot vinden,* to get no meal. **·hondekar, -rren,** *n.* cart (*drawn by dog(s)*). **·hondenasyl,** *n.n.* dogs' home. **·honden·baantje, -s,** *n.n.* dog's job. **·hondenbrood,** no pl., *n.n.* dog biscuit(s). **·hondenfokker, -s,** *n.* dog breeder, dog fancier. **·hondenhok, -kken,** *n.n.* (dog-) kennel. **·hondenkost,** no pl., *n.* dog's food. **·hondenleven,** no pl., *n.n.* dog's life. **·hondententoonstelling,** *n.* dog show. **·hondenwacht,** *n.* mid(dle) watch. **·hondenweer,** no pl., *n.n.* beastly weather. **·hondenziekte,** no pl., *n.* distemper.

·honderd, *num.* hundred. **~ tegen één,** hundred to one. ¶*n.n.* hundred. *in het ~ liggen,* to be at sixes and sevens; *in het ~ lopen,* to go wrong. **·honderdduizend,** *num.* hundred thousand. **·honderdjarig,** *a.* hundred years old, centenary. **·honderdmaal,** *adv.* hundred times. **·honderdtal, -llen,** *n.n.* hundred. **·honderdvoud,** *n.n.* multiple of hundred. **·honderdvoudig,** *a. & adv.* hundredfold, centuple. **·honderdwerf,** *adv.* hundredfold, centuple.

·**hondewagen, -s,** *n.* cart (drawn by dog(s)). **honds,** *a.* churlish. ·**hondsaap, -sapen,** *n.* baboon, cynocephalus. ·**hondsdagen,** pl. only, *n.* dog days. **honds·dolheid,** no pl., *n.* rabies; hydrophobia. ·**hondsdraf,** no pl., *n.* ground ivy. ·**hondshaai,** *n.* lesser spotted dogfish. ·**hondsheid,** no pl., *n.* churlishness. ·**hondsnetel, -s,** *n.* white nettle. ·**hondsroos, -rozen,** *n.* briar rose.

·**honen, hoon,** *v.i.* & *v.t.* to taunt; to jeer at. ·**honend,** *a.* scornful, derisive.

Hon·gaar, -garen, *n.* Hungarian. **Honga·rije,** *n.N.* Hungary.

·**honger,** no pl., *n.* hunger. ~ *hebben,* to be hungry; ~ *lijden,* to starve, go hungry; *van* ~ *sterven,* to die of starvation. ·**hongerdood,** no pl., *n.* death from hunger. *de* ~ *sterven,* to die of starvation. ·**hongeren,** *v.i.* to hunger. ~ *naar,* to hunger after *or* for. ·**hongerig,** *a.* hungry. ·**hongerlijder, -s,** *n.* starveling. ·**hongerloon, -lonen,** *n.n.* starvation wages. ·**hongersnood,** no pl., *n.* famine. **hongerstaking,** *n.* hunger-strike.

·**honig,** no pl., *n.,* ·**honing,** no pl., *n.* honey. ·**honingbeer, -beren,** *n.* honey bear. ·**honingbij,** *n.* honey bee. ·**honingdauw,** no pl., *n.* honeydew. ·**honingraat, -raten,** *n.* honeycomb. ·**honingrijk,** *a.* rich in honey. ·**honingzeem,** no pl., *n.n.* virgin honey. ·**honingzoet,** *a.* honey-sweet, honied; mellifluous.

honk, no pl., *n.n.* home (*in games*). *bij* ~ *blijven,* to stay at home.

·**honneponnig,** *a.,* ·**honnig,** *a.* dinky, sweet.

hon·neurs, pl. only, *n.* honours. *de* ~ *waarnemen,* to do the honours. **hono·rair,** *a.* honorary. **hono·rarium, -ia,** *n.n.* fee. **hono·reren, -reer,** *v.t.* to honour (*bill*). *niet* ~, to dishonour.

hoofd, *n.n.* head; chief. *een* ~ *groter,* taller by a head; *zoveel* ~*en zoveel zinnen,* many men many minds; *een zwaar* ~ *hebben in,* to be doubtful about the outcome of; *het* ~ *bieden aan,* to resist; *zich het* ~ *breken over,* to rack one's brain over; *het* ~ *in de schoot leggen,* to give in; *mijn* ~ *staat er niet naar,* I do not feel like it now; *ze staken de* ~*en bij elkaar,* they put their heads together; *zijn* ~ *stoten,* to knock one's head *or* to meet with a rebuff; *het* ~ *verliezen,* to lose one's head; *het* ~ *niet verliezen,* to keep one's head; *veel aan het* ~ *hebben,* to be terribly busy; *niet wel bij het* ~ *zijn,* not to be right in the head; *door het* ~ *gaan,* to slip one's mind; *iets over het* ~ *zien,* to overlook a thing; *uit het* ~, by heart. ¶*prefix.* chief, main, principal. ·**hoofdaanlegger, -s,** *n.* prime mover, instigator. ·**hoofdakte, -s,** *n.* head teacher's certificate. ·**hoofdaltaar, -taren,** *n.n.* high altar. ·**hoofdarbeid,** no pl., *n.* brainwork. ·**hoofdartikel, -s, *n.n.*** leading article, editorial. ·**hoofdbegrip,**

-**ppen,** *n.n.* fundamental principle. ·**hoofdbestuur, -sturen,** *n.n.* central committee. ·**hoofdbreken,** no pl., *n.n.* racking of the brain. ·**hoofdbrekend,** *a.* complicated. ·**hoofddeksel, -s, *n.n.*** head-dress; headgear. ·**hoofddoek,** *n.* head-cloth. ·**hoofddoel,** *n.n.* main object. ·**hoofdeinde, -n,** *n.n.* head (*of bed, table*). ·**hoofdelijk,** *a.* per capita. ~*e omslag,* poll-tax; ~*e stemming,* voting by roll call; ~ *onderwijs,* individual teaching. ¶*adv.* ~ *aansprakelijk,* severally liable. ·**hoofdeloos, -loze,** *a.* headless. ·**hoofdgeld,** *n.n.* head-money; capitation fee. ·**hoofdgeleiding,** *n.* main (*of gas, water, electricity*). ·**hoofdgetal, -llen,** *n.n.* cardinal number. ·**hoofdig,** *a.* obstinate, headstrong. ·**hoofdingenieur, -s,** *n.* chief engineer. ·**hoofdinspecteur, -s,** *n.* chief inspector. ·**hoofdkaas,** no pl., *n.* brawn (*cooked meat*). ·**hoofdknik, -kken,** *n.* nod. ·**hoofdkussen, -s,** *n.n.* pillow. ·**hoofdkwartier,** *n.n.* headquarters. ·**hoofdleiding,** *n.* general management. ·**hoofdletter, -s,** *n.* capital (letter). ·**hoofdlijn,** *n.* main line, trunk line. ·**hoofdmacht,** *n.* main body (*of army*). ·**hoofdonderwijzer, -s,** *n.* headmaster (*of primary school*). ·**hoofdpersoon, -sonen,** *n.* principal person *or* character. ·**hoofdpijn,** *n.* headache. ·**hoofdredacteur, -s,** *n.* editor-in-chief. ·**hoofdrol, -llen,** *n.* leading part. ·**hoofdschudden,** no pl., *n.n.* shake of the head. ·**hoofdstuk, -kken,** *n.n.* chapter. ·**hoofdtooisel, -s,** *n.n.* ornamental head-dress. ·**hoofdtrek, -kken,** *n.* main feature. *in hoofdtrekken,* in outline. ·**hoofdverdienste, -n,** *n.* chief merit; principal source of income. ·**hoofdverkeersweg,** *n.* arterial road. ·**hoofdwindstreken,** pl. only, *n.* cardinal points of the compass. ·**hoofdzaak, -zaken,** *n.* main point. *in* ~, on the whole, substantially. **hoofd·zakelijk,** *adv.* chiefly, mainly ·**hoofdzin, -nnen,** *n.* principal sentence.

hoofs, *a.* & *adv.* courtly. ·**hoofsheid,** no pl., *n.* courtliness.

hoog, hoge, *a.* high; tall; exalted. *het hoge Noorden,* the extreme North, the Arctic region; *de Hoge Raad,* the Supreme Court, *twee voet* ~, two foot deep (*snow*). ¶*adv.* highly. *of hij* ~ *of laag springt,* whether he likes it or no; *twee* ~, on the second floor. ·**hoogaars, -zen,** *n.* fishing smack. ·**hoogachten,** *v.t.* to esteem. ·**hoogachting,** no pl., *n.* esteem, regard. **hoog·adellijk,** *a.* most noble. ·**hoogbejaard,** *a.* very aged. **hoog·dravend,** *a.* highflown, high-falutin. **hoogedel·achtbaar, -bare,** *a.* (Right) Honourable (*title of burgomasters of big towns*). **hoogedelge·streng,** *a.* (Right) Honourable (*title of certain high officials and officers*). **hoogeer·waard,** *a.* Right Reverend (*title of certain high members of the clergy*). ·**hooggaand,** *a.* ~*e ruzie,* flaming quarrel. ·**hooggeacht,** *a.* highly esteemed. ·**hooggebergte, -n,** *n.n.* high mountain range. ·**hooggeboren,** *a.* Right Honourable (*ducal title*). ·**hooggeleerd,** *a.* (*title given to professors*). **hoogge·plaatst,** *a.* highly placed. **hoogge·schat, -tte,** *a.* highly valued. **hoogge·spannen,** *a.* highly strung. **hoog·hartig,** *a.* proud, haughty. **hoog·hartigheid,** no pl., *n.* haughtiness. ·**hoogheid, -heden,** *n.* highness; Highness (*title of prince*). ·**hooghouden,** *v.t.s.,* *irr.* to uphold, keep up. ·**hoogland,** *n.n.* highland. ·**hooglander, -s,** *n.* highlander. ·**hoogleraar, -s,** *n.* professor. ·**hoogleraars-ambt,** *n.n.* professorship. ·**Hooglied,** no pl., *n.n.* the Song of Songs. **hoog·lopend,** *a.* violent. ·**hoogmis, -ssen,** *n.* high Mass. ·**hoogmoed,** no pl., *n.* pride. **hoog·moedig,** *a.* proud, haughty. ·**hoogmoedswaanzin,** no pl., *n.* megalomania. **hoog·mogend,** *a.* High and Mighty (*title of Dutch Republic M.P.s*). **hoog·nodig,** *a.* urgently needed. ¶*adv.* urgently. **hoog·nodige,** no pl., *n.n.* *het ~,* the necessities. ·**hoogoven, -s,** *n.* blast furnace. ·**hoogrood, -rode,** *a.* bright red; flushed. ·**hoogschatten, schat hoog,** *v.t.s.* to esteem highly. ·**hoogschatting,** no pl., *n.* high esteem. ·**hoogspanning,** no pl., *n.* high tension. **hoogst,** *a.* highest; supreme; utmost. ¶*adv.* highly, extremely; most. ¶no pl., *n.n. op zijn ~,* at the most or at its height; *ten ~e,* at the most or extremely. ·**hoogstaand,** *a.* eminent, distinguished; of high moral character. **hoogst·aangeslagene, -n,** *n.* more highly taxed. ·**hoogsteigen,** *a. in ~ persoon,* in person, in the flesh. ·**hoogstens,** *adv.* at the most, at the outside. ·**hoogstwaar-schijnlijk,** *a.* highly probable. ¶*adv.* most probably. ·**hoogte, -n,** *n.* height; pitch; altitude; elevation. *de ~ ingaan,* to go up, rise; *in de ~ steken,* to praise, boost; *op de ~ blijven van,* to remain up-to-date with; *iemand op de ~ brengen,* to tell a person all about it; *op de ~ houden,* to keep informed; *zich op de ~ stellen van,* to gather full information about or to acquaint oneself with; *tot op zekere ~,* to a certain extent; *uit de ~,* haughtily, off-hand. ·**hoogtecirkel, -s,** *n.* circle of altitude. ·**hoogtelijn,** *n.* perpendicular. ·**hoogtem..ter, -s,** *n.* altimeter. ·**hoogtepunt,** no pl., *n.n.* culminating point, peak. ·**hoogteroer,** *n.n.* elevation rudder. ·**hoogtij,** no pl., *n.n. ~ vieren,* to reign supreme or to run riot. ·**hoogtijd,** *n.* high festival. ·**hoogveen, -venen,** *n.n.* moorland peat, peat-moor. ·**hoogverraad,** no pl., *n.n.* high treason. ·**hoogvlakte, -n,** *n.* plateau. **hoog·waardig,** *a.* venerable. **hoog·waardig-heid, -heden,** *n.* Eminence (*title of certain high prelates*). **hoog·waardigheidsbekleder, -s,** *n.* dignitary. **hoog·water,** no pl., *n.n.* high tide. *het is ~,* the tide is in; *met*

~, at high tide. **hoog·welgeboren,** *a.* Right Honourable (*title of certain members of nobility*).

hooi, no pl., *n.n.* hay. *~ keren,* to toss hay; *te ~ en te gras,* in a haphazard way; *te veel ~ op zijn vork nemen,* to bite off more than one can chew. ·**hooiberg,** *n.* haystack, hayrick. ·**hooiboter,** no pl., *n.* butter (*from hay-fed cattle*). ·**hooibouw,** no pl., *n.* haymaking. ·**hooibroei,** no pl., *n.* smouldering of hay. ·**hooien,** *v.t.* to make hay. ·**hooikist,** *n.* hay-box. ·**hooi-koorts,** no pl., *n.* hay fever. ·**hooimaand,** no pl., *n.* hay-month, July. ·**hooimijt,** *n.* hayrick. ·**hooiopper, -s,** *n.* haycock. ·**hooischelf, -ven,** *n.* haystack. ·**hooischuur, -schuren,** *n.* hay-barn. ·**hooistapel, -s,** *n.* haystack. ·**hooivork,** *n.* pitchfork. ·**hooi-wagen, -s,** *n.* hay waggon; daddy-long-legs; harvest-spider. ·**hooizolder, -s,** *n.* hayloft.

hoon, no pl., *n.* scorn, taunt(s), derision. ·**hoongelach,** no pl., *n.n.* scornful laughter.

hoop, hopen, *n.* heap, pile. *een hele ~,* heaps and heaps; *een ~ geld,* heaps of money; *een ~ leugens,* a pack of lies; *een ~ moeite,* lots of trouble; *te ~ lopen,* to gather in a crowd. ¶no pl., *n.* hope, hopes. *~ hebben op,* to have hopes of; *~ geven,* to give or hold out hope; *op ~ leven,* to live in hope; *op ~ van,* in the hope of. ·**hoopvol, -lle,** *a.* hopeful.

·**hoorbaar, -bare,** *a.* audible. ·**hoorbaarheid,** no pl., *n.* audibility. ·**hoorbuis, -zen,** *n.* ear-trumpet. ·**hoorder, -s,** *n.* hearer.

hoorn, -s, *n.* horn; bugle; mouthpiece or receiver (*telephone*). *~ van overvloed,* horn of plenty, cornucopia. ·**hoornachtig,** *a.* horny. ·**hoornblazer, -s,** *n.* bugler, trumpeter. ·**hoornen,** *a.* (made of) horn. ·**hoorngeschal,** no pl., *n.n.* flourish of trumpets, sound of bugles. ·**hoornig,** *a.* horny. ·**hoornslang,** *n.* horned viper. ·**hoornsnavel,** *n.* hornbill. ·**hoornuil,** *n.* horned owl. ·**hoornvee,** no pl., *n.n.* horned cattle. ·**hoornvlies, -zen,** *n.n.* cornea.

hoos, hozen, *n.* waterspout; bailer. ·**hoosvat,** *n.n.* bailer (*scoop*).

hop, no pl., *n.* hop; hops. ·**hopbouw,** no pl., *n.* hop-growing.

·**hopeloos, -loze,** *a.* hopeless. ¶*adv.* hopelessly; beyond hope. **hope·loosheid,** no pl., *n.* hopelessness. **hopen, hoop,** *v.t.* to hope; to heap. *het beste ~,* to hope for the best. ¶*v.i. ~ op,* to hope for.

·**hopje, -s,** *n.n.* (type of) caramel.

·**hopman, hoplieden,** *n.* captain; scout-master.

·**hoppen, hop,** *v.t.* to hop (*in brewing*).

·**hopper, -s,** *n.* hopper.

·**hopstaak, -staken,** *n.* hop pole.

·**horde, -n,** *n.* horde, troop.

·**horen, -s,** *n.* See **hoorn;** behoren. ¶**hoor,** *v.t.* to hear. *hoor!,* you see! or you know!;

hoor eens!, I say!; *laten* ~, to produce
(*sound*) *or* to send news; *laat eens* ~,
out with it; *het laat zich* ~ *dat*. one can
take it that . . .; *wie niet* ~ *wil moet
voelen*, let him learn from experience.
¶no pl., *n.n. een leven dat* ~ *en zien je
vergaan*, a noise fit to wake the dead.
·**horige, -n**, *n*. serf, villein.
·**horizon, -s**, *n*. horizon. *aan de* ~, on the
horizon; *onder de* ~, below the horizon.
horizon·taal, -tale, *a*. horizontal.
·**horlepijp**, *n*. hornpipe.
hor·loge, -s, *n.n*. watch. *op mijn* ~, by my
watch. **hor·logeveer, -veren**, *n*. watch-
spring. **hor·logewijzer, -s**, *n*. watch-
hand.
·**horrelvoet**, *n*. club-foot.
·**horretje, -s**, *n.n*. gauze window-screen.
hort, *n*. jolt, jerk. *met* ~*en en stoten*, jerkily,
by fits and starts. ·**horten**, *v.i*. to jolt;
to halt (*of conversation*).
hor·tensia, -'s, *n*. hydrangea.
·**horzel, -s**, *n*. hornet, gad-fly. ◢
·**hospita, -'s**, *n*. landlady. **·hospitaal, -talen**,
n.n. hospital, infirmary. *in het* ~, in hospital. **hospitaalsoldaat, -daten**, *n*. hospital
orderly.
·**hossen, hos**, *v.i*. to follow a band dancing
and shouting.
·**hostie, -tiën** *or* **-s**, *n*. host, consecrated
wafer.
hot, *int*. right! (*to horse*). ¶no pl., *n.n. hij
weet van* ~ *noch haar*, he is profoundly
ignorant; ~ *en haar door elkaar*, mixed up,
higgledy-piggledy.
·**hotsen**, *v.i*. to shake, jolt.
hou, *a*. ~ *en trouw*, loyal and true.
·**houdbaar, -bare**, *a*. tenable; maintainable.
·**houdbaarheid**, no pl., *n*. tenability.
·**houden**, *v.t., irr*. to hold (*in hand*); to
keep, retain; to hold, contain; to keep
(*promise*); to keep on (*course*); to keep
(*shop*); to hold (*meeting*); to keep, observe
(*feast day*); to make (*speech*). *niet te* ~,
not to be kept back; *het ervoor* ~ *dat*,
to take it that; ~ *voor*, to (mis)take for;
iets voor zich ~, to keep something
to oneself; *uit elkaar* ~, to distinguish.
¶*v.i., irr*. to hold, keep. *links or rechts* ~,
to keep to the left *or* to the right; ~ *met*,
to hold with; *het zal erom* ~, it will
be touch and go; ~ *van*, to like, love. ¶*v.r.
zich* ~ *alsof*, to pretend; *zich doof* ~,
to sham deaf; *zich goed* ~, to keep a
straight face *or* to bear up; *zich* ~ *aan*, to
keep to, abide by; *zich* ~ *bij*, to keep to.
·**houder, -s**, *n*. holder; bearer. ·**houding**,
n. carriage, attitude. *een* ~ *aannemen*,
to adopt an attitude; *in de* ~ *staan*, to
stand to attention; *zich een* ~ *geven*, to
cover one's confusion.
hout, no pl., *n.n*. wood, timber; wood, plantation. *alle* ~ *is geen timmerhout*, you can't
make a silk purse out of a sow's ear.

·**houtaankap**, no pl., *n*. timber-felling.
·**houtaanplant**, no pl., *n*. afforestation.
·**houtachtig**, *a*. woody. ·**houtblok, -kken**,
n.n. block *or* log of wood. ·**houtduif, -ven**,
n. wood-pigeon. ·**houten**, *a*. wooden.
·**houterig**, *a*. wooden, stiff. ·**houterigheid**,
no pl., *n*. woodenness. ·**houtgewas, -ssen**,
n.n. wood (*trees*). ·**houtgravure, -s**, *n.
wood*-engraving. ·**houthakker, -s**, *n*.
wood-cutter. ·**houthandel, -s**, *n*. timber-
trade; timber-yard. ·**houthandelaar, -s**, *n*.
timber-merchant. ·**houthouwer, -s**, *n*.
hewer of wood. ·**houtig**, *a*. woody. ·**houtje,
-s**, *n.n*. small stick. *op een* ~ *bijten*, to go
hungry; *iets op zijn eigen* ~ *doen*, to do
something off one's own bat. ·**houtkever,
-s**, *n*. death-watch beetle. ·**houtkrullen**,
pl. only, *n*. wood shavings. ·**houtluis, -zen**,
n. wood-louse. ·**houtmijt**, *n*. wood-pile.
·**houtmolm**, no pl., *n*. mould (*decayed
wood*). ·**houtrijk**, *a*. woody, wooded.
·**houtskool**, no pl., *n*. charcoal. ·**houtsne(d)e,
sneden**, *n*. woodcut. ·**houtsnijwerk**, no pl.,
n.n. woodcarving. ·**houtsnip, -ppen**, *n*.
woodcock. ·**houtspaander, -s**, *n*. chip of
wood. ·**houttuin**, *n*. timber-yard. ·**houtvester, -s**, *n*. forester. **houtveste·rij**, *n*.
forestry. ·**houtvlotter, -s**, *n*. raftsman,
lumberjack. ·**houtwagen, -s**, *n*. timber-
waggon. ·**houtwerf, -ven**, *n*. timber-yard.
·**houtworm**, *n*. woodworm. ·**houtzaag-
molen, -s**, *n*. wood-mill. ·**houtzager, -s**, *n.*
sawyer. **houtzage·rij**, *n*. saw-mill.
·**houvast**, no pl., *n.n*. hold, support; foothold.
geen ~ *hebben aan*, to have no grip on
or to have nothing to go by.
houw, *n*. cut, gash. ·**houwdegen, -s**, *n*.
broadsword. **hou·weel, -welen**, *n.n.*
pickaxe, mattock. ·**houwen**, *v.i., str*. to
hew; to quarry. ·**houwer, -s**, *n*. hewer.
ho·vaardig, *a*. proud, haughty. **hovaar·dij**,
no pl., *n*. pride, haughtiness.
·**hoveling**, *n*. courtier. **hove·nier, -s**, *n.*
gardener.
·**hozen, hoos**, *v.t*. to bail, scoop.
hu!, *int*. gee up.
hui, no pl., *n*. whey.
·**huichelaar, -s**, *n*. hypocrite. ·**huichelachtig**,
a. hypocritical, dissembling. **huichela·rij**,
n. hypocrisy, dissimulation. ·**huichelen**,
v.i. to dissemble. ¶*v.t*. to sham, simulate.
huid, *n*. skin; hide. *een dikke* ~ *hebben*,
to be thick-skinned; *iemand de* ~ *vol
schelden*, to hurl abuse at someone;
iemand op zijn ~ *geven*, to beat a person.
·**huidarts**, *n*. dermatologist. ·**huidenkoper,
-s**, *n*. fell-monger.
·**huidig**, *a*. present-day. *ten* ~*en dage*,
nowadays; *tot op de* ~*e dag* to this
day.
·**huidskleur**, *n*. colour of the skin, complexion.
·**huidvetten, vet**, *v.t*. to dress leather.
·**huidvetter, -s**, *n*. leather-dresser, currier.
huidvette·rij, *n*. curriery. ·**huidworm**, *n*.

Guinea worm. ·huidzenuw, *n.* cutaneous nerve. ·huidziekte, -n. *n.* skin disease.
huif, -ven, *n.* coif; tilt. ·huifkar, -rren, *n.* tilt cart.
huig, *n.* uvula.
huik, *n.* hooded cloak. *de ~ naar de wind hangen,* to temporize.
·huilbui, *n.* fit of crying. ·huilebalk, *n.* crybaby. ·huilen, *v.i.* to howl, whine; to cry, weep. *'t is om te ~,* it's enough to make the angels weep; *het ~ stond hem nader dan het lachen,* he could have cried. ·huilerig, *a.* tearful.
huis, -zen, *n.n.* house; home. *~ en haard,* hearth and home; *~ van bewaring,* detention prison; *heer or vrouw or zoon des huizes,* master *or* mistress *or* son of the house; *men kan huizen op hem bouwen,* he is utterly reliable; *met de deur in ~ vallen,* to plunge into a subject; *aan ~ gebonden,* tied to the house; *aan ~ komen bij,* to be on visiting terms with; *langs de huizen,* from door to door; *naar ~ gaan,* to go home; *te ~. See* thuis; *ten huize van,* at the home of; *te mijnen huize,* at my house; *van ~,* away from home; *van ~ gaan,* to leave home; *van goeden huize,* of good family; *van ~ uit,* by birth, originally. ·huisapotheek, -theken, *n.* medicine chest. ·huisarchitectuur, no pl., *n.* domestic architecture. ·huisarrest, no pl., *n.n. ~ hebben,* to be confined to quarters *or* (*fig.*) to have to stay at home. ·huisarts, *n.* family doctor. ·huisbaas, -bazen, *n.* landlord. ·huisbakken, *a.* home-made. ·huisbediende, -n, *n.* domestic. ·huisbel, -llen, *n.* door-bell. ·huisbewaarder, -s, *n.* caretaker. ·huisbezoek, *n.n.* district *or* parish visiting. ·huisbraak, no pl., *n.* housebreaking. ·huisbrand, no pl., *n.* household fuel. ·huisdier, *n.n.* domestic animal. ·huisdokter, -s, *n.* family doctor. ·huiselijk, *a.* domestic; homely, home-loving; domesticated. *het ~ leven,* home life; *de ~e kring,* the family circle. ¶ *adv.* in homely fashion. ·huiselijkheid, no pl., *n.* domesticity. ·huisgenoot, -noten, *n.* housemate, member of the family. ·huisgenote, -n, *n.* housemate, member of the family (*female*). ·huisgezin, -nnen, *n.n.* family, household. ·huisgoden, pl. only, *n.* household gods. ·huisheer, -heren, *n.* landlord; master of the house. huis·houdelijk, *a.* domestic; economical; informal. *voor ~ gebruik,* for household use. huis·houdelijkheid, no pl., *n.* economy. ·huishouden, *v.i.s., irr.* to keep house; to create havoc. *er is geen huis met hem te houden,* he is unmanageable; *vreselijk ~ onder,* to create terrible havoc among. ¶ -s, *n.n.* household. *het ~ doen,* to run the house; *een ~ opzetten,* to set up house; *een ~ van Jan Steen,* a Bohemian sort of household. ·huishouding, *n.* household;

housekeeping. ·huishoudkunde, no pl., *n.* economy, domestic science. ·huishoudschool, -scholen, *n.* school of domestic science. ·huishoudster, -s, *n.* housekeeper. ·huishuur, -huren, *n.* rent. ·huisje, -s, *n.n.* small house; shell (*of snail*); case. *elk ~ heeft z'n kruisje,* every family has a skeleton in the cupboard. ·huisjesmelker, -s, *n.* extortionate landlord of poor property, rack-renter. ·huisjesslak, -kken, *n.* snail. ·huiskamer, -s, *n.* living-room. ·huisknecht, *n.* manservant. ·huislook, no pl., *n.n.* houseleek. ·huismiddel, *n.n.* domestic remedy. ·huismarter, -s, *n.* stone-marten. ·huismoeder, -s, *n.* mother (of the family). ·huismus, -ssen, *n.* sparrow; stay-at-home. ·huisonderwijs, no pl., *n.n.* private tuition. ·huisraad, no pl., *n.n.* furniture; household effects. ·huissleutel, -s, *n.* front door key. ·huisvader, -s, *n.* father (of the family). ·huisvesten, *v.t.* to house, accommodate. ·huisvesting, no pl., *n.* housing, accommodation. *~ geven or verlenen,* to give house-room to, take in. ·huisvlijt, no pl., *n.* home industry. ·huisvrede, no pl., *n.* domestic peace. ·huisvredebreuk, no pl., *n.* disturbance of domestic peace. ·huisvriend, *n.* friend of the family. ·huisvrouw, *n.* housewife. ·huiswaarts, *adv.* homeward(s). ·huiswerk, no pl., *n.n.* homework; housework. ·huiszoeking, *n.* housesearch; house-to-house search. *~ doen,* to search a house; *machtiging tot ~,* search warrant. ·huiszwaluw, *n.* (house-) martin.
·huiveren, *v.i.* to shudder, shiver. *~ bij de gedachte,* to shudder at the thought; *~ voor,* to shrink from. ·huiverig, *a.* shivery; hesitant. ·huiverigheid, no pl., *n.* chilliness; hesitation. ·huivering, *n.* shudder; shiver. huivering·wekkend, *a.* horrible.
·huize, *n.n. See* huis. ·huizen, huis, *v.i. & v.t.* to house. ·huizenhoog, -hoge, *a.* towering. ·huizenkant, no pl., *n.* wall side of pavement. ·huizennood, -noden, *n.* housing shortage. ·huizing, *a.* habitation.
·hulde, no pl., *n.* homage; tribute. *~ brengen or doen or bewijzen aan,* to pay homage to. ·huldebetoon, no pl., *n.n.,* ·huldeblijk, *n.n.* token of homage, tribute. ·huldigen, *v.t.* to pay *or* render homage (to). ·huldiging, *n.* homage; inauguration.
hulk, *n.* vessel. *de ~ van staat,* the ship of state.
·hullen, hul, *v.t.* to envelop, wrap; to shroud (*in mystery*).
hulp, no pl., *n.* help, aid, assistance ; relief, succour. *~ in de huishouding,* lady help, lady companion ; *~ zoeken bij,* to seek the help of ; *om ~ roepen,* to call for help ; *te ~ komen,* to come to the rescue;

zonder ~, single-handed, unaided. ·hulp-akte, -s, *n.* assistant teacher's certificate. ·hulpbank, *n.* loan office. hulpbe·hoevend, *a.* needy, destitute. hulpbe·hoevendheid, no pl., *n.* destitution ; infirmity. ·hulp-betoon, no pl., *n.n.* assistance. ·hulpbron, -nnen, *n.* resource. ·hulpeloos, -loze, *a.* helpless. hulpe·loosheid, no pl., *n.* helpless-ness. ·hulpgebouw, *n.n.* temporary structure. ·hulpgeroep, no pl., *n.n.* cries for help. ·hulpkantoor, -toren, *n.n.* sub-office. ·hulpkas, -ssen, *n.* relief fund. ·hulpkruiser, -s, *n.* auxiliary cruiser. ·hulplijn, *n.* auxiliary line. ·hulpmiddel, *n.n.* remedy ; expedient. ·hulppersoneel, no pl., *n.n.* emergency staff. ·hulpspoorweg, *n.* auxiliary railway. hulp·vaardig, *a.* helpful, willing to help. hulp·vaardigheid, no pl., *n.* readiness to help. ·hulpwerk-woord, *n.n.* auxiliary (*verb*).
huls, -zen, *n.* pod, husk ; case ; cartridge *or* shell case. ·hulsel, -s, *n.n.* cover.
hulst, no pl., *n.* holly.
hum !, *int.* hem !
humani·ora, pl. only, *n.n.* humanistic studies. humani·teit, *n.* humaneness, humanity.
hu·meur, *n.n.* humour, mood. *in zijn* ~, in a good temper ; *uit zijn* ~, in a bad temper, out of sorts. hu·meurig, *a.* moody, capricious. hu·meurigheid, no pl., *n.* moodiness.
·hummel, -s, *n.* tot (*child*).
·humor, no pl., *n.* humour. humo·ristisch, *a.* humorous, humoristic.
hun, *pron.* their ; (to) them. *met* ~ *vieren*, (the) four of them ; *het hunne*, theirs ; *de hunnen*, theirs, their relatives.
·hunebed, -dden, *n.n.* barrow (*ancient tomb*).
·hunkeren, *v.i.* ~ *naar*, to hanker after, hunger for.
·hunne(n), *pron. See* hun. ·hunnent, *pron. te* ~ (*stil.*), at their house. ·hunnentwege, *adv.* on their behalf, for their sake. ·hunnentwil, *adv.* for their sake.
·huppelen, *v.i.* to hop.
hups, *a.* strapping.
·huren, huur, *v.t.* to hire, rent; to engage (*servant*).
·hurken, pl. only, *n. op de* ~ *zitten*, to squat. ¶*v.i.* to squat.
hut, -tten, *n.* hut, cottage; (ship's) cabin. ·hutkoffer, -s, *n.* cabin trunk.
·hutsen, *v.t.* to shake up. ·hutspot, no pl., *n.* stew; hotchpotch.
huur, huren, *n.* hire, rent. *te* ~, to be let. ·huurauto, -'s, *n.* taxi, hired car. ·huur-baas, -bazen, *n.* landlord. ·huurceel, -celen, *n.*, ·huurcontract, *n.n.* lease. ·huurcommissie, -s, *n.* rent restriction committee. ·huurder, -s, *n.* tenant. ·huurgeld, *n.n.* rent(-money), hire. ·huur-huis, -zen, *n.n.* rented house. ·huurkantoor, -toren, *n.n.* registry office (*for servants*). ·huurkoetsier, -s, *n.* cabman. ·huurkoop,

no pl., *n.* hire-purchase. ·huurleger, -s, *n.n.* army of mercenaries. ·huurling, *n.* hireling, mercenary. ·huurrijtuig, *n.n.* hackney carriage. ·huursom, -mmen, *n.* rent-money. ·huurster, -s, *n.* tenant (*female*). ·huurtijd, *n.* tenancy. ·huur-voorwaarde, -n, *n.* terms of the lease. ·huurwaarde, -n, *n.* rental value. ·huurwet, -tten, *n.* rent act.
·huwbaar, -bare, *a.* marriageable, nubile. ·huwelijk, *n.n.* marriage; wedlock; wedding. *een* ~ *aangaan* or *sluiten*, to contract a marriage; *in het* ~ *treden* or *zich in het* ~ *begeven*, to enter into matrimony; *ten* ~ *vragen*, to propose to; *uit het eerste* ~, (*child*) of the first marriage. ¶*a. de* ~*e staat*, the married state. ·huwelijks, *a.* ~*e voorwaarden*, marriage settlement. ·huwelijksaanzoek, *n.n.* proposal *or* offer of marriage. ·huwelijksadvertentie, -s, *n.* matrimonial advertisement. ·huwelijks-afkondiging, *n.* banns. *de* ~ *voorlezen*, to publish the banns. ·huwelijksakte, -n, *n.* marriage lines. ·huwelijksband, *n.* bond of marriage. ·huwelijksbootje, no pl., *n.n. in het* ~ *stappen*, to embark upon marriage. ·huwelijksfeest, *n.n.* wedding (-party). ·huwelijksgeluk, no pl., *n.n.* conjugal bliss. ·huwelijksleven, no pl., *n.n.* married life. ·huwelijksvoorwaarden, pl. only, *n.* marriage settlement. ·huwen, *v.t.* to wed, marry. ¶*v.i.* ~ *met*, to marry.
hu·zaar, -zaren, *n.* hussar. hu·zarensla, no pl., *n.* Russian salad.
hya·cint, *n.* hyacinth.
hy·draulisch, *a.* hydraulic. hydro·graaf, -grafen, *n.* hydrographer.
hyper·bool, -bolen, *n.* hyperbole.
hyp·nose, no pl., *n.* hypnosis. hypnoti·seren, -seer, *v.t.* to hypnotize. hypnoti·seur, -s, *n.* hypnotist.
hypothe·cair, *a.* ~*e acte*, mortgage deed; ~*e obligatie*, mortgage bond; ~*e schuld*, mortgage debt. hypo·theek, -theken, *n.* mortgage. *met* ~ *bezwaard* or *belast*, mortgaged. hypo·theekbank, *n.* mortgage bank. hypothe·keren, -keer, *v.t.* to mort-gage.
hypo·these, -n, *n.* hypothesis.
hyste·rie, no pl., *n.* hysteria. hys·terisch, *a.* hysterical.

I

·ibis, -ssen, *n.* ibis.
ide·aal, -dealen, *n.n.* ideal. *een* ~ *van een* … ; an ideal. … . ¶-deale, *a.* ideal. ideali·seren, -seer, *v.t.* to idealize. idea·lisme, no pl., *n.n.* idealism. idea·listisch, *a.* idealistic. ¶*adv.* idealistically. i·dee, -deeën, *n.n.* idea; notion; opinion. *ik heb zo'n* ~ *dat*, I have a vague idea that; *in het* ~ *dat*, under the

impression that; *naar mijn* ~, in my opinion; *iemand op het* ~ *brengen*, to put the thought into someone's head; *op het* ~ *komen*, to hit upon an idea. **ide·ëel, -deële,** *a.* ideal, imaginary, notional.
·idem, *adv.* item, likewise.
iden·tiek, *a.* identical. **identifi·ceren, -ceer,** *v.t.* to identify. **identi·teitsbewijs, -zen,** *n.n.* identity papers, identity card.
idi·oot, -ioten, *n.* idiot. **¶-iote,** *a.* idiotic. **¶***adv.* idiotically. **idi·oterig,** *a.* idiotic. **¶***adv.* idiotically. **idio·tisme,** no pl., *n.n.* idiocy.
ie, *pron.* (*coll.*) he.
·ieder, *pron.* every, each; any. *een* ~, everyone. **ieder·een,** *pron.* everyone, everybody.
·iegelijk, *pron. een* ~ (*stilted*), everybody.
·iemand, *pron.* somebody, anybody, someone, anyone. *zeker* ~, a certain person.
iep, *n.* **·iepenboom, -bomen,** *n.* elm(-tree).
·iepen, *a.* (*made of*) elm.
Ier, *N.* Irishman. **Ierland,** *n.N.,* Ireland. **Iers,** *a.* Irish.
iet, *pron. als iets komt tot* ~, *kent* ~ *zichzelve niet,* success has given (him) swelled head.
iets, *pron.* something, anything. *zo* ~, anything like it; *is er* ~?, anything the matter? **¶***adv.* somewhat, a little. **·ietsje,** no pl., *n.n. een* ~, a trifle, a shade; *met een* ~ . . ., with just a little. . . . **·ietwat,** *pron.* something, anything. **¶***adv.* somewhat.
·ijdel, *a.* vain; idle, empty. **·ijdelheid, -heden,** *n.* vanity; futility. **·ijdellijk,** *adv.* in vain. **·ijdeltuit,** *n.* vain person.
ijk, *n.* verification of weights and measures. **·ijker, -s,** *n.* inspector of weights and measures. **·ijkloon, -lonen,** *n.n.* fee for verification of weights and measures. **·ijkmaat, -maten,** *n.* standard measure. **·ijkmeester, -s,** *n. See* ijker.
ijl, no pl., *n. in aller* ~, post-haste. **¶***a.* thin, rarified. **·ijlbode, -n,** *n.* fast courier. **·ijlen,** *v.i.* to hasten; to rave, to be delirious. **·ijlgoed, -deren,** *n.n.* fast goods. **·ijlheid,** no pl., *n.* rarity, thinness. **ijl·hoofdig,** *a.* lightheaded, delirious. **·ijlings,** *adv.* in great haste. **·ijlkoorts,** *n.* delirium.
ijs, no pl., *n.n. ice. niet over een nacht* ~ *gaan,* not to act rashly; *zich op glad* ~ *wagen,* to tread on slippery ground; *beslagen ten* ~ *komen,* to come prepared. **·ijsbaan, -banen,** *n.* skating-rink. **·ijsbeer, -beren,** *n.* polar bear. **·ijsberen, -beer,** *v.i.* to pace up and down. **·ijsberg,** *n.* iceberg. **·ijsbloemen,** pl. only, *n.* frost-work. **·ijselijk,** *a.* horrible. **¶***adv.* horribly. **·ijsgang,** no pl., *n.* ice-drift. **·ijskamer, -s,** *n.* refrigerating chamber. **·ijskarretje, -s,** *n.n.* ice-cream barrow. **·ijskast,** *n.* refrigerator. **·ijskelder,** *n.* ice-house. **·ijskoud,** *a.* icy cold. **·IJsland,** *n.N.* Iceland. **·IJslands,** *a.* Icelandic. **·ijsmachine, -s,** *n.* freezing-machine. **·ijsschol, -llen,** *n.,* **ijsschots,** *n.*

icefloe. **·ijstap, -ppen,** *n.* icicle. **·ijstijd,** *n.* glacial period. **·ijsventer, -s,** *n.* ice-cream vendor. **·ijsvogel, -s,** *n.* kingfisher. **·ijswater,** no pl., *n.n.* iced water. **·ijszee, -zeeën,** *n.* polar sea. *Noordelijke* ~, Arctic; *Zuidelijke* ~, Antarctic.
·ijver, no pl., *n.* zeal, ardour; diligence. **·ijveraar, -s,** *n.* zealot. **·ijveren,** *v.i.* to be zealous, ~ *tegen,* to declaim against; ~*voor*; to advocate strongly. **·ijverig,** *a.* zealous, diligent. **·ijverzucht,** no pl., *n.* jealousy, envy. **ijver·zuchtig,** *a.* jealous, envious.
·ijzel, no pl., *n.* ice (*on roads, surfaces*). **·ijzelen,** *v. imp. het ijzelt,* the roads are covered with ice. **·ijzen, ijs,** *v.i.* to shudder. ~ *bij de gedachte,* to shudder at the thought; ~ *van,* to shudder with; ~ *voor,* to shudder at.
·ijzer, no pl., *n.n.* iron; horseshoe; shackle. *men moet het* ~ *smeden als het warm is,* strike while the iron is hot. **·ijzeraarde.** no pl., *n.* ferruginous earth. **·ijzerachtig,** *a,* ferruginous. **·ijzerdraad, -draden,** *n.* iron wire. **·ijzeren,** *a.* (*made of*) iron; cast-iron. **·ijzergaas,** no pl., *n.n.* wire-netting. **·ijzergaren,** no pl., *n.n.* sewing thread. **·ijzergiete·rij,** *n.* iron-foundry. **·ijzerhandel,** no pl., *n.* iron trade; iron-mongery. **·ijzerhandelaar, -s,** *n.* iron-monger. **·ijzerhard,** *a.* (as) hard as iron. **ijzer·houdend,** *a.* ferriferous; ferruginous. **·ijzerkruid,** no pl., *n.n.* verbena; ironwort. **·ijzeroer,** no pl., *n.n.* bog-ore. **·ijzerslakken,** pl. only, *n.* iron slag. **ijzersmelte·rij,** *n.* iron-foundry. **·ijzersterk,** *a.* (as) strong as iron. **·ijzervreter, -s,** *n.* fire-eater (*military man*). **·ijzerwaren,** pl. only, *n.* hardware, ironmongery.
·ijzig, *a.* icy; horrific. **¶***adv.* icily; horribly. **·ijzing,** *n.* shudder. **ijzing·wekkend,** *a.* gruesome, ghastly.
ik, *pron.* I. **ik·zelf,** *pron.* I myself.
il·lusie, -s, *n.* illusion. *iemand zijn* ~*s benemen,* to disillusion a person; *zich* ~*s maken over,* to entertain illusions about; *zich geen* ~*s maken,* to have no illusions about.
illus·tratie, -s, *n.* illustration. *ter* ~ *van,* in illustration of. **illus·treren, -treer,** *v.t.* to illustrate.
imagi·nair, *a.* imaginary.
imi·tatie, -s, *n.* imitation.
·imker, -s, *n.* apiarist, beekeeper.
·immer, *adv.* ever. **·immermeer,** *adv.* evermore. **immers,** *adv. hij is er* ~?, he is there, surely? **¶***c.* for.
im·muun, -mmune, *a.* immune. ~ *maken,* to immunize, render immune. **im·muun·making,** *n.* immunization.
impo·neren, -neer, *v.t.* to impress, overawe. **impo·nerend,** *a.* imposing, impressive.
·import, *n.* import. **impor·teren, -teer,** *v.t.* to import. **impor·teur, -s,** *n.* importer.

impo·sant, *a.* imposing.
improduc·tief, -ve, *a.* unproductive.
improvi·seren, -seer, *v.t.* to improvise, extemporize.
in, *prep.* in, into; at. ¶*adv.* in.
in·achtneming, no pl., *n.* observance. *met ~ van,* observing, with due consideration of.
·inademen, *v.t.s.* & *v.i.s.* to breathe in, inhale. **·inademing,** no pl., *n.* breathing in; intake of breath.
inaugu·reren, -reer, *v.t.* to inaugurate.
·inbaar, -bare, *a.* collectable.
·inbakeren, *v.t.s.* to swaddle. ¶*zich ~, v.r.* to wrap oneself up well.
·inbakken bak in, *v.i.* to lose weight (*in oven*).
·inbedroefd, *a.* very sad.
·inbeelden, zich, *v.r.s.* to imagine. *zich heel wat ~,* to fancy oneself too much. **·inbeelding,** *n.* imagination; conceit.
·inbegrepen, *a.* inclusive of, including. *niet ~,* exclusive of. **·inbegrip,** no pl., *n.n. met ~ van,* inclusive of.
inbe·slagneming, *n.* seizure, distress, distraint. **inbe·zitneming,** *n.* occupation, taking possession of. **inbe·zitstelling,** *n.* placing in possession of.
·inbijten, *v.i.s.,* *str.* to bite into.
·inbinden, *v.t.s.,* *str.* to bind (*books*).
·inblazen, blaas in, *v.t.s.,* *str.* to prompt, suggest. *nieuw leven ~,* to breathe new life into. **·inblazing,** *n.* instigation, prompting.
inboedel, -s, *n.* household effects, furniture.
·inboeken, *v.t.s.* to book.
·inboeten, *v.t.s.* *zijn leven* or *gezondheid erbij ~,* to lose one's life or health over it.
·inboezemen, *v.t.s.* to inspire (*confidence, etc.*); to strike (*terror*) into, fill with; to rouse (*suspicion*) in.
·inboorling, *n.* native.
·inborst, no pl., *n.* nature, character.
·inbouwen, *v.t.s.* to build in.
·inbraak, -braken, *n.* burglary.
·inbranden, *v.t.s.* to burn in(to).
·inbreken, breek in, *v.i.s.,* *str.* to burgle, break into. *~ bij X,* to burgle X's house. **·inbreker, -s,** *n.* burglar.
·inbreng, no pl., *n.* amount brought in (*capital, dowry*). **·inbrengen,** *v.t.s.,* *irr.* to bring or take in; to put forward. *hij heeft niets in te brengen,* he has no say in the matter or he has no objection; *iets ~ tegen,* to object to.
·inbreuk, no pl., *n.* infringement, transgression. *~ maken op.* to encroach upon, infringe.
·inbrokkelen, *v.t.s.* to lose gradually.
·inbuigen, *v.i.s.,* *str.* to bend inwards.
·inburgeren, *v.i.s.* to acclimatize. ¶*zich ~, v.r.s.* to become acclimatized.
incas·seren, -sseer, *v.t.* to cash; to collect. **incas·sering,** *n.* cashing; collection. **in·casso,**

no pl., *n.n.* collection. *ter ~,* for cashing.
in·cassobank, *n.* collecting agency.
inciden·teel, -tele, *a.* incidental.
incli·natie, -s, *n.* inclination.   **incli·natie-naald,** *n.* dipping-needle.
in·cluis, *adv.* included.
inconveni·ent, *n.n.* inconvenience, drawback.
in·dachtig, *a.* mindful of. *~ maken,* to put in mind of.
·indammen, dam in, *v.t.s.* to dam.
·indelen, deel in, *v.t.s.* to classify. *~ bij,* to incorporate in (*army*). **·indeling,** *n.* classification; incorporation.
·indenken, *v.r.t.s.·· irr. zich iets ~,* to imagine or realize something; *zich ergens ~,* to think oneself into.
inder·daad, *adv.* indeed, really. **inder·haast,** *adv.* in haste. **inder·tijd,** *adv.* at the time; in the past.
·indeuken, *v.t.s.* to dent.
·Indië, *n.N.* the Indies. *Achter ~,* Burma, Siam, etc.; *Oost ~,* the East Indies; *Voor ~,* Hindostan and Pakistan; *West ~.* the West Indies.
in·dien, *c.* if, in case.
·indienen, *v.t.s.* to introduce (*bill*); to present (*budget*); to tender, hand in (*resignation*); to lodge, prefer (*complaint, charge*). **·indiening,** *n.* introduction.
in·diensttreding, *n.* commencement of one's duties. *bij ~,* on starting (*new job*).
·indijken, *v.t.s.* to dyke (in, round), reclaim (*land*). **·indijking,** *n.* dyking, reclamation.
indivi·du, -en *and* **'s.** *n.n.* individual. **individu·eel, -uele,** *a.* individual.
·indommelen, *v.i.s.* to doze off.
·indompelen, *v.t.s.* to plunge in, immerse. **·indompeling,** *n.* immersion.
Indo·nesië, *n.* Malay Archipelago, Indonesia.
·indopen, doop in, *v.t.s.* to dip in(to).
·indraaien, *v.t.s.* to turn in(to). ¶*v.r.s. zich ergens ~,* to worm oneself in.
·indrijven, drijf in, *v.t.s.,* *str.* to drive in; to float in(to).
·indringen, *v.i.s.,* *str.* to force one's way into, penetrate. ¶*v.r.s. zich ~ bij,* to force oneself upon; to ingratiate oneself with. **·indringer, -s,** *n.* intruder. **·indringster, -s,** *n.* intruder (*female*). **·indringerig,** *a.* intrusive, importunate. **in·dringerigheid,** no pl., *n.* intrusiveness.
·indrinken, *v.t.s.,* *str.* to imbibe.
·indroevig, *a.* very sad.
·indrogen, droog in, *v.i.s.* to dry up.
·indruisen, *v.i.s. ~ tegen,* to clash with, be at variance with.
·indruk, -kken, *n.* impression; imprint. *~ maken op,* to impress; *de ~ maken van* to give the impression of; *onder de ~ van,* impressed by or with. **·indrukken, druk in,** *v.t.s.* to push in. **·indruksel, -s,** *n.n.* imprint, impression. **indruk·wekkend,** *a.* impressive.

industri·eel, -iële, *a.* industrial. ¶**-iëlen,** *n.* manufacturer, industrialist. **indus·trie-school, -scholen,** *n.* technical school. **indus·triestad, -steden,** *n.* manufacturing ·town.

·indutten, dut in, *v.i.s.* to doze off.

·induwen, *v.t.s.* to push in.

in·een, *adv.* & *prefix.* together, close together; into one another.

in·eendraaien, *v.t.s.* to twist together. **in·eengedrongen,** *a.* thickset. **in·eengrijpen,** *v.i.s., str.* to interlock; to gear into each other. **in·eenkrimpen,** *v.i.s, str.* to shrink, cower. ~ *van angst,* to shrink with fear. **in·eenlopen, loop ineen,** *v.i.s., str.* to run together, communicate.

in·eens, *adv.* at once, suddenly.

in·eenschuiven, schuif ineen, *v.t.s., str.* & *v.i.s., str.* to telescope. **in·eenstorten,** *v.i.s.* to collapse, topple over. **in·eenstorting,** *n.* collapse. **in·eenstrengelen,** *v.t.s.* to intertwine. **in·eenzakken, zak ineen,** *v.i.s.* to collapse, cave in.

inel·kaar, *adv. See* **ineen.**

·inenten, *v.t.s.* to inoculate, vaccinate. **·inenting,** *n.* inoculation, vaccination.

in·fante, -n, *n.* infanta. **infante·rie,** no pl., *n,* infantry. **infante·rist,** *n.* infantry-man.

infec·teren, -teer, *v.t.* to infect. **in·fectie, -s,** *n.* infection.

inferi·eur, *a.* inferior. ¶*n.* inferior, subordinate.

·influisteren, *v.t.s.* to whisper (*in person's ear*), prompt.

infor·matie, -s, *n.* information. ~*s inwinnen,* to make inquiries. **infor·meren, -meer,** *v.i.* to make inquiries. ~ *bij,* to inquire from; ~ *naar,* to inquire after.

in·fusie, -s, *n.* infusion. **in·fusiediertje, -s,** *n.n.* infusoria.

·ingaan, ga in, *v.t.s., irr.* to enter; to take, catch on. ¶*v.i.s., irr.* to commence. ~ *op;* to go into, discuss further *or* to agree to; ~ *tegen,* to go against. **·ingaand,** *a.* ~*e rechten,* import duty. **·ingang,** *n.* entrance, way in. ~ *vinden,* to find acceptance; ~ *vinden bij,* to go down with; *met* ~ *van,* (as) from.

·ingebeeld, *a.* imaginary; conceited. **·ingebeeldheid,** no pl., *n.* conceit.

·ingeboren, *a.* innate.

·ingehouden, *a.* subdued, restrained; bated (*breath*).

·ingekankerd, *a.* inveterate.

·ingekuild, *a.* ~ *veevoeder,* ensilage.

·ingeland, *n.* landowner (*in polder*).

·ingelegd, *a.* inlaid; preserved.

·ingemeen, -mene, *a.* vile.

ingeni·eur, -s, *n.* engineer (*graduate*).

·ingenomen, *a.* ~ *met,* taken with, keen on; *met zichzelf* ~ *zijn,* to fancy oneself. **·ingenomenheid,** no pl., *n.*, sympathy; infatuation.

·ingeschreven, *a.* entered.

·ingesloten, *a.* enclosed, contained.

·ingespannen, *a.* strenuous. ¶*adv.* strenuously; intently.

·ingetogen, *a.* modest, retiring. **inge·togenheid,** no pl., *n.* modesty.

inge·val, *c.* in case.

·ingevallen, *a.* hollow, sunken.

·ingeven, geef in, *v.t.s., str.* to administer (*medicine*); to suggest, prompt. **·ingeving,** *n.* inspiration.

inge·volge, *prep.* in accordance *or* compliance with.

·ingewand, *n.n.* intestine.

·ingewijde, -n, *n.* initiate, adept.

inge·wikkeld, *a.* complicated, involved. **inge·wikkeldheid, -heden,** *n.* intricacy, complication.

·ingeworteld, *a.* deep-rooted, deep-seated, inveterate.

inge·zetene, -n, *n.* resident, inhabitant.

·ingezonden, *a.* ~ *stuk,* letter to the editor.

·ingieten, *v.t.s., str.* to pour in; to infuse (*new life*).

·ingooien, *v.t.s.* to throw in; to smash (*windows*).

·ingraven, zich, graaf in, *v.r.s., str.* to dig oneself in.

·ingrijpen, *v.i.s., str.* to intervene, step in. **·ingrijpend,** *a.* thorough, far-reaching.

·inhakken, hak in, *v.i.s.* ~ *op,* to hit out at.

·inhalen, haal in, *v.t.s.* to draw *or* take *or* gather in; to receive in state; to overtake, catch up with. **in·halig,** *a.* grasping, greedy.

·inham, -mmen, *n.* inlet, bay.

in·hechtenisneming, *n.* arrest.

in·heems, *a.* native, indigenous.

·inhoud, no pl., *n.* contents; capacity. **·inhouden,** *v.t.s., irr.* to contain, hold; to hold back; to deduct. ¶*zich* ~, *v.r.s., irr.* to restrain oneself. **·inhouding,** *n.* deduction; stoppage. **·inhoudsmaat, -maten,** *n.* cubic measure. **·inhoudsopgave, -n,** *n.,* **·inhoudstabel, -llen,** *n.* table of contents.

·inhouwen, *v.i.s., str. See* **inhakken.**

initia·tief, no pl., *n.n.* initiative, enterprise.

·injagen, jaag in, *v.t.s., irr.* to drive into.

·inkankeren, *v.i.s.* to eat into.

inkar·naat, no pl., *n.n.* pink **inkar·naten,** *a.* pink, flesh-coloured.

·inkeep, -kepen, *n.* notch. **·inkepen, keep in,** *v.t.s.* to notch. **·inkeping,** *n.* notch.

·inkeer, no pl., *n.* repentance; residence. *tot* ~ *komen,* to repent; *zijn* ~ *nemen bij,* to go and live with. **·inkeren, keer in,** *v.i.s. tot zichzelf* ~, to repent *or* to collect oneself.

·inkijk, no pl., *n.* overlooking. *tegen de* ~, (*curtains*) to prevent people from seeing in. **·inkijken,** *v.i.s., str.* to look in. ¶*v.t.s., str.* to glance at, skim.

·inklaren, klaar in, *v.t.s.* to clear (*at customs*).

·inklaring, *n.* clearance, clearing (*incoming customs*).
·inkleden, kleed in, *v.t.s.* to clothe; to frame (*question*).
·inkomen, *v.i.s.*, *irr.* to enter, come in. *daar komt niets van in*, nothing doing. ¶-s, *n.n.* income. ·inkomend, *a.* incoming. *~e rechten*, import duty. ·inkomst, *n.* entry; income; receipts. ·inkomstenbelasting, *n.* income-tax.
·inkoop, -kopen, *n.* purchase. *inkopen doen*, to go shopping. ·inkoopboek, *n.n.* bought journal, purchases book. ·inkoopsprijs, -zen, *n.* purchasing price, cost price. ·inkopen, koop in, *v.t.s.*, *irr.* to purchase. ¶*zich ~*, *v.r.s.*, *irr.* to buy oneself in. ·inkoper, -s, *n.* buyer (*in firm*).
·inkorten, *v.t.s.* to shorten; to reduce (*debt*). ·inkorting, *n.* shortening; reduction.
·inkrimpen, *v.i.s.*, *str.* to shrink; to retrench. ·inkrimping, *n.* shrinking; retrenchment.
inkt, *n.* ink. *Oost-Indische ~*, Indian ink. ·inktpotlood, -loden, *n.n.* indelible pencil. ·inktvis, -ssen, *n.* squid, cuttle-fish; octopus.
·inkuilen, *v.t.s.* to ensilage. ·inkuiling, *n.* ensilage.
·inkwartieren, *v.t.s.* to billet, quarter. ·inkwartiering, *n.* billeting. ·inkwartieringsbiljet, -tten, *n.n.* billeting order.
·inlaat, -laten, *n.* inlet. ·inlaatduiker, -s, *n.*, ·inlaatsluis, -zen, *n.* sluice (*letting water into polder or canal*).
·inladen, laad in, *v.t.s.*, *irr.* to take in, load.
·inlage, -n, *n.* land between outer dykes.
·inlander, -s, *n.* native. ·inlands, *a.* native.
·inlas, -ssen, *n.* insertion, stop-press. ·inlassen, las in, *v.t.s.* to insert. ·inlassing, *n.* (*act of*) insertion.
·inlaten, laat in, *v.t.s.*, *str.* to let in, admit. ¶*v.r.*, *str. zich ~ met*, to have dealings with or to concern oneself with.
·inleg, no pl., *n.* deposit; tuck (*seam*). ·inleggeld, *n.n.* entrance money, stakes; deposit. ·inlegblad, *n.n.* extra leaf (*of table*). ·inleggen, leg in, *v.t.s.*, *irr.* to put in; to deposit; to preserve, pickle (*vegetables*); to take in. ·inlegger, -s, *n.* depositor. ·inlegwerk, *n.n.* inlaid work, marquetry.
·inleiden, *v.t.s.* to introduce, preface. ·inleider, -s, *n.* initiator. ·inleiding, *n.* introduction, preface.
·inleveren, *v.t.s.* to hand in, deliver up. ·inlevering, *n.* handing in, surrender.
·inlichten, *v.t.s.* to inform. *~ over or omtrent*, to inform on or about; *verkeerd ~*, to misinform. ·inlichting, *n.* information. *nadere ~en*, further information. ·inlichtingendienst, *n.* intelligence service. *geheime ~*, secret service.
·inliggend, *a.* enclosed.
inlijsten, *v.t.s.* to frame.
·inlijven, lijf in, *v.t.s.* to incorporate, annex (*country*); to draft into (*army unit*). ·inlijving, *n.* incorporation, annexation.

·inlopen, loop in, *v.i.s.*, *str.* to run or drop in. *~ bij*, to drop in on; *er ~*, to be caught.
·inlossen, los in, *v.t.s.* to redeem (*pledge*). ·inlossing, *n.* redemption.
·inluiden, *v.t.s.* to ring in (*new year*); to start off.
·inluizen, luis in, *v.i.s. er ~*, to be caught.
·inmaak, no pl., *n.* pickling, preserving. ·inmaakfles, -ssen, *n.* preserving-bottle. ·inmaken, maak in, *v.t.s.* to preserve, pickle.
·inmengen, *v.t.s.* to mix in. ¶*v.r.s. zich ergens ~*, to meddle with something or butt in on something. ·inmenging, *n.* interference.
·inmetselen, *v.t.s.* to immure, wall up.
in·middels, *adv.* meanwhile.
·innemen, neem in, *v.t.s.*, *str.* to take in; to take (*medicine*); to take, capture; to take up (*space*). *iemand tegen zich ~*, to prejudice a person against one; *iemand voor zich ~* to prepossess a person in one's favour. in·nemend, *a.* winning, fetching. ·inneming, *n.* capture (*of town*).
·innen, in, *v.t.* to collect, cash.
·innerlijk, *a.* inner, inward. ¶*adv.* inwardly. ·innerlijke, no pl., *n.n.* the inner self.
·innig, *a.* fervent, heartfelt. ¶*adv.* deeply. ·innigheid, no pl., *n.* fervour; affection.
·inning, *n.* collection (*of money*). *ter ~*, for collection. ·inningskosten, pl. only, *n.* cost of collection.
·inpakken, pak in, *v.t.s.* to pack. ¶*v.i.s.* to pack up. ¶*v.r.s. zich goed ~*, to wrap oneself up well. ·inpakking, *n.* wrapping(s).
·inpalmen, *v.t.s.* to haul in; to swipe, snaffle.
·inpeperen, *v.t.s. iemand iets ~* (*fig.*), to rub something in.
·inpikken, pik in, *v.t.s.* to pinch (*take*); to pinch (*arrest*). *het goed ~*, to set about it properly.
·inplanten, *v.t.s.* to implant.
·inpolderen, *v.t.s.* to reclaim (*land into polder*).
·inprenten, *v.t.s.* to inculcate. *iemand iets ~*, to impress something on someone.
·inproppen, prop in, *v.t.s.* to cram into.
·inrichten, *v.t.s.* to fit up; to arrange. *goed ingericht*, well-appointed. ·inrichting, *n.* fitting up; arrangement, disposition; institution, establishment.
·inrijden, *v.t.s.*, *str.* to ride in; to break in (*horse*).
·inrijgen, *v.t.s.*, *str.* to lace tightly.
·inrit, no pl., *n.* entrance (*for vehicles*).
·inroepen, *v.t.s.*, *str.* to call in, invoke. ·inroeping, *n.* invocation.
·inruilen, *v.t.s.* to exchange. *~ tegen*, to exchange for. ·inruiling, *n.* exchange.
·inruimen, *v.t.s. plaats ~*, to make room.
·inrukken, ruk in, *v.t.s.* to enter (*town by mili'ary*). ¶*v.i.s.* to dismiss, withdraw. *ingerukt, mars!*, dismiss!

·inschakelen, *v.t.s.* to switch on; to insert.
·inschenken, *v.t.s.*, *str.* to pour out.
·inschepen, scheep in, *v.t.s.* to ship, embark. ¶*v.r.s.* zich ~ *naar*, to embark for. ·inscheping, *n.* embarkation.
·inschieten, *v.t.s.*, *str.* to shoot into; to be lost, go by the board. *een batterij* ~, to find the range (*by guns of battery*); *het leven erbij* ~, to lose one's life in doing so; *geld erbij* ~, to lose money over it. ¶zich ~, *v.r.s.* to find one's target.
in·schikkelijk, *a.* obliging, accommodating. in·schikkelijkheid, no pl., *n.* readiness to oblige. ·inschikken, schik in, *v.i.s.* to make room.
·inschrift, *n.n.* inscription. ·inschrijven, schrijf in, *v.t.s.*, *str.* to book, enter; to register. ¶*v.i.s.* to subscribe. ~ *op*, to subscribe for or to send in a tender. ·inschrijver, -s, *n.* subscriber. *de laagste* ~, person submitting the lowest tender. ·inschrijving, *n.* registration; tender.
in·sect, *n.n.* insect.
·insgelijks, *adv.* likewise. ~ !, the same to you!
in·signe, -s, *n.* badge.
·inslaan, sla in, *v.t.s.*, *irr.* to drive in; to knock in, smash (*window*); to turn into (*road*). *de bodem* ~, to knock the bottom out of; *iemand de hersens* ~, to bash someone's brains out. ¶*v.i.s.*, *irr.* to strike (*lightning*); to hit (*shell*); to make a hit (*drama*). ·inslag, no pl., *n.* woof, weft. ¶*n.* provisions.
·inslapen, slaap in, *v.i.s.*, *str.* to fall asleep.
·inslikken, slik in, *v.t.s.* to swallow.
·insluimeren, *v.i.s.* to doze off.
·insluiten, *v.t.s.*, *str.* to enclose; to shut in; to encircle. ·insluiting, *n.* encirclement. *onder* ~ *van*, together with.
·insnijden, *v.t.s.*, *str.* to cut into, incise. ·insnijding, *n.* incision.
·inspannen, span in, *v.t.s.*, *irr.* to put (*horses*) to; to exert (*strength*). ¶zich ~, *v.r.s.*, *irr.* to make an effort, exert oneself. inspannend, *a.* strenuous, exacting. ·inspanning, *n.* exertion; effort; strain. *met* ~ *van alle krachten*, with the utmost exertion.
inspec·teur, -s, *n.* inspector. in·spectiereis, -zen, *n.* tour of inspection. inspec·trice, -s, *n.* inspectress.
·inspelen, speel in, *v.t.s.* to take the newness off (*musical instrument*). ¶zich ~, *v.r.s.* to get back into practice; to get one's hand or eye in (*music or games*).
·inspreken, spreek in, *v.t.s.*, *str.* iemand moed ~, to put heart in a person.
·inspringen, *v.i.s.*, *str.* to recede, stand back. ~ *voor iemand*, to take someone's place.
·inspuiten, *v.t.s.*, *str.* to inject. ·inspuiting, *n.* injection.
·instaan, sta in, *v.i.s.*, *irr.* ~ *voor*, to guarantee or to vouch or answer for.
instal·latie, -s, *n.* installation; appointment.

instal·leren, -leer, *v.t.* to install; to appoint, induct.
in·standhouden, houd instand, *v.t.s.*, *irr.* to maintain, preserve. in·standhouding, *n.* maintenance, upkeep.
in·stantie, -s, *n.* instance, resort. *ter* or *in eerste* ~, in the first instance.
·instappen, stap in, *v.i.s.* to get in.
·insteken, steek in, *v.t.s.*, *str.* to put in.
·instellen, stel in, *v.t.s.* to adjust; to set up, institute. ~ *op*, to tune in to. ·instelling, *n.* adjustment; institution.
·instemmen, stem in, *v.i.s.* ~ *met*, to agree or concur with. ·instemming, *n.* approval, agreement.
in·stinct, *n.n.* instinct.
insti·tuut, -tuten, *n.n.* institute, institution.
·instoppen, stop in, *v.t.s.* to put in; to tuck in (*bed*).
·instorten, *v.i.s.* to collapse. ·instorting, *n.* collapse; break-up.
in·structie, -s, *n.* instruction.
instrumen·teren, -teer, *v.t.* to orchestrate, instrument.'
·instuderen, -deer, *v.t.s.* to practise, study.
Insu·linde, *n.N.* (*poet.*) East Indies.
·inteelt, no pl., *n.* inbreeding.
in·tegendeel, *adv.* on the contrary.
inte·graal, -grale, *a.* integral. inte·graalrekening, *n.* integral calculus. integrerend, *a.* integral, integrant.
·intekenaar, -s, *n.* subscriber. ·intekenen, *v.i.s.* to subscribe to or for. ·intekening, *n.* subscription.
inten·dance, no pl., *n.* Army Service Corps.
in·tens, *a.* intense, forceful. inten·sief, -ve, *a.* intensive.
intercommu·naal, -nale, *a.* ~ *telefoongesprek*, long-distance or trunk call.
·interen, teer in, *v.i.s.* to use up one's capital.
interes·sant, *a.* interesting. ·interesse, no pl., *n.* interest, liking. intere·seren, -sseer, *v.t.* to interest. ¶*v.r.* zich ~ *voor*, to take an interest in. ·interest, *n.* interest (*on capital*). *tegen* ~, at interest.
intergealli·eerd, *a.* inter-allied.
interi·eur, *n.n.* interior; interior scene.
interlo·caal, -cale, *a. See* intercommunaal.
interlocu·toir, *a.* interlocutory.
intermit·terend, *a.* intermittent.
in·tern, *a.* resident; internal. in·ternaat, -naten, *n.n.* boarding-school. inter·neren, -neer, *v.t.* to intern. inter·nering, *n.* internment.
interpo·leren, -leer, *v.t.* to interpolate.
interpre·teren, -teer, *v.t.* to interpret.
interrum·peren, -peer, *v.t.* to interrupt. interveni·ëren, -ieer, *v.i.* to intervene. inter·ventie, -s, *n.* intervention.
in·tiem, *a.* intimate. ~ *zijn*, to be on terms of intimacy.
in·tijds, *adv.* in (good) time.
intimi·teit, *n.* intimacy.
·intocht, *n.* entry (*into place*).

·intomen, toom in, *v.t.s.* to curb, rein in.
·intrede, no pl., *n.*, ·intree, no pl., *n.* entry,
entrance; advent. ·intreden, treed in,
v.i.s., *str.* (*stilled*) to enter.
·intrek, no pl., *n.* zijn ~ nemen, to put up,
take up residence. ·intrekken, trek in,
v.t.s., *str.* to draw in; to retract; to withdraw. ·intrekking, *n.* withdrawal; repeal,
revocation.
·intrest, *n.* See interest.
intri·gant, *n.* schemer, intriguer. in·trige, -s,
n. intrigue. intri·geren, -geer. *v.i.* to scheme,
intrigue.
introdu·cé, -'s, *n.* guest (*at club or function*).
introdu·ceren, -ceer, *v.t.* to introduce.
intro·ductie, -s, *n.* introduction.
in·tussen, *adv.* meanwhile, in the meantime.
·inval, -llen, *n.* invasion; raid, inroad,
incursion; idea, brainwave. *het is daar
de zoete* ~, they keep open house. ·invallen,
val in, *v.t.s.*, *str.* to fall in(to); to collapse;
to set in (*frost*), come on (*night*); to occur
(*to one*); to take someone's place. ¶no
pl., *n.n. voor het* ~ *van de nacht*, before
nightfall. ·invalshoek, *n.* angle of incidence.
inva·lide, -n, *n.* invalid. invalidi·teit, no pl.,
n. disablement; non-validity. invalidi-
·teitsverzekering, *n.* health insurance.
invalidi·teitswet, -tten, *n.* national insurance act.
inven·taris, -ssen, *n.* inventory. *de* ~
opmaken, to take stock. inventari·satie,
-s, *n.* stock-taking.
·invetten, vet in, *v.t.s.* to grease.
invi·té, -'s, *n.* guest. invi·teren, -teer, *v.t.*
to invite.
·invliegen, *v.i.s.*, *str.* to fly in(to). ~ *op*. to
fly at; *er* ~ (*fig.*), to be caught.
·invloed, *n.* influence. ~ *uitoefenen bij*, to
exert one's influence with; ~ *op*, influence
on *or* over. ·invloedrijk, *a.* influential.
·invoegen, *v.t.s.* to insert. ·invoeging, *n.*
(*act of*) insertion. ·invoegsel, -s, *n.n.*
insert, insertion.
·invoer, *n.* import; importation. ·invoer-
der, -s, *n.* introducer. ·invoerdraad,
-draden, *n.* lead-in. ·invoeren, *v.t.s.* to
import; to introduce. ·invoering. *n.*
introduction. ·invoerrechten, pl. only,
n.n. import duty.
·invorderaar, -s, *n.* collector. ·invorderbaar,
-bare, *a.* collectable. ·invorderen, *v.t.s.*
to collect, recover (*debts*). ·invordering,
n. collection, recovery (*of debts*).
·invreten, vreet in, *v.i.s.*, *str.* to bite into,
corrode. ·invretend, *a.* corrosive.
in·vrijheidstelling, no pl., *n.* release.
·invullen, vul in, *v.t.s.*, to fill in *or* up. ·invul-
ling. *n.* filling in *or* up. ·invulsel, -s, *n.*
entry (*on form*).
·inwaarts, *a.* & *adv.* inward.
·inwachten, *v.t.s.* tc await.

·inwegen, weeg in, *v.i.s.*, *str.* to lose in weighing
out.
in·wendig, *a.* internal, interior. *de* ~*e mens*,
the inner man; *voor* ~ *gebruik*, to be taken
internally. ¶*adv.* inwardly, internally.
in·wendige, no pl., *n.n.* the interior part(s).
·inwerken, *v.i.s.* ~ *op*, to act upon. ¶*v.r.s.*
zich er ~, to work oneself in. ·inwerking,
n. influence.
·inwijden, *v.t.s.* to consecrate; to ordain.
~ *in*, to initiate into. ·inwijding, *n.*
consecration; initiation. ·inwijdingsrede,
-nen, *n.* inaugural address.
·inwikkelen, *v.t.s.* to wrap up.
·inwilligen, *v.t.s.* to grant, concede; to comply
with. ·inwilliging, *n.* granting. ~ *van*,
compliance with.
·inwinnen, win in, *v.t.s.*, *str.* to regain; to
gather (*information*).
·inwisselen, *v.t.s.* ~ *voor* or *tegen*, to
exchange for.
·inwonen, woon in, *v.i.s.* to live in. ~ *bij*,
to lodge with. ·inwoner, -s, *n.* inhabitant;
occupant. ·inwoning, no pl., *n. kost en* ~,
board and lodging.
·inwortelen, *v.i.s.* to strike root.
·inzage, no pl., *n.* ~ *nemen van*, to examine;
ter ~, for inspection *or* on approval *or*
open to the public (*document*).
·inzakken, zak in, *v.i.s.* to sag, cave in.
·inzamelen, *v.t.s.* to gather, collect. ·inzame-
ling, *n.* collection (*money*).
·inzegenen, *v.t.s.* to bless, consecrate. ·inze-
gening, *n.* blessing, consecration.
·inzenden, *v.t.s.*, *str.* to send in. ·inzender, -s,
n. contributor; exhibitor. ·inzending, *n.*
contribution; exhibit.
·inzepen, zeep in, *v.t.s.* to soap, lather.
·inzet, -tten, *n.* stake(s). ·inzetten, zet in,
v.t.s. to put in, insert; to set (*precious
stones*); to start (*song*). ·inzetter, -s, *n.*
first bidder.
·inzicht, *n.n.* insight. *naar mijn* ~, in my
opinion. ·inzien, zie in, *v.t.s.*, *irr.* to look
into, glance through; to understand;
to realize. ¶no pl., *n.n. bij nader* ~,
on second thoughts; *naar mijn* ~ or
mijns ~*s*, in my opinion.
·inzinken, *v.i.s.*, *str.* to sink in, sag.
·inzitten, zit in, *v.i.s.*, *str. er* (*erg*) *mee* ~ or *er
over* ~, to be very worried about it; *er
lelijk* ~, to be badly caught; *er warmpjes* ~,
to be warmly dressed *or* to be very well off.
in·zonderheid, *adv.* (*stilled*) especially.
·inzouten, *v.t.s.* to salt, pickle.
iro·nie, no pl., *n.* irony. i·ronisch, *a.* ironical.
irri·gatie, -s, *n.* irrigation. irri·geren, -geer.
v.t. to irrigate.
irri·teren, -teer, *v.t.* to irritate.
·ischias, no pl., *n.* sciatica.
iso·latie, no pl., *n.* isolation; insulation.
iso·latieband, no pl., *n.* insulating tape.
iso·lator, *n.* insulator. iso·leren, -leer.
v.t. to isolate; to insulate.

Itali·aan, -ianen, *n.* Italian. **Itali·aans,** *a.* Italian. *~e,* Italian woman. **I·talië,** *n.N.* Italy.

i·voor, no pl., *n.n.* ivory. **i·voren,** *a.* (*made of*) ivory.

J

ja, *int.* yes. ¶no pl., *n.n.* yea, yes.

·jaaggeld, *n.n.* towage (*with horses*). **·jaaglijn,** *n.* tow(ing)-line (*from boat to horse*). **·jaagpad,** *n.n.* tow(ing)-path.

jaap, japen, *n.* gash, cut.

jaar, jaren, *n.n.* year. *~ en dag,* a year and a day; *~ op ~,* year after year; *eens in 't ~,* once a year; *het ene ~ door het andere,* one year with another; *na ~ en dag,* after many years; *om het andere ~,* every other year; *om de vier ~,* every fourth year *sinds ~ en dag,* for many years; *van ~ tot ~,* year by year; *gisteren voor een ~,* a year ago yesterday. **·jaarbeurs, -zen,** *n.* annual trade fair. **·jaardag,** *n.* anniversary. **·jaarfeest,** *n.n.* annual feast. **·jaargang,** *n.* volume (*one year of periodical*). **·jaargetij, -den,** *n.n.,* **·jaargetijde, -n,** *n.* season (*spring summer, etc.*). **·jaarkring,** *n.* annual cycle; annual ring (*on tree*). **·jaarlijks,** *a.* yearly, annual. **·jaarling,** *n.* yearling. **·jaarloon, -lonen,** *n.n.* yearly wage, salary. **·jaarmarkt,** *n.* (annual) fair. **·jaarring,** *n.* annual ring (*on tree*). **·jaarstaat, -staten,** *n.* annual returns *or* statistics. **·jaartal, -llen,** *n.n.* date. **·jaartelling,** *n.* era. **·jaarwedde, -n,** *n.* (*stilted*) salary. **·jaarwisseling,** *n.* turn of the year.

·jabroer, -s, *n.* spineless person, yes-man.

jacht, no pl., *n.* hunt, chase; hunting, shooting; pursuit. *op (de) ~ gaan,* to go hunting *or* shooting; *op ~ naar,* in pursuit of; *~ maken op,* to hunt, pursue. ¶*n.n.* yacht. **·jachtakte, -n,** *n.* shooting licence. **·jachten,** *v.i.* & *v.t.* to hurry, hustle. **·jachthond,** *n.* sporting dog; hound. **·jachthoorn, -s,** *n.* hunting-horn. **·jachthuis, -zen,** *n.* shooting-box. **jachtig,** *a.* hurried, restless. **·jachtpaard,** *n.n.* hunter (*horse*). **jachtopziener, -s,** *n.* gamekeeper. **·jachtroer,** *n.n.* fowling-piece. **·jachtsneeuw,** *n.* snow-drift, driving snow. **·jachtspin, -nnen,** *n.* hunting-spider. **·jachtspriet,** *n.* hunting-spear. **·jachttijd,** *n.* shooting season. **·jachtvliegtuig,** *n.n.* fighter, fighting-plane. **·jachtwet, -tten,** *n.* game-law(s). **·jachtzweep, -zwepen,** *n.* hunting-crop.

·jagen, jaag, *v.t.,* irr. to hunt, shoot; to chase, drive on. *hem een kogel door het hoofd ~,* to put a bullet through his brain; *op kosten ~,* to run into expense. ¶*v.i., irr.* to hunt, shoot; to race, rush. *uit ~ gaan,* to go hunting *or* shooting; *~ naar (fig.),*

to hunt after; *~ op,* to hunt. **·jager, -s,** *n.* huntsman; towing-horse; driver of towing-horse; soldier in the Rifles. **·jagerslatijn,** no pl., *n.n.* sportsman's yarn. **·jagerstas, -ssen,** *n.* game-bag.

jak, -kken, *n.n.* jacket (*woman's*).

·jakhals, -zen, *n.* jackal.

·jakkeren, *v.i.* to tear along, race. ¶*v.t.* to urge along.

·jakkes, *int.* bah! (*disgust*).

ja·loers, *a.* jealous. **ja·loersheid,** no pl., *n.* jealousy. **jaloe·zie,** no pl., *n.* jealousy. *uit ~,* out of jealousy. **jaloe·zieën,** pl. only, *n.* Venetian blind(s).

·jambe, -n, *n.* iambus. **jambisch,** *a.* iambic.

·jammer, no pl., *n.* misery, distress. *~! or 't is ~!,* pity! *or* what a pity!; *'t is zo ~,* it is such a pity. **·jammeren,** *v.i.* to lament. **jammerklacht,** *n.* lamentation. **·jammerlijk,** *a.* miserable, pitiful. ¶*adv.* miserably; signally.

Jan, *N.* John. *~ en Alle man,* all the world and his wife; *~ Compagnie,* John Company; *~ Klaassen,* Punch; *~, Piet en Klaas,* Tom, Dick, and Harry; *~ Rap en z'n maat,* rag, tag, and bobtail; *~ Salie,* a spiritless fellow. **·janboel,** no pl., *n.* (*fig.*) mess. **jan·dorie!,** *int.* blimey! **jan·hagel,** no pl., *n.n.* mob, rabble. **jan-in-de-zak,** no pl., *n.* plum duff.

·janken, *v.i.* to yelp; to whine, whimper.

Jan·maat, -s, *n.* Jack tar. **janple·zier, -s,** *n.* charabanc. **Jantje, -s,** *n.* sailor (*navy*). *er zich met een ~ van Leiden afmaken,* to dismiss something lightly.

Japan·nees, -nnezen, *n.* Japanese. **Ja·pans,** *a.* Japanese.

·japen, jaap, *v.t.* to slash.

ja·pon, -nnen, *n.* dress, frock, gown.

·jarenlang, *a.* (*e.g. friendship*) of years. ¶*adv.* for years. **jarig,** *a.* having one's birthday. **·jarige, -n,** *n.* person having his *or* her birthday.

jas, -ssen, *n.* coat. *geklede ~,* frock-coat.

jas·mijn, no pl., *n.* jasmin.

jaspis, no pl., *n.* jasper.

·jassen, jas, *v.t.* (*slang*) to peel (*potatoes*). ¶*v.i.* to play a certain card game.

·jasses, *int. See* **jakkes.**

Ja·vaan, -vanen, *n.* Javanese. **Ja·vaans,** *a.* Javanese. *~e,* Javanese woman.

ja·wel, *int.* yes; yes (but . . .); very well. **·jawoord,** no pl., *n.n.* consent. *het ~ geven,* to consent *or* to say yes.

je, *pers. pron.* you (*sing. unemphatic*). ¶*poss. pron.* your; the (*emphatic*).

jee!, *int.* gee!

·jekker, -s, *n.* pilot-jacket, pea-jacket.

je·lui, *pron. See* **jullie.**

je·never, no pl., *n.* gin. **je·neverbes, -ssen,** *n.* juniper-berry. **je·neverboom, -bomen,** *n.* juniper(-bush). **je·neverbranderij,** *n.* gin distillery. **je·neverneus, -zen,** *n.* an expensive nose. **je·neverstoker, -s,** *n.* gin

distiller. je·neverstokerij, n. gin distillery.
je·neverstruik, n. juniper(-bush).
·jengelen, v.i. to whimper.
jeugd, no pl., n. youth. ·jeugdherberg, n.
youth hostel. ·jeugdig, a. youthful.
·jeugdigheid, no pl., n. youthfulness.
jeuk, no pl., n. itch. ·jeuken, v.i. to itch.
¶v.t. to itch; to scratch. de handen of
vingers ~ hem om, he is itching to.
·jeukerig, a. itchy.
·Jezus, N. Jesus.
jicht, no pl., n. gout. ·jichtig, a. gouty.
·jichtknobbel, -s, n. chalk-stone.
jij, pron. you (sing. fam.). ·jijen, v.t. ~ en
jouen, to address (over) familiarly.
·Jobsbode, -n, n. Job's messenger. ·Jobs-
trooster, -s, n. Job's comforter.
joch, -ies, n.n., ·jochie, -s, n.n. urchin, small
boy.
·jodelen, v.i. to yodel.
·Jodenbuurt, n. Jewish quarter. ·Jodendom,
no pl., n.n. Jewry; Judaism. ·Jodenkerk,
n. het lijkt wel een ~!, what a noise!
·Jodenlijm, no pl., n. bitumen; spittle.
·Jodenvervolger, n. Jew-baiter. ·Joden-
vervolging, n. Jew-baiting, persecution of
the Jews. Jo·din, -nnen, n. Jewess.
·jodium, no pl., n.n. iodine. jodo·form, no
pl., n.n. iodoform.
Joego-·Slavië, n.N. Yugoslavia. Joego-·Slaaf,
n. Yugoslav. Joego-·slavisch, a. Yugoslav.
·joelen, v.i. to shout (of children or crowd).
Jo·hannesbrood, no pl., n.n. locust bean.
Jo·hanneskever, -s, n. rose-chafer.
·jokkebrok, -kken, n. fibber. ·jokken, jok,
v.i. to fib, tell fibs. jokker·nij, n. jest.
jol, -llen, n. yawl, jolly-boat; dinghy.
·jolig, a. jolly, merry. ·joligheid, no pl., n.
jollity, jolliness.
·jolleman, -nnen, n. boatman, wherryman.
·jonassen, -nas, v.t. & v.i. to toss in blanket.
jong, a. young. ~e kaas, new cheese; van
~e datum, of recent date; ~ste berichten,
the latest news. ¶adv. young. ¶n.n. young
(one); cub. ~en krijgen of werpen, to
litter. jonge·dame, -s, n. young lady.
jonge·heer, -heren, n. young gentleman.
·jongeling, n. (stilted) young man. jonge-
·lui, pl. only, n. young people. ·jongen, -s,
n. boy; lad; old boy (fam. to friend). ¶v.i.
to litter. ·jongensjaren, pl. only, n.n.
boyhood (years). ·jongere, n. younger one;
disciple. ·jongetje, -s, n.n. small boy.
jongge·borene, -n, n. newly born. jongge-
·huwde, -n, n. newly married (usu. pl.).
jongge·zel, -llen, n. bachelor. jong·mens,
n.n. young man. jongs, adv. van ~ af
(aan), from childhood. jongst, a. ~e
bediende, junior (clerk); ~e berichten,
latest news; ~e dag, Day of Judgment;
~e gebeurtemissen, recent events. jongst-
·leden, a. last. ~ Maandag, last Monday.
jonk, n. junk (vessel).
·Jonker, -s, n. squire. ·Jonkheer, -heren, n.

title of lesser nobility. ·Jonkvrouw, n. title
of lesser nobility, female.
Jood, Joden, n. Jew. Joods, a. Jewish.
jool, jolen, n. fun, frolic.
joon, jonen, n. fishing buoy.
·jota, 's, n. iota. geen ~, not a jot.
jou, pron. you (object case, sing. fam.).
·jouen, v.t. See jijen.
·journaal, -nalen, n.n. log(-book). journalis-
·tiek, no pl., n. journalism. journa-
·listisch, a. journalistic.
jouw, pron. your (sing. fam.).
·jouwen, v.i. to boo.
jubel, -s, n. shout(s) of joy. ·jubelen, v.i.
to shout for joy, exult. ·jubelkreet,
-kreten, n. shout of joy. jubi·laris, -ssen,
n. person celebrating his of her jubilee.
jubi·leren, -leer, v.i. to celebrate one's
jubilee. jubi·leum, -s or -lea, n.n. jubilee.
·juchtleer, n.n. Russia leather. ·juchtleren,
a. (made of) Russia leather.
·Judaspenning, n. honesty (plant). ·judassen,
-das, v.t. to tease (cruelly).
juf, no pl., n. nurse, governess. ·juffer, -s,
n. young lady, girl; pole, pile; dragon-fly;
paving beetle, rammer. ·jufferachtig, a.
prim. ·juffershondje, -s, n.n. toy dog.
beven als een ~, to tremble like a leaf.
·juffrouw, n. Miss; Mrs. (lower middle
class). juffrouw!, Miss. ... (form of address).
·juichen, v.i. to cheer.
juin, n. onion.
juist, a. exact, correct; right, just. ¶adv.
just; exactly, precisely. daarom ~, for
that very reason. ·juister, a. te ~ tijd,
at the right time. ·juistheid, no pl., n.
exactness, precision.
juk, -kken, n.n. yoke; beam (of scales). in
het ~ spannen, to put to the yoke; onder
het ~ brengen, to subjugate. ·jukbeen,
-deren, n.n. cheekbone.
·juli, N. July. juli·aans, a. Julian.
·jullie, pers. pron. you (people). ¶poss. pron.
of you (people), your.
·juni, N. June.
ju·ridisch, a. juridical; judicial. jurispru-
·dentie, no pl., n. jurisprudence.
jurk, n. frock, dress.
·jurylid, -leden, n.n. member of the jury;
juror.
jus, no pl., n. gravy.
jus·titie, no pl., n. justice; the law.
Jut, N. het hoofd van ~, strength-testing
machine.
·jute, no pl., n. jute. ·jutezak, -kken, n.
jute bag, gunny bag.
·jutten, jut, v.t. to filch, pinch. ·jutter, -s,
n. beach-comber.
·juttepeer, -peren, n. juicy type of pear.
ju·weel, -welen, n.n. jewel, gem. ju·welen,
a. jewelled. ju·welenkistje, -s, n.n. jewel-
box. juwe·lier, -s, n. jeweller. juwe-
·lierswerk, no pl., n.n. jewellery. juwe-
·lierswinkel, -s, n. jeweller's (shop).

K

See C

ka, -den, *n.* quay. *See* **kade.**
kaag, kagen, *n.* flat-bottomed barge; polder; flat ground beyond dykes.
kaai, *n.* quay. *See* **kade.**
kaaiman, -nnen, *n.* caiman, alligator.
·kaaimeester, -s, *n.* wharfinger. **·kaaiwerker, -s,** *n.* dock-labourer.
kaak, kaken, *n.* jaw; gill; pillory; ship's biscuit. *met beschaamde kaken,* shamefaced; *aan de ~ stellen,* to hold up to ridicule. **·kaakje, -s,** *n.* small biscuit. **·kaakmes, -ssen,** *n.n.* gutting knife. **·kaakslag,** *n.* slap in the face. **·kaakton, -nnen,** *n.* biscuit barrel. **·kaakster, -s,** *n.* herring lass.
kaal, kale, *a.* bald; callow; bare (*fig.*); threadbare. *een kale jonker,* a gentleman without means; *er ~ afkomen,* to come away empty-handed. **·kaalachtig,** *a.* slightly bald. **·kaalgeschoren,** *a.* shorn. **·kaalheid,** no pl., *n.* baldness. **·kaal·hoofdig,** *a.* baldheaded. **·kaalkop, -ppen,** *n.* baldpate (*rude*).
·kaantjes, pl. only, *n.n.* chitterlings.
kaap, kapen, *n.* cape. *K~ de Goede Hoop,* Cape of Good Hope. **·Kaapstad,** *N.* Cape Town. **·kaapstander, -s,** *n.* capstan. **·kaapvaarder, -s,** *n.* privateer. **·kaapvaart,** no pl., *n.* privateering. **Kaap·verdische Eilanden,** pl. *n.N.* Cape Verde Islands.
kaar, karen, *n.* fish-slide.
·kaarde, -n, *n.* teasel; card, wool-comb. **·kaarden,** *v.t.* to card (*wool*). **·kaarder, -s,** *n.* carder. **·kaardster, -s,** *n.* carder (*female*). **·kaardwol,** no pl., *n.* carding-wool.
kaars, *n.* candle; dandelion clock. *in de ~ vliegen,* to come to grief. **·kaarsdief, -ven,** *n.* thief (*in candle*). **·kaarsepit, -tten,** *n.* wick (*of candle*). **·kaarsrecht,** *a. & adv.* (as) straight as a candle. **·kaarsvet,** no pl., *n.n.* candle grease, tallow.
kaart, *n.* card; (admission) ticket; map, chart. *een spel ~en,* a pack of cards; *een doorgestoken ~,* a put-up job; *iemand in de ~ kijken,* to discover a person's secrets; *de ~ leggen,* to tell fortune (*by cards*); *in iemands ~ spelen,* to play into a person's hands; *alles op één ~ zetten,* to put all one's eggs into one basket. **·kaartbrief, -ven,** *n.* letter-card. **·kaarten,** *v.i.* to play cards. **·kaartenhuis, -zen,** *n.n.* house of cards; chart-house. **·kaartenhut, -tten,** *n.,* **·kaartenkamer, -s,** *n.* chart-room. **·kaartje, -s,** *n.n.* small map; (visiting) card; ticket. *een ~ leggen,* to have a game of cards. **·kaartlegster, -s,** *n.* fortune-teller. **·kaartlezen,** no pl., *n.n.* map-reading. **·kaartspel,** *n.n.* card game. ¶**-llen,** *n.n.* pack of cards. **·kaartsysteem, -temen,** *n.n.* card-index system.
kaas, kazen, *n.* cheese. *zich de ~ niet van het brood laten eten,* not to be put upon;

hij heeft er geen ~ van gegeten, it is well beyond him. **·kaasachtig,** *a.* cheesy, cheese-like. **·kaasboer,** *n.* cheesemaker. **·kaasboor, -boren,** *n.* cheese-taster. **·kaashandel,** no pl., *n.* cheese trade. ¶**-s,** *n.* cheese shop. **·kaashandelaar, -s,** *n.* cheesemonger. **·kaasjeskruid,** no pl., *n.n.* mallow. **·kaaskoper, -s,** *n.* cheesemonger. **·Kaaskop, -ppen,** *n.* nickname given to Dutch by Belgians. **·kaasmade, -n,** *n.,* **·kaasmijt,** *n.* cheese mite. **·kaasschaaf, schaven,** *n.* cheesecutter. **·kaasstengel, -s,** *n.* cheese-straw(s). **·kaasstof,** no pl., *n.* caseine. **·kaasstolp,** *n.* cheese-cover. **·kaaswaag, -wagen,** *n.* (cheese) weigh-house. **·kaaswei,** no pl., *n.* whey. **·kaaswrongel,** no pl., *n.* curd.
·kaatsbaan, -banen, *n.* fives court. **·kaatsbal, -llen,** *n.* fives ball; rubber ball. **·kaatsen,** *v.i.* to play ball. *wie kaatst moet de bal verwachten,* if you play with fire, you must expect to be burnt.
ka·baai, *n.* jacket (*East Indies*).
ka·baal, no pl., *n.n.* (*coll.*) racket, row. *~ maken* or *schoppen,* to kick up a row. **ka·baalschopper, -s,** *n.* person making disturbance.
Ka·balla, no pl., *n.* cabbala.
·ka·bas, -ssen, *n.* shopping basket.
·kabbelen, *v.i.* to ripple, babble. **·kabbeling,** *n.* ripple.
·kabel, -s, *n.* cable. **·kabelbaan, -banen,** *n.* cable road. **·kabelballon, -s,** *n.* captive balloon, barrage balloon. **·kabelbericht,** *n.n.* cable(gram). **·kabelgat,** *n.n.* cable tier. **kabel·jauw,** *n.* cod. **·kabellengte, -n,** *n.* cable('s) length. **·kabelschip, -schepen,** *n.n.* cable-laying ship. **·kabeltouw,** *n.n.* cable.
kabi·net, -tten, *n.n.* cabinet; water-closet. **kabi·netsformateur, -s,** *n.* person who forms a cabinet. **kabi·netsraad, -raden,** *n.* cabinet council. **kabi·netwerker, -s,** *n.* cabinet-maker.
ka·bouter, -s, *n.* brownie; gnome, goblin.
ka·buiskool, -kolen, *n.* (head of) cabbage.
·kachel, -s, *n.* stove. **·kachelglans,** no pl., *n.* stove-polish. **·kachelhout,** no pl., *n.n.* firewood.
ka·daster, -s, *n.n.* land registry (office). **kadas·traal,** *a.* cadastral. **kadas·treren, -treer,** *v.t.* to survey; to register (*land*).
ka·daver, -s, *n.n.* cadaver, carrion.
·kade, -n, *n.* quay.
·kader, -s, *n.n.* cadre, staff; framework. **·kaderuimte,** no pl., *n.* wharfage (*space*).
ka·det, -tten, *n.* cadet. **ka·detje, -s,** *n.n.* roll (*bread*).
ka·duuk, -duke, *a.* rickety.
kaf, no pl., *n.n.* chaff.
Kaffer, -s, *n.* Kaffir. **Kaffer, -s,** *n.* boor, lout.
kaft, *n.* cover, jacket (*book*). **·kaften,** *v.t.* to cover (*book*). **·kaftpapier,** no pl., *n.n.* brown paper (*protective cover on book*).
kaja·poetolie, no pl., *n.* cajuput(ene).

ka·juit, *n.* (ship's) cabin. *eerste* ~, saloon (*on ship*).
kak, no pl., *n.* (*vulg.*) excrement.
·**kakebeen, -benen**, *n.n.* jaw-bone.
·**kakelaar, -s**, *n.* cackler, chatterer. ·**kakelaarster, -s**, *n.* cackler, chatterer (*female*). ·**kakelbont**, *a.* motley. ·**kakelen**, *v.i.* to cackle; to chatter.
·**kaken, kaak**, *v.t.* to gut (*herrings*). ·**kaker, -s**, *n.* gutter (*of herrings*).
kake·toe, -s, *n.* cockatoo.
·**kakken, kak**, *v.i.* to cack.
·**kakkerlak, -kken**, *n.* cockroach.
ka·lander, -s, *n.* corn-weevil.
kale·bas, -ssen, *n.* gourd, calabash.
ka·lender, -s, *n.* calendar.
kalf, -lveren, *n.n.* calf. *als het* ~ *verdronken is dempt men de put*, to lock the stable door after the horse is stolen; *het gemeste* ~, the fatted calf; *een nuchter* ~, a new-born calf. ·**kalfachtig**, *a.* calf-like.
kal·faatijzer, -s, *n.n.* caulking iron. **kal·faateraar, -s**, *n.* caulker. **kal·faten, -faat**, *v.t.*, **kal·faateren**, *v.t.* to caulk.
·**kalfsbouillon**, no pl., *n.* veal broth. ·**kalfsbout**, *n.* leg of veal. ·**kalfsgehakt**, no pl., *n.n.* minced veal. ·**kalfslapje, -s**, *n.n.* veal steak. ·**kalfsle(d)er**, no pl., *n.n.* calf(skin) (*leather*). ·**kalfsleren**, *a.* (made of) calf(skin). *in* ~ *band*, bound in calf. ·**kalfsoester, -s**, *n.* veal collop. ·**kalfsschenkel**, *n.* knuckle of veal. ·**kalfsvel, -llen**, *n.n.* calfskin; (*fig.*) drum. ·**kalfszwezerik, -kken**, *n.* sweetbread.
·**kali**, no pl., *n.* potassium. ¶·**'s**, *n.* river (*East Indies*).
ka·liber, no pl., *n.n.* calibre; (size of) bore. *van hetzelfde* ~, of a kidney (*fig.*). **kali·breren, -breer**, *v.t.* to calibrate.
·**kali(e)f**, *n.* caliph.
·**kalium**, no pl., *n.* potassium.
kalk, no pl., *n.* lime; mortar; plaster. *gebluste* ~, slaked lime; *ongebluste* ~, quicklime. ·**kalkaarde**, no pl., *n.* calcareous earth. ·**kalkachtig**, *a.* calcareous. ·**kalkbak, -kken**, *n.* hod. ·**kalkbrander, -s**, *n.* lime-burner. ·**kalkbranderij**, *n.* lime-kiln. ·**kalkei, -eren**, *n.n.* preserved egg. ·**kalken**, *v.t.* to plaster; to whitewash. ·**kalkgroef, -ven**, *n.* limestone quarry. ·**kalkhoudend**, *a.* calcareous. ·**kalkoven, -s**, *n.* lime-kiln. ·**kalksteen**, no pl., *n.* limestone.
kal·koen, *n.* turkey. **kal·koens**, *a.* ~*e haan*, turkey-cock; ~*e hen*, turkey-hen.
kalm, *a.* calm. ~ *blijven* or *zich* ~ *houden*, to keep calm. ¶*adv.* calmly. *het* ~ *aanleggen*, to go steady. **kal·meren, -meer**, *v.t.* to calm, soothe. **kal·merend**, *a.* soothing, sedative. ·**kalmoes**, no pl., *n.* calamus, sweet rush. ·**kalmpjes**, *adv.* calmly. ~ *aan*, steady on. ·**kalmte**, no pl., *n.* calmness, composure.
·**kalong, -s**, *n.* flying fox.
ka·lotje, -s, *n.n.* skull-cap.
·**kalven, kalf**, *v.i.* to calve (*of cows; glaciers*).

·**kalverachtig**, *a.* calf-like. ·**kalverliefde**, no pl., *n.* calf-love.
kam, -mmen, *n.* comb; comb, crest; crest, ridge; cog; bridge (*of violin*). *alles over één* ~ *scheren*, to treat everything in the same way.
ka·meel, -melen, *n.* camel. *eenbultige* ~, dromedary.
ka·meleon, -s, *n.* chameleon.
kame·nier, -s, *n.*, **kame·nierster, -s**, *n.* lady's maid. ·**kamer, -s**, *n.* room; chamber; ventricle. *op* ~*s wonen*, to live in digs *or* lodgings; *op mijn* ~, in my room; *Eerste K*~, First Chamber, Senate; *Tweede K*~, Second Chamber, Lower House; *K*~ *van Koophandel*, Chamber of Commerce. **kame·raad, -raden**, *n.* comrade, companion. **kame·raadschap**, no pl., *n.* comradeship, camaraderie. **kameraad·schappelijk**, *a.* comradely, companionable. ·**kamerarrest**, no pl. *n.n.* confinement to one's room. ~ *hebben*, to be confined to barracks, C.B. ·**kamerbehangsel, -s**, *n.n.* wall-paper. ·**kamerdienaar, -s** or **-naren**, *n.* groom, valet; chamberlain. ·**kamergeleerde, -n**, *n.* armchair philosopher. ·**kamergymnastiek**, no pl., *n.* indoor gymnastics. ·**kamerheer, -heren**, *n.* chamberlain. ·**kamerhuur, -huren**, *n.* rent (*for room*). ·**Kamerijk**, *n.N.* Cambrai. ·**kamerjapon, -nnen**, *n.* dressing-gown. ·**kamerlid, -leden**, *n.n.* member of parliament. ·**kamerling**, *n.* chamberlain. ·**kamermeisje, -s**, *n.n.* chambermaid. ·**kamerplant**, *n.* indoor plant. ·**kamerstrateeg, -tegen**, *n.* armchair strategist. ·**kamerverslag**, *n.n.* report of parliamentary debates.
·**kamfer**, no pl., *n.* camphor. ·**kamferachtig**, *a.* camphoric. ·**kamferballetje, -s**, *n.n.* camphor-ball. ·**kamferspiritus**, no pl., *n.* camphorated spirits.
·**kamgaren, -s**, *n.n.* worsted. ¶*a.* worsted. ·**kamhagedis, -ssen**, *n.* iguana.
ka·mille, -n, *n.* camomile.
kami·zool, -zolen, *n.* camisole.
·**kammen, kam**, *v.t.* to comb. ·**kammossel, -s** *or* **-en**, *n.* (e)scallop.
kamp, *n.n.* camp. *het* ~ *opbreken*, to break camp, strike tents; *het* ~ *opslaan*, to pitch one's tents. ¶*n.* field; lot, parcel; combat. ~ *geven*, to give in, throw up the sponge. ·**kam·panje, -s**, *n.* companion, poop.
kam·peerder, -s, *n.* camper. **kampe·ment, -s**, *n.n.* encampment. ·**kampen**, *v.i.* to fight, combat. *te* ~ *hebben met*, to have to contend with; ~ *om*, to contend for. **kam·peren, -peer**, *v.i.* to camp.
kamper·foelie, no pl., *n.* honeysuckle. *wilde* ~, woodbine.
kamper·noelie, no pl., *n.* mushroom.
kampi·oen, *n.* champion; advocate. **kampi·oenschap, -ppen**, *n.n.* championship. ·**kamprechter, -s**, *n.* umpire. ·**kampvechter, -s**, *n.* wrestler.

·kamrad, -eren, *n.n.* cog-wheel. ·kamschelp,
n. (e)scallop. ·kamsel, no pl., *n.n.* combings. ·kamwol, no pl., *n.n.* combing-wool.
kan, -nnen, *n.* jug. *wie het onderste uit de*
~ wil hebben, krijgt het lid op de neus,
grasp all lose all.
ka·naal, -nalen, *n.n.* canal; channel. *het K~,*
the Channel. Ka·naalboot, -boten, *n.*
cross-Channel steamer. ka·naalgeld, *n.n.*
canal dues. kanali·satie, no pl., *n.* canalization. kanali·seren, -seer, *v.t.* to canalize.
ka·nalje, no pl., *n.n.* rabble. ¶-s, *n.* low
person.
ka·narie, -s, *n.* canary. Ka·narisch, *a. de*
~e Eilanden, the Canaries.
kan·deel, no pl., *n.* caudle. kan·deelwijn,
no pl., *n.* negus.
·kandelaar, -s, *n.* candlestick. kande·laber,
-s, *n.* candelabrum.
kandi·daat, -daten, *n.* candidate.
kan·dij, no pl., *n.*, kan·dijsuiker, no pl., *n.*
sugar-candy.
ka·neel, no pl., *n.* cinnamon. ka·neelstokje,
-s, *n.n.* stick of cinnamon.
·kangoeroe, -s, *n.* kangaroo.
·kanis, -ssen, *n.* creel.
·kanjer, -s, *n.* whopper.
·kanker, no pl., *n.* cancer; canker. ·kankeraar,
-s, *n.* grouser, grumbler. ·kankerbloem, *n.*
poppy. ·kankeren, *v.i.* to grouse, grumble;
to canker. ·kankergezwel, -llen, *n.n.*
cancerous tumour.
·kano, -'s, *n.* canoe.
ka·non, -nnen, *n.n.* gun, cannon. ka·non-
gebulder, no pl., *n.n.* roar of cannon.
kano·niek, *a.* canonical. kanoni·seren, -seer,
v.t. to canonize.
kanon·neerboot, -boten, *n.* gunboat. ka·non-
nenvlees, no pl., *n.n.* cannon fodder.
kanon·neren, -nneer, *v.t.* to cannonade.
kanon·nier, -s, *n.* gunner. ka·nonskogel,
-s, *n.* cannon-ball. ka·nonspijs, no pl.,
n. gun-metal.
kans, *n.* chance; opportunity; probability.
~ op, a chance of; *er is geen ~ op,* there
is no chance of it; *~ hebben om,* to stand
a chance of; *de ~ kan keren,* luck may
turn; *de ~ krijgen om,* to have a chance
to; *~ lopen om,* to run the risk of; *de ~*
schoon zien om, to see one's way clear to;
de ~ waarnemen, to seize the opportunity;
de ~ wagen, to take a chance; *er ~ toe*
zien or *~ zien om,* to see a chance to.
·kansel, -s, *n.* pulpit. kansela·rij, *n.* chancery,
chancellery. ·kanse·lier, -s, *n.* chancellor.
·kanselrede, -nen, *n.* homily.
·kansje, -s, *n.n.* windfall; slender chance.
·kansrekening, *n.* theory of probability.
·kansspel, *n.n.* game of chance.
kant, *n.* side; edge, border, rim, margin;
way, direction; lace. *het raakt ~ noch wal,*
it is utterly ridiculous; *aan ~ doen,* to
tidy up; *aan de ene ~,* on the one hand;
aan or *langs de ~ van de weg,* by the side

of the road; *aan ~ leggen,* to lay aside;
naar alle ~en, in all directions; *iets over*
zijn ~ laten gaan, to take no notice of
something; *van alle ~en,* on all sides,
from all angles; *van mijn ~,* on my part;
van ~ maken, to make away with, kill;
zich van ~ maken, to commit suicide.
¶*a. ~ en klaar,* shipshape, all ready.
kan·teel, -telen, *n.n.* crenelated battlement.
·kantelen, *v.t.* to topple over. ·kanten, *a.*
(made of) lace. ¶*v.r. zich ~ tegen,* to set
one's face against. ·kantig, *a.* sharp-edged.
·kantje, -s, *n.n. op het ~ af,* a narrow
escape, close shave, by the skin of one's
teeth *or* risqué; *er de ~s aflopen,* to scamp.
·kantlijn, *n.* margin *(line).*
kan·tongerecht, *n.n.* district court. kanton-
·neren, -nneer, *v.t.* to canton *(soldiers).*
kanton·nier, -s, *n.* state roadmender.
kan·tonrechter, -s, *n.* local magistrate.
kan·toor, -toren, *n.n.* office. *niet aan het*
rechte ~ zijn, to have come to the wrong
place; *op een ~ zijn,* to work in an office;
ten kantore van, at the office(s) of. kan-
·toorbediende, -n, *n.* clerk. kan·toor-
behoeften, pl. only, *n.* stationery. kan·toor-
kruk, -kken, *n.* (office-)stool. kan·toor-
loper, -s, *n.* collecting clerk.
·kanttekening, *n.* marginal note. ·kantwerk,
no pl., *n.n.* lace(-work). ·kantwerkster,
-s, *n.* lacemaker.
ka·nunnik, -kken, *n.* canon, prebendary.
kap, -ppen, *n.* coif, hood; cowl; roof; coping.
de ~ op de tuin hangen, to run away *(of*
monk) or to lay down office. ·kapbeitel, -s,
n. chisel. ·kapblok, -kken, *n.n.* chopping-
block. ·kapdoos, -dozen, *n.* dressing-case.
ka·pel, -llen, *n.* chapel; band; butterfly.
kape·laan, -lanen, *n.* chaplain; curate
(Roman Catholic). ka·pelmeester, -s, *n.*
bandmaster.
·kapen, kaap, *v.t.* to privateer; to filch.
·kaper, -s, *n.* privateer, raider *(man, ship).*
er zijn ~s op de kust, the coast is not clear.
·kaperbrief, -ven, *n.* letter of marque.
·kaperschip, -schepen, *n.n.* privateer,
raider.
kapi·taal, -talen, *n.n.* capital, principal.
¶-tale, *a.* capital, substantial. kapitaal-
·krachtig, *a.* with considerable capital.
kapitali·seren, -seer, *v.t.* to capitalize.
kapi·teel, -telen, *n.n.* capital *(of column).*
kapi·tein, -s, *n.* captain. ka·pittel, -s, *n.n.*
chapter. ka·pittelen, *v.t.* to lecture, tell off.
ka·pittelheer, -heren, *n.* prebendary, dean.
ka·pittelkerk, *n.* cathedral, minster. ka-
·pittelsgewijs, *adv.* chapter by chapter.
kaplaars, -zen, *n.* top-boot. ·kapmantel,
-s, *n.* hooded cloak. ·kapmes, -ssen, *n.n.*
chopper.
ka·poen, *n.n.* capon.
ka·pok, no pl., *n.n.* capoc.
ka·pot, -tten, *n.* greatcoat. ¶-tte, *a.* broken,
out of order; with holes in; *(fig.)* cut up.

hij is er ~ *van,* he is terribly upset by it;
~ *gaan,* to go to pieces; ~ *slaan,* to smash.
ka·potjas, -ssen, *n.* greatcoat. **ka·pothoedje,**
-s, *n.n.* bonnet (*old woman's*).
·**kappen, kap,** *v.t.* to chop, cut down. ¶*v.i.*
to chop; to dress (*hair*). ·**kapper, -s,** *n.*
hairdresser; caper. **kappers·winkel, -s,** *n.*
hairdresser's.
kap·seizen, -seis, *v.i.* to capsize, turn turtle.
·**kapsel, -s,** *n.n.* coiffure. ·**kapspiegel, -s,** *n.*
dressing mirror. ·**kapstok, -kken,** *n.* hat-
rack, hall-stand. ·**kaptafel, -s,** *n.* dressing-
table.
Kapu·cijner, -s, *n.* Capuchin. **kapu·cijner,**
-s, *n.* Spanish pea.
·**kapverbod,** no pl., *n.n.* timber-felling prohibition.
·**kapwagen, -s,** *n.* tilted cart.
kar, -rren, *n.* cart; bike *or* car (*coll.*).
ka·raat, -raten, *n.* carat.
kara·bijn, *n.* carbine. **karabi·nier, -s,** *n.*
carabineer.
ka·raf, -ffen, *n.* carafe; decanter.
ka·rakter, -s, *n.n.* character. **karakteri·seren,**
-seer, *v.t.* to characterize. **karakteris·tiek,**
a. characteristic. ¶*adv.* characteristically.
¶*n.* characteristic. **ka·rakterloos, -loze,** *a.*
characterless.
kara·vaan, -vanen, *n.* caravan (*desert*).
kar·bies, -zen, *n.* shopping basket.
karbo·nade, -n, *n.* chop, cutlet.
kar·bonkel, -s, *n.* carbuncle.
kar·bouw, *n.* buffalo (*East Indies*).
kardi·naal, -nalen, *n.* cardinal. **kardi-**
naalschap, no pl., *n.n.* cardinalate.
kar·doen, *n.* cardoon.
kar·does, -zen, *n.* poddle; cartridge.
kare·kiet, *n.* reed-warbler.
·**Karel, *N.* Charles.** ~ *de Grote,* Charlemagne.
·**karig,** *a.* meagre; parsimonious. ~ *zijn*
met, to be sparing of. ¶*adv.* scantily.
·**karigheid,** no pl., *n.* scantiness.
kar·kas, -ssen, *n.n.* carcass; skeleton.
kar·kiet, *n.* reed-warbler.
kar·mijn, no pl., *n.n.* carmine. **kar·mijnen,**
a. carmine. **kar·mijnrood, -rode,** *a.*
crimson. **karmo·zijn,** no pl., *n.n.* crimson.
karn, *n.* churn. ·**karnemelk,** no pl., *n.* butter-
milk. ·**karnen,** *v.t.* & *v.i.,* to churn.
·**karnton, -nnen,** *n.* churn.
ka·ronje, -s, *n.n.* virago.
ka·ros, -ssen, *n.* state coach.
·**karper, -s,** *n.n.* carp.
·**kar·pet, -tten,** *n.n.* rug; small carpet.
·**karreman, -nnen,** *n.* carter; dustman.
·**karren, kar,** *v.t.* to cart. ¶*v.i.* to bike.
·**karrepaard,** *n.n.* cart-horse. ·**karrespoor,**
-sporen, *n.n.* cart-rut. ·**karrevracht,** *n.*
cart-load.
·**kartel, -s,** *n.* notch; mill (*coin*). ·**kartelen,**
v.t. to mill. ¶*v.i.* to curdle (*milk*). ·**karte-**
ling, *n.* milling (*of coin*).
kar·tets, *n.* (round of) grape-shot.
kar·ton, no pl., *n.n.* cardboard, pasteboard.

kar·tonnen, *a.* (*made of*) cardboard.
karton·neren, -neer, *v.t.* to bind in boards.
kar·wats, *n.* hunting-crop.
kar·wei, *n.* job.
kar·wij, no pl., *n.* caraway. **kar·wijzaad,**
-zaden, *n.n.* caraway-seed.
kas, -ssen, *n.* case (*of watch*); socket (*of eye,*
tooth); hothouse; glasshouse; cash-desk,
pay-desk. *goed bij* ~ *zijn,* to be in funds;
slecht bij ~ *zijn,* to be short of money,
hard up; *geld in* ~, money in hand.
·**kasboek,** *n.n.* cash-book. ·**kasdruif, -ven,**
n. hothouse grape(s). ·**kasgroente, -n,** *n.*
vegetables grown under glass. **kasioper,**
-s, *n.* collecting clerk. ·**kasmiddelen,** pl.
only, *n.n.* cash in hand.
·**Kaspisch,** *a.* ~*e Zee,* Caspian Sea.
·**kasplant,** *n.* hothouse plant. ·**kassa, -'s,** *n.*
See **cassa.** ·**kassen, kas,** *v.t.* to set (*jewels*).
kas·sier, -s, *n.* cashier; teller. **kas·siers-**
kantoor, -toren, *n.n.* banking office.
kas·siersrekening, *n.* banking account.
kast, *n.* cupboard; case (*for instrument*);
digs; jug, quod. *in de* ~ *zitten,* to be in
quod.
kas·tanje, -s, *n.* chestnut; chestnut(-tree).
wilde ~, horse-chestnut. **kas·tanjeboom,**
-bomen, *n.* chestnut(-tree). **kas·tanjelaan,**
-lanen, *n.* avenue of chestnut-trees.
kas·teel, -telen, *n.n.* castle; castle, rook
(*chess*).
·**kastegeest,** no pl., *n.n.* caste-spirit.
·**kastekort,** *n.n.* deficit.
·**kaste·lein,** *n.* innkeeper, publican.
·**kastenmaker, -s,** *n.* cabinet-maker.
kas·tijden, *v.t.* to chastise. **kas·tijding,** *n.*
chastisement.
·**kastje, -s,** *n.n.* small cupboard. *van het* ~
naar de muur zenden, to send from pillar
to post.
kas·toor, -toren, *n.* castor, beaver. **kas·toren,**
a. beaver.
·**kastpapier,** no pl., *n.n.* shelf-paper.
kas·trol, -llen, *n.* casserole.
kasu·aris, -ssen, *n.* cassowary.
kat, -tten, *n.* cat. *de* ~ *de bel aanbinden,* to
bell the cat; *de* ~ *uit de boom kijken,* to
see which way the cat jumps; *hij knijpt*
de ~ *in het donker,* he is a whited sepulchre; *leven als* ~ *en hond,* to lead a cat-
and-dog life; *als een* ~ *in een vreemd*
pakhuis, like a fish out of water; *een* ~ *in*
de zak kopen, to buy a pig in a poke.
·**katachtig,** *a.* cat-like.
kata·falk, *n.* catafalque.
·**kater, -s,** *n.* tom-cat; hangover.
ka·theder, -s, *n.* chair. **kathe·draal, -dralen,**
n. cathedral.
Katho·liek, *n.* & *a.* (Roman) Catholic.
·**katjang, -s,** *n.* pea-nut; half-caste (*insult*).
·**katje, -s,** *n.n.* kitten; catkin. *geen* ~ *om*
zonder handschoenen aan te pakken, a
spitfire.
ka·toen, no pl., *n.n.* cotton. *iemand van* ~

geven, to let him have it. **ka·toenbouw,** no pl., n. cotton-growing. **ka·toendrukkerij,** n. calico-printing works. **ka·toenen,** a. (ma:e of) cotton. **ka·toenfabriek,** n. cotton mill. **ka·toenfabrikant,** n. cotton manufacturer. **ka·toenolie, -liën,** n. cotton-seed oil. **ka·toenpit, -tten,** n. cotton seed. **ka·toenspinner, -s,** n. cotton-spinner. **ka·toenspinnerij,** n. cotton mill. **ka·toentje, -s,** n.n. cotton print. **ka·toenwaren,** pl. only, n. cottons, cotton fabrics. **ka·toenwever, -s,** n. cotton weaver. **ka·toenweverij,** n. cotton mill. **ka·toenwol,** no pl., n. wincey. **ka·toenzaad, -zaden,** n.n. cotton seed.

katoog, -togen, n.n. cat's-eye.
ka·trol, -llen, n. pulley. **ka·trolblok, -kken,** n.n. pulley block. **ka·trolschijf, -ven,** n. pulley sheave.
kattebak, -kken, n. dickey (seat). **katte·belletje, -s,** n.n. little note, scrap of paper. **kattekwaad,** no pl., n.n. monkey tricks, mischief. **kattenasyl, -s,** n.n. cats' home. **kattengeslacht,** no pl., n.n. feline race. **kattengespin,** no pl., n.n. purring. **katte·pult,** n. catapult. **katterig,** a. head-achy (morning-after). **katterigheid,** no pl., n. See **kater.** **kattesprong,** n. very short distance. **kattestaart,** n. cat's-tail. **kattetong,** n. cat's tongue (chocolate). **kattevel, -llen,** n.n. catskin. **kattig,** a. catty, cattish. **katuil,** n. screech owl. **katvis,** no pl., n. small fry.
kauri, -'s, n. cowrie.
kauw, n. jackdaw.
kauwen, v.i. to chew, masticate. ¶v.i. ~ op, to chew. **kauwgom,** no pl., n.n. chewing gum.
kavel, -s, n. lot, parcel. **kavelen,** v.t. to parcel out, divide into lots; to compute. **kaveling,** n. lot, parcel; parcelling-out.
kaze·mat, -tten, n. casemate.
kazen, kaas, v.i. to curdle.
ka·zerne, -s, n. barrack(s) (mil.). **ka·zerne·bouw,** no pl., n. building of (depressing) tenements. **ka·zerneachtig,** a. barrack-like.
ka·zuifel, -s, n. chasuble.
keel, no pl., n.n. gules. ¶**kelen,** n. throat. een ~ opzetten, to cry out loud, complain loudly; het hangt me de ~ uit, I am fed-up with it. **keelband,** n. chin-strap. **keelgat,** n.n. gullet. in het verkeerde ~, down the wrong way. **keelholte, -n,** n. pharynx. **keelklank,** n. guttural (sound). **keelontsteking,** n. laryngitis. **keelpijn,** no pl., n. sore throat. **keelspiegel, -s,** n. laryngoscope.
keep, kepen, n. notch; cape.
keer, keren, n. turn, change; time, times. één ~, once; twee ~, twice; een paar ~, a few times; in één ~, at one go; op een ~, some time, one day, once upon a time; ... per ~, ... a time (so much); voor één ~, for once; voor deze ene ~, for this once.

keerdam, -mmen, n. weir. **keerkring,** n. tropic. **keerpunt,** n.n. turning point, crisis. **keersluis, -zen,** n. sluice. **keertje, -s,** n.n. time. kom eens een ~ aanlopen, do drop in sometime. **keerzijde, -s,** n. reverse (side). zie ~, please turn over.
Kees, N. abbrev. of Cornelis. **keeshond,** n. Chow (dog).
keet, keten, n. salt-works; shed. ~ hebben, to have fun; een ~ schoppen, to kick up a row.
keffen, kef, v.i. to yap. **keffer, -s,** n. yapping dog.
keg, -ggen, n. wedge. **kegel, -s,** n. cone; icicle; ninepin. **kegelaar, -s,** n. skittles-player. **kegelbaan, -banen,** n. skittle-alley, bowling alley. **kegelen,** v.i. to play game of skittles or ninepins. **kegel·snede, -n,** n. conic section. **kegelspel,** no pl., n.n. game of skittles.
kei, n. cobble(-stone); pebble. een ~ van een ..., a terrifically hard ... **keihard,** a. as hard as stone.
keil, n. wedge. **keilen,** v.t. to pitch; to play at ducks and drakes. **keilschrift,** no pl., n.n. cuneiform writing.
·keizer, n. emperor. geef de ~ wat des ~s is, render unto Caesar that which is due unto Caesar; waar niets is verliest de ~ zijn recht, nothing breeds nothing. **keize·rin, -nnen,** n. empress. **keizerlijk,** a. imperial. **keizerrijk,** n.n. empire. **keizer·schap,** no pl., n.n. emperorship. **keizers·kroon, -kronen,** n. imperial crown; crown-imperial (plant).
·kelder, -s, n. cellar. naar de ~ gaan, to go to the bottom (ship). **kelderen,** v.t. to store (in cellar). ¶v.i. to slump, crash (shares). **keldergat,** n.n. manhole; vent-hole; cellar mouth. **kelderkeuken, -s,** n. basement kitchen. **kelderruimte,** no pl., n. cellarage. **keldertje, -s,** n.n. cellaret. **kelderwoning,** n. basement.
kelen, keel, v.t. to kill, cut throat of.
kelk, n. cup, chalice; calyx. **kelkblad,** n.n. sepal. **kelk·vormig,** a. cup-shaped.
·kelner, -s, n. waiter. **kelne·rin, -nnen,** n. waitress.
Kelt, n. Celt.
kemel, -s, n. (poet.) camel. **kemelshaar,** no pl., n.n. camel's-hair. **kemelsharen,** a. camel's-hair.
Kempen, pl., N. de ~, the Campine.
kemphaan, -hanen, n. fighting cock; game-cock.
kenbaar, -bare, a. distinguishable, recogniz-able. **kenbaarheid,** no pl., n. recogniz-ability. **kenmerk,** n.n. characteristic; distinguishing mark. **kenmerken,** v.t. to characterize. ¶v.r. zich ~ door, to be characterized by. **kenmerkend,** a. characteristic. **kennelijk,** a. apparent, visible. in ~e staat (van dronkenschap), drunk and incapable. ¶adv. apparently;

obviously. ·**kennen, ken,** *v.t.* to know, be
acquainted with; to know, understand;
to seek advice of. ~ *aan,* to know by;
van gezicht ~, to know by sight; *te* ~
geven, to give to understand, signify,
intimate; *uit elkaar* ~, to know apart;
zich aan iets laten ~ or *zich laten* ~, to
show oneself up, expose oneself; *zich doen*
~ *als,* to show oneself (as); *iemand in
iets* ~, to seek a person's advice concerning. ·**kenner, -s,** *n.* connoisseur.
·**kennersblik,** no pl., *n.* the eye of a
connoisseur. ·**kennis, -ssen,** *n.* acquaintance
(*person*). ¶no pl., *n.* knowledge; learning;
acquaintance (*knowledge*); acquaintanceship; consciousness. *met* ~ *van zaken,* with
expert knowledge, expertly; *bij* ~, conscious; *buiten* ~, unconscious; *buiten
iemands* ~, without a person's knowledge;
in ~ *brengen met,* to introduce to; ~ *geven
van,* to give notice of; ~ *hebben aan,* to be
acquainted with (*person*); ~ *hebben van,*
to have knowledge of; *ter* ~ *komen van,*
to come to the knowledge of; ~ *maken
met,* to make the acquaintance of; ~
nemen van, to note, take cognizance of;
in ~ *stellen met* or *van,* to inform of.
·**kennisgeving,** *n.* notice, intimation. *voor*
~ *aannemen,* to take as read, duly note.
·**kennismaking,** *n.* acquaintance (*becoming
acquainted*). *bij nadere* ~, on further
acquaintance. ·**kennisneming,** no pl., *n.*
cognizance. ·**kenschetsen,** *v.t.* to characterize (*describe*). ·**kenspreuk,** *n.* motto.
·**kenteken,** *n.n.* distinguishing mark.
·**kentekenen,** *v.t.* to characterize (*by token*).
·**kenteren,** *v.i.* to turn (*of tide, season*).
·**kentering,** *n.* turn (*of tide, season*).
·**kepen, keep,** *v.t.* to notch. ·**keper, -s,** *n.*
twill. *iets op de* ~ *beschouwen,* to examine
something closely. ·**keperen,** *v.t.* to twill.
·**kerel, -s,** *n.* fellow, chap. ·**kereltje, -s,**
n.n. little chap.
·**keren, keer,** *v.t.* to turn; to turn up (*card*);
to check, beat off (*attack*); to turn out,
sweep. ¶zich ~, *v.r.* to turn. *zich* ~
tegen, to turn against; *zich* ~ *naar,* to
turn towards. ·**kerend,** *a. per* ~*e post,*
by return of post.
kerf, -ven, *n.* notch. ·**kerfbank,** *n.* cutting-
bench (*tobacco*). ·**kerfstok, -kken,** *n.* tally
(*stick*). *veel op zijn* ~ *hebben,* to have a
great deal on one's conscience.
kerk, *n.* church; church, chapel, tabernacle.
een huis als een ~, a vast house; *de* ~ *in
het midden laten,* to give and take; *de* ~
gaat aan, church begins; *de* ~ *gaat uit,*
church is over; *ter* ~ *gaan,* to go to church.
·**kerkban,** no pl., *n.* excommunication.
·**kerkbank,** *n.* pew. ·**kerkbelasting,** no pl.,
n. church rate. ·**kerkbestuur, -sturen,** *n.n.*
church council. ·**kerkbezoek,** no pl., *n.n.*
church attendance. ·**kerkdienst,** *n.* church
service, divine service. ·**kerkdienaar, -s.**

n. verger, sexton. ·**kerkekamer, -s,** *n.*
vestry; consistory. ·**kerkekas, -ssen,** *n.*
church funds. ·**kerkelijk,** *a.* ecclesiastical;
church-. ~ *feest,* church festival; ~ *goed,*
church property. ·**kerker, -s,** *n.* dungeon.
·**kerkeraad, -raden,** *n.* church council;
consistory. ·**kerkerecht,** *n.n.* church law,
canon law. ~*en,* last sacraments. ·**ker-
keren,** *v.t.* to incarcerate. ·**kerkering,** *n.*
incarceration. ·**kerkezakje, -s,** *n.n.*
offertory bag. ·**kerkgang,** *n.* churchgoing;
churching. ~ *doen,* to be churched.
·**kerkganger, -s,** *n.* churchgoer, chapelgoer;
worshipper. ·**kerkgenootschap, -ppen,** *n.n.*
congregation; denomination. ·**kerkgezag,**
no pl., *n.n.* ecclesiastical authority. ·**kerkgezang,** *n.n.* church singing; hymn.
·**kerkhof, -ven,** *n.n.* churchyard. *op het* ~,
in the churchyard. ·**kerkklok, -kken,** *n.*
church bell; church clock. ·**kerkkraai,** *n.*
jackdaw. ·**kerkleer, -leren,** *n.* church
doctrine. ·**kerkmeester, -s,** *n.* churchwarden. ·**kerknieuws,** no pl., *n.n.* ecclesiastical news. ·**kerkrecht,** no pl., *n.n.* canon
law. ·**kerkroof,** no pl., *n.n.* church robbery.
kerks, *a.* churchy. ·**kerkschender, -s,** *n.*
sacrilegious person. ·**kerkschennis,** *n.*
sacrilege. ·**kerksge-zind,** *a.* churchy.
·**kerksge-zindheid,** no pl., *n.* churchiness.
·**kerktoren, -s,** *n.* church tower; steeple.
·**kerkvader, -s,** *n.* Church Father. *de
geschriften der* ~*s,* patristic writings.
·**kerkvoogd,** *n.* prelate. ·**kerkvorst,** *n.*
prelate; prince of the church.
·**kermen,** *v.i.* to moan.
·**kermis, -ssen,** *n.* fair. *het is niet alle dagen* ~,
Christmas comes but once a year; *het is*
~ *in de hel,* the devil is beating his wife;
van een koude ~ *thuiskomen,* to come
away with a flea in one's ear. ·**kermisbed,
-dden,** *n.n.* palliasse. ·**kermisdeun,** *n.*
street-song. ·**kermisganger, -s,** *n.* visitor
to the fair. ·**kermisgast,** *n.,* ·**kermisklant,**
n. showman. ·**kermistent,** *n.* booth (*at fair*).
·**kermisvolk,** no pl., *n.n.* show people (*of
fair*). ·**kermiswagen, -s,** *n.* caravan.
kern, *n.* core, nucleus; kernel, stone; gist.
een ~ *van waarheid,* a grain of truth.
·**kernachtig,** *a.* pithy, terse. ·**kernachtig-
heid,** no pl., *n.* pithiness. ·**kerngezond,** *a.*
perfectly healthy. ·**kernspreuk,** *n.* aphorism.
·**kerrie,** no pl., *n.* curry.
kers, *n.* cherry; cress. ·**kerseboom, -bomen,**
n. cherry-tree. ·**kersenbrandewijn,** no pl.,
n. cherry-brandy. ·**kersenhout,** no pl., *n.n.*
cherrywood. ·**kersenpluk,** no pl., *n.* cherry-
picking. ·**kersepit, -tten,** *n.* cherry-stone.
·**kerspel, -s,** *n.n.* parish.
·**Kerstavond,** *n.* Christmas eve. ·**Kerstboom,
-bomen,** *n.* Christmas-tree. ·**Kerstdag,** *n.*
Christmas day. *eerste* ~, Christmas day;
tweede ~, Boxing day; *in de* ~*en,* during
Christmas time. ·**kerstenen,** *v.t.* to

christianize. ·kerstening, n. christianiza-
tion. ·Kerstfeest, n.n. Christmas (celebration). ·Kerstkindje, no pl., n.n. Christ
child, Infant Christ. ·Kerstlied, -eren, n.n.
Christmas carol. ·Kerstmis, -ssen, n.
Christmas. ·Kerstmorgen, -s, n. Christmas
morning. ·Kerstnacht, n. Christmas night.
·Kerstroos, -rozen, n. Christmas rose.
·Kersttijd, no pl., n. Christmas-tide.
·kersvers, a. perfectly fresh; fresh as a daisy.
¶adv. fresh.
·kervel, no pl., n. chervil. dolle ~, hemlock.
·kerven, kerf, v.t., irr. to carve, notch; to cut
(tobacco). ·kerver, -s, n. cutter (of tobacco).
·ketel, -s, n. kettle; cauldron; boiler. ·ketel-
bikker, -s, n. boiler-scaler. ·ketelhuis, -zen,
n.n. boiler-house. ·ketellapper, -s, n.
tinker. ·ketelmuziek, no pl., n. charivari.
·ketelruim, n.n. boiler-room. ·ketelsteen,
no pl., n. scale, boiler-scale. ·keteltrom,
-mmen, n. kettledrum.
·keten, -s or -en, n. chain; range (mountain).
pl. bonds, fetters. ·ketenen, v.t. to chain,
shackle.
·ketsen, v.t. & v.i. to glance off; to misfire;
to turn down (proposal).
·ketter, -s, n. heretic. ·ketteren, v.i. to rage,
swear. ·kette·rij, n. heresy. ·ketterjacht,
n. heresy hunt. ·ketters, a. heretical.
·ketting, n. chain; warp. aan de ~, chained
up; aan de ~ leggen, to lay an embargo
on (ship); van de ~, off the chain, unrestrained. ·kettingbak, -kken, n. chain
locker. ·kettingbreuk, n. continued fraction
(maths.). ·kettingbrug, -ggen, n. suspension
bridge. ·kettingdraad, -draden, n. warp.
·kettingganger, -s, n. convict (in chain-
gang). ·kettinggaren, -s, n.n. warp-thread.
·kettinghandel, no pl., n. speculative
selling and reselling of goods. ·ketting-
handelaar, -s, n. speculative middleman.
·kettinghond, n. bandog. ·kettingkast, n.
gear-case. ·kettingloos, -loze, a. chainless.
·kettingsteek, -steken, n. chain stitch.
keu, -s, n. cue (billiards). ¶-en, n. pig.
·keuboer, n. belch.
·keuken, -s, n. kitchen. ¶no pl., n. cooking.
·keukenboter, no pl., n. cooking butter.
·keukenfornuis, -zen, n.n. cooking range.
·keukengerei, no pl., n.n. cooking utensils. ·keukenmeid, n. kitchenmaid, cook.
·keukenpiet, n. man who interferes in
kitchen matters. ·keukenprinses, -ssen,
n. (fac.) cook. ·keukenwagen, -s, n.
travelling kitchen.
·Keulen, n.N. Cologne. ~ en Aken zijn niet
op één dag gebouwd, Rome was not built
in a day; alsof hij het in ~ hoorde donderen,
thunderstruck (fig.). Keuls, a. from or of
Cologne. ~e pot, (traditional) earthenware
jar.
·keur, n. choice, pick; hall-mark; charter.
op ~, on approval; te kust en te ~, to
one's heart's content. ·keurbende, -n, n.

band of picked men. ·keurder, -s, n.
assayer. ·keuren, v.t. to examine, test,
inspect; to assay. ·keurig, a. neat, trim.
¶adv. excellently, exquisitely. ·keuring, n.
inspection; test, assay; medical examination (for army). ·keuringscommissie, -s,
n. medical board. ·keuringsdienst, n. food
inspection (service). ·keurkamer, -s, n.
assay hall. ·keurkorps, n.n. crack regiment.
·keurmeester, -s, n. assayer. ·keurmerk,
n.n. hall-mark.
·keurslijf, -ven, n.n. bodice.
·keurtroepen, pl. only, n. picked troops.
·keurvorst, n. elector (prince). ·keur-
vorstelijk, a. electoral. ·keurvorstendom,
-mmen, n.n. electorate (principality).
·keurvorstin, -nnen, n. electress (princess).
keus, -zen, n. choice, selection. een ~ doen,
to make a choice, take one's choice;
iemand de ~ laten, to give a person the
choice; iemand voor de ~ stellen, to offer
someone a choice; naar ~, at choice;
uit vrije ~, by or from choice.
·keuter, -s, n., ·keuterboer, n. small farmer.
·keuvela·rij, n. chat, chatting. ·keuvelen, v.i.
to chat.
·keuze, -n, n. See keus.
·kever, -s, n. beetle.
·kibbelaar, -s, n. person or child who
squabbles. ·kibbela·rij, n. squabbling,
bickering. ·kibbelen, v.t. to squabble.
·kibbelpartij, n. children's squabble.
kiek, n. snap, snapshot. ·kiekeboe!, int.
peep-bo! ·kieken, v.t. to take a snap.
¶-s, n.n. chicken. ·kiekendief, -ven, n.
kite (bird). ·kiekje, -s, n.n. See kiek.
kiel, n. keel; blouse, smock (of boy, workman).
·kielhalen, -haal, v.t. to keelhaul. ·kiellinie,
no pl., n. in ~, in line ahead.
·kielwater, no pl., n.n. wake. ·kielzwaard,
n.n. centre-board.
kiem, n.n. germ; seed (fig.). in de ~ doden
or smoren, to nip in the bud. ·kiemblad,
n.n. cotyledon. ·kiemcel, -llen, n. germ-
cell. ·kiemen, v.i. to shoot, germinate.
·kieming, n. germination. ·kiemkracht,
no pl., n. germinative power. ·kiem-
krachtig, a. germinative. ·kiempje, -s,
n.n. small shoot (from seed). ·kiemvrij, a.
germ-free. ·kiemwit, no pl., n.n. albumen.
·kienen, v.i. to play at lotto. ·kienspel,
-llen, n.n. lotto.
kier, n. crack (of light). op een ~ staan,
to be ajar; op een ~ zetten, to leave ajar.
kies, -zen, n. molar, tooth. een ~ laten
trekken, to have a tooth drawn. ¶no pl.,
n.n. pyrite(s). ¶a. considerate, delicate.
·kiesbaar, -bare, a. eligible. ·kiesbaarheid,
no pl., n. eligibility. ·kiesbevoegd, a.
entitled to vote. ·kiesbe·voegdheid, no pl.,
n. franchise. ·kiescollege, -s, n.n. electoral
college. ·kiesdeler, -s, n. electoral quota.
·kiesdistrict, n.n. constituency. kiesge-
·rechtigd, a. qualified or entitled to vote.

·**kiesheid,** no pl., *n.* delicacy, consideration. **kiesheids·halve,** *adv.* from motives of delicacy. ·**kieskauw,** *n.* dainty feeder. ·**kieskauwen,** *v.i.* to toy with one's food. **kies·keurig,** *a.* fastidious, squeamish. **kies·keurigheid,** no pl., *n.* fastidiousness. ·**kiespijn,** no pl., *n.* toothache. ·**kiesplicht,** no pl., *n.* compulsory suffrage. **kies·plichtig,** *a.* with legal obligation to vote. ·**kiesrecht,** no pl., *n.n.* suffrage. *het* ~, the vote; *algemeen* ~, universal suffrage; *het* ~ *geven,* to enfranchise; *van het* ~ *beroven,* to disfranchise. ·**kies·vereniging,** *n.* political club, electoral association. ·**kieswet, -tten,** *n.* electoral law.

·**kietelen,** *v.t.* to tickle.
kieuw, *n.* gill (*of fish*). ·**kieuwdeksel, -s,** *n.n.* gill cover.
·**kievit, -tten** or **-en,** *n.* peewit, lapwing. ·**kievitsbloem,** *n.* fritillary. ·**kievitsei, -eieren,** *n.* plover's egg.
·**kiezel,** no pl., *n.n.* gravel, shingle. ·**kiezel·aarde,** no pl., *n.* silica. ·**kiezelachtig,** *a.* siliceous. ·**kiezelpad,** *n.n.* gravelled path.
·**kiezen, kies,** *v.t.,* *str.* to choose, select, pick; to elect. ~ *tot,* to elect; *tot vriend* ~, to choose for or as a friend; *hij moet* ~ *of delen,* take it or leave it. ·**kiezer, -s,** *n.* voter, elector. *de* ~*s,* the electorate. ·**kiezerscorps,** no pl., *n.n.* electorate. ·**kiezerslijst,** *n.* voters' list, register of electors.

·**kijf,** no pl., *n. buiten* ~, beyond dispute. ·**kijfachtig,** *a.* quarrelsome. ·**kijfziek,** *a.* exceedingly quarrelsome.
·**kijk,** no pl., *n.* view, display; views, opinion; chance. *te* ~ *lopen met,* to make a show of; *te* ~ *staan* or *zijn,* to be on view; *een* ~ *geven op,* to shed light on; *een goede* ~ *hebben op,* to have sound views on or of; *er is geen* ~ *op,* there is no chance of it. ·**kijkdag,** *n.* view day (*before auction*). ·**kijken,** *v.i.,* *str.* to look, have a look. *kijk eens!,* look here!; *kijk eens even!,* just a moment!; *kijk eens aan,* there now, or well, well; *laat maar je* ~, get away with you; *hij komt pas* ~, he is still wet behind the ears; ~ *naar,* to look at; ~ *op,* to look at (*clock*); *niet op het geld* ~, not to be particular about the money; *ik sta ervan te* ~, I am amazed by it; *iemand de woorden uit de mond* ~, to hang on to someone's lips. ·**kijker, -s,** *n.* spectator; telescope, field-glass; peeper (*slang: eye*). ·**kijkgat,** *n.n.* peephole, spyhole. ·**kijk·graag, -grage,** *a.* eager to see. ·**kijkje, -s,** *n.n.* peep. *een* ~ *nemen,* to have a look round. ·**kijkkast,** *n.* raree-show. **kijk·lustig,** *a.* eager to see. **kijk·lustige, -n,** *n.* rubberneck. ·**kijkspel, -llen,** *n.n.* peep show.
·**kijven, kijf,** *v.i.,* *str.* to scold. ~ *op,* to scold someone.

kik, no pl., *n.* sound. *hij gaf geen* ~, he uttered no sound. ·**kikken, kik,** *v.i.* to breathe a word. ·**kikker, -s,** *n.* frog. ·**kikkerdril,** no pl., *n.* frogspawn. ·**kikker·kruid,** no pl., *n.n.* frogbit. ·**kikvors,** *n.* frog.
kil, -llen, *n.* channel. ¶**-lle,** *a.* chill, chilly. ·**killig,** *a.* chilly.
·**kilo, -'s,** *n.* kilogramme. ¶*prefix meaning* 1,000.
kim, -mmen, *n.* horizon. **kimkiel,** *n.* bilge-keel.
kin, -nnen, *n.* chin.
·**kina,** no pl., *n.* quinine. **kinabast,** no pl., *n.* cinchona bark. ·**kinaboom, -bomen,** *n.* cinchona(-tree).
·**kinband,** *n.* chin-strap.
kind, -eren, *n.n.* child. *een* ~ *in de wieg,* an infant in arms; *onschuldig als een pasgeboren* ~, innocent as a babe unborn; *een* ~ *des doods,* doomed person, a dead man (*fig.*); *het* ~ *van de rekening zijn,* to have to foot the bill; *het* ~ *bij zijn naam noemen,* to call a spade a spade; *als* ~ *in huis,* like one of the family; ~ *noch kraai,* neither chick nor child. ·**kindeke,** no pl., *n.n. het* ~ *Jezus,* the Infant Jesus. ·**kinderachtig,** *a.* childish, puerile. ·**kinderachtigheid, -heden,** *n.* childishness. ·**kinderarbeid,** no pl., *n.* child labour. ·**kinderdoop,** no pl., *n.* infant baptism. ·**kindergek, -kken,** *n.* person over-fond of children. ·**kindergoed,** no pl., *n.n.* baby clothes. ·**kinderhand,** *n.* child's hand. *een* ~ *is gauw gevuld,* little things please little minds. ·**kinderjaren,** pl. only, *n.n.* infancy. ·**kinderkaart,** *n.* child's half-fare. *twee en een* ~, two and a child. ·**kinderkamer, -s,** *n.* nursery. ·**kinderkolonie, -s,** *n.* children's holiday camp. ·**kinderkost,** *n.* children's food. ·**kinderleed,** no pl., *n.n.* childish grief. ·**kinderliefde,** no pl., *n.* love of children. ·**kinderlijk,** *a.* childlike, naïve; filial. ·**kinderlijkheid,** no pl., *n.* naïveté. ·**kinderloos, -loze,** *a.* childless. ·**kinderloosheid,** no pl., *n.* childlessness. ·**kindermeid,** *n.* nursemaid. ·**kindermeisje, -s,** *n.n.* nursemaid. ·**kindermoord,** *n.* infanticide (*act*). ·**kindermoorder, -s,** *n.* infanticide (*person*). ·**kindermoorderes, -ssen,** *n.* infanticide (*female*) ·**kinderpokken,** pl. only, *n.* smallpox. ·**kinderpostzegel, -s,** *n.* charity stamp. ·**kinderpraat,** no pl., *n.* childish prattle or talk. ·**kinderrijmpje, -s,** *n.n.* nursery rhyme. ·**kinderschoen,** *n.* child's shoe. *de* ~*en uittrekken* or *de* ~*en ontwassen zijn,* to cast off childish ways or to cease from childish play. ·**kinderschool, -scholen,** *n.* infant school. ·**kinderspel,** *n.n.* children's game; child's play. ·**kindersterfte,** no pl., *n.* infant mortality. ·**kinderstoel,** *n.* high-chair. ·**kinderverlamming,** *n.* infantile paralysis. ·**kinderwagen, -s,** *n.* perambulator, pram. ·**kinderziekte, -n.** *n.* infantile

complaint. ·**kinderzorg**, no pl., *n.* infant welfare. ·**kindje**, -s, *n.n.* baby. ·**kindlief**, no pl., *n.n.* my dear child. **kinds**, *a.* infantile; senile. *hij is* ~, he is in his dotage *or* second childhood; *in mijn* ~*e jaren*, in my childhood years. ·**kindsbeen**, no pl., *n.n. van* ~ *af*, from a child, from childhood. ·**kindsheid**, no pl., *n.* infancy, childhood; senility, second childhood, dotage. *eerste* ~, early childhood. ·**kindskind**, -eren, *n.n.* grandchild.

ki·nine, no pl., *n.* quinine.

kink, *n.* kink, twist. *er is een* ~ *in de kabel*, there is a hitch. ·**kinkel**, -s, *n.* lout. ·**kinkelachtig**, *a.* loutish. ·**kinkhoest**, no pl., *n.* whooping-cough. ·**kinkhoorn**, -s, *n.*, ·**kinkhoren**, -s, *n.* winkle.

·**kinnebak**, -kken, *n.* jaw.

kip, -ppen, *n.* chicken, hen. *zich zo lekker als* ~ *voelen*, to feel as fit as a fiddle; *er als de kippen bij zijn*, to be on it in a flash; *redeneren als een* ~ *zonder kop*, to talk through the back of one's neck; *met de kippen op stok gaan*, to turn in early. ·**kipkar**, -rren, *n.* tipcart.

·**kiplekker**, *adv.* as fit as a fiddle. ·**kippeboutje**, -s, *n.n.* drumstick (*of fowl*).

·**kippen**, kip, *v.t.* to tip up.

·**kippenboer**, *n.* poultry farmer. ·**kippenei**, -eren, *n.n.* chicken's egg. ·**kippengaas**, no pl., *n.n.* wire netting. ·**kippenhok**, -kken, *n.n.* poultry house, hen-house. ·**kippenloop**. -lopen, *n.*, ·**kippenren**, -nnen, *n.* poultry run. ·**kippenvel**, no pl., *n.n.* gooseflesh. *ik krijg er* ~ *van*, it makes my flesh creep. ·**kippenvoer**, no pl., *n.n.* chicken-food. ·**kippig**, *a.* shortsighted, nearsighted. ·**kippigheid**, no pl., *n.* shortsightedness.

·**kipwagen**, -s, *n.* tipcart.

·**kirren**, kir, *v.i.* to coo.

·**kiskassen**, -kas, *v.i.* to play ducks and drakes.

kist, *n.* packing case; chest; (large wooden) box; coffin. ·**kistdam**, -mmen, *n.* cofferdam. ·**kisten**, *v.t.* to place in coffin; to protect with cofferdam. *laat je niet* ~, don't put up with it. ·**kistje**, -s, *n.* small case; box (*of cigars*).

kit, -tten, *n.* jug; coal-scuttle; opium den. ·**kitlijm**, *n.* lute (*cement*).

·**kittelachtig**, *a.* ticklish. ·**kittelen**, *v.t.* to tickle. ·**kittelig**, *a.* ticklish. **kitte·lorig**, *a.* touchy.

·**kitten**, kit, *v.t.* to lute (*cement*).

·**kittig**, *a.* spruce.

·**klaaglied**, -eren. *n.n.* lament, dirge. ·**klaaglijk**, *a.* plaintive, doleful. ·**Klaagmuur**, *N.* Wailing Wall. ·**klaagschrift**, *n.n.* written complaint. ·**klaagstem**, -mmen, *n.* plaintive voice. ·**klaagtoon**, -tonen, *n.* plaintive note. ·**klaagvrouw**, *n.* wailing woman. ·**klaagzang**, *n.* lament, dirge.

klaar, klare, *a.* clear, transparent; clear, evident; ready, finished. *klare jenever*, neat gin; *klare onzin*, pure nonsense; *klare wijn schenken*, to make oneself perfectly clear; ~ *is Kees*, that is that; *zo* ~ *als een klontje*, as plain as a pikestaff. ¶*adv.* clearly. ~ *wakker*, wideawake. **klaarblijkelijk**, *a.* apparent, evident. **klaarblijkelijkheid**, no pl., *n.* obviousness. ·**klaarhebben**, heb klaar, *v.t.s.*, *irr.* to have ready *or* finished. ·**klaarheid**, no pl., *n.* clearness, clarity. ·**klaarhouden**, *v.t.s.*, *irr.* to keep ready. ·**klaarkomen**, *v.i.s.*, *irr.* to get ready (*in time*). ·**klaarkrijgen**, *v.t.s.*, *str.* to get ready. ·**klaarleggen**, leg klaar, *v.t.s.*, *irr.* to put ready. ·**klaarlicht**, *a.* bright. *op* ~*e dag*, in broad daylight. ·**klaarliggen**, lig klaar, *v.i.s.*, *str.* to lie ready. ·**klaarmaken**, maak klaar, *v.t.s.* to prepare; to make up (*prescription*). ¶*zich* ~, *v.r.s.* to get ready. ·**klaarspelen**, speel klaar, *v.t.s. het* ~, to manage it, pull it off. ·**klaarstaan**, sta klaar, *v.i.s.*, *irr.* to stand ready *or* by. ·**klaarzetten**, zet klaar, *v.t.s.* to place in readiness, set out. **klaar·ziend**, *a.* clearsighted.

kla·bak, -kken, *n.* rozzer, copper (*slang*).

klacht, *n.* complaint. *een* ~ *tegen iemand indienen or inbrengen*, to lodge a complaint against someone.

klad, -dden, *n.* blot, stain; (*coll.*) clothes. *de* ~ *erin brengen*, to spoil the market; *bij de kladden pakken*, to catch hold of a person. ¶no pl., *n.n.* draft, rough copy. *in het* ~, in rough. ·**kladden**, klad, *v.i.* to stain, blot. ·**kladje**, -s, *n.n.* rough copy. ·**kladderig**, *a.* splodged. ·**kladpapier**, no pl., *n.n.* rough paper (*for notes*); blotting paper. ·**kladschrift**, *n.n.* rough work book (*at school*). ·**kladwerk**, no pl., *n.n.* rough copy.

·**klagen**, klaag, *v.i.s.* to complain. *ik mag niet* ~, I mustn't grumble; ~ *bij*, to complain to; ~ *over*, to complain of; *zijn nood* ~, to pour out one's troubles; *steen en been* ~, to complain bitterly. ¶no pl., *n.n. geen* ~ *hebben*, to have no reason for complaint. ·**klagend**, *a.* plaintive. ·**klager**, -s, *n.* person complaining; plaintiff.

klakkeloos, -loze, *a.* unmotivated. ¶*adv.* haphazardly, thoughtlessly.

klam, -mme, *a.* clammy.

·**klamboe**, -s, *n.* mosquito net.

klamp, *n.* clamp; cleat. ·**klampen**, *v.t.* to clamp. *aan boord* ~, to buttonhole.

klan·dizie, no pl., *n.* custom; customers; goodwill. *iemand de* ~ *gunnen*, to give a person one's custom.

klank, *n.* sound. *zijn naam heeft een goede* ~, he is held in high repute. ·**klankbodem**, -s, *n.* sound-board. ·**klankbord**, *n.n.* sound-board (*over pulpit*). ·**klankkast**, *n.* sound box. ·**klankleer**, no pl., *n.* phonetics. ·**klankloos**, -loze, *a.* toneless. ·**klanknabootsend**, *a.* onomatopoeic. ·**klanknabootsing**, *n.* onomatopoeia. ·**klankrijk**.

a. sonorous. **·klankrijkheid, -heden,** *n.* sonority. **·klankwet, -tten,** *n.* sound law. **klant,** *n.* customer, client. *een ruwe* ~, a tough customer.

klap, -ppen, *n.* blow; clap, smack; slap; crack *(of whip)*. *een* ~ *krijgen,* to receive a blow *or* to be hard hit; *een* ~ *om de oren krijgen,* to have one's ears boxed. **·klapbes, -ssen,** *n.* gooseberry. **·klapbrug, -ggen,** *n.* drawbridge. **·klapdeur,** *n.* swing door. **·klapekster, -s,** *n.* shrike. **·klaphek, -kken,** *n.n.* swing gate. **·klaplopen,** *v.i.s.* ~ *bij,* to cadge from. **·klaploper, -s,** *n.* sponger, cadger. **klaplope·rij,** no pl., *n.* sponging, cadging. **klap·pei,** *n.* gossip. **·klappen, klap,** *v.i.* to clap; to gossip *(Flemish). in de handen* ~, to clap one's hands; *uit de school* ~, to tell tales out of school. ¶*n.n. hij kent het* ~ *van de zweep,* he has been through the mill. **·klapper, -s,** *n.* index, register; telltale; bone, castanet; coco-nut palm. **·klapperboom, -bomen,** *n.* coco-nut palm. **·klapperdop, -ppen,** *n.* coco-nut shell. **·klapperen,** *v.i.* to rattle; to play (type of) castanet. *zijn tanden* ~, his teeth are chattering. **·klapperman, -lui,** *n.* watchman *(old-fashioned)*. **·klappernoot, -noten,** *n.* coco-nut. **·klapperolie,** no pl., *n.* coco-nut oil. **·klappertanden,** *v.i. hij klappertandde van kou,* his teeth chattered with cold. **·klappertuin,** *n.* coco-nut plantation. **·klaproos, -rozen,** *n.* poppy. **·klapstoel,** *n.* folding chair; tip-up seat. **·klapstuk, -kken,** *n.n.* rib-piece. **·klapwieken,** *v.i.* to flap the wings.

·klare, no pl., *n.* gin. **·klaren, klaar,** *v.t.* to clear, clarify; to clear *(at customs). hij zal het wel* ~, he will manage. **·klaring,** *n.* clearing, clarification; clearance *(at customs).* **kla·roen,** *n.* clarion. **kla·roengeschal,** no pl., *n.n.* clarion call.

klas, -ssen, *n.,* **·klasse, -n,** *n.* class; class, form. *in de* ~ *zitten bij . . .,* to be in so-and-so's form. **·klasselokaal, -kalen,** *n.n.* classroom. **·klassenhaat,** no pl., *n.* class-hatred. **·klassenstrijd,** no pl., *n.* class-struggle. **klassi·kaal, -kale,** *a.* class- *(in school).* ~ *onderwijs,* class teaching.

·klaterabeel, -belen, *n.* asp(-tree). **·klateren,** *v.i.* to splash *(falling water).* to babble *(brook).* **·klatergoud,** no pl., *n.n.* tinsel.

·klauteraar, -s, *n.* one who clambers. **·klauteren,** *v.i.* to clamber, scramble. **·klautervis, -ssen,** *m.* climbing perch.

klauw, *n.* claw, talon; clutch(es) *(fig.);* *(slang)* hand; rake; fluke. **·klauwen,** *v.t.* to claw. **klau·wier,** *n.* shrike. **·klauwzeer,** no pl., *n.n.* foot-rot. *See* **mond- en klauwzeer.**

·klaver, no pl., *n.* clover; clubs *(cards).* **klaver·aas, -azen,** *n.* ace of clubs. **·klaverblad,** *n.* clover leaf. **·klaveren,** *a.* club, of clubs *(cards).* **klaver·vier, -s,** *n.* four-leaved clover; four of clubs. **·klaverzuring,** *n.* wood-sorrel.

kla·vier, *n.n.* keyboard. **·kleden, kleed,** *v.t.* to clothe, dress. *het kleedt haar goed,* it suits her very well. **·klededracht,** *n.* costume *(native).* **kle·dij,** *n.* raiment. **·kleding,** *n.* clothing. **·kledingmagazijn,** *n.n.* clothing store. **·kledingstuk, -kken,** *n.* article of dress, garment. **kleed, klederen** *or* **kleren,** *n.n.* garment, dress; carpet; *pl.* clothes. *het raakt zijn koude kleren niet,* it leaves him stone cold. **·kleedje, -s,** *n.n.* (small) carpet; (small) tablecloth. **·kleedkamer, -s,** *n.* dressing room.

Kleef, *n.N.* Cleves. **·kleefachtig,** *a.* sticky. **·kleefgaren, -s,** *n.* bird's nest. **·kleefkruid,** no pl., *n.n.* goose-grass. **·kleefmiddel,** *n.n.* adhesive. **·kleefpleister, -s,** *n.n.* sticking-plaster. **·kleefstof, -ffen,** *n.n.* gluten.

·kleerborstel, -s, *n.* clothes-brush. **·kleerkast,** *n.* wardrobe, clothes-press. **·kleerkoper, -s,** *n.* old-clothes man. **·kleermaker, -s,** *n.* tailor. **·kleerscheuren,** pl. only, *n. er zonder* ~ *afkomen,* to come off scot-free. **·kleerschuier, -s,** *n.* clothes-brush. **·kleerwinkel, -s,** *n.* ready-made shop.

klef, -ffe, *a.* sticky, clammy.

klei, no pl., *n.* clay; alluvial earth. **·kleiaarde,** no pl., *n.* alluvial earth. **·kleiachtig,** *a.* clayey. **·kleigrond,** *n.* clayey soil.

klein, *a.* little, small; slight. ~ *geld,* small change; *de* ~*e luiden,* the lower-middle class; *een* ~*e maand geleden,* not quite a month ago; *de* ~*e man,* the small man; ~ *tenue,* service dress; ~*e uitgaven,* petty expenses; *in een* ~ *uur,* in less than an hour; *de* ~*e vaart,* inland *or* coastal navigation. ¶*adv.* small. ¶*n.n. in het* ~, on a small scale *or* retail; *van* ~ *af aan,* from childhood. **Klein-·Azië,** *n.N.* Asia Minor. **·kleindochter, -s,** *n.* granddaughter. **Klein-·Duimpje,** *n.N.* Tom Thumb. **·kleineren, -neer,** *v.t.* to belittle, disparage. **klei·nering,** *n.* disparagement. **klein-geestig,** *a.* narrow-minded. **klein-goed,** no pl., *n.n.* small biscuits; small fry *(children).* **·kleinhandel,** no pl., *n.* retail trade. **·kleinhandelaar, -s,** *n.* retail trader. **klein·hartig,** *a.* pusillanimous. **klein-hartigheid,** no pl., *n.* pusillanimity. **·kleinheid, -heden,** *n.* smallness. **·kleinigheid, -heden,** *n.* trifle, small thing. **·kleinkind, -eren,** *n.n.* grandchild. **·kleinkinderschooltje, -s,** *n.n.* infant school. **·kleinkrijgen,** *v.t.s., str.* to break up, reduce; to tame *(person).* **·kleinmaken, maak klein,** *v.t.s.* to break up; to digest; to change *(into small change);* to humble **·kleinood, -noden** *or* **-nodiën,** *n.n.* jewel, gem. **klein·steeds,** *a.* provincial, suburban. **klein·steedsheid,** no pl., *n.* parochialism. **·kleintje, -s,** *n.n.* little one; small matter. *veel* ~*s maken een grote,* every little helps; *hij is voor geen* ~ *vervaard,* he dare tackle anything. **klein·zerig,** *a.* soon hurt. *hij is* erg ~, he soon cries out *or* he is a crybaby *or* physical coward. **klein·zerigheid,** no pl., *n.* physical cowardice. **klein·zielig,** *a.* petty, small-minded. **klein·zieligheid, -heden,** *n.* pettiness, smallness. **·kleinzoon, -s,** *n.* grandson.

·kleiweg, *n.* clayey road.

klem, -mmen, *n.* clip; trap. *in de ~ zitten,* to be in a scrape; *~ bijzetten,* to emphasize. ¶*no pl., n.* accent, emphasis; lock-jaw. *met ~ van redenen,* with forceful arguments. **·klemhaak, -haken,** *n.* bench hook. **·klemmen,** **klem,** *v.t.* to pinch, catch (*finger in door*); to clench (*teeth*); to press, clasp. ¶*v.i.* to stick, jam (*door*). **·klemschroef, -ven,** *n.* clamping screw. **·klemteken, -s,** *n.* stress mark. **·klemtoon, -tonen,** *n.* accent, stress.

klep, -ppen, *n.* valve; flap; peak (*of cap*); key (*of wind instrument*). **·klepel, -s,** *n.* clapper; bill (*of stork*). **·kleppen, klep,** *v.i.* to toll, clang; to clatter (*of stork*). **·klepper, -s,** *n.* night-watchman (*old-fashioned*); steed; rattlebone(s). **·klepperen,** *v.i.* to clatter. **·klepraam, -ramen,** *n.n.* fanlight.

·kleren-. *See* **kleed** *and* **kleer-.**

klerk, *n.* clerk. **·klerkenwerk,** no pl., *n.n.* clerical work.

klets, *n.* smack, slap. ¶*no pl., n.* twaddle, drivel. **·kletsen,** *v.i.* to pitch, dash; to talk rubbish; to gossip. *met de zweep ~,* to crack a whip. **·kletskop, -ppen,** *n.* baldpate; (type of) sweet biscuit. **·kletskous,** *n.* gossip, chatterbox. **·kletsmajoor, -s,** *n.,* **·kletsmeier, -s,** *n.* inveterate gossiper (*man*). **·kletsnat, -tte,** *a.* sopping wet, soaked to the skin. **·kletspraat,** no pl., *n.* rubbish, poppycock. **·kletspraatje, -s,** *n.n.* chat; *pl. See* **kletspraat**.

·kletteren, *v.i.* to clash, clatter.

·kleumen, *v.i.* to shiver. *van kou ~,* to shiver with cold.

kleur, *n.* colour; dye; complexion; suit (*cards*). *een ~ krijgen,* to blush, go red in the face; *~ bekennen,* to show one's true colours *or* to follow suit; *van ~ veranderen,* to change colour; *in ~en en geuren,* with a wealth of detail. **·kleurdoos, -dozen,** *n.* paint-box. **·kleuren,** *v.t.* to colour. ¶*v.i.* to colour, blush. **·kleurenblind,** *a.* colour-blind. **·kleurhoudend,** *a.* fast (*colour*). **·kleurig,** *a.* colourful. **·kleurling,** *n.* coloured person. **·kleurloos, -loze,** *a.* colourless. **·kleurloosheid,** no pl., *n.* drabness. **·kleurmiddel,** *n.n.,* **·kleursel, -s,** *n.n.* colouring matter. **·kleurstof, -ffen,** *n.* colouring matter, pigment, dyestuff. **·kleurtje, -s,** *n.n.* colour, tint.

·kleuter, -s, *n.* toddler. **·kleuterschool, -scholen,** *n.* kindergarten.

·kleven, kleef, *v.i.* to stick, adhere. *~ aan,* to stick to, cleave to.

·klewang, -s, *n.* East Indian sword.

kliek, *n.* clique. **·kliekje, -s,** *n.* left-overs,

odds and ends (*food*). **·kliekjesdag,** *n.* day in week on which the left-overs are eaten.

klier, *n.* gland; unbearable person. **·klierachtig,** *a.* glandulous; scrofulous. **·kliergezwel, -llen,** *n.n.* scrofulous tumour. **·klierziekte, -n,** *n.* glandular disease; scrofula.

·klieven, klief, *v.t.* to cleave. *de golven ~,* to plough the waves.

·klikken, klik, *v.i.* to tell tales. *van iemand ~* to tell on a person. ¶*v.t.* to tell. **·klikspaan, -spanen,** *n.* telltale.

klim, no pl., *n.* climb.

kli·maat, -maten, *n.n.* climate, clime. **kli·maatgordel, -s,** *n.* zone.

·klimboon, -bonen, *n.* scarlet runner. **·klimijzer, -s,** *n.n.* climbing-iron. **·klimmen, klim,** *v.i., str.* to climb. *aan de hemel ~,* to rise in the sky; *in een boom ~,* to climb up a tree. ¶*no pl., n.n.* climb; climbing. **·klimmend,** *a.* growing. **·klimmer, -s,** *n.* climber. **·klimming,** *n. rechte ~,* right ascension. **·klimop,** no pl., *n.n.* ivy. *met ~ begroeid,* ivy-clad. **·klimpartij,** *n. het was een hele ~,* there was a lot of climbing needed. **·klimplant,** *n.* climber, climbing plant. **·klimroos, -rozen,** *n.* rambler (rose).

kling, *n.* blade (*of sword*); sand-hill. *over de ~ jagen,* to put to the sword. **·klingelen,** *v.i.* to tinkle, jingle.

kli·niek, *n.* clinic. **·klinisch,** *a.* clinical.

klink, *n.* latch, catch. **·klinkbout,** *n.* rivet. **·klinkdicht,** *n.n.* sonnet. **·klinken,** *v.i., str.* to sound, ring; to ring out; to clink (*glasses*). *het klinkt als een klok,* it sounds fine. ¶*v.t., str.* to clinch, rivet. **·klinkend,** *a.* resonant; sonorous. *~e munt,* hard cash. **·klinker, -s,** *n.* riveter; brick; vowel. **·klinkhamer, -s,** *n.* riveting hammer. **·klinkklaar, -lare,** *a.* pure, absolute. **·klinknagel, -s,** *n.* rivet. **·klinkwerk,** no pl., *n.n.* riveting.

klip, -ppen, *n.* rock, reef. *blinde ~,* sunken rock; *tegen de klippen op,* shamelessly. **·klipper, -s,** *n.* clipper (*ship*). **·klipvis,** no pl., *n.* dried cod. **·klipzout,** no pl., *n.n.* rock-salt.

klis, -ssen, *n.* burr; burdock; tangle (*of hair*). **·kliskruid,** no pl., *n.n.* burdock. **·klissen, klis,** *v.i.* to become tangled.

klit, -tten, *n. See* **klis**.

·klodder, -s, *n.* lump, blob. **·klodderen,** *v.i.* to daub.

kloek, *n.* brooding hen. ¶*a.* stout, brave; stout, heavy (*volume*). **·kloekheid,** no pl., *n.* boldness, bravery. **kloek·hartig,** *a.,* **kloek·moedig,** *a.* bold, resolute.

kloet, *n.* punt-pole.

klok, -kken, *n.* clock; bell (*of church, ship*); bell-glass. *hij heeft de ~ horen luiden, maar hij weet niet vaar de klepel hangt,* a little learning is a dangerous thing; *het aan de grote ~ hangen,* to bruit it about; *het is . . . wat de* ~ *slaat,* . . . is the order of the day; *op de* ~ *af,* to the minute; *een man van de* ~, a punctual man. ·klokgelui, no pl., *n.n.* ringing of bells, bell-ringing. ·klokgieter, -s, *n.* bell-founder. ·klokhen, -nnen, *n.* See kloek. ·klokhuis, -zen, *n.n,* (apple) core. ·klokje, -s, *n.n.* small clock *or* bell; hare-bell. ·klokke, no pl., *n.* ~ *vijf,* on the stroke of five. ·klokken, klok, *v.i.* to cluck. ·klokkenhuis, -zen, *n.n.* bell-chamber. ·klokkenspel, -llen, *n.n.* carillon. ·klokketoren, -s, *n.* clock- *or* bell-tower; steeple; belfry. ·klokketouw, *n.n.,* ·klokkereep, -repen. *n.* bell-rope. ·klokslag, no pl., *n.* ~ *vijf* or *met* ~ *van vijf,* on the stroke of five. ·klokslot, *n.n.* time-lock. ·klokspijs, no pl., *n.* bell-metal. ·klokvormig, *a.* bell-shaped.

klomp, *n.* clog, wooden shoe; lump; nugget. *één* ~ *zenuwen,* a bundle of nerves; *hij komt op* ~*en,* it is obvious what he wants; *nu breekt mijn* ~, well, I'm bothered. ·klompenmaker, -s, *n.* clogmaker. klompenmake·rij, *n.* clogmaker's yard. ·klompvoet, *n.* club-foot.

klont, *n.* clot; lump; clod. ·klonter, -s, *n.* clot. ·klonteren, *v.i.* to clot, curdle. ·klonterig, *a.* clotted, lumpy. ·klontje, -s, *n.n.* lump (*of sugar*). ·klontjessuiker, no pl., *n.* loaf sugar (*lumps*).

kloof, kloven, *n.* cleft, crevice; chap(s) (*in skin*); gulf (*fig.*). ·kloofmes, -ssen, *n.n.* cleaver.

·klooster, -s, *n.n.* monastery; nunnery, convent; cloister. ·kloosterachtig, *a.* cloistral, monastic. ·kloosterbroeder, -s, *n.* friar; lay brother. ·kloostergang, *n.* cloister (*corridor*). ·kloostergelofte, -n, *n.* monastic vow. ·kloosterlijk, *a.* monastic. ·kloosterling, *n.* monk; nun. ·kloosterorde, -n, *n.* monastic order. ·kloosterwezen, no pl., *n.n.* monasticism.

kloot, kloten, *n.* ball, globe.

·klop, -ppen, *n.* knock, tap. *iemand* ~ *geven* to beat a person; ~ *krijgen,* to be beaten. ·klopgeest, *n.* rapping spirit, poltergeist. ·klophengst, *n.* ridgel (*horse*). ·klopjacht, *n.* rough-house, scrap. ·kloppen, klop, *v.i.* to knock, tap; to tally, agree. ¶*v.t.* to beat (*egg, carpet*); to beat (*person at game*). *iemand geld uit de zak* ~, to get money out of a person. ·klopper, -s, *n.* door-knocker. ·klopping, *n.* pulsation, throb. ·kloptor, -rren, *n.* death-watch beetle.

klos, -ssen, *n.* bobbin, spool, reel; coil. ·kloskant, no pl., *n.* bobbin lace. ·klossen, klos, *v.t.* to make (*lace*); to clump.

·klotsen, *v.i.* to beat, dash (*cf waves*). ¶no pl., *n.n.* lapping (*of waves*).

·kloven, kloof, *v.t.* to cleave, chop; to split (*diamonds*). klove·nier, -s, *n.* harquebusier.

klucht, *n.* farce; bevy. ·kluchtig, *a.* farcical.

·kluchtigheid, -heden, *n.* drollery. ·kluchtspel, *n.n.* farce.

kluif, -ven *n.* claw; knuckle (*of pork, etc.*). ¶no pl., *n. een hele* ~, a tough proposition. ·kluifje, -s, *n.n.* bone (*for gnawing*). *lekker* ~, titbit. ·kluiffok, -kken, *n.* fore spritsail. ·kluifhout, *n.n.* jibboom.

kluis, -zen, *n.* hermitage; strong-room, safe-deposit; hawse-hole. ·kluisgat, *n.n.* hawse-hole.

·kluister, -s, *n.* fetter, shackle. ·kluisteren, *v.t.* to fetter, trammel.

kluit, *n.* avocet; five-cent piece; lump, clod. *flink uit de* ~*en gewassen,* tall, strapping; *uit de* ~*en schieten,* to grow quickly. ·kluitje, -s, *n.n.* small lump. *met een* ~ *in het riet sturen,* to fob off.

·kluiven, kluif, *v.t. & v.i.* to gnaw, pick. ·kluiver, -s, *n.* jib. ·kluiverboom, -bomen, *n.* jibboom.

·kluizenaar, -s, *n.* hermit. ·kluizenaarskreeft, -s, *n.* hermit-crab.

·klungel, -s, *n.* lout. ·klungelaar, -s, *n.* bungler. ·klungelen, *v.t.* to bungle.

kluts, no pl., *n. de* ~ *kwijt raken,* to lose one's head; *de* ~ *kwijt zijn,* to be flustered. ·klutsen, *v.t.* to beat, whisk.

·kluwen, -s, *n.n.* ball, clew (*of wool, etc.*).

·knaagdier, *n.n.* rodent.

knaap, knapen, *n.* (stilted) boy, lad.

·knabbelen, *v.t. & v.i.* to nibble. ~ *aan* or *op,* to nibble (at).

·knagen, knaag, *v.i.* to gnaw. ~ *aan,* to gnaw (at). ·knager, -s, *n.* gnawer. ·knaging, *n.* gnawing; pangs (*of conscience*).

knak, *n.* snap, crack. *een* ~ *geven,* to deal a blow to; *een* ~ *krijgen,* to receive a blow. ·knakken, knak, *v.t.* to snap; to impair. ¶*v.i.* to snap, crack. ·knakworst, *n.* pork sausage; chipolata sausage.

knal, -llen, *n.* bang, detonation, report. ·knalgas, no pl., *n.n.* detonating gas. ·knalgoud, no pl., *n.n.* fulminate of gold. ·knalkwik, no pl., *n.n.* fulminate of mercury. ·knallen, knal, *v.i.* to bang; to crack (*rifle*). ·knalpatroon, -tronen, *n.* detonator. ·knalpot, -tten, *n.* silencer. ·knalsignaal, -nalen, *n.n.* detonator.

knap, -ppen, *n.* snap, crack. ¶-ppe, *a.* handsome; clever, smart; respectable. ·knapheid, no pl., *n.* good looks; cleverness; skill. ·knapjes, *adv.* cleverly, smartly; neatly.

·knapkers, *n.* bigaroo.

·knappen, knap, *v.i.* to snap, crack. *een uiltje* ~, to take forty winks.

·knapperd, -s, *n.* clever one.

·knapperen, *v.i.* to crackle (*fire*).

·knapzak, -kken, *n.* knapsack.

knar, -rren, *n.* gnarl, knot.

·knarpen, *v.i.* to scrunch, crunch.

·knarsen, *v.t.* to grate, creak. *op* or *met de tanden* ~, to gnash one's teeth. ·knarsetanden, *v.i.* to gnash one's teeth.

knauw, *n.* bite. *een ~ geven*, to damage, seriously; *een ~ krijgen*, to be hard hit. ·**knauwen**, *v.i.* to gnaw.

knecht, *n.* manservant; man, mate, boy. ·**knechten**, *v.t.* to enslave. ·**kneohtschap**, no pl., *n.* servitude.

·**kneden**, **kneed**, *v.t.* to knead. ·**kneedbaar**, -bare, *a.* malleable. ·**kneedmachine**, -s, *n.* kneading machine.

kneep, **knepen**, *n.* pinch; trick. *daar zit 'm de ~*, that's where the shoe pinches; *hij heeft er de ~ van weg*, he knows all the tricks.

·**knekelhuis**, -zen, *n.n.* charnel-house.

knel, no pl., *n. in de ~ zitten*, to be in a fix. ·**knellen**, **knel**, *v.t.* to pinch, squeeze. ¶*v.i.* to pinch (*of shoes*). ·**knellend**, *a.* oppressive.

·**knerpen**, *v.i.* to crunch, scrunch.

·**knersen**, *v.i.* See **knarsen**.

·**knetteren**, *v.t.* to crackle (*burning wood*, *rifle-fire*).

kneu, *n.* linnet.

·**kneukel**, -s, *n.* knuckle.

·**kneusje**, -s, *n.n.* damaged egg.

·**kneuterig**, *a.* despondent.

·**kneuzen**, **kneus**, *v.t.* to bruise. ·**kneuzing**, *n.* bruise, contusion.

·**knevel**, -s, *n.* big moustache. ·**knevelaar**, -s, *n.* extortioner. **knevela·rij**, *n.* extortion. ·**knevelen**, *v.t.* to gag; to extort money from. *de pers ~*, to muzzle the press.

·**knibbelaar**, -s, *n.* haggler. **knibbela·rij**, *n.* haggling. ·**knibbelen**, *v.i.* to haggle.

knie, -ieën, *n.* knee. *iets onder de ~ hebben*, to have mastered a subject; *over de ~ leggen*, to put across one's knee, spank; *tot aan de ~ën*, up to one's knees. ·**kniebroek**, *n.* knickerbockers, knee-breeches. ·**kniebuiging**, *n.* genuflection. ·**knielen**, *v.i.* to kneel. ·**knielkussen**, -s, *n.n.* hassock. ·**knieschijf**, -ven, *n.* knee-cap. ·**kniesoor**, -soren, *n.n.* surly person. ·**kniestuk**, -kken, *n.n.* knee-patch. ·**knieval**, -llen, *n.* prostration. *een ~ doen voor*, to prostrate oneself before.

·**kniezen**, **knies**, *v.i.* to mope. ·**kniezerig**, *a.* fretful.

·**knijpbril**, -llen, *n.* pince-nez. ·**knijpen**, *v.t.*, *str.* & *v.i.*, *str.* to pinch. *iemand in de arm ~*, to pinch a person's arm. ·**knijper**, -s, *n.* clip, fastener; pincer (*of crab*). ·**knijptang**, *n.* pair of pincers.

knik, -kken, *n.* nod. ·**knikkebenen**, -been, *v.i.* to give at the knees. ·**knikkebollen**, -bol, *v.i.* to nod (*with sleep*). ·**knikken**, **knik**, *v.i.* to nod; to shake (*of knees*). (*van*) *ja ~*, to nod assent; (*van*) *nee ~*, to shake one's head. ·**knikker**, -s, *n.* marble (*toy*); (*fac.*) pate. ·**knikkeren**, *v.i.* to play marbles. *iemand er uit ~*, to kick someone out. ·**knikkerspel**, *n.n.* game of marbles.

·**knip**, -ppen, *n.* snip, cut (*with scissors*);

snap (*with fingers*); (small) trap; catch (*on door*). *het is geen ~ voor de neus waard*, it isn't worth a button. ·**knipcursus**, -ssen, *n.* sewing class. ·**knipmes**, -ssen, *n.n.* penknife. *buigen als een ~*, to bow and scrape. ·**knipogen**, -oog, *v.i.* to wink; to blink. *~ tegen*, to wink at. ·**knipoogje**, -s, *n.n.* wink. ·**knippatroon**, -tronen, *n.n.* paper pattern. ·**knippen**, **knip**, *v.t.* to cut (*with scissors*); to punch *or* clip (*tickets*). ¶*v.i.* to blink. *met de oogleden ~*, to blink rapidly; *met de vingers ~*, to snap one's fingers. See **geknipt**. ·**knipschaar**, -scharen, *n.* (pair of) scissors, clippers. ·**knipsel**, -s, *n.n.* cutting, clipping. ·**kniptor**, -rren, *n.* snap beetle.

·**knobbel**, -s, *n.* knob; lump, bump. ·**knobbelig**, *a.* knobbly; gnarled.

·**knoedel**, -s, *n.* lump (*of dough*); dumpling.

·**knoei**, no pl., *n.* muddle. *in de ~ zitten*, to be in a muddle. ·**knoeiboel**, no pl., *n.* muddle, mess; swindle. ·**knoeien**, *v.i.* to mess about with; *~ met*, to tamper with, falsify. ·**knoeier**, -s, *n.* person who makes a mess; cheat. **knoeie·rij**, *n.* malversation. ·**knoeister**, -s, *n.* person who makes a mess; cheat (*female*). ·**knoeiwerk**, no pl., *n.n.* shoddy work.

knoest, *n.* knot, gnarl. ·**knoestig**, *a.* gnarled.

knoet, *n.* knout.

·**knoflook**, no pl., *n.n.* garlic.

knok, -kken, *n.* bone. ·**knokig**, *a.* bony. ·**knokkel**, -s, *n.* knuckle. ·**knokkelkoorts**, no pl., *n.* dengue fever. ·**knokken**, **knok**, *v.i.* to fight.

knol, -llen, *n.* tuber, swede; jade (*old horse*). *iemand knollen voor citroenen verkopen*, to lead a person up the garden path. ·**knolgewas**, -ssen, *n.n.* tuberous plant. ·**knollenland**, no pl., *n.n.* turnip field(s). ·**knollentuin**, no pl., *n. hij is in zijn ~*, he is as pleased as Punch. ·**knolraap**, -rapen, *n.* swede. ·**knolselderij**, no pl., *n.* celeriac. ·**knolvormig**, *a.* tuberous. ·**knolzaad**, no pl., *n.n.* turnip seed.

knook, **knoken**, *n.* bone.

knoop, **knopen**, *n.* knot; button, stud, node. *een ~ leggen*, to tie a knot; *een ~ losmaken*, to undo a knot; *in de ~ raken*, to get tangled up; *de ~ doorhakken*, to cut the knot; *daar zit 'm de ~*, there lies the difficulty; *er een ~ op leggen*, to swear, curse; *knopen draaien*, to make buttons; *iets achter de knopen hebben*, to wrap oneself round (food, drink). ·**knoopkruid**, no pl., *n.n.* knapweed. ·**knooplaers**, -zen, *n.* button-boot. ·**knooplijn**, *n.* nodal line. ·**knoopnaald**, *n.* netting-needle. ·**knooppunt**, *n.n.* nodal point; junction, crossing. *~ van spoorwegen*, railway centre. ·**knoopsgat**, *n.n.* button-hole. **knop**, -ppen, *n.* bud; knob, handle; button, bell-push, switch (*electric light*); pommel. ·**knopen**, **knoop**, *v.t.* to tie, knot; to button; to make, knot (*nets*). *iets in zijn oor* ~ to make a (mental) note of, not to forget. ·knopendraaier, -s, *n.* button-maker. ·knopenhaakje, -s, *n.n.* buttonhook. ·knopenschaar, -scharen, *n.* button-stick. ·knoppen, knop, *v.i.* to bud.

knor, -rren, *n.* grunt. *knorren krijgen*, to be scolded. ·knorbeen, no pl., *n.n.* cartilege, gristle. ·knorhaan, -hanen, *n.* gurnet. ·knorren, knor, *v.i.* to grunt; to grumble. ~ *op*, to scold, grumble at. ·knorrepot, -tten, *n.* grumbler, grouser. ·knorrig, *a.* peevish, grumpy.

knot, -tten, *n.* knot, skein, clew. knots, *n.* cudgel, club. ·knotten, knot, *v.t.* to pollard; to curtail; to truncate. ·knotwilg, *n.* pollard(-willow).

·knuffelen, *v.t.* to fondle, cuddle.

knuist, *n.* fist; hand (*fig.*).

knul, -llen, *n.* dull fellow; fellow, chap. ·knullig, *a.* clumsy, awkward.

·knuppel, -s, *n.* cudgel, bludgeon. *een* ~ *in het hoenderhok gooien*, to cause a flutter in the dovecotes. ·knuppelen, *v.t.* to cudgel.

knus, *a.* snug. ·knusjes, *adv.* snugly.

·knutselaar, -s, *n.* potterer, tinkerer. knut·sela·rij, *n.* pottering. ·knutselen, *v.i.* to potter, tinker. *in elkaar* ~, to put together. ·knutselwerk, *n.n.* tinkering job.

·koddebeier, -s, *n.* gamekeeper; rural policeman. ·koddig, *a.* droll. ·koddigheid, -heden, *n.* drollery.

koe, -ien, *n.* cow. *de* ~ *bij de horens vatten*, to seize the bull by the horns; *ouwe koeien uit de sloot halen*, to reopen old sores; *men kan nooit weten hoe een* ~ *een haas vangt*, you never can tell; *men noemt geen* ~ *bont of er is een vlekje aan*, no smoke without fire. ·koebeest, *n.n.* cow. ·koebrug, -ggen, *n.* gangway (*for loading cattle*). ·koehoorn, -s, *n.* cow's horn. ·koehuid, *n.* cow-hide. ·koeiekop, -ppen, *n.* cow's head.

koeio·neren, -neer, *v.t.* to bully, persecute.

koek, *n.* cake; gingerbread. *ze gaan als* ~, they sell like hot cakes; *het is alles* ~ *en ei*, everything in the garden is lovely; *ze zijn als* ~ *en ei*, they are as thick as thieves; *dat is ouwe* ~, that's ancient history now; *voor zoete* ~ *opeten*, to swallow (*fig.*). koeke·loeren, *v.i.* to gape. ·koekenbakker, -s, *n.* confectioner, pastry-cook. ·koekepan, -nnen, *n.* frying pan. ·koekje, -s, *n.n.* biscuit. ·koektrommel, -s, *n.* biscuit tin, cake tin.

·koekoek, *n.* cuckoo; (*euphemism*) devil; skylight. *dat haal je de* ~, I should think so (*iron.*); *loop naar de* ~, go to blazes; *het is altijd* ~ *één zang*, there is never any change. ·koekoeksbloem, *n.* ragged robin. ·koekoeksspog, no pl., *n.n.*, ·koekoeksspuug, no pl., *n.n.* cuckoo-spit.

koel, *a.* cool; cold (*fig.*); calm. *in* ~*en bloede*, in cold blood. ·koelbak, -kken, *n.* cooler. koel·bloedig, *a.* cold-blooded; cool-headed. ¶*adv.* in cold blood. koel·bloedigheid, no pl., *n.* cold-bloodedness. ·koelemmer, -s, *n.* wine-cooler. ·koelen, *v.t.* to cool; to ice. *zijn woede* ~ *aan*, to vent one's passion on. ¶*v.i.* to cool, freshen. ·koelheid, no pl., *n.* coolness. ·koelhuis, -zen, *n.n.* cold store. ·koelboter, no pl., *n.* butter from cold storage.

·koelie, -s, *n.* coolie. ·koeliewerk, no pl., *n.n.* drudgery.

·koelinrichting, *n.* refrigeration plant. ·koelkamer, -s, *n.*, ·koelkelder, -s, *n.* cold store. ·koelmiddel, *n.n.* refrigerant. ·koeloven, -s, *n.* cooling chamber. ·koelte, no pl., *n.* cool, coolness. ·koeltje, -s, *n.* (gentle) breeze. ·koeltjes, *adv.* coldly (*fig.*). ·koelvat, *n.n.* cooler. ·koelwater, no pl., *n.n.* cooling water. ·koelweg, *adv.* coolly.

koen, *a.* bold, daring. ·koenheid, no pl., *n.* boldness, daring.

·koepel, -s, *n.* dome, cupola; summer-house. ·koepelgewelf, -ven, *n.n.* dome.

·koepokken, pl. only, *n.* cowpox. ·koepokinenting, *n.* vaccination.

Koerd, *n.* Kurd.

·koeren, *v.t.* to coo.

koe·rier, -s, *n.* courier.

koers, *n.* course (*of ship, and fig.*); price, quotation (*on stock exchange*); rate (*of exchange*). ~ *houden* or *zetten naar*, to make for, head for; *uit de* ~ *raken*, to be driven out of one's course; *tegen de* ~ *van*, at the rate of. ·koersbericht, *n.n.* market report. ·koersen, *v.i.* to make for. ·koershoudend, *a.* steady, firm. ·koerslijst, *n.* list of quotations. ·koersnotering, *n.* quotation. ·koersschommeling, *n.* fluctuation.

koest, *int.* quiet! *zich* ~ *houden*, to keep quiet.

·koestal, -llen, *n.* cowshed, cowhouse.

·koesteren, *v.t.* to cherish; to entertain (*hope*), harbour (*suspicion*). ¶*zich* ~, *v.r.* to bask.

koet, *n.* coot.

·koeter, -s, *n.* cowherd.

·koeteren, *v.i.* to jabber, talk gibberish. ·koeterwaals, no pl., *n.n.* gibberish, double Dutch.

·koetje, -s, *n.n.* small cow. *over* ~*s en kalfjes praten*, to talk about nothing in particular.

koets, *n.* coach. koet·sier, -s, *n.* coachman; cab-driver. ·koetspoort, *n.* carriage entrance.

·koevoet, *n.* crowbar.

·koffer, -s, *n.* trunk; coffer. ·koffertje, -s, *n.n.* attaché case. ·koffervis, -ssen, *n.* trunkfish.

·koffie, no pl., *n.* coffee. ~ *zetten*, to make coffee. ·koffiebaal, -balen, *n.* bag of coffee (*sack*). ·koffiebrander, -s, *n.* coffee-roaster.

koffiebrande·rij, *n*. coffee-roaster's. ·koffie-
dik, no pl., *n.n.* coffee-grounds. *zo klaar
als* ～, as clear as mud. ·koffiedrinken,
v.i.s., str. to lunch. ¶no pl., *n.n.* bread and
butter lunch. ·koffiehuis, -zen, *n.n.* café.
·koffiekamer, -s, *n.* refreshment room.
·koffiekan, -nnen, *n.* coffee-pot. ·koffietafel,
-s, *n.* luncheon table. ·koffietuin, *n.*
coffee-plantation. ·koffieuur, no pl.,
n.n. lunch-time.
·kofschip, -schepen, *n.n.* koff.
·kogel, -s, *n.* bullet. *de* ～ *geven*, to shoot,
execute; *tot de* ～ *veroordelen*, to condemn
to be shot; *de* ～ *is door de kerk*, the die is
cast. ·kogelbaan, -banen, *n.* trajectory.
·kogelen, *v.i.* to throw, pelt. ·kogelflesje,
-s, *n.n.* lemonade bottle. ·kogelgewricht,
n.n. ball and socket joint. ·kogellager, -s,
n.n. ball-bearing. ·kogelpot, -tten, *n.*,
·kogelring, *n.* ball-race. ·kogelrond, *a.*
spherical. ·kogeltje, -s, *n.n.* pellet. ·kogel-
vormig, *a.* spherical.
ko·hier, *n.n.* ledger (*of tax-collector*).
kok, -s, *n.* cook (*male*), chef.
Ko·kanje, *n.N.* Cockaigne.
ko·karde, -s, *n.* cockade.
·koken, kook, *v.i.* to boil; to cook, do the
cooking. ～ *van verontwaardiging*, to
seethe with indignation. ¶*v.t.* to boil;
to cook. ·kokendheet, -hete, *a.* boiling hot.
·koker, -s, *n.* case (*long container*); quiver.
dat komt niet uit zijn ～, he never thought
of that himself.
koke·rij, *n.* boiling-works.
·kokerjuffer, -s, *n.* caddis.
·kokhalzen, -hals, *v.i.* to retch, heave.
·kokker(d), -s, *n.* (*coll.*) nose.
·kokmeeuw, *n.* blackheaded gull.
·kokosboom, -bomen, *n.* coco-nut tree.
·kokosmat, -tten, *n.* coco-nut matting.
·kokosnoot, -noten, *n.* coco-nut.
·koksjongen, -s, *n.* kitchen-boy. koks·maat,
-s, *n.* cook's mate.
kol, -llen, *n.* witch; star (*on horse's head*).
·kolder, -s, *n.* jerkin. ¶no pl., *n.* staggers.
de ～ *in de kop hebben*, to behave wildly.
·kolen, no pl., *n.* coal; coals. *op hete* ～ *zitten*,
to be on tenterhooks; *vurige* ～ *op iemands
hoofd stapelen*, to heap coals of fire on a
person's head. ·kolenbak, -kken, *n.*
coal-scuttle, coal-box. ·kolenbrander, -s,
n. charcoal-burner. ·kolendamp, no pl.,
n. coal-fumes; carbon monoxide. ·kolen-
drager, -s, *n.* coal-heaver. ·kolenemmer,
-s, *n.* coal-scuttle. ·kolengruis, no pl.,
n.n. coal-dust. ·kolenhaven, -s, *n.* coaling-
port. ·kolenhok. -kken, *n.n.* coalshed.
·kolenkit, -tten, *n.* coal-scuttle. ·kolenmijn,
n. coal-mine, colliery. ·kolenschip, -schepen,
n.n. collier.
kolf, -ven, *n.* club, bat; butt(-end); spadix,
spike; receiver (*distilling apparatus*).
·kolfje, -s, *n.n. het is een* ～ *naar zijn
hand*, it is just right for him.

koli·brie, -s, *n.* humming-bird.
ko·liek, no pl., *n.* colic.
kolk, *n.* eddy, whirlpool; lock-chamber.
·kolken, *v.i.* to eddy.
·kollen, kol, *v.t.* to poleaxe.
ko·lom, -mmen, *n.* column (*architectural;
mercury; newspaper*).
kolom·bijntje, -s, *n.n.* sponge-cake.
kolo·nel, -s, *n.* colonel. ·kolo·nelse, no pl., *n.*
colonel's wife.
koloni·aal, -iale, *a.* colonial. *koloniale waren*,
groceries. ¶-ialen, *n.* colonial (*soldier*).
ko·lonie, -s, *n.* colony, settlement. koloni-
·seren, -seer, *v.t.* to colonize.
kolo·riet, no pl., *n.n.* colouring.
ko·los, -ssen, *n.* colossus.
·kolsem, -s, *n.* kelson.
kom, -mmen, *n.* bowl, basin. *de* ～ *der
gemeente*, the built-up centre of the town
or village.
kom·aan, *int.* come along!; come, come!
kom·af, no pl., *n.* descent. *van hoge* ～,
high-born.
kom·buis, -zen, *n.n.* caboose, galley.
komedi·ant, *n.* comedian. ko·medie, -s, *n.*
comedy. *wat een* ～, what a farce; *naar
de* ～ *gaan*, to go to a show. ko·mediestuk,
-kken, *n.n.* comedy (*play*).
ko·meet, -meten, *n.* comet.
·komen, *v.i., irr.* to come. *wie eerst komt,
eerst maalt*, first come first served; ～
halen, to come for; *hoe kom je daaraan?*,
how did you get hold of it?; *erachter* ～,
to twig, find out; *aan geld* ～, to come by
money; *hoe kom je daarbij?*, what has put
that into your head?; *bij iemand* ～, to
visit *or* to go to see someone; ～ *op* to
amount to. ·komend, *a.* next.
kom·foor, -foren, *n.n.* chafing-dish.
ko·miek, *a.* comic(al). ¶*n.* low comedian.
ko·mijn, no pl., *n.* cumin. komijne·kaas,
-kazen, *n.* cumin cheese.
·komisch, *a.* comical.
kom·kommer, -s, *n.* cucumber. kom·kom-
mertijd, no pl., *n.* silly season.
·komma, -'s, *n.* comma; decimal point.
komma·punt, *n.* semicolon.
kommen·saal, -salen, *n.* lodger.
·kommer, no pl., *n.* distress, care. ·kommer-
lijk, *a.* pitiful, grievous. ·kommerloos, -loze,
a. carefree. ·kommervol, -lle, *a.* sorrowful.
·kommetje, -s, *n.n.* (small) bowl; bowlful.
kom·mies, -zen, *n.* customs officer; excise-
man. kom·miesbrood, -broden, *n.* ammunition bread.
kom·pas, -ssen, *n.n.* compass. kom·pasbeugel,
-s, *n.* gimbals. kom·pasdoos, -dozen, *n.*
compass-box. kom·pashuisje, -s, *n.n.*
binnacle. kom·pasroos, -rozen, *n.* compass
card. kom·passtreek, -streken. *n.* point
of the compass.
kom·plot, -tten, *n.n.* plot.
kom·pres, *n.n.* compress. *warm* ～, fomentation.

komst, no pl., *n.* arrival. *op ~ zijn,* to be at hand.

kond, no pl., *n. ~ doen* or *maken,* to make known.

kon·fijt, no pl., *n.n.* preserves. **kon·fijten,** *v.t.* to preserve (*in sugar*).

ko·nijn, *n.n.* rabbit. **ko·nijnenhok, -kken,** *n.n.* rabbit-hutch. **ko·nijnevel, -llen,** *n.n.* rabbit-skin.

·koning, *n.* king. *de ~ te rijk zijn,* to be in the seventh heaven. **konin·gin, -nnen,** *n.* queen. **konin·ginnedag,** *n.* queen's birthday. **konin·ginnepage, -s,** *n.* swallowtail. **·koningsarend,** *n.* royal eagle. **·koningschap,** no pl., *n.n.* kingship **·koningsgezind,** *a.* royalist. **·koningsgier,** *n.* king-vulture. **·koningsmoord,** *n.* regicide. **·koningswater,** no pl., *n.n.* aqua regia. **·koningszeer,** no pl., *n.n.* king's evil. **·koninklijk,** *a.* royal, regal. *K~ Besluit,* Order in Council; *de K~e,* the Royal Dutch. ¶*adv.* royally, regally. **·koninkrijk,** *n.n.* kingdom.

·konkelaar, -s, *n.* schemer. **konkela·rij,** *n.* underhand dealings, dirty work. **·konkelen,** *v.i.* to scheme.

kon·vooi, *n.n.* convoy. **kon·vooiloper, -s,** *n.* ship's agent.

kooi, *n.* cage; pen, fold; duck-decoy; berth, bunk. *naar ~ gaan,* to turn in. **·kooieend,** *n.* decoy-duck. **·kooien,** *v.t.* to cage. **·kooiker, -s,** *n.* decoy-man. **·kooihondje, -s,** *n.n.* dog (*used by duck catcher*).

kook, no pl., *n. aan de ~,* on the boil; *aan de ~ brengen,* to bring to the boil; *van de ~,* off the boil or indisposed. **·kookboek,** *n.n.* cookery-book. **·kookcursus, -ssen,** *n.* cookery-class. **·kookhitte,** no pl., *n.* boiling-heat. **·kookpan, -nnen,** *n.* saucepan. **·kookpunt,** *n.n.* boiling-point. **·kookschool, -scholen,** *n.* cookery-school. **·kooksel, -s,** *n.n.* boiling.

kool, kolen, *n.* cabbage; coal(s); carbon (*element*). *het is ~,* it is rubbish, nonsense; *iemand een ~ stoven,* to play a trick on someone; *dove ~,* dead coal; *gloeiende ~,* live coal. **·koolachtig,** *a.* carbonaceous; cabbagy. **·kooldraad, -draden,** *n.* carbon filament. **·koolhydraat, -draten,** *n.n.* carbohydrate. **·koolmees, -mezen,** *n.* great titmouse. **·koolraap, -rapen,** *n.* swede. **·koolrups,** *n.* caterpillar of cabbage-butterfly. **·koolschaaf, -schaven,** *n.* cabbage-grater. **·koolspits,** *n.* carbon (*electric*). **·koolstof,** no pl., *n.* carbon (*in chemistry*). **·koolstronk,** *n.* cabbage stalk. **·koolteer,** no pl., *n.* coaltar. **kool·waterstof,** no pl., *n.* carburetted hydrogen. **·koolwitje, -s,** *n.* cabbage-butterfly. **·koolzaad,** no pl., *n.n.* rapeseed, cole-seed. **·koolzuur,** no pl., *n.n.* carbonic acid.

·koon, konen, *n.* (*stilted*) cheek.

koop, no pl., *n.* purchase; bargain. *een ~*

sluiten, to strike a bargain; *op de ~ toe,* into the bargain; *te ~,* for sale; *te ~ gevraagd,* wanted for sale; *te ~ lopen met,* to show off, flaunt; *weten wat er te ~ is,* to know what is doing. **·koopakte, -s,** *n.* **·koopceel, -celen,** *n.* title-deed, deed of sale. **·koophandel,** no pl., *n.* commerce, trade. *~ drijven,* to carry on trade. **·koopje, -s,** *n.n.* bargain. *op een ~,* on the cheap; *een ~ hebben aan iets,* to have got something very cheap. **·koopkracht,** *n.* purchasing power. **·koopkrachtig,** *a.* with purchasing power. **·kooplieden,** *n.* See **koopman.** **·kooplust** no pl., *n.* inclination to buy. **·koop·lustig,** *a.* eager to buy. **·koopman. kooplieden,** *n.* merchant. **·koopmanschap,** no pl., *n.n.* trade, business. **·koopprijs, -zen,** *n.,* **·koopsom, -mmen,** *n.* purchase price. **·koopstad, -steden,** *n.* commercial town. **·koopvaarder, -s,** *n.* merchantman. **koopvaar·dij,** no pl., *n.* merchant service, mercantile marine. **koopvaar·dijschip, -schepen,** *n.n.* merchantman. **koopvaar·dijvloot, -vloten,** *n.* merchant fleet. **·koopvrouw,** *n.* trader (*female*). **·koopwaar -waren,** *n.* merchandise. **·koopziek,** *a.* unable to refrain from buying. **·koopzucht,** no pl., *n.* urge to buy.

koor, koren, *n.n.* choir; choir, chancel; chorus (*in drama*).

koord, *n.n.* cord, rope. *de ~en van de beurs,* the purse-strings; *op het slappe ~ dansen,* to walk on the slack rope; *hij moet op het slappe ~ komen,* he must show his paces, do his tricks; *het strakke ~,* the tight-rope. **·koorddansen,** no pl., *n.n.* rope-dancing. **·koorddanser, -s,** *n.* rope-dancer. **·koordje, -s,** *n.n.* piece of string.

·koorgestoelte, -n, *n.n.* choir stalls. **·koorgezang,** no pl., *n.* choral singing or song. **·koorheer, -heren,** *n.* canon. **·koorhemd,** *n.n.,* **·koorkleed, -kleden,** *n.n.* surplice. **·koorkap, -ppen,** *n.* pluvial. **·koorknaap, -knapen,** *n.* choirboy.

koorts, *n.* fever. *anderdaagse ~,* tertian fever; *derdendaagse ~,* tertian or quartan fever; *iemand de ~ op het lijf jagen,* to frighten the life out of someone. **·koortsachtig,** *a.* feverish, febrile. **·koortsig,** *a.* feverish, frenzied. **·koortsigheid,** no pl., *n.* feverishness. **·koortslijder, -s,** *n.* fever patient. **·koortsmiddel,** *n.n.* febrifuge. **·koortsstillend,** *a.,* **koortswerend,** *a.* febrifugal.

·koorzang, *n.* choral singing or song. **·koorzanger, -s,** *n.* chorister.

koot, koten, *n.* ankle-bone; knuckle-bone. **·kootje, -s,** *n.n.* finger-bone, phalanx.

kop, -ppen, *n.* head; head (*coll: of man*); large cup; bowl (*of pipe*). *met honderd koppen,* with a crew of a hundred; *daar is ~ noch staart aan te vinden,* one cannot make head or tail of it; *een ~ als vuur*

krijgen, to go red in the face; *de* ~ *indruk-ken*, to nip in the bud, squash; *op de* ~ *af*, exactly; *op de* ~ *tikken*, to pick up, get hold of; *zich op zijn* ~ *laten zitten*, to allow oneself to be sat upon; *over de* ~ *slaan*, to come a cropper *or* to turn a somersault.
·**kopal**, *n.n.* copal.
·**kopen, koop**, *v.t.*, *irr.* to buy, purchase. *bij iemand* ~, to deal with *or* to buy from a person. ·**koper**, -s, *n.* buyer, purchaser. ¶no pl., *n.n.* copper; brass. *geel* ~, brass; *rood* ~, copper. ·**koperachtig**, *a.* coppery, brassy. ·**koperdraad**, -**draden**, *n.* copper-wire, brass-wire. ·**koperdruk**, no pl., *n.* copperplate (*printing*). ·**koperen**, *a.* (made of) copper *or* brass. *¶v.t.* to copper. ·**kopererts**, *n.n.* copper ore. ·**kopergieter**, -s, *n.* brass-founder. ·**kopergoed**, no pl., *n.n.* copperware, brassware. ·**kopergroen**, no pl., *n.n.* verdigris. ·**koperhoudend**, *a.* cuprous. ·**koperrood**, -**rode**, *a.* copper-red. ¶no pl., *n.* copperas. ·**koperslager**, -s, *n.* coppersmith. ·**koperwerk**, no pl., *n.n.* copperware, brassware. ·**koperwiek**, *n.* redwing.
ko·pie, -ïeën, *n.* copy. *met twee kopieën*, in three copies (*typescript*). ·**kopieboek**, *n.n.* copybook. ·**kopi·eerinkt**, *n.* indelible ink. **kopi·eren, -ïeer**, *v.t.* to copy.
·**kopje**, -s, *n.n.* cup; small head. *een* ~ *kleiner maken*, to decapitate; ~ *duikelen*, to turn somersaults; ~ *krauw*, scratch-a-poll; ~ *onder gaan*, to go right under. ·**koplaag, -lagen**, *n.* top course. ·**koplicht**, *n.n.* headlight. ·**koploos, -loze**, *a.* ace-phalous.
·**koppel**, -s, *n.* belt (*for sword*). *¶n.n.* couple; brace; yoke; bevy; covey. ·**koppelaar**, -s, *n.* matchmaker; procurer. ·**koppelaar-ster**, -s, *n.* matchmaker; procuress. ·**koppela·rij**, no pl., *n.* matchmaking; procuring. ·**koppelband**, *n.* coupling-strap. ·**koppelbout**, *n.* coupling-pin. ·**koppelen**, *v.t.* to couple; to join. ·**koppeling** *n.* coupling; clutch (*of car*). ·**koppelriem**, *n.* belt. ·**koppelstang**, *n.* coupling-rod. ·**koppelteken**, -s, *n.n.* hyphen. ·**koppel-werkwoord**, *n.n.* copula. ·**koppelwoord**, *n.n.* copulative.
·**koppensnellen**, no pl., *n.n.* head-hunting. ·**koppensneller**, -s, *n.* head-hunter. ·**koppig**, *a.* obstinate, headstrong; heady. ·**koppig-heid, -heden**, *n.* obstinacy; headiness. ·**kopschool, -scholen**, *n.* central school. ·**kopstation**, -s, *n.n.* railway terminus. ·**kopstuk, -kken**, *n.n.* head-piece; leader. ·**koptelefoon**, *n.* earphone.
·**kopra**, no pl., *n.* copra.
ko·raal, -ralen, *n.n.* chorale. *¶no pl., n.n.* coral; coral bead. **ko·raalachtig**, *a.* coralline. **ko·raalbank**, *n.* coral-reef. **ko·raaldier**, *n.n.* coral polyp. **ko·raal-muziek**, no pl., *n.* choral music. **Ko·raalzee**, *N.* Coral Sea. **ko·ralen**, *a.* coral, coralline.

kor·beel, -belen, *n.* corbel.
kor·daat, -date, *a.* resolute, firm. **kor·daat-heid**, no pl., *n.* resolution, firmness.
·**koren**, no pl., *n.n.* corn, grain. *dat is* ~ *op zijn molen*, it suits him down to the ground, is grist to his mill. ·**korenaar, -naren**, *n.* ear of corn. ·**korenbeurs, -zen**, *n.* corn-exchange. ·**korenbloem**, *n.* cornflower. ·**korenbouw**, no pl., *n.* corn-growing. ·**koren-brand**, no pl., *n.* blight. ·**korenbrander**, -s, *n.* distiller. ·**korenmaat, -maten**, *n.* corn measure. *zijn licht onder de* ~ *zetten*, to hide one's light under a bushel. ·**koren-mijt**, *n.* cornstac... ·**korenroos, -rozen**, *n.* poppy. ·**korenschuur, -schuren**, *n.* granary. ·**korenzolder**, -s, *n.* corn loft.
·**korf, -ven**, *n.* basket, hamper; hive. ·**korfbal**, no pl., *n.* basket-ball.
·**korhaan, -hanen**, *n.* woodcock, blackcock. ·**korhoen, -ders**, *n.* woodcock (*female*).
·**korna·lijn**, *n.* cornelian.
·**kor·net, -tten**, *n.* cornet.
·**kor·noelje**, -s. *n.* cornel, dogwood; dogberry.
·**kor·nuit**, *n.* comrade; crony.
·**korpo·raal**, -s *or* -**ralen**, *n.* corporal. **korps**, *n.n.* corps (*army*); students' union.
·**korre, -n**, *n.* dredge-net.
·**korrel**, -s, *n.* grain; pellet; bead (*of rifle*). ·**korrelen**, *v.t. & v.i.* to granulate. ·**korrelig**, *a.* granular. ·**korreltje**, -s, *n.n.* (small) grain.
·**korren, kor**, *v.i.* to trawl.
·**korst**, *n.* crust; rind; scab. ·**korsten**, *v.i.* to form crust *or* scab. ·**korstig**, *a.* crusty; scabby. ·**korstigheid**, no pl., *n.* crustiness. ·**korstmos, -ssen**, *n.n.* lichen.
kort, *a.* short, brief. ~ *en goed*, in short; ~ *en klein slaan*, to smash to pieces; ~ *maar krachtig*, short and sweet; ~ *van stof*, short-tempered; *om* ~ *te gaan*, to be brief; *te* ~, short *or* too short; *te* ~ *doen*, to wrong; *te* ~ *komen*, to be short of; *erbij te* ~ *komen*, to lose by it; *te* ~ *schieten*, to fall short *or* to be lacking. ¶*adv.* shortly; briefly. ~ *daarna or daarop*, shortly afterwards; ~ *geleden*, a short time ago, recently; ~ *na* . . ., shortly after . . .; ~ *na elkaar*, in rapid succession; *tot voor* ~, until recently. ¶no pl., *n.n. in het* ~, in brief. **kort·ademig**, *a.* short-winded. **kort·af**, *a.* curt, abrupt. ·**kor-telijk**, *adv.* in short. ·**kortelings**, *adv.* recently, of late. ·**korten**, *v.t.* to shorten; to trim, clip; to deduct; to while away, beguile. *¶v.i.* to grow shorter. ·**kortheid**, no pl., *n.* shortness. ·**kortheidshalve**, *adv.* for the sake of brevity, for short. ·**kort-hoornvee**, no pl., *n.n.* short-horned cattle. ·**korting**, *n.* discount; deduction. *met een* ~ *van*, at a discount of. ·**kortom**, *adv.* in short, in fine. **Kortrijk**, *n.N.* Courtray. ·**kortsluiting**, *n.* short circuit. ·**kortstaart**, *n.* bobtail. ·**kortstaarten**, *v.t.* to dock. **kort·stondig**, *a.* shortlived, of short duration.

kort·stondigheid, no pl., *n.* briefness.
·kortswijl, no pl., *n.* (*stilted*) banter.
·kortweg, *adv.* in short. ·kortwieken, *v.t.*
to clip the wings of. kort·zichtig, *a.* shortsighted; near-sighted. kort·zichtigheid, no
pl., *n.* short-sightedness.
·korven, korf, *v.t.* to hive.
kor·vet, -tten, *n.* corvette.
·korzelig, *a.* short-tempered.
kost, no pl., *n.* food, fare; board; living,
livelihood. *ouwe* ~, stale news; *zware* ~,
strong meat (*fig.*); ~ *en inwoning,* board
and lodging; *de* ~ *verdienen,* to earn one's
living; *aan de* ~ *komen,* to earn a living;
iemand aan de ~ *helpen,* to help to earn
a living, give work to; *in de* ~ *doen,* to
put out to board; *in de* ~ *zijn bij,* to
board with. ·kostbaar, -bare, *a.* costly;
precious. ·kostbaarheid, no pl., *n.* costliness. ·kostbaarheden, pl. only, *n.* valuables.
·koste, no pl., *n.* *te mijnen* ~, at any
expense; *ten* ~ *van,* at the expense *or* cost
of; *ten* ~ *leggen aan,* to spend on. ·kostelijk,
a. costly; excellent, priceless. *die is* ~, how
funny! ¶*adv.* excellently. ·kostelijkheid,
-heden, *n.* costliness; priceless object (*lit.*
& *fig.*). ·kosteloos, -loze, *a.* & *adv.* free,
gratis. ·kosten, *v.t.* to cost. *tijd* ~, to
take time. ¶pl. only, *n.* cost, costs;
expense(s). ~ *maken,* to incur expenses;
~ *meebrengen,* to entail expense; *op eigen*
~, at one's own expense; *op* ~ *jagen,* to
put to expense; *op* ~ *van,* at the expense
of. ·kostend, *a.* ~*e prijs,* cost price.
·koster, -s, *n.* verger, sexton. koste·res, -ssen,
n. verger (*female*).
·kostganger, -s, *n.* boarder. ·kostgeld, *n.n.* cost
of board. ·kosthuis, -zen, *n.n.* boarding-
house. ·kostjuffrouw, *n.* landlady. ·kost-
school, -scholen, *n.* boarding-school.
kos·tuum, -tumes, *n.n.* costume; fancy dress.
·kostwinner, -s, *n.* breadwinner, wage-earner.
·kostwinning, *n.* livelihood.
kot, -tten, *n.n.* hovel, shack; cot, pen, kennel;
(*slang*) prison.
kote·let, -tten, *n.* cutlet.
·koteren, *v.t.* to prod, stir.
·kotsen, *v.i.* (*slang*) to vomit. *om van te* ~,
disgusting.
·kotter, -s, *n.* cutter.
kou, no pl., *n.* cold (*weather and indisposition*).
~ *vatten,* to catch a cold. ·koubeitel, -s,
n. cold chisel. koud, *a.* & *adv.* cold. ~*e*
drukte, swank; *vruchten van de* ~*e grond,*
fruit grown in the open; *het* ~ *hebben,* to
be cold; *het viel hem* ~ *op het lijf,* it made
him go cold all over; *ik werd er* ~ *van,*
it made my blood run cold; *het laat me* ~,
it leaves me cold; *hij is erom* ~, he's done
for. koud·bloedig, *a.* cold-blooded. ·koude,
κ. See kou. ·koudheid, no pl., *n.* coldness.
·koudjes, *a.* coldish. ¶*adv.* coldly. ·koud-
vuur, no pl., *n.n.* gangrene. ·koukleum, *n.*
person who feels the cold.

kous, *n.* stocking. *de* ~ *op de kop krijgen,*
to fail; *op zijn* ~*en,* in his stockinged feet
or without difficulty. ·kouseband, *n.*
garter. ·kousenbreien, no pl., *n.n.* knitting
(*of stockings*). ·kousenstoppen, no pl., *n.n.*
darning. ·kousevoet, *n.* *op* ~*en,* in his
stockinged feet. ·kousewinkel, -s, *n.*
hosier's shop. ·kousje, -s, *n.n.* small
stocking; wick; (gas-)mantle.
kout, no pl., *n.* (*stilted*) chat. ·kouten, *v.i.*
(*poet.*) to chat.
·kouter, -s, *n.* coulter.
·kouvatten, vat kou, *v.i.s.* to catch a cold.
·kouwe, *a. See* koud. ·kouwelijk, *a* chilly,
sensitive to cold.
Ko·zak, -kken, *N.* Cossack.
ko·zijn, *n.n.* window-sill; window-frame.
kraag, kragen, *n.* collar (*of coat or dress*).
een stuk in zijn ~ *hebben,* to be tipsy.
kraai, *n.* crow. *bonte* ~, hooded crow;
hij heeft kind noch ~, he has neither kith
nor kin. ·kraaien, *v.i.* to crow. *daar zal*
geen haan naar ~, no one need ever know.
·kraaienmars, *n. de* ~ *blazen,* to peg out.
·kraaiennest, *n.n.* crow's-nest.
·kraakamandel, -s, *n.* almond (*in shell*).
·kraakbeen, no pl., *n.n.* cartilage, gristle.
·kraakbeenachtig, *a.* cartilaginous, gristly.
·kraaknet, -tte, *a.* very neat. ·kraak-
porselein, no pl., *n.n.* egg-shell china.
·kraakstem, -mmen, *n.* creaky voice.
·kraakzindelijk, *a.* scrupulously clean.
kraal, kralen, *n.* bead; kraal (*S. Africa*);
corral (*S. America*). ·kraallijst, *n.* bead
moulding. ·kraaloogje, -s, *n.n.* beady eye.
kraam, kramen, *n.* stall, booth. *de hele* ~,
the whole caboodle; *het komt in zijn* ~ *te*
pas, it suits his book. ·kraambed, no pl.,
n.n. childbed. ·kraambezoek, *n.n.* lying-in
visit. ·kraamkind, -eren, *n.n.* new-born
baby. ·kraampje, -s, *n.* small stall.
·kraamverpleegster, -s, *n.* monthly nurse.
·kraamvrouw, *n.* woman in childbed.
·kraamvrouwenhospitaal, -talen, *n.n.* maternity hospital. ·kraamvrouwenkoorts,
no pl., *n.* puerperal fever.
kraan, kranen, *n.* crane (*bird; machine*); tap,
cock. *een* ~ *van een vent,* a clever fellow.
·kraanvogel, -s, *n.* crane (*bird*).
krab, -bben, *n.* crab; scratch. ·krabbedieven,
-dief, *v.t.* to pinch (*steal*). ·krabbekat,
-tten, *n.* scratch-cat. ·krabbel, -s, *n.*
scratch; scribble. ·krabbelaar, -s, *n.*
(clumsy) beginner (*on the ice*). ·krabbelen,
v.i. to scratch (*of kitten*); to scrawl; to
scramble (*to one's feet*); to skate badly (*of*
beginner). ·krabbelpootje, -s, *n.n.* scrawl.
·krabben, krab, *v.t.* to scratch; to claw; to
paw (*of horse*). ·krabber, -s, *n.* scraper,
scratcher. ·krabijzer, -s, *n.n.* scraping-iron.
·krabsel, -s, *n.n.* scrapings.
krach, no pl., *n.* crash, collapse.
kracht, *n.* strength, force; vigour; power,
energy. *volle* ~ *vooruit,* full speed ahead;

~ *bijzetten aan,* to enforce; ~ *hebben,* to stand, be valid; *boven zijn* ~*en,* beyond one's strength *or* means; *met alle* ~, with might and main; *met* ~ *van woorden,* by force of argument; *op* ~*en komen,* to regain one's strength; *uit* ~ *van,* by virtue of; *van* ~ *worden,* to come into force; *van* ~ *zijn,* to be in force. **kracht·dadig,** *a.* vigorous. **kracht·dadigheid,** no pl., *n.* vigour. **krachteloos, -loze,** *a.* powerless. ~ *maken,* to invalidate, nullify. **krachte·loosheid,** no pl., *n.* powerlessness. impotence. **krachtens,** *adv.* in virtue of. **krachtig,** *a.* powerful, strong; forceful, vigorous. ¶*adv.* strongly, forcibly. **krachtinstallatie, -s,** *n.* power-plant, power-station. **krachtlijn,** *n.* line of force. **krachtmeter, -s,** *n.* dynamometer. **kracht-patser, -s,** *n.* very strong man. **krachts-inspanning,** *n.* effort, exertion. **kracht-voe(de)r,** no pl., *n.n.* concentrate(d animal fodder).
krak, -kken, *n.* crack.
·Krakau, *n.N.* Cracow.
kra·kelen, -keel, *v.i.* to squabble, quarrel.
·krakeling, *a.* pretzel. **·kraken, kraak,** *v.i.* to crack, creak; to crunch, scrunch. *het vriest dat het kraakt,* it is freezing like anything; ~*de wagens lopen het langst,* creaking doors hang longest. ¶*v.t.* to crack.
·kralen, *a.* made of beads, beaded.
kram, -mmen, *n.* staple.
·kramer, -s, *n.* pedlar. **krame·rij,** *n.* (*pedlar's*) small wares. **·kramerslatijn,** no pl., *n.n.* dog latin.
·krammat, -tten, *n.* fascine; plaited straw (*on dykes*). **·krammen, kram,** *v.t.* to clamp, fasten with staples.
kramp, *n.* cramp. **kramp·achtig,** *s.* convulsive. ¶*adv.* convulsively. *iets* ~ *vasthouden,* to clutch like grim death.
·kramwerk, no pl., *n.n.* putting down fascines *or* straw (*on dykes*).
·kranig, *a.* plucky, smart. *een* ~ *stukje,* a fine feat. ¶*adv.* pluckily. *zich* ~ *houden,* to behave splendidly, bear up bravely. **·kranigheid,** no pl., *n.* pluck.
krank, *a.* (*poet.*) ill *or* puny. **krank·zinnig,** *a.* insane, mad. ~ *worden,* to go mad. **krank·zinnige, -n,** *n.* lunatic, madman. ¶no pl., *n.n. tot in 't* ~, to distraction. **krank·zinnigengesticht,** *n.n.* lunatic asylum. **krank·zinnigheid,** no pl., *n.* lunacy, madness.
krans, *n.* wreath. **·kransje, -s,** *n.n.* small wreath; circle, club.
krant, *n.* newspaper. **·krantenjongen, -s,** *n.* newspaper-boy, newsvendor.
krap, no pl., *n.* madder. ¶**-ppe,** *a.* tight, scanty. ¶*adv.* narrowly, tightly. *het* ~ *hebben,* to be only just able to manage; ~ *zitten,* to be cramped (for space) *or* to be short of (*staff or money*); ~ *aan,* barely enough. **·krapjes,** *adv.* tightly

kras, -ssen, *n.* scratch. ¶**-sse,** *a.* vigorous; hale and hearty; extreme, drastic. *een* ~ *verhaal,* a tall story; *dat is* ~, that is a bit thick. ¶*adv.* vigorously. *dat is* ~ *gesproken,* that is putting it strongly. **·krassen, kras,** *v.i.* to scratch, scrape; to jar (*the ear*); to caw, croak. *ergens op* ~, to scratch something. **·krasser, -s,** *n.* scraper.
krat, -tten, *n.n.* crate; tail-board.
·krater, -s, *n.* crater.
·kraton, -s, *n.* fortified royal compound (*East Indies*).
·krauw, *n.* scratch. **·krauwen,** *v.t.* to scratch. *kopje krauw,* scratch-a-poll.
kre·diet, *n.n.* credit. **kre·dietbrief, -ven,** *n.* letter of credit. **kre·dietinstelling,** *n.* credit bank. **·krediet,** no pl., *n.n. See* credit.
kreeft, *n.* lobster; crawfish, crayfish; cancer (*constellation*). **·kreeftengang,** no pl., *n. de* ~ *gaan,* to go backward. **·kreeftensla,** no pl., *n.* lobster salad. **·kreeftskeerkring,** no pl., *n.* tropic of Cancer.
kreek, kreken, *n.* creek.
kreet, kreten, *n.* (*stilted*) cry, shriek.
·kregel(ig), *a.* peevish, touchy. **·kregelheid,** no pl., *n.* peevishness.
krek, *adv.* exactly.
·krekel, -s, *n.* cricket (*insect*).
kreng, *n.n.* carrion; hateful person.
·krenken, *v.t.* to offend; to wound (*pride*); to injure. *zich gekrenkt voelen,* to feel hurt. **·krenkend,** *a.* insulting. **·krenking,** *n.* injury, offence.
krent, *n.* currant. **·krentenbaard,** *n.* herpes. **·krentenbroodje, -s,** *n.n.* currant bun. **·krenterig,** *a.* mean, niggardly. **·krenterig-heid, -heden,** *n.* meanness.
·Kreta, *n.N.* Crete. **Kre·tensisch,** *a.* Cretan.
kreuk, *n.* crease, wrinkle. **·kreukelen,** *v.t.*, **·kreuken,** *v.t.* to crease, crumple. **·kreuke-lig,** *a.* creased, wrinkled, crumpled.
·kreunen, *v.i.* to groan.
·kreupel, *a.* lame. ~ *aan,* lame in; ~ *worden,* to go lame. ¶*adv.* lamely. ~ *lopen,* to limp. **·kreupelbos, -ssen,** *n.n.* thicket. **·kreupele, -n,** *n.* lame person, cripple. **·kreupelhout,** no pl., *n.n.* brushwood, undergrowth.
krib, -bben, *n.,* **·kribbe, -n,** *n.* manger; groyne. **·kribbebijter, -s,** *n.* crib-biter. **·kribbig,** *a.* fretful; testy.
·kriebel, -s, *n.* itch, tickle. **kriebelachtig,** *a.* ticklish. **·kriebelen,** *v.t.* to tickle. ¶*v.i.* to itch, tickle. **·kriebelig,** *a.* ticklish; irritable. **·kriebeling,** *n.* itch, tickle.
kriek, *n.* black cherry; cherry. **·kriekeboom, -bomen,** *n.* black cherry tree; cherry tree. **·krieken,** *v.i.* to chirp. ¶no pl. *n.n. bij het* ~ *van de dag,* at daybreak.
kriel, *n.n.* small throw-out; creel. **·krielen,** *v.i.* to teem. **·krielhaan, -hanen,** *n.* dwarf cock. **·krielhen, -nnen,** *n.* dwarf hen. **·krielkip, -ppen,** *n.* dwarf chicken. **·krieltje, -s,** *n.n.* dwarf fowl.

167 krak — kroon

·**kriemelen**, *v.i.* to teem; to tickle.
krijg, no pl., *n.* (*stilted*) war.
·**krijgen**, *v.t.*, *str.* to receive; to get; to catch (*illness*). *gedaan* ~, to be given notice; *iets gedaan* ~, to manage (to do) something; *er genoeg van* ~, to be fed up with something; *het te kwaad* ~, to be unable to stand it *or* to be unable to remain serious any longer; *er van langs* ~, to be beaten; *een ongeluk* ~, to meet with an accident; *iemand ertoe* ~, to get a person to agree to; *iemand te spreken* ~, to manage to speak to a person.
·**krijger**, -**s**, *n.* warrior. ·**krijgertje**, no pl., *n.n.* ~ *spelen*, to play tag. ·**krijgsartikelen**, pl. only, *n.n.* articles of war. ·**krijgsbedrijf**, -**ven**, *n.n.* military exploit. ·**krijgsbehoeften** pl. only, *n.* munitions of war. ·**krijgsbeleid**, no pl., *n.n.* military skill. ·**krijgsbende**, -**n**, *n.* band of soldiers. ·**krijgsgevangene**, -**n**, *n.* prisoner of war. ·**krijgskans**, *n.* fortunes of war. ·**krijgskunde**, no pl., *n.* art *or* science of war. ·**krijgslist**, *n.* stratagem. ·**krijgslied**, -**eren**, *n.n.* warlike song. ·**krijgsman**, **krijgslieden**, *n.* warrior. ·**krijgsplan**, -**nnen**, *n.n.* plan of campaign. ·**krijgsraad**, -**raden**, *n.* council of war; court martial. ·**krijgsschool**, -**sscholen**, *n.* military academy. *hogere* ~, staff college. ·**krijgstocht**, *n.* campaign, expedition. ·**krijgsvolk**, no pl., *n.n.* soldiery. ·**krijgswet**, -**tten**, *n.* martial law. *de* ~ *afkondigen*, to proclaim martial [law. **krijgs·zuchtig**, *a.* warlike.
krijs, *n.* shriek, cry. ·**krijsen**, *v.i.*, *str.* to shriek, screech.
krijt, no pl., *n.n.* chalk (*writing material*); lists. *bij iemand in het* ~ *staan*, to be in debt to someone; *met dubbel* ~ *schrijven*, to overcharge *or* charge double; *in het* ~ *treden*, to enter the lists. ·**krijtachtig**, *a.* chalky. ·**krijten**, *v.i.*, *str.* (*stilted*) to weep; to chalk. ·**krijtgebergte**, -**n**, *n.n.* chalk-hills. ·**krijtgroeve**, -**n**, *n.* chalk-pit. ·**krijtje**, -**s**, *n.n.* piece of chalk. *met een* ~ *aan de balk schrijven*, to make a special note of (*memorable event*). ·**krijtrots**, *n.* chalk-cliff.
Krim, *N. de* ~, the Crimea. ·**Krimoorlog**, *N. de* ~, the Crimean War.
krimp, no pl., *n.* shrinkage; want. *iets op de* ~ *maken*, to allow for shrinking. ¶*a.* live; very fresh. ·**krimpen**, *v.i.*, *str.* to shrink; to writhe; to back (*of wind*). ¶*v.t.*, *str.* to shrink. ·**krimping**, no pl., *n.* shrinkage. ·**krimpvis**, no pl., *n.n.* crimped fish. ·**krimp-vrij**, *a.* unshrinkable.
kring, *n.* circle; ring; circle, set. ·**kringelen**, *v.t.* to coil. ·**kringetje**, -**s**, *n.n.* small circle or ring. ~**s** *blazen*, to blow smoke rings; ~**s** *spuwen*, to stand idle. ·**kringloop**, no pl., *n.* cycle (*course*). ·**kringsgewijze**, *adv.* in circular fashion. ·**kringvormig**, *a.* circular.

·**krinkel**, -**s**, *n.* crinkle. ·**krinkelen**, *v.i.* to crinkle.
kri·oelen, *v.i.*, to teem, swarm. ~ *van*, to teem with.
kris, -**ssen**, *n.* kris, creese. ¶*int. bij* ~ *en kras*, firmly, stoutly.
·**kriskras**, *adv.* criss-cross. ·**kriskrassen**, -**kras**, *v.i.* to criss-cross.
kris·tal, -**llen**, *n.n.* crystal. **kris·tallen**, *a.* crystal, crystalline. **kristalli·seren**, -**seer**, *v.t.* & *v.i.* to crystallize. **kris·talvormig**, *a.* crystalloid.
kri·tiek, *n.* criticism. *beneden* ~, below par. ¶*a.* critical, crucial. ·**kritisch**, *a.* critical.
krocht, *n.n.* cavern.
kroeg, *n.* public-house (*low-class*). ·**kroegbaas**, -**bazen**, *n.* publican. ·**kroegloper**, -**s**, *n.* pub-crawler.
kroep, no pl., *n.* croup (*disease*).
·**kroes**, -**zen**, *n.* mug; crucible. ¶*a.* fuzzy, crinkled. **kroes·harig**, *a.* crinkly-haired. ·**kroeskop**, -**ppen**, *n.* fuzzy head of hair; person with fuzzy hair. ·**kroezen**, **kroes**, *v.i.* to frizz.
kro·ketje, -**s**, *n.n.* croquette.
·**kroko·dil**, -**llen**, *n.* crocodile.
·**krokus**, -**ssen**, *n.* crocus.
·**krollen**, **krol**, *v.i.* to caterwaul.
krols, *a.* randy.
krom, -**mmen**, *a.* curved, crooked, bent. *kromme benen*, bow-legs; ~ *van*, doubled up with. ¶*adv.* crookedly. *zich* ~ *lachen*, to laugh one's head off; *zich* ~ *werken*, to work oneself to death; ~ *spreken*, to talk baby talk *or* to put words the wrong way round. **krom·benig**, *a.* bow-legged. ·**krombek**, -**kken**, *n.* crookbill. ·**kromhout**, *n.n.* knee (*timber*). ·**kromliggen**, **lig krom**, *v.i.s.*, *str.* to pinch and scrape. ·**kromme**, -**n**, *n.* curve (*line*). ·**krommen**, **krom**, *v.t.* to curve, bend; to crook. ·**krommes**, -**ssen**, *n.n.* hollowing knife. ·**kromming**, *n.* bend, curve. ·**krompasser**, -**s**, *n.* callipers. ·**kromsnavel**, -**s**, *n.* curlew. ·**kromtrekken**, **trek krom**, *v.i.*, *str.* to warp. ·**kromzwaard**, *n.n.* scimitar.
·**kronen**, **kroon**, *v.t.* to crown.
kro·niek, *n.* chronicle. **kro·niekschrijver**, -**s**, *n.* chronicler.
·**kroning**, *n.* coronation. ·**kroningsmantel**, -**s**, *n.* coronation-robe.
·**kronkel**, -**s**, *n.* coil, twist. ·**kronkeldarm**, *n.* ileum. ·**kronkelen**, *v.i.* to twist, turn, wind. ¶*zich* ~, *v.r.* to twist, coil, wind. ·**kronkelig**, *a.* winding; meandering. ·**kronkelpad**, *n.n.* winding path. ·**kronkelweg**, *n.* langs; ~*en gaan*, to follow crooked ways.
kroon, **kronen**, *n.* crown; corolla; chandelier. *de* ~ *neerleggen*, to abdicate; *de* ~ *spannen*, to come top; *iemand naar de* ~ *steken*, to rival someone; *de* ~ *zetten op*, to crown (*fig.*); *de* ~ *op het werk zetten*, to complete one's task. ·**kroondomein**, *n.n.* crown-land. ·**kroon·insignes** pl. only *n.n.* regalia.

·**kroonlijst**, *n.* cornice. ·**kroonluchter**, **-s** *n.* chandelier. ·**kroontjespen**, **-nnən**, *n.* crown nib.
kroos, no pl., *n.n.* duck-weed.
kroost, no pl., *n.n.* offspring.
kroot, **kroten**, *n.* beetroot; beet.
krop, **-ppen**, *n.* crop, gizzard; goitre; head (*of lettuce*). *een ~ in de keel hebben*, to have a lump in one's throat. ·**kropaar**, no pl., *n.* cocksfoot. ·**kropachtig**, *a.* goitrous. ·**kropduif**, **-ven**, *n.* pouter (pigeon). ·**kropgans**, **-zen**, *n.* (type of) pelican. ·**kropgezwel**, **-llen**, *n.n.* goitre. ·**kropje**, **-s**, *n.n.* head (*of lettuce*). ·**kroppen**, **krop**, *v.t.* to feed (*geese forcibly*). *ik kan het niet ~,* I can't swallow or stomach it. ¶*v.i.* to stick (*in one's throat*). ·**kropsla**, no pl., *n.* cabbage lettuce.
krot, **-tten**, *n.n.* hovel.
·**krozig**, *a.* overgrown (*of pond*).
kruid, *n.n.* herb. *~en*, herbs, spices; *er is geen ~ voor gewassen*, there is no remedy for it; *er is geen ~ voor hem gewaassen*, there is nothing one can do about him. ·**kruidachtig**, *a.* herbaceous. ·**kruidboek**, *n.n.* herbal. ·**kruiden**, *v.t.* to season, spice; to interlard (*story*). **kruide·nier**, **-s**, *n.* grocer. **kruide·nierswaren**, pl. only, *n.* groceries. **kruide·nierswinkel**, **-s**, *n.*, **kruide·nierszaak**, **-zaken**, *n.* grocer's shop. ·**kruidenlezer**, **-s**, *n.* herbalist. ·**kruidenwijn**, no pl., *n.* spiced wine. **kruide·rij**, *n.* spice(s). ·**kruidig**, *a.* spicy. ·**kruidje·roer-me-niet**, **-nieten** *or* **kruidjes-roer-me-niet**, *n.n.* sensitive plant. ·**kruidkaas**, **-kazen**, *n.* spiced cheese. ·**kruidkoek**, *n.* spiced gingerbread. ·**kruidnagel**, **-s**, *n.* clove. ·**kruidnagelboom**, **-bomen**, *n.* clove(-tree). ·**kruidnoot**, **-noten**, *n.* nutmeg. ·**kruidtuin**, *n.* botanical garden(s).
·**kruien**, *v.t.* to wheel (*wheel-barrow*). ¶*v.i.* to carry (*ice on river*). ·**kruier**, **-s**, *n.* (luggage-)porter; carrier. ·**kruiersloon**, **-lonen**, *n.n.* porterage.
kruik, *n.* pitcher, stone bottle.
kruim, no pl., *n.n.* crumb (*substance*). ·**kruimel**, **-s**, *n.* crumb. ·**kruimelen**, *v.t.* to crumble. ·**kruimelig**, *a.* crumby, crumbly.
kruin, *n.* top, crown. ·**kruinschering**, *n.* tonsure.
·**kruipelings**, *adv.* in creeping fashion. ·**kruipen**, *v.i.*, *str.* to creep, crawl; to grovel. ·**kruipend**, *a.* creeping; cringing. *~ dier*, reptile. ·**kruiper**, **-s**, *n.* creeper; toady. ·**kruiperig**, *a.* fawning. **kruipe·rij**, *n.* toadyism.
kruis, *n.n.* cross; sharp (*raised note*); trial, affliction. *~ of munt*, heads or tails; *een ~ slaan*, to make the sign of the cross; *aan het ~ slaan*, to nail to the cross. ·**kruisafneming**, *n.* descent from the cross. ·**kruisband**, *n.* postal wrapper. ·**kruisbeeld**, *n.n.* crucifix. ·**kruisbek**, **-kken**, *n.* crossbill.

·**Kruisberg**, *N.* (*Mount*) Calvary. ·**kruisbes**, **-ssen**, *n.* gooseberry. ·**kruisbloem**, *n.* finial. **kruis·bloemig**, *a.* cruciferous. ·**kruisboog**, **-bogen**, *n.* cross-bow; ogive. ·**Kruisdagen**, pl. only, *n.* Rogation days. ·**kruisdistel**, **-s**, *n.* sea-holly. ·**kruisdood**, no pl., *n.* death on the cross. ·**kruisdoorn**, **-s**, *n.* gooseberry-bush. ·**kruiselings**, *adv.* crosswise. ·**kruisen**, *v.t.* to cross; to crucify; to cross-breed. *elkaar ~,* to cross (*letters, roads*). ¶*v.i.* to cruise. ¶*zich ~, v.r.* to cross oneself. ·**kruiser**, **-s**, *n.* cruiser. ·**kruisgang**, *n.* cloister(s) (*covered walk*). ·**kruisgewelf**, **-ven**, *n.n.* cross-vaulting. ·**kruisgewijze**, *adv.* crosswise. ·**kruishout**, *n.n.* cross-beam; cross (*holy*). ·**kruisigen**, *v.t.* to crucify. ·**kruisiging**, *n.* crucifixion. ·**kruising**, *n.* cross-breeding; crossing. ·**kruisje**, **-s**, *n.n.* small cross. *de drie ~s achter de rug hebben*, to be past thirty. ·**kruismast**, *n.* mizzen-mast. ·**kruisnet**, **-tten**, *n.n.* square dipping-net. ·**kruispaal**, **-palen**, *n.* turnstile. ·**kruispunt**, *n.n.* crossing, intersection; junction (*roads, railways*). ·**kruisridder**, **-s**, *n.* knight of the cross. ·**kruissnelheid**, **-heden**, *n.* cruising speed. ·**kruisteken**, **-s**, *n.* sign of the cross. ·**kruistocht**, *n.* crusade; cruise. ·**kruisvaarder**, **-s**, *n.* crusader. ·**kruisvaart**, *n.* crusade. ·**kruisverband**, *n.n.* cross-bond; cross-bandage. ·**Kruisverheffing**, *n.* exaltation of the cross. ·**kruisverhoor**, **-horen**, *n.n.* cross-examination. *een ~ afnemen*, to cross-examine. ·**kruisvormig**, *a.* cruciform. ·**kruisweg**, *n.* cross-road; way of the cross. ·**kruiswijs**, *adv.* crosswise.
kruit, no pl., *n.n.* gunpowder. *zijn ~ drooghouden*, to stay prepared; *zijn ~ verschieten*, to shoot one's bolt; *zijn ~ verspillen*, to waste one's energy; *met los ~ schieten*, to fire blanks. ·**kruitdamp**, *n.* gunpowder smoke. ·**kruitfabriek**, *n.*, ·**kruitmolen**, **-s**, *n.* gunpowder-mill. ·**kruithoorn**, **-s**, *n.* powder-horn, powder-flask. ·**kruitkamer**, **-s**, *n.*, ·**kruitmagazijn**, *n.*, ·**kruittoren**, **-s**, *n.* powder-magazine.
·**kruiven**, **kruif**, *v.i.* to curl (*of waves*).
·**kruiwagen**, **-s**, *n.* wheelbarrow. *achter een ~ lopen*, to trundle a wheelbarrow; *een ~ hebben*, to make use of influence.
·**kruize·munt**, no pl., *n.* wild mint.
kruk, **-kken**, *n.* crutch; door-handle; crank (*of engine*); perch; stool; bungler. ·**krukas**, **-ssen**, *n.* crank-shaft. ·**krukken**, **kruk**, *v.i.* to be ailing.
krul, **-llen**, *n.* curl; flourish. *krullen*, woodshavings. ·**krulhaar**, no pl., *n.n.* curly hair. ·**krulhond**, *n.* poodle. ·**krullebol**, **-llen**, *n.* curly-pate. ·**krullen**, **krul**, *v.t.* & *v.i.* to curl, wave. ·**krullenjongen**, **-s**, *n.* carpenter's boy. ·**krulletje**, **-s**, *n.n.* ringlet (*hair*). ·**krulstaart**, *n.* curly tail. ·**krultabak**, no pl., *n.* fine-cut tobacco. ·**krultang**, *n.* curling-tongs.

·kubiek, *a.* cubic. ·kubus, -ssen, *n.* cube.
kuch, *n.* cough (*dry*). ·kuchen, *v.i.* to cough,
hem.
·kudde, -n, *n.* herd; flock. ·kuddegeest, no
pl., *n.* herd instinct.
·kuier, no pl., *n.* stroll. *op de* ~ *zijn*, to be
out for a stroll. ·kuieren, *v.i.* to stroll.
kuif, -ven, *n.* tuft (*over forehead*); forelock;
crest (*of bird*). ·kuifeend, *n.* tufted duck.
·kuifleeuwerik, -kken, *n.* crested lark.
·kuifmees, -mezen, *n.* crested titmouse.
·kuiken, -s, *n.n.* chick; silly person. ·kuiken-
dief, -ven, *n.* harrier.
kuil, *n.* pit, hole. ·kuilen, *v.t.* to ensilage.
·kuiltje, -s, *n.n.* small pit; dimple.
kuip, *n.* tub. *weten welk vlees in de* ~ *is*,
to know with whom one is dealing.
·kuipen, *v.t.* to put in tub. ¶*v.i.* to cooper;
to intrigue. ·kruiper, -s, *n.* cooper;
intriguer. ·kuiperij, *n.* cooperage, workshop; intrigue. ·kuiphout, no pl., *n.n.*
staves.
kuis, *a.* chaste. ·kuisen, *v.t.* to purify.
·kuisheid, no pl., *n.* chastity.
kuit, *n.* calf (*of leg*). ¶no pl., *n.n.* roe, spawn.
~ *schieten*, to spawn; *ergens haring of* ~
van willen hebben, to want to get to the
bottom of a thing. ·kuitbeen, -deren, *n.n.*
fibula. ·kuitbroek, *n.* knee-breeches.
·kuitenflikker, -s, *n.* *een* ~ *slaan*, to cut
a caper. ·kuiter, -s, *n.*, ·kuitvis, -ssen, *n.*
spawner.
kukele·ku, *int.* cock-a-doodle-doo.
kul, no pl., *n.* rot, nonsense. *flauwe* ~,
nonsense.
·kunde, no pl., *n.* scientific knowledge,
learning. ·kundig, *a.* learned; experienced,
skilful. ·kundigheid, -heden, *n.* knowledge,
skill. *kundigheden*, attainments.
·kunne, no pl., *n.* sex.
·kunnen, kan, *v. aux., irr.* to be able; can, may.
hij kon uren zitten kijken, he would sit and
stare for hours; *het zou* ~, it is possible;
hij kan er bij, he can reach it; *hij kan er
buiten*, he can do without it; *het kan er
niet mee door*, it is not good enough.
¶*v.i., irr.* to be possible. kunst, *n.* art;
trick. *beeldende* ~*en*, plastic arts; *schone*
~*en*, fine arts; *zwarte* ~, necromancy,
black magic; *dat is geen* ~, there is nothing
in it (*fig.*); ~*en maken* or *uithalen*, to do
tricks or to be troublesome; *met* ~ *en
vliegwerk*, somehow, only just. ·kunstarm,
n. artificial arm. ·kunstdraaier, -s, *n.*
(ivory-)turner. ·kunsteloos, -loze, *a.*
artless, naïve. ·kunsteloosheid, no pl., *n.*
artlessness. kunstenaar, -s, *n.* artist.
·kunstenares, -ssen, *n.* artist (*female*).
·kunstenmaker, -s, *n.* acrobat. ·kunstgebit,
-tten, *n.n.* denture, artificial teeth.
·kunstgewrocht, *n.n.* work of art. ·kunst-
greep, -grepen, *n.* trick, artifice. ·kunst-
handel, -s, *n.* art dealer's (shop). ·kunst-
handelaar, -s, *n.* art dealer. kunstig, *a.*

ingenious, clever. ¶*adv.* cleverly, artfully.
·kunstijs, no pl., *n.n.* artificial ice. ·kunstje,
-s, *n.n.* trick. ~*s doen*, to perform tricks.
·kunstjuweel, -welen, *n.n.* gem (*fig.*).
·kunstkenner, -s, *n.* connoisseur, art expert.
·kunstlicht, no pl., *n.n.* artificial light.
kunst·lievend, *a.* art-loving. kunst·matig,
a. artificial. kunst·matigheid, no pl., *n.*
artificiality. ·kunstmest, no pl., *n.* artificial
manure, fertilizer. ·kunstmiddel, *n.n.*
artificial means; trick. ·kunstnijverheid,
no pl., *n.* industrial art. ·kunstnijverheids-
school, -sscholen, *n.* school of arts and
crafts. ·kunstrijden, no pl., *n.n.* trick
riding; figure skating. ·kunstrijder, -s, *n.*
circus rider; figure skater. ·kunstschilder,
-s, *n.* painter, artist. ·kunstsmaak, no pl.,
n. artistic taste(s). ·kunststuk, -kken, *n.n.*
masterpiece; feat, tour de force. kunst-
vaardig, *a.* skilful. kunst·vaardigheid, no
pl., *n.* skill. ·kunstveiling, *n.* art sale.
·kunstvoorwerp, *n.n.* objet d'art. ·kunst-
werk, *n.n.* work of art. ·kunstzin, no pl.,
n. artistic sense. kunst·zinnig, *a.* artistically minded, artistic.
ku·ras, -ssen, *n.n.* cuirass. kuras·sier, -s, *n.*
cuirassier.
kurk, *n.* cork, stopper. ¶no pl., *n.* cork
(*bark*). ·kurkachtig, *a.* corky. ·kurkdroog,
-droge, *a.* cork-dry. ·kurkeik, *n.* cork-oak,
cork-tree. ·kurken, *a.* (made of) cork.
¶*v.t.* to cork. ·kurkengeld, *n.n.* corkage.
·kurketrekker, -s, *n.* corkscrew.
kus, -ssen, *n.* kiss. ·kushandje, -s, *n.n.*
een ~ *geven*, to blow a kiss to. ·kussen,
kus, *v.t.* to kiss. ¶-s, *n.n.* cushion; pillow.
op het ~ *zitten*, to be in office. ·kussen-
sloop, -slopen, *n.* pillow-case.
kust, *n.* coast, shore. *aan de* ~, on the
coast; *onder de* ~, in shore; *op de* ~ *zetten*,
to beach; *van de* ~, off shore. ¶no pl.,
n. te ~ *en te keur*, plenty, of every
description. ·kustbatterij, *n.* coastal
battery. ·kustgebied, *n.n.* coastal area.
·kuststreek, -streken, *n.* coastal district.
·kuststrook, -stroken, *n.* coastal strip.
·kus·vaarder, -s, *n.* coasting-vessel, coaster.
·kustversterking, *n.* coastal defence(s).
·kustvisser, -s, *n.* off-shore fisherman.
·kustvisserij, *n.* off-shore fishery. ·kust-
vuur, -vuren, *n.n.* coast light. ·kustwacht,
n. coastguard (*service*). ·kustwachter, -s,
n. coastguard (*official*).
kuur, kuren, *n.* whim, caprice; cure. *een* ~
doen or *volgen*, to take a cure.
kwaad, kwade, *a.* bad, ill, evil; angry.
te kwader ure, in an evil hour; *zich* ~
maken, to get angry. ¶*adv.* bad(ly);
angrily. *het niet* ~ *hebben*, not to be
badly off; *het te* ~ *krijgen*, to come to the
end of one's self-control; *het te* ~ *krijgen
met*, to fall foul of; *er* ~ *uitzien*, to look
bad (*ill*). ¶no pl., *n.n.* evil; harm, injury;
wrong. ~ *doen*, to do wrong; *iemand* ~

doen, to harm a person; *wie ~ doet,
~ vermoedt,* evil to him that evil thinks;
iemand iets ten kwade duiden, to blame
someone for something. **kwaad·aardig,** *a.*
malicious, ill-natured; malignant. **kwaad-
·aardigheid, -heden,** *n.* viciousness, malice;
malignancy, virulence. **kwaad·denkend,** *a.*
suspicious. **kwaadge·zind,** *a.* hostile, ill-
disposed. **·kwaadheid,** no pl., *n.* anger.
·kwaadschiks, *adv.* unwillingly. **·kwaad-
spreekster, -s,** *n.* slanderer (*female*).
·kwaadspreken, spreek kwaad, *v.i.s.,* *str.*
to talk scandal. **kwaad·sprekend,** *a.*
slanderous, backbiting. **·kwaadspreker,
-s,** *n.* slanderer, calumniator. **kwaad-
spreke·rij,** no pl., *n.* scandal, slander.
·kwaadstoken, stook kwaad, *v.i.s.* to make
mischief. **·kwaadstoker, -s,** *n.* mischief-
maker. **·kwaadstookster, -s,** *n.* mischief-
maker (*female*). **kwaad·willig,** *a.* ill-
disposed; unwilling. **kwaad·willige, -n,** *n.*
rebel. **kwaad·willigheid, -heden,** *n.*
unwillingness, unreliability.
kwaal, -llen, *n.* complaint, disease.
kwab, -bben, *n.* lobe; dewlap. **·kwabaal,
-balen,** *n.* eel-pout.
kwade, *See* **kwaad,** *n.n.* **kwader,** *See*
kwaad, *a.*
kwa·drast, draten, *n.n.* square (*power*). *in
het ~,* squared. **kwa·draatwortel, -s,** *n.*
square root.
kwa·jongen, -s, *n.* urchin; street arab.
kwa·jongensachtig, *a.* like a schoolboy.
kwak, *int.* smack, flop. **·kwaken, kwaak,**
v.i. to croak; to quack. **·kwakkel, -s,** *n.*
quail. **·kwakkelen,** *v.i.* to be ailing.
·kwakkelwinter, -s, *n.* mild winter.
·kwakken, kwak, *v.t.* to dash, smack,
slam. **¶***v.i.* to crash. **·kwakzalven, -zalf,**
v.i. to play the quack. **·kwakzalver, -s,**
n. quack, charlatan. **kwakzalve·rij,** *n.*
quackery. **·kwakzalversmiddel,** *n.n.* quack
medicine.
kwal, -llen, *n.* jelly-fish.
·kwalijk, *adv.* ill, amiss; sick, queer; hardly,
scarcely. *neem me niet ~,* I beg your
pardon, excuse me, I am sorry, sorry;
iets ~ nemen, to take offence at something.
kwalijk·riekend, *a.* evil-smelling.
kwali·teit, *n.* quality.
kwalm, no pl., *n.* thick sooty smoke.
·kwalmen, *v.i.* & *v.t.* to belch forth smoke.
·kwan·selaar, -s, *n.* barterer. **kwansela·rij,** *n.*
bartering. **·kwanselen,** *v.i.* to barter, truck.
kwan·suis, *adv.* in pretence.
kwant, *n.* jolly fellow.
kwanti·teit, *n.* quantity.
kwart, *n.n.* quarter; crotchet. *~ over één,*
a quarter past one; *~ voor één,* a quarter
to one. **kwar·taal, -talen,** *n.n.* quarter
(*three months*). **·kwartdraai,** *n.* quarter of
a turn.
·kwartel, -s, *n.* quail. **·kwartelkoning,** *n.*
corn-crake.

kwar·tet, -tten, *n.n.* quartette.
kwar·tier, *n.n.* quarter of an hour; quarter
(*of town; of moon*); quarters (*military*);
quarter, mercy. *vrij ~,* break (*at school*).
kwar·tierarrest, no pl., *n.n.* *~ hebben,* to be
confined to barracks. **kwar·tiermeester,
-s,** *n.* paymaster, quartermaster.
kwar·tiermuts, *n.* forage cap.
·kwartje, -s, *n.n.* 25 cents piece (*Dutch*).
·kwartjesvinder, -s, *n.* confidence man
(*small type*).
kwarts, no pl., *n.n.* quartz.
kwast, *n.* brush (*for paint*), mop (*washing
up*); tassel; knot (*in wood*); quaint person.
¶ no pl., *n.* lemon squash. **·kwasterig,** *a.*
foppish. **·kwastig,** *a.* knotty (*of wood*).
·kwebbel, -s, *n.* chatterbox. **·kwebbelen,** *v.i.*
to chatter.
kwee, kweeën, *n.* quince. **·kweeappel, -s,** *n.*
quince (*apple-shaped*).
·kweek(gras), no pl., *n.n.* couch-grass.
·kweekbed, -dden, *n.n.* seed-bed. **·kweek-
school, -scholen,** *n.* training college.
·kweektuin, *n.* nursery (garden).
kween, kwenen, *n.* barren cow.
·kweepeer, -peren, *n.* quince (*pear-shaped*).
·kwekeling, *n.* pupil-teacher. **·kweken,
kweek,** *v.t.* to grow, raise (*plants, vegetables*); to breed, rear (*animals*); to cultivate, breed, foster (*feelings, emotions*).
·kweker, -s, *n.* grower, nurseryman.
kweke·rij, *n.* nursery (garden.).
·kweldam, -mmen, *n.* inner dyke (*in polder*).
·kwelder, -s, *n.* salting, mud flat.
·kwelduivel, -s, *n.,* **·kwelgeest,** *n.* tormentor
(*fig.*).
·kwelen, kweel, *v.i.* to warble (*of birds*).
·kwellen, kwel, *v.t.* to torment; to vex,
worry. **·kweller, -s,** *n.* tormentor.
·kwelling, *n.* torment.
·kwelwater, no pl., *n.n.* seepage (*along dykes*).
·kwelziek, *a.* ever-tormenting. **·kwelzucht,**
no pl., *n.* passion for tormenting.
·kwestie, -s, *n.* question, matter under
discussion; quarrel. *een ~ van tijd,* a
matter of time; *de zaak in ~,* the matter
in question; *geen ~ van,* out of the
question; *buiten ~,* beyond all question;
buiten de ~, off the point.
kwetsbaar, -bare, *a.* vulnerable. **·kwetsbaar-
heid,** no pl., *n.* vulnerability. **·kwetsen,**
v.t. to injure, wound; to wound, offend.
iemand in zijn eer ~, to hurt a person's
pride. **kwet·suur, -suren,** *n.* wound, injury
(*lit.*).
·kwetteren, *v.i.* to twitter, chirrup.
·kwezel, -s, *n.* bigot. **·kwezelaar, -s,** *n.*
ditherer. **·kwezelachtig,** *a.* sanctimonious.
kwezela·rij, *n.* bigotry.
·kwibus, -ssen, *n.* jackanapes.
kwiek, *a.* nimble, alert; smart. **¶***adv.*
briskly.
kwijl, no pl., *n.n.* slaver (*dribble*). **·kwijlen,**
v.i. to slaver, dribble.

·**kwijnen,** *v.i.* to languish, pine away; to droop.

kwijt, *a.* lost. *ik ben het ~,* I have lost it; *~ raken,* to lose, get rid of, shake off. ·**kwijtbrief, -ven,** *n.* receipt. ·**kwijten,** *v.t., str.* to pay off, discharge (*debt*). ¶*v.r., str. zich ~ van,* to acquit oneself of. ·**kwijting,** *n.* discharge, payment (*of debt*). *ter ~ van,* in settlement of. ·**kwijtraken, raak kwijt,** *v.t.s.* to get rid of. ·**kwijtschelden,** *v.t.s., str.* to remit; to forgive, condone. ·**kwijtschelding,** *n.* remission; absolution.

kwik, -kke, *a. See* **kwiek.** ¶no pl., *n.n.* mercury, quicksilver. ·**kwikbad,** *n.n.* mercurial bath. ·**kwikbarometer, -s,** *n.* mercury barometer. ·**kwikdamp,** *n.* mercury vapour. ·**kwikstaart,** *n.* wagtail. ·**kwikzilver,** no pl., *n.n.* mercury, quicksilver.

kwinke·leren, -leer, *v.i.* to carol (*of birds*). ·**kwinkslag,** *n.* quip, sally.

kwint, *n.* quint.

·**kwintappel, -s,** *n.* colocynth.

kwin·tet, -tten, *n.n.* quintet(te).

·**kwispe(l)door, -doren,** *n.* spittoon, cuspidor. ·**kwispel, -s,** *n.* brush, tuft; sprinkler (*for holy water*). ·**kwispelen,** *v.i.* to wag. *met de staart ~,* to wag one's tail. ·**kwispelstaarten,** *v.i.* to wag one's tail.

·**kwistig,** *a.* lavish. *~ met,* lavish of (*money*), lavish with (*praise*), lavish in giving. ·**kwistigheid,** no pl., *n.* lavishness.

kwi·tantie, -s, *n.* receipt.

L

la, -den, *n.* drawer. *See* **laatje.**

·**laadboom, -bomen,** *n.* derrick. ·**laadruim,** *n.n.* cargo hold. ·**laadvermogen,** no pl., *n.n.* carrying capacity; dead weight.

·**laafdrank,** *n.* (*poet.*) refreshing drink.

laag, lagen, *n.* layer; coat (*paint*); broadside; ambush. *iemand de volle ~ geven,* to let someone have it (*fig.*). ¶**lage,** *a.* low; mean, vile. ¶*adv.* low. *~ neerzien op,* to look down upon. ¶*See* **lager,** *a. & adv.* **laag·hartig,** *a.* base, vile. **laag·hartigheid,** no pl., *n.* baseness. ·**laagheid, -heden,** *n.* lowness; meanness. ·**laagland,** *n.n.* lowland. ·**laagte, -n,** *n.* lowness; low place. *in de ~,* down below; *naar de ~ gaan,* to go down. **laag·veen,** no pl., *n.n.* bog-peat; peat-bog. ·**laagvlakte, -n,** *n.* (lowland) plain. **laag·water,** no pl., *n.n.* low tide. *bij ~,* at low tide.

·**laaie,** no pl., *n. in lichter ~ staan,* to blaze. ·**laaien,** *v.i.* to blaze. *~ van,* to be ablaze with (*fig.*).

·**laakbaar, -bare,** *a.* reprehensible. ·**laakbaarheid,** no pl., *n.* reprehensibility.

laan, lanen, *n.* avenue. *iemand de ~ uitsturen,* to fire, sack someone.

laars, -zen, *n.* boot. *iets aan zijn ~ lappen,* to ignore *or* be indifferent to something. ·**laarzenknecht,** *n.* bootjack.

laat, late, *a.* late, belated. (*om*) *hoe ~?,* (at) what time?; *hoe ~ is het?,* what is the time?; *hoe ~ heb je het?,* what time do you make it?; *is het weer zo ~?,* have we come to that again?; *op de late avond,* late in the evening; *te ~,* too late *or* late, overdue. ¶*adv.* late. *te ~,* too late, late; *~ op de dag,* late in the day.

laat·dunkend, *a.* conceited, overweening. **laat·dunkendheid,** no pl., *n.* arrogance.

·**laatje, -s,** *n.n.* small drawer; till. *aan het ~ zitten,* to handle the cash.

laatst, *a.* last; latest. *in de ~e tijd,* of late, recently. ¶*adv.* recently; lately. ¶no pl., *n.n. op het ~,* in the end; *op zijn ~,* at the latest; *voor het ~,* for the last time. ·**laatste, -n,** *n. & n.n.* last; latter. *dit ~,* the latter. ·**laatstelijk,** *adv.* lastly. **laatstgenoemd,** *a.* last-mentioned, latter. **laatsteleden,** *a.* last (*of date*).

labbekak, -kken, *n.* milksop.

labber·daan, no pl., *n.* salt cod.

la·biel, *a.* labile, unstable.

labora·torium, -ia, *n.n.* laboratory. **laboreren, -reer,** *v.i.* to labour.

lach, no pl., *n.* laugh, laughter. *in een ~ schieten,* to burst out laughing. ·**lachbui,** *n.* fit of laughter. ·**lachebek, -kken,** *n.* giggler. ·**lachen,** *v.i., irr.* to laugh. *~ met,* to laugh at (*scorn*); *~ om,* to laugh at *or* over; *~ tegen,* to laugh *or* smile at; *zich dood ~ or zich krom ~,* to double up with laughter; *~ als een boer die kiespijn heeft,* to laugh on the wrong side of one's face; *in zijn vuistje ~,* to laugh in one's sleeve. ¶*v.t., irr. zich een ongeluk ~ or zich een aap ~,* to split one's sides with laughter. ¶no pl., *n.n. barsten van het ~,* to die of laughing. ·**lachend,** *a.* laughing; smiling. ·**lacher, -s,** *n.* laugher. ·**lachgas,** no pl., *n.n.* laughing gas. ·**lachje, -s,** *n.n.* half-smile. ·**lachlust,** no pl., *n.* inclination to laugh. *de ~ opwekken,* to provoke laughter. ·**lachspier,** *n.* laughing muscle. *op de ~en werken,* to provoke laughter. **lach·wekkend,** *a.* laughable. ·**lachziek,** *a.* giggly.

la·cune, -s, *n.* gap.

·**ladder, -s,** *n.* ladder. *de maatschappelijke ~,* the social scale.

·**lade, -n,** *n.* drawer. *See* **la,** *n.* and **laatje,** *n.n.*

·**ladelichter, -s,** *n.* shop-lifter.

·**laden, laad,** *v.t., irr.* to load (*ship, vehicle*); to load (*fire-arm*); to charge (*with electricity*). ¶*v.i., irr.* to load, take in cargo. ·**lader, -s,** *n.* loader. ·**lading,** *n.* load, cargo; charge (*electric*); loading, charge (*of fire-arm*). ·**ladingmeester, -s,** *n.* loading clerk.

laf, -ffe, *a.* cowardly; insipid. ·**lafaard, -s,** *n.* coward. ·**lafbek, -kken,** *n.* milksop.

·**lafenis, -ssen.** *n.* (*poet.*) refreshment.

laf·hartig, *a.* cowardly. **laf·hartigheid**, no pl., *n.*, **lafheid, -heden**, *n.* cowardice.

·lager, *a.* lower. *~e akte*, primary teacher's certificate; *~ onderwijs*, primary education. ¶**-s**, *n.n.* bearing(s) (*of machine*). **·lagerbier**, *n.n.* lager. **lager·eind**, no pl., *n.n.* lower end, bottom. **lager·hand**, no pl., *n.* left (*of host*). **lager·huis, -zen**, *n.n.* Second Chamber, House of Commons. **lager·wal**, no pl., *n.* lee shore. *aan ~ geraken*, to go down in the world.

la·gune, -s, *n.* lagoon.

lak, -kken, *n.n.* sealing-wax; lacquer. ¶no pl., *n.n.* *~ hebben aan*, to care nothing about.

la·kei, *n.* lackey, footman.

·lakon, laak, *v.t.* to censure, blame. ¶*n.n.* cloth (*material*); (table-)cloth; sheet (*on bed*). *de ~s uitdelen*, to rule the roast; *van hetzelfde ~ een pak krijgen*, to be dealt with in the same way. **·lakenfabriek**, *n.* cloth factory. **·lakenfabrikant**, *n.* cloth manufacturer. **lakenhal, -llen**, *n.* Cloth Hall, drapers' hall. **lakens**, *a.* (made of) cloth. **·lakenscheerder, -s**, *n.* cloth shearer. **·lakenverver, -s**, *n.* cloth dyer. **·lakenvolder, -s**, *n.* fuller. **lakenwever, -s**, *n.* cloth weaver. **·lakenweverij**, *n.* cloth weaving mill.

·lakken, lak, *v.t.* to lacquer; to seal.

·lakmoes, no pl., *n.n.* litmus.

laks, *a.* slack, indifferent. **·laksheid**, no pl., *n.* slackness, laxity.

·lakschoenen, pl. only, *n.* patent leather shoes. **·lakwerk**, no pl., *n.n.* lacquer ware, japanned goods.

lam, -mmeren, *n.n.* lamb. ¶**-mme**, *a.* paralysed, paralytic; worn out (*of screw*); (*coll.*) wretched, boring. *iemand ~ slaan*, to beat a person to a jelly.

·lama, -'s, *n.* llama.

lambri·zeren, -zeer, *v.t.* to wainscot, panel. **lambri·zering**, *n.* wainscot(ting), panelling.

·lamheid, no pl., *n.* paralysis. **lam·lendig**, *a.* miserable, wretched. ¶*adv. zich ~ voelen*, to feel awful. **lam·lendigheid**, no pl., *n.* wretchedness. **·lammeling**, *n.* wretch. **lamme·nadig**, *a. & adv. See* **lamlendig**.

·lammeren, *v.i.* to lamb. ¶*See* **lam**. *n.n.* **·lammergier**, *n.* lammergeyer, bearded vulture.

la·moen, *n.n.* shafts (*of cart*).

lamp, *n.* lamp; lamp, bulb; valve (*wireless*). *naar de ~ rieken*, to smell of the lamp; *tegen de ~ lopen*, to be caught. **·lampeglas, -zen**, *n.n.* lamp-chimney. **·lampekap, -ppen**, *n.* lampshade. **·lampekousje, -s**, *n.n.* lamp-wick; (gas) mantle. **·lampenhok, -kken**, *n.n.* lamp-cabin. **lampe·nist**, *n.* lampman. **lampenkoorts**, no pl., *n.* stage fright. **la·m·petkan, -nnen**, *n.* ewer, water jug. **lam·petkom, -mmen**, *n.* wash-basin. **lampi·on, -s**, *n.* Chinese lantern. **lampisterij**, *n.* lamp-cabin

lam·prei, *n.* lamprey.

·lamsbout, *n.* leg of lamb. **·lamsvlees**, no pl., *n.n.* lamb (*meat*).

lan·ceerbuis, -zen, *n.* torpedo tube. **lanceren, -ceer**, *v.t.* to launch (*offensive; rumour*); to fire, discharge (*torpedo*). **lan·ceerinrichting**, *n.* firing gear (*for torpedoes*).

land, *n.n.* land; land, country; land, field. *het ~ hebben*, to be fed up; *het ~ hebben aan*, to have an aversion to; *het ~ krijgen*, to become fed up with; *'s ~s wijs 's ~s eer*, do in Rome as Rome does; *er valt geen ~ met hem te bezeilen*, one cannot get on with him; *aan ~ gaan*, to go ashore; *op het ~*, in the country(side); *te ~*, on land, by land; *te ~ komen*, to land, get to. **·landaard**, no pl., *n.* national character. **·landadel**, no pl., *n.* landed nobility. **·landarbeider, -s**, *n.* agricultural labourer. **lan·dauer, -s**, *n.* landau. **·landbezit**, no pl., *n.n.* landed property. **·landbouw**, no pl., *n.* agriculture. **·landbouwbedrijf, -ven**, *n.n.* agricultural enterprise. **·landbouwer, -s**, *n.* farmer. **·landbouwkunde**, no pl., *n.* agriculture (*science*). **landbouw·kundig**, *a.* agricultural. **·landdag**, *n.* diet (*parliament*). **·landelijk**, *a.* rural, rustic. **landelijkheid**, no pl., *n.* rusticity. **·landen**, *v.t. & v.i.* to land. **·landengte, -n**, *n.* isthmus. **·landerig**, *a.* depressed. *~ zijn*, to be in the dumps. **·landerigheid**, no pl., *n.* fedupness. **·lande·rijen**, pl. only, *n.* estates; fields and meadows. **·landgenoot, -noten**, *n.* fellow-countryman. **·landgenote, -n**, *n.* fellow-countrywoman. **·landgoed, -eren**, *n.n.* estate, country-seat. **·landgraaf, -graven**, *n.* landgrave. **·landhuis, -zen**, *n.n.* country-house, villa. **·landing**, *n.* landing, disembarkation. **·landingsmast**, *n.* mooring mast (*of airship*). **·landingstoestel, -llen**, *n.n.* undercarriage (*of aircraft*). **·landingstroepen**, pl. only, *n.* landing forces. **·landjonker, -s**, *n.* country squire. **·landkaart**, *n.* map. **·landklimaat**, no pl., *n.n.* continental climate. **·landlieden**, pl. *n. See* **landman**. **·landloper, -s**, *n.* tramp, vagabond. **landlope·rij**, no pl., *n.* vagrancy. **landmacht**, *n.* army (*in general*). **·landman, landlieden**, *n.* countryman, peasant. **·landmeter, -s**, *n.* surveyor; looper (*caterpillar*). **lan·douw**, *n.* (fruitful) region, pasture. **·landpaal, -palen**, *n.* boundary mark. **·landpacht**, *n.* ground rent. **·landraad, -raden**, *n.* district court (*East Indies*). **·landrat, -tten**, *n.* land-lubber. **·landschap, -ppen**, *n.n.* landscape; region. **·landsdrukkerij**, *n.* government stationery office. **·landsheer, -heren**, *n.* monarch. **·landskas, -ssen**, *n.* public treasury. **·landsknecht**, *n.* lansquenet. **·landsman, landslieden**, *n.* (fellow-)countryman. **·landstorm**, *n.* type of home guard *or* military reserve. **·landstreek, -streken**, *n.* region.

·**landsvrouw**, *n.* queen, sovereign lady. ·**landtong**, *n.* spit (*of land*). ·**landverhuizer**, ·**s**, *n.* emigrant. ·**landverhuizing**, *n.* emigrátion. ·**landverraad**, no pl., *n.n.* high treason. ·**landverrader**, ·**s**, *n.* traitor (*to his country*). ·**landvoogd**, *n.* governor, viceroy. **landvoog·des**, ·**ssen**, *n.* governess, vicereine. **landvoog·dij**, no pl., *n.* governorship. ·**landwaarts**, *adv.* landward. ·**landweer**, no pl., *n.* territorial army. ·**landweerman**, ·**nnen**, *n.* territorial. ·**landweg**, *n.* country road; overland route.

lang, *a.* long; tall. *het is zo ~ als het breed is*, it's six of one and half a dozen of the other; *een ~e tong hebben*, to be a scandalmonger; *iets op de ~ baan schuiven*, to put something off to the Greek kalends; *een werk van ~e adem*, a long job; *~ van stof*, long-winded. ¶*adv.* long; a long time. *al ~*, a long time, long ago, long; *nog zo ~*, ever so long; *een tijd ~*, for a time; *uren ~*, for hours; *~ geen . . .*, by no means . . .; *~ niet* or *bij ~e niet*, not nearly, far from; *in ~*, for a long time; *iets ~ en breed bespreken*, to discuss at great length; *hoe ~er hoe beter*, the longer the better; *op zijn ~st*, at the utmost. **lang·armig**, *a.* long-armed. ·**langbeen**, ·**benen**, *n.* longshanks. **lang·benig**, *a.* long-legged. ·**langbek**, ·**kken**, *n.* long-bill. **lang·dradig**, *a.* long-winded, prolix. **lang·durig**, *a.* protracted, lasting. **lang·durigheid**, no pl., *n.* long duration. ·**langgerekt**, *a.* long-drawn-out. **lang·halzig**, *a.* long-necked. **lang·harig**, *a.* long-haired. ·**langoor**, ·**goren**, *n.* long-ears. **langs**, *prep.* along; past. *iemand er van ~ geven*, to let someone have it (*fig.*); *~ iemand heen*, past someone. **langs·boord**, *adv.* alongside. ·**langslaper**, ·**s**, *n.* late riser. **langs·zij**, *adv.* alongside. ·**languit**, *adv.* full length. **lang·vingerig**, *a.* long-fingered. **lang·werpig**, *a.* oblong. **lang·wijlig**, *a.* tedious. ·**langzaam**, ·**zame**, *a.* slow. *~ vooruit*, easy ahead; *~ aan*, slowly, gently. ¶*adv.* slowly. ·**langzamerhand**, *adv.* gradually.

lank·moedig, *a.* long-suffering. **lankmoedigheid**, no pl., *n.* long-suffering. **lans**, *n.* lance. **lan·sier**, ·**s**, *n.* lancer. **lan·taarn**, ·**s**, *n.*, **lan·taren**, ·**s**, *n.* lantern, lamp; skylight. **lan·tarenopsteker**, ·**s**, *n.* lamplighter. **lan·tarenpaal**, ·**palen**, *n.* lamp-post. **lan·tarenplaatje**, ·**s**, *n.n.* lantern slide.

·**lanterfant**, *n.* idler, wastrel. ·**lanterfanten**, *v.i.* to idle, loaf. **lap**, ·**ppen**, *n.* cloth; piece (*of fabric, leather, skin*); rag; patch (*on clothes; of land*). *de lappen hangen erbij*, it is in rags; *alle lappen uithangen*, spread every stitch of canvas. ·**lapje**, ·**s**, *n.n.* small rag or patch; piece of steak, escalop. *iemand voor het ~ houden*, to pull a person's leg. ·**lapmiddel**,

n.n. palliative. ·**lappen**, **lap**, *v.t.* to patch, mend; to clean (*windows with chamois leather*). *het ~* (*fig.*), to do the trick; *iemand iets ~*, to play someone a trick; *iemand erbij ~*, to catch a person (*fig.*). ·**lappenmand**, *n.* ragbag. *in de ~*, ailing. ·**lapwerk**, no pl., *n.n.* patchwork.

lar·deren, ·**deer**, *v.t.* to lard. **larf**, ·**ven**, *n.* larva. ·**larie**, no pl., *n.*, ·**lariefarie**, no pl., *n.* nonsense. ·**lariks**, *n.*, ·**lariksboom**, ·**bomen**, *n.* larch. ·**larve**, ·**n**, *n.* larva, grub.

las, ·**ssen**, *n.* joint, seam, weld. ·**lasijzer**, ·**s**, *n.n.* welding iron. ·**lasplaat**, ·**platen**, *n.* fish-plate (*of rails*). ·**lassen**, **las**, *v.t.* to weld. ·**lasser**, ·**s**, *n.* welder.

last, *n.* load; cargo; burden, weight; trouble, nuisance; command; tax. *de ~ breken*, to break bulk; *op zware ~en zitten*, to be heavily encumbered; *ten ~e van*, chargeable to; *iemand iets ten ~e leggen*, to lay something to someone's charge; *iemand tot ~ zijn*, to be a burden on someone; *~ hebben van*, to be troubled with; *dan is Holland in ~*, then there will be real trouble; *~ krijgen*, to be troubled or to receive instructions; *op ~ van*, on instructions of. ¶*n.n.* last (*weight*). ·**lastdier**, *n.n.* beast of burden.

·**laster**, no pl., *n.* slander, libel. ·**lasteraar**, ·**s**, *n.* slanderer, libeller. ·**lasteren**, *v.t.* to slander. *God ~*, to blaspheme. ·**lastering**, *n.* slander; blasphemy. ·**lasterlijk**, *a.* slanderous, libellous. ·**lasterpraatje**, ·**s**, *n.n.* slanderous talk, scandal. ·**lasterproces**, ·**ssen**, *n.n.* slander suit, libel action.

·**lastezel**, ·**s**, *n.* pack-donkey. ·**lastgeefster**, ·**s**, *n.* (*female*) principal (*in transaction*). ·**lastgever**, ·**s**, *n.* principal (*in transaction*). ·**lastig**, *a.* difficult; troublesome; awkward. *iemand ~ vallen*, to trouble or importune someone. ¶*adv.* with difficulty. ·**lastlijn**, *n.* Plimsoll line. ·**lastpaard**, *n.n.* pack-horse. ·**lastpost**, *n.* nuisance (*person*).

lat, ·**tten**, *n.* lath. ·**latafel**, ·**s**, *n.* chest of drawers. ·**laten**, **laat**, *v. aux., str.* to let; to make, cause, have; to permit. ¶*v.t., str.* to leave off (*doing*); to leave. *het erbij ~*, to leave it at that; *~ vallen*, to drop; *~ zien*, to show. ·**lathyrus**, ·**ssen**, *n.* sweet pea. **La·tijn**, no pl., *n.n.* Latin. ·**latwerk**, no pl., *n.n.* trellis. **lau·rier**, *n.* laurel. **lau·rierblad**, ·**eren**, *n.* laurel leaf, bay leaf. **lau·rierkers**, *n.* bayberry.

lauw, *a.* tepid, lukewarm. ·**lauwheid**, no pl., *n.* lukewarmness. ·**lauwer**, ·**s** or ·**en**, *n.* laurel. ·**~en behalen**, to reap laurels. ·**lauwerkrans**, *n.* laurel wreath.

·**lavaglas**, no pl., *n.n.* obsidian. **lave·ment**, *n.n.* enema. **lave·mentspuit**, *n.* enema syringe.

·laven, laaf, *v.t.* to refresh. ¶zich ~, *v.r.* to refresh oneself. zich ~ *aan*, to drink from.
la·vendel, no pl., *n.* lavender.
la·veren, -veer, *v.i.* to tack (*of sailing ship*).
·laving, *n.* refreshment.
la·waai, no pl., *n.n.* noise, din, racket. la·waaierig, *a.* noisy, loud. la·waaimaker, -s, *n.*, noise-maker; swanker.
la·wine, -s, *n.* avalanche.
la·xeermiddel, -s *or* -en, *n.n.* laxative. la·xeren, -xeer, *v.t.* to purge.
·lazarus, no pl., *n.* ben je ~ ? (*vulg.*), are you mad?
la·zuren, *a.* azure. la·zuur, -zuren, *n.* lapis lazuli. la·zuurblauw, *a.* azure. la·zuursteen, -stenen, *n.* lapis lazuli.
leb, no pl., *n.* rennet. ·lebmaag, -magen, *n.* abomasum.
·lector, *n.* lecturer (*at university*). lecto·raat, -raten, *n.n.* lecturership. lec·tuur, no pl., *n.* reading (matter).
·ledematen, pl., *n.n.*, leden, pl., *n.n. See* lid. ·ledenlijst, *n.* members' register. ·ledental, *n.n.* membership (*number of members*).
·ledepop, -ppen, *n.* lay figure; puppet.
·leder, no pl., *n.n.* leather. *See* leer. ·lederbereider, -s, *n.* currier. ·lederen, *a.* (made of) leather. ·lederwaren, pl. only, *n.* leather goods.
·ledig, *a.* (*stilted*) empty. *See* leeg. ·ledigen, *v.t.* to empty. ·lediggang, *n.* idleness. ·ledigganger, -s, *n.* idler. ·ledigheid, no pl., *n.* emptiness; idleness. ~ *is des duivels oorkussen*, idleness is the root of all evil. ·lediging, no pl., *n.* emptying.
ledi·kant, *n.n.* bedstead.
leed, no pl., *n.n.* sorrow, grief; harm, hurt. ~ *doen*, to grieve, pain; *iemand zijn ~ klagen*, to unburden oneself to a person. ¶lede, *a.* met lede ogen, with envious eyes. ·leedvermaak, no pl., *n.n.* malicious pleasure. ·leedwezen, no pl., *n.n.* regret.
·leefregel, -s, *n.* rule of life. ·leeftijd, *n.* age. boven de ~, over age; op zijn ~, at his age; van dezelfde ~, of an age. ·leeftocht, no pl., *n.* victuals. ·leefwijze, -n, *n.* way of life.
leeg, lege, *a.* empty; spare (*time*). met lege handen, empty-handed; met een lege maag, on an empty stomach. ·leegbranden, *v.i.s.* to burn out. ·leegdrinken, *v.t.s.*, str. to empty, drain. ·leegeten, eet leeg, *v.t.s.*, irr. to clean (one's plate). ·leeggieten, *v.t.s.*, str. to empty (*liquid*). ·leeghalen, haal leeg, *v.t.s.* to empty, loot. ·leeglopen, loop leeg, *v.i.s.*, str. to run dry; to go flat (*of tyre*). laten ~, to deflate. ¶no pl., *n.n.* loafing. ·leegloper, -s, *n.* loafer. ·leegpompen, *v.t.s.* to pump dry. ·leegstaan, sta leeg, *v.i.s.*, irr. to stand empty. ·leegte, -n, *n.* emptiness, void.
leek, leken, *n.* layman.
leem, no pl., *n.n.* loam. ·leemachtig, *a.* loamy. ·leemgroeve, -n, *n.* loampit.

·leemte, -n, *n.* gap; lacuna, hiatus.
leen, lenen, *n.n.* fief; loan. in ~ *hebben*, to hold in fee *or* to have borrowed; *te ~*, on loan; *te ~ vragen*, to ask for the loan of. ·leenbank, *n.* loan office. ·leendienst, *n.* feudal service. ·leeneed, -neden, *n.* oath of allegiance. ·leengoed, -deren, *n.n.* fief. ·leenheer, -heren, *n.* feudal lord. ·leenman, -nnen, *n.* vassal. leen·plichtig, *a.* liege. ·leenrecht, no pl., *n.n.* feudal law. leen·roerig, *a.* feudal. ·leenstelsel, -s, *n.n.* feudal system.
leep, lepe, *a.* cunning, sly. ·leepheid, no pl., *n.* cunning.
leer, no pl., *n.n.* leather. ~ om ~, tit for tat; *van een andermans ~ is het goed riemen snijden*, it's easy to be free with someone else's money. ¶leren, *n.* ladder; doctrine, theory. in de ~ *doen bij*, to apprentice to. ·leerachtig, *a.* leathery. ·leerboek, *n.n.* textbook. ·leergang, *n.* course (*of study*). ·leergeld, *n.n.* fee (*for school; of apprentice*). leer·gierig, *a.* eager to learn, studious. leer·gierigheid, no pl., *n.* eagerness to learn. ·leerjaar, -jaren, *n.n.* year (*of curriculum*). *pl. also:* apprenticeship. ·leerjongen, -s, *n.* apprentice. ·leerkracht, *n.* teacher. ·leerling, *n.* pupil; disciple. ·leerlooien, no pl., *n.n.* tanning. ·leerlooier, -s, *n.* tanner. ·leerlooie·rij, *n.* tannery. ·leermeester, -s, *n.* master, teacher. ·leermiddel, *n.n.* educational appliance. ·leer·plan, -nnen, *n.n.* syllabus, curriculum. ·leerplicht, no pl., *n.* compulsory education. leer·plichtig, *a.* subject to compulsory education. ·leerrede, -denen, *n.* sermon. ·leerrijk, *a.* instructive. ·leerschool, -scholen, *n.* school (*fig.*). ·leerstelling, *n.* tenet; dogma. ·leerstelsel, -s, *n.* system. ·leerstoel, *n.* chair (*academic*). ·leerstof, no pl., *n.* subject-matter (*of teaching*). ·leerstuk, -kken, *n.n.* dogma. ·leertijd, no pl., *n.* apprenticeship. ·leerwerk, no pl., *n.n.* leather-work. ·leerzaam, -zame, *a.* docile, teachable; instructive. ·leerzaamheid, no pl., *n.* docility.
·leesbaar, -bare, *a.* readable, legible. ·leesbaarheid, no pl., *n.* readability; legibility. ·leesbeurt, *n.* turn to read. ·leesbibliotheek, -theken, *n.* lending library. ·leesboek, *n.n.* reader (*book*). ·leesgezelschap, -ppen, *n.n.* book club. ·leeslust, no pl., *n.* love of reading.
leest, *n.* last (*shoemaker's*); waist. op een andere ~ schoeien, to cast in a different mould.
·leesteken, -s, *n.n.* punctuation mark. ·leeswijzer, -s, *n.* bookmark. ·leeszaal, -zalen, *n.* reading-room.
leeuw, *n.* lion. ·leeuwenaandeel, no pl., *n.n.* lion's share. ·leeuwenbek, -kken, *n.* snapdragon. ·leeuwenkuil, *n.* lions' den. ·leeuwerik, -kken, *n.* !ark. skylark. leeuw·in, -nnen, *n.* lioness.

lef, no pl., *n.n.* pluck, courage. *als je ~ hebt,* if you dare.

leg, no pl., *n.* lay (*of poultry*). *aan de ~,* in lay.

le·gaat, -gaten, *n.n.* legacy, bequest. ¶**-gaten,** *n.* legate. **legali·satie, -s,** *n.* legalization. **legali·seren· -seer,** *v.t.* to legalize. **lega·taris, -ssen,** *n.* legatee. **lega·teren, -teer,** *v.t.* to bequeath. **le·gatie, -s,** *n.* embassy, legation.

legboor, -boren, *n.* ovipositor.

le·gende, -n, *n.* legend.

leger, -s, *n.n.* army; lair. *~ des heils,* Salvation Army. **legerafdeling,** *n.* division (*of army*). **legeren,** *v.i.* to encamp.

le·geren, -geer, *v.t.* to alloy. **le·gering,** *n.* alloy.

legerspits, *n.* spearhead (*of army*). **leger·trein,** *n.* military train. **legertros. -ssen,** *n.* baggage (*of army*).

leggen, leg, *v.t., irr.* to lay; to lay (*eggs*). **legger, -s,** *n.* layer (*person; chicken*); sleeper (*railway*); ledger.

legio, *a.* legion, numerous. **legi·oen,** *n.n.* legion.

legi·tiem, *a.* legitimate. **legiti·matie, -s,** *n.* legitimization. **legiti·matiebewijs, -zen,** *n.n.* identification papers.

legkaart, *n.* jig-saw puzzle. **legkip, -ppen,** *n.* laying hen. **legtijd,** *n.* laying season.

legu·aan, -uanen, *n.* iguana.

lei, *n.* slate. **leidekker, -s,** *n.* slater.

leiband, *n.* leading-strings. *aan de ~ lopen,* to be tied to (*somebody's*) apron strings. **leiboom, -bomen,** *n.* espalier.

·Leiden, *n.N.* Leyden.

·leiden, *v.t.* to lead, conduct. *zich laten ~ door,* to be guided by; *tot niets ~,* to lead nowhere. **leider, -s,** *n.* leader. **leiding,** no pl., *n.* guidance, conducting; leadership. *de ~ hebben,* to be in control; *de ~ op zich nemen,* to take charge. ¶*n.* main (*water, gas, electric*); conduit. **leiding-water.** no pl., *n.n.* tap water. **leidraad, -draden,** *n.* guiding principle.

Leids, *a.* (from *or* of) Leyden.

leidsel, -s, *n.n.* rein(s). **leidsman, -slieden,** *n.* guide, mentor. **leidster, -rren,** *n.* lodestar.

·leien, *a.* (made of) slate. *he' gaat als van een ~ dakje,* it all goes very smoothly. **leigroeve, -n,** *n.* slate quarry. **leikleurig,** *a.* slate-coloured.

!ek, -kke, *a.* leaky; punctured (*tyre*). *~ zijn,* to leak (*ship*). ¶**-kken,** *n.n.* leak, leakage; puncture. *een ~ krijgen,* to spring a leak. **lek·kage, -s,** *n.* leakage. **lekken, lek,** *a.* to leak; to lick.

·lekebroeder, -s, *n.* lay brother.

·lekker, *a.* nice, pleasant; dainty. *iemand ~ maken,* to rouse a person's interest; *iets ~ vinden,* to enjoy something; *zich niet ~ voelen,* not to feel well; *zo ~ als kip,* as fit as a fiddle. ¶*adv.* nicely. *~ warm,*

nice and warm; *~ eten,* to enjoy one's food; *dank je ~!,* no thanks (*ironical*). **lekkerbek, -kken,** *n.* gourmet. *hij is een ~,* he has a sweet tooth. **lekker·bekken, -bek,** *v.i.* to gormandize. **lekker·nij,** *n.* delicacy, titbit. **lekkers,** no pl., *n.n. iets ~,* something nice. **lekkertjes,** *adv.* nicely.

·leksteen, -stenen. *n.* dripstone.

lel, -llen, *n.* lobe (*of ear*); gill (*of cock*).

·lelie, -s *cr* **-liën,** *n.* lily. **·lelietje-van-dalen, -s-van-dalen,** *n.n.* lily of the valley.

·lelijk, *a.* ugly; nasty; awkward, inconvenient. *~ als de nacht,* ugly as sin. ¶*adv.* in an ugly way. *het ziet er ~ uit,* it looks ugly; *er ~ aan toe zijn,* to be in a sad state. **·lelijkerd, -s,** *n.* ugly *or* nasty person.

·lemen, *a.* (made of) loam.

·lemmer, -s, *n.n.,* **·lemme:, -s,** *n.n.* blade (*of sword, knife*).

·lende, -n *or* **-nen,** *n.* loin. **lendenpijn,** no pl., *n.,* **lendenschot,** no pl., *n.n.* lumbago. **lendenstuk, -kken,** *n.n.* loin, rump(steak).

·lenen, leen, *v.t.* to lend; to borrow. *~ aan,* to lend to; *~ van,* to borrow from. ¶*v.r. zich ~ tot,* to lend oneself to.

leng, *n.* ling. ¶*n.n.* sling (*for hoisting*).

·lengen, *v.t.* to lengthen. ¶*v.i.* to lengthen, become longer. **lengte, -n,** *n.* length; longitude. *in de ~,* lengthwise; *tot in ~ van dagen,* for years to come. **lengteas, -ssen,** *n.* longitudinal axis. **lengtecirkel, -s,** *n.* circle of longitude. **lengtedoorsnee, -sneden,** *n.* longitudinal section. **lengtemaat, -maten,** *n.* linear measure.

·lenig, *a.* supple, lithe. **lenigen,** *v.t.* to alleviate. **lenigheid,** no pl., *n.* suppleness. **·leniging,** *n.* alleviation.

·lening, *n.* loan. *een ~ sluiten,* to contract a loan.

lens, -zen, *n.* lens. ¶**-ze,** *a.* empty, dry (*of pump* or *ship's bilge*). *iemand ~ slaan,* to knock someone out. **lenspomp, -n.** bilge-pump. **lensvormig,** *a.* lens-shaped.

·lente, -s, *n.* spring (*season*). **lentebode, -n,** *n.* harbinger of spring. **lenteklokje, -s,** *n.n.* harebell. **·lentemaand,** *n.* March. **lente·nachtevening,** *n.* vernal equinox.

·lenzen, lens, *v.t.* to empty (*with pump*).

·lepel, -s, *n.* spoon; ladle. **lepelaar, -s,** *n.n.* spoonbill. **lepelblad,** *n.* chuck (*of lathe, etc.*). ¶no pl., *n.n.* spoonwort. **lepelboor, -boren,** *n.* shell-bit. **lepeldiefje, -s,** *n.n.* shepherd's purse. **lepelen,** *v.t.* to spoon, ladle. **lepelkost,** no pl., *n.* liquid food. **lepelvormig,** *a.* spoon-shaped.

leperd, -s, *n.* cunning person.

·lepra, no pl., *n.* leprosy. **le·proos, -prozen,** *n.* leper. **le·prozenhuis, -zen,** *n.n.* leper hospital.

·leraar, -raren *or* **-s,** *n.* teacher (*in secondary school*); minister (*of religion*). **leraars·kamer, -s,** *n.* staff room (*secondary school*).

lera·res, -ssen, *n.* teacher (*female; in secondary school*).
·leren, *a.* (made of) leather. ¶leer, *v.i.* to learn. ¶leer, *v.t.* to teach; to learn. *iemand ~ kennen*, to get to know a person. ·lering, *n.* instruction. ¶no pl., *n.* catechism class (*Roman Catholic*).
les, -ssen, *n.* lesson. ~ *geven*, to teach; *iemand de ~ lezen*, to lecture a person. ·lesgeld, no pl., *n.n.* fee (*for lesson*). ·lesje, -s, *n.n.* lesson. *iemand een ~ geven*, to teach a person a lesson. ·les-rooster, -s, *n.* time-table (*in school*).
·lessen, les, *v.t.* to quench; to slake. ·lessenaar, -s, *n.* desk.
lest, *a.* last. ·leste, no pl., *n.n. ten langen ~, at long last*.
Let, -tten, *N.* Latvian. ·Letland, *n.N.* Latvia· Lets, *a.* Latvian.
·letsel, no pl., *n.n.* hurt, injury. ~ *ondervinden*, to sustain an injury; *iemand ~ toebrengen*, to inflict an injury on someone. ·letten, let, *v.i. let wel*, note, mark you; ~ *op*, to pay attention to. ¶*v.t.* to hinder, prevent. *wat let me*, what is to prevent me.
·letter, -s, *n.* letter (*of alphabet*); type (*print*). *naar de ~*, to the letter. ¶-en, pl. only. *n.* letters, literature. *in de ~en studeren*, to study an arts subject. ·letteren, *v.t.*, to letter. ·lettergieter, -s, *n.* type founder. lettergiete·rij, *n.* type foundry. ·lettergreep, -grepen, *n.* syllable. ·letterkast, *n.* type case. ·letterkunde, no pl., *n.* literature. letter·kundig, *a.* literary. letter·kundige, -n, *n.* man of letters. ·letterlijk, *a.* literal. ·letterschrift, no pl., *n.n.* alphabetical writing. ·letterteken, -s, *n.n.* character (*letter*). ·letterzetten, no pl., *n.n.* type-setting. ·letterzetter, -s, *n.* compositor, type-setter. letterzette·rij, *n.* composing room. ·letterziften, no pl., *n.n.* hair-splitting.
·leugen, -s, *n.* lie. *een ~ om bestwil*, a white lie; ~*s verkopen*, to tell lies. ·leugenaar, -s, *n.* liar. ·leugenachtig, *a.* lying, mendacious. ·leugentje, -s, *n.n.* fib.
leuk, *a.* dry, humorous; nice; pleasant, jolly. ¶*adv.* amusingly. ·leukweg, *adv.* drily, humorously.
·leunen, *v.i.* to lean. ·leuning, *n.* rail, banister(s); back (*of chair*). ·leunstoel, *n.* armchair. ·leunstokje, -s, *n.n.* mahlstick.
leur, *n. te ~ stellen*, to disappoint. ·leurder, -s, *n.* hawker. ·leuren, *v.i.* to hawk. ~ *met*, to hawk.
leus, -zen, *n.* slogan, device, watchword. *voor de ~*, for the look of the thing.
leut, no pl., *n.* fun. *voor de ~*, for fun.
·leuteraar, -s, *n.* driveller. ·leuteren, *v.i.* to talk drivel. ·leuterpraat, no pl., *n.* twaddle.
·Leuven, *n.N.* Louvain.
·leuze, -n, *n.* See leus.
·leven, leef, *v.i.* to live; to be alive. *leve de Koningin*, long live the Queen; *van iets ~*,

to live on something; *wie dan leeft dan zorgt*, sufficient unto the day is the evil thereof. ¶no pl., *n.n.* life; living; quick; noise. *het ~ laten*, to lose one's life; *bij zijn ~*, during his lifetime; ~ *in de brouwerij brengen*, to make things hum; *naar het ~*, from the life; *om het ~ brengen*, to kill, make away with; *om het ~ komen*, to lose one's life; *een strijd op ~ en dood*, a fight to the death. ¶-s, *n.n.* life, biography. ·levend, *a.* alive, quick. ·levendig, *a.* lively, vivacious, sprightly; keen. ¶*adv.* in a lively manner. ·levendigheid, no pl., *n.* liveliness, vivacity. ·levenloos, -loze, *a.* lifeless, inanimate. ·levenmaker, -s, *n.* noisy person. ·levens·beschrijving, *n.* biography. ·levensduur, no pl., *n.* term of life. ·levensgeschiedenis, -ssen, *n.* life history. ·levensgevaar, no pl., *n.n.* danger. *met ~*, at the risk of one's life. levensge·vaarlijk, *a.* risky, perilous. ·levensgroot, -grote, *a.* life-size. ·levenskracht, *n.* vital energy. ·levenslang, *a.* lifelong. ~*e gevangenschap*, life sentence. ·levenslicht, no pl., *n.n. het ~ aanschouwen*, to behold the light of day. ·levensloop, no pl., *n.* career, course of life. ·levenslust, no pl., *n.* joie de vivre. levens·lustig, *a.* cheerful. ·levensmiddelen, pl. only, *n.n.* victuals. ·levensonderhoud, no pl., *n.* subsistence, livelihood. levens·vatbaar, -bare, *a.* viable. ·levensverzekering, *n.* life-assurance. *een ~ sluiten*, to take out a life-assurance. ·levenswandel, no pl., *n.* way of living. ·leventje, no pl., *n.n.* life.
·lever, -s, *n.* liver.
leveran·cier, -s, *n.* supplier, caterer; tradesman. leve·rantie, -s, *n.* delivery (*of goods*). ·leverbaar, -bare, *a.* deliverable. ·leveren, *v.t.* to furnish, supply; to deliver (*goods*). *hij zal het hem wel ~*, he will manage; *stof ~ tot*, to give rise to. ·leveringstermijn, *n.* time of delivery.
·leverkruid, no pl., *n.n.* liverwort. ·levertraan, no pl., *n.* (cod-)liver oil. ·leverworst, *n.* liver sausage.
·lezen, lees, *v.i.*, *str.* to read. *het kan ~ en schrijven*, it stands rough usage. ¶*v.t.*, *str.* to read; to gather, glean. ·lezenaar, -s, *n.* lectern. ·lezenswaard, *a.* worth reading. ·lezer, -s, *n.* reader; gleaner. leze·res, -ssen, *n.* reader (*female*). ·lezing, *n.* lecture, address; reading (*on scale*); version, account. *een ~ houden*, to give a lecture.
li·as, -ssen, *n.* bundle of papers.
li·bel, -llen, *n.* dragonfly. ¶*n.n.* libel, lampoon.
·lichaam, -chamen, *n.n.* body. *naar ~ en geest*, in body and mind. ·lichaamsarbeid, no pl., *n.* physical labour. ·lichaamsbeweging, *n.* bodily exercise. ·lichaamsbouw, no pl., *n.* build, frame. ·lichaamsgestel, no pl., *n.n.* constitution (*physical*). ·lichaamskracht, no pl., *n.* physical strength. li·chamelijk, *a.* corporal.

physical; bodily; material. ¶*adv.* physically.

licht, *n.n.* light. *een* ~, a great light (*iron.*); ~ *maken,* to put a light on; *er ging hem een* ~ *op,* he began to see daylight; *zijn* ~ *bij iemand opsteken,* to go to a person for information; *aan het* ~ *brengen,* to bring to light; *tussen* ~ *en donker,* in the twilight. ¶*a.* light; mild (*tobacco, etc.*). ~ *in het hoofd,* light-headed. ¶*adv.* lightly; easily. *See* **allicht.** **·lichtbeeld,** *n.n.* image of lantern slide. **·lichtboei,** *n.* light-buoy. **·lichtbrekend,** *a.* refractive. **·lichtbreking,** *n.* refraction (*of rays*). **·lichtbundel, -s,** *n.* beam of light. **·lichtekooi,** *n.* wanton. **lichte·laaie,** *adv. in* ~, ablaze. **·lichtelijk,** *adv.* slightly. **·lichten,** *v.t.* to lift, raise; to weigh (*anchor*); to raise (*ship*); to clear (*pillar-box*); to rifle (*till, etc.*). *iemand uit het bed* ~, to arrest someone at night. ¶*v.i.* to grow light (*dawn*); to lighten (*lightning*); to be phosphorescent. **·lichtend,** *a.* phosphorescent, luminous. **·lichter, -s,** *n.* lighter. **·lichtgas,** no *pl., n.n.* gas (*light*). **lichtge·lovig,** *a.* credulous, gullible. **lichtge·lovigheid,** no *pl., n.* credulity. **·licht·geraakt,** *a.* touchy. **licht·gevend,** *a.* luminous. **·lichtgranaat, -naten,** *n.* tracer shell. **·lichting,** *n.* collection (*postal*); class, levy. **·lichtkabel, -s,** *n.* electric-light cable. **·lichtkogel, -s,** *n.* tracer bullet. **·lichtmatroos, -trozen,** *n.* ordinary seaman. **·Lichtmis,** no *pl., n.* Candlemas. ¶**-ssen,** *n.* libertine. **·lichtpunt,** *n.n.* luminous point; ray of light (*fig.*). **·lichtreclame, -s,** *n.* illuminated sign. **·lichtschip, -schepen,** *n.* lightship. **·lichtsterkte,** no *pl., n.* candlepower. **licht·vaardig,** *a.* rash, thoughtless. **licht·vaardigheid, -heden,** *n.* rashness. **licht·zinnig,** *a.* frivolous; flighty. **licht·zinnigheid, -heden,** *n.* frivolity; flightiness.

lid, leden, *n.n.* lid; limb; member; member (*of a society*); paragraph. *een ziekte onder de leden hebben,* to be sickening for something; *uit het* ~, out of joint. ¶**ledematen,** *n.n.* member, limb. **·lidgras,** no *pl., n.n.* couchgrass. **·lidmaat, -maten,** *n.* member (*of congregation*). **·lidmaatschap,** no *pl., n.n.* membership. **·lidwoord,** *n.n.* article (*grammatica*).

·lied, -deren, *n.n.* song; hymn. **·liederboek,** *n.n.* song book.

·lieden, *pl.* only, *n.* people, folks.

·liederlijk, *a.* debauched; obscene. **·liederlijkheid, -heden,** *n.* dissoluteness; obscenity.

·liedje, -s, *n.n.* song, ditty. *het eind van het* ~, the end of the matter, the upshot; *een ander* ~ *zingen,* to change one's tune; *het oude* ~, the same old thing. **·liedjeszanger, -s,** *n.* street-singer.

lief, -ve, *a.* dear; sweet; nice. *lieve . . . my dearest . . .; meer dan hem* ~ *is,* more than he cares for; ~ *tegen,* sweet to; *Onze Lieve Heer,* Our Lord; *Onze Lieve*

Vrouw, the Virgin Mary, Our Lady; *de lieve lente,* sweet springtime. ¶*adv.* nicely. ~ *doen,* to pretend friendliness; *iets voor* ~ *nemen,* to put up with something; *net zo* ~, just as soon. ¶no *pl., n.n.* ~ *en leed,* weal and woe; *in* ~ *en leed,* in joy and sorrow. **lief·dadig,** *a.* charitable. **lief·dadigheid, -heden,** *n.* charity. **·liefde,** no *pl., n.* love. ~ *voor,* love of; *uit* ~, for *or* out of love. **·liefdeblijk,** *n.n.* love token. **·liefdedienst,** *n.* act of charity. **·liefdedrank,** *n.* love potion. **·liefdeloos, -loze,** *a.* uncharitable, unkind. **·liefdepand,** *n.n.* love token. **·liefderijk,** *a.* loving, charitable. **·liefdesverklaring,** *n.* proposal, declaration of love. **·liefdevol, -lle,** *a.* loving. **·liefdezuster, -s,** *n.* sister of charity, sister of mercy. **liefdoene·rij,** *n.* affected friendliness. **·liefelijk,** *a.* lovely, charming. **·liefelijkheid, -heden,** *n.* loveliness. **·liefelijkheden** (*iron.*), nice tricks. **·liefhebben, heb lief,** *v.t.s., irr.* to love, cherish. **·liefhebber, -s,** *n.* lover, amateur; prospective buyer. **·liefhebberen,** *v.i.* to dabble. **liefhebbe·rij,** *n.* hobby. *er bestaat grote* ~ *voor,* it is in great demand; *het is een* ~, it is a joy or treat. **·liefje, -s,** *n.n.* sweetheart (*female*). **·liefheid,** no *pl., n.* niceness, sweetness. **·liefkozen, -koos,** *v.t.* to fondle, caress. **·liefkozing,** *n.* caress. **liefst,** *n.n. See* **lief.** ¶*adv.* rather, preferably. *ik zou* ~ *. . .* I would prefer to . . .; (*het*) ~ *hebben,* to prefer. **·liefste,** no *pl., n.* lover. **lief·tallig,** *a.* lovable, sweet. **lief·talligheid,** no *pl., n.* charm, loveliness.

·liegen, *v.i., str.* to lie, tell lies. ¶*v.t., str.* to lie. *hij liegt het,* he lies.

lier, *n.* lyre; larch; winch. *het gaat als een* ~, it goes on wheels; *branden als een* ~, to burn like matchwood. **·lierdicht,** *n.n., ·lierzang,** *n.* lyric (poem). **·lierstaart,** *n.* lyre-bird.

lies, -zen, *n.* groin.

·lieveling, *n.* darling. **·lievelingskleur,** *n.* favourite colour. **lieve·moederen,** no *pl., n.n. daar helpt geen* ~ *aan,* it's no use crying over spilt milk. **lieve·heersbeestje, -s,** *n.n.* ladybird. **·liever,** *a.* nicer, dearer. *See* **lief.** ¶*adv.* rather; sooner. *iets* ~ *hebben,* to prefer something; *ik doe niets* ~. I like nothing better. **·lieverd, -s,** *n.* darling. **liever·lede,** *adv. van* ~, gradually. **lievevrouwen·bedstro,** no *pl., n.n.* Lady's bed straw. **·lievigheid, -heden,** *n.* sweet words (*usu. unfavourable*).

·liflafjes, *pl.* only, *n.n.* kickshaws.

·ligdag, *n.* day in port. **·liggeld,** *n.n.* harbour dues. **·liggen, lig,** *v.i., str.* to lie. *blijven* ~, to remain *or* to stay in bed; *gaan* ~, to lie down *or* to drop (*of wind*); *iets laten* ~, to leave something alone. **·liggend,** *a.* recumbent, prone. **·ligging,** no *pl., n.* situation; lie (*of the land*); bedding (*mil.*). **·ligplaats,** *n.* berth. **·ligstoel,** *n.*

chaise-longue. ·ligstro, no pl., *n.n.* litter (*straw*).
li·guster, -s, *n.* privet.
lij, no pl., *n.* lee. *aan* ~, on the lee side. ·lijboord, *n.n.* lee side.
·lijdbaar, -bare, *a.* bearable. ·lijdelijk, *a.* passive; patient. ·lijdelijkheid, no pl., *n.* passivity. ·lijden, *v.t., str.* to suffer, endure; to bear, stand. *iemand mogen* ~, to like someone; *schipbreuk* ~, to be shipwrecked. ¶*v.i., str.* to suffer. ~ *aan* or *te* ~ *hebben van*, to suffer from, labour under. ¶no pl., *n.n.* suffering; Passion (*of Christ*). *na* ~ *komt verblijden*, after rain comes sunshine. ·lijdend, *a.* suffering; passive. ·lijdens-beker, no pl., *n.* cup of bitterness. ·lijdens-geschiedenis, no pl., *n.* tale of woe; Passion. ·lijdenspreek, -preken, *n.* Passion sermon. ·lijdensweek, -weken, *n.* Holy Week. ·lijdensweg, no pl., *n.* way of the cross. ·lijder, -s, *n.* sufferer, patient. ·lijdzaam, -zame, *a.* meek, long-suffering. ·lijdzaam-heid, no pl., *n.* meekness, patience.
lijf, -ven, *n.n.* body; life; bodice. ~ *en goed*, life and property; *geen hart in het* ~ *hebben*, to be of little importance; *iemand op het* ~ *vallen*, to take a person unawares; *iemand te* ~ *gaan*, to attack a person; *iemand tegen het* ~ *lopen*, to come across a person; *iets aan den lijve voelen*, to experience something oneself; *in levenden lijve*, alive and well. ·lijfarts, *n.* court physician. ·lijfeigene, -n, *n.* serf. ·lijf-eigenschap, no pl., *n.* serfdom; bondage. ·lijfgarde, -n, *n.* bodyguard. ·lijtje, -s, *n.n.* bodice. ·lijfjonker, -s, *n.* page (*boy*).
·Lijfland, *n.N.* Livonia.
·lijfrente, -n, *n.* annuity. ·lijfsbehoud, no pl., *n.n.* preservation of life. ·lijfsgevaar, no pl., *n.n.* danger of life. ·lijfspreuk, *n.* favourite maxim. ·lijfstraf, -ffen, *n.* corporal punishment. ·lijftocht, no pl., *n.* provision, victuals. ·lijfwacht, *n.* body-guard.
lijk, *n.n.* corpse, dead body. ·lijkachtig, *a.* cadaverous. ·lijkbaar, -baren, *n.* bier. ·lijkbezorger, -s, *n.* undertaker. ·lijk-bidder, -s, *n.* undertaker's man. ·lijk-dienst, *n.* burial service.
·lijken, *v.i., str.* to look like, resemble; to seem, appear. *het lijkt uitstekend*, it is an excellent likeness; *nergens naar* ~, to look like nothing on earth; ~ *op*, to look like. ¶*v.t., str.* to please.
·lijkenhuis, -zen, *n.n.* mortuary. ·lijkenroof, no pl., *n.* body-snatching. ·lijkkleed, -kleden, *n.n.* shroud, winding-sheet. ·lijkkleurig, *a.* cadaverous, livid. ·lijkkoets, *n.* hearse. ·lijkopening, *n.* autopsy. ·lijkoven, -s, *n.* crematorium. ·lijkrede, -denen, *n.* funeral oration. ·lijkschouwer, -s, *n.* coroner. ·lijkschouwing, *n.* post-mortem. ·lijkverstijving, *n.* rigor mortis. ·lijkwade, -n, *n.* shroud. ·lijkzang, *n.* dirge.

lijm, no pl., *n.* glue. ·lijmen, *v.t.* to glue. *zich laten* ~, to be talked round. ·lijmerig, *a.* gluey. ¶*adv.* with a drawl. ·lijmstok, -kken, *n.* lime-twig. ·lijmwater, no pl., *n.n.* size.
lijn, *n.* line; line, cord; route (*bus, tram*). *één* ~ *trekken*, to pull together; *op één* ~, in a line; *over de hele* ~, all along the line. ·lijnbaan, -banen, *n.* rope-yard, rope-walk. ·lijndraaier, -s, *n.* ropemaker. ·lijnen, *v.t.* to rule.
·lijnkoek, *n.* linseed cake. ·lijnmeel, no pl., *n.n.* linseed meal. ·lijnolie, no pl., *n.* linseed oil.
·lijnrecht, *a.* (dead-)straight. ¶*adv.* ~ *ingaan tegen*, to be diametrically opposed to. ·lijnslager, -s, *n.* ropemaker. ·lijntekenen, no pl., *n.n.* geometrical drawing. ·lijntje, -s, *n.n.* short line. *iemand aan het* ~ *hebben*, to have a person on a string. ·lijntrekken, no pl., *n.n.* swinging the lead. ·lijntrekker, -s, *n.* shirker.
·lijnwaad, -waden, *n.n.* linen. ·lijnzaad, no pl., *n.n.* linseed.
lijs, -zen, *n.* dawdler. *lange* ~, long figure (*on china*).
lijst, *n.* list; frame, border; cornice. ·lijsten, *v.t.* to frame.
·lijster, -s, *n.* thrush. ·lijsterbes, -ssen, *n.* rowan; rowanberry.
·lijve, *n.* See lijf, *n.n.*
·lijvig, *a.* corpulent; hefty (*tome*). ·lijvigheid, no pl., *n.* corpulence.
·lijwaarts, *adv.* leeward. ·lijzeil, *n.n.* studding-sail.
·lijzig, *a.* slow.
lik, -kken, *n.* lick; swipe (*blow*).
·likdoorn, -s, *n.* corn (*on foot*).
li·keur, *n.* liqueur. li·keurstoker, -s, *n.* liqueur distiller. li·keurstokerij, *n.* liqueur distillery. li·keurtje, -s, *n.n.* (glass of) liqueur.
·likhout, *n.n.* polishing-stick. ·likkebaard, *n.* gourmet. ·likkebaarden, *v.i.* to lick one's lips. ·likken, lik, *v.t.* to lick. ·liksteen, -stenen, *n.* polishing-block.
·lila, no pl., *n.n.* lilac. ¶*a.* lilac.
·lillen, lil, *v.i.* to quiver.
li·miet, *n.* limit. limi·teren, -teer, *v.t.* to limit.
·limmetje, -s, *n.n.* sweet lime.
li·moen, *n.* lemon. limo·nade, -s, *n.* lemonade, soft drink.
·linde, -n, *n.*, ·lindeboom, -bomen, *n.* lime (-tree), linden.
lini·aal, -ialen, *n.n.* ruler (*instrument*). ·linie, -s, *n.* line (*of ships, of defence, of family*). ¶no pl., *n.* line, equator. lini·eren, -ieer, *v.t.* to rule (*with lines*). ·linie-schip, -schepen, *n.n.* ship of the line.
·linker, *a.* left; near (*of horses*). ·linkerhand, *n.* left-hand. *de* ~, the left. ·linkerkant, no pl.. *n.*, ·linkerzijde, no pl., *n.* left-hand side. *naar de* ~, to the left. links, *a.* left,

left-hand; left-handed; clumsy; left wing.
¶*adv.* to *or* at *or* on the left; awkwardly.
~ *laten liggen,* to give (*a person*) the cold
shoulder *or* to leave (*a place*) on the left.
·linksaf, *adv.* to the left. ·linksheid,
-heden, *n.* clumsiness. ¶no pl., *n.* left-
handedness. ·linksom, *adv.* to the left.
~ *keert!* left turn!
·linnen, -s, *n.n.* linen. *a.* ¶(*made of*) linen.
~ *band,* cloth binding. ·linnengoed, -deren,
n.n. linen (*articles*). ·linnenmand, *n.*
clothes-basket.
lint, *n.n.* ribbon. ·lintje, -s, *n.n.* (short *or*
narrow) ribbon; decoration, knighthood.
·lintjesregen, -s, *n.* (*fac.*) birthday honours.
·lintworm, *n.* tapeworm. ·lintzaag, -zagen,
n. band-saw.
·linze, -n, *n.* lentil. ·linzenmeel, no pl., *n.n.*
lentil flour.
lip, -ppen, *n.* lip. *zich op de lippen bijten,*
to bite one's lips. ·lipbloemig, *a.* labiate.
·lippenstift, *n.* lipstick.
liqui·datie, -s, *n.* liquidation. liqui·deren,
-deer, *v.t.* to liquidate.
lis, -ssen, *n.* flag, iris. ·lisbloem, *n.* flag, iris.
·lisdodde, -n, *n.* cat's-tail.
·lispelen, *v.i.,* ·lispen, *v.i.* to lisp.
·Lissabon, *n.N.* Lisbon.
list, *n.* ruse, trick. ·listig, *a.* wily, cunning,
artful. ·listigheid, -heden, *n.* cunning.
·liter, -s, *n.* litre.
lite·rair, *a.* literary.
·litteken, -s, *n.n.* scar.
Li·thauen, *n.N.* Lithuania Li·thaus, *a.*
Lithuanian.
·Livius, *N.* Livy.
Li·vorno, *n.N.* Leghorn.
li·vrei, *n.* livery.
lob, -bben, *n.* lobe.
·lobbes, *n.* large, kindly person *or* animal.
lo·caal, -cale, *a.* local. lo·caalspoorweg, *n.*
district railway.
·loco, *n.* spot, on the spot (*of goods*). ¶*prefix.*
acting-, deputy ~. ·locomo·biel, *n.*
transportable steam-engine. locomo·tief,
-ven, *n.* engine, locomotive.
·lodderogen, -roog, *v.i.* to make eyes. lode-
·reindoosje, -s, *n.n.* scent locket.
·loden, *a.* leaden, (*made of*) lead. *met* ~
schoenen, with leaden feet. ¶lood, *v.t.* to,
plumb, take soundings. ·loding, *n.*
sounding.
·Lodewijk, *N.* Louis.
·loeder, -s, *n.* low, despicable person.
loef, no pl., *n.* luff. *de* ~ *afsteken,* to luff;
iemand de ~ *afsteken* (*fig.*), to get the
better of a person, forestall a person.
·loefwaarts, *adv.* to windward.
·loeien, *v.i.* to low, moo, bellow; to roar
(*of wind*).
loens, *a.* squinting. ·loensen, *v.i.* to squint.
loep, *n.* magnifying glass.
loer, no pl., *n. op de* ~ *staan* or *liggen,* to
lie in wait; *iemand een* ~ *draaien,* to play

someone a nasty trick. ·loeren, *v.i.* to
peer; to spy. ~ *op,* to lie in wait for.
·loeven, loef, *v.i.* to luff. ·loevert, *adv. te* ~,
to windward.
lof, no pl., *n.* praise. *eigen* ~, self-praise *or*
praises; *boven alle* ~ *verheven,* beyond all
praise; *tot zijn* ~, in his praise. ¶loven,
n.n. vespers. ¶no pl., *n.n. Brussels* ~,
chicory. ·lofdicht, *n.n.* panegyric (*poem*).
·loffelijk, *a.* praiseworthy. ·loffelijkheid,
no pl., *n.* praiseworthiness.
Lo·fodden, pl. *N. de* ~, Lofoten Islands.
·lofpsalm, *n.* hymn of praise. ·lofrede, -denen,
n. panegyric (*oration*). ·loftuiting, *n.*
eulogy, encomium. lof·waardig, *a.* praise-
worthy. ·lofzang, *n.* hymn of praise.
log, -gge, *a.* heavy, cumbrous. ¶-ggen, *n.n.*
log. ·logboek, *n.n.* log, log-book.
·loge, -s, *n.* lodge (*freemasons*); box (*in*
theatre).
lo·gé, -'s, *n.* guest (*staying the night*). lo·geer-
kamer, -s, *n.* spare room. loge·ment, *n.n.*
hostelry, lodging-house. loge·menthouder,
-s, *n.* innkeeper.
·logen, loog, *v.t.* to steep in lye.
·logenstraffen, -straf, *v.t.* to belie, give the
lie to.
lo·geren, -geer, *v.i.* to stay (*as a guest*).
~ *bij,* to stay with.
·logger, -s, *n.* lugger, drifter.
·logheid, no pl., *n.* clumsiness.
·logzeil, *n.n.* lug-sail.
lo·gies, -zen, *n.n.* lodgings; fo'c'sle, crew's
quarters. ~ *met ontbijt,* bed and breakfast.
·logisch, *a.* logical. *dat is nogal* ~, that
goes without saying.
lok, -kken, *n.* lock (*hair*).
lo·kaal, -kalen, *n.n.* room (*large*), hall.
·lokaas, no pl., *n.n.* bait. ·lokduif, -ven, *n.*
stool-pigeon, decoy. ·lokeend, *n.* decoy-
duck.
lo·ket, -tten, *n.n.* booking-office, box-office
(*window*); pigeon-hole. *aan het* ~, at the
counter.
·lokken, lok, *v.t.* to lure, tempt; to decoy,
entice. ·lokmiddel, -s, *n.n.* lure, bait. ·lokspijs,
-zen, *n.* bait. ·lokstem, -mmen, *n.* siren
voice. ·lokster, -s, *n.* temptress. ·lokvink,
n. decoy. ·lokvogel, -s, *n.* decoy, call-bird.
lol, no pl., *n.* (*coll.*) fun. *voor de* ~, for fun.
·lolletje, -s, *n.n.* bit of fun, lark. *het leven*
is geen ~, life is not all beer and skittles.
·lollig, *a.* jolly.
·lomig, *a. & adv.* with lassitude.
·lommer, no pl., *n.* shade. ·lommerachtig, *a.*
shady.
·lommerd, -s, *n.* pawnbroker's (shop). *in de*
~, at the pawnbroker's, up the spout.
·lommerdbriefje, -s, *n.* pawn-ticket.
·lommerdhouder, -s, *n.* pawnbroker.
lomp, *a.* clumsy; unmannerly. ¶*n. usu. pl.*
rag, tatter. ·lompenkoper, -s, *n.* rag-
dealer, rag-and-bone man. ·lomperd, -s
n. clumsy person; clodhopper.

·**Londen**, *n.N.* London.
·**lonen**, loon, *v.t.* to pay, repay. *het loont de moeite,* it is worth while. ·**lonend**, *a.* remunerative.
·**long**, *n.* lung. ·**longkruid**, no pl., *n.n.* lungwort. ·**longontsteking**, *n.* pneumonia. ·**longpijp**, *n.* windpipe. ·**longtering**, no pl., *n.* pulmonary tuberculosis.
lonk, *n.* ogle, glad eye. ·**lonken**, *v.i.* to ogle.
lont, *n.* fuse. ~ *ruiken,* to smell a rat; *de* ~ *in 't kruit steken,* to put the match to the tinder. ·**lontstok**, -kken, *n.* linstock.
·**loochenaar**, -s, *n.* denier. ·**loochenen**, *v.t.* to deny, disavow. ·**loochening**, *n.* denial.
lood, no pl., *n.n.* lead. *het is* ~ *om oud ijzer,* much of a muchness; *met* ~ *in de schoenen,* with leaden feet; *ramen met glas in* ~, leaded windows; *uit het* ~, out of plumb. ¶**loden**, *n.n.* (sounding-)lead; plumb-line; weight of 10 grammes. *See* loodje. ·**loodachtig**, *a.* like lead. ·**loodfoelie**, no pl., *n.* lead foil. ·**loodgieter**, -s, *n.* plumber. **loodgieterij**, -rij, *n.* plumber's (shop); leadworks. ·**loodgieterswerk**, no pl., *n.n.* plumbing. ·**loodje**, -s, *n.n.* lead seal. *het* ~ *leggen,* to pay the piper; *de laatste* ~*s wegen het zwaarst,* it's the last straw that breaks the camel's back. ·**loodkleurig**, *a.* leaden, livid. ·**loodlijn**, *n.* perpendicular *(line).* ·**loodrecht**, *a.* perpendicular.
loods, *n.* shed; pilot. ·**loodsen**, *v.t.* to pilot. ·**loodsmannetje**, -s, *n.n.* pilot-fish. ·**loodswezen**, no pl., *n.n.* pilotage *(service).*
·**loodwit**, no pl., *n.n.* white lead. ·**loodzwaar**, -zware, *a.* heavy as lead.
loof, no pl., *n.n.* foliage, leaves. ·**loofboom**, -bomen, *n.* tree *(other than conifer).* ·**loofhout**, no pl., *n.n.* trees *(other than conifer);* hard wood. ·**loofhuttenfeest**, *n.n.* Feast of Tabernacles. ·**loofrijk**, *a.* leafy. ·**loofwerk**, no pl., *n.n.* leaf-work *(carving).*
loog, no pl., *n.n.* lye. ·**loogachtig**, *a.* alkaline. ·**loogkruid**, no pl., *n.n.* kelp. ·**loogwater**, no pl., *n.n.* lye. ·**loogzout**, *n.n.* alkali.
·**looien**, *v.t.* to tan. ·**looier**, -s, *n.* tanner. **looierij**, -rij, *n.* tannery. ·**looistof**, *n.* tannin. ·**looizuur**, no pl., *n.n.* tannic acid.
look, no pl., *n.n.* garlic; leek.
loom, lome, *a.* slow; languid; oppressive. *met lome schreden,* with dragging steps. ·**loomheid**, no pl., *n.* slowness, langour.
loon, lonen, *n.n.* wage(s); pay; reward, deserts. *het is zijn verdiende* ~, serve him right. ·**loonactie**, -s, *n.* campaign for higher wages. ·**loonarbeid**, no pl., *n.* manual labour. ·**loonarbeider**, -s, *n.* hired labourer. ·**loongeschil**, -llen, *n.n.* wage dispute. ·**loonstandaard**, *n.* rate of wages. ·**loonsverhoging**, *n.* rise in wages. ·**loonsvermindering**, *n.* wage cut. ·**loontrekker**, -s, *n.* wage-earner.
loop, no pl., *n.* course; walk, gait. *zijn* ~ *hebben,* to take its course; *iets de vrije* ~

laten, to allow something free play; *een andere* ~ *nemen,* to follow a different course; *op de* ~, on the run; *op de* ~ *gaan,* to take to one's heels. ¶**lopen**, *n.* barrel *(of fire-arm).* ·**loopbaan**, -banen, *n.* career; orbit. ·**loopbrug**, -ggen, *n.* footbridge. ·**loopgraaf**, -graven, *n.* trench *(military).* ·**loopje**, -s, *n.n.* short run; short walk *een* ~ *nemen met,* to make a fool of. ·**loopjongen**, -s, *n.* errand boy. ·**loopmare**, -n, *n.* tidings. ·**looppas**, no pl., *n.* doublequick time. *in de* ~, at the double. ·**loopplank**, *n.* gangway. **loops**, *a.* on heat, ·**loopspin**, -nnen, *n.* hunting spider. ·**looptijd**, *n.* currency *(of bill).* ·**loopvogel**, -s, *n.* walker *(bird).*
loor, no pl., *n. te* ~ *gaan,* to be lost.
loos, loze, *a.* cunning; empty *(of nut);* false *(alarm).* ·**loosheid**, no pl., *n.* cunning. ·**loospijp**, *n.* waste-pipe.
loot, loten, *n.* shoot, cutting.
·**lopen**, loop, *v.i.,* *str.* to walk; to run; to go. *laat hem* ~, leave him alone; *alles laten* ~, to let things drift. ¶*v.t.,* *str.* to walk, run. ¶*no pl., n.n.* een uur ~*(s),* an hour's walk; *het op een* ~ *zetten,* to break into a run. ·**lopend**, *a.* running, current. ~ *schrift,* cursive; *zich als een* ~ *vuurtje verspreiden,* to spread like wildfire. ·**loper**, -s, *n.* runner; messenger; stair- *or* hall-carpet; table-runner; pass-key.
lor, -rren, *n.* rag; worthless thing. *het kan me geen* ~ *schelen,* it leaves me cold.
lorgnet, -tten, *n.n.* pince-nez. **lorgnon**, -s, *n.n.* monocle; lorgnette.
·**lorkeboom**, -bomen, *n.* larch.
·**lorre**, no pl., *N.* Poll(y) (parrot).
·**lorregoed**, no pl., *n.n.* trash. ·**lorrig**, *a.* trashy.
·**lorrie**, -s, *n.* lorry, truck.
los, -ssen, *n.* lynx. ¶*a.* loose; disjointed, undone. *losse arbeider,* casual labourer; ~ *gerucht,* wild rumour; *met* ~ *kruit schieten,* to fire blanks; *losse patroon,* blank cartridge; *losse rib,* floating rib; *op losse schroeven,* on an unsound basis. ¶*adv.* loosely, *er op* ~ *slaan,* to hammer away at it; *er op* ~, happily, recklessly. ·**losbaar**, -bare, *a.* redeemable. **los-bandig**, *a.* dissolute, licentious. ·**los-bandigheid**, -heden, *n.* dissipation. ·**losbarsten**, *v.i.s.,* *irr.* to break out, break *(storm);* to burst forth. ·**losbarsting**, *n.* outbreak, burst. **los-bladig**, *a.* loose-leaf. ·**losbol**, -llen, *n.* rake, profligate. ·**losbreken**, breek los, *v.i.s.,* *str.* to break loose, break away. ·**losdag**, *n.* discharging day. ·**losdraaien**, *v.t.s.* to turn loose, unscrew. ·**los-en-laadsteiger**, -s, *n.* landing stage. ·**losgaan**, ga los, *v.i.s.,* *irr.* *erop* ~, to go for, make for. ·**losgeld**, *n.n.* ransom. ·**losgespen**, *v.t.s.* to unbuckle. ·**losgooien**, *v.i.s. & v.t.s.* to cast off. ·**loshaken**, haak los, *v.t.s.* to unhook. ·**loshangend**, *a.* dishevelled. ·**losheid**, no

pl., n. looseness. ·losjes, adv. loosely.
·losknopen, knoop los, v.t.s. to unbutton;
to untie. ·loskomen, kom los, v.i.s., irr.
to get loose; to get going. ·loskopen,
koop los, v.t.s., irr. to buy off. ·loskrijgen,
v.t.s., str. to unloosen, undo. ·loslaten,
laat los, v.t.s., str. to let go, set free,
release. niets ~, to let nothing out, be
reticent. los·lippig, a. flippant; indiscreet.
los·lippigheid, no pl., n. flippancy; indiscretion. ·loslopen, loop los, v.i.s., str.
to be at liberty. het zal wel ~, it won't
be so bad. ·losmaken, maak los, v.t.s.
to loosen, undo, untie. ~ van, to detach
from. ¶zich ~, v.r.s. to release oneself.
zich ~ van, to dissociate oneself from or
to get away from. ·losplaats, n. discharging berth. ·losprijs, -zen, n. ransom.
·losraken, raak los, v.i.s. to get loose.
·losrukken, ruk los, v.t.s. to tear loose.
zich ~, to tear oneself away. ·losscheuren,
v.t.s. to tear loose. ·losschroeven, schroef
los, v.t.s. to unscrew. ·lossen, los, v.t. to
unload; to fire (arms); to redeem (pledge).
·lossing, n. unloading. ·losslaan, sla los,
v.i.s., irr. to break away. ·losstormen,
v.i.s. ~ op, to rush at. ·lostijd, n. time
for unloading. ·lostornen, v.t.s. to unpick.
·lostrekken, trek los, v.t.s., str. to pull loose.
~ op, to march upon. ·losweken, week
los, v.t.s. to soak off. ·losweg, adv. off-hand,
lightly. ·loszitten, zit los, v.i.s., str. to be
loose. het zit los, it is coming off.
lot, n.n. lottery ticket. een ~ uit de loterij,
one in a thousand. ¶no pl., n.n. fate,
destiny, lot. iemand aan zijn ~ overlaten,
to leave a person to his fate. ·loteling, n.
conscript. ·loten, loot, v.i. to draw lots.
~ om, to draw for. lote·rij, n. lottery.
lote·rijbriefje, -s, n.n. lottery ticket.
·lotgenoot, -noten, n. companion (in
adventure or adversity). ·lotgeval, -llen,
n.n. adventure.
·Lotharingen, n.N. Lorraine.
·loting, n. drawing of lots; conscription (with
ballot). ·lotsverbetering, no pl., n. improvement of conditions.
·loupe, -s, n. magnifying glass. onder de ~
nemen, to scrutinize. ·louter, v.t. to
·louter, a. pure, sheer. ·louteren, v.t. to
refine; to purify. ·loutering, n. purification;
chastening.
·Louwmaand, N. January.
·loven, loof, v.t. to praise, extol. ~ en
bieden, to bargain.
·lover, no pl., n.n. foliage.
·lozen, loos, v.t. to drain.
·Lucas, N. Luke.
lucht, n. air; smell; sky. ~ geven aan, to
give vent to; uit de ~ gegrepen, invented;
de ~ krijgen van, to get wind of; uit de ~
komen vallen, to drop from the skies; in
de ~ vliegen, to explode, blow up. ·lucht-
aanval, -llen, n. air attack. ·lucht-

afweergeschut, no pl., n.n. anti-aircraft
guns. ·luchtballon, -s, n. balloon (aeronautic). ·luchtbelwaterpas, -ssen, n.n.
spirit-level. ·luchtdicht, a. air-tight. ¶adv.
hermetically. ·luchtdruk, no pl., n.
atmospheric pressure. ·luchten, v.t. to air,
to ventilate; to give vent to; to show off.
iemand niet mogen ~ of zien, to hate the
sight of a person.
·luchter, -s, n. chandelier.
·luchteskader, -s, n.n. air squadron. ·lucht-
geleiding, n. overhead wires. ·lucht-
gesteldheid, -heden, n. climate; condition
of the atmosphere.
lucht·hartig, a. light-hearted. lucht·hartig-
heid, no pl., n. light-heartedness.
·luchtig, a. airy, light. ¶adv. airily, lightly.
iets ~ opvatten, to make light of something.
·luchtje, -s, n.n. smell. een ~ scheppen,
to get a breath of air; er is een ~ aan,
there is something fishy about it. ·lucht-
kasteel, -telen, n.n. castle in the air.
·luchtkoker, -s, n. ventilating shaft.
·luchtledig, a. void of air. ~ maken, to
exhaust; ~e ruimte, vacuum. lucht·ledige,
no pl., n.n. vacuum. ·luchtpijp, n. windpipe. ·luchtpost, no pl., n. air mail.
·luchtruim, no pl., n.n. atmosphere, space.
·luchtschip, -schepen, n.n. airship. ·lucht-
spiegeling, n. mirage. ·luchtstreek, -streken,
n. zone, climate. ·luchtvaart, no pl., n.
aviation. ·luchtverversing, no pl., n.
ventilation. ·luchtwortel, -s, n. aerial root.
·lucifer, -s, n. match. ·lucifersdoosje, -s,
n.n. matchbox.
lu·guber, a. lugubrious.
lui, pl. only, n. people. ¶a. lazy. een ~
leventje, an easy life; ~e stoel, easy chair;
liever ~ dan moe, born tired. ·luiaard, -s,
n. lazy person; ai, sloth.
luid, a. loud. met ~er stem, in a loud voice.
·luiden, pl. only, n. people. de kleine ~,
the small man. ¶v.i. (stilted) to sound.
het luidt als volgt, it reads as follows.
¶v.t. to ring, toll. ·luidkeels, adv. at the
top of one's voice. luid·ruchtig, a. noisy.
luid·ruchtigheid, no pl., n. noise, loudness.
·luier, -s, n. diaper, napkin. ·luieren, v.i.
to laze, be idle. ·luiermand, n. layette.
·luierstoel, n. easy chair.
·luifel, -s, n. penthouse roof; glass
awning.
·luiheid, no pl., n. laziness.
Luik, n.N. Liège.
luik, n.n. hatch (over hold); shutter. ·luiken,
v.t., str. (stilted) to close.
·Luikerwaal, -walen, N. Walloon from Liège.
·luilak, -kken, n. lazy-bones. ·luilakken,
-lak, v.i. to laze. Lui·lekkerland, n.N.
the Land of Cockaigne.
luim, n. whim; humour, mood. ·luimig, a.
moody, capricious; humorous.
·luipaard, n.n. leopard.
luis, -zen, n. louse.

·**luister**, no pl., *n.* splendour. ~ *bijzetten aan*, to add splendour to.

·**luisteraar**, -s, *n.* listener. ·**luisteren**, *v.i.* to listen. ~ *naar*, to listen to *or* to respond to. ·**luisterdienst**, *n.* monitoring service (*radio*). ·**luisterpost**, *n.* listening-post.

·**luisterrijk**, *a.* glorious.

·**luistervink**, *n.* eavesdropper; listener (*to radio*).

luit, *n.* lute.

·**luitenant**, *n.* lieutenant.

·**luitjes**, pl. only, *n.n.* people.

·**luiwagen**, -s, *n.* broom (*for scrubbing floor*). ·**luiwammes**, -ssen, *n.* lazy-bones.

·**luizenmarkt**, *n.* old-clothes' market. ·**luizig**, *a.* lousy.

·**lukken**, **luk**, *v.i.* to succeed. ·**lukraak**, -rake, *a.* haphazard.

·**lummel**, -s, *n.* lout. ·**lummelachtig**, *a.* loutish. ·**lummelen**, *v.i.* to hang about. ·**lummelig**, *a.* loutish.

·**lunteren**, *v.i.* to dawdle.

lurf, -ven, *n. bij de lurven pakken*, to take (*person*) by the scruff of the neck.

lus, -ssen, *n.* loop; tab, tag, strap (*in vehicle*).

lust, *n.* inclination, liking; pleasure, delight; lust. *zijn ~ en zijn leven*, his greatest joy; ~ *hebben in . . .*, to feel like (*doing something*); ~ *krijgen in*, to begin to feel like; ~ *naar* or *tot*, zest for. ·**lusteloos**, -loze, *a.* listless. ·**lusteloosheid**, no pl., *n.* listlessness, apathy. ·**lusten**, *v.t.* to like, fancy. *het lust me niet*, I don't fancy it; *hij zal ervan* ~, he will catch it. ·**lustig**, *a.* merry, cheerful; vigorous. ¶*adv.* merrily. ·**lustigjes**, *adv.* merrily; vigorously.

·**Luthers**, *a.* Lutheran.

·**luttel**, *a.* little. ¶*adv.* little. ¶no pl., *n.n.* little.

luur, **luren**, *n. iemand in de luren leggen*, to bamboozle a person. *See* **luier**.

luw, *a.* sheltered (*from wind*); mild. ·**luwen**, *v.i.* to abate, die down. *het zal wel* ~, it will blow over. ·**luwte**, -n, *n.* lee, shelter.

·**luxe**, no pl., *n.* luxury. ·**luxeartikel**, -s *or* -en, *n.n.* fancy article, *pl.* fancy goods. ·**luxeuitgaaf**, -gaven, *n.* édition de luxe. **luxu·cus**, -euze, *a.* luxurious.

lu·zerne, no pl., *n.* lucern(e).

·**Lybië**, *n.N.* Libya. **Lybisch**, *a.* Libyan.

Ly·on, *n.N.* Lyons.

M

maag, **magen**, *n.* stomach; kinsman. *er mee in zijn* ~ *zitten*, to be landed with something. ·**maagbrij**, no pl., *n.* chyme. ·**maagmelksap**, no pl., *n.n.* chyle.

maagd, *n.* maiden, virgin. ·**maagdelijk**, *a.* virginal, maidenly. ·**maagdelijkheid**, no pl., *n.* virginity. ·**maagdenhonig**, no pl., *n.*

virgin honey. ·**maagdenpalm**, *n.* periwinkle (*plant*). ·**maagdenroof**, no pl., *n.* rape. ·**maagdepeer**, -peren, *n.* virgin pear. ·**maagdvlies**, -zen, *n.n.* hymen.

·**maagholte**, -n, *n.* pit of the stomach. ·**maagpijn**, *n.* stomach-ache. ·**maagsap**, -ppen, *n.n.* gastric juice. ·**maagschap**, no pl., *n.n.* kinship. ·**maagzuur**, no pl., *n.n.* heartburn. ·**maagzweer**, -zweren, *n.* gastric ulcer.

maai, *n. See* **made**.

·**maaien**, *v.t.* to mow, to reap, to cut. ·**maaier**, -s, *n.* mower, reaper. ·**maaimachine**, -s, *n.* mowing machine, reaper.

maak, no pl., *n. in de* ~, under repair; *iets in de* ~ *hebben*, to have something made. ·**maakloon**, -lonen, *n.n.* charge for making. ·**maaksel**, -s, *n.n.* make. ·**maakwerk**, no pl., *n.n.* mass-produced stuff.

maal, **malen**, *n.n.* meal (*repast*); mole (*on skin*); mail bag; time(s), occasion. *hoeveel* ~ or *hoeveel malen*, how many times; *een enkele* ~, once in a while; *ten enen male*, once and for all, absolutely; *ten tweeden male*, for the second time. ¶*suffix.* times.

·**maalgeld**, *n.n.* miller's fee.

·**maalstokje**, -s, *n.n.* mahlstick.

·**maalstroom**, -stromen, *n.* maelstrom, vortex. ·**maaltand**, *n.* molar.

·**maalteken**, -s, *n.n.* multiplication sign.

·**maaltijd**, *n.* meal (*repast*).

maan, **manen**, *n.* moon. *halve* ~, half-moon, crescent; *afnemende* ~, waning moon; *wassende* ~, waxing moon; *het is lichte* ~, there is a moon; *het is donkere* ~, there is no moon; *naar de* ~, lost; *loop naar de* ~, go to blazes.

·**maanbrief**, -ven, *n.* dunning letter.

maand, *n.* month.

·**maandag**, *n.* Monday.

·**maandbericht**, *n.n.* monthly report. ·**maandblad**, *n.n.* monthly (*publication*). ·**maandelijks**, *a.* monthly. ¶*adv.* monthly; once a month, every month. ·**maandenlang**, *adv.* for months. ·**maandgeld**, *n.n.* salary, monthly pay. ·**maandstaat**, -staten, *n.* monthly return. ·**maandstonden**, pl. only, *n.* monthly periods.

·**maankop**, -ppen, *n.* poppy; poppy-head. ·**maanlicht**, no pl., *n.n.* moonlight. ·**maansteen**, -stenen, *n.* moonstone. ·**maansverduistering**, *n.* moon eclipse. ·**maanvis**, -ssen, *n.* moon-fish. ·**maanzaad**, no pl., *n.n.* mawseed. ·**maanziek**, *a.* moonstruck, lunatic. ·**maanziekte**, no pl., *n.* lunacy.

maar, *c.* but. ¶*adv.* but, only. ~ *al te spoeding*, all too soon; *zo* ~, just like that; *was ik* ~, if only I were. ¶no pl., *n.n.* but, objection. ¶**maren**, *n.* tidings, report.

·**maarschalk**, *n.* marshal.

maart, *N.* March. **maarts**, *a.* March.

Maas, *N.* Meuse.

maas, **mazen**, *n.* mesh. *door de mazen*

kruipen, to slip through the mesh. ·maas-
bal, -llen, *n.* darning-ball. ·maaswerk, no
pl., *n.n.* tracery (*architectural*).
maat, -s, *n.* mate, companion. ¶maten, *n.*
measure; size, measurement; metre (*verse*);
time, measure (*music*); bar (*music*). op ~,
to measure; *de* ~ *nemen*, to take a person's
measure; *de* ~ *loopt over*, that is the last
straw; *met twee maten meten*, to show
favouritism; *de* ~ *aangeven*, to mark
time; ~ *houden*, to keep time; *de* ~ *slaan*,
to beat time; *met mate*, in moderation;
in hoge mate, to a large extent. ·maatglas,
-zen, *n.n.* graduated measure. ·maatje, -s,
n.n. small measure; friend. *goede* ~*s zijn*,
to be pals. ·maatjesharing, *n.* matie.
·maatjespeer, -peren, *n.* bergamot (*pear*).
·maatregel, -s *or* -en, *n.* measure. ~*en*
treffen, to take measures.
maat·schappelijk, *a.* social. ~ *kapitaal*,
registered capital. maatschap·pij, *n.*
society, company; society (*human*).
·maatslag, *n.* beat (*music*). ·maatstaf,
-staven, *n.* standard; criterion. *een* ~
aanleggen, to apply a standard. ·maatstok,
-kken, *n.* (carpenter's) rule. ·maatvast, *a.*
keeping time.
machi·naal, -nale, *a.* mechanical. ¶*adv.*
mechanically. ~ *bewerken*, to machine.
ma·chine, -s, *n.* machine, engine. ma-
·chinebedrijf, -ven, *n.n.* engineering trade.
ma·chinebouw, no pl., *n.* engine-building.
ma·chinefabriek, *n.* engineering works.
ma·chinegeweer, -weren, *n.n.* machine-
gun. ma·chinekamer, -s, *n.* engine-room.
ma·chineloods, *n.* engine-house. machine-
·rie, -ieën, *n.* machinery. ma·chinetekenen,
no pl., *n.n.* mechanical drawing. machi-
·nist, *n.* (ship's) engineer; engine-driver.
eerste ~, first engineer.
macht, *n.* power, might, force; authority;
power (*mathematical*). *de* ~ *in handen*
hebben, to be in power; *niet bij* ~*e*, not in
a position; *boven zijn* ~, beyond his
strength; *in zijn* ~, under his control *or*
in his power; *met* or *uit alle* ~, with might
and main; *een* ~ *van geld*, a power of
money; *tot de 4*ᵈᵉ ~ *verheffen*, to raise to
the 4th power. ·machtbrief, -ven, *n.*
power of attorney, proxy. ·machteloos,
-loze, *a.* powerless, helpless. ·machte-
·loosheid, no pl., *n.* helplessness. ·macht-
·hebbende, -n, *n.* person in power *or*
authority. ·machtig, *a.* powerful, mighty;
rich (*food*). *een taal* ~ *zijn*, to have a
language at one's command; *iets* ~
worden, to secure something. ¶*adv.*
mightily, mighty. ·machtigen, *v.t.* to
empower, authorize. ·machtiging, *n.*
authorization. ·machtsaanwijzer, -s, *n.*
exponent (*mathematical*). ·machtsbetoon,
no pl., *n.n.* display of power. ·machtspreuk,
n. soap-box argument. ·machtsverhouding,
n. relative power.

·made, -n, *n.* maggot.
made·liefje, -s, *n.n.* daisy.
·maffen, maf, *v.i.* (*coll.*) to sleep.
maga·zijn, *n.n.* warehouse; store(s) (*shop*);
magazine (*of fire-arms*). maga·zijnmeester,
-s, *n.* storekeeper.
·mager, *a.* lean; thin; meagre. ·magerheid,
no pl., *n.* leanness; thinness. ·magertjes,
adv. poorly.
ma·gie, no pl., *n.* magic. ·magiër, -s, *n.*
magician; magus.
magis·traal, -trale, *a.* magisterial.
mag·naat, -naten, *n.* magnate.
mag·neet, -neten, *n.* magnet. mag·netisch, *a.*
magnetic. magneti·seren, -seer, *v.t.* to
magnetize.
magni·fiek, *a.* magnificent, splendid.
·Mahomed, *N.* Mohammed. Mahome·daan,
-danen, *n.* Mohammedan.
ma·honiehout, no pl., *n.n.* mahogany.
ma·honiehouten, *a.* (made of) mahogany.
·mais, no pl., *n.* maize, corn. ·maiskolf,
-ven, *n.* corn-cob. mai·zena, no pl., *n.*
cornflour.
majesteit, *n.* majesty. ·majesteitsschennis,
n. lese-majesty. majestu·eus, -ze, *a.*
majestic.
ma·jeur, *a.* major (*music*).
ma·joor, -s, *n.* major (*rank*).
mak, -kke, *a.* tame, gentle.
·makelaar, -s, *n.* broker. ~ *in effecten*,
stockbroker. ·makelaarsloon, -lonen, *n.n.*,
·makelaarsprovisie, no pl., *n.* brokerage.
makela·rij, *n.* broking.
make·lij, *n.* (*stilted*) make. ·maken, maak,
v.t. to make; to make, render; to mend,
repair; to form (*idea*); to raise (*objection*);
to do (*exercises*). *hoe maakt U het?*, how
are you?; *maak dat je wegkomt!*, get away!
or get out!; *het maakt niets*, it doesn't
matter; *hij heeft er niets mee te* ~, it's no
business of his *or* he has nothing to do
with it; *hij heeft hier niets te* ~, he has
no business here. ·maker, -s, *n.* maker.
·makheid, no pl., *n.* tameness.
·maki, -'s, *n.* macaco.
·makkelijk, *a.* easy. ¶*adv.* easily. *See*
gemakkelijk.
·makker, -s, *n.* comrade, companion.
ma·kreel, -krelen, *n.* mackerel.
mal, -lle, *a.* foolish, mad. ¶*n. iemand voor*
de ~ *houden*, to make fun of a person.
Mala·diven, *N.* Maldive Islands.
mal·aise, no pl., *n.* slump, depression.
·male, *n. See* maal.
·malen, maal, *v.t.*, *irr.* to grind; to mill; to
pump. *die het eerst komt, het eerst maalt*, first
come, first served. ¶*v.i.* to wander (*in mind*);
to care. *door het hoofd* ~, to run through
one's mind; *wat maal ik er om?* what do
I care?
·malheid, -heden, *n.* foolishness.
·malie, -liën, *n.* mesh. ·maliebaan, -banen,
n. mall. ·maliënkolder, -s, *n.* coat of mail.

·maling, no pl., n. ~ hebben aan iets, not to care a rap about something; iemand in de ~ nemen, to pull a person's leg.

·mallejan,-s, n. timber wagon. ·mallemolen, -s, n. merry-go-round. ·mallen, mal, v.i. to romp. ·mallepraat, no pl., n. nonsense. ·malligheid. -heden, n. foolishness, foolish thing.

mals, a. tender; mellow. ·malsheid, no pl., n. tenderness.

·maluwe, -n, n., ·malve, -n, n. mallow.

·mammoet, n. mammoth.

man, -nnen, n. man; husband. de gaande en komende ~, the man in the street; de derde ~, the third party; mannen broeders, friends and brothers; een ~ een ~ een woord een woord, a bargain is a bargain; een ~ van zijn woord, as good as his word; zijn ~ vinden, to meet one's match; ~ en paard noemen, to give chapter and verse; aan de ~ brengen, to sell, dispose of; als de nood aan de ~ komt, in case of need; met ~ en muis vergaan, to be lost with all hands; op de ~ af, point-blank (fig.); een gevecht van ~ tegen ~, a hand-to-hand fight.

man·chet, -tten, n. cuff. man·chetknoop, -knopen, n. cuff-link.

·manco, no pl., n.n. shortage.

mand, n. basket; hamper. door de ~ vallen, to own up.

man·daat, -daten, n.n. mandate; power of attorney.

manda·rijn, n. mandarin. manda·rijntje, -s, n.n. tangerine.

·mandefles, -ssen, n. demijohn. ·mandenmaker, -s, n. basket-maker. ·mandje, -s, n.n. little basket; bed (fac.). naar zijn ~ gaan, to turn in.

·mandoer, -s, n. native foreman (East Indies).

ma·nege, -s, n. riding school. ma·negepaard, n.n. riding-school horse.

·manen, maan, v.t. to dun. ¶pl. only, n. mane (of horse, etc.); manes (myth.). ·maner, -s, n. dun.

·maneschijn, no pl., n. moonlight; moonshine

man·gaan, no pl., n.n. manganese. man·gaanijzer, no pl., n.n. ferro-manganese.

·mangat, n.n. manhole.

·mangel, -s, n. mangle; almond. ¶no pl., n.n. lack. ·mangelen, v.t. to (pass through) mangle. ·mangelgoed, no pl., n.n. linen to be mangled.

·mangelwortel, -s, n. mangelwurzel, mangold.

man·haftig, a. manly, brave. man·haftigheid, no pl. n. manliness, bravery.

ma·nie, -ieën, n. mania, craze.

ma·nier, n. manner, way; pl. only, manners. dat is geen ~ van doen, you can't do that sort of thing; bij ~ van spreken, in a manner of speaking; op die ~, in that way; op de een of andere ~, one way or another.

manifes·teren, -teer, v.i. to hold a demonstration.

mank, a. lame, crippled. ~ gaan, to limp. manke·ment, n.n. defect, fault, trouble. man·keren, -keer, v.i. to be lacking or absent; to fail. wat mankeert je?, what is the matter with you? or what has come over you?; ik mankeer niets, I'm all right; zonder ~, without fail. ¶v.t. to miss (train, etc.).

·manlief, no pl., n. dear! (to husband). man·moedig, a. manful. ·mannelijk, a. male; masculine; manly. ·mannelijkheid, -heden, n. masculinity; manhood; manliness. ·mannenklooster, -s, n.n. monastery. ·mannenkoor, -koren, n.n. male choir. ·mannenmoed, no pl., n. manly courage. ·mannentaal, no pl., n. manly speech. dat is ~, that's talking. ·mannetje, -s, n.n. little man; male (of animal). ·mannetjes . . ., prefix. male . . . (cock, bull). mannetjes·putter, -s, n. male goldfinch; he-man. mans, no pl., n. niet veel ~ zijn, not to be very strong; ~ genoeg zijn, to be strong enough.

man·sarde, -s, n. attic.

·manschap, n. sing. only, crew; pl. only, men (military). ·manshoog, -hoge, a. at or of man height. ·manshoogte, no pl., n. man's height. ·manskerel, -s, n. fellow. ·manslag, no pl., n. manslaughter. ·manslengte, no pl., n. man's height. ·mansoor, no pl., n.n. hazelwort. ·manspersoon, -sonen, n. man, male person.

·mantel, -s, n. cloak, mantle; coat (woman's); jacket, casing. ·mantelpak, -kken, n.n. suit (woman's two-piece).

manufac·turen, pl. only, n. soft goods. manufactu·rier, n. draper. manufac·tuurwinkel, -s, n. drapery (shop).

·Manusje, n.N. ~ van alles, odd-job man. man·ziek, a. ze is ~, she is a nymphomaniac. map, -ppen, n. portfolio.

marchan·deren, -deer, v.i. to bargain. mar·cheren, -cheer, v.i. to march. iets doen ~, to make something go.

marco·nist, n. wireless operator.

·mare, -n, n. See maar.

maréchaus·sée, -s, n. state policeman. ¶no pl., n. state police.

·marentak, -kken, n. mistletoe.

·marge, -s, n. margin.

Ma·ria, N. Mary. ~ Boodschap, Annunciation Day; ~ Lichtmis, Candlemas-Day.

ma·rine, no pl., n. navy. bij de ~, in the navy; het departement van ~, the Admiralty (ministry). ma·rineofficier, n. naval officer. ma·rineren, -neer, v.t. to pickle. ma·rinewerf, -ven, n. naval dockyard. mari·nier, -s, n. marine.

marjo·lein, no pl., n. marjoram.

mark, n. march (borderland); mark (coin). mar·kant, a. striking. mar·keren, -keer, v.t. to mark.

marke·tentster, -s, *n.* sutler.
mar·keur, -s, *n.* marker (*billiards*).
·markgraaf, -graven, *n.* margrave. ·markgronden, pl. only, *n.* common (land). mar·kies, -zen, *n.* marquis, marquess. markie·zin, -nnen, *n.* marchioness.
markt, *n.* market. *aan de ~ brengen,* to put on the market; *naar de ~ gaan,* to go to market; *op de ~,* in the market-place; *van alle ~en thuis zijn,* to be shrewd. ·marktbericht, *n.n.* market report. ·markten, *v.i.* to go marketing. ·marktgeld, *n.n.* market dues. ·marktplaats, *n.* marketsquare; market town. ·marktplein. *n.n.* market-square.
·marmer, no pl., *n.n.* marble. ·marmerachtig, *a.* like marble. ·marmeren, *a.* (*made of*) marble. ¶*v.t.* to marble, grain. ·marmerslijper, -s, *n.* marble-polisher.
mar·mot, -tten, *n.* marmot, guinea-pig.
maro·kijn. no pl., *n.n.* morocco (*leather*). maro·kijnen, *a.* morocco. Marok·kaan, *N.* Moroccan. Marok·kaans, *a.* Moroccan. Ma·rokko, *n.N.* Morocco.
mars, *n.* pack (*of pedlar*); march; top (*mast*). *hij heeft heel wat in zijn ~,* he is a man of many parts; *grote ~,* main-top. ¶*int.* march! ·marsoefening, *n.* route march. ·marsorde, no pl., *n.* order of march. ·marsorder, -s, *n.* marching orders. ·marsroute, -s, *n.* line of march.
marse·pein, *n.* marzipan. marse·peinen, *a.* (*made of*) marzipan.
marslantaren, -s, *n.* top-lantern. ·marssteng, *n.* top-mast. ··marszeil, *n.n.* topsail.
marskramer, -s, *n.* pedlar.
·martelaar, -s, *n.* martyr. ·martelaarschap, no pl., *n.n.* martyrdom. ·martela·res, -ssen, *n.* martyr (*female*). ·marteldood, no pl., *n.* martyr's death. *de ~ sterven,* to suffer martyrdom. ·martelen, *v.t.* to torture, torment. ·martelend, *a.* agonizing. ·marteling, *a.* torture. ·martelkamer -s, *n.* chamber of torture.
·marter, -s, *n.* marten.
mas·keren, *v.t.* to mask, camouflage. ·masker, -s, *n.n.* mask; disguise; larva. *iemand het ~ afrukken,* to unmask a person. maske·rade, *n.* masquerade. ·maskeren *v.t.* to mask. ¶*zich ~, v.r.* to put on a mask.
·massa, -'s, *n.* mass, crowd. *bij ~'s,* in large quantities, wholesale. mas·saal, -saale, *a.* in the mass; wholesale. ·massa-aanval, -llen, *n.* massed attack. mas·seren, -sseer, *v.t.* to massage. mas·sief, -ve, *a.* massive; solid (*not hollow*). ¶-ven, *n.n.* massif.
mast, *n.* mast. ·mastboom, -bomen, *n.* pine. ·mastbos, -ssen, *n.n.* fir-wood; forest of masts. ·masten, *v.t.* to mast. ·mastklimmen, no pl., *n.n.* climbing the greasy pole. ·mastkoker, -s, *n.* mast-hole. ·mastkorf, -ven, *n.* crow's-nest.
mat, -tten, *n.* mat; old Spanish coin. *zijn*

matten oprollen, to pack up one's traps. ¶-tte, *a.* weary, faint; dull, mat; dim. *de koning is ~,* checkmate; *~ geven,* to mate (*chess*).
·mate, *n. See* maat. ·mateloos, -loze, *a.* boundless, immense.
materi·aal, -ialen, *n.n.* material(s). ma·terie, -riën or -ries, *n.* matter. materi·eel, -iële, *a.* material. ¶no pl., *n.n.* material. *rollend ~,* rolling-stock.
·matglas, no pl., *n.n.* frosted glass. ·matheid, no pl., *n.* lassitude. ·mathoen, -ders or -deren, *n.n.* plover. ·matig, *a.* moderate; temperate, abstemious; indifferent (*of success*). ¶*adv.* moderately; indifferently. ¶*suffix.* in accordance with. ·matigen, *v.t.* to moderate, restrain. ·matigheid, no pl., *n.* moderation, temperance. ·matiging, *n.* moderation (*action*).
ma·tras, -ssen, *n.* mattress.
matriar·chaat, no pl., *n.n.* matriarchy. ma·trijs, -zen, *n.* matrix, mould.
ma·troos, -trozen, *n.* sailor. *vol ~,* A.B.; *~ 1ste klas,* leading seaman. ma·trozenpak. -kken, *n.n.* sailor suit.
·matten, *a.* rush-bottomed. ¶*mat, v.t.* to mend (*chairs*). ·mattenbies, -zen, *n.* bulrush. ·mattenkloppen, no pl., *n.n.* carpet beating. ·mattenklopper, -s, *n.* carpet beater.
Mat·theus, *N.* Matthew.
·matwerk, no pl., *n.n.* matting.
·mauwen, *v.i.* to mew.
·mazelen, pl. only, *n.* measles.
·mazen, maas, *v.t.* to darn invisibly.
me, *pron.* me; to me.
me·chanica, no pl., *n.* mechanics (*science*). mecani·cien, -s, *n.* mechanic. engineer. me·chanisch, *a.* mechanical.
Mechelen. *n.N.* Malines, Mechlin.
me·dalje, -s, *n.* medal. medal·jon, -s, *n.n.* medallion, locket.
·mede, no pl., *n.* madder; mead. ¶*adv.* (*stilted*) also, too. *See* mee. ¶*prefix.* fellow-, co-, joint. *often* mee. ·medeburger, -s, *n.* fellow-citizen. ·medadader, -s, *n.* accomplice. mede·deelzaam, -zame, *a.* communicative. ·mededelen, deel mede, *v.t.s. See* meedelen. ·mededeling, -s, *n. See* meedeling. ·meddingen, *v.i.s.* to compete. *~ naar,* to compete for. ·mededinger, -s, *n.* competitor. ·mededinging, *n.* competition, rivalry. *buiten ~,* hors concours. ·mededingster, -s, *n.* competitor (*female*). ·mededirecteur, -s, *n.* joint-manager. ·mededogen, no pl., *n.n. See* meedogen. ·medeeigenaar, -s, *n.* part-owner. ·medegerechtigd, *a.* also entitled. ·medegevangene, -n, *n.* fellow-prisoner. ·medegevoel, no pl., *n.n.* sympathy, fellow-feeling. ·medehelper, -s, *n.* assistant. ·medeklinker, -s, *n.* consonant. ·medelid, -leden, *n.n.* fellowmember. ·medelijden, no pl., *n.n.* pity, compassion. *~ hebben met,* to have pity

on *or* to be sorry for (*person*); *uit* ~, out of pity. **mede·lijdend,** *a.* compassionate. **·medemens,** *n.* fellow-human. **mede·plichtig,** *a.* accessory. ~ *aan,* accessory to, a party to. **mede·plichtige, -n,** *n.* accomplice. **mede·plichtigheid,** no pl., *n.* complicity. **·medeschepsel, -s,** *n.n.* fellow-creature. **mede·schuldige, -n,** *n.* accomplice. **·medewerken,** *v.i.s.* See **meewerken.** **·medewerker, -s,** *n.* collaborator; contributor (*to publication*). **·medewerking,** *n.* collaboration, assistance. **·medeweten,** no pl., *n.n.* (previous) knowledge. **mede·zeggenschap,** no pl., *n.* say. ~ *eisen,* to demand a voice (in the matter).

medica·ment, *n.n.* medicine (*remedy*). **medi·cijn,** *n.n.* medicine (*remedy*). ~*en,* medicine (*science*); *in de* ~*en studeren,* to study medicine. **·medicus, -ci,** *n.* medical man, physician. **·medisch,** *a.* medical.

mee, *adv.* also, too. ~ *van de partij zijn,* to join in *or* to belong to the party. ¶*prefix. See* **mede. ·meebrengen,** *v.t.s.,* *irr.* to bring along; to entail, involve. **·meedelen, deel mee,** *v.t.s.* to impart. *iemand iets* ~, to communicate something to somebody. **·meedeling,** *n.* communication; announcement. **·meedoen, doe mee,** *v.i.s., irr.* to join (in). *aan iets* ~, to join in something. **·meedogen,** no pl., *n.n.* compassion. **mee·dogend,** *a.* compassionate. **mee·dogenloos, -loze,** *a.* merciless, relentless.

·meeëten, eet mee, *v.i.s., irr.* to join (in a meal). **·meegaan, ga mee,** *v.i.s., irr.* to come along. ~ *met,* to accompany; ~ *met zijn tijd,* to move with the times. **·meegaand,** *a.* accommodating. **mee·gaandheid,** no pl., *n.* pliancy. **·meegeven, geef mee,** *v.t.s., str.* to give (*to take along*). **·meehebben, heb mee,** *v.t.s., irr.* to have with one. **·meekomen,** *v.i.s., irr.* to come along. **·meekrap,** no pl., *n.* madder. **·meekrijgen,** *v.t.s., str.* to be given (to take along).

meel, no pl., *n.n.* meal; flour. **·meelachtig,** *a.* mealy, floury. **·meelbak, -kken,** *n.* flour-bin. **·meeldauw,** no pl., *n.* mildew. **·meel·draad, -draden,** *n.* stamen.

meelachen, *v.i.s., irr.* to join in the laughter. **·meelij,** no pl., *n. See* **medelijden. ·meelopen, loop mee,** *v.i.s., str.* to accompany, walk along with. *als het meeloopt,* if all goes well. **·meeloper, -s,** *n.* hanger-on. **·meemaken, maak mee,** *v.t.s.* to experience. *veel* ~, to go through a lot. **·meenemen, neem mee,** *v.t.s., str.* to take along. **·meepraten, praat mee,** *v.i.s.* to join in the conversation. *ik kan er van* ~, I have had experience of it.

meer, meren, *n.n.* lake. ¶*indef. pron.* more. *steeds* ~, more and more. ¶*adv.* more; frequently. *te* ~, all the more; *des te* ~, all the more; *geen kind* ~, no longer a

child; *nooit* ~, never again; *er is niets* ~, there is nothing left.

·meerboei, *n.* mooring-buoy.

·meerder, *a.* greater. **·meerdere, -n,** *n.* superior. **·meerderheid, -heden,** *n.* majority; superiority. **meerder·jarig,** *a.* of age. **meerder·jarigheid,** no pl., *n.* majority (*age*).

·meerekenen, *v.t.s.* to count in, include. **·meerijden,** *v.i.s., str.* to ride along with. *mogen* ~, to be given a lift.

·meerkat, -tten, *n.* grivet. **·meerketting,** *n.* mooring chain. **·meerkoet,** *n.* coot.

·meermalen, *adv.* repeatedly.

·meerman, -nnen, *n.* merman. **meer·min, -nnen,** *n.* mermaid. **·meerschuim,** no pl., *n.n.* meerschaum. **·meerschuimen,** *a.* meerschaum.

meer·stemmig, *a.* polyphonic. ~ *gezang,* part-song. **·meervoud,** *n.n.* plural. **meer·voudig,** *a.* plural. **·meerwaarde, -n,** *n.* surplus value.

mees, mezen, *n.* tit, titmouse.

·meeslepen, sleep mee, *v.t.s.* to drag along; to carry away (*audience*).

·meesmuilen, *v.i.* to simper.

·meespreken, spreek mee, *v.i.s., str. See* **meepraten.**

meest, *a.* most. *de* ~*e tijd,* most of the time. ¶*adv.* most; greatest. ¶*n.n. het* ~, most; *op zijn* ~, at the most. ¶*pl.* only. *n. de* ~*en,* most of them, most people. **·meestal,** *adv.* mostly, usually. **·meestbegunstigd,** *a.* most favoured. **·meestbiedende, -n,** *n.* highest bidder.

·meester, -s, *n.* master. *een taal goed* ~ *zijn,* to have a good command of a language; *zich* ~ *maken van,* to conquer, possess oneself of; *iets* ~ *worden,* to master something; *zichzelf* ~ *worden,* to control oneself. **·meester·res, -ssen,** *n.* mistress. **meester·knecht, -s,** *n.* foreman. **·meester·lijk,** *a.* masterly. **·meesterschap,** no pl., *n.n.* mastership; mastery. **·meesterwerk,** *n.n.* masterpiece.

·meesttijds, *adv.* mostly.

meet, no pl. *n.* starting-line. *van* ~ *af aan,* from the beginning. **·meetbaar, -bare,** *a.* measurable. **·meetbrief, -ven,** *n.* certificate of registry (*of ship*).

·meetellen, tel mee, *v.i.s.* to count, be of importance.

·meetgeld, *n.n.* metage. **·meetkunde,** no pl., *n.* geometry. **·meetlat, -tten.** *n.* ruler (*instrument*).

·meetrekken, trek mee, *v.i.s., str.* to pull along; to join in pulling. **·meetronen, troon mee,** *v.t.s.* to coax along.

meeuw, *n.* (sea-)gull.

·meevallen, val mee, *v.i.s., str., imp.* to be a pleasant surprise, turn out better than expected. **·meevaller, -s,** *n.* windfall, piece of good luck. **·meevechten,** *v.i.s., str.* to join in fight. **mee·warig** *a.*

compassionate. **mee·warigheid,** no pl., *n.*
compassion. ·**meeewerken,** *v.i.s.* to co-
operate.
mei, *N.* May. ·**meiboom, -bomen,** *n.* maypole. ·**meiboter,** no pl., *n.* spring butter.
meid, *n.* maidservant; girl, wench. ~ *alleen,*
maid-of-all work; *tweede* ~, parlour-maid.
·**meidenkamer, -s,** *n.* maid's room. ·**meiden-**
praatje, -s, *n.n.* (*usu. pl.*) servants'
gossip.
·**Meidoorn, -s,** *n.* hawthorn, may tree.
·**meier, -s,** *n.* leaseholder (*farmer*); bailiff.
meie·rij, *n.* small farm; bailiwick.
·**Meikever, -s,** *n.* cockchafer.
·**meineed,** *n.* perjury. *een* ~ *doen,* to commit
perjury. **mein·edig,** *a.* perjured. **mein-**
·**edige, -n,** *n.* perjurer.
·**meisje, -s,** *n.n.* girl; fiancée. ·**meisjesachtig,**
a. girlish. ·**meisjesgek, -kken,** *n.* person
over-fond of girls.
·**Meitak, -kken,** *n.* flowering hawthorn, May
flower. ·**meizoentje, -s,** *n.n.* daisy.
Me·juffrouw, *n.* Miss; Mrs. (*lower middle-class*).
me·kaar, *pron.* each other.
·**Mekkaganger, -s,** *n.* pilgrim to Mecca.
me·laats, *a.* leprous. **me·laatse, -n,** *n.* leper.
me·laatsheid, no pl., *n.* leprosy
me·lange, -s, *n.* mixture, blend.
me·lasse, no pl., *n.* molasses.
·**melden,** *v.t.* to report, mention. ¶*zich* ~,
v.r. to report. **meldens·waardig,** *a.* worth
mentioning. ·**melding,** *n.* mention.
·**melig,** *a.* mealy, floury (*of potato*); sleepy (*of*
pear).
me·lisse, no pl., *n.* herb balm.
melk, no pl., *n.* milk. *hij heeft niets in de* ~
te brokken, he has no influence. ·**melk-**
achtig, *a.* milky. ·**melkboer,** *n.* milkman.
·**melkdistel, -s,** *n.* sow-thistle. ·**melken,** *v.t.*
str. to milk. ·**melker, -s,** *n.* milker; milter.
melke·rij, *n.* dairy farm. ·**melkgevend,** *a.*
milk-yielding. ·**melkinrichting,** *n.* dairy.
·**melkklier,** *n.* lacteal gland. ·**melkkoe,**
·**koeien,** *n.* milch cow, milker. ·**melkmeid,**
n. milkmaid, dairymaid. ·**melkmuil,** *n.*
milksop. ·**melksalon, -s,** *n.* milk bar.
·**melksap, -ppen,** *n.* latex; chyle. ·**melk-**
slijter, -s, *n.* milk retailer. ·**melkster, -s,**
n. milker (*female*). ·**melkvee,** no pl., *n.n.*
dairy cattle. ·**melkwagen, -s,** *n.* milk-cart,
milk-float. ·**Melkweg,** *N.* Milky Way,
galaxy. ·**melkweger, -s,** *n.* lactometer.
·**melkwit, -tte,** *a.* milky-white. **melkzuur,**
no pl., *n.n.* lactic acid.
me·loen, *n.* melon.
me·morie, *n.* memory; memorial; memorandum. ~ *van toelichting,* explanatory
memorandum.
men, *pron.* one; people; they, you, we;
a man. ~ *zegt,* they say.
mena·geren, -geer, *v.t.* to spare (*feelings*).
me·neer, -neren, *n.* sir; man, gentleman.
·**menen, meen** *v.t.* to mean; to intend; to
think, suppose. *hij meent het goed,* he

means well. ·**menens,** no pl., *n.n. het is* ~,
it is serious.
me·neren, -neer, *v.t.* to call a person "sir".
·**mengbaar, -bare,** *a.* mixable. ·**mengel-**
dichten, pl. only, *n.n.* miscellaneous poems.
·**mengelen,** *v.t.* to mingle, mix. ·**mengeling,**
no pl., *n.* mixture. ·**mengelmoes,** no pl.,
n.n. jumble, medley. ·**mengelwerk,** no pl.,
n.n. miscellaneous writings. ·**mengen,** *v.t.*
to mix, mingle, blend. *zich* ~ *in,* to
interfere in; *zich* ~ *onder,* to mingle with.
·**menger, -s,** *n.* mixer. ·**menging,** *n.*
mixture. ·**mengsel, -s,** *n.n.* mixture.
·**menie,** no pl., *n.* red lead; minimum.
·**meniën, -nie,** *v.t.* to (paint with) red
lead.
·**menig,** *pron.* many, many a. ·**menigen,**
pron. many a man. ·**menigerhande,** *a.,*
·**menigerlei,** *a.* various, of many kinds,
manifold. ·**menigmaal,** *adv.* many a time.
·**menigte, -n,** *n.* crowd, multitude. **menig-**
vuldig, *a.* manifold, frequent. ¶*adv.*
frequently, abundantly. **menig·vuldigheid,**
no pl., *n.* multiplicity, abundance. ·**menig-**
werf, *adv.* many a time.
·**mening,** *n.* opinion; intention. *naar mijn* ~,
in my opinion; *van* ~ *verschillen,* to differ
in opinion.
Me·nist, *N.* Mennonite.
·**mennen, men,** *v.t.* to drive, guide (*horse-*
drawn vehicle). ·**menner, -s,** *n.* driver (*of*
horse-drawn vehicle).
mens, *n.* man, human being. *de* ~*en,* people;
geen ~, nobody, no one; *onder de* ~*en,*
among people. ¶*n.n.* person (*with pity,*
dislike or condescension). *het oude* ~, the
old woman. ·**mensaap, -sapen,** *n.* anthro-
poid ape. ·**mensdom,** no pl., *n.n.* mankind.
·**menselijk,** *a.* human. ·**menselijkerwijze,**
a. humanly. ·**menselijkheid,** no pl., *n.*
humanity (*sentiment*). ·**menseneter, -s,** *n.*
cannibal, man-eater. ·**mensenhaat,** no pl.,
n. misanthropy. ·**mensenhater, -s,** *n.*
misanthropist. ·**mensenheugenis,** no pl.,
n. living memory. ·**mensenkenner, -s,** *n.*
judge of character. ·**mensenkind, -eren,**
n.n. human being. ·**mensenleeftijd,** *n.*
lifetime. ·**mensenliefde,** no pl., *n.* philanthropy. ·**mensenschuw,** *a.* shy, unsociable.
·**mensheid,** no pl., *n.* mankind; human
nature. ·**menslievend,** *a.* humane, philanthropic. **mens·lievendheid,** no pl., *n.*
philanthropy. **mens·waardig,** *a.* worthy
of a human being. ·**menswording,** *n.*
incarnation.
mep, -ppen, *n.* (*coll.*) biff, sock. ·**meppen,**
mep, *v.t.* (*coll.*) to biff.
·**merel, -s,** *n.* blackbird.
·**meren, meer,** *v.t.* to moor.
·**merendeel,** no pl., *n.n. het* ~, the greater
part. ·**merendeels,** *adv.* for the greater
part, mostly.
merg, no pl., *n.n.* marrow (*in bone*); pith.
door ~ *en been dringen,* to set one's teeth

on edge; *in ~ en been*, to the backbone, to the core. ·**mergachtig**, *a.* marrowy. ·**mergel**, no pl., *n.* marl. ·**mergelachtig**, *a.* marly. ·**mergelgroeve**, -**n**, *n.* marl-pit. ·**mergpijp**, *n.* marrowbone.

merk, *n.n.* mark; brand, make. ·**merkbaar**, -**bare**, *a.* noticeable, appreciable. ·**merkelijk**, *a.* marked, considerable. ¶*adv.* perceptibly. ·**merken**, *v.t.* to notice; to perceive; to mark. *niets laten ~*, to give no inkling, give nothing away. ·**merkijzer**, -**s**, *n.n.* branding iron. ·**merkinkt**, *n.* marking-ink. ·**merklap**, -**ppen**, *n.* sampler. ·**merkteken**, -**s**, *n.n.* mark, sign, token. **merk·waardig**, *a.* remarkable, noteworthy. **merk·waardigheid**, -**heden**, *n.* curiosity, remarkable thing; *pl.* the sights.

·**merrie**, -**s**, *n.* mare. ·**merrieveulen**, -**s**, *n.* filly. **mes**, -**ssen**, *n.n.* knife. *hij is onder 't ~*, he is being examined. ·**mesje**, -**s**, *n.n.* little knife; blade.

mes·jogge, *a.* (*slang*) mad. ·**messenlegger**, -**s**, *n.* knife-rest. ·**messen-lijper**, -**s**, *n.* knife-grinder. ·**messen-trekker**, -**s**, *n.* member of a razor gang. **Mes·sias**, *N.* Messiah.

·**messing**, no pl., *n.n.* brass. ·**messteek**, -**teken**, *n.* knife-thrust.

mest, no pl., *n.* dung, manure. ·**mestdier**, *n.n.* animal kept for fattening. ·**mesten**, *v.t.* to fatten, feed up; to dung, manure. ·**mesthoop**, -**hopen**, *n.* dunghill, manure heap.

mes·ties, -**zen**, *n.* mestizo.

·**mestkever**, -**s**, *n.* dung-beetle. ·**meststof**, -**ffen**, *n.* manure, fertilizer. ·**mestvaalt**, *n.* dunghill. ·**mestvee**, no pl., *n.n.* cattle kept for fattening.

met, *prep.* with; by. *~ dat al*, for all that; *~ den dag*, every day; *~ Pasen*, at Easter; *~ z'n vieren*, four of us *or* of them *or* of you. ¶*adv.* at that moment.

me·taal, -**talen**, *n.n.* metal. **me·taalachtig**, *a.* metallic. **me·taalbewerker**, -**s**, *n.* metal worker. **me·taaldraad**, -**draden**, *n.* metallic wire; metal filament. **me·taalschuim**, no pl., *n.n.* dross. **me·taalslak**, -**kken**, *n.* slag, scoria. **me·talen**, *a.* (made of) metal.

met·een, *adv.* immediately; at the same time; presently. *ik kom ~*, I shan't be long.

·**meten**, **meet**, *v.t.*, *str.* to measure; to gauge. *zich met iemand ~*, to match oneself against a person. ·**meter**, -**s**, *n.* godmother; measurer; meter; metre (*measure*). ·**metgezel**, -**llen**, *n.* companion. ·**metgezellin**, -**nnen**, *n.* companion (*female*).

me·thodisch, *a.* methodical.

·**meting**, *n.* measurement. **me·triek**, *a.* metric. ·**metrisch**, *a.* metrical. ·**metrum**, -**tra**, *n.n.* metre (*of verse*).

·**metselaar**, -**s**, *n.* bricklayer. **metselaars·baas**, -**bazen**, *n.* master-bricklayer. **metselaars·knecht**, *n.* journeyman bricklayer. **met·sela·rij**, no pl., *n.* brickwork, masonry.

·**metselen**, *v.i.* to lay bricks; to build. ·**metselkalk**, no pl., *n.*, ·**metselspecie**, no pl., *n.* mortar. ·**metselwerk**, no pl., *n.* brickwork, masonry.

·**metten**, pl. only, *n.* matins. *iemand de ~ lezen*, to lecture a person; *korte ~ maken met*, to make short work of.

metter·daad, *adv.* indeed, in fact. **metter·tijd**, *adv.* in time, in due course. **metter·woon**, *adv.* *zich ~ ergens vestigen*, to establish oneself somewhere.

·**metworst**, no pl., *n.* breakfast sausage.

·**meubel**, -**s** *or* -**en**, *n.n.* piece of furniture. *~en* or *~s*, furniture; *een lastig ~*, a troublesome individual; *een raar ~*, a queer customer. ·**meubelen**, *v.t.* to furnish. ·**meubelmagazijn**, *n.n.* furniture stores. ·**meubelmaker**, -**s**, *n.* cabinet-maker, joiner. ·**meubelmake·rij**, *n.* furniture works. ·**meubelpolitoer**, no pl., *n.n.* french polish. **meubi·lair**, no pl., *n.n.* furniture. **meubi·leren**, -**leer**, *v.t.* to furnish. **meubi·lering**, *n.* furnishing; furniture.

meug, no pl., *n.* liking. *ieder zijn ~*, every man to his taste; *tegen heug en ~*, against one's inclination.

me·vrouw, *n.* Mrs.; Madam; lady. **me·vrouwen**, *v.t.* to call a person Madam.

mi·auw, *int.* miaow. **mi·auwen**, *v.i.* to miaow, mew.

·**middag**, *n.* midday; afternoon. *heden ~ (stilted)*, this afternoon; *na de ~*, in the afternoon, after lunch; *van ~*, this afternoon; *voor de ~*, before lunch; *'s ~s*, in the afternoon(s). ·**middagdutje**, -**s**, *n.n.* after-dinner nap. ·**middageten**, no pl., *n.n.* midday meal. ·**middagmaal**, -**malen**, *n.n.* midday meal, dinner. **mid·dagmalen**, -**maal**, *v.i.* (*stilted*) to dine. ·**middaguur**, -**guren**, *n.n.* noon.

·**middel**, -**s**, *n.n.* waist, middle. ¶-**en**, *n.n.* means; remedy. ·**middelaar**, -**s**, *n.* mediator. ·**middelaarschap**, no pl., *n.n.* mediatorship. ·**middelbaar**, -**bare**, *a.* medium, middle, average, middling; secondary (*school*). ·**middeleeuwen**, pl. only, *n.* Middle Ages. ·**middeleeuws**, *a.* medieval. **middeler·wijl**, *adv.* meanwhile, in the meantime. ·**middelgroot**, -**grote**, *a.* medium(-sized). ·**Middellands**, *a.* *~e Zee*, the Mediterranean. ·**middellijk**, *a.* indirect. ·**middellijn**, *n.* diameter. ·**middelloop**, no pl., *n.* middle course, middle reaches. ·**middelmaat**, no pl., *n.* average. *gulden ~*, golden mean. **middel·matig**, *a.* mediocre, indifferent; medium. **middel·matigheid**, -**heden**, *n.* mediocrity. ·**middelpunt**, *n.n.* centre. **middelpunt·vliedend**, *a.* centrifugal. **middelpunt·zoekend**, *a.* centripetal. ·**middelrif**, -**ffen**, *n.n.* midriff. ·**middelschot**, -**tten**, *n.n.* partition. ·**middelslag**, no pl., *n.n.* average, medium. ·**middelsoort**, *n.* or *n.n.* average, medium. ·**middeltje**, -**s**, *n.n.* trick, device; remedy. ·**middelweg**, *n.* middle course,

mean. *de gulden* ~, the golden mean; *een* ~ *vinden*, to hit upon a compromise.
·midden, -s, *n.n.* middle, centre; midst.
iets in het ~ *brengen*, to put something forward; *iets in het* ~ *laten*, not to pronounce on something; *te* ~ *van*, in the midst of; *uit ons* ~, from our midst.
¶*adv.* ~ *in*, in the middle of; ~ *onder*, in the middle of, during; ~ *op*, in the middle of. ·middendoor, *adv.* in two, across. ·middenin, *adv.* in the middle.
·middenstand, no pl., *n.* (lower) middle class.
·middernacht, *n.* midnight. midder·nachtelijk, *a.* midnight.
·midscheeps, *adv.* amidships.
mier, *n.* ant. ·mieren, *v.i.* to fiddle, toy; to bother, fuss. ·miereneter, -s, *n.* ant-eater.
·mierenhonig, *n.* honeydew. ·mierenhoop, -hopen, *n.* ant-hill. ·mierenzuur, no pl., *n.n.* formic acid.
·mieriksworteI, -s, *n.* horse-radish.
·mieter, -s, *n.* (*vulg.*) body, backside; (*derogatory*) person. *iemand op zijn* ~ *geven* or *komen*, to beat a person. ·mieteren, *v.t.* (*vulg.*) to throw. ¶*v.i.* (*vulg.*) to fall.
mij, *pron.* me.
·mijden, *v.t.*, *str.* to avoid, shun.
mijl, *n.* mile; league. ·mijlenlang, *a.* mile(s)-long. ·mijlenver, -rre, *a.* for miles (and miles). ·mijlpaal, -palen, *n.* milestone.
mijmeraar, -s, *n.* one who muses *or* ponders.
·mijmeren, *v.i.* to muse, ponder, meditate.
mijme·rij, *n.*, ·mijmering, *n.* reverie.
mijn, *poss. a.* my. ¶*n.n. het* ~ *en het dijn*, mine and thine. *See* mijns. ¶*n.* auction market; mine, pit; mine (*explosive*).
·mijnarbeid, no pl., *n.* mining (*labour*).
·mijnbouw, no pl., *n.* mining (*industry*).
·mijnbouwkunde, no pl., *n.* mining (*science*).
·mijnbouwkundig, *a.* ~ *ingenieur*, mining engineer. ·mijnbouwschool, -scholen, *n.* school of mines.
·mijne, -n, *pron. & n. & n.n. het* ~, mine (*sing.*); *de* ~, mine (*sing.*); *de* ~*n*, mine (*pl.*), my family; *ik denk er het* ~ *van*, I have my own opinion about it.
·mijnen, *v.t.* to buy at public auction.
·mijnenlegger, -s, *n.* mine-layer. ·mijnenveger, -s, *n.* mine-sweeper. ·mijnenveld, *n.n.* mine-field.
·mijnent, *adv. te* ~, at my house. ·mijnenthalve, *adv.*, ·mijnentwege, *adv.* as for me; in my name. ·mijnentwille, *adv. om* ~, for my sake.
mijn·heer, mijne heren, Mr.; sir. *See* meneer, *n.*
·mijngang, *n.* gallery (*of mine*). ·mijngas, -ssen, *n.n.* fire-damp. ·mijnhout, no pl., *n.n.* pit-props. ·mijningenieur, -s, *n.* mining engineer. ·mijnlamp, *n.* safety-lamp. ·mijnstut, -tten, *n.* pit-prop.
·mijnwerker, -s, *n.* miner. ·mijnwezen, no pl., *n.n.* mining (*industry*). ·mijnworm, *n.* hookworm.

mijt, *n.* mite (*coin; insect*); (hay-)stack.
·mijten, *v.t.* to stack (*hay*).
·mijter, -s, *n.* mitre.
·mijterig, *a.* full of mites.
·mijterstad, -steden, *n.* episcopal town.
mij·zelf, *pron.* myself.
mik, -kken, *n.* fork, crutch; loaf. ·mikken, mik, *v.i.* to aim. ~ *op*, to take aim at.
·mikmak, no pl., *n.* caboodle; difficulty.
·mikpunt, *n.n.* aim; target, butt.
mild, *a.* liberal, generous; mild. *met* ~*e hand*, lavishly. mild·dadig, *a.* bounteous, liberal.
mild·dadigheid, no pl., *n.* liberality.
·mildheid, -heden, *n.* bounty.
mili·cien, -s, *n.* conscript. mili·tair, *a.* military. ¶*n.* soldier, man in uniform.
mi·litie, no pl., *n.* militia. militie·plichtig, *a.* liable to military service.
·mille, no pl., *n.* thousand. ·milligram, -mmen, *n.* milligramme. ·milliliter, -s, *n.* millilitre. ·millimeter, -s, *n.* millimetre.
·millimeteren, *v.t.* to crop closely. ·millioen, *n.n.* million.
milt, *n.* spleen (*organ*). ·miltvuur, no pl., *n.n.* anthrax. ·miltzucht, no pl., *n.* melancholia, spleen. milt·zuchtig, *a.* splenetic.
min, -nnen, *n.* wet-nurse. ¶no pl., *n.* (*stilted*) love. *iets in der minne schikken*, to come to a friendly arrangement. ¶-nne, *a.* despicable; bad, poor. *het is mij te* ~, it is beneath me. ¶*adv.* less; minus. ~ *of meer*, more or less, somewhat. ·minachten, *v.t.* to disdain; to disregard. ·minachtend, *a.* contemptuous, disdainful. ·minachtig, no pl., *n.* contempt, disdain. ·uit ~ *voor*, in contempt of. ·minder, *a.* smaller; less. *de* ~*e goden*, the lesser gods; *de* ~*e stand*, the lower orders. ¶*adv.* less. ·Minderbroeder, -s, *n.* Franciscan. ·mindere, -n, *n.* inferior. *de* ~*n*, the lower ranks. ·minderen, *v.t.* to diminish. *zeil* ~, to take in sail. ·minderheid, -heden, *n.* minority. ·mindering, *n.* diminution. minder·jarig, *a.* under age. minder·jarige, -n, *n.* minor. minder·jarigheid, no pl., *n.* minority (*in age*). minder·waardig, *a.* inferior. geestelijk ~, mentally deficient. minder·waardigheid, no pl., *n.* inferiority.
·mine, -s, *n.* pretence.
mi·neur, *n.* minor key. ¶*a.* minor.
mi·niem, *a.* minimal, slight.
mi·nister, -s, *n.* minister, secretary (cabinet). *Eerste* ~, Prime Minister. minis·terie, -s, *n.n.* ministry, department, office. *het Openbaar* ~, the Public Prosecutor, Director of Public Prosecutions. ministeri·eel, -iële, *a.* ministerial. mi·nister·presi·dent, *n.* Prime Minister. mi·nister·raad, no pl., *n.* cabinet council. mi·nister·schap, no pl., *n.n.* ministry (*tenure of office*).
·minnaar, -s, *n.* (*stilted*) lover. minna·res, -ssen, *n.* (*stilted*) love, mistress. ·minne, no pl., *n.* love. *See* min. ·minnebrief, -ven

n. love-letter. ·minnedicht, *n.n.* love poem. ·minnekozen, -koos, *r.i.* (*poet.*) to talk sweet nothings. ·minuelied, -eren, *n.n.* love-song. ·minnelijk, *a.* amicable. ¶*adv.* amicably. ·minnen, min, *v.t.* (*stilted*) to love. minnens·waardig, *a.* lovable. ·minnezanger, -s, *n.* minstrel.

·minnetjes, *adv.* poorly. minst, *a.* least, smallest, slightest. ¶*adv.* least. ¶*a.* & *n.n.* de ~e *zijn*, to yield; *het* ~*e*, the least; *het* ~, least of all, at all; *in het* ~ *niet*, not in the least, by no means; *op z'n* ~, at (the) least; *ten* ~*e*, at least; *voor het* ~, at all events. ·minstens, *adv.* at (the) least.

minuti·eus, -ze, *a.* painstaking; detailed. mi·nuut, -nuten, *n.* minute. mi·nuut-wijzer, -s, *n.* minute-hand.

minver·mogend, *a.* poor, indigent.

·minzaam, -zame, *a.* affable, gracious. ·minzaamheid, no pl., *n.* friendliness, graciousness.

mi·rakel, -s, *n.n.* miracle.

·mirre, no pl., *n.* myrrh.

mirt, *n.* myrtle. ·mirteboom, -bomen, *n.* myrtle(-tree).

mis, -ssen, *n.* mass. *stille* ~, low mass. ¶*a.* wrong. ~ *of raak*, hit or miss; *het* ~ *hebben*, to be mistaken; *het is lang niet* ~, it is far from negligible. ¶*adv.* inaccurately, badly, wrong.

mis·baar, no pl., *n.n.* clamour, uproar. ~ *maken*, to make a great fuss.

·misbaksel, -s, *n.n.* monstrosity.

·misboek, *n.n.* missal.

·misbruik, *n.n.* abuse; misuse. ~ *maken van*, to abuse, take advantage of; ~ *van vertrouwen*, breach of trust. mis·bruiken, *v.t.* to abuse, misuse. ·misdaad, -daden, *n.* crime, misdeed. mis·dadig, *a.* criminal, guilty. ·misdadiger, -s, *n.* criminal, evil-doer. mis·deeld, *a.* destitute. ~ *van*, lacking in.

·misdienaar, -s, *n.* acolyte, server.

·misdoen, doe mis, *v.t.s.*, *irr.* to do wrong, incorrectly, mis·doen, *v.t.*, *irr.* to do wrong, sin. mis·dragen, -draag, *v.i.*, *str.* to misbehave, behave badly. ·misdrijf, -ven, *n.n.* offence, misdemeanour. mis·drijven, -drijf, *v.t.*, *str.* to commit (*offence*). ·misdruk, -kken, *n.* macule, mackle. mis·duiden, *v.t.* to misinterpret, take ill.

mi·sère, -s, *n.* misery. *in de* ~ *zitten*, to be in trouble.

·misgaan, ga mis, *v.i.s.*, *irr.* to go wrong. ·misgooien, *v.i.s.* to miss (*throwing*). ·misgreep, -grepen, *n.* mistake, blunder. mis·gunnen, -gun, *v.t.* to begrudge. mis·hagen, -haag, *v.t.* to displease. ¶no pl., *n.n.* displeasure. mis·handelen, *v.t.* to ill-treat. mis·handeling, *n.* ill-treatment. mis·kennen, -ken, *v.t.* to misjudge, fail to appreciate. mis·kenning, no pl., *n.* failure to appreciate. mis·kocht, *a.* See bekocht.

·miskraam, -kramen, *n.* miscarriage. mis·leiden, *v.t.* to mislead. mis·leidend, *a.* misleading, deceptive. ·mislopen, loop mis, *v.i.s.*, *str.* to go wrong. ¶*v.t.s.*, *str.* to miss. mis·lukkeling, *n.* failure, misfit (*person*). mis·lukken, -luk, *v.i.* to fail. mis·maakt, *a.* deformed. mis·moedig, *a.* disheartened. mis·noegd, *a.* displeased, disgruntled. mis·noegdheid, no pl., *n.*, mis·noegen, no pl., *n.n.* discontent.

·mispel, -s, *n.* medlar.

mis·plaatst, *a.* misplaced, mistaken. ·mispunt, *n.n.* unpleasant person. ·misrekenen, *v.i.s.* to make a wrong calculation. mis·rekenen, *v.i.s.* to judge badly. mis·rekening, *n.* miscalculation.

mis·schien, *adv.* perhaps, maybe. *zoals U* ~ *weet*, as you may know.

·misselijk, *a.* sick, queasy; hateful. ·misselijkheid, no pl., *n.* sickness, nausea.

·missen, mis, *v.t.* to miss; to lack; to spare. *zij kunnen het slecht* ~, they can ill afford it. ¶*v.i.* to miss, fail.

·missie, -s, *n.* mission.

·misslaan, sla mis, *v.t.s.*, *irr.* to miss (*hitting*). ·misslag, *n.* miss; error. ·misstaan, sta mis, *v.t.s.*, *irr.* to be unbecoming. ·misstand, *n.* abuse. ·misstap, -ppen, *n.* false step, false move.

mist, *n.* fog, mist. ·misten, *v.i.* to be foggy *or* misty. ·mistig, *a.* foggy, misty.

·misteltak, -kken, *n.* mistletoe.

mis·troostig, *a.* disconsolate, dejected. mis·trouwen, no pl., *n.n.* distrust. ·mis·verstand, *n.n.* misunderstanding. mis·vormd, *a.* misshapen, deformed. ·mis·wijzing, *n.* error (*compass*).

mitrail·leur, -s, *n.* machine-gun; mach:ne-gunner.

mits, *c.* provided. ¶*prep.* ~ *dezen*, hereby. ·mits·dien, *adv.* consequently. mits·gaders, *adv.* together with.

mo·biel, *a.* mobile.

·modder, no pl., *n.* mud, mire. ·modderaar, -s, *n.* bungler. ·modderachtig, *a.* muddy. ·modderen, *v.i.* to flounder, bungle. ·modderig, *a.* muddy. ·modderplas, -ssen, *n.* puddle. ·modderpoel, *n.* slough. ·modder-schuit, *n.* hopper(-barge). ·moddersloot, -sloten, *n.* muddy ditch.

·mode, -s, *n.* fashion. *naar de* ~, after the fashion. ·modeartikel, *n.n.* novelty, fancy article.

mo·del, -llen, *n.n.* model; pattern. mo·del-uniform, *n.* or *n.n.* regulation uniform.

·modepop, -ppen, *n.* doll (*over-fashionable woman*). ·modewinkel, -s, *n.*, ·modezaak, -zaken, *n.* milliner's (shop). modi·eus, -ze, *a.* fashionable. mo·diste, -n, *n.* milliner, dressmaker.

moe, no pl., *n.* mummie (*mother*). ¶-de, *a.* tired. *hij is het* ~, he is tired of it; ~ *worden*, to tire, become tired.

moed, no pl., *n.* courage; cheer. *goede* ~

hebben, to be of good heart; *zijn* ~ *bijeenrapen*, to take one's courage in both hands; ~ *scheppen* or *vatten*, to pluck up courage; *blij te* ~*e*, in high spirits; *in arren* ~*e*, in angry mood. ·moede, *See* moe, *a. and* moed, *n.* ·moedeloos, -loze, *a.* despondent, disheartened. ·moedeloosheid, no pl., *n.* despondency, dejection. ·moeder, -s, *n.* mother; matron; dam·(*animal*). ~ *de vrouw* (*coll.*), the missus. ·moedergek, *a.* over-attached to mother. ·moederkoren, no pl., *n.n.* ergot. ·moederkruid, no pl., *n.n.* feverfew. ·moederlief, no pl., *n.* mother darling. ·moederlijk, *a.* motherly, maternal. ¶*adv.* in a motherly way. ·moedernaakt, *a.* stark naked. moeder·overste, -n, *n.* mother superior. ·moederrecht, no pl., *n.n.* matriarchy. ·moederschap, no pl., *n.n.* motherhood, maternity. ·moederschip, -schepen, *n.n.* aircraft tender, depot ship. ·moederskant, no pl., *n.*, ·moederszijde, no pl., *n. van* ~, on the mother's side. ·moederskindje, -s, *n.n.* mother's darling. ·moedervlek, -kken, *n.* birth-mark. ·moederzielalleen, *a. & adv.* all alone.

·moedig, *a.* courageous. ·moedwil, no pl., *n.*, moed·willigheid, no pl., *n.* wantonness, spite. *uit* ~, wantonly. ·moedwillig, *a.* wilful, wanton.

·moeheid, no pl., *n.* tiredness, fatigue.

·moeial, -llen, *n.* busybody. ·moeien, *v.t.* to trouble; *iemand* ~ *in*, to involve a person in. ¶*v.r. zich* ~ *in* or *met*, to interfere with, meddle with. ·moeilijk, *a.* difficult, hard. ¶*adv.* with difficulty. ·moeilijkheid, -heden, *n.* difficulty, trouble. *in moeilijkheden verkeren*, to be in trouble. ·moeite, no pl., *n.* trouble, pains, effort. *het is de* ~ *niet waard* or *het loont de* ~ *niet*, it isn't worth while; ~ *doen*, to take pains; *zich de* ~ *getroosten*, to take the trouble; *het gaat in één* ~ *door*, it will not give extra trouble. ·moeizaam, -zame, *a.* laborious.

moer, *n.* nut (*of screw*). ¶no pl., *n.* (*pejorative*) mother; lees, dregs.

moe·ras, -ssen, *n.n.* marsh; swamp. moe·rasachtig, *a.* marshy. moe·rasgas, -sen, *n.n.* marsh gas. moe·raskoorts, *n.* paludal fever. moe·raspalm, *n.* nipa palm. moe·rassig, *a.* marshy; swampy.

·moerbei, *n.*, ·moerbezie, -ziën, *n.* mulberry. ·moerbeiboom, -bomen, *n.* mulberry-tree.

·moerbout, *n.* nut-bolt. ·moeren, *v.t.* (*coll.*) to damage. ¶*v.i.* (*coll.*) to fiddle, toy. ·moerschroef, -ven, *n.* nut; female screw.

moes, no pl., *n.n.* stewed fruit *or* vegetables. ·moesgroente, -n, *n.* greens, pot-herbs.

·moesje, no pl., *n.n.* mummie (*mother*); patch, beauty-spot.

·moesson, -s, *n.* monsoon.

·moestuin, *n.* kitchen-garden.

·moeten, *v.i., irr. & v.t., irr.* to have to (*must*),

to be obliged *or* forced; to have got to. ~ *hebben*, to want; *wat moet dat*, what is the meaning of that; (*past tense also*) *je moest . . .*, you ought to . . . ¶no pl., *n.n.* ~ *is dwang*, ask politely!

Mof, -ffen, *N.* Jerry, Boche.

mof, -ffen, *n.* muff; sleeve (*engine*).

·moffel, -s, *n.* muffle (*in furnace*). ·moffelen, *v.t.* to enamel. ·moffeloven, -s, *n.* muffle furnace.

·mogelijk, *a.* possible. *alle* ~*e dingen*, all sorts of things; *best* ~, quite possible. ¶*adv.* possibly. *zo* ~, if possible. ·mogelijkerwijs, *adv.* possibly. ·mogelijkheid, -heden, *n.* possibility; eventuality. ·mogen, mag, *v.t., irr.* to be allowed (*may*); to like, be fond of. *graag* ~, to be very fond of; *het mocht wat!*, so what!; (*past tense also*) *mocht . . .*, should . . . ·mogendheid, -heden, *n.* power.

·moker, -s, *n.* sledge-hammer. ·mokeren, *v.t.* to hammer.

Moker·hei, *N.* Mook Heath. *ik wou dat hij op de* ~ *zat*, he can go to blazes.

Mokka, *n. N.* Mocha.

·mokkel, -s, *n.n.* buxom wench. ·mokkelen, *v.t.* to cuddle.

mol, -llen, *n.* flat; minor key; mole (*animal*). ·molen, -s, *n.* mill; windmill. ·molenaar, -s, *n.* miller; cockchafer. ·molenbeek, -beken, *n.* mill-stream, mill-race. ·molendijk, *n.* mill-dam. ·molentje, -s, *n.n.* little mill; toy windmill. *hij loopt met* ~*s*, he has a bee in his bonnet *or* bats in the belfry. ·molenwiek, *n.* sail (*of mill*).

mo·lest, no pl., *n.n.* average (*to ship*). moles·teren, -teer, *v.t.* to molest, annoy. mo·lestrisico, -'s, *n.n.* war risk (*shipping*). mo·lestverzekering, *n.* war-risk insurance.

·mollen, mol, *v.t.* (*slang*) to do in. ·mollenvanger, -s, *n.* mole-catcher. ·mollenvel, -llen, *n.n.* moleskin. ·molletje, -s, *n.n.* little mole; plump child. ·mollig, *a.* plump, chubby. ·molligheid, no pl., *n.* chubbiness.

molm, no pl., *n.* mould; peat-dust. ·molmen, *v.i.* to moulder away.

·molshoop, -hopen, *n.* mole-hill. ·molsla, no pl., *n.* dandelion (*salad*).

·molton, no pl., *n.n.* swan-skin.

mom, -mmen, *n.* or *n.n.* mask. *onder het* ~ *van*, under the cloak of. ·mombakkes, -ssen, *n.n.* mask.

momen·teel, -tele, *a.* momentary. ¶*adv.* momentarily; for the time being. mo·mentopname, -n, *n.* instantaneous photograph.

·mompelaar, -s, *n.* mutterer. ·mompelen, *v.i.* to, mutter, mumble.

mond, *n.* mouth; orifice; muzzle (*of fire-arm*). *zijn* ~ *houden*, to hold one's tongue; *een grote* ~ *hebben*, to have too much to say for oneself; *geen* ~ *opendoen*, not to say a word; *iemand de* ~ *snoeren*, to stop a person's mouth; *bij* ~*e van*, from the lips of; *met open* ~, open-mouthed; *met de* ~ *vol tanden*, tongue-tied; *iemand naar de* ~ *praten*, to flatter a person; *als uit één* ~, of one accord; *hij zegt wat hem voor de* ~ *komt*, he just says whatever comes into his head; *zijn* ~ *voorbijpraten*, to shoot off one's mouth, give the game away. ·mondbehoeften, pl. only, *n*. victuals, provisions. ·mondeling, *a*. oral, verbal. ~ *examen*, viva voce. mond-en-·klauwzeer, no pl., *n.n.* foot-and-mouth disease. ·mondharmonica, -'s, *n*. mouth-organ. ·moadig, *a*. of age. ·mondje, -s, *n.n.* little mouth. ~ *dicht*, mum's the word; *hij is niet op zijn* ~ *gevallen*, he has the gift of the gab, a ready tongue. ·mondjesmaat, no pl., *n*. scanty measure. ~ *krijgen*, to be on short commons. ·mondjevol, no pl., *n.n.* a smattering. ·mondklem, no pl., *n.n.* lockjaw. ·mondprop, -ppen, *n*. gag. ·mondvoorraad, no pl., *n*. provisions.

·monnik, *n*. monk, friar. *gelijke* ~*en gelijke kappen*, what is sauce for the goose is sauce for the gander. ·monnikachtig, *a*. monkish. ·monnikenleven, no pl., *n.n.* monastic life. ·monnikenwerk, no pl., *n.n.* endless useless task. ·monnikskap, -ppen, *n*. monk's-hood; aconite.

mono·loog, -logen, *n*. monologue, soliloquy.

·monster, -s, *n.n.* monster; freak; sample, pattern. ·monsterachtig, *a*. monstrous. ·monsterboek, *n.n.* book of samples. ·monsteren, *v.t.* to muster. inspect. ·monsterrol, -llen, *n*. muster-roll. ·monsterkist, *n*. sample-case. monstru·eus, -ze, *a*. monstrous.

mon·tage, no pl., *n*. assembling, erecting. mon·tagewerkplaats, *n*. assembling room, assembling shop. mon·tant, *n.n.* amount. ·monter, *a*. lively, gay, brisk.

mon·teren, -teer, *v.t.* to assemble, erect, mount. mon·tering, *n*. assembling, erecting, mounting. mon·teur, -s, *n*. fitter, assembler, mechanic. mon·tuur, -turen, *n*. frame, mount, setting. *met gouden* ~, gold-rimmed.

mooi, *a*. fine, beautiful, handsome, pretty. *daar ben je* ~ *mee*, that is a lot of use!; *dat is alles heel* ~, that's all very well. ¶*adv*. beautifully; nicely. ~ *doen*, to put on a show of friendliness; ~ *gelapt*, cleverly managed. ¶*n.n. het* ~*e van het geval*, the funny part of it; *iets* ~*s* or *wat* ~*s*, a pretty pickle; *op z'n* ~*st*, at best. mooidoene·rij, *n*. airs. ·mooiheid, no pl., *n*. prettiness, fineness. ·mooiigheid, -heden, *n*. fine things; fine doings. ·mooipraten, praat mooi, *v.t.s.* to flatter. ·mooiprater, -s, *n*. flatterer. ·mooitjes, *adv*. finely.

moord, *n*. murder. ~ *en brand schreeuwen*, to shout blue murder. ·moordaanslag, *n*. attempted murder. *een* ~ *doen op iemand*, to attempt a person's life. moord·dadig, *a*.

murderous. moord·dadigheid, no pl., *n*. murderousness. ·moorden, *v.t.* to kill. murder. ·moordenaar, -s, *n*. murderer. moordena·res, -ssen, *n*. murderess. moorde·rij, *n*. massacre. moord·gierig, *a*. bloodthirsty. ·moordhol, *n.n.* den of cutthroats. ·moordkuil, *n*. *van zijn hart een* ~ *maken*, to smother one's feelings. ·moordlust, *n*. thirst for blood. ·moordpartij, *n*. carnage, massacre.

Moors, *a*. Moorish.

moot, moten, *n*. slice (*of fish*).

mop, -ppen, *n*. joke; blot; (*type of*) biscuit. *ouwe* or *afgezaagde* ~, stale joke, chestnut; *moppen tappen*, to crack jokes. ·mopje, -s, *n.n.* joke; tune. ·mopneus, -zen, *n*. pugnose. ·moppentapper, -s, *n*. joker. ·mopperaar, -s, *n*. grumbler. ·mopperen, *v.i.* to grumble. ·mopperig, *a*. disgruntled. grumbly. ·mopshond, *n*. pug.

mo·raal, no pl., *n*. moral(s). mo·reel, -rele, *a*. moral. ¶no pl., *n.n.* morale.

mo·rel, -llen, *n*. morello. mo·relleboom, -bomen, *n*. morello-tree.

·mores, pl. only, *n*. *iemand* ~ *leren*, to teach a person manners.

mor·fine, no pl., *n*. morphine, morphia. morfi·nist, *n*. morphinomaniac.

·morgen, -s, *n*. or *n.n.* measure of land, one morning's ploughing. ¶*n*. morning. *'s* ~*s*, in the morning(s); *op een* ~, one morning; *van* ~, this morning; *van* ~ *vroeg*, early this morning. ¶*adv.* to-morrow. ~ *over acht dagen*, to-morrow week; *tot* ~, see you to-morrow; ~ *brengen!*, catch me! morgen·avond, *adv*. to-morrow evening. ·Morgenland, *n.N.* the Orient. ·Morgenlands, *a*. Oriental. morgenochtend, *adv*. to-morrow morning. ·morgenrood, no pl., *n.n.* (red of) dawn. ·morgenschemering, *n*. dawn. morgenstond, *n*. early morn(ing). *de* ~ *heeft goud in de mond*, the early bird catches the worm.

mori·aan, -ianen, *n*. blackamoor.

·mormel, -s, *n.n.* ugly creature. ·mormeldier, *n.n.* marmot.

·morrelen, *v.i.* to fumble. ~ *aan*, to fumble with.

·morren, mor, *v.i.* to grumble, murmur. ·morsboel, no pl., *n*. mess (*dirt*). ·morsdood, -dode, *a*. stone-dead. ·morsen, *v.i.* to make a mess. ¶*v.t.* to spill, slop. ·morsig, *a*. messy, grubby. ·morspot, -tten, *n*. muckworm (*fig.*).

·mortel, no pl., *n*. mortar (*substance*). ·mortelbak, -kken, *n*. hod. mor·tier, *n*. mortar (*vessel; fire-arm*).

·morzel, -s, *n.n.* smithereens.

mos, -ssen, *n.n.* moss. ·mosachtig, *a.*, ·mossig, *a*. mossy.

mos·kee, -keeën, *n*. mosque.

Mos·kovisch, *a*. Muscovite.

·mossel, -s. *n*. mussel. ·mosselvanger, *n.*

mussel-fisher. ·mosselvangst, no pl., n. mussel-fishing.
most, no pl., n. must (wine).
·mosterd, no pl., n. mustard. bruine ~, black mustard; gele ~, white mustard; hij weet waar Abraham de ~ haalt, he is in the know; ~ na de maaltijd, too late; het is dure ~, it is expensive. ·mosterdzuur, no pl., n.n. mustard pickles, piccalilli.
mot, -tten, n. moth. de ~ zit er in, it is moth-eaten or (fig.) the rot is setting in; de ~ in de maag, a gnawing in the stomach; ~ hebben, to quarrel.
·motie, -s, n. resolution (at meeting). een ~ aannemen, to pass a resolution; een ~ indienen, to bring forward a resolution; een ~ van vertrouwen, a vote of confidence; een ~ van afkeuring, a vote of censure; een ~ van wantrouwen, a vote of non-confidence. mo·tief, -ven, n.n. motive; motif. moti·veren, -veer, v.t. to motivate. moti·vering, n. motivation. ·motor, -s or -en, n. motor. ·motorpech, no pl., n. engine trouble. ·motorrijtuig, n.n. motor-vehicle.
·motregen, -s, n. drizzle. ·motregenen, v.i. to drizzle. ·mottig, a. moth-eaten; pock-marked; (coll.) awful.
mousse·line, -s, n. muslin.
mout, no pl., n.n. malt. ·moutbak, -kken, n. malt-bin. ·mouteest, n. malt-kiln. ·mouten, v.t. to malt. ·mouter, -s, n. maltster. moute·rij, n. malt-house.
mouw, n. sleeve. ergens een ~ aan passen, to find a way out; iemand iets op de ~ spelden, to make a person believe tall stories; iets uit de ~ schudden, to produce something without effort.
mud, -dden, n. or n.n. hectolitre.
muf, -ffe, a. musty.
·muffeldier, n.n. moufflon.
·muffig, a. musty. ·muffigheid, no pl., n. mustiness.
mug, -ggen, n. gnat, midge. ·muggebeet, -beten, n. gnat-bite. ·muggenziften, v.i. to split hairs. ·muggenzifter, -s, n. hair-splitter. muggenzifte·rij, n. hair-splitting.
muil, n. mule (slipper); mouth, snout. ·muilband, n. muzzle. ·muilbanden, v.t. to muzzle; to gag. ·muildier, n.n. mule. ·muilezel, -s, n. mule, hinny. ·muildrijver, -s, n. muleteer. ·muilkorf, -ven, n. muzzle. ·muilpeer, -peren, n. box on the ear.
muis, -zen, n. mouse; ball of the thumb. ·muisje, -s, n.n. little mouse. dat ~ zal een staartje hebben, you will hear more of this; pl. also: ~s, sugared caraway seeds. ·muiskleurig, a. mouse-coloured.
·muiteling, n. mutineer. ·muiten, v.i. to mutiny. ¶no pl., n.n. aan het ~ slaan, to mutiny. ·muiter, -s, n. mutineer. muite·rij, n. mutiny. ·muitziek, a. seditious, mutinous. ·muitzucht, n. mutinous spirit. muit·zuchtig, a. See muitziek.

muizen, muis, v.i. to mouse. het muist al wat van katten komt, what is bred in the bone will out in the flesh. ·muizenissen, pl. only, n. ~ in het hoofd hebben, to have lots of small worries. ·muizenkoren, no pl., n.n. rye-grass. ·muizentarwe, no pl., n. rat poison. ·muizenval, -llen, n. mouse-trap. ·muizenvanger, -s, n. mouser. ·muizerd, -s, n. buzzard.
mul, -lle, a. loose, sandy. ¶no pl., n. loose earth. ·mulder, -s, n. miller.
·Mulo, -'s, N. Central school.
·mummelen, v.i. to mumble.
·mummie, -s, n. mummy (corpse).
·München, n. N. Munich.
mu·nitie, no pl., n. munitions; ammunition.
·munster, -s, n.n., ·munsterkerk, n. minster.
munt, n. coin; coinage; mint. de Munt, the Mint; ~ slaan, to coin money; ~ slaan uit, to make capital out of; met gelijke ~ betalen, to pay back in a person's own coin; voor goede ~ aannemen, to take for gospel; kruis of ~, heads or tails. ¶no pl., n. mint (plant). ·muntafval, no pl., n. scissel. ·munteenheid, -heden, n. monetary unit(y). ·munten, v.t. to coin, mint. ~ op, to aim at; hij heeft het op mij gemunt, he's got it in for me. ·munter, -s, n. minter. valse ~, coiner. ·muntgasmeter, -s, n. penny (or shilling)-in-the-slot gasmeter. ·muntkabinet, -tten, n.n. numismatic cabinet. ·muntloon, -lonen, n.n. mintage. ·muntkenner, -s, n. numismatist. ·muntmeter, -s, n. slot-meter. ·muntspecie, -ciën, n. specie. ·muntstempel, -s, n. coin-stamp, die. ·muntstuk, -kken, n.n. coin, piece (of money). ·muntvoet, n. monetary standard. ·muntwezen, no pl., n.n. coinage, monetary system.
·murik, -kken, n. chickweed.
·murmelen, v.i. to murmur, purl. murmu·reren, -mureer, v.i. to murmur, grumble.
murw, a. soft, tender. ~ slaan, to beat to a jelly (fig.).
mus, -ssen, n. sparrow. zich blij maken met een dode ~, to rejoice foolishly over little.
musi·ceren, -ceer, v.i. to make music. musi·cienne, -s, n. musician (female). ·musicus, -ci, n. musician (male).
mus·kaat, -katen, n. nutmeg; muscadel. mus·kaatbloem, no pl., n. mace. mus·kaatboom, -bomen, n. nutmeg(-tree). mus·kaatnoot, -noten, n. nutmeg. mus·kaatwijn, no pl., n. muscatel (wine).
mus·ket, -tten, n.n. matchlock, musket. muske·tier, -s, n. musketeer.
mus·kiet, -s, n. mosquito.
·muskus, no pl., n. musk. ·muskusachtig, a. musky. ·muskusdier, n.n. musk-deer. ·muskuskat, -tten, n. civet (-cat). ·muskusrat, -tten, n. musk-rat, musquash.
·mussenei, -eieren, n.n. sparrow's egg. ·mussenhagel, no pl., n. small shot.

mu·tatie, -s, *n.* mutation; changes in staff.
muts, *n.* bonnet; woollen cap, tam-o'-shanter; (tea-)cosy. *met de* ~ *naar iets gooien,* to make a shot at something; *daar staat me de* ~ *niet naar,* I am not in the mood for it. **·mutsaard, -s,** *n.,* **·mutserd, -s,** *n.* faggot.
muur, muren, *n.* wall. *met het hoofd tegen de* ~ *lopen,* to knock one's head against a brick wall. ¶no pl., *n.* chickweed. **·muuranker, -s,** *n.n.* wall-tie, brace. **·muurbloem,** *n.* wallflower. **·muurkruid,** no pl., *n.n.* chickweed. **·muurkruiper, -s,** *n.* wall-creeper. **·muurschildering,** *n.* mural painting. **·muurvaren, -s,** *n.* wall-rue; stone-fern. **·muurvast,** *adv.* as firm as a rock. **·muurzwaluw,** *n.* swift; martin.
·muze, -n, *n.* muse.
·Muzelman, -nnen, *n.* Mussulman.
mu·ziek, no pl., *n.* music; band (*military*). *op de* ~, to the music; *op* ~ *zetten,* to set to music; ~ *maken,* to have music. **mu·ziekavondje, -s,** *n.n.* musical evening. **mu·ziekgezelschap, -ppen,** *n.n.* band, musical society. **mu·ziekhandel, -s,** *n.* music shop. **mu·ziekinstrument,** *n.n.* musical instrument. **mu·ziekkorps,** *n.n.* band (*military*). **mu·ziekstander, -s,** *n.* music-stand. **mu·ziektent,** *n.* bandstand. **muzi·kaal, -kale,** *a.* musical. **muzi·kant,** *n.* bandsman, musician.
mys·terie, -s *or* **-riën,** *n.n.* mystery. **mys·teriespel,** *n.n.* mystery, miracle play. **mysteri·eus, -ze,** *a.* mysterious.
·mythe, -n, *n.* myth.

N

na, *prep.* after; on, after. ¶*adv.* near; closely. *op vijf* ~, all but five; *te* ~ *komen,* to offend; *bij lange* ~ *niet,* not by a long chalk; *voor en* ~, time and again.
naad, naden, *n.* seam; suture. *zich uit de* ~ *werken,* to work oneself to death (*fig.*). **·naadje, -s,** *n.n.* little seam. *het* ~ *van de kous willen weten,* he wants to know every detail. **naadloos, -loze,** *a.* seamless, weldless.
naaf, -naven, *n.* nave, hub.
·naaidoos, -dozen, *n.* work-basket. **·naaien,** *v.t. & v.i.* to sew. **·naaikrans,** *n.* sewing-bee. **·naaister, -s,** *n.* seamstress; needle-woman. **·naaiwerk,** no pl., *n.n.* sewing, needlework.
naakt, *a.* naked, bare. ~*e feiten,* bald facts; ~*e figuur,* nude. **·naaktheid,** no pl., *n.* nakedness, nudity. **·naaktloper, -s,** *n.* nudist; Adamite. **·naaktzadig,** *a.* gymnospermous.
naald, -en, *n.* needle. **·naaldboom, -bomen,** *n.* conifer. **·naaldbos, -ssen,** *n.n.* pine-forest. **·naaldenkoker, -s** *n.* needle-case.

·naaldhout, no pl., *n.n.* wood *or* timber of coniferous trees. **·naaldvis, -ssen,** *n.* pipe-fish. **·naaldvormig,** *a.* needle-shaped.
naam, namen, *n.* name. *het heeft geen* ~, it is awful; *op mijn* ~, in my name; *uit mijn* ~, from me, in my name; *van* ~ *kennen,* to know by name; *met name noemen,* to mention by name; *met name,* particularly; *ten name van,* in the name of. **·naamcijfer, -s,** *n.n.* monogram, cipher. **·naamgenoot, -noten,** *n.* namesake. **·naamkaartje, -s,** *n.n.* (visiting-)card. **naamloos, -loze,** *a.* nameless, anonymous. *naamloze vennootschap,* limited company. **·naampje, -s,** *n.n.* name, pet name. **·naamval, -llen,** *n.* case (*grammatical*). **·naamwoord,** *n.n.* noun. *bijvoeglijk* ~, adjective; *zelfstandig* ~, noun.
·naäpen, aap na, *v.t.s.* to ape, imitate. **·naäper, -s,** *n.* mimic. **·naäperij,** *n.* aping.
naar, nare, *a.* disagreeable; horrid. *je wordt er* ~ *van,* it makes one feel sick. ¶*prep.* to, towards, for; according to; at; of; in; after. ~ *beneden,* downstairs *or* downwards *or* down; ~ *boven,* upstairs *or* upwards *or* up; ~ *huis gaan,* to go home; ~ *iemand toe,* up to a person. ¶*c.* ~ *men zegt,* it is said, as they say. **naar·geestig,** *a.* mournful, melancholy. **naar·geestigheid,** no pl., *n.* melancholy, gloom. **naarge·lang,** *prep.* according to. ¶*c.* as. **·naarheid, -heden,** *n.* unpleasantness. **naar·mate,** *c.* as.
·naarstig, *a.* (stilted) industrious. **·naarstigheid,** no pl., *n.* (stilted) diligence.
naast, *a.* nearest; next, next door. *de* ~*e toekomst,* the near future; *de* ~*e weg,* the shortest way. ¶*adv.* nearest. ¶*prep.* beside, next (to), alongside. *hier* ~, next door; *er* ~ *zijn,* to be mistaken. **·naastbestaande, -n,** *n.* next of kin. **naast·bijzijnd,** *a.* nearest. **·naaste,** *n.n. ten* ~ *bij,* approximately. ¶*n.* fellow-creature, neighbour. **·naasten,** *v.t.* to expropriate. **·naastenliefde,** no pl., *n.* love of one's neighbour. **naastgelegen,** *a.* nearest. **·naasting,** *n.* expropriation; seizure.
·na-avond, *n.* latter part of the evening. **·nabauwen,** *v.t.s.* to repeat parrotlike. **·nabehandeling,** *n.* after-treatment. **·nabestaande, -n,** *n.* relative. **·nabestellen,** *bestel na, v.t.s.* to give a repeat order. **·nabetalen, betaal na,** *v.i.s.* to pay afterwards. **·nabetrachting,** *n.* afterthought.
na·bij, *prep.* near; close to *or* by. ¶*adv. van* ~, from close by, closely. ¶*a.* near. **na·bijgelegen,** *a.* neighbouring, near by. **na·bijheid,** no pl., *n.* neighbourhood, vicinity. **na·bijkomen,** *v.t.s.* to approach, come near to.
·nablaffen, blaf na, *v.t.s.* to bark after. **·nablijven, blijf na,** *v.i.s., str.* to stay behind. **·nabloeden,** *v.i.s.* to go on bleeding. **·nabloeien,** *v.i.s.* to have a second bloom.

·nabootsen, *v.t.s.* to imitate. ·nabootsing, *n.* imitation. na·burig, *a.* neighbouring, near by. ·nabuur, -buren, *n.* neighbour. ·nabuurschap, no pl., *n.n.* neighbourhood.
nacht, *n.* night (*not evening*). de helé ~, all night (long); *bij* ~ *en ontij(d)*, at an unseasonable hour; *in de* ~, during the night; *in het holst van de* ~, at dead of night; *van* ~, last night *or* to-night. *des* ~*s or 's* ~*s*, at night. ·nachtasyl, *n.n.* night-shelter (*for down and outs*). ·nachtbezoek, *n.n.* nocturnal visit. ·nacht-braken, -braak, *v.i.* to turn night into day. ·nachtbraker, -s, *n.* reveller. ·nachtdienst, *n.* night-service; night-duty. ·nachtegaal, -galen, *n.* nightingale. ·nachtegaalsslag, *n.* jug of nightingale. ·nachtelijk, *a.* nocturnal, nightly. ~ *uur*, hour of night. ·nachtevening, *n.* equinox. ·nachtgoed, no pl., *n.n.* night-clothes. ·nachtjapon, -nnen, *n.* night-gown. ·nachtkaars, *n.* (bedroom) candle. *als een* ~ *uitgaan*, to fizzle out. ·nachtkastje, -s, *n.n.* night-stool, commode. ·nachtleger, -s, *n.n.* bivouac. ·nachtlogies, -zen, *n.n.* lodging. ·nachtmerrie, -s, *n.* nightmare. ·nachtpitje, -s, *n.n.* night-light. ·nachtpon, -nnen, *n.* See nachtjapon. ·nachtrust, no pl., *n.* night's rest. ·nachtschade, -n, *n.* nightshade. ·nachtschuit, *n.* night-boat. *met de* ~ *komen*, to be late. ·nachtslot, *n.n.* double-lock. *op het* ~ *doen*, to double-lock. ·nachtuil, *n.* screech-owl. ·nachtuiltje, -s, *n.n.* (night-)moth. ·nachtverblijf, -ven, *n.n.* accommodation for the night. ·nachtvlinder, -s, *n.* (night-) moth. ·nachtwaak, -waken, *n.* night-watch. ·nachtwacht, *n.* night-watchman; Midnight Round. ·nachtwaker, -s, *n.* night-watchman. ·nachtzoen, *n.* good-night kiss. ·nachtzwaluw, *n.* nightjar.
·nacijferen, *v.t.s.* to check, verify. na·dat, *c.* after. ·nadeel, -delen, *n.n.* disadvantage, drawback. *ten nadele van*, at the expense of, to the detriment of. na·delig, *a.* detrimental, harmful, prejudicial. ·naden-ken, *v.i.s.*, *irr.* to reflect, think. ~ *over*, to reflect upon, think about. ¶no pl., *n.n.* reflection, consideration. *bij* ~, on consideration; *iemand tot* ~ *stemmen*, to give a person food for thought; *zonder* ~, thoughtlessly. na·denkend, *a.* thoughtful, reflective. ·nader, *a.* nearer; further. *iets* ~*s*, further particulars; *bij* ~ *inzien*, on second thoughts; *tot* ~ *order*, until further notice. ¶*adv.* nearer, more closely *or* fully. nader·bij, *adv.* nearer, more closely. ·naderen, *v.i.* to approach, draw near. ¶*v.t.* to approach, draw near to. nader·hand, *adv.* afterwards, later on. ·nadering, *n.* approach. ·naderingswerken, pl. only, *n.n.* approaches (*military*). ·nadezen, *adv.* hereafter. na·dien, *adv.* thereafter. ·nadoen, doe na, *v.t.s.*, *irr.* to imitate. ·nadorst, no pl., *n.* afterthirst.

·nadraven, draaf na, *v.t.s.* to trot after. ·nadruk, no pl., *n.* emphasis, stress; reprint, pirated edition. *de* ~ *leggen op*, to emphasize; *met* ~, emphatically; ~ *verboden*, copyright reserved. ·na-drukkelijk, *a.* emphatically. ·nadrukken, druk na, *v.t.s.* to reprint, pirate. ·nagaan, ga na, *v.t.s.*, *irr.* to follow, keep an eye on; to trace, ascertain. ·nagalm, *n.* reverbera-tion. ·nagalmen, *v.i.s.* to reverberate. ·nagapen, gaap na, *v.t.s.* to gape after. ·nageboorte, -n, *n.* afterbirth. ·nagedachte, -n, *n.* afterthought. ·nagedachtenis, no pl., *n.* memory, remembrance. *ter* ~ *van*, in memory of.
·nagel, -s, *n.* nail (*finger, etc.*); claw; (large) nail, rivet. ·nagelbloem, *n.* gillyflower. ·nagelboom, -bomen, *n.* clove-tree. ·nagel-borstel, -s, *n.* nail-brush. ·nagelen, *v.t.* to nail. ·nagelhout, no pl., *n.n.* clove-wood. ·nagelkaas, no pl., *n.* clove cheese. ·nagel-kruid, no pl., *n.n.* avens. ·nagelvast, *a.* fixed with nails.
·nagemaakt, *a.* artificial, imitation. nage-·noeg, *a.* almost, nearly, all but. ·nage-recht, *n.n.* dessert. ·nageslacht, no pl., *n.n.* posterity; descendants. ·nageven, geef na, *v.t.s.*, *str.* to finish by saying, admit. ·nagewas, no pl., *n.n.* after-crop. ·na-gloeien, *v.i.s.* to continue glowing. *gloeien niet na*, no afterglow. ·nagooien, *v.t.s.* to throw after. ·naherfst, no pl., *n.* late autumn. ·nahollen, hol na, *v.t.s.* to tear after. ·nahouden, *v.t.s.*, *irr.* to keep in (*school boy*). *er op* ~, to keep.
na·ief, -ve, *a.* naïve, ingenuous. naïve·teit, no pl., *n.* naïveté.
·naijver, no pl., *n.* jealousy; emulation. na·ijverig, *a.* jealous, envious. ·najaar, -jaren, *n.n.* autumn.
na·jade, -n, *n.* naiad.
·najagen, jaag na, *v.t.* & *v.t.s.*, *str.* to pursue, chase *or* hunt after. ·najouwen, *v.t.s.* to hoot after.
·naken, naak, *v.i.* (*poet.*) to approach, draw near.
·nakend, *a.* naked.
·nakijken, *v.t.s.*, *str.* to look after, watch; to correct. ·naklank, *n.* echo. ·naklinken, *v.i.s.*, *str.* to carry on (*of sound*). ·na-komeling, *n.* descendant. ·nakomelingschap, no pl., *n.* offspring, issue, progeny. ·nakomen, *v.i.s.*, *irr.* to come afterwards. ¶*v.t.s.*, *irr.* to follow; to fulfil, perform, comply with. ·nakomertje, -s, *n.n.* late-comer (*child*). ·nakoming, *n.* fulfilment; compliance. ·nakroost, no pl., *n.n.* progeny, issue. ·nalaten, laat na, *v.t.s.*, *str.* to leave behind (*on death*); to neglect, omit. *ik kon niet* ~ . . ., I could not help . . . ·na·latenschap, -ppen, *n.* inheri-tance, estate. na·latig, *a.* negligent, remiss. na·latigheid, -heden, *n.* negligence, remiss-ness. ·nalating, *n.* omission. ·naleven,

leef na, *v.t.s.* to observe; to live up to. naleving, *n.* observance, fulfilment. nalezen, lees na, *v.t.s.*, *str.* to read over; to glean. nalopen, loop na, *v.t.s.*, *str.* to run after. ¶*v.i.s.*, *str.* to be slow (*timepiece*). naloper, -s, *n.* follower. namaak, no pl., *n.* imitation. namaaksel, -s, *n.n.* imitation, fake. namaken, maak na, *v.t.s.* to copy, imitate.

name, *n. See* naam. namelijk, *adv.* namely. ¶*c.* for, because. nameloos, -loze, *a.* nameless. namens, *prep.* on behalf of.

Namen, *n. N.* Namur.

nameten, meet na, *v.t.s.*, *str.* to measure again. na·middag, *n.* afternoon. *des ~s* or *'s ~s*, in the afternoon.

nan·king, no pl., *n.n.* nankeen.

naogen, oog na, *v.t.s.* to eye. naoogst, *n.* after-crop. na-oorlogs, *a.* post-war.

nap, -ppen, *n.* cup.

napleiten, *v.t.s.* to argue (*about settled matter*). napluizen, pluis na, *v.t.s.*, *str.* to investigate carefully.

Napole·ontisch, *a.* Napoleonic.

napraten, praat na, *v.i.s.* to imitate (*in speech*). napret, no pl., *n.* fun after the others have left.

nar, -rren, *n.* fool, jester.

narcis, -ssen, *n.* narcissus; daffodil.

nar·cose, no pl., *n.* narcosis. *onder ~*, under an anaesthetic.

narede, -denen, *n.* epilogue. narekenen, *v.t.s.* to check, verify; to calculate.

narigheid, -heden, *n.* trouble(s), unpleasantness.

narijden, *v.t.s.*, *str.* to ride *or* drive after. *iemand ~*, to spur someone on. naroepen, *v.t.s.*, *str.* to call after. naschilderen, *v.t.s.* to copy (*painting*). naschrift, *n.n.* postscript. naschrijven, schrijf na, *v.t.s.*, *str.* to copy (*writing*). naslaan, sla na, *v.t.s.*, *irr.* to look up. nasleep, no pl., *n.* train, aftermath. nasmaak, no pl., *n.* aftertaste, taste. naspel. no pl., *n.n.* afterplay; sequel. naspelen, speel na, *v.t.s.* to play after; to return (*in card game*). naspellen, spel na, *v.t.s.* to spell after. naspeuren, *v.t.s.* to detect, investigate. naspeuring, *n.* investigation, detection. nastaren, staar na, *v.t.s.* to gaze after. nastreven, streef na, *v.t.s.* to strive after, pursue.

nat, -tte, *a.* wet; damp, moist. *~ maken*, to wet, moisten; *~ van*, wet with; *hij is een broeder van de natte gemeente*, he lifts his elbow. ¶no pl., *n.n.* wet, liquid. *het is één pot ~*, it is all the same. natheid, no pl., *n.* wetness.

natafelen, *v.i.s.* to talk after dinner.

natie, -s, *n.* nation; Jewish nation. nationaliteit, *n.* nationality.

natrium, no pl., *n.n.* sodium.

nattig, *a.* wettish. nattigheid, no pl., *n.* wet, damp. *~ voelen*, to smell a rat.

na·tura, no pl., *n. in ~*, in kind. natu·raliën,

pl. only, *n.* natural produce. na·ture, *n. See* natuur. natu·rel, -llen, *n.* native, aboriginal. na·tuur, no pl., *n.* nature; scenery. *in de vrije ~*, in the open air; *naar de ~*, from nature. ¶-ren, *n.* nature. *van nature*, by nature. na·tuurboter, no pl., *n.* butter. na·tuurdrift, *n.* instinct. na·tuurgetrouw, *a.* true to nature. na·tuurhistoricus, -ci, *n.* naturalist. na·tuurkennis, no pl., *n.* natural science. na·tuurkunde, no pl., *n.* physics. natuur·kundig, *a.* physical. na·tuurlijk, *a.* natural. ¶*adv.* naturally; of course. natuur·lijker·wijze, *adv.* naturally. na·tuurlijkheid, no pl., *n.* naturalness, simplicity. na·tuurschoon, no pl., *n.n.* beautiful scenery. na·tuurspeling, *n.* freak of nature. na·tuurverschijnsel, -s, *n.n.* natural phenomenon. na·tuurwol, no pl., *n.* native wool.

nauw, *a.* narrow, tight; close. *~ van geweten*, scrupulous or conscientious. ¶*adv.* narrowly, tightly. *~ verwant*, closely related; *het niet ~ nemen*, not to be very particular; *~ merkbaar*, scarcely noticeable. ¶no pl., *n.* Straits. *~ van Calais*, Straits of Dover; *in het ~ zitten*, to be in a tight corner; *in het ~ drijven*, to press hard, bring to bay. nauwelijks, *adv.* hardly, scarcely. nauwge·zet, -tte, *a.* scrupulous, meticulous. nauwge·zetheid, no pl., *n.* punctuality, conscientiousness. nauwheid, -heden, *n.* narrowness, tightness. nauw·keurig, *a.* accurate, exact. *~ onderzoek*, close examination. nauw·keurigheid, -heden, *n.* accuracy. nauw·lettend, *a.* accurate, observant. nauw·lettendheid, no pl., *n.* accuracy. nauwte, -n, *n.* straits, narrows; defile.

navel, -s, *n.* navel. navelstreng, *n.* navelstring, umbilical cord.

nave·nant, *adv.* in proportion.

navergadering, *n.* after-meeting. navertellen, vertel na, *v.t.s.* to repeat. naverwant, *a.* closely related. naverwantschap, no pl., *n.* relationship. na·volgbaar, -bare, *a.* imitable. navolgen, *v.t.s.* to follow, imitate. navolgens·waardig, *a.* worth following. navolger, -s, *n.* follower, imitator. navolging, *n.* imitation. *ter ~ dienen*, to serve as a model. navorsen, *v.t.s.* to investigate. navorser, -s, *n.* investigator. navorsing, *n.* investigation, exploration. navraag, no pl., *n.* inquiries; demand. *bij ~*, on inquiry; *~ doen naar*, to inquire after; *er is veel ~ naar*, it is in great demand. navragen, vraag na, *v.t.s.*, *str.* to inquire. naweeën, pl. only, *n.n.* after-pains, after effects. nawegen, weeg na, *v.t.s.*, *str.* to weigh again. nawerken, *v.i.s.* to have after-effects. nawerking, *n.* after-effects. nawinter, -s, *n.* late winter. nazaat, -zaten, *n.* descendant. nazeggen, zeg na, *v.t.s.*, *irr.* to repeat, say after. nazenden, *v.t.s.*, *str.* to send after *or* on.

~ *s.v.p.*, please forward. ·**nazien, zie na,**
v.t.s., *irr.* to follow (*with eyes*); to examine,
check; to correct; to overhaul. ·**nazitten,**
zit na, *v.t.s.*, *str.* to pursue. ·**nazoeken,**
v.t.s. to look up (*in record*). ·**nazomer, -s,**
n. late summer.
neces·saire, -s, *n.* housewife (*sewing outfit*).
·**neder,** *adv.* (*stilted*) down. *See* **neer.** ¶*prefix.*
low, lower; down. *See* **neer.** ·**nederdalen,**
daal naar, *v.t.s.* (*stilted*) to descend.
·**Nederduits,** *a.* Low German. ·**nederig,** *a.*
humble; lowly. ·**nederlaag, -lagen,** *n.*
defeat. ·**Nederland,** *n.N.* Holland, the
Netherlands. *de* ~*en*, the Low Countries.
·**Nederlander, -s,** *n.* Dutchman. ·**Neder-**
lands, *a.* Dutch. *de* ~ *Hervormde Kerk,*
the Dutch State Church. ·**nederzetten,**
zet neder, zich, *v.r.s.* to settle (*of settler*).
·**nederzetting,** *n.* settlement (*of people*).
nee, *adv.* no. ~ *maar!*, oh, but *or* I say!;
wel ~!, certainly not! ¶no pl., *n.n.* no.
neef, neven, *n.* cousin (*male*); nephew.
neen, *adv.* (*stilted*) *See* **nee.**
neep, nepen, *n.* pinch. ·**neepjesmuts,** *n.*
mob-cap.
neer, *adv.* down. ¶*prefix.* down. ·**neer-**
buigend, *a.* condescending. ·**neerdoen,**
doe neer, *v.t.s.*, *irr.* to let down (*object*).
·**neerhaal, -halen,** *n.* down-stroke. ·**neer-**
halen, haal neer, *v.t.s.* to fetch down, pull
down. ·**neerkomen,** *v.i.s.*, *irr.* to come
down, descend; to land, alight (*from the*
air). ~ *op*, to amount to, boil down to.
·**neerleggen, leg neer,** *v.t.s.*, *irr.* to lay
down, put down. *zijn ambt* ~, to resign
from office; *een hert* ~, to shoot a stag;
de kroon ~, to abdicate. ¶*zich* ~, *v.r.s.*,
irr. to lie down. *zich* ~ *bij*, to put up
with, acquiesce in. ·**neerliggen, lig neer,**
v.i.s., *irr.* to lie down. ·**neerslaan, sla neer,**
v.t.s., *irr.* to knock down, strike down.
de ogen ~, to cast down one's eyes; *het*
stof ~, to lay the dust. ¶*v.i.s.*, *irr.* to
precipitate (*chemistry*). ·**neer·slachtig,** *a.*
depressed, downcast. ·**neer·slachtigheid,**
no pl., *n.* dejection. ·**neerslag,** no pl., *n.*
downfall (*of rain, snow, etc.*); precipitation,
deposit. ·**neerstorten,** *v.i.s.* to crash down;
to crash. ·**neervlijen, zich,** *v.r.s.* to lie
down, snuggle up.
neet, neten, *n.* nit.
nega·tief, -ve, *a.* negative. ¶*adv.* in the
negative. **ne·geeren,** *v.t.* to ignore, cut.
·**negen,** *num.* nine. ¶**-s,** *n.* nine. ·**negendaags,**
a. nine days. ·**negende,** *a.* ninth. *ten* ~,
in the ninth place. ·**negenderlei,** *a.* of
nine kinds. ·**negenen,** *num. bij* ~, just on
nine; *in* ~, into nine, *met hun* ~, the
nine of them; *met ons* ~, the nine of us;
met zijn ~, with eight others; *de trein*
van ~, the nine o'clock train. ·**negen-**
entwintig, *num.* twenty-nine. ·**negenmaal,**
adv. nine times. ·**negenoog, -nogen,** *n.*
lamprey; carbuncle, furuncle. ·**negental,**

·**lien,** *n.n.* nine. *een* ~, eight or nine.
·**negentig,** *num.* ninety. ·**negentiger,** *a.*
in de ~ *jaren*, in the 'nineties. ¶**-s,** *n.*
nonagenarian. ·**negentigste,** *a.* ninetieth.
·**negenvoud,** *n.n.* multiple of nine. ·**negen-**
voudig, *a.* ninefold. ·**negenwerf,** *adv.*
(*stilted*) nine times.
·**neger, -s,** *n.* negro. ·**negeren,** *v.t.* to bully.
ne·geren, -geer, *v.t.* to ignore. **nege·rij,**
n. See **negorij.** ·**nege·rin, -nnen,** *n.* negress.
·**negerkoren,** no pl., *n.* millet. ·**neger-**
schip, -schepen, *n.n.* slaver (*ship*). **negor·ij,**
n. negro village; backwater (*fig.*).
ne·gotie, -s, *n.* trade, business.
·**neigen,** *v.t.* to decline (*sun*). *geneigd zijn,*
to be inclined. ·**neiging,** *n.* inclination,
leaning(s), tendency.
nek, -kken, *n.* nape; (*coll.*) neck. *iemand met*
de ~ *aanzien*, to turn one's back on a
person, cold-shoulder a person; *iemand de*
~ *omdraaien*, to wring a person's neck.
·**nekken, nek.** *v.t.* to break the neck of.
·**nekkramp,** no pl., *n.* spotted fever;
cerebro-spinal meningitis. ·**nekslag,** *n.*
death-blow. ·**nekvel,** no pl., *n.n.* scruff of
the neck.
·**nemen, neem,** *v.t.*, *str.* to take; to capture.
iets op zich ~, to undertake something;
tot zich ~, to take (*food*); *iemand er tussen*
~, to play a joke on someone; *het er goed*
van ~, to do oneself well.
nerf, -ven, *n.* vein, nerve (*of leaf*); grain (*of*
wood).
nergens, *adv.* nowhere. ~ *om geven*, to
care for nothing; ~ *toe dienen*, to have no
purpose; ~ *goed voor*, good-for-nothing.
·**Nergenshuizen,** *n.N.* nowhere.
·**nering,** *n.* (retail) trade; custom. ~ *doen,*
to keep a shop. ·**neringdoende, -n,** *n.*
tradesman, shopkeeper.
ner·veus, -ze, *a.* nervous. **nervosi·teit,** no
pl., *n.* nervousness.
nest, *n.n.* nest; litter, nest; (*vulg.*) bed; small
place; horrid girl. ·**en uithalen,** to go
birds'-nesting. ·**nestelen,** *v.i.* to nestle;
to make one's nest. *zich ergens* ~, to
ensconce oneself. ·**nesthaar, -haren,** *n.n.*
first hair, down. ·**nestig,** *a.* snappy.
·**nestkuiken, -s,** *n.n.* nestling. ·**nestveren,**
pl. only, *n.* first feathers, down. ·**nestvol,**
nesten vol. *n.n.* nestful.
net, -tten, *n.n.* net; rack (*in railway carriage*);
network; toils, snare(s). *achter het* ~
vissen, to fish before the net; *in het* ~
vallen, to be trapped; *zijn netten spannen,*
to spread one's nets. ¶**-tte,** *a.* neat, tidy;
decent, respectable. ¶no pl., *n.n.* fair
copy. *in het* ~ *schrijven*, to make a fair
copy. ¶*adv.* neatly, tidily; decently,
respectably; just; precisely. ~ *op tijd,*
just in time; ~ *zo lang tot*, until; *daar* ~,
just now.
·**netel, -s,** *n.* nettle. ·**netelachtig,** *a.* urtica-
ceous. ·**neteldier,** *n.n.* pl. coelentera.

neteldoek, no pl., *n.n.* muslin. **neteldoeks,** *a.* (of) muslin. **netelig,** *a.* thorny, ticklish. **netelkoorts,** no pl., *n.,* **netelroos,** no pl., *n.* erysipelas, St. Anthony's fire.

netjes, *adv.* neatly; nicely. **netmaag, -magen,** *n.* reticulum. **netschrift,** *n.n.* fair-copy book. **nettenboeter, -s,** *n.* net-repairer. **nettenboetster, -s,** *n.* net-repairer (*female*). **nettenbreier, -s,** *n.* net-maker. **nettenbreister, -s,** *n.* net-maker (*female*). **nettenknopen, knoop netten,** *v.i.s.* to net. **netto,** *a.* & *adv.* net. **nettowinst,** no pl., *n.* net profits. **netvleugelig,** *a.* neuropterous. **netvlies, -zen,** *n.n.* retina. **netvormig,** *a.* reticulate. **netwerk,** no pl., *n.n.* network.

Neurenberg, *n. N.* Nuremberg.

neuken, *v.t.* (*coll.*) to bash.

neuriën, -rie, *v.i.* to hum (*sing*).

neus, -zen, *n.* nose; nozzle; toe-cap. *een wassen ~,* a blind, pretext; *wie zijn ~ schendt, schendt zijn aangezicht,* it's an ill bird that fouls its own nest; *de ~ ophalen voor,* to turn up one's nose at; *niet verder zien dan zijn ~ lang is,* not to see beyond one's own nose; *het gaat zijn ~ voorbij,* it is not for him; *iemand iets aan de ~ hangen,* to make a person believe an improbable tale; *iemand bij de ~ hebben,* to pull a person's leg; *iets langs zijn ~ weg zeggen,* to mention something just like that; *overal met zijn ~ bij zijn,* to poke one's nose into everything; *iemand iets onder de ~ wrijven,* to rub something into someone; *op zijn ~ kijken,* to look disappointed; *vlak voor zijn ~,* under his very nose. **neusaap, -sapen,** *n.* nose-ape, proboscis-monkey. **neusbeen, -deren,** *n.n.* nasal bone. **neusbloeding,** *n.* nose-bleed. **neusgat,** *n.n.* nostril. **neusholte, -n,** *n.* nasal cavity. **neushoorn, -s,** *n.* rhinoceros, **neushoornvogel, -s,** *n.* hornbill. **neusje, -s,** *n.n.* little nose. *het ~ van de zalm,* the pick of the bunch, the choicest piece. **neuswijs, -ze,** *a.* priggish, conceited. **neuzen, neus,** *v.i.* to nose.

nevel, -s, *n.* mist, haze. **nevelachtig,** *a.* misty, hazy; nebulous. **nevelvlek, -kken,** *n.* nebula.

nevengeschikt, *a.* co-ordinate. **nevenman, -nnen,** *n.* neighbour, next man (in row). **nevens,** *prep.* besides, next to. **nevenschikkend,** *a.* co-ordinate.

nicht, *n.* cousin (*female*); niece.

niemand, *pron.* nobody, no one. *~ niet?,* not anyone? **niemandsland,** no pl., *n.n.* no-man's-land. **niemen·dal,** *adv.* not at all. ¶no pl., *n.n.* nothing at all. **niemen·dalletje, -s,** *n.n.* a mere nothing.

nier, *n.* kidney. **nierontsteking,** *n.* nephritis. **niersteen, -stenen,** *n.* renal calculus. **niervet,** no pl., *n.n.* suet. **niervormig,** *a.* kidney-shaped. **nierziekte, -n,** *n.* kidney trouble.

nieskruid, no pl., *n.n.,* **nieswortel,** no pl., *n.* hellebore.

niet, *adv.* not. *~ beter,* not or no better; *~ eens,* not even. ¶no pl., *n.n.* nothing, nought; blank. *in het ~ verzinken,* to dwindle into nothingness; *te ~ doen,* to nullify, annul; *om ~ or voor ~,* for nothing. ¶*prefix.* non-. **nieteling,** *n.* nonentity. **nietig,** *a.* insignificant, paltry; null and void. **nietigheid, -heden,** *n.* futility; triviality; nullity. **nietigverklaring,** *n.* nullification; annulment. **niets,** *pron.* nothing. *~ anders dan,* nothing but; *hij heeft er ~ aan,* it is of no use to him. ¶*adv.* not at all. *~ te vroeg,* none too early. **nietsbeduidend,** *a.,* **nietsbetekenend,** *a.* insignificant. **nietsdoend,** *a.* idle. **nietsdoenerij,** *n.* idling. **nietszeggend,** *a.* meaningless; insignificant. **niettegenstaande,** *prep.* in spite of. ¶*c.* although, for all. . . . **niette·min,** *adv.* nevertheless, none the less.

nieuw, *a.* new; fresh; modern. *nieuwste berichten,* latest news. **nieuwbakken,** *a.* new-fangled. **nieuweling,** *n.* novice, beginner, tyro. **nieuwe·maan,** no pl., *n.* new moon. **nieuwen,** *v.t.* to interest. **nieuwer·wets,** *a.* new-fashioned. **nieuwheid,** no pl., *n.* newness. **nieuwigheid, -heden,** *n.* novelty; innovation. **nieuwjaar,** no pl., *n.n.* New Year. **nieuw·modisch,** *a.* fashionable. **Nieuwpoort,** *n. N.* Nieuport. **nieuws,** no pl., *n.n.* news, tidings. *iets ~,* something new; *van ~ af aan,* anew. **nieuwsbericht,** *n.n.* news item. **nieuwsblad,** *n.n.* newspaper. **Nieuw·Schotland,** *n. N.* Nova Scotia. **nieuws·gierig,** *a.* curious, inquisitive. *~ te weten,* anxious to know. **nieuws·gierigheid,** no pl., *n.* curiosity. **nieuwtje, -s,** *n.n.* piece of news, the latest. *het ~ is er af,* the novelty has worn off.

niezen, nies, *v.i.* to sneeze.

nihil, *pron.* nil.

nijd, no pl., *n.* envy. **nijdas, -ssen,** *n.* surly person. **nijdasserig,** *a.* surly, cross. **nijdig,** *a.* angry; venomous. *~ worden,* to get angry. **nijdigaard, -s,** *n.* surly person. **nijdigheid,** no pl., *n.* anger.

nijgen, *v.i., str.* to curtsey. **nijging,** *n.* curtsey.

Nijl, *N.* Nile. **Nijlpaard,** *n.n.* hippopotamus. **nijnagel, -s,** *n.* agnail.

nijpen, *v.t., str.* to pinch. *het begint te ~,* they are feeling the pinch. **nijpend,** *a.* biting (*cold*). **nijper, -s,** *n.* pincers, nippers. **nijptang,** *n.* (pair of) pincers.

nijver, *a.* industrious. **nijverheid, -heden,** *n.* industry.

nikkel, no pl., *n.n.* nickel. **nikkelen,** *a.* (of) nickel.

nikker, -s, *n.* nigger.

niks, *pron.* nothing. *een man van ~,* a worthless person.

nimf, *n.* nymph.

·nimmer, *adv. (stilted)* never. ·nimmermeer, *adv. (stilted)* nevermore.

·nippel, -s, *n.* nipple *(metal)*.

·nippen, nip, *v.t.* to sip.

·nippertje, no pl., *n.n. op het* ~, in the nick of time; *op het* ~ *aankomen* to cut it fine.

nis, -ssen, *n.* niche.

ni·veau, -'s, *n.n.* level, plane. nivel·leren, -lleer, *v.t.* to level. nivel·lering, *n.* levelling.

·Noach, *N.* Noah.

·nobel, *a.* noble, generous.

noch, *c.* ~ . . ., ~ . . ., neither . . . nor . . . noch·thans, *adv.* nevertheless, yet.

·node, *adv.* reluctantly. ~ *gaan,* to be loath to go; *van* ~ *hebben,* to need. ·nodeloos, -loze, *a.* needless. ·nodeloosheid, no pl., *n.* needlessness. ·noden, nood, *v.t. (stilted)* to invite. *hij laat zich niet* ~, he does not need much pressing. ·nodig, *a.* necessary. ~ *hebben,* to need, to want; *hij heeft er niets mee* ~, it is no business of his; ~ *maken,* to necessitate; *er is heel wat* ~ *om* . . ., it takes a lot to . . .; *blijf niet langer dan* ~, do not stay longer than you need; *zo* ~, if need be. ¶*adv.* necessarily. *iemand* ~ *moeten spreken,* to have to speak to someone. ·nodige, no pl., *n.n.* what is necessary; the needful. ·nodigen, *v.t. (stilted)* to invite.

·noembaar, -bare, *a.* mentionable. ·noemen, *v.t.* to name, call; to name, mention. noemens·waard(ig), *a.* worth mentioning *or* speaking of. *niet* ~, negligible. ·noemer, -s, *n.* denominator.

noen, no pl., *n. (stilted)* noon. ·noenmaal, -malen, *n.n. (stilted)* lunch.

noest, *a.* diligent. ~*e vlijt,* unwearying industry. ·noestheid, no pl., *n.* diligence, industry.

nog, *adv.* still; yet. ~ *een kopje?,* another cup?; ~ *eens,* once more; ~ *vele malen,* many more times; ~ *iemand,* somebody else, anybody else; *hoe lang* ~?, how much longer?; ~ *maar drie,* only three; ~ *wel,* at that.

·noga, no pl., *n.* nougat.

nog·al, *adv.* rather, fairly; rather a lot. ·nogmaals, *adv.* once more, once again.

nok, -kken, *n.* ridge *(of roof)*.

no·maden, pl. only, *n.* nomads. no·madisch, *a.* nomad(ic).

·nommer, -s, *n.n. See* nummer.

non, -nnen, *n.* nun.

nonac·tief, *a.* on half-pay, not on active service. *op* ~ *stellen,* to retire. ·nonactivi·teit, no pl., *n. op* ~ *zijn,* to be on half-pay.

·nonnenklooster, -s, *n.n.* convent, nunnery. ·nonnetje, -s, *n.n.* little nun; smew.

·nonsens, no pl., *n.* nonsense.

nood, noden, *n.* necessity, need; distress, want. *geen* ~!, no fear!; *het heeft geen* ~, there is no hurry; *in* ~ *verkeren,* to be in distress; *iemand uit de* ~ *helpen,* to help a person out; *als de* ~ *aan de man komt,* if the worst comes to the worst *or* in case of need. ·noodanker, -s, *n.n.* sheet-anchor. ·noodbrug, -ggen, *n.* temporary bridge. ·nooddeur, *n.* emergency door. ·nooddruft, no pl., *n. (stilted)* want, indigence. ·nood·druftig, *a. (stilted)* indigent, destitute. ·nooddwang, no pl., *n. (stilted)* compulsion. ·noodgedwongen, *a.* from sheer necessity, perforce. ·noodhulp, *n.* relief, temporary help *(assistant or servant)*. ·noodjaar, -jaren, *n.n.* year of distress. ·noodklok, -kken, *n.* tocsin. ·noodlanding, *n.* forced landing. ·nood·lijdend, *a.* necessitous, distressed. ·noodlot, no pl., *n.n.* fate, destiny. ·nood·lottig, *a.* fatal; ill-fated. ·nood·lottigheid, -heden, *n.* fatality. ·noodmast, *n.* jury-mast. ·noodpeil, no pl., *n.n.* danger mark. ·noodrantsoen, *n.n.* emergency ration. ·noodrem, -mmen, *n.* safety brake. ·noodschot, *n.n.* distress gun. ·noodsein, *n.n.* signal of distress, S.C.S. ·nooduitgang, *n.* emergency exit. ·nood·verband, *n.n.* first-aid dressing. ·noodvlag, -ggen, *n.* flag of distress. ·noodweer, no pl., *n.n.* severe weather. *bij* ~, in stress of weather. ¶no pl., *n.* self-defence. *uit* ~, in self-defence. nood·wendig, *a. (stilted)* necessary, ineluctable. nood·wendigheid, -heden, *n. (stilted)* necessity. ·noodzaak, no pl., *n.* necessity. *zonder* ~, unnecessarily. nood·zakelijk, *a.* necessary. ¶*adv.* necessarily, of necessity. ·nood·zakelijkheid, -heden, *n.* necessity. ·nood·zaken, -zaak, *v.t.* to oblige, to necessitate. *zich genoodzaakt zien,* to find oneself obliged.

nooit, *adv.* never. ~ *ofte nimmer,* never! never!

Noor, Noren, *N.* Norwegian. noord, no pl., *n.n.* North. ¶no pl., *n.* the north. *om de* ~ *varen,* to sail north about. ¶*adv.* north. ·noordelijk, *a.* northern; northerly. ~*st,* northernmost. ¶*adv.* northwards. ~ *van,* north of. ·noorden, no pl., *n.n.* north. *ten* ~ *van,* (to the) north of. ·noordenwind, no pl., *n.* north wind. ·noorder, *a.* northern. ·noorderbreedte, no pl., *n.* North latitude. ·noorderkeerkring, *n.* tropic of cancer ·noorderlicht, no pl., *n.n.* northern lights. ·noorderzon, no pl., *n. met de* ~ *vertrekken,* to abscond, do a moonlight flit. Noord·Holland, *n.N. (province of)* North Holland. noord·oost, *adv.* north-east. ~ *ten oosten,* N.E. by E. noord·oostelijk, *a.* north-east(erly). ¶*adv.* north-east. noord·oosten, no pl., *n.n.* north-east. Noordpool, no pl., *N.* North Pole. noord·poolgebied, *n.n.* arctic region(s). Noord·poolzee, *N.* Arctic Ocean. noords, *a.* northern. ·Noordster, no pl., *n.* North Star, pole-star. ·noord·waarts, *adv.* northward(s). noord·west, *adv.* north-west. noord·westelijk, *a.*

north-west(erly). ¶*adv.*north-west. **noord-**
·westen, no pl., *n.n.* north-west. **Noordˑzee,**
N. North Sea. **·Noorman, -nnen,** *N.*
Dane, Norseman. **Noors,** *a.* Norwegian.
·Noorwegen, *n.N.* Norway.

noot, noten, *n.* nut; note (*music*); note
(*writing*). *een harde ~,* a hard nut to
crack; *hele ~,* semibreve; *halve ~,* minim;
vierde ~, crotchet; *achtste ~,* quaver;
zestiende ~, semiquaver; *twee-en-dertigste*
~, demisemiquaver; *op noten zetten,* to set
to music; *veel noten op zijn zang hebben,*
to have too much to say for oneself.
·nootjeskolen, pl. only, *n.* nuts (*coal*).
nootmusˑkaat, no pl., *n.* nutmeg.

nop, -ppen, *n.* nap; burl.

·nopen, noop, *v.t.* to compel. *zich genoopt*
voelen, to feel obliged. **·nopens,** *prep.*
concerning.

·nopje, -s, *n.n. in zijn ~s zijn,* to be as
pleased as Punch.

nor, no pl., *n.* (*slang*) jug, quod.

norˑmaal, -male, *a.* normal. **normaliˑsering,**
n. normalization.

nors, *a.* gruff, surly. **·norsheid,** no pl., *n.*
gruffness.

·nota, -'s, *n.* note (*diplomatic*); account, bill.
notariˑaat, -iaten, *n.n.* notaryship. **notari-**
·eel, -iele, *a.* notarial. *notariele volmacht,*
power of attorney. **noˑtaris, -ssen,** *n.*
notary public.

·notebolster, -s, *n.* walnut-husk. **·noteboom,**
-bomen, *n.* walnut-tree. **·notedop, -ppen,**
n. nutshell. **notemusˑkaat,** no pl., *n.*
nutmeg. **·notenbalk,** *n.* staff, stave (*music*).
·notenhout, no pl., *n.n.* walnut (*wood*).
·notenhouten, *a.* (of) walnut. **·notenkraker,**
-s, *n.* nutcracker.

noˑteren, -teer, *v.t.* to note (down); to quote
(*prices*). **noˑtering,** *n.* noting, notation;
quotation, price. **·notie, -s,** *n.* notion.
noˑtitie, -s, *n.* note; notice. **notuˑleren,**
-leer, *v.t.* to take down, minute. **·notulen,**
pl. only, *n.* minutes. *de ~ goedkeuren,* to
adopt the minutes; *de ~ zonder voorlezen*
goedkeuren, to take the minutes as read;
iets in de ~ opnemen, to enter something
in the minutes; *de ~ houden,* to keep the
minutes; *de ~ maken,* to take the minutes.
·notulenboek, *n.n.* minute-book.

nou, *adv.* (*coll.*) now. *See* **nu.**

nouveauˑté, -'s, *n.* novelty, (*pl.*) fancy goods.
noˑvelle, -n, *n.* short story or novel.

nu, *adv.* now. *~ eerst,* not until now;
~ eens . . . dan weer . . . , now . . . now . . . ;
wat ~, what next; *tot ~ toe,* hitherto;
van ~ af (*aan*), henceforward. ¶*c.* now
that.

nuˑance, -s, *n.* shade (*of colour*). **nuanˑceren,**
-ceer, *v.t.* to shade. **nuanˑcering,** *a,*
nuance, shade.

·nuchter, *a.* sober (*not drunk*); sober, level-
headed; not yet having had breakfast.
op de ~e maag, on an empty stomach;

~ *kalf,* new-born calf. **·nuchterheid, no**
pl., *n.* sobriety; matter-of-factness.

nuf, -ffen, *n.* prude, prig. **·nuffig,** *a.* prudish,
priggish.

nuk, -kken, *v.t.* whim. **·nukkig,** *a.* capricious.

nul, -llen, *n.* zero, nought, cipher. *in het*
jaar ~, in the year dot *or* donkeys' years
ago; *~ op het rekest krijgen,* to come away
with a flea in one's ear. ¶*a.* valueless.
nulliˑteit, *n.* nonentity. **·nulpunt,** *n.n.* zero
(*on scale*).

·nummer, -s, *n.n.* number; size (*of gloves, etc.*);
turn (*performance*); copy (*of paper or*
periodical). *een oud ~,* a back number;
iemand op zijn ~ zetten, to put a person
in his place. **·nummerbord,** *n.n.* indicator.
·nummeren, -merde, *v.t.* to number. ¶*zich ~,*
v.r. to number off. **·nummering,** *n.*
numbering. **·nummerplaat, -platen,** *n.*
registration plate. **·nummerschijf, -ven,** *n.*
dial (*on telephone*).

·nuntius, -tii, *n.* nuncio.

nurks, *a.* grumpy, grouchy.

nut, no pl., *n.n.* benefit, use. *het heeft geen ~,*
it is of no use; *~ trekken uit,* to derive
profit from; *ten nutte van,* for the benefit
of; *zich iets ten nutte maken,* to turn
something to one's advantage. **·nutteloos,**
-loze, *a.* useless; in vain. ¶*adv.* uselessly;
in vain. **·nutteloosheid,** no pl., *n.* uselessness. **·nutten, nut,** *v.t.* (*stilted*) to be of use.
·nuttig, *a.* useful. **·nuttigen,** *v.t.* to partake
of (*food*). *iets ~,* to take nourishment.
·nuttigheid, no pl., *n.* utility. **·nuttiging,**
n. consumption; communion.

O

oˑase, -n, *n.* oasis.

·o-benen, pl. only, *n.n.* bow-legs.

·ober, -s, *n.* waiter.

obˑject, *n.n.* object, objective. **objecˑtief, -ve,**
a. objective. ¶**-ven,** *n.n.* object-lens.

obˑlaat, -laten, *n.* oblate; host, eucharist.

obliˑgaat, -gaten, *n.n.* obligato. **obliˑgatie,**
-s, *n.n.* debenture, bond. **obligaˑtoir,** *a.*
obligatory.

obserˑvatie, -s, *n.* observation. **obserˑvatie-**
korps, *n.n.* observer corps. **obserˑvator,** *n.*
observer.

obsteˑtrie, no pl., *n.* obstetrics.

obsˑtructie, -s, *n.* obstruction. *~ voeren,* to
carry out a policy of obstruction.

oceˑaan, -ceanen, *n.* ocean. *de Grote ~,* the
Pacific Ocean.

och!, *int.* oh! *~ arme,* poor thing; *~ kom,*
really? *or* don't you believe it!

·ochtend, *n.* morning. *des ~s or 's ~s,* in
the morning. **·ochtendgloˑren,** no pl., *n.n.*
(*poet.*) break of day. **·ochtendstond,** no pl.,
n. dawn. *de ~ heeft goud in de mond,*
the early bird catches the worm.

oc·taaf, -taven, *n.* octave.
oc·trooi, *n.n.* patent; charter; octroi. oc·trooibrief, -ven, *n.* letters patent. oc·trooibureau, -'s, *n.n.* patent office. octrooi·eren, -ieer, *v.t.* to patent.
ocu·lair, *n.n.* ocular.
o·deur, -s, *n.* perfume, scent.
oecono·mie, no pl., *n.* economics. *See* economie.
oecu·menisch, *a.* oecumenical.
oef!, *int.* ugh!
·oefenaar, -s, *n.* lay reader. ·oefenen, *v.t.* to train; to exercise, practise. ¶*v.r. zich* ~ (*in*), to train, practise. ·oefening, *n.* exercise, practise. ·oefenschool, -scholen. *n.* training school. ·oefenspel, *n.n.* practice game.
·oehoe, -s, *n.* horned owl.
Oekra·ine, *N.* Ukraine.
oer, no pl., *n.n.* bog-ore.
·Oeral, *N. de* ~, the Urals.
·oerdier, *n.n.* protozoon. ·oermens, *n.* primitive. ·oeros, -ssen, *n.* aurochs. ·oertijd, no pl., *n.* prehistoric times. ·oervorm, *n.* prototype. ·oerwoud, *n.n.* virgin forest.
·oester, -s, *n.* oyster. ·oesterkweker, -s, *n.* oyster-breeder. ·oesterkwekerij, *n.* oyster-farm. ·oesterput, -tten, *n.* oyster-bed (*cultivated*). ·oesterplaat, -platen, *n.* oyster-bank, scalp. ·oesterteelt, no pl., *n.* oyster-culture. ·oestervangst, no pl., *n.* oyster-fishery; oystering. ·oesterzaad, no pl., *n.n.* (oyster) spat.
·oever, -s, *n.* shore; bank. *buiten zijn* ~*s treden*, to overflow one's banks. ·oeveraas, no pl., *n.n.* day-fly, ephemerid. ·oeverkruid, no pl., *n.n.* shore-weed. ·oeverloper, -s, *n.* summer snipe. ·oeverpieper, -s, *n.* rock pipit, sea lark. ·oeverzwaluw, *n.* sand-martin.
of, *c.* or; whether, if; before, but; unless; as if. ~ ... ~ ..., either ... or ..., whether ... or ...; *al* ~ *niet* (*warm*), (warm) or not; *een jaar* ~ *vijf*, some four or five years; *en* ~!, rather!; ~ *het kan!*, I assure you it is possible.
offen·sief, -ven, *n.n.* offensive.
·offer, -s, *n.n.* sacrifice, offering; victim. *een* ~ *brengen*, to make a sacrifice; *ten* ~ *brengen*, to sacrifice. ·offeraar, -s, *n.* immolator. ·offe·rande, -s, *n.* offering. ·offerblok, -kken, *n.n.* offertory-box. ·offerdier, *n.n.* sacrificial animal. ·offeren, *v.t.* to sacrifice, offer (up). of·ferte, -s, *n.* offer. *een* ~ *doen*, to make an offer. offer·vaardig, *a.* prepared to make sacrifices. offer·vaardigheid, no pl., *n.* liberality.
offici·eel, -iele, *a.* official.
offi·cier, -en *or* -s, *n.* officer. ~ *van gezondheid*, medical officer; ~ *van Justitie*, public prosecutor. offi·cierskajuit, *n.* ward-room. offi·cierstafel, -s, *n.* officers' mess. officier·vlieger, -s, *n.* flight lieutenant.

offici·eus, -ze, *a.* semi-official.
of·freren, -reer, *v.t.* to offer.
of·schoon, *c.* though, although.
·ofte, *c.* (*stilted*) or.
·ogen, oog, *v.t.* to eye. ¶*v.i.* ~ *op*, to aim at. ·ogenblik, -kken, *n.n.* moment, instant. *in een* ~, in the twinkling of an eye; *op het* ~, at the moment; *elk* ~, at any moment. ·ogenblikje, -s, *n.n.* short moment. *een* ~!, half a mo'! ogen·blikkelijk, *a.* momentary; immediate. ¶*adv.* immediately, this instant. ogen·schijnlijk, *a.* apparent, seeming. ·ogenschouw, no pl., *n.* iets in ~ nemen, to review, take stock of. ·ogentroost, no pl., *n.* eyebright.
o·ho!, *int.* aha!
oir, no pl., *n.n.* issue, progeny.
·oker, no pl., *n.* ochre. ·okergeel, -gele, *a.* ochreous. ¶ no pl., *n.n.* yellow ochre.
·okkernoot, -noten, *n.* walnut.
ok·saal, -salen, *n.n.* organ-loft.
·oksel, -s, *n.n.* arm-pit; axil.
·okshoofd, *n.n.* hogshead.
·olie, -iën, *n.* oil. *heilige* ~, chrism. ·olie·achtig, *a.* oily, oleaginous. ·oliebol, -llen. *n.* doughnut. olie-en-a·zijnstel, -llen, *n.n.* cruet-stand. olie·houdend, *a.* oil-bearing, oleaginous. ·oliejas, -ssen, *n.* oilskin (*coat*). ·olieman, -nnen, *n.* oiler, greaser. ·olie·molen, -s, *n.* oil-press; oil-plant (*factory*). ·oliën, -lie, *v.t.* to oil. ·olienoot, -noten, *n.* peanut. ·oliepot, -tten, *n.* oil-box. ·oliesel, no pl., *n.n.* het laatste ~, extreme unction. ·olieslager, -s, *n.* oil manufacturer. ·olie·slage·rij, *n.* oil-plant (*factory*). ·oliesteca, -stenen, *n.* oil-stone, hone.
·olifant, *n.* elephant. ·olifantachtig, *a.* elephantine. ·olifantsziekte, no pl., *n.* elephantiasis.
o·lijf, -ven, *n.* olive. o·lijfachtig, *a.* olivaceous. O·lijfberg, *N.* Mount of Olives.
·olijk, *a.* arch, roguish, playful. ·olijkerd, -s, *n.* rogue. ·olijkheid, -heden, *n.* quip. roguishness.
olm, *n.*, ·olmboom, -bomen, *n.* elm. ·ol·menhout, no pl., *n.n.* elmwood.
om, *prep.* round, roundabout; about; at; for (*e.g. 5 for 6d.*); for, on account of. ~ *het vlugst*, quickest; ~ *en bij*, roundabout; ~ *de andere dag*, every other day; ~ *te*, to, in order to. ¶*adv.* round; out, passed, over. *hem* ~ *hebben*, to be tight. ¶*prefix.* round, about, over.
·oma, -'s, *n.* grandma.
om·armen, *v.t.* to embrace. om·arming, *n.* embrace.
·omber, no pl., *n.* umber. ¶no pl., *n.n.* ombre. ·omberen, *v.i.* to play at ombre. ·omberspel, *n.n.* (game of) ombre. ·ombervis, -ssen, *n.* bar (*fish*). ·omber·vogel, -s, *n.* umbrette, umber-bird.
·ombladeren, *v.t.s.* to turn over the leaves.
·omboordsel, -s, *n.n.* edging, trimming.

·ombrengen, *v.t.s.*, *irr.* to make away with. *de tijd* ~, to kill time.

om·cirkelen, *v.t.* to encircle.

om·dat, *c.* because, since, as.

om·dijken, *v.t.* to embank.

·omdoen, doe om, *v.t.s.*, *irr.* to put on, wrap round.

·omdraaien, *v.t.s.* to turn round *or* about. *iemand de hals* ~, to wring a person's neck; *de hoek* ~, to turn the corner. ¶*v.i.s.* to veer *or* swing round. ¶*zich* ~, *v.r.s.* to turn round.

·omgaan, ga om, *v.i.s.*, *irr.* to go round; to pass. *er gaat veel om*, a great deal is happening *or* they are very busy; *het gaat buiten hem om*, it does not concern *or* touch him; ~ *in*, to happen *or* to take place in *or* to feel; ~ *met*, to frequent, associate with *or* to have dealings with *or* to handle; *met bedrog* ~, to practise deceit. ¶*v.t.* to turn (*corner*). ·omgaande, *a.* *per* ~, by return. ·omgang, no pl., *n.* intercourse (*social*); procession; gallery, battlement. *lastig in de* ~, difficult to get on with. ·omgangstaal, no pl., *n.* colloquial speech *or* language.

·omgekeerd, *a.* turned round *or* over; upside down; reversed, inverted. *juist* ~, the other way round, just the reverse; *en* ~, and vice versa.

·omgelegen, *a.* surrounding.

om·geven, -geef, *v.t.*, *str.* to surround, encircle. om·geving, no pl., *n.* surroundings; entourage.

·omhaal, no pl., *n.* fuss; verbiage. *met* ~ *van woorden*, with great verbosity. ·omhalen, haal om, *v.t.s.* to pull down *or* over.

om·heen, *adv.* round.

om·heinen, *v.t.* to fence in. om·heining, *n.* fence.

om·helzen, -hels, *v.t.* to embrace. om·helzing, *n.* embrace.

om·hoog, *adv.* upwards; up, aloft. *naar* ~, upwards; *van* ~, from on high. ¶*prefix.* up, upwards.

om·hullen, -hul, *v.t.* to envelop; to enshroud. om·hulsel, -s, *n.n.* cover, wrapping, casing. *stoffelijk* ~, mortal remains.

·omkeer, no pl., *n.* See ommekeer. ·omkeren, keer om, *v.t.s.* to turn, turn round *or* over. *ieder dubbeltje* ~, to look twice at every penny. ¶*v.i.s.* to turn round *or* back. ¶*zich* ~, *v.r.s.* to turn (round).

·omkijken, *v.i.s.*, *str.* to look round. ~ *naar*, to look round for.

·omkippen, kip om, *v.t.s.* to tip over.

om·kleden, -kleed, *v.t.* to clothe. *met redenen* ~, to motivate. ·omkleden, kleed om, *v.t.s.* to change (*clothes*). om·kleedsel, -s, *n.n.* cover, casing.

·omkomen, *v.i.s.*, *irr.* to perish. ~ *van*, to perish with. ¶*v.t.s.*, *irr.* to come round (*corner*).

om·koopbaar, -bare, *a.* corruptible, open to

bribery. om·koopbaarheid, no pl., *n.* corruptibility. ·omkoopgeld, no pl., *n.n.* bribe. ·omkopen, koop om, *v.t.s.*, *irr.* to bribe. ·omkoper, -s, *n.* briber. omkope·rij, *n.* bribery.

·omkrullen, krul om, *v.t.s.* to curl up.

om·laag, *adv.* below, down. *naar* ~, down; *van* ~, from below.

·omlegsel, -s, *n.n.* edging.

om·liggend, *a.* surrounding.

om·lijsten, *v.t.* to frame.

·omloop, no pl., *n.* circulation; revolution (*of stars, etc.*). *in* ~ *brengen*, to circulate; *buiten* ~ *stellen*, to withdraw from circulation. ·omloopstijd, *n.* time of revolution (*of stars, etc.*); currency (*of bill*). ·omlopen, loop om, *v.i.s.*, *irr.* to go *or* veer round. *het hoofd loopt hem om*, his head reels. ¶*v.t.s.*, *str.* to walk round. *een straatje* ~, to go for a stroll.

·ommegang, *n.* See omgang.

·ommekeer, no pl., *n.* change, turn, reversal; revulsion. *een* ~ *brengen in*, to revolutionize.

·ommelanden, pl. only, *n.n.* surrounding countryside.

·ommestaand, *a.* overleaf.

·ommezien, no pl., *n.n. in een* ~, in a trice.

·ommezijde, -n, *n.* back. *zie* ~, see back *or* please turn over.

om·muren, -muur, *v.t.* to wall in.

·omploegen, *v.t.s.* to plough up.

·ompraten, praat om, *v.t.s.* to talk round *or* over.

om·rasteren, *v.t.* to rail *or* fence in. om·rastering, *n.* railing, wire-fence.

·omrekenen, *v.t.s.* to convert (*calculation*).

om·ringen, *v.t.* to surround, encircle.

·omroep, *n.* broadcast. ·omroepen, *v.t.s.*, *str.* to broadcast. ·omroeper, -s, *n.* town crier; broadcaster.

·omruilen, *v.t.s.* to exchange.

·omschakelen, *v.t.s.* to change *or* switch over.

·omschrift, *n.n.* legend (*on coin*). om·schrijfbaar, -bare, *a.* definable. om·schrijven, -schrijf, *v.t.*, *str.* to define, circumscribe. om·schrijving, *n.* definition, paraphrase.

om·singelen, *v.t.* to surround, invest. om·singeling, *n.* encirclement.

·omslaan, sla om, *v.t.s.*, *irr.* to knock down; to turn down *or* back; to wrap round; to turn (*corner*). ¶*v.i.s.*, *irr.* to capsize, be upset; to change (*weather*). *links* ~, to turn to the left.

om·slachtig, *a.* wordy; involved, overcomplicated. om·slachtigheid, no pl., *n.* prolixity; complicatedness.

·omslag, no pl., *n.* fuss, bother; taxation. *zonder* ~, without ceremony; *hoofdelijke* ~, poll-tax. ¶*n.* or *n.n.* jacket, dust-cover (*of book*); compress. ·omslagboor, -boren, *n.* hand-brace. ·omslagdoek, *n.* shawl, wrap.

om·sluiten, *v.t.*, *str.* to enclose, surround.

·**omspitten**, spit om, *v.t.s.* to dig up.
·**omspoelen**, *v.t.s.* to rinse round. **om·spoelen**, *v.t.* to wash (*shore*).
·**omspringen**, *v.i.s.*, *str.* ~ *met*, to handle, manage.
·**omstaan**, sta om, *v.i.s.*, *irr.* ~ *om*, to toss for.
·**omstander**, -s, *n.* bystander. **om·standig**, *a.* detailed, circumstantial. ¶*adv.* in detail. **om·standigheid**, -**heden**, *n.* circumstance; detail. *in de gegeven omstandigheden*, in or under the circumstances; *naar omstandigheden*, comparatively speaking or considering; *onder geen* ~, on no account.
·**omstreek**, -**streken**, *n.* (*usu. pl.*) surrounding country. *Rotterdam en omstreken*, the Rotterdam area. **om·streeks**, *prep. & adv.* about, in the neighbourhood of.
om·strengelen, *v.t.* to entwine, encircle.
om·stuwen, *v.t.* to crowd round.
·**omtoveren**, *v.t.s.* to transform.
·**omtrek**, -**kken**, *n.* outline, contour. ¶no pl., *n.* neighbourhood, vicinity. *binnen een* ~ *van*, within a radius of; *kilometers in de* ~, for miles around. ·**omtrekken**, **trek om**, *v.t.s.*, *str.* to pull over or down; to turn, outflank. *een* ~*de beweging*, an enveloping movement.
om·trent, *adv.* about. ¶*prep.* concerning; about.
om·tuinen, *v.t.* to enclose.
·**omvang**, no pl., *n.* extent; volume, bulk; size, magnitude; girth. **om·vangen**, *v.t.*, *str.* to encompass. **om·vangrijk**, *a.* extensive; bulky. **om·vangrijkheid**, no pl., *n.* (great) extent.
·**omvaren**, vaar om, *v.t.s.*, *str.* to circumnavigate.
om·vatten, -**vat**, *v.t.* to comprise, embrace, include. *veel* ~*d*, comprehensive.
om·ver, *adv. & prefix.* over, down, to the ground.
om·verwerpen, werp omver, *v.t.s.*, *str.* to overthrow. **om·verwerping**, no pl., *n.* overthrow.
om·wallen, -**wal**, *v.t.* to wall in or round.
·**omwas**, no pl., *n.* washing up. ·**omwassen**, **was om**, *v.t.s.*, *irr.* to wash up, rinse round.
·**omweg**, *n.* detour. *langs een* ~, by a roundabout way; *zonder* ~*en*, straight out, point-blank.
·**omwenteling**, *n.* revolution; rotation (*round axis*). *een* ~ *teweeg brengen in*, to revolutionize.
·**omwerken**, *v.t.s.* to remodel; to rewrite, recast. ·**omwerking**, *n.* remodelling; rewriting.
om·windsel, -**s**, *n.n.* wrapper.
·**omwisselen**, *v.t.s.* to change (round). ¶*v.i.s.* to alternate.
·**omwonend**, *a.* neighbouring. ·**omwoners**, pl. only, *n.* neighbours.
·**omzendbrief**, -**ven**, *n.* circular letter.

·**omzet**, no pl., *n.* turnover, sale. ·**omzetten**, **zet om**, *v.t.s.* to transpose; to turn over (*capital*). ~ *in*, to convert into. ·**omzetting**, *n.* transposition, reversal.
om·zichtig, *a.* cautious, circumspect.
on-, *prefix.* un-, in-, dis-, *etc.*
onaan·dachtig, *a.* inattentive.
on·aangenaam, -**name**, *a.* unpleasant, disagreeable. **on·aangenaamheid**, -**heden**, *n.* unpleasantness. *onaangenaamheden krijgen met*, to fall out with.
on·aangeraakt, *a.*, **on·aangeroerd**, *a.* untouched.
on·aangesproken, *a.* untapped.
on·aangetast, *a.* untouched.
on·aangevochten, *a.* unchallenged.
onaan·lokkelijk, *a.* unattractive.
onaan·nemelijk, *a.* unacceptable, inadmissible.
onaan·stotelijk, *a.* unobjectionable.
onaan·tastbaar, -**bare**, *a.* unassailable, unimpeachable. **onaan·tastbaarheid**, no pl., *n.* unassailability.
onaan·trekkelijk, *a.* unattractive.
onaan·vaardbaar, -**bare**, *a.* unacceptable.
onaan·vechtbaar, -**bare**, *a.* unassailable.
onaan·zienlijk, *a.* insignificant; inconsiderable. **onaan·zienlijkheid**, no pl., *n.* insignificance.
on·aardig, *a.* not nice. **on·aardigheid**, -**heden**, *n.* unkindness, unpleasantness.
on·achtzaam, -**zame**, *a.* inattentive. **on·achtzaamheid**, -**heden**, *n.* negligence, carelessness.
on·afgebroken, *a.* uninterrupted, continuous.
on·afgewerkt, *a.* unfinished.
onaf·hankelijk, *a.* independent. **onaf·hankelijkheid**, no pl., *n.* independence.
onaf·losbaar, -**bare**, *a.* irredeemable.
onaf·scheidbaar, -**bare**, *a.*, **onaf·scheidelijk**, *a.* inseparable. **onaf·scheidelijkheid**, no pl., *n.* inseparability.
onaf·wendbaar, -**bare**, *a.* ineluctable, unavoidable.
onaf·zienbaar, -**bare**, *a.* endless, immense.
onaf·tent, *a.* inattentive.
onbaat·zuchtig, *a.* unselfish, disinterested. **onbaat·zuchtigheid**, no pl., *n.* unselfishness.
onbarm·hartig, *a.* merciless. **onbarm·hartigheid**, no pl., *n.* mercilessness.
onbe·antwoord, *a.* unanswered.
onbe·daarlijk, *a.* uncontrollable, ungovernable (*laughter*, etc).
onbe·dacht, *a.*, **onbe·dachtzaam**, -**zame**, *a.* thoughtless, inconsiderate.
onbe·dekt, *a.* uncovered.
onbe·dorven, *a.* unspoilt, innocent. **onbe·dorvenheid**, no pl., *n.* innocence.
onbe·dreven, *a.* inexperienced.
onbe·drieglijk, *a.* unmistakable.
onbe·duidend, *a.* insignificant. **onbe·duidendheid**, -**heden**, *n.* insignificance.
onbe·dwingbaar, -**bare**, *a.* uncontrollable.
onbe·gaanbaar, -**bare**, *a.* impassable.

onbe·gonnen, *a. het is ∼ werk,* there is no end to it.

onbe·grensd, *a.* unlimited.

onbe·grijpelijk, *a.* incomprehensible. onbe·grijpelijkheid, -heden, *n.* incomprehensibility.

onbe·haaglijk, *a.* uncomfortable, uneasy. onbe·haaglijkheid, no pl., *n.* discomfort.

onbe·haard, *a.* hairless.

onbe·heerd, *a.* unattended.

onbe·holpen, *a.* clumsy. onbe·holpenheid, -heden, *n.* clumsiness.

onbe·hoorlijk, *a.* unseemly, improper. onbe·hoorlijkheid, -heden, *n.* impropriety.

onbe·houwen, *a.* unmannerly; ungainly.

onbe·hulpzaam, -zame, *a.* unhelpful.

onbe·kend, *a.* unknown, unacquainted. *ergens ∼ zijn,* not to know the way somewhere. onbe·kende, -n, *n.* stranger. onbe·kendheid, no pl., *n.* unfamiliarity; obscurity.

onbe·kommerd, *a.* unconcerned, carefree.

onbe·klemd, *a.* unconstrained. *met ∼e borst zingen,* to sing away happily.

onbe·kookt, *a.* rash, ill-considered.

onbe·krompen, *a.* not narrow-minded; liberal. onbe·krompenheid, no pl., *n.* liberality.

onbe·kwaam, -kwame, *a.* incapable, inefficient. onbe·kwaamheid, -heden, *n.* incompetence.

onbe·langrijk, *a.* unimportant. onbe·langrijkheid, -heden, *n.* unimportant matter; insignificance.

onbe·leefd, *a.* impolite, rude. onbe·leefdheid, -heden, *n.* impoliteness, rudeness.

onbe·legen, *a.* (too) new (*bread, etc.*).

onbe·lemmerd, *a.* unobstructed.

onbe·merkt, *a.* unnoticed.

onbe·middeld, *a.* impecunious.

onbe·mind, *a.* unloved. onbe·minnelijk, *a.* unlovely.

onbe·nullig, *a.* insignificant; inane.

onbe·paald, *a.* indefinite; unlimited. ∼ *vertrouwen,* implicit faith; *∼e wijs,* infinitive; *voor ∼e tijd,* indefinitely, sine die. onbe·palend, *a.* indefinite (*grammar*).

onbe·perkt, *a.* boundless, unlimited.

onbe·proefd, *a.* untried.

onbe·raden, *a.* ill-advised. onbe·radenheid, no pl., *n.* rashness.

onbe·recht, *a.* without extreme unction.

onbe·reden, *a.* unmounted.

onbe·rede·neerd, *a.* unreasoned.

onbe·reikbaar, -bare, *a.* inaccessible.

onbe·reisd, *a.* untravelled.

onbe·rekenbaar, -bare, *a.* incalculable.

onbe·rispelijk, *a.* irreproachable.

onbe·schaafd, *a.* uncivilized; ill-bred.

onbe·schaamd, *a.* shameless, unashamed; impudent. onbe·schaamdheid, -heden, *n.* impudence.

onbe·schadigd, *a.* undamaged.

onbe·scheiden, *a.* indiscreet, indelicate. onbe·scheidenheid, -heden, *n.* indiscretion.

onbe·schoft, *a.* impertinent, insolent. onbe·schoftheid, -heden, *n.* impertinence.

onbe·schreven, *a.* blank (*page*). onbe·schrijfelijk, *a.* indescribable.

onbe·schroomd, *a.* unabashed.

onbe·schut, -tte, *a.* unsheltered.

onbe·sefbaar, -bare, *a.* inconceivable.

onbe·slagen, *a.* unshod. ∼ *ten ijs komen,* to start unprepared.

onbe·slecht, *a.,* onbe·slist, *a.* undecided. ∼ *eindigen,* to end in a draw. onbe·slistheid, no pl., *n.* indecision.

onbe·sneden, *a.* uncircumcised.

onbe·sproken, *a.* blameless.

onbe·staanbaar, -bare, *a.* impossible. ∼ *met,* incompatible with.

onbe·stelbaar, -bare, *a.* undelivered, dead (*letter*).

onbe·stemd, *a.* indeterminate.

onbe·stendig, *a.* unstable, unsettled; fickle. onbe·stendigheid, -heden, *n.* inconstancy.

onbe·storven, *a.* too fresh, unhung (*meat*). ∼ *weduwe,* grass widow.

onbe·stuurbaar, -bare, *a.* ungovernable, out of control.

onbe·suisd, *a.* headlong; hot-headed.

onbe·taalbaar, -bare, *a.* priceless, invaluable. onbe·taald, *a.* unpaid, outstanding.

onbe·tamelijk, *a.* unseemly, indecent. onbe·tamelijkheid, -heden, *n.* unseemliness, indecency.

onbe·tekenend, *a.* insignificant.

onbe·teugeld, *a.* unbridled.

onbe·treurd, *a.* unlamented.

onbe·trouwbaar, -bare, *a.* unreliable, untrustworthy. onbe·trouwbaarheid, -heden, *n.* unreliability.

onbe·tuigd, *a. zich niet ∼ laten,* to do one's full share.

onbe·twist, *a.* undisputed. onbe·twistbaar, -bare, *a.* indisputable.

onbe·vaarbaar, -bare, *a.* unnavigable. onbe·vaarbaarheid, no pl., *n.* unnavigability.

onbe·vallig, *a.* ungraceful.

onbe·vangen, *a.* unprejudiced. onbe·vangenheid, no pl., *n.* impartiality.

onbe·varen, *a.* unnavigated.

onbe·vattelijk, *a.* slow on the uptake; incomprehensible.

onbe·vlekt, *a.* immaculate.

onbe·voegd, *a.* unqualified, incompetent. onbe·voegdheid, no pl., *n.* incompetence.

onbevoor·oordeeld, *a.* unprejudiced.

onbe·voorrecht, *a.* unprivileged.

onbe·vredigd, *a.* unsatisfied. onbe·vredigend, *a.* unsatisfactory.

onbe·vreesd, *a.* undaunted.

onbe·vroed, *a.* unsuspected.

onbe·waakt, *a.* unguarded.

onbe·waarheid, *a.* unverified.

onbe·weegbaar, -bare, *a.* immovable.

onbe·weeglijk, *a.* motionless, immobile. onbe·weeglijkheid, no pl., *n.* immobility.

onbe·werkt, *a.* plain.　*~e stoffen,* raw materials.
onbe·wezen, *a.* unproved.
onbe·wimpeld, *a.* undisguised.
onbe·wogen, *a.* unmoved; impassive.
onbe·woonbaar, -bare, *a.* uninhabitable. **onbe·woond,** *a.* uninhabited.
onbe·wust, *a.* unconscious, unaware. ¶*adv.* unconsciously, unawares.
onbe·zadigd, *a.* impetuous.
onbe·zet, -tte, *a.* vacant, unoccupied.
onbe·zield, *a.* inanimate.
onbe·zoedeld, *a.* undefiled.
onbe·zoldigd, *a.* unsalaried, honorary
onbe·zonnen, *a.* rash, thoughtless.　**onbe·zonnenheid,** no pl., *n.* rashness.
onbe·zorgd, *a.* carefree, light-hearted.
onbe·zwaard, *a.* unburdened; unencumbered.
on·billijk, *a.* unfair, unjust.　**on·billijkheid, -heden,** *n.* injustice, unfairness.
on·blusbaar, -bare, *a.* inextinguishable.
onboet·vaardig, *a.* impenitent.
on·brandbaar, -bare, *a.* incombustible.
on·breekbaar, -bare, *a.* unbreakable.
·onbruik, no pl., *n.n.* desuetude.　*in ~ geraken,* to become obsolete. **on·bruikbaar, -bare,** *a.* unusable, useless.
on·buigbaar, -bare, *a.* inflexible.　**on·buigzaam, -zame,** *a.* unyielding.
on·christelijk, *a.* unchristian.
·ondank, no pl., *n.* ingratitude.　*mijns ~s,* in spite of myself; *~ is 's werelds loon,* ingratitude is the way of the world. **on·dankbaar, -bare,** *a.* ungrateful.　**on·dankbaarheid, -heden,** *n.* ingratitude. **on·danks,** *adv.* in spite of.
on·deelbaar, -bare, *a.* indivisible.　*~ getal,* prime number; *een ~ ogenblik,* a fraction of a second. **on·deelbaarheid,** no pl., *n.* indivisibility.
on·degelijk, *a.* unsubstantial; superficial.
on·denkbaar, -bare, *a.* unthinkable.
·onder, *prep.* under; below; beneath; underneath; among, amidst; during.　*~ de wind,* to leeward; *~ andere,* among other things; *~ mij,* under me *or* in my keeping; *~ ons,* between ourselves. ¶*adv.* below; underneath.　*~ aan,* at the bottom *or* foot of; *~ in,* in the bottom of; *naar ~,* down; *ten ~ brengen,* to overcome; *ten ~ gaan,* to succumb. ¶*prefix.* under, lower.
onder·aan, *prep.* at the bottom *or* foot.
·onderaannemer, -s, *n.* sub-contractor.
onder·aards, *a.* subterranean.
·onderadjudant, *n.* warrant-officer.
·onderadmiraal, -ralen *or* **-s,** *n.* vice-admiral.
onder·af, *adv.* from the bottom.
·onderafdeling, *n.* subdivision, subsection.
·onderarm, *n.* forearm.
onderbe·licht, *a.* under-exposed.
·onderbevelhebber, -s, *n.* second in command.
onderbe·wust, *a.* subconscious.　**onderbe·wustzijn,** no pl., *n.n.* subconscious(ness).

·**onderblijven, blijf onder,** *v.i.s., str.* to stay under.
·**onderbootsman, -tslieden,** *n.* boatswain's mate.
·**onderbouw,** no pl., *n.* substructure.
onder·breken, -breek, *v.t., str.* to interrupt. **onder·breking,** *n.* interruption.
·**onderbrengen,** *v.t.s., irr.* to shelter.
·**onderbroek,** *n.* (pair of) pants (*underwear*)
·**onderbuur, -buren,** *n.* downstairs neighbour.
·**onderdaan, -danen,** *n.* subject (*of state*).
·**onderdak,** no pl., *n.n.* shelter, accommodation.
onder·danig, *a.* humble, obsequious.　**onder·danigheid,** no pl., *n.* submissiveness.
·**onderdeel, -delen,** *n.n.* fraction; (spare) part, *pl.* accessories, fittings.
·**onderdoen, doe onder,** *v.t.s., irr.* to put on (*skates, etc.*). ¶*v.i.s., irr. voor niemand ~,* to be second to none.
·**onderdompelen,** *v.t.s.* to immerse, submerge.
onder·door, *adv.* underneath.　*het kan er mee ~,* it will pass.
onder·drukken, -druk, *v.t.* to suppress, stifle; to oppress.　**onder·drukken,** *v.t.s.* to press under. **onder·drukker, -s,** *n.* suppressor; oppressor. **onder·drukking,** *n.* suppression; oppression.
·**onderduiken,** *v.i.s., str.* to dive under, disappear beneath the surface.
onder·een, *adv.* together.
·**onderen,** *adv. naar ~,* downward(s); *van ~,* at *or* from the bottom.
·**ondergaan, ga onder,** *v.i.s., irr.* to go down, sink; to perish. **onder·gaan, -ga,** *v.t.s., irr.* to undergo; to endure.　·**ondergang,** no pl., *n.* decline, ruin; setting (*of sun*).　*het was zijn ~,* it led to his undoing.
onderge·schikt, *a.* subordinate; subservient.　*van ~ belang,* of secondary importance; *~ maken aan,* to subordinate to. **onderge·schikte, -n,** *n.* subordinate, inferior. **onderge·schiktheid,** no pl., *n.* subordination; subservience.
·**ondergeschoven,** *a.,* ·**ondergestoken,** *a.* supposititious.
onderge·tekende, -n, *n.* undersigned.
·**ondergoed, -eren,** *n.n.* underwear, underclothing.
·**ondergrond,** *n.* subsoil.　**onder·gronds,** *a.* underground.
onder·handelen, *v.i.* to negotiate.　**onder·handeling,** *n.* negotiation.　*~en aanknopen,* to enter into negotiations. **onder·hands,** *a.* private (*sale, etc.*).
onder·havig, *a.* in question.　*het ~e geval,* the present case.
·**onderhemd,** *n.n.* undervest.
onder·hevig, *a. ~ aan,* subject to.
onder·horig, *a.* dependent.　**onder·horigheid, -heden,** *n.* dependence.
·**onderhoud,** no pl., *n.n.* keep, sustenance; upkeep; interview. **onderhouden,** *v.t.s., irr.* to keep under. **onder·houden,** *v.i., irr.* to

support, maintain; to keep up, entertain; to keep in repair; to entertain, amuse. ¶zich ~, *v.r.*, *irr.* to support oneself (*financially*). zich ~ met, to converse with. onder·houdend, *a.* entertaining. ·onder·houdskosten, pl. only, *n.* maintenance cost.
·onderhuid, no pl., *n.* cutis.
onder·in, *adv.* at *or* near the bottom.
·onderjurk, *n.* petticoat.
·onderkaak, -kaken, *n.* lower jaw.
·onderkant, *n.* bottom, lower side.
·onderkin, -nnen, *n.* double chin.
·onderkleren, pl. only, *n.n.* underclothes.
·onderkomen, no pl., *n.n.* shelter.
·onderkoning, *n.* viceroy.   onderkoningin, -nnen, *n.* vicereine.
·onderkruipen, *v.t.s.*, *str.* to creep under. onder·kruipen, *v.i.*, *str.* to undercut. onder·kruiper, -s, *n.* blackleg. onder·kruiping, *n.* undercutting.
·onderlaag, -lagen, *n.* substratum.
onder·langs, *adv.* along the bottom.
onder·legd, *a.* goed ~, well grounded. ·onderlegger, -s, *n.* writing-pad.
·onderlijf, -ven, *n.n.* lower part of the body. ·onderlijfje, -s, *n.n.* camisole.
·onderling, *a.* mutual, common.   ¶*adv.* mutually; together, with one another.
·onderlip, -ppen, *n.* lower lip.
·onderlopen, loop onder, *v.i.s.*, *str.* to be flooded. laten ~, to flood.
onder·maans, *a.* sublunary.
onder·mijnen, *v.t.* to undermine.
onder·nemen, -neem, *v.t.*, *str.* to undertake; to attempt. onder·nemend, *a.* enterprising. onder·nemer, -s, *n.* contractor; employer. onder·neming, *n.* enterprise, venture; concern (*firm*); estate. onder·nemingsgeest, no pl., *n.* spirit of enterprise.
·onderofficier, *n.* non-commissioned officer, N.C.O.; petty officer.
onder·onsje, -s, *n.n.* private affair.
·onderpand, *n.n.* pledge.
·onderra, -raas, *n.* lower yard.
·onderricht, no pl., *n.n.* instruction, tuition. onder·richten, *v.t.* to instruct.
·onderrok, -kken, *n.* underskirt, petticoat.
onder·schatten, -schat, *v.t.* to underestimate. onder·schatting, *n.* underestimation.
·onderscheid, no pl., *n.n.* distinction. de jaren des ~s, the years of discretion; ~ maken tussen, to distinguish between. onder·scheiden, *v.t.* to distinguish; to decorate, honour. ik kan ze niet ~, I can't tell them apart; niet te ~, indistinguishable. ¶zich ~, *v.r.* to distinguish oneself. ¶*a.* (*stilted*) distinct. onder·scheiding, *n.* distinction; decoration. onder·scheidingsvermogen, -s, *n.n.* power of discrimination. onder·scheidingsteken, *n.n.* distinctive make; decoration.
onder·scheppen, -schep, *v.t.* to intercept. onder·schepping, *n.* interception.
onder·schragen, -schraag, *v.t.* to shore up.

·onderschrift, *n.n.* legend, letter-press. onder·schrijven, -schrijf, *v.t.*, *str.* to endorse (*view*).
onders·hands, *adv.* by private sale.
·onderspit, no pl., *n.n.* het ~ delven, to lose the struggle.
·onderst, no pl., *n.n.* undermost.
·onderstand, no pl., *n.* assistance; relief; dole.
·ondersteboven, *adv.* upside down.
·onderstel, -llen, *n.n.* under-carriage. onder·stellen, -stel, *v.t.* to suppose. onder·stelling, *n.* supposition.
onder·steunen, *v.t.* to support; to relieve. onder·steuning, no pl., *n.* support.
onder·strepen, -streep, *v.t.* to underline.
·onderstuk, -kken, *n.n.* lower part.
onder·tekenaar, -s, *n.* subscriber, signatory. onder·tekenen, *v.t.* to sign. onder·tekening, *n.* signature.
·ondertitel, -s, *n.* sub-title.
·ondertoon, -tonen, *n.* undertone.
·ondertrouw, no pl., *n.* betrothal. ~ zijn to be betrothed (*banns published*).
onder·tussen, *adv.* meanwhile.
onder·vangen, *v.t.*, *str.* to intercept.
·onderveedelen, -deel, *v.t.* to subdivide. ·onderverdeling, *n.* subdivision.
onder·vinden, *v.t.*, *str.* to experience. onder·vinding, *n.* experience.
onder·voed, *a.* undernourished. onder·voeden, *v.t.* to underfeed. onder·voeding, no pl., *n.* malnutrition.
·ondervoorzitter, -s, *n.* deputy chairman.
onder·vragen, -vraag, *v.t.*, *str.* to interrogate. onder·vrager, -s, *n.* interrogator. onder·vraging, *n.* interrogation.
onder·weg, *adv.* on the way.
·onderwerp, *n.n.* subject; topic. onder·werpen, *v.t.*, *str.* to subject. ~ aan, to subject to. ¶zich ~, *v.r.*, *str.* to submit; to resign oneself. onder·werping, *n.* subjection; submission.
·onderwicht, *a.* underweight.
·onderwijs, no pl., *n.n.* education; teaching; schooling. ~ geven in, to teach; bij het ~, in education. onder·wijzen, -wijs, *v.t.*, *str.* & *v.i.*, *str.* to teach. onder·wijzer, -s, *n.* (primary school) teacher. onderwijze·res, -ssen, *n.* (primary school) teacher (*female*).
onder·worpeling, *n.* slave. onder·worpen *a.* submissive; resigned. ~ aan, subject to. onder·worpenheid, no pl., *n.* submissiveness; subjection.
onder·zeeboot, -boten, *n.*, onder·zeeër, -s, *n.* submarine. onder·zees, -zese, *a.* submarine.
·onderzoek, no pl., *n.n.* examination, investigation, inquiry, research. een ~ doen naar, to inquire into; bij nader ~, upon closer examination; in ~, under investigation. onder·zoeken, *v.t.*, *irr.* to examine, investigate, scrutinize. onder·zoeking, *n.* investigation; exploration. onder·zoekingsreis, -zen, *n.* journey of exploration. onder·zoekingsreiziger, -s, *n.* explorer.

ondes·kundig, *a.* inexpert.

·ondeugd, *n.* vice; mischievous little rogue.
¶no pl., *n.* mischief. on·deugdelijk, *a.*
unsound, unwholesome. on·deugend, *a.*
naughty, mischievous. on·deugendheid,
-heden, *n.* naughtiness, mischief.

on·dicht, *a.* leaky.

·ondienst, *n.* ill-service. on·dienstig, *a.*
unserviceable.

·ondiep, *a.* shallow. ·ondiepte, -n, *n.* shallow.

·ondier, *n.* monster, brute.

·onding, *n.n.* useless thing.

ondoel·matig, *a.* unsuitable. ondoel·treffend,
a. ineffectual.

on·doenlijk, *a.* unfeasible.

ondoor·dacht, *a.* thoughtless, rash. ondoor-
·dachtheid, -heden, *n.* thoughtlessness.

ondoor·dringbaar, -bare, *a.* impenetrable,
impervious. ondoor·dringbaarheid, no pl.,
n. impenetrability, imperviousness.

ondoor·grondelijk, *a.* inscrutable, unfathomable. ondoor·grondelijkheid, no pl., *n.*
inscrutability.

ondoor·schijnend, *a.* opaque.

ondoor·zichtig, *a.* untransparent.

on·draaglijk, *a.* unbearable, intolerable.

ondubbel·zinnig, *a.* unambiguous.

on·duidelijk, *a.* indistinct, not clear. on-
·duidelijkheid, -heden, *n.* indistinctness;
obscurity.

on·duldbaar, -bare, *a.* intolerable.

ondu·leren, -leer, *v.t.* & *v.i.* to wave,
undulate.

on·echt, *a.* not genuine, spurious; illegitimate
(*child*).

on·edel, *a.* base.

on·eens, *a.* het ~ zijn, to disagree; het met
zichzelf ~ zijn, to be in two minds.

·oneer, no pl., *n.* dishonour, disgrace. on·eer-
baar, -bare, *a.* indecent. on·eerbaarheid,
-heden, *n.* indecency. oneer·biedig, *a.*
disrespectful. oneer·biedigheid, -heden, *n.*
disrespect. on·eerlijk, *a.* dishonest.
on·eerlijkheid, -heden, *n.* dishonesty.
on·eervol, -lle, *a.* dishonourable.

on·eetbaar, -bare, *a.* uneatable.

on·effen, *a.* uneven, rough.

on·eindig, *a.* infinite, endless. ¶no pl., *n.n.*
tot in 't ~e, ad infinitum. on·eindigheid,
no pl., *n.* infinity.

on·enig, *a.* at variance. on·enigheid, -heden,
n. discord; quarrel.

oner·varen, *a.* inexperienced. oner·varenheid,
no pl., *n.* inexperience.

on·even, *a.* odd (*not even*). oneven·redig, *a.*
disproportionate. oneven·redigheid, -heden,
n. disproportion. oneven·wichtig, *a.*
unbalanced.

onfat·soenlijk, *a.* improper, indecent. onfat-
·soenlijkheid, -heden, *n.* impropriety,
indecency.

on·feilbaar, -bare, *a.* infallible. on·feilbaar-
heid, no pl., *n.* infallibility.

on·fraai, *a.* unlovely.

on·fris, -sse, *a.* not fresh.

on·gaarne, *adv.* (*stilted*) reluctantly. iets ~
zien, to frown upon something.

on·gangbaar, -bare, *a.* not current.

ongast·vrij, *a.* inhospitable.

onge·acht, *a.* unesteemed. ¶*prep.* in spite of.

onge·baand, *a.* unbeaten, untrodden.

onge·beden, *a.* unbidden.

onge·blust, *a.* unquenched. ~e kalk, unslaked lime, quicklime.

onge·bonden, *a.* unbound; dissolute. onge-
·bondenheid, -heden, *n.* dissoluteness.

onge·bruikt, *a.* unused.

onge·build, *a.* unbolted (*meal*).

onge·daan, -dane, *a.* unperformed, undone.
iets ~ maken, to live something down.

onge·deerd, *a.* unhurt.

onge·dekt, *a.* uncovered.

onge·desemd, *a.* unleavened.

·ongedierte, no pl., *n.n.* vermin.

onge·droomd, *a.* undreamt of.

·ongeduld, no pl., *n.n.* impatience. onge-
·duldig, *a.* impatient.

onge·durig, *a.* restless, fidgety. onge·durig-
heid, no pl., *n.* restlessness.

onge·dwongen, *a.* natural, unconstrained.
onge·dwongenheid, no pl., *n.* unconstraint.

onge·eerd, *a.* unhonoured.

ongeëven·aard, *a.* matchless, unparalleled.

ongefran·keerd, *a.* unstamped.

ongege·neerd, *a.* unceremonious, free-and-
easy. ongege·neerdheid, -heden, *n.* free-
and-easiness.

onge·grond, *a.* unfounded, groundless.

onge·gund, *a.* begrudged.

onge·hard, *a.* unhardened, untempered.

onge·havend, *a.* undamaged.

onge·hinderd, *a.* unhindered, unimpeded.

onge·hoopt, *a.* unhoped-for.

onge·hoord, *a.* unheard of.

onge·hoorzaam, -zame, *a.* disobediènt. onge-
·hoorzaamheid, -heden, *n.* disobedience.

onge·huwd, *a.* unmarried.

onge·kleed, *a.* unclothed.

onge·kleurd, *a.* plain, uncoloured.

onge·korven, *a.* uncut.

onge·krenkt, *a.* unhurt.

onge·kreukt, *a.* uncrumpled, unruffled.

onge·kunsteld, *a.* artless, unaffected.

onge·laden, *a.* unloaded.

onge·geldig, *a.* invalid. ~ maken, to invalidate;
~ verklaren, to annul. on·geldigheid, no
pl., *n.* invalidity, nullity. on·geldig-
verklaring, *n.* annulment.

onge·leerd, *a.* unlearned; ignorant.

onge·legen, *a.* inconvenient, inopportune.
kom ik ~?, am I intruding. onge·legenheid,
-heden, *n.* inconvenience, difficulty. in ~
verkeren, to be embarrassed.

onge·lijk, *a.* unequal; dissimilar. niet ~ aan,
not unlike. ¶*adv.* unequally; unevenly.
·ongelijk, no pl., *n.n.* wrong. ~ bekennen,
to admit oneself in the wrong; iemand ~
geven, to disagree with someone; iemand

geen ~ *geven,* not to blame a person; *iemand in 't* ~ *stellen,* to put a person in the wrong. **ongelijk·benig,** *a.* scalene *(angle, triangle).* **onge·lijkheid, -heden,** *n.* inequality; unevenness. **ongelijk·matig,** *a.* unequal, uneven. **ongelijk·soortig,** *a.* heterogenous. **ongelijk·soortigheid,** no pl., *n.* heterogeneity. **ongelijk·vormig,** *a.* dissimilar. **ongelijk·zijdig** *a.* scalene *(triangle).*

ongelini·eerd, *a.* unruled, without lines.

onge·lofelijk, *a.* incredible, unbelievable.

·ongeloof, no pl., *n.n.* unbelief, disbelief.

onge·loofbaar, -bare, *a.* unbelievable. **ongeloof·waardig,** *a.* not to be relied on *(information).* **onge·lovig,** *a.* unbelieving; incredulous. **onge·lovige, -n,** *n.* unbeliever, infidel.

onge·louterd, *a.* unrefined.

·ongeluk, -kken, *n.n.* unhappiness; ill-luck; misfortune; accident; wretch. *een* ~ *komt nooit alleen,* misfortunes never come singly; *een* ~ *krijgen,* to meet with an accident; *het zal z'n* ~ *zijn,* it will be his ruin; *zich een* ~ *begaan,* to do something to oneself; *zich een* ~ *eten,* to eat oneself nearly to burst. **·ongelukje, -s,** *n.n.* misfortune. **onge·lukkig,** *a.* unhappy; unfortunate; unlucky. ¶*adv.* unhappily; unfortunately; unluckily. **onge·lukkiger-wijs,** *adv.* unfortunately. **·ongeluksbode, -n,** *n.* bearer of bad news. **·ongeluksdag,** *n.* unlucky day. **·ongelukskind, -eren,** *n.n.* unlucky person. **·ongeluksvogel, -s,** *n.* bird of ill omen.

·ongemak, -kken, *n.n.* inconvenience, discomfort; trouble *(physical).* **onge·makkelijk,** *a.* uncomfortable. ¶*adv.* not easily.

ongema·nierd, *a.* unmannerly.

onge·meen, -mene, *a. (stilted)* uncommon, rare.

onge·merkt, *a.* unperceived; unmarked.

ongemeubi·leerd, *a.* unfurnished.

onge·moeid, *a.* undisturbed. *iemand* ~ *laten,* to leave a person alone.

onge·naakbaar, -bare, *a.* unapproachable.

·ongenade, no pl., *n.* disgrace, displeasure. *in* ~ *vallen bij,* to fall into disgrace with. **onge·nadig,** *a.* merciless.

onge·neeslijk, *a.* incurable.

onge·negen, *a.,* **onge·neigd,** *a.* disinclined.

onge·nietbaar, -bare, *a.* unpalatable; disagreeable.

·ongenoegen, no pl., *n.n.* displeasure. ~ *krijgen met,* to fall out with. **onge·noeglijk,** *a.* unpleasant. **onge·noegzaam, -zame,** *a.* inadequate.

onge·nood, -node, *a.* uninvited.

onge·oefend, *a.* untrained.

onge·oorloofd, *a.* unpermitted, unlawful.

onge·ordend, *a.* disorderly.

onge·past, *a.* improper, inappropriate.

onge·rechtig, *a.* iniquitous. **onge·rechtigd,** *a.*

unwarranted. **onge·rechtigheid, -heden,** *n.* iniquity.

onge·reddrd, *a.* disorderly.

onge·reed, -rede, *a.* unprepared. **onge·rede,** no pl., *n.n. in 't* ~ *raken,* to get into a tangle.

onge·regeld, *a.* irregular. *op* ~*e tijden,* at odd times; ~*e goederen,* job lot; ~*e klant,* chance customer. **onge·regeldheid, -heden,** *n.* irregularity.

onge·rekend, *a.* uncounted. ~ *. . .,* without taking . . . into account.

onge·rept, *a.* untouched, virgin.

·ongerief, no pl., *n.n.* inconvenience. **onge·riefelijk,** *a.* inconvenient. **onge·riefelijkheid, -heden,** *n.* inconvenience.

onge·rijmd, *a.* absurd, preposterous.

onge·rust, *a.* anxious, uneasy, worried. *zich* ~ *maken over,* to worry about. **onge·rustheid,** no pl., *n.* anxiety, uneasiness.

onge·schikt, *a.* unsuited; inconvenient.

onge·schoeid, *a.* unshod.

onge·schonden, *a.* undamaged.

onge·schoold, *a.* unschooled.

onge·schoren, *a.* unshaved.

onge·stadig, *a.* unsteady.

onge·steld, *a.* unwell, indisposed. **onge·steldheid, -heden,** *n.* indisposition.

onge·stoord, *a.* undisturbed.

onge·straft, *a.* unpunished. ¶*adv.* with impunity.

onge·tekend, *a.* unsigned.

onge·troost, *a.* uncomforted.

onge·trouw, *a.* unfaithful. **onge·trouwd,** *a.* unmarried, single.

onge·twijfeld, *a.* undoubted. ¶*adv.* undoubtedly, no doubt.

·ongeval, -llen, *n.n.* accident. **·ongevallenwet, -tten,** *n.* Workman's Compensation Act. **onge·vallig,** *a.* displeasing.

onge·veer, *adv.* about, approximately.

onge·veinsd, *a.* unfeigned.

onge·vleugeld, *a.* wingless.

onge·voelig, *a.* unfeeling; insensible. ~ *voor,* insensible to. **onge·voeligheid. -heden,** *n.* insensibility.

onge·wapend, *a.* unarmed.

onge·wassen, *a.* unwashed.

onge·wenst, *a.* undesirable, unwished for.

onge·wettigd, *a.* unauthorized.

onge·wijd, *a.* unhallowed.

onge·wijzigd, *a.* unaltered.

onge·wild, *a.* unintentional; not in demand. **onge·willig,** *a.* unwilling.

onge·woon, -wone, *a.* unusual, unfamiliar. **onge·woonheid, -heden,** *n.* unusualness. **·ongewoonte,** no pl., *n.* want of practice.

onge·wraakt, *a.* unchallenged.

onge·wroken, *a.* unavenged.

onge·zegd, *a.* unsaid.

onge·zeglijk, *a.* intractable.

onge·zellig, *a.* unsociable; not pleasant (to be).

onge·zien, *a.* unseen. ¶*adv.* in spite of.

onge·zocht, *a.* natural; unsought for.

onge·zond, a. unhealthy.
onge·zouten, a. unsalted. ¶adv. iemand ~ de waarheid zeggen, to tell someone the blunt truth.
onge·zuurd, a. unleavened.
ongods·dienstig, a. irreligious.
·ongunst, no pl., n. disfavour. **on·gunstig,** a. unfavourable; adverse.
on·guur, -gure, a. unsavoury.
on·handelbaar, -bare, a. unmanageable.
on·handig, a. clumsy, awkward. **on·handigheid, -heden,** n. clumsiness.
on·hebbelijk, a. disagreeable. **on·hebbelijkheid, -heden,** n. disagreeable habit or action.
·onheil, n.n. calamity. ~ stichten, to work mischief. **onheil·spellend,** a. ominous.
onher·bergzaam, -zame, a. inhospitable.
onher·kenbaar, -bare, a. unrecognizable.
onher·roepelijk, a. irrevocable.
onher·stelbaar, -bare, a. irreparable.
on·heuglijk, a. immemorial. sedert ~e tijden, since time immemorial.
on·heus, a. discourteous.
on·hoorbaar, -bare, a. inaudible.
on·houdbaar, -bare, a. untenable.
on·huiselijk, a. not like home.
on·ingewijd, a. uninitiated.
onin·schikkelijk, a. unaccommodating.
on·juist, a. incorrect, inaccurate. **on·juistheid, -heden,** n. inaccuracy.
on·kenbaar, -bare, a. unrecognizable.
on·kies, a. indelicate.
·onklaar, -klare, a. out of order, fouled.
·onkosten, no pl. n. expenses. iemand op ~ jagen, to run someone into expense; zonder ~, free of charge.
on·kreukbaar, -bare, a. unimpeachable. **on·kreukbaarheid,** no pl., n. integrity.
·onkruid, no pl., n.n. weed(s). ~ vergaat niet, ill weeds grow apace.
on·kuis, a. unchaste. **on·kuisheid, -heden,** n. unchastity.
·onkunde, no pl., n. ignorance. uit zuiver ~, from sheer ignorance. **on·kundig,** a. ignorant. ~ van, unaware of; iemand van iets ~ laten, not to inform someone of something.
on·kwetsbaar, -bare, a. invulnerable.
·onlangs, adv. recently, the other day.
on·ledig, a. zich ~ houden met, to occupy one's time with.
on·leesbaar, -bare, a. illegible. **on·leesbaarheid,** no pl., n. illegibility.
on·logisch, a. illogical.
on·loochenbaar, -bare, a. undeniable.
·onlusten, pl. only, n. disturbance, riot.
·onmacht, n. impotence. in ~ liggen, to lie in a swoon. **on·machtig,** a. impotent.
on·matig, a. immoderate.
onmee·dogend, a. merciless, ruthless.
on·meetbaar, -bare, a. immeasurable.
·onmens, n. brute. **on·menselijk,** a. inhuman.
on·merkbaar. -bare, a. imperceptible.

on·metelijk, a. immense. **on·metelijkheid,** no pl., n. immensity.
on·middellijk, a. immediate, direct. ¶adv. immediately, directly, at once, straightaway.
·onmin, no pl., n. discord, quarrel.
on·misbaar, -bare, a. indispensable. **on·misbaarheid,** no pl., n. indispensability.
onmis·kenbaar, -bare, a. unmistakable.
on·mogelijk, a. impossible; ridiculous. ¶adv. not possibly, impossibly. **on·mogelijkheid, -heden,** n. impossibility.
on·mondig, a. under age.
onna·denkend, a. thoughtless. **onna·denkendheid, -heden,** n. thoughtlessness.
onna·speurlijk, a. inscrutable.
onna·tuurlijk, a. unnatural.
onnauw·keurig, a. inaccurate, inexact.
on·nodig, a. unnecessary.
on·nozel, a. simple, silly; harmless; paltry. **Onnozele·kinderendag,** N. Innocents' Day.
on·nut, -tte, a. useless.
onom·koopbaar, -bare, a. incorruptible.
onom·stotelijk, a. irrefutable.
onom·wonden, a. frank, straight out.
onont·beerlijk, a. indispensable.
onont·gonnen, a. uncultivated.
onont·koombaar, -bare, a. ineluctable, inescapable.
onont·ploft, a. unexploded.
onont·vankelijk, a. unreceptive.
onont·warbaar, -bare, a. inextricable.
onont·wikkeld, a. undeveloped; uneducated.
on·ooglijk, a. unsightly.
onoordeel·kundig, a. injudicious.
on·opgelost, a. undissolved.
on·opgemerkt, a. unnoticed.
on·opgesmukt, a. unadorned, unembroidered.
onop·houdelijk, a. incessant.
onop·lettend, a. inattentive.
onop·losbaar, -bare, a. insoluble.
onop·recht, a. insincere.
onop·zettelijk, a. unintentional, inadvertent.
onover·gankelijk, a. intransitive.
onover·komelijk, a. insuperable.
onover·troffen, a. unsurpassed.
onover·winnelijk, a. invincible. **onover·winnelijkheid,** no pl., n. invincibility.
·onpaar, -pare, a. uneven.
onpar·tijdig, a. impartial. **onpar·tijdigheid, -heden,** n. impartiality.
·onpas, adv. te ~, out of season or amiss. **on·passelijk,** a. sick (vomiting).
on·peilbaar, -bare, a. unfathomable.
onper·soonlijk, a. impersonal.
on·practisch, a. unpractical.
·onraad, no pl., n.n. danger. er broeit ~, there is trouble brewing. **on·raadzaam, -zame,** a. inadvisable.
·onrecht, no pl., n.n. wrong, injustice. iemand ~ aandoen, to wrong a person; ten ~e, unjustly. **onrecht·matig,** a. unlawful, illegal. **onrecht·matigheid, -heden,** n.

illegality. **onrecht·vaardig**, *a.* unjust, unfair. **onrecht·vaardigheid, -heden**, *n.* injustice, unfairness. **onrecht·zinnig**, *a.* heterodox.

on·redelijk, *a.* unreasonable, irrational.

onregel·matig, *a.* irregular. **onregel·matigheid, -heden**, *n.* irregularity.

on·rein, *a.* unclean, impure.

on·ridderlijk, *a.* unchivalrous.

on·rijp, *a.* unripe.

on·roerend, *a.* immovable. *~e goederen*, immovables, real property.

·onrust, no pl., *n.* unrest; disturbance. ¶ *n.* fidget; balance (*in watch*). **onrust·barend**, *a.* alarming. **on·rustig**, *a.* restless, disturbed. **·onruststoker, -s**, *n.* mischief-maker.

ons, *n.n.* ounce (*of 100 grammes*). ¶ *pers. pron.* us, to us. ¶ **-nze**, *poss. pron.* our. *See* **onze**.

onsamen·hangend, *a.* incoherent, disjointed.

on·schadelijk, *a.* harmless.

on·schatbaar, -bare, *a.* invaluable.

on·scheidbaar, -bare, *a.* inseparable.

on·schendbaar, -bare, *a.* inviolable. **on·schendbaarheid**, no pl., *n.* inviolability; immunity (*parliamentary*).

on·schoon, -schone, *a.* lacking beauty. **·onschuld**, no pl., *n.* innocence. **on·schuldig**, *a.* innocent; harmless.

on·smakelijk, *a.* unpalatable, unsavoury.

onso·lide, *a.* unsubstantial; unsound (*company, etc.*).

onstand·vastig, *a.* inconstant.

on·sterfelijk, *a.* immortal. **on·sterfelijkheid**, no pl., *n.* immortality.

on·stichtelijk, *a.* unedifying.

on·stoffelijk, *a.* incorporeal.

on·stuimig, *a.* impetuous; turbulent. **on·stuimigheid, -heden**, *n.* impetuosity; turbulence.

onsympa·thiek, *a.* unlikeable.

ontaal·kundig, *a.* ungrammatical.

ont·aard, *a.* degenerate. **ont·aarden**, *v.i.* to degenerate, deteriorate. **ont·aarding**, *n.* degeneration, deterioration.

on·tastbaar, -bare, *a.* impalpable, intangible.

ont·beren, -beer, *v.t.* to lack, do without. **ont·bering**, *a.* privation, want, hardship.

ont·bieden, *v.t., str.* to summon, call.

ont·bijt, *n.n.* breakfast. **ont·bijten**, *v.i., str.* to breakfast. **ont·bijtkoek**, *n.* gingerbread.

ont·binden, *v.t., str.* to dissolve; to decompose, resolve. **ont·binding**, *n.* dissolution; decomposition. *~ van krachten*, resolution of forces; *tot ~ overgaan*, to decompose.

ont·bloot, -blote, *a.* bare; uncovered (*head*); devoid. **ont·bloten, -bloot**, *v.t.* to bare, uncover; to unsheathe. **ont·bloting**, *n.* denudation.

ont·boezemen, zich, *v.r.* to unbosom oneself. **ont·boezeming**, *n.* outpouring, effusion.

ont·bolsteren, *v.t.* to shell, hull.

ont·bossen, -bos, *v.t.* to disafforest.

ont·brandbaar, -bare, *a.* inflammable. **ont·brandbaarheid**, no pl., *n.* inflammability.

ont·branden, *v.i.* to catch fire, ignite. *doen ~*, to ignite. **ont·branding**, *n.* ignition (*process*).

ont·breken, -breek, *v.i., str.* to be lacking. ¶ *v.t., str. het ontbreekt ons aan . . .*, we lack . . .

ont·cijferen, *v.t.* to decipher, decode. **ont·cijfering**, *n.* decipherment, decoding.

ont·daan, -dane, *a.* upset, shaken.

ont·dekken, -dek, *v.t.* to discover; to uncover. **ont·dekker, -s**, *n.* discoverer. **ont·dekking**, *n.* discovery. **ont·dekkingsreis, -zen**, *n.* voyage *or* journey of discovery. **ont·dekkingsreiziger, -s**, *n.* explorer.

ont·doen, -doe, *v.t., irr. ~ van*, to strip of. ¶ *v.r., irr. zich ~ van*, to dispose of, divest oneself of.

ont·dooien, *v.i.* to thaw; to melt.

ont·duiken, *v.t., str.* to elude, dodge. **ont·duiking**, *n.* evasion.

ontegen·zeggelijk, *a.* undeniable, incontestable.

ont·eigenen, *v.t.* to dispossess; to expropriate (*property*). **ont·eigening**, *n.* dispossession, expropriation.

on·telbaar, -bare, *a.* innumerable, countless.

on·tembaar, -bare, *a.* indomitable.

ont·eren, -eer, *v.t.* to dishonour, desecrate. **ont·erend**, *a.* degrading. **ont·ering**, *n.* desecration.

ont·erven, -erf, *v.t.* to disinherit. **ont·erving**, *n.* disinheritance.

onte·vreden, *a.* dissatisfied, discontented. **onte·vredenheid**, no pl., *n.* dissatisfaction, discontent.

ont·fermen, *v.r. zich ~ over*, to have pity on. **ont·ferming**, no pl., *n.* pity.

ont·futselen, *v.t. iemand iets ~*, to sneak something away from someone.

ont·gaan, -ga, *v.t., irr.* to escape, elude.

ont·gelden, *v.t., str.* to suffer for. *het ~*, to suffer, pay for it (*fig.*).

ont·ginnen, -gin, *v.t., str.* to reclaim, clear (*land*); to develop, exploit (*mineral deposits*). **ont·ginning**, *n.* reclamation; development.

ont·glippen, -glip, *v.t.* to slip away from, escape.

ont·goochelen, *v.t.* to disillusion, undeceive. **ont·goocheling**, *n.* disillusionment.

ont·groeien, *v.t.* to outgrow.

ont·groenen, *v.t.* to rag (*freshmen*). **ont·groening**, *n.* ragging (*of freshmen*).

ont·haal, no pl., *n.n.* reception. *een goed ~ vinden*, to meet with a favourable reception. **ont·halen**, *v.t.* to treat, regale. *~ op*, to treat to, regale with.

ont·halzen, -hals, *v.t.* (*stilted*) to decapitate.

ont·heffen, -hef, *v.t., str.* to free; to exonerate. *~ van*, to free from (*blame, obligation*) *or* to relieve from (*post*). **ont·heffing**, *n.* exemption; exoneration; discharge, removal.

ont·heiligen, *v.t.* to desecrate. **ont·heiliging,** *n.* desecration.

ont·hoofden, *v.t.* to decapitate, behead. **ont·hoofding,** *n.* decapitation.

ont·houden, *v.t., irr.* to withhold, keep from, deny; to remember, bear in mind. ¶*v.r., irr. zich ~ van,* to abstain *or* refrain from. **ont·houdend,** *a.* abstinent. **ont·houder, -s,** *n.* abstainer. **ont·houding,** no pl., *n.* abstinence; abstention.

ont·hullen, -hul, *v.t.* to unveil; to reveal. **ont·hulling,** *n.* unveiling; disclosure.

ont·hutsen, *v.t.* to disconcert. **ont·hutst,** *a.* disconcerted.

·ontij(d), *n.* inopportune time. **on·tijdig,** *a.* inopportune, untimely.

ont·kennen, -ken, *v.t.* to deny. **ont·kennend,** *a.* negative. *~ antwoord,* answer in the negative. **ont·kenning,** *n.* negation.

ont·ketenen, *v.t.* to unchain.

ont·kiemen, *v.i.* to germinate. **ont·kieming,** *n.* germination.

ont·kleden, -kleed, *v.t. & v.r.* to undress.

ont·knopen, -knoop, *v.t.* to untie, unbutton. **ont·knoping,** *n.* denouement.

ont·komen, *v.i., irr.* to escape. *~ aan,* to elude *or* to get away from. **ont·koming,** *n.* escape.

ont·koppelen, *v.t.* to uncouple, disconnect.

ont·kurken, *v.t.* to uncork.

ont·laden, -laad, *v.t., irr.* to unload; to discharge (*electricity*).

ont·lasten, *v.t.* to unburden, relieve. ¶zich ~, *v.r.* to relieve oneself. **ont·lasting,** *n.* motion, evacuation.

ont·leden, -leed, *v.t.* to analyse; to dissect. **ont·leding,** *n.* analysis; dissection. **ont·leedkunde,** no pl., *n.* anatomy. **ont·leedmes, -ssen,** *n.n.* scalpel, dissecting knife.

ont·lenen, -leen, *v.i. ~ aan,* to borrow *or* derive from.

ont·loken, *a.* open (*flower*).

ont·lokken, -lok, *v.t.* to draw, coax, elicit.

ont·lopen, -loop, *v.t., str.* to escape; to avoid, shun.

ont·luiken, *v.i., str.* to open. **ont·luikend,** *a.* budding, nascent.

ont·luizen, -luis, *v.t.* to delouse.

ont·mantelen, *v.t.* to dismantle.

ont·maskeren, *v.t.* to unmask. **ont·maskering,** *n.* unmasking.

ont·masten, *v.t.* to dismast.

ont·moedigen, *v.t.* to discourage. **ont·moediging,** *n.* discouragement.

ont·moeten, *v·t.* to meet, come across; to encounter. *elkaar ~,* to meet (one another). **ont·moeting,** *n.* meeting; encounter.

ont·nemen, -neem, *v.t., str.* to take (away) from, deprive of. **ont·neming,** *n.* deprivation.

ont·nuchteren, *v.t.* to sober; to disillusion,

undeceive. **ont·nuchtering,** *n.* disillusionment.

ontoe·gankelijk, *a.* inaccessible. **ontoe·gankelijkheid,** no pl., *n.* inaccessibility.

ontoe·geeflijk, *a.* unaccommodating.

ontoe·laatbaar, -bare, *a.* inadmissible.

ontoe·passelijk, *a.* inappropriate.

ontoe·reikend, *a.* inadequate. **ontoe·reikendheid, -heden,** *n.* inadequacy.

ontoe·rekenbaar, -bare, *a.* irresponsible (*mad*).

on·toonbaar, -bare, *a.* not fit to be seen.

ont·plofbaar, -bare, *a.* explosive. **ont·ploffen, -plof,** *v.i.* to explode. **ont·ploffing,** *n.* explosion, detonation.

ont·plooien, *v.t.* to unfold, unfurl; to deploy. **ont·plooing,** *n.* deployment; maturity (*of faculties*).

ont·poppen, -pop, zich, *v.r.* (*lit.*) to leave the chrysalis; (*fig.*) to reveal oneself as, blossom out into.

ont·raden, -raad, *v.t., irr. & v.i., irr.* to dissuade, advise against.

ont·rafelen, *v.t.* to unravel.

ont·redderd, *a.* disabled, battered. **ont·reddering,** *n.* damage, confusion.

ont·rieven, -rief, *v.t.* to deprive.

ont·roerd, *a.* moved. **ont·roeren,** *v.t.* to move, affect. **ont·roering,** *n.* emotion.

ont·rollen, -rol, *v.t.* to unroll.

on·troostbaar, -bare, *a.* inconsolable.

·ontrouw, no pl., *n.* disloyalty; infidelity. ¶*a.* disloyal; unfaithful.

ont·roven, -roof, *v.t.* to rob of.

ont·ruimen, *v.t.* to evacuate, clear. **ont·ruiming,** *n.* evacuation.

ont·rukken, -ruk, *v.t.* to snatch (away) from.

ont·schepen, -scheep, *v.t.* to disembark. ¶zich ~, *v.r.* to disembark. **ont·scheping,** *n.* disembarkation.

ont·schieten, *v.t., str.* to escape, slip (away) from.

ont·sieren, *v.t.* to disfigure.

ont·slaan, -sla, *v.t., irr.* to dismiss, discharge. *~ van,* to relieve from *or* of. **ont·slag,** no pl., *n.* dismissal, discharge. (*zijn*) *~ aanvragen,* to ask to be released (*from post*); (*zijn*) *~ geven,* to dismiss; *zijn ~ indienen,* to hand in one's resignation; (*zijn*) *~ krijgen,* to be dismissed; (*zijn*) *~ nemen,* to resign. **ont·slagneming,** *n.* resignation (*from post*).

ont·slapen, *a.* (*stilted*) passed away.

ont·sluieren, *v.t.* to unveil.

ont·sluiten, *v.t., str.* (*stilted*) to open.

ont·smetten, -smet, *v.t.* to disinfect. **ont·smetting,** *n.* disinfection. **ont·smettingsmiddel,** *n.n.* disinfectant.

ont·snappen, -snap, *v.i.* to escape. *~ aan,* to escape from.

ont·spannen, -span, *v.t., irr.* to unbend (*bow*); to relax. ¶zich ~, *v.r., irr.* to relax; to seek recreation. **ont·spanning,** *n.* relaxation; recreation.

ont·spinnen, -spin, zich, v.r., str. to develop, arise (conversation).
ont·sporen, -spoor, v.i. to be derailed. doen ~, to derail. **ont·sporing,** n. derailment.
ont·springen, v.t., str. to jump away from. de dans ~, to escape scot-free.
ont·spruiten, v.i., str. to bud, sprout.
ont·staan, -sta, v.i., irr. to originate, arise. doen ~, to cause. ¶no pl., n.n. origin.
ont·steken, -steek, v.t., str. (stilted) to kindle. doen ~, to inflame. **ont·steking,** n. inflammation.
ont·steld, a. alarmed.
ont·stelen, -steel, v.t., str. to steal from.
ont·stellen, -stel, v.t. to alarm. **ont·steltenis,** no pl., n. alarm, consternation.
ont·stemd, a. out of tune; displeased. **ont··stemmen, -stem,** v.t. to put out of tune; to displease.
ont·stentenis, no pl., n. bij ~ van, in the absence of, in default of.
ont·stichten, v.t. to give offence.
ont·stoken, a. inflamed.
ont·takelen, v.t. to dismantle (ship).
ont·trekken, -trek, v.t., str. ~ aan, to withdraw from. ¶v.r., str. zich ~ aan, to back out of. **ont·trekking,** n. withdrawal.
ont·tronen, -troon, v.t. to dethrone.
·ontucht, no pl., n. immorality, prostitution. huis van ~, house of ill-fame. **on·tuchtig,** a. lewd.
·ontuig, no pl., n.n. riff-raff.
ont·vallen, -val, v.t., str. to fall from. zich geen woord laten ~, not to say a word about it; het is mij ~, it escaped me.
ont·vangbewijs, -zen, n.n. receipt. **ont·vang·dag,** n. reception day. **ont·vangen,** v.t., str. to receive. **ont·vangenis,** no pl., n. conception (impregnation). onbevlekte ~, immaculate conception. **ont·vanger, -s,** n. recipient; tax-collector. **ont·vangerskantoor, -toren,** n.n. tax-collector's office. **ont·vangkamer, -s,** n. reception room. **ont·vangst,** n. reception; receipt (the receiving); takings, receipts. in ~ nemen, to take, receive; na or bij ~ van, on receipt of. **ont·vangtoestel, -llen,** n.n. receiving set. **ont·vankelijk,** a. susceptible, receptive. ~ voor, amenable to. **ont··vankelijkheid, -heden,** n. susceptibility.
ont·veinzen, -veins, v.t. to dissemble, conceal.
ont·vellen, -vel, v.t. to skin.
ont·vetten, -vet, v.t. to remove the fat of.
ont·vlambaar, -bare, a. inflammable. **ont··vlammen, -vlam,** v.t. to inflame.
ont·vluchten, v.t. & v.i. to escape, flee.
·ont voeren, v.t. to abduct, carry off. **ont··voering,** n. abduction.
ont·volken, v.t. to depopulate. **ont·volking,** n. depopulation.
ont·vreemden, v.t. to misappropriate, embezzle.
ont·waken, -waak, v.i. (stilted) to awake.
ont·wapenen, v.t. to disarm.

ont·waren, -waar, v.t. (stilted) to perceive.
ont·warren, -war, v.t. to disentangle, unravel.
ont·wassen, -was, v.t. to grow out of.
ont·weien, v.t. to draw, eviscerate.
ont·wennen, -wen, v.t. to lose the habit of. iemand iets ~, to break a person of the habit of doing something.
ont·werp, n.n. design, project. ¶prefix. draft-. **ont·werpen,** v.t., str. to design, plan, draft. **ont·werper, -s,** n. designer.
ont·wijden, v.t. to desecrate. **ont·wijding,** n. desecration.
on·twijfelbaar, -bare, a. undoubted, unquestionable.
ont·wijken, v.t., str. to evade; to avoid, shirk. **ont·wijkend,** a. evasive, noncommittal. **ont·wijking,** n. evasion.
ont·wikkelaar, -s, n. developer. **ont·wikkeld,** a. developed; well-educated. **ont·wikkelen,** v.t. to develop; to generate. zich ~ tot, to develop into. **ont·wikkeling,** n. development; evolution; education.
ont·woekeren, v.i. (stilted) ~ aan, to wrest from.
ont·worstelen, v.t. to wrest from. zich ~ aan, to tear oneself away from.
ont·wortelen, v.t. to uproot.
ont·wrichten, v.i. to dislocate. **ont·wrichting,** n. dislocation.
ont·zag, no pl., n.n. respect, awe. ~ hebben voor, to be in awe of; er ~ onder hebben, to keep them in awe. **ont·zaglijk,** a. stupendous, tremendous. **ontzag·wekkend,** a. awe-inspiring.
ont·zeggen, -zeg, v.t., irr. to deny, forbid. iemand de toegang ~, to refuse a person admittance ¶v.r., irr. zich iets ~, to deny oneself something. **ont·zegging,** n. denial (of pleasure, etc.).
ont·zenuwen, v.t. to unnerve.
ont·zet, no pl., n.n. relief (of town, etc.). ¶-tte, a. appalled; horrified; dislocated. **ont·zetten, -zet,** v.t. to relieve (town, etc.); to dismiss; to horrify; to dislocate. iemand uit zijn ambt ~, to deprive a person of his office. **ont·zettend,** a. appalling, dreadful. **ont·zetting,** n. relief; dismissal; dislocation. ¶no pl., n. horror, dismay.
ont·zien, -zie, v.t., irr. to fear; to respect; to spare, consider. niets ~d, unscrupulous, brutal. ¶zich ~, v.r., irr. to take care of oneself.
ont·zinken, v.t., str. to sink away from.
on·uitgegeven, a. unpublished.
on·uitgemaakt, a. undecided.
on·uitgesproken, a. unspoken.
onuit·puttelijk, a. inexhaustible. **onuit··puttelijkheid,** no pl., n. inexhaustibility.
onuit·spreekbaar, -bare, a. unpronounceable. **onuit·sprekelijk,** a. unspeakable.
onuit·staanbaar, -bare, a. unbearable.
onuit·wisbaar, -bare, a. indelible.
on·vast, a. unsteady; unsettled.
on·vatbaar, -bare, a. ~ voor, impervious to;

~ *maken*, to immunize. **on·vatbaarheid, -heden,** *n.* insusceptibility; immunity.
on·veilig, *a.* unsafe.
onver·anderbaar, -bare, *a.* unchangeable. **onver·anderlijk,** *a.* invariable.
onver·antwoord, *a.* unwarranted. **onverant·woordelijk,** *a.* irresponsible.
onver·beterlijk, *a.* incorrigible.
onver·biddelijk, *a.* inexorable, relentless.
onver·bloemd, *a.* (*fig.*) unvarnished.
onver·brekelijk, *a.* indissoluble.
onver·dacht, *a.* unsuspected.
onver·dedigbaar, -bare, *a.* indefensible.
onver·deelbaar, -bare, *a.* indivisible. **onver·deeld,** *a.* undivided. ¶*adv.* whole-heartedly.
onver·diend, *a.* undeserved. **onver·dienstelijk,** *a.* undeserving.
onver·dorven, *a.* not depraved.
onver·draagzaam, -zame, *a.* intolerant. **onver·draagzaamheid,** no pl., *n.* intolerance.
onver·droten, *a.* (*stilted*) indefatigable.
onver·enigbaar, -bare, *a.* incompatible.
onver·flauwd, *a.* unabated.
onver·gankelijk, *a.* imperishable.
onver·geeflijk, *a.* unpardonable.
onver·getelijk, *a.* unforgettable, memorable.
onver·hinderd, *a.* unimpeded.
onver·hoeds, *a.* unexpected, sudden. ¶*adv.* unawares.
onver·holen, *a.* undisguised. ¶*adv.* openly.
onver·hoopt, *a.* unexpected.
onver·kiesbaar, -bare, *a.* ineligible. **onver·lieslijk,** *a.* undesirable.
onver·klaarbaar, -bare, *a.* unaccountable, inexplicable.
onver·krijgbaar, -bare, *a.* unobtainable.
onver·kwikkelijk, *a.* unpleasant, unsavoury. **·onverlaat, -laten,** *n.* (*stilted*) scoundrel; vandal.
onver·mengd, *a.* unmixed, unalloyed.
onver·mijdelijk, *a.* inevitable.
onver·minderd, *a.* undiminished, unabated.
onver·moeibaar, -bare, *a.* indefatigable. **onver·moeid,** *a.* untiring.
·onvermogen, no pl., *n.n.* inability, incapacity; indigence. **onver·mogend,** *a.* powerless, unable.
onver·murwbaar, -bare, *a.* unrelenting, adamant.
onver·poosd, *a.* unremitting.
onver·richt, *a.* unperformed. ~*er zake terugkeren*, to return without having succeeded.
onver·saagd, *a.* undaunted.
onver·schillig, *a.* indifferent; heedless. ~ *voor*, indifferent to; *een* ~*e hoeveelheid*, any quantity. **onver·schilligheid,** no pl., *n.* indifference.
onver·schrokken, *a.* undaunted.
onver·slapt, *a.* unflagging.
onver·staanbaar, -bare, *a.* unintelligible.
onver·standig, *a.* unwise.
onver·stoorbaar, -bare, *a.* imperturbable. **onver·stoord,** *a.* undisturbed.

onver·taalbaar, -bare, *a.* untranslatable.
onver·teerbaar, -bare, *a.* indigestible.
onver·togen, *a.* indelicate, indecent.
onver·vaard, *a.* fearless.
onver·valst, *a.* unadulterated.
onver·vreemdbaar, -bare, *a.* inalienable.
onver·vuld, *a.* unfulfilled.
onver·wacht, *a.* & *adv.* unexpected. **onver·wachts,** *adv.* unexpectedly.
onver·wijld, *a.* immediate. ¶*adv.* immediately, without delay.
onver·zadelijk, *a.* insatiable.
onver·zekerd, *a.* uninsured.
onver·zettelijk, *a.* stubborn, unyielding.
onver·zoenlijk, *a.* irreconcilable, implacable.
onver·zorgd, *a.* unprovided for, uncared for; untidy, unkempt.
onver·zwakt, *a.* unweakened, unimpaired.
on·vindbaar, -bare, *a.* unfindable. *het is* ~, it cannot be found.
on·voegzaam, -zame, *a.* unseemly.
on·voelbaar, -bare, *a.* intangible.
onvol·daan, -dane, *a.* unsatisfied; unpaid.
onvol·doend(e), *a.* insufficient.
onvol·komen, *a.* incomplete, imperfect.
onvol·ledig, *a.* incomplete.
onvol·maakt, *a.* imperfect. **onvol·maaktheid, -heden,** *n.* imperfection.
onvol·prezen, *a.* beyond praise.
onvol·tallig, *a.* incomplete (*insufficient number*).
onvol·tooid, *a.* unfinished, incomplete; imperfect (*tense*).
onvol·wassen, *a.* not fully grown.
on·voorbedacht, *a.* unpremeditated.
on·voorbereid, *a.* unprepared.
onvoor·delig, *a.* disadvantageous.
onvoor·spoedig, *a.* unpropitious.
onvoor·waardelijk, *a.* unconditional.
onvoor·zichtig, *a.* imprudent. **onvoor·zichtigheid, -heden,** *n.* imprudence.
onvoor·zien, *a.* unforeseen. **onvoor·ziens,** *adv.* unawares.
on·vriendelijk, *a.*, **onvriend·schappelijk,** *a.* unfriendly.
on·vrij, *a.* unfree. **on·vrije, -n,** *n.* serf, bondsman. **on·vrijheid,** no pl., *n.* serfdom, bondage. **onvrij·willig,** *a.* involuntary.
on·vruchtbaar, -bare, *a.* unfruitful, barren; unprofitable (*discussion*). **on·vruchtbaarheid,** no pl., *n.* barrenness.
on·waar, -ware, *a.* untrue.
·onwaarde, no pl., *n.* invalidity. *van* ~ *zijn*, to be null and void. **on·waardig,** *a.* unworthy.
on·waarheid, -heden, *n.* untruth. **onwaar·schijnlijk,** *a.* improbable. **onwaar·schijnlijkheid, -heden,** *n.* improbability.
on·wankelbaar, -bare, *a.* unwavering.
·onweer, -weren, *n.n.* thunder-storm. *er komt* ~, there is a storm brewing. **onweer·achtig,** *a.* thundery.
onweer·legbaar, -bare, *a.* incontrovertible, irrefutable.

·onweersbui, *n.* thunder-storm. ·onweerslucht, *n.* thundery *or* stormy sky.

onweer·staanbaar, -bare, *a.* irresistible.

·onweersvogel, -s, *n.* stormy petrel.

on·wel, *a.* unwell, indisposed.

on·welkom, *a.* unwelcome.

onwel·levend, *a.* discourteous.

onwel·luidend, *a.* unharmonious.

onwel·riekend, *a.* malodorous.

onwel·willend, *a.* disobliging.

·onweren, -weert, *v. imp.* to thunder.

on·wetend, *a.* ignorant. on·wetendheid, no pl., *n.* ignorance. on·wetens, *adv.* unknowingly, without my (*etc.*) knowledge.

onweten·schappelijk, *a.* unscientific.

on·wettelijk, *a.* illegal. on·wettig, *a.* unlawful, illegal; illegitimate.

on·wezenlijk, *a.* unreal.

on·wijs, -ze, *a.* unwise.

·onwil, no pl., *n.* unwillingness. onwillekeurig, *a.* involuntary. on·willig, *a.* unwilling; recalcitrant.

on·wrikbaar, -bare, *a.* unshakable.

on·zacht, *a.* ungentle; rough.

·onze, *pers. pron.* het ~, ours (*n.n. sing.*); de ~, ours (*n. sing.*); de ~n, ours (*n. & n.n. pl.*) or our family or party.

on·zedelijk, *a.* immoral, obscene. on·zedelijkheid, no pl., *n.* immorality, obscenity. on·zedig, *a.* immodest.

onzee·waardig, *a.* unseaworthy. onzee·waardigheid, no pl., *n.* unseaworthiness.

on·zeglijk, *a.* unutterable.

on·zeker, *a.* uncertain, doubtful; unsafe; shaky, unsteady. on·zekere, no pl., *n.n.* uncertainty. on·zekerheid, -heden, *n.* uncertainty.

onzelf·standig, *a.* dependent (on others).

onzelieve·heersbeestje, -s, *n.n.* lady-bird. onzelievevrouwen·bedstro, no pl., *n.n.* lady's bed straw.

·onzent, *adv.* te ~, at our place. ·onzenthalve, *adv.* (*stilted*) for our sake, as far as we are concerned. ·onzentwege, *adv.* ~ or van ~, on our behalf. ·onzentwil, *adv.* om ~, for our sake.

Onze·vader, -s, *n.n.* Lord's prayer.

on·zichtbaar, -bare, *a.* invisible. on·zichtbaarheid, no pl., *n.* invisibility.

on·zijdig, *a.* neutral. on·zijdigheid, no pl., *n.* neutrality.

·onzin, no pl., *n.* nonsense.

on·zindelijk, *a.* dirty. on·zindelijkheid, no pl., *n.* uncleanliness.

on·zinnig, *a.* nonsensical. on·zinnigheid, -heden, *n.* absurdity.

on·zuiver, *a.* impure. on·zuiverheid, -heden, *n.* impurity.

ooft, no pl., *n.n.* fruit (*in general*).

oog, ogen, *n.* eye. een blauw ~, a black eye; grote ogen opzetten, to open one's eyes wide; iets met lede ogen aanzien, to view something with envy; geen ~ dichtdoen, not to sleep a wink; zijn ogen de kost geven,

to feast one's eyes *or* to keep one's eyes skinned; iemand de ogen uitsteken, to make a person jealous; in het ~ lopen, to be obvious; in het ~ lopend, conspicuous, obvious; iets in het ~ houden, to keep an eye on something; iemand naar de ogen zien, to study a person's wishes; ~ om ~, an eye for an eye; onder vier ogen, privately (between two persons); iets onder de ogen zien, to face something, grapple with something; op het ~, on the face of it; iets op het ~ hebben, to have something in mind; uit het ~ verliezen, to lose sight of; uit het ~ uit het hart, out of sight out of mind; met iets voor ogen, with something in view. ·oogappel, -s, *n.* apple of the eye. ·ooggetuige, -n, *n.* eye-witness. ·ooghaar, -haren, *n.n.* eyelash. ·oogheelkunde, no pl., *n.* ophthalmology. ·oogholte, -n, *n.* (eye-)socket. ·oogje, -s, *n.n.* little eye. een ~ in het zeil houden, to keep a watchful eye. ·ooglid, -leden, *n.n.* eyelid. oogluikend, *adv.* iets ~ toelaten, to condone something, connive at something. ·oogmerk, *n.n.* object, aim. ·oogopslag, no pl., *n.* glance. in één ~ or bij de eerste ~, at a glance. ·oogpunt, *n.n.* point of view, viewpoint.

oogst, *n.* harvest; crop. ·oogsten, *v.t.* to harvest, reap, gather. ·oogster, -s, *n.* harvester. ·Oogstmaand, *N.* harvest month; August.

·oogtand, *n.* eye-tooth. ·oogvlies, -zen, *n.n.* cornea. ·oogwenk, *n.* wink, twinkling of an eye. ·oogzenuw, *n.* optic nerve.

ooi, *n.* ewe.

·ooievaar, -s, *n.* stork. ·ooievaarsbek, -kken, *n.* crane's bill.

ooit, *adv.* ever.

ook, *adv.* also, too, as well, likewise; even. ~ nog, still; ~ niet, neither, not . . . either; hoe ~, however; hoe dan ~, anyhow; waar ~, wherever; wanneer ~, whenever; wat ~, whatever; wie ~, whoever.

oom, -s, *n.* uncle. hoge ~, bigwig. ·oomzegger, -s, *n.* nephew, niece.

oor, oren, *n.n.* ear; handle (of cup, jug, etc.), ergens geen oren naar hebben, to refuse to hear of something; op één ~ na gevild, almost finished; tot over de oren in . . ., up to one's ears in . . .; iemand ter ore komen, to come to a person's ears.

·oorbaar, -bare, *a.* (*stilted*) seemly, proper.

·oorbel, -llen, *n.* ear-ring.

oord, *n.n.* (*stilted*) region; place.

·oordeel, -delen, *n.n.* judgment, opinion; sentence, verdict. een leven als een ~, a noise fit to wake the dead. oordeelkundig, *a.* judicious. ·oordeelsdag, *n.* judgment day. ·oordeelvelling, *n.* judgment. ·oordelen, -deel, *v.i.* to judge, deem. te ~ naar, judging from; ~ over, to judge of.

·oorijzer, -s, *n.n.* casque (gold or silver part

of Dutch female costume). ·oorknopje, -s, *n.n.* ear-drop.

·oorkonde, -n, *n.* charter, ancient document. ·oorkussen, -s, *n.n.* pillow. ·oorlam, -mmen, *n.n.* rum ration. ·oorlel, -llen, *n.* lobe of ear. ·oorlof, no pl., *n.n.* (*archaic*) permission; (*archaic*) farewell. ·oorlog, *n.* war. ~ *voeren,* to wage war; *in ~ zijn,* to be at war. ·oorlogsbehoeften, pl. only, *n.,* ·oorlogsbenodigdheden, pl. only, *n.* munitions of war. ·oorlogsbodem, -s, *n.* (*stilted*) warship. ·oorlogsbuit, no pl., *n.* booty. ·oorlogshaven, -s, *n.* naval port. ·oorlogsmisdadiger, -s, *n.* war criminal. ·oorlogsmoede, *a.* war-weary. ·oorlogsmolest, no pl., *n.n.* war risk. ·oorlogsschip, -schepen, *n.n.* man-of-war. ·oorlogsschuld, *n.* war debt; war guilt. ·oorlogsvloot, -vloten, *n.* navy, fleet. oorlog·voerend, *a.* belligerent, at war. ·oorlogvoering, no pl., *n.* conduct of war. oorlog·zuchtig, *a.* warlike, bellicose. oorlog-·zuchtigheid, no pl., *n.* bellicosity.

·oorspiegel, -s, *n.* ear speculum.

·oorsprong, *n.* origin, source. oor·spronkelijk, *a.* original. oor·spronkelijkheid, no pl., *n.* originality.

·oortje, -s, *n.n.* farthing. *hij kijkt alsof hij zijn laatste ~ versnoept heeft,* he looks taken aback.

·oortuiten, no pl., *n.n.* buzzing in the ears. ·ooruil, *n.* long-eared owl. ·oorveeg, -vegen, *n.* box on the ear. oorver·dovend, *a.* deafening. oorver·scheurend, *a.* ear-splitting. ·oorvijg, *n. See* oorveeg. ·oor-worm, *n.* earwig.

·oorzaak, -zaken, *n.* cause; root (*fig.*).

Oost, *n.* East. *de ~,* the East *or* the East Indies. ¶*a.* east. ¶*adv.* east. ·oostelijk, *a.* easterly, eastern. ~ *van,* (to the) east of, eastward of. ·Oosten, no pl., *n.n.* east. *het ~,* the East; *ten ~ van,* (to the) east of. ·Oostenrijk, *n.N.* Austria. ·Oostenrijker, -s, *N.* Austrian. ·Oosten-rijks, *a.* Austrian. Oostenrijk-Hon·gaars, *a.* Austro-Hungarian. ·oostenwind, *n.* east wind. ·ooster-, *prefix.* eastern. ·oosterling, *n.* Oriental. *vreemde ~en,* foreign Asiatics. ·oosters, *a.* oriental, eastern. ·Ooster-schelde, *N.* East Scheldt. Oost-·Goten, pl. only, *N.* Ostrogoths. Oost-Indië, *n. N.* East Indies. Oost-·Indiëvaarder, -s, *n.* East Indiaman. Oost-·Indisch, *a.* East Indian. ~ *doof,* pretending not to hear; ~*e kers,* nasturtium. ·Oostland, *n. N.* the Baltic countries. ·oostmoesson, -s, *n.* north-east *or* dry monsoon (*East Indies*). ·oostpassaat, no pl., *n.* north-east trade wind. ·oostwaarts, *a. & adv.* eastward. Oost·zee, *N.* Baltic.

ore, *n. See* oor.

·ootje, -s, *n.n.* small o. *iemand in het ~ nemen,* to pull a person's leg.

·ootmoed, no pl., *n.* humility, meekness. oot·moedig, *a.* humble, meek.

op, *prep.* on, upon; at; in. ~ *zijn Engels,* in the English way; ~ *een keer,* once upon a time. ¶*adv.* up; finished, gone, spent. ~ *en top,* every inch.

·opa, -'s, *n.* grandad.

o·paal, -palen, *n.* opal.

·opbellen, bel op, *v.t.s.* to ring up.

·opbergen, *v.t.s., str.* to put away, clear away. ·opbeuren, *v.t.s.* to lift up (*something heavy*); to clear up.

·opbiechten, *v.t.s.* to confess.

·opbieden, *v.i.s., str.* ~ *tegen,* to bid against. ·opblazen, blaas op, *v.t.s., str.* to blow up; to inflate.

·opblijven, blijf op, *v.i.s., str.* to stay up.

·opbloei, *n.* revival. ·opbloeien, *v.i.s.* to begin to flourish.

·opbod, no pl., *n.n. bij ~,* by auction.

·opborrelen, *v.i.s.* to bubble up.

·opbouw, no pl., *n.* building up. ·opbouwen, *v.t.s.* to build up; to construct.

·opbranden, *v.t.s.* to burn down *or* out.

·opbreken, breek op, *v.t.s., str.* to break up *or* open. *het beleg ~,* to raise the siege; *het kamp ~,* to break camp. ¶*v.i.s., str. het zal je zuur ~,* you will regret it.

·opbrengen, *v.t.s., irr.* to raise, bring up; to yield; to run in (*by police*). ·opbrengst, *n.* yield.

·opbruisen, *v.i.s.* to effervesce.

·opcenten, pl. only, *n.* additional tax.

·opdagen, daag op, *v.i.s.* to turn up, appear. op·dat, *c.* that, in order that. ~ *niet,* lest.

·opdelven, delf op, *v.t.s., str.* to dig up.

·opdienen, *v.t.s.* to dish *or* serve up.

·opdiepen, *v.t.s.* to deepen; to unearth.

·opdirken, *v.t.s.* to dress up. *zich ~,* to dress oneself up (*showily*).

·opdissen, dis op, *v.t.s.* to dish up.

·opdoeken, *v.t.s.* to gather; to pack up.

·opdoemen, *v.i.s.* to loom up.

·opdoen, doe op, *v.t.s., irr.* to lay in (*stock*); to gather (*knowledge*); to catch (*disease*). ¶*zich ~, v.r., irr.* to arise.

·opdokken, dok op, *v.t.s.* to fork out (*money*). ·opdonder, -s, *n.* (*vulg.*) blow. ·opdonderen, *v.i.s.* (*vulg.*) to go away.

·opdraaien, *v.t.s.* to turn up. ¶*v.i.s. ~ voor,* to be let in for; *ergens voor ~,* to have to pay the piper.

·opdracht, *n.* instruction, order; dedication. ~ *geven,* to commission, instruct. ·op-dragen, draag op, *v.t.s., str.* to carry up; to commission, instruct. *de mis ~,* to celebrate mass.

·opdrijven, drijf op, *v.t.s., str.* to force up.

·opdringen, *v.i.s., str.* to press on. ¶*v.t.s., str. iemand iets ~,* to thrust something on a person. ¶*zich ~, v.r.s., str.* to force oneself on a person. op·dringerig, *a.* obtrusive, importunate.

·opdrinken. *v.t.s., str.* to drink (up).

·opdrogen, droog op, *v.i.s.* to dry up.
·opdruk, -kken, *n.* surcharge.
·opduiken, *v.i.s.*, *str.* to emerge; to turn up.
·opduwen, *v.t.s.* to push up.
op·een, *adv.* one upon another. ¶*prefix.*
together op·eendrijven, drijf opeen, *v.t.s.*,
str. to round up. op·eenhopen, hoop opeen,
v.t.s., to accumulate. op·eenhoping, *n.*
accumulation. op·eens, *adv.* suddenly, all
at once. op·eenstapelen, *v.t.s.* to pile up.
·opeisen, *v.t.s.* to demand, claim. ·opeising,
·*n.* demand.
·open, *a.* open.
open·baar, -bare, *a.* public. ~ *maken*, to
make public, divulge. open·baarheid, no
pl., *n.* publicity. open·baarmaking, *n.*
publication, disclosure. open·baren, -baar,
v.t. to reveal, disclose. open·baring, *n.*
revelation; manifestation.
·openbreken, breek open, *v.t.s.*, *str.* to burst
open.
·opendoen, doe open, *v.t.s.*, *irr.* to open.
¶*v.i.s.*, *irr.* to answer the door.
·openen, *v.t.* to open.
·opengaan, ga open, *v.i.s.*, *irr.* to open.
·opengewerkt, *a.* open-work.
open·hartig, *a.* open-hearted, frank. open-
·hartigheid, -heden, *n.* open-heartedness.
·openheid, no pl., *n.* openness.
·openhouden, *v.t.s.*, *irr.* to keep *or* hold open.
·opening, *n.* opening; aperture. ·openingsrede,
-nen, *n.* inaugural address.
·openleggen, leg open, *v.t.s.*, *irr.* to lay open,
reveal.
·openliggen, lig open, *v.i.s.*, *str.* to lie open.
·openlijk, *a.* open, public.
open·lucht-, *prefix.* open air, outdoor.
·openmaken, maak open, *v.t.s.* to open.
·openrijten, *v.t.s.*, *str.* (*stilted*) to rip open.
·openslaan, sla open, *v.t.s.*, *irr.* to open (*book*,
door).
·openspalken, *v.t.s.*, ·opensperren, sper open,
v.t.s. to open wide (*eyes*, *mouth*).
·openspringen, *v.i.s.*, *str.* to burst open.
·openstaan, sta open, *v.i.s.*, *irr.* to stand open.
·openstellen, stel open, *v.t.s.* to (throw) open.
·openvallen, val open, *v.i.s.*, *str.* to fall open;
to become vacant.
·openzetten, zet open, *v.t.s.* to open (*and keep
open*).
ope·ratie, -s, *n.* operation. ope·ratietafel, -s,
n. operating table. ope·reerbaar, -bare, *a.*
operable. ope·reren, -reer, *v.i.* to operate.
¶*v.t.* to operate on.
ope·rette, -s, *n.* musical comedy.
·opeten, eet op, *v.t.s.*, *irr.* to eat (up). *zich
~ van nijd*, to be consumed with envy.
·opfleuren, *v.t.s.* & *v.i.s.* to brighten *or* cheer
up.
·opflikkeren, *v.i.s.* (*vulg.*) to go away.
·opfrissen, fris op. *v.t.s.* to freshen up, refresh,
revive. ¶*v.i.s.* to freshen up, revive.
·opgaaf, -gaven, *n. See* opgave.
·opgaan, ga op. *v.i.s.*. *irr.* to go up, rise.

het gaat niet op, it won't do *or* it doesn't
hold. ¶*v.t.s.*, *irr.* to ascend, climb. ·opgang,
n. rise. ~ *maken*, to catch on, be popular.
·opgave, -n, *n.* statement, returns; paper,
question (*in examination*). *met ~ van . . .,*
stating . . .; *zonder ~ van redenen*, without
reasons given.
·opgeblazen, *a.* puffed up, swollen.
·opgekropt, *a.* pent-up (*emotion*).
·opgeld, *n.n.* agio. ~ *doen*, to be in great
demand.
·opgelegd, *a.* laid up.
·opgepropt, *a.* crammed, packed.
·opgeruimd, *a.* cheerful.
·opgescheept, *a.* ~ *zijn met*, to be landed
with.
·opgeschoten, *a.* overgrown.
·opgesmukt, *a.* gaudy.
·opgetogen, *a.* elated. ~ *over* or *van*, elated
with.
·opgeven, geef op, *v.t.s.*, *str.* to hand up; to
give up, abandon; to cough up; to set
(*task*); to state (*particulars*). ¶*v.i.s.*, *str.*
~ *van*, to speak highly of.
·opgewassen, *a.* ~ *zijn tegen*, to be equal to,
be a match for.
·opgewekt, *a.* cheerful. opge·wektheid, no
pl., *n.* cheerfulness.
·opgewonden, *a.* excited. opge·wondenheid,
no pl., *n.* excitement, agitation.
·opgezet, -tte, *a.* swollen.
·opgooien, *v.t.s.* to throw *or* toss up.
·opgraven, graaf op, *v.t.s.*, *str.* to dig up; to
exhume.
·opgroeien, *v.i.s.* to grow up.
·ophaal, -halen, *n.* upstroke. ·ophaalbrug,
-ggen, *n.* drawbridge.
·ophakken, hak op, *v.t.s.* to chop up. ¶*v.i.s.*
to brag. ·ophakker, -s, *n.* braggart.
·ophalen, haal op, *v.t.s.* to pull up; to shrug;
to bring up; to weigh (*anchor*); to i·nale.
op·handen, *adv.* approaching, at hand.
·ophangen, *v.t.s.*, *str.* to hang (up).
·ophebben, heb op, *v.t.s.*, *irr.* to have on; to
have finished (*meal*). *een flink glas ~*, to
have had a drink or two; *niet veel met
iemand ~*, not to be very keen on a person.
·ophef, no pl., *n.* fuss, to-do. ·opheffen, hef
op, *v.t.s.*, *str.* to lift, raise; to abolish, annul;
to raise (*siege*); to call off (*strike*). ·op-
heffing, *n.* raising, elevation; abolition.
·ophelderen, *v.t.s.* to elucidate. ·opheldering,
n. elucidation.
·ophemelen, *v.t.s.* to extol.
·ophijsen, *v.t.s.*, *str.* to hoist (up).
·ophitsen, *v.t.s.* to set on, incite. ·ophitsing,
n. instigation.
·ophoepelen, *v.i.s.* (*coll.*) to hook it.
·ophogen, hoog op, *v.t.s.* to raise, bank up.
·ophoren, hoor op, *v.t.s.* er *vreemd van ~*, to
be surprised at something.
·ophouden, *v.t.s.*, *irr.* to hold up; to uphold;
to detain, keep. ¶*v.i.s.*, *irr.* to stop, cease.
~ *met*, to leave off, to cease to. ¶zich ~,

v.r.s., irr. to stay, stop, dwell. ¶no pl., *n.n. zonder* ~, without a break, on end, incessantly.

o·pinie, -s, *n.* opinion. *naar mijn* ~, in my opinion.

·opium, no pl., *n.* opium. ·opiumkit, -tten, *n.* opium-den. ·opiumschuiver, -s, *n.* opium smoker.

·opjagen, jaag op, *v.t.s., str.* to send *or* drive up; to start. ·opjager, -s, *n.* beater (*at shoot*).

·opkijken, *v.i.s., str.* to look up. ~ *naar*, to look up at; ~ *van*, to be surprised at.

·opkikkeren, *v.i.s.* (*coll.*) to perk up.

·opkisten, *v.t.s.* to coffer (*dyke*).

·opklaren, klaar op, *v.i.s.* to clear *or* brighten up. ¶*v.t.s.* to elucidate.

·opklimmen, klim op, *v.t.s., str.* to climb up, ascend.

·opknappen, knap op, *v.t.s.* to tidy *or* smarten up; to put right, manage. ¶*v.i.s.* to get better.

·opknopen, knoop op, *v.t.s.* to tie up; to hang.

·opkoken, kook op, *v.t.s.* to boil up.

·opkomen, *v.i.s., irr.* to come up *or* on; to come in (*tide*); to rise; to grow; to present oneself. *bij iemand* ~, to cross a person's mind; ~ *tegen*, to object to; ~ *voor*, to champion *or* to stand up for. ·opkomend, *a.* rising, coming. ·opkomst, no pl., *n.* rise; attendance.

·opkopen, koop op, *v.t.s., irr.* to buy up.

·opkroppen, krop op, *v.t.s.* to bottle (*emotions*).

·opkruipen, *v.t.s., str.* to creep *or* crawl up.

·opkunnen, kan op, *v.t.s., irr.* to be able to eat. *niet* ~ *tegen*, to be no match for; *ik kan m'n plezier wel op*, I'm not enjoying it; *het kan niet op*, there seems no end to it (*money*). ¶*v.i.s., irr.* to be able to get up.

·opweken, kweek op, *v.t.s.* to rear, raise.

·opkwikken, kwik op, *v.t.s.* to refresh. ¶*v.i.s.* to feel refreshed.

·oplaag, -lagen, *n. See* oplage.

·oplaaien, *v.i.s.* to flare up.

·oplage, -n, *n.* impression, edition.

·oplappen, lap op, *v.t.s.* to patch up.

·oplaten, laat op, *v.t.s., str.* to fly (*kite*).

·oplawaai, *n.* (*coll.*) blow.

·opleggen, leg op, *v.t.s., irr.* to lay on *or* up *or* by; to impose. *er een gulden* ~, to add a guilder to the price. ·oplegging, *n.* imposition (*of hands or fine*).

·opleiden, *v.t.s.* to lead *or* train up; to train. ·opleiding, *n.* training.

·oplepelen, *v.t.s.* to ladle out.

·opletten, let op, *v.i.s.* to attend, pay attention; to mind, look after. op·lettend, *a.* attentive. op·lettendheid, -heden, *n.* attention, attentiveness.

·opleven, leef op, *v.i.s.* to revive.

·opleveren, *v.t.s.* to yield, bring in; to result in. ·oplevering, *n.* delivery (*of work*).

·opleving, *n.* revival.

·oplichten, *v.t.s.* to lift up; to swindle, defraud.

·oplichter, -s, *n.* swindler. oplichte·rij, *n.* swindle, fraud.

·oploeven, loef op, *v.i.s.* to luff (up).

·oploop, -lopen, *n.* disturbance, tumult. ·oplopen, loop op, *v.t.s., str.* to walk up; to catch (*disease*), sustain (*injury*). ¶*v.i.s., str.* to rise, mount up. ~ *tegen*, to run into. ·oplopend, *a.* rising. op·lopend, *a.* quick-tempered.

op·losbaar, -bare, *a.* soluble. op·losbaarheid, no pl., *n.* solubility. ·oplossen, los op, *v.t.s. & v.i.s.* to dissolve; to solve. ·oplossing, *n.* solution. ·oplossingsmiddel, *n.n.* solvent.

·opluchten, *v.t.s.* to refresh, relieve. ·opluchting, *n.* relief.

·opluisteren, *v.t.s.* (*stilted*) to add lustre to. ·opluistering, *n.* embellishment. *ter* ~ *van*, to add lustre to.

·opmaken, maak op, *v.t.s.* to spend, squander; to draw up (*document*); to make (*bed*).

·opmarcheren, marcheer op, *v.i.s.* to advance; to go away. ·opmars, *n.* march, advance. ~ *tegen*, march on *or* against.

op·merkelijk, *a.* remarkable. ·opmerken, *v.t.s.* to notice, observe; to remark, observe, comment. opmerkens·waardig, *a.* remarkable, noteworthy. ·opmerking, *n.* remark. *een* ~ *maken over*, to comment on. op·merkzaam, -zame, *a.* observant. op·merkzaamheid, no pl., *n.* attentiveness.

·opmeten, meet op, *v.t.s., str.* to measure; to survey. ·opmeting, *n.* measurement; survey.

·opmonteren, *v.t.s.* to cheer up.

·opname, -n, *n.* survey. *een fotografische* ~, a photograph. ·opnemen, neem op, *v.t.s., str.* to pick *or* take up; to chart, survey; to take stock of, scrutinize; to photograph; to admit, adopt; to assimilate; to take up, borrow; to place, insert (*in publication*); to mop up. *het kalm* ~, to take it calmly; *het* ~ *tegen*, to try conclusions with; *het voor iemand* ~, to take up the cudgels for. ·opnemer, -s, *n.* surveyor. ·opneming, *n.* admission; survey.

op·nieuw, *adv.* again, afresh, once more. ~ *beginnen*, to make a fresh start.

·opnoemen, *v.t.s.* to name, enumerate.

·opoe, -'s, *n.* granny.

·opofferen, *v.t.s.* to sacrifice. ·opoffering, *n.* sacrifice.

·oponthoud, no pl., *n.n.* delay; temporary residence.

·oppakken, pak op, *v.t.s.* to pick up; to pack up.

·oppassen, pas op, *v.t.s.* to tend, look after. ¶*v.i.s.* to take care. ~ *voor*, to beware of, be careful of, mind. op·passend, *a.* steady (-going). ·oppasser, -s, *n.* attendant, keeper; batman. ·oppassing, no pl., *n.* nursing, care.

·opper, -s, *n.* haycock; lee. ¶*prefix.* upper, supreme.

·opperarmbeen, -benen, *n.n.* humerus.
·opperbest, *a.* excellent.
·opperbevel, no pl., *n.n.* supreme command.
·opperbevelhebber, -s, *n.* commander-in-chief.
·opperen, *v.t.* to cock (*hay*); to put forward, raise.
opperheerschap·pij, no pl., *n.* supremacy, sovereignty.
·opperhoofd, *n.n.* chieftain, head.
·opperhuid, no pl., *n.* epidermis.
·oppermacht, *n.* supremacy, supreme power. opper·machtig, *a.* supreme.
·opperman, opperlieden, *n.* hodman, bricklayer's labourer.
·oppermens, *n.* superman.
·opperrabijn, *n.* chief rabbi.
·opperste, *a.* supreme, uppermost. ¶-n, *n.* superior.
·oppervlak, -kken, *n.n.* upper surface. opper·vlakkig, *a.* superficial, shallow. ¶*adv.* superficially. ~ *beschouwd,* on the surface. opper·vlakkigheid, -heden, *n.* s<i>u</i>perficiality. ·oppervlakte, -n, *n.* surface; area.
·opperwachtmeester, -s, *n.* sergeant-major.
·oppeuzelen, *v.t.s.* to eat (*with relish*).
·oppikken, pik op, *v.t.s.* to pick up; to run in; to peck up.
·oppoetsen, *v.t.s.* to polish.
oppo·sitie, -s, *n.* opposition.
·opprikken, prik op, *v.t.s.* to pin up.
·oprakelen, *v.t.s.* to stir up (*fire*); to rake up (*fig.*).
·opraken, raak op, *v.i.s.* to give out, get low.
·oprapen, raap op, *v.t.s.* to pick up. ¶no pl., *n.n. niet voer het ~,* uncommon.
op·recht, *a.* upright; sincere, genuine. op·rechtheid, no pl., *n.* uprightness; sincerity.
·opredderen, *v.t.s.* to tidy up, straighten.
·oprichten, *v.t.s.* to erect, set up; to found, establish, float. ·oprichter, -s, *n.* founder. ·oprichting, *n.* establishment, formation.
·oprijden, *v.t.s., str.* to ride *or* drive up (*slope*); to ride *or* drive along *or* up *or* down (*street, etc.*).
·oprijlaan, -lanen, *n.* (carriage-)drive.
·oprijten, *v.t.s., str.* to rip up.
·oprijzen, rijs op, *v.i.s., str.* to rise.
·opril, -llen, *n.* ascent, uphill road.
·oprispen, *v.i.s.* to belch. ·oprisping, *n.* belch.
·oprit, -tten, *n. See* april.
·oproep, *n.* summons, call. ·oproepen, *v.t.s., str.* to summon; to call (up). ·oproeping, *n. See* oproep
·oproer, *n.n.* rebellion, revolt, insurrection; tumult. ~ *kraaien,* to stir up strife. op·roerig, *a.* rebellious, mutinous. ·oproer-kraaier, -s, *n.* agitator. ·oproerling, *n.* rebel, insurgent.
·oproken, rook op, *v.t.s.* to finish (smoking).
·oprollen, rol op, *v.t.s.* to roll up.

·opruien, *v.t.s.* to incite (*to rebellion*). ·op-ruiend, *a.* inflammatory, seditious (*words*). ·opruier, -s, *n.* agitator. ·opruiing, *n.* incitement, sedition.
·opruimen, *v.t.s.* to clear away; to clear (*stock*). ·opruiming, *n.* clearance, clearing-away; clearance sale.. ~ *houden,* to have a clear-up.
·oprukken, ruk op, *v.i.s.* to advance, march on; to go away.
·opscharrelen, *v.t.s.* to dig up (*fig.*).
·opschepen, scheep op, *v.t.s.* ~ *met,* to saddle with.
·opscheppen, schep op, *v.t.s.* to ladle out. ¶*v.i.s.* to swank, boast. ·opschepper, -s, *n.* braggart, swank-pot. op·schepperig, *a.* swanky. opschepperij, no pl., *n.* swank.
·opschieten, *v.i.s., str.* to get on, make headway. *met elkaar* ~, to get on together. ¶*v.t.s.* to fire (*upwards*).
·opschik, no pl., *n.* finery. ·opschikken, schik op, *v.i.s.* to move up. ¶*v.t.s.* to dress up.
·opschorsen, *v.t.s.,* ·opschorten, *v.t.s.* to suspend, reserve (*judgment*); to postpone, defer; to prorogue. ·opschorting, *n.* suspension; stay (*of execution*); prorogation.
·opschrift, *n.n.* inscription; heading. ·op-schrijven, schrijf op, *v.t.s., str.* to write down.
·opschrikken, schrik op, *v.i.s., str.* to be startled, start.
·opschroeven, schroef op, *v.t.s.* to screw up; to puff up.
·opschrokken, schrok op, *v.t.s.* to devour, gobble up.
·opschudden, schud op, *v.t.s.* to shake up. ·opschudding, *n.* commotion. ~ *veroor-zaken,* to create a stir.
·opschuiven, schuif op, *v.t.s., str.* to push up. ¶*v.i.s., str.* to move up.
·opsieren, *v.t.s.* to adorn, embellish.
·opslaan, sla op, *v.t.s., irr.* to turn up (*collar*); to raise (*eyes*); to turn up (*page*), open (*book*); to pitch (*tent*); to lay in (*stores*). ¶*v.i.s., irr.* to become dearer. ·opslag, *n.* facing (*of uniform*); cuff. ¶no pl., *n.* rise (*in salary*); glance; storage. ·opslagplaats, *n.* store, storage place.
·opslokken, slok op, *v.t.s.* to gobble up.
·opslorpen, *v.t.s.,* ·opslurpen, *v.t.s.* to drink noisily; to swallow (*profits*).
·opsluiten, *v.t.s., str.* to shut *or* lock up. ·opsluiting, *n.* incarceration.
·opsmuk, no pl., *n.* finery. ·opsmukken, smuk op, *v.t.s.* to adorn, embellish.
·opsnij(d)en, snij(d) op, *v.t.s., str.* to cut up. ¶*v.i.s., str.* to brag, boast. ·opsnij(d)er, -s, *n.* braggart, swank-pot. op·snij(d)erig, *a.* swanky. opsnij(d)e·rij, no pl., *n.* swank.
·opsnorren, snor op, *v.t.s.* to dig up (*fig.*).
·opsnuiven, snuif op, *v.t.s., str.* to sniff in *or* up.
·opsommen, som op, *v.t.s.* to sum up, enumerate.

·opsparen, spaar op, *v.t.s.* to save (up).
·opspelden, *v.t.s.* to pin up.
·opspelen, speel op, *v.i.s.* to speak angrily, make a row.
·opsporen, spoor op, *v.t.s.* to track, trace, run to earth. ·opsporing, *n.* tracing, tracking.
·opspraak, no pl., *n.* scandal. *iemand in ~ brengen*, to compromise someone; *in ~ komen*, to be talked about. ·opspreken, spreek op, *v.i.s.*, *str.* to speak up.
·opspringen, *v.i.s.*, *str.* to jump up, start.
·opstaan, sta op, *v.i.s.*, *irr.* to stand up; to get up; to rise, revolt.
·opstal, -llen, *n.* superstructure.
·opstand, *n.* rising, revolt. *in ~ komen*, to rise, rebel. ·opstandeling, *n.* rebel, insurgent. op·standig, *a.* rebel, insurgent.
·opstapelen, *v.t.s.* to pile up; to accumulate.
·opstappen, stap op, *v.i.s.* to mount (*cycle*); to go away.
·opsteken, steek op, *v.t.s.*, *str.* to hold up, put up; to sheathe; to light. *er niet veel van ~*, not to learn a great deal from it. ¶*v.i.s.*, *str.* to rise (*wind*).
·opstel, -llen, *n.n.* essay, composition. ·opstellen, stel op, *v.t.s.* to draft, draw up; to put up, erect; to draw up, align, place (*troops*). ·opstelling, *n.* disposition (*of troops*); framing; erection.
·opstijgen, *v.i.s.*, *str.* to ascend, rise.
·opstoken, stook op, *v.t.s.* to stoke; to incite, instigate. ·opstoker, -s, *n.* instigator. opstoke·rij, *n.* incitement, instigation.
·opstootje, -s, *n.n.* riot, disturbance.
·opstoppen, stop op, *v.t.s.* to pad, stuff. ·opstopper, -s, *n.* punch, dig. ·opstopping, *n.* stoppage; jam; bottle-neck.
·opstrijken, *v.t.s.*, *str.* to brush up; to pocket (*money*).
·opstropen, stroop op, *v.t.s.* to roll up (*sleeves*).
·opstuiven, stuif op, *v.i.s.*, *str.* to fly up (*dust*); to flare up (*in anger*).
·optekenen, *v.t.s.* to note down.
·optellen, tel op, *v.t.s.* to add up.
op·teren, -teer, *v.i.s.* ~ *voor*, to opt.
opti·cien, -s, *n.* optician.
·optie, no pl., *n.* option.
·optillen, til op, *v.t.s.* to lift up, raise.
·optisch, *a.* optical.
·optocht, *n.* procession.
·optooien, *v.t.s.* to adorn.
·optornen, *v.t.s.* to rip up. ¶*v.i.s.* ~ *tegen*, to run up against.
·optreden, treed op, *v.i.s.*, *str.* to appear, make one's appearance; to take action, assert oneself. ~ *als*, to act as. ¶no pl., *n.n.* appearance (*public*); attitude. *gezamenlijk ~*, joint action.
·optrekje, -s, *n.n.* chalet, beach hut. ·op·trekken, trek op, *v.t.s.*, *str.* to pull up, raise; to shrug; to raise (*building*). ¶*v.i.s.*, *str.* to lift (*fog*). ~ *tegen*, to march against.
·optuigen, *v.t.s.* to rig; to harness.

·opvallen, val op, *v.i.s.*, *str.* to strike (*become noticeable*). op·vallend, *a.* striking; conspicuous.
·opvangen, *v.t.s.*, *str.* to catch; to intercept; to absorb (*shock*).
·opvaren, vaar op, *v.t.s.*, *irr.* to sail up. ·opvarende, -n, *n.* those on board, passengers and crew.
·opvatten, vat op, *v.t.s.* to take up; to conceive (*plan*); to understand, interpret. *iets verkeerd ~*, to take something amiss; *weer ~*, to resume. ·opvatting, *n.* opinion, conception.
·opvegen, veeg op, *v.t.s.* to sweep up.
·opvijzelen, *v.t.s.* to lever or jack up; to crack up.
·opvissen, vis op, *v.t.s.* to fish up.
·opvliegen, *v.i.s.*, *str.* to fly up; to go up in the air (*fig.*). op·vliegend, *a.* quick-tempered. op·vliegendheid, no pl., *n.* irascibility.
·opvoeden, *v.t.s.* to bring up, educate. ·opvoeder, -s, *n.* educator. ·opvoeding, *n.* education, upbringing. ·opvoedkunde, no pl., *n.* pedagogy. opvoed·kundig, *a.* pedagogic.
·opvoeren, *v.t.s.* to force up, raise; to speed up; to perform, act, produce. ·opvoering, *n.* performance.
·opvolgen, *v.t.s.* to succeed (*follow*); to follow (*instructions*). ·opvolger, -s, *n.* successor. ·opvolging, *n.* succession.
op·vorderbaar, -bare, *a.* claimable; repayable. ·opvorderen, *v.t.s.* to claim.
·opvouwen, *v.t.s.* to fold up.
·opvreten, vreet op, *v.t.s.*, *str.* to eat (up) (*of animals*); (*vulg.*) to eat (up).
·opvrolijken, *v.t.s.* to cheer up, enliven.
·opvullen, vul op, *v.t.s.* to fill up, pad. ·opvulling, *n.*, ·opvulsel, -s, *n.n.* fill-up.
·opwaarts, *a.* upward. ¶*adv.* upward(s).
·opwachten, *v.t.s.* to wait for; to lie in wait for. ·opwachting, *n.* *zijn ~ maken bij*, to be received in audience.
·opwegen, weeg op, *v.i.s.*, *str.* ~ *tegen*, to counter-balance, offset.
·opwekken, wek op, *v.t.s.* to arouse; to resuscitate. ~ *tot*, to rouse to. op·wekkend, *a.* stimulating. ·opwekking, *n.* stimulation; resuscitation.
·opwellen, wel op, *v.i.s.* to well up; to surge, rise. ·opwelling, *n.* burst, access, wave. *de eerste ~*, the first impulse.
·opwerken, *v.t.s.* to work up. ¶*zich ~*, *v.r.s.* to work one's way up.
·opwerpen, *v.t.s.*, *str.* to throw up; to erect; to raise.
·opwinden, *v.t.s.*, *str.* to wind (up). ¶*zich ~*, *v.r.s.*, *str.* to get excited. ·opwinding, *n.* excitement.
op·zegbaar, -bare, *a.* terminable. ·opzeggen, zeg op, *v.t.s.*, *irr.* to say, recite; to terminate; to cancel. *iemand de dienst ~*, to give a person notice; *tot ~s toe*, until

further notice. ·opzegging, *n.* notice; termination.

·opzenden, *v.t.s., str.* to send on, forward.

·opzet, no pl., *n.* plan, framework; design, intention. met ∼, on purpose, deliberately; zonder ∼, unintentionally. op·zettelijk, *a.* intentional, deliberate. ¶*adv.* purposely, on purpose. ·opzetten, zet op, *v.t.s.* to put up; to put on. *een zaak* ∼, to set up in business. ¶*v.i.s. komen* ∼, to gather (*storm*) *or* to come along.

·opzicht, *n.n.* respect, point of view. *in elk* ∼, *in alle* ∼*en*, in every way; *ten* ∼*e van*, as regards, with respect to. ¶*n.n.* supervision. ·opzichter, -s, *n.* overseer, supervisor; surveyor. op·zichtig, *a.* showy, loud.

opzich·zelfstaand, *a.* isolated; apart.

·opzien, zie op, *v.i.s., irr* to look up. ∼ *naar*, to look up at; *ergens tegen* ∼, to dread, shrink from; *ergens (vreemd) van* ∼, to be surprised at. ¶no pl., *n.n.* surprise. ∼ *baren*, to create a stir. opzien·barend, *a.* startling, sensational. ·opziener, -s, *n.* overseer; inspector.

·opzitten, zit op, *v.i.s., str.* to sit up. *er zit niets anders op*, there is nothing left but to do it.

·opzoeken, *v.t.s., irr.* to seek, look for; to call on, call to see.

·opzouten, *v.t.s.* to pickle.

·opzwepen, zweep op, *v.t.s.* to whip up; to incite.

·opzwellen, zwel op, *v.i.s., str.* to swell. ·opzwelling, *n.* swelling.

orang·oetang, -s, *n.* orang-utan.

o·ranje, *a.* orange. ¶no pl., *n.n.* orange (*colour*). ¶*N.* Orange (*royal house*). *Oranje boven*, three cheers for Orange. o·ranjeachtig, *a.* orange-like. o·ranjeappel, -s, *n.* (*stilted*) orange. o·ranjebitter, -s, *n.* orange bitters. o·ranjeboom, bomen, *n.* orange-tree (*usu. symbolic*). o·ranjegezind, *a.* pro-Orange, loyal to Orange. Oranjege·zinde, -n, *n.* Orangist. O·ranjeklant, *n.* Orangeman. oranje·rie, -rieën, *n.* conservatory, greenhouse. o·ranjestrikje, -s, *n.n.* orange favour. Oranje·vrijstaat, *N.* Orange Free State.

orchi·dee, -deeën, *n.* orchid.

·orde, -n, *n.* order (*scientific division*); (*monastic*) order; style (*architectural*). ¶no pl., *n.* order (*arrangement*); order, discipline. *aan de* ∼ *komen*, to come up for discussion; *aan de* ∼ *zijn*, to be under discussion; *het is aan de* ∼ *van de dag*, that is the order of the day; *buiten de* ∼ *gaan*, to be out of order; *in* ∼, all right; *in* ∼ *brengen*, to put right, arrange; *het zal in* ∼ *komen*, it'll be all right; *niet goed in* ∼, not quite right; *op* ∼ *komen*, to get straight. ·ordebroeder, -s, *n.* brother, friar. ·ordekruis, *n.n.* cross (*of knight's order*). orda·lievend, *a.* orderly (*keen on*

order). ·ordelijk, *a.* orderly. ¶*adv.* in good order. ·ordelijkheid, no pl., *n.* orderliness. ·ordeloos, -loze, *a.* disorderly. ·ordeloosheid, no pl., *n.* disorderliness. ·ordenen, *v.t.* to arrange, regulate; to ordain. ·ordening, *n.* arrangement, regulation; ordination. or·dentelijk, *a.* decent, proper; reasonable.

·order, -s, *n.* order, command; order (*financial*). *tot nader* ∼, until further notice. ·orderbriefje, -s, *n.n.* note of hand.

·ordeteken, *n.n.* decoration; *pl.* insignia.

ordi·nair, *a.* vulgar, common.

ordon·nans, *n.* orderly (officer). ordon·nantie, -s, *n.* decree, ordinance.

o·reren, -reer, *v.i.* to orate, hold forth.

or·gaan, -ganen, *n.n.* organ (*not musical instrument*). organi·satie, -s, *n.* organization. organi·sator, *n.* organizer. or·ganisch, *a.* organic. organi·seren, -seer, *v.t.* to organize.

·orgel, -s, *n.n.* organ. *een* ∼ *draaien*, to grind an organ. ·orgeldraaier, -s, *n.* organ-grinder. ·orgelen, *v.i.* (*stilted*) to warble.

oriën·taal, -tale, *a.* oriental. oriën·teren, -teer, zich, *v.r.* to find one's bearings. oriën·tering, *n.* orientation.

origi·neel, -nele, *a.* original.

or·kaan, -kanen, *n.* hurricane.

or·kest, *n.n.* orchestra. orkes·treren, -treer, *v.t.* to orchestrate, score.

or·naat, -naten, *n.n.* vestments, official robes. *in vol* ∼, in full pontificals.

os, -ssen, *n.* ox, bullock.

oscil·leren, -leer, *v.i.* to oscillate.

·ossendrijver, -s, *n.* drover, ox-driver. ·ossenhaas, -hazen, *n.* fillet of beef, undercut. ·ossenvlees, no pl., *n.n.* beef. ·ossenweider, -s, *n.* grazier.

·otter, -s, *n.* otter.

oud, *a.* old, aged; ancient; stale. *zo* ∼ *als de weg naar Rome*, as old as the hills; ∼ *worden*, to grow old; *de* ∼*e heer*, the old man, the governor; *de* ∼*e lui*, the old folks, my parents. ¶*prefix* ex-, former. ¶*n.n.* old. ∼ *en nieuw vieren*, to see the new year in. ·oudachtig, *a.* oldish, elderly. ·oudbakken, *a.* stale. ·oude, -n, *n.* or *n.n.* *iets bij het* ∼ *laten*, to leave matters as they were before; *hij is weer de* ∼, he is his old self again; *de* ∼*n*, the ancients. ·oudejaar, no pl., *n.n.* New Year's Eve (*day*). oudejaars·avond, *n.* New Year's Eve (*evening*). oude·mannenhuis, -zen, *n.n.* almshouse (*for men*).

·ouder, *a.* older, elder. *hoe* ∼ *hoe gekker*, there is no fool like an old fool; ∼ *gewoonte*, as of old. ¶-s, *n.* parent. ·ouderdom, no pl., *n.* age; old age. *hoge* ∼, extreme old age. ·ouderliefde, no pl., *n.* parental *or* filial love. ·ouderlijk, *a.* parental. ·ouderling, *n.* elder (*church*). ·ouderloos, -loze, *a.* orphaned. ouder·wets, *a.* old-fashioned. ¶*adv.* in an old-fashioned way.

·**oudgast,** *n.* old colonial. **oudge·diende, -n,** *n.* ex-serviceman; old-timer. ·**oudheid, -heden,** *n.* antiquity. ·**oudheidkunde,** no pl., *n.* archaeology. **oudheid·kundig,** *a.* antiquarian, archaeological. ·**oudje, -s,** *n.n.* old man *or* woman. *de ~s,* the old folks. **oud·leerling,** *n.* old pupil, old boy. ·**oudoom, -s,** *n.* great-uncle. **oud·roest,** no pl., *n.n.* scrap iron. **ouds(·her),** *adv. van ~,* of old. **oudst,** *a.* oldest, eldest; senior. **oud·strijder, -s,** *n.* ex-serviceman. ·**oudtante, -s,** *n.* great-aunt. **oudtesta·mentisch,** *a.* Old Testament. ·**oudtijds,** *adv.* in olden times.

·**outer, -s,** *n.n.* (*poet.*) altar.
outil·lage, no pl., *n.* equipment, plant. **outil·leren, -leer,** *v.t.* to equip.
·**ouwe,** *a. & n. See* **oud(e).**
·**ouwel, -s,** *n.* wafer.
·**ouwelijk,** *a.* oldish. ·**ouwetje, -s,** *n.n. See* **oudje.**
o·**vatie, -s,** *n.* ovation. *een ~ brengen,* to give an ovation.
·**oven, -s,** *n.* oven. ·**ovengat,** *n.n.,* ·**ovenmond,** *n.* oven-mouth.
·**over,** *prep.* over; across; beyond; opposite; via, by; above; past; on, concerning, about. *~ een uur,* in an hour's time; *~ het geheel,* on the whole. *¶adv.* over; left. *rede te ~,* plenty of reason; *~ en weer,* to and fro. ·**overal,** *adv.* everywhere. *~ waar,* wherever.
·**overbekend,** *a.* familiar, widely known.
overbe·lasten, *v.t.s.* to overburden, overload.
overbe·leefd, *a.* too polite.
overbe·licht, *a.* over-exposed (*photograph*).
overbe·volkt, *a.* over-populated.
·**overblijfsel, -s** *or* **-en,** *n.n.* remainder, remnant, relic. ·**overblijven, blijf over,** *v.i.s., str.* to remain, be left.
over·bluffen, -bluf, *v.t.* to bluff.
over·bodig, *a.* superfluous. **over·bodigheid, -heden,** *n.* superfluity.
over·boord, *adv.* overboard.
·**overbrengen,** *v.t.s., irr.* to transfer, transport; to convey; to transmit; to translate. ·**overbrenger, -s,** *n.* bearer, carrier (*of disease*); tell-tale.
·**overbrieven, brief over,** *v.t.s.* to repeat, tell. ·**overbriever, -s,** *n.* tell-tale.
over·bruggen, -brug, *v.t.* to bridge.
·**overbuur, -buren,** *n.* neighbour (across the way).
overcom·pleet, -plete, *a.* surplus.
·**overdaad,** no pl., *n.* excess. **over·dadig,** *a.* excessive.
over·dag, *adv.* by day(light).
over·dekken, -dek, *v.t.* to cover.
over·denken, *v.t., irr.* to consider, think over.
·**overdoen, doe over,** *v.t.s., irr.* to do (over) again; to make over, dispose of; to put over.
·**over·donderen,** *v.t.* to overawe. *overdonderd,* dumbfounded.

·**overdracht,** *n.* transfer. **over·drachtelijk,** *a.* metaphorical. ·**overdragen, draag over,** *v.t.s., str.* to carry over; to transmit; to transfer, assign, delegate.
over·dreven, *a.* exaggerated; ~xcessive, extravagant. **over·drevenheid, -heden,** *n.* extravagance, exaggeration.
over·drijven, drijf, *v.t., str.* to exaggerate. ·**over·drijver, -s,** *n.* exaggerator. | **over·drijving,** *n.* exaggeration.
·**overdruk, -kken,** *n.* surcharge. *¶a.* extremely busy. *het ~ hebben,* to be too busy. ·**overdrukje, -s,** *n.n.* transfer (*picture*).
over·dwars, *a.* cross (*section*). *¶adv.* across.
over·een, *adv.* to the same. *~ uitkomen,* to agree, come to the same thing.
over·eenkomen, *v.i.s., irr.* to agree, to correspond, agree. *¶v.t.s., irr. iets ~,* to agree to something. **over·eenkomst,** *n.* agreement, similarity; conformity. *bij onderlinge ~,* by mutual consent. **over·een·komstig,** *a.* corresponding; equivalent, analogous. *¶prep.* in accordance with.
over·eenstemmen, stem overeen, *v.i.s.* to agree. *~ met,* to fit, correspond with. **over·eenstemming,** no pl., *n.* agreement (*of opinion*). *in ~ brengen met,* to reconcile with; *tot ~ komen,* to come to terms.
over·eind, *adv.* on end, upright. *~ staan,* to stand up.
over·erfelijk, *a.* hereditary. ·**overerven, -erf,** *v.t.s.* to inherit. *¶v.i.s.* to be transmitted (by inheritance).
·**overgaaf,** no pl., *n. See* **overgave.**
·**overgaan, ga over,** *v.i.s., irr.* to ring; to move (*to higher form*); to pass *or* wear off. *~ in,* to change into; *in elkaar ~,* to merge; *~ naar,* to go over to; *~ op,* to pass to; *~ tot,* to pass on to. *¶v.t.* to cross, go across. ·**overgang,** *n.* transition; crossing. ·**overgangsvorm,** *n.* intermediate form. **over·gankelijk,** *a.* transitive.
·**overgave, -n,** *n.* surrender; transfer.
·**overgelukkig,** *a.* most happy.
·**overgeven, geef over,** *v.t.s., str.* to hand over; to surrender. *¶v.i.s., str.* to vomit. *¶zich ~,* *v.r.s., str.* to surrender, give oneself up.
overge·voelig, *a.* over-sensitive.
·**overgieten,** *v.t.s., str.* to pour; to decant. **over·gieten,** *v.i., str. ~ met,* to cover *or* drench with.
·**overgroot, -grote,** *a.* vast.
·**overgrootmoeder, -s,** *n.* great-grandmother. ·**overgrootvader, -s,** *n.* great-grandfather.
over·haast, *a.* rash, precipitate, hasty. **over·haasting,** no pl., *n.* precipitation.
·**overhalen, haal over,** *v.t.s.* to pull (over); to persuade. *zich laten ~,* to be persuaded.
·**overhand,** no pl., *n. de ~ hebben,* to have the upper hand; *de ~ krijgen op,* to get the upper hand of. **over·handigen,** *v.t.* to

hand over; to present. **over·handiging**, *n.* delivery; presentation. **over·hands**, *a.* ~*e steek*, whip stitch. ¶*adv.* overhand.

·overhebben, heb over, *v.t.s.*, *irr.* to have left. *hij heeft er veel voor over*, it is worth a lot to him.

over·heen, *adv.* over, across. *er gingen jaren* ~, years went by.

over·heerlijk, *a.* delicious.

over·heersen, *v.t.* to dominate. ¶*v.i.* to predominate. **over·heerser, -s**, *n.* despot. **over·heersing**, *n.* domination.

·overheid, -heden, *n.* authority; (public) authorities. **·overheidspersoon, -sonen**, *n.* magistrate; *pl.* authorities.

·overhellen, hel over, *v.i.s.* to incline, lean over; to lean to. ~ *naar*, to incline towards.

·overhemd, *n.n.* shirt. **overhemdsknoopje, -s**, *n.n.* stud (*for shirt-front*).

over·hoop, *adv.* pell-mell, in a heap; in disorder; at sixes and sevens. ~ *liggen*, to be untidy (*room*) *or* to be at loggerheads; ~ *schieten*, to shoot down, kill.

over·horen, -hoor, *v.t.* to hear (*lessons*).

·overhouden, *v.t.s.*, *irr.* to have left.

·overig, *a.* remaining. **·overige**, no pl., *n.n.* rest, remainder. **overigens**, *adv.* for the rest, otherwise.

over·ijlen, zich, *v.r.* to hurry too much; to be precipitate. **over·ijling**, *n.* precipitance.

over·jarig, *a.*, more than one year old.

·overjas, -ssen, *n.* overcoat, topcoat.

·overkant, no pl., *n.* the opposite side. *aan de* ~, across (*street, water, etc.*); *aan de* ~ *van*, beyond.

over·kappen, -kap, *v.t.* to roof in.

·overkoken, kook over, *v.i.s.* to boil over.

over·komelijk, *a.* surmountable. **·overkomen**, *v.i.s.*, *irr.* to come over; to come through *or* across (*sound, signal*). **over·komen**, *v. imp.*, *irr.* to befall, happen to. **·overkomst**, no pl., *n.* coming, visit.

over·kropt, *a.* overburdened (*with emotion*). ~ *gemoed*, pent-up feelings, overburdened heart.

·overlaat, -laten, *n.* overflow, weir.

·overladen, laad over, *v.t.s.*, *irr.* to trans-ship, transfer load *or* cargo; to re-load. **over·laden, -laad**, *v.t.*, *irr.* to overload, burden; to surfeit. ¶*a.* overloaded, over-full.

over·land, *adv.* by land.

over·langs, *a.* longitudinal. ¶*adv.* lengthwise.

·overlast, no pl., *n.* inconvenience, trouble. ~ *aandoen* or *bezorgen* or *iemand tot* ~ *zijn*, to cause inconvenience.

·overlaten, laat over, *v.t.s.*, *str.* to leave. ~ *aan*, to leave to.

over·leden, *a.* deceased.

over·leg, no pl., *n.n.* consultation, deliberation, discussion; thought, judgment. ~ *plegen*, to consult together; ~ *plegen met*, to consult; *in* ~ *met*, in consultation *or* concert with; *met* ~, with discretion;

na rijp ~, on mature consideration. **·overleggen, leg over**, *v.t.s.*, *irr.* to produce (*document*); to put by (*money*). **over·leggen, -leg**, *v.t.*, *irr.* to deliberate, discuss; to consider. *iets met iemand* ~, to consult someone about something. **·overlegging**, no pl., *n. tegen* ~ *van*, on production of.

over·leven, -leef, *v.t.* to survive; to outlive. **over·levende, -n**, *n.* survivor.

·overleveren, *v.t.s.* to hand down (*tradition*); to hand over. *overgeleverd aan*, at the mercy of. **·overlevering**, *n.* tradition.

·overlezen, lees over, *v.t.s.*, *str.* to re-read.

·overligdagen, pl. only, *n.* (days of) demurrage. **·overliggeld**, *n.n.* demurrage. **·overliggen, lig over**, *v.i.s.*, *str.* to be on demurrage.

over·lijden, *v.i.*, *str.* to pass away. ¶no pl., *n.n.* decease, demise.

·overloop, -lopen, *n.* overflow; landing (*of stairs*). **·overlopen, loop over**, *v.i.s.*, *str.* to overflow, run over; to cross; to go over (*to the enemy*). **·overloper, -s**, *n.* deserter, turncoat.

over·luid, *a.* (*stilted*) aloud.

·overmaat, no pl., *n.* excess. *tot* ~ *van ramp*, to make matters worse.

·overmacht, no pl., *n.* superiority, superior forces; force majeure; Act of God. *voor de* ~ *bezwijken*, to yield to superior numbers. **over·machtig**, *a.* superior, stronger.

·overmaken, maak over, *v.t.s.* to remit; to transfer (*money*). **·overmaking**, *n.* remittance; transfer.

over·mannen, -man, *v.t.* to overpower; to overcome (*by sleep, fatigue*).

over·matig, *a.* excessive. ~ *gebruik*, excess.

over·meesteren, *v.t.* to overpower, conquer.

·overmoed, no pl., *n.* recklessness; presumption. **over·moedig**, *a.* reckless, over-bold; presumptuous.

·overmorgen, *adv.* the day after to-morrow.

over·nachten, *v.i.* to stay the night.

·overnemen, neem over, *v.t.s.*, *str.* to take over; to borrow, adopt.

over·oud, *a.* ancient.

over·peinzen, -peins, *v.t.* to reflect on.

·overplaatsen, *v.t.s.* to transfer; to translate (*bishop*). **overplaatsing**, *n.* transfer; translation (*bishop*).

·overplanten, *v.t.s.* to transplant.

over·prikkelen, *v.t.* to over-excite.

over·reden, -reed, *v.t.* to persuade, induce. **over·redend**, *a.* persuasive. **over·reding**, *n.* persuasion.

·overreiken, *v.t.s.* to hand, pass.

over·rijden, *v.t.*, *str.* to run over, knock down.

over·rompelen, *v.t.* to rush, take by surprise; to surprise. **over·rompeling**, *n.* surprise (attack).

over·schaduwen, *v.t.* to overshadow, eclipse.

·overschakelen, *v.i.s.* to switch over.

over·schatten, -schat, *v.t.* to overestimate.

·overschenken, *v.t.s.*, *str.* to decant.

·overschepen, **scheep over**, *v.t.s.* to transship.

·overschieten, *v.i.s.*, *str.* to remain, be left.

·overschoen, *n.* galosh.

·overschot, -tten, *n.* remainder, surplus.

over·schreeuwen, *v.t.* to shout down.

over·schrijden, *v.t.*, *str.* (*stilted*) to cross, step across; to exceed, overstep, transgress. over·schrijding, *n.* transgression.

·overschrijven, **schrijf over**, *v.t.s.*, *str.* to copy; to re-write. ·overschrijving, *n.* transcript, copy.

·overslaan, **sla over**, *v.t.s.*, *irr.* to omit, leave out, skip; to pass over. ¶*v.i.s.*, *irr.* to catch, break (*of voice*); to turn to.

over·spannen, *v.t.*, *irr.* to span. ¶**zich ~**, *v.r.*, *irr.* to over-exert oneself. ¶*a.* overwrought. over·spanning, *n.* over-exertion.

over·speelster, -s, *n.* adulteress. ·overspel, no pl., *n.n.* adultery. over·speler, -s, *n.* adulterer. over·spelig, *a.* adulterous.

·overspringen, *v.i.s.*, *str.* to jump across.

·overstaan, no pl., *n.n.* **ten ~ van**, in the presence of.

over·stag, *adv.* **~ gaan**, to put a ship about *or* to change one's tack.

·overstappen, **stap over**, *v.i.s.* to change (*on journey*).

·overste, -n, *n.* lieutenant-colonel; prior, prioress.

·oversteken, **steek over**, *v.t.s.*, *str.* to cross.

over·stelpen, *v.t.* to overwhelm. ¶*v.i.* **~ met**, to shower . . . upon, overwhelm with.

over·stemmen, -stem, *v.t.* to drown (*sound*).

over·stromen, -stroom, *v.t.* to flood, inundate. over·stroming, *n.* flood, inundation.

over·stuur, *a.* upset. ¶*adv.* out of order, upset.

over·tallig, *a.* supernumerary.

·overtekenen, *v.t.s.* to copy (*by drawing*). over·tekenen, *v.t.* to over-subscribe.

·overtocht, *n.* crossing, passage.

over·togen, *a.* **~ met**, suffused with.

over·tollig, *a.* superfluous, redundant. over·tolligheid, -heden, *n.* superfluity.

over·toog, *past tense only.* (*stilted*) suffused.

over·treden, -treed, *v.i.*, *str.* to transgress, infringe, break. over·treder, -s, *n.* transgressor. over·treding, *n.* transgression, infringement.

over·treffen, -tref, *v.t.*, *str.* to surpass, excel. **in aantal ~**, to outnumber.

·overtrek, -kken, *n.n.* slip, cover. ·overtrekken, **trek over**, *v.t.s.*, *str.* to cross; to pull (over); to trace. over·trekken, -trek, *v.t.*, *str.* to cover, upholster. ·overtrekpapier, no pl., *n.n.* tracing paper.

over·troeven, -troef, *v.t.* to over-trump.

over·tuigen, *v.t.*, to convince. ¶**zich ~**, *v.r.*, to convince *or* satisfy oneself. over·tuigend, *a.* convincing. over·tuiging, *n.* conviction. **uit ~**, from conviction.

·overuren, pl. only, *n.n.* overtime. **~ maken**, to work overtime.

·overvaart, *n.* crossing, passage.

·overval, -llen, *n.* raid, surprise attack; hold-up. over·vallen, -val, *v.t.*, *str.* to raid, attack unawares; to hold up.

·overvaren, **vaar over**, *v.t.s.*, *irr.* to cross (*by boat*). over·varen, -vaar, *v.t.*, *irr.* to run down.

overver·hitten, -hit, *v.t.* to overheat.

·oververtellen, **vertel over**, *v.t.s.* to repeat.

over·vleugelen, *v.t.* to outstrip, surpass.

·overvloed, no pl., *n.* plenty, abundance. **~ van . . .**, . . . galore; **ten ~e**, moreover. over·vloedig, *a.* plentiful, abundant, copious. ·overvloeien, *v.i.s.* to overflow. **~ van**, to abound with.

·overvol, -lle, *a.* brim-full.

over·vragen, -vraag, *v.t.*, *str.* to overcharge.

·overwaard, *a.* well worth. ·overwaarde, no pl., *n.* surplus value.

·overweg, *n.* level crossing. over·weg *adv.* **~ kunnen met**, to get on well with.

over·wegen, -weeg, *v.t.*, *str.* to consider. over·wegend, *a.* preponderant. over·weging, *n.* consideration. **in ~**, under consideration; **ter ~**, for reflection; **uit ~ van**, in consideration of.

over·weldigen, *v.t.* to overpower; to usurp. over·weldigend, *a.* overwhelming; stupendous. over·weldiger, -s, *n.* usurper. over·weldiging, *n.* conquest; usurpation.

over·welven, -welf, *v.t.* to vault.

·overwerk, no pl., *n.n.* overwork. ·overwerken, *v.i.s.* to work overtime. over·werken, zich, *v.r.* to overwork oneself.

·overwicht, no pl., *n.n.* overweight; preponderance.

over·winnaar, -s, *n.* conqueror, victor. over·winnen, -win, *v.i.*, *str.* to conquer; to overcome, vanquish; to gain the victory. over·winning, *n.* victory. ·overwinst, no pl., *n.* excess profit(s).

over·winteren, *v.i.* to hibernate.

over·zees, -zeese, *a.* oversea(s,) from Oversea(s).

·overzetboot, -boten, *n.* ferry. ·overzetten, **zet over**, *v.t.s.* to take *or* ferry across; to translate.

·overzicht, no pl., *n.n.* survey, summary, outline. over·zichtelijk, *a.* easily surveyed, well and logically arranged. over·zichtelijkheid, no pl., *n.* clarity, good arrangement. ·overzien, **zie over**, *v.t.s.*, *irr.* to look over. over·zien, -zie, *v.t.*, *irr.* to survey; to oversee. **niet te ~**, vast, incalculable.

·overzijde, no pl., *n.* (*stilted*) other *or* opposite side.

·overzwemmen, **zwem over**, *v.t.s.*, *str.* to swim across.

o.w-er, -s, *n.* profiteer.

oxy·deren, -deer, *v.t.* to oxidize.

P

pa, -'s, *n.* pa, dad.

·**paadje, -s,** *n.n.* small path.

·**paaien,** *v.i.* to grave (*ship*); to spawn. ¶*v.t.* to soothe. ·**paaitijd,** no pl., *n.* spawning season.

paal, palen, *n.* post, pile, pole, stake. *het staat als een ~ boven water,* it is perfectly clear; *~ en perk stellen aan . . .,* to put limits to . . . ·**paalbewoner, -s,** *n.* lake-dweller. ·**paaltje, -s,** *n.n.* picket, peg. ·**paalwoning,** *n.* lake-dwelling. ·**paalworm,** *n.* pile-worm.

paap, papen, *n.* papist. ·**paapsgezind,** *a.* popish.

paar, paren, *n.n.* pair, couple. *bij paren,* in twos *or* pairs; *een ~,* a pair, a few; *een ~ keer,* once or twice; *twee ~ schoenen,* two pairs of shoes.

paard, *n.n.* horse; knight (*chess*). *~ rijden,* to ride (on horseback); *men moet een gegeven ~ niet in de bek zien,* do not look a gift horse in the mouth; *het ~ achter de wagen spannen,* to put the cart before the horse; *iemand over het ~ tillen,* to make too much of a person; *te ~,* on horseback. ·**paardekracht,** *n.* horse-power. ·**paarden-bloem,** *n.* dandelion. ·**paardenboon, -bonen,** *n.* broad bean. ·**paardenfokker, -s,** *n.* horse-breeder. ·**paardenfokkerij,** no pl., *n.* horse-breeding. ¶*n.* stud-farm. ·**paarden-horzel, -s,** *n.* gad-fly. ·**paardenknecht,** *n.* ostler. ·**paardenkoper, -s,** *n.* horse-dealer, horse-coper. ·**paardenmiddel,** *n.n.* violent remedy. ·**paardenslachter, -s,** *n.* horsemeat butcher; knacker. **paardenslachte·rij,** *n.* knacker's yard. ·**paardenspel, -llen,** *n.n.* circus. ·**paardenstal, -llen,** *n.* stable. ·**paardenstamboek,** *n.n.* stud-book. ·**paar-denstoeterij,** *n.* stud, stud-farm. ·**paarden-vilder, -s,** *n.* knacker. ·**paardenvlees,** no pl., *n.n.* horseflesh. *hij heeft ~ gegeten,* he is restless. ·**paardenvolk,** no pl., *n.n.* cavalry, horse. ·**paardrijden,** *v.i.s.,* *str.* to ride (*on horseback*). ¶no pl., *n.n.* (horse-) riding.

·**paarle·moer,** no pl., *n.n.* mother-of-pearl. ·**paarle·moeren,** *a.* (made of) mother-of-pearl.

paars, *a.* violet, purple.

·**paarsgewijs,** *adv.* in pairs, in twos. ·**paartijd,** no pl., *n.* pairing time.

·**Paasavond,** *n.* Easter eve. ·**Paasbest,** no pl., *n.n.* Sunday best. ¶*adv.* in one's Sunday best. ·**Paasbloem,** *n.* primrose. ·**Paasbrood, -broden,** *n.n.* Easter loaf; matzos. ·**Paasdag,** *n.* Easter Day. ·**Paasfeest,** *n.n.* Easter. ·**Paaslam, -mmeren,** *n.n.* Pascal Lamb. ·**Paaslelie,** *n.* daffodil. ·**Paastijd,** no pl., *n.* Easter time.

·**paatje, -s,** *n.* daddy.
·**pacha, -'s,** *n.* pasha.

pacht, *n.* lease, rent. *in ~ geven,* to let *or* farm out; *in ~ hebben,* to hold on lease. ·**pachten,** *v.t.* to rent, farm. ·**pachter, -s,** *n.* tenant, farmer, leaseholder. ·**pachtgeld,** *n.n.* rent, rental. ·**pachthoeve, -n,** *n.* farm(-house). ·**pachtsom, -mmen,** *n.* rent.

pacifi·ceren, -ceer, *v.t.* to pacify.

pad, *n.n.* path. *op het ~ zijn,* to be abroad; *op het rechte ~ blijven,* to run straight. ¶**-dden,** *n.* toad. ·**padde(n)stoel,** *n.* toadstool. *eetbare ~,* mushroom. ·**padvinder, -s,** *n.* boy scout; pathfinder. **padvinde·rij,** no pl., *n.* boy scout movement. ·**padvindster, -s,** *n.* girl guide.

paf, *int.* bang! ¶*adv.* *hij stond er ~ van,* he was flabbergasted. ·**paffen, paf,** *v.i.* to pop (*shoot*); to puff (*smoke*). ·**pafferig,** *a.* puffy.

pa·gaai, *n.* paddle. **pa·gaaien,** *v.i.* to paddle.

·**pagger, -s,** *n.* fence (*East Indies*).

·**pagina, -'s,** *n.* page. **pagina·tuur, -turen,** *n.* pagination. **pagi·neren, -neer,** *v.t.* to paginate.

pa·gode, -s, *n.* pagoda.

pais, no pl., *n.* *alles is ~ en vree,* all is peace and quiet *or* everything in the garden is lovely.

·**pajong, -s,** *n.* umbrella (*East Indies*).

pak, -kken, *n.n.* parcel, packet; bundle, pack; suit (*of clothes*). *een ~ slaag,* a thrashing, drubbing; *een ~ voor de broek,* a (good) spanking; *een ~ van het hart,* a load off one's mind; *bij de pakken neerzitten,* to sit down in despair; *met ~ en zak,* with bag and baggage.

pa·ket, -tten, *n.n.* packet, parcel. **pa·ketboot, -boten,** *n.* packet, packet-boat. **pa·ketpost,** no pl., *n.* parcel post. **pa·ketvaart,** no pl., *n.* packet service.

·**pakezel, -s,** *n.* pack-mule. ·**pakgaren,** no pl., *n.n.* pack-thread. ·**pakhuis, -zen,** *n.n.* warehouse. ·**pakhuisknecht,** *n.* warehouseman. ·**pakijs,** no pl., *n.n.* pack ice. ·**pakje, -s,** *n.n.* parcel. ·**pakjesdrager, -s,** *n.* porter. ·**pakken, pak,** *v.t.* to pack; to seize, grasp, grip. *er eentje ~,* to have one; *iemand te ~ hebben or nemen,* to have caught someone; *het zwaar te ~ hebben,* to have caught it badly. ¶*v.i.* to pack. ·**pakkend,** *a.* moving, gripping. *een ~ bewijs,* a striking proof. ·**pakkerd, -s,** *n.* hug. **pak·ket, -tten,** *n.n. See* **paket.** ·**pakking,** no pl., *n.* packing. ·**pakkist,** *n.* packing case. ·**paknaald,** *n.* packing-needle. ·**pakpapier,** no pl., *n.n.* brown paper, wrapping paper. ·**paktouw,** no pl., *n.n.* twine. ·**pakzolder, -s,** *n.* warehouse loft.

pal, -llen, *n.* catch, pawl, ratchet. ¶*a.* firm. *sta ~,* hold fast. ¶*adv.* firmly; due, straight.

pa·leis, -leizen, *n.n.* palace. **pa·leisachtig,** *a.* palatial.

pa·let, -tten, *n.n.* palette.

palfre·nier, -s, *n.* groom.

·paling, *n.* eel.
·palis·sade, -n, *n.* palisade, stockade.
palis·sander(hout), no pl., *n.n.* palissander.
pal·jas, -ssen, *n.* clown, merry andrew; pallet (*mattress*).
palm, *n.* palm; palm(-tree). ·palmachtig, *a.* palmy. ·palmboom, -bomen, *n.* palm-tree. ·palmboompje, -s, *n.n.* box(-tree). ·palmen, *v.t.* to haul. Palm·pasen, *N.* Palm Sunday. ·palmpit, -tten, *n.* palm-kernel. ·palm·struik, *n.* box(-tree). Palm·zondag, *N.* Palm Sunday.
Palts, *N.* Palatinate. ·Paltsgraaf, -graven, *n.* Count Palatine. ·Paltsgraafschap, -ppen, *n.n.* County Palatine. ·Paltsgravin, -nnen, *n.* Countess Palatine.
·pampagras, no pl., *n.n.* pampas grass.
pampel·moes, -zen, *n.* grape-fruit.
pamper·noelje, -s, *n.* mushroom.
pan, -nnen, *n.* pan; tile; confusion, mess. *de hele ~,* the whole show; *in de ~ hakken,* to exterminate, slaughter.
pand, *n.n.* pawn, pledge; tail (*of shirt, coat*); premises; section. *~ verbeuren,* to play at forfeits. ·pandbeslag, no pl., *n.n.* distraint. ·pandbrief, -ven, *n.* mortgage bond. ·panden, *v.t.* to distrain, seize. ·pandgever, -s, *n.* pawner. ·pandhouder, -s, *n.* pawnee. ·pand(jes)huis, -zen, *n.n.* pawnshop. ·pandjesjas, -ssen, *n.* tails (*coat*). ·pandrecht, *n.n.* lien. ·pand·verbeuren, no pl., *n.n.* (game of) forfeits.
pa·neel, -nelen, *n.n.* panel.
pa·neermeel, no pl., *n.n.* bread-crumb (*for cooking*). pa·neren, -neer, *v.t.* to roll or cover in bread-crumb.
·panharing, *n.* fresh herring.
pa·niek, *n.* panic. ·panisch, *a.* panic.
·pannekoek, *n.* pancake. ·pannenbakker, -s, *n.* tile-maker. ·pannenbakke·rij, *n.* tile-works. ·pannendak, *n.n.* tiled roof. ·pannendekker, -s, *n.* tiler. ·pannetje, -s, *n.n.* small pan.
pan·toffel, -s, *n.* slipper. *onder de ~ zitten,* to be henpecked; *het op zijn ~tjes af kunnen,* to be able to do it with ease. pan·toffelheld, *n.* henpecked husband.
·pantser, -s, *n.n.* cuirass, armour; armour-plating. ·pantserauto, -'s, *n.* armoured car. ·pantserdek, -kken, *n.*·· armour-plating. ·pantserdier, *n.n.* armadillo. ·pantseren, *v.t.* to armour-plate. ·pantsergranaat, -naten, *n.* armour-piercing shell. ·pantser·hemd, *n.n.* coat of mail. ·pantserkruiser, -s, *n.* armoured cruiser. ·pantserschip, -schepen, *n.n.* iron-clad.
pap, -ppen, *n.* porridge. pap; poultice. *tot ~ koken,* to boil to a mash.
pa·pa, -'s, *n.* papa.
pa·paver, -s, *n.* poppy. pa·paverachtig, *a.* papaverous.
pape·gaai, *n.* parrot. pape·gaaienziekte, no pl., *n.* parrot disease, psittacosis.
pape·rassen, pl. only, *n.* papers, documents.

pa·pier, *n.n.* paper; *pl.* stocks and shares; identity papers, credentials. *in de ~en lopen,* to run into money; *het ~ is geduldig,* don't believe a thing because it is in print. pa·pierachtig, *a.* papery. pa·pierbloem, *n.* immortelle. pa·pieren, *a.* (of) paper. pa·pierfabriek, *n.* paper-mill. pa·piermand, *n.* waste-paper-basket. pa·piermerk, *n.n.* watermark. pa·piermolen, -s, *n.* paper-mill. pa·piertje, -s, *n.n.* small piece of paper.
papil·lot, -tten, *n.* curl-paper. *met papillotten in het haar,* her hair in curl-papers.
·paplepel, -s, *n.* porridge-spoon. *het ze met de ~ ingeven,* to spoon-feed them. ·pappen, pap, *v.t.* to poultice. ·Pappenheimers, pl. *N. hij kent zijn ~,* he knows his customers. ·pappot, -tten, *n.* porridge pot. *bij moeders ~ blijven,* to be a stay-at-home, to be tied to one's mother's apron-strings.
pa·raaf, -rafen, *n.* initials (*short signature*).
pa·raat, -rate, *a.* ready.
pa·rabel, -s, *n.* parable.
para·bool, -bolen, *n.* parabola.
pa·rade, -s, *n.* parade, review; parry. *~ maken,* to parade. pa·radepaard, *n.n.* parade-horse; (*fig.*) individual or thing one shows off. pa·radepas, -ssen, *n.* parade-step, goose-step. para·deren, -deer, *v.t.* to parade; to show off.
para·dijs, -zen, *n.n.* paradise. para·dijsvogel, -s, *n.* bird of paradise.
para·feren, -feer, *v.t.* to initial.
paraf·fine, no pl., *n.* paraffin wax. paraf·fine·kaars, *n.* paraffin wax-candle.
para·graaf, -grafen, *n.* section (*of chapter*).
paral·lel, -llen, *n.* parallel. ¶*a. & adv.* parallel. paral·lelklas, -ssen, *n.n.* duplicate class.
para·plu, -'s, *n.* umbrella. para·plubak, -kken, *n.* umbrella stand.
para·siet, *n.* parasite. parasi·teren, -teer, *v.i.* to parasitize. para·sitisch, *a.* parasitic.
para·sol, -s, *n.* sunshade.
par·doen, -s, *n.* backstay.
par·does, *int.* smack, bang.
par·don, *int.* sorry! I beg your pardon! excuse me! ¶no pl., *n.n.* pardon, mercy. pardon·nabel, *a.* excusable. pardon·neren, -neer, *v.t.* to pardon, excuse.
·parel, -s, *n.* pearl. ·parelachtig, *a.* pearly. ·parelduiken, no pl., *n.n.* pearl-diving. ·parelen, *v.i.* to pearl. *het zweet ~de op zijn voorhoofd,* beads of sweat appeared on his brow. ·parelgort, no pl., *n.* pearl-barley. ·parelhoen, -deren, *n.n.* guinea-fowl. parel·moer, no pl., *n.n.* mother-of-pearl. ·parelmos, no pl., *n.n.* Irish moss. ·parel·snoer, *n.n.* rope of pearls. ·parelzaad, no pl., *n.n.* seed-pearls.
·paren, paar, *v.t.* to pair. ¶*zich ~, v.r.* to mate. *zich ~ aan,* to be coupled with, go with.
pa·reren, -reer, *v.t.* to parry.

par·fum, -s, *n.n.* perfume, scent. parfu·
·meren, -meer, *v.t.* to perfume, scent.
·pari, *adv.* ~ *staan,* to be at par. ¶*no* pl.,
n.n. à ~, at par; *boven* ~, above par,
at a premium.
·paria, -'s, *n.* pariah.
Pa·rijs, *n.N.* Paris. ¶*a.* Parisian. Pa·rijze-
naar, -s, *N.* Parisian.
·paring, *n.* mating.
park, *n.n.* park. par·keerplaats, *n.* parking
place. par·keren, -keer, *v.t.* to park.
par·ket, -tten, *n.n.* bench, Public Prosecutor's
office. *in een lastig* ~ *zitten,* to be in a
nasty predicament. par·ketvloer, *n.*
parquet floor.
par·kiet, *n.* parakeet.
parle·ment, *n.n.* parliament. parlemen·tair,
a. parliamentary. ~*e vlag,* flag of truce.
parlemen·teren, -teer, *v.i.* to parley.
parle·vinken, *v.i.* to jabber.
par·mantig, *a.* pert, jaunty.
parochi·aan, -ianen, *n.* parishioner. pa-
·rochie, -s, *n.* parish.
paro·die, -dieën, *n.* parody. parodi·ëren,
-ieer, *v.t.* to parody.
pa·rool, -rolen, *n.n.* parole; password, watchword.
part, *n.n.* portion, share. *er* ~ *noch deel aan
hebben,* to have nothing to do with something; *voor mijn* ~, I for one. ¶*n. iemand
~en spelen,* to play s meone tricks, to
play someone false.
par·terre, -s, *n.n.* pit (*in theatre*); ground floor.
particu·lier, *a.* private. *in* ~ *bezit,* privately
owned. ¶*n.* private person.
par·tieel, -iele, *a.* partial (*in part*). ¶*adv.*
partially.
par·tij, *n.* part; quantity, lot; match
(*marriage*); party (*grouping*); party (*entertainment*); game (*cards, billiards, etc.*).
een goede ~ *doen,* to make a good match;
~ *kiezen,* to take sides; *bij* ~*en verkopen,*
to sell in lots; *van de* ~ *zijn,* to join in.
¶*no* pl., *n.* profit. ~ *trekken van,* to take
advantage of. par·tijdig, *a.* partial, biased.
¶*adv.* in a biased way. par·tijdigheid, no pl.,
n. partiality. par·tijganger, -s, *n.* partisan.
par·tijtje, -s, *n.n.* party (*entertainment*).
par·tijzucht, no pl., *n.* party spirit,
factiousness. parti·tuur, -turen, *n.* score.
·partje, -s, *n.n.* segment, quarter (*orange*).
parve·nu, -'s, *n.* upstart.
pas, -ssen, *n.* step, pace; pass (*mountain*);
passport. *de* ~ *aangeven,* to mark time
(*literal*); *iemand de* ~ *afsnijden,* to forestall
a person, bar a person's way; *in de* ~
lopen, to keep step; *in de* ~ *zien te komen
bij,* to curry favour with. ¶*no* pl., *n.n.*
op zijn ~, in (good) season; *te* ~ *en te
onpas,* in season and out of season; *te* ~
brengen, to introduce (into talk); *te* ~
komen, to come in handy, be useful; *niet
te* ~ *komen,* not to be the proper thing;
er aan te ~ *komen,* to be needed; *er bij*

te ~ *komen,* to be involved *or* concerned;
van ~ *komen,* to come at an opportune
moment. ¶*adv.* just, just now; hardly,
scarcely; only; freshly, newly.
·Pasen, *N.* Easter; Passover.
pasge·boren, *a.* new-born. pasge·huwd, *a.*
newly wed.
·pasgeld, no pl., *n.n.* (small) change.
·pasje, -s, *n.n.* transfer (*ticket*).
·paskamer, -s, *n.* fitting room. ·pasklaar,
-klare, *a.* ready (*for trying on*); ready-
made, cut-and-dried. ¶*adv. iets* ~ *maken,*
to get something ready (*for fitting*) *or* to
adapt something.
pas·kwil, -llen, *n.* lampoon; foolishness.
·paslood, -loden, *n.n.* plummet. ·pasmunt, *n.*
small coins. ·paspoort, *n.n.* passport.
pas·saat, -saten, *n.*, pas·saatwind, *n.* trade-
wind.
pas·sage, -s, *n.* passage (*in book, etc.*); passage,
voyage; arcade. pas·sagebiljet, -tten, *n.n.*
steamship ticket. passa·gier, -s, *n.*
passenger. passa·gieren, *v.i.* to go on
shore-leave.
passe·ment, *n.n.* braid, trimming. passe-
·mentwerker, -s, *n.* lacemaker.
·passen, pas, *v.t.* to fit; to fit on, try on; to
suit; to become, behove. ~ *en meten,* to
pinch and scrape. ¶*v.i.* to pass (*in cards*).
~ *bij,* to match, go (*well*) with; ~ *in,*
to fit into; ~ *op,* to mind *or* to beware of;
er voor ~, to decline. ·passend, *a.* suitable,
fitting, apposite. ·passer, -s, *n.* compasses;
market (*East Indies*). *een* ~, a pair
of compasses; *een kromme* ~, a pair of
callipers. ·passerdoos, -dozen, *n.* box of
mathematical instruments. pas·seren,
-seer, *v.t.* to pass. ¶*v.i.* to pass (by).
·passie, -s, *n.* passion, craze; Passion.
·passiebloem, *n.* passion flower.
pas·sief, -ve, *a.* passive. ¶passiva, *n.n.*
liability.
·passiespel, *n.n.* passion play.
·passiva, pl. *n. See* passief.
pas·tei, *n.* pie, pastry. pas·teibakker, -s, *n.*
pastry-cook. pas·teitje, -s, *n.n.* patty.
pasti·nak, *n.* parsnip.
pas·toor, -s, *n.* priest (*Roman Catholic*).
pasto·rie, -rieën, *n.* parsonage, rectory,
vicarage, presbytery.
pat, *a.* stalemate.
pa·tent, *n.n.* patent, license. ~ *nemen op,*
to patent, take out a patent for. ¶*a.*
capital, excellent. paten·teren, -teer, *v.t.*
to patent. pa·tenthouder, -s, *n.* patentee.
pa·tentolie, no pl., *n.* patent oil, rape oil.
pa·tentrecht, *n.n.* patent right. pa·tent-
·sluiting, *n.* patent lock *or* stopper.
·pater, -s, *n.* friar. ~ *goedleven,* epicure, one
who likes the good things of life. pater-
·noster, -s, *n.* & *n.n.* paternoster; (*slang*)
darbies. pa·tertje, -s, *n.n.* small friar.
~ *langs de kant,* ring-a-roses.
patho·loog, -logen, *n.* pathologist.

pati·ënt, *n.* patient.
·**patjakker**, -s, *n.* scoundrel, rascal.
·**patjol**, -s, *n.* mattock (*East Indies*).
pa·triciër, -s, *n.* patrician.
pa·trijs, -zen, *n.* partridge. **pa·trijspoort**, *n.* port-hole.
patro·naat, -naten, *n.n.* patronage; youth organization (*Roman Catholic*). **patro·nes**, -ssen, *n.* patron saint, patroness. **pa·troon**, -tronen, *n.* patron saint, patron; employer, boss; cartridge. *losse patronen,* blank cartridges; *scherpe patronen,* ball *or* live cartridges. ¶*n.n.* pattern, design. **pa·troonband**, *n.* feed-strip. **pa·troonhouder**, -s, *n.* clip. **pa·troonhuls**, -zen, *n.* cartridge-case. **pa·troontas**, -ssen, *n.* cartridge-box.
. **pa·trouille**, -s, *n.* patrol. **patrouil·leren**, -leer, *v.t. & v.i.* to patrol.
pats, *int.* smack. ¶*n.* smack. ·**patsen**, *v.t. & v.i.* to bang. *met zijn geld ~,* to throw one's money about. ·**patser**, -s, *n.* spendthrift; bounder. ·**patserig**, *a.* swanky.
pauk, *n.* kettle-drum. ·**pauken**, *v.i.* to beat the kettle-drum. **pauke·nist**, *n.* kettle-drummer.
paus, *n.* pope. ·**pausdom**, no pl., *n.n.* papacy. ·**pauselijk**, *a.* papal, pontifical.
pau·seren, -seer, *v.i.* to pause, stop.
pauw, *n.* peacock. ·**pauweveer**, -veren, *n.* peacock's feather. ·**pauwfazant**, *n.* argus pheasant. **pau·win**, -nnen, *n.* peahen. ·**pauwoog**, -wogen, *n.* peacock butterfly. ·**pauwstaart**, *n.* fantail pigeon.
·**pauze**, -n, *n.* pause; interval.
pavil·joen, *n.n.* pavilion; marquee.
pé, no pl., *n. er de ~ in hebben,* to be fed up.
pech, no pl., *n.* bad luck. *~ hebben,* to have a run of bad luck.
pe·daal, -dalen, *n.* pedal.
pe·dant, *n.* pedant. ¶*a.* pedantic. **pedante·rie**, -rieën, *n.* pedantry.
·**peddelen**, *v.i.* to pedal.
pe·del, -s, *n.* beadle.
pedi·cure, -s, *n.* chiropodist.
pee, **peeën**, *n.* beet. ·**peekoffie**, no pl., *n.* chicory.
peen, **penen**, *n.* carrot. *witte ~,* parsnip.
peer, **peren**, *n.* pear; reservoir. *met z'n gebakken peren zitten,* to be left in the lurch.
pees, **pezen**, *n.* tendon, sinew; string (*bow*).
peet, **peten**, *n.* godfather, godmother. ·**peetdochter**, -s, *n.* goddaughter. ·**peetoom**, -s, *n.* godfather. ·**peettante**, -s, *n.* godmother. ·**peetzoon**, -zonen, *n.* godson.
peil, no pl., *n.n.* level; gauge. *er valt geen ~ op hem te trekken,* one cannot rely on him; *beneden ~,* not up to the mark; *op ~,* at the right level; *op hoger ~ brengen,* to raise the standard. ·**peilen**, *v.t.* to gauge; to probe; to fathom, sound. ·**peilglas**, -zen, *n.n.* water-gauge. ·**peillood**, -loden, *n.n.* lead. ·**peiloos**, -lloze, *a.* unfathomable. ·**peilschaal**, -schalen, *n.* water-gauge, tide-gauge. ·**peilstok**, -kken, *n.* dipstick.

·**peinzen**, -peins, *v.i.* to ponder, meditate. ·**peinzend**, *a.* meditative, pensive.
peis, no pl., *n. See* pais.
pek, no pl., *n.n.* pitch. ·**pekbroek**, *n.* jack tar. ·**pekdraad**, -draden, *n.* waxed thread.
·**pekel**, no pl., *n.* brine, pickle. *in de ~ zitten,* to be in trouble. ·**pekelachtig**, *a.* briny. ·**pekelen**, *v.t.* to pickle, salt. ·**pekelharing**, *n.* salt herring. ·**pekelvlees**, no pl., *n.n.* salted meat.
·**pekken**, **pek**, *v.t.* to pitch, tar.
pel, -llen, *n.* shell (*egg, nut*); skin (*banana*).
·**pelgrim**, -s, *n.* pilgrim. ·**pelgrimstocht**, *n.* pilgrimage.
peli·kaan, -kanen, *n.* pelican.
·**pellen**, **pel**, *v.t.* to peel, shell, hull. ·**pelmolen**, -s, *n.* peeling-machine.
pelo·ton, -s, *n.n.* platoon.
pels, -zen, *n.* fur; fur coat. ·**pelsdier**, *n.n.* furred animal. ·**pelshandelaar**, -s, *n.* furrier. ·**pelsjager**, -s, *n.* fur-trapper. ·**pelsjas**, -ssen, *n.* fur coat. ·**pelswerk**, no pl., *n.n.* furriery, peltry. ·**pelte·rij**, *n.* furriery, peltry.
·**peluw**, *n.* bolster.
pen, -nnen, *n.* pen; nib; quill; peg; needle. *in de ~ blijven,* to remain unfinished.
pe·narie, no pl., *n. in de ~ zitten,* to be in a fix.
pen·dule, -s, *n.* timepiece.
pe·nibel, *a.* painful, embarrassing.
·**pennelikker**, -s, *n.* quill-driver. ·**pennemes**, -ssen, *n.n.* pocket-knife. ·**pennen**, **pen**, *v.t.* to pen. ·**penneschacht**, *n.* quill. ·**pennestreek**, -streken, *n.*, ·**pennetrek**, -kken, *n.* stroke of the pen. *met één ~,* at a stroke of the pen.
·**penning**, *n.* medal; official's identification disc. ·**penningkruid**, no pl., *n.n.* money-wort. ·**penningkunde**, no pl., *n.* numismatics. ·**penningmeester**, -s, *n.* treasurer.
pens, *n.* paunch, belly; rumen.
pen·seel, -selen, *n.n.* brush (*artist's*). ·**penseelaapje**, -s, *n.n.* wistiti. **pen·selen**, -seel, *v.t.* to paint.
pensi·oen, *n.n.* pension. *met ~ gaan,* to take one's pension, go on retired pay; *op ~ stellen,* to pension. **pensi·oensbijdrage**, -n, *n.* superannuation contribution. **pensi·on**, -s, *n.n.* boarding-house; board. *en ~ zijn,* to live in a boarding house. **pensio·naat**, -naten, *n.n.* boarding-school. **pension·neren**, -neer, *v.t.* to pension (off).
pentekenaar, -s, *n.* black-and-white artist. ·**pentekening**, *n.* pen-and-ink drawing.
·**peper**, no pl., *n.* pepper. ·**peperbus**, -ssen, *n.* pepperpot, pepper-castor. ·**peperduur**, -dure, *a.* very expensive. ·**peperen**, *v.t.* to pepper. **peper-en-zoutkleurig**, *a.* tinged with grey, pepper-and-salt. **peper-en-zoutstel**, -llen, *n.n.* cruet-stand. ·**peperhuisje**, -s, *n.n.* cornet, screw (of paper). ·**peperig**, *a.* peppery. ·**peperkers**, no pl., *n.* pepperwort. ·**peperkoek**, *n.* gingerbread,

ginger cake. ·**peperkorrel, -s,** *n.* pepper-corn. **peper·munt,** no pl., *n.* peppermint. **peper·muntje, -s,** *n.n.* peppermint (*sweet*). ·**pepernoot, -noten,** *n.* gingerbread nut. ·**pepertuin,** *n.* pepper plantation. ·**peper-vogel, -s,** *n.* toucan. ·**peperwortel, -s,** *n.* horse-radish.

·**peppel, -s,** *n.* poplar.

per, *prep.* per, by. *2 gulden ~ meter,* 2 guilders a metre.

per·ceel, -celen, *n.n.* premises; lot, parcel, plot. **per·ceelsgewijze,** *adv.* in lots..

per·cent, *n.n.* per cent. **percen·tage, -s,** *n.n.* percentage. **per·centsgewijze,** *adv.* pro rata, proportionally.

per·cussiedopje, -s, *n.n.* percussion cap.

·**pereboom, -bomen,** *n.,* ·**perelaar, -s,** *n.* pear-tree. ·**perenhout,** *n.n.* pear-wood.

pe·rikel, *n.n.* (*stilted*) danger.

peri·ode, -s *or* **-n,** *n.* period. **perio·diek,** *a.* periodical.

perk, *n.n.* (flower-)bed, plot; bound, limit. *binnen de ~en blijven,* to keep within bounds; *alle ~en te buiten gaan,* to go beyond all bounds.

perka·ment, *n.n.* parchment, vellum. **perka-menten,** *a.* (of) parchment *or* vellum. **perka·mentrol, -llen,** *n.* parchment scroll.

per·missie, -s, *n.* permission. *met ~,* by your leave. **permit·teren, -teer,** *v.t.* to permit, allow. *zich iets ~,* to permit oneself a liberty *or* to afford oneself a luxury.

per·plex, *a.* perplexed, baffled.

per·ron, -s, *n.n.* platform. **per·ronkaartje, -s,** *n.n.* platform ticket.

pers, *n.* press. *ter ~e,* in the press; *ter ~e gaan,* to go to press. ·**persbureau, -'s,** *n.n.* press agency.

per ·se, *adv.* by hook or by crook. *hij wil ~ . . .,* he insists on . . .

·**persen,** *v.t.* to press, squeeze. ·**perser, -s,** *n.* presser, squeezer. **persklaar, -klare,** *a.* ready for the press. ·**perskuip,** *n.* wine-press.

perso·nalia, pl. only, *n.n.* personal (*news-paper column*). **personali·teit,** *n.* person-ality, personal remark. **perso·neel, -nele,** *a.* personal. *personele belasting,* householder's tax. ¶ no pl., *n.n.* staff, personnel, servants. **per·sonenlift,** *n.* passenger lift. **per·sonen-trein,** *n.* passenger train. **personifi·ëren, -ieer,** *v.t.* to personify. **per·soon, -sonen,** *n.* person. *mijn ~,* I myself; *ik voor mijn ~,* I for one; *in ~,* personified; *per ~,* a head; *klein van ~,* small of stature. **per·soonlijk,** *a.* personal. ¶ *adv.* personally, in person. **per·soonlijkheid, -heden,** *n.* personality.

perspec·tief, -tieven, *n.n.* perspective, vista. ¶ no pl., *n.* perspective (*science*).

·**perspomp,** *n.* force pump. **perstribune, -s,** *n.* press gallery. **persvrijheid,** no pl., *n.* freedom of the press.

perti·nent, *a.* positive, categorical. ¶ *adv. ~ weigeren,* to refuse obstinately.

·**perubalm,** no pl., *n.* (*kind of*) balsam.

·**Perzië,** *n.N.* Persia. ·**Perzisch,** *a.* Persian.

·**perzik,** *n.* peach. ·**perzikkruid,** no pl., *n.n.* lady's thumb.

pest, *n.* plague, pestilence, pest. *iets haten als de ~,* to hate something like poison; *er de ~ in hebben,* to be fed up. ·**pestbuil,** *n.* plague sore. ·**pesten,** *v.t.* to tease, bait. **peste·rij,** *n.* malicious teasing. **pesti·lentie, -s,** *n.* pestilence, plague. ·**pestvogel, -s,** *n.* waxwing..

pet, -tten, *n.* (peaked) cap.

·**petekind, -eren,** *n.n.* godchild. ·**petemoei,** *n.* godmother.

peter·selie, no pl., *n.* parsley.

pe·tieterig, *a.* diminutive.

pe·titie, -s, *n.* petition, memorial. **petitio-naris, -ssen,** *n.* petitioner. **petition·neren, -neer,** *v.t.* to petition.

·**petje, -s,** *n.n.* small cap. *het is boven mijn ~,* it is too learned for me.

Pe·trarca, *N.* Petrarch.

pe·troleum, no pl., *n.* paraffin oil; petroleum. **pe·troleumbron, -nnen,** *n.* oil-well. **pe·troleumkachel, -s,** *n.* oil-stove. **pe·troleumveld,** *n.n.* oil-field.

·**Petrus,** *N.* Peter.

·**pettenmaker, -s,** *n.* capmaker.

·**petto,** no pl., *n. iets in ~ houden,* to keep something up one's sleeve.

peueraar, -s, *n.* sniggler. ·**peueren,** *v.i.* to sniggle (*for eels*).

peuk, *n.,* ·**peukje, -s,** *n.n.* fag-end.

peul, *n.* shell, pod, husk. ·**peulgewas, -ssen,** *n.n.,* legume. ·**peulschil, -llen,** *n.* pea-pod. *een peulschilletje,* a mere flea-bite. ·**peultjes,** pl. only, *n.n.* green peas. ·**peulvrucht,** *n.* leguminous plant; *pl.* pulse.

peur, *n.* bob (*worm*). ·**peurder, -s,** *n. See* **peueraar.** ·**peuren,** *v.i. See* **peueren.**

·**peuter, -s,** *n.* pipe-cleaner; tiny tot; biff. ·**peuteraar, -s,** *n.* pipe-cleaner; fiddler. ·**peuteren,** *v.i.* to toy, fiddle. *in zijn neus ~,* to pick one's nose. ·**peuterig,** *a.* niggly. ·**peuterwerk,** no pl., *n.n.* finicky job.

·**peuzelen,** *v.t.* to munch; to eat with relish.

·**pezerik, -kken,** *n.* bull's pizzle.

ph~, *see* **f~.**

·**pheno·meen, -menen,** *n.n.* phenomenon.

philan·troop, -tropen, *n.* philanthropist.

phi·lister. -s, *n.* philistine; non-student.

philo·soof, -sofen, *n.* philosopher.

pho·neticus, -ci, *n.* phonetician. **phone·tiek,** no pl., *n.* phonetics. **pho·netisch,** *a.* phonetic. ¶ *adv.* phonetically.

·**phosphor,** no pl., *n.,* ·**phosphorus,** no pl., *n.* phosphorus.

pi·ano, -'s, *n.* piano. *~ spelen,* to play the piano. **pi·anokrukje, -s,** *n.n.* piano-stool. **pi·anospel,** no pl., *n.n.* piano-playing. **pi·anostemmer, -s,** *n.* piano-tuner.

pi·as, -ssen, *n.* clown, buffoon. pi·asserig, *a.* clownish.

pi·aster, -s, *n.* piastre.

piccolo, -'s, *n.* piccolo (*flute*); page(-boy), buttons.

pief, *int.* ~ poef paf, whizz bang.

piek, *n.* pike; peak.

piekeraar, -s, *n.* worrier. ·piekeren, *v.i.* to worry, brood, fret. ·piekerig, *a.* wispy. ·piekfijn, *a.* tip-top, posh.

piel, *n.* duck.

pienter, *a.* clever, smart. ·pienterheid, -heden, *n.* cleverness.

piep, *int.* squeak! chirp! ·piepen, *v.i.* to squeak; to chirp; (*slang*) to sleep. ¶*v.t.* to roast (*potatoes in ashes*). ·pieper, -s, *n.* squeaker; pipit; (*coll.*) spud. ·pieperig, *a.* squeaky, shrill. ·piepjong, *a.* very young. ·piepkuiken, -s, *n.n.* spring chicken. ·piepzak, no pl., *n. in de* ~ *zitten*, to be in a blue funk.

pier, *n.* earthworm; pier, jetty. ·pierenbak, -kken, *n.* children's pool. ·pierenbakje, -s, *n.n.* worm-tin. ·pierenland, no pl., *n.n. naar het* ~ *gaan*, to be food for worms. ·pierewaaien, *v.i.* to be on the spree. ·pierewaaier, -s, *n.* rake, rip.

Piet, *N.* Peter; person. *een hele* ~, quite a big fellow; *zwarte* ~, the black servant of Santa Claus.

pieterman, -s, *n.* weever. *grote* ~, dragon weever; *kleine* ~, lesser weever.

pieter·selie, no pl., *n.* parsley.

piet·lut, -tten, *n.* small-minded person. *er voor* ~ *bijzitten*, to be superfluous. piet·luttig, *a.* small-minded, niggly.

pij, *n.* cowl. ·pijjekker, -s, *n.* peajacket.

pijl, *n.* arrow, bolt, shaft. ~ *en boog*, bow and arrow; *als een* ~ *uit de boog*, like an arrow. ·pijlbundel, -s, *n.* sheaf of arrows. ·pijler, -s, *n.* pillar, column. ·pijlkoker, -s, *n.* quiver. ·pijlkruid, no pl., *n.n.* arrowhead (*plant*); arrow grass. ·pijlriet, no pl., *n.n.* reed-grass. ·pijlstaart, *n.* pin-tail (*duck*). ·pijlstaartrog, -ggen, *n.* sting-ray. ·pijlstaartvlinder, -s, *n.* hawk-moth. ·pijlwortel, -s, *n.* arrowroot.

pijn, *n.* pain, ache; pine(-tree). ~ *doen*, to hurt, smart; ~ *hebben*, to have a pain, be in pain, ache. ·pijnappel, -s, *n.* fir-cone, pine-cone. ·pijnbank, *n.* rack (*for torture*). *op de* ~ *leggen*, to put to torture or to the rack. ·pijnboom, -bomen, *n.* pine(-tree). ·pijnigen, *v.t.* to torture, torment, rack. ·pijniger, -s, *n.* tormentor. ·pijniging, *n.* torture. ·pijnlijk, *a.* painful, sore. ·pijnloos, loze, *a.* painless. ·pijnstillend, *a.* pain-relieving, sedative. ~ *middel*, sedative, anodyne.

pijp, *n.* pipe; pipe, tube; leg (*of trousers*); funnel (*of steamship*); pipe, butt; fife; stick (*of wax*). ·pijpaarde, no pl., *n.* china clay. ·pijpbeen, -deren, *n.n.* long bone. ·pijpbloem, *n.* birthwort, snake-root. ·pijpedop,

-ppen, *n.* lid on pipe-bowl. ·pijpekoter, -s, *n.* pipe-digger. ·pijper, -s, *n.* fifer. ·pijpesteel, -stelen, *n.* pipe-stem. ·pijpkaneel, no pl., *n.n.* stick cinnamon. ·pijpleiding, *n.* pipe-line. ·pijpriet, no pl., *n.n.* reed(s). ·pijpzak, -kken, *n.* bagpipe.

pik, no pl., *n.n.* pitch. ¶no pl., *n. de* ~ *hebben op*, to have a down on. ¶-kken, *n.* pick, pickaxe.

pi·kant, *a.* piquant; spicy. pikante·rie, -rieën, *n.* piquancy.

pikbroek, *n.* jack tar. ·pikdonker, *a.* pitch-dark. ¶no pl., *n.n.* pitch-darkness.

pikdraad, -draden, *n.* waxed thread.

pi·keren, -keer, *v.t.* to pique, nettle.

pi·ket, -tten, *n.* picket (*in army*). *officier van* ~, picket officer. ¶*n.n.* piquet (*cards*). pi·ketpaal, palen, *n.* picket (*post*). pi·ketten, -ket, *v.i.* to play piquet.

pi·keur, -s, *n.* riding-master.

pikhouweel, -welen, *n.n.* pickaxe.

pikken, pik, *v.t.* to peck, pick; to (cover with) pitch.

·pikol, -s, *n.* picul (*East Indian weight*).

pikzwart, *a.* pitch-black.

pil, -llen, *n.* pill.

pi·laar, -laren, *n.* pillar. pi·larenbijter, -s, *n.* hypocrite.

pilledoos, -dozen, *n.* pill-box.

·pilo, no pl., *n.n.* corduroy.

pi·loot, -loten, *n.* pilot (*of aircraft*).

pi·ment, no pl., *n.* pimento; allspice.

pimpel, no pl., *n. aan de* ~ *zijn*, he's taken to lifting the elbow. ·pimpelaar, -s, *n.* toper, tippler. ·pimpelen, *v.i.* to tipple. ·pimpelmees, -mezen, *n.* titmouse. ·pimpelpaars, *a.* dark purple.

pin, -nnen, *n.* peg, pin.

·pinang, *n.* areca.

pin·cet, -tten, *n.n.* tweezers.

·pinda, -'s, *n.* pea-nut.

pingelaar, -s, *n.* haggler. ·pingelen, *v.t.* to haggle.

·pinguïn, -s, *n.* penguin.

pink, *n.* little finger; pink, fishing boat; heifer. *bij de* ~*en zijn*, to have one's wits about one, be quick on the uptake. ·pinken, *v.i.* to blink, wink.

·Pinkster, *N.* Whitsuntide, Whitsun; Pentecost. ~ *drie*, Whit Tuesday. Pinkster·avond, *N.* eve of Whit Sunday. ·Pinksterbloem, *n.* cuckoo-flower. ·Pinksterdag, *N.* Whit Sunday. *tweede* ~, Whit Monday. ·Pinksteren, *N. See* Pinkster. pinkster·nakel, -s, *n.* parsnip.

·pinnen, *v.t.* to peg, pin.

pi·oen, *n.*, pi·oenroos, -rozen, *n.* peony.

pi·on, -s, *n.* pawn (*chess*).

pio·nierswerk, no pl., *n.n.* pioneering.

pip, no pl., *n.* pip (*poultry disease*). *de* ~ *hebben*, to be fed up.

pi·pet, -tten, *n.* pipette.

·pippeling, *n.* pippin.

pips, *a.* peaky, off colour.

pi·raat, -raten, *n.* pirate.
pira·mide, -n, *n.* pyramid.
·pisang, -s, *n.* banana. *een rare* ~, a queer customer.
·pissebed, -dden, *n.* dandelion.
pis·tool, -tolen, *n.n.* pistol. **pis·tooltje,** -s, *n.n.* toy-pistol.
pit, -tten, *n.* kernel, stone, pip; pith; wick. *er zit geen* ~ *in hem,* he has no backbone. **·pittig,** *a.* pithy. **·pittigheid,** no pl., *n.* pithiness. **·pitvis,** -ssen, *n.* dragon-fish. **·pitvrucht,** *n.* pome; kernel fruit.
plaag, plagen, *n.* plague, nuisance, pest. **·plaaggeest,** *n.* tease. **·plaagziek,** *a.* fond of teasing. **·plaagzucht,** no pl., *n.* love of teasing.
plaat, platen, *n.* plate; sheet *(metal)*; slab *(marble)*; record *(gramophone)*; dial; plate, picture; sandbank. *de* ~ *poetsen,* to sling one's hook. **·plaatdruk,** no pl., *n.* copperplate *(engraving).* **·plaatje,** -s, *n.n.* picture; plate, disc.
plaats, *n.* place; room, space; square; courtyard; place *(town, village, farm)*; passage *(in book)*; post, job, seat, passage. ~ *grijpen,* to take place; ~ *hebben,* to take place *or* to have the space; ~ *innemen,* to take up room; ~ *maken,* to make room; ~ *nemen,* to take a seat, sit down; ~ *vinden,* to take place; *in* ~ *van,* instead of; *op enkele* ~*en,* in a few places; *op zijn* ~, in the right place; *op de* ~ *rust!,* stand easy!; *ter* ~*e,* on the spot; *van* ~ *verwisselen,* to change places. **·plaatsbekleder,** -s, *n.* substitute, locum tenens. **·plaatsbeschrijving,** *n.* topography. **·plaatsbespreking,** *n.* booking, reservation. **·plaatsbewijs,** -zen, *n.n.* ticket. **·plaatscommandant,** *n.* military commander *(garrison).* **·plaatselijk,** *a.* local. **·plaatsen,** *v.t.* to place, put; to station, post; to insert *(advertisement)*; to invest *(money.* **·plaatsgebrek,** no pl., *n.n.* lack of space. **·plaatsing,** *n.* placing *(appointment)*; insertion *(of advertisement).* **plaatsingsbureau, -'s,** *n.n.* employment bureau. **·plaatskaart,** *n.* ticket. **·plaatstroom,** no pl., *n.* anode current. **·plaatsruimte,** no pl., *n.* space, room, accommodation. **·plaatsvervangend,** *a.* deputy, acting. **·plaatsvervanger, -s,** *n.* deputy, substitute, supply, locum tenens. **·plaatsvervanging,** *n.* substitution.
·plaatwerk, *n.n.* plates, illustrated volume.
pla·dijs, -zen, *n.* plaice.
pla·fond, -s, *n.n.* ceiling.
plag, -ggen, *n.* sod *(of turf).*
·plagen, plaag, *v.t.* to tease. ~ *met,* to tease about; *zijn hersens* ~ *met,* to rack one's brains over; *mag ik U* ~ *met . . .,* may I disturb you with . . . **·plager, -s,** *n.* tease, teaser. **plage·rij,** *n.* teasing, chaff.
·plagge, -n, *n. See* plag. **·plaggen,** *a.* (of) turf. ¶*v.i.* to cut turf. **·plaggensteker, -s,** *n.* turf-cutter; turf spade.

plagi·aat, -iaten, *n.n.* plagiarism. **plagi·aris, -ssen,** *n.* plagiarist.
plak, -kken, *n.* slice; slab, bar; ferule. *onder de* ~ *zitten,* to be under someone's thumb. **plak·kaat, -katen,** *n.n.* placard; edict, proclamation. **·plakken, plak,** *v.t.* to stick, paste, glue. ¶*v.i.* to stick. *blijven* ~, to stay on and on. **·plakker, -s,** *n.* person who stays on and on. **·plakkerig,** *a.* sticky. **·plakmiddel,** *n.n.* adhesive. **·plakpleister, -s,** *n.n.* sticking plaster. **·plaksel, -s,** *n.n.* adhesive paste. **·plakzegel, -s,** *n.n.* revenue stamp; adhesive label.
pla·muren, -muur, *v.t.* to prime *(surface).* **pla·muur(sel),** no pl., *n.n.* priming. **pla·muurmes, -ssen,** *n.n.* putty knife.
plan, -nnen, *n.n.* plan; project; *pl.* designs.
pla·neet, -neten, *n.* planet.
plank, *n.* plank, board; shelf. *de* ~ *misslaan,* to be wide of the mark; *van de bovenste* ~, first-rate. **·planken,** *a.* (made of) boards, plank. **·plankenkoorts,** no pl., *n.* stage fright. **·plankenvloer,** *n.* boarded floor. **plan·kier,** *n.n.* platform.
·plannenmaker, -s, *n.* planner, schemer.
plant, *n.* plant. **·plantaarde,** no pl., *n.* vegetable mould. **plant·aardig,** *a.* vegetable, herbaceous. **plan·tage, -s,** *n.* plantation, estate. **·planten,** *v.t.* to plant. **·plantenetend,** *a.* herbivorous. **·planteneter, -s,** *n.* herbivore. **·plantengroei,** no pl., *n.* vegetation. **·plantenkweker, -s,** *n.* nurseryman. **plantenkweker·ij,** *n.* nursery (-garden). **·plantenluis, -zen,** *n.* greenfly. **·plantenrijk,** no pl., *n.n.* vegetable kingdom. **·plantentuin,** *n.* botanical garden. **·planter, -s,** *n.* planter. **plantkunde,** no pl., *n.* botany. **plant·kundige, -n,** *n.* botanist. **plant·soen,** *n.n.* gardens *(public),* park.
plas, -ssen, *n.* puddle, pool; lake. *de grote* ~, the sea. **·plasdankje, -s,** *n.n. om een* ~ *te verdienen,* in order to ingratiate oneself. **·plasje, -s,** *n.n.* puddle. *een* ~ *doen,* to wee-wee. **·plasregen, -s,** *n.* downpour. **·plasregenen,** *v.i., imp.* to pour (with rain). **·plassen, plas,** *v.i.* to splash. **plasse·rij,** *n.* splashing.
plas·tiek, *n.* plastics. **·plastisch,** *a.* plastic.
plat, -tte, *a.* flat; level; vulgar, coarse. *een platte beurs,* an empty purse; ~ *bord,* a plate; *het platte land,* the countryside; ~ *drukken,* to squeeze; ~ *lopen,* to trample, wear out; ~ *maken,* to flatten; ~ *schieten,* to shoot to pieces. ¶*adv.* flat; vulgarly. ¶-tten, *n.n.* flat (part).
pla·taan, -tanen, *n.* plane-tree.
·platboomd, *a.* flat-bottomed.
Plat·duits, *a.* Low German.
pla·teel, -telen, *n.n.* (object made of) glazed earthenware.
·platheid, -heden, *n.* flatness; vulgarity, coarseness.
·platina, no pl., *n.n.* platinum.

·**platlood**, no pl., *n.n.* sheet lead. **platte·grond,** *n.* ground-plan, map. **platte·land,** no pl., *n.n.* countryside. **platte·lander, -s,** *n.*, **platte·landsbewoner, -s,** *n.* countryman (*rural inhabitant*). **platte·landsgemeente, -n,** *n.* rural municipality. **platvis, -ssen,** *n.* flat-fish. ·**platvoet,** *n.* flat-foot. ~*en hebben,* to be flat-footed. ·**platvoetwacht,** *n.* dog-watch (*4 to 8 p.m.*). ·**platweg,** *adv.* flatly. ·**platzak,** *adv.* empty-handed; without a penny.

pla·vei, *n.* paving-stone. **pla·veien,** *v.t.* to pave. **pla·veisel, -s,** *n.n.* paved roadway. **pla·vuis, -zen,** *n.* flag(stone).

ple·bejer, -s, *n.* plebeian. **ple·bejisch,** *a.* plebeian. **plebs,** no pl., *n.n.* rabble.

plecht, *n.* forward *or* after deck (*small vessel*). ·**plechtanker, -s,** *n.n.* sheet-anchor. ·**plechtgewaad, -waden,** *n.n.* solemn robes. ·**plechtig,** *a.* solemn, stately. ·**plechtigheid, -heden,** *n.* solemnity; ceremony. **plecht·matig,** *a.,* **plecht·statig,** *a.* solemn. **plecht·statigheid, -heden,** *n.* solemnity.

plee, -'s, *n.* privy.

·**pleegkind, -eren,** *n.n.* foster-child. ·**pleegmoeder, -s,** *n.* foster-mother. ·**pleegouders,** pl. only, *n.* foster-parents. ·**pleegvader, -s,** *n.* foster-father. ·**pleegzuster, -s,** *n.* sick-nurse. ·**plegen, pleeg,** *v.t.* to commit. *overleg* ~, to consult (together). ¶*v.t., irr.* to be in the habit of... *hij placht* . . ., he used to . . . ·**pleger, -s,** *n.* perpetrator.

plei-dooi, *n.n.* plea; counsel's speech (*for the defence*). *een* ~ *houden,* to make a plea.

plein, *n.n.* square (*in town*).

·**pleister, -s,** *n.n.* plaster. ¶no pl., *n.* plaster, stucco. ·**pleisterbeeld,** *n.n.* plaster cast. ·**pleisteren,** *v.t.* to plaster. ¶*v.i.* to bait (*horses*). ·**pleisterkalk,** no pl., *n.* plaster, stucco. ·**pleisterplaats, -s,** *n.* baiting place, stage.

pleit, *n.n.* (law)suit; plea. *het* ~ *beslissen,* to decide; *het* ~ *is beslist* or *beslecht* or *voldongen,* the day is won; *het* ~ *winnen,* to carry the day. ·**pleitbezorger, -s,** *n.* counsel, barrister, lawyer. ·**pleiten,** *v.i.* to plead, argue. ~ *voor,* to speak well for; ~ *tegen,* to tell against. ·**pleiter, -s,** *n.* pleader. ·**pleitgeding,** *n.n.* lawsuit. ·**pleitrede, -nen,** *n.* plea, s:.·ech. **pleit·zuchtig,** *a.* litigious.

plei·zier, *n.n. See* **plezier.**

plek, -kken, *n.,* **plekje, -s,** *n.n.* (*coll.*) place, spot.

·**plempen,** *v.t.* to fill in, level. **plengen,** *v.t.* (*stilted*) to shed (*blood, etc.*); to pour (*libation*). ·**plengoffer, -s,** *n.n.* libation.

·**plethamer, -s,** *n.* flatting hammer. ·**pletmachine, -s,** *n.* flatting machine. ·**pletmolen, -s,** *n.* rolling mill. ·**pletrol, -llen,** *n.* flatting mill. ·**pletten, plet,** *v.t.* to roll out; to crush. ·**pletter, -s,** *n.* flatter. ¶no pl., *n. te* ~ *slaan,* to beat to pulp; *te* ~ *vallen,* to crash. **plette·rij,** *n.* rolling mill.

·**pleuris. -ssen,** *n.* pleurisy.

ple·zier, *n.n.* pleasure. ~ *doen,* to please; *iemand een* ~ *doen,* to do someone a favour; ~ *hebben,* to enjoy oneself, have a good time; ~ *hebben in,* to take pleasure in; ~ *krijgen in,* to begin to take pleasure in; ~ *maken,* to make merry; *ten* ~*e van,* for the pleasure of (*person*). ¶*n.* duty. **ple·zierboot, -boten,** *n.* pleasure steamer. **ple·zieren,** *v.t.* to please. **ple·zierig,** *a.* pleasant, entertaining. **ple·ziermaker, -s,** *n.* merry-maker, reveller. **ple·zierreis, -zen,** *n.* pleasure-trip.

plicht, *n.* duty, obligation. *iemand tot zijn* ~ *brengen,* to teach a person his duty, remind a person of his duty; *uit* ~ *tegenover,* in duty to; *volgens zijn* ~, according to one's conscience. **plicht·matig,** *a.* dutiful. ¶*adv.* dutifully, as in duty bound. ·**plichtpleging,** *n.* ceremony, compliment. *geen* ~*en,* don't stand on ceremony. ·**plichtsbesef,** no pl., *n.n.* sense of duty. ·**plichtsbetrachting,** no pl., *n.* devotion to duty. ·**plichtsgetrouw,** *a.* dutiful. ·**plichts·halve,** *adv.* as in duty bound. ·**plichtsvervulling,** *n.* discharge of one's duty. ·**plichtvergeten,** *a.* forgetful of one's duty. ·**plichtverzaker, -s,** *n.* shirker. ·**plichtverzuim,** no pl., *n.n.* neglect of duty.

plint, *n.* skirting board; plinth.

ploeg, *n.* plough; gang, shift; team. *de hand aan de* ~ *slaan,* to put one's hand to the plough; *van achter de* ~ *komen,* to have rustic manners. ·**ploegbaas, -bazen,** *n.* foreman, ganger. ·**ploegboom, -bomen,** *n.* plough-beam. ·**ploegen,** *v.t.* to plough. ·**ploeger, -s,** *n.* ploughman. ·**ploegijzer, -s,** *n.n.* coulter. ·**ploegschaaf, -schaven,** *n.* (carpenter's) plough. ·**ploegschaar, -scharen,** *n.* ploughshare. ·**ploegstaart,** *n.* plough-tail.

ploert, *n.* cad. *de koperen* ~, the sun (*East Indian slang*). ·**ploertachtig,** *a.* caddish. ·**ploertendoder, -s,** *n.* life-preserver. **ploerte·rij,** *n.* caddish trick. ·**ploertig,** *a.* caddish.

·**ploeteraar, -s,** *n.* plodder. ·**ploeteren,** *v.i.* to plod, splash; to drudge.

plof, *int.* thud, plop. ·**ploffen, plof,** *v.i.* to thud, plop.

·**plombe, -s,** *n.* filling (*of tooth*). ·**plom·beerloodje, -s,** *n.n.* lead seal. **plom·beersel, -s,** *n.n.* filling (*of tooth*).

plomp, *n.* waterlily. ¶*a.* clumsy, awkward. ¶*int.* splash, plop. ·**plompen,** *v.i.* to splash, plop. ·**plompheid, -heden,** *n.* clumsiness.

plons, *n.* splash. ¶*int.* splash! ·**plonzen, plons,** *v.i.* to splash.

plooi, *n.* fold; pleat, crease. *zijn gezicht in de* ~ *zetten,* to put on a serious expression. ·**plooibaar, -bare,** *a.* pliable, flexible. ·**plooibaarheid,** no pl., *n.* pliability, flexibility. ·**plooien,** *v.t.* to fold; to pleat, to crease. ·**plooiing,** *n.* folding (*geology*). ·**plooisel, -s,** *n.n.* pleating.

plots, *adv.* suddenly. ·plotseling, *a.* sudden. ¶*adv.* suddenly. ~ *stilhouden*, to pull up short.

·pluche, no pl., *n.* plush.

pluim, *n.* plume, feather; tail, tuft. plui·mage, -s, *n.* plumage. ·pluimen, *v.t.* to pluck. ·pluimpje, -s, *n.n.* small plume; compliment; feather in one's cap. ·pluimstaart, *n.* bushy tail. ·pluimstrijken, *v.t.* to flatter, fawn upon. ·pluimstrijker, -s, *n.* flatterer, toady. pluimstrijke·rij, *n.* flattery. ·pluimvaren, -s, *n.* royal fern. ·pluimvee, no pl., *n.n.* poultry.

pluis, no pl., *n.n.* fluff; oakum. ¶*a. het is daar niet* ~, there's something wrong there. ·pluisje, -s, *n.n.* bit of fluff. ·pluizen, pluis, *v.t., str.* to pick (*oakum*). ¶*v.i., str.* to produce fluff. ·pluizer, -s, *n.* person who ferrets out things. ·pluizig, *a.* fluffy.

pluk, no pl., *n.* gathering, picking. *een hele* ~, a long job. ·plukharen, -haar, *v.i.* to bicker. ·plukken, pluk, *v.t.* to gather, pick; to pluck; (*fig.*) to fleece. ¶*v.i.* ~ *aan*, to pick at. ·plukker, -s, *n.* gatherer, reaper. ·plukster, -s, *n.* gatherer, reaper (*female*). ·pluksel, no pl., *n.n.* picked threads. ·pluktijd, no pl., *n.* picking season.

plunderaar, -s, *n.* plunderer. ·plunderen, *v.t.* to plunder, pillage, loot, sack. ¶*v.i.* to plunder. ·plundering, *n.* pillage, sack. ·plunderziek, *a.* rapacious, drunk with plunder.

·plunje, no pl., *n.* kit; togs. ·plunjezak, -kken, *n.* kitbag.

plus, *adv.* plus. ~ *minus*, approximately.

plu·vier, *n.* plover.

pneu·matisch, *a.* pneumatic. pneumo·nie, no pl., *n.* pneumonia.

·pochen, *v.i.* to boast, brag. ~ *op*, to boast of. ·pocher, -s, *n.* boaster. poche·rij, *n.* boasting. ·pochhans, -zen, *n.* braggart.

·poedel, -s, *n.* poodle. ·poedelen, *v.i.* to miss; to puddle (*iron*). ·poedelnaakt, *a.* stark naked. ·poedelprijs, -zen, *n.* booby prize.

·poeder, -s, *n.n.* powder. *tot* ~ *malen*, to pulverize. *See* poeier. ·poederchocolade, no pl., *n.* chocolate powder. ·poederkwast, *n.* powder-puff. ·poedersuiker, no pl., *n.* castor sugar. ·poedervorm, *n. in* ~, in powder form.

poef, *int. pief* ~ *paf!*, bang, bang!

·poeier, -s, *n.n.* powder. *See* poeder. ·poeieren, *v.t.* to powder. ·poeierig, *a.* powdery.

poel, *n.* puddle; pool.

poelepe·taat, -taten, *n.* guinea-fowl. poe·let, no pl., *n.n.* breast of veal. poe·lier, -s, *n.* poulterer. poe·lierswinkel, -s, *n.* poulterer's (shop).

·poelsnip, -ppen, *n.* snipe.

·poema, -'s, *n.* puma.

poen, *n.* vulgarian. ·poenig, *a.* loud, boastful.

poes, *n.* puss; (*fur*) tippet. *voor de* ~ *zijn*, to be a goner; *lang niet voor de* ~, by no means negligible. ·poeslief, ve, *a.* as sweet as sweet can be; honeyed (*fig.*).

·poespas, no pl., *n.* hotchpotch.

·poesta, -'s, *n.* Puszta.

po·ëtisch, *a.* poetic(al).

poets, *n.* trick. *iemand een* ~ *bakken*, to play someone a trick. ·poetsdoek, *n.* polishing rag. ·poetsen, *v.t.* to polish, clean (*shoes, etc.*); to brush (*teeth*). *de plaat* ~, to desert, run away; *'m* ~, to hook it, scram. ·poetser, -s, *n.* polisher (*person*). ·poetsgerei, no pl., *n.n.*, ·poetsgoed, no pl., *n.n.* polishing things. ·poetskatoen, no pl., *n.n.* cotton waste. ·poetslap, -ppen, *n.* polishing rag. ·poetspommade, -s, *n.* polishing cream. ·poetswerk, no pl., *n.n.* polishing.

·poezelig, *a.* plump; chubby.

poë·zie, no pl., *n.* poetry.

pof, *int.* plunk! ¶no pl., *n. op de* ~ *kopen*, to buy on tick. ·pofbroek, *n.* knickerbockers. ·poffen, pof, *v.i.* to buy on tick; to pop (*shoot*). ¶*v.t.* to roast (*chestnuts*); to pop (*corn*). ·poffertje, -s, *n.n.* fritter. ·poffertjeskraam, -kramen, *n.n.* fritterbooth. ·pofmouw, *n.* leg-of-mutton sleeve.

·pogen, poog, *v.t.* to endeavour.

·poging, *n.* attempt, effort. *een* ~ *tot*, an attempt at; *een* ~ *om*, an attempt to.

pok, -kken, *n.* pock; vaccination mark. ¶-kken, pl. only, *n.* smallpox. *van de* ~ *geschonden*, pock-marked. pok·dalig, *a.* pock-pitted.

·poken, pook, *v.t.* to poke. *in het vuur* ~, to poke the fire. ·poker, -s, *n.* poker.

·pokhout, no pl., *n.* lignum vitæ. ·pokken, pl. only, *n. See* pok. ·pokkenbriefje, -s, *n.n.* vaccination certificate. ·pokkig, *a.* pocky. ·pokpuist, *n.* pock. ·pokput, -tten, pock-mark. ·pokstof, no pl., *n.* vaccine.

pol, -llen, *n.* clump (*of grass*), tussock.

·polder, -s, *n.* polder. ·polderbestuur, -sturen, *n.* polder-board. ·poldergast, *n.* navvy. ·poldergemaal, -malen, *n.n.* drainage mill. ·polderjongen, -s, *n.* navvy. ·polderwerker, -s, *n.* navvy.

po·lemisch, *a.* polemic. polemi·seren, -seer, *v.i.* to polemize, carry on controversy. pole·mist, *n.* controversialist.

·Polen, *n.N.* Poland.

po·liep, *n.* polyp; polypus.

po·lijsten, *v.t.* to polish, burnish. po·lijster, -s, *n.* polisher (*person*).

·polis, -ssen, *n.* policy (*insurance*).

po·liticus, -ci, *n.* politician.

po·litie, no pl., *n.* police. po·litieagent, *n.* policeman; police-officer. po·litieblad, *n.n.* police gazette. po·litiebureau, -'s, *n.n.* police-station. po·litievaartuig, *n.n.* police-launch.

poli·tiek, *a.* political; politic, diplomatic. ¶no pl., *n.* politics. *in* ~ (*stilted*), in civilian clothes.

po·litiemacht, no pl., *n.* body of police;

police-force. **po·litieman, -nnen,** *n.* policeofficer. **po·litiemuts,** *n.* forage-cap. **po·litierechter, -s,** *n.* police-magistrate. **po·litietroepen,** pl. only, *n.* military police. **po·litiewezen,** no pl., *n.n.* police; policesystem. **po·litiezaak, -zaken,** *n.* police matter.

poli·toer, no pl., *n.n.* french polish. **poli·toerder, -s,** *n.* french-polisher. **poli·toeren,** *v.t.* to french-polish.

pol·lak, -kk∈n, *n.* pollock.

pollepel, -s, *n.* ladle.

polospel, *n.n.* polo.

pols, *n.* wrist; pulse; jumping-pole. **polsarmband,** *n.* wristlet. **polsen,** *v.t.* to sound, throw out a feeler. *iemand ~ over,* to sound a person about. **polsgewricht,** *n.n.* wrist(-joint). **polsmofje, -s,** *n.n.* mitten. **polsslag,** no pl., *n.* pulse. **polsspringen,** no pl., *n.n.* pole-jumping. **polsstok, -kken,** *n.* jumping-pole.

pome·rans, *n.* bitter orange. **pome·ransbitter, -s,** *n.n.* orange bitters.

pom·made, *n.* pomatum; pomade. **pommaderen, -deer,** *v.t.* to pomade.

·Pommer, -s, *N.* Pomerania. **·Pommeren,** *n.N.* Pomerania. **·Pommers,** *a.* Pomeranian.

pomp, *n.* pump. *loop naar de ~!,* go and lose yourself! **·pompbak, -kken,** *n.* trough (*under pump*).

pompel·moes, -zen, *n.* grapefruit.

·pompen, *v.i.* & *v.t.* to pump. *~ of verzuipen,* do or die.

pomper·nikkel, -s, *n.* Pumpernickel.

pom·pier, -s, *n.* fireman (*in fire service*).

pom·poen, *n.* pumpkin, gourd.

·pompstation, -s, *n.n.* pumping station. **·pompzuiger, -s,** *n.* piston. **·pompzwengel, -s,** *n.* pump-handle.

pon, -nnen, *n.* nighty.

pond, -nnen, *n.n.* pound **·pondenbezit,** no pl., *n.n.* sterling holdings. **·ponder, -s,** *n.* pounder (*of . . . pounds*). **pondspondsge·wijze,** *adv.* pro rata.

·ponie, -s, *n.* *See* pony.

·ponjaard, -s, *n.* dagger.

pons, *n.* punch. **ponsen,** *v.t.* to punch.

pont, *n.* ferry (*boat*); (large) punt.

ponte·neur, no pl., *n.n.* *op zijn ~ staan,* to stand on his dignity.

·pontje, -s, *n.n.* punt. **pon·ton, -s,** *n.* pontoon, **ponton·nier, -s,** *n.* pontoneer. **·pontschipper, -s,** *n.* ferryman.

pony, -'s, *n.* pony; fringe (*of hair*).

·pooien, *v.i.* to tipple. **·pooier, -s,** *n.* tippler; scamp.

pook, poken, *n.* poker (*fire*).

Pool, Polen, *N.* Pole (*from Poland*). **Pools,** *a.* Polish.

pool, polen, *n.* pole. **·poolbeer, -beren,** *n.* polar bear. **·poolijs,** no pl., *n.n.* polar ice. **·poolkat, -tten,** *n.* Arctic fox. **·poolreiziger, -s,** *n.* Arctic explorer. **·poolschip, -schepen,**

n.n. polar exploration ship. **·poolshoogte,** no pl., *n.* elevation of the pole, latitude. *~ nemen,* to see how the land lies. **·Poolster,** *N.* Pole-star. **·poolvos, -ssen,** *n.* Arctic fox. **·poolzee, -zeeën,** *n.* polar sea.

poon, ponen, *n.* gurnard.

poort, *n.* gate; gateway. **·poortader, -s,** *n.* portal vein. **·poorter, -s,** *n.* citizen, burgher. **·poortje, -s,** *n.n.* back gate. **·poortwachter, -s,** *n.* gate-keeper.

poos, pozen, *n.* while, time. **·poosje, -s,** *n.n.* little while. *binnen een ~,* within a short while.

poot, poten, *n.* leg, foot, paw (*of animal*); leg (*of table, etc.*); (*slang*) hand. *~ aan spelen,* to put one's back into it; *op zijn ~ spelen,* to kick up rough; *op poten staan,* to be well put together; *op zijn achterste poten gaan staan,* to become shirty. **·pootaardappel, -s,** *n.* seed-potato. **·pootje, -s,** *n.n.* small leg *or* foot *or* paw (*of animal*); small leg (*of furniture*). *~s geven* (*coll.*), to shake hands; *met hangende ~s,* crestfallen, tail down. **·pootjesbaden,** no pl., *n.n.* paddling (*in shallow water*). **·pootstok, -kken,** *n.* dibber. **·pootvis,** no pl., *n.* seed-fish.

pop, -ppen, *n.* doll; puppet; pupa, nymph, chrysalis; (*coll.*) guilder. *de poppen waren aan het dansen,* the fur began to fly.

·popel, -s, *n.* poplar. **·popelen,** *v.i.* to flutter, quiver.

pope·line, no pl., *n.* poplin.

·poppengoed, no pl., *n.n.* doll's clothes. **·poppenhuis, -zen,** *n.n.* doll's house. **·poppenkast, -en,** *n.* puppet show, Punch and Judy show. **poppekaste·rij,** *n.* tomfoolery. **·poppekraam, -kramen,** *n.* booth with toys; rubbish. **·popperig,** *a.* doll-like, dollish. **·popperigheid,** no pl., *n.* dollishness. **·poppetje, -s,** *n.n.* little doll, mannikin. *~s tekenen,* to draw little figures. **·poppewagen, -s,** *n.* doll's pram.

popu·lair, *a.* popular.

popu·lier, -s, *n.* poplar.

por, -rren, *n.* prod, dig. **·porder, -s,** *n.* knocker-up.

po·reus, -ze, *a.* porous. **po·reusheid,** no pl., *n.* porousness.

por·fier, no pl., *n.* porphyry. **por·fieren,** *a.* (of) porphyry.

·porren, por, *v.t.* to prod, dig; to knock up (*wake*).

porse·lein, no pl., *n.n.* china, porcelain. ¶no pl., *n.* purslane. **porse·leinaarde,** no pl., *n.* china clay, kaolin. **porse·leinbloempje, -s,** *n.n.* London pride. **porseleinen,** *a.* (of) china.

port, no pl., *n.* port (*wine*). ¶*n.n.* postage. **por·taal, -talen,** *n.n.* landing (*of stairs*); porch. **porte·feuille, -s,** *n.* pocket-book, wallet; portfolio. *zijn ~ neerleggen,* to resign (*of cabinet minister*). **portemon·nee, -s,** *n.* purse.

·porti, pl., *n.n. See* porto.
·portie, -s, *n.* portion; helping.
por·tiek, *n.* portico.
por·tier, -s, *n.* hall-porter, door-keeper. ¶*n.n.* carriage-door.
·porto, -'s *or* -ti, *n.n.* postage.
por·tierswoning, *n.* porter's lodge.
por·tret, -tten, *n.n.* portrait; photograph. *zijn ~ laten maken,* to have one's portrait painted *or* photograph taken. portret·teren, -teer, *v.t.* to paint (person's) portrait, portray.
Portu·gees, -gese, *a.* Portuguese.
·portvrij, *a.* post-free.
·portwijn, *n.* portwine.
·portzegel, -s, *n.n.* postage-due stamp.
po·seren, -seer, *v.i.* to pose; to strike attitudes.
po·sitie, -s, *n.* position. *in de ~ staan,* to stand to attention; *in ~ zijn,* to be in the family way. posi·tief, -ve, *a.* positive. *positieve ideeën,* decided views. ¶*adv.* decidedly. *ik weet het ~,* I am absolutely sure. ¶-ven, *n.n.* positive. *niet bij zijn positieven zijn,* to be out of one's senses; *zijn positieven kwijtraken,* to lose one's wits.
post, *n.* (door-)post; post (*station*); sentry; post (*mail*). *~ vatten,* to take up one's position; *bij de ~,* in the post-office; *met* or *over de ~,* by post; *op ~ staan,* to stand sentry; *op zijn ~,* at his post; *een brief op de ~ doen,* to post a letter; *per ~,* by post. ·postadministratie, no pl., *n.* postal authorities. ·postambtenaar, -naren, *n.* postal official. ·postauto, -'s, *n.* mail van. ·postbeambte, -n, *n.* postal worker, post-office employee. ·postbode, -n, *or* -s, *n.* postman. ·postbus, -ssen, *n.* post-office box, private box. ·postcheque- en girodienst, *n.* postal cheque and transfer system. ·postdienst, no pl., *n.* postal service. ·postdirecteur, -s, *n.* postmaster. ·postduif, -ven, *n.* carrier-pigeon.
poste·lein, no pl., *n.n.* purslane.
·posten, *v.t.* to post (*letter*); to picket. poste·rijen, pl. only, *n.* postal service. ·postkantoor, -toren, *n.n.* post-office. ·postloper, -s, *n.* letter-carrier (*of office*). ·postmerk, *n.n.* postmark. *datum ~,* date as postmark. ·postpak(k)et, -tten, *n.n.* postal parcel. *als ~ verzenden,* to send by parcel post. ·postpapier, no pl., *n.n.* note- or letter-paper. ·postrekening, *n.* postal cheque account. ·postspaarbank, *n.* post-office savings bank.
postu·leren, -leer, *v.t.* to postulate.
pos·tuur, -turen, *n.* posture, attitude.
·postverbond, *n.n.* postal union. ·postverdrag, *n.n.* postal convention. ·postverkeer, no pl., *n.n.* mail traffic. ·postvliegtuig, *n.n.* mail plane. ·postwagen, -s, *n.* mail van. ·postwezen, no pl., *n.n.* postal service. ·postwissel, -s, *n.* money order,

postal order. ·postzak, -kken, *n.* mail bag.
·postzegel, -s, *n.* (postage) stamp.
pot, -tten, *n.* pot; jar; stake, pool. *eten wat de ~ schaft,* to take pot-luck; *de ~ verteren,* to spend the pool; *de ~ verwijt de ketel dat hij zwart is,* the pot calls the kettle black.
·potas, no pl., *n.* potash. ·potdicht, *a.* watertight; airtight. ·potdoof, -dove, *a.* stone-deaf.
·poteling, *n.* seedling; seed-fish. ·poten, poot, *v.t.* to plant. ·poter, -s, *n.* planter; seed-potato.
·pothuis, -zen, *n.n.* small half-basement house.
·potig, *a.* robust.
·potje, -s, *n.n.* small pot; glass (*of beer*); game (*billiards, cards*). *kleine ~s hebben ook oren,* little pitchers have long ears.
·potjeslatijn, no pl., *n.n.* dog-Latin. ·potkachel, -s, *n.* tubular stove. ·potlepel, -s, *n.* ladle. ·potloden, -lood, *v.t.* to blacklead.
·potlood, -loden, *n.n.* pencil; blacklead, plumbago. pot·nat, no pl., *n.n. het is één ~,* there is no difference between them. potpour·ri, -'s, *n.n.* medley.
·potscherf, -ven, *n.* potsherd.
pots, *n.* prank. ·potsenmaker, -s, *n.* wag.
pot·sierlijk, *a.* ludicrous.
·potten, pot, *v.t.* to pot; to hoard. save. ·pottenbakker, -s, *n.* potter. pottenbakke·rij, *n.* pottery (*factory*).
potver·dorie, *int.* gorblimey!
·potverteren, no pl., *n.n.* spending the pool. ·potvis, -ssen, *n.* cachalot.
·pover, *a.* meagre, poor. ·povertjes, *adv.* poorly.
·pozen, poos, *v.i.* to linger; to pause.
Praag, *n.N.* Prague.
·praaien, *v.t.* to hail (*ship*).
praal, no pl., *n.* pomp; lustre. ·praalbed, -dden, *n.n.* bed of state. ·praalgraf, -ven, *n.n.* mausoleum. ·praalhans, -zen, *n.* braggart. ·praalkoets, *n.* state-coach. ·praalvertoon, no pl., *n.n.* pomp, ostentation. ·praalwagen, -s, *n.* allegorical car (*in procession*). ·praalziek, *a.* ostentatious. ·praalzucht, no pl., *n.* ostentation.
praam, pramen, *n.* pram, praam.
praat, no pl., *n.* talk. *aan de ~ houden,* to keep talking; *veel ~s hebben,* to have a lot to say for oneself. ·praatachtig, *a.,* ·praatgraag, -grage, *a.* talkative, loquacious. ·praatje, -s, *n.n.* chat; rumour; scandal. *een ~ maken,* to have a chat; *het ~ gaat dat* or *er lopen ~s dat . . .,* there is a rumour that . . .; *mooie ~s,* soft words; *~s vullen geen gaatjes,* fair words butter no parsnips; *een ~ voor de vaak,* idie talk. ·praatjesmaker, -s, *n.* chatterer; conceited ass. praat·lustig, *a.* talkative. ·praatsmaker, -s, *n.* swankpot. ·praatstoel, no pl., *n. op zijn ~ zitten,* to be set for a long talk. ·praatvaar, -s, *n.* great talker.

·praatziek, *a.* loquacious, garrulous. ·praat-zucht, no pl., *n.* loquacity, garrulity.
pracht, no pl., *n.* splendour. *wat een ~ van een* . . .!; what a splendid . . .! *¶prefix.* splendid. ·prachtband, *n.* special binding (*book*). ·prachtexemplaar, -plar₃n, *n.n.* fine specimen; special edition, edition de luxe. ·prachtig, *a.* splendid. pracht-·lievend, *a.* fond of ostentation. pracht-·lievendheid, no pl., *n.* love of display.
·practisch, *a.* practical; practicable. *¶adv.* practically.
prae-, *prefix. See* pre-.
prakke·zeren, -zeer, *v.i.* to ponder. *¶v.t.* to think out.
prak·tijk, *n.* practice; practice (*of doctor, barrister*). *in de ~,* in practice; *kwade ~en,* evil practices. prakti·zeren, -zeer, *v.i.* to practise (*of doctor, barrister*). *~d geneesheer,* medical practitioner, practising doctor.
·pralen, praal, *v.i.* to be resplendent, shine. *~ met,* to flaunt, show off. ·praler, -s, *n.* person showing off. prale·rij, *n.* ostentation.
prat, *adv. ~ gaan* or *zijn op,* to be proud of, glory in.
·praten, praat, *v.i.* to talk. *~ met,* to talk to *or* with; *~ over,* to talk about *or* of; *ergens omheen ~,* to hedge; *~ als Brugman,* to talk the hind leg off a donkey; *iemand iets uit het hoofd ~,* to talk someone out of something; *er valt met hem te ~,* one can reason with him; *ik weet ervan te ~,* I have had experience of it. ·prater, -s, *n.* talker.
prauw, *n.* proa.
pre-, *prefix.* pre-.
pre·ad·vies, -zen, *n.n.* preliminary advice.
prea·label, *a.* previous.
pream·bule, -s, *n.* preamble.
pre·cair, *a.* precarious.
pre·cies, -ze, *a.* precise, exact. *¶adv.* precisely, exactly;. just so. *~ op tijd,* just in time; *om 10 uur ~,* at 10 o'clock sharp. preci-·seren, -seer, *v.t.* to specify.
predesti·natie, no pl., *n.* predestination.
·predikambt, *n.n.* ministry (*of clergyman*).
predi·kant, *n.* minister, clergyman, parson, vicar, curate (*not Roman Catholic*). predi·kantswoning, *n.* parsonage, vicarage. predi·katie, -s, *n.* sermon, homily. ·predik-beurt, *n.* turn to preach. ·prediken, *v.t.* & *v.i.* to preach. ·prediker, -s, *n.* preacher. *de P~,* Ecclesiastes. ·predikheer, -heren, *n.* Dominican. ·prediking, *n.* preaching.
preek, preken, *n.* sermon. *een ~ houden,* to preach *or* deliver a sermon. ·preekbeurt, *n. See* predikbeurt. ·preekstoel, *n.* pulpit. ·preektoon, -tonen, *n.* pulpit voice. ·preektrant, *n.* style of preaching.
prefe·reren, -reer, *v.t.* to prefer. *~ boven,* to prefer to. prefe·rent, *a.* preferential.

~e aandelen, preferred shares. prefe-·rentie, -s, *n.* preference.
·preken, preek, *v.i.* & *v.t.* to preach. ·prekerig, *a.* preachy.
prelimi·nair, *a.* preliminary.
prelu·deren, -deer, *v.i.* & *v.t.* to prelude. pre·ludium, -diën, *n.n.* prelude.
·premie, -s *or* -iën, *n.* premium; bonus; option. ·premiegeld, *n.n.* option money. ·premielening, *n.* lottery loan.
premi·ère, -s, *n.* first-night.
·premiestelsel, -s, *n.n.* bounty system.
pre·misse, -s, *n.* premise.
prent, *n.* print, engraving; picture. ·prent-briefkaart, *n.* picture-postcard. ·prenten, *v.t.* to imprint, impress. ·prentenboek, *n.n.* picture-book. ·prentenkabinet, -tten, *n.n.* print collection. ·prentje, -s, *n.n.* picture, small illustration. *~s kijken,* to look at pictures.
prepa·raat, -raten, *n.n.* preparation (*scientific*). prepa·reren, -reer, *v.t.* to prepare.
pre·senning, *n.* tarpaulin.
pre·sent, *n.n.* present. *¶a.* present. presen-·teerblad, *n.n.* tray, salver. presen·teren, -teer, *v.t.* to present; to offer. *het geweer ~,* to present arms; *zich ~,* to present oneself, occur. pre·sentexemplaar, -plaren, *n.n.* presentation *or* complimentary *or* free copy. pre·sentie, no pl., *n.* presence. pre·sentiegeld, *n.n.* attendance fee. pre-·sentielijst, *n.* attendance register, roll.
presi·dent, *n.* president, chairman; foreman (*jury*). president-commis·saris, -ssen, *n.* chairman of board of directors. presi-·dentschap, no pl., *n.n.* presidency, chairmanship. presi·dentszetel, no pl., *n.* (presidential) chair. presi·deren, -deer, *v.i.* to preside over; to preside, be in the chair.
·preskop, no pl., *n.* brawn (*jellied meat*).
pres·sant, *a.* urgent. ·pressen, pres, *v.t.* to press (*into service*). pres·seren, -seer, *v.t.* to press. *¶v.i.* to be urgent. ·pressie, no pl., *n.* pressure. *~ uitoefenen op,* to bring pressure to bear on.
pres·tatie, -s, *n.* achievement, feat. pres·teren, -teer, *v.t.* to achieve, perform.
pret, no pl., *n.* fun, pleasure. *~ hebben,* to enjoy oneself; *~ hebben over,* to be amused at; *~ maken,* to make merry; *huilen van de ~,* to cry with laughing; *voor de ~,* for fun.
preten·dent, *n.* pretender; claimant. pre-·tentie, -s, *n.* pretention.
·pretje, -s, *n.n.* bit of fun. ·prettig, *a.* pleasant, nice; jolly. ·pretmaker, -s, *n.* merry-maker, reveller.
·preutelen, *v.i.* to grumble.
preuts, *a.* prudish, prim. ·preutsheid, no pl., *n.* prudishness, prudery.
·prevelen, *v.t.* & *v.i.* to mutter.
preven·tief, -ve, *a.* preventive. *preventieve hechtenis,* detention on remand.

pri·eel, -iëlen, *n.n.* arbour, summerhouse.
priem, *n.* awl, bodkin; knitting-needle.
·priemen, *v.t.* to pierce. ·priemkruid, no pl., *n.n.* awlwort.
·priester, -s, *n.* priest. ·priesterambt, *n.n.* priestly office. ·priesterdom, no pl., *n.n.* priesthood (*the priests*). prieste·res, -ssen, *n.* priestess. ·priestergewaad, -waden, *n.n.* sacerdotal garb. ·priesterlijk, *a.* priestly. ·priesterorde, -n, *n.* order of priesthood. ·priesterschap, no pl., *n.n.* priesthood (*dignity*). priesterwijding, *n.* ordination.
·prijken, *v.i.* to shine, be resplendant. ~ *met*, to show off.
prijs, -zen, *n.* price; prize; praise. ~ *maken*, to capture; ~ *verklaren*, to confiscate; ~ *stellen op* or *op* ~ *stellen*, to appreciate; *tegen de* ~ *van*, at the price of; *tegen elke* ~, at any price; *tot elke* ~, at any cost; *voor geen* ~, not at any price. ·prijscourant, *n.* price list. ·prijsgeld, *n.n.* prize-money. ·prijsgerecht, *n.n.* prize-court. ·prijsgeven, geef prijs, *v.t.s.*, *str.* to give up; to abandon. ·prijshoudend, *a.* steady, firm (*in price*). ·prijskamp, *n.* (*stilted*) competition. ·prijsmaking, *n.* capture; seizure. ·prijsnotering, *n.* quotation (*of prices*). ·prijsnummer, -s, *n.n.* winning number. ·prijsopgave, -n, *n.* quotation (*of prices*). ·prijsrecht, no pl., *n.n.* prize law. ·prijsrechter, -s, *n.* prize judge; judge (*at match*). ·prijsschieten, no pl., *n.n.* shooting match. ·prijsvraag, -vragen, *n.* competition (*answers to question*). ·prijzen, prijs, *v.t.* to price, mark. ¶*v.t.*, *str.* to praise. *zich gelukkig* ~, to deem oneself happy. ·prijzenhof, -ven, *n.n.* prize-court. ·prijzens·waardig, *a.* praise-worthy. ·prijzig, *a.* high-priced.
prik, -kken, *n.* prick, sting; lamprey. ·prikje, -s, *n.n. voor een* ~, for a song. ·prikkel, -s, *n.* prickle, sting; goad; stimulus, incentive. ·prikkelbaar, -bare, *a.* irritable. ·prikkelbaarheid, no pl., *n.* irritability. ·prikkeldraad, no pl., *n.n.* barbed wire. ·prikkeldraadversperring, *n.* barbed-wire entanglement. ·prikkelen, *v.t.* to stimulate; to prickle; to irritate. ·prikkeling, *n.* prickling, tickling, irritation, stimulus. ·prikken, prik, *v.t.* to prick, sting. ·prikslee, -sleeën, *n.* sledge (*moved by spiked sticks*), priktol, -llen, *n.* peg-top.
pril, -lle, *a.* early, tender.
·prima, *a.* first-rate. pri·mair, *a.* primary. primi·tief, -ve, *a.* primitive. ·primo, *adv.* in the first place. ~ *Januari*, on the 1st of January. ·primula, -'s, *n.* primrose.
prin·cipe, -s, *n.n.* principle. *uit* ~, on principle. principi·eel, -iele, *a.* essential, fundamental. *om principiele redenen*, for reasons of principle, on principle; ~ *dienstweigeraar*, conscientious objector. ¶*adv.* on principle.

prins, *n.* prince. *de* ~ *gesproken hebben*, not to be quite sober; *van de* ~ *geen kwaad weten*, to be perfectly innocent. ·prinsdom, -mmen, *n.n.* principality. ·prinselijk, *a.* princely. prin·ses, -ssen, *n.* princess. prin·sessenboon, -bonen, *n.* French bean. prinsge·maal, -malen, *n.* prince consort. ·prinsgezind, *a.* Orangist.
priori·teit, *n.* priority.
·prisma, -'s, *n.n.* prism.
pri·vaat, -vate, *a.* private. ¶-vaten, *n.n.* privy. pri·vaatbezit, no pl., *n.n.* private property. pri·vaatdocent, *n.* unpaid university lecturer. pri·vaatrecht, no pl., *n.n.* civil law. pri·vaatrechtelijk, *a.* of *or* according to civil law. pri·vé, *a.* private.
pro·baat, -bate, *a.* efficacious, sovereign.
pro·beersel, -s, *n.n.* try, experiment. pro·beersteen, -stenen, *n.* touchstone. pro·beren, -beer, *v.t.* to try, have a try.
pro·bleem, -blemen, *n.n.* problem.
procé·dé, -'s, *n.n.* process. proce·deren, -deer, *v.i.* to litigate. *gaan* ~, to go to law.
proce·dure, -s, *n.* process; action, lawsuit.
pro·cent, *n.n.* per cent.
pro·ces, -ssen, *n.n.* action, lawsuit; process. *een* ~ *beginnen*, to go to law, institute legal proceedings; *een* ~ *voeren* or *in een* ~ *gewikkeld zijn*, to be involved in a lawsuit; *iemand een* ~ *aandoen*, to institute proceedings against someone. pro·cessie, -s, *n.* procession. pro·cessiegezang, *n.n.* processional. pro·cessievlinder, -s, *n.* procession moth. proces-ver·baal, pro·cessen-verbaal, *n.n.* official minutes; summons. ~ *opmaken tegen iemand*, to summons a person.
procla·matie, -s, *n.* proclamation. procla·meren, -meer, *v.t.* to proclaim.
procu·ratie, -s, *n.* power of attorney, proxy. procu·ratiehouder, -s, *n.* proxy; confidential clerk. procu·reur, -s, *n.* solicitor. procureur-gene·raal, procureurs-generaal, *n.* attorney-general.
produ·cent, *n.* producer (*of produce*). produ·ceren, -ceer, *v.t.* to produce. pro·duct, *n.n.* product; pl. produce. pro·ductie, no pl., *n.* production. ~ *op grote schaal*, mass production. produc·tief, -ve, *a.* productive, remunerative. *iets* ~ *maken*, to make something pay.
proef, -ven *n.* test, trial, experiment; proof, copy, specimen; proof. *de* ~ *op de som*, the final proof; *een* ~ *afleggen*, to pass a test; *een* ~ *doorstaan*, to pass a severe test; *proeven doen*, to make experiments; *proeven nemen met* ... to give a trial to ...; *op de* ~ *stellen*, to put to the test. ·proefbalans, *n.* trial balance. ·proefballon, -s, *n.* pilot balloon. *een* ~ *oplaten*, to put out a feeler. ·proefblad, *n.n.* specimen page, proof-sheet. ·proefhoudend, *a.* proof, standard. ·proefjaar, -jaren, *n.n.*

year of probation. ·proefje, -s, *n.n.* taste, sample. ·proefkonijn, *n.n.* rabbit (*for experimental purposes*); (*fig.*) guinea-pig. ·proefles, -ssen, *n.* trial lesson. ·proeflokaal, -kalen, *n.n.* bodega, bar. ·proefmonster, -s, *n.n.* testing sample. ·proefnaald, *n.* touch-needle. ·proefneming, *n.* experiment. ·proefnummer, -s, *n.n.* specimen copy. proefonder·vindelijk, *a.* experimental, empirical. ·proefrit, -tten, *n.* trial run (*with car*). ·proefschrift, *n.n.* thesis (*for degree*). ·proefsteen, -stenen, *n.* touchstone. ·proefstomen, no pl., *n.n.* steam trials. ·proeftijd, *n.* probationary period, apprenticeship. ·proeftocht, *n.* trial trip. ·proefvlieger, -s, *n.* test pilot. ·proefvlucht, *n.* test flight. ·proefwerk, *n.n.* test paper.

·proesten, *v.i.* to snort. ~ *van het lachen*, to burst out laughing (*smothered*).

·proeve, -n. *See* proef. ·proeven, proef, *v.t.* to taste; to sample. *laten* ~, to give a taste of. ¶*v.i.* to taste. ~ *naar*, to taste of. ·proever, -s, *n.* taster.

pro·feet, -feten, *n.* prophet. *een* ~ *die brood eet*, a worthless prophet.

professo·raal, rale, *a.* professorial. professo·raat, -raten, *n.n.* professorship. profe·teren, -teer, *v.t.* to prophesy. profe·tes, -ssen, *n.* prophetess. profe·tie, -s, *n.* prophecy.

pro·fiel, *n.n.* profile.

pro·fijt, *n.n.* profit, benefit. pro·fijtelijk, *a.* profitable. profi·teren, -teer, *v.i.* to profit. ~ *van*, to profit *or* benefit by, avail oneself of.

prog·nose, -s, *n.* prognosis.

pro·gramma, -'s, *n.n.* programme; syllabus; platform (*political*).

progres·sief, -ve, *a.* progressive.

projec·teren, -teer, *v.t.* to project. pro·jectie, -s, *n.* projection.

pro·leet, -leten, *n.* vulgarian. prole·tariër, -s, *n.* proletarian. prole·tarisch, *a.* proletarian.

prolon·gatie, -s, *n.* prolongation. *op* ~, on security. prolon·geren, -geer, *v.t.* to renew (*bill*).

pro·loog, -logen, *n.* prologue.

pro·messe, -s, *n.* promissory note.

pro·motie, -s, *n.* promotion; graduation. ~ *maken*, to be promoted, gain promotion. pro·motor, -s, *n.* promoter; professor (*supervising thesis*). promo·veren, -veer, *v.i.* to graduate. ¶*v.t.* to confer a degree on.

prompt, *a.* prompt, ready. ¶*adv.* promptly; punctually. ·promptheid, no pl., *n.* promptitude; punctuality.

pronk, no pl., *n.* show, ostentation; finery. *te* ~ *staan*, to be on show. ·pronkappel, -s, *n.* pumpkin. ·pronkbed, -dden, *n.n.* bed of state. ·pronkboon, -bonen, *n.* scarlet runner. ·pronken, *v.i.* to show off; to strut (*peacock*). ~ *met*, to show off,

flaunt. ·pronker, -s, *n.* dandy. ·pronkerig, *a.* showy, gaudy. pronke·rij, *n.n.* show, ostentation. ·pronkerwt, *n.* sweet pea. ·pronkjuweel, -welen, *n.* gem. ·pronkstuk, -kken, *n.n.* show-piece. ·pronkziek, *a.* fond of show. ·pronkzucht, no pl., *n.* ostentatiousness.

prooi, *n.* prey. *ten* ~ *vallen aan*, to fall a prey to.

proost, *n.* dean; provost. ¶*int.* cheerio (*a toast*).

prop, -ppen, *n.* ball, wad; plug (*of wadding*); swab; bung; gag; dottle. *een* ~ *in de keel*, a lump in one's throat; *op de proppen komen*, to turn up; *ergens mee op de proppen komen*, to come out with something.

propae·deutisch, *a.* propaedeutic; preliminary.

propa·geren, -geer, *v.t.* to propagate.

·proper, *a.* clean, neat. ·properheid, no pl., *n.* cleanliness, neatness. ·propertjes, *adv.* neatly, tidily.

propo·neren, -neer, *v.t.* to propose. propo·nent, *n.* postulant.

·proppen, prop, *v.t.* to cram; to fill. ·proppenschieter, -s, *n.* pop-gun. ·propvol, -lle, *a.* bung-full.

·prosit, *int.* cheerio (*a toast*).

prostitu·ee, -s, *n.* prostitute. prostitu·eren, -tueer, *v.t.* to prostitute.

pro·tectie, no pl., *n.* protection. prote·geren, -geer, *v.t.* to protect, patronize.

pro·test, *n.n.* protest; protestation. ~ *aantekenen tegen*, to protest against; *zonder* ~, without demur. protes·teren, -teer, *v.i.* to protest.

proto·plasma, no pl., *n.n.* protoplasm.

provi·and, no pl., *n.n.* victuals, stores. provian·deren, -deer, *v.t.* to victual, provision. provian·dering, *n.* victualling. provi·andmeester, -s, *n.* storekeeper.

pro·vincie, -s *or* -ciën, *n.* province.

pro·visie, -s, *n.* provision; commission (*of broker*). pro·visiekamer, -s, *n.* larder, pantry, store. pro·visiekast, *n.* storecupboard.

pro·voost, *n.* provost. ¶*n.n.* detention room.

·proza, no pl., *n.n.* prose. pro·zaïsch, *a.* prosaic.

pruik, *n.* wig. ·pruikebol, -llen, *n.* tousle-head. ·pruikentijd, no pl., *n.* days gone by. ·pruikerig, *a.* antiquated, outmoded.

·pruilen, *v.i.* to pout, sulk. ·pruiler, -s, *n.* one who pouts *or* sulks. ·pruilerig, *a.* sulky. ·pruilhoek, no pl., *n. in zijn* ~ *zitten*, to sulk in a corner.

pruim, *n.* plum; quid (*chewing tobacco*). *droge* ~, prune. ·pruimeboom, -bomen, *n.* plum-tree. ·pruimemondje, -s, *n.n. een* ~ *trekken*, to purse one's lips. ·pruimen, *v.t.* & *v.i.* to chew (*tobacco*). ·pruimepit, -tten, *n.* plum-stone. ·pruimtabak, no pl., *n.* chewing tobacco.

Pruis, *N.* Prussian. ·Pruisen, *n.N.* Prussia.

·Pruisisch, *a.* Prussian. ~ *zuur,* prussic acid.

prul, -llen, *n.n.* worthless thing; bauble, gimcrack. ·prulding, *n.n.* worthless thing. ·prullenboel, no *pl., n.* rubbish, trash. ·prullenmand, *n.* waste-paper-basket. ·prull(er)ig, *a.* rubbishy, trashy. ·prulschrijver, -s, *n.* trash writer.

pruts. *See* prul. ·prutsen, *v.i.* to potter, tinker.

·pruttelaar, -s, *n.* grumbler. ·pruttelen, *v.i.* to grumble; to simmer.

psychi·ater, -s, *n.* psychiatrist. psychi·atrisch, *a.* psychiatric. psycho·loog, -logen, *n.* psychologist. psy·chose, -s, *n.* psychosis.

puber·teit, no *pl., n.* puberty.

publi·catie, -s, *n.* publication. publi·ceren, -ceer, *v.t.* to publish; to give publicity to. publi·cist, *n.* publicist; journalist. publici·teit, no *pl., n.* publicity.

pu·bliek, *a.* public. ~ *geheim,* open secret; ~ *huis,* disorderly house; ~*e veiling,* auction sale. ¶*adv.* publicly, in public. ~ *verkopen,* to sell by auction. ¶no *pl., n.n.* public; audience. *het grote* ~, the general public; *in het* ~, in public. pu·bliekrecht, no *pl., n.n.* public law. publiek·rechtelijk, *a.* in or according to public law.

·puddelen, *v.t.* to puddle.

puf, no *pl., n.* (*coll.*) *ik heb er geen* ~ *in,* I do not feel like it. ·puffen, puf, *v.i.* to puff. ·pufferig, *a.* close, sultry.

pui, *n.* bottom of facade; steps of town hall.

puik, *a.* excellent, choice. ·puikje, no *pl., n.n.* pick, choice part *or* morsel.

·puilader, -s, *n.* varicose vein. ·puilen, *v.i.* to bulge, protrude. ·puiloog, -logen, *n.n.* goggle-eye. ·puil·ogig, *a.* goggle-eyed.

·puimen, *v.t.* to pumice. ·puimsteen, -stenen, *n.* pumice-stone.

puin, no *pl., n.* rubble. *in* ~ *vallen,* to fall to ruins. ·puinhoop, -hopen, *n.* heap of rubble; ruin.

·puist, *n.* pimple, pustule. *zich een* ~ *lachen* (*coll.*), to be vastly amused. ·puistachtig, *a.* pimply.

puit, *n.* eel-pout; frog.

·pukkel, -s, *n.* pimple.

pul, -llen, *n.* (large) jug.

·pulken, *v.i.* to pick.

pulp, no *pl., n.* pulp; beet-sugar pulp (*fodder*).

·pulver, no *pl., n.n.* (*stilted*) gunpowder.

·pummel, -s, *n.* yokel, boor, lout. ·pummelig, *a.* boorish, loutish.

pu·naise, -s, *n.* drawing-pin.

punt, *n.n.* point; mark (*for work*); unit (*in quotation*); tip; toe (*of shoe*); dot, full stop. *dubbele* ~, colon.

·puntboord, *n.n.* butterfly-collar.

·puntdicht, *n.n.* epigram. ·punten, *v.t.* to

sharpen (*point*). ·punter, -s, *n.* punt. ·punthouweel, -welen, *n.n.* pick (*tool*). ·puntig, *a.* pointed, sharp. ·puntje, -s, *n.n.* small point. *ergens een* ~ *aan zuigen,* to tell a tale to suit the occasion; *als* ~ *bij paaltje komt,* when it comes to the point; *in de* ~*s,* in apple-pie order; *in de* ~*s gekleed zijn,* to be dressed up to the nines; *in de* ~*s kennen,* to know pat; *de* ~*s op de i zetten,* to dot one's i's and cross one's t's. ·puntlijn, *n.* dotted line.

pu·pil, -llen, *n.* pupil (*of eye*); ward (*young person*).

·puren, puur, *v.t.* (*stilted*) to suck (*honey*).

pur·gatie, -s, *n.* purge. pur·geermiddel, *n.n.* purgative. pur·geren, -geer, *v.t.* to purge.

Puri·tein, *n.* Puritan.

·purper, no *pl., n.n.* purple. ·purperachtig, *a.* purplish. ·purperen, *a.* purple. ·purperkleurig, *a.* purple. ·purperrood, no *pl., n.* purple. ¶-rrode, *a.* purple. ·purperslak, -kken, *n.* murex.

put, -tten, *n.* pit, hole; well. *in de* ~ *zijn,* to be in the dumps. ·puthaas, -bazen, *n.* foreman (*of navvies*). ·puthaak, -haken, *n.* bucket-hook (*over well*). ·putjesschepper, -s, *n.* sewer-man.

·putoor, -toren, *n.* bittern.

puts, *n.* bucket.

·putten, put, *v.t.* to draw (*water*). ~ *uit,* to draw on. ·putter, -s, *n.* water-drawer; thistle-finch. ·putwater, no *pl., n.n.* well water.

puur, pure, *a.* pure.

py·jama, -'s, *n.* (pair of) pyjamas.

Q

See also k(w).

qua·draat, -draten, *n.n. See* kwadraat.

·quaestie, -s, *n. See* kwestie.

qualifi·ceeren, -ceer, *v.t.* to qualify.

quaran·taine, no *pl., n.* quarantine.

·quarto, -'s, *n.n.* quarto. ¶*adv.* fourthly.

queru·lant, *n.* professional grumbler.

·queue, -s, *n.* queue. *See also* keu.

qui·vive, no *pl., n.n. op zijn* ~ *zijn,* to be on the qui vive.

·quotum, -ta, *n.n.* quota.

R

ra, raas, *n.* yard (*of mast*). *See also* raden, *v.t.*

raad, no *pl., n.* advice, counsel. ~ *geven,* to advise; ~ *inwinnen,* to ask advice; ~ *weten,* to know a way out; *geen* ~ *weten,* to be at a loss *or* at one's wits' end; *er is wel* ~ *op,* we shall find a solution;

goede ~ was duur, it was difficult to know what to do; *met ~ en daad*, by word and deed. ¶**raden**, *n.* council, board; counsellor. *met iemand te rade gaan*, to consult a person. ·**raadgevend**, *a.* advisory, consultative. ·**raadgever**, -**s**, *n.* adviser. ·**raadgeving**, *n.* advice. ·**raadhuis**, -**zen**, *n.* town hall. **raadpensio·naris**, -**ssen**, *n.* State Pensionary. ·**raadplegen**, -**pleeg**, *v.t.* to consult. ·**raadpleging**, *n.* consultation. ·**raadsbesluit**, *n.n.* decision of town council; decree. ·**raadsel**, -**s**, *n.n.* riddle. ·**raadselachtig**, *a.* enigmatic. ·**raadsheer**, -**heren**, *n.* councillor; bishop (*chess*). ·**raadslid**, -**leden**, *n.n.* councillor, member of town council. ·**raadslieden**, pl. *n.* advisers. *See* **raadsman**. ·**raadsman**, -**slieden**, *n.* adviser. ·**raadsvergadering**, *n.* meeting of the (town) council. ·**raadsverslag**, *n.n.* report of the (town) council. ·**raadszitting**, *n.* session of the town council. ·**raadzaal**, -**zalen**, *n.* council chamber. ·**raadzaam**, -**zame**, *a.* advisable. ·**raadzaamheid**, no pl., *n.* advisability.

raaf, raven, *n.* raven. *witte ~*, white crow.
·**raagbol**, -**llen**, *n. See* **ragebol**.
·**raaigras**, no pl., *n.n.* darnel.
raak, rake, *a. het is ~*, it is a hit *or* it went home. ¶*adv. ~ schieten*, to hit the mark; *maar ~ praten*, to talk at random. ·**raaklijn**, *n.* tangent. ·**raakpunt**, *n.n.* point of contact.
raam, ramen, *n.n.* window; frame. ·**raamkoord**, *n.n.* sash-cord. ·**raamkozijn**, *n.n.* window-frame, window-sill.
raap, rapen, *n.* turnip, rape.
·**raapbord**, *n.n.* mortar-board.
·**raapkoek**, *n.* rape-cake. ·**raapolie**, no pl., *n.* rape-oil. ·**raapstelen**, pl. only, *n.* turnip-tops. ·**raapzaad**, no pl., *n.n.* rapeseed.
raar, rare, *a.* strange, curious, queer.
·**raaskallen**, -**kal**, *v.i.* to rave.
raat, raten, *n.* (honey)comb.
ra·barber, no pl., *n.* rhubarb.
ra·bat, no pl., *n.n.* rebate, discount.
·**rabbi**, -'**s**, *n.*, **rab·bijn**, *n.* rabbi.
rad, -**eren**, *n.n.* wheel. *iemand een ~ voor de ogen draaien*, to throw dust in a person's eyes. ¶*a.* -**dde**, *a.* glib. ·**radbraken**, -**braak**, *v.t.* to break on the wheel; to murder (*a language*). ·**raddraaier**, -**s**, *n.* ringleader.
·**rade**, no pl., *n. See* **raad**.
ra·deeren, *v.t.* to erase; to engrave. **ra·deernaald**, *n.* burin.
·**radeloos**, -**loze**, *a.* desperate, at one's wits' end. ·**radeloosheid**, no pl., *n.* desperation.
·**raden**, **raad**, *v.t.* to advise; to guess. *~ naar*, to guess at; *ra, ra, wat is dat?* guess what it is. ·**Radenrepubliek**, *n.* Soviet Republic.
·**raderboot**, -**boten**, *n.* paddle-steamer. ·**raderkast**, *n.* paddle-box. ·**raderwerk**, no pl., *n.n.* wheels (*of mechanism*).

·**radheid**, no pl., *n.* glibness, volubility.
radi·caal, -**cale**, *a.* radical.
ra·dijs, -**zen**, *n.* radish.
radio·loog, -**logen**, *n.* radiologist. ·**radio·omroep**, *n.* broadcast. ·**radium**, no pl., *n.n.* radium.
·**radja**, -'**s**, *n.* rajah.
·**rafel**, -**s**, *n.* ravel. ·**rafelen**, *v.t. & v.i.* to fray, to ravel out.
raffinade·rij, *n.* refinery. **raffina·deur**, -**s**, *n.* refiner. **raffi·neren**, -**neer**, *v.t.* to refine.
rag, no pl., *n.n.* cobweb. ·**ragebol**, -**llen**, *n.* ceiling mop; mop of hair. ·**ragfijn**, *a.* gossamer.
rail, -**s**, *n.* rail.
rak, -**kken**, *n.n.* rack; reach (*of waterway*).
·**rakel**, -**s**, *n.* rake. ·**rakelen**, *v.t.* to rake.
·**rakelings**, *adv. ~ voorbijgaan*, to graze, brush.
·**raken, raak**, *v.t.* to touch; to hit (*target*); to concern, touch. ¶*v.i.* to get, begin to.
ra·ket, -**tten**, *n.* rocket; hedge-mustard.
·**rakker**, -**s**, *n.* (young) rascal, mischievous boy.
ram, -**mmen**. *n.* ram.
·**ramen**, **raam**, *v.t.* to estimate.
rame·nas, -**ssen**, *n.* horse-radish.
·**raming**, *n.* estimate.
ram·meien, *v.t.* to batter.
·**rammelaar**, -**s**, *n.* rattle; buck rabbit. ·**rammelen**, *v.t. & v.i.* to rattle; to jingle, clank. ·**rammeling**, *n.* thrashing. ·**rammelkast**, *n.* rattle-trap.
·**rammen, ram**, *v.t.* to ram.
ramp, *n.* disaster, catastrophe.
rampo·neren, -**neer**, *v.t.* to damage.
·**rampspoed**, *n.* (*stilted*) adversity. ·**ramp·spoedig**, *a.* (*stilted*) disastrous. ·**ramp·zalig**, *a.* wretched, miserable. **ramp·zaligheid**, -**heden**, *n.* misery.
ran·cune, -**s**, *n.* rancour.
rand, *n.* edge, border; brim, brink, rim. *aan de ~ van*, on the verge of. ·**rand·gebergte**, -**n**, *n.n.* mountainous ridge (*of tableland*). ·**randschrift**, *n.n.* legend (*on coin*). ·**randversiering**, *n.* ornamental border. ·**randstaat**, -**staten**, *n.* border state.
rang, *n.* rank; position. *eerste ~*, first row. **ran·geerder**, -**s**, *n.* shunter. **ran·geerlocomotief**, -**ven**, *n.* shunting-engine. **ran·geerschijf**, -**ven**, *n.* turntable. **ran·geerspoor**, -**sporen**, *n.n.* siding. **ran·geerterrein**, *n.n.* shunting-yard. **ran·geren**, **geer**, *v.t.* to shunt. ·**ranglijst**, *n.* army list. ·**rangnummer**, -**s**, *n.n.* number (*on list*). ·**rangorde**, no pl., *n.* order. ·**rangschikken**, -**schik**, *v.t.* to arrange; to classify. ·**rangschikking**, *n.* arrangement; classification.
rank, *n.* tendril, clasper. ¶*a.* slender; crank, easily overturned (*vessel*). ·**rankheid**, no pl., *n.* slenderness; crankiness.
ra·nonkel, -**s**, *n.* ranunculus.
rans, *a.* rancid.

·ransel, -s, *n.n.* pack, knapsack; beating. *een pak* ~, a beating. ·ranselen, *v.t.* to beat, thrash.

·ransig, *a.* rancid.

ran·tsoen, *n.n.* ration; ransome. rantsoe·neren, -neer, *v.t.* to ration. rantsoe·nering, *n.* rationing.

rap, -ppe, *a.* nimble, agile.

ra·palje, no pl., *n.n.* riff-raff.

·rapen, raap, *v.t.* to pick up, gather.

·rapheid, no pl., *n.* agility.

rap·pel, no pl., *n.n.* recall. rappe·leren, -leer, *v.t.* to recall.

rap·port, *n.n.* report, statement. ~ *uitbrengen over*, to report on; *zich in* ~ *stellen met*, to communicate with. rappor·teren, -teer, *v.t.* to report.

·rarekiek, *n.* rare show. ·rarigheid, -heden, *n.* queer thing, oddity. rari·teit, *n.* curio.

ras, -ssen, *n.n.* race, breed. ¶-sse, *a.* (*stilted*) swift. ·rasecht, *a.* thoroughbred, pedigree. ·rashond, *n.* pedigree dog.

rasp, *n.* rasp; grater. ·raspen, *v.t.* to rasp; to grate.

·rassenhaat, no pl., *n.* racial hatred.

·raster, -s, *n.* lath. ·rasterdraad, no pl., *n.n.* barbed wire. ·rastering, *n.* railing. ·rasterwerk, no pl., *n.n.* trellis-work.

rat, -tten, *n.* rat.

·ratel, -s, *n.* rattle. ·ratelaar, -s, *n.* (child's) rattle. ·ratelboor, -boren, *n.* ratchet brace. ·ratelen, *v.i.* to rattle. ¶*v.t.* to rattle; to crash (*thunder*). ·ratelkous, *n.* prattler. ·ratelpopulier, *n.* aspen. ·ratelslag, *n.* peal of thunder. ·ratelslang, *n.* rattlesnake.

ratifi·ceren, -ceer, *v.t.* to ratify.

·ratjetoe, no pl., *n.* hotchpotch.

·rato, no pl., *n. naar* ~, pro rata.

rats, no pl., *n. in de* ~ *zitten*, to be in a blue funk.

·rattenkruid, no pl., *n.n.* arsenic. ·rattenvanger, -s, *n.* rat-catcher.

rauw, *a.* raw; harsh, raucous. ·rauwheid, no pl., *n.* rawness.

ra·vijn, *n.n.* ravine.

ra·votten, -vot, *v.i.* to romp.

·razeil, *n.n.* square sail.

·razen, raas, *v.i.* to rage, rave. ·razend, *a.* raving, furious; ravenous; terrific. *het is om* ~ *te worden*, it is enough to drive one crazy. ¶*adv.* terrifically, awfully. razer·nij, no pl., *n.* frenzy.

re, -'s, *n.* re.

re·aal, realen, *n.* real (*coin*).

re·actie, -s, *n.* reaction.

rea·geerbuis, -zen, *n.* test-tube. rea·geermiddel, *n.n.* reagent. rea·geerpapier, no pl., *n.n.* litmus-paper. rea·geren, -geer, *v.i.* to react.

re·alia, pl. only, *n.n.* realities. reali·seren, seer, *v.t.* to realize.

re·bel, -llen, *n.* rebel, mutineer. rebel·leren,

-leer, *v.i.* to rebel, mutiny. re·bels, *a.* mutinous.

recen·seren, -seer, *v.t.*, to review (*book, etc.*). recen·sent, *n.* reviewer. re·censie, -s, *n.* review (*of book, etc.*).

re·cept, *n.n.* recipe, receipt; prescription. re·ceptie, -s, *n.* reception.

re·ces, no pl., *n.n.* recess. *op* ~ *gaan*, to go into recess, adjourn; *op* ~ *zijn*, to be in recess.

re·cherche, -s, *n.* criminal investigation department. re·cherchevaartuig, *n.n.* revenue-cutter. recher·cheur, -s, *n.* detective.

recht, *a.* straight; just, right. ~ *maken*, to straighten; *te* ~*er tijd*, at the right time. ¶*adv.* quite; straight. ~ *toe* ~ *aan*, straight on. ¶*no pl., n.n.* law, justice. ~ *geven op*, to entitle to; ~ *hebben op*, to be entitled to; *tot zijn* ~ *komen*, to show to full advantage. ¶*n.n.* right, claim. *met* ~, rightly; *met welk* ~*?*, by what right? ¶*usu. pl., n.n.* law; duty, customs. *student in de* ~*en*, law student; *iemand in* ~*en aanspreken* or *vervolgen*, to sue a person. recht·aan, *adv.* straight on. ·rechtbank, *n.* court of law; tribunal; kitchen-dresser (*fixed*). ·rechtdraads, *adv.* with the grain. ·rechtelijk, *a.* judicial, legal. ·rechteloos, -loze, *a.* without rights. ·rechten, *v.t.* to straighten; to administer justice. ·rechtens, *adv.* by right(s), in justice. ·rechter, -s, *n.* judge, justice. ¶*a.* right(-hand). ·rechterambt, no pl., *n.n.* judgeship. ·rechterarm, *n.* right arm. rechter-commis·saris, -ssen, *n.* judge-commissioner. ·rechterhand, *n.* right hand. ·rechterkant, no pl., *n.* right-hand side. ·rechterlijk, *a.* judicial. *de* ~*e macht*, the judicature. ·rechtervleugel, -s, *n.* right wing. ·rechterzijde, no pl., *n.* (*stilted*) right-hand side. ·rechtgeaard, *a.* right-minded, upright. ·rechtge·lovig, *a.* orthodox. ·rechtge·lovigheid, no pl., *n.* orthodoxy. ·rechthebbende, -n, *n.* rightful claimant. ·rechtheid, no pl., *n.* straightness. ·rechthoek, *n.* rectangle. recht·hoekig, *a.* rectangular. ·rechtigen, *v.t.* to authorize, entitle. recht·lijnig, *a.* rectilinear. ·rechtmaken, maak recht, *v.t.s.* to straighten. recht·matig, *a.* rightful, lawful. recht·matigheid, -heden, *n.* rightfulness, legality. recht·op, *adv.* upright, erect. recht·opstaand, *a.* vertical, upright. recht·over, *adv.* (straight) opposite. rechts, *a.* right-handed; belonging to the Right (*in politics*). ¶*adv.* to or on the right. ~ *en averechts*, plain and purl; *naar* ~, (to the) right. ·rechtsaf, *adv.* to the right. ·rechtsbeginsel, *n.n.* principle of justice. ·rechtsbegrip, -ppen, *n.n.* concept of justice; sense of justice. ·rechtsbevoegd, *a.* competent. ·rechtsbevoegdheid, no pl., *n.* competence;

jurisdiction. **recht·schapen,** *a.* upright, honest. **recht·schapenheid,** no pl., *n.* uprightness. **rechtscollege, -s,** *n.n.* court, bench. **rechtsgebied,** *n.n.* jurisdiction. **·rechtsgeding,** *n.n.* lawsuit. **rechts·geldig,** *a.* legal, valid in law. **·rechtsgeleerd,** *a.* juridical. **rechtsgeleerde, -n,** *n.* lawyer, jurist. **rechtsgeleerdheid,** no pl., *n,* jurisprudence. **·rechtsgevoel,** no pl., *n.n.* sense of justice. **·rechtsingang,** no pl., *n.n.* ~ *verlenen aan,* to find a true bill for. **·rechtskosten,** pl. only, *n.* legal expenses. **rechts·kundig,** *a.* legal, juridical. **·rechtsom,** *adv.* to the right. **·rechtsom-keert,** *int.* about turn!. ~ *maken,* to turn tail. **·rechtspersoon, -sonen,** *n.* body corporate. *als* ~ *erkennen,* to incorporate. **·rechtspleging,** *n.* judicature, administration of justice. **·rechtspraak,** no pl., *n.* administration of justice, jurisdiction. **·rechtspreken, spreek recht,** *v.i.s., str.* to administer justice. ~ *cver,* to sit in judgment upon. **·rechtspraktijk,** *n.* legal practice. **recht·standig,** *a.* vertical, perpendicular. **·rechtsterm,** *n.* legal term. **·rechtstreeks,** *a.* direct. **·rechtsvervolging,** *n.* prosecution. **·rechtsvordering,** *n.* legal claim. **·rechtswege,** no pl., *n. van* ~, according to the law, by right(s). **·rechts-wezen,** no pl, *n.n.* judicature. **·rechtszaak, -zaken,** *n.* lawsuit. **·rechtszaal, -zalen,** *n.* court-room. **·rechtszitting,** *n.* session (*of the court*). **recht·toe,** *adv.* straight on. **recht·uit,** *adv.* straight on; frankly. **recht·vaardig,** *a.* just; righteous. **recht-vaardigen,** *v.t.* to justify. ¶*zich* ~, *v.r.* to vindicate oneself. **recht·vaardigheid,** no pl., *n.* justice; righteousness. **recht-vaardiging,** *n.* justification; vindication. **recht·zinnig,** *a.* orthodox. **recht·zinnig-heid,** no pl., *n.* orthodoxy.

re·clame, -s, *n.* advertising; advertisement; complaint. ~ *maken voor,* to advertise. **re·clamebureau, -'s,** *n.n.* advertising agency. **re·clameplaat, -platen,** *n.* picture poster. **recla·meren, -meer,** *v.i.* to complain.

reclas·seren, -seer, *v.t.* to reclaim (*in social work*). **reclas·sering,** *n.* reclamation (*in social work*).

recru·teren, -teer, *v.t.* to recruit. **re·cruut, -cruten,** *n.* recruit.

·rector, -s *or* **-toren,** *n.* headmaster, principal; director (*of religicus institution*). ~ *magnificus,* Chancellor, Provost, Principal (*of university*). **recto·raat, -raten,** *n.n.* headmastership; Chancellorship.

re·çu, -'s, *n.n.* receipt; ticket, check.

ɪedac·teur, -s, *n.* editor. **re·dactie, -s,** *n.* editoriɛl board; wording. **redactio·neel, -nele,** *a.* editorial. **redac·trice, -s,** *n.* woman editor.

·reddeloos, -loze, *a.* irretrievable. **redden, red,** *v.t.* to save, rescue. ¶*zich* ~, *v.r.* to

D.E.D.

save oneself; to manage, get along. **·redder, -s,** *n.* rescuer. **·redderen,** *v.t.* to put in order. **redding,** *n.* rescue; salvation. **·reddingsboei,** *n.* life-buoy. **·reddingsboot, -boten,** *n.* life-boat. **·reddingsgordel, -s,** *n.* life-belt. **·reddingstoestel, -llen,** *n.n.* life-saving apparatus.

·rede, no pl., *n.* reason, sense. *in de* ~ *liggen,* to stand to reason. ¶*-voeringen,* *n.* speech. *in de* ~ *vallen,* to interrupt. ¶*-n or* **-reeën.** roadstead, roads. **·rededeel, -delen,** *n.n.* part of speech. **·redekavelen,** *v.i.* (*stilted*) to argue, reason. **·redelijk,** *a.* rational; reasonable; moderate. ¶*adv.* in reason; moderately. **·redelijkerwijs,** *adv.* reasonably. **·redelijkheid,** no pl., *n.* reasonableness; rationality. **·redeloos, -loze,** *a.* unreasonable; brute (*of animals*). **·rede-loosheid,** no pl., *n.* irrationality; unreasonableness. **·reden,** *n.* reason, cause. *om* ~ *dat,* because. ¶*-s,* *n.* ratio. **redenaar, -s,** *n.* orator. **redenaarskunst,** *n.* oratorical art. **rede·neren, -neer,** *v.i.* to reason, argue. **rede·nering,** *n.* reasoning, argument. **·reder, -s,** *n.* shipowner. **rede·rij,** *n.* (firm of) shipowners. **rederijker, -s,** *n.* rhetorician. **·rederijkers-kamer, -s,** *n.* chamber of rhetoricians. **·rederijkerskunst,** no pl., *n.* rhetoric. **·redetwist,** *n.* disputation. **·redetwisten,** *v.i.* to argue, dispute. **redevoeren,** *v.i.* to make a speech. **redevoering,** *n.* speech. *een* ~ *houden,* to deliver a speech.

redi·geren, -geer, *v.t.* to edit; to word, frame.

redmiddel, *n.n.* remedy.

ree, reeën, *n.* roe, doe, hind. *See also* **rede.**

·reebok, -kken, *n.* roebuck. **·reebout,** *n.* haunch of venison.

reeds, *adv.* already. ~ *in . . .,* as early as . . .

re·ëel, reële, *a.* real (*of value*).

reef, reven, *n.n.* reef. *een* ~ *inbinden,* to take in a reef; *een* ~ *losmaken,* to let out a reef.

reekalf, -lveren, *n.n.* fawn.

reeks, *n.* series, sequence; progression.

reep, repen, *n.* strip; rope; bar (*chocolate*).

reet, reten, *n.* crevice, cleft.

refe·raat, -raten, *n.n.* report. **refe·reren, -reer,** *v.i.* to refer; to report.

re·frein, *n.n.* chorus, refrain.

re·geerder, -s, *n.* ruler.

·regel, -s *or* **-en,** *n.* rule, regulation; rule, line. *in de* ~, as a rule. **·regelaar, -s,** *n.* regulator. **·regelen,** *v.t.* to regulate, adjust; to arrange. ¶*v.r. zich* ~ *naar,* to conform to. **·regeling,** *n.* arrangement; regulation; adjustment. **·regelmaat,** no pl., *n.* regularity. **regel·matig,** *a.* regular, even. **regel·matigheid,** no pl., *n.* regularity. **regelrecht,** *a.* straight. ¶*adv.* ~ *ingaan tegen,* to be in flat contradiction of.

·regen, -s, *n.* rain. *blauwe* ~, wistaria; *gouden* ~, laburnum; *van de* ~ *in de drop,*

from the frying pan into the fire. ·regen-
achtig, a. rainy. ·regenbak, -kken, n.
cistern, water tank. ·regenboog, -bogen, n.
rainbow. ·regenboogvlies, -zen, n.n. iris
(of eye). ·regenbui, n. shower (of rain).
·regenen, v.imp. to rain. ·regenfluiter, -s, n.
curlew. ·regenjas, -ssen, n. mackintosh,
raincoat. ·regenloos, -loze, a. rainless.
·regenscherm, n.n. (stilted) umbrella.
re·gent, n. regent; governor; member of
ruling class (in Dutch Republic). re·gen-
tenregering, n. oligarchy (in Dutch
Republic). regen·tes, -ssen, n. regent,
governor (female). re·gentschap, -ppen,
n.n. regency.
·regenworm, n. earthworm. ·regenzon, no
pl., n. watery sun.
re·geren, -geer, v.i. to reign, rule; to rule,
govern. ¶v.t. to reign over, rule, govern.
re·gering, n. reign; government. aan de ∼
komen, to come to the throne or to come
into power. re·geringsbeleid, no pl., n.n.
policy, rule. re·geringspartij, n. party in
office. re·geringswege, no pl., n. van ∼,
for or on behalf of the government.
re·gie, no pl., n. stage-management; government monopoly.
re·gime, -s, n.n. regime; diet.
regis·seur, -s, n. stage manager.
re·gister, -s, n.n. register; index (of book);
stop (of organ). regis·tratie, -s, n. registration; registry. regis·tratiekantoor, -toren,
n.n. (fiscal) registrar's office.
regle·ment, n.n. regulation. reglemen·tair,
a. regulation.
re·gres, no pl., n.n. recourse.
rei, n. chorus (in classical play).
·reiger, -s, n. heron. ·reigerkolonie, -s or
-iën, n. heronry. ·reigersbek, -kken, n.
stork's-bill (plant).
·reiken, v.i. to reach, extend; to carry (voice).
¶v.t. to reach, hand. ·reikhalzen, hals, v.i.
∼ naar, to long for. ·reikhalzend, adv.
longingly.
·reilen, v.i. zoals het ·reilt en zeilt, lock, stock
and barrel.
Reims, n.N. Rheims.
rein, a. pure, clean. 't is je ∼ste onzin, it's
absolute nonsense. ·reine, no pl., n.n.
iets in 't ∼ brengen, to clear up, straighten
out. ·reinheid, no pl., n. purity. ·reinigen,
v.t. to clean, cleanse. ·reiniging, n.
cleansing, purification.
reis, -zen, n. journey; voyage; travel(s)
(stilted) time, occasion. een ∼ aanvaarden,
to start on a journey; op ∼, (away) on a
journey; op ∼ naar, on the way to.
·reisbeschrijving, n. book of travels.
·reisbeurs, -zen, n. travelling scholarship.
·reisbiljet, -tten, n.n. ticket (for journey).
·reisbureau, -'s, n.n. travel agency.
·reisdeken, -s, n. travelling rug. ·reisduif,
-ven, n. homing pigeon. ·reisgeld, n.n.
travelling expenses. ·reisgelegenheid,

-heden, n. means of transport. ·reisgezel-
schap, -ppen, n.n. conducted tour. met
een ∼, on a conducted tour. ·reisgoed,
-deren, n.n. (personal) luggage. ·reiskoffer,
-s, n. trunk. reis·vaardig, a. ready to start
(on journey).
·reizang, n. chorus (in classical play).
·reizen, reis, v.i. to travel, journey, voyage.
·reiziger, -s, n. traveller.
rek, no pl., n. stretch, elasticity. ¶-kken, n.n.
rack; reach (of waterway); roost. ·rekbaar,
-bare, a. elastic, extensible. ·rekbaarheid,
no pl., n. elasticity. ·rekbank, n. drawing
bench.
·rekel, -s, n. dog, cur; (young) rascal.
·rekelachtig, a. ill-mannered.
·rekenaar, -s, n. calculator. ·rekenboek, n.n.
arithmetic book. ·rekenbord, n.n. abacus.
·rekenen, v.i. to calculate, reckon. ∼ met,
to reckon by; ∼ op, to count upon, rely
on; ∼ maar!, you bet! ¶v.t. to charge;
to reckon, estimate. door elkaar gerekend,
on an average; ∼ onder, to count among.
·rekenfout, n. error in calculation.
·rekening, n. bill, account; calculation.
∼ en veraniwoording doen, to render an
account (treasurer); ∼ houden met, to take
into account; ∼ maken op, to rely on;
een ∼ vereffenen, to settle a score; zijn ∼
vinden bij, to make a profit out of; in
∼ brengen, to charge; op ∼ kopen, to
buy on credit; op ∼ stellen van, to put
down to. ·rekening-courant, -gen-courant,
n. current account. ·rekenkamer, no pl.,
n. audit office. ·rekenkunde, no pl., n.
arithmetic. reken·kundig, a. arithmetical.
·rekenles, -ssen, n. arithmetic lesson.
·rekenmachine, -s, n. calculating machine.
reken·plichtig, a. responsible. ·rekenschap,
no pl., n. account. ∼ afleggen van, to
account for, render an account of; zich ∼
geven van, to realize. ·rekensom, -mmen,
n. sum, problem.
·rekken, rek, v.t. to stretch, draw out; to
protract. ·rekstok, -kken, n. horizontal
bar (gymnastic apparatus).
re·laas, -lazen, n.n. account, story. re·latie,
-s, n. connection, relation.
·reling, -s, n. rail (of ship).
·relletje, -s, n.n. disturbance, riot.
·relmuis, -zen, n. dormouse.
rem, -mmen, n. brake. ·remblok, -kken,
n.n. brake-block.
rem·bours, no pl., n.n. onder ∼, C.O.D.
re·mise, -s, n. remittance; coach-house;
engine-shed.
remit·teren, -teer, v.t. to remit.
·remmen, rem, v.i. to brake, put on the
brake(s). ·remmer, -s, n. brakesman.
rempla·çant, n. substitute (person).
·remschoen, n. brake, drag. ·remwagen, -s,
n. brake-van.
ren, -nnen, n. gallop; (chicken-)run. ·ren-
baan, -banen, n. racecourse, race-track.

ren·dabel, *a.* remunerative. ren·deren,-deer,
v.i. to pay, yield a profit. rende·ment,
no pl., *n.n.* yield, profit. ren·derend, *a.*
remunerative.
·rendier, *n.n.* reindeer.
re·net, -tten, *n.* rennet (*apple*).
·rennen, ren, *v.i.* to gallop; to rush. ·ren-
paard, *n.n.* racehorse.
·rente, no pl., *n.* interest. *op ~*, out at
interest; *van zijn ~ leven*, to be of
independent means. ·rentegevend, *a.*
interest-bearing. ·rentekaart, *n.* insurance
card. ·renteloos, -loze, *a.* interest-free.
~ kapitaal, dead capital; *~ voorschot*, free
loan. ·renten, *v.t.* to yield interest.
rente·nier, -s, *n.* rentier, person of independent means. rente·nieren, *v.i.* to live on
one's private means. ·rentestandaard, *n.*
rate of interest. ·rentevoet, no pl., *n.* rate
of interest. ·rentezegel, -s, *n.* insurance
stamp. ·rentmeester, -s, *n.* steward,
bailiff. ·rentmeesterschap, no pl., *n.n.*
stewardship.
rep, no pl., *n. in ~ en roer*, in an uproar,
in confusion.
repara·teur, -s, *n.* repairer. repa·ratie, -s,
n. repair(s). repa·reren, -reer, *v.t.* to
repair, mend.
·repel, -s, *n.* brake (*for flax*). ·repelen, *v.t.*
to brake (*flax*).
repe·teren, -teer, *v.t.* to rehearse. repe·titie,
-s, *n.* rehearsal. *grote ~*, dress rehearsal.
repe·titor, *n.* private tutor.
re·pliek, *n.* answer, rejoinder. *van ~ dienen*,
to reply.
·reppen, rep, *v.i. ~ van*, to mention. ¶zich ~,
v.r. to bestir oneself.
repre·saille, -s, *n.* reprisal.
repu·bliek, *n.* republic. republi·kein, *n.*
republican. republi·keins, *a.* republican.
repu·tatie, no pl., *n.* reputation.
re·quest, *n.n.* petition, memorial.
requi·reren, -reer, *v.t.* to requisition. requi-
·sitie, -s, *n.* requisition. requisi·toir, *n.n.*
requisitory.
·reseda, -'s, *n.* mignonette.
reser·vaat, -vaten, *n.n.* reservation. re·ser-
vedeel, -delen, *n.n.* spare part. reser-
·veren, -veer, *v.t.* to reserve.
resi·dent, *n.* commissioner (*East Indies*).
respec·tief, -ve, *a.* respective, several.
respec·tievelijk, *adv.* respectively,
severally.
res·pijt, no pl., *n.n.* respite. res·pijtdagen,
pl. only, *n.* days of grace.
res·sort, no pl., *n.n.* jurisdiction, province;
diocese. ressor·teren, -teer, *v.i. ~ onder*,
to be within (someone's) jurisdiction *or*
province.
rest, *n.* rest, remainder. res·tant, *n.n.*
remainder.
restau·ratiewagen, -s, *n.* dining car.
res·teren, -teer, *v.i.* to remain, be left.
·resten, *v.t.* to be left.

restitu·eren, -eer, *v.t.* to refund, make
restitution of.
resul·taat, -taten, *n.n.* result. resul·teren,
-teer, *v.i.* to result.
resu·meren, -meer, *v.t.* to summarize.
reti·rade, -s, *n.* lavatory.
re·tour, *n.* return. re·tourbiljet, -tten, *n.n.*,
re·tourtje, -s, *n.n.* return-ticket.
re·traite, -s, *n.* retreat. *de ~ blazen*, to
sound the retreat.
reu, *n.* (male) dog.
reuk, *n.* smell; scent; fragrance. *de ~ van
iets krijgen*, to get wind of something.
·reukaltaar, -taren, *n.n.* incense altar.
·reukeloos, -loze, *a.* odourless. ·reukflesje,
-s, *n.n.* scent bottle. ·reukje, no pl., *n.n.*
smell. *er is een ~ aan*, there is something
fishy about it. ·reukoffer, -s, *n.n.* incense
offering. ·reukvat, *n.n.* censer. ·reukwerk,
n.n. perfumes. ·reukzenuw, *n.* olfactory
nerve.
reus, -zen, *n.* giant. reus·achtig, *a.* gigantic,
enormous, huge.
·reutel, no pl., *n.* death-rattle. ·reutelen,
v.i. to rattle, gurgle.
·reuzel, no pl., *n.* lard.
·reuzen, *prefix.* giant, gigantic. ·reuzenhaai,
n. basking-shark. ·reuzenslang, *n.* boa-
constrictor. ·reuzenzwaai, *n.* grand swing.
reu·zin, -nnen, *n.* giantess.
re·vanche, -s, *n.* revenge. re·vanchepartij, *n.*
return match.
·reven, reef, *v.t.* to reef, shorten sail.
re·vers, *invar., n.n.* back (*of coin*); facing,
lapel.
revo·lutie, -s, *n.* revolution.
re·vue, -s, *n.* review; revue. *de ~ laten
passeren*, to pass in review.
rhe·torisch, *a.* rhetorical.
rheuma·tiek, *n.* rheumatism. rheu·matisch,
a. rheumatic.
·rhythme, -n, *n.n.* rhythm.
ri·ant, *a.* pleasant, charming.
rib, -bben, *n.* rib. ·ribbel, -s, *n.* (small)
ridge. ·ribbelig, *a.* ridgy, ribbed. ·ribbeling,
n. ripple-mark. ·ribbenkast, *n.* chest
(*bones of*). ·ribstuk, -kken, *n.* rib (*of beef,
etc.*).
·richel, -s, *n.* ledge, ridge.
·richten, *v.t.* to direct, aim. *~ naar*, to
direct towards; *~ op or tegen*, to aim at;
~ tot, to address to. ¶*v.r. zich ~ naar*,
to conform to, be guided by; *zich ~ tot*,
to address oneself to. ·richter, -s, *n.*
judge (*biblical*). ·richting, *n.* direction;
persuasion. ·richtlijn, *n.* line of sight.
·richtschroef, -ven, *n.* adjusting screw.
·richtsnoer, *n.n.* line of conduct.
ri·cinusboom, -bomen, *n.* castor-oil plant.
ri·cinusolie, no pl., *n.* castor-oil.
·ridder, -s, *n.* knight. *iemand tot ~ slaan*,
to create a person a knight. ·ridderen,
v.t. to knight. ·ridderkruis, *n.n.* decoration
in order(s) of knighthood. ·ridderlijk, *a.*

knightly; chivalrous. ·ridderlijkheid, no
pl., *n.* chivalry. ·ridderorde, -n, *n.* order
of knighthood. ·ridderschap, -ppen, *n.*
knighthood, chivalry. ·ridderslag, no pl.,
n. accolade. ·ridderspel, *n.n.* tournament
(*knightly*). ·riddertijd, *n.* age of chivalry.
·ridderzaal, -zalen, *n.* hall (*of castle*).
riek, *n.* (2, 3, or 4-pronged) fork (*agri-cultural*).
·rieken, *v.i.*, *str.* (*stilted*) to smell.
riem, *n.* strap, thong; belt; oar; ream.
riet, no pl., *n.n.* reed; rush, thatch; cane.
een ~je, a drinking straw. ·rietbos, -ssen,
n.n. reed-marsh. ·rietdekker, -s, *n.*
thatcher. ·rieten, *a.* thatched; cane,
wicker. ·rietgans, -zen, *n.* bean goose.
·rietgors, *n.* reed-bunting, reed-sparrow.
·riethoen, -ders, *n.n.* moorhen. ·rietmolen,
-s, *n.* (sugar-)cane mill. ·rietmus, -ssen, *n.*
See rietgors. ·rietsnip, -ppen, *n.* snipe.
·rietsuiker, no pl., *n.* cane-sugar. ·riettuin,
n. sugar-cane field. ·rietveld, *n.n.* reedland.
·rietvink, *n.* *See* rietgors. ·rietvoorn, -s,
n. rudd. ·rietzanger, -s, *n.* sedge-warbler.
rif, -ffen, *n.n.* reef.
rij, *n.* row; range (*hills, etc.*). *op ~en,* in rows.
·rijbaan, -banen, *n.* riding track. ·rijbewijs,
-zen, *n.n.* driving licence. ·rijbroek, *n.*
riding breeches. ·rijden, *v.i.*, *str.* to ride;
to drive. *schaatsen ~,* to skate; *~ en
rossen,* to rush or career around. ¶*v.t.*, *str.*
to drive. ·rijder, -s, *n.* rider, horseman.
·rijdier, *n.n.* mount.
rijf, -ven, *n.* rake.
·rijgdraad, -draden, *n.* tacking-cotton. ·rijgen,
v.t., *str.* to tack; to string (*beads*); to lace.
·rijglaars, -zen, *n.* lace-up boot. ·rijgnaald,
n. bodkin. ·rijgsnoer, *n.n.* lace.
rijk, *a.* (of) wealthy. *~ aan,* rich in. ¶*n.n.*
state, realm, empire, kingdom. *zijn ~ is
uit,* his reign is at an end; *het ~ alleen
hebben,* to have the place to oneself.
·rijkaard, *n.* rich person (*derogatory*).
·rijkdom, -mmen, *n.* wealth, riches.
·rijkelijk, *adv.* richly, copiously. rijke·lui,
pl. only, *n.* rich people.
·rijkleed, -kleden, *n.n.* riding-habit. ·rij-
knecht, *n.* groom.
rijks·ambtenaar, -naren, *n.* government
official; civil servant. ·rijksappel, -s, *n.*
imperial orb. ·rijksarchief, -ven, *n.* public
record office. ·rijksbelasting, *n.* tax.
·rijksbewind, no pl., *n.n.* government.
rijks·daalder, -s, *n.* rix-dollar. ·Rijksdag,
n. Reichstag. ·rijksgrens, -zen, *n.* frontier.
·rijkskosten, pl. only, *n. op ~,* at government expense. ·rijksmuseum, -sea, *n.n.*
national museum. rijks·opvoedings-
gesticht, *n.n.* approved school. ·rijks-
verzekering, *n.* national insurance. ·rijks-
wege, no pl., *n. van ~,* on government
account.
·rijkunst, no pl., *n.* horsemanship. ·rijlaars,
-zen, *n.* riding-boot.

rijm, no pl., *n.* hoar-frost. ¶*n.n.* rhyme.
op ~, in rhyme. ·rijmelaar, -s, *n.* versifier,
poetaster. rijmela·rij, *n.* doggerel. ·rijme-
len, *v.i.* to write doggerel. ·rijmen, *v.i.*
to rhyme; to agree. *~ op,* to rhyme with;
~ met, to tally with. ·rijmloos, -loze, *a.*
rhymeless. ·rijmpje, -s, *n.n.* jingle.
Rijn, *N.* Rhine. ·Rijnaak, -naken, *n.* Rhine
barge. ·Rijnland, *n.N.* Rhineland. ·Rijn-
lands, *a.* Rhineland, Rhenish. ·Rijnvaart,
no pl., *n.* Rhine traffic or transport.
·Rijnwijn, *n.* Rhine wine.
rijp, no pl., *n.* hoar-frost. ¶*a.* ripe. *~ en
groen,* ripe and unripe; *~ worden,* to
ripen; *na ~ beraad,* after mature consideration.
·rijpaard, *n.n.* mount, riding-horse. ·rijpad,
n.n. bridle-path.
·rijpelijk, *adv. iets ~ overwegen,* to give
something careful consideration. ·rijpen,
v.i. to ripen. *~ tot,* to ripen into. ¶*v.imp.
het heeft gerijpt,* there has been a hoar-frost.
·rijpheid, no pl., *n.* ripeness, maturity.
·rijpwording, no pl., *n.* ripening.
rijs, -zen, *n.n.* osier; twig. ·rijshout, no pl.,
n.n. osier.
·rijschool, -scholen, *n.* riding academy.
·Rijssel, *n.N.* Lille, Lisle.
rijst, no pl., *n.* rice. ·rijstblok, -kken, *n.n.*
rice-pounder. ·rijstbouw, no pl., *n.* rice-
growing. ·rijstebrij, no pl., *n.* rice-pudding.
·rijstepap, no pl., *n.* rice-milk. ·rijstpel-
machine, -s, *n.* rice-huller. ·rijstpelmolen,
-s, *n.* rice-hulling mill. ·rijstvogel, -s, *n.*
paddy-bird.
·rijswerk, no pl., *n.n.* osier-work.
·rijten, *v.t.*, *str.* (*stilted*) to rend.
·rijtoer, *n.* drive, ride. ·rijtuig, *n.n.* carriage.
·rijtuigfabriek, *n.* coach-works. ·rijtuig-
maker, -s, *n.* coach-builder. ·rijweg, *n.*
carriage-way. ·rijwiel, *n.n.* bicycle.
·rijwielhersteller, -s, *n.* cycle repairer.
·rijzen, rijs, *v.i.*, *str.* to rise; to arise. ·rijzig,
a. tall. ·rijzigheid, no pl., *n.* tallness.
·rijzweep, -zwepen, *n.* riding-crop.
rikke·tik, *int.* tick-tack, pitter-patter.
riks, *n.* *See* rijksdaalder.
·rillen, ril, *v.i.* to shiver; to shudder. *~ van,*
to shudder at. ·rillerig, *a.* shivery. ·rilling,
n. shiver; shudder.
·rimboe, no pl., *n.* jungle.
·rimpel, -s, *n.* wrinkle; ripple. ·rimpelen,
v.t. to wrinkle, pucker. ·rimpelig, *a.*
wrinkled, wrinkly. ·rimpeling, *n.* wrinkling,
ripple.
ring, *n.* ring. ·ringbaan, -banen, *n.* loop-
railway. ·ringdijk, *n.* circular dyke.
·ringelen, *v.t.* to ring, band. ·ringeling, *n.*
ring finger. ·ringelmus, -ssen, *n.* tree-
sparrow. ·ringeloren, -loor, *v.t.* to bully.
·ringen, *v.t.* to ring, band. ·ringetje, -s,
n.n. small ring; smoke ring. *je kunt hem
door een ~ halen,* he looks as if he's just
come out of a band-box. ·ringsteken, no

pl., *n.n.* tilting at the ring. ·**ringvaart,** *n.* circular canal. **ring·vormig,** *a.* annular, ring-shaped. ·**ringwerpen,** no pl., *n.n.* playing at quoits.

·**rinkelbel, -llen,** *n.* jingling-bells.

rins, *a.* sourish, tart.

rio·leren, -leer, *v.t.* to drain. **ri·ool, riolen,** *n.* sewer, drain. **ri·oolstelsel, -s,** *n.n.* system of drainage, sewers. **ri·oolwater,** no pl., *n.n.* sewage.

rips, no pl., *n.n.* rep.

ris, -ssen, *n.* row, string.

·**risico, -'s,** *n.n.* risk. *voor ~ van,* at the risk of; *op eigen ~,* at one's own risk.

ris·kant, *a.* risky. **ris·keren, -keer,** *v.t.* to risk.

·**rissen, ris,** *v.t.* to string. **rist,** *n.* *See* **ris.** ·**risten,** *v.t.* *See* **rissen.**

rit, -tten, *n.,* ·**ritje, -s,** *n.* ride, drive. ·**rit·meester, -s,** *n.* cavalry captain.

·**ritnaald,** *n.* wireworm.

·**ritselen,** *v.i.* to rustle.

·**ritsijzer, -s,** *n.n.* gouge.

ritu·eel, -uelen, *n.n.* ritual.

ri·vier, *n.* river. **ri·vierdonderpad, -dden,** *n.* miller's thumb.

rob, -bben, *n.* seal. **robbe·does, -zen,** *n.* tomboy. ·**robbenjacht,** *n.* seal-hunt(ing). ·**robbentraan,** no pl., *n.* seal-oil.

·**robber, -s,** *n.* rubber (*cards*).

ro·bijn, *n.* ruby. **ro·bijnen,** *a.* (of) ruby.

·**rochelen,** *v.i.* to expectorate (*noisily*); to rattle (*before death*).

roe, *n.* *See* **roede.**

·**roebel, -s,** *n.* rouble.

·**roede, -n,** *n.* rod, pole; wand; 10 metres.

roef, -ven, *n.* deck-house. ¶*int.* whizz.

·**roeibank, -s** *n.* thwart. ·**roeiboot, -boten,** *n.* rowing-boat. ·**roeien,** *v.i.* to row; to scull. *men moet ~ met de riemen die men heeft,* one must use the means one has. ·**roeier, -s,** *n.* rower, oarsman. ·**roeiriem,** *n.,* ·**roeispaan, -spanen,** *n.* oar.

roek, *n.* rook.

·**roekeloos, -loze,** *a.* reckless. ·**roekeloosheid, -heden,** *n.* recklessness.

roe·koeken, *v.i.* to coo.

roem, no pl., *n.* fame, glory.

Roe·meens, *a.* Roumanian.

·**roemen,** *v.t.* to praise. ¶*v.i.* to boast. *~ op,* to boast (of).

·**roemer, -s,** *n.* rummer.

·**roemrijk,** *a.,* **roem·ruchtig,** *a.,* **roemvol, -lle,** *a.* glorious, renowned. **roem·zuchtig,** *a.* vainglorious.

roep, *n.* call, cry; repute. *de ~ hebben van* or *in de ~ staan van,* to have the reputation of; *in kwade ~ brengen,* to bring into bad repute. ·**roepen,** *v.t., str.* to call. *iemand laten ~,* to send for a person; *zich geroepen voelen,* to feel called upon to. ¶*v.i., str.* to call, cry. *~ om,* to call (for); *~ over,* to praise. ·**roeper, -s,** *n.* crier; megaphone. ·**roeping,** no pl., *n.* call(ing), vocation. ·**roepletters,** pl. only, *n.* call-sign

(*radio*). ·**roepstem, -mmen.** *n.* voice, call (*of duty*).

roer, *n.n.* rudder; helm, wheel; stem (*of pipe*); tube, pipe; firelock. *uit het ~ lopen,* not to answer the wheel. ¶no pl., *n. in rep en ~,* in confusion. ·**roerdomp,** *n.* bittern. ·**roerei, -eieren,** *n.n.* scrambled egg. ·**roeren,** *v.t.* to stir; to move; to beat (*drum*); to stir, move, affect (*emotions*). ¶*v.i. ~ aan,* to touch; *~ in,* to stir. ¶*zich ~,* *v.r.* to stir, bestir oneself. ·**roerend,** *a.* moving, touching. *~e goederen,* movables. ·**roerganger, -s,** *n.* helmsman, man at the wheel. ·**roerig,** *a.* restless; turbulent. ·**roering,** *n.* stir, motion. ·**roerloos, -loze,** *a.* motionless. ·**roerpen, -nnen,** *n.* helm, tiller. ·**roersel,** *n.n.* (*stilted*) motive, prompting. ·**roerspaan, -spanen,** *n.* wooden spoon; spatula. ·**roervink,** *n.* decoy (*bird*); ring-leader.

roes, -zen, *n.* drunken fit, inebriation. *in de ~ der overwinning,* in the flush of victory; *zijn ~ uitslapen,* to sleep off the effects of drink.

roest, no pl., *n.* or *n.n.* rust; roost. *oud ~,* old iron. ¶no pl., *n.* blight. ·**roesten,** *v.i.* to rust, get rusty; to roost. ·**roestig,** *a.* rusty. ·**roestvogel, -s,** *n.* perching bird. ·**roestvrij,** *a.* rustless, stainless. ·**roest·werend,** *a.* rust-preventing.

roet, *n.n.* soot. *~ in 't eten gooien,* to be a spoilsport. ·**roetachtig,** *a.,* ·**roetig,** *a.* sooty. ·**roetzwart,** *a.* black as soot. ¶no pl., *n.n.* bistre, lamp-black.

·**roezemoezen, -moes,** (*used in pl. only*). to bustle; to bumble. ·**roezemoezig,** *a.* boisterous; bumbling.

·**roffel, -s,** *n.* roll, ruffle; jack-plane. ·**roffelen,** *v.t.* to roll (the drum); to rough-plane. ·**roffelschaaf, -schaven,** *n.* jack-plane. ·**roffelvuur,** no pl., *n.n.* drum-fire, barrage.

rog, -**gen,** *n.* ray, thornback.

rogge, no pl., *n.* rye.

rok, -kken, *n.* skirt; dress-coat, tails.

rokeloos, -loze, *a.* smokeless. ·**roken, rook,** *v.t.* to smoke. ¶*v.i.* to smoke. *~ van,* to reek with. ·**roker, -s,** *n.* smoker. ·**rokerig,** *a.* smoky. **roke·rij,** *n.* smoke-house.

·**rokken, -s,** *n.n.* distaff.

rol, -llen, *n.* roll; roller; part, role; list, panel, (muster) roll. *de rollen omkeren,* to turn the tables; *uit zijn ~ vallen,* to act out of character; *zijn ~ kennen,* to know one's lines. ·**rolgordijn,** *n.n.* roller-blind. ·**rollaag, -lagen,** *n.* upright course of bricks. **rol·lade, -s,** *n.* collared beef or veal (*etc.*). ·**rollebollen, -bol,** *v.i.* to turn somersaults. ·**rollen, rol,** *v.t.* to roll. *zakken ~,* to pick pockets. ¶*v.i.* to roll, tumble. ·**roller, -s,** *n.* roller. ·**rolletje, -s,** *n.n.* (*small*) roll; castor. *het ging op ~s,* it went very smoothly. ·**rolluik** *n.n.* roller-shutter. ·**rolpens,** no pl., *n.* minced beef in tripe. ·rolprent, n. (stilled) film. ·rolrond, a. cylindrical. ·rolschaats, n. roller-skate. ·rolvast, a. word-perfect. ·rolveger, -s, n. carpet-sweeper.

Ro·maans, a. Romance; Norman (archit.). ro·man, -s, n. novel. roman·cier, -s, n. novelist. roma·nesk, a. romantic. ro·man·schrijfster, -s, n. novelist (female). ro·man·schrijver, -s, n. novelist (male). ro·man·ticus, -ci, n. romanticist. roman·tiek, a. romantic. ¶no pl., n. romanticism. ro·mantisch, a. romantic.

Ro·mein, N. Roman. Ro·meins, a. Roman. ·romen, room, v.t. to cream.

·rommel, no pl., n. rubbish; stuff; mess. ouwe ~, old junk. ·rommelen, v.i. to rumble; to rummage. ·rommelig, a. untidy. ·rommelkamer, -s, n. lumber room. ·rommelpot, -tten, n. primitive rumbling Dutch musical instrument.

romp, n. trunk (of body); hull (of ship); body (of plane).

·rompslomp, no pl., n. to-do; caboodle.

rond, a. round; straightforward. goed Zeeuws goed ~, Zeelanders are straightforward. ¶adv. round(ly); openly. ¶prep. round; about. ¶no pl., n.n. in het ~, around, roundabout. ¶prefix about, (a)round. ·rondbazuinen, v.t.s. to trumpet forth. rond·borstig, a. open-hearted. rond·borstigheid, no pl., n. open-heartedness. ·rondbrengen, v.t.s., irr. to take round. ·rondbrieven, brief rond, v.t.s. to spread about. ·ronddobberen, v.i.s. to drift around (in small craft). ·ronddraaien, v.t.s. to turn (round). ¶v.i.s. to turn (round). ·ronde, -s, n. round (military); beat (police). ·rondedans, n. round dance. ron·deel, -delen, n. bastion. ·ronden, v.t. to round. ¶v.i. to become round. ·rondgaan, ga rond, v.i.s., irr. to go about; to go round, circulate. laten ~, to hand round. ·rondgang, n. circuit. ·rondheid, no pl., n. roundness. ·rondhout, n.n. spar, (round) timber. ·ronding, n. rounding. ·rondje, -s, n.n. round (of drinks). een ~ geven, to stand a round. rondkijken, v.i.s., str. to look round. ·rondkomen, v.i.s., irr. to come round; to make ends meet. ~ met, to manage on. ·rondlopen, loop rond, v.i.s., str. to walk about or round. vrij ~, to be at large. rond·om, adv. all round, roundabout. ¶prep. roundabout. ·rondreis, -zen, n. circular tour. ·rondreizen, reis rond, v.t.s. to travel about. ·rondreizend, a. itinerant. ·rond·schrift, no pl., n.n. round hand. ·rond·schrijven, no pl., n.n. circular letter. ·rondsel, -s, n.n. pinion. ·rondslingeren, v.t.s. to fling around. ¶v.i.s. to lie around. ·rondsluipen, v.i.s., str. to steal about. ·rondsturen, stuur rond, v.t.s. to send round or out. ·rondte, -n, n. in de ~, round; de ~ doen, to go round. ·ronduit,

adv. roundly, frankly, bluntly. ~ spreken, to speak one's mind; ~ gezegd, frankly (speaking). ·rondvertellen, vertel rond, v.t.s. to spread. ·rondvoeren, v.t.s. to lead about. ·rondvraag, no pl., n. question (to meeting). iets in ~ brengen, to put the question. ·rondwaren, waar rond, v.i.s. to walk (of spirits). ergens ~, to haunt a place.

rong, n. rung.

·ronken, v.i. to snore; to whirr, drone.

·ronselaar, -s, n. crimp. ·ronselen, v.t. to crimp, press.

·Röntgenstralen, pl. only, n. X-rays.

rood, rode, a. red. ~ maken, to redden; ~ worden, to go red, redden; rode hond, prickly heat. ·roodaarde, no pl., n. ruddle. ·roodachtig, a. reddish. ·roodbont, a. red and white. ·roodborstje, -s, n.n. robin. ·roodbruin, a. reddish-brown, russet. ·roodgloeiend, a. red-hot. ·roodharig, a. red-haired. Rood·kapje, n.N. Little Red Riding-Hood. ·roodkoper, n.n. copper. ·roodkoperen, a. (of) copper. ·roodvonk, no pl., n.n. scarlet fever. ·roodvos, -ssen, n. bay (horse).

roof, roven, n. scab. ¶no pl., n. robbery; plunder. op ~ uitgaan, to go out in search of prey. ·roofachtig, a. rapacious. ·roof·bouw, no pl., n. overcropping; exhaustive cultivation. ·roofdier, n.n. beast of prey. roof·gierig, a. rapacious. ·roofnest, n.n. den of robbers. ·roofridder, -s, n. robber baron. ·roofschip, -schepen, n.n. pirate ship. ·rooftocht, n. raid. ·roofziek, a. rapacious. ·roofzucht, no pl., n. rapacity.

·rooien, v.t. to dig (potatoes); to clear (of roots and shrub). ·rooilijn, n. alignment. ·rooimeester, -s, n. surveyor.

rook, no pl., n. smoke. ·rookartikelen, pl. only, n.n. smokers' requisites. ·rookloos, -loze, a. smokeless. ·rooksalon, -s, n. smoking room. ·rooktabak, no pl., n. pipe tobacco. rook·vlees, no pl., n.n. smoked beef. ·rookworst, n. smoked sausage. ·rookzwart, no pl., n.n. lamp-black.

room, no pl., n. cream. ·roomachtig, a. creamy. ·roomboter, no pl., n. (dairy-)butter. ·roomijs, no pl., n.n. ice-cream.

Rooms, a. Roman Catholic. ·Roomsgezind, a. pro-Roman Catholic, papist. ·Rooms-Katholiek, a. Roman Catholic.

·roomsoes, -zen, n. cream puff.

roos, rozen, n. rose; card (of compass); bull's eye. ¶no pl., n. erysipelas; dandruff. roos·kleurig, a. rose-coloured, rosy.

·roosten, v.t. to roast; to toast. ·rooster, -s, n. grill, gridiron; grid; rota, time-table. ·roosteren, v.t. to roast, grill; to toast. ·roosterwerk, no pl., n.n. grating.

ros, -ssen, n.n. steed. ¶-sse, a. ruddy.

·rosbief, no pl., n. roast beef.

·rose, a. pink.

·roskam, -mmen, n. curry-comb. ·roskam·men, -kam, v.t. to curry-comb.

rosma·rijn, no pl., *n.* rosemary.
·rossen, ros, *v.i.* to rush (around).
·rossig, *a.* ruddy; sandy (*hair*).
rot, -tten, *n.* stack (*of arms*). *aan rotten zetten*, to stack. ¶no pl., *n.n.* rot. ¶-tte, *a.* rotten, decayed. ¶*adv.* *zich* ~ *werken*, to work oneself to death.
·rotan, no pl., *n.* or *n.n.* rattan.
·roten, root, *v.t.* to ret. rote·rij, *n.* rettery.
ro·teren, -teer, *v.i.* to rotate.
·rotgans, -zen, *n.* wild goose.
·rotheid, no pl., *n.* rottenness.
rots, *n.* rock; cliff. ·rotsachtig, *a.* rocky.
·rotsblok, -kken, *n.n.* boulder. ·Rots-gebergte, *n.N.* Rocky Mountains, Rockies.
·rotspartij, *n.* (mass of) rocks; rockery.
·rotspunt, *n.* (rocky) peak. ·rotsvast, *a.* (as) firm as a rock.
·rotten, rot, *v.i.* to rot, putrefy. ·rotting, *n.* putrefaction; cane.
rouw, no pl., *n.* mourning. *in de* ~ *voor*, in mourning for. ·rouwbeklag, no pl., *n.n.* condolence. ·rouwdienst, *n.* memorial service. ·rouwen, *v.i.* to mourn. ¶*v.t.* to regret, rue. ·rouwfloers, no pl., *n.n.* crape. ·rouwig, *a.* sorry. ·rouwklacht, *n.* lamentation.
·roven, roof, *v.t.* & *v.i.* to rob. ·rover, -s, *n.* robber. rove·rij, no pl., *n.* robbery.
ro·yaal, -yale, *a.* liberal, generous. ¶*adv.* generously, freely.
ro·yeren, -yeer, *v.t.* to strike off, expel.
·rozeblad, -eren, *n.n.* rose-leaf. ·rozeboom, -bomen, *n.* rose-tree, rose-bush. ·rozebottel, -s, *n.* (rose) hip. ·rozelaar, -s, *n.* rose-tree. rozema·rijn, no pl., *n.* rosemary. ·rozengeur, no pl., *n.* perfume of roses. *alles was* ~ *en maneschijn*, everything in the garden was lovely. rozen·hoedje, -s, *n.n.* chaplet (*Roman Catholic prayer*). ·rozenhout, no pl., *n.n.* rosewood. ·rozenkrans, *n.* garland of roses; rosary. ·Rozenkruiser, -s, *N.* Rosicrucian. ·rozerood, -rode, *a.* rose-red. ·rozestok, -kken, *n.* pedicle (*of antlers*). ro·zet, -tten, *n.* rosette.
·rozig, *a.* rosy.
ro·zijn, *n.* raisin.
·rubber, no pl., *n.* rubber.
ru·briek, *n.* heading, column.
·ruchtbaar, -bare, *a.* (*stilted*) public. ~ *maken*, to make known; ~ *worden*, to transpire. ·ruchtbaarheid, no pl., *n.* (*stilted*) publicity.
rug, -ggen, *n.* back; ridge. *iemand de* ~ (*toe*)*keren*, to turn one's back upon someone; *het is achter de* ~, it is over and done with; *iemand met de* ~ *aanzien*, to give a person the cold shoulder; *het groeit me niet op de* ~, I'm not made of money. ·ruggegraat, -graten, *n.* backbone, spine. ·ruggelings, *adv.* backwards; back to back. ·ruggemerg, no pl., *n.n.* spinal marrow. ·ruggespraak, no pl., *n.* consultation. ~ *houden met*, to consult with. ·ruggesteun, no pl., *n.* support, backing.

·rugvin, -nnen, *n.* dorsal fin. ·rugwaarts, *a.* & *adv.* backward(s). ·rugzijde, -n, *n.* back.
rui, no pl., *n.* moulting. ·ruien, *v.i.* to moult.
ruif, -ven, *n.* rack (*in stable*).
ruig, *a.* shaggy; rough. ·ruigte, -n, *n.* underwood.
·ruiken, *v.t.*, *str.* to smell; to scent (*game*). *lont* ~, to smell a rat. ¶*v.i.*, *str.* to smell. ~ *aan*, to smell (at); ~ *naar*, to smell of; *het kan er niet naar* ~, it isn't a patch on it. ·ruiker, -s, *n.* nosegay.
ruil, *n.* exchange, barter. ·ruilbaar, -bare, *a.* exchangeable. ·ruilen, *v.t.* to exchange, barter; to swop. ·ruilhandel, no pl., *n.* barter. ·ruilmiddel, *n.n.* medium of exchange. ·ruilverkaveling, *n.* redistribution of multiple allotments (*land*).
ruim, *a.* roomy, spacious; wide, broad, ample. ¶*adv.* largely, amply. ~ *zes weken geleden*, more than six weeks ago. ¶*n.n.* hold (*of ship*); nave (*of church*). ·ruimen, *v.t.* to vacate; to clear (away); to empty (*cesspools*). ·ruimschoots, *a.* ample. ¶*adv.* amply, plentifully. ~ *gelegenheid hebben*, to have ample opportunity. ·ruimte, no pl., *n.* room, space. *iemand de* ~ *geven*, to give a person a wide berth. ·ruimtemaat, -maten, *n.* cubic measure. ·ruimtevrees, no pl., *n.* agoraphobia.
ruin, *n.* gelding.
ru·ïne, -s, *n.* ruin. ruï·neren, -neer, *v.t.* to ruin.
·ruisen, *v.i.* to rustle, murmur.
·ruisvoorn, -s, *n.* rudd.
ruit, *n.* diamond, lozenge; pane (*glass*); rue (*plant*). ·ruiten, pl. only, *n.* diamonds (*cards*).
·ruiter, -s, *n.* horseman, rider. *Spaanse* ~ or *Friese* ~, chevaux-de-frise. ruite·rij, no pl., *n.* cavalry. ·ruiterlijk, *a.* chivalrous. ·ruiterpad, *n.n.* bridle-path.
·ruitijd, *n.* moulting time.
·ruitje, -s, *n.n.* check. *See also* ruit. ·ruitjesgoed, -eren, *n.n.* checked material. ·ruitvormig, *a.* lozenge-shaped.
ruk, -kken, *n.* wrench; tug, jerk. ·rukken, ruk, *v.i.* to wrench; to tug, snatch. *te velde* ~, to go to war, take the field. ·rukwind, *n.* gust of wind, squall.
rul, -lle, *a.* bumpy.
·rumboon, -bonen, *n.* chocolate liqueur.
ru·moer, no pl., *n.n.* noise, uproar, clamour. ru·moerig, *a.* noisy.
run, no pl., *n.* tan (*bark*).
rund, -eren, *n.n.* cow, bull, ox. ·runderaas, -dazen, *n.* gadfly. ·runderlapje, -s, *n.n.* beefsteak. ·rundvee, no pl., *n.n.* (horned) cattle. ·rundvet, no pl., *n.n.* beef suet. ·rundvlees, no pl., *n.n.* beef.
·rune, -s, *n.* rune. ·runenschrift, no pl., *n.n.* runic writing.
·runkleurig, *a.* tan-coloured. ·runmolen, -s, *n.* bark-mill.

·runnen, run, v.i. to curdle.
rups, n. caterpillar. ·rupsbandwiel, n.n. caterpillar wheel.
rus, -ssen, n. rush.
Rus, -ssen, n. Russian. ·Rusland, n.N. Russia. ·Russisch, a. Russian. Rus·sin, -nnen, N. Russian (woman).
·russen, a. (of) rush; rush-bottomed.
rust, no pl., n. rest, quiet. *plaats ~!*, stand easy!; ~ *en vrede*, peace and quiet; ~ *noch duur hebben*, to be restless; *geen* ~ *hebben*, not to be at ease; ~ *houden*, to take rest; *met* ~ *laten*, to leave in peace, leave alone; *tot* ~ *brengen*, to quiet; *tot* ~ *komen*, to quiet down; *wel te* ~*e!*, goodnight; *zich ter* ~*e begeven*, to go to rest, turn in. ·rustbank, n., ·rustbed, -dden, n. couch. ·rusteloos, -loze, a. restless. ruste·loosheid, no pl., n. restlessness. ·rusten, v.i. to rest. ·rustend, a. emeritus.
rus·tiek, a. rustic.
·rustig, a. quiet, restful. ·rustigheid, no pl., n. restfulness. ·rustjes, adv. quietly.
·rusting, n. armour.
·rustjaar, -jaren, n.n. sabbatical year. ·rustverstoorder, -s, n. disturber of the peace.
·rutschbaan, -banen, n. switchback railway.
ruw, a. rough ; raw (*of materials*), crude. ruw·harig, a. wire-haired. ·ruwheid, -heden, n. roughness.
·ruzie, -s, n. quarrel. ~ *hebben* or *maken*, to quarrel; ~ *krijgen*, to fall out. ·ruzieachtig, a. quarrelsome. ·ruziemaker, -s, n. quarrelsome person.

S

·saai, no pl., n. serge. ¶*a.* dull, tedious. ·saaiheid, no pl., n. dullness.
·sabbelen, v.i. to slaver.
·sabel, no pl., n.n. sable. ¶-s, n. sword, sabre. ·sabelbek, -kken, n. avocet. ·sabelbont, n.n. sable fur. ·sabeldier, n.n. sable. ·sabeltas, -ssen, n. sabretache.
sacris·tein, n. sacristan. sacris·tie, -tieën, n. vestry, sacristy.
saffi·aan, no pl., n.n. morocco (*leather*).
saf·fier, n. sapphire (*gem*). ¶no pl., n.n. sapphire (*substance*). saf·fieren, a. (of) sapphire.
saf·fraan, no pl., n. saffron.
sa·gaai, n. assegai.
·sage, -n, n. legend, saga.
·sail·lant, n. salient.
sa·jet, no pl., n. or n.n. worsted. sa·jetten, a. (of) worsted.
sakker·loot, *int.* by Jove !
·Saksen n.N. Saxony. ·Sakser, -s, N. Saxon. ·Saksisch, a. Saxon.

sa·lade, -n, n. salad.
salari·ëren, -ieer, v.t. to salary. salari·ëring, n. (payment of) salary. ·sa·laris, -ssen, n.n. salary. sa·larisregeling, n. scale of pay.
·saldo, -'s or -di, n.n. balance. *batig* or *voordelig* ~, surplus, balance in hand; *nadelig* ~, deficit.
sa·letjonker, -s, n. carpet-knight.
·salie, no pl., n. sage.
salmi·ak, no pl., n. sal-ammoniac.
sa·lon, -s, n. drawing-room; saloon. sa·lonmuziek, no pl., n. chamber music.
sal·peter, no pl., n.n. saltpetre. sal·peterzuur, no pl., n.n. nitric acid.
salu·eren, -eer, v.t. & v.i. to salute. sa·luut, -luten, n.n. salute, salutation. sa·luutschot, n.n. ~*en lossen*, to fire a salute.
·salvo, -'s, n.n. volley, round.
·samen, adv. together. ¶*prefix.* together.
·samenbinden, v.t.s., str. to tie together, tie up.
·samendrukken, druk samen, v.t.s. to press together, compress.
·samengaan, ga samen, v.i.s., irr. to go together, agree.
·samengesteld, a. compound, complex. ·samengesteldheid, -heden, n. complexity.
·samenhang, no pl., n. connection. ·samenhangen, v.i.s., str. to hang together, cohere. ~ *met*, to be connected with. ·samenhangend, a. coherent.
·samenhokken, hok samen, v.i.s. to herd or crowd together.
·samenhoren, hoor samen, v.i.s. to belong together. samen·horigheid, no pl., n. solidarity.
·samenkomen, v.i.s., irr. to come together, meet, gather. ·samenkomst, n. meeting, gathering.
·samenkoppelen, v.t.s. to couple.
·samenleving, n. society; cohabitation.
·samenloop, no pl., n. concourse; confluence. ·samenlopen, loop samen, v.i.s., str. to run together; to run into each other, converge.
·samenpersen, v.t.s., to compress.
·samenraapsel, -s, n.n. hotchpotch. ~ *van leugens*, tissue of lies.
·samenscholen, school samen, v.i.s. to assemble, gather (*of crowd*). ·samenscholing, n. assembly, gathering (*unfavourable*).
·samensmelten, v.t.s., str. to melt together, fuse. ·samensmelting, n. fusion, amalgamation.
·samenspannen, span samen, v.i.s., irr. to plot (together).
·samenspraak, -spraken, n. dialogue. ·samenspreking, n. (*stilted*) conversation.
·samenstel, no pl., n.n. structure. ·samenstellen, stel samen, v.t.s. to compose. ·samensteller, -s, n. composer. ·samenstelling, n. composition.

·samentreffen, **tref samen,** *v.i.s.,* *str.* to coincide.

·samentrekken, **trek samen,** *v.t.s.,* *str.* to pull together, to concentrate; to contract. ¶zich ~, *v.r.s.,* *str.* to contract. ·samentrekking, *n.* contraction; concentration.

·samenvallen, **val samen,** *v.i.s.,* *str.* to coincide.

·samenvatten, **vat samen,** *v.t.s.* to summarize, recapitulate. ·samenvatting, *n.* summary, précis.

·samenweefsel, -s, *n.n.* tissue, web.

·samenwerken, *v.i.s.* to work together, collaborate, co-operate. ·samenwerking, *n.* collaboration, co-operation.

·samenwonen, **woon samen,** *v.i.s.* to live together; to cohabit.

·samenzijn, no pl., *n.n.* being together; gathering.

·samenzweren, **zweer samen,** *v.i.s.,* *str.* to plot. ·samenzwering, *n.* plot, conspiracy.

·sanctie, -s, *n.* sanction.

san·daal, -dalen, *n.* sandal.

·sandelhout, *n.n.* sandal-wood.

·sani·tair, *a.* sanitary.

·santekraam, no pl., *n.* de hele ~, the whole caboodle.

sap, -ppen, *n.n.* sap, juice. ·saploos, -loze, *a.* sapless.

sapper·loot, *int.* See **zakkerloot.**

·sappig, *a.,* ·saprijk, *a.* sappy, juicy; luscious.

sar·dijn, *n.* sardine.

·sarren, **sar,** *v.t.* to bait, tease. ·sarrig, *a.* teasing.

sas, -ssen, *n.* lock(-chamber). *in zijn ~ zijn,* to be in high spirits.

·sater, -s, *n.* satyr.

sa·tijn, *n.n.* satin. sa·tijnen, *a.* (of) satin.

sau·cijzebroodje, -s, *n.n.* sausage roll.

saus, *n.* sauce, gravy. ·sausen, *v.t.* to sauce. ·sauskom, -mmen, *n.* sauceboat.

savoye·kool, -kolen, *n.* savoy (cabbage).

·sawah, -s, *n.* rice field, paddy field.

scapu·lier, -s, *n.n.* scapulary.

·scène, -s, *n.* scene.

·scepticus, -ci, *n.* sceptic. ·sceptisch, *a.* sceptical. ~ *staan tegenover iets,* to be sceptical about something.

schaaf, schaven, *n.* plane; shredder. ·schaafbank, *n.* carpenter's bench. ·schaafbeitel, -s, *n.* ·schaafmes, -ssen, *n.n.* plane-iron. ·schaafsel, no pl., *n.n.* shavings.

schaak, no pl., *n.n.* chess. ~ *spelen,* to play chess. ¶*int.* check! ~ *zetten,* to checkmate; ~ *staan,* to be in check. ·schaakbord, *n.n.* chessboard. ·schaakfiguur, -guren, *n.* chessman, piece. ·schaakmat, *a.* checkmate, stalemate. ~ *zetten,* to mate, checkmate. ·schaakpartij, *n.* game of chess. ·schaakspel, -llen, *n.n.* (game of) chess; set of chessboard and chessmen. ·schaakspeler, -s, *n.* chess player.

schaal, schalen, *n.* dish, bowl; (collecting) plate; shell (*of egg, shellfish, beetle*); (pair of) scales; scale (*tonal*); scale (*of balance*); scale, proportion. *de ~ doen overslaan,* to tip the balance; *gewicht in de ~ leggen,* to be of great importance; *op ~,* to scale; *op grote ~,* large-scale. ·schaaldier, *n.n.* crustacean. ~en, shellfish. ·schaalverdeling, *n.* graduation; graduated scale.

·schaamachtig, *a.* bashful. ·schaambeen, -deren, *n.n.* os pubis. ·schaamdelen, pl. only, *n.n.* genitals. ·schaamrood, no pl., *n.n.* (*stilted*) blush. *iemand het ~ op de kaken jagen,* to bring a blush to a persons cheeks. ¶-rode, *a.* blushing. ·schaamte, no pl., *n.* shame. ·schaamtegevoel, -ens, *n.n.* sense *or* feeling of shame. ·schaamteloos, -loze, *a.* shameless, impudent. ·schaamteloosheid, no pl., *n.* shamelessness.

schaap, schapen, *n.n.* sheep. *onnozel ~,* silly goose; *als er één ~ over de dam is volgen er meer,* come one come all. ·schaapachtig, *a.* sheepish. ·schaapherder, -s, *n.* shepherd. ·schaapje, -s, *n.n.* (little) sheep. *zijn ~s op het droge hebben,* to have feathered one's nest. ·schaapskooi, *n.* sheep-fold. ·schaapskop, -ppen, *n.* sheep's-head; blockhead.

schaar, scharen, *n.* (pair of) scissors *or* shears; share (*of plough*); pincers, claws. *See also* **schare.** ·schaarbek, -kken, *n.* scissor-bill.

schaard, *n.* notch, chip; shard.

schaars, *a.* scarce, scanty. ·schaarsheid, no pl., *n.,* ·schaarste, *n.* scarcity, dearth, shortage.

schaats, *n.* skate. ·schaatsenrijden, *r.i.s.,* *str.* to skate. ·schaatsenrijder, -s, *n.* skater.

·schacheraar, -s, *n.* See **sjacheraar.** ·schacheren, *v.i.* See **sjacheren.**

schacht, *n.* shaft; quill; shank.

·schade, no pl., *n.* damage; harm, injury. *door ~ en schande wordt men wijs,* live and learn; *tot ~ van,* to the detriment of; *zonder ~ aan,* without detriment to. ·schadelijk, *a.* harmful. ·schadelijkheid, no pl., *n.* harmfulness. ·schadeloos, -loze, *a.* harmless. ~ *stellen,* to compensate, indemnify. ·schadeloosstelling, *n.* compensation, indemnification, reparation. ·schaden, **schaad,** *v.t.* to harm, injure. ·schadepost, *n.* loss (*financial*). ·schadevergoeding, *n.* compensation, damages.

·schaduw, *n.* shade; shadow. *ze kunnen niet in zijn ~ staan,* they cannot be compared to him. ·schaduwen, *v.t.* to shade. ·schaduwrijk, *a.* shady, shaded. ·schaduwzijde, -n, *n.* shady side.

·schaffen, **schaf,** *v.t.* to procure.

·schaften, *v.i.* to eat (*of workmen between hours of work*). ·schaftlokaal, -kalen, *n.n.* refreshment room (*popular*). ·schafttijd, *n.* (workers') meal-time.

·schakel, -s, n. link, shackle. ·schakelaar, -s, n. switch. ·schakelbord, n.n. switchboard. ·schakelen, v.t. to link; to switch, connect. ·schakeling, n. linking. ·schakelnet, -tten, n.n. trammel-net.

·schaken, schaak, v.i. to play at chess. ¶v.t. to carry off; to elope with (of man). ·schaker, -s, n. chess player; abductor. ·schaking, n. abduction; elopement.

scha·keren, -keer, v.t. to variegate. scha·kering, n. shade, gradation.

schalk, n. (funny) rogue. schalks, a. roguish. ·schalksheid, no pl., n. roguishness.

·schallen, schal, v.i. to sound, resound.

schalm, n. link, shackle.

schal·mei, n. shawm.

·schamel, a. humble, meagre.

·schamen, schaam, zich, v.r. to be ashamed. zich ~ over, to be ashamed of; zich dood ~, to die of shame.

schamp, n. graze. ·schampen, v.t. to graze (touch). ·schamper, a. scornful, sarcastic. ·schamperheid, -heden, n. sarcasm. ·schampschot, n.n. glancing shot.

schan·daal, -dalen, n.n. scandal. wat een ~, how awful! schan·dalig, a. scandalous. schandali·seren, -seer, v.t. to scandalize. ·schanddaad, -ddaden, n. outrage. ·schande, no pl., n. shame, disgrace. te ~ maken, to disgrace. ·schandelijk, a. shameful, disgraceful. ·schandelijkheid, -heden, n. infamy. ·schandmerk, n.n. stigma. ·schandpaal, -palen, n. pillory. ·schandvlek, -kken, n. stigma. schandvlekken, -vlek, v.t. to disgrace.

schans, n. earthwork, entrenchment. ·schansgraver, -s, n. sapper. ·schansloper, -s, n. great-coat.

·schapebout, n. leg of mutton. ·schapenfokker, -s, n. sheep-farmer. ·schapenwolkjes, pl. only, n. cirri; mackerel sky. ·schaper, -s, n. shepherd. ·schapevacht, n. fleece. ·schapevel, -llen, n.n. sheepskin. ·schapevlees, no pl., n.n. mutton.

·schappelijk, a. fair, tolerable.

schar, -rren, n. dab.

schare, -n, n. (stilted) host, multitude. ·scharen, schaar, v.t. to draw up. ¶zich ~, v.r. to range oneself.

·scharensliep, n., ·scharenslijper, -s, n. knife-grinder.

schar·laken, a. scarlet. ¶no pl., n.n. scarlet. schar·lakens, a., schar·lakenrood, -rode, a. scarlet.

schar·minkel, -s, n. skeleton. schar·minkelig, a. scraggy.

schar·nier, n.n. hinge.

·scharrelaar, -s, n. potterer; beginner. ·scharrelen, v.i. to potter; to grub; to flirt.

schat, -tten, n. treasure; wealth; dear, darling. ·schatbaar, -bare, a. taxable, ratable.

·schateren, v.i. ~ van 't lachen, to roar with laughter. ·schaterlach, no pl., n. burst of laughter, guffaw. ·schaterlachen, v.i. to roar with laughter.

·schatgraver, -s, n. treasure-hunter. ·schatkamer, -s, n. treasury (room). ·schatkist, n. exchequer, treasury. ·schatkistbiljet, -tten, n.n. treasury bill. schat·plichtig, a. tributary. ·schatrijk, a. wealthy. ·schattebout, n. darling. ·schatten, schat, v.t. to estimate, assess. ~ op, to value at; te hoog ~, to overestimate; iets naar waarde ~, to appreciate something. ·schatter, -s, n. valuer. ·schattig, a. sweet. ·schatting, n. estimate, valuation. naar ~, approximatel·, at a rough estimate.

·schaven, schaaf, v.t. to plane.

scha·vot, -tten, n.n. scaffold.

scha·vuit, n. rascal. scha·vuitenstreek, -streken, n. knavish trick.

·schede, -n, n. sheath; scabbard; vagina. in de ~ steken, to sheathe.

·schedel, -s, n. skull, cranium. ·schedelboor, -boren, n. trepan. ·schedelboring, n. trepanation.

scheef, -scheve, a. crooked; slanting, askew. een scheve verhouding, a false position; ~ trekken to warp. ·scheefhals, -zen, n. wryneck. ~

scheel, schele, a. cross-eyed, squinting. ¶adv. ~ zien, to squint. ·scheelzien, no pl., n.n. strabismus, squinting.

scheen, schenen, n. shin.

scheep, adv. ~ gaan, to go on board, embark. scheeps-, prefix. ship's-, ship-, naval. ·scheepsbehoeften, pl. only, n. ship's stores. ·scheepsbeschuit, n.n. hard tack. ·scheepsbouw, no pl., n. ship-building. scheepsbouw·kundig, a. ship-building. ·scheepsbouwmeester, -s, n. ship-builder. ·scheepsbouwwerf, -ven, n. ship-yard. ·scheepsgelegenheid, -heden, n. shipping opportunity. per ~, by ship. ·scheepsgezel, -llen, n. shipmate. ·scheepst·elling, n. slipway. ·scheepsjongen, -s, n. cabin boy. ·scheepsjournaal, -nalen, n.n. log (-book). ·scheepsmakelaar, -s, n. shipbroker. ·scheepsrecht, no pl., n.n. maritime law. ·scheepsroeper, -s, n. mega phone. ·scheepsruim, n.n. hold (of ship). ·scheepsruimte, no pl., n. tonnage, shipping. ·scheepstijdingen, pl. only, n. shipping intelligence. scheeps·timmerwerf, -ven, n. ship-yard. ·scheepsvolk, no pl., n.n. sailors. ·scheepswant, no pl., n.n. rigging. ·scheepvaart, no pl., n. navigation. ·scheepvaartmaatschappij, n. shipping company.

·scheerbekken, -s, n.n. shaving basin or bowl. ·scheerkwast, n. shaving brush. ·scheerling, n. hemlock. ·scheermes, -ssen, n.n. razor. ·scheertijd, n. shearing time. ·scheerwinkel, -s, n. barber's shop. ·scheerzeep, no pl., n. shaving soap.

scheg, -ggen, n. cutwater.

·scheidbaar, -bare, a. separable. ·scheiden,

_v.t._ to separate, divide; to part; to get divorced. ¶_v.i._ to part. ~ _van_, to divorce or to part from. ¶_zich_ ~, _v.r._ to part. ·scheiding, _n._ separation, division, parting; divorce. ·scheidsgerecht, _n.n._ court of arbitration. ·scheidsmuur, -muren, _n._ partition wall. ·scheidsrechter, -s, _n._ arbiter, arbitrator; referee, umpire. ·scheikunde, no pl., _n._ chemistry. ·scheikundig, _a._ chemical. scheikundige, -n, _n._ chemist (_scientific_).

schel, -lle, _a._ shrill, piercing. ¶-llen, _n._ bell; scales (_Biblical_).

·Schelde, _N._ Scheldt.

·schelden, _v.i._, _str._ to use abusive language call names. ~ _op_, to abuse, inveigh against. ·scheldnaam, -namen, _n._ nickname (_abusive_). ·scheldpartij, _n._ slanging match. ·scheldwoord, _n.n._ abusive word.

·schelen, scheelt, _v.imp._ to differ. _het kan me niet_ ~, it doesn't matter to me; _het scheelt niet veel_, it doesn't make a great difference; _wat scheelt eraan?_, what is the matter?; _het scheelt hem in het hoofd_, he is not all there.

schelf, -ven, _n._ stack, rick.

·schelheid, no pl., _n._ shrillness.

·schelkruid, no pl., _n.n._ greater celandine.

·schellak, no pl., _n._ shellac.

·schellen, schel, _v.i._ to ring (the bell).

·schellinkje, -s, _n.n._ gallery, gods.

schelm, _n._ rascal, rogue. ·schelmachtig, _a._ roguish (_unfavourable_). schelmerij, _n._ roguery. schelms, _a._ roguish (_favourable_).

schelp, _n._ shell; scallop. ·schelpdier, _n.n._ shell-fish.

·schelvis, -ssen, _n._ haddock.

·schema, -'s, _n.n._ scheme, outline.

·schemer, no pl., _n._ dusk, twilight. ·schemerachtig, _a._ dim. ·schemeravond, _n._ twilight. ·schemerdonker, no pl., _n.n._ twilight. ·schemeren, _v.i._ to dawn; to grow dark; to sit in the twilight. _het schemert mij voor de ogen_, my head is beginning to reel ·schemering, _n._ twilight, dusk. ·schemerlamp, _n._ reading-lamp. ·schemeruurtje, -s, _n.n._ hour of twilight.

·schenden, _v.t._, _str._ to damage, disfigure; to violate; to transgress. ·schender, -s, _n._ violator. ·schending, _n._ violation, transgression.

·schenkblad, _n.n._ tray.

·schenkel, -s, _n._ femur. ·schenkelvlees, no pl., _n.n._ shin of beef, _etc._

·schenken, _v.t._, _str._ to pour; to give, present. _het leven_ ~ _aan_, to give birth to; _vergiffenis_ ~, to pardon; _vertrouwen_ ~, to show confidence. ·schenking, _n._ donation.

·schennis, no pl., _n._ violation.

schep, -ppen, _n._ scoop; spoonful. ·schepel, -s, _n._ bushel.

·schepeling, _n._ member of crew.

·schepen, _n._ alderman. ¶·scheep, _v.t._ to ship.

·schepnet, -tten, _n.n._ landing net. ·scheppen, schep, _v.t._ to ladle, scoop; to create. _adem_ ~, to draw breath; _moed_ ~, to take courage; _vreugde_ ~ _in_, to find pleasure in. ·scheppend, _a._ creative. ·schepper, -s, _n._ creator; scoop. ·schepping, _n._ creation. ·scheprad, -eren, _n.n._ paddle-wheel. ·schepsel, -s, _n.n._ creature.

·schepter, -s, _n._ sceptre. _de_ ~ _zwaaien_, to wield the sceptre.

·schepvat, _n.n._ bailer.

·scheren, scheer, _v.t._ to shave; to shear. _langs het water_ ~, to skim the water. ¶_zich_ ~, _v.r._ to shave.

scherf, -ven, _n._ sherd; splinter, fragment; shrapnel.

·schering, _n._ warp; shearing. ~ _en inslag_, warp and woof; _dat is_ ~ _en inslag_, it is an everyday occurrence.

scherm, _n.n._ screen; curtain (_stage_). _achter de_ ~_en_, behind the scenes. ·schermbloemig, _a._ umbelliferous. ·schermdegen, -s, _n._ foil. ·schermen, _v.i._ to fence; to flourish. ·schermer, -s, _n._ fencer. ·schermles, -ssen, _n._ fencing lesson. ·schermutselen, _v.i._ to skirmish. ·schermutseling, _n._ skirmish.

scherp, _a._ sharp; keen, clear-cut; acute; caustic. ¶no pl., _n.n._ edge. _met_ ~ _schieten_, to fire ball cartridges; _op_ ~, rough-shod. ·scherpen, _v.t._ to sharpen, whet. ·scherpheid, no pl., _n._ sharpness, keenness. ·scherprechter, -s, _n._ executioner. ·scherpschutter, -s, _n._ sharp-shooter. ·scherpte, no pl., _n._ sharpness; edge. ·scherpziend, _a._ sharpsighted, perspicacious. ·scherpzinnig, _a._ acute. scherpzinnigheid, no pl., _n._ acuteness, discernment.

scherts, no pl., _n._ jest, banter. ·schertsen, _v.i._ to jest, banter. ·schertsenderwijze, _adv._ jokingly.

·schervengerecht, _n.n._ ostracism.

schets, _n._ sketch; outline. ·schetsen, _v.t._ to sketch.

·schetteren, _v.i._ to blare.

scheur, _n._ tear, rent. ·scheurbuik, no pl., _n._ scurvy. ·scheuren, _v.t._ to tear (up), rend; to plough (up) (_grassland_). ¶_v.i._ to tear. ·scheuring, _n._ split, schism; ploughing up (_of grassland_). ·scheurkalender, -s, _n._ tear-off calendar. ·scheurmaker, -s, _n._ schismatic. ·scheurmand, _n._ waste-paper-basket. ·scheurpapier, no pl., _n._ waste paper.

scheut, _n._ shoot, sprig; dash (_of liquid_). ·scheutig, _a._ lavish.

schicht, _n._ dart; flash (_of lightning_). ·schichtig, _a._ shy, skittish (_of horse_). ~ _worden voor_, to shy at (_of horse_).

·schielijk, _a._ swift. ·schielijkheid, no pl., _n._ swiftness.

schier, _adv._ almost. ·schiereiland, _n.n._ peninsula.

·schietbaan, -banen, _n._ shooting-range,

rifle-range. **schieten**, *v.i.*, *str.* to shoot, fire. *laten* ~, to let go of; ~ *op*, to fire at; *in z'n kleren* ~, to hurry into one's clothes; *voorover* ~, to pitch forward. ¶*v.t.* to shoot. *geld* ~, to lend money; *wortel* ~, to strike root; *het schiet me door het hoofd*, it occurs to me; *iemand dadelijk* ~, to size a person up at once. **schietgat**, *n.n.* embrasure, loophole. **schietgebed**, *n.n.* ejaculatory prayer. **schietkatoen**, no pl., *n.n.* gun-cotton. **schietmasker**, -s, *n.n.* humane killer. **schietschijf**, -ven, *n.* target. **schietspoel**, *n.* shuttle. **schiettent**, *n.* shooting-gallery. **schietvoorraad**, no pl., *n.* (store of) ammunition. **schietwond** *n.* shot-wound.

schiften, *v.t.* to sort, sift; to curdle. **schifting**, *n.* sorting; curdling.

schijf, -ven, *n.* disc; slice. **schijfschieten**, no pl., *n.n.* target practice.

schijn, no pl., *n.* shine; appearance, semblance. *het heeft de* ~ *alsof*, it looks as if; *naar allen* ~, to all appearances; *onder de* ~ *van*, under the show of. **schijnaanval**, -llen, *n.* feint (*attack*). **schijnbaar**, -bare, *a.* seeming, apparent. **schijnbeeld**, *n.n.* illusion. **schijnbeweging**, *n.* feint (*military movement*). **schijndode**, -n, *n.* person apparently dead. **schijndood**, no pl., *n.* apparent death. ¶-dode, *a.* apparently dead. **schijnen**, *v.i.*, *str.* to shine; to seem, appear. *het schijnt dat*, it seems that *or* it would seem that; *naar het schijnt*, it appears. **schijngeleerde**, -n, *n.* pseudo-scholar. **schijngeleerdheid**, no pl., *n.* pseudo-learning. **schijngestalte**, -n, *n.* phase (*of moon*). **schijngevecht**, *n.n.* sham fight. **schijnheilig**, *a.* hypocritical. **schijnheilige**, -n, *n.* hypocrite. **schijnheiligheid**, no pl., *n.* hypocrisy. **schijnsel**, -s, *n.n.* glimmer, glow. **schijntje**, no pl., *n.n. geen* ~, not the least little bit. **schijnvroom**, -vrome, *a.* sanctimonious. **schijnwerper**, -s, *n.n.* dazzle lamp, flood-light.

schik, no pl., *n.* ~ *hebben*, to have fun; *in z'n* ~ *zijn*, to be pleased. **schikkelijk**, *a.* accommodating. **schikken**, **schik**, *v.t.* to arrange, order. ¶*v.imp.* to suit. *als het U schikt*, when it is convenient to you. ¶*zich* ~, *v.r.* to come right. *zich* ~ *in*, to resign oneself to; *zich* ~ *naar*, to conform to; *zich* ~ *om*, to arrange oneself round. **schikking**, *n.* arrangement. *een* ~ *treffen*, to come to an arrangement.

schil, -llen, *n.* rind, peel, skin.

schild, *n.n.* shield, scutcheon; coat of arms; wing-case. *iets in het* ~ *voeren*, to be up to mischief. **schilder**, -s, *n.* painter. **schilderachtig**, *a.* picturesque. **schilderen**, *v.t.* to paint. ¶*v.i.* to stand sentry; to walk up and down. **schilderhuisje**, -s, *n.n.* sentry box. **schilderij**, *n.* or *n.n.* painting, picture. **schildering**, *n.* portrayal.

schilderkunst, no pl., *n.* art of painting. **schilderkwast**, *n.* paint-brush. **schilderstok**, -kken, *n.* mahlstick. **schildersverdriet**, no pl., *n.n.* saxifrage. **schilderwerk**, no pl., *n.n.* painting. **schilderwinkel**, -s, *n.* (house-)painter's workshop. **schildklier**, *n.* thyroid gland. **schildknaap**, -knapen, *n.* squire, page. **schildkrab**, -bben, *n.* hermit crab. **schildluis**, *n.* scale insect. **schildpad**, -dden, *n.* tortoise; turtle. **schildpadden**, *a.* tortoise-shell. **schildpadsoep**, no pl., *n.* turtle soup. **schildwacht**, *n.* sentry.

schilfer, -s, *n.* flake, scale. **schilferen**, *v.i.* to flake, peel off.

schillen, schil, *v.t.* to peel, pare. **schilmesje**, -s, *n.n.* paring-knife.

schim, -mmen, *n.* shade, shadow, spectre; silhouette. **schimachtig**, *a.* shadowy.

schimmel, -s, *n.* mould, mildew; dapple-gray (horse). **schimmelachtig**, *a.* mouldy. **schimmelen**, *v.i.* to grow mouldy. **schimmelig**, *a.* mouldy. **schimmelplant**, *n.* fungus.

schimmenrijk, no pl., *n.n.* spirit world. **schimmenspel**, *n.n.* shadow-play.

schimp, *n.* taunt(s), jeer. **schimpdicht**, *n.n.* satire. **schimpen**, *v.i.* to scoff. ~ *op*, to scoff at. **schimper**, -s, *n.* scoffer. **schimperij**, *n.* scoffing. **schimpnaam**, -namen, *n.* (abusive) nickname. **schimpscheut**, *n.* gibe, jeer. **schimpwoord**, *n.n.* abusive word.

schip, schepen, *n.n.* ship, vessel; nave (*of church*). *schoon* ~ *maken*, to make a clean sweep. **schipbreuk**, *n.* shipwreck. ~ *lijden*, to be shipwrecked, be cast away *or* to miscarry. **schipbreukeling**, *n.* shipwrecked person, castaway. **schipbrug**, -ggen, *n.* floating-bridge. **schipper**, -s, *n.* master (*of sailing ship*); bargee. **schipperaar**, -s, *n.* compromiser (*habitual*). **schipperen**, *v.t.* to manage; to compromise. **schipperij**, no pl., *n.* inland navigation. **schippershond**, *n.* watch-dog (*on barge*). **schippersknecht**, *n.* barge-hand.

schisma, -'s, *n.n.* schism.

schitteren, *v.i.* to glitter, shine, sparkle. **schitterend**, *a.* splendid, glittering.

schmink, no pl., *n.n.* make-up. **schminken**, *v.t.* to make up. ¶*zich* ~, *v.r.* to make up.

schobbejak, -kken, *n.* scoundrel.

schoeien, *v.i.* to shoe. **schoeisel**, no pl., *n.n.* footwear.

schoelje, -s, *n.* low scoundrel.

schoen, *n.* shoe. *de stoute schoenen aantrekken*, to pluck up courage; *wie de* ~ *past, trek hem aan*, let whom the cap fits wear it; *met loden schoenen*, with leaden feet.

schoener, -s, *n.* schooner.

schoenlapper, -s, *n.* cobbler. **schoenmaker**, -s, *n.* shoemaker. **schoenpoetser**, -s, *n.* boot-black. **schoensmeer**, no pl., *n.* boot-polish.

·schoffel, -s, n. hoe.
schoft, n. rascal, hooligan. ~en, withers.
·schofterig, a. rude, ill-mannered. ·schoftje, -s, n.n. street arab.
schok, -kken, n. shock, jerk. ·schokbreker, -s, n. bumper. ·schokbuis, -zen, n. percussion fuse. ·schokken, schok, v.t. to shake, jerk; to give a shock to; to shatter (fig.). ·schokker, -s, n. (type of) fishing-boat. ·schokschouderen, v.i. to shrug one's shoulders.
schol, -llen, n. plaice; floe (of ice). ·scholekster, -s, n. oyster-catcher.
·scholen, school, v.i. to flock together; to shoal. scho·lier, n. pupil, scholar.
·schollevaar, -s, n. cormorant.
·schommel, -s, n. swing. ·schommelen, v.i. to swing; to rock, roll. ·schommeling, n. fluctuation. ·schommelstoel, n. rocking-chair.
·schone, -n, n. beauty (woman).
schoof, schoven, n. sheaf.
·schooien, v.i. to beg; to cadge. ·schooier, -s, n. beggar, tramp; cadger.
school, scholen, n. school. op ~, at school; van ~ afgaan, to leave school. ·schoolbank, n. form, desk. ·schoolblijven, v.i.s., str. to stay in. ¶no pl., n.n. detention. ·schoolgebruik, no pl., n.n. voor ~, for use in school(s). ·schooljaar, -jaren, n.n. scholastic year. ·schooljeugd, no pl., n. schoolchildren. ·schooljuffrouw, n. schoolmistress. ·schoolmeester, -s, n. schoolmaster. schools, a. scholastic. ·schooltas, -ssen, n. satchel. ·schooltijd, n. school hours. ·schooltje, -s, n.n. little school. ~ spelen, to play school. ·schoolvos, -ssen, n. pedant.
schoon, schone, a. clean; beautiful. ¶adv. clean(ly); beautifully. ¶c. though. ·schoonbroe(de)r, -s, n. brother-in-law. ·schoondochter, -s, n. daughter-in-law. ·schoonheid, -heden, n. beauty. ·schoonheidsleer, no pl., n. æsthetics. ·schoonheidszin, no pl., n. æsthetic sense. ·schoonhouden, v.t.s., irr. to keep clean. ·schoonklinkend, a. melodious, fine-sounding. ·schoonmaak, no pl., n. cleaning, clean-up. ·schoonmaakster, -s, n. charwoman, cleaner. ·schoonmoeder, -s, n. mother-in-law. ·schoonouders, pl. only, n. parents-in-law. ·schoontjes, adv. neatly, nicely. ·schoonvader, -s, n. father-in-law. ·schoonvegen, veeg schoon, v.t.s. to sweep clean. ·schoonzoon, -s, n. son-in-law. ·schoonzuster, -s, n. sister-in-law.
schoor, schoren, ·n. prop, buttress. ·schoorsteen, -stenen, n. chimney; funnel (of steamship). ·schoorsteengek, -kken, n. cowl (chimney). ·schoorsteenmantel, -s, n. mantelpiece. ·schoorsteenveger, -s, n. chimney-sweep.
·schoorvoeten, v.i. to hesitate. ·schoorvoetend, a. reluctant.

schoot, schoten, n. lap; (fig.) womb, bosom, fold; shoot, sprig; sheet (ship's rope); bolt (of lock). in de ~ der aarde, in the bowels of the earth. ·schoothondje, -s, n.n. lapdog. ·schootsvel, -llen, n.n. (leather) apron. ·schootsveld, n.n. field of fire. ·schootsverheid, no pl., n. range of fire. ·schootvrij, a. See schotvrij.
schop, -ppen, n. spade, shovel, scoop; kick. ·schoppen, schop, v.t. to kick. ¶pl. only, n. spades (cards). schoppen·aas, -azen, n.n. ace of spades. ·schopstoel, n. op de ~ zitten, to be ready to go at any moment.
schor, -rre, a. hoarse. ¶-rren, n. salting(s); mud flat.
·schorem, no pl., n.n. populace.
·schoren, schoor, v.t. to shore up.
·schorheid, no pl., n. hoarseness.
schorpi·oen, n. scorpion.
·schorrimorrie, no pl., n.n. populace.
schors, n. bark, rind. ·schorsen, v.t. to suspend (from membership); to adjourn (meeting). schorse·neel, -nelen, n., schorse·neer, -neren, n. scorzonera, salsify. ·schorsing, n. suspension; adjournment.
schort, n. apron, pinafore. ·schorten, v.t. to suspend (payment). ¶v.imp. wat schort er aan?, what is the matter?
schot, n.n. shot, report; partition (wooden); bulkhead; movement. een ~ doen, to fire a shot; er vielen schoten, shots rang out; zich buiten ~ houden, to keep out of harm's way; onder ~, within range; er zit geen ~ in, things won't move.
Schot, N. Scot, Scotsman.
·schotel, -s, n. dish. ·schoteldoek, n. dishcloth. ·schoteltje, -s, n.n. saucer.
schots, n. (ice-)floe. ¶adv. rudely. ~ en scheef, higgledy-piggledy, topsy-turvy.
Schots, a. Scottish.
·schotschrift, n.n. lampoon.
·schotvaars, -zen, n. heifer.
·schotvrij, a. bomb-proof; scot-free.
·schouder, -s, n. shoulder. de ~s ophalen, to shrug one's shoulders; ~ aan ~, shoulder to shoulder; iemand over de ~ aanzien, to give a person the cold shoulder. ·schouderblad, n.n. shoulder-blade.
schout, n. sheriff, bailiff. schout-bij-·nacht, n. rear-admiral.
schouw, n. chimney; inspection, survey. ·schouwburg, n. theatre. ·schouwen, v.t. to survey. een lijk ~, to hold an inquest, perform a post-mortem. ·schouwspel, n.n. spectacle.
·schoven, schoof, v.t. to sheave.
schraag, schragen, n. trestle. ·schraagbeeld, n.n. caryatid. ·schraagpijler, -s, n. buttress.
schraal, schrale, a. meagre, scanty; lean, thin; poor (of soil). ·schraalhans, n. miser. ~ is keukenmeester, there is not much to eat. ·schraalheid, no pl., n. poverty, thinness.
·schraapachtig, a. miserly. ·schraapijzer, -s,

n.n., **schraapmes, -ssen**, *n.n.* scraper.
schraapsel, no pl., *n.n.* scrapings. **schraapzucht**, no pl., *n.* miserliness, avarice.
schraap·zuchtig, *a.* miserly.
schrab, -bben, *n.* scratch. **schrabben, schrab**,
v.t. to scratch; to scrape. **schrabber, -s**,
n. scraper.
schragen, schraag, *v.t.* to support, prop up.
schram, -mmen, *n.* scratch, graze. **schrammen, -schram**, *v.t.* to scratch, graze.
schrander, *a.* shrewd, smart. **schranderheid**,
no pl., *n.* cleverness, discernment.
schransen, *v.i.* to gorge, stuff (*favourable*).
schrap, -ppen, *n.* to scratch. *er een ~
doorhalen*, to strike out. ¶*adv. zich ~
zetten*, to dig one's feet in. **schrapen**,
schraap, *v.t.* to scrape. **schraper, -s**, *n.*
miser. **schraperig**, *a.* miserly. **schrappen**,
schrap, *v.t.* to scrape; to cross out. **schrap-
sel**, no pl., *n.n.* scrapings.
schrede, -n, *n.* step, pace. *met rasse ~n.*
with rapid strides.
schreef, schreven, *n.* line, stroke. *een ~je
voor hebben*, to be a favourite.
schreeuw, *n.* cry, shout, scream. **schreeuwen**,
v.i. to cry, shout; to squeal. **schreeuwend**,
a. crying; loud. **schreeuwerig**, *a.* loud,
blatant. **schreeuwlelijk**, *n.* bawler.
schreien, *v.i.* to cry, weep. *~ van vreugde*,
to weep for joy. **scheierig**, *a.* tearful.
schriel, *a.* meagre. **schrieltjes**, *adv.* meagrely.
schrift, no pl., *n.n.* (hand)writing. *op ~
brengen*, to put in writing. ¶*n.n.* writing-
book. ¶no pl., *n.* Scripture, Writ. **schriftelijk**, *a.* written, in writing. ¶*adv.* in
writing. ¶no pl., *n.n.* written part (of
examination). **schriftgeleerde, -n**, *n.*
scribe. **schrif·tuur**, no pl., *n.* scripture.
schrif·tuurlijk, *a.* scriptural.
schrijdelings, *adv.* astride. **schrijden**, *v.i.*,
str. to stride.
schrijfbehoeften, pl. only, *n.* writing
materials, stationery. **schrijfmachine, -s**,
n. typewriter. **schrijfster, -s**, *n.* (woman)
writer, authoress. **schrijftaal**, no pl., *n.*
written language. **schrijfteken, -s**, *n.n.*
character, symbol, letter. **schrijftrant**,
no pl., *n.* style of writing.
schrijlings, *adv.* See **schrijdelings**.
schrijn, *n.* chest, cabinet.
schrijnen, *v.t.* to graze (*skin*). **schrijnend**,
a. smarting.
schrijnwerk, no pl., *n.n.* joiner's work.
schrijnwerker, -s, *n.* cabinet-maker,
joiner.
schrijven, schrijf, *v.t.*, *str.* to write. ¶*v.i.*, *str.*
to write. *~ aan*, to write to; *~ op een
advertentie*, to answer an advertisement.
¶no pl., *n.n.* written communication,
letter. **schrijver, -s**, *n.* writer, author; clerk.
schrijve·rij, no pl., *n.* writing, scribbling.
schrik, no pl., *n.* fight, shock. *er de ~ in
brengen*, to put the fear of God into them;
met ~ vervullen, to strike terror into;

met ~ wakker worden, to wake with a
start. **schrikaanjagend**, *a.* terrifying.
schrikachtig, *a.* jumpy, nervous. **schrik-
barend**, *a.* terrific. **schrikbeeld**, *n.n.*
bogey. **schrikbewind**, *n.n.* terror.
schrikkeldag, *n.* intercalary day.
schrikkelijk, *a.* awful.
schrikkeljaar, -jaren, *n.n.* leap year.
schrikkelmaand, *n.* February.
schrikken, schrik, *v.i.*, *str.* to be frightened,
start. *doen ~*, to frighten. **schrik·wekkend**,
a. frightening.
schril, -lle, *a.* shrill.
schrobben, schrob, *v.t.* to scrub. **schrobber,
-s**, *n.* scrubbing-brush. **schrob·beren,
-beer**, *v.t.* to give a dressing-down.
schrobnet, -tten, *n.n.* trawl-net.
schroef, -ven, *n.* screw; vice; propeller.
~ zonder eind, worm-gear. **schroefas,
-ssen**, *n.* propeller-shaft. **schroefboor,
-boren**, *n.* auger. **schroefgang**, no pl., *n.*
thread of screw. **schroefsluiting**, *n.*
screw-top. **schroefvormig**, *a.* spiral.
schroeien, *v.t.* to scorch, singe.
schroevedraaier, -s, *n.* screw-driver. **schroeven, schroef**, *v.t.* to screw.
schrokken, schrok, *v.t. & v.i.* to bolt, eat
gluttonously. **schrokker, -s**, *n.* glutton.
schrokk(er)ig, *a.* gluttonous. **schrokkig-
heid**, no pl., *n.* gluttony.
schromelijk, *a.* terrible, awful. *zich ~
vergissen*, to be grossly mistaken.
schromen, schroom, *v.t.* to dread; to
hesitate.
schrompelen, *v.i.* to shrivel up.
schroom, no pl., *n.* diffidence; scruple.
schroom·vallig, *a.* diffident, timid.
schroot, no pl., *n.n.* grape-shot.
schub, -bben, *n.* scale. **schubben, schub**,
v.t. to scale (*fish*). **schubbig**, *a.* scaly.
schubdier, *n.n.* armadillo.
schuchter, *a.* bashful, timid. **schuchterheid**,
no pl., *n.* bashfulness, timidity.
schuddebollen, -bol, *v.i.* to be constantly
nodding. **schudden, schud**, *v.t.* to shake;
to shuffle (*cards*). ¶*v.i.* to shake. *~ van
't lachen*, to rock with laughter. **schudding**,
n. shaking.
schuier, -s, *n.* brush. **schuieren**, *v.t.* to
brush.
schuif, -ven, *n.* slide; sliding-lid. **schuifdeur**,
n. sliding-door. **schuifelen**, *v.i.* to shuffle
(*walk*). **schuifladder, -s**, *n.* extension-
ladder. **schuiftrompet, -tten**, *n.* trombone.
schuilen, *v.i.*, *str. & v.t.*, *str.* to shelter.
~ voor, to shelter from. **schuilevinkje**,
no pl., *n.n. ~ spelen*, to play hide and
seek. **schuilgaan, ga schuil**, *v.i.s.*, *irr.*
to hide. **schuilhoek**, *n.* hiding-place.
schuilhouden, zich, *v.r.s.*, *irr.* to lie low,
remain in hiding. **schuilnaam, -namen**,
n. pseudonym. **schuilplaats**, *n.* shelter;
hiding-place. *een ~ verlenen*, to shelter,
harbour.

schuim, no pl., *n.n.* foam, froth; scum; lather. ·**schuimachtig**, *a.* foamy, frothy. ·**schuimbekken**, -ben, *v.i.* to foam at the mouth. ·**schuimen**, *v.i.* to foam, froth; to sparkle (*wine*); to skim; to sponge. ·**schuimer**, -s, *n.* sponger; pirate. ·**schuimig**, *a.* foamy. ·**schuimpje**, -s, *n.n.* meringue. ·**schuimspaan**, -spanen, *n.* skimmer.

schuin, *a.* slanting, oblique; dirty (*joke*). ~ **houden**, to tilt. ·**schuinen**, *v.t.* to bevel, slant off. ·**schuinsmarcheerder**, -s, *n.* loose liver.

schuit, *n.* barge; boat (*derog.*). ·**schuitenhuis**, -zen, *n.n.* boat-house. ·**schuitje**, -s, *n.n.* little barge; basket (*of balloon*); pig (*of tin*). *wie in 't ~ zit moet varen*, there is no going back now; *in 't zelfde ~ zitten*, all to be in the same boat. ·**schuitjevaren**, no pl., *n.n.* boating.

·**schuiven**, schuif, *v.t.*, *str.* to push, shove; to slide. *de schuld op een ander ~*, to lay the blame on someone else; *opium ~*, to smoke opium.

schuld, *n.* debt; guilt; fault. *achterstallige ~*, arrears; ~ *hebben*, to be guilty or to owe money; *iemand de ~ geven van*, to blame someone for; *er de ~ van krijgen*, to be blamed for it. ·**schuldbekentenis**, -ssen, *n.* confession of guilt; promissory note. ·**schuldbrief**, -ven, *n.* debenture. ·**schuldeiser**, -s, *n.* creditor. ·**schuldeloos**, -loze, *a.* innocent, blameless. ·**schuldenaar**, -s *or* -naren, *n.* debtor. ·**schuldig**, *a.* guilty. ~ *zijn*, to be guilty or to owe; *het antwoord ~ blijven*, to make no answer; *zich ~ maken aan*, to be guilty of. ·**schuldige**, -n, *n.* culprit, offender. ·**schuldvordering**, *n.* claim.

schulp, *n.* shell. *in zijn ~ kruipen*, to draw in one's horns.

·**schunnig**, *a.* shabby, scurvy.

·**schuren**, schuur, *v.t.* to scour, scrub.

schurft, no pl., *n.* scabies, itch, mange. ·**schurftig**, *a.* mangy, scabby.

schurk, *n.* scoundrel. ·**schurkenstreek**, -streken, *n.* knavery, dirty trick.

·**schut**, -tten, *n.n.* partition; fence. ·**schutblad**, *n.n.* fly-leaf; bract. ·**schutdeur**, *n.* lockgate. ·**schutkolk**, *n.* lock-chamber. ·**schutsengel**, -s, *n.* guardian angel. ·**schutsheer**, -heren, *n.* patron. ·**schutsluis**, -zen, *n.* lock (*canal*). ·**schutsvrouw**, *n.* patroness. ·**schutten**, schut, *v.t.* to go through lock (*canal*).

·**schutter**, -s, *n.* marksman, shot; militiaman. ·**schutterig**, *a.* awkward, clumsy. **schutterij**, *n.* militia (*local*).

·**schutting**, *n.* hoarding.

schuur, schuren, *n.* barn.

·**schuurborstel**, -s, *n.* scrubbing-brush. ·**schuurgerei**, no pl., *n.n.* scouring-things. ·**schuurlinnen**, no pl., *n.n.*, ·**schuurpapier**, no pl., *n.n.* emery cloth, sandpaper.

schuw, *a.* shy, timorous. ·**schuwen**, *v.t.* to

shun. ·**schuwheid**, no pl., *n.* shyness. ·**schuwlelijk**, *a.* awfully ugly.

scru·pule, -s, *n.* scruple, qualm.

se·conde, -n, *n.* second (1/60 *minute*).

secre·taire, -s, *n.* writing-desk. **secreta·resse**, -n, *n.* secretary (*female*). **secreta·rie**, -rieën, *n.* town clerk's office. **secre·taris**, -ssen, *n.* secretary (*male*); town clerk.

·**sectie**, -s, *n.* section; dissection; autopsy.

secu·lair, *a.* secular. **seculari·seren**, -seer, *v.t.* to secularize.

se·cunde, -n, *n.* See **seconde**.

·**sedert**, *prep.* since. ~ *enige dagen*, for some days past; ~ 2 *jaar*, for the last 2 years. ¶*adv.* since. ¶*c.* since.

se·grijn, no pl., *n.n.* shagreen.

sein, *n.n.* signal. *een ~ geven*, to make a signal. ·**seinen**, *v.i.* to signal. ·**seiner**, -s, *n.* signaller. ·**seinfout**, *n.* transmission error. ·**seinpaal**, -palen, *n.* semaphore. ·**seintoestel**, -llen, *n.n.* signalling apparatus, transmitter.

sei·zoen, *n.n.* season.

·**sekse**, -n, *n.* sex. ·**sekte**, -n, *n.* sect.

se·kuur, -kure, *a.* accurate, precise.

·**selderie**, no pl., *n.*, ·**selderij**, no pl., *n.* celery.

se·naat, -naten, *n.* senate; students' union committee.

·**seneblad**, *n.n.*, ·**seneplant**, *n.* senna.

sen·satie, -s, *n.* sensation. ~ *maken*, to create a stir. **sen·satiestuk**, -kken, *n.n.* thriller (*play*).

se·quester, -s, *n.* sequestrator; sequestration. **seques·tratie**, -s, *n.* sequestration. **seques·treren**, -treer, *v.t.* to sequestrate.

sera·fijn, *n.* seraph.

ser·geant, *n.* sergeant. **sergeant·-vlieger**, -s, *n.* sergeant-pilot; flight-sergeant.

·**serie**, -s, *n.* series.

·**serienummer**, -s, *n.* serial number.

seri·eus, -ze, *a.* serious.

se·ring, *n.* lilac. **se·ringeboom**, -bomen, *n.* lilac-tree.

ser·pent, *n.n.* shrew, viper (*fig.*). **serpen·tine**, -s, *n.* paper streamer.

·**serre**, -s, *n.* conservatory; enclosed verandah.

ser·veren, -veer, *v.t.* to serve. **ser·vet**, -tten, *n.* napkin. *tussen ~ en tafellaken*, betwixt and between.

·**Servië**, *n.N.* Serbia. ·**Servi·ër**, -s, *N.* Serbian. **ser·vies**, -zen, *n.n.* set (*of china*).

·**Servisch**, *a.* Serbian.

·**sesam**, no pl., *n.* sesame.

·**sessie**, -s, *n.* session.

sext, *n.* sixth (*interval*).

sfeer, sferen, *n.* sphere; domain, province. ·**sferisch**, *a.* spherical.

sfinx, *n.* sphinx.

Sicili·aans, *a.* Sicilian. **Si·cilië**, *n.N.* Sicily.

·**sidderaal**, -ralen, *n.* electric eel. ·**sidderen**, *v.i.* to shake, tremble. ·**siddering**, *n.* shudder, quiver.

·**side·raal**, -rale, *a.* siderial.

·siepelen, *v.i.* to trickle, ooze.

sier, no pl., *n.* cheer; ornament. ·sieraad, -raden, *n.n.* ornament. ·sierheester, -s, *n.* ornamental shrub. ·sierlijk, *a.* elegant, graceful.

si·gaar, -garen, *n.* cigar. si·garenkist, *n.* cigar-box. si·garenwinkel, -s, *n.* tobacconist's. siga·ret, -tten, *n.* cigarette.

sig·naal, -nalen, *n.n.* signal. signa·leren, -leer, *v.i.* to signal. zich ~, to distinguish oneself. signale·ment, *n.n.* personal description.

·sijpelen, *v.i.* to trickle, ooze.

sijs, -zen, *n.* siskin. *een rare* ~, a queer customer. ·sijsje, -s, *n.n.* siskin.

sik, -kken, *n.* goat; goat's beard; goatee.

·sikkel, -s, *n.* sickle, reaping-hook; sickle, crescent; shekel.

sikke·neurig, *a.* peevish.

·sikkepit, no pl., *n.* geen ~, not a jot.

·simpel, *a.* simple, plain. ¶*adv.* simply. ·simpelheid, no pl., *n.* simplicity. ·simpeltjes, *adv.* simply.

simu·lant, *n.* simulator, malingerer. simu·leren, -leer, *v.i.* to simulate.

·sinaasappel, -s *or* -en, *n.* orange.

sinds, *adv., prep., & c. See* sedert. sinds·dien, *adv.* since.

·singel, -s, *n.* girdle; girth; moat; rampart.

sin·jeur, -s, *n.* fellow.

sint, *a.* saint. ¶*n.* saint; Santa Claus.

·sintel, -s, *n.* cinder. ·sintelbaan, -banen, *n.* dirt-track.

Sinter·klaas, *N.* Santa Claus. Sinter·klaaspop, -ppen, *n.* gingerbread mannikin. Sint-·Janskruid, no pl., *n.n.* St. John's wort. Sint-·Joris, *N.* St. George. Sint-·Juttemis, *N.* met ~, at the Greek calends.

sip, *adv.* glum.

·Sire, no pl., *n.* Your Majesty.

si·rene, -n, *n.* siren.

si·roop, -ropen, *n.* syrup.

·sisklank, *n.* hissing sound. ·sissen, sis, *v.i.* to hiss; to sizzle. ·sisser, -s, *n.* squib. met een ~ aflopen, to fizzle out.

sits, *n.n.* chintz.

situ·atie, -s, *n.* situation.

Six·tijns, *a.* Sistine.

sjaal, -s, *n.* shawl.

·sjacheraar, -s, *n.* haggler, shady trader. ·sjacheren, *v.i.* to trade, bargain (*usu. unfavourable*).

sja·ko, -'s, *n.* shako.

sja·lot, -tten, *n.* shallot.

·sjamberloek, *n.* dressing-gown.

·sjampie, no pl., *n.* (*vulg.*) champagne.

sjees, sjezen, *n.* gig. ·sjezen, sjees, *v.i.* to plough (*exam.*).

sjerp, *n.* sash.

·sjoelbak, -kken, *n.* shovel-board.

·sjofel, *a.* shabby. ·sjofelheid, no pl., *n.* shabbiness. ·sjofeltjes, *adv.* shabbily.

·sjokken, sjok, *v.i.* to trudge.

·sjorren, sjor, *v.t.* to lash.

sjouw, no pl., *n.* (tough) job. aan de ~ gaan, to go on the spree. ·sjouwen, *v.i.* to carry, drag, lug; to toil. ·sjouwer, -s, *n.,* ·sjouwerman, -lui, *n.* casual labourer; dock-hand.

sla, no pl., *n.* salad.

Slaaf, Slaven, *N.* Slav.

slaaf, slaven, *n.* slave. slaafs, *a.* servile; slavish. ·slaafsheid, no pl., *n.* servility; slavishness.

slaag, no pl., *n.* een pak ~, a beating; ~s zijn, to have joined battle.

slaan, sla, *v.t., irr.* to beat, strike; to beat, defeat. een brug ~ over, to throw a bridge over; olie ~, to make oil; touw ~, to lay ropes. ¶*v.i., irr.* to beat; to sing, warble. aan het kruis ~, to nail to the cross; aan het muiten ~, to mutiny; zich er doorheen ~, to fight one's way through; om zich heen ~, to lay about one *or* to wrap round one.

slaap, slapen, *n.* temple (*head*). ¶no pl., *n.* sleep. ~ hebben, to be sleepy; de ~ niet kunnen vatten, to be unable to get to sleep; in ~ vallen, to fall asleep; in ~ zijn, to be asleep. ·slaapbeen, -deren, *n.n.* temporal bone. ·slaapbroek, *n.* pyjamatrousers. ·slaapdronken, *a.* overcome with sleep. ·slaapgelegenheid, -heden, *n.* sleeping accommodation. ·slaapgoed, no pl., *n.n.* night-garments. ·slaaphuis, -zen, *n.n.* doss-house. ·slaapje, -s, *n.n.* nap. ·slaapkamer, -s, *n.* bedroom. ·slaapkop, -ppen, *n.* sleepy fellow. ·slaapliedje, -s, *n.n.* lullaby. ·slaapmiddel, *n.n.* opiate, narcotic. ·slaapmuts, *n.* night-cap. ·slaapster, -s, *n.* sleeper (*female*). de Schone S~, the Sleeping Beauty. ·slaapwandelaar, *n.* sleepwalker, somnambulist. ·slaapwandelen, no pl., *n.n.* sleepwalking, somnambulism. slaap·wekkend, *a.* soporific. siaap·werend, *a.* sleepdispelling. ·slaapzaal, -zalen, *n.* dormitory. ·slaapziekte, no pl., *n.* sleepy sickness. ·slaapzucht, no pl., *n.* lethargy.

·slaatje, -s, *n.* salad. ergens een ~ uit slaan, to make a good profit out of something.

slab, -bben, *n.,* ·slabbetje, -s, *n.n.* bib.

sla·bakken, -bak, *v.i.* to laze. sla·bakker, -s, *n.* slacker.

·slaboontjes, pl. only, *n.n.* French beans.

·slachtbank, *n.* shambles. ter ~ leiden, to lead to the slaughter. ·slachtbeest, *n.n.* slaughter cattle. ·slachten, *v.t.* to kill, slaughter. ·slachter, -s, *n.* butcher. slachte·rij, *n.* butcher's shop; slaughterhouse. ·slachthamer, -s, *n.* pole-axe. ·slachthuis, -zen, *n.n.* slaughter-house, abattoir. ·slachting, *n.* slaughter. ·slachtmaand, *n.* November. ·slachtmasker, -s, *n.n.* humane killer. ·slachtoffer, -s, *n.n.* victim. ·slachtplaats, *n.* slaughter-house. ·slachtvee, no pl., *n.n.* cattle for slaughter.

sla·dood, no pl., *n.* very tall person.

slag, *n.* blow; beat, stroke; report, crash; note, call (*of birds*); turn; knack; battle. *een ~ doen*, to strike a blow; *geen ~ doen*, not to do a stroke (of work); *een ~ om de arm houden*, to keep something up one's sleeve; *ergens een ~ naar slaan*, to have a shot at something; *zijn ~ slaan*, to make one's coup *or* to see one's chance; *aan de ~ gaan*, to set to work; *aan de ~ komen*, to get a look in; *op ~ komen*, to get one's hand in; *zonder ~ of stoot*, without striking a blow. ¶no pl., *n.n.* type. ·**slagader, -s**, *n.* artery. ·**slagaderlijk**, *a.* arterial. ·**slagaderverkalking**, *n.* arteriosclerosis. ·**slagboom, -bomen**, *n.* barrier. ·**slagen, slaag**, *v.i.* to succeed; to pass (*exam.*). ·**slager, -s**, *n.* butcher. ·**slage·rij**, *n.* butcher's shop. ·**slaghamer, -s**, *n.* mallet. ·**slaghoedje, -s**, *n.n.* percussion-cap. ·**slagkwik**, no pl., *n.n.* fulminate of mercury. ·**slagorde, -n**, *n.* order of battle, battle-array. ·**slagpen, -nnen**, *n.* quill. ·**slagpin, -nnen**, *n.* firing-pin. ·**slagregen, -s**, *n.* downpour. ·**slagroom**, no pl., *n.* whipped cream. ·**slagschip, -schepen**, *n.n.* battleship. ·**slagtand**, *n.* fang; tusk. ·**slag·vaardig**, *a.* ready for battle. ·**slag·vaardigheid**, no pl., *n.* readiness, preparedness. ·**slagveld**, *n.n.* field of battle. ·**slagzee, -zeeën**, *n.* crashing wave. **slag·zij**, no pl., *n.* list. ·**slag ~ hebben**, to list. ·**slag·zwaard**, *n.n.* broadsword.

slak, -kken, *n.* snail; slug; slag, scoria. ·**slaken, slaak**, *v.t.* to heave (*sigh*); (*stilted*) break (*chains*).

·**slakkengang**, *n.* snail's pace. ·**slakkenmeel**, no pl., *n.n.* ground slag. ·**slakkensteker, -s**, *n.* (*fac.*) bayonet.

slam·pamper, -s, *n.* boozer.

slang, *n.* snake; tube, hosepipe. ·**slangachtig**, *a.* snaky. ·**slangenbezweerder, -s**, *n.* snake-charmer. ·**slangenkruid**, no pl., *n.* snake-weed. ·**slangenmens**, *n.* contortionist.

slank, *a.* slim, slender. *voor de ~e lijn*, in order to slim. ·**slankheid**, no pl., *n.* slimness.

·**slaolie, -liën**, *n.* salad oil.

slap, -ppe, *a.* slack, soft, limp; weak; spineless. *zich ~ lachen*, to be helpless with laughter. ·**slapeloos, -loze**, *a.* sleepless. **slape·loosheid**, no pl., *n.* sleeplessness. ·**slapen, slaap**, *v.i.*, *str.* to sleep; be asleep. *mijn voet slaapt*, I have pins and needles. ·**slaper, -s**, *n.* sleeper; second dyke. ·**slaperig**, *a.* sleepy, drowsy. ·**slaperigheid**, no pl., *n.* sleepiness. ·**slapheid**, no pl., *n.* limpness; spinelessness. ·**slapjes**, *adv.* poorly. ·**slapte**, no pl., *n.* slackness.

·**Slaven**, *pl. N.* Slavs.

·**slaven, slaaf**, *v.i.* to slave. ·**slavenarbeid**, no pl., *n.* slavery. ·**slavenhandel**, no pl., *n.* slave-trade. ·**slavenjuk**, no pl., *n.n.* yoke of bondage. ·**slavenschip, -schepen**, *n.n.*

slaver. **slaver·nij**, *n.* slavery, bondage. **sla·vin, -nnen**, *n.* slave (*female*). ·**Slavisch**, *a.* Slavonic, Slavic. **Sla·vonisch**, *a.* Slavonian.

slecht, *a.* bad; evil. *er ~ aan toe zijn*, to be in a bad state; *~er*, worse; *~st*, worst. ·**slechten**, *v.t.* to raze, level. ·**slechtheid**, -**heden**, *n.* badness. ·**slechting**, no pl., *n.* razing, levelling. **slechts**, *adv.* merely, only, but. ·**slechtweg**, *adv.* without ceremony.

·**slede, -n**, *n.*, **slee, sleeën**, *n.* sledge, sleigh. ·**sledevaart**, *n.* sleigh-ride.

·**sleedoorn, -s**, *n.* blackthorn, sloe.

sleep, slepen, *n.* train (*of garment*); string (*of barges*). ·**sleepboot, -boten**, *n.* tug. ·**sleepbootdienst**, *n.* towing service. ·**sleephelling**, *n.* slipway. ·**sleeploon, -lonen**, *n.n.* towage. ·**sleepnet, -tten**, *n.n.* dragnet. ·**sleeptouw**, *n.n.* hawser, tow-rope. *op ~ hebben*, to have in tow. ·**sleepvaart**, no pl., *n.* towing service.

·**sleet**, no pl., *n.* wear (and tear).

slemp, no pl., *n.* saffron-milk. ·**slempen**, *v.i.* to carouse. ·**slemper, -s**, *n.* carouser. ·**slenteraar, -s**, *n.* lounger. ·**slenteren**, *v.i.* to lounge.

·**slendang**, *n.* Malay shawl.

·**slepen, sleep**, *v.t.* to drag; to haul; to tow. ·**sleper, -s**, *n.* haulage contractor. ·**slepers·paard**, *n.n.* dray-horse. **slepers·wagen, -s**, *n.* dray.

·**slet, -tten**, *n.* slut.

·**sleuf, -ven**, *n.* slot, groove.

sleur, no pl., *n.* routine. ·**sleuren**, *v.t.* to drag.

·**sleutel, -s**, *n.* key; regulator; clef. *Franse ~*, monkey-wrench. ·**sleutelbeen, -deren**, *n.n.* collar bone. ·**sleutelbloem**, *n.* primula, primrose.

slib, no pl., *n.* or *n.n.* mud, slime, alluvium. ·**slibberachtig**, *a.* slippery. ·**slibberen**, *v.i.* to slither. ·**slibberig**, *a.* slippery.

slier, *n.* string, long row. ·**slieren**, *v.i.* to slide. **sliert**, *n. See* slier.

slijk, no pl., *n.n.* mud, mire. ·**slijkbord**, *n.n.* mudguard. ·**slijkerig**, *a.* muddy. ·**slijkgronden**, pl. only, *n.* mud flats. ·**slijknat, -tte**, *a.* soaking wet.

slijm, *n.n.* slime, mucus, phlegm. ·**slijmdiertje, -s**, *n.n.* amoeba. ·**slijmerig**, *a.* slimy. ·**slijmvis, -ssen**, *n.* shanny. ·**slijmvlies, -zen**, *n.n.* mucous membrane.

·**slijpen**, *v.t.*, *str.* to grind, sharpen; to cut *or* polish (*diamonds*). ·**slijper, -s**, *n.* grinder; cutter, polisher (*of diamonds*). ·**slijpe·rij**, *n.* grinding-shop. ·**slijpmolen, -s**, *n.* grinding-mill. ·**slijpplank**, *n.* knife-board. ·**slijppoeder**, no pl., *n.n.* knife-powder. ·**slijpsel, -s**, *n.n.* grindings. ·**slijpsteen, -stenen**, *n.* grindstone.

slij·tage, no pl., *n.* wear (and tear). ·**slijten**, *v.i.*, *str.* to wear (out). ¶*v.t.*, *str.* to wear out *or* down; to retail. ·**slijter, -s**, *n.*

retailer. **slijte·rij**, *n.* licensed shop, small pub.

slik, no pl., *n.n. See* **slijk**. ·**slikken, slik**, *v.t.* to swallow; to put up with.

slim, **-mme**, *a.* clever; artful. ·**slimheid**, no pl., *n.* cleverness. ·**slimmerd, -s**, *n.* clever one. ·**slimmigheid, -heden**, *n.* clever trick.

·**slinger**, **-s**, *n.* pendulum; swing, lurch; sling (*weapon*); cranking-handle; festoon. *een ~ om de arm houden*, to keep something up one's sleeve. ·**slingeraap, -rapen**, *n.* spider-monkey. ·**slingeren**, *v.i.* to swing, oscillate; to sway, lurch; to meander, wind; to lie about. ¶*v.t.* to fling, hurl. ·**slingering**, *n.* oscillation; lurch, roll. ·**slingerplant**, *n.* climber, trailer (*plant*). ·**slingerwijdte**, **-n**, *n.* amplitude (*of oscillation*).

·**slinken**, *v.i., str.* to shrink, dwindle. ·**slinking**, *n.* shrinkage; dwindling. **slinks**, *a.* cunning, underhand. ·**slinksheid, -heden**, *n.* cunning (trick).

slip, -ppen, *n.* flap; tail (*of coat*). ·**slipjas, -ssen**, *n.* tail-coat, tails. ·**slippedrager, -s**, *n.* pall-bearer. ·**slippen, slip**, *v.i.* to slip; to skid. ·**slippertje, -s**, *n.n. een ~ maken*, to slip away unnoticed.

·**slobber**, no pl., *n.* thick mud; pigwash. ·**slobberen**, *v.i.* to slobber. ·**slobberig**, *a.* dirty. ·**slobeend**, *n.* shoveller (*duck*). ·**slobkous**, *n.* gaiter; spat.

·**slodderachtig**, *a.* slovenly. ·**slodderen**, *v.i.* to flop. ·**sloddervos, -ssen**, *a.* slovenly person.

·**sloeber, -s**, *n.* low scoundrel.

sloep, *n.* sloop; long-boat.

·**sloerie, -s**, *n.* slut.

slof, **-ffen**, *n.* slipper. *het op z'n ~jes afkunnen*, to be able to do it easily. ·**sloffen, slof**, *v.i.* to shuffle.

slok, -kken, *n.* draught, gulp; swig. ·**slok·darm**, *n.* gullet. ·**slokken, slok**, *v.t. & v.i.* to swallow, guzzle. ·**slokker, -s**, *n.* guzzler.

slons, *n.* slut. ·**slonzig**, *a.* sluttish.

sloof, sloven, *n.* drudge.

sloom, slome, *a.* drowsy.

sloop, slopen, *n.* pillow-case, slip.

sloot, sloten, *n.* ditch, dyke. ·**slootje, -s**, *n.n.* small ditch. ·**slootjespringen**, no pl., *n.n.* leaping over ditches.

slop, -ppen, *n.* blind alley (*in slum*).

·**slopen, sloop**, *v.t.* to demolish, pull down. *een ~de ziekte*, a wasting disease. ·**sloper, -s**, *n.* housebreaker, ship-breaker. **slope·rij**, *n.* ship-breaking yard.

·**slordig**, *a.* careless, slipshod, untidy. *een ~e 100 gulden*, about a hundred guilders.

·**slorpen**, *v.i.* to drink noisily.

slot, *n.n.* lock (*on door, etc.*); castle; conclusion, end. *~ volgt*, to be concluded; *achter ~ en grendel*, under lock and key; *op ~ doen*, to lock; *per ~ van rekening*, all said and done; *ten slotte*, finally; *tot ~*, in conclusion. ·**slotakkoord**, *n.n.* final chord. ·**slotenmaker, -s**, *n.* locksmith. ·**slotkoers**, *n.* closing rate. ·**slotplein**, *n.n.* castle yard. ·**slotsom, -mmen**, *n.* (final) conclusion. ·**slotsteen, -stenen**, *n.* keystone. ·**slotvoogd**, *n.* castellan.

·**sloven, sloof**, *v.i.* to drudge, toil.

Slo·waak, -waken, *N.* Slovak. **Slo·waaks**, *a.* Slovak. **Slowa·kije**, *n.N.* Slovakia. **Slo·ween, -wenen**, *N.* Slovene.

·**sluier, -s**, *n.* veil. ·**sluieren**, *v.t.* to veil.

sluif, -ven, *n.* (*umbrella*) cover.

sluik, *a.* lanky, sleek. ·**sluikhandel**, no pl., *n.* smuggling. ·**sluikhandelaar, -s**, *n.* smuggler. **sluik·harig**, *a.* sleek-haired.

·**sluimer**, no pl., *n.* slumber. ·**sluimeraar, -s**, *n.* slumberer. ·**sluimering**, *n.* slumber.

·**sluipen**, *v.i., str.* to creep stealthily. ·**sluiper, -s**, *n.* one who creeps stealthily. ·**sluipmoord**, *n.* assassination. ·**sluipmoordenaar, -s,** *n.* assassin. **sluipwesp**, *n.* ichneumon fly.

sluis, -zen, *n.* lock, sluice; flood-gates. ·**sluisdeur**, *n.* lock-gate. ·**sluisgeld**, *n.n.* lock-dues. ·**sluiskolk**, *n.* lock-chamber. ·**sluiswachter, -s**, *n.* lock-keeper.

·**sluitboom, -bomen**, *n.* barrier, swing-gate; boom. ·**sluiten**, *v.t., str.* to close, shut; to shut up; to lock; to conclude, contract. *de rekening sluit met een verlies van . . .*, the account shows a loss of . . . ·**sluitend**, *a.* close-fitting; balanced. ·**sluiter, -s**, *n.* shutter. ·**sluiting**, *n.* fastening; method of closing. ·**sluitingsuur, -suren**, *n.n.* closing-time. ·**sluitrede, -nen**, *n.* syllogism. ·**sluitring**, *n.* washer. ·**sluitsteen, -stenen**, *n.* keystone. ·**sluitstuk**, *n.n.* breech-block. ·**sluitzegel, -s**, *n.n.* adhesive stamp (*not for postage*).

·**slungel, -s**, *n.* lout. ·**slungelachtig**, *a.* loutish. ·**slungelen**, *v.i.* to hang about. ·**slungelig**, *a.* loutish.

slurf, -ven, *n.* trunk (*of elephant*).

·**slurpen**, *v.i.* to drink noisily.

sluw, *a.* shy, cunning, wily. ·**sluwheid, -heden**, *n.*, ·**sluwigheid, -heden**, *n.* slyness, cunning.

smaad, no pl., *n.* scorn, opprobrium, shame. ·**smaadschrift**, *n.n.* libel.

smaak, smaken, *n.* taste; relish, flavour. *~ krijgen in*, to get a taste for; *in de ~ vallen bij*, to become a favourite with; *~ hebben in*, to have a liking for; *er is een ~je aan*, there is something wrong with it. ·**smaakvol, -lle**, *a.* tasteful.

·**smaaldicht**, *n.n.*, ·**smaalschrift**, *n.n.* lampoon.

·**smachten**, *v.i.* to languish. *~ van*, to languish for (*thirst*); *~ naar*, to yearn for. ·**smachtend**, *a.* languishing, langorous.

·**smadelijk**, *a.* scornful, humiliating. ·**smadelijkheid, -heden**, *n.* ignominy. ·**smaden, smaad**, *v.t.* to scorn, revile, malign.

smak, -kken, *n.* smack; crash.

·**smakelijk**, *a.* tasteful, tasty. ¶*adv.* tastefully; heartily. *eet ~*, enjoy your meal.

·smakeloos, -loze, *a.* tasteless; insipid. ·smakeloosheid, no pl., *n.* tastelessness. ·smaken, smaak, *v.t.* to taste. *smaakt het?*, do you like it?; ~ *naar*, to taste of.

·smakken, smak, *v.i.* to smack. *met de lippen* ~, to smack one's lips. ¶*v.t.* to dash, fling.

smal, -lle, *a.* narrow. ·smaldeel, -delen, *n.n.* squadron (*naval*). ·smalen, smaal, *v.i.* to rail. ~ *op*, to rail at. ·smalend, *a.* scornful. ·smalheid, no pl., *n.* narrowness. ·smalspoor, no pl., *n.n.* narrow-gauge railway. ·smalte, no pl., *n.* narrowness.

sma·ragd, *n.* emerald. sma·ragden, *a.* (of) emerald.

smart, *n.* grief, sorrow, pain. ·smartelijk, *a.* painful. ·smarteloos, -loze, *a.* painless. ·smarten, *v.i.* to grieve, pain.

·smeden, smeed, *v.t.* to forge; to weld; to hatch (*plot*). smede·rij, *n.* forge. ·smeedbaar, -bare, *a.* malleable. ·smeedijzer, no pl., *n.n.* wrought iron. ·smeedwerk, no pl., *n.n.* wrought ironwork.

·smeekbede, -n, *n.* prayer, supplication. ·smeekschrift, *n.n.* petition.

smeer, no pl., *n.n.* grease, fat. ~ *geven*, to thrash. ¶smeren, *n.* smear. ·smeerboel, no pl., *n.* mess. ·smeerbus, -ssen, *n.* grease-box. ·smeerder, -s, *n.* greaser. ·smeerlap, -ppen, *n.* dirty person. smeer·lappe·rij, no pl., *n.* filth. ·smeerpoes, *n.* dirty person. ·smeersel, -s, *n.n.* ointment. ·smeerwortel, no pl., *n.* orpine, stonecrop.

smeet, smeten, *n.* throw.

·smekeling, *n.* supplicant. ·smeken, smeek, *v.t.* & *v.i.* to entreat, implore.

smeltbaar, -bare, *a.* liquefiable. ·smeltbaarheid, no pl., *n.* capacity of liquefying. ·smelten, *v.t.* to melt; to smelt. ¶*v.i.* to melt. ·smelter, -s, *n.* smelter. smelte·rij, *n.* smelting works. ·smeltkroes, -zen, *n.* melting-pot, crucible. ·smeltpunt, *n.n.* melting-point.

·smeren, smeer, *v.t.* to smear, lubricate. *'m* ~, to do a bunk; *een boterham* ~, to butter a slice of bread; *iemand de handen* ~, to use palm-oil (*bribe*). ·smerig, *a.* filthy. ·smerigheid, -heden, *n.* filth.

·smeris, -ssen, *n.* copper (*policeman*).

smet, -tten, *n.* taint, blemish. ·smetstof, -ffen, *n.* virus, infectious matter. ·smetteloos, -loze, *a.* spotless, impeccable. ·smetten, smet, *v.t.* to stain.

·smeulen, *v.i.* to smoulder.

smid, smeden, *n.* (black)smith. ·smidse, -n, *n.* smithy, forge. ·smidsknecht, *n.* blacksmith's man. ·smidsoven, -s, *n.* forge. ·smidswinkel, -s, *n.* smithy.

smient, *n.* widgeon.

·smiezen, pl. only, *n. in de* ~ *krijgen*, to twig. ·smijdig, *a.* supple.

·smijten, *v.t.*, *str.* to fling; to chuck. ¶*v.i.*, *str.* ~ *met*, to waste.

·smisse, -n, *n. See* smidse.

smoel,. *n.n.* (*vulg.*) face, mouth.

·smoesje, -s, *n.n.* excuse, pretext. ·smoezen, smoes, *v.i.* to whisper.

·smoken, smook, *v.i.* to smoke (*thick smoke*). ·smoking, *n.* dinner-jacket.

·smokkelaar, -s, *n.* smuggler. smokkela·rij, *n.* smuggling. ·smokkelen, *v.t.* & *v.i.* to smuggle. ·smokkelwaar, -waren, *n.* contraband.

smook, no pl., *n.* sooty smoke.

smoor, no pl., *n. er de* ~ *in hebben*, to be fed up. ·smoordronken, *a.* blind drunk. ·smoorheet, -hete, *a.* broiling hot. ·smoorklep, -ppen, *n.* throttle; choke. ·smoorlijk, *adv.* madly. ·smoorspoel, *n.* choke coil. ·smoren, smoor, *v.i.* to smother; to stifle; to stew.

smout, no pl., *n.* lard.

smuk, no pl., *n.* finery.

·smullen, smul, *v.i.* to eat with relish. ·smulbroer, -s, *n.*, ·smulpaap, -papen, *n.* gourmet, epicure. ·smulpartij, *n.* a good meal.

·snaaien, *v.t.* to snatch.

snaak, snaken, *n.* joker. snaaks, *a.* playful. ·snaaksheid, -heden, *n.* drollery.

snaar, snaren, *n.* string (*on musical instrument*); chord. ·snaarinstrument, *n.n.* stringed instrument.

·snakken, snak, *v.i.* to gasp. ~ *naar*, to gasp for *or* to long for.

·snappen, snap, *v.t.* to snap; to understand. ¶*v.i.* to babble.

snarenpijpe·rij, *n.* trifles. ·snarenspel, no pl., *n.n.* string music.

snars, *n. geen* ~, nothing whatsoever.

·snater, -s, *n.* (*coll.*) mouth. *hou je* ~, shut up. ·snateren, *v.i.* to quack (*duck*).

·snauwen, *v.i.* to snarl (*fig.*). ·snauwerig, *a.* snarly.

·snavel, -s, *n.*, sneb, -bben, *n.* bill, beak.

·snede, -n, *n.*, snee, sneeën, *n.* cut; slice; cutting edge. ·snedig, *a.* witty, smart. ·snedigheid, no pl., *n.* ready wit.

sneeuw, no pl., *n.* snow. *onder de* ~, deep in snow. ·sneeuwbal, -llen, *n.* snowball; Guelder rose. ·sneeuwberg, *n.* snowcapped mountain. ·sneeuwen, *v.imp.* to snow. ·sneeuwgrens, -zen, *n.* snow-line. ·sneeuwhaas, -hazen, *n.* mountain hare. ·sneeuwhoen, -ders, *n.n.* ptarmigan. ·sneeuwklopje, -s, *n.n.* snowdrop. ·sneeuwpop, -ppen, *n.* snowman. ¶sneeuw·witje, *n.N.* Snow-White.

snel, -lle, *a.* swift, fast. ·snelheid, -heden, *n.* speed. ·snellen, snel, *v.i.* to rush. ·sneltrein, *n.* express; fast train. ·snelvuur, no pl., *n.n.* rapid fire. ·snelvuurgeschut, no pl., *n.n.* quick-firing guns.

·snerpen, *v.i.* to cut, bite (*of wind, cold*). ·snerpend, *a.* biting.

snert, no pl., *n.* (*coll.*) pea soup; rubbish, nonsense. ·snertvent, *n.* worthless fellow.

sneu, *a.* sad, disappointing.

·sneuvelen, *v.i.* to be killed (*in action*).
snib, -bben, *n.* shrew. ·snibbig, *a.* sharp (*of answer*).
·snijbloem, *n.* cut flower(s). ·snijboon, -bonen, *n.* French bean. *een rare* ~, a queer customer. ·snijden, *v.t., str.* to cut; to carve; to geld; to dilute. *elkaar* ~, to intersect; *in stukken* ~, to cut to pieces. ¶ *zich* ~, *v.r., str.* to cut oneself. ·snijdend, *a.* sharp, cutting, biting. ·snijder, -s, *n.* tailor. ·snijding, *n.* intersection. ·snijlijn, *n.* intersecting line. ·snijpunt, *n.n.* point of intersection. ·snijtand, *n.* incisor. ·snijwerk, no pl., *n.n.* carving.
snik, -kken, *n.* sob. ¶ *a. niet recht* ~, not all there. ·snikheet, -hete, *a.* stifling. ·snikken, snik, *v.i.* to sob.
snip, -ppen, *n.* snipe. ·snippenjacht, no pl., *n.* snipe shooting.
·snipper, -s, *n.* scrap, shred.
snit, -tten, *n.* cut, fashion.
·snodaard, -s, *n.* (*stilted*) villain.
·snoeren, *v.t.* to prune, clip, lop, trim. ·snoeimes, -ssen, *n.n.* pruning-knife, shears. ·snoeisel, -s, *n.n.* prunings, trimmings.
snoek, *n.* pike.
·snoepcenten, pl. only, *n.* child's pocket-money. ·snoepen, *v.i.* to eat sweets. ·snoeper, -s, *n.* one who eats sweets. ·snoeperig, *a.* sweet, charming. ·snoepgoed, no pl., *n.n.* sweets. ·snoeplust, no pl., *n.* over-fondness for sweets. ·snoepreisje, -s, *n.n.* trip. ·snoepster, -s, *n.* one who eats sweets (*female*). ·snoepwinkel, -s, *n.* sweetshop, tuckshop.
snoer, *n.n.* cord; line; string (*of beads, etc.*). ·snoeren, *v.t.* to tie; to string.
snoes, -zen, *n.* darling.
·snoeshaan, -hanen, *n.* *een vreemde* ~, a quaint fellow, a curious foreigner.
snoet, *n.* snout.
·snoeven, snoef, *v.i.* to boast, brag. ·snoever, -s, *n.* braggart. ·snoeverij, *n.* bragging.
·snoezig, *a.* sweet, lovely.
snol, -llen, *n.* tart.
snood, snode, *a.* (*stilted*) base, wicked.
snor, -rren, *n.* moustache. ·snorbaard, *n.*, ·snorrebaard, *n.* large moustache. ·snorren, snor, *v.i.* to purr; to whizz. snorrepijperij, no pl., *n.* gimcrackery.
·snotaap, -tapen, *n.*, ·snotjongen, -s, *n.*, ·snotneus, -zen, *n.* urchin; whippersnapper. ·snotje, no pl., *n.n.* *iets in het* ~ *krijgen*, to get wind of something. ·snotteren, *v.i.* to snivel.
·snuffelaar, -s, *n.* Paul Pry. ·snuffelen, *v.i.* to sniff; to ferret. ·snufje, -s, *n.n.* novelty.
·snugger, *a.* bright, smart.
snuif, no pl., *n.* snuff. ·snuifje, -s, *n.n.* pinch of snuff.
·snuisterij, *n.* trinket.
·snuit, *n.* snout; trunk (*of elephant*). ·snuiten, *v.i., str.* to snuff (*candle*). *de neus* ~, to blow one's nose. ·snuiter, -s, *n.* chap, fellow.
·snuiven, snuif, *v.i., str.* to sniff; to snort; to take snuff.
·snurken, *v.i.* to snore.
·sober, *a.* sober. ·soberheid, no pl., *n.* sobriety, frugality. ·sobertjes, *adv.* poorly.
sociali·satie, no pl., *n.* socialization. sociali·seren, -seer, *v.t.* to socialize. socië·teit, *n.* club. socio·loog, -logen, *n.* sociologist.
·soebatten, -bat, *v.i.* to beg and pray.
soep, *n.* soup. *niet veel* ~*s*, not up to much.
·soepel, *a.* supple. ·soepelheid, no pl., *n.* suppleness.
·soeplepel, -s, *n.* ladle.
soes, -zen, *n.* dotard; cream puff.
·soesa, no pl., *n.* bother.
·soezen, soes, *v.i.* to doze. ·soezerig, *a.* drowsy.
·soja, no pl., *n.* soya.
sok, -kken, *n.* sock. *ouwe* ~, old fogey; *op zijn sokken*, in one's socks; *iemand van z'n sokken slaan*, to knock a person down.
sol·daat, -daten, *n.* soldier.
sol·deer, no pl., *n.n.*, sol·deersel, no pl., *n.n.* solder. sol·deerlamp, *n.* blow-lamp. sol·deren, -deer, *v.t.* to solder.
sol·dij, *n.* (soldier's) pay.
soli·dair, *a.* solidary. *zich* ~ *verklaren met*, to express solidarity with. solidari·teit, *n.* solidarity. so·lide, *a.* strong; reliable, sound.
so·list, *n.* soloist.
·sollen, sol, *v.i.* ~ *met*, to romp or have a game with.
solli·citant, *n.* applicant. solli·citatie, -s, *n.* application. solli·citeren, -teer, *v.i.* ~ *naar*, to apply for.
so·lutie, -s, *n.* solution.
sol·vabel, *a.* solvent. solvabili·teit, *n.* solvency.
som, -mmen, *n.* sum; problem. *sommen maken*, to do sums.
·somber, *a.* gloomy, sombre. ·somberheid, no pl., *n.* gloom.
som·matie, -s, *n.* summons. som·meren, -meer, *v.t.* to summon; to call upon.
·sommetje, -s, *n.n.* small sum. *een aardig* ~, a tidy little sum.
·sommige, *pron.* some. ~*n*, some (people).
soms, *adv.* sometimes; perhaps. ~ . . . ~ . . ., at times . . . then again. . . .
·sonde, -s, *n.* probe.
Sont, *N. de* ~, the Sound.
soort, *n.* or *n.n.* sort, kind; species. *een* ~ . . ., a kind of . . .; ~ *zoekt* ~, like calls to like; *in zijn* ~, of its kind. ~ *gewicht*, specific gravity. soortge·lijk, *a.* similar. ·soortnaam, -namen, *n.* generic name.
soos, no pl., *n.* club. *op de* ~, at the club.
sop, -ppen, *n.* or *n.n.* suds. *het ruime* ~, the briny ocean; *het* ~ *is de kool niet*

waard, the game is not worth the candle.
·**soppen, sop,** *v.t.* to steep, dip.
so·praan, -pranen, *n.* soprano.
sor·teerder, -s, *n.* sorter. **sor·teren, -teer,**
v.t. to sort. **sor·tering,** *n.* sorting.
souf·fleren, -fleer, *v.i.* to prompt. **souf·fleur,**
-s, *n.* prompter.
sour·dine, -s, *n.* mute (*on violin, etc.*).
souve·rein, *n.* sovereign, ruler. **souvereini-**
·**teit,** *n.* sovereignty.
spaak, spaken, *n.* spoke. ¶ *adv.* ~ *lopen* to
go wrong. ·**spaakbeen, -deren,** *n.n.* radius
(*bone*).
spaan, spanen, *n.* chip (*of wood*); scoop, pat.
·**spaander, -s,** *n.* chip, shaving.
Spaans, *a.* Spanish. ~*e ruiters,* chevaux-de-
frise.
·**spaarbank,** *n.* savings-bank. ·**spaarder, -s,** *n.*
depositor. ·**spaarcenten,** pl. only, *n.,*
·**spaarduiten,** pl. only, *n.,* ·**spaargeld,** no
pl., *n.n.* savings. ·**spaarkas, -ssen,** *n.*
savings-bank. ·**spaarpot, -tten,** *n.* money-
box. ·**spaarzaam, -zame,** *a.* economical,
thrifty; sparing. ·**spaarzaamheid,** no pl.,
n. economy, thrift.
spaar, no pl., *n.n.* spar (*mineral*).
·**spade, -n,** *n.* spade.
spa·lier, *n.* espalier; trellis-work.
spalk, *n.* splint. ·**spalken,** *v.t.* to put in splints.
span, -nnen, *n.* span. ¶ *n.n.* team, yoke;
couple.
span·deren, -deer, *v.t.* to spend. ~ *aan,* to
spend on.
·**spanen,** *a.* chip.
·**Spanjaard,** *N.* Spaniard. ·**Spanje,** *n.N.* Spain.
Span·jool, -jolen, *N.* Spaniard (*derog.*).
·**spankracht,** *n.* elasticity. ·**spannen, span,**
v.t., irr. to stretch; to strain; to bend,
draw (*bow*); to put (*horse in vehicle*).
¶ *v.i., irr.* to be tight. *het zal er* ~, things
will get lively. ·**spannend,** *a.* exciting,
thrilling. ·**spanning,** *n.* tension, strain;
tension, voltage; suspense. ·**spanrups,** *n.*
looper (*caterpillar*).
spant, *n.* joist, timber.
spar, -rren, *n.* spruce-fir. ·**sparappel, -s,** *n.*
fir-cone.
·**sparen, spaar,** *v.t.* to save; to spare. ¶ *v.i.*
to save.
·**sparreboom, -bomen,** *n.* spruce-fir, fir-tree.
·**sparrenbos, -bossen,** *n.* fir-wood.
·**spartelen,** *v.i.* to flounder, struggle. ·**sparte-**
ling, *n.* floundering, struggle.
·**spat, -tten,** *n.* spavin; speck, spot. ·**spatader,**
-s, *n.* varicose vein. ·**spatbord,** *n.n.* mudguard.
·**spatel, -s,** *n.* spatula.
spati·ëren, -eer, *v.t.* to space.
·**spatten, spat,** *v.i.* to splash, spatter.
spece·rij, *n.* spice.
specht, *n.* woodpecker. *blauwe* ~, nut-
hatch; *groene* ~, rain-bird.
speci·aal, -ale, *a.* special. ·**specie, -s** *or* **-ciën,**
n. specie, cash.

specu·lant, *n.* speculator. **specu·leren, -leer,**
v.i. to speculate. ~ *op,* to trade *or* gamble
on.
·**speeksel,** no pl., *n.n.* saliva, spittle.
·**speekselklier,** *n.* salivary gland.
·**speelbal, -llen,** *n.* ball, plaything. ~ *van*
de golven, at the mercy of the waves.
·**speelbank,** *n.* gaming-house. ·**speeldoos,**
-dozen, *n.* musical box. ·**speelduivel, -s,**
n. demon of gambling. ·**speelgenoot,**
·**noten,** *n.* playfellow, playmate. ·**speelgoed,**
-eren, *n.n.* toy. *een stuk* ~, a toy. ·**speelhol,**
n.n. gambling den. ·**speeljacht,** *n.n.*
pleasure yacht. ·**speelkaart,** *n.* playing
card. ·**speelkwartier,** *n.n.* break (*at school*).
·**speelplaats,** *n.* playground. **speels,** *a.*
playful. **speelse·wijs,** *adv.* playfully.
·**speelterrein,** *n.n.* recreation ground.
·**speeltuig,** *n.n.* musical instrument. **speel-**
werk, *n.n.* chime (*of clock*). ·**speelziek,** *a.*
playful. ·**speelzucht,** no pl., *n.* passion for
gambling.
speen, spenen, *n.n.* teat; comforter. ·**speen-**
kruid, no pl., *n.n.* pilewort. ·**speenvarken,**
-s, *n.n.* sucking-pig.
speer, speren, *n.* spear. ·**speerpunt,** *n.* spear-
head. ·**speerwerpen,** no pl., *n.n.* throwing
the javelin.
spek, no pl., *n.n.* bacon. *er voor* ~ *en bonen*
bijzitten, to be entirely superfluous; *dat*
is geen ~ *voor jouw bek,* that is not for
you. ·**spekbokking,** *n.* fat bloater. ·**spek-**
eend, *n.* widgeon. ·**spekken, spek,** *v.t.*
to lard. *zijn beurs* ~, to line one's purse.
·**speknaald,** *n.* larding-pin. ·**spekslager, -s,**
n. pork-butcher. ·**speksteen,** no pl., *n.*
soap-stone.
spek·takel, -s, *n.n.* racket. ~ *maken,* to
kick up a row.
·**spekvet,** no pl., *n.n.* bacon fat.
spel, *n.n.* game, play. *het* ~ *in handen*
hebben, to hold the trumps; *iemand vrij* ~
laten, to give a person free play; *iemand*
buiten ~ *laten,* to leave a person out of
it; *op het* ~ *staan,* to be at stake; *alles op*
het ~ *zetten,* to stake everything. ¶ **-llen,**
n.n. pack (*of cards*); set (*of dominoes, etc.*);
show, booth. ¶ no pl., *n.n.* play, performance (*sport*); playing (*music*); acting.
·**spelbreker, -s,** *n.* spoil-sport.
speld, *n.* pin. *er is geen* ~ *tussen te krijgen,*
you cannot get a word in edgeways.
·**speldekop, -ppen,** *n.* pin's head. ·**spelde-**
prik, -kken, *n.* pin-prick.
·**spelen, speel,** *v.i.* to play; to gamble. *door*
het hoofd ~, to run through one's head;
naar binnen ~, to dispatch (*eat*); ~ *om,*
to play for. ·**spelenderwijs,** *adv.* without
effort, in fun. ·**speler, -s,** *n.* player; actor;
musician. ·**spelerijden,** no pl., *n.n.* pleasure-
drive, joy-ride. ·**spelevaren,** no pl., *n.n.*
boating, yachting. ·**speling,** *n.* play,
looseness; lassitude; freak, sport.
·**spellen, spel,** *v.t.* to spell.

spelletje, -s, *n.n.* game.
spelling, *n.* spelling.
spe·lonk, *n.* cave, cavern.
spen·deren, -deer, *v.t.* *See* spanderen.
spenen, speen, *v.t.* to wean.
sperboom, -bomen, *n.* barrier. sperren,
sper, *v.t.* to bar. spervuur, no pl., *n.n.*
barrage (*gunfire*).
sperwer, -s, *n.* sparrow-hawk.
sperzieboon, -bonen, *n.* French bean.
speten, speet, *v.t.* to skewer.
speurder, -s, *n.* detective. speuren, *v.t.*
to track. speurhond, *n.* bloodhound.
speurzin, no pl., *n.* flair.
spichtig, *a.* lank, spiky, wispy.
spie, -eën, *n.* peg; (*coll.*) cent, money.
spieden, *v.i.* to spy.
spiegat, *n.n.* scupper.
spiegel, -s, *n.* mirror, looking-glass; stern
(*of ship*); level (*of sea*). spiegelbeeld,
n.n. image. spiegelei, -eren, *n.n.* fried
egg. spiegelen, *v.t.* to mirror, reflect.
¶zich ~, *v.r.* to look at oneself (*in mirror*).
zich ~ aan, to take example by. spiegelgevecht, *n.n.* mimic battle. spiegelglad,
-dde, *a.* as smooth as a mirror. spiegelglas,
no pl., *n.n.* plate glass. spiegeling, *n.*
reflection. spiegelruit, *n.* plate glass
window. spiegelzaal, -zalen, *n.* hall of
mirrors.
spieken, *v.i.* to crib.
spier, *n.* muscle; blade, shoot.
spiering, *n.* smelt. *een ~ uitwerpen om
een kabeljauw te vangen,* to throw a sprat
to catch a whale.
spierkracht, no pl., *n.* muscular strength.
spiernaakt, *a.* stark naked. spierwit,
-tte, *a.* snow-white.
spies, -zen, *n.* pike, javelin.
spijbelaar, -s, *n.* truant. spijbelen, *v.i.*
to play truant.
spijker, -s, *n.* nail (*iron*). *~s met koppen
slaan,* to get down to brass tacks. spijkeren, *v.t.* to nail. spijkerschrift, no pl.,
n.n. cuneiform writing.
spijl, *n.* bar, spike.
spijs, -zen, *n.* food. spijskaart, *n.* bill of
fare. spijsvertering, no pl., *n.* digestion.
spijt, no pl., *n.* regret; spite. *tot mijn ~ . . .,*
I regret that . . .; *ik heb er ~ van,* I am
sorry for it. spijten, *v.i., str. het spijt
me,* I am sorry. spijtig, *a.* spiteful.
het is ~, it's a pity.
spijzigen, *v.t.* (*stilted*) to feed.
spikkel, -s, *n.* speckle. spiksplinternieuw,
a. brand-new.
spil, -llen, *n.* axis, pivot; axle. spillebeen,
-benen, *n.* spindle-legged person. spille-
leen, -lenen, *n.* female fief. spillen,
spil, *v.t.* to spill, waste. spilziek, *a.*
extravagant. spilzucht, no pl., *n.* extravagance.
spin, -nnen, *n.* spider.
spi·nazie, no pl., *n.* spinach.

spinnekop, -ppen, *n.* spider. spinnen, spin,
v.t., str. to spin; to purr. spinne·rij, *n.*
spinning-mill. spinneweb, -bben, *n.n.*
cobweb. spinnewiel, *n.n.* spinning-wheel.
spinrag, no pl., *n.n.* cobweb. spinrokken,
-s, *n.n.* distaff. spinsel, no pl., *n.n.*
spinnings; web.
spi·on, -nnen, *n.* spy; mirror (*outside window*).
spion·nage, no pl., *n.* espionage. spionneren, -neer, *v.i.* to spy.
spiritu·aliën, no pl. only, *n.* alcoholic liquor,
spirits. spiritu·eel, -ele, *a.* witty. spiritus,
no pl., *n.* methylated spirits.
spit, -tten, *n.n.* spit (*for roasting*); spadeful.
¶no pl., *n.n.* lumbago.
spits, *n.* point; pinnacle; spear-head. *de ~
afbijten,* to bear the brunt; *aan de ~
stellen,* to place at the head; *aan de ~
staan,* to be in the van; *op de ~ drijven,*
to bring matters to a head. ¶*a.* sharp,
pointed. spitsboef, -ven, *n.* rascal. spitsboog, -bogen, *n.* pointed arch. spitsen,
v.t. to point, sharpen. spitsmuis, -zen,
n. shrew (*mouse*). spitsroede, -n, *n. door
de ~n lopen,* to run the gauntlet. spitsvondig, *a.* subtle. spits·vondigheid,
-heden, *n.* subtlety.
spitten, spit, *v.t.* to dig.
spleet, spleten, *n.* cleft, crack. splijtbaar,
-bare, *a.* cleavable. splijten, *v.t., str.*
to split, cleave. splijting, *n.* cleavage.
splijtzwam, -mmen, *n.* schizomycete;
(*fig.*) seed of disruption.
splinter, -s, *n.* splinter. splinteren, *v.i.* to
splinter. splinternieuw, *a.* brand-new.
splitsen, *v.t.* to split (up); to splice. ¶zich ~,
v.r. to split up. splitsing, *n.* splitting
(up); bifurcation.
splitvrucht, *n.* dehiscent fruit.
spoed, no pl., *n.* speed, haste. spoedbestelling,
n. express delivery. spoedcursus, -ssen,
n. concentrated course. spoedeisend,
a. urgent, pressing. spoeden, zich, *v.r.*
to hurry, hasten. spoedig, *a.* speedy.
¶*adv.* soon, before long; speedily, quickly.
spoel, *n.* spool, bobbin. spoelbak, -kken,
n. rinsing tub. spoeldrank, *n.* gargle.
spoelen, *v.t.* to rinse; to wash (*of sea*).
spoeling, no pl., *n.* hog-wash. spoelkom,
-mmen, *n.* slop-basin.
spoken, spook, *v.i.* to haunt; to be very
rough (*of sea*).
spon, -nnen, *n.* bung. sponde, -n, *n.* (*fig.*)
bedside. spongat, *n.n.* bung-hole. spon-
ning, *n.* groove.
spons, -en *or* -zen, *n.* sponge. sponsachtig, *a.*
spongy. sponsen, *v.t.* to sponge.
spon·taan, -tane, *a.* spontaneous.
spook, spoken, *n.n.* ghost, spectre. spookachtig, *a.* ghostly, spectral. spookgestalte,
-n, *n.* phantom. spookhuis, -zen, *n.n.*
haunted house. spooksel, -s, *n.n.* phantom.
spoor, sporen, *n.* spur; spore. *de sporen
geven,* to set spurs to. ¶*n.n.* spoor, track,

trail; trace; railway, rails, track. *enkel* ~, single line; *smal* ~, narrow gauge; *het* ~ *bijster zijn*, to have lost one's way, to be at sea *(fig.)*; *per* ~, by rail. ¶*prefix.* railway-. ·**spoorloos, -loze,** *a.* & *adv.* without trace. ~ *verdwijnen,* to vanish. ·**spoorslags,** *adv.* at full speed. ·**spoorweg,** *n.* railway. ·**spoorwegnet, -tten,** *n.n.* railway-system. **spo·radisch,** *a.* sporadic. ·**spore, -n,** *n.* spore. ·**sporen, spoor,** *v.i.* to go by train. ¶no pl., *n.n.* railway travel. *één uur* ~*s,* one hour by train.
sport, *n.* rung. ¶no pl., *n.* sport. ·**sportarti-kelen,** pl. only, *n.n.* sports requisites. ·**sportblad,** *n.n.* sporting paper. ·**sportief, -ve,** *a.* sportsmanlike. ·**sportkar, -rren,** *n.* mail-cart.
spot, no pl., *n.* mockery, ridicule; laughing-stock. *de* ~ *drijven met,* to ridicule. ·**spotachtig,** *a.* mocking, derisive. ·**spotdicht,** *n.n.* satirical poem. ·**spotgoedkoop, -kope,** *a.* dirt-cheap. ·**spotlach,** no pl., *n.* mocking laugh. ·**spotlijster, -s,** *n.* mocking-bird. ·**spotnaam, -namen,** *n.* nickname. ·**spot-prent,** *n.* caricature. ·**spotprijs, -zen,** *n.* bargain price. ·**spotrede, -nen,** *n.* diatribe *(mocking).* ·**spotschrift,** *n.n.* lampoon. ·**spotten, spot,** *v.i.* to mock, jeer. ~ *met,* to scoff at; *hij laat niet met zich* ~, he stands no nonsense. ·**spottenderwijs,** *adv.* mock-ingly. ·**spotter, -s,** *n.* mocker, scoffer. **spotter·nij,** *n.* mockery. ·**spotvogel, -s,** *n.* mocking-bird. ·**spotziek,** *a. See* **spotachtig.** ·**spotzucht,** no pl., *n.* love of mockery.
·**spouwen,** *v.t.irr.* to split.
spraak, spraken, *n.* speech, language. ·**spraakgebrek,** *n.n.* defect of speech. ·**spraakgebruik,** no pl., *n.n.* usage *(linguis-tic).* ·**spraakkunst,** *n.* grammar. ·**spraak-zaam, -zame,** *a.* talkative, loquacious. ·**spraakzaa·nheid,** no pl., *n.* loquacity. ·**sprake,** no pl., *n. er was* ~ *van,* there was some talk of it; *er is geen* ~ *van,* it is out of the question; *ter* ~ *brengen,* to raise *(a point); ter* ~ *komen,* to come up for discussion. ·**sprakeloos, -loze,** *a.* speech-less. **sprake·loosheid,** no pl., *n.* speechless-ness.
sprank, *n.* spark; brook *(small).*
·**spreekbeurt,** *n.* lecture, sermon. *een* ~ *vervullen,* to deliver a lecture. ·**spreekbuis, -zen,** *n.* speaking-tube. ·**spreekcel, -llen,** *n.* call-box. ·**spreekfout,** *n.* slip of the tongue. ·**spreekgestoelte, -n,** *n.* pulpit, platform. ·**spreekkamer, -s,** *n.* consulting room. ·**spreekster, -s,** *n.* speaker *(female).* ·**spreektaal,** no pl., *n.* colloquial language. ·**spreekuur, -kuren,** *n.n.* consulting hour, ·**spreekwijze, -n,** *n.* expression, phrase. ·**spreekwoord,** *n.n.* proverb. **spreek-·woordelijk,** *a.* proverbial.
spreeuw, *n.* starling.
sprei, *n.* bedstead. ·**spreiden,** *v.t.* to spread.

·**spreken, spreek,** *v.i.* to speak, talk. *niet te* ~ *zijn,* not to be at home (to someone); *niet te* ~ *zijn over,* to be displeased at; *het spreekt vanzelf,* it stands to reason; *het spreekt voor zichzelf,* it is obvious; *iemand* ~, to speak to someone; ~ *met,* to talk to or with; ~ *over,* to talk of or about *or* on; ~ *tot, (lit.)* to speak to or *(fig.)* to appeal to; ~ *van,* to talk of; ~ *voor,* to talk to on behalf of. ·**sprekend,** *a.* speaking, telling. ·**spreker, -s,** *n.* speaker.
·**sprengen,** *v.t.* to sprinkle. ·**sprengkwast,** *n.* aspergillum. ·**sprenkel, -s,** *n.* spark; speck. ·**sprenkelen,** *v.t.* to sprinkle. ·**sprenkeling,** *n.* sprinkling.
spreuk, *n.* motto; proverb.
spriet, *n.* blade *(grass);* antenna, feeler. ·**sprietzeil,** *n.n.* spritsail.
·**springen,** *v.i., str.* to jump, leap; to spring; to explode; to break *(string). laten* ~, to spring *(mine).* ·**spring-in-'t-veld,** no pl., *n.* lively young person. ·**springkever, -s,** *n.* spring beetle. ·**springkruid,** no pl., *n.n.* spurge. ·**springlevend,** *a.* alive and kicking. ·**springplank,** *n.* spring-board. ·**springstof, -ffen,** *n.* explosive. ·**springtij,** *n.n.* spring tide. ·**springtor, -rren,** *n.* spring beetle. ·**springtouw,** *n.n.* skipping-rope. ·**springveer, -veren,** *n.* spiral spring. ·**sprinkhaan, -hanen,** *n.* grasshopper.
sprits, no pl., *n.n.* (kind of) shortbread.
·**sproeien,** *v.t.* to sprinkle, spray. ·**sproei-wagen, -s,** *n.* sprinkler-van.
sproet, *n.* freckle. ·**sproeterig,** *a.* freckled.
·**sprokkel, -s,** *n.* dry twig. ·**sprokkelaar, -s,** *n.* wood-gatherer. ·**sprokkelen,** *v.t.* to gather dead wood. ·**sprokkelhout,** no pl., *n.n.* dead wood. ·**Sprokkelmaand,** *N.* February.
sprong, *n.* leap, jump. *een* ~ *doen,* to take a leap; *kromme* ~*en maken,* to cut capers; *de* ~ *wagen,* to take the plunge; *op* ~ *staan om . . .,* to be on the point of. . . . ·**sprongsgewijs,** *adv.* by leaps.
·**sprookje, -s,** *n.n.* fairy tale.
sprot, -tten, *n.* sprat.
spruit, *n.* sprout, shoot; offspring. ·**spruiten,** *v.i., str.* to sprout, shoot. ·**spruitjes,** pl. only, *n.n.* Brussels sprouts.
spui, *n.n.* sluice *(for letting out water).* ·**spuien,** *v.i.* to let out water; to ventilate. ·**spuigat,** *n.n.* scupper. *het loopt de* ~*en uit,* it goes too far.
spuit, *n.* syringe, squirt; (fire-)engine; gamp. ·**spuiten,** *v.i., str.* to spout, squirt. ·**spuitfles, -ssen,** *n.* siphon. ·**spuitgast,** *n.* fireman *(of fire-engine).* ·**spuitslang,** *n.* hose. ·**spuitwater,** no pl., *n.n.* soda-water.
spul, -llen, *n.n.* stuff; belongings; togs; booth. ·**sputteren,** *v.i.* to splutter; to grouse.
spuug, no pl., *n.n.* spit, spittle.
·**spuwen,** *v.i.* to spit; to vomit, spew.
staaf, staven, *n.* bar; stave; ingot.
staak, staken, *n.* stake, pole.
staal, stalen, *n.n.* sample, pattern. ¶no pl.,

n.n. steel. ·**staalachtig,** *a.* steely. ·**staal-
blauw,** *a.* steely blue. ·**staaldraad, -draden,**
n. steel wire. ·**staalfabriek,** *n.* steel-
works. ·**staalmeester, -s,** *n.* syndic. ·**staaltje,**
-s, *n.n.* sample, example.
staan, sta, *v.i., irr.* to stand; to stand still;
to be; to reside (*of clergyman*); to suit,
become; to insist. *gaan* ~, to get up;
wat staat er?, what does it say?; *het staat
aan jou,* it's up to you; *hoe staat het met* . . .*?,*
how is . . .*?; wat hem te doen staat,* what he
must do; *het komt te* ~ *op,* it amounts to;
~ *op,* to insist on; *tot* ~ *brengen,* to
bring to a standstill; *ergens vóór* ~,
to be faced by something; *er slecht vóór* ~,
to be in a bad way; *nergens voor* ~, to
stick at nothing. **staand,** *a.* standing; upright, perpendicular. *~e hond,* setter,
pointer; *iemand ~e houden,* to stop a
person; *zich ~e houden,* to maintain
oneself. ·**staandevoets,** *adv.* then and there.
·**staangeld,** *n.n.* market dues. ·**staanplaats,**
n. standing-room.
staar, no pl., *n.* cataract (*of eye*).
staart, *n.* tail; pigtail. ·**staartbeen, -deren,**
n.n. coccyx. ·**staartmees, -mezen,** *n.*
longtailed titmouse.
staat, staten, *n.* list, statement; State. *Staten
Generaal,* States General; *Raad van State,*
Council of State. ¶no pl., *n.* state, condition; rank; style. *in* ~ *stellen,* to enable;
in ~ *zijn,* to be able; *tot alles in* ~ *zijn,*
to be capable of anything; ~ *maken op,*
to rely on. **staat·huishoudkunde,** no pl.,
n. political economy. **staathuishoud-
·kunde,** *a.* politico-economic. ·**staatkunde,**
no pl., *n.* politics, statesmanship. **staat-
·kundig,** *a.* political. ·**staatsambtenaar,
-naren,** *n.* civil servant, government
official. ·**staatsbedrijf, -ven,** *n.n.* government undertaking. ·**staatsbeheer,** no pl.,
n.n. (state) administration. ·**staatsbeleid,**
no pl., *n.n.* statesmanship. ·**staatsblad,**
no pl., *n.n.* paper publishing laws and
decrees. ·**staatsburger, -s,** *n.* citizen.
·**staatsburgerschap,** no pl., *n.n.* citizenship. ·**staatscourant,** *n.* official state
gazette. ·**staatsdienst,** no pl., *n.* government service. ·**staatsdomein,** *n.n.* crown-
land. ·**staatsexamen, -s,** *n.n.* matriculation.
·**staatsgelden,** pl. only, *n.n.* public money.
·**staatsgezinde, -n,** *n.* adherent of the
States. ·**staatsgreep, -grepen,** *n.* coup
d'état. ·**staatsinrichting,** *n.* polity, form
of government. ·**staatskas, -ssen,** *n.*
Treasury, exchequer. ·**staatslichaam,**
no pl., *n.n.* body politic. ·**staatsman,
-lieden,** *n.* statesman. ·**staatsmansbeleid,**
no pl., *n.n.* statesmanship. ·**staatsmis-
dadiger, -s,** *n.* political offender. ·**staats-
papieren,** pl. only, *n.n.* government
securities. ·**staatsrecht,** no pl., *n.n.* constitutional law. **staats·rechtelijk,** *a.*
·constitutional. ·**staatsschuld,** *n.* national

debt. ·**staatswege,** *adv. van* ~, on behalf
of the government. ·**staatswetenschappen,**
pl. only, *n.* political science.
sta·biel, *a.* stable. **stabili·seren, -seer,** *v.t.*
to stabilize.
stad, steden, *n.* town, city. **stade,** *adv.
te* ~ *komen,* to stand in good stead.
·**stadgenoot, -noten,** *n.* fellow townsman.
·**stadhouder, -s,** *n.* stadtholder. **stad-
·houderlijk,** *a.* of a stadtholder. ·**stad-
houderloos, -loze,** *a.* stadtholderless.
·**stadhouderschap,** no pl., *n.n.* stadtholder-
ate. **stad·huis, -zen,** *n.n.* town hall.
stad·huistaal, no pl., *n.* pompous *or*
stilted language.
·**stadion, -s,** *n.n.* stadium. ·**stadium, -dia,**
stage, phase. *in een* ~, at a stage.
·**stadsbestuur, -sturen,** *n.n.* municipality,
corporation; town council. ·**stadsmens,**
n. ~**en,** townspeople, townsfolk. ·**stads-
schouwburg,** *n.* municipal theatre. ·**stad-
waarts,** *a. & adv.* townward(s).
staf, staven, *n.* staff; mace, staff. ·**stafkaart,**
n. ordnance map. ·**stafrijm,** *n.n.* alliteration.
stag, *n.* stay (*rope*). *over* ~ *gaan,* to stay,
go about *or* (*fig.*) to change one's tack.
·**stage,** no pl., *n.* term of probation.
·**sta-in-de-weg,** no pl., *n.* impediment,
obstacle.
·**stagzeil,** *n.n.* staysail.
·**staken, staak,** *v.i.* to stop. *de arbeid* ~,
to go on strike; *de betaling* ~, to suspend
payment. ¶*v.i.* to go on strike, be out on
strike. *de stemmen* ~, the votes are
equally divided. ·**staker, -s,** *n.* striker.
sta·ket, -tten, *n.n.,* **sta·ketsel, -s,** *n.n.* fence
palisade.
·**staking,** *n.* strike; cessation, suspension.
bij ~ *van stemmen,* in case of an equal
division.
·**stakker(d), -s,** *n.* poor wretch.
stal, -llen, *n.* stable; cowshed, byre; fold;
sty. *op* ~ *zetten,* to stable, house *or* to
shelve; *van* ~ *halen,* to trot out.
·**stalen,** *a.* (of) steel, steely. ¶**staal,** *v.t.* to
steel.
stalhoude·rij, *n.* livery stable. ·**stalknecht,**
n. stableman; groom. ·**stalkruid,** no pl.,
n.n. cammock. ·**stallen,** *stal, v.t.* to stable;
to garage. ·**stalles,** pl. only, *n.* stalls
(*theatre*). ·**stalletje, -s,** *n.n.* stall (*market*).
·**st·alling,** *n.* stable. ¶no pl., *n.* stabling.
·**stalmeester, -s,** *n.* equerry, master of the
horse.
s·am, -mmen, *n.* stem; stem, trunk; tribe.
·**stamboek,** *n.n.* stud-book, herd-book;
pedigree. ·**stamboom, -bomen,** *n.* genealogical tree, pedigree.
·**stamelaar, -s,** *n.* stammerer. ·**stamelen,** *v.i.*
to stammer.
·**stamgast,** *n.* habitué (*of café, etc.*). ·**stam-
houder, -s,** *n.* son and heir. ·**stamhuis,
-zen,** *n.n.* dynasty. ·**stammen, stam,**

v.i. ~ *uit*, to date from; ~ *van*, to descend *or* be descended from. ·**stamouders**, pl. only, *n.* ancestors.

stamp, *n.* stamp (*with foot*). ·**stampen,** *v.i.* to stamp; to pitch (*ship*). *met zijn voet* ~, to stamp one's foot. ¶*v.t.* to stamp, ram; to pound. ·**stamper, -s,** *n.* stamper; pestle; pistil. ·**stamppot,** no pl., *n.* hotchpotch. ·**stampvoeten,** *v.i.* to stamp one's foot. ·**stampvol,-lle,** *a.* crowded, bung-full.

·**stamtafel, -s,** *n.* regular table (*at café*). ·**stamverwant,** *a.* cognate. ·**stamverwantschap,** no pl., *n.* (*racial*) affinity.

stand, *n.* attitude, position; height, level; state (*barometer*); score; class, station, rank, status. *de burgerlijke* ~, register of births, deaths and marriages; ~ *ophouden*, to keep up one's position; *boven zijn* ~, above one's social position; *in alle* ~*en*, in every walk of life. ¶no pl., *n.* state, condition. ~ *van zaken*, state of affairs; ~ *houden*, to stand firm; *in* ~ *houden*, to keep up, maintain; *tot* ~ *brengen*, to bring about; *tot* ~ *komen*, to be brought about. ·**standaard.** *n.* standard. ·**standbeeld.** *n.n.* statue. ·**stander. -s,** *n.* stand. ·**standje, -s,** *n.n.* scolding; scene. *een* ~ *krijgen*, to be ticked off. ·**standplaats,** *n.* stand; pitch; station, post; living (*clergyman*). ·**standpunt,** *n.n.* point of view. ·**standrecht,** no pl., *n.n.* summary justice. **stand·rechtelijk,** *a.* summary. **stand·vastig,** *a.* steadfast. **stand·vastigheid,** no pl., *n.* steadfastness. ·**standvogel, -s,** *n.* resident bird.

stang, *n.* rod, bar; perch. *iemand op* ~ *jagen*, to provoke a person for fun.

stank, *n.* stink.

stanni·ool, no pl., *n.n.* tin foil.

stap, -ppen, *n.* step, footstep. *een* ~ *doen*, to take a step; *bij elke* ~, at every step; *op* ~ *gaan*, to set out; ~ *voor* ~, step by step.

·**stapel, -s,** *n.* pile, stack; stocks (*of shipyard*). *op* ~ *staan*, to be on the stocks; *op* ~ *zetten*, to lay down the keel of; *van* ~ *laten lopen*, to launch. ·**stapelen,** *v.t.* to pile (up). ·**stapelgek, -kke,** *a.* raving mad. ·**stapelgoederen,** pl. only, *n.n.* staple commodities. ·**stapelplaats,** *n.* staple town. ·**stapelwolk,** *n.* cumulus.

·**stappen, stap,** *v.i.* to step. ·**stapvoets,** *adv.* at a walking pace.

star, -rre, *a.* stiff; fixed. ·**staren, staar,** *v.i.* to gaze, stare. ·**starogen, -oog,** *v.i.* to stare.

·**state,** *n.* See **staat.** ·**statenbijbel, -s,** *n.* Dutch Authorized Version of the Bible.

·**statie, -s,** *n.* Station of the Cross. ¶no pl., *n.* pomp, ceremony. ·**statiegewaad, -waden,** *n.n.* robes of state. ·**statietrap, -ppen,** *n.* accommodation ladder.

·**statig,** *a.* stately, solemn. ·**statigheid,** no pl., *n.* stateliness, solemnity.

stati·on, -s, *n.n.* station. **station·nair,** *a.* stationary. **station·neren, -neer,** *v.t.* to station, place. **stati·onschef, -s,** *n.* station-master.

·**statisch,** *a.* static. **sta·tisticus, -ci,** *n.* statistician. **statis·tiek,** *n.* statistics. **sta·tistisch,** *a.* statistical.

statu·tair, *a.* statutory. **sta·tuut, -tuten,** *n.n.* statute.

sta·vast, *adv.* *een man van* ~, a resolute man.

staven, staaf, *v.t.* to confirm, substantiate. ·**staving,** *n.* confirmation, substantiation.

·**stede,** no pl., *n.* (*stilted*) town; stead. (*hier*) *ter* ~ *or te dezer* ~, in this town; *in* ~ *van*, instead of. ·**stedehouder, -s,** *n.* (*stilted*) lieutenant. ~ *van Christus,* Vicar of Christ. ·**stedelijk,** *a.* municipal, urban. ·**stedeling,** *n.* town-dweller. ·**stedemaagd,** *n.* patroness (*of town*).

steeds, *a.* town-. ¶*adv.* always, ever. *nog* ~, still; ~ *groter*, bigger and bigger; ~ *meer*, evermore.

steeg, stegen, *n.* alley, lane.

steek, steken, *n.* stab, thrust; dig; sting; stitch; three-cornered hat. *geen* ~, nothing at all; *het houdt geen* ~, it does not hold water; *een* ~ *onder water*, a sly dig; *in de* ~ *laten*, to leave in the lurch; *er is een* ~*je aan los*, there is something wrong about it. ·**steekappel, -s,** *n.* thorn apple. ·**steekbeitel, -s,** *n.* paring-chisel. ·**steekdoorn, -s,** *n.* gooseberry. ·**steekhevel, -s,** *n.* plunging-siphon. ·**steekhoudend,** *a.* valid. ·**steekpan, -nnen,** *n.* bed-pan. ·**steekpasser, -s,** *n.* (pair of) dividers. ·**steekproef, -ven,** *n.* random sample. ·**steekspel,** *n.n.* tournament. ·**steekvlam, -mmen,** *n.* blow-torch. ·**steekvlieg,** *n.* gadfly. ·**steekwagen, -s,** *n.* hand-cart. ·**steekwond,** *n.* stab-wound.

steel, stelen, *n.* handle, shaft; stem, stalk.

steels, *a.* stealthy. ·**steelsgewijs,** *adv.* stealthily, by stealth.

steen, stenen, *n.* stone; brick. *een* ~ *van mijn hart,* a weight off my mind; ~ *en been klagen,* to complain bitterly. ·**steenaarde,** no pl., *n.* brick clay. ·**steenachtig,** *a.* stony. ·**steenader, -s,** *n.* rocky vein. ·**steenarend,** *n.* golden eagle, osprey. ·**steenbakker, -s,** *n.* brickmaker. ·**steenbakkerij,** *n.* brick-yard. ·**steenbok, -kken,** *n.* ibex. ·**Steenbokskeerkring,** no pl., *N.* tropic of Capricorn. ·**steenbreke,** no pl., *n.* saxifrage. ·**steenbreker, -s,** *n.* stone-crusher. ·**steendruk,** no pl., *n.* lithography. ·**steendrukkerij,** *n.* lithographic printing-works. ·**steenduif, -ven,** *n.* rock-pigeon. ·**steeneik,** *n.* holm-oak. ·**steengroeve, -n,** *n.* quarry. ·**steengruis,** no pl., *n.n.* stone-dust; brick-dust. ·**steenhouwer, -s,** *n.* stone-mason. ·**steenhouwerij,** *n.* stone-mason's yard. ·**steenkolen,** pl. only, *n.* coal, pit-coal. ·**steenkolenmijn,**

n. coal-mine, colliery. **·steenkool,** no pl., *n.* See steenkolen. **·steenkreeft,** *n.* crayfish. **·steenkruid,** no pl., *n.n.* saxifrage. **·steenmarter, -s,** *n.* stone-marten. **·steenmos,** no pl., *n.* rock lichen. **·steenpuist,** *n.* boil. **·steenrood, -rode,** *a.* brick-red. **·steenrots,** *n.* rock. **·steenslag,** no pl., *n.* road metal. **·steenuil,** *n.* barn-owl. **·steenweg,** *n.* paved road. **·steenworp,** *n.* stone's throw. **·steenzout,** no pl., *n.n.* rock-salt. **·steenzwaluw,** *n.* swift. **·steenzweer, -zweren,** *n.* boil.

·steevast, *a.* regular.

steg, no pl., *n. weg noch ~ weten,* to be a perfect stranger.

·steiger, -s, *n.* scaffolding; landing stage. **·steigeren,** *v.i.* to rear, prance.

steil, *a.* steep. **·steilheid,** no pl., *n.* steepness. **·steiloor, -oren,** *n.* donkey. **steil·orig,** *a.* stubborn. **·steilschrift,** no pl., *n.n.* perpendicular writing. **·steilte,** no pl., *n.* steepness.

stek, -kken, *n.* cutting, slip.

·stekeblind, *a.* blind as a bat.

·stekel, -s, *n.* prickle, spine. **·stekelachtig,** *a.* prickly. **·stekelbaars, -zen,** *n.* stickleback, tiddler. **stekel·huidig,** *a.* echinoderm. **·stekelig,** *a.* prickly. **·stekelrog, -ggen,** *n.* thornback. **·stekelvarken, -s,** *n.n.* porcupine.

·steken, steek, *v.i., str.* to sting; to smart; to burn *(of sun). er steekt wat achter,* there is something at the back of it. ¶*v.t., str.* to sting, prick; to spear; to put, stick.

·stekken, stek, *v.t.* to slip, set *(plants).* **·stekker, -s,** *n.* (wall-)plug.

stel, -llen, *n.n.* set; cooker. ¶no pl., *n.n. op ~ zijn,* to be settled; *op ~ en sprong,* abruptly.

·stelen, steel, *v.t., str.* to steal. *het kan me gestolen worden,* it leaves me indifferent. ¶*v.i., str.* to steal. *uit ~ gaan,* to go on a burgling expedition.

·stelkunde, no pl., *n.* algebra. **stel·lage, -s,** *n.* scaffolding. **·stellen, stel,** *v.t.* to place, put; to adjust, regulate, focus; to compose; to postulate, suppose. *voorwaarden ~,* to make conditions; *tevreden ~,* to satisfy; *het goed kunnen ~,* to be well off; *het te ~ hebben met,* to have difficulties with; *~ op,* to fix at; *het ~ zonder,* to do without; *ter hand ~ (stilted)* to hand to. **·stellig,** *a.* positive, decided. **·stelligheid,** no pl., *n.* positiveness, certainty. **·stelling,** *n.* thesis; position *(military)*; scaffolding. *~ nemen tegen,* to take a stand against. **·stelpen,** *v.t.* to staunch.

·stelregel, -s, *n.* fixed rule. **·stelschroef, -ven,** *n.* adjustable screw. **·stelsel, -s,** *n.n.* system. **·stelselloos, -loze,** *a.* unmethodical. **·stelsel·matig,** *a.* systematical. **·stelsel·matigheid,** no pl., *n.* thoroughness.

stelt, *n.* stilt. *alles op ~en zetten,* to put

everything in a turmoil. **·steltloper, -s,** *n.* stilt-walker. **·steltwortel, -s,** *n.* prop-root.

stem, -mmen, *n.* voice; part *(in singing)*; vote. *met luide ~,* in a loud voice; *bij ~ zijn,* to be in good form *(singing).* **·stembanden,** pl. only, *n.* vocal chords. **·stembiljet, -tten,** *n.n.* voting- or ballot-paper. **·stembureau, -'s,** *n.n.* polling booth. **·stembus, -ssen,** *n.* poll; ballot-box. **·stemgeluid,** *n.n.* sound of the voice. **·stemgerechtigd,** *a.* entitled to vote. **·stemgerechtigde, -n,** *n.* voter. **·stemhebbend,** *a.* voiced. **·stemloos, -loze,** *a.* voiceless. **·stemmen, stem,** *v.t.* to tune. ¶*v.i.* to vote; to put in a mood. *~ op,* to vote for; *~ over,* to vote on; *treurig ~,* to put in a sad mood, make (one) feel sad; *gunstig ~ voor,* to predispose in favour of. **·stemmer, -s,** *n.* voter; tuner. **·stemmig,** *a.* sober, quiet, sedate. **·stemmigheid,** no pl., *n.* quietness, demureness. **·stemming,** *n.* ballot; polling; division; mood, frame of mind. *~ maken,* to create an atmosphere; *in ~ komen,* to be put to the vote.

·stempel, -s, *n.n.* stamp *(tool)*; die; postmark. **·stempelbeeld,** *n.n.* effigy. **·stempelen,** *v.t.* to postmark; to stamp, hall-mark. **·stempelinkt,** *n.* ink for rubber-stamp. **·stempelkussen, -s,** *n.n.* inking pad.

·stemplicht, no pl., *n.* compulsory voting. **·stemrecht,** no pl., *n.n.* suffrage, franchise, vote. **·stemsleutel, -s,** *n.* tuning-key. **·stemvork,** *n.* tuning-fork.

stenen, *a.* (of) stone; (of) brick. **·stenigen,** *v.t.* to stone to death, lapidate. **·steniging,** *n.* lapidation.

steng, *n.* topmast. **·stengel, -s,** *n.* stalk, stem. **·stengelknoop, -knopen,** *n.* node.

steno·graaf, -grafen, *n.* stenographer. **stenoty·piste, -n,** *n.* shorthand-typist.

steppenhoen, -ders, *n.n.* sand-grouse.

ster, -rren, *n.* star.

·sterfbed, -dden, *n.n.* death-bed. **·sterfdag,** *n.* dying day. **·sterfelijk,** *a.* mortal. **·sterfelijkheid,** no pl., *n.* mortality. **·sterfgeval, -llen,** *n.n.* a) death. **·sterfhuis, -zen,** *n.n.* house of mourning. **·sterfte,** no pl., *n.* mortality, death. **·sterftecijfer, -s,** *n.n.* death-rate.

ste·riel, *a.* sterile. **sterili·seren, -seer,** *v.t.* to sterilize.

sterk, *a.* strong. *~e drank,* liquor; *dat is ~,* that's a bit thick; *100 man ~,* (of) a 100 men; *zich ~ maken,* to be certain. **·sterken,** *v.t.* to strengthen, invigorate. **·sterking,** no pl., *n.* strengthening. **·sterkte,** no pl., *n.* strength, power; establishment *(of unit). op ~ houden,* to keep up to strength.

stern, *n.* tern.

·sterrebaan, -banen, *n.* orbit of star. **·sterrejaar, -jaren,** *n.n.* siderial year. **·sterrekers,** no pl., *n.* garden-cress. **·sterrekroos,** no pl., *n.n.* water starwort. **·sterremuur,**

no pl., *n.* starwort. ·**sterrenbeeld**, *n.n.* constellation. ·**sterrenhemel**, no pl., *n.* starry sky. ·**sterrenkijker**, **-s**, *n.* stargazer; telescope. ·**sterrenkunde**, no pl., *n.* astronomy. ·**sterrenkundig**, *a.* astronomical. ·**sterrenwacht**, *n.* observatory. ·**sterrenwichelaar**, **-s**, *n.* astrologer. **sterrenwichela·rij**, no pl., *n.* astrology. ·**sterretje**, **-s**, *n.n.* little star; asterisk; pip (*on uniform*).
·**sterveling**, *n.* mortal. *geen* ~, not a soul. ·**sterven**, **sterf**, *v.i.*, *str.* to die. ~ *aan*, to die of; *van honger* ~, to starve to death. ¶*v.t.*, *str.* to die. ¶no pl., *n.n.*, death. *op* ~ *liggen*, to be on the point of death; *op* ~ *na dood*, all but dead. ·**stervend**, *a.* dying, moribund. ·**stervensnood**, no pl., *n.* agony of death. ·**stervensuur**, **-uren**, *n.n.* hour of death, last hour.
·**stervormig**, *a.* star-shaped.
steun, no pl., *n.* support; comfort; relief, dole. *tot* ~ *van*, in support of; ~ *trekken*, to be on the dole; ~ *verlenen aan*, to support. ·**steuncomité**, **-'s**, *n.n.* relief committee. ·**steunen**, *v.i.* to moan, groan. ~ *op*, to lean on *or* to be based on. ¶*v.t.* to support, prop (up); to second, support. ·**steunfonds**, *n.n.* relief fund. ·**steunpilaar**, **-laren**, *n.* pillar. ·**steunpunt**, *n.n.* point of support; fulcrum. ·**steuntrekkend**, *a.* on the dole. ·**steuntrekker**, **-s**, *n.* recipient of relief. ·**steunuitkering**, *n.* unemployment benefit.
steur, *n.* sturgeon. ·**steurkrab**, **-bben**, *n.* prawn.
·**stevel**, **-s**, *n.* boot.
·**steven**, **-s**, *n.* prow, stem. *de* ~ *wenden* (*stilted*), to put about (*ship*); *de* ~ *wenden naar* (*stilted*), to make for. ·**stevenen**, *v.i.* to sail, steer.
·**stevig**, *a.* firm, strong, stout; substantial. *een* ~*e bries*, a stiff breeze; *een* ~ *uur gaans*, an hour's brisk walk. ¶*adv.* firmly. ~ *doorstappen*, to walk at a stiff pace; ~ *inpakken*, to wrap up well; ~ *staan*, to stand firm. ·**stevigheid**, no pl., *n.* firmness.
sticht, *n.n.* bishopric. *het S*~, the bishopric of Utrecht. ·**stichtelijk**, *a.* edifying; devotional. ¶*adv. dank je* ~, thank you for nothing. ·**stichtelijkheid**, **-heden**, *n.* edification. ·**stichten**, *v.i.* to edify. ¶*v.t.* to found, establish. *brand* ~, to raise a fire; *tweedracht* ~, to stir up strife. ·**stichter**, **-s**, *n.* founder. ·**stichting**, *n.* foundation; edification.
·**stiefbroe(de)r**, **-s**, *n.* stepbrother. ·**stiefdochter**, **-s**, *n.* stepdaughter. ·**stiefkind**, **-eren**, *n.n.* stepchild. ·**stiefmoeder**, **-s**, *n.* stepmother. **stief·moederlijk**, *a.* stepmotherly. ·**stiefvader**, **-s**, *n.* stepfather. ·**stiefzoon**, **-s** *or* **-zonen**, *n.* stepson. ·**stiefzuster**, **-s**, *n.* stepsister.
·**stiekem**, *adv.* on the sly. *er* ~ *van door gaan*,

to sneak off. ·**stiekemerd**, **-s**, *n.* sneak. ·**stiekemweg**, *adv.* on the sly.
stier, *n.* bull. ·**stierengevecht**, *n.n.* bullfight. ·**stierkalf**, **-veren**, *n.n.* bull-calf. ·**stierlijk**, *adv.* excessively. *zich* ~ *vervelen*, to be bored to distraction.
·**Stiermarken**, *n.N.* Styria.
stift, *n.n.* peg, pin.
stigmati·seren, **-seer**, *v.t.* to stigmatize.
stijf, **-ve**, *a.* stiff, rigid. ~ *worden*, to stiffen. ¶*adv.* stiffly. *iets* ~ *en strak volhouden*, stoutly to maintain something. **stijf·harig**, *a.* wire-haired. ·**stijfheid**, no pl., *n.* stiffness. **stijf·hoofdig**, *a.* *See* **stijfkoppig**. ·**stijfkop**, **-ppen**, *n.* obstinate person. **stijf·koppig**, *a.* obstinate, headstrong. **stijf·koppigheid**, no pl., *n.* obstinacy. ·**stijfsel**, no pl., *n.n.* starch. ·**stijfselen**, *v.t.* to starch. ·**stijf·selkwast**, *n.* paste-brush. ·**stijfte**, no pl., *n.* stiffness.
·**stijgbeugel**, **-s**, *n.* stirrup. ·**stijgen**, *v.i.*, *str.* to rise, go up. *doen* ~, to send up; *naar het hoofd* ~. to go to one's head; *te paard* ~, to mount (*one's horse*). ·**stijging**, *n.* rise; increase. ·**stijgkracht**, no pl., *n.*, ·**stijgvermogen**, no pl., *n.n.* climbing power.
stijl, *n.* style; post, jamb, support. ·**stijlbloempje**, **-s**, *n.n.* flower of speech. ·**stijlfiguur**, **-guren**, *n.* figure of speech. ·**stijlloos**, **-loze**, *a.* without style.
·**stijven**, **stijf**, *v.t.*, *str.* to stiffen; to starch. *de kas* ~, to swell the funds.
·**stikdonker**, *a.* pitch-dark. ¶no pl., *n.n.* pitch-darkness. ·**stikgas**, **-ssen**, *n.n.* chokedamp. ·**stikken**, **stik**, *v.i.* to stifle, choke, suffocate; be suffocated. *stik!*, go to blazes; *het was om te* ~, it was stifling *or* it was screamingly funny. ¶*v.t.* to stitch. ·**stiksel**, no pl., *n.n.* stitching. ·**stiknaald**, *n.* stitching-needle. ·**stikstof**, no pl., *n.* nitrogen. ·**stikstofhoudend**, *a.* nitrogenous. ·**stikvol**, **-lle**, *a.* chock-full. ·**stikwerk**, no pl., *n.n.* stitching.
stil, **-lle**, *a.* still, quiet, silent. *stille diender*, a detective; *stille mis*, low mass; *stille vennoot*, sleeping partner; *stille week*, Holy Week; *stille Zaterdag*, Saturday before Easter; *Stille Zuidzee* or *Stille Oceaan*, Pacific Ocean.
sti·leren, **-leer**, *v.i.* to compose (*writing*); to stylize.
sti·let, **-tten**, *n.n.* stiletto.
·**stilhouden**, *v.i.s.*, *irr.* to stop, come to a stop; to draw up. ¶*v.t.s.*, *irr.* to keep quiet. ¶*zich* ~, *v.r.*, *irr.* to keep quiet. ·**stilleggen**, **leg stil**, *v.t.s.* to stop. ·**stillen**, **stil**, *v.t.* to still, appease, silence; to allay. ·**stilletjes**, *adv.* silently; secretly. ·**stilleven**, **-s**, *n.n.* still life. ·**stilliggen**, **lig stil**, *v.i.s.*, *str.* to lie still; to lie idle. ·**stilstaan**, **sta stil**, *v.i.s.*, *irr.* to stand still; to be at a standstill. *blijven* ~, to stop, pull up; *laten* ~, to stop; ~ *bij*, to dwell on. ·**stilstaand**, *a.* stagnant, dead. ·**stilstand**, no pl., *n.*

standstill; stagnation. ·stilte, no pl., n. stillness, silence. in ~, silently. ·stil-zitten, zit stil, v.i.s., str. to sit still; to remain idle. ·stilzwijgen, v.i.s., str. to remain silent. ¶no pl., n.n. silence. stil-zwijgend, a. silent; tacit; taciturn. stil·zwijgenheid, no pl., n. silence, taci-turnity.

·stinkdier, n.n. skunk. ·stinken, v.i., str. to stink. ·stinkstok, -kken, n. stinker (cigar).

stip, -ppen, n., ·stippel, -s, n. dot. ·stippelen, v.i. to dot, stipple. ·stippellijn, n. dotted line. stipt, a. punctual; strict. ·stiptheid, no pl., n. punctuality; strictness.

·stoeien, v.i. to romp. ·stoeipartij, n. romp, rough-and-tumble. ·stoeiziek, a. romping.

stoel, n. chair. het niet cnder ~en of banken steken, to make no secret of it; voor ~en en banken spelen, to play to an empty house. ·stoelendraaier, -s, n. chair-maker. ·stoelengeld, no pl., n.n. pew-rent. ·stoelenmatter, -s, n. chair-mender. ·stoelenzetster, -s, n. pew-opener. ·stoel-gang, no pl., n. defecation.

stoep, n. stoep, (private) pavement.

stoer, a. stalwart, sturdy.

stoet, n. procession.

stoete·rij, n. stud; stud-farm.

stof, -ffen, n. substance, matter; subject-matter; material (textile), stuff. kort van ~, brief, to the point; lang van ~, long-winded; ~ tot nadenken, food for thought. ¶no pl., n.n. dust. ~ afnemen, to dust (clean); onder het ~ zitten, to be covered in dust. ·stofbril, -llen, n. (pair of) goggles. ·stofdeeltje, -s, n.n. particle of dust. ·stofdicht, a. dust-proof. ·stofdoek, n. duster. stof·fage, -s, n. stuff, material (textile). stof·feerder, -s, n. upholsterer. ·stoffel, -s, n. clumsy person, blockhead. ·stoffelijk, a. material. ~ overschot, mortal remains. ·stoffen, stof, v.i. to boast. ¶v.t. to dust (room). ¶a. (of) cloth. ·stoffer, -s, n. feather-brush. stof·feren, -feer, v.t. to upholster. stof·fering, n. upholstery. ·stoffig, a. dusty. ·stofgoud, no pl., n.n. gold-dust. ·stofje, -s, n.n. speck of dust. ·stofnaam, -namen, n. name of material. ·stofregen, -s, n. drizzle. ·stofregenen, v.i. to drizzle. ·stofwisseling, no pl., n. metabolism. ·stofzuiger, -s, n. vacuum cleaner.

stoï·cijn, n. stoic. stoï·cijns, a. stoic(al).

stok, -kken, n. stick; perch; pole, staff (for flag); stock (of anchor); stocks. het aan de ~ krijgen met, to fall out with; op ~ gaan, to go to roost. ·stokboon, -bonen, n. runner bean. ·stokdoof, -dove, a. stone-deaf. ·stokdweil, n. (floor) mop.

·stokebrand, n. mischief-maker. ·stoken, stook, v.t. to stoke; to burn; to distil; to pick (teeth). kwaad ~, to brew mischief. ·stoker, -s, n. stoker, fireman; distiller. stoke·rij, n. distillery.

·stokje, -s, n.n. little stick. ergens een ~ voor steken, to put a stop to something; van z'n ~ vallen, to faint. ·stokken, stok, v.i. to cease to circulate. z'n adem stokte, his breath caught. ·stokkerig, a. halting; woody. ·stokoud, a. very old. ·stok-paardje, -s, n.n. hobby-horse; hobby. ·stokroos, -rozen, n. hollyhock. ·stokslag, n. blow (with a stick). ·stokstijf, -ve, a. as stiff as a poker. ·stokstil, -lle, a. stock-still. ·stokvis, no pl., n. stockfish.

·stollen, stol, v.i. to coagulate, congeal, clot; to curdle. ·stolling, n. coagulation.

stolp, n. (bell-shaped glass) cover.

stom, -mme, a. dumb, speechless; stupid. stomme film, silent film; geen ~ woord, not a word. ·stomdronken, a. dead drunk.

·stomen, stoom, v.i. to steam.

·stommeknecht, n. dumb-waiter.

·stommelen, v.i. to clump.

·stommeling, n., ·stommerik, -kken, n. blockhead. ·stommigheid, -heden, n., stommi·teit, n. stupidity; blunder.

stomp, a. blunt, dull; obtuse. ~e toren, tower. ¶n. punch (with fist). ·stompen, v.t. to punch, pummel. ·stompheid, no pl., n. bluntness. ·stomphoekig, a. obtuse-angled. ·stompje, -s, n.n. stub, stump. ·stompneus, -zen, n. snub-nose. stomp-zinnig, a. obtuse (of perception).

·stomvervelend, a. terribly dull.

stond, n. (stilted) hour, moment. ~en, menses.

stoof, stoven, n. footstool. ·stoofappel, -s, n. cooking apple. ·stoofpan, -nnen, n. stewing pan.

·stookmiddel, n.n. fuel. ·stookolie, -liën, n. liquid fuel (oil). ·stookoven, -s, n. furnace. ·stookplaats, n. fireplace; stokehold.

stoom, no pl., n. steam. onder eigen ~, under her own power. ·stoombarkas, -ssen, n. steam-launch. ·stoomboot, -boten, n. steamer, steamship. ·stoomcurcus, -ssen, n. concentrated course. ·stoomfiets, n. motor-bike. ·stoomgemaal, -malen, n.n. pumping station. ·stoomketel, -s, n. boiler. ·stoomtram, -s, n. local railway. ·stoomvaart, no pl., n. steam navigation. ·stoornis, -ssen, n. disturbance.

stoot, -stoten, n. shock, push; stab; blast (on siren); stroke, shot (at billiards). ·stootblok, -kken, n.n. buffer. ·stootje, -s, n.n. push, nudge. ·stootkar, -rren, n. push-cart. ·stootkussen, -s, n.n. buffer.

stop, -ppen, n. plug; stopper. ·stopcontact, n.n. plug connection. ·stopfles, -ssen, n. stoppered bottle. ·stoplap, -ppen, n. sampler (of darning stitches); stop-gap. ·stopmes, -ssen, n.n. putty knife. ·stop-middel, n. astringent. ·stopnaald, n. darning-needle. ·stoppel, -s, n. stubble. ·stoppelig, a. stubbly. ·stoppen, stop, v.t. to stop; to darn; to fill (pipe); to put. ¶v.i. to stop. ·stopplaats, n. stop, halt.

·**stopster, -s,** *n.* darner (*female*). ·**stopverf,** no pl., *n.* putty. ·**stopwoord,** *n.n.* stop-gap; expletive. ·**stopzetten, zet stop,** *v.t.s.* to stop; to close down. ·**stopzetting,** *n.* stoppage.

·**storen, stoor,** *v.t.* to disturb. ¶ *v.r. zich ~ aan,* to mind, be disturbed by; *zich niet ~ aan,* to take no notice of. ·**storing,** *n.* disturbance, interruption.

s'**orm,** *n.* storm (*of wind*). ·**stormaanval, -llen,** *n.* assault (*military*). ·**stormachtig,** *a.* stormy. ·**stormband,** *n.* chin-strap. ·**stormen,** *v.i.* to storm. ·**stormklok, -kken,** *n.* tocsin. ·**stormladder, -s.** *n.* scaling-ladder. ·**stormlamp,** *n.* hurricane lamp. ·**stormloop,** no pl., *n.* assault (*military*). ·**stormlopen, loop storm,** *v.i.s., str.* to rush, assault. ·**stormram, -mmen,** *n.* battering-ram. ·**stormtroepen,** pl. only, *n.* shock troops. ·**stormvogel, -s,** *n.* stormy petrel. ·**stormweer,** no pl., *n.* stormy weather.

·**stortbad,** *n.n.* shower-bath. *een ~ geven,* to pour cold water on. ·**stortbui,** *n.* downpour. ·**storten,** *v.t.* to shed; to spill; to dump, tip; to deposit, pay in. *zich ~ in,* to throw oneself into, plunge into; *zich ~ op,* to throw oneself upon; *tranen ~,* to shed tears. ·**stortgoederen,** pl. only, *n.n.* goods stowed in bulk. ·**storting,** *n.* payment, deposit. ·**stortkar, -rren,** *n.* tip-cart. ·**stortplaats,** *n.* rubbish-tip, rubbish-dump. ·**stortregen, -s,** *n.* downpour. ·**stortregenen,** *v.imp.* to pour (with rain). ·**stortvloed,** *n.* torrent. ·**stortzee, -zeeën,** *n. een ~ krijgen,* to ship a heavy sea.

·**stoten, stoot,** *v.i.* to push, knock. *aan de grond ~,* to touch ground (*ship*); *ergens op ~,* to strike upon something (*ship*) or to come across something. ¶*v.t.* to bump, stub; to push; to thrust; to shock. *iemand voor het hoofd ~,* to affront a person. ¶*v.r. zich ~ aan,* to bump into; to be shocked at.

·**stotteraar, -s,** *n.* stammerer, stutterer. ·**stotteren,** *v.i.* to stammer, stutter.

stout, *a.* bold, daring; naughty. ·**stouterd, -s,** *n.* naughty child. ·**stoutheid,** no pl., *n.* naughtiness. ·**stoutigheid, -heden,** *n.* naughty action. **stout·moedig,** *a.* bold. **stout·moedigheid,** no pl., *n.* daring. ·**stoutweg,** *adv.* boldly.

·**stouwen,** *v.t.* to stow, trim. ·**stouwer, -s,** *n.* stevedore, stower.

·**stoven, stoof,** *v.t. & v.i.* to stew. ·**stovenzetster, -s,** *n.* pew-opener (*female*).

straal, stralen, *n.* ray; jet; radius. ·**straalbrekend,** *a.* refractive. ·**straalbreking,** *n.* refraction. ·**straalbundel, -s,** *n.* pencil of rays. ·**straaldier,** *n.n.* radiate (*animal*). ·**straalsgewijs,** *adv.* radially.

straat, straten, *n.* street, road; straits (*in geography*). *op ~,* in the street(s); *iemand op ~ zetten,* to turn a person out. ·**straatarm,** *a.* very poor. ·**straatjongen, -s,** *n.*

street arab. ·**Straatsburg,** *n.N.* Strasbourg. ·**straatschender, -s,** *n.* hooligan. ·**straatschenderij,** *n.* hooliganism. ·**straatslijper, -s,** *n.* loafer. ·**straatslijperij, -s,** *n.* loafing. ·**straatsteen, -stenen,** *n.* paving-stone. ·**straatvuil,** no pl., *n.n.* town refuse. ·**straatweg,** *n.* highway.

straf, -ffen, *n.* punishment. *~ krijgen,* to be punished. *op straffe van,* on penalty of. ¶*a.* severe, stiff. ·**strafbaar, -bare,** *a.* punishable. ·**strafbepaling,** *n.* penal provision. ·**strafexpeditie, -s,** *n.* punitive expedition. ·**straffe,** *n. See* straf. ·**straffeloos, loze,** *a.* with impunity. ·**straffeloosheid,** no pl., *n.* impunity. ·**straffen, straf,** *v.t.* to punish. ·**strafkolonie, -s,** *n.* penal settlement. ·**strafmaatregel,** *n.* punitive measure. ·**strafoefening,** *n.* execution (*of sentence*). ·**strafpeloton, -s,** *n.n.* firing squad. ·**strafport,** *n.* surcharge. ·**strafportzegel, -s,** *n.n.* postage-due stamp. ·**strafprediker, -s,** *n.* hell-fire preacher. ·**strafrecht,** no pl., *n.n.* criminal law. **straf·rechtelijk,** *a.* criminal, penal. ·**strafrechter, -s,** *n.* criminal judge. ·**strafregel, -s,** *n.* (*usu. pl.*) lines (*for punishment*). ·**strafschop, -ppen,** *n.* penalty kick. ·**straftijd,** *n.* term of imprisonment. ·**strafvordering,** *n.* criminal procedure. ·**strafwerk,** no pl., *n.n.* imposition (*at school*). ·**strafwet, -tten,** *n.* criminal law, penal law. ·**strafwetboek,** *n.n.* penal code. ·**strafzaak, -zaken,** *n.* criminal case.

strak, -kke, *a.* tight, taut; intent. ·**strakheid,** no pl., *n.* tightness; intentness. ·**strakjes,** *adv.,* **straks,** *adv.* presently; just now. *tot ~!,* see you later!

·**stralen, straal,** *v.i.* to beam, radiate; to be ploughed (*in exam.*). ·**stralenbundel, -s,** *n.* pencil of rays. ·**stralenkrans,** *n.* halo. ·**straling,** *n.* radiation.

stram, -mme, *a.* stiff. ·**stramheid,** no pl., *n.* stiffness.

strand, *n.n.* (sandy) beach. *op het ~ zetten,* to beach. ·**stranden,** *v.i.* to strand, run aground. ·**strandgoed, -eren,** *n.n.* wrecked goods; flotsam and jetsam. ·**strandhut, -tten,** *n.* beach-hut. ·**strandjutter, -s,** *n.* wrecker; beach-comber. ·**strandjutterij,** *n.* wrecking; beach-combing. ·**strandloper, -s,** *n.* sanderling. ·**strandpluvier, -s,** *n.* sea-plover. ·**strandrecht,** *n.n.* right of salvage. ·**strandvonder, -s,** *n.* wreck-master.

stra·teeg, -tegen, *n.* strategist. ·**stratenmaker, -s,** *n.* roadmender.

streek, streken, *n.* stroke, line; region, district; point (of the compass); trick. *rare streken,* foolish pranks; *op ~ komen,* to get into one's stride; *van ~,* not too well *or* upset.

streep, strepen, *n.* line, stripe; dash, hyphen. *een ~ halen door,* to strike out; *er loopt een ~ door,* there's a screw loose; *het is* *een* ~ *door de rekening,* it upsets all calculations. ·**streepjesgoed,** no pl., *n.n.* striped material(s).

·**strekdam, -mmen,** *n.* breakwater. ·**strekgras,** no pl., *n.n.* dog-grass. ·**strekken, -strek,** *v.i.* to stretch, extend. *zolang de voorraad strekt,* as long as stocks last; ~ *om,* to serve to; ~ *tot,* to be conducive to; *tot eer* ~, to do credit to. ·**strekking,** *n.* tendency, purport. ·**strekkingsroman, -s,** *n.* novel with a purpose. ·**strekspier,** *n.* tensor *(muscle).*

·**strelen, streel,** *v.t.* to stroke, caress. *de zinnen* ~, to gratify the senses. ·**strelend,** *a.* flattering. ·**streling,** *n.* caress.

stremmen, strem, *v.i.* to curdle, coagulate. ¶*v.t.* to curdle; to· obstruct *(traffic).* ·**stremming,** *n.* coagulation; obstruction. ·**stremsel, -s,** *n.n.,* ·**stremstof, -ffen,** *n.* coagulant; rennet.

streng, *n.* strand *(of rope);* trace *(rope);* skein. ¶*a.* severe; stern, strict, rigorous. ·**strengel, -s,** *n.* strand *(of plait).* ·**strengelen,** *v.t.* to twine. *(zich) in elkaar* ~, to intertwine. ·**strengheid,** no pl., *n.* severity.

·**strepen, streep,** *v.t.* to stripe.

·**streven, streef,** *v.i.* to strive. ~ *naar,* to strive *or* aspire after. ¶no pl., *n.n.* endeavour(s), aspiration.

·**stribbelen,** *v.i.* to struggle, resist.

striem, *n.* weal. ·**striemen,** *v.t.* to lash. ·**striemend,** *a.* biting.

strijd, *n.* combat, fight. ~ *voeren tegen,* to wage war against; *in* ~ *met,* contrary to, conflicting with; *om* ~, vying *(with one another); zich ten* ~*e rusten,* to prepare for battle. ·**strijdbaar, -bare,** *a.* capable of bearing arms. ·**strijdbaarheid,** no pl., *n.* ability to fight. ·**strijdbijl,** *n.* battle-axe. ·**strijden,** *v.i., str.* to combat, fight. ~ *met,* to clash with *or* to fight with *or* against; *er valt niet over te* ~, there can be no two opinions about it. ·**strijder, -s,** *n.* combatant. ·**strijdend,** *a.* fighting; conflicting. *de* ~*e kerk,* the church militant. ·**strijdgenoot, -noten,** *n.* comrade in arms. ·**strijdig,** *a.* conflicting, contradictory; incompatible. ·**strijdigheid, -heden,** *n.* contradiction; incompatibility. ·**strijdkrachten,** pl. only, *n.* (military) forces. ·**strijdkreet, -kreten,** *n.* battle-cry. ·**strijdlust.** no pl., *n.* pugnacity, warlike spirit. **strijd·lustig,** *a.* bellicose, aggressive. ·**strijdmiddel,** *n.n.* weapon. ·**strijdperk,** *n.n.* arena. ·**strijdros, -ssen,** *n.n.* charger. ·**strijdschrift,** *n.n.* polemic writing. **strijd·vaardig,** *a.* ready to fight. **strijd vaardigheid,** no pl., *n.* readiness to fight. ·**strijdvraag, -vragen,** *n.* controversial point.

strijk, no pl., *n.* ironing. ·**strijkage, -s,** *n.* bowing and scraping. ·**strijkdeken, -s,** *n.* ironing-cloth. ·**strijkelings,** *adv.* ~ *voorbijgaan,* to skim *or* brush past. ·**strijken,** *v.i., str.* to stroke; to iron. ~ *langs,* to

brush past; *gaan* ~ *met,* to walk off with. ¶*v.t., str.* to iron; to lower *(boat);* to strike *(sail).* ·**strijkgoed,** no pl., *n.n.* laundry *(to be ironed).* ·**strijkijzer, -s,** *n.n.* flat-iron. ·**strijkinstrument,** *n.n.* string instrument. ·**strijkje, -s,** *n.n.* string-band. ·**strijkorkest,** *n.n.* string-orchestra. ·**strijkplank,** *n.* ironing-board. ·**strijkster, -s,** *n.* ironer, laundress. ·**strijkstok, -kken,** *n.* bow *(violin).*

strik, -kken, *n.* bow, knot; snare. *een* ~ *spannen,* to lay a snare. ·**strikken, strik,** *v.t.* to tie *(into a knot);* to snare.

strikt, *a.* strict. ·**striktheid, -heden,** *n.* strictness.

·**strikvraag, -vragen,** *n.* catch question.

·**stripgoed,** no pl., *n.n.* strip-leaf. ·**strippen, strip,** *v.t.* to strip *(tobacco).*

stro, no pl., *n.n.* straw. ·**stroachtig,** *a.* strawy. ·**strobloem,** *n.* immortelle. ·**strobos, -ssen,** *n.* bundle of straw. ·**strodak,** *n.n.* thatched roof. ·**strodekker, -s,** *n.* thatcher.

stroef, -ve, *a.* not smooth, jerky; stiff. ·**stroefheid, -heden,** *n.* stiffness.

·**strohalm,** *n.* blade of straw. ·**strokarton,** no pl., *n.n.* strawboard.

·**stroken, strook,** *v.i.* ~ *met,* to tally with, fit in with.

·**stroman, -nnen,** *n.* puppet, figure-head.

·**stromen, stroom,** *v.i.* to stream, flow, pour. ·**stroming,** *n.* current; tend, drift.

strompelen, *v.i.* to hobble, limp. ·**strompelig,** *a.* doddering, clumsy.

stronk, *n.* stump *(tree);* stalk *(cabbage).*

stront, *n.n. (vulg.)* faeces. ·**strontje, -s,** *n.* stye *(eye.).*

·**strooibiljet, -tten,** *n.n.* leaflet, handbill. ·**strooien,** *v.t.* to strew, scatter. ¶*a.* (of) straw. ·**strooier, -s,** *n.* caster, dredger. ·**strooisel,** no pl., *n.n.* that which is strewn; litter. ·**strooizand,** no pl., *n.n.* fine sand.

strook, stroken, *n.* strip; flounce; counterfoil.

stroom, stromen, *n.* stream; current *(water and electricity);* flow. *bij stromen,* in streams; *op* ~ *liggen,* to lie in the current; *onder* ~, live. ·**stroomafwaarts,** *adv.* downstream. ·**stroombed, -dden,** *n.n.* riverbed, channel. ·**stroombreker, -s,** *n.* breakwater, groyne. ·**stroomgebied,** *n.n.* (river-)basin; catchment area. ·**stroomkring,** *n.* (electric) circuit. ·**stroomlevering,** *n.* electric supply. ·**stroomloos, -loze,** *a.* dead *(electricity).* ·**stroomopwaarts,** *adv.* upstream. ·**stroomrijk,** *a.* rich in rivers. ·**stroomsterkte, -n,** *n.* strength of current. ·**stroomversnelling,** *n.* rapid. ·**stroomwisselaar, -s,** *n.* switch.

stroop, stropen, *n.* syrup, treacle. ·**stroopachtig,** *a.* treacly. ·**strooppot, -tten,** *n.* treacle-jar. ·**stroo ocht,** *n.* marauding expedition, raid.

·**strootje, -s,** *n.n.* little straw; cigarette *(East Indies).* ~ *trekken,* to draw lots.

strop, -ppen, *n.* halter. *een lelijke* ~, a bad

loss or disappointment. ·stropdas, -ssen, n. stock (tie). ·stropen, stroop, v.i. to poach (game); to pillage, maraud. ¶v.t. to poach; to skin. ·stroper, -s, n. poacher; marauder. ·stroperig, a. treacly. strope·rij, n. poaching; robbery.
·stropop, -ppen, n. puppet; figure-head.
·stroppen, strop, v.t. to snare.
strot, -tten, n. throat. ·strotklep, -ppen, n. epiglottis. ·strottenhoofd, n.n. larynx.
·strozak, -kken, n. straw mattress, palliasse.
·strubbeling, n. difficulty, trouble.
struif, -ven, n. omelette.
struik, n. bush, shrub. ·struikelblok, -kken, n. stumbling block, obstacle. ·struikelen, v.i. to stumble. ·struikeling, n. stumble, trip-up. ·struikgewas, -ssen, n.n. brushwood, bushes. ·struikrover, -s, n. footpad, highwayman. struikrove·rij, n. (highway) robbery.
struis, n. ostrich. ¶a. sturdy. ·struisvogel, -s, n. ostrich.
stru·weel, -welen, n.n. brushwood.
stu·deerkamer, n. study. stu·dent, n. student, undergraduate. stu·dentencorps, n.n. students' union. stu·dentenhaver, no pl., n. mixed almonds and raisins. stu·dentendagen, pl. only, n. college days. studenti·koos, -koze, a. student-like. stu·deren, -deer, v.i. to study. ~ in, to study. ·studie, -diën, n. study (scholarly, scientific). in ~ nemen, to take into consideration. ¶-s, n. study, studying. op ~ zijn, to be at college. ¶no pl., n. zeal, application. ·studiebeurs, -zen, n. scholarship, exhibition. ·studiecommissie, -s, n. committee of inquiry. studi·eus, -ze, a. studious.
stuf, no pl., n. rubber, eraser.
stug, -gge, a. surly. ·stugheid, no pl., n. surliness.
·stuifaarde, no pl., n. dry-mould. ·stuifmeel, no pl., n.n. pollen. ·stuifzand, no pl., n.n. drift-sand. ·stuifzwam, -mmen, n. puffball.
stuip, n. convulsion. ~en, fit(s). ·stuipachtig, a. convulsive. ·stuiptrekken, -trek, v.i. to be convulsed, twitch. ·stuiptrekking, n. convulsive movement, twitch.
·stuitbeen, ·-deren, n.n. coccyx. ·stuiten, v.i. to bounce. ~ op, to strike against, meet with; ~ tegen, to strike. ¶v.t. to stop, check. iemand tegen de borst ~, to shock or offend someone. ·stuiter, -s, n. big marble.
·stuiven, stuif, v.i., str. to dash. het stuift, the dust flies about. ·stuiver, -s, n. penny. een aardige ~, a pretty penny.
stuk, -kken, n.n. piece; object; document. ingezonden ~, a letter to the editor; een stout ~, a bold feat; een ~ in z'n kraag hebben, to be half-seas over; aan or in stukken slaan, to knock to pieces; aan or in één ~ door, without a break; bij stukken en brokken, piecemeal; op het ~ van, in the matter of; op geen stukken na,

not by a long chalk; op z'n ~ blijven staan, to stick to one's guns; groot van ~, of large stature; van z'n ~ brengen, to fluster; uit één ~, of one piece; ~ voor ~, one by one. ¶-kken or -s, n.n. piece, item. per ~ or het ~, a piece; bij het ~, singly; een ~ of zes, some five or six. ¶-kke, a. broken.
stuka·door, -s, n. plasterer.
·stukbreken, breek stuk, v.t.s., str. to break to pieces. ·stukgaan, ga stuk, v.i.s., irr. to break. ·stukgoed, -eren, n.n. general cargo. ·stukloon, no pl., n.n. op ~, on piece rates. ·stuksgewijs, adv. one by one. ·stukslaan, sla stuk, v.t.s., irr. to break to pieces, smash. ·stukwerk, no pl., n.n. piece-work.
stulp, n. bell-glass; (lit.) hut.
·stumper(d), -s, n. (poor) wretch. ·stumperig, a. wretched.
·sturen, stuur, v.i. to steer. ~ om, to send for. ¶v.t. to send; to steer.
stut, -tten, n. prop, support. ·stutmuur, -muren, n. buttress. ·stutten, stut, v.t. to prop, shore.
stuur, sturen, n.n. helm, tiller; (steering-) wheel; handle-bar; (driving-)wheel. ·stuuras, -ssen, n. steering-shaft. ·stuurboord, no pl., n.n. starboard. ·stuurhuis, -zen, n.n. wheelhouse. ·stuurloos, -loze, a. out of control. ·stuurman, -lieden or -lui, n. mate (on ship); man at the wheel or helm, steersman. ·stuurmanskunst, no pl., n. art of navigation. ·stuurrad, -eren, n.n. steering-wheel; driving-wheel. ·stuurreep, -repen, n. tiller-rope.
stuurs, a. surly. ·stuursheid, no pl., n. surliness.
·stuurstok, -kken, n. tiller; joy-stick. ·stuurvlak, -kken, n.n. aileron.
stuw, n. weir, dam. ·stuwa·door, -s, n. stevedore (not workman). stuwa·doorsbaas, -bazen, n. warehouse foreman. stu·wage, no pl., n. stowage. ·stuwdam, -mmen, n. weir, dam ·stuwen, v.t. to stow; to propel; to dam up. ·stuwkracht, no pl., n. propelling force. ·stuwplan, -nnen, n.n. plan of stowage.
subli·meren, -meer, v.t. to sublimate.
subsidi·air, a. with the alternative or option of. subsidi·ëren, -dieer, v.t. to subsidize. subsidi·ëring, n. subsidization.
substi·tuut, -tuten, n. substitute, deputy.
sub·tiel, a. subtle.
suc·ces, -ssen, n.n. success. veel ~, good luck!; geen ~ hebben, to be unsuccessful. suc·cessierechten, pl. only, n.n. death duties.
succur·sale, -n, n. branch(-office).
suf, -ffe, a. dull, sleepy. ·suffen, suf, v.i. to be dull, be far away. ·suffer(d), -s, n. stupid fellow.
sugge·reren, -reer, v.t. to suggest. sug·gestie, -s, n. suggestion.

·**suiker, -s,** *n.* (type of) sugar. ¶*no* pl., *n.* sugar. ·**suikerachtig,** *a.* sugary. ·**suikerbiet,** *n.* sugar-beet. ·**suikerboon, -bonen,** *n.* butter bean. ·**suikeren,** *v.t.* to sugar. ·**suikergast,** *n.* sugar-mite. ·**suikergoed,** no pl., *n.n.* sweets, confectionery. ·**suikerig,** *a.* sugary. ·**suikerpot, -tten,** *n.* sugar-basin. ·**suikerraffinaderij,** *n.* sugar-refinery. ·**suikerraffinadeur, -s,** *n.* sugar-refiner. ·**suikerriet,** no pl., *n.n.* sugar-cane. ·**suikerwater,** no pl., *n.n.* sugar and water. ·**suikerwerk,** no pl., *n.n.* sweets, confectionery. ·**suikerziekte,** no pl., *n.* diabetes. ·**suikerzoet,** *a.* as sweet as sugar. ·**suizebollen, -bol,** *v.i.* to be dizzy. ·**suizelen,** *v.i.* to rustle. ·**suizelig,** *a.* dizzy. ·**suizeling,** *n.* rustle; dizzy feeling. ·**suizen, suis,** *v.i.* to rustle; to whizz, buzz. *mijn oren ~,* my ears are singing.

·**suja!,** *excl.* hushaby.

su·jet, -tten, *n.n.* individual (*pejorative*).

su·kade, no pl., *n.* (candied) peel. **su·kade-koek,** *n.* gingerbread with peel.

·**sukkel, -s,** *n.,* ·**sukkelaar, -s,** *n.* poor soul. *aan de ~ zijn,* to be ailing. **sukkelachtig,** *a.* ailing. **sukkela·rij,** *n.* bungling. ·**sukkeldraf,** no pl., *n.* jog-trot. ·**sukkelen,** *v.i.* to be ailing, to have trouble; to trudge, get along slowly. *achter iemand aan ~,* to come lagging behind. **sukkelgangetje,** no pl., *n.n. het gaat een ~,* things go jogging along.

sul, -llen, *n.* kindly simpleton.

sul·faat, -faten, *n.n.* sulphate.

·**sullen, sul,** *v.i.* to slide.

sum·mair, *a.,* **sum·mier,** *a.* summary. ·**summum,** no pl., *n.n.* summit, height.

superi·eur, *a.* superior. ¶*n.* superior.

sup·pletietroepen, pl. only, *n.* supports, reserves. **supple·toir,** *a.* supplementary.

sup·poost, *n.* doorkeeper, turnkey.

suppri·meren, -meer, *v.t.* to suppress.

·**sure, -n,** *n.* surah.

surname·rair, *a.* supernumary.

surro·gaat, -gaten, *n.n.* substitute.

sursé·ance, no pl., *n. ~ van betaling,* suspension of payment.

surveil·leren, -leer, *v.t.* to supervise; to invigilate.

·**sussen, sus,** *v.t.* to soothe; to hush up.

symbo·liek, no pl., *n.* symbolism. **sym·bool, -bolen,** *n.n.* symbol.

sympa·thie, *n.* fellow-feeling, sympathy, liking. *~ voelen voor,* to be in sympathy with. **sympa·thiek,** *a.* congenial, pleasant. **sym·pathisch,** *a.* sympathetic (*nerves*). **sympathi·seren, -seer,** *v.i.* to sympathize.

·**Syrië,** *n.N.* Syria. ·**Syrisch,** *a.* Syrian.

sys·teem, -temen, *n.n.* system.

T

Taag, *N.* Tagus.

taai, *a.* tough; tenacious. *hou je ~!,* keep

your pecker up! ·**taaiheid,** no pl., *n.* toughness; tenacity. **taai-·taai,** no pl., *n.n.* tough gingerbread.

taak, taken, *n.* task.

taal, talen, *n.* language, tongue, speech. *~ noch teken geven,* to give no sign of life. ·**taaleigen,** no pl., *n.n.* idiom. ·**taalfout,** *n.* grammatical mistake. ·**taalgebruik,** no pl., *n.n.* usage (*linguistic*). ·**taalgeleerde, -n,** *n.* linguist, philologist. ·**taalgevoel,** no pl., *n.n.* linguistic feeling. ·**taalkenner, -s,** *n.* linguist. ·**taalkunde,** no pl., *n.* philology. ·**taalkundig,** *a.* linguistic, grammatical. **taal·kundige, -n,** *n. See* taalgeleerde. ·**taalschat,** no pl., *n.* vocabulary. ·**taaltje, -s,** *n.n.* jargon; lingo.

taan, no pl., *n.* tan. ·**taander, -s,** *n.* tanner. **taande·rij,** *n.* tannery, tanning-yard. ·**taankleurig,** *a.* tan-coloured, tawny.

taart, *n.* tart; fancy pastry. ·**taartebakker, -s,** *n.* pastry-cook. ·**taartpunt,** *n.* wedge of cake. ·**taartje, -s,** *n.* pastry (*fancy*).

ta·bak, no pl., *n.* tobacco. **ta·baksonderneming,** *n.,* **ta·baksplantage, -s,** *n.* tobacco plantation.

·**tabbaard,** *n.,* ·**tabberd,** *n.* gown, robe.

ta·bel, -llen, *n.* table, list, index. **tabel·leren, -leer,** *v.t.* to tabulate.

taber·nakel, -s, *n.n.* tabernacle. *iemand op z'n ~ komen,* to give a person a drubbing.

·**tachtig,** *num.* eighty. ·**tachtiger, -s,** *n.* octogenarian. ¶*in de ~ jaren,* in the eighties. ·**tachtigjarig,** *a.* octogenarian. *~e oorlog,* the Eighty Years' War. ·**tachtigmaal,** *adv.* eighty times. ·**tachtigste,** *a.* eightieth. ·**tachtigvoud,** *n.n.* multiple of eighty.

taf, -ffen, *n.* taffeta.

·**tafel, -s,** *n.* table. *aan ~ gaan,* to sit down to dinner. *etc.; na ~,* after the meal; *ter ~ brengen,* to bring on the tapis. ·**tafelappel, -s,** *n.* dessert apple. ·**tafeldekken,** no pl., *n.n.* laying the table. ·**tafelen,** *v.i.* to sit at table. ·**tafelgerei,** no pl., *n.n.* table ware. ·**tafelkleed, -kleden,** *n.n.* table-cloth (*not for meal*); table-cover. ·**tafellaken, -s,** *n.n.* table-cloth (*for meal*). ·**tafelschuimer, -s,** *n.* sponger.

tafe·reel, -relen, *n.n.* scene, picture.

·**taffen,** *a.* (of) taffeta.

·**taille, -s,** *n.* waist. **tail·leren, -leer,** *v.t.* to tailor. **tail·leur, -s,** *n.* tailor; tailor-made.

tak, -kken, *n.* branch, bough.

·**takel, -s,** *n.* pulley, tackle. ·**takelaar, -s,** *n.* rigger. **take·lage,** no pl., *n.* rigging. ·**takelblok, -kken,** *n.n.* (tackle-)block. ·**takelen,** *v.t.* to rig; to hoist (up). ·**takelwagen, -s,** *n.* breakdown lorry. ·**takelwerk,** no pl., *n.n.* rigging, cordage.

takje, -s, *n.n.* twig. ·**takkenbos, -ssen,** *n.* faggot.

takt, no pl., *n.* tact. **tak·tiek,** no pl., *n.* tactic(s). ·**taktisch,** *a.* tactical. ·**taktloos,**

-loze, *a.* tactless. ·taktloosheid, -heden, *n.* tactlessness. ·taktvol, -lle, *a.* tactful.
tal, no pl., *n.n.* number. ~ *van,* a (great) number of; *zonder* ~, innumerable.
·tale, -n, *n.* (*bibl.*). *See* taal.
ta·lentvol, -lle, *a.* talented.
·talhout, *n.n.* billet (*wood*).
·talie, -s, *n.* tackle. ·taliën, talie, *v.t.* to tackle. ·taliereep, -repen, *n.* lanyard.
talk, no pl., *n.* tallow; talcum. ·talkvet, no pl., *n.n.* tallow.
·talloos, -loze, *a.* countless.
·talmen, *v.i.* to linger, dawdle. talme·rij, no pl., *n.* lingering, delay.
ta·lon, -s, *n.* stub, counterfoil.
·talreep, -repen, *n.* lanyard.
·talrijk, *a.* numerous. ·talrijkheid, no pl., *n.* numerousness.
tam, -mme, *a.* tame. *tamme kastanje,* sweet chestnut; ~ *maken,* to tame.
tama·rinde, -n, *n.* tamarind.
tama·risk, *n.* tamarisk.
·tamboer, -s, *n.* drummer. tam·boeren, *v.i.* to drum. ~ *op* (*fig.*), to hammer at.
tamboe·rijn, *n.* tambourine. tamboerma·joor, -s, *n.* drum-major.
·tamelijk, *a.* tolerable. ¶*adv.* tolerably, fairly, pretty.
·tamheid, no pl., *n.* tameness.
·tamtam, -s, *n.* tomtom.
tand, *n.* tooth; prong; cog. *de* ~ *des tijds,* the ravages of time; ~*en krijgen,* to cut one's teeth; *iemand aan de* ~ *voelen,* to test a person; *met lange* ~*en eten,* to eat without appetite; *op de* ~*en bijten,* to set one's teeth. ·tandarts, *n.* dentist. ·tandbeen, no pl., *n.n.* dentine. ·tandeloos, -loze, *a.* toothless. ·tanden, *v.t.* to cog; to indent. ·tandheelkunde, no pl., *n.* dentistry. ·tandheelkundig, *a.* dental. ·tandkas, -ssen, *n.* alveolus, socket. ·tandmiddel, -s, *n.n.* dentifrice. ·tandpijn, no pl., *n.* toothache. ·tandrad, -eren, *n.n.* cog-wheel. ·tandradbaan, -banen, *n.* rack-railway. ·tandsteen, no pl., *n.* tartar, scale. ·tandvlees, no pl., *n.n.* gums.
·tanen, taan, *v.t.* to tan. ¶*v.i.* to fade, tarnish.
tang, *n.* (pair of) tongs *or* pincers; shrew. *het slaat als een* ~ *op een varken,* it does not apply in the least; *met geen* ~ *aanraken,* not to touch with a barge-pole.
·tangens, *n.* tangent.
·tanig, *a.* tawny.
·tante, -s, *n.* aunt.
tanti·ème, -s, *n.* bonus.
tap, -ppen, *n.* tap; bung. ·tapgat, *n.n.* tap-hole; bung-hole.
ta·pijt, *n.n.* carpet. ·tapissi·ère, -s, *n.* furniture van.
·tappelen, *v.i.* to trickle; to gush. ·tappelings, *adv.* in a trickle *or* gush. ·tappen, tap, *v.t.* to tap, draw; to crack (*jokes*). ·tapper, -s, *n.* publican. ·tappe·rij, *n.* public-house.

taps, *a.* conical. ·taptemelk, no pl., *n.* skimmed milk. ·taptoe, -s, *n.* tattoo, last post. tap·uit, *n.* wheatear (*bird*). ·tapverbod, *n.n.* prohibition.
·tarbot, -tten, *n.* turbot.
ta·rief, -ven, *n.n.* tariff.
ta·rok, no pl., *n.n.* tarot.
·tarra, no pl., *n.* tare.
·tarten, *v.t.* to dare, challenge, defy.
·tarwe, no pl., *n.* wheat. *Turkse* ~, maize.
tas, -ssen, *n.* pile, heap; (hand-)bag. ~*je,* hand-bag. ·tasjeskruid, no pl., *n.n.* shepherd's purse. ·tassen, tas, *v.t.* to heap, stack.
tast, no pl., *n. bij* or *op de* ~, by touch; *z'n weg op de* ~ *vinden,* to grope one's way along. ·tastbaar, -bare, *a.* tangible, palpable. ·tastbaarheid, no pl., *n.* tangibility. ·tasten, *v.i.* to grope, feel, fumble. ~ *naar,* to grope for. ¶*v.t.* to touch, feel. *iemand in zijn eer* ~. to injure a person's honour. ·tastzin, no pl., *n.* tactile sense.
·tateren, *v.i.* to prattle.
·taxateur, -s, *n.* valuer. ta·xatie, -s, *n.* valuation. ta·xatieprijs, -zen, *n.* valuation price. *tegen* ~, at valuation. ta·xeren, -xeer, *v.t.* to value, appraise.
·taxis, -ssen, *n.*, ·taxisboom, -bomen, *n.* yew(-tree).
te, *prep.* at, in, on. ¶*adv.* too; to (*before infinitive*).
·technicus, -ci, *n.* technician.
·teder, *a.* tender; delicate. ·tederheid, no pl., *n.* tenderness; delicacy.
teef, teven, *n.* bitch; vixen.
teek, teken, *n.* tick.
·teelaarde, no pl., *n.* vegetable earth, mould. ·teelbal, -llen, *n.* testicle. ·teelgewas, -ssen, *n.n.* cultivated plant(s). ·teelt, no pl., *n.* cultivation, culture. ·teeltvis, no pl., *n.* fry.
·teemachtig, *a.* drawling. ·teemkous, *n.* drawler.
teems, *n.* hair-sieve. ·teemsen, *v.t.* to sieve.
teen, tenen, *n.* toe; osier. *op de tenen lopen,* to walk on tiptoe; *op de tenen getrapt,* offended, huffy. ·teenganger, -s, *n.* digitigrade. ·teenhout, no pl., *n.n.* osier. ·teenwilg, *n.* osier-willow.
teer, tere, *a. See* teder. ¶no pl., *n.* or *n.n.* tar. ·teerachtig, *a.* tarry. teerge·voelig, *a.* sensitive. teerge·voeligheid, no pl., *n.* sensitivity. teer·hartig, *a.* tender-hearted. teer·hartigheid, no pl., *n.* tender-heartedness. ·teerkleed, -kleden, *n.n.* tarpaulin.
·teerling, *n.* die (*pl.* dice).
·teerzeep, no pl., *n.* coal-tar soap.
·tegel, -s, *n.* tile. ·tegelbakker, -s, *n.* tile-maker. ·tegelbakkerij, *n.* tile-works.
tege·lijk, *adv.*, tege·lijkertijd, *adv.* at the same time, at once, together, simultaneously. *één* ~, one at a time.
·tegelvloer, *n.* tiled floor.
tege·moet-, *prefix.* towards. tege·moetgaan,

ga tegemoet, *v.i.s.*, *irr.* to go to meet, head for. tege·moetkomen, *v.i.s.*, *irr.* to (come to) meet, fall in with. tege·moetkoming, *n.* accommodating spirit; compensation. tege·moetkomend, *a.* accommodating.

·tegen, *prep.* against; towards, by; at; for; to. ¶*adv.* against. ¶no pl., *n.n.* het voor en ~, the pros and cons. ¶*prefix.* against, counter.

tegen·aan, *adv.* (close) against.

·tegenaanval, -llen, *n.* counter-attack.

·tegenbeeld, *n.n.* counterpart; contrast.

·tegenbericht, *n.n.* advice to the contrary.

·tegenbevel, *n.n.* counter-order. ~ geven, to countermand.

·tegenbezoek, *n.n.* return visit.

·tegendeel, no pl., *n.n.* opposite, reverse. in ~, on the contrary.

tegen·draads, *adv.* against the grain.

·tegengeschenk, *n.n.* return gift.

·tegengesteld, *a.* opposite, contrary. ~ aan, opposite to. ·tegengestelde, no pl., *n.n.* opposite, contrary, reverse.

·tegengif, -ten, *n.n.*, ·tegengift, *n.n.* antidote.

·tegenhanger, -s, *n.* counterpart; pendant.

·tegenhouden, *v.t.s.*, *irr.* to check, stop.

·tegenkanten, *v.t.s.* to oppose. ·tegenkanting, *n.* opposition.

·tegenkomen, *v.t.s.*, *irr.* to meet, come across.

·tegenlopen, loop tegen, *v.t.s.*, *str.* to run to meet; to go badly.

·tegenmaatregel, *n.* counter-measure.

·tegenmiddel, *n.n.* antidote.

·tegennatuurlijk, *a.* unnatural.

tegen·over, *prep.* opposite; (as) against; towards. hier ~, across the way. tegen·overgesteld, *a.* opposite.

·tegenpartij, *n.* opponent.

·tegenprestatie, -s, *n.* service in return, quid pro quo.

·tegenslag, *n.* piece of bad luck, reverse.

·tegenspartelen, *v.i.* to resist, struggle.

·tegenspoed, no pl., *n.* adversity.

·tegenspraak, no pl., *n.* contradiction. ·tegenspreken, spreek tegen, *v.t.s.*, *str.* to contradict.

·tegensputteren, *v.i.s.* to mutter objections.

·tegenstaan, sta tegen, *v.t.s.*, *irr.* to be repugnant. ·tegenstand, no pl., *n.* resistance, opposition. ·tegenstander, -s, *n.* opponent.

·tegenstellend, *a.* adversative. ·tegenstelling, *n.* contrast.

·tegenstreven, streef tegen, *v.t.s.* to oppose.

·tegenstribbelen, *v.i.s.* to resist.

·tegenstrijd, no pl., *n.* contradiction. tegen·strijdig, *a.* contradictory, conflicting. tegen·strijdigheid, -heden, *n.* contradiction.

·tegenvallen, val tegen, *v.i. & v.t.*, *str.* to be a disappointment (to). ·tegenvaller, -s, *n.* disappointment.

·tegenvergif, -ten, *n.n.*, ·tegenvergift, *n.n.* antidote.

·tegenvoeter, -s, *n.* antipode.

·tegenwaarde, -n, *n.* equivalent.

·tegenweer, no pl., *n.* resistance.

·tegenwerken, *v.t.s.* to oppose. obstruct. ·tegenwerking, *n.* opposition.

·tegenwicht, *n.n.* counter-weight. een ~ vormen tegen, to counterbalance.

·tegenwind, head wind.

tegen·woordig, *a.* present. ~ zijn bij, to attend. ¶*adv.* at present, nowadays. tegen·woordigheid, no pl., *n.* presence.

·tegenzang, *n.* antiphon.

·tegenzin, no pl., *n.* dislike, aversion, reluctance. met ~, reluctantly.

te·goed, *adv.* ~ hebben, to have a credit of. ¶no pl., *n.n.* balance.

te·huis, *adv.* at home. ¶-zen, *n.n.* home. See thuis.

teil, *n.* basin.

teint, no pl., *n.* complexion.

·teisteren, *v.t.* to ravage; to infest.

·teken, -s, *n.n.* sign; signal. ten ~ van, in token of. ·tekenaar, -s, *n.* draughtsman. ·tekenbehoeften, pl. only, *n.* drawing materials. ·tekenen, *v.i.* to draw; to sign. ¶*v.t.* to draw; to sign; to mark, characterize. ·tekenhaak, -haken, *n.* T-square. ·tekening, *n.* drawing; marking(s); signing. ·tekenleraar, -s, *n.* art master.

te·kort, *n.n.* shortage; deficit. te·kortkoming, *n.* imperfection.

tekst, *n.* text; letterpress. ~ en uitleg geven, to give chapter and verse. ·tekstboekje, -s, *n.n.* libretto. ·tekstcritiek, *n.* textual criticism. ·tekstverbetering, *n.* emendation.

tel, no pl., *n.* count. niet in ~ zijn, to be of no account. ¶-llen, *n.* pas op je tellen, watch your step. ·telbaar, -bare, *a.* countable.

tele·fooncel, -llen, *n.* (public) call-box. tele·fooncentrale, -s, *n.* telephone exchange. telefo·niste, -n, *n.* telephone operator (female).

telegra·feren, -feer, *v.i.* to wire, telegraph. tele·grafisch, *a.* telegraphic.

·telen, teel, *v.t.* to grow, cultivate; to breed. ·teler, -s, *n.* grower; breeder.

te·leurstellen, stel teleur, *v.t.s.* to disappoint. te·leurstelling, *n.* disappointment.

telg, *n.* (stilted) scion.

·telgang, no pl., *n.* amble. ·telganger, -s, *n.* ambler.

·teling, *n.* growing; breeding.

·telkenmale, *adv.* time and time again. ·telkens, *adv.* (stilted) every time. ~ als, whenever.

·tellen, tel, *v.t.* to count; to number. ~ onder, to count among. ·teller, -s, *n.* teller, counter. ·telling, *n.* count; census. ·telpas, no pl., *n.* amble. ·telraam, -ramen, *n.n.* abacus, ball-frame. telwoord, *n.n.* numeral.

·tembaar, -bare, *a.* tamable. ·tembaarheid, no pl., *n.* tamability.

·temen, teem, *v.i.* to drawl. ·temer, -s, *n.*
drawler. teme·rij, no pl., *n.* drawling.
te·met, *adv.* (*stilted*) sometimes.
·temmen, tem, *v.t.* to tame. ·temmer, -s, *n.*
tamer. ·temming, *n.* taming.
·tempel, -s, *n.* temple. ·tempelheer, -heren,
n. templar. tempe·lier, -s, *n.* templar.
drinken als een ~, to drink like a
fish. ·tempelridder, -s, *n.* Knight
Templar.
·tempera, no pl., *n.* distemper (*paint*).
tempera·tuur, -turen, *n.* temperature.
·temperen, *v.t.* to temper; to damp.
·tempermes, -ssen, *n.n.* palette knife.
·temperoven, -s, *n.* tempering furnace.
·tempo, -'s, *n.n.* time, tempo; rate.
ten, *prep.* at (the). ~ *eerste*, first(ly).
ten·dens, *n.* tendency; purpose.
·tender, -s, *n.* tender.
·tenen, *a.* osier; wicker-work.
·tengel, -s, *n.* lath.
·tenger, *a.* slender; delicate. ·tengerheid,
no pl., *n.* slenderness.
tenge·volge, *adv.* ~ *van*, as a result of.
te·nietdoen, doe teniet, *v.t.s.*, *irr.* to undo,
nullify. te·nietgaan, ga teniet, *v.t.s.*, *irr.*
to perish.
tent, *n.* tent; booth. *iemand uit zijn* ~
lokken, to draw a person out.
ten·tamen, -s, *n.* preliminary examination.
·tentdoek, no pl., *n.n.* canvas.
ten·toonspreiden, *v.t.s.* to display. ten-
·toonstellen, stel tentoon, *v.t.*°. to show,
exhibit. ten·toonstelling, *n.* exhibition.
te·nue, -n, *n.* or *n.n.* uniform. *in groot* ~,
in full dress *or* uniform.
ten·uitvoerbrenging, *n.* execution (*of something*).
ten·ware, *adv.* (*stilted*) unless.
ten·zij, *adv.* unless.
·tepel, -s, *n.* nipple; teat.
ter, *prep.* at (the), to (the), in (the).
ter·aardebestelling, *n.* interment.
ter·dege, *adv.* thoroughly.
ter·doodbrenging, *n.* execution (*of person*).
te·recht, *adv.* rightly, properly; deservedly.
te·rechtbrengen,*v.t.s.*, *irr. het* ~, to arrange
matters; *er niets van* ~, to make a mess
of things. te·rechthelpen, *v.t.s.*, *irr.* to
set right, direct. te·rechtkomen, *v.t.s.*,
irr. to right itself; to be found again, turn
up again. *niet* ~, to miscarry; *op z'n
voeten* ~, to land on one's feet. te·recht-
staan, sta terecht, *v.i.s.*, *irr.* to be on
trial. te·rechtstellen, stel terecht, *v.t.s.*
to put on trial; to execute. te·rechtstelling,
n. trial; execution. te·rechtwijzen, wijs
terecht, *v.t.s.*, *str.* to correct, reprimand.
te·rechtwijzing, *n.* reprimand.
·teren, teer, *v.t.* to tar. ¶*v.i.* to consume.
achteruit ~, to eat into one's capital;
~ *op*, to live on.
·tergen, *v.t.* to tease, irritate. ·terging, *n.*
provocation.

ter·hand, *adv.* in hand. ter·handstelling, *n.*
delivery.
·tering, *n.* consumption, phthisis. *de* ~
naar de nering zetten, to live in accordance
with one's means. ·teringachtig, *a.*
consumptive. ·teringlijder, -s, *n.* consumptive.
ter·leen, *adv.* as a loan.
ter·loops, *a.* casual. ¶*adv.* incidentally, in
passing.
term, *n.* term. *volgens de* ~*en der wet*,
within the meaning of the act.
ter·miet, *n.* termite.
ter·mijn, *n.n.* term, time; instalment. *op* ~
verkopen, to sell forward; *op korte* ~,
at short notice, short-term. ter·mijn-
handel, no pl., *n.* business in futures.
ter·nauwernood, *adv.* scarcely, hardly.
ter·ne(d)er, *adv.* down. ter·neergeslagen, *a.*
downcast, dejected.
terp, *n.* mound (*prehistoric*).
terpen·tijn, no pl., *n.* turpentine.
ter·ras, -ssen, *n.n.* terrace. ter·rasvormig,
a. terraced.
ter·rein, *n.n.* ground, field. *het* ~ *verkennen*
to reconnoitre.
ter·rine, -s, *n.* tureen.
ter·sluiks, *adv.* by stealth.
ter·stond, *adv.* at once, forthwith.
terti·air, *a.* tertiary.
terts, *n.* third (*music*).
te·rug, *adv.* back; backward(s). ¶*prefix.*
back, re-.
te·rugbetaalbaar, -bare, *a.* repayable. te·rug-
betalen, betaal terug, *v.t.s.* to repay,
refund. te·rugbetaling, *n.* refund.
te·rugblik, no pl., *n.* retrospect.
te·rugbrengen, *v.t.s.*, *irr.* to take back. ~
tot, to reduce to.
te·rugdeinzen, deins terug, *v.i.s.* to shrink
back.
te·ruggave, no pl., *n.* restitution, return,
restoration.
te·ruggetrokken, *a.* retiring.
te·ruggeven, geef terug, *v.t.s.*, *str.* to give
back, return.
te·rughouden, *v.t.s.*, *irr.* to hold *or* keep
back, retain. terug·houdend, *a.* reserved,
reticent. terug·houdendheid, no pl., *n.*
reserve.
te·rugkaatsen, *v.t.s.* to throw back; to reflect;
to reverberate. ¶*v.i.s.* to bounce back.
te·rugkaatsing, *n.* reflection; reverbera-
tion.
te·rugkeer, no pl., *n.* return. te·rugkeren,
keer terug, *v.i.s.* to turn back; to return.
te·rugkomen, *v.i.s.*, *irr.* to come back; to
return. ~ *op*, to revert to; ~ *van*, to
come back on. te·rugkomst, no pl., *n.*
return.
te·rugkoop, -kopen, *n.* repurchase. te·rug-
kopen, koop terug, *v.t.s.*, *irr.* to repurchase.
te·rugkoopwaarde, -n, *n.* surrender value.
te·rugkoppelingsspoel, *n.* reaction coil.

te·rugkrabbelen, *v.i.s.* to back out.
te·rugloop, no pl., *n.* recoil.
te·rugnemen, neem terug, *v.t.s., str.* to take back; to retract.
te·rugplaatsen, *v.t.s.* to put back, replace.
te·rugreis, -zen, *n.* return journey.
te·rugrit, -tten, *n.* drive back.
te·rugroepen, *v.t.s., str.* to call back, recall. **te·rugroeping,** *n.* recall.
te·rugschrikken, schrik terug, *v.i.s., str.* to shrink back. ~ *voor,* to recoil from.
te·rugslaan, sla terug, *v.t.s., irr.* to beat back; to repulse. ¶*v.i.s., irr.* to backfire. **te·rug-slag,** no pl., *n.*, **te·rugsprong,** no pl., *n.*, **te·rugstoot,** no pl., *n.* rebound, recoil; repercussion. **te·rugstotend,** *a.* repulsive. **te·rugstuit,** no pl., *n. See* **terugslag.**
te·rugtocht, *n.* retreat.
te·rugtraprem, -mmen, *n.* back-pedal brake.
te·rugtrekken, trek terug, *v.t.s., str.* to pull or draw back, withdraw. ¶*v.i.s., str.* to retreat, withdraw. ¶**zich ~,** *v.r.s., str.* to retreat, retire, withdraw.
te·rugwerken, *v.i.s.* to react. **te·rugwerkend,** *a.* ~*e kracht,* retrospective effect. **te·rug-werking,** *n.* reaction, retroaction.
te·rugwijken, *v.i.s., str.* to recede.
te·rugwinnen, win terug, *v.t.s., str.* to win back, regain.
ter·wijl, *c.* while, whilst; while, whereas. ¶*adv.* meanwhile, in the meantime.
ter·wille, *adv.* ~ *van,* for the sake of.
ter·zelfder, *pron.* ~ *tijd,* at the same time.
ter·zijde, *adv.* aside. **ter·zijdestelling,** no pl., *n. met* ~ *van,* putting aside.
·**Tessel,** *n.N.* Texel.
test, *n.* chafing-dish.
testa·ment, *n.n.* will, last will and testament; Testament. **tes·teren, -teer,** *v.t.* to bequeath.
teug, *n.* draught, pull.
·**teugel, -s,** *n.* rein, bridle. *de* ~ *strak houden,* to keep a tight hand over. ·**teugelen,** *v.t.* to bridle. ·**teugelloos, -loze,** *a.* unbridled, unrestrained. ·**teugelloosheid,** no pl., *n.* unrestraint.
·**teunisbloem,** *n.* evening primrose.
teut, *n.* spout (*tea-* or *coffee-pot*); dawdler. ·**teuten,** *v.i.* to dawdle.
·**tevens,** *adv.* at the same time.
tever·geefs, *adv.* in vain, vainly.
te·vreden, *a.* satisfied, contented. **te·vreden-heid, no** pl., *n.* satisfaction, contentment. **te·vredenstellen, stel tevreden,** *v.t.s.* to satisfy.
te·waterlating, *n.* launching.
te·weegbrengen, *v.t.s., irr.* to bring about.
tex·tiel, *a.* textile.
thans, *adv.* (*stilted*) at present.
thea·traal, -trale, *a.* theatrical.
thee, theeën, *n.* tea. ~ *zetten,* to make tea; *op de* ~, to tea. ·**theebus, -ssen,** *n.* tea-caddy. ·**theelichtje, -s,** *n.n.* spirit stove. ·**theelood,** no pl., *n.n.* tinfoil.

Theems, *N.* Thames.
·**theemuts,** *n.* tea-cosy. ·**theeschepje, -s,** *n.n.* tea(-caddy) spoon. ·**theezeefje. -s.** *n.n.* tea-strainer.
·**thema, -'s,** *n.n.* exercise; theme.
theo·logisch, *a.* theological. **theo·loog, -logen,** *n.* theologian, divine.
theo·reticus, -ci, *n.* theorist. **theo·retisch,** *a.* theoretical. **theoreti·seren, -seer,** *v.i.* to theorize. **theo·rie, -rieën,** *n.* theory.
theo·soof, -sofen, *n.* theosophist.
thuis, *adv.* at home. *handen* ~, hands off; *van iets niet* ~ *zijn* to be against something. ¶no pl., *n.n.* home. *See* **huis.** ·**thuishoren, hoor thuis,** *v.i.s.* to belong. ·**thuiskomst,** no pl., *n.* home-coming. ·**thuisreis, -zen,** *n.* homeward journey.
·**tichel, -s,** *n.* tile. ·**tichelaar, -s,** *n.* tile-maker.
tien, *num.* ten. ¶*n.* ten. **tiend,** *n.n.* tithe. ·**tiendaags,** *a.* ten-day. ·**tiende,** *a.* tenth. ¶**-n,** *n.n.* tenth; tithe. ·**tiendelig,** *a.* consisting of ten parts; decimal. ·**tiend-heffer, -s,** *n.* tithe-owner, tithe-gatherer. ·**tiend·plichtig,** *a.* tithable. ·**tiendrecht,** *n.n.* right to levy tithes. ·**tiendubbel,** *a.* tenfold. ·**tiendduizend,** *num.* ten thousand. ·**tienen,** *num.* ten. *de trein van* ~, the ten o'clock train; *bij* ~, just on ten; *in* ~, into ten; *met hun* ~, the ten of them; *met ons* ~, the ten of us: *met z'n* ~, with nine others. ·**tienhoek,** *n.* decagon. **tien·hoekig,** *a.* decagonal. ·**tienjarig,** *a.* (of) ten years, decennial. ·**tiental, -llen,** *n.n.* (*number of*) ten. **tien·tallig,** *a.* decimal. ·**tientje, -s,** *n.n. gouden* ~, gold ten-guilder coin. ·**tienvoud,** *n.n.* decuple. ·**tienvoudig,** *a.* tenfold. ·**tienwerf,** *a.* (*stilted*) tenfold.
tier, no pl., *n.* growth.
tiere·lieren, *v.i.* to warble.
·**tieren,** *v.i.* to thrive, flourish; to rage, storm.
tierlan·tijntje, -s, *n.n.* flourish, twiddly bit.
tij, *n.n.* tide. *het* ~ *is verlopen,* the tables are turned. **tijd,** *n.* time, times, days; season, period; tense. ~ *kosten,* to take time; *de* ~ *is om,* time is up; *het is mijn* ~, it is time for me to go; *de hele* ~, all the time; *een* ~ *geleden,* some time ago; *lieve* ~!, dear me!; *bij* ~ *en wijle* (*stilted*), in due time or now and then; *bij* ~*en* (*stilted*), at times; *bij* ~*s,* in (good) time; *in lange* ~, for a long time past; *in geen* ~*en,* not for ages; *met de* ~, as time goes on; *na korter of langer* ~, sooner or later; *op* ~, in time; *te dien* ~*e* (*stilted*), at that time; *te zijner* ~, in due time; *ten* ~*e van,* at or in the time of; *tegen die* ~, by that time; *uit de* ~, out of date; *voor de* ~, before time or ahead of time. ·**tijdbuis, -zen,** *n.* time-fuse. ·**tijdelijk,** *a.* temporary; temporal. ·**tijdens,** *prep.* during. ·**tijdgeest,**

no pl., *n.* spirit of the age. ·tijdgenoot,
-noten, *n.* contemporary. ·tijdig, *a.*
timely, opportune. ¶*adv.* in good time.
·tijding, *n.* news, tidings. *een goede* ∼,
a piece of good news. ·tijdje, no pl., *n.n.*
short time, little while. ·tijdkring, *n.*
cycle. ·tijdlang, *adv. een* ∼, for some time.
·tijdopname, -n, *n.* time exposure. ·tijdperk,
n.n. period. ·tijdrekening, *n.* chronology;
era. ·tijd·rovend, *a.* taking up time.
·tijdruimte, -n, *n.,* ·tijdsbestek, no pl.,
n.n. space of time. ·tijdschrift, *n.n.*
periodical (*publication*). ·tijdstip, -ppen,
n.n. (point of) time. ·tijdsverloop, no pl.,
n.n. course of time. ·tijdvak, -kken,
n.n. period. ·tijdverdrijf, no pl., *n.n.*
pastime.
·tijgen, *v.i.str.* to hie.
·tijger, -s, *n.* tiger. ·tijgerachtig, *a.* tigerish.
tijge·rin, -nnen, *n.* tigress. ·tijgerwolf,
-ven, *n.* spotted hyena.
·tijhaven, -s, *n.* tidal harbour.
tijk, *n.* tick (*bedding*).
·tijloos, -lozen, *n.* jonquil.
tijm, *n.* thyme. ·tijmachtig, *a.* thymy.
tik, -kken, *n.* tap, rap, flick. ·tijke, -s, *n.n.*
touch, trace. ·tikken, tik, *v.i.* to tap,
tick; to type. *iemand op de vingers* ∼,
to rap a person's knuckles. ·tikker, -s,
n. ticker. ·tikkertje, -s, *n.n.* death-watch
beetle. ·tiktak, no pl., *n.n.* tick-tock.
til, -llen, *n.* (dove-)cote. *op* ∼ *zijn*, to be in
the wind *or* in the offing. ¶no pl., *n.*
een hele ∼, heavy to lift.
·tilda, -'s, *n.* tilde.
·tillen, til, *v.t.* to lift.
·timmeren, *v.i.* to do carpentering; to
hammer. *niet hoog* ∼, to be no shining
light; ∼ *op*, to hammer at; *aan de weg* ∼,
to be in the limelight. ·timmergereedschap,
no pl., *n.n.* carpenter's tools. ·timmerman,
-lui *or* (*stilted*) -lieden, *n.* carpenter.
·timmerwerf, -ven, *n.* carpenter's yard.
·timmerwerk, no pl., *n.n.* carpentering.
·timmerwinkel, -s, *n.* carpenter's workshop.
tin, no pl., *n.n.* tin (metal). *See also* tinne.
·tingelen, *v.i.* to jingle. tinge·ling, *excl.*
ting-a-ling. ·tingeltangel, -s, *n.* (low-class)
music hall. ·tinkelen, *v.i.* to tinkle.
·tinne, -n, *n.* pinnacle; battlement. ·tinne-
gieter, -s, *n.* pewterer. ·tinnen, *a.* (of)
pewter. ·tinschuitje, -s, *n.n.* pig of tin.
tint, *n.* tint, shade. ·tintelen, *v.i.* to twinkle,
scintillate, sparkle; to tingle. ·tinteling,
n. twinkling; tingling. ·tinten, *v.t.* to
tinge. ·tintje, -s, *n.* tinge.
tip, -ppen, *n.* tip (*point, corner*). ·tippel,
no pl., *n. een hele* ∼, quite a walk. ·tip-
pelen. *v.i.* to trip (*walk quickly*). ·tippen,
tip, *v.t.* to clip, trim.
tirail·leren, -leer, *v.i.* to skirmish. tirail·leur,
-s, *n.* rifleman. tirail·leurvuur, no pl.,
n.n. independent fire.

ti·ran, -nnen, *n.* tyrant.
·titel, -s, *n.* title.
·tittel, -s, *n.* tittle, jot.
titu·lair, *a.* titular. titu·laris, -ssen, *n.*
holder (*of an office*). titula·tuur, -turen,
n. title. titu·leren, -leer, *v.i.* to (use) title,
address.
tjalk, *n.* spritsail barge.
·tjangelen, *v.i.* to strum.
·tjiftjaf, -ffen, *n.* chiff-chaff.
·tjilpen, *v.i.* to chirp.
·tjokvol, -lle, *a.* chockfull.
·tjotter, -s, *n.* small sailing boat.
·tobbe, -n, *n.* tub. ·tobben, tob, *v.i.* to worry;
to toil. ∼ *over*, to worry about. ·tobber
-s, *n.* worrier, brooder. tobbe·rij, no pl.
n. worrying.
toch, *c.* yet, still, nevertheless, all the same.
maar ∼, yet. ¶*adv.* (*remains untranslated*).
kom ∼, do come; *je weet* ∼, you do know;
wat bedoelt hij ∼, what can he mean.
tocht, *n.* expedition, journey; draught (*air*).
op de ∼ *zitten*, to sit in a draught. ·tochten,
v. imp. het tocht, there is a draught, it is
draughty. ·tochtgat, *n.n.* vent-hole.
·tochtgenoot, -noten, *n.* fellow-traveller.
·tochtig, *a.* draughty. ·tochtje, -s, *n.n.*
trip, excursion. ·tochtlat, -tten, *n.* draught-
excluder (*lath*). ·tochtsloot, -sloten, *n.*
ditch (*running water*).
toe, *adv.* shut, closed; to. *naar* ∼, to, towards; *tot nu* ∼, until now; *tot daar* ∼,
that far; *er nog niet aan* ∼ *zijn*, not to be
that far yet; *maar* ∼, on and on; ∼!, come
on!; ∼ *maar!*, attaboy!; ∼ *nou!*, please do!
·toebedeelen, *v.t.s.* to allot.
·toebehoren, behoor toe, *v.t.s.* to belong to.
¶no pl., *n.n. met* ∼, with appurtenances.
·toebereiden, *v.t.s.,* to prepare. ·toebereiding,
n. preparation. ·toebereidsel, *n.n.* preparations.
·toebijten, *v.i.s.,* *str.* to bite (*of fish*).
·toebinden, *v.t.s.,* *str.* to tie up.
·toeblijven, blijf toe, *v.t.s.,* *str.* to remain
shut.
·toebrengen, *v.t.s.,* *irr.* to deal, inflict.
·toebulderen, *v.t.s.* to roar at.
·toedekken, dek toe, *v.t.s.* to cover.
·toedenken, *v.t.s.,* *irr.* to destine for.
·toedienen, *v.t.s.* to administer.
·toedoen, doe toe, *v.t.s.,* *irr.* to close, shut.
¶no pl., *n.n.* intermediary, action. *door*
zijn ∼, through him.
·toedraaien, *v.t.s.* to turn off (*tap*).
·toedracht, no pl., *n. de ware* ∼, the way it
happened. ·toedragen, draag toe, *v.t.s.,*
str. to bear. *achting* ∼, to hold in esteem.
¶*zich* ∼, *v.r.s.,* *str.* to happen.
·toedrinken, *v.t.s.,* *str. iemand* ∼, to drink
a person's health.
·toeduwen, *v.t.s.* to push to.
·toeëigenen, *v.t.s. zich iets* ∼, to appropriate
something. ·toeëigening, *n.* appropriation.

·toegaan, ga toe, *v.i.s., irr.* to close, shut; to happen. **·toegang,** *n.* admittance, admission; entrance; access. *verboden ~,* no admittance. **·toegangsprijs, -zen,** *n.* admission fee. **toe·gangelijk,** *a.* accessible. **toe·gangelijkheid,** no pl., *n.* accessibility.

·toegedaan, *adv. iemand ~ zijn,* to be attached to a person; *een mening ~ zijn,* to hold a view.

toe·geeflijk, *a.* indulgent, lenient. **toe·geeflijkheid,** no pl., *n.* indulgence.

·toegenegen, *a.* affectionate. **·toegenegenheid,** no pl., *n.* affection.

·toegepast, *a.* applied.

·toegeven, geef toe, *v.t.s., str.* to admit, concede, grant; to throw in. ¶*v.i.s., str.* to give in. **toe·gevend,** *a.* indulgent. **toe·gevendheid,** no pl., *n.* indulgence.

·toehalen, haal toe, *v.t.s.* to draw tight.

·toehoorder, -s, *n.* hearer. **·toehoren, hoor toe,** *v.i.s.* to listen.

·toehouden, *v.t.s., irr.* to keep shut.

·toejuichen, *v.t.s.* to cheer. **toejuiching,** *n.* cheer(s), shouts.

·toekan, -s, *n.* toucan.

·toekennen, ken toe, *v.t.s.* to award, confer upon, *~ aan,* to attribute to. **·toekenning,** *n.* award, adjudication.

·toekeren, keer toe, *v.t.s.* to turn to.

·toekijken, *v.i.s., str.* to look on.

·toeknopen, knoop toe, *v.t.s.* to button up.

·toekomen, *v.i.s., irr.* to be or have sufficient; to make ends meet. ¶*v.t.s., str.* to be due to. *doen ~,* to forward. **·toekomend,** *a.* future; due. **·toekomst,** no pl., *n.* future. **toe·komstig,** *a.* future.

·toekrijgen, *v.t.s., str.* to get shut; to get extra.

·toekunnen, kan toe, *v.i.s., irr.* to be able to shut. *~ met,* to be able to do with.

toe·laatbaar, -bare, *a.* permissible.

·toelachen, *v.t.s.* to smile at or on or upon.

·toelage, -n, *n.* allowance, subsidy.

·toelaten, laat toe, *v.t.s., str.* to permit, allow; to admit, let in. **·toelating,** *n.* permission; admission. **·toelatingsexamen, -s,** *n.n.* matriculation or entrance examination.

·toeleg, no pl., *n.* design, purpose. **·toeleggen, leg toe,** *v.t.s., irr. er geld op ~,* to be out of pocket by it; *het erop ~,* to aim at. ¶*v.r.s., irr. zich ~ op,* to apply oneself to.

·toelichten, *v.t.s.* to elucidate. **·toelichting,** *n.* elucidation. *ter ~ van,* in elucidation of.

·toeloop, no pl., *n.* concourse. **·toelopen, loop toe,** *v.i.s., str. ~ op,* to run up to.

·toemeten, meet toe, *v.t.s., str.* to mete out to.

toen, *adv.* then. ¶*c.* when, as.

·toenaam, -namen, *n.* surname.

·toenadering, *n.* approach; rapprochement.

·toenemen, neem toe, *v.i.s., str.* to increase. *in kracht ~,* to gather strength. **·toeneming,** *n.* increase.

·toenmaals, *adv. (stilted)* then, at the time. **·toenmalig,** *a. (stilted)* of the time. **·toentertijd,** *adv. (stilted)* at the time.

toe·passelijk, *a.* appropriate, suitable. *~ zijn op,* to apply to; *niet ~ zijn op,* to be irrelevant to. **toe·passelijkheid,** no pl., *n.* applicability. **·toepassen, pas toe,** *v.t.s.* to apply. **·toepassing,** *n.* application. *in ~ brengen,* to practise.

toer, *n.* turn; tour. *~en doen,* to perform tricks; *een hele ~,* quite a job.

·toerechten, *v.t.s.* to prepare.

·toereiken, *v.t.s.* to hand. ¶*v.i.s.* to be sufficient. **toe·reikend,** *a.* sufficient, adequate.

toe·rekenbaar, -bare, *a.* responsible; accountable. **toe·rekenbaarheid,** no pl., *n.* responsibility. **·toerekenen,** *v.t.s. iemand iets ~,* to impute something to somebody.

·toeren, *v.i.* to tour.

toer·nooi, *n.n.* tournament.

·toeroepen, *v.t.s., str.,* to call to.

·toerusten, *v.t.s.* to equip.

toe·schietelijk, *a.* forthcoming. **toeschieten,** *v.i.s., str. ~ op,* to rush at.

·toeschijnen, *v.t.s., str.* to seem, appear.

·toeschouwer, -s, *n.* spectator.

·toeschrijven, schrijf toe, *v.t.s., str. ~ aan,* to ascribe or attribute to.

·toeschuiven, schuif toe, *v.t.s., str.* to push to, draw *(curtains).*

·toeslaan, sla toe, *v.t.s., irr.* to slam *(door).* ¶*v.i.s., irr. erop ~,* to hit out. **·toeslag,** *n.* extra allowance.

·toespeling, *n.* allusion.

·toespijs, -zen, *n.* dessert.

·toespraak, -spraken, *n.* address, speech. **·toespreken, spreek toe,** *v.t.s., str.* to address, speak to.

·toestaan, sta toe, *v.t.s., irr.* to allow, permit.

·toestand, *n.* state of affairs, condition.

·toesteken, steek toe, *v.t.s., str.* to extend, hold out.

·toestel, -llen, *n.n.* (piece of) apparatus, machine.

·toestemmen, stem toe, *v.i.s.* to consent, agree. *~ in,* to consent to. **·toestemming,** *n.* consent, permission.

·toestromen, stroom toe, *v.i.s.* to flow towards, come flocking to.

toet, *n.* knot, bun *(hair) (coll.)* face.

·toetakelen, *v.t.s.* to rig out *(fig.);* to manhandle.

·toetasten, *v.i.s.* to fall to, help oneself.

·toeten, *v.i.* to toot. *op de hoorn ~,* to sound the horn. **·toeter, -s,** *n.* hooter. **·toeteren,** *v.i.* to hoot.

·toetje, -s, *n.n.* dessert.

·toetreden, treed toe, *v.i.s., str. ~ tot,* to join.

·toetrekken, trek toe, *v.t.s., str.* to pull to.

toets, *n.* key *(piano);* test, assay. **·toetsen,** *v.t.* to test, assay; to put to the test. **·toetssteen, -tenen,** *n.* touchstone.

·toeval, -llen, *n.n.* accident, chance; fit. *het ~ wilde*, luck would have it. ·toevallen, val toe, *v.i.s., str.* to fall to. ¶*v.t.s., str.* to devolve upon. toe·vallig, *a.* accidental. ¶*adv.* accidentally, by chance. toevalliger-wijs, *adv.* accidentally, by chance. toe·valligheid, -heden, *n.* chance.

·toeven, toef, *v.i.* (*lit.*) to linger.
·toeverlaat, no pl., *n.* refuge, support.
·toevertrouwen, *v.t.s. iemand iets ~*, to entrust a person with something; *het is hem toevertrouwd*, trust him to do it.
·toevloed, no pl., *n.* affluence.
·toevlucht, no pl., *n.* refuge. *zijn ~ nemen tot*, to have recourse to. ·toevluchtsoord, *n.n.* (haven of) refuge.
·toevoegen, *v.t.s.* to add; to adjoin. ·toevoeging, *n.* addition. ·toevoegsel, -s, *n.n.* addition, supplement.
·toevoer, *n.* supply. ·toevoeren, *v.t.s.* to supply.
·toevouwen, *v.t.s.* to fold up.
·toewan, -s, *n.* tuan.
·toewas, no pl., *n.* increase.
·toewensen, *v.t.s.* to wish.
·toewijden, *v.t.s. ~ aan*, to dedicate to. ¶ *v.r.s. zich ~ aan*, to devote oneself to.
·toewijzen, wijs toe, *v.t.s., str.* to assign, allot, award. ·toewijzing, *n.* assignment, award.
·toezeggen, zeg toe, *v.t.s., irr.* to promise.
·toezenden, *v.t.s., str.* to send, forward.
·toezicht, *n.n.* supervision, inspection. *~ houden op*, to superintend. ·toezien, zie toe, *v.i.s., irr.* to look on; to survey, superintend.
·toga, -'s, *n.* gown; toga.
·toi·let, -tten, *n.n.* toilet; dress. *~ maken*, to dress. toi·letkamer, -s, *n.* dressing-room.
·tokkelen, *v.t.* to thrum.
·toko, -'s, *n.* store (*East Indies*).
·tol, -llen, *n.* top; toll. ·tolbeambte, -n, *n.* custom-house officer. ·tolboom, -bomen, *n.* turnpike.
·tolk, *n.* interpreter.
·tolkantoor, -toren, *n.n.* custom-house. ·tollen, tol, *v.i.* to spin (*of top*). *in het rond ~*, to whirl round. ·tollenaar, -s, *n.* publican (*bibl.*). tol·plichtig, *a.* liable to toll. ·tolverbond, *n.n.* customs union. ·tolvrij, *a.* customs free.
to·maat, -maten, *n.* tomato.
·tomeloos, -loze, *a.* unbridled. ·tomeloosheid, no pl., *n.* unrestrainedness. ·tomen, toom, *v.t.* to bridle; to bridle, curb.
·ton, -nnen, *n.* barrel, tun; ton.
·tondel, no pl., *n.* tinder. ·tondeldoos, -dozen, *n.* tinderbox.
ton·deuse, -s, *n.* (pair of) clippers.
to·neel, -nelen, *n.n.* stage; scene; theatre. *bij het ~*, on the stage; *ten tonele*, on the scene. to·neelcriticus, -ci, *n.* dramatic critic. to·neeldirecteur, -s, *n.* theatrical

manager. to·neelgezelschap, -ppen, *n.n.* theatrical company. to·neelkijker, -s, *n.* opera glasses. to·neelknecht, *n.* stage-hand. to·neelschool, -scholen, *n.* school of acting. to·neelschrijver, -s, *n.* playwright. to·neelspeelster, -s, *n.* actress. to·neelspel, *n.n.* play; acting. to·neelspeler, -s, *n.* actor. to·neelstuk, -kken, *n.n.* play.
·tonen, toon, *v.t.* to show.
tong, *n.* tongue; sole (*fish*). *een gladde ~*, a glib tongue; *het lag me op de ~*, it was on the tip of my tongue. ·tongeworst, *n.* tongue-sausage. ·tongklier, *n.* lingual gland. ·tongval, -llen, *n.* accent; dialect.
to·nijn, *n.* tunny(-fish).
·tonneboei, *n.* barrel-buoy. ·tonnemaat, no pl., *n.*, ·tonnenmaat, no pl., *n.* tonnage. ·tonnetje, -s, *n.* little cask.
·tooi, *n.* array; finery. ·tooien, *v.t.* to adorn.
·toom, tomen, *n.* bridle, reins. *in ~ houden*, to keep in check.
·toon, tonen, *n.* tone. *de ~ aangeven*, to set the fashion; *~ houden*, to keep in tune; *op vriendelijke ~*, in a friendly tone. ¶ no pl., *n.* *ten ~ stellen*, to display, exhibit. toonaan·gevend, *a.* leading, influential. ·toonaard, *n.* (musical) key. ·toonbaar, -bare, *a.* presentable, fit to be seen. ·toonbank, *n.* (shop) counter. ·toonbeeld, *n.n.* model, example. ·toonder, -s, *n.* bearer. ·toondichter, -s, *n.* composer. ·toonhoogte, no pl., *n.* pitch (*musical*). ·toonkunst, no pl., *n.* music (*art*). ·toonladder, -s, *n.* scale (*musical*). ·toonloos, -loze, *a.* toneless. ·toonsoort, *n.* key, mode. ·toontje, no pl., *n.n.* tone. *een ~ lager zingen*, to pipe down. ·toonval, -llen, *n.* modulation. ·toonvast, *a.* keeping in tune.
toorn, no pl., *n.* wrath. ·toornen, *v.i.* to be wrathful. ·toornig, *a.* wrathful, irate.
toorts, *n.* torch.
top, *excl.* done!, agreed! ¶ -ppen, *n.* top, summit, apex; top (*toy*). *~ van de mast*, masthead; *met de vlag in ~*, the flag flying at the masthead; *iets ten ~ voeren*, to carry something to extremes.
to·paas, -pazen, *n.* topaz.
topo·graaf, -grafen, *n.* topographer.
·toppen, top, *v.t.* to top, lop. ·toppunt, *n.n.* apex; culminating point; height, acme.
·topzeil, *n.n.* topsail. ·topzwaar, -zware, *a.* top-heavy.
tor, ··rren, *n.* beetle.
·toren, -s, *n.* tower, steeple; castle (*chess*). ·torenblazer, -s, *n.* watchman (*on tower*). ·torenklok, -kken, *n.* church-bell; church-clock. ·torentje, -s, *n.n.* turret. ·torenuil, *n.* barn-owl. ·torenvalk, *n.* kestrel. ·torenwachter, -s, *n.* watchman (*on tower*). ·torenzwaluw, *n.* swift.
torn, *n.* tear, rent; unravelled seam. *een hele ~*, quite a job. ·tornen, *v.t.* to unstitch, unpick. ¶ *v.i.* *~ aan*, to meddle

with; *er valt niet aan te* ~, you can't alter it now.

torpe·deren, -deer, *v.t.* to torpedo (*sink*). **tor·pedo,** *n.* torpedo. **tor·pedojager, -s,** *n.* (torpedo-boat) destroyer. **torpedolan-·ceerbuis, -zen,** *n.* torpedo-tube.

tors, *n.* torso. **·torsen,** *v.t.* to bear, carry (*heavy weight*).

·torsie, no pl., *n.* torsion.

·tortelduif, -ven, *n.* turtle-dove.

tot, *prep.* to, as far as; till, until; as, for. ~ *aan,* up to; ~ *voor,* up to . . . ago; ~ *nog toe* or ~ *nu toe,* till now, up to now, as yet; ~ *en met,* up to . . . inclusive; ~ *hier,* thus far; ~ *morgen,* see you to-morrow. ¶ *adv.* till, until.

to·taal, -tale, *a.* total. ¶ *adv.* totally, utterly. ¶ **-talen,** *n.n.* total, sum total.

tot·dat, *c.* till, until.

·totok, -s, *n.* European (*East Indies*).

tot·standkoming, *n.* realization.

tour·née, -s, *n.* tour.

·touter, -s, *n.* swing. **·touteren,** *v.i.* to swing.

touw, *n.n.* rope; string, twine; loom. ~ *pluizen,* to pick oakum; ~ *slaan,* to lay ropes; *je kunt er geen* ~ *aan vastknopen,* you can't make head or tail of it; *in* ~ *zijn,* to be in harness; *op* ~ *zetten,* to set on foot. **·touwbaan, -banen,** *n.* rope-walk. **·touwslager, -s,** *n.* ropemaker. **touwslage-·rij,** *n.* rope-yard. **·touwtje, -s,** *n.n.* piece of string. ~ *springen,* to skip. **·touw-trekken,** no pl., *n.n.* tug of war. **·touw-werk,** no pl., *n.n.* cordage, rigging.

·tovenaar, -s, *n.* sorcerer, magician. **tovena-res, -ssen,** *n.* sorceress. **tovena·rij,** *n.* sorcery, witchcraft. **·toverachtig,** *a.* magic, enchanting. **·toverboek,** *n.n.* conjuring book. **·toverdokter, -s,** *n.* witch-doctor. **·toverdrank,** *n.* potion, philtre. **·toveren,** *v.i.* to practise witch-craft; to conjure. ¶ *v.t.* to conjure. **·tover-formule, -s,** *n.* charm, spell, magic formula. **·toverheks,** *n.* witch. **tover·kol, -llen,** *n.* witch, hag. **·toverkunst,** no pl., *n.* art of magic. **·toverlantaarn,** *n.* magic lantern. **·tover-middel,** *n.n.* charm, spell. **·toverslag,** *adv.* *als door* or *bij* or *met* ~, as if by magic. **·toverspreuk,** *n.* incantation.

traag, trage, *a.* slow, sluggish. **·traagheid,** no pl., *n.* slowness; inertia.

traan, tranen, *n.* tear; train-oil. *tranen met tuiten schreien,* to weep one's eyes out. **·traanachtig,** *a.* trainy. **·traanbuis, -zen,** *n.* tear-duct. **·traanklier,** *n.* lachrymal gland. **traankoke·rij,** *n.* try-works. **·traanogen, -oog,** *v.i. hij traanoogde,* his eyes watered.

tra·ceren, -ceer, *v.t.* to trace (out).

·trachten, *v.t.* to try. ~ *naar,* to strive after.

·tractie, no pl., *n.* traction.

tra·ditie, -s, *n.* tradition.

tra·giek, no pl., *n.* tragedy, tragic element. **·tragisch,** *a.* tragic(al).

tra·ject, *n.n.* stretch, stage, section.

trak·taat, -taten, *n.n.* treaty; tract. **trak·tatie, -s,** *n.* treat. **trakte·ment,** *n.n.* salary, **trak·teren,** *v.t.* & *v.i.* to treat. *ik trakteer,* it's my treat; ~ *op,* to treat to.

·tralie, -s, *n.* bar (*metal*). **·traliehek, -kken,** *n.n.* grille. **·traliën, -lie,** *v.t.* to trellis. **·tralievenster, -s,** *n.n.* lattice window.

tram, -s, *n.* tram; local railway. **·trammen** tram, *v.i.* to go by tram.

tramon·tane, no pl., *n. de* ~ *kwijtraken,* to lose one's bearings.

·tranen, traan, *v.i.* to water. **·tranig,** *a.* trainy.

trans, *n.* battlement.

transfor·mator, -s or **-en,** transformer.

tran·sito, no pl., *n.n.* transit. **tran·sitohandel,** no pl., *n.n.* transit-trade, through-trade. **transi·toir,** *a.* transitory.

transpi·reren, -reer, *v.i.* to perspire. **transpi·ratie,** no pl., *n.* perspiration.

transpo·neren, -neer, *v.t.* to transpose.

trans·port, *n.n.* transport, carriage. **transpor·teren, -teer,** *v.t.* to transport, convey. **trans·portschip, -schepen,** *n.n.* troop-ship. **trans·portvliegtuig,** *n.n.* troop-carrier (*plane*). **trans·portwezen,** no pl., *n.n.* transport.

trant, *n.* manner, style. *in de* ~ *van,* after the style of.

trap, -ppen, *n.* step; step, degree; stairs, staircase; kick. *de* ~ *opgaan,* to go up-stairs; *op de* ~, on the staircase; ~ *op,* ~ *af,* up and down the stairs; *van* ~ *tot* ~, by degrees. **·trapas, -ssen,** *n.* crank axle. **·trapgans, -zen,** *n.* bustard. **·trapgevel, -s,** *n.* stepped gable. **·trapladder, -s,** *n.* stepladder. **·trapleuning,** *n.* banisters. **·traploper, -s,** *n.* stair-carpet. **·trappelen,** *v.i.* to trample, stamp. **·trappenhuis, -zen,** *n.n.* well of staircase. **·trapper, -s,** *n.* treadle; pedal. **·trapsgewijs,** *adv.* gradually, step by step.

tra·ra, *excl.* tra-di-da.

tras, no pl., *n.n.* trass.

tra·want, *n.* henchman.

·trechter, -s, *n.* funnel (*for filling*); crater (*from explosion*). **·trechtervormig,** *a.* funnel-shaped.

tred, *n.* step, pace. *gelijke* ~ *houden met,* to keep pace with. **·trede, -n,** *n.* step; rung; step, pace. **·treden, treed,** *v.i., str.* (*stilted*) to tread, step. *in de plaats* ~ *van,* to take the place of; *in bizonder-heden* ~, to enter into detail; *naar voren* ~, to come forward. **·tredmolen, -s,** *n.* treadmill. **tree, treeën,** *n. See* **trede**. **·treeplank,** *n.* running-board.

tref, no pl., *n.* chance, luck. **·treffelijk,** *a.* excellent. **·treffen, tref,** *v.t., str.* to hit, strike; to touch, move; to meet with, come across. *het doel* ~, to hit the mark;

een vergelijk ~, to reach a compromise;
je treft het, you are in luck. ¶ no pl.,
n.n. clash, encounter. ·**treffend**, *a.* striking;
touching. ·**treffer**, **-s**, *n.* hit. ·**trefkans**,
n. probability of hitting. ·**trefpunt**, *n.n.*
point of impact.

treil, *n.* trawl. ·**treilen**, *v.i.* to trawl. ·**treiler**,
-s, *n.* trawler.

trein, *n.* train; retinue. *met de* ~, by train.
·**treinconducteur**, **-s**, *n.* railway guard.
·**treinenloop**, no pl., *n.* train service.
·**treiteraar**, **-s**, *n.* (malicious) tease. ·**treiteren**,
v.t. to tease (*maliciously*).

trek, **-kken**, *n.* pull, haul; draught; trick
(*card*); stroke (*pen*); trait, feature; groove,
rifling; migration. *er zit geen* ~ *in*,
it does not draw well; *op de* ~ *zitten*, to
sit in a draught; *in brede trekken*, in broad
outline. ¶ no pl., *n.* longing, appetite.
~ *hebben in . . .*, to feel like . . .; *in* ~ *bij*,
in request with. ·**trekbank**, *n.* draw-
bench. ·**trekdier**, *n.n.* beast of draught.
·**trekhond**, *n.* (cart-pulling) dog. ·**trekje**,
-s, *n.n.* pull, whiff. ·**trekkebenen**, **-been**,
v.i. to drag one's leg. ·**trekkebekken**,
-bek, *v.i.* to bill and coo. ·**trekken**, **trek**,
v.t., *str.* to pull, draw; to attract. *één lijn* ~
met, to be in agreement with. ¶ *v.i.*, *str.*
to draw (*tea*); to march, go. *met een
been* ~, to limp. ‖ *v.imp.*, *str.* to be
draughty. ·**trekker**, **-s**, *n.* drawer (*of
bill*); trigger. ·**trekking**, *n.* draw. ·**treklijn**,
n. tow-line. ·**treknet**, **-tten**, *n.n.* drag-net.
·**trekpaard**, *n.n.* draught-horse. ·**trekpen**,
-nnen, *n.* drawing-pen. ·**trekpleister**, **-s**,
n.n. vesicatory; attraction. ·**trekschuit**, *n.*
horse-drawn barge. ·**treksel**, **-s**, *n.n.*
infusion. ·**trekvogel**, **-s**, *n.* migratory
bird.

·**trema**, **-'s**, *n.n.* diaeresis.
·**tremmen**, **trem**, *v.t.* to trim (*coal*). ·**tremmer**,
-s, *n.* trimmer.

tres, **-ssen**, *n.* tress, plait.
·**treurboom**, **-bomen**, *n.* weeping tree. ·**treur-
dicht**, *n.n.* elegy. ·**treuren**, *v.i.* to mourn,
grieve. ·**treurig**, *a.* sad. ·**treurigheid**, no
pl., *n.* sadness. ·**treurmars**, *n.* funeral
march. ·**treurspel**, *n.n.* tragedy. ·**treurwilg**,
n. weeping willow. ·**treurzang**, *n.* dirge;
elegy.

·**treuzel**, **-s**, *n.* ·**treuzelaar**, **-s**, *n.* dawdler.
·**treuzelachtig**, *a.* dawdling. ·**treuzela·rij**, *n.*
dawdling. ·**treuzelen**, *v.i.* to dawdle.

tri·bune, **-s**, *n.* platform, tribune.
·**triest(ig)**, *a.* dreary, depressing.
trijp, no pl., *n.n.* mock velvet. ·**trijpen**, *a.*
(of) mock velvet.
·**trijsblok**, **-kken**, *n.n.* brace block. ·**trijsen**,
v.t. to trice.
·**trildiertje**, **-s**, *n.n.* vibrio. ·**trilgras**, **-ssen**, *n.n.*
quaking-grass. ·**trillen**, **tril**, *v.i.* to vibrate;
to tremble, quake; to quaver, trill. ·**triller**,
-s, *n.* trill, quaver. ·**trilling**, *n.* vibration.
·**trilpopulier**, *n.* aspen.

tri·mester, **-s**, *n.n.* quarter, term.
tri·omf, *n.* triumph.   **triom·fantelijk**, *a.*
triumphant.   **tri·omfboog**, **-bogen**, *n.*
triumphal arch.   **triom·feren**, **-feer**, *v.i.*
to triumph.
·**triplo**, *adv. in* ~, in triplicate.
·**trippelaar**, **-s**, *n.* tripper (*not holiday maker*).
·**trippelen**, *v.i.* to trip.
trip·tiek, *n.* triptych.
·**troebel**, *a.* turbid; troubled, muddy. ·**troebe-
len**, pl. only, *n.* riot(s), disturbance(s).
·**troebelheid**, no pl., *n.* turbidity.
troef, **-ven**, *n.* trump(s).   ~ *bekennen*, to
follow suit; *iemand* ~ *geven*, to give
someone a drubbing. **troef·aas**, **-azen**, *n.n.*
ace of trumps.
troep, *n.* troupe; body (*of soldiers*); crowd;
herd, flock. ~*en*, troops. ·**troepenmacht**,
no pl., *n.* military forces. ·**troepenwijs**,
adv. in groups.
·**troetelen**, *v.t.* to pamper.   ·**troetelkind**,
-eren, *n.n.* pet; spoilt child.
·**troeven**, **troef**, *n.* trump.
·**troffel**, **-s**, *n.* trowel.
trog, **-ggen**, *n.* trough.   **troggelaar**, **-s**, *n.*
wheedler. ·**troggelen**, *v.i.* to wheedle.
trom, **-mmen**, *n.* drum. *Turkse* ~, big drum;
de ~ *roeren*, to beat the big drum; *met
slaande* ~, with drums beating. ·**trom-
geroffel**, no pl., *n.n.* roll of drums.
·**trommel**, **-s**, *n.* drum; tin, canister.
·**trommelaar**, **-s**, *n.* drummer. ·**trommelen**,
v.i. to drum; to bang.   *bij elkaar* ~,
to get together. ·**trommelslag**, *n.* drum-
beat. ·**trommelslager**, **-s**, *n.* drummer.
·**trommelvlies**, **-zen**, *n.n.* ear-drum.
tromp, *n.* horn, trump; trunk (*elephant*).
tromp·pet, **-tten**, *n.* trumpet. **trom·petblazer**,
-s, *n.* trumpeter. **trom·petgeschal**, no pl.,
n.n. flourish of trumpets. **trom·petten**,
-pet, *v.i.* to trumpet. **trom·petter**, **-s**, *n.*
trumpeter.
·**tronen**, **troon**, *v.i.* to throne, be enthroned;
to allure.
·**tronie**, **-s**, *n.* face, mug.
tronk, *n.* trunk (*tree*).
troon, **tronen**, *n.* throne. ·**troonhemel**, **-s**, *n.*
canopy. ·**troonopvolger**, **-s**, *n.* heir to the
throne, successor. ·**troonopvolging**, *n.*
succession. ·**troonrede**, **-denen**, *n.* speech
from the throne. ·**troonsafstand**, no pl., *n.*
abdication. ·**troonsbestijging**, no pl., *n.*
accession (to the throne).
troost, no pl., *n.* consolation, comfort.
·**troosteloos**, **-loze**, *a.* disconsolate; dreary.
·**troosteloosheid**, no pl., *n.* dreariness.
·**troosten**, *v.t.* to console, comfort. ·**troost-
rijk**, *a.*, ·**troostvol**, **-lle**, *a.* comforting.
tropen, pl. only, *n.* tropics. **tropisch**, *a.*
tropical.
tros, **-ssen**, *n.* bunch, cluster; hawser; train,
baggage (*army*).
trots, no pl., *n.* pride. ¶ *a.* proud, haughty.
~ *zijn op*, to be proud of. ¶ *c.* in spite of.

trot·seren, -seer, *v.t.* to defy; to brave.
trot·sering, *n.* defiance.
trot·toir, -s, *n.n.* pavement, side-walk.
trot·toirband, *n.* kerb-stone.
trouw, no pl., *n.* fidelity, loyalty; faith.
~ *zweren,* to swear allegiance; *te goeder* ~,
in good faith. ¶*a.* faithful, true; trusty.
·**trouwbreuk,** no pl., *n.* breach of faith.
·**trouwdag,** *n.* wedding-day. ·**trouwelijk,**
adv. faithfully. ·**trouweloos, -loze,** *a.*
faithless. ·**trouweloosheid,** no pl., *n.*
faithlessness. ·**trouwen,** *v.i.* to marry.
~ *met,* to get married to. ¶ *v.t.* to marry,
wed. ·**trouwens,** *adv.* for that matter.
trouw·hartig, *a.* true-hearted. ·**trouwjapon,**
-nnen, *n.* wedding dress. ·**trouwpak,**
-kken, *n.n.* wedding suit.
truc, -s, *n.* trick.
·**truffel, -s,** *n.* truffle.
·**trui,** *n.* jersey, sweater.
tru·weel, -welen, *n.n.* trowel.
Tsjech, *N.* Czech. **Tsjechoslo·waaks,** *a.*
Czechoslovak. **Tsjechoslowa·kije,** *n.N.*
Czechoslovakia.
·**tsjirpen,** *v.i.* to chirrup.
·**tuberoos, -rozen,** *n.* tuberose.
tucht, no pl., *n.* discipline. ·**tuchteloos, -loze,**
a. undisciplined, unruly. ·**tuchteloosheid,**
no pl., *n.* want of discipline; licence.
·**tuchthuis, -zen,** *n.n.* house of correction.
·**tuchthuisboef, -ven,** *n.* convict. ·**tucht-
huisstraf, -ffen,** *n.* hard labour. ·**tuchtigen,**
v.t. to chastise. ·**tuchtiging,** *n.* chastisement. ·**tuchtmiddel,** *n.n.* means of
correction. ·**tuchtschool, -scholen,** *n.*
reformatory.
·**tuffen, tuf,** *v.i.* (*coll.*) to motor.
tui, *n.* rope. ·**tuianker, -s,** *n.n.* boweranchor. ·**tuien,** *v.t.* to moor.
tuig, *n.n.* harness (*horse*). ¶ no pl., *n.n.*
tools; rigging. **tui·gage,** no pl., *n.* rigging.
·**tuigen,** *v.t.* to rig; to harness (*horse*).
·**tuiger, -s,** *n.* rigger. ·**tuighuis, -zen,** *n.n.*
arsenal. ·**tuigkamer, -s,** *n.* harness-room.
tuil, *n.* nosegay. ~*tje,* posy.
·**tuimel, -s,** *n.* tumble. ·**tuimelaar, -s,** *n.*
tumbler; tumbler (*pigeon*). ·**tuimelen,** *v.i.*
to tumble. ·**tuimeling,** *n.* tumble; somersault.
tuin, *n.* garden. *iemand om de* ~ *leiden,*
to mislead a person, lead a person up the
garden path. ·**tuinaarde,** no pl., *n.*
vegetable mould. ·**tuinbaas, -bazen,** *n.*
(head-)gardener. ·**tuinboon, -bonen,** *n.*
broad bean. ·**tuinbouw,** no pl., *n.* horticulture. ·**tuinbouwschool, -scholen,** *n.*
horticultural college. ·**tuinder, -s,** *n.*
market gardener. **tuinde·rij,** *n.* market
garden. ·**tuindorp,** *n.n.* garden suburb.
·**tuinfluiter, -s,** *n.* garden-warbler. ·**tuin-
gereedschap,** no pl., *n.n.* gardening tools.
·**tuingewassen,** pl. only, *n.n.* garden plants.
·**tuinhuisje, -s,** *n.n.* summer-house. **tui·nier,
-s,** *n.* gardener. **tui·nieren,** *v.i.* to do some

gardening. ·**tuinkers,** no pl., *n.* mustard
and cress. ·**tuinknecht,** *n.* (under-)
gardener. ·**tuinman, -lieden** *or* **-lui,** *n.*
gardener. ·**tuinslak, -kken,** *n.* slug.
tuit, *n.* spout. *tranen met* ~*en schreien,* to
cry one's eyes out. ·**tuiten,** *v.i. mijn oren* ~,
my ears are singing. ·**tuitkan, -nnen,** *n.*
pitcher.
tuk, *a.* ~ *op,* keen on. ·**tukje, -s,** *n.n.* doze.
een ~ *doen,* to have a nap.
·**tulband,** *n.* turban; currant loaf (*of traditional
shape*).
·**tule,** no pl., *n.* tulle.
tulp, *n.* tulip. ·**tulpebol, -llen,** *n.* tulip bulb.
·**Tunis,** *n.N.* Tunis; Tunisia.
ture·luur, -luren *or* **-s,** *n.* redshank. **ture·luurs,**
a. frantic, mad. ·**turen, tuur,** *v.i.* to gaze,
peer.
turf, no pl., *n.* peat. *in het veen ziet men op
geen* ~*je,* when there is plenty one doesn't
count. ¶ **-ven,** *n.* block of peat. ·**turfachtig,** *a.* peaty. ·**turfboer,** *n.* peatman.
·**turfgraverij,** *n.* peat-digging. ·**turfmolm,**
no pl., *n.* peat-dust. ·**turfsteken, steek turf,**
v.i.s., str. to cut peat. ·**turfstrooisel,** no
pl., *n.n.* peat-litter. ·**turftrapper, -s,** *n.*
peat-labourer; (*coll.*) boot.
Tur·kije, *n.N.* Turkey.
tur·koois, -zen, *n.* turquoise. **tur·kooizen,** *a.*
(of) turquoise.
Turks, *a.* Turkish.
turma·lijn, *n.* tourmaline.
·**turnen,** *v.i.* to do gymnastics. ·**turner, -s,**
n. athlete.
·**turven, turf,** *v.i. er op los* ~, to lay about
one; *iemand er uit* ~, to throw someone
out.
tussen, *prep.* between, among, amidst.
iemand er ~ *nemen,* to pull a person's leg;
er van ~ *gaan,* to clear out; *er* ~ *door,*
in between.
·**tussenbedrijf, -ven,** *n.n.* entr'acte.
tussen·beide, *adv.* between whiles. **tussen-
beidekomen,** *v.i.s., irr.* to intervene,
interfere. **tussen·beidetreden, treed tussenbeide** *v.i.s., irr.* to intervene, interfere.
·**tussendek, -kken,** *n.n.* between-decks.
tussen·deks, *adv.* between-decks, (in the)
steerage.
·**tussendeur,** *n.* communicating door.
·**tussengelegen,** *a.* intermediate, intervening.
tussen·in, *adv.* in between.
·**tussenkomst,** no pl., *n.* intervention.
·**tussenmuur, -muren,** *n.* party-wall.
·**tussenpersoon, -sonen,** *n.* intermediary;
mediator; middleman.
·**tussenpoos, -pozen,** *n.* interval.
·**tussenruimte, -n,** *n.* interval, intervening
space.
·**tussenschot,** *n.n.* partition.
·**tussenspel,** *n.n.* interlude.
·**tussentijd,** *n. in die* ~, in the meantime,
meanwhile. ·**tussentijds,** *a.* interim. ~*e
verkiezing,* by-election.

tussen·uit, adv. er ~ gaan, to get out.
·**tussenvoegen,** v.t.s. to insert, interpolate.
·**tussenvoeging,** n. insertion, interpolation.
·**tussenvoegsel,** -s, n.n. insert.
·**tussenvorm,** n. intermediate form.
·**tussenwerpsel,** -s, n.n. interjection.
·**tussenzin,** -nnen, n. parenthesis.
twaalf, num. twelve. ¶-ven, n. twelve.
·**twaalfde,** a. twelfth. ·**twaalftal,** -llen, n.n.
dozen. ·**twaalftallig,** a. duodecimal.
·**twaalven,** num. twelve. de trein van ~,
the twelve o'clock train; bij ~, just on
twelve; in ~, into twelve; met hun ~,
the twelve of them; met ons ~, the twelve
of us; met z'n ~, with eleven others.
twaalf·vingerig, a. duodenal. ~e darm,
duodenum. ·**twaalfvoud,** n.n. multiple of
twelve.
twee, num. two. ¶**tweeën,** n. two. ~ aan ~,
two by two. ·**tweedaags,** a. two-day.
·**tweede,** a. second. **tweede·hands,** a.
second-hand. ·**tweedekker,** -s, n. biplane.
tweede·rangs, a. second-rate. ·**tweedracht,**
no pl., n. discord. ·**tweeën,** num. two.
de trein van ~, the two o'clock train;
bij ~, just on two; in ~, into two;
met hun ~, the two of them; met ons ~,
the two of us; met z'n ~, with someone
else. ·**tweeërhande,** a., ·**tweeërlei,** a. of
two kinds. ·**tweegesprek,** -kken, n.
dialogue. **twee·hoofdig,** a. two-headed.
twee·jarig, a. biennial. **tweeklank,** n.
diphthong. **twee·ledig,** a. dual, double.
·**tweeling** n. twin(s). ·**tweemaandelijks,**
a. bimonthly. ·**tweemanschap,** -ppen, n.n.
duumvirate. ·**tweepersoons,** a. double, for
two. **twee·slachtig,** a. bisexual, hermaphrodite. **tweespalt,** no pl., n. discord.
·**tweespan,** -nnen, n. two-horse team.
·**tweespraak,** -spraken, n. dialogue. ·**twee-**
sprong, n. bifurcation. op de ~, at the
parting of the ways. **twee·stemmig,** a.
for two voices. ·**tweestrijd,** n. uncertainty,
inner conflict. in ~ staan, to be in two
minds. ·**tweetal,** -llen, n.n. two, pair (of).
twee·talig, a. bilingual. **twee·voudig,** a.
twofold, double. **twee·zijdig,** a. two-sided.
·**twijfel,** no pl., n. doubt. er is geen ~ aan
or het lijdt geen ~, it is beyond doubt;
aan ~ onderhevig, open to doubt; boven
alle ~ verheven, beyond all doubt. ·**twijfe-**
laar, -s, n. doubter. ·**twijfelachtig,** a.
doubtful, dubious. ·**twijfel·achtigheid,**
-heden, n. doubtfulness. ·**twijfelen,** v.i. to
doubt. ~ aan, to doubt (of). ·**twijfeling,**
n. doubt, hesitation. **twijfel·moedig,** a.
irresolute.
twijg, n. twig.
twijn, no pl., n. twine.
·**twintig,** num. twenty. ·**twintiger,** -s, n.
person in his twenties. ·**twintigste,** a.
twentieth. ·**twintigtal,** -llen, n.n. twenty,
score. ·**twintigvoud,** n.n. multiple of
twenty. **twintig·voudig,** a. twentyfold.

twist, n. quarrel, dispute. ~ zoeken, to pick
a quarrel. ·**twistappel,** -s, n. apple of
discord, bone of contention. ·**twisten,** v.i.
to quarrel, dispute. ·**twistgeding,** n.n.
lawsuit. ·**twistgesprek,** -kken, n.n. disputation. ·**twistvraag, -vragen,** n. controversial
question. ·**twistzoeker,** -s, n. quarrelsome
person.
·**type,** -s, n.n. type; character, card. **ty·peren,**
peer, v.t. to be typical of. **ty·perend,** a.
~ voor, characteristic of. ·**typen,** v.t. &
v.i. to type.
·**typhus,** no pl., n. typhoid (fever). vlek ~,
typhus. ·**typhuslijder,** -s, n. typhoid case.
·**typisch,** a. typical; quaint, picturesque.

U

U, pron. you (formal sg. and pl.).
ui, n. onion; joke.
·**uier, -s,** n. udder.
·**uiig,** a. oniony; funny.
uil, n. owl. elk meent zijn ~ een valk te zijn,
everyone thinks his own geese swans.
·**uilachtig,** a. owlish. ·**uilskuiken, -s,** n.n.
owlet; stupid person. ·**uiltje, -s,** n.n. owlet;
owl moth. een ~ knappen, to have a nap.
uit, prep. out of, from; for; through. ¶ adv.
out. het moet er ~, it must go out; hij
is erop ~ om . . ., he is out after . . .
¶ prefix. out.
·**uitademen,** v.i.s. to breathe out, exhale.
·**uitbaggeren,** v.t.s. to dredge.
·**uitbannen, ban uit,** v.t.s., irr. to banish; to
exorcise.
·**uitbarsten,** v.i.s., irr. to burst out; to
explode. ·**uitbarsting,** n. outburst;
explosion; eruption.
·**uitbeelden,** v.t.s. to depict. ·**uitbeelding,** n.
representation.
·**uitbesteden, besteed uit,** v.t.s. to board out;
to put out to contract. ·**uitbesteding,** n.
boarding-out; putting out to contract.·
·**uitbetaling,** n. payment.
·**uitbijten,** v.t.s., str. to corrode.
·**uitblazen, blaas uit,** v.t.s., str. to blow out.
de laatste adem ~, to breathe one's last.
·**uitblijven, blijf uit,** v.i.s., str. to stay away;
to fail to come.
·**uitblinken,** v.i.s., str. to shine, excel.
·**uitbloeien,** v.i.s. to cease flowering.
·**uitbouw,** n. annex (building).
·**uitbraaksel, -s,** n.n. vomit. ·**uitbraken,**
braak uit, v.t.s. to vomit; to spew forth,
belch.
·**uitbrander, -s,** n. scolding.
·**uitbreiden,** v.t.s. to extend, enlarge. ¶ zich
~, v.r.s. to expand; to spread. ·**uit-**
breiding, n. extension, spread.
·**uitbreken, breek uit,** v.i.s., str. to break out.
¶ no pl., n.n. outbreak.
·**uitbrengen,** v.t.s., irr. to bring out. een
rapport ~, to make a report.

·uitbrullen, brul uit, *v.i.s.* to roar (out).
·uitbuiten, *v.t.s.* to exploit. ·uitbuiter, -s, *n.* exploiter. ·uitbuiting, *n.* exploitation.
uit·bundig, *a.* exuberant; excessive. uit·bundigheid, -heden, *n.* exuberance.
·uitdagen, daag uit, *v.t.s.* to challenge, defy. ·uitdagend, *a.* defiant. ·uitdager, -s, *n.* challenger. ·uitdaging, *n.* challenge.
·uitdampen, *v.t.s.* to evaporate.
·uitdelen, deel uit, *v.t.s.* to distribute, hand out. ·uitdeling, *n.* distribution.
·uitdenken, *v.t.s., irr.* to think out, devise.
·uitdijen, *v.i.s.* (*lit.*) to expand.
·uitdoen, doe uit, *v.t.s., irr.* to put out; to take off.
·uitdoven, doof uit, *v.t.s.* to extinguish, put out.
·uitdossen, dos uit, *v.t.s.* to attire, bedeck.
·uitdraaien, *v.t.s.* to turn out, switch off. *op niets* ~, to come to nothing.
·uitdrager, -s, *n.* second-hand dealer. ·uit·dragerswinkel, -s, *n.* second-hand shop.
·uitdrijven, drijf uit, *v.t.s., str.* to drive out, expel.
·uitdrogen, droog uit, *v.t.s. & v.i.s.* to dry out, dessicate.
uit·drukkelijk, *a.* express, positive, explicit. uit·drukkelijkheid, no pl., *n.* explicitness. ·uitdrukken, druk uit, *v.t.s.* to express; to squeeze (out). ·uitdrukking, *n.* expression.
uit·een, *adv.* asunder.
uit·eenbarsten, *v.i.s.* to explode.
uit·eendrijven, drijf uiteen, *v.t.s., str.* to disperse, scatter.
uit·eengaan, ga uiteen, *v.i.s., irr.* to disperse, separate.
uit·eenlopen, loop uiteen, *v.i.s., str.* to diverge. uit·eenlopend, *a.* divergent.
uit·eennemen, neem uiteen, *v.t.s., str.* to take to pieces, dismantle.
uit·eenrafelen, *v.t.s.* to unravel.
uit·eenvallen, val uiteen, *v.i.s., str.* to fall to pieces.
uit·eenzetten, zet uiteen, *v.t.s.* to expound, set forth. uit·eenzetting, *n.* exposition.
·uiteinde, -n, *n.n.* extreme end, extremity. uit·eindelijk, *a.* ultimate.
·uiten, *v.t.* to utter, voice. ¶ zich ~, *v.r.* to express oneself.
uiten·treuren, *adv.* on and on.
uiter·aard, *adv.* by nature.
·uiterlijk, *a.* external, outward. ¶ *adv.* outwardly; at the latest. ¶ no pl., *n.n.* (outward) appearance, looks. ·uiterlijkheid, -heden, *n.* exterior; *pl.* externals. ·uitermate, *adv.* excessively.
·uiterst, *a.* out(er)most, utmost, utter, extreme. ¶ *adv.* extremely. ·uiterste, -n, *n.n.* extreme; extremity. *in* ~*n vervallen*, to go to extremes; *tot het* ~, to the utmost.
·uiterwaard, *n.* foreland.
·uitfluiten, *v.t.s., str.* to jeer at.
·uitfoeteren, *v.t.s.* to swear at.
·uitgaaf, -gaven, *n.* expense; edition.

·uitgaan, ga uit, *v.i.s., irr.* to go out. ~ *op,* to end in; ~ *van,* to start from. ·uitgaand, *a.* going out. ~*e rechten,* export duties. ·uitgaansdag, *n.* day off. ·uitgang, *n.* exit. *punt van* ~, starting point.
·uitgave, -n, *n.* See uitgaaf.
uitge·breid, *a.* extensive, comprehensive. uitge·breidheid, -heden, *n.* extent.
·uitgehongerd, *a.* ravenous.
uitge·laten, *a.* exuberant. uitge·latenheid, no pl., *n.* exuberance.
·uitgeleefd, *a.* decrepit.
·uitgeleerd, *a.* having finished studies *or* apprenticeship.
·uitgeleide, no pl., *n.n. iemand* ~ *doen,* to show a person out.
·uitgelezen, *a.* select, picked.
·uitgemaakt, *a.* settled.
·uitgeslapen, *a.* wide-awake.
·uitgesteld, *a.* deferred.
·uitgestorven, *a.* extinct; deserted.
·uitgestreken, *a.* demure. *een* ~ *gezicht,* a straight face.
uitge·strekt, *a.* extensive. uitge·strektheid, -heden, *n.* extent; expanse.
·uitgeteerd, *a.* emaciated.
·uitgeven, geef uit, *v.t.s., str.* to spend; to publish, edit; to utter, issue. ~ *voor,* to pass off as; *zich* ~ *voor,* to pose as. ·uitgever, -s, *n.* publisher. ·uitgeversfirma, -'s, *n.* publishing house.
·uitgewekene, -n, *n.* refugee.
·uitgewezene, -n, *n.* exile.
·uitgewoond, *a.* in bad repair.
·uitgezocht, *a.* excellent.
·uitgezonderd, *c.* except, save.
·uitgifte, -n, *n.* issue, emission.
·uitglijden, *v.i.s., str.,* ·uitglippen, glip uit, *v.i.s.* to slip.
·uitgraven, graaf uit, *v.t.s.* to dig up; to excavate.
·uitgroeien, *v.t.s.* to outgrow.
·uithalen, haal uit, *v.t.s.* to draw or pull out; to do, carry out (*prank*).
·uithangbord, *n.n.* signboard. ·uithangen, *v.t.s., str.* to hang out. *de grote heer* ~, to put on airs.
uit·heems, *a.* foreign.
·uithoek, *n.* remote corner.
·uithollen, hol uit, *v.t.s.* to hollow (out).
·uithongeren, *v.t.s.* to starve (out).
·uithoren, hoor uit, *v.t.s.* to pump. *iemand* ~, to pump a person.
·uithouden, *v.t.s., irr.* to hold out; to bear, stand. ·uithoudingsvermogen, no pl., *n.n.* staying power, stamina.
uit·huizig, *a.* from home.
·uiting, *n.* utterance, expression. ~ *geven aan,* to voice; *tot* ~ *komen,* to find expression.
·uitjouwen, *v.t.s.* to jeer at, boo.
·uitkeren, keer uit, *v.t.s.* to pay (out). ·uitkering, *n.* payment; dividend; benefit.
·uitkiezen, kies uit, *v.t.s., str.* to choose, select.

·uitkijk, no pl., *n.* look-out. *op de* ~ *staan*, to be on the look-out. ·uitkijken, *v.i.s.*, *str.* to look out. ·uitkijktoren, -s, *n.* watchtower.

·uitklaren, klaar uit, *v.t.s.* to clear (*ship*).

·uitkleden, kleed uit, *v.t.s.* to undress. ¶ zich ~, *v.r.s.* to undress.

·uitkloppen, klop uit, *v.t.s.* to beat, shake, (*carpet*).

·uitknijpen, *v.t.s.*, *str.* to squeeze out. ¶ *v.i.s.*, *str. er* ~, to hook it.

·uitknipsel, -s, *n.n.* cutting, clipping.

·uitkomen, *v.i.s.*, *irr.* to come out; to appear; to hatch; to be brought to light; to come true; to work out, turn out. *het komt uit*, it is correct; *verkeerd* ~, to turn out wrong; *doen* ~, to emphasize; *doen* ~ *alsof*, to make it appear as if; ~ *met*, to have sufficient with; ~ *op*, to give on, look out over; ~ *voor*, to admit, ·uitkomst, *n.* result; solution. ~ *geven*, to bring a solution.

·uitkunnen, kan uit, *v.i.s.*, *irr.* to get out. ¶ no pl., *n.* godsend; deliverance.

·uitlaat, -laten, *n.* exhaust. ·uitlaatgassen, pl. only, *n.n.* exhaust fumes.

·uitlachen, *v.t.s.*, *irr.* to laugh at.

·uitlaten, laat uit, *v.t.s.*, *str.* to let out; to omit. ¶ *v.r.s.*, *str. zich* ~ *over*, to speak of; *zich niet* ~ *over*, to refuse to give an opinion on. ·uitlating, *n.* omission; utterance. ·uitlatingsteken, -s, *n.n.* apostrophy.

·uitleg, no pl., *n.* explanation; interpretation. ·uitleggen, leg uit, *v.t.s.*, *str.* or *irr.* to explain; to interpret. ·uitlegging, *n.* See uitleg.

·uitleven, leef uit, zich, *v.r.s.* to live one's life to the full.

·uitleveren, *v.t.s.* to extradite. ·uitlevering, *n.* extradition.

·uitlokken, lok uit, *v.t.s.* to provoke, call forth.

·uitloop, -lopen, *n.* outlet. ·uitlopen, loop uit, *v.i.s.*, *str.* to run out; to sprout. ~ *in*, to run into; ~ *op*, to lead to. ·uitloper, -s, *n.* offshoot; spur (*mountain*).

·uitlozen, loos uit, *v.i.s.* to empty.

·uitloven, loof uit, *v.t.s.* to offer.

·uitmaken, maak uit, *v.t.s.* to break off (*engagement*); to settle; to constitute. *iemand* ~ *voor* . . ., to call a person a . . .; *het maakt niets uit*, it is immaterial.

·uitmergelen, *v.t.s.* to exhaust.

·uitmeten, meet uit, *v.t.s.*, *str.* to measure.

·uitmonden, *v.i.s.* ~ *in*, to debauch into. ·uitmonding, *n.* mouth, outlet.

·uitmoorden, *v.t.s.* to massacre.

·uitmunten, *v.i.s.* to excel. uit·muntend, *a.* excellent.

uit·nemend, *a.* excellent. uit·nemendheid, no pl., *n. bij* ~, par excellence.

·uitnodigen, *v.t.s.* to invite. ·uitnodiging, *n.* invitation.

·uitoefenen, *v.t.s.* to exercise, practise, carry on. *drang* ~, to bring pressure to bear; *kracht* ~, to exert strength; *macht* ~, to wield power. ·uitoefening, no pl., *n.* exercise, pursuit, discharge.

·uitpakken, pak uit, *v.t.s.* to unpack; to boast; to let rip.

·uitpluizen, pluis uit, *v.t.s.*, *str.* to sift, thresh out.

·uitpraten, praat uit, *v.i.s.* to finish talking.

·uitproesten, *v.t.s. het* ~, to burst out laughing.

·uitpuilend, *a.* bulging, protruding.

·uitputten, put uit, *v.t.s.* to exhaust. ·uitputting, no pl., *n.* exhaustion. ·uitputtingsoorlog, *n.* war of attrition.

·uitrafelen, *v.t.s.* to fray.

·uitrakelen, *v.t.s.* to rake out.

·uitrazen, raas uit, *v.i.s.* to cease raging.

·uitreiken, *v.t.s.* to distribute, issue. ·uitreiking, *n.* distribution, issue.

·uitreis, -zen, *n.* outward journey *or* voyage. ·uitreizen, reis uit, *v.i.s.* to set out.

·uitrekenen, *v.t.s.* to calculate. ·uitrekening, *n.* calculation.

·uitrekken, rek uit, *v.t.s.* to stretch (out).

·uitrichten, *v.t.s.* to do, perform.

·uitroeien, *v.t.s.* to exterminate, eradicate. ·uitroeiing, *n.* extermination; extirpation.

·uitroep, *n.* exclamation. ·uitroepen, *v.t.s.*, *str.* to exclaim; to proclaim, call. ·uitroepteken, -s, *n.n.* exclamation mark.

·uitrukken, ruk uit, *v.t.s.* to tear out. ¶ *v.i.s.* to turn out, sally forth.

·uitrusten, *v.t.s.* to equip, fit out. ¶ *v.i.s.* to rest, take a rest. ·uitrusting, *n.* equipment; outfit.

·uitschakelen, *v.t.s.* to switch off; to eliminate. ·uitschakeling, *n.* switching off; elimination.

·uitscheiden, *v.i.s.* to stop, leave off. ¶ *v.t.s.* to excrete.

·uitschelden, *v.t.s.* to abuse, call names.

·uitschieten, *v.t.s.*, *str.* to shoot out; to slip (off). ·uitschot, no pl., *n.n.* throw-outs, rejects.

·uitschrijven, schrijf uit, *v.t.s.*, *str.* to write out; to call (*meeting*).

·uitschuren, schuur uit, *v.t.s.* to scour (out). ·uitschuring, no pl., *n.* erosion.

·uitslaan, sla uit, *v.t.s.*, *irr.* to beat out; to spread, stretch out. ¶ *v.i.s.*, *irr.* to burst out (*flames*); to sweat (*wall*). ·uitslag, no pl., *n.* rash; damp (*on wall*); result.

·uitslapen, slaap uit, *v.i.s.*, *str.* to have a good long sleep.

·uitsliepen, *v.t.s.* to jeer at.

·uitsloven, sloof uit, zich, *v.r.s.* to work oneself to death.

·uitsluiten, *v.t.s.*, *str.* to exclude, preclude, debar. uit·sluitend, *a.* exclusive. ·uitsluiting, *n.* exclusion. ·uitsluitsel, no pl., *n.n.* decisive answer.

·uitsmijten, *v.t.s.*, *str.* to throw out. ·uitsmijter, -s, *n.* chucker-out; meat sandwich with fried egg.

·uitspannen, span uit, *v.t.s.*, *irr.* to stretch out; to take out (*horse*). ·uitspanning, *n.* baiting-place. ·uitspansel, no pl., *n.n.* firmament.

·uitsparen, spaar uit, *v.t.s.* to save. ·uitsparing, *n.* saving.

·uitspatting, *n.* dissipation.

·uitspelen, speel uit, *v.t.s.* to finish play *or* game. *tegen elkaar* ~, to play one against the other.

·uitspraak, -spraken, *n.* pronunciation; pronouncement; sentence, verdict. ~ *doen*, to pass judgment. ·uitspreken, spreek uit, *v.t.s.*, *str.* to pronounce. ¶ *v.i.s.*, *str.* to finish speaking.

·uitspringen, *v.i.s.*, *str.* to project.

·uitspuiten, *v.t.s.*, *str.* to syringe.

·uitstaan, sta uit, *v.t.s.*, *irr.* to bear, endure; to stand, stick. *niets uit te staan hebben met*, to have nothing to do with. ¶ *v.i.s.*, *irr.* to be put out (at interest).

·uitstalkast, *n.* showcase. ·uitstallen, stal uit, *v.t.s.* to display. ·uitstalling, *n.* display.

·uitstapje, -s, *n.n.* excursion, trip. ·uitstappen, stap uit, *v.i.s.* to get out.

·uitsteeksel, -s, *n.n.* projection. ·uitstek, no pl., *n.n. bij* ~, par excellence. ·uitsteken, steek uit, *v.t.s.*, *str.* to hold out; to gouge out. ¶ *v.i.s.*, *str.* to stick out, protrude. ·uitstekend, *a.* protruding. uit·stekend, *a.* excellent.

·uitstel, no pl., *n.n.* delay; deferment. ~ *van betaling*, extension of payment; ~ *van executie*, stay of execution; ~ *verlenen*, to grant a respite. ·uitsteldagen, pl. only, *n.* days of grace. ·uitstellen, stel uit, *v.t.s.* to put off, postpone.

·uitstoten, *v.t.s.*, *str.* to push out, expel.

·uitstorten, *v.t.s.* to pour out *or* forth. *zijn hart* ~, to unburden one's heart.

·uitstralen, straal uit, *v.t.s.* to radiate.

·uitstrekken, strek uit, *v.t.s.* to stretch; to reach out. ¶ *zich* ~, *v.r.s.* to extend.

·uitstrooien, *v.t.s.* to strew, scatter. ·uitstrooisel, -s, *n.n.* (false) rumour.

·uittocht, *n.* exodus.

·uittreden, treed uit, *v.i.s.*, *str.* to withdraw, retire. ·uittreding, *n.* withdrawal, resignation.

·uittrekken, trek uit, *v.t.s.*, *str.* to pull out, extract. ¶*v.i.s.*, *str. er op* ~, to set out. ·uittreksel, -s, *n.n.* extract.

·uitvaagsel, -s, *n.n.* sweepings; scum, dregs (*fig.*).

·uitvaardigen, *v.t.s.* to issue, proclaim. ·uitvaardiging, *n.* issue, promulgation.

·uitvaart, *n.* obsequies.

·uitval, -llen, *n.* sally; outburst. ·uitvallen, val uit, *v.i.s.*, *str.* to fall *or* drop out; to fly out (*anger*).

·uitvaren, vaar uit, *v.i.s.*, *str.* to sail (out), put to sea. ~ *tegen*, to inveigh against.

·uitverkoop, -kopen, *n.* clearance sale.

·uitverkoren, *a.* chosen, elect.

·uitvinden, *v.t.s.*, *str.* to invent. ·uitvinder, -s, *n.* inventor. ·uitvinding, *n.* invention. ·uitvindsel, -s, *n.n.* invention, device.

·uitvissen, vis uit, *v.t.s.* to ferret out.

·uitvlakken, vlak uit, *v.t.s.* to rub out.

·uitvloeisel, -s, *n.n.* outcome.

·uitvloeken, *v.t.s.* to swear at.

·uitvlucht, *n.* subterfuge, pretext.

·uitvoer, *n.* export. *ten* ~ *brengen*, to execute, perform. uit·voerbaar, -bare, *a.* practicable. uit·voerbaarheid, no pl., *n.* feasibility. ·uitvoeren, *v.t.s.* to execute, carry out; to export. *iets* ~, to be up to mischief; *niets* ~, to slack. uit·voerig, *a.* detailed. ¶ *adv.* in detail. ·uitvoering, *n.* performance; execution.

·uitvragen, vraag uit, *v.t.s.*, *str.* to ask out; to pump.

·uitwaarts, *a.* & *adv.* outward(s).

·uitwas, -ssen, *n.* excrescence.

·uitwasemen, *v.i.s.* to evaporate.

·uitwateren, *v.i.s.* ~ *in*, to discharge into. ·uitwatering, *n.* outlet. ·uitwateringskanaal, -nalen, *n.* drainage canal.

·uitweg, *n.* way out, outlet.

·uitweiden, *v.i.s.* to expatiate; to digress. ·uitweiding, *n.* expatiation; digression.

uit·wendig, *a.* external.

·uitwerken, *v.t.s.* to work out, elaborate. *iemand er* ~, to get a person out. ·uitwerking, *n.*, ·uitwerksel, -s, *n.n.* effect, result.

·uitwerpsel, -s *or* -en, *n.n.* excrement.

·uitwijken, *v.i.s.*, *str.* to give way; to go into exile.

·uitwijzen, wijs uit, *v.t.s.*, *str.* to show, prove.

·uitwissen, wis uit, *v.t.s.* to obliterate.

·uitwisselen, *v.t.s.* to exchange.

·uitzenden, *v.t.s.*, *str.* to send out. ¶ *v.i.s.*, *str.* to broadcast. ·uitzending, *n.* broadcast.

·uitzet, -tten, *n.* trousseau. ·uitzetten, zet uit, *v.i.s.* to expand. ¶ *v.i.s.* to put out (*money*); to evict; to lower (*boat*). ·uitzetting, *n.* expansion; eviction.

·uitzicht, *n.n.* view; prospect.

·uitzieken, *v.i.s.* to convalesce.

·uitzien, zie uit, *v.i.s.*, *irr.* to look out. *er* ~, to look; *er goed* ~, to look well; ~ *naar*, to look out for *or* to look forward to; ~ *op*, to face, look out upon.

·uitzingen, *v.t.s.*, *str.* to sing to the end. *het* ~, to hold out to the end.

·uitzoeken, *v.t.s.*, *irr.* to sort.

·uitzonderen, *v.t.s.* to except. ·uitzondering, *n.* exception. ·uitzonderingsgeval, -llen, *n.n.* exceptional case.

·uitzweten, zweet uit, *v.t.s.* to exude.

·ulevel, -llen, *n.* Cupid's kiss (*sweet*).

ultrama·rijn, no pl., *n.n.* ultramarine.

ultra·rood, -rode, *a.* infra-red.

una·niem, *a.* unanimous.

·unie, -s, *n.* union.

u·niek, *a.* unique.

·ure. *See* uur.
u·sance, -s, *n.* (trade) custom, usage (of the trade).
utilita·ristisch, *a.* utilitarian.
uur, uren, *n.n.* hour. *om twee* ~, at two o'clock; *om het* ~, every hour; *over een* ~, in an hour's time; *te goeder ure*, in a happy hour. ·uurwerk, *n.n.* timepiece. ·uurwijzer, -s, *n.* hour hand.
Uw, *poss. pron.* your. *de* or *het* ~*e*, yours. ·uwent, *adv. ten* ~ (*stilted*), at your house. ·uwenthalve, *adv.*, ·uwentwege, *adv.* for your sake, on your behalf. ·uwerzijds, *adv.* on your part.

V

vaag, vage, *a.* vague. ·vaagheid, no pl., *n.* vagueness.
vaak, no pl., *n.* sleepiness. *Klaas V*~, the Sandman. ¶*adv.* frequently, often.
vaal, vale, *a.* drab; dun. ·vaalbleek, -bleken, *a.* sallow.
vaalt, *n.* dungheap.
vaam, vamen, *n.* fathom.
vaan, vanen, *n.* banner. ·vaandel, -s, *n.n.* banner, standard. ·vaandrig, *n.* ensign, cornet.
·vaardig, *a.* ready; proficient, dexterous. ·vaardigheid, no pl., *n.* skill.
·vaargeul, *n.* channel.
vaars, -zen, *n.* heifer.
vaart, *n.* voyage; canal. ¶ no pl., *n.* speed; course; navigation. *er* ~ *achter zetten*, to get a move on; *het zal zo'n* ~ *niet lopen*, it won't come to that; *de grote* ~, ocean-going trade; *de kleine* ~, coastal trade; *in de* ~ *brengen*, to put into service. ·vaartje, -s, *n.n.* father. *See* aardje. ·vaartuig, *n.n.* vessel. ·vaarwater, -s or -en, *n.n.* waterway. *iemand in het* ~ *zitten*, to cross a person's path; *uit iemands* ~ *blijven*, to give a person a wide berth. ·vaarweg, *n.* channel, fairway. vaar·wel, *int.* farewell. ¶ no pl., *n.n.* farewell.
vaas, vazen, *n.* vase.
·vaatdoek, *n.* dishcloth. ·vaatje, -s, *n.n.* keg, small barrel *or* cask. *uit een ander* ~ *tappen*, to change one's tune. ·vaatstelsel, -s, *n.n.* vascular system. ·vaatwerk, no pl., *n.n.* dishes.
va·cantie, -s, *n.* holiday(s). *de grote* ~, long vacation, summer holidays; *met* ~ *zijn*, to be on holiday. va·cantiekaart, *n.* excursion ticket. va·cantieoord, *n.n.* holiday resort. vaca·ture, -s, *n.* vacancy.
vacci·neren, -neer, *v.t.* to vaccinate.
vacht, *n.* fleece.
·vadem, -s, *n.* fathom. ·vademen, *v.t.* to fathom; to cord.
·vader, -s, *n.* father *het Onze V*~, the Lord's Prayer. ·vaderhuis, no pl., *n.n.*

paternal home. ·vaderland, no pl., *n.n.* fatherland. ·vaderlander, -s, *n.* patriot vaderland·lievend, *a.* patriotic. ·vaderlands, *a.* native, national; patriotic. ·vaderlandsliefde, no pl., *n.* patriotism. ·vaderlief, no pl., *n.* father dear. ·vaderliefde, no pl., *n.* father-love. ·vaderlijk, *a.* paternal, fatherly. ·vaderloos, -loze, *a.* fatherless. ·vadermoord, *n.* patricide. ·vaderschap, no pl., *n.n.* paternity. ·vaderstad, no pl., *n.* native town.
vadsig, *a.* lazy. ·vadsigheid, no pl., *n.* laziness.
·vagebond, *n.* vagabond.
·vagelijk, *adv.* vaguely.
·vagevuur, no pl., *n.n.* purgatory.
vak, -kken, *n.n.* compartment, pigeon-hole; profession, trade; branch (*of study*). ·vakarbeider, -s, *n.* skilled labourer. ·vakbeweging, *n.* trade-union movement, trade-unionism. ·vakbond, *n.* trade-union. ·vakgenoot, -noten, *n.* colleague. vak·kundig, *a.* skilled, competent. ·vakman, -lieden, *n.* expert. ·vakonderwijs, no pl., *n.n.* vocational training. ·vakterm, *n.* technical term. ·vakvereniging, *n.* trade-union (*congress*).
val, -llen, *n.* fall, drop; trap. *ten* ~ *brengen*, to overthrow. ·valbijl, *n.* guillotine. ·valbrug, -ggen, *n.* drawbridge. ·valdeur, *n.* trapdoor. ·valhek, -kken, *n.n.* portcullis.
va·lies, -zen, *n.n.* portmanteau.
valk, *n.* falcon. valke·nier, -s, *n.* falconer. ·valkenjacht, no pl., *n.* hawking.
valkuil, *n.* pit (*trap*).
val·lei, *n.* valley.
·vallen, val, *v.i.*, *str.* to fall; to drop; to be. *laten* ~, to drop; *het valt me zwaar*, I find it hard; *er valt niet over te klagen*, there is no reason for complaint; ~ *onder*, to fall *or* come under; ~ *over*, to take objection to. ¶no pl., *n.n.* fall. *het* ~ *van de avond*, nightfall. ·vallend, *a.* ~*e ster*, shooting star; ~*e ziekte*, epilepsy. ·valluik, *n.n.* trapdoor. ·valpoort, *n.* portcullis. ·valreep, -repen, *n.* man-rope. *een glaasje op de* ~, stirrup-cup.
vals, *a.* false; vicious; forged. ~*e munter*, coiner. ¶*adv.* falsely. ~ *spelen*, to cheat (at play). ·valsaard, -s, *n.* treacherous person.
·valscherm, *n.n.* parachute.
·valsheid, -heden, *n.* falseness.
·valstrik, -kken, *n.* snare; trap.
va·luta, -'s *n.* rate (of exchange); currency.
valwind, *n.* squall.
·vampier, -s, *n.* vampire.
van, *prep.* of, from; with; for. ~ *de week*, this week; *ik meen* ~ *ja*, I think so. ¶-nnen, *n.* family name. van·af, *prep.* from. van·avond, *adv.* to-night, this evening. van·daag, *adv.* to-day. van·daan, *adv.* from. *van . . .* ~, away from . . . van·daar, *adv.* from there, thence; hence.

vande·hands, *a.* off (*horse*). van·door, *adv.* off. *er* ~ *zijn*, to have skipped. van·een, *adv.* asunder. *ver* ~, wide apart.
·vangarm, *n.* tentacle. ·vangen, *v.t.*, *str.* to catch. ·vanger, -s, *n.* catcher. ·vangertje, no pl., *n.n.* ~ *spelen*, to play he. ·vanglijn, *n.* painter (*rope*). vangst, *n.* catch; haul.
van·hier, *adv.* from here.
va·nille, no pl., *n.* vanilla.
van·nacht, *adv.* to-night (*not evening*); last night (*not evening*). van·ouds, *adv.* of old.
van·waar, *adv.* from where, whence. van·wege, *prep.* on account of, because of; on behalf of. van·zelf, *adv.* of itself, of its own accord. vanzelf·sprekend, *a.* self-evident.
·varen, -s, *n.* fern, bracken. ¶vaar, *v.i.*, *str.* to sail, navigate. *hoe vaart U?*, how are you?; *laten* ~, to give up, abandon; *er goed bij* ~, to do well out of it; *de duivel is in hem gevaren*, the devil has entered into him. ·varensgast, *n.*, ·varensgezel, -llen, *n.* seaman.
vari·ëren, -eer, *v.t.* & *v.i.* to vary.
·varken, -s, *n.n.* pig. ·varkensdraf, no pl., *n.* hog-wash. ·varkenshoeder, -s, *n.* swine-herd. ·varkenskarbonade, -s, *n.* pork chop. ·varkenskot, -tten, *n.n.* pigsty. ·varkenslapje, -s, *n.n.* pork-steak. ·varkensvlees, no pl., *n.n.* pork. ·varkensziekte, no pl., *n.n.* swine-fever.
vast, *a.* firm, steady; solid; fixed; permanent, regular. ~*e goederen*, real property; ~*e kleur*, fast colour; ~*e uitdrukking*, standing phrase. ¶*adv.* firmly, fast; certainly; in the meantime. ~ *en zeker*, most certainly.
vastbe·raden, *a.* determined, resolute. vastbe·radenheid, no pl., *n.* determination, firmness.
·vastbinden, *v.t.s.*, *str.* to tie up, fasten.
vaste·land, *n.n.* continent.
·vasten, *v.i.* to fast. ¶no pl., *n.* Lent. vasten·avond, *n.* Shrove Tuesday. ·vasten·dag, *n.* fast-day, day of abstinence. ·vastentijd, no pl., *n.* Lent.
·vastgespen, *v.t.s.* to buckle.
·vastgrijpen, *v.t.s.*, *str.* to seize, catch hold of.
·vastgroeien, *v.i.s.* to grow together.
·vasthechten, *v.t.s.* to fasten, attach.
·vastheid, no pl., *n.* firmness.
·vasthouden, *v.t.s.*, *irr.* to hold, keep hold of; to detain. ¶*v.r.s.*, *irr.* or *v.i.s.*, *irr.* (*zich*) ~ *aan*, to hold on to, stick to. vast·houdend, *a.* tenacious. vast·houdendheid, no pl., *n.* tenacity.
·vastigheid, no pl., *n.* certainty.
·vastklampen, zich, *v.r.s.* zich ~ *aan*, to cling to.
·vastklemmen, klem vast, *v.t.s.* to fix. zich ~ *aan*, to cling to.
·vastkleven, kleef vast, *v.i.s.* & *v.t.s.* to stick.
·vastklinken, *v.t.s.*, *str.* to rivet.

·vastknopen, knoop vast, *v.t.s.* to button up; to tie.
·vastkoppelen, *v.t.s.* to couple.
·vastleggen, leg vast, *v.t.s.* to fasten; to lay down.
·vastliggen, lig vast, *v.i.s.*, *str.* to lie firm; to be fastened or moored; to be tied up.
·vastlopen, loop vast, *v.i.s.*, *str.* to run aground; to get stuck.
·vastmaken, maak vast, *v.t.s.* to fasten; to attach; to furl.
·vastraken, raak vast, *v.i.s.* See vastlopen.
·vastroesten, *v.i.s.* to rust up
·vastschroeven, schroef vast, *v.t.s.* to lash, strap.
·vaststaan, sta vast, *v.i.s.*, *irr.* to stand firm; to be an established fact.
·vaststellen, stel vast, *v.t.s.* to establish; to determine, settle.
·vastzetten, zet vast, *v.t.s.* to fasten.
·vastzitten, zit vast, *v.i.s.*, *str.* to stick; to be aground; to be stuck or jammed.
vat, *n.n.* barrel, cask, vat; vessel (*container*). ~*en wassen*, to wash up; *wat in 't* ~ *is verzuurt niet*, it will keep. ¶no pl., *n.n.* hold, grip. ·vatbaar, -bare, *a.* ~ *voor*, susceptible of, prone to. ·vatbaarheid, no pl., *n.* liability, susceptibility. ·vatten, vat, *v.t.* to seize; to catch; to understand.
va·zal, -llen, *n.* vassal. va·zalstaat, -staten, *n.* vassal state; puppet state.
·vechten, *v.i.*, *str.* to fight. ~ *met*, to fight (with); ~ *tegen*, to fight (with). ·vechter, -s, *n.* fighter. ·vechtersbaas, -bazen, *n.* pugnacious person. ·vechtjas, -ssen, *n.* real fighter. vecht·lustig, *a.* pugnacious. ·vechtpartij, *n.* fight, scrap.
·veder, -s or -en, *n.* See veer. ·vederbos, -ssen, *n.* tuft, plume.
vee, no pl., *n.n.* cattle. See beesten. ·veearts, *n.* veterinary surgeon. veeartse·nij, no pl., *n.* veterinary science. ·veeboer, *n.*, ·veefokker, -s, *n.* stock-breeder. veefokke·rij, *n.* stock-farm. ¶no pl., *n.* cattle breeding.
veeg, vegen, *n.* wipe; slap, swipe; witch. *iemand een* ~ *uit de pan geven*, to tell a person off. ¶vege, *a.* ominous.
·veehoeder, -s, *n.* herdsman.
veel, vele, *pron.* much, many; a lot. ¶*adv.* much. ~ *te* . . ., far too . . .; ~ *te* ~, far too much or many. ·veelal, *adv.* mostly.
veelbe·lovend, *a.* promising.
veelbe·tekenend, *a.* significant.
veelbe·wogen, *a.* eventful.
veel·eer, *adv.* rather.
veel·eisend, *a.* exacting.
·veelhoek, *n.* polygon. veel·hoekig, *a.* polygonous.
·veelmeer, *adv.* rather. ·veelmin, *adv.* much less.
veelom·vattend, *a.* comprehensive.
veel·soortig, *a.* manifold, multifarious.
veel·stemmig, *a.* polyphonous.

veels·zins, *adv.* in many respects.
veelver·mogend, *a.* powerful.
·veelvoet, *n.* polypod.
·veelvoud, *n.n.* multiple. **veel·voudig**, *a.* manifold.
·veelvraat, **-vraten**, *n.* glutton.
veel·vuldig, *a.* frequent. **veel·vuldigheid**, no pl., *n.* frequency.
veelwijve·rij, *n.* polygamy.
veel·zeggend, *a.* significant.
veel·zijdig, *a.* many-sided; versatile; catholic (*taste*). **veel·zijdigheid**, no pl., *n.* versatility.
veem, **vemen**, *n.n.* storage company.
·veemarkt, *n.* cattle market.
·veemgericht, *n.n.* secret tribunal, vehmic court.
veen, **venen**, *n.n.* peat; bog, peat-bog. **·veenachtig**, *a.* peaty, boggy. **·veenbaas**, **-bazen**, *n.*, **·veenboer**, *n.* peat-cutter, peat dealer. **veende·rij**, *n.* peat-digging. **·veengrond**, *n.* peat-land, bog. **·veenkolonie**, **-s** *or* **-niën**, *n.* village in peat-land. **·veenmol**, **-llen**, *n.* mole cricket. **·veenmos**, no pl., *n.n.* sphagnum.
·veepest, no pl., *n.* cattle-plague, murrain.
veer, **veren**, *n.* feather; spring (*metal*). ¶ *n.n.* ferry. **·veerboot**, **-boten**, *n.* ferry. **·veerdienst**, *n.* ferry-service. **·veerkracht**, *n.* elasticity, resilience. **veer·krachtig**, *a.* elastic, resilient; springy. **·veerman**, **-lieden** *or* **-lui**, *n.* ferryman. **·veerpont**, *n.* ferry.
·veertien, *num.* fourteen. ~ *dagen*, a fortnight; *over* ~ *dagen*, in a fortnight. **·veertiendaags**, *a.* fortnightly. **·veertiende**, *a.* fourteenth. ¶**-n**, *n.* fourteenth (part).
·veertig, *num.* forty. **·veertiger**, **-s**, *n.* (person of) forty. **·veertigste**, *a.* fortieth. **·veertigtal**, **-llen**, *n.n.* (about) forty.
veest, *n.* (*vulg.*) flatus.
·veestal, **-llen**, *n.* cattle shed. **·veestapel**, no pl., *n.* live stock (*of country*). **·veeteelt**, no pl., *n.* cattle breeding.
·vegen, **veeg**, *v.t.* to sweep; to wipe (*feet*). **·veger**, **-s**, *n.* brush; sweeper.
vege·tariër, **-s**, *n.* vegetarian. **vege·tarisch**, *a.* vegetarian. **vege·teren**, **-teer**, *v.i.* to vegetate.
veil, *a.* venal, corruptible. *zijn leven* ~ *hebben*, to be ready to lay down one's life. **·veildag**, *n.* auction day. **·veilen**, *v.t.* to sell by auction, put up to auction. **·veiler**, **-s**, *n.* auctioneer. **·veilheid**, no pl., *n.* venality. **·veilig**, *a.* safe, secure. ~ *voor*, secure from. ¶*adv.* safely, with safety. **·veiligheid**, no pl., *n.* safety, security. **·veiligheidshalve**, *adv.* for safety's sake. **·veiligsheidsspeld**, *n.* safety-pin. **·veiling**, *n.* auction.
·veine, no pl., *n.* luck.
·veinzaard, **-s**, *n.* dissembler, hypocrite. **·veinzen**, **veins**, *v.i.* to dissemble. ¶*v.t.* to

simulate, feign. **veinze·rij**, *n.* dissimulation, hypocrisy.
vel, **-llen**, *n.n.* skin, hide; sheet (*paper*). ~ *over been*, skin and bone; *in losse vellen*, in sheets; *het* ~ *over de oren halen*, to fleece; *uit z'n* ~ *springen*, to burst with anger.
veld, *n.n.* field. *het* ~ *ruimen*, to retire, give way; ~ *winnen*, to gain ground; *op het* ~, in the fields; *te* ~*e*, in the field; *te* ~*e trekken*, to take the field; *uit het* ~ *geslagen*, taken aback. **·veldbed**, **-dden**, *n.n.* camp-bed. **·veldbloem**, *n.* wild flower. **·veldfles**, **-ssen**, *n.* travelling flask. **·veldheer**, **-heren**, *n.* general. **·veldheerschap**, no pl., *n.n.* generalship. **·veldhoen**, **-ders**, *n.n.* partridge. **·veldleeuwerik**, **-kken**, *n.* skylark. **·veldmus**, **-ssen**, *n.* tree-sparrow. **·veldoverste**, **-n**, *n.* general. **·veldprediker**, **-s**, *n.* chaplain to the forces. **·veldsla**, no pl., *n.* dandelion salad. **·veldslag**, *n.* battle. **·veldspaat**, no pl., *n.n.* feldspar. **·veldtenue**, no pl., *n.n.* battle-dress. **·veldtocht**, *n.* campaign. **·veldwachter**, **-s**, *n.* rural constable.
·velen, *v.t.*, *inf. only*, to bear, stand.
·velerhande, *a.*, **·velerlei**, *a.* various, many kinds of.
velg, *n.* rim (*wheel*).
ve·lijn, no pl., *n.n.* vellum.
·vellen, **vel**, *v.t.* to fell, cut down; to pass (*sentence*); to couch (*spear*).
·vellenkoper, **-s**, *n.* fellmonger.
ven, **-nnen**, *n.* fen.
·vendel, **-s**, *n.n.* company.
ven·duhouder, **-s**, *n.* auctioneer. **ven·duhuis**, **-zen**, *n.n.* auction room. **ven·dutie**, **-s**, *n.* auction.
·venen, **veen**, *v.i.* to cut peat.
ve·nerisch, *a.* venereal.
ve·nijn, no pl., *n.n.* venom. **ve·nijnig**, *a.* venomous; vicious.
·venkel, no pl., *n.* fennel.
·vennoot, **-noten**, *n.* partner. *stille* ~, sleeping partner. **·vennootschap**, **-ppen**, *n.* company, partnership. *commanditaire* ~, limited partnership; *naamloze* ~, limited liability company.
·venster, **-s**, *n.n.* window. **·vensterbank**, *n.* windowsill. **·vensterglas**, **-zen**, *n.n.* window-pane. ¶no pl., *n.n.* window glass. **·vensterkozijn**, *n.n.* window-frame.
vent, *n.* fellow, chap, bloke. **·venten**, *v.t.* to hawk. **·venter**, **-s**, *n.* hawker.
ven·tiel, *n.n.* valve (*air*). **ven·tielslang**, *n.* valve-tubing. **venti·leren**, **-leer**, *v.t.* to ventilate.
·Venushaar, no pl., *n.n.* maidenhair.
ver, **-rre**, *a.* far, distant, remote. *op verre na niet*, not by far.
ver·aangenamen, **-naam**, *v.t.* to make pleasant.
veraan·schouwelijking, *n.* illustration.
ver·achtelijk, *a.* despicable, contemptible.

ver·achtelozen, -loos, *v.t.* to neglect.
ver·achten, *v.t.* to despise, scorn. **ver·achting,** no pl., *n.* contempt, scorn.
ver·ademen, *v.i.* to breathe again. **ver·ademing,** no pl., *n.* relief.
veraf, *adv.* far (away).
·verafgelegen, *a.* remote.
ver·afgoden, -good, *v.t.* to idolize. **ver·afgoding,** *n.* idolization.
ver·afschuwen, *v.t.* to abhor, loathe.
ver·anderen, *v.t.* to change, alter. ¶*v.i.* to change, alter. ∼ *van* . . ., to change (in)to another . . . **ver·andering,** *n.* change, alteration. **ver·anderlijk,** *a.* changeable, variable. **ver·anderlijkheid,** no pl., *n.* variability.
ver·ankeren, *v.t.* to anchor.
verant·woordelijk, *a.* responsible. **verant·woordelijkheid, -heden,** *n.* responsibility.
ver·antwoorden, *v.t.* to answer for; to justify. *het hard te* ∼ *hebben,* to have a tough time. **ver·antwoording,** *n.* justification; responsibility. *ter* ∼ *roepen,* to call to account.
ver·armen, *v.t.* to impoverish, reduce to poverty. **ver·arming,** *n.* impoverishment.
ver·assen, -as, *v.t.* to cremate.
ver·baal, -bale, *a.* verbal. *proces* ∼, summons.
ver·baasd, *a.* surprised, amazed. **ver·baasdheid,** no pl., *n.* surprise, amazement.
ver·babbelen, *v.t.* to waste (*time*) chatting.
verbali·seren, -seer, *v.t.* to summons.
ver·band, *n.n.* bandage, dressing; connection, relation; context. *hypothecair* ∼, mortgage; ∼ *houden met,* to be connected with. **ver·bandgaas,** no pl., *n.n.* gauze bandage. **ver·bandkist,** *n.* first-aid box. **ver·bandwatten,** pl. only, *n.* sterilized cotton wool.
ver·banneling, *n.* exile. **ver·bannen, -ban,** *v.t., irr.* to exile, banish. **ver·banning,** *n.* exile, banishment.
ver·basterd, *a.* degenerate. **ver·basteren,** *v.i.* to degenerate. **ver·bastering,** *n.* degeneration.
ver·bazen, -baas, *v.t.* to amaze, astonish. *her verbaast me,* I am surprised. **ver·bazend,** *a.* amazing. **ver·bazing,** no pl., *n.* amazement, surprise. **verbazing·wekkend,** *a.* amazing, stupendous.
ver·beelden, *v.t.* to represent. ¶*zich* ∼, *v.r.* to imagine, fancy. **ver·beelding,** *n.* imagination; conceit. **ver·beeldingskracht,** no pl., *n.* imaginative power.
ver·beiden, *v.t.* to await. ¶*v.i.* to abide.
ver·bergen, *v.t., str.* to hide, conceal.
ver·beten, *a.* restrained, pent up.
ver·beteraar, -s, *n.* corrector. **ver·beteren,** *v.t.* to improve; to ameliorate; to correct. ¶*zich* ∼, *v.r.* to reform, mend one's ways. **ver·betering,** *n.* improvement, betterment; correction. **ver·beteringsgesticht,** *n.n.* reformatory.
ver·beurd, *a.* forfeited. **ver·beurdverklaren, verklaar verbeurd,** *v.t.s.* to confiscate,

seize. **ver·beurdverklaring,** *n.* confiscation, seizure. **ver·beuren,** *v.t.* to forfeit. *pand* ∼, to play at forfeits.
ver·beuzelen, *v.t.* to fritter away.
ver·bieden, *v.t., str.* to forbid, prohibit. *verboden toegang,* no admittance.
ver·bijsterd, *a.* bewildered. **ver·bijsteren,** *v.t.* to bewilder. **ver·bijstering,** no pl., *n.* bewilderment.
ver·bijten, *v.t., str.* to suppress. ¶*v.r., str.* *zich* ∼ *van woede,* to burn (inwardly) with rage.
ver·binden, *v.t., str.* to connect, link; to combine; to bandage. ¶*v.r., str.* *zich* ∼ *tot,* to bind *or* commit oneself to. **ver·binding,** *n.* connection; combination. *zich in* ∼ *stellen met,* to communicate with. **ver·bindingslijn,** *n.* line of communication. **ver·bindingsofficier,** *n.* signals officer. **ver·bindingspunt,** *n.n.* junction. **ver·bindingsteken, -s,** *n.n.* hyphen. **ver·bintenis, -ssen,** *n.* contract, agreement; undertaking.
ver·bitterd, *a.* embittered; grim. **ver·bitteren,** *v.t.* to embitter, sour.
ver·bleken, -bleek, *v.i.* to grow pale; to fade, pale.
ver·blijd, *a.* delighted. **ver·blijden,** *v.t.* to gladden, delight. ¶*zich* ∼, *v.r.* to rejoice.
ver·blijf, -ven, *n.n.* residence; stay. **ver·blijfkosten,** pl. only, *n.* hotel expenses. **ver·blijven, -blijf,** *v.i., str.* to reside; to remain.
ver·blinden, *v.t.* to blind, dazzle.
ver·bloemd, *a.* veiled. **ver·bloemen,** *v.t.* to disguise.
ver·bluffen, -bluf, *v.t.* to dumbfound, stagger. **ver·bluffend,** *a.* startling.
ver·bod, no pl., *n.n.* prohibition, ban.
ver·boemelen, *v.t.* to dissipate.
ver·bolgen, *a.* incensed. **ver·bolgenheid,** no pl., *n.* wrath.
ver·bond, *n.n.* alliance; union; covenant. *het Oude V*∼, the Old Testament.
ver·borgen, *a.* hidden, concealed.
·verbouw, no pl., *n.* cultivation. **ver·bouwen,** *v.t.* to cultivate.
verbouwe·reerd, *a.* flabbergasted. **verbouwe·reerdheid,** no pl., *n.* consternation.
ver·branden, *v.t.* to burn. **ver·branding,** *n.* combustion; cremation. **ver·brandingsoven, -s,** *n.* incinerator.
ver·brassen, -bras, *v.t.* to dissipate.
ver·breden, -breed, *v.t.* to broaden.
ver·breiden, *v.t.* to spread, propagate. **ver·breiding,** *n.* spread(ing).
ver·breken, -breek, *v.t., str.* to break; to cut off.
ver·brijzelen, *v.t.* to smash, shatter. **ver·brijzeling,** *n.* smashing.
ver·broddelen, *v.t.* to bungle.
ver·broederen, *v.i.* to fraternize. **ver·broedering,** *n.* fraternization.
ver·brokkelen, *v.t. & v.i.* to crumble (away). **ver·brokkeling,** *n.* disintegration.

ver·bruid, *a.* dashed, damned. **ver·bruien,** *v.t.* het ~ *bij,* to incur the displeasure of.
ver·bruik, no pl., *n.n.* consumption, expenditure. **ver·bruiken,** *v.t.* to consume. **ver·bruiker, -s,** *n.* consumer.
ver·buigbaar, -bare, *a.* declinable. **ver·buigen,** *v.t., str.* to bend, twist; to decline. **ver·buiging,** *n.* declension.
ver·dacht, *a.* suspected, suspicious, questionable. ~ *maken,* to fasten suspicion on; ~ *zijn op,* to be prepared for. **ver·dachtmaking,** *n.* insinuation.
ver·dagen, -daag, *v.t.* to adjourn, prorogue.
ver·dampen, *v.t. & v.i.* to evaporate.
ver·dedigen, *v.t.* to defend, protect. **ver·dediger, -s,** *n.* defender; counsel for the defence. **ver·dediging,** *n.* defence.
ver·deelbaar, -bare, *a.* divisible. **ver·deeld,** *a.* divided.
ver·dekt, *a.* concealed, under cover.
ver·delen, -deel, *v.t.* to divide; to share out. ~ *in,* to divide into; ~ *onder,* to divide among; ~ *over,* to spread over. **ver·deler, -s,** *n.* divider. **ver·deling,** *n.* division, distribution.
ver·delgen, *v.t.* to exterminate. **ver·delger, -s,** *n.* destroyer. **ver·delging,** *n.* extermination.
ver·denken, *v.t., irr.* to suspect. **ver·denking,** *n.* suspicion. ~ *krijgen,* to become suspicious; *aan* ~ *onderhevig,* open to suspicion; *in* ~ *brengen,* to throw suspicion on.
·verder, *a.* farther, further. ¶*adv.* farther, further; besides, moreover. *ga* ~, go on.
ver·derf, no pl., *n.n.* ruin, destruction. *in het* ~ *storten,* to ruin, undo. **ver·derfelijk,** *a.* pernicious. **ver·derfelijkheid,** no pl., *n.* pernicious influence. **ver·derfenis,** no pl., *n.* damnation. **ver·derven, -derf,** *v.t., str.* to corrupt, pervert.
ver·dicht, *a.* fictitious. **ver·dichten,** *v.t.* to invent. **ver·dichtsel, -s,** *n.n.* fabrication, fiction.
ver·dienen, *v.t.* to earn; to deserve, merit. ~ *aan,* to earn out of. **ver·dienste, -n,** *n.* earnings, wages; merit, deserts. *naar* ~, deservedly. **ver·dienstelijk,** *a.* meritorious. **ver·dienstelijkheid,** no pl., *n.* merit.
ver·diepen, *v.t.* to deepen. ¶*v.r. zich* ~ *in,* to be absorbed in, lose oneself in. **ver·dieping,** *n.* floor, story.
ver·dierlijken, *v.t.* to brutalize. ¶*v.i.* to become brutalized. **ver·dierlijking,** *n.* brutalization.
ver·dikkel, *excl.* blimey!
ver·dikken, -dik, *v.t.* to thicken. **ver·dikking,** *n.* thickening.
ver·doemd, *a.* damned, cursed, doomed. **ver·doemelijk,** *a.* damnable. **ver·doemeling,** *n.* cursed person. **ver·doemen,** *v.t.* to curse.
ver·doen, -doe, *v.t., irr.* to do away with.
ver·doezelen, *v.t.* to blur.

ver·dolen, -dool, *v.i.* to lose one's way.
ver·domd, *a.* damned.
verdonkere·manen, -maan, *v.t.* to purloin.
ver·dorren, -dor, *v.t.* to wither.
ver·dorven, *a.* depraved.
ver·doven, -doof, *v.t.* to deafen; to deaden; to numb; to anaesthetize. ~*d middel,* opiate, dope. **ver·doving,** *n.* stupor; anæsthesia. **ver·dovingsmiddel,** *n.n.* narcotic.
ver·draaglijk, *a.* bearable, tolerable. **ver·draagzaam, -zame,** *a.* tolerant. **ver·draagzaamheid,** no pl., *n.* tolerance.
ver·draaid, *a.* distorted. ¶*adv.* damn. **ver·draaien,** *v.t.* to twist, distort. **ver·draaiing,** *n.* distortion.
ver·drag, *n.* treaty. **ver·dragen, -draag,** *v.t., str.* to bear, endure. **·verdragend,** *a.* long-range; carrying.
verdrie·dubbelen, *v.t.* to treble.
ver·driet, no pl., *n.n.* grief, sorrow. ~ *hebben over,* to grieve over. **ver·drietelijk,** *a.* annoying, vexatious. **ver·drietelijkheid, -heden,** *n.* vexation. **ver·drieten,** *v.t., str.* to grieve, vex. **ver·drietig,** *a.* sad, sorrowful.
verdrie·voudigen, *v.t.* to treble.
ver·drijven, -drijf, *v.t., str.* to drive away, dispel; to dislodge. *tijd* ~, to pass the time.
ver·dringen, *v.t., str.* to jostle; to crowd out; to supersede. *zich* ~ *om,* to crowd round.
ver·drinken, *v.t., str.* to drown; to spend on drink. ¶*v.i., str.* to drown, be drowned. **ver·drinking,** *n.* drowning.
ver·drukken, -druk, *v.t.* to oppress. **ver·drukker, -s,** *n.* oppressor. **ver·drukking,** *n.* oppression.
ver·dubbelen, *v.t.* to double. **ver·dubbeling,** *n.* doubling.
ver·duidelijken, *v.t.* to elucidate. **ver·duidelijking,** *n.* elucidation.
ver·duisteren, *v.t.* to darken, obscure; to black-out; to embezzle. **ver·duistering,** *n.* darkening, black-out; eclipse; embezzlement.
ver·duiveld, *a.* devilish. ¶*adv.* devilish, jolly.
ver·dunnen, -dun, *v.t.* to thin (out); to dilute; to rarefy.
ver·duren, -duur, *v.t.* to endure, bear.
ver·duurzamen, -zaam, *v.t.* to preserve.
ver·duwen, *v.t.* to push away; to stomach.
ver·dwaald, *a.* lost, strayed.
ver·dwaasd, *a.* besotted, foolish.
ver·dwalen, -dwaal, *v.i.* to lose one's way, get lost.
ver·dwazing, *n.* infatuation.
ver·dwijnen, *v.i., str.* to disappear, vanish. **ver·dwijning,** *n.* disappearance.
ver·edelen, *v.t.* to ennoble, elevate. **ver·edeling,** no pl., *n.* ennoblement, refinement.
ver·eelt, *a.* callous, horny. **ver·eelten,** *v.t.* to make callous. ¶*v.i.* to grow callous.
vereen·voudigen, *v.t.* to simplify. **vereen·voudiging,** *n.* simplification.

vereen·zelvigen, *v.t.* to identify. vereen·zelviging, *n.* identification.

ver·eeuwigen, *v.t.* to perpetuate. ver·eeuwiging, *n.* perpetuation.

ver·effenen, *v.t.* to settle, square. ver·effening, *n.* settlement.

ver·eis, no pl., *n.n.* naar ~ van omstandigheden, as circumstances require. ver·eisen, *v.t.* to require. ver·eist, *a.* required, essential. ver·eiste, -n, *n.* requirement, requisite.

·veren, veer, *v.i.* to be elastic *or* springy. ¶*a.* (of) feather(s).

ver·engelsen, *v.t.* to anglicize.

ver·engen, *v.t.* to narrow.

ver·enigbaar, -bare, *a.* compatible. ~ met, consistent with. ver·enigd, *a.* united, combined. ver·enigen, *v.t.* to unite, join. ~ met, to join to *or* with *or* to reconcile to; niet te ~ met, irreconcilable with. ¶zich ~, *v.r.* to unite. zich ~ met, to join *or* to agree with. ver·eniging, *n.* union, society, association. ver·enigingsleven, no pl., *n.n.* corporate life. ver·enigingslokaal, -kalen, *n.n.* club room.

ver·ergeren, *v.t.* to worsen, aggravate. ¶*v.i.* to become worse. ver·ergering, *n.* worsening, deterioration.

ver·etteren, *v.i.* to fester.

verf, -ven, *n.* paint, colour. ·verfhout, no pl., *n.n.* dye-wood. ·verfkuip, *n.* dyeing tub.

ver·fijnen, *v.t.* to refine.

·verflaag, -lagen, *n.* coat of paint.

ver·flauwen, *v.i.* to slacken, flag. ver·flauwing, no pl., *n.* slackening, abatement.

ver·flensen, *v.i.* to fade, wilt.

·verflucht, no pl., *n.* smell of paint.

ver·foeien, *v.t.* to abhor, abominate. ver·foeiing, *n.* abomination. ver·foeilijk, *a.* detestable.

ver·fomfaaien, *v.t.* to crumple, dishevel.

ver·fraaien, *v.t.* to embellish.

ver·fransen, *v.t.* to frenchify.

ver·frissen, -fris, *v.t.* to refresh. ver·frissing, *n.* refreshment.

·verfstof, -ffen, *n.* dye(-stuff), colour. ·verfwaren, pl. only, *n.* dye-stuffs, paints.

ver·gaan, -ga, *irr.* to perish; to be lost (ship). ¶*v.t., irr.* het zal hem slecht ~, he will fare badly; het zal hem ernaar ~, he will get his deserts. ¶*a.* wrecked, lost; perished, decayed. ·vergaand, *a.* far-going.

ver·gaarbak, -kken, *n.* reservoir, tank. ver·gaderen, *v.t.* to gather. ¶*v.i.* to meet, assemble. ver·gadering, *n.* meeting, assembly. ver·gaderplaats, *n.* meeting-place.

ver·gallen, -gal, *v.t.* to embitter, sour; to spoil (pleasure).

vergalop·peren, -peer, zich, *v.r.* to make a gaffe.

ver·gankelijk, *a.* transitory, transient. ver·gankelijkheid, no pl., *n.* transitoriness.

ver·gapen, -gaap, zich, *v.r.* zich ~ aan, to become infatuated with.

ver·gassen, -gas, *v.t.* to gasify.

ver·gasten, *v.t.* ~ op, to treat to, regale with; zich ~ aan, to feast upon.

ver·geeflijk, *a.* pardonable. ver·geefs, *a.* fruitless. ¶*adv.* in vain. te ~, in vain.

ver·geetachtig, *a.* forgetful. ver·geetachtigheid, no pl., *n.* forgetfulness. ver·geetboek, no pl., *n.n.* in het ~ raken, to fall into oblivion. ver·geet-mij-nietje, -s, *n.n.* forget-me-not.

ver·gelden, *v.t., str.* to repay, requite. ver·gelding *n.* retribution; retaliation. ter ~ van, in return for.

verge·lijk, *n.n.* compromise. verge·lijkbaar, -bare, *a.* comparable. verge·lijken, *v.t., str.* to compare. ~ bij, to compare to. verge·lijkenderwijs, *adv.* in comparison. verge·lijking, *n.* comparison; equation.

verge·makkelijken, *v.t.* to simplify, make easy. verge·makkelijking, *n.* facilitation.

·vergen, *v.t.* to demand, require.

verge·noegd, *a.* contented. verge·noegdheid, no pl., *n.* contentment. verge·noegen, *v.t.* to content.

ver·getelheid, no pl., *n.* oblivion; forgetfulness.

ver·geten, -geet, *v.t., str.* to forget. ik ben z'n naam ~, I forget his name.

ver·geven, -geef, *v.t., str.* to forgive, pardon; to give away; to misdeal; to poison. ver·gevensgezind, *a.* forgiving. ver·geving, no pl., *n.* pardon.

·vergevorderd, *a.* (far) advanced.

verge·wissen, -wis, zich, *v.r.* zich ~ van, to ascertain.

verge·zellen, -zel, *v.t.* to accompany.

·vergezicht, *n.n.* prospect, vista.

verge·zocht, *a.* far-fetched.

ver·giet, *n.n.* strainer. ver·gieten, *v.t., str.* to shed, spill.

ver·giffenis, no pl., *n.* forgiveness, pardon.

ver·gif, -ten, *n.n.*, ver·gift, *n.n.* poison; venom. ver·giftig, *a.* poisonous; venomous. ver·giftigen, *v.t.* to poison. ver·giftiging, *n.* poisoning.

ver·gissen, -gis, zich, *v.i.* to make a mistake. zich ~ in, to be mistaken in. ver·gissing, *n.* mistake, error.

ver·goddelijken, *v.t.* to deify. ver·goden, -good, *v.t.* to idolize.

ver·goeden, *v.t.* to compensate, indemnify, reimburse. ver·goeding, *n.* compensation. ver·goelijken, *v.t.* to excuse, explain away. ver·goelijking, *n.* extenuation. ter ~ van, in excuse of.

ver·gokken, -gok, *v.t.* to gamble away.

ver·gooien, -gooi, *v.t.* to throw away. ¶*v.r.* zich ~ aan, to throw oneself away on.

ver·grijp, *n.n.* offence; outrage. ver·grijpen, zich, *v.r., str.* zich ~ aan, to infringe, offend against.

ver·groeien, *v.i.* to grow out of shape.

ver·grootglas, -zen, *n.n.* magnifying glass.
ver·groten, -groot, *v.t.* to enlarge, magnify.
ver·groting, *n.* enlargement.
ver·gruizelen, *v.t.* to crush.
ver·guizen, -guis, *v.t.* (*stilted*) to vilify, revile.
ver·guizing, *n.* revilement.
ver·guld, *a.* gilt. ~ *op snee*, gilt-edged; *ergens mee* ~ *zijn*, to be highly pleased with something. **ver·gulden,** *v.t.* to gild.
ver·gunnen, -gun, *v.t.* to permit, grant. **ver·gunning,** *n.* permission; permit, licence.
ver·haal -halen, *n.n.* story, account. *op zijn* ~ *komen*, to recover, collect oneself. ¶no pl., *n.n.* redress, remedy. *er is geen* ~ *op*, there is no redress. **ver·haaltrant,** no pl., *n.* narrative style.
ver·haasten, *v.t.* to hasten, accelerate, precipitate.
ver·halen, -haal, *v.t.* to tell, relate; to shift (*vessel*); to recover, recoup (*loss*); to recover. **ver·halend,** *a.* narrative. **ver·halenderwijs,** *adv.* in a narrative manner.
ver·handelbaar, -bare, *a.* negotiable. **ver·handelen,** *v.t.* to deal in; to transact, negotiate; to discuss. **ver·handeling,** *n.* treatise, discourse.
ver·hangen, *v.t.*, *str.* to hang in different place.
ver·harden, *v.t.* to harden; to metal (*road*). ¶*v.i.* to grow hardened. **ver·harding,** *n.* hardening.
ver·haren, -haar, *v.i.* to moult.
ver·haspelen, *v.t.* to spoil; to garble.
ver·heerlijken, *v.t.* to glorify. **ver·heerlijking,** *n.* glorification.
ver·heffen, -hef, *v.t.*, *str.* to raise, lift, elevate; to exalt. ¶*zich* ~, *v.r.*, *str.* to rise. **ver·heffing,** *n.* elevation.
ver·heimelijken, *v.t.* to keep secret.
ver·helderen, *v.t.* to clarify, clear. ¶*v.i.* to clear up, light up. **ver·heldering,** *n.* clarification; brightening.
ver·helen, -heel, *v.t.* to conceal, hide, disguise. **ver·heling,** *n.* concealment.
ver·helpen, *v.t.*, *str.* to remedy.
ver·hemelte, -n, *n.n.* palate; canopy.
ver·heugd, *a.* pleased. **ver·heugen,** *v.t.* to gladden, delight. ¶*zich* ~, *v.r.* to rejoice. *zich* ~ *op*, to look forward to; *zich* ~ *over*, to rejoice at. **ver·heugenis, -ssen,** *n.*, **ver·heuging,** *n.* joy.
ver·heven, *a.* exalted, lofty.
ver·hinderen, *v.t.* to prevent. **ver·hindering,** *n.* hindrance.
ver·hitten, -hit, *v.t.* to heat. ¶*zich* ~, *v.r.* to overheat oneself.
ver·hoeden, *v.t.* to prevent.
ver·hogen, -hoog, *v.t.* to heighten, raise; to increase, enhance. ~ *met*, to increase by. **ver·hoging,** *n.* heightening; increase.
ver·holen, *a.* secret, hidden.
verhonderd·voudigen, *v.t.* to increase a hundredfold.
ver·hongeren, *v.t.* to starve (to death), to die

of hunger. **ver·hongering,** no pl., *n.* starvation.
ver·hoor, -horen, *n.n.* hearing, trial. *in* ~ *nemen*, to interrogate. **ver·horen, -hoor,** *v.t.* to hear (*prayer*); t examine, interrogate.
verho·vaardigen, zich, *v.r.* to pride oneself, be proud.
ver·houden, zich, *v.r.*, *irr.* to be in proportion. **ver·houding,** *n.* relation; proportion; ratio. *naar* ~, in proportion, proportionately.
ver·huisbiljet, -tten, *n.n.* removal notice (*local registration*). **ver·huisdag,** *n.* moving day. **ver·huiswagen, -s,** *n.* furniture (removal) van. **ver·huizen, -huis,** *v.i.* to (re)move. ¶*v.t.* to remove. **ver·huizer, -s,** *n.* removal man. **ver·huizing,** *n.* removal.
ver·huren, -huur, *v.t.* to let; to hire out. ¶*zich* ~, *v.r.* to hire oneself out. **ver·huurder, -s,** *n.* lessor. **ver·huurkantoor, -toren,** *n.n.* employment agency.
verhypothe·keren, -keer, *v.t.* to mortgage.
verifica·teur, -s, *n.* verifier; auditor. *kommies* ~, preventive officer. **verifi·ëren, -eer,** *v.t.* to verify.
ver·ijdelen, *v.t.* to frustrate, defeat. **ver·ijdeling,** *n.* frustration.
·vering, *n.* spring-action.
ver·jaard, *a.* superannuated. **ver·jaardag,** *n.* birthday; anniversary. **ver·jaargeschenk,** *n.n.* birthday present.
ver·jagen, -jaag, *v.t.*, *str.* to chase *or* drive away; to expel; to dispel. **ver·jaging,** *n.* expulsion.
ver·jaren, -jaar, *v.i.* to celebrate a birthday; to become superannuated. **ver·jaring,** *n.* superannuation. **ver·jaringsrecht,** no pl., *n.n.* statute of limitations. **ver·jarings·termijn,** *n.* term of limitation.
ver·jongen, *v.t.* to rejuvenate.
ver·kalken, *v.i.* to calcify. **ver·kalking,** *n.* calcification.
ver·kapt, *a.* disguised, in disguise.
ver·kavelen, *v.t.* to parcel out. **ver·kaveling,** *n.* parcelling out.
ver·keer, no pl., *n.n.* traffic; (social) intercourse. **ver·keerd,** *a.* wrong. ¶*adv.* wrong(ly), amiss, ill. ~ *begrijpen*, to misunderstand; ~ *lopen*, to miss one's way; ~ *opnemen*, to take amiss. **ver·keerdelijk,** *adv.* wrong(ly). **ver·keersheuveltje, -s,** *n.n.* traffic island. **ver·keersmiddel,** *n.n.* means of transport. **ver·keersweg,** *n.* arterial road; trade route.
ver·kennen, -ken, *v.t.* to reconnoitre. **ver·kenning,** *n.* reconnoitring; reconnaissance.
ver·keren, -keer, *v.i.* to associate, have intercourse; to change. **ver·kering,** *n.* courtship.
ver·kerven, -kerf, *v.t.*, *str. het* ~ *bij*, to incur the displeasure of. **ver·keuvelen,** *v.t.* to chatter away.
ver·kiesbaar, -bare, *a.* eligible. *zich* ~ *stellen*, to seek election. **ver·kiesbaarheid,** no pl.,

n. eligibility. **ver·kiezen, -kies,** *v.t., str.* to prefer; to elect, choose; to choose, wish. **ver·kiezing,** *n.* election; choice. *naar* ~, at pleasure, at will.

ver·kijken, *v.t., str.* to lose. ¶**zich** ~, *v.r., str.* to be mistaken.

ver·kikkerd, *a.* keen, struck.

ver·klaarbaar, -bare, *a.* explicable. **ver·klaard,** *a.* professed, declared.

ver·klappen, -klap, *v.t.* to blab, give away. *de boel* ~, to give the show away. **ver·klapper, -s,** *n.* telltale.

ver·klaren, -klaar, *v.t.* to declare; to explain, elucidate. ¶**zich** ~, *v.r.* to declare oneself, come out into the open. **ver·klaring,** *n.* declaration; deposition; explanation.

ver·kleden, -kleed, *v.t.* to change clothes; to disguise. ¶**zich** ~, *v.r.* to change (one's clothes). **ver·kleding,** *n.* disguise.

ver·kleefd, *a.* attached, devoted. **ver·kleefdheid,** no pl., *n.* attachment, devotion.

ver·kleinbaar, -bare, *a.* reducible. **ver·kleinen,** *v.t.* to reduce, diminish; to belittle. **ver·kleining,** *n.* reduction. **ver·kleinwoord,** *n.n.* diminutive.

ver·kleumen, *v.i.* to grow numb *(with cold).*

ver·kleuren, *v.i.* to discolour. **ver·kleuring,** *n.* discoloration.

ver·klikken, -klik, *v.t.* to tell (tales). **ver·klikker, -s,** *n.* telltale; indicator.

ver·klungelen, *v.t.* to waste.

ver·kneuteren, zich, *v.r.* to rejoice, gloat. *zich* ~ *in,* to gloat over.

ver·kniezen, -knies, zich, *v.r.* to mope.

ver·knippen, -knip, *v.t.* to cut to pieces.

ver·knocht, *a.* attached, devoted. **ver·knochtheid,** no pl., *n.* devotion.

ver·knoeien, *v.t.* to spoil, bungle.

ver·koelen, *v.t.* to cool; to damp.

ver·koken, -kook, *v.t.* & *v.i.* to boil away.

ver·kolen, -kool, *v.t.* to carbonize. ¶*v.i.* to char.

ver·kondigen, *v.t.* to proclaim, declare. **ver·kondiging,** *n.* proclamation.

ver·koop, -kopen, *n.* sale. **ver·koopbaar, -bare,** *a.* salable. **ver·koopbaarheid,** no pl., *n.* salability. **·verkoophuis, -zen,** *n.n.* sale-room. **ver·koopster, -s,** *n.* saleswoman. **·verkoopwaarde, -n,** *n.* market value. **ver·kopen, -koop,** *v.t., irr.* to sell. *publiek* ~, to sell ·by auction; *grappen* ~, to tell jokes. **ver·koper, -s,** *n.* salesman; seller. **ver·koping,** *n.* sale; auction.

ver·koperen, *v.t.* to copper, copper-bottom.

ver·koren, *a.* chosen, elect.

ver·korten, *v.t.* to shorten; to abbreviate, abridge. **ver·kortenderwijs,** *adv.* for short. **ver·korting,** *n.* shortening; abbreviation.

ver·kouden, *a.* ~ *zijn,* to have a cold; ~ *worden,* to catch a cold. **ver·koudheid, -heden,** *n.* cold *(in the head). een* ~ *opdoen,* to catch a cold.

ver·kozen, *a.* chosen, elected.

ver·krachten, *v.t.* to violate; to rape. **ver·krachting,** *n.* violation; rape.

ver·kreukelen, *v.t.* to crumple.

ver·krijgbaar, -bare, *a.* procurable. ~ *bij,* obtainable from. **ver·krijgen,** *v.t., str.* to obtain. **ver·krijging,** *n.* acquisition.

ver·kroppen, -krop, *v.t.* to swallow stomach.

ver·kruimelen, *v.t.* to crumble (away).

ver·kwanselen, *v.t.* to fritter away.

ver·kwijnen, *v.i.* to pine (away).

ver·kwikkelijk, *a.* invigorating. **ver·kwikken, -kwik,** *v.t.* to refresh. **ver·kwikking,** *n.* refreshment.

ver·kwisten, *v.t.* to waste, squander. **ver·kwister, -s,** *n.* spendthrift. **ver·kwisting,** *n.* waste, wastefulness.

ver·laat, -laten, *n.n.* lock weir.

ver·lagen, -laag, *v.t.* to reduce, lower. **ver·laging,** *n.* reduction.

ver·lak, no pl., *n.n.* lacquer. **ver·lakken, -lak,** *v.t.* to lacquer; to bamboozle. **ver·lakke·rij,** no pl., *n.* bamboozlement. **ver·lakt,** *a.* lacquered; patent leather.

ver·lammen, -lam, *v.t.* to paralyse. **ver·lamming,** *n.* paralysis.

ver·langen, *v.t.* to desire, want. ¶*v.i.* ~ *naar,* to long for. ¶*n.n.* longing, desire. *op* ~ *van,* by desire of. **ver·langend,** *a.* desirous. **ver·langlijst,** *n.* list of presents wanted. **ver·langst,** *n. See* **verlangen,** *n.n.*

ver·laten, -laat, *v.t., str.* to leave; to desert, forsake. ¶*v.r. zich* ~ *op,* to depend on. ¶*a.* deserted, lonely, forsaken. **ver·latenheid,** no pl., *n.* loneliness.

ver·leden, *a.* last; past. ¶*adv.* recently. ¶no pl., *n.n.* past.

ver·legen, *a.* bashful, shy; embarrassed. *er mee* ~ *zijn,* not to know what to do with it; ~ *zijn om,* to be at a loss for. **ver·legenheid,** no pl., *n.* bashfulness; embarrassment, difficulty.

ver·leggen, -leg, *v.t., irr.* to shift.

ver·leidelijk, *a.* tempting. **ver·leidelijkheid, -heden,** *n.* temptation. **ver·leiden,** *v.t.* to tempt; to seduce. **ver·leider, -s,** *n.* tempter; seducer. **ver·leiding,** *n.* temptation; seduction.

ver·lenen, -leen, *v.t.* to grant; to afford, render *(help).* **ver·lening,** *n.* granting; bestowal; rendering.

ver·lengde, -n, *n.n.* produced part of line. **ver·lengen,** *v.t.* to prolong, extend; to produce *(line).* **ver·lenging,** *n.* prolongation, extension; production. **ver·lengstuk, -kken,** *n.n.* piece for lengthening.

ver·leppen, -lep, *v.i.* to wilt.

ver·leren, -leer, *v.t.* to unlearn.

ver·let, no pl., *n.n.* delay.

ver·levendigen, *v.t.* to revive.

ver·licht, *a.* illuminated; enlightened; relieved. **ver·lichten,** *v.t.* to light; to lighten, relieve. **ver·lichting,** *n.* lighting; alleviation.

ver·liefd, *a.* in love; amorous. ~ *op,* in love

with; ~ *worden*, to fall in love. **ver·liefdheid, -heden**, *n.* infatuation.
ver·lies, -zen, *n.n.* loss, bereavement; *pl.* casualties. **ver·liezen, -lies**, *v.t.*, *irr.* to lose. **ver·liezer, -s**, *n.* loser.
ver·lijden, *v.t.*, *str.* to draw up.
ver·lof, -ven, *n.n.* leave, permission; leave, furlough; licence. *met* ~, on leave. **ver·lofganger, -s**, *n.* soldier on leave.
ver·lokken, -lok, *v.t.* to entice. **ver·lokking**, *n.* temptation.
ver·loochenen, *v.t.* to deny, repudiate. ¶*zich* ~, *v.r.* to deny oneself. **ver·loochening**, *n.* denial.
ver·loofde, -n, *n.* fiancé(e).
ver·loop, no pl., *n.n.* course, progress; falling off (*business*). *na* ~ *van tijd*, in course of time. **ver·lopen, -loop**, *v.i.*, *str.* to elapse, go by; to go downhill; to pass, go off.
ver·loren, *a.* lost. *de* ~ *zoon*, the prodigal son; ~ *gaan*, to be lost.
ver·loskunde, no pl., *n.* obstetrics. **verlos·kundige, -n**, *n.* obstetrician. **ver·lossen, -los**, *v.t.* to deliver; to release. **ver·losser, -s**, *n.* deliverer; saviour. **ver·lossing**, *n.* deliverance; delivery.
ver·loten, -loot, *v.t.* to dispose of by lottery. **ver·loting**, *n.* lottery, raffle.
ver·loven, -loof, *v.t.* to betroth. ¶*zich* ~, *v.r.* to become engaged. **ver·loving**, *n.* engagement.
ver·luchten, *v.t.* to illuminate.
ver·luiden, *v.i. naar verluidt*, it is rumoured.
ver·lustigen, zich, *v.r.* to disport oneself.
ver·maak, -maken, *n.n.* pleasure, amusement.
ver·maard, *a.* celebrated, renowned. **ver·maardheid**, no pl., *n.* fame, renown; celebrity.
ver·mageren, *v.i.* to grow thin. **ver·mageringskuur, -kuren**, *n.* slimming course.
ver·makelijk, *a.* amusing. **ver·maken, -maak**, *v.t.* to amuse, divert; to mend; to bequeath. ¶*zich* ~, *v.r.* to amuse *or* enjoy oneself.
vermale·dijen, *v.t.* to curse.
ver·malen, -maal, *v.t.* to grind, pulverize.
ver·manen, -maan, *v.t.* to admonish. **ver·maning**, *n.* admonition.
ver·mannen, -man, zich, *v.r.* to brace oneself.
ver·meerderen, *v.t.* & *v.i.* to increase. **ver·meerdering**, *n.* increase.
ver·meien, zich, *v.r.* to disport oneself.
ver·melden, *v.t.* to mention, state. **ver·melding**, *n.* mention.
ver·menen, -meen, *v.t.* to be of the opinion.
ver·mengen, *v.t.* to mix; to blend.
vermenig·vuldigen, *v.t.* to multiply. **vermenig·vuldiging**, *n.* multiplication.
ver·metel, *a.* audacious. **ver·metelheid**, no pl., *n.* audacity.
ver·mijden, *v.t.*, *str.* to avoid, evade. **ver·mijding**, no pl., *n.* avoidance.
vermil·joen, no pl., *n.n.* vermilion.
ver·minderen, *v.t.* & *v.i.* to decrease, lessen,

reduce. **ver·mindering**, *n.* decrease, diminution.
ver·minken, *v.t.* to maim, mutilate. **ver·minking**, *n.* mutilation. **ver·minkte, -n**, *n.* cripple.
ver·missen, -mis, *v.t.* to miss. **ver·mist**, *a.* missing.
ver·mits, *c.* whereas, since, as.
ver·moedelijk, *a.* probable, presumable. ¶*adv.* probably, presumably. **ver·moeden**, *v.t.* to suppose, presume, suspect. ¶*-s*, *n.n.* suspicion; surmise. *kwade* ~*s hebben op*, to suspect.
ver·moeid, *a.* tired. ~ *van*, tired with. **ver·moeidheid**, no pl., *n.* tiredness, fatigue. **ver·moeien**, *v.t.* to tire. **ver·moeienis, -ssen**, *n.* fatigue.
ver·mogen, -mag, *v.t.*, *irr.* to be able. *niets* ~, to be powerless. ¶*-s*, *n.n.* fortune; ability, power; capacity. *naar zijn beste* ~, to the best of his ability. **ver·mogend**, *a.* wealthy, of substance.
ver·molmen, *v.i.* to moulder (away).
ver·mommen, -mom, *v.t.* to disguise. **ver·momming**, *n.* disguise.
ver·moorden, *v.t.* to murder.
ver·morsen, *v.t.* to waste.
ver·morzelen, *v.t.* to crush.
ver·murwen, *v.t.* to soften, mollify.
ver·nauwen, *v.t.* to narrow. **ver·nauwing**, *n.* narrowing.
ver·nederen, *v.t.* to humiliate, humble. **ver·nedering**, *n.* humiliation.
ver·neembaar, -bare, *a.* audible, perceptible.
ver·nemen, -neem, *v.t.*, *str.* to hear, understand, learn.
ver·nielen, *v.t.* to destroy, smash. **ver·nieler, -s**, *n.* destroyer, one who destroys. **ver·nieling**, *n.* destruction. **ver·nielzucht**, no pl., *n.* destruction, love of destruction.
ver·nietigen, *v.t.* to destroy, annihilate; to annul. **ver·nietigend**, *a.* destructive. **ver·nietiging**, *n.* destruction, annihilation.
ver·nieuwbaar, -bare, *a.* renewable. **ver·nieuwen**, *v.t.* to renew. **ver·nieuwing**, *n.* renewal.
ver·nikkelen, *v.t.* to nickel-plate.
ver·nis, -ssen, *n.* varnish; veneer. **ver·nissen, -nis**, *v.t.* to varnish.
ver·nuft, no pl., *n.n.* genius, intelligence. **ver·nuftig**, *a.* ingenious. **ver·nuftigheid**, no pl., *n.* ingenuity.
veron·achtzamen, -zaam, *v.t.* to neglect, disregard.
veronder·stellen, -stel, *v.t.* to suppose, assume. **veronder·stelling**, *n.* supposition.
ver·ongelijken, *v.t.* to wrong.
ver·ongelukken, -luk, *v.i.* to meet with an accident; to perish.
veront·heiligen, *v.t.* to desecrate.
veront·reinigen, *v.t.* to pollute.
veront·rusten, *v.t.* to alarm, perturb. ¶*v.r. zich* ~ *over*, to be alarmed at. **veront·rusting**, *n.* alarm, perturbation.

veront·schuldigen, *v.t.* to excuse. ¶**zich ~,** *v.r.* to apologize, excuse oneself. **veront-·schuldiging,** *n.* excuse, apology.
veront·waardigd, *a.* indignant; outraged. **veront·waardigen,** *v.t.* to fill with indignation. **veront·waardiging,** no pl., *n.* indignation.
ver·oordeelde, -n, *n.* person condemned. **ver·oordelen, -deel,** *v.t.* to condemn; to sentence. **ver·oordeling,** *n.* condemnation, conviction.
ver·oorloofd, *a.* permitted; permissible. **ver·oorloven, -loof,** *v.t.* to permit, allow. ¶*v.r.* **zich ~ om,** to take the liberty to.
ver·oorzaken, -zaak, *v.t.* to cause, bring about.
veroot·moedigen, *v.t.* to humble.
ver·orberen, *v.t.* to eat, polish off.
ver·ordenen, *v.t.* to decree; to ordain.
ver·ouderd, *a.* antiquated, obsolete, out-of-date. **ver·ouderen,** *v.i.* to age, grow old. ¶*v.t.* to make older. **ver·ouwelijken,** *v.i.* to begin to look old.
ver·overaar, -s, *n.* conqueror. **ver·overen,** *v.t.* to conquer, capture. **ver·overing,** *n.* conquest; capture.
ver·pachten, *v.t.* to lease, farm out.
ver·pakken, -pak, *v.t.* to pack, wrap up. **ver·pakking,** *n.* packing.
ver·panden, *v.t.* to pawn, mortgage.
ver·patsen, *v.t.* to squander.
verper·soonlijken, *v.t.* to personify.
ver·pesten, *v.t.* to infect; to spoil.
ver·plaatsbaar, -bare, *a.* movable. **ver-·plaatsen,** *v.t.* to move, transfer. **ver-·plaatsing,** *n.* move, transfer.
ver·planten, *v.t.* to transplant.
ver·pleegster, -s, *n.* (trained) nurse. **ver-·plegen, -pleeg,** *v.t.* to nurse. **ver·pleging,** *n.* nursing. **ver·pleger, -s,** *n.* male nurse.
ver·pletteren, *v.t.* to crush, squash. **ver-·pletterend,** *a.* crushing, overwhelming.
ver·plicht, *a.* compulsory, obligatory. **~ aan,** indebted to; under an obligation to; **~ zijn om,** to have to. **ver·plichten,** *v.t.* to oblige, compel; to oblige, put under obligation. **ver·plichting,** *n.* obligation; commitment.
ver·poppen, -pop, zich, *v.r.* to pupate.
ver·poten, -poot, *v.t.* to transplant.
ver·potten, -pot, *v.t.* to repot.
ver·praten, -praat, *v.t.* to waste (*time*) talking.
ver·raad, no pl., *n.n.* treason, treachery. **ver·raden, -raad,** *v.t., str.* to betray, give away. **ver·rader, -s,** *n.* traitor, betrayer. **ver·raderlijk,** *a.* treacherous; insidious.
ver·rassen, -ras, *v.t.* to surprise, take unawares. **ver·rassend,** *a.* surprising, startling. **ver·rassing,** *n.* surprise.
·**verre,** *a.* See **ver. verre·gaand,** *a.* extreme, excessive.
ver·rekenen, *v.t.* to settle. ¶**zich ~,** *v.r.* to miscalculate.
·**verrekijker, -s,** *n.* telescope, field-glasses.

ver·rekken, -rek, *v.t.* to sprain. *verrek!,* go to blazes!
·**verreweg,** *adv.* by far.
ver·richten, *v.t.* to perform, carry out.
ver·rijken, *v.t.* to enrich.
ver·rijzen, -rijs, *v.i., str.* to rise; to spring up. **ver·rijzenis,** no pl., *n.* resurrection.
ver·roeren, zich, *v.r.* to move, stir.
ver·roesten, *v.i.* to rust (away).
ver·rotten, -rot, *v.i.* to rot (away).
ver·ruilen, *v.t.* to exchange.
ver·ruimen, *v.t.* to enlarge, expand.
ver·rukkelijk, *a.* delightful, ravishing. **ver-·rukken, -ruk,** *v.t.* to delight. **ver·rukking,** *n.* delight, transport.
vers, -zen, *n.n.* poem; verse; couplet. ¶*a.* fresh, new-laid, new.
ver·saagd, *a.* faint-hearted. **ver·sagen, -saag,** *v.i.* to grow faint-hearted.
ver·schaffen, -schaf, *v.t.* to procure, provide.
ver·schalen, -schaal, *v.i.* to go flat.
ver·schalken, *v.t.* to outwit, foil.
ver·schansen, zich, *v.r.* to entrench oneself. **ver·schansing,** *n.* entrenchment; bulwark (*ship*).
ver·scheiden, *v.i.* (*stilted*) to depart, pass away. ¶*a.* divers, several. **ver·scheiden-heid, -heden,** *n.* diversity.
ver·schepen, -scheep, *v.t.* to ship.
ver·scherpen, *v.t.* to make sharper; to tighten up (*regulation*); to intensify.
ver·scheuren, *v.t.* to tear up, tear to pieces.
ver·schiet, no pl., *n.n.* horizon. **in het ~,** in the distance, in the offing. **ver·schieten,** *v.t., str.* to use up (*ammunition*); to advance (*money*). ¶*v.i., str.* to fade; to turn pale.
ver·schijnen, *v.i., str.* to appear, turn up. **ver·schijning,** *n.* appearance; figure; apparition. **ver·schijnsel,** *n.n.* phenomenon; sympton.
ver·schikken, -schik, *v.t.* to arrange differently.
ver·schil, -llen, *n.n.* difference, distinction; remainder. **ver·schillen, -schil,** *v.i.* to differ, vary. **ver·schillend,** *a.* different; various.
ver·scholen, *a.* hidden, tucked away.
ver·schonen, -schoon, *v.t.* to put on clean linen; (*stilted*) to excuse. **ver·schoning,** *n.* change of linen; (*stilted*) excuse, apology. **~ vragen,** to apologize.
ver·schoppeling, *n.* outcast. **ver·schoppen, -schop,** *v.t.* to kick away.
ver·schoten, *a.* faded.
ver·schrijven, -schrijf, zich, *v.r., str.* to make a mistake (*in writing*).
ver·schrikkelijk, *a.* terrible, frightful. **ver-·schrikken, -schrik,** *v.i., str.* to have a shock, be frightened. ¶*v.t., str.* to frighten.
ver·schroeien, *v.t.* to scorch, singe.
ver·schrompelen, *v.t.* to shrivel, wither.
ver·schuilen, zich, *v.r., str.* to hide, conceal oneself.
ver·schuiven, -schuif, *v.t., str.* to shove **or** push away; to postpone.

ver·schuldigd, *a.* due, owing.　~ *zijn aan,* to owe to.

ver·sieren, *v.t.* to adorn.　**ver·siering**, *n.* ornament, decoration.　**ver·siersel**, **-s**, *n.n.* ornament.

ver·slaafd, *a.*　~ *aan,* addicted to.　**ver·slaafdheid**, no pl., *n.* addiction.

ver·slaan, **-sla**, *v.t., irr.* to defeat, beat; to quench.　**ver·slag**, *n.n.* report, account.　**ver·slagen**, *a.* beaten; dejected.　**ver·slaggever**, **-s**, *n.* reporter.

ver·slapen, **-slaap**, zich, *v.r., str.* to oversleep.

ver·slappen, **-slap**, *v.i.* to become limp.　¶*v.t.* to relax.

ver·sleten, *a.* worn (out).　**ver·slijten**, *v.t., str.* to wear out.　*iemand* ~ *voor,* to take a person for.　¶*v.i., str.* to wear (out).

ver·slikken, **-slik**, zich, *v.r.* to choke, swallow the wrong way.

ver·slinden, *v.t., str.* to devour.

·**versmaat**, **-maten**, *n.* metre (*poetry*).

ver·smachten, *v.i.* to languish.　~ *van dorst,* to be parched with thirst.

ver·smaden, **-smaad**, *v.t.* to spurn, scorn.

ver·smelten, *v.i., str.* to melt away; to blend.　*in tranen* ~, to dissolve in tears.

ver·smoren, **-smoor**, *v.t.* to smother.

ver·snapering, *n.* sweet, titbit.

ver·snellen, **-snel**, *v.t.* to speed up, accelerate.　**ver·snelling**, *n.* acceleration; gear, speed.　**ver·snellingsbak**, **-kken**, *n.* gear-box.

ver·snijden, *v.t., str.* to spoil (*by cutting*); to dilute (*wine*).

ver·snipperen, *v.t.* to cut into small pieces, disperse.

ver·spelen, **-speel**, *v.t.* to lose.

ver·sperren, **-sper**, *v.t.* to bar, obstruct.　**ver·sperring**, *n.* obstruction.

ver·spieden, *v.t.* (*stilted*) to spy out.

ver·spillen, **-spil**, *v.t.* to waste.

ver·splinteren, *v.t.* & *v.i.* to break into splinters.

ver·spreiden, *v.t.* to spread, scatter, disperse.　¶zich ~, *v.r.* to spread.　**ver·spreiding**, *n.* spread(ing), propagation.

ver·spreken, **-spreek**, zich, *v.r., str.* to make a slip of the tongue.

ver·springen, *v.t., str.* to move up, skip.

ver·staan, **-sta**, *v.t., irr.* to understand.　*wel te* ~, that is to say; *verkeerd* ~, to misunderstand; *zich* ~ *met,* to come to an understanding with; ~ *onder,* to understand by; *zich* ~ *op,* to be well up in.　**ver·staanbaar**, **-bare**, *a.* understandable, intelligible.　~ *maken,* to explain.　**ver·staander**, **-s**, *n.* one who understands.　**ver·stand**, no pl., *n.n.* intelligence; understanding.　*gezond* ~, common sense; ~ *genoeg hebben om,* to have the sense to; *iemand iets aan het* ~ *brengen,* to make a person see a thing; *met dien* ~e, on the understanding.　**ver·standelijk**, *a.* intellectual.　**ver·standhouding**, no pl., *n.* understanding; relations.　**ver·standig**, *a.* intelligent; sensible, wise.　**ver·standskies**, **-zen**, *n.* wisdom-tooth.

ver·starren, **-star**, *v.i.* to become rigid.

ver·steend, *a.* petrified.

ver·stek, no pl., *n.n. bij* ~, by default, in one's absence.　**ver·stekeling**, *n.* stowaway.

ver·stelbaar, **-bare**, *a.* adjustable.　**ver·steld**, *a.* mended; dumbfounded.　~ *staan van,* to be taken aback by.　**ver·stellen**, **-stel**, *v.t.* to mend; to adjust.　**ver·stelwerk**, no pl., *n.n.* mending.

ver·sterken, *v.t.* to strengthen; to fortify.　**ver·sterking**, *n.* strengthening; fortification; reinforcement.

ver·sterven, **-sterf**, *v.i., str.* to die out.

ver·stijven, **-stijf**, *v.i., str.* to stiffen; to grow numb.　¶*v.t., str.* to stiffen; to benumb.

ver·stikken, **-stik**, *v.i.* to suffocate.　**ver·stikking**, no pl., *n.* suffocation.

ver·stoken, *a.*　~ *van,* destitute *or* deprived of.

ver·stokken, **-stok**, *v.t.* to harden.　**ver·stokt**, *a.* hardened, obdurate.

ver·stommen, **-stom**, *v.t.* to silence.　¶*v.i.* to become silent.

ver·stompen, *v.t.* to blunt, dull.

ver·stoord, *a.* disturbed; cross.

ver·stoppen, **-stop**, *v.t.* to stop up; to hide.　**ver·stoppertje**, no pl., *n.n.*　~ *spelen,* to play hide-and-seek.

ver·storen, **-stoor**, *v.t.* to disturb; to upset, annoy.

ver·stoteling, *n.* outcast.　**ver·stoten**, **stoot**, *v.t., str.* to cast off, repudiate.

ver·stouten, zich, *v.r.* to make bold.

ver·strekken, **-strek**, *v.t.* to provide with; procure; to supply; to render.

·**verstrekkend**, *a.* far-reaching.

ver·strijken, *v.i., str.* to go by, to elapse.

ver·strikken, **-strik**, *v.t.* to ensnare, entangle.

ver·strooid, *a.* scattered; absent-minded.　**ver·strooidheid**, **-heden**, *n.* absent-mindedness.　**ver·strooien**, *v.t.* to scatter, disperse.　¶zich ~, *v.r.* to scatter, disperse.　**ver·strooiing**, *n.* dispersal; distraction, diversion.

ver·stuiken, *v.t.* to sprain, wrick (*ankle*).

ver·suft, *a.* stupefied, dazed.

ver·taalbaar, **-bare**, *a.* translatable.　**ver·taalster**, **-s**, *n.* translator (*woman*).

ver·takken, **-tak**, zich, *v.r.* to branch, ramify.　**ver·takking**, *n.* fork, ramification.

ver·talen, **-taal**, *v.t.* to translate.　**ver·taler**, **-s**, *n.* translator.　**ver·taling**, *n.* translation.

·**verte**, no pl., *n.* (far) distance.　*er niet in de verste* ~ *aan denken,* not to have the remotest idea of doing it.

ver·tederen, *v.t.* to mollify.　**ver·tedering**, *n.* mollification.　**ver·teerbaar**, **-bare**, *a.* digestible.

vertegen·woordigen, *v.t.* to represent.　**vertegen·woordiger**, **-s**, *n.* representative.　**vertegen·woordiging**, *n.* representation.

ver·tellen, -tel, *v.t.* to tell. ¶**zich ~,** *v.r.* to miscount. **ver·teller, -s,** *n.* narrator. **ver·telling,** *n.* story, narration. **ver·telsel, -s,** *n.n.* story, tale.

ver·teren, -teer, *v.t.* to consume; to digest; to corrode. ¶*v.i.* to digest. **ver·tering,** *n.* digestion; expenses, score.

ver·tienvoudigen, *v.t.* to increase tenfold.

ver·tier, no pl., *n.n.* activity, bustle.

ver·tikken, -tik, *v.t.* to refuse point-blank.

ver·tinnen, -tin, *v.i.* to coat with tin.

ver·toeven, -toef, *v.i.* to stay.

ver·tolken, *v.t.* to interpret.

)**er·tonen, -toon,** *v.t.* to produce, exhibit, display. **ver·toning,** *n.* show, display.

ver·toog, -togen, *n.n.* treatise; expostulation.

ver·toon, no pl., *n.n.* show, ostentation; display. *op ~,* on production.

ver·toornd, *a.* incensed.

ver·tragen, -traag, *v.t.* to retard, delay. **ver·traging,** *n.* delay. *~ hebben,* to be late (*train*).

ver·trappen, -trap, *v.t.* to trample down, crush.

ver·trek, -kken, *r.n.* room, apartment. ¶no pl., *n.n.* departure; sailing. **ver·trekken, -trek,** *v.i.,* *str.* to leave, start. ¶*v.t.,* *str.* to distort.

ver·troetelen, *v.t.* to spoil, pamper.

ver·troosten, *v.t.* to comfort. **ver·troosting,** *n.* comfort, solace.

ver·trouwbaar, -bare, *a.* dependable, trustworthy. **ver·trouwd,** *a.* trusted, trusty; safe. *~ met,* conversant with. **ver·trouwdheid,** no pl., *n.* familiarity. **ver·trouwelijk,** *a.* confidential. **ver·trouwelijkheid, -heden,** *n.* intimacy. **ver·trouweling,** *n.* confidant(e). **ver·trouwen,** *v.t.* to trust; to entrust. ¶*v.i. ~ op,* to rely on. ¶no pl., *n.n.* trust, faith, confidence. *met ~,* confidently.

ver·twijfeld, *a.* desperate. **ver·twijfelen,** *v.t.* to despair. **ver·twijfeling,** *n.* desperation.

ver·vaard, *a.* (*stilted*) alarmed.

ver·vaardigen, *v.t.* to manufacture. **ver·vaardiging,** *n.* manufacture.

ver·vaarlijk, *a.* frightful, tremendous.

ver·val, no pl., *n.n.* decline, falling-off, decadence; fall, drop. *~ van krachten,* (senile) decay. **ver·valdatum,** *n.* date when due. **ver·vallen, -val,** *v.i.,* *str.* to fall into decay; to become due (*bill*); to terminate, lapse. *~ in,* to fall *or* lapse into. ¶*a.* ramshackle, dilapidated; overdue, expired.

ver·valsen, *v.t.* to falsify, adulterate; to forge. **ver·valsing,** *n.* falsification, adulteration.

ver·vangen, *v.t.,* *str.* to replace. **ver·vanging,** *n.* replacement, substitution.

ver·vat, *a. ~ in,* couched in.

ver·velen, -veel, *v.t.* to bore; to annoy.

¶**zich ~,** *v.r.* to be bored. ¶no pl., *n. tot ~s toe,* ad nauseam. **ver·velend,** *a.* boring, tedious; annoying. **ver·veling,** *n.* boredom.

ver·vellen. -vel, *v.i.* to get a new skin, peel. ·**verveloos, -loze,** *a.* paintless. ·**verven, verf,** *v.t.* to paint, dye. **verve·rij,** *n.* dyeworks.

ver·versen, *v.t.* to refresh, change. **ver·versing,** *n.* refreshment.

·**ververwijderd,** *a.* far distant.

ver·vetting, no pl., *n.* fatty degeneration.

vervier·dubbelen, *v.t.* to quadruple.

ver·vliegen, *v.i.,* *str.* to evaporate, volatilize; to vanish.

ver·vloeken, *v.t.* to curse. **ver·vloeking,** *n.* curse, malediction. **ver·vloekt,** *a.* cursed; damned; blasted.

ver·voegen, *v.t.* to conjugate. **ver·voeging,** *n.* conjugation.

ver·voer, no pl., *n.n.* transport; removal. **ver·voerbaar, -bare,** *a.* conveyable. **ver·voerbewijs, -zen,** *n.n.* railway warrant. **ver·voeren,** *v.t.* to transport, convey. **ver·voering,** *n.* transport, rapture. **ver·voermiddel,** *n.n.* conveyance, means of transport.

ver·volg, *n.n.* continuation, sequel. *in 't ~,* in future, henceforth. **ver·volgen,** *v.t.* to continue, proceed; to pursue; to persecute; to prosecute. **ver·volgens,** *adv.* then, next, afterwards. **ver·volger, -s,** *n.* pursuer; persecutor; prosecutor. **ver·volging,** *n.* pursuit; persecution; prosecution. **ver·volgingswaanzin,** no pl., *n.* persecution mania.

ver·vormen, *v.t.* to transform. **ver·vorming,** *n.* transformation.

ver·vreemd, *a.* alienated. **ver·vreemden,** *v.t.* to alienate, estrange. ¶*v.r. zich ~ van,* to become estranged from. **ver·vreemding,** *n.* alienation, estrangement.

ver·vroegen, *v.t.* to make earlier.

ver·vuild, *a.* filthy. **ver·vuilen,** *v.t.* to make filthy.

ver·vullen, -vul, *v.t.* to fill; to fulfil. **ver·vulling,** *n.* fulfilment; performance, execution. *in ~ gaan,* to be realized.

ver·waand, *a.* conceited. **ver·waandheid,** no pl., *n.* conceit.

ver·waardigen, *v.t.* to deem worthy of, vouchsafe. ¶*zich ~, v.r.* to condescend.

ver·waarloosd, *a.* neglected. **ver·waarlozen, -loos,** *v.t.* to neglect. **ver·waarlozing,** no pl., *n.* neglect.

ver·wachten, *v.t.* to expect, anticipate. **ver·wachting,** *n.* expectation. *in blijde ~,* with child; *boven ~,* beyond expectation; *buiten ~* or *tegen alle ~,* contrary to expectation.

ver·want, *a.* related; cognate; kindred. ¶*n.* relative, relation. **ver·wantschap,** no pl., *n.* relation(ship); affinity.

ver·ward, *a.* confused. *~ raken in,* to get

entangled in. **ver·wardheid,** no pl., *n.*
confusion.

ver·warmen, *v.t.* to heat. **ver·warming,** *n.*
heating.

ver·warren, -war, *v.t.* to mix up, confuse,
entangle. *met elkaar* ∼, to confuse.
¶**zich** ∼, *v.r.* to get confused. **ver·warring,**
n. confusion, muddle.

ver·weer, no pl., *n.n.* resistance, defence.

ver·weerd, *a.* weather-beaten.

ver·weermiddel, *n.n.* means of defence.
ver·weerschrift, *n.n.* (written) defence,
apology.

ver·wekken, -wek, *v.t.* tó produce, cause,
rouse; to beget.

ver·welken, *v.i.* to fade, wilt.

ver·welkomen, *v.t.* to welcome. **ver·welkom-
ing,** *n.* welcome.

ver·wend, *a.* spoilt. **ver·wennen, -wen,** *v.t.*
to spoil (*child*). .

ver·wensen, *v.t.* to curse. **ver·wensing,** *n.*
curse, malediction.

ver·weren, -weer, *v.i.* to weather, become
weather-beaten. ¶**zich** ∼, *v.r.* to defend
oneself. **ver·wering,** *n.* weathering.

ver·werkelijken, *v.t.* to realize (*make real*).

ver·werken, *v.t.* to use up. *kunnen* ∼, to
cope with, assimilate; ∼ *tot,* to work into.
ver·werking, *n. bij de* ∼ *van,* in dealing with.

ver·werpelijk, *a.* objectionable, reprehensible.
ver·werpen, *v.t., str.* to reject.

ver·werven, -werf, *v.t., str.* to acquire, obtain.

ver·wezen, *a.* dumbfounded.

ver·wezenlijken, *v.t.* to realize (*make real*).

ver·wijderd, *a.* distant, remote. **ver·wijderen,**
v.t. to remove; to eliminate. ¶**zich** ∼,
v.r. to withdraw, retire. **ver·wijdering,** *n.*
removal, elimination.

ver·wijfd, *a.* effeminate. **ver·wijfdheid,** no
pl., *n.* effeminacy.

ver·wijl, no pl., *n.n.* delay. **ver·wijlen,** *v.i.*
(*stilted*) to tarry, linger.

ver·wijt, *n.n.* reproach. *iemand een* ∼ *maken
van,* to reproach a person with. **ver·wijten,**
v.t., str. to reproach. **ver·wijtend,** *a.*
reproachful.

ver·wijzen, -wijs, *v.t., str.* to refer. **ver-
·wijzing,** *n.* (cross-)reference. *onder* ∼
naar, with reference to.

ver·wikkelen, *v.t.* to involve. **ver·wikkeling,**
n. complication.

ver·wilderd, *a.* neglected; unkempt. **ver-
·wilderen,** *v.i.* to run wild, become a
wilderness.

ver·wisselbaar, -bare, *a.* interchangeable.
ver·wisselen, *v.t.* to exchange, change,
interchange. ∼ *met* or *tegen,* to exchange
for; *van plaats* ∼, to change places.
ver·wisseling, *n.* change, exchange.

ver·wittigen, *v.t.* (*stilted*) to inform, advise.
ver·wittiging, *n.* notice.

ver·woed, *a.* furious.

ver·woesten, *v.t.* to destroy, devastate, lay
waste, ruin. **ver·woestend,** *a.* devastating.

ver·woester, -s, *n.* destroyer. **ver·woesting,**
n. destruction, devastation, havoc.

ver·wonden, *v.t.* to wound, injure.

ver·wonderd, *a.* astonished, surprised. **ver-
·wonderen,** *v.t.* to astonish, surprise. *het
is niet te* ∼, no wonder. ¶**zich** ∼, *v.r.* to
wonder. **ver·wondering,** no pl., *n.* astonishment, surprise. **ver·wonderlijk,** *a.* astonishing, queer.

ver·wonding, *n.* wound, injury.

ver·wonen, -woon, *v.t.* to pay for rent.

ver·worden, *v.i., str.* to decay, degenerate. **ver-
·wording,** no pl., *n.* degeneration.

ver·worpeling, *n.* outcast.

ver·wrikken, -wrik, *v.t.* to wrench.

ver·wringen, *v.t., str.* to distort.

ver·zachten, *v.t.* to soften, ease. **ver·zachtend,**
a. softening; mitigating. **ver·zachting,** *n.*
alleviation; mitigation.

ver·zadigen, *v.t.* to satisfy; to satiate.

ver·zaken, -zaak, *v.t.* to renounce, forsake.

ver·zakken, -zak, *v.i.* to subside.

ver·zamelaar, -s, *n.* collector. **ver·zamelen,**
v.t. to collect, gather. *zijn moed* ∼, to
pluck up courage. ¶**zich** ∼, *v.r.* to assemble, gather. **ver·zameling.** *n.* collection.
ver·zamelplaats, *n.* meeting-place.

ver·zanden, *v.i.* to silt up.

ver·zegelen, *v.t.* to seal (up), put under seal.
ver·zegeling, *n.* sealing (up).

ver·zeilen, *v.i.* to lose one's course, land in
the wrong place. *verzeild raken onder,* to
fall among.

ver·zekeraar, -s, *n.* insurer, underwriter.
ver·zekerbaar, -bare, *a.* insurable. **ver-
·zekerd,** *a.* assured; insured, assured.
ver·zekeren, *v.t.* to assure; to guarantee;
to assure, insure, underwrite. ¶**zich** ∼,
v.r. to ascertain, make sure; to secure;
to insure oneself. **ver·zekering,** *n.* assurance; insurance, assurance.

ver·zenden, *v.t., str.* to dispatch, forward,
remit. **ver·zending,** *n.* consignment, shipment; dispatch.

·verzenen, pl. only, *n. de* ∼ *tegen de prikkels
slaan,* to kick against the pricks.

ver·zengen, *v.t.* to singe, scorch.

ver·zet, no pl., *n.n.* resistance; diversion.
∼ *aantekenen,* to protest. **ver·zetten, -zet,**
v.t. to move, shift. ¶**zich** ∼, *v.r.* to resist;
to take some recreation.

ver·zien, -zie, *v.i., irr. het* ∼ *hebben op,*
to have it in for. **verziend,** *a.* long-sighted;
far-seeing.

ver·zilveren, *v.t.* to silver-plate; to cash.

ver·zinken, *v.i., str.* to sink (away); to lose
oneself (*in thought*).

ver·zinnen, -zin, *v.t., str.* to invent. **ver·zinsel,
-s,** *n.n.* invention, concoction.

ver·zoek, *n.n.* request. *op* ∼, by request;
ten ∼*e van,* at the request of. **ver·zoeken,**
v.t., irr. to request; to tempt. **ver·zoeking,**
n. temptation. **ver·zoekschrift,** *n.n.*
petition, memorial.

ver·zoenbaar, -bare, a. reconcilable. Ver·zoendag, n. Grote ~, Day of Atonement. ver·zoenen, v.t. to reconcile. met elkaar ~, to reconcile; zich met elkaar ~, to become reconciled. ver·zoenend, a., ver·zoeningsgezind, a. conciliatory.

ver·zolen, -zool, v.t. to resole.

ver·zorgen, v.t. to look after, tend. ¶zich ~, v.r. to take care of oneself. ver·zorging, n. care.

ver·zot, a. ~ op, enamoured of.

ver·zuchten, v.i. to sigh; to long. ver·zuchting, n. sigh, lamentation.

ver·zuim, n.n. oversight, omission; nonattendance, absenteeism. ver·zuimen, v.t. to neglect, omit.

ver·zuipen, v.t., str. (vulg.) to drown; to booze away. ¶v.i., str. (vulg.) to be drowned.

ver·zwakken, -zwak, v.t. & v.i. to weaken. ver·zwakking, n. weakening.

ver·zwaren, -zwaar, v.t. to make heavier. ver·zwelgen, v.t., str. to swallow up, engulf. ver·zwijgen, v.t., str. to keep secret, hush up. ver·zwikken, -zwik, v.t. to sprain.

·vesper, -s, n.n. vespers.

vest, n.n. waistcoat.

·veste, -n, n. (stilted) stronghold, fort. ·vestigen, v.t. to establish, set up. de aandacht ~ op, to call attention to; de ogen ~ op, to fix one's eyes upon. ¶zich ~, v.r. to settle, establish oneself. ·vestiging, n. establishment. ·vesting, n. fortress. ·vestingwerk, n.n. fortification.

vet, -tten, n.n. fat, grease. ¶a. fat, greasy. vette druk, bold print; vette grond, rich soil. ·vetachtig, a. fatty, greasy.

·vete, -n, n. feud.

·veter, -s, n. lace (boot, etc.). ·veterband, n. tape; braid. ·vetergat, n.n. eyelet.

vete·raan, -ranen, n. veteran.

·vetheid, no pl., n. fatness. ·vetkaars, n. tallow-candle. ·vetkruid, no pl., n.n. stonecrop. ·vetleer, no pl., n.n. greased leather. ·vetleren, a. (of) greased leather. ·vetmesten, v.t.s. to fatten (up). ·vetplant, n. succulent plant. ·vetpotje, -s, n.n. fairy-lamp (oil). ·vetten, vet, v.t. to fatten, grease. ·vettig, a. fatty, greasy. ·vetvrij, a. greaseproof. ·vetweiden, v.t. to fatten. ·vetweider, -s, n. grazier. vetweide·rij, n. graziery.

·veulen, -s, n.n. foal; colt, filly.

·vezel, -s, n. fibre; filament. ·vezelachtig, a. fibrous. ·vezelen, v.t. to fray, ravel. ·vezelig, a. fibrous; stringy.

vic·torie, -s, n. victory. ~ kraaien, to triumph.

victu·aliën, pl. only, n. victuals.

vief, -ve, a. lively.

vier, num. four. onder ~ ogen, in private. vier·bladig, a. four-leaved. ·vierdaags, a. four day. ·vierde, a. fourth. ¶-n, n.n. fourth (part). ten ~, in the fourth place.

vier·delig, a. fourfold. ·vierdemachtswortel, -s, n. fourth root. ·vierderangs, a. fourthrate. ·vierdubbel, a. fourfold, quadruple. ·vieren, num. four. de trein van ~, the four o'clock train; bij ~, just on four; in ~, into four; met hun ~, the four of them; met ons ~, the four of us; met z'n ~, with three others.

·vieren, v.t. to celebrate; to pay out, slacken.

·vierendeel, -delen, n.n. fourth part. ·vierendelen, v.t. to quarter. ·vierhoek, n. quadrangle. vier·hoekig, a. quadrangular.

·viering, n. celebration.

vier·jarig, a. four-year-old. ·vierkaart, n. sequence of four (cards). ·vierkant, n.n. square, quadrangle. in het ~, square. ¶a. square. ¶adv. squarely; squarely, flatly. ·vierkantswortel, -s, n. square root. vier·kleurig, a. four-coloured. ·vierkwartsmaat, no pl., n. quadruple time. vier·ledig, a. quadripartite. ·vierling, n. quadruplet(s). ·viermaal, adv. four times. ·vierman, -nnen, n. one of four magistrates. ·vierpersoons, a. four-seated. ·vierschaar, -scharen, n. tribunal of four magistrates. ·viersprong, n. cross-roads. op de ~, at the parting of the ways. vier·stemmig, a. for four voices. ·viertal, -llen, n.n. number or set of four. ·viertalig, a. in four languages. ·viervoeter, -s, n. quadruped. vier·voetig, a. four-footed. ·viervoud, n.n. quadruple; multiple of four. vier·voudig, a. fourfold. vier·zijdig, a. quadrilateral.

vies, -ze, a. filthy, dirty; foul, nauseating; fastidious, dainty. er ~ van zijn, to be disgusted by or averse to it; een ~ gezicht trekken, to turn up one's nose. ·viezerik, -kken, n. dirty pig (fig.). ·viezigheid, -heden, n. filth; smut.

vigi·lante, -s, n. four-wheeler.

·vijand, n. enemy; fiend, foe. tot ~ maken, to make an enemy of. vij·andelijk, a. hostile, enemy; inimical. vij·andelijkheid, -heden, n. hostility. vij·andig, a. hostile, inimical. ~ gezind, ill-disposed. vij·andigheid, -heden, n. hostility, enmity. vijanden, -nnen, n. enemy (female). ·vijandschap, -ppen, n. enmity, animosity.

vijf, num. five. ¶-ven, n. five. geef me de ~, shake hands. See vijven, num. ·vijfde, a. fifth. ¶-n, n.n. fifth (part). ·vijfderlei, a. of five kinds. ·vijfdubbel, a. fivefold. ·vijfhoek, n. pentagon. vijf·hoekig, a. pentagonal. ·vijfling, n. quintuplet(s). ·vijftal, -llen, n.n. number or set of five. ·vijftien, num. fifteen. ·vijftiende, a. fifteenth. ¶-n, n.n. fifteenth (part). ·vijftig, num. fifty. ·vijftigste, a. fiftieth. ¶-n, n.n. fiftieth (part). ·vijfvoud, n.n. multiple of five. vijf·voudig, a. fivefold.

vijg, n. fig; pellet of horse-dung. ·vijgeblad, n.n. fig-leaf. ·vijgeboom, -bomen, n. fig-tree. vijgendistel, -s, n. prickly pear. ·vijgeneter, -s, n. fig-eater, beccafico.

vijl, *n.* file. **·vijlen,** *v.t.* to file. **·vijlsel,** no pl., *n.n.* filings.

·vijven, *num.* five. *de trein van* ~, the five o'clock train; *bij* ~, just on five; *in* ~, into five; *met hun* ~, the five of them; *met ons* ~, the five of us; *met z'n* ~, with four others.

vijver, -s, *n.* pond.

·vijzel, -s, *n.* mortar; jack(-screw). **·vijzelen,** *v.t.* to jack (up).

·vilder, -s, *n.* skinner; (horse-)knacker. **vilde·rij,** *n.* knacker's yard. **·villen, vil,** *v.t.* to skin, flay.

vilt, no pl., *n.n.* felt. **·viltachtig,** *a.* felty. **·vilten,** *a.* (of) felt.

vin, -nnen, *n.* fin. *geen* ~ *verroeren,* not to lift a finger.

·vinden, *v.t., str.* to find, come across; to find, think. *hoe vind je het?,* what do you think of it?; *er niets aan* ~, to think it unattractive; *het goed met elkaar* ~, to get on well together; *er is wel iets op te* ~, there is bound to be a solution; *hij is er voor te* ~, he'll be willing. **·vinder, -s,** *n.* finder. **·vinding,** *n.* find, discovery. **·vindingrijk,** *a.* inventive, ingenious. **vinding·rijkheid,** no pl., *n.* inventiveness, ingenuity. **·vindplaats,** *n.* place where . . . is found.

·vinger, -s, *n.* finger. *lange* ~*s hebben,* to be light-fingered; *iets door de* ~*s zien,* to let something pass; *iemand op de* ~*s kijken,* to keep an eye on a person; *iemand op de* ~*s tikken,* to tick a person off. **·vingerafdruk, -kken,** *n.* fingerprint. **·vingerdier,** *n.n.* aye-aye. **·vingerdoekje, -s,** *n.n.* small napkin. **·vingeren,** *v.t.* to finger. **·vingergras,** no pl., *n.n.* panic grass. **·vingerhoed,** *n.* thimble. **·vingerhoedskruid,** no pl., *n.n.* foxglove. **·vingerling,** *n.* finger-stall. **·vingerwijzing,** *n.* hint. **·vingerzetting,** *n.* fingering (*music*).

vink, *n.* finch. **·vinken,** *v.i.* to catch finches. **·vinkeslag,** *n.* finch-trap; note of the finch.

·vinnig, *a.* sharp, cutting, biting. **·vinnigheid,** no pl., *n.* sharpness. **·vinvis, -ssen,** *n.* rorqual.

vio·let, -tte, *a.* violet. ¶no pl., *n.n.* violet. **vio·lier, -s,** *n.* stock-gillyflower. **vio·list,** *n.* violinist. **vi·ool, -iolen,** *n.* violin; violet (*flower*). *op de* ~ *spelen,* to play the violin. **vi·ooltje, -s,** *n.n.* violet, pansy.

vis, -ssen, *n.* fish. **·visachtig,** *a.* fishy. **·visarend,** *n.* osprey. **·visboer,** *n.* fishman. **·visdiefje, -s,** *n.n.* tern. **·visgerei,** no pl., *n.n.* fishing-tackle. **·visgraat, -graten,** *n.* fish-bone. **·viskweker, -s,** *n.* fish-farmer. **·viskwekerij,** *n.* fish-farm, hatchery. **·vislepel, -s,** *n.* fish-slice. **·visotter, -s,** *n.* otter. **·visplaats,** *n.* fishing-ground. **·visreiger, -s,** *n.* heron. **·visrijk,** *a.* abounding in fish. **·visteelt,** no pl., *n.* pisciculture. **·visvangst,** no pl., *n.* fishing,

fishery. **·viswijventaal,** no pl., *n.* Billingsgate.

vi·seren, -seer, *v.t.* to visa. **·visie,** no pl., *n.* ter ~ liggen, to lie open for inspection. **visi·oen,** *n.n.* vision. **vision·nair, -s,** *n.* visionary.

visi·tatie, -s, *n.* customs examination. **vi·site, -s,** *n.* visit, call; visitors, company. *een* ~ *maken,* to pay a visit. **visi·teren, -teer,** *v.t.* to examine, search. **vi·sitekaartje. -s,** *n.n.* visiting card. **visi·teur. -s,** *n.* custom-house officer.

·vissen, vis, *v.i.* to fish, angle. **·visser, -s, n.** fisherman; angler. **visse·rij,** *n.* fishing-industry, fishery. **·vissersbedrijf,** no pl., *n.n.* fishing-industry.

·visum, -s *or* **visa,** *n.n.* visa.

vi·trage, -s, *n.* curtaining. **vi·trine -s,** *n.* shop-window.

·vitten, vit, *v.i.* to find fault, cavil. ~ *op,* to carp at. **·vitter, -s,** *n.* fault-finder, caviller. **·vitterig,** *a.* censorious. **vitte·rij,** *n.* cavilling.

vi·vat, no pl., *n.n.* cheers.

vi·zier, -s, *n.* vizier; visor. *in het* ~ *krijgen* to sight, spot. **vi·zierhoogte, -n,** *n.* elevation. **vi·zierkijker, -s,** *n.* telescopic sights. **vi·zierkorrel, -s,** *n.* bead. **vi·zierlijn,** *n.* line of sight.

vla, vlaas, *n.* custard.

vlaag, vlagen, *n.* squall, gust of wind; shower; access, fit; paroxysm.

Vlaams, *a.* Flemish. ~*e,* Flemish woman. **·Vlaanderen,** *n.N.* Flanders.

vlag, -ggen, *n.* flag, colours. *als een* ~ *op een modderschuit,* out of place; *met* ~ *en wimpel,* with flying colours. **·vlaggedoek,** no pl., *n.n.* bunting. **·vlaggen, vlag,** *v.i.* to put out the flag(s). **·vlaggeschip, -schepen,** *n.n.* flagship. **·vlaggestok, -kken,** *n.* flagstaff. **·vlagvertoon,** no pl., *n.n.* showing the flag.

vlak, -kke, *a.* flat, level. ¶*adv.* flatly; close; immediately; straight, smack, bang. ~ *bij,* close to, near by; *tot* ~ *bij,* right up to; ~ *voor,* right in front of. ¶-kken, *n.n.* plane; flat. *hellend* ~, inclined plane *or* slippery slope. **·vlakgom, -mmen,** *n.n.* india-rubber. **·vlakheid, -heden,** *n.* flatness. **·vlakte, -n,** *n.* plain; sheet (*of water*). *tegen de* ~ *slaan,* to knock down. **·vlaktemaat, -maten,** *n.* square measure. **·vlakuit,** *adv.* flatly.

vlam, -mmen, *n.* flame; grain (*in wood*). *vlammen schieten,* to flame, blaze; *in volle* ~ *staan,* to be ablaze; ~ *vatten,* to catch fire.

·Vlaming, *n.* Fleming.

vlam·kleurig, *a.* flame-coloured. **·vlammen, vlam,** *v.i.* to flame, blaze (up). ¶*v.t.* to water (*silk*). **·vlammenwerper, -s,** *n.* flame-thrower. **·vlampijp,** *n.* boiler-tube, flue. **·vlampijpketel, -s,** *n.* flue-boiler.

vlas, no pl., *n.n.* flax. **·vlasachtig,** *a.* flaxy,

flaxen. **vlasbek, -kken,** *n.* toadflax. **·vlasboer,** *n.* flax-grower. **·vlasbouw,** no pl., *n.* flax-growing. **·vlasbraken,** no pl., *n.n.* braking of flax. **·vlaskoper, -s,** *n.* flax-dealer. **·vlaskruid,** no pl., *n.n.* toadflax. **·vlassen,** *a.* flaxen. ¶ **vlas,** *v.i.* ~ *op,* to look forward to. **·vlasteelt,** no pl., *n.* flax-growing. **·vlasvink,** *n.* linnet. **·vlaszaad,** no pl., *n.n.* flax-seed, linseed.

vlecht, *n.* plait, tress. **·vlechten,** *v.t.* to plait. **·vlechtwerk,** no pl., *n.n.* wicker-work.

·vleermuis, -zen, *n.* bat (*animal*).

vlees, -zen, *n.n.* flesh; meat. *in den vleze,* in the flesh; *het gaat hem naar den vleze,* he is doing well. **·vleesetend,** *a.* carnivorous. **·vleeseter, -s,** *n.* carnivora. **·vleeshal, -llen,** *n.* meat market. **·vleeshouwer, -s,** *n.* butcher. **·vleeshouwe·rij,** *n.* butcher's shop. **vlees·kleurig,** *a.* flesh-coloured. **·vleesloos, -loze,** *a.* meatless. **·vleesmolen, -s,** *n.* mincer. **·vleesnat,** no pl., *n.n.* gravy. **·vleespot, -tten,** *n.* fleshpot.

vleet, vleten, *n.* herring-net. *bij de* ~, in plenty.

·vlegel, -s, *n.* flail; lout, rascal. **·vlegelachtig,** *a.* loutish. **·vlegeljaren,** pl. only, *n.n.* awkward age.

·vleien, *v.t.* to flatter. **·vleier, -s,** *n.* flatterer. **vleie·rij,** *n.* flattery. **·vleister, -s,** *n.* flatterer (*female*). **·vleitaal,** no pl., *n.* flattering words.

vlek, -kken, *n.* spot, blot; stain; village. **·vlekkeloos, -loze,** *a.* spotless. **·vlekken, vlek,** *v.t.* to spot, stain. **·vlektyphus,** no pl., *n.* typhus; spotted fever. **·vlekvrij,** *a.* stainless.

vlerk, *n.* wing; pinion; boor. **·vlerkprauw,** *n.* outrigger canoe.

·vleselijk, *a.* carnal.

vlet, -tten, *n.n.* flat-bottomed boat.

vleug, *n.,* **vleugje, -s,** *n.n.* flicker, spark; waft.

·vleugel, -s, *n.* wing; grand piano. **·vleugeldeur,** *n.* folding-doors. **·vleugelen,** *v.t.* to pinion. **·vleugelloos, -loze,** *a.* wingless. **·vleugelmoer,** *n.* butterfly-nut.

·vleze, *n.n.* See **vlees.** **·vlezig,** *a.* fleshy, meaty.

·vlieden, *v.i.,* str. (*stilted*) to flee, fly.

vlieg, *n.* fly. *iemand een* ~ *afvangen,* to steal a march on a person; *twee* ~*en in één klap vangen,* to kill two birds with one stone. **·vliegboot, -boten,** *n.* flying-boat. **·vliegdienst,** *n.* flying-service, command. **·vliegen,** *v.i.,* str. to fly. *hij ziet ze* ~, he is not all there; *in de lucht* ~, to explode; *in brand* ~, to catch fire; *erin* ~, to get caught. **·vliegend,** *a.* flying. *in* ~*e haast,* in a tearing hurry. **vliege·nier, -s,** *n.* airman. **·vliegenkast,** *n.* meat-safe. **·vliegensvlug,** *adv.* with lightning speed. **·vliegenvanger, -s,** *n.* fly-catcher. **·vlieger, -s,** *n.* kite (*toy*); airman, flyer. **·vliegkamp,**

n.n. aerodrome. **·vliegkampschip, -schepen,** *n.n.* aircraft-carrier. **·vliegkorps, *n.n.*** flying corps. **·vliegmachine, -s,** *n.,* **·vliegtuig,** *n.n.* aeroplane; pl. aircraft. **·vliegwerk,** *n.n.* *met kunst en* ~, by hook or by crook. **·vliegwezen,** no pl., *n.n.* aviation. **·vliegwiel,** *n.n.* fly-wheel.

vlier, *n.* elder. **·vlierbes, -ssen,** *n.* elderberry. **·vliering,** *n.* loft.

vlies, -zen, *n.n.* membrane, skin; fleece. **·vliesridder, -s,** *n.* Knight of the Golden Fleece. **vlies·vleugelig,** *a.* hymenopterous.

vliet, *n.* brook. **·vlieten,** *v.i.,* str. to flow.

·vliezig, *a.* filmy.

·vlijen, *v.t.* to lay down; to nestle.

·vlijm, *n.* lancet. **·vlijmscherp,** *a.* razor-edged.

vlijt, no pl., *n.* industry, diligence. **·vlijtig,** *a.* diligent.

·vlinder, -s, *n.* butterfly. **vlinder·bloemig,** *a.* papilionaceous.

Vlissingen, *n.N.* Flushing.

vloed, *n.* river, stream; flood, high tide; flow, torrent. **·vloedgolf, -ven,** *n.* tidal wave, bore. **vloei,** *n.n.* piece of blotting paper. **·vloeibaar, -bare,** *a.* liquid. ~ *maken,* to liquify. **·vloeibaarheid,** no pl., *n.* fluidity. **·vloeien,** *v.i.* to flow, stream; to blot (*with blotting paper*). **·vloeiend,** *a.* flowing, fluent, smooth. **·vloeipapier,** no pl., *n.n.* blotting paper. **·vloeistof, -ffen,** *n.* liquid.

vloek, *n.* oath, swear word; curse. *in een* ~ *en een zucht,* in the twinkling of an eye. **·vloeken,** *v.i.* to curse, swear; to clash (*colours*).

vloer, *n.* floor. **·vloeren,** *v.t.* to floor. **·vloerkleed, -kleden,** *n.n.* carpet. **·vloerzeil,** *n.n.* linoleum.

vlok, -kken, *n.* flake; flock, tuft. **·vlokkig,** *a.* flaky; flocky.

·vlonder, -s, *n.* plank bridge.

vlo, vlooien, *n.* flea. **·vlooien,** *v.t.* to catch fleas.

vloot, vloten, *n.* fleet; navy. **·vlootbasis, -ases,** *n.* naval base. **·vlootje, -s,** *n.n.* butter dish. **·vlootvoogd,** *n.* (*stilted*) admiral of the fleet.

vlot, -tten, *n.n.* raft. ¶ **-tte,** *a.* afloat; fluent; smooth, easy. **·vlotheid,** no pl., *n.* fluency; smoothness. **·vlotten, vlot,** *v.t.* to raft. ¶ *v.i.* to go smoothly. **·vlottend,** *a.* floating; liquid. **·vlotter, -s,** *n.* raftsman; float.

vlucht, *n.* flight (*through air*); flight, escape; wingspan; flock, bevy. *de* ~ *nemen,* to take to flight; *op de* ~ *jagen,* to put to flight; *op de* ~ *slaan,* to take to flight. **·vluchteling,** *n.* fugitive; refugee. **·vluchten,** *v.i.* to fly, flee. ~ *voor,* to fly from. **·vluchthaven, -s,** *n.* port of refuge. **·vluchtheuvel, -s,** *n.* mound, refuge; traffic island. **·vluchtig,** *a.* fleeting, cursory, casual; volatile. **·vluchtigheid,** no pl., *n.* volatility. **·vluchtplaats,** *n.* asylum, refuge.

vlug, -gge, *a.* quick, fast. ~ *bij,* quick, nimble. **·vluggerd, -s,** *n.* smart boy. **·vlugheid,** no pl., *n.* quickness. **·vlugschrift,** *n.n.* pamphlet. **·vlugzand,** *n.n.* quicksand(s). **·vlugzout,** no pl., *n.n.* sal volatile.

vocht, *n.n.* damp, moisture; liquid, fluid. **·vochtig,** *a.* damp, moist. **·vochtigheid,** no pl., *n.* dampness.

vod, -dden, *n.n.* rag; rubbish. *iemand bij de vodden krijgen,* to get hold of someone. **·voddenkoper, -s,** *n.* rag-and-bone merchant. **·voddenraper, -s,** *n.* rag-picker. **·vodje, -s,** *n.n.* rag; scrap (*of paper*).

voeden, *v.t.* to feed, nourish; to cherish. *zich ~ met,* to feed on. **·voeder,** no pl., *n.n.* fodder. **·voederen,** *v.t.* to feed (*cattle*). **·voeding,** *n.* feeding, nutrition. **·voedingskanaal, -nalen,** *n.n.* alimentary canal. **·voedingsmiddel,** *n.n.* foodstuff. **·voedingswaarde, -n,** *n.* food value. ~ *geven aan,* to strengthen. **·voedster, -s,** *n.* wet-nurse; foster-mother. **·voedsterkind, -eren,** *n.n.* foster-child. **·voedstervader, -s,** *n.* foster-father. **·voedzaam, -zame,** *a.* nourishing, nutritious.

voeg, *n.* joint, seam. *in dier ~e,* in such manner; *uit de ~en rukken,* to put out of joint. **·voegen,** *v.t.* to join; to point (*brickwork*). ~ *bij,* to add to; *zich ~ bij,* to join; *zich ~ naar,* to conform to, comply with. ¶*v.imp.* to become, be fitting. **·voegijzer, -s,** *n.n.* pointing-iron. **·voeglijk,** *a.* becoming, suitable. **·voegwoord,** *n.n.* conjunction. **·voegzaam, -zame,** *a.* suitable, decent. **·voegzaamheid, -heden,** *n.* propriety.

·voelbaar, -bare, *a.* tangible, palpable. **·voelen,** *v.t.* to feel. ~ *voor,* to like, favour. **·voeler, -s,** *n.* **·voelhoorn, -s,** *n.,* **·voelspriet,** *n.* feeler, tentacle. **·voeling,** no pl., *n.* touch, contact. ~ *hebben met,* to be in touch with.

voer, *n.n.* cart-load. ¶no pl., *n.n.* fodder. **·voeren,** *v.t.* to feed; to lead, conduct; to transport; to fly (*flag*); to line. *het bevel ~,* to be in command; *het woord ~,* to be the spokesman, speak. **·voering,** *n.* lining. **·voerman, -lieden** *or* **-lui,** *n.* carter, wagoner; carrier. **·voertaal, -talen,** *n.* medium, vehicle (*language*). **·voertuig,** *n.n.* vehicle, conveyance.

voet, *n.* foot; footing, terms; style. *vijf ~,* five feet; *vaste ~ krijgen,* to obtain a foothold; ~ *bij stuk houden,* to stick to one's guns; *het heeft veel ~en in de aarde,* it takes some doing; *het gaat zover als het ~en heeft,* it is all right as far as it goes; *iemand de ~ lichten,* to oust a person; *met ~en treden,* to trample underfoot; *onder de ~ lopen,* to overrun; *op ~ van oorlog,* on a war footing; *op staande ~,* instantly; *op vrije ~,* at liberty; *op de ~ volgen,* to follow closely; *te ~,* on foot; *ten ~en uit,*

full length; *zich uit de ~en maken,* to take to one's heels; *iemand iets voor de ~en gooien,* to cast something in a person's teeth. **·voetangel, -s,** *n.* mantrap. ~*s en klemmen (fig.),* pitfalls. **·voetbal, -llen,** *n.* football. **·voetballen, -bal,** *v.i.* to play football. **·voetboeien,** pl. only, *n.* fetters. **·voetboog, -bogen,** *n.* crossbow. **·voetbreed,** no pl., *n.n. geen ~ wijken,* not to give an inch. **·voetenbankje, -s,** *n.n.* footstool. **·voetganger, -s,** *n.* pedestrian. **·voetje, -s,** *n.n.* little foot. ~ *voor ~,* step by step; *bij iemand een wit ~ krijgen,* to get into a person's good books. **·voetknecht,** *n.* foot-soldier. **·voetlicht,** *n.n.* footlights. **·voetspoor, -sporen,** *n.n.* footstep; footprint. **·voetstuk, -kken,** *n.n.* pedestal. **·voetval, -llen,** *n.* prostration. **·voetvolk,** no pl., *n.n.* foot-soldiers, foot.

·vogel, -s, *n.* bird. *een slimme ~,* a wily bird. **·vogelaar, -s,** *n.* fowler. **·vogelbekdier,** *n.n.* platypus, duck-mole. **·vogelen,** *v.t.* to catch birds. **·vogellijm,** no pl., *n.* birdlime; mistletoe. **·vogelnest,** *n.n.* bird's nest. **·vogelroer,** *n.n.* fowling-piece. **·vogeltje, -s,** *n.n.* little bird. ~*s die vroeg zingen zijn voor de poes,* don't rejoice too soon. **·vogelverschrikker, -s,** *n.* scarecrow. **·vogelvlucht,** *n.* bird's-eye view. **·vogelvrij,** *a.* outlawed. ~ *verklaren,* to outlaw. **·vogelvrijverklaring,** *n.* outlawry.

Vo·gezen, pl. only, *N.* Vosges.

·voile, -s, *n.* veil.

vol, -lle, *a.* full; full-time. *volle melk,* full-cream milk; *volle neef,* cousin german; *ten volle,* fully, in full; ~ *met,* full of; *iemand niet voor ~ aanzien,* not to take a person quite seriously. **·volbloed,** *a.* thoroughbred. **vol·bloedig,** *a.* full-blooded. **vol·brengen,** *v.t., irr.* to perform, accomplish, achieve. **vol·brenging,** *n.* fulfilment. **vol·daan, -dane,** *a.* satisfied; paid, receipted.

·volder, -s, *n.* fuller. *See* **voller.**

voldoen, doe vol, *v.t.s., irr.* to fill (up). **vol·doen, -doe,** *v.i., irr.* to satisfy. ~ *aan,* to fulfil, comply with, meet. **vol·doend(e),** *a.* satisfactory, sufficient. **vol·doening,** *n.* satisfaction. *ter ~ van,* in settlement of.

vol·dongen, *a.* ~ *feit,* fait accompli.

·volgaarne, *adv.* (*stilted*) with great pleasure.

·volgeling, *n.* adherent, follower. **·volgen,** *v.t.* to follow; to pursue. *colleges ~,* to attend lectures. ¶*v.i.* to follow, ensue. *wie volgt?,* who's next?; ~ *op,* to follow. **·volgend,** *a.* following, next. **·volgenderwijs,** *adv.* as follows. **·volgens,** *prep.* according to; as per.

·volgieten, *v.t.s., str.* to fill (*pour*).

·volgkoets, *n.* mourning coach. **·volgnummer, -s,** *n.n.* serial number.

·volgooien, *v.t.s.* to fill (*throw*).

·volgorde, no pl., *n.* order, sequence. *in ~*, consecutive. ·volgwagen, -s, *n.* trailer (*car*). ·volgzaam, -zame, *a.* docile.
vol·harden, *v.i.* to persevere, persist. vol·harding, *n.* perseverance, tenacity.
·volheid, no pl., *n.* fullness. ·volhouden, *v.t.s.*, *irr.* to keep up, maintain; to sustain. ¶*v.i.*, *irr.* to persevere.
voli·ère, -s, *n.* aviary.
volk, *n.n.* people, nation; people, populace; work-people. *onder het ~ brengen*, to popularize; *een man uit het ~*, a man of the people. ·volkenbond, *n.* See volkerenbond. ·volkenkunde, no pl., *n.* ethnology. ·volkenrecht, no pl., *n.n.* international law. ·volkerenbond, *n.* league of nations. ·volkje, s, *n.n.* people; young people.
vol·komen, *a.* perfect, complete. vol·komenheid, no pl., *n.* perfection, completeness.
·volkplanter, -s, *n.* settler. ·volkplanting, *n.* settlement (*colony*). ·volkrijk, *a.* populous. volks-, *prefix.* people's, popular, national, public. ·volksklasse, -n, *n.* lower classes. ·volksleider, -s, *n.* demagogue. ·volkslied, -eren, *n.n.* popular song; national anthem. ·volkslogies, -zen, *n.n.* fo'c'sle. ·volksmenigte, -n, *n.* crowd, multitude. ·volksmenner, -s, *n.* demagogue. ·volksmond, *n.* *in de ~*, in popular parlance. ·volksoploop, -lopen, *n.* street crowd. ·volksoproer, *n.n.* riot. ·volksrubber, no pl., *n.* native rubber. ·volksstam, -mmen, *n.* native tribe. ·volkstelling, *n.* census. ·volkstuintje, -s, *n.n.* allotment. ·volksverhuizing, *n.* migration of the nations. ·volksvertegenwoordiger, -s, *n.* member of parliament.
·volle, *a.* See vol. vol·ledig, *a.* complete, full. vol·ledigheid, no pl., *n.* completeness. vol·ledigheidshalve, *adv.* for the sake of completeness. vol·leerd, *a.* accomplished; proficient; thorough; past-master. ·vollemaan, -manen, *n.* full moon. ·vollemaansgezicht, *n.n.* pudding face.
·vollen, vol, *v.t.* to full. ·voller, -s, *n.* fuller. volle·rij, *n.* fulling-mill.
·vollopen, loop vol, *v.i.s.*, *str.* to fill, become filled. vol·maakt, *a.* perfect. vol·maaktheid, no pl., *n.* perfection. ·volmacht, *n.* full powers. *bij ~*, by proxy. ·volmachtigen, *v.t.* to empower, authorize. vol·making, *n.* perfection. vol·mondig, *a.* frank, wholehearted. ·volop, *adv.* in plenty; plenty of ...,... galore. ·volproppen, prop vol, *v.t.s.* to stuff. ·volschenken, *v.t.s.*, *str.* to fill (*pour*). ¶ol·slagen, *a.* complete, utter. vol·staan, -sta, *v.i.*, *irr.* to suffice. ·volstorten, *v.t.s.* to pay up (in full). vol·strekt, *a.* absolute. *~ niet*, by no means, not at all. vol·tallig, *a.* complete; up to strength. vol·talligheid, no pl., *n.* completeness. ·volte, no pl., *n.* fullness; crowd, press. vol·tekend, *a.* fully subscribed. vol·tooien, *v.t.* to complete.

vol·tooiing, *n.* completion. ·voltreffer, -s, *n.* direct hit. vol·trekken, -trek, *v.t.*, *str.* to execute, carry into effect; to solemnize (*marriage*). vol·trekking, *n.* execution, accomplishment, solemnization. ·voluit, *adv.* in full. ·volvet, -tte, *a.* full-cream. vol·voeren, *v.t.* (*stilted*) to perform. vol·wassen, *a.* fully-grown, adult. vol·wassene, -n, *n.* adult, grown-up. ·volzin, -nnen, *n.* sentence.
·vondeling, *n.* foundling.
·vonder, -s, *n.* plank bridge.
vondst, *n.* find, discovery.
vonk, *n.* spark. ·vonkelen, *v.i.* to sparkle. ·vonken, *v.i.* to emit sparks. ·vonkvrij, *a.* sparkless.
·vonnis, -ssen, *n.* sentence, judgment. ·vonnissen, -nis, *v.t.* to sentence.
vont, *n.* font.
voogd, *n.* guardian. voog·des, -ssen, *n.* guardian (*female*). voog·dij, *n.* guardianship.
voor, voren, *n.* furrow. ¶*prep.* for, to; for, in favour of; by. *gisteren ~ een week*, yesterday week; *~ een week*, a week ago. ¶*adv.* in (the) front; fast, ahead. *er ~*, for it. ¶no pl., *n.n.* *het ~ en tegen*, the pros and cons. ¶*prefix.* pre-.
voor·aan, *adv.*, in front. voor·aanstaand, *a.* prominent, leading.
voor·af, *adv.* beforehand, previously. voor·afgaan, ga vooraf, *v.i.s.*, *irr.* to precede. voor·afgaand, *a.* preceding, previous, preliminary.
voor·al, *adv.* especially, above all; by all means. *~ niet*, by no means. vooral·eer, *c.* (*stilted*) before. voorals·nog, *adv.* as yet.
·voorarm, *n.* fore-arm.
·voorarrest, *n.n.* detention on remand. *in ~*, on *or* under remand.
·vooravond, *n.* early part of evening; eve.
·voorbaat, no pl., *n.* *bij ~*, in anticipation.
voor·barig, *a.* premature; hasty. voor·barigheid, -heden, *n.* prematureness, hastiness.
·voorbedacht, *a.* premeditated, wilful. *met ~en rade*, with malice aforethought; *~ zijn op*, to be prepared for. ·voorbedachtheid, no pl., *n.* premeditation.
·voorbeeld, *n.n.* example; instance. *een ~ stellen*, to make an example; *bij ~*, for instance; *ten* or *tot ~ stellen*, to hold up as an example. voor·beeldeloos, -loze, *a.* matchless. voor·beeldig, *a.* exemplary.
·voorbehoedmiddel, *n.n.* preservative.
·voorbehoud, no pl., *n.n.* proviso, reservation. *met ~ van*, without prejudice to; *onder ~*, with the proviso; *zonder ~*, unreservedly. ·voorbehouden, *v.t.s.*, *irr.* to reserve. *ongelukken ~*, barring accidents.
·voorbereiden, *v.t.s.* to prepare. *iemand ~*

op, to prepare someone for. ·voorbereidend, *a.* preparatory, preliminary. ·voorberei-ding, *n.* preparation (*action*). *~en treffen*, to make preparations. ·voorbereidsel, *n.n.* preparative.

·voorbericht, *n.n.* preface, foreword.
·voorbeschikken, beschik voor, *v.t.s.* to predestine, pre-ordain. ·voorbeschikking, *n.* predestination.
·voorbestemmen, bestem voor, *v.t.s.* to predestine.
·voorbidden, bid voor, *v.i.s.*, *str.* to lead in prayer.
voor·bij, *prep.* past, beyond. ¶*adv.* past, at an end, over. voor·bijgaan, ga voorbij, *v.i.s.*, *irr.* to go past, go by; to pass, roll by. ¶*v.t.s.*, *irr.* to pass, go past. ¶no pl., *n.n.* in het *~*, in passing; met *~ van*, over the head of. voor·bijgaand, *a.* temporary, transient. voor·bijganger, -s, *n.* passer-by.
·voorbode, -n, *n.* forerunner, harbinger.
·voorchristelijk, *a.* pre-Christian.
·voordacht, no pl., *n.* premeditation. *met ~*, deliberately.
·voordat, *c.* before.
·voordeel, -delen, *n.n.* advantage; profit. *zijn ~ doen met* or *~ trekken uit*, to profit by; *ten voordele van*, for the benefit of. voor·delig, *a.* advantageous, profitable. voor·deligheid, no pl., *n.* advantageousness.
·voordeur, *n.* front door.
·voordoen, doe voor, *v.t.s.*, *irr.* to put on (*in front*). het *~*, to show (*by example*). ¶zich *~*, *v.r.s.*, *irr.* to present itself, arise, crop up. zich *~ als*, to pass oneself off as.
·voordracht, *n.* lecture, address; delivery, diction; nomination. *een ~ indienen*, to submit a list of names. ·voordragen, draag voor, *v.t.s.*, *str.* to recite; to propose (*candidate*).
voor·eerst, *adv.* to begin with; for the time being. *~ niet*, not just yet.
·voorgaan, ga voor, *v.i.s.*, *irr.* to go before; to have precedence; to be fast, gain (*time-piece*). ¶*v.t.s.*, *irr.* iemand *~*, to lead the way. ·voorgaand, *a.* preceding. ·voorganger, -s, *n.* predecessor.
·voorgebergte, -n, *n.n.* promontory, head-land.
·voorgeborchte, no pl., *n.n.* limbo.
·voorgenomen, *a.* contemplated.
·voorgerecht, *n.n.* entrée.
·voorgeschiedenis, no pl., *n.* prehistory; antecedents.
·voorgeslacht, no pl., *n.n.* ancestors, for-bears.
·voorgevallene, no pl., *n.n.* the occurrence, happenings.
·voorgevel, -s, *n.* façade.
·voorgeven, geef voor, *v.t.s.*, *str.* to pretend, profess, purport.
·voorgevoel, -ens, *n.n.* premonition.

voor·goed, *adv.* once and for all; altogether.
·voorgrond, *n.* foreground. *op de ~ treden*, to come to the fore.
voor·handen, *a.* available, in store.
·voorhaven, -s, *n.* outer harbour.
·voorhebben, heb voor, *v.t.s.*, *irr.* to have on (*in front*); to intend; to have the advantage. het goed *~*, to mean well.
voor·heen, *adv.* formerly.
·voorhistorisch, *a.* prehistoric.
·voorhoede, -n, *n.* vanguard, van.
·voorhoofd, *n.n.* forehead.
·voorhouden, *v.t.s.*, *irr.* to hold before. *iemand iets ~*, to expostulate with a person about something.
·voorhuid, *n.* foreskin, prepuce.
·voorin, *adv.* in (the) front, at the beginning.
Voor-·Indië, *n.N.* India and Pakistan.
voor·ingenomen, *a.* prepossessed, prejudiced.
·voorjaar, -jaren, *n.n.* spring. ·voorjaars-nachtevening, *n.* vernal equinox.
·voorkamer, -s, *n.* front room.
·voorkauwen, *v.t.s.* iemand iets *~*, to spoon-feed a person.
·voorkennis, no pl., *n.* foreknowledge, prescience. *buiten mijn ~*, without my knowledge.
·voorkeur, no pl., *n.* preference; first refusal.
·voorkomen, *v.i.s.*, *irr.* to come to the front or head; to appear in court; to happen, occur. *het komt me voor*, it seems to me. ¶no pl., *n.n.* (outward) appearance; presence. voor·komen, *v.t.*, *irr.* to prevent, obviate, avert. ·voorkomend, *a.* occurring. voor·komend, *a.* affable, obliging. voor·koming, no pl., *n. ter ~ van*, for the prevention of.
·voorlaatst, *a.* last but one.
·voorleggen, leg voor, *v.t.s.*, *irr.* to place before; to submit.
·voorletter, -s, *n.* initial.
·voorlezen, lees voor, *v.t.s.*, *str.* to read out.
·voorlichten, *v.t.s.* to light (a person's way); to enlighten. ·voorlichting, no pl., *n.* enlightenment.
·voorliefde, no pl., *n.* predilection.
·voorloper, -s, *n.* precursor. voor·lopig, *a.* provisional, preliminary. ¶*adv.* provisionally, for the time being.
voor·malig, *a.* former.
·voorman, -nnen, *n.* foreman; man in front.
·voormars, -sen, *n.* foretop.
voor·meld, *a.* above-mentioned.
voor·middag, *n.* morning, forenoon.
voorn, *n.* roach, minnow.
voor·naam, -namen, *n.* Christian name, first name. voor·naam, -name, *a.* eminent, distinguished; prominent. ·voornaam-woord, *n.n.* pronoun. voor·namelijk, *adv.* chiefly, principally.
·voornemen, neem voor, zich, *v.r.s.*, *str.* to intend, propose. ¶-s, *n.n.* intention, resolution. *~s zijn*, to have the intention.

voor·noemd, *a.* above-mentioned.
voor·onder, -s, *n.n.* fo'c'sle.
voor·oordeel, -delen, *n.n.* prejudice.
voor·oorlogs, *a.* pre-war.
voor·op, *adv.* in front.
voor·opgaan, ga voorop, *v.i., irr.* to lead the way, walk at the head.
voor·opgezet, -tte, *a.* preconceived.
vooropleiding, *n.* preliminary training.
voorouders, pl. only, *n.* ancestors. **voorouderlijk,** *a.* ancestral.
voor·over, *adv.* forward; prone.
voorpost, *n.* outpost.
voorproef, -ven, *n.* foretaste. **voorproever,** -s, *n.* taster.
·voorraad, -raden, *n.* provision, store, stock. **voor·radig,** *a.* in stock.
voorrang, *n.* precedence; priority.
voorrecht, *n.n.* privilege.
voorrede, -nen, *n.* preface.
voorrijder, -s, *n.* outrider.
voorruim, *n.n.* forehold.
·voorschieten, *v.t.s., str.* to advance, lend.
·voorschijn, *adv.* te ~ brengen, to produce; te ~ komen, to appear.
·voorschoot, -schoten, *n.* apron, pinafore. **·voorschot,** -tten, *n.n.* advance (*money*).
·voorschrift, *n.n.* prescription; regulation.
·voorschrijven, schrijf voor, *v.t.s., str.* to prescribe.
voors·hands, *adv.* (*stilted*) for the time being.
·voorslaan, sla voor, *v.t.s., irr.* to propose. **·voorslag,** *n.* grace note; proposal.
·voorsnijden, *v.t.s., str.* to carve.
·voorspel, *n.n.* prelude. **voor·spellen,** -spel, *v.t.* to foretell, prophesy, forebode. **voor·spelling,** *n.* prophecy, forecast.
·voorspiegelen, *v.t.s.* to hold out (*deceitfully*). zich iets ~, to delude oneself.
·voorspoed, *n.* prosperity. **voor·spoedig,** *a.* prosperous.
·voorspraak, -spraken, *n.* mediator, advocate. ¶no pl., *n.* intercession. **·voorspreken,** spreek, voor, *v.t.s., str.* to say first; to speak in favour of.
·voorsprong, *n.* start, advantage.
·voorstaan, sta voor, *v.t.s., irr.* to advocate. ¶*v.i.s., irr.* to stand in front; to be present in one's memory.
·voorstad, -steden, *n.* suburb.
·voorstander, -s, *n.* advocate, supporter. **voorstanderklier,** *n.* prostate gland.
·voorste, *a.* first, foremost.
·voorstel, -llen, *n.n.* proposal; motion. **·voorstellen,** stel voor, *v.t.s.* to propose, move; to introduce; to represent. ¶zich ~, *v.r.s.* to introduce oneself; to imagine; to visualize. **·voorsteller,** -s, *n.* proposer, mover. **·voorstelling,** *n.* introduction; representation, performance; notion.
·voorsteven, -s, *n.* stem, prow.
voort, *adv.* forward, on.
·voortaan, *adv.* in future.

·voortbestaan, besta voort, *v.i.s., irr.* to continue to exist.
·voortbewegen, beweeg voort, *v.t.s., str.* to move on. **·voortbeweging,** *n.* locomotion.
·voortbrengen, *v.t.s., irr.* to produce. **·voortbrengsel,** -s, *n.n.* product, result; produce.
·voortduren, duur voort, *v.i.s.* to continue, last.
·voorteken, -s *or* -en, *n.n.* sign, omen.
·voortgaan, ga voort, *v.i.s., irr.* to continue, go on. **·voortgang,** no pl., *n.* progress. ~ maken, to proceed, get on.
·voortmaken, maak voort, *v.i.s.* to make haste.
·voortplanten, *v.t.s.* to propagate; to transmit. **·voortplanting,** *n.* propagation; reproduction; transmission.
voor·treffelijk, *a.* excellent. **voor·treffelijkheid,** -heden, *n.* excellence.
·voortrekken, trek voor, *v.t.s., str.* to favour.
voorts, *adv.* moreover, besides.
·voorttrekken, trek voort, *v.t.s., str.* to drag along. ¶*v.i.s., irr.* to march on.
voort·varend, *a.* go-ahead, energetic.
voort·vluchtig, *a.* fugitive.
·voortzetten, zet voort, *v.t.s.* to continue, prosecute, proceed on. **·voortzetting,** *n.* continuation.
voor·uit, *adv.* forward; ahead; beforehand, in advance. **voor·uitgaan, ga vooruit,** *v.i.s., irr.* to lead the way; to get on, improve. **voor·uitgang,** *n.* progress. **voor·uit·strevend,** *a.* progressive. **voor·uitzicht,** *n.n.* prospect.
·voorvader, -s, *n.* ancestor.
·voorval, -llen, *n.n.* incident, occurrence. **·voorvallen, val voor,** *v.i.s., str.* to occur, happen.
·voorvechter, -s, *n.* champion.
·voorvoegsel, -s, *n.n.* prefix.
voor·waar, *adv.* truly, indeed.
·voorwaarde, -n, *n.* condition; *pl.* terms. onder geen ~, on no account. **voor·waardelijk,** *a.* conditional.
·voorwaarts, *a. & adv.* forward, onward(s).
·voorwenden, *v.t.s.* to pretend, profess. **·voorwendsel,** -s, *n.n.* pretext, pretence.
voor·wereldlijk, *a.* prehistoric.
·voorwerp, *n.n.* object. **·voorwerpen,** *v.t.s., str.* to throw before.
·voorzaat, -zaten, *n.* (*stilted*) ancestor.
·voorzanger, -s, *n.* precentor.
voor·zegd, *a.* aforesaid.
·voorzetsel, -s, *n.n.* preposition.
voor·zichtig, *a.* careful, cautious. **voor·zichtigheid,** no pl., *n.* prudence, care, caution. **voor·zichtigheidshalve,** *adv.* as a precaution.
voor·zien, -zie, *v.t., irr.* to foresee, expect. ~ van, to provide *or* furnish with. ¶*v.i., irr.* ~ in, to supply, meet, cater for. **voor·zienigheid,** no pl., *n.* providence. **voor·ziening,** *n.* provision, supply.
·voorzitten, zit voor, *v.i.s., str.* to preside, be

in the chair. ·voorzitter, -s, *n.* president, chairman. ·voorzitterschap, -ppen, *n.* presidency, chairmanship.
voorzo·ver, *c.* insofar.
voos, -voze, *a.* rotten; woolly (*radish*).
·vorderen, *v.t.* to demand, claim. ¶*v.i.* to progress. ·vordering, *n.* demand, claim; progress, advance.
·vore, -n, *n.* furrow.
voren, *adv.* naar ∼, forward, to the front; *te* ∼, beforehand; *van* ∼, in front; *van* ∼ *af* (*aan*), from the beginning, afresh; *van te* ∼, beforehand.
·vorig, *a.* former, previous.
vork, *n.* fork. *weten hoe de* ∼ *in de steel zit*, to know what's what. ·vorkbeen, -deren, *n.n.* wishbone.
vorm, *n.* form, shape; formality; convention; mould. *naar de* ∼, in due form. ·vormelijk, *a.* formal, conventional. ·vormeling, *n.* confirmee. ·vormen, *v.t.* to form, shape, frame; to confirm (*Roman Catholic*). ∼ *naar*, to model upon. ¶*zich* ∼, *v.r.* to form. ·vorming, *n.* formation. ·vormleer, no pl., *n.* elementary geometry; accidence (*grammar*). ·vormloos, -loze, *a.* shapeless. ·vormloosheid, no pl., *n.* shapelessness.
vors, *n.* frog.
·vorsen, *v.i.* ∼ *naar*, to investigate.
vorst, *n.* frost; monarch, prince; ridge (*roof*). ·vorstelijk, *a.* princely, royal; munificent. ·vorstendom, -mmen, *n.n.* principality. ·vorstenhuis, -zen, *n.n.* dynasty. ·Vorstenlanden, pl. only, *n.n.* Principalities (*Oriental*). vors·tin, -nnen, *n.* queen, empress. ·vorstvrij, *a.* frost-proof.
vos, -ssen, *n.* fox; sorrel. ·vossen, vos, *v.i.* to swot (*study*). ·vossenjacht, no pl., *n.* fox-hunting.
vouw, *n.* fold, crease. *uit de* ∼, uncreased. ·vouwbaar, -bare, *a.* foldable, pliable. ·vouwbeen, -benen, *n.n.* paper-knife. ·vouwblad, *n.n.* folder. ·vouwdeur, *n.* folding-door(s). ·vouwen, *v.t.* to fold. ·vouwstoel, *n.* deck-chair.
vraag, vragen, *n.* question; demand (*commercial*). ∼ *en aanbod*, supply and demand; *dat is de* ∼, that remains to be seen; ∼ *naar*, to ask for. ·vraagbaak, -baken, *n.* oracle. ·vraaggesprek, -kken, *n.n.* interview. ·vraagsgewijs, *adv.* by way of question and answer. ·vraagstuk, -kken, *n.n.* problem. ·vraagteken, *n.n.* question mark.
vraat, vraten, *n.* glutton. ·vraatzucht, no pl., *n.* voracity, gluttony. vraat·zuchtig, *a.* voracious.
vracht, *n.* load, cargo, freight; freight(age). ·vrachtauto, -'s, *n.* lorry. ·vrachtboot, -boten, *n.* freighter. ·vrachtbrief, -ven, *n.* bill of lading; consignment note. ·vrachtcontract, *n.n.* charter-party. ·vrachtdienst, *n.* cargo-service. ·vrachtgoed, -deren, *n.n.* cargo, goods. ·vrachtlijst, *n.* manifest.

·vrachtrijder, -s, *n.* carrier, carter. ·vrachtvaarder, -s, *n.* freighter; freighter captain. ·vrachtvaart, no pl., *n.* carrying trade. ·vrachtwagen, -s, *n.* truck, van.
vragen, vraag, *v.t.*, *str.* to ask. ∼ *naar*, to ask after, inquire for *or* after; ∼ *om*, to ask for. ·vragend, *a.* inquiring, interrogative. ·vragenlijst, *n.* questionnaire. ·vrager, -s, *n.* inquirer.
·vrede, -s, *n.* peace. ∼ *sluiten*, to make *or* conclude peace; ∼ *stichten*, to bring about peace; ∼ *hebben met*, to be content with. vrede·lievend, *a.* peace-loving, peaceful. vrede·lievendheid, no pl., *n.* love of peace, peaceableness. ·vrederechter, -s, *n.* justice of the peace. ·vredesnaam, *adv.* *in* ∼, for goodness sake. ·vredestichter, -s, *n.* peacemaker. ·vredig, *a.* peaceful, quiet. ·vreedzaam, -zame, *a.* peaceable; pacific.
vreemd, *a.* strange; foreign; queer. *ergens* ∼ *zijn*, to be a stranger somewhere. ·vreemde, -n, *n.* stranger. *in de* ∼, abroad, in foreign parts. ·vreemdeling, *n.* stranger; foreigner. ·vreemdelingenbureau, -'s, *n.n.* tourist office. ·vreemdelingenlegioen, *n.n.* foreign legion. ·vreemdheid, -heden, *n.* queerness. vreemd·soortig, *a.* peculiar, singular.
vrees, vrezen, *n.* fear, dread. ∼ *voor*, fear of *or* for. vreesaan·jagend, *a.* terrifying. vrees·achtig, *a.* timid. vrees·wekkend, *a.* terrifying.
·vreetzak, -kken, *n.* glutton.
vrek, -kken, *n.* miser. ·vrekachtig, *a.* miserly.
·vreselijk, *a.* terrible, dreadful, awful.
·vreten, vreet, *v.t.*, *str.* to eat (*of animal*); to eat voraciously, gorge. ·vreter, -s, *n.* greedy eater.
·vreugde, no pl., *n.* joy. ·vreugdeloos, -loze, *a.* joyless. ·vreugdeschot, *n.n.* salute (*shot*). ·vreugdevol, -lle, *a.* full of joy.
·vreze, *n.* See vrees. ·vrezen, vrees, *v.t.* & *v.i.* to fear, dread.
vriend, *n.* friend. *iemand te* ∼ *houden*, to keep in well with. ·vriendelijk, *a.* friendly, kind. ·vriendelijkheid, -heden, *n.* friendliness, kindness. ·vriendendienst, *n.* friendly service. vrien·din, -nnen, *n.* friend (*female*). ·vriendschap, no pl., *n.* friendship. vriendschappelijk, *a.* friendly, amicable.
·vriespunt, no pl., *n.n.* freezing point. ·vriesweer, no pl., *n.n.* frosty weather. ·vriezen, vries, *v.imp.*, *irr.* to freeze.
vrij, *a.* free. *de* ∼*e kunsten*, the liberal arts; ∼ *kwartier*, break (*at school*); ∼*e tijd*, spare time, leisure; *een* ∼*e dag*, a day off; ∼ *krijgen*, to get time off; ∼ *van*, free from. ¶*adv.* freely; rather, pretty, fairly. ·vrijaf, *a.* ∼ *hebben*, to have time off.
vrij·age, no pl., *n.* courtship.
·vrijblijvend, *a.* free, without prejudice. ·vrijbrief, -ven, *n.* passport, permit. ·vrijbuiter, -s, *n.* freebooter. vrijbuite·rij, *n.* privateering.

·vrijdag, *n.* Friday. *'s* ~*s*, on Friday(s). ·vrijdags, *a.* Friday.

·vrijdenker, -s, *n.* free-thinker. vrijdenke·rij, *n.* free-thinking. ·vrijdom, -mmen, *n.* exemption. ·vrije, -n, *n.* freeman. ·vrijelijk, *adv.* freely.

·vrijen, *v.i.* to court, make love, spoon. ·vrijer, -s, *n.* sweetheart, suitor. ·vrije-rij, *n.* courting.

·vrijgeleide, -n, *n.n.* safe-conduct. ·vrijgeven, geef vrij, *v.t.s.*, *str.* to release; to give time off. vrij·gevig, *a.* liberal, generous. vrij·gevigheid, no pl., *n.* liberality. vrijge-·zel, -llen, *n.* bachelor. ·vrijhandel, no pl., *n.* free trade. ·vrijheer, -heren, *n.* baron. ·vrijheid, no pl., *n.* freedom, liberty. *dichterlijke* ~, poetic licence; *de* ~ *nemen*, to make free; *zich een* ~ *veroorloven*, to take a liberty; *in* ~, at liberty. ¶-heden, *n.* charter, privilege. ·vrijheid·lievend, *a.* freedom-loving. ·vrijheidsliefde, no pl., *n.* love of freedom. ·vrijheidsoorlog, *n.* war of independence. ·vrijhouden, *v.t.s.*, *irr.* to keep free; to pay for someone's entertainment. ·vrijkaart, *n.* complimentary ticket, free pass. ·vrijlaten, laat vrij, *v.t.s.*, *str.* to release. ·vrijlating, *n.* release. ·vrijmaken, maak vrij, *v.t.s.* to free, emancipate. ·vrijmaking, *n.* liberation, emancipation. vrij·metselaar, -s, *n.* freemason. vrij·metselaarsloge, -s, *n.* masonic lodge *or* hall. vrijmetsela·rij, no pl., *n.* freemasonry. vrij·moedig, *a.* frank, candid. vrij·moedigheid, -heden, *n.* frankness, boldness. ·vrijpleiten, *v.t.s.* to exculpate, exonerate. vrij·postig, *a.* bold, forward. vrij·postigheid, -heden, *n.* boldness. ·vrijspraak, -spraken, *n.* acquittal. ·vrijspreken, spreek vrij, *v.t.s.*, *str.* to acquit. ·vrijstaan, sta vrij, *v.i.s.*, *irr.* to stand by oneself; to be permitted. *het staat U vrij*, you are free to. ·vrijstellen, stel vrij, *v.t.s.* to exempt. ·vrijstelling, *n.* exemption.

·vrijster, -s, *n.* sweetheart (*female*). *ouwe* ~, old maid.

·vrijuit, *adv.* freely, openly. ·vrijwaren, -waar, *v.t.* to safeguard. ~ *voor* or *tegen*, to safeguard from or against. ·vrijwaring, *n.* safeguard(ing). ·vrijwel, *adv.* practically. vrij·willig, *a.* voluntary. vrij·zinnig, *a.* liberal, progressive. vrij·zinnigheid, no pl., *n.* liberalism.

vrind, *n.* *See* vriend.

vroed, *a.* wise, prudent. *de* ~*e vaderen*, the city fathers. ·vroedkunde, no pl., *n.* midwifery. ·vroedschap, -ppen, *n.* town council. ·vroedvrouw, *n.* midwife.

vroeg, *a.* early. ¶*adv.* early. *te* ~, (too) early; *niets te* ~, none too soon; ~ *of laat*, sooner or later. ·vroeger, *a.* earlier, former, previous. ¶*adv.* earlier, sooner; formerly. ·vroegmetten, pl. only, *n.* matins. ·vroeg-mis, -ssen, *n.* early mass. ·vroegrijp, *a.*

precocious, premature. vroeg·rijpheid, no pl., *n.* precocity. ·vroegte, no pl., *n.* *in de* ~, early in the morning. vroeg-·tijdig, *a.* early. ¶*adv.* betimes, at an early hour.

·vrolijk, *a.* merry, jolly, gay, cheerful. ·vrolijkheid, no pl., *n.* mirth, gaiety, cheerfulness.

·vromelijk, *adv.* piously. vroom, vrome, *a.* pious, devout. ·vroomheid, no pl., *n.* piety.

vrouw, *n.* woman; wife; queen (*cards*). *de* ~ *des huizes*, the mistress of the house; *moeder de* ~, the old girl; ~ *Jansen*, Mrs. Jansen (*working class*). ·vrouw-achtig, *a.* womanish. ·vrouwelijk, *a.* feminine; female; womanly. ·vrouwelijkheid, no pl., *n.* femininity. ·vrouwenarts, *n.* gynaecologist. ·vrouwengek, -kken, *n.* philanderer. ·vrouwenklooster, -s, *n.n.* nunnery, convent. ·vrouwenmunt, no pl., *n.* alecost mint, costmary. ·vrouwen-regering, no pl., *n.* petticoat government. ·vrouwenroof, no pl., *n.* abduction. ·vrouwenschoentje, -s, *n.n.* lady's slipper. ·vrouwlief, no pl., *n.* my dear wife. ·vrouwmens, *n.n.*, ·vrouwspersoon, -sonen, *n.* woman, female. ·vrouwvolk, no pl., *n.n.* womenfolk.

vrucht, *n.* fruit. *met* ~, with success; *zonder* ~, fruitless. ·vruchtafdrijvend, *a.* abortifacient. ·vruchtafdrijving, *n.* abortion. ·vruchtbaar, -bare, *a.* fruitful; fertile; prolific. ·vruchtbaarheid, no pl., *n.* fruitfulness; fertility; fecundity. ·vruchtbeginsel, -s, *n.n.* ovary (*plants*). ·vruchtbekleedsel, -s, *n.n.* capsule (*plants*). ·vruchtdragend, *a.* fruit-bearing. ·vruchteloos, -loze, *a.* fruitless; vain, futile. ·vruchteloosheid, no pl., *n.* futility. ·vruchtengelei, *n.* jam. ·vruchtgebruik, no pl., *n.n.* usufruct. ·vruchtkiem, *n.* germ, embryo. ·vruchtvorming, no pl., *n.* fructification.

vuig, *a.* vile, base.

vuil, *a.* dirty; smutty. ~*e was*, dirty linen. ¶no pl., *n.n.* dirt. ·vuilbek, -kken, *n.* foul-mouthed person. ·vuiligheid, -heden, *n.* dirty, smut. ·vuilik, -kken, *n.* dirty-minded person. ·vuilmaken, maak vuil, *v.t.s.* to dirty, soil. ·vuilnis, no pl., *n.* refuse, dirt. ·vuilnisbak, -kken, *n.* dustbin. ·vuilnisbelt, *n.* rubbish-dump. ·vuilpoes, -zen, *n.* dirty person. ·vuilte, no pl., *n.* dirt. ·vuiltje, -s, *n.n.* speck of dirt. *er was geen* ~ *aan de lucht*, everything in the garden was lovely.

vuist, *n.* fist. *met ijzeren* ~, with a grip of iron; *voor de* ~, unprepared, extempore. ·vuistje, -s, *n.n.* little fist. *in zijn* ~ *lachen*, to laugh up one's sleeve; *uit het* ~ *eten*, to have an impromptu meal. ·vuistrecht, no pl., *n.n.* club-law.

·vulhaard, *n.* anthracite stove.

vul·kaan, -kanen, *n.* volcano.

·vullen, vul, *v.t.* to fill; to stuff. ·vulling, *n.* filling; stuffing; stopping. ·vulpen, -nnen, *n.* fountain pen. ·vulsel, -s, *n.n.* stuffing.
vuns, -ze, *a.*, ·vunzig, *a.* musty, fusty, stale. ·vuren, vuur, *v.i.* to fire. ~ op, to fire at *or* on. ¶no pl., *n.n.* firing. ·vurenhout, no pl., *n.n.* deal. ·vurenhouten, *a.* (of) deal. ·vurig, *a.* fiery; ardent, fervent. ·vurigheid, no pl., *n.* fieriness, ardour, spirit. vuur, vuren, *n.n.* fire, fire-place; beacon, light. ¶ no pl., *n.n.* fire (*element*); fire (*shooting*); zeal; blight; gangrene. ~ en licht, heating and lighting; ~ slaan, to strike a light; het ~ na aan de schenen leggen, to press a person hard; zich het ~ uit de sloffen lopen, to run oneself off one's legs; in het ~ van, in the heat of; in ~ en vlam, ablaze; te ~ en te zwaard, with fire and sword. ·vuurdood, no pl., *n.* death by fire. ·vuurdoop, no pl., *n.* baptism of fire. ·vuurgloed, no pl., *n.* fiery glow, blaze. ·vuurgoudhaantje, -s, *n.n.* crested wren. ·vuurkever, -s, *n.* firefly. ·Vuurland, *n.N.* Terra del Fuego. ·Vuurlander, -s, *N.* Fuegian. ·vuurleiding, *n.* fire-control. ·vuurlinie, -s, *n.* line of fire. ·vuurmaker, -s, *n.* fire-lighter. ·vuurmond, *n.* gun, cannon. ·vuurpeloton, -s, *n.n.* firing squad. ·vuurpijl, *n.* rocket. ·vuurproef, -ven, *n.* trial by fire, ordeal. de ~ doorstaan, to stand the test. ·vuurrood, -rode, *a.* flaming red. ~ worden, to blush scarlet. ·vuurschip, -schepen, *n.n.* lightship. ·vuursnelheid, -heden, *n.* rate of fire. ·vuurspuwend, *a.* fire-spitting. ~e berg, volcano. ·vuursteen, -stenen, *n.* flint. ·vuurtoren, -s, *n.* lighthouse. ·vuurvast, *a.* fireproof. ~e steen, fire-brick. ·vuurvreter, -s, *n.* fire-eater. ·vuurwerk, no pl., *n.n.* firework(s). ·vuurzee, -zeeën, *n.* sea *or* sheet of fire.

W

·waadbaar, -bare, *a.* fordable. ·waadvogel, -s, *n.* wading-bird.
waag, wagen, *n.* balance; weigh-hou_e. een hele ~, a risky business. ·waaghals, -zen, *n.* daredevil. ·waaghalze·rij, *n.* daredevilry. ·waagschaal, schalen, *n.* scale. in de ~ liggen, to tremble in the balance. ·waagstuk, -kken, *n.n.* risky undertaking.
·waaien, *v.t.*, irr. to blow (of *wind*); to fly, flutter (*flag*). laat maar ~, never mind. ·waaier, -s, *n.* fan. waaier·vormig, *a.* fan-shaped.
waak, waken, *n.* vigil. ·waakhond, *n.* watchdog. waaks, *a.* watchful. ·waakzaam, -zame, *a.* watchful, vigilant, alert. ·waakzaamheid, no pl., *n.* watchfulness.
Waal, *N.* Waal (*river*). ¶ Walen, *n.* Walloon. Waals, *a.* Walloon.
waan, no pl., *n.* delusion, false belief. in de

~ brengen, to lead to think; in de ~ verkeren, to labour under the delusion. ·waanwijs, -ze, *a.* conceited, bumptious. ·waanzin, no pl., *n.* madness, insanity. waan·zinnig, *a.* mad, insane, crazy. waan·zinnige, -n, *n.* madman, lunatic.
waar, ware, *a.* true. ~ maken, to prove. ¶ adv. truly; where. ~ ook, wherever. ¶ c. where. ¶ waren, *n.* ware(s). ~ voor z'n geld, value for money. waar·aan, adv. to *or* on which, of whom; to *or* of what. waar·achter, adv. behind which, behind whom, behind what. waar·achtig, *a.* true, veritable. ¶ adv. truly; sure enough. waar·bij, adv. by *or* near which. ·waarborg, *n.* guarantee; security. ·waarborgen, v.t. to guarantee. ~ tegen, to secure against. ·waarborgsom, -mmen, *n.* security. waar·boven, adv. above whom *or* which *or* what.
waard, *a.* worth; worthy, dear. ¶ *n.* innkeeper, landlord; drake; holm. zoals de ~ is vertrouwt hij zijn gasten, people suspect others of their own failings. ·waarde, -n, *n.* worth, value; pl. stocks, shares, securities. ~ hechten aan, to set store by; naar ~ schatten, to estimate at its true value; ter ~ van, to the value of; van nul en gener ~, null and void. ·waardeloos, -loze, *a.* worthless. ·waarderecht, *n.n.* ad valorem duty. ·waarderen, -deer, v.t. to appreciate; to value. waar·derend, *a.* appreciative. waar·dering, *n.* appreciation, esteem; valuation. ·waardevol, -lle, *a.* valuable. ·waardig, *a.* worthy, dignified. ·waardigheid, -heden, *n.* dignity; dignity, office. ·waardigheidsbekleder, -s, *n.* dignitary.
waar·din, -nnen, *n.* landlady, innkeeper (*female*).
waar·door, adv. through *or* by which *or* what. waar·heen, adv. where, where to, whither. ·waarheid, -heden, *n.* truth; veracity. een ~ als een koe, a truism; achter de ~ komen, to find out the truth; naar ~, truthfully. waarheid·lievend, *a.* truthful.
waar·in, adv. in which *or* what. waar·langs, adv. along which *or* what.
·waarlijk, adv. truly, indeed.
waar·mee, adv. with which *or* whom *or* what. ·waarmerk, *n.n.* hall-mark, stamp. ·waarmerken, v.t. to stamp, authenticate; to hall-mark.
waar·na, adv. after which. waar·naar, adv. at which *or* whom *or* what. waar·naast, adv. beside which *or* whom *or* what.
waar·neembaar, -bare, *a.* perceptible. ·waarnemen, neem waar, v.t.s., str. to observe, perceive; to perform, attend to. de praktijk ~ van, to deputize for (*doctor*). ·waarnemend, *a.* acting, deputy. ·waarnemer, -s, *n.* observer; deputy, locum tenens. ·waarneming, *n.* observation; deputizing.

waar·om, *adv.* round which; why. **waarom-**
·trent, *adv.* about which. **waar·onder,** *adv.*
under *or* among which *or* whom. **waar·op,**
adv. on which; whereupon. **waar·over,**
adv. about which.
waar·schijnlijk, *a.* probable, likely. **waar-**
·schijnlijkheid, -heden, *n.* probability.
·waarschuwen, *v.t.* to warn. **·waarschuwing,**
n. warning; demand notice.
waar·tegen, *adv.* against which *or* whom *or*
what. **waar·toe,** *adv.* for which, for what.
waar·tussen, *adv.* between which *or* whom
or what. **waar·uit,** *adv.* from which *or*
what. **waar·voor,** *adv.* why; for which *or*
whom.
·waarzeggen, zeg waar, *v.i.s.,* *irr.* to tell
fortunes. **·waarzegger, -s,** *n.* fortune-
teller, soothsayer. **·waarzegster, -s,** *n.*
fortune-teller (*female*).
waas, no pl., *n.n.* haze; bloom.
wacht, *n.* watchman, sentry; watch, guard;
guard-house. *de* ~ *hebben,* to be on guard
or watch; *de* ~ *houden,* to keep watch;
~ *lopen,* to stand watches; *in de* ~ *slepen,*
to collar.
·wachtel, -s, *n.* quail.
·wachten, *v.i.* to wait. *het staat hem te* ~,
it is in store for him; ~ *op,* to wait for.
¶ *v.t.* to await. ¶ *v.r. zich* ~ *voor,* to be
on one's guard against. **·wachter, -s,** *n.*
watchman. **·wachtgeld,** *n.n.* half-pay.
·wachtgelder, -s, *n.* person on half-pay.
·wachthond, *n.* watchdog. **·wachthuisje, -s,**
n.n. sentry-box. **·wachtkamer, -s,** *n.*
waiting room. **·wachtmeester, -s,** *n.*
sergeant-major (*cavalry*). **·wachtwoord,**
n.n. password, watchword.
wad, -dden, *n.n.* mud-flat, shallow.
·Waddeneiland, *n.N.* Frisian Island.
·wade, -n, *n.* shroud.
·waden, waad, *v.i.* to wade. ~ *door,* to ford.
waf, *int.* ~ ~, bow-wow.
·wafel, -s, *n.* waffle.
·wagen, -s, *n.* cart, wagon. *krakende* ~*s*
lopen het langst, creaking doors hang
longest. ¶ **waag,** *v.t.* to venture, risk.
wie waagt die wint, faint heart never won
fair lady; *ze zijn aan elkaar gewaagd,* it is
diamond cut diamond. ¶ **waag, zich,** *v.r.*
zich ~ *aan,* to venture on. **·wagenhuis,**
-zen, *n.n.* cartshed, coach-house. **·wagen-**
maker, -s, *n.* cartwright; coachbuilder.
·wagenmenner, -s, *n.* charioteer. **·wagen-**
smeer, no pl., *n.n.* cart-grease. **·wagenwijd,**
adv. wide. **·wagenziek,** *a.* train-sick.
·waggelen, *v.i.* to waddle; to totter, toddle.
wa·gon, -s, *n.* (*railway*) carriage or truck.
·wajang, -s, *n.* wayang.
wak, -kken, *n.n.* air-hole (*in ice*).
·wake, -n, *n.* vigil. **·waken, waak,** *v.i.* to
watch. ~ *bij,* to sit up with; ~ *tegen,*
to guard against; *er voor* ~ *dat,* to take
care that. **·waker, -s,** *n.* watcher; outer
dyke. **·wakker,** *a.* awake; alert, brisk.

~ *maken,* to wake; ~ *worden,* to wake up.
·wakkeren, *v.i.* to freshen. **·wakkerheid,**
no pl., *n.* briskness.
wal, -llen, *n.* rampart; shore; embankment.
aan ~, ashore, on shore; *aan lager* ~
geraken, to get into low water; *van de* ~
in de sloot, from the frying-pan into the
fire; *van* ~ *steken,* to push off, go
ahead. **·walbaas, -bazen,** *n.* wharfinger.
·waldhoorn, -s, *n.* French horn.
·walgelijk, *a.* loathsome, nauseating. **·walgen,**
v.i. to nauseate. ~ *van,* to be nauseated
by, loathe. ¶ no pl., *n.n. tot* ~*s toe,*
ad nauseam. **·walging,** *n.* loathing,
disgust; nausea.
·walkapitein, -s, *n.* shore superintendent.
walm, *n.* oily *or* sooty smoke. **·walmen,** *v.i.*
to smoke.
·walnoot, -noten, *n.* walnut.
·walrus, -ssen, *n.* walrus.
wals, *n.* waltz; (rolling) cylinder. **·walsen,**
v.i. to waltz. ¶ *v.t.* to roll (*steel*). **·walser,**
-s, *n.* waltzer.
·walstro, no pl., *n.n.* bedstraw (*plant*).
·walvis, -ssen, *n.* whale. **·walvisbaard,** *n.*
whalebone, baleen. **·walvisspek,** no pl.,
n.n. blubber. **·walvistraan,** no pl., *n.*
train-oil. **·walvisvaarder, -s,** *n.* whaler.
wam, -mmen, *n.* dewlap. **·wambuis, -zen,**
n.n. jerkin, doublet.
·wanbedrijf, -ven, *n.n.* crime. **·wanbegrip,**
-ppen, *n.n.* false notion. **·wanbeheer,** no
pl., *n.n.,* **·wanbeleid,** no pl., *n.n.,* **·wan-**
bestuur, no pl., *n.n.* maladministration,
mismanagement. **·wanbetaler, -s,** *n.*
defaulter. **·wanbetaling,** *n.* non-payment.
·wanbof, no pl., *n.* bad luck. **·wanboffen,**
-bof, *v.i.* to be out of luck.
wand, *n.* wall.
·wandaad, -daden, *n.* crime.
·wandel, no pl., *n.* walk; behaviour, conduct.
aan or *op de* ~, out walking. **·wandelaar,**
-s, *n.* walker. **·wandelen,** *v.i.* to walk.
gaan ~, to go for a walk. ¶ *n.n. uit* ~
gaan, to go walking. **·wandelhoofd,** *n.n.*
promenade pier. **·wandeling,** *n.* walk,
stroll. *een* ~ *doen,* to take a walk; *in de* ~,
popularly. **·wandelstok, -kken,** *n.* walking-
stick.
·wandgedierte, no pl., *n.n.* bugs. **·wandluis,**
-zen, *n.* bug.
·wanen, waan, *v.t.* to imagine.
wang, *n.* cheek.
·wangedrag, no pl., *n.n.* bad conduct.
·wangedrocht, *n.n.* monster. **·wangunst,**
no pl., *n.* envy.
·wangzak, -kken, *n.* cheek-pouch.
·wanhoop, no pl., *n.* despair. *uit* ~, in
despair. **·wanhopen, -hoop,** *v.i.* to despair.
wan·hopig, *a.* desperate, despairing.
·wankel, *a.* unsteady, shaky. **·wankelbaar,**
-bare, *a.* unsteady; labile. **·wankelen,** *v.i.*
to totter, rock; to waver. **wankel·moedig,**
a. vacillating, irresolute.

·wanklank, *n.* discordant note.
·wanmolen, -s, *n.* winnowing mill.
wan·neer, *adv.* when. ¶ *c.* whenever.
·wannen, wan, *v.t.* to winnow.
·wanorde, no pl., *n.* disorder. wan·ordelijk, *a.* disorderly. wan·ordelijkheid, no pl., *n.* disorderliness. wan·schapen, *a.* misshapen. ·wansmaak, no pl., *n.* bad taste, lack of taste. wan·smakelijk, *a.* in bad taste. wan·staltig, *a.* misshapen.
want, *n.n.* rigging. ¶ *n.* mitten. ¶ *c.* for.
·wantrouwen, no pl., *n.n.* distrust; suspicion. wan·trouwend, *a.* distrustful, suspicious. ·wanverhouding, *n.* disproportion; bad state of affairs.
·wapen, -s *or* -en, *n.n.* weapon. ¶ -s, *n.n.* arm (*military · service*); (coat of) arms. *onder de ~s roepen,* to call to the colours. ·wapenbroeder, -s, *n.* comrade in arms. ·wapendos, no pl., *n.* full armour *or* panoply. ·wapenen, *v.t.* to arm. ·wapenfabriek, *n.* arms-factory. ·wapenfeit, *n.n.* feat of arms. ·wapenhandel, no pl., *n.* use of arms. ·wapening, no pl., *n.* arming. ·wapenkunde, no pl., *n.* heraldry. ·wapenmagazijn, *n.n.* arsenal. ·wapenrok, -kken, *n.* tunic. ·wapenrusting, *n.* armour. ·wapenschild, *n.n.* scutcheon. ·wapensmid, -smeden, *n.* armourer. ·wapenspreuk, *n.* heraldic device. ·wapenstilstand, *n.* armistice.
·wapperen, *v.i.* to fly, wave (*flag*). *doen ~,* to fly (*flag*).
war, no pl., *n. in de ~,* disarranged, untidy; *in de ~ raken,* to get confused; *in de ~ sturen,* to upset, disarrange.
wa·rande, -s, *n.* pleasure garden.
·warboel, no pl., *n.* muddle, confusion.
wa·rempel, *adv.* See waarachtig.
·waren, waar, *v.i.* to wander.
·warenhuis, -zen, *n.n.* (department) stores.
·warhoofd, *n.n.* muddle-head. war·hoofdig, *a.* muddle-headed.
wa·ringin, -s, *n.* banyan-tree.
·warkruid, no pl., *n.n.* dodder.
warm, *a.* warm, hot. *~ lopen,* to (over-)heat (*machinery*). ·warmen, *v.t.* to warm, heat.
·warmoes, no pl., *n.n.* vegetables, pot-herbs. warmoeze·nier, -s, *n.* market-gardener.
·warmpjes, *adv.* warmly, cosily. ·warmte, no pl., *n.* warmth, heat.
·warnet, -tten, *n.n.* tangle. ·warrelen, *v.i.* to whirl. ·warreling, *n.* whirl. ·warrelwind, *n.* whirlwind.
wars, *a. ~ van,* averse from *or* to.
·Warschau, *n.N.* Warsaw.
·warwinkel, *n.* See warboel.
was, -ssen, *n.* wash, laundry. *in de ~ doen,* to send to the laundry. ¶ no pl., *n.* wax; rise (*water*); growth. *slappe ~,* dubbing. ·wasachtig, *a.* waxy. ·wasbaar, -bare, *a.* washable. ·wasbeer, -beren, *n.* raccoon. ·wasdoek, no pl., *n.* oil-cloth. ·wasdom,

no pl., *n.* growth. ·wasdraad, -draden, *n.* waxed thread. ·wasecht, *a.* fast (*colour*). ·wasgoed, no pl., *n.n.* laundry, washing. ·waskaars, . *n.* taper. ·wastafel, -s, *n.* wash-stand. ·wastafeltje, -s, *n.n.* wax tablet. ·wassen, was, *v.t.* to wax. ¶ *v.t., irr.* to wash; to wash (up). ¶ *v.i., str.* to wax, grow; to rise (*water*). ¶ zich ~, *v.r.* to wash. *zich schoon ~,* to whitewash oneself. ¶ *a.* waxen, (of) wax. ·wassen·beeld, *n.n.* wax figure. ·wasse·rij, *n.* laundry.
wat, *pron. interr.* what? what! *~ voor,* what (sort of). ¶ *pron. rel.* what, which, that. *alles ~,* all (that). ¶ *pron. indef.* something, anything; some, any. ¶ *adv.* a little; very.
wat·blief, *int.* beg pardon!
·water, -s *or* -en, *n.n.* water; dropsy. *als ~ en vuur,* at daggers drawn; *hoog ~,* high tide; *laag ~,* low tide; *sterk ~,* spirits; *onder ~ zetten,* to flood, inundate; *te ~,* by sea or water; *te ~ laten,* to launch. ·waterachtig, *a.* watery. ·waterbak, -kken, *n.* tank, cistern; urinal. ·waterbel, -llen, *n.* bubble. ·waterblaas, -blazen, *n.* urinary vessel. ·waterbouwkunde, no pl., *n.* hydraulic engineering. waterbouw·kundig, *a.* hydraulic (*engineering*). ·waterdamp, *n.* vapour. ·waterdicht, *a.* waterproof, watertight. *~ beschot,* bulkhead. ·waterdier, *n.n.* aquatic animal. ·wateren, *v.t.* to water. ¶ *v.i.* to make water. ·watergang, *n.* water-course. ·watergeus, -zen, *n.* sea beggar. ·waterglas, -zen, *n.n.* drinking glass. ¶ no pl., *n.n.* water-glass. ·waterhoen, -ders, *n.n.* moorhen. ·waterhoofd, *n.n.* hydrocephalus. ·waterhoos, -hozen, *n.* water-spout. water·houdend, *a.* aqueous. ·waterig, *a.* watery. ·watering, *n.* water-course. ·waterjuffer, -s, *n.* dragonfly. ·waterkant, *n.* water-side, water-front. ·waterkers, no pl., *n.* watercress. ·waterkruik, *n.* pitcher. ·waterlaars, -zen, *n.* wader(s). ·waterleiding, *n.* waterworks; water system. ·waterlis, -ssen, *n.* (water-)flag. ·waterloos, -loze, *a.* waterless. ·waterlozing, *n.* drainage. ·waterpas, -ssen, *n.n.* water-level (*instrument*). ¶ -sse, *a.* level. ·waterpassen, -pas, *v.t.* to level, grade. ·waterpers, *n.* hydraulic press. ·waterpokken, pl. only, *n.* chicken-pox. ·waterpot, -tten, *n.* chamber-pot. ·waterproef, -ven, *n.* ordeal by water. ·waterrijk, *a.* abounding with water. ·waterschap, -ppen, *n.n.* polder. ·waterscheerling, *n.* water-hemlock. ·waterscheiding, *n.* watershed. ·waterschildpad, -dden, *n.* turtle. ·waterschout, *n.* water-bailiff. ·waternsoed, -no̅den, *n.* flood, inundation. ·waterstaat, no pl., *n.* department for roads and waterways. ·waterstand, *n.* water-level (*height*). ·waterstof, no pl., *n.* hydrogen. ·watertanden, *v.i. ik watertand ervan* or *het doet me ~,* it makes my mouth water.

·waterverf, -ven, n. water-colour(s). ·water-verplaatsing, no pl., n. displacement, tonnage. ·watervlak, -kken, n.n. sheet of water. ·watervliegtuig, n.n. sea-plane. ·watervrees, no pl., n. hydrophobia. ·watervrij, a. anhydrous. ·waterweg, n. waterway. ·waterzucht, no pl., n. dropsy. water·zuchtig, a. dropsical.

·watje, -s, n.n. wad of cotton-wool. wat·teren, -teer, v.t. to quilt. ·watten, a. cotton-wool.

·wauwelaar, -s, n. tattler, chatterbox. ·wauwelen, v.i. to chatter.

·wazig, a. hazy. ·wazigheid, no pl., n. haziness.

we, pron. See wij.

web, -bben, n.n. web.

wed, -dden, n.n. watering place, horse pond. ·wedde, -n, n. (stilted) salary.

·wedden, wed, v.i. to bet, wager. ·wedden-schap, -ppen, n. wager. ·wedder, -s, n. betting man, gambler.

·weder, no pl., n.n. (stilted). See weer. ¶adv. (stilted). See weer. ¶prefix re-, again, back. ·wederdienst, n. service in return. tot ~ bereid, ready to reciprocate. ·weder-doop, -dopen, n. re-baptism. ·wederdoper, -s, n. anabaptist. wederdope·rij, no pl., n. anabaptism. ·wedergeboorte, -n, n. rebirth, regeneration. ·wederhelft, n. better half. ·wederik, -kken, n. loosestrife.

weder·invoer, no pl., n. re-importation. weder·kerig, a. mutual, reciprocal. weder-·kerigheid, -heden, n. reciprocity. weder-·opbouw, no pl., n. reconstruction. weder-·rechtelijk, a. illegal, unlawful. weder-·varen, no pl., n.n. experience, adventure. ¶-vaar, v.t. to befall. weder·waardigheid, -heden, n. vicissitude. ·wederzijds, a. mutual.

·wedijver, no pl., n. rivalry, competition. ·wedijveren, v.i. to compete. ·wedloop, -lopen, n. race. ·wedren, -nnen, n. (horse-) race. ·wedstrijd, n. match, competition.

·weduwe, -n, n. widow. ·weduwnaar, -s, n. widower.

wee, weeën, n.n. woe; pl. labour pains, birth pangs. ¶weeë, a. faint.

·weefgetouw, n.n. loom. ·weefsel, -s, n.n. tissue. ·weefspoel, n. shuttle.

·weegbree, no pl., n. plantain.

·weegbrug, -ggen, n. weigh-bridge. ·weegloon, -lonen, n.n. weighage.

·weegluis, -zen, n. bug.

weegs, n. See weg.

·weegschaal, -schalen, n. (pair of) scales, balance.

week, weken, n. week. om de ~, every week; om de andere ~, every other week; over een ~, in a week's time; voor een ~, a week ago. ¶no pl., n. soak. in de ~ staan, to be in soak. ¶weke, a. weak, soft. ·weekblad, n.n. weekly (paper). ·weekdier, n.n. mollusc. ·weekgeld, n.n. weekly wage(s). week·hartig, a. tender-hearted. ·weekheid, no pl., n. tenderness, softness.

·weeklacht, n. lamentation. ·weeklagen, -klaag, v.i. to lament. ~ over, to bewail.

·weekloon, -lonen, n.n. weekly wage(s). ·weekstaat, -staten, n. weekly return.

·weelde, -n, n. luxury. ·weelderig, a. luxurious.

·weemoed, no pl., n. melancholy. wee-·moedig, a. melancholy.

weer, weren, n. wether. ¶no pl., n. defence. in de ~ zijn, to be busy; zich te ~ stellen, to defend oneself. ¶no pl., n.n. weather. bij gunstig ~, weather permitting; in ~ en wind, wet or dry, in rain or sunshine. ¶adv. again, once more. heen en ~ or over en ~, to and fro, up and down, back and forth. ·weerbaar, -bare, a. able-bodied. ·weerbaarheid, no pl., n. state of defence. weer·barstig, a. obstinate, recalcitrant. weer·barstigheid, no pl., n. obstinacy. ·weerbericht, n.n. weather report. ·weerga, no pl., n. equal, match; devil. loop naar de ~, go to blazes; om de ~ niet, like hell you won't. ·weergaas, -gase, a. devilish. ·weergaloos, -loze, a. matchless. weer·galmen, v.i. to echo, reverberate. ·weergeven, geef weer, v.t.s., str. to render. ·weerhaan, -hanen, n. weather-vane. weer·houden, v.t., irr. to keep or hold back, restrain. weer·kaatsen, v.t. to reflect, echo. ¶v.i. to rebound. weer·klinken, v.t.s., str. to echo, resound. weer·kundig, a. meteorological. weer-·leggen, -leg, v.t. to refute, disprove. weer-·legging, n. refutation. ·weerlicht, no pl., n.n. summer lightning. als de ~, hell for leather. ·weerlichten, v.imp. to lighten (lightning). ·weerloos, -loze, a. defenceless. ·weerloosheid, no pl., n. defencelessness. ·weermacht, n. military forces. ·weer-middelen, pl. only, n.n. means of defence. weer·om, adv. back; again, once again. weer·omslag, no pl., n., weer·omstuit, no pl., n. recoil; rebound. van de ~, as a reaction. ·weerschijn, no pl., n. reflection. ·weersgesteldheid, -heden, n. state of the weather. weers·kanten, pl. only, n. both sides. weer·spannig, a. refractory, recalcitrant. weer·spiegelen, v.t. to mirror. weer·staan, -sta, v.t., irr. to resist, oppose. ·weerstand, no pl., n. resistance, opposition. weer·streven, -streef, v.t. to oppose. weers·zijden, pl. only, n. both sides. ·weervoorspelling, n. weather forecast. ·weerwil, no pl., n. in ~ van, in spite of, despite. ·weerwolf, -ven, n. werewolf. ·weerwraak, no pl., n. retaliation, reprisal. ·weerzien, no pl., n.n. meeting again. tot ~s, au revoir. ·weerzin, no pl., n. reluctance, aversion. weerzin·wekkend, a. repulsive, revolting.

wees, wezen, n. orphan. ·weeshuis, -zen, n.n. orphanage. ·weesmoeder, -s, n. matron (of orphanage).

·weesge·groetje, -s, n.n. Ave Maria (prayer).

weet, no pl., *n.* ~ *van iets hebben*, to be in the know, be aware of something. ·weetal, -llen, *n.* know-all. weet·gierig, *a.* eager to learn. weet·gierigheid, no pl., *n.*, ·weetlust, no pl., *n.* desire for knowledge.

weeuw, *n.* widow. ·weeuwtje, -s, *n.n.* smew.

weg, *n.* way, road; route, avenue, channel. *onder* ~, on the way; *zich op* ~ *begeven*, to set out; *op de slechte* ~ *brengen*, to lead astray; *zijns weegs gaan*, to go one's way *or* their several ways. ¶*adv.* away; gone, lost. ~ *met*, down with. ¶*prefix.* away, off. ·wegbrengen, *v.t.s.*, *irr.* to put away; to sink (*for insurance money*). ·wegcijferen, *v.t.s.* to eliminate. -wege, *suffix* on behalf of; on account of, by reason of. ·wegen, weeg, *v.t.*, *str.* to weigh. ·wegens, *prep.* on account of. ·wegkomen, *v.i.s.*, *irr.* to get away. *maak dat je wegkomt*, get away with you, make yourself scarce. ·weg-kunnen, kan weg, *v.i.s.*, *irr.* to be able to go *or* get away. ·wegkwijnen, *v.i.s.* to languish, pine away. ·weglaten, laat weg, *v.t.s.*, *str.* to leave out, omit. ·weglating, *n.* omission. ·wegleggen, leg weg, *v.t.s.*, *irr.* to lay away *or* by. ·weglopen, loop weg, *v.i.s.*, *str.* to run away *or* off. ·wegmoeten, *v.i.s.*, *irr.* to have to go away. ·weg-moffelen, *v.t.s.* to spirit away. ·wegnemen, neem weg, *v.t.s.*, *str.* to take away. *dat neemt niet weg dat*, it does not alter the fact that. ·wegraken, raak weg, *v.i.s.* to get lost. ·wegtrekken, trek weg, *v.t.s.*, *str.* to pull *or* draw away. ¶*v.i.s.*, *str.* to march off. ·wegtronen, troon weg, *v.t.s.* to entice away. ·wegwerken, *v.t.s.* to eliminate, get rid of. ·wegwerker, -s, *n.* roadmender. ·wegwijs, -ze, *a.* knowing one's way; au courant. ·wegwijzer, -s, *n.* finger-post.

wei, *n.* meadow. *in de* ~ *sturen*, to put out to grass. ¶ no pl., *n.* whey; serum (*of blood*).

·Weichsel, *N.* Vistula.

·weide, -n, *n.* meadow. *See* wei. ·weide-bloem, *n.* daisy. ·weidegrond, *n.* pasture land. ·weiden, *v.i.* to graze. ¶ *v.t.* *zijn ogen* ~ *aan*, to feast one's eyes on. ·weiderecht, *n.n.* grazing rights.

weids, *a.* grand; stately.

·weifelaar, -s, *n.* waverer. ·weifelachtig, *a.* wavering. ·weifelen, *v.i.* to waver. weifel-moedig, *a.* irresolute, vacillating.

·weigeraar, -s, *n.* person who refuses. ·weigerachtig, *a.* unwilling to grant. ·weigeren, *v.t.* to refuse, deny. ¶ *v.i.* to fail (to act). ·weigering, *n.* refusal.

·weiland, *n.n.* meadow; meadow land.

·weinig, *pron.* (a) little, (a) few. ¶ *adv.* little. *één te* ~, one short. ·weinigje, no pl., *n.n.* small quantity.

weit, no pl., *n.* wheat.

·weitas, -ssen, *n.* game-bag.

·weitebloem, no pl., *n.* flower of wheat.

·wekelijk, *a.* soft, tender.

·wekelijks, *a.* & *adv.* weekly.

·wekeling, *n.* weakling. ·weken, week, *v.t.* & *v.i.* to soak, soften.

·wekken, wek, *v.t.* to wake, waken, awaken; to cause. ·wekker, -s, *n.* alarum-clock.

wel, -llen, *n.* fountain, spring. ¶ *a.* well. ¶ *adv.* well; very much; indeed, truly. *als ik me* ~ *herinner* or *als ik het* ~ *heb*, if I remember rightly; ~ *tien*, ten at least; *hij zal* ~ *komen*, I daresay he'll come *or* he is sure to come. ¶ *excl.* well!, why! ~ *nee*, oh no *or* don't you believe it. ¶ no pl., *n.n.* ~ *en wee*, weal and woe. wel·aan, *excl.* (*stilted*) well then. ·wel-bedacht, *a.* well thought-out. ·wel-begrepen, *a.* well understood. ·welbehagen, no pl., *n.n.* pleasure. ·welbekend, *a.* well-known, familiar. ·welbemind, *a.* dearly beloved. ·welbespraakt, *a.* fluent. ·weldaad, -daden, *n.* boon, benefit. wel·dadig, *a.* salutary; charitable. wel·dadigheid, -heden, *n.* charity, beneficence. wel·denkend, *a.* right-thinking. ·weldoen, doe wel, *v.i.s.*, *irr.* to do good. ·weldoener, -s, *n.* benefactor. ·weldoenster, -s, *n.* benefactress. ·weldra, *adv.* soon, before long. wel·edel, *a. to address gentleman: den* ~*en heer* . . ., (to) . . . Esq.; ~*e heer*, dear sir. wel·edelgeboren, *a. to address physicians, certain magistrates and educationists.* wel·edelgestreng, *a. to address certain magistrates, legal officers and educationists.* wel·edelzeergeleerd, *a. to address holders of Doctor's degree.* wel·eer, *adv.* (*stilted*) of old. weleer·waard, *a. to address certain priests and clergymen.*

Welf, *N.* Guelph.

welge·aard, *a.* good-natured. welge·boren, *a.* high-born. welge·daan, -dane, *a.* well-fed. welge·steld, *a.* well-to-do, well-off. ·wel-gevallen, *v.t. zich iets laten* ~, to put up with something. ¶ No pl., *n.n.* satisfaction, pleasure. welge·vallig, *a.* pleasing. welge-zind, *a.* well-disposed. wel·haast, *adv.* (*stilted*) soon.

·welig, *a.* luxuriant. ·weligheid, no pl., *n.* luxuriance.

·welijzer, no pl., *n.n.* puddled iron.

welis·waar, *adv.* it is true.

welk, *pron. interr.* which, what; which one. ¶ *pron. rel.* who, which, that. ~ *ook*, what(so)ever.

·welkom, *a.* welcome. *iemand* ~ *heten*, to bid a person welcome. ·welkomst, no pl., *n.* welcome. ·welkomstgroet, *n.* welcome.

·wellen, wel, *v.t.* to weld. ¶ *v.i.* to well up. ·welletjes, *adv.* good enough. *het is* ~, that will do. wel·levend, *a.* courteous. wel·levendheid, -heden, *n.* courtesy, politeness. wel·licht, *adv.* perhaps. wel·luidend, *a.* melodious, harmonious. ·wellust, no pl., *n.* voluptuousness, lust; delight. wel·lusteling, *n.* voluptuary, lecher. wel·lustig, *a.* voluptuous, sensual. ·welmachine, -s, *n.*

welding apparatus. ·welnaad, -naden, *n.*
weld. wel·nu, *excl.* well then.
welp, *n.* whelp, cub...
wel·riekend, *a.* fragrant, sweet-smelling.
·welslagen, no pl., *n.n.* success. wel-
·sprekend, *a.* eloquent. wel·sprekendheid,
no pl., *n.* eloquence. ·welstand, no pl., *n.*
prosperity, comfort; well-being. ·welste,
no pl., *n.n. van je* ~, like anything.
·weltevreden, *a.* well-contented. ·welvaart,
no pl., *n.* prosperity. ·welvaren, no pl., *n.n.*
prosperity. ¶ vaar wel, *v.i.s., str.* to
prosper. wel·varend, *a.* prosperous; in
good health.
·welven, welf, *v.t.* to vault, arch.
wel·voeglijk, *a.* becoming, decent. wel-
·voeglijkheid, no pl., *n.* propriety, decency.
wel·willend, *a.* obliging, kind. wel-
·willendheid, no pl., *n.* kindness, sympathy.
·welzijn, no pl., *n.n.* welfare, well-being.
·wemelen, *v.i.* to teem, swarm. ~ *van,* to
crawl with.
·wenden, *v.t.* to turn. ¶ zich ~, *v.r.* to turn.
zich ~ *tot,* to apply to, address oneself to;
men kan er zich ~ *noch keren,* there is no
room to swing a cat. ·wending, *n.* turn.
·wenen, ween, *v.i.* to weep. ~ *over,* to
bewail; ~ *van vreugde,* to weep for joy.
·Wenen, *n.N.* Vienna.
wenk, *n.* wink, nod; hint. ·wenkbrauw, *n.*
eyebrow. ·wenken, *v.t.* to beckon.
·wennen, wen, *v.t.* to accustom. ¶ *v.i.* ~ *aan,*
to become accustomed to.
wens, *n.* wish, desire. *naar* ~, smoothly,
according to wish. ·wenselijk, *a.* desirable.
·wenselijkheid, no pl., *n.* desirability.
·wensen, *v.t.* to wish, desire, want.
·wentelen, *v.t.* to roll over. *zich* ~ *om,* to
revolve round. ·wenteling, *n.* turn,
revolution. ·wentelteefje, -s, *n.n.* bread
fried in batter. ·wenteltrap, -ppen, *n.*
spiral staircase.
werda, *excl.* halt! who goes there?
·wereld, *n.* world. *op de* ~ *of ter* ~, in the
world; *waarom ter* ~, why on earth; *ter* ~
komen, to be born. ·wereldbeschouwing, *n.*
conception of the world, philosophy.
·wereldbeschrijving, *n.* cosmography. ·we-
reldbol, no pl., *n.* globe (*earth*). ·werelddeel,
-delen, *n.n.* part of the world, continent.
·wereldgericht, no pl., *n.n.* last judgment.
wereld·kundig, *a.* generally known. *iets* ~
maken, to make something public. ·wereld-
lijk, *a.* worldly, secular. ·wereldreiziger, -s,
n. globe-trotter. ·werelddruim, no pl., *n.n.*
(infinite) space. ·werelds, *a.* worldly.
·wereldstad, -steden, *n.* metropolis. ·wereld-
streek, -streken, *n.* zone. ·wereldwijs, -ze,
a. worldly-wise. ·wereldzee, -zeeën, *n.*
ocean.
·weren, weer, *v.t.* to keep off, avert. ¶ zich ~,
v.r. to defend oneself; to exert oneself.
werf, -ven, *n.* ship-building yard; yard.
·werfkantoor, -toren, *n.n.* recruiting office.

·wering, no pl., *n.* prevention,·exclusion.
werk, *n.n.* work. ~ *aan de winkel,* work to
be done; *lang* ~ *hebben met,* to take a long
time over; *ergens* ~ *van maken,* to take a
matter up; *alles in het* ~ *stellen,* to make
every effort; *te* ~ *gaan,* to proceed. ¶ no
pl., *n.n.* oakum. ~ *pluizen,* to pick oakum.
·werkbaas, -bazen, *n.* foreman. ·werkbank,
n. work-bench. ·werkbij, *n.* worker-bee.
werk·dadig, *a.* active. ·werkdag, *n.*
working-day. ·werkelijk, *a.* real, true.
·werkelijkheid, -heden, *n.* reality. *in* ~,
actually. ·werkeloos, -loze, *a.* idle, inactive.
·werke·loosheid, no pl., *n.* idleness, inactivity. ·werken, *v.i.* to work; to warp.
~ *op,* to affect. ·werkend, *a.* working,
active. ·werker, -s, *n.* worker. ·werkezel,
-s, *n.* drudge. ·werkgever, -s, *n.* employer.
·werking, *n.* working, action; effect.
buiten ~, out of action, no longer
operative; *buiten* ~ *stellen,* to suspend;
in ~ *treden,* to come into force. ·werk-
kracht, *n.* energy; workman. ·werkkring,
n. sphere of action. ·werklieden, *pl.* See
werkman. ·werkloos, -loze, *a.* unemployed.
·werkloosheid, no pl., *n.* unemployment.
·werkloze, -n, *n.* unemployed (*person*).
·werklust, no pl., *n.* enthusiasm for work.
·werkman, -lui *or* -lieden, *n.* workman,
labourer. ·werknemer, -s, *n.* employee.
·werkplaats, *n.* workshop. ·werkrooster,
-s, *n.* time-table. ·werkstaking, *n.* strike.
·werkster, -s, *n.* worker (*female*); charwoman. ·werktuig, *n.n.* tool, implement.
·werktuigkunde, no pl., *n.* mechanics.
werktuig·kundig, *a.* mechanical (*engineering*). werk·tuiglijk, *a.* mechanical.
·werkverschaffing, no pl., *n.* provision of
work (*for unemployed*). ·werkwijze, -n, *n.*
method, procedure. werk·willige, -n, *n.*
non-striker. ·werkwoord, *n.n.* verb.
·werkzaam, -zame, *a.* active; operative.
~ *zijn bij,* to be employed with. ·werk-
zaamheid, -heden, *n.* activity; *pl.* operations. ·werkzuster, -s, *n.* ward-maid.
·werpanker, -s, *n.n.* bow-anchor. ·werp-
draad, -draden, *n.* woof. ·werpen, *v.t., str.*
to throw, cast, fling; to drop (*young*).
·werpgaren, no pl., *n.n.* woof. ·werplijn, *n.*
line, painter. ·werplood, no pl., *n.n.*
sounding-lead. ·werpnet, -tten, *n.n.*
casting-net. ·werpspies, -zen, *n.* javelin
·werptuig, *n.n.* projectile.
werst, *n.* verst.
·wervel, -s, *n.* vertebra. ·werveldier, *n.n.*
vertebrate (animal). ·wervelen, *v.i.* to
whirl. ·wervelwind, *n.* whirlwind.
·werven, werf, *v.t., str.* to recruit; to enrol.
·werving, *n.* recruitment.
·werwaarts. *adv.* whither.
wes·halve, *c.* wherefore.
wesp, *n.* wasp. ·wespendief, -ven, *n.* bee-
hawk, honey-buzzard. ·wespennest, *n.n.*
wasps' nest; (*fig.*) hornets' nest.

West, no pl., *n.n.* west. ¶ *N.* West Indies. ¶ *adv.* west. ·**westelijk**, *a.* western, westerly. ·**Westen**, no pl., *n.n.* west. *naar het ~*, westward(s); *ten ~ van*, west of; *buiten ~ zijn*, to be unconscious. ·**wester-**, *prefix* west(ern). ·**westers**, *a.* occidental, western. **West·faals**, *a.* Westphalian. **West·falen**, *n.N.* Westphalia. ·**Westgoten**, pl. only, *N.* Visigoths. **West·Indiëvaarder**, **-s**, *n.* West Indiaman. **West·-Indisch**, *a.* West Indian. ·**westwaarts**, *a.* westward(s).

wet, **-tten**, *n.* law; act. *iemand de ~ stellen*, to lay down the law to a person; *bij de ~ bepalen*, to enact; *buiten de ~ stellen*, to outlaw. ·**wetboek**, *n.n.* code (of law). ·**weten**, **weet**, *v.t.*, *irr.* to know; to be aware of. *weet ik veel*, ask me another; *weet je wat*, I'll tell you; *naar ik weet*, to my knowledge; *het goed samen ~*, to get on well; *dat moet hij ~*, that's his look-out; *willen ~*, to admit; *niets willen ~ van*, not to want any dealings with; *er iets op weten*, to find a remedy; *te ~*, namely. ¶ no pl., *n.n.* knowledge. *tegen beter ~ in*, against (my) better judgment. ·**wetens**, *adv.* knowingly. ·**wetenschap** **-ppen**, *n.* science; knowledge. **weten·schappelijk**, *a.* scientific. **wetens·waardig**, *a.* interesting, worth knowing.

·**wetering**, *n.* water-course. ·**wetgeleerde**, **-n**, *n.* jurist. ·**wetgeleerdheid**, no pl., *n.* legal science. ·**wetgevend**, *a.* legislative. ·**wetgeving**, no pl., *n.* legislation. ·**wethouder**, **-s**, *n.* alderman. **wets-**, *prefix* legal, of the law. ·**wetsontwerp**, *n.n.* bill. ·**wetstaal**, **-stalen**, *n.n.* whetting-steel. ¶ no · pl., *n.* legal phraseology. ·**wetsteen**, **-stenen**, *n.* whetstone, hone. ·**wetsvoorstel**, **-llen**, *n.n.* (draft) bill. ·**wettelijk**, *a.* legal, statutory. ·**wettelijkheid**, **-heden**, *n.* legality. ·**wetteloos**, **-loze**, *a.* lawless. ·**wetten**, **wet**, *v.t.* to whet, sharpen. ·**wettig**, *a.* lawful, legitimate. ·**wettigen**, *v.t.* to legitimatize, legalize. ·**wettigheid**, no pl., *n.* legitimacy. ·**wettiging**, no pl., *n.* legalization.

·**weven**, **weef**, *v.t.* to weave. ·**wever**, **-s**, *n.* weaver. **weve·rij**, *n.* weaving-mill. ·**wezel**, **-s**, *n.* weasel. ·**wezen**, *v.i.*, *infin. only.* to be. *hij mag er ~*, he's not a bad sort. ¶ **-s**, *n.n.* being, existence; being, creature; essence; countenance. *in ~ houden*, to keep in being; *in ~ zijn*, to exist. ·**wezenlijk**, *a.* real; essential. ·**wezenlijkheid**, no pl., *n.* reality. ·**wezenloos**, **-loze**, *a.* vacant, blank. ·**wichelaar**, **-s**, *n.* diviner. ·**wichela·rij**, *n.* divination, augury. ·**wichelen**, *v.i.* to divine. ·**wichelroede**, **-n**, *n.* divining rod; dowsing rod. ·**wicht**, *n.n.* infant, babe. ¶ no pl., *n.n.* weight. ·**wichtig**, *a.* weighty.

wie, *pron. interr.* who(m). *van ~*, whose. ¶ *pron.*, *rel.* who, he who. ¶ *pron. indef.* *~ ook*, who(so)ever. ·**wiebelen**, *v.i.* to wobble. ·**wieden**, *v.t.* to weed. ·**wieder**, **-s**, *n.* weeder. ·**wiedes**, *a.* '*t is nogal ~*, it's obvious. ·**wiedster**, **-s**, *n.* weeder (*female*). **wieg**, *n.* cradle. *in de ~ gelegd zijn voor*, to be destined to become; *in de ~ smoren*, to nip in the bud. ·**wiegelen**, *v.i.* to rock. ·**wiegelied**, **-eren**, *n.n.* lullaby. ·**wiegen**, *v.t.* to rock. **wiek**, *n.* wing; sail (*mill*); wick. *in z'n ~ geschoten*, hurt in his pride. **wiel**, *n.n.* wheel. *iemand in de ~en rijden*, to put a spoke in someone's wheel. ·**wielen**, *v.i.* to wheel, turn. ·**wielenbaan**, **-banen**, *n.* cycling track. ·**wielewaal**, **-walen**, *n.* golden oriole. ·**wieling**, *n.* eddy. ·**wielrijden**, *v.i.*, *infin. only.* (*stilted*) to cycle. ·**wielrijder**, **-s**, *n.* (*stilted*) cyclist. ·**wiemelen**, *v.i.* to fidget. ·**wier**, no pl., *n.n.* seaweed(s). ·**wierook**, no pl., *n.* incense. *iemand ~ toezwaaien*, to praise a person to the skies. ·**wierookvat**, *n.n.* censer, thurible. **wig**, **-ggen**, *n.* wedge. **wij**, *pron.* we. **wijd**, *a.* wide; ample. ¶ *adv.* wide(ly). *~ en zijd*, far and wide. ·**wijdberoemd**, *a.* far-famed. ·**wijden**, *v.t.* to consecrate; to ordain (*priest*). *~ aan*, to dedicate to, devote to. ·**wijding**, *n.* consecration; ordination; devotion. **wijd-lopig**, *a.* prolix. ·**wijdte**, **-n**, *n.* width. ·**wijdvertakt**, *a.* widespread. **wijf**, **-ven**, *n.n.* woman, female (*derog.*). ·**wijfje**, **-s**, *n.n.* female, hen. ·**wijfjesvaren**, **-s**, *n.* female fern. **wijk**, *n.* district. *de ~ nemen naar*, to fly to. ·**wijken**, *v.i.str.* to give way. ·**wijkplaats**, *n.* refuge. **wijl**, *n.* while. *bij ~en*, sometimes; *bij tijd en ~e*, now and then. ¶ *c.* as, since. ·**wijlen**, *a.* late (*dead*). ¶ *v.i.* to stay. **wijn**, *n.* wine. *klare ~ schenken*, to be frank. ·**wijnberg**, *a.* vineyard. ·**wijnbergslak**, **-kken**, *n.* escargot, edible snail. ·**wijnbouw**, no pl., *n.* viticulture. ·**wijngaard**, *n.* vineyard. ·**wijnluis**, **-zen**, *n.* philloxia. ·**wijnlezing**, *n.* vintage (*harvest*). ·**wijnmaand**, *n.* October. ·**wijnproever**, **-s**, *n.* wine-taster. ·**wijnruit**, *n.* rue. ·**wijnsteen**, no pl., *n.* tartar. ·**wijnsteenzuur**, no pl., *n.n.* tartaric acid. ·**wijnstok**, **-kken**, *n.* vine. ·**wijntapper**, **-s**, *n.* vintner. ·**wijnzak**, **-kken**, *n.* wineskin.

wijs, **-ze**, *a.* wise. *niet recht ~* (*silly*); *er niet uit ~ worden*, to make no sense of it. ¶ **-zen**, *n.* manner, way, fashion; air, tune. *bij ~ van*, by way of or in a manner of; *op deze ~*, in this way or to this tune; *van de ~ raken*, to be put off, lose one's head. ·wijsbegeerte, no pl., n. philosophy. ·wijselijk, adv. wisely. ·wijsgeer, -geren, n. philosopher. ·wijsheid, -heden, n. wisdom. ·wijsje, -s, n.n. tune. ·wijsmaken, maak wijs, v.t.s. to make believe. ·wijsneus, -zen, n. prig, know-all. wijs·neuzig, a. stuck-up.

·wijten, v.t., str. iets ~ aan, to blame for something; het is te ~ aan, it is the fault of. ·wijting, n. whiting.

·wijwater, no pl., n.n. holy water. ·wijwaterbakje, -s, n.n. holy water stoup, aspersorium. ·wijwaterkwast, n. aspergillum.

·wijze, -n, n. sage. de Wijzen uit het Oosten, the Magi. See also wijs, n. ·wijzen, wijs, v.t., str. to point out, show. ¶ v.i., str. ~ naar, to point at; ~ op, to point out, point to. ·wijzer, -s, n. pointer, hand. grote ~, minute hand; kleine ~, hour hand. ·wijzerplaat, -platen, n. dial, face. ·wijzigen, v.t. to alter, modify. ·wijziging, n. alteration, modification.

wik, -kken, n. vetch.

·wikkelen, v.t. to wrap (up), envelop, swathe. gewikkeld in, involved in.

·wikken, wik, v.t. to weigh. ~ en wegen, to weigh the pros and cons.

wil, no pl., n. will, wish. laatste or uiterste ~, last will and testament; 's mensen ~ 's mensen leven, live and let live; buiten zijn ~, without his consent; om 's hemels ~, for heaven's sake; tegen ~ en dank, against one's will, willy-nilly; elk wat ~s, something for every taste; ter wille van, for the sake of; ter wille zijn, to oblige.

wild, a. wild; unruly. ~e boot, tramp (steamer); ~e staking, runaway strike. ¶ no pl., n.n. game; venison. grof ~, big game; in 't ~, wild, at random. ·wildbraad, no pl., n.n. venison. ·wilde, a. savage. ·wildebras, -ssen, n. tom-boy. ·wildeman, -nnen, n. rough and wild person. ·wildernis, -ssen, n. wilderness. ·wildheid, -heden, n. wildness. ·wildvreemd, a. ergens ~ zijn, to be a perfect stranger somewhere. ·wildzang, no pl., n. singing of birds.

wilg, n. willow. ·wilgeboom, -bomen, n. willow(-tree).

·wille, n. See wil. ·willekeur, no pl., n. arbitrariness. naar ~, at one's own discretion. wille·keurig, a. arbitrary; haphazard, random. ·willen, wil, v.t., irr. to want, wish; to be willing; to say. er niet aan ~, not to want to hear of it; het toeval wilde, chance would have it; men wil, it is said. ·willens, adv. purposely, deliberately. ·willig, a. willing, docile. ·willoos, -loze, a. will-less. ·wilskracht, no pl., n. will-power.

·wimpel, -s, n. pennant, streamer. ·wimper, -s, n. eyelash.

wind, n. wind. de Eilanden beneden de W~, Leeward Isles; de Eilanden boven de W~,

Windward Isles; een ~ laten, to break wind; in de ~ slaan, to neglect, ignore (advice); de ~ van voren krijgen, to get it in the neck; het gaat hem voor de ~, he is prospering; met alle ~en waaien, to be a time-server. ·windas, -ssen, n. windlass. ·windbuil, n. gas-bag. ·winde, -n, n. bindweed, convolvulus. ·winden, v.t., str. to wind. ¶ zich ~, v.r., str. to wind (road). ·winderig, a. windy, blowy. ·windgat, n.n. vent-hole. ·windhaver, no pl., n. wild oats. ·windhoek, n. windy corner. ·windhond, n. greyhound. ·windhoos, -hozen, n. whirlwind. ·windje, -s, n.n. breath of air. ·windketel, -s, n.n. air-chamber. ·windmeter, -s, n. wind-gauge. ·windmolen, -s, n. windmill. ·windpokken, pl. only, n. chicken-pox. ·windroos, -rozen, n. compass-card. ·windsel, -s, n.n. bandage, band. ·windspil, -llen, n. capstan. ·windstil, -lle, a. calm. ·windstilte, -n, n. calm. ·windstreek, -streken, n. point of the compass. ·windvaan, -vanen, n. weathervane. ·windwaarts, adv. (to) windward.

·wingerd, n. vineyard; vine. wilde ~, Virginia creeper.

·wingewest, n.n. conquered country.

·winkel, -s, n. shop; (work)shop. ·winkelbediende, -s or -n, n. shop-assistant. ·winkeldief, -ven, n. shop-lifter. ·winkelen, v.i. to shop, go shopping. ·winkelhaak, -haken, n. (carpenter's) square; tear (three-cornered). ·winkelhuis, -zen, n.n. shop. ·winke·lier, -s, n. shopkeeper. ·winke·lierster, -s, n. shopkeeper (female). ·winkeljuffrouw, n. shop-assistant (female). ·winkelnering, n. custom. ·winkelopstand, no pl., n. shop-fittings. ·winkelprijs, -zen, n. retail price.

·winnaar, -s, n. winner. ·winnen, win, v.t., str. to win, gain; to win, gather; to make (hay). zo gewonnen zo geronnen, easy come easy go; aan iemand ~, to find a person much better. ·winner, -s, n. winner. ·winning, no pl., n. production, extraction. winst, n. profit(s), gain. ·winstbejag, no pl., n.n. love of profit. uit ~, from motives of gain. ·winstderving, no pl., n. loss of profit. ·winstgevend, a. remunerative, lucrative.

·winter, -s, n. winter. des ~s or 's ~s, in winter. ·winterachtig, a. wintry. ·winteren, v.imp. to be frosty. het begint al te ~, it is getting wintry. ·winterhanden, pl. only, n. ~ hebben, to have chilblains (on hands). ·winterkoninkje, -s, n.n. wren. ·winterkraai, n. hooded crow. ·winterling, n. hemlock. ·wintermaand, n. December; pl. winter months. ·winters, a. wintry. ·winterslaap, no pl., n. winter-sleep, hibernation. ·wintervoeten, pl. only, n. ~ hebben, to suffer from chilblains (on feet).

wip, -ppen, n. jump; see-saw; beam (scales). in een ~, in a jiffy; op de ~ staan, to be uncertain about one's job. **·wipneus, -zen,** n. tip-tilted nose. **·wippen, wip,** v.i. to see-saw; to jump, bob. **·wipplank,** n. see-saw. **·wipstaart,** n. wagtail. **·wipstoel,** n. rocking-chair.

·wirwar, no pl., n. tangle, mix-up.

wis, -sse, a. certain. **~ en zeker,** as sure as eggs is eggs. ¶ **-ssen,** n. wisp.

·wisjewasje, -s, n.n. trifle, footling matter.

·wiskunde, no pl., n. mathematics. **·wiskundig,** a. mathematical. **·wiskundige, -n,** n. mathematician.

wispel·turig, a. fickle. **wispel·turigheid,** no pl., n. fickleness.

·wissel, -s, n. bill (of exchange); points (railway).

·wissen, wis, v.t. to wipe. **·wisser, -s,** n. wiper.

·wisselaar, -s, n. money-changer. **·wissel-agent,** n. exchange-broker. **·wisselbaar, -bare,** a. changeable. **·wisselbank,** n. discount-bank. **·wisselbeker, -s,** n. challenge cup. **·wisselbouw,** no pl., n. rotation of crops. **·wisselbrief, oven,** n. bill of exchange. **·wisselen,** v.t. to change; to give change for; to exchange. ¶ v.i. to change; to shed one's teeth (milk teeth). **·wisselgeld,** no pl., n.n. (small) change. **·wisseling,** n. change, exchange. **·wisselkoers,** n. rate of exchange. **·wisselprovisie,** no pl., n. commission. **·wisselrijm,** n.n. alternate rhyme. **·wisselspoor, -sporen,** n.n. siding. **·wisselstroom,** no pl., n. alternating current. **wissel·vallig,** a. uncertain, changeable. **·wisselwachter, -s,** n. points-man. **·wisselwerking,** n. interplay, interaction.

wit, -tte, a. white. Witte Donderdag, Maundy Thursday; **~ maken,** to whiten. ¶ **-tten,** n.n. white. **·witgepleisterd,** a. whitewashed. **·witgloeiend,** a. white-hot. **·witheid,** no pl., n. whiteness. **·withouten,** a. whitewood. **·witje, -s,** n.n. white (butterfly). **·witjes,** adv. sweetly. **·witkalk,** no pl., n. whitewash. **·witkiel,** n. (railway) porter. **·witlo(o)f,** no pl., n.n. chicory, endive(s). **·wittebrood, -broden,** n.n. white bread. **·wittebroodsweken,** pl. only, n. honeymoon. **·wittekool, -kolen,** n. white cabbage. **·witten, wit,** v.t. to whitewash. **·witvis, -ssen,** n. whiting, whitebait.

·woede, no pl., n. anger, fury, rage. **·woeden,** v.i. to rage. **·woedend,** a. furious. **~ maken,** to infuriate; zich **~ maken op,** to become enraged with.

·woeker, no pl., n. usury. **~ drijven,** to practise usury. **·woekeraar, -s,** n. usurer. **·woekerachtig,** a. usurious. **·woekeren,** v.i. to practise usury; to grow parasitically. **~ met,** to make the most of. **·woekerplant,** n. parasite (plant). **·woekerzucht,** no pl., n. passion for usury.

·woelen, v.i. to turn and toss; to root, grub. **~ in,** to rummage in. **·woelig,** a. turbulent, restless. **~e zee,** choppy sea. **·woeling,** n.

agitation; pl. disturbances. **·woelwater. -s,** n. fidget.

·woensdag, n. Wednesday. 's **~s,** on Wednesdays. ¶ u. Wednesday.

woerd, n. drake. **·woerhaan, -hanen,** n. cock-pheasant.

woest, a. wild, savage; wild, waste, desolate. **·woesteling,** n. rough and violent person. **woeste·nij,** n. wilderness. **·woestheid,** no pl., n. wildness, violence. **woes·tijn,** n. desert.

wol, -llen, n. wool. onder de **~,** between the sheets; veel geschreeuw maar weinig **~,** much ado about nothing. **·wolachtig,** a. woolly.

wolf, -ven, n. wolf; weevil; caries. **·wolfachtig,** a. wolfish.

·wolfabriek, n. woollen mill.

·wolfsangel, -s, n. wolf-trap. **·wolfskers,** no pl., n. deadly nightshade. **·wolfsklauw,** no pl., n. club-moss. **·wolfsmelk,** no pl., n. spurge. **·wolfswortel, -s,** n. aconite, wolf's-bane.

·wolgras, no pl., n.n. cotton-grass.

wolk, n. cloud. een kind als een **~,** a fine child; in de **~en zijn,** to be beside oneself with joy.

·wolkaarder, -s, n. wool-carder.

·wolkachtig, a. cloudy. **·wolkbreuk,** n. cloud-burst. **·wolkenhemel, -s,** n. sky (with clouds). **·wolkenkrabber, -s.** n. sky-scraper. **·wolkeloos, -loze,** a. cloudless. **·wolkig,** a. cloudy.

·wolkruid, no pl., n.n. mullein. **·wollegoed,** no pl., n.n. woollens. **·wollig,** a. woolly. **wol·vin, -nnen,** n. she-wolf.

wond, -en, n. wound, injury. de vinger op de **~ leggen,** to point out the weak spot; oude **~en,** old sores. ¶ a. sore. de **~e plek,** the sore spot. **·wondbaar, -bare,** a. vulnerable. **·wonde, -n,** n. See wond. **·wonden,** v.t. to wound, injure; to hurt.

·wonder, -s, n.n. wonder, miracle; prodigy, marvel. geen **~,** no wonder; **~ boven ~,** strange to say. ¶ a. strange. **·wonderbaar, -bare,** a. miraculous, prodigious. **·wonderbaarlijk,** a. miraculous; strange. **·wonderboom, -bomen,** n. castor-oil plant. **·wonderdadig,** a. miraculous. **·wonderdoener, -s,** n. miracle worker. **·wonderdoktor, -s,** n. quack; medicine man. **·wondergoed,** a. remarkably well. **·wonderkind, -eren,** n.n. infant prodigy. **·wonderklein,** a. wondrously small. **·wonderkracht,** n. miraculous power. **·wonderkruid,** no pl., n.n. St.·John's-wort. **·wonderolie,** no pl., n. castor-oil. **·wonderschoon, -schone,** a. remarkably beautiful. **·wonderspreuk,** n. magic formula.

·wondheelkunde, no pl., n. surgery (art). **·wondijzer, -s,** n.n. probe. **·wondroos,** no pl., n. erysipelas.

·wonen, woon, v.i. to live, dwell, reside. **~ bij,** to live with (in house of). **·woning,**

n. dwelling, residence. ·woningbureau, -'s, *n.n.* house agency. woon·achtig, *a.* resident. ·woonbuurt, *n.* residential quarter. ·woonhuis, -zen, *n.n.* (dwelling-) house. ·woonkamer, -s, *n.* living-room. ·woonplaats, *n.* (place of) residence, home, abode. ·woonschip, -schepen, *n.n.* houseboat. ·woonwagen, -s, *n.* caravan (*on wheels*).

woord, *n.n.* word. *geen stom ~*, not a word; *het hoge ~ is eruit*, the truth is out; *het hoogste ~ hebben*, to shout loudest; *het ~ alleen hebben*, to monopolize the conversation; *het ~ geven aan*, to call upon . . . (*to speak*); *het ~ nemen*, to begin to speak; *het ~ richten tot*, to address; *het ~ bij de daad voegen*, to suit the action to the word; *~en vuil maken over*, to waste words about. ·woordbreker, -s, *n.* promise breaker. ·woordbreuk, *n.* breach of faith. ·woordelijk, *a.* literal, verbatim. ·woordenboek, *n.n.* dictionary. ·woordenschat, no pl., *n.* wealth of vocabulary. ·woordenwisseling, *n.* altercation. woordenzifterij, *n.* word-splitting. ·woordje, -s, *n.* (*little*) word. *een ~*, just a word. ·woordspeling, *n.* pun. ·woordvoerder, -s, *n.* spokesman.

·worden, *v.i.*, *str.* to become, get, grow. ·wording, no pl., *n.* origin.

·worgen, *v.t.* to strangle. ·worging, *n.* strangulation. ·worgpaal, -palen, *n.* garotting-post.

worm, *n.* worm; maggot. ·wormig, *a.* wormy, worm-eaten. ·wormkruid, no pl., *n.n.* tansy. worm·stekig, *a.* worm-eaten. worm·vormig, *a.* vermiform. *~ aanhangsel*, appendix.

worp, *n.* throw.

worst, *n.* sausage. ·worstebroodje, -s, *n.n.* sausage-roll.

·worstelaar, -s, *n.* wrestler. ·worstelen, *v.i.* to wrestle; to struggle. ·worsteling, *n.* struggle.

·wortel, -s, *n.* root; carrot. *~ schieten*, to strike root; *~ trekken*, to extract the root of (*number*). ·wortelboom, -bomen, *n.* mangrove. ·wortelen, *v.i.* to take root. ·wortelknol, -llen, *n.* tuber. ·wortelteken, -s, *n.n.* radical sign.

woud, *n.n.* forest. ·woudduivel, -s, *n.* mandrill. ·woudhoen, -ders, *n.n.* woodcock. ·woudloper, -s, *n.* woodsman.

wouw, *n.* kite.

wraak, no pl., *n.* revenge, vengeance. *uit ~*, in revenge. ·wraakbaar, -bare, *a.* blamable; objectionable (*witness*). wraak·gierig, *a.* vindictive. ·wraaklust, no pl., *n.*, ·wraakneming, *n.* vindictiveness. ·wraakoefening, *n.* revenge, retaliation. ·wraakzucht, no pl., *n.* vindictiveness.

wrak, -kken, *n.n.* wreck. ¶ -kke, *a.* rickety. ·wraken, wraak, *v.t.* to take exception to, challenge.

·wrakgoederen, pl. only, *n.n.* wreck (*goods*).

wrang, *a.* tart, acid. ·wrangheid, no pl., *n.* tartness.

wrat, -tten, *n.* wart. ·wrattig, *a.* warty.

wreed, wrede, *a.* cruel. ·wreedheid, -heden, *n.* cruelty. ·wreedaard, -s, *n.* cruel person, brute. wreed·aardig, *a.* cruel.

·wreken, wreek, *v.t.* to avenge, revenge. ·wreker, -s, *n.* avenger.

·wrevel, no pl., *n.* annoyance, resentment. ·wrevelig, *a.* peevish.

·wriemelen, *v.i.* to wriggle, fidget.

·wrijfhout, *n.n.* fender (*ship's*). ·wrijfpaal, -palen, *n.* rubbing-post. ·wrijven, wrijf, *v.t.*, *str* to rub. ·wrijving, *n.* friction; (*fig.*) clash.

·wrikken, wrik, *v.t.* to wrench; to scull.

·wringen, *v.t.*, *str.* to wring. ¶ zich ~, *v.r.*, *str.* to wriggle, squirm. ·wringing, no pl., *n.* torsion.

·wrochten, *v.t.* (*stilted*) to work.

·wroegen, *v.t.* to prick (*conscience*). ·wroeging, *n.* remorse.

·wroeten, *v.i.* to root, grub; to burrow; to scratch (*chicken*).

wrok, no pl., *n.* rancour, grudge. *~ koesteren*, to bear a grudge. ·wrokken, wrok, *v.i.* to sulk; to have a grudge.

wrong, *n.* knot, bun (*hair*). ·wrongel, no pl., *n.* curds.

wuft, *a.* frivolous. ·wuftheid, -heden, *n.* frivolity.

·wuiven, wuif, *v.i.* to wave (*hand*).

wulk, *n.* whelk.

wulp, *n.* curlew.

wulps, *a.* playful; wanton, lascivious. ·wulpsheid, no pl., *n.* lasciviousness.

·wurgen, *v.t. See* worgen.

wurm, *n. See* worm. ·wurmen, *v.i.* to wriggle.

X

x-benen, pl. only, *n.n. ~ hebben*, to be knock-kneed.

Y

See IJ.

Z

zaad, zaden, *n.n.* seed. *op zwart ~ zitten*, to be hard-up. ·zaadkiem, *n.* germ.

zaag, zagen, *n.* saw; bore (*person*). ·zaagbek, -kken, *n.* sawbill. ·zaagbok, -kken, *n.* trestle. ·zaagmeel, no pl., *n.n.*, ·zaagmolm, no pl., *n.* or *n.n.*, ·zaagsel, no pl., *n.n.* sawdust.

zaaibed, -dden, *n.n.* seed-bed. **zaaien**, *v.t.* to sow. **zaaier, -s**, *n.* sower. **zaaigoed**, no pl., *n.n.* sowing-seed. **zaaikoren**, no pl., *n.n.* seed-corn. **zaailing**, *n.* seedling. **zaaisel**, no pl., *n.n.* sowings. **zaaitijd**, *n.* sowing season.

zaak, zaken, *n.* matter, affair; thing; business; shop; law-suit. *het is ~ or de ~ is*, it is advisable; *gedane zaken nemen geen keer*, it's no use crying over spilt milk; *gemene ~ maken met*, to make common cause with; *er een ~ van maken*, to go to law about it; *niet veel ~s*, nothing much; *ter zake van* or *in zake*, in the matter of; *ter zake!*, to the point!; *niets ter zake doen*, to be neither here nor there. **zaakbezorger, -s**, *n.* agent, proxy. **zaakgelastigde, -n**, *n.* agent, proxy; chargé d'affaires. **zaakje, -s**, *n.n.* (little) affair; business, show, caboodle. **zaakkennis**, no pl., *n.* practical knowledge. **zaak·kundig**, *a.* expert. **zaaks**, *n. See* zaak. **zaakwaarnemer, -s**, *n.* representative, solicitor.

zaal, zalen, *n.* hall, room.

zabbelen, *v.i.* to suck.

zacht, *a.* soft; gentle; slow. **zacht·aardig**, *a.* gentle, mild. **zachtheid, -heden**, *n.* softness. **zachtjes**, *adv.* softly; slowly; gently. *~ aan*, gently, slowly or gradually. **zacht·moedig**, *a.* gentle, mild.

zadel, -s, *n.n.* saddle. *uit het ~ lichten*, to unseat, oust. **zadeldek, -kken**, *n.n.* saddle-cloth. **zadelen**, *v.t.* to saddle. **zadelknop, -ppen**, *n.* pommel. **zadelmaker, -s**, *n.* saddler. **zadelriem, -s**, *n.* saddle-girth. **zadeltas, -ssen**, *n.* saddle-bag; tool-bag.

zagen, zaag, *v.t.* to saw; to talk boringly. **zager, -s**, *n.* sawyer. **zage·rij**, *n.* saw-mill.

zak, -kken, *n.* sack, bag; pouch; pocket. *in ~ en as*, in sackcloth and ashes; *in de ~ tasten*, to put one's hand in one's pocket; *op ~*, in one's pocket, about one. **zakboekje, -s**, *n.n.* note-book. **zakdoek, n.** (pocket-)handkerchief.

zake, n. *See* zaak. **zakelijk**, *a.* matter-of-fact, to the point; objective. *~e inhoud*, précis, gist. **zakelijkheid, -heden**, *n.* conciseness; objectivity. **zaken-**, *prefix*, business-.

zakken, zak, *v.t.* to sack, bag. ¶ *v.i.* to fall, sink, drop; to fail (*in exam.*). *laten ~*, to lower or to plough (*in exam.*). **zakkenrollen**, no pl., *n.n.* picking pockets. **zakkenroller, -s**, *n.* pickpocket. **zaklantaarn, -s**, *n.*, **zaklantaren, -s**, *n.* electric torch.

zalf, -ven, *n.* ointment, salve.

zalig, *a.* blessed; glorious; divine, heavenly. *~ maken*, to save. **zaligen**, *v.t.* to beatify. **zaliger**, *a.* late, of blessed memory. **zaligheid, -heden**, *n.* salvation; bliss; beatitude. **zaligmakend**, *a.* sanctifying.

Zaligmaker, no pl., *n.* Saviour. **zaligmaking**, *n.* salvation. **zaligverklaring**, *n.* beatification.

zalm, *n.* salmon. *het neusje van de ~*, the pick of the lot.

zalven, zalf, *v.t.* to anoint. **zalvend**, *a.* unctuous. **zalving**, *n.* anointing; unction. **zalvingsolie**, **-liën**, *n.* chrismal oil.

zamen, *adv. te ~*, together. *See* samen.

zand, *n.n.* sand; dust, grit. **zandachtig**, *a.* sandy. **zandbank**, *n.* sand-bank, shoal; *pl.* flats. **zandblad**, *n.n.* sand-leaf. **zanderig**, *a.* sandy, gritty. **zanderigheid**, no pl., *n.* sandiness, grittiness. **zandgebak**, no pl., *n.n.* shortbread. **zandglas, -glazen**, *n.n.* hour-glass. **zandgoed**, no pl., *n.n.* sand-leaf. **zandgras**, no pl., *n.n.* lyme-grass. **zandgroeve, -n**, *n.* sand-pit. **zandgrond**, *n.* sandy soil. **zandhaas, -hazen**, *n.* white hare. **zandig**, *a.* sandy. **zandkever, -s**, *n.* tiger-beetle. **zandkoekje, -s**, *n.n.* shortcake biscuit. **zandloper, -s**, *n.* hour-glass. **Zandmannetje**, *n.N.* the Sandman. **zandplaat, -platen**, *n.* sand-bank. **zandruiter, -s**, *n.* *~ worden*, to be thrown or unhorsed. **zandsteen**, no pl., *n.* sandstone. **zandstuiving**, *n.* sand-drift. **zandweg**, *n.* sandy road. **zandwesp**, *n.* digger-wasp. **zandzuiger, -s**, *n.* suction-dredger.

zang, *n.* song, singing; canto. **zanger, -s**, *n.* singer. **zange·res, -ssen**, *n.* singer (*female*). **zangerig**, *a.* melodious, sing-song. **zangkoor, -koren**, *n.n.* choir. **zangnummer, -s**, *n.n.* song(-item). **zangsleutel, -s**, *n.* clef. **zangwedstrijd**, *n.* singing competition.

zanik, no pl., *n.* bore. **zaniken**, *v.i.* to be a bore, nag.

zat, -tte, *a.* satiated; (*vulg.*) drunk. *zich ~ eten*, to eat one's fill.

zaterdag, *N.* Saturday. *'s ~s*, on Saturdays. **zaterdags**, *a.* Saturday.

zatheid, no pl., *n.* satiety.

zavel, no pl., *n.* sandy clay. **zavelboom, -bomen**, *n.* savin.

ze, *pron.* she, her; they, them. *See* zij.

zeboe, -s, *n.* zebu.

zede, -n, *n.* custom; *pl.* morals, manners. *~n en gewoonten*, manners and customs. **zedelijk**, *a.* moral. **zedelijkheid**, no pl., *n.* morality. **zedelijkheidsgevoel**, no pl., *n.n.* moral sense. **zedeloos, -loze**, *a.* immoral. **zedeloosheid**, no pl., *n.* immorality. **zedenbederf**, no pl., *n.n.* corruption of morals; depravity. **zedenkunde**, no pl., *n.* moral philosophy. **zeden·kundig**, *a.* moral. **zedenleer**, no pl., *n.* ethics. **zedenmeester, -s**, *n.* moralist. **zedig**, *a.* modest, demure. **zedigheid**, no pl., *n.* modesty.

zee, zeeën, *n.* sea; (*large*) wave; (*fig.*) ocean, flood. *~ kiezen* or *in ~ steken*, to put out to sea; *recht door ~ gaan*, to steer a straight course; *in volle ~*, on the open sea; *op ~*, at sea; *over ~*, by sea, across

the sea; *ter* ~, by sea, of the navy.
·zeearend, *n.* sea eagle, osprey. ·zeearm, *n.*
inlet, estuary. ·zeeassurantie, -s, *n.*
marine insurance. ·zeeaster, -s, *n.* sea-
starwort. ·zeebanket, no pl., *n.n.* herring.
·zeebarbeel, -belen, *n.* red mullet. ·zee-
boezem, -s, *n.* gulf, bay. ·zeebonk, *n.*
old salt. ·zeebreker, -s, *n.* breakwater.
·zeedier, *n.n.* marine animal. ·zeedistel, -s,
n. sea-holly. ·zeedrift, no pl., *n.* flotsam.
·zeeduiker, -s, *n.* diver (*bird*). ·zeeëgel, -s,
n. sea-urchin. ·zeeëngte, -n, *n.* strait(s),
narrows.
zeef, zeven, *n.* sieve, strainer. ·zeefdoek, *n.n.*
straining cloth.
zeeg, zegen, *n.* sheer.
·zeegat, *n.n.* harbour-mouth; estuary. *het* ~
uitgaan, to put to sea. ·zeegezicht, *n.n.*
seascape. ·zeegier, *n.* frigate-bird. ·zeegras,
no pl., *n.n.* seaweed(s), alga(e). ·zeehandel,
no pl., *n.* oversea trade. ·zeeheld, *n.* naval
hero. ·zeehond, *n.* seal. ·zeehoofd, *n.n.*
pier, jetty. ·zeekaart, *n.* (sea-)chart.
·zeekasteel, -telen, *n.n.* (*lit.*) large (sea-)
vessel. ·zeeklaar, *a.* ready for sea. ~
maken, to refit. ·zeekoet, *n.* guillemot.
·zeekraal, no pl., *n.* marsh samphire.
·zeekwal, -llen, *n.* jelly-fish. ·zeelieden, *n.*,
·zeelui, *n.* See zeeman.
zeelt, *n.* tench.
zeem, zemen, *n.n.* wash-leather.
·zeemacht, no pl., *n.* navy, naval forces.
·zeeman, -lieden, *or* -lui, *n.* seaman,
sailor. ·zeemanschap, no pl., *n.n.* seamanship. ~ *gebruiken*, to give-and-take.
·zeemeermin, -nnen, *n.* mermaid. ·zee-
meeuw, *n.* sea-mew, gull.
·zeemleer, no pl., *n.* wash-leather, chamois-
leather. ·zeemleren, *a.* (of) wash-leather.
·zeemogendheid, -heden, *n.* maritime power.
·zeemtouwer, -s, *n.* leather-dresser.
·zeeofficier, -s *or* -en, *n.* naval officer.
zeep, zepen, *n.* soap.
·zeepaap, -papen, *n.* stargazer (*fish*).
·zeepachtig, *a.* soapy. ·zeepkruid, no pl.,
n.n. soapwort.
·zeeprotest, *n.n.* ship's protest.
·zeepsop, no pl., *n.n.* soapsuds. ·zeepzieden,
no pl., *n.n.* soap-boiling. ·zeepzieder, -s,
n. soap-maker. zeepziede·rij, *n.* soap-
works.
zeer, no pl., *n.n.* pain. ~ *doen*, to hurt, pain.
¶ *zere*, *a.* sore. ¶ *adv.* very, (very) much,
greatly.
·zeeraaf, -raven, *n.* cormorant. ·zeerecht,
no pl., *n.n.* maritime law.
zeereer·waard, *a.* *to address certain higher
Catholic priests.* zeerge·leerd, *a.* *to address
person with Doctor's degree.*
·zeerob, -bben, *n.* seal; old salt. ·zeeroof,
no pl., *n.* piracy. ·zeerot, -tten, *n.* water
rat; old salt. ·zeerover, -s, *n.* pirate.
zeerst, no pl., *n.n.* *om het* ~, as much as
possible; *ten* ~*e*, to the utmost.

·zeeschildpad, -dden, *n.* turtle. ·zeeschuimen,
no pl., *n.n.* piracy. ·zeeschuimer, -s, *n.*
pirate. ·zeespiegel, no pl., *n.* sea-level.
·zeester, -rren, *n.* starfish. ·zeestraat,
-straten, *n.* strait(s). ¦zeetocht, *n.*
voyage.
Zeeuw, *N.* Zeelander. Zeeuws, *a.* Zeeland.
·zeevaarder, -s, *n.* navigator. ·zeevaart, no
pl., *n.* navigation. ·zeevaartkunde, no pl.,
n. art of navigation, seamanship. ·zee-
varend, *a.* seafaring. ·zeevast, *a.* well-
secured. ·zeeverklaring, *n.* See zeeprotest.
·zeevracht, *n.* freight. zee·waardig, *a.*
seaworthy. zee·waardigheid, no pl., *n.*
seaworthiness. ·zeewaarts, *a.* seaward.
·zeeweg, *n.* sea-route. ·zeewering, *n.*
sea-wall, sea defences. ·zeewezen, no pl.,
n.n. maritime affairs. ·zeewier, no pl., *n.n.*
seaweed. ·zeeziek, *a.* sea-sick. ·zeeziekte,
no pl., *n.* sea-sickness.
·zege, no pl., *n.* (*literary*) victory, triumph.
·zegel, -s, *n.n.* seal, stamp. *op* ~, on stamped
paper. ·zegelen, *v.t.* to seal. ·zegelkosten,
pl. only *n.* stamp duties. ·zegellak, no
pl., *n.n.* sealing-wax. ·zegelring, *n.* signet
ring.
·zegen, -s, *n.* drag-net. ¶ no pl., *n.* blessing;
godsend. ·zegenen, *v.t.* to bless. ·zegening,
n. blessing, benediction. ·zegenrijk, *a.*
blessed. ·zegepoort, *n.* triumphal arch.
·zegepraal, -pralen, *n.* triumph, victory.
·zegepralen, -praal, *v.i.*, zegevieren, *v.i.* to
triumph.
·zegge, no pl., *n.* sedge.
·zeggen, zeg, *v.t.*, *irr.* to say, tell. *zegge*, that
is to say; *zo gezegd zo gedaan*, no sooner
said than done; *dat zegt wat*, that means
a lot; *wat U zegt!*, you don't say so!;
er valt niets op te ~, there is nothing to be
said against it. ¶ no pl., *n.n.* saying.
naar zijn ~, according to what he says.
·zeggenschap, no pl., *n.* say, control.
·zegsman, zegslieden, *n.* spokesman; informant. ·zegswijze, -n, *n.* expression,
phrase.
zeil, *n.n.* sail; tarpaulin; floor-cloth. *alle* ~*en
bij hebben*, to have all sails set, do one's
utmost; *met opgestoken* ~, in high
dudgeon; *met volle* ~*en*, all sails set.
·zeildoek, no pl., *n.n.* sailcloth, canvas.
·zeilen, *v.i.* to sail.
zeis, *n.* scythe.
·zeker, *a.* certain; safe, reliable. *een* ~*e
plaats*, the lavatory (*euphemism*). ¶ *adv.*
certainly, positively; no doubt. *ik weet
niet* ~, I'm not sure; *toch* ~, surely.
¶ *pron.* certain. ·zekere, no pl., *n.n.*
het ~ *voor het onzekere nemen*, to prefer
the certain to the uncertain. ·zekerheid,
no pl., *n.* certainty; security. ~ *hebben*,
to be certain. zekerheids·halve, *adv.* for
safety's sake. ·zekering, *n.* fuse.
·zelden, *adv.* rarely, seldom. ~ *of nooit*,
hardly ever. ·zeldzaam, -zame, *a.* rare.

¶ *adv.* exceptionally. ·**zeldzaamheid, -heden,** *n.* rarity.

zelf, *pron.* self. *ik* ~, I myself; *zij* ~, they themselves; *uit zich* ~, of one's own accord. ·**zelfbedrog,** no pl., *n.n.* self-deceit. ·**zelfbedwang,** no pl., *n.n.* self-control, restraint. ·**zelfbehagen,** no pl., *n.n.* complacency. ·**zelfbeheersing,** no pl., *n.* self-control. *zijn* ~ *verliezen,* to lose control of oneself. ·**zelfbespiegeling,** *n.* introspection. ·**zelfbewust,** *a.* self-assured, self-confident. ·**zelfbe·wustheid,** no pl., *n.* self-assurance, self-confidence. ·**zelfde,** *pron.* same. ·**zelfge·noegzaam, -zame,** *a.* self-sufficient. ·**zelfge·noegzaamheid,** no pl., *n.* self-sufficiency. ·**zelfgevoel,** no pl., *n.n.* self-respect. ·**zelfkant,** *n.* selvage; seamy side. ·**zelfmoord,** *n.* suicide. ·**zelfmoorden, zich** *v.r.* to commit suicide. ·**zelfmoordenaar, -s,** *n.* suicide (*male*). ·**zelfmoordenares, -ssen,** *n.* suicide (*female*). ·**zelfontbranding,** no pl., *n.* spontaneous combustion. **zelfs,** *adv.* even. **zelf·standig,** *a.* independent; self-supporting. ~ *naamwoord,* noun, substantive. **zelf·standigheid,** no pl., *n.* independence. ·**zelfstrijd,** no pl., *n.* inward struggle. ·**zelfvertrouwen,** no pl., *n.n.* self-confidence. ·**zelfvoldaan, -dane,** *a.* complacent. ·**ze:·voldoening,** no pl., *n.* satisfaction. ·**zelfzucht,** no pl., *n.* egoism, egotism. **zelf·zuchtig,** *a.* selfish, self-seeking.

·**zemelen,** pl. only, *n.* bran. ·**zemelig,** *a.* . (*full of*) bran.

·**zemen, zeem,** *v.t.* to rub with wash-leather. ·**zemen·lap, -ppen,** *n.* (piece of) wash-leather.

·**zendbrief, -ven,** *n.* epistle. ·**zendeling,** *n.* missionary. ·**zenden,** *v.t., str.* to send. ~ *om,* to send for. ·**zender, -s,** *n.* sender; transmitter. ·**zending,** *n.* shipment, consignment; mission. ·**zendtijd,** *n.* transmission time.

·**zeneblad, -eren,** *n.n.* senna-leaf.

·**zengen,** *v.t.* to scorch, singe.

·**zenuw,** *n.* nerve. *het op de* ~*en hebben,* to have an attack of nerves. ·**zenuwachtig,** *a.* nervous. ·**zenuwachtigheid,** no pl., *n.* nervousness. ·**zenuwgestel, -llen,** *n.n.* nervous system. ·**zenuwknoop, -knopen,** *n.* ganglion. ·**zenuwlijder, -s,** *n.* neurasthenic. ·**zenuwontsteking,** *n.* neuritis. ·**zenuwpijn,** *n.* neuralgia. ·**zenuwtoeval, -llen,** *n.* nervous attack. ·**zenuwziek,** *a.* neurasthenic.

·**zepen, zeep,** *v.t.* to soap. ·**zeperig,** *a.* soapy. **zerk,** *n.* tombstone.

zes, *num.* six. ¶ **-ssen,** *n.* six. ·**zesdaags,** *a.* six days'. ·**zesde,** *num.* sixth. ¶ **-n,** *n.n.* sixth (part). *ten* ~, in the sixth place. ·**zesdehalf,** *a.* five and a half. ·**zesderlei,** *a.* of six kinds. ·**zesdubbel,** *a.* sixfold. ·**zeshoek,** *n.*·hexagon. ·**zeshonderd,** *num.* six hundred. ·**zesmaal,** *adv.* six times.

·**zessen,** *num.* six. *de trein van* ~, the six o'clock train; *bij* ~, just on six; *in* ~, into six; *met hun* ~, the six of them; *met ons* ~, the six of us; *met z'n* ~, with five others; *van* ~ *klaar,* good all round. ·**zestal, -llen,** *n.n.* half-a-dozen. ·**zestien** *num.* sixteen. ·**zestiende,** *a.* sixteenth. ¶ **-n,** *n.n.* sixteenth (part). ·**zestig,** *num.* sixty. ·**zestiger, -s,** *n.* person in his sixties. ·**zestigtal, -llen,** *n.n.* about sixty, some sixty. ·**zestigste,** *a.* sixtieth. ·**zesvoet,** *n.* hexameter. ·**zesvoud,** *n.n* multiple of six. ·**zesvoudig,** *a.* sixfold.

zet, -tten, *v.t.* move (*in game*); push, shove. *een gemene* ~, a dirty trick; *een stoute* ~, a bold stroke. ·**zetbaas, -bazen,** *n.* manager (*of public-house*).

·**zetel, -s,** *n.* seat (*fig.*). ·**zetelen,** *v.i.* to reside. ·**zetfout,** *n.* misprint. ·**zethaak, -haken,** *n.* composing-stick. ·**zetmachine, -s,** *n.* composing-machine. ·**zetmeel,** no pl., *n.n.* starch; amyl. ·**zetsel, -s,** *n.n.* brew; set-up type. ·**zetten, zet,** *v.t.* to put, place; to set, mount; to set up, compose; to make (*tea, coffee*). *iets niet kunnen* ~, to resent *or* dislike something. ¶ **zich** ~, *v.r.* to take a seat. ·**zetter, -s,** *n.* compositor. **zette·rij,** *n.* compositors' room. ·**zetting,** *n.* arrangement, orchestration.

zeug, *n.* sow. *platte* ~, woodlouse.

·**zeulen,** *v.t.* to drag, lug.

·**zeuren,** *v.i.* to worry. ~ *om,* to keep on asking for. ·**zeurig,** *a.* tedious. ·**zeurkous,** *n.,* ·**zeurpiet,** *n.* one who keeps on asking; bore.

·**zeven,** *num.* seven. ¶ **zeef,** *v.t.,* to sieve, strain. ·**Zevenbergen,** *n.N.* Transylvania. ·**zevenblad,** *n.n.* bishop's weed. ·**zevende,** *a.* seventh. ¶ **-n,** *n.n.* seventh (part). ·**zevenderlei,** *a.* of seven kinds. ·**zeven·dubbel,** *a.* sevenfold. ·**zevenen,** *num.* seven. *de trein van* ~, the seven o'clock train; *bij* ~, just on seven; *in* ~, into seven; *met hun* ~, the seven of them; *met ons* ~, the seven of us; *met z'n* ~, with six others. ·**zevenhonderd,** *num.* seven hundred. ·**zevenhoek,** *n.* heptagon. ·**zevenklapper, -s,** *n.* squib. ·**zeven·mijlslaarzen,** pl. only, *n.* seven-league boots. ·**zevenslaper, -s,** *n.* dormouse. ·**zevenster,** no pl., *n.* Pleiades. ·**zeventál, -llen,** *n.n.* (number of) six. ·**zeventien,** *num.* seventeen. ·**zeventiende,** *a.* seventeenth. ¶ **-n,** *n.n.* seventeenth (part). ·**zeventig,** *num.* seventy. ·**zeventiger, -s,** *n.* septuagenarian. ·**zeventigste,** *a.* seventieth. ¶ **-n,** *n.n.* seventieth (part). ·**zevenvoud.** *n.n.* multiple of seven. ·**zevenvoudig,** *a.* sevenfold.

·**zeveraar, -s,** *n.* driveler. ·**zeveren,** *v.i.* to drivel.

zich, *pron.* oneself; him(self); her(self); it(self); you(rself); them(selves).

zicht, no pl., *n.n.* sight. *in* ~, (with)in

sight; *op* ~, at sight. ·zichtbaar, -bare, *a.* visible. ·zichtbaarheid, no pl., *n.* visibility. ·zichtzending, *n.* consignment on approval. zich·zelf, *pron.* *op* ~, in itself; *uit* ~, of one's own accord. *See* zich.
zie·daar, *int.* behold, there. ~ *hoe*, that is how.
·zieden, *v.t.* or *v.t.*, *str.* to boil; to seethe.
zie·hier, *int.* behold, here. ~ *hoe*, this is how.
ziek, *a.* ill, sick; diseased. ~ *worden*, to fall ill. ·zieke, -n, *n.* ill person, patient, sufferer. ·ziekelijk, *a.* sickly, ailing; morbid. ·ziekenboeg, *n.* sick-bay, sick-berth. ·ziekenbus, -ssen, *n.* sick-fund. ·ziekendrager, -s, *n.* stretcher-bearer. ·ziekenhuis, -zen, *n.n.* hospital. ·ziekenoppasser, -s, *n.* male nurse; hospital orderly. ·ziekenwagen, -s, *n.* ambulance. ·ziekte, -n, *n.* illness; complaint; disease, blight. ·ziektebeeld, *n.n.* syndrome. ·ziektenleer, no pl., *n.* pathology. ·ziekteverschijnsel, -s, *n.n.* symptom.
ziel, *n.* soul; bore (*gun*). *tut z'n* ~ *onder z'n arm lopen*, to be bored to death; *iemand op z'n* ~ *geven*, to thrash a person; *ter* ~*e*, dead and buried. ·zieleleven, no pl., *n.n.* spiritual life. ·zieleadel, 10 pl., *n.* nobility of soul. ·zielig, *a.* pitiful. ·zielkunde, no pl., *n.* psychology. ·ziolloos, -loze, *a.* soulless. ·zielmis, -ssen, *n.* mass for the dead. ·zielsangst, *n.* agony, anguish. ·zielsbedroefd, *a.* deeply afflicted. ·zielsblij, *a.* intensely pleased. ·zielsgesteldheid, -heden, *n.* state of mind. ·zielsveel, *adv.* dearly. ·zielsverhuizing, *n.* transmigration of souls. ·zieltogen, -toog, *v.i.* to agonize. ·zieltoging, *n.* agony of death.
zien, zie, *v.t.*, *irr.* to see. *laten* ~, to show; *niet te* ~, not visible; ~ *te slapen*, to try and sleep; *over het hoofd* ~, to overlook. ¶ *v.i.*, *irr.* to look. *scheel* ~, to squint; *goed* ~, to have good eyesight; ~ *naar*, to look at; ~ *op*, to mind. ¶ no pl., *n.n.* seeing, sight. *tot* ~*s!*, so long! ·ziende, *a.* seeing. *ze zijn* ~*de blind*, they have eyes but cannot see. ·zienderogen, *adv.* perceptibly. ·ziener, -s, *n.* seer. ·zienersblik, no pl., *n.* prophetic eye. ·zienlijk, *a.* visible. ziens, no pl., *n.n.* *See* zien. ·zienswijze, -n, *n.* view, opinion.
zier, no pl., *n.* whit, jot. *een* ~*tje*, a trifle, particle.
zie·zo, *int.* that's that.
zift, *n.* sieve. ·ziften, *v.t.* to sift.
Zi·geuner, -s, *n.* gipsy. Zigeune·rin, -nnen, *n.* gipsy (-woman).
zig·zagsgewijze, *adv.* zigzag fashion.
zij, *pron.* she; they. ¶ *n.* *See* zijde. ·zij·aanval, -llen, *n.* flank attack. ·zijaanzicht, *n.n.* side elevation, side-view. ·zijd, *adv.* *wijd en* ~, far and wide. ·zijde, -n, *n.* side. *op* ~, aside, on one side, by one's side, at the side, alongside, to one side;

ter ~, aside; *van alle zijden*, from or on all sides; *van de* ~ *van*, on the part of, from the side of. ¶ no pl., *n.* silk. ·zij(de)achtig, *a.* silky. ·zijdelings, *a.* sidelong. ¶ *adv.* sideways, sidelong. ·zijden, *a.* silk. ·zijdepapier, no pl., *n.n.* tissue-paper. ·zijdeplant, *n.* swallow-wort. ·zijderups, *n.* silkworm. ·zijdestaart, *n.* waxwing. ·zijdeteelt, no pl., *n.* silk-culture.
·zijgen, *v.i.*, *str.* to strain, filter; (*literary*) to sink.
zijn, *pron.* his; its; one's. ¶ ben, *v.i.*, *irr.* & copula. to be. ¶ no pl., *n.n.* being, existence. ·zijne, -n, *n.n. de* or *het* ~, his. ·zijnent, *adv.* (*stilted*) *te* ~, at his house. ·zijnenthalve, *adv.* (*stilted*) for his sake. ·zijnentwege, *adv.* (*stilted*) for his sake; on his behalf. ·zijnentwil, *adv. om* ~, for his sake. ·zijnerzijds, *adv.* on his part.
·zijpelen, *v.i.* to seep, ooze.
·zijrivier, *n.* tributary (*river*). ·zijspan, -nnen, *n.n.* side-car. ·zijspoor, -sporen, *n.n.* siding (*railway*). ·zijsprong, *n.* leap aside.
zilt, *a.* brackish. *het* ~*e nat*, the briny ocean. ·ziltig, *a.* brackish.
·zilver, no pl., *n.n.* silver. ·zilverachtig, *a.* silvery. ·zilverbon, -nnen, *n.* currency note. ·zilveren, *a.* (of) silver; silvery. ·zilvergoed, no pl., *n.n.* silver, plate. ·zilverling, *n.* piece of silver; silverling. ·zilverpopulier, *n.* white poplar, abele. ·zilverreiger, -s, *n.* egret. ·zilverschoon, -schonen, *n.n.* silver-weed. ·zilverstuk, -kken, *n.n.* silver coin. ·zilverwerk, no pl., *n.n.* silverware, plate.
zin, -nnen, *n.* sense; meaning; sentence; inclination, mind. *iemand zijn* ~ *geven*, to let a person do what he likes; *iemands* ~ *doen*, to do what a person wants; *ik heb* ~ *in*, I feel like *or* I should like; ~ *hebben om*, to have a mind to, to feel like; *geen* ~ *hebben*, to make no sense *or* not to feel like; *niet goed bij zinnen*, not in one's right senses; *zijn zinnen bij elkaar hebben*, to have one's wits about one; *iets in de* ~ *hebben*, to be up to something; *zijn zinnen zetten op*, to set one's heart on. ·zindelijk, *a.* clean. ·zindelijkheid, no pl., *n.* cleanliness.
·zingen, *v.t.*, *str.* to sing.
zink, no pl., *n.n.* zinc. ·zinken, *a.* (of) zinc. ¶ *v.i.*, *str.* to sink. *doen* ~, to sink. ¶ no pl., *n.n. tot* ~ *brengen*, to sink. ·zinking, *n.* catarrh. ·zinklood, -loden, *n.n.* lead-sinker. ·zinkput, -tten, *n.* cesspool. ·zinksel, -s, *n.n.* dregs, sediment. ·zinkstuk, -kken, *n.n.* mattress (*dyke-building*).
zin·ledig, *a.* meaningless. ·zinnebeeld, *n.n.* emblem, symbol. ·zinne·beeldig, *a.* emblematic, symbolic. ·zinnelijk, *a.* sensuous; sensual. ·zinnelijkheid, -heden, *n.* sensualism; sensuality. ·zinneloos, -loze, *a.* insane. ·zinneloosheid, no pl., *n.* insanity. ·zinnen, zin, *v.i.*, *str.* to ponder, meditate. ~ *op*, to brood on (*revenge*).

·zinnespel, *n.n.* morality (*drama*). ·zinrijk, *a.* significant. ·zinsbedrog, no pl., *n.n.* illusion. ·zinsbedwelming, no pl., *n.* intoxication. ·zinsnede, -n, *n.* phrase, words (*of sentence*). ·zinspelen, -speel, *v.i.* to allude. ~ *op*, to hint at. ·zinspeling, *n.* allusion. ·zinspreuk, *n.* motto. ·zins-verbijstering, no pl., *n.* mental derangement. ·zinswending, *n.* turn of phrase. ·zintuig, *n.n.* organ (*of the senses*). ·zintuiglijk, *a.* sensory. ·zinverwant, *a.* synonymous.

zit, no pl., *n. een hele* ~, a long journey (*sitting down*); ~*je*, cosy seat. ·zitkamer, -s, *n.* sitting-room. ·zitplaats, *n.* seat. ·zitten, zit, *v.i.*, *str.* to sit; to be; to be in prison; to fit, suit. *hoe zit dat?*, how is that?; *dat zit nog*, that remains to be seen; *gaan* ~, to sit down; *blijven* ~, to remain seated *or* not to get a remove to a higher class at school; *er zit wat achter*, there is more in it than meets the eye; *ergens mee* ~, to have something on one's hands; *onder iets* ~, to be covered by something; *er zit niets anders op dan*, there is nothing for it but. ·zitting, *n.* session; seat, bottom (*chair*). ·zitvlak, -kken, *n.n.* seat, bottom (*person*).

zo, *adv.* so, like this *or* that, thus; presently, directly. ~ . . . *als* . . ., as . . . as . . .; ~ *een*, such a (one); ~ *iets*, such a thing, something like that; ~ *nu en dan*, now and again; ~ *maar*, just like that; *om* ~ *en* ~ *laat*, at such and such a time. ¶ *int.* oh!; really! ~ ~, well, well. ¶ *c.* as. ¶ zooien. *See* zooi. zo·al, *adv.* among other things. zo·als, *c.* as, such as, like. zo·danig, *pron.* such. ¶ *adv.* in such a manner. zo·dat, *c.* so that.

·zode, -n, *n.* sod. ~*n aan de dijk brengen*, to bring grist to the mill. zo·doende, *adv.* thus; consequently. zo·dra, *adv.* as soon as, no sooner.

zoek, *adv.* lost, mislaid. ¶ no pl., *n. op* ~ *naar*, in search of. ·zoekbrengen, *v.t.s.*, *irr.* to pass. *de tijd* ~, to kill time. ·zoeken, *v.t.*, *irr.* to look for, seek. ¶ *v.i.*, *irr.* ~ *naar*, to look for. ·zoeker, -s, *n.* seeker. ·zoeklicht, *n.n.* searchlight. ·zoekmaken, maak zoek, *v.t.s.* to lose, mislay. ·zoek-raken, raak zoek, *v.i.s.* to get lost *or* mislaid.

zoel, *a.* balmy (*weather*).
·zoemen, *v.i.* to buzz, hum.
zoen, *n.* kiss. ·zoenen, *v.t. & v.i.* to kiss. *om te* ~, lovely. ·zoengeld, no pl., *n.n.* blood-money. ·zoenoffer, -s, *n.n.* peace offering, expiatory sacrifice.
zoet, *a.* sweet. ~ *water*, fresh water; ~*e woordjes*, honeyed words; ~ *houden*, to keep quiet *or* be well-behaved. ·zoet-achtig, *a.* sweetish. ·zoetekauw, *n.* sweet-tooth. ·zoetekoek, no pl., *n. alles voor* ~ *opeten*, to swallow it all. ·zoetelaar, -s, *n.*

sutler. ·zoetelaarster, -s, *n.* sutler (*female*). ·zoetemelks, *a.* ~*e kaas*, cream cheese. ·zoetheid, no pl., *n.* sweetness. ·zoethout, no pl., *n.n.* liquorice root. ·zoetig, *a.* sweetish. ·zoetigheid, -heden, *n.* sweets. ·zoetjes, *adv.* gently, slowly. ~ *aan*, gradually. zoet·sappig, *a.* sugary, mealy-mouthed. ·zoetwaterdier, *n.n.* freshwater animal. ·zoetwaterkreeft, *n.* crayfish, crawfish.

zo·éven, *adv.* just now.
zog, no pl., *n.n.* milk, suck; wake (*ship's*). ·zogen, zoog, *v.t.* to suckle, give suck, nurse.
zoge·naamd, *a.* so-called, would-be, alleged. ¶ *adv.* ostensibly, supposedly. zo·haast, *adv.* (*stilted*). *See* zodra. zo·lang, *adv.* as long as, so long as.
·zolder, -s, *n.* attic, loft; ceiling. ·zolderen, *v.t.* to store. ·zoldering, *n.* ceiling. ·zolderluik, *n.n.* trap-door. ·zolderschuit, *n.* barge (*cargo on deck only*).
·zolen, zool, *v.t.* to (re)sole.
·zomen, zoom, *v.t.* to hem.
·zomer, -s, *n.* summer. *des* ~*s* or *'s* ~*s*, in summer; *van de* ~, this *or* last *or* next summer. ·zomerachtig, *a.* summery. ·zomeren, *v.i. het begint te* ~, it is getting summer(y). ·Zomermaand, *N.* June. ·zomers, *a.* summery. ·zomertarwe, no pl., *n.* spring-wheat.
zo·min, *adv.* no more than.
zon, -nnen, *n.* sun. *door de* ~ *verbrand*, sunburnt; *hij kan de* ~ *niet in 't water zien schijnen*, he is envious of the good fortune of others.
·zondaar, -s *or* -daren, *n.* sinner. ·zondaarsbankje, -s, *n.n.* penitent's form. *op het* ~ *zitten*, to be had up on the carpet.
·z'ondag, *N.* Sunday. *des* ~*s* or *'s* ~*s*, on Sunday(s). ·zondags, *a.* Sunday. *op zijn* ~, in his Sunday best. ·zondagsgezicht, *n.n.* sanctimonious face.
zonda·res, -ssen, *n.* sinner (*female*). ·zonde, -n, *n.* sin. *'t is* ~, it's a pity *or* shame. ·zondenbok, -kken, *n.* scapegoat.
·zonder, *prep.* without; but for.
·zonderling, *a.* singular, peculiar. ¶ *n.* eccentric.
·zondeval, no pl., *n.* fall of man. ·zondig, *a.* sinful. ·zondigen, *v.i.* to sin. ·zondvloed, no pl., *n.* deluge, Flood.
·zonnebad, *n.n.* sunbath. ·zonnebloem, *n.* sunflower. ·zonnekever, -s, *n.* lady-bird. ·zonnekijker, -s, *n.* helioscope. ·zonneklaar, -klare, *a.* as plain as a pikestaff. ·zonnekruid, no pl., *n.n.* sun-rose. ·zonnemaand, *n.* solar month. ·zonnen, zich, *v.r.* to sun oneself. ·zonnescherm, *n.n.* sunshade. ·zonnestand, *n.* sun's altitude. ·zonnesteek, -steken, *n.* sunstroke. ·zonnestilstand, *n.* solstice. ·zonnestraal, -stralen, *n.* sunbeam. ·zonnevis, -ssen, *n.* moonfish. ·zonnevogel, -s, *n.* bird of paradise. ·zonnewijzer, -s, *n.*

sun-dial. ·zonnig, *a.* sunny. ·zonsonder-gang, *n.* sunset. ·zonsopgang, *n.* sunrise, dawn. ·zonsverduistering, *n.* eclipse (*sun*). ·zoogdier, *n.n.* mammal. ·zoogtijd, *n.* period of lactation.

zooi, *n.* lot, heap. *wat een* ~, what a lot of rubbish, what a mess.

zool, zolen, *n.* sole (*foot*). ·zoolganger, -s, *n.* plantigrade.

room, zomen, *n.* hem; fringe, edge.

zoon, -s *or* zonen, *n.* son. *de verloren* ~, the prodigal son.

·zootje, -s, *n.n.* lot; boiling (*of fish*). *See* zooi.

zorg, *n.* care; anxiety, worry. *mijn* ~*!*, do I care!; ~ *baren*, to cause anxiety; ~ *dragen voor*, to look after; *goede* ~*en*, good offices. ·zorgelijk, *a.* critical. ·zorge-loos, -loze, *a.* care-free; careless. ·zorge-loosheid, no *pl.*, *n.* improvidence. ·zorgen, *v.i.* ~ *voor*, to look after, take care of, see to. zorg·vuldig, *a.* careful. zorg-·wekkend, *a.* alarming, critical. ·zorgzaam, -zame, *a.* careful, considerate.

zot, -tte, *a.* foolish. ¶ -tten, *n.* fool. ·zotheid, -heden, *n.* folly. ·zotteklap, no *pl.*, *n.* silly talk. zotter·nij, *n.* tomfoolery.

zou. *See* zullen, zal.

zout, *n.n.* salt; salted. ¶ *a.* salt; salted. ·zoutachtig, *a.* salty. ·zouteloos, -loze, *a.* saltless, insipid. ·zouten, *v.t., irr.* to salt. ·zoutevis, no *pl.*, *n.* salt cod. ·zoutheid, no *pl.*, *n.* saltness. ·zoutig, *a.* salty. ·zoutkeet, -keten, *n.* saltworks. ·zoutpan, -nnen, *n.* salt-pan. ·zouttuin, *n.* salt-pan. ·zout-vaatje, -s, *n.n.* salt-cellar. ·zoutzak, -kken, *n.* bag of salt. *als een* ~ *ineenzakken*, to fall like a log. ·zoutzieden, no *pl.*, *n.n.* salt-making. zoutziede·rij, *n.* salt-works. ·zoutzuur, no *pl.*, *n.n.* hydrochloric acid.

zo·veel, *num.* so much *or* many. *vijf* ~, five and something. ¶ *adv.* as much. ~ *te meer*, all the more. ¶ *c.* ~ *als*, as much as. zo·veelste, *num.* *voor de* ~ *keer*, for the umptieth time; *het* ~ *jaar*, in the year so and so. zo·ver, *adv.* so far, thus far; as far as, so far as. *tot* ~, that far, as far as; *voor* ~, in as far as. zo·waar, *adv.* actually, sure enough. zo·wat, *adv.* about, approximately. zo·wel, *c.* ~ *als*, as well as; ~ ... *als* ..., both ... and ... zo·zeer, *adv.* so much.

zucht, *n.* sigh. ~ *naar*, desire *or* craving *or* thirst for. ·zuchten, *v.i.* to sigh; to moan. ·zuchtje, -s, *n.n.* (*little*) sigh; light breeze, breath of air.

zuid, *adv.* south. Zuid, *N.* South. ·zuidelijk, *a.* southern, south; southerly. ¶ *adv.* southward(s). ~ *van*, (to the) south of. ·Zuiden, *n.N.* South. *ten* ~ *van*, south of. ·zuider-, *prefix.* southern, south. ·zuider-breedte, no *pl.*, *n.* south latitude. ·Zuider-kruis, *n.N.* Southern Cross. Zuid-·Holland, *n.N.* South Holland (*province*). zuid·oost,

adv. south-east. zuid·oostelijk, *a.* south-east. Zuid-Oosten, *n.N.* South-East. ·Zuidpoolzee, *N.* Antartic (Ocean). zuid-·west, *adv.* south-west. zuid·westelijk, *a.* south-west. Zuid·Westen, *n.N.* South-West.

·zuigeling, *n.* baby, suckling. ·zuigen, *v.i., str.* to suck. ~ *op* or *aan*, to suck. ·zuiger, -s, *n.* sucker; piston. ·zuigfles, -ssen, *n.* feeding-bottle. ·zuiging, *n.* sucking; suction. ·zuigworm, *n.* fluke.

zuil, *n.* pillar, column. ·zuilengalerij, *n.* colonnade.

·zuinig, *a.* economical, thrifty. ·zuinigheid, -heden, *n.* economy, thrift. ·zuinigjes, *adv.* thriftily.

·zuipen, *v.i., str. & v.t., str.* to drink, booze. ·zuiper, -s, *n.*, ·zuiplap, -ppen, *n.* boozer.

·zuivel, no *pl.*, *n.n.* dairy-produce. ·zuivel-boerderij, *n.* dairy-farm.

·zuiver, *a.* pure; clear. ·zuiveraar, -s, *n.* cleaner, purifier. ·zuiveren, *v.t.* to clean(se), purify. ·zuiverheid, no *pl.*, *n.* purity. ·zuivering, *n.* purification, cleansing. ·zuiveringszout, no *pl.*, *n.n.* aperient salt.

zulk, *pron.* such. zulks, *pron.* such (a thing), that.

·zullen, zal, *v.aux.* (*for future tense or probability*) shall, will. zou, should, would; *hij zou gezegd hebben*, he is supposed to have said; *wat zou het?*, what of it?

·zullie, *pron.* (*coll.*) they.

zult, *n.* brawn (*meat*).

·zulte, -n, *n.* sea-aster.

·zulten, *v.t.* to pickle.

·zundgat, *n.n.* touch-hole.

·zuren, zuur, *v.i.* to turn sour. ·zuring, *n.* sorrel. ·zuringzuur, no *pl.*, *n.n.* oxalic acid.

zus, *adv.* thus. ~ *of zo*, one thing *or* the other; *het staat* ~ *of zo*, it is touch and go. ¶ -ssen, *n.* sister; little girl. ·zuster, -s, *n.* sister; nurse, sister. ·zusterliefde, no *pl.*, *n.* sisterly love. ·zusterlijk, *a.* sisterly. ·zusterschool -scholen, *n.* convent school.

zuur, zure, *a.* sour, acid. *een* ~ *stukje brood*, a hard-earned living; ~ *worden*, to turn sour. ¶ zuren, *n.n.* acid; heartburn. *in 't* ~, pickled. ·zuurachtig, *a.* sourish. ·zuurbes, -ssen, *n.* barberry. ·zuurdeeg, no *pl.*, *n.n.*, ·zuurdesem, no *pl.*, *n.* leaven. ·zuurheid, no *pl.*, *n.* sourness. ·zuurkast, *n.* fume cupboard. ·zuurkool, no *pl.*, *n.* sauerkraut. ·zuurpruim, *n.* kill-joy, wet-blanket. ·zuurstof, no *pl.*, *n.* oxygen. ·zuurtje, -s, *n.n.* acid-drop. ·zuurverdiend, *a.* hard-earned. ·zuurvrij, *a.* free from acid.

zwaai, *n.* swing, flourish, turn. ·zwaaien, *v.t.* to swing; to wield. ¶ *v.i.* ~ *met*, to wave.

zwaan, zwanen, *n.* swan.

zwaar, zware, *a.* heavy, severe. ~ *op de hand*, dull, stodgy. ¶ *adv.* heavily; seriously, badly. ·zwaarbeladen, *a.* heavily laden.

zwaard, *n.n.* sword; leeboard. ·zwaardleen,

-lenen, *n.n.* male fief. zwaardlelie, -s, *n.* gladiolus. zwaardvechter, -s, *n.* gladiator.
zwaarhoofd, *n.* pessimist. zwaarhoofdig, *a.* pessimistic, gloomy. zwaarlijvig, *a.* corpulent. zwaarmoedig, *a.* melancholy. zwaarmoedigheid, no pl., *n.* melancholy. zwaarte, no pl., *n.* weight, heaviness. zwaartekracht, no pl., *n.* (force of) gravity. zwaartelijn, *n.* median. zwaartepunt, *n.n.* centre of gravity. zwaartillend, *a.* taking things too seriously. zwaarwichtig, *a.* weighty, ponderous.
zwabber, -s, *n.* mop, swab. zwabberen, *v.t.* to mop, swab.
zwachtel, -s, *n.* (roller-)bandage. zwachtelen, *v.t.* to bandage.
zwager, -s, *n.* brother-in-law. zwagerin, -nnen, *n.* sister-in-law.
zwak, -kke, *a.* weak, feeble; faint. ¶ no pl., *n.n.* weakness, foible. zwakheid, -heden, *n.* weakness. zwakhoofdig, *a.* weak-minded. zwakjes, *adv.* weakly, faintly. zwakkelijk, *a.* weakly. zwakkeling, *n.* weakling. zwakte, no pl., *n.* weakness, delicacy. zwakzinnig, *a.* feeble-minded, mentally deficient.
zwalken, *v.i.* to drift about.
zwaluw, *n.* swallow (*bird*). zwaluwstaart, *n.* dovetail.
zwam, -mmen, *n.* fungus. zwammen, zwam, *v.i.* to gas. zwamneus, -zen, *n.* gas-bag (*fig.*).
zwanebloem, *n.* flowering rush. zwanebrood, no pl., *n.n.* sweet flag.
zwang, no pl., *n. in* ~, in vogue. zwanger, *a.* pregnant. zwangerschap, -ppen, *n.* pregnancy.
zwarigheid, -heden, *n.* difficulty, scruple. *zwarigheden maken,* to raise objections.
zwart, *a.* black. ¶ no pl., *n.n.* black. ¶ *adv.* gloomily. zwartbont, *a.* black and white, mottled. zwartgallig, *a.* melancholy. zwartkapje, -s, *n.n.* black-cap (*bird*). zwartkopmees, -mezen, *n.* marsh titmouse. zwartlakens, *a.* (of) black cloth. zwartogig, *a.* black-eyed. zwartoog, -ogen, *n.* black-eyed person. zwartrok, -kken, *n.* black-coat (*clergyman*); rook, crow. zwartsel, no pl., *n.n.* blacking.
zwavel, no pl., *n.* sulphur. zwavelachtig, *a.* sulphurous. zwavelbloem, no pl., *n.* flowers of sulphur. zwavelen, *v.t.* to fumigate (*with sulphur*). zwaveligzuur, no pl., *n.n.* sulphurous acid. zwavelstok, -kken, *n.* sulphur match. zwavelwaterstof, no pl., *n.* sulphuretted hydrogen. zwavelzuur, no pl., *n.n.* sulphuric acid.
Zweden, *n.N.* Sweden. Zweed, Zweden, *N.* Swede. Zweeds, *a.* Swedish.
zweefmolen, -s, *n.* whirligig (*in fair*). zweefrek, -kken, *n.n.* flying trapeze zweefvliegtuig, *n.n.* glider (*aeroplane*). zweefvlucht, *n.* volplane.
zweem, no pl., *n.,* zweempje, -s, *n.n.* touch,

shade. *geen* ~ *van waarleid,* not a semblance of truth.
zweep, zwepen, *n.* whip, horsewhip. zweeptol, -llen, *n.* whipping-top.
zweer, zweren, *n.* sore, ulcer, boil.
zweet, no pl., *n.n.* sweat; moisture. zweetdoek, *n.* sudarium. zweetmiddel, *n.n.* sudorific. zweetvoeten, pl. only, *n.* sweaty feet. zweetziekte, no pl., *n.* sweating sickness.
zwelgen, *v.t., str.* to swallow; to guzzle. zwelger, -s, *n.* glutton.
zwellen, zwel, *v.i., str.* to swell. zwelling, *n.* swelling.
zwembad, *n.n.* swimming bath.
zwemen, zweem, *v.i.* ~ *naar,* to border upon.
zwemmen, zwem, *v.i., str.* to swim. zwemmer, -s, *n.* swimmer. zwemmerig, *a.* watery. zwemvest, *n.n.* life-jacket. zwemvlies, -zen, *n.n.* web (*of foot*).
zwendel, -s, *n.* swindle. zwendelaar, -s, *n.* swindler. zwendelarij, *n.* swindle.
zwengel, -s, *n.* pump-handle; flax-brake, swingle, scutcher. zwengelaar, -s, *n.* scutcher. zwengelarij, *n.* scutching mill.
zwengelen, *v.t.* to swingle, scutch.
zwenken, *v.t.* to swerve, wheel round. zwenkgras, no pl., *n.n.* fescue (*grass*). zwenking, *n.* turn.
zwepen, zweep, *v.t.* to whip, lash.
zweren, zweer, *v.i., str.* to ulcerate, fester. ¶ *v.t., str.* to swear. ~ *op,* to swear at *or* on.
zwerfblok, -kken, *n.n.,* zwerfkei, *n.* erratic block *or* boulder. zwerflust, no pl., *n.* roving spirit. zwerftocht, *n.* wandering. zwerfvogel, -s, *n.* nomadic bird. zwerfziek, *a.* of a roving disposition.
zwerk, no pl., *n.n.* welkin.
zwerm, *n.* swarm. zwermen, *v.i.* to swarm. zwermtijd, *n.* swarming season.
zwerveling, *n.* wanderer. zwerven, zwerf, *v.i., str.* to wander, roam. zwerver, -s, *n.* vagabond, tramp.
zweten, zweet, *v.i.* to sweat. zweterig, *a.* sweaty.
zwetsen, *v.i.* to brag. zwetser, -s, *n.* braggart. zwetserij, *n.* bragging.
zweven, zweef, *v.i.* to float (in); to glide (*aeroplane*); to hover.
zwezerik, -kken, *n.* sweetbread.
zwichten, *v.i.* to give way. ~ *voor,* to yield to.
zwiepen, *v.i.* to swish.
zwier, no pl., *n.* flourish; pomp. *aan de* ~ *gaan,* to go on the spree. zwierbol, -llen, *n.* wild spark. zwieren, *v.i.* to reel. zwierig, *a.* dashing; flamboyant.
zwijgen, *v.i., str.* to be silent, keep silent. ¶ no pl., *n.n.* silence. *iemand het* ~ *opleggen,* to impose silence on; *tot* ~ *brengen,* to silence. zwijgend, *a.* silent. Zwijger, *N. Willem de* ~, William the Silent. zwijgzaam, -zame, *a.* taciturn.

zwijm, no pl., *n.* swoon. *in ~ vallen*, to swoon. ·zwijmelen, *v.i.* to become *or* feel dizzy.

zwijn, *n.n.* hog; swine. *wild ~*, wild boar. ·zwijnachtig, *a.* swinish. ·zwijnenboel, no pl., *n.* (*fig.*) pigsty. ·zwijnenhoeder, -s, *n.* swineherd. ·zwijnenstal, -llen, *n.* pigsty, piggery. zwijne·rij, *n.* filth. ·zwijntje, -s, *n.n.* little pig; piece of luck.

·zwikken, zwik, *v.t.* to sprain.
·zwingel, -s, *n. See* zwengel.
·Zwitser, -s, *N.* Swiss. ·Zwitserland, *n.N.* Switzerland. ·Zwitsers, *a.* Swiss.
·zwoegen, *v.i.* to toil. ·zwoeger, -s, *n.* toiler.
zwoel, *a.* sultry. ·zwoelheid, no pl., *n.* sultriness.
zwoerd, no pl., *n.n.* bacon-rind.

A

a, *indef. art.* een; per.
aback, *adv.* terug. *to be taken* ~, verbluft staan *irr.*
abacus, *n.* telraam *n.n.*
abaft, *adv.* achter; op het achterschip.
abandon, *v.t.* aan zijn lot *n.n.* overlaten *str.*, laten *str.* varen. ¶ *v.r. to* ~ *oneself to,* zich overgeven *str.* aan. ¶ *n.* ongedwongenheid *n.*, nonchalance *n.* **abandoned,** *a.* ongegeneerd; verdorven. **abandonment,** *n.* achterlating *n.*, afstand *n.*; verlaten *n.n.*
abase, *v.t.* vernederen, verlagen. **abasement,** *n.* vernedering *n.*
abash, *v.t.* beschamen. **abashed,** *a.* verlegen, onthutst. **abashment,** *n.* beschaming *n.*
abate, *v.t.* afnemen *str.*, verzwakken, verminderen; gaan *irr.* liggen. **abatement,** *n.* vermindering *n.*
abbess, *n.* abdis *n.* **abbey,** *n.* abdij *n.* **abbot,** *n.* abt *n.*
abbreviate, *v.t.* afkorten, verkorten, bekorten. **abbreviation,** *n.* afkorting *n.*
abdicate, *v.t. & v.i.* afstand *n.* doen *irr.* (van). **abdication,** *n.* afstand (van de troon) *n.*
abdomen, *n.* buik *n.*; achterlijf *n.n.* (*insect*). **abdominal,** *a.* buik-.
abduct, *v.t.* ontvoeren. **abduction,** *n.* ontvoering *n.* **abductor,** *n.* ontvoerder *n.*
abeam, *adv.* dwarsscheeps. ~ *of,* vlak tegenover.
abed, *adv.* in *or* te bed.
aberrant, *a.* afwijkend, afdwalend. **aberration,** *n.* aberratie *n.* (*optical*); afdwaling *n.*
abet, *v.t.* bijstand *n.* verlenen; ophitsen. **abettor,** *n.* opstoker *n.*
abeyance, *n. in* ~, onbeheerd (*estate*), opgeschort.
abhor, *v.t.* verfoeien, verafschuwen. **abhorrence,** *n.* afschuw *n.* **abhorrent,** *a.* onverdragelijk.
abide, *v.t. & v.i.* verwijlen, (ver)toeven; wachten op. *to* ~ *by,* zich houden *irr.* aan. **abiding,** *a.* duurzaam.
ability, *n.* bekwaamheid *n.*, vermogen *n.n. to the best of my* ~, naar mijn beste vermogen.
abject, *a.*, ~**ly,** *adv.* verachtelijk; nederig. **abjection,** *n.* vernedering *n.*
abjuration, *n.* afzwering *n.* **abjure,** *v.t.* afzweren *str.*
ablative, *n.* ablatief *n.*
ablaze, *a.* in vuur *n.n.* en vlam *n.* vlammend, in lichte(r) laaie.
able, *a.* bekwaam, knap; bij machte. *to be* ~ *to,* kunnen *irr.*, vermogen *irr.*; ~ *seaman,*

vol matroos *n.*; ~*bodied,* weerbaar, gezond van lijf *n.n.* en leden *pl.n.n.*
ablet, *n.* alvertje *n.n.*
ablution, *n.* ablutie *n.*, reiniging *n.*
ably, *adv.* bekwaam, knap, kundig.
abnegate, *v.t.* verloochenen, afzweren *str.* **abnegation,** *n.* zelfverloochening *n.*
abnormal, *a.*, ~**ly,** *adv.* abnormaal. **abnormality,** *n.* abnormaliteit *n.*
aboard, *adv.* aan boord.
abode, *n.* woonplaats *n.*, verblijf *n.n.*
abolish, *v.t.* afschaffen, opheffen *str.* ~**abolishment,** *n.*, **abolition,** *n.* afschaffing *n.*
abominable, *a.*, -**bly,** *adv.* afschuwelijk. **abominate,** *v.t.* verafschuwen, verfoeien. **abomination,** *n.* verafschuwing *n.* (*emotion*); schanddaad *n.* (*action*). *to hold in* ~, verafschuwen, gruwen van.
aboriginal, *a.* inheems; oorspronkelijk. **aborigine,** *n.* inboorling *n.*
abort, *v.i.* ontijdig bevallen *str.*; avorteren. **abortion,** *n.* ontijdige geboorte *n.*; vruchtafdrijving *n.* **abortive,** *a.* vergeefs, mislukt, vruchteloos.
abound, *v.i.* overvloedig zijn. *to* ~ *with,* vol zijn van, wemelen van.
about, *prep.* om, rondom; overal in; ongeveer, omstreeks, omtrent; betreffende, over, aangaande. *what* ~ . . ., hoe zit het met . . . ¶ *adv.* om; in omloop. *to be* ~, bij de hand zijn; *round* ~, rondom, er omheen.
above, *prep.* boven, meer dan; over. ~*board,* eerlijk, open, oprecht. ¶ *a.* bovengenoemd. ¶ *adv.* boven; hierboven, daarboven. ~ *all,* vooral, in de eerste plaats; ~*mentioned,* bovenvermeld. ¶ *n.* bovenstaande *n.* or *n.n.*; bovengenoemde *n.* or *n.n.*; bovenvermelde *n.* or *n.n.*
abrade, *v.t.* afschuren, afslijten *str.*; schaven. **abrasion,** *n.* schuring *n.*, geschaafde plek *n.*
abreast, *adv.* naast elkaar, zij aan zij. *to keep* ~ *of* or *with,* op de hoogte blijven *str.* van.
abridge, *v.t.* bekorten. **abridgement,** *n.* bekorting *n.*
abroad, *adv.* buitenslands; buitenshuis. *from* ~, uit het buitenland; *to get* ~, de ronde doen *irr.* (*rumour*).
abrogate, *v.t.* afschaffen, opheffen *str.*, herroepen *str.*, **abrogation,** *n.* afschaffing *n.*, opheffing *n.*
abrupt, *a.*, ~**ly,** *adv.* plotseling, onverwacht; bruusk. **abruptness,** *n.* plotseling afbreken *n.n.*; bruuskheid *n.*, kortheid *n.*
Absalom, *N.* Absalon *N.*
abscess, *n.* abces *n.n.*, gezwel *n.n.*
abscond, *v.i.* er van door gaan *irr.*, zich uit de voeten maken.
absence, *n.* afwezigheid *n.*, gebrek *n.n.*

~ of mind, verstrooidheid n. **absent,** v.t.
to ~ oneself, wegblijven str. ¶ a., ~ly,
adv. afwezig; verstrooid. **absentee,** n.
afwezige n. **absenteeism,** n. arbeidsver-
zuim n.n. **absent-minded,** a. verstrooid.
absolute, a., ~ly, adv. volkomen, volstrekt,
volslagen, absoluut.
absorb, v.t. in zich opnemen str., absorberen,
opslorpen. **absorbed,** a. verdiept. **absor-
bent,** n. absorberende stof n. **absorbing,** a.
boeiend (story). **absorption,** n. absorptie
n.; verdiept zijn n.n.
abstain, v.i. to ~ from, zich onthouden irr.
van. **abstainer,** n. (geheel)onthouder n.
abstemious, a. matig. **abstemiousness,** n.
matigheid n.
abstention, n. onthouding n.
abstinence, n. (geheel)onthouding n., matigheid n. **abstinent,** a. zich onthoudend,
matig.
abstract, v.t. onttrekken str., aftrekken str.;
ontvreemden. ¶ a. abstract; afgetrokken.
¶ n. korte inhoud n., uittreksel n.n.
abstracted, a., ~ly, adv. in gedachten pl.n.
verzonken, afgetrokken. **abstraction,** n.
abstractie n.; afgetrokkenheid n.; ont-
vreemding n.
abstruse, a., ~ly, adv. diepzinnig, duister.
absurd, a., ~ly, adv. onzinnig, ongerijmd,
belachelijk. **absurdity,** n. onzinnigheid n.,
dwaasheid n.
abundance, n. overvloed n., menigte n.
in ~, volop. **abundant,** a. overvloedig.
~ in, rijk aan. ¶ ~ly, adv. overvloedig,
rijkelijk.
abuse, v.t. misbruiken, misbruik maken van;
uitschelden str. beschimpen. ¶ n. misbruik
n.n.; misstand n.; scheldwoorden pl.n.n.
abusive, a., ~ly, adv. grof; beledigend.
abut, v.i. to ~ on, grenzen aan, belenden. **abutment,** n. stenen beer n., schraag-
pijler n.
abysmal, a. bodemloos, grondeloos. **abyss,** n.
(bodemloze) afgrond n.
acacia, n. acacia n.
academic(al), a., ~ly, adv. academisch.
academician, n. lid n.n. van een academie n.
academy, n. academie n.; genootschap n.n.,
instituut n.n.
accede, v.i. to ~ to, instemmen met; aanvaarden, inwilligen, voldoen irr. aan;
bestijgen str. (throne).
accelerate, v.t. versnellen, bespoedigen.
acceleration, n. versnelling n., bespoediging
n. **accelerator,** n. versneller n.
accent, v.t. accentueren, de nadruk leggen op.
¶ n. accent n.n., klemtoon n., nadruk n.
accentuate, v.t. doen uitkomen. **accentuation,** n. nadruk n., klemtoon n.
accept, v.t. aanvaarden, aannemen str.;
accepteren. **acceptability,** n. aannemelijkheid n. **acceptable,** a., ~ly, adv. aannemelijk,
aanvaardbaar; welkom. **acceptance,** n.
aannemen n.n., aanneming n., acceptatie n.

acceptation, n. aanneming n.; aangenomen
betekenis n. **acceptor,** n. acceptant n.
access, n. toegang n.; genaakbaarheid n.;
vlaag n., opwelling n. **accessibility,** n.
toegankelijkheid n.; genaakbaarheid n.,
vatbaarheid n. **accessible,** a. toegankelijk;
genaakbaar, vatbaar.
accession, n. aanwinst n.; aanvaarding n.
(office); bestijging n. (throne).
accessory, a. bijkomstig; medeplichtig. ¶ n.
bijzaak n.; medeplichtige n. accessories,
onderdelen pl. n.n., benodigdheden pl. n.
accidence, n. vormleer n., buigingsleer n.
accident, n. toeval n.n.; ongeluk n.n., ongeval
n.n. **accidental,** a., ~ly, adv. toevallig;
bijkomstig.
acclaim, v.t. toejuichen. **acclamation,** n.
acclamatie n.; bijval n.
acclimatization, n. acclimatisatie n. **acclimatize,** v.t. acclimatiseren.
acclivity, n. helling n.
accolade, n. accolade n.
accommodate, v.t. aanpassen; plaats n.
hebben voor, onderdak n.n. verlenen aan.
to ~ with, voorzien irr. van; to ~ oneself to,
zich aanpassen aan, zich voegen naar.
accommodating, a. inschikkelijk. **accommodation,** n. aanpassing n., inschikkelijkheid n.; onderdak n.n., onderkomen n.n.
~ladder, staatsietrap n., valreepstrap n.
accompaniment, n. begeleiding n., ac-
compagnement n.n. **accompanist,** n.
begeleider n. **accompany,** v.t. begeleiden,
vergezeld doen gaan; accompagneren.
to accompany with or by, begeleiden van,
begeleiden met.
accomplice, n. medeplichtige n.
accomplish, v.t. vervullen; verwezenlijken,
tot stand brengen irr. **accomplished,** a.
ontwikkeld, beschaafd. **accomplishment,**
n. vervulling n., voltooiing n.; talent n.n.
accord, v.i. overeenstemmen. ¶ v.t. toestaan
irr., verlenen. ¶ n. overeenstemming n.
with one ~, eenstemmig; of one's own ~,
uit eigen beweging n. **accordance,** n.
overeenstemming n. in ~ with, overeenkomstig. **accordant,** a. ~ with or to,
volgens, in overeenstemming met.
according, adv. ~ to, volgens; ~ as,
al naar gelang. **accordingly,** adv. dus,
dienovereenkomstig.
accordion, n. harmonica n.
accost, v.t. aanspreken str.
accouchement, n. verlossing n. **accoucheur,**
n. verloskundige n.
account, v.i. to ~ for, rekenschap n. geven
str. van, verklaren; to be ~ed, geacht
worden str. ¶ n. rekening n.; rekenschap n.;
verslag n.n., verklaring n.; conto n.n.,
krediet n.n. of no ~, van geen belang n.n.;
on one's own ~, op eigen verantwoordelijkheid n., voor eigen rekening; on no ~,
in geen geval n.n.; on ~ of, vanwege,
wegens, ter wille van; to call to ~, ter

verantwoording *n.* roepen; *to close an* ∼,
een conto sluiten *str.*; *to take* ∼ *of*, rekening
houden *irr.* met; *to take into* ∼, meetellen,
meerekenen; *to give a good* ∼ *of oneself*,
zich kranig gedragen *str.*; *to keep* ∼*s*,
boekhouden *irr.*; *to open an* ∼ *with*, een
krediet openen bij; *to turn something into*
∼, partij trekken *str.* van iets, iets ten
nutte maken. **accountability,** *n.* verantwoordelijkheid *n.*; toerekenbaarheid *n.*
accountable, *a.* verantwoordelijk. **accountancy,** *n.* boekhouden *n.n.* **accountant,** *n.*
boekhouder *n. chartered* ∼, accountant *n.*
accoutre, *v.t.* uitrusten; uitdossen. **accoutre-
ments,** *pl.n.* uitrusting *n.*
accredit, *v.t.* machtigen, van geloofsbrieven
pl.n. voorzien; krediet *n.n.* verschaffen;
toeschrijven *str.* **accredited,** *a.* geaccredi-
teerd.
accretion, *n.* aanwas *n.*
accrue, *v.t.* toenemen *str.*, oplopen *str.*
accumulate, *v.t. & v.i.* ophopen, opeenstapelen. **accumulation,** *n.* ophoping *n.*,
opeenstapeling *n.* **accumulative,** *a.* zich
opeenstapelend. **accumulator,** *n.* accu
(mulator) *n.*; ophoper *n.* (*person*).
accuracy, *n.* nauwkeurigheid *n.* **accurate,** *a.*,
∼ly, *adv.* nauwkeurig, stipt.
accursed, *a.* vervloekt.
accusation, *n.* beschuldiging *n.*, aanklacht *n.*
accusative, *n.* accusatief *n.* **accusatory,**
a. beschuldigend. **accuse,** *v.t.* beschuldigen,
aanklagen. *the* ∼*d*, de beschuldigde, de
beklaagde. **accuser,** *n.* beschuldiger *n.*,
aanklager *n.*
accustom, *v.t. to* ∼ *to*, gewennen aan;
to be ∼*ed to*, gewoon zijn aan.
ace, *n.* aas *n.*; kampioen vlieger *n. within
an* ∼ *of*, op een haar *n.n.* na.
acephalous, *a.* koploos.
acerbity, *n.* wrangheid *n.*, scherpte *n.*
acetate, *n.* acetaat *n.n.*, azijnzuurzout *n.n.*
acetic, *a.* azijnzuur. **acetify,** *v.t.* zuur
maken. ¶ *v.i.* zuur worden *str.* **acetous,** *a.*
azijn-. **acetylene,** *n.* acetyleen *n.n.*
ache, *n.* pijn *n.* ¶ *v.i.* pijn doen *irr.*
achievable, *a.* uitvoerbaar. **achieve,** *v.t.*
volbrengen *irr.*, verrichten; behalen.
achievement, *n.* prestatie *n.*, succes
n.n.
achromatic, *a.* achromatisch.
acid, *a.* zuur. ∼ *-drops*, zuurballetjes *pl. n.n.*
¶ *n.* zuur *n.n.* **acidify,** *v.t.* verzuren.
acidity, *n.* zuurheid *n.* **acidulated,** *a.*
zuurachtig. **acidulous,** *a.* zuurachtig.
acknowledge, *v.t.* erkennen; bekennen;
ontvangst *n.* berichten van (*receipt*).
acknowledgement, *n.* erkenning *n.*; bekentenis *n.*; bericht *n.n.* van ontvangst *n.*
acme, *n.* hoogtepunt *n.n.*, toppunt *n.n.*
acne, *n.* puistje(s) *n.n.*
acolyte, *n.* misdienaar *n.*
aconite, *n.* akoniet *n.*, monnikskap *n.*
acorn, *n.* eikel *n.*

acoustic, *a.* acoustisch, gehoor-. **acoustics,**
pl.n. acoustiek *n.*
acquaint. *v.t.* bekend maken. *to* ∼ *oneself
with*, zich op de hoogte stellen van, zich
vertrouwd maken met. **acquaintance,** *n.*
bekendheid *n.*; kennis *n.*, bekende *n.*
(*person*). *to make the* ∼ *of*, kennis maken
met. **acquaintanceship,** *n.* kennis *n.*,
bekendheid *n.*
acquiesce, *v.i. to* ∼ *in*, zich neerleggen bij,
berusten in, berusten bij, inwilligen.
acquiescence, *n.* berusting *n.*, inwilliging *n.*
acquiescent, *a.* geduldig, toegevend.
acquire, *v.t.* verkrijgen *str.*, verwerven. *str.*
acquired, *a.* aangeleerd. **acquirement,** *n.*
verwerving *n.* ∼*s*, kundigheden *pl.n.*
acquisition, *n.* aanwinst *n.*; verkregene *n.n.*
acquisitive, *a.*, ∼ly, *adv.* hebzuchtig.
acquisitiveness, *n.* hebzucht *n.*;
acquit, *v.t.* vrijspreken *str.*; vrijstellen.
acquittal, *n.* vrijspraak *n.* **acquittance,** *n.*
vereffening *n.*; quittering *n.*
acre, *n.* 4047 M²., $\pm$ 0·4 H.A. **acreage,** *n.*
oppervlakte *n.*
acrid, *a.* scherp, bijtend.
acrimonious, *a.*, ∼ly, *adv.* bitter, bits.
acrimony, *n.* scherpheid *n.*, bitsheid *n.*
acrobat, *n.* acrobaat *n.* **acrobatics,** *pl.n.*
acrobatiek *n.*
across, *adv.* dwars, dwars over, dwars door.
to come ∼, tegenkomen *irr.*, (toevallig)
ontmoeten.
acrostic, *n.* naamdicht *n.n.*
act, *v.i.* handelen; acteren (*of actor*). ¶ *v.t.*
spelen, opvoeren (*drama*). ¶ *n.* daad *n.*,
handeling *n.*; wet *n.* (*law*); bedrijf *n.n.*
(*theatre*). ∼ *of God*, force majeure *n.*
A ∼*s of Apostles*, Handelingen *pl.n.*; *to be
caught in the* ∼, op heterdaad betrapt
worden *str.* **acting,** *n.* acteren *n.n.*, spel
n.n. ¶ *a.* waarnemend.
actinic, *a.* actinisch. **actinism,** *n.* actiniteit *n.*
action, *n.* daad *n.*, handeling *n.*; werking *n.*;
mechaniek *n.*; proces *n.n.*, aanklacht *n.*
actionable, *a.* vervolgbaar.
active, *a.*, ∼ly, *adv.* bedrijvig, werkzaam;
actief, levendig. **activity,** *n.* bedrijvigheid
n., werkzaamheid *n.*; levendigheid *n.*
actor, *n.* toneelspeler *n.* **actress,** *n.* toneelspeelster *n.*
actual, *a.*, ∼ly, *adv.* werkelijk, wezenlijk;
tegenwoordig. **actuality,** *n.* werkelijkheid
n.
actuary, *n.* actuaris *n.*
actuate, *v.t.* aansporen, in beweging *n.*
brengen *irr.*
acuity, *n.* scherpheid *n.* **acumen,** *n.* scherpzinnigheid *n.*
acute, *a.*, ∼ly, *adv.* scherp; scherpzinnig,
schrander; hevig, intens. **acuteness,** *n.*
scherpheid *n.*; scherpzinnigheid *n.*
adage, *n.* gezegde *n.n.*
Adam's apple, *n.* Adamsappel *n.*
adamant, *a.*, **adamantine,** *a.* onvermurwbaar.

adapt, *v.t.* aanpassen, geschikt maken; bewerken. **adaptability,** *n.* aanpassingsvermogen *n.n.* **adaptable,** *a.* buigzaam. **adaptation,** *n.* aanpassing *n.*; bewerking *n.* **adaptive,** *a.* geschikt tot aanpassen.

add, *v.t.* & *v.i.* bijvoegen, toevoegen; optellen. *to* ~ *to,* vermeerderen.

adder, *n.* adder *n.* **adder's-wort,** *n.* slangenkruid *n.n.*

addict, *v.r. to addict oneself to,* zich wijden aan; ~*ed to,* verslaafd aan. **addiction,** *n.* verslaafdheid *n.*

addition, *n.* bijvoeging *n.*, toevoeging *n.*; optelling *n.* **additional,** *a.,* ~*ly, adv.* bijkomend, extra.

addle, *a.* bedorven. ¶ *v.t.* bederven *str.* **addle-brained,** *a.,* **addle-pated,** *a.* warhoofdig.

address, *v.t.* aanspreken *str.,* toespreken *str.*; adresseren. ¶ *n.* toespraak *n.*; adres *n.n.*; handigheid *n.* **addressee,** *n.* geadresseerde *n.* **addressograph,** *n.* adresseermachine *n.*

adduce, *v.t.* aanvoeren, aanhalen. **adducible,** *a.* aanvoerbaar.

adenoids, *pl.n.* adenoïden *pl.n.*

adept, *a.* bedreven, kundig. ¶ *n.* deskundige *n.,* ingewijde *n.*

adequacy, *n.* voldoendheid *n.* **adequate,** *a.,* ~*ly, adv.* gepast, geschikt.

adhere, *v.i.* kleven, hangen *str. to* ~ *to,* trouw blijven *str.* aan. **adherence,** *n.* aanhankelijkheid *n.,* trouw *n.* **adherent,** *n.* aanhanger *n.* **adhesion,** *n.* adhesie *n.*; gehechtheid *n.* **adhesive,** *a.,* ~*ly, adv.* kleverig. ~ *label,* gegomd etiket *n.n.*; ~ *plaster,* hechtpleister *n.n.* **adhesiveness,** *n.* kleverigheid *n.*

adipose, *a.* vet.

adjacency, *n.* nabijheid *n.* **adjacent,** *a.* naburig, aangrenzend.

adjectival, *a.,* ~*ly, adv.* bijvoeglijk. **adjective,** *n.* bijvoeglijk naamwoord *n.n.*

adjoin, *v.t. to* ~ *to,* toevoegen aan. ¶ *v.i.* grenzen aan, belenden.

adjourn, *v.t.* verdagen. ¶ *v.i.* uiteengaan *irr.* **adjournment,** *n.* verdaging *n.*

adjudge, *v.t.,* **adjudicate,** *v.t.* toewijzen *str.* **adjudication,** *n.* toewijzing *n.,* vonnis *n.n.*

adjunct, *n.* aanhangsel *n.n.,* toevoegsel *n.n.*

adjuration, *n.* bezwering *n.* **adjure,** *v.t.* bezweren *str.*

adjust, *v.t.* regelen; (ver)stellen. *to* ~ *to,* in overeenstemming *n.* brengen *irr.* met. **adjustable,** *a.* verstelbaar. **adjustment,** *n.* aanpassing *n.,* schikking *n.*

adjutancy, *n.* adjudantsrang *n.* **adjutant,** *n.* adjudant *n.*

admeasure, *v.t.* toemeten *str.* **admeasurement,** *n.* toemeting *n.*

administer, *v.t.* besturen, beheren. *to* ~ *an oath to,* een eed *n.* afnemen *str.*; *to* ~ *justice,* recht spreken *str.* **administration,** *n.* bestuur *n.n.,* beheer *n.n.*; administratie *n.* **administrative,** *a.* administratief.

administrator, *n.* administrateur *n.,* bestuurder *n.,* beheerder *n.* **administratrix,** *n.* bestuurster *n.*

admirable, *a.,* ~*bly, adv.* bewonderenswaardig.

admiral, *n.* admiraal *n.* **admiralty,** *n.* admiraliteit *n. First Lord of the A*~ (Britse) Minister van Marine. ,

admiration, *n.* bewondering *n.* **admire,** *v.t.* bewonderen. **admirer,** *n.* bewonderaar *n.* **admiringly,** *adv.* met bewondering.

admissibility, *n.* toelaatbaarheid *n.*; aannemelijkheid *n.* **admissible,** *a.,* ~*bly, adv.* toelaatbaar; aannemelijk. **admission,** *n.* toelating *n.,* toegang *n.*; aanvaarding *n.*

admit, *v.t.* toelaten *str.*; toegeven *str.*; toegang *n.* verschaffen. **admittance,** *n.* toegang *n. no* ~, verboden toegang *n.* **admittedly,** *adv.* toegegeven.

admixture, *n.* toevoegsel *n.n.,* bijmengsel *n.n.*

admonish, *v.t.* vermanen, berispen, terechtwijzen *str.* **admonition,** *n.* vermaning *n.* **admonitory,** *a.* vermanend.

ado, *n.* ophef *n.,* omslag *n. much* ~ *about nothing,* veel drukte *n.* om niets.

adobe, *n.* in de zon gebakken klei *n.*

adolescence, *n.* jongelingschap *n.n.* **adolescent,** *a.* opgroeiend. ¶ *n.* aankomende jongen *n.*; aankomend meisje *n.n.*

adopt, *v.t.* aannemen *str.,* overnemen *str.* **adoption,** *n.* aanneming *n.* **adoptive,** *a.* aangenomen.

adorable, *a.,* ~*bly, adv.* aanbiddelijk. **adoration,** *n.* aanbidding *n.* **adore,** *v.t.* aanbidden *str.* **adorer,** *n.* aanbidder *n.*

adorn, *v.t.* versieren, tooien. **adornment,** *n.* versiering *n.,* tooi *n.*

adrenalin, *n.* adrenaline *n.*

Adriatic, *a.* Adriatisch.

adrift, *a.* aan wind *n.* en golven *pl.n.* prijsgegeven *str. to break* ~, op drift *n.* raken; *to cut oneself* ~ *from,* zich losmaken van; *to turn* ~, aan zijn lot *n.n.* overlaten *str.*

adroit, *a.,* ~*ly, adv.* behendig. **adroitness,** *n.* behendigheid *n.*

adulation, *n.* (kruiperige) vleierij *n.* **adulator,** *n.* kruiper *n.* **adulatory,** *a.* kruiperig, vleiend.

adult, *a.* volwassen. ¶ *n.* volwassene *n.*

adulterate, *v.t.* vervalsen. **adulteration,** *n.* vervalsing *n.* **adulterer,** *n.* echtbreker *n.,* overspelige *n.* **adulteress,** *n.* echtbreekster *n.,* overspelige *n.* **adulterous,** *a.* overspelig. **adultery,** *n.* echtbreuk *n.,* overspel *n.n.*

adumbrate, *v.t.* schetsen, een vaag beeld *n.n.* geven *str.* van.

advance, *v.t.* naar voren brengen *str.*; opperen; bevorderen; voorschieten *str.* ¶ *v.i.* vooruitkomen *irr.,* vorderen. ¶ *n.* vordering *n.*; bevordering *n.*; vooruitgang *n.*; hoger bod *n.n. in* ~, vooraf, vooruit. **advancement,** *n.* promotie *n.*; vordering *n.*

advantage, *n.* voordeel *n.n. to take* ~ *of,* profiteren van, partij *n.* trekken *str.* van, misbruik *n.n.* maken van. **advantageous,** *a.* voordelig.

advent, *n.* komst *n.*; advent *n.*

adventitious, *a.* toevallig.

adventure, *v.t.* wagen. ¶ *n.* avontuur *n.n.*; gewaagde onderneming *n.* **adventurer,** *n.* avonturier *n.* **adventuresome,** *a.* avontuurlijk, vermetel. **adventuress,** *n.* avonturierster *n.* **adventurous,** *a.* avontuurlijk.

adverb, *n.* bijwoord *n.n.* **adverbial,** *a.*, ~ly, *adv.* bijwoordelijk.

adversary, *n.* tegenstander *n.* **adverse,** *a.*, ~ly, *adv.* tegengesteld; ongunstig. **adversity,** *n.* tegenspoed *n.*

advert, *v.i.* to ~ to, wijzen *str.* op, terugkomen *irr.* op.

advertise, *v.t.* & *v.i.* adverteren; reklame *n.* maken voor. **advertisement,** *n.* advertentie *n.*; reklame *n.* **advertiser,** *n.* adverteerder *n.*; reklameblad *n.n.* **advertising,** *a.* advertentie-, publiciteits-.

advice, *n.* raad *n.*, advies *n.n.*; bericht *n.n.* at the ~ of, op raad van. **advisability,** *n.* raadzaamheid *n.* **advisable,** *a.* raadzaam.

advise, *v.t.* raadgeven *str.*; raden, aanraden, adviseren; berichten. **advised,** *a.* doordacht, welberaden. **advisedly,** *adv.* willens en wetens, na rijp beraad *n.n.*, met opzet *n.* **adviser,** *n.* raadgever *n.*, raadsman *n.*

advocacy, *n.* pleidooi *n.n.*, voorspraak *n.* **advocate,** *v.t.* verdedigen, pleiten voor, voorstaan *irr.* ¶ *n.* verdediger *n.*, voorspreker *n.*

advowson, *n.* collatierecht *n.n.*

adze, *n.* dissel *n.*

Aegean, *a.* Aegeïsch.

aegis, *n.* aegis *n.*, schild *n.n.*, bescherming *n.*

Aeolian, *a.* Aeolisch.

aerated, *a.* koolzuurhoudend.

aerial, *a.* lucht-. ¶ *n.* antenne *n.*

aerodrome, *n.* vliegveld *n.n.*

aerolite, *n.* meteoorsteen *n.*

aeronaut, *n.* luchtschipper *n.* **aeronautic,** *a.* luchtvaart-. **aeronautics,** *n.* luchtvaart *n.*

aeroplane, *n.* vliegtuig *n.n.*

aerostatics, *pl.n.* aërostatica *sg.n.*

Aesop, *N.* Esopus *N.*

aesthete, *n.* aestheticus *n.* **aesthetic,** *a.*, -ally, *adv.* aesthetisch. **aesthetics,** *pl.n.* aesthetica *sg.n.*, schoonheidsleer *n.*

afar, *adv.* ver, in de verte. from ~, uit de verte.

affability, *n.* minzaamheid *n.*, vriendelijkheid *n.* **affable,** *a.*, ~bly, *adv.* minzaam, vriendelijk.

affair, *n.* zaak *n.*, aangelegenheid *n.*; kwestie *n.*; liefdesgeschiedenis *n.*

affect, *v.t.* invloed *n.* hebben op; roeren, bewegen *str.*; aandoen *irr.* **affectation,** *n.* geaffecteerdheid *n.* **affected,** *a.*, ~ly, *adv.* geaffecteerd; geroerd, aangedaan. **affection,** *n.* genegenheid *n.*; aandoening *n.* **affectionate,** *a.*, ~ly, *adv.* toegenegen, hartelijk.

affidavit, *n.* beëdigde (schriftelijke) verklaring *n.*

affiliate, *v.t.* als lid *n.n.* opnemen *str.* ¶ *v.i.* to ~ with, zich aansluiten *str.* bij. **affiliation,** *n.* aansluiting *n.*; opnemen *n.n.* ~ order, echtingsbewijs *n.n.*

affinity, *n.* affiniteit *n.*; overeenkomst *n.*

affirm, *v.t.* verzekeren; bevestigen, bekrachtigen. **affirmation,** *n.* bevestiging *n.* **affirmative,** *a.*, ~ly, *adv.* bevestigend. ¶ *n.* in the ~, bevestigend.

affix, *v.t.* vasthechten.

afflict, *v.t.* bedroeven; kwellen. **affliction,** *n.* droefenis *n.*, leed *n.n.*; bezoeking *n.*

affluence, *n.* overvloed *n.* **affluent,** *a.*, ~ly, *adv.* overvloedig. ¶ *n.* zijrivier *n.*

afflux, *n.* toevloed *n.*

afford, *v.t.* verschaffen, opleveren; kunnen *irr.* betalen.

afforest, *v.t.* bebossen. **afforestation,** *n.* bebossing *n.*

affray, *n.* vechtpartij *n.*

affront, *v.t.* beledigen. ¶ *n.* belediging *n.*

afield, *adv.* op het veld. far ~, ver weg, ver van huis *n.n.*

afire, *adv.* in brand *n.*

aflame, *adv.* in lichte(r) laaie.

afloat, *adv.* drijvend; op zee *n.*

afoot, *adv.* op de been. to be ~, bestaan *irr.*; to set ~, aan de gang brengen *irr.*, op touw zetten.

afore, *prep.* voor. **aforementioned,** *a.*, aforesaid, *a.* voornoemd.

afraid, *a.* bang, bevreesd.

afresh, *adv.* opnieuw.

Africa, *N.* Afrika *n.N.*

aft, *adv.* achteruit; op het achterschip. fore and ~, voor en achter.

after, *prep.* achter, achteraan; na; naar, volgens. ~ all, per slot *n.n.* van rekening *n.* ¶ *adv.* daarna; achteraan. ¶ *c.* nadat. ¶ *a.* later, volgend.

afterbirth, *n.* nageboorte *n.*

after-crop, *n.* tweede oogst *n.*

after-dinner, *a.* voor na den eten.

afterglow, *n.* nagloed *n.*

aftermath, *n.* nagras *n.n.*; (*fig.*) nasleep *n.*

afternoon, *n.* (na)middag *n.*

aftertaste, *n.* nasmaak *n.*

afterthought, *n.* nader inzien *n.n.*, nadere overweging *n.*

afterwards, *adv.* later, naderhand.

again, *adv.* opnieuw, weer; nogmaals; terug. ~ and ~, telkens weer; twice as much ~, driemaal zoveel.

against, *prep.* tegen; strijdig met.

agape, *adv.* met open mond.

agaric, *n.* vliegenzwam *n.*

agate, *n.* agaat *n.* ¶ *a.* agaten.

agave, *n.* agave *n.*, Amerikaanse aloë *n.*

age, *n.* leeftijd *n.*, ouderdom *n.*; tijdperk *n.n.*; eeuwigheid *n.* of ~, meerderjarig, volmondig; under ~, minderjarig, onmondig; old ~, oude dag *n.* ¶ *v.t.* oud

maken. ¶ *v.i.* oud worden *str.* **aged,** *a.*
bejaard, oud. **ageless,** *a.* nooit verouderend.
agency, *n.* agentschap *n.n.*; bemiddeling *n.*,
tussenkomst *n.*
agenda, *n.* agenda *n.*
agent, *n.* agent *n.*; middel *n.n.*
agglomerate, *v.t.* & *v.i.* (zich) opeenstapelen,
(zich) opeenhopen. **agglomeration,** *n.*
agglomeraat *n.n.*; opeenhoping *n.*
agglutinate, *v.t.* samenkleven. **agglutination,**
n. agglutinatie *n.*; samenvoeging *n.*
aggrandize, *v.t.* vergroten, verheerlijken.
aggrandisement, *n.* vergroting *n.*, verheerlijken *n.n.*
aggravate, *v.t.* verergeren, verzwaren;
ergeren. **aggravating,** *a.* verzwarend;
ergerlijk. **aggravation,** *n.* verergering *n.*,
verzwaring *n.*
aggregate, *a.* gezamenlijk. ¶ *n. in the ~,*
in totaal *n.n.*, globaal. ¶ *v.t.* samenvoegen.
aggregation, *n.* aggregatie *n.*; opeenhoping
n.
aggression, *n.* aanval *n.*, aggressie *n.* **aggressive,** *a.* strijdlustig, aggressief. **aggressor,**
n. aanvaller *n.*
aggrieved, *a.* bedroefd; gekrenkt.
aghast, *a.* ontdaan, ontsteld; verbauwereerd.
agile, *a.* behendig; lenig. **agility,** *n.* behendigheid *n.*; lenigheid *n.*
agio, *n.* agio *n.*
agitate, *v.t.* bewegen *str.*; in beroering *n.*
brengen *irr.* ¶ *v.i.* agiteren; propaganda *n.*
maken. **agitation,** *n.* beroering *n.*, woeling
n.; gemoedsbeweging *n.*, agitatie *n.*;
campagne *n.* **agitator,** *n.* opruier *n.*,
volksmenner *n.*
aglow, *a.* gloeiend.
agnail, *n.* nijnagel *n.*
agnate, *a.* bloedverwant *n.* van vaderszijde *n.*
agnostic, *a.* agnostisch. ¶ *n.* agnosticus *n.*
ago, *adv.* geleden.
agog, *adv.* verlangend, belust.
agonize, *v.i.* vergaan *irr.* van pijn *n.*, vergaan
irr. van smart *n.* **agony,** *n.* zielesmart *n.*;
foltering *n.*; doodsstrijd *n.*
agrarian, *a.* agrarisch. ¶ *n.* agrariër *n.*
agree, *v.i.* overeenstemmen, het eens zijn;
overeenkomen *irr.*; kloppen. **agreeable,** *a.*,
~ly, *adv.* aangenaam, prettig. *to be ~ to
something,* iets goedvinden. **agreeableness,**
n. aangenaamheid *n.* **agreement,** *n.*
overeenstemming *n.*; overeenkomst *n.*,
afspraak *n.*
agricultural, *a.* landbouw-; landbouwkundig.
agriculture, *n.* landbouw *n.* **agriculturist,** *n.*
landbouwkundige *n.*; landbouwer *n.*
agrimony, *n.* agrimonie *n.*, leverkruid *n.n.*
aground, *a.* aan de grond, gestrand.
ague, *n.* wisselkoorts *n.*, koude koorts *n.*
ah, *int.* Ah! O! **aha,** *int.* aha! oho!
ahead, *adv.* vooraan; voor, vooruit. *go ~!,*
vooruit!
ahem, *int.* h'm!
ahoy, *int.* ehoi.

aid, *v.t.* helpen *str.*; bijstand *n.* verlenen.
¶ *n.* hulp *n.*, bijstand *n.*
aide-de-camp, *n.* ordonnans *n.*; adjudant *n.*
aigrette, *n.* aigrette *n.*; kleine witte reiger *n.*
ail, *v.t.* schelen, mankeren. **ailing,** *a.* ziekelijk. **ailment,** *n.* ongesteldheid *n.*
aim, *v.i.* mikken. ¶ *v.t. to ~ at,* aanleggen
irr. op. ¶ *n.* doel *n.n.*; oogmerk *n.n.*,
bedoeling *n.* **aimless,** *a.*, **~ly,** *adv.* doelloos.
air, *n.* lucht *n.*; luchtje *n.n.*; wijs *n.*, wijsje
n.n.; voorkomen *n.n.*, schijn *n.* *to give
oneself ~s,* zich airs *pl.n.n.* geven *str.*
¶ *v.t.* luchten; bespreken *str.*; te koop
lopen *str.* met.
aircraft, *n.* vliegtuig *n.n.* **aircraft-carrier,** *n.*
vliegdekschip *n.n.*, vliegkampschip *n.n.*
aircushion, *n.* windkussen *n.n.* **airgun,** *n.*
windbuks *n.* **airhole,** *n.* wak *n.n.*; luchtgat
n.n. **airily,** *adv.* luchtig; luchthartig.
airiness, *n.* luchtigheid *n.*; luchthartigheid
n. **airing,** *n.* luchten *n.n.* *to take an ~,*
een luchtje scheppen. **airless,** *a.* bedompt;
windstil. **air line,** *n.* luchtroute *n.*; luchtvaart maatschappij *n.* **airliner,** *n.*
passagiersvliegtuig *n.n.* **airmail,** *n.* lucht-
post *n.* **airman,** *n.* vliegenier *n.*, vlieger *n.*
airminded, *a.* geïnteresseerd in vliegtuigen
pl.n.n. **airpipe,** *n.* luchtbuis *n.* **airport,** *n.*
vlieghaven *n.* **airpump,** *n.* luchtpomp *n.*
airraid, *n.* luchtaanval *n.* **airshaft,** *n.*
luchtkoker *n.* **airship,** *n.* luchtschip *n.n.*
air-tight, *a.* luchtdicht. **airway,** *n.* lucht-
vaartroute *n.* **airy,** *a.* luchtig; luchthartig.
aisle, *n.* zijbeuk *n.*
ajar, *adv.* op een kier *n.*
akimbo, *adv. with arms ~,* met de handen
pl.n. op de heupen *pl.n.*
akin, *a.* verwant.
alabaster, *n.* albast *n.n.* ¶ *a.* albasten.
alack, *int.* helaas! o wee!
alacrity, *n.* bereidwilligheid *n.*, monterheid *n.*
alarm, *v.t.* verontrusten, verontstellen;
alarmeren. ¶ *n.* alarm *n.n.*; verontrusting
n., ongerustheid *n.*; misbaar *n.n.* **alarm-
bell,** *n.* alarmklok *n.* **alarm-clock,** *n.*
wekker(klok) *n.* **alarm-post,** *n.* alarm-
plaats *n.* **alarmist,** *n.* alarmist *n.*, bang-
maker *n.*
alarum, *n.* alarm *n.n.*; wekker *n.*
alas, *int.* helaas.
alb, *n.* albe *n.*
Albanian, *N.* Albanees *N.* ¶ *a.* Albanisch.
albatross, *n.* albatros *n.*
albeit, *c.* ofschoon, al . . . ook.
albino, *n.* albino *n.*
album, *n.* album *n.n.*
albumen, *n.* eiwit *n.n.*, eiwitstof *n.* **albuminous,** *a.* eiwithoudend.
alchemic, *a.* alchimistisch. **alchemist,** *n.*
alchimist *n.* **alchemy,** *n.* alchimie *n.*
alcohol, *n.* alkohol *n.* **alcoholic,** *a.* alkoholisch.
alcove, *n.* alkoof *n.*; nis *n.*
alder, *n.* els *n.*
alderman, *n.* wethouder *n.*, schepen *n.*

ale, *n.* (Engels) bier *n.n.* **alehouse,** *n.* bierhuis *n.n.*
alembic, *n.* distilleerkolf *n.*
alert, *a.,* ~ly, *adv.* waakzaam. *to be on the* ~, op z'n qui-vive *n.n.* zijn. **alertness,** *n.* waakzaamheid *n.*
algae, *pl.n.* zeewier *n.n.*
algebra, *n.* algebra *n.* **algebraic,** *a.* algebraïsch.
alias, *n.* alias *n.n.* ¶ *a.* alias, anders genoemd.
alibi, *n.* alibi *n.n.*
alien, *a.* vreemd, uitheems. ¶ *n.* vreemdeling *n.,* buitenlander *n.* **alienable,** *a.* vervreemdbaar. **alienate,** *v.t.* vervreemden. **alienation,** *n.* vervreemding *n.;* overdracht *n.* **alienist,** *n.* krankzinnigendokter *n.;* psychiater *n.*
alight, *v.i.* afstappen, uitstappen. ¶ *a.* aangestoken, aan; in brand.
align, *v.t.* richten, in één lijn brengen *irr.* **alignment,** *n.* opstelling *n.,* lijn *n.*
alike, *a.* gelijk. ¶ *adv.* gelijk(elijk), op dezelfde manier.
aliment, *n.* voedsel *n.n.,* spijs *n.* **alimentary,** *a.* voedings-. **alimentation,** *n.* voeding *n.*
alimony, *n.* alimentatie *n.,* uitkering *n.* (aan een gescheiden vrouw).
aliquot, *a.* evenmatig.
alive, *a.* levend, in leven; opgewekt, levendig. ~ *to,* vatbaar, gevoelig voor.
alkali, *n.* loogzout *n.n.* **alkaline,** *a.* alkalisch. **alkalization,** *n.* alkalisering *n.*
all, *a.* heel, geheel, gans; al, alle; ieder, enig, elk. ~ *kinds of,* allerhande; *on* ~ *fours,* op handen *pl.n.* en voeten *pl.n.;* *with* ~ *speed,* in aller ijl *n.;* *with* ~ *my heart,* van ganser harte. ¶ *adv.* helemaal, geheel, volkomen. ~ *along,* aldoor; ~ *around,* overal om . . . heen; ~ *at once,* tegelijk; ~ *but,* bijna; ~ *over,* overal in . . ., voorbij; ~ *right,* in orde; ~ *the better,* des te beter; ~ *the same,* toch; *it's* ~ *the same to me,* 't is mij eender. ¶ *pron.* *after* ~, per slot *n.n.* van rekening *n.;* *at* ~, soms; *not at* ~, helemaal niet, geenszins, in 't geheel niet; *once for* ~, eens vooral; *for* ~ *I know,* voor zover ik weet; *for* ~ *I care,* wat mij betreft; *in* ~, ~ *in* ~, alles bij elkaar, in 't geheel; ~ *of us,* wij allen, wij allemaal. ¶ *n.* al *n.n.,* alles *n.n.* ¶ *prefix* al-, alles-. ~*in wrestling,* (Amerikaans) worstelen *n.n.;* ~*-round,* overal goed in.
allay, *v.t.* stillen, doen bedaren; matigen.
allegation, *n.* bewering *n.* **allege,** *v.t.* beweren.
allegiance, *n.* trouw *n.,* aanhankelijkheid *n.*
allegoric(al), *a.,* ~ally, *adv.* allegorisch, zinnebeeldig. **allegorize,** *v.t.* allegorisch voorstellen. **allegory,** *n.* allegorie *n.*
alleviate, *v.t.* verlichten, verzachten. **alleviation,** *n.* verlichting *n.,* verzachting *n.*
alley, *n.* steeg *n.,* gang *n.* *blind* ~, doodlopende steeg.
All-Hallows, *N.* Allerheiligen *n.*

alliance, *n.* verbond *n.n.,* bondgenootschap *n.n.;* huwelijksband *n.* **allied,** *a.* verbonden, geallieerd.
alligator, *n.* krokodil *n.,* alligator *n.,* kaaiman *n.*
alliterate, *v.i.* allitereren. **alliteration,** *n.* alliteratie *n.,* stafrijm *n.n.* **alliterative,** *a.* allittererend.
allocate, *v.t.* toewijzen *str.,* toedelen. **allocation,** *n.* toewijzing *n.,* toedeling *n.*
allodial, *a.* allodiaal. **allodium,** *n.* vrij erfgoed *n.n.,* allodium *n.n.*
allopathic, *a.* allopathisch. **allopathist,** *n.* allopaath *n.* **allopathy,** *n.* allopathie *n.*
allot, *v.t.* toedelen. **allotment,** *n.* toedeling *n.;* volkstuintje *n.n.*
allow, *v.t.* toestaan *irr.,* veroorloven; goedkeuren. **allowable,** *a.* geoorloofd, rechtmatig. **allowance,** *n.* toelage *n.* *to make* ~*s for,* in aanmerking *n.* nemen *str.* dat.
alloy, *n.* allooi *n.n.;* gehalte *n.n.;* alliage *n.* ¶ *v.t.* legeeren.
All Saints' Day, *N.* Allerheiligen *n.* **All Souls' Day,** *N.* Allerzielen *n.*
allspice, *n.* piment *n.n.*
allude, *v.i.* *to* ~ *to,* zinspelen op, doelen op.
allure, *v.t.* verlokken; aanlokken. **allurement,** *n.* verlokking *n.,* aanlokking *n.;* lokmiddel *n.n.* **alluring,** *a.,* ~ly, *adv.* aanlokkelijk, verleidelijk.
allusion, *n.* toespeling *n.,* zinspeling *n.* **allusive,** *a.* zinspelend.
alluvial, *a.* alluviaal, aangeslibd. **alluvium,** *n.* alluvium *n.n.;* aangeslibd land *n.n.*
ally, *v.t.* *to* ~ *with,* verbinden *str.* met. ¶ *n.* bondgenoot *n.*
almanac, *n.* almanak *n.*
almightiness, *n.* almacht *n.* **almighty,** *a.* almachtig.
almond, *n.* amandel *n.*
almoner, *n.* aalmoezenier *n.*
almost, *adv.* bijna, nagenoeg.
alms, *pl.n.* aalmoes *n.* **alms-house,** *n.* armenhuis *n.n.,* hofje *n.n.*
aloe, *n.* aloë *n.,* agave *n.* **aloes,** *n.* aloë *n.,* aloësap *n.n.*
aloft, *adv.* omhoog; (naar) boven.
alone, *a.* & *adv.* alleen, eenzaam; op zichzelf staand. *to leave* ~, met rust *n.* laten *str.*
along, *prep.* langs; door, over. ¶ *adv.* voort, vooruit. ~ *with,* mee, met, samen met. **alongshore,** *adv.* langs de kust. **alongside,** *adv.* langszij. ~ *of,* naast.
aloof, *adv.* op een afstand; gereserveerd. **aloofness,** *n.* gereserveerdheid *n.*
aloud, *a.* hardop, luide.
alp, *n.* (hoge) berg *n.* *the Alps,* de Alpen *pl.N.*
alpaca, *n.* alpaca *n.*
alphabet, *n.* alphabet *n.n.* **alphabetical,** *a.* alphabetisch.
alpine, *a.* Alpen-. **alpinist,** *n.* bergbeklimmer *n.*
already, *adv.* al, reeds.
Alsace, *N.* Elzas *N.* **Alsatian,** *N.* Elzasser *N.*

also, *adv.* ook, eveneens.
altar, *n.* altaar *n.n.* altar-cloth, *n.* altaar-
kleed *n.n.* altar-piece, *n.* altaarstuk *n.n.*
alter, *v.t.* veranderen; wijzigen. alterability,
n. veranderlijkheid *n.* alterable, *a.*
veranderlijk. alteration, *n.* verandering *n.*;
wijziging *n.*
altercation, *n.* woordenwisseling *n.*, twist *n.*
alternate, *v.t. & v.i.* afwisselen. ¶ *a.*, ~ly,
adv. afwisselend, beurtelings. alternation,
n. afwisseling *n.* alternative, *a.* afwisselend,
beurtelings. ¶ *n.* alternatief *n.n.* alterna-
tor, *n.* wisseldynamo *n.*
although, *c.* ofschoon, alhoewel.
altimeter, *n.* hoogtemeter *n.*
altitude, *n.* hoogte *n.*
alto, *n.* alt *n.*; altviool *n.*
altogether, *adv.* in het geheel, helemaal,
volkomen.
altruism, *n.* altruïsme *n.n.*, onzelfzuchtigheid
n. altruist, *n.* altruïst *n.*
alum, *n.* aluin *n.*
aluminium, *n.* aluminium *n.n.*
alveolar, *a.* tand-. alveolus, *n.* tandkas *n.*
always, *adv.* altijd, altoos, steeds.
amalgam, *n.* amalgaam *n.n.*; mengelmoes *n.n.*
amalgamate, *v.t.* amalgameren; samensmelten *str.* amalgamation, *n.* amalgamatie
n., vermenging *n.*
amanuensis, *n.* secretaris *n.*
amaryllis, *n.* amarillis *n.*
amass, *v.t.* ophopen.
amateur, *n.* amateur *n.*; dilettant *n.*
amateurish, *a.* dilettantachtig.
amatory, *a.* liefdes-.
amaze, *v.t.* verbazen. amazement, *n.*
verbazing *n.* amazing, *a.* verbazend,
verbazingwekkend.
Amazon, *N.* Amazone *N.*
ambassador, *n.* gezant *n.*, ambassadeur *n.*
ambassadorial, *a.* gezantschaps-. ambassa-
dress, *n.* ambassadrice *n.*
amber, *n.* amber *n.n.*, barnsteen *n.* ¶ *a.*
barnstenen. ambergris, *n.* ambergrijs *n.n.*
ambidextrous, *a.* vaardig in het gebruik van
beide handen *pl.n.*
ambient, *a.* omringend.
ambiguity, *n.* dubbelzinnigheid *n.* ambiguous,
a., ~ly, *adv.* dubbelzinnig.
ambition, *n.* eerzucht *n.*, ambitie *n.* ambitious, *a.*, ~ly, *adv.* eerzuchtig, ambitieus.
to be ~ *of*, ambiëren.
amble, *v.i.* de telgang gaan *irr.* ¶ *n.* telgang
n. ambler, *n.* telganger *n.*
ambrosia, *n.* ambrozijn *n.n.* ambrosial, *a.*
ambrozijnen.
ambulance, *n.* ambulance *n.*, ziekenwagen *n.*
ambulate, *v.i.* wandelen. ambulatory, *a.*
wandel-.
ambuscade, *n.*, ambush. *n.* hinderlaag *n.*
¶ *v.t.* in hinderlaag leggen *irr.*
ameliorate, *v.t.* verbeteren. amelioration, *n.*
verbetering *n.*
amen, *int.* amen. ¶ *n.* amen *n.n.*

amenable, *a.* vatbaar, ontvankelijk; handelbaar, gedwee.
amend, *v.t.* verbeteren. ¶ *v.i.* zich beteren.
amendable, *a.* vatbaar voor verbetering *n.*
amendment, *n.* verbetering *n.*; amendement
n.n. amends, *pl.n.* vergoeding *n.* *to make*
~ *for something*, iets goedmaken.
amenity, *n.* voordeel *n.n.*, aantrekkelijkheid
n.
America, *N.* Amerika *n.N.* American, *N.*
Amerikaan *N.*, Amerikaanse, *N.*
amethyst, *n.* amethist *n.*
amiability, *n.* beminnelijkheid *n.* amiable,
a., ~bly, *adv.* beminnelijk; vriendelijk.
amianthus, *n.* amiant *n.n.*, steenvlas *n.n.*
amicable, *a.*, ~bly, *adv.* vriendschappelijk.
amid(st), *prep.* te midden van, midden in,
onder. amidships, *adv.* midscheeps.
amiss, *adv.* kwalijk; te onpas. *nothing comes*
~ *to him*, alles is van zijn gading *n.*
amity, *n.* vriendschappelijkheid *n.*
ammeter, *n.* ampèremeter *n.*
ammonia, *n.* ammonia(k) *n.* liquid ~,
salmiakgeest *n.*; sal ~c, salmiak *n.*
ammonite, *n.* ammoniet *n.*
ammunition, *n.* ammunitie *n.*, schietvoorraad *n.*
amnesia, *n.* geheugenverlies *n.n.*
amnesty, *n.* amnestie *n.* *to give* ~ *to*, amnestie
verlenen aan.
among(st), *prep.* onder; te midden van.
amoral, *a.* amoreel.
amorous, *a.* minziek; liefdes-. amorousness,
n. verliefdheid *n.*
amorphous, *a.* amorph, vormloos.
amortisation, *n.* amortisatie *n.*, delging *n.*
amortise, *v.t.* amortiseren, delgen.
amount, *v.i.* *to* ~ *to*, bedragen *str.*, neerkomen *irr.* op. ¶ *n.* bedrag *n.n.*
amour, *n.* liefdesgeschiedenis *n.*
ampere, *n.* ampère *n.*
ampersand, *n.* teken & *n.n.*
amphibia, *pl.n.* amphibie *n.*, tweeslachtig
dier *n.n.* amphibian, *a.*, amphibious, *a.*
amphibisch, tweeslachtig, amfibie . . .
amphitheatre, *n.* amphitheater *n.*
ample, *a.* ruim, ampel. amplification, *n.*
vergroting *n.*; uitbreiding *n.*; nadere
toelichting *n.* amplifier, *n.* versterker *n.*
amplify, *v.t.* versterken; uitbreiden; nader
toelichten. amplitude, *n.* grootte *n.*;
omvang *n.*; amplitudo *n.* amply, *adv.*
ruim, ruimschoots, rijkelijk.
amputate, *v.t.* afzetten, amputeren. amputation, *n.* amputatie *n.*
amuck, *adv.* amok.
amulet, *n.* amulet *n.n.*
amuse, *v.t.* amuseren, vermaken. amusement,
n. amusement *n.n.*, vermaak *n.n.*; tijd-
verdrijf *n.n.* amusing, *a.*, ~ly, *adv.*
vermakelijk, amusant.
an, *art.* een.
anabaptist, *n.* wederdoper *n.*
anachronism, *n.* anachronisme *n.n.*

anæmia, *n.* bloedarmoede *n.* **anæmic,** *a.* bloedarm, bleekzuchtig.
anæsthesia, *n.* anæsthesie *n.*, verdoving *n.*, gevoelloosheid *n.* anæsthetic, *a.* gevoelloos. ¶ *n.* verdovend middel *n.n.* anæsthetize, *v.t.* verdoven, wegmaken.
anagram, *n.* anagram *n.n.*
anal, *a.* anaal, aars-.
analogical, *a.* analogisch. analogous, *a.* analoog, overeenkomstig. analogy, *n.* analogie *n.*, overeenstemming *n.*
analyse, *v.t.* ontleden, analyseren. analysis, *n.* ontleding *n.*, analyse *n.* analyst, *n.* scheikundige *n.* analytic(al), *a.* ontledend, analytisch.
anarchic(al), *a.* anarchistisch. anarchism, *n.* anarchisme *n.n.* anarchist, *n.* anarchist *n.* anarchy, *n.* anarchie *n.*
anathema, *n.* banvloek *n.* anathemize, *v.t.* de banvloek uitspreken *str.* over.
anatomical, *a.* anatomisch. anatomize, *v.t.* ontleden. anatomist, *n.* anatomist *n.* anatomy, *n.* anatomie *n.*, ontleedkunde *n.*
ancestor, *n.* voorvader *n.* ~s, voorouders *n.* ancestral, *a.* voorvaderlijk. ancestry, *n.* voorgeslacht *n.n.*; afkomst *n.*
anchor, *n.* anker *n.n.* ¶ *v.t.* ankeren. ¶ *v.i.* voor anker liggen *irr.* anchorage, *n.* ankerplaats *n.*, ankergrond *n.*; ankergeld *n.n.*
anchorite, *n.* anachoreet *n.*, kluizenaar *n.*
anchovy, *n.* ansjovis *n.*
ancient, *a.*, ~ly *adv.* oud, aloud; eerwaardig. ¶ *n.* oude *n.* van dagen *pl.n.* the ~s, de klassieken.
ancillary, *a.* dienstbaar, ondergeschikt.
and, *c.* en.
andiron, *n.* haardijzer *n.n.*
androgynous, *a.* hermaphroditisch, twee-slachtig.
anecdotal, *a.* anecdotisch. anecdote, *n.* anecdote *n.*
anemone, *n.* anemoon *n.*
aneroid, *n.* aneroïde barometer *n.*
aneurism, *n.* slagaderbreuk *n.*
anew, *adv.* opnieuw.
angel, *n.* engel *n.* angelic, *a.* engelachtig. angelica, *n.* engelwortel *n.*
anger, *v.t.* boos maken, vertoornen. ¶ *n.* boosheid *n.*, toorn *n.*
angina, *n.* angina *n.*
angle, *v.i.* hengelen. ¶ *n.* hoek *n.* angler, *n.* hengelaar *n.* angling, *n.* hengelen *n.n.* to go ~, uit hengelen gaan *irr.*
Anglican, *a.* Anglikaans. anglicise, *v.t.* verengelsen. anglicism, *n.* anglicisme *n.n.* anglophile, *a.* Engelsgezind. Anglo-Saxon, *a.* Angelsaksisch. ¶ *N.* Angelsakser *N.*
angrily, *adv.* boos, toornig. angry, *a.* boos, toornig.
anguish, *n.* smart *n.*, zielesmart *n.*
angular, *a.*, ~ly, *adv.* hoekig, kantig. angularity, *n.* hoekigheid *n.*, kantigheid *n.*
anhydrous, *a.* watervrij.

anil, *n.* indigo *n.* aniline, *n.* aniline *n.*
animadversion, *n.* aanmerking *n.*, critiek *n.* animadvert, *v.i.* to ~ on, laken, berispen.
animal, *n.* dier *n.n.* the ~ kingdom, het dierenrijk. animalcule, *n.* oerdiertje *n.n.* animalism, *n.* dierlijkheid *n.*
animate, *v.t.* bezielen. animated, *a.* bezield; opgewekt, geanimeerd. animation, *n.* bezieling *n.*
animosity, *n.* vijandigheid *n.*, verbitterdheid *n.* animus, *n.* animositeit *n.*, vijandelijke gezindheid *n.*
anise, *n.* anijs *n.* aniseed, *n.* anijszaad *n.n.*
anker, *n.* anker *n.n.* (wine).
ankle, *n.* enkel *n.* anklet, *n.* enkelring *n.*; enkelbeschermer *n.*
annals, *pl.n.* annalen *pl.n.*
anneal, *v.t.* temperen; brandverven.
annex, *v.t.* aanhechten, toevoegen; annexeren. ¶ *n.* bijlage *n.*; bijgebouw *n.n.* annexation, *n.* annexatie *n.*
annihilate, *v.t.* vernietigen. annihilation, *n.* vernietiging *n.*
anniversary, *n.* (ver)jaardag *n.*; gedenkdag *n.*
annotate, *v.t.* van aantekeningen voorzien. annotation, *n.* aantekening *n.* annotator, *n.* maker van aantekeningen.
announce, *v.t.* aankondigen, bekend maken. announcement, *n.* aankondiging *n.*, bekendmaking *n.*
annoy, *v.t.* ergeren, irriteren. annoyance, *n.* ergernis *n.*, last *n.* annoying, *a.* vervelend, ergerlijk.
annual, *a.*, ~ly, *adv.* jaarlijks; éénjarig. annuitant, *n.* lijfrentetrekker *n.* annuity, *n.* lijfrente *n.*, jaargeld *n.n.*
annul, *v.t.* ongeldig verklaren, te niet doen *irr.*
annular, *a.* ringvormig.
annulment, *n.* vernietiging *n.*, ongeldig verklaring *n.*
annunciation, *n.* aankondiging *n.* A~-day, Maria Boodschap *N.*
anode, *n.* anode *n.*, positieve pool *n.*
anodyne, *a.* pijnstillend.
anoint, *v.t.* zalven. the Lord's Anointed, de Gezalfde des Heren. anointment, *n.* zalven *n.n.*
anomalous, *a.* abnormaal, afwijkend. anomaly, *n.* abnormaliteit *n.*, afwijking *n.*
anon, *adv.* aanstonds.
anonymous, *a.*, ~ly, *adv.* anoniem.
anopheles, *n.* malariamuskiet *n.*
another, *a.* een ander; nog een, een tweede. one ~, elkaar.
answer, *v.t.* beantwoorden, antwoorden (op); beantwoorden aan. to ~ to a name, luisteren naar een naam *n.*; to ~ back, tegenpraten. ¶ *v.i.* to ~ for, instaan *irr.* voor; boeten voor. ¶ *n.* antwoord *n.n.* answerable, *a.* verantwoordelijk, aan-sprakelijk.
ant, *n.* mier *n.*
antagonism, *n.* antagonisme *n.n.*, vijandschap

n. **antagonist,** *n.* tegenstander *n.* **antagonize,** *v.t.* vijandig maken.
Antarctic, *a.* Zuidpool-.
ant-eater, *n.* miereneter *n.*
antecedence, *n.* voorafgaan *n.n.* **antecedent,** *a.*, ~ly, *adv.* voorafgaand. ¶ ~s, *pl.n.* antecedenten *pl.n.n.*
antechamber, *n.* antichambre *n.*, wachtkamer *n.*
antedate, *v.t.* vroeger dateren.
antediluvian, *a.* antidiluviaans.
antelope, *n.* antilope *n.*
antemeridian, *a.* vóór de middag.
antenatal, *a.* vóór de geboorte.
antenna, *n.* antenne *n.*; voelhoorn *n.*, voelspriet *n.*
anterior, *a.* voorafgaand, voor-.
anteroom, *n.* voorkamer *n.*, wachtkamer *n.*
anthem, *n.* hymne *n.* *national* ~, volkslied *n.n.*
anther, *n.* helmknop *n.*
ant-hill, *n.* mierenhoop *n.*
anthology, *n.* bloemlezing *n.*
Anthony, *N.* Antonius. *St.* ~'s fire, Sint Antoniesvuur *n.n.*, roos *n.*
anthracite, *n.* anthraciet *n.*
anthrax, *n.* miltvuur *n.n.*
anthropologist, *n.* anthropoloog *n.* **anthropology,** *n.* anthropologie *n.*
anthropophagi, *pl.n.* menseneters *pl.n.*
anti-, *prefix* anti-, tegen-.
anti-aircraft, *prefix* luchtafweer-.
antic, *a.* kluchtig. ¶ -s, *pl.n.* dolle sprongen *pl.n.*
anticipate, *v.t.* voorzien *irr.*, verwachten; vooruitlopen *str.* op. **anticipation,** *n.* verwachting *n.*; voorgevoel *n.n.* *in* ~, bij voorbaat. **anticipatory,** *a.* vooruitlopend; bij voorbaat.
antidote, *n.* tegengif *n.n.*
antimony, *n.* antimonium *n.n.*
antipathetic, *a.* antipathiek. **antipathy,** *n.* antipathie *n.*
antipodes, *pl.n.* tegenvoeters *pl.n.*
antiquarian, *a.* oudheidkundig. **antiquary,** *n.* oudheidkundige *n.*
antiquated, *a.* verouderd.
antique, *a.* antiek, ouderwets. ¶ *n.* antikiteit *n.* **antiquity,** *n.* oudheid *n.* *antiquities,* antikiteiten *n.*
antiseptic, *a.* antiseptisch. ¶ *n.* antiseptisch middel *n.n.*
antithesis, *n.* tegenstelling *n.*
antitoxin, *n.* tegengif *n.n.*
antler, *n.* tak *n.* van het gewei *n.* *antlers,* gewei *n.n.*
antonym, *n.* antoniem *n.n.*, tegengesteld begrip *n.n.*
Antwerp, *N.* Antwerpen *n.N.*
anus, *n.* anus *n.*
anvil, *n.* aanbeeld *n.n.*
anxiety, *n.* bezorgdheid *n.*; angst *n.* **anxious,** *a.*, ~ly, *adv.* bezorgd; angstig.

any, *pron.* enig; een; welk . . . ook; ieder, elk; ook, ook soms, wat. *not* ~, geen.
anybody, *pron.* iemand; iedereen, een ieder; 't is gelijk wie.
anyhow, *adv.* hoe dan ook, in elk geval; onverschillig hoe, op een of andere manier.
anything, *pron.* iets, wat dan ook. ~ *but,* allesbehalve; *not* ~, niets.
anyway, *adv.* hoe dan ook, in elk geval.
anywhere, *adv.* waar . . . ergens; 't is gelijk waar, onverschillig waar; overal.
apace, *adv.* snel, hand over hand. *ill weeds grow* ~, onkruid *n.n.* vergaat niet.
apanage, *n.* apanage *n.*, deel *n.n.*
apart, *adv.* afzonderlijk, ter zijde; uiteen. ~ *from,* afgezien van; *to set* ~, afzonderen.
apartment, *n.* vertrek *n.n.*, kamers *pl.n.*
apathetic, *a.* apathisch, onverschillig; lusteloos. **apathy,** *n.* apathie *n.*, onverschilligheid *n.*; lusteloosheid *n.*
ape, *n.* aap *n.* ¶ *v.t.* naäpen.
aperient, *n.* laxeermiddel *n.n.*
aperture, *n.* opening *n.*
apex, *n.* toppunt *n.n.*; top *n.*, spits *n.*
aphis, *n.* bladluis *n.*
aphorism, *n.* aphorisme *n.*
aphrodisiac, *n.* prikkelend middel *n.n.*
apiary, *n.* bijenstal *n.*
apiculture, *n.* imkerij *n.*
apish, *a.*, ~ly, *adv.* aapachtig. **apishness,** *n.* aapachtigheid *n.*
aplomb, *n.* zelfvertrouwen *n.n.*, aplomb *n.n.*
Apocalypse, *N.* Openbaring *N.*, Apocalypse *N.* **Apocalyptic,** *a.* als een Apocalypse.
apocrypha, *pl.n.* apocriefe boeken *pl.n.n.* **apocryphal,** *a.* apocrief.
apogee, *n.* hoogtepunt *n.n.*
apologetic, *a.*, ~ally, *adv.* verontschuldigend. **apologist,** *n.* apologeet *n.* **apologize,** *v.i.* zich verontschuldigen.
apologue, *n.* fabel *n.*
apology, *n.* excuus *n.n.*; apologie *n.*, verweerschrift *n.n.*
apoplectic, *a.*, ~ally, *adv.* beroerteachtig. ~ *fit,* beroerte *n.* **apoplexy,** *n.* beroerte *n.*
apostasy, *n.* afvalligheid *n.* **apostate,** *n.* afvallige *n.* **apostatize,** *v.i.* afvallig worden *str.*
apostle, *n.* apostel *n.* **apostolic,** *a.* apostolisch.
apostrophe, *n.* toespraak *n.*; afkappingsteken *n.n.* **apostrophize,** *v.t.* zich tot iemand wenden.
apothecary, *n.* apotheker *n.*
apotheosis, *n.* verheerlijking *n.*, apotheose *n.*
appal, *v.t.* ontstellen. **appalling,** *a.* verschrikkelijk.
apparatus, *n.* toestel *n.n.*; uitrusting *n.*, hulpmiddelen *pl.n.n.*
apparel, *n.* kleding *n.*, tooi *n.* ¶ *v.t.* tooien.
apparent, *a.* blijkbaar; ogenschijnlijk; zichtbaar. *heir* ~, troonsopvolger. **apparently,** *adv.* blijkbaar; ogenschijnlijk.
apparition, *n.* (geest)verschijning *n.*
appeal, *v.i.* aantrekkelijk zijn; appelleren.

to ~ *against*, protest *n.n.* aantekenen tegen; *to* ~ *to*, een beroep *n.n.* doen *irr.* op. ¶ *n.* hoger beroep *n.n.*, appel *n.n.*

appear, *v.i.* verschijnen *str.*; ten tonele verschijnen *str.*; blijken *str.*; schijnen *str.* **appearance,** *n.* verschijnen *n.n.*; voorkomen *n.n.*, uiterlijk *n.n. to keep up* ~*s*, de schijn redden; *to put in an* ~, zich vertonen.

appease, *v.t.* bevredigen, kalmeren. **appeasement,** *n.* bevrediging *n.*

appellant, *n.* appellant *n.* **appellation,** *n.* benaming *n.* **appellative,** *n.* naam *n.*, benaming *n.*

append, *v.t.* aanhangen *str.*, toevoegen. **appendage,** *n.* aanhangsel *n.n.* **appendicitis,** *n.* blindedarmontsteking *n.* **appendix,** *n.* aanhangsel *n.n.*; blinde darm *n.*

appertain, *v.i.* toebehoren.

appetite, *n.* eetlust *n.* **appetizer,** *n.* iets voor de eetlust. **appetizing,** *a.* aantrekkelijk.

applaud, *v.t.* toejuichen, applaudisseren. **applause,** *n.* applaus *n.n.*, bijval *n.*

apple, *n.* appel *n.* **apple-core,** *n.* klokhuis *n.n.* **apple-dumpling,** *n.* appelbol *n.* **apple-pie,** *n.* appeltaart *n. in* ~ *order*, alles in de puntjes. **apple-sauce,** *n.* appelmoes *n.n.*

appliance, *n.* toestel *n.*, hulpmiddel *n.n.*

applicability, *n.* toepasselijkheid *n.* **applicable,** *a.* toepasselijk. **applicant,** *n.* sollicitant *n.* **application,** *n.* toepassing *n.*, aanwending *n.*; toewijding *n.*, ijver *n.*; sollicitatie *n.* **apply,** *v.t.* aanbrengen *irr.*; toepassen, aanwenden. ¶ *v.t. to* ~ *oneself to*, zich toeleggen op.

appoint, *v.t.* bepalen, vaststellen; benoemen, aanstellen; inrichten. **appointment,** *n.* afspraak *n.*; benoeming *n.*, aanstelling *n.*; toerusting *n.*, inrichting *n.*

apportion, *v.t.* toewijzen *str.*, toedelen. **apportionment,** *n.* toewijzing *n.*, toedeling *n.*

apposite, *a.*, ~**ly**, *adv.* toepasselijk. **appositeness,** *n.* toepasselijkheid *n.* **apposition,** *n.* aanhechting *n.*; bijvoeging *n.*; bijstelling *n.*

appraisal, *n.* schatting *n.* **appraise,** *v.t.* schatten, taxeren. **appraiser,** *n.* schatter *n.*, taxateur *n.*

appreciable, *a.*, ~**bly,** *adv.* merkbaar. **appreciate,** *v.t.* waarderen; hoogschatten, op prijs stellen. **appreciation,** *n.* waardering. **appreciative,** *a.* waarderend.

apprehend, *v.t.* begrijpen *str.*, vatten; in hechtenis *n.* nemen *str.*; vrezen. **apprehensible,** *a.* bevattelijk. **apprehension,** *n.* bevatting *n.*, begrip *n.n.*; aanhouding *n.*; beduchtheid *n.*, vrees *n.* **apprehensive,** *a.*, ~**ly,** *adv.* beducht, bevreesd.

apprentice, *n.* leerjongen *n.*, leerling *n.* ¶ *v.t. to* ~ *to*, in de leer doen *irr.* bij. **apprenticeship,** *n.* leertijd *n.*, leerjaren *pl.n.n.*

apprise, *v.t.* berichten, kennis geven.

approach, *v.t.* naderen; benaderen. ¶ *n.*

nadering *n.*; toegang *n.*, toegangsweg *n.* **approachable,** *a.* toegankelijk.

approbation, *n.* goedkeuring *n.* **approbatory,** *a.* goedkeurend.

appropriate, *v.t.* zich toeëigenen; besteden. ¶ *a.* geschikt, passend. **appropriateness,** *n.* geschiktheid *n.* **appropriation,** *n.* toeëigening *n.*

approval, *n.* goedkeuring *n. on* ~, op zicht. **approve,** *v.t.* goedkeuren. ¶ *v.i. to* ~ *of*, goedkeuren. **approvingly,** *adv.* goedkeurend.

approximate, *a.* bijna gelijk, benaderend. ¶ ~**ly,** *adv.* bij benadering *n.* ¶ *v.t.* benaderen.

appurtenance, *n.* toebehoren *n.n.*, bijbehoren *n.n.* **appurtenant,** *a.* bijbehorend.

apricot, *n.* abrikoos *n.*

April, *N.* april *N.* **April Fool,** *N.* aprilgek *n.*

apron, *n.* schort *n.*, boezelaar *n.*; schootsvel *n.n.* **apron-string,** *n. to be tied to the* ~*s of*, onder de plak zitten van.

apse, *n.* apsis *n.*

apt, *a.*, ~**ly,** *adv.* bekwaam, geschikt; geneigd. **aptitude,** *n.* bekwaamheid *n.*, geschiktheid *n.*; neiging *n.*

aquarium, *n.* aquarium *n.n.* **aquatic,** *a.* in het water levend; water-. **aqueduct,** *n.* (bovengrondse) waterleiding *n.* **aqueous,** *a.* waterig, waterachtig.

aquiline, *a.* arends-, haviks-.

Arab, *N.* Arabier *N. street arab*, straatjongen *n.* ¶ *a.* Arabisch. **Arabia,** *N.* Arabië *n.N.* **Arabic,** *a.* Arabisch.

arabesque, *n.* arabesk *n.*

arable, *a.* bebouwbaar.

arachnoid, *a.* spinachtig.

arbiter, *n.* scheidsrechter *n.* **arbitrarily,** *adv.* willekeurig, grillig. **arbitrariness,** *n.* willekeur *n.* **arbitrary,** *a.* willekeurig, grillig. **arbitrate,** *v.t.* beslechten. **arbitration,** *n.* arbitrage *n.* **arbitrator,** *n.* scheidsrechter *n.*

arboraceous, *a.* boomachtig; bosrijk. **arboriculture,** *n.* boomkweken *n.n.*

arbour, *n.* priëel *n.n.*

arc, *n.* (cirkel)boog *n.*

arcade, *n.* zuilengang *n.*; winkelgalerij *n.*

Arcadia, *N.* Arcadië *n.N.* **Arcadian,** *a.* Arcadisch.

arcanum, *n.* geheim *n.n.*

arch, *n.* boog *n.*, gewelf *n.n.* ¶ *v.t.* zich welven. ¶ *prefix,* aarts-. ¶ *a.*, ~**ly,** *adv.* schalks, snaaks.

archæological, *a.* oudheidkundig. **archæologist,** *n.* archæoloog *n.*, oudheidkundige *n.* **archæology** *n.* archæologie *n.*, oudheidkunde *n.*

archaic, *a.* verouderd. **archaism,** *n.* verouderde uitdrukking *n.*

archangel, *n.* aartsengel *n.*

archbishop, *n.* aartsbisschop *n.* **archbishopric,** *n.* aartsbisdom *n.n.*

archduchy, *n.* aartshertogdom *n.n.* archduke, *n.* aartshertog *n.*
archer, *n.* boogschutter *n.* archery, *n.* boogschieterij *n.*
archiepiscopal, *a.* aartsbisschoppelijk.
archipelago, *n.* archipel *n.*
architect, *n.* architect *n.* architecture, *n.* architectuur *n.*
archives, *pl.n.* archief *n.n.*
archness, *n.* schalksheid *n.*, snaaksheid *n.*
archway, *n.* verwelfde gang *n.*
arc-lamp, *n.* booglicht *n.n.*
arctic, *a.* Noordpool-.
ardent, *a.*, ~ly, *adv.* vurig. ardour, *n.* vuur *n.n.*, ijver *n.*
arduous, *a.* moeilijk, zwaar, moeizaam. arduousness, *n.* moeilijkheid *n.*, moeizaamheid *n.*
area, *n.* oppervlak *n.n.*, oppervlakte *n.*; gebied *n.n.*; open ruimte *n.* vóór souterrain *n.n.*
arena, *n.* arena *n.*, strijdperk *n.n.*
areometer, *n.* luchtmeter *n.*
argent, *n.* zilver *n.n.* ¶ *a.* zilveren.
Argentine, *N.* Argentinië *n.N.*
argillaceous, *a.* kleiachtig.
argosy, *n.* (antiek) koopvaardijschip *n.n.*
argue, *v.i.* redeneren, redetwisten. ¶ *v.t.* beweren, betogen. argument, *n.* argument *n.n.*, redenering *n.*; redetwist *n.* argumentation, *n.* redenering *n.* argumentative, *a.* twistgraag.
aria, *n.* aria *n.*
arid, *a.* dor, droog. aridity, *n.* dorheid *n.*
aright, *adv.* recht, juist.
arise, *v.i.* oprijzen *str.*, zich verheffen *str.*
aristocracy, *n.* aristocratie *n.* aristocrat, *n.* aristocraat *n.* aristocratic, *a.*, ~ally, *adv.* aristocratisch.
arithmetic, *n.* rekenkunde *n.* arithmetical, *a.*, ~ally, *adv.* rekenkundig. arithmetician, *n.* rekenkundige *n.*; rekenaar *n.*
ark, *n.* ark *n.* ~ *of bulrushes,* biezen mandje *n.n.*; *A* ~ *of the Covenant,* Arke des Verbonds *n.*
arm, *n.* arm *n.*; wapen *n.n.* *at* ~'s *length,* op eerbiedige afstand *n.*; *small* ~s, draagbare vuurwapenen *n.n.*; *to rise in* ~s, de wapens opvatten; *to* ~s, te wapen; *under* ~s, onder de wapenen; *coat of* ~s, familiewapen *n.n.*, wapenrok *n.*; *man-at-* ~s, krijgsman *n.* ¶ *v.t.* (be)wapenen.
armada, *n.* vloot *n.* *A* ~, Armada *N.*
armadillo, *n.* gordeldier *n.n.*
armament, *n.* krijgstoerusting *n.*, wapenen *pl.n.n.* ~-*works,* wapenfabriek *n.*
armature, *n.* bewapening *n.*; anker *n.n.*
arm-chair, *n.* leuningstoel *n.*, fauteuil *n.*
arm-hole, *n.* armsgat *n.n.*
armistice, *n.* wapenstilstand *n.*
armlet, *n.* armring *n.*, brassard *n.*
armorial, *a.* wapen-. ~ *bearings,* wapenschild *n.n.*
armour, *n.* wapenrusting *n.*, harnas *n.n.*;

pantser *n.n.* armour-bearer, *n.* schildknaap *n.* armour-clad, *a.* gepantserd.
armourer, *n.* wapensmid *n.* armourplated, *a.* gepantserd. armoury, *n.* arsenaal *n.n.*
armpit, *n.* oksel *n.*
army, *n.* leger *n.n.* army contractor, *n.* leverancier *n.* van het leger. army list, *n.* ranglijst *n.*
aroma, *n.* aroma *n.n.* aromatic, *a.* aromatisch.
around, *adv.* rondom, om . . . heen; in het rond; rond, om. ¶ *prep.* rondom.
arouse, *v.t.* wekken; opwekken, wakker schudden.
arrack, *n.* arak *n.*
arraign, *v.t.* voor het gerecht dagen, beschuldigen. arraignment, *n.* aanklacht *n.*
arrange, *v.t.* in orde maken, in orde brengen *irr.*; schikken; arrangeren. arrangement, *n.* schikking *n.*; overeenkomst *n.*
arrant, *a.*, ~ly, *adv.* doortrapt, aarts-.
arras, *n.* (wand)tapijt *n.n.*
array, *v.t.* opstellen, scharen; uitdossen. ¶ *n.* slagorde *n.*
arrear, *n.* achterstand *n.*, achterstallige schuld *n.*
arrest, *v.t.* arresteren, aanhouden *irr.*; stuiten. ¶ *n.* arrestatie *n.*, inhechtenisneming *n.* arresting, *a.* boeiend.
arrival, *n.* aankomst *n.*; aangekomene *n.* arrive, *v.i.* aankomen *irr.*
arrogance, *n.* aanmatiging *n.* arrogant, *a.*, ~ly, *adv.* aanmatigend.
arrogate, *v.t.* zich aanmatigen. *to* ~ *to oneself,* zich aanmatigen.
arrow, *n.* pijl *n.* arrow-root, *n.* pijlwortelmeel *n.n.*, arrowroot *n.n.* arrowy, *a.* pijlvormig.
arse, *n.* aars *n.n.*
arsenal, *n.* arsenaal *n.n.*
arsenic, *n.* arsenicum *n.n.*, rattenkruid *n.n.* arsenic(al), *a.* arseen-.
arson, *n.* brandstichting *n.*
art, *n.* kunst *n.*; kunstgreep *n.*
arterial, *a.* slagaderlijk. ~ *road,* hoofdverkeersweg *n.*
arteriosclerosis, *n.* aderverkalking *n.*
artery, *n.n.* slagader *n.*
artesian, *a.* artesisch.
artful, *a.*, ~ly, *adv.* listig. artfulness, *n.* listigheid *n.*
arthritis, *n.* jicht *n.n.*
artichoke, *n.* artisjok *n.*
article, *n.* artikel *n.n.*; lidwoord *n.n.* ~s, contract *n.n.* ¶ *v.t.* contractueel verbinden *str.*
articulate, *a.*, ~ly, *adv.* geleed; zich duidelijk uitsprekend. ¶ *v.t.* duidelijk uitspreken *str.* articulation, *n.* geleding *n.*; articulatie *n.*, duidelijke uitspraak *n.*
artifice, *n.* list *n.*, kunstgreep *n.* artificer, *n.* ambachtsman *n.*; schepper *n.* artificial, *a.* kunstmatig; gekunsteld; kunst-. artificiality, *n.* onnatuurlijkheid *n.*, gekunsteldheid *n.*

artillery, *n.* artillerie *n.*, geschut *n.n.* **artillery-**
man, *n.* artillerist *n.*
artisan, *n.* handwerksman *n.*
artist, *n.* kunstenaar *n.* **artiste,** *n.* artiest *n.*;
toneelspeler *n.*, toneelspeelster *n.* **artistic,**
a. artistiek. **artistry,** *n.* kunstenaarstalent.
artless, *a.* ongekunsteld; onbedreven; smakeloos. **artlessness,** *n.* ongekunsteldheid *n.*;
kunsteloosheid *n.*
arum (lily), *n.* Aronskelk *n.*
Aryan, *a.* Arisch. ¶ *N.* Ariër *N.*
as, *adv.* als, evenals, zoals, alsof. ~ *soon* ~,
zodra. ¶ *c.* als, zoals; toen, terwijl,
wanneer; naarmate; aangezien, daar.
~ *it were,* als het ware; ~ *for,* ~ *to,*
wat betreft; ~ *yet,* totnogtoe, voorlopig.
¶ *pron. such* ~, zij die.
asbestos, *n.* asbest *n.n.*
ascend, *v.i.* (op)klimmen *str.*, (op)stijgen *str.*
¶ *v.t.* opvaren *str.*, opklimmen *str.* **ascend-**
ancy, *n.* overwicht *n.n.*; invloed *n.*, gezag
n.n. **ascendant,** *a.* stijgend; overheersend.
¶ *n. in the* ~, toenemend. **ascension,** *n.*
beklimming *n. A* ~ *Day,* Hemelvaartsdag
N. **ascent,** *n.* beklimming *n.*; steilte *n.*,
helling *n.*
ascertain, *v.t.* vaststellen; zich vergewissen
van. **ascertainable,** *a.* vast te stellen.
ascertainment, *n.* vaststelling *n.*
ascetic, *a.* ascetisch. ¶ *n.* asceet *n.* **asceticism,**
n. ascetisme *n.n.*
ascribable, *a.* ~ *to,* toe te schrijven aan.
ascribe, *v.t.* toeschrijven *str.*
aseptic, *a.* aseptisch.
asexual, *a.* geslachtloos.
ash, *n.* as *n.* (*burnt substance*); es *n.*, essen-
boom *n.* ~*es,* as *n.*
ashamed, *a.* beschaamd. *to be* ~ *of,* zich
schamen over; *to be* ~ *for,* zich schamen
voor.
ashen, *a.* doodsbleek; essen, van essenhout.
ashlar, *n.* hardsteen *n.* ¶ *a.* hardstenen.
ashore, *adv.* aan wal *n. to run* ~, (doen *irr.*)
stranden.
ashpan, *n.* asbak *n.* **ash-pit,** *n.* askuil *n.*
ash-tray, *n.* asbakje *n.n.* **Ash-Wednesday,**
A. Asdag *N.* **ashy,** *a.* asachtig; doodsbleek.
Asia, *N.* Azië *n.N.* **Asiatic,** *a.* Aziatisch.
¶ *N.* Aziaat *N.*
aside, *adv.* ter zijde, op zij. ¶ *n.* terzijde *n.n.*,
terzijdespraak *n.*
asinine, *a.* ezelachtig.
ask, *v.t.* vragen *str.*; eisen; verzoeken *irr.*
askance, *adv.* schuin, van terzijde.
askew, *adv.* scheef, schuin.
aslant, *adv.* schuin, dwarsover.
asleep, *a.* in slaap *n.*
asp, *n.* adder *n.*; esp *n.*, espeboom *n.*
asparagus, *n.* asperge *n.*
aspect, *n.* aanblik *n.*, voorkomen *n.n.*;
oogpunt *n.n.*; ligging *n.*
aspen, *a.* espen.
asperge, *v.t.* besprenkelen. **aspergillum,** *n.*
wijwaterkwast *n.*

asperity, *n.* ruwheid *n.*, onevenheid *n.*
asperse, *v.t.* belasteren. **aspersion,** *n.*
besprenkeling *n.*; laster *n.*
asphalt, *n.* asfalt *n.n.*
asphyxia, *n.* verstikking *n.* **asphyxiate,** *v.t.*
verstikken. **asphyxiation,** *n.* verstikking *n.*
aspic, *n.* spijklavendel *n.*; aspisadder *n.*;
aspic *n.*
aspirant, *n.* aspirant *n.*, candidaat *n.* **aspirate,**
v.t. aspireren. ¶ *n.* geaspireerde letter *n.*
aspiration, *n.* streven *n.n.*, aspiratie *n.*
aspire, *v.i. to* ~ *after, for, to,* streven naar.
aspirin, *n.* aspirine *n.*
aspiring, *a.* eerzuchtig.
ass, *n.* ezel *n. to make an* ~ *of oneself,* zich
ezelachtig gedragen *str.*
assail, *v.t.* aanvallen *str.*; overstelpen.
assailable, *a.* aantastbaar. **assailant,** *n.*
aanvaller *n.*
assassin, *n.* moordenaar *n.*, sluipmoordenaar
n. **assassinate,** *v.t.* verraderlijk vermoorden. **assassination,** *n.* sluipmoord *n.*,
(politieke) moord *n.*
assault, *v.t.* aanvallen *str.*, bestormen;
aanranden. ¶ *n.* bestorming *n.*, stormaanval *n.*; aanranding *n.*
assay, *v.t.* toetsen, onderzoeken *irr.*, essay-
eren. ¶ *n.* analyse *n.*, onderzoek *n.n.*
assayer, *n.* essayeur *n.*
assemblage, *n.* verzameling *n.*, samenkomst *n.*
assemble, *v.t.* verzamelen, bijeenbrengen
irr. ¶ *v.i.* bijeenkomen *irr.*, zich verzamelen. **assembly,** *n.* bijeenkomst *n.*;
verzameling *n.*; montage *n.* ~ *line,*
lopende band *n.*; ~ *works,* montage-
afdeling *n.* **assembly room,** *n.* balzaal *n.*
assent, *v.i. to* ~ *to,* toestemmen in, goedkeuren. ¶ *n.* toestemming *n.*, instemming
n., goedkeuring *n.*
assert, *v.t.* beweren. ¶ *v.i. to* ~ *oneself,*
zich doen *irr.* gelden. **assertion,** *n.* bewering
n. **assertive,** *a.*, ~ly, *adv.* stellig; zelfbewust.
assess, *v.t.* schatten, aanslaan *irr.*, taxeren.
assessable, *a.* belastbaar. **assessment,** *n.*
schatting *n.*; aanslag *n.* **assessor,** *n.*
schatter *n.*, assessor *n.*
asset, *n.* bezit *n.n.*, voordeel *n.n.*; creditpost
n. ~*s,* activa *pl. n.n.*
asseverate, *v.t.* betuigen, plechtig verzekeren.
asseveration, *n.* plechtige verzekering *n.*
assiduity, *n.* onverdroten ijver *n.* **assiduous,**
a., ~ly, *adv.* onverdroten; volhardend.
assign, *v.t.* aanwijzen *str.*, toewijzen *str.*;
toeschrijven *str.*; overdragen *str.* **assign-**
able, *a.* toewijsbaar. **assignation,** *n.*
aanwijzing *n.*; toeschrijving *n.*; overdracht
n.; afspraak *n.* **assignee,** *n.* gevolmachtigde *n.* **assignment,** *n.* aanwijzing *n.*;
toewijzing *n.*; overdracht *n.*
assimilate, *v.t.* assimileren; gelijk maken.
¶ *v.i.* gelijk worden *str.* **assimilation,** *n.*
assimilatie *n.*
assist, *v.t.* bijstaan *irr.*, steunen, helpen *str.*

¶ *v.i.* to ~ *at*, bijwonen. **assistance,** *n.* bijstand *n.*, hulp *n.* **assistant,** *n.* assistent *n.*; hulp *n.*, helper *n.*

assize, *n.* zitting *n.* van rondgaande rechters.

associate, *v.t.* verenigen. ¶ *v.i.* to ~ *with*, omgaan *irr.* met, verkeren met. ¶ *a.* geassocieerd, mede-. ¶ *n.* compagnon *n.*; deelgenoot *n.*

assonance, *n.* assonantie *n.* **assonant,** *a.* assonerend.

assort, *v.t.* sorteren. **assortment,** *n.* assortiment *n.n.*

assuage, *v.t.* stillen, bevredigen; lenigen. **assuagement,** *v.t.* verzachting *n.*; leniging *n.*

assume, *v.t.* onderstellen, aannemen *str.*; zich aanmatigen. **assuming,** *a.* aanmatigend. **assumption,** *n.* onderstelling *n.*; aanmatiging *n.*

assurance, *n.* verzekering *n.*; zekerheid *n.*; zelfvertrouwen *n.n.* **assure,** *v.t.* verzekeren; assureren. **assured,** *a.*, ~**ly,** *adv.* verzekerd; vol zelfvertrouwen; zeker. **assurer,** *n.* verzekeraar *n.*; assuradeur *n.*

Assyria, *N.* Assyrië *n.N.*

aster, *n.* aster *n.*

asterisk, *n.* sterretje *n.n.*

astern, *adv.* achter; achteruit.

asthma, *n.* aamborstigheid *n.*, asthma *n.n.* **asthmatic** *a.* aamborstig, asthmatisch.

astir, *adv.* op de been, in de weer.

astonish, *v.t.* verwonderen, verbazen. to be ~*ed*, zich verbazen. **astonishing,** *a.*, ~**ly,** *adv.* verbazend. **astonishment,** *n.* verbazing *n.*

astound, *v.t.* verbazen.

astraddle, *adv.* schrijlings.

astral, *a.* sterre-.

astray, *adv.* verdwaald. to go ~, verdwalen.

astride, *adv.* schrijlings.

astringency, *n.* samentrekkende eigenschap *n.* **astringent,** *a.* samentrekkend. ¶ *n.* samentrekkend middel *n.n.*, (bloed)-stelpend middel *n.n.*

astrologer, *n.* sterrenwichelaar *n.* **astrological,** *a.* astrologisch. **astrology,** *n.* sterrenwichelarij *n.*

astronomer, *n.* sterrenkundige *n.* **astronomical,** *a.* sterrenkundig. **astronomy,** *n.* sterrenkunde *n.*

astute, *a.*, ~**ly,** *adv.* sluw, geslepen. **astuteness,** *n.* sluwheid *n.*, geslepenheid *n.*

asunder, *adv.* uiteen, uit elkaar.

asylum, *n.* toevluchtsoord *n.n.* *lunatic* ~, krankzinnigengesticht *n.n.*

at, *prep.* aan; te, tot, ter; om; op; in; tegen, voor. ~ *not* ~ *all*, helemaal niet; ~ *first*, in 't begin; ~ *last*, ten slotte, ten laatste; ~ *least*, minstens, ten minste; ~ *length*, tenslotte; ~ *once*, dadelijk, onmiddellijk, terstond.

atavism, *n.* atavisme *n.n.* **atavistic,** *a.* atavistisch.

atheism, *n.* atheïsme *n.n.* **atheist,** *n.* atheïst *n.*

Athenian, *a.* Atheens. **Athens,** *N.* Athene *n.N.*

athirst, *adv.* dorstig; dorstend.

athlete, *n.* athleet *n.* **athletic,** *a.* athletisch. **athletics,** *pl.n.* athletiek *n.*

at home, *n.* ontvangdag *n.*

athwart, *prep.* dwarsover, dwarsvoor. ¶ *adv.* dwarsscheeps.

Atlantic, *a.* Atlantisch.

atlas, *n.* atlas *n.*

atmosphere, *n.* atmosfeer *n.*; dampkring *n.* **atmospheric,** *a.* atmosferisch, dampkrings-.

atoll, *n.* atol *n.*, koraaleiland *n.n.*

atom, *n.* atoom *n.n.* **atomic,** *a.* atomisch, atoom-.

atone, *v.i.* boeten voor, goedmaken. **atonement,** *n.* boete *n.*, verzoening *n.n.* *Day of A*~, Grote Verzoendag N.

atonic, *a.* toonloos.

atrabilious, *a.* zwartgallig.

atrocious, *a.* gruwelijk, afgrijselijk. **atrocity,** *n.* gruwelijkheid *n.*; gruweldaad *n.*

atrophy, *v.i.* afsterven *str.* ¶ *n.* atrophie *n.*, afsterving *n.*

attach, *v.t.* vastmaken. to ~ *to*, vastmaken aan; to be ~*ed to*, gehecht zijn aan. **attachable,** *a.* aanhechtbaar. **attachment,** *n.* band *n.*, aanhankelijkheid *n.*, gehechtheid *n.*

attack, *v.t.* aanvallen *str.*; aantasten. ¶ *n.* aanval *n.*

attain, *v.t.* bereiken, verkrijgen *str.* ¶ *v.i.* to ~ *to*, bereiken. **attainable,** *a.* bereikbaar.

attainder, *n.* ontering *n.*

attainment, *n.* talent *n.n.* ~*s*, kundigheden *pl. n.*

attar, *n.* essence *n.* ~ *of roses*, rozenolie *n.*

attempt, *v.t.* pogen, proberen, trachten. ¶ *n.* poging *n.*; aanslag *n.*

attend, *v.t.* begeleiden, vergezellen; verzorgen, verplegen; bijwonen, bezoeken *irr.* ¶ *v.i.* to ~ *to*, aandacht *n.* schenken *str.* aan; letten op. **attendance,** *n.* bediening *n.*; behandeling *n.*; tegenwoordigheid *n.*, aanwezigheid *n.*; opkomst *n.* **attendant,** *a.* aanwezig; bijbehorend. ¶ *n.* bediende *n.*, oppasser *n.* **attention,** *n.* aandacht *n.*, oplettendheid *n.* **attentive,** *a.*, ~**ly,** *adv.* aandachtig; oplettend; attent.

attenuate, *v.t.* verzachten; verzwakken. **attenuated,** *a.* vermagerd, verzwakt. **attenuation,** *n.* verzachting *n.*

attest, *v.t.* getuigen, verklaren. **attestation,** *n.* getuigenis *n.*

attic, *n.* vliering *n.*, dakkamertje *n.n.*

Attic, *a.* Attisch.

attire, *v.t.* tooien, uitdossen. ¶ *n.* tooi *n.*, dos *n.*

attitude, *n.* houding *n.* **attitudinize,** *v.i.* poseren.

attorney, *n.* procureur *n.*, gevolmachtigde *n.* *power of* ~, volmacht *n.*, procuratie *n.*; ~-*general*, procureur-generaal *n.*

attract, *v.t.* aantrekken *str.* **attraction,** *n.*

aantrekkingskracht *n.* **attractive,** *a.,* ~ly, *adv.* aantrekkelijk. **attractiveness,** *n.* aantrekkelijkheid *n.*
attribute, *v.t.* toeschrijven *str.* ¶ *n.* eigenschap *n.,* attribuut *n.n.* **attributive,** *a.* attributief.
attrition, *n.* wrijving *n.,* afschuring *n.;* berouw *n.n. war of* ~, uitputtingsoorlog *n.*
attune, *v.t.* in overeenstemming *n.* brengen *irr.,* doen *irr.* harmonieren.
auburn, *a.* kastanjebruin.
auction, *n.* veiling *n.* (bij opbod *n.n.*). *Dutch* ~, veiling (bij afslag *n.*). ¶ *v.t.* veilen. **auctioneer,** *n.* venduhouder *n.*
audacious, *a.,* ~ly, *adv.* stoutmoedig, vermetel; brutaal. **audacity,** *n.* vermetelheid *n.*
audibility, *n.* hoorbaarheid *n.* **audible,** *a.,* ~bly, *adv.* hoorbaar.
audience, *n.* gehoor *n.n.,* toehoorders *pl.n.;* audientie *n.*
audit, *v.t.* verifiëren, nazien *irr.* ¶ *n.* verificatie *n.,* nazien *n.n.*
audition, *n.* gehoor *n.n.* **auditive,** *a.* gehoor-. **auditor,** *n.* toehoorder *n.;* verificateur *n.* **auditorium,** *n.* gehoorzaal *n.;* gehoor *n.n.* **auditory,** *n.* toehoorders *pl.n.* ¶ *a.* gehoor-.
auger, *n.* avegaar *n.;* aardboor *n.*
aught, *pron.* iets, wat ook. *for* ~ *I care,* wat mij betreft; *for* ~ *I know,* voor zover ik weet.
augment, *v.t.* vermeerderen. ¶ *v.i.* vermeerderen, toenemen *str.* **augmentation,** *n.* vermeerdering *n.*
augur, *v.t.* voorspellen. **augury,** *n.* voorspelling *n.;* voorteken *n.n.*
august, *a.* doorluchtig.
August, *N.* augustus *N.* **Augustan,** *a.* van Augustus. **Augustine,** *a.* Augustijner.
auk, *n.* alk *n.*
aunt, *n.* tante *n.*
aura, *n.* aura *n.,* emanatie *n.,* uitstraling *n.*
aural, *a.* oor-.
aureola, *n.* aureool *n.,* stralenkrans *n.*
auricle, *n.* hartkamer *n.;* oorschelp *n.*
auricula, *n.* aurikel *n.*
auricular, *a.* oor-.
auriferous, *a.* goudhoudend.
aurora, *n.* ochtendgloren *n.n.,* dageraad *n.* ~ *australis,* zuiderlicht; ~ *borealis,* noorderlicht.
auscultation, *n.* auscultatie *n.*
auspices, *pl.n.* voortekenen *pl.n.n. under the* ~ *of,* onder bescherming *n.* van.
auspicious, *a.,* ~ly, *adv.* gunstig, veelbelovend.
austere, *a.,* ~ly, *adv.* streng, sober, eenvoudig. **austerity,** *n.* strengheid *n.,* eenvoud *n.*
austral, *a.* zuidelijk. **Australia,** *N.* Australië *n.N.* **Australian,** *a.* Australisch. ¶ *N.* Australiër *N.;* Australische *N.*
Austria, *N.* Oostenrijk *n.N.* **Austrian,** *a.*

Oostenrijks. ¶ *N.* Oostenrijker *N.;* Oostenrijkse *N.*
authentic, *a.,* ~ally, *adv.* echt, geloofwaardig. **authenticate,** *v.t.* waarmerken, bekrachtigen. **authenticity,** *n.* echtheid *n.*
author, *n.* schrijver *n.,* auteur *n.;* schrijfster *n.;* schepper *n.* **authoress,** *n.* schrijfster *n.* **authoritative,** *a.,* ~ly, *adv.* gebiedend; gezaghebbend. **authority,** *n.* gezag *n.n.;* aanzien *n.n.;* autoriteit *n.,* deskundige *n. authorities,* overheid *n.,* autoriteiten *pl.n.* **authorization,** *n.* volmacht *n.,* machtiging *n.* **authorize,** *v.t.* machtigen.
authorship, *n.* auteurschap *n.n.*
autobiography, *n.* autobiografie *n.*
autocracy, *n.* alleenheerschappij *n.* **autocrat,** *n.* autocraat *n.* **autocratic,** *a.* autocratisch.
autograph, *n.* eigenhandig geschreven stuk *n.n.*
automatic, *a.* automatisch, werktuiglijk. **automatically,** *adv.* automatisch, werktuiglijk, van zelf. **automaton,** *n.* automaat *n.*
automobile, *n.* automobiel *n.*
autonomy, *n.* autonomie *n.,* zelfbestuur *n.n.* **autopsy,** *n.* lijkopening *n.,* lijkschouwing *n.*
autotype, *n.* autotypie *n.*
autumn, *n.* herfst *n.,* najaar *n.n.* **autumnal,** *a.* herfst-, najaars-.
auxiliary, *a.* hulp-. ¶ *n.* helper *n. auxiliaries,* hulptroepen *n.*
avail, *v.t.* & *v.i.* baten, helpen *str.* ¶ *n.* nut *n.n.,* baat *n. without* ~, vruchteloos. **availability,** *n.* beschikbaarheid *n.* **available,** *a.* beschikbaar, voorhanden.
avalanche, *n.* lawine *n.*
avarice, *n.* gierigheid *n.,* schraapzucht *n.;* hebzucht *n.* **avaricious,** *a.,* ~ly *adv.* gierig; hebzuchtig.
avenge, *v.t.* wreken *str.* **avenger,** *n.* wreker *n.*
avenue, *n.* laan *n.;* boulevard *n.;* toegang *n.*
aver, *v.t.* beweren, verzekeren.
average, *n.* gemiddelde *n.n.,* doorsnee *n.; averij n. on an* ~, gemiddeld, in doorsnee, door elkaar gerekend; *general* ~, averij grosse; *particular* ~, averij particulier. ¶ *v.t.* gemiddeld bedragen *str.,* gemiddeld komen *irr.* op.
averse, *a.,* ~ly, *adv.* afkerig. ~ *to,* ~ *from,* afkerig van. **aversion,** *n.* afkeer *n.,* afkerigheid *n.,* weerzin *n.*
avert, *v.t.* afwenden, afkeren.
aviary, *n.* volière *n.*
aviation, *n.* vliegwezen *n.n.,* luchtvaart *n.;* vliegsport *n.* **aviator,** *n.* vlieger *n.;* vliegenier *n.*
avid, *a.* gretig, begerig. **avidity,** *n.* gretigheid *n.,* begeerte *n.*
avocation, *n.* roeping *n.;* beroep *n.n.*
avocet, *n.* kluit *n.*
avoid, *v.t.* vermijden *str.;* ontwijken *str.* **avoidable,** *a.* te vermijden. *not* ~, onvermijdelijk. **avoidance,** *n.* vermijding *n. in* ~ *of,* ter vermijding van.

avoirdupois, *n.* *not translated.*
avow, *v.t.* erkennen, toegeven *str.* **avowal,** *n.* erkentenis *n.* **avowedly,** *adv.* onomwonden, openlijk.
avuncular, *a.* een oom betreffend.
await, *v.t.* wachten op, verwachten; te wachten staan *irr.*
awake, *v.t.* wekken, wakker maken. ¶ *v.i.* ontwaken, wakker worden *str.* *to* ~ *to, tot het besef komen irr.* van. ¶ *a.* wakker.
awaken, *v.t.* wakker maken. ¶ *v.i.* wakker worden *str.* **awakening,** *n.* ontwaken *n.n.*; ontnuchtering *n.*
award, *v.t.* toekennen, toewijzen *str.* ¶ *n.* uitspraak *n.*, vonnis *n.n.*; toegekende beloning *n.*, onderscheiding *n.*
aware, *a.* gewaar, bewust. *to be* ~ *of,* weten *irr.*
awash, *adv.* bespoeld door het water.
away, *adv.* weg, heen; er op los.
awe, *v.t.* ontzag inboezemen. ¶ *n.* ontzag *n.n.*; eerbiedige vrees *n.* **awe-struck,** *a.* met ontzag *n.n.* **awful,** *a.,* ~ly, *adv.* ontzaglijk, vreselijk; afschuwelijk. **awfulness,** *n.* afschuwelijkheid *n.*
awhile, *adv.* een poosje.
awkward, *a.,* ~ly, *adv.* onhandig, links; verlegen; lastig. **awkwardness,** *n.* onhandigheid *n.*; verlegenheid *n.*
awl, *n.* els *n.*
awning, *n.* zonnetent *n.*
awry, *a.* & *adv.* scheef, schuin.
axe, *n.* bijl. *he has an* ~ *to grind,* hij heeft zelfzuchtige belangen *n.n.* **axe-head,** *n.* blad *n.n.* (van de bijl.).
axillary, *a.* okselstandig, oksel-.
axiom, *n.* axioma *n.n.* **axiomatic,** *a.,* ~ally, *adv.* axiomatisch.
axis, *n.* as *n.*, spil *n.*
axle, *n.* as *n.* **axle-tree,** *n.* wagenas *n.*
ay, *adv.* ja. *the* ~*es have it,* het is aangenomen.
ayah, *n.* baboe *n.*
azalea, *n.* azalea *n.*
azimuth, *n.* azimuth *n.n.*
azure, *n.* azuur *n.n.*, hemelsblauw *n.n.* ¶ *a.* azuren.

B

baa, *v.i.* blaten. ¶ *n.* geblaat. **baa-lamb,** *n.* schaapje *n.n.*, lammetje *n.n.*
babble, *v.i.* babbelen; kabbelen. ¶ *n.* gebabbel *n.n.*; gekabbel *n.n.* **babbler,** *n.* wauwelaar *n.*
babe, *n.* kindje *n.n.*, zuigeling *n.*
baboon, *n.* baviaan *n.*
baby, *n.* klein kind *n.n.*, baby *n.* **babyhood,** *n.* eerste kindsheid *n.* **baby-linen,** *n.* kindergoed *n.n.*, luiers *pl.n.* **babyish,** *a.* kinderachtig.
bachelor, *n.* vrijgezel *n.* ~ *of arts,* bacca-

laureus *n.* **bachelor's button,** *n.* dubbele boterbloem *n.*
bacillus, *n.* bacil *n.*
back, *n.* rug *n.*; achterkant *n.*; achterspeler *n.* ~ *to front,* achterstevoren; *to put a person's* ~ *up,* iemand nijdig maken. ¶ *v.t.* achteruitbewegen *str.*; de rug versterken van; steunen; wedden op. *to* ~ *out of something,* ergens uitdraaien. ¶ *adv.* achteruit, terug, achterwaarts.
backbite, *v.t.* belasteren. **backbiter,** *n.* lasteraar *n.*
backbone, *n.* ruggegraat *n.* *to the* ~, door en door.
backdoor, *n.* achterdeur *n.*
backer, *n.* helper *n.*; wedder *n.*
backfire, *v.i.* terugslaan *irr.*
backgammon, *n.* triktrak *n.n.*
background, *n.* achtergrond *n.*
backhand, *n.* vandehandse slag *n.* **backhanded,** *a.* dubbelzinnig, indirect.
backing, *n.* steun *n.*
back number, *n.* oud nummer *n.n.*
backside, *n.* achterkant *n.*; achterwerk *n.n.* achterste *n.n.*
backslide, *v.i.* afvallig worden *str.*, minder geestdrift *n.* vertonen. **backslider,** *n.* afvallige *n.* **backsliding,** *n.* afvalligheid *n.*, verslapping *n.*, vermindering *n.* van geestdrift *n.*
back stairs, *n.* achtertrap *n.* ¶ *a.* heimelijk, oneerlijk.
backstitch, *n.* voor- en achtersteek *n.*
backward, *a.* achterwaarts; achterlijk. ¶ *adv.* achterwaarts, terug. **backwards,** *adv.* achterwaarts, terug. **backwardness,** *n.* achterlijkheid *n.*
backwater, *n.* dood water *n.n.*; vergeten hoekje *n.n.*
backwoods, *pl.n.* afgelegen oerwoud *n.n.*; binnenland *n.n.*
bacon, *n.* spek *n.n.*
bacterium, *n.* bacterie *n.*
bad, *a.,* ~ly, *adv.* slecht, kwaad; stout; bedorven; vals. *to go* ~, bederven *str.*; *to be* ~ly *off,* er slecht aan toe zijn.
badge, *n.* insigne *n.*
badger, *n.* das *n.* ¶ *v.t.* plagen, voortdurend lastig vallen *str.*
badness, *n.* slechtheid *n.*
baffle, *v.t.* verwarren; verijdelen.
bag, *n.* tas *n.*; weitas *n.*; zak *n.* ~ *and baggage,* met pak *n.* en zak. ¶ *v.t.* in zakken doen *irr.* ¶ *v.i.* puilen.
bagatelle, *n.* kleinigheid *n.*, bagatel *n.*
baggage, *n.* bagage *n.*; lichtekooi *n.*
bagginess, *n.* zakachtig hangen *n.n.*; gezwollenheid *n.* **baggy,** *a.* zakkerig, zakachtig; gezwollen.
bagman, *n.* handelsreiziger *n.*
bagpipe, *n.* doedelzak *n.*
bail, *n.* borg *n.*, borgtocht *n.*; staket *n.n.* ¶ *v.t.* borg blijven *str.* voor. *to* ~ *out,* vrijkrijgen *str.* door borgstelling *n.* ¶ *v.i.*

hozen. **bailee,** *n.* borgtochthouder *n.*
bailer, *n.* hoosvat *n.n.*
bailiff, *n.* deurwaarder *n.*; opzichter · *n.*;
baljuw *n.*
bairn, *n.* kind *n.n.*
bait, *v.t.* van lokaas *n.n.* voorzien *irr.*; tergen,
kwellen; laten *str.* pleisteren. ¶ *v.i.*
pleisteren. ¶ *n.* lokaas *n.n.*; verversing
n.; pleisteren · *n.n.*
baize, *n.* baai *n.*
bake, *v.t.* & *v.i.* bakken *irr.*; braden *irr.*
bakehouse, *n.* bakkerij *n.* **baker,** *n.* bakker
n. **bakery,** *n.* bakkerij *n.*
balance, *n.* balans *n.*; weegschaal *n.*; evenwicht *n.n.*; onrust *n.*; saldo *n.n.* ~ *of*
power, staatkundig evenwicht. ¶ *v.t.* in
evenwicht houden *irr.*, in evenwicht
brengen *irr.* ¶ *v.i.* in evenwicht zijn.
balance-sheet, *n.* balans *n.*
balcony, *n.* balkon *n.n.*
bald, *a.,* ~**ly,** *adv.* kaal; naakt.
balderdash, *n.* onzin *n.*
baldness, *n.* kaalheid *n.*
baldric, *n.* bandelier *n.,* schouderband *n.*
bale, *n.* baal *n.* ¶ *v.t.* in balen verpakken.
baleful, *a.,* ~**ly,** *adv.* onheilspellend; ellendig.
balk, *v.t.* dwarsbomen; verijdelen. ¶ *v.i.*
to ~ *at,* blijven *str.* steken voor.
Balkan, *N.* the ~*s,* de Balkan, de Balkan-
staten.
ball, *n.* bal *n.*; kogel *n.*; bal *n.n.* (*dance*)
to keep the ~ *rolling,* het gesprek gaande
houden *irr.*
ballad, *n.* ballade *n.,* lied *n.n.*
ballast, *n.* ballast *n,* ¶ *v.t.* ballasten. ¶ *v.i.*
ballast innemen *str.*
ball-bearing, *n.* kogellager *n.n.*
ballet, *n.* ballet *n.n.* **ballet-dancer,** *n.* ballet-
danser(es) *n.*
balloon, *n.* ballon *n.*; luchtballon *n.* ¶ *v.i.*
opbollen.
ballot, *n.* geheime stemming *n.*; stemballetje
n.n. **ballot-box,** *n.* stembus *n.*
balm, *n.* balsem *n.*; troost *n.* ¶ *v.t.* balsemen.
balmy, *a.* balsemachtig.
Baltic, *a.* Oostzee-. ~ *Republics,* Oostzee-
staten *pl. N.,* Randstaten *pl. N.* ¶ *N.*
Oostzee *N.*
baluster, *n.* baluster *n.,* stijl *n.* **balustrade,**
n. balustrade *n.*
bamboo, *n.* bamboe *n.n.* ¶ *a.* bamboe,
bamboezen.
bamboozle, *v.t.* bedotten, beetnemen *str.*
ban, *v.t.* verbannen *irr.*; vervloeken; in de
ban doen *irr.* ¶ *n.* afkondiging *n.*;
ban(vloek) *n.*
banal, *a.* banaal. **banality,** *n.* banaliteit *n.*
banana, *n.* banaan *n.,* pisang *n.*
band, *n.* band *n.,* lint *n.n.*; drijfriem *n.*;
troep *n.,* bende *n.*; muziekkorps *n.n.,*
orkestje *n.n.* ¶ *v.i.* *to* ~ *together,* zich
verenigen.
bandage, *n.* verband *n.n.,* zwachtel *n.* ¶ *v.t.*
verbinden *str.,* zwachtelen.

bandbox, *n.* hoedendoos *n.,* lintendoos *n.*
he looks as if he came out of a ~, je kon
hem door een ringetje halen.
bandicoot, *n.* buideldas *n.*
bandit, *n.* bandiet *n.*
bandmaster, *n.* kapelmeester *n.*
bandog, *n.* kettinghond *n.,* bandrekel *n.*
bandsman, *n.* muzikant *n.* **bandstand,** *n.*
muziektent *n.*
bandy, *a.* met O-benen; krom. ¶ *v.t.* over
en weer slaan *irr.,* wisselen.
bane, *n.* vergif *n.n.*; verderf *n.n.* **baneful,** *a.*
giftig; verderfelijk.
bang, *v.t.* slaan (met) *irr.,* bonzen (met).
¶ *v.i.* knallen. ¶ *n.* slag *n.,* knal *n.*
bangle, *n.* armring *n.*; enkelring *n.*
banish, *v.t.* verbannen *irr.* **banishment,** *n.*
verbanning *n.*; ballingschap *n.*
banisters, *pl.n.* trapleuning *n.*
banjo, *n.* banjo *n.*
bank, *n.* bank *n.*; oever *n.*; (zand)bank *n.*;
berm *n.* ¶ *v.t.* op de bank zetten; in-
dammen; ophopen. ¶ *v.i.* *to* ~ *on,*
rekenen op. **bank-bill,** *n.* bankaanwijzing
n. **bank clerk,** *n.* bankbediende *n.* **bank
credit,** *n.* bankkrediet *n.n.* **banker,** *n.*
bankier *n.* **bank-holiday,** *n.* beursvacantie
(dag) *n.* **banking account,** *n.* banksaldo
n.n. **banking house,** *n.* bank *n.,* bankiers-
firma *n.* **bank-note,** *n.* bankbiljet *n.n.*
bank-rate, *n.* bankdisconto *n.n.* **bankrupt,**
a. bankroet, failliet. ¶ *n.* bankroetier *n.*
bankruptcy, *n.* bankroet *n.n.,* faillissement
n.n. **bank stock,** *n.* bankkapitaal *n.n.*
banner, *n.* banier *n.*
banns, *pl.n.* huwelijksafkondiging *n.*
banquet, *n.* banket *n.n.,* feestmaal *n.n.*
banshee, *n.* weeklagend spook *n.n.*
bantam, *n.* krielhaan *n.,* krielkip *n.*
banter, *v.i.* gekscheren, schertsen. ¶ *n.*
gekkernij *n.,* scherts *n.*
banyan, *n.,* **banyan-tree,** *n.* waringin *n.*
baptism, *n.* doop *n.* **baptismal,** *a.* doop-.
baptist, *n.* doper *n.* **Baptist,** *n.* Doops-
gezinde, *n.*; Wederdoper *n.* **baptize,** *v.t.*
dopen.
bar, *n.* staaf *n.*; tralie *n.*, spijl *n.*; baar *n.*;
(slag)boom *n.*; drempel *n.,* zandbank *n.*;
bar *n.,* café *n.n.*; balie *n.* ¶ *v.t.* afsluiten
str.; versperren.
barb, *n.* weerhaak *n.* ¶ *v.t.* van weerhaken
voorzien *irr.*
barbarian, *n.* barbaar *n.* ¶ *a.* barbaars.
barbaric, *a.* barbaars. **barbarism,** *n.*
barbaarsheid *n.* **barbarity,** *n.* barbaarsheid
n. **barbarous,** *a.* barbaars.
barbed, *a.* van weerhaken voorzien *irr.*
~*wire,* prikkeldraad *n.n.*
barbel, *n.* barbeel *n.*
barber, *n.* barbier *n.*
bard, *n.* bard *n.,* zanger *n.*
bare, *a.* naakt, bloot, kaal. **bareback,** · *adv.*
zonder zadel *n.n.* **barefaced,** *a.* onbeschaamd. **barefoot,** *a.* barrevoets.

bareheaded, *a.* blootshoofds. **barelegged,** *a.* met blote benen *n.n.* **barely,** *adv.* nauwelijks, ter nauwernood. **bareness,** *n.* naaktheid *n.*, kaalheid *n.*

bargain, *n.* koopje *n.n.*; overeenkomst. *into the* ~, bovendien. ¶ *v.i.* loven en bieden *str.*; onderhandelen.

barge, *n.* binnenschip *n.n.*; aak *n.* ¶ *v.i.* *to* ~ *into*, aanbonzen tegen. **bargee,** *n.* binnenschipper *n.*

baritone, *n.* bariton *n.*

barium, *n.* barium *n.n.*

bark, *n.* schors *n.*; bast *n.*; run *n.*; geblaf *n.n.*; bark *n.* ¶ *v.t.* afschorsen. ~ *v.i.* blaffen.

barley, *n.* gerst *n.* **barley-corn,** *n.* gerstekorrel *n.*; gerst *n.* *John B*~, de Alkohol. **barley-sugar,** *n.* gerstesuiker *n.* **barleywater,** *n.* gerstewater *n.n.*

barm, *n.* gist *n.*

barmaid, *n.* buffetjuffrouw *n.* **barman,** *n.* buffetknecht *n.*

barn, *n.* schuur *n.*

barnacle, *n.* eendenmossel *n.* ~ *goose*, boomgans *n.*

barn-floor, *n.* deel *n.*

barometer, *n.* barometer *n.*

baron, *n.* baron *n.* **baroness,** *n.* barones *n.* **baronet,** *n.* baronet *n.* **baronetcy,** *n.* baronetschap *n.n.* **baronial,** *a.* van een baron *n.* **barony,** *n.* baronie *n.*

baroque, *a.* barok. ¶ *n.* barokke *n.n.*, barokke stijl *n.*

barrack, *n.* barak *n.* ~*s*, kazerne *n.*

barrage, *n.* waterdam *n.*; spervuur *n.n.* **barrage-balloon,** *n.* kabelballon *n.*

barratry, *n.* schelmerij *n.*

barrel, *n.* ton *n.*, vat *n.n.*; loop *n.* (*of rifle*). ¶ *v.t.* inkuipen. **barrel-organ,** *n.* draaiorgel *n.n.*

barren, *a.* onvruchtbaar, kaal. **barrenness,** *n.* onvruchtbaarheid *n.*

barricade, *n.* barricade *n.*

barrier, *n.* barrière *n.*; slagboom *n.*, sluitboom *n.*; hindernis *n.* ~*-reef*, koraalrif *n.n.*

barring, *prep.* behalve, behoudens.

barrister, *n.* advocaat *n.*

bar-room, *n.* gelagkamer *n.*

barrow, *n.* handkar *n.*, berrie *n.*; grafheuvel *n.*

barter, *n.* ruilhandel *n.* ¶ *v.i.* ruilen.

basalt, *n.* bazalt *n.n.* ¶ *a.* bazalten. **basaltic,** *a.* bazaltachtig.

base, *n.* basis *n.*, grondslag *n.*; bas *n.*; base *n.* ¶ *a.* laag, gemeen; vals. ¶ *v.t.* baseren, grondvesten.

baseball, *n.* Amerikaans balspel *n.n.*

baseless, *a.* ongegrond.

base-line, *n.* grondlijn *n.*

basely, *adv.* laag, gemeen.

basement, *n.* benedenverdieping *n.*, souterrain *n.n.*

baseness, *n.* laagheid *n.*

bash, *v.t.* beuken, slaan *irr.*

bashful, *a.*, ~*ly*, *adv.* bedeesd, schuchter.

bashfulness, *n.* bedeesdheid *n.*, schuchterheid *n.*

basic, *a.* basisch; fundamenteel.

basil, *n.* basilicum *n.n.*, balsemkruid *n.n.*

basilica, *n.* basiliek *n.*

basilisk, *n.* draak *n.*

basin, *n.* kom *n.*, bekken *n.n.*; havenkom *n.*; stroomgebied *n.n.*

basis, *n.* basis *n.*, grondslag *n.*

bask, *v.i.* zich koesteren.

basket, *n.* mand *n.*

bass, *n.* bas *n.*; baars *n.*

bassoon, *n.* fagot *n.*

bast, *n.* bast *n.*; touw van bast *n.n.*

bastard, *n.* bastaard *n.* ¶ *a.* basterd-, bastaard-, onecht. **bastardy,** *n.* bastaardij *n.*

baste, *v.t.* bedruipen *str.*; afranselen.

bastinado, *n.* bastonnade *n.*, pak *n.n.* slaag.

bastion, *n.* bastion *n.n.*, bolwerk *n.n.*

bat, *n.* vleermuis *n.*; kolf *n.*, slaghout *n.n.* ¶ *v.i.* terugslaan *irr.*

batch, *n.* baksel *n.n.*; partij *n.*

bated, *a.* ingehouden.

bath, *n.* bad *n.n.*, ~*-chair*, rolstoel *n.* **bathe,** *v.t.* baden; zich baden; betten. ¶ *n.* bad *n.n.* **bathing-machine,** *n.* badkoets *n.*

bathos, *n.* belachelijke anticlimax *n.*

batiste, *n.* batist *n.n.*

batman, *n.* oppasser *n.*

baton, *n.* dirigeerstok *n.*; stok *n.*; staf *n.*

batrachian, *a.* kikvorsachtig.

battalion, *n.* bataljon *n.n.*

batten, *n.* lat *n.*, klamp *n.* ¶ *v.t.* *to* ~ *down*, (de presennings) schalmen.

batter, *v.t.* beuken; rammeien; havenen. ¶ *n.* beslag *n.n.*

battering-ram, *n.* stormram *n.*

batter-pudding, *n.* (soort) pannekoek *n.*

battery, *n.* batterij *n.*; geweldpleging *n.*; accu *n.*

battle, *n.* slag *n.*, veldslag *n.*, zeeslag *n.*; strijd *n.* ¶ *v.i.* strijden *str.* **battle-array,** *n.* slagorde *n.* **battledore,** *n.* raket *n.n.* **battledress,** *n.* veldtenue *n.* **battlefield,** *n.* slagveld *n.n.* **battlement,** *n.* ~*s*, kantelen *n.n.*

battue, *n.* klopjacht *n.*, drijfjacht *n.*

bauble, *n.* snuisterij *n.*, prul *n.n.*

baulk, *v.t.* & *v.i.* *See* **balk.**

bawd, *n.* koppelaarster *n.* **bawdy,** *a.* liederlijk.

bawl, *v.t.* luidkeels schreeuwen.

bay, *n.* golf *n.*, baai *n.*, bocht *n.*; nis *n.*, erker *n.*; laurierboom *n.*; vos *n.* *to be at* ~, in het nauw zitten *str.*; *to hold at* ~, in bedwang *n.n.* houden *irr.* ¶ *a.* vaalbruin. ¶ *v.i.* blaffen.

bayonet, *n.* bajonet *n.* ¶ *v.t.* met de bajonet doorsteken *str.*

bay-window, *n.* erker *n.*

bazaar, *n.* bazaar *n.*

be, *copula.* zijn.

beach, *n.* strand *n.n.*, kust *n.* ¶ *v.t.* op het strand zetten.

beacon, *n.* baken *n.n.*

bead, *n.* kraal *n.*; (vizier)korrel *n.* ~*s*, rozenkrans *n.*

beadle, *n.* pedel *n.*; bode *n.*

beagle, *n.* brak *n.*

beak, *n.* snavel *n.*

beaker, *n.* beker *n.*

beam, *n.* balk *n.*; juk *n.n.*; lichtstraal *n.*; stralenbundel *n.* ¶ *v.t.* uitstralen. ¶ *v.i.* stralen. **beam-ends,** *pl.n. to be on her* ~, op z'n zij liggen *str.*; *to be on one's* ~, (*fig.*) in verlegenheid *n.* zitten *str.* **beamy,** *a.* stralend.

bean, *n.* boon *n.* *broad* ~, tuinboon *n.*; *butter* ~, (grote) witte boon; *French* ~, prinsessenboon *n.*; *haricot* ~, witte boon; *runner* ~, snijboon *n.*

bear, *v.t.* dragen *str.*; baren, voortbrengen *irr.*; verdragen *str.* ¶ *v.i.* aanhouden *irr.* *to* ~ *against*, steunen op; *to* ~ *down*, overmannen; *to* ~ *off*, wegdragen *str.*; *to* ~ *on*, betrekking *n.* hebben op; *to* ~ *up*, zich moedig gedragen *str.* ¶ *v.r. to* ~ *oneself*, zich gedragen *str.* ¶ *n.* beer *n.* *she-*~, berin *n.* **bearable,** *a.*, ~**ly,** *adv.* dragelijk.

beard, *n.* baard *n.*; weerhaak *n.* ¶ *v.t.* trotseren. **beardless,** *a.* baardeloos.

bearer, *n.* drager *n.* *to* ~, aan toonder *n.* **bearing,** *n.* houding *n.*, gedrag *n.n.*; richting *n.*, strekking *n.* *to find one's* ~*s*, zich oriënteren; ~*s*, lager *n.n.* (*machinery*).

bear-skin, *n.* berenvel *n.n.*; berenmuts *n.*

beast, *n.* beest *n.n.*, dier *n.n.* **beastlike,** *a.* beestachtig. **beastliness,** *n.* beestachtigheid *n.* **beastly,** *a.* beestachtig; vreselijk.

beat, *v.t.* slaan *irr.*; kloppen; klotsen; klutsen; verslaan *irr.* *to* ~ *about the bush*, ergens omheen draaien; *to* ~ *down the price*, afdingen *str.*; *to* ~ *off*, afslaan *irr.* ¶ *n.* slag *n.*; maatslag *n.*; ronde *n.* **beaten,** *a.* geplet, gedreven. ~ *track*, begane weg *n.* **beater,** *n.* drijver *n.*

beatific, *a.* gelukzalig; zaligmakend. **beatification,** *n.* zaligmaking *n.* **beatify,** *v.t.* zaligmaken, zalig verklaren. **beatitude,** *n.* zaligheid *n.* *the B*~*s*, de Zaligsprekingen *pl.N.*

beau, *n.* galant *n.*

beauteous, *a.*, ~**ly,** *adv.* schoon. **beautiful,** *a.*, ~**ly,** *adv.* mooi, schoon. **beautify,** *v.t.* fraai maken, mooi maken. **beauty,** *n.* schoonheid *n.*; prachtexemplaar *n.n.*

beaver, *n.* bever *n.*; vilten hoed *n.*

becalm, *v.i.* stillen, bedaren. *to be* ~*ed*, door windstilte worden *str.* overvallen.

because, *c.* omdat.

beck, *n.* wenk *n.* *to be at someone's* ~ *and call*, op iemands wenken gereed staan *irr.* **beckon,** *v.t.* & *v.i.* wenken, een wenk geven *str.*

becloud, *v.i.* bewolken.

become, *v.t.* (goed) staan *irr.*; passen. ¶ *v.i.* worden *str.* **becoming,** *a.*, ~**ly,** *adv.* passend, gepast; bevallig.

bed, *n.* bed *n.n.* ¶ *v.t.* te bed leggen; in een bed planten.

bedaub, *v.t.* bekladden.

bed-clothes, *pl.n.* beddegoed *n.n.*, dekens *pl.n.* **bedding,** *n.* beddegoed *n.n.*

bedeck, *v.t.* tooien, versieren.

bedevil, *v.t.* beheksen.

bedew, *v.t.* bedauwen, bevochtigen.

bedfellow, *n.* slaapkameraad *n.*

bedim, *v.t.* benevelen.

bedizen, *v.t.* opschikken.

bedlam, *n.* gekkenhuis *n.n.*

bedpan, *n.* steekpan *n.* **bedpost,** *n.* beddepost *n.*

bedraggle, *v.t.* bemodderen.

bedridden, *a.* bedlegerig. **bedrock,** *n.* grondgesteente *n.n.*; grondslag *n.* **bedroom,** *n.* slaapkamer *n.* **bedside,** *n.* *at his* ~, aan zijn bed *n.n.* **bedstead,** *n.* ledikant *n.n.* **bed-time,** *n.* bedtijd *n.*

bee, *n.* bij *n.* *to have a* ~ *in one's bonnet*, een idee-fixe *n.* hebben.

beech, *n.* beuk *n.* *copper* ~, rode beuk. ¶ *a.* beuken.

beef, *n.* rundvlees *n.n.*; os *n.* *beeves*, slachtvee *n.n.* **beef-eater,** *n.* soldaat *n.* van de Tower. **beef-steak,** *n.* biefstuk *n.*, runderlapje *n.n.* **beef-tea,** *n.* bouillon *n.*

bee-hive, *n.* bijenkorf *n.* **bee-line,** *n.* rechte lijn *n.* *to make a* ~ *for*, recht afstevenen op. **bee-master,** *n.* imker *n.*

beer, *n.* bier *n.n.* *small* ~, dun bier *n.n.* **beery,** *a.* bierachtig, bier-.

beet, *n.* biet *n.*; beetwortel *n.*

beetle, *n.* tor *n.*, kever *n.*; stamper *n.*, heiblok *n.n.* ¶ *v.t.* stampen. **beetle-brows,** *pl.n.* vooruitstekende wenkbrauwen *pl.n.*

beetroot, *n.* kroot *n.* **beetsugar,** *n.* bietensuiker *n.*

befall, *v.t.* overkomen *irr.*, wedervaren *str.* ¶ *v.i.* gebeuren.

befit, *v.t.* passen, voegen, betamen.

befog, *v.t.* benevelen.

befool, *v.t.* voor den gek houden *irr.*, bedotten.

before, *prep.* vóór. ~ *long*, eerlang. ¶ *adv.* voorop, vooruit; voorheen. ¶ *c.* voor, alvorens. **beforehand,** *adv.* vooruit, vooraf.

befoul, *v.t.* bevuilen.

befriend, *v.t.* helpen *str.* vriendschap *n.* betonen.

beg, *v.t.* bidden *str.*, smeken. ~ *for*, vragen *str.* om; *to* ~ *the question*, de vraag omzeilen; *I* ~ *your pardon*, neem me niet kwalijk. ¶ *v.i.* bedelen.

beget, *v.t.* verwekken.

beggar, *n.* bedelaar *n.*; kerel *n.* ¶ *v.t.* tot de bedelstaf brengen *irr.* *it* ~*s description*, het gaat alle beschrijving *n.* te boven. **beggarliness,** *n.* armoedigheid *n.* **beggarly,** *a.* armoedig, armzalig. **beggary,** *n.*

bedelarij *n.* *reduced to* ~, tot de bedelstaf gebracht.

begin, *v.t.* & *v.i.* beginnen *str.*, aanvangen *str.* *to* ~ *with,* om te beginnen. **beginner,** *n.* beginner *n.* **beginning,** *n.* begin *n.n.,* aanvang *n.*

begone, *int.* weg! voort!

begonia, *n.* begonia *n.*

begrudge, *v.t.* misgunnen.

beguile, *v.t.* bedriegen *str.* *to* ~ *the time,* de tijd verdrijven *str.*

behalf, *n.* *on* ~ *of,* namens, van wege; ten bate van; *on his* ~, om zijnentwil.

behave, *v.i.* zich gedragen *str.* ¶ *v.r.* zich gedragen *str.* **behaviour,** *n.* gedrag *n.n.,* houding *n.*

behead, *v.t.* onthoofden.

behest, *n.* opdracht *n.*

behind, *prep.* & *adv.* achter. ¶ *a.* achterstallig. ¶ *n.* achterste *n.n.* **behindhand,** *adv.* achterna, te laat.

behold, *v.t.* aanschouwen. **beholder,** *n.* aanschouwer *n.*

behove, *v.i.* betamen.

being, *n.* wezen *n.n.* *to bring into* ~, in het leven roepen *str.*

belabour, *v.t.* afrossen.

belated, *a.* achteraankomend ; verlaat.

belay, *v.t.* vastmaken. **belaying-pin,** *n.* klamp *n.*

belch, *v.i.* een boertje laten. *to* ~ *forth,* uitbraken. ¶ *n.* oprisping *n.;* boertje *n.n.*

beldam, *n.* oud wijf *n.n.*

beleaguer, *v.t.* belegeren. **beleaguerer,** *n.* belegeraar *n.*

belfry, *n.* klokketoren *n.;* klokkehuis *n.n.*

Belgian, *n.* Belgisch. ¶ *N.* Belg *n.;* Belgische *n.* (*woman*). **Belgium,** *N.* België *n.N.*

Belgrade, *N.* Belgrado *n.N.*

belie, *v.t.* logenstraffen.

belief, *n.* geloof *n.n.;* overtuiging *n.* **believable,** *a.* geloofbaar, geloofelijk. **believe,** *v.t.* geloven. *I don't* ~ *in* . . ., ik ben geen voorstander *n.* van . . . **believer,** *n.* gelovige *n.*

belittle, *v.t.* kleineren.

bell, *n.* bel *n.;* klok *n.* (*church*); glas *n.n.* (*nautical*). *to ring the* ~, bellen. ¶ *v.i.* bulken (*stag*).

belladonna, *n.* (vergiftige) nachtschade *n.*

bell-clapper, *n.* klepel *n.*

belle, *n.* schone *n.*

bell-flower, *n.* klokje *n.n.* **bell-founder,** *n.* klokkengieter *n.*

bellicose, *a.* oorlogzuchtig. **belligerent,** *a.* oorlogvoerend. ¶ *n.* oorlogvoerende *n.*

bell-metal, *n.* klokspijs *n.*

bellow, *v.i.* loeien; bulderen.

bellows, *n.* blaasbalg *n.*

bell-pull, *n.* schellekoord *n.n.* **bell-rope,** *n.* klokketouw *n.n.* **bell-wether,** *n.* belhamel *n.*

belly, *n.* buik *n.* ¶ *v.i.* zwellen *str.* ¶ *v.t.* doen *irr.* zwellen.

belong, *v.i.* *to* ~ *to,* behoren aan; *to* ~ *with,* behoren bij. **belongings,** *n.* eigendom *n.n.;* toebehoren *n.n.*

beloved, *a.* bemind.

below, *prep.* onder, beneden. ¶ *adv.* naar beneden; hier onder.

belt, *n.* gordel *n.;* riem *n.;* drijfriem *n.*

belvedere, *n.* belvedère *n.,* uitzichttoren *n.*

bemoan, *v.t.* bejammeren.

bench, *n.* bank *n.;* draaibank *n.;* gerechtshof *n.n.;* rechters *pl.n.,* magistraten *pl.n.* **bencher,** *n.* rechter *n.,* magistraat *n.*

bend, *v.t.* buigen *str.* ¶ *v.i.* zich buigen *str.* ¶ *n.* bocht *n.,* kromming *n.* **bendable,** *a.* buigbaar.

beneath, *prep.* onder, beneden. ¶ *adv.* onder, beneden; hierbeneden.

benediction, *n.* zegening *n.,* zegen *n.*

benefaction, *n.* weldaad *n.* **benefactor,** *n.* weldoener *n.* **benefactress,** *n.* weldoenster *n.*

benefice, *n.* predikantsplaats *n.* **beneficence,** *n.* weldadigheid *n.* **beneficent,** *a.* weldadig. **beneficial,** *a.* voordelig, heilzaam. **beneficiary,** *n.* beneficiant *n.* **benefit,** *n.* baat *n.n.,* voordeel *n.n.* *for the* ~ *of,* ten bate van, in het belang van; ~ *society,* ziekenbus *n.;* ~ *performance,* liefdadigheidsvoorstelling *n.*

benevolence, *n.* welwillendheid *n.* **benevolent,** *a.,* ~**ly,** *adv.* welwillend.

Bengal, *N.* Bengalen *n.N.* ~ *light,* Bengaals vuur. ¶ *a.* Bengaals. **Bengali,** *n.* Bengalees *n.* (*person*); Bengalees *n.n.* (*language*).

benighted, *a.* door de nacht overvallen; achterlijk (*fig.*).

benign, *a.,* ~**ly,** *adv.* vriendelijk, minzaam. **benignity,** *n.* welwillendheid *n.,* goedheid *n.*

benison, *n.* zegening *n.,* zegen *n.*

bent, *n.* neiging *n.,* aanleg *n.;* richting *n.* ¶ *a.* gebogen. *to be* ~ *on* . . ., er op uit zijn om . . .

benumb, *v.t.* verkleumen.

benzene, *n.,* **benzine,** *n.* benzine *n.* **benzoin,** *n.* benzoë *n.* benzol(e), *n.* benzol *n.*

bequeath, *v.t.* *to* ~ *to,* vermaken aan.

bequest, *n.* legaat *n.n.*

berberry, *n.* berberis *n.*

bereave, *v.t.* beroven. **bereaved,** *a.* diepbedroefd. **bereavement,** *n.* (zwaar) verlies *n.n.*

bergamot, *n.* bergamot *n.*

Berlin, *N.* Berlijn *n.N.* ~ *wool,* fijne breiwol *n.*

berry, *n.* bes *n.*

berth, *n.* ligplaats *n.,* ankerplaats *n.* (*of ship*). *to give a person a wide* ~, iemand de ruimte geven *str.* ¶ *v.t.* vastleggen *irr.*

beseech, *v.t.* smeken. **beseeching,** *a.,* ~**ly,** *adv.* smekend.

beseem, *v.t.* betamen, voegen. **beseeming,** *a.* welvoeglijk, passend.

beset, *v.t.* insluiten *str.,* omringen; bestoken.

besetting sin, zonde *n.* waartoe men lichtelijk vervalt.
beside, *prep.* naast; behalve. ~ *oneself,* buiten zichzelf. **besides,** *prep.* behalve. ¶ *adv.* bovendien.
besiege, *v.t.* belegeren.
besmear, *v.t.* besmeuren.
besom, *n.* bezem *n.*
besot, *v.t.* verdwazen. **besotted,** *a.* verdwaasd.
bespangle, *v.t.* bezaaien (met lovertjes).
bespatter, *v.t.* bespatten.
bespeak, *v.t.* bestellen, bespreken *str.*
bespoke, *a.* op maat.
besprinkle, *v.t.* besprenkelen, bezaaien.
best, *a.* & *adv.* best. ~ *man,* bruidjonker *n.*; *at* ~, op zijn best; *to make the* ~ *of it,* er zich in schikken; *to make the* ~ *of a bad job,* maken wat er van te maken valt. **bested,** *a. he was* ~, hij moest het afleggen.
bestial, *a.* beestachtig. **bestiality,** *n.* beestachtigheid *n.*
bestir, *v.r. to* ~ *oneself,* zich reppen.
bestow, *v.t. to* ~ *on,* schenken *str.* aan. **bestowal,** *n.* schenking *n.*
bestrew, *v.t.* bestrooien.
bestride, *v.t.* beschrijden *str.*; schrijlings zitten *str.* op.
bet, *n.* weddenschap *n.* ¶ *v.i.* wedden.
betake, *v.r. to* ~ *oneself to,* zich begeven *str.* naar.
bethink, *v.r. to* ~ *oneself,* zich bedenken *irr.; to* ~ *oneself of,* zich herinneren.
betide, *v.t.* overkomen *irr.,* wedervaren *str.*
betimes, *adv.* op tijd, bijtijds.
betoken, *v.t.* aanduiden; betekenen.
betray, *v.t.* verraden *str.;* bedriegen *str.* **betrayal,** *n.* verraad *n.n.*
betroth, *v.t.* verloven. **betrothal,** *n.* verloving *n.*
better, *a.* & *adv.* beter. *all the* ~, *so much the* ~, des te beter; *to get the* ~ *of a person,* iemand te slim af zijn; *to think* ~ *of . . .,* zich bedenken *irr.; you had* ~ *go,* je moest nu maar gaan; *you had* ~ *not go,* je moest maar liever niet gaan; *to be* ~ *off,* er beter aan toe zijn. ¶ *n.* ~*s,* meerderen *pl.n.* ¶ *v.t.* verbeteren. **betterment,** *n.* verbetering *n.*
between, *prep.* tussen. ~ *ourselves,* onder ons.
betwixt, *prep.* ~ *and between,* half en half.
bevel, *a.* schuin. ¶ *n.* schuinte *n.* ¶ *v.t.* afkanten; schuin slijpen *str.*
beverage, *n.* drank *n.*
bevy, *n.* vlucht *n.;* troepje *n.n.*
bewail, *v.t.* bejammeren; weeklagen over.
beware, *n.* oppassen. ~ *of,* zich hoeden voor.
bewilder, *v.t.* verbijsteren. **bewilderment,** *n.* verbijstering *n.*
bewitch, *v.t.* betoveren, beheksen.
bey, *n.* bei *n.*
beyond, *prep.* voorbij; buiten, over, boven; behalve. *adv.* verder.
bezel, *n.* schuin geslepen kant *n.;* kas *n.* (*of set jewel*).

bias, *n.* .neiging *n.,* vooroordeel *n.n.;* effect *n.n.* ¶ *v.t.* naar één kant doen *irr.* overhellen; bevooroordelen. **biassed,** *a.* vooringenomen.
bib, *n.* slabbetje *n.n.*
Bible, *n.* Bijbel *n.* **biblical,** *a.* bijbels.
bibliographer, *n.* bibliograaf *n.* **bibliographical,** *a.* bibliografisch. **bibliography,** *n.* bibliografie *n.* **bibliomania,** *n.* bibliomanie *n.* **bibliophile,** *n.* boekenliefhebber *n.*
bibulous, *a.* aan de drank verslaafd; dronken.
bicarbonate, *n.* dubbelkoolzuurzout *n.n.* ~ *of soda,* dubbelkoolzure soda *n.*
biceps, *n.* biceps *n.*
bicker, *v.i.* kibbelen. **bickering,** *n.* gekibbel *n.n.*
bicycle, *n.* fiets *n.;* rijwiel *n.n.*
bid, *v.t.* verzoeken *irr. to* ~ *farewell,* vaarwel zeggen *irr.; to* ~ *welcome,* welkom heten; *to* ~ *fair,* beloven. ¶ *v.i. to* ~ *for,* bieden *str.* op. ¶ *n.* bod *n.n. to make a* ~ *for,* een poging *n.* doen *irr.* om. **bidder,** *n.* bieder *n.* *highest* ~, meestbiedende *n.* **bidding,** *n.* verzoek *n.n.;* bevel *n.n.;* bod *n.n.*
bide, *v.t.* (ver)beiden, afwachten.
biennial, *a.* tweejarig.
bier, *n.* draagbaar *n.,* lijkbaar *n.*
bifurcated, *a.* gevorkt.
big, *a.* groot; dik, zwaar; zwanger. *to talk* ~, opscheppen.
bigamy, *n.* bigamie *n.*
bight, *n.* bocht, *n.,* baai *n.*
bigness, *n.* grootte *n.,* grootheid *n.*
bigot, *n.* kwezelaar *n.;* kwezel *n.* (*woman*). **bigoted,** *a.* kwezelachtig. **bigotry,** *n.* kwezelarij *n.*
bigwig, *n.* hoge ome *n.*
bilabial, *a.* tweelippig.
bilateral, *a.* tweezijdig.
bilberry, *n.* blauwe bosbes *n.*
bile, *n.* gal *n.*
bilge, *n.* buik *n.* (*of ship*). **bilge-keel,** *n.* kimkiel *n.* **bilge-pump,** *n.* lenspomp *n.* **bilge-water,** *n.* water *n.n.* in 't ruim.
bilingual, *a.* tweetalig.
bilious, *a.* galachtig.
bilk, *v.t.* bedriegen *str.,* oplichten.
bill, *n.* snavel *n.,* bek *n.* (*bird*); snoeimes *n.n.* (*implement*); rekening *n.* (*account*); aanplakbiljet *n.n.* (*poster*); wetsontwerp *n.n.* (*draft bill*). ~ *of exchange* wisselbrief *n.;* ~ *of fare,* menu *n.n.;* ~ *of lading,* cognossement *n.n.;* ~ *of sale,* koopbrief *n.* ¶ *v.t. to* ~ *and coo,* trekkebekken. **billboard,** *n.* aanplakbord *n.n.* **bill-broker,** *n.* wisselmakelaar *n.*
billet, *n.* kwartier *n.n.;* blok hout *n.n.*
bill-hook, *n.* snoeimes *n.n.*
billiards, *n.* biljart *n.n.,* biljartspel *n.n.* **billiard-table,** *n.* biljart *n.n.*
billow, *n.* baar *n.,* golf *n.*
bill-sticker, *n.* aanplakker *n.*
bin, *n.* bak *n.,* kist *n.;* wijnrek *n.n.*

bind, *v.t.* binden *str.*; verbinden *str.*; inbinden *str.*; verplichten. *he is bound to*, hij moet, hij is gedwongen, hij zal ongetwijfeld; *he is bound over*, hij moet beloven. binder, *n.* (boek)binder *n.*; binder *n.* binding, *n.* band *n.* ¶ *a.* bindend, verplicht. bindweed, *n.* akkerwinde *n.*

bine, *n.* rank *n.*

binnacle, *n.* kompashuisje *n.n.*

binocular, *a.* binoculair. ¶ *n.* ~s, kijker *n.*

binomial, *a.* binominaal, tweeledig. ¶ *n.* binomium *n.n.*

binominal, *a.* tweenamig.

biographer, *n.* biograaf *n.* biographical, *a.* biografisch. biography, *n.* biografie *n.*, levensbeschrijving *n.*

biological, *a.* biologisch. biologist, *n.* bioloog *n.* biology, biologie *n.*

bipartite, *a.* tweedelig.

biped, *n.* tweevoetig dier *n.n.*

biplane, *n.* tweedekker *n.*

birch, *n.* berk *n.* (*tree*); berkenhout *n.n.* (*substance*); (berken)roe(de) *n.* ¶ *v.t.* met de roe(de) bestraffen.

bird, *n.* vogel *n.* bird-cage, *n.* vogelkooi *n.* bird-fancier, *n.* vogelliefhebber *n.*; vogelkoopman *n.* bird's-eye, *n.* (soort) tabak *n.*; blauwe veronica *n.* ~ *view of* . . ., . . . in vogelvlucht gezien.

birth, *n.* geboorte *n.*; afkomst *n.* birthday, *n.* verjaardag *n.* ~ *suit*, Adamskostuum *n.n.* birthmark, *n.* moedervlek *n.* birthplace, *n.* geboorteplaats *n.* birthrate, *n.* geboortecijfer *n.n.*

biscuit, *n.* beschuit *n.n.*; biscuitje *n.n.*

bisect, *v.t.* in tweeën snijden *str.*, halveren.

bisexual, *a.* tweeslachtig.

bishop, *n.* bisschop *n.*; raadsheer *n.* (*chess*). bishopric, *n.* bisdom *n.n.*

bismuth, *n.* bismuth *n.n.*

bison, *n.* bizon *n.*

bistre, *a.* roetbruin.

bit, *n.* stuk(je) *n.n.*; beetje *n.n.*; boorijzer *n.n.* (*drill*); baard *n.*(*key*); gebit *n.n.* (*horse*). ~ *by* ~, stukje bij beetje.

bitch, *n.* teef *n.*

bite, *v.t.* bijten *str.* *to* ~ *off*, afbijten *str.* ¶ *n.* beet *n.*, hap *n.* biter, *n.* bijter *n.* *the* ~ *bit*, leer om leer.

bitter, *a.*, ~ly, *adv.* bitter; verbitterd. ¶ *n.* bitter bier *n.n.* ~s, bitter (*in gin*).

bittern, *n.* roerdomp *n.*

bitterness, *n.* bitterheid *n.*

bitumen, *n.* aardpek *n.n.*, aardhars *n.* bituminous, *a.* aardpekachtig.

bivalve, *n.* tweeschalig weekdier *n.n.*

bivouac, *n.* bivak *n.n.* ¶ *v.i.* bivakeren.

bizarre, *a.* bizar, grillig.

blab, *v.i.* (uit de school) klappen.

black, *a.* zwart; donker, duister. ~ *eye*, blauw oog *n.n.*; ~ *and white*, zwart op wit; ~ *letter*, Gothische druk *n.*; ~ *pudding*, bloedworst *n.* ¶ *v.t.* zwart maken. blackball, *v.t.* uitsluiten *str.*, deballoteren.

black-beetle, *n.* zwarte tor *n.* blackberry, *n.* braam *n.* *to go* ~*ing*, bramen plukken. blackbird, *n.* merel *n.* blackboard, *n.* bord *n.n.* blackcock, *n.* korhaan *n.*, korhoen *n.* blacken, *v.t.* zwart maken. blackguard, *n.* schoft *n.* blackhead, *n.* wurmpje *n.n.* blacking, *n.* schoensmeer *n.*; zwartsel *n.n.* blackish, *a.* zwartachtig. blackjack, *n.* ploertendoder *n.* blacklead, *n.* potlood *n.n.* blackleg, *n.* onderkruiper *n.* blackmail, *n.* chantage *n.* blackmailer, *n.* chanteur *n.* blackness, *n.* zwartheid *n.* blacksmith, *n.* smid *n.* blackthorn, *n.* sleedoorn *n.*

bladder, *n.* blaas *n.*

blade, *n.* halm *n.*, spriet *n.*; lemmet *n.n.* (*knife*), kling *n.* (*sword*).

blain, *n.* blaar *n.*

blame, *n.* blaam *n.*, schuld *n.* ¶ *v.t.* de schuld geven (aan); laken, afkeuren. blameless, *a.*, ~ly, *adv.* onberispelijk. blameworthy, *a.* afkeurenswaardig, laakbaar.

blanch, *v.i.* bleken, verbleken.

blancmange, *n.* blanc-manger *n.*

bland, *a.*, ~ly, *adv.* zacht, vriendelijk. blandish, *v.t.* vleien, strelen; verlokken. blandishment, *n.* verlokking *n.*

blank, *a.* wit; blank; blanco; sprakeloos, wezenloos. ~ *cartridge*, losse patroon *n.*; ~ *verse*, rijmloze verzen *pl.n.n.*; ~ *wall*, blinde muur *n.* ¶ *n.* leemte *n.*; blanco formulier *n.n.*; losse patroon *n.* *to draw a* ~, een niet trekken *str.*

blanket, *n.* deken *n.* ¶ *v.t.* bedekken.

blankly, *adv.* botweg; wezenloos.

blare, *n.* geschal *n.n.*, geschetter *n.n.* ¶ *v.i.* schallen, schetteren.

blarney, *n.* mooie praatjes *pl.n.n.*

blaspheme, *v.t.* God lasteren. blasphemer, *n.* godlasteraar *n.* blasphemous, *a.*, ~ly, *adv.* godlasterlijk. blasphemy, *n.* godlastering *n.*

blast, *n.* rukwind *n.*, windstoot *n.*; ontploffing *n.*; luchtstroom (van hoogoven) *n.*; stoot *n.* (*trumpet*); brand *n.* (*corn*). ¶ *v.t.* laten springen; vernietigen; verzengen. blasted, *a.* vervloekt. blast-furnace, *n.* hoogoven *n.* blast-pipe, *n.* afvoerpijp *n.*

blatant, *a.* schreeuwerig; in 't oog lopend; onverholen.

blaze, *n.* brand *n.*, vuurgloed *n.*; gloed *n.* ¶ *v.i.* in lichtelaaie staan *irr.* *to* ~ *away*, erop los schieten *str.*; *to* ~ *up*, oplaaien.

blazer, *n.* flanellen sportjas *n.*

blazon, *n.* blazoen *n.n.* ¶ *v.t.* blazoeneren; uitbazuinen (*fig.*). blazonry, *n.* heraldiek *n.*

bleach, *v.t.* bleken; verbleken. bleacher, *n.* bleker. bleaching-powder, *n.* bleekpoeder *n.n.* bleaching-works, *n.* blekerij *n.*

bleak, *n.* alvertje *n.n.* ¶ *a.* kil, troosteloos, baar. bleakness, *n.* kilheid *n.*, troostelooosheid *n.*

blear, *a.* leep; dof. blear-eyed, *a.* druipogig. bleary, *a.* *See* blear.

bleat, *v.i.* blaten.
bleed, *v.i.* bloeden. **bleeding,** *n.* aderlating *n.*
blemish, *n.* smet *n.*; fout *n.* ¶ *v.t.* bevlekken.
blench, *v.i.* terugdeinzen.
blend, *v.t.* & *v.i.* mengen. ¶ *n.* mengsel *n.n.*,
mélange *n.*
bless, *n.* zegenen; wijden. **blessed,** *a.* gezegend; (geluk)zalig. **blessing,** *n.* zegen *n.*,
zegening *n.* **blest,** *a.* gelukzalig.
blight, *n.* brand *n.*, roest *n.*, meeldauw *n.*
blind, *a.* blind; blind lopend, doodlopend.
~ *coal,* glanskool *n.*; ~ *nettle,* dove netel
n.; ~ *side,* zwakke zijde *n.* ¶ *adv.* ~ *drunk,*
stomdronken. ¶ *n.* rolgordijn *n.n.*; voorwendsel *n.n.* **blindly,** *adv.* blind. **blindfold,**
a. & *adv.* geblinddoekt; blindelings (*fig.*).
¶ *v.t.* blinddoeken. **blindman's buff,** *n.*
blindemannetje *n.n.* **blindness,** *n.* blindheid *n.* **blindworm,** *n.* hazelworm *n.*
blink, *v.i.* knipogen. ¶ *n.* knipoogje *n.n.*
blinkers, *pl.n.* oogkleppen *pl.n.*
bliss, *n.* (geluk)zaligheid *n.* **blissful,** *a.*, ~ly,
adv. (gelug)zalig.
blister, *n.* blaar *n.*, blaas *n.*
blithe, *a.*, ~ly, *adv.* blij, monter.
blizzard, *n.* verblindende sneeuwstorm *n.*,
jachtsneeuw *n.*
bloat, *v.t.* doen *irr.* zwellen. ¶ *v.i.* opzwellen
str. **bloated,** *a.* gezwollen, opgeblazen.
bloater, *n.* bokking *n.*
blob, *n.* mop *n.*, bobbel *n.*
block, *n.* blok *n.n.*; katrol *n.*, takel *n.n.*
verkeersopstopping *n.*, stremming *n.*
~ *letters,* vette druk. ¶ *v.t.* versperren,
stremmen; blokkeren. **blockade,** *n.*
blokkade *n.* ~ *runner,* blokkadebreker *n.*;
to run a ~, door een blokkade heenbreken.
¶ *v.t.* blokkeren. **blockhead,** *n.* domkop *n.*
blockhouse, *n.* blokhuis *n.n.*
bloke, *n.* vent *n.*, kerel *n.*
blond, *a.* blond. **blonde,** *a.* blond. ¶ *n.*
blondine *n.*
blood, *n.* bloed *n.n.*; volbloed *n.* (*horse*).
his ~ *was up,* zijn bloed kookte; ~ *is
thicker than water,* bloed kruipt waar het
niet gaan kan. ¶ *v.t.* aderlaten. **bloodcurdling,** *a.* die de haren te berge doet
rijzen. **bloodhorse,** *n.* volbloed (paard) *n.n.*
bloodhound, *n.* bloedhond *n.* **bloodily,** *a.*
bloedig. **bloodless,** *a.* bloedeloos. **bloodletting,** *n.* aderlating *n.* **blood-poisoning,** *n.*
bloedvergiftiging *n.* **bloodshed,** *n.* bloedvergieten *n.n.* **bloodshot,** *a.* met bloed *n.n.*
belopen. **bloodthirsty,** *a.* bloeddorstig.
bloodvessel, *n.* bloedvat *n.n.* **bloody,** *a.*
bloederig, bloedig; bloeddorstig; verdomd
(*vulgar*).
bloom, *n.* bloem *n.*, bloesem *n.*; waas *n.n.*,
bloem *n.* ¶ *v.i.* bloeien. **bloomer,** *n.*
bloeier *n.*; flater *n.* **blooming,** *a.* bloeiend;
blozend (van gezondheid); (*vulg.*)
verduveld.
blossom, *n.* bloesem *n.* ¶ *v.i.* bloeien. *to* ~
out as, zich ontpoppen als.

blot, *n.* vlek *n.*, klad *n.*; smet *n.* ¶ *v.t.*
bekladden. *to* ~ *out,* uitwissen
blotch, *n.* klad *n.*, smeer *n.* ¶ *v.t.* bekladden.
blotchy, *a.* kladderig; vol vlekken.
blotter, *n.* vloeiblok *n.n.* **blotting-pad,** *n.*
vloeiblok *n.n.* **blotting-paper.** *n.* vloei
(papier) *n.n.*
blouse, *n.* blouse *n.* (*woman's*); kiel *n.* (*boy's
or man's*).
blow, *n.* slag *n.*, stoot *n.* *in full* ~, in volle
bloei *n.*; *without a* ~, zonder slag of stoot.
¶ *v.i.* blazen *str.*; hijgen *str.*; waaien *str.*
¶ *v.t.* b'azen *str.*; blazen *str.* op. *be* ~*ed!*;
loop naar de maan; *to* ~ *hot and cold,*
uit twee monden *n.* spreken *str.*; *to* ~ *a
kiss,* een kus(hand) toewerpen *str.*; *to* ~
one's nose, zich snuiten *str.*; *to* ~ *away,*
wegwaaien *str.*, wegblazen *str.*; *to* ~ *down,*
omwaaien *str.*; *to* ~ *in,* inwaaien *str.*;
aanwaaien *str.*; *to* ~ *off,* afwaaien *str.*,
afblazen *str.*; (stoom) aflaten *str.*; *to* ~ *out,*
opblazen *str.*; *to* ~ *up,* opblazen *str.*; doen
springen; *to* ~ *one's brains out,* zich voor
de kop schieten *str.* **blower,** *n.* blazer *n.*
blowfly, *n.* vleesvlieg *n.* **blowhole,** *n.*
neusgat *n.* (*of whale*); luchtgat *n.n.*
blown, *n.* uitgebloeid; buiten adem.
blowpipe, *n.* blaaspijp *n.*, blaasroer *n.n.*
blowzy, *a.* slonsig.
blubber, *n.* walvisspek *n.n.* ¶ *v.i.* snottebellen.
bludgeon, *n.* knuppel *n.* ¶ *v.t.* knuppelen.
blue, *a.* blauw; terneergeslagen, gedrukt.
¶ *n.* blauw *n.n.*; blauwsel *n.n.* ¶ *v.t.*
blauwverven. **blue book,** *n.* blauwboek
n.n. **bluebottle,** *n.* bromvlieg *n.* **bluejacket,** *n.* Jantje *n.n.* **blueness,** *n.* blauwheid *n.* **bluestocking,** *n.* blauwkous *n.*
bluff, *a.* bars, bruusk; gulhartig, goedmoedig.
¶ *n.* steile kaap *n.*; bluffen *n.n.*, grootspraak *n.* ¶ *v.t.* overbluffen.
bluish, *a.* blauwachtig.
blunder, *n.* flater *n.*, misslag *n.* ¶ *v.i.* een
misslag begaan *irr.*; stommelen. *to make
a* ~, een bok schieten *str.* **blunderbuss,** *n.*
donderbus *n.* **blunderer,** *n.* domkop *n.*;
iemand die stommiteiten begaat.
blunt, *a.* stomp; bot; lomp. ¶ *v.t.* afstompen,
stomp maken. **bluntness,** *n.* stompheid *n.*;
botheid *n.*
blur, *n.* vlek *n.*, smeer *n.*; onduidelijkheid *n.*
¶ *v.t.* benevelen, onduidelijk maken.
blurt, *v.t.* *to* ~ *something out,* iets eruit
flappen.
blush, *n.* blos *n.*, kleur *n.* *without a* ~,
zonder blikken of blozen. ¶ *v.i.* blozen,
een kleur krijgen *str.*
bluster, *v.i.* bulderen, razen. stormen.
blusterer, *n.* snoever *n.*
boa, *n.* boa *n.*
boar, *n.* mannetjesvarken *n.n.*, beer *n.*
(*wild*) ~, wild zwijn *n.n.*, everzwijn *n.n.*
board, *n.* plank *n.*; boord *n.n.*; kost *n.*;
kostgeld *n.n.*; raad *n.* *B*~ *of Trade,*
Ministerie *n.n.* van Handel *n.*; *on* ~.

aan boord; ~ *and lodging*, kost en inwoning
n. ¶ *v.t.* beschieten *str.*, dichtspijkeren;
enteren, aanklampen; in de kost nemen
str. ¶ *v.i.* *to* ~ *with*, in de kost zijn bij.
boarder, *n.* kostganger *n.*; kostjongen *n.*
boarding-house, *n.* kosthuis *n.n.*, pension
n.n. **boarding-school**, *n.* kostschool *n.*
board-school, *n.* volksschool *n.* **board-
wages**, *pl.n.* kostgeld *n.n.*
boast, *v.i.* bluffen, pochen, opscheppen.
¶ *v.t.* bogen op. ¶ *n.* grootspraak *n.*;
roem *n.*, trots *n.* **boaster**, *n.* pocher *n.*,
bluffer *n.* **boastful**, *a.* blufferig, opschepperig.
boat, *n.* boot *n.*; (saus)kom *n.* ¶ *v.i.* roeien;
zeilen; spelevaren. **boat-hook**, *n.* bootshaak
n. **boating**, *n.* spelevaren *n.n.* **boatswain**, *n.*
bootsman *n.*
bob, *n.* knik *n.*; shilling *n.*; melodie *n.* (*bells*).
¶ *v.i.* op en neer gaan *irr.*; dobberen.
bobbed, *a.* kortgeknipt.
bobbin, *n.* spoel *n.*, klos *n.*
bobtail, *n.* kortstaart *n.*
bode, *v.t.* voorspellen.
bodice, *n.* keurslijf *n.n.*, lijfje *n.n.*
bodily, *a.* & *adv.* lichamelijk; compleet.
bodkin, *n.* priem *n.*; rijgpen *n.*
body, *n.* lichaam *n.n.*, lijf *n.n.*; lijk *n.n.*
(*corpse*); troep *n.* (*men*); kracht *n.*, sterkte
n.; karosserie *n.* *in a* ~, allen te zamen.
hodyguard, *n.* lijfwacht *n.*
bog, *n.* moeras *n.n.*; laagveen *n.n.* **bogged**, *a.*
to be ~, in de modder blijven *str.* steken.
boggy, *a.* moerassig, veenachtig.
bogey, *n.* boeman *n.*
boggle, *v.t.* aarzelen. *it* ~*s the imagination*,
het gaat de verbeelding te boven.
bogus, *a.* vals, nagemaakt.
Bohemia, *N.* Bohemen *n.N.* **Bohemian**, *N.*
Bohemer *N.* ¶ *a.* Boheems.
boil, *n.* steenpuist *n.* ¶ *v.i.* & *v.t.* koken.
to ~ *down*, inkoken, verkoken. **boiler**, *n.*
stoomketel *n.* **boiling point**, *n.* kookpunt
n.n.
boisterous, *a.*, ~*ly*, *adv.* onstuimig, rumoerig.
bold, *a.*, ~*ly*, *adv.* stout(moedig); vrijpostig.
as ~ *as brass*, zo brutaal als de raven;
to make ~ *to*, zich verstouten. **boldness**,
n. stoutmoedigheid *n.*; durf *n.*
bole, *n.* stam *n.*
bollard, *n.* bollard *n.*
bolster, *n.* peluw *n.*, kussen *n.n.* ¶ *v.t.*
to ~ (*up*), met kussens steunen; rug-
steunen.
bolt, *n.* grendel *n.*, bout *n.*; (bliksem)straal *n.*
a ~ *from the blue*, een donderslag *n.* uit
onbewolkte hemel *n.* ¶ *v.t.* grendelen;
builen (*flour*); schrokken (*food*). ¶ *v.i.* op
hol slaan *irr.* (*horse*); er van door gaan
irr.
bolus, *n.* grote pil *n.*
bomb, *n.* bom *n.* ¶ *v.t.* bombarderen.
bombard, *v.t.* bombarderen; bekogelen.
bombardment *n.* bombardement *n.n.*

bombast, *n.* bombast *n.* **bombastic**, *a.*
bombastisch.
bomber, *n.* bommenwerper *n.* **bomb-proof**,
a. bomvrij. **bombshell**, *n.* bom *n.*; donderslag *n.*
bond, *n.* band *n.*; verbond *n.n.*, contract *n.n.*;
obligatie *n.*; boeien *n.*; *in* ~, in
entrepôt *n.n.* **bondage**, *n.* slavernij *n.*,
lijfeigenschap *n.* **bonded**, *a.* ~ *warehouse*,
entrepôt *n.n.* **bondholder**, *n.* obligatie-
houder *n.* **bondman**, *n.* slaaf *n.*, lijfeigene
n. **bondsman**, *n.* borg *n.*
bone, *n.* been *n.n.*; graat *n.* (*fish*). **bone-dry**,
a. kurkdroog. **bone-meal**, *n.* beendermeel
n.n. **bonesetter**, *n.* heelmeester *n.*
bonfire, *n.* vreugdevuur *n.*; vuurtje *n.n.*
bonnet, *n.* muts *n.*; kap *n.* (*car*).
bonny, *a.* lief, aardig.
bonus, *n.* gratificatie *n.*, premie *n.*
bony, *a.* benig; gratig.
booby, *n.* domoor *n.*, sukkel *n.*
book, *n.* boek *n.n.* ~ *post*, als drukwerk *n.n.*
¶ *v.t.* boeken; opschrijven *str.*, inschrijven
str. *to* ~ *a seat*, een plaats *n.* bespreken
str.; een kaartje *n.n.* kopen *irr.* **bookable**,
a. te boeken; te bespreken. **bookbinder**, *n.*
boekbinder *n.* **bookcase**, *n.* boekenkast *n.*
booking office, *n.* plaatsbureau *n.n.*; loket
n.n. **bookish**, *a.* boekachtig; geleerd;
pedant. **book-keeper**, *n.* boekhouder *n.*
book-keeping *n.* boekhouden *n.n.*; boek-
houding *n.* ~ *by double* (or *single*) *entry*,
dubbel (*or* enkel) boekhouden. **bookmaker**,
n. boekmaker *n.* **bookseller**, *n.* boek-
handelaar *n.* **bookshelf** *n.* boekenplank *n.*
bookstall, *n.* boekenstalletje *n.n.* **book-
worm**, *n.* boekenworm *n.*
boom, *n.* (haven)boom *n.* (*harbour*); spriet
n., spier *n.* (*ship*); gedaver *n.n.*, gedreun
n.n. ¶ *v.i.* daveren, dreunen; in de hoogte
gaan *irr.*
boomerang, *n.* boemerang *n.*
boon, *n.* gunst *n.*; weldaad *n.* ¶ *a.* vrolijk,
lustig.
boor, *n.* pummel *n.*, boerekinkel *n.* **boorish**,
a. lomp.
boost, *v.t.* reclame *n.* maken voor.
boot, *n.* laars *n.* *to* ~, op de koop toe;
Puss in B ~*s*, de Gelaarsde Kat *n.* ¶ *v.t.*
trappen. **booted**, *a.* gelaarsd.
booth, *n.* kraam *n.*, tent *n.*
bootlace, *n.* (schoen)veter *n.* **bootlegger**, *n.*
dranksmokkelaar *n.* **bootless**, *a.* vruchteloos. **boots**, *n.* schoenpoetser *n.* **boot-tree**,
n. leest *n.*
booty, *n.* buit *n.*
booze, *n.* drank *n.* ¶ *v.i.* zuipen *str.* **boozy**,
a. dronken.
boracic, *a.* ~ *acid*, boorzuur *n.n.*
border, *n.* rand *n.*; zoom *n.*; grens *n.* ¶ *v.t.*
omzomen. ¶ *v.i.* *to* ~ *on*, grenzen aan.
borderland, *n.* grensgebied *n.n.*
bore, *v.t.* boren; (*fig.*) vervelen. ¶ *n.* boorgat
n.n.; kaliber *n.n.*; ziel *n.* (*fire-arm*);

vervelend iets *n.n.*, vervelende persoon *n.*; vloedgolf *n.*
boreal, *a.* noorder... **boreas,** *n.* noorderwind *n.*
boredom, *n.* verveling *n.*
borer, *n.* boorder *n.*
born, *a.* geboren.
borough, *n.* stad *n.*; stedelijke gemeente *n.*
borrow, *v.t.* lenen; borgen. *to ~ from,* lenen van, ontlenen aan. **borrower,** *n.* lener *n.*
bosh, *n.* onzin *n.*, nonsens *n.*
bosom, *n.* boezem *n.*, borst *n.*; schoot *n.* (*fig.*).
boss, *n.* baas *n.*; knop *n.* ¶ *v.t.* de baas spelen over. **bossy,** *a.* bazig.
botanic(al), *a.* botanisch. **botanist,** *n.* botanist *n.*, plantkundige *n.* **botany,** *n.* botanie *n.*, plantkunde *n.*
botch, *v.t.* knoeien, verknoeien. **botcher,** *n.* knoeier *n.*
both, *a.* beide; allebei. *~ ... and ...,* zowel ... als ...; *~ of us,* wij beiden.
bother, *n.* last *n.*, gezanik *n.n.* ¶ *v.t.* lastig vallen *str. to ~ about,* zich zorgen *n.* maken over.
bottle, *n.* fles *n.* ¶ *v.t.* bottelen; inmaken.
bottom, *n.* bodem *n.*; achterste *n.n.*, zitvlak *n.n. at ~,* in de grond; *to be at the ~ of something,* ergens achter zitten. **bottomless,** *a.* bodemloos, grondeloos. **bottomry,** *n.* bodemerij *n.*
bough, *n.* tak *n.*
boulder, *n.* kei *n.*, grote rolsteen *n.*
bounce, *v.i.* bonzen; terugkaatsen. *to ~ into,* binnenstormen. ¶ *n.* terugstoot *n.*; veerkracht *n.* **bouncer,** *n.* uitsmijter *n.*
bound, *v.i.* springen *str.* ¶ *v.t.* begrenzen. ¶ *n.* sprong *n. ~s,* grenzen; *out of ~s,* verboden; *within ~s,* binnen de perken *n.n.* ¶ *a.* gebonden. *~ for,* met bestemming *n.* naar; *to be ~ to,* moeten *irr.*; *homeward ~,* op de terugreis. **boundary,** *n.* grens *n.*, grenslijn *n.*
bounder, *n.* patser *n.*
boundless, *a.* onbegrensd, grenzeloos.
bounteous, *a.*, **bountiful,** *a.* vrijgevig, weldadig. **bounty,** *n.* gave *n.*; premie *n.*
bouquet, *n.* bouquet *n.n.*, ruiker *n.*
bourn, *n.* beekje *n.n.*
bourn(e), *n.* grens *n.*
bout, *n.* ronde *n.*; partij *n.*; aanval *n.*
bovine, *a.* runderachtig ; dom, traag.
bow, *n.* buiging *n.*; boog *n.* (*weapon or instrument*); boeg *n.* (*of ship*). ¶ *v.t.* doen *irr.* buigen. *to ~ a person in,* iemand buigende inlaten *str.* ¶ *v.i.* buigen *str. to ~ to,* zich buigen voor.
bowdlerize, *v.t.* zuiveren.
bowel, *n.* ingewand *n.n.*
bower, *n.* priëel *n.*
bowie-knife, *n.* dolkmes *n.n.*
bowl, *n.* kom *n.*, bekken *n.n.*, schaal *n.*; (houten) bal *n. ~s,* kegelspel *n.n.*, bolspel *n.n.*; *to play at ~s,* kegelen. ¶ *v.i.* kegelen;

de bal werpen *str.* **bowler,** *n.* speler *n.*; bolhoed *n.* **bowler-hat,** *n.*, bolhoed *n.*
bow-legged, *a.* met kromme benen *n.n.* **bowline,** *n.* boelijn *n.*
bowling green, *n.* kegelbaan *n.*, bollebaan *n.*
bowsprit, *n.* boegspriet *n.* **bow-window,** *n.* erker *n.*
box, *n.* doos *n.* (*wooden or cardboard container*); kist *n.* (*wooden container*); kistje *n.n.* (*small metal or wooden container*); koffer *n.* (*luggage*); bus *n.* (*for letters*); bok *n.* (*of carriage*); loge *n.* (*in theatre*); hokje *n.n.* (*of porter*); buksboom *n.* (*tree*); bank *n.* (*of witness*); oorveeg *n.*, klap *n.* (*blow*); fooi *n.* (*tip*). ¶ *v.i.* boksen. ¶ *v.t.* pakken, in een doos (*or* kist) doen *irr. to ~ a person's ears,* iemand een oorveeg geven *str.* **boxer,** *n.* bokser *n.* **boxing,** *n.* boksen *n.n.* **Boxing-Day,** *N.* Tweede Kerstdag *N.* **box-office,** *n.* plaatsbureau *n.n.* **boxwood,** *n.* palmhout *n.n.*
boy, *n.* jongen *n.*, knaap *n.*
boycott, *v.t.* boycotten; uitsluiten. ¶ *n.* boycot.
boyhood, *n.* jongensjaren *pl.n.n.* **boyish,** *a.*, *~ly, adv.* jongensachtig, kinderachtig.
brace, *n.* boor *n.* (*drill*); bras *n.* (*naut.*); draagband *n.*, koppel *n.* (*band*); paar *n.n.* (*two*). *~s or pair of ~s,* bretel *n.* ¶ *v.t.* verankeren; brassen (*naut.*). *to ~ oneself,* zijn krachten *n.* inspannen, zich schrap zetten.
bracelet, *n.* armband *n.*
brachial, *a.* arm ... , armvormig. **brachycephalic,** *a.* rondhoofdig, breedschedelig.
bracing, *a.* versterkend, opfrissend.
bracken, *n.* (adelaars)varen *n.*
bracket, *n.* kram *n.*, klamp *n.*; console *n.*; gasarm *n. between ~s,* tussen haakjes *n.n.* ¶ *v.t.* tussen haakjes plaatsen; in één adem noemen.
brackish, *a.* brak.
brad, *n.* spijker *n.* zonder kop *n.* **bradawl,** *n.* els *n.*
brag, *v.i.* snoeven, bluffen. **braggart,** *n.* snoever *n.*
brahmin, *n.*, **brahman,** *n.* brahmaan *n.*
braid, *v.t.* vlechten *str.* ¶ *n.* vlecht *n.*; boordsel *n.n.*
brain, *n.* hersenen *pl.n.*, hersens *pl.n.*; brein *n.n.*, verstand *n.n.* ¶ *v.t.* de hersens inslaan *irr.* **brainless,** *a.* hersenloos, onbezonnen.
brake, *n.* braambos *n.*; (vlas)braak *n.*; rem *n.* (*on wheel*); brik *n.* (*carriage*). *to put the ~(s) on,* remmen. ¶ *v.t.* braken (*flax*). ¶ *v.i.* remmen. **brakesman,** *n.* remmer *n.*
bramble, *n.* braam(struik) *n.*; doornbos *n.*
bran, *n.* zemelen *pl.n.*
branch, *n.* tak *n.*; filiaal *n.n.* ¶ *v.i.* zich vertakken. **branchless,** *a.* takkeloos. **branchy,** *a.* getakt, takkig.
brand, *n.* brandend stuk *n.n.* hout *n.n.*; merk *n.n.*; soort *n.*; brandmerk *n.n.* (*stigma*). ¶ *v.t.* brandmerken.

brandish, *v.t.* zwaaien.
brand-new, *a.* (spik)splinternieuw.
brandy, *n.* brandewijn *n.*, cognac *n.*
brass, *n.* geel koper *n.n.*, messing *n.n.*; geld *n.n.*; onbeschaamdheid *n.* **brass-band,** *n.* fanfare *n.*, fanfarekorps *n.n.* **brass-founder,** *n.* kopergieter *n.* **brassy,** *a.* koperachtig; koperkleurig; onbeschaamd.
brat, *n.* blaag *n.*, kind *n.n.*, jong *n.n.*
bravado, *n.* bravade *n.*
brave, *a.*, ~ly, *adv.* moedig, dapper; flink. ¶ *n.* dappere. ¶ *v.t.* trotseren, braveren.
bravery, *n.* dapperheid *n.*
bravo, *int.* bravo! ¶ *n.* (gehuurde) sluipmoordenaar *n.*
brawl, *v.i.* ruzie maken, tieren. ¶ *n.* ruzie *n.*, standje *n.n.* **brawler,** *n.* lawaaimaker *n.*, ruziemaker *n.*
brawn, *n.* spierkracht *n.* (*muscle*); hoofdkaas *n.* (*meat*). **brawny,** *a.* gespierd.
bray, *v.i.* balken; schetteren. ¶ *n.* gebalk *n.n.*; geschetter *n.n.*
brazen, *a.*, ~ly, *adv.* bronzen, geelkoperen; onbeschaamd (*fig.*). **brazenfaced,** *a.* onbeschaamd. **brazenness,** *n.* onbeschaamdheid *n.*
brazier, *n.* koperslager *n.*; komfoor *n.n.*
Brazil, *N.* Brazilië *n.N.* **brazil,** *n.* Paranoot *n.* **Brazilian,** *a.* Braziliaans.
breach, *n.* bres *n.*; overtreding *n.*, inbreuk *n.* ~ *of promise,* verbreking *n.* van de trouwbelofte.
bread, *n.* brood *n.n.* *slice of* ~ *and butter,* boterham *n.*
breadth, *n.* breedte *n.*; ruime opvatting *n.*
break, *v.t.* doen *irr.* springen (*bank*); casseren (*military career*). to ~ *wind,* een wind *n.* laten *str.* ¶ *v.t.* breken. *to* ~ *away,* losbreken *str.*; *to* ~ *down,* blijven *str.* steken; *to* ~ *with,* vriendschap verbreken *str.* met. ¶ *n.* breuk *n.*; onderbreking *n.*; serie *n.* (*billiards*). **breakable,** *a.* breekbaar. **breakage,** *n.* breken *n.n.* **breakdown,** *n.* mislukking *n.*, ineenstorting *n.*; panne *n.* (*car*). ~ *lorry,* takelwagen *n.* **breaker,** *n.* stortzee *n.* ~*s,* branding *n.* **breakfast,** *n.* ontbijt *n.n.* ¶ *v.i.* ontbijten *str.* **breakneck,** *a.* halsbrekend. *at* ~ *speed,* in dolle vaart *n.* **breakthrough,** *n.* doorbraak *n.* **break-up,** *n.n.*, uiteenvallen *n.n.* **breakwater,** *n.* golfbreker *n.*
bream, *n.* brasem *n.* ~ *v.t.* schoonbranden.
breast, *n.* borst *n.*; boezem *n.*; hart *n.n.* ¶ ~ *v.t.* het hoofd bieden *str.* aan; ingaan *irr.* tegen. **breastwork,** *n.* borstwerk *n.*
breath, *n.* adem *n.* *to get a* ~ *of air,* een luchtje scheppen. **breathe,** *v.i.* ademen; inademen, uitademen; fluisteren. *to* ~ *again,* weer vrij ademhalen. **breather,** *n.* *to take a* ~, even uitblazen *str.* **breathless,** *a.* ademloos.
breech, *n.* sluitstuk *n.n.* (*of gun*). *pair of* ~*es,* korte broek *n.*

breed, *v.t.* fokken, kweken; grootbrengen *irr.* ¶ *n.* ras *n.n.*, soort *n.* **breeder,** *n.* fokker *n.*; fokdier *n.n.* (*animal*). **breeding,** *n.* fokken *n.n.*; opvoeding *n.*
breeze, *n.* bries *n.*, koeltje *n.n.* **breezy,** *a.* winderig; luidruchtig.
brethren, *pl.n.* broeders *pl.n.*
breve, *n.* brève *n.*; twee hele noten *pl.n.*
brevet, *n.* brevet *n.n.* ¶ *v.t.* de titulaire rang verlenen (van).
breviary, *n.* brevier *n.n.*
brevity, *n.* kortheid *n.*, bondigheid *n.*
brew, *v.t.* brouwen *irr.* ¶ *n.* brouwsel *n.n.* **brewery,** *n.* brouwerij *n.*
briar, *n.* wilde roos *n.*; wit heidekruid *n.n.*; pijp *n.* van witte heidewortel *n.* *sweet* ~, eglantier *n.*
bribable, *a.* omkoopbaar. **bribe,** *n.* omkoopprijs *n.*, steekpenning *n.* ¶ *v.t.* omkopen *irr.* **briber,** *n.* omkoper *n.* **bribery,** *n.* omkoperij *n.*
brick, *n.* baksteen *n.*; blok *n.* (*toy*). ¶ *v.t. to* ~ *up,* dichtmetselen. **brick-kiln,** *n.* steenoven *n.* **bricklayer,** *n.* metselaar *n.* **brickwork,** *n.* metselwerk *n.n.* ~*s,* steenbakkerij *n.*
bridal, *a.* bruids-. **bride,** *n.* bruid *n.*; jonggehuwde *n.* **bridegroom,** *n.* bruidegom *n.* **bridesmaid,** *n.* bruidsmeisje *n.n.*
bridge, *n.* brug *n.*; kam *n.* (*of violin*). ¶ *v.t.* overbruggen. **bridgehead,** *n.* bruggehoofd *n.n.*
bridle, *n.* teugel *n.*, breidel *n.*, toom *n.n.* ¶ *v.t.* beteugelen. **bridle-path,** *n.* ruiterpad *n.n.*, jaagpad *n.n.*
brief, *a.*, ~ly, *adv.* kort, bondig, beknopt. *to be* ~, om kort te gaan. ¶ *n.* instructie *n.* **briefless,** *a.* zonder praktijk *n.* **briefness,** *n.* bondigheid *n.*
brier, *n.* *See* **briar.**
brig, *n.* brik *n.*
brigade, *n.* brigade *n.* **brigadier,** *n.* brigade-generaal *n.*
brigand, *n.* rover *n.* **brigandage,** *n.* roverij *n.*
brigantine, *n.* brigantijn *n.*
bright, *a.*, ~ly, *adv.* helder, klaar; schitterend; levendig, opgewekt. **brighten,** *v.t.* opvrolijken. **brightness,** *n.* helderheid *n.*; opgewektheid *n.*
brill, *n.* griet *n.*
brilliance, *n.* glans *n.*; luister *n.*, pracht *n.* **brilliant,** *a.*, ~ly, *adv.* glansrijk, schitterend ¶ *n.* briljant *n.*
brim, *n.* rand *n.* ¶ *v.t.* tot de rand vol zijn. **brimful,** *a.* boordevol. **brimstone,** *n.* zwavel *n.*
brindled, *a.* gespikkeld, gestreept.
brine, *n.* pekel *n.*; zilte nat *n.n.* (*fig.*). ¶ *v.t.* pekelen.
bring, *v.t.* brengen *irr. to* ~ *about,* tot stand brengen; *to* ~ *back,* (weer) terugbrengen *irr.*; *to* ~ *down,* neerhalen, neerschieten *str.*; *to* ~ *down the house,* geweldig geapplaudisseerd worden *str.*; *to* ~

forward, transporteren; *to* ~ *in guilty*, schuldig verklaren; *I brought it off*, ik heb het hem geleverd; *to* ~ *out*, te voorschijn halen, aan den dag brengen *irr.*; *to* ~ *over*, overhalen; *to* ~ *round*, tot bewustzijn brengen; bepraten, overhalen; *to* ~ *to*, bijbrengen *irr.*; *to* ~ *up*, grootbrengen *irr.*; braken.

brink, *n.* rand *n.*

briny, *a.* zout. *the* ~ *ocean*, het zilte nat.

briquette, *n.* briket *n.n.*

brisk, *a.*, ~**ly,** *adv.* kwik, levendig; fris. ¶ *v.i.* *to* ~ *up*, verlevendigen.

brisket, *n.* borststuk *n.n.*

briskness, *n.* levendigheid *n.*

bristle, *n.* borstel *n.*; stijf haar *n.n.* ¶ *v.i.* overeind (gaan) staan. **bristly,** *a.* borstelig.

Britain, *N.* Brittanje *n.N.* **British,** *a.* Brits. **Briton,** *N.* Brit *N.*; Engelsman *N.* **Brittany,** *N.* Bretagne *n.N.*

brittle, *a.* bros.

broach, *n.* (braad)spit *n.n.* ¶ *v.t.* aansteken *str.* (*barrel*); ter sprake brengen *irr.* (*conversation*).

broad, *a.*, ~**ly,** *adv.* breed, wijd; ruim; algemeen. ~ *daylight*, helder daglicht *n.n.* **broadcast,** *v.t.* & *v.i.* omroepen *str.*, uitzenden *str.*; wijd uitzaaien. ¶ *n.* uitzending *n.* ¶ *adv.* *to sow* ~, met de hand uitzaaien. **broadcloth,** *n.* fijn zwart laken *n.n.* **broaden,** *v.t.* verbreden. ¶ *v.i.* breder worden *str.* **broadness,** *n.* grofheid *n.* **broadsheet,** *n.* schotschrift *n.n.*, vlugschrift *n.n.*; rijmprent *n.* **broadside,** *n.* volle laag *n.* **broadsword,** *n.* slagswaard *n.n.*

brocade, *n.* brocade *n.*

broccoli, *n.* groene bloemkool *n.*

brochure, *n.* brochure *n.*

brogue, *n.* grove schoen *n.*; Iers accent *n.n.*

broil, *n.* twist *n.* ¶ *v.t.* braden, roosteren.

broken, *a.* gebroken. **broken-hearted,** *a.* met een gebroken hart *n.n.* **broken-winded,** *a.* dampig.

broker, *n.* makelaar *n.*, agent *n.*; (soort) deurwaarder *n.* **brokerage,** *n.* makelarij *n.*, courtage *n.*

bromide, *n.* bromide *n.n.*

bromine, *n.* broom *n.n.*, bromium *n.n.*

bronchial, *a.* van de luchtpijptakken *pl.n.* **bronchitis,** *n.* bronchitis *n.*

bronze, *n.* brons *n.n.* ¶ *a.* van brons, bronzen; bronskleurig. ¶ *v.t.* bronzen.

brooch, *n.* broche *n.*

brood, *n.* broedsel *n.n.*, gebroed *n.n.*; kroost *n.n.* ¶ *v.i.* broeden. ¶ *v.t.* (uit)broeden.

brook, *n.* beek *n.* ¶ *v.t.* dulden, verdragen *str.*

broom, *n.* bezem *n.*; brem *n.* (*plant*). **broomstick,** *n.* bezemsteel *n.*

broth, *n.* bouillon *n.*

brothel, *n.* bordeel *n.n.*

brother, *n.* broer *n.*, broeder *n.* **brotherhood,** *n.* broederschap *n.* **brother-in-law,** *n.* schoonbroer *n.* **brotherly,** *a.* broederlijk.

brougham, *n.* (soort) gesloten rijtuig *n.n.*

brow, *n.* wenkbrauw *n.*; voorhoofd *n.n.*; kruin *n.* **browbeat,** *v.t.* overdonderen, op de kop zitten *str.*

brown, *a.* bruin. ~ *paper*, pakpapier *n.n.*; *in a* ~ *study*, in somber gepeins verzonken. **brownie,** *n.* kabouter *n.*, aardmannetje *n.n.*

browse, *v.i.* grazen; grasduinen (*fig.*).

bruise, *v.t.* kneuzen. ¶ *n.* kneuzing *n.* **bruiser,** *n.* ruwe vechtersbaas *n.*

Brummagem, *a.* namaak, vals.

brunette, *n.* brunette *n.*

brunt, *n.* schok *n.* *to bear the* ~, de stoot opvangen *str.*

brush, *n.* borstel *n.*; kwast *n.* (*large*), penseel *n.n.* (*small*); staart *n.* (*fox*). ¶ *v.t.* borstelen; vegen. *to* ~ *aside*, ter zijde schuiven *str.*; *to* ~ *up*, oppoetsen. **brushwood,** *n.* kreupelhout *n.n.*

brusque, *a.* brusk; kortaf.

brutal, *a.*, ~**ly,** *adv.* onmenselijk, beestachtig; ruw. **brutality,** *n.* beestachtigheid *n.*, onmenselijkheid *n.* **brutalize,** *v.t.* verdierlijken, verwilderen. **brute,** *n.* redeloos dier *n.n.*; bruut *n.*, onmens *n.* ¶ *a.* redeloos; bruto. **brutish,** *a.* dierlijk, zinnelijk. **brutishness,** *n.* dierlijkheid *n.*

bubble, *n.* bel *n.*, bobbel *n.* ¶ *v.i.* borrelen, pruttelen.

bubonic, *a.* ~ *plague*, builenpest *n.*

buccaneer, *n.* boekanier *n.*, vrijbuiter *n.*

buck, *n.* mannetje *n.*, mannetjesdier *n.n.*; rammelaar *n.* (*rabbit*); (ree)bok *n.*, damhert *n.n.*; aalkorf *n.* ¶ *v.i.* bokken. *to* ~ *up*, opschieten *str.* **buck-bean,** *n.* boksboon *n.*

bucket, *n.* emmer *n.* *to kick the* ~, het hoekje omgaan *irr.*; ~-*shop*, gokkantoor *n.n.*

buck-hound, *n.* jachthond *n.*

buckle, *n.* gesp *n.* ¶ *v.t.* gespen; ombuigen *str.*, krullen.

buckler, *n.* beukelaar *n.*

buckram, *n.* stijf linnen *n.n.*

buckshot, *n.* grove hagel *n.* **buckskin,** *n.* boksvel *n.n.*; zacht geel leer *n.n.* **buckwheat,** *n.* boekweit *n.n.*

bucolic, *a.* herderlijk, landelijk.

bud, *n.* knop *n.* ¶ *v.i.* (uit)botten.

Buddha, *N.* Boedha *N.*

budge, *v.i.* (zich) bewegen *str.*, (zich) verroeren.

budget, *n.* budget *n.n.*, begroting *n.* ¶ *v.i.* uittrekken. *to* ~ *for something*, iets op de begroting zetten, met iets rekening houden *irr.*

buff, *a.* geelbruin, zeemkleurig.

buffalo, *n.* buffel *n.*; karbouw *n.*

buffer, *n.* stootkussen *n.*, stootblok *n.n.*

buffet, *n.* buffet *n.n.* (*furniture*); restauratiezaal *n.*, buffet *n.n.*; stoot *n.* (*wind*); slag *n.* ¶ *v.t.* slaan *irr.*, beuken.

buffoon, *n.* hansworst *n.*; nar *n.* **buffoonery,** *n.* grappenmakerij *n.*

bug, *n.* kever *n.*, tor *n.*; wandluis *n.* bugbear, *n.* boeman *n.*
buggy, *n.* licht rijtuig *n.n.* op twee wielen *n.n.* ¶ *a.* vol wandluizen *n.*
bugle, *n.* hoorn *n.* ¶ *v.i.* op een hoorn blazen. **bugler,** *n.* hoornblazer *n.*
bugloss, *n.* slangenkruid *n.n.*
buhl, *n.* ingelegd werk *n.n.*, boulewerk *n.n.*
build, *v.t.* bouwen; stichten, aanleggen. *to* ~ *up,* opbouwen. ¶ *v.i. to* ~ *on,* bouwen op, zich verlaten *str.* op. ¶ *n.* bouw. *n.*, lichaamsbouw *n.* **builder,** *n.* bouwmeester *n.*; aannemer *n.* **building,** *n.* gebouw *n.n.* ~-*site,* bouwterrein *n.n.*
bulb, *n.* (bloem)bol *n.*; lamp *n.*, lampje *n.n.* (*light*). **bulbous,** *a.* knolvormig.
bulge, *n.* buik *n.*; uitpuiling *n.* ¶ *v.i.* uitpuilen; opzwellen *str.*
bulk, *n.* massa *n.*, volume *n.n.*; merendeel *n.n. to break* ~, beginnen *str.* te lossen; *in* ~, in losse massa, in het groot; *loaded in* ~, met stortgoederen *n.n.* geladen. ¶ *v.i.* groot lijken *str.*; veel plaats innemen *str.* **bulkhead,** *n.* dwarsschot *n.n.*, waterdicht schot *n.n.* **bulky,** *a.* van grote omvang *n.*; lijvig.
bull, *n.* stier *n.*; speculant *n.* à la hausse; bul *n.* (*papal*). **bulldog,** *n.* bulhond *n.*, bullebijter *n.*
bullet, *n.* kogel *n.* ~-*headed,* met een ronde kop *n.*
bulletin, *n.* bulletin *n.n.*
bullfight, *n.* stierengevecht *n.n.* **bullfinch,** *n.* goudvink *n.*, bloedvink *n.* **bullfrog,** *n.* brulkikvors *n.*
bullion, *n.* ongemunt goud *n.n. or* zilver *n.n.*
bullock, *n.* os *n.* **bull's eye,** *n.* roos *n.* (*target*); rond venster *n.n.*; dievenlantaarn *n.*
bully, *n.* (laffe) treiteraar *n.* ¶ *v.t.* door vrees *n.* tot iets dwingen *str.*; treiteren, koeionneren, negeren.
bulrush, *n.* grote lisdodde *n.*; bies *n.*
bulwark, *n.* bolwerk *n.n.*; verschansing *n.* (*of ship*).
bum, *n.* achterste *n.n.*
bumble-bee, *n.* hommel *n.*
bumboat, *n.* provisieboot *n.*
bump, *n.* bons *n.*, stoot *n.*, schok *n.*; buil *n.*, knobbel *n.* ¶ *v.i.* bonzen, stoten *str.* **bumper,** *n.* bokaal *n.*; boordevol glas *n.n.* ¶ *a.* rijk.
bumpkin, *n.* pummel *n.*, boerekinkel *n.*
bumptious, *a.* aanmatigend.
bumpy, *a.* hobbelig.
bun, *n.* krentebroodje *n.n.*; wrong *n.*, dotje *n.n.* (*hair*).
bunch, *n.* bos *n.* (*flowers*); tros *n.* (*grapes*); hoop *n.*, troep *n.* ¶ *v.t. to* ~ *together,* bijeendoen *irr.*, in bosjes verenigen.
bundle, *n.* bundel *n.*, bos *n.* ¶ *v.t.* samenbinden *str.*
bung, *n.* spon *n.*, bom *n.* ¶ *v.t.* smijten *str.* ¶ *adv.* pal, prop.
bungalow, *n.* landhuisje *n.n.*

bunghole, *n.* spongat *n.n.*
bungle, *v.t.* verknoeien. **bungler,** *n.* prutser *n.*, klungelaar *n.*
bunion, *n.* eeltgezwel *n.n.*
bunk, *n.* kooi *n.*, slaapbank *n. to do a* ~, er vandoor gaan *irr.*
bunker, *n.* kolenruim *n.n.*, kolenbunker *n.*; kuil *n.* (*golf*). ¶ *v.t. & v.i.* kolen innemen *str.*, bunkeren.
bunkum, *n.* onzin *n.*
bunny, *n.* konijntje *n.n.*
bunting, *n.* vlaggen *pl.n.*; vlaggedoek *n.n.*; ortolaan *n.* (*bird*).
buoy, *n.* boei *n.*, ton *n.* ¶ *v.t.* betonnen. *to* ~ *up,* drijvende houden *irr.*, hoog geven *str.* **buoyancy,** *n.* drijfvermogen *n.n.*; veerkracht (van geest) *n.* **buoyant,** *a.* drijvend; opgewekt.
bur(r), *n.* kleefkruid *n.n.*, klit *n.*, klis *n.*
burbot, *n.* kwabaal *n.*
burden, *n.* last *n.*, vracht *n.*; lading *n.*; tonnenmaat *n.*; refrein *n.n.* ¶ *v.t.* belasten; drukken. **burdensome,** *a.* drukkend, zwaar.
burdock, *n.* klit *n.*, klis *n.*
bureau, *n.* schrijftafel *n.*; organisatie *n.* **bureaucracy,** *n.* bureaucratie *n.* **bureaucrat,** *n.* bureaucraat *n.* **bureaucratic,** *a.* bureaucratisch.
burgeon, *n.* knop *n.* ¶ *v.i.* (uit)botten.
burgess, *n.,* **burgher,** *n.* burger *n.*, poorter *n.*
burglar, *n.* inbreker *n.* **burglary,** *n.* inbraak *n. to commit a* ~, inbreken *str.*, inbraak doen *irr.*
burgomaster, *n.* burgemeester *n.*
Burgundian, *a.* Bourgondisch. **Burgundy,** *N.* Bourgondië *n.N.* ¶ *n.* bourgogne *n.* (*wine*).
burial, *n.* begrafenis *n.*
burin, *n.* etsnaald *n.*, graveerstift *n.*
burlesque, *n.* klucht *n.*, burlesk *n.* ¶ *v.t.* belachelijk maken.
burly, *a.* stoer, potig.
Burma, *N.* Birma *n.N.* **Burmese,** *a.* Birmaans.
burn, *v.t.* verbranden. *to* ~ *down,* afbranden. ¶ *v.i.* branden. ¶ *n.* brandwond *n.*; beek *n.* (*brook*). **burner,** *n.* brander *n.* **burning-glass,** *n.* brandglas *n.n.*
burnish, *v.t.* polijsten. **burnisher,** *n.* polijster *n.*
burnous, *n.* burnoe *n.*
burr, *n.* ruwe kant *n.* (*of metal*); wetsteen *n.*; uitspraak *n.* met krachtige R. *n.*
burrow, *n.* hol *n.n.* ¶ *v.i.* graven *str.*, wroeten.
bursar, *n.* thesaurier *n.* (*official*); beursstudent *n.*
burst, *n.* breuk *n.*, barst *n.*; uitbarsting *n.* ¶ *v.i.* barsten *irr. to* ~ *open,* openvliegen *str.*
bury, *v.t.* begraven *str.* **burying place,** *n.* begraafplaats *n.*
bus, *n.* (omni)bus *n.*, (auto)bus *n.*
busby, *n.* kolbak *n.*
bush, *n.* struik *n.*; vossestaart *n.* ~-*es,* kreupelhout *n.n.*, kreupelbos *n.n.*

bushel, *n.* schepel *n.*
Bushman, *N.* Bosjesman *N.*
bushy, *a.* ruig.
busily, *adv.* druk; vlijtig, ijverig. **business,** *n* zaak *n.;* zaken *pl.n.;* bedrijf *n.n.,* beroep *n.n.;* gedoe *n.n.*   *on* ~, voor zaken; ~ *relations,* handelsbetrekkingen *pl. n.* **businesslike,** *a.* practisch. **business man,** *n.* zakenman *n.*
busk, *n.* balein *n.*
buskin, *n.* kothurn *n.*
bust, *n.* buste *n.;* borstbeeld *n.n.;* fuif *n.* ¶ *a.* kapot.
bustard, *n.* trapgans *n.*
bustle, *v.i.* druk in de weer zijn. ¶ *v.t.* aansporen. ¶ *n.* bedrijvigheid *n.,* drukte *n.* **bustler,** *n.* bedrijvig iemand.
busy, *a.* druk. *to be* ~, het druk hebben. ¶ *v.t.* bezighouden *irr.* **busybody,** *n.* bemoeial *n.*
but, *c.* maar. ¶ *prep.* behalve. ~ *for,* ware het niet dat. ¶ *adv.* slechts. ¶ *n.* maar *n.n.* ¶ *v.t.* ~ *me no buts,* geen maren.
butcher, *n.* slager *n.;* wreedaard *n.* ¶ *v.t.* slachten; wreedaardig vermoorden. **butchery,** *n.* slagerij *n.;* slachting *n.,* slachtpartij *n.*
butler, *n.* chef-huisknecht *n.;* bottelier *n.* (*bibl.*).
butt, *n.* van *n.n.,* pijp *n.;* kolf *n.* (*gun*); mikpunt *n.n.* (*target*); peuk *n.* (*cigar*). ¶ *v.t.* met de kop stoten. **butt-end,** *n.* kolf *n.*
butter, *n.* boter *n.* ¶ *v.t.* boteren, smeren. *to* ~ *up,* vleien. **buttercup,** *n.* boterbloem *n.* **butterdish,** *n.* botervlootje *n.n.* **butterfly,** *n.* vlinder *n.,* kapel *n.* ~ *nut,* vleugelmoer *n.* **butter-milk,** *n.* karnemelk *n.* **buttery,** *n.* provisiekamer *n.* ¶ *a.* boterachtig.
buttock, *n.* bil *n.* ~*s,* achterste *n.*
button, *n.* knoop *n.;* knop *n.* (*press*). ~*s,* chasseur *n.,* page *n.,* piccolo *n.* ¶ *v.t.* *to* ~ (*up*), toeknopen, dichtknopen. **buttonhole,** *n.* knoopsgat *n.n.;* bloem *n.* in 't knoopsgat. ¶ *v.t.* aanklampen. **buttonhook,** *n.* knoopenhaakje *n.n.*
buttress, *n.* steun;   r *n.;* beer *n.* ¶ *v.t.* schragen, steunen.
buxom, *a.* mollig, welgedaan.
buy, *v.t.* kopen *irr. to* ~ *dearly,* duur betalen. **buyer,** *a.* koper *n.*
buzz, *v.i.* zoemen, gonzen. ¶ *n.* gezoem *n.n.,* gegons *n.n.*
buzzard, *n.* buizerd *n.*
by, *prep.* bij, nabij; met, per, door; langs, voorbij; om. ~ *heart,* van buiten; ~ *all means,* toch vooral; ~ *no means,* geenszins; ~ *oneself,* alleen; op z'n eentje; ~ *reason of,* vanwege; ~ *that time,* tegen die tijd *n.;* ~ *way of,* als. ¶ *adv.* erbij; voorbij. ~ *and large,* over het geheel (genomen); ~ *and* ~, straks, dadelijk; ~ *the by(e),*

tussen haakjes *n.n.; to lay* ~, in reserve *n.* houden *irr.*
bye, *int.* ~ - ~, da-ag! ¶ *adv. See* **by.**
by-election, *n.* tussentijdse verkiezing *n.*
bygone, *a.* vervlogen. **by-law,** *n.* plaatselijke verordening *n.* **by-pass,** *n.* omgelegde verkeersweg *n.* ¶ *v.t.* omheen trekken *str.* **by-path,** *n.* zijpad *n.n.* **by-play,** *n.* bijhandeling *n.,* stil spel *n.n.* **by-product,** *n.* bijproduct *n.n.,* nevenproduct *n.n.* **bystander,** *n.* toeschouwer *n.* **by-way,** *n.* zijweg *n.* **byword,** *n.* spreekwoord *n.n.;* voorwerp *n.n.* van spot *n.*
Byzantine, *a.* Byzantijns.

C

cab, *n.* huurijtuig *n.n.;* bril *n.* (*of engine*).
cabal, *n.* intrige *n.*
cabbage, *n.* kool *n.* ~ *butterfly,* koolwitje *n.n.*
Cabbala, *N.* Kabbalah *N.* **Cabbalistic,** *a.* Kabbalistisch.
cabby, *n.,* **cab-driver,** *n.* koetsier *n.*
cabin, *n.* kajuit *n.,* hut *n.;* hutje *n.n.* **cabinboy,** *n.* kajuitsjongen *n.*
cabinet, *n.* kastje *n.n.;* kaoinet *n.n.,* ministerraad *n.;* kabinet *n.n.* (*room*). **cabinetmaker,** *n.* schrijnwerker *n.,* meubelmaker *n.*
cable, *n.* kabel *n.;* kabelbericht *n.n.* ¶ *v.t.* seinen, berichten. **cablegram,** *n.* kabelbericht *n.n.*
cabman, *n.* koetsier *n.* **cabstand,** *n.* standplaats *n.*
cachalot, *n.* potvis *n.*
cachexy, *n.* ongezonde toestand *n.*
cachinnation, *n.* schaterlach *n.*
cackle, *v.i.* kakelen; gaggelen, snateren. ¶ *n.* gekakel *n.n.;* gesnater *n.n.*
cacophony, *n.* cacophonie *n.,* onwelluidendheid *n.*
cactus, *n.* kaktus *n.*
cad, *n.* ploert *n.*
cadastral, *a.* kadastraal. ~ *survey,* topografische opmeting *n.*
cadaverous, *a.* lijkkleurig.
caddie, *n.* golf-jongen *n.*
caddy, *n.* theebuisje *n.n.*
cadence, *n.* kadans *n.,* rhythme *n.n.*
cadet, *n.* kadet *n.;* jongste zoon *n.,* jongere *or* jongste broer *n.*
cadge, *v.t.* (af)bedelen. **cadger,** *n.* bedelaar *n.,* klaploper *n.*
cadmium, *n.* cadmium *n.n.*
caduceus, *n.* staf (van Mercurius) *n.*
café, *n.* koffiehuis *n.n.*
caffeine, *n.* kaffeïne *n.*
cage, *n.* kooi *n.;* liftkooi *n.* ¶ *v.t.* in een kooi opsluiten *str.*
cairn, *n.* steenhoop *n.*
caisson, *n.* caisson *n.*
caitiff, *n.* schelm *n.*

cajole, *v.t.* vleien. cajolery, *n.* vleierij *n.*
cake, *n.* koek *n.*; cake *n.*; stuk *n.n.* (*soap*).
¶ *v.i.* een koek vormen.
calabash, *n.* kalebas *n.*
calamitous, *a.* rampspoedig. calamity, *n.*
ramp *n.*, onheil *n.n.*
calash, *n.* calèche *n.*
calcareous, *a.* kalkhoudend. calcify, *v.i.*
verkalken. calcination, *n.* verkalking *n.*;
volkomen verbranding *n.* calcine, *v.t.*
verkalken; door vuur *n.n.* verteren.
calcium, *n.* calcium *n.n.*
calculable, *a.* berekenbaar. calculate, *v.t.*
berekenen. ¶ *v.i.* rekenen. calculation, *n.*
berekening *n.* calculator, *n.* rekenmachine
n. calculus, *n.* rekening *n.* (*maths.*); steen *n.*
differential ~, differentiaalrekening *n.*
Caledonian, *a.* Caledonisch, Schots.
calendar, *n.* kalender *n.*
calf, *n.* kalf *n.n.*; kalfleer *n.n.*
calibrate, *v.t.* kalibreren. calibration, *n.*
kalibrering *n.*
calibre, *n.* kaliber *n.n.*
calico, *n.* gedrukt katoen *n.n.*
caliph, *n.* kalif *n.*
calk, *v.t.* op scherp zetten (*of horse*).
call, *v.t.* roepen *str.*; noemen; beroepen *str.*
to ~ *to the bar*, tot advocaat *n.* toelaten *str.*
¶ *v.i.* roepen *str.*; een bezoek *n.n.* brengen
irr. *to* ~ *after*, noemen naar; *to* ~ *at*,
aanlopen *str.* bij; aandoen *irr* (*port*); *to* ~
back, terugroepen *str.*; *to* ~ *for*, afhalen,
komen *irr.* halen; vragen *str.* naar; *to* ~
forth, uitlokken; *to* ~ *in at*, aanlopen *str.* bij;
to ~ *off*, afgelasten; *to* ~ *on*, een bezoek
n.n. afleggen bij, een beroep *n.n.* doen *irr.*
op; *to* ~ *out*, uitroepen *str.*; *to* ~ *to*,
toeroepen *str.*; *to* ~ *up*, oproepen *str.*;
voor de geest roepen *str.* ¶ *n.* roep *n.*,
geroep *n.n.*; bezoek *n.n.* (*visit*); roep *n.*,
zang *n.* (*birds, etc.*); appel *n.n.* (*roll*-);
beroep *n.n.* (*clergy*); aanleiding *n.*, noodzaak *n.* (*need*). caller, *n.* bezoeker *n.*
calligraphy, *n.* schoonschrijven *n.n.*
calling, *n.* beroep *n.n.*, roeping *n.* call-
office, *n.* (publiek) telefoonstation *n.n.*
callosity, *n.* eeltigheid *n.* callous, *a.* eeltig,
vereelt; hardvochtig, ongevoelig. callous-
ness, *n.* hardvochtigheid *n.*, gevoelloosheid
n.
callow, *a.* kaal; onervaren.
callus, *n.* eelt *n.n.*
calm, *a.*, ~ly, *adv.* kalm, rustig. ¶ *n.* kalmte
n., windstilte *n.* ¶ *v.t.* stillen, kalmeren,
doen *irr.* bedaren. calmness, *n.* kalmte *n.*
calomel, *n.* calomel *n.n.*
caloric, *n.* warmte *n.n.* calorie, *n.* calorie *n.*
calorific, *a.* warmte . . .
calumniate, *v.t.* (be)lasteren. calumniation,
n. lastering *n.* calumniator, *n.* lasteraar *n.*
calumnious, *a.* lasterlijk. calumny, *n.*
laster(ing) *n.*
Calvary, *N.* Calvarieberg *n.*; Kruisweg *N.*
calve, *v.i.* kalven.

calyx, *n.* bloemkelk *n.*
cam, *n.* kam *n.*
camber, *n.* welving *n.*
cambric, *n.* batist *n.n.*
camel, *n.* kameel *n.*
camellia, *n.* camelia *n.*
cameo, *n.* camee *n.*
camera, *n.* camera *n.*; kiektoestel *n.n.*
camiknickers, *pl.n.* hemdbroek *n.*
camisole, *n.* kamizool *n.*
camomile, *n.* kamille *n.*
camouflage, *n.* camouflage *n.* ¶ *v.t.* camou-
fieren.
camp, *n.* kamp *n.n.* ¶ *v.i.* kamperen.
campaign, *n.* veldtocht *n.*; campagne *n.*
campaigner, *n.* veteraan *n.*
campanula, *n.* klokje *n.n.*
camper, *n.* kampeerder *n.* camp-follower, *n.*
legerparasiet *n.*
camphor, *n.* kamfer *n.* camphorated, *a.*
gekamferd.
camp-stool, *n.* vouwstoeltje *n.n.*
can, *n.* kan *n.* ¶ *v.t.* inmaken. ¶ *aux.v.*
kunnen *irr.*
Canadian, *a.* & *N.* Canadees *N.*
canal, *n.* kanaal *n.n.*, gracht *n.*, vaart *n.*
canalization, *n.* kanalisatie *n.* canalize,
v.t. kanaliseren.
canary, *n.* kanarie *n.*
cancel, *v.t.* herroepen *str.*, intrekken *str.*;
doorhalen, laten *str.* wegvallen. cancella-
tion, *n.* intrekken *n.n.*; doen vervallen *n.n.*
cancer, *n.* kanker *n.* Cancer, *N.* de Kreeft.
tropic of ~, Kreeftskeerkring *N.* cancerous
a. kankerachtig.
candelabrum, *n.* luchter *n.*
candid, *a.*, ~ly, *adv.* oprecht, openhartig.
candidate, *n.* candidaat *n.* candidature, *n.*
candidatuur *n.*
candidness, *n.* oprechtheid *n.*, openhartigheid
n.
candied, *a.* geconfijt, geglaceerd. ~ *peel*,
sucade *n.*
candle, *n.* kaars *n.* Candlemas, *N.* Maria
Lichtmis *N.* candlestick, *n.* kandelaar *n.*
candour, *n.* oprechtheid *n.*
candy, *n.* kandij *n.*; suikergoed *n.n.* ¶ *v.t.*
konfijten.
cane, *n.* riet *n.*; rotting *n.* ¶ *v.t.* afranselen.
cane-bottomed, *a.* met rieten zitting *n.*
canine, *a.* honds. ¶ *n.* hoektand *n.*
canister, *n.* (blikken) bus *n.*
canker, *n.* brand *n.*, roest *n.*; mondkanker
n. ¶ *v.i.* invreten *str.*, verkankeren.
cankered, *a.* aangetast, verkankerd. can-
kerous, *a.* kankerachtig.
cannibal, *a.* kannibaal *n.*, menseneter *n.*
¶ *a.* kannibalistisch. cannibalism, *n.* kan-
nibalisme *n.n.*
cannon, *n.* kanon *n.n.*; carambole *n.* ¶ *v.i.*
caramboleren. cannonball, *n.* kanonskogel
n.
cannot, *aux.v.* See can.
canny, *a.* omzichtig.

canoe, *n.* kano *n.*

canon, *n.* kanon *n.*; kanunnik *n.*, domheer *n.* ~ *law,* kanonieke wet *n.* **canonical,** *a.* kanoniek. ~*s,* kerkelijk gewaad *n.n.* **canonization,** *n.* heiligverklaring *n.* **canonize,** *v.t.* heilig verklaren. **canonry,** *n.* domheerschap *n.n.*

canopy. *n.* baldakijn *n.*, troonhemel *n.* ¶ *v.t.* met een baldakijn bedekken.

cant, *n.* preektoon *n.*; hoogdravende onzin *n.*; bargoens *n.n.*; schuine kant *n.* ¶ *v.i.* overhellen.

can't (cannot), *aux.v. See* **can.**

Cantab, *a.* van Cambridge.

cantankerous, *a.* wrevelig, vitterig, brommerig.

canteen, *n.* kantine *n.*; veldmenage *n.*

canter, *v.i.* (in korte galop) rijden *str.* ¶ *n.* korte galop *n.*

cantharides, *pl.n.* Spaanse vlieg *n.*

canticle, *n.* lofzang *n. the C*~*s,* het Hooglied *n.N.*

cantilever, *n.* ~ *bridge,* bascule brug *n.*

canto, *n.* zang *n.*

canton, *n.* kanton *n.n.* ¶ *v.t.* kantonneren. **cantonment,** *n.* kantonnement *n.n.*

canvas, *n.* zeildoek *n.n.*; doek *n.n. under* ~, onder zeil *n.*; in tenten *n.*

canvass, *v.t.* werven *str.*; grondig onderzoeken *irr.* ¶ *n.* stemmenwerving *n.* **canvasser,** *n.* stemmenwerver *n.*; colporteur *n.*

canyon, *n.* cañon *n.*

cap, *n.* pet *n.*; muts *n.*; baret *n.n.*; dopje *n.n.*, hoedje *n.n. to set one's* ~ *at,* hengelen naar. ¶ *v.t.* overtroeven.

capability, *n.* bekwaamheid *n.*, vermogen *n.n.* **capable,** *a.* bekwaam, geschikt.

capacious, *a.,* ~ly, *adv.* ruim.

capacitate, *v.t.* bevoegd maken. **capacity,** *n.* bevoegdheid *n.*, bekwaamheid *n.*; inhoud *n.,* (berg)ruimte *n.*

cap-à-pie, *adv.* van top tot teen.

caparison, *n.* schabrak *n.n.* ¶ *v.t.* bedekken, optuigen.

cape, *n.* kap *n.,* pelerine *n. (clothing)*; kaap *n.* **caper,** *n.* kapriool *n. (leap)*; kappertje *n.n. (bean).* ¶ *v.i.* rondspringen *str.*

capercailye, *n.,* **capercailzie,** *n.* auerhaan *n.*

Cape Town, *N.* Kaapstad *N.*

capillary, *a.* capillair. ¶ *n.* haarbuisje *n.n.,* haarvat *n.n.*

capital, *a.,* ~ly, *adv.* voornaamst, hoofd ... ~ *punishment,* doodstraf *n.* ¶ *n.* hoofdstad *n. (town)*; hoofdletter *n. (writing)*; kapiteel *n.n. (architecture)*; kapitaal *n.n. (finance).* **capitalism,** *n.* kapitalisme *n.n.* **capitalist,** *n.* kapitalist *n.* **capitalization,** *n.* kapitalisatie *n.* **capitalize,** *v.t.* kapitaliseren; met hoofdletters schrijven *str.* **capitation,** *n.* hoofdelijke belasting *n.,* hoofdelijke omslag *n.*

capitular, *n.* kapittel ... **capitulary,** *a.* kapittel ...

capitulate, *v.i.* kapituleren. **capitulation,** *n.* kapitulatie *n.*

capon, *n.* kapoen *n.n.*

caprice, *n.* gril *n.* **capricious,** *a.,* ~ly, *adv.* grillig, wispelturig.

Capricorn, *.N.* Steenbok *N. Tropic of* ~ Steenbokskeerkring *N.*

capsicum, *n.* Spaanse peper *n.*

capsize, *v.i.* kapseizen, omslaan *irr.*

capstan, *n.* kaapstander *n.*

capsule, *n.* capsule *n.*

captain, *n.* kaptein *n.*, kapitein *n.*, gezagvoerder *n.* **captaincy,** *n.* kapiteinschap *n.n.,* bevelhebberschap *n.n.* **captainship,** *n.* rang *n.* van kapitein *n.*; leiding *n.*

caption, *n.* opschrift *n.n.,* onderschrift *n.n.* **captious,** *a.,* ~ly, *adv.* misleidend, spitsvondig.

captivate, *v.t.* bekoren, boeien. **captive,** *n.* gevangene *n.* ¶ *a.* gevangen. ~ *balloon,* kabelballon *n.* **captivity,** *n.* gevangenschap *n.* **captor,** *n.* persoon *n.* die gevangen neemt *n.*; vanger *n.* **capture,** *v.t.* buitmaken, prijsmaken, opbrengen *irr.* ¶ *n.* vangst *n.*; buitmaken *n.n.,* kapen *n.*

Capuchin, *N.* Kapucijner *N.*

car, *n.* auto *n.*; tram *n.*

carafe, *n.* karaf *n.*

caramel, *n.* karamel *n.*

carapace, *n.* rugschild *n.n.*

carat, *n.* karaat *n.n.*

caravan, *n.* karavaan *n.*; woonwagen *n.* **caravansery,** *n.* karavansera *n.*

caraway, *n.* karwij *n.*

carbide, *n.* karbied *n.n.*

carbine, *n.* karabijn *n.*

carbolic, *a.* karbol ...

carbon, *n.* koolstof *n.*; koolspits *n.*; copieerpapier *n.n.* **carbonaceous,** *a.* koolhoudend. **carbonate,** *n.* carbonaat *n.n.* **carbonic,** *n.* ~ *acid,* koolzuur *n.n.* **carbonize,** *v.t.* carboniseren, verkolen.

carboy, *n.* mandfles *n.*

carbuncle, *n.* karbonkel *n.,* steenpuist *n.*

carburetter, *n.* carburateur *n.*

carcase, *n.* kreng *n.n.,* karkas *n.n.*; romp *n. (slaughtered meat).*

card, *n.* kaart *n.*; naamkaartje *n.n.*; (wol)kaarde *n.* ¶ *v.t.* kaarden. **cardboard,** *n.* karton *n.n.* **carder,** *n.* kaarder *n.*

cardiac, *a.* hart ...

cardigan, *n.* gebreid jasje *n.n.*

cardinal, *n.* kardinaal *n.* **cardinalate,** *n.* kardinaalschap *n.*

cardsharper, *n.* valse speler *n.* **card-table,** *n.* speeltafeltje *n.n.*

care, *n.* zorg *n.,* bezorgdheid *n. (worry)*; zorg *n.,* toezicht *n.n. (supervision)*; voorzichtigheid *n. (carefulness). with* ~, voorzichtig; *to take* ~, voorzichtig zijn; *to take* ~ *of,* zorg dragen *str.* voor; *to take* ~ *to,* er voor zorgen dat; ~ *of* (= *c/o*), per adres (= p.a.). ¶ *v.i.* geven *str.* om *(affection)*; bezorgd zijn *(worry)*; **lust**

hebben (*want*). to ~ *for*, geven *str.* om, houden *irr.* van.

careen, *v.t.* krengen, kielen.

career, *n.* carrière *n.*, loopbaan *n.*; vaart *n.* ¶ *v.i.* voortsnellen.

careful, *a.*, ~ly, *adv.* voorzichtig; zorgvuldig.

carefulness, *n.* voorzichtigheid *n.* **careless,** *a.*, ~ly, *adv.* slordig, nalatig; zorgeloos.

carelessness, *n.* slordigheid *n.*; zorgeloosheid *n.*

caress, *n.* liefkozing *n.* ¶ *v.t.* liefkozen, strelen.

caretaker, *n.* huisbewaarder *n.*, concierge *n.* **careworn,** *a.* afgetobd, door zorgen *pl. n.* verteerd.

cargo, *n.* lading *n.*

caricature, *n.* karikatuur *n.*, spotprent *n.* ¶ *v.t.* bespottelijk voorstellen. **caricaturist,** *n.* karikaturist *n.*

caries, *n.* wolf *n.* **carious,** *a.* door wolf aangetast.

carking, *a.* ~ *care,* knagende zorg *n.*

carman, *n.* voerman *n.*

Carmelite, *N.* Karmeliet *N.*

carminative, *n.* windafdrijvend middel *n.n.*

carmine, *n.* karmozijn *n.n.*, karmijn *n.n.*

carnage, *n.* slachting *n.*, bloedbad *n.n.*

carnal, *a.*, ~ly, *adv.* vleselijk; zinnelijk.

carnation, *n.* anjelier *n.* ¶ *a.* rose.

carnelian, *n.* kornalijn *n.* (*stone*) & *n.n.* (*substance*).

carnival, *n.* karnaval *n.n.*

carnivorous, *a.* vleesetend. **carnivore,** *n.* vleeseter *n.*

carol, *n.* lied *n.n.*, zang *n.* ¶ *v.i.* zingen *str.*

carotid, *n.* halsslagader *n.*

carousal, *n.* drinkgelag *n.n.* **carouse,** *v.i.* fuiven.

carp, *n.* karper *n.* ¶ *v.i.* vitten, bedillen. to ~ *at,* vitten op.

carpenter, *n.* timmerman *n.* ¶ *v.i.* timmeren. **carpentry,** *n.* timmerwerk *n.n.*; timmermansambacht *n.n.*

carper, *n.* vitter *n.*

carpet, *n.* vloerkleed *n.n.*, tapijt *n.n.* ¶ *v.t.* met een tapijt beleggen. **carpet-bag,** *n.* valies *n.n.* **carpeting,** *n.* tapijtgoed *n.n.*

carriage, *n.* rijtuig *n.n.* (*vehicle*); vervoer *n.n.* (*transport*); vracht *n.*, vrachtgeld *n.n.* (*payment*); houding *n.*, gedrag *n.n.* (*attitude*). **carriage-drive,** *n.* oprijlaan *n.* **carriage forward,** *a.* tegen rembours *n.* **carriage free,** *a.*, **carriage paid,** *a.* franco, vrachtvrij. **carrier,** *n.* vrachtrijder *n.*, voerman *n.*, bode *n.*; vrachtvaarder *n.*, bagagedrager *n.* (*on bicycle*).

carrion, *n.* aas *n.n.*, kreng *n.n.*

carrot, *n.* wortel *n.*, worteltje *n.n.* **carroty,** *a.* geelrood.

carry, *v.t.* dragen *str.*, vervoeren; bevatten; winnen *str.*, behalen; aannemen *str.*; overbrengen *irr.* ¶ *v.i.* (ver)dragen *str.* ¶ *v.r.* zich gedragen *str.* to ~ *coals to Newcastle,* overbodig werk doen *irr.*,

water naar zee dragen *str.*; to ~ *the day,* de overwinning behalen; to ~ *one's mind back to,* terugdenken *irr.* aan; to ~ *one's point,* zijn wil n. gedaan krijgen *str.*; to ~ *tales,* uit de school klappen; to ~ *weight,* gewicht *n.n.* in de schaal leggen; to ~ *one's years well,* jong zijn voor z'n jaren; to ~ *about,* (met zich) ronddragen *str.*; to ~ *away,* meeslepen; to ~ *forward,* overbrengen *irr.*; to ~ *off,* behalen, wegvoeren; to ~ *on,* zijn gang gaan, opspelen, doorslaan *irr.*; to ~ *through,* doorzetten.

cart, *n.* kar *n.*, wagen *n.* to put the ~ *before the horse,* het paard achter de wagen spannen *irr.* ¶ *v.t.* met een kar vervoeren. to ~ *around,* rondslepen. **cartage,** *n.* sleeploon *n.n.*

cartel, *n.* kartel *n.n.*

carter, *n.* vrachtrijder *n.* **cart-horse,** *n.* karrepaard *n.n.*, sleperspaard *n.n.*

Carthusian, *a.* Karthuizer.

cartilage, *n.* kraakbeen *n.n.* **cartilaginous,** *a.* kraakbeen . .

cart-load, *n.* karrevracht *n.*

cartoon, *n.* spotprent *n.* **cartoonist,** *n.* tekenaar *n.* van spotprenten *n.*

cartridge, *n.* patroon *n.* **cartridge-case,** *n.* (patroon)huls *n.* **cartridge-paper,** *n.* sterk (teken)papier *n.n.*

carve, *v.t.* voorsnijden *str.*; snijden *str.*; beeldhouwen. **carver,** *n.* voorsnijder *n.*; voorsnijmes *n.n.* **carving,** *n.* beeldhouwwerk *n.n.*, snijwerk *n.n.* ~ *knife,* voorsnijmes *n.n.*, vleesmes *n.n.*; ~ *fork,* vleesvork *n.*

cascade, *n.* (kleine) waterval *n.*

case, *n.* kist *n.*, bak *n.*, kast *n.*, doos *n.*, étui *n.n.*, koker *n.* (*container*); geval *n.n.* (*occurrence*); rechtszaak *n.*, proces *n.n.* (*lawsuit*). in ~, in geval (dat); *in the* ~ *of,* in geval van. ¶ *v.t.* in een étui (*etc.*) doen *irr.* **case-hardened,** *a.* verstokt.

casein, *n.* kaasstof *n.*, caseine *n.*

case-knife, *n.* hartsvanger *n.* **case law,** *n.* recht *n.n.* op precedent gegrond *n.n.*

casemate, *n.* kazemat *n.*

casement, *n.* openslaand venster *n.n.*

caseous, *a.* kaasachtig.

cash, *n.* geld *n.n.*, contanten *pl.n.n.* ~ *on delivery,* rembours *n.n.*; ~ *payment,* contante betaling *n.* ¶ *v.t.* inwisselen, innen, inkasseren, verzilveren. **cashbook,** *n.* kasboek *n.n.*

cashew, *n.* cachou *n.*

cashier, *n.* kassier *n.* ¶ *v.t.* afdanken.

cashmere, *n.* cachemir *n.*

casing, *n.* omhulsel *n.n.*, bekleding *n.*, mantel *n.*

cask, *n.* vat *n.n.*, ton *n.* **casket,** *n.* kistje *n.n.*, cassette *n.*

cassation, *n.* cassatie *n.*

casserole, *n.* vuurvaste pan *n.*

cassia, *n.* cassia *n.*

cassock, *n.* soutane *n.*

cassowary, *n.* casuaris *n.*
cast, *v.t.* werpen *str.* (*throw*); gieten *str.* (*pour*); uitbrengen *irr.* (*of vote*); uitrekenen (*accounts*). to ~ *a horoscope*, een horoscoop trekken *str.*; to ~ *the skin*, vervellen; to ~ *in one's lct with*, verkiezen *str.* het lot te delen met; to be ~ *away*, schipbreuk lijden *str.*; to ~ *up*, optellen; to ~ *off*, van zich af werpen *str.*, losgooien. ¶ *n.* worp *n.*, gooi *n.* (*throw*); uitwerpen *n.n.* (*throwing*); vorm *n.* (*mould*); afgietsel *n.n.* (*object from mould*); bezetting *n.* (*play*). to have a ~ *in one's eye*, scheel zien *irr.* ¶ *a.* gegoten; geworpen. ~ *iron*, gietijzer *n.n.;* ~ *steel*, gietstaal *n.n.;* ~ *off*, verstoten.
castanet, *n.* castagnet *n.*
castaway, *n.* schipbreukeling *n.*
caste, *n.* kaste *n.* to lose ~, stand *n.* verliezen *irr.*
castellan, *n.* slotvoogd *n.* **castellated**, *a.* gekanteeld.
caster sugar, *n.* strooisuiker *n.*, meelsuiker *n.*
castigate, *v.t.* kastijden. **castigation**, *n.* kastijding *n.*
casting vote, *n.* beslissende stem *n.*
castle, *n.* kasteel *n.n.*, slot *n.n.* ~ *in the air*, luchtkasteel *n.n.*
castor, *n.* bever *n.* (*animal*); kastoren hoed *n.* (*hat*); strooier *n.* (*utensil*); wieltje *n.n.* (*wheel*). ~ *oil*, wonderolie *n.*
castrate, *v.t.* castreren, lubben. **castration**, *n.* castratie *n.*
casual, *a.*, ~ly, *adv.* toevallig, terloops. ~ *labourer*, los werkman *n.* **casualty**, *n.* ongeluk *n.n.*, ongeval *n.n.* casualties, verliezen *pl.n.n.*
casuist, *n.* casuist *n.* **casuistic**, *a.* casuistisch. **casuistry**, *n.* casuistiek *n.*, haarkloverij *n.*
cat, *n.* kat *n.;* karwats *n.* ~ *o' nine tails*, (soort) karwats.
cataclysm, *n.* (natuur)ramp *n.;* omwenteling *n.*
catacomb, *n.* katakombe *n.*
catalepsy, *n.* catalepsie *n.* **cataleptic**, *n.* lijder *n.* aan catalepsie *n.*
catalogue, *n.* catalogus *n.* ¶ *v.t.* catalogiseren.
catapult, *n.* katapult *n.*, kattepult *n.*
cataract, *n.* waterval *n.n.*, cataract *n.;* grauwe staar *n.*
catarrh, *n.* catarrhe *n.*, zinking *n.* **catarrhal**, *a.* catarrhaal.
catastrophe, *n.* catastrophe *n.* **catastrophic**, *a.* catastrophaal.
catcall, *n.* gefluit *n.n.;* gejouw *n.n.* ¶ *v.t.* uitfluiten *str.*
catch, *v.t.* vangen *str.*; opvangen *str.*; grijpen *str.*; halen; betrappen. to ~ *it*, er van langs krijgen *str.*; to ~ *a person out*, iemand betrappen. ¶ *v.i.* blijven *str.* haken, blijven *str.* haperen; vuur vatten; stokken (*voice*). to ~ *on*, populair worden *str.*, ingang vinden *str.*; to ~ *up with*, inhalen. ¶ *n.* vangst *n.;* aanwinst *n.;* klink *n.*, knip *n.* *he had a* ~ *in his voice*,

z'n stem *n.* stokte. **catcher**, *n.* vanger *n.* **catching**, *a.* aanstekelijk; besmettelijk.
catchment, *n.* ~ *area*, neerslaggebied *n.n.*
catchpenny, *a.* bedrieglijk. **catchword**, *n.* slagwoord *n.n.*
catechism, *n.* catechismus *n.* **catechist**, *n.* catechist *n.*, catechiseermeester *n.* **catechize**, *v.t.* catechiseren.
categorical, *a.*, ~ly, *adv.* categorisch. **category**, *n.* categorie *n.*
cater, *v.i.* approvianderen. to ~ *for*, ... verschaffen. **caterer**, *n.* leverancier.
caterpillar, *n.* rups *n.*
caterwaul, *v.i.* krollen.
catfish, *n.* katvis *n.;* gestreepte haal *n.* catgut, *n.* snaar *n.*, darmsnaar *n.*
cathartic, *a.* purgerend, zuiverend.
cathedral, *n.* kathedraal *n.*
catheter, *n.* katheter *n.*
cathode, *n.* kathode *n.*
catholic, *a.* katholiek; Rooms Katholiek. **catholicism**, *n.* catholicisme *n.n.*
catkin, *n.* katje *n.n.*
cattle, *n.* vee *n.n.* **cattle plague**, *n.* veepest *n.* **cattle-show**, *n.* veetentoonstelling *n.*
catty, *a.* kattig, katachtig.
caucus, *n.* voorvergadering *n.;* kiescomité *n.n.*
caudal, *a.* staart ...
caul, *n.* helm *n.*
cauldron, *n.* (grote) ketel *n.*
cauliflower, *n.* bloemkool *n.*
caulk, *v.t.* kalefateren, breeuwen.
causal, *a.* causaal. **causality**, *n.* causaliteit *n.*, oorzakelijk verband *n.n.* **causation**, *n.* veroorzaking *n.*, oorzakelijkheid *n.* **cause**, *n.* oorzaak *n.* ¶ *v.t.* veroorzaken; teweegbrengen *irr.* **causeless**, *a.*, ~ly, *adv.* zonder oorzaak, ongegrond.
causeway, *n.* straatweg *n.;* dam *n.*
caustic, *a.* bijtend; scherp. ¶ *n.* bijtend middel *n.n.*
cauterisation, *n.* uitbranden *n.n.* **cauterise**, *v.t.* uitbranden. **cautery**, *n.* brandijzer *n.n.;* bijtend middel *n.n.*
caution, *n.* waarschuwing *n.;* berisping *n.;* omzichtigheid *n.* ¶ *v.t.* waarschuwen. **cautionary**, *a.* waarschuwend. **cautious**, *a.*, ~ly, *adv.* omzichtig. **cautiousness**, *n.* omzichtigheid *n.*
cavalcade, *n.* ruiterstoet *n.* **cavalier**, *n.* ridder *n.* C~, aanhanger *n.* van Karel I. **cavalry**, *n.* cavalerie *n.*, paardenvolk *n.n.*, ruiterij *n.*
cave, *n.* hol *n.n.*, grot *n.* ¶ *v.i.* to ~ *in*, instorten.
caveat, *n.* protest *n.n.*
cavern, *n.* spelonk *n.*, hol *n.n.* **cavernous**, *a.* spelonkachtig.
caviar(e), *n.* kaviaar *n.*
cavil, *v.i.* to ~ *at*, vitten op. **caviller**, *n.* vitter *n.*
cavity, *n.* holte *n.*
cavort, *v.i.* rondspringen *str.*

caw, *v.i.* krassen.
cayenne, *n.* Cayenne(peper) *n.*
cayman, *n.* kaaiman *n.*
cease, *v.i.* ophouden *irr.*, staken. ¶ *v.t.* doen irr. ophouden. ¶ *n. without* ~, onophoudelijk. ceaseless, *a.*, ~ly, *adv.* onophoudelijk.
cedar, *n.* ceder *n.*
cede, *v.t.* opgeven *str.*, afstand doen *irr.* van, afstaan *irr.*; toegeven *str.*
ceiling, *n.* plafond *n.n.*, zoldering *n.*
celandine, *n.* stinkende gouwe *n.*; speenkruid *n.n.*
celebrant, *n.* celebrant *n.* celebrate, *v.t.* vieren; voltrekken *str.* celebrated, *a.* vermaard, beroemd. celebration, *n.* viering *n.* celebrity, *n.* roem *n.*; beroemd persoon *n.*
celerity, *n.* spoed *n.*, snelheid *n.*
celery, *n.* selderie *n.*
celestial, *a.*, ~ly, *adv.* hemels.
celibacy, *n.* ongehuwde staat *n.* celibate, *n.* celibatair *n.*, vrijgezel *n.*
cell, *n.* cel *n.*; kluis *n.*
cellar, *n.* kelder *n.* cellarage, *n.* kelderhuur *n.* cellaret, *n.* likeurkeldertje *n.n.*
cellular, *a.* cel . . ., cellulair.
celluloid, *n.* celluloïde *n.n.* cellulose, *n.* cellulose *n.*
Celt, *N.* Kelt *N.* ¶ *n.* bronzen (*or* stenen) beitel. Celtic, *a.* Keltisch.
cement, *n.* cement *n.n.* ¶ *v.t.* cementeren.
cemetery, *n.* begraafplaats *n.*
cenotaph, *n.* gedenkteken *n.n.*, grafmonument *n.n.*
censer, *n.* wierookvat *n.n.*
censor, *n.* censor *n. the* ~*s*, de censuur *n.* ¶ *v.t.* censureren. censorious, *a.*, ~ly, *adv.* vitterig. censorship, *n.* censuur *n.*
censurable, *a.* afkeurenswaardig. censure, *n.* veroordeling *n.*, afkeuring *n.*; berisping *n.* ¶ *v.t.* afkeuren, critiek *n.* uitoefenen op; berispen.
census, *n.* volkstelling *n.*
cent, *n.* honderd *n.n.*; cent *n. per* ~, procent, ten honderd.
centaur, *n.* centaur *n.*, paardmens *n.n.*
centenarian, *n.* honderdjarige *n.* centenary, *n.* eeuwfeest *n.n.* centennial, *n.* eeuwfeest *n.n.* ¶ *a.* honderdjarig. centesimal, *a.* honderddelig. ¶ *n.* honderdste gedeelte *n.n.* centigrade, *a.* honderddelig. *10 degrees* ~, 10 graden *pl.n.* Celsius. centimeter, *n.* centimeter *n.* centipede, *n.* duizendpoot *n.*
central, *a.*, ~ly, *adv.* centraal. centralization, *n.* centralisatie *n.* centralize, *v.t.* centraliseren. centre, *n.* middelpunt *n.n.*, centrum *n.n.* ~ *of gravity*, zwaartepunt *n.n.*; dead ~, dode punt *n.n.* ¶ *a.* midden . . . ¶ *v.t.* concentreren. ¶ *v.i.* samenkomen *irr.* centre-bit, *n.* centerboor *n.* centrifugal, *a.* centrifugaal, middelpuntvliedend. centripetal, *a.* centripetaal, middelpuntzoekend.

centuple, *a.* honderdvoud. century, *n.* eeuw *n.*; honderdtal *n.n.* (*cricket*).
cephalic, *a.* hoofd . . . .
ceramic, *a.* ceramisch. ~*s*, pottebakkerskunst *n.*
cereal, *a.* graan . . . ¶ *n.* graansoort *n.* ~*s*, graangewassen *pl.n.n.*
cerebellum, *n.* kleine hersenen *pl.n.* cerebral, *a.* hersen . . . cerebrum, *n.* grote hersenen *pl.n.*
cerement, *n.* lijkwa *n.*
ceremonial, *a.*, ~ly, *adv.* ceremonieel, plechtig. ¶ *n.* ceremonieel *n.n.* ceremonious, *a.*, ~ly, *adv.* plechtstatig, vormelijk. ceremony, *n.* plechtigheid *n.*; plichtpleging *n.*
certain, *a.*, ~ly, *adv.* zeker, vast, stellig. ¶ *pron.* zeker. certainty, *n.* zekerheid *n.*
certificate, *n.* certificaat *n.n.*, bewijs *n.n.*, attest *n.n.*; getuigschrift *n.n.* ¶ *v.t.* een certificaat verlenen (aan), diplomeren. certification, *n.* certificaat *n.n.* certified, *a.* ~ *copy*, gewaarmerkt afschrift *n.n.*, kopie *n.* konform. certify, *v.t.* attesteren, verklaren.
certitude, *n.* zekerheid *n.*
cerulean, *a.* hemelsblauw.
cervical, *a.* hals . . ., nek . . .
cessation, *n.* ophouden *n.n.*
cession, *n.* afstand *n.*, cessie *n.*
cesspool, *n.* beerput *n.*, zinkput *n.*
cetacean, *n.* walvisachtig.
chafe, *v.t.* wrijven *str.*, schaven. ¶ *v.i.* wrijven *str.*, schaven; zich ergeren.
chaff, *n.* kaf *n.n.*, haksel *n.n.*; gekscheren *n.n.* ¶ *v.t.* voor de gek houden *irr.* ¶ *v.i.* gekheid *n.* maken. chaff-cutter, *n.* hakmes *n.n.*; kafmolen *n.*
chaffer, *v.i.* dingen *str.*
chaffinch, *n.* boekvink *n.*
chagrin, *n.* verdriet *n.n.*, hartzeer *n.n.*
chain, *n.* keten *n.*, ketting *n.*; reeks *n.* ¶ *v.t.* ketenen; aan de ketting leggen *irr.*
chair, *n.* stoel *n.*; zetel *n.*; leerstoel *n. to address the* ~, de voorzitter toespreken *str.*; *to take the* ~, presideren. ¶ *v.t.* op de schouders *pl.n.* ronddragen *str.* chairman, *n.* voorzitter *n.* ~ *of the board*, presidentcommissaris *n.* chairmanship, *n.* voorzitterschap *n.n.*
chaise, *n.* sjees *n.*
chalcedony, *n.* chalcedoon *n.* (*stone*), *n.n.* (*substance*).
chalice, *n.* beker *n.*, kelk *n.*
chalk, *n.* krijt *n.n. not by a long* ~, op geen stukken na. ¶ *v.t.* (met krijt) schrijven *str.*; aankalken. chalky, *a.* krijtachtig, vol krijt.
challenge, *v.t.* uitdagen; aanroepen *str.* (*by sentry*). ¶ *n.* uitdaging *n.*; aanroeping *n.* ~ *cup*, wisselbeker *n.* challenger, *n.* uitdager *n.*
chalybeate, *a.* ijzerhoudend.
chamber, *n.* vertrek *n.n.*, kamer *n.*, zaal *n.*

~*s*, kantoor *n.n. (lawyer's)*. **chamberlain,** *n.* kamerheer *n.* **chambermaid,** *n.* kamermeisje *n.n.*; kamenier *n.* **chamber music,** *n.* kámermuziek *n.*

chameleon, *n.* kameleon *n.n.*

chamois, *n.* gems *n.* ~ *leather,* zeemleer *n.n.*

champ, *v.t.* kauwen. ¶ *n.* kauwen *n.n.*

champagne, *n.* champagne *n.*

champion, *n.* kampioen *n.* ¶ *v.t.* verdedigen.

chance, *n.* kans *n.*, toeval *n.n. to take one's* ~, de kans waarnemen *str.*, het erop wagen; *to stand a good* ~, kans hebben. ¶ *a.* lukraak; toevallig. ¶ *v.t.* wagen; toevallig plaatsvinden *str.*

chancel, *n.* koor *n.n.*

chancellery, *n.* kanselarij *n.* **chancellor,** *n.* kanselier *n.* **chancery,** *n.* kanselarij *n. Court of C* ~, afdeling *n.* van het hoogste gerechtshof.

chancre, *n.* sjanker *n.*

chandelier, *n.* kroonluchter *n.*

chandler, *n.* kaarsenmaker *n.*

change, *v.t.* veranderen; overstappen; wisselen; zich verkleden. *to* ~ *colour,* van kleur *n.* verschieten *str.*; *to* ~ *places with,* van plaats *n.* ruilen met. ¶ *n.* verandering *n.*; overgang *n.*; klein geld *n.n.*; verschoning *n. a* ~ *for the better,* een verbetering *n.*; *for a* ~, voor de variatie. **changeable,** *a.* veranderlijk. **changeability,** *n.* veranderlijkheid *n.* **changeless,** *a.* onveranderlijk. **changeling,** *n.* wisselkind *n.n.*

channel, *n.* bedding *n.*, vaarwater *n.n. the (English) C* ~, het Kanaal.

chant, *n.* lied *n.n.*, kerkgezang *n.n.* ¶ *v.t.* zingen *str.* **chanter,** *n.* (voor) zanger *n.*

chantry, *n.* kapel *n.*

chaos, *n.* chaos *n.* **chaotic,** *a.* chaotisch.

chap, *n.* kerel *n.*, vent *n. (man)*; kloof *n. (skin).* ¶ *v.t. & v.i.* scheuren, splijten *str.*

chap-book, *n.* volksboekje *n.n.*

chapel, *n.* kapel *n.*; kerk *n.*

chaperon, *n.* chaperon(n)e *n.* ¶ *v.t.* chaperonneren.

chaplain, *n.* (huis)kapelaan *n.*; aalmoezenier *n.* ~ *to the forces,* veldprediker *n.* **chaplaincy,** *n.* waardigheid *n.* van (huis)kapelaan *or* aalmoezenier.

chaplet, *n.* (rozen)krans *n.*

chapter, *n.* hoofdstuk *n.n. (of book)*; kapittel *n.n. (of bible)*; kapittel *n.n. (of cathedral). to give* ~ *and verse,* tekst *n.* en uitleg *n.* geven *str.*

char, *v.t.* verkolen.

character, *n.* karakter *n.n.*; kenteken *n.n.*, karaktertrek *n.*; reputatie *n.*, goede naam *n.*; getuigschrift *n.n.*; excentrieke persoon *n.* **characteristic(al),** *a.* karakteristiek, kenschetsend. **characterization,** *n.* kenschetsing *n.* **characterize,** *v.t.* karakteriseren, kenschetsen, kenmerken.

charade, *n.* charade *n.*

charcoal, *n.* houtskool *n.* **charcoal-burner,** *n.* kolenbrander *n.*

charge, *v.t.* beladen *irr.*, belasten; vullen; laden *irr.*; berekenen, in rekening *n.* brengen *irr.*; aanklagen; aanvallen *str.* ¶ *n.* lading *n.*; opdracht *n.*, last *n.*; kosten *n.*; beschuldiging *n.*; aanval *n.*; taak *n.*, plicht *n.*; ambt *n.n.*; pupil *n. free of* ~, gratis; *no* ~ *for* . . ., franco thuis; *officer in* ~, dienstdoend officier *n.*; *to be in* ~, de leiding hebben; *to take* ~ *of,* waarnemen *str.*, zich belasten met. **chargeable,** *a.* ten laste komend.

charger, *n.* strijdros *n.n.*

chariot, *n.* wagen *n.*, strijdwagen *n.* **charioteer,** *n.* wagenmenner *n.*

charitable, *a.,* ~**bly,** *adv.* weldadig, liefdadig. **charity,** *n.* liefdadigheid *n.*; naastenliefde *n.*; liefdadigheidsinstelling *n.* ~ *school,* armenschool *n.*

charlatan, *n.* kwakzalver *n.*, charlatan *n.* **charlatanism,** *n.* kwakzalverij *n.*

charlock, *n.* wilde mosterd *n.*

charlotte, *n.* (soort) pudding *n.*

charm, *v.t.* betoveren; bekoren. ¶ *n.* tovermiddel *n.n.*, toverspreuk *n.*; betovering *n.*; bekoring *n.*; amulet *n.n.* **charmer,** *n.* bekoorster *n.* **charming,** *a.* charmant, bekoorlijk.

charnel house, *n.* knekelhuis *n.n.*

chart, *n.* (zee)kaart *n.*; tabel *n.* ¶ *v.t.* in kaart *n.* brengen *irr.*

charter, *n.* charter *n.*, handvest *n.n.*; octrooi *n.n.* ¶ *v.t.* bij charter instellen; bevrachten, charteren. **charter party,** *n.* chertepartij *n.*

charwoman, *n.* werkvrouw *n.*, werkster *n.*

chary, *a.* karig; behoedzaam.

chase, *v.t.* jagen, achtervolgen; ciseleren, drijven *str.* ¶ *n.* jacht *n.*; vervolging *n.* **chaser,** *n.* najager *n.*; graveur *n.*, drijver *n.*

chasm, *n.* kloof, afgrond *n.*

chassis, *n.* chassis *n.n.*, onderstel *n.n.*

chaste, *a.,* ~**ly,** *adv.* kuis, zuiver. **chasten,** *v.t.* kuisen; verootmoedigen.

chastise, *v.t.* kastijden. **chastisement,** *n.* kastijding *n.* **chastiser,** *n.* kastijder *n.*

chastity, *n.* kuisheid *n.*, eerbaarheid *n.*

chasuble, *n.* kazuifel *n.*

chat, *v.i.* keuvelen. ¶ *n.* praatje *n.*

chattel, *n.* roerend goed *n.n.*, bezitting *n. goods and* ~, have *n.* en goed *n.n.*

chatter, *v.i.* snateren, kakelen; kwetteren; snappen. ¶ *n.* gesnater *n.n.*; gekwetter *n.n.*; gebabbel *n.n.* **chatterbox,** *n.* kletskous *n.* **chatterer,** *n.* babbelaar *n.* **chatty,** *a.* babbelziek; vlot geschreven.

chauffeur, *n.* chauffeur *n.*

cheap, *a.,* ~**ly,** *adv.* goedkoop; verachtelijk. **cheapen,** *v.t.* afdingen *str.*; in waarde *n.* doen *irr.* dalen. **cheapness,** *n.* goedkoopte *n.*

cheat, *v.i.* bedriegen *str.*, beetnemen *str.* ¶ *n.* bedrieger *n.* **cheater,** *n.* bedrieger *n.* **cheating,** *n.* bedrog *n.n.*

check, *n.* schaak *n.*; plotselinge stilstand *n.*, tegenstand *n.*, échec *n.n.* ;beteugeling *n.*, contrôle *n.*; fiche *n.*, bonnetje *n.n.*; geruite stof *n.* ¶ *v.t.* schaakmat zetten; tegenhouden *irr.*, beteugelen; controleren. **checkmate,** *a.* schaakmat. **check-nut,** *n.* contramoer *n.*

cheek, *n.* wang *n.*; brutaliteit *n.* ¶ *v.t.* brutaliseren. **cheekbone,** *n.* jukbeen *n.n.* **cheeky,** *a.* brutaal.

cheer, *n.* opgeruimdheid *n.*, vrolijkheid *n.* onthaal *n.n.* *to be of good* ~, goedsmoeds zijn. ¶ *v.i.* hoera roepen *str.* *to* ~ *up,* vrolijker worden *str.* ¶ *v.t.* toejuichen. *to* ~ *up,* opvrolijken. **cheerful,** *a.,* ~**ly,** *adv.* opgewekt, opgeruimd, vrolijk. **cheerfulness,** *n.* opgeruimdheid *n.,* blijmoedigheid *n.* **cheeriness,** *n.* blijmoedigheid *n.* **cheerless,** *a.* ongezellig, somber, troosteloos. **cheery,** *a.,* ~**ily,** *adv.* opgeruimd.

cheese, *n.* kaas *n.* **cheesemonger,** *n.* kaaskoper *n.* **cheeseparing,** *a.* krenterig. ¶ *n.* kaaskorstje *n.n.* **cheese-scoop,** *n.* kaasboor *n.*

cheetah, *n.* (soort) luipaard *n.n.*

chemical, *a.* chemisch. ¶ *n.* ~*s,* chemicaliën *pl.n.*

chemise, *n.* vrouwenhemd *n.n.*

chemist, *n.* scheikundige *n.* (*researcher*); apotheker *n.* (*pharmacist*); ~'*s shop,* apotheek *n.* **chemistry,** *n.* scheikunde *n.*

cheque, *n.* cheque *n.* **cheque-book,** *n.* chequeboekje *n.n.*

chequer, *v.t.* in ruitjes *pl.n.n.* verdelen. **chequered,** *a.* veelbewogen.

cherish, *v.t.* liefhebben; koesteren.

cheroot, *n.* (manilla)sigaar *n.*

cherry, *n.* kers *n.* (*fruit*); kersehout *n.n.* (*wood*). ~ *brandy,* Kirsch *n.n.* **cherrystone,** *n.* kersepit *n.* **cherry-tree,** *n.* kerseboom *n.*

cherub, *n.* cherubijn *n.* **cherubic,** *a.* engelachtig.

chervil, *n.* kervel *n.*

chess, *n.* schaakspel *n.n.* *to play* ~, schaken; *a game of* ~, een spel *n.n.* schaak *n.n.* **chessboard,** *n.* schaakbord *n.n.* **chesspiece,** *n.* stuk *n.n.*

chest, *n.* kist *n.*; koffer *n.*, kas *n.*; borstkas *n.* ~ *of drawers,* latafel *n.*

chestnut, *n.* kastanje *n.*; kastanjeboom *n.*; kastanjebruin paard *n.n.*; ouwe mop *n.* (*joke*).

cheval-glass, *n.* staande spiegel *n.*

chevalier, *n.* ridder *n.*, ruiter *n.*

cheviot, *n.* cheviot *n.n.*

chew, *v.t.* kauwen; pruimen. *to* ~ *the cud,* herkauwen. **chewing gum,** *n.* kauwgom *n.n.*

chicane, *n.* chicane *n.* ¶ *v.i.* chicaneren. **chicanery,** *n.* chicanes *pl.n.*

chick, *n.* kuiken *n.n.* **chicken,** *n.* kip *n.* **chicken-hearted,** *a.* lafhartig. **chickenpox,** *n.* windpokken *pl.n.* **chick-pea,** *n.* keker *n.* **chickweed,** *n.* sterremuur *n.*

chicory, *n.* cichorei *n.*; witlof *n.n.*

chide, *v.t.* bekijven *str.*, beknorren.

chief, *n.* chef *n.*, hoofd *n.n.* ¶ *a.* voornaamste, eerste, hoofd . . . **chiefly,** *adv.* voornamelijk, hoofdzakelijk. **chieftain,** *n.* opperhoofd *n.n.*

chilblain, *n.* winter *n.* aan de handen; winter *n.* aan de voeten. *to suffer from* ~*s,* winterhanden *pl.n. or* wintervoeten *pl.n.* hebben.

child, *n.* kind *n.n.* **childbed,** *n.* kraambed *n.n.* **childbirth,** *n.* bevalling *n.* **childhood,** *n.* kindsheid *n.* **childish,** *a.,* ~**ly,** *adv.* kinderachtig. **childishness,** *n.* kinderachtigheid *n.* **childless,** *a.* kinderloos. **childlike,** *a.* kinderlijk. **children,** *pl. of* child.

chill, *a.* kil, koel. ¶ *n.* kilte *n.*; verkoudheid *n.* *to take off the* ~, de eerste kou eraf nemen *str.* ¶ *v.t.* koud maken; bevriezen *irr.*; temperen (*steel*). ~*ed meat,* bevroren vlees *n.n.* **chilliness,** *n.* kilheid *n.* **chilly,** *a.* kil; huiverig.

Chiltern Hundreds, *pl.N.* *to apply for the* ~ ~, verzoeken *irr.* als parlementslid ontslagen te worden; *to accept the* ~ ~, als parlementslid aftreden *str.*

chime, *n.* klokkenspel *n.n.,* klokkenmelodie *n.* ¶ *v.t.* luiden. ¶ *v.i.* harmoniëren. *to* ~ *in with,* instemmen met.

chimera, *n.* schrikbeeld *n.n.,* hersenschim *n.* **chimerical,** *a.,* ~**ly,** *adv.* hersenschimmig.

chimney, *n.* schoorsteen *n.*; lampeglas *n.n.* **chimney-pot,** *n.* schoorsteen(pot) *n.* **chimney sweep,** *n.* schoorsteenveger *n.*

chimpanzee, *n.* chimpansé *n.*

chin, *n.* kin *n.*

china, *n.* porselein *n.n.* ~ *clay,* porseleinaarde *n.* ¶ *a.* porseleinen. **China,** *N.* China *n.N.* **Chinese,** *a.* Chinees. ~ *lantern,* lampion *n.* ¶ *N.* Chinees *n.*

chine, *n.* ruggestuk *n.n.*

chink, *n.* spleet *n.,* reet *n.*; gerinkel *n.n.* ¶ *v.t.* rinkelen.

chintz, *n.* sits *n.n.*

chip, *n.* spaander *n.*; schilfer *n.,* splintertje *n.n.*; gebraden aardappelsnipper *n.* *he is a* ~ *of the old block,* hij heeft een aartje *n.n.* naar zijn vaartje. ¶ *v.t.* afkerven *str.*; afschilferen.

chipmunk, *n.* aardeekhoorntje *n.n.*

chipped, *a.* geschaard (*blade*); met stukjes eraf.

chiromancy, *n.* chiromantie *n.,* handwaarzeggerij *n.*

chiropodist, *n.* pedicure *n.,* likdoornsnijder *n.* **chiropody,** *n.* likdoornsnijden *n.n.*

chirp, *v.i.,* tsjilpen, sjirpen. **chirrup,** *v.i.* tsjilpen; kwelen.

chisel, *n.* beitel *n.* ¶ *v.t.* beitelen.

chit, *n.* briefje *n....,* kattebelletje *n.n.*; klein ding *n.n.*

chit-chat, *n.* gekeuvel *n.n.*

chitterlings, *pl.n.* kaantjes *pl.n.n.*

chivalrous, *a.* ridderlijk. **chivalry,** *n.* ridderschap *n.n.* (*historical*); ridderlijkheid *n.* (*behaviour*).

chive, *n.* bieslook *n.n.*
chlorate, *n.* chloraat *n.n.* **chloride,** *n.*
chloride *n.n.* ~ *of lime,* chloorkalk *n.;*
~ *of soda,* chloornatrium *n.n.* **chlorine,** *n.*
chloor *n.n.*
chloroform, *n.* chloroform *n.* ¶ *v.t.* chloro-
formiseren.
chlorophyll, *n.* chlorophyl *n.n.,* bladgroen *n.n.*
chlorosis, *n.* bleekzucht *n.*
chock, *n.* klos *n.,* blok *n.* ~ *full,* tjokvol.
chocolate, *n.* chocolade *n.*
choice, *n.* keus *n.* ¶ *a.,* ~ly, *adv.* uitgelezen.
choir, *n.* koor *n.n.* **choirboy,** *n.* koorknaap *n.*
choke, *v.t.* doen *irr.* stikken, verstikken;
verstoppen, opstoppen. *to* ~ *off,* afschrikken. ¶ *v.i.* stikken. ¶ *n.* smoorklep
n. **chokedamp,** *n.* mijngas *n.n.*
choker, *n.* stropdas *n.*
choler, *n.* gal *n.;* toorn *n.* **choleric,** *a.* driftig,
toornig.
cholera, *n.* cholera *n.*
choose, *v.t.* & *v.i.* kiezen *str.,* verkiezen *str.*
chop, *n.* kotelet *n.,* karbonade *n.;* kaak *n.*
¶ *v.t.* & *v.i.* hakken, kappen, kloven.
to ~ *up,* fijnhakken. **chopper,** *n.* hakmes
n.n. **chopping block,** *n.* hakblok *n.n.*
choppy, *a.* woelig.
chopstick, *n.* eetstokje *n.n.*
choral, *n.* koraal *n.*
chord, *n.* snaar *n.,* pees *n.;* akkoord *n.n.*
chorister, *n.* koorzanger *n.*
chorus, *n.* refrein *n.n.;* koor *n.n.* ~ *girl,*
danseresje *n.n.*
chough, *n.* kauw *n.*
chrism, *n.* chrisma *n.n.,* zalfolie *n.,* heilige
olie *n.*
Christ, *N.* Christus *N.*
christen, *v.t.* dopen; een naam geven *str.*
Christendom, *N.* Christenheid *N.* **christening,** *n.* doop *n.* **Christian,** *N.* Christen *N.*
¶ *a.* Christelijk, Christen . . . ~ *name,*
voornaam *n.* **Christianize,** *v.t.* kersteuen.
Christianity, *n.* Christendom *n.n.,* Christenheid *n.* **Christmas,** *N.* Kerstmis *N.* ¶ *a.*
Kerst . . . **Christmas-box,** *n.* nieuwjaarsfooi
n.
chromatic, *a.* chromatisch.
chrome, *n.,* **chromium,** *n.* chromium *n.n.*
chromolithography, *n.* chromolithografie *n.,*
kleurensteendruk *n.*
chronic, *a.* chronisch.
chronicle, *n.* kroniek *n.* ¶ *v.t.* boekstaven.
chronicler, *n.* kroniekschrijver *n.*
chronological, *a.,* ~ly, *adv.* chronologisch.
chronology, *n.* chronologie *n.,* tijdreken-
kunde *n.* **chronometer,** *n.* chronometer *n.*
chrysalis, *n.* pop *n.*
chrysanthemum, *n.* chrysant *n.*
chrysolite, *n.* chrysoliet *n.*
chub, *n.* kopvoorn *n.*
chubby, *a.* mollig.
chuck, *v.t.* aaien, strijken *str. to* ~ *away,*
wegsmijten *str.* ¶ *v.i.* klappen met de
tong, klokken.

chuckle, *v.i.* grinniken; inwendig lachen.
¶ *n.* half onderdrukt gelach *n.n.*
chum, *n.* kameraad *n.* ¶ *v.i. to* ~ *up with,*
maatjes worden *str.* met.
chump, *n.* blok *n.n.,* homp *n.;* dik eind *n.n.*
van lendenen *pl.n.*
chunk, *n.* brok *n.,* klomp *n.*
church, *n.* kerk *n.* **churching,** *n.* kerkgang *n.*
churchman, *n.* geestelijke *n.;* lid *n.n.* van
de Engelse staatskerk. **churchwarden,** *n.*
kerkmeester *n.,* kerkvoogd *n.* **churchy,** *a.*
kerks. **churchyard,** *n.* kerkhof *n.n.*
churl, *n.* boerenkinkel *n.* **churlish,** *a.,* ~ly,
adv. vlegelachtig. **churlishness,** *n.* vlegel-
achtigheid *n.*
churn, *n.* karn *n.* ¶ *v.t.* karnen; roeren.
chutney, *n.* Indische kruiderij *n.*
chyle, *n.* chijl *n.,* maagmelksap *n.n.*
chyme, *n.* maagbrij *n.*
cicada, *n.* cicade *n.,* (soort) krekel *n.*
cicatrice, *n.* lidteken *n.n.* **cicatrize,** *v.t.*
dichtgaan *irr.,* een lidteken *n.n.* vormen.
cider, *n.* appelwijn *n.*
cigar, *n.* sigaar *n.* **cigarette,** *n.* sigaret *n.*
cincture, *n.* gordel *n.*
cinder, *n.* sintel *n.,* slak *n.* **Cinderella,** *N.*
Assepoester *N.*
cinema, *n.* bioscoop *n.,* cinema *n.* **cinemato-
graph,** *n.* kinematograaf *n.*
cinerary, *a.* as . . .
cinnabar, *n.* cinnaber *n.n.;* vermiljoen
n.n.
cinnamon, *n.* kaneel *n.* or *n.n.*
Cinque, *num.* ~ *Ports,* de Vijf Havensteden
pl.n.
cipher, *n.* nul *n.;* onbetekenend iemand *n.n.;*
cijfer *n.n.;* cijferschrift *n.n.;* monogram *n.n.*
¶ *v.i.* cijferen, rekenen.
circle, *n.* cirkel *n.;* kring *n.* ¶ *v.i.* ronddraaien.
¶ *v.t.* omringen. **circlet,** *n.* cirkeltje *n.n.,*
band *n.*
circuit, *n.* omtrek *n.;* kringloop *n.;* rondgang
n.; rechtsgebied *n.n.;* stroomkring *n.*
short ~, kortsluiting *n.; out of* ~, uit-
geschakeld. **circuitous,** *a.* met een'omweg;
wijdlopig.
circular, *a.,* ~ly, *adv.* cirkelvormig; krings-
gewijs. ~ *letter,* circulaire *n.;* ~ *saw,*
cirkelzaag *n.;* ~ *staircase,* wenteltrap *n.;*
~ *ticket,* rondreisbiljet *n.n.* ¶ *n.* circulaire
n. **circulate,** *v.i.* circuleren, in omloop
zijn. ¶ *v.t.* laten *str.* circuleren, in omloop
brengen *irr.* **circulating,** *a.* ~ *decimal,*
repeterende breuk *n.;* ~ *library,* leen-
bibliotheek *n.* **circulation,** *n.* circulatie *n.,*
omloop *n.* ~ *of the blood,* bloedsomloop *n.*
circumcise, *v.t.* besnijden *str.* **circumcision,**
n. besnijdenis *n.*
circumference, *n.* omtrek *n.*
circumflex, *n.* circonflex *n.* ~ *accent,*
samentrekkingsteken *n.n.*
circumlocution, *n.* omschrijving *n,* **cir-
cumlocutory,** *a.* omschrijvend, omslachtig.
circumnavigate, *v.t.* omzeilen, omvaren *str.*

circumnavigation, *n.* omzeiling *n.*, omvaart *n.* circumnavigator, *n.* omzeiler *n.*
circumscribe, *v.t.* omschrijven *str.*; beperken. circumscription, *n.* omschrijving *n.*; beperking *n.*
circumspect, *a.*, ~ly, *adv.* omzichtig. circumspection, *n.* omzichtigheid *n.*
circumstance, *n.* omstandigheid *n.* circumstanced, *a.* geplaatst. circumstantial, *a.*, ~ly, *adv.* omstandig. ~ evidence, derivatief bewijs *n.n.*
circumvent, *v.t.* misleiden.
circus, *n.* circus *n.n.*; rond plein *n.n.*
cirrus, *n.* vederwolk *n.*
cisalpine, *a.* Cisalpijns.
Cistercian, *a.* Cistercienser.
cistern, *n.* regenbak *n.*, reservoir *n.n.*
citadel, *n.* citadel *n.*
citation, *n.* dagvaarding *n.*; aanhaling *n.* cite, *v.t.* dagvaarden; citeren, aanhalen.
citizen, *n.* burger *n.* citizenship, *n.* burgerschap *n.n.*; burgerrecht *n.n.*
citrate, *n.* citraat *n.n.* citric, *a.* ~ acid, citroenzuur *n.n.* citron, *n.* (grote) citroen *n.*
city, *n.* stad *n.*, grote stad *n.*
civet, *n.* civetkat *n.*
civic, *a.* burger . . ., stads . . .
civil, *a.*, ~ly, *adv.* beleefd; civiel, burger . . . ~ servant, ambtenaar *n.* bij het burgerlijk bestuur; ~ service, civiele dienst *n.* civilian, *n.* niet-militair *n.*, burger *n.* civility, *n.* beleefdheid *n.* civilization, *n.* beschaving *n.* civilize, *v.t.* beschaven.
clack, *v.i.* klappen, klapperen. ¶ *v.t.* klappen met. ¶ *n.* geklepper *n.n.*; geratel *n.n.*
clad, *a.* gekleed.
claim, *v.t.* aanspraak *n.* maken op, eisen, vorderen; beweren. ¶ *n.* vordering *n.*, eis *n.*, aanspraak *n.*; bewering *n.* to lay ~ to, aanspraak maken op. claimable, *a.* opeisbaar. claimant, *n.* eiser *n.*
clairvoyant, *n.* clairvoyant(e) *n.* ¶ *a.* clairvoyant(e), helderziend.
clam, *n.* (soort) mossel *n.*; gaapschelp *n.*
clamber, *v.i.* klauteren, klimmen *str.*
clammy, *a.* klef, klam.
clamorous, *a.* luidruchtig, rumoerig. clamour, *n.* luidruchtigheid *n.*, rumoer *n.n.*, misbaar *n.n.* ¶ *v.i.* roepen *str.* to ~ for, roepen *str.* om.
clamp, *n.* klamp *n.*, kram *n.* ¶ *v.t.* klampen.
clan, *n.* stam *n.*, geslacht *n.n.*
clandestine, *a.*, ~ly, *adv.* clandestien, heimelijk.
clang, *n.* schelle klank *n.*; gekletter *n.n.* ¶ *v.i.* luid klinken *str.* ¶ *v.t.* luid doen *irr.* klinken. clangour, *n.* geschetter *n.n.*, geschal *n.n.*
clank, *v.t.* rinkelen, kletteren. ¶ *n.* gerinkel *n.n.*, gekletter *n.n.*
clannish, *a.* kliekerig.
clap, *n.* klap *n.*, slag *n.* ¶ *v.i.* klappen. ¶ *v.t.* slaan *irr.* to ~ eyes on, zien *irr.*;

to ~ into gaol, in de gevangenis stoppen. clapper, *n.* klepel *n.*; ratel *n.*
claptrap, *n.* bombast *n.*, kletspraat *n.*
claret, *n.* Bordeau wijn *n.*
clarification, *n.* klaring *n.*; verduidelijking *n.* clarify, *v.t.* verduidelijken. ¶ *v.i.* helder worden *str.*
clarinet, *n.* klarinet *n.*
clarion, *n.* klaroen *n.*
clarity, *n.* helderheid *n.*, klaarheid *n.*
clash, *v.i.* botsen, stoten *str.*; rinkelen; in strijd zijn. to ~ with, in botsing *n.* komen *irr.* met, tegenstrijdig zijn. ¶ *n.* botsing *n.*; gekletter *n.n.*; conflict *n.n.*
clasp, *v.t.* omklemmen; vatten. ¶ *n.* knip *n.*, gesp *n.*; greep *n.* clasp-knife, *n.* knipmes *n.n.*
class, *n.* klasse *n.*; klas *n.* ¶ *v.t.* classificeren, rangschikken. classic, *a.* klassiek. ¶ *n.* the ~s, de klassieken. classical, *a.*, ~ly, *adv.* klassiek. classification, *n.* classificatie *n.* classify, *v.t.* classificeren.
clatter, *v.i.* klateren; kletteren, rammelen. ¶ *n.* geklater *n.n.*; gekletter *n.n.*; geratel *n.n.*
clause, *n.* clausule *n.*, artikel *n.n.*; bijzin *n.*, zin *n.*
claustral, *a.* kloosterachtig, klooster . . .
claustrophobia, *n.* claustrophobie *n.*
clavichord, *n.* clavecordium *n.n.*
clavicle, *n.* sleutelbeen *n.n.*
claw, *n.* klauw *n.*; klemhaak *n.*; poot *n.*, schaar *n.* ¶ *v.t.* krabben, krauwen.
clay, *n.* klei *n.*, leem *n.n.* ¶ *a.* aarden. clayey, *a.* kleiachtig.
clean, *a.*, ~ly, *adv.* schoon, zuiver, zindelijk. ¶ *v.t.* schoonmaken. cleaner, *n.* schoonmaakster *n.* cleanliness, *n.* zindelijkheid *n.* cleanly, *a.* zindelijk. cleanse, *v.t.* zuiveren.
clear, *a.*, ~ly, *adv.* klaar, helder, duidelijk; netto; vrij, onbelast, onbezwaard. ¶ *v.t.* opklaren, ophelderen (*difficulty*); inklaren, uitklaren (*of ship or cargo*); niet raken (*obstacle*); van blaam zuiveren (*reputation*); lichten (*pillar-box*); vereffenen (*account*). ¶ *v.i.* opklaren (*weather*); helder worden. to ~ away, opruimen; to ~ off, weggaan *irr.*; to ~ out, verwijderen; to ~ up, ophelderen. clearance, *n.* opklaring *n.*; uitverkoop *n.*, opruiming *n.* clear-headed, *a.* helder, met helder hoofd *n.n.* clearing, *n.* open ruimte *n.* (*in forest*); vereffening *n.*, verrekening *n.* (*account*). clearing-house, *n.* verrekenkantoor *n.n.* clearness, *n.* klaarheid *n.*, helderheid *n.*, duidelijkheid *n.* clear-sighted, *a.* helderziend.
cleat, *n.* klamp *n.*, wig *n.* ¶ *v.t.* (met een klos *n.*) bevestigen.
cleavage, *n.* kloof *n.*, afscheuring *n.* cleave, *v.t.* kloven, splijten *str.* ¶ *v.i.* to ~ to, aankleven. cleaver, *n.* hakbijl *n.*
clef, *n.* (muziek)sleutel *n.*
cleft, *n.* kloof *n.*, spleet *n.*
clematis, *n.* clematis *n.*

clemency, *n.* goedertierenheid *n.*, genade *n.*
clement, *a.* goedertieren, genadig.
clench, *v.t.* ballen, klemmen.
clerestory, *n.* rij *n.* kerkvensters *n.n.*
clergy, *n.* geestelijkheid *n.*, de geestelijken *pl.n.* clergyman, *n.* geestelijke *n.*, dominee *n.* cleric, *a.* geestelijk. ¶ *n.* geestelijke *n.*
clerical, *a.* geestelijk, clericaal.
clerk, *n.* klerk *n.*; secretaris *n.*; griffier *n.* clerkship, *n.* klerkenbaantje *n.n.*
clever, *a.*, ~ly, *adv.* slim, knap; handig. cleverness, *n.* slimheid *n.*; handigheid *n.*
clew, *n.* kluwen *n.n.*
cliché, *n.* cliché *n.n.*
click, *v.i.* tikken; klappen. ¶ *v.t.* doen *irr.* tikken, (doen *irr.*) klappen. ¶ *n.* tik *n.*
client, *n.* klant *n.*; cliënt *n.*
cliff, *n.* steile rots(wand) *n.*; klip *n.*
climacteric, *a.* climacterisch. ¶ *n.* kritieke levensjaar *n.n.*
climate, *n.* klimaat *n.n.*   climatic, *a.* klimaats . . .
climax, *n.* climax, *n.*, toppunt *n.n.*
climb, *v.i.* klimmen *str.*; stijgen *str.* to ~ down, een toontje lager zingen *str.* ¶ *v.t.* beklimmen *str.*; klimmen *str.* op. climbable, *a.* beklimbaar. climber, *n.* klimmer *n.*; klimplant *n.* climbing-power, *n.* stijgvermogen *n.n.* climbing-rate, *n.* stijgsnelheid *n.*
clime, *n.* klimaat *n.n.*
clinch, *v.t.* klinken *str.*; beklinken *str.* *that* ~es the matter, dat maakt het definitief. ¶ *n.* klinknagel *n.*; greep *n.* clincher, *n.* klinknagel *n.*; dooddoener *n.*
cling, *v.i.* hangen *str.*, kleven. *to* ~ *to*, zich houden *irr.* aan, zich vastklemmen aan.
clinic, *n.* kliniek *n.*   clinic(al), *a.*, ~ally, *adv.* klinisch.
clink, *v.t.* klinken *str.*, doen *irr.* klinken. ¶ *n.* klinken *n.n.*   clinker, *n.* klinker *n.*; hamerslag *n.*
clip, *n.* haak *n.*; knijper *n.*, houder *n.*, klem *n.*; slag *n.* ¶ *v.t.* knijpen *str.*; (be)snoeien; kortwieken; afbijten *str.*; scheren *str.*; (aaneen)hechten; een klap geven *str.* clipper, *n.* klipper *n.*; scheerder *n.* ~*s*, tondeuse *n.*, wolschaar *n.*; schaartje *n.n.* clippings, *pl.n.* uitknipsels *pl.* *n.* afsnijdsel *n.n.*
clique, *n.* kliek *n.*, coterie *n.*
cloak, *n.* mantel *n.*; dekmantel *n.* (*fig.*). ¶ *v.t.* bemantelen, omhullen. cloakroom, *n.* vestiaire *n.*, garderobe *n.*; bagagedepôt *n.n.*
clock, *n.* klok *n.*   *two o'* ~, twee uur *n.n.* clockwise, *adv.* met de wijzers mee.   counter ~, tegen de wijzers in. clockwork, *n.* uurwerk *n.*, slagwerk *n.n.*
clod, *n.* kluit *n.*, klont *n.*; lomperd *n.* clodhopper, *n.* kinkel *n.*, pummel *n.*
clog, *n.* blok *n.n.*; klomp *n.* ¶ *v.t.* belemmeren, doen *irr.* steken, verstoppen.
cloister, *n.* open kloostergang *n.*, wandelgang

n.; klooster *n.n.*   ¶ *v.t.* kloosteren, afzonderen.
close, *v.t.* sluiten *str.*; eindigen, besluiten *str.*; handgemeen worden *str.*   *to* ~ *down*, stopzetten, sluiten *str.* ¶ *v.i.* zich sluiten *str.*, dichtgaan *irr.*   *to* ~ *in*, de gelederen sluiten; vallen *str.* (*night*). ¶ *a.* gesloten; besloten; bedompt, drukkend; achterhoudend; gierig; nauwsluitend; getrouw. *at* ~ *quarters*, van zeer nabij. ¶ *adv.* dicht bijeen. ¶ *n.* einde *n.n.*, besluit *n.n.* close by, *adv.* dichtbij. closely, *adv.* dicht (op elkaar); van nabij. closeness, *n.* geslotenheid *n.*; bedomptheid *n.*; achterhoudendheid *n.*; gierigheid *n.*
closet, *n.* kabinet *n.n.*; privaat *n.n.*; studeerkamer *n.*   ¶ *v.t.* *to be* ~*ed together*, een geheim onderhoud *n.n.* hebben.
closure, *n.* sluiting *n.*; besluit *n.n.*, slot *n.n.*
clot, *n.* klonter *n.*, klodder *n.* ¶ *v.i.* klonteren, stollen.   ~*ted cream*, dikke room *n.*
cloth, *n.* doek *n.n.*; laken *n.n.*; stof *n.* *the* ~, de geestelijkheid.   clothe, *v.t.* kleden; bekleden.   clothes, *pl.n.* kleren *pl.n.n.*, kleding *n.*   clothes-basket, *n.* vuillinnenmand *n.*   clothes-brush, *n.* kleerborstel *n.*   clothes-horse, *n.* droogrek *n.n.*   clothes-line. *n.* drooglijn *n.*   clothes-peg, *n.* knijpertje *n.n.*   clothes-press, *n.* kleerkast *n.*   clothes-prop, *n.* stut *n.n.* onder drooglijn *n.*   clothier, *n.* lakenfabrikant *n.*; lakenkoper *n.*   clothing, *n.* kleding *n.*   cloth-worker, *n.* lakenwerker *n.*
cloud, *n.* wolk *n.*; grote menigte *n.*   *to be under a* ~, in de druk zitten; uit de gratie zijn; *every* ~ *has a silver lining*, geen ongeluk zo groot of er is een geluk bij. ¶ *v.t.* bewolken, verduisteren. ¶ *v.i.* *to* ~ *over*, betrekken *str.* cloudless, *a.* onbewolkt. cloudy, *a.*, ~ily, *adv.* bewolkt; somber, duister.
clout, *n.* vaatdoek *n.*, lap *n.*
clove, *n.* kruidnagel *n.*   *oil of* ~*s*, kruidnagelolie *n.*
cloven, *a.* gespleten.
clover, *n.* klaver *n.*   *to be in* ~, een goed leventje leiden.
clown, *n.* clown *n.*, hansworst *n.* clownish, *a.*, ~ly, *adv.* clownachtig.
cloy, *v.t.* overladen.
club, *n.* knots *n.*, kalf *n.*; club *n.*; klaver *n.* ¶ *v.t.* knuppelen. ¶ *v.i.* *to* ~ *together*, gezamenlijk de kosten dragen *str.* clubfoot, *n.* horrelvoet *n.*   club-law, *n.* recht *n.n.* van de sterkste.
cluck, *v.i.* klokken.
clue, *n.* kluwen *n.n.*; leiddraad *n.*
clump, *n.* brok *n.*; groep *n.*; slag *n.* ¶ *v.i.* klossen.
clumsiness, *n.* onhandigheid *n.*, lompheid *n.* clumsy, *a.*, ~ly, *adv.* onhandig, lomp.
cluster, *n.* tros *n.*, bos *n.* ¶ *v.i.* in trossen groeien; zich verzamelen.
clutch, *v.t.* grijpen *str.* ¶ *v.i.* zich vastklampen

aan. ¶ *n.* greep *n.*; klauw *n.*; haak *n.*; broedsel *n.n.*

clutter, *v.i. to ~ up,* met rommel bedekken. ¶ *n.* warboel.

coach, *n.* rijtuig *n.n.*, koets *n.*; spoorwagen *n.*, personenwagen *n.*; repetitor *n.* ¶ *v.t.* lessen geven *str.*, africhten. **coach-box,** *n.* bok *n.* **coach-house,** *n.* koetshuis *n.n.* **coachman,** *n.* koetsier *n.*

coadjutor, *n.* coadjutor *n.*; ambtgenoot *n.*

coagulate, *v.i.* stollen, stremmen. **coagulation,** *n.* stolling *n.*, stremming *n.*

coal, *n.* steenkool *n.*, kolen *pl.n. (pit-coal)*; kool *n. (live coal).* ¶ *v.i.* kolen innemen *str.* **coal-dust,** *n.* gruiskool *n.*

coalesce, *v.i.* zich verenigen, samensmelten *str.* **coalescence,** *n.* samengroeiing *n.*, samensmelting *n.*

coal-hole, *n.* kolenhok *n.n.*; stortgat *n.n.*

coalition, *n.* coalitie *n.*

coalman, *n.* kolendrager *n.* **coalmine,** *n.*, **coalpit,** *n.* (steen)kolenmijn *n.*

coarse, *a.*, ~ly, *adv.* grof, ruw. **coarseness,** *n.* grofheid *n.*, ruwheid *n.*

coast, *n.* kust *n.* ¶ *v.i.* langs de kust varen *str.*; vrijwielen. **coaster,** *n.* kustvaarder *n.* **coastguard,** *n.* kustwacht *n.* **coasting trade,** *n.* kustvaart *n.*

coat, *n.* jas *n.*; mantel *n.*; vacht *n.*, pels *n.*; laag *n.* ~ *of arms,* wapenschild *n.n.*; ~ *of mail,* maliënkolder *n.* ¶ *v.t.* bekleden, bedekken. **coating,** *n.* bekleding *n.*, laag *n.*

coax, *v.t.* overhalen, bepraten; vleien.

cob, *n.* (maïs)kolf *n. (maize);* zware hit *n. (horse);* (soort) hazelnoot *n. (fruit).*

cobalt, *n.* kobalt *n.n.*

cobble, *n.* keisteen *n.* ¶ *v.t.* bekeien *(road);* lappen *(shoe).* **cobbler,** *n.* schoenlapper *n.*

cobweb, *n.* spinneweb *n.n.*, spinrag *n.n.*

cocaine, *n.* cocaïne *n.*

cochineal, *n.* cochenille *n.*

cock, *n.* haan *n. (bird, part of firearm);* mannetje *n.n. (male bird);* kraan *n. a ~ and bull story,* een ongerijmd verhaal. ¶ *v.t.* spannen *irr.*; opheffen *str.*, opzetten.

cockade, *n.* kokarde *n.*

cock-a-doodle-doo, *excl.* kukeleku! **cock-a-hoop,** *a.* vol uitgelaten vreugde *n.*

cockatoo, *n.* kaketoe *n.*

cockatrice, *n.* basilisk *n.*

cockchafer, *n.* meikever *n.*

cockcrow, *n.* hanegekraai *n.n. at ~,* bij het eerste ochtendgloren.

cocked, *a.* ~ *hat,* steek *n.*

cocker, *n.* ~ *spaniel,* (soort) patrijshond *n.*

cockerel, *n.* jonge haan *n.*

cock-eyed, *a.* loens; scheef, verkeerd. **cockhorse,** *n.* stokpaardje *n.*

cockle, *n.* haantje *n.n.*, (soort) mossel *n.*

Cockney, *N.* echte Londenaar *N.* ¶ *a.* plat Londens.

cockpit, *n.* stuurstoel *n.*

cockroach, *n.* kakkerlak *n.*

cocksure, *a.* al te zeker, absoluut zeker.

cocktail, *n.* cocktail *n.*

cocoa, *n.* cacao *n.*

coconut, *n.* kokosnoot *n.* ~ *tree,* kokospalm *n.*

cocoon, *n.* pop *n.*, cocon *n.*

cod, *n.* kabeljauw *n.* *dried ~,* stokvis *n.*; ~ *-liver oil,* levertraan *n.*

coddle, *v.t.* vertroetelen.

code, *n.* code *n.*; wetboek *n.n.* ¶ *v.t.* in code overbrengen *irr.*

codger, *n.* slimmerik *n.*

codicil, *n.* codicil *n.n.*, aanhangsel *n.n.*

codification, *n.* codificatie *n.* **codify,** *v.t.* codificeren.

co-education, *n.* coëducatie *n.*

coefficient, *n.* coëfficiënt *n.*

coerce, *v.t.* dwingen *str.* **coercion,** *n.* dwang *n.* **coercive,** *a.* dwang . . .

coeval, *a.* gelijktijdig. ¶ *n.* tijdgenoot *n.*

coexist, *v.i.* gelijktijdig bestaan *irr.* **coexistence,** *n.* gelijktijdig bestaan *n.n.*

co-executor, *n.* medeëxecuteur *n.*

coffee, *n.* koffie *n. black ~,* koffie zonder melk. **coffee-bean,** *n.* koffieboon *n.* **coffee-grounds,** *n.* koffiedik *n.n.* **coffee-pot,** *n.* koffiepot *n.* **coffee-room,** *n.* gelagkamer *n.*

coffer, *n.* koffer *n.*; caisson *n.*, waterdichte kist *n.* **coffer-dam,** *n.* kistdam *n.*

coffin, *n.* doodkist *n.* ¶ *v.t.* kisten.

cog, *n.* tand *n.*, kam *n.*

cogency, *n.* overtuigende kracht *n.* **cogent,** *a.*, ~ly, *adv.* overtuigend, klemmend.

cogitate, *v.i.* denken *irr.*, peinzen. ¶ *v.t.* overpeizen. **cogitation,** *n.* overpeinzing *n.*

cognate, *a.* verwant.

cognition, *n.* kennis *n.* **cognizance,** *n.* kennis *n.*, kennisneming *n.*; competentie *n.* **cognizant,** *a.* kennis dragend.

cognomen, *n.* familienaam *n.*; bijnaam *n.*

cog-wheel, *n.* tandrad *n.n.*

cohabit, *v.i.* samenwonen. **cohabitation,** *n.* samenwoning *n.*

co-heir, *n.* medeërfgenaam *n.* **co-heiress,** *n.* medeërfgename *n.*

cohere, *v.i.* samenhangen *str.* **coherence,** *n.* samenhang *n.* **coherent,** *a.* samenhangend.

cohesion, *n.* samenhang *n.*, cohesie *n.* **cohesive,** *a.* samenhangend.

cohort, *n.* cohorte *n.*

coif, *n.* muts *n.*, kap *n.*

coil, *n.* spiraal *n.*; kronkeling *n.*; spoel *n.* ¶ *v.t.* winden *str.*, kronkelen.

coin, *n.* munt *n.*, geldstuk *n.n.* ¶ *v.t.* munten; verzinnen *str.* **coinage,** *n.* muntstelsel *n.n.*

coincide, *v.i.* samenvallen *str.*; overeenstemmen. **coincidence,** *n.* samenloop *n.* van omstandigheden, toeval *n.n.* **coincident,** *a.* samenvallend. **coincidental,** *a.* toevallig.

coiner, *n.* (valse) munter *n.*

coir, *n.* kokosvezel *n.*

coition, *n.* copulatie *n.*

coke, *n.* cokes *n.*

colander, *n.* vergiet *n.n.*

cold, *a.,* ~**ly,** *adv.* koud. ~ *comfort,* schrale troost *n.;* ~*blooded,* koelbloedig; ~*hearted,* ongevoelig; ~ *cream,* huidzalf *n.; in* ~ *storage,* in de koelkamer; *to* ~*shoulder,* negeren. ¶ *n.* verkoudheid *n.,* kou *n. to catch (a)* ~, kou vatten. **coldish,** *a.* koudachtig. **coldness,** *n.* kou(de) *n.*

cole-, *prefix,* kool-. **coleseed,** *n.* koolzaad *n.n.*

colic, *n.* koliek *n.,* buikpijn *n.*

collaborate, *v.i.* samenwerken. **collaboration,** *n.* samenwerking *n.* **collaborator,** *n.* medewerker *n.*

collapse, *v.i.* ineenstorten, invallen *str.*

collar, *n.* kraag *n. (of coat);* boord *n.n. (of shirt);* halsband *n. (of dog).* ~ *bone,* *n.* sleutelbeen *n.n.*

collate, *v.t.* vergelijken *str.*

collateral, *a.* evenwijdig; zijdelings. ¶ *n.* zijdelingse bloedverwant *n.*

collation, *n.* vergelijking *n.;* lichte maaltijd *n.;* begeving *n.*

colleague, *n.* collega *n.*

collect, *v.t.* verzamelen; innen; ophalen, afhalen; zich verzamelen. ¶ *v.r. to* ~ *oneself,* zich zelf meester worden *irr.* ¶ *n.* collecte *n.,* kort gebed *n.n.* **collected,** *a.* bedaard, zich zelf meester. **collection,** *n.* verzameling *n.;* collecte *n.;* (bus)lichting *n.* **collective,** *a.,* ~**ly,** *adv.* collectief, gezamenlijk. ¶ *n.* collectieve *n.* **collector,** *n.* verzamelaar *n.;* controleur *n;*

college, *n.* (afdeling *n.* van) universiteit *n.;* school *n.* **collegiate,** *a.* van een "college".

collide, *v.i.* in botsing *n.* komen *irr.*

collie, *n.* (Schotse) herdershond *n.*

collier, *n.* (kolen)mijnwerker *n.;* kolenschip *n.n.* **colliery,** *n.* kolenmijn *n.*

collision, *n.* botsing *n.;* aanvaring *n.*

collocation, *n.* plaatsing *n.,* rangschikking *n.*

colloid, *n.* colloïde *n.* **colloidal,** *a.* colloïdaal.

collop, *n.* lapje (vlees) *n.n.*

colloquial, *a.* tot de omgangstaal behorend, gemeenzaam. **colloquialism,** *n.* gemeenzame zegswijze *n.*

colloquy, *n.* samenspraak *n.*

collusion, *n.* geheime verstandhouding *n.* **collusive,** *a.,* ~**ly,** *adv.* heimelijk.

colocynth, *n.* kolokwint *n.,* bitterappel *n.*

Cologne, *N.* Keulen *n.N. eau de* ~, eau de Cologne.

colon, *n.* dikke darm *n.*

colonel, *n.* kolonel *n.* **colonelcy,** *n.* kolonelschap *n.n.*

colonial, *a.* koloniaal. **colonist,** *n.* kolonist *n.* **colonization,** *n.* kolonisatie *n.* **colonize,** *v.t.* koloniseren.

colonnade, *n.* zuilenrij *n.*

colony, *n.* kolonie *n.*

colophon, *n.* colophon *n.n.,* slottitel *n.*

colossal, *a.* kolossaal. **colossus,** *n.* kolos *n.;* gevaarte *n.n.*

colour, *n.* kleur *n.;* verf *n.* ~*s,* vlag *n.,* vaandel *n.n.; to change* ~, van kleur verschieten *str.;" to give* ~ *to,* een schijn

van waarheid geven *str.* aan; *to show one's true* ~, zich in z'n ware gedaante tonen; *off* ~, niet al te lekker. ¶ *v.t.* kleuren, verven. ¶ *v.i.* een kleur krijgen *str.* **colourable,** *a.* aannemelijk. **colouration,** *n.* kleur *n.* **colour-blind,** *a.* kleurenblind. **colourblindness,** *n.* kleurenblindheid *n.* **colouring,** *n.* kleur *n.,* kleursel *n.n.* **colourless,** *a.* kleurloos.

colt, *n.* (hengst)veulen *n.n.* **coltsfoot,** *n.* klein hoefblad *n.n.*

columbine, *n.* akelei *n.*

column, *n.* zuil *n.,* pilaar *n.,* kolom *n.;* kolonne *n.* (men). **columnar,** *a.* zuilvormig.

coma, *n.* slaapziekte *n.;* lethargie *n.* **comatose,** *a.* slaapzuchtig; schijndood.

comb, *n.* kam *n.;* (honig)raat *n.* ¶ *v.t.* kammen.

combat, *n.* strijd *n.,* gevecht *n.n.* ¶ *v.t.* bestrijden *str.* **combatant,** *n.* strijder *n.* **combative,** *a.* strijdlustig.

comber, *n.* kammer *n.;* lange krulgolf *n.*

combination, *n.* combinatie *n.,* verbinding *n.,* bijeenvoeging *n.* ~*s,* hemdbroek *n.* **combine,** *v.t.* combineren; verbinden *str.;* doen *irr.* samengaan. ¶ *v.i.* zich combineren.

combings, *pl.n.* uitkamsel *n.n.*

combustibility, *n.* brandbaarheid *n.* **combustible,** *a.* brandbaar; ontvlambaar. ¶ *n.* brandstof *n.* **combustion,** *n.* verbranding *n.*

come, *v.i.* komen *irr. to* ~ *it strong,* overdrijven *str.;* ~ *what may,* wat er ook gebeuren moge; *to* ~ *about,* gebeuren; *to* ~ *across,* toevallig aantreffen *str.; to* ~ *along,* meegaan *irr.; to* ~ *by,* voorbijkomen *irr.; to* ~ *down,* naar beneden komen *irr.,* vallen *str.; to* ~ *for,* komen *irr.* halen, afhalen; *to* ~ *forth,* te voorschijn komen *irr.; to* ~ *forward,* zich (aan)melden; *to* ~ *in,* binnenkomen *irr.; to* ~ *in for,* op tijd komen *irr.* voor; *to* ~ *off,* (er) afkomen *irr.,* (er) afraken; *to* ~ *on,* aankomen *irr.;* opschieten *str.;* gedijen; *to* ~ *out,* verschijnen *str.; to* ~ *round,* bijkomen *irr.,* bijdraaien; *to* ~ *to,* (weer) bijkomen *irr.;* komen *irr.* op; *to* ~ *under,* vallen *str.* onder; *to* ~ *up,* opkomen *irr.;* ter sprake komen *irr.*

comedian, *n.* komediant *n.* **comedy,** *n.* komedie *n.,* blijspel *n.n.*

comeliness, *n.* bevalligheid *n.* **comely,** *a.* bevallig.

comer, *n.* bezoeker *n. all* ~*s,* iedereen.

comestibles, *pl.n.* eetwaren *pl.n.*

comet, *n.* komeet *n.*

comfort, *n.* troost *n.,* vertroosting *n.;* gemak *n.n.,* gerief *n.n.* ¶ *v.t.* troosten, opbeuren. **comfortable,** *a.,* ~**ably,** *adv.* gerieflijk; behaaglijk. **comforter,** *n.* trooster *n.;* fopspeen *n. (baby's).* **comfortless,** *a.* troosteloos; ongerieflijk.

comic, *n.* komiek *n.* **comic(al),** *a.,* ~**ally,** *adv.* komiek, komisch, grappig.

coming, *n.* komst *n.* ¶ *a.* komend. **coming-of-age,** *n.* meerderjarigheid *n.*
comma, *n.* komma *n.*
command, *v.t.* bevelen *str.*, gebieden *str.*; commanderen; bestrijken *str.* (*strategically*); halen (*of prices*). ¶ *n.* bevel *n.n.* *to have at one's* ~, beschikken over; *to be in* ~ *of,* het bevel voeren over. **commandant,** *n.* commandant *n.* **commandeer,** *v.t.* opvorderen, requireren. **commander,** *n.* bevelhebber *n.*; commandant *n.*; commandeur *n.* ~*-in-chief,* opperbevelhebber *n.* **commanding,** *a.* indrukwekkend. **commandment,** *n.* gebod *n.n.*
commemorate, *v.t.* herdenken *irr.* **commemoration,** *n.* herdenking *n.* *in* ~ *of,* ter herdenking van. **commemorative,** *a.* gedenk . . ., herdenkings . . .
commence, *v.t. & v.i.* aanvangen *str.* **commencement,** *n.* aanvang *n.*
commend, *v.t.* aanbevelen *str.*; prijzen *str.* **commendable,** *a.*, ~**ably,** *adv.* aanbevelenswaardig, prijzenswaardig. **commendation,** *n.* aanbeveling *n.*; lof *n.* **commendatory,** *a.* aanbevelend ; lovend.
commensurable, *a.* (onderling) meetbaar. **commensurate,** *a.* evenredig, gelijkmatig.
comment, *n.* commentaar *n.n.*, opmerking *n.*; critiek *n.* ¶ *v.i.* (een) opmerking maken. *to* ~ *on,* commentaar leveren op. **commentary,** *n.* commentaar *n.n.* **commentator,** *n.* commentator *n.*
commerce, *n.* handel *n.*; verkeer *n.n.*, omgang *n.* **commercial,** *a.* handels . . ., commercieel.
comminatory, *a.* dreigend.
commingle, *v.t.* vermengen.
commiserate, *v.t.* *to* ~ *with,* beklagen, medelijden hebben met. **commiseration,** *n.* medelijden *n.n.*
commissariat, *n.* intendance *n.*; commissariaat *n.n.* **commissary,** *n.* commissaris *n.*
commission, *n.* opdracht *n.*; commissie *n.*, commissieloon *n.n.*, provisie *n.*; (officiers) aanstelling *n.*; commissie *n.* *to put into* ~, in dienst *n.* stellen. ¶ *v.t.* bestellen; opdracht geven *str.* voor; aanstellen.
commissionaire, *n.* portier *n.*; kruier *n.*
commissioner, *n.* hoofdcommissaris *n.*; gevolmachtigde *n.*
commit, *v.t.* begaan *irr.*, plegen. *to* ~ *to,* toevertrouwen aan; *to* ~ *oneself,* zich compromitteren; zich verbinden *str.*; *to* ~ *for trial,* naar een rechtbank verwijzen *str.* **commitment,** *n.* bevel *n.n.* tot inhechtenisneming *n.*; verplichting *n.* **committal,** *n.* toewijzing *n.*; begaan *n.n.*, bedrijven *n.n.*
committee, *n.* comité *n.n.*
commode, *n.* latafel *n.*
commodious, *a.*, ~**ly,** *adv.* gerieflijk.
commodity, *n.* handelsartikel *n.n.* **commodities,** waren *n.*, goederen *n.n.*

commodore, *n.* bevelhebber *n.* van een eskader *n.n.*
common, *a.*, ~**ly,** *adv.* gezamelijk, gemeen, gemeenschappelijk; algemeen, alledaags; ordinair. ~ *law,* gewoonterecht *n.n.*; ~ *room,* gemeenschappelijk vertrek *n.n.*; ~ *sense,* gezond verstand *n.n.* ¶ *n.* gemeenteweide *n.*, meent *n.* *House of C*~*s,* Lagerhuis *n.N.* **commonalty,** *n.* burgerij *n.*, gemeenschap *n.* **commoner,** *n.* burger *n.*; meentgenoot *n.* **commonplace,** *n.* gemeenplaats *n.* ¶ *a.* gewoon. **commonwealth,** *n.* gemenebest *n.n.*, staatslichaam *n.n.*; republiek *n.*
commotion, *n.* beroering *n.*, opschudding *n.*, commotie *n.*
communal, *a.* gemeenschappelijk, communaal. **commune,** *n.* gemeente *n.* ¶ *v.i.* overleggen *irr.* **communicable,** *a.* mededeelbaar. **communicant,** *n.* communicant *n.* **communicate,** *v.t.* me(d)edelen. ¶ *v.i.* *to* ~ *with,* in verbinding *n.* staan *irr.* met. **communication,** *n.* me(d)edeling *n.*; verbinding *n.*, verbindingsweg *n.* **communicative,** *a.* mededeelzaam. **communion,** *n.* gemeenschap *n.*; communie *n.* **communism,** *n.* communisme *n.n.* **communist,** *n.* communist *n.* **communistic,** *a.* communitisch. **community,** *n.* gemeenschap *n.*
commutability, *n.* verwisselbaarheid *n.* **commutable,** *a.* verwisselbaar. **commutation,** *n.* verwisseling *n.*; omschakeling *n.*; commutatie *n.*
commute, *v.t.* veranderen.
compact, *n.* verdrag *n.n.*, overeenkomst *n.*; tabletje *n.n.* ¶ *a.*, ~**ly,** *adv.* dicht, opeengedrongen. **compactness,** *n.* dichtheid *n.*
companion, *n.* (met)gezel *n.*, kameraad *n.*, makker *n.*; gezellin *n.* (*female*); kampanje *n.* (*on ship*). **companionable,** *a.*, ~**ably,** *adv.* gezellig. **companionship,** *n.* kameraadschap *n.* **company,** *n.* maatschappij *n.*, compagnie *n.*; gezelschap *n.n.*; visite *n.* *ship's* ~, bemanning *n.*
comparable, *a.*, ~**bly,** *adv.* vergelijkbaar. **comparative,** *a.*, ~**ly,** *adv.* vergelijkend. ¶ *n.* vergrotende trap *n.* **compare,** *v.t.* vergelijken *str.* ¶ *n.* vergelijking *n.* **comparison,** *n.* vergelijking *n.* *beyond* ~, niet te vergelijken; *by* ~ *with,* in vergelijking met.
compartment, *n.* afdeling *n.*, vak *n.n.*; coupé *n.*
compass, *v.t.* omvatten, insluiten *str.*; bereiken; beramen. ¶ *n.* omvang *n.*, omtrek *n.*; bestek *n.n.*; kompas *n.n.* ~*es,* passer *n.*; ~ *card,* kompasroos *n.*
compassion, *n.* erbarmen *n.n.*, medelijden *n.n.* **compassionate,** *a.* meewarig, medelijdend.
compatibility, *n.* verenigbaarheid *n.* **compatible,** *a.*, ~**bly,** *adv.* verenigbaar. ~ *with,* strokend met.

compatriot, *n.* landgenoot *n.*
compeer, *n.* gelijke *n.*; kornuit *n.*
compel, *v.t.* dwingen *str.*, verplichten.
compendious, *a.* beknopt. **compendium,** *n.* (beknopt) handboek *n.n.*
compensate, *v.t.* vergoeden, schadeloos stellen, compenseren. **compensation,** *n.* vergoeding *n.*, schadeloosstelling *n.*, compensatie *n.* **compensatory,** *a.* compenserend.
compete, *v.i.* wedijveren; concurreren. *to ~ for,* mededingen *str.* naar.
competence, *n.*, **competency,** *n.* bevoegdheid *n.*; bekwaamheid *n.* **competent,** *a.* bevoegd; bekwaam, competent.
competition, *n.* concurrentie *n.*; wedstrijd *n.*; competitie *n.* **competitive,** *a.* concurrerend; vergelijkend *(exam.).* **competitor,** *n.* mededinger *n.*, concurrent *n.*
compilation, *n.* compilatie *n.* **compile,** *v.t.* verzamelen, compileren. **compiler,** *n.* compilator *n.*
complacence, *n.*, **complacency,** *n.* voldoening *n.* (wel)behagen *n.n.*; inschikkelijkheid *n.* **complacent,** *a.* (zelf)voldaan, met zichzelf ingenomen; inschikkelijk.
complain, *v.i.* klagen. *to ~ of,* klagen over. **complaint,** *n.* klacht *n.*; kwaal *n. (illness).*
complaisance, *n.* inschikkelijkheid *n.*, hoffelijkheid *n.* **complaisant,** *a.* inschikkelijk; hoffelijk.
complement, *v.t.* aanvullen, voltallig maken. ¶ *n.* aanvulling *n.*; getalssterkte *n.* **complementary,** *a.* aanvullend, complementair.
complete, *a.*, ~*ly, adv.* volledig, volkomen, kompleet; voltallig. ¶ *v.t.* afmaken, voltooien. **completeness,** *n.* volledigheid *n.* **completion,** *n.* voltooiing *n.*; aanvulling *n.*
complex, *a.* samengesteld; ingewikkeld. ¶ *n.* samenstel *n.n.*, complex *n.n.*
complexion, *n.* gelaatskleur *n.*, teint *n.n.*; voorkomen *n.n.*, aanzien *n.n.*
complexity, *n.* samengesteldheid *n.*, ingewikkeldheid *n.*
compliance, *n.* inschikkelijkheid *n.*, meegaandheid *n.*, toegevendheid *n.* **compliant,** *a.*, ~*ly, adv.* inschikkelijk, meegaand, toegevend.
complicate, *v.t.* ingewikkeld maken; verwikkelen. ¶ *a.* ingewikkeld. **complicated,** *a.* ingewikkeld. **complication,** *n.* verwikkeling *n.*, complicatie *n.*
complicity, *n.* medeplichtigheid *n. to act in ~,* medeplichtig zijn.
compliment, *n.* kompliment *n.n.*; plichtpleging *n.* ¶ *v.t.* komplimenteren, een komplimentje maken. *to ~ on,* gelukwensen met. **complimentary,** *a.* complimenteus. ~ *copy,* presentexemplaar *n.n.*; ~ *ticket,* vrijkaart *n.*
compline, *n.* completen *pl.n.*
comply, *v.i.* zich schikken. *to ~ with,*

nakomen *irr.,* naleven, voldoen *irr.* aan, zich voegen naar.
component, *a.* samenstellend. ~ *part,* onderdeel *n.n.* ¶ *n.* bestanddeel *n.n.*
comport, *v.r. to ~ oneself,* zich gedragen *str.*
compose, *v.t.* samenstellen; componeren; zetten; tot bedaren brengen *irr.* ¶ *v.r. to ~ oneself,* tot bedaren komen *irr.* **composed,** *a.*, ~*bly, adv.* bedaard, kalm. **composer,** *n.* componist *n.* **composing-stick,** *n.* zethaak *n.* **composite,** *a.* samengesteld, gemengd. **composition,** *n.* samenstelling *n.*, compositie *n.*; opstel *n.n.* **compositor,** *n.* letterzetter *n.*
compost, *n.* compost *n.*, mengmest *n.*
composure, *n.* bezadigdheid *n.*, kalmte *n.*
compound, *a.* samengesteld. ¶ *n.* samenstelling *n.*; mengseltje *n.n.*; erf *n.n.*
comprehend, *v.t.* begrijpen *str.*; omvatten. **comprehensible,** *a.*, ~*bly, adv.* begrijpelijk. **comprehension,** *n.* begrip *n.n.*; verstand *n.n.*; omvang *n.* **comprehensive,** *a.*, ~*ly, adv.* veelomvattend; uitgebreid.
compress, *v.t.* samenpersen, samendrukken. ¶ *n.* kompres *n.n.*, natte omslag *n.* **compressibility,** *n.* samendrukbaarheid *n.* **compressible,** *n.* samendrukbaar. **compression,** *n.* samendrukking *n.* samenpersing *n.*
comprise, *v.t.* omvatten, bevatten.
compromise, *n.* compromis *n.n.*, minnelijke schikking *n.* ¶ *v.i.* tot een minnelijke schikking komen *irr.,* in der minne schikken; schipperen; in opspraak brengen *irr.*
compulsion, *n.* dwang *n.* **compulsory,** *a.* ~*ily, adv.* gedwongen, verplicht.
compunction, *n.* wroeging *n.*, spijt *n.*, gewetensknaging *n.*
computable, *a.* berekenbaar. **computation,** *n.* berekening *n.*, raming *n.* **compute,** *v.t.* berekenen, ramen.
comrade, *n.* kameraad *n.*, makker *n.* **comradeship,** *n.* kameraadschap *n.*
con, *v.t.* nauwkeurig nagaan *irr.*, onderzoeken *irr.* ¶ *adv. pro and ~,* voor en tegen.
concatenate, *v.t.* aaneenschakelen. **concatenation,** *n.* aaneenschakeling *n.*
concave, *a.* hol, concaaf. **concavity,** *n.* holte *n.*, holheid *n.*
conceal, *v.t.* verbergen *str.*; verzwijgen *str.* geheim houden *irr.* **concealable,** *a.* verbergbaar. **concealment,** *n.* verborgenheid *n.*; heimelijkheid *n.*
concede, *v.t.* toegeven *str.*, inwilligen.
conceit, *n.* verwaandheid *n.*, verbeelding *n.*; inval *n.*, grilligheid *n.* **conceited,** *a.* verwaand.
conceivability, *n.* denkbaarheid *n.* **conceivable,** *a.*, ~*bly, adv.* denkbaar, begrijpelijk. **conceive,** *v.t.* zich voorstellen *(idea),* begrijpen *str.*; ontvangen *str.*, zwanger worden *str. (pregnancy),* opvatten *(plan).*

concentrate, *v.t.* samentrekken *str.*; concentreren. **concentration,** *n.* samentrekking *n.*; concentratie *n.*; dichtheid *n.*
concentre, *v.i.* in één middelpunt samenkomen *irr.* **concentric,** *a.* concentrisch.
concept, *n.* begrip *n.n.* **conception,** *n.* voorstelling *n.*, begrip *n.n.*, opvatting *n.*; ontvangenis *n.*
concern, *v.t.* betreffen *str.*, aangaan *irr.*; verontrusten. **to ~ oneself with,** zich inlaten *str.* met. ¶ *n.* aangelegenheid *n.*, zaak *n.*; onderneming *n.*, concern *n.n.*; bezorgdheid *n.* **concerned,** *a.*, **~ly,** *adv.* bezorgd. **~ in,** betrokken bij. **concerning,** *prep.* betreffende. **concernment,** *n.* deelneming *n.*
concert, *n.* concert *n.n.*; overeenstemming *n.*, harmonie *n.* **in ~ with,** in overleg met. **concerted,** *a.* **~ action,** gezamenlijk optreden *n.n.*
concertina, *n.* (soort) harmonica *n.*
concession, *n.* concessie *n.*; toestemming *n.*
conch, *n.* oorschelp *n.*, zeeschelp *n.*
conciliate, *v.t.* verzoenen; voor zich innemen *str.* **conciliation,** *n.* verzoening *n.* **conciliator,** *n.* bemiddelaar *n.* **conciliatory,** *a.* verzoenend; bemiddelend.
concise, *a.*, **~ly,** *adv.* beknopt; bondig. **conciseness,** *n.* beknoptheid *n.*; bondigheid *n.*
conclave, *n.* conclave *n.* **in secret ~,** bij geheime zitting *n.*
conclude, *v.t. & v.i.* besluiten *str.*, beslissen; eindigen, sluiten *str.* **conclusion,** *n.* besluit *n.n.*; gevolgtrekking *n.*; einde *n.n.* **conclusive,** *a.*, **~ly,** *adv.* afdoende, beslissend.
concoct, *v.t.* bereiden; beramen, smeden (*fig.*). **concoction,** *n.* brouwsel *n.n.*
concomitant, *a.*, **~ly,** *adv.* begeleidend, vergezellend. ¶ *n.* bijkomende omstandigheid *n.*
concord, *n.* overeenstemming *n.*, eendracht *n.*; harmonie *n.* **concordance,** *n.* overeenstemming *n.*; concordantie *n.*, index *n.* **concordant,** *a.* overeenstemmend.
concordat, *n.* concordaat *n.n.*
concourse, *n.* samenloop *n.*; toeloop *n.*, menigte *n.*
concrete, *n.* beton *n.n.* ¶ *a.*, **~ly,** *adv.* concreet; van beton, betonnen. ¶ *v.t.* betonneren. **concreteness,** *n.* concreetheid *n.*
concretion, *n.* samengroeiing *n.*; verharding *n.*
concubine, *n.* bijzit *n.*; bijwijf *n.n.*
concupiscence, *n.* zondige begeerte *n.*, vleselijke lust *n.* **concupiscent,** *a.* begerend.
concur, *v.i.* samenvallen *str.*; overeenstemmen; het ééns zijn. **concurrence,** *n.* samentreffen *n.n.*; medewerking *n.* **concurrent,** *a.*, **~ly,** *adv.* gelijktijdig; overeenkomend, overeenstemmend.
concuss, *v.t.* schokken. **concussion,** *n.* schok *n.*; hersenschudding *n.*

condemn, *v.t.* veroordelen; afkeuren; onbewoonbaar verklaren. **condemnable,** *a.* verwerpelijk, laakbaar. **condemnation,** *n.* veroordeling *n.*; afkeuring *n.* **condemnatory,** *a.* veroordelend, afkeurend.
condensable, *a.* verdichtbaar. **condensation,** *n.* condensatie *n.*, samenpersing *n.* **condense,** *v.t.* condenseren; concentreren. ¶ *v.i.* zich condenseren. **condenser,** *n.* condensator *n.*
condescend, *v.i.* zich verwaardigen. **condescending,** *a.*, **~ly,** *adv.* genadig, neerbuigend. **condescension,** *n.* genadigheid *n.*
condign, *a.* verdiend.
condiment, *n.* kruiderij *n.*
condition, *n.* toestand *n.*, staat *n.*; voorwaarde *n.* ¶ *v.t.* bedingen *str.*, bepalen; afhankelijk maken. **conditional,** *a.*, **~ly,** *adv.* voorwaardelijk. **~ on,** afhankelijk van. ¶ *n.* voorwaardelijke wijs *n.* **conditioned,** *a.* ... geaard, ... gezind. **~ reflex,**
condolatory, *a.* condoleantie . . . **condole,** *v.i.* **to ~ with a person on** . . ., iemand condoleren met . . . **condolence,** *n.* condoleantie *n.*, rouwbeklag *n.n.*
condonation, *n.* vergiffenis *n.*, kwijtschelding *n.* **condone,** *v.t.* vergeven *str.*, kwijtschelden *str.*
condor, *n.* condor *n.*, Zuid-Amerikaanse gier *n.*
conduce, *v.t.* bijdragen *str.*, strekken. **conducive,** *a.* bevorderlijk. **~ to,** strekkend tot.
conduct, *v.t.* leiden, voeren; dirigeren. ¶ *n.* gedrag *n.n.*, houding *n.* **conduction,** *n.* geleiding *n.* **conductive,** *a.* geleidend. **conductivity,** *n.* geleidingsvermogen *n.n.* **conductor,** *n.* bestuurder *n.*; dirigent *n.*; conducteur *n.*; geleider *n.*; (bliksem)afleider *n.* **conductress,** *n.* leidster *n.*; bestuurster *n.*; conductrice *n.*
conduit, *n.* leiding *n.*, kanaal *n.n.*
cone, *n.* kegel *n.*; denappel *n.*
confabulate, *v.i.* vertrouwelijk praten. **confabulation,** *n.* vertrouwelijk gesprek *n.n.*
confection, *n.* suikergoed *n.n.*; bereiding *n.* **confectioner,** *n.* suikerbakker *n.*; banketbakker *n.*; handelaar *n.* in suikergoed *n.n.* **confectionery,** *n.* suikerbakkerij *n.*; suikergoed *n.n.*
confederacy, *n.* verbond *n.n.* **confederate,** *n.* bondgenoot *n.* ¶ *a.* verbonden. ¶ *v.i.* een verbond aangaan *irr.* **confederation,** *n.* bondgenootschap *n.*; statenbond *n.*
confer, *v.i.* beraadslagen *str.* ¶ *v.t.* verlenen. **to ~ upon,** verlenen aan. **conference,** *n.* conferentie *n.*; bespreking *n.*
confess, *v.i.* bekennen, biechten. ¶ *v.t.* (op)biechten. **confessedly,** *adv.* ontegenzeggelijk; volgens eigen bekentenis *n.* **confession,** *n.* biecht *n.*; bekentenis *n.*; (geloofs)belijdenis *n.* **confessional,** *n.* biechtstoel *n.*

confidant, *n.* vertrouweling *n,* **confide,** *v.t.*
to ~ to, toevertrouwen aan. ¶ *v.i. to ~ in,*
vertrouwen op. **confidence,** *n.* vertrouwen
n.n.; **confident,** *a.,* ~ly, *adv.* vol. vertrouwen, *n.n.;* zeker, overtuigd. **confidential,**
a., ~ly, *adv.* vertrouwelijk.
:onfiguration, *n.* gedaante *n.;* (planeten)stand
n.
confine, *n.* grens *n.;* grensgebied *n.n.* ¶ *v.t.*
beperken; opsluiten *str.* ¶ *v.i. to be ~d,*
in de kraam zijn. ¶ *v.r. to ~ oneself to,*
zich beperken tot. **confinement,** *n.*
opsluiting *n.;* bevalling *n.*
confirm, *v.t.* bevestigen; bekrachtigen;
vormen (*Roman Catholic*); als lidmaat *n.*
aannemen *str.* (*Protestant*). **confirmation,**
n. bevestiging *n.;* bekrachtiging *n.;*
vormsel *n.n.* (*Roman Catholic*); aanneming
n., belijdenis *n.* (*Protestant*). **confirmatory,**
a. bevestigend, bekrachtigend. **confirmed,**
a. verstokt, onverbeterlijk.
confiscate, *v.t.* beslag *n.n.* leggen op, verbeurd
verklaren, aanhalen. **confiscation,** *n.*
verbeurdverklaring *n.*
conflagration, *n.* grote brand *n.*
conflict, *n.* strijd *n.,* geschil *n.n.,* conflict *n.n.*
¶ *v.i.* in tegenspraak *n.* zijn; in botsing *n.*
komen *irr.* **conflicting,** *a.* tegenstrijdig.
confluence, *n.* samenvloeiing *n.* **confluent,** *n.*
zijrivier *n.,* bijrivier *n.* ¶ *a.* samen-
vloeiend.
conform, *v.i.* zich richten, zich schikken.
to ~ with, zich voegen naar. ¶ *v.t.* overeenkomstig maken. **conformable,** *a.,* ~bly,
adv. overeenkomstig; meegaand. **con-
formation,** *n.* overeenstemming *n.;* inrichting *n.,* aard *n.,* bouw *n.* **conformity,**
n. overeenstemming *n.* *in ~ with,*
overeenkomstig.
confound, *v.t.* verwarren, in de war brengen
irr., beschaamd maken; vernietigen.
confounded, *a.,* ~ly, *adv.* verduiveld,
vervloekt.
confront, *v.t.* confronteren; staan *irr.*
tegenover. **confrontation,** *n.* confrontatie
n.
confuse, *v.t.* verwarren, verbijsteren. **confused,**
a., ~ly, *adv.* verward; verlegen. **confusion,**
n. verwarring *n.;* warboel *n.;* verlegenheid
n.
confutable, *a.* weerlegbaar. **confutation,** *n.*
weerlegging *n.* **confute,** *v.t.* weerleggen.
congé, *n.* congé *n.n.*
congeal, *v.i.* stollen; stremmen; bevriezen *irr.*
¶ *v.t.* doen *irr.* stollen; doen *irr.* bevriezen.
congealment, *n.* stollen *n.n.;* bevriezing
n.
congenial, *a.* sympathiek, geestverwant.
congeniality, *n.* sympathie *n.,* geestver-
wantschap *n.*
congenital, *a.* aangeboren.
congeries, *n.* opeenstapeling *n.,* samenloping
n.
conger (eel), *n.* zeepaling *n.*

congest, *v.t.* ophopen, congestie *n.* veroorzaken. **congested,** *a.* overvol. **congestion,**
n. ophoping *n.,* congestie *n.*
conglomerate, *v.t.* samenvoegen, opéénhopen,
conglomereren. ¶ *a.* opééngehoopt, samen-
gepakt. ¶ *n.* conglomeraat *n.n.,* opeenhoping *n.* **conglomeration,** *n.* opéénhoping
n.
conglutinate, *v.t.* samenkleven. **conglutina-
tion,** *n.* samenkleving *n.*
congratulate, *v.t.* & *v.i.* gelukwensen,
feliciteren. **congratulation,** *n.* gelukwens *n.*
congratulatory, *a.* felicitatie . . .
congregate, *v.i.* bijeenkomen *irr.* ¶ *v.t.*
bijeenbrengen *irr.* **congregation,** *n.*
gemeente *n.,* congregatie *n.*
congress, *n.* congres *n.n.;* parlement *n.n.*
Trade Union C~, Vakverbond *n.n.*
congruence, *n.* congruentie *n.* **congruent,** *a.*
congruent.
congruity, *n.* overeenkomst *n.,* overeenstemming *n.* **congruous,** *a.,* ~ly, *adv.*
overeenkomstig; consequent.
conic(al), *a.,* ~ally, *adv.* kegelvormig,
conisch. *~ section,* kegelsnede *n.* **conics,**
pl.n. leer *n.* van de kegelsneden.
conifer, *n.* conifeer *n.,* naaldboom *n.*
conjectural, *a.* vermoedelijk, conjecturaal.
conjecture, *n.* gissing *n.,* conjectuur *n.*
¶ *v.t.* gissen.
conjoin, *v.t.* samenvoegen, verbinden *str.*
conjoint, *a.* gezamenlijk; mede . . . **con-
jointly,** *adv.* in vereniging met, gemeenschappelijk.
conjugal, *a.,* ~ly, *adv.* echtelijk, huwelijks . . .
conjugate, *v.t.* vervoegen, conjugeren. **conjugation,** *n.* vervoeging *n.,* conjugatie
n.
conjunction, *n.* verbinding *n.;* samenwerking
n.; voegwoord *n.n.*
conjunctiva, *n.* bindvlies *n.n.*
conjunctive, *n.* aanvoegende wijs *n.* ¶ *a.,*
~ly, *adv.* verbindend.
conjuncture, *n.* samenloop *n.* (van omstandigheden); crisis *n.*
conjuration, *n.* bezwering *n.,* toverspreuk *n.*
conjure, *v.t.* bezweren *str.;* smeken.
to ~ up, bezweren *str.* oproepen *str.*
¶ *v.i.* goochelen, toveren. **conjurer,** *n.*
goochelaar *n.*
connect, *v.t.* verbinden *str.,* aanéénsluiten *str.*
in verbinding brengen *irr.;* koppelen.
¶ *v.i.* in verbinding staan *irr.* **connection,**
n. verbinding *n.;* verband *n.n.;* aansluiting *n.;* connectie *n.*
conning tower, *n.* commandotoren *n.*
connivance, *n.* oogluikende toelating *n.*
connive, *v.i. to ~ at,* oogluikend toelaten
str.
connoisseur, *n.* (kunst)kenner *n.*
connotation, *n.* (bij)betekenis *n.* **connote,**
v.t. betekenen, in zich sluiten *str.*
connubial, *a.* echtelijk, huwelijks . . .
conquer, *v.t.* veroveren onderwerpen *str.*

¶ v.i. een verovering n. behalen; overwinnen str. **conquerable,** a. overwinnelijk. **conqueror,** n. veroveraar n.
conquest, n. verovering n.; overwinning n.
consanguinity, n. bloedverwantschap n.
conscience, n. geweten n.n.; bewustheid n. in (all) ~, redelijkerwijs; voorwaar; for ~' sake, om des gewetens wille. **consciencestricken,** a. gekweld door het geweten. **conscientious,** a., ~ly, adv. nauwgezet; gewetens . . . **conscientiousness,** n. nauwgezetheid n.
conscious, a., ~ly, adv. bewust, gewaar; bij kennis. to be ~ of, zich bewust zijn van. **consciousness,** n. bewustzijn n.n.
conscript, n. dienstplichtige n., militien n., loteling n. **conscription,** n. dienstplicht n.
consecrate, v.t. wijden, heiligen, consacreren. **consecration,** n. wijding n., heiliging n., consacratie n.
consecutive, a., ~ly, adv. opeenvolgend, achtereenvolgend.
consensus, n. overeenstemming n.; algemeen gevoelen n.n.
consent, v.t. toestemmen; berusten. ¶ n. toestemming n., inwilliging n. silence gives ~, die zwijgt stemt toe.
consequence, n. gevolg n.n.; gevolgtrekking n.; belang n.n. in ~, dientengevolge; in ~ of, ten gevolge van, bijgevolg; of no ~, van geen belang. **consequent,** a., ~ly, adv. consequent. ~ on, voortvloeiend uit. **consequential,** a. consequent, daaruit volgend.
conservancy, n. raad n. van toezicht n.n.
conservation, n. behoud n.n., bewaring n. **conservatism,** n. conservatisme n.n. **conservative,** a. conservatief. ¶ n. conservatief n. **conservator,** n. conservator n., bewaarder n. **conservatory,** n. serre n., broeikas n.; conservatoire n.n. **conserve,** v.t. conserveren.
consider, v.t. overwegen str., rekening n. houden irr. met; ontzien irr. **considerable,** a., ~bly, adv. aanzienlijk, belangrijk. **considerate,** a., ~ly, adv. attent, zorgzaam. **consideration,** n. overweging n.; beschouwing n.; achting n.; vergoeding n. to take into ~, in aanmerking n. nemen str.; in ~ of, met het oog op. **considering,** adv. aangezien.
consign, v.t. toewijzen str.; overdragen str.; consigneren. **consignee,** n. geconsigneerde n., geadresseerde n. **consignor,** n. afzender n. **consignment,** n. zending n., consignatie n.
consist, v.i. to ~ in, berusten op; to ~ of, bestaan irr. uit. **consistence,** n., **consistency,** n. consistentie n., dichtheid n., samenhang n. **consistent,** a., ~ly, adv. samenhangend, consistent, consequent.
consistory, n. consistorie n., kerkeraad n.
consolable. a. troostbaar. **consolation,** n.

troost n. ~ prize, poedelprijs n. **consolatory,** a. troostend, troost . . . **console,** v.t. troosten.
consolidate, v.t. versterken, hechter maken; consolideren. ¶ v.i. hard worden str. **consolidation,** n. versterking n.; vast worden n.n.; consolidering n.
consols, pl.n. Engelse Werkelijke Schuld n., Engelse geconsolideerde staatschuld n.
consonance, n. gelijkluidendheid n., harmonie n. **consonant,** a. gelijkluidend; overeenstemmend. ¶ n. medeklinker n.
consort, v.i. to ~ with, omgaan met. ¶ n. gemaal n.; gemalin n.; vergezellend schip n.n.
conspicuous, a., ~ly, adv. in het oog lopend; opzichtig; treffend.
conspiracy, n. samenzwering n., complot n.n.
conspirator, n. samenzweerder n. **conspire,** v.i. samenzweren str., samenspannen irr. ¶ v.t. beramen.
constable, n. politieagent n. **constabulary,** n. politiemacht n.
constancy, n. standvastigheid n.; bestendigheid n. **constant,** a., ~ly, adv. standvastig; bestendig; vast; voortdurend, aanhoudend. ¶ n. constante n.
constellation, n. sterrenbeeld n.n., gesternte n.n.
consternated, a. to be ~, ontsteld zijn. **consternation,** n. ontsteltenis n.
constipate, v.t. constiperen. **constipation,** n. constipatie n., hardlijvigheid n.
constituency, n. kiesdistrict n.
constituent, a. samenstellend; kies . . . ~ part, bestanddeel n.n. ¶ n. kiezer n.
constitute, v.t. uitmaken, vormen, samenstellen. ¶ v.r. to ~ oneself, zich opwerpen str. als. **constitution,** n. samenstelling n., vorming n.; (lichaams)gestel n.n.; grondwet n., constitutie n. **constitutional,** a., ~ly, adv. natuurlijk, aangeboren; grondwettelijk, grondwettig, constitutioneel. ¶ n. gezondheidswandeling n.
constrain, v.t. bedwingen str.; dwingen str.; nopen, noodzaken. **constrained,** a., ~ly, adv. gedwongen, onnatuurlijk. **constraint,** n. dwang; gedwongenheid n.
constrict, v.t. samentrekken str. **constriction,** n. samentrekking n. **constrictive,** a. samentrekkend. **constrictor,** n. sluitspier n.
construct, v.t. bouwen, oprichten; construeren. **construction,** n. bouw n., samenstelling n. aanleg n.; zinsbouw n.; verklaring n., uitlegging n. **constructive,** a., ~ly, adv. opbouwend, constructief.
construe, v.t. uitleggen, verklaren; mondeling vertalen.
consuetude, n. gewoonte n., gebruik n.n.
consul, n. consul n. **consular,** a. consulair. **consulate,** n. consulaat n.n.
consult, v.t. raadplegen, consulteren. ¶ v.i. beraadslagen. **consultant,** n. consultant n.; consulterend geneesheer n. **consultation,** n.

raadpleging *n.*, beraadslaging *n.*; consult *n.n.* **consultative,** *a.* raadgevend.

consumable, *a.* verteerbaar. **consume,** *v.t.* verteren; vernietigen. **consumer,** *n.* verbruiker *n.*, afnemer *n.*, consument *n.*

consummate, *a.* volkomen, doortrapt. ¶ *v.t.* voltrekken, vervullen. **consummation,** *n.* voltrekking *n.*

consumption, *n.* verbruik *n.n.*, consumptie *n.*; tering *n.* **consumptive,** *a.* teringachtig. ¶ *n.* teringlijder *n.*

contact, *n.* aanraking *n.*, contact *n.n.* *to come into* ~ *with,* voeling verkrijgen met. ¶ *v.t.* contact maken met.

contagion, *n.* besmetting *n.*, aansteking *n.* **contagious,** *a.* besmettelijk, aanstekelijk. **contagiousness,** *n.* besmettelijkheid *n.*, aanstekelijkheid *n.*

contain, *v.t.* bevatten, omvatten, inhouden *irr.*, behelzen; bedwingen *str.*, beheersen. *to* ~ *oneself,* zich beheersen. **container,** *n.* blik *n.n.*, bus *n.*, doos *n.*, vat *n.n.*, zakje *n.n.*

contaminate, *v.t.* besmetten; bezoedelen. **contaminated,** *a.* bedorven. **contamination,** *n.* besmetting *n.*; bederf *n.n.*

contango. *n.* contango *n.n.*, prolongatie-premie *n.*

contemn, *v.t.* verachten.

contemplate, *v.t.* beschouwen, overpeinzen; aanschouwen; van plan zijn. ¶ *v.i.* peinzen. **contemp.ation,** *n.* beschouwing *n.*; overpeinzing *n.* **contemplative,** *a.*, ~ly, *adv.* bespiegelend, contemplatief.

contemporaneous, *a.* gelijktijdig; even oud. **contemporary,** *a.*, ~ily, *adv.* gelijktijdig. ¶ *n.* tijdgenoot *n.*

contempt, *n.* verachting *n.*, minachting *n.* ~ *of court,* belediging van het hof. **contemptible,** *a.*, ~bly, *adv.* verachtelijk. **contemptuous,** *a.*, ~ly, *adv.* minachtend. ~ *of,* met minachting voor.

contend, *v.t.* beweren; betwisten. ¶ *v.i.* strijden *str.*, worstelen.

content, *a.* tevreden, voldaan. ¶ *n.* tevreden-heid *n.*, genoegen *n.n.*; inhoud *n.* ¶ *v.t.* tevreden stellen. ¶ *v.r.* *to* ~ *oneself,* zich tevreden stellen. **contented,** *a.* tevreden. **contentedness,** *n.* tevredenheid *n.*

contention, *n.* strijd *n.*, twist *n.*; bewering *n.* **contentious,** *a.*, ~ly, *adv.* twistziek.

contentment, *n.* tevredenheid *n.*

contents, *pl.n.* inhoud *n.*

contest, *n.* wedstrijd *n.*; strijd *n.* ¶ *v.t.* betwisten, bestrijden *str.* **contestable,** *a.* strijdig, betwistbaar.

context, *n.* samenhang *n.*

contiguity, *n.* nabijheid *n.*; aanraking *n.* **contiguous,** *a.*, ~ly, *adv.* aangrenzend; belendend.

continence, *n.* zelfbeheersing *n.*; kuisheid *n.* **continent,** *a.*, ~ly, *adv.* matig; kuis. ¶ *n.* werelddeel *n.n.*; vasteland *n.n.* *the C*~,

het vasteland van Europa. **continental,** *a.* continentaal.

contingency, *n.* toevalligheid *n.*, onvoorziene omstandigheid *n.* **contingent,** *a.* toevallig, eventueel. ¶ *n.* contingent *n.n.*

continual. *a.*, ~ly, *adv.* voortdurend, onophoudelijk. **continuance,** *n.* voort-during *n.*; bestendiging *n.* **continuation,** *n.* voortzetting *n.*; prolongatie *n.*; vervolg *n.n.* **continue,** *v.t.* voortzetten, vervolgen; prolongeren. *to be* ~*d,* wordt vervolgd. **continuity,** *n.* verband *n.n.*, samenhang *n.*; continuïteit *n.* **continuous,** *a.*, ~ly, *adv.* aanhoudend, onafgebroken.

contort, *v.t.* verwringen *str.*, verdraaien. **contortion,** *n.* verwringing *n.*, verdraaiing *n.* **contortionist,** *n.* slangenmens *n.n.*

contour, *n.* omtrek *n.*, contour *n.n.*

contra, *prep.* tegen. ¶ *n.* creditzijde *n.*

contraband, *n.* contrabande *n.*, smokkelwaar *n.*

contract, *n.* contract *n.n.*, overeenkomst *n.* ¶ *v.t.* samentrekken *str.*; inkrimpen *str.*; contracteren, een contract sluiten *str. or* maken *or* aangaan *irr.*; vatten, oplopen *str.* ¶ *v.i.* zich samentrekken *str.*, inkrimpen *str.* **contraction,** *n.* samentrekking *n.* **contractor,** *n.* aannemer *n.*; sluitspier *n.* **contractual,** *a.* contractueel, bij contract *n.n.*

contradict, *v.t.* tegenspreken, in tegenspraak *n.* zijn met. **contradiction,** *n.* tegenspraak *n.*; tegenstrijdigheid *n.* **contradictoriness,** *n.* tegenstrijdigheid *n.*; zucht *n.* tot tegenspreken *n.n.* **contradictory,** *a.*, ~ily, *adv.* tegenstrijdig; strijdig.

contradistinction, *n.* tegenstelling *n.* **contra-distinguish,** *v.t.* door tegenstelling *n.* onderscheiden.

contralto, *n.* tweede sopraan *n.*

contraption, *n.* toestel *n.n.*, uitvindsel *n.n.*

contrapuntal, *a.* van contrapunt *n.n.*, in contrapunt *n.n.*

contrariety, *n.* tegenstrijdigheid *n.*; onver-enigbaarheid *n.* **contrarily,** *adv.* op tegenovergestelde wijze; dwars. **contrari-ness,** *n.* dwarsheid *n.* **contrary,** *a.* tegen-gesteld; strijdig; dwars. ~ *to,* in strijd met. ¶ *adv.* tegen. ¶ *n.* tegenovergestelde *n.n.*, tegendeel *n.n.* *on the* ~, integendeel; *to hear to the* ~, tegenbericht *n.n.* krijgen *str.*

contrast, *n.* tegenstelling *n.*, contrast *n.n.* ¶ *v.t.* stellen tegenover. ¶ *v.i.* een tegen-stelling *n.* vormen. *to* ~ *with,* afsteken *str.* bij.

contravene, *v.t.* overtreden *str.*, inbreuk maken op. **contravention,** *n.* overtreding *n.*, inbreuk *n.*

contribute, *v.t.* bijdragen *str.* ¶ *v.i.* me(d)e-werken. **contribution,** *n.* bijdrage *n.* **contributive,** *a.* bijdragend. **contributor,** *n.* bijdrager *n.*, medewerker *n.* **contributory,** *a.* bijdragend; bevorderlijk.

contrite, *a.*, ~ly, *adv.* berouwvol. boetvaardig. **contrition**, *n.* diep berouw *n.n.*, boetvaardigheid *n.*

contrivance, *n.* uitvindsel *n.n.*, apparaat *n.n.*; bedenksel *n.n.* **contrive**, *v.t.* bedenken *irr.*, overleggen; het weten klaar te spelen. **contriver**, *n.* intrigant *n.*

control, *v.t.* toezicht *n.n.*, contrôle *n.*; bestuur *n.n.* *to be in* ~ *of*, het toezicht voeren over, beheersen; *to have something in* ~, iets meester zijn; *out of* ~, niet te besturen, stuurloos. ¶ *v.t.* controleren; in bedwang *n.n.* houden, beheersen. **controllable**, *a.* te controleren. **controller**, *n.* verificateur *n.*; controleur *n.*; chef *n.*

controversial, *a.* polemisch, betwist. **controversy**, *n.* dispuut *n.n.*, geschil *n.n.*, redetwist *n.* **controvert**, *v.t.* betwisten. **controvertible**, *a.* betwistbaar.

contumacious, *a.*, ~ly, *adv.* weerspannig, weerbarstig. **contumacy**, *n.* weerbarstigheid *n.*

contumelious, *a.*, ~ly, *adv.* honend, schimpend, verachtend. **contumely**, *n.* smaad *n.*, hoon *n.*

contusion, *n.* kneuzing *n.*

conundrum, *n.* woordraadsel *n.n.*

convalescence, *n.* herstel *n.n.*, genezing *n.*, beterschap *n.* **convalescent**, *a.* herstellend.

convene, *v.t.* samenroepen *str.*, bijeenroepen *str.*

convenience, *n.* gemak *n.n.*, gerieflijkheid *n.*; gelegen tijd *n.* *at your* ~, als het U gelegen valt; *at your earliest* ~, zodra het U gelegen valt. **convenient**, *a.*, ~ly, *adv.* geschikt, gelegen; gemakkelijk.

convent, *n.* (vrouwen)klooster *n.n.*

conventicle, *n.* geheime godsdienstoefening *n.*; bidstond *n.*; bedehuis *n.n.*

convention, *n.* samenkomst *n.*, conventie *n.*; verdrag *n.n.*; gebruik *n.n.*, conventie *n.* **conventional**, *a.* overeengekomen; gebruikelijk. **conventionalism**, *n.* conventionalisme *n.n.* **conventionality**, *n.* gebruikelijkheid *n.*

conventual, *a.* klooster . . .

converge, *v.t.* in een punt *n.n.* samenkomen *irr.*, convergeren. **convergence**, *n.* convergentie *n.* **convergent**, *a.* convergerend.

conversant, *a.* vertrouwd. ~ *in*, bedreven in.

conversation, *n.* gesprek *n.n.*; omgang *n.* **conversational**, *a.* conversatie . . .; spraakzaam. **converse**, *v.i.* converseren, zich onderhouden *irr.* ¶ *a.*, ~ly, *adv.* omgekeerd. ¶ *n.* omgekeerde *n.n.*, tegenstelde *n.n.*

conversion, *n.* bekering *n.*; omzetting *n.*, verandering *n.*; conversie *n.* **convert**, *v.t.* bekeren; omzetten; converteren. ¶ *n.* bekeerling *n.*; bekeerlinge *n.* (*woman*). **convertibility**, *n.* verwisselbaarheid *n.*, converteerbaarheid *n.* **convertible**, *a.* veranderbaar; converteerbaar.

convex, *a.* convex, bol. **convexity**, *n.* bol(rond)heid *n.*

convey, *v.t.* overbrengen *irr.*, overdragen *str.*: vervoeren, verschepen; uitdrukken. **conveyance**, *n.* vervoermiddel *n.n.*; (acte van) overdracht *n.* **conveyancer**, *n.* (soort) notaris *n.* **conveyer**, *n.* overbrenger *n.* ~ *belt*, lopende band *n.*

convict, *v.t.* veroordelen, schuldig verklaren. ¶ *n.* dwangarbeider *n.* **conviction**, *n.* overtuiging *n.*; veroordeling *n.*

convince, *v.t.* overtuigen. **convincing**, *a.*, ~ly, *adv.* overtuigend.

convivial, *a.* gezellig, feestelijk. **conviviality**, *n.* gezelligheid *n.*, feestelijkheid *n.*

convocation, *n.* oproeping *n.*; synode *n.*; (universitair) kiezerslichaam *n.n.* **convoke**, *v.t.* samenroepen *str.*, bijeenroepen *str.*

convolution, *n.* kronkeling *n.*

convolvulus, *n.* winde *n.*

convoy, *n.* konvooi *n.n.*; kolonne *n.* ¶ *v.t.* begeleiden, konvooieren.

convulse, *v.t.* krampachtig samentrekken *str.*, stuiptrekken *str.* **convulsion**, *n.* stuip *n.*, stuiptrekking *n.* **convulsive**, *a.*, ~ly, *adv.* stuiptrekkend, krampachtig.

cony, *n.* konijn *n.n.*

coo, *v.i.* kirren.

cook, *n.* kok *n.*; kokin *n.* (*female*); keukenmeid *n.* ¶ *v.t.* koken; (toe)bereiden; vervalsen. **cookery**, *n.* kookkunst *n.*; koken *n.n.* ~ *book*, kookboek *n.n.*

cool, *a.*, ~ly, *adv.* koel; kalm; onbeschaamd. ¶ *n.* koelte *n.* **cooler**, *n.* koelvat *n.n.*

coolie, *n.* koelie *n.*

coolness, *n.* koelheid *n.*; koelte *n.*; aplomb *n.n.*

coop, *n.* (kippen)hok *n.n.*; korf *n.* ¶ *v.t.* opsluiten *str.* **cooper**, *n.* kuiper *n.* ¶ *v.i.* kuipen. **cooperage**, *n.* kuipersloon *n.n.*

co-operate, *v.i.* samenwerken, medewerken. **co-operation**, *n.* samenwerking *n.*, medewerking *n.*, coöperatie *n.* **co-operative**, *a.* medewerkend, coöperatief. **co-operator**, *n.* medewerker *n.*

coopery, *n.* kuiperij *n.*

co-opt, *v.t.* co-opteren.

co-ordinate, *a.* nevenschikkend. ¶ *v.t.* met elkaar in overeenstemming brengen *irr.*; coördineren.

coot, *n.* koet *n.*, meerkoet *n.*

copal, *n.* copal *n.n.*

co-partner, *n.* compagnon *n.*, deelgenoot *n.* **co-partnership**, *n.* vennootschap *n.*, deelgenootschap *n.n.*

cope, *n.* muurkap *n.*, vorst *n.*; koorhemd *n.n.* ¶ *v.t.* bekappen; bedekken. ¶ *v.i.* *to* ~ *with something*, iets aankunnen *irr.*; voldoen *irr.* aan iets.

coper, *n.* paardekoper *n.*

coping, *n.* muurkap *n.* ~ *stone*, deksteen *n.*

copious, *a.*, ~ly, *adv.* overvloedig, rijkelijk. **copiousness**, *n.* overvloed *n.*, overvloedigheid *n.*

copper, *n.* rood koper *n.n.*; (grote) ketel *n.*; koperen munt *n.* ¶ *a.* (rood)koperen. ¶ *v.t.* verkoperen. **copperas**, *n.* ijzersulfaat

n.n., koperrood *n.n.* **coppered,** *a.* verkoperd. **copperplate,** *n.* kopergravure *n.*
~ *writing,* mooi geschreven oude hand *n.*
copper-works, *pl.n.* koperpletterij *n.*
coppery, *a.* koperachtig.
coppice, *n.* kreupelhout *n.n.*, kreupelbos *n.n.*
copra, *n.* kopra *n.*
copse, *n. See* coppice.
copulate, *v.i.* zich paren, copuleren. **copulation,** *n.* paring *n.*, copulatie *n.* **copulative,**
a. parings . . .
copy, *n.* afschrift *n.n.*, copie *n.*; exemplaar
n.n.; nabootsing *n.* ¶ *v.t.* overschrijven
str., copiëren; nadoen *irr.*, nabootsen.
copy-book, *n.* schrift *n.n.* **copyhold,** *n.*
erfpacht *n.* **copying-press,** *n.* copieerpers *n.*
copyist, *n.* copiïst *n.* **copyright,** *n.* kopijrecht *n.n.*, copierecht *n.n.*, auteursrecht
n.n.
coquet, *a.* coquet. ¶ *v.i.* coquetteren.
coquetry, *n.* coquetterie *n.*, behaagzucht *n.*
coquette, *n.* coquette *n.* **coquettish,** *a.*
coquet, behaagziek.
coral, *n.* koraal *n.n.* ¶ *a.* koralen; koraalrood.
coralline, *a.* koraalachtig.
corbel, *n.* draagsteen *n.*
cord, *n.* snoer *n.n.*, streng *n.*, touw *n.n.*.
koord *n.n.*; geribde stof *n.* ¶ *v.t.* samenbinden *str.* **cordage,** *n.* touwwerk *n.n.*
cordial, *a.*, ~ly, *adv.* hartelijk. ¶ *n.* hartsterkend middel *n.n.*; likeur *n.* **cordiality,**
n. hartelijkheid *n.*
cordite, *n.* kordiet *n.n.*
cordon, *n.* cordon *n.n.*, koord *n.n.*; keten *n.*
corduroy, *n.* geribd bombazijn *n.n.* ~s,
broek *n.* van geribd bombazijn.
core, *n.* hart *n.n.*, kern *n.*; klokhuis *n.n.*
co-respondent, *n.* mede-aangeklaagde *n.* in
echtscheidingsproces *n.n.*
coriaceous, *a.* taai.
coriander, *n.* koriander *n.*
cork, *n.* kurk *n.n.* (*substance*), *n.* (*stopper*).
¶ *v.t.* kurken. **corkage,** *n.* kurkengeld *n.n.*
corkscrew, *n.* kurketrekker *n.*
cormorant, *n.* aalscholver *n.*
corn, *n.* koren *n.n.*, graan *n.n.*; mais *n.*;
korrel *n.*; likdoorn *n.* **corncrake,** *n.*
kwartelkoning *n.*
cornea, *n.* hoornvlies *n.n.*
corned, *a.* gepekeld. ~ *beef,* vlees *n.n.*, in
blik *n.n.*
cornel, *n.* kornoelje *n.*
cornelian, *n.* kornalijn *n.n.* (*substance*), *n.*
(*jewel*). ¶ *a.* kornalijnen.
corneous, *a.* hoornachtig.
corner, *n.* hoek *n.*; opkopersgroep *n.* *at the* ~,
op de hoek; *to drive into a* ~, in 't nauw
drijven *str.*; *in a tight* ~, in 't nauw.
¶ *v.t.* in 't nauw drijven *str.*; opkopen *irr.*
cornet, *n.* kornet *n.*, hoorn *n.*; peperhuis *n.n.*
corn-factor, *n.* korenkoper *n.* **cornflour,** *n.*
maïzena *n.* **cornflower,** *n.* korenbloem *n.*
corn-salad, *n.* veldsla *n.*
cornice, *n.* kroonlijst *n.*

cornucopia, *n.* hoorn *n.* des overvloeds.
corollary, *n.* gevolgtrekking *n.*
corona, *n.* corona *n.*, lichtkrans *n.*
coronation, *n.* kroning *n.*
coroner, *n.* lijkschouwer *n.* ~'s *inquest,*
lijkschouwing *n.*
coronet, *n.* kroon *n.*; diadeem *n.n.*
corporal, *a.* lichamelijk. ¶ *n.* korporaal
n.
corporate, *a.* een rechtspersoon *n.* vormend.
~ *body,* lichaam *n.n.*, rechtspersoon *n.*
corporation, *n.* corporatie *n.*, rechtspersoon
n.; buikje *n.n.*
corporeal, *a.* lichamelijk, stoffelijk.
corps, *n.* korps *n.n.*
corpse, *n.* lijk *n.n.*
corpulence, *n.* zwaarlijvigheid *n.* **corpulent,**
a. zwaarlijvig, corpulent.
Corpus Christi, *N.* Heilige Sacramentsdag *N.*
corpuscle, *n.* (bloed)lichaampje *n.n.*
corral, *n.* veekraal *n.*, omheining *n.* ¶ *v.t.*
opsluiten *str.*
correct, *v.t.* verbeteren; corrigeren; tuchtigen.
¶ *a.*, ~ly, *adv.* juist, precies; correct.
correction, *n.* verbetering *n.*; tuchtiging *n.*
house of ~, verbeteringsgesticht *n.n.*
corrective, *a.* correctief, verbeterings . . .
correctness, *n.* correctheid *n.* **corrector,** *n.*
verbeteraar *n.*; corrector *n.*
correlate, *v.t.* met elkaar in overeenstemming
brengen *irr.* ¶ *n.* correlaat *n.n.* **correlation,**
n. correlatie *n.* **correlative,** *a.* correlatief.
correspond, *v.i.* corresponderen; overeenstemmen, kloppen. **correspondence,** *n.*
briefwisseling *n.*, correspondentie *n.*;
overeenstemming *n.* **correspondent,** *n.*
correspondent *n.* ¶ *a.*, ~ly, *adv.* overeenstemmend.
corridor, *n.* gang *n.*, corridor *n.*
corrigible, *a.* verbeterlijk.
corroborate, *v.t.* bevestigen. **corroboration,** *n.*
bevestiging *n.* **corroborative,** *a.* bevestigend.
corrode, *v.t.* wegvreten *str.*, uitbijten *str.*
¶ *v.i.* verteren, verroesten. **corrosion,** *n.*
wegvreting *n.* **corrosive,** *a.*, ~ly, *adv.*
bijtend, invretend. ¶ *n.* bijtend middel
n.n.
corrugate, *v.t.* golven, rimpelen. **corrugated,**
a. ~ *iron,* gegolfd plaatijzer *n.n.*
corrupt, *v.t.* bederven *str.*; omkopen *irr.*
¶ *a.*, ~ly, *adv.* verdorven; bedorven;
omkoopbaar, veil. **corruptibility,** *n.*
verderfelijkheid *n.*; omkoopbaarheid *n.*,
veilheid *n.* **corruptible,** *a.*, ~bly, *adv.*
omkoopbaar. **corruption,** *n.* bederf *n.n.*;
verdorvenheid *n.* **corruptive,** *a.* bedervend.
corruptness, *n.* bedorvenheid *n.*
corsage, *n.* corsage *n.n.*, lijfje *n.n.*
corsair, *n.* zeerover *n.*
cors(e)let, *n.* borstharnas *n.n.*
corset, *n.* korset *n.n.*
cortex, *n.* schors *n.*; buitenlaag *n.* **cortical,** *a.*
schors . . .

coruscate, *v.t.* schitteren. **coruscation**, *n.* schittering *n.*, glans *n.*
corvette, *n.* korvet *n.n.*
corvine, *a.* raafachtig.
cosine, *n.* cosinus *n.*
cosily, *adv. See* cosy, *a.* **cosiness**, *n.* gezelligheid *n.*
cosmetic, *a.* schoonheids . . . ¶ *n.* cosmetiek *n.*, schoonheidsmiddel *n.n.*
cosmic, *a.* kosmisch, wereld . . . **cosmography**, *n.* kosmografie *n.* **cosmopolitan**, *a.* cosmopolitisch. ¶ *n.* cosmopoliet *n.* **cosmos**, *n.* kosmos *n.*; heelal *n.n.*
Cossack, *N.* Kozak *N.*
cost, *v.t.* kosten; de kosten vaststellen. ¶ *n.* kosten *pl.n.*; prijs *n.*
coster(monger), *n.* venter *n.*
costive, *a.* hardlijvig.
costliness, *n.* kostbaarheid *n.* **costly**, *a.* kostbaar, duur.
costume, *n.* kostuum *n.n.*; klederdracht *n.*
cosy, *a.* gezellig, knus. ¶ *n.* (thee)muts *n.*
cot, *n.* hok *n.n.*; til *n.*; kinderbedje *n.n.*
cote, *n.* hok *n.n.*, til *n.*
coterie, *n.* coterie *n.*, kliek *n.*
cottage, *n.* huisje *n.n.*; hut *n.*, hutje *n.n.*; villatje *n.n.* **cottager**, *n.* eenvoudig landman *n.*
cotton, *n.* katoen *n.n.*; garen *n.n.* ~ *wool*, watten *pl.n.*; *needle and* ~, naald *n.* en draad *n.* ¶ *v.i.* *to* ~ *on to*, snappen. **cotton-gin**, *n.* pelmachine *n.* **cotton-mill**, *n.* katoenfabriek *n.* **cotton-plant**, *n.* katoenstruik *n.*, katoenplant *n.* **cotton-spinner**, *n.* katoenspinner *n.* **cotton-waste**, *n.* katoenafval *n.*
couch, *n.* divan *n.*, rustbed *n.n.* ¶ *v.t.* vellen. *to* ~ *in*, uitdrukken in.
cough, *v.i.* hoesten. *to* ~ *up*, opgeven *str.*; te voorschijn brengen *irr.* ¶ *n.* hoest *n.*
could, *aux.v. See* can.
coulter, *n.* kouter *n.n.*, ploegijzer *n.n.*
council, *n.* raad *n.*; raadsvergadering *n.* *C~ of State*, Raad van State; ~ *of war*, krijgsraad *n.* **councillor**, *n.* raadslid *n.n.*
counsel, *n.* raad *n.*, advies *n.n.*; advocaat *n.*, raadgever *n.* *to keep one's own* ~, zijn mond *n.* houden *irr.*
count, *v.t.* tellen. ¶ *v.i.* achten. *to* ~ *in*, meetellen; *to* ~ *on*, rekenen op; *to* ~ *out*, buitensluiten *str.* ¶ *n.* tel *n.*, telling *n.*; berekening *n.*; punt *n.n.*; graaf *n.* *to keep* ~ *of*, tellen; *to leave out of* ~, buiten rekening laten *str.*; *to lose* ~, de tel kwijt raken.
countenance, *n.* gelaat *n.n.*; steun *n.* ¶ *v.t.* steunen.
counter, *n.* penning *n.*; damstuk *n.n.*; toonbank *n.*; teller *n.*; boeg *n.* ¶ *adv.* tegen, tegenover. ¶ *v.t.* tegenwerken. **counteract**, *v.t.* tegenwerken. **counter-action**, *n.* tegenwerking *n.* **counter-balance**, *v.t.* opwegen tegen. ¶ *n.* tegengewicht *n.n.* **counterblast**, *n.* tegenstoot *n.*;

hevig antwoord *n.n.* **countercharge**, *v.t.* een tegenklacht *n.* indienen. ¶ *n.* tegenaanklacht *n.* **counter-claim**, *n.* tegeneis *n.*
counterfeit, *v.t.* namaken, vervalsen; huichelen. ¶ *a.* namaak; nagemaakt. ¶ *n.* namaak *n.*
counterfoil, *n.* contrôlestrook *n.*
countermand, *v.t.* afzeggen, afbestellen; herroepen *str.*
counter-order, *n.* tegenbevel *n.n.*
counterpane, *n.* sprei *n.*; gestikte deken *n.*
counterpart, *n.* tegenpartij *n.*; tegenhanger *n.* **counterplea**, *n.* tegenpleidooi *n.n.* **counter-plot**, *n.* tegenlist *n.*
counterpoint, *n.* contrapunt *n.n.*
counterpoise, *n.* tegenwicht *n.n.* **countersign**, *n.* wachtwoord *n.n.*; mede-ondertekening *n.* ¶ *v.t.* contrasigneren.
countess, *n.* gravin *n.*
counting-house, *n.* kantoor *n.n.* **countless**, *a.* talloos.
countrified, *a.* landelijk, boers. **country**, *n.* land *n.n.*; platteland *n.n.*, buiten *n.n.* ~ *dance*, landelijke dans *n.* **country-house**, *n.* landhuis *n.n.* **countryman**, *n.* landgenoot *n.*; buitenman *n.*, landman *n.* **country seat**, *n.* buitenplaats *n.*, landgoed *n.n.* **countryside**, *n.* platteland *n.n.*
county, *n.* graafschap *n.n.*, provincie *n.*
coup, *n.* gelukkige zet *n.*
couple, *n.* paar *n.n.*; koppel *n.n.*, span *n.n.* ¶ *v.t.* koppelen. **couplet**, *n.* paar *n.n.*; versregels *pl.n.* **coupling**, *n.* koppeling *n.*
coupon, *n.* bon *n.*, coupon *n.*
courage, *n.* moed *n.* *to take one's* ~ *in both hands*, zich vermannen. **courageous**, *a.*, ~ly, *adv.* moedig, dapper.
courier, *n.* koerier *n.*
course, *n.* loop *n.*; stroom *n.*; richting *n.*, koers *n.*; lange jacht *n.*; renbaan *n.*; laag stenen *n.*; cursus *n.*; kuur *n.* *of* ~, natuurlijk; *in due* ~, mettertijd; te bekwamer tijd, te zijnder tijd; *it's a matter of* ~, het spreekt van zelf. ¶ *v.i.* lopen *str.*; jagen *str.* **courser**, *n.* renpaard *n.n.* **coursing**, *n.* lange jacht *n.*
court, *n.* hof *n.n.*; gerechtshof *n.n.*; opwachting *n.*; plein *n.n.*, hofje *n.n.* *to pay* ~ *to*, het hof maken aan. ¶ *v.t.* het hof maken; zoeken *irr.* **courteous**, *a.*, ~ly, *adv.* hoffelijk, wellevend.
courtesan, *n.* courtisane *n.*
courtesy, *n.* hoffelijkheid *n.*, wellevendheid *n.* *by* ~, uit hoffelijkheid. **courtier**, *n.* hoveling *n.* **courtliness**, *n.* hoffelijkheid *n.* **courtly**, *a.* hoffelijk, hoofs. **court-martial**, *n.* krijgsraad *n.* *to be* ~*ed*, voor de krijgsraad gebracht worden *str.*
court-plaster, *n.* Engelse pleister *n.*
courtship, *n.* hofmakerij *n.*, vrijage *n.* **courtyard**, *n.* binnenhof *n.n.*, binnenplaats *n.*, achterplaats *n.*
cousin, *n.* neef *n.* (*male*), nicht *n.* (*female*).

~ *german*, volle neef. **cousinship**, *n.* neefschap *n.n.*

cove, *n.* kreek *n.*, inham *n.*; kerel *n.*, vent *n. (coll.).*

covenant, *n.* verbond *n.n.*, verdrag *n.n.* ¶ *v.i.* zich verbinden *str.* **Covenanter**, *N.* Schotse Presbyteriaan *N.*

Coventry, *N.* Coventry *n.N.* *to send to* ~, dood verklaren.

cover, *v.t.* bedekken, toedekken; dekken; omvatten. ¶ *n.* bedekking *n.*; dekking *n.*; bescherming *n.*; schuilplaats *n.*; deksel *n.n.*; omslag *n.*; enveloppe *n.*, couvert *n.n. under ~ of*, verborgen door, onder de schijn van. **covering**, *n.* bedekking *n.*; dekmantel *n.* **coverlet**, *n.* sprei *n.* **covert**, *n.* schuilplaats *n.*; struikgewas *n.n.*; leger *n.n.* ¶ *a.*, ~ly, *adv.* verborgen, geheim.

covet, *v.t.* begeren. **covetous**, *a.*, ~ly, *adv.* begerig, hebzuchtig. **covetousness**, *n.* begerigheid *n.*, begeerte *n.*, hebzucht *n.*

covey, *n.* vlucht *n.*; troep *n.*

cow, *n.* koe *n.* ¶ *v.t.* bang maken, vrees inboezemen.

coward, *n.* lafaard *n.* **cowardice**, *n.* lafhartigheid *n.*, lafheid *n.* **cowardly**, *a.* laf, lafhartig.

cow-boy, *n.* koejongen *n.*; bereden veeherder *n.* **cow-catcher**, *n.* koeienvanger *n.*

cower, *v.i.* ineenkrimpen *str.*

cowherd, *n.* koeherder *n.* **cowhide**, *n.* rundleer *n.n.* **cowhouse**, *n.* koestal *n.*

cowl, *n.* monnikskap *n.*; gek *n. (on chimney).*

cow-pox, *n.* koepokken *pl.n.*

cowrie, *n.* porseleinslak *n.*

cowslip, *n.* sleutelbloem *n.*

coxcomb, *n.* hanekam *n.*

coxswain, *n.* stuurman *n.*

coy, *a.*, ~ly, *adv.* schuchter, bedeesd.

coyote, *n.* prairiewolf *n.*

coyness, *n.* bedeesdheid *n.*

cozen, *v.t.* bedriegen *str.* **cozenage**, *n.* bedriegerij *n.*

crab, *n.* krab *n.* **crab-apple**, *n.* wilde appel *n.* **crabbed**, *a.* stuurs, nors.

crack, *v.t.* kraken; barsten *irr.* ¶ *v.i.* kraken; barsten *irr.*; afknappen. ¶ *a.* eersterangs. ¶ *n.* barst *n.*, breuk *n.*; slag *n.*; knal *n.* **crack-brained**, *a.* niet goed snik.

cracker, *n.* pistache *n.*, knalbonbon *n.*; zevenklapper *n.*; hard beschuitje *n.n.*

crackle, *v.i.* knetteren; knappen. **crackling**, *n.* geknetter *n.*; bros zwoerd *n.n.* **cracknel**, *n.* krakeling *n.*

cradle, *n.* wieg *n.*; bakermat *n.* ¶ *v.t.* wiegen; in de wieg leggen *irr.*

craft, *n.* ambacht *n.n.*; handwerk *n.n.*; sluwheid *n.*, listigheid *n.*; vaartuig *n.n.* **craftiness**, *n.* sluwheid *n.*, listigheid *n.* **craftsman**, *n.* (bekwaam) handwerksman *n.* **crafty**, *a.*, ~ily, *adv.* listig, sluw.

crag, *n.* steile rots *n.* **craggy**, *a.* steil, grillig.

crake, *n.* kwartelkoning *n.*

cram, *v.t.* volstoppen, volproppen; klaarstomen *(for exam.).* **cram-full**, *a.* stampvol, propvol. **crammer**, *n.* repetitor *n.*

cramp, *n.* kramp *n.*; kram *n.* ¶ *v.t.* met kramp aandoen *irr.* *to be* ~*ed*, geen bewegingsvrijheid *n.* hebben.

cranberry, *n.* veenbes *n.*, vossenbes *n.*

crane, *n.* kraanvogel *n.*; kraan *n.*; hevel *n.* ¶ *v.t.* *to* ~ *one's neck*, reikhalzen, de hals uitstrekken. **crane's-bill**, *n.* ooievaarsbek *n.*, reigersbek *n.*

cranial, *a.* schedel . . .

crank, *n.* kruk *n.*, slinger *n.*; dwaas *n.*, excentriek *n.* ¶ *a.* rank. ¶ *v.t.* buigen *str.*; vastmaken. *to* ~ *up*, aanzetten. **crankiness**, *n.* excentriciteit *n.* **cranking-handle**, *n.* slinger *n.* **cranky**, *a.* raar, excentriek.

crannied, *a.* vol spleten. **cranny**, *n.* scheur *n.*, spleet *n.*

crape, *n.* floers *n.n.*; rouwband *n.*

crash, *v.t.* neerslaan *irr.* ¶ *v.i.* neerstorten; te pletter vallen *str.* ¶ *n.* ineenstorting *n.*; krach *n.*; zware slag *n.*; botsing *n.*; vliegongeluk *n.n.*

crass, *a.* grof.

crate, *n.* krat *n.n.*

crater, *n.* krater *n.*

cravat, *n.* stropdas *n.*

crave, *v.t.* smeken. ¶ *v.i.* *to* ~ *for*, hartstochtelijk verlangen naar, begeren.

craven, *a.* lafhartig.

craving, *n.* hartstochtelijk verlangen *n.n.*

craw, *n.* krop *n.* **crawfish**, *n.* zoetwaterkreeft *n.*

crawl, *v.i.* kruipen *str.* *to* ~ *with*, krioelen van. ¶ *n.* kruipen *n.n.*; viskaar *n.*, vigelante *n.*

crayfish, *n.* zoetwaterkreeft *n.*

crayon, *n.* pastel *n.n.*, tekenkrijt *n.n.*

craze, *n.* manie *n.*, rage *n.* ¶ *v.t.* gek maken. **craziness**, *n.* krankzinnigheid *n.* **crazy**, *a.*, ~ily, *adv.* gek; wrak. ~ *pavement*, pad *n.n.* (met stenen van verschillende grootte).

creak, *v.i.* kraken, knarsen, piepen.

cream, *n.* room *n.*; crème *n.*; bloem *n. (fig.). cold* ~, coldcream *n.*; ~ *of tartar*, wijnsteenzuur *n.n.* ¶ *a.* crème. ¶ *v.t.* romen, afromen; met crème inwrijven *str.* ¶ *v.i.* dik worden *str.* **cream-laid**, *a.* geel geribd. **creamy**, *a.* romig, roomachtig.

crease, *v.t.* kreuken; vouwen. ¶ *n.* kreuk *n.*; vouw *n.*, plooi *n.* **creasy**, *a.* verkreukeld; geplooid.

create, *v.t.* scheppen *str.*; aanstellen tot. **creation**, *n.* schepping *n.* **creative**, *a.*, ~ly, *adv.* scheppend, oorspronkelijk. **creator**, *n.* schepper *n.* **creature**, *n.* schepsel *n.n.*, werktuig *n.n.*

credence, *n.* geloof *n.n.* **credentials**, *pl.n.* geloofsbrieven *pl.n.* **credibility**, *n.* geloofwaardigheid *n.* **credible**, *a.*, ~bly, *adv.* geloofwaardig.

credit, *n.* krediet *n.n.*; credit *n.n.*; geloof *n.n.*,

vertrouwen *n.n.* *to do* ~ *to a person,* iemand tot eer strekken; *to give a person* ~ *for,* iemand de eer geven; *to his* ~, te zijnen gunste. ¶ *v.t.* geloven, geloof *n.n.* hechten aan; crediteren. **creditable,** *a.,* ~bly, *adv.* eervol. **creditor,** *n.* crediteur *n.,* schuldeiser *n.*
credo, *n.* credo *n.n.*
credulity, *n.* lichtgelovigheid *n.* **credulous,** *a.* lichtgelovig.
creed, *n.* geloof *n.n.*; geloofsbelijdenis *n.*
creek, *n.* kreek *n.*; inham *n.*
creel, *n.* (tenen) mand *n.*
creep, *v.i.* kruipen *str.* *my flesh began to* ~, ik kreeg kippevel *n.n.* ¶ *n.* *it gives me the* ~*s,* ik krijg er kippevel *n.n.* van. **creeper,** *n.* klimplant *n.*; rank *n.* **creepy,** *a.* griezelig.
cremate, *v.t.* verbranden. **cremation,** *n.* lijkverbranding *n.* **crematorium,** *n.* lijkoven *n.*; crematorium *n.n.*
crenellated, *a.* gekanteeld ; gekarteld.
crenate(d), *a.* gekerfd, getand.
Creole, *N.* Kreool *N.* ¶ *a.* Kreools.
creosote, *n.* creosoot *n.n.*
crepitate, *v.i.* knetteren.
crepuscular, *a.* schemer . . .
crescent, *n.* (maan)sikkel *n.* ¶ *a.* wassend. ~ *moon,* wassende maan *n.,* halve maan *n.*
cress, *n.* waterkers *n.,* tuinkers *n.*
crest, *n.* kam *n.,* kuif *n.*; helmteken *n.n.*; top *n.,* kruin *n.* **crested,** *a.* gekuifd, kuif . . . **crestfallen,** *a.* terneergeslagen.
cretin, *n.* kretijn *n.n.*
cretonne, *n.* creton(ne) *n.n.*
crevasse, *n.* kloof *n.,* scheur *n.,* spleet *n.*
crevice, *n.* scheur *n.,* spleet *n.*
crew, *n.* bemanning *n.*; scheepsvolk *n.n.*
crewel, *n.* borduurwol *n.*
crib, *n.* kribbe *n.*; spiekvertaling *n.* ¶ *v.t.* spieken; gappen.
cribbage, *n.* (soort) kaartspel *n.n.*
crick, *n.* kramp *n.,* stijfheid *n.*
cricket, *n.* krekel *n.*; cricketspel *n.n.* *to play* ~, cricketten.
crier, *n.* omroeper *n.*
crime, *n.* misdaad *n.* **criminal,** *a.,* ~ly, *adv.* misdadig; crimineel, strafrechtelijk. ~ *law,* strafrecht *n.n.*; *C.I.D.* (*C*~ *Investigation Department*), recherche *n.* ¶ *n.* misdadiger *n.* **criminality,** *n.* misdadigheid *n.*
crimp, *v.t.* krullen; krimpen.
crimson, *n.* karmozijn; donkerrood.
cringe, *v.i.* kruipen *str.,* vleien. **cringer,** *n.* kruiper *n.*
crinkle, *v.i.* rimpelen. ¶ *v.t.* rimpelen, ineenfrommelen. **crinkly,** *a.* rimpelig, verfrommeld.
crinoline, *n.* crinoline *n.,* hoepelrok *n.*
cripple, *n.* kreupele *n.*; gebrekkige *n.,* verminkte *n.* ¶ *v.t.* kreupel maken; verminken.
crisis, *n.* crisis *n.*; keerpunt *n.n.*

crisp, *a.* bros, brokkelig; gekruld. ¶ *v.t.* krullen. *to* ~ *up,* bros maken.
criss-cross, *a.* kriskras.
criterion, *n.* maatstaf *n.,* criterium *n.n.*
critic, *n.* criticus *n.* **critical,** *a.,* ~ly, *adv.* kritiek; critisch. **criticize,** *v.t.* beoordelen, critiseren; becritiseren; recenseren. **criticism,** *n.* critiek *n.,* beoordeling *n.*; recensie *n.* **critique,** *n.* critiek *n.*
croak, *v.i.* kwaken; krassen. ¶ *n.* gekwaak *n.n.,* gekras *n.n.*
crochet, *n.* haakwerk *n.n.* ¶ *v.t. & v.i.* haken.
crock, *n.* pot *n.*; oud meubel *n.n.* ¶ *v.i.* *to* ~ *up,* ziek worden *str.* **crockery,** *n.* aardewerk *n.n.*
crocodile, *n.* krokodil *n.*
crocus, *n.* krokus *n.*
croft, *n.* klein boerderijtje *n.n.* **crofter,** *n.* keuterboer *n.*
cromlech, *n.* prehistorische monumentsteen *n.*
crone, *n.* oud wijf *n.n.*
crony, *n.* kornuit *n.n.,* kameraad *n.*
crook, *n.* bocht *n.,* kromte *n.*; oplichter *n.,* dief *n.* ¶ *v.t.* buigen *str.,* krommen. **crooked,** *a.,* ~ly, *adv.* krom, scheef; oneerlijk.
croon, *v.i. & v.t.* neuriën.
crop, *n.* krop *n.* (*of bird*); oogst *n.* (*harvest*); jachtzweep *n.* (*hunting*-); knipsel *n.n.* (*hair*). ¶ *v.t.* oogsten; afgrazen, afvreten *str.*; afknippen; kortstaarten; de oren knippen. ¶ *v.i.* *to* ~ *up,* zich voordoen *irr.,* opduiken *str.* **cropper,** *n.* kropduif *n.,* kropper *n.* *to come a* ~, over de kop gaan *irr.*
croquet, *n.* croquetspel *n.n.*
cross, *n.* kruis *n.n.*; kruising *n.*; gekruist ras *n.n.* ¶ *a.* elkaar kruisend; dwars; kwaad, boos, slecht gehumeurd. *to be at* ~ *purposes,* elkaar misverstaan *irr.* ¶ *v.t.* kruisen. ¶ *v.i.* elkaar kruisen. ¶ *v.r.* *to* ~ *oneself,* een kruis slaan. **cross-bar,** *n.* dwarshout *n.n.* **cross-bow,** *n.* kruisboog *n.* **cross-bred,** *a.* gekruist. **cross-breed,** *n.* gekruist ras *n.n.* **cross-examination,** *n.* kruisverhoor *n.* **cross-examine,** *v.t.* door de tegenpartij ondervragen; aan een scherp verhoor onderwerpen. **cross-grained,** *a.* tegen de draad in; lastig. **cross-hatch,** *v.t.* arceren. **crossing,** *n.* kruising *n.*; overweg *n.* **crossly,** *adv.* kwaad. **crossness,** *n.* kwaadheid *n.* **cross-road,** *n.* kruisweg *n.* **crosswise,** *adv.* kruisgewijs; kruiselings.
crotchet, *n.* haakje *n.n.*; kwartnoot *n.*; gril *n.,* nuk *n.* **crotchety,** *a.* grillig, nukkig.
crouch, *v.i.* hurken, ineenduiken *str.*
croup, *n.* kruis *n.n.,* croupe *n.*; kroep *n.*
crow, *n.* kraai *n.* *a white* ~, een witte raaf *n.*; *as the* ~ *flies,* in rechte lijn *n.*; *hooded* ~, bonte kraai *n.* ¶ *v.i.* kraaien. **crow's-nest,** *n.* kraaiennest *n.n.*
crowbar, *n.* koevoet *n.,* breekijzer *n.n.*

crowd, *n.* menigte *n.*; hoop *n.* ¶ *v.i.* zich
verdringen *str.* ¶ *v.t.* vullen; dringen *str.*
crown, *n.* kroon *n.*; kruin *n.* ¶ *v.t.* kronen;
bekronen. *to ~ it all,* als toppunt *n.n.*
crown prince, *n.* kroonprins *n.*
crozier, *n.* bisschopsstaf *n.*
crucial, *a.* kruisgewijs; beslissend, critiek.
crucible, *n.* smeltkroes *n.*
crucifix, *n.* kruisbeeld *n.n.* crucifixion, *n.*
kruisiging *n.* cruciform, *a.* kruisvormig.
crucify, *v.t.* kruisigen.
crude, *a.,* ~ly, *adv.* ruw, grof, onbereid.
crudity, *n.* ruwheid *n.,* grofheid *n.*
cruel, *a.,* ~ly, *adv.* wreed. cruelty, *n.*
wreedheid *n.*
cruet, *n.* olieflesje *n.n.,* azijnflesje *n.n.*
cruet-stand, *n.* olie- en azijnstel *n.n.*
cruise, *v.i.* kruisen. ¶ *n.* kruisen *n.n.*; reis *n.*
cruiser, *n.* kruiser *n.* cruising speed, *n.*
kruissnelheid *n.*
crumb, *n.* kruimel *n.*; kruim *n.n.* ¶ *v.t.*
kruimelen; paneren. crumble, *v.i.* af-
brokkelen. crumbly, *a.* kruimelig. crumby,
a. kruimig.
crumpet, *n.* plaatkoek *n.*
crumple, *v.t.* kreukelen. ~d up, ineen-
gefrommeld.
crunch, *v.t.* kraken; knarsen.
crupper, *n.* kruis *n.n.*
crusade, *n.* kruistocht *n.,* kruisvaart *n.*
crusader, *n.* kruisvaarder *n.*
crush, *v.t.* verpletteren; verkreukelen; onderdrukken. ¶ *n.* gedrang *n.n.*; hartstochte-
lijke bewondering *n.* crushing-mill, *n.*
pletmolen *n.*
crust, *n.* korst *n.*; schaal *n.* ¶ *v.i.* een korst
n. vormen. crustaceous, *a.* geschaald;
schaal . . . crustiness, *n.* korstigheid *n.,*
korzeligheid *n.* crusty, *a.,* ~ily, *adv.*
korstig; korzelig.
crutch, *n.* kruk *n.*
crux, *n.* moeilijkheid *n.*
cry, *n.* schreeuw *n.,* kreet *n.,* gil *n.*; roep *n.*;
geblaf *n.n. a far ~ from,* heel anders dan,
een hele sprong *n.*; *in full ~,* blaffend het
wild achterna. ¶ *v.i.* schreeuwen, roepen
str.; gillen; huilen, schreien, wenen. ¶ *v.t.*
roepen *str.,* uitroepen *str. to ~ down,*
afbreken *str.,* afkammen; *to ~ off,* zich
terugtrekken *str.*; *to ~ out,* uitroepen *str.*
crypt, *n.* grafkelder *n.*; onderaardse kapel *n.*
cryptogram, *n.* kryptogram *n.n.,* in geheim-
schrift geschreven stuk *n.n.*
crystal, *n.* kristal *n.n.* ¶ *a.* kristallen.
crystalline, *a.* kristalachtig; helder.
crystallization, *n.* kristallisatie *n.* crystallize, *v.i.* kristalliseren. ¶ *v.t.* laten
kristalliseren.
cub, *n.* jong *n.n.,* welp *n.*
cube, *n.* kubus *n.*; derdemacht *n.* ~ root,
derdemachtswortel *n.* cubic, *a.* kubiek;
kubusvormig.
cubicle, *n.* hokje *n.n.*; afgeschoten kamertje
n.n.

cubit, *n.* voorarm *n.*; ellepijp *n.*; elleboogs-
lengte *n.*
cuckold, *n.* horendrager *n.*
cuckoo, *n.* koekoek *n.*
cucumber, *n.* komkommer *n.*
cud, *n.* voedsel *n.n.* in de voormaag. *to chew
the ~,* herkauwen.
cuddle, *v.t.* knuffelen, liefkozen.
cudgel, *n.* knuppel *n.* ¶ *v.t.* knuppelen.
to ~ one's brains, zich het hoofd breken
str.; *to take up the ~s for,* het voor (iemand)
opnemen *str.*
cue, *n.* slagwoord *n.n.*; aanwijzing *n.*; keu *n.*
cuff, *n.* oorveeg *n.*; manchet *n.* ¶ *v.t.* klappen
geven *str.*
cuirass, *n.* kuras *n.n.* cuirassier, *n.* kurassier
n.
culinary, *a.* keuken . . ., kook . . .
cull, *v.t.* plukken, lezen *str.*
cullender, *n. See* colander.
culm, *n.* kolengruis *n.n.*; glanskool *n.*; stro
n.n.
culminate, *v.i.* culmineren, het toppunt
bereiken. culmination, *n.* culminatie *n.*
hoogtepunt *n.n.,* hoogste stand *n.*
culpability, *n.* schuldigheid *n.* culpable, *a.,*
~bly, *adv.* schuldig. culprit, *n.* schuldige *n.*
cult, *n.* eredienst *n.*; verering *n.,* aanbidding *n.*
cultivate, *v.t.* bebouwen; verbouwen; aankweken, ontwikkelen. cultivation, *n.*
bebouwing *n.*; verbouwen *n.n.*; beoefening
n. cultivator, *n.* bebouwer *n.*
culture, *n.* cultuur *n.,* aankweking *n.*;
cultuur *n.,* beschaving *n. physical ~.*
lichamelijke ontwikkeling *n.*
culvert, *n.* duiker *n.*
cumber, *v.t.* last veroorzaken. cumbersome,
a. lastig, hinderlijk. cumbrous, *a.* log,
onhandelbaar.
cumin, *n.* komijn *n.*
cumulative, *a.* ophopend.
cumulus, *n.* stapelwolk *n.*
cuneiform, *a.* wigvormig. ~ writing,
spijkerschrift *n.n.*
cunning, *a.,* ~ly, *adv.* listig, sluw, geslepen.
¶ *n.* sluwheid *n.,* listigheid *n.*; handigheid *n.*
cup, *n.* kop *n.,* kopje *n.n.*; beker *n. in his ~s,*
boven z'n theewater *n.n.*
cupboard, *n.* kast *n.* ~ love, zelfzucht *n.*
cupidity, *n.* hebzucht *n.*
cupola, *n.* koepel *n.*; geschuttoren *n.*
cupreous, *a.* koperachtig; koperkleurig.
cur, *n.* rekel *n.*; (*fig.*) ploert *n.*
curability, *n.* geneeslijkheid *n.* curable, *a.*
geneeslijk.
curacy, *n.* predikantsplaats *n.* curate, *n.*
(hulp)predikant *n.*; kapelaan *n.*
curative, *a.* genezend.
curator, *n.* curator *n.,* beheerder *n.*
curb, *v.t.* in bedwang houden *irr.,* beteugelen.
¶ *n. See* kerb.
curd, *n.* wrongel *n.* ~s, wrongel *n.*
curdle, *v.i.* klonteren, stremmen. ¶ *v.t.*
stremmen, doen *irr.* stollen.

cure, *v.t.* genezen *str.*, herstellen; roken, zouten, pekelen. ¶ *n.* genezing *n.*, herstel *n.n.*; kuur *n.*; geneesmiddel *n.n.*; zielzorg *n.*, predikantsplaats *n.*

curfew, *n.* avondklok *n.* *to impose a* ~, verbieden *str.* om zich na . . . op straat te begeven.

curio, *n.* rariteit *n.* **curiosity**, *n.* nieuwsgierigheid *n.*; curiositeit *n.* **curious**, *a.*, ~ly, *adv.* nieuwsgierig; merkwaardig, curieus.

curl, *n.* krul *n.*; kronkeling *n.* ¶ *v.t. & v.i.* krullen; kronkelen.

curlew, *n.* wulp *n.*

curling, *n.* balspel *n.n.* (op het ijs). **curling-iron**, *n.* krultang *n.*, friseertang *n.* **curl-paper**, *n.* papiljot *n.* **curly**, *a.* gekruld.

curmudgeon, *n.* gierigaard *n.*, vrek *n.*

currant, *n.* krent. *red* ~, rode (aal)bes *n.*; *white* ~, witte (aal)bes *n.*; *black*~, zwarte (aal)bes *n.*

currency, *n.* betaalmiddel *n.n.*, valuta *n.*; gangbaarheid *n.*; looptijd *n.* **current**, *a.*, ~ly, *adv.* gangbaar, algemeen verspreid; in omloop; courant. ¶ *n.* stroom *n.*, stroming *n.*; loop *n.*

curriculum, *n.* leerstof *n.*

currier, *n.* leertouwer *n.*, leerbereider *n.*

curry, *v.t.* roskammen; met kerrie *n.* kruiden; (leer) touwen, (leer) bereiden. *to* ~ *favour with*, flikflooien, zoeken *irr.* de gunst te winnen van. ¶ *n.* kerrie *n.* **currycomb**, *n.* roskam *n.*

curse, *n.* vloek *n.*, vervloeking *n.* ¶ *v.i.* vloeken. ¶ *v.t.* vervloeken; uitvloeken. **cursed**, *a.* vervloekt.

cursive, *a.* cursief, lopend.

cursorily, *adv.* terloops. **cursory**, *a.* vluchtig, haastig.

curt, *a.*, ~ly, *adv.* kortaf, bits.

curtail, *v.t.* beperken, besnoeien.

curtain, *n.* gordijn *n.n.*; scherm *n.n.* ¶ *v.t.* behangen *str.* met gordijnen. *to* ~ *off*, afschieten *str.* (met een gordijn). **curtain fire**, *n.* spervuur *n.n.* **curtain-rod**, *n.* gordijnroe(de) *n.*

curtsy, *n.* buiging *n.* ¶ *v.i.* een buiging maken.

curvature, *n.* kromming *n.* **curve**, *v.t.* buigen *str.*, ombuigen *str.* ¶ *v.i.* een bocht maken, buigen *str.* ¶ *n.* kromming *n.*; kromme *n.*

curvet, *n.* bokkesprong *n.*

curvilinear, *a.* kromlijnig.

cushion, *n.* kussen *n.n.*; buffer *n.*; biljartband *n.*; wrijfkussen *n.n.* ¶ *v.t.* van kussens voorzien *irr.*

custard, *n.* vla *n.*, vlade *n.*

custodian, *n.* custos *n.*, bewaarder *n.* **custody**, *n.* bewaring *n.*; hechtenis *n.*

custom, *n.* gewoonte *n.*, gebruik *n.n.*; inkomend recht *n.n.*; klandizie *n.*, nering *n.* ~s, douane . . . **customary**, *a.*, ~ily, *adv.* gebruikelijk, gewoon. **customer**, *n.* klant *n.* **custom-house**, *n.* douanekantoor

n.n. ~ *officer*, douanebeambte *n.*, kommies *n.*

cut, *v.t.* snijden *str.*; afsnijden *str.*; knippen (*with scissors*); maaien (*grass*); steken *str.* (*turf*); slijpen *str.* (*glass*); couperen (*castrate*); grieven, striemen (*feelings*); verlagen (*price*); negeren (*ignore*). *to* ~ *it fine*, weinig marge overlaten *str.*; *to* ~ *it short*, het kort maken; *to* ~ *capers*, bokkesprongen maken; *to* ~ *its teeth*, tanden krijgen *str.*; *to* ~ *both ways*, voor- en nadelen hebben; ~ *and dried*, pasklaar (gemaakt); *to* ~ *and run*, zich uit de voeten maken; *to* ~ *down*, vellen, besnoeien; *to* ~ *out*, uitknippen; (*fig.*) knippen; *to* ~ *off with a shilling*, onterven; ~ *up*, stuksnijden *str.*; *to be* ~ *up* (*fig.*), ontdaan zijn. ¶ *n.* snee *n.*, snede *n.*; houw *n.* (*with sword*); houtsnee *n.* (*wood engraving*); verlaging *n.* (*in payment*); kortere weg *n.* (*road*); snit *n.n.* (*of clothes*).

cutaneous, *a.* huid . . .

cute, *a.* lief.

cuticle, *n.* opperhuid *n.*

cutlass, *n.* hartsvanger *n.*

cutler, *n.* messenmaker *n.* **cutlery**, *n.* messenmakersvak *n.n.*; messen *pl.n.n.* en scharen *pl.n.*; eetgerei *n.n.*

cutlet, *n.* kotelet *n.*

cutpurse, *n.* zakkenroller *n.*

cutter, *n.* snijder *n.*; coupeur *n.*; snijmes *n.n.*; kotter *n.* **cut-throat**, *n.* moordenaar. ¶ *a.* moorddadig. **cutting**, *n.* stek *n.*; uitknipsel *n.*; snijwerk *n.n.* ¶ *a.* scherp, bijtend.

cuttle-fish, *n.* inktvis *n.*

cwt, *n.* *See* **hundredweight.**

cycle, *n.* kringloop *n.*; tijdkring *n.*; cyclus *n.*; fiets *n.*, rijwiel *n.n.* **cycling**, *n.* fietsen *n.n.* ~ *track*, fietspad *n.n.* **cyclist**, *n.* fietser *n.*

cyclone, *n.* cycloon *n.*

cyclops, *n.* cycloop *n.*

cygnet, *n.* jonge zwaan *n.*, zwaantje *n.n.*

cylinder, *n.* cylinder *n.*; rol *n.*, wals *n.* **cylindrical**, *a.* cylindrisch.

cymbal, *n.* cymbaal *n.*, bekken *n.n.*

cynic, *n.* cynicus *n.* ¶ *a.* cynisch.

cypress, *n.* cypres *n.*

cyst, *n.* gezwel *n.n.*, ettergezwel *n.n.*

czar, *n.* czaar *n.*, tsaar *n.* **czarina**, *n.* czarina *n.*, tsarina *n.*

Czech, *N.* Tsjech *N.* ¶ *a.* Tsjechisch. **Czechoslovakia**, *N.* Tsjechoslowakije *n.N.* **Czechoslovakian**, *a.* Tsjechoslowaaks.

D

dab, *v.t.* tikken; betten. ¶ *v.i.* bestrijken *str.* ¶ *n.* tikje *n.n.*; schar *n.* (*fish*).

dabble, *v.i.* plassen; knoeien; liefhebberen. *to* ~ *in*, een beetje doen *irr.* aan. **dabbler**, *n.* knoeier *n.*

dace, *n.* serpeling *n.*, witvis *n.*

dactyl, *n.* dactylus *n.*
dad, *n.,* **daddy,** *n.* paatje *n.n.,* papa *n.*
daddy-long-legs, *n.* hooiwagen *n.* (*spider*); glazenmaker *n.* (*large mosquito*).
dado, *n.* lambrizering *n.*
daffodil, *n.* gele narcis *n.*
daft, *n.* gek. **daftness,** *n.* gekheid *n.*
dagger, *n.* dolk. *to look* ~*s at,* iemand met de ogen doorboren; *to be at* ~*s drawn,* elkaar niet kunnen uitstaan.
dahlia, *n.* dahlia *n.*
daily, *a.* & *adv.* dagelijks. ¶ *n.* dagblad *n.n.*
daintiness, *n.* fijnheid *n.*; kieskeurigheid *n.* **dainty,** *a.,* ~**ily,** *adv.* fijn; kieskeurig. ¶ *n.* lekkernij *n.*
dairy, *n.* melkwinkel *n.*   ~*farm,* melkboerderij *n.* **dairymaid,** *n.* melkmeid *n.* **dairyman,** *n.* melkboer *n.*; zuivelboer *n.* **dairy produce,** *n.* zuivelproducten *pl.n.n.*
dais, *n.* estrade *n.*; baldakijn *n.n.*
daisy, *n.* madeliefje *n.n.*
dale, *n.* dal *n.n.*
dalliance, *n.* gedartel *n.n.*; getalm *n.n.* **dally,** *v.i.* dartelen; talmen.
dam, *n.* dam *n.,* dijk *n.*; moer *n.*; wijfje *n.n.* ¶ *v.t.* afdammen.
damage, *n.* schade *n.*; nadeel *n.n.*; averij *n.* ~*s,* schadevergoeding *n.* ¶ *v.t.* beschadigen; havenen.
damascene, *a.* gedamasceerd. **damask,** *n.* damast *n.n.* ¶ *v.t.* damasceren.
dame, *n.* Vrouwe *N.*; (oude) vrouw *n.*
damn, *v.t.* verdoemen; veroordelen, afkeuren; vloeken. ¶ *n.* vloek *n.* **damnable,** *a.,* ~**bly,** *adv.* verdoemelijk; vervloekt. **damnation,** *n.* verdoemenis *n.* **damnatory,** *a.* veroordelend.
damp, *a.* vochtig. ¶ *n.* vochtigheid *n.*; nevel *n.*; (mijn)gas *n.n.* ¶ *v.t.* vochtig maken; bekoelen, temperen. *to* ~ *down,* dekken (*fire*). **damper,** *n.* demper *n.,* sleutel *n.* **dampish,** *a.* ietwat vochtig. **dampness,** *n.* vochtigheid *n.*
damsel, *n.* jonkvrouw *n.*
damson, *n.* damastpruim *n.*
dance, *v.i.* & *v.t.* dansen. *to* ~ *attendance on,* iemand achterna lopen *str.* ¶ *n.* dans *n.*; bal *n.n.* **dancer,** *n.* danser *n.*
dandelion, *n.* paardebloem *n.*   ~ *salad,* molsla *n.*
dandle, *v.t.* laten *str.* wippen.
dandruff, *n.* roos *n.*
dandy, *n.* fat *n.* ¶ *a.* fijn.
Dane, *N.* Deen *N.   Great* ~, Deense dog *n.*
danger, *n.* gevaar *n.n.* **dangerous,** *a.,* ~**ly,** *adv.* gevaarlijk.
dangle, *v.i.* bengelen, slingeren.
Danish, *a.* Deens.
dank, *a.* vochtig.
dapper, *a.* flink, parmant.
dapple, *v.t.* (be)spikkelen. ¶ *a.* gevlekt, gespikkeld. ~ *grey,* appelgrauw.
dare, *v.t.* durven, het wagen; uitdagen, tarten. *I* ~ *say,* ik denk *irr.* wel. **daring,** *a.,* ~**ly,**

adv. gedurfd, gewaagd, stout. ¶ *n.* durf *n.,* vermetelheid *n.*
dark, *a.,* ~**ly,** *adv.* donker, duister. *to keep* ~, verborgen houden *irr.*; *the* ~ *ages,* de duistere middeleeuwen *pl.n.*; *a* ~ *horse,* een onbekend renpaard *n.n.,* (*fig.*) een ondoorgrondelijk karakter *n.n.*; ~ *lantern,* dievenlantaren *n.* ¶ *n.* donker *n.n.,* duister *n.n.,* duisternis *n.*; onwetendheid *n.* **darken,** *v.t.* donker maken. *never* ~ *my doors again,* zet hier nooit weer een voet over de drempel. ¶ *v.i.* donker worden *str.* **darkish,** *a.* vrij donker. **darkling,** *adv.* in het duister. **darkness,** *n.* donker *n.n.,* duisternis *n.*
darling, *n.* lieveling *n.*; schat *n.* ¶ *a.* geliefd, bemind.
darn, *v.t.* stoppen; mazen.   *See also* **damn.** ¶ *n.* gestopte plaats *n.*
darnel, *n.* dolik *n.*
darning-ball, *n.* maasbal *n.* **darning-needle,** *n.* stopnaald *n.*
dart, *n.* (werp)spies *n.*; (plotselinge) sprong *n. to play* ~*s,* met pijltjes *pl.n.n.* werpen *str.* ¶ *v.i.* schieten *str.,* vliegen *str. to* ~ *at,* aanvliegen *str.* op; *to* ~ *away,* wegschieten *str.*
dash, *v.t.* gooien, slaan *irr.,* stoten *str.,* te pletter slaan *irr.*; (*fig.*) teleurstellen, de bodem inslaan *irr.* ~ *it,* verdorie! ¶ *v.i.* hollen, stuiven *str. to* ~ *away,* wegschieten *str.; to* ~ *off,* er van door gaan *irr.* ¶ *n.* slag *n.,* stoot *n.*; loopje *n.n.*; zwier *n.,* élan *n.n.*; tikje *n.n.,* scheutje *n.n.* **dashboard,** *n.* spatbord *n.n.* **dashing,** *a.* onstuiming; zwierig.
dastard, *n.* lafaard *n.* **dastardly,** *a.* lafhartig.
data, *pl.n.* gegevens *pl.n.n.*
date, *n.* datum *n.*; afspraakje *n.n.*; dadel *n.* (*fruit*). *out of* ~, uit de tijd, ouderwets; *up to* ~, bij; op de hoogte. ¶ *v.t.* dateren.
dative, *n.* datief *n.,* derde naamval *n.*
daub, *n.* kladschilderij *n.* or *n.n.* ¶ *v.t.* kladden, smeren.
daughter, *n.* dochter *n.* **daughter-in-law,** *n.* schoondochter *n.*
daunt, *v.t.* afschrikken *str.,* ontmoedigen. **dauntless,** *a.* onversaagd.
davenport, *n.* klein schrijftafeltje *n.n.*
davit, *n.* davit *n.*
daw, *n.* kauw *n.*
dawdle, *v.i.* treuzelen. **dawdler,** *n.* treuzel *n.*
dawn, *n.* dageraad *n.*; het aanbreken van de dag. ¶ *v.i.* dagen; licht worden *str. it* ~*ed upon me,* er ging me een licht op.
day, *n.* dag *n.*   ~ *and night,* nacht *n.* en dag *n.*; ~ *by* ~, dag aan dag; ~ *of grace,* respijtdag *n.*; *one* ~, eens op een dag; *the other* ~, onlangs; *every other* ~, om de andere dag; *some* ~, op een goede dag; *to lose the* ~, de slag verliezen *str.*; ~*'s work,* dagwerk *n.n.* **day-book,** *n.* journaal *n.n.* **day-boy,** *n.* externe *n.* **daybreak,** *n.* dageraad *n.* **daydream,** *n.* mijmering *n.*

¶ *v.i.* wakend dromen. **day-labourer,** *n.* dagloner *n.* **daylight,** *n.* daglicht *n.n.* **day nursery,** *n.* bewaarschool *n.* **daytime,** *n. in the ~,* overdag.

daze, *v.t.* verdoven, versuffen; in de war brengen *irr.* ¶ *n.* verbijstering *n.,* verwarring *n.*

dazzle, *v.t.* verblinden. ¶ *n.* verblinding *n.*

deacon, *n.* diaken *n.*

dead, *a.* dood; doods, mat. *~ centre,* dood punt *n.n.; ~ certainty,* absolute zekerheid *n.; ~ coal,* dove kool *n.; ~ letter,* onbestelbare brief *n.: ~ level,* volkomen vlak, op hetzelfde peil, gelijk; *~ season,* stille seizoen *n.n.; to be a ~ shot,* nooit missen; *to come to a ~ stop,* niet verder kunnen *irr.* ¶ *adv.* dood. *~ against . . .,* vlak tegen . . . in; *~ drunk,* smoordronken. ¶ *n.* dode *n.* or *n.n. at ~ of night,* in het holle van de nacht. **deaden,** *v.t.* dempen; verdoven; verstompen. **deadliness,** *n.* doodsheid *n.;* afschuwelijke verveling *n.;* dodelijke ernst *n.* **deadlock,** *n.* impasse *n.* **deadly,** *a.* dodelijk; vreselijk. ¶ *adv.* dodelijk; doods . . .; vreselijk. **deadness,** *n.* doodsheid *n.*

deaf, *a.* doof. *~ and dumb,* doofstom; *as ~ as a post,* zo doof als een kwartel. **deafen,** *v.t.* verdoven, doof maken. **deafness,** *n.* doofheid *n.*

deal, *n.* hoeveelheid *n.;* (handels)transactie *n.;* geven *n.n. (of cards);* grenenhout *n.n.,* vurenhout *n.n. a great (of good) ~,* heel wat; *my ~,* ik moet geven. ¶ *a.* grenen, vurenhouten. ¶ *v.t.* handelen; te doen hebben; geven *str. (cards). to ~ with,* handelen met, de doen *irr.* hebben met, omspringen *str.* met, klein krijgen *str.* **dealer,** *n.* handelaar *n.,* koopman *n.;* gever *n. (at cards).* **dealing,** *n.* omgang *n.;* handeling *n. ~s,* transacties *pl.n.*

dean, *n.* deken *n.;* doyen *n.;* president van een faculteit *n.* **deanery,** *n.* dekenschap *n.;* kapittelhuis *n.*

dear, *a.* duur, kostbaar; dierbaar; lief. *~ sir,* Geachte Heer *n.* ¶ *n.* lieveling *n.* **dearly,** *adv.* duur; innig. **dearness,** *n.* duurheid *n.;* innigheid *n.,* genegenheid *n.*

dearth, *n.* schaarste *n.,* gebrek *n.n.*

death, *n.* dood *n. to be in at the ~,* het eind meemaken; *to bore to ~,* dodelijk vervelen; *to put to ~,* ter dood brengen *irr.; like grim ~,* als de weerga; *tired to ~,* doodmoe; *~ penalty,* doodstraf *n.* **death-bed,** *n.* sterfbed *n.n.* **death duties,** *pl.n.* successierechten *pl.n.n.* **deathless,** *a.* onsterfelijk. **deathlike,** *a.* doods. **deathly,** *a.* dodelijk; doods. **death-mask,** *n.* dodenmasker *n.* **death-rate,** *n.* sterftecijfer *n.n.* **death-trap,** *n.* val *n. it is a ~,* het is levensgevaarlijk. **death-watch beetle,** *n.* doodkloppertje *n.n.*

debar, *v.t.* uitsluiten *str.*

debase, *v.t.* verlagen, vernederen; vervalsen.

debasement, *n.* vernedering *n.;* vervalsing *n.*

debatable, *a.* betwistbaar. **debate,** *n.* debat *n.n.,* twistgesprek *n.n.;* discussie *n.*

debauch, *v.t.* bederven *str.* **debauchery,** *n.* losbandigheid *n.*

debenture, *n.* obligatie *n. ~ stock,* obligatiekapitaal *n.n.*

debilitate, *v.t.* verzwakken. **debility,** *n.* zwakheid *n.*

debit, *n.* debet *n.n.;* debetzijde *n.* ¶ *v.t.* debiteren.

debonair, *a.* joviaal.

debouch, *v.i.* uitmonden; deboucheren.

debris, *n.* puin *n.n.*

debt, *n.* schuld *n. to run into ~,* schuld maken. **debtor,** *n.* schuldenaar *n.,* debiteur *n.*

decade, *n.* tiental *n.n.* jaren.

decadence, *n,* verval *n.n.,* achteruitgang *n.* **decadent,** *a.* decadent.

decagon, *n.* tienhoek *n.*

decalogue, *n.* de tien geboden *pl.n.n.*

decamp, *v.i.* opbreken *str.;* heengaan *irr.* **decampment,** *n.* opbreken *n.n.;* vertrek *n.n.*

decant, *v.t.* overgieten *str.,* overschenken *str.* **decanter,** *n.* (wijn)karaf *n.*

decapitate, *v.t.* onthoofden. **decapitation,** *n.* onthoofding *n.*

decay, *v.i.* vervallen *str.,* verrotten; achteruitgaan *irr.* ¶ *n.* verval *n.n.;* achteruitgang *n. to fall into ~,* in verval geraken.

decease, *v.i.* overlijden *str.* **deceased,** *a.* overledene *n.*

deceit, *n.* bedrog *n.n.;* bedrieglijkheid *n.* **deceitful,** *a., ~ly, adv.* bedrieglijk. **deceive,** *v.t.* bedriegen *str.;* misleiden; teleurstellen. **deceiver,** *n.* bedrieger *n.*

December, *N.* december *N.*

decency, *n.* betamelijkheid *n.,* fatsoen *n.n.*

decennial, *a.* tienjarig, tienjaarlijks.

decent, *a., ~ly, adv.* betamelijk; fatsoenlijk; behoorlijk.

decentralization, *n.* decentralisatie *n.* **decentralize,** *v.t.* decentraliseren.

deception, *n.* bedrog *n.n.,* misleiding *n.* **deceptive,** *a., ~ly, adv.* bedrieglijk.

decide, *v.t.* beslissen, besluiten *str.* **decided,** *a., ~ly, adv.* beslist, bepaald.

decimal, *a.* tientallig; tiendelig.

decimate, *v.t.* decimeren, een slachting *n.* aanrichten onder. **decimation,** *n.* slachting *n.*

decipher, *v.t.* ontcijferen, ontraadselen.

decision, *n.* beslissing *n.,* besluit *n.n.;* beslistheid *n.* **decisive,** *a., ~ly, adv.* beslissend, afdoend.

deck, *n.* dek *n.n.;* spel *n.n.* (kaarten). *~ chair,* vouwstoel *n.* ¶ *v.t.* tooien, versieren.

declaim, *v.t.* voordragen *str.,* declameren. **declaimer,** *n.* hoogdravend spreker *n.* **declamation,** *n.* hoogdravende rede *n.* **declamatory,** *a.* hoogdravend.

declaration, *n.* verklaring *n.,* declaratie *n.*

383 daze — degradation

declaratory, *a.* verklarend. **declare,** *v.t.* verklaren; aangeven *str.*; melden. ¶ *v.r. to ~ oneself,* zich nader verklaren, zijn mening *n.* zeggen *irr.*

declension, *n.* verbuiging *n.* **declinable,** *a.* verbuigbaar. **declination,** *n.* afwijking *n.*, declinatie *n.* **decline,** *v.i.* hellen; afnemen *str.*, achteruitgaan *irr.* ¶ *v.t.* verbuigen *str.*; afwijzen *str.*, weigeren, van de hand wijzen *str.* ¶ *n.* achteruitgang *n.*, verval *n.n.*

declivity, *n.* helling *n.*, glooiing *n.* **declivitous,** *a.* hellend.

decoction, *n.* afkooksel *n.n.*

decode, *v.t.* ontcijferen.

decompose, *v.t.* ontbinden *str.* ¶ *v.i.* tot ontbinding overgaan *irr.* **decomposition,** *n.* ontbinding *n.*

decontrol, *v.t.* vrijlaten *str.*

decorate, *v.t.* versieren; schilderen; decoreren. **decoration,** *n.* versiering *n.*; schilderen *n.n.*; decoratie *n.* **decorative,** *a.*, ~ly, *adv.* decoratief. **decorator,** *n.* huisschilder *n.*; decorateur *n.*

decorous, *a.*, ~ly, *adv.* welvoeglijk. **decorticate,** *v.t.* ontschorsen.

decorum, *n.* welvoeglijkheid *n.*; decorum *n.n.*

decoy, *v.t.* verlokken, in de val lokken. *n.* lokmiddel *n.n.*; lokaas *n.n.*; lokvogel *n.n.* ~ *duck,* lokeend.

decrease, *v.i.* verminderen, afnemen *str.* ¶ *v.t.* verminderen, doen *irr.* afnemen. ¶ *n.* vermindering *n.*; afneming *n.*, afname *n.*

decree, *n.* decreet *n.n.*; verordening *n.* ¶ *v.t.* bepalen, verordenen, decreteren.

decrepit, *a.* afgeleefd, aftands. **decrepitude,** *n.* gebrekkigheid *n.*

decrescent, *a.* afnemend.

decry, *v.t.* afbreken *str.*, afkeuren.

decuple, *a.* tienvoudig. ¶ *n.* tienvoud *n.n.*

dedicate, *v.t.* opdragen *str.*, wijden. **dedication,** *n.* opdracht *n.*; toewijding *n.* **dedicatory,** *a.* als opdracht *n.*

deduce, *v.t.* afleiden. *to ~ from,* opmaken uit. **deducible,** *a.* af te leiden.

deduct, *v.t.* aftrekken *str.*, afnemen *str.* **deduction,** *n.* aftrekking *n.*; gevolgtrekking *n.* **deductive,** *a.*, ~ly, *adv.* deductief.

deed, *n.* daad *n.*; acte *n.*, document *n.n.*

deem, *v.t.* achten, oordelen.

deep, *a.*, ~ly, *adv.* diep; diepzinnig; geheim; sluw; donker. *a ~ voice,* een zware stem *n.*; ~ *sea,* zee *n.* ¶ *n.* zee *n.*; diepte *n.* **deepen,** *v.t.* verdiepen, uitdiepen. ¶ *v.i.* dieper worden *str.* **deep-laid,** *a.* wel overlegd. **deepness,** *n.* diepte *n.*

deer, *n.* hert *n.* **deer-stalking,** *n.* sluipjacht *n.* op herten.

deface, *v.t.* schenden *str.*, ontsieren. **defacement,** *n.* schending *n.*

defalcate, *v.t.* verduisteren. **defalcation,** *n.* verduistering *n.*

defamation, *n.* smaad *n.*, laster *n.*, eerroving

n. **defamatory,** *a.* lasterlijk. **defame,** *v.t.* lasteren, onteren.

default, *v.i.* zijn verplichtingen niet nakomen; niet betalen. ¶ *n.* gebrek *n.n.*; verzuim *n.n. in ~ of,* bij gebreke van; *by ~,* bij verstek. **defaulter,** *n.* wanbetaler *n.*; verduisteraar *n.*

defeat, *v.t.* verslaan *irr.*; verwerpen *str.* ¶ *n.* nederlaag *n.* **defeatism,** *n.* defaitisme *n.n.*

defecate, *v.i.* afgaan *irr.* **defecation,** *n.* ontlasting *n.*

defect, *n.* gebrek *n.n.*, mankement *n.n.* **defection,** *n.* afvalligheid *n.* **defective,** *a.* gebrekkig; defect. **defectiveness,** *n.* onvolkomenheid *n.*

defence, *n.* verdediging *n.*; verweer *n.n. in ~ of,* ter verdediging van; *witness for the ~,* getuige à décharge. **defenceless,** *a.*, ~ly, *adv.* weerloos. **defend,** *v.t.* verdedigen. **defendant,** *n.* beschuldigde *n.* **defender,** *n.* verdediger *n.* **defensible,** *a.* verdedigbaar. **defensive,** *a.*, ~ly, *adv.* defensief. ¶ *n. to be on the ~,* een verdedigende houding *n.* aannemen *str.*

defer, *v.t.* uitstellen. ¶ *v.i. to ~ to,* zich onderwerpen *str.* aan. **deference,** *n.* eerbied *n. in ~ to,* uit achting *n.* voor. **deferment,** *n.* uitstel *n.n.* **deferred,** *a.* ~ *shares,* uitgestelde aandelen *pl.n.n.*

defiance, *n.* uitdaging *n.* **defiant,** *a.* uitdagend, tartend.

deficiency, *n.* gebrek *n.n.*, tekort *n.n.* **deficient,** *a.* ontoereikend; gebrekkig. *mentally ~,* achterlijk.

deficit, *n.* deficit *n.n.*, tekort *n.n.*

defile, *v.t.* bezoedelen, verontreinigen. ¶ *n.* pas *n.*, défilé *n.n.* **defilement,** *n.* bezoedeling *n.* **defiler,** *n.* bezoedelaar *n.*

define, *v.t.* omschrijven *str.*; definiëren. **definite,** *a.*, ~ly, *adv.* bepaald; duidelijk omschreven. **definition,** *n.* omschrijving *n.*, definitie *n.* **definitive,** *a.*, ~ly, *adv.* bepalend; onherroepelijk.

deflate, *v.t.* laten *str.* leeglopen; deflatie veroorzaken. **deflation,** *n.* laten leeglopen *n.n.*; deflatie *n.*

deflect, *v.t.* doen *irr.* afwijken. **deflection,** *n.* afwijking *n.*

deflower, *v.t.* onteren.

deform, *v.t.* misvormen. **deformed,** *a.* mismaakt; wanstaltig. **deformity,** *n.* mismaaktheid *n.*

defraud, *v.t.* bedriegen *str. to ~ of,* onthouden *irr.* **defrauder,** *n.* bedrieger *n.*

defray, *v.t.* bekostigen, dragen *str.*

deft, *a.*, ~ly, *adv.* handig; aardig.

defunct, *a.* overleden. ¶ *n.* overledene *n.*

defy, *v.t.* uitdagen, tarten; trotseren.

degeneracy, *n.* ontaarding *n.* **degenerate,** *v.i.* ontaarden. ¶ *a.* ontaard, gedegenereerd. ¶ *n.* gedegenereerde *n.* **degeneration,** *n.* ontaarding *n. fatty ~,* vervetting *n.*

degradation, *n.* degradatie *n.*; **verwording**

n. **degrade,** *v.t.* degraderen; doen *irr.* ontaarden.

degree, *n.* graad *n.*; rang *n.*; mate *n.* *to a ~,* buitenmate; *by ~s,* geleidelijk; *~s of comparison,* trappen *n.* van vergelijking *n.*

deification, *n.* vergoding *n.* **deify,** *v.t.* vergoden, vergoddelijken.

deign, *v.t.* zich verwaardigen.

deism, *n.* deïsme *n.n.* **deist,** *n.* deïst *n.* **deity,** *n.* godheid *n.*, goddelijkheid *n.*

deject, *v.t.* ontmoedigen. **dejected,** *a.* ontmoedigd, neerslachtig **dejection,** *n.* neerslachtigheid *n.*

delay, *v.t.* vertragen; uitstellen. ¶ *v.i.* talmen, dralen. ¶ *n.* uitstel *n.n.*

delectable, *a.,* *~bly,* *adv.* verrukkelijk, heerlijk.

delegate, *v.t.* afvaardigen, delegeren, volmachtigen. ¶ *n.* afgevaardigde *n.*, gedelegeerde *n.*, gevolmachtigde *n.* ¶ *a.* gedelegeerd. **delegation,** *n.* delegatie *n.*

delete, *v.t.* doorhalen, uitschrappen.

deleterious, *a.* schadelijk, verderfelijk.

deliberate, *a.,* *~ly,* *adv.* opzettelijk; bedaard, langzaam. ¶ *v.i.* delibereren, beraadslagen. ¶ *v.t.* overwegen *str.* **deliberateness,** *n.* beradenheid *n.* **deliberation,** *n.* beraadslaging *n.*; beraad *n.n.* **deliberative,** *a.* beraadslagend.

delicacy, *n.* kiesheid *n.*, fijngevoeligheid *n.*; lekkernij *n.* **delicate,** *a.,* *~ly,* *adv.* kies, delicaat; fijn, teder ; lekker.

delicious, *a.,* *~ly,* *adv.* heerlijk, lekker.

delight, *n.* genot *n.n.*; verrukking *n.* *to take ~ in,* behagen *n.n.* scheppen in. ¶ *v.t.* verheugen, verrukken. ¶ *v.i.* genot vinden, behagen scheppen. **delightful,** *a.,* *~ly,* *adv.* verrukkelijk, heerlijk.

delineate, *v.t.* schetsen; beschrijven *str.* **delineation,** *n.* schets *n.*; beschrijving *n.*

delinquency, *n.* overtreding *n.*, plichtverzuim *n.n.* **delinquent,** *n.* overtreder *n.*; schuldige *n.* ¶ *a.* schuldig.

delirious, *a.* ijlhoofdig; waanzinnig. **delirium,** *n.* ijlen *n.n.*; waanzin *n.*

deliver, *v.t.* bevrijden; verlossen; afleveren; inleveren, uitleveren; houden *irr. (speech):* overbrengen *irr. (message).* **deliverance,** *n.* bevrijding *n.*; uitspraak *n.*, vonnis *n.n.* **deliverer,** *n.* bevrijder *n.*, verlosser *n.* **delivery,** *n.* bevrijding *n.*, verlossing *n.*; levering *n.*, leverantie *n.*; voordracht *n.*

dell, *n.* dal *n.n.*

delta, *n.* delta *n.*

delude, *v.t.* misleiden.

deluge, *n.* zondvloed *n.*; stortvloed *n.* ¶ *v.t.* overstromen; *(fig.)* overstelpen.

delusion, *n.* zinsbegoocheling *n.*; dwaling *n.* **delusive,** *a.,* *~ly,* *adv.* bedrieglijk.

delve, *v.t.* delven.

demagogic, *a.* demagogisch. **demagogue,** *n.* demagoog *n.*, volksmenner *n.*

demand, *v.t.* eisen, vorderen, vragen *str.*

¶ *n.* eis *n.*, vordering *n.*; vraag *n.*, behoefte *n.*

demarcate, *v.t.* afbakenen; de grenzen vaststellen van. **demarcation,** *n.* grens *n.*

demean, *v.r.* *to ~ oneself,* zich gedragen, zich verlagen. **demeanour,** *n.* gedrag *n.n.*, houding *n.*

demented, *a.* waanzinnig.

demerit, *n.* gebrek *n.n.*, tekortkoming *n.*, nadeel *n.n.*

demesne, *n.* domein *n.n.*

demi-, *prefix,* half.

demise, *n.* overlijden *n.n.*

demisemiquaver, *n.* 32ste noot *n.*

demission, *n.* ontslag *n.n.*

demobilize, *v.t.* demobiliseren.

democracy, *n.* democratie *n.* **democrat,** *n.* democraat *n.* **democratic,** *a.* democratisch.

demolish, *v.t.* afbreken *str.*, slopen. **demolition,** *n.* afbreken *n.n.*, afbraak *n.*, sloping *n.*

demon, *n.* demon *n.*, boze geest *n.* **demoniac,** *a.* demonisch.

demonstrable, *a.,* *~bly,* *adv.* bewijsbaar. **demonstrate,** *v.t.* bewijzen *str.*, aantonen; betogen. ¶ *v.i.* een demonstratie *n.* houden *irr.* **demonstration,** *n.* betoging *n.*, demonstratie *n.* **demonstrative,** *a.,* *~ly,* *adv.* aanschouwelijk; overdreven. *~ pronoun,* aanwijzend voornaamwoord *n.n.* **demonstrator,** *n.* betoger *n.*; assistent *n.*

demoralization, *n.* demoralisatie *n.* **demoralize,** *v.t.* demoraliseren.

demur, *v.i.* bezwaar maken; bedenkingen maken. ¶ *n.* bezwaar *n.n.*; bedenking *n.*; aarzeling *n.*

demure, *a.,* *~ly,* *adv.* preuts, zedig. **demureness,** *n.* preutsheid *n.*, zedigheid *n.*

demurrage, *n.* overliggdagen *pl.n.*

demurrer, *n.* exceptie *n.*

den, *n.* hol *n.n.*; kamer *n.*

deniable, *a.* loochenbaar. **denial,** *n.* ontkenning *n.*, verloochening *n.*; weigering *n.*

denim, *n.* grof katoen *n.n.*

denizen, *n.* bewoner *n.*

denominate, *v.t.* aanwijzen *str.* **denomination,** *n.* benaming *n.*; soort *n.*; sekte *n.*; coupure *n.* **denominational,** *a.* confessioneel. **denominator,** *n.* noemer *n.*

denote, *v.t.* aanwijzen *str.*, aanduiden.

denounce, *v.t.* aanklagen, aangeven *str.*; opzeggen *irr.* **denouncement,** *n.* aanklacht *n.*

dense, *a.* dicht; dom. **denseness,** *n.* dichtheid *n.*; domheid *n.* **density,** *n.* dichtheid *n.*

dent, *n.* deuk *n.*, bluts *n.* ¶ *v.t.* indeuken.

dental, *a.* tand ... **dentifrice,** *n.* tandpasta *n.*, tandpoeder *n.n.* **dentist,** *n.* tandarts *n.* **dentistry,** *n.* tandheelkunde *n.* **dentition,** *n.* tandstelsel *n.n.*; tanden krijgen *n.n.* **denture,** *n.* kunstgebit *n.n.*

denudation, *n.* ontbloting *n.*; beroving *n.* **denude,** *v.t.* ontbloten; ontdoen *irr.*

denunciation, *n.* aanklacht *n.*

deny, *v.t.* ontkennen; ontzeggen; weigeren; loochenen.

deodorant, n. reukverdrijvend middel n.n.
deodorize, v.t. reukeloos maken. **deodorizer,**
n. *See* **deodorant.**
depart, v.i. vertrekken *str.*, heengaan *irr.*
to ~ from, afwijken *str.* van. ¶ *v.t. to ~ this
life,* overlijden *str.* **department,** n. afdeling
n., departement n.n. **departure,** n. vertrek
n.n.; afwijking n.
depend, v.i. afhangen *str. to ~ on,* vertrouwen
op; *it ~s,* het hangt ervan af. **dependant,**
n. ondergeschikte n. **dependence,** n.
afhankelijkheid n. **dependency,** n.
afhankelijkheid n.; onderhorigheid n.,
wingewest n.n. **dependent,** a. afhankelijk.
~ from, afhangend van; *~ on,* afhankelijk
van. ¶ n. afhankelijke persoon n.
depict, v.t. schilderen; beschrijven *str.*
depilation, n. ontharing n. **depilatory,** n.
ontharingsmiddel n.n.
deplete, v.t. uitputten, verminderen. **deple-
tion,** n. uitputting n.
deplorable, a., ~bly, adv. betreurenswaardig,
jammerlijk. **deplore,** v.t. betreuren.
deploy, v.t. ontplooien; deployeren. **deployment,** n. deployeren n.n.
deponent, n. getuige n.
depopulate, v.t. ontvolken. **depopulation,** n.
ontvolking n.
deport, v.t. deporteren. **deportation,** n.
deportatie n.
deportment, n. houding n.
depose, v.t. afzetten, onttronen; getuigen,
verklaren.
deposit, v.t. neerleggen; deponeren; bezinken
str. ¶ n. deposito n.n.; storting n.;
bezinksel n.n., neerslag n. **depositary,** n.
bewaarder n. **deposition,** n. getuigen-
verklaring n.; afneming n. van het Kruis;
afzetting n. **depositor,** n. storter n.
depository, n. bewaarplaats n.
depot, n. depot n.n.
deprave, v.t. verderven *str.*, bederven *str.*
~d, verdorven. **depravity,** n. verdorvenheid n.
deprecate, v.t. afkeuren, diep betreuren.
deprecation, n. afkeuring n. **deprecatory,** a.
afkeurend.
depreciate, v.i. in waarde dalen. ¶ v.t. de
waarde verminderen van. **depreciation,** n.
waardevermindering n.
depredate, v.t. leegplunderen; verwoesten.
depredation, n. plundering n., verwoesting
n. **depredator,** n. plunderaar n.
depress, v.t. neerdrukken; (fig.) terneer-
drukken, terneerslaan *irr.* **depression,** n.
neerdrukking n.; depressie n.; daling n.;
neerslachtigheid n., gedruktheid n.
deprivation, n. beroving n., verlies n.n.
deprive, v.t. beroven; ontzetten.
depth, n. diepte n. *~ of winter,* hartje n.n.
van de winter; *he is out of his ~,* het
gaat hem te boven; *~ charge,* dieptebom n.
deputation, n. deputatie n., afvaardiging n.
depute, v.t. afvaardigen; overdragen *str.*

deputize, v.i. *to ~ for,* optreden *str.* voor.
deputy, n. afgevaardigde n., gevolmachtigde n.; plaatsvervanger n. ¶ a.
vice . . ., onder . . ., adjunct . . .
deracinate, v.t. ontwortelen.
derail, v.i. ontsporen, derailleren. ¶ v.t. doen
irr. ontsporen. **derailment,** n. ontsporing n.
derange, v.t. storen. **deranged,** a. niet goed
wijs. **derangement,** n. storing n.
derelict, a. onbeheerd; verlaten. **dereliction,**
n. verzuim n.n., verzaking n.
deride, v.t. bespotten, uitlachen. **derision,** n.
spot n., bespotting n. **derisive,** a., ~ly,
adv. spottend, honend.
derivable, a. afleidbaar. **derivation,** n.
afleiding n. **derivative,** a., ~ly, adv.
afgeleid. ¶ n. derivaat n.n. **derive,** v.t.
voortspruiten *str. to ~ from,* afleiden van
(or uit).
derogate, v.t. benadelen; afbreuk doen *irr.*
aan. **derogation,** n. afbreuk n. **derogatory,**
a. afbreuk doende, nadeel n.n. toe-
brengend.
derrick, n. laadboom n.; kraan n.
dervish, n. derwis n.
descant, n. discant n. ¶ v.i. zingen *str.* in
variaties n.; (fig.) uitweiden.
descend, v.i. dalen, afdalen; afstammen; zich
verlagen. *to ~ on,* onverwacht bezoeken
irr. **descendant,** n. nakomeling n. **descent,**
n. afdaling n., neerdaling n.; helling n.;
afstamming n.; inval n.
describe, v.t. beschrijven *str.* **description,** n.
beschrijving n.; signalement n.n. **descriptive,** a., ~ly, adv. beschrijvend.
descry, v.t. gewaarworden *str.*, bespeuren.
desecrate, v.t. ontheiligen, ontwijden.
desecration, n. ontheiliging n., ontwijding
n.
desert, n. woestijn n.; woestenij n.; verdienste
n., verdiende loon n.n. ¶ a. verlaten,
onbewoond. ¶ v.i. deserteren. **deserter,** n.
deserteur n. verlatenheid n.; **desertion,** n. verlatenheid n.;
desertie n.
deserve, v.t. verdienen. *to ~ of,* zich verdienstelijk maken jegens. **deservedly,** adv.
terecht. **deserving,** a. verdienstelijk.
deshabille, n. négligé n.n.
desiccate, v.t. drogen. ¶ v.i. opdrogen.
desiccated, a. (uit)gedroogd. **desiccation,**
n. opdroging n.
desiderate, v.t. wensen. **desideratum,** n.
desideratum n.n.
design, v.t. ontwerpen *str.*; bedoelen. ¶ n.
plan n.n., ontwerp n.n.; opzet n., bedoeling
n.
designate, v.t. aanduiden, aanwijzen *str.*
designation, n. aanduiding n., aanwijzing
n.; benaming n.
designedly, adv. opzettelijk. **designer,** n.
ontwerper n.; intrigant. **designing,** a.
intrigerend.
desirability, n. wenselijkheid n. **desirable,** a.
wenselijk, begeerlijk. **desire,** v.t. wensen,

begeren. ¶ *n.* wens *n.*, begeerte *n.* *by* ~,
op verzoek *n.n.* **desirous,** *a.,* ~**ly,** *adv.*
begerig. ~ *of,* verlangend naar.
desist, *v.t.* ophouden *irr.* *to* ~ *from,* nalaten
str.
desk, *n.* lessenaar *n.*
desolate, *v.t.* verwoesten, ontvolken. ¶ *a.*
woest, verlaten, eenzaam, troosteloos.
desolation, *n.* verwoesting *n.,* troosteloosheid *n.*
despair, *v.i.* wanhopen. *to* ~ *of,* wanhopen
aan. ¶ *n.* wanhoop *n.* *in* ~, wanhopig.
despairingly, *adv.* wanhopig.
despatch, *v.t.* & *n.* *See* **dispatch.**
desperado, *n.* wanhopige woesteling *n.*
desperate, *a.,* ~**ly,** *adv.* wanhopig, ver-
twijfeld; hopeloos. **desperation,** *n.*
vertwijfeling *n.*
despicable, *a.,* ~**bly,** *adv.* verachtelijk.
despise, *v.t.* verachten; versmaden.
despite, *prep.* trots, in weerwil van.
despoil, *v.t.* plunderen, beroven.
despond, *v.i.* moedeloos worden *str.* **des-
pondence,** *n.,* **despondency,** *n.* moedeloos-
heid *n.* **despondent,** *a.* moedeloos.
despot, *n.* despoot *n.,* dwingeland *n.* **despotic,**
a., ~**ally,** *adv.* despotisch. **despotism,** *n.*
despotisme *n.n.,* dwingelandij *n.*
dessert, *n.* dessert *n.n.,* nagerecht *n.n.*
destination, *n.* (plaats *n.* van) bestemming *n.*
destine, *v.t.* bestemmen. **destiny,** *n.*
bestemming *n.;* lot *n.n.,* noodlot *n.n.*
destitute, *a.* behoeftig, hulpbehoevend. ~ *of,*
verstoken van. **destitution,** *n.* armoede *n.,*
hulpbehoevendheid *n.*
destroy, *v.t.* vernietigen; verdelgen. **destroyer,**
n. vernieler *n.;* torpedojager *n.* **destruction,**
n. vernieling *n.,* vernietiging *n.;* verdelging
n.; ondergang *n.* **destructive,** *a.,* ~**ly,** *adv.*
vernietigend; afbrekend. **destructiveness,**
n. vernietigingslust *n.*
desuetude, *n.* onbruik *n.n.*
desultoriness, *n.* oppervlakkigheid *n.* **desul-
tory,** *a.* onsamenhangend; oppervlakkig,
vluchtig.
detach, *v.t.* losmaken; afzonden; detacheren.
detachable, *a.* afneembaar. **detachment,** *n.*
onbevangenheid *n.;* onverschilligheid *n.*
detail, *n.* bijzonderheid *n.,* bizonderheid *n.;*
detail *n.n.* *in* ~, omstandig; *to go into* ~,
in bijzonderheden treden. ¶ *v.t.* opsommen; detacheren.
detain, *v.t.* ophouden *irr.;* gevangen houden
irr. **detainer,** *n.* bevel *n.n.* tot inhechtenisneming *n.*
detect, *v.t.* ontdekken; opsporen. **detection,**
n. ontdekking *n.;* opsporing *n.* **detective,** *a.*
opsporings . . ¶ *n.* rechercheur *n.,*
detective *n.* **detector,** *n.* verklikker *n.*
detention, *n.* gevangenzetting *n.;* school-
blij ven *n.n.*
deter, *v.t.* afschrikken *str.*
detergent, *n.* zuiverend middel *n.n.*
deteriorate, *v.i.* ontaarden, in kwaliteit *n.*

achteruitgaan *irr.* **deterioration,** *n.*
achteruitgang *n.,* bederf *n.n.*
determinable, *a.* bepaalbaar. **determinate,**
v.t. vaststellen. ¶ *a.,* ~**ly,** *adv.* bepaald,
beslist. **determination,** *n.* vaststelling *n.;*
vastberadenheid *n.* **determinative,** *a.*
bepalend. **determine,** *v.t.* bepalen, vaststellen; besluiten *str.;* eindigen.
detest, *v.t.* verfoeien, verafschuwen. **detestable,** *a.,* ~**bly,** *adv.* verfoeilijk, afschuwelijk
detestation, *n.* verfoeiing *n.*
dethrone, *v.t.* onttronen. **dethronement,** *n.*
onttroning *n.*
detonate, *v.t.* doen *irr.* ontploffen. ¶ *v.i.*
ontploffen. **detonation,** *n.* ontploffing *n.,*
slag *n.,* knal *n.* **detonator,** *n.* slaghoedje
n.n., schokbuisje *n.n.*
detour, *n.* omweg *n.*
detract, *v.t.* kleineren; kwaadspreken *str.* van.
¶ *v.i.* *to* ~ *from,* afbreuk *n.* doen *irr.* aan.
detraction, *n.* kleinering *n.;* kwaadsprekerij
n. **detractive,** *a.* lasterlijk. **detractor,** *n.*
lasteraar *n.*
detriment, *n.* nadeel *n.n.* **detrimental,** *a.,*
~**ly,** *adv.* nadelig, schadelijk.
deuce, *n.* twee *n.;* duivel *n.* **deuced,** *a.*
verduiveld.
devastate, *v.t.* verwoesten. **devastation,** *n.*
verwoesting *n.*
develop, *v.t.* ontwikkelen; zich ontwikkelen.
developer, *n.* ontwikkelaar *n.* **development,**
n. ontwikkeling *n.*
deviate, *v.i.* afwijken *str.* **deviation,** *n.*
afwijking *n.*
device, *n.* plan *n.n.,* list *n.;* uitvinding *n.,*
apparaat *n.n.;* zinspreuk *n.* *left to his
own* ~*s,* aan zijn lot overgelaten.
devil, *n.* duivel *n.;* duivelstoejager *n.* *between
the* ~ *and the deep sea,* tussen twee vuren;
to play the ~ *with,* in de war sturen.
¶ *v.t.* kruiden en roosteren. **devilish,** *a.*
duivels. **devilment,** *n.* geduvel *n.n.;*
kattekwaad *n.n.* **devilry,** *n.* roekeloze
moed *n.*
devious, *a.* kronkelend, een omweg volgend.
by ~ *ways,* langs een omweg *n.*
devise, *v.t.* verzinnen *str.,* ontwerpen *str.;*
nalaten *str.* **deviser,** *n.* plannenmaker *n.*
devisor, *n.* erflater *n.*
devoid, *a.* verstoken.
devolution, *n.* devolutie *n.* **devolve,** *v.i.*
to ~ *upon,* neerkomen *irr.* op.
devote, *v.t.* wijden, toewijden. **devoted,** *a.,*
~**ly,** *adv.* (toe)gewijd; verknocht. **devotee,**
n. aanbidder *n.* **devotion,** *n.* toewijding *n.;*
godsvrucht *n.,* vroomheid *n.;* gehechtheid
n., verknochtheid *n.* **devotional,** *a.* vroom,
stichtelijk.
devour, *v.t.* verslinden *str.*
devout, *a.,* ~**ly,** *adv.* godvruchtig; oprecht.
devoutness, *n.* godsvrucht *n.*
dew, *n.* dauw *n.* ¶ *v.t.* bedauwen. **dewy, a.**
bedauwd.
dewlap, *n.* halskwabbe *n.*

dexterity, *n*. handigheid *n*., behendigheid *n*., vaardigheid *n*. **dexterous**, *a*., ~ly, *adv*. handig, behendig, vaardig.

diabetes, *n*. suikerziekte *n*. **diabetic**, *a*. suikerziekte ... ¶ *n*. lijder *n*. aan suikerziekte *n*.

diabolic(al), *a*., ~ally, *adv*. duivels.

diadem, *n*. diadeem *n.n*.

diaeresis, *n*. trema *n.n*., deelteken *n.n*.

diagnosis, *n*. diagnose *n*. **diagnostic**, *a*. diagnostiek.

diagonal, *a*., ~ly, *adv*. diagonaal. ¶ *n*. diagonaal *n*., hoeklijn *n*.

diagram, *n*. diagram *n.n*.; schema *n.n*. **diagrammatic**, *a*. schematisch.

dial, *n*. wijzerplaat *n*.; zonnewijzer *n*. ¶ *v.t*. draaien.

dialect, *n*. dialekt *n.n*. **dialectical**, *a*., ~ly, *adv*. dialectisch. **dialectics**, *pl.n*. dialektiek *n*.

dialogue, *n*. dialoog *n*., tweespraak *n*.

diameter, *n*. diameter *n*., middellijn *n*. **diametrical**, *a*., ~ly, *adv*. diametraal; lijnrecht.

diamond, *n*. diamant *n*.; ruit *n*. *it is ~ cut ~*, ze zijn aan elkaar gewaagd; ~*s* (*cards*), ruit, ruiten.

diapason, *n*. diapason *n*., toonomvang *n*.

diaper, *n*. luier *n*.

diaphanous, *a*. doorzichtig.

diaphragm, *n*. middenrif *n.n*.; diaphragma *n.n*.

diarist, *n*. schrijver *n*. van een dagboek *n.n*.

diarrhoea, *n*. diarrhee *n*.

diary, *n*. dagboek *n.n*.; agenda *n*.

diatribe, *n*. schimprede *n*.

dibble, *n*. pootstok *n*. ¶ *v.t*. poten.

dice, *pl.n*. dobbelstenen *pl.n*.; dobbelspel *n.n*. ¶ *v.i*. dobbelen. ¶ *v.t*. *to ~ away*, verdobbelen. **dice-box**, *n*. dobbelkroes *n*.

dickens, *n*. drommel *n*.

dick(e)y, *n*. kattebak *n*.; frontje *n.n*.

dictate, *v.t*. dicteren; voorschrijven *str*. ¶ *n*. voorschrift *n.n*.; inspraak *n*. **dictation**, *n*. dictee *n.n*. **dictator**, *n*. dictator *n*. **dictatorial**, *a*. dictoriaal, gebiedend. **dictatorship**, *n*. dictatuur *n*.

diction, *n*. voordracht *n*., dictie *n*. **dictionary**, *n*. woordenboek *n.n*.

didactic, *a*. didactisch.

diddle, *v.t*. bedotten.

die, *v.i*. sterven *str*., dood gaan *irr*.; sneuvelen. *to ~ away*, afsterven *str*., wegsterven *str*.; *to ~ off*, uitsterven *str*.; *to be dying to* ..., branden van verlangen om te ... ¶ *v.t*. sterven. ¶ *n*. dobbelsteen *n*.; muntstempel *n*. **die-hard**, *n*. persoon *n*. die de strijd niet opgeeft.

diet, *n*. dieet *n.n*.; dieet *n.n*., rijksdag *n*. ¶ *v.i*. een dieet volgen. **dietary**, *a*. het dieet betreffend, dieet ... **dietetic**, *a*. diëtetisch. ¶ *n*. ~*s*, voedingsleer *n*.

differ, *v.i*. verschillen; het niet eens zijn.

difference, *n*. verschil *n.n*. **different**, *a*., ~ly, *adv*. verschillend; anders. **differential**, *a*. differentiaal. ~ *calculus*, differentiaalrekening *n*. **differentiate**, *v.i*. onderscheiden.

difficult, *a*. moeilijk, lastig. **difficulty**, *n*. moeilijkheid *n*.

diffidence, *n*. gebrek *n.n*. aan zelfvertrouwen *n.n*.; schroomvalligheid *n*. **diffident**, *a*., ~ly, *adv*. schroomvallig.

diffraction, *n*. straalbreking *n*.

diffuse, *v.t*. verspreiden. ¶ *a*. diffuus; wijdlopig. **diffusion**, *n*. verspreiding *n*.; diffusie *n*. **diffusive**, *a*. verspreid; wijdlopig.

dig, *v.t*. graven *str*. ¶ *n*. ~*s*, kamer *n*., kast *n*.

digest, *v.t*. verteren; verwerken; kroppen. ¶ *n*. digesten *pl.n.n*.; kort verslag *n.n*. **digester**, *n*. Papiniaanse pot *n*. **digestible**, *a*. verteerbaar. **digestion**, *n*. spijsvertering *n*. **digestive**, *a*. spijsverterings ...

digger, *n*. graver *n*.; graafmachine *n*. **diggings**, *pl.n*. goudveld *n.n*.

digit, *n*. vinger *n*.; teen *n*.; cijfer *n.n*.

digitalis, *n*. vingerhoedskruid *n.n*.

dignified, *a*. waardig. **dignify**, *v.t*. tot een waardigheid *n*. verheffen *str*.; deftig noemen. **dignitary**, *n*. waardigheidsbekleder *n*. **dignity**, *n*. waardigheid *n*.

digress, *v.i*. afdwalen, uitweiden. **digression**, *n*. afdwaling *n*., uitweiding *n*. **digressive**, *a*. uitweidend.

dike, *n*. *See* **dyke**.

dilapidate, *v.i*. vervallen *str*., in verval *n.n*. raken. **dilapidated**, *a*. bouwvallig. **dilapidation**, *n*. verval *n.n*.

dilatation, *n*. uitzetting *n*. **dilate**, *v.t*. doen irr. uitzetten; openspalken. ¶ *v.i*. zich uitzetten. *to ~ upon*, uitweiden over.

dilatoriness, *n*. nalatigheid *n*. **dilatory**, *a*. nalatig, tot uitstellen geneigd.

dilemma, *n*. dilemma *n.n*.

diligence, *n*. ijver *n*., vlijt *n*. **diligent**, *a*., ~ly, *adv*. vlijtig, naarstig.

dill, *n*. venkel *n*.; dille *n*.

dilly-dally, *v.i*. treuzelen, beuzelen.

dilute, *v.t*. verdunnen. ¶ *a*. verdund. **dilution**, *n*. verdunning *n*.

diluvial, *a*. diluviaal. **diluvium**, *n*. diluvium *n.n*.

dim, *a*., ~ly, *adv*. vaag, dof, onduidelijk; mat. ¶ *v.i*. dof worden *str*. ¶ *v.t*. dof maken; overschaduwen.

dime, *n*. 1/10 dollar *n*.

dimension, *n*. afmeting *n*.; omvang *n*.

diminish, *v.t*. verminderen. ¶ *v.i*. verminderen, afnemen *str*. **diminution**, *n*. vermindering *n*.; afname *n*., afneming *n*. **diminutive**, *a*., ~ly, *adv*. zeer klein; miniatuur ... ¶ *n*. verkleinwoord *n*.

dimity, *n*. diemit *n.n*. ¶ *a*. diemiten.

dimness, *n*. dofheid *n*.; duisterheid *n*.

dimple, *n*. kuiltje *n.n*. ¶ *v.t*. & *v.i*. kuiltjes (in de wangen) krijgen *str*.

din, *n*. lawaai *n.n*.; geraas *n.n*. ¶ *v.t*. *to ~*

something into someone's ears, iemand voortdurend iets zeggen *irr.*
dine, *v.i.* dineren, eten *str.* *to* ~ *out*, uit eten gaan *irr.* ¶ *v.t.* mee uit eten *n.n.* nemen *str.*, op een maaltijd *n.* trakteren.
ding-dong, *n.* gebeier *n.n.*
dingy, *a.* groezelig, goor; dof.
dining-car, *n.* restauratiewagen *n.* **dining-room**, *n.* eetkamer *n.*; eetzaal *n.* **dinner**, *n.* middagmaal *n.n.*, middageten *n.n.*; diner *n.n.* ~ *jacket*, smoking *n.*; ~ *service*, eetservies *n.n.*
dint, *n.* kracht *n.* *by* ~ *of*, door (middel van)
diorama, *n.* diorama *n.n.*
dip, *v.t.* dopen, dompelen; wassen. *to* ~ *the flag*, de vlag strijken *str.*, met de vlag salueren. ¶ *v.i.* duiken *str.*; inclineren. *to* ~ *into*, vluchtig inkijken *str.*; *to* ~ *into one's purse*, met de hand in de zak tasten.
diphtheria, *n.* diphtheritis *n.*
diphthong, *n.* tweeklank *n.*
diploma, *n.* diploma *n.n.*
diplomacy, *n.* diplomatie *n.* **diplomat**, *n.* diplomaat *n.* **diplomatic**, *a.*, ~ally, *adv.* diplomatisch.
dipper, *n.* duiker *n.*; schep *n.*; dompelaar *n.*
dipsomania, *n.* drankzucht *n.* **dipsomaniac**, *n.* drankzuchtige *n.*
dipstick, *n.* peilstok *n.*
dire, *a.* verschrikkelijk.
direct, *a.* direct, rechtstreeks; onmiddellijk. ¶ *v.t.* richten; besturen, richten; dirigeren; de weg wijzen *str.*; voorschrijven *str.* **direction**, *n.* richting *n.*; leiding *n.*, aanwijzing *n.* **directive**, *a.* besturend, richt ... ¶ *n.* richtlijn *n.* **directly**, *adv.* rechtstreeks; onmiddellijk, aanstonds; zodra. **director**, *n.* directeur *n.*; leider *n.*; commissaris *n.* **directory**, *n.* adresboek *n.n.* **directress**, *n.* directrice *n.*
dirge, *n.* lijkzang *n.*, treurzang *n.*
dirigible, *a.* bestuurbaar.
dirk, *n.* ponjaard *n.*, dolk *n.*
dirt, *n.* vuil *n.n.* ~ *cheap*, spotgoedkoop. **dirtiness**, *n.* vuilheid *n.*, vuiligheid *n.* **dirty**, *a.*, ~ily, *adv.* vuil; laag.
disability, *n.* onvermogen *n.n.*; onbekwaamheid *n.* **disable**, *v.t.* ongeschikt maken; buiten gevecht stellen. **disabled**, *a.* buiten gevecht gesteld. ~ *soldier*, invaliede.
disabuse, *v.t.* ontnuchteren; uit de droom helpen *str.*
disadvantage, *n.* nadeel *n.n.*; verlies *n.n.* **disadvantageous**, *a.* ~ly, *adv.* nadelig, onvoordelig.
disaffect, *v.t.* ontrouw maken. **disaffection**, *n.* ontrouw *n.*, ontevredenheid *n.*
disagree, *v.i.* het oneens zijn; niet overeenkomen *irr.* *it* ~*s with me*, het bekomt me niet goed. **disagreeable**, *a.*, ~bly, *adv.* onaangenaam. **disagreement**, *n.* verschil *n.n.*, onenigheid *n.*; meningsverschil *n.n.*

disallow, *v.t.* niet toestaan *irr.*, niet goedkeuren; (zijn) goedkeuring onthouden *irr.* aan.
disappear, *v.i.* verdwijnen *str.* **disappearance**, *n.* verdwijning *n.*
disappoint, *v.t.* teleurstellen; verijdelen. **disappointment**, *n.* teleurstelling *n.*
disapprobation, *n.*, **disapproval**, *n.* afkeuring *n.* **disapprove**, *v.t.* afkeuren. ¶ *v.i.* *to* ~ *of*, afkeuren.
disarm, *v.t.* ontwapenen; onschadelijk maken. **disarmament**, *n.* ontwapening *n.*
disarrange, *v.t.* in wanorde *n.* brengen *irr.* **disarrangement**, *n.* verwarring *n.*
disarray, *n.* wanorde *n.*, verwarring *n.* ¶ *v.t.* in wanorde brengen *irr.*
disaster, *n.* ramp *n.*, onheil *n.n.* **disastrous**, *a.*, ~ly, *adv.* rampspoedig.
disavow, *v.t.* loochenen; niet erkennen. **disavowal**, *n.* loochening *n.*; ontkenning *n.*
disband, *v.t.* ontbinden *str.*; afdanken. ¶ *v.i.* uiteengaan *irr.*
disbelief, *n.* ongeloof *n.n.* **disbelieve**, *v.t.* niet geloven. **disbeliever**, *n.* ongelovige *n.*
disburse, *v.t.* uitgeven *str.*; voorschieten *str.* **disbursement**, *n.* uitgave *n.*; voorschot *n.n.*
disc, *n.* schijf *n.*; discus *n.*
discard, *v.t.* verwerpen *str.*, ter zijde leggen; uittrekken *str.*
discern, *v.t.* ontwaren; onderscheiden. **discernible**, *a.*, ~bly, *adv.* waarneembaar, zichtbaar. **discerning**, *a.* oordeelkundig. **discernment**, *n.* onderscheidingsvermogen *n.n.*; scherpzinnigheid *n.*
discharge, *v.t.* ontladen, lossen; kwijtschelden *str.*; ontslaan *irr.*; afschieten *str.*; etteren. ¶ *n.* lossing *n.*; vrijlating *n.*; ontslag *n.n.*; salvo *n.n.*; lozing *n.* **discharger**, *n.* ontlader *n.*
disciple, *n.* discipel *n.* **disciplinarian**, *a.* disciplinair, tucht ... ¶ *n.* ordehouder *n.* **disciplinary**, *a.* disciplinair. **discipline**, *n.* discipline *n.*; tucht *n.*; tuchtiging *n.*, kastijding *n.* ¶ *v.t.* tuchtigen, kastijden.
disclaim, *v.t.* ontkennen; verwerpen *str.*; van zich wijzen *str.* **disclaimer**, *n.* ontkenning *n.*; verwerping *n.*
disclose, *v.t.* bekend maken; onthullen; blootleggen. **disclosure**, *n.* onthulling *n.*
discoloration, *n.* verkleuring *n.*, verandering *n.* van kleur *n.* **discolour**, *v.i.* verkleuren, verschieten *str.* ¶ *v.t.* doen *irr.* verkleuren, doen *irr.* verschieten.
discomfit, *v.t.* verslaan *irr.*; verijdelen. **discomfiture**, *n.* nederlaag *n.*; mislukking *n.*
discomfort, *n.* ongemak *n.n.* ¶ *v.t.* onbehaaglijk maken.
discompose, *v.t.* doen *irr.* ontstellen, in verwarring *n.* brengen *irr.* **discomposure**, *n.* ontsteltenis *n.*; verwarring *n.*
disconcert, *v.t.* in de war brengen *irr.*, uit het veld slaan.
disconnect, *v.t.* uitschakelen; afkoppelen.
disconsolate, *a.* troosteloos; somber.

discontent, *n.* ontevredenheid *n.*, misnoegen *n.n.* ❡ *v.t.* ontevreden maken. **discontented,** *a.* ontevreden, misnoegd.

discontinuance, *n.*, discontinuation, *n.* afbreking *n.*, storing *n.*, staking *n.* discontinue, *v.t.* afbreken *str.*, storen, staken.

discord, *n.* wanklank *n.*; tweedracht *n.* discordance, *n.* strijdigheid *n.*; onenigheid *n.* discordant *a.* vals; onenig.

discount, *v.t.* disconteren, aftrekken *str.*; buiten rekening laten *str.*, niet veel waarde hechten aan. ❡ *n.* disconto *n.n.*, korting *n.*, rabat *n.n. at a ~*, beneden pari, niet in trek *n.*

discountenance, *v.t.* afkeuren, niet aanmoedigen.

discourage, *v.t.* ontmoedigen; afschrikken *str.* discouragement, *n.* ontmoediging *n.*

discourse, *v.i.* spreken *str.*; redeneren. *to ~ on* or *of,* spreken over. ❡ *n.* rede *n.*; onderhandeling *n.*

discourteous, *a.*, *~ly, adv.* onhoffelijk, onbeleefd. discourtesy, *n.* onhoffelijkheid *n.*

discover, *v.t.* ontdekken; blootleggen. discoverable, *a.* zichtbaar. discoverer, *n.* ontdekker *n.* discovery, *n.* ontdekking *n.*

discredit, *v.t.* geen geloof *n.n.* hechten aan; het geloof schokken *str.* ❡ *n.* oneer *n.*, diskrediet *n.n.* discreditable, *a.*, *~bly, adv.* schandelijk.

discreet, *a.*, *~ly, adv.* taktvol, discreet.

discrepancy, *n.* verschil *n.n.*; tegenstrijdigheid *n.* discrepant, *a.* tegenstrijdig.

discretion, *n.* takt *n.*, overleg *n.n.*; goeddunken *n. at the ~ of,* naar goedvinden *n.n.* van. discretionary, *a.* onbeperkt, naar believen *n.n.*

discriminate, *v.i.* onderscheiden, onderscheid *n.n.* maken. ❡ *a.* onderscheidend; oordeelkundig. discrimination, *n.* onderscheid *n.n.*; onderscheidingsvermogen *n.n.* discriminatory, *a.* onderscheidend; oordeelkundig. *~ law,* uitzonderingswet *n.*

discursive, *a.* beredenerend; afdwalend.

discuss, *v.t.* bespreken *str.* discussion, *n.* bespreking *n.*; discussie *n.*

disdain, *v.t.* minachten, versmaden. ❡ *n.* minachting *n.*, versmading *n.* disdainful, *a.*, *~ly, adv.* minachtend.

disease, *n.* ziekte *n.*, kwaal *n.* diseased, *a.* ziek, ziekelijk.

disembark, *v.t.* ontschepen, landen. ❡ *v.i.* (zich) ontschepen, landen. disembarkation, *n.* ontscheping *n.*, landing *n.*

disembodiment, *n.* losmaking *n.* (van het lichaam). disembody, *v.t.* bevrijden van het lichaam.

disembowel, *v.t.* de buik opensnijden *str.*

disenchant, *v.t.* ontgoochelen. disenchantment, *n.* ontgoocheling *n.*

disencumber, *v.t.* vrijmaken.

disengage, *v.t.* vrijmaken, losmaken. ❡ *v.i.* het gevecht afbreken *str.* disengaged, *a.*

vrij. disengagement, *n.* vrijmaking *n.*; vrij zijn *n.n.*

disentangle, *v.t.* ontwarren, losmaken.

disestablish, *v.t.* scheiden, van de staat losmaken.

disfavour, *n.* ongenade *n.*; nadeel *n.n.* ❡ *v.t.* niet begunstigen.

disfiguration, *n.* schending *n.*, ontsiering *n.* disfigure, *v.t.* schenden *str.*, ontsieren.

disfranchise, *v.t.* van burgerrechten *pl.n.n.* beroven; van het kiesrecht beroven. disfranchisement, *n.* beroving *n.* van het kiesrecht.

disgorge, *v.t.* uitbraken; (*fig.*) teruggeven *str.*

disgrace, *n.* ongenade *n.*; schande *n.*; schandvlek *n.* ❡ *v.t.* onteren; in ongenade brengen *irr.*; schande brengen *irr.* over. disgraceful, *a.*, *~ly, adv.* schandelijk.

disgruntled, *a.* ontevreden, ontstemd.

disguise, *v.t.* vermommen. ❡ *n.* vermomming *n.*; voorwendsel *n.n.*

disgust, *v.t.* doen *irr.* walgen. *to be ~ed at,* walgen van. ❡ *n.* afkeer *n.*, walging *n.* disgusting, *a.*, *~ly, adv.* walgelijk; stuitend.

dish, *n.* schotel *n.*; gerecht *n.* ❡ *v.t.* opdissen. *to ~ up,* opdissen. dishcloth, *n.* schoteldoek *n.*, vaatdoek *n.*

dishearten, *v.t.* ontmoedigen.

dishevel, *v.t.* het haar in de war brengen *irr.*

dishonest, *a.*, *~ly, adv.* oneerlijk. dishonesty, *n.* oneerlijkheid *n.*

dishonour, *n.* oneer *n.*, schande *n.* ❡ *v.t.* onteren, te schande maken. dishonourable, *a.*, *~bly, adv.* onterend, eerloos.

dish-washer, *n.* bordenwasser *n.* dish-water, *n.* bordenwater *n.n.*

disillusion, *v.t.* ontgoochelen, ontnuchteren. ❡ *n.* ontgoocheling *n.*, desillusie *n.* disillusionment, *n.* ontgoocheling *n.*, desillusie *n.*

disinclination, *n.* ongeneigdheid *n.*, afkerigheid *n.* disincline, *v.t.* afkerig maken. *~d to,* afkerig van of niet geneigd om.

disinfect, *v.t.* ontsmetten. disinfectant, *n.* ontsmettingsmiddel *n.n.* disinfection, *n.* ontsmetting *n.*

disingenuous, *a.* onoprecht, geveinsd.

disinherit, *v.t.* onterven.

disintegrate, *v.i.* uit elkaar vallen *str.*, tot ontbinding overgaan *irr.*; verweren. disintegration, *n.* ontbinding *n.*; uit elkaar vallen *n.n.*; verwering *n.*

disinter, *v.t.* opgraven *str.*

disinterested, *a.*, *~ly, adv.* belangeloos, onbaatzuchtig; onpartijdig. *~ in,* niet geïnteresseerd bij.

disjoin, *v.t.* losmaken. disjoint, *v.t.* ontwrichten. disjointed, *a.* onsamenhangend, los.

disjunct, *a.* gescheiden.

disk, *n. See* disc.

dislike, *v.t.* niet houden *irr.* van. ❡ *n.* afkeer *n.*; tegenzin *n.*

dislocate, *v.t.* ontwrichten; verwrikken. **dislocation,** *n.* ontwrichting *n.*

dislodge, *v.t.* verdrijven *str.*, verjagen *str.*

disloyal, *a.*, ~ly, *adv.* ontrouw, ongetrouw; trouweloos. **disloyalty,** *n.* ontrouw *n.*; trouweloosheid *n.*

dismal, *a.*, ~ly, *adv.* somber, naar.

dismantle, *v.t.* ontmantelen; onttakelen.

dismast, *v.t.* ontmasten.

dismay, *v.t.* ontmoedigen; verschrikken *str.* ¶ *n.* schrik *n.*, ontsteltenis *n.*; verslagenheid *n.*

dismember, *v.t.* uiteenrukken; ontleden.

dismiss, *v.t.* ontslaan *irr.*; afdanken; ontbinden *str.*; van zich afzetten. **dismissal,** *n.* ontslag *n.n.*; afdanking *n.*

dismount, *v.i.* afstijgen *str.* ¶ *v.t.* uit het zadel werpen *str.*; demonteren.

disobedience, *n.* ongehoorzaamheid *n.* **disobedient,** *a.*, ~ly, *adv.* ongehoorzaam. **disobey,** *v.t.* niet gehoorzamen.

disoblige, *v.t.* onwelwillend behandelen.

disorder, *v.t.* in verwarring *n.* brengen *irr.* ¶ *n.* wanorde *n.*, verwarring *n.*; uitspatting *n.*; kwaal *n.* **disordered,** *a.* verward; ongeregeld. **disorderly,** *a.* wanordelijk; liederlijk.

disorganization, *n.* desorganisatie *n.* **disorganize,** *v.t.* desorganiseren; ontwrichten.

disown, *v.t.* niet erkennen, verloochenen.

disparage, *v.t.* zich kleinerend uitlaten *str.* over; afkeuren. **disparagement,** *n.* kleinering *n.*

disparity, *n.* ongelijkheid *n.*

dispassionate, *a.*, ~ly, *adv.* kalm, bezadigd.

dispatch, *v.t.* verzenden *str.*; afdoen *irr.*, afmaken; bespoedigen. ¶ *n.* verzending *n.n.*; bericht *n.n.*

dispel, *v.t.* verdrijven *str.*

dispensary, *n.* apotheek *n.*; armenapotheek *n.*

dispensation, *n.* dispensatie *n.*; ontheffing *n.*, vrijstelling *n.* **dispense,** *v.t.* uitdelen; toedienen; klaarmaken. ¶ *v.i.* to ~ with, het doen *irr.* zonder; *he can* ~ *with it*, hij kan er buiten.

dispenser, *n.* apotheker *n.*

dispersal, *n.* verstrooiing *n.*; verspreiding *n.* **disperse,** *v.t.* verspreiden, verstrooien; uiteenjagen *str.* ¶ *v.i.* uiteengaan *irr.* **dispersion,** *n.* verstrooiing *n.*; verspreiding *n.*

dispirit, *v.t.* ontmoedigen.

displace, *v.t.* verplaatsen; verdringen *str.*; vervangen *str.* **displacement,** *n.* verplaatsing *n.*; waterverplaatsing *n.*; vervanging *n.*

display, *v.t.* tentoonspreiden, uitstallen; vertonen. ¶ *n.* vertoning *n.*

displease, *v.t.* mishagen; onaangenaam aandoen *irr.* **displeased,** *a.* misnoegd. **displeasure,** *n.* misnoegen *n.n.*

disport, *v.r.* to ~ *oneself*, zich vermaken, dartelen.

disposable, *a.* beschikbaar. **disposal,** *n.* beschikking *n.*; van de hand doen *n.n.*,

zich ontdoen van *n.n.* **dispose,** *v.i.* beschikken. to ~ *of*, beschikken over; zich ontdoen *irr.* van. ¶ *v.t.* schikken, ordenen; opstellen; regelen. *man proposes, God* ~s, de mens wikt, God beschikt. **disposed,** *a.* geneigd. **disposition,** *n.* gesteldheid *n.*; opstelling *n.*; regeling *n.*; neiging *n.*, aanleg *n.*

dispossess, *v.t.* onteigenen; uit (zijn) bezit verdrijven *str.* **dispossession,** *n.* onteigening *n.*; beroving *n.*

disproportion, *n.* wanverhouding *n.*, onevenredigheid *n.* **disproportionate,** *a.*, ~ly, *adv.* onevenredig, niet in verhouding *n.*

disprove, *v.t.* weerleggen; logenstraffen.

disputable, *a.* betwistbaar. **disputant,** *n.* redetwister *n.* **disputation,** *n.* redetwist *n.*, dispuut *n.n.* **dispute,** *v.i.* redetwisten, disputeren. ¶ *v.t.* betwisten. ¶ *n.* dispuut *n.n.*; geschil *n.n.* *in* ~, in kwestie *n.*; *without* ~, buiten kijf *n.*

disqualification, *n.* uitsluiting *n.*, disqualificatie *n.* **disqualify,** *v.t.* onbevoegd verklaren, uitsluiten *str.*; disqualificeren.

disquiet, *v.t.* verontrusten. ¶ *n.* onrust *n.*

disquisition, *n.* uiteenzetting *n.*, verhandeling *n.*

disregard, *v.t.* veronachtzamen, in de wind slaan *irr.* ¶ *n.* veronachtzaming *n.*; geringschatting *n.*

disrepair, *n.* verval *n.n.*

disreputable, *a.*, ~ly, *adv.* berucht; schandelijk. **disrepute,** *n.* kwade naam *n.*, oneer *n.*, schande *n.*

disrespect, *n.* oneerbiedigheid *n.* **disrespectful,** *a.*, ~ly, *adv.* oneerbiedig.

disrobe, *v.i.* zich ontkleden. ¶ *v.t.* ontkleden.

disrupt, *v.t.* verbreken *str.*; ontwrichten. **disruption,** *n.* verbreking *n.*; ontwrichting *n.*

dissatisfaction, *n.* ontevredenheid *n.*; misnoegen *n.n.* **dissatisfy,** *v.t.* niet bevredigen, ontevreden stemmen.

dissect, *v.t.* ontleden. ~*ing-room*, ontleedkamer *n.* **dissection,** *n.* ontleding *n.*, sectie *n.* **dissector,** *n.* ontleder *n.*, anatoom *n.*

dissemble, *v.i.* veinzen, huichelen. ¶ *v.t.* ontveinzen, verhelen. **dissembler,** *n.* veinzer *n.*, huichelaar *n.*

disseminate, *v.t.* uitzaaien, verspreiden.

dissension, *n.* onenigheid *n.*, verdeeldheid *n.*; tweedracht *n.* **dissent,** *v.i.* verschillen van mening *n.*; zich afscheiden. ¶ *n.* verschil *n.n.* van mening *n.*; afscheiding *n.* **Dissenter,** *N.* Afgescheidene *N.* **dissentient,** *a.* andersdenkend. ¶ *n.* andersdenkende *n.*; tegenstemmer *n.*

dissertation, *n.* verhandeling *n.*; proefschrift *n.n.*, dissertatie *n.*

disservice, *n.* ondienst *n.*

dissever, *v.t.* scheiden; afsnijden *str.*

dissidence, *n.* onenigheid *n.*, meningsverschil *n.n.*; afscheiding *n.* **dissident,** *a.* andersdenkend.

dissimilar, *a.* ongelijk, verschillend. **dissimilarity,** *n.* ongelijkheid *n.*, verschil *n.n.*
dissimulate, *v.i.* veinzen, huichelen. ¶ *v.i.* ontveinzen; verbergen *str.* **dissimulation,** *n.* veinzerij *n.*; dissimulatie *n.*
dissipate, *v.t.* verdrijven *str.*; verstrooien; doen *irr.* optrekken *str.*; verkwisten. ¶ *v.i.* zich verstrooien, optrekken *str.* **dissipated,** *a.* losbandig. **dissipation,** *n.* verkwisting *n.*; losbandigheid *n.*
dissociate, *v.t.* afzonderen, scheiden. ¶ *v.r.* to ~ oneself from, zich losmaken van.
dissolubility, *n.* oplosbaarheid *n.* **dissoluble,** *a.* oplosbaar.
dissolute, *a.*, ~ly, *adv.* losbandig.
dissolution, *n.* wegsmelting *n.*, vervloeiing *n.*; ontbinding *n.*
dissolvable, *a.* oplosbaar; ontbindbaar. **dissolve,** *v.t.* oplossen; ontbinden *str.* ¶ *v.i.* zich oplossen. to be ~d in tears, in tranen wegsmelten *str.*
dissonance, *n.* wanklank *n.*, dissonant *n.*
dissuade, *v.t.* ontraden. to ~ from, overhalen niet te. **dissuasion,** *n.* ontrading *n.* **dissuasive,** *a.*, ~ly, *adv.* ontradend, afradend.
dissyllabic, *a.* tweelettergrepig.
distaff, *n.* spinrokken *n.n.* ~ side, vrouwelijke linie *n.*
distance, *n.* afstand. long ~ call. intercommunaal gesprek *n.n.*; in the ~, in de verte. ¶ *v.t.* achter zich laten *str.*, voorbijstreven. **distant,** *a.*, ~ly, *adv.* ver verwijderd, afgelegen.
distaste, *n.* afkeer *n.*, walging *n.* **distasteful,** *a.*, ~ly, *adv.* onsmakelijk, walgelijk.
distemper, *n.* ziekte *n.*; hondenziekte *n.*; kalkverf *n.* ¶ *v.t.* met kalkverf *n.* schilderen.
distend, *v.i.* uitzetten, opzetten. ¶ *v.t.* doen *irr.* uitzetten. **distention,** *n.* uitzetting *n.*
distich, *n.* tweeregelig vers *n.n.*
distil, *v.t.* distilleren. **distillation,** *n.* distillatie *n.* distiller, *n.* distillateur *n.*, brander *n.* **distillery,** *n.* distilleerderij *n.*, branderij *n.*, stokerij *n.*
distinct, *a.*, ~ly, *adv.* verschillend; apart; duidelijk. as ~ from, in tegenstelling met. **distinction,** *n.* onderscheid *n.n.*; onderscheiding *n.*; voornaamheid *n.*, distinctie *n.* **distinctive,** *a.*, ~ly, *adv.* kenmerkend. **distinctness,** *n.* duidelijkheid *n.*
distinguish, *v.t.* onderscheiden; kenmerken. ¶ *v.i.* to ~ between, verschil *n.n.* maken tussen. **distinguishable,** *a.* te onderscheiden. **distinguished,** *a.* aanzienlijk, voornaam, gedistingeerd.
distort, *v.t.* verwringen *str.*; verdraaien. **distortion,** *n.* verdraaiing *n.*; verwrongenheid *n.*
distract, *v.t.* afleiden; storen. **distracted,** *a.*, ~ly, *adv.* verward; razend; buiten zich zelf. **distraction,** *n.* verwarring *n.*;

afgetrokkenheid *n.*; afleiding *n.* to ~, tot gekwordens toe.
distrain, *v.t.* beslag *n.n.* leggen *irr.*; aanslaan *irr.* **distrainable,** *a.* waarop beslag *n.n.* gelegd kan worden. **distraint,** *n.* beslaglegging *n.*, beslag *n.n.*
distress, *n.* nood *n.*; ellende *n.*; angst *n.*; beslaglegging *n.* ¶ *v.t.* bedroeven, kwellen; beslag *n.n.* leggen *irr.* op, in beslag *n.n.* nemen *str.*
distribute, *v.t.* uitdelen; verdelen; distribueren. **distribution,** *n.* uitdeling *n.*; verdeling, verspreiding *n.*; distributie *n.* **distributive,** *a.*, ~ly, *adv.* verdelend, distributief. **distributor,** *n.* uitdeler *n.*; stroomverdeler *n.*
district, *n.* district *n.n.*; arrondissement *n.n.*; buurt *n.*, wijk *n.*
distrust, *v.t.* wantrouwen. ¶ *n.* wantrouwen *n.n.* **distrustful,** *a.*, ~ly, *adv.* wantrouwend.
disturb, *v.t.* storen; verontrusten. **disturbance,** *n.* storing *n.*, verstoring *n.*, stoornis *n.*; opschudding *n.*
disunion, *n.* onenigheid *n.* **disunite,** *v.t.* verdelen. ¶ *v.i.* onenig worden *str.*
disuse, *v.i.* to be ~d, in onbruik zijn. ¶ *n.* onbruik *n.n.* to fall into ~, in onbruik geraken.
ditch, *n.* sloot *n.*, gracht *n.*, greppel *n.* ¶ *v.i.* sloten graven *str.* to be ~ed, in een sloot *n.* geraken.
ditto, *adv.* dito; dezelfde, hetzelfde.
ditty, *n.* liedje *n.n.*, deuntje *n.n.*
diuretic, *a.* urineafdrijvend. ¶ *n.* urineafdrijvend middel *n.n.*
diurnal, *a.* dagelijks, dag . . .
divagate, *v.i.* afdwalen. **divagation,** *n.* afdwaling *n.*
divan, *n.* divan *n.*
dive, *v.i.* duiken *str.*; doordringen *str.* (fig.). **diver,** *n.* duiker *n.*
diverge, *v.i.* afwijken *str.* **divergence,** *n.* afwijking *n.* **divergent,** *a.* afwijkend; uiteenlopend.
divers, *a.* ettelijke, verscheidene. **diverse,** *a.*, ~ly, *adv.* verscheiden, verschillend. **diversification,** *n.* afwisseling *n.*, verandering *n.* **diversify,** *v.t.* afwisselen, variëren. **diversion,** *n.* afleiding *n.*; verzetje *n.n.*; verlegging *n.* **diversity,** *n.* verscheidenheid *n.* **divert,** *v.t.* afleiden, afwenden; verleggen; amuseren.
divest, *v.t.* ontkleden; ontbloten, ontdoen *irr.* ¶ *v.r.* to ~ oneself of, zich ontdoen *irr.* van.
divide, *v.t.* verdelen. ¶ *v.i.* zich splitsen; uiteengaan *irr.* **dividend,** *n.* dividend *n.n.*; deeltal *n.n.* **divider,** *n.* deler *n.* ~s, steekpasser *n.*
divination, *n.* waarzeggerij *n.*; voorspelling *n.* **divine,** *v.t.* waarzeggen *irr.*; voorspellen. ¶ *a.*, ~ly, *adv.* goddelijk, hemels. ~ service, godsdienstoefening *n.* ¶ *n.* geestelijke *n.*; godgeleerde *n.*
diving bell, *n.* duikerklok *n.*

divining rod, *n.* wichelroede *n.* **divinity,** *n.* godheid *n.*; goddelijkheid *n.*
divisibility, *n.* deelbaarheid *n.* **divisible,** *a.* deelbaar. **division,** *n.* verdeling *n.*; deling *n.*; verdeeldheid *n.*; stemming *n.* **divisor,** *n.* deler *n.*
divorce, *n.* echtscheiding *n.* ¶ *v.t.* scheiden, zich laten scheiden. ¶ *v.i.* scheiden. **divorcee,** *n.* gescheiden vrouw *n.*
divulge, *v.t.* onthullen.
dizziness, *n.* duizeligheid *n.*, duizeling *n.* **dizzy,** *a.*, ~ily, *adv.* duizelig; duizelingwekkend.
do, *v.t.* doen *irr.*; maken; verrichten; uitoefenen; bereiden; beetnemen *str.*; uithangen *str.* to ~ up, inpakken; repareren. ¶ *v.i.* doen *irr.*; dienen; klaar zijn, ophouden *irr.* met. *I* ~ *believe,* ik geloof beslist; ~ *come,* kom toch; *so* ~ *I,* ik ook; *that will* ~, dat is genoeg; *that won't* ~, dat kan zo niet, dat gaat zo niet; *to* ~ *for,* dienen als; *I could* ~ *with . . .,* ik zou wel . . . lusten; *to* ~ *without,* het stellen zonder; *how* ~ *you* ~?, hoe maakt U het?; *to* ~ *away with,* afschaffen. ¶ *n.* fuif *n.*; geschiedenis *n.*
docile, *a.* gewillig, volgzaam, gedwee. **docility,** *n.* gewilligheid *n.*
dock, *n.* dok *n.n.*; bank *n.* (van de beschuldigden); wilde zuring *n.*; stompje *n.n.* ¶ *v.t.* dokken; kortstaarten. **docker,** *n.* dokwerker *n.*
docket, *n.* borderel *n.n.*; etiket *n.n.* ¶ *v.t.* merken en nummeren.
dockyard, *n.* scheepswerf *n.*
doctor, *n.* dokter *n.*; doctor *n.* ¶ *v.t.* knoeien met, vervalsen. **doctorate,** *n.* doctoraat *n.n.* **doctrinal,** *a.* leerstellig. **doctrine,** *n.* leer *n.*, leerstelling *n.*
document, *n.* akte *n.*, document *n.n.* ¶ *v.t.* documenteren. **documentary,** *a.* gedocumenteerd. ~ *evidence,* geschreven bewijsstukken *n.n.*
dodder, *n.* warkruid *n.n.*, trilgras *n.n.* ¶ *v.i.* strompelen.
dodge, *v.t.* ontwijken *str.*, ontzeilen; opzijspringen *str.* ¶ *n.* kunstgreep *n.*, list *n.* **dodger,** *n.* slimmerik *n.*, draaier *n.*
doe, *n.* ree *n.*, hinde *n.*; wijfje *n.n.*
doer, *n.* dader *n.*; man *n.* van de daad.
doff, *v.t.* afnemen *str.*
dog, *n.* hond *n.*; reu *n.* *lucky* ~, geluksvogel *n.* ¶ *v.t.* op de voet volgen. **dogcart,** *n.* tweewielig rijtuigje *n.n.* **dog-days,** *n.* hondsdagen *pl.n.*
doge, *n.* doge *n.*
dog-ear, *n.* ezelsoor *n.n.* **dog-fish,** *n.* doornhaai *n.* **dogged,** *a.*, ~ly, *adv.* taai, vasthoudend. **doggedness,** *n.* vasthoudendheid *n.*
doggerel, *n.* kreupelrijm *n.*; rijmelarij *n.*
doggish, *a.* honds. **dog-latin,** *n.* potjeslatijn *n.n.*
dogma, *n.* dogma *n.n.*, leerstuk *n.n.* **dogmatic,**

a., ~ally, *adv.* dogmatisch. **dogmatism,** *n.* dogmatisme *n.n.* **dogmatist,** *n.* dogmaticus *n.* **dogmatize,** *v.i.* dogmatiseren.
dog-rose, *n.* hondsroos *n.* **dog-sleep,** *n.* hazenslaap *n.* **dog-weary,** *a.* bekaf.
doily, *n.* onderleggertje *n.n.*, linnen tafelmatje *n.n.*
doing, *a.* *there's nothing* ~, er gebeurt niets. ¶ *n.* ~s, doen en laten *n.n.*; boel *n.*
doit, *n.* duit *n.*
doldrums, *pl.n.* streek *n.* van de windstilten *pl.n.* *to be in the* ~, landerig zijn.
dole, *n.* aalmoes *n.*; steun *n.*, werklozenuitkering *n.* ¶ *v.t.* to ~ out, uitdelen.
doleful, *a.*, ~ly, *adv.* treurig, smartelijk.
dolichocephalic, *a.* langschedelig.
doll, *n.* pop *n.*
dollar, *n.* dollar *n.*
dolman, *n.* dolman *n.*
dolomite, *n.* dolomiet *n.*
dolorous, *a.* pijnlijk, smartelijk.
dolphin, *n.* dolfijn *n.*; dukdalf *n.*
dolt, *n.* domkop *n.*, sukkel *n.* **doltish,** *a.*, ~ly, *adv.* dom, sukkelachtig.
domain, *n.* domein *n.n.*, gebied *n.n.*; macht *n.*
dome, *n.* koepel *n.* **domed,** *a.* koepelvormig.
Domesday Book, *N.* Kadaster *n.n.* van Willem de Veroveraar.
domestic, *a.* huishoudelijk; huiselijk; huis . . .; binnenlands. ~ *economy,* huishoudkunde *n.*; ~ *servant,* bediende *n.*, dienstbode *n.* ¶ *n.* bediende *n.*, dienstbode *n.* **domesticate,** *v.t.* temmen, tam maken. **domesticity,** *n.* huiselijkheid *n.*
domicile, *n.* domicilie *n.n.*, woonplaats *n.* ¶ *v.t.* domiciliëren. **domiciled,** *a.* woonachtig. **domiciliary,** *a.* huis . . . ~ *visit,* huiszoeking *n.* **domiciliate,** *v.i.* domiciliëren.
dominance, *n.* overheersing *n.*; beheersing *n.* **dominant,** *a.* overheersend. ¶ *n.* dominant *n.* **dominate,** *v.t.* beheersen. ¶ *v.i.* heersen. **domineer,** *v.i.* de baas spelen, overheersen.
Dominican, *N.* Dominikaan *N.*
dominion, *n.* heerschappij *n.*; gebied *n.n.*; Dominion *N.*
domino, *n.* domino *n.*, dominosteen *n.*; dominospel *n.n.*
don, *n.* professor. ¶ *v.t.* aantrekken *str.*
donation, *n.* schenking *n.*
donkey, *n.* ezel. **donkey-engine,** *n.* hulpmachine *n.*, donkie *n.* **donkey-man,** *n.* donkieman *n.*
donor, *n.* schenker *n.*
doom, *n.* oordeel *n.n.*; ondergang *n.* ¶ *v.t.* veroordelen, doemen. **doomsday,** *n.* dag *n.* des oordeels. *till* ~, voor eeuwig.
door, *n.* deur *n.* *within* ~s, binnenshuis; *out of* ~s, buitenshuis. **doorkeeper,** *n.* portier *n.* **door-plate,** *n.* naamplaatje *n.n.* **doorstep,** *n.* drempel *n.*; stoep *n.* **doorway,** *n.* ingang *n.*

dope, *n.* verdovend middel *n.n.* ¶ *v.t.* verdovende middelen geven *str.*
dormant, *a.* slapend, sluimerend, latent. ~*partner,* stille vennoot *n.*
dormer, *n.* dakvenster *n.n.*
dormitory, *n.* slaapzaal *n.*
dormouse, *n.* relmuis *n.,* hazelmuis *n.*
dorsal, *a.* dorsaal, rug ...
dosage, *n.* dosis *n.,* dosering *n.* dose, *n.* dosis *n.;* portie *n.* ¶ *v.t.* voorschrijven *str.;* toedienen, ingeven *str.*
doss, *v.i.* (*slang*) slapen *str.* doss-house, *n.* (*slang*) slaaphuis *n.n.*
dot, *n.* punt *n.,* stip *n.* ¶ *v.t.* stippelen.
dotage, *n.* kindsheid *n.;* verzotheid *n.*
dotard, *n.* kindse grijzaard *n.* dote, *v.t.* kinds worden *str. to* ~ *on,* verzot zijn op.
doting, *a.* kinds; dol, gek.
dottle, *n.* propje *n.n.,* klokhuis *n.n.*
double, *a.* dubbel; tweeledig; tweepersoons ... ~ *or quits,* kiet of dubbel; ~ *entry,* dubbel boekhouden *n.n.;* ~ *time,* looppas *n.* ¶ *v.t.* verdubbelen; omzeilen; terugkeren. *to* ~ *up,* dubbelvouwen. ¶ *v.i.* (zich) verdubbelen. ¶ *n.* dubbele *n.n.;* dubbelganger *n.;* duplicaat *n.n.* double-barrelled, *a.* dubbelloops, tweeloops. double-breasted, *a.* met twee rijen knopen. double-dealing, *n.* huichelarij *n.* double-quick, *a.* versneld. ~ *time,* looppas *n.*
doublet, *n.* wambuis *n.n.;* doublet *n.n.*
doubt, *n.* twijfel *n.,* onzekerheid *n. beyond a* ~, boven alle twijfel verheven, ongetwijfeld. ¶ *v.t.* betwijfelen. doubtful, *a.,* ~ly, *adv.* twijfelachtig; verdacht; dubbelzinnig. doubtless, *a.* ongetwijfeld.
dough, *n.* deeg *n.n.*
doughty, *a.,* ~ily, *adv.* geducht.
douse, *v.t.* onderdompelen; uitdoven.
dove, *n.* duif *n.,* tortelduif *n.* dove-cote, *n.* duiventil *n.,* duivenhok *n.n.*
dovetail, *n.* zwaluwstaart *n.* ¶ *v.t.* met een zwaluwstaart verbinden *str.*
dowager, *n.* douairière *n.*
dowdy, *a.* slonzig; slecht gekleed.
dowel, *n.* treknagel *n.;* houten pen *n.*
dower, *n.* bruidschat *n.*
down, *n.* dons *n.n.;* heuvel *n.* ~*s,* heuvelland *n.n.* ¶ *prep.* langs; naar beneden langs, af, neer. ~ *stroke,* neerhaal *n.* ¶ *adv.* (naar) beneden, neer, onder. *money* ~, contant. ¶ *v.t.* er onder houden *irr.;* neergooien; doen *irr.* vallen. downcast, *a.* neerslachtig. downfall, *n.* ondergang *n.,* val *n.* downhill, *a.* bergafwaarts. downpour, *n.* stortbui *n.,* slagregen *n.* downright, *a.* rechtstreeks; openhartig, rechtuit (gezegd). downstairs, *a.* (naar) beneden. ¶ *adv.* naar beneden. down-train, *n.* trein *n.* (van de hoofdstad). downtrodden, *a.* vertrapt. downward(s), *a. & adv.* naar beneden, nederwaarts. downy, *a.* donzig.
dowry, *n.* bruidschat *n.*
dowser, *n.* roedeloper *n.* dowsing, *n.* wichelen

n.n.; rhabdomantie *n.* dowsing rod, *n.* wichelroede *n.*
doze, *v.i.* dutten, soezen, dommelen. ¶ *n.* dutje *n.n.,* tukje *n.n.*
dozen, *n.* dozijn *n.n.*
drab, *a.* vaalbruin ; saai. ¶ *n.* slons *n.*
drachm, *n.* drachma *n.*
draft, *n.* wissel *n.,* traite *n.;* eerste ontwerp *n.n.;* lichting *n.;* detachement *n.n.;* diepgang *n.* ¶ *a.* ontwerp ..., concept ... ¶ *v.t.* ontwerpen *str.;* detacheren.
drag, *v.t.* slepen, sleuren; trekken *str. to* ~ *along,* voortslepen; *to* ~ *for,* dreggen naar; *to* ~ *out,* rekken. ¶ *v.i.* slepen. ¶ *n.* dreg *n.;* haak *n.* drag-chain, *n.* remketting *n.* drag-net, *n.* sleepnet *n.n.*
draggle, *v.t.* bemodderen, door 't slijk sleuren.
dragoman, *n.* drogman *n.,* tolk *n.*
dragon, *n.* draak *n.* dragon-fly, *n.* waterjuffer *n.,* libel *n.*
dragoon, *n.* dragonder *n.* ¶ *v.t.* met geweld *n.n.* dwingen *str.*
drain, *n.* riool *n.;* greppel *n.;* afvoerbuis *n.* ¶ *v.t.* rioleren, draineren; uitputten. drainage, *n.* drooglegging *n.;* riolering *n.,* draineren *n.* drainer, *n.* vergiet *n.n.*
drainpipe, *n.* draineerbuis *n.*
drake, *n.* woerd *n.*
dram, *n.* drachme *n.;* slokje *n.n.*
drama, *n.* drama *n.n.;* toneelstuk *n.n.*
dramatic, *a.,* ~ally, *adv.* dramatisch.
dramatist, *n.* toneelschrijver *n.*
drape, *v.t.* bekleden; hullen; draperen
draper, *n.* lakenkoper *n.;* manufacturier *n.*
drapery, *n.* laken *n.n.,* stof *n.;* draperie *n.*
drastic, *a.* drastisch.
draught, *n.* haal *n.;* teug *n.;* drankje *n.n.;* tocht *n.;* vangst *n.;* kladje *n.n.,* ontwerp *n.n.;* diepgang *n.* ~ *s,* damspel *n.n.; on* ~, op 't vat. ¶ *v.t. See* draft. ¶ *a.* trek ... draughtboard, *n.* tekenbord *n.n.* draught-horse, *n.* trekpaard *n.n.* draughtsman, *n.* tekenaar *n.* draughty, *a.* tochtig.
draw, *v.t.* trekken *str.;* putten; aantrekken *str.* (af)tappen; spannen *irr.;* tekenen; een diepgang hebben van. *to* ~ *lots,* loten. ¶ *v.i.* aantrekken *str.;* de sabel trekken *str.;* tekenen. *to* ~ *near,* naderen; *to* ~ *out,* lengen. ¶ *n.* trekking *n.,* loterij *n.;* onbeslist spel *n.n.;* succes *n.n.* drawback, *n.* nadeel *n.n.,* bezwaar *n.n.* drawbridge, *n.* ophaalbrug *n.* drawer, *n.* la(de) *n.;* trekker *n.* ~*s,* onderbroek *n.* drawing, *n.* tekening *n.* drawing-board, *n.* tekenplank *n.* drawing-pin, *n.* punaise *n.* drawing-room, *n.* salon *n.*
drawl, *v.t.* temerig spreken *str.* ¶ *n.* temerige spraak *n.*
dray, *n.* slepersswagen *n.,* brouwerswagen *n.* dray-horse, *n.* slepersspaard *n.n.* drayman, *n.* sleper *n.*
dread, *n.* vrees *n.,* schrik *n.* ¶ *a.* gevreesd, geducht. ¶ *v.t.* vrezen, duchten. dreadful,

a., ∼ly, *adv.* vreselijk. **dreadnought,** *n.* groot pantserschip *n.n.*

dream, *n.* droom *n.*; droombeeld *n.n.* ¶ *v.i.* & *v.t.* dromen. **dreamer,** *n.* dromer *n.* **dreamy,** *a.*, ∼ily, *adv.* dromerig.

drear, *a. See* dreary. **dreariness,** *n.* akeligheid *n.*, somberheid *n.* **dreary,** *a.*, ∼ily, *adv.* akelig, naar, somber, woest.

dredge, *v.i.* baggeren; dreggen; met een sleepnet *n.n.* vissen. ¶ *v.t.* (uit)baggeren; strooien. ¶ *n.* baggermolen *n.*; sleepnet *n.n.*; strooibus *n.* **dredger,** *n.* baggermolen *n.*; baggerman *n.*; strooibus *n.* **dredging machine,** *n.* baggermachine *n.*

dregs, *pl.n.* droesem *n.*; bezinksel *n.n.* *to the* ∼*s,* tot op de bodem.

drench, *v.t.* doornat maken; drenken.

dress, *v.t.* kleden; bereiden; bewerken; verbinden *str. to* ∼ *down,* een schrobbering geven *str.; to* ∼ *up,* costumeren. ¶ *v.i.* zich aankleden. ¶ *n.* kleding *n.*; kleed *n.n.*; japon *n.*, toilet *n.n.* **dress clothes,** *pl.n.* avondtenue *n.* or *n.n.* **dress-circle,** *n.* balkon *n.n.* **dresser,** *n.* aanrechtbank *n.*; dressoir *n.*; kleder *n.*, kapper *n.* **dressing,** *n.* verband *n.n.*; saus *n.*; pap *n.*, stijfsel *n.* **dressing-gown,** *n.* kamerjapon *n.* **dressing-room,** *n.* kleedkamer *n.* **dressing-table,** *n.* toilettafel *n.*, kaptafel *n.* **dressmaker,** *n.* naaister *n.* **dressy,** *a.* chic; zwierig.

dribble, *v.i.* kwijlen; druppelen. ¶ *v.t.* zachtjes trappen. ¶ *n.* straaltje *n.n.* **driblet,** *n.* klein beetje *n.n.* *by* ∼*s,* bij stukjes *pl. n.n.* en brokjes *pl. n.n.*

drift, *v.i.* drijven *str.*, afdrijven *str.*; opwaaien, zich opeenhopen. ¶ *n.* drift *n.*; stroming *n.*; strekking *n.*; betekenis *n.*; opeenhoping *n.* **drifter,** *n.* haringbuis *n.* **drift-ice,** *n.* drijfijs *n.n.* **drift-sand,** *n.* stuifzand *n.n.* **driftwood,** *n.* drijfhout *n.n.*

drill, *n.* boor *n.*; zaaimachine *n.*; exerceren *n.n.*; dril *n. (linen).* ¶ *v.t.* boren; exerceren. **drill-plough,** *n.* zaaimachine *n.*

drily, *adv.* droog.

drink, *v.t.* drinken *str.* ¶ *n.* drank *n.*; dronk *n.* **drinkable,** *a.* drinkbaar. **drinker,** *n.* drinker *n.*; drinkebroer *n.* **drinking bout,** *n.* drinkgelag *n.n.*

drip, *v.t.* & *v.i.* druipen *str.* ¶ *n.* druppel *n.*, drop *n.* **dripping,** *n.* braadvet *n.n.* **dripping-pan,** *n.* druippan *n.*

drive, *v.t.* drijven *str.*; voortdrijven *str.*; rijden *str.*; mennen. *to* ∼ *away,* wegjagen *str.* ¶ *v.i.* rijden *str. to* ∼ *away,* wegrijden *str.* ¶ *n.* ritje *n.n.*; rijweg *n.*; oprijlaan *n.*; campagne *n.*; stuwkracht *n.*

drivel, *n.* gebazel *n.*, onzin *n.* ¶ *v.t.* bazelen. **driveller,** *n.* suffer *n.*

driver, *n.* koetsier *n.*; bestuurder *n.*; chauffeur *n.* **driving-box,** *n.* bok *n.*

drizzle, *v.i.* motregenen. ¶ *n.* motregen *n.* **drizzly,** *a.* mottig.

droll, *a.* kluchtig, grappig, koddig. **drollery,** *n.* grappenmakerij *n.*

dromedary, *n.* dromedaris *n. (one hump).*

drone, *n.* dar *n.*; hommel *n.*; gegons *n.n.*; gesnor *n.n.* ¶ *v.i.* gonzen; snorren.

droop, *v.i.* neerhangen *str.*; het hoofd laten *str.* hangen; kwijnen; moedeloos zijn. ¶ *n.* laten hangen *n.n.*

drop, *v.i.* vallen *str.*; druppelen, druipen *str. to* ∼ *away,* afvallen *str.; to* ∼ *in,* aanlopen *str.; to* ∼ *off,* verminderen. ¶ *v.t.* laten *str.* vallen; opgeven *str.*, laten *str.* varen. *to* ∼ *a curtsey,* een neiging *n.* maken; *to* ∼ *a hint,* een wenk *n.* geven *str.; to* ∼ *a line,* een woordje *n.n.* schrijven *str.; to* ∼ *one's voice,* zachter spreken *str.* ¶ *n.* val *n.*; vallen *n.n.*; druppel *n.*, drop *n.*; drupje *n.n.*; valluik *n.n.* **drop-scene,** *n.* toneelscherm *n.n.*

dropsical, *a.* waterzuchtig. **dropsy,** *n.* waterzucht *n.*

dross, *n.* metaalschuim *n.n.*; slakken *pl.n.*; droesem *n.*; waardeloos goed *n.n.* **drossy,** *a.* onzuiver.

drought, *n.* droogte *n.* **droughty,** *a.* droog, dor.

drove, *n.* drom *n.*, kudde *n.* **drover,** *n.* veedrijver *n.*

drown, *v.i.* verdrinken *str.* ∼*ing man,* drenkeling *n.* ¶ *v.t.* verdrinken *str.*; overstemmen. *to be* ∼*ed,* verdrinken *str.*

drowsiness, *n.* slaperigheid *n.* **drowsy,** *a.*, ∼ily, *adv.* soezerig, dommelig.

drub, *v.t.* ranselen, afrossen. **drubbing,** *n.* ransel *n.n.*, pak *n.n.* slaag.

drudge, *v.i.* sloven, zich afsloven, zwoegen. ¶ *n.* zwoeger *n.*, werkezel *n.* **drudgery,** *n.* geslaaf *n.n.*, gezwoeg *n.n.*

drug, *n.* drogerij *n.*; narcotisch middel *n.n.* ¶ *v.t.* bedwelmen. ¶ *v.i.* narcotische middelen gebruiken.

drugget, *n.* karpetje *n.n.*, loper *n.*

druggist, *n.* drogist *n.*

druid, *n.* druïde *n.*

drum, *n.* trommel *n.*, trom *n.*; tamboer *n.* ¶ *v.t.* & *v.i.* trommelen. **drum-fire,** *n.* roffelvuur *n.n.* **drum-head,** *n.* trommelvel *n.n.* ∼ *court-martial,* krijgsraad *n.* te velde. **drum-major,** *n.* tamboermajoor *n.* **drummer,** *n.* trommelslager *n.*, tamboer *n.* **drumstick,** *n.* trommelstok *n.*; boutje *n.n.*

drunk, *a.* dronken. **drunkard,** *n.* dronkaard *n.* **drunken,** *a.*, ∼ly, *adv.* dronken; dronkemans . . . **drunkenness,** *n.* dronkenschap *n.*

drupe, *n.* steenvrucht *n.*

dry, *a.*, ∼ly, *adv.* droog; niet zoet. ∼ *goods,* ellegoed *n.n.*; manufacturen *pl.n.* ¶ *v.t.* drogen; afdrogen. ¶ *v.i.* uitdrogen, opdrogen.

dryad, *n.* dryade *n.*

dry-clean, *v.t.* stomen. **dry-dock,** *n.* droogdok *n.n.* **dryness,** *n.* droogheid *n.* **dry-nurse,** *n.* baker *n.* **dry-salter,** *n.* handelaar *n.* in drogerijen *pl.n.*

dual, *a.* tweevoudig, tweeledig. **duality,** *n.* tweevoudigheid *n.*
dub, *v.t.* (tot ridder) slaan *irr.*
dubious, *a.,* ~ly, *adv.* twijfelachtig, onzeker.
ducal, *a.* hertogelijk.
ducat, *n.* dukaat *n.*
duchess, *n.* hertogin *n.* **duchy,** *n.* hertogdom *n.n.*
duck, *n.* eend *n.;* grof linnen *n.n.* ¶ *v.i.* duiken *str.* ¶ *v.t.* ontduiken *str.;* onderdompelen. **duckweed,** *n.* eendekroos *n.n.* **duckling,** *n.* eendje *n.n.*
duct, *n.* (afvoer)buis *n.,* pijp *n.* **ductile,** *a.* handelbaar; buigzaam. **ductility,** *n.* buigzaamheid *n.* **ductless,** *a.* zonder afvoerbuis.
dud, *a.* waardeloos. ¶ *n.* prul *n.n.;* niet ontploft projectiel *n.n.*
dudgeon, *n.* *to retire in* ~, kwaad weggaan *irr.*
due, *a.* schuldig; verplicht; behoorlijk, gepast. *to be* ~, moeten *irr.* aankomen; *to become* ~, vervallen *str.; in* ~ *course,* te zijner tijd *n.; in* ~ *form,* in de juiste vorm. ¶ *n.* recht *n.n.* ~s, gelden *pl.n.n.*
duel, *n.* duel *n.n.,* tweegevecht *n.n.* ¶ *v.i.* duelleren. **duellist,** *n.* duellist *n.*
duet, *n.* duet *n.n.*
duffer, *n.* suffer *n.,* domoor *n.*
dug, *n.* tepel *n.*
dug-out, *n.* kano *n.;* (uitgegraven) schuilkelder *n.*
duke, *n.* hertog *n.* **dukedom,** *n.* hertogdom *n.n.*
dulcimer, *n.* hakkebord *n.n.*
dull, *a.* dof; mat; suf; dom; vervelend, saai; slap; stomp, bot. ¶ *v.t.* afstompen; dof maken. ¶ *v.i.* afstompen; verflauwen. **dullard,** *n.* sufferd. **dullness,** *n.* botheid *n.;* matheid *n.;* saaiheid *n.*
duly, *adv.* behoorlijk.
dumb, *a.,* ~ly, *adv.* stom; sprakeloos. **dumb-bells,** *pl.n.* halters *pl.n.* **dumbfound,** *v.t.* doen *irr.* verstomd staan. **dumbness,** *n.* stomheid *n.* **dumb-show,** *n.* gebarenspel *n.n.* **dumb-waiter,** *n.* dientafeltje *n.n.*
dummy, *n.* pop *n.;* etalagedoos *n.;* exerceerpatroon *n.n.;* blinde *n.* (*whist*).
dump, *n.* stortplaats *n.,* vuilnisbelt *n.;* opslagplaats *n.* *to be down in the* ~s, terneergeslagen zijn. ¶ *v.t.* neerploffen, storten; de markt overvoeren, onder de markt verkopen *irr.* **dumping,** *n.* dumping *n.n.* **dumping-cart,** *n.* stortkar *n.,* kipkar *n.* **dumping ground,** *n.* stortplaats *n.,* vuilnisbelt *n.*
dumpling, *n.* knoedel *n.*
dumpy, *a.* kort en dik.
dun, *a.* vaalbruin, grauw, somber. ¶ *n.* schuldeiser *n.* ¶ *v.t.* manen.
dunce, *n.* ezel *n.;* domkop *n.*
dune, *n.* duin *n.n.,* zandheuvel *n.*
dung, *n.* mest *n.* ¶ *v.t.* bemesten.
dungeon, *n.* kerker *n.*

dungfork, *n.* mestvork *n.* **dunghill,** *n.* mesthoop *n.*
duo, *n.* duo *n.n.,* duet *n.n.*
dupe, *n.* dupe *n.,* bedrogene *n.* ¶ *v.t.* duperen.
duplicate, *n.* duplicaat *n.n.* ¶ *a.* dubbel; in duplo. ¶ *v.t.* verdubbelen; een afschrift *n.n.* maken. **duplicity,** *n.* dubbelhartigheid *n.*
durability, *n.* duurzaamheid *n.* **durable,** *a.,* ~bly, *adv.* duurzaam. **duration,** *n.* duur *n.*
duress, *n.* dwang *n.;* gevangenschap *n.*
during, *prep.* gedurende, onder, in de loop van.
dusk, *n.* schemering *n.* ¶ *a.* duister, schemerig. **dusky,** *a.* schemerachtig; zwart.
dust, *n.* stof *n.n.* *to kick up a* ~, herrie schoppen. ¶ *v.t.* bestuiven *str.;* bestrooien. ¶ *v.i.* stof *n.n.* afnemen *str.* **dustbin,** *n.* vuilnisbak *n.* **dustcart,** *n.* vuilniswagen *n.* **dust-cover,** *n.* omslag *n.* **duster,** *n.* stofdoek *n.* **dustman,** *n.* vuilnisman *n.* **dust-sheet,** *n.* stoflaken *n.n.* **dustpan,** *n.* blik *n.n.* *brush and* ~, veger *n.* en blik.
dusty, *a.* stoffig, stofferig.
Dutch, *a.* Hollands, Nederlands. *the* ~, de Nederlanders; ~ *auction,* verkoping *n.* bij afslag *n.;* ~ *courage,* moed *n.* uit het glas; ~ *treat,* ieder voor zichzelf betalen; *to talk like a* ~ *uncle,* iemand de les lezen *str.;* ~ *wife,* sluimerrol *n.,* slaaprol *n.* ¶ *N.* Nederlands *n.N.* *double* ~, koeterwaals. **Dutchman,** *N.* Hollander *N.,* Nederlander *N.*
dutiable, *a.* aan rechten *pl. n.n.* onderhevig.
dutiful, *a.,* ~ly, *adv.* eerbiedig; plichtsgetrouw. **duty,** *n.* plicht *n.;* rechten *pl.n.n.* *to be off* ~, geen dienst *n.* hebben; *to be on* ~, van dienst *n.* zijn.
dwarf, *n.* dwerg *n.* **dwarfish,** *a.* dwergachtig.
dwell, *v.i.* wonen; verblijven *str.* *to* ~ *on,* stilstaan *irr.* bij. **dweller,** *n.* bewoner *n.* **dwelling,** *n.* woning *n.*
dwindle, *v.i.* afnemen *str.,* minder worden *str.*
dye, *v.t.* verven. ¶ *n.* verfstof *n.* **dyer,** *n.* verver *n.* **dyestuff,** *n.* verfstof *n.* **dyeworks,** *n.* ververij *n.*
dying, *n.* sterven *n.n.* ¶ *a.* stervende; doods . . .
dyke, *n.* sloot *n.;* dijk, *n.,* dam *n.*
dynamic(al), *a.,* ~ly, *adv.* dynamisch. **dynamics,** *n.* dynamica *n.*
dynamite, *n.* dynamiet *n.n.*
dynamo, *n.* dynamo *n.*
dynastic, *a.* dynastiek. **dynasty,** *n.* dynastie *n.*
dysentery, *n.* dysenterie *n.*
dyspepsia, *n.* slechte spijsvertering *n.* **dyspeptic,** *a.* dispeptisch.

E

each, *pron.* elk, ieder. ~ *other,* elkaar.
eager, *a.,* ~ly, *adv.* vurig, ongeduldig; belust, verlangend. **eagerness,** *n.* verlangen *n.n.,* ongeduld *n.n.*

eagle, *n*. arend *n*., adelaar *n*. **eaglet**, *n*. jonge arend *n*.

ear, *n*. oor *n.n.*; gehoor *n.n.*; aar *n*. **eardrum**, *n*. trommelvlies *n.n.*

earl, *n*. graaf *n*. **earldom**, *n*. graafschap *n.n.*

earliness, *n*. vroegheid *n*., vroegtijdigheid *n*. **early**, *a*. & *adv*. vroeg; vroegtijdig.

earmark, *v.t.* merken; bestemmen. ¶ *n*. kenmerk *n.n.*

earn, *v.t.* verdienen; verwerven *str.*

earnest, *a*., ~ly, *adv*. ernstig; dringend. *in good* ~, in volle ernst *n*.; ~ *money*, handgeld *n.n.*, godspenning *n*. **earnestness**, *n*. ernst *n*.

earnings, *pl.n.* verdienste *n*., loon *n.n.*

ear-ring, *n*. oorbel *n*., oorring *n*. **ear-shot**, *n*. *within* ~, te beroepen, binnen gehoorsafstand *n*.

earth, *n*. aarde *n*.; grond *n*.; hol *n.n.* ¶ *v.t.* in de grond stoppen; aanaarden. **earthen**, *a*. aarden. **earthenware**, *n*. aardewerk *n.n.* **earthly**, *a*. aardsgezind. *of no* ~ *use*, van hoegenaamd geen nut *n.n.* **earthquake**, *n*. aardbeving *n*. **earthworm**, *n*. aardworm *n*. **earthy**, *a*. aardsgezind, werelds; grond . . .

ear-trumpet, *n*. spreekhoorn *n*. **earwig**, *n*. oorworm *n*.

ease, *n*. gemak *n.n.*; ongedwongenheid *n*. *at* ~, ongedwongen. ¶ *v.t.* vergemakkelijken, verlichten. *to* ~ *off*, vieren.

easel, *n*. ezel *n*.

easiness, *n*. gemakkelijkheid *n*. ~ *of mind*, gemoedsrust *n*.

east, *n*. oosten *n.n.* ¶ *a*. oost, oostelijk. *E*~ *Indiaman*, Oostinjevaarder *n*. ¶ *adv*. ten oosten; naar het oosten.

Easter, *N*. Pasen *N*.

easterly, *a*. & *adv*. oostelijk, oosten . . . **eastern**, *a*. oosters; oostelijk; oost . . ., oosten . . . **eastward**, *a*. & *adv*. oostwaarts.

easy, *a*., ~ily, *adv*. gemakkelijk; gerust; welgesteld. ~ *chair*, leunstoel *n*., fauteuil *n*. **easy-going**, *a*. gemakzuchtig; (de zaken) gemakkelijk opnemend.

eat, *v.t.* eten *str.*; opeten *str.*; vreten *str.* ¶ *v.i. to* ~ *into*, invreten *str.*, wegvreten *str.* **eatable**, *a*. eetbaar. ~*s*, eetwaar *n*. **eater**, *n*. eter *n*. **eating-house**, *n*. eetgelegenheid *n*.

eaves, *n*. dakrand *n*.

eavesdrop, *v.t.* afluisteren. **eavesdropper**, *n*. luistervink *n*.

ebb, *n*. eb *n*., ebbe *n*. *at a low* ~, op een laag peil *n.n.*; aan lager wal *n*. ¶ *v.i.* ebben. *to* ~ *away*, ebben; afnemen *str.*

ebon, *a*. ebbenhouten. **ebonite**, *n*. eboniet *n.n.* ¶ *a*. ebonieten. **ebony**, *n*. ebbenhout *n.n.* ¶ *a*. ebbenhouten.

ebullition, *n*. koken *n.n.*; opwelling *n*., opborreling *n*.

eccentric, *a*. excentrisch; (*fig.*) excentriek. ¶ *n*. excentriek *n*. **eccentricity**, *n*. excentriciteit *n*.

Ecclesiastes, *N*. Prediker *N*. **ecclesiastic(al)**, *a*. kerkelijk, kerk . . .; geestelijk. ¶ *n*. geestelijke *n*.

echelon, *n*. échelon *n.n.*

echo, *n*. echo *n*.; weerklank *n*. ¶ *v.i.* weerklinken *str.*; terugkaatsen; herhalen.

eclectic, *a*. eclectisch; uitzoekend. ¶ *n*. eclecticus *n*. **eclecticism**, *n*. eclecticisme *n.n.*

eclipse, *n*. eclips *n*., verduistering *n*. ¶ *v.t.* verduisteren. **ecliptic**, *n*. ecliptica *n*.

eclogue, *n*. herdersdicht *n.n.*

economic(al), *a*., ~ly, *adv*. economisch; huishoudelijk; zuinig, spaarzaam. **economics**, *n*. economie *n*., (staat)huishoudkunde *n*. **economist**, *n*. economist *n*.; econoom *n*. **economize**, *v.t.* bezuinigen, besparen, sparen. ¶ *v.i.* bezuinigen. **economy**, *n*. huishoudkunde *n*.; zuinigheid *n*., spaarzaamheid *n*.; bezuiniging *n*., besparing *n*. *domestic* ~, huishoudkunde *n*.; *political* ~, staathuishoudkunde *n*.

ecstasy, *n*. extase *n*., (geest)vervoering *n*. **ecstatic**, *a*. extatisch, verrukt.

eczema, *n*. eczeem *n.n.*

eddy, *n*. draaikolk *n*.; maalstroom *n*. ¶ *v.t.* wervelen, draaien.

edge, *n*. kant *n*., rand *n*.; scherpe kant *n*.; snede *n*. *on* ~, op z'n kant; overspannen; *to set the teeth on* ~, door merg *n.n.* en been *n.n.* gaan *irr.* ¶ *v.t.* slijpen *str.*; zomen, omzomen. ¶ *v.i.* geleidelijk dringen *str.* **edge-tool**, *n*. snijdend werktuig *n.n.* **edgeways**, *adv*. schuin; met de scherpe kant naar voren. *not to get a word in* ~, er geen woord *n.n.* tussen kunnen *irr.* krijgen. **edging**, *n*. rand *n*.; franje *n*.

edibility, *n*. eetbaarheid *n*. **edible**, *a*. eetbaar

edict, *n*. edict *n.n.*

edification, *n*. stichting *n*.

edifice, *n*. gebouw *n.n.*, bouwwerk *n.n.*

edify, *v.t.* opbouwen; stichten. **edifying**, *a*. stichtelijk.

edit, *v.t.* bezorgen, persklaar maken; uitgeven *str.* **edition**, *n*. uitgave *n*., editie *n*.; druk *n*. **editor**, *n*. redacteur *n*.; bewerker *n*., bezorger *n*. **editorial**, *a*. redactioneel, redactie . . . ¶ *n*. hoofdartikel *n.n.* **editorship**, *n*. redacteurschap *n.n.*

educate, *v.t.* opvoeden. **educated**, *a*. beschaafd, ontwikkeld. **education**, *n*. opvoeding *n*.; ontwikkeling *n*.; onderwijs *n.n.* **educational**, *a*. onderwijs . . . **educator**, *n*. opvoeder *n.n.* (*male*), opvoedster *n*. (*female*).

educe, *v.t.* te voorschijn brengen *irr.*

eel, *n*. aal *n*., paling *n*. **eelbuck**, *n*. aalkorf *n*.

eerie, *a*. huiveringwekkend, spookachtig.

efface, *v.t.* uitwissen. ¶ *v.r. to* ~ *oneself*, zich op de achtergrond houden *irr.* **effacement**, *n*. doen verdwijnen *n.n.*

effect, *n*. uitwerking *n*.; indruk *n*.; effect *n.n.* *to give* ~ *to*, ten uitvoer brengen *irr.*; gehoor *n.n.* geven *str.* aan; *in* ~, in

werkelijkheid *n.*; *to no* ~, tevergeefs; ~*s*, bezittingen *pl.n.* ¶ *v.t.* teweegbrengen *irr.*, tot stand brengen *irr.*
effective, *a.*, ~ly, *adv.* werkzaam; doeltreffend. **effectual**, *a.*, ~ly, *adv.* doelmatig.
effectuate, *v.t.* bewerkstelligen.
effeminacy, *n.* verwijfdheid *n.* **effeminate**, *a.*, ~ly, *adv.* verwijfd.
effervesce, *v.i.* opbruisen. **effervescence**, *n.* opbruising *n.n.* **effervescent**, *a.* opbruisend. ~ *powder*, bruispoeder *n.n.*
effete, *a.* afgeleefd, uitgeput.
efficacious, *a.*, ~ly, *adv.* doeltreffend, krachtdadig. **efficacy**, *n.* doeltreffendheid *n.*
efficiency, *n.* werking *n.*, doelmatigheid *n.*; nuttig effect *n.n.* **efficient**, *a.*, ~ly, *adv.* doeltreffend; werkzaam.
effigy, *n.* beeltenis *n.*; beeldenaar *n.*
efflorescence, *n.* ontluiking *n.*, bloei *n.* **efflorescent**, *a.* bloeiend.
effluence, *n.* uitvloeisel *n.n.*; uitstraling *n.* **effluent**, *a.* uitvloeiend; uitstralend.
effluvium, *n.* uitwaseming *n.*
effort, *n.* inspanning *n.*; poging *n.* **effortless**, *a.* zonder inspanning *n.*
effrontery, *n.* onbeschaamdheid *n.*; brutaliteit *n.*
effulgence, *n.* glans *n.* **effulgent**, *a.* glanzend, stralend.
effusion, *n.* uitstorting *n.*; (*fig.*) ontboezeming *n.* **effusive**, *a.*, ~ly, *adv.* overdreven; buitengewoon hartelijk.
eft, *n.* watersalamander *n.*
egg, *n.* ei *n.n.* ¶ *v.t.* *to* ~ *on*, aanzetten, ophitsen. **eggcup**, *n.* eierdopje *n.n.* **eggflip**, *n.* warm bier *n.n.* met eieren. **egg-nog**, *n.* advokaat *n.* **egg-plant**, *n.* eierplant *n.* **eggshell**, *n.* eierdop *n.*; eierschaal *n.*
eglantine, *n.* egelantier *n.*; hondsroos *n.*
egoism, *n.* egoïsme *n.n.*, zelfzucht *n.* **egoistic**, *a.*, ~ally, *adv.* egoïstisch. **egotism**, *n.* eigenliefde *n.*; zelfgenoegzaamheid *n.* **egotist**, *n.* egoïst *n.* **egotistic**, *a.*, ~ally, *adv.* zelfzuchtig.
egregious, *a.*, ~ly, *adv.* uitmuntend, voortreffelijk.
egress, *n.* uitgang *n.*
egret, *n.* kleine zilverreiger *n.*
Egypt, *N.* Egypte *n.N.* **Egyptian**, *a.* Egyptisch. ¶ *n.* Egyptenaar *n.* (*male*), Egyptische *n.* (*female*).
eh, *int.* he! wat?
eiderdown, *n.* eiderdons *n.n.*; donzen deken *n.* **eiderduck**, *n.* eidergans *n.*
eight, *num.* acht. *the* ~ *of us*, wij achten; met ons achten. **eighteen**, *num.* achttien. **eighteenth**, *a.* achttiende. **eightfold**, *a.* achtvoudig. **eighth**, *a.* achtste. ¶ *n.* achtste *n.n.* **eightieth**, *a.* tachtigste. **eighty**, *num.* tachtig.
either, *pron.* één van beide; beide. ~ *of us*, één van ons. ¶ *c.* ~ . . . *or* . . ., of(wel) . . . of(wel) . . . ¶ *adv.* ook.

ejaculate, *v.t.* uitroepen *str.*; uitstoten *str.* **ejaculation**, *n.* uitroep *n.*; uitwerpen *n.n.* **ejaculatory**, *a.* ~ *prayer*, schietgebed *n.n.*
eject, *v.t.* uitwerpen *str.*; verdrijven *str.* **ejection**, *n.* verdrijving *n.*; uitstoting *n.*
eke, *v.t.* *to* ~ *out*, aanvullen.
elaborate, *v.t.* uitwerken; ontwikkelen. ¶ *a.*, ~ly, *adv.* uitvoering, uitgebreid. **elaboration**, *n.* ontwikkeling *n.*
eland, *n.* eland *n.*
elapse, *v.i.* verstrijken *str.*, verlopen *str.*
elastic, *a.* elastisch, veerkrachtig. **elasticity**, *n.* elasticiteit *n.*, veerkracht *n.*
elate, *v.t.* opgetogen maken. ¶ *a.* opgetogen. **elation**, *n.* opgetogenheid *n.*; overmoed *n.*
elbow, *n.* elleboog *n.* *to be out at* ~*s*, met de ellebogen door de mouwen steken *str.* ¶ *v.t.* duwen, dringen *str.* **elbow-room**, *n.* ruimte *n.* om zich te bewegen.
elder, *a.* ouder, oudste. ¶ *n.* oudere *n.*, oudste *n.*; ouderling *n.*; vlier *n.* **elderly**, *a.* ietwat bejaard. **eldest**, *a.* oudste.
elect, *v.t.* kiezen *str.*; verkiezen *str.* ¶ *a.* uitverkoren; gekozen. ¶ *n.* uitverkorene *n.* **election**, *n.* verkiezing *n.* **electioneer**, *v.i.* stemmen werven. **electioneering**, *n.* verkiezingswerk *n.n.* **elective**, *a.* kies . . . ~ *affinity*, affiniteit *n.* **elector**, *n.* kiezer *n.* *E*~, Keurvorst *N.* **electoral**, *a.* kies . . ; keurvorstelijk. ~ *reform*, herziening *n.* van het kiesrecht; ~ *truce*, politieke godsvrede *n.* **electorate**, *n.* gezamenlijke kiezers *pl.n.*; keurvorstendom *n.n.*
electric, *a.* electrisch. **electrical**, *a.* electrisch. ~ *engineer*, electrotechnicus. **electricity**, *n.* electriciteit *n.* **electrification**, *n.* electrificatie *n.*; electrisering *n.* **electrify**, *v.t.* electriseren. **electrocute**, *v.t.* door electriciteit *n.* terechtstellen. **electrocution**, *n.* electrocutie *n.* **electrolyse**, *v.t.* electrolyseren. **electrolysis**, *n.* electrolyse *n.* **electro-plate**, *v.t.* galvanisch verzilveren. **electrotype**, *n.* electrotypie *n.*, galvano *n.*
electuary, *n.* likkepot *n.*
eleemosynary, *a.* liefdadigheids . . .
elegance, *n.* sierlijkheid *n.*, bevalligheid *n.*, elegance *n.* **elegant**, *a.*, ~ly, *adv.* sierlijk, bevallig, elegant.
elegiac, *a.* elegisch. **elegy**, *n.* elegie *n.*, treurzang *n.*
element, *n.* element *n.n.*; bestanddeel *n.n.* **elemental**, *a.* van de elementen. **elementary**, *a.* elementair; eenvoudig.
elephant, *n.* olifant *n.* *white* ~, iets waar men mee zit. **elephantine**, *a.* olifantachtig.
elevate, *v.t.* verheffen *str.*; veredelen. **elevated**, *a.* verheven. ~ *railway*, luchtspoorweg *n.* **elevation**, *n.* opheffing *n.*; verhevenheid *n.*; hoogte *n.*, elevatie *n.* **elevator**, *n.* hijskraan *n.*; lift *n.*
eleven, *num.* elf. ¶ *n.* elftal *n.n.* **eleventh**, *a.* elfde.
elf, *n.* elf *n.*; fee *n.*; kabouter *n.* **elfin**, *a.* elfachtig.

elicit, *v.t.* uitlokken, aan het licht brengen *irr.*

elide. *v.t.* weglaten *str.*

eligibility, *n.* verkiesbaarheid *n.* eligible, *a.* verkiesbaar; geschikt.

eliminate, *v.t.* elimineren, uitschakelen, uit de weg ruimen. elimination, *n.* eliminatie *n.*, verwijdering *n.*

elision, *n.* weglating *n.*

elixir, *n.* elixer *n.*

elk, *n.* eland *n.*; wapiti *n.*

ell, *n.* el *n.*

ellipse, *n.* ellips *n.* ellipsis, *n.* uitlating *n.* elliptical, *a.* elliptisch.

elm, *n.* olm *n.*, iep *n.*

elocution, *n.* voordracht *n.*, dictie *n.* elocutionist, *n.* voordrachtskunstenaar *n.*

elongate, *v.t.* verlengen, rekken. elongation, *n.* verlenging *n.*

elope, *v.i.* weglopen *str.* to ~ with, ontvoeren, schaken. elopement, *n.* ontvoering *n.*, schaking *n.*

eloquence, *n.* welsprekendheid *n.* eloquent, *a.*, ~ly, *adv.* welsprekend.

else, *adv.* anders. *everybody* ~, ieder ander; alle anderen. elsewhere, *adv.* ergens anders, elders.

elucidate, *v.t.* toelichten, verduidelijken, ophelderen. elucidation, *n.* toelichting *n.*, verklaring *n.* elucidatory, *a.* verklarend.

elude, *v.t.* ontsnappen (aan), ontwijken *str.* aan. elusive, *a.* moeilijk te bereiken, ontwijkend.

emaciate, *v.t.* vermageren, uitteren. emaciated, *a.* uitgeteerd, uitgemergeld. emaciation, *n.* vermagering *n.*

emanate, *v.i.* to ~ from, voortkomen *irr.* uit, afkomstig zijn van. emanation, *n.* uitstraling *n.*; uitwaseming *n.*

emancipate, *v.t.* vrij maken, emanciperen. emancipation, *n.* vrijmaking *n.*, emancipatie *n.*

emasculate, *v.t.* ontmannen, lubben; ontzenuwen.

embalm, *v.t.* balsemen.

embank, *v.t.* indijken, afdammen. embankment, *n.* kade *n.*, wal *n.*; (spoor)dijk *n.*

embargo, *n.* beslag *n.n.*, embargo *n.n.*

embark, *v.t.* inschepen. ¶ *v.i.* aan boord gaan *irr.*, zich inschepen. to ~ on, zich wagen in. embarkation, *n.* inscheping *n.*

embarrass, *v.t.* verlegen maken; hinderen, generen. embarrassment, *n.* verlegenheid *n.*, verwarring *n.*; moeilijkheid *n.*

embassy, *n.* gezantschap *n.n.*, ambassade *n.*

embed, *v.t.* in een bedding *n.* leggen *irr.* to ~ in, omgeven door.

embellish, *v.t.* verfraaien, versieren. embellishment, *n.* verfraaiing *n.*, versiering *n.*

ember, *n.* gloeiende sintel *n.* ~ days, quatertemper *n.n.*

embezzle, *v.t.* verduisteren. embezzlement, *n.* verduistering *n.* embezzler, *n.* verduisteraar *n.*

embitter, *v.t.* verbitteren.

emblazon, *v.t.* blazoeneren.

emblem, *n.* zinnebeeld *n.n.*, embleem *n.n.* emblematic, *a.*, ~ally, *adv.* zinnebeeldig, emblematisch.

embodiment, *n.* belichaming *n.* embody, *v.t.* belichamen, omvatten.

embolden, *v.t.* verstouten.

embolism, *n.* embolie *n.*

emboss, *v.t.* drijven *str.*, opwerken. embossment, *n.* reliëfwerk *n.n.*

embrace, *v.t.* omhelzen; aannemen *str.*; overgaan *irr.* tot. ¶ *n.* omhelzing *n.*

embrasure, *n.* schietgat *n.n.*

embrocation, *n.* wrijfmiddel *n.n.*

embroider, *v.t.* & *v.i.* borduren. embroidery, *n.* borduursel *n.n.*, borduurwerk *n.n.*

embroil, *v.t.* verwikkelen. embroilment, *n.* verwikkeling *n.*

embryo, *n.* embryo *n.n.*, kiem *n.*

emend, *v.t.* verbeteren, emenderen. emendation, *n.* (tekst)verbetering *n.* emendator, *n.* emendator *n.*

emerald, *n.* smaragd *n.* (*gem*), *n.n.* (*stone*).

emerge, *v.i.* oprijzen *str.*, te voorschijn komen *irr.* emergence, *n.* verschijning *n.* emergency, *n.* verschijning *n.*; onverwachte gebeurtenis *n.* emergent, *a.* opkomend.

emery, *n.* amaril *n.* emery-cloth, *n.* schuurlinnen *n.n.* emery-paper, *n.* schuurpapier *n.n.*

emetic, *a.* braakwekkend. ¶ *n.* braakmiddel *n.n.*

emigrant, *n.* emigrant *n.*, landverhuizer *n.* emigrate, *v.i.* emigreren, uitwijken *str.* emigration, *n.* emigratie *n.*

eminence, *n.* verhevenheid *n.*; hoogte *n.*; voortreffelijkheid *n.*, eminentie *n.* eminent, *a.* verheven; voortreffelijk. eminently, *adv.* verheven; voortreffelijk; bij uitnemendheid *n.* bij uitstek *n.*

emissary, *n.* gezant *n.*, afgezant *n.*

emission, *n.* uitzending *n.*; emissie *n.* uitgifte *n.* emit, *v.t.* uitzenden *str.*; voortbrengen *irr.*

emollient, *a.* verzachtend.

emolument, *n.* salaris *n.n.*, honorarium *n.n.*

emotion, *n.* ontroering *n.*, aandoening *n.*, emotie *n.* emotional, *a.*, ~ly, *adv.* ontroerend; gemoeds . . .

empanel, *v.t.* samenstellen.

emperor, *n.* keizer *n.*

emphasis, *n.* nadruk *n.* emphasize, *v.t.* de nadruk leggen *irr.* op. emphatic, *a.*, ~ally, *adv.* nadrukkelijk.

empire, *n.* keizerrijk *n.n.*; rijk *n.n.*; heerschappij *n.*

empiric(al), *a.*, ~ly, *adv.* empirisch. ¶ *n.* empiricus *n.* empiricism, *n.* empirie *n.*

emplacement, *n.* opstelling *n.*, emplacement *n.n.*

employ, *v.t.* gebruiken, bezigen, aanwenden. ¶ *n.* dienst *n.* in the ~ of, in dienst bij. employee, *n.* employé *n.* employer, *n.* werkgever *n.*; patroon *n.* employment, *n.*

aanwending *n.*; bezigheid *n.*; dienst *n.*, beroep *n.n.*
emporium, *n.* stapelplaats *n.*; wereldmarkt *n.*; magazijn *n.n.*
empower, *v.t.* machtigen; in staat *n.* stellen.
empress, *n.* keizerin *n.*
emptiness, *n.* leegheid *n.*, leegte *n.* **empty,** *a.* leeg; vergeefs, ijdel. ¶ *v.t.* ledigen, leeg maken. ¶ *v.i.* leeg worden *str.*
empurple. *v.t.* purperrood maken.
empyrean, *a.* hemels.
emu, *n.* emoe *n.*, casuaris *n.*
emulate, *v.t.* nastreven, wedijveren met. **emulation,** *n.* wedijver *n.* **emulous,** *a.*, ∼**ly.** *adv.* naijverig. ∼ *of,* strevend naar.
emulsion, *n.* emulsie *n.*
enable, *v.t.* in staat *n.* stellen.
enact, *v.t.* bepalen, vaststellen; tot wet *n.* verheffen *str.*; spelen. **enactment,** *n.* verordening *n.*, wet *n.*; wetsbekrachtiging *n.*
enamel, *n.* émail *n.n.*; glazuur *n.n.* ¶ *v.t.* emailleren; verglazen.
enamoured, *a.* ∼ *of,* or *with,* verliefd op.
encage, *v.t.* opsluiten *str.*
encamp, *v.i.* kamperen. **encampment,** *n.* kamp *n.n.*, legerplaats *n.*
encase, *v.t.* omsluiten *str.*
encaustic, *a.* encaustisch. ∼ *tile,* verglaasde tegel *n.*
enchain, *v.t.* ketenen; boeien.
enchant, *v.t.* bekoren, verrukken; betoveren. **enchanter,** *n.* tovenaar *n.* **enchantment,** *n.* bekoring *n.* **enchantress,** *n.* bekoorster *n.*; tovenares *n.*
encircle, *v.t.* omcirkelen; omsingelen. **encirclement,** *n.* omsingeling *n.*
enclose, *v.t.* insluiten *str.*; omheinen; omgeven *str.* **enclosure,** *n.* omheining *n.*; omheinde plaats *n.*; ingesloten stuk *n.n.*; bijlage *n.*
encomium, *n.* lof *n.*, loftuiting *n.*
encompass, *v.t.* omgeven *str.*, omringen.
encore, *int.* bis! ¶ *v.t.* bisseren. ¶ *n.* bis-nummer *n.n.*
encounter, *v.t.* ontmoeten, treffen *str.* ¶ *n.* ontmoeting *n.*; gevecht *n.n.*, treffen *n.n.*
encourage, *v.t.* aanmoedigen. **encouragement,** *n.* aanmoediging *n.*
encroach, *v.i.* indringen *str.*, veld winnen *str.* *to* ∼ *on,* inbreuk *n.* maken op. **encroachment,** *n.* indringing *n.*; inbreuk *n.*
encrust, *v.i.* incrusteren; omkorsten.
encumber, *v.t.* belasten; hinderen; met een hypotheek *n.* bezwaren, met schulden *pl.n.* belasten. **encumbrance,** *n.* last *n.*, hindernis *n.*; hypotheek *n.*
encyclical, *n.* encycliek *n.*
encyclopædia, *n.* encyclopedie *n.* **encyclopædic,** *a.* encyclopedisch.
end, *n.* eind *n.n.*, einde *n.n.*; slot *n.n.*, besluit *n.n.*, afloop *n.*; oogmerk *n.n.*, doel *n.n. at an* ∼, ten einde; *to no* ∼, tevergeefs; *no* ∼ *of,* massa's *pl. n.*; een hele boel *n.*; *'n the* ∼, tenslotte; *on* ∼, overeind;

∼ *to* ∼, (in de lengte) achter elkaar; *there's an* ∼ *of it,* en daarmee uit; *to be at a loose* ∼, niets om handen *n.* hebben; *to make both* ∼*s meet,* rondkomen *irr.*; *to keep one's* ∼ *up,* zich niet op de kop laten *str.* zitten. ¶ *v.t.* eindigen; afmaken; een eind maken aan. ¶ *v.i.* eindigen; aflopen *str.*; ophouden *irr.*
endanger, *v.t.* in gevaar *n.n.* brengen *irr.*
endear, *v.t.* dierbaar maken, bemind maken. **endearment,** *n.* liefkozing *n.*
endeavour, *v.i.* pogen, streven. ¶ *n.* poging *n.*, inspanning *n.*; streven *n.n.*
endemic, *a.* endemisch.
ending, *n.* einde *n.n.*
endive, *n.* andijvie *n.*
endless, *a.*, ∼**ly,** *adv.* eindeloos.
endorse, *v.t.* endosseren; steunen; onderschrijven *str.* **endorsee,** *n.* geëndosseerde *n.* **endorsement,** *n.* endossement *n.n.*; goedkeuring *n.* **endorser,** *n.* endossant *n.*
endow, *v.t.* begiftigen, beschenken *str.* **endowment,** *n.* begiftiging *n.*, schenking *n.*
endurable, *a.* verdraaglijk. **endurance,** *n.* uithoudingsvermogen *n.n.*; lijdzaamheid *n.*, geduld *n.n.* **endure,** *v.t.* verdragen *str.*, dulden. ¶ *v.i.* voortduren.
endways, *adv.*, **endwise,** *adv.* rechtop, overeind.
enema, *n.* klisteer *n.*
enemy, *n.* vijand *n.*; vijandin *n.*
energetic, *a.*, ∼**ally,** *adv.* energiek, krachtig. **energy,** *n.* energie *n.*; arbeidsvermogen *n.n.*
enervate, *v.t.* ontzenuwen, verslappen.
enfeeble, *v.t.* verzwakken.
enfeoff, *v.t.* belenen, overdragen *str.*
enfilade, *v.t.* enfileren, bestrijken *str.* ¶ *n.* flankvuur *n.n.*
enfold, *v.t.* omvatten.
enforce, *v.t.* kracht *n.* bijzetten aan, doorzetten; doen *irr.* eerbiedigen. **enforcement,** *n.* handhaving *n.*; bevestiging *n.*
enfranchise, *v.t.* vrij maken; het kiesrecht geven *str.* aan. **enfranchisement,** *n.* bevrijding *n.*; verlening *n.* van het kiesrecht.
engage, *v.t.* verbinden *str.*; aanwerven *str.*, engageren; de strijd aanbinden *str.* met. *to be* ∼*d,* bezet zijn; geëngageerd zijn. ¶ *v.i. to* ∼ *in,* zich mengen in; beginnen *str.*, aanknopen. **engaged,** *a.* verloofd, geëngageerd; bezet. **engagement,** *n.* verplichting *n.*; afspraak *n.*; engagement *n.n.*, verloving *n.*; gevecht *n.n.*, treffen *n.n.* **engaging,** *a.* innemend.
engender, *v.t.* verwekken; veroorzaken.
engine. *n.* machine *n.*; locomotief *n.*; brandspuit *n.* **engine-driver,** *n.* machinist *n.* **engineer,** *n.* ingenieur *n.*, werktuigkundige *n.*; machinist *n.*; soldaat *n.* (*or* officier *n.*) van de genie. ¶ *v.t.* weten *irr.* te bewerken. **engineering,** *n.* ingenieurswerk *n.n.*; machinebouw *n.* **engine-house,** *n.* loods *n.*, huisje *n.n.*

England, N. Engeland n.N. **English,** a.
Engels. ¶ N. Engels n.N. **Englishman,** N.
Engelsman N., pl. Engelsen. **Englishwoman,** N. Engelse N.
engrain, v.t. in de wol verven; inwortelen.
engrave, v.t. graveren; imprenten. **engraver,**
n. graveur n. **engraving,** n. gravure n.;
graveerkunst n.
engross, v.t. geheel in beslag n.n. nemen str.
~ed in, verdiept in; to be ~ed in, opgaan
irr. in. **engrossment,** n. diepe belangstelling
n.
engulf, v.t. verzwelgen str., opslokken.
enhance, v.t. vermeerderen, verhogen.
enigma, n. enigma n.n., raadsel n.n.
enigmatic(al), a., ~ly, adv. enigmatisch,
raadselachtig.
enjoin, v.t. gelasten, bevelen str.; op het hart
drukken.
enjoy, v.t. genieten (van). ¶ v.r. to ~ oneself,
zich amuseren. **enjoyable,** a. genietbaar;
genoeglijk. **enjoyment,** n. genot n.n.,
genoegen n.n.
enlarge, v.t. vergroten, uitbreiden. ¶ v.i.
to ~ upon, uitweiden over. **enlargement,**
n. vergroting n.
enlighten, v.t. inlichten, voorlichten.
enlist, v.t. inschrijven str.; aanwerven str.;
winnen str. ¶ v.i. dienst n. nemen str.
enlistment, n. indiensttreding n.; aan-
werving n.
enliven, v.t. opvrolijken.
enmesh, v.t. verstrikken.
enmity, n. vijandschap n.
ennoble, v.t. adelen, veredelen.
enormity, n. ongehoorde n.n. **enormous,** a.,
~ly, adv. kolossaal, enorm; ontzettend.
enough, a. & adv. genoeg; voldoende. well ~
heel goed.
enounce, v.t. uitspreken str., uiten.
enquire, v.i. & v.t. See inquire.
enrage, v.t. woedend maken.
enrapture, v.t. verrukken, in verrukking n.
brengen irr.
enrich, v.t. verrijken.
enrol, v.t. inschrijven str.; aanwerven str.
¶ v.i. zich laten str. inschrijven.
ensconce, v.r. to ~ oneself. zich verschansen,
zich verdekt opstellen.
enshrine, v.t. in een schrijn n. plaatsen.
ensign, n. standaard n., vlag n.; vaandrig n.
blue ~, vlag van de Engelse vlootreserve
n.; red ~, Engelse koopvaardijvlag n.;
white ~, Engelse marinevlag n.
ensilage, v.t. inkuilen. ¶ n. ingekuild voeder
n.n.
enslave, v.t. tot slaaf n. maken, onderwerpen
str. **enslaver,** n. onderdrukker n.
ensnare, v.t. verstrikken, in de val lokken.
ensue, v.i. volgen. to ~ from, voortvloeien
uit. **ensuing,** a. komend, volgend.
entail, v.t. vermaken, onvervreemdbaar
maken; met zich meebrengen irr. ¶ n.
onvervreemdbaar erfgoed n.n.

entangle, v.t. verstrikken, verwarren. **entanglement,** n. verwikkeling n.; versperring
n.
enter, v.t. binnengaan irr., binnentreden str.;
betreden str.; inschrijven str.; aantekenen.
¶ v.i. binnengaan irr. to ~ into, aanknopen,
aangaan irr.; to ~ upon, betreden str.;
beginnen str.
enteric, a. ingewands . . . ~ fever, darm-
typhus n. **enteritis,** n. ingewandsont-
steking n.
enterprise, n. onderneming n.; onder-
nemingszin n. **enterprising,** a. ondernemend ; vermetel.
entertain, v.t. onderhouden irr.; onthalen;
amuseren, vermaken; koesteren. **entertainment,** n. onthaal n.n.; vermakelijkheid n.
enthral, v.t. tot slaaf n. maken; (fig.)
betoveren. **enthralling,** a. boeiend.
enthrone, v.t. op de troon plaatsen;
wijden.
enthusiasm, n. enthousiasme n.n., geestdrift
n. **enthusiast,** n. enthousiast n. **enthusiastic,** a., ~ally, adv. enthousiast,
geestdriftig.
entice, v.t. verleiden, verlokken. **enticement,**
n. verlokking n.
entire, a., ~ly, adv. geheel, volkomen.
entirety, n. geheel n.n.
entitle, v.t. to ~ to, aanspraak n. geven str.
op.
entity, n. geheel n.n.; zijn n.n.; wezen
n.n.
entomb, v.t. begraven str.
entomologist, n. entomoloog n. **entomology,**
n. entomologie n., insectenleer n.
entrails, pl.n. ingewanden pl.n.n.; (fig.)
binnenste n.n.
entrain, v.t. in een trein n. laden; met zich
meeslepen. ¶ v.i. instappen.
entrance, n. ingang n.; intrede n.; toegang n.
en·trance, v.t. verrukken; in vervoering
brengen irr.
entrap, v.t. in de val lokken.
entreat, v.t. smeken, bidden str. **entreaty,** n.
smeekbede n.; dringend verzoek n.n.
entrench, v.t. verschansen. **entrenchment,** n.
verschansing n.
entrust, v.t. toevertrouwen.
entry, n. intrede n.; intocht n.; ingang n.,
toegang n.; inschrijving n.
entwine, v.t. omstrengelen.
enumerate, v.t. opsommen. **enumeration,** n.
opsomming n.
enunciate, v.t. verkondigen. **enunciation,** n.
verkondiging n.; voordracht n.
envelop, v.t. omhullen, omwikkelen; omsingelen. **envelope,** n. enveloppe n.,
couvert n.n.; omslag n.; omhulsel n.n.
envelopment, n. omhulsel n.n.; om-
trekkende beweging n.
envenom, v.t. vergiftigen.
enviable, a., ~bly, adv. benijdenswaardig.
envious, a., ~ly, adv. afgunstig, jaloers.

environ, *v.t.* omringen, omgeven *str.* environment, *n.* omgeving *n.* environs, *n.* omstreken *pl.n.*

envisage, *v.t.* onder de ogen zien *irr.*

envoy, *n.* gezant *n.*, afgezant *n.*; slotvers *n.n.*

envy, *n.* afgunst *n.*, nijd *n.*, jaloezie *n.*

epaulet(te), *n.* epaulet *n.*

epergne, *n.* middenstuk *n.n.* (op tafel *n.*).

ephemera, *pl.n.* ééndagsvlieg *n.*; vergankelijk iets *n.n.* ephemeral, *a.* kortstondig.

epic, *n.* heldendicht *n.n.*, epos *n.n.* ¶ *a.* episch.

epicure, *n.* epicurist *n.* epicurean, *a.* epicurisch.

epidemic, *a.* epidemisch. ¶ *n.* epidemie *n.*

epidermis, *n.* opperhuid *n.*

epigram, *n.* epigram *n.n.*, puntdicht *n.n.* epigrammatic, *a.* epigrammatisch.

epilepsy, *n.* vallende ziekte *n.* epileptic, *a.* epileptisch.

epilogue, *n.* epiloog *n.*, narede *n.*, slotrede *n.*

Epiphany, *N.* Driekoningen *N.*

episcopacy, *n.* bisschoppelijke kerkregering *n.*; gezamenlijke bisschoppen *pl.n.* episcopal, *a.* bisschoppelijk. episcopate, *n.* bisdom *n.n.*; bisschoppelijke waardigheid *n.*

episode, *n.* episode *n.*; voorval *n.n.*

epistle, *n.* epistel *n.n.*; brief *n.* epistolary, *a.* brief . . .

epitaph, *n.* grafschrift *n.n.*

epithet, *n.* epitheton *n.n.*, benaming *n.*

epitome, *n.* kort begrip *n.n.*, korte inhoud *n.*; samenvatting *n.* epitomize, *v.t.* verkort weergeven *str.*

epoch, *n.* tijdperk *n.n.* ~ making, opzienbarend.

Epsom salts, *pl.n.* Engels zout *n.n.*

equable, *a.*, ~bly, *adv.* gelijkmatig.

equal, *a.* gelijk; gelijkvormig; dezelfde, hetzelfde. ¶ *n.* gelijke *n.* or *n.n.* without ~, zonder weerga *n.* ¶ *v.t.* gelijk zijn aan, evenaren; gelijk maken. equality, *n.* gelijkheid *n.*; gelijkvormigheid *n.* equalization, *n.* gelijkmaking *n.* equalize, *v.t.* gelijk maken. equally, *adv.* gelijk; gelijkelijk.

equanimity, *n.* gelijkmoedigheid *n.*

equate, *v.t.* gelijkstellen; tot een gemiddelde brengen *irr.* equation, *n.* vergelijking *n.* equator, *n.* evenaar *n.*, evennachtslijn *n.*, aequator *n.* equatorial, *a.* aequatoriaal.

equerry, *n.* stalmeester *n.*

equestrian, *a.* ruiter . . ¶ *n.* ruiter, *n.* paardrijder *n.*

equilateral, *a.* gelijkzijdig.

equilibrist, *n.* koorddanser *n.* equilibrium, *n.* evenwicht *n.n.*

equine, *a.* paarden . . .

equinoctial, *a.* evennachts . . . equinox, *n.* dag- en nachtevening *n.*

equip, *v.t.* uitrusten. equipage, *n.* equipement *n.n.*; equipage *n.* equipment, *n.* uitrusting *n.*; toerusting *n.*

equipoise, *n.* evenwicht *n.n.*

equitable, *a.*, ~bly, *adv.* billijk; onpartijdig. equity, *n.* billijkheid *n.*; billijkheidsrecht *n.n.* in ~, billijkerwijs.

equivalence, *n.* gelijkwaardigheid *n.* equivalent, *a.* gelijkwaardig. ¶ *n.* equivalent *n.n.*

equivocal, *a.*, ~ly, *adv.* dubbelzinnig; onzeker. equivocate, *v.i.* dubbelzinnig spreken *str.* uitvluchten *pl. n.n.* zoeken *irr.* equivocation, *n.* dubbelzinnigheid *n.*; draaierij *n.* equivoque, *n.* woordspeling *n.*

era, *n.* tijdperk *n.n.*; jaartelling *n.*

eradicate, *v.t.* verdelgen, uitroeien.

erase, *v.t.* uitschrappen; doorhalen. eraser, *n.* inktgom *n.n.* erasure, *n.* uitschrapping *n.*; doorhaling *n.*

ere, *c. & prep.* eer, voordat, vóór. ~ long, eerlang.

erect, *v.t.* oprichten; bouwen; opheffen *str.* ¶ *a.* rechtop, overeind; kaarsrecht. erection *n.* oprichting *n.*; erectie *n.* erectness. *n.* rechte houding *n.*; oprechtheid *n.*

eremite, *n.* kluizenaar *n.*, heremiet *n.*

ergot, *n.* moederkoorn *n.n.*

ermine, *n.* hermelijn *n.* (animal), *n.n.* (material). ¶ *a.* hermelijnen. ermined, *a.* met hermelijn getooid.

erode, *v.t. & v.i.* wegvreten, uitslijten *str.* erosion, *n.* uitslijting *n.*, erosie *n.*

erotic, *a.* erotisch, liefde(s) . . . eroticism. *n.* erotisme *n.n.*

err, *v.i.* dwalen, dolen.

errand, *n.* boodschap *n.* to run ~s, boodschappen doen *irr.* errand-boy, *n.* loopjongen *n.*

errant, *a.* dwalend; zwervend.

erratic, *a.*, ~ally, *adv.* dwalend; onberekenbaar, onvast.

erratum, *n.* drukfout *n.*

erroneous, *a.*, ~ly, *adv.* foutief, onjuist. error, *n.* fout *n.*, vergissing *n.*; dwaling *n.*

eructation, *n.* oprisping *n.*

erudite, *a.*, ~ly, *adv.* geleerd. erudition, *n.* geleerdheid *n.*

eruption, *n.* uitbarsting *n.*

erysipelas, *n.* roos *n.*

escalade, *n.* escalade *n.*, beklimming *n.*

escalator, *n.* rollende trap *n.*

escapade, *n.* dolle streek *n.*

escape, *v.i.* ontsnappen; ontvluchten; ontduiken *str.* to ~ from, ontkomen *irr.* aan. ¶ *n.* ontsnapping *n.*, ontkoming *n.* to make one's ~, ontsnappen. escapement, *n.* ontsnapping *n.*; gang *n.* escape-valve, *n.* veiligheidsklep *n.*

escarpment, *n.* steile glooiing *n.*

escheat, *v.i.* vervallen *str.* ¶ *v.t.* verbeurd verklaren.

eschew, *v.t.* schuwen.

escort, *v.t.* escorteren, begeleiden. escort, *n.* escorte *n.n.*, begeleiding *n.*

escutcheon, *n.* wapenschild *n.n.*

esoteric, *a.* esoterisch, geheim.

espalier, *n.* spalier *n.n.*, leiboom *n.*

esparto, *n.* esparto *n.n.*, Spaans gras *n.n.*

especial, *a.*, ~ly, *adv.* bijzonder, speciaal.
espionage, *n.* spionnage *n.*
esplanade, *n.* esplanade *n.*, boulevard *n.*; glacis *n.n.*
espousal(s), *n.* huwelijk *n.n.*; verloving *n.* espouse, *v.t.* huwen; (*fig.*) omhelzen.
espy, *v.t.* bespeuren, bespieden.
esquire, *n.* schildknaap *n.* ... *Esq.*, den Weledel Geb. Heer ...
·essay, *n.* proef *n.*, proefneming *n.*; opstel *n.n.*, verhandeling *n.* es·say, *v.t.* toetsen; beproeven.
essence, *n.* wezen *n.*, substantie *n.*; grondbestanddeel *n.n.*; essence *n.*, uittreksel *n.n.*
essential, *a.*, ~ly, *adv.* werkelijk; noodzakelijk, onmisbaar. ~ *oil,* vluchtige olie *n.*
establish, *v.t.* oprichten, stichten; vaststellen. Established Church, *N.* Staatskerk *N.* establishment, *n.* stichting *n.*; handelshuis *n.n.*; vaststelling *n.*
estate, *n.* rang *n.*, klasse *n.*; landgoed *n.n.*; bezit *n.n.*, fortuin *n.n. fourth* ~, vierde stand *n.n.*; *man's* ~, mannelijke leeftijd *n.*; *real* ~, onroerende goederen *pl.n.n.*
esteem, *v.t.* achten, hoogachten; waarderen, op prijs *n.* stellen. estimable, *a.* achtenswaardig. estimate, *v.t.* schatten, ramen, begroten. ¶ *n.* schatting *n.*, raming *n.*, begroting *n.* estimation, *n.* achting *n.*; schatting *n.*; oordeel *n.n.* estimator, *n.* taxateur *n.*
estrange, *v.t.* vervreemden. estrangement, *n.* vervreemding *n.*
estuary, *n.* zeearm *n.*, brede riviermonding *n.*
etch, *v.t.* etsen. etcher, *n.* etser *n.* etching, *n.* ets *n.*
eternal, *a.*, ~ly, *adv.* eeuwig, eeuwigdurend, onveranderlijk. eternity, *n.* eeuwigheid *n.*
ether, *n.* ether *n.* ethereal, *a.* etherisch; vluchtig.
ethical, *a.*, ~ly, *adv.* ethisch. ethics, *pl.n.* ethica *n.*, zedenleer *n.*
ethnography, *n.* land- en volkenkunde *n.*
ethnology, *n.* ethnologie *n.*, volkenkunde *n.*
etiquette, *n.* etiquette *n.*
etymological, *a.*, ~ly, *adv.* etymologisch. etymology, *n.* etymologie *n.*
eucharist, *n.* Eucharistie *N*; hostie *n.*
eulogist, *n.* lofredenaar *n.* eulogize, *v.t.* loven. eulogy, *n.* lofrede *n.*
eunuch, *n.* eunuch *n.*
euphemism, *n.* euphemisme *n.n.*
euphonic, *a.* welluidend. euphony, *n.* welluidendheid *n.*
euphuism, *n.* gezochte taal *n.*
Europe, *N.* Europa *n.N.* European, *a.* Europeaans.
evacuate, *v.t.* ontruimen, evacueren; zich ontlasten. evacuation, *n.* ontruiming *n.*; ontlasting *n.*
evade, *v.t.* ontwijken *str.*, ontduiken *str.*
evaluate, *v.t.* de waarde bepalen van. evaluation, *n.* schatting *n.*

evanescent, *a.* voorbijgaand.
evangelical, *a.* evangelisch. evangelist, *n.* evangelieprediker *n.* evangelize, *v.t.* kerstenen. ¶ *v.i.* het evangelie prediken.
evaporate, *v.i.* verdampen. ¶ *v.t.* (doen *irr.*) verdampen. evaporation, *n.* verdamping *n.*
evasion, *n.* ontwijking *n.*, ontduiking *n.* evasive, *a.*, ~ly, *adv.* ontwijkend.
eve, *n.* vóóravond *n.*; (*poet.*) avond *n.*
even, *a.* gelijk, gelijkmatig; effen; quitte. ¶ *adv.* zelfs. *not* ~, zelfs niet; ~ *now,* zoëven; ~ *so,* juist! ¶ *v.t.* gelijkmaken, effenen; gelijkstellen.
evening, *n.* avond *n. in the* ~, 's avonds; ~ *dress,* avondtoilet *n.n.*
evenly, *adv.* gelijkmatig; gelijkelijk. evenness, *n.* gelijkheid *n.*, gelijkmatigheid *n.*
evensong, *n.* avondlied *n.n.*; vesper *n.*
event, *n.* gebeurtenis *n.*; sportnummer *n.n. after the* ~, achteraf; *in the* ~ *of,* voor het geval dat; *at all* ~*s,* in elk geval *n.n.* eventful, *a.* veelbewogen; belangrijk.
eventide, *n.* avondstond *n.*
eventual, *a.* eventueel; mogelijk. eventuality, *n.* mogelijke gebeurtenis *n.* eventually, *adv.* ten slotte.
eventuate, *v.i.* aflopen *str.*; uitlopen *str.*
ever, *adv.* ooit; steeds. ~ *since,* van toen af aan; *for* ~ *so long,* heel lang. evergreen, *a.* altijd groen. ¶ *n.* altijd groene plant *n.*
everlasting, *a.*, ~ly, *adv.* eeuwig(durend). evermore, *adv.* voor altijd.
every, *a.* elk, ieder. ~ *other day,* om de andere dag. everybody, *pron.* iederen. everyday, *a.* alledaags. everyone, *pron.* iedereen. everything, *pron.* alles. everywhere, *adv.* overal.
evict, *v.t.* uitzetten. eviction, *n.* uitzetting *n.*
evidence, *n.* bewijsmateriaal *n.n. in* ~, op de voordrond; *to give* ~, getuigenis afleggen. ¶ *v.t.* aan den dag leggen *irr.* evident, *a.*, ~ly, *adv.* klaarblijkelijk, blijkbaar. evidential, *a.* tot bewijs *n.n.* dienend.
evil, *a.*, ~ly, *adv.* kwaad, boos, slecht. *the* ~ *one,* de Boze *N.* ¶ *n.* kwaad *n.n.*
evince, *v.t.* aan den dag leggen *irr.*
evocation, *n.* oproeping *n.*; bezwering *n.* evoke, *v.t.* oproepen *str.*; uitlokken.
evolution, *n.* evolutie *n.*, ontwikkeling *n.*; beweging *n.* evolve, *v.t.* ontwikkelen. ¶ *v.i.* zich ontvouwen.
ewe, *n.* ooi *n.*
ewer, *n.* lampetkan *n.*
exacerbate, *v.t.* verscherpen, verbitteren.
exact, *a.*, ~ly, *adv.* nauwkeurig, precies; stipt. ¶ *v.t.* vorderen, eisen, vergen. exacting, *a.* veeleisend. exaction, *n.* afpersing *n.* exactitude, *n.*, exactness, *n.* nauwkeurigheid *n.*, nauwgezetheid *n.*
exaggerate, *v.t.* overdrijven *str.* exaggeration, *n.* overdrijving *n.*
exalt, *v.t.* verheffen *str.*; ophemelen. exaltation, *n.* verheffing *n.*; geestvervoering *n.*

examination, n. onderzoek n.n.; verhoor n.n.;
examen n.n. **examine,** v.t. onderzoeken
irr.; ondervragen str.; exâmineren. **examiner,** n. examinator n.; inspecteur n.
example, n. voorbeeld n.n., model n.n.
for ~, bij voorbeeld n.n.
exasperate, v.t. ergeren, razend maken.
exasperation, n. ergernis n.
excavate, v.t. uitgraven str. **excavation,** n.
uitgraving n. **excavator,** n. graafmachine
n.
exceed, v.t. overtreffen str.; te buiten gaan
irr. **exceedingly,** adv. buitengewoon.
excel, v.t. overtreffen. ¶ v.i. uitmunten.
excellence, n. uitmuntendheid n., uitste-
kendheid n.; excellentie n. **excellency,** n.
excellentie n. **excellent,** a., ~ly, adv.
uitstekend, uitmuntend.
except, v.t. uitzonderen. ¶ prep. behalve.
excepting, prep. uitgezonderd. **exception,**
n. uitzondering n.; tegenwerping n.,
bezwaar n.n. **exceptionable,** a. aanstotelijk; betwistbaar. **exceptional,** a.,
~ly, adv. zeldzaam.
exerpt, n. uittreksel n.n. ¶ v.t. een uittreksel
maken.
excess, n. overdaad n., buitensporigheid n.
~ fare, toeslag n.; ~ luggage, overvracht
n.; E~ Profits Tax, Oorlogswinst-
belasting n. **excessive,** a., ~ly, adv.
buitensporig.
exchange, v.t. ruilen, wisselen. ¶ v.i. om-
ruilen. ¶ n. ruil n., verwisseling n.;
wisselkoers n.; beurs n. foreign ~,
buitenlandse valuta n. **exchangeable,** a.
verwisselbaar.
exchequer, n. schatkist n.
excise, v.t. uitsnijden str.; veraccijnzen.
¶ n. accijns n. **excision,** n. uitsluiting n.
excitability, n. prikkelbaarheid n. **excitable,**
a. licht opgewonden. **excitation,** n.
prikkeling n. **excitement,** n. opgewonden-
heid n.
exclaim, v.t. uitroepen str. to ~ against,
uitvaren str. tegen. **exclamation,** n.
uitroep n., uitroeping n. **exclamatory,** a.
uitroepend.
exclude, v.t. uitsluiten str. **exclusion,** n.
uitsluiting n. **exclusive,** a., ~ly, adv.
uitsluitend; exclusief.
excommunicate, v.t. excommuniceren, in de
ban doen irr. **excommunication,** n.
excommunicatie n., kerkelijke ban n.
excoriation, n. ontvelling n.
excrement, n. uitwerpsel n.n.
excrescence, n. uitwas n. **excrescent,** a.
overtollig.
excretion, n. afscheiding n.
excruciating, a. ondragelijk.
exculpate, v.t. verschonen, verontschuldigen.
exculpation, n. verontschuldiging n.
exculpatory, a. verontschuldigend.
excursion, n. tocht n., uitstapje n.n.;
afdwaling n. ~ train, pleiziertrein n.

excursionist, n. pleizierreiziger n. **excursive,**
a., ~ly, adv. afdwalend.
excusable, a. verschoonbaar. **excuse,** r.t.
verontschuldigen; rechtvaardigen. ¶ n.
verontschuldiging n., excuus n.n.
execrable, a., ~ly, adv. verfoeilijk, afschuwelijk. **execrate,** v.t. verfoeien,
verwensen. **execration,** n. verfoeiïng n.;
gruwel n.
execute, v.t. uitvoeren, volbrengen irr.;
uitoefenen; terechtstellen. **execution,** n.
volbrenging n.; voltrekking n.; terecht-
stelling n. **executioner,** n. beul n. **executive,**
a. uitvoerend. ¶ n. bestuur n.n., uitvoerend
lichaam n.n. **executor,** n. executeur n.
executrix, n. executrice n.
exemplar, n. voorbeeld n.n. **exemplary,** a.,
~ily, adv. voorbeeldig.
exemplification, n. verklaring n.; gewaarmerkt
afschrift n.n. **exemplify,** v.t. verklaren,
toelichten; een afschrift n.n. maken.
exempt, v.t. vrijstellen. ¶ a. vrijgesteld.
exemption, n. vrijstelling n.
exercise, v.t. oefenen; beoefenen; uitoefenen;
bezighouden irr. to be ~d in one's mind,
zich zorgen maken. ¶ v.i. (zich) oefenen.
¶ n. oefening n.; uitoefening n.
exert, v.t. aanwenden, inspannen irr., uitoefenen. **exertion,** n. inspanning n.
exhalation, n. uitwaseming n. **exhale,** v.t.
uitwasemen; uitademen.
exhaust, v.t. uitputten; leegmaken. ¶ n.
uitlaat n. **exhausted,** a. uitgeput; (lucht-)
ledig. **exhaustible,** a. uitputbaar. **exhaustion,** n. uitputting n.
exhibit, v.t. tentoonstellen, aan den dag
leggen irr. ¶ n. inzending n.; tentoon-
gesteld stuk n.n. **exhibition,** n. tentoon-
stelling n.; vertoning n.; studiebeurs n.
exhibitioner, n. beursstudent n. **exhibitor,**
n. exposant n.
exhilarate, v.t. opvrolijken. **exhilaration,** n.
opvrolijking n.
exhort, v.t. aansporen, vermanen. **exhorta-
tion,** n. aansporing n.
exhumation, n. opgraving n. **exhume,** v.t.
opgraven str.
exigence, a., **exigency,** n. noodzakelijkheid
n., vereiste n.
exile, v.t. verbannen. ¶ n. balling n.;
ballingschap n.
exist, v.i. bestaan irr.; leven. **existence,** n.
bestaan n.n. **existent,** a., **existing,** a.
bestaand.
exit, n. uitgang n. ¶ v.t. ~, af!
exodus, n. uittocht n. Exodus, N. Exodus
N.
exonerate, v.t. van blaam n. ontheffen str.
exoneration, n. zuivering n., ontheffing n.
exorbitance, n. buitensporigheid n. **exorbi-
tant,** a., ~ly, adv. buitensporig.
exorcise, v.t. uitdrijven str.; bezweren
str. **exorcism,** n. (geesten)bezwering n. **exorcist,** n. (geesten)bezweerder n.

exordium, *n.* aanhef *n.*
exotic, *a.* exotisch, uitheems.
expand. *v.t.* uitbreiden; doen *irr.* uitzetten. ¶ *v.i.* uitzetten; loskomen *irr.* **expanse,** *n.* uitgestrektheid *n.* **expansibility,** *n.* uitzetbaarheid *n.* **expansible,** *a.* uitzetbaar. **expansion,** *n.* uitzetting *n.*; uitbreiding *n.* **expansive,** *a.* uitzettings . . .; mededeelzaam.
expatiate, *v.i.* uitweiden.
expatriate, *v.t.* verbannen. ¶ *v.r.* *to ∼ oneself,* zijn land *n.n.* verlaten *str.* ¶ *n.* banneling *n.*; uitgewekene *n.* **expatriation,** *n.* verbanning *n.*; uitwijking *n.*
expect, *v.t.* verwachten; rekenen op. **expectancy,** *n.* verwachting *n.* **expectant,** *a.*, **∼ly,** *adv.* verwachtend, vol verwachting *n.*; in blijde verwachting *n.* **expectation,** *n.* verwachting *n.*; vooruitzicht *n.n.*
expectorate, *v.i.* opgeven *str.*; ophoesten; spuwen. **expectoration,** *n.* opgeving *n.*; slijm *n.n.*
expedience, *n.,* **expediency,** *n.* dienstigheid *n.*; doelmatigheid *n.*, doeltreffendheid *n.*; raadzaamheid *n.* **expedient,** *a.*, **∼ly,** *adv.* raadzaam, wenselijk; doelmatig.
expedite, *v.t.* verhaasten, bevorderen. **expedition,** *n.* expeditie *n.*, tocht *n.*; haast *n.*, spoed *n.* **expeditionary,** *a.* expeditie . . . **expeditious,** *a.*, **∼ly,** *adv.* snel, voortvarend.
expel, *v.t.* verjagen *str.*, verdrijven *str.*
expend, *v.t.* verbruiken. **expenditure,** *n.* uitgaaf *n.*; uitgeven *n.n.*; verbruik *n.n.* **expense,** *n.* uitgaaf *n.*, onkosten *pl.n.* **expensive,** *a.*, **∼ly,** *adv.* duur, kostbaar.
experience, *n.* ervaring *n.*, ondervinding *n.* ¶ *v.t.* ervaren, ondervinden *str.* **experienced,** *a.* ervaren.
experiment, *n.* proefneming *n.*, experiment *n.n.* ¶ *v.i.* proeven *pl. n.* nemen *str.*, experimenteren. **experimental,** *a.* proefondervindelijk.
expert, *a.,* **∼ly,** *adv.* bedreven; deskundig. **∼ at,** bedreven in. ¶ *n.* deskundige *n.*, expert *n.* **expertness,** *n.* bedrevenheid *n.*
expiable, *a.* weer goed te maken. **expiate,** *v.t.* boeten, goed maken. **expiation,** *n.* boete *n.* **expiatory,** *a.* boete . . ., zoen . . .
expiration, *n.* afloop *n.*, beëindiging *n.*; vervallen *n.n.*, vervaltijd *n.* **expire,** *v.i.* uitademen; vervallen *str.*; de geest geven *str.*
explain, *v.t.* uitleggen *irr.*, verklaren. *to ∼ away,* goedpraten. **explanation,** *n.* uitlegging *n.*, verklaring *n.*, opheldering *n.* **explanatory,** *a.* verklarend.
expletive, *a.* aanvullend. ¶ *n.* stopwoord *n.n.*; vloek *n.*
explicable, *a.*, **∼bly,** *adv.* verklaarbaar.
explicit, *a.*, **∼ly,** *adv.* uitdrukkelijk; uitvoerig.
explode, *v.i.* ontploffen, springen *str.* ¶ *v.t.*

doen *irr.* ontploffen, doen *irr.* springen; *(fig.)* ter zijde stellen. **exploded,** *a.* ontploft; verouderd.
exploit, *v.t.* exploiteren; uitbuiten. ¶ *n.* daad *n.*; wapenfeit *n.n.* **exploitation,** *n.* exploitatie *n.*; uitbuiting *n.*
exploration, *n.* onderzoeking *n.*, navorsing *n.* *journey of ∼,* ontdekkingsreis *n.* **exploratory,** *a.* onderzoekings . . . **explore,** *v.t.* nasporen, onderzoeken *irr.* **explorer,** *n.* ontdekkingsreiziger *n.*
explosion, *n.* ontploffing *n.*, uitbarsting *n.* **explosive,** *a.,* **∼ly,** *adv.* ontploffend, ontploffings . . . ¶ *n.* springstof *n.*
exponent, *n.* exponent *n.*; vertolker *n.*
ex.port, *v.t.* uitvoeren, exporteren. **·export,** *n.* uitvoer *n.*, export *n.* **exportation,** *n.* uitvoer *n.* **exporter,** *n.* exporteur *n.*
expose, *v.t.* tentoonstellen; blootleggen *irr.*; blootstellen; aan de kaak stellen; belichten. **exposition,** *n.* uiteenzetting *n.*, verklaring *n.*
expostulate, *v.i.* een ernstig vertoog *n.n.* doen *irr.* *to ∼ with someone on,* iemand onderhouden *irr.* over. **expostulation,** *n.* vertoog *n.n.*, vermaning *n.*
exposure, *n.* blootstelling *n.*; het blootgesteld zijn; belichting *n.*
expound, *v.t.* uitleggen *irr.*, vertolken. **expounder,** *n.* verklaarder *n.*
express, *v.t.* uitdrukken; uitpersen. ¶ *a.* **∼ly,** *adv.* uitdrukkelijk; bepaald; opzettelijk. **∼ train,** sneltrein *n.* **expressible,** *a.* uit te drukken. **expression,** *n.* uitdrukking *n.*; uitpersing *n.* **expressionless,** *a.* zonder uitdrukking *n.* **expressive,** *a.*, **∼ly,** *adv.* veelzeggend, vol uitdrukking *n.* **expressiveness,** *n.* uitdrukking *n.*; uitdrukkingsvermogen *n.n.*
expropriate, *v.t.* onteigenen. **expropriation,** *n.* onteigening *n.*
expulsion, *n.* wegjagen *n.n.*; uitdrijving *n.*
expunge, *v.t.* uitwissen.
expurgate, *v.t.* zuiveren. **expurgation,** *n.* zuivering *n.* **expurgator,** *n.* zuiveraar *n.*
exquisite, *a.*, **∼ly,** *adv.* uitgezocht, fijn, volmaakt. **exquisiteness,** *n.* fijnheid *n.*
extant, *a.* bestaande, in wezen.
extemporaneous, *a.*, **extemporary,** *a.*, **extempore,** *a.* onvoorbereid, voor de vuist weg. **extemporize,** *v.i.* improviseren.
extend, *v.t.* uitstrekken; uitbreiden; doortrekken, *str.*, verlengen; uitsteken *str.*; doen *irr.* toekomen. ¶ *v.i.* zich uitstrekken. **extensibility,** *n.* rekbaarheid *n.* **extensible,** *a.* rekbaar. **extension,** *n.* uitbreiding *n.*; verlenging *n.* **extensive,** *a.*, **∼ly,** *adv.* uitgebreid, veelomvattend. **extent,** *n.* uitgebreidheid *n.*, uitgestrektheid *n.*, omvang *n.* *to such an ∼,* zozeer; *to a large ∼,* grotendeels.
extenuate, *v.t.* verzachten, verminderen. **extenuating,** *a.* verzachtend. **extenuation,** *n.* verzachting *n.*

F

exterior, *a.* buitenste; uiterlijk; uitwendig; van buiten, buiten ... ¶ *n.* buitenkant *n.*; uiterlijk *n.n.*
exterminate, *v.t.* uitroeien, verdelgen. extermination, *n.* uitroeiing *n.*, verdelging *n.*
external, *a.*, ~ly, *adv.* uitwendig; uiterlijk; extern. ¶ *n.* ~s, uiterlijkheden *pl.n.*
extinct, *a.* uitgedoofd; uitgestorven. extinction, *n.* uitdoving *n.*; vernietiging *n.*, ondergang *n.* extinguish, *v.t.* uitdoven; blussen; vernietigen. extinguisher, *n.* blusapparaat *n.n.*
extirpate, *v.t.* uitroeien, verdelgen. extirpation, *n.* uitroeiing *n.*
extol, *v.t.* verheffen *str.*; prijzen *str.*
extort, *v.t.* afpersen. extortion, *n.* afpersing *n.*; afzetterij *n.* extortionate, *a.* buitensporig. extortioner, *n.* uitbuiter *n.*, afperser *n.*
extra, *a.* extra. ¶ *n.* iets extra's *n.n.* no ~s, alles inbegrepen.
extract, *v.t.* trekken *str.*; uittrekken *str.* extract, *n.* extract *n.n.*, uittreksel *n.n.* extraction, *n.* uittreksel *n.n.*; afkomst *n.*
extradite, *v.t.* uitleveren. extradition, *n.* uitlevering *n.*
extrajudicial, *a.*, ~ly, *adv.* wederrechtelijk.
extra-mural, *a.* buiten de universiteit.
extraneous, *a.* vreemd.
extraordinary, *a.*, ~ily, *adv.* buitengewoon.
extravagance, *n.* buitensporigheid *n.*; overdaad *n.*, verkwisting *n.*; overdrijving *n.* extravagant, *a.*, ~ly, *adv.* buitensporig; overdreven.
extreme, *a.*, ~ly, *adv.* uiterst; laatst; verst. ¶ *n.* uiterste *n.n.* to go to ~s, in het uiterste vervallen. extremity, *n.* uiterste *n.n.*; uiteinde *n.n.*
extricate, *v.t.* ontwarren, losmaken.
extrinsic, *a.*, ~ally, *adv.* uiterlijk.
extrude, *v.t.* verdrijven *str.* extrusion, *n.* verdrijving *n.*
exuberance, *n.* weelderigheid *n.*; overvloed *n.*; uitbundigheid *n.* exuberant, *a.*, ~ly, *adv.* weelderig; uitbundig.
exude, *v.t.* uitzweten.
exult, *v.i.* jubelen, juichen. exultant, *a.* opgetogen, triomfantelijk. exultation, *n.* gejubel *n.n.*; opgetogenheid *n.*
eye, *n.* oog *n.n.* to clap one's ~s on, te zien krijgen *str.*; to see ~ to ~ with, het eens zijn met; up to one's ~s, tot over de oren. ¶ *v.t.* bekijken *str.*, gadeslaan *irr.* eyeball, *n.* oogappel *n.* eyebrow, *n.* wenkbrauw *n.* eyeglass, *n.* monocle *n.* eyelash, *n.* wimper *n.*, ooghaar *n.n.* eyelid, *n.* ooglid *n.n.* eye-opener, *n.* iets wat iemand de ogen doet opengaan. eyepiece, *n.* oculair *n.n.* eyesight, *n.* gezicht *n.n.*, gezichtsvermogen *n.n.* eyesore, *n.* doorn *n.* in 't oog. eyewash, *n.* oogwater *n.n.* all ~, allemaal sinoesjes *pl.n.n.* eye-witness, *n.* ooggetuige *n.*
eyrie, *n.* nest *n.n.*

fable, *n.* fabel *n.*
fabric, *n.* weefsel *n.n.*; stof *n.*; structuur *n.* fabricate, *v.t.* vervaardigen; verzinnen *str.* fabrication, *n.* verzinsel *n.n.* fabricator, *n.* verzinner *n.*
fabulist, *n.* fabeldichter *n.* fabulous, *a.*, ~ly, *adv.* fabelachtig.
facade, *n.* vóórgevel *n.*
face, *n.* gezicht *n.n.*; voorkant *n.*; wijzerplaat *n.*; uiterlijk *n.n.*; onbeschaamdheid *n.* to save one's ~, z'n prestige *n.n.* redden; to set one's ~ against, zich verzetten tegen; in ~ of, tegenover; in the ~ of, tegen ... in; ~ to ~, tegenover elkaar. ¶ *v.t.* staan *irr.* tegenover; onder de ogen zien *irr.*; trotseren. ¶ *v.i.* to ~ about, zich omkeren. facer, *n.* moeilijk iets *n.n.*
facet, *n.* facet *n.*
facetiae, *pl.n.* humoristische lectuur *n.* facetious, *a.*, ~ly, *adv.* grappig, niet ernstig.
facial, *a.* gelaats ...
facile, *a.* gemakkelijk; goedkoop. facilitate, *v.t.* vergemakkelijken. facility, *n.* gemak *n.n.*, gerieflijkheid *n.*; faciliteit *n.*; vaardigheid *n.*
facing, *n.* revers *n.*; bekleding *n.* ¶ *a.* uitziend op.
facsimile, *n.* facsimile *n.n.*
fact, *n.* feit *n.n.*, werkelijkheid *n.*
faction, *n.* (politieke) partij *n.*, factie *n.* factious, *a.* partijzuchtig; oproerig.
factitious, *a.* kunstmatig.
factor, *n.* factor *n.*; agent *n.*
factory, *n.* fabriek *n.*; faktorij *n.*
factotum, *n.* factotum *n.*, duivelstoejager *n.*
faculty, *n.* vermogen *n.n.*, gave *n.*; bevoegdheid *n.*; faculteit *n.*
fad, *n.* gril *n.*; manie *n.*; liefhebberij *n.* faddist, *n.* iemand die er een gril op nahoudt. faddy, *a.* vol grillen.
fade, *v.i.* verwelken; verschieten *str.* fadeless, *a.* kleurhoudend, wasecht.
faeces, *pl.n.* uitwerpselen *pl.n.n.*
fag, *n.* baar *n.*; jongere leerling *n.*; last *n.*; (*slang*) sigaret *n.* ¶ *v.i.* zich afsloven. fag-end, *n.* zelfkant *n.*; uiteinde *n.n.* fagged, *a.* doodop. fagging, *n.* gezwoeg *n.n.*
faggot, *n.* takkebos *n.*
fail, *v.i.* ontbreken *str.*; mislukken; te kort schieten *irr.*; achteruitgaan *irr.*; failleren, bankroet gaan *irr.* ¶ *v.t.* in de steek laten *str.* ¶ *n.* without ~, absoluut zeker. failing, *n.* tekortkoming *n.*, gebrek *n.n.* ¶ *prep.* ontbrekend. failure, *n.* mislukking *n.*; faillissement *n.n.*
fain, *adv.* (*poet.*) gaarne.
faint, *a.*, ~ly, *adv.* zwak; flauw; onduidelijk. ¶ *v.i.* flauw vallen *str.* to ~ away, bezwijmen. ¶ *n.* bezwijming *n.*, flauwte *n.* faint-hearted, *a.* lafhartig. fainting-fit, *n.*

flauwte *n.* **faintness,** *n.* zwakheid *n.*,
flauwheid *n.*
fair, *a.* schoon; blond; rechtvaardig, eerlijk;
vrij goed; vrij groot. ~ *and square,*
eerlijk; *he bids* ~, hij heeft een goede
kans *n.* ¶ *n.* jaarmarkt *n.*; kermis *n.*
fairish, *a.* tamelijk goed. **fairly,** *adv.*
tamelijk; vrij. *See also* **fair,** *a.* **fairness,** *n.*
schoonheid *n.*; blondheid *n.*; rechtvaardigheid *n.*, eerlijkheid *n.* **fair-spoken,** *a.*
beleefd. **fairway,** *n.* vaarwater *n.n.*
fairy. *n.* fee *n.* **fairyland,** *n.* feeënrijk *n.n.*
fairy-tale, *n.* sprookje *n.n.*
faith, *n.* vertrouwen *n.n.*; trouw *n.*; geloof
n.n. in good ~, te goeder trouw. **faithful,**
a., ~**ly,** *adv.* trouw; oprecht. *yours* ~*ly,*
Uw dw. dr.; hoogachtend. ¶ *n. the* ~,
de gelovigen *pl.n.* **faithless,** *a.* trouweloos.
fake, *v.t.* namaken, vervalsen. ¶ *n.* namaak
n., namaaksel *n.n.*
fakir, *n.* fakir *n.*
falcon, *n.* valk *n.* **falconer,** *n.* valkenier *n.*
falconry, *n.* valkerij *n.*; valkenjacht *n.*
fall, *v.i.* vallen *str.*; neerkomen *str.*; dalen;
ten val komen *irr.*; zondigen. *to* ~ *due,*
vervallen *str.*; *to* ~ *off,* afvallen *str.*,
achteruitgaan *irr.*; *to* ~ *out,* ruzie krijgen
str.; *to* ~ *short,* te kort schieten *str.* ¶ *n.*
val *n.*; vallen *n.n.*; daling *n.*; ondergang
n.
fallacious, *a.,* ~**ly,** *adv.* bedrieglijk. **fallacy,**
n. dwaalbegrip *n.n.*, drogreden *n.*
fallibility, *n.* feilbaarheid *n.* **fallible,** *a.*,
~**bly,** *adv.* feilbaar.
fallow, *a.* vaalbruin; braak. ¶ *n.* braakland
n.n. **fallow-deer,** *n.* damhert *n.n.*
false, *a.*, ~**ly,** *adv.* vals; bedrieglijk; onjuist.
~ *step,* misstap *n.* **falsehood,** *n.* valsheid
n., leugen *n.*, bedrog *n.n.*
falsetto, *n.* falset *n.n.*; falsetstem *n.*
falsification, *n.* vervalsing *n.* **falsify,** *v.t.*
vervalsen; beschamen. **falsity,** *n.* valsheid
n.; onjuistheid *n.*
falter, *v.i.* weifelen; stamelen.
fame, *n.* roem *n.*; faam *n.*; vermaardheid *n.*
famed, *a.* beroemd, vermaard.
familiar, *a.*, ~**ly,** *adv.* vertrouwd; vertrouwelijk; gemeenzaam, familiaar. **familiarity,** *n.*
vertrouwdheid *n.*; vertrouwelijkheid *n.*;
familiariteit *n.* **familiarize,** *v.t.* vertrouwd
maken.
family, *n.* familie *n.*; gezin *n.n.* **family
allowance,** *n.* gezinstoelage *n.*
famine, *n.* hongersnood *n.*; schaarste *n.*
famish, *v.t.* uithongeren. ¶ *v.i.* verhongeren.
famous, *a.*, ~**ly,** *adv.* beroemd; prachtig.
fan, *n.* waaier *n.*; ventilator *n.*; bewonderaar
n. ¶ *v.t.* waaien; aanwakkeren.
fanatic, *n.* fanaticus *n.*, dweper *n.* **fanatic(al),**
a., ~**ly,** *adv.* fanatiek, dweepziek. **fanaticism,** *n.* fanatisme *n.n.*
fancier, *n.* liefhebber *n.*, kweker *n.* **fanciful,**
a., ~**ly,** *adv.* grillig, fantastisch. **fancy,** *n.*
fantasie *n.*; verbeelding *n.*; inval *n.*,

luim *n.*; zin *n.*, lust *n.* ¶ *v.t.* zich verbeelden; zin hebben in. **fancy-dress,** *n.*
kostuum *n.n.* **fancy-goods,** *pl.n.* galan-
terieeën *pl.n.* **fancy-price,** *n.* fabelachtige
prijs *n.* **fancy-work,** *n.* fraaie handwerken
pl.n.n.
fanfare, *n.* fanfare *n.*
fang, *n.* hoektand *n.*, slagtand *n.*
fanlight, *n.* waaiervormig bovenlicht *n.n.*
fantail, *n.* pauwstaart(duif) *n.*
fantastic, *a.*, ~**ally,** *adv.* grillig, fantastisch.
fantasy, *n.* fantasie *n.*
far, *a.* ver. *the F*~ *East,* het Verre Oosten.
¶ *adv.* ver. *by* ~, verreweg; ~ *and wide,*
wijd en zijd; ~ *off,* ver weg; *as* ~ *as,*
tot aan; *so* ~, tot zover.
farce, *n.* klucht *n.* **farcical,** *a.* kluchtig.
fare, *n.* kost *n.*; gerecht *n.n.*; vrachtprijs *n.*;
passagier *n.* ¶ *v.i.* varen, zich bevinden
str. to ~ *badly,* er slecht afkomen *irr.*
farewell, *excl.* vaarwel! ¶ *n.* vaarwel *n.n.*,
afscheid *n.n.*
farinaceous, *a.* meel . . .
farm, *n.* boerderij *n.*, hoeve *n.* ~ *yard,*
(boeren)erf *n.n.* ¶ *v.t.* bebouwen. *to* ~ *out,*
uitboeren, verpachten. **farmer,** *n.* boer *n.*
farm-house, *n.* boerenwoning *n.* **farming,**
n. landbouw *n.*
farrago, *n.* mengelmoes *n.n.*
farrier, *n.* hoefsmid *n.* **farriery,** *n.* hoef-
smederij *n.*
farrow, *v.i.* biggen, biggen *pl. n.* werpen *str.*
farsighted, *a.* verziend. **farther,** *a.* & *adv.*
verder. **farthest,** *a.* verst.
farthing, *n.* ¼ stuiver *n.*
fascinate, *v.t.* bekoren, boeien. **fascination,**
n. bekoring *n.*, betovering *n.*
fashion, *n.* mode *n.*; manier *n.*, wijze *n.*;
vorm *n.* ¶ *v.t.* vormen, fatsoeneren.
fashionable, *a.*, ~**bly,** *adv.* modieus; naar
de mode.
fast, *a.* onbeweeglijk, vast; hecht, stevig;
snel, vlug; losbandig. ¶ *adv.* snel; stevig;
dicht; los. ¶ *v.i.* vasten. ¶ *n.* vasten *n.*,
vastendag *n.* **fasten,** *v.t.* vastmaken;
bevestigen. **fastener,** *n.* haak *n.*, knip *n.*
fastidious, *a.*, ~**ly,** *adv.* kieskeurig.
fastness, *n.* stevigheid *n.*; vastheid *n.*;
vesting *n.*, sterkte *n.*
fat, *a.* vet; dik. ~ *stock,* mestvee *n.n.*
¶ *n.* vet *n.n. the* ~ *is in the fire,* de
poppen zijn aan 't dansen. ¶ *v.t. See*
fatten.
fatal, *a.*, ~**ly,** *adv.* noodlottig; dodelijk.
fatalism, *n.* fatalisme *n.n.* **fatalist,** *n.*
fatalist *n.* ¶ *a.* fatalistisch. **fatality,** *n.*
fataliteit *n.*; dodelijk ongeluk *n.n.* fate, *n.*
noodlot *n.n.*; lot *n.n.* **fated,** *a.* voorbestemd.
fateful, *a.* noodlottig; onheilspellend.
fathead, *n.* domkop *n.*
father, *n.* vader *n.*; pater *n.* ¶ *v.t.* vader
zijn voor; voorstaan *irr.* **fatherhood,** *n.*
vaderschap *n.n.* **father-in-law,** *n.* schoon-
vader *n.* **fatherland,** *n.* vaderland *n.n.*

fatherless, a. vaderloos. **fatherly,** a. vaderlijk.

fathom, n. vadem n. ¶ v.t. vademen; omvatten; peilen; doorgronden. **fathomless,** a. peilloos, grondeloos.

fatigue, n. vermoeidheid n., afmatting n.; korvee n. ¶ v.t. vermoeien, afmatten. **fatigue party,** n. korveepeloton n.n.

fatling, n. jong gemest dier n.n. **fatness,** n. vetheid n. **fatten,** v.t. vetmesten. ¶ v.i. vet worden str. **fatty,** a. vettig. ~ degeneration, vervetting n.

fatuity, n. dwaasheid n. **fatuous,** a. dwaas, onzinnig.

fault, n. fout n.; afbreking n.; schuld n. to find ~ with, aanmerking n. maken op. **faultiness,** n. gebrekkigheid n. **faultless,** a. feilloos. **faulty,** a., ~ily, adv. gebrekkig.

faun, n. faun n., bosgod n.

favour, n. gunst n.; begunstiging n.; souvenir n.n.; (old-fashioned) brief n. in ~ of, ten gunste van; in ~, in de gunst; out of ~, uit de gunst. ¶ v.t. begunstigen; steunen, ten gunste zijn van. **favourable,** a., ~bly, adv. gunstig; bevorderlijk. **favoured,** a. begunstigd. **favourite,** n. gunsteling n. ¶ a. lievelings . . . **favouritism,** n. favoritisme n.n.

fawn, n. reekalf n.n. ¶ a. lichtbruin. ¶ v.i. to ~ on, vleien, pluimstrijken. **fawningly,** adv. vleierig.

fay, n. fee n.

fealty, n. trouw n. (aan de leenheer).

fear, n. vrees n., angst n.; ontzag n.n. ¶ v.t. vrezen; duchten. **fearful,** a., ~ly, adv. vreselijk; angstig. **fearless,** a. onbevreesd.

feasibility, n. doenlijkheid n.; mogelijkheid n. **feasible,** a., ~bly, adv. doenlijk, uitvoerbaar.

feast, n. feest n.n. ¶ v.i. feestvieren; smullen. to ~ on, zich te goed doen irr. aan. ¶ v.t. onthalen.

feat, n. daad n.; prestatie n. ~ of arms, wapenfeit n.n.

feather, n. veer n., pluim n. birds of a ~ flock together, soort zoekt soort n.; a ~ in one's cap, een pluim (op iemands hoed); ~ bed, veren bed n.n. ¶ v.t. bevederen; schuinleggen irr. to ~ one's nest, zijn schaapjes n.n. op het droge brengen irr. **feather-brained,** a. wuft. **feather-weight,** n. lichtste bokser n. **feathery,** a. vederachtig, gevederd.

feature, n. gelaatstrek n.; trek n.; voornaamste stuk n.n. ¶ v.t. op de eerste plaats staan.

febrifuge, n. koortsverdrijvend middel n.n. **febrile,** a. koortsig, koorts . . .

February, N. februari N.

feculent, a. troebel.

fecundate, v.t. bevruchten, vruchtbaar maken. **fecundation,** n. bevruchting n. **fecundity,** n. vruchtbaarheid n.

federal, a. federaal, bonds . . . **federate,** v.i. een (staten)bond n. vormen. ¶ a. gefedereerd. **federation,** n. (staten)bond n.; federatie n. **federative,** a. federatief, bonds . . .

fee, n. honorarium n.n.; betaling n.; contributie n.; . . . geld n.n.

feeble, a., ~bly, adv. zwak, krachteloos. ~minded, zwakzinnig. **feebleness,** n. zwakte n., zwakheid n.

feed, v.t. voeden; voeren. ¶ v.i. voeden. to ~ on, leven van, zich voeden met. ¶ n. maal n.n. **feeder,** n. eter n.; aanvoer . . . **feeding-bottle,** n. zuigfles n.

feel, v.t. voelen; betasten. ¶ v.i. zich voelen. ¶ n. gevoel n.n.; aanvoelen n.n. **feeler,** n. voelhoorn n.; (fig.) proefballon n. **feeling,** n. gevoel n.n.; stemming n. ¶ a. gevoelvol.

feet, pl.n. See foot.

feign, v.t. & v.i. veinzen, huichelen. **feigned,** a. gefingeerd.

feint, n. schijnbeweging n.

felicitate, v.t. to ~ on, feliciteren met. **felicitation,** n. felicitatie n., gelukwens n. **felicitous,** a. gelukkig gekozen. **felicity,** n. geluk n.n.; gelukzaligheid n.; toepasselijkheid n.

feline, a. katachtig.

fell, n. vel n.n., huid n.; kale heuvel n. ¶ a. fel, wreed. ¶ v.t. vellen, omhakken. **fellmonger,** n. huidenkoopman n.

fellow, n. metgezel n.; ouder lid n.n. van een universiteit n.; kerel n.; mede . . . **fellow-citizen,** n. medeburger n. **fellow-creature,** n. medemens n. **fellow-feeling,** n. medegevoel n.n. **fellowship,** n. gemeenschap n.; broederschap n.; beurs n. voor gevorderde universitaire studie n.; waardigheid n. van ouder student n.

felo de se, n. zelfmoord n.

felon, n. misdadiger n., booswicht n. **felonious,** a. misdadig. **felony,** n. zware misdaad n.

felt, n. vilt n.n. ¶ v.t. met vilt bekleden.

female, a. vrouwelijk. ~ screw, moerschroef n. ¶ n. vrouw n.; wijfje n.n.

feminine, a. vrouwelijk. **femininity,** n. vrouwelijkheid n.

femur, n. dijbeen n.n.

fen, n. moeras n.n., moerasland n.n.

fence, n. schutting n.; omheining n.; heler n. ¶ v.t. omheinen. ¶ v.i. schermen. **fenceless,** a. onbesloten. **fencer,** n. schermer n. **fencing,** n. schermkunst n., schermen n.n. **fencing master,** n. schermmeester n.

fend, v.t. afweren.

fender, n. haardrand n.; wrijfhout n.n., kurkezak n.

fennel, n. venkel n.

feral, a. wild.

ferment, v.i. gisten. ¶ v.t. doen irr. gisten. ¶ n. gisting n. **fermentation,** n. gisting n.

fern, n. varen n.

ferocious, a., ~ly, adv. woest, wild; verscheurend. **ferocity,** n. wildheid n.

ferret, *n.* fret *n.* ¶ *v.t.* to ~ out, uitvissen.
ferruginous, *a.* ijzerhoudend.
ferrule, *n.* metalen ring *n.*
ferry, *n.* veer *n.n.*; veerboot *n.* ferryman, *n.* veerman *n.*
fertile, *a.* vruchtbaar. fertility, *n.* vruchtbaarheid *n.* fertilization, *n.* bevruchting *n.* fertilize, *v.t.* bevruchten; vruchtbaar maken.
ferule, *n.* plak *n.*
fervency, *n.* gloed *n.*, vuur *n.n.* fervent, *a.*, ~ly, *adv.* vurig. fervid, *a.* gloeiend, vurig; innig. fervour, *n.* gloed *n.*, vuur *n.n.*
festal, *a.*, festive, *a.* feestelijk, feest . . .
fester, *v.i.* zweren, etteren.
festival, *n.* feestdag *n.*; festival *n.n.* festivity, *n.* feestelijkheid *n.*; feestvreugde *n.*
festoon, *n.* slinger *n.*, guirlande *n.*
fetch, *v.t.* halen, brengen *irr.*; te voorschijn brengen *irr.*; aantrekken *str.* fetching, *a.* aantrekkelijk, bekoorlijk.
fête, *n.* feest *n.n.*
fetid, *a.* stinkend.
fetish, *n.* fetisch *n.* fetishism, *n.* fetischisme *n.n.*
fetlock, *n.* kluister *n.*; vetlok *n.*
fetter, *v.t.* boeien; belemmeren. ¶ *n.* boei *n.*, kluister *n.*
feud, *n.* vete *n.*
feudal, *a.* feudaal, feodaal. feudalism, *n.* feudalisme *n.n.* feudatory, *a.* leenroerig. ¶ *n.* leen *n.n.*; leenman *n.*
fever, *n.* koorts *n.* feverish, *a.* koortsig, koortsachtig.
few, *a.* weinig. a ~, enkele, een paar; ~ and far between, zeldzaam.
fey, *a.* veeg; de dood nabij.
fiancé(e), *n.*, fiancé(e), *n.* verloofde *n.*
fiasco, *n.* fiasco *n.n.*
fiat, *n.* fiat *n.n.*, goedkeuring *n.*
fib, *n.* leugentje *n.n.*, jokkentje *n.n.* ¶ *v.i.* jokken. fibber, *n.* jokker *n.*
fibre, *n.* vezel *n.* fibrous, *a.* vezelig, vezelachtig.
fickle, *a.* wispelturig; onbestendig. fickleness, *n.* wispelturigheid *n.*
fictile, *a.* kneedbaar; lemen.
fiction, *n.* romanliteratuur *n.*; verdichting *n.*, verzinsel *n.n.* fictitious, *a.*, ~ly, *adv.* verzonnen, gefingeerd.
fiddle, *n.* fiedel. as fit as a ~, kiplekker. ¶ *v.i.* fiedelen; peuteren. fiddler, *n.* vioolspeler *n.* fiddlestick, *n.* strijkstok *n.* ~s!, onzin!
fidelity, *n.* trouw *n.*; getrouwheid *n.*
fidget, *v.i.* wriemelen; zenuwachtig peuteren. fidgety, *a.* ongedurig.
fiduciary, *a.* fiduciair. ¶ *n.* pandhouder *n.*
fie, *int.* foei!
fief, *n.* leengoed *n.n.*
field, *n.* veld *n.n.*; akker *n.*; terrein *n.*; in the ~, op het terrein; te velde. field-glasses, *pl.n.* veldkijker *n.* field-marshal, *n.* veldmaarschalk *n.* fielder, *n.* fielder *n.*

fiend, *n.* duivel *n.* the F~, de Boze. fiendish, *a.*, ~ly, *adv.* duivels.
fierce, *a.*, ~ly, *adv.* fel; heftig, verwoed; woest.
fiery, *a.* vurig.
fife, *n.* pijp *n.*, fluit *n.* ¶ *v.t.* & *v.i.* pijpen.
fifteen, *num.* vijftien. fifteenth, *a.* vijftiende. fifth, *a.* vijfde. fifthly, *adv.* ten vijfde. fiftieth, *a.* vijftigste. fifty, *num.* vijftig.
fig, *n.* vijg *n.*
fight, *v.i.* vechten *str.*, strijden *str.* ¶ *v.t.* bevechten *str.*, bestrijden *str.* ¶ *n.* gevecht *n.n.*, strijd *n.* fighter, *n.* vechter *n.*; jachtvliegtuig *n.n.*
figment, *n.* verdichtsel *n.n.*
fig-tree, *n.* vijgeboom *n.*
figurant, *n.* figurant *n.* (male); figurante *n.* (female). figurative, *a.*, ~ly, *adv.* figuurlijk, overdrachtelijk.
figure, *n.* figuur *n.*; voorkomen *n.n.*, gestalte *n.*; cijfer *n.n.*; prijs *n.* ¶ *v.t.* berekenen; voorstellen. ¶ *v.i.* figureren. figured, *a.* gewerkt. figure-head, *n.* schegbeeld *n.n.*, galjoenbeeld *n.n.*
filament, *n.* vezel *n.*; draad *n.*
filbert, *n.* (soort) hazelnoot *n.*
filch, *v.t.* gappen. filcher, *n.* gapper *n.*
file, *n.* vijlen, afvijlen; rangschikken, in een dossier *n.n.* plaatsen. ¶ *n.* vijl *n.*; rij *n.*, rot *n.*; lias *n.*, dossier *n.n.* file-cutter, *n.* vijlmaker *n.*
filial, *a.*, ~ly, *adv.* kinderlijk.
filibuster, *n.* vrijbuiter *n.* ¶ *v.i.* roven.
filigree, *n.* filigraan *n.n.*
filings, *pl.n.* vijlsel *n.n.*
fill, *v.t.* vullen; vervullen; bekleden. to ~ up, opvullen; invullen. ¶ *v.i.* zich vullen, vol raken. ¶ *n.* vulling *n.* to eat one's ~, zich zat eten.
fillet, *n.* lendestuk *n.n.*; plak *n.*; netje *n.n.* ¶ *v.t.* van het been (or van de graat) afsnijden *str.*
fillip, *n.* knip *n.*; prikkel *n.* ¶ *v.t.* aansporen.
filly, *n.* merrieveulen *n.n.*
film, *n.* vlies *n.n.*; film *n.* ¶ *v.t.* filmen, verfilmen.
filter, *n.* filter *n.* ¶ *v.t.* filtreren. filter-paper, *n.* filtreerpapier *n.n.*
filth, *n.* vuil *n.n.*; vuiligheid *n.*, viezigheid *n.* filthy, *a.*, ~ily, *adv.* vuil, vies.
filtrate, *v.t.* filtreren. ¶ *n.* filtraat *n.n.*
fin, *n.* vin *n.*
final, *a.*, ~ly, *adv.* finaal, eind . . ., slot . . . ¶ *n.* finale *n.* ~s, (universitair) eindexamen *n.n.* finale, *n.* finale *n.* finality, *n.* eindresultaat *n.n.*; afdoendheid *n.*; beslistheid *n.*
finance, *n.* financiën *pl.n.*; financiewezen *n.n.* ~s, geldmiddelen *pl.n.n.* ¶ *v.t.* geldelijk steunen, van geld *n.n.* voorzien *irr.* financial, *a.*, ~ly, *adv.* financieel; geldelijk. financier, *n.* financier *n.*
finch, *n.* vink *n.*
find, *v.t.* vinden *str.*; ontdekken; verklaren,

uitspreken *str. all found,* alles inbegrepen.
¶ *n.* vondst *n.;* ontdekking *n.* **finder,** *n.*
vinder *n.* **finding,** *n.* uitspraak *n.*
fine, *a.,* ~**ly,** *adv.* mooi, fraai; fijn. ¶ *n.*
boete *n.* ¶ *v.t.* beboeten; zuiveren. **fine-**
draw, *v.t.* mazen. **fineness,** *n.* fijnheid *n.*
finery, *n.* tooi *n.,* opschik *n.*
finesse, *n.* finesse *n.;* geslepenheid *n.*
finger, *n.* vinger *n.;* vingerbreedte *n.* ¶ *v.t.*
betasten, bevingeren. **fingering,** *n.*
vingerzetting *n.;* vingervaardigheid *n.*
fingerpost, *n.* wegwijzer *n.* **fingerprint,** *n.*
vingerafdruk *n.* **finger-stall,** *n.* vingerling
n.
finial, *n.* kruisbloem *n.*
finical, *a.,* ~**ly,** *adv.* overdreven nauwkeurig,
peuterig.
finish, *v.t.* eindigen, voltooien. ¶ *v.i.* eindigen,
ophouden *irr.* ¶ *n.* eind *n.n.,* slot *n.n.,*
besluit *n.n.;* afwerking *n.*
finite, *a.,* ~**ly,** *adv.* eindig.
fir, *n.* den *n.,* denneboom *n.*
fire, *n.* vuur *n.n.;* brand *n.;* gloed *n.,* hartstocht *n. to hang* ~, niet vorderen;
to miss ~, ketsen; *to set on* ~, in brand
steken *str.* ¶ *v.t.* in brand steken *str.*
¶ *v.i.* vuren, schieten *str.* **fire-alarm,** *n.*
brandschel *n.* **firearms,** *pl.n.* vuurwapenen *pl.n.n.* **firebrand,** *n.* (*fig.*) stoke-
brand. *n.* **firebrick,** *n.* vuurvaste steen *n.*
fire brigade, *n.* brandweer *n.* **firedamp,** *n.*
mijngas *n.n.* **fire-eater,** *n.* vuurvreter *n.*
fire-engine, *n.* brandspuit *n.* **fire-escape,** *n.*
brandladder *n.* **firefly,** *n.* glimworm *n.*
fire-irons, *pl.n.* haardstel *n.n.* **fireman,** *n.*
brandweerman *n.;* stoker *n.* **fireplace,** *n.*
haard *n.* **fire policy,** *n.* brandpolis *n.*
fireproof, *a.* vuurvast; brandvrij. **fire-ship,**
n. brander *n.* **fireside,** *n.* haard *n.,* haardstede *n.* **firewood,** *n.* brandhout *n.n.*
fireworks, *pl.n.* vuurwerk *n.n.* **firing,** *n.*
vuren *n.n.;* brandstof *n.* **firing-squad,** *n.*
executiepeloton *n.n.*
firkin, *n.* vaatje *n.n.*
firm, *a.,* ~**ly,** *adv.* vast, stevig; vastberaden.
¶ *n.* firma *n.*
firmament, *n.* firmament *n.n.*
firmness, *n.* vastheid *n.;* vastberadenheid *n.*
first, *a.* eerste; voornaamste. ~ *night,*
première *n.; at* ~, in 't begin; *from the* ~,
al dadelijk. **first-born,** *n.* eerstgeborene *n.*
firstling, *n.* eersteling *n.* **firstly,** *adv.*
eerst; in de eerste plaats; ten eerste.
first-rate, *a.* eerste klas *n.*
fiscal, *a.* fiskaal.
fish, *n.* vis *n.* ¶ *v.t.* vissen. **fishbone,** *n.*
graat *n.* **fisherman,** *n.* visser *n.* **fishery,** *n.*
visserij *n.* **fishing rod,** *n.* hengel *n.* **fishing**
smack, *n.* visserspink *n.* **fishing tackle,** *n.*
vistuig *n.n.* **fishmonger,** *n.* vishandelaar *n.*
fishy, *a.* visachtig; visrijk; verdacht.
fissure, *n.* spleet *n.,* barst *n.* ¶ *v.t.* splijten *str.*
fist, *n.* vuist *n.* **fisticuffs,** *n.* bokspartij *n.*
fistula, *n.* fistel *n.*

fit, *v.t.* passen; uitrusten; monteren. ¶ *v.i.*
passen. ¶ *a.,* ~**ly,** *adv.* passend; geschikt;
gezond. ¶ *n.* toeval *n.;* vlaag *n.;* bevlieging
n. it's a good ~, het past goed. **fitful,** *a.,*
~**ly,** *adv.* grillig. **fitness,** *n.* geschiktheid *n.*
fitter, *n.* passer *n.;* monteur *n.;* fitter *n.*
fitting, *a.,* ~**ly,** *adv.* passend, gepast.
¶ *n.* passen *n.n.*
five, *num.* vijf. **fiver,** *n.* bankje *n.n.* van vijf.
fivefold, *a.* vijfvoudig. ¶ *n.* vijfvoud *n.n.*
fives, *pl.n.* (soort) balspel *n.n.*
fix, *v.t.* vastmaken, vasthechten; voorstellen;
regelen. ¶ *n.* moeilijkheid *n.* **fixation,** *n.*
vastlegging *n.,* fixering *n.* **fixed,** *a.,* ~**ly,**
adv. vast; constant; strak. **fixings,** *pl.n.*
gerei *n.n.* **fixture,** *n.* garnituur *n.n.;*
spijkervast voorwerp *n.n.;* vast nummer
n.n.; afspraak *n.*
fizz, *v.i.* bruisen; sissen. **fizzle,** *v.i.* sissen.
to ~ *out,* op niets uitlopen *str.*
flabbergast, *v.t.* van zijn stuk *n.n.* brengen *irr.*
flabbiness, *n.* slapheid *n.,* weekheid *n.*
flabby, *a.* slap, week.
flaccid, *a.* slap.
flag, *n.* vlag *n.;* trottoirsteen *n.;* lis *n.,*
lisdodde *n.* ¶ *v.i.* vlaggen; kwijnen,
verslappen. ¶ *v.t.* seinen.
flagellate, *v.t.* geselen. **flagellation,** *n.*
geseling *n.*
flageolet, *n.* flageolet *n.*
flagon, *n.* fles, *n.,* flacon *n.*
flagrancy, *n.* schaamteloosheid *n.* **flagrant,**
a., ~**ly,** *adv.* schaamteloos, flagrant.
flagship, *n.* vlaggeschip *n.n.* **flagstaff,** *n.*
vlaggestok *n.*
flail, *n.* (dors)vlegel *n.*
flake, *n.* schilfer *n.;* schots *n.,* schol *n.;*
vlok *n.* ¶ *v.i.* (af)schilferen. ¶ *v.t.* doen
irr. schilferen. **flaky,** *a.* schilferachtig;
vlokkig.
flamboyant, *a.* kleurrijk, opzichtig.
flame, *n.* vlam *n.* ¶ *v.i.* opvlammen.
flamingo, *n.* flamingo *n.*
Flanders, *N.* Vlaanderen *n.N.*
flange, *n.* flens *n.*
flank, *n.* flank *n.;* zijde *n.* ¶ *v.t.* flankeren.
flannel, *n.* flanel *n.n.* ¶ *a.* flanellen. ~*s,*
flanellen broek *n.* **flannelette,** *n.* katoen-
flanel *n.n.*
flap, *n.* pand *n.n.;* klep *n.;* klap *n.,* slag *n.*
¶ *v.t.* slaan *irr.,* klapwieken. ¶ *v.i.*
flappen.
flapper, *n.* vin *n.;* bakvis *n.*
flare, *n.* gloed *n.;* lichtsignaal *n.n.;* (parachute)
fakkel *n.* ¶ *v.i.* flakkeren. *to* ~ *up,*
opvlammen.
flash, *n.* straal *n.;* flikkering *n.;* strik *n.*
¶ *v.i.* flikkeren, flitsen. **flashlight,** *n.*
magnesiumlicht *n.n.* **flashy,** *a.,* ~**ily,** *adv.*
flikkerend; opzichtig.
flask, *n.* fles *n.,* flacon *n.*
flat, *a.* plat, vlak; vervelend. ¶ ~**ly,** *adv.*
ronduit; botweg. *See also* **fiat.** *a.* ¶ *n.*
vlak land *n.n.;* ondiepte *n.;* étage *n.*

flat-footed, a. met platvoeten pl.n. **flat-iron**, n. strijkijzer n.n. **flatness**, n. vlakheid n. **flatten**, v.t. plat maken.
flatter, v.t. vleien; flatteren. **flatterer**, n. vleier n. **flattery**, n. vleierij n.
flattish, a. platachtig.
flatulence, n. winderigheid n. **flatulent**, a. winderig; opgeblazen.
flaunt, v.t. pronken met.
flavour, n. aroma n.n.; smaak n. ¶ v.t. smaak geven str. aan.
flaw, n. gebrek n.n., fout n. **flawless**, a. vlekkeloos; zonder gebreken.
flax, n. vlas n.n. **flax-comb**, n. hekel n. **flaxen**, a. vlaskleurig.
flay, v.t. villen; martelen. **flayer**, n. vilder n.
flea, n. vlo n. to send a person away with a ~ in his ear, iemand afschepen. **flea-bite**, n. vlooiebeet n.; bagatel n.
fleck, n. vlek n., plek n., spikkel n.
fledge, v.t. van veren voorzien, bevederen.
flee, v.i. vlieden str., vluchten. ¶ v.t. ontvluchten.
fleece, n. vacht n.; vlies n.n. ¶ v.t. scheren str.; het vel over de oren halen. **fleecy**, a. wollig.
fleet, a. snel, vlug. ¶ n. vloot n.
Fleming, N. Vlaming N. **Flemish**, a. Vlaams.
flesh, n. vlees n.n. in the ~, in levenden lijve; to lose ~, mager worden str. **fleshless**, a. vleesloos; mager. **fleshly**, a. vleselijk, zinnelijk. **fleshy**, a. vlezig, gevleesd.
flexibility, n. buigzaamheid n. **flexible**, a., ~bly, adv. buigzaam; handelbaar, inschikkelijk. **flexion**, n. buiging n.
flick, n. tik n. ¶ v.t. tikken; wegknippen.
flicker, v.t. flikkeren. ¶ n. flikkering n.
flier, n. See **flyer**.
flight, n. vlucht n.; vliegafstand n. ~ of stairs, trap n.; to put to ~, op de vlucht drijven str.; to take ~, op de vlucht slaan irr. **flighty**, a. vluchtig; lichtzinnig.
flimsiness, n. dunheid n., lichtheid n. **flimsy**, a. dun, licht. ¶ n. dun papier n.n., copie n.
flinch, v.i. terugdeinzen. to ~ from, opzien irr. tegen.
fling, v.t. slingeren; gooien, smijten str. ¶ v.i. vliegen str., stormen. ¶ n. worp n., gooi n.; (soort) dans n. to have a ~ at someone, iemand een veeg uit de pan geven str.
flint, n. vuursteen n. **flint-glass**, n. flintglas n.n. **flinty**, a. hard; hardvochtig.
flip, n. tik n. ¶ v.t. tikken, (weg)knippen.
flippancy, n. luchtigheid n. **flippant**, a. luchthartig, onbezonnen.
flirt, v.i. flirten, coquetteren. to ~ with, (fig.) spelen met. ¶ n. coquette n., flirt n. **flirtation**, n. geflirt n.n.
flit, v.i. fladderen, vliegen str.
flitch, n. zijde n.; moot n., schijf n.
flitter, v.i. fladderen.
float, v.i. drijven str., zweven; wapperen. ¶ v.t. vlot maken, vlotten; oprichten;

uitschrijven str. ¶ n. vlot n.n.; kurk n.; wagentje n.n., kar n.; drijvende brandspuit n. **floating**, a. drijvend; vlottend. ~ bridge, schipbrug n.; ~ capital, vlottend kapitaal n.; ~ dock, drijvend dok n.n.
flock, n. kudde n.; vlucht n.; zwerm n.; vlok n., vlokwol n. ¶ v.i. to ~ together, samenscholen. **flocky**, a. vlokkig.
floe, n. schots n., schol n.
flog, v.t. geselen, ranselen. **flogging**, n. geseling n.
flood, n. vloed n.; overstroming n.; stroom n. ¶ v.t. overstromen; onder water n.n. zetten. **flood-gate**, n. sluisdeur n. **flood-light**, n. schijnwerper n. **floodlit**, a. het verlicht.
floor, n. vloer n.; grond n.; verdieping n. to get the ~, het woord krijgen str.; to take the ~, het woord voeren. ¶ v.t. bevloeren; tot zwijgen brengen irr. **flooring**, n. bevloering n.n.
flop, v.i. ploffen; mislukken. ¶ n. plof n.; mislukking n.
floral, a. bloemen . . ., bloem . . . **florid**, a., ~ly, adv. bloemrijk; blozend. **floridity**, n. bloemrijkheid n.
florin, n. gulden n.; twee shilling stuk n.n.
florist, n. bloemist n.
floss, n. floretzijde n.
flotsam, n. zeedrift n., drijvend wrakgoed n.n.
flounce, n. brede strook n., volant n. ¶ v.i. spartelen. to ~ out, (de kamer) uitstuiven str.
flounder, n. bot n. ¶ v.i. spartelen; baggeren; in de war raken.
flour, n. bloem n.; meel n.n. ¶ v.t. met bloem insmeren.
flourish, v.i. bloeien, gedijen. ¶ v.t. zwaaien met. ¶ n. zwaai n.; zwier n.; geschal n.n.
flout, v.t. bespotten, met verachting n. behandelen.
flow, v.i. vloeien, stromen. ¶ n. vloed n.; stroom n.
flower, n. bloem n.; bloesem n. ¶ v.i. bloeien. ¶ v.t. met bloemen versieren. **flowerpot**, n. bloempot n. **flowery**, a. bloemrijk.
fluctuate, v.i. op en neer gaan irr.; golven, schommelen. **fluctuation**, n. schommeling n.; weifeling n.
flue, n. schoorsteen n., vuurgang n.
'flu, n. influenza, n., griep n.
fluency, n. welbespraaktheid n.; vlotheid n. **fluent**, a., ~ly, adv. welbespraakt; vloeiend.
fluff, n. pluis n.; dons n.n. **fluffy**, a. pluizig, wollig.
fluid, a. vloeibaar. ¶ n. vloeistof n. **fluidity**, n. vloeibaarheid n.
fluke, n. zuigworm n.; ankerblad n.n.; bof n.; gelukje n.n. ¶ v.i. boffen.
flummery, n. onzin n., geleuter n.n.
flunkey, n. lakei n.
flurry, n. windstoot n.; gejaagdheid n. ¶ v.t. in de war sturen.
flush, n. blos n.; opwelling n.; stroom n.;

volgkaart *n.*   ¶ *a.* vol; goed bij kas.
~ *with,* gelijk met. ¶ *v.t.* blozen, kleuren;
doorspoelen; glad maken.
Flushing, *N.* Vlissingen *n.N.*
fluster, *v.t.* in de war brengen *irr.*   ¶ *n.*
verwarring *n.*
flute, *n.* fluit *n.*   ¶ *v.t.* groeven. **flutist,** *n.*
fluitist *n.,* fluitspeler *n.*
flutter, *v.i.* fladderen; wapperen; popelen.
¶ *n.* gefladder *n.n.;* speculatie *n.*
flux, *n.* vloed *n.,* stroom *n.*
fly, *v.i.* vliegen *str.;* vluchten. ¶ *v.t.* voeren;
ontvluchten.   ¶ *n.* vlieg *n.;* vigilante *n.*
fly-catcher, *n.* vliegenvanger *n.* **flyer,** *n.*
vlieger *n.,* vliegenier *n.* **fly-fishing,** *n.*
hengelen *n.n.* met kunstvliegen. *pl. n.* **flying,**
n. vliegen *n.n.*   ¶ *a.* vliegend.   ~ *artillery,*
rijdende artillerie *n.;* ~ *boat,* vliegboot *n.;*
~ *field,* vliegveld *n.* **fly-leaf,** *n.* schutblad
n.n. **flywheel,** *n.* vliegwiel *n.n.*
foal, *n.* hengsteveulen *n.n.*
foam, *n.* schuim *n.n.*   ¶ *v.i.* schuimen.
to ~ *at the mouth,* schuimbekken. **foamy,**
a. schuimend.
fob, *n.* horlogezakje *n.n.*   ¶ *v.t.* *to* ~ *off,*
afschepen; met een kluitje *n.n.* in 't riet
sturen.
focal, *a.* brandpunts . . . **focus,** *n.* brandpunt
n.n.
fodder, *n.* voeder. ¶ *v.t.* voederen.
foe, *n.* vijand *n.*
fog, *n.* mist *n.*   **fog-signal,**
n. misthoorn *n.*
fog(e)y, *n.* ouderwets persoon *n.*
foible, *n.* zwak punt *n.n.,* zwakke zijde *n.*
foil, *n.* foeliesel *n.n.;* schermdegen *n.,* floret *n.*
¶ *v.t.* verijdelen.
foist, *v.t.* *to* ~ *something on someone,* iemand
iets aansmeren.
fold, *v.t.* vouwen; plooien. *to* ~ *back,*
omvouwen.   ¶ *n.* vouw *n.;* (schaaps)kooi
n.; kudde *n.* **folder,** *n.* (gevouwde)
circulaire *n.;* map *n.* **folding-chair,** *n.*
vouwstoel *n.* **folding-doors,** *pl.n.* dubbele
deur *n.* **folding table,** *n.* klaptafel *n.*
foliage, *n.* gebladerte *n.n.,* loof *n.n.;* loofwerk
n.n.
folio, *n.* foliant *n.;* folio *n.n.*
folk, *n.* volk *n.n.;* mensen *pl.n.,* luitjes *pl.n.*
folklore, *n.* volkskunde *n.,* folklore *n.*
follow, *v.t.* volgen; nazetten, vervolgen;
uitoefenen.   *to* ~ *suit,* kleur bekennen;
het voorbeeld volgen. **follower,** *n.*
volgeling *n.,* aanhanger *n.*
folly, *n.* dwaasheid *n.*
foment, *v.t.* betten; (*fig.*) aanstoken, aanhitsen. **fomentation,** *n.* behandeling *n.*
met hete omslagen *pl.n.* **fomenter,** *n.*
opruier *n.*
fond, *a.,* ~**ly,** *adv.* toegevend. ~ *of,* verzot
op.
fondle, *v.t.* liefkozen.
fondness, *n.* tederheid *n.;* genegenheid *n.*
font, *n.* doopvont *n.*

food, *n.* voedsel *n.n.;* voeder *n.n.;* (*fig.*)
stof *n.*
fool, *n.* dwaas *n.,* gek *n.;* nar *n.;* vla *n.*
to make a ~ *of,* voor de gek houden *irr.;*
to play the ~, zich gek aanstellen; *to live
in a* ~'s *paradise,* zichzelf bedriegen *str.;*
to send a person on a ~'s *errand,* iemand
voor de gek laten *str.* lopen. ¶ *v.t.* voor
de gek houden *irr.* ¶ *v.i.* gekheid *n.* maken.
to ~ *about with,* zijn tijd *n.* verkwisten
met. **foolery,** *n.* dwaasheid *n.* **foolhardy,**
a. roekeloos, doldriest. **foolish,** *a.,* ~**ly,**
adv. dwaas, gek, mal. **foolproof,** *a.*
absoluut veilig. **foolscap,** *n.* lang folio
papier *n.n.*
foot, *n.* voet *n.;* voetvolk *n.n.,* infanterie *n.*
on ~, te voet; *to put one's* ~ *in it,* een
flater *n.* begaan *irr.* ¶ *v.t.* *to* ~ *the bill,*
de rekening betalen; *to* ~ *it,* lopen *str.*
football, *n.* voetbal *n.* **foot-board,** *n.*
treeplank *n.* **footbridge,** *n.* vlonder *n.,*
voetbrug *n.* **footgear,** *n.* schoeisel *n.n.*
foothold, *n.* vaste voet *n.* **footing,** *n.*
houvast *n.n.* *on an equal* ~, op voet van
gelijkheid *n.* **footlights,** *pl.n.* voetlicht *n.n.*
footman, *n.* livreiknecht *n.* **foot-pace,** *n.*
wandelpas *n.* **footpad,** *n.* struikrover *n.*
footpath, *n.* voetpad *n.n.* **footprint,** *n.*
indruk van de voet *n.,* spoor *n.n.* **footstep,**
n. voetstap *n.,* tred *n.* **footstool,** *n.*
voetenbankje *n.n.* **footwarmer,** *n.* voet-
stoof *n.*
fop, *n.* kwast *n.,* modegek *n.,* fat *n.* **foppery,**
n. kwasterij *n.* **foppish,** *a.* fatterig.
for, *prep.* voor; om; gedurende; naar. ~ *all
that,* in weerwil van dat alles; ~ *all I care,*
voor mijn part *n.;* ~ *all I know,* voor
zover ik weet. ¶ *c.* want.
forage, *n.* fourage *n.,* (vee)voeder *n.n.*
¶ *v.i.* fourageren; ¶ *v.t.* doorzoeken *irr.*
forage-cap, *n.* politiemuts *n.*
foray, *n.* rooftocht *n.* ¶ *v.i.* röven, plunderen.
for·bear, *v.t.* verdragen *str.;* nalaten; zich
onthouden *irr.* van. ·**forbear,** *n.* voorvader
n. **forbearance,** *n.* verdraagzaamheid *n.,*
toegevendheid *n.*
forbid, *v.t.* verbieden *str.* *Heaven* ~, dat
verhoede God!
force, *n.* kracht *n.;* strijdmacht *n.* *to come
into* ~, van kracht worden *str.* ¶ *v.t.*
dwingen *str.,* noodzaken; forceren. **forcedly,**
adv. gedwongen. **forceful,** *a.,* ~**ly,** *adv.*
krachtig.
forcemeat, *n.* gehakt *n.n.*
forceps, *n.* forceps *n.,* tang *n.*
forcible, *a.,* ~**bly,** *adv.* krachtig; gewelddadig.
forcing-frame, *n.* broeiraam *n.n.* **forcing-
house,** *n.* broeikas *n.* **forcing-pump,** *n.*
perspomp *n.*
ford, *n.* doorwaadbare plaats *n.* **fordable,** *a.*
doorwaadbaar.
fore, *a.* voor . . . ¶ *adv.* vooraan. ¶ *n.*
to the ~, vooraan; op de voorgrond.
forebode, *v.t.* voorspellen.

forecabin, *n.* voorkajuit *n.*
forecast, *v.t.* voorspellen; beramen. ¶ *n.* voorspelling *n.*
foreclose, *v.t.* tegenhouden *irr.* **to ~ a** *mortgage,* een hypotheek *n.* vervallen verklaren. **foreclosure,** *n.* executie *n.*
foredoom, *v.t.* doemen.
forefather, *n.* voorvader *n.*
forefinger, *n.* wijsvinger *n.*
forego, *v.t.* voorafgaan *irr.* **foregone,** *a. a ~ conclusion,* een uitgemaakte zaak *n.*
foreground, *n.* voorgrond *n.*
forehead, *n.* voorhoofd *n.n.*
foreign, *a.* vreemd, buitenlands. **F~** *Office,* Ministerie *n.N.* van Buitenlandse Zaken. **foreigner,** *n.* vreemdeling *n.,* buitenlander *n.*
foreknowledge, *n.* vooruitweten *n.n.*
foreland, *n.* landtong *n.,* kaap *n.*
forelock, *n.* voorlok *n.* **to take time by the ~,** van de gelegenheid gebruik *n.n.* maken.
foreman, *n.* voorman *n.,* meesterknecht *n.;* voorzitter *n.*
foremast, *n.* fokkemast *n.*
foremost, *a.* voorste, eerste. ¶ *adv.* voorop.
forensic, *a.* gerechtelijk.
forepart, *n.* voorste deel *n.n.*
forerunner, *n.* voorloper *n.,* voorbode *n.*
foresail, *n.* fokkezeil *n.n.*
foresee, *v.t.* voorzien *irr.,* vooraf weten *irr.*
foreshadow, *v.t.* (voor)beduiden.
foreshorten, *v.t.* verkorten, in verkorting *n.* tekenen.
foresight, *n.* overleg *n.n.;* vooruitziendheid *n.*
forest, *n.* woud *n.n.;* bos *n.n.*
forestall, *v.t.* vóór zijn; voorkomen *irr.*
forester, *n.* houtvester *n.* **forestry,** *n.* bosbouw *n.;* boswezen *n.n.*
foretaste, *n.* voorsmaak *n.*
foretell, *v.t.* voorspellen.
forethought, *n.* voorbedachtheid *n.;* voorzorg *n.*
foretop, *n.* vóórmars *n.*
forewarn, *v.t.* vooraf waarschuwen.
forfeit, *v.t.* verbeuren. ¶ *n.* pand *n.n.;* verbeurde *n.n.* **forfeiture,** *n.* verbeuring *n.*
forge, *v.t.* smeden; maken; namaken, vervalsen. ¶ *v.i.* valsheid *n.* in geschrifte plegen. **to ~ ahead,** vooruitkomen *irr.* ¶ *n.* smidse *n.;* smederij *n.;* smeltoven *n.* **forger,** *n.* vervalser *n.,* falsaris *n.* **forgery,** *n.* valsheid *n.* in geschrifte.
forget, *v.t.* vergeten *str.* **forgetful,** *a.* vergeetachtig. **forgetfulness,** *n.* vergeetachtigheid *n.* **forget-me-not,** *n.* vergeetmij-nietje *n.n.*
forgive, *v.t.* vergeven *str.;* kwijtschelden *str.* **forgiveness,** *n.* vergevingsgezindheid *n.*
forgo, *v.t.* afzien *irr.* van, zich ontzeggen *irr.*
fork, *n.* vork *n.;* gaffel *n.;* vertakking *n.,* tweesprong *n.* ¶ *v.i.* zich vertakken. ¶ *v.t.* **to ~ out,** opdokken. **forked,** *a.* gevorkt.

forlorn, *a.* verlaten; hopeloos. **~** *hope,* wanhopige onderneming *n.*
form, *n.* vorm *n.;* gedaante *n.;* conditie *n.;* formulier *n.n.;* klasse *n.;* schoolbank *n.* ¶ *v.t.* vormen. **formal,** *a., ~ly, adv.* formeel; vormelijk. **formality,** *n.* formaliteit *n.;* vormelijkheid *n.* **formation,** *n.* vorming *n.;* formatie *n.*
former, *n.* vormer *n.,* schepper *n.* **the ~,** de eerste. ¶ *a.* vroeger; vorig. **formerly,** *adv.* vroeger.
formic, *a.* **~** *acid,* mierenzuur *n.n.*
formidable, *a., ~bly, adv.* geducht.
formless, *a.* vormeloos.
formula, *n.* formule *n.* **formulate,** *v.t.* formuleren.
fornicate, *v.i.* hoereren. **fornication,** *n.* overspel *n.n.,* ontucht *n.* **fornicator,** *n.* overspelige *n.*
forsake, *v.t.* verlaten *str.,* in de steek laten *str.*
forsooth, *adv.* voorwaar.
forswear, *v.t.* afzweren *str.* ¶ *v.r.* **to ~ oneself,** meineed *n.* plegen.
fort, *n.* fort *n.n.,* vesting *n.*
forth, *adv.* voort, vooruit, voorwaarts; te voorschijn. **and so ~,** enzovoorts. **forthcoming,** *a.* op handen (zijnd), aanstaande. **forthright,** *a.* oprecht. **forthwith,** *adv.* aanstonds, terstond.
fortieth, *a.* veertigste.
fortification, *n.* versterking *n.* **fortify,** *v.t.* versterken.
fortitude, *n.* zedelijke moed *n.,* zielskracht *n.*
fortnight, *n.* veertien dagen *pl.n.* **to-morrow ~,** morgen over veertien dagen.
fortress, *n.* fort *n.n.,* vesting *n.*
fortuitous, *a.* toevallig. **fortuitously,** *adv.* toevallig, toevalligerwijs. **fortuity,** *n.* toeval *n.n.*
fortunate, *a.* gelukkig. **fortunately,** *adv.* gelukkig, gelukkigerwijs. **fortune,** *n.* geluk *n.n.;* fortuin *n.n.;* lot *n.n.* **fortune-hunter,** *n.* gelukzoeker *n.* **fortune-teller,** *n.* waarzegger *n.* (*male*), waarzegster *n.* (*female*).
forty, *num.* veertig.
forum, *n.* forum *n.n.,* rechtbank *n.*
forward, *a.* voorste; vergevorderd; vooruitstrevend; vroegrijp; vrijpostig. ¶ *adv.* vooruit; voorwaarts. ¶ *v.t.* doorzenden *str.;* bevorderen. **forwarding,** *n.* verzending *n.* **~** *agent,* expediteur *n.* **forwardness,** *n.* vroegtijdigheid *n.;* brutaliteit *n.* **forwards,** *adv. See* **forward.**
fosse, *n.* sloot *n.,* gracht *n.*
fossil, *n.* fossiel *n.n.*
foster, *v.t.* bevorderen, aankweken. **fosterbrother,** *n.* zoogbroeder *n.* **foster-child,** *n.* voedsterkind *n.n.;* pleegkind *n.n.* **fosterdaughter,** *n.* voedsterdochter *n.,* pleegdochter *n.* **foster-father,** *n.* pleegvader *n.* **foster-mother,** *n.* pleegmoeder *n.* **fostersister,** *n.* zoogzuster *n.*
foul, *a., ~ly, adv.* vuil, onzuiver; bedorven; onklaar; (*fig.*) gemeen. ¶ *v.t.* bezoedelen,

bevuilen; onklaar maken; oplopen *str.* tegen. **foulness,** *n.* vuilheid *n.*; gemeenheid *n.*, laagheid *n.*

found, *v.t.* stichten, oprichten. **foundation,** *n.* stichting *n.*; grondslag *n.*, fundering *n.* **founder,** *n.* stichter *n.*, oprichter *n.* ¶ *v.i.* zinken *str.*, vergaan *irr.* ¶ *v.t.* doen *irr.* vergaan.

foundling, *n.* vondeling *n.* **foundling hospital,** *n.* vondelingenhuis *n.n.*

foundress, *n.* stichtster *n.*

foundry, *n.* (metaal)gieterij *n.*

fount, *n.* bron *n.*; type *n.n.*, lettersoort *n.* **fountain,** *n.* bron *n.*; fontein *n.* **fountainhead,** *n.* bron *n.*, oorsprong *n.* **fountainpen,** *n.* vulpen *n.*

four, *num.* vier. *on all* ~*s*, op handen *pl.n.* en voeten *pl.n.* **fourfold,** *n.* viervoud. ¶ *a.* viervoudig. **four-in-hand,** *n.* vierspan *n.n.* **fourposter,** *n.* groot ledikant *n.n.* met hemel *n.* **fourscore,** *a.* tachtig. **fourteen,** *num.* veertien. **fourteenth,** *a.* veertiende. **fourth,** *a.* vierde. **fourthly,** *adv.* ten vierde.

fowl, *n.* kip *n.*, eend *n.*, vogel *n.n.*; gevogelte *n.n.* ¶ *v.i.* vogels vangen *str.* **fowler,** *n.* vogelaar *n.* **fowling,** *n.* vogeljacht *n.* **fowling-piece,** *n.* ganzenroer *n.n.*

fox, *n.* vos *n.* **foxed,** *a.* verkleurd, vergeeld. **foxglove,** vingerhoedskruid *n.n.* **fox-hunt,** *n.* vossenjacht *n.* **fox-terrier,** *n.* foxterrier *n.* **foxy,** *a.* sluw.

fracas, *n.* ruzie *n.*, opschudding *n.*

fraction, *n.* breuk *n.*; onderdeel *n.n.* **fractional,** *a.* breuk . . .; onbeduidend.

fractious, *a.*, ~ly, *adv.* lastig, weerspannig.

fracture, *n.* breuk *n.* ¶ *v.t.* breken *str.*

fragile, *a.* bros, breekbaar. **fragility,** *n.* brosheid *n.*, breekbaarheid *n.*

fragment, *n.* brokstuk *n.n.* **fragmentary,** *a.* fragmentarisch.

fragrance, *n.* geur *n.*, welriekendheid *n.* **fragrant,** *a.* geurig, welriekend.

frail, *a.* zwak, teer, bros. **frailty,** *n.* zwakheid *n.*, brosheid *n.*

frame, *n.* raam *n.n.*; lijst *n.*; montuur *n.*; broeibrak *n.*; chassis *n.n.*; lichaamsbouw *n.* ¶ *v.t.* inlijsten, omlijsten. **framework,** *n.* kader *n.n.*

France, *N.* Frankrijk *n.N.*

franchise, *n.* burgerrecht *n.n.*; stemrecht *n.n.*

frank, *a.*, ~ly, *adv.* openhartig, oprecht. ¶ *v.t.* frankeren.

frankincense, *n.* wierook *n.*

frankness, *n.* openhartigheid *n.*, oprechtheid *n.*

frantic, *a.*, ~ally, *adv.* razend, waanzinnig.

fraternal, *a.*, ~ly, *adv.* broederlijk. **fraternity,** *n.* broederschap *n.* **fraternization,** *n.* verbroedering *n.* **fraternize,** *v.i.* zich verbroederen. **fratricide,** *n.* broedermoord *n.* (*act*); broedermoordenaar *n.*

fraud, *n.* bedrog *n.n.* (*act*); bedrieger *n.* **fraudulence,** *n.* bedrieglijkheid *n.*, bedrog *n.n.* **fraudulent,** *a.*, ~ly, *adv.* bedrieglijk.

fraught, *a.* vol; overstelpt.

fray, *n.* strijd *n.*, gevecht *n.n.*; kale plek *n.* ¶ *v.t.* rafelen.

freak, *n.* gril *n.*, kuur *n.*

freckle, *n.* sproet *n.* ¶ *v.i.* sproeten krijgen *str.* **freckled,** *a.* sproeterig.

free, *a.* vrij; gratis; onbezet. ~ *lance,* wilde *n.*; ~ *trade,* vrijhandel *n.* **freedom,** *n.* vrijheid *n.*; ereburgerschap *n.n.* **freehold,** *n.* vrij eigendom *n.n.* **freeholder,** *n.* bezitter *n.* van vrij eigendom *n.n.* **freely,** *adv.* vrij, vrijuit, vrijelijk. **freeman,** *n.* burger *n.* **freemartin,** *n.* onvruchtbare koe *n.* **freemason,** *n.* vrijmetselaar *n.* **freemasonry,** *n.* vrijmetselarij *n.* **freestone,** *n.* zandsteen *n.* **freethinker,** *n.* vrijdenker *n.* **freewheel,** *n.* vrijwiel *n.n.*, vrijloop *n.*

freeze, *v.i.* vriezen *irr.*, bevriezen *irr.* ¶ *v.t.* doen *irr.* bevriezen. **freezing mixture,** *n.* koudmakend mengsel *n.n.* **freezing point,** *n.* vriespunt *n.n.*

freight, *n.* vracht *n.*, lading *n.* **freighter,** *n.* vrachtschip *n.n.*; bevrachter *n.*

French, *a.* Frans. *f*~ *windows,* openslaande glazen deur *n.* **french-polish,** *v.t.* politoeren. ¶ *n.* politoer *n.n.* **frenchify,** *v.t.* verfransen. **Frenchman,** *N.* Fransman *N.* **Frenchwoman,** *N.* Franse *N.*

frenzied, *a.* waanzinnig, razend. **frenzy,** *N.* waanzin *n.*, razernij *n.*

frequency, *n.* veelvuldigheid *n.*; frequentie *n.* **frequent,** *a.*, ~ly, *adv.* herhaaldelijk; veelvuldig. **fre·quent,** *v.t.* bezoeken *irr.*; omgaan *irr.* met. **frequentation,** *n.* omgang *n.*, verkeer *n.n.* **frequenter,** *n.* bezoeker *n.*

fresh, *a.*, ~ly, *adv.* fris; vers; zoet. **freshen,** *v.t.* opfrissen, verversen. ¶ *v.i.* fris worden *str.*; aanwakkeren. **freshet,** *n.* zoetwaterstroom *n.* **freshman,** *n.* groen *n.* **freshness,** *n.* frisheid *n.*; versheid *n.* **freshwater,** *n.* zoet water *n.n.*

fret, *v.i.* zich ergeren, zich onnodige zorgen *pl.n.* maken. ¶ *v.t.* uitzagen, uitsnijden *str.* **fretful,** *a.*, ~ly, *adv.* gemelijk, knorrig.

fretsaw, *n.* figuurzaag *n.* **fretwork,** *n.* lijstwerk *n.n.*

friability, *n.* brosheid *n.* **friable,** *a.* bros, broos.

friar, *n.* kloosterbroeder *n.*, frater *n.* **friary,** *n.* klooster *n.n.*

friction, *n.* wrijving *n.*

Friday, *N.* vrijdag *N.*

friend, *n.* vriend *n.* (*male*); vriendin *n.* (*female*). **friendliness,** *n.* vriendelijkheid *n.* **friendly,** *a.* vriendelijk; vriendschappelijk; bevriend. ~ *society,* vereniging tot onderlinge steun *n.* **friendship,** *n.* vriendschap *n.*

frieze, *n.* fries *n.*

frigate, *n.* fregat *n.n.*

fright, *n.* vrees *n.*, schrik *n.*, ontsteltenis *n.* **frighten,** *v.t.* doen *irr.* schrikken, bang maken. **frightful,** *a.,* ~**ly,** *adv.* vreselijk, afschuwelijk.

frigid, *a.,* ~**ly,** *adv.* koud, kil; stijf. **frigidity,** *n.* koudheid *n.*; stijfheid *n.*

frill, *n.* geplooide strook *n.*; jabot *n.*, ruche *n.* ¶ *v.t.* plooien.

fringe, *n.* franje *n.*; rand *n.* ¶ *v.t.* van een franje voorzien *irr.*; als een franje omgeven *str.*

frippery, *n.* prullegoed *n.n.*

Frisia, *N.* Friesland *n.N.*

Frisian, *a.* Fries. ¶ *N.* Fries *N.* (*male*); Friezin *N.* (*female*).

frisk, *v.i.* dartelen, vrolijk rondhuppelen *str.* **friskiness,** *n.* dartelheid *n.* **frisky,** *a.* dartel, vrolijk.

fritillary, *n.* keizerskroon *n.*

fritter, *n.* beignet *n.*, poffertje *n.n.* ¶ *v.t. to ~ away,* verbeuzelen, verkwisten.

frivolity, *n.* wuftheid *n.*, lichtzinnigheid *n.*; luchthartigheid *n.* **frivolous,** *a.,* ~**ly,** *adv.* wuft; luchthartig.

frizzle, *v.t.* krullen, kroezen; sissen.

fro, *adv. to and ~,* heen en weer.

frock, *n.* japon *n.*, jurk *n.*; pij *n.*

frog, *n.* kikvors *n.*, kikker *n.*

frolic, *n.* pretje *n.n.*, grap *n.* ¶ *v.i.* pret maken; dartelen. **frolicsome,** *a.* jolig.

from, *prep.* van. vanuit, vandaan; sedert; door.

frond, *n.* palmblad *n.n.*; varenblad *n.n.*

front, *n.* voorkant *n.*; front *n.n.*; frontje *n.n. in ~,* voorop, vooraan; *in ~ of,* voor; tegenover; *~ room,* voorkamer *n.* ¶ *v.i.* gericht zijn naar, uitzien *irr.* op. **frontage,** *n.* voorzijde *n.*; voorgevel *n.* **frontal,** *a.* front . . . **frontier,** *n.* grens *n.* **frontispiece,** *n.* titelplaat *n.*

frost, *n.* vorst *n.*; mislukking *n.* ¶ *v.t.* glaceren; mat slijpen *str.* **frost-bitten,** *a.* bevroren. **frosted,** *a.* mat. **frosty** *a.,* ~**ily,** *adv.* vorstig; ijzig.

froth, *n.* schuim *n.n.* ¶ *v.i.* schuimen. ¶ *v.t.* doen *irr.* schuimen. **frothy,** *a.,* ~**ily,** *adv.* schuimend; ijdel.

frown, *v.i.* fronsen; misnoegd kijken *str.*

frowsy, *a.* goor, vuil, slordig.

frozen, *a.* bevroren.

fructification, *n.* bevruchting *n.*; vrucht-vorming *n.* **fructify,** *v.t.* bevruchten.

frugal, *a.,* ~**ly,** *adv.* spaarzaam. matig. **frugality,** *n.* spaarzaamheid *n.*, matigheid *n.*

fruit, *n.* vrucht *n.*; fruit *n.n.* **fruiterer,** *n.* fruithandelaar *n.* **fruitful,** *a.,* ~**ly,** *adv.* vruchtbaar. **fruition,** *n.* rijpheid *n.*; vruchtgebruik *n.n.* **fruitless,** *a.,* ~**ly,** *adv.* vruchteloos.

frump, *n.* ouwe sok *n.*

frustrate, *v.t.* verijdelen. **frustration,** *n.* verijdeling *n.*; onmacht *n.*

fry, *v.t.* bakken *irr.*, braden *irr. fried egg,* spiegelei *n.n.* ¶ *n.* jong goedje *n.n.*; jonge volkje *n.n.* **frying pan,** *n.* bakpan *n.*; koekepan *n.*

fuchsia, *n.* foksia *n.*

fuddle, *v.t.* verwarren, benevelen.

fudge, *n.* fondant *n.*; (*fig.*) onzin *n.*

fuel, *n.* brandstof *n.* ¶ *v.t.* van brandstof voorzien *irr.*

fug, *n.* mufheid *n.*, bedomptheid *n.*

fugitive, *a.* vluchtig, voorbijgaand; voort-vluchtig ¶ *n.* vluchteling *n.*

fugleman, *n.* leider *n.*

fugue, *n.* fuga *n.*

fulcrum, *n.* steunpunt *n.n.*

fulfil, *v.t.* vervullen, uitvoeren, volbrengen *irr.* **fulfilment,** *n.* vervulling *n.*

full, *a.* vol; gevuld; volledig. *~ stop,* punt *n.*; *~ up,* vol. ¶ *adv.* heel; ten volle. ¶ *v.t.* vollen. **full-blown,** *a.* geheel ont-wikkeld. **full-blooded,** *a.* volbloed. **full dress,** *a.* gala . . . **fuller,** *n.* volder *n.* **fulling mill,** *n.* volmolen *n.* **full length,** *a.* ten voeten uit. **fullness,** *n.* volheid *n.* **fully,** *adv.* ten volle; geheel.

fulminate, *v.i.* donderen; ontploffen; ful-mineren. **fulminating powder,** *n.* knal-poeder *n.n.* **fulmination,** *n.* knal *n.*, ontploffing *n.*; fulminatie *n.*

fulsome, *a.* overdreven.

fumble, *v.i.* rondtasten; morrelen; onzeker doen *irr.* **fumbler,** *n.* knoeier *n.n.*, morrelaar *n.*

fume, *n.* damp *n.*, uitwaseming *n.*, rook *n.* ¶ *v.i.* dampen; koken (van woede *n.*). **fumigate,** *v.t.* uitroken. **fumigation,** *n.* uitroking *n.*

fun, *n.* aardigheid *n.*, grappigheid *n. for ~,* voor de grap; *like ~,* dat het een aardigheid heeft; *to make* or *poke ~ at,* voor de gek houden *irr.*

function, *n.* functie *n.*; werking *n.*; plechtig-heid *n.*; ambt *n.n.*; ambtsvervulling *n.* ¶ *v.i.* werken; fungeren. **functionary,** *n.* ambtenaar *n.*, beambte *n.*

fund, *n.* fonds *n.n.*, kapitaal *n.n. ~s,* fondsen, *pl.n.n.*, effecten *pl.n.n.*; voorraad *n.*; *in ~s,* bij kas.

fundament, *n.* fondement *n.n.* **fundamental,** *a.,* ~**ly,** *adv.* fundamenteel, grond . . .

funeral, *n.* begrafenis *n.* ¶ *a,* lijk . . ., begrafenis . . . *~ procession,* lijkstoet *n.*; *~ pile,* brandstapel *n.* **funereal,** *a.* treurig, somber.

fungous, *a.* zwamachtig. **fungus,** *n.* zwam *n.*

funicular, *a.* kabel . . .

funk, *n.* vrees *n.* ¶ *v.t.* niet aandurven *irr.*

funnel, *n.* trechter *n.*; schoorsteen(pijp) *n.*

funny, *a.* grappig.

fur, *n.* bont *n.n.*; pels *n.*, pelswerk *n.n.*; beslag *n.n.*; ketelsteen *n.* ¶ *a.* bonten.

furbelow, *n.* geplooide strook *n.*

furbish, *v.t.* oppoetsen; polijsten. **furbisher,** *n.* polijster *n.*

furcate, *a.* gevorkt.

furious, *a.,* ~**ly,** *adv.* woedend, razend.

furl, *v.t.* inhalen, oprollen.

furlong, *n.* 1/8 Engelse mijl (201 Meter) *n.*

furlough, *n.* verlof *n.n.*
furnace, *n.* stookoven *n.*
furnish, *v.t.* leveren, verschaffen; meubileren.
   furnisher, *n.* leverancier *n.*; stoffeerder *n.*
   furniture, *n.* meubilair *n.*; meubelen *pl.n.n.*
furred, *a.* beslagen. **furrier**, *n.* bontwerker *n.*
furrow, *n.* voor *n.*; groef *n.*, rimpel *n.*
furry, *a.* bonten.
further, *a.* verder. ¶ *adv.* verder; nader.
   ¶ *v.t.* bevorderen. **furtherance**, *n.* bevordering *n.* **furthermore**, *adv.* bovendien,
   en ook. **furthest**, *n.* verste.
furtive, *a.*, ~ly, *adv.* steelsgewijs, sluiks.
fury, *n.* woede *n.*; razernij *n.*
furze, *n.* brem *n.*; gaspeldoorn *n.*
fuse, *v.t.* versmelten *str.*; samensmelten *str.*
   to ~ the light, kortsluiting *n.* veroorzaken.
   ¶ *v.i.* (door)smelten *str.*, doorslaan *irr.*
   ¶ *n.* lont *n.*; tijdbuis *n.*; zekering *n.* **fusee**,
   n. lont *n.*; windlucifer *n.*
fusel, *a.* ~ *oil*, foezelolie *n.*
fuselage, *n.* geraamte *n.n.*
fusilier, *n.* fuselier *n.* **fusillade**, *n.* geweervuur
   n.n., fusillade *n.*
fusion, *n.* samensmelting *n.*, fusie *n.*
fuss, *n.* (onnodige) drukte *n.*; ophef *n.* ¶ *v.i.*
   zich nodeloos zorgen *n.* maken; druk doen
   irr. **fussy**, *a.* druk; nodeloos bezorgd.
fustian, *n.* bombazijn *n.n.*, fustein *n.n.*
fusty, *a.* muf.
futile, *a.* beuzelachtig; nutteloos, vergeefs.
futility, *n.* beuzelachtigheid *n.*, futiliteit
   n.; bagatel *n.*
future, *a.* toekomstig; aanstaand. ¶ *n.*
   toekomst *n.*; toekomende tijd *n.* **futurity**,
   n. toekomst *n.*, toekomstigheid *n.*
fuzz, *n.* pluis *n.n.*, dons *n.n.* **fuzzy**, *a.*
   donzig; kroes.

G

gab, *v.i.* wauwelen. ¶ *n. he has the gift of
   the* ~, hij kan praten als Brugman.
   gabble, *v.t.* brabbelen; aframmelen. **gabbler**,
   n. brabbelaar *n.*
gaberdine, *n.* gabardine *n.*
gable, *n.* puntgevel *n.*; geveltop *n.*
gaby, *n.* sukkel *n.*
gad, *n.* horzel *n.* ¶ *v.i. to ~ about*, lanterfanten. **gadfly**, *n.* paardevlieg *n.*, horzel *n.*
gadget, *n.* apparaatje *n.n.*, dingetje *n.n.*
gaff, *n.* gaffel *n.* *to blow the* ~, een geheim
   n.n. verklappen.
gaffe, *n.* blunder *n.*, flater *n.*
gaffer, *n.* ouwe baas *n.*
gag, *n.* prop *n.*; tussenvoegsel *n.n.*; grap *n.*
   ¶ *v.t.* een prop in de mond stoppen;
   improviseren.
gage, *n.* onderpand *n.n.* ¶ *v.t.* verbeuren.
gaggle, *v.i.* snateren. ¶ *n.* vlucht *n.*
gaiety, *n.* vrolijkheid *n.* **gaily**, *adv.* vrolijk,
   opgewekt; kleurig.

gain, *n.* winst *n.*, aanwinst *n.*; voordeel *n.n.*
   ¶ *v.t.* winnen *str.*, verkrijgen *str.* ¶ *v.i.*
   winnen *str. to ~ upon*, inhalen. **gainer**, *n.*
   winner *n.* **gainful**, *a.*, ~ly, *adv.* voordelig,
   winstgevend.
gainsay, *v.t.* tegenspreken *str.*
gait, *n.* gang *n.*, pas *n.*
gaiter, *n.* slobkous *n.*
gala, *n.* gala *n.n.*
galaxy, *n.* melkweg *n.*; schitterende verzameling *n.*
gale, *n.* storm *n.*
gall, *n.* gal *n.*; galnoot *n.*, bitterheid *n.*
   ¶ *v.t.* verbitteren.
gallant, *a.*, ~ly, *adv.* galant; dapper; fier.
   ¶ *n.* galant *n.* **gallantry**, *n.* galanterie *n.*;
   dapperheid *n.*
galleon, *n.* galjoen *n.*
gallery, *n.* galerij *n.*, gaanderij *n.*; tribune *n.*;
   schellinkje *n.n.*; (schilderijen)museum *n.n.*
galley, *n.* galei *n.*; kombuis *n.n.*; zetraam *n.n.*
gallipot, *n.* zalfpotje *n.*
gallon, *n.* 4,54 Liter *n.*
gallop, *v.i.* galopperen. ¶ *v.t.* doen *irr.*
   galopperen. ¶ *n.* galop *n.*
gallows, *pl.n.* galg *n.* **gallows-tree**, *n.* galg *n.*
galore, *adv.* bij de vleet, in overvloed *n.*
galosh, *n.* overschoen *n.*
galvanic, *a.* galvanisch. **galvanism**, *n.*
   galvanisme *n.n.* **galvanize**, *v.t.* galvaniseren.
gambit, *n.* gambiet *n.*
gamble, *v.i.* spelen, dobbelen; gokken. ¶ *n.*
   gokspel *n.n.* **gambler**, *n.* speler *n.*
gamboge, *n.* guttegom *n.*
gambol, *v.i.* huppelen, dartelen. ¶ *n.*
   kromme sprong *n.*
game, *n.* spel *n.n.*; wild *n.n.*; wildbraad *n.n.*
   ¶ *a.* flink, moedig. ¶ *v.i.* spelen, dobbelen.
   gamecock, *n.* kemphaan *n.* **gamekeeper**, *n.*
   jachtopziener *n.* **gamester** *n.* speler *n.*
   dobbelaar *n.*
gammon, *n.* gerookte ham *n.*
gamut, *n.* toonladder *n.*, toonschaal *n.*
gander, *n.* gent *n.*
gang, *n.* bende *n.*; ploeg *n.* **ganger**, *n.*
   ploegbaas *n.*
gangrene, *n.* koudvuur *n.n.*
gangster, *n.* bandiet *n.*
gangway, *n.m.* doorgang *n.*; loopplank *n.*;
   gangboord *n.n.*
gaol, *n.* gevangenis *n.* **gaoler**, *n.* cipier *n.*
gap, *n.* gat *n.n.*, opening *n.*; lacune *n.*; poort
   n.
gape, *v.i.* staren. *to ~ at*, aangapen.
garage, *n.* garage *n.* ¶ *v.t.* in de garage
   stallen.
garb, *n.* kleding *n.*, gewaad *n.n.* ¶ *v.t.* kleden.
garbage, *n.* afval *n.*; vuilnis *n.*
garble, *v.t.* verminken, door elkaar haspelen.
   garbled, *a.* verminkt, onherkenbaar.
garden, *n.* tuin *n*, ¶ *v.i.* tuinieren. **gardener**,
   n. tuinier *n.*
gardenia, *n.* gardenia *n.*

gardening, *n.* tuinieren *n.n.*
gargle, *v.i.* gorgelen. ¶ *n.* gorgeldrank *n.*
gargoyle, *n.* waterspuwer *n.*
garish, *a.*, ~ly, *adv.* opzichtig, schel.
garland, *n.* guirlande *n.*, bloemenkrans *n.*
garlic, *n.* knoflook *n.n.*
garment, *n.* gewaad *n.n.*; kledingstuk *n.n.*
garner, *v.t.* opslaan *irr.* ¶ *n.* graanzolder *n.*
garnet, *n.* granaat *n.*
garnish, *v.t.* garneren. ¶ *n.* garnering *n.*, garnituur *n.* garniture, *n.* garnering *n.*, garnituur *n.*
garret, *n.* zolderkamertje *n.n.*, vliering *n.*
garrison, *n.* garnizoen *n.n.* ¶ *v.t.* een garnizoen leggen *irr.* in.
garrotte, *n.* worgtoestel *n.n.* ¶ *v.t.* worgen. garrotter, *n.* worger *n.*
garrulity, *n.* praatachtigheid *n.* garrulous, *a.* praatziek.
garter, *n.* kouseband *n.*
gas, *n.* gas *n.n.* ¶ *v.t.* door gas bedwelmen; door gas doen *irr.* stikken. gaselier, *n.* gaskroon *n.* gaseous, *a.* gasachtig. gas-fitter, *n.* gasfitter *n.*
gash, *v.t.* snijden *str.*, japen. ¶ *n.* gapende wond *n.*
gas-jet, *n.* gaspit *n.*
gasket, *n.* pakking *n.*
gas-main, *n.* gasleiding *n.* gas man, *n.* kwitantieloper *n.* gas-meter, *n.* gasmeter *n.* gasometer, *n.* gashouder *n.* gas-oven, *n.* gasfornuis *n.n.*
gasp, *v.i.* hijgen; naar adem *n.* snakken. ¶ *n.* snik *n.*, hijging *n.*
gaspipe, *n.* gasbuis *n.* gas stove, *n.* gaskachel *n.*; gasfornuis *n.n.*
gastric, *a.* maag . . . gastronomy, *n.* gastronomie *n.*
gas-works, *pl.n.* gasfabriek *n.*
gate, *n.* poort *n.*; hek *n.n.* gateway, *n.* poort *n.*; toegangsweg *n.*
gather, *v.t.* verzamelen, bijeenbrengen *irr.*; innemen *str.* to ~ *from*, opmaken uit. ¶ *v.i.* vergaderen. ¶ *n.* inneemsel *n.n.*
gatherer, *n.* inzamelaar *n.*; oogster *n.* gathering, *n.* verzameling *n.*; bijeenkomst *n.*
gaudiness, *n.* opzichtigheid *n.* gaudy, *a.*, ~ily, *adv.* opzichtig, bont.
gauge, *v.t.* peilen; schatten. ¶ *n.* peilstok *n.*; peilglas *n.n.*; maatstaf *n.*; wijdte *n.* narrow ~, nauw spoor *n.n.*; wide ~, wijd spoor *n.n.* gauger, *n.* peiler *n.*; meter *n.*
gaunt, *a.*, ~ly, *adv.* schraal, mager.
gauntlet, *n.* handschoen *n.*
gauze, *n.* gaas *n.n.*
gavel, *n.* voorzittershamer *n.*
gawky, *a.* onhandig.
gay, *a.* vrolijk, opgeruimd, levendig.
gaze, *v.i.* staren, turen. ¶ *n.* starende blik *n.*
gazelle, *n.* gazelle *n.*
gazette, *n.* nieuwsblad *n.n.*; courant *n.*

¶ *v.t.* bekend maken. gazetteer, *n.* klapper *n.*
gear, *n.* tuig *n.n.*, gerei *n.n.*; tuigage *n.*; koppeling *n.*; versnelling *n.* to change ~, overschakelen; *to reverse* ~, terugschakelen, in de achteruit zetten; low ~, eerste versnelling; *reverse* ~, achteruitversnelling *n.* ¶ *v.t.* koppelen; een versnelling geven *str.* gearbox, *n.* versnellingsbak *n.* gearing, *n.* drijfwerk *n.n.*
geisha, *n.* geisha *n.*
gelatine, *n.* gelatine *n.* gelatinous, *a.* gelatineachtig.
geld, *v.t.* snijden *str.*, castreren. gelding, *n.* ruin *n.*; gesneden dier *n.n.*
gem, *n.* juweel *n.n.*, kleinood *n.n.*, edelgesteente *n.n.* ¶ *v.t.* met edelgesteenten tooien.
gender, *n.* geslacht *n.n.*
genealogical, *a.* genealogisch. ~ *tree*, stamboom *n.n.*
general, *a.* algemeen. ¶ *n.* algemeen *n.n.*; generaal *n.* generality, *n.* algemeenheid *n.*; gemeenplaats *n.* generalization, *n.* generalisatie *n.* generalize, *v.i.* generaliseren. generally, *adv.* in het algemeen, over 't algemeen. generalship, *n.* generaalschap *n.n.*; beleid *n.n.*
generate, *v.t.* voortbrengen *irr.*; opwekken, ontwikkelen. generation, *n.* voortbrenging *n.*; voortplanting *n.*; geslacht *n.n.* generator, *n.* voortbrenger *n.*; dynamo *n.*
generic, *a.* algemeen; geslachts . . .
generosity, *n.* edelmoedigheid *n.*; vrijgevigheid *n.* generous, *a.*, ~ly, *adv.* edelmoedig; vrijgevig; overvloedig, rijk.
genesis, *n.* wording *n.* G~, Genesis *N.*
genial *a.*, ~ly, *adv.* gul, joviaal; geniaal; weldadig. geniality, *n.* jovialiteit *n.*; genialiteit *n.*; weldadigheid *n.*
genital, *a.* voortplantings . . . genitals, *pl.n.* geslachtsdelen *pl.n.*
genitive, *n.* genitief *n.*, tweede naamval *n.*
genius, *n.* geest *n.*; genie *n.n.*; aanleg *n.*
genteel, *a.*, ~ly, *adv.* voornaam, deftig; fijn.
gentian, *n.* gentiaan *n.*
gentile, *a.* heidens, ongelovig; niet-Joods.
gentility, *n.* voorname mensen *pl.n.*; goede manieren *pl.n.* gentle, *a.* zacht, teder; adellijk. gentlefolk, *pl.n.* lieden *pl.n.* van deftigen huize. gentleman. *n.* heer *n.*; man *n.* gentlemanly, *a.* heerachtig; fatsoenlijk. gentleness, *a.* zachtheid *n.*; zachtzinnigheid *n.* gentlewoman, *n.* vrouw *n.* van aanzienlijke geboorte *n.* gently, *adv.* zachtjes; geleidelijk. gentry, *pl.n.* de deftige stand.
genuflexion, *n.* kniebuiging *n.*, knieval *n.*
genuine, *a.*, ~ly, *adv.* echt, onvervalst.
genus, *n.* geslacht *n.n.*, soort *n.*, klasse *n.*
geographer, *n.* aardrijkskundige *n.* geographical, *a.*, ~ly, *adv.* aardrijkskundig. geography, *n.* aardrijkskunde *n.*

geological, *a.* geologisch. **geologist**, *n.* geoloog *n.* **geology**. *n.* geologie *n.*
geometric(al), *a.* meetkundig. **geometrician**, *n.* meetkundige *n.* **geometry**, *n.* meetkunde *n. solid* ~, stereometrie *n.*
geranium, *n.* geranium *n.*
gerfalcon, *n.* giervalk *n.*
germ, *n.* kiem *n.*; ziektekiem *n.*
German, *a.* Duits. ~ *band*, straatmuzikanten *pl.n.*; ~ *silver*, pleetzilver *n.n.*; ~ *woman*, Duitse *N.* ¶ *N.* Duitser *N.*
germane, *a.* verwant; bloedeigen.
germinal, *a.* kiem . . . **germinate**, *v.i.* ontkiemen. **germination**, *n.* ontkieming *n.*
gerund, *n.* gerundium *n.n.*
gestation, *n.* zwangerschap *n.*
gesticulate, *v.i.* gesticuleren, gebaren maken. **gesticulation**, *n.* gebaar *n.n.*; gebarenspel *n.n.*
gesture, *n.* gebaar *n.n.*
get, *v.t.* krijgen *str.*; halen; overhalen tot; begrijpen *str.* ¶ *v.i.* worden *str.*; komen *irr.* *to* ~ *away*, wegkomen *irr.*; *to* ~ *back*, terugkomen *irr.*; teruggaan *irr.*; *to* ~ *down*, uitstappen; *to* ~ *hold of*, te pakken krijgen *str.*; *to* ~ *in*, binnenkomen *irr.*; gekozen worden *str.*; *to* ~ *off*, zich wegmaken; *to* ~ *on*, vooruitkomen *irr.*; *to* ~ *out* wegkomen *irr.*; *to* ~ *over*, te boven komen *irr.*; *to* ~ *round*, omzeilen; *to* ~ *together*, bijeenbrengen *irr.*; *to* ~ *through*, er door komen *irr.*; het eraf brengen *irr.*; *to* ~ *up steam*, opstoken. **get-at-able**, *a.* te krijgen; bereikbaar. **get-up**, *n.* kleding *n.*; uiterlijk *n.n.*
geyser, *n.* geiser *n.*; verwarmingstoestel *n.n.*
gewgaw, *n.* prul *n.n.*
ghastliness, *n.* afgrijselijkheid *n.* **ghastly**, *a.* doodsbleek; spookachtig; afgrijselijk, ijzingwekkend.
gherkin, *n.* augurkje *n.n.*
ghost, *n.* spook *n.n.*, geestverschijning *n.* **ghostly**, *a.* spookachtig; geestelijk.
ghoul, *n.* boze geest *n.* **ghoulish**, *a.* demonisch.
giant, *n.* reus *n.* **giantess**, *n.* reuzin *n.*
gibber, *v.i.* brabbelen. **gibberish**, *n.* brabbeltaal *n.*
gibbet, *n.* galg *n.*
gibbon, *n.* gibbon *n.*
gibe, *v.i.* honen, schimpen. *to* ~ *at*, beschimpen.
giblets, *pl.n.* afval *n.* (van gevogelte *n.n.*).
giddiness, *n.* duizeligheid *n.*; onbezonnenheid *n.* **giddy**, *a.*, ~ily, *adv.* duizelig, draaierig; onbezonnen.
gift, *n.* gaaf *n.*, gift *n.*, geschenk *n.n.* **gifted**, *a.* begaafd.
gig, *n.* cabriolet *n.*; giek *n.*
gigantic, *a.* reusachtig.
giggle, *v.i.* giechelen.
gild, *v.t.* vergulden. **gilder**, *n.* vergulder *n.* **gilding**, *n.* verguldsel *n.n.*
gill, *n.* kieuw *n.*; 0,14 Liter *n.*
gillyflower, *n.* muurbloem *n.*; anjelier *n.*

gilt, *n.* verguldsel *n.n.* **gilt-edged**, *a.* verguld op snee *n.*; soliede.
gimcrack, *a.* prullig, prullerig.
gimlet, *n.* schroefboor *n.*
gin, *n.* jenever *n.*; strik *n.*
ginger, *n.* gember *n.* ¶ *v.t.* *to* ~ *up*, opkikkeren. **gingerbread**, *n.* peperkoek *n.* **gingerly**, *adv.* voorzichtig, behoedzaam.
gipsy, *n.* zigeuner *n.*
giraffe, *n.* giraffe *n.*
gird, *v.t.* omgorden, aangorden. **girder**, *n.* (stalen) balk *n.* **girdle**, *n.* gordel *n.*
girl, *n.* meisje *n.n.* **girlhood**, *n.* meisjesjaren *pl.n.n.* **girlish**, *a.*, ~ly, *adv.* meisjesachtig, meisjes . . .
girth, *n.* buikriem *n.*; omvang *n.*
gist, *n.* hoofdpunt *n.n.*
give, *v.t.* geven *str.*; meegeven *str.*; verlenen. *to* ~ *away*, weggeven *str.*; verklappen, verraden; *to* ~ *forth*, uitzenden *str.*, uitstralen; *to* ~ *in*, inleveren; *to* ~ *out*, uitdelen; verklaren; *to* ~ *up*, laten *str.* varen. ¶ *v.i.* doorbuigen *str.*; bezwijken *str.* *to* ~ *in*, het opgeven *str.*; *to* ~ *on*, uitzien *irr.* op; *to* ~ *out*, opraken; *to* ~ *up*, zich gewonnen geven *str.* ¶ *n.* veerkracht *n.* **giver**, *n.* gever *n.*
gizzard, *n.* spiermaag *n.*
glacial, *a.* ijzig, ijs . . . **glacier**, *n.* gletscher *n.*
glad, *a.* verheugd, blij, vrolijk. **gladden**, *v.t.* verblijden, verheugen.
glade, *n.* open plaats *n.* (in een bos *n.n.*).
gladiator, *n.* zwaardvechter *n.*
gladiolus, *n.* zwaardlelie *n.*
gladly, *adv.* gaarne.
glamorous, *a.* betoverend. **glamour**, *n.* betovering *n.*, aantrekkingskracht *n.*
glance, *n.* blik *n.*; oogopslag *n.* ¶ *v.i.* kijken *str.*; afschampen. *to* ~ *at*, een blik werpen *str.* op.
gland, *n.* klier *n.*
glanders, *pl.n.* droes *n.*
glare, *v.i.* hel schijnen *str.*; woest kijken *str.* ¶ *n.* schittering *n.*; felle gloed *n.*; kwade blik *n.* **glaring**, *a.* schreeuwend.
glass, *n.* glas *n.n.*; spiegel *n.*; barometer *n.*; bel *n.*, ~es, bril *n.* ¶ *a.* glazen. ¶ *v.t.* glazeren. **glass-blower**, *n.* glasblazer *n.* **glass-cutter**, *n.* glassnijder *n.*; glazenmakersdiamant *n.* **glass-house**, *n.* broeikas *n.*; bak *n.* **glass-works**, *pl.n.* glasfabriek *n.* **glassy**, *a.* glasachtig; spiegelglad.
glaze, *v.t.* ruiten *pl.n.* inzetten; verglazen; glaceren. ~ed *paper*, geglaceerd papier *n.n.* ¶ *n.* glazuur *n.n.*; glans *n.* **glazier**, *n.* glazenmaker *n.*
gleam, *n.* glans *n.*, schijn *n.* ¶ *v.i.* glanzen, blinken *str.*
glean, *v.t.* lezen *str.*; oppikken. **gleaner**, *n.* arenlezer *n.*; arenleesster *n.* (*female*).
glebe, *n.* land *n.n.*, aarde *n.*
glee, *n.* vrolijkheid *n.*; meerstemmig lied *n.n.*
glen, *n.* bergdal *n.n.*

glib, *a.,* ~**ly,** *adv.* rad, vloeiend.
glide, *v.i.* glijden *str.;* zweven. **glider,** *n.* zweefvliegtuig *n.n.*
glimmer, *v.i.* blinken *str.,* glimmen *str.;* schemeren. ¶ *n.* zwak schijnsel *n.n.;* schemerlicht *n.n.*
glimpse, *n.* glimp *n.* ¶ *v.t.* even zien *irr.*
glint, *n.* schijnsel *n.n.,* glinstering *n.* ¶ *v.i.* glinsteren.
glisten, *v.i.* glanzen, blinken *str.,* fonkelen.
glitter, *v.i.* flonkeren, fonkelen. ¶ *n.* fonkeling *n.*
gloaming, *n.* schemering *n.*
gloat, *v.i.* met duivels leedvermaak *n.n.* toezien *irr. to* ~ *over,* zich vermeien in.
globe, *n.* aardbol *n.;* ballon *n.;* stolp *n.*
globular, *a.* bolvormig. **globule,** *n.* bolletje *n.n.*
gloom, *n.* donkerte *n.;* somberheid *n.;* neerslachtigheid *n.* **gloomy,** *a.,* ~**ily,** *adv.* donker, somber; neerslachtig.
glorification, *n.* verheerlijking *n.* **glorify,** *v.t.* verheerlijken. **glorious,** *a.,* ~**ly,** *adv.* glorierijk, roemrijk; heerlijk, verrukkelijk. **glory,** *n.* roem *n,* glorie *n.;* zaligheid *n.*
gloss, *n.* glans *n.;* glosse *n.,* commentaar *n.n.* ¶ *v.i.* doen *irr.* glanzen; glosseren. *to* ~ *over,* wegredeneren. **glossary,** *n.* woordenlijst *n.* **glossiness,** *n.* glans *n.* **glossy,** *a.* glanzend.
glove, *n.* handschoen *n.* **glover,** *n.* handschoenmaker *n.*
glow, *v.i.* gloeien. ¶ *n.* gloed *n.*
glower, *v.i.* dreigend kijken *str.*
glow-worm, *n.* glimworm *n.*
glucose, *n.* glucose *n.,* druivensuiker *n.*
glue, *n.* lijm *n.* ¶ *v.t.* lijmen.
glum, *a.* somber; stuurs.
glut, *n.* overvoering *n.* ¶ *v.t.* oververzadigen.
glutinous, *a.* kleverig, lijmerig.
glutton, *n.* gulzigaard *n.* **gluttonous,** *a.,* ~**ly,** *adv.* gulzig; vraatzuchtig. **gluttony,** *n.* gulzigheid *n.;* vraatzucht *n.*
glycerine, *n.* glycerine *n.*
gnarl, *n.* knoest *n.* **gnarled,** *a.* knoestig.
gnash, *v.t.* knarsen.
gnat, *n.* mug *n.*
gnome, *n.* kabouter *n.*
gnu, *n.* gnoe *n.,* wildebeest *n.n.*
go, *v.i.* gaan *irr.;* lopen *str.;* verlopen *str.;* vertrekken *str.;* gangbaar zijn. *to* ~ *to law,* een proces *n.n.* aangaan *irr.; to* ~ *mad,* gek worden *str.; to* ~ *wrong,* mislopen *str.* ¶ *n.* vuur *n.n.,* élan *n.n.;* vaart *n.*
goad, *n.* prikkel *n.* ¶ *v.t.* prikkelen, aanzetten.
go-ahead, *a.* voortvarend.
goal, *n.* doel *n.;* goal *n.* **goalkeeper,** *n.* doelverdediger *n.*
goat, *n.* geit *n.;* bok *n. the sheep and the* ~*s,* de schapen *n.n.* en de bokken. **goatish,** *a.* bokachtig; geil.
gobble, *v.t.* schrokken, opslokken. **gobbler,** *n.* opslokker *n.*

go-between, *n.* tussenpersoon *n.,* bemiddelaar *n.*
goblet, *n.* beker *n.,* kroes *n.*
goblin, *n.* kabouter *n.*
go-cart, *n.* loopwagentje *n.n.*
God, *N.* God *N.* **godchild,** *n.* petekind *n.n.* **goddess,** *n.* godin *n.* **godfather,** *n.* peetoom *n.* **godhead,** *n.* godheid *n.;* goddelijkheid *n.* **godless,** *a.* goddeloos. **godlike,** *a.* goddelijk. **godliness,** *n.* godsvrucht *n.* **godly,** *a.* vroom, godvruchtig. **godmother,** *n.* peettante *n.* **godsend,** *n.* uitkomst *n.*
goffer, *v.t.* pijpen, plooien.
goggle, *v.i.* staren, met puilende ogen *pl. n.n.* kijken *str.* ¶ *n.* ~*s,* stofbril *n.*
going, *n.* gaan *n.n. comings and* ~*s,* doen *n.n.* en laten *n.n.*
goitre, *n.* kropgezwel *n.n.* **goitrous,** *a.* lijdende aan kropgezwel.
gold, *n.* goud *n.n.* ¶ *a.* gouden. **goldbeater,** *n.* goudslager *n.,* goudpletter *n.* **goldbeater's skin,** *n.* goudvlies *n.n.* **golddigger,** *n.* gouddelver *n.* **golden,** *a.* gouden. **goldfinch,** *n.* distelvink *n.;* puttertje *n.n.* **goldleaf,** *n.* goudblad *n.n.* **goldsmith,** *n.* goudsmid *n.*
golliwog, *n.* (grappige) pop *n.*
gondola, *n.* gondel *n.* **gondolier,** *n.* gondelier *n.*
gong, *n.* gong *n.*
good, *a.* goed; braaf, zoet. *G*~ *Friday,* Goede Vrijdag *N.; to make* ~*,* vergoeden; goed terechtkomen *irr.* ¶ *n.* goed(e) *n.n.,* welzijn *n.n.;* goed *n.n.* ~*s,* goederen *pl. n.n.;* ~*s train,* goederentrein *n.* **good-bye,** *adv.* tot ziens! gegroet! ¶ *n.* afscheid *n.n.,* vaarwel *n.n.* **goodliness,** *n.* goedheid *n.;* voortreffelijkheid *n.* **good-looking,** *a.* knap. **goodly,** *a.* flink, aanmerkelijk. **good-natured,** *a.* goedaardig; goedhartig. **goodness,** *n.* goedheid *n.;* deugdelijkheid *n. for* ~' *sake,* om 's Hemels wil; ~ *gracious,* lieve Hemel! **goodwill,** *n.* welwillendheid *n.;* klandizie *n.*
goose, *n.* gans *n.* **gooseberry,** *n.* kruisbes *n. to play* ~*,* in de weg zijn. **gooseflesh,** *n.* kippevlees *n.n.* **goosestep,** *n.,* paradepas *n.*
Gordian, *a.* Gordiaans.
gore, *n.* geronnen bloed *n.n.* ¶ *v.t.* verwonden.
gorge, *n.* keel *n.,* strot *n.;* nauwe bergpas *n.* ¶ *v.i.* schrokken. ¶ *v.t.* volproppen.
gorgeous, *a.,* ~**ly,** *adv.* prachtig.
gorilla, *n.* gorilla *n.*
gormandize, *v.i.* lekkerbekken.
gorse, *n.* brem *n.*
gory, *a.* bloederig.
goshawk, *n.* havik *n.*
gosling, *n.* gansje *n.n.*
gospel, *n.* evangelie *n.n.*
gossamer, *n.* herfstdraad *n.;* ragfijn weefsel *n.n.*
gossip, *n.* kletskous *n.;* buurvrouw *n.;* buurpraatje *n.n.* ¶ *v.i.* kletsen; kouten.

Gothic, a. gothisch.
gouge, n. guts n. ¶ v.t. gutsen; uitsteken str.
gourd, n. pompoen n.; waterfles n.
gourmand, n. smulpaap n.
gout, n. jicht n. **gouty,** a. jichtig.
govern, v.t. besturen; regeren. ¶ v.i. regeren, heersen. **governable,** a. bestuurbaar; volgzaam. **governance,** n. bestuur n.n. **governess,** n. gouvernante n. **government,** n. regering n.; bestuur n.n. **governor,** n. gouverneur n.; bestuurder n.; ouwe heer n.; regulateur n.
gown, n. japon n.; toga n, tabberd n.
grab, v.t. pakken, grijpen str. ¶ n. greep n.
grace, n. genade n.; gunst n.; bevalligheid n.; gebed n.n. **to say** ~, bidden str. (before meal); danken (after meal); the year of ~, het jaar onzes Heren. ¶ v.t. versieren, bekoring n. verlenen aan. **graceful,** a., ~ly, adv. gratieus, bevallig. **graceless,** a., ~ly, adv. onbevallig, lomp. **gracious,** a. ~ly, adv. genadig. **goodness** ~, goeie genade!
gradation, n. gradatie n., graadverdeling n.; trapsgewijze overgang n. **grade,** n. graad n., kwaliteit n.; helling n. ¶ v.t. graderen; sorteren. **gradient,** n. helling n.
gradual, a., ~ly, adv. geleidelijk; trapsgewijs.
graduate, v.t. graderen; titreren. ¶ v.i. promoveren. ¶ n. gepromoveerde n. **graduation,** n. (schaal)verdeling n.; promotie n.
graft, v.t. enten; omkopen irr. ¶ n. ent n.; omkoperij n.
grain, n. korrel n.; graan n.n., koren n.n.; grein n., korrel n., draad n. ¶ v.t. greineren.
grammar, n. spraakkunst n.; spraakleer n. **grammarian,** n. grammaticus n. **grammatical,** a., ~ly, adv. taalkundig, grammatikaal.
gramme, n. gram n.
gramophone, n. gramofoon n. ~ record, gramofoonplaat n.
grampus, n. bruinvis n.
granary, n. graanschuur n., graanzolder n.
grand, a. groot; groots. ~ duchess, groothertogin n.; ~ duchy, groothertogdom n.n.; ~ duke, groothertog n. **grandchild,** n. kleinkind n.n. **granddaughter,** n. kleindochter n. **grandee,** n. grande n. **grandeur,** n. grootsheid n., pracht n. **grandfather,** n. grootvader n. **grandiloquence,** n. hoogdravendheid n.; grootspraak n. **grandiloquent,** a. hoogdravend; grootsprakig. **grandiose,** a. groots, grandioos. **grandmother,** n. grootmoeder n. **grandson,** n. kleinzoon n.
grange, n. landhuis n.n., herenboerderij n.
granite, n. graniet n.n.
granny, n. oma n.; grootje n.n.
grant, v.t. toestaan irr., vergunnen; schenken str., verlenen. ¶ n. subsidie n.n. **grantor,** n. schenker n.

granulate, v.i. korrelen. ~d sugar, korrelsuiker n. **granule,** n. korrel n.
grape, n. druif n. bunch of ~s, druiventros n. **grape-shot,** n. schroot n.n.
graphic, a. graphisch. **graphite,** n. grafiet n.n.
grapnel, n. dreg n.; enterhaak n.; werpanker n.n.
grapple, v.t. aanklampen; enteren. ¶ v.i. to ~ with, worstelen met. ¶ n. See grapnel n.
grasp, v.t. grijpen str.; vatten; begrijpen str. ¶ n. greep n.; bereik n.n.; bevattingsvermogen n.n. **grasping,** a. inhalig, hebzuchtig.
grass, n. gras n.n. **grasshopper,** n. sprinkhaan n. **grass-widow,** n., onbestorven weduwe n. **grassy,** a. grazig; grasachtig.
grate, n. rooster n.; traliewerk n.n. ¶ v.t. raspen; knarsen; traliën.
grateful, a., ~ly, adv. dankbaar; erkentelijk.
grater, n. rasp n.
gratification, n. bevrediging n., voldoening n.; gratificatie n. **gratify,** v.t. bevredigen, voldoen irr., voldoening schenken str.
grating, a. knarsend. ¶ n. traliewerk n.n.; rooster n.
gratis, a. & adv. gratis.
gratitude, n. dankbaarheid n.
gratuitous, a., ~ly, adv. kosteloos; ongemotiveerd. **gratuity,** n. gratificatie n.; fooi n.
gravamen, n. bezwaarschrift n.n.; hoofdpunt n.n. van een aanklacht n.
grave, n. graf n.n.n., grafkuil n. ¶ a., ~ly, adv. ernstig; plechtig. **gravedigger,** n. doodgraver n.
gravel, n. kiezel n.n.n., grint n.n.; graveel n.n. ¶ v.t. begrinten. **gravelly,** a. kiezelachtig, grintachtig.
graver, n. graveerstift n.
gravestone, n. grafsteen n.
gravitate, v.i. graviteren. to ~ towards, aangetrokken worden str. door. **gravitation,** n. zwaartekracht n.
gravity, n. gewicht n.n.; ernst n.; zwaartekracht n. specific ~, soortelijk gewicht n.n.
gravy, n. jus n., vleesnat n.n. **gravy-boat,** n. sauskom n.
gray, a. See grey.
graze, v.i. grazen, weiden. ¶ v.t. laten str. grazen; schaven; schampen; rakelings voorbijgaan irr. **grazier,** n. vetweider n.
grease, n. vet n.n.; smeer n.; consistentvet n.n. ¶ v.t. smeren; invetten. **greasegun,** n. vetspuit n. **greasy,** a., ~ily, adv. vettig; vet.
great, a. groot; aanzienlijk; knap. **greataunt,** n. oudtante n. **greatcoat,** n. overjas n.; kapotjas n. **great-grand-aunt,** n. overoudtante n. **great-grandchild,** n. achterkleinkind n.n. **great-grandfather,** n. overgrootvader n. **great-grandmother,** n. overgrootmoeder n. **great-grandson,** n.

achterkleinzoon *n.* **greatly,** *adv.* grotelijks; zeer. **greatness,** *n.* grootheid *n.,* grootte *n.* **great-uncle,** *n.* oudoom *n.*

grebe, *n.* fuut *n.*

greed, *n.,* **greediness,** *n.* hebzucht *n.,* begerigheid *n.;* gulzigheid *n.* **greedy,** *a.,* ~ily, *adv.* hebzuchtig, begerig; gulzig.

green, *a.* groen; onrijp; onervaren. ~ *crop,* groenvoer *n.n.* ¶ *n.* groen *n.n.;* grasveld *n.n.* ~s, groente *n.* **greengage,** *n.* reine claude *n.,* groene pruim *n.* **greengrocer,** *n.* groenteboer *n.* **greenhorn,** *n.* nieuweling *n.* **greenhouse,** *n.* broeikast *n.;* oranjerie *n.* **greenish,** *a.* groenig, groenachtig. **Greenland,** *N.* Groenland *n.N.* **greenness,** *n.* groenheid *n.* **green room,** *n.* acteurskamer *n.*

greet, *v.t.* groeten, begroeten. **greeting,** *n.* groet *n.;* begroeting *n.*

gregarious, *a.,* ~ly, *adv.* gezellig; kudde. . . .

grenade, *n.* (hand)granaat *n.* **grenadier,** *n.* grenadier *n.*

grey, *a.* grijs; grauw. ¶ *n.* grijs *n.n.;* grauw *n.n.* ¶ *v.i.* beginnen *str.* te grijzen. **greybeard,** *n.* grijsaard *n.* **greyhound,** *n.* hazewind *n.* **greyish,** *a.* grijsachtig.

grid, *n.* rooster *n.;* net *n.n.* **gridiron,** *n.* rooster *n.*

grief, *n.* smart *n.* droefheid *n. to come to* ~, een ongeluk *n.n.* krijgen *str.* **grievance,** *n.* grief *n.* **grieve,** *v.t.* bedroeven, verdrieten *str.;* berouwen. **grievous,** *a.,* ~ly, *adv.* smartelijk; deerlijk.

griffin, *n.* griffioen *n.*

griffon, *n.* affenpinscher *n.*

grig, *n.* zandaal *n.;* krekel *n. as merry as a* ~, zo blij als een vogeltje *n.n.*

grill, *n.* rooster *n.;* traliedeur *n.* ¶ *v.t.* roosteren. ~ *room,* restaurant *n.n.*

grim, *a.,* ~ly, *adv.* grimmig; onverbiddelijk.

grimace, *n.* grijns *n.,* grimas *n.* ¶ *v.i.* grijnzen.

grime, *n.* vuil *n.n.,* roet *n.n.* ¶ *v.t.* vuil maken.

grimness, *n.* grimmigheid *n.*

grimy, *a.* vuil, roetig.

grin, *n.* grijns *n.* ¶ *v.i.* grijnzen.

grind, *v.t.* malen; slijpen *str.;* draaien. *to* ~ *the faces of the poor,* de armen *n.* onderdrukken; *to* ~ *down,* fijn maken. ¶ *n.* karwei *n.* **grinder,** *n.* slijper *n.;* maaltand *n.* **grindstone,** *n.* slijpsteen *n.*

grip, *v.t.* grijpen *str.;* beet houden *irr.* ¶ *n.* greep *n.;* handtas *n.*

gripe(s), *n.* koliek *n.*

grisly, *a.* griezelig; afgrijselijk.

grist, *n.* maalkoren *n.n. to bring* ~ *to the mill,* zaken aanbrengen *irr.*

gristle, *n.* kraakbeen *n.n.* **gristly,** *a.* kraakbeenachtig.

grit, *n.* steengruis *n.n.;* vastberadenheid *n.* ¶ *v.t.* malen. *to* ~ *one's teeth,* tandenknarsen. **gritty,** *a.* zanderig.

grizzled, *a.* grijs, grauw. **grizzly,** *a.* ~ *(bear),* grijze beer *n.*

groan, *v.i.* steunen, kreunen, kermen. ¶ *n.* gesteun *n.n.,* gekreun *n.n.*

groat, *n.* groot *n.* ~s, grutten *pl. n.*

grocer, *n.* kruidenier *n.* **groceries,** *pl. n.* kruidenierswaren *pl. n.,* koloniale waren *pl. n.*

grog, *n.* grok *n.* **groggy,** *a.* slap op de benen *pl. n.n.*

groin, *n.* lies *n.;* graatrib *n.*

groom, *n.* stalknecht *n.;* kamerheer *n.;* bruidegom *n.* ¶ *v.t.* roskammen, verzorgen.

groove, *n.* groef *n.* ¶ *v.t.* groeven.

grope, *v.i.* tasten, in 't duister zoeken *irr.*

gross, *a.,* ~ly, *adv.* grof, ruw; bruto. ¶ *n.* gros *n.n.* (144); gros *n.n.,* massa *n. in the* ~, in 't algemeen. **grossness,** *n.* grofheid *n.*

grotesque, *a.,* ~ly, *adv.* potsierlijk, grotesk.

grotto, *n.* grot *n.*

ground, *n.* grond *n.,* aarde *n.;* terrein *n.n.;* grond *n.,* reden *n.* ~s, koffiedik *n.n.; to break new* ~, het terrein ontginnen *str.; to gain* ~, veld winnen *str.;* ~ *floor,* benedenverdieping *n.; on the* ~ *floor,* gelijkvloers. ¶ *v.t.* gronden; grondvesten; aan de grond zetten. **grounding,** *n.* grondslag *n. with a good* ~, goed onderlegd. **groundless,** *a.,* ~ly, *adv.* ongegrond. **groundsel,** *n.* kruiskruid *n.n.* **groundwork,** *n.* onderbouw *n.;* grondslag *n.*

group, *n.* groep *n.* ¶ *v.t.* groeperen.

grouse, *n.* hazelhoen *n.n.;* bezwaar *n.n.* ¶ *v.i.* mopperen, kankeren. **grouser,** *n.* brompot *n.,* kankeraar *n.*

grout, *n.* gruttemeel *n.n.* ~s, bezinksel *n.n.*

grove, *n.* bosje *n.n.,* bossage *n.*

grovel, *v.i.* kruipen *str.,* zich vernederen.

grow, *v.i.* groeien; wassen *str. to* ~ *up,* opgroeien; groot worden *str.* ¶ *v.t.* verbouwen, kweken, telen.

growl, *v.i.* brommen, grommen. **growler,** *n.* brompot *n.*

grown-up, *n.* volwassene *n.* **growth,** *n.* groei *n.,* wasdom *n.;* aanwas *n.;* gezwel *n.n.*

groyne, *n.* krib *n.,* golfbreker *n.*

grub, *n.* larve *n.;* eten *n.n.,* kost *n.* ¶ *v.i.* graven *str.,* wroeten.

grudge, *n.* wrok *n. to have* (or *bear*) *a* ~ *against,* een wrok koesteren tegen.

gruel, *n.* pap *n.,* brij *n.*

gruelling, *a.* afmattend.

gruesome, *a.* gruwzaam, ijzingwekkend.

gruff, *a.,* ~ly, *adv.* bars, nors. **gruffness,** *n.* barsheid *n.,* norsheid *n.*

grumble, *v.i.* brommen, knorren. **grumbler,** *n.* brombeer *n.,* knorrepot *n.* **grumpy,** *a.* brommerig, knorrig.

grunt, *v.i.* knorren. ¶ *n.* geknor *n.n.*

guano, *n.* guano *n.*

guarantee, *n.* waarborg *n.,* zekerheid *n.,* garantie *n.* ¶ *v.t.* waarborgen, garanderen.

guard, *n.* wacht *n.;* bewaker *n.;* garde *n.;*

conducteur *n.*; scherm *n.n.*, stootplaat *n.*
~*s.* gardetroepen *pl. n.* ¶ *v.t.* beschermen,
behoeden. ¶ *v.i.* to ~ against, zich hoeden
voor. **guarded**, *a.* gereserveerd, voorzichtig, omzichtig. **guardian**, *n.* voogd *n.*;
bewaarder *n.* **guardianship**, *n.* voogdij
n. **guardsman**, *n.* officier (*or* soldaat)
van de garde.
gudgeon, *n.* grondel *n.* (*fish*); pen *n.*, spil *n.*
~ *pin*, zuigerpen *n.*
guerdon, *n.*, loon *n.n.*
guess, *v.t. & v.i.* raden *irr.*, gissen. ¶ *n.* gis *n.*,
gissing *n.* by ~, op de gis.
guest, *n.* gast *n.* paying ~, betalend logé *n.*
guffaw, *v.i.* luidkeels lachen *irr.* ¶ *n.* luid
gelach *n.n.*
guidance, *n.* leiding *n.*; geleide *n.n.* **guide**,
n. gids *n.*; leidraad *n.* girl ~, padvindster
n. ¶ *v.t.* leiden; besturen. **guide-book**,
n. reisgids *n.*
guild, *n.* gilde *n.n.* **Guildhall**, *N.* gildehuis
n.n.
guilder, *n.* gulden *n.*
guile, *n.* list *n.*, bedrog *n.n.* **guileful**, *a.*,
~ly, *adv.* arglistig, vals. **guileless**, *a.*,
~ly, *adv.* argeloos, onschuldig.
guillotine, *n.* valbijl *n.*, guillotine *n.* ¶ *v.i.*
guillotineren.
guilt, *n.* schuld *n.* **guiltless**, *a.*, ~ly, *adv.*
onschuldig; schuldeloos. **guilty**, *a.*, ~ily,
adv. schuldig.
guinea, *n.* guinje *n.* **Guinea**, *N.* Guinea *n.N.*
guinea-corn, *n.* negerkoren *n.n.* **guinea-**
fowl, *n.* paarlhoen *n.n.* **guinea-pig**, *n.*
marmot *n.*
guise, *n.* uiterlijk *n.n.*, voorkomen *n.n.*
in the ~ of, bij wijze van.
guitar, *n.* guitaar *n.*
gulf, *n.* golf *n.*; afgrond *n.*; (*fig.*) kloof *n.*
gull, *n.* meeuw *n.*
gullet, *n.* slokdarm *n.*
gullibility, *n.* lichtgelovigheid *n.* **gullible**,
a. lichtgelovig.
gully, *n.* geul *n.*; goot *n.*; bergkloof *n.*
gulp, *v.t.* inslikken, slokken. ¶ *n.* slok *n.*;
slokkend geluid *n.n.*
gum, *n.* gom *n.*; tandvlees *n.n.* ¶ *v.t.* gom-
men. **gummy**, *a.* gommig, gomachtig.
gumption, *n.* gezond verstand *n.n.*, initiatief *n.n.*
gun, *n.* kanon *n.n.*; geweer *n.n.* ¶ *v.i.*
schieten *str.* **gunboat**, *n.* kanonneerboot *n.*
gun-carriage, *n.* affuit *n.n.* **gun-cotton**,
n. schietkatoen *n.n.* **gun-metal**, *n.* kanon-
spijs *n.* **gunner**, *n.* kanonnier *n.*, artillerist
n. **gunnery**, *n.* artillerie *n.*; ballistiek *n.*
gunpowder, *n.* buskruit *n.n.* **gunshot**, *n.*
geweerschot *n.n.*; kanonschot *n.n.* within
~, binnen schot *n.n.* **gunsmith**, *n.*
geweermaker *n.* **gunstock**, *n.* geweer-
lade *n.*
gunwale, *n.* dolboord *n.n.*
gurgle, *v.i.* klokken, gorgelen. ¶ *n.* geklok
n.n., gegorgel *n.n.*

gurnard, *n.* knorhaan *n.*, poon *n.*
gush, *v.i.* gutsen, krachtig uitstromen;
overdreven praten. ¶ *n.* gulp *n.*, stroom
n.; gedweep *n.n.*
gusset, *n.* inzetsel *n.n.*
gust, *n.* windvlaag *n.*, windruk *n.*
gustatory, *a.* smaak. . . .
gusto, *n.* animo *n.n.*
gusty, *a.* winderig, buiig.
gut, *n.* darm *n.* ~*s*, ingewanden *pl. n.n.*;
durf *n.* ¶ *v.t.* uithalen; leegbranden,
uitbranden.
gutter, *n.* goot *n.* ¶ *v.i.* aflopen *str.* **gutter-**
snipe, *n.* straatjongen *n.*
guttural, *a.* keel. . . . ¶ *n.* keelklank *n.*
guy, *n.* touw *n.n.*, reep *n.*; pop *n.*, vogelverschrikker *n.* ¶ *v.t.* bespotten.
guzzle, *v.i.* zwelgen *str.*
gymkhana, *n.* sportfeest *n.n.*
gymnasium, *n.* gymnastiekschool *n.*; gym-
nastiekzaal *n.* **gymnastic**, *a.*, ~ally, *adv.*
gymnastisch. **gymnastics**, *n.* gymnastiek
n.
gypsum, *n.* gips *n.n.*
gyrate, *v.i.* ronddraaien. **gyration**, *n.* rond-
draaiing *n.*, omwenteling *n.*
gyroscope, *n.* gyroscoop *n.*
gyve, *n.* (voet)boei *n.*, keten *n.*

H

haberdasher, *n.* winkelier *n.* in garen en
band. **haberdashery**, *n.* garen- en band-
winkel *n.*
habiliment, *n.* kleding *n.*
habit, *n.* gewoonte *n.*; kleed *n.n.*, gewaad
n.n. by ~, uit gewoonte; to fall into a ~,
een gewoonte aannemen *str.* **habitable**,
a. bewoonbaar. **habitat**, *n.* natuurlijke
woonplaats *n.* **habitation**, *n.* bewoning
n.; woonplaats *n.* **habitual**, *a.*, ~ly, *adv.*
gewoon, gebruikelijk. **habituate**, *v.t.*
wennen, gewennen.
hack, *v.t.* hakken; houwen *str.* ¶ *n.* huur-
paard *n.n.*; knol *n.* **hacking**, *a.* ~ cough,
droge hoest *n.*
hackle, *n.* nekveren *pl. n.*; hekel *n.* ¶ *v.t.*
hekelen.
hackney, *n.* rijpaard *n.n.*; hakkenei *n.*
hackney coach, *n.* huurkoets *n.* **hack-**
neyed, *a.* afgezaagd.
haddock, *n.* schelvis *n.*
hæmorrhage, *n.* bloeduitstorting *n.* **hæmor-**
rhoids, *pl. n.* aambeien *pl. n.*
haft, *n.* heft *n.n.*, handvat *n.n.* ¶ *v.t.* van
een heft voorzien *irr.*
hag, *n.* heks *n.*; oud wijf *n.n.*
haggard, *a.* bleek en vermagerd.
haggis, *n.* Schotse vleespudding *n.*
haggle, *v.i.* dingen *str.*, afdingen *str.*
hail, *v.t.* aanroepen *str.*; verwelkomen, begroeten. ¶ *v.i.* to ~ from, afkomstig zijn van.

¶ *v. imp.* hagelen. ¶ *n.* hagel *n.*; roep *n.*
¶ *int.* heil! **hailstone,** *n.* hagelkorrel *n.*
hair, *n.* haar *n.n. to a* ~, haarfijn. **hair-**
dresser, *n.* kapper *n.*, coiffeur *n.* **hairless**,
a. onbehaard. ` **hair-splitting,** *n.* haar-
kloverij *n.* **hair-trigger,** *n.* sneller *n.*
hairy, *a.* behaard.
hake, *n.* dors *n.*
halberd, *n.* hellebaard *n.* **halberdier,** *n.*
hellebaardier *n.*
halcyon, *n.* ijsvogel *n.* ¶ *a.* rustig.
hale, *a.* flink, gezond. ¶ *v.t.* sleuren,
slepen.
half, *a.* half. ~ *past five,* half zes; ~ *past*
twelve, half een. ¶ *n.* helft *n. too clever*
by ~, veel te slim. **half-blood,** *n.* halfbloed
n. **half-calf,** *n.* halfleer *n.n.* **half-caste,** *n.*
halfbloed *n.* **half-hearted,** *a.* weifelend,
onverschillig. **half-mast,** *a.* halfstok.
half-pay, *n.* wachtgeld *n.n. on* ~, op
nonactiviteit *n.* **halfpenny,** *n.* halve
stuiver *n.* **half-witted,** *a.* halfgaar, half
wijs.
halibut, *n.* heilbot *n.*
hall, *n.* zaal *n.*; vestibule *n.*, gang *n.*; eetzaal
n.; gebouw *n.n.*; herenhuis *n.n.* **hall-mark,**
n. ijk *n.*, keurmerk *n.n.* ¶ *v.t.* ijken,
keurmerken.
halloo, *n.* hallo *n.n.* ¶ *v.i.* roepen *str.*
hallow, *v.t.* heiligen, wijden.
hallstand, *n.* (gang)kapstok *n.*
hallucination, *n.* zinsbegoocheling *n.*, halluci-
natie *n.*
halo, *n.* stralenkrans *n.*; lichtkring *n.*
halt, *n.* halte *n.*; stilstand *n.* ¶ *a.* mank,
kreupel. ¶ *v.i.* halt houden *irr.*; mank
lopen *str.* ¶ *v.t.* halt laten *str.* houden;
tot staan brengen *irr.*
halter, *n.* halster *n.*; strop *n.*
halve, *v.t.* halveren.
halyard, *n.* val *n.*
ham, *n.* ham *n.*; bil *n.*
hames, *n.* haam *n.*
hamlet, *n.* gehucht *n.n.*
hammer, *n.* hamer *n.* ¶ *v.t.* hameren. ¶ *v.i.*
hameren. *to* ~ *away at,* loshameren op.
hammock, *n.* hangmat *n.*
hamper, *n.* sluitmand *n.* ¶ *v.t.* belemmeren.
hamster, *n.* hamster *n.*
hamstring, *n.* kniepees *n.* ¶ *v.t.* verlammen.
hand, *n.* hand *n.*; wijzer *n. at* ~, op handen;
at first ~, uit de eerste hand; *to go* ~ *in* ~,
samengaan *irr.*; *off* ~, voor de vuist (weg);
on ~, voorradig; *on all* ~*s,* van alle
kanten *n.*; *on the one* ~, enerzijds; *on the*
other ~, anderzijds; *out of* ~, niet te
beheersen; *to have a free* ~, vrij zijn;
to lay ~*s on,* te pakken krijgen *str.*;
to lend a ~, een handje *n.n.* helpen *str.*
¶ *v.t.* overhandigen; aanreiken. *to* ~
down, overleveren; *to* ~ *in,* inleveren;
to ~ *out,* uitreiken. **handbag,** *n.* handtasje
n.n. **hand-barrow,** *n.* handkar *n.* **hand-**
bell, *n.* tafelbel *n.* **handbill,** *n.* strooibiljet,

n.n. **handbook,** *n.* handboek *n.n.* **hand-**
breadth, *n.* handbreedte *n.* **handcuff,** *n.*
handboei *n.* ¶ *v.t.* boeien. **handful,** *n.*
handvol *n.*, handjevol *n.n.* **handicap,** *n.*
handicap *n.*; nadeel *n.n.* ¶ *v.t.* handicappen; belemmeren. **handicraft,** *n.*
handwerk *n.n.*, ambacht *n.n.* **handi-**
craftsman, *n.* handwerksman, *n.* ambachtsman *n.* **handiness,** *n.* handigheid *n.*
handwork, *n.* werk *n.n.* **handkerchief,** *n.*
zakdoek *n.* **handle,** *n.* handvat *n.n.*;
hengsel *n.n.*; heft *n.n.*; oor *n.n.*; greep *n.*;
kruk *n.*; knop *n.* ¶ *v.t.* hanteren; omspringen *str.* met; manoeuvreren. **handle-**
bar, *n.* stuur *n.n.* **hand-made,** *a.* met de
hand gemaakt. **handmaid,** *n.* dienares *n.*
handrail, *n.* leuning *n.* **handshake,** *n.*
handdruk *n.*
handsome, *a.*, ~ly, *adv.* knap; aanzienlijk,
royaal.
handwriting, *n.* (hand)schrift *n.n.* **handy,**
a., ~ily, *adv.* handig; bij de hand.
hang, *v.t.* hangen *str.*, ophangen *str.*; behangen
str. to ~ *fire,* niet opschieten *str.* ¶ *v.i.*
hangen *str. to* ~ *behind,* achterblijven *str.*;
to ~ *on,* vasthangen *str.*; volhouden *irr.*
¶ *n.* aard *n.*, slag *n. to get the* ~ *of a thing,*
de slag te pakken krijgen *str.*
hangar, *n.* hangar *n.*
hang-dog, *a. a* ~ *expression,* een arme-
zondaarsgezicht *n.n.*
hanger, *n.* hanger *n.*; kapstokje *n.n.* **hanger-**
on, *n.* trawant *n.*; klaploper *n.* **hanging(s),**
n. wandtapijt *n.n.* **hangman,** *n.* beul
n.
hank, *n.* streng *n.*
hanker, *v.i.* hunkeren. *to* ~ *after,* hunkeren
naar.
hansom, *n.* tweewielig huurrijtuig *n.n.*
haphazard, *a.* lukraak.
hapless, *a.* rampzalig, ongelukkig.
happen, *v.i.* gebeuren, plaats hebben. *I* ~*ed*
to be there, ik was daar toevallig.
happiness, *n.* geluk *n.n.* **happy,** *a.*, ~ily,
adv. gelukkig, blij; tevreden.
harangue, *n.* toespraak *n.* ¶ *v.t.* toespreken
str.
harass, *v.t.* uitputten; bestoken; niet met
rust *n.* laten *str.*
harbinger, *n.* bode *n.*, voorloper *n.*
harbour, *n.* haven *n.*; schuilplaats *n.* ¶ *v.t.*
herbergen, een schuilplaats *n.* verlenen
aan; koesteren.
hard, *a.* hard; zwaar, moeilijk; moeizaam.
~ *cash,* klinkende munt *n.*; ~ *labour,*
dwangarbeid *n.*; *to call a person* ~ *names,*
iemand scherp veroordelen; *a* ~ *and fast*
rule, een vaste regel *n.* ¶ *adv.* hard; vlak,
dicht. ~ *at it,* druk bezig; ~ *up,* slecht
bij kas; ~ *set,* onbuigzaam. **hard-bitten,** *a.*
taai. **harden,** *v.t.* verharden; harden.
¶ *v.i.* hard worden *str.* **hard-headed,** *a.*
practisch, nuchter. **hard-hearted,** *a.*
hardvochtig. **hardihood,** *n.* onversaagdheid

n., koenheid *n.* **hardiness,** *n.* onversaagdheid *n.*; gehardheid *n.* **hardly,** *adv.* nauwelijks. **hardness,** *n.* hardheid *n.* **hardship,** *n.* ontbering *n.*; ongemak *n.n.* **hardware,** *n.* ijzerwaar *n.* **hardy,** *a.*, ~ily, *adv.* onversaagd; gehard.

hare, *n.* haas *n.* **harebell,** *n.* grasklokje *n.n.* **harebrained,** *a.* onbesuisd. **harelip,** *n.* hazelip *n.*

harem, *n.* harem *n.*

haricot-bean, *n.* witte boon *n.*

hark, *v.i.* luisteren. *to* ~ *back to,* teruggaan *irr.* tot; terugkomen *irr.* op.

harlequin, *n.* harlekijn *n.*; hansworst *n.*

harlot, *n.* hoer *n.*

harm, *n.* schade *n.*, kwaad *n.n.*; letsel *n.n.* ¶ *v.t.* kwaad doen *irr.* (aan). **harmful,** *a.*, ~ly, *adv.* schadelijk, nadelig. **harmless,** *a.*, ~ly, *adv.* onschadelijk; onschuldig.

harmonic, *a.* harmonisch; welluidend. **harmonica,** *n.* mondharmonica *n.* **harmonics,** *pl.n.* harmonieleer *n.* **harmonious,** *a.* harmonieus; overeenstemmend. **harmonize,** *v.t.* harmoniseren; in overeenstemming *n.* brengen *irr.* ¶ *v.i.* harmoniëren; overeenstemmen. **harmonium,** *n.* harmonium *n.n.* **harmony,** *n.* harmonie *n.*; overeenstemming *n.*

harness, *n.* harnas *n.n.*; tuig *n.n.* *in* ~, in 't gareel. ¶ *v.t.* harnassen; het tuig aandoen *irr.*

harp, *n.* harp *n.* ¶ *v.i. to* ~ *on,* voortdurend spreken *str.* over. **harpist,** *n.* harpenist *n.*

harpoon, *n.* harpoen *n.* ¶ *v.t.* harpoeneren.

harpy, *n.* harpij *n.*

harridan, *n.* ouwe tang *n.*

harrier, *n.* hond *n.* (voor de hazenjacht).

harrow, *n.* eg *n.* ¶ *v.t.* eggen; pijnigen, kwellen.

harry, *v.t.* plunderen, teisteren.

harsh, *a.*, ~ly, *adv.* hard; streng, hardvochtig; schril, scherp. **harshness,** *n.* hardheid *n.*; hardvochtigheid *n.*; schrilheid *n.*

hart, *n.* hert *n.n.* **hartshorn,** *n.* hertshoorn *n.*

harum-scarum, *a.* wild, onbesuisd.

harvest, *n.* oogst *n.* ~ *home,* oogstfeest *n.n.* ¶ *v.t.* oogsten. **harvester,** *n.* oogster *n.*

hash, *v.t.* hakken. ¶ *n.* ragoût *n.*; mengelmoes *n.n.*

hasp, *n.* wervel *n.*; beugel *n.* ¶ *v.t.* (met een wervel *n.*) sluiten *str.*

hassock, *n.* knielkussen *n.n.*

haste, *n.* haast *n.*, spoed *n.* *more* ~ *less speed,* haastige spoed is zelden goed. **hasten,** *v.i.* zich haasten. **hastiness,** *n.* haastigheid *n.*, gehaastheid *n.* **hasty,** *a.*, ~ily, *adv.* haastig; gehaast; overhaastig, overijld.

hat, *n.* hoed *n.* **hatbox,** *n.* hoedendoos *n.*

hatch, *n.* luik *n.n.*; schuif *n.*, poortje *n.n.*; broedsel *n.n.* ¶ *v.t.* uitbroeden; beramen; arceren. **hatchery,** *n.* viskwekerij *n.*

hatchet, *n.* bijl *n.*

hatchway, *n.* luikopening *n.*

hate, *v.t.* haten; verafschuwen. *to* ~ *to* . . ., niet houden *irr.* van. ¶ *n.* haat *n.* **hateful,** *a.*, ~ly, *adv.* hatelijk, verfoeilijk. **hatred,** *n.* haat *n.*; afschuw *n.*

hatter, *n.* hoedenmaker *n.* *as mad as a* ~, stapelgek.

haughtiness, *n.* hooghartigheid *n.* **haughty,** *a.*, ~ily, *adv.* hooghartig, hoogmoedig.

haul, *v.t.* halen, trekken *str.*, slepen. *to* ~ *over the coals,* een uitbrander *n.* geven *str.* ¶ *n.* haal *n.*; trek *n.*; vangst *n.*

haunch, *n.* dij *n.*; lendestuk *n.n.*; bout *n.*

haunt, *v.i.* spoken. ¶ *v.t.* rondwaren door, rondspoken in; voortdurend bezoeken *irr,* ¶ *n.* verblijfplaats *n.* **haunted,** *a.* ~ *house,* spookhuis *n.n.*; *the house is* ~, het spookt in het huis.

hautboy, *n.* hobo *n.*

have, *v.t.* hebben *irr.*; bezitten *str.*; gebruiken; beetnemen *str.*

haven, *n.* veilige haven *n.*, schuilplaats *n.n.*

haversack, *n.* knapzak *n.*; ransel *n.n.*

havoc, *n.* verwoesting *n.* *to play* ~ *with,* huishouden *irr.* onder.

haw, *n.* hagedoornbes *n.*; hapering *n.* ¶ *v.i.* haperen.

hawk, *n.* havik *n.*; valk *n.* ¶ *v.i.* op de valkenjacht gaan *irr.*, met valken jagen *str.* ¶ *v.t.* venten. **hawker,** *n.* venter *n.*, leurder *n.*

hawse, *n.* kluis *n.* **hawse-hole,** *n.* kluisgat *n.n.* **hawser,** *n.* tros *n.*, kabel *n.*

hawthorn, *n.* hagedoorn *n.*

hay, *n.* hooi *n.n. to make* ~, hooien; *to make* ~ *of,* in de war sturen; *make* ~ *while the sun shines,* smeed het ijzer als het heet is. **haycock,** *n.* hooiopper *n.* **haymaker,** *n.* hooier *n.* **hayrick,** *n.*, **haystack,** *n.* hooimijt *n.*, hooiberg *n.*

hazard, *n.* toeval *n.n.*, kans *n.*; risico *n.n.*; hazardspel *n.n.* ¶ *v.t.* wagen, riskeren. **hazardous,** *a.*, ~ly, *adv.* gewaagd.

haze, *n.* mist *n.*, nevel *n.*; waas *n.n.* ¶ *v.t.* benevelen.

hazel, *n.* hazelaar *n.* ¶ *a.* hazelbruin. **hazel-nut,** *n.* hazelnoot *n.*

hazy, *a.*, ~ily, *adv.* beneveld; wazig, vaag.

he, *pron.* hij.

head, *n.* hoofd *n.n.*; directeur *n.*; kop *n.*; kruin *n.*, top *n.*; bron *n.*; beeldenaar *n.* ~ *wind,* tegenwind *n.*; *8* ~ *of cattle,* 8 stuks vee *n.n.*; ~*s or tails,* kruis *n.n.* of munt *n.*; ~ *over heels,* hals *n.* over kop; *from* ~ *to foot,* van top tot teen *n.*; *I can't make* ~ *or tail of it,* ik kan er geen touw *n.* aan vastknopen; *to lose one's* ~, de kluts kwijtraken; *over the* ~*s of,* te hoog over. ¶ *v.t.* aan het hoofd staan *irr.* van; aanvoeren. *to* ~ *for,* koers *n.* zetten naar; *to* ~ *off,* afwenden. **headache,** *n.* hoofdpijn *n.* **head-dress,** *n.* kapsel *n.n.*; hoofdtooi *n.* **header,** *n.* duikeling *n.*, buiteling *n.n.* **head-hunter,** *n.* koppensneller *n.* **headiness,** *n.* hoofdigheid *n.*; koppigheid *n.* **heading,** *n.* opschrift *n.n.*, titel *n.*, kop *n.* **headland,** *n.* voorgebergte *n.n.*, kaap *n.* **headless,** *a.* zonder hoofd *n.n.* **headlight,** *n.* koplicht *n.n.* **headlong,** *a.* onstuimig; onbezonnen. ¶ *adv.* onstuimig: hals *n.* over kop *n.* **headmaster,** *n.* hoofdonderwijzer *n.*; directeur *n.*; rector *n.* **headmistress,** *n.* hoofdonderwijzeres *n.*; directrice *n.* **headquarters,** *pl.n.* hoofdkwartier *n.n.*; rectoraat *n.n.* **headship,** *n.* directeurschap *n.n.*; rectoraat *n.n.* **headstrong,** *a.* koppig. **headway,** *n.* vooruitgang *n.* *to make ~,* opschieten *str.* **heady,** *a.* hoofdig, koppig.

heal, *v.t.* helen, genezen *str.*, gezond maken. ¶ *v.i.* helen, genezen *str.*, gezond worden *str. to ~ up,* dichtgroeien. **healer,** *n.* heler *n.* **health,** *n.* gezondheid *n.* *~ resort,* gezondheidsoord *n.n.* **healthiness,** *n.* gezondheid *n.* **healthy,** *a.*, *~ily, adv.* gezond.

heap, *n.* hoop *n.*; menigte *n.*, massa *n.* ¶ *v.t.* ophopen. *to ~ up,* opstapelen, opeenhopen; *to ~ with,* overladen met.

hear, *v.t.* horen; verhoren. *to ~ from,* horen van; *to ~ of,* horen van (*or* over). **hearer,** *n.* toehoorder *n.* **hearing,** *n.* gehoor *n.n.*; verhoor *n.n. in his ~,* zodat hij het horen kon; *within ~,* op gehoorsafstand *n.*

hearken, *v.i.* luisteren. *to ~ to,* luisteren naar.

hearsay, *n. by* (or *from* or *on*) *~,* van horen zeggen *n.n.*

hearse, *n.* lijkwagen *n.*

heart, *n.* hart *n.n.*; moed *n.*; binnenste *n.n. ~(s),* harten (*cards*); *at ~,* in de grond; *by ~,* van buiten; *out of ~,* moedeloos; *to take ~,* moed *n.* scheppen *str.* **heartbreaking,** *a.* hartverscheurend. **heartburn,** *n.* zuur *n.n.* **heartburning,** *n.* ergernis *n.*; afgunst *n.* **hearten,** *v.t.* aanmoedigen, bemoedigen. **heartfelt,** *a.* oprecht, innig.

hearth, *n.* haard *n.*; haardstede *n.* **hearthrug,** *n.* karpetje *n.n.*, haardkleedje *n.n.*

heartiness, *n.* hartelijkheid *n.*, animo *n.* or *n.n.* **heartless,** *a.*, *~ly, adv.* harteloos; lafhartig. **heartrending,** *a.* hartverscheurend. **heartsease,** *n.* (driekleurig) viooltje *n.n.* **heart-whole,** *a.* gezond van harte. **hearty,** *a.*, *~ily, adv.* hartelijk; hartig.

heat, *n.* hitte *n.*, warmte *n.*; vuur *n.n.*, gloed *n.*; loop *n.* (*sport*). *on ~,* loops. ¶ *v.t.* verhitten; verwarmen. **heated,** *a.*, *~ly, adv.* driftig; opgewonden. **heater,** *n.* verwarmingstoestel *n.n.*

heath, *n.* hei(de) *n.* **heathen,** *n.* heiden *n.* ¶ *a.* heidens. **heathenish,** *a.* heidens. **heather,** *n.* heide(plant) *n.*

heave, *v.t.* oplichten; slaken. *to ~ down,* neerhalen; *to ~ overboard,* overboord werpen *str.*; *to ~ to,* bijdraaien. ¶ *v.i.* deinen; op en neer gaan *irr.*; kokhalzen.

heaven, *n.* hemel *n.*; lucht *n.* **heavenly,** *a. & adv.* hemels.

---

heaviness, *n.* zwaarte *n.*; zwaarheid *n.*; zwaarmoedigheid *n.* **heavy,** *a.*, *~ily, adv.* zwaar; gedrukt; sloom, traag.

Hebrew, *a.* Hebreeuws. ¶ *N.* Hebreeër *N.*

hecatomb, *n.* hecatombe *n.*

heckle, *v.t.* hekelen.

hectic, *a.*, *~ally, adv.* koortsig.

hector, *v.t.* overdonderen; koejeneren.

hedge, *n.* haag *n.*, heg *n.* ¶ *v.t.* omheinen. ¶ *v.i.* een ontwijkend antwoord *n.n.* geven *str.* **hedgehog,** *n.* egel *n.* **hedger,** *n.* heggemaker *n.*; haagsnoeier *n.* **hedgerow,** *n.* haag *n.*

heed, *n.* behoedzaamheid *n.*, omzichtigheid *n.* *to take ~,* oppassen; *to pay ~ to,* acht slaan *irr.* op. **heedful,** *a.*, *~ly, adv.* behoedzaam; opmerkzaam. **heedless,** *a.*, *~ly, adv.* achteloos; onverschillig.

heel, *n.* hiel *n.*; hak *n.* *to be down at ~,* er armoedig uitzien *irr.*; *to lay by the ~s,* gevangen zetten; *to take to one's ~s,* het op een lopen setten. ¶ *v.i. to ~ over,* overhellen. ¶ *v.t.* een hak *n.* zetten aan.

hefty, *a.* zwaar.

hegemony, *n.* hegemonie *n.*

heifer, *n.* vaars *n.*

heigh-ho, *int.* och! ach!

height, *n.* hoogte *n.*; toppunt *n.n.* **heighten,** *v.t.* verhogen.

heinous, *a.* gruwelijk.

heir, *n.* erfgenaam *n.* *~ apparent,* rechtmatige troonopvolger *n.*; *~ presumptive,* vermoedelijke erfgenaam. **heiress,** *n.* erfgename *n.* **heirless,** *a.* zonder erfgenaam *n.* **heirloom,** *n.* erfstuk *n.n.*

heliograph, *n.* heliograaf *n.* **heliogravure,** *n.* heliogravure *n.* **heliotrope.** *n.* heliotroop *n.*

helium, *n.* helium *n.n.*

hell, *n.* hel *n.* **Hellene,** *N.* Helleen *N.* **Hellenic,** *a.* Helleens. **hellish,** *a.*, *~ly, adv.* hels.

helm, *n.* helmstok *n.*; roer *n.n.*

helmet, *n.* helm *n.*

helmsman, *n.* roerganger *n.*

helot, *n.* heloot *n.*, slaaf *n.*

help, *v.t.* helpen *str.*; bijstaan *irr.*; bedienen. *I cannot ~ it,* ik kan er niets aan doen *irr.* ¶ *n.* hulp *n.*; bijstand *n.*; helper *n.*; helpster *n.* **helper,** *n.* helper *n.* (*male*); helpster *n.* (*female*). **helpful,** *a.* hulpvaardig; behulpzaam. **helpless,** *a.*, *~ly, adv.* hulpeloos. **helpmate,** *n.* echtgenoot *n.* (*male*); echtgenote *n.* (*female*).

helter-skelter, *adv.* holderdebolder.

hem, *v.t.* zomen; hummen. ¶ *n.* zoom *n.*

hemisphere, *n.* halfrond *n.n.*

hemlock, *n.* dolle kervel *n.*

hemp, *n.* hennep *n.* **hempen,** *a.* hennepen, van hennep *n.*

hemstitch, *v.t.* met à jour steek *n.* zomen. ¶ *n.* zoomsteek *n.*; à jour steek *n.*

hen, *n.* hen *n.*, kip *n.*; wijfje *n.n.* **henbane,** *n.* bilzenkruid *n.n.*

hence, *adv.* hiervandaan; daarvandaan, daarom. **henceforth.** *adv.* voortaan.
henchman, *n.* handlanger *n.*
hencoop, *n.* hoenderhok *n.n.* **henpecked,** *a.* onder de pantoffel. **henroost,** *n.* hoenderrek *n.n.*
her, *pron.* haar, ze. ¶ *poss.a.* haar.
herald, *n.* heraut *n.;* voorloper *n.* **heraldic,** *a.* heraldisch. **heraldry,** *n.* heraldiek *n.*
herb, *n.* kruid *n.n.* **herbaceous,** *a.* kruidachtig, kruid . . . **herbage,** *n.* groen *n.n.* **herbal,** *a.* kruiden-. ¶ *n.* herbarium *n.n.* **herbalist,** *n.* kruidenkenner *n.;* drogist *n.*
herbivorous, *a.* plantenetend.
Herculean, *a.* herculisch.
herd, *n.* kudde *n.;* hoeder *n.,* herder *n.* ¶ *v.i.* in kudden leven; samenscholen. ¶ *v.t.* samendrijven *str.* **herdsman,** *n.* veehoeder *n.*
here, *adv.* hier. ~ *and now,* onmiddelijk; *it's neither* ~ *nor there,* dat heeft er niets mee te maken. **hereafter,** *adv.* hierna, voortaan. ¶ *n.* hiernamaals *n.n.* **hereby,** *adv.* hierbij; hierdoor.
hereditary, *a.* erfelijk; erf . . . **heredity,** *n.* erfelijkheid *n.;* overerving *n.*
herein, *adv.* hierin. **hereof,** *adv.* hiervan, hierover. **hereon,** *adv.* hierop.
heresy, *n.* ketterij *n.* **heretic,** *n.* ketter *n.* **heretical,** *a.,* ~ly, *adv.* ketters.
heretofore, *adv.* hiertevoren, voorheen. **hereupon,** *adv.* hierop. **herewith,** *adv.* hiermee, hierbij, bij deze.
heritage, *n.* erfenis *n.;* erfdeel *n.n.*
hermaphrodite, *n.* hermaphrodiet *n.* **hermaphroditic,** *a.* tweeslachtig.
hermetic, *a.,* ~ally, *adv.* hermetisch; luchtdicht.
hermit, *n.* kluizenaar *n.* **hermitage,** *n.* kluis *n.*
hernia, *n.* breuk *n.*
hero, *n.* held *n.* **heroic,** *a.,* ~ally, *adv.* heldhaftig; helden . . . **heroine,** *n.* heldin *n* **heroism,** *n.* heldhaftigheid *n.;* heldenmoed *n.*
heron, *n.* reiger *n.* **heronry,** *n.* reigerkolonie *n.*
hero-worship, *n.* heldenverering *n.*
herring, *n.* haring *n.* red ~, gerookte bokking; *(fig.)* iets om de aandacht af te leiden. **herring bone,** *n.* haringgraat *n.*
hers, *pron.* de hare, het hare; van haar.
herself, *pron.* zijzelf; haarzelf; zichzelf, zich.
hesitate, *v.i.* aarzelen; weifelen. **hesitation,** *n.* aarzeling *n.;* weifeling *n.*
heterodox, *a.* andersdenkend, onrechtzinnig. **heterodoxy,** *n.* andersdenkendheid *n.,* onrechtzinnigheid *n.* **heterogenous,** *a.* heterogeen.
hew, *v.t.* houwen *str.,* hakken.
hexagon, *n.* zeshoek *n.* **hexagonal,** *a.* zeshoekig. **hexameter,** *n.* hexameter *n.,* zesvoet *n.*
hey, *int.* hei!

heyday, *n.* bloeitijd *n.,* toppunt *n.n.*
hiatus, *n.* hiaat *n.n.;* gaping *n.,* leemte *n.*
hibernate, *v.i.* overwinteren; de winterslaap houden *irr.*
hiccough, *v.i.,* **hiccup,** *v.i.* hikken, de hik hebben. ¶ *n.* hik *n.*
hickory, *n.* Noord-Amerikaanse walnoot *n.*
hide, *n.* huid *n.,* vel *n.n.* *to play* ~ *and seek* verstoppertje *n.n.* spelen. ¶ *v.t.* verbergen *str.;* verstoppen. *to* ~ *from,* verbergen voor. ¶ *v.i.* zich verbergen *str.* **hidebound,** *a.* bekrompen.
hideous, *a.,* ~ly, *adv.* afzichtelijk, afschuwelijk.
hiding, *n.* pak slaag *n.n.* **hiding-place,** *n.* schuilplaats *n.*
hierarchy, *n.* hiërarchie *n.;* priesterregering *n.* **hierarchic,** *a.* hiërarchisch.
hieroglyph. *n.* hiëroglief *n.* **hieroglyphic,** *a.* hiëroglyphisch.
higgledy-piggledy, *a.* overhoop, onderlsteboven.
high, *a.* hoog; verheven; lang. ~ *and mighty,* aanmatigend; ~ *life,* de grote wereld. **High Church,** *N.* ritualistisch gezinde richting *n.* van de Engelse staatskerk. **high-flown,** *a.* hoogdravend. **highland,** *n.* hoogland *n.n.* ¶ *a.* hooglands. **highly,** *adv.* hoogst, buitengewoon. **highness,** *n.* hoogheid *n.,* verhevenheid *n.* **highroad,** *n.* highway, *n.* grote weg *n.,* straatweg *n.* **highwayman,** *n.* struikrover *n.*
hilarious, *a.* vrolijk; uitgelaten. **hilarity,** *n.* vrolijkheid *n.,* hilariteit *n.*
hill, *n.* heuvel *n.;* berg *n.* **hillock,** *n.* heuvel *n.,* heuveltje *n.n.;* hoop *n.* **hilly,** *a.* heuvelachtig; bergachtig.
hilt, *n.* gevest *n.n.,* hecht *n.n.,* heft *n.n.*
him, *pron.* hem. **himself,** *pron.* hemzelf, zichzelf; zich.
hind, *n.* hinde *n.* ¶ *a.* achter . . . **hinder,** *a.* achterste.
hinder, *v.t.* belemmeren, (ver)hinderen, beletten.
hindermost, *a.* achterste. **hind-quarters,** *pl.n.* achterdeel *n.n.,* achterpoten *pl.n.*
hindrance, *n.* belemmering *n.,* hindernis *n.,* beletsel *n.n.*
hinge, *n.* scharnier *n.n.;* spil *n.;* hengsel *n.n.* ¶ *v.t.* van scharnieren voorzien *irr.* ¶ *v.i. to* ~ *on,* draaien om.
hint, *n.* aanwijzing *n.,* wenk *n.;* toespeling *n.* ¶ *v.t.* een wenk geven *str. to* ~ *at,* zinspelen op; toespelingen maken op.
hip, *n.* heup *n.;* rozebottel *n.* ¶ *int.* ~, ~, *hurray!,* hiep! hiep! hoera! **hip-bath,** *n.* zitbad *n.n.*
hippodrome, *n.* renbaan *n.*
hippopotamus, *n.* nijlpaard *n.n.*
hire, *n.* huur *n.;* loon *n.n.* *on* ~, te huur. ¶ *v.t.* huren; in dienst nemen *str.* **hireling,** *n.* huurling *n.*
hirsute, *a.* behaard; ruig.
his, *pron.* zijn; de zijne, het zijne, van hem.

hispid, *a.* borstelig.

hiss, *v.i.* sissen. ¶ *v.t.* uitfluiten *str.*

historian, *n.* historicus *n.*, geschiedschrijver *n.* **historical**, *a.*, ~ly, *adv.* historisch, geschiedkundig. **historiographer**, *n.* geschiedschrijver *n.* **history**, *n.* geschiedenis *n.*, historie *n.*; verhaal *n.n.*

histrionic, *a.* dramatisch.

hit, *v.t.* slaan *irr.*; treffen *str.*, raken. *to* ~ *it off with*, goed overweg kunnen met. ¶ *v.i. to* ~ *upon*, vinden *str.*, treffen *str.* · ¶ *n.* stoot *n.*, slag *n.*; succesnummer *n.n.*

hitch, *v.i.* horten, blijven *str.* steken. ¶ *v.t.* aanhaken, vastmaken. ¶ *n.* hapering *n.*

hither, *adv.* herwaarts, hierheen. ~ *and thither*, her- en derwaarts. **hitherto**, *adv.* tot nog toe, tot dusver.

hive, *n.* (bijen)korf *n.*; zwerm *n.* bijen. ¶ *v.t.* korven. ¶ *v.i. to* ~ *off*, wegzwermen.

hoar, *a.* grijs, grauw.

hoard, *n.* (verborgen) schat *n.*; (verborgen) voorraad *n.* ¶ *v.t.* opsparen; hamsteren. **hoarding**, *n.* schutting *n.*

hoar-frost, *n.* rijp *n.*, rijm *n.* **hoariness**, *n.* grijsheid *n.*

hoarse, *a.*, ~ly, *adv.* schor, hees. **hoarseness**, *n.* schorheid *n.*, heesheid *n.*

hoary, *a.* grijs (van ouderdom).

hoax, *v.t.* voor de gek houden *irr.* ¶ *n.* beetnemerij *n.*

hob, *n.* zijplaatje *n.n.* aan de haard; pin *n.*

hobble, *v.i.* hobbelen, strompelen. ¶ *v.t.* kluisteren. **hobbledehoy**, *n.* aankomende jongen *n.*

hobby, *n.* stokpaardje *n.n.*; liefhebberij *n.* **hobby-horse**, *n.* stokpaardje *n.n.*

hobgloblin, *n.* kabouter *n.*

hobnail, *n.* zoolspijker *n.*

hobnob, *v.i.* vertrouwelijk omgaan *irr.*

hobo, *n.* landloper *n.*

hock, *n.* Rijnwijn *n.*; hakpees *n.* ¶ *v.t.* de hakpees doorsnijden *str.*

hockey, *n.* hockey *n.n.*

hocus-pocus, *n.* hocus-pocus *n.*

hod, *n.* trog *n.*

hodge-podge, *n.* hutspot *n.*, allegaartje *n.n.*

hodman, *n.* opperman *n.*

hoe, *n.* schoffel *n.* ¶ *v.t.* schoffelen.

hog, *n.* zwijn *n.* ¶ *v.t.* hebzuchtig te pakken krijgen *str.* **hoggish**, *a.*, ~ly, *adv.* zwijnachtig; gulzig. **hogshead**, *n.* okshoofd *n.n.*

hoist, *n.* hijstoestel *n.n.*; kraan *n.* ¶ *v.t.* hijsen *str.*

hoity-toity, *a. to be* ~, uit de hoogte doen *irr.*, aanstellerig zijn.

hold, *v.t.* houden *irr*; behouden *irr*; vasthouden *irr*; tegenhouden *irr*; inhouden *irr.*, bevatten; boeien; bewaren; bekleden; vieren. ¶ *v.i.* het uithouden *irr.*; niet breken *str.*; blijven *str.* duren; van kracht zijn. *to* ~ *forth*, uitweiden; *to* ~ *good*, nog steeds van toepassing *n.* zijn; *to* ~ *with*, goedkeuren. ¶ *n.* vat *n.*, greep *n.*, houvast *n.n.*; invloed *n.*, macht *n.*;

(scheeps)ruim *n.n.* **hold-all**, *n.* nécessaire *n.* **holder**, *n.* houder *n.*; bezitter *n.* **holding**, *n.* bezit *n.n.*; aandeel *n.n.*; houvast *n.n.*; pachthoeve *n.*

hole, *n.* gat *n.n.*; moeilijkheid *n.* ¶ *v.t.* een gat maken in.

holiday, *n.* vacantiedag *n.*; feestdag *n. on* ~, met vacantie *n.*; ~s, vacantie *n.*

holiness, *n.* heiligheid *n.*

Hollands, *N.* linnen *n.n.*; Schiedammer *n.*

hollow, *a.* hol; vals. ¶ *n.* holte *n.*; dal *n.n.* ¶ *v.t.* uithollen. **hollowness**, *n.* holheid *n.*; valsheid *n.*

holly, *n.* hulst *n.* **hollyhock**, *n.* stokroos *n.*

holm, *n.* steeneik *n.*; waard *n.*

holocaust, *n.* brandoffer *n.n.*; slachting *n.*

holograph, *n.* eigenhandig geschreven (document *n.n.*).

holster, *n.* holster *n.*

holy, *a.*, ~ily, *adv.* heilig. ~ *water*, wijwater *n.n.*; *H* ~ *Week*, Passieweek *N.*

homage, *n.* hulde *n. to do* ~, huldigen.

home, *n.* huis *n.n.*, tehuis *n.n.*, thuis *n.n.*; woning *n.*, woonstee *n.*; vaderland *n.n. at* ~, thuis. ¶ *a.* binnenlands. *H* ~ *Office*, Ministerie . van Binnenlandse Zaken; ~ *rule*, autonomie *n.* ¶ *adv.* naar huis; raak. *to drive* ~, vastslaan *irr.*; kracht bijzetten. **home-bred**, *a.* inheems. **homeless**, *a.* dakloos. **homeliness**, *n.* huiselijkheid *n.* **homely**, *a.* huiselijk; eenvoudig. **homesick**, *a. to be* ~, heimwee *n.n.* hebben. **homesickness**, *n.* heimwee *n.n.* **homestead**, *n.* woonstee *n.* **homeward(s)**, *a. & adv.* huiswaarts. ~ *bound*, op de thuisreis.

homicidal, *a.* moorddadig. **homicide**, *n.* manslag *n.*; moordenaar *n.*

homily, *n.* zedepreek *n.*; kanselrede *n.*

homing pigeon, *n.* postduif *n.*

hominy, *n.* grof gemalen maïs *n.*; maïspap *n.*

homœopathic, *a.* homeopathisch. **homœopathy**, *n.* homeopathie *n.*

homogeneous, *a.* gelijksoortig.

homogenous, *a.* homogeen.

hone, *n.* wetsteen *n.* ¶ *v.t.* aanzetten.

honest, *a.*, ~ly, *adv.* eerlijk; oprecht. **honesty**, *n.* eerlijkheid *n.*; Judaspenning *n.*

honey, *n.* honing *n.*, honig *n.* **honeycomb**, *n.* honingraat *n.* **honeycombed**, *a.* vol gangen *pl.n.* en holen *pl.n.n.* **honeyed**, *a.* (honing) zoet, lieflijk. **honeymoon**, *n.* wittebroodsweken *pl.n.* **honeysuckle**, *n.* kamperfoelie *n.*

honorarium, *n.* honorarium *n.n.* **honorary**, *a.* honorair; ere . . .

honour, *n.* eer *n.*; aanzien *n.n. Your H* ~, *title not translated; in writing:* Edelachtbare Heer. **honourable**, *a.*, ~bly, *adv.* eervol; eerzaam; eerbaar. *the H* ~, *the Right H* ~, *titles not translated.*

hood, *n.* kap *n.*; huif *n.* ¶ *v.t.* met een kap bedekken. ~*ed crow*, bonte kraai *n.* **hoodwink**, *v.t.* misleiden, verschalken.

hoof, *n.* hoef *n.*
hook, *n.* haak *n.*; sikkel *n.* *by* ~ *or by crook,* hoe dan ook. ¶ *v.t.* aanhaken.
hooligan, *n.* straatschender *n.*
hoop, *n.* hoepel *n.*; beugel *n.* ¶ *v.t.* met hoepels beslaan *irr.* ¶ *v.i.* roepen *str.* **hooper,** *n.* kuiper *n.* **hooping-cough,** *n.* kinkhoest *n.*
hoot, *v.i.* toeteren; jouwen. ¶ *n.* stoot *n.*; gejouw *n.n.* ~s *of laughter,* uitbundig gelach *n.n.* **hooter,** *n.* toeter *n.*; hoorn *n.*
hop, *v.i.* huppelen; hinken. ~ *it!*, smeer 'm! ¶ *n.* sprongetje *n.n.*; hop *n.*
hope, *n.* hoop *n.* ¶ *v.t.* hopen. **hopeful,** *a.,* ~ly, *adv.* hoopvol; veelbelovend. **hopeless,** *a.,* ~ly, *adv.* hopeloos.
hopper, *n.* hopper *n.*; zaadbak *n.*; modderschuit *n.*
horde, *n.* horde *n.*
horizon, *n.* horizon *n.* **horizontal,** *a.,* ~ly, *adv.* horizontaal.
hormone, *n.* hormoon *n.*
horn, *n.* hoorn *n.,* horen *n.*; punt *n.*; hoorn *n.n.* (*material*). ¶ *a.* hoornen. **hornbeam,** *n.* haagbeuk *n.* **hornblende,** *n.* hoornblende *n.* **hornbook,** *n.* A.B.C. boekje *n.n.* **horned,** *a.* gehoornd; hoorn . . .
hornet, *n.* horzel *n.*
hornpipe, *n.* horlepijp *n.* **horny,** *a.* hoornachtig.
horoscope, *n.* horoscoop *n.*
horrible, *a.,* ~bly, *adv.* verschrikkelijk, vreselijk; akelig.
horrid, *a.,* ~ly, *adv.* afschuwelijk, ontzettend.
horrify, *v.t.* met afschuw vervullen. **horror,** *n.* afschrik *n.,* afschuw *n.,* afgrijzen *n.n,* ontzetting *n.*
horse, *n.* paard *n.n.*; paardevolk *n.n.*; schraag *n.,* ezel *n.* **horseback,** *n.* *on* ~, te paard. **horsebox,** *n.* boks *n.* **horsebreaker,** *n.* pikeur *n.,* dresseerder *n.* **horse-chestnut,** *n.* paardekastanje *n.* **horse-coper,** *n.* paardenkoper *n.* **horse-fly,** *n.* paardevlieg *n.* **Horse Guards,** *pl.N.* bereden lijfwacht *n.* **horse-laugh,** *n.* luide lach *n.* **horseman,** *n.* ruiter *n.,* paardrijder *n.* **horsemanship,** *n.* rijkunst *n.* **horseplay,** *n.* ruw spel *n.n.* **horsepond,** *n.* paardenwed *n.n.* **horsepower,** *n.* paardekracht *n.* **horserace,** *n.* wedren *n.* **horseradish,** *n.* ramenas *n.* **horseshoe,** *n.* hoefijzer *n.n.* **horsewoman,** *n.* paardrijdster *n.*
horticultural, *a.* tuinbouwkundig, tuinbouw . . . **horticulture,** *n.* tuinbouw *n.*
hose, *n.* kous *n.*; slang *n.* ~*pipe,* brandslang *n.* **hosier,** *n.* handelaar *n.* in gebreide en wollen goederen *pl.n.n.* **hosiery,** *n.* gebreide en wollen goederen *pl.n.n.*
hospitable, *a.,* ~bly, *adv.* herbergzaam, gastvrij.
hospital, *n.* ziekenhuis *n.n.*; hospitaal *n.n.*
hospitality, *n.* gastvrijheid *n.*
host, *n.* gastheer *n.*; waard *n.*; leger *n.n.,* heirschaar *n.*

hostage, *n.* gijzelaar *n.*
hostel, *n.* tehuis *n.n.,* kosthuis *n.n.* **hostelry,** *n.* herberg *n.*
hostess, *n.* gastvrouw *n.*
hostile, *a.,* ~ly, *adv.* vijandig, vijandelijk. **hostility,** *n.* vijandigheid *n.,* vijandelijkheid *n.*
hot, *a.,* ~ly, *adv.* warm; heet; gepeperd, pikant. **hotbed,** *n.* broeibak *n.*; (*fig.*) broeinest *n.n.* **hot-blooded,** *a.* heetbloedig.
hotchpotch, *n.* hutspot *n.*; mengelmoes *n.n.*
hotel, *n.* hotel *n.n.* ~ *and travelling expenses,* reis- en verblijfkosten *pl.n.*
hothouse, *n.* broeikast *n.* **hotpot,** *n.* (soort) jachtschotel *n.* **hot-press,** *n.* gloeipers *n.* ¶ *v.t.* heet glanzen, heet persen.
hough, *n.* hakpees *n.* ¶ *v.t.* verlammen, de hakpees doorsnijden *str.*
hound, *n.* hond *n.,* jachthond *n.* ¶ *v.t.* achtervolgen.
hour, *n.* uur *n.n.* **hourglass,** *n.* zandloper *n.* **hour-hand,** *n.* uurwijzer *n.* **hourly,** *a.* (van) ieder uur *n.n.* ¶ *adv.* om het uur.
house, *n.* huis *n.n.*; herberg *n.*; gehoor *n.n.*; Kamer *N.* ~ *full,* uitverkocht. ¶ *v.t.* onder dak brengen *irr.,* herbergen. **housebreaker,** *n.* inbreker *n.*; sloper *n.* **household,** *n.* huishouding *n.*; huisgezin *n.n.* **householder,** *n.* hoofd *n.n.* van een gezin *n.n.* **housekeeper,** *n.* huishoudster *n.* **housemaid,** *n.* tweede meid *n.* **housemaster,** *n.* intern leraar *n.* **housewarming,** *n.* feestje *n.n.* bij het betrekken van een nieuwe woning *n.* **housewife,** *n.* huisvrouw *n.*; naainécessaire *n.* **housewifery,** *n.* huishouding *n.*; huishoudelijkheid *n.* **housework,** *n.* huiswerk *n.n.* **housing,** *n.* huisvesting *n.*; benedenmast *n.*; dekkleed *n.n.*
hovel, *n.* krot *n.n.*; hut *n.*
hover, *v.i.* zweven, blijven *str.* hangen.
how, *adv.* hoe. ~ *about* . . .? hoe staat het met . . .? ¶ **however,** *adv.* echter, evenwel; niettemin. ¶ *c.* hoe . . . ook, hoe dan ook.
howitzer, *n.* houwitser *n.*
howl, *v.i.* huilen, schreeuwen, brullen; janken. ¶ *n.* gehuil *n.n.,* geschreeuw *n.n.,* gejank *n.n.* **howler,** *n.* bok *n.,* stommiteit *n.*
howsoever, *adv.* hoe . . . ook.
hoy, *n.* (soort) lichter *n.*
hoyden, *n.* robbedoes *n.,* wildzang *n.*
hub, *n.* naaf *n.*; (*fig.*) middelpunt *n.n.,* spil *n.*
hubbub, *n.* rumoer *n.n.,* verwarring *n.*
hub-cap, *n.* naafdop *n.*
huckaback, *n.* grof linnen *n.n.,* handdoekengoed *n.n.*
huckster, *n.* venter *n.,* marskramer *n.*
huddle, *v.t.* opeendringen *str.* ¶ *v.i.* *to* ~ *together,* bij elkaar kruipen *str.* ¶ *n.* gedrang *n.n.* *to go into a* ~, de koppen *n.* samen steken *str.*
hue, *n.* tint *n.,* schakering *n.* *to raise a* ~ *and cry,* luid alarm roepen; de achtervolging beginnen *str.*

huff, *n.* geraaktheid *n. in a ~*, geraakt. ¶ *v.t.* in z'n wiek *n.* schieten *str.*; blazen *str. (draughts).* ¶ *v.i. to feel ~ed, to be ~ed*, geraakt zijn. **huffy**, *a.* geraakt, gepiqueerd.

hug, *v.t.* tegen zich aandrukken, omhelzen; knuffelen. ¶ *n.* liefkozende druk *n.*

huge, *a.*, *~ly*, *adv.* reusachtig, geweldig, kolossaal.

hugger-mugger, *a.* geheel door · elkaar, verward.

hulk *n.* afgetakeld schip *n.n.*

hull, *n.* schil *n.*, dop *n.*, schaal *n.*; romp *n.* ¶ *v.t.* pellen.

hullaballoo, *n.* lawaai *n.n.*, herrie *n.*

hullo. *int.* hallo!

hum, *n.* gesnor *n.n.*, geronk *n.n.*, gegons *n.n.*, gebrom *n.n.* ¶ *v.t. & v.i.* snorren, ronken, gonzen, brommen; neuriën.

human, *a.*, *~ly*, *adv.* menselijk, mensen . . . **humane**, *a.*, *~ly*, *adv.* menslievend, humaan. **humanity**, *n.* mensheid *n.*; menselijkheid *n*; menslievendheid *n.* **humanitarian**, *a.* menslievend.

humble, *a.*, *~bly*, *adv.* nederig, onderdanig; bescheiden. **humble-bee**, *n.* hommel *n.* **humbleness**, *n.* nederigheid *n.*

humbug, *n.* (soort) pepermuntbal *n.*; (*fig.*) lak *n.*, kool *n.*, larie *n.*

humdrum, *a.* eentonig, saai, alledaags.

humid, *a.* vochtig. **humidity**, *n.* vocht *n.n.*; vochtigheid *n.*

humiliate, *v.t.* vernederen; verootmoedigen. **humiliation**, *n.* vernedering *n.*; verootmoediging *n.* **humility**, *n.* nederigheid *n.*; ootmoed *n.*

humming bird, *n.* kolibri *n.* **humming-top**, *n.* bromtol *n.*

humorist, *n.* humorist *n.* **humorous**, *a.*, *~ly*, *adv.* geestig, humoristisch. **humour**, *n.* vocht *n.n.*; humeur *n.n.*; luim *n.*, stemming *n. in good ~*, goed geluimd; *out of ~*, slecht gehumeurd. ¶ *v.t.* tevreden stellen, z'n zin *n.* geven *str.*

hump, *n.* bult *n.*, bochel *n.*; uitsteeksel *n.n.* ¶ *v.t.* krommen. **humpback**, *n.* bultenaar *n.*, gebochelde *n.* **humpty-dumpty**, *n.* kleine dikzak *n.*

hunch, *n.* bult *n.*, bochel *n.*; gevoel *n.n.*, ingeving *n.* ¶ *v.t.* krommen. **hunchback**, *n.* bultenaar *n.*, gebochelde *n.* **hunch-backed**, *a.* gebocheld.

hundred, *num.* honderd. **hundredth**, *a.* honderdste. **hundredweight**, *n.* centenaar (112 Engelse ponden).

Hungarian, *a.* Hongaar *N.* (*male*); Hongaarse *N.* (*female*). **Hungary**, *N.* Hongarije *n.N.*

hunger, *n.* honger *n.* ¶ *v.i. to ~ after* (or *for*), hongeren naar. **hungry**, *a.*, *~ily*, *adv.* hongerig.

hunk, *n.* homp *n.*, brok *n.*

hunt, *n.* jacht *n.*; gezelschap *n.n.* jagers jachtgebied *n.n.* ¶ *v.t.* jagen. ¶ *v.i.* jagen. *to ~ for*, jacht maken op. **hunter**, *n.* jager *n.*; jachtpaard *n.n.* **hunting**, *n.* jacht

n., jagen *n.n.* **hunting-box**, *n.* jachthuis *n.n.* **huntress**, *n.* jagerin *n.* **huntsman**, *n.* jager *n.*; jachtknecht *n.*

hurdle, *n.* horde *n.*; hek *n.n.*

hurdy-gurdy, *n.* lier *n.*, draaiorgeltje *n.n.*

hurl, *v.t.* slingeren, werpen *str.*

hurly-burly, *n.* opschudding *n.*, verwarring *n.*

hurrah, *int.*, **hurray**, *int.* hoera. ¶ *v.i.* hoera roepen *str.*

hurricane, *n.* orkaan *n. ~ lamp*, stormlamp *n.*

hurry, *v.i.* zich haasten. *to ~ along*, zich voorthaasten. ¶ *v.t.* haasten, verhaasten. ¶ *n.* haast *n.* **hurry-scurry**, *adv.* holderdebolder, hals *n.* over kop *n.*

hurt, *v.i.* pijn doen *irr.* ¶ *v.t.* pijn doen *irr.*; bezeren; kwetsen; benadelen. ¶ *n.* letsel *n.n.*, wond *n.*; nadeel *n.n.*; schade *n.* **hurtful**, *a.*, *~ly*, *adv.* nadelig, schadelijk.

hurtle, *v.t.* slingeren. ¶ *v.i.* vliegen *str.*

husband, *n.* man *n.*, echtgenoot *n.* ¶ *v.t.* ontzien *irr.*, zuinig omspringen *str.* met. **husbandman**, *n.* landman *n.* **husbandry**, *n.* landbouw *n.*; zuinig beheer *n.n.*

hush, *n.* diepe stilte *n.*, zwijgen *n.n.* ¶ *v.t.* tot zwijgen brengen *irr.*, sussen. *to ~ up*, in de doofpot stoppen. ¶ *int.* still, st! **hushmoney**, *n.* steekpenning *n.*

husk, *n.* dop *n.*, schil *n. ~s*, doppen, schillen, kaf *n.n.* ¶ *v.t.* pellen, doppen, schillen. **husky**, *a.* vol schillen; schor, hees. ¶ *n.* Eskimohond *n.* **huskily**, *adv.* schor, hees.

hussar, *n.* huzaar *n.*

hussy, *n.* deern *n.*; ondeugd *n.*

hustings, *pl.n.* tribune *n.* van candidaat *n.*

hustle, *v.t.* voortdringen *str.*, aansporen. ¶ *v.i.* zich haasten, jachten. ¶ *n.* gejacht *n.n.*

hut, *n.* hut *n.*

hutch, *n.* hok *n.n.*

hyacinth, *n.* hyacint *n.*

hybrid, *n.* bastaard *n.*

hydrangea, *n.* hortensia *n.*

hydrant, *n.* hydrant *n.*, standpijp *n.*

hydraulic, *a.* hydraulisch.

hydrogen, *n.* waterstof *n.* **hydrography**, *n.* hydrographie *n.* **hydropathic**, *a.* hydropathisch. **hydropathy**, *n.* hydropathie *n.*, watergeneeskunde *n.* **hydrophobia**, *n.* watervrees *n.*, hondsdolheid *n.* **hydroplane**, *n.* watervliegtuig *n.n.*

hyena, *n.* hyena *n.*

hygiene, *n.* gezondheidsleer *n.*, hygiëne *n.* **hygienic**, *a.* hygiënisch.

hymen, *n.* maagdvlies *n.n.*

hymn, *n.* gezang *n.n.*; lofzang *n.* **hymnal**, *n.* gezangboek *n.n.*

hyperbole, *n.* hyperbool *n.* **hyperbolical**, *a.*, *~ly*, *adv.* hyperbolisch.

hypercritical, *a.*, *~ly*, *adv.* overcritisch.

hyphen, *n.* koppelteken *n.n.*, verbindingsstreepje *n.n.* **hyphenated**, *a.* door een koppelteken *n.n.* verbonden.

hypnosis, *n.* hypnose *n.* **hypnotic,** *a.* hypnotisch. **hypnotize,** *v.t.* hypnotiseren. **hypnotism,** *n.* hypnotisme *n.n.*
hypochondriac, *a.* zwaarmoedig.
hypocrisy, *n.* huichelarij *n.*, veinzerij *n.* **hypocrite,** *n.* huichelaar *n.*, veinzer *n.*, hypocriet *n.*
hypodermic, *a.* onderhuids.
hypothesis, *n.* hypothese *n.*, veronderstelling *n.* **hypothetical,** *a.* hypothetisch.
hyssop, *n.* hysop *n.*
hysteria, *n.* hysterie *n.* **hysterical,** *a.* hysterisch. **hysterics,** *n.* hysterie *n.*; zenuwaanval *n.*

I

I, *pron.* ik.
iambic, *a.* jambisch. ¶ *n.* jambe *n.*
ibex, *n.* steenbok *n.*
ibis, *n.* ibis *n.*
ice, *n.* ijs *n.n.* ¶ *v.t.* met ijs afkoelen; frapperen; met ijs bedekken, glaceren. **iceberg,** *n.* ijsberg *n.* **ice-bound,** *a.* ingevroren. **icebox,** *n.* ijskast *n.* **ice-house,** *n.* ijskelder *n.*, ijspakhuis *n.n.* **ice-breaker,** *n.* ijsbreker *n.* **ice-cream,** *n.* roomijs *n.n.* **ice-field,** *n.* ijsveld *n.n.* **Iceland,** *N.* IJsland *n.N.* **Icelandic,** *a.* IJslands.
ichneumon, *n.* pharaonsrat *n.*; sluipwesp *n.*
icicle, *n.* ijskegel *n.* **iciness,** *n.* ijskoude *n.*, ijzige kou *n.* **icing,** *n.* suikerglazuur *n.*
iconoclasm, *n.* beeldenstorm *n.* **iconoclast,** *n.* beeldstormer *n.*
icy, *a.*, ∼ily, *adv.* ijzig; ijskoud.
idea, *n.* idee *n.* or *n.n.*, gedachte *n.*; denkbeeld *n.n.*, begrip *n.n.*; opvatting *n.*; mening *n.*
ideal, *n.* ideaal *n.n.* ¶ *a.*, ∼ly, *adv.* ideaal. **idealism,** *n.* idealisme *n.n.* **idealist,** *n.* idealist *n.* **idealize,** *v.t.* idealiseren.
identical, *a.*, ∼ly, *adv.* identiek; dezelfde, hetzelfde. **identify,** *v.t.* identificeren; vereenzelvigen. **identity,** *n.* identiteit *n.*; individualiteit *n.*
ideology, *n.* ideologie *n.*
idiocy, *n.* idiootheid *n.*
idiom, *n.* idioom *n.n.*, taaleigen *n.n.* **idiomatic,** *a.* idiomatisch.
idiosyncracy, *n.* persoonlijke eigenaardigheid *n.*; persoonlijke gevoeligheid *n.* **idiosyncratic,** *a.* persoonlijk, eigenaardig.
idiot, *n.* idioot *n.* **idiotic,** *a.* idioot.
idle, *a.* nietsdoend, niet aan 't werk; lui; ongegrond; nutteloos. ¶ *v.i.* leeglopen *str.*, luieren. ¶ *v.t.* to ∼ away, verluieren. **idleness,** *n.* ledigheid *n.*, luiheid *n.*; nutteloosheid *n.* **idler,** *n.* leegloper *n.*, nietsdoener *n.*
idol, *n.* afgod *n.*; afgodsbeeld *n.n.* **idolater,** *n.* afgodendienaar *n.* **idolatrous,** *a.* afgodisch.

idolatry, *n.* afgodendienst *n.*; vergoding *n.* **idolize,** *v.t.* verafgoden.
idyll, *n.* idylle *n.* **idyllic,** *a.* idyllisch.
if, *c.* als, indien, ingeval, wanneer.
igloo, *n.* ijswoning *n.*
igneous, *a.* vurig; door vuur *n.n.* voortgebracht.
ignis fatuus, *n.* dwaallicht *n.n.*
ignite, *v.t.* aansteken *str.*, doen *irr.* ontbranden. ¶ *v.i.* vuur *n.n.* vatten, ontvlammen. **ignition,** *n.* ontbranding *n.*, ontsteking *n.*
ignoble, *a.*, ∼bly, *adv.* laag, verachtelijk.
ignominious, *a.*, ∼ly, *adv.* schandelijk; smadelijk. **ignominy,** *n.* schande *n.*, smaad *n.*
ignoramus, *n.* weetniet *n.*, domoor *n.* **ignorance,** *n.* onwetendheid *n.*, onkunde *n.* **ignorant,** *a.*, ∼ly, *adv.* onwetend; onkundig. **ignore,** *v.t.* niet weten *irr.*; niet willen *irr.* weten, negeren.
iguana, *n.* leguaán *n.*, kamhagedis *n.*
ilk, *pron.* elk. ¶ *n.* of that ∼, van die soort *n.*
ill, *a.* slecht; kwaad; ziek. to take it ∼, het kwalijk nemen. ¶ *adv.* slecht, kwaad; kwalijk. ¶ *n.* kwaad *n.n.* **ill-advised,** *a.* onberaden, onbezonnen. **ill-bred,** *a.* ongemanierd, onopgevoed.
illegal, *a.*, ∼ly, *adv.* onwettig, onrechtmatig. **illegality,** *n.* onwettigheid *n.*
illegibility, *n.* onleesbaarheid *n.* **illegible,** *a.*, ∼bly, *adv.* onleesbaar.
illegitimacy, *n.* onwettigheid *n.* **illegitimate,** *a.*, ∼ly, *adv.* onwettig; onecht.
ill-fated, *a.* ongelukkig; rampspoedig.
ill-feeling, *n.* kwaad bloed *n.n.*
illiberal, *a.*, ∼ly, *adv.* kleingeestig; niet royaal. **illiberality,** *n.* kleingeestigheid *n.*; karigheid *n.*
illicit, *a.* onwettig; ongeoorloofd.
illimitable, *a.*, ∼bly, *adv.* onbegrensd.
illiteracy, *n.* ongeletterdheid *n.* **illiterate,** *a.* ongeletterd. ¶ *n.* analphabeet *n.*
illnatured, *a.* boosaardig.
illness, *n.* ziekte *n.*
illogical, *a.*, ∼ly, *adv.* onlogisch.
ill-timed, *a.* ongelegen.
ill-treat, *v.t.* mishandelen.
illuminate, *v.t.* verlichten; illumineren; verluchten. **illumination,** *n.* verlichting *n.*; illuminatie *n.* **illumine,** *v.t.* verlichten, ophelderen.
illusion, *n.* illusie *n.*; hersenschim *n.* **illusive,** *a.*, **illusory,** *a.* denkbeeldig, illusoir.
illustrate, *v.t.* toelichten; illustreren. **illustration,** *n.* toelichting *n.*; illustratie *n.*, plaat *n.* **illustrative,** *a.*, ∼ly, *adv.* verduidelijkend, ophelderend.
illustrious, *a.*, ∼ly, *adv.* doorluchtig, beroemd.
ill-will, *n.* kwaadwilligheid *n.*
image, *n.* beeld *n.n.*; voorstelling *n.* ¶ *v.t.* afbeelden; afspiegelen. **imagery,** *n.* beeldwerk *n.n.*; beeldrijkheid *n.* **imaginable,** *a.* denkbaar; denkbeeldig. **imaginary,** *a.*

ingebeeld, denkbeeldig. **imagination**, *n.*
verbeelding *n.*; verbeeldingskracht *n.*
imaginative, *a.*, ~**ly**, *adv.* rijk aan verbeelding *n.* **imagine**, *v.t.* & *v.i.* (zich)
verbeelden.
imago, *n.* ontwikkeld insect *n.n.*
imbecile, *a.* zwakhoofdig, zwakzinnig. ¶ *n.*
imbeciel *n.* **imbecility**, *n.* zwakhoofdigheid
n., zwakzinnigheid *n.*
imbibe, *v.t.* indrinken *str.*, in zich opnemen
str.
imbroglio, *n.* verwikkeling *n.*, verwarring
n.
imbue, *v.t.* doordringen *str.* *to* ~ *with*,
drenken met.
imitate, *v.t.* navolgen, nabootsen; namaken.
imitation, *n.* navolging *n.*; namaak *n.*
imitative, *a.* nabootsend. **imitator**, *n.*
navolger *n.*; nabootser *n.*
immaculate, *a.*, ~**ly**, *adv.* onbevlekt,
onbesmet, smetteloos.
immanent, *a.* immanent.
immaterial, *a.*, ~**ly**, *adv.* onstoffelijk,
onlichamelijk; onverschillig. **immateri-**
ality, *n.* onstoffelijkheid *n.*, onwezenlijk-
heid *n.*
immature, *a.* onrijp; ontijdig. **immaturity**, *n.*
onrijpheid *n.*; ontijdigheid *n.*
immeasurable, *a.*, ~**bly**, *adv.* onmeetbaar.
immediate, *a.* onmiddellijk; rechtstreeks.
immediately, *adv.* onmiddellijk, dadelijk.
immemorial, *a.* onheuglijk; oeroud.
immense, *a.*, ~**ly**, *adv.* onmetelijk; oneindig.
immensity, *n.* onmetelijkheid *n.*; oneindigheid *n.*
immerse, *v.t.* onderdompelen. *to be* ~*d in*,
geheel opgaan *irr.* in. **immersion**, *n.*
onderdompeling *n.*
immigrant, *n.* immigrant *n.* **immigrate**, *v.i.*
immigreren. **immigration**, *n.* immigratie *n.*
imminence, *n.* (iets wat) op het punt staat
te gebeuren. **imminent**, *a.* dreigend, op
handen.
immobile, *a.* onbeweeglijk. **immobility**, *n.*
onbeweeglijkheid *n.*
immoderate, *a.*, ~**ly**, *adv.* buitensporig,
mateloos.
immodest, *a.*, ~**ly**, *adv.* onbescheiden;
onbetamelijk. **immodesty**, *n.* onbe-
scheidenheid *n.*; onbetamelijkheid *n.*
immolate, *v.t.* (op)offeren. **immolation**, *n.*
offer *n.n.*
immoral, *a.* onzedelijk. **immorality**, *n.*
onzedelijkheid *n.*
immortal, *a.*, ~**ly**, *adv.* onsterfelijk; onvergankelijk. **immortality**, *n.* onsterfelijk-
heid *n.* **immortalize**, *v.t.* onsterfelijk
maken, vereeuwigen.
immovable, *a.*, ~**bly**, *adv.* onbeweeglijk;
onwrikbaar. ¶ **-s**, *pl.n.* onroerende
goederen *pl.n.n.*
immune, *a.* immuun. ~ *from*, onvatbaar
voor. **immunity**, *n.* immuniteit *n.*;
onvatbaarheid *n.*

immure, *v.t.* ommuren, insluiten *str.*
immutability, *n.* onveranderlijkheid *n.*
immutable, *a.*, ~**bly**, *adv.* onveranderlijk.
imp, *n.* speelse geest *n.*
impact, *n.* botsing *n.*; stoot *n.*, schok *n.*
impair, *v.t.* benadelen; verzwakken.
impale, *v.t.* spietsen.
impalpable, *a.* onvoelbaar, ontastbaar.
impart, *v.t.* verlenen, verstrekken; bijbrengen *irr.*
impartial, *a.*, ~**ly**, *adv.* onpartijdig. **im-**
partiality, *n.* onpartijdigheid *n.*
impassable, *a.* ontoegankelijk; onbegaanbaar.
impasse, *n.* impasse *n.*
impassibility, *n.* onaandoenlijkheid *n.* **im-**
passible, *a.* onaandoenlijk.
impassioned, *a.* hartstochtelijk.
impassive, *a.* onverstoorbaar.
impatience, *n.* ongeduld *n.n.* **impatient**, *a.*,
~**ly**, *adv.* ongeduldig. *to be* ~ *of something*,
iets niet kunnen *irr.* dulden.
impeach, *v.t.* aanklagen, beschuldigen.
impeachment, *n.* aanklacht *n.*, beschuldiging *n.*
impecunious, *a.* onbemiddeld, zonder geld
n.n.
impede, *v.t.* belemmeren, tegenhouden *irr.*
impediment, *n.* belemmering *n.*, beletsel
n.n. ~ *of speech*, spraakgebrek *n.n.*
impel, *v.t.* voortdrijven *str.*, aanzetten,
bewegen *str.*
impend, *v.i.* boven het hoofd hangen *str.*, op
komst *n.* zijn.
impenetrability, *n.* ondoordringbaarheid *n.*;
(*fig.*) ondoorgrondelijkheid *n.* **impenetrable**,
a., ~**bly**, *adv.* ondoordringbaar; (*fig.*)
ondoorgrondelijk.
impenitence, *n.* onboetvaardigheid *n.*, verstoktheid *n.* **impenitent**, *a.*, ~**ly**, *adv.*
onboetvaardig, verstokt.
imperative, *a.*, ~**ly**, *adv.* gebiedend; dringend
noodzakelijk. ¶ *n.* gebiedende wijs *n.*
imperceptible, *a.* onmerkbaar.
imperfect, *a.*, ~**ly**, *adv.* onvolmaakt; onvol-
komen. ¶ *n.* onvoltooid verleden tijd *n.*
imperfection, *n.* onvolmaaktheid *n.*
imperial, *a.*, ~**ly**, *adv.* keizerlijk, rijks . . .
¶ *n.* imperiaal(papier) *n.n.* **imperialism**, *n.*
imperialisme *n.n.* **imperialist**, *n.* imperialist
n.
imperil, *v.t.* in gevaar *n.n.* brengen *irr.*
imperious, *a.*, ~**ly**, *adv.* gebiedend, heerszuchtig.
imperishable, *a.* onvergankelijk.
impermeability, *n.* ondoordringbaarheid *n.*
impermeable, *a.* ondoordringbaar.
impersonal, *a.*, ~**ly**, *adv.* onpersoonlijk.
impersonate, *v.t.* verpersoonlijken; voorstellen, belichamen. **impersonation**, *n.*
verpersoonlijking *n.*; vertolking *n.*
impertinence, *n.* onbeschaamdheid *n.*,
brutaliteit *n.* **impertinent**, *a.* onbeschaamd,
vrijpostig; niet ter zake.
imperturbable, *a.*, ~**bly**, *adv.* onverstoorbaar.

impervious, *a.* ondoordringbaar. ~ *to,* niet vatbaar voor.

impetigo, *n.* baardschurft *n.*

impetuosity, *n.* onstuimigheid *n.,* heftigheid *n.* **impetuous,** *a.,* ~**ly,** *adv.* onstuimig, heftig.

impetus, *n.* drijfkracht *n.;* aandrang *n.;* vaart *n.*

impiety, *n.* goddeloosheid *n.*

impinge, *v.i. to* ~ (*up*)*on,* inbreuk *n.* maken op.

impious, *a.,* ~**ly,** *adv.* goddeloos.

impish, *a.,* ~**ly,** *adv.* speels, ondeugend.

implacable, *a.* onverbiddelijk, onverzoenlijk.

implant, *v.t.* inprenten.

implement, *v.t.* uitvoeren. ¶ *n.* werktuig *n.n.* ~*s,* gereedschap *n.n.*

implicate, *v.t. to* ~ *in,* betrekken *str.* bij. **implication,** *n.* gevolgtrekking *n. by* ~, stilzwijgend.

implicit, *a.,* ~**ly,** *adv.* stilzwijgend, als vanzelf sprekend; onvoorwaardelijk.

implore, *v.t.* smeken, bidden *str.*

imply, *v.t.* te verstaan geven *str.,* insinueren; insluiten *str.*

impolite, *a.* onbeleefd, onwellevend. **impoliteness,** *n.* onbeleefdheid *n.,* onwellevendheid *n.*

imponderable, *a.* onweegbaar. ¶ *n.* ~*s,* imponderabilia *pl.n.n.*

import, *v.t.* invoeren, importeren; betekenen, beduiden. ¶ *n.* invoer *n.,* import *n.;* belang *n.n.,* betekenis *n.* **importance,** *n.* belang *n.n.* **important,** *a.* belangrijk. **importation,** *n.* invoer *n.,* invoering *n.* **importer,** *n.* importeur *n.*

importunate, *a.* opdringerig, lastig. **importune,** *v.t.* lastig vallen *str.* **importunity,** *n.* overlast *n.*

impose, *v.t.* opleggen *irr.* ¶ *v.i. to* ~ *on,* imponeren; bedriegen *str.,* misleiden. **imposing,** *a.* imposant, indrukwekkend. **imposition,** *n.* oplegging *n.;* last *n.;* strafwerk *n.n.*

impossibility, *n.* onmogelijkheid *n.* **impossible,** *a.,* ~**bly,** *adv.* onmogelijk.

impostor, *n.* bedrieger *n.*

impotence, *n.* onmacht *n.,* machteloosheid *n.;* impotentie *n.* **impotent,** *a.,* ~**ly,** *adv.* onmachtig, machteloos; impotent.

impound, *v.t.* beslag *n.n.* leggen *irr.* op.

impoverish, *v.t.* verarmen.

impracticability, *n.* onuitvoerbaarheid *n.,* ondoenlijkheid *n.* **impracticable,** *a.* onuitvoerbaar, ondoenlijk.

imprecate, *v.t.* vervloeken, verwensen. **imprecation,** *n.* verwensing *n.*

impregnable, *a.,* ~**bly,** *adv.* onneembaar.

impregnate, *v.t.* doortrekken *str.,* verzadigen; bevruchten. **impregnation,** *n.* verzadiging *n.;* bevruchting *n.*

impress, *v.t.* imprenten; op het hart drukken; imponeren, indruk *n.* maken op; pressen. ¶ *n.* indruk *n.,* afdruk *n.* **impression,** *n.*

indruk *n.;* druk *n.* **impressionable,** *a.* voor indrukken *pl.n.* vatbaar. **impressive,** *a.,* ~**ly,** *adv.* indrukwekkend.

imprint, *v.t.* drukken; imprenten. ¶ *n.* (af)druk *n.;* stempel *n.n.*

imprison, *v.t.* gevangenschap *n.;* gevangenzetting *n.*

improbability, *n.* onwaarschijnlijkheid *n.* **improbable,** *a.,* ~**bly,** *adv.* onwaarschijnlijk.

impromptu, *a.* geïmproviseerd.

improper, *a.,* ~**ly,** *adv.* ongepast; onbehoorlijk. **impropriety,** *n.* ongepastheid *n.;* onbetamelijkheid *n.*

improvable, *a.* vatbaar voor verbetering *n.* **improve,** *v.t.* verbeteren. ¶ *v.i.* beter worden *str.,* vooruitgaan *irr.* **improvement,** *n.* verbetering *n.;* beterschap *n.,* vooruitgang *n.*

improvidence, *n.* zorgeloosheid *n.* **improvident,** *a.,* ~**ly,** *adv.* zorgeloos.

improvise, *v.v.i.* improviseren.

imprudence, *n.* onvoorzichtigheid *n.* **imprudent,** *a.,* ~**ly,** *adv.* onvoorzichtig.

impudence, *n.* onbeschaamdheid *n.* **impudent,** *a.,* ~**ly,** *adv.* onbeschaamd.

impugn, *v.t.* aanvallen *str.*

impulse, *n.* opwelling *n.,* aandrang *n.;* stoot *n.* **impulsive,** *a.* impulsief.

impunity, *n.* straffeloosheid *n.*

impure, *a.,* ~**ly,** *adv.* onzuiver; onkuis. **impurity,** *n.* onzuiverheid *n.;* onkuisheid *n.*

imputable, *a.* toerekenbaar. **imputation,** *n.* betichting *n.* **impute,** *v.t.* toeschrijven *str.,* ten laste leggen *irr.*

in, *prep.* in; te; op; bij; aan; naar; uit. ¶ *adv.* aan; binnen; thuis. ¶ *n. the* ~*s and outs,* de finesses *pl.n.*

inability, *n.* onvermogen *n.n.;* onbekwaamheid *n.*

inaccessible, *a.,* ~**bly,** *adv.* ongenaakbaar, ontoegankelijk.

inaccuracy, *n.* onnauwkeurigheid *n.* **inaccurate,** *a.,* ~**ly,** *adv.* onnauwkeurig.

inaction, *n.* werkeloosheid *n.* **inactive,** *a.,* ~**ly,** *adv.* werkeloos; traag, flauw. **inactivity,** *n.* werkeloosheid *n.,* ledigheid *n.*

inadequacy, *n.* ontoereikendheid *n.* **inadequate,** *a.* ontoereikend.

inadmissible, *a.* ontoelaatbaar.

inadvertence, *n.* onachtzaamheid *n.* **inadvertent,** *a.,* ~**ly,** *adv.* onachtzaam.

inalienable, *a.* onvervreemdbaar.

inane, *a.* zinloos; onbeduidend.

inanimate, *a.* onbezield, levenloos.

inanition, *n.* uitputting *n.*

inanity, *n.* zinloosheid *n.;* onbeduidendheid *n.*

inapplicable, *a.* ontoepasselijk; niet van toepassing *n.*

inapposite, *a.* ontoepasselijk, ongepast.

inappreciable, *a.,* ~**bly,** *adv.* onbeduidend, nauwelijks merkbaar.

inapproachable, *a.* ongenaakbaar, ontoegankelijk.

inappropriate, *a.*, ~ly, *adv.* ongeschikt, ongepast.
inapt, *a.* ongeschikt, onbekwaam. inaptitude, *n.* onbekwaamheid *n.*
inarticulate, *a.*, ~ly, *adv.* sprakeloos; ongeleed.
inasmuch, *adv.* voor zoverre als, aangezien.
inattention, *n.* onoplettendheid *n.*, achteloosheid *n.* inattentive, *a.*, ~ly, *adv.* onoplettend, achteloos.
inaudible, *a.*, ~bly, *adv.* onhoorbaar.
inaugural, *a.* inauguraal, openings . . . inaugurate, *v.t.* inaugureren, openen, inwijden. inauguration, *n.* inauguratie *n.*, plechtige opening *n.*, inwijding *n.*
inauspicious, *a.*, ~ly, *adv.* ongunstig, weinig goeds voorspellend.
inborn, *a.* ingeboren, aangeboren.
inbred, *a.* ingeteeld; te veel onder elkaar getrouwd.
incalculable, *a.* onberekenbaar.
incandescence, *n.* gloeiing *n.* incandescent, *a.* witgloeiend. ~ *light*, gloeilicht *n.n.*
incantation, *n.* bezwering *n.*, toverformulier *n.n.*
incapability, *n.* onbekwaamheid *n.*; onbevoegdheid *n.* incapable, *a.* onbekwaam; onbevoegd. incapacitate, *v.t.* onbekwaam maken. incapacity, *n. See* incapability.
incarcerate, *v.t.* gevangen zetten.
incarnate, *a.* vlees *n.n.* geworden, verlichamelijkt. ¶ *v.t.* vlees worden *str.*; mens *n.* worden *str.* incarnation, *n.* vleeswording *n.*; verpersoonlijking *n.*
incautious, *a.*, ~ly, *adv.* onvoorzichtig.
incendiarism, *n.* brandstichting *n.* incendiary, *a.* brand . . .; vurig. ~ *bomb*, brandbom *n.* ¶ *n.* brandstichter *n.*
incense, *n.* wierook *n.* ¶ *v.t.* bewieroken; vertoornen (*anger*).
incentive, *n.* aansporing *n.*, prikkel *n.*
inception, *n.* begin *n.n.*
incertitude, *n.* onzekerheid *n.*
incessant, *a.*, ~ly, *adv.* aanhoudend, onophoudelijk.
incest, *n.* bloedschande *n.* incestuous, *a.*, ~ly, *adv.* bloedschendig.
inch, *n.* Engelse duim (2,54 cm.). ~ *by* ~, voet voor voet *n.*; *every* ~, op en top; *by* ~*es*, geleidelijk.
incidence, *n.* gebied *n.n.*, verbreiding *n.*; inval *n. angle of* ~, invalshoek *n.*
incident, *n.* voorval *n.n.* ¶ *a.* bijkomstig. ~ *to*, voortvloeiend uit. incidental, *a.*, ~ly, *adv.* bijkomstig; toevallig. ¶ *n.* bijkomstigheid *n.*
incinerate, *v.t.* (tot as) verbranden. incinerator, *n.* verbrandingsoven *n.*
incipient, *a.* eerste, begin . . .
incise, *v.t.* (in)snijden *str.*, (in)kerven *str.* incision, *n.* insnijding *n.*, inkerving *n.* incisor, *n.* snijtand *n.*
incite, *v.t.* aansporen, ophitsen. incitement, *n.* aansporing *n.*, prikkel *n.*

incivility, *n.* onbeleefdheid *n.*
inclemency, *n.* onbarmhartigheid *n.*; guurheid *n.* inclement, *a.* onbarmhartig; guur.
inclination, *n.* neiging *n.*; helling *n.*; inclinatie *n.* incline, *v.t.* neigen; doen *irr.* hellen. ¶ *v.i. to* ~ *to*, overhellen naar, geneigd zijn tot. ¶ *n.* helling *n.*
include, *v.t.* bevatten, omhelzen. inclusion, *n.* omvatting *n.*, inbegrip *n.n.* inclusive, *a.*, ~ly, *adv.* insluitend; veelomvattend. ~ *of*, met inbegrip *n,n.* van.
incognito, *a.* incognito.
incoherence, *n.* onsamenhangendheid *n.* incoherent, *a.*, ~ly, *adv.* onsamenhangend.
income, *n.* inkomen *n.n.*, inkomsten *pl.n.* income-tax, *n.* inkomstenbelasting *n.* incoming, *a.* inkomend; nieuw.
incommensurability, *n.* (onderlinge) onmeetbaarheid *n.* incommensurable, *a.* (onderling) onmeetbaar. incommensurate, *a.* (onderling) onmeetbaar; ongeëvenredigd.
incommode, *v.t.* lastig vallen *str.*, storen, hinderen. incommodious, *a.*, ~ly, *adv.* hinderlijk.
incommutable, *a.* onveranderlijk.
incomparable, *a.*, ~bly, *adv.* onvergelijkelijk, weergaloos.
incompatibility, *n.* onverenigbaarheid *n.* incompatible, *a.* onverenigbaar.
incompetence, *n.* onbekwaamheid *n.*; onbevoegdheid *n.* incompetent, *a.*, ~ly, *adv.* onbekwaam; onbevoegd.
incomplete, *a.*, ~ly, *adv.* onvolledig, niet volledig.
incomprehensible, *a.*, ~bly, *adv.* onverstaanbaar, onbegrijpelijk.
inconceivable, *a.*, ~bly, *adv.* onbegrijpelijk.
inconclusive, *a.* niet afdoend, niet beslissend, niet overtuigend.
incongruity, *n.* ongerijmdheid *n.* incongruous, *a.*, ~ly, *adv.* onverenigbaar; ongerijmd.
inconsequent, *a.*, ~ly, *adv.* niet consequent; onlogisch.
inconsiderable, *a.*, ~bly, *adv.* onbelangrijk.
inconsiderate, *a.*, ~ly, *adv.* achteloos; onbezonnen; onattent.
inconsistency, *n.* tegenstrijdigheid *n.* inconsistent, *a.*, ~ly, *adv.* tegenstrijdig.
inconsolable, *a.*, ~bly, *adv.* ontroostbaar.
inconspicuous, *a.*, ~ly, *adv.* niet in 't oog vallend.
inconstancy, *n.* onstandvastigheid *n.*, wispelturigheid *n.* inconstant, *a.* onstandvastig, wispelturig.
incontestable, *a.*, ~bly, *adv.* onbetwistbaar.
incontinence, *n.* gebrek *n.n.* aan zelfbeheersing *n.* incontinent, *a.* zonder zelfbeheersing *n.*
incontrovertible, *a.* onbetwistbaar.
inconvenience, *n.* ongemak *n.n.*, ongerief *n.n.* ¶ *v.t.* lastig vallen *str.*, tot last *n.* zijn. inconvenient, *a.*, ~ly, *adv.* ongelegen, lastig.
incontrovertible, *a.* onverwisselbaar, niet wisselbaar.

incorporate, *v.t.* inlijven; opnemen *str.*; rechtspersoonlijkheid *n.* verlenen aan ¶ *a.* rechtspersoonlijk. **incorporation,** *n.* inlijving *n.*; opname *n.*

incorporeal, *a.*, ~ly, *adv.* onlichamelijk.

incorrect, *a.*, ~ly, *adv.* onjuist, onnauwkeurig.

incorrigible, *a.*, ~bly, *adv.* onverbeterlijk.

incorruptibility, *n.* onomkoopbaarheid *n.*; onvergankelijkheid *n.* **incorruptible,** *a.* onomkoopbaar; onvergankelijk.

increase, *v.t.* vermeerderen, doen *irr.* toenemen. ¶ *v.i.* toenemen *str.* (aan)groeien. ¶ *n.* toename *n.*, groei *n.*, vermeerdering *n.*

incredibility, *n.* ongelooflijkheid *n.* **incredible,** *a.*, ~bly, *adv.* ongelooflijk.

incredulity, *n.* ongelovigheid *n.* **incredulous,** *a.*, ~ly, *adv.* ongelovig.

increment, *n.* vermeerdering *n.*; verhoging *n.*

incriminate, *v.t.* beschuldigen. **incrimination,** *n.* beschuldiging *n.* **incriminatory,** *a.* beschuldigend, incriminerend.

incrustation, *n.* omkorsting *n.*; ketelsteen *n.*

incubate, *v.t.* (uit)broeden; incuberen. **incubation,** *n.* broeding *n.*; incubatie *n.* **incubator,** *n.* broedmachine *n.*

incubus, *n.* nachtmerrie *n.*; incubus *n.*

inculcate, *v.t.* imprenten.

inculpate, *v.t.* beschuldigen.

incumbency, *n.* predikantsplaats *n.*; verplichting *n.* **incumbent,** *n.* predikant *n.* ¶ *a.* *it is* ~ *on you to,* het is Uw plicht om.

incunabula, *pl.n.* wiegedruk *n.*

incur, *v.t.* oplopen *str.*, zich op den hals *n.* halen.

incurability, *n.* ongeneeslijkheid *n.* **incurable,** *a.*, ~bly, *adv.* ongeneeslijk; hopeloos.

incursion, *n.* inval *n.*, strooptocht *n.*

indebted, *a.* verplicht; schuldig.

indecency, *n.* onbetamelijkheid *n.* **indecent,** *a.*, ~ly, *adv.* onbetamelijk, onfatsoenlijk.

indecision, *n.* besluiteloosheid *n.* **indecisive,** *a.* besluiteloos; onbeslist.

indeclinable, *a.* onverbuigbaar.

indecorous, *a.* onwelvoeglijk.

indeed, *adv.* inderdaad; werkelijk.

indefatigable, *a.*, ~bly, *adv.* onvermoeid.

indefeasible, *a.* onaantastbaar.

indefensible, *a.* onverdedigbaar.

indefinable, *a.* niet te beschrijven.

indefinite, *a.*, ~ly, *adv.* onbepaald; onbegrensd; vaag.

indelible, *a.*, ~bly, *adv.* onuitwisbaar.

indelicacy, *n.* onkiesheid *n.* **indelicate,** *a.*, ~ly, *adv.* onkies; grof.

indemnification, *n.* schadeloosstelling *n.* **indemnify,** *v.t.* schadeloosstellen. **indemnity,** *n.* schadeloosstelling *n.*; vergoeding *n.*

indent, *v.t.* deuken, indrukken; laten *str.* inspringen. *to* ~ *to,* in de leer doen *irr.* bij. **indentation,** *n.* deuk *n.*; insnijding *n.*

indenture, *n.* leercontract *n.n.* ¶ *v.t.* in de leer doen *irr.*

independence, *n.* onafhankelijkheid *n.* **independent,** *a.*, ~ly, *adv.* onafhankelijk.

indescribable, *a.*, ~bly, *adv.* onbeschrijfelijk.

indestructible, *a.* onverwoestbaar, onverdelgbaar.

indeterminable, *a.* onbepaalbaar, niet uit te maken. **indeterminate,** *a.*, ~ly, *adv.* onbepaald, vaag.

index, *n.* wijsvinger *n.*; inhoudsopgaaf *n.*; klapper *n.*; index *n.* ¶ *v.t.* van een index voorzien *irr.*

India, *N.* Indië *n.N.*; Voor-Indië *n.N.* **Indiaman,** *n.* Oostinjevaarder *n.* **Indian,** *a.* Indisch; Voor-Indisch. ~ *file,* achter elkaar; ~ *ink,* Oostindische inkt *n.*; ~ *summer,* mooie nazomer *n.* **india-rubber,** *n.* gomelastiek *n.n.*

indicate, *v.t.* aanwijzen *str.*, aanduiden; te kennen geven *str.* **indication,** *n.* aanwijzing *n.*, aanduiding *n.* **indicative,** *a.* aantonend. ¶ *n.* aantonende wijs *n.* **indicator,** *n.* indicateur *n.*, nummerbord *n.n.*

indict, *v.t.* aanklagen, beschuldigen. **indictment,** *n.* aanklacht *n.*, beschuldiging *n.*

Indies, *N.* Indië *n.N. East* ~, Oost Indië *n.N.*; *West* ~, West Indië *n.N.*

indifference, *n.* onverschilligheid *n.*; onbeduidendheid *n.* **indifferent,** *a.*, ~ly, *adv.* onverschillig; onbeduidend.

indigence, *n.* behoeftigheid *n.*, armoede *n.*, nooddruft *n.*

indigenous, *a.* inheems, inlands; aangeboren.

indigent, *a.*, ~ly, *adv.* behoeftig, arm.

indigestible, *a.* onverteerbaar. **indigestion,** *n.* indigestie *n.*, slechte spijsvertering *n.*

indignant, *a.*, ~ly, *adv.* verontwaardigd. **indignation,** *n.* verontwaardiging *n.* **indignity,** *n.* belediging *n.*, smaad *n.*; vernedering *n.*

indigo, *n.* indigo *n.n.*

indirect, *a.*, ~ly, *adv.* indirect, niet rechtstreeks.

indiscernible, *a.* niet te onderscheiden.

indiscreet, *a.*, ~ly, *adv.* onbescheiden, indiscreet; onvoorzichtig, onberaden. **indiscretion,** *n.* indiscretie *n.*; onberadenheid *n.*

indiscriminate, *a.*, ~ly, *adv.* onoordeelkundig, zonder onderscheid *n.n.* te maken.

indispensable, *a.*, ~bly, *adv.* onmisbaar, noodzakelijk.

indispose, *v.t.* *to* ~ *to* or *towards,* ongunstig stemmen tegenover; ~*d,* ongesteld; niet gezind. **indisposition,** *n.* ongesteldheid *n.*; afkerigheid *n.*, ongeneigdheid *n.*

indisputable, *a.*, ~bly, *adv.* onbetwistbaar.

indissoluble, *a.*, ~bly, *adv.* onoplosbaar; onverbreekbaar.

indistinct, *a.*, ~ly, *adv.* onduidelijk, verward. **indistinctness,** *n.* onduidelijkheid *n.*, verwardheid *n.*

indistinguishable, *a.* niet te onderscheiden.
individual, *a.,* ~**ly,** *adv.* individueel, persoonlijk; afzonderlijk. ¶ *n.* persoon *n;* individu *n.n.* **individuality,** *n.* persoonlijkheid *n.;* individualiteit *n.*
indivisibility, *n.* ondeelbaarheid *n.* **indivisible,** *a.,* ~**bly,** *adv.* ondeelbaar.
indolence, *n.* traagheid *n.* **indolent,** *a.,* ~**ly,** *adv.* traag, ijdel.
indomitable, *a.,* ~**bly,** *adv.* ontembaar.
indoor, *a.* huis . . ., binnen . . . **indoors,** *adv.* binnenshuis; thuis.
indubitable, *a.,* ~**bly,** *adv.* ontwijfelbaar.
induce, *v.t.* bewegen *str.,* er toe brengen *irr.;* induceren (*electricity*). **inducement,** *n.* aansporing *n.*
induct, *v.t.* inwijden, introduceren. **induction,** *n.* introductie *n.;* inductie *n.* (*electrical*). **inductive,** *a.,* ~**ly,** *adv.* inductief.
indulge, *v.i. to* ~ *in something,* zich iets permitteren. ¶ *v.t.* zijn zin geven *str.;* verwennen. **indulgence,** *n.* toegevendheid *n.;* aflaat *n.* **indulgent,** *a.,* ~**ly,** *adv.* toegeeflijk; inschikkelijk.
industrial, *a.* industrieel; nijverheids . . ., fabrieks . . . **industrious,** *a.,* ~**ly,** *adv.* nijver, vlijtig, werkzaam. **industry,** *n.* ijver *n.,* vlijt *n.;* nijverheid *n.,* industrie *n.*
inebriate, *v.t.* dronken maken. **inebriation,** *n.* dronkenschap *n.*
ineffable, *a.,* ~**bly,** *adv.* onuitsprekelijk.
ineffective, *a.,* ~**ly,** *adv.,* **ineffectual,** *a.,* ~**ly,** *adv.* zonder uitwerking *n.,* vruchteloos.
inefficacious, *a.,* ~**ly,** *adv.* ondoeltreffend. **inefficiency,** *n.* ondoeltreffendheid *n.* **inefficient,** *a.,* ~**ly,** *adv.* ondoeltreffend, slecht georganiseerd.
inelegant, *a.,* ~**ly,** *adv.* onbevallig.
ineligibility, *n.* onverkieslijkheid *n.* **ineligible,** *a.* onverkieslijk; niet verkiesbaar.
ineluctable, *a.* onafwendbaar.
inept, *a.* onzinnig. **ineptitude,** *n.* onzinnigheid *n.*
inequality, *n.* ongelijkheid *n.*
inequitable, *a.* onbillijk.
inert, *a.,* ~**ly,** *adv.* traag; bewegingloos. **inertia,** *n.* traagheid *n.*
inessential, *a.* niet noodzakelijk.
inestimable, *a.* onschatbaar.
inevitable, *a.,* ~**bly,** *adv.* onvermijdelijk.
inexact, *a.* onnauwkeurig.
inexcusable, *a.,* ~**bly,** *adv.* onvergeeflijk.
inexhaustible, *a.* onuitputtelijk.
inexorable, *a.,* ~**bly,** *adv.* onverbiddelijk.
inexpediency, *n.* onraadzaamheid *n.* **inexpedient,** *a.* onraadzaam.
inexpensive, *a.,* ~**ly,** *adv.* goedkoop.
inexperience, *n.* onervarenheid *n.* **inexperienced,** *a.* onervaren.
inexpiable, *a.,* ~**bly,** *adv.* onverzoenlijk.
inexplicable, *a.,* ~**bly,** *adv.* onverklaarbaar.
inexpressible, *a.,* ~**bly,** *adv.* onuitsprekelijk. **inexpressive,** *a.* zonder uitdrukking *n.*
inextinguishable, *a.* onblusbaar.

inextricable, *a.* niet te ontwarren.
infallibility, *n.* onfeilbaarheid *n.* **infallible,** *a.,* ~**bly,** *adv.* onfeilbaar.
infamous, *a.,* ~**ly,** *adv.* schandelijk. **infamy,** *n.* schande *n.*
infancy, *n.* kindsheid *n.* **infant,** *n.* kind *n.n.,* zuigeling *n.* **infanta,** *n.* infante *n.* **infanticide,** *n.* kindermoord *n.;* kindermoordenaar *n.* (*person*). **infantile,** *a.* kinderlijk, kinderachtig; kinder . . . **infantry,** *n.* infanterie *n.*
infatuated, *a.* ~ *with,* dwaas ingenomen met. **infatuation,** *n.* blinde ingenomenheid *n.*
infect, *v.t.* besmetten, aansteken *str.* **infection,** *n.* besmetting *n.,* aansteking *n.,* infectie *n.* **infectious,** *a.* besmettelijk; aanstekelijk.
infelicitous, *a.* ongelukkig gekozen.
infer, *v.t.* opmaken, afleiden. **inference,** *n.* gevolgtrekking *n.*
inferior, *a.* minder (goed); ondergeschikt. ¶ *n.* mindere *n.,* inferieur *n.* **inferiority,** *n.* minderwaardigheid *n.;* ondergeschiktheid *n.*
infernal, *a.* hels, duivels.
infest, *v.t.* onveilig maken. *to be* ~*ed with,* wemelen van.
infidel, *a.* ongelovig. ¶ *n.* ongelovige *n.,* heiden *n.* **infidelity,** *n.* ongelovigheid *n.;* ontrouw *n.*
infiltrate, *v.i.* langzaam doordringen *str.*
infinite, *a.,* ~**ly,** *adv.* oneindig, grenzeloos. **infinitive,** *n.* onbepaalde wijs *n.* **infinitude,** *n.,* **infinity,** *n.* oneindigheid *n.;* onbegrensdheid *n.*
infirm, *a.* gebrekkig, zwak. **infirmary,** *n.* gasthuis *n.n.;* armenapotheek *n.* **infirmity,** *n.* gebrek *n.n.,* zwakte *n.*
inflame, *v.t.* doen *irr.* ontvlammen; doen *irr.* ontsteken. **inflammability,** *n.* ontvlambaarheid *n.* **inflammable,** *a.* ontvlambaar. **inflammation,** *n.* ontsteking *n.* **inflammatory,** *a.* opruiend, oproerig.
inflate, *v.t.* opblazen; opdrijven *str.* ~*d,* gezwollen. **inflation,** *n.* inflatie *n.*
inflect, *v.t.* buigen *str.;* verbuigen *str.* **inflection,** *n.* buiging *n.;* verbuiging *n.*
inflexibility, *n.* onbuigbaarheid *n.;* onbuigzaamheid *n.* **inflexible,** *a.,* ~**bly,** *adv.* onbuigbaar; onbuigzaam.
inflict, *v.t.* doen *irr.* ondergaan; opleggen *irr.;* toebrengen *irr.* **infliction,** *n.* oplegging *n.;* toebrengen *n.n.;* bezoeking *n.*
influence, *n.* invloed *n.* ¶ *v.t.* invloed hebben op, beïnvloeden. **influential,** *a.* invloedrijk.
influenza, *n.* griep *n.*
influx, *n.* toevloed *n.*
inform, *v.t.* berichten, me(d)edelen; inlichten. ¶ *v.i. to* ~ *against,* een (verraderlijke) aanklacht indienen tegen.
informal, *a.,* ~**ly,** *adv.* niet formeel. **informality,** *n.* informaliteit *n.*
informant, *n.* zegsman *n.* **information,** *n.* kennisgeving *n.;* inlichting *n.,* inlichtingen

pl.n. **informative,** *a.* leerzaam. **informer,** *n.* aanklager *n.*
infraction, *n.* inbreuk *n.*
infrequent, *a.* zeldzaam.
infringe, *v.i.* inbreuk maken op. **infringement,** *n.* inbreuk *n.*
infuriate, *v.t.* woedend maken.
infuse, *v.t.* laten *str.* trekken; imprenten. **infusion,** *n.* aftreksel *n.n.*
infusoria, *pl.n.* infusiediertjes *pl.n.n.*
ingenious, *a.*, ∼ly, *adv.* vernuftig, vindingrijk. **ingenuity,** *n.* vindingrijkheid *n.*
ingenuous, *a.*, ∼ly, *adv.* ongekunsteld, naïef.
ingle, *n.* haard *n.*
inglorious, *a.*, ∼ly, *adv.* roemloos.
ingot, *n.* baar *n.*, staaf *n.*
ingrained, *a.* ingeworteld; verstokt.
ingratiate, *v.r.* to ∼ oneself with, zich bij iemand in de gunst werken.
ingratitude, *n.* ondankbaarheid *n.*
ingredient, *n.* bestanddeel *n.n.*
ingress, *n.* toegang *n.*
ingrowing, *a.* in het vlees groeiend.
inhabit, *v.t.* bewonen. **inhabitable,** *a.* bewoonbaar. **inhabitant,** *n.* inwoner *n.*, bewoner *n.*
inhale, *v.t.* & *v.i.* inademen.
inharmonious, *a.* onwelluidend.
inherent, *a.* inhaerent, onafscheidelijk verbonden.
inherit, *v.t.* & *v.i.* erven. **inheritance,** *n.* erfenis *n.*; overerving *n.*
inhibit, *v.t.* tegenhouden *irr.*, onderdrukken.
inhospitable, *a.*, ∼bly, *adv.* onherbergzaam; ongastvrij.
inhuman, *a.*, ∼ly, *adv.* onmenselijk. **inhumanity,** *n.* onmenselijkheid *n.*
inimical, *a.* vijandig, vijandelijk.
inimitable, *a.*, ∼bly, *adv.* onnavolgbaar.
iniquitous, *a.* ongerechtig, onbillijk. **iniquity,** *n.* ongerechtigheid *n.*, onbillijkheid *n.*
initial, *a.*, ∼ly, *adv.* eerste, aanvangs . . ., begin . . . ¶ *n.* voorletter *n.* ¶ *v.t.* paraferen.
initiate, *v.t.* inwijden; ondernemen. **initiation,** *n.* inwijding *n.* **initiative,** *n.* initiatief *n.n.*
inject, *v.t.* inspuiten *str.* **injection,** *n.* inspuiting *n.*, injectie *n.*
injudicious, *a.*, ∼ly, *adv.* onverstandig, onoordeelkundig.
injunction, *n.* rechterlijk bevel *n.n.*
injure, *v.t.* wonden, kwetsen; onrecht aandoen *irr.*, verongelijken. (*also:*) ∼d, beledigd.
injurious, *a.*, ∼ly, *adv.* schadelijk, nadelig. **injury,** *n.* letsel *n.n.*; verwonding *n.*; nadeel *n.n.*, schade *n.*
injustice, *n.* onrecht *n.n.*, onrechtvaardigheid *n.*
ink, *n.* inkt *n.* ¶ *v.t.* inkten.
inkling, *n.* flauw idee *n.n.*
inkstand, *n.* inktstel *n.n.* **inky,** *a.* inktachtig; vol inkt.
inlaid, *a.* ingelegd.
inland, *a.* binnenlands. ¶ *adv.* landwaarts.

inlay, *v.t.* inleggen *irr.* ¶ *n.* inlegsel *n.n.*
inlet, *n.* inham *n.*
inmate, *n.* bewoner *n.*
inmost, *a.* hinnenste.
inn, *n.* herberg *n.*; college *n.n.* en verblijfplaats *n.* van advocaten *pl.n.*
innate, *a.*, ∼ly, *adv.* ingeboren, aangeboren.
inner, *a.* binnenste; inwendig. ∼ tube, binnenband *n.*
innings, *pl.n.* beurt *n.* om te spelen. to get one's ∼, aan de beurt komen *irr.*
innkeeper, *n.* herbergier *n.*
innocence, *n.* onschuld *n.*; onnozelheid *n.* **innocent,** *a.*, ∼ly, *adv.* onschuldig; onnozel.
innocuous, *a.*, ∼ly, *adv.* onschadelijk.
innovate, *v.t.* nieuwigheden *pl.n.* invoeren, veranderingen *pl.n.* aanbrengen *irr.* **innovation,** *n.* nieuwigheid *n.*, verandering *n.* **innovator,** *n.* invoerder *n.* van nieuwigheden.
innoxious, *a.*, ∼ly, *adv.* onschadelijk.
innuendo, *n.* (hatelijke) toespeling *n.*
innumerable, *a.*, ∼bly, *adv.* ontelbaar, talloos.
inoculate, *v.t.* inenten, enten. **inoculation,** *n.* inenting *n.*, enting *n.*
inodorous, *a.* reukloos.
inoffensive, *a.*, ∼ly, *adv.* onschadelijk, ongevaarlijk.
inoperative, *a.* zonder uitwerking *n.*
inopportune, *a.*, ∼ly, *adv.* ongelegen, ontijdig.
inordinate, *a.*, ∼ly, *adv.* buitensporig, bovenmatig.
inorganic, *a.*, ∼ally. *adv.* anorganisch.
in-patient, *n.* (inwonend) patiënt *n.*
inquest, *n.* (gerechtelijk) onderzoek *n.n.*; lijkschouwing *n.*
inquietude, *n.* ongerustheid *n.*
inquire, *v.i.* navraag *n.* doen *irr.*, informeren. to ∼ after, vragen *str.* naar; to ∼ into, onderzoeken *irr.*; to ∼ of, vragen *str.* aan. **inquiry,** *n.* vraag *n.*; navraag *n.*; onderzoek *n.n.*
inquisition, *n.* inquisitie *n.*; (gerechtelijk) onderzoek *n.n.*
inquisitive, *a.*, ∼ly, *adv.* nieuwsgierig.
inquisitor, *n.* inquisiteur *n.* **inquisitorial,** *a.* onderzoekend.
inroad, *n.* inval *n.*; strooptocht *n.*
insalubrious, *a.* ongezond. **insalubrity,** *n.* ongezondheid *n.*
insane, *a.* krankzinnig. **insanity,** *n.* krankzinnigheid *n.*
insatiable, *a.*, ∼bly, *adv.* onverzadelijk.
inscribe, *v.t.* inschrijven *str.*; graveren; opdragen *str.* **inscription,** *n.* inschrift *n.n.*, opschrift *n.n.*; opdracht *n.n.*
inscrutable, *a.*, ∼bly, *adv.* ondoorgrondelijk, onnaspeurlijk.
insect, *n.* insect *n.n.* **insecticide,** *n.* insectenpoeder *n.n.* **insectivorous,** *a.* insectenetend.
insecure, *a.*, ∼ly, *adv.* onzeker, onvast

onveilig. **insecurity,** *n.* onzekerheid *n.*, onveiligheid *n.*

insensate, *a.* gevoelloos, ongevoelig; zinneloos.

insensibility, *n.* ongevoeligheid *n.*; gevoelloosheid *n.* **insensible,** *a.*, ~**bly,** *adv.* ongevoelig; gevoelloos; onmerkbaar. ~ *of* or *to,* ongevoelig voor.

inseparable, *a.*, ~**bly,** *adv.* onafscheidelijk, onscheidbaar.

insert, *v.t.* invoegen, inlassen; plaatsen. **insertion,** *n.* invoeging *n.*, inlassing *n.*; plaatsing *n.*

inshore, *adv.* bij de kust; naar de kust toe.

inside, *prep.* binnen. ¶ *adv.* binnen. ¶ *n.* binnenkant *n.* ~ *out,* binnenste buiten.

insidious, *a.*, ~**ly,** *adv.* verraderlijk, bedrieglijk.

insight, *n.* inzicht *n.*, begrip *n.n.*

insignia, *n.* onderscheidingstekenen *pl.n.n.*, kentekenen *pl.n.n.*

insignificance, *n.* onbetekenendheid *n.* **insignificant,** *a.*, ~**ly,** *adv.* onbetekenend.

insincere, *a.*, ~**ly,** *adv.* onoprecht, huichelachtig. **insincerity,** *n.* onoprechtheid *n.* ,

insinuate, *v.t.* te verstaan geven *str.* insinueren. ¶ *v.i. to* ~ *oneself into,* zich indringen *str.* bij. **insinuation,** *n.* insinuatie *n.*, bedekte toespeling *n.*

insipid, *a.*, ~**ly,** *adv.* smakeloos, flauw; zouteloos. **insipidity,** *n.* smakeloosheid *n.*

insist, *v.i.* aanhouden *irr.*, aandringen *str.*; volhouden *irr. if you* ~, als U er op staat. **insistence,** *n.* aanhouden *n.n.*, aandringen *n.n.*, aandrang *n.* **insistent,** *a.* dringend.

insolence, *n.* onbeschaamdheid *n.*; brutaliteit *n.* **insolent,** *a.*, ~**ly,** *adv.* onbeschaamd; brutaal.

insolubility, *n.* onoplosbaarheid *n.* **insoluble,** *a.* onoplosbaar; onverklaarbaar.

insolvency, *n.* staat *n.* van onvermogen *n.n.* **insolvent,** *a.* onvermogend.

insomnia, *n.* slapeloosheid *n.*

insomuch, *adv.* ~ *as,* in zoverre als; ~ *that,* zodat.

inspect, *v.t.* onderzoeken *irr.*, nagaan *irr.*; inspecteren. **inspection,** *n.* onderzoek *n.n.*; inzage *n.*; inspectie *n.* **inspector,** *n.* opziener *n.*, inspecteur *n.*

inspiration, *n.* ingeving *n.*, inspiratie *n.* **inspire,** *v.t.* bezielen, inboezemen, inspireren.

inspirit, *v.t.* bezielen, moed *n.* geven *str.*

inspissate, *v.t.* verdikken, indampen.

instability, *n.* onbestendigheid *n.*, veranderlijkheid *n.*

install, *v.t.* installeren. **installation,** *n.* installatie *n.*; aanleg *n.*

instalment, *n.* aflevering *n.*; termijn *n.* *in* ~s, bij gedeelten *pl.n.n.*

instance, *n.* voorbeeld *n.n.*; aandrang *n.*, dringend verzoek *n.n.*; instantie *n. for* ~, bij voorbeeld. ¶ *v.t.* als voorbeeld aanhalen. **instant,** *a.*, ~**ly,** *adv.* onmiddellijk. *the 5th inst(ant),* de vijfde dezer. ¶ *n.*

ogenblik *n.n.* **instantaneous,** *a.*, ~**ly,** *adv.* ogenblikkelijk, onmiddellijk.

instead, *prep.* in plaats *n.* daarvan. ~ *of,* in plaats *n.* van.

instep, *n.* wreef *n.*

instigate, *v.t.* aansporen, ophitsen. **instigation,** *n.* aansporing *n.* *at the* ~ *of,* op aandrang *n.* van. **instigator,** *n.* aanzetter *n.*, ophitser *n.*

instil, *v.t.* inboezemen; (langzaam) imprenten.

instinct, *n.* instinct *n.n.* **instinctive,** *a.*, ~**ly,** *adv.* instinctmatig.

institute, *v.t.* instellen, stichten; beginnen *str.* ¶ *n.* instituut *n.n.* **institution,** *n.* instelling *n.*; institutie *n.*

instruct, *v.t.* onderwijzen *str.*; last *n.* geven *str.* **instruction,** *n.* onderwijs *n.n.*; opdracht *n.* **instructive,** *a.* leerzaam. **instructor,** *n.* instructeur *n.*

instrument, *n.* instrument *n.n.*; werktuig *n.n.*; acte *n.*, document *n.n.* **instrumental,** *a.*, ~**ly,** *adv.* instrumentaal; dienstig, bevorderlijk. *to be* ~ *in,* behulpzaam zijn in; *to be* ~ *to,* strekken tot. **instrumentality,** *n.* toedoen *n.n.*, bemiddeling *n.*

insubordinate, *a.* weerbarstig. **insubordination,** *n.* weerbarstigheid *n.*; insubordinatie *n.*

insufferable, *a.*, ~**bly,** *adv.* onduldbaar.

insufficiency, *n.* ontoereikendheid *n.*; onbekwaamheid *n.* **insufficient,** *a.*, ~**ly,** *adv.* onvoldoende, ontoereikend.

insular, *a.* eiland . . .; bekrompen. **insularity,** *n.* eiland *n.n.* zijn *n.n.*; bekrompenheid *n.*

insulate, *v.t.* isoleren. **insulation,** *n.* isolering *n.*; isolement *n.n.* **insulator,** *n.* isolator *n.*

insult, *v.t.* beledigen. ¶ *n.* belediging *n.*

insuperable, *a.*, ~**bly,** *adv.* onoverkomelijk.

insupportable, *a.*, ~**bly,** *adv.* ondragelijk.

insurance, *n.* verzekering *n.*, assurantie *n.* ~ *broker,* assuradeur *n.*; ~ *company,* verzekeringsmaatschappij *n.* **insure,** *v.t.* verzekeren. **insurer,** *n.* verzekeraar *n.*

insurgent, *n.* opstandeling *n.*

insurmountable, *a.*, ~**bly,** *adv.* onoverkomelijk.

insurrection, *n.* opstand *n.*; oproer *n.n.* **insurrectionary,** *a.* oproerig; muitziek. **insurrectionist,** *n.* opstandeling *n.*

intact, *a.* onaangeroerd.

intaglio, *n.* ingesneden steen *n.*

intangible, *a.*, ~**bly,** *adv.* ontastbaar; onmerkbaar.

integer, *n.* geheel getal *n.n.* **integral,** *a.* geheel, volledig; integraal. ¶ *n.* integraal *n.* **integrate,** *v.t.* integreren; volledig maken. **integrity,** *n.* volledigheid *n.*; integriteit *n.*, onkreukbaarheid *n.*

intellect, *n.* intellect *n.n.*, verstand *n.n.* **intellectual,** *a.*, ~**ly,** *adv.* intellectueel, verstandelijk. ¶ *n.* intellectueel *n.*

intelligence, *n.* verstand *n.n.*; bericht *n.n.*; officiële inlichtingen *pl.n.*, spionnage *n.* ~ *service,* inlichtingendienst *n.* **intelligent,**

a., ~**ly,** *adv.* verstandig; vlug. **intelligentzia,** *n.* intellectuelen *pl.n.*
intemperance, *n.* onmatigheid *n.* **intemperate,** *a.,* ~**ly,** *adv.* onmatig, ongematigd.
intend, *v.t.* van plan *n.n.* zijn, voornemens zijn; bedoelen. ¶ *v.i. to* ~ *well,* het goed menen. **intendant,** *n.* intendant *n.* **intended,** *a.* voorgenomen, opzettelijk. ¶ *n.* aanstaande *n.*
intense, *a.,* ~**ly,** *adv.* intens; fel, hevig. **intensify,** *v.t.* versterken, intenser maken. **intensity,** *n.* intensiteit *n.,* hevigheid *n.* **intensive,** *a.,* ~**ly,** *adv.* krachtig, intens, intensief.
intent, *a.,* ~**ly,** *adv.* ingespannen, aandachtig. ~ *on,* belust op; verdiept in. ¶ *n.* doel *n.n.*; voornemen *n.n.,* plan *n.n. to all* ~*s and purposes,* in alle opzichten *pl.n.n.* **intention,** *n.* bedoeling *n.* **intentional,** *a.* opzettelijk.
inter, *v.t.* ter aarde bestellen.
interact, *v.i.* op elkaar inwerken. **interaction,** *n.* wisselwerking *n.*
intercede, *v.i.* tussenbeide komen *irr. to* ~ *for,* voorspreken *str.*
intercept, *v.t.* onderscheppen, opvangen *str.* **intercession,** *n.* tussenkomst *n.*; voorspraak *n.* **intercessor,** *n.* bemiddelaar *n.*
interchange, *v.t.* ruilen, wisselen. ¶ *n.* ruil *n.,* wisseling *n.*
intercourse, *n.* omgang *n.,* verkeer *n.n.*; betrekking *n.*
interdict, *v.t.* verbieden *str.* ¶ *n.* verbod *n.n.* **interdiction,** *n.* verbod *n.n.,* interdict *n.n.* **interdictory,** *a.* verbiedend, verbods . . .
interest, *v.t.* interesseren, belang *n.n.* inboezemen. ¶ *v.r. to* ~ *oneself in,* belang *n.n.* stellen in, zich interesseren voor. ¶ *n.* belangstelling *n.,* interesse *n.n.*; interest *n.,* rente *n.*; belang *n.n.,* voordeel *n.n.* **interested,** *a.* belangstellend; belang *n.n.* hebbend. *to be* ~ *in,* belang *n.n.* stellen in. **interesting,** *a.* interessant.
interfere, *v.i.* tussenbeide komen *irr.*; interfereren. *to* ~ *in,* zich mengen in. **interference,** *n.* inmenging *n.*; tussenkomst *n.*; interferentie *n.*
interim, *n.* tussentijd *n.* ¶ *adv.* voorlopig.
interior, *a.* binnen . . ., binnenste. ¶ *n.* binnenste *n.*; binnenland *n.n.*
interjection, *n.* tussenwerpsel *n.n.*
interlace, *n.* dooreen strengelen, dooreen vlechten *str.*
interleave, *v.t.* doorschieten *str.* met witte vellen *pl.n.n.*
interline, *v.t.* interliniëren. **interlinear,** *a.* interlineair.
interlock, *v.t.* in elkaar grijpen *str.*
interlocutor, *n.* persoon *n.* met wie men spreekt.
interlope, *v.i.* zich op andermans terrein *n.n.* begeven *str.* **interloper,** *n.* indringer *n.,* beunhaas *n.*

interlude, *n.* tussenspel *n.n.*; intermezzo *n.n.*
intermarriage, *n.* onderling huwelijk *n.n.*; huwelijk *n.n.* tussen bloedverwanten *pl.n.* **intermarry,** *v.i.* onder elkaar trouwen.
intermediary, *a.* tussenliggend, tussen . . . ¶ *n.* tussenpersoon *n.,* bemiddelaar *n.*; tussenkomst *n.* **intermediate,** *a.,* ~**ly,** *adv.* tussenliggend; indirect.
interment, *n.* teraardebestelling *n.*
interminable, *a.,* ~**bly,** *adv.* eindeloos, oneindig.
intermingle, *v.t.* mengen, vermengen. ¶ *v.i.* zich vermengen.
intermission, *n.* onderbreking *n.,* tussenpoos *n.* intermit, *v.i.* afbreken *str.,* staken. **intermittent,** *a.* onderbroken. ~ *fever,* intermitterende koorts *n.*
intern, *v.t.* interneren.
internal, *a.,* ~**ly,** *adv.* inwendig; innerlijk; binnenlands.
international, *a.* internationaal. ~ *law,* volkenrecht *n.n.*
internecine, *a.* moorddadig, elkaar verdelgend.
interpellate, *v.t.* interpelleren. **interpellation,** *n.* interpellatie *n.*
interpolate, *v.t.* interpoleren, tussenvoegen, inlassen. **interpolation,** *n.* interpolatie *n.,* tussenvoeging *n.*
interpose, *v.t.* tussenplaatsen; tussenbeide brengen *irr.* ¶ *v.i.* in de rede vallen *str.* **interposition,** *n.* tussenkomst *n.,* bemiddeling *n.*
interpret, *v.t.* vertolken; verklaren. **interpretation,** *n.* vertolking *n.*; verklaring *n.* **interpreter,** *n.* tolk *n.*; vertolker *n.*
interrogate, *v.t.* ondervragen *str.* **interrogation,** *n.* ondervraging *n.* **interrogative,** *a.,* ~**ly,** *adv.* vragend. **interrogatory,** *a.* vragend. ¶ *n.* ondervraging *n.,* verhoor *n.n.*
interrupt, *v.t.* onderbreken *str.*; in de rede vallen *str.* **interruption,** *n.* onderbreking *n.,* storing *n.*
intersect, *v.t.* snijden *str.*; doorkruisen. **intersection,** *n.* doorsnee *n.*; kruispunt *n.n.*
intersperse, *v.t.* hier en daar tussenwerpen *str.*
interstice, *n.* tussenruimte *n.*; spleet *n.*
intertwine, *v.t.* ineenstrengelen, dooreenvlechten *str.*
interval, *n.* tussenpoos *n.*; tussenruimte *n.*; interval *n.n.*
intervene, *v.i.* tussenbeide komen *irr.,* interveniëren. **intervention,** *n.* bemiddeling *n.*; interventie *n.*
interview, *n.* onderhoud *n.n.,* interview *n.n.* ¶ *v.t.* een onderhoud hebben met.
interweave, *v.t.* dooreenweven *irr.*
intestate, *a.* zonder testament *n.n.*
intestine, *n.* darm. ~*s,* ingewanden *pl.n.n.*
intimacy, *n.* vertrouwelijkheid *n.,* intimiteit *n.* **intimate,** *a.,* ~**ly,** *adv.* vertrouwelijk, intiem; innerlijk. ¶ *v.t.* te kennen geven *str.* **intimation,** *n.* kennisgeving *n.*; wenk *n.*

intimidate, *v.t.* vrees aanjagen *str.*, bang maken, intimideren. **intimidation,** *n.* bangmakerij *n.*, intimidatie *n.*

into, *prep.* in.

intolerable, *a.*, ~**bly,** *adv.* ondragelijk; onuitstaanbaar. **intolerance,** *n.* onverdraagzaamheid *n.* **intolerant,** *a.* onverdraagzaam.

intonation, *n.* intonatie *n.*, stembuiging *n.* **intone,** *v.t.* intoneren; aanheffen *str.*

intoxicate, *v.t.* bedwelmen; dronken maken. **intoxication,** *n.* bedwelming *n.*; roes *n.*; dronkenschap *n.*

intractable, *a.* weerspannig, onhandelbaar.

intransigent, *a.* intransigent.

intransitive, *a.* onovergankelijk.

intrepid, *a.*, ~**ly,** *adv.* onversaagd, onverschrokken. **intrepidity,** *n.* onversaagdheid *n.*

intricacy, *n.* ingewikkeldheid *n.* **intricate,** *a.*, ~**ly,** *adv.* ingewikkeld; netelig.

intrigue, *n.* intrige *n.* ¶ *v.i.* intrigeren, kuipen.

intrinsic, *a.*, ~**ally,** *adv.* intrinsiek, wezenlijk.

introduce, *v.t.* inleiden; indienen; voorstellen. **introduction,** *n.* inleiding *n.*; voorstelling *n.* **introductory,** *a.* inleidend.

introspection, *n.* zelfonderzoek *n.n.*, zelfbespiegeling *n.* **introspective,** *a.* zelfbespiegelend.

introverted, *a.* (tot zichzelf) ingekeerd.

intrude, *v.i.* zich opdringen *str.*; lastig vallen *str.* ¶ *v.t.* opdringen *str.* **intruder,** *n.* indringer *n.* **intrusion,** *n.* indringing *n.*; opdringing *n.* **intrusive,** *a.* binnengedrongen.

intuition, *n.* intuïtie *n.*, ingeving *n.* **intuitive,** *a.* intuïtief. **intuitively,** *adv.* intuïtief, als bij ingeving *n.*

inundate, *v.t.* onder water *n.n.* zetten; overstelpen. **inundation,** *n.* overstroming *n.*

inure, *v.t.* harden.

invade, *v.t.* binnenvallen *str.*, een inval *n.* doen *irr.* in. **invader,** *n.* aanvaller *n.*, binnendringer *n.*

in·valid, *a.* ongeldig. ·**invalid** *a.* gebrekkig, gebrekkelijk. ¶ *n.* zieke *n.*, gebrekkige *n.*; invalide *n.* ¶ *v.t.* wegens invaliditeit *n.* (uit de dienst) ontslaan *irr.* **invalidate,** *v.t.* ongeldig maken. **invalidity,** *n.* ongeldigheid *n.*

invaluable, *a.* onschatbaar.

invariable, *a.*, ~**bly,** *adv.* onveranderlijk; constant.

invasion, *n.* inval *n.*; invasie *n.*

invective, *n.* scheldwoorden *pl.n.n.*

inveigh, *v.i.* uitvaren *str.*

inveigle, *v.t.* verlokken.

invent, *v.t.* uitvinden *str.*; verzinnen *str.* **invention,** *n.* uitvinding *n.*; verzinsel *n.n.* **inventive,** *a.* vindingrijk. **inventor,** *n.* uitvinder *n.*

inventory, *n.* inventaris *n.*; boedelbeschrijving *n.*

inverse, *a.*, ~**ly,** *adv.* omgekeerd. **inversion,** *n.* omzetting *n.*; inversie *n.* **invert,** *v.t.* omzetten, omkeren. ~**ed commas,** aanhalingstekens *pl.n.n.*

invertebrate, *a.* ongewerveld.

invest, *v.t.* beleggen; omsingelen; hullen.

investigate, *v.t.* navorsen, nauwkeurig onderzoeken *irr.* ¶ *v.i.* to ~ into, een onderzoek *n.n.* instellen naar. **investigation,** *n.* onderzoek *n.n.* **investigator,** *n.* onderzoeker *n.*, naspeurder *n.*

investiture, *n.* investituur *n.*; ambtsbekleding *n.*

investment, *n.* belegging *n.* **investor,** *n.* belegger *n.*

inveterate, *a.* onverbeterlijk, aarts . . .

invidious, *a.*, ~**ly,** *adv.* hatelijk; onbenijdenswaardig; netelig.

invigilate, *v.i.* surveilleren.

invigorate, *v.t.* versterken, kracht *n.* geven *str.* aan.

invincible, *a.*, ~**bly,** *adv.* onoverwinnelijk.

inviolability, *n.* onschendbaarheid *n.* **inviolable,** *a.*, ~**bly,** *adv.* onschendbaar. **inviolate,** *a.* ongeschonden.

invisibility, *n.* onzichtbaarheid *n.* **invisible,** *a.*, ~**bly,** *adv.* onzichtbaar.

invitation, *n.* uitnodiging *n.* by ~, op uitnodiging *n.* **invite,** *v.t.* uitnodigen; verzoeken *irr.* om. **inviting,** *a.* aanlokkelijk.

invocation, *n.* aanroeping *n.*

invoice, *n.* factuur *n.* ¶ *v.t.* factureren.

invoke, *v.t.* aanroepen *str.*; inroepen *str.*

involuntary, *a.*, ~**ly,** *adv.* onwillekeurig.

involution, *n.* inwikkeling *n.*; machtsverheffing *n.*

involve, *v.t.* verwikkelen; insluiten *str.*, omvatten. ~**d,** ingewikkeld.

invulnerable, *a.* onkwetsbaar.

inward, *a.* inwendig; innerlijk; naar binnen. ¶ *adv.* naar binnen, binnenwaarts. **inwardly,** *adv.* inwendig, innerlijk. **inwards,** *adv.* naar binnen, binnenwaarts.

odine, *n.* jodium *n.n.*

I.O.U., *N.* schuldbekentenis *n.*

ipecacuanha, *n.* braakwortel *n.*

irascibility, *n.* opvliegendheid *n.* **irascible,** *a.* opvliegend, driftig.

irate, *a.* toornig, verbolgen. **ire,** *n.* toorn *n.*, gramschap *n.*

Ireland, *N.* Ierland *n.N.*

iridescent, *a.* regenboogkleurig.

iris, *n.* iris *n.*, regenboogvlies *n.n.*; zwaardlelie *n.*

Irish, *a.* Iers. **Irishman,** *N.* Ier *N.*

irk, *v.t.* ergeren, verdrieten *str.* **irksome,** *a.* vervelend, verdrietig.

iron, *n.* ijzer *n.n.*; strijkijzer *n.n.*; golfstok *n.* ¶ *a.* ijzeren. ~ *ration,* noodrantsoen *n.n.* ¶ *v.t.* strijken *str.* **iron-bound,** *a.* met ijzeren banden *pl.n.* beslagen. **iron-clad,** *a.* gepantserd.

ironic(al), *a.*, ~**ly,** *adv.* ironisch.

ironmonger, *n.* ijzerhandelaar *n.* **iron-mould,**

n. ijzermaal *n.n.* **ironside**, *N.* soldaat *n.* van Cromwell. **iron-works**, *pl.n.* ijzergieterij *n.*; ijzersmelterij *n.*; ijzerpletterij *n.*

irony, *n.* ironie *n.*

irradiate, *v.t.* bestralen.

irrational, *a.*, ~**ly**, *adv.* onredelijk. **irrationality**, *n.* onredelijkheid *n.*

irreclaimable, *a.* onherstelbaar.

irreconcilable, *a.*, ~**bly**, *adv.* onverzoenlijk; onverenigbaar.

irrecoverable, *a.*, ~**bly**, *adv.* onherroepelijk; onherstelbaar.

irredeemable, *a.* onaflosbaar; onherstelbaar.

irreducible, *a.* onherleidbaar; onoverwinnelijk.

irrefutable, *a.*, ~**bly**, *adv.* onweerlegbaar, onomstotelijk.

irregular, *a.*, ~**ly**, *adv.* onregelmatig; ongeregeld. ¶ *n.* ~*s*, ongeregelde troepen *pl.n.* **irregularity**, *n.* onregelmatigheid *n.*

irrelevancy, *n.* ontoepasselijkheid *n.* **irrelevant**, *a.*, ~**ly**, *adv.* ontoepasselijk. *it is* ~ *to . . .*, het heeft niets uit te staan met . . .

irreligious, *a.*, ~**ly**, *adv.* ongodsdienstig.

irremediable, *a.*, ~**bly**, *adv.* onherstelbaar.

irremissible, *a.*, ~**bly**, *adv.* onvergeeflijk.

irremovable, *a.* onwrikbaar; niet verwijderbaar.

irreparable, *a.*, ~**bly**, *adv.* onherstelbaar.

irrepressible, *a.*, ~**bly**, *adv.* onbedwingbaar.

irreproachable, *a.*, ~**bly**, *adv.* onberispelijk.

irresistibility, *n.* onweerstaanbaarheid *n.* **irresistible**, *a.*, ~**bly**, *adv.* onweerstaanbaar.

irresolute, *a.*, ~**ly**, *adv.* besluiteloos. **irresolution**, *n.* besluiteloosheid *n.*

irrespective, *a.* niets ontziend. ~ *of*, zonder aanzien van. **irrespectively**, *adv.* ongeacht. ~ *of*, zonder aanzien van.

irresponsible, *a.* onverantwoordelijk.

irretrievable, *a.*, ~**bly**, *adv.* onherstelbaar, onherroepelijk.

irreverence, *n.* oneerbiedigheid *n.* **irreverent**, *a.*, ~**ly**, *adv.* oneerbiedig.

irrevocable, *a.*, ~**bly**, *adv.* onherroepelijk.

irrigate, *v.t.* besproeien; irrigeren. **irrigation**, *n.* irrigatie *n.*

irritability, *n.* prikkelbaarheid *n.* **irritable**, *a.*, ~**bly**, *adv.* prikkelbaar; lichtgeraakt. **irritant**, *a.* prikkelend. ¶ *n.* prikkelend middel *n.n.* **irritate**, *v.t.* prikkelen. **irritation**, *n.* prikkeling *n.*; geprikkeldheid *n.*, ergernis *n.*

irruption, *n.* inval *n.*, binnendrijven *n.n.*

isinglass, *n.* vislijm *n.*

island, *n.* eiland *n.n.*; vluchtheuvel *n.* **islander**, *n.* eilandbewoner *n.* **isle**, *n.* eiland *n.n.* **islet**, *n.* eilandje *n.n.*

isolate, *v.t.* afzonderen, isoleren. **isolation**, *n.* afzondering *n.*, isolering *n.*

issue, *v.i.* te voorschijn komen *irr.* *to* ~ *from*, ontspruiten *str.* uit; voortspruiten *str.* uit. ¶ *v.t.* uitvaardigen; in omloop brengen *irr.* ¶ *n.* resultaat *n.n.*; uitweg *n.*; nakomelingschap *n.*; uitgifte *n.*; circulatie *n.*; nummer *n.n.*

isthmus, *n.* landengte *n.*

it, *pron.* het; hij, zij; dit, dat. *with* ~, daarmee.

Italian, *a.* Italiaans. ¶ *N.* Italiaan. **Italy**, *N.* Italië *n.N.*

italicize, *v.t.* cursief schrijven *str.* **italics**, *pl.n.* cursief *n.n.*

itch, *v.i.* jeuken. ¶ *n.* jeuk *n.*; schurft *n.*

item, *adv.* eveneens. ¶ *n.* post *n.*; artikel *n.n.*; bijzonderheid *n.*; bericht *n.n.* **itemize**, *v.t.* specificeren.

iterate, *v.t.* herhalen.

itinerant, *a.* rondreizend. **itinerary**, *n.* reisroute *n.*; reisplan *n.n.* ¶ *a.* reis . . ., weg . . .

its, *pron.* zijn, haar. **itself**, *pron.* zichzelf. *in* ~, op zichzelf; *by* ~, alleen.

ivory, *n.* ivoor *n.n.* ~ *black*, ivoorzwart *n.n.* ¶ *a.* ivoren.

ivy, *n.* klimop *n.n.*

J

jab, *v.t.* steken *str.*, porren. ¶ *n.* steek *n.*, por *n.*

jabber, *v.i.* wauwelen. **jabbering**, *n.* gewauwel *n.n.*

jack, *n.* dommekracht *n.*, vijzel *n.*; boer *n.* *every man* ~, iedereen; ~ *tar*, pekbroek *n.*

jackal, *n.* jakhals *n.*

jackanapes, *n.* aap *n.*

jack-ass, *n.* mannetjesezel *n.* **jack-boots**, *pl.n.* waterlaarzen *pl.n.*

jackdaw, *n.* kauw *n.*

jacket, *n.* jas *n.*, jasje *n.n.*; jekker *n.*; omslag *n.*

Jack-of-all-trades, *n.* twaalf ambachten *pl.n.n.* dertien ongelukken *pl.n.n.*

jade, *n.* nephriet *n.*, bittersteen *n.*; slet *n.* **jaded**, *a.* afgemat; blasé.

jag, *v.t.* kerven *str.* **jagged**, *a.* gepunt, getand.

jail, *n.* gevangenis *n.* ¶ *v.t.* in de gevangenis zetten. **jailer**, *n.* cipier *n.*

jam, *n.* jam *n.*, gelei *n.*; opeenhoping *n.*, opstopping *n.*, gedrang *n.n.* ¶ *v.t.* persen. ¶ *v.i.* vastlopen *str.*, blijven *str.* steken.

jamb, *n.* post *n.*, stijl *n.*

jangle, *v.t.* rammelen, tjingelen.

janitor, *n.* portier *n.*, concierge *n.*

Janissary, *N.* Janitsaar *n.*

January, *N.* januari *N.*

japan, *n.* japans lakwerk *n.n.* ¶ *v.t.* verlakken. **Japan**, *N.* Japan. **Japanese**, *a.* Japans. ¶ *N.* Japanner *N.*, Japannees *N.* (*male*); Japanse *N.* (*female*). **japanner**, *n.* verlakker *n.*

jar, *n.* pot *n.*, fles *n.*; schok *n.* ¶ *v.i.* knarsen, krassen. *to* ~ *with*, niet harmoniëren met; strijden tegen. ¶ *v.t.* stoten *str.*

jargon, *n.* koeterwaals *n.n.*; eigen taaltje *n.n.*

jasmine, *n.* jasmijn *n.*

jasper, *n.* jaspis *n.n.* (*material*), *n.* (*jewel*).

jaundice, *n.* geelzucht *n.* **jaundiced**, *a.* geelzuchtig; pessimistisch.

jaunt, *n.* uitstapje *n.n.* **jaunty**, *a.*, ~ily, *adv.* zwierig.

javelin, *n.* werpspies *n.*

jaw, *n.* kaak *n.*; kaakbeen *n.n.*; (*coll.*) brutaliteit *n.* ¶ *v.i.* (*coll.*) kletsen.

jay, *n.* Vlaamse gaai *n.*

jealous, *a.*, ~ly, *adv.* jaloers; angstvallig; bezorgd. **jealousy**, *n.* jaloersheid *n.*; naijver *n.*

jeer, *v..i.* honen, spotten. to ~ at, bespotten, honen.

jejune, *a.* flauw; schraal.

jelly, *n.* gelei *n.* **jelly-fish**, *n.* kwal *n.*

jemmy, *n.* (kort) breekijzer *n.n.*

jenny, *n.* spinmachine *n.*

jenny-ass, *n.* ezelin *n.*

jeopardize, *v.t.* op het spel zetten. **jeopardy**, *n.* gevaar *n.n.*

jerk, *v.t.* stoten *str.*, rukken. ¶ *n.* stoot *n.*, ruk *n.*, hort *n.* by ~s, met horten en stoten.

jerkin, *n.* wambuis *n.n.*

jerry-building, *n.* revolutiebouw *n.*

jersey, *n.* sporttrui *n.*

jest, *n.* grap *n.*, kwinkslag *n.* in ~, voor de grap; uit de grap. ¶ *v.i.* schertsen, grapjes *pl.n.n.* maken. **jester**, *n.* hofnar *n.*; grappenmaker *n.* **jestingly**, *a.* schertsenderwijs.

Jesuit, *N.* Jezuïet *N.* **jesuitical**, *a.*, ~ly, *adv.* Jezuïetisch.

Jesus, *N.* Jezus *N.*

jet, *n.* git *n.n.*; straal *n.*; sproeier *n.*; vlam *n.* **jet-plane**, *n.* schroefloos vliegtuig *n.n.* **jet-black**, *a.* pikzwart.

jetsam, *n.* strandgoed *n.n.*, wrakgoed *n.n.*

jettison, *v.t.* overboord werpen *str.*

jetty, *n.* pier *n.*, havenhoofd *n.n.*

Jew, *N.* Jood *N.* **Jew's-harp**, *n.* mondharp *n.*

jewel, *n.* juweel *n.n.* ¶ *v.t.* van stenen *pl.n.* voorzien *irr.* **jeweller**, *n.* juwelier *n.* **jewellery**, *n.* juwelen *pl.n.n.*

Jewess, *N.* Jodin *N.* **Jewish**, *a.* Joods. **Jewry**, *N.* Jodendom *n.N.*

jib, *n.* kluiver *n.*; kraanarm *n.* ¶ *v.i.* niet aandurven.

jiffy, *n* ogenblikje *n.n.*. tikje *n.n.* in a ~, in een wip *n.*

jig, *n.* horlepijp *n.* ¶ *v.i.* (de horlepijp) dansen.

jigger, *n.* pottenbakkersschijf *n.*; biljartbok *n.*; mesje *n.n.*

jigsaw, *n.* rondzaag *n.* ~ puzzle, legkaart *n.*

jilt, *v.t.* de bons geven *str.*, laten *str.* zitten. ¶ *n.* coquette *n.*

jingle, *v.i.* rinkelen. ¶ *v.t.* (laten *str.*) rinkelen. ¶ *n.* gerinkel *n.n.*

jingo, *n.* chauvinist *n.* by ~, verdikke! **jingoism**, *n.* chauvinisme *n.n.*

job, *n.* baantje *n.n.*; karwei *n.* odd ~s, allerlei karweitjes *pl.n.n.* ¶ *a.* a ~ lot, een rommelzootje *n.n.* ¶ *v.t.* scharrelen; verhuren; knoeien. **jobber**, *n.* makelaar;

effectenhandelaar *n.* **jobbery**, *n.* knoeierij *n.*

jockey, *n.* jockey *n.*, pikeur *n.* ¶ *v.t.* verdringen *str.*; met kunstgrepen *pl.n.* bereiken.

jocose, *a.*, ~ly, *adv.* grappig, vol scherts.

jocular, *a.*, ~ly, *adv.* grappig.

jocund, *a.*, ~ly, *adv.* blij, vrolijk.

jog, *v.t.* schudden; porren. ¶ *v.i.* horten, sjokken. ¶ *n.* stootje *n.n.* **joggle**, *v.i.* sjokken. to ~ along, voortsukkelen. **jog-trot**, *n.* sukkeldrafje *n.n.*

John Bull, *N.* de Engelsman *N.*

join, *v.t.* samenvoegen, verbinden *str.*; zich aansluiten *str.* bij. to ~ battle, de strijd aanbinden *str.* ¶ *v.i.* lid *n.n.* worden *str.* to ~ in, meedoen *irr.*; to ~ up, onder dienst *n.* gaan *irr.* ¶ *n.* aaneenvoeging *n.*, koppeling *n.*, las *n.* **joiner**, *n.* schrijnwerker *n.* **joint**, *n.* voeg *n.*; gewricht *n.n.*; scharnier *n.*; bout *n.*, groot stuk *n.n.* vlees *n.n.* ¶ *a.* verenigd. on ~ account, voor gezamenlijke rekening *n.* ¶ *v.t.* voegen; verbinden *str.* **joint-heir**, *n.* mede-erfgenaam *n.* **jointly**, *adv.* gezamenlijk. **joint-stock company**, *n.* maatschappij *n.* op aandelen *pl.n.n.*

jointure, *n.* weduwgoed *n.n.*

joist, *n.* dwarsbalk *n.*; rib *n.*

joke, *n.* grap *n.*; aardigheid *n.* beyond a ~, al te mal; it is no ~, 't is geen gekheid *n.* ¶ *v.i.* grappen maken. joking apart, alle gekheid *n.* op een stokje *n.n.* **joker**, *n.* grappenmaker *n.*; troefkaart *n.*

jollification, *n.* fuifje *n.n.* **jollity**, *n.* pret *n.*, vrolijkheid *n.* **jolly**, *a.*, ~ily, *adv.* vrolijk; lollig, aardig; leuk. **jolly-boat**, *n.* jol *n.*

jolt, *v.i.* horten, hotsen, stoten *str.*, schudden. ¶ *v.t.* doen *irr.* schudden. ¶ *n.* hort *n.*, stoot *n.*

jonquil, *n.* jonquille *n.*

jostle, *v.t.* (ver)dringen *str.*, duwen.

jot, *n.* jota *n.* not a ~, geen zier *n.* ¶ *v.t.* to ~ down, optekenen.

journal, *n.* dagboek *n.n.*; journaal *n.n.*; tijdschrift *n.n.* **journalism**, *n.* journalistiek *n.* **journalist**, *n.* journalist *n.*, dagboekschrijver *n.*

journey, *n.* reis *n.* ¶ *v.i.* reizen, trekken *str.* **journeyman**, *n.* dagloner *n.*; gezel *n.*, knecht *n.* ~ tailor, kleermakersgezel *n.*

joust, *n.* tournooi *n.n.*, steekspel *n.n.* ¶ *v.i.* aan een tournooi *n.n.* deelnemen *str.*

Jove, *N.* Jupiter *N.* by ~, sapperloot!

jovial, *a.*, ~ly, *adv.* opgewekt, joviaal, gezellig. **joviality**, *n.* opgewektheid *n.*, jovialiteit *n.*

jowl, *n.* kaak *n.* cheek by ~ with, vlak naast.

joy, *n.* vreugde *n.*, blijdschap *n.*, genoegen *n.n.* **joyful**, *a.*, ~ly, *adv.* vreugdevol, blij. **joyless**, *a.*, ~ly, *adv.* treurig, verdrietig. **joyous**, *a.*, ~ly, *adv.* vreugdevol, blij, verheugd. **joy-ride**, *n.* uitstapje *n.n.*, plezierrit *n.* **joy-stick**, *n.* stuurknuppel *n.*

jubilant, *a.* jubelend, uitbundig blij. **jubilation,** *n.* gejubel *n.n.*, vreugdebetoon *n.n.*
jubilee, *n.* jubileum *n.n.*
Judaic, *a.* Joods. **Judaism,** *N.* Jodendom *n.N.*
judge, *n.* rechter *n.* *J~s,* Richteren *pl.N.*
¶ *v.i.* rechtspreken *str.;* oordelen. ¶ *v.t.*
vonnissen; achten; schatten. **judgment,** *n.*
oordeel *n.n.;* vonnis *n.n.,* uitspraak *n.*
J~ Day, dag *n.* des Oordeels.
judicature, *n.* rechterlijke macht *n.;* rechtspleging *n.,* rechtspraak *n.* **judicial,** *a.*
~ly, *adv.* rechterlijk, gerechtelijk; oordeelkundig. **judicious,** *a.,* ~ly, *adv.* oordeelkundig; weloverlegd.
jug, *n.* kruik *n.,* kan *n.;* kannetje *n.n.;* (*coll.*)
doos *n.* ¶ *v.t.* in de pot koken. ~ged
hare, hazenpeper *n.*
juggle, *v.i.* goochelen. **juggler,** *n.* goochelaar *n.*
jugular, *a.* ~ *vein,* halsader *n.*
juice, *n.* sap *n.n.* **juiciness,** *n.* sappigheid *n.*
juicy, *a.,* ~ily, *adv.* sappig.
jujube, *n.* jujube *n.*
julep, *n.* koeldrank *n.*
July, *N.* juli *N.*
jumble, *n.* warboel *n.* ~ *sale,* bazaar *n.*
¶ *v.t.* door elkaar gooien, dooreenhaspelen.
jump, *v.i.* springen *str.;* opspringen *str.*
to ~ at, afspringen *str.* op. ¶ *v.t.* springen
str. over *or* uit; wegkapen. ¶ *n.* sprong *n.*
jumper, *n.* springer *n.;* jumper *n.,* wollen
jakje *n.n.* **jumping beetle,** *n.* springtor *n.*
jumpy, *a.* zenuwachtig.
junction, *n.* verbinding *n.;* verenigingspunt
n.n.
juncture, *n.* ogenblik *n.n.;* samenloop *n.* van
omstandigheden *pl.n.*
June, *N.* juni *N.*
jungle, *n.* rimboe *n.;* oerwoud *n.n.*
junior, *a.* jongere, jongste. ¶ *n.* junior *n.,*
jongere *n.* *he is my ~,* hij is jonger dan
ik; hij is later aangesteld dan ik.
juniper, *n.* jeneverstruik *n.* **juniper-berry,** *n.*
jeneverbes *n.*
junk, *n.* jonk *n.;* rommel *n.*
junket, *n.* (soort) wrongel *n.*
juridical, *a.,* ~ly, *adv.* gerechtelijk, juridisch.
jurisdiction, *n.* rechtsmacht *n.;* rechtsgebied *n.n.;* rechtshandeling *n.;* jurisdictie
n. **jurisprudence,** *n.* jurisprudentie *n.,*
rechtsgeleerdheid *n.* **jurist,** *n.* jurist *n.,*
rechtsgeleerde *n.* **juror,** *n.* gezworene *n.,*
jurylid *n.n.* **jury,** *n.* jury *n.,* rechtbank *n.*
van gezworenen *pl.n.* **jury-box,** *n.* bank *n.*
der gezworenen *pl.n.* **juryman,** *n.* gezworene *n.,* jurylid *n.n.* **jury-mast,** *n.*
noodmast *n.*
just, *a.* juist, rechtvaardig; welverdiend.
¶ *adv.* juist, even; juist, precies. ~ *as,*
even als; ~ *as well,* net even goed;
~ *fancy!,* verbeeld je!; ~ *now,* daarnet,
zoëven; *it's ~ possible,* de mogelijkheid
bestaat; *not ~ yet,* vooreerst niet. **justice,**
n. rechtvaardigheid *n.;* gerechtigheid *n.;*
magistraat *n.,* rechter *n.*

justifiable, *a.,* ~bly, *adv.* verdedigbaar, te
rechtvaardigen. **justification,** *n.* recht-
vaardiging *n.;* verantwoording *n.* **justify,**
v.t. rechtvaardigen; wettigen, verantwoorden.
justly, *adv* rechtvaardig; terecht, met recht.
justness, *n.* juistheid *n.;* rechtvaardigheid
n.; rechtmatigheid *n.*
jut, *v.i.* uitsteken *str.,* vooruitspringen *str.*
jute, *n.* jute *n.*
juvenile, *a.* jeugdig, kinder . . .
juxtaposition, *n.* naast elkaar plaatsing *n.*

K

kale, *n.* kool *n.* *curly ~,* boerenkool *n.*
kaleidoscope, *n.* kaleidoscoop *n.*
kangaroo, *n.* kangoeroe *n.*
kedge, *n.* werpanker *n.n.*
keel, *n.* kiel *n.* *false ~,* loze kiel *n.* ¶ *v.i.*
to ~ over, omslaan *irr.,* kantelen.
keen, *a.,* ~ly, *adv.* scherp; levendig; scherpzinnig; gesteld, belust. **keenness,** *n.*
scherpheid *n.;* scherpzinnigheid *n.;* belust-
heid *n.*
keep, *v.t.* houden *irr.;* bewaren; vervullen;
behoeden; onderhouden *irr.;* vieren. *to ~*
from, verborgen houden *irr.* voor; *to ~ off,*
van 't lijf houden *irr.;* *to ~ on,* ophouden
irr.; aanhouden *irr.;* *to ~ under,* er onder
houden *irr.;* *to ~ up,* onderhouden *irr.;*
volhouden *irr.* ¶ *v.i.* goed blijven *str.;*
zich houden *irr.* *to ~ walking,* blijven *str.*
lopen; *to ~ at,* volhouden *irr.* met; *to ~*
away, wegblijven *str.;* *to ~ off,* afblijven
str. van; *to ~ on,* doorgaan *irr.* met. ¶ *n.*
onderhoud *n.n.;* kost *n.;* bewaring *n.;*
slottoren *n.* **keeper,** *n.* bewaarder *n.;*
jachtopzichter *n.;* curator *n.* **keeping,** *n.*
bewaring *n.* *in ~ with,* in overeenstemming
n. met. **keepsake,** *n.* aandenken *n.n.,*
gedachtenis *n.*
keg, *n.* vaatje *n.n.*
ken, *n.* gezichtskring *n.* *within ~,* zichtbaar.
kennel, *n.* hondenhok *n.n.*
kerb, *n.,* **kerbstone,** *n.* trottoirband *n.*
kerchief, *n.* (hoofd)doek *n.*
kernel, *n.* kern *n.;* pit *n.*
ketch, *n.* kaag *n.*
ketchup, *n.* pikante saus *n.*
kettle, *n.* ketel *n.* **kettle-drum,** *n.* pauk *n.*
keteltrom *n.*
key, *n.* sleutel *n.;* toets *n.;* toonaard *n.*
keyboard, *n.* klavier *n.n.* **keyhole,** *n.*
sleutelgat *n.n.* **keynote,** *n.* grondtoon *n.*
keystone, *n.* sluitsteen *n.*
khaki, *n.* khaki *n.n.* ¶ *a.* khaki.
kick, *v.t.* schoppen, trappen. *to ~ out,* eruit
trappen; *to ~ up a row,* herrie maken.
¶ *n.* schop *n.,* trap *n.;* terugstoot *n.*
to get a ~ out of, genoegen *n.n.* scheppen
str. in.

kid, *n.* jonge geit *n.*; geitenleer *n.n.*; glacé *n.n.*; kind *n.n.* ¶ *a.* van geitenleer *n.n.* ¶ *v.t.* voor de gek houden *irr.* **kid gloves,** *pl.n.* glacé-handschoenen *pl.n.*

kidnap, *v.t.* ontvoeren; pressen. **kidnapper,** *n.* kinderdief *n.*

kidney, *n.* nier *n.* **kidney-bean,** *n.* witte boon *n.*

kill, *v.t.* doden; slachten; verdoven. *to be ~ed,* gedood worden *str.*; sneuvelen. ¶ *n.* doden *n.n.* *to be in at the ~,* bij het einde aanwezig zijn. **killing,** *a.* dodelijk; onweerstaanbaar; buitengewoon grappig. **kill-joy,** *n.* spelbederver *n.*

kiln, *n.* kalkoven *n.*; eest *n.* **kiln-dry,** *v.t.* in een kalkoven *or* eest drogen.

kilt, *n.* Schotse rok *n.*

kin, *n.* bloedverwanten *pl.n.*, magen *pl.n.* **kinship,** *n.* (bloed)verwantschap *n.*

kind, *n.* soort *n.* or *n.n.*; aard *n.*, natuur *n.* *in ~,* in natura; in dezelfde munt. ¶ *a.* vriendelijk; welwillend.

kindergarten, *n.* Fröbelschool *n.*

kindle, *v.t.* aansteken *str.*, doen *irr.* ontvlammen; opwekken.

kindliness, *n.* goedheid *n.*, welwillendheid *n.* **kindly,** *a.* goed, goedaardig, welwillend. **kindness,** *n.* vriendelijkheid *n.*, goedheid *n.*

kindred, *n.* aanverwant; soortgelijk.

kine, *pl.n.* koeien *pl.n.*

kinetic, *a.* kinetisch, bewegings . . .

king, *n.* koning *n.* **kingcup,** *n.* dotterbloem *n.* **kingdom,** *n.* koninkrijk *n.n.*, rijk *n.n.* **kingfisher,** *n.* ijsvogel *n.* **kinglike,** *a.*, **kingly,** *a.* koninklijk. **King's Bench,** *N.* (vroeger) Hoog Gerechtshof *n.N.*

kink, *n.* kink *n.*, slag *n.*, kronkel *n.*

kinsfolk, *pl.n.* verwanten *pl.n.* **kinship,** *n.* verwantschap *n.* **kinsman,** *n.* bloedverwant *n.*

kipper, *n.* (soort) gerookte en gezouten vis *n.*

kirk, *n.* (Schotse) kerk *n.*

kiss, *n.* kus *n.*, zoen *n.* ¶ *v.t.* kussen, zoenen. ¶ *v.i.* (elkaar) kussen.

kit, *n.* gereedschap *n.n.*; uitrustingsmateriaal *n.n.* **kitbag,** *n.* gereedschapstas *n.*; plunjezak *n.*

kitchen, *n.* keuken *n.* **kitchen-dresser,** *n.* aanrecht *n.*, rechtbank *n.* **kitchen-garden,** *n.* moestuin *n.* **kitchen-maid,** *n.* tweede keukenmeid *n.* **kitchen-range,** *n.* (kook)-fornuis *n.n.*

kite, *n.* wouw *n.*; vlieger *n.*

kith, *n.* ~ *and kin,* vrienden *pl.n.* en magen *pl.n.*

kitten, *n.* katje *n.n.*, poesje *n.n.* ¶ *v.i.* jongen *pl.n.n.* krijgen *str.* **kittenish,** *a.* speels.

kleptomania, *n.* kleptomanie *n.* **kleptomaniac,** *n.* kleptomaan *n.*

knack, *n.* handigheid *n.*, slag *n.*; gewoonte *n.*

knacker, *n.* paardenvilder *n.*

knapsack, *n.* ransel *n.n.*; knapzak *n.*

knave, *n.* schurk *n.*, schelm *n.*; boer *n.* (*card*).

knavery, *n.* schurkerij *n.*; schelmenstreken *pl.n.* **knavish,** *a.*, ~**ly,** *adv.* schurkachtig, schelmachtig.

knead, *v.t.* kneden. **kneading-trough,** *n.* (bakkers)trog *n.*

knee, *n.* knie *n.* **knee-cap,** *n.* knieschijf *n.*

kneel, *v.i.* knielen.

knell, *n.* doodsklok *n.* ¶ *v.i.* de doodsklok luiden.

knickerbockers, *pl.n.* wijde kniebroek *n.* **knickers,** *pl.n.* onderbroek *n.*, pantalon *n.*

knick-knacks, *pl.n.* snuisterijen *pl.n.*

knife, *n.* mes *n.n.* ¶ *v.t.* (dood)steken *str.* **knife-grinder,** *n.* scharenslijper *n.* **knife-sharpener,** *n.* mesaanzetter *n.*

knight, *n.* ridder *n.*; paard *n.n.* (*chess*). ¶ *v.t.* tot ridder slaan *irr.* **knight-errant,** *n.* dolende ridder *n.* **knighthood,** *n.* ridderschap *n.* *order of ~,* ridderorde *n.* **knightly,** *a.* ridderlijk.

knit, *v.i.* breien; knopen. ¶ *v.t.* breien; knopen. *to ~ one's brows,* de wenkbrauwen *pl.n.* fronsen. **knitter,** *n.* breister *n.* **knitting,** *n.* breiwerk *n.n.* **knitting-needle,** *n.* breinaald *n.*, breipen *n.*

knob, *n.* knop *n.*; knobbel *n.* **knobby,** *a.* knobbelig.

knock, *v.t.* kloppen, bonzen; slaan *irr.* *to ~ down,* neerslaan *irr.*; toewijzen *str.* ¶ *v.i.* *to ~ about,* rondzwerven *str.* ¶ *n.* klop *n.*; slag *n.* **knocker,** *n.* klopper *n.* **knock-kneed,** *a.* met X-benen. **knock-out,** *n.* knockout *n.*

knoll, *n.* heuveltje *n.n.*

knot, *v.t.* aaneenknopen. ¶ *n.* knoop *n.*; klompje *n.n.* **knotty,** *a.*, ~**ily,** *adv.* ingewikkeld, netelig.

knout, *n.* knoet *n.*

know, *v.t.* weten *irr.*; kennen; kunnen *irr.* ¶ *n.* *to be in the ~,* weet *n.* hebben (van . . .). **knowing,** *a.* geslepen; veelbetekenend. **knowingly,** *adv.* met opzet *n.*; met kennis *n.* van zaken *pl.n.* **knowledge,** *n.* kennis *n.*; kunde *n.*; wetenschap *n.*, medeweten *n.n.* *it is common ~,* 't is algemeen bekend; *without my ~,* zonder mijn voorkennis *n.*

knuckle, *n.* knokkel *n.*; schenkel *n.* ¶ *v.i.* *to ~ down to,* zwichten *irr.* voor. **knuckleduster,** *n.* boksijzer *n.n.*

kowtow, *v.i.* *to ~ to,* zich onderdanig gedragen voor, flikflooien.

kudos, *n.* eer *n.*, roem *n.*

L

label, *n.* etiket *n.n.* ¶ *v.t.* van een etiket voorzien *irr.*; een naam *n.* geven *str.*

labial, *a.* lip . . . ¶ *n.* lipklank *n.*

laboratory, *n.* laboratorium *n.n.*

laborious, *a.*, ~**ly,** *adv.* werkzaam; omslachtig. **labour,** *n.* arbeid *n.*; werkkrachten

pl.n.; barensweeën *pl.n.n.* *hard* ~,
dwangarbeid *n.*; *L*~ or *the L*~ *Party*,
de Arbeiderspartij *N.* ¶ *v.i.* arbeiden,
werken. *to* ~ *under a misapprehension*,
onder een dwaling *n.* verkeren. ¶ *v.t.*
to ~ *a point*, ergens verder op ingaan *irr.*
labourer, *n.* arbeider *n.* **labour exchange,**
n. arbeidsbeurs *n.*
laburnum, *n.* gouden regen *n.*
labyrinth, *n.* doolhof *n.*
lace, *n.* veter *n.*; kant *n.n.* ¶ *v.t.* (dicht)-
rijgen *str.*; (met kant *n.n.*) afzetten.
lacerate, *v.t.* scheuren, openscheuren. **lacera-**
tion, *n.* openscheuring *n.*
lachrymose, *a.* huilerig.
lack, *v.t.* gebrek *n.n.* hebben aan, een tekort
n.n. hebben aan. ¶ *n.* gebrek *n.n.*, gemis
n.n., tekort *n.n.*
lackadaisical, *a.* smachtend, geaffecteerd.
lackey, *n.* lakei *n.*
laconic, *a.* laconisch.
lacquer, *n.* lak *n.n.*; vernis *n.n.* ¶ *v.t.* verlakken.
lactation, *n.* melkafscheiding *n.*; zogen *n.n.*
lacteal, *a.* melk . . .
lacuna, *n.* leemte *n.*, gaping *n.*
lad, *n.* knaap *n.*, jongen *n.*
ladder, *n.* ladder *n.*
lade, *v.t.* beladen. **lading,** *n.* lading *n.*
bill of ~, vrachtbrief *n.*, cognossement *n.n.*
ladle, *n.* pollepel *n.*; soeplepel *n.* ¶ *v.t.*
to ~ *out*, oplepelen, uitscheppen.
lady, *n.* dame *n.*; mevrouw *n.*; vrouw *n.*
~'*s maid*, kamenier *n.* **lady-bird,** *n.*
lieveheersbeestje *n.n.* **Lady Day,** *N.* Maria
Boodschap *N.* **ladylike,** *a.* damesachtig;
als een dame *n.* **ladyship,** *n.* (*titel van
een adellijke dame*).
lag, *v.i.* dralen. *to* ~ *behind*, achterblijven
str. ¶ *n.* boef *n.* **laggard,** *n.* treuzelaar *n.*
lagoon, *n.* lagune *n.*
laic, *a.*, ~*ally*, *adv.* leken . . . ¶ *n.* leek *n.*
laid, *a.* ~ *mould*, papiervorm *n.* met koperdraad *n.n.*; ~ *paper*, geribd papier *n.n.*
lair, *n.* leger *n.n.*; hol *n.n.*
laird, *n.* (Schotse) grondbezitter *n.*
laity, *n.* leken *pl.n.*
lake, *n.* meer *n.n.*, vijver *n.*
lamb, *n.* lam *n.n.*
lambent, *a.* stralend.
lambkin, *n.* lammetje *n.n.* **lamblike,** *a.*
zacht als een lam *n.n.*
lame, *a.*, ~*ly*, *adv.* mank, kreupel. ¶ *v.t.*
kreupel maken; verminken. **lameness,** *n.*
mankheid *n.*
lament, *v.i.* weeklagen, jammeren. ¶ *v.t.*
betreuren. ¶ *n.* weeklacht *n.* **lamentable,**
a., ~*bly*, *adv.* betreurenswaardig, jammerlijk. **lamentation,** *n.* weeklacht *n.* *L*~*s*,
Klaagliederen *pl.n.n.*
lamina, *pl.n.* dunne plaat *n.*, lamelle *n.*
Lammas, *N.* 1 Augustus *N.*
lamp, *n.* lamp *n.*; lantaarn *n.*, lantaren *n.*
lampoon, *n.* schotschrift *n.n.*

lamp-post, *n.* lantarenpaal *n.* **lamp-shade,** *n.*
lampekap *n.*
lamprey, *n.* lamprei *n.*
lance, *n.* lans *n.* ~ *corporal*, soldaat *n.*
eerste klasse *n.* ¶ *v.t.* lanceren. **lancer,** *n.*
lansier *n.* **lancet,** *n.* lancet *n.*
land, *n.* land *n.n.* *to see how the* ~ *lies*,
poolshoogte nemen *str.*; *by* ~, over land
n.n.; *on* ~, aan land *n.n.*; aan wal *n.*
¶ *v.i.* landen. *to* ~ *on*, terechtkomen *irr.*
op. ¶ *v.t.* landen; aan wal *n.* zetten.
landed, *a.* landerijen *pl.n.* bezittende.
~ *gentry*, (groot)grondbezitters *pl.n.*;
~ *property*, grondbezit *n.n.* **land-forces,**
pl.n. landmacht *n.* **landgrave,** *n.* landgraaf
n. **landing,** *n.* landing *n.*; portaal *n.n.*,
overloop *n.* ~ *place*, aanlegplaats *n.*;
~ *stage*, steiger *n.* **landlady,** *n.* kostjuf-
frouw *n.* hospita *n.*; waardin *n.* **landlord,** *n.*
huisbaas *n.*; kostbaas *n.*; herbergier *n.*,
waard *n.*, kastelein *n.* **landlubber,** *n.*
landrot *n.* **landmark,** *n.* baken *n.n.*;
mijlpaal *n.* **landowner,** *n.* grondbezitter *n.*
landscape, *n.* landschap *n.n.* **landslide,** *n.*
aardverschuiving *n.* **land-tax,** *n.* grondbelasting *n.*
lane, *n.* landweg *n.*; nauwe straat *n.*; vaargeul
n.
language, *n.* taal *n.* *bad* ~, scheldwoorden
pl.n.n., vloeken *pl.n.*
languid, *a.*, ~*ly*, *adv.* loom, lusteloos.
languish, *v.i.* kwijnen; verflauwen. *to* ~
for, smachten naar. **languor,** *n.* matheid
n., loomheid *n.*, lusteloosheid *n.*
lank, *a.*, **lanky,** *a.* sluik; schraal. **lankness,** *n.*
schraalheid *n.*
lansquenet, *n.* lansknecht *n.*
lantern, *n.* lantaarn *n.*, lantaren *n.* *Chinese*
~, lampion *n.*; *dark* ~, dievenlantaren *n.*
lantern-jawed, *a.* met een lang, mager
gezicht *n.n.*
lap, *n.* schoot *n.*; ronde *n.* ¶ *v.t.* likken,
oplikken. **lap-dog,** *n.* schoothondje *n.n.*
lapel, *n.* lapel *n.*
lapidary, *n.* steensnijder *n.* **lapidation,** *n.*
steniging *n.*
lapis-lazuli, *n.* lazuursteen *n.*
lapse, *v.i.* vervallen *str.*, verlopen *str.* ¶ *n.*
verloop *n.n.*; afdwaling *n.*, misstap *n.*
lapwing, *n.* kievit *n.*
larboard, *n.* bakboord *n.n.*
larceny, *n.* diefstal *n.*
larch, *n.* lariks *n.*, lorkenboom *n.*
lard, *n.* (varkens)reuzel *n.* ¶ *v.t.* larderen;
(door)spekken.
larder, *n.* provisiekamer *n.*, provisiekast *n.*
larding-needle, *n.* lardeerpriem *n.*
large, *a.* groot; ruim, wijd. ¶ *n.* *at* ~, op
vrije voeten *pl.n.*; *the public at* ~, het
grote publiek. **largely,** *adv.* grotendeels;
in 't algemeen. **largeness,** *n.* grootheid *n.*;
grootte *n.*
largesse, *n.* vrijgevigheid *n.*, mildheid *n.*;
gave *n.*

lark, *n.* leeuwerik *n.*; lolletje *n.n.*
larkspur *n.* ridderspoor *n.*
larva, *n.* larve *n.*, pop *n.*
larynx, *n.* strottenhoofd *n.n.*
Lascar, *N.* Laskaar *N.*
lascivious, *a.*, ~ly, *adv.* wellustig.
lash, *n.* zweepslag *n.*; gesel *n.* ¶ *v.i.* slaan *irr.*
  to ~ *out,* slaan *irr.*, achteruitslaan *irr.*
  ¶ *v.t.* slaan *irr.*; vastbinden *str.*, vast-
  sjorren.
lass, *n.* meisje *n.n.*
lassitude, *n.* moeheid *n.*, afmatting *n.*
lasso, *n.* lasso *n.* ¶ *v.t.* met een lasso vangen;
  str.
last, *n.* leest *n.* (*shoemaker*); last *n.* (*weight*);
  duur *n.*, uithoudingsvermogen *n.n.*;
  laatst(e) *n.n. at* ~, tenslotte; *at long* ~,
  ten langen leste. ¶ *v.i.* duren; het uithouden *irr.* ¶ *a.* laatst(e); vorig, verleden;
  jongstleden. ¶ *adv.* tenslotte. lasting, *a.*
  duurzaam; bestendig. lastly, *adv.* ten
  laatste, tenslotte.
latch, *n.* klink *n.* ¶ *v.t.* op de klink doen *irr.*
latchkey, *n.* huissleutel *n.*
late, *a.* laat; te laat; wijlen. ¶ *adv.* laat; te
  laat. *as* ~ *as,* tot aan; tot in. lately, *adv.*
  onlangs; in de laatste tijd.
latent, *a.* verborgen; latent.
lateral, *a.*, ~ly, *adv.* zijdelings, zij . . .
latex, *n.* melksap *n.n.*
lath, *n.* lat *n.* ~ *and plaster,* bepleisterde
  latten *pl.n.*
lathe, *n.* draaibank *n.*
lather, *n.* schuim *n.n.*, zeepsop *n.n.* ¶ *v.i.*
  schuimen. ¶ *v.t.* inzepen.
Latin, *N.* Latijn *n.N.* ¶ *a.* latijns.
latitude, *n.* breedte *n.*; vrijheid *n.* (van
  handelen *n.n.*), speling *n.* latitudinarian,
  n. vrijzinnige *n.*
latrine, *n.* latrine *n.*
latter, *a.* laatste. ¶ *n. the* ~, de laatste,
  deze.
lattice, *n.* latwerk *n.n.*, traliewerk *n.n.* ¶ *v.t.*
  van traliewerk *n.n.* voorzien *irr.*
laud, *v.t.* prijzen *str.* laudable, *a.*, ~bly,
  adv. prijzenswaardig.
laudanum, *n.* laudanum *n.n.*, opiumtinctuur
  n.
laudatory, *a.* lovend, prijzend.
laugh, *v.i.* lachen *irr. to* ~ *at,* lachen om,
  uitlachen *irr.* ¶ *n.* gelach *n.n.*; lach *n.*
  laughable, *a.* belachelijk; lachwekkend.
  laughing stock, *n.* mikpunt *n.n.* van
  spotternij *n.* laughter, *n.* gelach *n.n.*
launch, *v.t.* van stapel *n.* laten *str.* lopen, te
  water *n.n.* laten *str.*; lanceren. ¶ *v.i.*
  to ~ *forth,* in zee *n.* steken *str.*; *to* ~ *into,*
  beginnen *str.* aan. ¶ *n.* sloep *n.*
laundress, *n.* wasvrouw *n.* laundry, *n.*
  wasserij *n.*; was *n.*
laureate, *a.* gelauwerd. *Poet L* ~, hofdichter
  n.
laurel, *n.* laurier *n.* ~*s,* lauweren *pl.n.*
lava, *n.* lava *n.*

lavatory, *n.* toilet *n.n.*, toiletkamer *n.*,
  retirade.
lave, *v.t.* baden, wassen.
lavender, *n.* lavendel *n.*
lavish, *a.*, ~ly, *adv.* kwistig. ¶ *v.t.* kwistig
  uitdelen.
law, *n.* wet *n.*; recht *n.n. to go to* ~,
  procederen; *to lay down the* ~, de wet
  stellen. law-abiding, *a.* ordelievend.
  law court, *n.* rechtbank *n.* lawful, *a.*,
  ~ly, *adv.* wettig; wettelijk; rechtmatig.
  lawless, *a.*, ~ly, *adv.* wetteloos; ongebreideld.
lawn, *n.* grasveld *n.n.*, grasperk *n.n.*; batist
  n.n. lawn-tennis, *n.* tennis *n.n.*
lawsuit, *n.* proces *n.n.*, rechtsgeding *n.n.*
  lawyer, *n.* advocaat *n.*; rechtsgeleerde *n.*
lax, *a.*, ~ly, *adv.* laks, slordig; slap. laxative,
  a. laxerend. ¶ *n.* laxeermiddel *n.n.* laxity,
  n. laksheid *n.*
lay, *v.t.* leggen *irr.*; bezweren *str.*; stillen,
  lessen. *to* ~ *the table,* tafel *n.* dekken;
  to ~ *by,* wegleggen *irr.*; op zij leggen *irr.*;
  to ~ *it on,* overdrijven *str.*; het er dik
  opleggen *irr.* ¶ *v.i. to* ~ *off,* ophouden *irr.*
  ¶ *n.* ballade *n.*, lied *n.n.*; ligging *n.*;
  karwei *n.* ¶ *a.* leken . . . layer, *n.* laag *n.*;
  leghen *n.* lay-figure, *n.* ledepop *n.*,
  mannequin *n.* or *n.n.* layman, *n.* leek *n.*
laze, *v.i.* luieren. laziness, *n.* luiheid *n.*
  lazy, *a.*, ~ily, *adv.* lui.
lea, *n.* wei(de) *n.*; braak *n.*
lead, *n.* lood *n.n.* (*metal*); witlijn *n.* (*printing*);
  dieplood *n.n.* (*casting lead*); leiding *n.*,
  eerste plaats *n.* (*prominence*); hoofdrol *n.*
  (*theatrical*); voorhand *n.* (*cards*). *it is his* ~,
  hij moet *irr.* uitkomen. ¶ *v.t.* leiden, de
  weg wijzen *str.*; aanvoeren; eerst spelen.
  leaden, *a.* loden. leader, *n.* leider *n.*,
  aanvoerder *n.*; hoofdartikel *n.n.* leadership, *n.* leiding *n.*; beleid *n.n.* leading, *a.*
  ~ *aircraftsman,* korporaal *n.* vliegtuig-
  maker *n.*; ~ *article,* hoofdartikel *n.n.*;
  ~ *question,* vraag die op een bepaald
  antwoord *n.n.* doelt; ~ *seaman,* matroos *n.*
  eerste klasse *n.* leading-strings, *pl.n.*
  leiband *n.* lead-pencil, *n.* potlood *n.n.*
leaf, *n.* blad *n.n.* leafless, *a.* bladerloos.
  leaflet, *n.* strooibiljet *n.n.* leafy, *a.*
  bladerrijk, bebladerd.
league, *n.* verbond *n.n.*; zeemijl *n.* (*measure*).
  ¶ *v.i.* een verbond *n.n.* aangaan *irr.*
  leaguer, *n.* verbondene *n.*
leak, *v.i.* lekken, lek zijn. ¶ *n.* lek *n.n.*
  to spring a ~, lek worden *str.*; lek slaan
  irr. leakage, *n.* lek *n.n.*, lekkage *n.*
  leaky, *a.* lek.
lean, *a.* mager, dun; schraal. ¶ *n.* mager
  vlees *n.n.* ¶ *v.i.* leunen; overhellen.
  leaning, *n.* neiging *n.* leanness, *n.* mager-
  heid *n.*; schraalheid *n.*
leap, *v.i.* springen *str.*; opspringen *str.* ¶ *n.*
  sprong *n.* leap-frog, *n.* haasje-over *n.n.*
  leap-year, *n.* schrikkeljaar *n.n.*

learn, *v.i.* & *v.t.* leren; vernemen *str.* **learned,**
a., ~**ly,** *adv.* geleerd. **learner,** *n.* leerling *n.;*
beginner *n.* **learning,** *n.* geleerdheid *n.,*
kunde *n.*
lease, *n.* huurcontract *n.n.;* huurtijd *n.;*
pacht *n.* *long* ~, erfpacht *n.;* ~ *of life,*
levensduur *n.; to gain a new* ~ *of life,*
als verjongd zijn. ¶ *v.t.* huren, pachten;
verhuren, verpachten. **leasehold,** *n.* pacht
n. **leaseholder,** *n.* pachter *n.,* huurder *n.*
leash, *n.* koppel *n.,* riem *n. to strain at the* ~,
van ongeduld *n.n.* branden.
least, *a.* minste, geringste. ¶ *n.* minst *n.n.,*
minste *n.* or *n.n.* *at* ~, ten minste;
minstens; *at the* ~, op z'n minst; *(not) in
the* ~, allerminst (niet).
leather, *n.* leer *n.,* leder *n.n.* **leathern,** *a.*
leren. **leathery,** *a.* leerachtig, taai.
leave, *v.i.* vertrekken *str.,* weggaan *irr.*
¶ *v.t.* verlaten *str.;* achterlaten *str.;*
nalaten *str. to* ~ *alone,* met rust *n.* laten
str.; to ~ *it at that,* er verder niets meer over
zeggen *irr.; to* ~ *go of,* loslaten *str.* ¶ *n.*
verlof *n.n.;* permissie *n. by your* ~, met
Uw verlof *n.n.*
leaven, *n.* zuurdeeg *n.n.,* zuurdesem *n.*
¶ *v.t.* desemen; doordringen *str.*
leavings, *pl.n.* overblijfsel *n.n.;* kliekjes
pl.n.n.
lecher, *n.* wellusteling *n.* **lecherous,** *a.*
wellustig. **lechery,** *n.* ontucht *n.*
lecture, *n.* lezing *n.;* college *n.n.* ¶ *v.i.* een
lezing *n.* houden *irr.;* college *n.n.* geven
str. to ~ *on,* spreken *str.* over. ¶ *v.t.* de
les lezen *str.* **lecturer,** *n.* lector *n.,* docent
n.; persoon *n.* die een lezing *n.* houdt.
lectureship, *n.* lectoraat *n.n.*
ledge, *n.* richel *n.,* rand *n.*
ledger, *n.* grootboek *n.n.*
lee, *n.* luwte *n.*
leech, *n.* bloedzuiger *n.;* geneesheer *n.*
leek, *n.* prei *n.*
leer, *v.i.* schuin kijken *str. to* ~ *at,* toelonken.
¶ *n.* schuine blik *n.*
lees, *pl.n.* droesem *n.*
leeway, *n. to make* ~, afvallen *str.*
left, *a.* over; links, linker. ¶ *adv.* links. ¶ *n.*
linkerkant *n.,* linkerhand *n. to the* ~,
aan de linkerkant; naar links; *the L*~, de
Linksen *pl.n.*
leg, *n.* been *n.n.;* poot *n.;* bout *n.;* pijp *n.*
legacy, *n.* legaat *n.n.*
legal, *a.,* ~**ly,** *adv.* wettig, wettelijk. **legality,**
n. wettigheid *n.* **legalize,** *v.t.* wettigen,
legaliseren.
legate, *n.* legaat *n.*
legatee, *n.* legataris *n.*
legation, *n.* gezantschap *n.n.;* legatie *n.*
legend, *n.* legende *n.;* opschrift *n.n.* **legend-
ary,** *a.* legendarisch.
legerdemain, *n.* goochelarij *n.*
leggings, *pl.n.* beenkappen *pl.n.*
legibility, *n.* leesbaarheid *n.* **legible,** *a.,*
~**bly,** *adv.* leesbaar.

legion, *n.* legioen *n.n.* ¶ *a.* legio.
legislate, *v.i.* wetten *pl. n.* maken. **legislation,**
n. wetgeving *n.* **legislative,** *a.* wetgevend.
legislator, *n.* wetgever *n.* **legislature,** *n.*
wetgevende macht *n.*
legitimacy, *n.* wettigheid *n.* **legitimate,** *a.,*
~**ly,** *adv.* wettig; gewettigd; echt; normaal.
legitimation, *n.* wettiging *n.,* legitimatie *n.*
legitimize, *v.t.* wettigen.
leguminous, *a.* peul . . .
leisure, *n.* vrije tijd *n. at your* ~, als het U
gelegen valt. ¶ *a.* vrij. ,**leisurely,** *a.* & *adv.*
langzaam, op z'n gemak *n.n.*
lemon, *n.* citroen *n.* ¶ *a.* citroengeel.
lemonade, *n.* (citroen)limonade *n.* **lemon-
squash,** *n.* kwast *n.,* citroenlimonade
n.
lend, *v.t.* lenen; verlenen. *to* ~ *oneself to,*
zich lenen tot.
length, *n.* lengte *n.;* afstand *n.;* duur *n.;*
stuk *n.n.;* eindje *n.n.* *at* ~, tenslotte,
eindelijk; uitvoerig. **lengthen,** *v.t.* verlengen. **lengthwise,** *adv.* in de lengte.
lengthy, *a.* langgerekt, langdradig, langdurig.
leniency, *n.* zachtzinnigheid *n.* **lenient,** *a.*
zachtzinnig, toegevend. **lenitive,** *a.*
verzachtend. **lenity,** *n.* zachtheid *n.*
lens, *n.* lens *n.*
Lent, *N.* vasten *n.,* vastentijd *n.* ~ *term,*
collegetermijn van Kerstmis tot Pasen.
lenticular, *a.* lensvormig.
lentil, *n.* linze *n.*
leonine, *a.* leeuwachtig, leeuwen . . .
leopard, *n.* luipaard *n.*
leper, *n.* melaatse *n.* **leprosy,** *n.* melaatsheid
n. **leprous,** *a.* melaats.
lese-majesty, *n.* majesteitsschennis *n.*
less, *a.* minder; min, minus. ¶ *adv.* minder.
lessee, *n.* huurder *n.,* pachter *n.*
lessen, *v.t.* verminderen. ¶ *v.i.* verminderen,
afnemen *str.* **lesser,** *a.* minder, kleiner.
lesson, *n.* les *n.*
lessor, *n.* verhuurder *n.,* verpachter *n.*
lest, *c.* opdat niet, uit vrees dat.
let, *v.t.* laten *str.;* toestaan *irr.;* verhuren,
verpachten; verhinderen, belemmeren.
¶ *n.* beletsel *n.n.*
lethal, *a.* dodelijk.
lethargic, *a.* slaperig, loom, lethargisch.
lethargy, *n.* slaapzucht *n.*
letter, *n.* letter *n.;* brief *n.* ~*s,* letteren *pl.n.*
(literature); ~ *of marque,* kaperbrief *n.*
¶ *v.t.* letteren. **letter-balance,** *n.* brievenweger *n.* **letterbox,** *n.* brievenbus *n.*
letter-card, *n.* postblad *n.n.* **lettered,** *a.*
geletterd, geleerd; met letters *pl.n.*
lettering, *n.* opschrift *n.n.;* titel *n.* **letter-
press,** *n.* tekst *n.*
lettuce, *n.* kropje *n.n.* sla.
levant, *v.i.* met de Noorderzon vertrekken *str.*
levee, *n.* ochtendreceptie *n.*
level, *n.* waterpas *n.n.;* peil *n.n.,* niveau *n.n.*
water ~ waterspiegel *n.; on a* ~ *with,*

P

gelijkstaand met. ¶ *a.* effen, vlak; waterpas; gelijk. *to get* ~, quitte worden *str.*
¶ *v.t.* gelijk maken; slechten; vellen.
to ~ *at*, richten op.
lever, *n.* hefboom *n.* **leverage,** *n.* hefboom-
werking *n.* **lever-watch,** *n.* ankerhorloge *n.n.*
leveret, *n.* haasje *n.n.*
levity, *n.* lichtheid *n.,* lichtzinnigheid *n.*
levy, *n.* heffing *n.;* lichting *n.* ¶ *v.t.* heffen
str.; lichten.
lewd, *a.,* ~ly, *adv.* liederlijk, ontuchtig.
lexicon, *n.* woordenboek *n.n.*
liability, *n.* aansprakelijkheid *n.;* verantwoordelijkheid *n. liabilities,* passief *n.n.*
liable, *a.* aansprakelijk. ~ *to,* onderhevig
aan; blootgesteld aan; vatbaar voor.
liar, *n.* leugenaar *n.*
libation, *n.* plengoffer *n.n.* ·
libel, *n.* smaadschrift *n.n.;* laster *n.* ¶ *v.t.*
belasteren. **libeller,** *n.* belasteraar *n.*
libellous, *a.* lasterlijk.
liberal, *a.,* ~ly, *adv.* vrij, vrijzinnig; vrijgevig, royaal; liberaal. **liberality,** *n.*
vrijgevigheid *n.;* vrijzinnigheid *n.*
liberate, *v.t.* bevrijden. **liberation,** *n.*
bevrijding *n.*
libertine, *n.* libertijn *n.*
liberty, *n.* vrijheid *n.*
libidinous, *a.* wellustig.
librarian, *n.* bibliothecaris *n.* **library,** *n.*
bibliotheek *n.*
licence, *n.* vergunning *n.,* verlof *n.n.;* vrijheid
n.; patent *n.n.* **license,** *v.t.* vergunnen;
patenteren.
licentiate, *n.* licentiaat *n.*
licentious, *a.,* ~ly, *adv.* losbandig.
lichen, *n.* korstmos *n.n.*
lick, *v.t.* likken; afranselen. ¶ *n.* lik *n.*
veegje *n.n.* **licking,** *n.* pak *n.n.* slaag.
lid, *n.* deksel *n.n.;* lid *n.n.*
lie, *v.i.* liegen *str.* (*tell lies*); liggen *irr. to* ~
down, gaan *irr.* liggen. ¶ *n.* leugen *n.*
(*untruth*); ligging *n. to tell a* ~, liegen *str.*
lief, *adv.* lief. *as* ~, net zo lief.
liege, *n.* leenheer *n.;* leenman *n.*
lien, *n.* pandrecht *n.n.*
lieu, *n. in* ~ *of,* in plaats *n.* van.
lieutenancy, *n.* stadhouderschap *n.n.;* luite-
nantschap *n.n.* **lieutenant,** *n.* luitenant *n.*
(*army*); luitenant ter zee *n.* tweede klasse *n.*
~ *commander,* luitenant ter zee eerste
klasse.
life, *n.* leven *n.n.* ~ *annuity,* lijfrente *n.;*
~ *assurance* or ~ *insurance,* levens-
verzekering *n.; as large as* ~, levensgroot;
for ~, levenslang; *from* ~, naar de
natuur. **lifebelt,** *n.* reddingsgordel *n.*
life-blood, *n.* levensbloed *n.n.* **lifeboat,** *n.*
reddingsboot *n.* **lifebuoy,** *n.* reddingsboei
n. **lifeless,** *a.,* ~ly, *adv.* levenloos. **lifeline,**
n. reddingslijn *n.* **lifepreserver,** *n.*
ploertendoder *n.* **lifesize,** *a.* (op) natuurlijke grootte *n.* **lifetime,** *n.* levensduur *n.,*
mensenleven *n.n.*

lift, *v.t.* optillen, opheffen *str.;* opslaan *irr.;*
rooien. ¶ *v.i.* optrekken *str.* ¶ *n.* lift *n.;*
hijskooi *n.*
ligament, *n.* band *n.* **ligature,** *n.* verband *n.n.*
light, *a.,* ~ly, *adv.* licht. ¶ *n.* licht *n.n.;*
vlammetje *n.n.,* lucifer *n. Northern L*~*s,*
Noorderlicht *n.N.;* ~*s,* longen *pl.n.*
(*animal food*); *according to their* ~*s,* naar
hun beste inzicht *n.n.* ¶ *v.t.* aansteken *str.*
¶ *v.i. to* ~ *up,* opsteken *str.; to* ~ *upon,*
toevallig vinden *str.;* vallen *str.* op. **lighten,**
v.t. verlichten. ¶ *v.i.* bliksemen, (weer)-
lichten. **lighter,** *n.* lichter *n.* (*vessel*);
aansteker *n.* ¶ *v.t.* vervoeren met lichters
pl.n. **lighthearted,** *a.* luchthartig. **lighthouse,** *n.* vuurtoren *n.* **lighting,** *n.* verlichting *n.* **lightness,** *n.* lichtheid *n.;*
luchtigheid *n.* **lightning,** *n.* bliksem *n.*
lightning-conductor, *n.,* **lightning-rod,** *n.*
bliksemafleider *n.*
ligneous, *a.* houtachtig.
lignite, *n.* bruinkool *n.*
like, *a.* gelijk. ¶ *adv.* zoals. ¶ *c.* zoals. ¶ *v.t.*
houden *irr.* van, geven *str.* om. ¶ *n.*
voorliefde *n.* **likelihood,** *n.* waarschijnlijkheid *n.* **likely,** *a.* vermoedelijk, waarschijnlijk. *he is not* ~ *to come,* hij zal
wel niet komen. **liken,** *v.t.* vergelijken *str.*
likeness, *n.* gelijkenis *n.,* overeenkomst *n.*
likewise, *adv.* eveneens; insgelijks. **liking,**
n. zin *n.,* smaak *n.,* trek *n. a* ~ *for,*
zin in.
lilac, *n.* sering *n.* ¶ *a.* lila.
lilt, *v.i.* vrolijk zingen *str.*
lily, *n.* lelie *n.*
limb, *n.* lid *n.n.*
limber, *a.* lenig.
limbo, *n.* voorgeborchte *n.n.* van de hel;
vergetelheid *n.*
lime, *n.* lindeboom *n.* (*tree*); kalk *n.* (*stone*);
lijm *n.* (*glue*). **limekiln,** *n.* kalkoven *n.*
limelight, *n.* kalklicht *n.n. tc be in the* ~,
in 't midden van de belangstelling staan
irr. **limestone,** *n.* kalksteen *n.*
limerick, *n.* vijfregelig rijmpje *n.n.*
limit, *n.* grens *n.,* limiet *n.* ¶ *v.t.* beperken;
begrenzen. ~*ed company,* naamloze
vennootschap *n.* **limitation,** *n.* beperking
n. **limitless,** *a.* onbegrensd.
limn, *v.t.* malen.
limp, *a.* slap. ¶ *v.i.* hinken, mank gaan *irr.*
¶ *n. to have a* ~, mank lopen *str.*
limpet, *n.* pok *n.*
limpid, *a.* helder, doorzichtig. **limpidity,** *n.*
helderheid *n.,* doorzichtigheid *n.*
linchpin, *n.* lunspen *n.*
linden, *n.* linde *n.,* lindeboom *n.*
line, *n.* lijn *n.;* regel *n.;* snoer *n.n.;* evenaar *n.*
in ~ *ahead,* in kiellinie *n.; hard* ~*s,* wat
een pech *n.* ¶ *v.t.* voeren; bezetten.
to ~ *the road,* langs de weg staan *irr.*
lineage, *n.* geslacht *n.n.,* afkomst *n.*
lineal, *a.,* ~ly, *adv.* lijnrecht; direct.
linear, *a.* lijnvormig, lineair.

linen, *n.* linnen *n.n.*; ondergoed *n.n.* ¶ *a.* (van) linnen. **linendraper,** *n.* manufacturier *n.* **linenpress,** *n.* linnenkast *n.*

liner, *n.* passagierschip *n.n.*

linger, *v.i.* talmen, dralen.

lingo, *n.* taaltje *n.n.*, brabbeltaal *n.* **lingual,** *a.* tong . . . **linguist,** *n.* taalkundige *n.* **linguistic,** *a.* taalkundig.

liniment, *n.* smeersel *n.n.*

lining, *n.* voering *n.* *the darkest cloud has a silver ~,* geen ongeluk *n.n.* of er is een geluk *n.n.* bij.

link, *n.* schakel *n.* *~s,* golfbaan *n.* ¶ *v.t.* aaneenschakelen, verbinden *str.* **link-boy,** *n.* toortsdrager *n.*

linnet, *n.* vlasvink *n.*

linseed, *n.* lijnzaad *n.n.* **linseed oil,** *n.* lijnolie *n.*

lint, *n.* pluksel *n.n.*

lintel, *n.* bovendrempel *n.*

lion, *n.* leeuw *n.*; gefêteerd man *n.* **lioness,** *n.* leeuwin *n.* **lionize,** *v.t.* fêteren.

lip, *n.* lip *n.*; *(coll.)* brutale praatjes *pl.n.n.* **lipstick,** *n.* lippenstift *n.n.*

liquefaction, *n.* smelten *n.n.*, smelting *n.* **liquefiable,** *a.* smeltbaar. **liquefy,** *v.t.* smelten, vloeibaar maken. ¶ *v.i.* vloeibaar worden *str.* **liqueur,** *n.* likeur *n.* **liquid,** *a.* vloeibaar. ¶ *n.* vloeistof *n.* **liquidate,** *v.t.* liquideren; afwikkelen. **liquidation,** *n.* liquidatie *n.*; afwikkeling *n.* **liquor,** *n.* (sterke) drank *n.*

liquorice, *n.* zoethout *n.n.*, drop *n.*

Lisbon, *N.* Lissabon *n.N.*

lisp, *v.t.* & *v.i.* lispelen. ¶ *n.* *to have a ~,* lispelen.

lissom, *a.* lenig.

list, *n.* lijst *n.*; slagzij *n.n.* *~s,* strijdperk *n.n.* ¶ *v.t.* op een lijst plaatsen, opschrijven *str.*; opsommen. ¶ *v.i.* overhellen, slagzij hebben.

listen, *v.i.* luisteren. *to ~ to,* luisteren naar; *to ~ for,* wachten op; *to ~ in,* luisteren. **listener,** *n.* luisteraar *n.*

listless, *a.*, *~ly,* *adv.* lusteloos.

litany, *n.* litanie *n.*

literal, *a.*, *~ly,* *adv.* letterlijk.

literary, *a.* literair, letterkundig. **literature,** *n.* literatuur *n.*

lithe, *a.* lenig.

lithograph, *n.* lithografie *n.*, steendrukplaat *n.* **lithographer,** *n.* steendrukker *n.* **lithography,** *n.* lithografie *v.*, steendruk *n.*

litigant, *n.* procederende partij *n.* **litigate,** *v.t.* & *v.i.* procederen. **litigation,** *n.* procederen *n.n.*; rechtsgeding *n.n.* **litigious,** *a.* pleitziek.

litmus, *n.* lakmoes *n.n.*

litre, *n.* liter *n.*

litter, *n.* draagbaar *n.* *(conveyance)*; (stro)-strooisel *n.n.* *(for cattle)*; nest *n.n.*, worp *n.* *(of young)*; rommel *n.* *(mess)*. ¶ *v.t.* bestrooien; met een warboel *n.* bedekken. ¶ *v.i.* (jongen *pl.n.n.*) werpen *str.*

little, *a.* klein; weinig. ¶ *adv.* weinig. ¶ *n.* weinig(e) *n.n.* *~ by ~,* beetje *n.n.* bij beetje *n.n.* **littleness,** *n.* kleinzieligheid *n.*

littoral, *a.* kust . . .

live, *v.i.* leven; blijven *str.* leven; wonen. ¶ *v.t.* leven, leiden. *to ~ down,* goedmaken. ¶ *a.* levend; onder stroom; scherp. *~ coal,* gloeiende kool *n.* **livelihood,** *n.* bestaan *n.n.*, levensonderhoud *n.n.* **liveliness,** *n.* levendigheid *n.* **livelong,** *a.* *~ day,* godganse dag *n.* **lively,** *a.* levendig.

liver, *n.* lever *n.* *(organ)*; levende *n.* *(person)*.

livery, *n.* livrei *n.*; onderhoud *n.n.* van paarden *pl.n.n.* **livery company,** *n.* Londens gilde *n.n.* **liveryman,** *n.* lid *n.n.* van een Londens gilde *n.n.*; stalhouder *n.* **livery stable,** *n.* stalhouderij *n.*

livestock, *n.* levende have *n.*, vee *n.n.*

livid, *a.* doodsbleek.

living, *a.* levend. *within ~ memory,* bij mensenheugenis *n.* ¶ *n.* levensonderhoud *n.n.*; predikantsplaats *n.* *for a ~,* voor de kost; om den brode. **living-room,** *n.* woonkamer *n.*, huiskamer *n.*

Livy, *N.* Livius *N.*

lizard, *n.* hagedis *n.*

llama, *n.* lama *n.*

lo! *int.* zie!

loach, *n.* bermpje *n.n.*

load, *v.t.* laden *irr.*; overladen *irr.* ¶ *n.* vracht *n.*, lading *n.*; last *n.* *~s,* massa's. **loader,** *n.* lader *n.*, bevrachter *n.* **loadline,** *n.* lastlijn *n.* **loadstone,** *n.* zeilsteen *n.*, magneet *n.*

loaf, *n.* brood *n.n.* ¶ *v.i.* slenteren. **loafer,** *n.* leegloper *n.*

loam, *n.* leem *n.n.* **loamy,** *a.* lemig.

loan, *n.* lening *n.*; lenen *n.n.* *on ~,* te leen; *out on ~,* uitgeleend. ¶ *v.t.* lenen.

loath, *a.* ongenegen, afkerig. **loathe,** *v.t.* verafschuwen, een afkeer *n.* hebben van, walgen van. **loathing,** *n.* walging *n.*; afkeer *n.* **loathsome,** *a.* weerzinwekkend, walgelijk.

lob, *v.t.* onderhands werpen *str.* ¶ *n.* onderhandse worp *n.*

lobby, *n.* wandelgang *n.*, couloir *n.*

lobe, *n.* lel *n.*

lobster, *n.* (zee)kreeft *n.*

local, *a.* plaatselijk. ¶ *n.* lokaaltrein *n.*; (plaatselijke) herberg *n.* **locality,** *n.* plaats *n.*, localiteit *n.* **localization,** *n.* plaatselijke beperking *n.* **localize,** *v.t.* beperken, localiseren. **locally,** *adv.* plaatselijk, ter plaatse. **locate,** *v.t.* de plaats bepalen van; opsporen, vinden *str.*; opstellen. **location,** *n.* plaatsbepaling *n.*; woonplaats *n.*

loch, *n.* (Schots) meer *n.n.*

lock, *n.* slot *n.n.* *(apparatus)*; sluis *n.*, kolk *n.* *(shipping)*; lok *n.* *(hair).* ¶ *v.t.* op slot doen *irr.* ¶ *v.i.* in elkaar grijpen *str.*, koppelen. **lock-chamber,** *n.* schutkolk *n.*

locker, *n.* kastje *n.n.*

locket, *n.* medaljon *n.n.*

lockjaw, *n.* klem *n.* **lockkeeper,** *n.* **sluis-**
wachter *n.* **lock-out,** *n.* lock-out *n.*,
uitsluiting *n.* **locksmith,** *n.* slotenmaker *n.*
lock-up, *n.* arrestantenlokaal *n.n.* ¶ *a.*
~ *shop,* winkel *n.* zonder woonhuis *n.n.*
locomotion, *n.* beweging *n.*, verplaatsing *n.*
locomotive, *a.* bewegings . . . ¶ *n.* locomotief *n.*
locust, *n.* sprinkhaan *n.*; cicade *n.*
locution, *n.* spreekwijze *n.*, uitdrukking *n.*
lode, *n.* (metaal)ader *n.* **lodestar,** *n.* poolster
n. **lodestone,** *n. See* loadstone.
lodge, *n.* portierswoning *n.*; jachthuis *n.n.*;
loge *n.* ¶ *v.t.* huisvesten, herbergen;
indienen. *to* ~ *oneself,* zich nestelen. ¶ *v.i.*
to ~ *with,* in de kost zijn bij; inwonen bij.
lodge-keeper, *n.* portier *n.* **lodger,** *n.*
kostganger *n.* **lodging-house,** *n.* logement
n.n. **lodgings,** *pl.n.* kosthuis *n.n. in* ~,
op kamers *pl.n.*
loft, *n.* vliering *n.*, zolder *n.*
loftiness, *n.* verhevenheid *n.* **lofty,** *a.*, **~ily,**
adv. verheven; trots.
log, *n.* blok *n.n.* (*wood*); log *n.n.* (*nautical*);
logboek *n.n.*, scheepsjournaal *n.n.* ¶ *v.t.*
(in het logboek) optekenen.
loganberry, *n.* braamframboos *n.*
logarithm, *n.* logarithme *n.* **logarithmic,** *a.*
logarithmisch.
logbook, *n.* logboek *n.n.*, scheepsjournaal
n.n.
log-cabin, *n.* blokhuis *n.n.*
loggerheads, *pl.n. to be at* ~ *with,* het oneens
zijn met.
logic, *n.* logica *n.* **logical,** *a.*, **~ly,** *adv.*
logisch. **logician,** *n.* logicus *n.*
logwood, *n.* campêche-hout *n.*
loin, *n.* lende *n.*; lendestuk *n.n.*
loiter, *v.i.* treuzelen; rondslenteren. **loiterer,**
n. treuzelaar *n.*; lanterfanter *n.*
loll, *v.i.* hangen *str.*; bungelen, lummelen.
lollipop, *n.* (soort) snoepgoed *n.n.*
London, *N.* Londen *n.N.* ¶ *a.* Londens.
lone, *a.* eenzaam, verlaten. **loneliness,** *n.*
eenzaamheid *n.* **lonely,** *a. & adv.* eenzaam.
lonesome, *a.* eenzaam.
long, *a.* lang; langdurig, gerekt. ¶ *adv.* lang;
al day ~, de hele dag; *I shan't*
be ~, ik blijf niet lang weg. ¶ *n. before* ~,
eerlang; *to take* ~, lang duren. ¶ *v.i.*
to ~ *for,* verlangen naar. **longboat,** *n.*
sloep *n.* **long-bow,** *n.* handboog *n. to draw*
the ~, met spek *n.n.* schieten *str.* **longevity,**
n. hoge ouderdom *n.*; lange levensduur *n.*
longing, *n.* begeerte *n.* ~ *for* or *after,*
verlangen *n.n.* naar. **longhand,** *n.* gewoon
handschrift *n.n.* **longish,** *a.* vrij lang.
longitude, *n.* lengte *n.* **longitudinal,** *a.*,
~ly, *adv.* lengte . . ., in de lengte. **long-**
shoreman, *n.* baliekluiver *n.* **longsighted,**
a. verziend; vooruitziend. **longsuffering,** *a.*
lankmoedig. **longtailed,** *a.* langstaartig.
~ *duck,* ijseend *n.*; ~ *tit,* staartmees *n.*
long-term, *a.* ~ *policy,* plan *n.n.* met het

oog op de toekomst. **longwinded,** *a.*
langdradig.
look, *v.i.* kijken *str.*; er uitzien *irr. to* ~ *at,*
kijken naar; aankijken *str.; to* ~ *for,*
zoeken *irr.* naar; *to* ~ *forward to,* uitzien
irr. naar. ¶ *v.t.* er uitzien *irr.* ¶ *n.* blik *n.*;
voorkomen *n.n.*; uiterlijk *n.n.* **looker-on,**
n. toeschouwer *n.* **look-in,** *n.* kijkje *n.*
looking-glass, *n.* spiegel *n.* **look-out,** *n.*
uitkijk *n.*
loom, *n.* weefgetouw *n.n.* ¶ *v.i.* opdoemen.
loon, *n.* dwaas *n.*
loop, *n.* lus *n.*; bocht *n.* ¶ *v.i.* kronkelen;
omduikelen. ¶ *v.t. to* ~ *the* ~, een
duikeling *n.* maken. **loophole,** *n.* kijkgat
n.n.; schietgat *n.n.*; uitweg *n.*
loose, *a.*, **~ly,** *adv.* los; loszinnig. **loosen,** *v.t.*
los maken; losgooien. **looseness,** *n.* losheid
n.
loot, *v.t.* plunderen. ¶ *n.* buit *n.*
lop, *v.t.* knotten; afhakken, snoeien.
lop-sided, *a.* scheef; eenzijdig.
loquacious, *a.* praatziek, spraakzaam.
loquacity, *n.* spraakzaamheid *n.*
lord, *n.* heer *n.*, lord *n. House of L~s,*
Hogerhuis *n.N.; first L~ of,* Minister van;
the L~, de Heer; *the L~'s Prayer,* het Onze
Vader; *the L~'s Day,* de dag des Heren;
the L~'s Supper, het laatste Avondmaal.
lordliness, *n.* voornaamheid *n.* **lordling,** *n.*
onbeduidende lord *n.* **lordly,** *a.* voornaam;
trots. **lordship,** *n.* lordschap *n.n.*; heerschappij *n.*
lore, *n.* kunde *n.*, wetenschap *n.*, kennis *n.*
lorgnette, *n.* lorgnon *n.*, face à main *n.*
loriot, *n.* wielewaal *n.*
lorry, *n.* vrachtauto *n.*
lose, *v.t.* verliezen *irr.*, kwijt raken. *to* ~
one's way, verdwalen; *to* ~ *sight of,* uit het
oog verliezen *irr.* ¶ *v.i.* achterlopen *str.*
loser, *n.* verliezer *n.* **loss,** *n.* verlies *n.n.*
lot, *n.* lot *n.n.* (*in lottery*); levenslot *n.n.* (*in*
life); partij *n.* (*in sale*); hoop *n.* (*quantity*).
a ~, heel veel; *the* ~, de hele boel.
lotion, *n.* wasmiddeltje *n.n.*, lotie *n.*
lottery, *n.* loterij *n.*
lotus, *n.* lotus *n.*
loud, *a.* luid; luidruchtig; opzichtig, schreeuwerig. **loud(ly),** *adv.* hardop. *See also* loud.
loudness, *n.* (geluids)kracht *n.*; opzichtigheid *n.* **loudspeaker,** *n.* luidspreker *n.*
loudspoken, *a.* luidsprekend.
lounge, *n.* (grote) zitkamer *n.*; voorhal *n.*
(van hotel *n.n.*). ¶ *v.i.* luieren, flaneren.
lounger, *n.* flaneur *n.* **lounge-suit,** *n.*
colbert-costuum *n.*
louse, *n.* luis *n.* **lousy,** *a.* luizig; miserabel.
lout, *n.* lummel *n.* **loutish,** *a.*, **~ly,** *adv.*
lummelachtig.
lovable, *a.* lieftallig, beminnenswaardig. **love,**
n. liefde *n.*; geliefde *n.*; schat *n. in* ~
with, verliefd op; *to make* ~ *to,* het hof
maken aan; *for* ~, uit liefde; voor niets;
for the ~ *of God,* om Godswil *n.; to send*

one's ~ *to*, de hartelijke groeten *pl.n.* doen *irr.* aan. ¶ *v.t.* beminnen, liefhebben *irr.*; houden *irr.* van. **love affair,** *n.* liefdesgeschiedenis *n.*, amourette *n.* **love-bird,** *n.* parkiet *n.* **love-letter,** *n.* minnebrief *n.* **loveliness,** *n.* lieflijkheid *n.* **lovelorn,** *a.* dodelijk verliefd. **lovely,** *a.* lieflijk, heerlijk. **love match,** *n.* huwelijk *n.n.* uit liefde *n.* **lover,** *n.* minnaar *n.* ~*s*, minnend paar *n.n.* **lovesick,** *a.* smachtend verliefd. **love-token,** *n.* minnepand *n.n.* **loving,** *a.* liefhebbend, liefderijk, teder.

low, *a.* & *adv.* laag; gering; zacht; nederig; plat, ordinair. ¶ *v.i.* loeien, bulken. **lower,** *a.* lager ¶ *v.t.* laten *str.* zakken; strijken; verlagen, verminderen. ¶ *v.i.* somber zien *irr.*; dreigen. **lowlands,** *pl.n.* lage land *n.n.* van Schotland. **lowliness,** *n.* nederigheid *n.*; geringheid *n.* **lowly,** *a.* & *adv.* nederig, bescheiden. **low-necked,** *a.* met laag uitgesneden hals *n.* **lowness,** *n.* laagte *n.*; geringheid *n.* **low-spirited,** *a.* neerslachtig, gedrukt.

loyal, *a.*, ~ly, *adv.* loyaal; trouw, verkleefd. **loyalist,** *n.* trouw aanhanger *n.* **loyalty,** *n.* trouw *n.*, verkleefdheid *n.*, loyaliteit *n.*

lozenge, *n.* ruit *n.*; pastille *n.*

lubber, *n.* onbevaren zeeman *n.* **lubberly,** *a.* onhandig.

lubricant, *n.* smeersel *n.n.*, smeerolie *n.* **lubricate,** *v.t.* smeren, oliën. **lubricator,** *n.* smeerpot *n.*, oliepot *n.*

lubricity, *n.* geilheid *n.*

luce, *n.* snoek *n.*

lucerne, *n.* honingklaver *n.*, luzerneklaver *n.* **lucid,** *a.* helder; duidelijk, begrijpelijk. **lucidity,** *n.* helderheid *n.*; begrijpelijkheid *n.* **luck,** *n.* toeval *n.n.*; geluk *n.n.* *bad* ~, pech *n.*; *good* ~, veel succes *n.n.*; *worse* ~, ongelukkigerwijs; *to be in* ~, geluk *n.n.* hebben. **luckless,** *a.* ongelukkig. **lucky,** *a.*, ~ily, *adv.* gelukkig.

lucrative, *a.* voordelig, winstgevend. **lucre,** *n.* voordeel *n.n.*, winst *n.*

lucubration, *n.* overpeinzing *n.*, verhandeling *n.*

ludicrous, *a.*, ~ly, *adv.* belachelijk, bespottelijk.

luff, *n.* loef *n.* ¶ *v.i.* loeven. ¶ *v.t.* de loef afsteken *str.*

lug, *v.t.* sleuren, slepen.

luggage, *n.* bagage *n.* **luggage van,** *n.* bagagewagen *n.*

lugger, *n.* logger *n.*

lugubrious, *a.*, ~ly, *adv.* luguber, naargeestig.

lug-sail, *n.* breefok *n.*

lugworm, *n.* zeepier *n.*

lukewarm, *a.* lauw; (*fig.*) onverschillig.

lull, *v.t.* sussen, kalmeren, bedaren. ¶ *n.* (tijdelijke) windstilte *n.* **lullaby,** *n.* wiegelied(je) *n.n.*

lumbago, *n.* lendenschot *n.n.*, spit *n.n.* **lumbar,** *a.* lenden . . .

lumber, *n.* (oude) rommel *n.*; zaaghout *n.n.*,

timmerhout *n.n.* **lumberman,** *n.* houtkapper *n.* **lumber-room,** *n.* rommelkamer *n.*

luminary, *n.* lichtgevend hemellichaam *n.n.*, licht *n.n.* **luminous,** *a.* lichtgevend, stralend.

lump, *n.* klomp *n.*, brok *n.*; klontje *n.n.*; buil *n.*, bobbel *n.* *in the* ~, en bloc. ¶ *a.* rond. ¶ *v.t.* *to* ~ *together*, bij elkaar gooien. **lump-sugar,** *n.* klontjessuiker *n.* **lumpy,** *a.* klonterig.

lunacy, *n.* krankzinnigheid *n.*

lunar, *a.* maans . . .; van de maan. ~ *eclipse*, maansverduistering *n.*

lunatic, *a.* krankzinnig. ~ *asylum*, krankzinnigengesticht *n.n.* ¶ *n.* krankzinnige *n.*

lunch, *n.* lunch *n.*, middagmaal *n.n.* ¶ *v.i.* lunchen.

lung, *n.* long *n.*

lunge, *n.* uitval *n.*, stoot *n.* ¶ *v.i.* een uitval doen *irr.*

lupin, *n.* lupine *n.*

lurch, *v.i.* (plotseling zijwaarts) slingeren; wankelen. ¶ *n.* slingering *n.* *to leave in the* ~, in de steek laten *str.*

lure, *n.* lokaas *n.n.*, lokspijs *n.* ¶ *v.t.* verlokken, lokken.

lurid, *a.* sensationeel; schril.

lurk, *v.i.* op de loer liggen *str.*

luscious, *a.*, ~ly, *adv.* sappig.

lush, *a.* weelderig; sappig.

lust, *n.* zucht *n.*, begeerte *n.*; wellust *n.* ¶ *v.t.* *to* ~ *for, to* ~ *after*, dorsten naar.

lustful, *a.*, ~ly, *adv.* wellustig.

lustre, *n.* luister *n.*, glans *n.*; lustrum *n.n.* **lustrous,** *a.* glansrijk.

lusty, *a.*, ~ily, *adv.* lustig, stevig, ferm.

lute, *n.* luit *n.* (*instrument*); kit *n.n.*, kleefdeeg *n.n.* (*substance*). ¶ *v.t.* kitten.

Lutheran, *N.* Lutheraan *N.* ¶ *a.* Luthers.

luxuriance, *n.* weelderigheid *n.* **luxuriant,** *a.*, ~ly, *adv.* weelderig, overvloedig. **luxuriate,** *v.i.* welig tieren; zich vermeien. **luxurious,** *a.*, ~ly, *adv.* weelderig, luxueus. **luxury,** *n.* weelde *n.*; wulpsheid *n.*

lycanthropy, *n.* weerwolfsziekte *n.*

lye, *n.* loog *n.n.*

lying-in, *n.* kraambed *n.n.* **lying-in hospital,** *n.* kraaminrichting *n.*

lymph, *n.* lymphe *n.* **lymphatic,** *a.* lymphatisch.

lynch, *v.t.* lynchen.

lynx, *n.* los *n.*

lyre, *n.* lier *n.* **lyric,** *a.* lyrisch. ¶ *n.* lyrisch gedicht *n.n.*

lysol, *n.* lysol *n.*

M

macabre, *a.* griezelig, macabre.

macadam, *n.* macadam *n.n.*, steenslag *n.* **macadamize,** *v.t.* macadamiseren.

macaroni, *n.* macaroni *n.*
macaroon, *n.* macaron *n.*, bitterkoekje *n.n.*
mace, *n.* staf *n.*, scepter *n.* (*object*); foelie *n.* (*spice*).
macerate, *v.t.* laten *str.* weken.
machinate, *v.t.* beramen, smeden. **machination**, *n.* intrige *n.*, kuiperij *n.*
machine, *n.* machine *n.*, werktuig *n.n.*, toestel *n.n.* **machine-gun**, *n.* mitrailleur *n.*
machinery, *n.* machinerie *n.* **machine-tool**, *n.* gereedschapswerktuig *n.n.* **machinist**, *n.* machineconstructeur *n.*; machinist *n.*; machinenaaister *n.*
mackerel, *n.* makreel *n.*
mackintosh, *n.* regenjas *n.*
macrocosm, *n.* heelal *n.n.*
mad, *a.*, ~ly, *adv.* krankzinnig; gek, dol.
madam, *n.* mevrouw *n.*
madcap, *n.* dolzinnig iemand *n.* ¶ *a.* dolzinnig. **madden**, *v.t.* dol maken; woedend maken.
madder, *n.* meekrap *n.*
madhouse, *n.* gekkenhuis *n.n.* **madman**, *n.* gek *n.*; dolleman *n.* **madness**, *n.* krankzinnigheid *n.*
maelstrom, *n.* maalstroom *n.*
magazine, *n.* magazijn *n.n.* (*of rifle*); kruitkamer *n.*; tijdschrift *n.*
magenta, *a.* roodpaars.
maggot, *n.* wormpje *n.n.*, made *n.*
magi, *pl.n.* *the three* ~, de drie wijzen *pl.n.* uit het Oosten.
magic, *a.* magisch; tover . . . ¶ *n.* toverkunst *n.* **magical**, *a.* magisch; tover . . . **magically**, *adv.* bij toverslag *n.* **magician**, *n.* tovenaar *n.*; goochelaar *n.*
magisterial, *a.*, ~ly, *adv.* magistraal; gebiedend. **magistrate**, *n.* magistraat *n.*, overheidspersoon *n.*; politierechter *n.*
magnanimity, *n.* grootmoedigheid *n.* **magnanimous**, *a.*, ~ly, *adv.* grootmoedig.
magnate, *n.* magnaat *n.*
magnesia, *n.* talkaarde *n.*
magnesium, *n.* magnesium *n.n.*
magnet, *n.* magneet *n.* **magnetic**, *a.*, ~ally, *adv.* magnetisch. **magnetism**, *n.* magnetisme *n.n.* **magnetize**, *v.t.* magnetiseren. **magneto**, *n.* magneet . . . *n.*, magneto . . . *n.*
magnification, *n.* vergroting *n.*
magnificence, *n.* luister *n.*, pracht *n.* **magnificent**, *a.*, ~ly, *adv.* prachtig.
magnifier, *n.* vergroter *n.* **magnify**, *v.t.* vergroten. ~*ing glass*, vergrootglas *n.n.*, loupe *n.* **magnitude**, *n.* grootte *n.*, omvang *n.*
magnolia, *n.* magnolia *n.*
magnum, *n.* dubbele fles *n.*
magpie, *n.* ekster *n*
magus, *n.* magiër *n.* *See also* **magi**.
mahogany, *n.* mahoniehout *n.n.*
maid, *n.* meid *n.*; meisje *n.n.*; maagd *n.* *old* ~, ouwe vrijster *n.* **maiden**, *n.* meisje *n.n.*; maagd *n.* ¶ *a.* ~ *speech*, eerste redevoering *n.* **maidenhair**, *n.* venushaar

n.n. **maidenhead**, *n.* maagdelijkheid *n.* **maidenly**, *a.* zedig; maagdelijk.
mail, *n.* malie *n.*; post *n.*, mail *n.* *coat of* ~, maliënkolder *n.* ¶ *v.t.* met de post verzenden *str.* **mail-bag**, *n.* postzak *n.* **mailboat**, *n.* mailboot *n.*, pakketboot *n.* **mailcoach**, *n.* postwagen *n.* **mail-train**, *n.* posttrein *n.*
maim, *v.t.* verminken.
main, *a.* voornaamst, hoofd . . . ~ *brace*, grote bras *n.*; *to splice the* ~ *brace*, grog *n.* uitdelen; ~ *deck*, opperdek *n.n.*; ~ *force*, geweld *n.n.*; *the* ~ *force*, de hoofdmacht *n.*; ~ *sheet*, grote schoot *n.*; ~ *yard*, grote ra *n.* ¶ *n.* kracht *n.*; zee *n.*, oceaan *n.*; hoofdleiding *n.* *in the* ~, hoofdzakelijk. **mainland**, *n.* vasteland *n.n.* **mainly**, *adv.* voornamelijk. **mainmast**, *n.* grote mast *n.* **mainsail**, *n.* grootzeil *n.n.* **mainspring**, *n.* grote veer *n.*; drijfveer *n.* **mainstay**, *n.* grootstag *n.n.*; steunpilaar *n.*
maintain, *v.t.* handhaven, instandhouden *irr.*; onderhouden *irr.*; bewaren. **maintenance**, *n.* handhaving *n.*; onderhoud *n.n.*
main-top, *n.* grote mars *n.* **main-topgallant**, *n.* grootbram . . . **main-topmast**, *n.* grootmarssteng *n.* **main-topsail**, *n.* grootmarszeil *n.n.*
maize, *n.* maïs *n.*
majestic, *a.*, ~ally, *adv.* majestueus. **majesty**, *n.* majesteit *n.*
major, *n.* majoor *n.*; oudere *n.*, senior *n.*; meerderjarige *n.* ¶ *a.* zeer groot. **majority**, *n.* meerderheid *n.*; meerderjarigheid *n.*
make, *v.t.* maken; vervaardigen; doen *irr.*, houden *irr.*; zetten; bereiken; voeren. *to* ~ *out*, onderscheiden; begrijpen *str.*; *to* ~ *up*, samenstellen; verzinnen *str.* ¶ *v.i.* *to* ~ *for*, afgaan *irr.* op; *to* ~ *away with*, afschaffen. ¶ *n.* maaksel *n.n.*; vorm *n.* **make-believe**, *n.* voorwendsel *n.n.*; voor de leus. **makepeace**, *n.* vredestichter *n.* **maker**, *n.* maker *n.*; fabrikant *n.* **makeshift**, *n.* hulpmiddel *n.n.*, noodhulp *n.* **makeweight**, *n.* toegift *n.*, aanvulling *n.* **making**, *n.* vervaardiging *n.* *in the* ~, in de maak; *to have the* ~*s of*, aanleg *n.* hebben om.
maladjusted, *a.* slecht aangepast. **maladjustment**, *n.* slechte regeling *n.*
maladministration, *n.* wanbeheer *n.n.*, wanbestuur *n.n.*
malady, *n.* ziekte *n.*, kwaal *n.*
malaria, *n.* malaria *n.*
Malay, *N.* Maleier *N.* (*person*); Maleis *n.N.* (*language*). ¶ *a.* Maleis.
malcontent, *n.* ontevreden. ¶ *n.* ontevredene *n.*
male, *a.* mannelijk. ~ *screw*, vaarschroef *n.* ¶ *n.* mannetje *n.n.*; mannelijke persoon *n.*, man *n.*
malediction, *n.* vervloeking *n.* **malefactor**, *n.* boosdoener *n.* **malevolence**, *n.* boosaardigheid *n.* **malevolent**, *a.*, ~ly, *adv.* boosaardig.

malformation, *n*. misvorming *n*.
malice, *n*. kwaadaardigheid *n*. *with* ~ *aforethought*, met voorbedachten rade.
malicious, *a*., ~ly, *adv*. kwaadaardig.
malign, *a*. boosaardig; kwaadaardig; verderfelijk. ¶ *v.t.* kwaad *n.n.* spreken *str.* van. **malignancy**, *n*. kwaadaardigheid *n*. **malignant**, *a*., ~ly, *adv*. kwaadaardig.
malinger, *v.i.* simuleren. **malingerer**, *n*. simulant *n*. **mallard**, *n*. wilde eend *n*., woerd *n*.
malleability, *n*. smeedbaarheid *n*.; kneedbaarheid *n*. **malleable**, *a*. smeedbaar; kneedbaar.
mallet, *n*. (houten) hamer *n*.
mallow, *n*. maluwe *n*.
malmsey, *n*. malvezij *n*.
malnutrition, *n*. ondervoeding *n*.
malodorous, *a*. onwelriekend.
malpractice, *n*. ~*s*, kwade praktijken *pl.n*.
malt, *n*. mout *n.n.* ¶ *v.t.* mouten.
maltreat, *v.t.* mishandelen.
mama, *n*. mama *n*.
mammal, *n*. zoogdier *n.n*.
mammoth, *n*. mammoet *n*.
man, *n*. man *n*.; mens *n*.; knecht *n*.; werkman *n*. ~ *of war*, oorlogschip *n.n.* ¶ *v.t.* bemannen.
manacle, *n*. handboei *n*. ¶ *v.t.* boeien, kluisteren.
manage, *v.t.* besturen, beheren, leiden; het zo aanleggen *irr*. ¶ *v.i.* het klaarspelen. **manageable**, *a*. handelbaar. **management**, *n*. directie *n*., administratie *n*.; behandeling *n*. **manager**, *n*. administrateur *n*.; directeur *n*., chef *n*.
Manchuria, *N*. Mantsjoerije *n.N*.
mandarin, *n*. mandarijn *n*.
mandatary, *n*. mandataris *n*. **mandate**, *n*. mandaat *n.n.* **mandatory**, *a*. lastgevend.
mandible, *n*. kaak *n*.
mandolin, *n*. mandoline *n*.
mandrake, *n*. alruin *n*.
mane, *n*. manen *pl.n*.
manes, *pl.n.* schimmen *pl.n*.
manful, *a*., ~ly, *adv*. manhaftig.
manganese, *n*. mangaan *n.n*.
mange, *n*. schurft *n*.
mangelwurzel, *n*. mangelwortel *n*.
manger, *n*. kribbe *n*. *a dog in the* ~, een afgunstig iemand.
mangle, *n*. mangel *n*. ¶ *v.t.* mangelen; havenen.
mango, *n*. mangga *n*.
mangy, *a*. schurftig.
man-handle, *v.t.* toetakelen, ruw behandelen.
man-hole, *n*. mangat *n.n.* **manhood**, *n*. mannelijkheid *n*.
mania, *n*. manie *n*.; waanzin *n*. **maniac**, *n*. waanzinnige *n*.
manifest, *a*., ~ly, *adv*. duidelijk; klaarblijkelijk. ¶ *n*. (scheeps)manifest *n.n.* ¶ *v.r.* *to* ~ *oneself*, zich openbaren. **manifestation**, *n*. manifestatie *n*., uiting *n*.

manifesto, *n*. manifesto *n.n*.
manifold, *a*. veelvuldig, velerhande, velerlei.
manikin, *n*. mannetje *n.n.*; ledepop *n*.
manipulate, *v.t.* hanteren; bewerken. **manipulation**, *n*. manipulatie *n*.
mankind, *n*. mensheid *n*., mensdom *n.n*.
manlike, *a*. mannelijk, manachtig. **manliness**, *n*. mannelijkheid *n*. **manly**, *a*. mannelijk.
manner, *n*. manier *n*.; wijze *n*.; soort *n*. ~*s and customs*, zeden *pl.n.* en gewoonten *pl.n.*; *in a* ~, in zeker opzicht *n.*; *in a* ~ *of speaking*, als het ware; *all* ~ *of*, allerhande. **mannered**, *a*. gemanierd; gemaniëreerd. **mannerism**, *n*. gemaniëreerdheid *n*. **mannerly**, *a*. welgemanierd, beleefd.
mannish, *a*. manachtig.
manœuvre, *n*. manoeuvre *n*. ¶ *v.i.* manoeuvreren.
manometer, *n*. manometer *n*.
manor, *n*. heerlijkheid *n*.; landhuis *n.n.*, kasteel *n.n.* **manor-house**, *n*. landhuis *n.n.*, kasteel *n.n.* **manorial**, *a*. heerlijk.
man-power, *n*. arbeidskrachten *pl.n.*; mensenmateriaal *n.n.* **man-servant**, *n*. knecht *n*.
mansion, *n*. herenhuis *n.n.*; étagewoning *n*.
manslaughter, *n*. manslag *n*.
mantelpiece, *n*., **mantelshelf**, *n*. schoorsteenmantel *n*.
mantilla, *n*. mantille *n*.
mantle, *n*. mantel *n*.; (gloei)kousje *n.n.* ¶ *v.t.* bemantelen.
mantrap, *n*. voetangel *n*.
manual, *a*. hand . . . ¶ *n*. handboek *n.n.*; manuaal *n.n*.
manufactory, *n*. fabrikage *n*.; fabrikaat *n.n.* **manufacture**, *n*. fabrikage *n*.; fabrikaat *n.n.*; fabriceren *n.n.* ¶ *v.t.* fabriceren. **manufacturer**, *n*. fabrikant *n*.
manumission, *n*. vrijlating *n*.
manure, *n*. mest *n*. ¶ *v.t.* bemesten.
manuscript, *n*. manuscript *n.n.*; handschrift *n.n*.
many, *pron*. veel, vele. ~ *a time*, menigmaal; *as* ~ *as*, wel.
map, *n*. (land)kaart *n*. ¶ *v.t.* in kaart brengen *irr. to* ~ *out*, ontwerpen *str*.
maple, *n*. ahorn *n*., esdoorn *n*.
mar, *v.t.* bederven *str*.
marauder, *n*. plunderaar *n*.
marble, *n*. marmer *n.n.*; knikker *n*. ¶ *a*. marmeren. ¶ *v.t.* marmeren.
March, *N*. maart *N*. ¶ *a*. maarts. **march**, *v.i.* marcheren. ¶ *v.t.* laten *str*. marcheren. ¶ *n*. mars *n*.; loop *n*., gang *n*.; mark *n*., grensland *n.n*.
marchioness, *n*. markiezin *n*.
marconigram, *n*. draadloos telegram *n.n*.
mare, *n*. merrie *n*. ~*'s nest*, iets wat tot niets leidt; ~*'s tail*, paardestaart *n*.
margarine, *n*. margarine *n*.
margin, *n*. marge *n*., kantlijn *n*. **marginal**, *a*. marginaal.
margrave, *n*. markgraaf *n*.

marigold, *n.* goudsbloem *n.*
marine, *n.* zee . . . ¶ *n.* vloot *n* , marine *n.*; marinier *n.* mariner, *n.* matroos *n.,* zeeman *n.*
marital, *a.* huwelijks . . ., echtelijk.
maritime, *a.* maritiem, zee . . .
marjoram, *n.* marjolein *n.*
mark, *n.* merk *n.n.,* teken *n.n.* (*sign*); blijk *n.n.* (*proof*); cijfer *n.n.* (*at school*); mark *n.* (*coin*). ¶ *v.t.* merken; punten *pl.n.n.* geven *str.*; onthouden *irr.*
market, *n.* markt *n.* ¶ *v.t.* op de markt brengen *irr.* marketable, *a.* verkoopbaar. market-garden, *n.* warmoezerij *n.,* moestuin *n.* market-gardener, *n.* warmoezenier *n.* market-gardening, *n.* tuinderij *n.* market-place, *n.* marktplein *n.n.*
marking-iron, *n.* brandijzer *n.n.*
marksman, *n.* scherpschutter *n.*
marl, *n.* mergel *n.*
marmalade, *n.* marmelade *n.*
marmot, *n.* marmot *n.*
maroon, *n.* (soort) vuurwerk *n.n.* ¶ *a.* kastanjebruin. ¶ *v.t.* (op een onbewoond eiland) achterlaten *str.*
marquee, *n.* grote tent *n.*
marquess, *n.,* marquis, *n.* markies *n.*
marquetry, *n.* inlegwerk *n.n.*
marquisate, *n.* markiezaat *n.n.*
marriage, *n.* huwelijk *n.n.* *by* ~, aangetrouwd (*relative*); *to ask in* ~, ten huwelijk vragen *str.*; ~ *lines,* trouwbewijs *n.n.* marriageable, *a.* huwbaar. married, *a.* getrouwd.
marrow, *n.* merg *n.* (*of bone*). *vegetable* ~, Engelse kalebas *n.* marrow-bone, *n.* mergpijp *n.* marrowy, *a.* vol merg *n.n.*
marry, *v.t.* trouwen; uithuwelijken. ¶ *v.i.* trouwen.
marsh, *n.* moeras *n.n.*
marshal, *n.* maarschalk *n.* ¶ *v.t.* rangschikken, ordenen.
marshmallow, *n.* heemst *n.* marsh-marigold, *n.* dotterbloem *n.* marshy, *a.* moerassig, drassig.
marsupial, *n.* buideldier *n.n.*
mart, *n.* markt *n.*; verkooplokaal *n.n.*
marten, *n.* marter *n.*
martial, *a.* krijgshaftig; krijgs . . .
martin, *n.* huiszwaluw *n.*
martinet, *n.* dienstklopper *n.*
martyr, *n.* martelaar *n.* martyrdom, *n.* martelaarschap *n.n.*; marteling *n.*
marvel, *n.* wonder *n.n.* ¶ *v.i.* *to* ~ *at,* zich verwonderen over. marvellous, *a.,* ~ly, *adv.* verbazend, wonderbaar(lijk).
mascot, *n.* mascotte *n.*
masculine, *n.* mannelijk.
mash, *v.t.* fijnstampen, moezen. ¶ *n.* mengelmoes *n.n.*; gestampte groente *n.*
mask, *n.* masker *n.n.*; mom *n.n.* ¶ *v.t.* maskeren, vermommen; verbergen *str.*
mason, *n.* steenhouwer *n.*; vrijmetselaar *n.,*

macon *n.* masonic, *a.* maconniek, vrijmetselaars . . . masonry, *n.* metselwerk *n.n.*; vrijmetselarij *n.*
masquerade, *n.* maskerade *n.* ¶ *v.i.* zich vermommen.
mass, *n.* massa *n.,* hoeveelheid *n.*; menigte *n.*; mis *n.* (*church*). ¶ *v.t.* verzamelen, samenhopen.
massacre, *n.* bloedbad *n.n.,* slachting *n.,* moordpartij *n.* ¶ *v.t.* ombrengen *irr.,* een slachting *n.* aanrichten onder.
massage, *n.* massage *n.* ¶ *v.t.* masseren.
massive, *a.* massief.
mass-produce, *v.t.* in serie *n.* vervaardigen.
mast, *n.* mast *n.* (*of ship*); mast *n.,* eikels *pl.n.*
master, *n.* meester *n.*; baas *n.*; schipper *n.,* gezagvoerder *n.* ¶ *v.t.* meester worden *str.,* zich meester maken van. master-builder, *n.* aannemer *n.,* bouwmeester *n.* masterful, *a.* bazig, heerszuchtig. master-key, *n.* loper *n.* masterly, *a.* & *adv.* meesterlijk. masterpiece, *n.* meesterstuk *n.n.,* meesterwerk *n.n.* mastership *n.* leraarschap *n.n.* mastery, *n.* heerschappij *n.,* meerderheid *n.*; vaardigheid *n.,* bedrevenheid *n.*
mast-head, *n.* top *n.* van de mast.
mastic, *n.* masti(e)k *n.* or *n.n.*
mastication, *n.* kauwen *n.n.* masticate, *v.t.* kauwen.
mastiff, *n.* bulhond *n.*
mat, *n.* mat *n.* ¶ *v.t.* dooreenvlechten *str.* ¶ *v.i.* verward raken.
match, *n.* lucifer *n.* (*stick*); lont *n.* (*fuse*); gelijke *n.,* weerga *n.* (*equal*); huwelijk *n.n.* (*marriage*); match *n.,* wedstrijd *n.* (*contest*). ¶ *v.t.* evenaren, zich kunnen *irr.* meten met; paren; doen *irr.* passen, in overeenstemming *n.* brengen *irr.* matchbox, *n.* lucifersdoosje *n.n.* matchless, *a.,* ~ly, *adv.* onvergelijkelijk, weergaloos. matchmaker, *n.* koppelaar *n.* (*male*), koppelaarster *n.* (*female*); lucifersfabrikant *n.*
mate, *n.* maat *n.*; kameraad *n.,* makker *n.*; gade *n.*; mannetje *n.n.,* wijfje *n.n.*; stuurman *n.*; schaakmat *n.n.* (*chess*). ¶ *v.t.* paren; schaakmat zetten (*chess*). ¶ *v.i.* zich paren.
material, *a.,* ~ly, *adv.* stoffelijk; gewichtig, belangrijk; wezenlijk. ¶ *n.* materiaal *n.n.,* bouwstof *n.*; materieel *n.n.* raw ~, grondstof *n.* materialism, *n.* materialisme *n.n.* materialist, *n.* materialist *n.* materialistic, *a.* materialistisch. materialize, *v.i.* zich verwezenlijken.
maternal, *a.,* ~ly, *adv.* moederlijk; moeders . . . maternity, *n.* moederschap *n.n.* ~ *hospital,* kraaminrichting *n.*; ~ *benefit,* uitkering *n.* bij bevalling *n.*
mathematical, *a.* mathematisch, wiskunstig. mathematician, *n.* mathematicus *n.,* wiskundige *n.* mathematics, *pl.n.* wiskunde *n.*
matins, *pl.n.* metten *pl.n.,* vroegmis *n.*

matricide, *n.* moedermoord *n.* (*act*); moedermoordenaar *n.* (*person*).
matriculate, *v.i.* zich (als student *n.*) laten *str.* inschrijven; toelatingsexamen *n.n.* afleggen *irr.* voor de universiteit. matriculation, *n.* inschrijving *n.*; toelatingsexamen *n.n.*
matrimonial, *a.*, ~ly, *adv.* huwelijks . . . matrimony, *n.* huwelijk *n.n.*, echtelijke staat *n.*
matrix, *n.* matrijs *n.*, gietvorm *n.*
matron, *n.* matrone *n.*; directrice *n.*
matter, *n.* stof *n.* (*substance*); (*fig.*) zaak *n.*, aangelegenheid *n.*; etter *n.* (*pus*). *what's the* ~?, wat scheelt eraan?; *a* ~ *of* . . ., een kwestie *n.* van . . . ; *a* ~ *of course*, iets vanzelfsprekends; *a* ~ *of fact*, een feit *n.n.*; ~*-of-fact*, practisch. ¶ *v.i.* van belang *n.n.* zijn.
matting, *n.* matwerk *n.n.*
mattock, *n.* houweel *n.n.*
mattress, *n.* matras *n.*
mature, *a.*, ~ly, *adv.* rijp; gerijpt. ¶ *v.i.* rijpen, tot rijpheid *n.* komen *irr.*; vervallen *str.* maturity, *n.* rijpheid *n.*; vervaldag *n.*
matutinal, *a.* morgen . . .
maudlin, *a.* sentimenteel.
maul, *v.t.* toetakelen.
maulstick, *n.* schildersstok *n.*
maunder, *v.i.* leuteren.
mausoleum, *n.* praalgraf *n.n.*
mauve, *a.* licht paars, mauve.
mavis, *n.* zanglijster *n.*
maw, *n.* maag *n.*; bek *n.*
mawkish, *a.* sentimenteel.
maxim, *n.* leerspreuk *n.*
maximum, *n.* maximum *n.n.*
may, *v.i.* mogen *irr.*; kunnen *irr.* ¶ *n.* meidoorn *n.* May, *N.* mei *N.* May-Day, *N.* erste mei *n.* mayfly, *n.* kokerjuffer *n.*
mayor, *n.* burgemeester *n.* mayoralty, *n.* burgemeesterschap *n.n.* mayoress, *n.* burgemeestersvrouw *n.*; (vrouwelijke) burgemeester *n.*
maypole, *n.* meiboom *n.*
maze, *n.* doolhof *n.* (*fig.*) *in a* ~, verbijsterd.
me, *pron.* mij, me.
mead, *n.* mee; (*poet.*) beemd *n.n.*, weide *n.*
meadow, *n.* wei(de) *n.*
meagre, *a.*, ~ly, *adv.* mager, schraal.
meal, *n.* maal *n.n.*, maaltijd *n.*; meel *n.* mealy, *a.* melig. mealy-mouthed, *a.* zoetsappig.
mean, *a.*, ~ly, *adv.* gemiddeld; middelmatig, laag, gemeen. ¶ *n.* gemiddelde *n.n.*, middelmaat *n.*; middel *n.n. by all* ~*s*, zeker; (*also:*) ~*s*, middelen *pl.n.n.*; vermogen *n.n.* ¶ *v.t.* menen; bedoelen; betekenen.
meander, *n.* kronkeling *n.* ¶ *v.i.* kronkelen, zich slingeren.
meaning, *n.* betekenis *n.*, zin *n.* ¶ *a.* veelbetekenend. meanness, *n.* geringheid *n.*; gemeenheid *n.* meantime, *adv. in the* ~,

ondertussen. meanwhile, *adv.* ondertussen, inmiddels.
measles, *pl.n.* mazelen *pl.n. German* ~, rode hond *n.*
measurable, *a.*, ~bly, *adv.* meetbaar. measure, *n.* maat *n.*; maatstaf *n.*; maatregel *n. made to* ~, op maat; *to take* ~*s*, maatregelen treffen *str.* ¶ *v.t.* meten *str.*; opmeten *str.* ¶ *v.i.* meten *str.* measurement, *n.* maat *n.*; afmeting *n.*
meat, *n.* vlees *n.n.* meat-safe, *n.* vliegenkast *n.*
mechanic, *a.* mechanisch; machinaal. ¶ *n.* handwerksman *n.*; mecanicien *n.* ~*s*, werktuigkunde *n.* mechanical, *a.*, ~ly, *adv.* mechanisch, werktuiglijk; machinaal. mechanize, *v.t.* mechaniseren. mechanization, *n.* mechanisatie *n.* mechanism, *n.* mechanisme *n.*
medal, *n.* medalje *n.*; penning *n.*
meddle, *v.i. to* ~ *with*, zich bemoeien met; zich inlaten *str.* met. meddler, *n.* bemoeial *n.* meddlesome, *a.* bemoeiziek.
medial, *a.* midden . . ., tussen . . . mediate, *v.i.* bemiddelen, bemiddelend optreden *str.* median, *n.* bemiddeling *n.* mediator, *n.* bemiddelaar *n.*
medical, *a.*, ~ly, *adv.* medisch, geneeskundig. ~ *man*, dokter *n.* medicament, *n.* medicament *n.n.*, geneesmiddel *n.n.* medicate, *v.t.* geneeskundig behandelen; geneeskundig bereiden. medicinal, *a.*, ~ly, *adv.* geneeskrachtig, geneeskundig. medicine, *n.* medicijn *b.*, geneesmiddel *n.n.*; geneeskunde *n.*
medieval, *a.* middeleeuws.
mediocre, *a.* middelmatig. mediocrity, *n.* middelmatigheid *n.*
meditate, *v.i.* nadenken *irr.*, peinzen. ¶ *v.t.* overpeinzen. meditation, *n.* overpeinzing *n.* meditative, *a.*, ~ly, *adv.* peinzend.
Mediterranean, *N.* Middellandse Zee *N.*
medium, *a.* gemiddeld; van middelbare grootte *n.* ¶ *n.* middelslag *n.n.*, middelsoort *n.*; middenstof *n.*; tussenkomst *n.*; medium *n.n.*
medlar, *n.* mispel *n.*
medley, *n.* mengelmoes *n.n.*; potpourri *n.* or *n.n.*
meek, *a.*, ~ly, *adv.* zachtzinnig, zachtmoedig; gedwee; ootmoedig. meekness, *n.* zachtzinnigheid *n.*; gedweeheid *n.*; ootmoed *n.*
meerschaum, *n.* meerschuim *n.n.* ¶ *a.* meerschuimen.
meet, *v.t.* ontmoeten; tegemoet komen *irr.*; afhalen; voldoen *irr.* aan, bevredigen. ¶ *v.i.* bijeenkomen *irr.* ¶ *n.* bijeenkomst *n.* (van jagers *pl.n.*). ¶ *a.* gepast. meeting, *n.* bijeenkomst *n.*; ontmoeting *n.* meeting-house, *n.* bedehuis *n.n.*
megalomania, *n.* grootheidswaanzin *n.*
melancholic, *a.* melancholiek, zwaarmoedig. melancholy, *n.* zwaarmoedigheid *n.* ¶ *a.* zwaarmoedig, droefgeestig.

meliorate, *v.t.* verbeteren.
mellifluous, *a.* zoetvloeiend.
mellow, *a.* rijp, mals, vol. ¶ *v.t.* doen *irr.*
rijpen; temperen. ¶ *v.i.* rijp worden *str.*
mellowness, *n.* rijpheid *n.*
melodious, *a.*, ~ly, *adv.* melodieus. melodic,
a. melodisch. melodrama, *n.* melodrama
n.n. melody, *n.* melodie *n.*, zangwijze *n.*
melon, *n.* meloen *n.*
melt, *v.t.* smelten *str.*; vertederen. ¶ *v.i.*
smelten *str.* melter, *n.* smelter *n.* melting-
pot, *n.* smeltkroes *n.*
member, *n.* lid *n.n.*; lidmaat *n.* membership,
n. lidmaatschap *n.n.*; ledental *n.n.*
membrane, *n.* vlies *n.n.*
memento, *n.* gedachtenis *n.*
memoir, *n.* gedenkschrift *n.n.*; verhandeling
n. ~s, memoires *pl.n.*
memorable, *a.*, ~bly, *adv.* gedenkwaardig,
heuglijk.
memorandum, *n.* nota *n.*
memorial, *a.* gedenk . . . ¶ *n.* memorie *n.*;
gedenkstuk *n.n.* memorialize, *v.t.* een
verzoekschrift richten tot.
memorize, *v.t.* van buiten leren. memory, *n.*
geheugen *n.n.*; herinnering *n.*; gedachtenis
n.
men, *pl.n. See* man.
menace, *v.t.* bedreigen. ¶ *n.* bedreiging *n.*;
dreigend gevaar *n.n.*
menagerie, *n.* beestenspel *n.n.*
mend, *v.t.* herstellen, vermaken, repareren;
stoppen; verbeteren. ¶ *v.i.* beter worden
str., zich verbeteren. ¶ *n.* verstelde plaats
n. to be on the ~, beterende zijn.
mendacious, *a.*, ~ly, *adv.* leugenachtig.
mendacity, *n.* leugenachtigheid *n.*
mender, *n.* hersteller *n.*
mendicancy, *n.* bedelarij *n.* mendicant, *n.*
bedelaar *n.*; bedelmonnik *n.*
menial, *a.* dienstbaar; laag. ¶ *n.* dienstknecht
n.; ondergeschikte *n.*
meningitis, *n.* hersenvliesontsteking *n.*
menstrual, *a.* menstruatie . . . menstruation,
n. menstruatie *n.*
mental, *a.*, ~ly, *adv.* geestelijk, geestes . . .
~ arithmetic, hoofdrekenen *n.n.*
mention, *v.t.* melden, noemen; gewag *n.n.*
maken van. ¶ *n.* vermelding *n.* mentionable, *a.* noemenswaard.
mentor, *n.* mentor *n.*
menu, *n.* menu *n.n.*, spijskaart *n.*
mephitic, *a.* stinkend.
mercantile, *a.* handels . . . ~ marine,
handelsvloot *n.*
mercenary, *a.* baatzuchtig. ¶ *n.* huursoldaat
n.
mercer, *n.* manufacturier *n.* (in wollen en
zijden goederen *pl.n.n.*). mercerize, *v.t.*
merceriseren. mercery, *n.* manufactuur-
zaak *n.*: manufacturen *pl.n.*
merchandise, *n.* koopwaar *n.* merchant, *n.*
koopman *n.* ~ service, koopvaardijvloot
n. merchantman, *n.* koopvaardijschip *n.n.*

merciful, *a.*, ~ly, *adv.* genadig; barmhartig.
merciless, *a.*, ~ly, *adv.* meedogenloos.
mercurial, *a.* kwikzilverachtig; levendig.
mercury, *n.* kwikzilver *n.n.*
mercy, *n.* genade *n.*, barmhartigheid *n.*
mere, *a.* louter, enkel. ¶ *n.* meer *n.n.*
merely, *adv.* enkel, alleen.
meretricious, *a.*, ~ly, *adv.* opzichtig.
merge, *v.i.* verzinken *str.*; opgaan *irr.* in.
merger, *n.* fusie *n.*, samensmelting *n.*
meridian, *n.* meridiaan *n.*; middaghoogte *n.*;
toppunt *n.n.* meridional, *a.*, ~ly, *adv.*
meridionaal, zuidelijk.
merino, *n.* merinos *n.*
merit, *v.t.* verdienen, waard zijn. ¶ *v.i.*
to ~ of, zich verdienstelijk maken jegens.
¶ *n.* verdienste *n.* meritorious, *a.*, ~ly,
adv. verdienstelijk.
mermaid, *n.* (zee)meermin *n.* merman, *n.*
meerman *n.*
merriment, *n.* vrolijkheid *n.* merry, *a.*, ~ily,
adv. vrolijk; aangeschoten. to make ~,
vrolijk zijn; feest *n.n.* vieren. merry-
andrew, *n.* paljas *n.* merry-go-round, *n.*
mallemolen *n.*
mesh, *n.* maas *n.* ¶ *es*, netwerk *n.n.* ¶ *v.t.*
knopen; verstrikken.
mesmerism, *n.* mesmerisme *n.n.* mesmerize,
v.t. magnetiseren.
mess, *n.* schotel *n.*; tafel *n.*, bak *n.*; vuile
boel *n.* verwarring *n.* ¶ *v.i.* morsen,
knoeien. to ~ with, samen eten *str.* met.
message, *n.* boodschap *n.* messenger, *n.*
bode *n.*; boodschapper *n.*
Messiah, *N.* Messias *N.*
messmate, *n.* baksmaat *n.*; tafelgenoot *n.*
messroom, *n.* eetkamer *n.*
Messrs, *pl.N.* de Heren *pl.N.*, de Firma.
metal, *n.* metaal *n.n.* ~s, spoorstaven *pl.n.*
¶ *a.* metalen. metallic, *a.* metalen;
metaalachtig. metalliferous, *a.* metaal-
houdend. metallurgy, *n.* metallurgie *n.*
metamorphose, *v.t.* omscheppen *str.*, herscheppen *str.* metamorphosis, *n.* metamorphose *n.*, gedaanteverwisseling *n.*
metaphor, *n.* metaphoor *n.*; beeldspraak *n.*
metaphorical, *a.*, ~ly, *adv.* overdrachtelijk,
figuurlijk.
metaphysical, *a.*, ~ly, *adv.* metaphysisch.
metaphysics, *pl.n.* metaphysica *n.*
mete, *v.t.* to ~ out, uitdelen.
meteor, *n.* meteoor *n.* meteoric, *a.* meteoor
. . . meteorology, *n.* meteorologie *n.*,
weerkunde *n.*
meter, *n.* meter *n.*
method, *n.* methode *n.*, werkwijze *n.*
methodical, *a.*, ~ly, *adv.* methodisch.
Methodist, *N.* Methodist *n.*
methylated, *a.* ~ spirits, spiritus *n.*
meticulous, *a.*, ~ly, *adv.* nauwgezet,
angstvallig.
metre, *n.* metrum *n.*; Meter *N.* metric(al),
a. metrisch, metriek.
metropolis, *n.* wereldstad *n.* metropolitan, *a.*

van de wereldstad; aartsbisschoppelijk-
¶ *n.* metropolitaan *n.*, aartsbisschop *n.*
mettle, *n.* vuur *n.n.*, temperament *n.*
to put a person on his ~, iemand op de
proef stellen. **mettlesome,** *a.* vurig.
mew, *n.* meeuw *n.* (*bird*). ~*s*, achterstraatje
n.n. met stallen *pl.n.* ¶ *v.i.* miauwen.
miasma, *n.* miasme *n.n.*
mica, *n.* mica *n.n.*
microbe, *n.* microbe *n.*
microcosm, *n.* microcosmos *n.*
micrometre, *n.* micrometer *n.*
microphone, *n.* microphoon *n.*
microscope, *n.* microscoop *n.* **microscopic,** *a.*,
~**ally,** *adv.* microscopisch.
mid, *a.* midden. *in* ~ . . ., midden in . . .
midday, *n.* middag *n.*
midden, *n.* vaalt *n.*, mesthoop *n.*
middle, *n.* midden *n.n.*; middel *n.n.* (*waist*).
¶ *a.* midden . . ., middel . . ., tussen . . .;
middelbaar. **middling,** *a.* middelmatig.
¶ *adv.* tamelijk.
middy, *n.* adelborst *n.*
midge, *n.* mug *n.*
midget, *n.* dwerg *n.*
midnight, *n.* middernacht *n.*   ¶ *a.* midder-
nachtelijk. **midriff,** *n.* middenrif *n.n.*
midship, *adv.* midscheeps. **midshipman,** *n.*
adelborst *n.* **midst,** *n.* midden *n.n. in the*
~ *of,* te midden van. **midsummer,** *n.*
hartje *n.n.* (van de) zomer. **midway,** *adv.*
halverwege.
midwife, *n.* vroedvrouw *n.* **midwifery,** *n.*
verloskunde *n.*
midwinter, *n.* hartje *n.n.* (van de) winter.
mien, *n.* uiterlijk *n.n.*, voorkomen *n.n.*
might, *n.* macht *n.*; kracht *n.* **mightiness,** *n.*
machtigheid *n.*; hoogheid *n.* **mighty,** *a.*,
~**ily,** *adv.* machtig; krachtig; geweldig.
mignonette, *n.* reseda *n.*
migrant, *n.* trekvogel *n.*, zwerfvogel *n.*
migrate, *v.i.* (naar een ander land *n.n.*)
verhuizen; trekken *str.* **migration,** *n.*
verhuizing *n.*; trek *n.* **migratory,** *a.*
zwervend.
milch-cow, *n.* melkkoe *n.*
mild, *a.*, ~**ly,** *adv.* zacht; zachtaardig; licht.
mildew, *n.* schimmel *n.*
mildness, *n.* zachtheid *n.*; zachtaardigheid *n.*;
lichtheid *n.*
mile, *n.* mijl *n.* **mileage,** *n.* afstand *n.* in
mijlen *pl.n.*
milfoil, *n.* duizendblad *n.n.*
militant, *a.* strijdend; strijdlustig. **militarism,**
n. militarisme *n.n.* **military,** *a.* militair.
militate, *v.i.* strijdend zijn. **militia,** *n.*
landweer *n.*
milk, *n.* melk *n.* ¶ *v.t.* melken. **milkfloat,** *n.*
melkkar *n.* **milkman,** *n.* melkboer *n.*
milksop, *n.* melkmuil *n.* **milky,** *a.* melk-
achtig. *M* ~ *Way,* Melkweg *n.*
mill, *n.* molen *n.*; fabriek *n.*; spinnerij *n.*
¶ *v.t.* malen; kartelen. ¶ *v.i.* in 't rond
tollen. **millboard,** *n.* (dik) karton *n.n.*,

bordpapier *n.n.* **milldam,** *n.* molendijk *n.*
miller, *n.* molenaar *n.*
millenium, *n.* duizendjarig rijk *n.n.*
millet, *n.* gierst *n.*
milliner, *n.* modiste *n.* **millinery,** *n.* modear-
tikelen *pl.n.n.*
million, *n.* millioen *n.n.*, miljoen *n.n.*
millionaire, *n.* millionnair *n.*
mill-owner, *n.* fabrikant *n.* **mill-pond,** *n.*
molenkolk *n.*
milt, *n.* . milt *n.*
mime, *n.* gebarenspel *n.n.* ¶ *v.t.* nabootsen.
¶ *v.i.* door gebaren *pl.n.n.* voorstellen.
mimic, *a.* mimisch; nabootsend; schijn . . .
¶ *v.t.* nabootsen; naäpen. **mimicry,** *n.*
mimiek *n.*
minatory, *a.* dreigend.
mince, *v.t.* fijn hakken. *not to* ~ *matters,*
er geen doekjes *pl.n.n.* om winden *str.*;
~*ed meat,* gehakt *n.n.* ¶ *n.* gehakt *n.n.*
mincemeat, *n.* fijngehakte gedroogde
vruchten *pl.n.* **mincepie,** *n.* pasteitje *n.n.*
met *mincemeat* gevuld. **mincer,** *n.*,
mincing-machine, *n.* vleesmolen *n.*
mincingly, *adv.* geaffecteerd.
mind, *n.* geest *n.*; gemoed *n.n.*; verstand *n.n.*;
gedachte *n.* *in one's right* ~, bij z'n volle
verstand; *out of one's* ~, niet recht bij
z'n verstand; *to be in two* ~*s*, weifelen;
presence of ~, tegenwoordigheid *n.* van
geest; *to know one's own* ~, weten *irr.* wat
men wil; *to bear in* ~, bedenken *irr.*;
to make up one's ~, besluiten *str.* ¶ *v.t.*
denken *irr.* om; passen op. ~ *your own
business,* bemoei je met je eigen zaken
pl.n.; *never* ~, het doet er niet toe.
minded, *a.* gezind. **mindful,** *a.* indachtig.
~ *of,* gedachtig aan.
mine, *pron.* de mijne, het mijne; van mij.
¶ *n.* mijn. ¶ *v.t.* ondermijnen; mijnen *pl.n.*
leggen *irr.* in. **minelayer,** *n.* mijnenlegger
n. **miner,** *n.* mijnwerker *n.* **minesweeper,**
n. mijnenveger *n.*
mineral, *a.* mineraal, delfstoffen . . . ¶ *n.*
delfstof *n.* **mineralogy,** *n.* mineralogie *n.*
mingle, *v.t.* vermengen. ¶ *v.i. to* ~ *with,*
zich mengen onder.
miniature, *n.* minjatuur *n.* ¶ *a.* miniatuur.
minim, *n.* halve noot *n.*; kleine hoeveelheid *n.*
minimal, *a.* minimaal. **minimize,** *v.t.* tot een
minimum terugbrengen *irr.*; verkleinen.
minimum, *n.* minimum *n.n.*
mining, *n.* mijnbouw *n.*
minion, *n.* favoriet *n.*, gunsteling *n.*
minister, *n.* minister *n.*; gezant *n.*; predikant
n. ¶ *v.i. to* ~ *to,* hulp *n.* verlenen aan;
verzorgen. **ministerial,** *a.*, ~**ly,** *adv.*
ministerieel. **ministration,** *n.* bediening *n.*;
(geestelijke) bijstand *n.* **ministry,** *n.*
ministerie *n.n.*; predikantschap *n.n.*
minium, *n.* rode menie *n.*
mink, *n.* Amerikaans stinkdier *n.n.*
minnow, *n.* stekelbaarsje *n.n.*, voorntje *n.n.*
minor, *a.* minder, kleiner; mineur.   ¶ *n.*

minderjarige *n.* **minority,** *n.* minderheid *n.*; minderjarigheid *n.*
minster, *n.* domkerk *n.*
minstrel, *n.* minstreel *n.*; negerzanger *n.*
mint, *n.* munt *n.* (*plant & coin*). a ~ of, een hoop. ¶ *v.t.* munten, slaan *irr.* **mintage,** *n.* munten *n.n.* **mint-sauce,** *n.* kruizemuntsaus *n.*
minuet, *n.* menuet *n.n.*
minus, *prep.* min, minus. ¶ *n.* minusteken *n.n.*
minute, *n.* minuut *n.* this ~, op staande voet *n.*; ~s, notulen *pl.n.* ¶ *a.*, ~ly, *adv.* klein, gering. ¶ *v.t.* notuleren. **minutiae,** *pl.n.* kleinigheden *pl.n.*
minx, *n.* kat *n.*
miracle, *n.* wonder *n.n.*, mirakel *n.n.* **miraculous,** *a.*, ~ly, *adv.* wonderbaarlijk.
mirage, *n.* luchtspiegeling *n.*
mire, *n.* modder *n.*, slijk *n.n.*
mirror, *n.* spiegel *n.* ¶ *v.t.* weerspiegelen.
mirth, *n.* vrolijkheid *n.* **mirthful,** *a.*, ~ly, *adv.* vrolijk.
miry, *a.* modderig.
misadventure, *n.* ongeluk *n.n.*, wederwarigheid *n.*
misalliance, *n.* huwelijk *n.n.* beneden zijn stand *n.*
misanthrope, *n.* mensenhater *n.* **misanthropy,** *n.* mensenhaat *n.*
misapplication, *n.* verkeerde toepassing *n.* **misapply,** *v.t.* verkeerd toepassen.
misapprehend, *v.t.* misverstaan *irr.* **misapprehension,** *n.* misverstand *n.n.*
misappropriate, *v.t.* zich onrechtmatig toeëigenen. **misappropriation,** *n.* onrechtmatige toeëigening *n.*
misbehave, *v.i.* zich misdragen *str.* **misbehaviour,** *n.* wangedrag *n.n.*
misbelief, *n.* wangeloof *n.n.*, ongeloof *n.n.* **misbeliever,** *n.* ongelovige *m.*; dwaler *n.*
miscalculate, *v.i. & v.t.* misrekenen.
miscarriage, *n.* mislukking *n.*; miskraam *n.* ~ of justice, gerechtelijke dwaling *n.* **miscarry,** *v.i.* verloren gaan *irr.*; mislukken; een miskraam *n.* krijgen *str.*
miscellaneous, *a.* gemengd. **miscellany,** *n.* mengelwerk *n.n.*, mengeling *n.*
mischance, *n.* ongeluk *n.n.*, ongeval *n.n.*
mischief, *n.* kwaad *n.n.*; kattekwaad *n.n.* to make ~, stoken; kwaad stichten. **mischief-maker,** *n.* kwaadstichter *n.* **mischievous,** *a.*, ~ly, *adv.* moedwillig; ondeugend.
misconceive, *v.t.* verkeerd opvatten. **misconception,** *n.* verkeerd begrip *n.n.*
misconduct, *n.* wangedrag *n.n.* ¶ *v.t.* slecht beheren. ¶ *v.r.* zich slecht gedragen *str.*
misconstruction, *n.* verkeerde uitleg *n.* **misconstrue,** *v.t.* verkeerd opvatten; misduiden.
miscount, *v.t.* verkeerd (op)tellen. ¶ *n.* verkeerde telling *n.*
miscreant, *n.* snodaard *n.*

misdeal, *v.t. & v.i.* verkeerd geven *str.*; vergeven *str.* ¶ *n.* verkeerd geven *n.n.*
misdeed, *n.* misdaad *n.*; wandaad *n.*
misdemeanour, *n.* wangedrag *n.n.*; vergrijp *n.n.*, misdrijf *n.n.*
misdirect, *v.t.* verkeerd adresseren; verkeerd richten; verkeerde aanwijzingen geven *str.*
miser, *n.* vrek *n.*, gierigaard *n.*
miserable, *a.*, ~bly, *adv.* ellendig; armzalig; diep ongelukkig.
miserly, *a.* vrekkig, gierig.
misery, *n.* ellende *n.*
misfire, *v.i.* ketsen; overslaan *irr.*
misfit, *n.* iets wat niet past.
misfortune, *n.* ongeluk *n.n.*
misgiving, *n.* angstig voorgevoel *n.n.*
misgovern, *v.t.* slecht regeren.
misguide, *v.t.* misleiden.
mishap, *n.* ongeval *n.n.*, ongelukje *n.n.*
misinform, *v.t.* verkeerd inlichten.
misinterpret, *v.t.* verkeerd uitleggen *irr.* **misinterpretation,** *n.* verkeerde uitlegging *n.*
misjudge, *v.t.* verkeerd beoordelen.
mislay, *v.t.* verleggen *irr.*, zoek maken.
mislead, *v.t.* misleiden.
mismanage, *v.t.* slecht beheren; verkeerd behandelen. **mismanagement,** *n.* wanbeheer *n.n.*; verkeerd optreden.
misname, *v.t.* een verkeerde naam *n.* geven *str.* aan.
misnomer, *n.* verkeerde benaming *n.*
misogynist, *n.* tegenstander *n.* van het huwelijk.
misplace, *v.t.* misplaatsen.
misprint, *v.t.* verkeerd drukken. ¶ *n.* drukfout *n.*
mispronounce, *v.t.* verkeerd uitspreken *str.*
misquotation, *n.* verkeerde aanhaling *n.* **misquote,** *v.t.* verkeerd aanhalen.
misrepresent, *v.t.* verkeerd voorstellen; een valse voorstelling *n.* geven *str.* van.
misrule, *n.* wanbestuur *n.n.*
miss, *v.t.* missen; niet raken; mislopen *str.*; verzuimen; ontbreken *str.* ¶ *v.i.* to be ~ing, vermist worden *str.* ¶ *n.* misslag *n.* **Miss,** *N.* Juffrouw; Mejuffrouw (*form of address*).
missal, *n.* misboek *n.n.*
misselthrush, *n.* mistellijster *n.*
misshapen, *a.* mismaakt, wanstaltig.
missile, *n.* werptuig *n.n.*, projectiel *n.n.*
missing, *a.* vermist; weg.
mission, *n.* zending *n.*, missie *n.*; gezantschap *n.n.* **missionary,** *n.* zendeling *n.*, missionaris *n.*
missive, *n.* missive *n.*, zendbrief *n.*
misspell, *v.t.* verkeerd spellen.
misstatement, *n.* onjuiste verklaring *n.*
mist, *n.* nevel *n.*; mist *n.*
mistake, *n.* vergissing *n.*, fout *n.* to make a ~, zich vergissen. ¶ *v.t.* misverstaan *irr.* to ~ for, aanzien *irr.* voor; to be ~n, zich vergissen.

mister, *n.* meneer *n.* *Mr. R.*, meneer R. (*speech*); De Heer R. (*in writing*).
mistimed, *a.* ontijdig, misplaatst.
mistletoe, *n.* marentakken *pl.n.*
mistranslate, *v.t.* verkeerd vertalen.
mistress, *n.* meesteres *n.*; juffrouw *n.*; maîtresse *n.* *Mrs. R.*, Mevrouw R. (*speech and in writing*).
mistrust, *v.t.* wantrouwen. ¶ *n.* wantrouwen *n.n.*, achterdocht *n*, **mistrustful**, *a.*, ~ly, *adv.* wantrouwig, achterdochtig.
misty, *a.*, ~ily, *adv.* nevelig, mistig.
misunderstand, *v.t.* misverstaan *irr.*; verkeerd begrijpen *str.* **misunderstanding**, *n.* misverstand *n.n.*
misuse, *v.t.* misbruiken. ¶ *n.* misbruik *n.n.*
mite, *n.* mijt *n.* (*insect*); penning *n.* (*coin*); zier *n.n.* (*trifle*); peuter *n.* (*child*).
mitigate, *v.t.* lenigen; verzachten. **mitigation**, *n.* leniging *n.*; verzachting *n.*
mitre, *n.* mijter *n.*
mitt(en), *n.* want *n.*
mix, *v.t.* mengen, vermengen. ~*ing chamber*, verbrandingskamer *n.* ¶ *v.i.* zich vermengen. *to* ~ *with*, omgaan *irr.* met. **mixture**, *n.* mengsel *n.n.*
mizzen, *n.* bezaan. ¶ *a.* bezaans . . .
mnemonic, *n.* geheugenkunstje *n.n.* ~*s*, geheugenleer *n.*
moan, *v.i.* kreunen. ¶ *n.* gekreun *n.n.*
moat, *n.* gracht *n.*
mob, *n.* volksmenigte *n.*; gepeupel *n.n.*; menigte *n.*, bende *n.* ¶ *v.t.* omringen.
mobile, *a.* beweeglijk; mobiel. beweegbaar. **mobility**, *n.* beweeglijkheid *n.*; beweegbaarheid *n.*
mobilization, *n.* mobilisatie *n.* **mobilize**, *v.t.* mobiliseren.
mock, *v.t.* spotten met, voor de gek houden *irr.* ¶ *a.* nagemaakt; zogenaamd. ¶ *n.* *to make* (*a*) ~ *of*, de spot drijven *str.* met. **mocker**, *n.* spotter *n.* **mockery**, *n.* spot *n.*, spotternij *n.*, bespotting *n.*
modal, *a.* modaal. **modality**, *n.* modaliteit *n.*
mode, *n.* wijze *n.*, manier *n.*; toonsoort *n.*
model, *n.* model *n.n.*, toonbeeld *n.n.* ¶ *v.t.* modelleren, boetseren. *to* ~ *on*, vormen naar.
moderate, *a.*, ~ly, *adv.* matig, gematigd. ¶ *v.t.* matigen. **moderation**, *n.* matigheid *n.*; matiging *n.*
modern, *a.* modern; hedendaags. **modernize**, *v.t.* moderniseren.
modest, *a.*, ~ly, *adv.* bescheiden; zedig. **modesty**, *n.* bescheidenheid *n.*; zedigheid *n.*
modicum, *n.* bescheiden hoeveelheid *n.*
modification, *n.* wijziging *n.* **modify**, *v.t.* wijzigen.
modish, *a.*, ~ly, *adv.* modieus.
modulate, *v.t.* moduleren.
mohair, *n.* Angorawol *n.*
moiety, *n.* helft *n.*
moil, *n.* zware arbeid *n.* *to toil and* ~, sloven en zwoegen.

moist, *a.* vochtig. **moisten**, *v.t.* vochtig maken, bevochtigen. **moisture**, *n.* vocht *n.n.*
molar, *n.* kies *n.*, maaltand *n.*
molasses, *pl.n.* melasse *n.*
mole, *n.* mol *n.* (*animal*); pier *n.*, havendam *n.* (*jetty*); moedervlek *n.* (*mark*).
molecular, *a.* moleculair. **molecule**, *n.* molecule *n.*
mole-cricket, *n.* veenmol *n.* **moleskin**, *n* mollevel *n.n.* ¶ *a.* mollevellen.
molest, *v.t.* molesteren, overlast *n.* aandoen *irr.* **molestation**, *n.* molestatie *n.*, overlast *n.*
mollify, *v.t.* verzachten; vermurwen, vertederen.
mollusc, *n.* weekdier *n.n.*
mollycoddle, *v.t.* vertroetelen.
molten, *a.* gesmolten.
moment, *n.* ogenblik *n.n.*; belang *n.n.*, gewicht *n.n.* (*importance*); **momentarily**, *adv.* (voor) een ogenblik *n.n.*; ogenblikkelijk. **momentary**, *a.* kortstondig, van korten duur *n.* **momentous**, *a.* gewichtig, belangrijk.
momentum, *n.* moment *n.n.*; gang *n.*, vaart *n.*
monarch, *n.* monarch *n.*; vorst *n.* (*male*), vorstin *n.* (*female*). **monarchical**, *a.* monarchaal. **monarchy**, *n.* monarchie *n.*
monastery, *n.* klooster *n.* **monastic**, *a.* kloosterlijk; klooster . . .
Monday, *N.* maandag *N.*
monetary, *a.* geldelijk, financieel; geld . . .; munt . . . **money**, *n.* geld *n.n.* *ready* ~, baar geld; ~'*s worth*, waar *n.* voor z'n geld. **money-bag**, *n.* geldbuidel *n.* **moneyed**, *a.* bemiddeld, vermogend. **moneylender**, *n.* geldschieter *n.* **money-lending**, *n.* geldschieten *n.n.* **money-order**, *n.* postbewijs *n.n.*
mongoose, *n.* ichneumon *n.*
mongrel, *n.* straathond *n.*, bastaard *n.* ¶ *a.* van gemengd ras *n.n.*
monitor, *n.* monitor *n.* (*ship*); vermaner *n.*; censor *n.*; klasseleider *n.*
monitory, *a.* vermanend.
monk, *n.* monnik *n.*
monkey, *n.* aap *n.* ¶ *v.i.* morrelen. **monkey-puzzle**, *n.* apenboom *n.*, araucaria *n.* **monkey-wrench**, *n.* schroefsleutel *n.*
monkish, *a.* monnikachtig.
monocle, *n.* monocle *n.*
monogram, *n.* naamcijfer *n.n.*
monologue, *n.* alleenspraak *n.*
monomania, *n.* monomanie *n.* **monomaniac**, *n.* monomaan *n.*
monophthong, *n.* éénklank *n.*
monoplane, *n.* ééndekker *n.*
monopolize, *v.t.* monopoliseren. **monopoly**, *n.* monopolie *n.*; alleenhandel *n.*
monosyllabic, *a.* éénlettergrepig. **monosyllable**, *n.* éénlettergrepig woord *n.n.*
monotonous, *a.*, ~ly, *adv.* eentonig. **monotony**, *n.* eentonigheid *n.*

monsoon, *n.* moesson *n.*
monster, *n.* monster *n.n.*, gedrocht *n.n.*
monstrance, *n.* monstrans *n.*
monstrosity, *n.* monsterachtigheid *n.*, gedrochtelijkheid *n.* **monstrous,** *a.*, ~ly, *adv.* monsterachtig; afschuwelijk.
month, *n.* maand *n.* **monthly,** *a.* & *adv.* maandelijks. ~ *period,* maandstonden *pl.n.* ¶ *n.* maandblad *n.n.*
monument, *n.* monument *n.n.*, gedenkteken *n.n.* **monumental,** *a.* ~ly, *adv.* monumentaal.
mood, *n.*...stemming *n.*; luim *n.*; wijs *n.* (*grammar*). **moodiness,** *n.* zwaarmoedigheid *n.* **moody,** *a.*, ~ily, *adv.* zwaarmoedig; humeurig.
moon, *n.* maan *n.* *once in a blue* ~, een enkele keer *n.* ¶ *v.i.* dromen. *to* ~ *around,* lopen *str.* rondsuffen. **mooncalf,** *n.* maankalf *n.n.* **moonlight,** *n.* maanlicht *n.n.* **moonlit,** *a.* door de maan verlicht. **moonshine,** *n.* maneschijn *n.* **moonstruck,** *a.* maanziek, sentimenteel.
Moor, *N.* Moor *N.*; Moriaan *N.* (*blackamoor*). **Moorish,** *a.* Moors.
moor, *n.* heide *n.*; hoogveen *n.n.* ¶ *v.t.* (vast)meren. **moor-hen,** *n.* waterhoen *n.n.*; korhoen *n.n.* **mooring,** *n.* ligplaats *n.*
moose, *n.* eland *n.*
moot, *a.* betwistbaar, onbeslecht.
mop, *n.* zwabber *n.*, stokdweil *n.*; ragebol *n.* ¶ *v.t. to* ~ *up,* opdweilen; *to* ~ *up the enemy,* het terrein van vijanden *pl.n.* zuiveren.
mope, *v.i.* druilen, kniezen.
moraine, *n.* moraine *n.*, morene *n.*
moral, *a.*, ~ly, *adv.* zedelijk, moreel. ¶ *n.* zedeles *n.*; zedeleer *n.*, moraal *n.* ~s, zeden *pl.n.* **morale,** *n.* moreel *n.n.* **morality,** *n.* zedelijkheid *n.* **moralize,** *v.i.* moraliseren
morass, *n.* moeras *n.n.*
morbid, *a.* ziekelijk; ziekte . . .
more, *a.* & *adv.* meer. *once* ~, nog eens; *one* ~, nog één; *two* ~, nog twee; *much* ~, veel meer; *no* ~, niet meer; niet langer; ~ *or less,* min of meer; *the* ~ *the better,* hoe meer hoe beter.
morella, *n.* morel *n.*
moreover, *adv.* bovendien, daarenboven.
moribund, *a.* zieltogend.
morn, *n.* (*poet.*). *See* morning. **morning,** *n.* morgen *n.*; ochtend *n.* *of a* ~, 's morgens; ~ *dress,* ochtendkostuum *n.n.*
morocco, *n.* marokijn *n.* ¶ *a.* marokijnen.
morose, *a.*, ~ly, *adv.* gemelijk.
morphia, *n.* morphine *n.*
morris dance, *n.* volksdans *n.*
morrow, *n.* volgende dag *n.*
morse, *n.* walrus *n.*
Morse, *N.* Morse *n.N.*
morsel, *n.* brokje *n.n.*
mortal, *a.*, ~ly, *adv.* sterfelijk; dodelijk. ¶ *n.* sterveling *n.* **mortality,** *n.* sterfelijkheid *n.*; sterfte *n.*

mortar, *n.* vijzel *n.* (*vessel*); mortier *n.* (*fire-arm*); mortel *n.* (*substance*). **mortarboard,** *n.* mortelplank *n.*; baret *n.*
mortgage, *v.t.* hypothekeren, verpanden. ¶ *n.* hypotheek *n.* **mortgage-bond,** *n.* pandbrief *n.* **mortgage-deed,** *n.* hypothecaire acte *n.* **mortgagee,** *n.* hypotheekhouder *n.* **mortgager,** *n.* hypotheeknemer *n.*
mortification, *n.* afsterving *n.*, koudvuur *n.n.*; vernedering *n.*, beschaming *n.* **mortify,** *v.t.* vernederen, beschamen; kastijden.
mortice, *n.* tapgat *n.n.*
mortmain, *n.* dode hand *n.*
mortuary, *n.* lijkenhuis *n.n.* ¶ *a.* graf . . .
mosaic, *n.* mozaïek *n.n.*
Moslem, *N.* Mohammedaan *N.* ¶ *a.* Mohammedaans.
mosque, *n.* moskee *n.*
mosquito, *n.* muskiet *n.*; mug *n.*
moss, *n.* mos *n.n.* **mossy,** *a.* mossig, bemost.
most, *a.* meest. ¶ *adv.* meest; zeer, bizonder. *at* (*the*) ~, op z'n hoogst; hoogstens. ¶ *n.* meeste *n.n.*; meesten *pl.n.n.* *to make the* ~ *of,* zoveel mogelijk profiteren van. **mostly,** *adv.* meestal, meestendeels.
mote, *n.* stofje *n.n.*
moth, *n.* mot *n.*; nachtvlinder *n.* **motheaten,** *a.* met de mot erin.
mother, *n.* moeder *n.*; moer *n.*, droesem *n.* ¶ *v.t.* moeder spelen over. **motherhood,** *n.* moederschap *n.n.* **mother-in-law,** *n.* schoonmoeder *n.* **motherless,** *a.* moederloos. **motherly,** *a.* moederlijk.
mother-of-pearl, *n.* paarlemoer *n.n.* ¶ *a.* paarlemoeren.
motion, *n.* beweging *n.*; voorstel *n.n.*, motie *n.*; stoelgang *n.* ¶ *v.t.* wenken. **motionless,** *a.* onbeweeglijk.
motive, *n.* beweegreden *n.*, motief *n.n.* ¶ *a.* bewegings . . ., beweeg . . . ~ *power* drijfkracht *n.*
motley, *a.* bont, veelkleurig. ¶ *n.* narrenpak *n.n.*
motor, *n.* motor *n.* ¶ *a.* drijf . . . **motor-car,** *n.* auto *n.* **motor-cycle,** *n.* motorfiets *n.* **motoring,** *n.* autorijden *str.* **motorist,** *n.* automobilist *n.*
mottled, *a.* gevlekt.
motto, *n.* motto *n.n.*, zinspreuk *n.*
mould, *n.* aarde *n.*, teelaarde *n.* (*earth*); schimmel *n.* (*decay*); gietvorm *n.*, matrijs *n.* (*vessel*). ¶ *v.t.* gieten *str.*; vormen. **moulder** *v.i.* vermolmen, vergaan *irr.* ¶ *n.* vormer *n.* **mouldiness,** *n.* schimmeligheid *n.* **moulding,** *n.* vorming *n.*; lijst *n.*; fries *n.* **mouldy,** *a.* beschimmeld ; vermolmd.
moult, *v.i.* ruien, verharen. ¶ *n.* ruien *n.n.*
mound *n.* heuveltje *n.n.*; hoop *n.*
mount, *n.* berg *n.*; rijpaard *n.n.* ¶ *v.i.* stijgen *str.*, rijzen *str.*, naar boven gaan *irr.* *to* ~ *up,* oplopen *str.* ¶ *v.t.* beklimmen *str.*, bestijgen *str.*, opgaan *irr.* *to* ~ *guard,* de wacht betrekken *str.* **mountain,** *n.* berg *n.*

mountain-ash, *n.* lijsterbes *n.*; ratel-populier *n.* **mountain-chain,** *n.* bergketen *n.* **mountaineer,** *n.* bergbewoner *n.*; bergbeklimmer *n.* **mountaineering,** *n.* bergbeklimmen *n.n.* **mountainous,** *a.* bergachtig.

mountebank, *n.* kwakzalver *n.*

mounting, *n.* montuur *n.*; affuit *n.n.*

mourn, *v.i.* rouwen, treuren. ¶ *v.t.* betreuren. **mourner,** *n.* rouwdrager *n.* **mournful,** *a.*, ~ly, *adv.* droevig, treurig. **mourning,** *n.* rouw *n.*; rouwkleding *n.*

mouse, *n.* muis *n.* **mousehole,** *n.* muizengat *n.n.* **mouser,** *n.* muizenvanger *n.*

moustache, *n.* snor *n.*; knevel *n.*

mouth, *n.* mond *n.*; muil *n.*, bek *n.*; opening *n.* *by word of* ~, mondeling; *down in the* ~, neerslachtig. ¶ *v.t.* declameren. **mouthful,** *n.* mondvol *n.* **mouth-organ,** *n.* mondharmonica *n.* **mouthpiece,** *n.* mondstuk *n.n.*; woordvoerder *n.*

movable, *a.*, ~bly, *adv.* beweegbaar; beweeglijk. ¶ *n.* ~*s,* roerende goederen *pl.n.n.* **move,** *v.i.* zich bewegen *str.*, een beweging *n.* maken; verhuizen. *to* ~ *off,* wegtrekken *str.* ¶ *v.t.* bewegen *str.*; verplaatsen, verzetten; voorstellen. ¶ *n.* beweging *n.*; zet *n.* *to get a* ~ *on,* opschieten *str.* **movement,** *n.* beweging *n.*; mechaniek *n.* **mover,** *n.* beweger *n.*; beweegkracht *n.* **movies,** *pl.n.* bioscoop *n.* **moving,** *a.*, ~ly, *adv.* roerend, aandoenlijk.

mow, *v.t.* maaien. ¶ *n.* hooiberg *n.*; opper *n.* **mower,** *n.* maaier *n.*

much, *a.* veel. *I thought as* ~, dat dacht ik wel; *as* ~ *again,* ééns zoveel. ¶ *adv.* zeer, veel, erg; vrijwel, nagenoeg.

mucilage, *n.* (vloeibare) gom *n.*

muck, *n.* mest *n.*; vuil *n.n.*, smeerlapperij *n.* ¶ *v.t.* (*coll.*) *to* ~ *it up,* de boel verknoeien. ¶ *v.i.* (*coll.*) *to* ~ *around,* knoeien.

mucous, *a.* slijmig; slijm . . . **mucus,** *n.* slijm *n.n.*

mud, *n.* modder *n.*, slijk *n.n.*

muddle, *n.* warboel *n.*

muddy, *a.* modderig. **mudguard,** *n.* spatbord *n.n.* **mudscraper,** *n.* voetenschraper *n.*

muff, *n.* mof *n.* ¶ *v.t.* verknoeien.

muffin, *n.* verse beschuitbol *n.*

muffle, *v.t.* dempen. ¶ *n.* moffeloven *n.*

muffler, *n.* halsdoek *n.*

mufti, *n.* burgerkleding *n.* *in* ~, in politiek.

mug, *n.* kroes *n.*; (*fig.*) suffer. **muggy,** *a.* gedrukt; bedompt.

mulatto, *n.* mulat *n.*

mulberry, *n.* moerbei *n.*

mulct, *v.t.* beboeten.

mule, *n.* muilezel *n.*, muildier *n.n.* **muleteer,** *n.* muilezeldrijver *n.* **mulish,** *a.*, ~ly, *adv.* koppig.

mull, *v.t.* kruiden. ~*ed wine,* kandeel *n.*

mullet, *n.* poon *n.*, mul *n.*

multifarious, *a.* veelsoortig, veelvuldig. **multiform,** *a.* veelvormig. **multiple,** *a.*

veelvoudig. ¶ *n.* veelvoud *n.n.* *least common* ~, kleinste gemene veelvoud. **multiplication,** *n.* vermenigvuldiging *n.* **multiplicity,** *n.* menigvuldigheid *n.* **multiply,** *v.t.* vermenigvuldigen. **multitude,** *n.* menigte *n.*; massa *n.* **multitudinous,** *a.* talrijk.

mum, *int.* ~*'s the word,* mondjedicht!; *to keep* ~, geen woord *n.n.* zeggen *irr.*

mumble, *v.t.* & *v.i.* mompelen, prevelen.

mummer, *n.* gemaskerd comediant *n.* **mummery,** *n.* poppekasterij *n.*

mummy, *n.* maatje *n.n.*, moesje *n.n.*; mummie *n.*

mumpish, *a.* landerig. **mumps,** *pl.n.* bof *n.*

munch, *v.t.* knabbelen.

mundane, *a.* werelds.

municipal, *a.* gemeentelijk; gemeente . . . **municipality,** *n.* gemeente *n.*

munificence, *n.* vrijgevigheid *n.*, milddadigheid *n.* **munificent,** *a.*, ~ly, *adv.* vrijgevig, mild(dadig).

muniment, *n.* oorkonde *n.*

munition, *n.* krijgsvoorraad *n.*

mural, *a.* muur . . . ¶ *n.* muurschildering *n.*

murder, *n.* moord *n.* ¶ *v.t.* vermoorden. **murderer,** *n.* moordenaar *n.* **murderess,** *n.* moordenares *n.* **murderous,** *a.*, ~ly, *adv.* moorddadig.

murky, *a.* donker, duister.

murmur, *v.i.* mompelen; murmelen, ruisen. ¶ *n.* gemompel *n.n.*; gemurmel *n.n.*, geruis *n.n.*

murrain, *n.* veepest *n.*

muscatel, *n.* muskaatdruif *n.*

muscle, *n.* spier *n.* **muscular,** *a.* gespierd, spier . . .

muse, *n.* muze *n.* ¶ *v.i.* peinzen.

museum, *n.* museum *n.n.*

mushroom, *n.* champignon *n.*

mushy, *a.* brijig.

music, *n.* muziek *n.* **musical,** *a.*, ~ly, *adv.* muzikaal. **music-hall,** *n.* variététheater *n.n.* **musician,** *n.* muzikant *n.*; musicus *n.* **music-stand,** *n.* muziekstander *n.* **music-stool,** *n.* pianokrukje *n.n.*

musk, *n.* muskus *n.*

musket, *n.* musket *n.n.* **musketeer,** *n.* musketier *n.* **musketry,** *n.* geweeroefeningen *pl.n.*

musky, *a.* muskusachtig.

muslin, *n.* mousseline *n.*, neteldoek *n.n.* ¶ *a.* mousselinen.

mussel, *n.* mossel *n.*

Mussulman, *N.* Muzelman *N.*

must, *v.i.* moeten *irr.* ¶ *n.* most *n.*

mustard, *n.* mosterd *n.* ~ *and cress,* waterkers *n.*

muster, *v.t.* monsteren; bijeenbrengen *irr.* ¶ *n.* monstering *n.* *to pass* ~, de toets doorstaan *irr.*

mustiness, *n.* dufheid *n.* **musty,** *a.*, ~ily, *adv.* duf, schimmelig.

mutability, *n.* veranderlijkheid *n.* **mutable,**

a. veranderlijk, wispelturig. **mutation,** *n.*
mutatie *n.*

mute, *a.,* ~**ly,** *adv.* stom, sprakeloos. ¶ *n.*
stomme *n.;* bidder *n.;* sourdine *n.*

mutilate, *v.t.* verminken. **mutilation,** *n.*
verminking *n.*

mutineer, *n.* muiter *n.,* oproermaker *n.*

mutinous, *a.,* ~**ly,** *adv.* muitziek, oproerig.

mutiny, *n.* muiterij *n.,* oproer *n.n.* ¶ *v.i.*
aan het muiten slaan *irr.*

mutter, *v.i. & v.t.* mompelen. ¶ *n.* gemompel
n.n.

mutton, *n.* schapenvlees *n.n.* ~ *chop,*
lamskotelet *n.*

mutual, *a.,* ~**ly,** *adv.* wederkerig, wederzijds.

muzzle, *n.* muil *n.,* bek *n.,* snuit *n.;* muilkorf
n., muilband *n.;* mond *n.* (*of fire-arm*).
¶ *v.t.* muilbanden.

my, *pron.* mijn.

myopia, *n.* bijziendheid *n.* **myopic,** *a.*
bijziend.

myriad, *n.* tienduizendtal *n.n.,* myriade *n.*

myrmidon, *n.* handlanger *n.,* dienaar *n.*

myrrh, *n.* mirre *n.*

myrtle, *n.* mirt *n.*

myself, *pron.* zelf; ikzelf, mijzelf.

mysterious, *a.,* ~**ly,** *adv.* geheimzinnig.
mystery, *n.* geheim *n.n.,* mysterie *n.n.*
mystic(al), *a.,* ~**ly,** *adv.* mystiek. **mysti-**
cism, *n.* mystiek *n.,* mysticisme *n.n.*
mystification, *n.* mystificatie *n.,* geheim-
zinnigheid *n.* **mystify,** *v.t.* mystificeren.

myth, *n.* mythe *n.* **mythological,** *a.* mytho-
logisch. **mythology,** *n.* mythologie *n.,*
godenleer *n.*

N

nab, *v.t.* inrekenen, snappen; op de kop
tikken.

nacre, *n.* paarlemoer *n.n.* ¶ *a.* paarlemoeren.

nadir, *n.* nadir *n.n.*

nag, *v.t.* zeuren, vitten. ¶ *n.* hit *n.,* paard *n.n.*

naiad, *n.* najade *n.,* waternimf *n.*

nail, *n.* nagel *n.;* spijker *n.* ¶ *v.t.* (vast)
spijkeren. *to* ~ *down,* dichtspijkeren;
vastzetten.

naive, *a.,* ~**ly,** *adv.* naïef. **naivety,** *n.*
naïveteit *n.*

naked, *a.,* ~**ly,** *adv.* naakt; bloot. *stark* ~,
spiernaakt. **nakedness,** *n.* naaktheid *n.*

name, *n.* naam *n. by* ~, met name; *Christian*
~, voornaam *n.* ¶ *v.t.* noemen. **nameless,**
a. naamloos; nameloos; onnoemelijk.
namely, *adv.* namelijk. **namesake,** *n.*
naamgenoot *n.*

nankeen, *n.* nanking *n.n.*

nanny-goat, *n.* geit *n.*

nap, *n.* dutje *n.n.* (*doze*); nop *n.* (*on cloth*);
soort kaartspel *n.n.*

nape, *n.* nek *n.*

napkin, *n.* servet *n.;* luier *n.*

napoleonic, *a.* Napoleontisch.

narcosis, *n.* narcose *n.* **narcotic,** *a.* verdovend, slaapwekkend. ¶ *n.* verdovend
middel *n.n.*

narrate, *v.t.* verhalen. **narration,** *n.* verhaal
n.n., relaas *n.n.* **narrative,** *a.* verhalend.
¶ *n.* verhaal *n.n.,* relaas *n.n.*

narrow, *a.,* ~**ly,** *adv.* nauw, eng, smal;
kleingeestig. *a* ~ *majority,* een geringe
meerderheid *n.;* ~ *gauge,* smalspoor *n.n.*
¶ *v.t.* vernauwen. ¶ *n.* ~*s,* zeeëngte *n.*
narrowminded, *a.* kleingeestig, kleinzielig.
narrowness, *n.* nauwheid *n.;* bekrompenheid *n.*

nasal, *a.* neus . . . ¶ *n.* neusklank *n.*

nastiness, *n.* viezigheid *n.;* onprettigheid *n.*
nasty, *a.,* ~**ily,** *adv.* vies, vuil; onprettig.

natal, *a.* geboorte . . .

nation, *n.* volk *n.n.,* natie *n.* **national,** *a.,*
~**ly,** *adv.* nationaal; vaderlands; staats . . .
¶ *n.* landgenoot *n.* in den vreemde.
nationality, *n.* nationaliteit *n.* **nationalize,**
v.t. nationaliseren; onteigenen.

native, *a.* aangeboren; oorspronkelijk;
inheems. ~ *country,* land *n.n.* van
geboorte *n.;* ~ *tongue,* moedertaal *n.;*
~ *soil,* geboortegrond *n.* ¶ *n.* inboorling
n., inlander *n.;* inlandse oester *n.* **nativity,**
n. geboorte *n.*

natrium, *n.* natrium *n.n.*

natron, *n.* natron *n.n.*

natter, *v.i.* zeuren.

natty, *a.* keurig.

natural, *a.,* ~**ly,** *adv.* natuurlijk. ~ *re-*
sources, bodemrijkheid *n.* ¶ *n.* idioot *n.*
naturalist, *n.* natuurhistoricus *n.;* opzetter
n. **naturalization,** *n.* naturalisatie *n.*
naturalize, *v.t.* naturaliseren. **nature,** *n.*
natuur *n.;* aard *n.,* karakter *n.n. by* ~,
van nature; *in the* ~ *of things,* uit den
aard der zaak *n.; true to* ~, natuurgetrouw.

naught, *n.* niets *n.n.;* nul *n. to come to* ~,
mislukken; op niets uitlopen *str.; to set*
at ~, in de wind slaan *irr.*

naughty, *a.,* ~**ily,** *adv.* stout, ondeugend.

nausea, *n.* walging *n.* **nauseate,** *v.t.* doen *irr.*
walgen. **nauseous,** *a.* walgelijk.

nautical, *a.* zee . . ., scheeps . . .

naval, *a.* zee . . ., scheeps . . .; scheepvaart . . .;
vloot . . ., marine. . . . ~ *officer,* zee-
officier *n.*

nave, *n.* naaf *n.* (*of wheel*); schip *n.n.* (*of*
church).

navel, *n.* navel *n.*

navigability, *n.* bevaarbaarheid *n.* **navigable,**
a. bevaarbaar. **navigate,** *v.i.* varen. ¶ *v.t.*
bevaren; besturen. **navigation,** *n.* scheepvaart *n.;* navigatie *n.;* zeemanschap *n.,*
stuurmanskunst *n.* **navigator,** *n.* zee-
vaarder *n.*

navvy, *n.* polderjongen *n.,* grondwerker *n.*

navy, *n.* vloot *n.;* marine *n.*

nay, *adv.* nee(n); wat meer is; ja zelfs. ¶ *n.*
to say ~, weigeren

neap, *n.* dood tij *n.n.* ~ *tide,* dood tij *n.n.*
near, *a.* nabij, dichtbijzijnd; bijdehands. *the* ~ *future,* de naaste toekomst; *to have a* ~ *escape,* ter nauwernood ontsnappen; ~ *miss,* neventreffer *n.* ¶ *prep.* nabij, naast. ¶ *adv.* bij; bijna. ¶ *v.t.* & *v.i.* naderen. **nearly,** *adv.* bijna. **near-sighted,** *a.* bijziend.
neat, *a.*, ~ly, *adv.* net(jes); zindelijk, proper. **neatness,** *n.* netheid *n.*; zindelijkheid *n.*
nebulous, *a.* nevelachtig, nevelig; vaag.
necessaries, *pl.n.* benodigdheden *pl.n.* **necessary,** *a.*, ~ily, *adv.* noodzakelijk, vereist, benodigd. **necessitate,** *v.t.* noodzakelijk maken. **necessitous,** *a.* behoeftig. **necessity,** *n.* noodzaak *n.*; behoeftigheid *n.*
neck, *n.* hals *n.*, nek *n.* **necklace,** *n.* collier *n.* halssnoer *n.n.* **necktie,** *n.* das *n.*
necrology, *n.* doodsbericht *n.n.*
necromancer, *n.* tovenaar *n.*, geestenbezweerder *n.* **necromancy,** *n.* zwarte kunst *n.*
nectar, *n.* nektar *n.*
nectarine, *n.* (soort) perzik *n.*
need, *n.* nood *n.*, behoefte *n.*; noodzaak *n.*; ellende *n. to be in* ~ *of,* van node hebben. ¶ *v.t.* nodig hebben, behoeven; (be)hoeven. **needful,** *a.* noodzakelijk, vereist. **neediness,** *n.* behoeftigheid *n.*
needle, *n.* naald *n.*; wijzer *n.*; obelisk *n.* **needle-case,** *n.* naaldenkoker *n.*
needless, *a.* nodeloos.
needlewoman, *n.* naaister *n.* **needlework,** *n.* naaiwerk *n.n.*; handwerkje *n.n.*
needs, *adv.* noodzakelijk, noodwendig.
needy, *a.*, ~ily, *adv.* behoeftig.
nefarious, *a.* snood, schandelijk
negation, *n.* ontkenning *n.* **negative,** *a.*, ~ly, *adv.* ontkennend; negatief.
neglect, *v.t.* verwaarlozen; verzuimen. ¶ *n.* verwaarlozing *n.* **neglectful,** *a.* onverschillig, achteloos, nalatig. **negligence,** *n.* nalatigheid *n.*, achteloosheid *n.* **negligent,** *a.*, ~ly, *adv.* achteloos, nalatig.
negotiable, *a.* verhandelbaar. **negotiate,** *v.i.* onderhandelen; handel *n.* drijven *str.* ¶ *v.t.* verhandelen; sluiten *str.*; nemen *str.* **negotiation,** *n.* onderhandeling *n.* **negotiator,** *n.* onderhandelaar *n.*
negress, *n.* negerin *n.* **negro,** *n.* neger *n.*
negus, *n.* gekruide wijn *n.*
neigh, *v.i.* hinniken. ¶ *n.* gehinnik *n.n.*
neighbour, *n.* buur *n.*, buurman *n.*, buurvrouw *n.* ¶ *v.i. to* ~ *upon,* grenzen aan. **neighbourhood,** *n.* buurt *n.*; nabijheid *n.* **neighbourly,** *a.* buur . . . *in* ~ *fashion,* als goede buren *pl.n.*
neither, *pron.* geen van beiden. ~ . . . *nor* . . . , noch . . . noch . . .
neolithic, *a.* neolithisch.
neologism, *n.* neologisme *n.n.*
neophyte, *n.* neophiet *n.*, nieuweling *n.*
nephew, *n.* neef *n.*
nepotism, *n.* nepotisme *n.n.*
nerve, *n.* zenuw *n.*; durf *n.* ¶ *v.t.* stalen.

¶ *v.r.* *to* ~ *oneself,* zich vermannen.
nerveless, *a.* slap, zwak. **nervous,** *a.*, ~ly, *adv.* zenuwachtig, nerveus. **nervousness,** *n.* zenuwachtigheid *n.*
nest, *n.* nest *n.n.* ¶ *v.i.* nesten, nestelen. **nest-egg,** *n.* spaarduitje *n.n.* **nestle,** *v.i.* zich nestelen. **nestling,** *n.* nestkuiken *n.n.*
net, *n.* net *n.n.* ¶ *v.t.* in een net vangen *str.*; binnenhalen. ¶ *a.* netto.
nether, *a.* beneden, onderste.
netting, *n.* netwerk *n.n.*
nettle, *n.* netel *n.* ¶ *v.t.* netelen, ergeren. ~d, gepikeerd.
network, *n.* net *n.n.*, netwerk *n.n.*
neural, *a.* zenuw . . . **neuralgia,** *n.* zenuwpijn *n.* **neuralgic,** *a.* neuralgisch. **neurasthenia,** *n.* neurasthenie *n.*, zenuwzwakte *n.* **neurasthenic,** *a.* neurasthenisch. **neuritis,** *n.* zenuwontsteking *n.* **neurology,** *n.* zenuwleer *n.* **neurosis,** *n.* neurose *n.*, zenuwziekte *n.* **neurotic,** *a.* zenuwziek. ¶ *n.* zenuwlijder *n.*
neuter, *a.* onzijdig. **neutral,** *a.*, ~ly, *adv.* onzijdig, neutraal. **neutrality,** *n.* onzijdigheid *n.*, neutraliteit *n.* **neutralize,** *v.t.* neutraliseren.
never, *adv.* nooit. *well I* ~, heb ik van m'n leven!; ~ *mind,* laat maar; 't geeft niets. **nevertheless,** *adv.* niettemin; desondanks.
new, *a.* nieuw; vers, fris. **newborn,** *a.* pasgeboren. **newcomer,** *n.* nieuweling *n.*; pas (aan)gekomene *n.* **newfangled,** *a.* nieuwerwets. **newfashioned,** *a.* nieuwmodisch. **newly,** *adv.* kort geleden, onlangs. **newness,** *n.* nieuwheid *n.*, nieuwigheid *n.*
news, *n.* nieuws *n.n.* **newsagent,** *n.* krantenhandelaar *n.* ~'s *shop,* krantenwinkel *n.* **newspaper,** *n.* krant *n.*, dagblad *n.n.* **newspaper-boy,** *n.* krantenjongen *n.* **news-sheet,** *n.* nieuwsblad *n.n.* **newsvendor,** *n.* krantenjongen *n.*
newt, *n.* (water)salamander *n.*
New Year, *N.* Nieuwjaar *n.N.* **New Year's Eve,** *N.* oudejaarsavond *n.*
next, *a.* volgend, eerstvolgend; aanstaand. ~ *of kin,* naaste bloedverwant *n.* ¶ *adv.* daarna, vervolgens. **next-door,** *adv.* hiernaast; daarnaast.
nib, *n.* pen *n.*, punt *n.*
nibble, *v.i.* knabbelen.
nice, *a.*, ~ly, *adv.* aardig; lief; mooi; net; kieskeurig. **niceness,** *n.*, **nicety,** *n.* fijnheid *n.*; nauwkeurigheid *n.*; kieskeurigheid *n.*
niche, *n.* nis *n.*
nick, *n.* kerf *n.*, inkerving *n. in the* ~ *of time,* op het nippertje. ¶ *v.t.* kerven *str.*
nickel, *n.* nikkel *n.n.* ¶ *a.* nikkelen. ~ *plated,* vernikkeld.
nickname, *n.* bijnaam *n.*, spotnaam *n.* ¶ *v.t.* een spotnaam geven *str.*
nicotine, *n.* nicotine *n.*
niece, *n.* nicht *n.*

niggard, *n.* vrek *n.*, gierigaard *n.* **niggardly,** *a. & adv.* vrekkig, gierig; schraal, mager.

nigger, *n.* nikker *n.*

nigh, *prep.* nabij. ¶ *adv.* bijna. ~ *on,* bij de.

night, *n.* nacht *n.*; avond *n.* *at* ~, *by* ~, 's nachts; *late at* ~, 's avonds laat; *last* ~, gisteravond; de afgelopen nacht. **nightcap,** *n.* slaapmuts *n.*; (*fig.*) slaapmutsje *n.n.* **nightfall,** *n.* het vallen van den avond. **nightgown,** *n.* nachtjapon *n.*

nightingale, *n.* nachtegaal *n.*

night-jar, *n.* geitenmelker *n.*

nightly, *a.* nachtelijk. ¶ *adv.* 's nachts; iedere nacht *n.*, iedere avond *n.* **nightmare,** *n.* nachtmerrie *n.* **night-primrose,** *n.* Teunisbloem *n.* **nightshade,** *n.* nachtschade *n.* **nightwatchman,** *n.* nachtwaker *n.*

nil, *n.* niets *n.n.*

nimble, *a.*, ~**bly,** *adv.* vlug, vaardig. **nimbleness,** *n.* vlugheid *n.*, vaardigheid *n.*

nimbus, *n.* stralenkrans *n.*; regenwolk *n.*

nincompoop, *n.* onnozele *n.*, sul *n.*

nine, *num.* negen; negenen. **ninefold,** *a.* negenvoudig.

ninepin, *n.* kegel *n.*

nineteen, *num.* negentien. **nineteenth,** *a.* negentiende.

ninetieth, *a.* negentigste. **ninety,** *num.* negentig.

ninny, *n.* sukkel *n.*, hals *n.*

ninth, *a.* negende. **ninthly,** *adv.* ten negende.

nip, *n.* neep *n.*, kneep *n.*; beet *n.*; steek *n.* ¶ *v.t.* nijpen *str.*, knijpen *str.*; bijten *str.*; steken *str.* ¶ *v.i.* wippen.

nipper, *n.* jongen *n.*

nipple, *n.* tepel *n.*

nit, *n.* neet *n.*

nitrate, *n.* nitraat *n.n.* **nitre,** *n.* salpeter *n.n.* **nitric acid,** *n.* salpeterzuur *n.n.* **nitrous,** *a.* salpeterachtig.

nitrogen, *n.* stikstof *n.*

no, *adv.* nee(n). ~ *more,* niet meer. ¶ *a.* geen. ¶ *n.* stem *n.* tegen.

nobility, *n.* adel *n.*, adelstand *n.* **noble,** *a.*, ~**bly,** *adv.* edel; adellijk. ¶ *n.* edelman *n.* **nobleman,** *n.* edelman *n.* **nobleness,** *n.* adellijkheid *n.*

nobody, *pron.* niemand.

nocturnal, *a.* nachtelijk; nacht . . .

nod, *v.i.* knikken; knikkebollen. ¶ *v.t.* knikken. *to* ~ *one's head,* met het hoofd knikken. ¶ *n.* knikje *n.n.*

noddle, ¶ *n.* bol *n.*

node, *n.* knoop *n.*; knoest *n.*

noggin, *n.* maatje *n.n.*

noise, *n.* leven *n.*, lawaai *n.n.* ¶ *v.t.* *to* ~ *it abroad,* het ruchtbaar maken. **noiseless,** *a.*, ~**ly,** *adv.* geluidloos, stil.

noisome, *a.*, ~**ly,** *adv.* stinkend; hinderlijk.

noisy, *a.*, ~**ily,** *adv.* luidruchtig; lawaaierig.

nomad, *n.* nomade *n.* **nomadic,** *a.* nomadisch.

nomenclature, *n.* nomenclatuur *n.*, terminologie *n.*

nominal, *a.* nominaal. **nominally,** *adv.* nominaal, in naam. **nominate,** *v.t.* kandidaatstellen; aanstellen. **nomination,** *n.* nominatie *n.*, kandidaatstelling *n.*, voordracht *n.* **nominative,** *n.* nominatief *n.*, eerste naamval *n.* **nominee,** *n.* genoemde *n.*, benoemde *n.*

non-acceptance, *n.* non-acceptatie *n.*

nonage, *n.* minderjarigheid *n.*

nonagenarian, *n.* negentigjarige *n.*

non-appearance, *n.* ontstentenis *n.*

nonce, *n. for the* ~, voor deze keer *n.*

nonce-word, *n.* slechts éénmaal voorkomend woord *n.n.*

non-commissioned, *a.* ~ *officer,* onderofficier *n.*

non-committal, *a.* tot niets verbindend, vaag.

non-compliance, *n.* weigering *n.*; nalatigheid *n.*

noncomformist, *n.* afgescheidene *n.*

non-conductor, *n.* slechte geleider *n.*

nondescript, *a.* onbenullig, onbeduidend.

none, *pron. & a.* geen; niets; niemand. ¶ *adv.* niets. ~ *too,* niet al te.

nonentity, *n.* onbeduidend iets *or* iemand.

non-intervention, *n.* niet tussenbeide treden *n.n.*, non-interventie *n.*

non-payment, *n.* nietbetaling *n.*

nonplus, *v.t.* uit het veld slaan *irr.*

nonsense, *n.* onzin *n.*, nonsens *n.* **nonsensical,** *a.*, ~**ly,** *adv.* onzinnig.

non-smoker, *n.* coupé *n.n.* niet roken.

nonsuit, *v.t.* royeren.

noodle, *n.* knoedel *n.*; uilskuiken *n.n.*

nook, *n.* hoek *n.*, hoekje *n.n.*

noon, *n.* middag *n.*, twaalf uur *n.n.* **noonday,** *a.* middag . . . **noontide,** *n.* middag *n.*

noose, *n.* lus *n.*, strik *n.*

nor, *c.* noch; en ook niet, en evenmin.

norm, *n.* norm *n.* **normal,** *a.* normaal. **normally,** *adv.* normaal; gewoonlijk.

Norse, *a.* oud-Noors. **Norseman,** *N.* Noorman *N.*

north. *n.* Noorden *n.N.* ¶ *a. & adv.* noord . . ., noordelijk. **north-east,** *n.* noordoosten *n.n.* ¶ *a.* noordoost . . ., noordoostelijk. **northerly,** *a.* noordelijk. **northern,** *a.* noordelijk, uit het Noorden. **northerner,** *n.* bewoner *n.* van het Noorden. **northward,** *a. & adv.* noordwaarts.

Norway, *N.* Noorwegen *n.N.* **Norwegian,** *a.* Noors. ¶ *N.* Noor *N.*

nose, *n.* neus *n.* *to pay through the* ~, te duur betalen. ¶ *v.t.* snuffelen. *to* ~ *something out,* iets uitvissen. **nosegay,** *n.* ruiker *n.*

nostalgia, *n.* heimwee *n.n.*

nostril, *n.* neusgat *n.n.*

nostrum, *n.* kwakzalversmiddel *n.n.*

nosy, *a.* nieuwsgierig.

not, *adv.* niet.

notable, *a.*, ~**bly,** *adv.* opmerkelijk; waarneembaar; merkwaardig. ¶ *n.* notabele *n.*

notarial, *a.* notarieel. **notary,** *n.*, **notary public,** *n.* notaris *n.*

notation, *n.* notering *n.*; voorstellingswijze *n.*
notch, *n.* inkeping *n.*, kerf *n.* ¶ *v.t.* inkepen, kerven *str.*
note, *n.* noot *n.* (*music*); toon *n.*, klank *n.* (*sound*); nota *n.*, aantekening *n.* (*memo*). ¶ *v.t.* aantekenen, optekenen, noteren. **noted,** *a.*, ~ly, *adv.* beroemd, vermaard; berucht. **notebook,** *n.* notitieboek *n.n.* **notecase,** *n.* portefeuille *n.* **notepaper,** *n.* postpapier *n.n.* **noteworthy,** *a.* merkwaardig.
nothing, *pron.* niets. ¶ *adv.* volstrekt niet. ¶ *n.* niets *n.n.*; ding *n.n.* van niets. **nothingness,** *n.* onbeduidendheid *n.*
notice, *n.* aandacht *n.*, oplettendheid *n.*; bericht *n.n.*, bekendmaking *n.*, kennisgeving *n.* *to give* ~, . . . opzeggen *irr.*; *to take* ~ *of*, kennis nemen *str.* van; letten op; *at a moment's* ~, op staande voet *n.*; *until further* ~, tot nader order *n.* ¶ *v.t.* opmerken; letten op. **noticeable,** *a.*, ~bly, *adv.* merkbaar, waarneembaar. **noticeboard,** *n.* aanplakbord *n.n.*
notifiable, *a.* waarvan kennis *n.* gegeven moet worden. **notification,** *n.* kennisgeving *n.* **notify,** *v.t.* kennis *n.* geven *str.* van, verwittigen.
notion, *n.* denkbeeld *n.n.*, begrip *n.n.*; notie *n.*
notoriety, *n.* beruchtheid *n.* **notorious,** *a.*, ~ly, *adv.* bekend, berucht.
notwithstanding, *prep.* niettegenstaande; trots. ¶ *c.* desondanks. ¶ *adv.* desniettemin.
nought, *n.* *See* **naught.**
noun, *n.* zelfstandig naamwoord *n.n.*
nourish, *v.t.* voeden; koesteren. **nourishment,** *n.* voedsel *n.n.*; voeding *n.*
novel, *a.* nieuw, ongewoon. ¶ *n.* roman *n.* **novelist,** *n.* romanschrijver *n.* **novelty,** *n.* nieuwigheid *n.*; nieuwtje *n.n.*
November, *N.* november *N.*
novice, *n.* novice *n.*; beginneling *n.* **noviciate,** *n.* noviciaat *n.n.*
now, *adv.* nu; thans. *by* ~, tegen deze tijd *n.* ¶ *c.* nu. **nowadays,** *adv.* tegenwoordig.
nowhere, *adv.* nergens.
nowise, *adv.* geenszins.
noxious, *a.* schadelijk, verderfelijk.
nozzle, *n.* mondstuk *n.n.*, tuit *n.*, pijp *n.*
nubile, *a.* huwbaar.
nucleus, *n.* kern *n.*
nude, *a.* naakt. ¶ *n.* naakt *n.n.* *in the* ~, naakt.
nudge, *v.t.* even aanstoten *str.*
nudity, *n.* naaktheid *n.*
nugatory, *a.* nietszeggend.
nugget, *n.* klomp *n.*
nuisance, *n.* last *n.*; hinder *n.*; overlast *n.*; lastpost *n.* *commit no* ~, verontreiniging *n.* verboden.
null, *a.* ongeldig. **nullify,** *v.t.* ongeldig verklaren. **nullity,** *n.* ongeldigheid *n.*, nietigheid *n.*
numb, *a.* gevoelloos, verkleumd, verdoofd.

number, *n.* getal *n.n.*; aantal *n.n.*; nummer *n.n.*; aflevering *n.* ¶ *v.t.* nummeren; rekenen, tellen; bedragen *str.* **numberless.** *a.* talloos.
numbness, *n.* gevoelloosheid *n.*; verdoving *n.*; verkleumdheid *n.*
numeral, *a.* getal. ¶ *n.* telwoord *n.n.* **numeration,** *n.* telling *n.*; talstelsel *n.n.* **numerator,** *n.* teller *n.* **numerical,** *a.*, ~ly, *adv.* numeriek. ~ *superiority*, grotere getalsterkte *n.* **numerous,** *a.* talrijk.
numismatics, *pl.n.* numismatiek *n.*, penningkunde *n.*
numskull, *n.* uilskuiken *n.n.*
nun, *n.* non *n.* **nunnery,** *n.* (nonnen)klooster *n.*
nuncio, *n.* nuntius *n.*, pauselijk gezant *n.*
nuptial, *a.* huwelijks . . ., bruids . . . ¶ *n.* ~s, bruiloft *n.*, huwelijk *n.n.*
nurse, *n.* verpleegster *n.*; ziekenoppasser *n.*; baker *n.*; kinderjuffrouw *n.* *wet* ~, min *n.* ¶ *v.t.* verplegen; verzorgen, oppassen; (*fig.*) koesteren: **nursemaid,** *n.* kindermeisje *n.* **nursery,** *n.* kinderkamer *n.*; bewaarschool *n.*; kwekerij *n.* **nurseryman,** *n.* kweker *n.* **nursery rhyme,** *n.* bakerrijmpje *n.n.* **nursery tale,** *n.* sprookje *n.n.* **nursing,** *n.* (zieken)verplegen *n.n.* **nursing home,** *n.* particuliere verpleeginrichting *n.* **nursling,** *n.* bakerkind *n.n.*
nurture, *v.t.* voeden; opkweken. ¶ *n.* voedsel *n.n.*; opvoeding *n.*
nut, *n.* noot *n.* (*fruit*); moer *n.* (*on bolt*). *not . . . for* ~s, absoluut niet . . .; ~ *screw*, stelschroef *n.* ¶ *v.i.* noten *pl.n.* plukken. **nutcracker,** *n.* notenkraker *n.* **nutgall,** *n.* galnoot *n.* **nutmeg,** *n.* notenmuskaat *n.*
nutriment, *n.* voedsel *n.n.* **nutrition,** *n.* voeding *n.*; voedsel *n.n.* **nutritious,** *a.* voedzaam.
nutshell, *n.* notedop *n.* *in a* ~, in 't kort; in enkele woorden *pl.n.n.*
nymph, *n.* nimf *n.*; pop *n.* (*of insect*). **nymphomania,** *n.* manziekte *n.*

O

oaf, *n.* pummel *n.*
oak, *n.* eik *n.*; eikenhout *n.n.* ¶ *a.* eiken, eikenhouten. **oak-apple,** *n.* galnoot *n.* **oaken,** *a.* eikenhouten.
oakum, *n.* werk *n.n.* *to pick* ~, touw *n.n.* pluizen *str.*
oar, *n.* riem *n.* *to put in one's* ~, z'n neus *n.* erin steken *str.* **oarsman,** *n.* roeier *n.*
oasis, *n.* oase *n.*
oast, *n.* eest *n.*
oath, *n.* eed *n.* *on* ~, onder ede; *to take the* ~, beëdigd worden *str.*
oatmeal, *n.* havermeel *n.n.* **oats,** *pl.n.* haver *n.* *he has sown his wild* ~, z'n wilde haren *pl.n.n.* zijn uitgevallen.

obduracy, n. verstoktheid n. **obdurate,** a., ~**ly,** adv. verstokt; onverbiddelijk.

obedience, n. gehoorzaamheid n. **obedient,** a., ~**ly,** adv. gehoorzaam. your ~ servant, Uw dienstwillige dienaar n.

obeisance, n. diepe buiging n.; (fig.) hulde n.

obese, a. corpulent, zwaarlijvig. **obesity,** n. corpulentie n.

obey, v.t. gehoorzamen.

obituary, n. bericht n.n. van overlijden n.n.; necrologie n.

object, n. voorwerp n.n.; doel n.n. no ~, bijzaak n. ¶ v.i. bezwaar maken. to ~ to, bezwaar maken tegen. **object-lesson,** n. aanschouwingsles n. **objection,** n. bezwaar n.n., tegenwerping n. **objectionable,** a. afkeurenswaardig. **objective,** a., ~**ly,** adv. objectief. ¶ n. doel n.n.; objectief n.n. **objectivity,** n. objectiviteit n.

obligation, n. verplichting n.; obligatie n. **obligatory,** a. verplicht. **oblige,** v.t. verplichten; een dienst bewijzen str. **obliging,** a. voorkomend, dienstvaardig.

oblique, a., ~**ly,** adv. schuin; indirect, zijdelings. **obliquity,** n. schuinheid n.; indirectheid n.

obliterate, v.t. uitwissen; doen irr. verdwijnen.

oblivion, n. vergetelheid n. **oblivious,** a. vergeetachtig. to be ~ of, vergeten.

oblong, a. langwerpig. ¶ n. langwerpig vierkant n.n., rechthoek n.

obloquy, n. smaad n., schande n.

obnoxious, a., ~**ly,** adv. schadelijk; hinderlijk.

oboe, n. hobo n.

obscene, a. onkuis, ontuchtig. **obscenity,** n. onkuisheid n., ontuchtige woorden pl.n.n.; ontuchtige voorstellingen pl.n.

obscuration, n. verduistering n. **obscure,** a., ~**ly,** adv. duister; nederig. ¶ v.t. verduisteren; overschaduwen. **obscurity,** n. duisternis n.; duisterheid n. to live in ~, in teruggetrokkenheid n. leven.

obsequies, pl.n. (plechtige) begrafenis n.

obsequious, a., ~**ly,** adv. onderdanig, kruiperig.

observable, a. waarneembaar. **observance,** n. naleving n., inachtneming n.; gebruik n.n. **observant,** a. oplettend, opmerkzaam. **observation,** n. waarneming n.; opmerking n. **observatory,** n. observatorium n.n., sterrenwacht n. **observe,** v.t. waarnemen str.; opmerken; in acht nemen str., naleven. **observer,** n. waarnemer n.

obsessed, a. bezeten. **obsess,** v.t. achtervolgen, kwellen. **obsession,** n. kwellende gedachte n., obsessie n.

obsolete, a. verouderd, in onbruik n.n. geraakt.

obstacle, n. hindernis n., hinderpaal n.; beletsel n.n.

obstinacy, n. halsstarrigheid n., koppigheid n. **obstinate,** a., ~**ly,** adv. halsstarrig, koppig.

obstreperous, a., ~**ly,** adv. luidruchtig; weerbarstig.

obstruct, v.t. versperren; (de voortgang) belemmeren; obstructie n. voeren tegen. **obstruction,** n. versperring n.; opstopping n.; obstructie n. **obstructive,** a. verhinderend.

obtain, v.t. verkrijgen str. ¶ v.i. heersen, gelden str. **obtainable,** a. verkrijgbaar.

obtrude, v.i. zich opdringen str. **obtrusive,** a., ~**ly,** adv. indringend, opdringend.

obtuse, a., ~**ly,** adv. stomp; stompzinnig. **obtuseness,** n. stompheid n.

obverse, a. tegengesteld. ¶ n. voorzijde n.

obviate, v.t. voorkomen irr., afwenden.

obvious, a., ~**ly,** adv. voor de hand liggend, duidelijk.

occasion, n. gelegenheid n.; aanleiding n. ¶ v.t. veroorzaken, aanleiding n. geven str. tot. **occasional,** a. toevallig; gelegenheids . . . ~ table, salontafeltje n.n. **occasionally,** adv. toevallig; zo nu en dan.

occident, n. westen n.n. **occidental,** a. westelijk; westers.

occult, a. verborgen, geheim; occult. **occultism,** n. occultisme n.n.

occupancy, n. bewoning n. **occupant,** n. bewoner n., huurder n. **occupation,** n. beroep n.n.; bezigheid n.; bezetting n. **occupier,** n. See occupant. **occupy,** v.t. bezig houden irr.; in beslag n.n. nemen str.; bewonen; bekleden; innemen str.; bezetten.

occur, v.i. vóórkomen irr., voorvallen str.; invallen str. **occurrence,** n. voorval n.n., gebeurtenis n.

ocean, n. oceaan n.

ochre, n. oker n.

o'clock, n. ten ~, tien uur n.n.

octagon, n. achthoek n. **octagonal,** a. achthoekig.

octave, n. octaaf n.

octavo, n. octavo (formaat) n.n.

October, N. oktober n.

octogenarian, n. tachtigjarige n.

octopus, n. achtarmige poliep n.

ocular, a. zichtbaar; oog . . . ¶ n. oculair n.n. **oculist,** n. oculist n., oogarts n.

odd, a., ~**ly,** adv. oneven; overblijvend; vreemd, zonderling. ~ jobs, allerhande karweitjes pl.n.n.; ~ moments, verloren ogenblikjes pl.n.n. **oddity,** n. zonderling iets n.n. **odds,** pl.n. ongelijkheid n., overmacht n.; voordeel n.n. the ~ are (that), er is alle kans n. op dat.

odious, a., ~**ly,** adv. hatelijk, afschuwelijk. **odium,** n. blaam n., afkeer n.

odorant, a., **odoriferous,** a. geurig, welriekend. **odour,** n. geur n.; reuk n. to be in bad ~, in kwade reuk staan irr.

of, prep. van. ~ age, meerderjarig; ~ an evening, op een avond n.; ~ late, de laatste tijd.

off, prep. van; in de buurt van, op de hoogte

van. ¶ *adv.* af, er af, weg; hiervandaan. ¶ *a.* ander, verder; vrij; slecht, bedorven.

offal, *n.* afval *n.*; lever *n.*, nieren *pl.n.* enz.

offence, *n.* overtreding *n.*; aanstoot *n.*, ergernis *n.* **offend,** *v.t.* beledigen; aanstoot geven *str.* ¶ *v.i.* to ~ *against,* overtreden *str.* **offender,** *n.* overtreder *n.*; schuldige *n.* **offensive,** *a.,* ~ly, *adv.* beledigend; aanstoot gevend; onaangenaam; aanvallend, aanvals . . . ¶ *n.* offensief *n.n.*

offer, *v.t.* aanbieden *str.*; voorslaan *irr.*; ten beste geven *str.*; uitoefenen. ¶ *v.i.* zich aanbieden *str.* ¶ *n.* aanbod *n.n.* ~ of *marriage,* huwelijksaanzoek *n.n.* **offering,** *n.* offerande *n.* **offertory,** *n.* collecte *n.*

offhand, *adv.* op slag, zonder meer. ¶ *a.* hooghartig.

office, *n.* kantoor *n.n.*; ambt *n.n.*, functie *n.*; dienst *n.*; (kerk)dienst *n.*; ministerie *n.n.*; privaat *n.n.* to be in ~, aan het bewind zijn; *kind* ~, vriendelijkheid *n.* **officer,** *n.* officier *n.*; (politie)agent *n.*; ambtenaar *n.*; comitélid *n.n.* ¶ *v.t.* aanvoeren; van officieren voorzien *irr.* **official,** *a.,* ~ly, *adv.* officieel; ambtelijk. ~ *secret,* ambtsgeheim *n.n.* ¶ *n.* ambtenaar *n.* **officialdom,** *n.* bureaucratie *n.* **officiate,** *v.i.* fungeren; officiëren. **officious,** *a.,* ~ly, *adv.* overgedienstig; bemoeiziek.

offing, *n.* open zee *n.* in the ~, voor de boeg.

offish, *a.* gereserveerd, uit de hoogte.

off-licence, *n.* vergunning *n.* (voor verkoop *n.* per fles *n.*).

off-print, *n.* afdruk *n.*

offscourings, *pl.n.* uitvaagsel *n.n.*

offset, *v.t.* opwegen *str.* tegen; compenseren. ¶ *n.* tegenwicht *n.n.*

offshoot, *n.* uitloper *n.*; zijtak *n.*

offspring, *n.* kroost *n.n.*; voortbrengsel *n.n.*

oft, *adv.* (*poet.*) vaak. **often,** *adv.* dikwijls.

ogive, *n.* kruisboog *n.*, spitsboog *n.*

ogle, *v.t.* toelonken.

ogre, *n.* menseneter *n.*

oh, *int.* ach! och! o!

oil, *n.* olie *n.*; petroleum *n.* in ~s, met olieverf geschilderd. ¶ *v.t.* oliën, smeren. **oil-cake,** *n.* raapkoek *n.* **oilcloth,** *n.* wasdoek *n.n.*, zeildoek *n.n.* **oil-colour.** *n.* olieverf *n.* **oilfield,** *n.* petroleumveld *n.n.* **oiliness,** *n.* oliachtigheid *n.* **oil-mill,** *n.* oliemolen *n.* **oil painting,** *n.* schilderij *n.* or *n.n.* in olieverf *n.* **oilskin,** *n.* oliejas *n.* **oilstove,** *n.* petroleumkachel *n.* **oilwell,** *n.* petroleumbron *n.* **oily,** *a.* olieachtig; vet; gesmeerd; zalvend, glad.

ointment, *n.* zalf *n.*, smeer *n.*

old, *a.* oud; vroeger. **olden,** *a.* aloud. **old-fashioned,** *a.* ouderwets. **oldish,** *a.* oudachtig; ouwelijk.

oleaginous, *a.* oliehoudend.

oleander, *n.* oleander *n.*

olfactory, *a.* reuk . . .

oligarchic, *a.* oligarchisch. **oligarchy,** *n.* oligarchie *n.*

olive, *n.* olijf *n.* **olive oil,** *n.* olijfolie *n.*

omelet(te), *n.* omelet *n.*

omen, *n.* voorteken *n.n.* **ominous,** *a.,* ~ly, *adv.* onheilspellend, dreigend.

omission, *n.* weglating *n.*; verzuim *n.n.*, nalatigheid *n.* **omit,** *v.t.* weglaten *str.*; verzuimen.

omnibus, *n.* omnibus *n.*

omnipotence, *n.* almacht *n.* **omnipotent,** *a.* almachtig, alvermogend.

omnipresent, *a.* alomtegenwoordig.

omniscience, *n.* alwetendheid *n.* **omniscient,** *a.* alwetend.

omnivorous, *a.* allesetend, alverslindend.

on, *prep.* op; aan, in, bij, tegen. ¶ *adv.* aan; door, voort. *and so* ~, enzovoort.

once, *adv.* eens, eenmaal. ~ *and again,* af en toe; ~ *in a while,* een hoogst enkele maal *n.* *at* ~, onmiddellijk. ¶ *c.* zodra.

one, *num.* een, één. ¶ *pron.* men. ~ *another,* elkaar.

onerous, *a.* bezwaarlijk, drukkend.

onesided, *a.* eenzijdig.

onion, *n.* ui *n.*

onlooker, *n.* toeschouwer *n.*

only, *a.* enig, enigst. ¶ *adv.* alleen, enig, enkel; maar. ¶ *c.* alleen.

onrush, *n.* stormloop *n.*

onset, *n.* aanval *n.*; aanvang *n.*

onslaught, *n.* aanval *n.*, bestorming *n.*

onus, *n.* last *n.*, verplichting *n.*

onward, *a.* & *adv.* voorwaarts.

onyx, *n.* onyx *n.*

ooze, *v.i.* sijpelen. ¶ *v.t.* uitzweten. ¶ *n.* zachte modder *n.* **oozy,** *a.* modderig; uitslaand.

opacity, *n.* ondoorzichtigheid *n.*

opal, *n.* opaal *n.* (*jewel*), *n.n.* (*substance*).

opaque, *a.* ondoorzichtig, ondoorschijnend.

open, *a.* open; openbaar; openhartig. ¶ *n.* open lucht *n.*; open veld *n.n.* ¶ *v.t.* openen, openmaken, opendoen *irr.* ¶ *v.i.* opengaan *irr.*, zich openen. **open-eyed,** *a.* met open ogen *pl.n.n.* **open-handed,** *a.* royaal. **opening,** *n.* opening *n.* ~s, vooruitzichten *pl.n.n.* **openly,** *adv.* openlijk. **open-mouthed,** *a.* met open mond *n.* **openness,** *n.* openheid *n.*; openhartigheid *n.* **openwork,** *a.* à jour.

opera, *n.* opera *n.* **opera-cloak,** *n.* sortie *n.* **opera-glasses,** *pl.n.* toneelkijker *n.* **opera-hat,** *n.* klakhoed *n.*

operate, *v.i.* werken; opereren. *to* ~ *on,* opereren.

operatic, *a.* opera . . .

operation, *n.* handeling *n.*; werking *n.*; operatie *n.*

operative, *a.* werkzaam. *to become* ~, in werking *n.* treden *str.* ¶ *n.* werkman *n.* **operator,** *n.* operateur *n.*; telefonist(e)

ophthalmia, *n.* oogontsteking *n.*

opiate, n. verdovend middel n.n.; slaapwekkend middel n.n.
opine, v.t. van mening n. zijn. opinion, n. mening n., oordeel n.n. opinionated, a. eigenzinnig.
opium, n. opium n.
opponent, n. tegenstander n.
opportune, a., ~ly, adv. gelegen; gunstig. opportunity, n. gelegenheid n.
oppose, v.t. zich verzetten tegen, bestrijden str.; tegenover elkaar stellen. opposite, a., ~ly, adv. tegenovergesteld; tegengesteld. ¶ prep. daar tegenover. ¶ n. tegenovergestelde n.n.; tegendeel n.n. opposition, n. tegenstand n.; oppositie n. in ~ to, in strijd n. met.
oppress, v.t. onderdrukken; verdrukken; drukken op, bezwaren. oppression, n. onderdrukking n., verdrukking n.; druk n. oppressive, a., ~ly, adv. drukkend; benauwend. oppressor, n. onderdrukker n.
opprobrious, a., ~ly, adv. smadelijk; schandelijk. opprobrium, n. smaad n.; schande n.
opt, v.t. opteren.
optic(al), a., ~ly, adv. optisch; gezichts . . . optician, n. opticien n. optics, pl.n. optiek n.
optimism, n. optimisme n.n. optimist, n. optimist n. optimistic, a., ~ally. adv. optimistisch.
option, n. keus n., voorkeur n.; optie n. optional, a. naar keuze.
opulence, n. weelde n., overvloed n. opulent, a., ~ly, adv. weelderig, overvloedig.
or, c. of.
oracle, n. orakel n.n. oracular, a. raadselachtig, duister.
oral, a., ~ly, adv. mondeling.
orange, a. oranje. ¶ n. oranje n.n. (colour); sinaasappel n. (fruit). orangeade, n. orangeade n.
orang-utan, n. orang-oetan n.
oration, n. rede n., redevoering n. orator, n. redenaar n. oratorical, a. oratorisch, redenaars . . . oratorio, n. oratorium n.n. oratory, n. rhetoriek n.; bidkapel n.
orb, n. schijf n.; kring n.; rijksappel n.
orbit, n. baan n., loopbaan n.; oogholte n., oogkas n.
orchard, n. boomgaard n.
orchestra, n. orkest n.n. orchestrate, v.t. orkestreren.
orchid, n. orchidee n.
ordain, v.t. beschikken; verordenen; wijden, ordenen.
ordeal, n. godsoordeel n.n., godsgericht n.n.; vuurproef n.; (fig.) beproeving n.
order, n. orde n.; soort n., orde n.; bevel n.n.; bestelling n. in ~ to, teneinde; to enter holy ~s, zich tot priester n. laten str. wijden. ¶ v.t. ordenen, regelen; bevelen str.; bestellen. orderly, a. ordelijk. ¶ n. oppasser n.; ordonnans n.
ordinal, a. rangschikkend.

ordinance, n. verordening n., ordonnantie n.
ordinary, a., ~ily, adv. gewoon, alledaags. ~ seaman, matroos n. (derde klasse n.). ¶ n. gaarkeuken n.n.; misboek n.n.
ordination, n. wijding n.
ordnance, n. geschut n.n. ~ factory, geschutgieterij n., artillerie werkplaats n.; ~ map, stafkaart n.; ~ survey, topografische opname n.
ordure, n. vuilnis n.
ore, n. erts n.n.
organ, n. orgaan n.n.; orgel n.n. organgrinder, n. orgeldraaier n. organic, a., ~ally, adv. organisch. organism, n. organisme n.n. organist, n. organist n.
organization, n. organisatie n. organize, v.t. organiseren. organizer, n. organisator n.
orgy, n. orgie n.
oriel, n. erker n.
Orient, N. Oosten n.N. orient, v.r. to ~ oneself, zich oriënteren. oriental, a. oostelijk; oosters. Oriental, N. Oosterling N.
orifice, n. opening n.
origin, n. oorsprong n.; afkomst n. original, a., ~ly, adv. oorspronkelijk; origineel. ~ sin, erfzonde n. originality, n. oorspronkelijkheid n.; originaliteit n. originate, v.i. voortspruiten str. to ~ from, afkomstig zijn van. ¶ v.t. voortbrengen irr. originator, n. ontwerper n., schepper n.
orlop, n. laagste dek n.n.
ormolu, n. verfgoud n.n.
ornament, n. sieraad n.n.; versiersel n.n. ¶ v.t. versieren, tooien. ornamental, a.. ~ly, adv. tot sieraad dienend; decoratief. ornate, a. overladen.
ornithology, n. vogelkunde n., ornithologie n.
orphan, n. wees n. orphanage, n. weeshuis n.n. orphaned, a. verweesd, ouderloos.
orrary, n. planetarium n.n.
orthodox, a. orthodox, rechtzinnig. orthodoxy, n. rechtzinnigheid n.
orthographic, a. orthografisch. orthography, n. spelling n.
orthopædic, a. orthopædisch.
ortolan, n. ortolaan n.
oscillate, v.i. schommelen; weifelen. oscillation, n. schommeling n. oscillatory, a. schommelend, slinger . . .
osculation, n. osculatie n., kus n.
osier, n. teenwilg n. ¶ a. tenen. osier-work. n. mandewerk n.n.
osprey, n. visarend n.
osseous, a. beenachtig, been . . . ossification, n. verbening n. ossify, v.i. tot been worden str.; verstenen.
ossuary, n. knekelhuis n.n.
ostensible, a., ~bly, adv. ogenschijnlijk.
ostentation, n. vertoon n.n. ostentatious, a,, ~ly, adv. praalziek; pronkerig.
ostler, n. stalknecht n.
ostracize, v.t. doodverklaren; uitsluiten str.
ostrich. n. struisvogel n.

other, *pron.* ander(s). *each* ~, elkaar. ¶ *a.* ander. *the* ~ *day*, onlangs. otherwise, *adv.* anders.

otter, *n.* otter *n.*

ought, *pron.* iets. ¶ *v.i.* behoren.

ounce, *n.* (Engels) ons *n.n.* = 28,35 Gram.

our, *pron.* ons, onze. ours, *pron.* de onze, het onze, van ons. ourself, *pron.*, ourselves, *pron.* wij(zelf); ons(zelf).

ousel, *n.* merel *n.*

oust, *v.t.* verdringen *str.*

out, *adv.* uit, naar buiten; eruit; buiten. ¶ *prep.* uit, buiten. ¶ *n. the ins and* ~*s*, alle bizonderheden *pl.n.* out-and-out, *a.* doortrapt; echt; door dik en dun.

outbid, *v.t.* meer bieden *str.* dan . . .

outbreak, *n.* uitbarsting *n.*; uitbreken *n.n.*

outbuilding, *n.* bijgebouw *n.n.*

outburst, *n.* uitbarsting *n.*; uitval *n.*

outcast, *n.* balling *n.*; verschoppeling *n.*, verworpeling *n.*

outcome, *n.* gevolg *n.n.*, resultaat *n.n.*

outcry, *n.* protest *n.n.*

outdo, *v.t.* overtreffen *str.*

outer, *a.* buiten . . ., buitenste. outmost, *a.* uiterste, buitenste.

outface, *v.t.* trotseren.

outfit, *n.* uitrusting *n.* outfitter, *n.* leverancier *n.* van uitrustingen *pl.n.*

outflank, *v.t.* omtrekken *str.*; overvleugelen.

outgoing, *a.* uitgaand.

outgrow, *v.t.* ontgroeien. outgrowth, *n.* uitgroeisel *n.n.*

outhouse, *n.* schuur *n.*, bijgebouw *n.n.*

outing, *n.* uitstapje *n.n.*

outlandish, *a.* zonderling, ongewoon.

outlast, *v.t.* langer duren dan . . .

outlaw, *v.t.* vogelvrij verklaren, buiten de wet stellen. ¶ *n.* vogelvrij verklaarde *n.* outlawry, *n.* vogelvrijverklaring *n.*

outlay, *n.* onkosten *pl.n.*

outlet, *n.* afvoerkanaal *n.n.*; uitweg *n.*; uitlaat *n.*

outline, *n.* omtrek *n.* ~*s*, hoofdtrekken *pl.n.* ¶ *v.t.* schetsen, aftekenen.

outlive, *v.t.* overleven.

outlook, *n.* vooruitzicht *n.n.*

outlying, *a.* afgelegen.

outmost, *a.* buitenste, uiterste.

outnumber, *v.t.* in getal *n.n.* overtreffen *str.*

out-of-date, *a.* verouderd; ouderwets. out-of-the-way, *a.* afgelegen; ongewoon. out-of-work, *a.* arbeidloos.

out-patient, *n.* buitenpatient *n.*

outpost, *n.* voorpost *n.*

output, *n.* productie *n.*

outrage, *n.* gewelddaad *n.*, vergrijp *n.n.* ¶ *v.t.* geweld *n.n.* aandoen *irr.*, beledigen.

outrageous, *a.*, ~*ly*, *adv.* buitensporig; schandelijk.

outrider, *n.* voorrijder *n.*

outrigger, *n.* uithouder *n.*

outright, *adv.* zonder voorbehoud *n.n.* helemaal.

outrun, *v.t.* voorbijlopen *str.*; voorbijstreven.

outsail, *v.t.* voorbijzeilen.

outset, *n.* aanvang *n.*, begin *n.n.*

outshine, *v.t.* in glans *n.* overtreffen *str.*, in de schaduw stellen.

outside, *n.* buitenkant *n. at the* ~, op z'n hoogste *n.n.*; *from the* ~, van buiten. ¶ *adv.* buiten; naar buiten. ¶ *prep.* buiten. ¶ *a.* van buiten; buiten . . .; maximum. outsider, *n.* buitenstaander *n.*

outskirts, *pl.n.* zoom *n.*, grens *n.*; buitenwijken *pl.n.*

outspoken, *a.* onbewimpeld; ronduit.

outstanding, *a.* in 't oog springend; onafgedaan, onbetaald.

outstep, *v.t.* overschrijden *str.*

outstrip, *v.t.* voorbijstreven.

outvote, *v.t.* overstemmen.

outward, *a.* uitwendig, uiterlijk. ¶ *adv.* naar buiten. outwardly, *adv.* uitwendig, uiterlijk; naar buiten. outwards, *adv.* buitenwaarts.

outweigh, *v.t.* zwaarder wegen *str.* dan; overtreffen *str.*

outwit, *v.t.* verschalken.

ouzel, *n. See* ousel *n.*

oval, *a.* ovaal, eirond.

ovarian, *a.* van de eierstok; van het vruchtbeginsel. ovary, *n.* eierstok *n.*; vruchtbeginsel *n.n.*

ovation, *n.* ovatie *n.*, hulde *n.*

oven, *n.* oven *n.*

over, *prep.* over, boven; aan de overkant van; over, betreffende, bij. ¶ *adv.* over, voorbij; omver. ~ *again*, nogmaals, opnieuw; ~ *and again*, keer *n.* op keer *n.*; *all* ~, van top tot teen; *it's all* ~, het is uit; *twice* ~, tweemaal.

overact, *v.i.* overdrijven *str.*

overall, *n.*, overalls, *pl.n.* werkbroek *n.*

overanxious, *a.*, ~*ly*, *adv.* al te bezorgd.

overawe, *v.t.* imponeren; overdonderen.

overbalance, *v.i.* het evenwicht verliezen *irr.*

overbearing, *a.* aanmatigend, heerszuchtig.

overboard, *adv.* overboord.

overburden, *v.t.* overladen.

overcast, *v.t.* bewolken; verdonkeren. ¶ *a.* betrokken.

overcharge, *v.t.* te veel vragen *str.*, overvragen *str.*

overcloud, *v.t.* met wolken *pl.n.* bedekken.

overcoat, *n.* overjas *n.*

overcome, *v.t.* overwinnen *str.*, te boven komen *irr.* ¶ *a.* overmand. ~ *by*, aangegrepen door.

overdo, *v.t.* overdrijven *str.* overdone, *a.* (al) te gaar.

overdraft, *n.* tekort *n.n.*, bankschuld *n.* overdraw, *v.i.* zijn krediet *n.n.* overschrijden *str.*

overdrive, *v.t.* afjakkeren.

overdue, *a.* over z'n tijd *n.*; achterstallig.

overestimate, *v.t.* overschatten. ¶ *n.* overschatting *n.*

overexpose, v.t. te lang belichten.
overfatigue, v.t. oververmoeien.
overflow, v.i. overvloeien; overlopen str.
¶ v.t. overstromen. to ~ its banks, buiten
de oevers pl.n. treden str. ¶ n. overstroming n.; overlaat n.; overloop n.
overgrown, a. begroeid; verwilderd; uit z'n
kracht n. gegroeid. overgrowth, n. te
welige groei n.
overhaul, v.t. inhalen; grondig nazien irr.,
inspecteren.
overhead, a. bovengronds. ~ expenses,
exploitatiekosten pl.n. ¶ adv. boven (het
hoofd).
overhear, v.t. afluisteren, bij toeval n.n.
horen.
overheat, v.t. oververhitten.
overjoyed, a. verrukt, buiten zichzelf van
vreugde n.
overlap, v.t. elkaar gedeeltelijk dekken,
gedeeltelijk over elkaar heenliggen str.
overlay, v.t. bedekken.
overleap, v.t. springen str. over.
overload, v.t. overladen; overbelasten.
overlook, v.t. heenzien irr. over; over het
hoofd zien irr.
overlord, n. opperheer n.
overmuch, a. al te veel. ¶ adv. al te zeer.
overnight, adv. de avond tevoren; de
nacht.
overpay, v.t. te veel betalen.
overpower, v.t. overweldigen, overmeesteren.
overproof, a. boven de normale sterkte.
overrate, v.t. overschatten.
overreach, v.r. to ~ oneself, het doel voorbijstreven; boven z'n krachten pl.n. gaan
irr.
override, v.t. afjakkeren; ter zijde stellen,
zich niet storen aan.
overrule, v.t. verwerpen str., vernietigen.
to be ~d, overstemd wo—den str.
overrun, v.t. binnenvallen str.; zich verspreiden over. we are ~ with mice, het
wemelt bij ons van de muizen.
oversea, a. overzees. ¶ adv. over zee n.
overseer, n. opzichter n., opziener n.,
controleur n.
overshoot, v.t. voorbijschieten str. to ~ the
mark, het doel voorbijstreven.
oversight, n. onoplettendheid n., vergissing n.
oversleep, v.i. zich verslapen.
overstatement, n. overdrijving n.
overstep, v.t. overschrijden str. to ~ all
bounds, de perken te buiten gaan irr.
overstrained, a. overspannen.
oversubscribe, v.t. meer dan voltekenen.
overt, a., ~ly, adv. open, openlijk.
overtake, v.t. inhalen, achterhalen.
overtax, v.t. te zwaar belasten. to ~ one's
strength, te veel vergen van zijn krachten
pl.n.
overthrow, v.t. omverwerpen str.; ten val n.
brengen irr. ¶ n. omverwerping n.; val n.
overtime, n. overuren pl.n.n.

overtone, n. boventoon n.
overture, n. ouverture n.   to make ~s,
toenadering n. zoeken irr.
overturn, v.i. omslaan irr., omvallen str.
¶ v.t. omwerpen str., omverwerpen str.
overweening, a. aanmatigend.
overweight, n. over(ge)wicht n.n.
overwhelm, v.t. overstelpen.   to ~ by,
bedelven met or onder.
overwork, v.t. te veel laten str. werken. ¶ n.
overwerk n.n., te veel werk n.n.
oviparous, a. eierleggend.
owe, v.t. schuldig zijn; te danken hebben.
owing, a. te betalen, schuldig. ~ to, te
danken aan (favourable); te wijten aan
(unfavourable); toe te schrijven aan
(noncommittal).
owl, n. uil n. owlet, n. uiltje n.n. owlish, a.
uilachtig.
own, a. eigen. ¶ v.t. bezitten str.; toegeven
str. ¶ v.i. to ~ to, bekennen dat; to ~ up,
bekennen. owner, n. eigenaar n., bezitter
n.; reder n. ownership, n. bezitterschap
n.n., eigendomsrecht n.n.
ox, n. os n.
oxalic, a. oxaal . . . ~ acid, zuringzuur
n.n.
oxidate, v.t. oxyderen. oxide, n. oxyde n.n.;
zuurstofverbinding n. oxygen, n. zuurstof
n. oxygenate, v.t. met zuurstof verbinden
str.
oyez!, excl. hoort!
oyster, n. oester n.   oyster-catcher, n.
scholekster n.   oyster-farm, n. oester-
kwekerij n.
ozone, n. ozon n.n. ozonize, v.t. ozoniseren.

P

pace, n. stap n., pas n.; gang n.; tempo n.n.
to keep ~ with, gelijke tred n. houden irr.
met. ¶ v.i. stappen. ¶ v.t. op en neer
lopen str. pacemaker, n. gangmaker n.
pacer, n. telganger n.
pacific, a. vreedzaam.   P~ Ocean, Stille
Zuidzee N., Grote Oceaan N. pacification,
n. vredestichting n.; bevrediging n.;
pacificatie n. pacifier, n. vredestichter n.
pacify, v.t. bevredigen, stillen, kalmeren.
pack, n. pak n.n.; ransel n.n. (soldier's);
spel n.n. (cards); troep n. (wolves, etc.).
¶ v.t. inpakken; verpakken.   ~ed, dicht
opeen gepakt. package, n. pakket n.n.
packer, n. pakker n. packet, n. pakket n.n.
packet-boat, n. pakketboot n. pack-ice, n.
pakijs n.n. packing, n. pakking n.n. pack-
thread, n. pakgaren n.n.
pact, n. verbond n.n., verdrag n.n.
pad, n. kussen(tje) n.n.; eeltkussen n.n.;
onderligger n.; blocnote n. ¶ v.t. opvullen,
watteren. ¶ v.i. tippelen.
paddle, n. pagaai n.; blad n.n., schoep n.

¶ *v.i.* pagaaien; pootje *n.n.* baden. **paddle-box**, *n.* raderkast *n.* **paddle-steamer**, *n.* raderboot *n.* **paddle-wheel**, *n.* scheprad *n.n.*
paddock, *n.* stoeterijpark *n.n.*
padlock, *n.* hangslot *n.n.* ¶ *v.t.* met een hangslot vastmaken.
pagan, *n.* heiden *n.* ¶ *a.* heidens. **paganism**, *n.* heidendom *n.n.*
page, *n.* page *n.* (*boy*); bladzij(de) *n.* (*paper*). ¶ *v.t.* door een page *n.* laten *str.* roepen; pagineren.
pageant, *n.* praalvertoning *n.* **pageantry**, *n.* praalvertoon *n.n.*
pail, *n.* emmer *n.*
pain, *n.* pijn *n.*; smart *n.* *for his* ~*s*, voor z'n moeite *n.*; *on* ~ *of*, op straffe van. ¶ *v.t.* pijn *n.* doen *irr.*; leed *n.n.* doen *irr.* **painful**, *a.*, ~*ly*, *adv.* pijnlijk. **painless**, *a.*, ~*ly*, *adv.* pijnloos. **painstaking**, *a.* nauwgezet; ijverig.
paint, *n.* verf *n.* ¶ *v.t.* schilderen, verven; beschrijven *str.* **painter**, *n.* schilder *n.*; vanglijn *n.* (*rope*). **painting**, *n.* schilderkunst *n.*; schilderij *n.* or *n.n.*
pair, *n.* paar *n.n.* ~ *of* . . . *used for single object remains untranslated e.g.* ~ *of trousers*, broek *n.* ¶ *v.t.* paren. ¶ *v.i.* zich paren.
pal, *n.* kameraad *n.*, maat *n.*
palace, *n.* paleis *n.n.*
palanquin, *n.* palankijn *n.*
palatable, *a.* smakelijk.
palatal, *a.* verhemelte . . . **palate**, *n.* verhemelte *n.n.*
palatial, *a.* vorstelijk.
palatinate, *n.* paltsgraafschap *n.n.* **palatine**, *a.* paltsgrafelijk. *count* ~, paltsgraaf *n.*
palaver, *n.* onderhandeling *n.*; geklets *n.n.* ¶ *v.i.* onderhandelen; kletsen.
pale, *a.*, ~*ly*, *adv.* bleek; licht. ¶ *n.* paal *n.*; spijl *n.* **paleness**, *n.* bleekheid *n.*
palette, *n.* palet *n.n.*
palfrey, *n.* damespaard *n.n.*
paling, *n.* staketsel *n.n.*, omheining *n.*
palisade, *n.* palissade *n.*, paalwerk *n.n.*
pall, *n.* lijkkleed *n.n.*; mantel *n.* ¶ *v.i.* tegenstaan *irr.* **pall-bearer**, *n.* slippendrager *n.*
pallet, *n.* stromatras *n.*
palliate, *v.t.* lenigen, verzachten; bewimpelen, verbloemen. **palliation**, *n.* leniging *n.*; verbloeming *n.* **palliative**, *n.* lapmiddel *n.n.*
pallid, *a.*, ~*ly*, *adv.* (doods)bleek. **pallor**, *n.* bleekheid *n.*
palm, *n.* palm *n.* (*of hand*); palm *n.*, palmboom *n.*; palmtak *n.* ¶ *v.t.* betasten. *to* ~ *off*, aansmeren. **palmer**, *n.* pelgrim *n.*
palmiped, *a.* met zwemvliezen *pl.n.*
palmistry, *n.* handkijkerij *n.*, handwaarzeggerij *n.*
palmy *a.* gelukkig. ~ *days*, bloeitijd *n.*
palpable, *a.*, ~*bly*, *adv.* tastbaar, voelbaar.
palpate, *v.t.* betasten.

palpitate, *v.i.* popelen. **palpitation**, *n.* hartklopping *n.*
palsied, *a.* verlamd. **palsy**, *n.* verlamming *n.*
paltry, *a.* onbetekenend; verachtelijk.
pampas, *n.* pampa's *pl.n.*
pamper, *v.t.* vertroetelen; te veel toegeven *str.* aan.
pamphlet, *n.* pamflet *n.n.*, brochure *n.* **pamphleteer**, *n.* pamfletschrijver *n.*
pan, *n.* pan. ¶ *v.t.* (goud)wassen *irr.*
panacea, *n.* panacee *n.*
pancake, *n.* pannekoek *n.*
pancreas, *n.* alvleesklier *n.*
pandemonium, *n.* hels lawaai *n.n.*
pander, *v.i.* *to* ~ *to*, zich dienstbaar stellen aan.
pane, *n.* ruit *n.*
panegyric, *a.* lofrede *n.* **panegyrist**, *n.* lofredenaar *n.*
panel, *n.* paneel *n.n.*; lijst *n.*, naamrol *n.*; rooster *n.*
panelling, *n.* lambrisering *n.*
pang, *n.* steek *n.*; kwelling *n.*
panic, *n.* paniek *n.* **panic-grass**, *n.* vingergras *n.n.* **panicky**, *a.* paniekachtig.
panicle, *n.* pluim *n.*
pannier, *n.* draagmand *n.*
panoply, *n.* volle wapenrusting; wapentrofee *n.*
panorama, *n.* panorama *n.n.*
pansy, *n.* driekleurig viooltje *n.n.*
pant, *v.i.* hijgen. *to* ~ *for*, snakken naar. ¶ *n.* hijging *n.* ~*s*, onderbroek *n.*
pantaloon, *n.* hanswort *n.*
pantechnicon, *n.* verhuiswagen *n.*
panther, *n.* panther *n.*
pantomime, *n.* pantomime *n.*
pantry, *n.* provisiekamer *n.*
pap, *n.* pap *n.*
papa, *n.* papa *n.*
papacy, *n.* pausdom *n.n.*; pauselijke waardigheid *n.* **papal**, *a.* pauselijk.
paper, *n.* papier *n.n.*; krant *n.*; verhandeling *n.*; examenopgave *n.* ¶ *a.* papieren. ¶ *v.t.* behangen *str.* **paper-clip**, *n.* knijpertje *n.n.* **paperhanger**, *n.* behanger *n.* **papermill**, *n.* papiermolen *n.* **paperweight**, *n.* presse-papier *n.*
Papist, *a.* pausgezind, Roomsgezind.
pappy, *a.* papperig.
par, *n.* gelijkheid. *to be on a* ~, gelijk staan *irr.*
parable, *n.* parabel *n.*
parabola, *n.* parabool *n.*, kegelsnede *n.* **parabolic**, *a.* parabolisch.
parachute, *n.* parachute *n.*, valscherm *n.n.* **parachutist**, *n.* parachutist *n.*
parade, *n.* parade *n.*; défilé *n.n.*, optocht *n.*; appel *n.n.*; paradeplein *n.n.*; promenade *n.* ¶ *v.i.* paraderen; trekken *str.*; aantreden *str.* ¶ *v.t.* parade *n.* laten *str.* maken; pronken met.
paradigm, *n.* paradigma *n.n.*, voorbeeld *n.n.*
Paradise, *N.* Paradijs *n.N.*

paradox, *n.* paradox *n.*
paraffin, *n.* petroleum *n.* ∼*-oil*, petroleum *n.*; ∼*-wax*, paraffine *n.*; *liquid* ∼, paraffine-olie *n.*
paragon, *n.* toonbeeld *n.n.*
paragraph, *n.* alinea *n.*; paragraaf *n.*
parallel, *n.* evenwijdig. ∼ *to*, evenwijdig met. ¶ *n.* parallel *n.*; breedtecirkel *n.* ¶ *v.t.* evenaren. **parallelogram,** *n.* parallelogram *n.n.*
paralyse, *v.t.* verlammen; met lamheid *n.* slaan *irr.* **paralysis,** *n.* verlamming *n.* **paralytic,** *a.* lam. ∼ *stroke*, beroerte *n.* ¶ *n.* lamme *n.*, verlamde *n.*
paramount, *a.* hoogst, opperst.
paramour, *n.* minnaar *n.* (*male*), minnares *n.* (*female*).
parapet, *n.* borstwering *n.*
paraphernalia, *pl.n.* toebehoorselen *pl.n.n.*
paraphrase, *n.* paraphrase *n.* ¶ *v.t.* para-phraseren.
parasite, *n.* parasiet *n.* **parasitic,** *a.* para-siterend, woeker . . .
parasol, *n.* parasol *n.*
parboil, *v.t.* ten dele koken.
parcel, *n.* pakje *n.n.*; deel *n.*; partij *n.*, kaveling *n.* ¶ *v.t.* *to* ∼ *out*, in percelen *pl.n.n.* verdelen. **parcel post,** *n.* pakketpost *n.*
parch, *v.t.* verdrogen; verschroeien. *to be* ∼*ed with thirst*, van dorst *n.* versmachten.
parchment, *n.* perkament *n.n.* ¶ *a.* perkamen-ten.
pardon, *n.* vergiffenis *n.*; pardon *n.n.* *beg* ∼, wat blieft U?; *I beg your* ∼, Neem me niet kwalijk! ¶ *v.t.* vergeven *str.*, ver-giffenis *n.* schenken *str.* **pardonable,** *a.*, ∼**bly,** *adv.* vergeeflijk.
pare, *v.t.* schillen (*fruit*); knippen (*nails*). **parer,** *n.* schilmes *n.n.*
parent, *n.* vader *n.*, moeder *n.* ∼*s*, ouders *pl.n.* **parentage,** *n.* afkomst *n.*, oorsprong *n.* **parental,** *a.* ouderlijk. **parenthood,** *n.* ouderschap *n.n.*
parenthesis, *n.* tussenzin *n.* *within* ∼, tussen haakjes *pl.n.n.* **parenthetical,** *a.* terloops.
paring, *n.* schil *n.*
Paris, *N.* Parijs *n.N.* **Parisian,** *a.* Parijs. ¶ *N.* Parijzenaar *N.*
parish, *n.* parochie *n.*; gemeente *n.* **parishioner,** *n.* parochiaan *n.*
parity, *n.* gelijkheid *n.*, pariteit *n.*
park, *n.* park *n.n.* ¶ *v.t.* parkeren. **parking-place,** *n.* parkeerterrein *n.*
parlance, *n.* taal *n.*, spraak *n.*
parley, *n.* onderhandeling *n.* ¶ *v.t.* onder-handelen.
parliament, *n.* parlement *n.n.* **parliamentary,** *a.* parlementair, parlements . . .
parlour, *n.* voorkamer *n.*; spreekkamer *n.*; salon *n.*
parochial, *a.* parochiaal; kleinsteeds; be-krompen.

parody, *n.* parodie *n.*
parole, *n.* erewoord *n.n.*, parool *n.n.* *on* ∼, op z'n erewoord *n.n.*
paroxysm, *n.* vlaag *n.*, heftige aanval *n.*
parquet, *n.* parket *n.n.*
parricide, *n.* vadermoord *n.* (*act*); vader-moordenaar *n.* (*person*).
parrot, *n.* papegaai *n.* ¶ *v.t.* nabauwen.
parry, *v.t.* afweren.
parse, *v.t.* taalkundig ontleden.
parsimonious, *a.*, ∼**ly,** *adv.* karig, spaarzaam. **parsimony,** *n.* karigheid *n.*, spaarzaamheid *n.*
parsley, *n.* pieterselie *n.*, peterselie *n.*
parsnip, *n.* pastinaak *n.*
parson, *n.* dominee *n.*, predikant *n.* **parson-age,** *n.* pastorie *n.*, predikantshuis *n.n.*
part, *n.* deel *n.n.*, gedeelte *n.n.*; aandeel *n.n.*; rol *n.* *private* ∼*s*, schaamdelen *pl.n.n.*; *in those* ∼*s*, in die streek *n.*; *to take* ∼, deelnemen *str.*; *to take in good* ∼, goed opnemen *str.*; *for my* ∼, wat mij betreft. ¶ *v.i.* scheiden *irr.*; uiteengaan *irr.*; breken *str.* ¶ *v.t.* scheiden *irr.*
partake, *v.i.* deelnemen *str.* *to* ∼ *of* or *in*, deelnemen aan *or* in. **partaker,** *n.* deel-nemer *n.*, deelgenoot *n.*
partial, *a.*, ∼**ly,** *adv.* gedeeltelijk; partijdig, eenzijdig. **partiality,** *n.* partijdigheid *n.*, eenzijdigheid *n.*; voorliefde *n.*
participant, *n.* deelnemer *n.* **participate,** *v.i.* *to* ∼ *in*, deelnemen *str.* in *or* aan. **participa-tion,** *n.* deelneming *n.* **participator,** *n.* deelnemer *n.*
participle, *n.* deelwoord *n.n.*
particle, *n.* deeltje *n.n.*
particoloured, *a.* bont.
particular, *a.*, ∼**ly,** *adv.* bizonder; speciaal; merkwaardig; kieskeurig, veeleisend. **par-ticularity,** *n.* bizonderheid *n.*; eigenaardig-heid *n.* **particularize,** *v.t.* in bizonderheden *pl.n.* treden *str.*
parting, *n.* scheiding *n.* *in* ∼, tot afscheid *n.n.*
partisan, *n.* aanhanger *n.*, partijganger *n.*; guerillastrijder *n.* ∼ *warfare*, guerilla-oorlog *n.*
partition, *n.* deling *n.*, verdeling *n.*; schot *n.n.*, tussenschot *n.n.* ¶ *v.t.* verdelen. *to* ∼ *off* afschieten *str.*
partitive, *a.* delend, partitief.
partly, *adv.* gedeeltelijk, deels.
partner, *n.* compagnon *n.*, vennoot *n.*; partner *n.* **partnership,** *n.* compagnonschap *n.n.*, vennootschap *n.*
partridge, *n.* patrijs *n.*
part-song, *n.* meerstemmige zang *n.*
party, *n.* partij *n.*; gezelschap *n.n.*; partijtje *n.n.*; deelnemer *n.* **party-truce,** *n.* godsvrede *n.* **party-wall,** *n.* tussenmuur *n.*
Paschal, *a.* Paas . . .
pasha, *n.* pacha *n.*
pasquinade, *n.* paskwil *n.*
pass, *v.i.* passeren, voorbijgaan *irr.*; slagen

(*exam.*); passen (*cards*). *to* ~ *for*, doorgaan
irr. voor. ¶ *v.t.* passeren, voorbijgaan *irr.*
overtrekken *str.*, overgaan *irr.*; overtreffen
str.; aannemen *str.*, goedkeuren. *to* ~
comments, aanmerkingen *pl.n.* maken. ¶ *n.*
pas *n.*, bergpas *n.*; gat *n.n.* (*channel*);
pas *n.*, verlofpas *n.*; staat *n.* van zaken
pl.n. **passable**, *a.*, ~**bly**, *adv.* tamelijk,
draagbaar. **passage**, *n.* doortocht *n.*;
overtocht *n.*; gang *n.*; passage *n.* **pass-book**,
n. kassiersboekje *n.n.* **pass degree**, *n.*
universiteitsgraad *n.* **passenger**, *n.*
passagier *n.*; reiziger *n.* ~ *train*, personen-
trein *n.* **passer-by**, *n.* voorbijganger *n.*
passing, *a.* voorbijgaand. ¶ *adv.* tamelijk.
¶ *n.* voorbijgaan *n.n.*; overlijden *n.n.*
in ~, in 't voorbijgaan; terloops.
passion, *n.* hartstocht *n.*, drift *n.*; lijden *n.n.*,
passie *n.* *to fly into a* ~, woedend worden
str. **passionate**, *a.*, ~**ly**, *adv.* hartstochtelijk.
passion-flower, *n.* passiebloem *n.* **passion
week**, *n.* lijdensweek *n.*
passive, *a.*, ~**ly**, *adv.* passief, lijdelijk.
passivity, *n.* lijdelijkheid *n.*
pass-key, *n.* loper *n.*
Passover, *N.* Joods Paasfeest *n.N.* ~ *bread*,
jodenpaasbrood *n.n.*
passport, *n.* paspoort *n.n.*
password, *n.* parool *n.n.*, wachtwoord *n.n.*
past, *a.* verleden, vorig; vroeger; geleden.
~*master in*, volleerd in. ¶ *prep.* voorbij,
over. *it is* ~ *crying for*, er helpt niets
meer aan; ~ *hope*, hopeloos. ¶ *adv.*
voorbij. ¶ *n.* verleden *n.n.*; verleden tijd *n.*
paste, *n.* deeg *n.n.*; pasta *n.*; valse steen *n.*
¶ *v.t.* plakken, opplakken. **pasteboard**, *n.*
bordpapier *n.n.*
pastel, *n.* pastel *n.n.*
pastepot, *n.* lijmpot *n.*
pastern, *n.* koot *n.*
pastille, *n.* pastille *n.*
pastor, *n.* herder *n.*; zieleherder *n.* **pastoral**,
a. herderlijk; landelijk, pastoraal. ¶ *n.*
herderlijk schrijven *n.n.*; herdersstuk
n.n.
pastry, *n.* gebak *n.n.*; pastei *n.* **pastry-board**,
n. rolplank *n.* **pastrycook**, *n.* banketbakker
n.
pasturable, *a.* geschikt voor weiland *n.n.*
pasture, *n.* weiland *n.n.*, grasland *n.n.*
¶ *v.i.* weiden, grazen. ¶ *v.t.* weiden, doen
irr. grazen.
pasty, *n.* pastei *n.* ¶ *a.* papperig, bleek.
pat, *n.* tikje *n.n.*; klompje *n.n.* ¶ *v.t.* tikken,
kloppen. *to* ~ *oneself on the back*, met
zichzelf tevreden zijn. ¶ *adv.* vlot.
patch, *n.* lap *n.*; lapje *n.n.* grond *n.* ¶ *v.t.*
oplappen. *to* ~ *up*, opknappen; *to* ~ *it up*,
het bijleggen *irr.* **patchy**, *a.* ongelijk.
pate, *n.* kop *n.*
paten, *n.* schaal *n.*
patent, *n.* octrooi *n.n.*, patent *n.n.* *letters* ~,
brevet *n.n.* ¶ *a.* duidelijk, zichtbaar.
¶ *v.t.* patenteren, octrooi nemen *str.* op.

patentee, *n.* patenthouder *n.* **patent-
leather**, *n.* patentleer *n.n.*
paternal, *a.*, ~**ly**, *adv.* vaderlijk. **paternity**,
n. vaderschap *n.n.*
path, *n.* pad *n.n.*
pathetic, *a.*, ~**ally**, *adv.* pathetisch, aandoenlijk, meelijwekkend.
pathless, *a.* ongebaand.
pathologic, *a.* pathologisch. **pathologist**, *n.*
patholoog *n.* **pathology**, *n.* pathologie *n.*,
ziekteleer *n.*
pathos, *n.* pathos *n.*
pathway, *n.* voetpad *n.n.*
patience, *n.* geduld *n.n.*; patience *n.* (*cards*).
patient, *a.*, ~**ly**, *adv.* geduldig. ¶ *n.*
patient *n.*; lijder *n.*
patina, *n.* patina *n.n.*
patriarch, *n.* patriarch *n.*, aartsvader *n.*
patriarchal, *a.* patriarchaal, aartsvaderlijk.
patrician, *n.* patriciër *n.* ¶ *a.* patricisch.
patrimony, *n.* vaderlijk erfdeel *n.n.*
patriot, *n.* patriot *n.*, vaderlander *n.* **patriotic**,
a. vaderlandslievend. **patriotism**, *n.*
vaderlandsliefde *n.*
patrol, *n.* patrouille *n.* ¶ *v.t. & v.i.* patrouille-
ren.
patron, *n.* patroon *n.*; beschermheer *n.*;
begunstiger *n.*; geregelde klant *n.* ~ *saint*,
schutspatroon *n.* **patronage**, *n.* bescherming *n.*; klandisie *n.*; patronaat *n.n.*
patroness, *n.* beschermvrouw *n.* **patronize**,
v.t. beschermen; begunstigen.
patten, *n.* trip *n.*
patter, *v.t.* kletteren; trippelen. ¶ *n.* gekletter
n.n.; getrippel *n.n.*; (erbij behorende)
woorden *pl.n.n.*
pattern, *n.* patroon *n.n.*; voorbeeld *n.n.*
patty, *n.* pasteitje *n.*
paucity, *n.* geringheid *n.*, schaarste *n.*
paunch, *n.* buik *n.*, pens *n.*, balg *n.*
pauper, *n.* armlastige *n.* **pauperism**, *n.*
pauperisme *n.n.*
pause, *n.* rust *n.*; pauze *n.*; onderbreking *n.*
¶ *v.i.* pauseren; even ophouden *irr.*
pave, *v.t.* bestraten, plaveien. **pavement**, *n.*
trottoir *n.n.* **paving-stone**, *n.* straatsteen *n.*
pavilion, *n.* paviljoen *n.n.*
paw, *n.* poot *n.* ¶ *v.t.* stampen. *to* ~
something, ergens aanzitten *str.*
pawn, *n.* pand *n.n.*, onderpand *n.n.*; pion *n.*
(*chess*); damschijf *n.* (*draughts*). ¶ *v.t.*
verpanden. **pawnbroker**, *n.* lommerd-
houder *n.* **pawnshop**, *n.* lommerd *n.*,
pandjeshuis *n.n.* **pawnticket**, *n.* lommerd-
briefje *n.n.*
pay, *v.t.* betalen; geven *str.*, brengen *irr.*;
teren. *to* ~ *attention to*, aandacht *n.*
schenken *str.* aan; *to* ~ *a visit*, een bezoek
n.n. afleggen *irr.*; *to* ~ *out*, vieren (*rope*).
¶ *v.i.* betalen; de moeite waard zijn. ¶ *n.*
loon *n.n.*; soldij *n.*; betaling *n.* **payable**, *a.*
betaalbaar. **payee**, *n.* nemer *n.* **payer**, *n.*
betaler *n.* **paymaster**, *n.* betaalmeester *n.*
payment, *n.* betaling *n.* **pay-office**, *n.*

betaalkantoor *n.n.* **pay-sheet,** *n.* betaalsrol *n.*

pea, *n.* erwt *n.* ~ *pod,* erwtenpeul *n.;* *sweet* ~, pronkerwt *n.*

peace, *n.* vrede *n.* **peaceable,** *a.,* ~**bly,** *adv.* vreedzaam; vredelievend. **peaceful,** *a.,* ~**ly,** *adv.* vreedzaam; vredig. **peace-offering,** *n.* zoenoffer *n.n.*

peach, *n.* perzik *n.* ¶ *v.i.* klikken. ¶ *v.t.* verklappen.

peacock, *n.* pauw *n.* ~ *butterfly,* pauwoog *n.* **peahen,** *n.* pauwin *n.*

pea-jacket, *n.* pijjekker *n.*

peak, *n.* piek *n.;* spits *n.,* top *n.;* toppunt *n.n.* **peaked,** *a.* puntig; smalletjes.

peal, *v.t.* luiden. ¶ *v.i.* luiden, schallen. ¶ *n.* gelui *n.n.* (*bells*); slag *n.* (*thunder*). ~ *of laughter,* schaterend gelach *n.n.*

peanut, *n.* aardnoot *n.,* grondnoot *n.;* apenoot *n.*

pear, *n.* peer *n.*

pearl, *n.* parel *n.* ¶ *v.t.* beparelen; parelen. ¶ *v.i.* (zich) parelen. **pearl-barley,** *n.* parelgort *n.* **pearled,** *a.* bepareld. **pearly,** *a.* parelachtig; parelgrijs.

pear-tree, *n.* pereboom *n.*

peasant, *n.* boer *n.* **peasantry,** *n.* boerenstand *n.,* boerenbevolking *n.*

peascod, *n.* erwtepeul *n.* **pease,** *pl.n.* erwten *pl.n.* **pea-shooter,** *n.* proppeschieter *n.*

peat, *n.* turf *n.* **peat-bog,** *n.* veen *n.n.,* laagveen *n.n.* **peat-cutter,** *n.* turfsteker *n.* **peaty,** *a.* turfachtig; veenrijk.

pebble, *n.* kiezelsteen *n.* **pebbly,** *a.* vol kiezelstenen.

peccadillo, *n.* zondetje *n.n.*

peck, *n.* ± 9,09 Liter; (*fig.*) hoop *n.;* pik *n.* ¶ *v.t.* pikken.

pecker, *n. to keep one's* ~ *up,* er de moed in houden *irr.*

peckish, *a.* hongerig. *to be* ~, trek *n.* hebben.

pectorial, *a.* borst . . .

peculate, *v.i.* verduistering *n.* plegen. ¶ *v.t.* verduisteren. **peculation,** *n.* verduistering *n.* **peculator,** *n.* verduisteraar *n.*

peculiar, *a.,* ~**ly,** *adv.* eigenaardig; vreemd. **peculiarity,** *n.* eigenaardigheid *n.*

pecuniary, *a.* geldelijk.

pedagogue, *n.* paedagoog *n.*

pedal, *n.* pedaal *n.n.* ¶ *v.i.* peddelen.

pedant, *n.* pedant *n.,* schoolvos *n.* **pedantic,** *a.* pedant. **pedantry,** *n.* pedanterie *n.*

peddle, *v.t.* venten.

pedestal, *n.* voetstuk *n.n.*

pedestrian, *a.* voet . . .; laag bij de grond. ¶ *n.* voetganger *n.*

pedicle, *n.* steeltje *n.n.*

pedicure, *n.* pedicuur *n.*

pedigree, *n.* stamboom *n.* ~ *cattle,* stamboekvee *n.n.*

pediment, *n.* kroonlijst *n.*

pedlar, *n.* venter *n.*

peek, *v.i.* kijken *str.,* gluren. ¶ *n.* kijkje *n.n.*

peel, *n.* schil *n.* *candied* ~, sucade *n.* ¶ *v.t.* schillen.

peep, *v.i.* piepen; een steelse blik *n.* werpen *str.* op. ¶ *n.* kijkje *n.n.* **peep-hole,** *n.* kijkgat *n.n.* **peepshow,** *n.* rarekiek *n.,* kijkkast *n.*

peer, *v.i.* turen, gluren. ¶ *n.* evenknie *n.;* gelijke *n.;* rijksgrote *n.* **peerage,** *n.* (hogere) adelstand *n.* **peeress,** *n.* vrouw van een *peer.* **peerless,** *a.,* ~**ly,** *adv.* weergaloos.

peevish, *a.,* ~**ly,** *adv.* kribbig, korzelig. **peevishness,** *n.* korzeligheid *n.*

peg, *n.* pen *n.,* pin *n.;* schroef *n.* (*of violin*). ¶ *v.i.* vastpinnen. ¶ *v.i.* ploeteren. *to* ~ *out,* eruit knijpen *str.* **peg-top,** *n.* priktol *n.*

pelican, *n.* pelikaan *n.*

pellet, *n.* balletje *n.n.;* pilletje *n.n.;* hagelkorrel *n.*

pellicle, *n.* vliesje *n.n.*

pell-mell, *a.* door elkaar.

pellucid, *a.* helder, doorschijnend.

pelt, *n.* huid *n.* ¶ *v.t.* bombarderen met; gooien. ¶ *v.i.* neerkletteren. ~*ing rain,* slagregen *n.;* kletsregen *n.*

pelvis, *n.* bekken *n.n.*

pen, *n.* pen *n.* (*writing*); schaapskooi *n.,* hok *n.n.* (*enclosure*). ¶ *v.t.* pennen (*write*); opsluiten *str.*

penal, *a.* straf . . . ~ *code,* wetboek *n.n.* van strafrecht *n.n.;* ~ *colony,* strafkolonie *n.;* ~ *law,* strafwet *n.;* ~ *servitude,* dwangarbeid *n.;* ~ *settlement,* strafkolonie *n.* **penalize,** *v.t.* straffen; handicappen. **penalty,** *n.* straf *n.,* boete *n. on* ~ *of,* op straffe van.

penance, *n.* boete *n.,* boetedoening *n.*

pence, *pl.n. See* penny.

pencil, *n.* potlood *n.n.* ¶ *v.t.* tekenen.

pendant, *n.* hanger *n.* **pendent,** *a.* hangend.

pending, *a.* hangende, lopende, onbeslist. ¶ *adv.* in afwachting *n.* van.

pendulum, *n.* slinger *n.*

penetrable, *a.* doordringbaar. **penetrate,** *v.t.* doordringen *str.;* doorgronden. *to* ~ *with,* doordringen *str.* van. ¶ *v.i.* binnendringen *str.* **penetration,** *n.* doordringen *n.n.;* binnendringen *n.n.;* scherpzinnigheid *n.*

penguin, *n.* pinguin *n.,* vetgans *n.*

peninsula, *n.* schiereiland *n.n.*

penitence, *n.* boete *n.,* boetedoening *n.;* berouw *n.n.* **penitent,** *a.,* ~**ly,** *adv.* boetvaardig. ¶ *n.* boeteling *n.* **penitentiary** *n.* boete . . .; verbeteringsgesticht *n.n.*

penman, *n.* schoonschrijver *n.* **penmanship,** *n.* schrijfkunst *n.*

pennant, *n.,* **pennon,** *n.* wimpel *n.,* bannier *n.*

penniless, *a.* zonder een cent *n.* **penny,** *n.* stuiver *n. to a* ~, tot op de laatste cent. **penny-dreadful,** *n.* (goedkope) sensatieroman *n.* **penny-in-the-slot machine,** *n.* muntautomaat *n.* **pennyroyal,** *n.* polei *n.* **penny-whistle,** *n.* fluitje *n.n.* **pennyworth,** *n. a* ~ *of* . . ., voor een stuiver . . .

pension, *n.* pensioen *n.n.* (*payment*); pension

n.n. (boarding-house). ¶ *v.t.* pensionneren.
pensionable, *a.* pensioengerechtigd. **pensionary.** *n.* pensionaris *n. Grand P~,* Raadpensionaris *N.* **pensioner,** *n.* gepensionneerde *n.*
pensive, *a.,* **~ly,** *adv.* peinzend, nadenkend.
pent, *a. ~ up,* opgesloten.
pentagon, *n.* vijfhoek *n.*
Pentecost, *N.* Pinkster *N.*
penthouse, *n.* afdak *n.n.*
penumbra, *n.* bijschaduw *n.*
penurious, *a.,* **~ly,** *adv.* behoeftig, armoedig. **penury,** *n.* diepe armoede *n.*
peony, *n.* pioen *n.,* pioenroos *n.*
people, *n.* volk *n.n.;* mensen *pl.n.;* men. ¶ *v.t.* bevolken.
pepper, *n.* peper *n.* **peppermint,** *n.* pepermunt *n.* **peppery.** *a.* peperachtig, peperig.
per, *prep.* per; door. *~ cent,* percent, ten honderd.
peradventure, *adv.* toevallig; misschien.
perambulate, *v.i.* doorwandelen. **perambulator,** *n.* kinderwagen *n.*
perceivable, *a.,* **~bly,** *adv.* merkbaar, waarneembaar. **perceive,** *v.t.* waarnemen *str.,* ontwaren.
percentage, *n.* percentage *n.n.*
perceptibility, *n.* waarneembaarheid *n.* **perceptible,** *a.,* **~bly,** *adv.* waarneembaar. **perception,** *n.* waarneming *n.,* gewaarwording *n.* **perceptive,** *a.* waarnemings . . .
perch, *n.* baars *n. (fish);* rek *n.n.,* stok *n.,* roest *n. (stick);* roede *n.* = 5½ yard. ¶ *v.i. to ~ on,* neerstrijken *str.* op; zitten *str.* op.
perchance, *adv.* bij geval, misschien.
percolate, *v.i.* doorsiepelen. ¶ *v.t.* filtreren. **percolator,** *n.* filter *n.,* filtreerkan *n.*
percuss, *v.t.* bekloppen; percuteren. **percussion,** *n.* slag *n.;* percutatie *n. instrument of ~,* slaginstrument *n.n.; ~ cap,* slaghoedje *n.n.*
perdition, *n.* ondergang *n.,* verderf *n.n.*
peregrin (falcon), *n.* edelvalk *n.*
peregrination, *n.* zwerftocht *n.*
peremptoriness, *n.* beslistheid *n.* **peremptory,** *a.,* **~ily,** *adv.* beslissend; gebiedend, geen tegenspraak *n.* duldend.
perennial, *a.* voortdurend; veeljarig. ¶ *n.* overblijvende plant *n.*
perfect, *a.,* **~ly,** *adv.* volmaakt, volkomen, perfect. ¶ *n.* voltooid tegenwoordige tijd *n.* ¶ *v.t.* (ver)volmaken. **perfection,** *n.* volmaaktheid *n. to ~,* in de perfectie.
perfidious, *a.,* **~ly,** *adv.* trouweloos, verraderlijk. **perfidy,** *n.* trouweloosheid *n.,* verraderlijkheid *n.*
perforate, *v.t.* perforeren. **perforation,** *n.* perforatie *n.*
perforce, *adv.* noodzakelijkerwijs; gewelddadig.
perform, *v.t.* vervullen, volbrengen *irr.;* ten uitvoer brengen *irr.;* verrichten; vertonen; spelen. ¶ *v.i.* optreden *str. ~ing dogs,*

gedresseerde honden *pl.n.* **performance,** *n.* vervulling *n.,* nakoming *n.,* tenuitvoerbrenging *n.;* prestatie *n.;* vertoning *n.,* uitvoering *n.* **performer,** *n.* uitvoerder *n.;* speler *n.,* acteur *n.,* zanger *n.*
perfume, *n.* geur *n.;* parfum *n.n.* ¶ *r.t.* doorgeuren; parfumeren. *~d,* geurig, welriekend. **perfumer,** *n.* parfumeur *n.* **perfumery,** *n.* reukwerk *n.n.*
perfunctoriness, *n.* vluchtigheid *n.,* oppervlakkigheid *n.* **perfunctory,** *a.,* **~ily,** *adv.* nonchalant, oppervlakkig, vluchtig, slordig.
pergola, *n.* berceau *n.n.*
perhaps, *adv.* misschien.
pericarditis, *n.* hartzakontsteking *n.* **pericardium,** *n.* hartzak *n.*
pericarp, *n.* zaadvlies *n.n.*
peril, *n.* gevaar *n.n.;* risico *n.n.* **perilous,** *a.,* **~ly,** *adv.* gevaarlijk, hachelijk.
period, *n.* periode *n.,* tijdperk *n.n.;* volzin *n. monthly ~s,* maandstonden *pl.n.* **periodical,** *a.,* **~ly,** *adv.* periodiek; geregeld terugkerend. ¶ *n.* tijdschrift *n.n.* **periodicity,** *n.* periodiek terugkeren *n.n.*
periphrasis, *n.* periphrase *n.,* omschrijving *n.* **periphrastic,** *a.* omschrijvend.
periscope, *n.* periscoop *n.*
perish, *v.i.* omkomen *irr.;* vergaan *irr.* **perishable,** *a.* aan bederf *n.n.* onderhevig.
peristyle, *n.* zuilengalerij *n.*
peritoneum, *n.* buikvlies *n.n.* **peritonitis,** *n.* buikvliesontsteking *n.*
periwig, *n.* pruik *n.*
periwinkle, *n.* alikruik *n.,* kreukel *n.*
perjure, *v.r. to ~ oneself,* een meineed *n.* doen *irr.,* vals zweren *str.* **perjured,** *a.* meinedig. **perjurer,** *n.* meinedige *n.* **perjury,** *n.* meineed *n.;* woordbreuk *n.*
perk, *v.i. to ~ up,* weer opkikkeren. **perky,** *a.* astrant, brutaal.
permanence, *n.* duurzaamheid *n.,* bestendigheid *n.* **permanent,** *a.,* **~ly,** *adv.* duurzaam, bestendig.
permeability, *n.* doordringbaarheid *n.* **permeable,** *a.* doordringbaar. **permeate,** *v.t.* doordringen *str.*
permissible, *a.* toelaatbaar, te veroorloven. **permission,** *n.* toestemming *n.,* permissie *n.* **permit,** *v.t.* veroorloven, toestaan *irr.;* permitteren. ¶ *n.* vergunning *n.,* verlof *n.n.;* pas *n.*
permutation, *n.* permutatie *n.*
pernicious, *a.,* **~ly,** *adv.* verderfelijk.
peroration, *n.* peroratie *n.,* redevoering *n.;* slot *n.n.* van de redevoering *n.*
perpendicular, *a.,* **~ly,** *adv.* loodrecht. ¶ *n.* loodlijn *n.;* schietlood *n.n.*
perpetrate, *v.t.* plegen, begaan *irr.* **perpetration,** *n.* plegen *n.n.,* begaan *n.n.* **perpetrator,** *n.* dader *n.,* schuldige *n.*
perpetual, *a.,* **~ly,** *adv.* eeuwigdurend; levenslang. *~ screw,* schroef *n.* zonder eind *n.n.* **perpetuate,** *v.t.* bestendigen,

vereeuwigen. **perpetuation**, *n.* bestendiging *n.*, vereeuwiging *n.* **perpetuity**, *n.* eeuwigheid *n.*

perplex, *v.t.* onthutsen; verwarren. **perplexity**, *n.* verlegenheid *n.*; verwarring *n.*

perquisite, *n.* bijverdienste *n.*

persecute, *v.t.* vervolgen. **persecution**, *n.* vervolging *n.* ~ *mania*, vervolgingswaanzin *n.* **persecutor**, *n.* vervolger *n.*

perseverance, *n.* volharding *n.*, doorzettingsvermogen *n.n.* **persevere**, *v.i.* volharden, doorzetten. **persevering**, *a.*, ~**ly**, *adv.* volhardend.

Persia, *N.* Perzië *n.N.* **Persian**, *a.* Perzisch. ¶ *N.* Perziër *N.* (*man*), Perzische *N.* (*woman*).

persimmon, *n.* dadelpruim *n.*

persist, *v.i.* volhouden *irr.*, aanhouden *irr.* **persistence**, *n.* hardnekkigheid *n.*; hardnekkig volhouden *irr.* **persistent**, *a.*, ~**ly**, *adv.* hardnekkig; gedurig, aanhoudend.

person, *n.* persoon *n.* in ~, in eigen persoon. **personage**, *n.* gewichtig persoon *n.* **personal**, *a.*, ~**ly**, *adv.* persoonlijk. **personality**, *n.* persoonlijkheid *n.* **personalty**, *n.* persoonlijk bezit *n.n.* **personate**, *v.t.* voorstellen, de rol spelen van. **personation**, *n.* voorstellen *n.n.*, spelen *n.n.* **personification**, *n.* verpersoonlijking *n.* **personify**, *v.t.* verpersoonlijken. **personnel**, *n.* personeel *n.n.*

perspective, *n.* perspectief *n.n.* (*view*); perspectief *n.* (*science*). ¶ *a.*, ~**ly**, *adv.* perspectivisch.

perspicacious, *a.*, ~**ly**, *adv.* scherpzinnig. **perspicacity**, *n.* scherpzinnigheid *n.* **perspicuity**, *n.* helderheid *n.*, klaarheid *n.* **perspicuous**, *a.* helder, duidelijk.

perspiration, *n.* transpiratie *n.*, zweet *n.n.* **perspire**, *v.i.* transpireren, zweten.

persuade, *v.t.* overtuigen; overhalen. **persuasion**, *n.* overreding *n.*, overredingskracht *n.*; gezindte *n.*, richting *n.* **persuasive**, *a.*, ~**ly**, *adv.* overtuigend.

pert, *a.*, ~**ly**, *adv.* monter; bij de hand; vrijpostig.

pertain, *v.i.* *to* ~ *to*, behoren bij *or* tot.

pertinacious, *a.*, ~**ly**, *adv.* halsstarrig, hardnekkig, koppig. **pertinacity**, *n.* halsstarrigheid *n.*

pertinence, *n.* toepasselijkheid *n.* **pertinent**, *a.*, ~**ly**, *adv.* toepasselijk. *to be* ~ *to*, van toepassing *n.* zijn op.

pertness, *n.* monterheid *n.*; vrijpostigheid *n.*

perturb, *v.t.* verontrusten; verstoren. **perturbation**, *n.* verontrusting *n.*; verstoring *n.*

peruke, *n.* pruik *n.*

perusal, *n.* nauwkeurige lezing *n.* **peruse**, *v.t.* lezen *str.*, doorlezen *str.*

pervade, *v.t.* doordringen *str.*, doortrekken *str.* **pervasive**, *a.* doordringend.

perverse, *a.*, ~**ly**, *adv.* verdorven, pervers; dwars, onhandelbaar. **perversion**, *n.* verdraaiing *n.*; verdorvenheid *n.*; perversie

n. **perversity**, *n.* perversiteit *n.*; dwarsheid *n.* **pervert**, *v.t.* verderven *str.* ¶ *n.* afvallige *n.*; verdorven iemand *n.*

pervious, *a.* doordringbaar; toegankelijk. ~ *to*, vatbaar voor.

pessimism, *n.* pessimisme *n.n.* **pessimist**, *n.* pessimist *n.* **pessimistic**, *a.* pessimistisch.

pest, *n.* plaag *n.*; pest *n.*; kwelgeest *n.*; hinderlijk onkruid *n.n. or* ongedierte *n.n.* **pester**, *v.t.* lastig vallen *str.* **pestiferous**, *a.* verpestend; ondragelijk, lastig.

pestilence, *n.* pestilentie *n.*, pest *n.* **pestilent**, *a.* pestilent. **pestilential**, *a.* pestachtig; verderfelijk.

pestle, *n.* stamper *n.*

pet, *a.* lievelings ... ~ *name*, troetelnaam *n.* ¶ *n.* huisdier *n.n.*; lieveling *n.* ¶ *v.t.* vertroetelen; liefkozen, aanhalen.

petal, *n.* bloemblad *n.n.*

petard, *n.* voetzoeker *n.* *hoist with one's own* ~, wie een put graaft voor een ander valt er zelf in.

petition, *n.* petitie *n.*, verzoekschrift *n.n.*; rekest *n.n.* ¶ *v.t.* een verzoekschrift indienen aan. **petitioner**, *n.* verzoeker *n.*

petrel, *n.* stormvogeltje *n.n.*

petrifaction, *n.* verstening *n.* **petrify**, *v.t.* verstenen.

petrol, *n.* benzine *n.* **petroleum**, *n.* petroleum *n.*

petticoat, *n.* onderrok *n.* ~ *government*, vrouwenregering *n.*

pettifogger, *n.* chicaneur *n.*

pettiness, *n.* kleinheid *n.*, kleinzieligheid *n.*

pettish, *a.*, ~**ly**, *adv.* humeurig, nukkig.

petty, *a.* klein; onbetekenend; kleinzielig. ~ *cash*, som *n.* voor lopende onkosten *pl.n.*; ~ *officer*, onderofficier *n.*, sergeant *n.*, korporaal *n.*

petulance, *n.* prikkelbaarheid *n.* **petulant**, *a.*, ~**ly**, *adv.* prikkelbaar; opvliegend.

pew, *n.* kerkbank *n.* ~ *opener*, stovenzetter *n.* (*male*), stovenzetster *n.* (*female*).

pewter, *n.* tin *n.n.* ¶ *a.* tinnen. **pewterer**, *n.* tinnegieter *n.*

phantasm, *n.* hersenschim *n.*, drogbeeld *n.n.* **phantasmagoria**, *n.* fantasmagorie *n.*

phantom, *n.* spooksel *n.n.*, spook *n.n.*, geest *n.*; droombeeld *n.n.* ~ *ship*, spookschip *n.n.*

pharaoh, *N.* Pharaoh *N.*

pharisaical, *a.*, ~**ly**, *adv.* farizees, schijnheilig. **Pharisee**, *N.* Farizeër *N.*, schijnheilige *n.*

pharmaceutical, *a.* pharmaceutisch. **pharmaceutics**, *pl.n.* pharmaceutica *n.* **pharmacy**, *n.* pharmacie *n.*; apotheek *n.*

pharynx, *n.* keelholte *n.*

phase, *n.* faze *n.*, stadium *n.n.*

pheasant, *n.* fazant *n.* ~ *cock*, fazantehaan *n.*

phenomenal, *a.*, ~**ly**, *adv.* phenomenaal; buitengewoon, merkwaardig. **phenomenon**, *n.* verschijnsel *n.n.*

phial, *n.* flool *n.*, flesje *n.n.*
philander, *v.i.* flirten; vrouwen *pl.n.* achterna lopen *str.*
philanthropic, *a.* philanthropisch, menslievend, weldadig.   **philanthropist,** *n.* philanthroop *n.*   **philanthropy,** *n.* philanthropie *n.*, mensenliefde *n.*, menslievendheid *n.*
philatelist, *n.* postzegelverzamelaar *n.*, philatelist *n.*
Philistine, *N.* Filistijn *N.*
philological, *a.* philologisch.   **philologist,** *n.* philoloog *n.*   **philology,** *n.* philologie *n.*
philosopher, *n.* philosoof *n.*, wijsgeer *n.* ~'s *stone,* steen *n.* der wijzen *pl.n.*   **philosophical,** *a.*, ~ly, *adv.* philosophisch, wijsgerig.   **philosophize,** *v.i.* bespiegelen.   **philosophy,** *n.* philosophie *n.*, wijsbegeerte *n.*
philter, *n.* minnedrank *n.*
phlebotomy, *n.* aderlating *n.*
phlegm, *n.* flegma *n.n.*; slijm *n.n.*   **phlegmatical,** *a.*, ~ly, *adv.* flegmatisch; flegmatiek.
phlox, *n.* phlox *n.*
phœnix, *n.* feniks *n.*
phone, *n.* *See* telephone.
phonetician, *n.* phoneticus *n.*   **phonetics,** *pl.n.* phonetica *n.*
phosphate, *n.* phosphaat *n.n.*
phosphor, *n.* phosphorus *n.*   **phosphoresce,** *v.i.* phosphoriseren, lichten.   **phosphorescence,** *n.* phosphorescentie *n.*, lichten *n.n.*   **phosphorus,** *n.* phosphorus *n.*
photo, *n.* foto *n.*   **photograph,** *n.* fotografie *n.*   ¶ *v.t.* fotograferen.   **photographer,** *n.* fotograaf *n.*   **photographic,** *a.*, ~ally, *adv.* fotographisch.   **photography,** *n.* fotographie *n.*   **photogravure,** *n.* fotogravure *n.*   **photolithograph,** *n.* fotolithografie *n.*
phrase, *n.* zinsnede *n.*; uitdrukking *n.*; phrase *n.*   ¶ *v.t.* uitdrukken.   **phraseology,** *n.* phraseologie *n.*; spreektrant *n.*, schrijftrant *n.*
phrenology, *n.* phrenologie *n.*, schedelleer *n.*
phthisis, *n.* longtering *n.*
phylloxera, *n.* druifluis *n.*
physic, *n.* geneesmiddel *n.n.*   ¶ *v.t.* medicijn *n.n.* ingeven *str.*   **physical,** *a.*, ~ly, *adv.* natuurkundig; stoffelijk; lichamelijk; lichaams . . .   **physician,** *n.* geneesheer *n.*, arts *n.*   **physicist,** *n.* natuurkundige *n.*   **physics,** *pl.n.* natuurkunde *n.*
physiognomy, *n.* physionomie *n.*; gelaat *n.n.*, voorkomen *n.n.*
physiological, *a.*, ~ly, *adv.* physiologisch.   **physiologist,** *n.* physioloog *n.*   **physiology,** *n.* physiologie *n.*
pianist, *n.* pianist *n.* *(male),* pianiste *n.* *(female).*   **piano,** *n.* piano *n.* *grand* ~, (concert)vleugel *n.*
picaresque, *a.* ~ *novel,* schelmenroman *n.*
pick, *v.t.* pikken; prikken; (af)kluiven *str.*; uitpeuteren; plukken.   *to* ~ *pockets,* zakken *pl.n.* rollen; *to* ~ *a quarrel,* ruzie *n.*
zoeken *irr.*; *to* ~ *one's way,* voorzichtig lopen *str.*   ¶ *n.* punthouweel *n.n.*; keus *n.*
pick-a-back, *adv.* op de rug *n.* *or* schouders *pl.n.* pickaxe, *n.* houweel *n.n.* **picked,** *a.* uitgelezen. **picker,** *n.* plukker *n.*
picket, *n.* staak *n.*; piket *n.n.*   ¶ *v.t.* afzetten; posten.
pickle, *n.* pekel *n.*, zuur *n.n.*   ~*s,* . . . in het zuur.   ¶ *v.t.* pekelen, inmaken.
picklock, *n.* loper *n.*   **pickpocket,** *n.* zakkenroller *n.*
picnic, *n.* picnic *n.*, picknick *n.*   ¶ *v.t.* picnicken.
pictorial, *a.*, ~ly, *adv.* geïllustreerd; uitbeeldend.   **picture,** *n.* schilderij *n.* *or n.n.*; afbeelding *n.*; toonbeeld *n.n.*   *the* ~*s* de bioscoop *n.*; ~ *postcard,* prentbriefkaart, *n.*   ¶ *v.t.* voorstellen.   **picture-gallery,** *n.* museum *n.n.* van schilderijen *pl.n.* *or n.n.*   **picture-palace,** *n.* bioscoop *n.*   **picturesque,** *a.*, ~ly, *adv.* schilderachtig.
piddle, *v.i.* piemelen; prutsen.   **piddling,** *a.* onbeduidend.
Pidgin-English, *N.* Pidgin-Engels *n.N.*
pie, *n.* pastei *n.*, taart *n.*   *to eat humble* ~, een toontje *n.n.* lager zingen *str.*   **piebald,** *a.* bont.
piece, *n.* stuk *n.n.*   ~ *of bread and butter,* boterham *n.*; . . . *a* ~, . . . per stuk; *in* (or *to*) ~*s,* aan stukken; *of one* ~, uit één stuk; ~ *by* ~, stuk voor stuk.   ¶ *v.t. to* ~ *together,* samenlappen.   **piece-goods,** *pl.n.* stukgoederen *pl.n.*   **piecemeal,** *adv.* bij stukken *pl.n.n.* en brokken *pl.n.*
pied, *a.* bont.
pier, *n.* pier *n.*, hoofd *n.n.*; pijler *n.*, beer *n.*
pierce, *v.t.* doorboren, doordringen *str.*
pier-glass, *n.* damspiegel *n.*, penantspiegel *n.*
piety, *n.* vroomheid *n.*
piffle, *n.* kletspraat *n.*   **piffling,** *a.* onbenullig, onbeduidend.
pig, *n.* varken *n.n.*; gieteling *n.*; partje *n.n.*   *to buy a* ~ *in a poke,* een kat in de zak kopen *irr.*
pigeon, *n.* duif *n.*   **pigeon-breasted,** *a.* met een kippeborst *n.*   **pigeon-fancier,** *n.* duivenhouder *n.*   **pigeonhole,** *n.* loket *n.n.*, vakje *n.n.*   ¶ *v.t.* in z'n geest *n.* classificeren; op de lange baan schuiven *str.*
pig-headed, *a.* koppig, eigenwijs.   **pig-iron,** *n.* ruw ijzer *n.n.*
pigment, *n.* pigment *n.n.*
pigmy, *n.* dwerg *n.*
pignut, *n.* aardaker *n.*
pigsticker, *n.* pierensteker *n.*   **pigsty,** *n.* varkenshok *n.n.*   **pigtail,** *n.* staartpruik *n.*; staart *n.*   **pigwash,** *n.* spoeling *n.*
pike, *n.* piek *n.* *(weapon);* tolboom *n.* *(barrier);* snoek *n.* *(fish).*
pikestaff, *n.* *as plain as a* ~, zo klaar als een klontje *n.n.*
pilaster, *n.* pilaster *n.*
pilchard, *n.* grote schardijn *n.*
pile, *n.* stapel *n.*, hoop *n.* *(heap);* bouwwerk

n.n. (*building*); element *n.n.*, batterij *n.* (*electric*); heipaal *n.* (*post*); rotte *n.* (*rifles*); munt *n.* (*of coin*); nop *n.*, pluis *n.n.* (*hair or textile*); aambei *n.* (*hæmorrhoids*). *funeral* ∼, brandstapel *n.*; *to make one's* ∼, fortuin *n.n.* maken. ¶ *v.t.* *to* ∼ *up*, opstapelen; *to* ∼ *it on*, overdrijven *str.*
piledriver, *n.* heimachine *n.*; heiblok *n.*
pilewort, *n.* speenkruid *n.n.*
pilfer, *v.t. & v.i.* stelen *str.*, gappen. **pilferer,** *n.* dief *n.*, gapper *n.*
pilgrim, *n.* pelgrim *n.* **pilgrimage,** *n.* pelgrimstocht *n.*, bedevaart *n.*
pill, *n.* pil *n.*
pillage, *n.* plundering *n.* ¶ *v.t.* plunderen. **pillager,** *n.* plunderaar *n.*
pillar, *n.* zuil *n.*, pilaar *n.*; (*fig.*) steunpilaar *n.* *from* ∼ *to post*, van 't kastje naar de muur.
pillarbox, *n.* brievenbus *n.*
pillion, *n.* duo-zadel *n.*
pillory, *n.* schandpaal *n.* ¶ *v.t.* aan de kaak stellen.
pillow, *n.* hoofdkussen *n.n.*, oorkussen *n.n.* ¶ *v.t.* met kussens *pl.n.n.* ondersteunen. **pillowcase,** *n.* kussensloop *n.*
pilot, *n.* loods *n.* (*of ship*): piloot *n.* (*of aircraft*). ¶ *v.t.* loodsen; besturen. **pilotage,** *n.* loodswezen *n.n.*; loodsgeld *n.n.* **pilot-balloon,** *n.* proefballon *n.* **pilot-fish,** *n.* loodsmannetje *n.n.*
pimento, *n.* piment *n.n.*
pimp, *n.* koppelaar *n.*
pimpernel, *n.* pimpernel *n.*
pimple, *n.* puistje *n.n.* **pimpled,** *a.* puisterig.
pin, *n.* speld *n.*; pin *n.*, pen *n.*, stift *n.* ¶ *v.t.* spelden, prikken. *to* ∼ *one's faith on*, alle vertrouwen *n.n.* stellen in.
pinafore, *n.* boezelaar *n.*
pincers, *pl.n.* nijptang *n.*; schaar *n.* (*of lobster*).
pinch, *v.t.* nijpen *str.*, knijpen *str.* ¶ *v.i.* zich bekrimpen *str.* ¶ *n.* kneep *n.* *at a* ∼, als 't er op aan komt; in geval *n.n.* van nood *n.*
pinchbeck, *n.* pinsbek *n.n.*, namaak *n.*
pincushion, *n.* speldenkussen *n.n.*
pine, *n.* den *n.*, pijnboom *n.* ¶ *v.i.* kwijnen. *to* ∼ *for*, smachten naar; *to* ∼ *away*, verkwijnen. **pineapple,** *n.* ananas *n.* **pine-cone,** *n.* pijnappel *n.*
pinfold, *n.* schuthok *n.n.*
ping-pong, *n.* pingpong *n.n.*, tafeltennis *n.*
pinion, *n.* wiek *n.*, vlerk *n.*; slagpen *n.*; (klein) tandrad *n.n.* ¶ *v.t.* kortwieken; boeien.
pink, *a.* rose, rozerood. ¶ *n.* anjelier *n.* *in the* ∼, opperbest.
pinnacle, *n.* toppunt *n.n.*
pinpoint, *n.* speldepunt *n.* ¶ *v.t.* nauwkeurig de plaats bepalen van. **pinprick,** *n.* speldeprik *n.*
pint, *n.* pint *n.*; 0,568 Liter *N.*
pioneer, *n.* pionier *n.*; baanbreker *n.*
pious, *a.*, ∼ly, *adv.* vroom, godvruchtig.

pip, *n.* pip *n.* (*disease*); pit *n.* (*of fruit*); oog *n.n.* (*on dice*); ster *n.* (*on uniform*).
pipe, *n.* pijp *n.*; buis *n.*, pijp *n.*; fluitje *n.n.* ¶ *v.i.* pijpen, fluiten *str.* *to* ∼ *up*, z'n stem *n.* verheffen *str.*; meespreken *str.* **pipeclay,** *n.* pijpaarde *n.* **pipe-cleaner,** *n.* pijpekeuter *n.* **pipe-line,** *n.* pijpleiding *n.* **piper,** *n.* pijper *n.*; doedelzakblazer *n.* **piping,** *n.* galon *n.*, bies *n.*; buizen *pl.n.* ¶ *a.* ∼ *hot*, kokend heet.
pipkin, *n.* pannetje *n.n.*
pippin, *n.* pippeling *n.*
piquancy, *n.* pikante *n.n.* **piquant,** *a.*, ∼ly, *adv.* pikant.
pique, *n.* gepikeerdheid *n.*, spijtigheid *n.* **piqued,** *a.* gepikeerd.
piquet, *n.* piket *n.n.*
piracy, *n.* zeeroverij *n.*; nadruk *n.* **pirate,** *n.* zeerover *n.*; roofschip *n.n.*; letterdief *n.* **piratical,** *a.* zeerovers . . .
piscatorial, *a.* vis . . ., vissers . . .
pish, *int.* ba!
piss, *n.* pis *n.* ¶ *v.i.* pissen.
pistil, *n.* stamper *n.*
pistol, *n.* pistool *n.n.* **pistolcase,** *n.* pistoolholster *n.*
pistole, *n.* pistool *n.*
piston, *n.* zuiger *n.* **piston-rod,** *n.* zuigerstang *n.*
pit, *n.* put *n.*; kuiltje *n.n.*; holte *n.*; kolenmijn *n.*; parterre *n.n.* *bottomless* ∼, afgrond *n.* ¶ *v.t.* kuilen. *to* ∼ *against one another*, tegen elkaar stellen; ∼*ted with the smallpox*, van de pokken *pl.n.* geschonden.
pit-a-pat, *adv.* tiktak, rikketik.
pitch, *n.* pik *n.*, pek *n.* (*tar*); graad *n.*, trap *n.*; hoogte *n.*; toonhoogte *n.*; standplaats *n.* ¶ *v.t.* pekken; opstellen, opslaan *irr.*, gooien. *to* ∼ *a tale*, een verhaal *n.n.* doen *irr.* ¶ *v.i.* stampen. *to* ∼ *into*, te lijf gaan *irr.*; zich werpen *str.* op; terechtkomen *irr.* in. **pitch-dark,** *a.* pikdonker.
pitcher, *n.* kruik *n.*, kan *n.*
pitchfork, *n.* hooivork *n.*, riek *n.* ¶ *v.t.* gooien.
pitchpine, *n.* grenenhout *n.*
pitchy, *a.* pikachtig; pikzwart.
piteous, *a.*, ∼ly, *adv.* jammerlijk, erbarmelijk, deerniswekkend.
pitfall, *n.* val *n.*, (verborgen) gevaar *n.n.*
pith, *n.* pit *n.*, kern *n.* **pith-helmet,** *n.* helmhoed *n.* **pithy,** *a.*, ∼ily, *adv.* pittig, kernachtig.
pitiable, *a.*, ∼bly, *adv.* beklagenswaardig, erbarmelijk. **pitiless,** *a.*, ∼ly, *adv.* meedogenloos, onbarmhartig.
pittance, *n.* schrale portie *n.*; klein beetje *n.n.*
pituitary, *a.* slijm . . .
pity, *n.* medelijden *n.n.* *it's a* ∼, het is jammer; *what a* ∼, hoe jammer; *to take* ∼ *on*, medelijden *n.n.* hebben met. ¶ *v.t.* medelijden *n.n.* hebben met.
pivot, *n.* spil *n.n.* ¶ *v.i.* om een spil draaien.
pixy, *n.* elf *n.*, fee *n.*, kabouter *n.*

placard, n. plakkaat n.n. ¶ v.t. beplakken.
placate, v.t. verzoenen; bevredigen.
place, n. plaats n. at your ~, bij jou (thuis).
¶ v.t. plaatsen; beleggen. I cannot ~ him,
ik kan hem niet thuisbrengen irr. **placer,**
n. goudwasserij n.
placid, a., ~ly, adv. onbewogen; kalm.
placidity, n. onbewogenheid n.
plagiarism, n. plagiaat n.n. **plagiarist,** n.
plagiaris n., plagiator n. **plagiarize,** v.t. &
v.i. plagiëren.
plague, n. plaag n.; pest n. ¶ v.t. plagen,
kwellen. **plague-sore,** n. pestbuil n.
plague-spot, n. pestvlek n.; pesthaard n.
plaice, n. schol n.
plaid, n. Schotse sjaal n.; reisdeken n.
plain, n. vlakte n. ¶ a., ~ly, adv. eenvoudig;
effen; duidelijk; ongekleurd; alledaags.
plaindealing, a. oprecht, eerlijk. **plainness,**
n. eenvoud n.; duidelijkheid n. **plainsong,**
n. koraalgezang n.n. **plainspoken,** a.
openhartig, rondborstig.
plaint, n. weeklacht n. **plaintiff,** n. klager n.,
eiser n. **plaintive,** a., ~ly, adv. klagend,
klagelijk.
plait, n. vlecht n. ¶ v.t. vlechten str.
plan, n. plan n.n.; ontwerp n.n. ¶ v.t. een
plan maken; ontwerpen str.; bedenken irr.
plane, n. plataan n. (tree); schaaf n. (tool);
vlak n.n. (surface); plan n.n., niveau n.n.
(level); vliegtuig n.n. (aeroplane). ¶ a. vlak.
¶ v.t. schaven; zweven.
planet, n. planeet n. **planetary,** a. planeta-
risch. ~ system, zonnestelsel n.n.
planish, v.t. planeren, gladschaven; polijsten.
plank, n. plank n. ¶ v.t. beplanken, bevloeren.
plant, n. plant n.; installatie n.; komplot n.n.
¶ v.t. planten; plaatsen.
plantain, n. weegbree n.
plantation, n. plantage n.; plantsoen n.n.
planter, n. planter n.
plantigrade, n. zoolganger n.
plaque, n. plaat n.
plasm, n. plasma n.n.
plaster, n. pleister n. (on wound); pleister
n.n., pleisterwerk n.n. ~ of Paris, gips
n.n. ¶ v.t. een pleister n. leggen op;
bepleisteren; bedekken. **plasterer,** n.
stukadoor n.
plastic, a. plastisch; kneedbaar; beeldend.
¶ n. ~s, plastisch materiaal n.n. **plasticity**
n. plasticiteit n., kneedbaarheid n.
plate, n. bord n.n.; (metaal)plaat n.; zilverwerk n.n.; tafelzilver n.n. ¶ v.t. met
platen pl.n. bedekken; verzilveren. **plate-
glass,** n. spiegelglas n. ~ window,
spiegelruit n. **plate-layer,** n. wegwerker n.
platerack, n. bordenrek n.n. **plate-shears,**
n. blikschaar n.
platform, n. podium n.n. (in hall); perron n.n.
(railway); emplacement n.n. (of gun);
balkon n.n. (of vehicle); (politiek) programma n.n. turning ~, draaischijf n.
platinum, n. platina n.n.

platitude, n. gemeenplaats n., banaliteit n.
platitudinous, a. banaal.
platoon, n. peloton n.n.
platter, n. platte schotel n., houten schaal n.
plaudit, n. toejuiching n.
plausibility, n. aannemelijkheid n. **plausible,**
a., ~bly, adv. aannemelijk; innemend.
play, v.i. spelen. ¶ v.t. spelen (op), bespelen;
op en neer (or heen en weer) laten str.
gaan. to ~ off against each other, tegen
elkaar uitspelen. ¶ n. spel n.n.; toneelstuk
n.n.; speling n., speelruimte n. **playbill,** n.
affiche n. **player,** n. (toneel)speler n.
playfellow, n. speelmakker n. **playful,** a.,
~ly, adv. speels, dartel. **playfulness,** n.
speelsheid n. **playgoer,** n. schouwburg-
bezoeker n. **playground,** n. speelplaats n.
playhouse, n. theater n.n., schouwburg n.
plaything, n. (stuk) speelgoed n.n. **playwright,** n. toneelschrijver n.
plea, n. pleidooi n.n. on the ~ of, onder
voorwendsel n.n. dat. **plead,** v.i. pleiten.
¶ v.t. aanvoeren. to ~ guilty, schuld n.
bekennen. **pleader,** n. pleiter n.
pleasant, a., ~ly, adv. aangenaam, genoeglijk. **pleasantry,** n. aardigheid n., scherts n.
please, v.t. genoegen doen irr.; bevallen str.,
aanstaan irr. ~!, alstublieft!; alsjeblieft!.
to be ~d at, zich verheugen over. **pleasing,**
a., ~ly, adv. aangenaam, behaaglijk;
pleasurable, a., ~bly, adv. aangenaam,
genoeglijk. **pleasure,** n. genoegen n.n.;
genot n.n.; vermaak n.n.; plezier n.n.,
welgevallen n.n.
pleat, n. plooi n. ¶ v.t. plooien.
plebeian, a. plebejisch. ¶ n. plebejer n.
plebiscite, n. plebisciet n.n.
pledge, n. pand n.n., onderpand n.n.; gelofte
n. ¶ v.t. verpanden; geven str. ¶ v.r. zich
verbinden str.
plenary, a. volledig; voltallig.
plenipotentiary, a. gevolmachtigd. ¶ n.
gevolmachtigde n.
plenitude, n. volheid n., overvloed n.
plenteous, a., ~ly, adv. overvloedig.
plentiful, a., ~ly, adv. overvloedig, ruim.
plenty, n. overvloed n. in ~, overvloedig;
~ of, een hele boel n.; volop.
pleonasm, n. pleonasme n.n.
plethora, n. overvloed n. **plethoric,** a.
volbloedig.
pleurisy, n. pleuris n., borstvliesontsteking n.
pliable, a. buigzaam; meegaand. **pliancy,** n.
buigzaamheid n. **pliant,** a., ~ly, adv.
buigzaam; meegaand.
pliers, pl.n. buigtang n.; combinatietang n.
a pair of ~, een buigtang n.
plight, n. toestand n. ¶ v.t. geven str.,
beloven.
plimsoll line, n. lastlijn n.
plinth, n. plint n.
plod, v.i. moeizaam voortgaan irr. to ~ along,
voortsjouwen, doorploeteren. **plodder,** n.
ploeteraar n.; zwoeger n.

plot, *n.* stukje *n.n.* grond *n.*; komplot *n.n.*, intrige *n.* ¶ *v.t.* in tekening *n.* brengen *irr.* ¶ *v.i.* plannen *pl.n.n.* smeden, intrigeren. **plotter**, *n.* samenzweerder *n.*

plough, *n.* ploeg *n.*; ploegschaaf *n.* the P~, de Grote Beer. ¶ *v.t.* ploegen, omploegen; laten *str.* zakken. to ~ through, doorworstelen. **ploughman**, *n.* ploeger *n.*, boer *n.* **ploughshare**, *n.* ploegschaar *n.*

plover, *n.* pluvier *n.*

pluck, *v.t.* plukken; tokkelen. to ~ up courage, z'n moed *n.* bijeenrapen. **plucky**, *a.*, ~ily, *adv.* moedig, dapper.

plug, *n.* prop *n.*; stopcontact, *n.n.*; bougie *n.* ¶ *v.t.* dichtstoppen; erin hameren.

plum, *n.* pruim *n.*

plumage, *n.* gevederte *n.n.*

plumb, *n.* schietlood *n.n.* out of ~, niet in het lood. ¶ *a.* absoluut. ¶ *v.t.* peilen.

plumbago, *n.* potlood *n.n.*

plumduff, *n.* Jan-in-de-zak *n.*

plumber, *n.* loodgieter *n.* **plumbing**, *n.* loodgieterswerk *n.n.*

plume, *n.* pluim *n.*, veer *n.* ¶ *v.r.* to ~ oneself on, zich laten *str.* voorstaan op.

plummet, *n.* dieplood *n.n.*

plump, *a.* mollig, poezelig; gevuld; pardoes. ¶ *v.i.* ploffen. to ~ for, kiezen *str.*; to ~ up, opschudden. **plumpness**, *n.* molligheid *n.*, dikheid *n.*

plum-pudding, *n.* rozijnenpudding *n.* **plum-tree**, *n.* pruimeboom *n.*

plumy, *a.* gevederd.

plunder, *n.* buit *n.*, roof *n.* ¶ *v.t.* plunderen, leegroven. **plunderer**, *n.* plunderaar *n.*

plunge, *v.i* duiken *str.*; stampen (of ship); achteruitslaan *irr.* (of horse). ¶ *v.t.* onderdompelen. ¶ *n.* indompeling *n.*, bad *n.n.* to take the ~, de sprong wagen. **plunger**, *n.* dompelaar *n.*; zuiger *n.*

pluperfect, *n.* voltooid verleden tijd *n.*

plural, *a.* meervoudig, meervouds . . . ¶ *n.* meervoud *n.n.* **pluralist**, *n.* geestelijke *n.* in meer dan een gemeente *n.* **plurality**, *n.* meerderheid *n.*; merendeel *n.n.*

plus, *prep.* plus. ¶ *n.* plusteken *n.n.* **plus-fours**, *pl.n.* golfbroek *n.*

plush, *n.* pluche *n.n.*

ply, *n.* vouw *n.*; draad *n.* ¶ *v.t.* hanteren (tool); uitoefenen (trade); bestoken (enemy); voeren (with food or drink). to ~ with, bestormen met. ¶ *v.i.* (heen en weer) varen *str.*

plywood, *n.* triplex *n.n.*

pneumatic, *a.*, ~ally, *adv.* pneumatisch; lucht . . .

pneumonia, *n.* longontsteking *n.*

poach, *v.i.* stropen. to ~ on someone's preserves, onder iemands duiven *pl.n.* schieten *str.* ¶ *v.t.* pocheren. **poacher**, *n.* stroper *n.*

pock, *n.* pok *n.*

pocket, *n.* zak *n.* to be out of ~, erop toeleggen *irr.* **pocket-book**, *n.* portefeuille *n.*;

zakboekje *n.n.* **pocket-handkerchief**, *n.* zakdoek *n.*

pock-marked, *a.*, **pock-pitted**, *a.* pokdalig, van de pokken geschonden.

pod, *n.* peul *n.* ¶ *v.t.* doppen.

podgy, *a.* dik.

poem, *n.* gedicht *n.n.* **poet**, *n.* dichter *n.* **poetic(al)**, *a.*, ~ly, *adv.* dichterlijk. **poetry**, *n.* dichtkunst *n.*, poëzie *n.*; gedichten *pl.n.n.*

poignancy, *n.* aangrijpendheid *n.* **poignant**, *a.*, ~ly, *adv.* aangrijpend; bitter, smartelijk.

point, *n.* punt *n.* (of object); punt *n.n.* (abstract); decimaalteken *n.n.*; percent *n.n.*; aardigheid *n.*; streek *n.* (compass). a case in ~, een voorbeeld *n.n.*; to the ~, ter zake. ¶ *v.t.* een punt *n.* maken aan. to ~ out, aanduiden. ¶ *v.i.* wijzen *str.* to ~ at, wijzen op. **pointblank**, *a.* à bout portant; op de man af. **point-duty**, *n.* dienst *n.* als verkeersagent *n.* **pointed**, *a.*, ~ly, *adv.* puntig, scherp; ad rem. **pointer**, *n.* wijzer *n.*; aanwijzing *n.*, vingerwijzing *n.*; staande hond *n.* **pointless**, *a.*, ~ly, *adv.* zonder punt *n.* it is ~, het heeft geen zin *n.* **pointsman**, *n.* wisselwachter *n.*

poise, *n.* evenwicht *n.n.*; houding *n.* ¶ *v.t.* in evenwicht houden *irr.* ¶ *v.i.* in evenwicht zijn.

poison, *n.* vergift *n.n.*, gif(t) *n.n.* ¶ *v.t.* vergiftigen. **poisoner**, *n.* gif(t)menger *n.* **poisonous**, *a.*, ~ly, *adv.* giftig, vergiftig.

poke, *n.* buidel *n.* ¶ *v.t.* stoten *str.*, porren (prod); oppoken (fire).

poke-bonnet, *n.* tuithoed *n.*

poker, *n.* pook *n.*, poker *n.* (object); poker *n.n.* (cards).

poky, *a.* nauw.

Poland, *N.* Polen *n.N.*

polar, *a.* pool . . . ~ bear, ijsbeer *n.* **polarity**, *n.* polariteit *n.* **polarize**, *v.t.* polariseren.

pole, *n.* pool *n.* (extremity); paal *n.*, staak *n.* (stake). **Pole**, *N.* Pool *N.*

pole-axe, *n.* slachtbijl *n.*

polecat, *n.* bunzing *n.*

polemic, *a.* polemisch. ¶ *n.* ~s, polemiek *n.*

pole-star, *n.* poolster *n.*

police, *n.* politie *n.* ¶ *v.t.* toezicht *n.n.* houden *irr.* op. **police-court**, *n.* politierechtbank *n.* **policeman**, *n.* politieagent *n.* **police-station**, *n.* politiebureau *n.*

policy, *n.* beleid *n.n.*; politiek *n.*

polish, *v.t.* polijsten, politoeren; poetsen (metal), boenen (wood). ¶ *n.* politoer *n.n.*; glans *n.*

Polish, *a.* Pools.

polisher, *n.* polijster *n.*, politoerder *n.*

polite, *a.*, ~ly, *adv.* beleefd. **politeness**, *n.* beleefdheid *n.*

politic, *a.* politiek; diplomatiek. ¶ *n.* ~s, politiek *n.* **political**, *a.*, ~ly, *adv.* politiek, staatkundig. ~ economy, staatshuishoudkunde *n.*; ~ science, staatswetenschappen

pl.n. **politician,** *n.* politicus *n.*, staatsman *n.* **polity,** *n.* staatsregeling *n.*; staat *n.*
poll, *n.* bol *n.*, hoofd *n.n.*; verkiezing *n.*, stemming *n.* ¶ *v.t.* knotten (*trees*); stemmen *pl.n.* verwerven *str.*
pollard, *n.* knotwilg *n.* ¶ *v.t.* knotten.
pollen, *n.* stuifmeel *n.n.*
polling-booth, *n.* stembureau *n.* **polling-clerk,** *n.* stemopnemer *n.* **poll-tax,** *n.* hoofdelijke omslag *n.*
pollinate, *v.t.* bestuiven *str.*
pollute, *v.t.* bezoedelen; verontreinigen. **pollution,** *n.* bezoedeling *n.*; verontreiniging *n.*
poltroon, *n.* lafaard *n.*
polyandry, *n.* veelmannerij *n.*
polychrome, *a.* veelkleurig. **polychromy,** *n.* veelkleurigheid *n.*, polychromie *n.*
polygamy, *n.* polygamie *n.*, veelwijverij *n.*
polyglot, *a.* veeltalig. ¶ *n.* polyglotte *n.*
polygon, *n.* veelhoek *n.* **polygonous,** *a.* veelhoekig.
polyp, *n.* poliep *n.* **polypus,** *n.* poliep *n.*
polysyllabic, *a.* veellettergrepig. **polysyllable,** *n.* veellettergrepig woord *n.n.*
polytechnic, *a.* polytechnisch.
polytheism, *n.* veelgoderij *n.*, polytheïsme *n.n.*
Pom, *N.* spitshond *n.*
pomatum, *n.* pomade *n.*
pomegranate, *n.* granaatappel *n.*
Pomerania, *N.* Pommeren *n.N.* **Pomeranian,** *a.* Pommers.
pommel, *n.* (degen)knop *n.*; (zadel)knop *n.* ¶ *v.t.* beuken.
pomp, *n.* praal *n.*, luister *n.*
pompom, *n.* snelvuurkanon *n.n.*
pomposity, *n.* hoogdravendheid *n.* **pompous,** *a.*, ~**ly,** *adv.* hoogdravend; deftigdoend.
pond, *n.* poel *n.*, vijver *n.*
ponder, *v.i.* peinzen, nadenken *irr.* ¶ *v.t.* overwegen *str.* **ponderable,** *a.* weegbaar.
ponderous, *a.*, ~**ly,** *adv.* zwaar, zwaarwichtig.
poniard, *n.* dolk *n.*
pontiff, *n.* hogepriester *n.*; paus *n.* **pontifical,** *a.*, ~**ly,** *adv.* pauselijk; pontificaal. ¶ *n.* ~**s,** vol ornaat *n.n.*
pontoon, *n.* ponton *n.*
pony, *n.* hit *n.*; (*coll.*) £25.
poodle, *n.* poedel *n.*
pooh, *int.* bah! **pooh-pooh,** *v.t.* als onzin *n.* verwerpen *str.*
pool, *n.* poel *n.*, plas *n.* (*water*); pot *n.* (*in game*); potspel *n.n.* (*billiards*); combinatie *n.* (*business*). ¶ *v.t.* samenleggen *irr.*, samendoen *irr.*
poop, *n.* achtersteven *n.*
poor, *a.*, ~**ly,** *adv.* arm; armelijk. **poor-box,** *n.* armenbus *n.* **poor-house,** *n.* armenhuis *n.n.* **poor-law,** *n.* armenwet *n.* **poorness,** *n.* armzaligheid *n.* **poor-rate,** *n.* armenbelasting *n.* **poor-relief,** *n.* armenzorg *n.*
pop, *v.i.* ploffen, knallen. **to ~ out,** te

voorschijn komen *irr.* ¶ *v.t.* afschieten *str.* ¶ *n.* knal *n.*
pope, *n.* pope *n.* **Pope,** *N.* Paus *N.* **popedom,** *n.* pausdom *n.n.*; pausschap *n.n.* **popery,** *n.* papisme *n.*
popgun, *n.* kinderpistooltje *n.n.*
popinjay, *n.* (*fig.*) kwast *n.*
popish, *a.* pausgezind.
poplar, *n.* populier *n.*
poplin, *n.* popeline *n.*
poppy, *n.* papaver *n.*; klaproos *n.* **poppycock,** *n.* onzin *n.*, nonsens *n.* **poppyseed,** *n.* maanzaad *n.*
populace, *n.* gepeupel *n.n.*, grauw *n.n.* **popular,** *a.*, ~**ly,** *adv.* populair, volks . . . **popularity,** *n.* populariteit *n.* **popularize,** *v.t.* populariseren. **populate,** *v.t.* bevolken. **population,** *n.* bevolking *n.* **populous,** *a.* dicht bevolkt.
porcelain, *n.* porselein *n.n.* ¶ *a.* porseleinen.
porch, *n.* voorportaal *n.n.*, portiek *n.*
porcupine, *n.* stekelvarken *n.n.*
pore, *n.* porie *n.* ¶ *v.i.* turen, staren. **to ~ over,** bestuderen.
pork, *n.* varkensvlees *n.n.* **porker,** *n.* big *n.* (*young pig*); mestvarken *n.n.*
porous, *a.* poreus. **porousness,** *n.* poreusheid *n.*
porphyry, *n.* porfier *n.n.*
porpoise, *n.* bruinvis *n.*
porridge, *n.* pap *n.* **porringer,** *n.* papbord *n.n.*, soepkommetje *n.n.*
port, *n.* haven *n.* (*harbour*); havenstad *n.* (*harbour town*); bakboord *n.n.* (*left side*); port(wijn) *n.* ¶ *a.* bakboords . . .
portable, *a.* draagbaar.
portal, *n.* portaal *n.n.*
portcullis, *n.* valpoort *n.*
portend, *v.t.* voorspellen, beduiden. **portent,** *n.* voorteken *n.n.*; wonder *n.n.* **portentous,** *a.* onheilspellend; vervaarlijk.
porter, *n.* drager *n.*, sjouwer *n.* (*carrier*); portier *n.* (*at gate*); porterbier *n.n.* **porterage,** *n.* draagloon *n.n.*
portfolio, *n.* portefeuille *n.*
port-hole, *n.* patrijspoort *n.*
portico, *n.* portiek *n.*; overdekte zuilengang *n.*
portion, *n.* deel *n.n.*; aandeel *n.n.*; portie *n.* ¶ *v.t.* verdelen. **to ~ off,** toebedelen; **to ~ out,** verdelen.
portliness, *n.* deftigheid *n.*; welgedaanheid *n.* **portly,** *a.* deftig; welgedaan.
portmanteau, *n.* valies *n.n.*
portrait, *n.* portret *n.n.*
portray, *v.t.* afbeelden, schilderen.
Portugal, *N.* Portugal *n.N.* **Portuguese,** *a.* & *N.* Portugees *N.*; *n.n.* (*language*).
pose, *n.* pose *n.*, houding *n.*; aanstellerij *n.* ¶ *v.i.* poseren. ¶ *v.t.* stellen. **poser,** *n.* lastige vraag *n.* **position,** *n.* positie *n.*; houding *n.*; stand *n.*; ligging *n.*; toestand *n.*
positive, *a.*, ~**ly,** *adv.* stellig; positief. ¶ *n.* positief *n.n.* (*mechanical*); positief *n.* (*speech*).

posse, *n.* gewapende politiemacht *n.*
possess, *v.t.* bezitten *str.* *what ~es him?,* wat bezielt hem? **possession,** *n.* bezit *n.n.,* bezitting *n.,* eigendom *n.n.* *to be in ~ of,* in het bezit zijn van. **possessive,** *a.,* ~ly, *adv.* bezittend; bezittelijk. **possessor,** *n.* bezitter *n.,* eigenaar *n.*
possibility, *n.* mogelijkheid *n.* **possible,** *a.* mogelijk. **possibly,** *adv.* mogelijk, mogelijkerwijs.
post, *n.* paal *n.* (*wood*); post *n.,* wachtpost *n.* (*guard*); ambt *n.* (*job*); post *n.,* postdienst *n.* (*mail*). *by ~,* per post; *by return of ~,* per ommegaande; *last ~,* taptoe *n.* ¶ *v.t.* aanplakken (*notice*); overplaatsen, aanstellen (*to job*); posten (*letter*). ¶ *prefix* na.
postage, *n.* port *n.n.* *~ due,* strafport *n.n.;* *~ stamp,* postzegel *n.* **postal,** *a.* post . . . *~ order,* postwissel *n.* **postcard,** *n.* briefkaart *n.* **postdate,** *v.t.* later dagtekenen.
poster, *n.* aanplakbiljet *n.n.*
posterior, *n.* achterste *n.n.*
posterity, *n.* nageslacht *n.n.*
postern, *n.* poortje *n.n.*
post-free, *a.* franco per post *n.* **posthaste,** *adv.* met grote spoed *n.,* in aller ijl *n.*
posthumous, *a.,* ~ly, *adv.* posthuum.
postman, *n.* postbode *n.,* brievenbesteller *n.* **postmark,** *n.* postmerk *n.n.,* stempel *n.n.* **postmaster,** *n.* postdirecteur *n.* *~ general,* directeur-generaal *n.* der posterijen *pl.n.*
post-mortem, *n.* *~ examination,* lijkschouwing *n.*
post-office, *n.* postkantoor *n.n.* **postpaid,** *a.* franco.
postpone, *v.t.* uitstellen. **postponement,** *n.* uitstel *n.n.*
postscript, *n.* naschrift *n.n.*
postulant, *n.* candidaat *n.* **postulate,** *v.t.* postuleren; aannemen *str.* ¶ *n.* postulaat *n.n.,* grondstelling *n.*
posture, *n.* houding *n.* ¶ *v.i.* een houding aannemen *str.,* poseren.
post-war, *a.* na-oorlogs.
posy, *n.* ruiker *n.*
pot, *n.* pot *n.* ¶ *v.t.* potten. ¶ *v.i.* *to ~ at,* schieten *str.* op.
potable, *a.* drinkbaar.
potash, *n.* potas *n.,* kaliumcarbonaat *n.n.*
potation, *n.* dronk *n.*
potassium, *n.* kali *n.,* kalium *n.*
potato, *n.* aardappel *n.* *~ blight,* aardappelziekte *n.*
potency, *n.* kracht *n.,* vermogen *n.n.;* potentie *n.* **potent,** *a.,* ~ly, *adv.* krachtig, sterk; potent. **potentate,** *n.* potentaat *n.* **potential,** *a.,* ~ly, *adv.* potentieel. ¶ *n.* potentiaal *n.n.* **potentiality,** *n.* potentialiteit *n.*
pother, *n.* drukte *n.*
potherb, *n.* moeskruid *n.n.*
pothole, *n.* gat *n.n.*
pothook, *n.* hanepoot *n.*
pothouse, *n.* kroeg *n.*

potion, *n.* drank *n.*
pot-luck, *n.* *to take ~,* meeëten *str.* wat de pot schaft.
potsherd, *n.* potscherf *n.*
pot-shot, *n.* lukraak schot *n.n.*
potter, *n.* pottebakker *n.* ¶ *v.i.* prutselen, knoeien. **pottery,** *n.* aardewerk *n.n.*
pouch, *n.* zak *n.;* buidel *n.;* wangzak *n.*
poulterer, *n.* poelier *n.*
poultice, *n.* warme omslag *n.* ¶ *v.t.* pappen.
poultry, *n.* gevogelte *n.n.;* pluimvee *n.n.*
pounce, *v.i.* *to ~ upon,* neerschieten *str.* op.
pound, *n.* pond *n.n.* (*weight and money*); schuthok *n.n.* (*for cattle*). ¶ *v.t.* fijnstampen; slaan *irr.;* opsluiten *str.* (*of cattle*). **poundage,** *n.* pondgeld *n.n.* **pounder,** *n.* . . . ponder *n.* (*weight*); stamper *n.*
pour, *v.t.* schenken *str.;* gieten *str.* *to ~ out,* (in)schenken *str.* ¶ *v.i.* *to ~ with rain,* slagregenen.
pout, *v.i.* pruilen; de lippen *pl.n.* vooruitsteken *str.* ¶ *n.* gepruil *n.n.*
pouter, *n.* kropduif *n.*
poverty, *n.* armoe(de) *n.;* schaarste *n.*
powder, *n.* poeier *n.n.;* poeder *n.n.;* kruit *n.n.* (*gunpowder*). ¶ *v.t.* tot poeder maken; poeieren; besprenkelen, bestrooien. **powder-puff,** *n.* poeierdons *n.* **powdery,** *a.* poeierachtig; stoffig.
power, *n.* macht *n.;* gezag *n.n.;* volmacht *n.;* kracht *n.,* energie *n.* **powerful,** *a.,* ~ly, *adv.* machtig; krachtig. **power-house,** *n.* (electrische) centrale *n.* **powerless,** *a.* machteloos. **power-loom,** *n.* mechanisch weefgetouw *n.n.*
pow-wow, *n.* gewichtige bespreking *n.*
pox, *n.* syphilis *n.*
practicability, *n.* uitvoerbaarheid *n.,* doenbaarheid *n.* **practicable,** *a.,* ~bly, *adv.* uitvoerbaar, doenbaar.
practical, *a.,* ~ly, *adv.* practisch. *~ joke,* toer *n.*
practice, *n.* praktijk *n.;* gebruik *n.n.;* gewoonte *n.* *in ~,* in de praktijk. **practise,** *v.i.* (zich) oefenen. ¶ *v.t.* uitoefenen; beoefenen; handelen. **practitioner,** *n.,* **general practitioner,** *n.* praktizerend geneesheer *n.*
pragmatic, *a.,* ~ally, *adv.* pragmatisch, pragmatiek.
prairie, *n.* prairie *n.*
praise, *n.* lof *n.* ¶ *v.t.* prijzen *str.,* loven. **praiseworthy,** *a.* prijzenswaardig.
pram, *n.* kinderwagen *n.*
prance, *v.i.* trots stappen, trappelen. **prancer,** *n.* paradepaard *n.*
prank, *n.* streek *n.,* toer *n.*
prate, *v.i.* babbelen; kletsen.
prattle, *v.i.* babbelen. ¶ *n.* gebabbel *n.n.* **prattler,** *n.* babbelaar *n.*
prawn, *n.* steurkrab *n.*
pray, *v.t.* & *v.i.* bidden *str.,* smeken. **prayer,** *n.* gebed *n.n.* *the Lord's P~,* het Onze Vader; *to say one's ~s,* bidden *str.*

preach, *v.t. & v.i.* preken, prediken. **preacher**, *n.* prediker *n.*; predikant *n.*

preamble, *n.* inleiding *n.*; considerans *n.*

prebend, *n.* prebende *n.* **prebendary**, *n.* domheer *n.*

precarious, *a.*, ~**ly**, *adv.* hachelijk, onzeker, precair. **precariousness**, *n.* onzekerheid *n.*

precaution, *n.* voorzorg *n.* **precautionary**, *a.* voorzorgs . . .

precede, *v.i.* voorafgaan *irr.* ¶ *v.t.* voorafgaan *irr.* aan; de voorrang hebben boven. **precedence**, *n.* voorrang *n.* **precedent**, *n.* precedent *n.n.*

precentor, *n.* voorzanger *n.*, koorleider *n.*

precept, *n.* stelregel *n.*, voorschrift *n.n.* **preceptor**, *n.* leermeester *n.*

precinct, *n.* terrein *n.n.*

preciosity, *n.* precieusheid *n.* **precious**, *a.*, ~**ly**, *adv.* kostbaar; (*ironical*) mooi. ~ *metals*, edele metalen *pl.n.n.* **preciousness**, *n.* kostbaarheid *n.*

precipice, *n.* afgrond *n.*

precipitancy, *n.* overhaasting *n.*, overijling *n.* **precipitate**, *a.* overhaast, overijld; voorbarig. ¶ *v.t.* precipiteren, doen *irr.* neerslaan; bespoedigen. ¶ *n.* precipitaat *n.n.*, neerslag *n.* **precipitation**, *n.* overhaasting *n.*

precipitous, *a.*, ~**ly**, *adv.* steil (*steep*); overhaast (*hasty*).

precis, *n.* résumé *n.n.*, uittreksel *n.n.*

precise, *a.*, ~**ly**, *adv.* nauwkeurig; juist; precies. **precision**, *n.* nauwkeurigheid *n.*

preclude, *v.t.* uitsluiten *str.*, verhinderen.

precocious, *a.*, ~**ly**, *adv.* vroeg rijp; (*fig.*) vroeg wijs. **precocity**, *n.* vroegrijpheid *n.*

preconceive, *v.t.* vooraf opvatten. ~**d** *notion*, vooropgezette mening *n.*

precursor, *n.* voorloper *n.*

predatory, *a.* roofzuchtig.

predecessor, *n.* voorganger *n.*

predestinate, *v.t.* voorbeschikken, voorbestemmen. **predestination**, *n.* voorbeschikking *n.*, voorbestemming *n.* **predestine**, *v.t. See* predestinate.

predetermine, *v.t.* van te voren bepalen.

predicament, *n.* moeilijke toestand *n.*, critiek geval *n.n.*

predicate, *n.* predicaat *n.n.*, gezegde *n.n.*

predict, *v.t.* voorspellen. **prediction**, *n.* voorspelling *n.*

predilection, *n.* voorkeur *n.*, voorliefde *n.*

predispose, *v.t. to* ~ *to*, ontvankelijk maken voor. **predisposition**, *n.* vatbaarheid *n.*, ontvankelijkheid *n.*; neiging *n.*, aanleg *n.*

predominance, *n.* overhand *n.*; overheersing *n.*, heerschappij *n.* **predominant**, *a.*, ~**ly**, *adv.* overwegend; overheersend. **predominate**, *v.i.* de overhand hebben; overheersen.

pre-eminence, *n.* voorrang *n.* **pre-eminent**, *a.* voortreffelijk, uitmuntend. **pre-eminently**, *adv.* bij uitnemendheid *n.*

pre-emption, *n.* recht *n.n.* van voorkoop *n.*

preen, *v.t.* gladstrijken. ¶ *v.r.* zich mooi maken.

pre-engage, *v.t.* vooraf verbinden *str.*

pre-establish, *v.t.* vooraf vaststellen.

pre-exist, *v.i.* van te voren bestaan *irr.* **pre-existence**, *n.* voorbestaan *n.n.*

preface, *n.* voorrede *n.*, inleiding *n.* ¶ *v.t.* van een voorrede voorzien *irr. to* ~ *with*, laten *str.* voorafgaan door. **prefatory**, *a.* inleidend.

prefect, *n.* prefect *n.*; monitor *n.* **prefecture**, *n.* prefectuur *n.*

prefer, *v.t.* verkiezen *str.*, de voorkeur geven *str.* aan, liever hebben dan; verheffen *str.*, bevorderen (*promote*). *to* ~ *to*, verkiezen boven; verheffen tot. **preferable**, *a.* verkieslijk, te verkiezen. **preferably**, *adv.* bij voorkeur *n.*, liefst. **preference**, *n.* voorkeur *n.*; voorliefde *n. in* ~, bij voorkeur; *in* ~ *to*, liever dan; ~ *bonds*, prioriteitsobligaties *pl.n.* **preferential**, *a.* bevoorrecht; preferentieel. ~ *shares*, preferente aandelen *pl.n.n.* **preferment**, *n.* bevor .ring *n.*

prefix, *v.t.* vooraf laten *str.* gaan. ¶ *n.* voorvoegsel *n.n.*

pregnancy, *n.* zwangerschap *n.* **pregnant**, *a.* zwanger; veelzeggend. (*fig.*) ~ *with*, zwanger van.

prehensile, *a.* grijp . . .

prejudge, *v.t.* vooraf oordelen; vooruit veroordelen.

prejudice, *n.* vooroordeel *n.n.* (*opinion*); afbreuk *n.*, schade *n.* (*harm*). ¶ *v.t.* voorinnemen *str.*; afbreuk doen *irr.* aan. **prejudicial**, *a.*, ~**ly**, *adv.* nadelig, schadelijk.

prelacy, *n.* prelaatschap *n.n.* **prelate**, *n.* prelaat *n.*, kerkvoogd *n.*, kerkvorst *n.*

preliminary, *a.* voorlopig; voorafgaand; voor . . .

prelude, *n.* voorspel *n.n.*; preludium *n.n.* ¶ *v.t.* een inleiding *n.* vormen tot.

premature, *a.*, ~**ly**, *adv.* voorbarig, ontijdig. **prematurity**, *n.* voorbarigheid *n.*

premeditate, *v.t.* beramen, overleggen. ~**d**, met voorbedachten rade. **premeditation**, *n.* voorbedachtheid *n.*

premier, *n.* eerste minister *n.*, premier *n.*

premise, *n.* premisse *n.*, voorop gezette stelling *n.* ~**s**, huis *n.n.* en erve *n.* ¶ *v.t.* vooropstellen.

premium, *n.* premie *n. to be at a* ~, boven pari *n.n.* staan *irr.*; opgeld *n.n.* doen *irr.*

premonition, *n.* waarschuwing *n.*, voorgevoel *n.n.* **premonitory**, *a.* waarschuwend.

preoccupation, *n.* afgetrokkenheid *n.*, bezorgdheid *n.* **preoccupied**, *a.* in gedachten *pl.n.* verzonken; bezorgd. **preoccupy**, *v.t.* in beslag *n.n.* nemen *str.*

preordain, *v.t.* vooraf beschikken.

preparation, *n.* voorbereiding *n.*, voorbereidsel *n.n.*; toebereiding *n.*; preparaat *n.n.* ~**s**, aanstalten *pl.n.n.*, toebereidselen *pl. n.n.* **preparative,** *a.* voorbereidend. ~ *to,* ter voorbereiding *n.* van. ¶ *n.* voorbereidsel *n.n.* **preparatory,** *a.* voorbereidend. ~ *to,* bij wijze van voorbereiding *n.* tot. **prepare,** *v.t.* voorbereiden; toebereiden, klaarmaken. ¶ *v.r.* to ~ *oneself,* zich voorbereiden.

prepay, *v.t.* vooruitbetalen. **prepayment,** *n.* vooruitbetaling *n.*

prepense, *a.* voorbedacht. *of malice* ~, met voorbedachten rade.

preponderance, *n.* overwicht *n.n.* **preponderant,** *a.,* ~*ly, adv.* overwegend. **preponderate,** *v.t.* het overwicht hebben, overwegend zijn.

preposition, *n.* voorzetsel *n.n.*

prepossess, *v.t.* innemen *str.* to ~ *in favour of,* innemen voor. **prepossessing,** *a.* innemend. **prepossession,** *n.* vooringenomenheid *n.*

preposterous, *a.,* ~*ly, adv.* bespottelijk, ongerijmd.

prepuce, *n.* voorhuid *n.*

prerogative, *n.* voorrecht *n.n.,* prerogatief *n.n.*

presage, *n.* voorteken *n.n.*

Presbyterian, *a.* Presbyteriaans. ¶ *N.* Presbyteriaan *N.*

prescience, *n.* voorwetenschap *n.;* vooruitziendheid *n.* **prescient,** *a.* vooruitwetend; vooruitziend.

prescribe, *v.t.* voorschrijven *str.* ¶ *v.i.* to ~ *to,* (geneeskundig) behandelen. **prescription,** *n.* voorschrift *n.n.;* recept *n.n.*

presence, *n.* tegenwoordigheid *n.,* aanwezigheid *n.;* persoonlijkheid *n.,* voorkomen *n.n.* ~ *of mind,* tegenwoordigheid van geest *n.* **present,** *a.* aanwezig, tegenwoordig, present; huidig; onderhavig, in kwestie *n. the* ~ *day,* de huidige dag; *at the* ~ *hour,* op dit uur *n.n.* ¶ *n.* tegenwoordige tijd *n.,* heden *n.n.;* present *n.n.,* geschenk *n.n.,* cadeau *n.n. at* ~, tegenwoordig; *for the* ~, voor 't ogenblik, momenteel. ¶ *v.t.* presenteren (*general & of arms*); aanbieden *str.* (*offer*); voorstellen (*people*) opleveren (*difficulties*). ¶ *v.r.* to ~ *oneself,* zich voordoen *irr.* **presentable,** *a.* presentabel, toonbaar. **presentation,** *n.* aanbieding *n.* (*gift*); voorstelling *n.* (*at court*). ~ *of prizes,* prijsuitdeling *n.;* ~ *copy,* presentexemplaar *n.n.*

presentiment, *n.* voorgevoel *n.n.*

presently. *adv.* zo meteen, dadelijk, aanstonds, straks.

preservation, *n.* bewaring *n.,* redding *n.* **preservative,** *a.* bederfwerend. **preserve,** *v.t.* bewaren, behoeden; inmaken, inleggen (*food*). ¶ *n.* ~*s,* conserven *pl.n.;* gereserveerd (jacht)terrein *n.n.* **preserver,** *n.* bewaarder *n.,* beschermer *n.*

preside, *v.i.* voorzitten *str.,* presideren. to ~ *over,* als voorzitter *n.* leiden. **presidency,** *n.*

presidentschap *n.n.* **president,** *n.* voorzitter *n.;* president *n.* **presidential,** *a.* van de president.

press, *v.t.* drukken; persen (*compress*); dringen *str.* (*push*); aandringen *str.* bij (*insist*); pressen (*into service*). to be ~*ed for time,* tijd *n.* tekort komen *irr.* ¶ *n.* pers *n.;* drukpers *n.;* gedrang *n.n.* (*of people*); kast *n.* (*cupboard*). **press-agency,** *n.* persbureau *n.n.* **presscutting,** *n.* krantenuitknipsel *n.n.* **presser,** *n.* perser *n.* **press-gallery,** *n.* perstribune *n.* **pressgang,** *n.* presgang *n.* **pressing,** *a.* dringend. **pressman,** *n.* journalist *n.* **press-stud,** *n.* drukknoopje *n.n.* **pressure,** *n.* druk *n.;* spanning *n.;* drang *n.*

prestige, *n.* prestige *n.n.,* aanzien *n.n.*

presumable, *a.,* ~*bly, adv.* vermoedelijk. **presume,** *v.t.* vermoeden, veronderstellen. to ~ *to,* de vrijheid nemen *str.* ¶ *v.i.* aanmatigend zijn. **presumption,** *n.* vermoeden *n.n.,* veronderstelling *n.;* aanmatiging *n.,* inbeelding *n.* **presumptive,** *a.,* ~*ly, adv.* vermoedelijk, gepresumeerd. **presumptuous,** *a.,* ~*ly, adv.* arrogant, aanmatigend.

presuppose, *v.t.* vooraf onderstellen. **presupposition,** *n.* voorafgaande veronderstelling *n.*

pretence, *n.* schijn *n.;* voorwendsel *n.n. under false* ~*s,* onder valse voorspiegeling *n.* **pretend,** *v.t.* voorgeven *str.;* beweren; doen *irr.* alsof. **pretender,** *n.* pretendent *n.*

pretension, *n.* pretentie *n.* **pretentious,** *a.,* ~*ly, adv.* pretentieus.

preterite, *n.* verleden tijd *n.*

preternatural, *a.,* ~*ly, adv.* onnatuurlijk.

pretext, *n.* voorwendsel *n.n.*

prettiness, *n.* aardigheid *n.,* mooiigheid *n.* **pretty,** *a.,* ~*ily, adv.* aardig, mooi, lief. ¶ *adv.* vrij, tamelijk.

prevail, *v.i.* de overhand hebben; uitwerking *n.* hebben; heersen. to ~ *on,* overhalen; to ~ *against,* zegevieren. **prevailing,** *a.* heersend. **prevalence,** *n.* algemeenheid *n.,* algemeen voorkomen *n.n.* **prevalent,** *a.,* ~*ly, adv.* heersend, algemeen.

prevaricate, *v.i.* uitvluchten *pl.n.n.* zoeken *irr.;* draaien. **prevarication,** *n.* draaierij *n.* **prevaricator,** *n.* draaier *n.*

prevent, *v.t.* voorkomen *str.,* beletten, verhinderen. **preventative,** *n.* voorbehoedmiddel *n.n.* **prevention,** *n.* voorkoming *n.,* verhindering *n.* **preventive,** *a.,* ~*ly, adv.* voorbehoedend, preventief.

previous, *a.,* ~*ly, adv.* vroeger, vorig, voorafgaand.

prevision, *n.* vooruitzien *n.n.;* voorzorg *n.*

pre-war, *a.* vooroorlogs, van voor den oorlog.

prey, *n.* prooi *n.* ¶ *v.i.* to ~ *on,* azen op, loeren op.

price, *n.* prijs *n. at any* ~, tegen elke prijs; *cost* ~, kostende prijs. ¶ *v.t.* prijzen.

priceless, *a.* onbetaalbaar. **price-list**, *n.* prijscourant *n.*

prick, *n.* prik *n.*, steek *n.*; wroeging *n.*, knaging *n.* *to kick against the* ∼*s*, de verzenen *pl.n.* tegen de prikkels *pl.n.* **slaan** *irr.* ¶ *v.t.* prikken, steken *str.*; prikkelen. *to* ∼ *the ears*, de oren *pl.n.n.* spitsen. **pricker**, *n.* prikker *n.*; prikkel *n.* **prickle**, *n.* prikkel *n.*, stekel *n.* ¶ *v.t.* prikkelen. **prickly**, *a.* prikkelig, stekelig. ∼ *heat*, warmtepuistjes *pl.n.n.*; ∼ *pear*, vijgdistel *n.*

pride, *n.* trots *n.*; hoogmoed *n.* ¶ *v.r. to* ∼ *oneself on,* trots zijn op, zich laten *str.* voorstaan op.

priest, *n.* geestelijke *n.*, priester *n.*, pastoor *n.* **priestess**, *n.* priesteres *n.* **priesthood**, *n.* priesterschap *n.n.* **priestlike**, *a.* priesterachtig. **priestly**, *a.* priesterlijk. **priestridden**, *a.* onder de hiel van de priesters *pl.n.*

prig, *n.* brave Hendrik *n.*; neuswijs iemand *n.n.* **priggish**, *a.*, ∼*ly*, *adv.* eigenwijs, neuswijs; braaf.

prim, *a.* preuts, stijf.

primacy, *n.* primaatschap *n.n.* **primarily**, *adv.* in de eerste plaats, voornamelijk. **primary**, *a.* primair, eerste. ∼ *education*, lager onderwijs *n.n.* **primate**, *n.* primaat *n.*, aartsbisschop *n.* **prime**, *a.* eerste, voornaamste; prima. *P*∼ *Minister*, Eerste Minister *n.*, premier *n.* ¶ *n.* begin *n.n.*; bloei *n.* van het leven. ¶ *v.t.* het antwoord ingeven *str.*; africhten; in de grondverf zetten; van kruit *n.n.* voorzien *irr.* **primer**, *n.* inleiding *n.*, boek *n.n.* voor beginners *pl.n.*

primeval, *a.* oorspronkelijk, uit de voortijd.

priming, *n.* grondverf *n.*; kruit *n.n.*

primitive, *a.*, ∼*ly*, *adv.* primitief; oorspronkelijk.

primness, *n.* preutsheid *n.*, stijfheid *n.*

primogeniture, *n.* eerstegeboorte *n.*

primrose, *n.* sleutelbloem *n.*

prince, *n.* vorst *n.*, prins *n.* (*monarch*); prins *n.* (*son of royalty & noble title*). **princely**, *a.* prinselijk, vorstelijk. **princess**, *n.* prinses *n.* ∼ *royal*, kroonprinses *n.*

principal, *a.* voornaamste, eerste, hoofd . . . ¶ *n.* chef *n.*; hoofd *n.n.*, directeur *n.*; lastgever *n.*, principaal *n.*; kapitaal *n.n.* hoofdsom *n.*

principality, *n.* vorstendom *n.n.*

principally, *adv.* voornamelijk, vooral.

principle, *n.* beginsel *n.n.*, principe *n.n.*; grondslag *n.* *on* ∼, uit principe.

print, *v.t.* drukken; afdrukken; in drukletters *pl.n.* schrijven *str.* ∼*ed matter*, drukwerk *n.n.* ¶ *n.* prent *n.*, gravure *n.*; indruk *n.*; afdruk *n.*; gedrukte katoenen stof *n.* *out of* ∼, uitverkocht. **printer**, *n.* drukker *n.* **printing**, *n.* drukken *n.n.*; drukkunst *n.* **printing ink**, *n.* drukinkt *n.* **printing press**, *n.* drukpers *n.* **printing-works**, *n.* drukkerij *n.*

prior, *n.* prior *n.*, overste *n.* ¶ *a.* vroeger, voorafgaand. ∼ *to*, vroeger dan, voorafgaand aan. **prioress**, *n.* priores *n.* **priority** *n.* voorrang *n.*, prioriteit *n.*

prism, *n.* prisma *n.n.*

prison, *n.* gevangenis *n.* **prisoner**, *n.* gevangene *n.*; arrestant *n.* *to take* ∼, gevangen nemen *str.*

pristine, *a.* oorspronkelijk, voormalig.

privacy, *n.* afzondering *n.*; privé vertrek *n.n.* **private**, *a.*, ∼*ly*, *adv.* privé, privaat; vertrouwelijk; persoonlijk; particulier. ¶ *n.* (gemeen) soldaat *n.*

privateer, *n.* kaper *n.*, kaperschip *n.n.* **privateering**, *n.* kaperij *n.*, kaapvaart *n.*

privation, *n.* ontbering *n.*; gemis *n.n.*

privet, *n.* liguster *n.*

privilege, *n.* voorrecht *n.n.*, gunst *n.*; privilegie *n.n.* ¶ *v.t.* bevoorrechten.

privily, *adv.* heimelijk. **privy**, *a.* geheim, heimelijk. *P*∼ *Council*, Geheime Raad *N.*, Raad *N.* van State; ∼ *purse*, civiele lijst *n.*; *Lord P*∼ *Seal*, Geheimzegelbewaarder *N.*; ∼ *to*, ingewijd in.

prize, *n.* prijs *n.* (*reward*); prijs *n.*, prijsschip *n.n.*, buit *n.* (*booty*). ¶ *v.t.* hoogschatten, op prijs schatten; prijsmaken; forceren. *to* ∼ *open*, openbreken *str.* **prize-court**, *n.* prijsgerecht *n.n.* **prize day**, *n.* prijsuitdeling *n.* **prizefighter**, *n.* bokser *n.*

probability, *n.* waarschijnlijkheid *n.* *in all* ∼, naar alle waarschijnlijkheid. **probable**, *a.*, ∼*bly*, *adv.* waarschijnlijk, vermoedelijk.

probate, *n.* gerechtelijke verificatie *n.* (van een testament *n.n.*). ¶ *v.t.* (een testament) laten *str.* verifiëren. **probation**, *n.* proeftijd *n.*; onderzoek *n.n.* **probationer**, *n.* aspirant *n.*; leerling-verpleegster *n.n.*

probe, *n.* sonde *n.* ¶ *v.t.* sonderen; onderzoeken *irr.*

probity, *n.* rechtschapenheid *n.*, oprechtheid *n.*

problem, *n.* probleem *n.n.*, vraagstuk *n.n.* **problematic**, *a.*, ∼*ally*, *adv.* problematisch; onzeker.

proboscis, *n.* slurf *n.*, snuit *n.*

procedure, *n.* werkwijze *n.*, methode *n.*; rechtspleging *n.* **proceed**, *v.i.* voortgaan *irr.*; vervolgen; vorderen. *to* ∼ *against,* in rechten *pl.n.n.* vervolgen. **proceeding**, *n.* voortgang *n.*; handelwijze *n.*; actie *n.* ∼*s*, handelingen *pl.n.*, werkzaamheden *pl.n.*; *to institute* ∼*s against*, een actie *n.* instellen tegen. **proceeds**, *pl.n.* opbrengst *n.*

process, *n.* voortgang *n.*, verloop *n.n.*, loop *n.*; procédé *n.n.*; bereidingswijze *n.* *in* ∼ *of . . .*, aan het . . . ¶ *v.t.* verduurzamen.

procession, *n.* processie *n.*, stoet *n.*, omgang *n.*

proclaim, *v.t.* uitroepen *str.*; verkondigen, afkondigen. *to* ∼ *the banns*, de huwelijksafkondiging doen *irr.* **proclamation**, *n.* proclamatie *n.*; afkondiging *n.*

proclivity, *n.* neiging *n.*; overhelling *n.*

procrastinate, *v.i.* uitstellen. **procrastination**, *n.* uitstel *n.n.* **procrastinator**, *n.* uitsteller *n.*

procreate, *v.t.* voortbrengen *irr.*; voortplanten. **procreation,** *n.* voortbrenging *n.*; voortplanting *n.*

proctor, *n.* procureur *n.* *King's P~,* procureur-generaal *n.*

procurable, *a.* verkrijgbaar. **procuration,** *n.* verschaffing *n.*; procuratie *n.*, volmacht *n.* **procurator,** *n.* zaakbezorger *n.*, gevolmachtigde, procureur *n.* **procure,** *v.t.* bezorgen, verschaffen, verkrijgen *str.* ¶ *v.i.* koppelen. **procurement,** *n.* bezorging *n.*, verwerving *n.* **procurer,** *n.* bezorger *n.*; koppelaar *n.* **procuress,** *n.* koppelaarster *n.*

prod, *v.t.* porren. ¶ *n.* por *n.*

prodigal, *a.*, ~**ly,** *adv.* kwistig. *~ of,* kwistig met; ~ *son,* verloren zoon *n.* **prodigality,** *n.* kwistigheid *n.*

prodigious, *a.*, ~**ly,** *adv.* wonderbaar, verbazend; ontzaglijk. **prodigy,** *n.* wonder *n.n.* *infant ~,* wonderkind *n.n.*

produce, *v.t.* voortbrengen *irr.*; te voorschijn brengen *irr.*; aanvoeren; teweegbrengen *irr.*; regisseren (*a play*); verlengen (*line*). ¶ *n.* opbrengst *n.*; voortbrengselen *pl.n.n.*; producten *pl.n.n.* **producer,** *n.* producent *n.*; regisseur *n.* **product,** *n.* product *n.n.*, voortbrengsel *n.n.*; resultaat *n.n.* **production,** *n.* productie *n.*; overlegging *n.* (*documents*); opvoering *n.*; regie *n.* **productive,** *a.*, ~**ly,** *adv.* productief; vruchtbaar.

profanation, *n.* ontwijding *n.*, ontheiliging *n.*; schennis *n.* **profane,** *a.*, ~**ly,** *adv.* profaan; goddeloos; werelds. ¶ *v.t.* ontheiligen. **profanity,** *n.* goddeloosheid *n.*; godslasterlijke taal *n.*

profess, *v.t.* belijden *str.*; verklaren; uitoefenen. **professed,** *a.* beweerd, voorgewend. **professedly,** *adv.* naar beweerd wordt, ogenschijnlijk. **profession,** *n.* belijdenis *n.*; beroep *n.n.* *by ~,* van beroep. **professional,** *a.*, ~**ly,** *adv.* beroeps . . ., vak . . . ~ *secret,* ambtsgeheim *n.n.*

professor, *n.* professor *n.*, hoogleraar *n.* **professorship,** *n.* professoraat *n.n.*

proffer, *v.t.* aanbieden *str.*; toereiken, toesteken *str.*

proficiency, *n.* vaardigheid *n.*, bedrevenheid *n.* **proficient,** *a.* vaardig, bedreven.

profile, *n.* profiel *n.n.*

profit, *n.* voordeel *n.n.*, winst *n.*; profijt *n.n.* ¶ *v.i.* voordeel trekken *str.* uit. *to ~ by or from,* profiteren van. ¶ *v.t.* baten. **profitable,** *a.*, ~**bly,** *adv.* voordelig, winstgevend. **profiteer,** *n.* O.W.ër *n.* **profitless,** *a.* onvoordelig.

profligacy, *n.* losbandigheid *n.* **profligate,** *n.* losbandig. ¶ *n.* losbol *n.*

profound, *a.*, ~**ly,** *adv.* diep; diepzinnig. **profundity,** *n.* diepzinnigheid *n.*

profuse, *a.*, ~**ly,** *adv.* kwistig, overvloedig. **profuseness,** *n.* kwistigheid *n.* **profusion,** *n.* overvloed *n.*

progenitor, *n.* voorvader *n.*; verwekker *n.* **progeny,** *n.* nakomelingschap *n.n.*; kroost *n.n.*

prognosis, *n.* prognose *n.* **prognostic,** *n.* voorteken *n.n.*; ziekteverschijnsel *n.n.* **prognosticate,** *v.t.* voorspellen. **prognostication,** *n.* voorteken *n.n.*; voorspelling *n.*

programme, *n.* programma *n.n.*

progress, *v.i.* vorderen; opschieten *str.* ¶ *n.* vordering *n.*, voortgang *n.*; loop *n.*, verloop *n.n.*; tocht *n.*; ontwikkelingsgang *n.* **progression,** *n.* (opklimmende) reeks *n.* **progressive,** *a.* toenemend; opklimmend; vooruitstrevend. **progressively,** *adv.* gaandeweg.

prohibit, *v.t.* verbieden *str.* **prohibition,** *n.* verbod *n.n.*; drankverbod *n.n.* **prohibitive,** *a.* buitensporig hoog. ~ *duties,* beschermende rechten *pl.n.n.*

project, *v.t.* ontwerpen *str.*; vooruit werpen *str.*; projecteren. ¶ *n.* plan *n.n.*, ontwerp *n.n.* **projectile,** *a.* voortdrijvend, stuw . . . ¶ *n.* projectiel *n.n.* **projection,** *n.* vooruitsteken *n.n.*; voortwerpen *n.n.*; projectie *n.* **projector,** *n.* ontwerper *n.*; projectie-apparaat *n.n.*

prolapse, *n.* verzakking *n.*

proletarian, *a.* proletarisch. ¶ *n.* proletariër *n.*, proleet *n.* **proletariat,** *n.* proletariaat *n.n.*

prolific, *a.*, ~**ally,** *adv.* vruchtbaar.

prolix, *a.* langdradig, wijdlopig. **prolixity,** *n.* langdradigheid *n.*, wijdlopigheid *n.*

prologue, *n.* proloog *n.*, inleiding *n.*

prolong, *v.t.* verlengen. **prolongation,** *n.* verlenging *n.*; prolongatie *n.*

promenade, *n.* promenade *n.*

prominence, *n.* uitsteeksel *n.n.*, onderscheiding *n.* **prominent,** *a.*, ~**ly,** *adv.* vooruitstekend; treffend; vooraanstaand. *to become ~,* op de voorgrond treden *str.*

promiscuity, *n.* (al te) vrij verkeer *n.n.* **promiscuous,** *a.*, ~**ly,** *adv.* gemengd, verward.

promise, *v.t.* beloven; toezeggen *irr.* ¶ *n.* belofte *n.*

promissory, *a.* ~ *note,* promesse *n.*

promontory, *n.* voorgebergte *n.n.*; kaap *n.*

promote, *v.t.* bevorderen; aankweken; in de hand werken. *to be ~d,* promotie *n.* maken. **promoter,** *n.* bevorderaar *n.*; oprichter *n.* **promotion,** *n.* bevordering *n.*; promotie *n.*

prompt, *a.*, ~**ly,** *adv.* prompt; stipt; vlug. ¶ *v.t.* voorzeggen *irr.*; inblazen *str.*; souffleren. **prompt-box,** *n.* souffleurshokje *n.n.* **prompt-copy,** *n.* souffleursboek *n.n.* **prompter,** *n.* souffleur *n.* **prompting,** *n.* souffleren *n.n.* ~*s,* ingeving *n.*, stem *n.* **promptitude,** *n.*, **promptness,** *n.* promptheid *n.*; stiptheid *n.*

promulgate, *v.t.* afkondigen, uitvaardigen. **promulgation,** *n.* afkondiging *n.*, uitvaardiging *n.*

prone, *a.* voorover; geneigd. **proneness,** *n* neiging *n.,* aanleg *n.*
prong, *n.* tand *n.,* vork *n.*
pronominal, *a.* voornaamwoordelijk.
pronoun, *n.* voornaamwoord *n.n.*
pronounce, *v.t.* uitspreken *str.*; uitspraak *n.* doen *irr.* van, verklaren. *to ~ against,* zich uitspreken *str.* tegen. **pronounced,** *a.* uitgesproken, geprononceerd. **pronounceable,** *a.* uit te spreken. **pronunciation,** *n.* uitspraak *n.*
proof, *n.* bewijs *n.n.*; blijk *n.n.*; proef *n.,* drukproef *n.*; sterktegraad *n.* ¶ *a.* *~ against,* bestand tegen. ¶ *v.t.* waterproef maken; vuurvast maken. **proof-sheet,** *n.* drukproef *n.*
prop, *n.* stut *n.,* schoor *n.* ¶ *v.t.* stutten. *to ~ up,* stutten.
propaganda, *n.* propaganda *n.*
propagate, *v.t.* verspreiden. ¶ *v.r.* zich voortplanten. **propagation,** *n.* voortplanting *n.,* verbreiding *n.* **propagator,** *n.* verbreider *n.,* verspreider *n.*
propel, *v.t.* voortdrijven *str.*; voortstuwen. **propellent,** *a.* voortdrijvend. ¶ *n.* drijfkracht *n.* **propeller,** *n.* schroef *n.*
propensity, *n.* neiging *n.*
proper, *a.* eigen; eigenlijk, juist; fatsoenlijk, behoorlijk. **properly,** *adv.* eigenlijk; fatsoenlijk, behoorlijk; terecht.
property, *n.* eigendom *n.n.*; eigenschap *n.,* hoedanigheid *n.*
prophecy, *n.* profetie *n.,* voorspelling *n.* **prophesy,** *v.t.* voorspellen. **prophet,** *n.* profeet *n.* **prophetic,** *a.,* ~ally, *adv.* profetisch.
prophylactic, *a.* prophylactisch. ¶ *n.* voorbehoedmiddel *n.n.*
propinquity, *n.* nabijheid *n.*
propitiate, *v.t.* gunstig stemmen; verzoenen. **propitiation,** *n.* verzoening *n.* **propitiatory,** *a.* gunstig stemmend; verzoenend.
propitious, *a.,* ~ly, *adv.* gunstig.
proportion, *n.* verhouding *n.*; evenredigheid *n.* *in ~,* naar verhouding; *in ~ to,* in verhouding tot. ¶ *v.t.* evenredig maken; afmeten. **proportional,** *a.* evenredig. **proportionate,** *a.* evenredig. **proportionately,** *adv.* naar verhouding *n.*
proposal, *n.* voorstel *n.n.*; aanbod *n.n.* **propose,** *v.t.* voorstellen,; aanbieden *str.* ¶ *v.i.* een huwelijksaanzoek *n.n.* doen *irr.* **proposition,** *n.* voorstel *n.n.,* aanbod *n.n.*; stelling *n.* (*mathematical*); probleem *n.n.*
propound, *v.t.* voorleggen *irr.*
proprietary, *a.* eigendoms . . . *~ medicine,* patentmiddel *n.n.* **proprietor,** *n.* eigenaar *n.* **proprietress,** *n.* eigenares *n.*
propriety, *n.* gepastheid *n.,* welvoeglijkheid *n.* *proprieties,* decorum *n.n.*
propulsion, *n.* voortstuwing *n.*; drijfkracht *n.*
prorogation, *n.* opschorting *n.,* verdaging *n.* **prorogue,** *v.t.* opschorten, verdagen.
prosaic, *a.* prozaïsch.

proscribe, *v.t.* in de ban doen *irr.*; buiten de wet stellen; vogelvrij verklaren. **proscription,** *n.* verbanning *n.*
prose, *n.* proza *n.n.*
prosecute, *v.t.* voortzetten; uitoefenen; gerechtelijk vervolgen. **prosecution,** *n.* voortzetting *n.*; uitoefening *n.*; gerechtelijke vervolging *n.* *counsel for the ~,* ambtenaar *n.* van het Openbaar Ministerie. **prosecutor,** *n.* vervolger *n.*; aanklager *n.*
proselyte, *n.* proseliet *n.,* bekeerling *n.* **proselytism,** *n.* bekeeringszucht *n.* **proselytize,** *v.i.* proselieten *pl.n.* maken. ¶ *v.t.* bekeren.
prosody, *n.* prosodie *n.,* versleer *n.*
prospect, *n.* uitzicht *n.n.*; vergezicht *n.n.*; vooruitzicht *n.n.,* hoop *n.* ¶ *v.t.* prospecteren, onderzoeken *irr.* **prospective,** *a.* te verwachten; toekomstig. **prospector,** *n.* mijnonderzoeker *n.* **prospectus,** *n.* prospectus *n.n.*
prosper, *v.i.* voorspoedig zijn; bloeien, gedijen. **prosperity,** *n.* welvaart *n.,* voorspoed *n.* **prosperous,** *a.,* ~ly, *adv.* welvarend, voorspoedig.
prostitute, *v.t.* prostitueren; misbruiken. *to ~ oneself to,* zich dienstbaar maken aan. ¶ *n.* prostituée *n.* **prostitution,** *n.* prostitutie *n.*
prostrate, *a.* ter aarde *n.* geworpen; uitgeput. *to lie ~,* plat neerliggen *str.* ¶ *v.t.* ter aarde werpen *str.*; vernederen; uitputten. **prostration,** *n.* ternederwerping *n.*; vernedering *n.*; uitputting *n.*
prosy, *a.* prozaïsch; nuchter; saai.
protect, *v.t.* beschermen; behoeden. *to ~ from,* beschermen voor. **protection,** *n.* bescherming *n.*; protectie *n.* **protectionism,** *n.* protectionisme *n.n.* **protective,** *a.,* ~ly, *adv.* beschermend. **protector,** *n.* beschermer *n.* **protectorate,** *n.* protectoraat *n.n.*
protest, *v.t.* betuigen, verklaren. ¶ *v.i.* protesteren. ¶ *n.* protest *n.n. deed of ~,* protestakte *n.* **Protestant,** *N.* Protestant *N.* **Protestantism,** *N.* Protestantisme *n.N.*
protocol, *n.* protocol *n.n.*
protoplasm, *n.* protoplasma *n.n.*
prototype, *n.* model *n.n.,* oorspronkelijk type *n.n.*
protozoa, *pl.n.* protozoön *n.n.*
protract, *v.t.* verlengen; rekken. **protraction,** *n.* verlenging *n.*; rekking *n.* **protractor,** *n.* graadboog *n.*
protrude, *v.t. & v.i.* uitsteken *str.*; uitpuilen. **protuberance,** *n.* uitsteeksel *n.n.*; uitwas *n.* **protuberant,** *a.* vooruitstekend, uitpuilend.
proud, *a.,* ~ly, *adv.* trots; fier; prachtig.
prove, *v.t.* bewijzen *irr.,* aantonen.
provender, *n.* fourage *n.*; proviand *n.*
proverb, *n.* spreekwoord *n.n. P~s,* Spreuken *pl.N.* **proverbial,** *a.,* ~ly, *adv.* spreekwoordelijk; in spreekwoorden *pl.n.n.* neergelegd.
provide, *v.t.* zorgen voor. *to ~ with,* voorzien *irr.* van; *to ~ oneself,* zich voorzien *irr.*;

to ~ *for oneself*, in z'n eigen onderhoud *n.n.* voorzien *irr.*· ¶ *v.i. to* ~ *for*, zorgen voor; *to* ~ *against*, maatregelen *pl.n.* nemen *str.* tegen. **provided**, *a.* mits. **providence**, *n.* vooruitziendheid *n.* *P*~, de Voorzienigheid *N.* **provident**, *a.*, ~ly, *adv.* vooruitziend, zorgzaam. *P*~ *Society*, vereniging *n.* van onderling hulpbetoon *n.n.* **providential**, *a.*, ~ly, *adv.* wonderbaarlijk. **provider**, *n.* verzorger *n.*; leverancier *n.*

province, *n.* provincie *n.*; gebied *n.n.*, sfeer *n.* **provincial**, *a.*, ~ly, *adv.* provinciaal. **provincialism**, *n.* provincialisme *n.n.*

provision, *n.* voorziening *n.*, voorzien *n.n.*; voorzorg *n.*; bepaling *n.*; voorraad *n.* ~*s*, proviand *n.*, mondvoorraad *n.* ¶ *v.t.* provianderen. **provisional**, *a.*, ~ly, *adv.* voorlopig; tijdelijk.

proviso, *n.* voorbehoud *n.n.* **provisory**, *a.* voorwaardelijk; voorlopig.

provocation, *n.* uitdaging *n.* *on the slightest* ~, bij de minste aanleiding *n.*; *under severe* ~, ergerlijk geprovoceerd. **provocative**, *a.* uitdagend; prikkelend. **provoke**, *v.t.* uitdagen, uitlokken; opwekken, te voorschijn roepen *str.* **provoking**, *a.* tartend, tergend.

provost, *n.* provoost *n.*; rector *n.*

prow, *n.* boeg *n.*, voorsteven *n.*

prowess, *n.* dapperheid *n.*; heldendaad *n.*

prowl, *v.i.* rondsluipen *str.* ¶ *n. to be on the* ~, op roof *n.* uitzijn. **prowler**, *n.* zwerver *n.*, stroper *n.*

proximity, *n.* onmiddellijke nabijheid *n.*

proxy, *n.* volmacht *n.* (*instrument*); gevolmachtigde *n.* (*person*).

prude, *n.* preutse vrouw *n.*; preuts meisje *n.n.*, nuf *n.*

prudence, *n.* voorzichtigheid *n.*, bedachtzaamheid *n.* **prudent**, *a.*, ~ly, *adv.* voorzichtig, bedachtzaam. **prudential**, *a.* wijs, beraden.

prudery, *n.* preutsheid *n.* **prudish**, *a.*, ~ly, *adv.* preuts; nuffig.

prune, *n.* gedroogde pruim *n.* ¶ *v.t.* snoeien.

prunella, *n.* prunel *n.*

pruning-hook, *n.*, **pruning-knife**, *n.* snoeimes *n.n.*

prurience, *n.* wulpsheid *n.*, geilheid *n.* **prurient**, *a.* wulps, pikant.

Prussia, *N.* Pruisen *n.N.* **Prussian**, *a.* Pruisisch. ¶ *N.* Pruis *N.*

prussic, *a.* ~ *acid*, blauwzuur *n.n.*

pry, *v.i.* turen, gluren. *to* ~ *into*, neuzen in; *to* ~ *upon*, beloeren. **prying**, *a.* nieuwsgierig.

psalm, *n.* psalm *n.* **psalmist**, *n.* psalmdichter *n.* **psalmodic**, *a.* psalmodisch. **psalmody**, *n.* psalmodie *n.*, psalmgezang *n.n.*

psalter, *n.* psalmboek *n.n.*

pseudo, *a.* pseudo, vals.

pseudonym, *n.* pseudoniem *n.n.* **pseudonymous**, *a.* pseudoniem.

pshaw, *int.* ba!

psyche, *n.* psyche *n.*, ziel *n.*

psychiatric, *a.* psychiatrisch. **psychiatrist**, *n.* psychiater *n.* **psychiatry**, *n.* psychiatrie *n.*

psychic, *a.* psychisch, ziels . . .; spiritualistisch

psychological, *a.*, ~ly, *adv.* psychologisch, zielkundig. **psychologist**, *n.* psycholoog *n.* **psychology**, *n.* psychologie *n.*

psychopath, *n.* psychopaath *n.*

psychosis, *n.* psychose *n.*

psychotherapeutics, *pl.n.*, **psychotherapy**, *n.* psychotherapie *n.*

ptarmigan, *n.* sneeuwhoen *n.n.*

pterodactyl, *n.* pterodactylus *n.*

ptomaine, *n.* ptomaïne *n.*

pub, *n.* herberg *n.*

puberty, *n.* puberteit *n.* **pubes**, *pl.n.* schaamdelen *pl.n.n.* **pubescence**, *n.* geslachtsrijpheid *n.* **pubescent**, *a.* geslachtsrijp.

public, *a.*, ~ly, *adv.* publiek, openbaar. ~ *debt*, staatsschuld *n.*; ~ *health*, volksgezondheid *n.*; ~ *house*, herberg *n.*; ~ *school*, particuliere school *n.*; ~ *spirit*, burgerzin *n.* ¶ *n.* publiek *n.n.* in ~, in 't openbaar. **publican**, *n.* herbergier *n.* **publication**, *n.* bekendmaking *n.*, afkondiging *n.*; publicatie *n.*; uitgave *n.* **publicity**, *n.* openbaarheid *n.*; publiciteit *n.* **public-spirited**, *a.* met burgerzin *n.*

publish, *v.t.* openbaar maken; publiceren; uitgeven *str.* **publishable**, *a.* voor uitgeven *n.n.* vatbaar. **publisher**, *n.* uitgever *n.* **publishing**, *n.* uitgeversbedrijf *n.n.* **publishing house**, *n.* uitgeversfirma *n.*

puce, *a.* puce, purperbruin.

puck, *n.* kaboutermannetje *n.n.*

pucker, *v.t.* rimpelen, plooien; fronsen. ¶ *n.* rimpel *n.*; fronsel *n.n.*

pudding, *n.* pudding *n.*

puddle, *n.* (modder)plas *n.* ¶ *v.i.* plassen, ploeteren (*in mud*). ¶ *v.t.* puddelen (*metal*). **puddling-furnace**, *n.* puddeloven *n.*

puerile, *a.* kinderachtig. **puerility**, *n.* kinderachtigheid *n.*

puff, *n.* puffen; paffen; hijgen, blazen *str.* ¶ *v.t.* uitblazen *str.*; reclame *n.* maken voor. ¶ *n.* (wind)stootje *n.n.*; rook(wolkje) *n.n.*; reclame *n.* **puff-adder**, *n.* pofadder *n.* **puffball**, *n.* stuifzwam *n.*

puffin, *n.* papegaaiduiker *n.*

puffiness, *n.* opgeblazenheid *n.*

puffpaste, *n.* bladerdeeg *n.n.*

puffy, *a.* opgeblazen.

pug, *n.* puk *n.*, mopshond *n.*

pugilism, *n.* boksen *n.n.* **pugilist**, *n.* bokser *n.*

pugnacious, *a.*, ~ly, *adv.* twistziek, strijdlustig. **pugnacity**, *n.* strijdlust *n.*

pug-nosed, *a.* met een mopsneus *n.*

puisne, *a.* jonger.

puissant, *a.* machtig, hoogmogend.

puke, *v.i.* braken.

pule, *v.i.* blèren.

pull, *v.t.* trekken *str.*, trekken *str.* aan. ¶ *v.i.* trekken *str. to* ~ *down*, neerhalen; *to* ~ *through*, er bovenop komen *irr.*; *to* ~ *oneself*

together, zich vermannen; *to* ~ *to bits*, aan stukken *pl.n.n.* trekken *str.* ¶ *n.* ruk *n.*; trek *n.*; proef *n.*; dronk *n.*; invloed *n.*
pullet, *n.* jonge kip *n.*
pulley, *n.* katrol *n.*; talie *n.*, takel *n.*
pull-over, *n.* trui *n.*
pulmonary, *a.* long . . .
pulp, *n.* vlees *n.n.*; weke massa *n.*; brij *n.*; pulp *n.* ¶ *v.t.* tot pulp maken; moezen.
pulpit, *n.* preekstoel *n.*, kansel *n.*
pulpy, *a.* zacht, vlezig.
pulsate, *v.i.* kloppen, slaan *irr.* **pulsation**, *n.* klopping *n.*, slag *n.*
pulse, *n.* pols *n.*, polsslag *n.*; peulvrucht(en) *n.* (*pl.n.*).
pulverization, *n.* vermaling *n.*; vernietiging *n.* **pulverize**, *v.t.* fijnmaken; vermorzelen.
pumice(-stone), *n.* puimsteen *n.*
pump, *n.* pomp *n.*; dansschoen *n.* ¶ *v.t.* pompen; leegpompen; uithoren (*information*). **pump-brake**, *n.* pompzwengel *n.*
pumpkin *n.* pompoen *n.*
pump-room, *n.* koerzaal *n.*
pun, *n.* woordspeling *n.* ¶ *v.i.* woordspelingen maken.
punch, *v.t.* stompen; knippen; perforeren; ponsen. ¶ *n.* stomp *n.*; kniptang *n.*; pons *n.*; letterstempel *n.n.*; punch *n.* *P* ~ *and Judy*, Jan Klaassen en Katrijn; *P* ~ *and Judy show*, poppenkast *n.*
puncheon, *n.* priem *n.*; vat *n.n.*
punctilio, *n.* overdreven vormelijkheid *n.* **punctilious**, *a.* vormelijk, nauwgezet.
punctual, *a.*, ~**ly**, *adv.* stipt (op tijd). **punctuality**, *n.* stiptheid *n.*
punctuate, *v.t.* punctueren; accentueren, kracht *n.* bijzetten. *to* ~ *with*, doorspekken met. **punctuation**, *n.* punctuatie *n.*; leestekens *pl.n.n.*
puncture, *n.* gaatje *n.n.* ¶ *v.t.* prikken. ~*d*, lek.
pundit, *n.* geleerde *n.*
pungency, *n.* scherpheid *n.* **pungent**, *a.*, ~**ly**, *adv.* scherp, bijtend, bitter.
punish, *v.t.* straffen, bestraffen; afstraffen, er van langs geven *str.*; (*fig.*) flink aanspreken *str.* **punishable**, *a.* strafbaar. **punishment**, *n.* straf *n.*, bestraffing *n.*; afstraffing *n.*
punster, *n.* iemand die woordspelingen *pl.n.* maakt.
punt, *n.* platboomde schuit *n.*, pont *n.* ¶ *v.t.* voortbomen. ¶ *v.i.* in een pont varen *str.*; tegen de bank spelen. **punter**, *n.* iemand die in een pont vaart; beroepswedder *n.*
puny, *a.* klein, pieterig.
pup *n.* jonge hond *n.* ¶ *v.i.* jongen *pl.n.n.* werpen *str.*
pupa, *n.* pop *n.*
pupil, *n.* leerling *n.*; pupil *n.*; pupil *n.*, oogappel *n.* **pupillage**, *n.* onmondigheid *n.*
puppet, *n.* pop *n.*; marionet *n.*, **puppet-show**, *n.* poppenspel *n.n.*
puppy, *n.* jonge hond *n.*

purblind, *a.* halfblind.
purchase, *v.t.* kopen *irr.*, aankopen *irr.*; winden *str.*, lichten (*anchor*). ¶ *n.* aankoop *n.*; houvast *n.n.* (*grip*). **purchaser**, *n.* koper *n.* **purchasing power**, *n.* koopkracht *n.*
pure, *a.*, ~**ly**, *adv.* zuiver; echt, onvervalst.
purgation, *n.* zuivering *n.* **purgative**, *a.* zuiverend; purgerend. ¶ *n.* purgeermiddel *n.n.* **Purgatory**, *N.* Vagevuur *n.N.* **purge**, *v.t.* zuiveren; purgeren. ¶ *n.* purgatie *n.*
purification, *n.* zuivering *n.*, reiniging *n.* **purify**, *v.t.* zuiveren, reinigen. **purism**, *n.* purisme *n.n.* **purist**, *n.* purist *n.*; taalzuiveraar *n.*
Puritan, *a.* puriteins. ¶ *N.* Puritein *N.*
purity, *n.* zuiverheid *n.*, reinheid *n.*
purl, *n.* garneerkoord *n.n.* (*bordering*); averechts breiwerk *n.n.* (*knitting*); gekabbel *n.n.* (*of brook*). ¶ *v.t.* averechts breien; ronddraaien, doen *irr.* omslaan (*turn*). ¶ *v.i.* kabbelen.
purler, *n.* buiteling *n.* *to come a* ~, over de kop gaan *irr.*
purlieu, *n.* omtrek *n.* ~*s*, omgeving *n.*
purloin, *v.t.* ontvreemden, zich toeëigenen.
purple, *n.* purper *n.n.*, purperrood *n.n.* ¶ *a.* purper, purperrood.
purport, *v.t.* voorgeven *str.*, beweren. ¶ *n.* zin *n.*, strekking *n.*
purpose, *n.* doel *n.n.*; voornemen *n.n.*, plan *n.n.* *it serves no* ~, het dient tot niets; *for that* ~, te dien einde; *on* ~, met opzet *n.*; *to the* ~, ter zake; *to little* ~, met weinig succes *n.n.*; *to no* ~, tevergeefs; *to some* ~, niet tevergeefs. ¶ *v.t.* zich voornemen *str.* **purposeless**, *a.* doelloos. **purposeful**, *a.*, ~**ly**, *adv.* doelbewust. **purposely**, *adv.* met opzet *n.*
purr, *v.i.* spinnen, snorren. ¶ *n.* spinnen *n.n.*
purse, *n.* beurs *n.* ¶ *v.t.* samentrekken *str.* **purseproud**, *a.* trots op zijn geld *n.n.* **purser**, *n.* administrateur *n.*; hofmeester *n.* **purse-strings**, *pl.n.* koorden *pl.n.n.* van de beurs.
purslane, *n.* postelein *n.*
pursuance, *n.* voortzetting *n.*, vervolging *n.* *in* ~ *of*, ingevolge, naar aanleiding *n.* van. **pursuant**, *a.* overeenkomstig. ~ *to*, ingevolge. **pursue**, *v.t.* vervolgen, voortzetten; najagen *str.* *to* ~ *one's advantage*, z'n voordeel *n.n.* weten *irr.* te benutten. **pursuit**, *n.* vervolging *n.*; jacht *n.* *in* ~ *of*, op jacht naar; ~*s*, bezigheden *pl.n.*
purulence, *n.* ettering *n.* **purulent**, *a.* etterend.
purvey, *v.t.* verstrekken, verschaffen. *to* ~ *with*, voorzien *irr.* van. **purveyance**, *n.* voorziening *n.*, leverantie *n.* **purveyor**, *n.* leverancier *n.*
purview, *n.* gebied *n.n.* *within the* ~ *of*, binnen het kader van.
pus, *n.* etter *n.*
push, *v.t.* duwen, stoten *str.*; schuiven *str.*; dringen *str.* ¶ *n.* duw *n.*; aanval *n.*; ambitie *n.*, energie *n.* **push-bike**, *n.*

fiets *n.* **push-cart,** *n.* handkar *n.* **pushing,** *a.* energiek, ambitieus; indringerig.

pusillanimity, *n.* kleinmoedigheid *n.*

pusillanimous, *a.* kleinmoedig.

puss, *n.* poes *n.*

pustule, *n.* puist *n.*, puistje *n.n.*

put, *v.t.* doen *irr.*; zetten, leggen *irr.*, plaatsen; uitdrukken (*in words*); voorstellen (*proposal*). to ~ *about*, rondstrooien; to ~ *by*, op zij *n.* leggen *irr.*; to ~ *down*, neerleggen *irr.*; opschrijven *str.*; to ~ *forth*, opperen; to ~ *forward*, indienen; opperen; to ~ *off*, uitstellen; hinderen; een tegenzin *n.* geven *str.* in; to ~ *on*, aandoen *irr.* (*clothes*); aannemen *str.* (*attitude*); opvoeren (*play*); voorzetten (*clock*); to ~ *out*, uitdoen *irr.*; uitstrooien; van de wijs brengen *irr.*; to ~ *oneself out*, zich moeite getroosten; to ~ *through*, aansluiten *str.* (*telephone*); to ~ *one to it*, iemand er toe dwingen *str.*; to ~ *up*, opsteken *str.*; opzenden *str.* (*price*); onderdak *n.n.* verlenen aan; to ~ *up with*, berusten in; to be ~ *upon*, het slachtoffer zijn; to ~ *the weight*, een kogel *n.* werpen *str.* See also **put(t).**

putative, *a.* vermeend.

putrefaction, *n.* bederf *n.n.*, (ver)rotting *n.* **putrefy,** *v.i.* (ver)rotten. ¶ *v.t.* doen (ver)rotten; bederven *str.* **putrescence,** *n.* (ver)rotting *n.*; rotheid *n.* **putrid,** *a.* rot, rottend; bedorven; vreselijk slecht.

put(t), *v.i. & v.t.* golfbal *n.* bij kuiltje *n.n.* slaan *irr.*

puttee, *n.* beenwindsel *n.n.*

putter, *n.* (soort *n.n.*) kolf *n.* **putting-green,** *n.* gras *n.n.* van een golfterrein *n.n.*

putty, *n.* stopverf *n.* ¶ *v.t.* stoppen.

put-up, *a. a* ~ *job*, doorgestoken kaart *n.*

puzzle, *n.* ingewikkeld raadsel *n.n.*; legkaart *n.* ¶ *v.t.* verwarren, verbijsteren. to be ~*d about*, zich afvragen *str.* of; to ~ *out*, ontcijferen, ontwarren. ¶ *v.i.* to ~ *over*, zich het hoofd breken *str.* over. **puzzlement,** *n.* perplexheid *n.*

pygmy, *n.* dwerg *n.*

pyjamas, *pl.n.* pyjama *n.*

pyramid, *n.* pyramide *n.*

pyre, *n.* brandstapel *n.*

pyrites, *n.* pyriet *n.n.*

pyrotechnics, *pl.n.* pyrotechniek *n.*, vuurwerkkunst *n.*

pyrrhonic, *a.* pyrrhonisch, sceptisch.

python, *n.* python *n.*

pythoness, *n.* priesteres *n.* van Apollo *N.*

pyx, *n.* monstrans *x.*

Q

quack, *v.i.* kwaken. ¶ *n.* gekwaak *n.n.* (*o' bird*); kwakzalver *n.* ~ *medicine*, kwakzalversmiddel *n.n.* **quackery,** *n.* kwakzalverij *n.*

quadrangle, *n.* vierkant *n.n.*, vierhoek *n.*; binnenplein *n.n.* **quadrangular,** *a.* vierkant, vierhoekig.

quadrant, *n.* kwadrant *n.n.*

quadrate, *a.* vierkant. ¶ *v.t.* kwadrateren.

quadratic, *a.* vierkant, vierkants . . .

quadrature, *n.* kwadratuur *n.*

quadrennial, *a.* vierjarig; vierjaarlijks.

quadrilateral, *a.* vierzijdig.

quadrille, *n.* quadrille *n.*

quadroon, *n.* quadrone *n.*

quadruped, *n.* viervoetig dier *n.n.*

quadruple, *a.* viervoudig. ¶ *n.* viervoud *n.n.*, vierdubbele *n.n.* ¶ *v.t.* verviervoudigen. **quadruplet,** *n.* viertal *n.n.*; vierling *n.* (*children*).

quaff, *v.t. & v.i.* leegdrinken *str.* ¶ *n.* grote teug *n.*

quaggy, *a.* moerassig, drassig. **quagmire,** *n.* moeras *n.n.*, drasland *n.n.*

quail, *n.* kwartel *n.* ¶ *v.i.* versagen; de moed verliezen *irr.*

quaint, *a.*, ~**ly,** *adv.* zonderling, eigenaardig. **quaintness,** *n.* eigenaardigheid *n.*

quake, *v.i.* beven, sidderen. **quaking grass,** *n.* trilgras *n.n.*

qualification, *n.* hoedanigheid *n.*; bevoegdheid *n.*; beperking *n.* **qualified,** *a.* bevoegd, gediplomeerd; bekwaam; beperkt, niet zonder voorbehoud *n.n.* **qualify,** *v.i.* zich bekwamen; de bevoegdheid verwerven *str.* voor. ¶ *v.t.* nader bepalen.

qualitative, *a.* qualitatief. **quality,** *n.* eigenschap *n.*; hoedanigheid *n.*; kwaliteit *n.*; hoge stand *n.*

qualm, *n.* walging *n.*; gewetensbezwaar *n.n.* **qualmish,** *a.* misselijk.

quandary, *n.* verlegenheid *n.*, moeilijk parket *n.n.*

quantitative, *a.* quantitatief. **quantity,** *n.* hoeveelheid *n.*, kwantiteit *n. in any* ~, veel.

quantum, *n.* hoeveelheid *n.*, quantum *n.n.*

quarantine, *n.* quarantaine *n.*

quarrel, *v.i.* ruzie *n.* maken, twisten. to ~ *with* (*also:*), bezwaar *n.n.* hebben tegen. ¶ *n.* ruzie *n.*, twist *n.* **quarreller,** *n.* ruziemaker *n.*, twistzoeker *n.* **quarrelsome,** *a.* twistziek.

quarry, *n.* steengroeve *n.* (*workings*); wild *n.n.*, prooi *n.* (*prey*). **quarryman,** *n.* steenhouwer *n.*

quart, *n.* pot *n.* bier *n.n.*; 1,136 Liter. ·

quartan, *a.* vierdedaags. ~ *fever*, aerdedaagse koorts *n.*

quarter, *n.* kwart *n.n.*, vierde deel *n.n.*, vierendeel *n.n.*; kwartier *n.n.*, wijk *n.*, buurt *n.* (*of town*); kwartier *n.n.* (*of army*), kwartaal *n.n.* (*3 months*); achterstuk *n.n.* (*rump*); kwartier *n.n.*, genade *n.* (*mercy*). ~ *of an hour*, kwartier *n.n.*; *from that* ~, van die kant *n.*; *at close* ~*s*, van dichtbij. ¶ *v.t.* in vieren (ver)delen; vierendelen (*punishment*). **quarter day,** *n.* betaaldag *n.*

termijn *n.* **quarter-deck,** *n.* achterdek *n.n.*
quarterly, *a.* kwartaal . . ., driemaande-
lijks. **quarter-master,** *n.* kwartiermeester *n.*
quarfern, *n.* van vier pond *n.n.*
quartet, *n.* kwartet *n.n.*
quarto, *n.* kwarto *n.n.*
quartz, *n.* kwarts *n.n.*
quash, *v.t.* casseren, nietig verklaren.
quasi, *a.* quasi. ¶ *adv.* als het ware.
quaver, *n.* achtste noot *n.*; triller *n.*; trilling *n.*
¶ *v.t.* trillen. **quavery,** *a.* beverig.
quay, *n.* kaai *n.*, kade *n.*
queasiness, *n.* misselijkheid *n.* **queasy,** *a.*
misselijk. *a* ~ *conscience,* een over-
gevoelig geweten *n.n.*
queen, *n.* koningin *n.*; vrouw *n.* (*cards*).
¶ *v.t. to* ~ *it,* de koningin spelen **queen
bee,** *n.* bijenkoningin *n.* **queen-consort,** *n.*
gemalin *n.* van de koning *n.* **queenlike,** *a.*,
queenly, *a.* als een koningin *n.*
queer, *a.*, ~ly, *adv.* raar, vreemd, zonderling;
raar, niet lekker (*not well*). ¶ *v.t.* in de
war sturen. *to* ~ *someone's pitch,* de boel
voor iemand bederven *str.* **queerness,** *n.*
vreemdheid *n.*
quell, *v.t.* onderdrukken, bedwingen *str.*
quench, *v.t.* blussen, doven; lessen.
querulous, *a.*, ~ly, *adv.* klagerig, ontevreden.
query, *n.* vraag *n.* ¶ *v.t.* in twijfel *n.* trekken
str.
quest, *n.* zoeken *n.n.*, nasporing *n.* ~ *for,*
avontuurlijke tocht *n.* tot opsporing *n.*
van; *in* ~ *of,* op zoek naar.
question, *n.* vraag *n.*; kwestie *n.*, vraagstuk
n.n. leading ~, vraag die het antwoord
ingeeft; *it is beside the* ~, het heeft er niets
mee te maken; *it is out of the* ~, er is geen
sprake van; *to beg the* ~, een feit *n.n.* als
vanzelfsprekend aannemen *str.* ¶ *v.t.*
ondervragen *str.*; betwijfelen. **questionable,**
a. twijfelachtig; bedenkelijk. **questioner,** *n.*
ondervrager *n.* **question-mark,** *n.* vraag-
teken *n.n.*
queue, *n.* queue *n.*; rij *n.*, file *n. to form a* ~
queue maken. ¶ *v.i.* queue maken.
quibble, *v.i.* muggenziften; chicaneren. ¶ *n.*
spitsvondigheid *n.* **quibbler,** *n.* chicaneur *n.*
quick, *a.*, ~ly, *adv.* vlug, snel; levend. ¶ *n.*
levend vlees *n.n. to the* ~, tot in 't vlees;
(*fig.*) tot in de ziel. **quicken,** *v.t.* verlevendigen; verhaasten. ¶ *v.i.* levend
worden *str.*
quicklime, *n.* ongebluste kalk *n.*
quickness, *n.* vlugheid *n.*, levendigheid *n.*
quicksands, *pl.n.* drijfzand *n.n.*
quickset, *a.* levend.
quicksighted, *a.* scherpziend.
quicksilver, *n.* kwikzilver *n.*
quid, *n.* (tabaks)pruim *n.*; (*coll.*) pond *n.n.*, £.
quidnunc, *n.* nieuwsgierigaard *n.*
quiescence, *n.* kalmte *n.*, rust *n.* **quiescent,** *a.*
kalm, rustig, stil.
quiet, *a.*, ~ly, *adv.* stil (*noise*); rustig,
bedaard, kalm (*behaviour*); mak (*animal*);

gerust (*mind*); stemmig (*colour*). ¶ *n.* rust
n., stilte *n.* ¶ *v.t.* kalmeren. ¶ *v.i. to* ~
down, bedaren, kalmeren. **quieten,** *v.t. &*
v.i. kalmeren, bedaren. **quietness,** *n.*,
quietude, *n.* stilte *n.*, rust *n.*; rustigheid *n.*
quietus, *n.* kwijtschelding *n.*
quill, *n.* schacht *n.*, pen *n.*; stekel *n.* **quill-
driver,** *n.* pennelikker *n.*
quilt, *n.* gewatteerde sprei *n.* ¶ *v.t.* watteren.
quince, *n.* kweepeer *n.*
quinine, *n.* kinine *n.*
quinquennial, *a.* vijfjarig; vijfjaarlijks.
quinsy, *n.* angina *n.*
quint, *n.* kwint *n.*, quint *n.*
quintal, *n.* centenaar *n.*, 100 pond *n.n.*
quintessence, *n.* wezen *n.n.*, kern *n.*
quintet, *n.* kwintet *n.n.*, quintet *n.n.*
quintuple, *n.* vijfvoudig. ¶ *n.* vijfvoud *n.n.*
¶ *v.t.* vervijfvoudigen.
quip, *n.* kwinkslag *n.*, geestigheid *n.*
quire, *n.* boek *n.n.*, 24 vel *n.n.*
quirk, *n.* streek *n.*, rare gewoonte *n.*
quit, *v.t. & v.i.* verlaten *str.* ¶ *a.* vrij.
quite, *adv.* helemaal, geheel; nogal. ~ *so,*
precies.
quits, *adv.* quitte, kiet.
quittance, *n.* kwijtschelding *n.*; voldoening *n.*
quiver, *v.i.* siddaren, trillen. ¶ *n.* siddering *n.*;
pijlkoker *n.* **quiverful,** *n.* koker *n.* vol;
hele boel *n.*
Quixote, *N.* Quichotte *N.* **quixotic,** *a.*
Donquichotachtig. **quixotism,** *n.* Don-
quichoterie *n.*
quiz, *v.t.* voor de gek houden *irr.* ¶ *n.*
vragenspel *n.n.*
quoit, *n.* werpschijf *n.*, werpring *n.*
quorum, *n.* voldoend aantal *n.n.* leden *pl.n.n.*
quota, *n.* quotum *n.n.*; aandeel *n.n.*
quotation, *n.* aanhaling *n.*, citaat *n.n.*;
prijsnotering *n.* **quote,** *v.t.* aanhalen,
citeren; noteren. ¶ *n.* aanhaling *n.*,
citaat *n.n.*
quoth, *v.t.* zei(de), sprak.
quotient, *n.* quotiënt *n.*

R

rabbi, *n.* rabbijn *n.* **rabbinical,** *a.* rabbijns.
rabbit, *n.* konijn *n.n. See* rarebit. **rabbity,** *a.*
konijnachtig.
rabble, *n.* grauw *n.n.*, gepeupel *n.n.*; bende *n.*
rabid, *a.* dol; heftig.
rabies, *n.* hondsdolheid *n.*
race, *n.* ras *n.n.* (*people*); geslacht *n.n.*
(*family*); wedren *n.*, wedloop *n.*, wedstrijd
n. (*match*); loop *n.* (*course*); beek *n.* (*water*).
¶ *v.i.* rennen; hard lopen *str.* ¶ *v.t.* om
het hardst lopen *str.* met. **race course,** *n.*
renbaan *n.* **racer,** *n.* renner *n.*; renpaard
n.n. **raciness,** *n.* pittigheid *n.*
rack, *n.* rek *n.n.*; ruif *n.*; netje *n.n.*; pijnbank
n. to go to ~ *and ruin,* ten gronde gaan *irr.*

¶ *v.t.* folteren, pijnigen. *to ~ one's brain*, zich het hoofd breken *str.*

racket, *n.* raket *n.n.*; (*coll.*) lawaai *n.n.*, kabaal *n.n.* (*noise*). ¶ *v.i.* kabaal maken. **rackety**, *a.* lawaaierig.

racoon, *n.* wasbeer *n.*

racy, *a.* pittig.

radiance, *n.* glans *n.* **radiant**, *a.* stralend. **radiate**, *v.i.* uitstralen, bestralen. ¶ *v.i.* stralen. **radiation**, *n.* uitstraling *n.*, bestraling *n.* **radiator**, *n.* radiateur *n.*, radiator *n.*

radical, *a.*, ~ly, *adv.* radikaal, ingrijpend; wortel ... ¶ *n.* wortel *n.*; radikaal *n.*

radio, *n.* radio *n.* **radio-active**, *a.* radioactief. **radiogram**, *n.* radiogram *n.* **radiograph**, *n.* radiografie *n.* **radiolocation**, *n.* radioplaatsbepaling *n.*

radish, *n.* radijs *n.* *black ~*, ramenas *n.*

radium, *n.* radium *n.n.*

radius, *n.* straal *n.*; kring *n.*

raffle, *v.t.* verloten. ¶ *n.* verloting *n.*

raft, *n.* vlot *n.n.* ¶ *v.t.* vlotten.

rafter, *n.* dakspar *n.*

raftsman, *n.* vlotter *n.*

rag, *n.* vod *n.n.*, lomp *n.*; lapje *n.n.*; studentenjool *n. in ~s*, in lompen, aan flarden *pl.n.* ¶ *v.t.* plagen. ¶ *v.i.* jool *n.* maken. **ragamuffin**, *n.* schooiertje *n.n.*, schoftje *n.n.*

rage, *n.* woede *n.*; rage *n.* (*fashion*). ¶ *v.i.* woeden, razen, tieren.

ragged, *a.* haveloos; gescheurd. **ragtag**, *a. ~ and bobtail*, janhagel *n.n.* **ragtime**, *n.* gesyncopeerde maat *n.* **ragwheel**, *n.* tandrad *n.n.*

raid, *n.* strooptocht *n.*, overval *n.*; razzia *n.* ¶ *v.t.* overvallen *str.* **raider**, *n.* deelnemer *n.* aan een overval *n.*; kaperschip *n.n.*

rail, *n.* leuning *n.*; rail *n.*, spoorstaaf *n. by ~*, per spoor *n.n.* ¶ *v.i. to ~ at*, schimpen op. **railhead**, *n.* eindstation *n.n.* **railing**, *n.* reling *n.* (*ship's*); hekwerk *n.n.*; geschimp *n.n.* (*jeering*). **railroad**, *n. See* **railway**. **railway**, *n.* spoorweg *n.*; spoor ... **railway-guard**, *n.* (trein)conducteur *n.* **railway-guide**, *n.* (spoor)gids *n.*, spoorboekje *n.n.*

raiment, *n.* dos *n.*, gewaad *n.n.*

rain, *n.* regen *n.* ¶ *v.t. & v.i.* regenen. *it never ~s but it pours*, een ongeluk *n.n.* komt zelden alleen; *to ~ cats and dogs*, slagregenen. **rainbow**, *n.* regenboog *n.* **rainfall**, *n.* regenval *n.*, neerslag *n.* **rainy**, *a.* regenachtig.

raise, *v.t.* opheffen *str.*; verhogen; rechtop zetten; lichten (*ship*); oproepen *str.* (*spirits*); opslaan *irr.* (*eyes*); opwerpen *str.* (*objections*); opwekken (*from death*); telen, fokken (*cattle*); grootbrengen *irr.* (*family*). ¶ *n.* verhoging *n.*

raisin, *n.* rozijn *n.*

rake, *n.* hark *n.*; losbol *n.*, lichtmis *n.* ¶ *v.t.* harken; rakelen (*fire*); enfileren (*firing*).

to ~ in, opstrijken *str.* **rakish**, *a.*, ~ly, *adv.* zwierig.

rally, *v.t.* samentrekken *str.*, verzamelen. ¶ *v.i.* weer op krachten *pl.n.* komen *irr.* ¶ *n.* hereniging *n.*; bijeenkomst *n.*

ram, *n.* ram *n.*; rammei *n.* (*instrument*). ¶ *v.t.* rammen; rammeien.

ramble, *v.i.* ronddolen. *to ~ from*, afdwalen van. ¶ *n.* zwerftocht *n.* **rambler**, *n.* klimroos *n.* **rambling**, *a.* verward, onsamenhangend; onregelmatig.

ramification, *n.* vertakking *n.* **ramify**, *v.t.* vertakken.

rammer, *n.* heiblok *n.n.*

ramp, *n.* helling *n.*; zwendelarij *n.*

rampage, *v.t.* als een dolle *n.* te keer gaan *irr.*

rampant, *a.* klimmend (*heraldry*); algemeen, heersend.

rampart, *n.* wal *n.*, bolwerk *n.n.*

rampion, *n.* rapunzel *n.*

ramrod, *n.* laadstok *n.*

ramshackle, *a.* bouwvallig.

ranch, *n.* veehouderij *n.* **rancher**, *n.* veefokker *n.*

rancid, *a.* ranzig, sterk. **rancidity**, *n.* ranzigheid *n.*

rancorous, *a.*, ~ly, *adv.* haatdragend, bitter. **rancour**, *n.* wrok *n.*, rancune *n.*

random, *n. at ~*, op goed geluk *n.n.* af, in den blinde. ¶ *a.* lukraak.

range, *n.* rij *n.*; aaneenschakeling *n.*; keten *n.*; schietbaan *n.*; fornuis *n.n.*; graasland *n.n.*; omvang *n.*; draagwijdte *n.*; gebied *n.n. out of ~*, buiten schot *n.n.* ¶ *v.t.* zwerven *str.*, dwalen. *to ~ oneself*, zich scharen. **range-finder**, *n.* afstandsmeter *n.* **ranger**, *n.* jager *n.*; houtvester *n.*

rank, *n.* rang *n.*; gelid *n.n.*; standplaats *n. the ~ and file*, de grote hoop; *to be reduced to the ~s*, gedegradeerd worden *str.* ¶ *v.i.* indelen, plaatsen. *to ~ with*, gelijk staan *irr.* met; *to ~ next to*, onmiddellijk volgen op. ¶ *a.* weelderig, welig; stinkend; absoluut. *~ nonsense*, je reinste onzin *n.*

rankle, *v.i.* zweren *str.*; knagen.

rankness, *n.* weligheid *n.*

ransack, *v.t.* plunderen; doorzoeken *irr.*

ransom, *n.* losgeld *n.n.*, afkoopsom *n.* ¶ *v.t.* vrijkopen *irr.*

rant, *v.i.* hoogdravend spreken *str.*

ranunculus, *n.* ranonkel *n.*

rap, *v.i.* tikken, kloppen. ¶ *n.* tik *n.*

rapacious, *a.*, ~ly, *adv.* roofgierig, hebzuchtig. **rapacity**, *n.* roofzucht *n.*, hebzucht *n.*

rape, *v.t.* verkrachten. ¶ *n.* verkrachting *n.*

rapeseed, *n.* raapzaad *n.n.*, koolzaad *n.n.*

rapid, *a.*, ~ly, *adv.* snel. ¶ *n.* stroomversnelling *n.* **rapidity**, *n.* snelheid *n.*

rapier, *n.* rapier *n.n.*

rapping spirit, *n.* klopgeest *n.*

rapt, *a.* verrukt. **rapture**, *n.* verrukking *n.* **rapturous**, *a.* verrukt, opgetogen.

rare, *a.* zeldzaam; buitengewoon; ijl, dun.

rarebit, *n.* geroosterde kaas *n.* op toast *n.*
raree-show, *n.* rarekiek *n.*
rarefaction, *n.* verdunning *n.* **rarefy,** *v.t.* verdunnen.
rarely, *adv.* zelden. **rareness,** *n.*, **rarity,** *n.* zeldzaamheid *n.*
rascal, *n.* schelm *n.*, schavuit *n.* **rascality,** *n.* schelmenstreek *n.*; schelmerij *n.* **rascally,** *a.* schelms.
rash, *a.*, ~**ly,** *adv.* onbezonnen, overijld. ¶ *n.* uitslag *n.*
rasher, *n.* sneetje *n.n.* spek *n.n.*
rashness, *n.* onbezonnenheid *n.*, overijling *n.*
rasp, *n.* rasp *n.* ¶ *v.t.* raspen. ¶ *v.i.* knarsen, krassen.
raspberry, *n.* framboos *n.*
rat, *n.* rat *n.* *to smell a* ~, lont *n.* ruiken *str.* ¶ *v.i.* ratten *pl.n.* vangen *str.*; (*coll.*) ervandoor gaan *irr.*
ratable, *a.* schatbaar, belastbaar.
ratchet, *n.* pal *n.*
rate, *n.* graad *n.*, mate *n.*; prijs *n.*; vaart *n.*; (gemeente)belasting *n.* ~ *of exchange,* wisselkoers *n.*; ~ *of interest,* rentevoet *n.*; ~ *of pay,* loonstandaard *n.*; *at any* ~, in elk geval *n.n.* ¶ *v.t.* berekenen; aanslaan *irr.*, taxeren; berispen. ¶ *v.i.* gerekend worden *str.* **ratepayer,** *n.* belastingbetaler *n.*
rather, *adv.* nogal, tamelijk; liever, eerder; en of!
ratification, *n.* bekrachtiging *n.*, ratificatie *n.* **ratify,** *v.t.* bekrachtigen, ratificeren.
rating, *n.* aanslag *n.*; rang *n.*; niet-officier *n.*
ratio, *n.* verhouding *n.*
ration, *n.* rantsoen *n.n.* ¶ *v.t.* rantsoeneren.
rational, *a.*, ~**ly,** *adv.* redelijk; verstandelijk. **rationalism,** *n.* rationalisme *n.n.* **rationalization,** *n.* verstandelijke verklaring *n.* **rationalize,** *v.t.* een redelijke verklaring vinden *str.* voor . . .
rationing, *n.* distributie *n.*
rattan, *n.* rottan *n.* or *n.n.*
rattle, *n.* ratel *n.*; ratelaar *n.* (*toy*); geratel *n.n.* ¶ *v.t.* ratelen, rammelen. **rattlesnake,** *n.* ratelslang *n.* **rattling,** *a.* drommels.
raucous, *a.* hees, schor.
ravage, *n.* verwoesting *n.* *the* ~*s of time,* de tand des tijds. ¶ *v.t.* verwoesten; plunderen.
rave, *v.i.* ijlen; razen.
ravel, *n.* rafel *n.* ¶ *v.i.* rafelen.
raven, *n.* raaf *n.* ¶ *a.* gitzwart.
ravenous, *a.*, ~**ly,** *adv.* vraatzuchtig; uitgehongerd.
ravine, *n.* ravijn *n.n.*
raving, *n.* ~*s,* ijlen *n.n.*; geraaskal *n.n.* ¶ *a.* dol.
ravish, *v.t.* ontvoeren; ontroven; meeslepen; verrukken. **ravisher,** *n.* ontvoerder *n.* **ravishing,** *a.* verrukkelijk. **ravishment,** *n.* verrukking *n.*
raw, *a.* rauw, ongekookt; ruw, onbewerkt;

onbedreven. ~ *materials,* grondstoffen *pl.n.* **rawness,** *n.* rauwheid *n.*; ruwheid *n.*
ray, *n.* straal *n.* (*light*); rog *n.* (*fish*).
raze, *v.t.* slechten. *to* ~ *to the ground,* met de grond gelijk maken.
razor, *n.* scheermes *n.n.* **razor-bill,** *n.* alk *n.* **razor-strop,** *n.* aanzetriem *n.*
re, *n.* re *n.* (*note*). ¶ *prep.* betreffende.
reach, *v.t.* bereiken; toereiken. ¶ *v.i.* reiken; zich uitstrekken. ¶ *n.* bereik *n.n.*; omvang *n.*; rak *n.n.* (*river*), pand *n.n.* (*canal*). *within* ~ *of,* binnen het bereik van; *out of* ~, niet te bereiken.
react, *v.i.* reageren; terugwerken. *to* ~ *against,* ingaan *irr.* tegen. **reaction,** *n.* reactie *n.* **reactionary,** *a.* reactionnair.
read, *v.i.* lezen *str.* ¶ *v.t.* lezen *str.*; doorzien *irr.*; verklaren. *to* ~ *law,* in de rechten *pl.n.n.* studeren. **readable,** *a.* leesbaar. **reader,** *n.* lezer *n.*; lector *n.*; adviseur *n.* (*of publisher*).
readily, *adv.* grif, geredelijk; gemakkelijk. **readiness,** *n.* gereedheid *n.*; bereidwilligheid *n.*
reading, *n.* lezing *n.*; lectuur *n.* **reading-room,** *n.* leeszaal *n.*
re-adjourn, *v.t.* opnieuw verdagen.
readjust, *v.t.* opnieuw regelen.
readmission, *n.* wedertoelating *n.* **readmit,** *v.t.* opnieuw toelaten *str.*
ready, *a.* gereed; klaar; bereid; bij de hand. ~ *money,* contant geld *n.n.*; ~ *wit,* gevatheid *n.* **ready-made,** *a.* confectie-.
reagent, *n.* reagens *n.*, reageermiddel *n.n.*
real, *a.*, ~**ly,** *adv.* echt; werkelijk. **realism,** *n.* realisme *n.n.* **reality,** *n.* werkelijkheid *n.* **realization,** *n.* verwezenlijking *n.*; bewustzijn *n.n.*, besef *n.n.* **realize,** *v.t.* beseffen, zich voorstellen; realiseren, te gelde maken; opbrengen *irr.* **really,** *adv.* werkelijk, waarlijk.
realm, *n.* (konink)rijk *n.n.*
ream, *n.* riem *n.*
reap, *v.t.* oogsten, maaien. **reaper,** *n.* oogster *n.*, maaier *n.*; maaimachine *n.* **reaping-hook,** *n.* sikkel *n.*, zicht *n.*
reappear, *v.i.* opnieuw verschijnen *str.* **reappearance,** *n.* opnieuw verschijnen *n.n.*
rear, *n.* achterhoede *n.*; achterkant *n.*; achterste *n.n.* ¶ *v.t.* grootbrengen *irr.*, opkweken. ¶ *v.i.* steigeren. **rear-admiral,** *n.* schout-bij-nacht *n.* **rearguard,** *n.* achterhoede *n.*
reason, *n.* reden *n.*; rede *n.*, verstand *n.n.*; billijkheid *n.* *by* ~ *of,* wegens, van wege; *it stands to* ~, het spreekt vanzelf; *within* ~, redelijk. ¶ *v.t. & v.i.* redeneren, beredeneren. **reasonable,** *a.* redelijk. **reasonably,** *adv.* redelijk, redelijkerwijs **reasoning,** *n.* redenering *n.*
reassemble, *v.t.* weer bijeenbrengen *irr* ¶ *v.i.* weer bijeenkomen *irr.*
reassert, *v.t.* weer doen *irr.* gelden.

reassure, *v.t.* gerust stellen.
rebate, *n.* rabat *n.n.*, korting *n.*
rebel, *n.* oproerling *n.* ¶ *a.* oproerig, opstandig. **re·bel**, *v.i.* in opstand komen *irr.* **rebellion**, *n.* opstand *n.* **rebellious**, *a.*, ~ly, *adv.* opstandig, oproerig.
rebore, *v.t.* uitslijpen *str.*
rebound, *v.i.* terugstuiten. ¶ *n.* weeromstuit *n.*
rebuff, *v.t.* afstoten *irr.*, afwijzen *str.* ¶ *n.* afwijzing *n.*; weigering *n.*
rebuild, *v.t.* herbouwen, weer opbouwen.
rebuke, *v.t.* terechtwijzen *str.*, berispen. ¶ *n.* terechtwijzing *n.*, berisping *n.*
rebus, *n.* rebus *n.*
rebut, *v.t.* terugslaan *irr.*, afstoten *irr.*
recalcitrance, *n.* weerbarstigheid *n.* **recalcitrant**, *a.* weerbarstig.
recall, *v.t.* terugroepen *str.*; zich herinneren; herroepen *str.*, intrekken *str.* ¶ *n.* terugroeping *n.* *beyond* ~, onherroepelijk.
recant, *v.i.* zijn woorden terugnemen *str.*; zijn dwaalleer *n.* afzweren *str.* **recantation**, *n.* herroeping *n.*, afzwering *n.*
recapitulate, *v.t.* samenvatten, in 't kort herhalen. **recapitulation**, *n.* samenvatting *n.*
recapture, *v.t.* heroveren; weer gevangen nemen *str.* ¶ *n.* herovering *n.*
recast, *v.t.* opnieuw gieten *str.*; omwerken.
recede, *v.i.* teruglopen *str.*
receipt, *n.* ontvangst *n.*; reçu *n.n.*, kwitantie *n.*; recept *n.n.* ¶ *v.t.* kwiteren.
receivable, *a.* ontvangbaar. **receive**, *v.t.* ontvangen *str.*; helen (*stolen property*). **receiver**, *n.* ontvanger *n.*; hoorn *n.* (*telephone*); heler *n.* *official* ~, curator *n.*
recent, *a.* recent. **recently**, *adv.* onlangs, kort geleden.
receptacle, *n.* vat *n.n.*; vergaarbak *n.*
reception, *n.* ontvangst *n.*; receptie *n.* **receptive**, *a.* ontvankelijk.
recess, *n.* alkoof *n.*; opschorting *n.*, vacantie *n.* **recession**, *n.* achteruitgang *n.*; teruglopen *n.n.*
recipe, *n.* recept *n.n.*
recipient, *n.* ontvanger *n.*
reciprocal, *a.*, ~ly, *adv.* wederkerig, wederzijds. **reciprocate**, *v.i.* een wederdienst *n.* bewijzen *str.* ¶ *v.t.* beantwoorden. **reciprocation**, *n.* beantwoording *n.* **reciprocity**, *n.* wederkerigheid *n.*
recital, *n.* opsomming *n.*, verhaal *n.n.*; concert *n.n.* **recitation**, *n.* voordracht *n.* **recitative**, *n.* recitatief *n.n.* **recite**, *v.t.* voordragen *str.*, opsommen.
reckless, *a.*, ~ly, *adv.* roekeloos; vermetel. **recklessness**, *n.* roekeloosheid *n.*; vermetelheid *n.*
reckon, *v.t.* rekenen; berekenen. ¶ *v.i.* rekenen. *to* ~ *with*, rekening houden *irr.* met. **reckoner**, *n.* rekenaar *n.* **reckoning**, *n.* afrekening *n.*; gissing *n.*, bestek *n.n.* (*at sea*).

reclaim, *v.t.* herwinnen *str.*; op het rechte pad brengen *irr.*; ontginnen *str.*, drooglegggen. **reclaimable**, *a.* ontginbaar.
reclamation, *n.* eis *n.*, vordering *n.*; ontginning *n.*, drooglegging *n.*
recline, *v.i.* achteroverleunen; rusten.
recluse, *n.* kluizenaar *n.*
recognition, *n.* erkenning *n.* (*fact*); herkenning *n.* (*person*). *in* ~ *of*, ter erkenning van.
recognizance, *n.* borgtocht *n.*
recognize, *v.t.* erkennen; herkennen.
recoil, *v.i.* terugspringen *str.*; terugdeinzen. ¶ *n.* terugstoot *n.*
recollect, *v.t.* zich herinneren. ¶ *v.i.* het zich herinneren. **recollection**, *n.* herinnering *n.*
recommend, *v.t.* aanbevelen *str.* **recommendable**, *a.* aanbevelenswaardig. **recommendation**, *n.* aanbeveling *n.* **recommendatory**, *a.* aanbevelings ...
recompense, *v.t.* belonen; vergoeden. ¶ *n.* beloning *n.*; vergoeding *n.*
reconcilable, *a.* verzoenbaar, verenigbaar. **reconcile**, *v.t.* verzoenen; doen *irr.* overeenstemmen. **reconciliation**, *n.* verzoening *n.*
recondite, *a.* verborgen, diepzinnig.
reconnaissance, *n.* verkenning *n.* ¶ *a.* verkennings ...
reconnoitre, *v.t.* verkennen. ¶ *v.i.* het terrein verkennen.
reconsider, *v.t.* opnieuw overwegen *str.*
reconstruct, *v.t.* opnieuw bouwen, herbouwen, reconstrueren. **reconstruction**, *n.* wederopbouw *n.*; reconstructie *n.*; herstel *n.n.*
re·cord, *v.t.* opschrijven *str.*; te boek stellen. **·record**, *n.* document *n.n.*; (officeel) stuk *n.n.* gramofoonplaat *n.*; record *n.n.* (*sport*). ~ *of service*, dienststaat *n.* **recorder**, *n.* griffier *n.* **record office**, *n.* rijksarchief *n.n.*
recount, *v.t.* verhalen; overtellen.
recoup, *v.t.* weer goed maken. ¶ *v.r. to* ~ *oneself for*, zich schadeloos stellen voor.
recourse, *n.* *to have* ~ *to*, toevlucht *n.* nemen *str.* tot.
recover, *v.i.* herstellen, beter worden *str.*; zich herstellen. ¶ *v.t.* herwinnen *str.*, herkrijgen *str.*; droogleggen; weer bedekken *to* ~ *one's breath*, weer op adem komen *irr.* **recoverable**, *a.* verhaalbaar. **recovery**, *n.* herstel *n.n.* *past* ~, onherstelbaar; ongeneeslijk.
recreant, *a.* lafhartig.
re-create, *v.t.* herscheppen *str.* **recreation**, *n.* ontspanning *n.*
recrimination, *n.* tegenbeschuldiging *n.*; verwijt *n.n.*
recrudescence, *n.* opleving *n.*, weer uitbreken *n.n.*
recruit, *v.t.* recruteren, aanwerven *str.*; herstellen, versterken. ¶ *n.* rekruut *n.* **recruitment**, *n.* recrutering *n.*
rectangle, *n.* rechthoek *n.* **rectangular**, *a.* rechthoekig.
rectifiable, *a.* te verbeteren, te herstellen. **rectification**, *n.* verbetering *n.*; rectificatie

n. **rectify,** *v.t.* verbeteren, herstellen; rectificeren, zuiveren.

rectilinear, *a.* rechtlijnig.

rectitude, *n.* rechtschapenheid *n.*; juistheid *n.*

rector, *n.* predikant *n.* **rectory,** *n.* predikants-woning *n.*

recumbent, *a.* achteroverleunend; rustend.

recuperate, *v.t.* herstellen. ¶ *v.i.* weer op krachten *pl. n.* komen *irr.*

recur, *v.i.* zich weer voordoen *irr.*; repeteren (*fraction*). to ~ to, terugkomen *irr.* op.

recurrence, *n.* herhaling *n.*, terugkeer *n.*

recurrent, *a.* zich herhalend, terugkerend; repeterend.

recusant, *n.* weigeraar *n.*

red, *a.* rood. ~ *deer*, edelhert *n.n.*; ~ *herring*, iets wat de aandacht afleidt; ~ *lead*, menie *n.*; ~ *mullet*, zeebarbeel *n.*; ~ *rag*, rode lap *n.*; ~ *tape*, bureaucratie *n.* ¶ *n.* rood *n.n.* a ~, een rooie (*political*).

redaction, *n.* opstellen *n.n.*

redden, *v.t.* rood maken. ¶ *v.i.* rood worden *str.*; blozen, een kleur *n.* krijgen *str.*

reddish, *a.* roodachtig.

redeem, *v.t.* aflossen; vervullen. **redeemable,** *a.* aflosbaar. **Redeemer,** *N.* Verlosser *N.*, Heiland *N.* **redemption,** *n.* aflossing *n.*; redding *n.*

red-haired, *a.* roodharig. **red-handed,** *a.* to be caught ~, op heterdaad betrapt worden *str.* **red-hot,** *a.* gloeiend heet.

redirect, *v.t.* nazenden *str.*

red-letter, *a.* ~ *day*, gelukkige dag *n.* **redness,** *n.* roodheid *n.*

redolence, *n.* welriekendheid *n.* **redolent,** *a.* welriekend. ~ *of*, bezwangerd met.

redouble, *v.t.* verdubbelen.

redoubt, *n.* redoute *n.*

redoubtable, *a.* geducht.

redound, *v.i.* strekken. *it ~s to his credit*, het strekt hem tot eer *n.*

redress, *v.t.* herstellen, goedmaken. ¶ *n.* herstel *n.n.*, redres *n.n.*

reduce, *v.t.* terugbrengen *irr.*; herleiden; brengen *irr.*; klein krijgen *str.*; reduceren. *in ~d circumstances,* aan lager wal *n.*, verarmd. **reducible,** *a.* reduceerbaar, herleidbaar. **reduction,** *n.* reductie *n.*; prijsvermindering *n.*; verlaging *n.*; inkrimping *n.*; bedwinging *n.*

redundancy, *n.* overtolligheid *n.* **redundant** *a.* overtollig.

reduplicate, *v.t.* verdubbelen.

reed, *n.* riet *n.n.*, rietstengel *n.* *broken* ~, iemand waar men niet op aan kan. **reed-bed,** *n.* rietveld *n.n.* **reed-grass,** *n.* pijlriet *n.n.* **reed-warbler,** *n.* karekiet *n.*, rietvink *n.* **reedy,** *a.* rietachtig; schraal.

reef, *n.* klip *n.*, rif *n.n.* (*rock*); reef *n.n.*, rif *n.n.* (*in sail*). ¶ *v.t.* reven. **reefer,** *n.* jekker *n.* **reef-knot,** *n.* platte knoop *n.*

reek, *n.* sterke lucht *n.*, stank *n.* ¶ *v.i.* to ~ *with*, sterk ruiken *str.* naar.

reel, *n.* haspel *n.*, klos *n.*; filmrol *n.*; (soort)

dans *n.* ¶ *v.t.* haspelen, winden *str.* to ~ off, afdraaien; aan één stuk opnoemen; *it made my brain* ~, het deed me duizelen. ¶ *v.i.* wankelen.

re-elect, *v.t.* herkiezen *irr.* **re-election,** *n.* herkiezing *n.*

re-eligible, *a.* herkiesbaar.

re-establish, *v.t.* herstellen, weer oprichten.

reeve, *n.* baljuw *n.*

refectory, *n.* eetzaal *n.*

refer, *v.t.* to ~ to, verwijzen *str.* naar; betrekking *n.* hebben op; raadplegen. ¶ *v.i.* to ~ to, zich beroepen *str.* op; zinspelen op. **referee,** *n.* scheidsrechter *n.* **reference,** *n.* verwijzing *n.*; referentie *n.* (*recommendation*). *with* ~ *to*, met betrekking *n.* tot. **reference book,** *n.* boek *n.n.* om iets in na te slaan *irr.*, handboek *n.n.* **reference library,** *n.* bibliotheek *n.* van handboeken.

refill, *v.t.* opnieuw vullen. ¶ *n.* nieuwe vulling *n.*

refine, *v.t.* verfijnen; raffineren, zuiveren. **refined,** *a.* gezuiverd; geraffineerd; verfijnd (*fig.*). **refinement,** *n.* raffinage *n.*; verfijning *n.* (*fig.*). **refiner,** *n.* raffinadeur *n.*; verfijner *n.* (*fig.*). **refinery,** *n.* raffinaderij *n.*

refit, *v.t.* opnieuw uitrusten; repareren.

reflect, *v.t.* weerkaatsen, weerspiegelen; overpeinzen. *~ed glory*, ontleende luister *n.* ¶ *v.i.* overpeinzen, nadenken *irr.*; een blaam *n.* werpen *str.* op. **reflection,** *n.* terugkaatsing *n.*; weerspiegeling *n.*; overdenking *n.*; verwijt *n.n.*, critiek *n.* **reflective,** *a.* nadenkend; bespiegelend. **reflector,** *n.* reflector *n.*, reflecteur *n.*

reflex, *n.* reflexbeweging *n.* **reflexive,** *a.* wederkerend.

reform, *v.t.* hervormen. ¶ *v.i.* zich verbeteren. ¶ *n.* hervorming *n.*; verbetering *n.* **reformation,** *n.* hervorming *n.*; verbetering *n.* **reformatory,** *a.* verbeterings . . . ¶ *n.* tuchtschool *n.*, verbeteringsgesticht *n.n.* **reformed,** *a.* hervormd; gereformeerd. **reformer,** *n.* hervormer *n.*

refract, *v.t.* breken *str.* **refraction,** *n.* (straal)-breking *n.*

refractoriness, *n.* weerbarstigheid *n.* **refractory,** *a.*, ~*ily*, *adv.* weerbarstig, weerspannig; vuurvast.

refrain, *v.t.* in toom houden *irr.*, beteugelen. ¶ *v.i.* zich bedwingen *str.* to ~ *from*, zich onthouden *irr.* van. ¶ *n.* refrein *n.n.*

refresh, *v.t.* verfrissen; verversen. **refresher,** *n.* opfrissing *n.* **refreshing,** *a.* opwekkend; verfrissend. **refreshment,** *n.* verversing *n.* **refreshment room,** *n.* restauratie *n.*, buffet *n.n.*

refrigerate, *v.t.* verkoelen; bevriezen *irr.* **refrigerator,** *n.* ijskast *n.*; koelkamer *n.*

refuge, *n.* toevlucht *n.*; vluchtheuvel *n.* (*traffic*). **refugee,** *n.* vluchteling *n.*, refugié *n.*

refulgence, *n.* glans *n.* **refulgent,** *a.* stralend.

refund, *v.t.* terugbetalen, rembourseren. ¶ *n.* terugbetaling *n.*, rembours(ement) *n.n.*

refusal, *n.* weigering *n.*; afwijzing *n.* re·fuse, *v.t.* weigeren; afwijzen *str.* ¶ *v.i.* weigeren. ·refuse, *n.* vuilnis *n.*, afval *n.*

refutation, *n.* weerlegging *n.* refute, *v.t.* weerleggen.

regain, *v.t.* herwinnen *str.*

regal, *a.*, ~ly, *adv.* koninklijk, vorstelijk.

regale, *v.t.* onthalen. ¶ *v.r. to ~ oneself with,* zich te goed doen *irr.* aan.

regalia, *pl.n.* tekenen *pl.n.n.* der waardigheid *n.*; insignes *pl.n.n. in full ~,* in vol ornaat *n.n.*

regard, *v.t.* beschouwen; achten; betreffen *str.,* aangaan *irr. as ~s,* wat betreft. ¶ *n.* opzicht *n.n.*; aanzien *n.n. to have ~ to,* achting *n.* hebben voor; *kind ~s,* vriendelijke groeten *pl.n.*; *in this ~,* in dit opzicht; *in ~ to,* te aanzien van; *without ~ to,* zonder rekening *n.* te houden *irr.* met. **regarding,** *adv.* betreffende, met betrekking *n.* tot. **regardless,** *a.* achteloos, onachtzaam. *~ of,* niet lettend op, onverschillig voor.

regatta, *n.* roeiwedstrijd *n.*, zeilwedstrijd *n.*

regency, *n.* regentschap *n.n.*

regenerate, *a.* herboren. ¶ *v.t.* herscheppen *str.,* doen *irr.* herleven. **regeneration,** *n.* wedergeboorte *n.*

regent, *n.* regent *n.*; regentes *n. (female).*

regicide, *n.* koningsmoord *n. (act);* koningsmoorder *n. (person).*

regime, *n.* regime *n.n.*, reglem *n.n.*

regimen, *n.* bewind *n.n.*; leefregel *n.*

regiment, *n.* regiment *n.n.* **regimental,** *a.* regiments . . . *~s,* uniform *n.n.* or

region, *n.* streek *n.*, gewest *n.n.*, gebied *n.n.* **regional,** *a.* gewestelijk.

register, *n.* register *n.n.*; (kiezers)lijst *n.* ¶ *v.t.* inschrijven *str.,* registreren; aantekenen *(letter).* ¶ *v.i.* zich laten *str.* inschrijven. **register ton,** *n.* register ton *n.* (2,8316 M³). **registered,** *a.* aangetekend.

registrar, *n.* ambtenaar *n.* van de burgerlijke stand; secretaris *n.* **registration,** *n.* inschrijving *n.*, **registry,** *n.* inschrijving *n.* *~ office,* bureau *n.n.* van de burgerlijke stand; kantoor *n.n.* van registratie *n.*

regret, *v.t.* betreuren; spijt *n.* hebben van. *I ~ to say,* het spijt me te moeten zeggen. ¶ *n.* spijt *n.*, leedwezen *n.n.*; berouw *n.n. with ~,* tot mijn spijt. **regretful,** *a.* vol spijt *n.*, vol berouw *n.n.* **regrettable,** *a.,* ~bly, *adv.* betreurenswaardig.

regular, *a.,* ~ly, *adv.* geregeld, regelmatig; vast; *(coll.)* echt. *~ army,* staand leger *n.n.* ¶ *n.* vaste klant *n. ~s,* geregelde troepen *pl.n.* **regularity,** *n.* regelmaat *n.*; gelijkmatigheid *n.* **regularization,** *n.* regeling *n.* **regularize,** *v.t.* regelen, regulariseren.

regulate, *v.t.* regelen. **regulation,** *n.* regeling

n.; reglement *n.n.*, verordening *n.*, voorschrift *n.n.* ¶ *a.* model . . .; voorgeschreven.

regulator, *n.* regelaar *n.*, regulateur *n.*

regurgitate, *v.t.* weer uitbraken. **regurgitation,** *n.* wederuitbraking *n.*

rehabilitate, *v.t.* rehabiliteren; herstellen. **rehabilitation,** *n.* rehabilitatie *n.*; herstel *n.n.*

rehearsal, *n.* repetitie *n.*; verhaal *n.n. dress ~,* grote repetitie. **rehearse,** *v.t.* repeteren.

reign, *n.* regering *n.*; gezag *n.n.*, macht *n. in the ~ of,* onder de regering van. ¶ *v.i.* regeren; heersen; heersend zijn.

reimburse, *v.t.* vergoeden, rembourseren. **reimbursement,** *n.* vergoeding *n.*, rembours(ement) *n.*

rein, *n.* teugel *n.*; leidsel *n.n.* ¶ *v.t.* teugelen; intomen; beteugelen. *to give a horse the ~(s),* een paard *n.n.* de vrije teugel geven *str.*

reindeer, *n.* rendier *n.n.*

reinforce, *v.t.* versterken. *~d concrete,* gewapend beton *n.n.* **reinforcement,** *n.* versterking *n.*

reinstate, *v.t.* weer in ere herstellen.

reinsure, *v.t.* herverzekeren.

reiterate, *v.t.* telkens weer herhalen. **reiteration,** *n.* voortdurende herhaling *n.*

reject, *v.t.* verwerpen *str.*; afwijzen *str.* ¶ *n.* afgekeurd voorwerp *n.n. ~s,* uitschot *n.n.* **rejection,** *n.* verwerping *n.*; afwijzing *n.*

rejoice, *v.i.* zich verheugen. **rejoicing,** *n.* vreugdebetoon *n.n.*, feestelijkheid *n.*

rejoin, *v.t.* zich weer voegen bij; weer verenigen; antwoorden. *to ~ the army,* weer onder dienst *n.* gaan *irr.* **rejoinder,** *n.* antwoord *n.n.*, dupliek *n.*

rejuvenate, *v.t.* verjongen. **rejuvenation,** *n.* verjonging *n.*

relapse, *v.i.* weer vervallen *str. to ~ into,* weer vervallen tot. *~ n.* wedervervalling *n.*; wederinstorting *n.*

relate, *v.t.* verhalen. *to ~ to or with,* in verband *n.n.* brengen *irr.* met; *to be ~d to,* in verband staan *irr.* met; verwant zijn aan. **relation,** *n.* betrekking *n.*, relatie *n.*; verhouding *n.*; bloedverwant *n.* **relationship,** *n.* verhouding *n.*; verwantschap *n.* **relative,** *a.,* ~ly, *adv.* betrekkelijk. *~ to,* betrekking hebbend op. ¶ *n.* verwant *n.* **relativity,** *n.* relativiteit *n.*, betrekkelijkheid *n.*

relax, *v.t.* ontspannen *irr.*; verslappen, minder streng doen *irr.* zijn. ¶ *v.i.* zich ontspannen *irr.* **relaxation,** *n.* verzachting *n.*; ontspanning *n.*, uitspanning *n.*

relay, *n.* vers span *n.n. (horses);* verse ploeg *n. (men);* relais *n.n. (radio). ~ race,* estafettenloop *n.; in ~s,* bij gedeelten *pl.n.n.* ¶ *v.t.* relayeren *(radio);* doorgeven *str.;* opnieuw bestraten *(road).*

release, *v.t.* vrijlaten *str.*; verlossen. *to ~ from,* ontheffen *str.* van. ¶ *n.* bevrijding *n.*; vrijlating *n.*; loslating *n.*; verlossing *n.*

relegate, *v.t.* verbannen *irr.*

relent, *v.i.* zich laten *str.* vermurwen, zwichten. **relentless,** *a.*, ~ly, *adv.* meedogenloos, onmeedogend.

relevance, *n.* toepasselijkheid *n.* **relevant,** *a.* toepasselijk; pertinent.

reliability, *n.* betrouwbaarheid *n.* **reliable,** *a.* betrouwbaar. **reliance,** *n.* vertrouwen *n.n.*

relic, *n.* reliquie *n.*; overblijfsel *n.n.*

relict, *n.* weduwe *n.*

relief, *n.* verlichting *n.*; leniging *n.*; opluchting *n.*; relief *n.n.* (*sculpture*). **relieve,** *v.t.* verlichten; lenigen; bevrijden; opluchten; aflossen.

religion, *n.* godsdienst *n.* **religious,** *a.*, ~ly, *adv.* godsdienstig. **with ~ care,** met de grootste zorg.

relinquish, *v.t.* opgeven *str.*, laten *str.* varen, afstand *n.* doen *irr.* van. **relinquishment,** *n.* afstand *n.*

reliquary, *n.* reliquieënkastje *n.n.*

relish, *v.t.* genieten *str.* van, genoegen *n.n.* scheppen *str.* in. ¶ *n.* smaak *n.*; zin *n.*, lust *n.*; aantrekkelijkheid *n.* **relishable,** *a.* smakelijk.

reluctance, *n.* tegenzin *n.*, weerzin *n.* **reluctant,** *a.*,⸱ ~ly, *adv.* onwillig, afkerig.

rely, *v.i.* **to ~ on,** vertrouwen op, steunen op.

remain, *v.i.* blijven *str.*; overblijven *str.* **it ~s to be seen,** dat moet nog blijken; **het staat nog te bezien;** *it ~s with him,* **het staat aan hem.** ¶ *n.* ~s, overblijfsel *n.n.*; *mortal* ~s, stoffelijk overschot *n.n.* **remainder,** *n.* overschot *n.n.*; restant *n.n.*; fondsrestant *n.n.* ¶ *v.t.* als restant van de hand doen *irr.*

remand, *v.t.* (in preventieve hechtenis *n.*) terugzenden *str.*

remark, *v.t.* opmerken; aanmerken. ¶ *n.* opmerking *n.*; aanmerking *n.* **remarkable,** *a.*, ~bly, *adv.* merkwaardig, opmerkelijk.

remediable, *a.* herstelbaar. **remedy,** *n.* geneesmiddel *n.n.*; middel *n.n.* **beyond ~,** onherstelbaar. ¶ *v.t.* verhelpen *str.*

remember, *v.t.* zich herinneren; denken *irr.* aan, gedenken *irr.* **~ me to . . .,** doe m'n groeten *pl.n.* aan . . . **remembrance,** *n.* herinnering *n.*; aandenken *n.n.*

remind, *v.t.* herinneren. **to ~ of,** doen *irr.* denken aan. **reminder,** *n.* herinnering *n.*; aanmaning *n.* **a gentle ~,** een zachte wenk *n.*

reminiscence, *n.* herinnering *n.* ~s, memoires *pl.n.*

remiss, *a.* nalatig. **remission,** *n.* kwijtschelding *n.* **with ~ of sins,** met aflaat *n.* van zonden *pl.n.* **remit,** *v.t.* doen *irr.* toekomen; kwijtschelden *str.*, vrijstellen van. ¶ *v.i.* afnemen *str.*,' verflauwen. **remittal,** *n.* kwijtschelding *n.* **remittance,** *n.* overmaking *n.*, remise *n.*

remnant, *n.* overblijfsel *n.n.*; restant *n.n.*, lap *n.*

remodel, *v.t.* opnieuw bewerken.

remonstrance, *n.* vermaning *n.*; vertoog *n.n.* **remonstrate,** *v.i.* tegenwerpingen *pl.n.* maken. **to ~ with someone against something,** bij iemand tegen iets protesteren.

remorse, *n.* berouw *n.n.*, wroeging *n.* **remorseful,** *a.*, ~ly, *adv.* vol berouw *n.n.*, berouwhebbend. **remorseless,** *a.*, ~ly, *adv.* meedogenloos, onbarmhartig.

remote, *a.* ver verwijderd, verafgelegen. **remotely,** *adv.* ver. **remoteness,** *n.* verheid *n.*; eenzaamheid *n.*

remount, *v.t.* weer bestijgen *str.*; opnieuw monteren. ¶ *n.* remontepaard *n.n.*; nieuwe zetting *n.*

removable, *a.* afneembaar; weg te nemen. **removal,** *n.* verwijdering *n.*; verhuizing *n.*; opheffing *n.* **remove,** *v.t.* verwijderen, wegnemen *str.* **to be ~d,** overgaan *irr.* (*at school*). ¶ *v.i.* verhuizen. ¶ *n.* graad *n.*; bevordering *n.*

remunerate, *v.t.* vergelden *str.*; belonen, betalen. **remuneration,** *n.* betaling *n.* **remunerative,** *a.* voordelig, lonend.

renaissance, *n.* renaissance *n.*

renal, *a.* nier . . .

renascence, *n.* wedergeboorte *n.*, herleving *n.* **rend,** *v.t.* uiteenscheuren. **to ~ from,** ontrukken aan.

render, *v.t.* geven *str.*, overleveren; weergeven *str.*, vertolken. **to ~ judgment,** een oordeel *n.n.* uitspreken *str.*; **to ~ a service,** een dienst *n.* bewijzen *str.*; **to ~ down,** uitsmelten *str.*, klaren. **rendering,** *n.* weergave *n.*, vertolking *n.*

renegade, *n.* afvallige, *n.*, renegaat *n.*

renew, *v.t.* hernieuwen. **renewal,** *n.* hernieuwing *n.*

rennet, *n.* kaasstremsel *n.n.*; renet *n.* (*apple*).

renounce, *v.t.* afstand *n.* doen *irr.* van, laten *str.* varen; verloochenen; renonceren (*cards*).

renovate, *v.t.* vernieuwen. **renovation,** *n.* vernieuwing *n.*

renown, *n.* vermaardheid *n.* **renowned,** *a.* vermaard.

rent, *n.* scheur *n.* (*tear*); huur *n.*, pacht *n.* (*payment*). ¶ *v.t.* huren, pachten; verhuren, verpachten. **rental,** *n.* (huis)huur *n.*; (land)pacht *n.*

renunciation, *n.* zelfverloochening *n.*; verzaking *n.*,⸱ verloochening *n.*

reopen, *v.t.* weer open doen *irr.* ¶ *v.i.* weer open gaan *irr.*

reorganization, *n.* reorganisatie *n.* **reorganize,** *v.t.* reorganiseren.

rep, *n.* rips *n.n.*

repair, *v.t.* repareren; herstellen; vergoeden. ¶ *v.i.* **to ~ to,** zich begeven *str.* naar; zich ophouden *irr.* ¶ *n.* reparatie *n.*; verblijfplaats *n.* **in bad ~,** slecht onderhouden. **repairable,** *a.*, reparable, *a.* herstelbaar. **reparation,** *n.* reparatie *n.*; schadeloosstelling *n.*, herstel *n.n.*

repartee, *n.* gevat antwoord *n.n.*

repast, *n.* maal *n.n.*, maaltijd *n.*
repatriate, *v.t.* repatriëren.
repay, *v.t.* terugbetalen. **repayable,** *a.* terugbetaalbaar. **repayment,** *n.* terugbetaling *n.*
repeal, *v.t.* herroepen *str.*, intrekken *str.* ¶ *n.* herroeping *n.*, intrekking *n.* **repealable,** *a.* herroepelijk.
repeat, *v.t.* herhalen; nazeggen *irr.*; oververtellen. *to ~ oneself,* in herhalingen *pl.n.* vervallen *str.* ¶ *v.i.* repeteren (*fraction*); oprispen (*food*). ¶ *n.* verhaling *n.* *~ order,* nabestelling *n.* **repeatedly,** *adv.* herhaaldelijk. **repeater,** *n.* repetitiehorloge *n.n.*
repel, *v.t.* keren, afslaan *irr.*; afstoten *str.* **repellent,** *a.* afstotend.
repent, *v.i.* berouw *n.n.* hebben. ¶ *v.t.* berouwen, berouw hebben over. **repentance,** *n.* berouw *n.n.* **repentant,** *a.*, ~ly, *adv.* berouwvol, boetvaardig.
repercussion, *n.* terugkaatsing *n.*, terugslag *n.*, reactie *n.*
repertory, *n.* repertoire *n.n.*
repetition, *n.* herhaling *n.*
repine, *v.i.* klagen. *to ~ at,* misnoegd zijn over.
replace, *v.t.* terugplaatsen; de plaats innemen *str.* van; *to ~ by* or *with,* vervangen door. **replant,** *v.t.* verplanten.
replenish, *v.t.* aanvullen. **replenishment,** *n.* aanvulling *n.*
replete, *a.* vol, (over)verzadigd. **repletion,** *n.* overlading *n.*
replica, *n.* kopie *n.*; evenbeeld *n.n.*
reply, *v.i.* antwoorden. *to ~ to,* antwoorden op, beantwoorden. ¶ *v.t.* antwoorden. ¶ *n.* antwoord *n.n.*; repliek *n.* (*parliamentary*).
report, *v.t.* rapporteren, melden, berichten. ¶ *v.i.* rapport *n.n.* uitbrengen *irr.*; zich melden. ¶ *n.* rapport *n.n.*; gerucht *n.n.*; slag *n.*, knal *n.* **reporter,** *n.* verslaggever *n.*
repose, *v.i.* rusten. *to ~ on,* zich verlaten *str.* op. ¶ *v.t.* laten *str.* rusten; stellen. ¶ *n.* rust *n.*
repository, *n.* bewaarplaats *n.*, bergplaats *n.*
reprehend, *v.t.* berispen. **reprehensible,** *a.*, ~bly, *adv.* berispelijk, laakbaar. **reprehension,** *n.* berisping *n.*; blaam *n.* **reprehensive,** *a.* laakbaar.
represent, *v.t.* vertegenwoordigen; voorstellen, weergeven *str.* **representation,** *n.* vertegenwoordiging *n.*; protest *n.*; voorstelling *n.*, opvoering *n.*; afbeelding *n.* **representative,** *a.*, ~ly, *adv.* vertegenwoordigend; typisch. *to be ~ of,* vertegenwoordigen. ¶ *n.* vertegenwoordiger *n.*
repress, *v.t.* onderdrukken; bedwingen *str.* **repression,** *n.* onderdrukking *n.*; bedwinging *n.*; repressie *n.* **repressive,** *a.* onderdrukkend; onderdrukkings . . .
reprieve, *v.t.* gratie *n.* verlenen aan; uitstellen. ¶ *n.* gratie *n.*; uitstel *n.n.*

reprimand, *n.* reprimande *n.*, terechtwijzing *n.* ¶ *v.t.* een reprimande geven *str.* aan, terechtwijzen *str.*
reprint, *v.t.* herdrukken; nadrukken. ¶ *n.* herdruk *n.*; nadruk *n.*
reprisal, *n.* represaille *n.*; weerwraak *n.* *in ~ for,* als represaillemaatregel *n.* voor.
reproach, *v.t.* verwijten *str.* *to ~ oneself for,* zich een verwijt *n.n.* maken van. ¶ *n.* verwijt *n.n.*; schande *n.*, oneer *n.* **reproachful,** *a.* verwijtend.
reprobate, *n.* verstokte zondaar *n.*
reproduce, *v.t.* reproduceren; opnieuw voortbrengen *irr.*; zich voortplanten. **reproduction,** *n.* reproductie *n.*; weergeving *n.*; voortplanting *n.* **reproductive,** *a.* voortplantings . . .
reproof, *n.* berisping *n.*, terechtwijzing *n.* **reprove,** *v.t.* berispen, terechtwijzen *str.*
reptile, *n.* reptiel *n.n.*, kruipend dier *n.n.* **reptilian,** *a.* kruipend; laag.
republic, *n.* republiek *n.* **republican,** *a.* republikeins. ¶ *n.* republikein *n.*
republication, *n.* hernieuwde uitgaaf *n.*, herdruk *n.*
repudiate, *v.t.* verstoten *str.*, verwerpen *str.*; verloochenen. **repudiation,** *n.* verstoting *n.*, verwerping *n.*; verloochening *n.*
repugnance, *n.* afkeer *n.*, weerzin *n.*, tegenzin *n.* **repugnant,** *a.* weerzinwekkend. *to be ~ to,* strijdig zijn met; tegen de borst stuiten.
repulse, *v.t.* afslaan *irr.*; terugdrijven *str.* ¶ *n.* afslaan *n.n.*; weigering *n.* **repulsion,** *n.* afstoting *n.*; weerzin *n.* **repulsive,** *a.*, ~ly, *adv.* weerzinwekkend.
reputable, *a.*, ~bly, *adv.* achtenswaardig, geacht, gunstig bekend staand. **reputation,** *n.* reputatie *n.*, (goede) naam *n.* **repute,** *v.t.* houden *irr.* voor. ¶ *n.* reputatie *n.*, (goede) naam *n.*
request, *v.t.* verzoeken *irr.* ¶ *n.* verzoek *n.n.*; vraag *n.* *at the ~ of,* op verzoek van; *in great ~,* zeer gezocht.
require, *v.t.* vorderen, eisen; nodig hebben. **requirement,** *n.* eis *n.*; vereiste *n.*
requisite, *a.* vereist, benodigd. ¶ *n.* vereiste *n.* **requisition,** *n.* opvordering *n.*, requisitie *n.* ¶ *v.t.* requireren.
requital, *n.* vergelding *n.* **requite,** *v.t.* vergelden *str.*, belonen.
reredos, *n.* altaarscherm *n.n.*
rescind, *v.t.* intrekken *str.*, herroepen *str.*
rescue, *v.t.* redden; bevrijden. ¶ *n.* redding *n.*; bevrijding *n.* *to come to the ~,* te hulp *n.* komen *irr.*
research, *v.t.* onderzoeken *irr.* ¶ *n.* onderzoek *n.n.*, nasporing *n.*
reseat, *v.t.* van nieuwe zitting(en) *pl.n.* voorzien *irr.*
resemblance, *n.* gelijkenis *n.*, overeenkomst *n.* **resemble,** *v.t.* gelijken *str.* op.
resent, *v.t.* kwalijk nemen *str.*, zich beledigd voelen door. **resentful,** *a.*, ~ly, *adv.* geraakt; wrokkig. **resentment,** *n.* wrok *n.*

reservation, *n.* terughouding *n.*; voorbehoud *n.n.*; reservatie *n.*; gebied *n.n.* **reserve,** *v.t.* reserveren; bewaren; voorbehouden *irr.* ¶ *n.* reserve *n.*; voorbehoud *n.n.*; terughoudendheid *n.*; limiet *n.* (*price*). ~*s,* aanvullingstroepen *pl.n.* **reserved,** *a.,* ~ly, *adv.* gereserveerd; terughoudend.

reservoir, *n.* reservoir *n.n.*

reset, *v.t.* opnieuw zetten.

reside, *v.i.* verblijven *str.,* verblijf *n.n.* houden *irr.* **residence,** *n.* verblijfplaats *n.,* woning *n.*; residentie *n.* **resident,** *a.* woonachtig; inwonend. ¶ *n.* ingezetene *n.* **residual,** *a.* overgebleven. **residuary,** *a.* overgebleven. ~ *legatee,* algemeen erfgenaam *n.*

residue, *n.* residu *n.n.*; saldo *n.n.*

resign, *v.i.* ontslag *n.n.* nemen *str.*; uittreden *str.* ¶ *v.r.* to ~ *oneself to,* zich neerleggen *irr.* bij. ¶ *v.t.* neerleggen *irr.,* opgeven *str.* **resignation,** *n.* ontslag *n.n.*; uittreden *n.n.*; berusting *n.,* gelatenheid *n.* **resigned,** *a.,* ~ly, *adv.* gelaten.

resilience, *n.* veerkracht *n.,* elasticiteit *n.* **resilient,** *a.* zich snel herstellend; elastisch.

resin, *n.* hars. **resinous,** *a.* harsachtig.

resist, *v.t.* weerstaan *irr.,* weerstand *n.* bieden *str.* aan, zich verzetten tegen. ¶ *v.i.* weerstand *n.* bieden *str.,* tegenstand *n.* bieden. **resistance,** *n.* verzet *n.n.,* tegenstand *n.*; weerstand *n.*

resolute, *a.,* ~ly, *adv.* vastberaden; vastbesloten. **resolution,** *n.* vastberadenheid *n.*; vastbeslotenheid *n.*; resolutie *n.,* motie *n.*; besluit *n.n.*; oplossing *n.*

resolvable, *a.* oplosbaar. **resolve,** *v.t.* oplossen. ¶ *v.i.* besluiten *str.*

resonance, *n.* weerklank *n.*; resonantie *n.* **resonant,** *a.* weerklinkend, resonerend.

resort, *v.i.* to ~ *to,* toevlucht *n.* nemen *str.* tot, zich begeven *str.* naar. ¶ *n.* toevlucht *n.*; redmiddel *n.n.*; verblijf *n.n.*; oord *n.n.*; instantie *n.*

resound, *v.i.* weerklinken *str.,* weergalmen. to ~ *with,* weerklinken van.

resource, *n.* hulpbron *n.*; uitkomst *n.*; vindingrijkheid *n.* ~*s,* hulpbronnen *pl.n.,* geldmiddelen *pl.n.n.*; *natural* ~*s,* bodemrijkheid *n.* **resourceful,** *a.,* ~ly, *adv.* vindingrijk. **resourcefulness,** *n.* vindingrijkheid *n.*

respect, *n.* eerbied *n.*; achting *n.,* aanzien *n.n.*; opzicht *n.n.* ~*s,* beleefde groeten *pl.n.*; *in every* ~, in alle opzichten. ¶ *v.t.* respecteren, (hoog)achten; eerbiedigen. **respectability,** *n.* aanzien *n.n.*; fatsoen *n.n.* **respectable,** *a.,* ~bly, *adv.* achtbaar, achtenswaardig; fatsoenlijk; respectabel. **respectful,** *a.,* ~ly, *adv.* eerbiedig. **respecting,** *adv.* aangaande. **respective,** *a.* respectief. *our* ~ *ways,* elk ons eigen weg. **respectively,** *adv.* respectievelijk.

respiration, *n.* ademhaling *n.* **respiratory,** *a.*

ademhalings . . . **respire,** *v.i.* herademen, weer op adem *n.* komen *irr.*

respite, *n.* uitstel *n.n.,* verademing *n.* ¶ *v.t.* uitstel verlenen.

resplendence, *n.* glans *n.,* luister *n.* **resplendent,** *a.,* ~ly, *adv.* glansrijk, luisterrijk.

respond, *v.i.* to ~ *to,* reageren op, gehoor *n.n.* geven *str.* aan. **respondent,** *n.* verdediger *n.,* beklaagde *n.* **response,** *n.* antwoord *n.n.*; reactie *n.* *in* ~ *to,* ingevolge.

responsibility, *n.* verantwoordelijkheid *n.* **responsible,** *a.,* ~bly, *adv.* verantwoordelijk.

responsive, *a.* sympathiek. *to be* ~ *to,* beantwoorden.

rest, *v.i.* rusten, uitrusten; steunen; overblijven *str.* (*remain*). to ~ *assured,* verzekerd zijn; *it* ~*s with you,* het staat aan U. ¶ *v.t.* steunen; doen *irr.* rusten; berusten. ¶ *n.* rustpauze *n.*; rustpunt *n.n.*; nachtrust *n.*; rest *n.,* overschot *n.n.* (*remainder*). *to have a* ~, even rusten; *to set at* ~, geruststellen.

restaurant, *n.* restaurant *n.n.*

resting place, *n.* rustplaats *n.*

restitution, *n.* teruggave *n.*; vergoeding *n.,* schadeloosstelling *n.*

restive, *a.* ongeduldig, ongedurig. **restless,** *a.,* ~ly, *adv.* rusteloos, onrustig. **restlessness,** *n.* rusteloosheid *n.,* onrustigheid *n.*

restoration, *n.* restauratie *n.*; herstel *n.n.* **restorative,** *n.* versterkend middel *n.n.* **restore,** *v.t.* restaureren, herstellen.

restrain, *v.t.* beteugelen, terughouden *irr.* ¶ *v.r.* to ~ *oneself,* zich inhouden *irr.* **restraint,** *n.* dwang *n.*; zelfbedwang *n.n.*; terughoudendheid *n.* *without* ~, ongestoord.

restrict, *v.t.* beperken. **restriction,** *n.* beperking *n.* **restrictive,** *a.* beperkend.

result, *n.* uitslag *n.*; gevolg *n.n.,* resultaat *n.n.* ¶ *v.i.* to ~ *from,* ontstaan *irr.* uit, voortvloeien uit; *to* ~ *in,* uitlopen *str.* op.

resume, *v.t.* hervatten; weer opvatten. **resumption,** *n.* hervatting *n.*; wederopneming *n.*

resurrect, *v.t.* doen *irr.* herleven; weer oprakelen. **resurrection,** *n.* opstanding *n.*; herrijzenis *n.*

resuscitate, *v.t.* doen *irr.* herleven. **resuscitation,** *n.* herleving *n.*

ret, *v.t.* roten.

retail, *n.* kleinhandel *n.* *in* ~, in het klein. ¶ *v.t.* in het klein verkopen *irr.*; in kleuren *pl.n.* en geuren *pl.n.* vertellen. **retailer,** *n.* kleinhandelaar *n.*

retain, *v.t.* behouden *irr.*; aanhouden *irr.* **retainer,** *n.* bediende *n.*; voorlopig honorarium *n.n.*

retake, *v.t.* opnieuw nemen *str.*; heroveren.

retaliate, *v.i.* weerwraak *n.* nemen *str.*; antwoorden. **retaliation,** *n.* weerwraak *n.*

retard, *v.t.* vertragen; uitstellen. **retardation,** *n.* vertraging *n.*

retch, v.i. kokhalzen.
retention, n. behoud n.n.; achterhouding n.
retentive, a. vasthoudend.
reticence, n. terughoudendheid n.; verzwijging n. **reticent,** a., ~ly, adv. terughoudend, gesloten.
reticule, n. reticule n.
retina, n. netvlies n.n.
retinue, n. gevolg n.n., hofstoet n.
retire, v.i. terugtrekken str.; zich terugtrekken str.; zijn ontslag n.n. nemen str. ¶ v.t. terugtrekken str.; pensionneren. **retired,** a. teruggetrokken. on ~ pay, on the ~ list, met pensioen n. **retirement,** n. teruggetrokkenheid n.; afzondering n.
retort, v.t. terugwerpen str., scherp antwoorden. ¶ n. scherp antwoord n.n.; kolffles n., retort n.n. (vessel).
retouch, v.t. retoucheren.
retrace, v.t. weer volgen, opsporen.
retract, v.t. terugtrekken str., intrekken str. **retraction,** n. intrekking n., herroeping n.
retreat, v.i. terugtrekken str. ¶ n. terugtocht n., aftocht n.
retrench, v.i. bezuinigen, zich bekrimpen str. **retrenchment,** n. bezuiniging n.
retribution, n. vergelding n.
retrievable, a. herstelbaar, terug te vinden. **retrieve,** v.t. terugvinden str. **retriever,** n. (soort) jachthond n.
retroactive, a., ~ly, adv. terugwerkend.
retrograde, a. achteruitgaand, teruglopend.
retrogression, n. achteruitgang n., ontaarding n.
retrospect, n. terugblik n. in ~, terugziend. **retrospective,** a., ~ly, adv. terugziend; met terugwerkende kracht n.
return, v.i. terugkeren; terugkomen irr. ¶ v.t. terugzenden str.; opgeven str. (state); afvaardigen (representative). to ~ thanks, dank n. betuigen. ¶ n. terugkeer n.; terugkomst n.; opgave n.; retourbiljet n.n. by ~ of post, per omgaande; in ~ for, in ruil n. voor; ~s, opbrengst n.; many happy ~s, hartelijk gelukgewenst. ¶ prefix terug . . . **returnable,** a. terug te zenden; herverkiesbaar. **returning officer,** n. voorzitter n. van een stembureau n.n.
reunion, n. reunie n., bijeenkomst n. **reunite,** v.t. opnieuw verenigen.
revaluation, n. nieuwe schatting n. **revalue,** v.t. opnieuw schatten.
reveal, v.t. openbaren; doen irr uitkomen.
reveille, n. reveille n.n.
revel, n. feestelijkheid n.; braspartij n. ¶ v.i. brassen. to ~ in, zich verlustigen in.
revelation, n. openbaring n.
reveller, n. pretmaker n. **revelry,** n. feestvreugde n.
revenge, v.t. wreken str. ¶ v.r. to ~ oneself for . . . on . . ., zich wreken over . . . op . . . ¶ n. wraak n.; revanche n. in ~ for, uit wraak over. **revengeful,** a., ~ly, adv. wraakzuchtig, wraakgierig.

revenue, n. inkomsten pl.n. **revenue-cutter,** n. recherchevaartuig n.n. **revenue officer,** n. belastingambtenaar n.
reverberate, v.i. weergalmen. ¶ v.t. weerkaatsen. **reverberation,** n. weerkaatsing n.
revere, v.t. hoogachten. **reverence,** n. hoogachting n., eerbied n. Your ~, Uw eerwaarde n.; his ~, zijn eerwaarde n. **reverend,** a. eerwaard. the R~ XYZ, Ds. XYZ. **reverent,** a., ~ly, adv. eerbiedig, nederig. **reverential,** a. eerbiedig.
reverie, n. mijmering n.
reversal, n. ommekeer n.; omzetting n. (of machine); cassatie n. (in law). **reverse,** v.t. omkeren; omgooien, omzetten; ongedaan maken. ¶ a. omgekeerd tegengesteld. ~ gear, achteruitversnelling n. ¶ n. omgekeerde n.n.; tegendeel n.n.; tegenslag n. (misfortune). **reversible,** a. omkeerbaar, draaibaar.
reversion, n. terugvalling n.; recht n.n. van opvolging n. **reversionary,** a. terugvallend. **revert,** v.i. terugvallen str. to ~ to, teruggaan irr. tot. **revertible,** a. terugvallend.
review, v.t. herzien irr.; in ogenschouw n. nemen str.; recenseren (book); laten str. paraderen (troops). ¶ n. overzicht n.n., recensie n.; revue n.; inspectie n., parade n. **reviewer,** n. recensent n.
revile, v.t. beschimpen, smalen op.
revise, v.t. herzien irr.; corrigeren. **reviser,** n. corrector n. **revision,** n. herziening n.
revisit, v.t. opnieuw bezoeken irr.
revival, n. wederopleving n., wederopbloei n. **revive,** v.i. herleven; bijkomen irr. ¶ v.t. doen irr. herleven.
revocable, a. herroepelijk. **revocation,** n. herroeping n. **revoke,** v.t. herroepen str., intrekken str. ¶ v.i. renonceren.
revolt, n. opstand n., oproer n.n. ¶ v.i. in opstand komen irr. ¶ v.t. in opstand brengen irr. **revolting,** a. weerzinwekkend, walgelijk. **revolution,** n. revolutie n.; omwenteling n.; toer n. **revolutionary,** n. revolutionnair n. ¶ a. revolutionnair. **revolutionize,** v.t. een ommekeer n. teweeg brengen irr. in.
revolve, v.i. (om)wentelen.
revolver, n. revolver n. **revolving** prefix draai . . .
revulsion, n. afkeer n.; ommekeer n.
reward, v.t. belonen. ¶ n. beloning n.
rewrite, v.t. opnieuw schrijven str.; omwerken.
rhapsody, n. rhapsodie n.
Rhenish, a. Rijn . . .
rhetoric, n. rhetorica n.; rhetoriek n. **rhetorical,** a., ~ly, adv. rhetorisch. **rhetorician,** n. rederijker n.
rheumatic, a. rheumatisch. **rheumatics,** pl.n. rheumatiek n. **rheumatism,** n. rheumatiek n.
Rhine, N. Rijn N.

rhinoceros, *n.* neushoorndier *n.n.*, rhinoceros *n.*

rhododendron, *n.* rhododendron *n.*

rhomb, *n.* ruit *n.* **rhombic**, *a.* ruitvormig.

rhubarb, *n.* rabarber *n.*

rhyme, *n.* rijm *n.n.* *without ~ or reason*, zonder slot *n.n.* of zin *n.* ¶ *v.t.* rijmen. *to ~ with*, rijmen op. **rhymster**, *n.* rijmelaar *n.*

rhythm, *n.* rhythme *n.n.* **rhythmic(al)**, *a.* rhythmisch.

rib, *n.* rib *n.*; ribbestuk *n.n.* (*meat*); rib *n.*, nerf *n.* (*of leaf*); ribbel *n.* (*on material*). ¶ *v.t.* ribben; ribbelen.

ribald, *a.* schuin, vrolijk; ongepast. **ribaldry**, *n.* schuine vrolijkheid *n.*

ribbon, *n.* lint *n.n.*; lintje *n.n.*

rice, *n.* rijst *n.*

rich, *a.* rijk; vol, warm; machtig (*food*). **riches**, *pl.n.* rijkdom *n.* **richly**, *adv.* rijk; rijkelijk. **richness**, *n.* rijkheid *n.*

rick, *n.* mijt *n.*, opper *n.*

rickets, *pl.n.* Engelse ziekte *n.*, rachitis *n.* **rickety**, *a.* rachitisch; wankel, wrak.

ricochet, *v.i.* ketsen.

rid, *v.t.* bevrijden, verlossen. *to get ~ of*, afkomen *irr.* van, kwijtraken. ¶ *v.t* *to ~ oneself of*, zich ontdoen *irr.* van. **riddance**, *n.* verlossing *n.* *good ~*, daar zijn we gelukkig van af.

ridden, *suffix. bed~*, bedlegerig.

riddle, *n.* raadsel *n.n.*; zeef *n.* (*sieve*). ¶ *v.t.* ziften; doorzeven.

ride, *v.i.* rijden *str.* *to ~ at anchor*, voor anker *n.n.* liggen *str.*; *to ~ for a fall*, zijn ondergang *n.* tegemoet gaan *irr.* ¶ *v.t.* berijden *str.* *to ~ a bicycle*, fietsen; *to ~ down*, omverrijden *str.* ¶ *n.* rit *n.* *to go for a ~*, een rijtoertje *n.n.* maken. **rider**, *n.* rijder *n.*, ruiter *n.* **riderless**, *n.* ruiterloos.

ridge, *n.* rug *n.*, kam *n.*; vorst *n.*, nok *n.* (*roof*); richel *n.*

ridicule, *n.* spot *n.* ¶ *v.t.* spot drijven *str.* met, belachelijk maken. **ridiculous**, *a.*, *~ly*, *adv.* bespottelijk, belachelijk.

riding, *n.* district *n.n.*

riding-crop, *n.* rijzweep *n.*, karwats *n.* **riding-hood**, *n.* *Red ~*, Roodkapje *n.N.* **riding-light**, *n.* ankerlicht *n.n.*

rife, *a.* algemeen. *~ with*, vol (van).

riffraff, *n.* gepeupel *n.n.*, gespuis *n.n.*

rifle, *n.* geweer *n.n.* ¶ *v.t.* groeven, trekken *str.* **rifle-range**, *n.* schietbaan *n.*

rift, *n.* scheur *n.*; barst *n.* *there is a ~ in the lute*, de vriendschap begint gevaar *n.n.* te lopen.

rig, *n.* tuig *n.n.*; plunje *n.* (*clothes*). ¶ *v.t.* optuigen. *to ~ out*, toetakelen. **rigger**, *n.* optakelaar *n.* **rigging**, *n.* tuigage *n.*

right, *n.* recht *n.n.*; rechterkant *n.* *the R~*, de Rechtsen *pl.N.*; *the ~s of it*, het ware van de zaak; *to have a ~ to*, recht hebben op; *by ~s*, rechtens, eigenlijk; *to be in* *the ~*, gelijk hebben; *in her own ~*, van zichzelf, niet door huwelijk *n.n.*; *to the ~ of*, rechts van; *to put to ~s*, in orde maken, in het reine brengen *irr.* ¶ *a.* rechts, rechter; recht (*angle*); juist, correct; billijk, behoorlijk. *all ~*, in orde; *on the ~ side of fifty*, nog geen vijftig. ¶ *adv.* juist; recht, billijk; (naar) rechts; vlak, onmiddellijk. *~ about turn*, rechtsomkeert; *~ away*, op staande voet; *~ enough*, zeker. ¶ *v.t.* overeind zetten; in orde maken. *to ~ oneself*, weer in orde *n.* komen *irr.* **right-angled**, *a.* rechthoekig.

righteous, *a.*, *~ly*, *adv.* gerecht; rechtschapen. **righteousness**, *n.* gerechtheid *n.*; rechtschapenheid *n.*

rightful, *a.*, *~ly*, *adv.* rechtmatig; rechtvaardig. **righthand**, *n.* rechts, rechter. **righthanded**, *a.* rechts. **rightness**, *n.* rechtheid *n.*, juistheid *n.*

rigid, *a.*, *~ly*, *adv.* stijf, onbuigbaar. **rigidity**, *n.* stijfheid *n.*, onbuigbaarheid *n.*

rigmarole, *n.* onsamenhangend verhaal *n.n.*

rigorous, *a.*, *~ly*, *adv.* gestreng; streng; guur. **rigour**, *n.* strengheid *n.*

rill, *n.* beekje *n.n.*

rim, *n.* rand *n.*; band *n.*; velling *n.* ¶ *v.t.* omranden. *gold ~med spectacles*, een gouden bril *n.*

rime, *n.* rijm *n.*, rijp *n.*; rijm *n.n.* ¶ *v.r.* berijpen. **rimy**, *a.* berijpt.

rind, *n.* korst *n.* (*cheese*); zwoerd *n.n.* (*bacon*).

ring, *n.* ring *n.*; kringetje *n.n.*; kliek *n.* (*people*); bokstrijdperk *n.n.*; klank *n.* *there is a ~ at the door*, er wordt gebeld; *to have a false ~*, vals klinken *str.*; *to give two ~s*, tweemaal bellen. ¶ *v.t.* ringen, een ring aandoen *irr.* *to ~ the bell*, bellen; *to ~ the bell(s)*, luiden; *to ~ at the door*, aanbellen; *to ~ up*, opbellen; *to ~ off*, afbellen; *to ~ with*, weerklinken *str.* van. ¶ *v.i.* klinken *str.*; weergalmen. **ringing**, *n.* gelui *n.n.* **ringleader**, *n.* belhamel *n.* **ringlet**, *n.* ringetje *n.n.* **ringworm**, *n.* ringworm *n.*, dauwworm *n.*

rink, *n.* ijsbaan *n.*, kunstbaan *n.*

rinse, *v.t.* spoelen, omspoelen. *to ~ out*, uitspoelen.

riot, *n.* oproer *n.n.*, muiterij *n.* *to run ~*, uit de band springen *str.*; paal noch perk kennen; *a ~ of colour*, een kleurenpracht *n.* ¶ *v.i.* oproerig worden *str.*; *to read the R~ Act*, de menigte sommeren uiteen te gaan *irr.* **rioter**, *n.* oproermaker *n.* **riotous**, *a.*, *~ly*, *adv.* oproerig; bandeloos, losbandig.

rip, *v.t.* lostornen. *to ~ off*, afscheuren; *to ~ up*, openrijten *str.* ¶ *v.i.* tornen; scheuren. *to let ~*, laten *str.* gaan. ¶ *n.* scheur *n.*; deugniet *n.*

ripe, *a.*, *~ly*, *adv.* rijp. **ripen**, *v.i.* rijpen, rijp worden *str.* ¶ *v.t.* doen *irr.* rijpen. **ripeness**, *n.* rijpheid *n.*

riposte, *n.* riposte *n.*, vaardig antwoord *n.n.*

ripping, *a.* heerlijk.
ripple, *n.* kabbeling *n.*; rimpeling *n.*; repel *n.* (*for flax*). ¶ *v.i.* kabbelen; rimpelen.
rise, *v.i.* stijgen *str.*; rijzen *str.*; opstaan *irr.*, verrijzen *str.* (*from death*); opsteken *str.* (*wind*). *to ~ from*, voortspringen *str.* uit. ¶ *n.* stijging *n.*; opkomst *n.*; verhoging *n.*, opslag *n.*; helling *n. to give ~ to*, aanleiding *n.* geven *str.* tot; *to take a ~ out of*, beetnemen *str.*
risible, *a.* lachwekkend.
rising, *n.* opstand *n.* ¶ *a.* opkomend.
risk, *n.* risico *n.n.*, gevaar *n.n. to run a ~*, gevaar lopen *str.*; *to take a ~*, iets riskeren. ¶ *v.t.* riskeren; wagen. **risky**, *a.* riskant, gewaagd.
rite, *n.* ritus *n.*, gebruikelijke plechtigheid *n.*
ritual, *a.*, ~ly, *adv.* ritueel. ¶ *n.* ritueel *n.n.*, rituaal *n.n.*
rival, *n.* mededinger *n.*, concurrent *n.*; medeminnaar *n. without ~*, zonder weerga *n.* ¶ *a.* mededingend, concurrerend. ¶ *v.t.* wedijveren met. **rivalry**, *n.* wedijver *n.*, concurrentie *n.*
river, *n.* rivier *n.*; stroom *n. the ~ Thames*, de rivier de Theems.
rivet, *n.* klinknagel *n.* ¶ *v.t.* (vast)klinken *str.*; vestigen.
rivulet, *n.* beek *n.*, stroompje *n.n.*
roach, *n.* voorn *n.*, blankvoorn *n.*
road, *n.* weg *n. by ~*, over land *n.n.*; *to take the ~*, op weg gaan *irr.*; ~*s*, rede (*shipping*). **road-hog**, *n.* woeste automobilist *n.*, kilometervreter *n.* **roadstead**, *n.* rede *n.* **roadster**, *n.* (type) rijwiel *n.n.*, (type) auto *n.*
roam, *v.i.* (rond)zwerven *str.*
roan, *n.* roodbont rund *n.n.*; bazaanleer *n.n.*
roar, *v.i.* brullen; bulderen. *to ~ with laughter*, brullen van 't lachen. ¶ *v.t.* brullen; bulderen. ¶ *n.* gebrul *n.n.*, gebulder *n.n. a ~ of laughter*, een schaterend gelach *n.n.*
roast, *v.t.* braden *irr.*; branden (*coffee*). ¶ *n.* gebraden vlees *n.n. ~ beef*, rosbief *n.* **roaster**, *n.* braadkip *n.*; koffiebrander *n.*
rob, *v.t.* bestelen *str.*, plunderen. **robber**, *n.* rover *n.*, dief *n.* **robbery**, *n.* roof *n.*; diefstal *n.*
robe, *n.* toga *n.*, gewaad *n.n.* ¶ *v.t.* kleden.
robin, *n.* roodborstje *n.n.*
robust, *a.* fors, krachtig.
rock, *n.* rots *n.*; steen *n.*; suikerstok *n. to be on the ~s*, op zwart zaad *n.n.* zitten *str.*; *the R~*, Gibraltar *n.N.* ¶ *v.t.* & *v.i.* schommelen, wiegen. **rockbottom**, *n.* rotsbodem *n.* ¶ *a. ~ price*, allerlaagste prijs *n.* **rockbound**, *a.* door rotsen omsloten. **rock crystal**, *n.* bergkristal *n.n.* **rocker**, *n.* schommelstoel *n.*; hobbelpaard *n.n.*; goudwasmachine *n.* **rockery**, *n.* rotstuin *n.*
rocket, *n.* vuurpijl *n.*; raket *n.n.*; damastbloem *n.* ¶ *v.i.* naar boven schieten *str.*

rocking chair, *n.* schommelstoel *n.* **rocking horse**, *n.* hobbelpaard *n.n.*
rock pigeon, *n.* klipduif *n.* **rock salt**, *n.* klipzout *n.n.* **rock-tar**, *n.* steenolie *n.* **rocky**, *a.* rotsachtig; onvast, wankelend. *the R~ Mountains, the Rockies*, het Rotsgebergte *n.N.*
rococo, *a.* rococo.
rod, *n.* roede *n.*; stang *n.*; roede *n.* = 16½ voet *n.* (*fishing-*)~, hengel *n.*
rodent, *n.* knaagdier *n.n.*
rodeo, *n.* veekamp *n.n.*
rodomontade, *n.* grootspraak *n.*
roe, *n.* ree *n.*, hinde *n. hard ~*, kuit *n.*; *soft ~*, hom *n.* **roebuck**, *n.* reebok *n.*
rogation, *n.* smeekbede *n. R~ days*, de drie dagen *pl.n.* voor Hemelvaart *N.*
rogue, *n.* schavuit *n.*, schelm *n. ~ elephant*, kwade alleenzwervende olifant *n.* **roguery**, *n.* schelmerij *n.*, schurkenstreek *n.* **roguish**, *a.*, ~ly, *adv.* schalks, guitig.
roister, *v.i.* pret *n.* maken.
roll, *v.i.* rollen; slingeren (*ship*). *to ~ in money*, in weelde *n.* baden. ¶ *v.t.* rollen; walsen. ¶ *n.* rol *n.*; wals *n.*; broodje *n.n.*; gerol *n.n.*, slingeren *n.n.*; geroffel *n.n.*; rol *n.*, lijst *n.*, register *n.n. to call the ~*, appèl *n.n.* houden *irr.* **roll-call**, *n.* appèl *n.n.* **roller**, *n.* rolletje *n.n.*; zware golf *n.n.* **roller-blind**, *n.* rolgordijn *n.n.* **roller-skates**, *pl.n.* rolschaatsen *pl.n.* **roller-towel**, *n.* rolhanddoek *n.*
rollick, *v.i.* pret *n.* maken, dartelen.
rolling-mill, *n.* pletmolen *n.* **rolling-pin**, *n.* rolstok *n.* **rolling-stock**, *n.* rollend materiaal *n.n.* **roll-top**, *a. ~ desk*, cylinderbureau *n.n.*
roly-poly, *n.* gerolde geleipudding *n.*
Roman, *a.* Romeins. *~ Catholic*, Rooms-Katholiek *n.* ¶ *N.* Romein *N.*
romance, *n.* romance *n.*; ridderroman *n.*; puur verzinsel *n.n.* ¶ *v.i.* maar wat verzinnen *str.* **romancer**, *n.* verteller *n.* van verzinsels *pl.n.n.*
romanesque, *a.* romanesk.
romantic, *a.*, ~ally, *adv.* romantisch.
romish, *a.* Paaps.
romp, *v.i.* stoeien, dartelen. ¶ *n.* stoeipartij *n.* **rompers**, *pl.n.* babypakje *n.n.*
rood, *n.* roede *n.*, 0,1 Are *n.*
roof, *n.* dak *n.n. ~ of the mouth*, verhemelte *n.n.* **roofing**, *n.* dakwerk *n.n.* **roofless**, *a.* dakloos.
rook, *n.* roek *n.*; kasteel *n.n.* (*chess*). ¶ *v.t.* afzetten. **rookery**, *n.* roekenkolonie *n.*; krottenbuurt *n.*
room, *n.* kamer *n.*; ruimte *n.*; gelegenheid *n.*, aanleiding *n. to give ~ to*, plaats *n.* maken voor. **roomy**, *a.*, ~ily, *adv.* ruim.
roost, *n.* roest *n. to go to ~*, op stok *n.* gaan *irr.*; *to come home to ~*, op zijn eigen hoofd *n.n.* neerkomen *irr.* ¶ *v.i.* op stok gaan *irr.*
rooster, *n.* haan *n.*

root, *n.* wortel *n.*   *square* ~, vierkantswortel *n.*; *to strike* ~, wortel schieten *str.* ¶ *v.i.* wortelen. *to* ~ *about*, rondsnuffelen. ¶ *v.t. to* ~ *out*, uitroeien; *to* ~ *up*, met wortel *n.* en al uittrekken *str.*   **root-crop**, *n.* knolgewassen *pl.n.n.* **rooted**, *a.* diep geworteld.
rope, *n.* touw *n.n.*; koord *n.n.*; snoer *n.* (*pearls*). *to know the* ~*s*, zijn weg *n.* kennen. ¶ *v.t.* (vast)binden *str. to* ~ *in*, inpalmen. **rope-dancer**, *n.* koorddanser *n.* **ropeladder**, *n.* touwladder *n.* **ropemaker**, *n.* touwslager *n.* **ropewalk**, *n.* lijnbaan *n.* **ropy**, *a.* draderig. **ropeyard**, *n.* touwslagerij *n.* **ropeyarn**, *n.* kabelgaren *n.n.*
rosary, *n.* rozenkrans *n.*; rozenhoedje *n.n.*
rose, *n.* roos *n.* ¶ *a.* rose; rozerood. **roseate**, *a.* rozig. **rosebud**, *n.* rozeknop *n.* **rosebush**, *n.* rozestruik *n.* **rosemary**, *n.* rozemarijn *n.* **rosette**, *n.* rozet *n.* **rosewood**, *n.* rozenhout *n.n.*
rosin, *n.* hars *n.n.*
rosiness, *n.* rooskleurigheid *n.*
rostrum, *n.* spreekgestoelte *n.n.*
rosy, *a.* rooskleurig.
rot, *v.i.* rotten, verrotten. ¶ *v.t.* doen *irr.* rotten. ¶ *n.* rot *n.n.*; verrotting *n.*; nonsens *n.*
rota, *n.* rooster *n.*
rotary, *a.* draaiend, roterend, draai . . . **rotate**, *v.i.* wentelen, draaien. *to* ~ *crops*, wisselbouw *n.* toepassen. **rotation**, *n.* wenteling *n.*; wisselbouw *n.*
rote, *n. by* ~, uit het hoofd, van buiten.
rotten, *a.* rot, bedorven; (*coll.*) beroerd. **rottenness**, *n.* rotheid *n.* **rotter**, *n.* verachtelijk individu *n.n.*
rotund, *a.* rond; welgedaan. **rotundity**, *n.* rondheid *n.* **rotunda**, *n.* rotonde *n.*
rouble, *n.* roebel *n.*
rouge, *n.* rouge *n.n.*
rough, *a.*, ~ly, *adv.* ruw; ruig; bars. ~ *copy*, kladje *n.n.* ¶ *n.* ruwe klant *n. to take the* ~ *with the smooth*, het nemen *str.* zoals het valt *str.* ¶ *v.t. to* ~ *it*, zich behelpen *str.*; *to* ~ *something out*, een plan *n.n.* in ruwe trekken *pl.n.* opstellen. **rough-cast**, *n.* beraping *n.*; ruwe pleisterkalk *n.* ¶ *v.t.* in ruwe trekken *pl.n.* schetsen. **roughen**, *v.t.* ruw maken. **rough-hewn**, *a.* ruw behouwen. **roughness**, *n.* ruwheid *n.* **roughrider**, *n.* pikeur *n.* **roughshod**, *a.* ruw beslagen. *to ride* ~ *over*, zich niet storen aan.
round, *a.* rond; flink, stevig. ¶ *adv.* rond, in het rond, rondom; om, langs een omweg. ¶ *prep.* om, om . . . heen. ¶ *n.* rond *n.n.*; schijf *n.* (*disc*); rondedans *n.*; sport *n.* (*ladder*); rondje *n.* (*drinks*); serie *n.*; salvo *n.n.*, schot *n.n.*, patroon *n.n. to go the* ~*s*, rondgaan *irr.* ¶ *v.t.* afronden; omzeilen. ¶ *v.i.* rond worden *str.* **roundabout**, *a.* indirect. ¶ *n.* draaimolen *n.* **rounders**, *pl.n.* honkbal *n.n.* **roundhand**, *n.* rondschrift *n.n.* **Roundhead**, *N.* Rondkop

N. **roundly**, *adv.* rond; ronduit. **roundness**, *n.* rondheid *n.* **round-robin**, *n.* stuk *n.n.* met de namen in een cirkel *n.* ondertekend. **roundsman**, *n.* loopknecht *n.*; -bezorger *n.*
roup, *n.* pip *n.*
rouse, *v.t.* opwekken; wakker schudden; aansporen.
rout, *n.* verwarde aftocht *n.*, wilde vlucht *n.* ¶ *v.t.* op de vlucht jagen *str.* ¶ *v.i.* wroeten; rondsnuffelen.
route, *n.* route *n.* **route-march**, *n.* marsoefening *n.*
routine, *n.* routine *n.*; sleur *n.*
rove, *v.i.* rondzwerven *str.* ¶ *v.t.* afzwerven *str.* **rover**, *n.* zwerver *n.*
row, *n.* rij *n. in a* ~, op een rij. ¶ *v.t.* & *v.i.* roeien.
row, *n.* herrie *n.*; ruzie *n.*; standje *n.n.* ¶ *v.i.* herrie maken; ruzie maken. ¶ *v.t.* een standje geven *str.*
rowan, *n.* lijsterbes *n.*
rowdy, *a.* luidruchtig, lawaaierig. **rowdyism**, *n.* straatschenderij *n.*
rowel, *n.* spoorradje *n.*
rower, *n.* roeier *n.* **rowing-boat**, *n.* roeiboot *n.* **rowlock**, *n.* dol *n.*; dolpen *n.*
royal, *a.*, ~ly, *adv.* koninklijk, vorstelijk; royaal (*paper*). ~ *sail*, bovenbramzeil *n.n.*; ~ *mast*, bovenbramsteng *n.*; *the* ~ *road*, de brede weg. **royalist**, *n.* royalist *n.* **royalty**, *n.* koningschap *n.n.*; vorstelijke personen *pl.n.*; tantième *p.n.*; auteursrechten *pl.n.n.*
rub, *v.t.* wrijven *str. to* ~ *shoulders with*, in aanraking *n.* komen *irr.* met. ¶ *n. that's the* ~, daar schuilt de moeilijkheid *n.*
rubber, *n.* rubber *n.*; gom *n.n.*; robber *n.* (*bridge*).
rubbish, *n.* vuil *n.n.*, afval *n.n.*; nonsens *n.*
rubble, *n.* puin *n.n.*, afbraak *n.*
rubicund, *a.* rood; met rode wangen *pl.n.*
rubric, *n.* rubriek *n.*
ruby, *n.* robijn *n.*
ruck, *n.* plooi *n.*; kreukel *n.* ¶ *v.t.* plooien; kreukelen. *to* ~ *up*, opkruipen *str.*
ruction, *n.* herrie *n.*
rudd, *n.* ruisvoorn *n.*
rudder, *n.* roer *n.n.*
ruddiness, *n.* rossige kleur *n.*
ruddle, *n.* rossige kleur *n.*
ruddy, *a.* rossig, rood; (*coll.*) verduveld.
rude, *a.*, ~ly, *adv.* ruw, grof; onbeleefd. *in* ~ *health*, in blakende welstand *n.* **rudeness**, *n.* ruwheid *n.*, grofheid *n.*; onbeleefdheid *n.*
rudiment, *n.* rudiment *n.n.*, grondbeginsel *n.n.* **rudimentary**, *a.* rudimentair.
rue, *n.* wijnruit *n.* (*herb*). ¶ *v.t.* berouwen; betreuren. **rueful**, *a.*, ~ly, *adv.* droevig, treurig; deerniswekkend.
ruff, *n.* geplooide kraag *n.*
ruffian, *n.* schurk *n.*, woesteling *n.* **ruffianly**, *a.* woest, brutaal.

ruffle, *v.t.* opzetten (*feathers*); door de war halen (*hair*); verstoren (*feelings*).
rug, *n.* kleedje *n.n.*; deken *n.*
ragged, *a.* ruig, ruw; stoer.
rugger, *n.* Rugby voetbalspel *n.n.*
ruin, *n.* ruïne *n.*, bouwval *n.*; ondergang *n.*, val *n.*; verderf *n.n.* *to fall to* ~, tot puin *n.n.* vervallen *str.* ¶ *v.t.* verwoesten, vernielen; bederven *str.*; in 't verderf storten, te gronde richten; ruïneren. **ruination,** *n.* ondergang *n.* **ruinous,** *a.*, ~ly, *adv.* bouwvallig; verderfelijk.
rule, *n.* regel *n.*; liniaal *n.n.* (*instrument*); reglement *n.n.*; bewind *n.n.*, bestuur *n.n.*; heerschappij *n.* *as a* ~, in de regel; *by* ~, volgens de regel; *by* ~ *of thumb*, volgens de praktijk. ¶ *v.t.* besturen; bepalen, beslissen; liniëren. ~*d out*, uitgesloten, buiten kwestie *n.* ¶ *v.i.* heersen. **ruler,** *n.* vorst *n.*; liniaal *n.n.* **ruling,** *a.* heersend. ¶ *n.* uitspraak *n.*
rum, *n.* rum *n.* ¶ *a.* (*coll.*) raar, zonderling.
rumble, *v.i.* rommelen; dreunen. ¶ *n.* (dof) gedreun *n.n.* ~ *seat,* kattebak *n.*
ruminant, *a.* herkauwend. ¶ *n.* herkauwend dier *n.n.* **ruminate,** *v.i.* herkauwen; overpeinzen. **rumination,** *n.* herkauwing *n.*; overpeinzing *n.*
rummage, *v.i.* scharrelen, graaien. *to* ~ *in,* doorzoeken *irr.* **rummage sale,** *n.* opruiming *n.*
rummer, *n.* roemer *n.*
rumour, *n.* gerucht *n.n.* ¶ *v.t.* *it is* ~*ed that,* er loopt een gerucht dat.
rump, *n.* kruis *n.n.*; staartstuk *n.n.* ~ *steak,* biefstuk *n.*
rumple, *v.t.* kreuken.
rumpus, *n.* herrie *n.*, opschudding *n.*
run, *v.i.* lopen *str.*; hardlopen *str.*; vloeien; doorlopen *str.* (*colour*); luiden (*text*). *to* ~ *dry,* droog vallen *str.*; ophouden *irr.*; *to* ~ *low,* opraken; *to* ~ *aground,* aan de grond raken; *to be* ~ *down,* oververmoeid zijn; *to* ~ *in the family,* in de familie zitten. ¶ *v.t.* laten *str.* lopen; drijven *str.* (*business*); exploiteren (*enterprise*); smokkelen; brengen *irr.*, leiden, voeren. *to* ~ *a race,* racen; *to* ~ *the show,* de baas zijn; *to* ~ *to earth,* opsporen, te pakken krijgen *str.*; *to* ~ *one's eye over,* het oog laten *str.* gaan over; *to* ~ *down,* omvèrrijden *str.*, overrijden *str.*; becritiseren; *to* ~ *in,* inrekenen; *to* ~ *out of* ·. ·., heenraken door; *to* ~ *through,* doorstéken (*stab*); *to* ~ *to,* kunnen *irr.* bekostigen (*expense*). ¶ *n.* loop *n.*; lange reeks *n.*; rit *n.*; ren *n.* (*chicken*); run *n.* (*cricket*). *a* ~ *on,* een grote navraag naar; *to have the* ~ *of,* vrije toegang *n.* hebben tot; *in the long* ~, op de lange duur; *out of the common* ~, ongewoon. **runaway,** *a.* ~ *horse,* hollend paard *n.n.*, paard op hol *n.*; ~ *knock,* beldeurtje *n.n.* ¶ *n.* vluchteling *n.*
rune, *n.* rune *n.*

rung, *n.* sport *n.*
runic, *a.* runen . . .
runnel, *n.* goot *n.*
runner, *n.* loper *n.*, boodschapper *n.*; blokkadebreker *n.* ~ *bean,* klimboon *n.* ~ *up,* tweede *n.* in de wedstrijd. **running,** *a.* lopend. ~ *account,* rekening *n.* courant; *three days* ~, drie dagen *pl.n.* achterelkaar. ¶ *n.* *to be in the* ~, in aanmerking *n.* komen *irr.*
runt, *n.* kriel *n.*
runway, *n.* startbaan *n.*
rupee, *n.* ropij *n.*
rupture, *n.* breuk *n.*; scheuring *n.* ¶ *v.t.* breken *str.* ¶ *v.i.* breken *str.* *to be* ~*d.* een breuk krijgen *str.*
rural, *a.*, ~ly, *adv.* landelijk; plattelands . . .
ruse, *n.* list *n.*
rush, *v.i.* vliegen *str.*, stuiven *str.*, snellen; stormen. *to be* ~*ed,* het vreselijk druk hebben. ¶ *v.t.* bestormen; overrompelen; overhaast afdoen *irr.*; matten (*chair*). ¶ *n.* onstuimige loop *n.*; hoop *n.*; bies *n.* (*stalk*). *to make a* ~ *for,* losstormen op. ¶ *a.* ~ *hour,* drukste uur *n.n.* **rush-mat,** *n.* biezenmat *n.*
rusk, *n.* beschuit *n.n.*
russet, *a.* roodbruin.
Russia, *N.* Rusland *n.N.* ¶ *a.* ~ *leather,* juchtleer *n.n.* **Russian,** *a.* Russisch. ¶ *N.* Rus *N.* (*man*); Russin *N.*, Russische *N.* (*woman*).
rust, *n.* roest *n.* ¶ *v.i.* roesten, roestig worden *str.*
rustic, *a.*, ~ally, *adv.* landelijk, boers. ¶ *n.* landman *n.*, plattelandsbewoner *n.* **rusticate,** *v.t.* naar 't land verbannen. **rustication,** *n.* verblijf *n.n.* op het land. **rusticity,** *n.* landelijkheid *n.*
rustiness, *n.* roestigheid *n.*
rustle, *v.i.* ritselen; ruisen. ¶ *v.t.* doen *irr.*, ritselen; doen *irr.* ruisen. ¶ *n.* geritsel *n.n.*; geruis *n.n.*
rusty, *a.*, ~ily, *adv.* roestig; knarsend.
rut, *n.* spoor *n.n.*, wagenspoor *n.n.*; sleur *n.*, routine *n.* (*fig.*); bronstijd *n.* (*of animals*). ¶ *v.i.* bronsten, bronstig zijn.
ruthless, *a.*, ~ly, *adv.* meedogenloos, onbarmhartig.
rutilant, *a.* vuurrood.
rye, *n.* rogge *n.* **ryegrass,** *n.* raaigras *n.n.*

S

Sabbatarian, *N.* Zondagsvierder *N.* **Sabbath,** *N.* Sabbat *N.*, rustdag *N.*
sable, *n.* sabeldier *n.n.*; sabelbont *n.n.* ¶ *a.* zwart.
sabotage, *n.* sabotage *n.* **saboteur,** *n.* saboteur *n.*
sabre, *n.* sabel *n.* ¶ *v.t.* sabelen, neersabelen.
saccharine, *n.* saccharine *n.* ¶ *a.* suikerzoet.

sacerdotal, *a*. priesterlijk.
sack, *n*. zak *n*.; plundering *n*. *to get the ~*, de bons krijgen *str*. ¶ *v.t*. in zakken doen *irr*.; de bons geven *str*.; plunderen. **sack-cloth**, *n*. *in ~ and ashes*, in zak *n*. en as *n*. **sackful**, *n*. zakvol *n*. **sacking**, *n*. zakkengoed *n.n*.
sacrament, *n*. sacrament *n.n*.
sacred, *a*. gewijd, heilig; geestelijk. *~ service*, godsdienstoefening *n*.; *~ from*, veilig voor.
sacrifice, *n*. offer *n.n*., offerande *n*.; slachtoffer *n.n*. *at the ~ of*, ten koste van; *at any ~*, wat het ook koste: **sacrificial**, *a*. offer . . .
sacrilege, *n*. heiligschennis *n*. **sacrilegious**, *a*., *~ly*, *adv*. heiligschennend.
sacristan, *n*. koster *n*.; sacristein *n*. **sacristy**, *n*. sacristie *n*.
sad, *a*., *~ly*, *adv*. treurig, droef. **sadden**, *v.t*. bedroeven, treurig maken.
saddle, *n*. zadel *n.n*.; lendestuk *n.n*. ¶ *v.t*. zadelen. *to ~ with*, opschepen met; *to be ~d with*, opgescheept zitten *str*. met. **saddle-back**, *n*. zadelrug *n*. **saddle-bag**, *n*. zadeltas *n*. **saddle-cloth**, *n*. zadeldoek *n.n*. **saddle-horse**, *n*. rijpaard *n.n*. **saddler**, *n*. zadelmaker *n*.
sadness, *n*. droefheid *n*.; droefenis *n*.
safe, *a*., *~ly*, *adv*. veilig; betrouwbaar. *~ and sound*, gezond en wel; *~ from*, vrij van, gevrijwaard voor; *~ conduct*, vrijgeleide *n.n*. ¶ *n*. brandkast *n*. *meat ~*, vliegenkast *n*. **safeguard**, *n*. bescherming *n*. beveiliging *n*.; waarborg *n*. ¶ *v.t*. beschermen; waarborgen. *to ~ against*, vrijwaren tegen. **safeness**, *n*. veiligheid *n*.; zekerheid *n*. **safety**, *n*. veiligheid *n*. *with ~*, zonder gevaar *n.n*. **safety-belt**, *n*. reddingsgordel *n*. **safety-curtain**, *n*. brandscherm *n.n*. **safety-pin**, *n*. veiligheidsspeld *n*.
saffron, *n*. saffraan *n*. ¶ *a*. geel.
sag, *v.i*. doorzakken, doorbuigen *str*.
sagacious, *a*. scherpzinnig. **sagacity**, *n*. scherpzinnigheid *n*.
sage, *a*. wijs. ¶ *n*. wijze *n*., wijsgeer *n*.; salie *n*. (*herb*).
sago, *n*. sago *n*.
sail, *n*. zeil *n.n*.; wiek *n*. (*mill*). *in full ~*, met volle zeilen. ¶ *v.i*. zeilen; varen *str*.; afvaren *str*. ¶ *v.t*. bevaren *str*.; varen *str*. met. **sailing**, *n*. zeilen *n.n*.; afvaart *n*. *~ orders*, instructies *pl.n*. **sailor**, *n*. matroos *n*. *to be a good ~*, geen last *n*. van zeeziekte *n*. hebben.
saint, *a*. heilig. ¶ *n*. heilige *n*. **sainted**, *a*. heilig; zaliger. **saintly**, *a*. heilig, vroom.
sake, *n*. *for the ~ of*, ter wille van; *for God's ~*, om Gods wil *n*.; *for your ~*, om uwentwil, voor je eigen wil *n*.
salaam, *n*. oosterse buiging *n*. ¶ *v.i*. diep buigen *str*.
salable, *a*. verkoopbaar.
salacious, *a*., *~ly*, *adv*. geil.
salad, *n*. sla *n*. *~ dressing*, sla-aanmaaksel *n.n*.; *~ oil*, sla-olie *n*.

salamander, *n*. salamander *n*.
salaried, *a*. gesalarieerd, bezoldigd. **salary**, *n*. salaris *n.n*., bezoldiging *n*.
sale, *n*. verkoop *n*.; veiling *n*. *for ~*, te koop; *on ~*, te koop. **sale-room**, *n*. verkooplokaal *n.n*. **salesman**, *n*. verkoper *n*.; winkelbediende *n*.; handelsagent *n*. **saleswoman**, *n*. verkoopster *n*.; winkeljuffrouw *n*.
salient, *a*. (voor)uitspringend; sterk uitkomend. ¶ *n*. saillant *n*.
saline, *a*. zouthoudend; zout . . . ¶ *n*. zoutpan *n*. **salinity**, *n*. zoutheid *n*., zoutgehalte *n.n*.; ziltheid *n*.
saliva, *n*. speeksel *n.n*. **salivary**, *a*. speeksel . . . **salivate**, *v.i*. speeksel afscheiden; kwijlen. **salivation**, *n*. speekselafscheiding *n*.
sallow, *a*. vuilgeel, vaal. **sallowness**, *n*. ongezonde bleekheid *n*.; vaalheid *n*.
sally, *n*. uitval *n*.; kwinkslag *n*. ¶ *v.i*. een uitval doen *irr*. *to ~ forth*, er op uit trekken *str*.
salmon, *n*. zalm *n*. *~ coloured*, zalmkleurig.
saloon, *n*. grote kajuit *n*. **saloon-bar**, *n*. (duurdere) bar *n*. **saloon-car**, *n*. luxewagon *n*., salonrijtuig *n.n*.
salsify, *n*. schorseneer *n*.
salt, *n*. zout *n.n*. *old ~*, oude zeerob *n*.; *to be worth one's ~*, z'n loon *n.n*. waard zijn. ¶ *a*. zout; zilt. ¶ *v.t*. zouten; inzouten. *to ~ away*, oppotten; *to ~ down*, opzouten. **salt-cellar**, *n*. zoutvaatje *n.n*. **saltfish**, *n*. zoutevis *n*. **salt-glaze**, *n*. zoutverglaassel *n.n*. **saltiness**, *n*. zoutheid *n*. **salting**, *n*. wadden *pl.n.n*. **saltish**, *a*. zoutig, zoutachtig. **salt-maker**, *n*. zoutzieder *n*. **saltpetre**, *n*. salpeter *n.n*. **salt-works**, *n*. zoutkeet *n*. **salty**, *a*. zoutig, zilt.
salubrious, *a*. gezond; heilzaam. **salubrity**, *n*. gezondheid *n*.; heilzaamheid *n*.
salutariness, *n*. heilzaamheid *n*., weldadigheid *n*. **salutary**, *a*. heilzaam weldadig.
salutation, *n*. groet *n*., begroeting *n*. **salute**, *n*. groet *n*., begroeting *n*.; saluut *n.n*. ¶ *v.t*. groeten, begroeten; salueren.
salvage, *n*. berging *n*.; bergloon *n.n*. ¶ *v.t*. bergen.
salvation, *n*. zaligmaking *n*.; redding *n*. *S~ Army*, Leger *n.N*. des Heils. **salvationist**, *n*. heilsoldaat *n*.; heilsoldate *n*. (*female*). **salve**, *n*. zalf *n*., balsem *n*. ¶ *v.t*. zalven; bergen *str*. (*property*).
salver, *n*. presenteerblad *n.n*.
salvo, *n*. salvo *n.n*.
sal-volatile, *n*. vlugzout *n.n*.
same, *a*., *pron*. zelfde. *the ~*, dezelfde *n*., hetzelfde *n.n*.; *it is all the ~ to me*, 't is mij eender. ¶ *adv*. *the ~*, op dezelfde wijze, eender; *all the ~*, toch, hoe dan ook. **sameness**, *n*. eentonigheid *n*.
Samoyed, *N*. Samojeed *N*.
samphire, *n*. zeevenkel *n*.
sample, *n*. monster *n.n*., staal *n*.; voorbeeld *n.n*. ¶ *v.t*. bemonsteren; proeven, keuren. **sampler**, *n*. merklap *n*.; staalboek *n.n*.

sanatorium, *n.* sanatorium *n.n.*
sanctification, *n.* heiliging *n.* sanctify, *v.t.* heiligen.
sanctimonious, *a.*, ~ly, *adv.* schijnheilig. sanctimony, *n.* schijnheiligheid *n.*
sanction, *n.* goedkeuring *n.*, bekrachtiging *n.*; sanctie *n.* ¶ *v.t.* bekrachtigen, bevestigen.
sanctity, *n.* heiligheid *n.*; onschendbaarheid *n.*
sanctuary, *n.* heiligdom *n.n.*; toevluchtsoord *n.n.*
sand, *n.* zand *n.n.* ~s, strand *n.n.*, zandvlakte *n.* ¶ *v.t.* met zand bestrooien.
sandal, *n.* sandaal *n.*
sandalwood, *n.* sandelhout *n.n.*
sand-bag, *n.* zandzak *n.* sandbank, *n.* zandbank *n.*, zandplaat *n.* sand-blast, *n.* zandstraal *n.* sandboy, *n.* as happy as a ~, zo blij as een kind *n.n.* sand-glass, *n.* zandloper *n.* sandgrouse, *n.* steppenhoen *n.n.* sandhill, *n.* duin *n.n.* sandmartin, *n.* oeverzwaluw *n.* sandpaper, *n.* schuurpapier *n.n.* ¶ *v.t.* met schuurpapier gladwrijven *str.* sandpiper, *n.* oeverloper *n.*
sandwich, *n.* sandwich *n.*, belegde boterham *n.* ¶ *v.t.* plakken tussen.
sandy, *a.* zandig; rossig.
sane, *a.*, ~ly, *adv.* gezond van geest *n.*; verstandig.
sanguinary, *a.* bloedig; bloeddorstig. sanguine, *a.*, ~ly, *adv.* volbloedig; optimistisch, hoopvol.
sanitary, *a.* sanitair, gezondheids . . . ~ inspector, inspecteur *n.* van de gezondheidsdienst. sanitation, *n.* hygiëne *n.*; hygiënische maatregelen *pl.n.*
sanity, *n.* gezondheid *n.* van geest *n.*
Sanscrit, *N.* Sanskriet *n.N.*
Santa Claus, *N.* Sinterklaas *N.*
sap, *n.* sap *n.n.*; (*coll.*) onnozele dwaas *n.* ¶ *v.t.* het sap onttrekken *str.* aan; ondermijnen.
sapience, *n.* wijsheid *n.* sapient, *a.*, ~ly, *adv.* wijs.
sapless, *a.* saploos.
sapling, *n.* jonge boom *n.*
saponaceous, *a.* zeepachtig. saponification, *n.* verzeping *n.* saponify, *v.t.* verzepen.
sapper, *n.* sappeur *n.*
sapphire, *n.* saffier *n.* or *n.n.* ¶ *a.* saffieren.
sappy, *a.* sappig.
sapwood, *n.* spint *n.n.*
Saracen, *N.* Saraceen *N.*
sarcasm, *n.* sarcasme *n.n.* sarcastic, *a.*, ~ally, *adv.* sarcastisch.
sarcophagus, *n.* sarcophaag *n.*
sardine, *n.* sardine *n.*
sardonic, *a.* sardonisch.
sartorial, *a.* kleermakers . . .
Sarum, *a.* van Salisbury.
sash, *n.* gordel *n.*, sjerp *n.*; schuifraam *n.n.* ~ cord, raamkoord *n.n.*
Satanic, *a.* satanisch.
satchel, *n.* schooltas *n.*, boekentas *n.*
satchet, *n.* zakje *n.n.*

sate, *v.t.* verzadigen. ~d, verzadigd, geblaseerd.
sateen, *n.* satinet *n.*
satellite, *n.* satelliet *n.n.*
satiability, *n.* verzadigbaarheid *n.* satiable, *a.* verzadigbaar. satiate, *v.t.* verzadigen. satiety, *n.* verzadigdheid *n.*
satin, *n.* satijn *n.n.* satinette, *n.* satinet *n.n.* satinwood, *n.* satijnhout *n.n.* satiny, *a.* satijnachtig.
satire, *n.* satire *n.*; hekelschrift *n.n.*, hekeldicht *n.n.* satirical, *a.*, ~ly, *adv.* satirisch. satirist, *n.* satiricus. satirize, *v.t.* hekelen.
satisfaction, *n.* tevredenheid *n.*; bevrediging *n.*, voldoening *n.* satisfactory, *a.* bevredigend. satisfactorily, *adv.* op bevredigende wijze. satisfy, *v.t.* bevredigen; tevreden stellen, voldoen *irr.*; verzadigen, stillen. ¶ *v.r.* to ~ oneself of, zich overtuigen van.
saturate, *v.t.* verzadigen. to ~ with, doortrekken *str.* met or van. saturation, *n.* verzadiging *n.*
Saturday, *N.* zaterdag *N.* ¶ *a.* zaterdags.
saturnine, *a.* somber.
sauce, *n.* saus; (*coll.*) onbeschaamdheid *n.*, brutaliteit *n.* ~-boat, sauskom *n.*
saucepan, *n.* pan *n.*, pannetje *n.n.*
saucer, *n.* schoteltje *n.n.*
sauciness, *n.* brutaliteit *n.* saucy, *a.*, ~ily, *adv.* onbeschaamd, brutaal.
saunter, *v.i.* drentelen. ¶ *n.* drentelgang *n.*
saurian, *a.* saurisch. ¶ *n.* krokodil *n.*
sausage, *n.* worst *n.* ~ roll, saucijzebroodje *n.n.*
savage, *a.*, ~ly, *adv.* wild, woest; barbaars. ¶ *n.* wilde *n.* ¶ *v.t.* bijten *str.* savageness, *n.* woestheid *n.* savagery, *n.* woestheid *n.*; barbaarsheid *n.*
savannah, *n.* savanne *n.*
save, *v.t.* redden; bewaren; (be)sparen, opsparen. to ~ from, behoeden voor; to ~ one's face, zijn figuur *n.* redden. ¶ *v.i.* sparen. ¶ *prep.* behalve. ~ for, met uitzondering *n.* van.
saveloy, *n.* cervelaatworst *n.*
saver, *n.* redder *n.*; spaarder *n.* saving, *n.* redden *n.n.*; sparen *n.n.*; besparing *n.*; redding *n.*, behoud *n.n.* ~s, spaarpenningen *pl.n.*; ~s, bank spaarbank *n.* ¶ *a.* ~ clause, uitzonderingsbepaling *n.*; ~ grace, reddende eigenschap *n.* ¶ *prep.* behalve, behoudens.
Saviour, *N.* Heiland *N.*, Zaligmaker *N.*
savour, *n.* smaak *n.*, geur *n.* ¶ *v.i.* to ~ of, smaken naar, doen *irr.* denken aan. savoury, *a.* smakelijk, geurig.
savoy, *n.* savoyekool *n.*
saw, *n.* zaag *n.*; oud gezegde *n.n.*, spreuk *n.* ¶ *v.t.* & *v.i.* zagen. sawdust, *n.* zaagsel *n.n.*, zaagmeel *n.n.* sawmill, *n.* zaagmolen *n.* sawpit, *n.* zaagkuil *n.* sawyer, *n.* zager *n.*
sawder, *n.* soft ~, mooie praatjes *pl.n.n.*
saxifrage, *n.* steenbreke *n.*

Saxon, *a.* Saksisch. ¶ *N.* Sakser *N.* **Saxony,** *N.* Saksen *n.N.*

saxophone, *n.* saxophoon *n.*

say, *v.t.* zeggen *irr.*; opzeggen *irr. to ~ grace,* bidden *str. (before meal)*; danken *(after meal)*; *to ~ mass,* de mis lezen *str.*; *it ~s . . .,* er staat; *it ~s so,* dat staat er; *~ on!,* ga door; *I ~,* hoor eens!, zeg!; *you don't ~,* och kom! ¶ *n.* woord *n.n. to have one's ~,* zeggen *irr.* wat men te zeggen heeft; *to have some ~,* medezeggenschap *n.* hebben. **saying,** *n.* gezegde *n.n.,* zegswijze *n. it goes without ~,* het spreekt vanzelf.

scab, *n.* roofje *n.n.,* korstje *n.n.*; schurft *n. (sheep)*; *(coll.)* onderkruiper *n.*

scabbard, *n.* schede *n.*

scabby, *a.* korstig; schurftig.

scabies, *n.* schurft *n.* **scabious,** *a.* schurftig.

scabrous, *a.* gewaagd, scabreus.

scaffold, *n.* schavot *n.n.* ¶ *v.t.* schragen; van een stellage *n.* voorzien *irr.* **scaffolding,** *n.* stellage *n.,* steiger *n.*

scald, *v.t.* (met hete vloeistof) branden; heet maken. ¶ *n.* brandwonde *n.* **scalding hot,** *a.* kokend heet, gloeiend heet.

scale, *n.* schaal *n.*; weegschaal *n.*; maatstaf *n.*; graadverdeling *n. (graduated)*; ladder *n. (social)*; toonladder *n.*; schub *n. (skin)*; schilfer *n.*; ketelsteen *n. pair of ~s,* weegschaal *n.*; *to turn the ~,* de weegschaal doen *irr.* overslaan; *on a large ~,* op grote schaal; *the ~s fell from my eyes,* de schellen vielen me van de ogen. ¶ *v.t.* wegen *str.*; beklimmen *str.*; schilferen; krabben, bikken. **scale-beam,** *n.* unster *n.* **scaled,** *a.* geschubd, schubbig. **scaler,** *n.* krabber *n.,* bikker *n.*

scallop, *n.* St. Jacobskam *n.* ¶ *v.t.* uitschulpen; in broodkruim *n.n.* bakken *irr.*

scalp, *n.* schedelhuid *n.* ¶ *v.t.* scalperen.

scalpel, *n.* ontleedmes *n.n.,* scalpel *n.n.*

scaly, *a.* geschubd, schubbig.

scamp, *n.* schalk *n.,* deugniet *n.*

scamper, *v.i.* er van door gaan *irr.*; hollen.

scan, *v.t.* onderzoeken *irr.*; scanderen. ¶ *v.i.* lopen *str.*

scandal, *n.* schandaal *n.n.*; schande *n.*; aanstoot *n.*; kwaadsprekerij *n.* **scandalize,** *v.t.* ergenis *n.* geven *str.* aan. *to be ~d,* gechokeerd zijn. **scandalmonger,** *n.* kwaadspreker *n.* **scandalous,** *a.,* ~ly, *adv.* schandalig; ergerlijk; lasterlijk.

scant, *a.* karig, schraal. **scantily,** *adv.* karig; ternauwernood. **scantiness,** *n.* karigheid *n.*; spaarzaamheid *n.* **scanty,** *a.* karig, spaarzaam.

scapegoat, *n.* zondebok *n.* **scapegrace,** *n.* deugniet *n.*

scapulary, *n.* scapulier *n.n.*

scar, *n.* lidteken. ¶ *v.t.* schrammen; met lidtekens bedekken.

scarab, *n.* tor *n.*; scarabee *n.*

scarce, *a.* zeldzaam; schaars. **scarcely,** *adv.*

nauwelijks, ternauwernood. **scarceness,** *n.* schaarsheid *n.,* schaarste *n.* **scarcity,** *n.* schaarste *n.* ~ *of,* gebrek *n.n.* aan.

scare, *v.t.* doen *irr.* schrikken; bang maken, schrik *n.* aanjagen *str.* ¶ *n.* schrik *n.,* paniek *n.* **scarecrow,** *n.* vogelverschrikker *n.*; *(fig.)* schrikbeeld *n.n.*

scarf, *n.* das *n.,* sjerp *n.*

scarification, *n.* insnijding *n.* **scarify,** *v.t.* kerven *str.,* insnijdingen maken.

scarlatina, *n.* rode hond *n.*

scarlet, *a.* scharlaken, scharlakens. ~ *fever,* roodvonk *n.n.*; ~ *runner,* pronkboon *n.*

scarp, *n.* steile helling *n.*

scathe, *v.t.* deren. **scathing,** *a.* vernietigend.

scatter, *v.t.* verstrooien; uitstrooien. ¶ *v.i.* uiteengaan *irr.,* zich verspreiden.

scavenger, *n.* straatveger *n.*; reiniger *n.* ~ *beetle,* aaskever *n.*; ~ *vulture,* aasgier *n.*

scene, *n.* toneel *n.n.,* tafereel *n.n.*; scène *n. (row). behind the ~s,* achter de schermen *pl.n.n.* **scenery,** *n.* toneel *n.n.*; toneeldecoraties *pl.n.*; landschap *n.n.* **scene-shifter,** *n.* toneelknecht *n.* **scenic,** *a.* toneel . . . ~ *railway,* miniatuurbaan *n.*

scent, *n.* geur *n.,* parfum *n.n.*; (reuk)spoor *n.n.*; reukzin *n. to get ~ of,* de lucht krijgen *str.* van; *to put off the ~,* van het spoor brengen *irr.* ¶ *v.t.* parfumeren; ruiken *str. to ~ out,* opsporen, ontdekken **scent-bottle,** *n.* odeurflesje *n.n.* **scentless,** *a.* reukeloos.

sceptic, *a.* sceptisch. ¶ *n.* scepticus *n.,* twijfelaar *n.* **scepticism,** *n.* scepticisme *n.n.*

sceptre, *n.* schepter *n.,* rijksstaf *n.*

schedule, *n.* tabel *n.*; plan *n.n.,* regeling *n.* ¶ *v.t.* vaststellen, regelen.

schematic, *a.* schematisch. **scheme,** *n.* schema *n.n.*; plan *n.n.* ¶ *v.t.* beramen. ¶ *v.i.* intrigeren. **schemer,** *n.* intrigant *n.*

schipperke, *n.* keeshond *n.*

schism, *n.* schisma *n.n.,* scheuring *n.* **schismatic,** *a.* schismatiek. ¶ *n.* scheurmaker *n.*

scholar, *n.* scholier *n.,* schooljongen *n.*; beursstudent *n.*; geleerde *n.* **scholarly,** *a.* geleerd. **scholarship,** *n.* geleerdheid *n.*; studiebeurs *n.* **scholastic,** *a.,* ~ally, *adv.* scholastisch; schools; school . . ., onderwijs . . . **scholasticism,** *n.* scholastiek *n.* **school,** *n.* school *n. at ~,* op school. ¶ *v.t.* onderwijzen *str.*; africhten; oefenen. ¶ *v.i.* scholen *pl.n.* vormen *(fish).* ¶ *v.r.* zich scholen. **school-board,** *n.* schoolcommissie *n.* **schoolboy,** *n.* schooljongen *n.* **schoolfellow,** *n.* schoolmakker *n.* **schoolgirl,** *n.* schoolmeisje *n.n.* **schooling,** *n.* opleiding *n.*; leerschool *n.* **schoolman,** *n.* scholasticus *n.* **schoolmaster,** *n.* onderwijzer *n.* **schoolmistress,** *n.* onderwijzeres *n.*

schooner, *n.* schoener *n.*

sciatica, *n.* ischias *n.,* (heup)jicht *n.*

science, *n.* wetenschap *n.*; kunde *n.*; wis- en

natuurkunde *n.* **scientific,** *a.,* ~**ally,** *adv.*
wetenschappelijk. **scientist,** *n.* natuurkundige *n.;* man *n.* van de wetenschap.
scimitar, *n.* (Turkse) kromme sabel *n.*
scintilla, *n.* sprankje *n.n.,* zweempje *n.n.*
scintillate, *v.i.* fonkelen, tintelen, flonkeren.
scintillation, *n.* fonkeling *n.,* tinteling *n.*
scion, *n.* loot *n.,* spruit *n.*
scission, *n.* scheuring *n.,* splitsing *n.*
scissor-bill, *n.* schaarbek *n.* **scissors,** *pl.n.*
schaar *n. pair of* ~, schaar *n.*
scoff, *v.i.* schimpen, spotten. ¶ *n.* spot *n.;*
schimpscheut *n.* **scoffer,** *n.* spotter *n.*
scoffing, *a.,* ~**ly,** *adv.* spottend.
scold, *v.i.* kijven *str.* ¶ *v.t.* bekijven *str.,*
een uitbrander *n.* geven *str.* ¶ *n.* kijfster *n.*
sconce, *n.* kaarshouder *n.*
scone, *n.* plaatkoekje *n.n.*
scoop, *n.* hoosvat *n.n.;* schep *n.;* kaasboor *n.;*
haal *n.,* schep *n.;* buitenkansje *n.n.* ¶ *v.t.*
uithozen; uitscheppen. **scooper,** *n.* boor *n.*
scoopnet, *n.* schepnet *n.n.*
scooter, *n.* vliegende Hollander *n.,* autoped
n.
scope, *n.* omvang *n.;* kader *n.n.,* bestek *n.n.;*
(*fig.*) terrein *n.n.,* gebied *n.n.;* bewegingsvrijheid *n.*
scorbutic, *a.* aan scheurbuik *n.* lijdend. ¶ *n.*
scheurbuiklijder *n.*
scorch, *v.i.* schroeien. ¶ *v.t.* (ver)schroeien.
score, *n.* kerf *n.;* streepje *n.n.;* aantal *n.n.*
behaalde punten *pl.n.n.;* twintigtal *n.n.;*
partituur *n.* (*music*). *four* ~, tachtig;
on that ~, wat dat betreft; *on the* ~ *of,*
op grond *n.* van; *old* ~*s,* oude schulden
pl.n. ¶ *v.t.* inkerven *str.;* onderstrepen;
behalen; op noten *pl.n.* zetten. **scorer,** *n.*
markeur *n.*
scoria, *pl.n.* slakken *pl.n.,* metaalschuim *n.n.*
scorn, *n.* verachting *n.,* minachting *n.;*
bespotting *n. to hold up to* ~, aan de
verachting prijsgeven *str.; to put to* ~,
beschamen. ¶ *v.t.* verachten, minachten,
versmaden. **scornful,** *a.,* ~**ly,** *adv.*
verachtend.
scorpion, *n.* schorpioen *n.*
scorzonera, *n.* schorseneer *n.*
scot, *n.* belasting *n. to pay* ~ *and lot,* schot
en lot betalen.
Scot, *N.* Schot *N.*
scotch, *v.t.* verijdelen. *to* ~ *something,*
ergens een stokje *n.n.* voor steken *str.*
Scotch, *a.* Schots. **Scotchman,** *N.* Schot *N.*
Scotchwoman, *N.* Schotse *N.*
scot-free, *a.* ongedeerd. *to get off* ~, *te*
zonder kleerscheuren *pl.n.* afkomen *irr.*
Scots, *a.* Schots. **Scotsman,** *N.* Schot *N.*
Scotswoman, *N.* Schotse *N.* **Scottish,** *a.*
Schots.
scoundrel, *n.* schurk *n.* **scoundrelly,** *a.*
schurkachtig.
scour, *v.t.* schuren; schrobben, boenen;
afzoeken *irr. to* ~ *the seas,* de zee

afzwalken. **scourer,** *n.* boender *n.;*
schuurder *n.*
scourge, *n.* gesel *n.,* zweep *n.;* plaag *n.* ¶ *v.t.*
geselen; kastijden, tuchtigen.
scout, *n.* verkenner *n.;* oppasser *n. boy* ~,
padvinder *n.* ¶ *v.i.* verkennen, op verkenning *n.* uitgaan *irr.* ¶ *v.t.* verwerpen *str.*
scoutmaster, *n.* troepleider *n.*
scowl, *v.i.* (de wenkbrauwen *pl.n.*) fronsen,
zuur kijken *str.* ¶ *n.* frons *n.,* zuur gezicht
n.n.
scrabble, *v.i.* krabbelen.
scrag, *n.* mager beest *n.n.* ~ *end of neck,*
mager halsstuk *n.n.* ¶ *v.t.* de nek
omdraaien. **scraggy,** *a.* mager.
scramble, *v.i.* grabbelen; tuimelen, klauteren.
¶ *v.t.* roeren (*eggs*). ~*d egg,* roerei *n.n.*
¶ *n.* gegrabbel *n.n.;* vechtpartij *n.*
scrap, *v.t.* weggooien; afkeuren. ¶ *v.i.*
bakkeleien, vechten *str.* ¶ *n.* stukje *n.n.,*
brokje *n.n.* **scrapbook,** *n.* album *n.n.,*
boek *n.n.* met uitknipsels *pl.n.n.*
scrape, *v.t.* schrapen, afkrabben; schuren;
krassen. *to* ~ *one's feet,* met de voeten
pl.n. schuifelen; *to* ~ *together,* bijeenschrapen. ¶ *v.i. to* ~ *along,* met moeite *n.*
voortkomen *irr.; to* ~ *through,* zich er net
doorheenslaan *irr.* ¶ *n.* verlegenheid *n.;*
vechtpartij *n. to be in a* ~, in de knel
zitten *str.; to get into a* ~, in de knel raken;
to help someone out of a ~, iemand uit de
brand helpen *str.* **scraper,** *n.* krabber *n.,*
schrabber *n.,* schraapijzer *n.n.*
scrap-heap, *n.* hoop oud roest *n.n. to cast cn*
the ~, aan kant *n.* doen *irr.* **scrap-iron,** *n.*
oud ijzer *n.n.,* oud roest *n.n.* **scrappiness,**
n. onsamenhangendheid *n.* **scrappy,** *a.,*
~**ily,** *adv.* onsamenhangend, los.
scratch, *v.t.* krabben, krauwen; doorhalen,
schrappen. *to* ~ *together,* bijeenscharrelen.
¶ *n.* krab *n.,* schram *n. to start from* ~,
van meet *n.* af aan beginnen *str.; not up*
to ~, niet goed genoeg. ¶ *a.* bijeengeraapt.
scrawl, *v.t.* slordig schijven *str.* ¶ *n.* slordig
schrift *n.n.,* hanepoten *pl.n.*
scream, *v.t. & v.i.* gillen, schreeuwen.
screech, *v.i.* gillen; krijsen *str.* **screech-owl,**
n. kerkuil *n.,* torenuil *n.*
screen, *n.* scherm *n.n.;* gordijn *n.n.* (*smoke*);
doek *n.n.* (*cinema*); rooster *n.,* zeef *n.*
(*sieve*). ¶ *v.t.* verbergen *str.;* maskeren;
zeven.
screw, *n.* schroef *n.;* peperhuisje *n.n.* (*paper*);
(*coll.*) loon *n.n.,* salaris *n.n.* ¶ *v.t.* schroeven
to ~ *up one's courage,* zich vermannen.
screwbolt, *n.* schroefbout *n.* **screw-driver,**
n. schroevendraaier *n.* **screwjack,** *n.*
dommekracht *n.* **screw-nut,** *n.* moer *n.*
scribble, *v.i.* krabbelen. **scribbler,** *n.* krabbelaar *n.,* prulschrijver *n.*
scribe, *n.* schriftgeleerde *n.;* copieerder *n.*
scrimmage, *n.* schermutseling *n.;* worsteling
n.
script, *n.* geschrift *n.n.;* schrift *n.n.*

scriptural, *a.* bijbels, schriftuurlijk. **Scripture**, *N. the Holy* ~(s), de Heilige Schrift.

scrofula, *n.* klierziekte *n.*   **scrofulous**, *a.* klierachtig.

scroll, *n.* rol *n.*; krul *n.* (*ornament*).

scrub, *v.t.* schrobben, schuren, boenen. ¶ *n.* kreupelhout *n.n.* **scrubber**, *n.* schrobber *n.*, boender *n.*   **scrubby**, *a.* dwergachtig, nietig; ruig.

scruff, *n.* ~ *of the neck*, nekvel *n.n.*

scrumptious, *a.* (*coll.*) heerlijk.

scrunch, *v.i.* knarsen, kraken. ¶ *v.t.* doen *irr.* knarsen, doen *irr.* kraken.

scruple, *n.* gewetensbezwaar *n.n.*, zwarigheid *n. to make no* ~ *to*, niet aarzelen om. ¶ *v.i. to* ~, bezwaar *n.n.* maken tegen. **scrupulous**, *a.*, ~ly, *adv.* nauwgezet, angstvallig.

scrutinize, *v.t.* nagaan *irr.*, nauwkeurig onderzoeken *irr.* **scrutiny**, *n.* contrôle *n.*, nauwkeurig onderzoek *n.n.*

scud, *v.i.* hard lopen *str.*; jagen *str.*; lenzen (*ship*).

scuffle, *n.* verward handgemeen *n.n.*; geschuifel *n.n.* ¶ *v.t.* schuifelen.

scull, *n.* roeiriem *n.*; wrikriem *n.* ¶ *v.i.* roeien; wrikken.

scullery, *n.* bijkeuken *n.* ~ *maid*, tweede keukenmeid *n.* **scullion**, *n.* vatenwasser *n.*

sculptor, *n.* beeldhouwer *n.*   **sculptural**, *a.* beeldhouw . . ., sculptureel. **sculpture**, *n.* beeldhouwkunst *n.*; beeldhouwwerk *n.n.*

scum, *n.* schuim *n.n.* ¶ *v.t.* afschuimen.

scurf, *n.* roos *n.* **scurfy**, *a.* vol roos.

scurrility, *n.* grofheid *n.* **scurrilous**, *a.*, ~ly, *adv.* grof, schunnig.

scurry, *v.i. to* ~ *away*, er gauw vandoor gaan *irr.* ¶ *n.* haast *n.*, verwarring *n.*

scurvy, *n.* scheurbuik *n.* ¶ *a.* gemeen.

scut, *n.* pluim *n.*

scutcheon, *n.* wapenschild *n.n.*

scuttle, *n.* kolenbak *n.*; klep *n.* ¶ *v.t.* doen *irr.* zinken.

scythe, *n.* zeis *n.* ¶ *v.t.* maaien.

sea, *n.* zee *n. at* ~, op zee; *to be at* ~, in de war zijn. **seaboard**, *n.* kust *n.*, kuststreek *n.* **seaborne**, *a.* overzees; over zee vervoerd. **sea-bound**, *a.* door de zee omringd. **sea-breeze**, *n.* zeewind *n.* **sea-brief**, *n.* zeebrief *n.* **sea-buckthorn**, *n.* duindoorn *n.* **seachest**, *n.* plunjekist *n.* **sea-eagle**, *n.* visarend *n.* **seafarer**, *n.* zeeman *n.* **seafaring**, *a.* zeevarend. **seafront**, *n.* zeeboulevard *n.* **sea-going**, *a.* zee . . . **sea-kale**, *n.* zeekool *n.*

seal, *n.* zeehond *n.*, rob *n.*; zegel *n.n.*; stempel *n.n.* ¶ *v.t.* verzegelen; (*fig.*) bezegelen.

sea-lane, *n.* vaargeul *n.* **sea-lawyer**, *n.* chicaneur *n.*, querulant *n.* **sea-legs**, *pl.n.* zeebenen *pl.n.n. to have got one's* ~, op dek *n.n.* kunnen *irr.* wandelen. **sea-level**, *n.* zeespiegel *n.*

sealing-wax, *n.* zegellak *n.*

sealskin, *n.* robbevel *n.n.*

seam, *n.* naad *n.*; zoom *n.*; mijnader *n.*

seaman, *n.* zeeman *n.* *able* ~, matroos *n.* (tweede klasse *n.*). **seamanship**, *n.* zeemanschap *n.* **seamark**, *n.* zeebaken *n.n.* **seamarker**, *n.* markeerboei *n.*

seamstress, *n.* naaister *n.*

seamy, *a.* lelijk.

sea-needle, *n.* geep *n.* **sea-plane**, *n.* watervliegtuig *n.n.*

sear, *v.t.* verschroeien; verdorren. ¶ *a.* droog, dor.

search, *v.i.* zoeken *irr. to* ~ *for*, zoeken naar; *to* ~ *into*, onderzoeken *irr.* ¶ *v.t.* doorzoeken *irr.*; fouilleren. ¶ *n.* zoeken *n.n.*; doorzoeking *n. in* ~ *of*, op zoek naar. **searcher**, *n.* visiteur *n.* **searchlight**, *n.* zoeklicht *n.n.* **search party**, *n.* groep mannen op zoek. **search-warrant**, *n.* machtiging *n.* tot huiszoeking *n.*

sea-risk, *n.* zeegevaar *n.n.* **seasick**, *a.* zeeziek. **seasickness**, *n.* zeeziekte *n.* **seaside**, *n.* aan de zeekant (gelegen). *at the* ~, aan zee; *to go to the* ~, naar een badplaats *n.* gaan *irr.*

season, *n.* jaargetijde *n.n.*; seizoen *n.n.*; geschikte tijd *n. silly* ~, komkommertijd *n.*; *strawberries are in* ~, het is de tijd van de aardbeien; *in and out of* ~, te pas en te onpas; *in good* ~, tijdig. ¶ *v.t.* kruiden. **seasonable**, *a.* gepast, geschikt. **seasonal**, *a.* van 't seizoen. **seasoned**, *a.* gekruid; gehard, beproefd. **seasoning**, *n.* kruiden *pl.n.n.* **season-ticket**, *n.* abonnementskaart *n.*

seat, *n.* zitplaats *n.*; zitting *n.*; zitvlak *n.n.*; zetel *n.*; (*fig.*) toneel *n.n.* ¶ *v.t.* doen *irr.* zitten. ¶ *v.i.* zitplaatsen bevatten voor.

sea-wall, *n.* zeewering *n.* **seaward**, *a. & adv.* zeewaarts. **seaweed**, *n.* zeewier *n.n.* **seaworthiness**, *n.* zeewaardigheid *n.* **seaworthy**, *a.* zeewaardig.

secede, *v.i.* zich afscheiden. *to* ~ *from*, uittreden *str.* uit *or* van. **secession**, *n.* afscheiding *n.*

seclude, *v.t. to* ~ *from*, uitsluiten *str.* van; *to* ~ *oneself*, zich afzonderen. **secluded**, *a.* afgezonderd, afgesloten. **seclusion**, *n.* afzondering *n.*

second, *a.* tweede. *every* ~ *week*, om de andere week; *to be* ~ *to none*, voor niemand onderdoen *irr.*; *at* ~*hand*, uit de tweede hand; *on* ~ *thoughts*, bij nader inzien *n.n.* ¶ *adv. the* ~ *best*, op één na de beste. ¶ *n.* seconde *n.*, secunde *n.*; tweede *n.* or *n.n.*; secondant *n.* ¶ *v.t.* helpen *str.*, bijstaan *irr.*; steunen. **secondary**, *a.* secundair; ondergeschikt. **seconder**, *n.* ondersteuner *n.* **secondhand**, *a.* tweedehands; antiquair. ¶ *adv.* uit de tweede hand. **secondly**, *adv.* in de tweede plaats, ten tweede. **second-rate**, *a.* tweederangs.

secrecy, *n.* geheimhouding *n.* **secret**, *a.*, ~ly, *adv.* geheim. ¶ *n.* geheim *n.n. in* ~, in 't geheim, stilletjes; *to keep a* ~, een geheim bewaren.

secretarial, a. secretaris . . . **secretariat**, n. secretariaat n.n., secretarie n. **secretary**, n. secretaris n.; secretaresse n. (*female*). S~ of . . ., Minister van . . . **secretaryship**, n. secretarisschap n.n., secretarisambt n.n.
secrete, v.t. afscheiden. to ~ from, verbergen str. voor. **secretion**, n. afscheiding n., afscheidsel n.n.
secretive, a. onmeedeelzaam, terughoudend, gesloten. **secretiveness**, n. onmeedeelzaamheid n.
sect, n. sekte n.; gezindte n. **sectarian**, a. sekte . . .
section, n. sectie n., afdeling n.; sectie n. (*medical*); paragraaf n. **sectional**, a. tot een sectie n. behorend; uit secties bestaande.
sector, n. sector n.
secular, a. wereldlijk, werelds; eeuwenoud. ¶ n. seculier n. **secularity**, n. wereldsheid n. **secularize**, v.t. seculariseren.
secure, a., ~ly, adv. zeker, verzekerd; vast; gerust. ¶ v.t. vastmaken; beveiligen; de hand leggen irr. op, zich meester n. maken van; to ~ from, vrijwaren tegen. **security**, n. veiligheid n.; waarborg n., pand n.n. *securities*, obligaties pl.n.; *government securities*, staatsfondsen pl.n.n.
sedate, a., ~ly, adv. bezadigd, rustig. **sedateness**, n. bezadigdheid n.
sedative, a. kalmerend, pijnstillend. ¶ n. kalmerend middel n.n.
sedentary, a. zittend.
sedge, n. zegge n., bies n. **sedge-warbler**, n. rietzanger n.
sediment, n. neerslag n., bezinksel n.n.
sedition, n. opstand n., muiterij n. **seditious**, a., ~ly, adv. oproerig, opruiend.
seduce, v.t. verleiden; verlokken. **seducer**, n. verleider n. **seduction**, n. verleiding n. **seductive**, a., ~ly, adv. verleidelijk, verlokkelijk. **seductress**, n. verleidster n.
sedulity, n. naarstigheid n.; angstvalligheid n. **sedulous**, a., ~ly, adv. naarstig; angstvallig.
see, n. (aarts)bisdom n.n.; (aarts)bisschopszetel n. the S~ of Rome, de Heilige Stoel. ¶ v.i. zien irr. to ~ about something, ergens voor zorgen; to ~ into something, iets onderzoeken irr.; to ~ through, doorzien irr. ¶ v.t. zien irr.; inzien irr., begrijpen str.; spreken str. I ~, jawell, ik begrijp het!; to ~ someone home, iemand naar huis brengen irr.
seed, n. zaad n.n. to run to ~, (lit.) in 't zaad schieten str., (fig.) verlopen str. ¶ v.i. in 't zaad schieten. **seed-bed**, n. zaaibed n.n. **seed-box**, n. zaadbak n. **seedcake**, n. kruidkoek n. **seed-corn**, n. zaaikoren n.n. **seedling**, n. zaaiplant n. **seed-pearl**, n. zaadparel n. **seed-pod**, n. zaadhuls n. **seed-potato**, n. pootaardappel n. **seedsman**, n. zaadhandelaar n. **seedy**, a. vol zaad n.n.; sjofel (*looks*); beroerd (*feeling*).
seeing, c. aangezien.

seek, v.t. zoeken irr.; trachten. ¶ v.i. to ~ after, streven naar, zoeken irr. **seeker**, n. zoeker n.
seem, v.i. schijnen str., lijken str.; er uitzien irr. alsof. it ~s to me, het schijnt me toe, het komt me voor. **seeming**, a. schijnbaar, ogenschijnlijk. **seemingly**, adv. schijnbaar, ogenschijnlijk; naar het schijnt.
seemliness, n. betamelijkheid n., gepastheid n. **seemly**, a. betamelijk, gepast; bevallig.
seep, v.i. sijpelen.
seer, n. helderziende n.; profeet n.
seesaw, n. wip n., wipplank n. ¶ v.i. wippen; op en neer gaan irr.
seethe, v.t. & v.i. koken, zieden str. to ~ with, koken van. **seething**, a. ziedend.
segment, n. segment n.n. **segmentary**, a. segmentarisch.
segregate, v.t. afzonderen. ¶ v.i. zich afzonderen. **segregation**, n. afzondering n.
seignorial, a. heerlijk.
seine, n. zegen n., sleepnet n.
seismic, a. seismisch. **seismograph**, n. seismograaf n.
seizable, a. waar beslag n.n. op gelegd kan worden. **seize**, v.t. vatten, grijpen str.; beslag n.n. leggen irr. op, confiskeren; aangrijpen str., bevangen str. to ~ upon, zich meester n. maken van; ~d with, bevangen door. **seizure**, n. beslaglegging n.; aanval n., beroerte n.
seldom, adv. zelden, zeldzaam.
select, v.t. (uit)kiezen str. ¶ a. uitgelezen; exclusief. **selection**, n. keus n., keur n.
selenium, n. selenium n.n.
self, pron. zelf. ¶ n. love of ~, eigenliefde n.; my former ~, mijn vroeger ik n.n.; his former ~, zijn ander ik n.n. ¶ prefix zelf. **self-acting**, a. automatisch. **self-adjusting**, a. zichzelf stellend. **self-assertive**, a. aanmatigend. **self-assurance**, n. zelfvertrouwen n.n. **self-centred**, a. in zichzelf opgaand. **self-command**, n. zelfbeheersing n. **self-confidence**, n. zelfvertrouwen n.n. **self-confident**, a. vol zelfvertrouwen. **self-conscious**, a. zelfbewust; verlegen. **self-contained**, a. afgesloten; in zichzelf besloten. **self-control**, n. zelfbeheersing n. **self-evident**, a. vanzelfsprekend, klaarblijkelijk. **selfish**, a., ~ly, adv. zelfzuchtig, egoïstisch. **selfishness**, n. zelfzuchtigheid n. egoïsme n.n. **self-possessed**, a. kalm, beheerst. **self-respect**, n. gevoel n.n. van eigenwaarde n. **selfsame**, a. zelfde. **self-taught**, a. zelf onderwezen. ~ man, autodidact n. **self-will**, n. eigenzinnigheid n. **self-willed**, a. eigenzinnig, koppig.
sell, v.t. verkopen irr. to ~ off, uitverkopen irr.; to ~ out, liquideren. ¶ v.i. verkocht worden str. to ~ well, veel aftrek n. vinden str. ¶ n. (coll.) beetnemerij n. **seller**, n. verkoper n.
selvage, n. zelfkant n.
semblance, n. schijn n., voorkomen n.n.

semi-, *prefix* half . . . semibreve, *n.* hele
noot *n.* semicircle, *n.* halve cirkel *n.*
semicolon, *n.* kommapunt *n.* semi-
detached, *a.* half vrijstaand. semi-final, *n.*
voorlaatste ronde *n.*
seminal, *a.* zaad . . ., kiem . . .
seminar, *n.* seminarium *n.n. (university).*
seminary, *n.* seminarium *n.n.,* kweekschool *n.*
semiquaver, *n.* zestiende noot *n.* semivowel,
n. halfklinker *n.*
semolina, *n.* griesmeel *n.n.*
sempiternal, *a.* eeuwig(durend).
sempstress, *n.* naaister *n.*
senate, *n.* senaat *n.* senator, *n.* senator *n.,*
senaatslid *n.n.* senatorial, *a.* senatoriaal,
senaats . . .
send, *v.t.* zenden *str.,* sturen. ¶ *v.i.* to
~ *for,* laten *str.* halen. sender, *n.*
zender *n.* send-off, *n.* feestelijk afscheid
n.n.
senile, *a.* seniel; ouderdoms . . . senility, *n.*
seniliteit *n.,* ouderdom *n.*
senior, *a.* ouder, oudste; hoger in rang *n.*
¶ *n.* oudere *n.*; hogere *n.* in rang *n.*
seniority, *n.* ancienniteit *n. by* ~, volgens
ancienniteit.
senna, *n.* senebladeren *pl.n.n.*
sensation, *n.* gevoel *n.n.,* gewaarwording *n.*;
opschudding *n.,* sensatie *n. to cause a* ~,
opzien *n.n.* baren, een opschudding
teweegbrengen *irr.* sensational, *a.*
sensationeel, opzienbarend.
sense, *n.* zintuig *n.n.,* zin *n.*; gevoel *n.n.*;
begrip *n.n.,* besef *n.n.,* bewustzijn *n.n.*;
(gezond) verstand *n.n.*; verstandige taal *n.*;
zin *n.,* betekenis *n.* ~ *of,* zin voor; ~ *of
smell,* reukzin *n.*; *common* ~, gezond
verstand *n.n.*; *in a* ~, in zekeren zin;
in every ~, in elk opzicht *n.n.*; *it doesn't
make* ~, *there's no* ~ *in it,* het heeft geen
zin; *he had the* ~, hij was zo verstandig;
to lose one's ~*s,* z'n bezinning *n.* verliezen
irr.; *to bring a person to his* ~*s,* iemand
tot bezinning *n.* brengen *irr.*; *in his* (right)
~*s,* bij zijn zinnen; *frightened out of one's*
~*s,* half dood van schrik *n.*; *to have taken
leave of one's* ~*s,* niet goed snik zijn.
¶ *v.t.* voelen, zich gewaar worden *str.* van.
senseless, *a.,* ~ly, *adv.* gevoelloos; ongevoelig; bewusteloos, buiten bezinning *n.*;
dwaas, onzinnig. senselessness, *n.* gevoelloosheid *n.*; dwaasheid *n.*
sensibility, *n.* gevoeligheid *n.*; vatbaarheid *n.*
sensible, *a.* gevoelig; merkbaar; verstandig.
to be ~ *of,* beseffen. sensibly, *adv.*
merkbaar; verstandig.
sensitive, *a.* gevoelig, fijngevoelig. ~ *plant,*
kruidje-roer-me-niet *n.n.*; ~ *to,* gevoelig
voor. sensitivity, *n.* (fijn)gevoeligheid
n.
sensory, *a.* zintuiglijk.
sensual, *a.,* ~ly, *adv.* zinnelijk. sensualism,
n. zinnelijkheid *n.,* wellust *n.* sensualist, *n.*

zinnelijk mens *n.n.* sensuality, *n.* zinnelijkheid *n.* sensualize, *v.t.* verzinnelijken.
sensuous, *a.* zinnelijk; weldadig.
sentence, *n.* zin *n.*; vonnis *n.n.,* oordeel *n.n.,*
uitspraak *n.* ¶ *v.t.* vonnissen, veroordelen.
sententious, *a.,* ~ly, *adv.* diepzinnig klinkend.
sentient, *a.* voelend. ~ *of,* bewust van.
sentiment, *n.* gevoel *n.n.*; gevoelen; gevoeligheid *n.* sentimental, *a.,* ~ly, *adv.*
sentimenteel. sentimentality, *n.* senti-
mentaliteit *n.*
sentry, *n.* schildwacht *n. to keep* ~, de
wacht houden *irr.*; *to be on* ~, op wacht
staan *irr.,* schilderen. sentry-box, *n.*
schilderhuisje *n.n.*
sepal, *n.* kelkblad *n.n.*
separable, *a.* scheidbaar. separate, *v.t.*
scheiden. ¶ *v.i.* scheiden; uiteengaan *irr.
to* ~ *from,* scheiden van. ¶ *a.,* ~ly, *adv.*
afzonderlijk; gescheiden. separation, *n.*
scheiding *n.* separator, *n.* afscheider *n.*;
roomafscheider *n.*
sepia, *n.* inktvis *n.*; sepia *n. (colour).*
Sepoy, *n.* Brits-Indisch soldaat *n.*
septangular, *a.* zevenhoekig.
September, *N.* september *N.*
septennial, *a.* zevenjarig.
septic, *a.* septisch.
septuagenarian, *n.* zeventigjarige *n.*
sepulchral, *a.* graf . . . sepulchre, *n.* graf *n.n.*
sepulture, *n.* teraardebestelling *n.*
sequel, *n.* vervolg *n.n.*; uitvloeisel *n.n.*
sequence, *n.* volgorde *n.*; opeenvolging *n.*;
suite *n.* (cards).
sequester, *v.t.* sequestreren, beslag *n.n.* leggen
irr. op. sequestration, *n.* sequestratie *n.,*
inbeslagneming *n.* sequestrator, *n.*
beslaglegger *n.*; beheerder *n.*
sequin, *n.* lovertje *n.n.*
seraglio, *n.* serail *n.n.,* harem *n.*
seraph, *n.* serafijn *n.* seraphic, *a.* engelachtig.
sere, *a.* dor, droog.
serenade, *n.* serenade *n.* ¶ *v.t.* een serenade
brengen *str.*
serene, *a.,* ~ly. *adv.* onbewogen, kalm;
helder, onbewolkt (*sky*); doorluchtig
(*title*). serenity, *n.* onbewogenheid *n.*;
wolkenloze stilte *n.*; doorluchtigheid *n.*
serf, *n.* lijfeigene *n.*; horige *n.* serfdom, *n.*
lijfeigenschap *n.*
serge, *n.* serge *n,* ¶ *a.* (van) serge.
sergeant, *n.* sergeant *n.* ~ *drummer,* tamboer
majoor *n.*; ~ *major,* sergeant-majoor *n.*
serial, *a.* tot een reeks *n.* behorend. ¶ *n.*
feuilleton *n.* serialist, *n.* feuilletonschrijver
n.
series, *n.* serie *n.,* reeks *n.*
serious, *a.,* ~ly, *adv.* ernstig; bedenkelijk.
to take something ~ly, iets ernstig
opnemen *str.*
serjeant, *n.* ~ *at law,* (soort) advokaat *n.*;
~-*at-arms,* intendant *n.,* deurwaarder *n.*
sermon, *n.* preek *n.* sermonize, *v.i.* preken
pl.n. houden *irr.*

serous, *a.* sereus.
serpent, *n.* slang *n.* **serpentine,** *a.* kronkelend; slangachtig.
serrated, *a.* gezaagd.
serried, *a.* aaneengesloten. ~ *ranks*, gesloten gelederen *pl.n.n.*
serum, *n.* serum *n.n.*
servant, *n.* bediende *n.*; knecht *n.* (*male*); dienstbode *n.*, meid *n.* (*female*). *domestic* ~, dienstbode *n.*; *public* ~, staatsdienaar *n.*; ~ *girl*, dienstmeisje *n.n.* **serve,** *v.t.* dienen, bedienen; fungeren; voldoende zijn; betekenen (*writ*); serveren (*tennis*). *to* ~ *the purpose*, geschikt zijn voor het doel; *to* ~ *a sentence*, zijn tijd *n.* uitzitten *str.*; *to* ~ *the table*, opdienen; *dinner is* ~*d*, het eten is op tafel *n.*; *if my memory* ~*s me* (*right*), als m'n geheugen *n.n.* me niet bedriegt; *it* ~*s you right*, 't is je verdiende loon *n.n.* ¶ *v.i.* dienen; dienstig zijn. **service,** *n.* dienst *n.*; servies *n.n.* (*china*). **serviceable,** *a.*, ~**bly,** *adv.* dienstbaar; bruikbaar, practisch.
servile, *a.* kruiperig, slaafs. **servility,** *n.* kruiperigheid *n.*, slaafsheid *n.* **servitude,** *n.* slavernij *n.*, dienstbaarheid *n.*
sesame, *n.* sesamkruid *n.n.* ~ *oil*, sesamolie *n.*
session, *n.* zitting *n.*
set, *v.t.* zetten, plaatsen; vaststellen; aanhitsen (*dog*). *to* ~ *going*, aan de gang brengen *irr.* ¶ *v.i.* stollen (*liquid*); beklinken (*masonry*); ondergaan *irr.*, zinken *str.* (*sun*). *to* ~ *about something*, iets aanpakken; *to* ~ *forth*, op reis *n.* gaan *irr.*; *to* ~ *in*, intreden *str.*, invallen *str.*; *to be* ~ *on*, verzot zijn op; *to* ~ *out*, op reis *n.* gaan *irr.* ¶ *a.* gezet, geregeld. ~ *books*, voorgeschreven boeken *pl.n.n.*; *to be hard* ~ *to*, het moeilijk vinden *str.* . . . ¶ *n.* stel *n.n.*; servies *n.n.* (*china*); kring *n.* (*people*). ~ *of teeth*, (kunst)gebit *n.n.*
setback, *n.* tegenslag *n.*
set-out, *n.* omhaal *n.*, geschiedenis *n.*
settee, *n.* sofa *n.*; rustbank *n.*
setter, *n.* staande hond *n.*
setting, *n.* montuur *n.*, montering *n.*; omgeving *n.*
settle, *v.i.* zich vestigen, zich nederzetten; bezinken *str.*; tot bedaren komen *irr.* *to* ~ *down*, zich installeren; bedaren. ¶ *v.t.* vaststellen; beslissen, beslechten; regelen; afrekenen; koloniseren. **settled,** *a.* vast; geregeld. **settlement,** *n.* nederzetting *n.*; volksplanting *n.*; regeling *n.*; schikking *n.*; afrekening *n.* *to make a* ~ *on*, geld *n.n.* vastzetten op. **settler,** *n.* kolonist *n.*
set-to, *n.* kloppartij *n.*
seven, *num.* zeven. ¶ *n.* zeven *n.*; zevental *n.n.* **sevenfold,** *a.* zevenvoudig. **seventeen,** *num.* zeventien. **seventeenth,** *a.* zeventiende. ¶ *n.* zeventiende *n.n.* **seventh,** *a.* zevende. ¶ *n.* zevende *n.n.* **seventieth,** *a.* zeventigste. ¶ *n.* zeventigste *n.n.* **seventy,** *num.* zeventig.

sever, *v.t.* afsnijden *str.*; afbreken *str.*
several, *a.* verscheiden. *they went their* ~ *ways*, zij gingen elk huns weegs. **severally,** *adv.* elk voor zich, ieder afzonderlijk.
severance, *n.* scheiding *n.*; afbreken *n.n.*
severe, *a.*, ~**ly,** *adv.* streng, straf. **severity,** *n.* strengheid *n.*
sew, *v.t.* naaien.
sewage, *n.* rioolwater *n.n.* ~ *farm*, zuiveringsinstallatie voor rioolslijk *n.n.* **sewer,** *n.* riool *n.* **sewerage,** *n.* riolering *n.*; rioolwater *n.n.*
sewing, *n.* naaien *n.n.*; naaiwerk *n.n.* **sewing-machine,** *n.* naaimachine *n.* **sewing-needle,** *n.* naald *n.*
sex, *n.* geslacht *n.n.*, sexe *n.*, kunne *n.*
sexagenarian, *n.* zestigjarige *n.*
sexless, *a.* geslachtloos.
sextant, *n.* sextant *n.*
sexton, *n.* koster *n.*, sacristein *n.*
sextuple, *a.* zesvoudig.
sexual, *a.*, ~**ly,** *adv.* sexueel, geslachts . . . **sexuality,** *n.* sexualiteit *n.*
shabbiness, *n.* kaalheid *n.* **shabby,** *a.*, ~**ily,** *adv.* haveloos, kaal; (*fig.*) gemeen, laag.
shack, *n.* loods *n.*, keet *n.*
shackle, *n.* boei *n.*; schakel *n.*, koppeling *n.* ¶ *v.t.* boeien, ketenen; koppelen.
shad, *n.* elft *n.*
shade, *n.* schaduw *n.*, lommer *n.*; schim *n.* (*ghost*); kap *n.*, scherm *n.n.*; nuance *n.*; tikje *n.n.* ¶ *v.t.* overschaduwen; schaduwen **shadow,** *n.* schaduw *n.*; schaduwbeeld *n.n.* **shadowy,** *a.* schaduwachtig; schaduwrijk; somber; vaag. **shady,** *a.* schaduwrijk; twijfelachtig, verdacht.
shaft, *n.* schacht *n.*; as *n.* *main* ~, krukas *n.*, drijfas *n.*
shag, *n.* pluis *n.n.*; sjektabak *n.* **shaggy,** *a.* ruig.
shagreen, *n.* segrijnleer *n.n.* ¶ *a.* segrijnleren.
shake, *v.t.* schudden; schokken; van streek brengen *irr.* *to* ~ *hands*, (elkaar) de hand geven *str.* ¶ *v.i.* schudden, trillen. ¶ *n.* schudding *n.*; scheur *n.* (*in wood*). *in a* ~, in een wip *n.* **shake-down,** *n.* kermisbed *n.n.* **shakiness,** *n.* onvastheid *n.*; beverigheid *n.* **shaky,** *a.*, ~**ily,** *adv.* beverig; onvast, wankel.
shall, *aux. v.* zullen *irr.*
shallot, *n.* sjalot *n.*
shallow, *a.* ondiep; oppervlakkig. ¶ *n.* ondiepte *n.*, zandbank *n.* **shallowness,** *n.* ondiepheid *n.*
sham, *v.t.* veinzen, voorwenden. ¶ *a.* voorgewend, gefingeerd. ¶ *n.* voorwendsel *n.n.*; bedrog *n.n.*; namaak *n.*
shamble, *v.i.* schuifelen, sloffen.
shambles, *pl.n.* slachtbank *n.*; bloedbad *n.n.*
shame, *n.* schaamte *n.*; schande *n.* *to put to* ~, beschamen. ¶ *v.t.* beschamen, beschaamd maken. *to* ~ *someone into* . . ., iemand door schaamte brengen *irr.* tot . . .
shamefaced, *a.* verlegen; beschaamd.

shameful, *a.*, ~ly, *adv.* schandelijk.
shameless, *a.*, ~ly, *adv.* schaamteloos.
sham-fight, *n.* spiegelgevecht *n.n.*;
shammy-leather, *n.* gemsleer *n.n.*; zeemleer *n.n.*
shampoo, *n.* shampoo *n.* ¶ *v.t.* een shampoo geven *str.*
shamrock, *n.* Ierse klaver *n.*
shandy, *n.* bier *n.n.* met gemberbier *n.n.*
shanghai, *v.t.* dronken aan boord brengen *irr.*
shank, *n.* schacht *n.*
shantung, *n.* shantung *n.n.*
shanty, *n.* keet *n.*, loods *n.*; matrozenliedje *n.n.*
shape, *n.* vorm *n.*; gedaante *n.* *to take* ~, vaste vorm aannemen *str.*; *in good* ~, in goede conditie *n.* ¶ *v.t.* vormen. *to* ~ *a course for*, koers *n.* zetten naar; *things are shaping well*, het ziet er veelbelovend uit.
shapeless, *a.* vormeloos. shapely, *a.* goedgevormd; bevallig.
share, *n.* ploegschaar *n.*; aandeel *n.n.*; portie *n.* *ordinary* ~, gewoon aandeel; *preference* ~, preferent aandeel; *registered* ~, aandeel op naam *n.*; *to go* ~*s in*, meedoen *irr.* aan; half om half doen *irr.* ¶ *v.t.* delen; verdelen. ¶ *v.i.* delen; deelnemen *str.*
shareholder, *n.* aandeelhouder *n.* sharer, *n.* deelnemer *n.*, deelgenoot *n.*
shark, *n.* haai *n.*; (*fig.*) afzetter *n.*
sharp, *a.*, ~ly, *adv.* scherp; spits, puntig; schel; bijdehand, gevat; bits, bijtend; dur (*music*). ~ *practice*, kwade praktijken *pl.n.* ¶ *n.* kruis *n.n.* sharpen, *v.t.* scherp maken; een punt *n.* slijpen *str.* aan. ¶ *v.i.* scherper worden *str.* sharper, *n.* afzetter *n.*, bedrieger *n.* sharpness, *n.* scherpte *n.*, scherpheid *n.* sharpshooter, *n.* scherpschutter *n.* sharpsighted, *a.* scherpziend. sharpwitted, *a.* scherpzinnig.
shatter, *v.t.* versplinteren, verbrijzelen; (*fig.*) de bodem inslaan *irr.* ¶ *v.i.* uiteenvallen *str.*
shave, *v.t.* scheren *str.*; schaven. ¶ *v.i.* zich scheren *str.* ¶ *n.* scheren *n.n.* *to have a* ~, zich scheren; zich laten *str.* scheren.
shaver, *n.* *young* ~, jong broekje *nn.*
shaving-brush, *n.* scheerkwast *n.* shaving-soap, *n.* scheerzeep *n.*
shavings, *pl.n.* krullen *pl.n.*
shawl, *n.* sjaal *n.*
she, *pron.* zij, ze.
sheaf, *n.* schoof *n.*; bundel *n.* ¶ *v.t.* tot schoven *pl.n.* binden *str.*
shear, *v.t.* scheren *str.* ¶ *n.* scheerwol *n.* (*pair of*) ~*s*, grote schaar *n.* shear-bill, *n.* schaarbek *n.* shearer, *n.* scheerder *n.* shearling, *n.* geschoren schaap *n.n.*
sheath, *n.* schede *n.*; (vleugel)schild *n.n.* sheathe, *v.t.* in de schede steken *str.*; bekleden.
sheave, *n.* schijf *n.* ¶ *v.t. See* sheaf.
shed, *n.* loods *n.*, schuurtje *n.n.*; afdak *n.n.*;

scheiding *n.* ¶ *v.t.* storten, vergieten *str.*; afwerpen *str.*, verliezen *irr.*
sheen, *n.* glans *n.* sheeny, *a.* glanzend.
sheep, *n.* schaap *n.n.* *the black* ~, het schurftige schaap; *the* ~ *and the goats*, de bokken *pl.n.* en de schapen; ~*'s eye*, verliefde blik *n.* sheep-dip, *n.* wasmiddel *n.n.* sheepdog, *n.* herdershond *n.* sheepfarmer, *n.* schapenfokker *n.* sheepfold, *n.* schaapskooi *n.* sheepish, *a.*, ~ly, *adv.* schaapachtig, onnozel. sheep-pen, *n.* schaapskooi *n.* sheep-shearing, *n.* schapenscheren *n.n.* sheepskin, *n.* schapevel *n.n.* sheepwalk, *n.* schapenweide *n.*
sheer, *a.* zuiver, louter; loodrecht. *by* ~ . . ., louter door . . . ¶ *v.i.* gieren. *to* ~ *off*, zich wegscheren; (*fig.*) er vandoor gaan *irr.* sheer-hulk, *n.* bok *n.*
sheet, *n.* laken *n.n.* (*linen*); vel *n.n.*, blad *n.n.* (*paper*); plaat *n.* (*metal*). ~ *of ice*, ijsvlakte *n.* ¶ *v.t.* bekleden. sheet-anchor, *n.* plechtanker *n.n.* sheet-copper, *n.* bladkoper *n.n.* sheet-iron, *n.* plaatijzer *n.n.* sheet-lightning, *n.* weerlicht *n.n.* sheet-mill, *n.* pletmolen *n.*
sheik(h), *n.* sjeik *n.*
shekel, *n.* sikkel *n.*
shelf, *n.* plank *n.*; terras *n.n.*; bank *n.*
shell, *n.* schaal *n.*, dop *n.* (*egg*); schelp *n.* (*mollusc*); schil *n.*, peul *n.*, dop *n.*, huls *n.* (*pulse*); pel *n.* (*shrimp*); geraamte *n.n.* (*ruin*); schild *n.n.* (*tortoise*); granaat *n.* (*explosive*); lijkkist *n.* (*coffin*). ¶ *v.t.* schillen, doppen, pellen; beschieten *str.*, bombarderen.
shellac, *n.* schellak *n.*
shell-fire, *n.* granaatvuur *n.n.*
shellfish, *n.* schaaldier *n.n.*
shellproof, *a.* bomvrij. shellshock, *n.* zenuwschok *n.* door granaatvuur *n.n.*
shelter, *n.* schuilplaats *n.*; onderkomen *n.n.* *to take* ~, schuilen; *under the* ~ *of*, in de luwte van. ¶ *v.i.* een schuilplaats zoeken *irr.*, schuilen. *to* ~ *from*, schuilen tegen, schuilen voor. ¶ *v.t.* beschutten, beschermen, behoeden.
shelve, *v.t.* op een plank *n.* zetten; (*fig.*) op de lange baan schuiven *str.* ¶ *v.i.* zacht hellen. shelving, *n.* planken *pl.n.* ¶ *a.* hellend.
shepherd, *n.* (schaap)herder *n.* ~*'s purse*, herderstasje *n.n.*, lepelblad *n.n.* ¶ *v.t.* hoeden; leiden. shepherdess, *n.* herderin *n.*
sherbert, *n.* sorbet *n.n.*
sheriff, *n.* schout *n.*
sherry, *n.* sherry *n.*
shield, *n.* schild *n.n.* ¶ *v.t.* beschermen, beschutten.
shift, *n.* verandering *n.*, beweging *n.*; schoft *n.* (*time*); ploeg *n.* (*men*); uitvlucht *n.* *to work double* ~*s*, met twee ploegen werken. ¶ *v.t.* verplaatsen, verleggen. ¶ *v.i.* zich verplaatsen. shifter, *n.* machinist *n.*

shiftless, a. onbeholpen, hulpeloos. shifty,
a. onbetrouwbaar.

shilling, n. shilling n.

shilly-shally, v.i. weifelen, besluiteloos zijn.

shin, n. scheen n. ¶ v.i. to ~ up a tree,
tegen een boom opklimmen str.

shindy, n. (coll.) standje n.n., herrie n.

shine, v.i. schijnen str.; glimmen str., blinken
str.; schitteren.

shingle, n. kiezelsteen n.; kiezel n.n.; kort
(vrouwen) haar n.n. ¶ v.t. kort knippen.

shingles, pl.n. gordelroos n.

shiny, a. glimmend, blinkend, glanzend.

ship, n. schip n.n. ~'s articles, monsterrol n.;
~'s clerk, waterklerk n.; ~'s papers,
scheepspapieren pl.n.n.; ~'s protest,
zeeprotest n.n. ¶ v.t. inschepen; verschepen; innemen str., binnenhalen (oars).
to ~ a sea, een stortzee n. overkrijgen str.
shipboard, n. scheepsboord n.n. on ~,
aan boord n.n. shipbreaker, n. sloper n.
shipbroker, n. scheepsmakelaar n.; scheeps-
bevrachter n., cargadoor n. shipbuilder, n.
scheepsbouwmeester n. shipbuilding, n.
scheepsbouw n. shipbuilding-yard, n.
scheepsbouwwerf n. ship-canal, n.
scheepvaartkanaal n.n. shipchandler, n.
handelaar n. in scheepsbehoeften pl.n.
shipload, n. scheepslading n. shipmate, n.
scheepskameraad n. shipment, n. verscheping n.; lading n. ship-owner, n.
reder n. shipper, n. verscheper n. shipping,
n. scheepvaart n.; scheepsgelegenheid n.
shipping-agent, n. expediteur n. shipping-
firm, n. rederij n. shipshape, a. netjes, in
orde n.; in de puntjes. shipwreck, n.
schipbreuk n. shipwrecked, a. to be ~,
scheepbreuk n. lijden str.; a ~ sailor, een
scheepbreukeling n. shipwright, n. scheeps-
timmerman n. shipyard, n. scheeps-
timmerwerf n.; scheepsbouwwerf n.

shire, n. graafschap n.n. shire-horse, n.
zwaar trekpaard n.n.

shirk, v.t. ontwijken str., zich onttrekken str.
aan. shirker, n. lijntrekker n.; plichtverzaker n.

shirt, n. hemd n.n., overhemd n.n. ~ of mail,
maliënkolder n. shirting, n. stof n. voor
hemden pl.n.n. shirtsleeve, n. hemdsmouw
n.

shiver, v.i. huiveren, rillen, sidderen; aan (or
in) gruzelementen pl.n.n. vallen str. ¶ v.t.
verbrijzelen, versplinteren. ¶ n. rilling n.,
huivering n.; splinter n. shivery, a.
beverig, huiverig.

shoal, n. zandbank n., ondiepte n.; school n.
in ~s, bij drommen pl.n., bij de vleet.

shock, n. schok n., stoot n.; botsing n.;
zenuwschokking n.; stuik n. (sheaves); bos
n.(hair). ¶ v.t. tegen de borst stuiten str.,
choqueren. to be ~ed at, aanstoot n.
nemen str. aan. shock-absorber, n.
schokbreker n. shocker, n. sensatieroman
n. shockheaded, a. met een dichte haarbos

n. shocking, a., ~ly, adv. aanstotelijk,
ergerlijk. shock-tactics, pl.n. taktiek van
de massa-aanval n. shock-troops, pl.n.
stormtroepen pl.n.

shoddy, n. lompenwol n. ¶ a. prullig,
prullerig.

shoe, n. schoen n.; hoefijzer n.; remschoen n.
(brake). a pair of ~s, een paar n.n.
schoenen. ¶ v.t. schoeien (people); beslaan
irr. (horse). shoe-black, n. schoenpoetser n.
shoe-blacking, n. shoensmeer n. shoehorn,
n. schoenhoorn n. shoelace, n. schoenveter
n. shoemaker, n. schoenmaker n.

shoo, v.t. to ~ away, wegjagen str.

shoot, v.i. schieten str.; jagen str. to ~ up,
opschieten str., omhoogschieten str. ¶ v.t.
afschieten str., afvuren; doodschieten str.;
storten (rubbish). to ~ a bridge, onder een
brug n. doorschieten str.; to ~ the bolt,
(de deur) grendelen. ¶ n. jachtterrein n.n.;
jachtpartij n.; stortkoker n.; stortplaats n.
the whole ~, de hele zooi n. shooting, n.
jagen n.n. ¶ a. schietend. ~ box, jacht-
huisje n.n.; ~ gallery, schiettent n.;
~ licence, jachtakte n.; ~ range, schietbaan n.; ~ star, vallende ster n.

shop, n. winkel n.; werkplaats n., atelier n.n.
to talk ~, over zijn vak n.n. praten;
to shut up ~, de winkel sluiten str. ¶ v.i.
winkelen. shop-assistant, n. winkelbediende n. shopkeeper, n. winkelier n.
shoplifter, n. winkeldief n. shopper, n.
winkelende n. shopping, n. winkelen n.n.
to do one's ~, winkelen. shop-soiled, a.
verkleurd. shop-steward, n. chef n. (van
de werkplaats). shopwalker, n. winkelchef
n. shopwindow, n. winkelraam n.n.;
étalage n.

shore, n. oever n., kust n.; wal n.; stut n.n.,
schraagbalk n. (support). on ~, aan land
n.n. ¶ v.t. stutten, schragen. shore-leave,
n. verlof n.n. om te passagieren.

short, a. kort; te kort; krap; kortaf (in
speech); bros (cake). ~ sight, bijziendheid
n.; ~ of breath, buiten adem n.; ~ of
money, niet goed bij kas n.; little ~ of . . .,
het grenst aan . . .; to be ~ of, gebrek n.n.
hebben aan; to fall ~ of, minder zijn dan;
to go ~, niet genoeg hebben; to run ~ of,
gebrek n.n. krijgen str. aan; to stop ~,
plotseling ophouden irr. ¶ n. ~s, korte
broek n. shortbread, n. zandgebak n.n.
short circuit, n. kortsluiting n. ¶ v.t.
kortsluiting veroorzaken (in). short-
coming, n. tekortkoming n., gebrek n.n.
shorten, v.t. korter maken, bekorten,
afkorten. to ~ sail, zeil verminderen.
shorthand, n. stenografie n. ¶ a. stenogra-
fisch. short-handed, a. to be ~, gebrek n.n.
hebben aan personeel n. shortish, a.
nogal kort. short-lived, a. kortstondig;
niet van langen duur n. shortly, adv. kort,
kortweg; binnenkort (soon). shortness, n.
kortheid n.; gebrek n.n. shortsighted, a.

bijziend; kortzichtig. **short-tempered,** *a.*
kort aangebonden. **shortwinded,** *a.*
kortademig.

shot, *n.* schot *n.n.*; stoot *n.*; slag *n.* (*in games*);
schop *n.* (*football*); hagel *n.* (*pellets*).
a dead ~, een uitstekend schutter *n.*;
to have a ~ at something, iets proberen;
naar iets raden.

shoulder, *n.* schouder *n.* *to give a person the
cold* ~, iemand met de nek aanzien *irr.*;
~ *of mutton,* schapebout *n.* ¶ *v.t.* op de
schouder nemen *str.*; verdringen *str.*,
wegduwen. **shoulder-belt,** *n.* bandelier *n.*
shoulder-strap, *n.* schouderlint *n.n.*

shout, *v.i.* roepen *str.*, schreeuwen. *to ~ for
joy,* het uitschreeuwen van vreugde *n.*;
to ~ with laughter, schaterlachen. ¶ *v.t.*
roepen *str.*, uitroepen *str.* ¶ *n.* kreet *n.*,
schreeuw *n.*

shove, *v.t.* duwen, schuiven *str.* ¶ *v.i.* duwen.
to ~ off, afduwen, van wal steken; (*fig.*)
weggaan *irr.* ¶ *n.* duw *n.*

shovel, *n.* schop *n.*; schepper *n.* **shovelful,** *n.*
schopvol *n.*

show, *v.t.* laten *str.*, zien, doen *irr.* zien,
tonen; aan den dag leggen. *to ~ something
up,* iets aan de kaak stellen. ¶ *v.i.* zich
tonen; zich voordoen *irr.* *it does not* ~,
het is niet te zien; *to ~ off,* opscheppen,
geuren. ¶ *n.* vertoning *n.*; vertoon *n.n.*;
voorstelling *n.* (*theatrical*); zaak *n.*,
geschiedenis *n.* *to make a poor* ~, een
armzalig figuur *n.n.* slaan *irr.* **show-case,**
n. uitstalkast *n.*, vitrine *n.*

shower, *n.* regenbui *n.*; stortvloed *n.* ¶ *v.t.*
to ~ upon, overstelpen met. **showerbath,**
n. stortbad *n.n.* **showery,** *a.* buiig.

showiness, *n.* opzichtigheid *n.* **showman,** *n.*
spullebaas *n.* **showpiece,** *n.* spektakelstuk
n.n.; paradepaard *n.n.* **show-room,** *n.*
toonzaal *n.* **showy,** *a.*, ~ily, *adv.* opzichtig,
pronkerig.

shrapnel, *n.* granaatkartets *n.* *a piece cf* ~,
een granaatscherf *n.*

shred, *v.t.* snipperen. ¶ *n.* snipper *n.*; (*fig.*)
ziertje *n.n.* *in* ~s, aan flarden *pl.n.n.*

shrew, *n.* helleveeg *n.*; spitsmuis *n.*

shrewd, *a.*, ~ly, *adv.* schrander, slim; loos;
scherpzinnig. *a ~ suspicion,* een sterk
vermoeden *n.n.* **shrewdness,** *n.* schranderheid *n.*

shrewish, *a.* kijfziek.

shrewmouse, *n.* spitsmuis *n.*

shriek, *v.t. & v.i.* gillen; gieren. ¶ *n.* gil *n.*;
schreeuw *n.*

shrift, *n.* *to give short* ~ *to,* korte metten
maken met.

shrill, *a.*, ~ly, *adv.* schel, schril.

shrimp, *n.* garnaal *n.* **shrimper,** *n.* garna-
lenvisser *n.* **shrimping,** *n.* garnalenvangst *n.*

shrine, *n.* reliquieënkastje *n.n.*; tempel *n.*;
altaar *n.n.*

shrink, *v.i.* krimpen *str.*, inkrimpen *str.*;
slinken *str.* *to ~ from,* terugdeinzen voor.

¶ *v.t.* doen *irr.* krimpen. **shrinkage,** *n.*
inkrimping *n.*

shrivel, *v.i.* verschompelen, rimpelen. ¶ *v.t.*
doen *irr.* verschrompelen.

shroud, *n.* lijkwade *n.*; omhulsel *n.n.* ~s,
staand want *n.n.* ¶ *v.t.* omhullen.

Shrovetide, *N.* dagen *pl.n.* vóór Vastenavond
N. **Shrove-Tuesday,** *N.* Vastenavond
N.

shrub, *n.* struik *n.*; heester *n.* **shrubbery,** *n.*
struikgewas *n.n.*, bosje *n.n.*

shrug, *v.t.* *to ~ one's shoulders,* de schouders
pl.n. ophalen. ¶ *n.* schouderophaling *n.*

shuck, *n.* dop *n.*, bolster *n.*

shudder, *v.i.* huiveren, rillen. *to ~ at,*
huiveren voor. ¶ *n.* huivering *n.*, rilling *n.*

shuffle, *v.i.* schuifelen; uitvluchten *pl.n.*
zoeken *irr.* ¶ *v.t.* schuifelen; schudden,
wassen (*cards*). *to ~ one's feet,* met de
voeten schuifelen. ¶ *n.* geschuifel *n.n.*
shuffling, *n.* wassen *n.n.*

shun, *v.t.* schuwen, vermijden *str.*

shunt, *v.t.* rangeren. *to ~ on to a siding,*
op een zijspoor *n.n.* brengen *irr.* ¶ *n.*
zijspoor *n.n.* **shunting-engine,** *n.* rangeer-
locomotief *n.*

shut, *v.t.* sluiten *str.*, dichtdoen *irr.*, toedoen
irr. *to ~ up,* dichtdoen *irr.*; ~ *up!,*
houd je mond! ¶ *v.i.* dichtgaan *irr.*

shutter, *n.* sluiter *n.*; sluiting *n.* (*camera*);
luik *n.n.*, blind *n.n.*

shuttle, *n.* schietspoel *n.* ¶ *v.i.* heen en weer
gaan *irr.* **shuttlecock,** *n.* pluimbal *n.*
shuttle-service, *n.* dienst *n.* heen en weer.

shy, *a.*, ~ly, *adv.* schuw; verlegen,
beschroomd; schichtig; huiverig. *once
caught, twice* ~, gebrande kinderen
schuwen het vuur. ¶ *v.i.* schichtig worden
str., op zij *n.* springen *str.* ¶ *v.t.* gooien. ¶ *n.*
werptent *n.* **shyness,** *n.* schuwheid *n.*;
verlegenheid *n.*

sibilant, *a.* sissend. ¶ *n.* sisklank *n.*

sibyl, *n.* sybille *n.*

siccative, *a.* opdrogend, siccatief.

Sicily, *N.* Sicilië *n.N.*

sick, *a.* ziek; onpasselijk, misselijk. *to be ~
of something,* iets beu zijn; ~ *at heart,*
vol hartzeer *n.n.* **sicken,** *v.i.* kwijnen, ziek
worden *str.* *to be ~ing for,* iets onder de
leden *pl.n.n.* hebben; vurig verlangen
naar . . .

sickle, *n.* sikkel *n.*

sickliness, *n.* ziekelijkheid *n.* **sickly,** *a.*
ziekelijk. *a ~ smile,* een flauwe glimlach
n. **sickness,** *n.* ziekte *n.*; misselijkheid *n.*

side, *n.* zij(de) *n.*; kant *n.*; partij *n.*; kantje
n.n. (*of paper*); (*coll.*) airs *pl.n.n.* *a ~ of
bacon,* een zij spek *n.n.*; *to take* ~s, partij
kiezen *irr.*; ~ *by* ~, naast elkaar, zij aan
zij; *on one* ~, op zij; *to one* ~, op zij,
ter zijde; *on both* ~s, *on either* ~, aan
weerskanten. **sideboard,** *n.* buffet *n.n.*;
aanrecht *n.* (*in kitchen*). **side-car,** *n.*
zijspan *n.n.* **side-face,** *adv.* in profiel *n.n.*

side-glance, *n.* blik *n.* van terzijde. **side-issue**, *n.* bijzaak *n.*, nevenkwestie *n.* **sidelight**, *n.* eigenaardig licht *n.n.* **sidelong**, *a. & adv.* zijdelings. **sideplay**, *n.* nevenspel *n.n.*

sidereal, *a.* sterren . . .

sideshow, *n.* bijkomstigheid *n.* **sidetrack**, *n.* wisselspoor *n.n.*, zijspoor *n.n.* ¶ *v.t.* op een zijspoor brengen *irr.* **sidewalk**, *n.* trottoir *n.n.* **sideways**, *a. & adv.* zijdelings, van terzijde. **sidewhiskers**, *pl.n.* bakkebaarden *pl.n.* **siding**, *n.* zijspoor *n.n.*, wisselspoor *n.n.*

sidle, *v.i.* zich zijdelings bewegen *str.*

siege, *n.* beleg *n.n.*, belegering *n.* *to lay* ∼ *to*, het beleg slaan *irr.* voor; *to raise the* ∼, het beleg opbreken *str.*

sieve, *n.* zeef *n.* ¶ *v.t.* zeven, ziften.

sift, *v.t.* zeven, ziften; builen (*flour*); uitpluizen *str.* (*evidence*).

sigh, *n.* zucht *n.* ¶ *v.i.* zuchten.

sight, *n.* gezicht *n.n.*, aanblik *n.*, schouwspel *n.n.*; zicht *n.*; korrel *n.* (*rifle*). ∼*s*, bezienswaardigheden *pl.n.* *to catch* ∼ *of*, in 't oog krijgen *str.*; *to lose* ∼ *of*, uit het oog verliezen *irr.*; *it looks a* ∼, 't ziet er vreselijk uit; *I can't bear the* ∼ *of it*, ik kan het niet luchten of zien; *at* ∼, op zicht; *at first* ∼, op het eerste gezicht; *out of* ∼ *out of mind*, uit het oog uit het hart; *within* ∼, in zicht. ¶ *v.t.* te zien krijgen *str.*; richten (*gun*). **sightless**, *a.* blind. **sightseer**, *n.* toerist *n.* **sightseeing**, *n.* bezienswaardigheden *pl.n.* bezoeken *irr.*

sign, *n.* teken *n.n.*; wenk *n.*; uithangbord *n.n.* *the* ∼ *of the cross*, het teken des kruises. ¶ *v.t.* tekenen, ondertekenen.

signal, *n.* sein *n.n.*, signaal *n.n.* ¶ *v.t.* seinen, signaleren. ¶ *a.* schitterend. **signal-box**, *n.* seinhuisje *n.n.* **signalize**, *v.t.* te kennen geven *str.* *to be* ∼*d*, zich onderscheiden. **signaller**, *n.* seiner *n.* **signalman**, *n.* seinwachter *n.*

signatory, *a.* ondertekenend. ¶ *n.* ondertekenaar *n.* **signature**, *n.* ondertekening *n.*, handteken *n.n.*

signboard, *n.* uithangbord *n.n.*

signet-ring, *n.* zegelring *n.*

significance, *n.* betekenis *n.*; belang *n.n.*, gewicht *n.n.* **significant**, *a.*, ∼**ly**, *adv.* veelbetekenend; veelzeggend; van betekenis *n.* **signification**, *n.* aanduiding *n.* **signify**, *v.t.* te verstaan geven *str.*; beduiden.

signpost, *n.* wegwijzer *n.*

silence, *n.* stilte *n.*; stilzwijgen *n.n.*; stilzwijgendheid *n.* *to keep* ∼, zwijgen *str.*; ∼ *gives consent*, die zwijgt stemt toe. ¶ *v.t.* tot zwijgen *n.n.* brengen *irr.*, het zwijgen opleggen *irr.* aan. **silencer**, *n.* (slag)demper *n.*; knalpot *n.* **silent**, *a.*, ∼**ly**, *adv.* stil, (stil)zwijgend. ∼ *partner*, stille vennoot *n.*; *to remain* ∼, zwijgen *str.*

silex, *n.* vuursteen *n.*

silhouette, *n.* silhouet *n.* ¶ *v.t.* *to be* ∼*d against*, zich aftekenen tegen.

silica, *n.* kiezelaarde *n.*

silk, *n.* zij(de) *n.* *to take* ∼, Queen's Counsel worden *str.* ¶ *a.* van zij(de), zijden. ∼ *hat*, hoge hoed *n.* **silken**, *a.* van zij(de), zijden. **silkiness**, *n.* zijdeachtigheid *n.* **silkworm**, *n.* zijderups *n.* **silky**, *a.* zijden; zijdeachtig; poeslief.

sill, *n.* drempel *n.* *window* ∼, vensterbank *n.*

silliness, *n.* dwaasheid *n.*; flauwiteit *n.* **silly**, *a.*, ∼**ily**, *adv.* onnozel; flauw. *the* ∼ *season*, de komkommertijd.

silo, *n.* silo *n.*; kuil *n.* ¶ *v.t.* inkuilen.

silt, *n.* slib *n.n.*, aanslibsel *n.n.* ¶ *v.t.* dichtslibben, verzanden.

silver, *n.* zilver *n.n.*; zilvergeld *n.n.*; zilverwerk *n.n.*; tafelzilver *n.n.* ¶ *a.* zilveren. ¶ *v.t.* verzilveren. **silverfish**, *n.* zilvervis *n.*; suikergast *n.* **silver fox**, *n.* zilvervos *n.* **silverleaf**, *n.* bladzilver *n.n.* **silverling**, *n.* zilverling *n.* **silverplated**, *a.* verzilverd. **silverside**, *n.* beste gedeelte *n.n.* van een runderschijf *n.* **silversmith**, *n.* zilversmid *n.* **silvery**, *a.* zilverwit, zilverblank.

simian, *a.* aapachtig.

similar, *a.* gelijksoortig, overeenkomstig. **similarity**, *n.* gelijksoortigheid *n.*, overeenkomst *n.* **similarly**, *adv.* op gelijksoortige manier *n.*; insgelijks.

simile, *n.* vergelijking *n.*

similitude, *n.* gelijkenis *n.*, overeenkomst *n.*

simmer, *v.i.* zachtjes koken, pruttelen. ¶ *v.t.* zacht laten *str.* koken.

simper, *v.i.* onnozel lachen. **simpering**, *a.* geaffecteerd.

simple, *a.* eenvoudig; gewoon; onnozel. **simpleminded**, *a.* naïef. **simpleton**, *n.* hals *n.*, onnozele bloed *n.* **simplicity**, *n.* eenvoud *n.*; onnozelheid *n.* **simplification**, *n.* vereenvoudiging *n.* **simplify**, *v.t.* vereenvoudigen. **simply**, *adv.* eenvoudig; gewoonweg; alleen maar, enkel.

simulate, *v.t.* voorwenden, fingeren, simuleren. **simulation**, *n.* voorwending *n.*; simulatie *n.*

simultaneous, *a.*, ∼**ly**, *adv.* gelijktijdig. **simultaneousness**, *n.* gelijktijdigheid *n.*

sin, *n.* zonde *n.* ¶ *v.i.* zondigen.

since, *adv.* sedert, sinds. *ever* ∼, van toen af; *long* ∼, al lang. ¶ *prep.* sedert, sinds. ¶ *c.* sedert, sinds; aangezien.

sincere, *a.*, ∼**ly**, *adv.* oprecht. *yours* ∼*ly* (*friendly*), je toegenegen, (*more formal*) met mijn beste groeten *pl.n.* **sincerity**, *n.* oprechtheid *n.*

sine, *n.* sinus *n.*

sinecure, *n.* sinecure *n.*

sinew, *n.* pees *n.*; (*fig.*) kracht *n.* **sinewy**, *a.* pezig; gespierd.

sinful, *a.*, ∼**ly**, *adv.* zondig. **sinfulness**, *n.* zondigheid *n.*

sing, *v.i.* zingen *str.*; tuiten, suizen (*ears*). ¶ *v.t.* zingen *str.*; bezingen *str.* *to* ∼ *out*, luide zingen; hard roepen *str.*

singe, *v.t.* (ver)schroeien. ¶ *v.i.* schroeien, verzengen.

singer, *n.* zanger *n.* **singing**, *n.* zingen *n.n.*; getuit *n.n.*, gesuis *n.n.*

single, *a.* enkel; ongetrouwd, ongehuwd; enig, enigst; éénpersoons . . . ~ *combat*, tweegevecht *n.n.* ¶ *n.* enkele reis *n.*; enkelspel *n.n.* ¶ *v.t.* to ~ *out*, uitkiezen *str.*, uitpikken. **single-breasted**, *a.* met één rij *n.* knopen *pl.n.* **singlehanded**, *a.* alleen, zonder hulp *n.* **singleness**, *n.* oprechtheid *n.*

singlet, *n.* borstrok *n.*

singly, *adv.* alleen; afzonderlijk, één voor één.

singsong, *n.* dreun *n.*; zangavondje *n.n.* ¶ *a.* eentonig.

singular, *a.*, ~**ly**, *adv.* enkelvoudig; eigenaardig, zonderling; merkwaardig. **singularity**, *n.* eigenaardigheid *n.*

sinister, *a.* onheilspellend; ongunstig.

sink, *v.i.* zinken *str.*; zakken, dalen, vallen *str.*; verzinken *str.* ~ *or swim*, erop of eronder. ¶ *v.t.* doen *irr.* zinken, tot zinken *n.n.* brengen *irr.*; graven *str*, boren; graveren *(die)*; laten *str.* varen *(differences).* ¶ *n.* gootsteen *n.* **sinker**, *n.* zinklood *n.n.* **sink-hole**, *n.* zinkput *n.*

sinking fund, *n.* amortisatiefonds *n.n.*

sinner, *n.* zondaar *n.*; zondares *n.* *(female).*

sinuosity, *n.* bochtigheid *n.*; kronkeling *n.* **sinuous**, *a.* bochtig, kronkelig.

sinus, *n.* holte *n.*; sinus *n.*

sip, *v.t.* met kleine teugjes *pl.n.n.* drinken *str.* ¶ *n.* klein teugje *n.n.*

siphon, *n.* hevel *n.*; sifon *n.* *plunging* ~, steekhevel *n.* ¶ *v.t.* overhevelen.

sir, *n.* meneer. *dear* ~, geachte heer, waarde heer; ~*s*, mijne heren; *S*~, *untranslated.*

sire, *n.* vader *n.*; stamvader *n.*; sire *(title).* ¶ *v.t.* fokken.

siren, *n.* sirene *n.*

sirloin, *n.* (runder)lendestuk *n.n.*

sister, *n.* zuster *n.* ~*-in-law*, schoonzuster *n.* **sisterhood**, *n.* zusterschap *n.* **sisterly**, *a.* zusterlijk.

sit, *v.i.* zitten *str.*; zitting *n.* hebben *(meeting).* *to* ~ *for an examination*, examen *n.n.* doen *irr.*; *to* ~ *for a portrait*, poseren; *to* ~ *down*, gaan *irr.* zitten; *to* ~ *out*, niet meedoen *irr.*

site, *n.* terrein *n.n.*; ligging *n.*; emplacement *n.n.*

sitting, *n.* zitting *n.* **sitting-room**, *n.* zitkamer *n.*, huiskamer *n.*

situated, *a.* gelegen; geplaatst. *well* ~, in een goede positie *n.* **situation**, *n.* positie *n.*, toestand *n.*; situatie *n.*; ligging *n.*; betrekking *n.*, plaats *n.*

six, *num.* zes. ¶ *n.* zes *n.* *at* ~*es and sevens*, overhoop. **sixfold**, *n.* zesvoud *n.n.* ¶ *a.* zesvoudig, zesdubbel.

sixteen, *num.* zestien. **sixteenth**, *a.* zestiende. ¶ *n.* zestiende *n.n.*

sixth, *a.* zesde. ¶ *n.* zesde *n.n.*

sixtieth, *a.* zestigste. ¶ *n.* zestigste *n.n.*

sixty, *num.* zestig. ¶ *n.* *the sixties*, de zestiger jaren *pl.n.n.*

sizable, *a.* behoorlijk, tamelijk groot. **size**, *n.* grootte *n.*, omvang *n*; maat *n.*; pap *n.*, lijmwater *n.n.* ¶ *v.t.* pappen. *to* ~ *up*, taxeren, naar waarde *n.* schatten.

sizzle, *v.i.* sissen.

skate, *n.* rog *n.* *(fish)*; schaats *n.* *(for ice).* ¶ *v.i.* schaatsen, schaatsenrijden *str.* *to* ~ *over thin ice*, zich op gevaarlijk ijs *n.n.* begeven *str.* **skater**, *n.* schaatsenrijder *n.* **skating-rink**, *n.* ijsbaan *n.*

skedaddle, *v.i.* *(coll.)* zich uit de voeten *pl.n.* maken.

skein, *n.* streng *n.*

skeleton, *n.* geraamte *n.n.*, skelet *n.n.* ~*key*, loper *n.*

sketch, *n.* schets *n.* ¶ *v.t. & v.i.* schetsen. **sketch-map**, *n.* schetskaartje *n.n.* **sketchy**, *a.* vluchtig.

skew, *a.* scheef. **skewbald**, *a.* gevlekt.

skewer, *n.* vleespen *n.* ¶ *v.t.* vaststeken *str.*

ski, *n.* ski *n.* ¶ *v.i.* skilopen *str.*

skid, *v.i.* slippen; doorglijden *str.* ¶ *n.* remketting *n.*; remslof *n.*; slippen *n.n.* *to put the* ~*s on*, remmen.

skiff, *n.* bootje *n.n.*, skiff *n.*

skilful, *a.* ~**ly**, *adv.* bekwaam, handig; ervaren. **skill**, *n.* bekwaamheid *n.*, handigheid *n.* **skilled**, *a.* bekwaam; geschoold.

skillet, *n.* metalen kookpannetje *n.n.*

skim, *v.t.* afschuimen; afromen *(milk)*; scheren *str.* langs *(movement)*; vluchtig doorlópen *str.* ~ *milk*, taptemelk *n.* **skimmer**, *n.* schuimspaan *n.*

skimp, *v.t.* beknibbelen. ¶ *v.i.* bezuinigen. **skimpy**, *a.* krap.

skin, *n.* huid *n.*, vel *n.n.*; vlies *n.n.* ¶ *v.t.* villen, stropen; pellen. **skin-deep**, *a.* oppervlakkig. **skinflint**, *n.* vrek *n.* **skinner**, *n.* vilder *n.* **skintight**, *a.* zeer nauw, engsluitend. **skinny**, *a.* broodmager.

skip, *v.i.* huppelen, touwtje *n.n.* springen *str.* ¶ *v.t.* overslaan *irr.* **skip-jack**, *n.* kniptor *n.* **skipper**, *n.* schipper *n.*, kapitein *n.* ¶ *v.t.* gezag *n.n.* voeren over. **skipping-rope**, *n.* springtouw *n.n.*

skirl, *v.i.* snerpen.

skirmish, *n.* schermutseling *n.* ¶ *v.t.* schermutselen. **skirmisher**, *n.* tirailleur *n.*

skirt, *n.* rok *n.* ¶ *v.t.* langs de rand gaan *irr.*; lopen *str.* langs.

skit, *n.* parodie *n.*

skittish, *a.*, ~**ly**, *adv.* dartel, grillig.

skittle, *n.* kegel *n.* ~*s*, kegelspel *n.n.*; ~ *alley*, kegelbaan *n.*

skulk, *v.i.* loeren, rondhangen *str.* ¶ *v.t.* ontwijken *str.* **skulker**, *n.* malinger *n.*

skull, *n.* schedel *n.* **skull-cap**, *n.* kalotje *n.n.*

skunk, *n.* bunzing *n.*; stinkdier *n.n.*

sky, *n.* hemel *n.*; lucht *n.*; uitspansel *n.n.* *in the* ~, aan de hemel; *to praise to the* *skies,* hemelhoog verheffen *str.* **sky-blue,** *a.* hemelsblauw. **skyhigh,** *a.* hemelhoog. **skylark,** *n.* (akker)leeuwerik *n.* ¶ *v.i.* lolletjes *pl.n.n.* uithalen. **skylight,** *n.* vallicht *n.n.;* lantaarn *n.;* dakraam *n.n.* **skyline,** *n.* gezichtseinder *n.,* horizon *n.* **sky-pilot,** *n.* hemeldragonder *n.* **sky-scraper,** *n.* wolkenkrabber *n.*

slab, *n.* plaat *n.,* platte steen *n.;* plak *n.*

slack, *a.* slap, los; laks. ∼ *water,* doodtij *n.n.;* kentering *n.;* *to be* ∼, het niet druk hebben. ¶ *n.* loos *n.* (*of rope*); gruiskolen *pl.n.;* *the* ∼ *of the trousers,* het zitvlak; ∼*s,* flanellen broek *n.* ¶ *v.i.* luieren. **slacken,** *v.t.* vieren. *to* ∼ *speed,* vaart *n.* verminderen. ¶ *v.i.* verslappen. **slacker,** *n.,* lijntrekker *n.;* uitdraaier *n.*

slag, *n.* slak *n.,* metaalschuim *n.n.* ¶ *v.i.* slakken *pl.n.* vormen.

slake, *v.t.* lessen (*thirst*); blussen (*lime*). ∼*d lime,* gebluste kalk *n.*

slam, *v.t.* bonzen, smijten *str.;* dichtgooien. *to* ∼ *down,* neerkwakken. ¶ *n.* bons *n.,* harde slag *n.;* slem *n.* (*whist*).

slander, *v.t.* (be)lasteren. ¶ *n.* laster *n.* **slanderer,** *n.* lasteraar *n.* **slanderous,** *a.,* ∼ly, *adv.* lasterlijk.

slang, *n.* argot *n.n.,* bargoens *n.n.* ¶ *v.t.* uitschelden *str.;* afbreken *str.* **slangy,** *a.* bargoens.

slant, *n.* helling *n.;* schuinte *n.* *a different* ∼, een ander aspect *n.n.* ¶ *a.* schuin, zijdelings. ¶ *v.i.* hellen; schuin aflopen *str.;* schuin invallen *str.* ¶ *v.t.* doen *irr.* hellen. **slanting,** *a.* hellend, schuin. **slantwise,** *a.* & *adv.* schuin, scheef.

slap, *v.t.* een klap *n.* geven *str.* ¶ *n.* klap *n.;* pats *n.* ¶ *adv.* pats, pardoes, vierkant. **slapdash,** *a.* overhaast, nonchalant. **slap-up,** *a.* (*coll.*) prima, rijk.

slash, *v.t.* houwen *str.;* japen, snijden *str.* ¶ *v.i.* houwen *str.,* hakken. ¶ *n.* houw *n.* (*sword*); jaap *n.* (*knife*).

slat, *n.* lat *n.*

slate, *n.* leisteen *n.;* lei *n.* ¶ *a.* leien; leikleurig. ¶ *v.t.* met leien *pl.n.* bedekken; afbreken *str.* (*criticise*). **slate-pencil,** *n.* griffel *n.* **slate-quarry,** *n.* leigroeve *n.*

slater, *n.* leidekker *n.*

slattern, *n.* slons *n.* ¶ *a.* slonzig.

slaughter, *n.* slachten *n.n.* (*cattle*); slachting *n.,* bloedbad *n.n.* ¶ *v.t.* slachten; afmaken, vermoorden. **slaughterer,** *n.* moordenaar *n.,* beul *n.* **slaughter-house,** *n.* slachthuis *n.n.,* abattoir *n.n.*

Slav, *a.* slavisch. ¶ *N.* Slaaf *N.*

slave, *n.* slaaf *n.;* slavin *n.* (*female*). ¶ *v.i.* slaven, sloven. **slaver,** *n.* slavenhandelaar *n.;* kwijl *n.* (*saliva*). ¶ *v.i.* kwijlen. **slavery,** *n.* slavernij *n.* **slavey,** *n.* slonzig dienstmeisje *n.n.*

Slavic, *a.* Slavisch.

slavish, *a.,* ∼ly, *adv.* slaafs.

Slavonic, *a.* Slavonisch.

slay, *v.t.* doden, doodslaan *irr.* **slayer,** *n.* moordenaar *n.*

sledge, *n.* slede *n.,* slee *n.* ¶ *v.i.* sleeën. **sledge-hammer,** *n.* voorhamer *n.*

sleek, *a.,* ∼ly, *adv.* glad; glanzend; sluik; zalvend. ¶ *v.t.* gladstrijken *str.*

sleep, *n.* slaap *n.* *my foot has gone to* ∼, mijn voet slaapt; *I'm dying with* ∼, ik val om van slaap. ¶ *v.i.* slapen. *the S∼ing Beauty,* de Schone Slaapster; ∼*ing partner,* stille vennoot *n.* **sleeper,** *n.* slaper *n.;* dwarsligger *n.* (*railway*). **sleepiness,** *n.* slaperigheid *n.* **sleeping-car,** *n.* slaapwagon *n.* **sleeping sickness,** *n.* slaapziekte *n.* **sleepless,** *a.,* ∼ly, *adv.* slapeloos. **sleeplessness,** *n.* slapeloosheid *n.* **sleepwalker,** *n.* slaapwandelaar *n.* **sleepwalking,** *n.* slaapwandelen *n.n.* **sleepy,** *a.* ∼ily, *adv.* slaperig.

sleet, *n.* sneeuw *n.* en regen *n.* ¶ *v.i.* sneeuwen en regenen. **sleety,** *a.* met sneeuw *n.* en regen *n.*

sleeve, *n.* mouw *n.;* voering *n.* (*technical*). *to laugh in one's* ∼, in z'n vuistje *n.n.* lachen *irr.;* ∼ *valve,* schuifklep *n.* **sleeveless,** *a.* zonder mouwen *pl.n.* *to send a person on a* ∼ *errand,* iemand voor gek *n.* laten *str.* lopen.

sleigh, *n.* slede *n.,* slee *n.* ¶ *v.i.* sledevaren. **sleight,** *n.* list *n.* ∼ *of hand,* kunstgreep *n.*

slender, *a.* ∼ly, *adv.* slank; tenger; schraal, gering. **slenderness,** *n.* slankheid *n.;* tengerheid *n.;* onbeduidendheid *n.*

sleuth, *n.* speurhond *n.;* detective *n.* ¶ *v.t.* opspeuren.

slice, *n.* plak *n.,* schijf *n.,* snee *n.,* sneetje *n.n.* ∼ *of bread and butter,* boterham *n.;* ∼ *of luck,* gelukje *n.n.* ¶ *v.t.* aan plakjes snijden *str.*

slick, *a.* glad, handig. ¶ *v.t.* glad maken. **slickness,** *n.* handigheid *n.*

slide, *v.i.* & *v.t.* glijden *str.;* schuiven *str. sliding door,* schuifdeur *n.; sliding knot,* slipknoop *n.; sliding scale,* wisselende schaal *n.; sliding seat,* glijdoft *n.* ¶ *n.* glijden *n.n.;* glijbaan *n.;* schuif *n.;* plaatje *n.n.,* glaasje *n.n.* (*microscope*); lantaarnplaatje *n.n.* (*lantern*). **slider,** *n.* glijder *n.;* schuif *n.* **sliding-rule,** *n.* rekenlineaal *n.n..*

slight, *a.* ∼ly, *adv.* licht; gering, onbeduidend. *not in the* ∼*est,* in 't minst niet. ¶ *n.* geringschatting *n.;* minachtende bejegening *n.* **slighting,** *a.* ∼ly, *adv.* minachtend, geringschattend. **slightness,** *n.* onbeduidendheid *n.;* lichtheid *n.*

slily, *adv.* sluw, listig.

slim, *a.* slank; dun. ¶ *v.i.* vermageren.

slime, *n.* slijm *n.n.;* slijk *n.n.,* slib *n.n.* **sliminess,** *n.* slijmerigheid *n.* **slimy,** *a.* slijmerig; glibberig.

sling, *n.* slinger *n.;* leng *n.n.* (*nautical*); draagband *n.;* riem *n.* ¶ *v.t.* slingeren;

gooien. *to ~ one's hook* (*coll.*), er van door gaan *irr.*

slink, *v.i.* sluipen *str.*

slip, *v.i.* glippen, slippen, uitglijden *str. to ~ across*, eventjes overwippen; *to ~ away*, ongemerkt weggaan *irr.* ¶ *v.t.* ontglippen; toestoppen. *to ~ off*, afschuiven *str.*; gauw uittrekken *str.*; *to ~ on*, aanschieten *str.* (*clothes*). ¶ *n.* vergissing *n.*, abuis *n.n.*; (kussen)sloop *n.*; strook *n.* (*paper*); helling *n.* (*yard*); stek *n.* (*shoot*); onderjurk *n. to make a ~*, zich vergissen; *to make a ~ of the tongue* (*pen*), zich verspreken *str.* (verschrijven *str.*); *a ~ of a girl*, een jong ding *n.n.* **slip-knot**, *n.* schuifknoop *n.*

slipper, *n.* pantoffel *n.*

slipperiness, *n.* gladheid *n.* **slippery**, *a.* glad, glibberig. **slippy**, *a.* glibberig; vlug, gewiekst. **slip-ring**, *n.* onderlegring *n.* **slipshod**, *a.* slordig. **slipway**, *n.* (scheeps)helling *n.*

slit, *n.* spleet *n.*; sleuf *n.* ¶ *v.t.* splijten *str.*; scheuren (*clothes*); doorsnijden *str.*

slither, *v.i.* slieren; glibberen.

slither, *v.i.* slieren; glibberen.

sliver, *n.* splinter *n.*

slobber, *v.i.* kwijlen. ¶ *v.t.* slobberen. ¶ *n.* kwijl *n.n.*

sloe, *n.* sleedoorn *n.*

slog, *v.i.* zwoegen, ploeteren. **slogger**, *n.* ploeteraar *n.*

slogan, *n.* leus *n.*, motto *n.n.*

sloop, *n.* sloep *n.*; korvet *n.*

slop, *v.i.* & *v.t.* morsen. ¶ *n.* spoeling *n.* ~*s*, spoelwater *n.n.*; lepelkost *n.* **slop-basin**, *n.* spoelkom *n.*

slope, *n.* helling *n.*; glooiing *n.* ¶ *v.i.* hellen, glooien. ¶ *v.t.* schuin houden *irr.* **sloping**, *a.* hellend, schuin.

slop-pail, *n.* toiletemmer *n.*; vuilwateremmer *n.* **sloppy**, *a.* morsig, slordig.

slot, *n.* gleuf *n.*, sleuf *n.*

sloth, *n.* luiheid *n.*, traagheid *n.*, vadsigheid *n.*; luiaard *n.* (*animal*). **slothful**, *a.* ~ly, *adv.* lui, traag, vadsig.

slot-machine, *n.* automaat *n.*

slouch, *v.i.* slungelen, slap lopen *str.* ¶ *n.* slappe gang *n.* **slouch-hat**, *n.* hoed *n.* met brede rand *n.*

slough, *n.* moeras *n.n.*

Slovak, *a.* Slowaaks. ¶ *N.* Slowaak *N.* **Slovakia**, *N.* Slowakije *n.N.* **Slovene**, *a.* Sloweens. ¶ *N.* Sloween *N.*

slovenliness, *n.* slordigheid *n.* **slovenly**, *a.* slordig.

slow, *a.* ~ly, *adv.* langzaam, traag; vervelend; achter (*clock*). ¶ *v.i. to ~ down*, langzamer (laten) *str.* gaan. **slowcoach**, *n.* treuzelaar *n.* **slowness**, *n.* traagheid *n.* **slow-witted**, *a.* traag van begrip *n.n.* **slowworm**, *n.* blindworm *n.*

sludge, *n.* dikke modder *n.*, bagger *n.* **sludgy**, *a.* modderig.

slug, *n.* slak *n.*; loden kogel *n.* ¶ *v.t.* (*coll.*) bewusteloos slaan *irr.*

sluggard, *n.* luiaard *n.*, luilak *n.* **sluggish**, *a.* ~ly, *adv.* traag.

sluice, *n.* sluis *n.* ¶ *v.t.* spuien; doorspoelen.

slum, *n.* slop *n.n.*, achterbuurt *n.* ¶ *v.i.* achterbuurten bezoeken *irr.*

slumber, *v.i.* sluimeren. ¶ *n.* sluimer *n.*

slump, *v.i.* plotseling dalen. ¶ *n.* plotselinge daling *n.*; krach *n.*; malaise *n*, depressie *n.*

slur, *v.t.* onduidelijk uitspreken *str.*, slepen. ¶ *n.* blaam *n.*; onduidelijke uitspraak *n. to cast a ~ on*, een smet *n.* werpen *str.* op.

slush, *n.* sneeuwslijk *n.n.* **slushy**, *a.* slikkerig, vol sneeuwslijk *n.n.*

slut, *n.* slons *n.*, slet *n.* **sluttish**, *a.*, ~ly, *adv.* slonzig.

sly, *a.*, ~ily, *adv.* sluw, listig. ¶ *n. on the ~*, stiekem. **slyness**, *n.* sluwheid *n.*

smack, *v.t.* smakken, patsen. *to ~ one's lips*, met de lippen *pl. n.* smakken. ¶ *n.* klap *n.*, pats *n.*; tikje *n.n.*; smak *n.* (*boat*). *to have a ~ at someone*, iemand een veeg *n.* uit de pan geven *str.* **smacker**, *n.* (*coll.*) klapzoen *n.*

small, *a.* klein; gering; weinig; kleingeestig. ~ *arms*, draagbare wapenen *pl.n.n.*; ~ *beer*, licht bier *n.n.*; ~ *change*, kleingeld *n.n.*; ~ *fry*, klein goed *n.n.*; *into the ~ hours* tot na middernacht; ~ *shot*, hagel *n.*; ~ *talk*, lichte conversatie *n.* ¶ *n. the ~ of the back*, de lendenstreek. **small-holder**, *n.* keuterboer *n.* **smallish**, *a.* kleintjes, nogal klein. **smallness**, *n.* kleinheid *n.*, kleinte *n.*

smallpox, *n.* pokken *pl.n.*

smart, *a.*, ~ly, *adv.* scherp, vinnig; flink, vlug; gevat; chic, modieus. ¶ *v.i.* pijn *n.* doen *irr.*; smarten. ¶ *n.* scherpe pijn *n.* **smarten**, *v.t.* mooi maken. *to ~ oneself up*, zich mooi maken. **smartness**, *n.* scherpheid *n.*; flinkheid *n.*; gevatheid *n.*; chic *n.*

smash, *v.t.* breken *str.*; stukslaan *irr.*; verbrijzelen; inslaan *irr.* (*windows*); bankroet *n.n.* gaan *irr.* ¶ *n.* slag *n.*, botsing *n.*; bankroet *n.n.*

smattering, *n.* oppervlakkige kennis *n.*

smear, *v.t.* smeren; besmeren. ¶ *n.* veeg *n.* **smeary**, *a.* vettig, morsig.

smell, *v.i.* ruiken *str.*; slecht ruiken *str. to ~ of*, ruiken *str.* naar. ¶ *v.t.* ruiken *str.*; ruiken *str.* aan, beruiken *str. to ~ a rat*; lont *n.* ruiken *str.* ¶ *n.* reuk *n.*; luchtje *n.n.* **smelling salts**, *pl.n.* reukzout *n.n.*

smelt, *v.t.* smelten *str.* ¶ *n.* spiering *n.* (*fish*). **smelter**, *n.* smelter *n.* **smelting-furnace**, *n.* smeltoven *n.* **smelting-works**, *pl.n.* ijzersmelterij *n.*

smew, *n.* nonnetje *n.n.*

smile, *v.i.* glimlachen. *to ~ at*, glimlachen tegen (*person*), om (*thing*). ¶ *n.* glimlach *n.*

smirch, *v.t.* bezoedelen, bekladden. ¶ *n.* klad *n.*, smet *n.*

smirk, *v.i.* onnozel lachen; vies lachen. ¶ *n.* onnozel lachje *n.n.*

smite, *v.t.* slaan *irr.*, treffen *str.*

smith, *n.* smid *n.*

smithereens, *pl.n.* gruizelementen *pl.n.n.*

smithy, *n.* smidse *n.*, smederij *n.*

smitten, *a.* getroffen. ~ *with*, verrukt over (*enthusiastic*).

smock, *n.* kiel *n*

smoke, *n.* rook *n.*; damp *n.*; walm *n.* *have a* ~, steek eens op! ¶ *v.i.* roken; dampen; walmen. ¶ *v.t.* beroken, uitroken. **smokeless**, *n.* rokeloos. **smoker**, *n.* roker *n.*; rookcoupé *n.n.* (*train*). **smoke-screen**, *n.* rookgordijn *n.n.*, rookscherm *n.n.* **smokiness**, *n.* rokerigheid *n.* **smoky**, *a.* rokerig.

smooth, *a.*, ~ly, *adv.* glad, vlak, effen; plausibel. *it runs* ~ly (*fig.*), het gaat van een leien dakje *n.n.* **smoothe**, *v.t.* glad maken, gladstrijken *str.*; stillen. *to* ~ *over*, vereffenen. **smoothness**, *n.* gladheid *n.*, vlakheid *n.*; plausibiliteit *n.* **smoothtongued**, *a.* mooipratend.

smother, *v.t.* smoren, verstikken; dempen.

smoulder, *v.i.* smeulen.

smudge, *v.t.* vuil maken, een smeer *n.* maken op. ¶ *n.* vuiltje *n.n.*

smug, *a.* zelfgenoegzaam; uitgestreken.

smuggle, *v.t.* & *v.i.* smokkelen. ~*d goods*, smokkelwaar *n.* **smuggler**, *n.* smokkelaar *n.* **smuggling**, *n.* smokkelen *n.n.*, smokkelarij *n.*, sluikhandel *n.*

smugness, *n.* zelfgenoegzaamheid *n.*

smut, *n.* vuiltje *n.n.*, roetvlokje *n.n.*; vuile taal *n.* **smuttiness**, *n.* vuiligheid *n.* **smutty**, *a.*, ~ily, *adv.* vuil.

snack, *n.* haastig maal *n.n.*

snaffle, *v.t.* inpikken.

snag, *n.* knoest *n.*, kwast *n.*; (*fig.*) moeilijkheid *n.*

snail, *n.* (huisjes)slak *n.*; snekrad *n.n.* (*wheel*).

snake, *n.* slang *n.* ~ *in the grass*, adder *n.* in het gras. **snake-charmer**, *n.* slangenbezweerder *n.* **snaky**, *a.* slangachtig.

snap, *v.i.* happen, snappen; snauwen. *to* ~ *at*, toesnauwen. ¶ *v.t.* (af)knappen; klappen, knippen. *to* ~ *one's fingers at*, maling *n.* hebben aan; *to* ~ *up*, wegsnappen. ¶ *n.* hap *n.*, snap *n.*; knip *n.* *we're having a cold* ~, 't is opeens koud geworden. **snapdragon**, *n.* leeuwenbek *n.* **snappy**, *a.*, ~ily, *adv.* vlug; bits. **snapshot**, *n.* kiek *n.*

snare, *n.* strik *n.*, valstrik *n.* ¶ *v.t.* strikken; (*fig.*) verstrikken.

snarl, *v.i.* grauwen, snauwen, grommen. *to* ~ *at*, afsnauwen. ¶ *v.t.* toesnauwen. ¶ *n.* grauw *n.*, snauw *n.*

snatch, *v.t.* grijpen *str.*; rukken. ¶ *v.i.* grijpen *str.*, grissen. ¶ *n.* ruk *n.*, greep *n.*; eindje *n.n.* (*song*). , ~es, stukken *pl.n.n.* en brokken *pl.n.*

sneak, *v.i.* sluipen *str.*; klikken. *to* ~ *away*, wegsluipen *str.*; wegkapen. ¶ *n.* klikspaan *n.*; gluiper *n.* **sneakthief**, *n.* gauwdief *n.*

sneer, *v.i.* honend lachen; grijnslachen. *to* ~ *at*, spotten met. ¶ *n.* hoongelach *n.n.*, spottende lach *n.* **sneering**, *a.* spottend, honend.

sneeze, *v.i.* niezen. *not to be* ~*d at*, niet te versmaden. ¶ *n.* niezen *n.n.*

snick, *v.t.* knippen; kerven *str.*

sniff, *v.i.* snuiven *str.*; snuffelen. ¶ *v.t.* ruiken *str.*; opsnuiven *str.* ¶ *n.* snuiven *n.n.*; luchtje *n.n.*

snigger, *v.i.* grinniken, gnuiven. ¶ *n.* gegrinnik *n.n.*

sniggle, *v.i.* aalsteken.

snip, *v.t.* (af)knippen. ¶ *n.* snipper *n.*

snipe, *n.* snip *n.* ¶ *v.i.* (verdekt) beschieten *str.* **sniper**, *n.* scherpschutter *n.*

snippet, *n.* snipper *n.*

snivel, *v.i.* snotteren. **sniveller**, *n.* snotteraar *n.*; huilebalk *n.*

snob, *n.* schoenlapper *n.*; snob *n.* **snobbery**, *n.* snobisme *n.n.* **snobbish**, *a.* snobachtig.

snook, *n.* *to cock a* ~ *at*, een neus *n.* maken tegen.

snooker, *n.* potspel *n.n.*

snoop, *v.i.* neuzen. **snooper**, *n.* bemoeial *n.*, nieuwsgierigaard *n.*

snooze, *v.i.* dutten. ¶ *n.* dutje *n.n.*

snore, *v.i.* snurken, ronken. ¶ *n.* gesnurk *n.n.*

snort, *v.i.* snuiven *str.*, briesen. ¶ *n.* gesnuif *n.n.*

snout, *n.* snuit *n.*; neus *n.*

snow, *n.* sneeuw *n.* ¶ *v.i.* sneeuwen. *to* ~ *under*, onder de sneeuw bedolven raken; ~*ed under*, bedolven (*fig.*), overstelpt. **snowball**, *n.* sneeuwbal *n.* ¶ *v.i.* met sneeuwballen gooien. **snowbound**, *a.* ingesneeuwd. **snowcapped**, *a.* met besneeuwde top *n.* **snowdrift**, *n.* sneeuwbank *n.*, sneeuwjacht *n.* **snowdrop**, *n.* sneeuwklokje *n.n.* **snowman**, *n.* sneeuwpop *n.* **snow-white**, *a.* sneeuwwit. **snowy**, *a.* sneeuwachtig; sneeuwwit.

snub, *v.t.* terechtwijzen *str.*, op de vingers *pl.n.* tikken. ¶ *n.* terechtwijzing *n.* **snub-nose**, *n.* stompneus *n.* **snub-nosed**, *a.* stompneuzig.

snuff, *n.* snuif *n.n.*, snuiftabak *n.* *to take* ~, snuiven *str.* ¶ *v.i.* snuiven *str.* (*tobacco*). ¶ *v.t.* snuiten *str.* (*candle*). **snuff-box**, *n.* snuifdoos *n.*

snuffle, *v.i.* snuffelen.

snug, *a.*, ~ly, *adv.* gezellig, knus.

snuggle, *v.i.* lekker liggen *str.* *to* ~ *close to*, zich aanvlelen tegen.

so, *adv.* zo; zozeer. *how* ~, hoezo; *and* ~ *was I*, en ik ook; *I think* ~, ik meen van wel; ~ *long*, tot ziens. ¶ *c.* dus. ~ *that*, zodat; opdat. ¶ *a.* *so-so*, matigjes.

soak, *v.i.* in de week staan *irr.* ¶ *v.t.* in de week zetten, weken. *to be* ~*ed*, doornat zijn. **soaking**, *a.* kletsnat, drijfnat, doornat.

soap, *n.* zeep *n.* ¶ *v.t.* (in)zepen. **soap-boiler,** *n.* zeepzieder *n.* **soap-bubble,** *n.* zeepbel *n.*
soapsuds, *n.* zeepsop *n.n.* **soapy,** *a.* zeperig, zeepachtig.
soar, *v.i.* hoog opstijgen *str.*
sob, *v.i.* snikken. ¶ *n.* snik *n.*
sober, *a.,* ~ly, *adv.* nuchter; sober, matig. **sobriety,** *n.* nuchterheid *n.;* matigheid *n.*
soccer, *n.* voetbalspel *n.n.*
sociability, *n.* gezelligheid *n.* **sociable,** *a.,* ~bly, *adv.* gezellig. **social,** *a.,* ~ly, *adv.* maatschappelijk; gezellig. ~ *services,* sociale voorziening *n.;* ~ *welfare,* maatschappelijk werk *n.n.* **socialism,** *n.* socialisme *n.n.* **socialist,** *n.* socialist *n.* **socialization,** *n.* socialisatie *n.* **socialize,** *v.t.* socialiseren. **society,** *n.* maatschappij *n.,* samenleving *n.;* maatschappij *n.,* vereniging *n.;* de (grote) wereld.
sock, *n.* sok *n.;* mep *n.* (*blow*). *to pull up one's* ~*s,* zich wat inspannen. ¶ *v.t.* (*coll.*) een opdonder *n.* geven *str.*
socket, *n.* kas *n.,* holte *n.*
sod, *n.* zo(de) *n.*
soda, *n.* soda *n.* **soda-water,** *n.* spuitwater *n.n.* **soda-fountain,** *n.* spuitwaterfles *n.,* sifon *n.*
sodden, *a.* doorweekt; drijfnat.
sofa, *n.* sofa *n.*
soft, *a.* zacht; mals; slap; halfgaar. ~ *drink,* niet-alkoholische drank *n.;* ~ *goods,* wollen en katoenen goederen *pl.n.n.;* ~ *soap,* groene zeep *n.;* (*fig.*) vleierij *n.;* ~ *spot,* zwakke plaats *n.* **soften,** *v.t.* zacht maken, verzachten; vermurwen. ¶ *v.i.* zacht worden *str.* **softener,** *n.* verzachter *u.* **soft-hearted,** *a.* teerhartig. **softly,** *adv.* zacht, zachtjes. **softness,** *n.* zachtheid *n.*
soggy, *a.* doorweekt; drassig.
soil, *n.* bodem *n.;* grond *n.,* aarde *n.;* smet *n.,* vlek *n.* ¶ *v.t.* bezoedelen; bevuilen.
sojourn, *n.* verblijf *n.n.* ¶ *v.i.* vertoeven, zich ophouden *irr.*
solace, *v.t.* troosten, vertroosten. ¶ *n.* troost *n.,* verlichting *n.*
solar, *a.* zonne . . . ~ *plexus,* (*pop.*) maagstreek *n.*
solder, *v.t. & v.i.* solderen. ¶ *n.* soldeersel *n.n.*
soldier, *n.* soldaat *n.* **soldierly,** *a.* krijgshaftig; soldaten . . . **soldiership,** *n.* krijgsmanschap *n.n.* **soldiery,** *n.* krijgsvolk *n.n.n.,* soldaten *pl.n.*
sole, *a.,* ~ly, *adv.* alleen; enig, enigst. ¶ *n.* zool *n.* (*of foot*); tong *n.* (*fish*). ¶ *v.t.* verzolen.
solecism, *n.* solecisme *n.n.;* flater *n.*
solemn, *a.,* ~ly, *adv.* plechtig. **solemnity,** *n.* plechtigheid *n.* **solemnization,** *n.* voltrekking *n.* **solemnize,** *v.t.* plechtig vieren; voltrekken *str.* (*marriage*).
solicit, *v.i.* lastig vallen *str.* (*of prostitute*). ¶ *v.t.* vragen *str.,* verzoeken *irr. to* ~ *for,* vragen om. **solicitation,** *n.* verzoek *n.n.,* aanzoek *n.n.;* aandringen *n.n.*

solicitor, *n.* notaris *n.;* procureur *n.* S~ *General,* Procureur Generaal.
solicitous, *a.,* ~ly, *adv.* bezorgd; begerig. **solicitude,** *n.* bezorgdheid *n.,* zorg *n.*
solid, *a.,* ~ly, *adv.* stevig, hecht; soliede, degelijk (*reliable*); massief (*not hollow*). ~ *contents,* kubieke inhoud *n.;* ~ *geometry,* stereometrie *n.;* ~ *hours,* volle uren *pl.n.n.* **solidarity,** *n.* solidariteit *n.* **solidify,** *v.i.* stollen; consolideren. ¶ *v.t.* doen *irr.* stollen. **solidity,** *n.* stevigheid *n.;* soliditeit *n.*
soliloquize, *v.i.* een alleenspraak *n.* houden *irr.* **soliloquy,** *n.* alleenspraak *n.*
solitaire, *n.* één enkele diamant *n.;* patiencespel *n.n.*
solitary, *a.,* ~ily, *adv.* eenzaam; verlaten; enkel, op zichzelfstaand. **solitude,** *n.* eenzaamheid *n.*
solo, *n.* solo *n.* **soloist,** *n.* solist *n.;* soliste *n.* (*female*).
solstice, *n.* zonnestilstand *n.*
solubility, *n.* oplosbaarheid *n.* **soluble,** *a.* oplosbaar; ontbindbaar. **solution,** *n.* oplossing *n.* **solvability,** *n.* oplosbaarheid *n.;* solvabiliteit *n.* **solvable,** *a.* oplosbaar; solvent (*financial*). **solve,** *v.t.* oplossen; ontraadselen. **solvency,** *n.* solvabiliteit *n.* **solvent,** *a.* solvent. ¶ *n.* oplossingsmiddel *n.n.*
sombre, *a.* somber, donker.
some, *pron.* enige, wat; sommige. ¶ *a.* een, de een of andere, het een of ander. ~ 10 *or* 12 *guilders,* een gulden of 10–12. **somebody,** *pron.* iemand. **somehow,** *adv.* op een of andere manier; hoe dan ook. **someone,** *pron.* iemand.
somersault, *n.* buiteling *n.* *to turn* ~*s,* buitelen.
something, *pron.* iets; wat. ¶ *adv.* zowat, wel wat. **sometime,** *adv.* soms; voorheen. ¶ *a.* vroeger, voormalig. **sometimes,** *adv.* soms. **somewhat,** *adv.* enigszins, enigermate. **somewhere,** *adv.* ergens; hier of daar.
somnambulism, *n.* somnambulisme *n.n.,* slaapwandelen *n.n.* **somnambulist,** *n.* slaapwandelaar *n.* **somnolence,** *n.* slaperigheid *n.* **somnolent,** *a.* slaperig. **somniferous,** *a.* slaapwekkend.
son, *n.* zoon *n.* **son-in-law,** *n.* schoonzoon *n.*
sonata, *n.* sonate *n.*
song, *n.* zang *n.;* lied *n.n.* *for a* ~, voor een appel en een ei *n.n.* **songster,** *n.* zanger *n.*
sonnet, *n.* sonnet *n.n.*
sonny, *n.* zoontjelief *n.n.*
sonorous, *a.,* ~ly, *adv.* klankvol, klankrijk, sonoor.
soon, *adv.* spoedig; weldra; gauw. *as* ~ *as,* zodra; *I would just as* ~ . . . , ik zou net zo lief . . .; *no* ~*er* . . . *than* . . . , nauwelijks . . . of . . .; *no* ~*er said than done,* zo gezegd zo gedaan.
soot, *n.* roet *n.n.*

sooth, *n.* waarheid *n.*
soothe, *v.t.* stillen, kalmeren. **soother**, *n.* kalmerend middel *n.n.*
soothsayer, *n.* waarzegger *n.*
sooty, *a.* roetig; roetkleurig.
sop, *v.t.* soppen, dopen. *~ping wet*, druipnat. ¶ *n.* sopje *n.n.*; concessie *n.*
sophism, *n.* sophisme *n.n.*, drogreden *n.*
sophist, *n.* sophist *n.*, drogredenaar *n.*
sophistic, *a.* sophistisch. **sophisticated**, *a.* wereldwijs. **sophistication**, *n.* wereldwijsheid *n.* **sophistry**, *n.* sophisterij *n.*
soporific, *a.* slaapwekkend.
soprano, *n.* sopraan *n.*
sorb, *n.* lijsterbes *n.*
sorcerer, *n.* tovenaar *n.* **sorceress**, *n.* tovenares *n.* **sorcery**, *n.* tovenarij *n.*
sordid, *a.*, *~ly*, *adv.* armzalig; laag.
sore, *a.* zeer, pijnlijk. *to have a ~ throat*, keelpijn *n.* hebben. ¶ *n.* rauwe plek *n.*, open plek *n.* **sorely**, *adv.* zeer, bizonder. **soreness**, *n.* pijnlijkheid *n.*
sorrel, *n.* zuring *n.* (*plant*); vos *n.* (*horse*). ¶ *a.* ros.
sorrow, *n.* smart *n.*, droefheid *n.*; leedwezen *n.n.* ¶ *v.i.* *to ~ at* or *over*, treuren over. **sorrowful**, *a.*, *~ly*, *adv.* treurig, bedroefd.
sorry, *a.*, *~ily*, *adv.* bedroefd; armzalig, ellendig. *I am ~ (for)*, het spijt me (voor).
sort, *n.* soort *n.* *all ~s*, allerlei slag *n.n.*; *not a bad ~*, geen kwaaie vent *n.*; *. . . of ~s*, een soort (van) *. . .*; *out of ~s*, slecht gehumeurd. ¶ *v.t.* sorteren. **sorter**, *n.* sorteerder *n.*
sortie, *n.* uitval *n.*
sorting, *a.* sorteer *. . .*
sot, *n.* dwaas *n.* **sottish**, *a.*, *~ly*, *adv.* verzopen.
sough, *v.i.* suizen, ruisen.
soul, *n.* ziel *n.* *not a ~*, geen levende ziel. **soulful**, *a.*, *~ly*, *adv.* gevoelvol; overdreven. **soulless**, *a.* zielloos.
sound, *n.* geluid *n.n.*; klank *n.*, toon *n.*; sont *n.*, zee-engte *n.* (*straits*); sonde *n.* (*instrument*); loding *n.* (*depth*). ¶ *a.*, *~ly*, *adv.* gezond; ongeschonden; soliede, betrouwbaar. *~ asleep*, vast in slaap *n.* ¶ *v.i.* klinken *str.*, luiden. ¶ *v.t.* doen *irr.* weerklinken; ausculteren (*chest*); sonderen (*wound*); peilen (*water*); polsen (*opinion*). *to ~ an alarm*, alarm *n.n.* blazen *str.* or slaan *irr.* **soundboard**, *n.* klankbord *n.n.*, klankbodem *n.* **sound-hole**, *n.* klankgat *n.n.*, galmgat *n.n.* **sounding-lead**, *n.* dieplood *n.n.* **sounding-line**, *n.* loodlijn *n.*, schietlood *n.n.* **soundings**, *pl.n.* peiling *n.* *to take ~*, peilen, loden. **soundless**, *a.* geluidloos. **soundness**, *n.* gezondheid *n.*; soliditeit *n.*
soup, *n.* soep *n.* **soupy**, *a.* soeperig.
sour, *a.*, *~ly*, *adv.* zuur; wrang. ¶ *v.t.* zuur maken; verbitteren.
source, *n.* bron *n.*; oorsprong *n.*
sourish, *a.* zuurachtig.

souse, *n.* pekel *n.*; saus *n.* ¶ *v.t.* pekelen; sausen.
south, *adv.* zuidelijk; in zuidelijke richting *n.*; zuidwaarts, naar het zuiden. *~ of*, ten zuiden van, bezuiden. ¶ *a.* zuidelijk; zuid-*. . .* ¶ *n.* zuiden *n.n.* **southbound**, *a.* naar het zuiden. **south-east**, *a.* zuidoost. ¶ *adv.* in (naar van) het zuidoosten. ¶ *n.* zuidoosten *n.n.* **south-easterly**, *a.* zuidoosten. ¶ *adv.* zuidoostwaarts. **southern**, *a.* zuidelijk. *S~ Cross*, Zuiderkruis *n.N.* **southward**, *a.* zuidelijk. ¶ *adv.* zuidwaarts. **south-west**, *a.* zuidwest. ¶ *adv.* in (naar van) het zuidwesten. ¶ *n.* zuidwesten *n.n.* **south-westerner**, *n.* zuidwesten wind *n.*; zuidwester *n.*
sovereign, *n.* vorst *n.*, souverein *n.*; gouden pond *n.n.* ¶ *a.* soeverein; oppermachtig. **sovereignty**, *n.* soevereiniteit *n.*
Soviet, *N.* Sowjet *N.*
sow, *n.* zeug *n.* ¶ *v.t.* zaaien; uitstrooien. **sower**, *n.* zaaier *n.*; zaaimachine *n.*
spa, *n.* badplaats *n.*
space, *n.* ruimte *n.*, plaats *n.*; afstand *n.* *~ of time*, tijdruimte *n.*, tijdsbestek *n.n.* ¶ *v.t.* ruimte *n.* laten *str.* tussen; spatiëren. **spacious**, *a.*, *~ly*, *adv.* ruim; uitgestrekt.
spade, *n.* schop *n.*; schoppen *n.* (*cards*). *to call a ~ a ~*, het kind bij z'n naam *n.* noemen. **spadework**, *n.* graafwerk *n.n.*; pionierswerk *n.n.*
Spain, *N.* Spanje *n.N.*
span, *n.* span *n.n.* *~ of time*, spanne *n.* tijds. ¶ *v.t.* overspannen.
spangle, *n.* lovertje *n.n.* ¶ *v.t.* met lovertjes versieren.
Spaniard, *N.* Spanjaard *N.*
spaniel, *n.* patrijshond *n.*
Spanish, *a.* Spaans.
spank, *v.t.* afranselen. **spanker**, *n.* bezaan. **spanking**, *a.* groot.
spanner, *n.* moersleutel *n.*; Engelse sleutel *n.*
spar, *n.* spar *n.*, boom *n.*, spriet *n.*, rondhout *n.n.* ¶ *v.i.* boksen; redetwisten.
spare, *v.t.* sparen, ontzien *irr.*; missen. *to ~*, te over. ¶ *a.* reserve; extra; schraal, mager. *~ room*, logeerkamer *n.* ¶ *n.* reservedeel *n.n.* **sparing**, *a.*, *~ly*, *adv.* spaarzaam, karig.
spark, *n.* vonk *n.*; sprankje *n.n.* ¶ *v.i.* vonken. **sparking-plug**, *n.* bougie *n.*
sparkle, *v.i.* fonkelen, flonkeren, tintelen. ¶ *n.* gefonkel *n.n.*, flikkering *n.*; glans *n.*
sparrow, *n.* mus *n.* **sparrow-hawk**, *n.* sperwer *n.*
sparse, *a.*, *~ly*, *adv.* dun; ver uit elkaar.
spasm, *n.* krampachtige beweging *n.*; stuiptrekking *n.*; vlaag *n.* **spasmodic**, *a.*, *~ally*, *adv.* krampachtig; bij vlagen *pl.n.*
spat, *n.* (oester)zaad *n.n.* *~s*, slobkousen *pl.n.*
spate, *n.* stortvloed *n.*; massa *n.*
spatial, *a.* ruimte *. . .*
spatter, *v.t.* bespatten, bekladden.
spatula, *n.* spatel *n.*

spavin, n. spat n.

spawn, n. broed n.n., broedsel n.n., gebroed n.n. ¶ v.i. kuit n. schieten str., paaien; zich vermenigvuldigen. **spawner,** n. kuiter n.

speak, v.i. spreken str.; een rede n. houden irr. so to ~, om zo te zeggen; it ~s for him, het pleit voor hem; it ~s for itself, het is vanzelfsprekend; to ~ of, spreken str. van or over; nothing to ~ of, niets van betekenis n.; to ~ to, spreken str. met, tegen or tot; to ~ up, hard spreken str.; to ~ with, spreken str. met. ¶ v.t. spreken str.; uitspreken str.; uiten; praaien (ship). **speaker,** n. spreker n. the S~, de voorzitter n. (House of Commons). **speaking,** a. ~ distance, afstand waarop men elkaar bespreken kan. not to be on ~ terms, elkaar niet meer spreken str. **speaking-tube,** n. spreekbuis n.

spear, n. speer n.; spies n. ¶ v.t. met een speer doorboren, doorspiesen. **spear-head,** n. speerpunt n.; spits n.

spearmint, n. pepermunt n.

spearwort, n. egelboterbloem n.

special, a., ~ly, adv. bizonder, speciaal; extra-. . . **specialist,** n. specialist n. **speciality,** n. specialiteit n. **specialization,** n. specialisering n. **specialize,** v.i. specialiseren.

specie, n. specie n., contanten pl.n.n.

species, n. soort n.n.; geslacht n.n.

specific, a., ~ally, adv. specifiek; soortelijk. ¶ n. middel n.n. **specification,** n. specificatie n. **specify,** v.t. specificeren, in bizonderheden pl.n.n. vermelden.

specimen, n. exemplaar n.n.; voorbeeld n.n.

specious, q., ~ly, adv. schoonschijnend; ogenschijnlijk.

speck, n. vlekje n.n., stip n., spikkel n. ¶ v.t. (be)spikkelen. **speckle,** n. spikkel n. ¶ v.t. (be)spikkelen.

spectacle, n. schouwspel n.n.; vertoning n. pair of ~s, bril n.; ~ frame, montuur n. **spectacular,** a. grandioos, op effect n.n. berekend. **spectator,** n. toeschouwer n.

spectral, a. spookachtig; van het spectrum. **spectre,** n. spook n.n.; geestverschijning n. **spectroscope,** n. spectroscoop n.

spectrum, n. spectrum n.n.

speculate, v.i. overpeinzen; speculeren. to ~ on, theoretiseren over; speculeren op. **speculation,** n. bespiegeling n., overpeinzing n.; speculatie n. **speculative,** a., ~ly, adv. bespiegelend; speculatief, speculerend. **speculator,** n. speculant n.

speculum, n. speculum n.n., spiegel n.

speech, n. spraak n., taal n.; rede n., redevoering n. part of ~, rededeel n.n.; ~ from the Throne, troonrede n. **speechify,** v.i. toespraken pl.n. houden irr. **speechless,** a., ~ly, adv. sprakeloos. ~ with, sprakeloos van.

speed, n. snelheid n.; spoed n.; vaart n.

at full ~, met volle kracht n., in volle vaart n. ¶ v.i. zich spoeden. to ~ up, versnellen. ¶ v.t. bespoedigen, verhaasten. God ~ (thee), God zij met U; to ~ up, vaart n. zetten achter. **speedometer,** n. snelheidsmeter n.

speedwell, n. ereprijs n.

speedy, a., ~ily, adv. spoedig, snel.

spell, v.i. spellen. ¶ v.t. spellen; voorspellen, betekenen. ¶ n. toverspreuk n.; toverkracht n.; bekoring n.; poosje n.n. (time). to cast a ~ on, begoochelen betoveren; to be under a ~, onder een betovering n. zijn; at a ~, achtereen. **spellbound,** a. betoverd. **spelling,** n. spelling n. **spelling-bee,** n. spelwedstrijd n.

spend, v.t. uitgeven str.; doorbrengen irr. (time); besteden. ¶ v.r. to ~ oneself, zich uitputten, afmatten. **spendthrift,** n. verkwister n. **spent,** a. uitgeput, op.

sperm, n. sperma n.n., zaad n.n. **spermato-zoon,** n. spermatozoïde n. **sperm-oil,** n. spermaceti-olie n. **sperm-whale,** n. potvis n.

spew, v.i. braken. ¶ v.t. uitbraken.

sphere, n. sfeer n.; werkkring n. **spherical,** a. bolvormig, sferisch.

sphinx, n. sphynx n.

spice, n. kruid n.n., specerij n. ¶ v.t. kruiden.

spick-and-span, a. piekfijn, keurig.

spicy, a. gekruid; kruiden . . .; pikant.

spider, n. spin n., spinnekop n. ~'s web, spinneweb n.n., spinrag n.n.

spigot, n. zwikje n.n.; spie n., tap n.

spike, n. tand n.; spijl n. ¶ v.t. vernagelen. **spiky,** a. puntig.

spill, n. spil n.; val n., tuimeling n. ¶ v.t. storten, morsen; vergieten str.; omgooien. **spin,** v.t. spinnen str.; doen irr. draaien. to ~ a yarn, een verhaal n.n. doen irr.; to ~ out, rekken. ¶ n. rit n., toertje n.n.

spinach, n. spinazie n.

spinal, a. ruggemerg . . ., ruggegraat . . . ~ column, ruggegraat n.

spindle, n. spoel n.; spil n., as n. **spindle-legs,** pl.n. spillebenen pl.n.n. **spindly,** a. spichtig.

spine, n. doorn n., prikkel n.; ruggegraat n.; rug n.

spinet, n. spinet n.n.

spinner, n. spinner n.

spinney, n. bosje n.n.

spinning-jenny, n. spinmachine n. **spinning-wheel,** n. spinnewiel n.n.

spinster, n. ongehuwde vrouw n.; jonge dochter n.; ouwe vrijster n.

spiral, a. spiraalvormig. ~ staircase, wenteltrap n. ¶ n. spiraal n. **spirally,** adv. spiraalsgewijs. . .

spire, n. (spitse) toren n.; torenspits n.

spirit, n. geest n.; geestverschijning n.; bezieling n., vuur n.n. ~s, alcohol n.; sterke drank n., spiritualiën pl.n.; animal ~s, levenslust n.; ~s of wine, wijngeest *n.;* ~*s of wood,* houtgeest *n.; in good* ~*s,* in een goed humeur *n.n.;* geanimeerd. ¶ *v.t. to* ~ *away,* wegmoffelen. **spirited,** *a.,* ~**ly,** *adv.* bezield, levendig. **spirit-lamp,** *n.* spirituslamp *n.* **spiritless,** *a.* terneergeslagen. **spirit-level,** *n.* waterpas *n.n.* **spiritual,** *a.,* ~**ly,** *adv.* geestelijk; geestrijk. **spiritualism,** *n.* geestelijkheid *n.;* spiritualisme *n.n.* **spiritualist,** *n.* spiritualist *n-* **spirituality,** *n.* geestelijkheid *n.,* onstoffelijkheid *n.* **spirituous,** *a.* alcoholisch.

spit, *v.i.* spuwen; blazen *str.* (*cat*). ¶ *v.t.* spuwen; aan het spit steken *str.* ¶ *n.* (braad)spit *n.n.;* landtong *n.;* spuug *n.n.* (*saliva*); sprekend evenbeeld *n.n.* ~ *and polish,* poetsen *n.n.* en boenen *n.n.*

spite, *n.* wrok *n.;* kwaadaardigheid *n. in* ~ *of,* ondanks, trots, in weerwil van; *out of* ~, uit wrok. ¶ *v.t.* dwarsbomen. **spiteful,** *a.,* ~**ly,** *adv.* afgunstig; kwaadaardig.

spitfire, *n.* driftkop *n.*

spittle, *n.* speeksel *n.n.* **spittoon,** *n.* spuwbak *n.*

splash, *v.i.* spatten; plonzen, plassen. ¶ *v.t.* bespatten. ¶ *n.* plons *n. to go a* ~, flink spenderen; *to make a* ~, opzien *n.n.* baren. **splash-board,** *n.* slijkbord *n.n.*

splay, *a.* scheef, schuin. ~ *foot,* ganzenvoet *n.*

spleen, *n.* milt *n.;* zwaarmoedigheid *n.* **spleeny,** *a.* zwaarmoedig.

splendid, *a.,* ~**ly,** *adv.* prachtig, schitterend. **splendour,** *n.* pracht *n.;* luister *n.,* praal *n.*

splenetic, *a.* zwaarmoedig.

splice, *v.t.* splitsen; (*coll.*) trouwen. ¶ *n.* splitsing *n.*

splint, *n.* spalk *n.* ¶ *v.t.* spalken.

splinter, *n.* splinter *n.* ¶ *v.i.* splinteren. ¶ *v.t.* versplinteren.

split, *n.* spleet *n.;* scheuring *n.,* splitsing *n.* ¶ *v.t.* splijten *str.;* klieven; delen. *to* ~ *hairs,* haarkloven; *to* ~ *one's sides,* zich kromlachen. ¶ *v.i.* splijten *str.,* barsten *irr.* ~*ting headache,* barstende hoofdpijn *n.* **split-peas**(e), *pl.n.* spliterwten *pl.n.*

splutter, *v.i.* sputteren. ¶ *n.* gesputter *n.n.*

spoil, *v.i.* bederven *str. to* ~ *for,* hunkeren naar. ¶ *v.t.* bederven; plunderen. ¶ *n.* ~**s,** buit *n.* **spoiler,** *n.* plunderaar *n.* spoilt, *a.* bedorven.

spoke, *n.* spaak *n.*

spokesman, *n.* woordvoerder *n.*

spoliation, *n.* beroving *n.,* plundering *n.*

sponge, *n.* spons *n. to throw up the* ~, zich gewonnen geven *str.* ¶ *v.t.* (af)sponsen. ¶ *v.i.* klaplopen *str.* **sponge-cake,** *n.* moscovisch gebak *n.n.* **sponger,** *n.* klaploper *n.* **sponginess,** *n.* sponsigheid *n.* **spongy,** *a.* sponsig, sponsachtig.

sponsor, *n.* peet *n. to stand* ~ *for,* instaan *irr.* voor.

spontaneity, *n.* spontaneïteit *n.,* natuurlijkheid *n.* **spontaneous,** *a.,* ~**ly,** *adv.* spontaan, vanzelf. ~ *combustion,* zelfontbranding *n.;* zelfverbranding *n.*

spoof, *v.i.* beetnemen *str.*

spook, *n.* spook *n.n.*

spool, *n.* spoel *n.,* klos *n.*

spoon, *n.* lepel *n.* ¶ *v.i.* vrijen. **spoonbill,** *n.* lepelaar *n.* **spoonbilled duck,** *a.* slobeend *n.* **spoonfeed,** *v.t.* met de lepel voeden. **spoonful,** *n.* lepelvol *n.,* lepel *n.*

spoor, *n.* spoor *n.n.*

sporadic, *a.,* ~**ally,** *adv.* sporadisch.

spore, *n.* spoor *n.*

sporran, *n.* Schotse tas *n.*

sport, *n.* sport *n.;* speling *n. old* ~, ouwe jongen *n.* ¶ *v.i.* dartelen, zich verlustigen. ¶ *v.t.* ten toon spreiden. **sporting,** *a.* sport(s) . . . ; royaal. *to take a* ~ *chance,* een twijfelachtige kans *n.* nemen *str.* **sportive,** *a.,* ~**ly,** *adv.* speels; sportief. **sportsman,** *n.* sportliefhebber *n.*

spot, *n.* plaats *n.,* plek *n.;* vlek *n.;* puistje *n.n. in* ~*s,* hier en daar. ¶ *a.* loco. ¶ *v.t.* vlekken; (op)merken. **spot-cash,** *n.* contante betaling *n.* **spotless,** *a.,* ~**ly,** *adv.* vlekkeloos, smetteloos. **spotted,** *a.* gevlekt, bont. ~ *dog,* Jan in de zak; ~ *fever,* vlektyphus *n.* **spotty,** *a.* gevlekt; met puistjes *pl.n.n.*

spouse, *n.* eega *n.;* echtgenoot *n.,* echtgenote *n.* (*female*); gemaal *n.,* gemalin *n.* (*female*).

spout, *n.* tuit *n.;* regenpijp *n.;* waterstraal *n. up the* ~, in de lommerd. ¶ *v.t.* spuiten *str.* ¶ *v.i.* spuiten *str.;* declameren.

sprain, *v.t.* verstuiken, verrekken. ¶ *n.* verstuiking *n.,* verrekking *n.*

sprat, *n.* sprot *n.,* schardijn *n. to throw a* ~ *to catch a whale,* een spiering *n.* uitgooien om een kabeljauw *n.* te vangen.

sprawl, *v.i.* verspreid liggen *str.;* languit liggen *str.*

spray, *v.t.* besproeien; bestuiven *str.* ¶ *n.* sproeier *n.;* vaporisateur *n.;* buiswater *n.n.* (*at sea*); takje *n.n.;* bouquetje *n.n.*

spread, *v.t.* verspreiden; uitspreiden; uitstrooien; spannen *str.* (*sail*); uitslaan *irr.* (*wings*). ¶ *v.i.* zich verspreiden, zich uitspreiden. ¶ *n.* verspreiding *n.;* uitbreiding *n.;* omvang *n.;* vlucht *n.* (*wings*); sprei *n.* (*bedcover*).

spread-eagled, *a.* met armen *pl.n.* en benen *pl.n.n.* uit elkaar.

spree, *n.* fuif *n. on the* ~, aan de boemel *n.*

sprig, *n.* takje *n.n.*

sprightliness, *n.* levendigheid *n.* **sprightly,** *a.* levendig, opgewekt.

spring, *v.i.* springen *str.;* opspringen *str. to* ~ *from,* voortspruiten *str.* uit; afstammen van; *to* ~ *to,* dichtslaan *irr; to* ~ *up,* opspringen *str.;* opkomen *irr.;* ontstaan *irr.* ¶ *v.t.* doen *irr.* springen. *to* ~ *something on someone,* iemand met iets op het lijf vallen *str.* ¶ *n.* bron *n.;* oorsprong *n.;* lente *n.* (*season*); veer *n.;* (*fig.*) drijfveer *n.* **spring-balance,** *n.* veerbalans *n.* **springbed,** *n.* springmatras *n.* **springboard,** *n.*

springplank *n.* **spring-chicken,** *n.* piepkuiken *n.n.* **spring-clean,** *v.i.* voorjaarsschoonmaak *n.* houden *irr.* **springiness,** *n.* veerkracht *n.*, elasticiteit *n.* **springtide,** *n.* springtij *n.n.* *(tide)*; lentetijd *n.* *(season).* **springtime,** *n.* lentetijd *n.* **springwater,** *n.* welwater *n.n.*, bronwater *n.n.* **springwheat,** *n.* zomertarwe *n.* **springy,** *a.* veerkrachtig, elastisch.

sprinkle, *v.i.* sprenkelen. ¶ *v.t.* besprenkelen. ¶ *n.* sprenkeling *n.* **sprinkler,** *n.* sprenkelaar *n.*; strooibus *n.* **sprinkling,** *n.* *with a ~ of . . .*, met hier en daar wat . . .

sprint, *v.i.* sprinten, spurten. ¶ *n.* sprint *n.* **sprinter,** *n.* deelnemer *n.* aan een sprintwedstrijd *n.*

sprit, *n.* (boeg)spriet *n.*

sprite, *n.* geest *n.*; elf *n.*, kabouter *n.*

spritsail, *n.* sprietzeil *n.n.*

sprocket, *n.* tandwiel *n.n.*

sprout, *v.i.* spruiten *str.* *to ~ up*, opschieten *str.* ¶ *n.* spriet *n.* *Brussels ~s*, spruitjes *pl.n.n.*

spruce, *n.* den *n.*, denneboom *n.* ¶ *a.* net. ¶ *v.i.* opdirken. ¶ *v.r.* *to ~ oneself up*, zich opdirken. **spruceness,** *n.* netheid *n.*

spry, *a.* kwiek, bij de hand.

spume, *n.* schuim *n.n.* ¶ *v.i.* schuimen.

spunk, *n.* fut *n.n.*; tondel *n.n.*

spur, *n.* spoor *n.*; prikkel *n.*; uitloper *n.* *on the ~ of the moment*, voor de vuist weg, impulsief. ¶ *v.t.* sporen, de sporen *pl.n.* geven. *to ~ on*, aansporen, aanzetten. ¶ *v.i.* *to ~ on*, spoorslags voortrijden *str.*

spurge, *n.* wolfsmelk *n.*

spurious, *a.*, *~ly*, *adv.* vals, nagemaakt.

spurn, *v.t.* versmaden, verwerpen *str.*

spurt, *v.i.* spuiten *str.*, gutsen; spurten *(sport).* ¶ *n.* gulp *n.*, straal *n.*; vlaag *n.*; spurt *n.* *(sport).*

sputter, *v.i.* sputteren. ¶ *n.* gesputter *n.*

spy, *n.* spion *n.* ¶ *v.t.* bespieden, bespionneren; in 't oog krijgen *str.* ¶ *v.i.* spionneren. **spy-glass,** *n.* verrekijker *n.* **spy-hole,** *n.* kijkgat *n.n.*

squabble, *v.i.* kibbelen; harrewarren.¶ *n.* getwist *n.n.*; ruzietje *n.n.*

squad, *n.* sectie *n.*

squadron, *n.* escadron *n.n.* *(army)*; eskader *n.n.* *(navy)*; escadrille *n.* *(aircraft).*

squalid, *a.* armelijk; goor, smerig.

squall, *n.* bui *n.*, windvlaag *n.* ¶ *v.i.* gillen, schreeuwen. **squally,** *a.* builg. **squalor,** *n.* armzaligheid *n.*; smerigheid *n.*

squander, *v.t.* verkwisten; verspreiden. **squanderer,** *n.*, verkwister *n.*

square, *a.* vierkant; rechthoekig; in het vierkant. *a ~ meal*, een flink maal *n.n.*; *~ root*, vierkantswortel *n.*; *to be ~*, gelijk staan *irr.*, afgerekend hebben. ¶ *n.* vierkant *n.n.*; kwadraat *n.n.* *(power)*; plein *n.n.* *(town)*; carré *n.n.* *(soldiers).* *on the ~*, eerlijk, betrouwbaar; *out of ~*, ontzet. ¶ *v.t.* vierkant maken; in het

kwadraat verheffen *str.*; vereffenen; omkopen *str.* *to ~ with*, in overeenstemming *n.* brengen *irr.* met; *to ~ oneself*, zich in postuur *n.* stellen. **squarely,** *adv.* vierkant; *(fig.)* botweg. **square-rigged,** *a.* met razeilen *pl.n.n.* **squaresail,** *n.* razeil *n.n.* **square-shouldered,** *a.* vierkant gebouwd.

squash, *v.t.* verpletteren; plat drukken. ¶ *n.* pulp *n.*, moes *n.n.*; raketspel *n.n.* **squashy,** *a.* drassig, week.

squat, *v.i.* hurken; zich neerzetten, zich vestigen. ¶ *a.* gedrongen. **squatter,** *n.* kolonist *n.*

squaw, *n.* Indianenvrouw *n.*

squeak, *v.i.* piepen, krijsen *str.* ¶ *n.* gepiep *n.n.*; gilletje *n.n.* **squeaker,** *n.* pieper *n.*; schreeuwlelijk *n.* **squeaky,** *a.* pieperig; krakend.

squeal, *v.i.* gillen, janken; verklappen. ¶ *n.* gil *n.* **squealing,** *n.* gegil *n.n.*, gejank *n.n.*

squeamish, *a.*, *~ly*, *adv.* overdreven kieskeurig.

squeeze, *v.t.* persen; uitdrukken. ¶ *n.* druk *n.*; persing *n.* *a tight ~*, een heel gedrang *n.n.* **squeezer,** *n.* perser *n.*, **lemon ~,** citroenknijper *n.*

squelch, *v.i.*, plassen, modderen. ¶ *n.* smak *n.*

squib, *n.* voetzoeker *n.*; schotschrift *n.n.*

squid, *n.* inktvis *n.*

squill, *n.* zeeajuin *n.*

squint, *v.i.* scheel zien *irr.*, scheel zijn. *to ~ at*, een blik *n.* werpen *str.* op. ¶ *n.* schele blik *n.* *to have a ~*, scheel zijn.

squire, *n.* schildknaap *n.*; landjonker *n.*, landheer *n.*

squirm, *v.i.* wriemelen; zich in bochten *pl.n.* wringen *str.*

squirrel, *n.* eekhoorn *n.*

squirt, *v.t.* spuiten *str.* ¶ *n.* spuit *n.*

squish, *v.i.* zuigen *str.*

stab, *v.t.* steken *str.* ¶ *n.* (dolk)steek *n.*

stability, *n.* stabiliteit *n.*; standvastigheid *n.*, duurzaamheid *n.* **stabilization,** *n.* stabilisatie *n.* **stabilize,** *v.t.* stabiliseren.

stable, *a.* stabiel; bestendig, duurzaam. ¶ *n.* stal *n.* *racing ~*, renstal *n.* **stabling,** *n.* stalling *n.*

stack, *n.* mijt *n.*, tas *n.*, opper *n.*; stapel *n.*; rot *n.* *(rifles).* groep schoorstenen *pl.n.* ¶ *v.t.* opstapelen.

staff, *n.* staf *n.*; (leger)staf *n.*; personeel *n.n.* ¶ *v.t.* van personeel *n.n.* voorzien *irr.*

stag, *n.* (mannetjes)hert *n.n.*, hertebok *n.* **stag-beetle,** *n.* vliegend hert *n.n.*

stage, *n.* toneel *n.n.*; steiger *n.*; stellage *n.*; stadium *n.n.*; rustpunt *n.n.*; pleisterplaats *n.* *by slow ~s*, geleidelijk. ¶ *v.t.* opvoeren, ten tonele brengen *irr.*; monteren. **stage-coach,** *n.* diligence *n.* **stage-fright,** *n.* plankenkoorts *n.* **stage-hand,** *n.* toneelknecht *n.* **stage-manager,** *n.* regisseur *n.*

stager, *n.* (ouwe) gediende *n.*

stagger, *v.i.* wankelen. ¶ *v.t.* verbluffen. **staggers**, *pl.n.* kolder *n.*, draaiziekte *n.*

stagnant, *a.* stilstaand. **stagnate**, *v.i.* stilstaan *irr.*, stagneren. **stagnation**, *n.* stilstand *n.*, stagnatie *n.*

stag-party, *n.* herenfuif *n.*

stagy, *a.* theatraal.

staid, *a.* sober, bezadigd. **staidness**, *n.* soberheid *n.*, bezadigdheid *n.*

stain, *n.* vlek *n.*; smet *n.*; verf *n.*; beits *n.* ¶ *v.t.* bevlekken; bezoedelen; verven; beitsen. ~*ed glass*, beschilderd (*or* gekleurd) glas *n.n.* **stainless**, *a.* onbevlekt; roestvrij.

stair, *n.* trap *n.*, trede *n.* *below* ~*s*, in de keuken; (*flight of*) ~*s*, trap *n.* **stair-carpet** *n.* traploper *n.* **staircase**, *n.* trap *n.*; trappenhuis *n.n.* **stairway**, *n.* trap *n.*

stake, *n.* staak *n.*, paal *n.*; brandstapel *n.*; inzet *n.*, aandeel *n.n.* *at the* ~, op de brandstapel; *to be at* ~, op het spel staan *irr.*; *to have a* ~ *in*, geïnteresseerd zijn bij. ¶ *v.t.* afpalen, afzetten; inzetten. *to* ~ *a claim*, een eis *n.* naar voren brengen *irr.*

stalactite, *n.* druipsteen *n.*, stalactiet *n.* **stalagmite**, *n.* druipsteen *n.*, stalagmiet *n.*

stale, *a.* oudbakken; (*fig.*) afgezaagd. ¶ *n.* gier *n.*

stalemate, *a.* schaakmat. ¶ *v.t.* schaakmat zetten.

stalk, *n.* steel *n.*, stengel *n.* ¶ *v.t.* besluipen *str.* ¶ *v.i.* schrijden *str.* **stalking-horse**, *n.* voorwendsel *n.n.*, dekmantel *n.*

stall, *n.* kraam *n.*, stalletje *n.n.*; box *n.* ~*s*, stalles *pl.n.* (*theatre*). ¶ *v.t.* stallen. ¶ *v.i.* blijven *str.* steken, vastlopen *str.*; afglijden *str.* (*plane*); uitvluchten *pl.n.* zoeken *irr.*

stallion, *n.* hengst *n.*

stalwart, *a.* stoer. ¶ *n.* trouw volgeling *n.*

stamen, *n.* meeldraad *n.*

stamina, *n.* uithoudingsvermogen *n.n.*

stammer, *v.i.* stotteren, stamelen. ¶ *n.* *he has a bad* ~, hij stamelt erg. **stammerer**, *n.* stotteraar *n.* stamelaar *n.*

stamp, *v.i.* stampen, trappen. ¶ *v.t.* fijnstampen; stempelen (*cancel*); frankeren (*with postage stamp*); zegelen (*with other stamp*). ¶ *n.* stamp *n.*, trap *n.*; (post)zegel *n.*; zegel *n.n.*; stempel *n.* **stamp-duty**, *n.* zegelrecht *n.n.*

stampede, *v.i.* plotseling op de vlucht gaan *irr.* ¶ *n.* wilde vlucht *n.*; grote toeloop *n.*

stamper, *n.* stamper *n.*; stempelaar *n.*

stance, *n.* stand *n.*, houding *n.*

stanchion, *n.* schoor *n.*; stut *n.* ¶ *v.t.* stutten.

stand, *v.i.* staan *irr.*; gaan *irr.* staan; blijven *str.* staan; van kracht *n.* zijn; zich candidaat *n.* stellen. *as it* ~*s*, zoals het nu is; *it* ~*s to reason*, het is nogal logisch; *where do I* ~ ?, waar ben ik aan toe?; ~ *and deliver*, je geld *n.n.* of je leven *n.n.*; ~ *at ease*, op de plaats rust; *to* ~ *to win*, een kans *n.* hebben om te winnen; *to* ~

corrected, een berisping *n.* aanvaarden; *to* ~ *aloof*, zich afzijdig houden *irr.*; *to* ~ *by*, gereed staan *irr.*; terzijde staan *irr.*; *to* ~ *down*, gaan *irr.* zitten; zich terugtrekken *str.*; *to* ~ *out*, uitsteken *str.*; volhouden *irr.* ¶ *v.t.* doen *irr.* staan; zetten; verdragen *str.*, uithouden *irr.*, uitstaan *irr.* *to* ~ *treat*, trakteren. ¶ *n.* stand *n.*; stilstand *n.*; standpunt *n.n.*; stand *n.*, stalletje *n.n.*; tribune *n.*; rek *n.n.*, rekje *n.n.* *to make a* ~, zich schrap zetten; *to take one's* ~, post *n.* vatten.

standard, *n.* standaard *n.*; vaandel *n.n.*; maatstaf *n.* ~ *of living*, levensstandaard *n.* ¶ *a.* standaard ... ~ *lamp*, staande lamp *n.* **standardization**, *n.* normalisering *n.* **standardize**, *v.t.* normaliseren.

standing, *a.* vast. ~ *orders*, vast reglement *n.n.* ¶ *n.* positie *n.* *of high* ~, zeer gezien. **stand-offish**, *a.* zich op een afstand *n.* houdend. **standpoint**, *n.* standpunt *n.n.* **standstill**, *n.* stilstand *n.* *to come to a* ~, tot staan *n.n.* komen *irr.* **stand-up**, *a.* staand. ~ *fight*, een echte kloppartij *n.*

stanza, *n.* stanza *n.*, couplet *n.n.*

staple, *n.* stapelplaats *n.*; hoofdproduct *n.n.*; hoofdbestanddeel *n.n.*; draad *n.*, vezel *n.* (*fibre*); kram *n.*, klemband *n.*

star, *n.* ster *n.* ¶ *v.t.* met sterren *pl.n.* tooien; van een sterretje *n.n.* voorzien *irr.* ¶ *v.i.* een hoofdrol *n.* spelen. **starboard**, *n.* stuurboord *n.n.* ¶ *adv.* aan stuurboord *n.n.*

starch, *n.* stijfsel *n.*; zetmeel *n.n.* ¶ *v.t.* stijfselen, stijven *str.* **starchy**, *a.* stijfselachtig; stijf, vormelijk.

stare, *v.i.* staren; grote ogen *pl.n.n.* opzetten. ¶ *n.* starre blik *n.*

starfish, *n.* zeester *n.* **starflower**, *n.* sterremuur *n.* **stargazer**, *n.* sterrenwichelaar *n.*

stark, *a.* strak, streng. ¶ *adv.* volslagen ~ *naked*, moedernaakt, spiernaakt.

starlight, *n.* sterrenlicht *n.*

starling, *n.* spreeuw *n.*

starlit, *a.* ~ *night*, heldere sterrenhemel *n.* **starry**, *a.* met sterren *pl.n.* bezaaid. **starshell**, *n.* lichtgranaat *n.*

start, *v.i.* beginnen *str.*; opschrikken *str.*, opspringen *str.*; starten (*sport*). *to* ~ *off*, beginnen; *to* ~ *out*, beginnen, vertrekken; *to* ~ *with*, om te beginnen. ¶ *v.t.* beginnen *str.*; in beweging *n.* zetten, op gang *n.* brengen *irr.*; beginnen *str.* met (*or* aan). ¶ *n.* begin *n.n.*, aanvang *n.*; start *n.* (*sport*); sprongetje *n.n.*; vlaag *n.* *to give a* ~, doen *irr.* opspringen; *a false* ~, een verkeerd begin *n.n.*; *at the* ~, in 't begin; *from* ~ *to finish*, van 't begin tot het einde. **starter**, *n.* starter *n.* ~ *self*, automatische starter. **starting-point**, *n.* uitgangspunt *n.n.* **starting-post**, *n.* afrijpaal *n.* **starting-wheel**, *n.* aanzetwiel *n.n.*

startle, *v.t.* doen *irr.* schrikken; verbazen.

starvation, *n.* verhongering *n.*, hongerlijden *n.n.* **starve**, *v.i.* honger *n.* lijden *str.* *to* ~

to death, van honger omkomen *irr.* ¶ *v.t.*
honger *n.* laten *str.* lijden, laten *str.* verhongeren. **starveling,** *n.* hongerlijder *n.*
state, *n.* staat *n.*, toestand *n.*; staat *n.*, rijk
n.n.; statie *n.*, luister *n.*; afdruk *n.* (*etching*).
The United S~s, de Verenigde Staten
pl.N.; *to be in a* (*terrible*) ~, vreselijk
opgewonden zijn; er vreselijk uitzien *irr.*;
to lie in ~, op een praalbed *n.n.* liggen
str. ¶ *a.* statie . . . , gala . . . ¶ *v.t.*
verklaren, opgeven *str.*, te kennen geven
str. **stated,** *a.* vast, bepaald.
stateliness, *n.* statigheid *n.* **stately,** *a.* statig.
statement, *n.* verklaring *n.*
state-room, *n.* statiezaal *n.*; luxehut *n.*
statesman, *n.* staatsman *n.* **statesmanship,**
n. staatkundig beleid *n.n.*
static, *a.* statisch. ~ *energy*, arbeidsvermogen *n.n.* van plaats *n.* **statics,** *pl.n.*
leer *n.* van het evenwicht, statica *n.*
station, *n.* stand *n.*, rang *n.*; post *n.*; station
n.n. (*railway*); statie *n.* (*of the Cross*);
walinrichting *n.* (*naval*). ¶ *v.t.* station-
neren, posteren. **stationary,** *a.* stationnair,
stilstaand.
stationer, *n.* verkoper *n.* van schrijfbehoeften
pl.n. **stationery,** *n.* schrijfbehoeften *pl.n.*
station-master, *n.* stationschef *n.*
statistical, *a.* ~ly, *adv.* statistisch. **statistician,** *n.* statisticus *n.* **statistics,** *pl.n.*
statistiek *n.*; statistieke gegevens *pl.n.n.*
statuary, *n.* beeldhouwwerk *n.n.*; beeldhouwer *n.* **statue,** *n.* standbeeld *n.n.*;
beeld *n.n.* **statuette,** *n.* beeldje *n.n.*
stature, *n.* gestalte *n.*; grootte *n.*
status, *n.* staat *n.*; positie *n.*
statute, *n.* statuut *n.n.*, ordonnantie *n.*;
wet *n. to place on the S~ Book*, tot wet *n.*
verheffen *str.* **statute-law,** *n.* geschreven
wet *n.* **statutory,** *a.* wettelijk voorgeschreven, bij de wet bepaald.
staunch, *a.* hecht; waterdicht. ¶ *v.t.* stelpen.
stave, *n.* staf *n.*; duig *n.* (*of barrel*); notenbalk
n. ¶ *v.t.* in duigen slaan *irr. to* ~ *off*,
afwenden.
stay, *v.i.* blijven *str.*; verblijven *str.*; logeren.
it has come to ~, het is nu ingeburgerd;
to ~ *put*, op z'n plaats *n.* blijven. ¶ *v.t.*
tegenhouden *irr.*; volhouden *irr.*; overstag
gooien. *to* ~ *the night*, blijven *str.* logeren.
¶ *n.* verblijf *n.n.*; uitstel *n.n.*; stag *n.*
(*nautical*); stut *n.*, steun *n.* ~s, korset *n.n.*
stayer, *n.* blijver *n.*; volhouder *n.* **staying-
power,** *n.* uithoudingsvermogen *n.n.*
staysail, *n.* stagzeil *n.n.*
stead, *n.* plaats *n.n. to stand one in good* ~,
iemand goed te pas komen *irr.* **steadfast,**
a., ~ly, *adv.* standvastig, onwrikbaar.
steadiness, *n.* vastheid *n.* **steady,** *a.*, ~ily,
adv. vast; bestendig; standvastig; geregeld.
¶ *v.t.* vastheid *n.* geven *str.* aan; kalmeren;
steunen; koers *n.* doen *irr.* houden. **steady-
going,** *a.* oppassend.
steak, *n.* lapje *n.n.*

steal, *v.i.* stelen *str.*; sluipen *str.* ¶ *v.t.* stelen
str. to ~ *a glance at*, een steelse blik *n.*
werpen *str.* op; *to* ~ *a march on someone*,
iemand te vlug af zijn.
stealth, *n. by* ~, tersluiks, steelsgewijze.
stealthy, *a.*, ~ily, *adv.* heimelijk.
steam, *n.* stoom *n.*; damp *n.* ¶ *v.i.* stomen;
dampen. ¶ *v.t.* stomen; uitstomen.
steamer, *n.* stoomboot *n.*; stoomkoker *n.*
steam-gauge, *n.* manometer *n.* **steam-
navigation,** *n.* stoomvaart *n.* **steam-trials,**
pl.n. proefstomen *n.n.* **steamy,** *a.* stomend;
beslagen (*window*).
stearin, *n.* stearine *n.*
steed, *n.* ros *n.n.*
steel, *n.* staal *n.n.*; wetstaal *n.n.* ¶ *a.* stalen,
van staal. ¶ *v.t.* stalen, harden. **steely,** *a.*
staalachtig; stalen.
steep, *a.*, ~ly, *adv.* steil; (*fig.*) kras. ¶ *v.t.*
onderdompelen. ¶ *v.i.* weken.(*fig.*) ~*ed in*,
doorkneed in. **steepen,** *v.i.* steiler worden
str.
steeple, *n.* (spitse) toren *n.* **steeplechase,** *n.*
| wedren *n.* met hindernissen *pl.n.* **steeple-
jack,** *n.* torenbeklimmer *n.*, schoorsteen-
beklimmer *n.*
steepness, *n.*, steilte *n.*
steer, *n.* stierkalf *n.n.*, var *n.* ¶ *v.i.* sturen;
naar het roer luisteren. *to* ~ *for*, koers
zetten naar; *to* ~ *clear of*, ontzeilen. ¶ *v.t.*
sturen. **steerage,** *n.* tussendek *n.n.* **steersman,** *n.* roerganger *n.*
stellar, *a.* sterren . . .
stem, *n.* stengel *n.*, steel *n.*; boeg *n.*, voorsteven *n.* ¶ *v.t.* stuiten, tegenhouden *irr.*
stench, *n.* stank *n.*
stencil, *n.* merkplaat *n.*, sjabloon *n.n.*;
stencil *n.* ¶ *v.t.* merken.
stenographer, *n.* stenograaf *n.* **stenography,**
n. stenografie *n.*
stentorian, *a.* Stentor . . .
step, *n.* stap *n.*, pas *n.*, schrede *n.*; trede *n.*,
tree *n.*; treeplank *n.* ¶ *v.i.* stappen.
stepfather, *n.* stiefvader *n.*
stepladder, *n.* trapladder *n.* **stepping-stone,**
n. middel *n.*; stijgblok *n.n.*
stereoscope, *n.* stereoscoop *n.* **stereoscopic,** *a.*
stereoscopisch.
stereotype, *n.* vaste vorm *n.*; stereotypie *n.*
sterile, *a.* steriel; onvruchtbaar. **sterility,** *n.*
steriliteit *n.*; onvruchtbaarheid *n.* **sterilize,**
v.t. steriliseren.
sterling, *a.* onvervalst, degelijk; sterling.
stern, *a.*, ~ly, *adv.* streng; hardvochtig.
¶ *n.* achtersteven *n.* **sternness,** *n.* strengheid *n.*
sternum, *n.* borstbeen *n.n.*
stern-wheel, *n.* hekwiel *n.n.*
stertorous, *a.* snurkend.
stethoscope, *n.* stethoscoop *n.*
stevedore, *n.* havenarbeider *n.*; **stuwadoor**
n.
stew, *v.t. & v.i.* stoven. ¶ *n.* gestoofde pot *n.*
steward, *n.* hofmeester *n.* (*ship*); rentmeester

n. (estate); ceremoniemeester *n.* **stewardess,**
n. hofmeesteres *n.*
stick, *n.* stok *n.*; pijp *n.* ¶ *v.t.* steken *str.*;
plakken, aanplakken; volhouden *irr.*
I can't ~ him, ik kan hem niet luchten.
¶ *v.i.* kleven, blijven *str.* hangen; blijven
str. steken; klemmen. *to ~ at nothing,*
nergens voor terugdeinzen; *to ~ up for,*
opkomen *irr.* voor. **stickiness,** *n.* kleverigheid *n.* **sticking-plaster,** *n.* hechtpleister *n.*
stick-in-the-mud, *n.* zeurpiet *n.*
stickleback, *n.* stekelbaars *n.*
stickler, *n.* voorstander *n.* *he is a great ~ for,*
hij is erg gesteld op.
sticky, *a.,* ~**ily,** *adv.* kleverig, plakkerig;
lastig.
stiff, *a.,* ~**ly,** *adv.* stijf; stram; flink; moeilijk.
stiffen, *v.t.* stijven *str.,* stijf maken; aanwakkeren (*wind*). **stiffnecked,** *a.* halsstarrig;
hooghartig. **stiffness,** *n.* stijfheid *n.*
stifle, *v.i.* stikken, smoren. ¶ *v.t.* verstikken,
smoren; onderdrukken.
stigma, *n.* schandvlek *n.*; stigma *n.n.* stig-
matization, *n.* stigmatisatie *n.* **stigmatize,**
v.t. brandmerken; stigmatiseren.
stile, *n.* naald *n.*; stijl *n.*; overstap *n.*
still, *a.* stil; kalm. *~ life,* stilleven *n.n.* ¶ *n.*
distilleertoestel *n.n.*; distilleerderij *n.*
¶ *v.t.* distilleren (*essence*); stillen, kalmeren;
tot bedaren *n.n.* brengen *irr.* ¶ *adv.* nog,
nog altijd; toch, maar toch. **still-born,** *a.*
doodgeboren. **stillness,** *n.* stilte *n.* **still-**
room, *n.* provisiekamer *n.*
stilt, *n.* stelt *n.*
stilted, *a.* hoogdravend.
stiltwalker, *n.* steltloper *n.*
stimulant, *n.* opwekkend, stimulerend. ¶ *n.*
opwekkend middel *n.n.*; stimulans *n.,*
prikkel *n.* **stimulate,** *v.t.* stimuleren;
aansporen. **stimulation,** *n.* prikkel *n.*
stimulus, *n.* aansporing *n.*
sting, *n.* angel *n.*; stekel *n.,* prikkel *n.*;
prik *n.*; knaging *n.* ¶ *v.t.* steken *str.,*
bijten *str.*; branden. ¶ *v.i.* tintelen.
stinginess, *n.* vrekkigheid *n.*
stinging-nettle, *n.* brandnetel *n.* **sting-ray,** *n.*
pijlstaartrog *n.*
stingy, *a.* vrekkig, gierig.
stink, *v.i.* stinken *str.* ¶ *n.* stank *n.* **stink-**
weed, *n.* doornappel *n.*
stint, *v.i.* zich bekrimpen *str.* ¶ *v.t.* karig zijn
met, karig toemeten *str.* ¶ *n.* kleine strandloper *n.* (*bird*). *without ~,* royaal.
stipend, *n.* (jaar)wedde *n.* **stipendiary,** *a.*
bezoldigd.
stipulate, *v.t.* bedingen *str.,* stipuleren.
stipulation, *n.* voorwaarde *n.*; overeenkomst *n.*
stir, *v.t.* roeren; oppoken; bewegen *str.*;
aanzetten. ¶ *v.i.* zich verroeren; zich
roeren; in beweging *n.* komen *irr.* ¶ *n.*
beroering *n.,* drukte *n.*; sensatie *n.* *to
cause a ~,* opzien *n.n.* baren. **stirring,** *a.*
levendig; bezielend; vol emotie *n.*

stirrup, *n.* stijgbeugel *n.* **stirrup-cup,** *n.*
glaasje *n.n.* op de valreep.
stitch, *v.t.* stikken. *to ~ up,* dichtnaaien,
hechten. ¶ *n.* steek *n.*
stoat, *n.* (soort) wezel *n.*
stock, *n.* stam *n.*; stronk *n.*; blok *n.n.*;
schandpaal *n.*; lade *n.* (*rifle*); cravate *n.*;
zweepstok *n.*; ras *n.n.*; voorraad *n.*; bouillon
n.; violier *n.* ~*s,* effecten *pl.n.n.* (*values*).
stapel *n.* (*of shipyard*); *on the ~s,* op stapel
n.; *to lay in a ~,* een vooraad opdoen *irr.*;
to take ~, de inventaris opmaken; (*fig.*) *to
take ~ of,* opnemen *str.* ¶ *a.* vast,
stereotiep. ¶ *v.t.* in voorraad *n.* hebben;
van voorraden *pl.n.* voorzien *irr.*; inslaan
irr., opdoen *irr.*; van vee *n.n.* voorzien *irr.*
stockade, *n.* palissade *n.*
stock-breeder, *n.* veefokker *n.*
stockbroker, *n.* makelaar *n.* in effecten
pl.n.n. **stock-company,** *n.* maatschappij *n.*
op aandelen *pl.n.n.* **stock-exchange,** *n.*
effectenbeurs *n.* **stock-holder,** *n.* effecten-
bezitter *n.*
stockiness, *n.* gezetheid *n.*
stockinet, *n.* tricot *n.n.*
stocking, *n.* kous *n.* **stockinged,** *a.* *in his ~
feet,* met kousen aan.
stock-in-trade, *n.* inventaris *n.*
stockjobber, *n.* speculatieve effectenhandelaar
n. **stockjobbing,** *n.* agiotage *n.*
stock-pot, *n.* bouillonpot *n.*
stockstill, *a.* stokstil, doodstil.
stocktaking, *n.* inventarisering *n.,* inven-
tarisatie *n.*
stocky, *a.* gezet, dik, stevig.
stockyard, *n.* veekamp *n.n.*
stodge, *n.* zware kost *n.* **stodgy,** *a.* onverteerbaar; pappig; zwaar op de hand.
stoic, *n.* Stoïcijn *n.* **stoic(al),** *a.,* ~**ly,** *adv.*
Stoïcijns. **stoicism,** *n.* Stoïcisme *n.n.*
stoke, *v.t.* stoken. **stokehole,** *n.* stookplaats *n.*
stoker, *n.* stoker *n.*
stole, *n.* stola *n.*
stolid, *a.,* ~**ly,** *adv.* onaandoenlijk, flegmatiek. **stolidity,** *n.* onaandoenlijkheid *n.*
stomach, *n.* maag *n.*; buik *n.*; (*fig.*) zin *n.*
¶ *v.t.* verduwen, verkroppen.
stone, *n.* steen *n.*; pit *n.*; edelsteen *n.*;
niersteen *n.*; gewicht van 14 engelse
ponden = ± 6,35 kg. ~*'s throw,* steen-
worp *n.*; *to leave no ~ unturned,* niets onbeproefd laten *str.* ¶ *a.* stenen, van steen
n. ¶ *v.t.* stenigen; van pitten *pl.n.* ontdoen
irr. **stone-blind,** *a.* stekeblind. **stonebreak,**
n. steenbreek *n.* **stone-cold,** *a.* steenkoud.
stonecrop, *n.* muurpeper *n.* **stonecutter,** *n.*
steenhouwer *n.* **stonedead,** *a.* morsdood.
stone-deaf, *a.* stokdoof. **stone-mason,** *n.*
steenhouwer *n.* **stone quarry,** *n.* steengroeve *n.* **stonework,** *n.* steenwerk *n.n.,*
metselwerk *n.n.* **stony,** *a.,* ~**ily,** *adv.*
steenachtig; stenen; hardvochtig.
stool, *n.* kruk *n.,* bankje *n.n.*; ontlasting *n.*
stool-pigeon, *n.* lokvogel *n.*

stoop, *v.i.* bukken; gebukt lopen *str.* ¶ *n.* voorovergebogen houding *n.*; stoop *n.*, kruik *n.*

stop, *v.i.* stoppen; ophouden *irr.*; stilstaan *irr.*, stilhouden *irr.* *to ~ short*, plots afbreken *str.*; *to ~ short at*, zich beperken tot; *to ~ short of*, zich onthouden *irr.* van; *to ~ at nothing*, nergens voor staan *irr*; *to ~ away*, wegblijven *str.* ¶ *vt.* stoppen; tot staan brengen *irr.*; stopzetten; dichtstoppen; vullen (*tooth*); versperren. *to ~ a person's mouth*, iemand de mond stoppen; *to ~ payment*, z'n betalingen *pl.n.* staken; *~ thief!*, houdt de dief!; *to ~ up*, verstoppen, dichtstoppen. ¶ *n.* stilstand *n.*; halte *n.*; register *n.n.*, klep *n.* (*full*) *~*, punt *n.*; *to be at a ~*, stilstaan *irr.*; *to put a ~ to*, een eind *n.n.* maken aan; *without a ~*, zonder ophouden *n.n.* **stop-cock**, *n.* afsluitkraan *n.* **stopgap**, *n.* stoplap *n.*; noodhulp *n.* **stoppage**, *n.* stopzetting *n.*; inhouding *n.* **stopper**, *n.* stop *n.*, stopper *n.* **stopping-place**, *n.* halte *n.* **stop-press**, *n.* nagekomen berichten *pl. n.n.* **stopwatch**, *n.* controleerhorloge *n.n.*

storage, *n.* opslaan *n.n.*, berging *n.*; opslagruimte *n.* *cold ~*, koelkamer *n.*, vrieskamer *n.* **storage-battery**, *n.* accumulator *n.* **store**, *v.t.* opslaan *irr.*; opbergen *str.*; provianderen. *~d with*, voorzien van. ¶ *n.* voorraad *n.*; opslagplaats *n.* magazijn *n.n.* *~s*, voorraad *n.*; warenhuis *n.n.*, winkel *n.*; *to set great ~ by*, ergens grote waarde *n.* aan hechten; *to be in ~ for one*, iemand te wachten staan *irr.* **storecupboard**, *n.* provisiekast *n.* **storehouse**, *n.* pakhuis *n.n.* bergplaats *n.* **storekeeper**, *n.* pakhuismeester *n.* **storeroom**, *n.* provisiekamer *n.*

storey, *n.* verdieping *n.* **storied**, *a.* met verdiepingen *pl.n.*

stork, *n.* ooievaar *n.*

storm, *n.* storm *n.*; vlaag *n.*, bui *n.*; bestorming *n.* *by ~*, stormenderhand. ¶ *v.i.* stormen; razen, tieren. ¶ *v.t.* bestormen. **storm-tossed**, *a.* heen en weer geslingerd door de storm. **stormy**, *a.* stormachtig; onstuimig. *~ petrel*, stormvogeltje *n.n.*

story, *n.* verhaal *n.n.*; geschiedenis *n.* *to tell stories*, jokken. *See* storey. **storybook**, *n.* vertelselboek *n.n.* **story-teller**, *n.* verteller *n.*, verhaler *n.*

stout, *a.*, *~ly*, *adv.* flink, dapper; dik, gezet. ¶ *n.* stout *n.n.*, donker bier *n.n.* **stoutness**, *n.* flinkheid *n.*; gezetheid *n.*

stove, *n.* kachel *n.*, fornuis *n.n.* **stove-pipe**, *n.* kachelpijp *n.*

stow, *v.t.* stouwen, stuwen. *to ~ something away*, iets opbergen *str.* **stowage**, *n.* stouwen *n.n.*, stuwage *n.*; bergruimte *n.* **stowaway**, *n.* blinde passagier *n.*

straddle, *v.t.* schrijlings zitten *str.* op; aan weerszijden *pl.n.* neerkomen *irr.* van.

straggle, *v.i.* verspreid raken, verdwaald raken. **straggler**, *n.* achterblijver *n.* **straggling**, *q.* verspreid, onregelmatig.

straight, *a.* recht; in orde *n.*; eerlijk. *to put ~*, in orde brengen *irr.* ¶ *a.* recht; ronduit, openhartig. *~ in front of*, vlak voor; *~ off*, zonder aarzeling *n.*; *~ out*, ronduit. **straightaway**, *adv.* onmiddellijk, op staande voet. **straighten**, *v.t.* recht maken; in orde *n.* brengen *irr.* **straightforward**, *a.* rechtstreeks; oprecht.

strain, *v.t.* overspannen *irr.*; (te zeer) inspannen; spannen; verrekken; forceren; filtreren. ¶ *v.i.* zich inspannen *irr.* *to ~ after*, streven naar. ¶ *n.* spanning *n.*; inspanning *n.*; verrekking *n.*; element *n,n.*; ras *n.n.* *~s*, melodie *n.*; *in the same ~*, op dezelfde toon. **strainer**, *n.* vergiet *n.n.*; filter *n.*

strait, *a.*, *~ly*, *adv.* nauw, eng. ¶ *n.* *~s*, zeeëngte *n.*, straat *n.*; verlegenheid *n.* **straiten**, *v.t.* nauw(er) maken. *to be in ~ed circumstances*, het niet breed hebben. **strait-jacket**, *n.* dwangbuis *n.n.* **straitlaced**, *a.* preuts. **straitness**, *n.* nauwheid *n.*

strand, *n.* strand *n.n.*; oever *n.*; streng *n.*, draad *n.* ¶ *v.i.* stranden, op het strand lopen *str.* ¶ *v.t.* doen *irr.* stranden. *to be ~ed*, hoog en droog zitten *str.*; (*fig.*) (ergens) beland zijn.

strange, *a.*, *~ly*, *adv.* vreemd; zonderling, raar. *~ to*, niet vertrouwd met. **strangeness**, *n.* vreemdheid *n.* **stranger**, *n.* vreemdeling *n.*

strangle, *v.t.* worgen. ¶ *n.* *~s*, droes *n.* **stranglehold**, *n.* *to have a ~ on somebody*, iemand in z'n macht *n.* hebben. **strangler**, *n.* worger *n.* **strangulation**, *n.* worging *n.*

strap, *n.* riem *n.*; band *n.*, lint *n.n.*; beugel *n.* ¶ *v.t.* vastbinden *str.* **straphanger**, *n.* lushanger *n.* **strapping**, *a.* stevig, flink.

stratagem, *n.* krijgslist *n.*, list *n.*

strategic, *a.* strategisch. **strategist**, *n.* strateeg *n.* **strategy**, *n.* strategie *n.*

stratification, *n.* laagvorming *n.* **stratify**, *v.t.* tot lagen *pl.n.* vormen. **stratum**, *n.* laag *n.*

straw, *n.* stro *n.n.*; strootje *n.n.* *I don't care a ~*, 't kan me geen lor *n.* schelen; *to draw ~s*, strootje trekken *str.*; *cheese ~*, kaasstengel *n.* ¶ *a.* strooien, van stro.

strawberry, *n.* aardbei *n.*

strawboard, *n.* strokarton *n.n.* **strawcutter**, *n.* hakselbank *n.*

stray, *v.i.* afdwalen; zwerven *str.* ¶ *a.* afgedwaald, verdwaald; toevallig. ¶ *n.* verdwaald dier *n.*; dakloze *n.*

streak, *n.* streep *n.*; veeg *n.* ¶ *v.t.* strepen. **streaky**, *a.* streperig; doorregen.

stream, *v.i.* stromen. ¶ *n.* stroom *n.*; beek *n.* *up ~*, stroom op; *down ~*, stroom af. **streamer**, *n.* wimpel *n.*; serpentine *n.* **stream-line**, *a.* stroomlijn.

street, *n.* straat *n.* *in the ~*, op straat; *to be in queer ~*, in geldverlegenheid *n.* zitten *str.* **street-arab**, *n.* straatjongen *n.* **street-corner**, *n.* hoek *n.* van de straat.

streetlamp, *n.* straatlantaren *n.* **street-walker,** *n.* prostituée *n.*

strength, *n.* kracht *n.*; sterkte *n.* *in full* ∼, in groten getale; *up to* ∼, op sterkte. **strengthen,** *v.t.* versterken; doen *irr.* toenemen.

strenuous, *a.,* ∼ly, *adv.* energiek; onverdroten.

stress, *n.* spanning *n.*; nadruk *n.*; accent *n.n.*, klemtoon *n.*; benardheid *n.* ¶ *v.t.* de nadruk leggen *irr.* op.

stretch, *v.t.* rekken; uitspreiden. *to* ∼ *a point,* toeschietelijk zijn, zich niet aan de letter houden *irr.* ¶ *v.i.* rekken; reiken; zich uitstrekken. ¶ *n.* uitgestrektheid *n.* *at a* ∼, achtereen, aan één stuk *n.n.* door.

stretcher, *n.* draagbaar *n.* **stretcher-bearer,** *n.* ziekendrager *n.*

strew, *v.t.* strooien, uitstrooien.

stricken, *a.* getroffen; zwaar beproefd.

strict, *a.,* ∼ly, *adv.* strikt; nauwgezet; nauwkeurig. **strictness,** *n.* striktheid *n.*; nauwgezetheid *n.*

stricture, *n.* strictuur *n.*, vernauwing *n.*; critiek *n.*

stride, *v.i.* schrijden *str.*, grote stappen *pl.n.* doen *irr.*

strident, *a.* doordringend, schel.

strife, *n.* strijd *n.*; twist *n.*, tweedracht *n.*

strike, *v.t.* slaan *irr.*, een slag *n.* geven *str.*; treffen *str.*, stoten *str.* op; aanslaan *irr.* *(note)*; aansteken *str.* *(match).* *to* ∼ *an attitude,* poseren; *to* ∼ *a balance,* een balans *n.* opmaken; *to* ∼ *a bargain,* een koop *n.* sluiten *str.*; *to* ∼ *oil,* olie *n.* aanboren; *to* ∼ *root,* wortel *n.* schieten *str.*; *to* ∼ *camp,* het kamp opbreken *str.*; *to* ∼ *something out,* iets doorhalen; *to* ∼ *up,* aanheffen *str.*; *to* ∼ *with pity,* met medelijden *n.n.* vervullen; *it* ∼*s me that* . . ., het komt me voor dat . . .; *het lijkt me* . . . ¶ *v.i.* slaan *irr.*; staken *(work).* *to* ∼ *at,* slaan *irr.* naar. ¶ *n.* staking *n.*, werkstaking *n.* *to be on* ∼, staken; *to go out on* ∼, gaan *irr.* staken. **strikebreaker,** *n.* onderkruiper *n.* **striker,** *n.* staker *n.*; slagpin *n.* (*in gun*). **striking,** *a.,* ∼ly, *adv.* opvallend, frappant.

string, *n.* touw *n.n.*; snaar *n.* (*musical*); snoer *n.n.* (*pearls*); ris *n.*, rij *n.* (*also :*) ∼s, strijkinstrumenten *pl.n.n.*, strijkorkest *n.n.*; *a piece of* ∼, een touwtje *n.n.*; *to pull* ∼*s,* invloed *n.* gebruiken. ¶ *v.t.* rijgen *str.* *to* ∼ *up,* opknopen. **string-band,** *n.* strijkje *n.n.* **string-bean,** *n.* snijboon *n.*

stringency, *n.* dringendheid *n.*; bindende kracht *n.*; scherpte *n.*, strengheid *n.* **stringent,** *a.,* ∼ly, *adv.* dringend; bindend; scherp, streng.

stringiness, *n.* vezeligheid *n.* **string-orchestra,** *n.* strijkorkest *n.n.* **stringy,** *a.* vezelig, draderig.

strip, *n.* reep *n.*; reepje *n.n.*, strookje *n.n.*

¶ *v.t.* stropen; afstropen; uitkleden; onttakelen; kaalvreten. *to* ∼ *of,* ontnemen *str.*, beroven van. ¶ *v.i.* zich ontkleden.

stripe, *n.* streep *n.*; striem *n.*; chevron *n.* ¶ *v.t.* strepen.

stripling, *n.* jongeling *n.*

stripy, *a.* gestreept.

strive, *v.i.* zich inspannen, *to* ∼ *after,* streven naar; *to* ∼ *against,* strijden *str.* met.

stroke, *v.t.* strelen, aaien. ¶ *n.* slag *n.*; stoot *n.*; zet *n.*; beroerte *n.* (*paralytic*); achterste roeier *n.* ∼ *of the pen,* pennestreek *n.*; ∼ *of luck,* veine *n.*; *at one* ∼, met één slag *n.*; *on the* ∼ *of eleven,* op slag van elven.

stroll, *v.i.* kuieren, rondwandelen. ∼*ing player,* rondreizend komediant *n.*

strong, *a.,* ∼ly, *adv.* sterk, krachtig; zwaar (*tobacco*). **strong-box,** *n.* geldkist *n.*, kleine brandkast *n.* **stronghold,** *n.* bolwerk *n.n.* **strongish,** *a.* vrij sterk. **strongminded,** *a.* energiek, resoluut. **strong-point,** *n.* mitrailleurnest *n.n.*; klein fort *n.n.* **strongroom,** *n.* kluis *n.*

strop, *n.* scheerriem *n.*, aanzetriem *n.* ¶ *v.t.* aanzetten.

structural, *a.,* ∼ly, *adv.* constructie . . ., structuur . . . **structure,** *n.* structuur *n.*, bouw *n.*; bouwwerk *n.n.*; samenstel *n.n.*

struggle, *v.t.* worstelen; strijden *str.* ¶ *n.* worsteling *n.*; strijd *n.* ∼ *for life,* strijd om het bestaan.

strum, *v.t.* tokkelen; rammelen.

strumpet, *n.* slet *n.*, hoer *n.*

strut, *v.i.* trots stappen; stutten (*support*). ¶ *n.* trotse gang *n.*; stut *n.*

strychnine, *n.* strychnine *n.*

stub, *n.* stomp *n.*, stompje *n.n.*; eindje *n.n.* (*cigar*); souche *n.* (*cheque book*). ¶ *v.t.* stoten.

stubble, *n.* stoppels *pl.n.* **stubble-field,** *n.* stoppelveld *n.n.* **stubbly,** *a.* stoppelig.

stubborn, *a.,* ∼ly, *adv.* halsstarrig; koppig; hardnekkig.

stubby, *a.* stomp.

stucco, *n.* pleisterkalk *n.*, gips *n.n.*

stuck-up, *a.* verwaand.

stud, *n.* beslagnagel *n.*; knop *n.*; knoopje *n.n.*; stoeterij *n.* (*horses*). ¶ *v.t.* met spijkers *pl.n.* beslaan *irr.*; bezaaien. **stud-bolt,** *n.* tapbout *n.* **stud-book,** *n.* stamboek *n.n.*

studding-sail, *n.* lijzeil *n.n.*

student, *n.* student *n.*; beoefenaar *n.*

stud-farm, *n.* stoeterij *n.* **stud-horse,** *n.* dekhengst *n.*

studied, *a.* bestudeerd, geleerd; gewild, opzettelijk.

studio, *n.* atelier *n.n.*

studious, *a.,* ∼ly, *adv.* leergierig; ijverig, vlijtig; zorgvuldig; overlegd. *with* ∼ *care,* met angstvallige zorg *n.* **study,** *n.* studie *n.*; étude *n.* (*music*); studeerkamer *n.*, studeervertrek *n.n.* *in a brown* ∼, in

gedachten *pl.n.* verzonken. ¶ *v.i.* studeren.
¶ *v.t.* studeren, bestuderen; instuderen;
rekening *n.* houden *irr.* met. *to* ~ *medicine*,
in de medicijnen *pl.n.* studeren.
stuff, *n.* stof *n.*; goed *n.n.*; spul *n.n.* ~ *and
nonsense*, allemaal onzin *n.* ¶ *v.t.*
volstoppen; farceren (*poultry*), opzetten
(*by naturalist*). ¶ *v.i.* gulzig eten *str.*
stuffing, *n.* opvulsel *n.n.*; farce *n.* **stuffy**, *a.*
benauwd, dompig; saai.
stultify, *v.t.* bespottelijk maken; ongerijmd
maken; te niet doen *irr.*, verijdelen.
stumble, *v.i.* struikelen. ¶ *n.* struikeling *n.*;
misstap *n.* **stumbling-block**, *n.* struikelblok
n.n., hinderpaal *n.*
stump, *n.* stomp *n.*; stronk *n.*; paaltje *n.n.*
¶ *v.t.* afknotten; afstompen; te moeilijk
zijn voor. **stumpy**, *a.* kort en dik.
stun, *v.t.* wezenloos slaan *irr.*; overdonderen.
stunning, *a.* verbazend.
stunt, *n.* toer *n.*, krachtstukje *n.n.*; boeren-
bedrog *n.n.* ¶ *v.i.* toeren *pl.n.* doen *irr.*
¶ *v.t.* de groei *n.* belemmeren van.
stunted, *a.* dwerg . . .
stupefaction, *n.* bedwelming *n.*; verbijstering
n. **stupefy**, *v.t.* bedwelmen, verdoven;
verbijsteren.
stupendous, *a.*, ~**ly**, *adv.* wonderbaarlijk,
kolossaal.
stupid, *a.*, ~**ly**, *adv.* dom, stom; dwaas.
stupidity, *n.* domheid *n.*; stommiteit *n.*
stupor, *n.* verdoving *n.*, bedwelming *n.*;
versuffing *n.*
sturdiness, *n.* stoerheid *n.* **sturdy**, *a.*, ~**ily**,
adv. stoer, fors.
sturgeon, *n.* steur *n.*
stutter, *v.i.* & *v.t.* stotteren. ¶ *n.* gestotter
n.n. stutterer, *n.* stotteraar *n.*
sty, *n.* varkenshok *n.n.*; strontje *n.n.* (*on eye*).
style, *n.* stijl *n.*; stilus *n.* (*monument*);
tijdrekening *n.* **stylish**, *a.* modisch,
zwierig. **stylize**, *v.t.* stiliseren, stileren.
styptic, *a.* bloedstelpend.
suave, *a.*, ~**ly**, *adv.* vriendelijk, zacht.
suavity, *n.* vriendelijkheid *n.*
sub-, *prefix* onder-, sub-.
subaltern, *a.* subaltern, ondergeschikt. ¶ *n.*
officier *n.* (onder de rang van kapitain *n.*).
sub-committee, *n.* sub-commissie *n.*
subconscious, *a.*, ~**ly**, *adv.* onderbewust.
¶ *n.* onderbewuste *n.n.*
subcutaneous, *a.* onderhuids. . . .
sub-deacon, *n.* onderdiaken *n.*
subdivide, *v.t.* onderverdelen. **subdivision**, *n.*
onderafdeling *n.*
subdue, *v.t.* bedwingen *str.*; onderwerpen *str.*;
temperen, dempen.
sub-editor, *n.* redacteur *n.*, secretaris *n.* van
de redactie.
subject, *v.t.* onderwerpen *str.*, blootstellen.
to ~ *to*, onderwerpen *str.* aan. ¶ *a.*
onderworpen. ~ *to*, onderworpen aan;
vatbaar voor; ~ *to the approval of*,
behoudens de goedkeuring van. ¶ *n.*

onderdaan *n.* (*of State*); onderwerp *n.n.*
on the ~ *of* . . ., inzake . . . **subjection**, *n.*
onderwerping *n.* **subjective**, *a.*, ~**ly**, *adv.*
subjectief. **subject-matter**, *n.* stof *n.*
subjugate, *v.t.* onderwerpen *str.* **subjugation**
n. onderwerping *n.*
subjunctive, *n.* aanvoegende wijs *n.*
sublet, *v.t.* onderverhuren.
sublimate, *v.t.* sublimeren, vervluchtigen.
¶ *n.* sublimaat *n.n.* **sublimation**, *n.*
sublimering *n.*
sublime, *a.*, ~**ly**, *adv.* subliem, verheven.
sublimity, *n.* verhevenheid *n.*
sublunar, *a.* ondermaans.
submarine, *a.* onderzees. ¶ *n.* duikboot *n.*,
onderzeeër *n.*
submerge, *v.t.* onderdompelen; overstromen.
¶ *v.i.* wegzinken *str.*, onderduiken *str.*
submersion, *n.* onderdompeling *n.*; overstroming *n.*
submission, *n.* onderwerping *n.*; voorlegging
n.; (bescheiden) mening *n.* **submissive**, *a.*,
~**ly**, *adv.* onderdanig, nederig. **submit**, *v.t.*
onderwerpen *str.*; voorleggen *irr.*; menen.
¶ *v.i.* zich onderwerpen *str.*
subordinate, *a.*, ~**ly**, *adv.* ondergeschikt.
~ *clause*, bijzin *n.* ¶ *n.* ondergeschikte *n.*
subordination, *n.* ondergeschiktheid *n.*
suborn, *v.t.* omkopen *irr.*
subpoena, *n.* dagvaarding *n.* met straf-
bedreiging *n.* ¶ *v.t.* dagvaarden.
subscribe, *v.i.* ondertekenen. *to* ~ *to*, zich
abonneren op; het eens zijn met. ¶ *v.t.*
intekenen voor. **subscriber**, *n.* ondertekenaar *n.*; abonné *n.* **subscription**, *n.*
onderschrift *n.n.*; contributie *n.*; abonne-
ment *n.n.*
subsequent, *a.* (na)volgend. **subsequently**,
adv. nadien, daarna; vervolgens.
subservience, *n.* dienstbaarheid *n.*; onder-
danigheid *n.* **subservient**, *a.* dienstbaar;
ondergeschikt; onderdanig, kruiperig.
subside, *v.i.* zinken *str.*, zakken; tot bedaren
n.n. komen *irr.*
subsidiary, *a.* ondergeschikt, afhankelijk.
~ *subject*, bijvak *n.n.*
subsidize, *v.t.* subsidiëren. **subsidy**, *n.*
subsidie *n.n.*
subsist, *v.i.* bestaan *irr.*, blijven *str.* bestaan.
subsistence, *n.* bestaan *n.n.*; (levens)
onderhoud *n.n.* ~ *allowance*, onder-
houdstoelage *n.*
subsoil, *n.* ondergrond *n.*
substance, *n.* stof *n.* (*matter*); wezen *n.n.*
(*essence*); hoofdzaak *n.* (*principal*); vermogen *n.n.* (*money*). **substantial**, *a.*
stoffelijk; wezenlijk; degelijk; welgesteld.
substantially, *adv.* stoffelijk; wezenlijk;
degelijk; welgesteld; in hoofdzaak *n.*
substantiate, *v.t.* verwezenlijken; met
bewijzen *pl.n.n.* staven.
substantive, *n.* zelfstandig naamwoord *n.n.*
substitute, *v.t.* vervangen. *to* ~ *for*, in de
plaats stellen van. ¶ *v.i. to* ~ *for*, de

plaats vervullen van. ¶ *a.* plaatsvervangend. ¶ *n.* substituut *n.* (*person*), *n.n.* (*thing*); remplaçant *n.* **substitution**, *n.* vervanging *n.*; onderschuiving *n.*
substratum, *n.* onderlaag *n.*; grondslag *n.*
substructure, *n.* onderbouw *n.*
subtenant, *n.* onderhuurder *n.*
subterfuge, *n.* uitvlucht *n.*
subterranean, *a.* onderaards.
subtilize, *v.t.* subtiliseren; ijl maken. **subtle**, *a.*, ~tly, *adv.* subtiel; spitsvondig. **subtlety**, *n.* subtiliteit *n.*; spitsvondigheid *n.*
subtract, *v.t.* & *v.i.* aftrekken *str.* to ~ from, aftrekken *str.* van; afdoen *irr.* van. **subtraction**, *n.* aftrekking *n.*
suburb, *n.* voorstad *n.*, buitenwijk *n.* **suburban**, *a.* voorstads . . .
subversion, *n.* omverwerping *n.* **subversive**, *a.* omverwerpend, afbrekend. **subvert**, *v.t.* omverwerpen *str.*, verstoren.
subway, *n.* tunnel *n.*, ondergrondse verbinding *n.*
succeed, *v.i.* slagen, succes *n.n.* hebben; opvolgen. ¶ *v.t.* volgen op, komen *irr.* na; opvolgen. **success**, *n.* succes *n.n.*; goed gevolg *n.n.* **successful**, *a.*, ~ly, *adv.* geslaagd; gelukkig. **succession**, *n.* successie *n.*, opvolging *n.*; opeenvolging *n.*, reeks *n.* in ~, achtereenvolgens; in ~ to, als opvolger *n.* van. **successive**, *a.*, ~ly, *adv.* achtereenvolgend. two ~ days, twee dagen *pl.n.* achtereen. **successor**, *n.* opvolger *n.*
succinct, *a.*, ~ly, *adv.* bondig; beknopt.
succour, *v.t.* bijstaan *irr.*, te hulp *n.* komen *irr.* ¶ *n.* bijstand *n.*, hulp *n.*
succulence, *n.* sappigheid *n.* **succulent**, *a.* sappig.
succumb, *v.i.* bezwijken *str.*, zwichten.
such, *a.* zulk, zodanig zo. ~ a thing, zo iets; no ~ thing, niets van dien aard *n.*; ~ as, zoals; ~like, dergelijk(e). ¶ *pron.* as ~, als zodanig; ~ and ~, zo en zo; ~ a one as, een zoals.
suck, *v.i.* & *v.t.* zuigen *str.* ¶ *n.* zuigen *n.n.* to give ~ to, zogen. **sucker**, *n.* zuiger *n.*; zuignap *n.*; uitloper *n.* (*shoot*). **suckingpig**, *n.* speenvarken *n.n.* **suckle**, *v.t.* zogen, de borst geven *str.* **suckling**, *n.* zuigeling *n.*
suction, *n.* zuiging *n.* ~ pump, zuigpomp *n.*
sudden, *a.* plotseling; onverhoeds. **suddenly**, *adv.* plotseling, eensklaps. **suddenness**, *n.* onverwachtheid *n.*
suds, *pl.n.* (zeep)sop *n.n.*
sue, *v.t.* vervolgen, aanspreken *str.* ¶ *v.i.* eisen; dingen *str.* to ~ for, verzoeken *irr.* om.
suet, *n.* niervet *n.n.*
suffer, *v.i.* lijden *str.* to ~ for it, ervoor boeten; to ~ from, lijden *str.* aan. ¶ *v.t.* lijden *str.*; verdragen *str.*; dulden, uitstaan *irr.*; toelaten *str.* **sufferable**, *a.* dragelijk, uit te houden *irr.* **sufferance**, *n.* lijdelijke toestemming *n.* to be admitted on ~,

geduld worden *str.* **sufferer**, *n.* lijder *n.*; patiënt *n.*; slachtoffer *n.n.* **suffering**, *n.* lijden *n.n.*
suffice, *v.i.* voldoen *irr.* ~ it to say, we kunnen *irr.* volstaan met te zeggen. ¶ *v.t.* voldoende zijn voor. **sufficiency**, *n.* voldoend aantal *n.n.*, voldoende hoeveelheid *n.* **sufficient**, *a.*, ~ly, *adv.* voldoend(e); toereikend.
suffix, *v.t.* achtervoegen. ¶ *n.* achtervoegsel *n.n.*
suffocate, *v.t.* & *v.i.* verstikken, smoren. **suffocation**, *n.* verstikking *n.*
suffragan, *a.* suffragaan. ¶ *n.* wijbisschop *n.*
suffrage, *n.* kiesrecht *n.n.*, stemrecht *n.n.*
suffuse, *v.t.* overdekken. ~d with blushes, met blosjes *pl.n.n.* overtogen.
sugar, *n.* suiker *n.* moist ~, bruine suiker. ¶ *v.t.* suikeren. **sugar-bowl**, *n.* suikerpot *n.* **sugar-candy**, *n.* kandijsuiker *n.* **sugar-cane**, *n.* suikerriet *n.n.* **sugar-castor**, *n.* suikerstrooier *n.* **sugared**, *a.* suikerzoet. **sugary**, *a.* suikerachtig, zoet.
suggest, *v.t.* voorstellen; ingeven *str.*, influisteren. to ~ itself, vanzelf opkomen *irr.* **suggestible**, *a.* voor suggestie *n.* vatbaar. **suggestion**, *n.* suggestie *n.*; voorstel *n.n.*, aanraden *n.n.*; wenk *n.* **suggestive**, *a.*, ~ly, *adv.* suggestief; veelbetekenend; gewaagd. to be ~ of, doen *irr.* denken aan.
suicidal, *a.* zelfmoord . . . **suicide**, *n.* zelfmoord *n.*; zelfmoordenaar *n.* (*person*).
suit, *n.* proces *n.n.* (*law*); aanzoek *n.n.* (*request*); kleur *n.* (*cards*); pak *n.n.* (*clothes*). ~ of armour, wapenrusting *n.* ¶ *v.t.* passen, gelegen komen *irr.*; schikken; staan *irr.* to ~ the action to the word, de daad bij het woord voegen; it ~s my purpose, het komt me goed uit. ¶ *v.i.* passen. to ~ with, overeenkomen *irr.* met. **suitability**, *n.* gepastheid *n.*, geschiktheid *n.* **suitable**, *a.*, ~bly, *adv.* gepast, geschikt. **suitcase**, *n.* koffer *n.*, koffertje *n.n.*
suite, *n.* gevolg *n.n.*; suite *n.* (*music*). ~ of furniture, ameublement *n.n.*
suited, *a.* geschikt.
suiting, *n.* costuumstof *n.*
suitor, *n.* partij *n.* (*law*); minnaar *n.*
sulk, *v.i.* pruilen, mokken. ¶ *n.* the ~s, het land. **sulky**, *a.*, ~ily, *adv.* pruilerig.
sullen, *a.* nors, zuur, gemelijk. **sullenness**, *n.* norsheid *n.*
sully, *v.t.* bezoedelen, besmeuren.
sulphate, *n.* sulfaat *n.n.* **sulphur**, *n.* zwavel *n.* **sulphuretted**, *a.* gezwaveld. ~ hydrogen, zwavelwaterstof *n.* **sulphuric**, *a.* zwavelig. ~ acid, zwavelzuur *n.n.* **sulphurous**, *a.* zwavelachtig, zwavel . . . **sulphury**, *a.* zwavelachtig, zwavel . . .
sultan, *n.* sultan *n.*
sultana, *n.* (sultana)rozijn *n.*
sultriness, *n.* zwoelheid *n.* **sultry**, *a.* zwoel, drukkend heet.

sum, *n.* som *n.*; bedrag *n.n.*; toppunt *n.n.* ~ *total*, totaal *n.n.*; *to be good at* ~*s*, goed kunnen *irr.* rekenen. ¶ *v.t. to* ~ *up*, optellen; opsommen; *to* ~ *a person up*, iemand beoordelen.

summarily, *adv.* summier, zonder vorm *n.* van proces *n.n.*; kort en bondig. **summarize**, *v.t.* resumeren, kort samenvatten. **summary**, *a.* beknopt; summier. ¶ *n.* kort overzicht *n.n.*

summer, *n.* zomer *n. in* ~, 's zomers. ¶ *v.i.* de zomer doorbrengen *irr.* **summerhouse**, *n.* tuinhuis *n.n.* **summery**, *a.* zomers.

summit, *n.* top *n.*; kruin *n.*; toppunt *n.n.*

summon, *v.t.* dagvaarden; sommeren; bijeenroepen *str.*; ontbieden *str. to* ~ *up one's courage*, zijn moed *n.* verzamelen. **summoner**, *n.* dagvaarder *n.* **summons**, *n.* dagvaarding *n.*, sommatie *n.*; bekeuring *n.* ¶ *v.t.* dagvaarden; bekeuren.

sump, *n.* vergaarbak *n.*

sumptuary, *a.* de uitgaven betreffend. ~ *law*, wet tegen de weelde.

sumptuous, *a.*, ~**ly**, *adv.* weelderig, kostbaar.

sun, *n.* zon *n.*; zonneschijn *n.* ¶ *v.r. to* ~ *oneself*, zich zonnen. **sunbeam**, *n.* zonnestraal *n.* **sunblind**, *n.* rolgordijn *n.n.* **sunburnt**, *a.* gebruind, getaand. **sunburst**, *n.* plotseling doorbreken *n.n.* van de zon.

Sunday, *N.* zondag *N.* ~ *best*, zondagskleren *pl.n.n.* ¶ *a.* zondags.

sun-deck, *n.* tentdek *n.n.*

sunder, *v.t.* scheiden.

sundew, *n.* zonnedauw *n.* **sundial**, *n.* zonnewijzer *n.*

sundry, *a.* diverse, allerhande. ¶ *n. sundries*, diversen *pl.n.n.*

sunflower, *n.* zonnebloem *n.*

sunken, *a.* gezonken; ingevallen. ~ *rock*, blinde klip *n.*

sunlight, *n.* zonlicht *n.n.* **sunlit**, *a.* zonnig. **sunny**, *a.* zonnig. **sunrise**, *n.* zonsopgang *n.* **sunset**, *n.* zonsondergang *n.* **sunshade**, *n.* parasol *n.* **sunshine**, *n.* zonneschijn *n.* **sunspot**, *n.* zonnevlek *n.* **sunstroke**, *n.* zonnesteek *n.*

sup, *v.i.* souperen. ¶ *n.* teugje *n.n.*, slokje *n.n.*

super, *a.* (*coll.*) bizonder. ¶ *prefix* boven, over, super, opper.

superable, *a.* overkomelijk.

superabound, *v.i. to* ~ *with*, overvloedig voorzien zijn van. **superabundant**, *a.*, ~**ly**, *adv.* overvloedig.

superannuate, *v.t.* op pensioen *n.n.* stellen. **superannuation**, *n.* pensioen *n.n.*

superb, *a.*, ~**ly**, *adv.* prachtig.

supercargo, *n.* supercarga *n.*

supercharger, *n.* compressor *n.*

supercilious, *a.*, ~**ly**, *adv.* verwaand, uit de hoogte.

supererogation, *n.* overdaad *n.* **supererogatory**, *a.* overtollig.

superficial, *a.*, ~**ly**, *adv.* oppervlakkig;

vlakte ... **superficiality**, *n.* oppervlakkigheid *n.*

superfine, *a.* prima.

superfluity, *n.* overtolligheid *n.*, overbodigheid *n.* **superfluous**, *a.* overtollig, overbodig.

superhuman, *a.* bovenmenselijk.

superintend, *v.t.* surveilleren. **superintendence**, *n.* toezicht *n.n.* **superintendent**, *n.* opziener *n.*, opzichter *n.*

superior, *a.* superieur; beter; hooghartig; arrogant. ~ *numbers*, overmacht *n.*; ~ *officer*, hoofdofficier *n.* ¶ *n.* superieur *n.*, meerdere *n.* **superiority**, *n.* superioriteit *n.*

superlative, *a.*, ~**ly**, *adv.* voortreffelijk. ~ *degree*, overtreffende trap *n.*

supernatural, *a.* bovennatuurlijk.

supernumerary, *a.* surnumerair.

superscribe, *v.t.* adresseren. **superscription**, *n.* opschrift *n.n.*

supersede, *v.t.* vervangen *str.*, te niet doen *irr.*

superstition, *n.* bijgeloof *n.n.* **superstitious**, *a.*, ~**ly**, *adv.* bijgelovig.

superstructure, *n.* bovenbouw *n.*

supertax, *n.* extra-belasting *n.*

supervene, *v.i.* er tussen komen *irr.*; intreden *str.*

supervise, *v.t.* toezicht *n.n.* houden *irr.* op. **supervision**, *n.* toezicht *n.n.* **supervisor**, *n.* opzichter *n.*; inspecteur *n.*

supine, *a.*, ~**ly**, *adv.* achterover(liggend); nalatig.

supper, *n.* avondeten *n.n.*, avondmaal *n.n.*; souper *n.n. the Last S*~, het laatste Avondmaal.

supplant, *v.t.* verdringen *str.*

supple, *a.* soepel, buigzaam; lenig.

supplement, *n.* supplement *n.n.* ¶ *v.t.* aanvullen. **supplementary**, *a.* aanvullend: suppletoir.

suppleness, *n.* soepelheid *n.*

supplicant, *n.* smekeling *n.* **supplicate**, *v.i.* smeken. *to* ~ *for*, smeken om. **supplication**, *n.* smeekbede *n.* **supplicatory**, *a.* smekend.

supplier, *n.* leverancier *n.* **supply**, *v.t.* leveren; verschaffen; aanvullen. *to* ~ *with*, voorzien *irr.* van. ¶ *n.* levering *n.*, leverantie *n.*; aanvoer *n.*, toevoer *n.*; voorziening *n.*; plaatsvervanger *n.* (*also :*) *supplies*, gelden *pl.n.n.*, credieten *pl.n.n.*; ~ *and demand*, vraag *n.* en aanbod *n.n.*

support, *v.t.* steunen; onderhouden *irr.*; verdragen, dulden. ¶ *v.r. to* ~ *oneself*, in z'n eigen onderhoud *n.n.* voorzien *irr.* ¶ *n.* steun *n.*; ondersteuning *n.*; onderhoud *n.n. in* ~ *of*, tot steun van. **supportable**, *a.* dragelijk, te verduren. **supporter**, *n.* helper *n.*; verdediger *n.*; supporter *n.*

suppose, *v.t.* (ver)onderstellen, vermoeden. **supposed**, *a.* vermeend. **supposition**, *n.* veronderstelling *n.* **supposititious**, *a.* denkbeeldig, verondersteld.

suppress, *v.t.* onderdrukken; verzwijgen *str.*;

bedwingen *str.* **suppression,** *n.* onderdrukking *n.*; verzwijging *n.* **suppressor,** *n.* onderdrukker *n.*

suppurate, *v.i.* etteren. **suppuration,** *n.* ettering *n.*

supremacy, *n.* oppermacht *n.*, heerschappij *n.*; suprematie *n.* **supreme,** *a.* hoogst(e); opperst(e). ~ *hour,* critieke ogenblik *n.n.*; ~ *folly,* grootste dwaasheid *n.* **supremely,** *adv.* hoogst, uiterst.

surcharge, *n.* extra-betaling *n.*; strafport *n.n.*; opdruk *n.*

sure, *a.* zeker; ongetwijfeld; veilig; betrouwbaar. *to be* ~*!,* voorzeker; *to make* ~ *of,* zich verzekeren van. **surely,** *adv.* zeker; veilig; stellig. **sureness,** *n.* zekerheid *n.*

surety, *n.* borgtocht *n.*, onderpand *n.n.*

surf, *n.* branding *n.*

surface, *n.* oppervlak *n.n.*; oppervlakte *n.* *on the* ~ (*also* :), op 't eerste gezicht. ¶ *a.* oppervlakkig. ¶ *v.t.* beleggen; aan de oppervlakte komen *irr.*

surfeit, *n.* oververzadiging *n.* ¶ *v.i.* zich de maag overladen. ~*ed with,* beu van.

surge, *n.* golf *n.*, baar *n.*; golving *n.* ¶ *v.i.* woelen; aanzwellen; dringen *str.*

surgeon, *n.* chirurg *n.*; scheepsdokter *n.* **surgery,** *n.* operatiekamer *n.*; spreekkamer *n.* **surgical,** *a.* heelkundig.

surly, *a.* nors, knorrig.

surmise, *v.t.* vermoeden, gissen. ¶ *n.* vermoeden *n.n.*

surmount, *v.t.* te boven komen *irr.*, overwinnen *str.* **surmountable,** *a.* overkomelijk.

surname, *n.* familienaam *n.* ¶ *v.t.* ~*d,* bijgenaamd.

surpass, *v.t.* overtreffen *str*

surplice, *n.* koorhemd *n.n.*

surplus, *n.* overschot *n.n.* ¶ *a.* overtollig.

surprise, *n.* verrassing *n.*; overrompeling *n.* *to my* ~, tot m'n verrassing *n.*; *to take by* ~, verrassen. ¶ *v.t.* verrassen; verbazen. **surprise-attack,** *n.* verrassing *n.* **surprise-visit,** *n.* onverwacht bezoek *n.n.* **surprising,** *a.*, ~*ly,* *adv.* verrassend, verwonderlijk.

surrender, *v.t.* overgeven *str.*, overleveren; afstand *n.* doen *irr.* van. ¶ *v.i.* zich overgeven *str.* ¶ *n.* overgave *n.*; afstand *n.*

surreptitious, *a.*, ~*ly,* *adv.* heimelijk, slinks.

surrogate, *a.* surrogaat. ¶ *n.* surrogaat *n.n.*

surround, *v.t.* omringen; omsingelen. ¶ *n.* rand *n.* **surroundings,** *pl.n.* omgeving *n.*

surtax, *n.* extra belasting *n.*

survey, *v.t.* overzien *irr.*; opnemen *str.*, opmeten *str.* ¶ *n.* overzicht *n.n.*; opmeting *n.* **surveyor,** *n.* opziener *n.*, opzichter *n.*; landmeter *n.*

survival, *n.* overblijfsel *n.n.*, voortbestaan *n.n.* **survive,** *v.i.* voortleven, in leven *n.n.* blijven *str.* ¶ *v.t.* overléven. **survivor,** *n.* overlevende *n.*; geredde *n.*

susceptibility, *n.* vatbaarheid *n.*; fijngevoeligheid *n.* **susceptible,** *a.* vatbaar; fijngevoelig; kwalijknemend. ~ *to,* vatbaar voor.

suspect, *v.t.* verdenken *irr.*; wantrouwen ¶ *a.* verdacht. ¶ *n.* verdachte *n.*

suspend, *v.t.* ophangen *str.*; schorsen (*member*); opschorten (*judgement*); staken (*payment*). *to be* ~*ed,* hangen *str.*; zweven; ~*ed animation,* schijndood *n.*

suspender, *n.* (sok)ophouder *n.* ~ *belt,* jarretellegordeltje *n.n.*

suspense, *n.* onzekerheid *n.*, afwachting *n.* *in* ~, in spanning *n.*

suspension, *n.* ophanging *n.*; opschorting *n.*; schorsing *n.*; uitstel *n.n.*, staking *n.* *to hold in* ~, in opgeloste toestand *n.* bevatten. **suspension-bridge,** *n.* hangbrug *n.*

suspicion, *n.* verdenking *n.*; achterdocht *n.n.*, wantrouwen *n.n.*; argwaan *n.*; (*coll.*) tikje *n.n.* **suspicious,** *a.*, ~*ly,* *adv.* verdacht; achterdochtig, wantrouwend.

sustain, *v.t.* steunen, stutten; volhouden *irr.*; verduren. *to* ~ *a loss,* een verlies *n.n.* lijden *str.* **sustained,** *a.* volgehouden, ononderbroken. **sustaining,** *a.* voedzaam. **sustenance,** *n.* voeding *n.*, levensonderhoud *n.n.*

sutler, *n.* zoetelaar *n.*; marketentster *n.*

suture, *n.* naad *n.*; hechting *n.*

suzerain, *n.* suzerein *n.*, leenheer *n.* **suzerainty,** *n.* suzereiniteit *n.*

swab, *n.* zwabber *n.*; propje *n.n.* (watten). ¶ *v.t.* zwabberen; opnemen *str.*

swaddle, *v.t.* zwachtelen; inbakeren. **swaddling-clothes,** *pl.n.* luiers *pl.n.*, windselen *pl.n.*

swag, *n.* (*coll.*) buit *n.*

swagger, *v.i.* pochen, snoeven, branie *n.* maken; parmantig rondstappen. ¶ *n.* branie *n.* **swaggerer,** *n.* pocher *n.*, snoever *n.* **swagger-stick,** *n.* badinetje *n.n.*

swain, *n.* jonge boer *n.*; vrijer *n.*, minnaar *n.*

swallow, *n.* zwaluw *n.* (*bird*); slok *n.* ¶ *v.i.* slikken. ¶ *v.t.* slikken, inslikken, doorslikken.

swamp, *n.* moeras *n.n.* ¶ *v.t.* vol water *n.n.* doen *irr.* lopen. *to be* ~*ed,* onderlopen *str.*; in de menigte opgaan *irr.*; overstelpt worden *str.* **swampy,** *a.* moerassig, drassig.

swan, *n.* zwaan *n.* **swan-neck,** *n.* zwanenhals *n.*

swan-mussel, *n.* eendenmossel *n.*

swank, *v.i.* opscheppen, geuren. **swank-pot,** *n.* opschepper *n.* **swanky,** *a.* opschepperig.

sward, *n.* grasveld *n.n.*

swarm, *n.* zwerm *n.* ¶ *v.i.* zwermen; krioelen. *to* ~ *with,* wemelen van.

swarthiness, *n.* donkerheid *n.* **swarthy,** *a.* donker, bruin.

swashbuckler, *n.* snoever *n.*

swathe, *n.* windsel *n.n.*, zwachtel *n.* ¶ *v.t.* zwachtelen.

sway, *v.i.* zwaaien, slingeren; overhellen. ¶ *v.t.* zwaaien; hanteren; bewegen *str.*, doen *irr.* overhellen. *to be ~ed by*, onder de invloed staan *irr.* van. ¶ *n.* zwaai *n.*; heerschappij *n.*, overwicht *n.n.*

swear, *v.i.* zweren *str.*, een eed *n.* afleggen; vloeken. *to ~ at*, uitvloeken; *to ~ to*, zweren op. ¶ *v.t.* zweren *str.*, onder ede beloven; bezweren *str. to ~ an oath*, een eed *n.* doen *irr.*; *to swear . . . in*, beëdigen. **swear-word**, *n.* vloek *n.*, vloekwoord *n.n.*

sweat, *v.i.* zweten. ¶ *v.t.* exploiteren, uitbuiten. ¶ *n.* zweet *n.n.*; (*coll.*) hard werk *n.n.* **sweated**, *a. ~ labour, ~ industry*, huisindustrie *n.* **sweater**, *n.* dikke sporttrui *n.* **sweating-shop**, *n.* werkplaats *n.* waar voor hongerloon *n.n.* gewerkt wordt. **sweating-system**, *n.* exploitatie *n.* van de arbeider *n.* in de huisindustrie. **sweaty**, *a.* bezweet, zweterig.

sweep, *v.t.* vegen; bestrijken *str.*; afzoeken *irr. to ~ the board*, alles winnen *str.* ¶ *v.i. to ~ across*, vliegen *str.* over. ¶ *n.* veeg *n.*; (schoorsteen)veger *n.*; slag *n. to make a clean ~*, opruiming *n.* houden *irr.*; *at a ~*, met één slag. **sweeper**, *n.* veger *n.* **sweeping**, *a.* wijd, ruim. *~ majority*, verpletterende meerderheid *n.*; *~ measure*, radikale maatregel *n.*; *~ statement*, generalisatie *n.* **sweepstake**, *n.* prijs *n.* bestaande uit de gezamenlijke inleg.

sweet, *a., ~ly, adv.* zoet; lieflijk; charmant; vers, fris. *to be ~ on*, verliefd zijn op; *~ briar*, egelantier *n.*; *~ chestnut*, tamme kastanje *n.*; *~ pea*, pronkerwt *n.*; *~ violet*, welriekend viooltje *n.n.*; *~ william*, duizendschoon *n.n.* ¶ *n.* zoetigheid *n.*, lekkertje *n.n. ~s*, snoepgoed *n.n.* **sweetbread**, *n.* zwezerik *n.* **sweeten**, *v.t.* zoet maken; verzoeten, veraangenamen. **sweetener**, *n.* zoet makend middel *n.n.*; douceurtje *n.n.* **sweetheart**, *n.* geliefde *n.*; meisje *n.n.*; schat *n.* **sweetmeats**, *pl.n.* suikergoed *n.n.* **sweetness**, *n.* zoetheid *n.*; liefheid *n.* **sweet-rush**, *n.* kalmoes *n.n.*

swell, *v.i.* zwellen *str. to ~ into*, aangroeien tot; *to ~ out*, aanzwellen *str.* ¶ *v.t.* doen *irr.* zwellen. ¶ *n.* deining *n.* (*sea*). **swelled**, *a. to have a ~ head*, verwaand zijn. **swelling**, *n.* gezwel *n.n.*

swelter, *v.i.* stikken van de hitte, liggen *str.* te blakeren. **sweltering**, *a. ~ heat*, smoorhitte *n.*

swerve, *v.i.* afwijken *str.*; zwenken. *to ~ from*, afdwalen van. ¶ *n.* zwenking *n.*

swift, *a., ~ly, adv.* snel. ¶ *n.* gierzwaluw *n.*, torenzwaluw *n.* **swiftness**, *n.* snelheid *n.*

swig, *n.* (*coll.*) slok *n.*

swill, *v.t.* spoelen; afspoelen; doorspoelen. ¶ *n.* spoelsel *n.n.*; varkensdraf *n.*

swim, *v.i.* zwemmen *str.*; duizelen. *to ~ with the tide*, met de stroom meegaan *irr.*; *sink or ~*, pompen of verzuipen. ¶ *v.t.* overzwemmen *str.*; doen *irr.* zwemmen. ¶ *n.* zwemmen *n.n. to be in the ~*, tot de ingewijden *pl.n.* behoren, goed op de hoogte zijn. **swimmer**, *n.* zwemmer *n.* **swimmingly**, *adv.* van een leien dakje *n.n.*

swindle, *v.i.* zwendelen. ¶ *v.t.* afzetten, oplichten. ¶ *n.* zwendelarij *n.*, oplichterij *n.* **swindler**, *n.* zwendelaar *n.*, oplichter *n.*

swine, *n.* zwijn *n.n.*; varken *n.n.* **swine-fever**, *n.* varkensziekte *n.* **swineherd**, *n.* zwijnenhoeder *n.* **swinepox**, *n.* vlekziekte *n.*

swing, *v.i.* zwaaien; schommelen; slingeren, bengelen. ¶ *v.t.* zwaaien; doen *irr.* schommelen; slingeren. ¶ *n.* zwaai *n.*; schommel *n.*; slingering *n. to get into the ~*, de slag te pakken krijgen *str.* **swing-door**, *n.* tochtdeur *b.*, doorslaande deur *n.* **swinging-bridge**, *n.* draaibrug *n.*

swingle, *n.* zwengel *n.* ¶ *v.t.* zwengelen.

swinish, *a.* zwijnachtig.

swipe, *v.t.* (*coll.*) slaan *irr.* **swipes**, *pl.n.* dunbier *n.n.*

swirl, *v.i.* dwarrelen, warrelen. ¶ *n.* dwarrelpoel *n.*, warreling *n.*

swish, *v.i.* zwiepen, suizen. ¶ *n.* gezwiep *n.n.*

Swiss, *a.* Zwitsers. ¶ *N.* Zwitser *N.*

switch, *v.t.* omschakelen. *to ~ on*, inschakelen; aandraaien; *to ~ off*, uitschakelen; uitdraaien. ¶ *n.* rijsje *n.n.*; karwats *n.*; schakelaar *n.*, knopje *n.n.* (*electric*). **switchback**, *n.* rutschbaan *n.* **switchboard**, *n.* schakelbord *n.n.*

Switzerland, *N.* Zwitserland *n.N.*

swivel, *v.i.* draaien. **swivel-chair**, *n.* draaistoel *n.*

swoon, *v.i.* bezwijmen, in zwijm *n.* vallen *str.* ¶ *n.* bezwijming *n.*, onmacht *n.*

swoop, *v.i.* neerschieten *str.*, neerstrijken *str.* ¶ *n.* neerschieten *n.n. at a ~*, met één slag *n.*

swop, *v.t.* ruilen. ¶ *n.* ruil *n.*

sword, *n.* zwaard *n.n.*, sabel *n.*, degen *n. to cross ~s*, de degen kruisen. **swordfish**, *n.* zwaardvis *n.* **sword-flag**, *n.* gele lis *n.* **sword-play**, *n.* schermen *n.n.* **swordsmanship**, *n.* schermkunst *n.* **swordstick**, *n.* degenstok *n.* **sword-swallower**, *n.* degenslikker *n.*

sworn, *a.* gezworen, beëdigd.

swot, *v.i.* vossen, blokken. ¶ *v.t.* doodslaan *irr.* (*fly*).

sycamore, *n.* esdoorn *n.*; ahorn *n.*

sycophant, *n.* sycophant *n.*; pluimstrijker *n.* **sycophantic**, *a.* vleierig, kruiperig.

syllabic, *a.* lettergreep . . . **syllable**, *n.* lettergreep *n.*

syllabus, *n.* programma *n.n.*

syllogism, *n.* syllogisme *n.n.*, sluitrede *n.* **syllogistic**, *a.* syllogistisch.

sylph, *n.* sylphe *n.*, luchtgeest *n.* **sylphide**, *n.* sylphide *n.*

sylvan, *a.* bos . . .

symbol, *n.* symbool *n.n.*, zinnebeeld *n.n.* **symbolic(al)**, *a., ~ly, adv.* symbolisch, zinnebeeldig. **symbolism**, *n.* symbolisme *n.n.*, symboliek *n.* **symbolize**, *v.t.* symboliseren, zinnebeeldig voorstellen.

symmetrical, *a.*, ~ly, *adv.* symmetrisch. **symmetry**, *n.* symmetrie *n.*

sympathetic, *a.*, ~ally, *adv.* sympathetisch; medegevoelend; medelijdend. ~ *strike*, sympathiestaking *n.*, solidariteitsstaking *n.*

sympathize, *v.i.* sympathiseren; medelijden *n.n.* hebben. **sympathiser**, *n.* volgeling *n.*; medelijdend persoon *n.* **sympathy**, *n.* sympathie *n.* ~ *with*, sympathie voor; *to be in* ~ *with*, voelen voor; ~ *for* or *with*, medelijden *n.n.* met.

symphonic, *a.* symphonisch. **symphony**, *n.* symphonie *n.*

symptom, *n.* symptoom *n.n.*, verschijnsel *n.n.* **symptomatic**, *a.* symptomatisch, kentekenend.

synagogue, *n.* synagoge *n.*

synchronism, *n.* synchronisme *n.n.*, gelijktijdigheid *n.* **synchronize**, *v.t.* synchroniseren. ¶ *v.i.* gelijktijdig zijn, (in tijd) overeenstemmen.

syncopate, *v.t.* syncoperen. **syncopation**, *n.* syncopering *n.*

syncope, *n.* syncope *n.*; onmacht *n.*

syndic, *n.* syndicus *n.* ¶ *n. the* ~*s*, de staalmeesters *pl.n.* **syndicalism**, *n.* syndicalisme *n.n.* **syndicalist**, *n.* syndicalist *n.* **syndicate**, *n.* syndicaat *n.n.* ¶ *v.t.* tot een syndicaat verenigen.

synod, *n.* synode *n.*, kerkvergadering *n.*

synonym, *n.* synoniem *n.n.* **synonymous**, *a.* synoniem, zinverwant.

synopsis, *n.* synopsis *n.*, overzicht *n.n.* **synoptic**, *a.*, ~ally, *adv.* synoptisch. overzichtelijk.

syntactic(al), *a.*, ~ly, *adv.* syntactisch. **syntax**, *n.* syntaxis *n.*; zinsbouw *n.*

synthesis, *n.* synthese *n.* **synthetic(al)**, *a.*, ~ly, *adv.* synthetisch; kunst . . .

syphilis, *n.* syphilis *n.* **syphilitic**, *a.* syphilitisch. ¶ *n.* syphilislijder *n.*

syphon, *n.* syphon *n.*

Syria, *N.* Syrië *n.N.* **Syrian**, *a.* Syrisch. ¶ *N.* Syriër *N.*

syringa, *n.* boerenjasmijn *n.*; sering *n.*

syringe, *n.* spuitje *n.n.* ¶ *v.t.* bespuiten *str.*; uitspuiten *str.*

syrup, *n.* stroop *n.*; siroop *n.* **syrupy**, *a.* stroopachtig, stroperig.

system, *n.* systeem *n.n.*, stelsel *n.n.*; gestel *n.n.* **systematic(al)**, *a.*, ~ly, *adv.* systematisch, stelselmatig; methodisch. **systematize**, *v.t.* systematiseren; systematisch indelen.

systole, *n.* systole *n.*, samentrekking *n.* (van het hart).

T

taal, *n.* Zuid-Afrikaans *n.N.*
tab, *n.* tongetje *n.n.*; etiket *n.n.*

tabby, *n.* getijgerde kat *n.*

tabernacle, *n.* tabernakel *n.n.*; bedehuis *n.n.*; tent *n.*

table, *n.* tafel *n.*; tabel *n.* ~ *of contents*, inhoudsopgave *n.*; *the* ~*s are turned*, de bordjes *pl.n.n.* zijn verhangen; *to wait at* ~, bedienen. ¶ *v.t.* ter tafel *n.* brengen *irr.*; tabelleren. **tablecloth**, *n.* tafelkleed *n.n.*; tafellaken *n.n.* (*for meals*). **tablespoon**, *n.* eetlepel *n.* **table-ware**, *n.* tafelgerei *n.n.*

tablet, *n.* tablet *n.n.* ~ *of soap*, stuk *n.n.* zeep *n.*

tabloid, *a.* in tabletvorm *n.* ¶ *n.* tablet *n.n.*

taboo, *n.* taboe *n.n.* ¶ *a.* taboe. ¶ *v.t.* taboe verklaren.

tabor, *n.* kleine trom *n.*

tabouret, *n.* taboeret *n.n.*

tabular, *a.* tabel . . . , tabellarisch. **tabulate**, *v.t.* tabellarisch rangschikken, in een tabel *n.* opnemen *str.*

tacit, *a.*, ~ly, *adv.* stilzwijgend. **taciturn**, *a.* zwijgzaam. **taciturnity**, *n.* zwijgzaamheid *n.*

tack, *n.* spijkertje *n.n.*; boeg *n.*, koers *n.*, gang *n.* (*ship*). *to try another* ~, het over een andere boeg gooien. ¶ *v.t.* vastspijkeren; laveren (*ship*). ¶ *v.i.* over stag *n.* gaan *irr.*

tackle, *n.* takel *n.*; tuig *n.n.*, gerei *n.n.* ¶ *v.t.* aanpakken, onder handen *pl.n.* nemen *str.*

tact, *n.* takt *n.*

tactical, *a.*, ~ly, *adv.* tactisch. **tactician**, *n.* tacticus *n.* **tactics**, *pl.n.* taktiek *n.*; krijgskunde *n.*

tactile, *a.* tast . . .

tactless, *a.*, ~ly, *adv.* taktloos.

tadpole, *n.* donderpad *n.*

taffeta, *n.* taf *n.*

taffrail, *n.* hekreling *n.*

tag, *n.* aanhangsel *n.n.*; etiket *n.n.*; refrein *n.n.* *to play* ~, krijgertje *n.n.* spelen. ¶ *v.i. to* ~ *behind*, achternalopen *str.*; *to* ~ *on to*, (zich) aansluiten *str.* bij.

tail, *n.* staart *n.*; pand *n.n.*, slip *n.* *heads or* ~*s*, kruis *n.n.* of munt *n.* ¶ *v.t.* de staart afsnijden *str.* *to top and* ~, de puntjes *pl.n.n.* afsnijden *str.* ¶ *v.i.* een staart *n.* vormen, achteraan komen *irr.* **tailboard**, *n.* achterschot *n.n.* **tail-light**, *n.* achterlicht *n.n.*

tailor, *n.* kleermaker *n.* **tailoring**, *n.* kleermakerswerk *n.n.* **tailormade**, *a.* gemaakt ¶ *n.* tailleur *n.*

tailpiece, *n.* staartstuk *n.n.*; slotvignet *n.n.*

taint, *v.t.* bevlekken; besmetten, bederven *str.* ¶ *n.* vlek *n.*; smet *n.* **taintless**, *a.* vlekkeloos, smetteloos.

take, *v.t.* nemen *str.*; beschouwen (*consider*); nodig zijn. *to* ~ *aim*, mikken, aanleggen; *to* ~ *cover*, dekking *n.* zoeken *irr.*; *to* ~ *shape*, vorm *n.* aannemen *str.*; *to* ~ *time*, tijd *n.* vergen; *it* ~*s time*, er is tijd *n.* mee gemoeid; *to* ~ *a person at his word*, op iemands woord *n.n.* afgaan *irr.*; *to* ~

one's breath away, iemand de adem benemen *str.*; *to ~ down*, neerhalen; opschrijven *str.*, noteren; *to ~ for*, houden *irr.* voor; *to ~ in*, binnenbrengen *irr.*; begrijpen *str.*; beetnemen *str.*; *to ~ off*, afzetten, afdoen *irr.*, uittrekken *str.*; nadoen *irr.*; *to ~ it out of someone*, het iemand betaald zetten; *to ~ up*, opnemen *str.*; aannemen *str.*; innemen *str.*; beginnen *str.* ¶ *v.i. to ~ after*, aarden naar; *to ~ off*, opstijgen *str.*; *to ~ to*, gaan *irr.* voelen voor, gaan *irr.* houden van; *to ~ to one's bed*, gaan *irr.* liggen; *to ~ to the boats*, in de boten *pl.n.* gaan *irr.*; *to ~ up with*, bevriend worden *str.* met; *to be ~n ill*, ziek worden *str.*; *to be ~n up with*, in beslag *n.n.* genomen worden *str.* door; *to be ~n with*, ingenomen zijn met. ¶ *v.r. to ~ oneself off*, weggaan *irr.*, zich uit de voeten *pl.n.* maken. ¶ *n.* vangst *n.*; opname *n.* **take-off**, *n.* startpunt *n.*; imitatie *n.* **taker**, *n.* nemer *n.* **taking**, *a.* innemend. ¶ *n. ~s*, ontvangst *n.*, recette *n.*

talc, *n.* talk *n.* **talcum**, *n. ~ powder*, talkpoeder *n.*

tale, *n.* verhaal *n.n.*; vertelsel *n.n.*; sprookje *n.n.*

talent, *n.* talent *n.n.* **talented**, *a.* begaafd, talentvol.

talion, *n.* vergelding *n.*

talisman, *n.* talisman *n.*

talk, *v.i.* praten; spreken *str.* *to ~ scandal*, kwaadspreken *str.*; *to ~ about*, praten over; *to ~ at*, praten tegen; *to ~ back*, (brutaal) antwoorden; *to ~ down*, overschreeuwen; *to ~ of*, praten over; *to ~ over*, bespreken *str.* ¶ *n.* praatje *n.n.*; causerie *n.* *~s*, besprekingen *pl.n.*; *small ~*, praatjes *pl.n.n.* over koetjes en kalfjes. **talkative**, *a.* spraakzaam; praatziek. **talker**, *n.* prater *n.* **talking**, *n.* gepraat *n.n.*

tall, *a.* lang; hoog, groot. *a ~ order*, geen kleinigheid *n.*; *~ story*, overdrijving *n.*, verzinsel *n.n.* **tallish**, *a.* vrij lang. **tallness**, *n.* lengte *n.*; hoogte *n.*, grootte *n.*

tallow, *n.* talk *n.*; kaarsvet *n.n.* **tallow-dip**, *n.* vetkaarsje *n.n.* **tallowy**, *a.* talkachtig.

tally, *n.* kerfstok *n.*; merk *n.n.*, teken *n.n.* *to take ~ of*, tellen. ¶ *v.i.* overeenstemmen. *to ~ with*, passen bij. ¶ *v.t.* aanstrepen. **tallyman**, *n.* ladingcontroleur *n.*

tally-ho, *int.* halali *n.n.*

talon, *n.* klauw *n.*

tamable, *a.* tembaar.

tamarind, *n.* tamarinde *n.*

tamarisk, *n.* tamarisk *n.*

tambour, *n.* tamboer *n.*; trommel *n.* **tambourine**, *n.* tamboerijn *n.*

tame, *a.*, *~ly*, *adv.* tam; mak; flauw, saai. ¶ *v.t.* temmen. **tamer**, *n.* temmer *n.*

tammy, *n.* stamijn *n.* **tammy-cloth**, *n.* zeefdoek *n.*

tam o' shanter, *n.* Schotse muts *n.*

tamp, *v.t.* aanstampen.

tamper, *v.i. to ~ with*, knoeien met, peuteren aan.

tan, *n.* run *n.*; looistof *n.*; taan *n.*; **taankleur** *n.* ¶ *a.* taankleurig. ¶ *v.t.* looien; **tanen**; verbranden; ranselen.

tandem, *n.* tandem *n.*

tang, *n.* bijsmaak *n.*; scherpte *n.*

tangent, *n.* tangens *n.* *to fly off at a ~*, over iets heel anders beginnen *str.*

tangerine, *n.* mandarijntje *n.n.*

tangibility, *n.* tastbaarheid *n.* **tangible**, *a.* tastbaar, voelbaar.

Tangiers, *N.* Tanger *n.N.*

tangle, *v.t.* in de war maken; verwarren. *to get ~d*, in de war raken. ¶ *n.* warboel *n.*, warhoop *n.*; wirwar *n.* *in a ~*, in de war. **tangly**, *a.* verward.

tango, *n.* tango *n.*

tank, *n.* bak *n.*, reservoir *n.n.*; tank *n.*

tankard, *n.* bierkroes *n.*

tank-car, *n.* tankwagen *n.* **tanker**, *n.* tankschip *n.n.*

tan-mill, *n.* runmolen *n.* **tanner**, *n.* leerlooier *n.*; taander *n.*; (*coll.*) zesstuiversstuk *n.n.* **tannery**, *n.* leerlooierij *n.*; taanderij *n.*

tannin, *n.* tannine *n.*, looizuur *n.n.*

tansy, *n.* boerenwormkruid *n.n.*

tantalize, *v.t.* tantaliseren.

tantalus, *n.* likeurstel *n.n.*

tantamount, *a. to be ~ to*, gelijkstaan *irr.* met.

tantrum, *n.* kwade luim *n.*

tanyard, *n.* leerlooierij *n.*

tap, *n.* kraan *n.*; tap *n.* (*beer*); tik *n.*, klop *n.* (*knock*). *on ~*, op de tap. ¶ *v.t.* tappen, aftappen; tikken. ¶ *v.i.* tikken, kloppen.

tape, *n.* lint *n.n.*, band *n.*; telegramstrook *n.* *red ~*, bureaucratisch gedoe *n.n.* ¶ *v.t.* binden *str.*; meten *str.* **tape-measure**, *n.* meterrolletje *n.n.*

taper, *n.* waslicht *n.n.*, kaars *n.* ¶ *v.i.* spits toelopen *str.* **tapering**, *a.* gepunt, spits toelopend.

tapestry, *n.* wandtapijt *n.n.*, tapisserie *n.*; tapijtwerk *n.n.*

tapeworm, *n.* lintworm *n.*

tapioca, *n.* tapioca *n.*

tapir, *n.* tapir *n.*

tappet-valve, *n.* kleplichter *n.*

tap-room, *n.* gelagkamer *n.*

tap-root, *n.* hoofdwortel *n.*

tapster, *n.* tapper *n.*

tar, *n.* teer *n.* or *n.n.*; pekbroek *n.* (*sailor*). ¶ *v.t.* teren.

tarantula, *n.* tarantula *n.*

tardiness, *n.* traagheid *n.*; nalatigheid *n.* **tardy**, *a.*, *~ily*, *adv.* traag, langzaam; nalatig.

tare, *n.* voederwikke *n.* (*plant*); tarra *n.* ¶ *v.t.* tarreren.

target, *n.* schietschijf *n.*; doelpunt *n.n.* **target-practice**, *n.* schijfschieten *n.n.*

tariff, *n.* tarief *n.n.*

tarn, *n.* bergmeertje *n.n.*

tarnish, *v.i.* dof worden *str.*, **aanslaan** *irr.*

¶ *v.t.* dof maken; doen *irr.* aanslaan; ontluisteren.

tarpaulin, *n.* dekzeil *n.n.*; presenning *n.* (*ship's*).

tarry, *a.* teerachtig. ¶ *v.i.* toeven, dralen.

tart, *n.* (vruchten)taart *n.*; (*vulgar*) snol *n.* ¶ *a.* wrang; bits.

tartan, *n.* Schots geruite wol *n.*

Tartar, *N.* Tartaar *N.* ¶ *a.* Tartaars.

tartar, *n.* wijnsteen *n.* **tartaric,** *a.* wijnsteen . . .

tartlet, *n.* taartje *n.n.*

tartness, *n.* wrangheid *n.*; bitsheid *n.*

task, *n.* taak *n.* *to take a person to* ~, iemand onder handen *pl.n.* nemen *str.* ¶ *v.t.* hard laten *str.* werken, veel vergen van. **taskmaster,** *n.* baas *n.*; werkgever *n.*

tassel, *n.* kwast *n.*; pluim *n.*

taste, *v.t.* smaken, proeven. ¶ *v.i.* *to* ~ *of,* smaken naar. ¶ *n.* smaak *n.*; voorproefje *n.n.* *in bad* ~, smakeloos; onkies; *in good* ~, smaakvol; kies; *to one's* ~, naar z'n zin *n.* **tasteful,** *a.,* ~ly, *adv.* smaakvol. **tasteless,** *a.* smakeloos. **taster,** *n.* proever *n.* **tasty,** *a.* ~ily, *adv.* smakelijk.

tatter, *n.* flard *n.*, vod *n.n.*, lomp *n.* *in* ~*s,* aan flarden. ¶ *v.t.* aan flarden *pl.n.* scheuren. ~ **ed,** aan flarden. **tatterdemalion,** *n.* vagebond *n.*, haveloos iemand.

tattle, *v.i.* babbelen, kakelen. **tattler,** *n.* babbelaar *n.*

tattoo, *n.* taptoe *n.n.*; tatoeëring *n.* ¶ *v.t.* tatoeëren.

taunt, *v.t.* honen, beschimpen. *to* ~ *with,* verwijten *str.* ¶ *n.* hoon *n.*, smaad *n.*, schimp *n.*

taut, *a.* strak, gespannen.

tavern, *n.* herberg *n.*

tawdry, *a.* prullerig, waardeloos.

tawny, *a.* taankleurig, tanig.

tax, *n.* belasting *n.*; last *n.*, zware proef *n.* *to be a* ~ *on,* veel vergen van. ¶ *v.t.* belasten; schatten, taxeren; veel vergen van, zwaar op de proef stellen. **taxable,** *a.* belastbaar. **taxation,** *n.* belasting *n.*; schatting *n.* **tax-collector,** *n.* ontvanger *n.* der belastingen *pl.n.* **tax-free,** *a.* vrij van belasting *n.*

taxi, *n.* taxi *n.* ¶ *v.i.* taxiën. **taxi-cab,** *n.* taxi *n.*

taxidermist, *n.* opzetter *n.* (van dieren *pl.n.n.*). **taxidermy,** *n.* kunst *n.* van dieren *pl.n.n.* op te zetten.

taxi-driver, *n.* taxichauffeur *n.*

tea, *n.* thee *n.* *at* ~, bij de thee; *to make* ~, thee zetten; *cup of* ~, kopje *n.n.* thee *n.* **tea-caddy,** *n.* theekistje *n.n.*, theebus *n.*

teach, *v.t.* onderwijzen *str.*; leren; les *n.* geven *str.* ¶ *v.i.* les *n.* geven *str.* **teachable,** *a.* te onderwijzen. **teacher,** *n.* onderwijzer *n.*; leraar *n.* **teaching,** *n.* lesgeven *n.n.*; onderwijs *n.n.* ~(*s*) leer *n.*

tea-cloth, *n.* theedoek *n.* **tea-cosy,** *n.* theemuts *n.* **teacup,** *n.* theekopje *n.n.* **teagown,** *n.* namiddag japon *n.*

teak, *n.* djatiehout *n.n.* ¶ *a.* djatiehouten.

teal, *n.* taling *n.*

team, *n.* span *n.n.*; stel *n.n.*; ploeg *n.*; elftal *n.n.* (*football*). ¶ *v.t.* inspannen. ¶ *v.i.* *to* ~ *up,* gaan *irr.* samenwerken. **teamster,** *n.* voerman *n.* **team-work,** *n.* samenwerking *n.*

tear, *n.* traan *n.* (*eye*); scheur *n.* (*in material*). ¶ *v.t.* scheuren; rukken. *to* ~ *to pieces,* aan stukken *pl.n.n.* scheuren. ¶ *v.i.* rukken; rennen, vliegen *str.* *to* ~ *along,* komen *irr.* aanstuiven, voortjagen *str.* ¶ *v.r.* *to* ~ *oneself away,* zich wegrukken.

tearful, *a.* huilerig; beschreid. **tearing,** *a.* razend; vliegend. **tearstained,** *a.* beschreid.

tease, *v.t.* plagen; kaarden (*wool*). ¶ *n.* plaaggeest *n.*

teasel, *n.* kaarde *n.*, kaarddistel *n.*

teat, *n.* tepel *n.*

tea-things, *pl.n.* theegerei *n.n.*

technical, *a.,* ~ly, *adv.* technisch; vak . . . **technicality,** *n.* technische bizonderheid *n.* **technique,** *n.* techniek *n.* **technology,** *n.* technologie *n.* **technological,** *a.* technologisch.

teddy-bear, *n.* beertje *n.n.*

tedious, *a.,* ~ly, *adv.* vervelend, saai. **tedium,** *n.* verveling *n.*

tee, *n.* aardhoopje *n.n.*

teem, *v.i.* wemelen. *to* ~ *with,* krioelen van. ¶ *v.t.* werpen *str.* **teeming,** *n.* wemelend; overvloedig, vruchtbaar.

teens, *pl.n.* jaren *pl.n.n.* van 13 tot 19.

teeny, *a.* (heel) klein.

teeter, *v.i.* onzeker zijn.

teeth, *pl.n.* *see* **tooth.** **teethe,** *v.i.* tanden *pl.n.* krijgen *str.*

teetotaler, *n.* geheelonthouder *n.*

tegument, *n.* omhulsel *n.n.*; zaadhuls *n.*

telegram, *n.* telegram *n.n.* **telegraph,** *n.* telegraaf *n.* ¶ *v.t. and v.i.* telegraferen. **telegraphic,** *a.* telegrafisch. **telegraphist,** *n.* telegrafist *n.*; telegrafiste *n.* (*female*) **telegraphy,** *n.* telegrafie *n.*

telephone, *n.* telefoon *n.* ¶ *v.t. and v.i.* telefoneren. **telephonic,** *a.* telefonisch. **telephonist,** *n.* telefonist *n.*; telefoniste *n.* (*female*). **telephony,** *n.* telefonie *n.*

telescope, *n.* telescoop *n.* ¶ *v.t.* ineenschuiven *str.* **telescopic,** *a.* telescopisch.

television, *n.* televisie *n.*

tell, *v.t.* vertellen; zeggen *irr.*; kennen; stemmen *pl.n.* opnemen *str.* *to* ~ *one's beads,* een rozekrans *n.* bidden *str.*; *to* ~ *tales,* verklappen; *to* ~ *apart,* onderscheiden; *to* ~ *off,* een standje *n.n.* geven *str.*; *all told,* alles bij elkaar. ¶ *v.i.* verklappen, klikken. *you can't* ~, je kunt het niet weten; *to* ~ *in favour of,* pleiten voor. **teller,** *n.* verteller *n.*; stemopnemer *n.* **tell-tale,** *n.* verklikker *n.* ¶ *a.* verradend.

temerity, *n.* vermetelheid *n.*

temper, *n.* temperament *n.n.,* geaardheid *n.;* humeur *n.n.* ‾¶ *v.t.* temperen, matigen; harden (*steel*). **to ~** *justice with mercy,* genade *n.* voor recht *n.n.* laten *str.* gelden.

temperament, *n.* temperament *n.n.,* gemoedsgesteldheid *n.* **temperamental,** *a.* van het temperament; met veel temperament.

temperance, *n.* matigheid *n.;* gematigdheid *n.* **temperate,** *a.* matig; gematigd.

temperature, *n.* temperatuur *n.*

tempered, *a.* getemperd, gehard.

tempest, *n.* storm *n.* **tempestuous,** *a.* stormachtig.

Templar, *N.* Tempelier *N.*

temple, *n.* tempel *n.;* Protestantse kerk *n.*

temporal, *a.,* ~**ly,** *adv.* tijdelijk; wereldlijk; tijd(s) ... **~** *bone,* slaapbeen *n.n.* **temporality,** *n.* wereldlijke macht *n.*

temporize, *v.i.* zich naar de omstandigheden *pl.n.* schikken; schipperen; tijd *n.* trachten te winnen; dralen. **temporizer,** *n.* draler *n.*

temporary, *a.,* ~**ily,** *adv.* tijdelijk.

tempt, *v.t.* in verzoeking *n.* brengen *irr.;* verleiden; tarten, trotseren. **temptation,** *n.* verleiding *n.;* verzoeking *n.* **tempter,** *n.* verleider *n.* **tempting,** *a.* verlokkelijk, aanlokkelijk, verleidelijk. **temptress,** *n.* verleidster *n.;* bekoorster *n.*

ten, *num.* tien. **~** *to one,* tien tegen één.

tenable, *a.* houdbaar, verdedigbaar.

tenacious, *a.,* ~**ly,** *adv.* taai, vasthoudend; hardnekkig. **tenacity,** *n.* vasthoudendheid *n.*

tenancy, *n.* huurtermijn *n.;* pachttermijn *n.;* bekleden *n.n.* van een ambt *n.n.* **tenant,** *n.* huurder *n.;* pachter *n.* ¶ *v.t.* bewonen. **tenantless,** *a.* onbewoond, leegstaand. **tenantry,** *n.* (gezamenlijke) pachters *pl.n.*

tench, *n.* zeelt *n.*

tend, *v.t.* passen op, verzorgen; ‑hoeden (*cattle*). ¶ *v.i.* in zekere richting *n.* gaan *irr.* **to ~** *to,* geneigd zijn (om); er toe bijdragen *str.* om, leiden tot. **tendency,** *n.* neiging *n.;* aanleg *n.;* strekking *n.*

tendentious, *a.,* ~**ly,** *adv.* tendencieus.

tender, *v.t.* aanbieden *str.;* indienen. **to ~** *for,* inschrijven *str.* op. ¶ *n.* oppasser *n.* (*person*); wachtschip *n.n.,* bevoorradingsschip *n.n.;* tender *n.* (*railway*); offerte *n.;* inschrijvingsbiljet *n.n.;* betaalmiddel *n.n.* **to invite ~s** *for,* aanbesteden; **by ~,** bij aanbesteding *n.* ¶ *a.,* ~**ly,** *adv.* teder, teer; mals; gevoelig. **~** *conscience,* bezwaard geweten *n.n.* **tenderness,** *n.* tederheid *n.;* malsheid *n.*

tendon, *n.* pees *n.*

tendril, *n.* hechtrank *n.*

tenebrous, *a.* duister.

tenement, *n.* huurkazerne *n.*

tenet, *n.* leerstelling *n.*

tenfold, *a.* tienvoudig.

tennis, *n.* tennis *n.n.* **tennis-court,** *n.* tennisbaan *n.*

tenon, *n.* pin *n.,* pen *n.*

tenor, *n.* tenor *n.* (*singer*); loop *n.* even **~,** kalm verloop *n.n.*

tense, *a.,* ~**ly,** *adv.* strak, gespannen. ¶ *v.t.* spannen *irr.* ¶ *n.* tijd *n.*

tensile, *a.* rekbaar. **~** *force,* spankracht *n.*

tension, *n.* spanning *n.* high **~,** hoogspanning *n.;* **~** *rod,* trekstang *n.;* **~** *spring,* spanveer *n.*

tensor, *n.* strekspier *n.*

tent, *n.* tent *n.*

tentacle, *n.* vangarm *n.*

tentative, *a.,* ~**ly,** *adv.* voorzichtig; schuchter; bij wijze *n.* van proef *n.*

tenter, *n.* spanraam *n.n.* **tenterhook,** *n.* spanhaak *n.* **to be on ~s,** op hete kolen *pl. n.* zitten *str.*

tenth, *a.* tiende. ¶ *n.* tiende deel *n.n.* **tenthly,** *adv.* ten tiende, in de tiende plaats.

tenuity, *n.* fijnheid *n.,* dunheid *n.,* ijlheid *n.* **tenuous,** *a.* fijn, dun, ijl.

tenure, *n.* bezit *n.n.*

tepid, *a.* lauw. **tepidity,** *n.* lauwheid *n.*

tercentenary, *n.* derde eeuwfeest *n.n.*

tergiversate, *v.i.* uitvluchten *pl.n.* zoeken *irr.* **tergiversation,** *n.* uitvlucht *n.*

term, *n.* uitdrukking *n.;* bewoording *n.;* termijn *n.;* duur *n.,* tijd *n.;* semester *n.n.,* collegetijd *n.* **~s** (*also*), voorwaarden *pl.n.;* condities *pl.n.;* **to be on good ~s** *with,* op goeden voet staan *irr.* met; **to make ~s,** tot een vergelijk *n.n.* komen *irr.;* **not to be on** *speaking* **~s,** elkaar niet toespreken *str.* ¶ *v.t.* noemen.

termagant, *n.* helleveeg *n.*

terminable, *a.* opzegbaar. **terminal,** *a.* eind ...; termijn ... ¶ *n.* eindpunt *n.n.;* poolklem *n.* **terminate,** *v.t.* beëindigen; opzeggen *irr.* ¶ *v.i.* eindigen; afloopn *str.* **termination,** *n.* beëindiging *n.;* slot *n.n.*

terminology, *n.* terminologie *n.*

terminus, *n.* eindpunt *n.n.;* kopstation *n.n.*

termite, *n.* termiet *n.*

tern, *n.* stern *n.,* visdiefje *n.n.*

terrace, *n.* terras *n.n.* ¶ *v.t.* van een terras voorzien *irr.,* tot een terras maken.

terra-cotta, *n.* terracotta *n.*

terrapin, *n.* (kleine) waterschildpad *n.*

terrestrial, *a.* aards; aard ...

terrible, *a.,* ~**bly,** *adv.* vreselijk, verschrikkelijk.

terrier, *n.* terrier *n.*

terrific, *a.,* ~**ally,** *adv.* schrikwekkend; verschrikkelijk. **terrify,** *v.t.* schrik *n.* aanjagen *str.;* met schrik *n.* vervullen.

territorial, *a.* territoriaal. ¶ *n.* soldaat *n.* van het territoriale leger. **territory,** *n.* (grond) gebied *n.n.*

terror, *n.* schrik *n.,* vrees *n.,* angst *n.;* terreur *n.,* schrikbewind *n.n.* **terrorism,** *n.* terrorisme *n.;* schrikbewind *n.n.* **terrorist,** *n.* terrorist *n.* **terrorize,** *v.t.* terroriseren, schrik *n.* aanjagen *str.*

terse, *a.,* ~**ly,** *adv.* kort en bondig.

tertian, *a.* derdedaags, anderdaags. **tertiary,** *a.* tertiair.

tesselated, *a.* mozaïek; betegeld.

test, *v.t.* toefsen; op de proef stellen; testen, keuren. ¶ *n.* proef *n.*; test *n.*, keuring *n. to put to the ~,* op de proef stellen; *~ match,* bekerwedstrijd *n.; ~ paper,* reageerpapier *n.n.;* proefwerk *n.n.; ~ tube,* reageerbuis *n.*

testacean, *n.* schaaldier *n.n.* **testaceous,** *a.* schaal . . . , schelp . . .

testament, *n.* testament *n.n.* **testamentary,** *a.* testamentair. **testator,** *n.* erflater *n.*

testatrix, *n.* erflaatster *n.*

tester, *n.* keurder *n.;* hemel *n.* *(bed).*

test-flight, *n.* proefvlucht *n.*

testicle, *n.* teelbal *n.*

testifier, *n.* getuige *n.* **testify,** *v.i.* getuigen, getuigenis *n.* afleggen. ¶ *v.t.* betuigen, plechtig verklaren.

testimonial, *n.* getuigschrift *n.n.* **testimony,** *n.* getuigenis *n.*

testiness, *n.* wreveligheid *n.* **testy,** *a.,* ~ily, *adv.* wrevelig, prikkelbaar.

tetanus, *n.* tetanus *n.,* klem *n.*

tether, *v.t.* vastbinden *str.,* tuieren. ¶ *n.* tuier *n.* *to be at the end of one's ~,* niet meer kunnen *irr.*

tetra, *prefix* vier . . . , tetra . . .

text, *n.* tekst *n.* **textbook,** *n.* leerboek *n.n.*

textile, *a.* geweven, textiel. ¶ *n.* textielstof *n.*

textual, *a.* tekstueel; letterlijk, woordelijk.

texture, *n.* weefsel *n.n.;* bouw *n.*

Thames, *N.* Theems *N.*

than, *c.* dan.

thank, *v.t.* danken, bedanken. *~ you,* alstublieft; *no, ~ you,* dank U; *~ God,* God zij dank *n.* ¶ *n.* ~s, dank *n.* **thankful,** *a.,* ~ly, *adv.* dankbaar. **thankless,** *a.* ondankbaar. **thanksgiving,** *n.* dankzegging *n. T~ Day,* Dankdag *N.*

that, *pron.* die; dat. *after ~,* daarna; *before ~,* daarvoor; *all ~,* dat alles; *~'s ~,* dat is in orde; *like ~,* zó; *in ~ . . . ,* in zover als . . . ¶ *adv.* zo. *~ far,* zover. ¶ *c.* dat; opdat.

thatch, *n.* dakstro *n.n.,* riet *n.n.* ¶ *v.t.* met riet dekken. *~ed roof,* rieten dak *n.n.* **thatcher,** *n.* rietdekker *n.*

thaw, *v.imp.* dooien. ¶ *v.i.* loskomen *irr.* ¶ *v.t.* ontdooien. ¶ *n.* dooi *n.*

the, *def.art.* de, het. ¶ *adv. ~ sooner ~ better,* des te gauwer des te beter; *~ more so because,* te meer omdat.

theatre, *n.* schouwburg *n.;* toneel *n.n.* **theatrical,** *a.* theatraal; toneel . . . ¶ *n.* ~s, toneelvoorstelling *n.*

thee, *pron.* U.

theft, *n.* diefstal *n.*

their, *pron.* hun. **theirs,** *pron.* de hunne; het hunne.

them, *pron.* hen; hun *(to them);* ze.

theme, *n.* thema *n.n.*

themselves, *pron.* zich; zichzelf; zelf.

then, *adv.* dan, toen; destijds. *before ~,*

voordien; *from ~ onwards,* van toen af aan; *till ~,* tot dan; *not until ~,* toen pas; *~ and there,* op staande voet; *now and ~,* nu en dan. ¶ *c.* dan, dus. *~ why did he . . . ,* maar waarom heeft hij dan . . . ¶ *a.* toenmalig. **thence,** *adv.* daarvandaan; vandaar.

theocracy, *n.* Godsbestuur *n.n.* **theocratic,** *a.* theocratisch.

theodolite, *n.* theodoliet *n.*

theologian, *n.* theoloog *n.,* godgeleerde *n.* **theological,** *a.* theologisch. **theology,** *n.* theologie *n.,* godgeleerdheid *n.*

theorem, *n.* theorema *n.n.,* stelling *n.*

theoretical, *a.,* ~ly, *adv.* theoretisch. **theorize,** *v.i.* theoretiseren. **theorist,** *n.* theoreticus *n.* **theory,** *n.* theorie *n.*

theosophy, *n.* theosophie *n.*

therapeutic, *a.* therapeutisch. ¶ *n.* ~s, therapie *n.* **therapy,** *n.* therapie *n.*

there, *adv.* daar; er; daarheen. *~ and back,* heen en weer; *~ you are!,* ziedaar!; klaar is Kees. **thereabouts,** *adv.* in die buurt *n.* **thereafter,** *adv.* daarna. **thereby,** *adv.* daarbij; daardoor. **therefore,** *adv.* daarom, derhalve, dus. **thereof,** *adv.* daarvan.

therm, *n.* warmteëenheid *n.* **thermal,** *a.* warmte . . . *~ baths,* hete bronbaden *pl.n.n.* **thermic,** *a.* warmte . . .

thermometer, *n.* thermometer *n.*

thermos-flask, *n.* thermosfles *n.*

these, *pron.* deze.

thesis, *n.* thesis *n.,* stelling *n.*

they, *pron.* zij; ze. *~ say,* men zegt.

thick, *a.,* ~ly, *adv.* dik; dicht. *~ as thieves,* dikke vrienden *pl.n.* ¶ *adv. ~ and fast,* in groten getale. ¶ *n.* dikke *n.n.;* dikte *n. through ~ and thin,* door dik *n.n.* en dun *n.n.* **thicken,** *v.t.* verdikken, dik(ker) maken. ¶ *v.i.* dik(ker) worden *str.;* dichter worden *str.;* nevelig worden *str. the plot ~s,* de verwikkelingen *pl.n.* nemen *str.* toe.

thicket, *n.* kreupelbos *n.n.*

thick-headed, *a.* dom. **thickish,** *a.* nogal dik, dikachtig. **thickness,** *n.* dikte *n.* **thickset,** *a.* gedrongen. **thickskinned,** *a.* dikhuidig; ongevoelig.

thief, *n.* dief *n.* **thieve,** *v.i.* dieven. **thievery,** *n.* dieverij *n.,* diefstal *n.* **thievish,** *a.* diefachtig.

thigh, *n.* dij *n.*

thimble, *n.* vingerhoed *n.*

thin, *a.,* ~ly, *adv.* dun; mager; ijl. ¶ *v.t.* verdunnen. ¶ *v.i.* dun worden *str.*

thine, *pron.* de Uwe; het Uwe; de Uwen *pl.*

thing, *n.* ding *n.n.;* zaak *n. not a ~,* niets; *a ~ or two,* het een en ander; *another ~,* iets ander; *first ~ to-morrow,* het eerste wat ik morgen doe; *a good ~ too,* maar goed ook; *the great ~,* waar het op aankomt; *the latest ~,* het laatste snufje; *such a ~,* zo iets; *my ~s,* m'n spullen *pl.n.n.*

think, *v.i.* denken *irr.;* menen. *to ~ much of,*

een hoog idee *n.n.* hebben van. ¶ *v.t.*
vinden *str.*; geloven, menen. **thinker**, *n.*
denker *n.* **thinking**, *a.* denkend. ¶ *n.*
denken *n.n.* *way of* ~, denkwijze *n.*,
mening *n.*
third, *a.* derde. ~ *best*, op twee na de beste.
¶ *n.* derde *n.* or *n.n.*, derde deel *n.n.*;
terts *n.* (*music*).
thirst, *n.* dorst *n.* ¶ *v.i.* dorsten. *to* ~ *for* or
after, dorsten naar. **thirsty**, *a.*, ~**ily**, *adv.*
dorstig.
thirteen, *num.* dertien. **thirteenth**, *a.* der-
tiende.
thirtieth, *a.* dertigste. **thirty**, *num.* dertig.
this, *pron.* dit; deze. *like* ~, zó; *to* ~ *day*,
tot op heden.
thistle, *n.* distel *n.* **thistledown**, *n.* distel-
pluis *n.n.*
thither, *adv.* derwaarts.
thole, *n.* dol *n.*, roeipen *n.*
thong, *n.* riem *n.*
thorax, *n.* borstkas *n.*
thorn, *n.* doorn *n.*; doornstruik *n.* **thorn-
apple**, *n.* doornappel *n.* **thorny**, *a.* doornig,
doornachtig.
thorough, *a.* grondig; flink; doortastend;
doortrapt (*unfavourable*); door en door.
thoroughbred, *a.* volbloed. ¶ *n.* volbloed *n.*
thoroughfare, *n.* doorgang *n.* *no* ~, voor het
verkeer gesloten.
thoroughgoing, *a.* radikaal. **thoroughness**, *n.*
grondigheid *n.*; doortastendheid *n.*
those, *pron.* die. ~ *who*, zij die.
thou, *pron.* gij.
though, *c.* ofschoon, (al)hoewel, al. *as* ~,
alsof; *even* ~, zelfs al. ¶ *adv.* toch;
trouwens; echter, evenwel.
thought, *n.* gedachte *n.*; denken *n.n.*; ietsje
n.n. (*little*); opinie *n.* *to give it a* ~, er
over denken *irr.*; *lost in* ~, in gedachten
pl.n. verdiept; *at the* ~ *of*, bij de gedachte
aan. **thoughtful**, *a.*, ~**ly**, *adv.* nadenkend;
bedachtzaam; attent. ~ *of*, bedacht op;
attent voor. **thoughtless**, *a.*, ~**ly**, *adv.*
onnadenkend; onbezonnen.
thousand, *num.* duizend. **thousandfold**, *a.*
duizendvoudig. ¶ *n.* duizendvoud *n.n.*
thousandth, *a.* duizendste. ¶ *n.* duizendste
deel *n.n.*
thraldom, *n.* slavernij *n.* **thrall**, *n.* slaaf *n.*
thrash, *v.t.* dorsen; afranselen. *to* ~ *something out*, iets uitvoerig behandelen. ¶ *v.i.*
in 't ronde slaan *irr.* **thrasher**, *n.* dorser *n.*;
dorsmachine *n.*; zeevos *n.* (*shark*). **thrashing**, *n.* dorsen *n.n.*; pak *n.n.* slaag.
thread, *n.* draad *n.*; garen *n.n.* ¶ *v.t.* rijgen *str.*;
een schroefdraad *n.* trekken *str.* in. *to* ~ *a
needle*, de draad door de naald steken *str.*;
to ~ *one's way*, zich een weg *n.* banen.
threadbare, *a.* kaal, versleten.
threat, *n.* bedreiging *n.*; dreigement *n.n.*
threaten, *v.t.* bedreigen; dreigen met.
¶ *v.i. to* ~ *with*, dreigen met.
three, *num.* drie. **three-cornered**, *a.* driekantig.

~ *hat*, steek *n.* **three-decker**, *n.* driedekker
n. **threefold**, *a.* drievoudig. ¶ *n.* drievoud
n.n. **threepence**, *n.* drie stuivers *pl.n.*
three-ply, *n.* triplex *n.n.* **three-score**, *a.*
zestig.
threshold, *n.* drempel *n.*
thrice, *adv.* driemaal.
thrift, *n.* spaarzaamheid *n.*; grasanjelier *n.*
thriftless, *a.* verkwistend. **thrifty**, *a.*, ~**ily**,
adv. spaarzaam.
thrill, *v.t.* aangrijpen *str.*, opwinden *str.* ¶ *n.*
sensatie *n.*; opwindend gevoel *n.n.* **thriller**,
n. sensatieroman *n.*; sensatiestuk *n.n.*
thrilling, *a.* aangrijpend, opwindend.
thrive, *v.i.* gedijen, tieren; floreren. **thriving**,
a. bloeiend, voorspoedig.
throat, *n.* keel *n.*; strot *n.* *to clear one's* ~,
zich de keel schrapen; *to cut one's* ~, zich
de keel afsnijden *str.*; *to cut one's own* ~,
zichzelf ruïneren. **throaty**, *a.* schor.
throb, *v.i.* kloppen, bonzen; stampen, trillen
(*engine*). ¶ *n.* klopping *n.*
throes, *pl.n.* barensweeën *pl.n.n.*, barensnood *n.* *in the* ~ *of*, in het midden van.
throne, *n.* troon *n.* ¶ *v.i.* tronen.
throng, *n.* gedrang *n.n.*, menigte *n.* ¶ *v.i.*
zich verdringen *str.* in.
throstle, *n.* lijster *n.*
throttle, *n.* strot *n.*; smoorklep *n.* (*engine*).
¶ *v.t.* worgen.
through, *prep.* door; doorheen. ¶ *adv.* door;
tot het einde toe. *to be wet* ~, doornat
zijn. ¶ *a.* doorgaand. **throughout**, *adv.*
geheel en al, door en door, in alle opzichten.
¶ *prep.* door heel. ~ *the day*, de hele dag
door.
throw, *v.t.* gooien, werpen *str.*; draaien
(*potter's clay*). *to* ~ *a bridge across*, een
brug *n.* slaan *irr.* over; *to* ~ *off*, van zich
afwerpen *str.*; uittrekken *str.*; *to* ~ *over*,
overboord gooien; *to* ~ *up*, opwerpen *str.*;
uitbraken; laten *str.* varen. ¶ *v.r. to* ~
oneself on, zich werpen *str.* op, zich storten
op. ¶ *n.* worp *n.*, gooi *n.* **throwback**, *n.*
atavistische terugkeer *n.*
thrush, *n.* lijster *n.*
thrust, *v.t.* stoten *str.*, steken *str.*; duwen.
¶ *v.r. to* ~ *oneself upon*, zich opdringen
str. aan. ¶ *n.* stoot *n.*, steek *n.*; duw *n.*
thud, *n.* plof *n.*, doffe slag *n.*
thumb, *n.* duim *n.* *to be all* ~s, vreselijk
onhandig zijn. ¶ *v.t.* beduimelen. **thumb-
nail**, *n.* nagel *n.* van de duim. ~ *sketch*,
penkrabbeltje *n.n.* **thumb-screw**, *n.*
vleugelschroef *n.*; duimschroef *n.* **thumb-
stall**, *n.* duimeling *n.*
thump, *v.t.* bonzen; slaan *irr.* op. ¶ *n.* bons
n., bonk *n.* **thumping**, *a.* reusachtig,
kolossaal.
thunder, *n.* donder *n.*, onweer *n.n.* ¶ *v.imp.*
donderen, onweren. ¶ *v.i.* bulderen.
thunderbolt, *n.* bliksemflits *n.* **thunderclap**,
n. donderslag *n.* **thundering**, *a.* donders;
kolossaal. **thunderstorm**, *n.* onweer *n.n.*,

onweersbui *n.* **thunderstruck**, *a.* (als) door
de bliksem getroffen; (*fig.*) verbaasd.
thurible, *n.* wierookvat *n.n.*
Thursday, *N.* donderdag *N. Holy* ~, Witte
Donderdag.
thus, *adv.* zo; dus, aldus; ~ *far*, tot zover.
thwack, *n.* pats *n.*
thwart, *v.t.* dwarsbomen. ¶ *n.* doft *n.* (*boat*).
thy, *pron.* Uw.
thyme, *n.* tijm *n.*
thyself, *pron.* U, Uzelf.
tiara, *n.* tiara *n.*
Tibet, *N.* Thibet *n.N.* **Tibetan**, *a.* van Thibet.
tibia, *n.* scheenbeen *n.n.*
tic, *n.* zenuwtrekking *n.*
tick, *v.i.* tikken. ¶ *v.t. to* ~ *off*, aanstippen;
(*fig.*) berispen, een standje *n.n.* geven *str.*
¶ *n.* tik *n.*; streepje *n.n.* (*mark*); teek *n.*
(*mite*); tijk *n.* (*cover*). *on* ~, op de pof.
ticker, *n.* tikker *n.*
ticket, *n.* etiket *n.n.* (*label*); kaartje *n.n.*
(*travel*); plaatsbewijs *n.n.* (*show*). **ticket-
collector**, *n.* controleur *n.* **ticket-office**,
n. plaatskaartenbureau *n.n.* **ticket-punch**,
n. kaartjestang *n.*
ticking, *n.* tikken *n.n.*, getik *n.n.*
tickle, *v.t.* kietelen; prikkelen. ¶ *v.i.* kietelen,
kriebelen. *to be* ~*d by*, geamuseerd worden
str. door. **ticklish**, *a.* kittelachtig; netelig,
delicaat.
tidal, *a.* getij . . . ~ *wave*, vloedgolf *n.*
tide, *n.* getij *n.n.*, tij *n.n.*; stroom *n.*;
seizoen *n.n.* *high* ~, hoog tij *n.n.*, hoog-
water *n.n.*; *low* ~, laag tij *n.n.*, laagwater
n.n. ¶ *v.i.* met de stroom drijven *str.*
¶ *v.t. to* ~ *over*, dóórkomen *irr.*
tidiness, *n.* netheid *n.*, ordelijkheid *n.*
tidings, *pl.n.* tijding *n.*, bericht *n.n.*
tidy, *a.*, ~**ily**, *adv.* net, netjes; behoorlijk,
flink, aardig. ¶ *v.t.* opruimen, aan kant
maken.
tie, *v.t.* binden *str.*; knopen; meren (*ship*).
to ~ *down*, vastbinden *str.*; beperken;
to ~ *up*, opbinden *str.*, bijeenbinden *str.*;
verwarren. ¶ *n.* band *n.*; das *n.*
tier, *n.* rij *n.*
tiff, *n.* ruzietje *n.n.* ¶ *v.i.* kibbelen.
tiffin, *n.* lunch *n*
tiger, *n.* tijger *n.* **tigerish**, *a.* tijgerachtig.
tiger-lily, *n.* tijgerlelie *n.*
tight, *a.*, ~**ly**, *adv.* nauw; strak; dicht;
aangeschoten. *it is a* ~ *fit*, het zit erg
krap; *to be in a* ~ *corner*, in het nauw
zitten. **tighten**, *v.t.* aanhalen; verscherpen.
tight-fitting, *a.* nauwsluitend. **tightlaced**, *a.*
puriteins. **tightness**, *n.* nauwheid *n.*
tights, *pl.n.* spanbroek *n.*; tricot *n.n.*
tigress, *n.* tijgerin *n.*
tile, *n.* tegel *n.*; dakpan *n.* ¶ *v.t.* betegelen;
met pannen *pl.n.* dekken. **tile-burner**, *n.*
pannenbakker *n.* **tiler**, *n.* pannendekker *n.*
till, *n.* geldla *n.* ¶ *prep.* tot, tot aan. ¶ *c.*
tot(dat). ¶ *v.t.* bebouwen, bewerken.
tillage, *n.* akkerbouw *n.*

tiller, *n.* akkerman *n.*; helmstok *n.* (*of
rudder*); uitloper *n.*, scheut *n.* (*plant*).
tilt, *v.i.* overhellen; toernooien. ¶ *v.t.* doen
irr. overhellen; schuin zetten; doen *irr.*
kantelen. ¶ *n.* overhelling *n. at full* ~,
in volle vaart *n.*
tilth, *n.* bebouwing *n.*; akkerbouw *n.*
tilting-wagon, *n.* kipkar *n.*
timbal, *n.* pauk *n.*
timber, *n.* timmerhout *n.n.*; bomen *pl.n.*
¶ *v.t.* met hout *n.n.* beschieten *str.* **timber-
merchant**, *n.* houtkoopman *n.* **timber-
yard**, *n.* houttuin *n.*; houtloods *n.*
time, *n.* tijd *n.*; maat *n.*, tempo *n.n. two* ~*s
three*, twee keer drie, twee maal drie;
what is the ~?, hoe laat is het?; *to pass the
~ of day*, elkaar een woordje *n.n.* spreken
str.; ~ *and* ~ *again*, telkens weer; *all
the* ~, de hele tijd; *at a* ~, tegelijk; *at
one* ~, vroeger; *at* ~*s*, soms; *by this* ~, nu;
by that ~, dan; *for a* ~, een tijdlang;
in ~, op tijd; *in due* ~, te zijner tijd;
in good ~, bijtijds; *to* ~, precies op tijd.
¶ *v.t.* de duur bepalen van, timen; stellen,
reguleren. ¶ *v.r. to* ~ *oneself*, nagaan *irr.*
hoeveel tijd *n.* men nodig heeft. **time-
keeper**, *n.* uurwerk *n.*; chronometer *n.*;
tijdopnemer *n.* **timely**, *a.* tijdig; te gele-
gener tijd *n.* (komend). ~ *joke*, grapje *n.n.*
op zijn tijd *n.* **timepiece**, *n.* uurwerk *n.n.*
timeserver, *n.* ja-broer *n.* **timetable**, *n.*
dienstregeling *n.* **time-worn**, *a.* aloud.
timid, *a.*, ~**ly**, *adv.* beschroomd, bedeesd.
timidity, *n.* beschroomdheid *n.*, bedeesdheid *n.* **timorous**, *a.* vreesachtig; angstvallig.
tin, *n.* tin *n.n.*; blik *n.n.*; blikje *n.n.*, busje *n.*
¶ *v.t.* vertinnen; in blik *n.n.* inmaken.
tincture, *n.* tinctuur *n.*
tinder, *n.* tondel *n.n.* **tinder-box**, *n.*
tondeldoos *n.*
tinfoil, *n.* bladtin *n.n.*, stanniool *n.n.*
tinge, *n.* tint *n.*; tikje *n.n.* ¶ *v.t.* tinten.
tingle, *v.i.* tintelen.
tinker, *n.* ketellapper *n.* ¶ *v.i.* prutsen.
tinkle, *v.i.* rinkelen, tingelen. ¶ *n.* gerinkel
n.n., getingel *n.n.*
tin-opener, *n.* blikkenmesje *n.n.* **tin-plate**, *n.*
blik *n.n.*
tinsel, *n.* klatergoud *n.n.*
tint, *n.* tint *n.*, kleur *n.* ¶ *v.t.* tinten, kleuren.
tin-tack, *n.* spijkertje *n.n.*
tiny, *a.* heel klein.
tip, *n.* tipje *n.n.*, puntje *n.n.*; spits *n.*; fooi *n.*
(*money*); wenk *n.* (*hint*); vuilnisbelt *n.*
(*refuse*). ¶ *v.t.* van een punt *n.* voorzien
irr.; een fooi geven *str.*; een wenk geven
str.; doen *irr.* kantelen, schuin zetten.
to ~ *the scales*, de schaal doen *irr.* door-,
slaan; *to* ~ *over*, omkippen; *to* ~ *up*,
opwippen. **tip-cart**, *n.* kipkar *n.*
tippet, *n.* bonten kraag *n.*
tipple, *v.i.* pimpelen. ¶ *n.* borreltje *n.n.*
tippler, *n.* pimpelaar *n.*

tipstaff, *n.* (beslagen) staf *n.*

tipsy, *a.* aangeschoten.

tiptoe, *v.i.* op de tenen *pl.n.* lopen *str.* ¶ *n. on* ~, op de tenen.

tiptop, *a.* prima.

tirade, *n.* tirade *n.*, uitval *n.*

tire, *v.i.* moe worden *str.* ¶ *v.t.* vermoeien. *to* ~ *out*, afmatten. **tired**, *a.* moe, vermoeid. **tiredness**, *n.* vermoeidheid *n.* **tiresome**, *a.* vervelend.

tissue, *n.* weefsel *n.n.* **tissue-paper**, *n.* zijdepapier *n.n.*

tit, *n.* meesje *n.n.* (*bird*); borst *n.* ~ *for tat*, lap om leer. **titbit**, *n.* lekkernijtje *n.n.*

tithe, *n.* tiende *n.*

titillate, *v.t.* prikkelen. **titillation**, *n.* prikkeling *n.*

titlark, *n.* graspieper *n.*

title, *n.* titel *n.*; eigendomsbewijs *n.n.* ¶ *v.t.* betitelen, tituleren. **title-deed**, *n.* eigendomsbewijs *n.n.* **titlepage**, *n.* titelblad *n.n.*

titmouse, *n.* mees *n.*

titter, *v.i.* giechelen.

tittle, *n.* tittel *n. jot or* ~, tittel of jota *n.* **tittle-tattle**, *n.* gebabbel *n.n.*; geklets *n.n.* ¶ *v.i.* babbelen; kletsen.

titular, *a.* titulair. ¶ *n.* titularis *n.*

to, *prep.* naar; naar ... toe; tot, tot aan, tot op; voor; bij; om, om te. ¶ *particle.* te. ¶ *adv.* toe, dicht. ~ *and fro*, heen en weer.

toad, *n.* pad *n.* **toadstool**, *n.* paddestoel *n.* **toady**, *n.* pluimstrijker *n.*

toast, *n.* toast *n.*, heildronk *n.*; geroosterd brood *n.n. to have a person on* ~, iemand te pakken hebben. ¶ *v.t.* toasten op (*drink*); roosteren (*bread*); warmen. **toasting-fork**, *n.* roostervork *n.*

tobacco, *n.* tabak *n.* ~ *pouch*, tabakzak *n.* **tobacconist**, *n.* sigarenhandelaar *n.* **tobacconist's**, *n.* tabakswinkel *n.*

toboggan, *n.* tobogansiede *n.*

tocsin, *n.* alarmklok *n.*

to-day, *adv.* vandaag; heden.

toddle, *v.i.* waggelen. **toddler**, *n.* kleuter *n.*

toddy, *n.* grok *n.*

to-do, *n.* drukte *n.*

toe, *n.* teen *n.* ¶ *v.t. to* ~ *the line*, bij de streep gaan *irr.* staan; (*fig.*) doen *irr.* zoals de anderen.

toff, *n.* fijne meneer *n.*

toffee, *n.* toffee *n.*

tog, *v.i. to* ~ *up*, uitdossen. ¶ *n.* ~s, plunje *n.*

together, *adv.* samen, tezamen; bijeen, bij elkaar.

toggle, *n.* pin *n.* **toggle-bolt**, *n.* schuifbout *n.*

toil, *v.i.* zwoegen; hard werken. *to* ~ *and moil*, werken en zwoegen. ¶ *n.* gezwoeg *n.n.*; hard werk *n.n. in the* ~*s of*, verstrikt door. **toiler**, *n.* zwoeger *n.*

toilet, *n.* toilet *n.n.* **toilet-case**, *n.* nécessaire *n.* **toilet-paper**, *n.* closetpapier *n.n.* **toilet-table**, *n.* toilettafel *n.*, kaptafel *n.*

token, *n.* teken *n.n.*; blijk *n.n.*; aandenken *n.n.*; rekenmunt *n.*

tolerable, *a.*, ~bly, *adv.* dragelijk, duldbaar. **tolerance**, *n.* verdraagzaamheid *n.*; gehardheid *n.*, verdragen *n.n.* (*medicine*). **tolerant**, *a.* verdraagzaam. **tolerate**, *v.t.* verdragen *str.*; dulden.

toll, *n.* tol *n.*; tolgeld *n.n. to take* ~ *of*, tol heffen *str.* van. ¶ *v.t. & v.i.* luiden, kleppen. **toll-free**, *a.* tolvrij.

tomato, *n.* tomaat *n.*

tomb, *n.* graf *n.n.*: graftombe *n.*

tomboy, *n.* robbedoes, *n.*

tombstone, *n.* grafsteen *n.*, zerk *n.*

tom-cat, *n.* kater *n.*

tome, *n.* boekdeel *n.n.*

tomfoolery, *n.* poppenkasterij *n.*

tommy-gun, *n.* handmitrailleur *n.*

tommy-rot, *n.* nonsens *n.*

to-morrow, *adv.* morgen. *the day after* ~, overmorgen.

tomtit, *n.* koolmees *n.*

tomtom, *n.* tamtam *n.*

ton, *n.* ton *n.* ... *register* ~*s*, ... registerton *n.*; ... *gross* ~*s*, ... bruto registerton *n.*; ... ~*s deadweight*, laadvermogen *n.n.* van ... ton: *metric* ~, ton van 1.000 K.G.; *long* ~, 2.400 Engelse ponden *pl.n.n.*; *short* ~, 2.240 Engelse ponden *pl.n.n.*

tonal, *a.* toon ... **tonality**, *n.* tonaliteit *n.*, toonaard *n.* **tone**, *n.* toon *n.*; klank *n.*; geest *n.*, stemming *n.*; tonus *n.* (*medical*). *in a low* ~, op zachte toon. ¶ *v.i.* harmoniëren. ¶ *v.t. to* ~ *down*, temperen, verzachten.

tongs, *pl.n.* tang *n. pair of* ~, tang *n.*

tongue, *n.* tong *n.*; taal *n.*, spraak *n.* ~ *of land*, landtong *n.*; *to give* ~, aanslaan *irr.*; *to hold one's* ~, z'n mond *n.* houden *irr.*; *with one's* ~ *in one's cheek*, ironisch. **tongue-tied**, *a.* sprakeloos, met de mond vol tanden *pl.n.* **tongue-twister**, *n.* moeilijk uit te spreken woord *n.n.*

tonic, *a.* tonisch. ¶ *n.* tonicum *n.n.*, versterkend middel *n.n.*; grondtoon *n.*

to-night, *adv.* vanavond; deze nacht *n.*

tonnage, *n.* tonnemaat *n.*, scheepsruimte *n.*; tonnegeld *n.n.*

tonsil, *n.* amandel *n.* **tonsilitis**, *n.* amandelontsteking *n.*

tonsure, *n.* tonsuur *n.*

too, *adv.* ook, eveneens; te, al te.

tool, *n.* werktuig *n.n.* ~*s*, gereedschap *n.n.* ¶ *v.t.* bewerken. **tool-box**, *n.* gereedschapskist *n.* **tooling**, *n.* stempels *pl.n.n.*

toot, *v.i.* toeteren, blazen *str.*

tooth, *n.* tand *n.*; kies *n.* ~ *and nail*, met hand *n.* en tand; *artificial teeth*, kunstgebit *n.n.*; *in the teeth of*, trots, tegen ... in. **toothache**, *n.* tandpijn *n.*, kiespijn *n.* **toothbrush**, *n.* tandenborstel *n.* **toothless**, *a.* tandeloos. **toothpaste**, *n.* tandpasta *n.* **toothpick**, *n.* tandenstoker *n.* **toothsome**, *a.* smakelijk.

top, *n.* top *n.*; toppunt *n.*; kruin *n.*, spits *n.*; hoofd *n.n. at the* ~, bovenaan; *at the* ~ *of one's voice*, luidkeels; *from* ~ *to bottom*, van boven tot onder; *on* ~, bovenop; bovendien. ¶ *a.* bovenste. ¶ *v.t.* overtreffen *str.*; uitsteken *str.* boven; aftoppen. *to* ~ *the poll*, de meeste stemmen hebben.

topaz, *n.* topaas *n.*

top-boot, *n.* kaplaars *n.* **top-coat**, *n.* overjas *n.* **top-dog**, *n.* winnaar *n.* **top-dressing**, *n.* bovenmest *n.*

tope, *v.i.* pimpelen. **toper**, *n.* pimpelaar *n.*

topee, *n.* (helm)hoed *n.*

top-gallant (mast), *n.* bramstong *n.* **top-gallant sail**, *n.* bramzeil *n.n.* **top-hat**, *n.* hoge hoed *n.* **top-heavy**, *a.* topzwaar.

topic, *n.* onderwerp *n.n.* **topical**, *a.*, ~ly, *adv.* actueel.

topmast, *n.* steng *n.* **topmost**, *a.* bovenste, hoogste.

topographer, *n.* topograaf *n.* **topographic**, *a.* topografisch. **topography**, *n.* topografie *n.*

topper, *n.* (*coll.*) hoge hoed *n.*

topping, *a.* heerlijk.

topple, *v.i.* omvallen *str. to* ~ *over*, voorover vallen *str.*

topsail, *n.* marszeil *n.n.*

topsyturvy, *a.* ondersteboven.

torch, *n.* toorts *n.*, fakkel *n. electric* ~, zaklantaarn *n.*

torment, *v.t.* kwellen, plagen. ¶ *n.* kwelling *n.* **tormentor**, *n.* kwelgeest *n.*, plager *n.*

tornado, *n.* tornado *n.*, wervelstorm *n.*

torpedo, *n.* torpedo *n.* ¶ *v.t.* torpederen. **torpedo-boat**, *n.* torpedoboot *n.* (torpedo-boat)-destroyer, *n.* torpedojager *n.* **torpedo-tube**, *n.* torpedolanceerbuis *n.*

torpid, *a.* loom, traag. **torpor**, *n.* loomheid *n.*, traagheid *n.*

torrefaction, *n.* uitdroging *n.* **torrefy**, *v.t.* uitdrogen.

torrent, *n.* bergstroom *n.*; stortvloed *n.* **torrential**, *a.* in stromen *pl.n.* neerkomend; onstuimig.

torrid, *a.* verzengend; heet.

torsion, *n.* torsie *n.*, wringing *n.*

torsk, *n.* dors *n.*

torso, *n.* torso *n.n.*; romp *n.*

tort, *n.* ongelijk *n.n.*

tortoise, *n.* schildpad *n.* **tortoiseshell**, *n.* schildpad *n.n.* ¶ *a.* schildpadden.

tortuous, *a.* kronkelig; met omwegen *pl.n.*

torture, *n.* marteling *n.*, foltering *n.* ¶ *v.t.* martelen, folteren. **torturer**, *n.* folteraar *n.*; beul *n.*

Tory, *N.* Conservatief *n.* ¶ *a.* Conservatief.

tosh, *n.* (*coll.*) onzin *n.*

toss, *v.t.* werpen *str.*; heen en weer slingeren. *to* ~ *up*, omhooggooien. ¶ *v.i.* woelen; opgooien. *to* ~ *up for it*, er om opgooien. ¶ *n.* worp *n.* **toss up**, *n. it's a* ~, 't is een dubbeltje *n.n.* op z'n kant *n.*

tot, *n.* borreltje *n.* (*glass*); peuter *n.* (*child*);

optelling *n.* (*addition*). ¶ *v.t. to* ~ *up*, optellen.

total, *a.* totaal, (ge)heel; volslagen. ¶ *n.* totaal *n.n.*; totaal bedrag *n.n.* ¶ *v.t.* optellen. ¶ *v.i.* een totaal *n.n.* vormen, bedragen *str.* **totally**, *adv.* totaal; volslagen, geheel en al. **totality**, *n.* totaal *n.n.* **totalizator**, *n.* totalisator *n.* **totalize**, *v.t.* een totaal *n.n.* maken (van).

tote, *n. See* totalizator. ¶ *v.t.* sjouwen.

totem, *n.* totem *n.*

totter, *v.i.* wankelen.

touch, *v.t.* raken, aanraken; betreffen *str.* (*concern*); roeren, aandoen *irr.* (*move*); innen, toucheren (*money*). *don't* ~ *it*, kom er niet aan; ~ *wood!*, even afkloppen!; *to* ~ *up*, bijwerken. ¶ *v.i.* elkaar raken. *it was* ~ *and go*, het was net op 't nippertje; *to* ~ *at . . .*, aandoen *irr.* ¶ *n.* aanraking *n.*; aanslag *n.* (*music*); tikje *n.n.* (*little*). *in* ~, in voeling *n.* **touchiness**, *n.* lichtgeraaktheid *n.* **touching**, *a.* roerend, aandoenlijk. **touchline**, *n.* zijlijn *n.* **touchstone**, *n.* toetssteen *n.* **touchy**, *a.*, ~ily, *adv.* lichtgeraakt; gevoelig.

tough, *a.*, ~ly, *adv.* taai; lastig. ¶ *n.* ruwe klant *n.* **toughen**, *v.t.* taai maken; harden. ¶ *v.i.* taai worden *str.* **toughness**, *n.* taaiheid *n.*

tour, *n.* toer *n.*, rondreis *n.* ¶ *v.t.* afreizen. ¶ *v.i.* een rondreis *n.* doen *irr.* **tourism**, *n.* toerisme *n.n.* **tourist**, *n.* toerist *n.* ~ *agency*, reisbureau *n.n.*

tournament, *n.* toernooi *n.n.*

tousle, *v.t.* in wanorde *n.* brengen *irr.* ~*d*, verward.

tout, *v.i.* klanten *pl.n.* werven *str.* ¶ *n.* agent *n.*

tow, *n.* werk *n.n.* (*rope*). *to take in* ~, op sleeptouw nemen *str.* ¶ *v.t.* slepen. **towage**, *n.* sleeploon *n.n.*

toward(s), *prep.* naar . . . toe; tegenover, jegens.

towel, *n.* handdoek *n.* ¶ *v.t.* afdrogen. **towelling**, *n.* handdoekengoed *n.n.*

tower, toren *n. a* ~ *of strength*, een vaste burcht *n.* ¶ *v.i. to* ~ *above* or *over*, hoog uitsteken *str.* boven.

tow-line, *n.* jaaglijn *n.*

town, *n.* stad *n.*; gemeente *n.* **townbred**, *a.* stads . . . **town-clerk**, *n.* gemeentesecretaris *n.* **town-council**, *n.* gemeenteraad *n.* **town-councillor**, *n.* gemeenteraadslid *n.n.* **town-hall**, *n.* stadhuis *n.n.*; raadhuis *n.n.* **town-planning**, *n.* stedenaanleg *n.* **townsfolk**, *pl.n.* stedelingen *pl.n.* **township**, *n.* gemeente *n.*

tow-path, *n.* jaagpad *n.n.* **tow-rope**, *n.* sleeptouw *n.n.*

toxic, *a.* vergiftig. **toxicity**, *n.* vergiftigheid *n.* **toxin**, *n.* toxine *n.*, giftstof *n.*

toxophily, *n.* boogschutterij *n.*

toy, *n.* stuk *n.n.* speelgoed. ~*s*, speelgoed *n.n.* ¶ *v.i.* spelen. ¶ *a.* speelgoed . . .

trace, *n.* spoor *n.n.*; streng *n.* (*rope*). ¶ *v.t.* nasporen, opsporen; traceren, overtrekken *str.*; calqueren. **traceable,** *a.* naspeurbaar. **tracer-shell,** *n.* lichtspoorgranaat *n.* **tracery** *n.* ornamentiek *n.*; netwerk *n.n.*
trachea, *n.* luchtpijp *n.*
tracing, *n.* tracé *n.n.* **tracing-paper,** *n.* calqueerpapier *n.n.*
track, *n.* spoor *n.n.*; baan *n.* *to keep ~ of,* nagaan *irr.*; *to make ~s,* er vandoor gaan *irr.* ¶ *v.t.* volgen, nasporen. **trackless,** *a.* spoorloos; ongebaand.
tract, *n.* uitgestrektheid *n.*; streek *n.*; tractaatje *n.n.*
tractable, *a.* handelbaar, volgzaam, gewillig.
traction, *n.* tractie *n.*; voorttrekking *n.* **tractor,** *n.* tractor *n.*
trade, *n.* handel *n.*; ambacht *n.n.*, bedrijf *n.n.*, vak *n.n.* *Board of T~,* Ministerie *n.N.* van Handel *N.* ¶ *v.i.* handel *n.* drijven *str. to ~ on,* speculeren op. **trademark,** *n.* handelsmerk *n.n.* **trade-price,** *n.* grossiersprijs *n.* **trader,** *n.* handelaar *n.,* koopman *n.* **trade-secret,** *n.* fabrieksgeheim *n.n.* **tradesman,** *n.* winkelier *n.,* neringdoende *n.* **tradespeople,** *pl.n. See* tradesman. **trade union,** *n.* vakvereniging *n.,* vakbond *n.* **trade unionism,** *n.* vakbeweging *n.* **trade unionist,** *n.* aanhanger *n.* van de vakbeweging. **trade-wind,** *n.* passaat *n.* **trading company,** *n.* handelmaatschappij *n.*
tradition, *n.* traditie *n.,* overlevering *n.* **traditional,** *a.* traditioneel.
traduce, *v.t.* belasteren.
traffic, *n.* verkeer *n.n.*; koophandel *n.* ¶ *v.i.* handel *n.* drijven *str.* **trafficker,** *n.* handelaar *n.*
tragedian, *n.* treurspeldichter *n.*; acteur *n.* in treurspelen *pl.n.n.* **tragedy,** *n.* treurspel *n.n.*; tragedie *n.* **tragic,** *a.,* *~ally, adv.* tragisch.
trail, *n.* spoor *n.n.*; pad *n.n.*; sliert *n.* ¶ *v.t.* achterna slepen. ¶ *v.i.* kruipen *str.* (*plant*). **trailer,** *n.* kruipplant *n.*; aanhangwagen *n.*
train, *n.* trein *n.*; sleep *n.*; nasleep *n.* *~ of thought,* gedachtengang *n.*; *by ~,* per spoor; met de trein; *it will bring . . . in its ~,* het zal . . . met zich meeslepen. ¶ *v.i.* oefenen, zich trainen. ¶ *v.t.* oefenen, trainen, opleiden, africhten; leiden (*tree*). **trainer,** *n.* trainer *n.*; dresseur *n.* **train-ferry,** *n.* spoorpont *n.* **training,** *n.* trainen *n.n.*; opleiding *n.* *~ college,* kweekschool *n.*; *~ ship,* opleidingsvaartuig *n.n.* **train-oil,** *n.* walvistraan *n.* **train-service,** *n.* treinenloop *n.* **trainsick,** *a.* wagenziek.
trait, *n.* trek *n.*
traitor, *n.* verrader *n.* **traitorous,** *a.* verraderlijk. **traitress,** *n.* verraadster *n.*
trajectory, *n.* (kogel)baan *n.*
tram, *n.* tram *n.*

trammel, *n.* sleepnet *n.n.* *~s,* kluister *n.,* boei *n.* ¶ *v.t.* kluisteren; belemmeren.
tramp, *n.* landloper *n.*; voetreis *n.,* wandeltocht *n.*; gestamp *n.n.* ¶ *v.i.* rondtrekken *str.*; stampen. **trample** *v.t.* vertrappen. *to ~ something underfoot,* iets met voeten *pl.n.* treden *str.* ¶ *v.i.* trappen. *to ~ upon,* stampen op.
tramway, *n.* tram *n.*
trance, *n.* trance *n.*; schijndood *n.*
tranquil, *a.* rustig, stil. **tranquillity,** *n.* rust *n.,* kalmte *n.* **tranquillize,** *v.t.* tot bedaren *n.n.* brengen *irr.,* kalmeren; geruststellen.
transact, *v.t.* verhandelen, afdoen *irr.* **transaction,** *n.* verhandeling *n.*; transactie *n.* **transactor,** *n.* bemiddelaar *n.*
transalpine, *a.* transalpijns.
transatlantic, *a.* transatlantisch.
transcend, *v.t.* uitsteken *str.* boven. **transcendent,** *a.* voortreffelijk, uitmuntend. **transcendental,** *a.* transcendentaal.
transcribe, *v.t.* kopiëren, overschrijven *str.* **transcript,** *n.,* **transcription,** *n.* kopie *n.,* afschrift *n.n.*
transept, *n.* dwarsschip *n.*
transfer, *v.t.* overdragen *str.,* overbrengen *irr.*; overplaatsen; calqueren. ¶ *n.* overdracht *n.,* overbrenging *n.*; overplaatsing *n.*; calqueerplaatje *n.n.* **transferable,** *a.* verhandelbaar.
transfiguration, *n.* transfiguratie *n.,* gedaanteverwisseling *n.* **transfigure,** *v.t.* van gedaante *n.* doen *irr.* veranderen.
transfix, *v.t.* doorbóren, doorstéken *str. to stand ~ed,* als aan de grond genageld staan *irr.*
transform, *v.t.* vervormen, omvormen; van gedaante *n.* veranderen. **transformation.** *n.* vervorming *n.,* gedaanteverwisseling *n.* **transformer,** *n.* transformator *n.*
transfuse, *v.t.* overgieten *str.*; overbrengen *irr.* **transfusion,** *n.* transfusie *n.*
transgress, *v.t.* overtreden; zondigen tegen. **transgression,** *n.* overtreding *n.* **transgressor,** *n.* overtreder *n.*; zondaar *n.*
transient, *a.* vergankelijk, kortstondig.
transit, *n.* transito *n.n.*; doorgang *n.,* doorvoer *n.* *in ~,* onderweg. **transition,** *n* overgang *n.* **transitional,** *a.* overgangs . . **transitive,** *a.* overgangelijk, transitief **transitoriness,** *n.* vergankelijkheid *n* ransitory, *a.* vergankelijk.
translatable, *a.* vertaalbaar. **translate,** *v.t.* vertalen; overplaatsen (*bishop*). **translation,** *n.* vertaling *n.*; overplaatsing *n* (*bishop*). **translator,** *n.* vertaler *n.*
translucent, *a.* doorschijnend, helder.
transmarine, *a.* overzees.
transmigrate, *v.i.* verhuizen. **transmigration,** *n.* verhuizing *n.* *~ of souls,* zielsverhuizing *n.*
transmissible, *a.* overdraagbaar; overerfelijk. **transmission,** *n.* overbrenging *n.*; overdracht *n.*; uitzending *n.* (*radio*). **transmit**

v.t. overbrengen *irr.*; doorgeven *str.*; uitzenden *str.* (*radio*). **transmitter,** *n.* zendstation *n.n.*, zender *n.*

transmutable, *a.* omzetbaar. **transmutation,** *n.* transmutatie *n.*, vormverandering *n.* **transmute,** *v.t.* omzetten.

transoceanic, *a.* overzeesch.

transom, *n.* dwarsbalk *n.* ~ *window*, raam *n.n.* boven deur *n.*

transparency, *n.* doorzichtigheid *n.* **transparent,** *a.*, ~**ly,** *adv.* doorzichtig, transparant.

transpire, *v.t.* uitwasemen; ruchtbaar worden *str.*

transplant, *v.t.* overplanten.

transport, *v.t.* vervoeren, transporteeren. ~*ed with joy,* verrukt. ¶ *n.* vervoer *n.n.*, transport *n.n.*; transportwezen *n.n.*; vervoering *n.*, verrukking *n.*; transportschip *n.n.* **transportation,** *n.* transportatie *n.*

transpose, *v.t.* omzetten; transponeeren. **transposition,** *n.* omzetting *n.*; transpositie *n.*

transubstantiate, *v.i.* transubstantiatie *n.* ondergaan *irr.* **transubstantiation,** *n.* transubstantiatie *n.*

transverse, *a.*, ~**ly,** *adv.* dwars, transversaal.

trap, *n.* val *n.*; valstrik *n.*; valdeur *n.*, luik *n.n.* ~*s,* bagage *n.* ¶ *v.t.* vangen *str.*; in de val doen *irr.* lopen; optuigen. **trapdoor,** *n.* valluik *n.n.*

trapeze, *n.* zweefrek *n.n.*

trapper, *n.* pelsjager *n.*

trappings, *pl.n.* tooi *n.*; bagage *n.*

trash, *n.* uitschot *n.n.*; prulleboel *n.* **trashy,** *a.* waardeloos, prullerig.

travail, *n.* barensnood *n.*; arbeid *n.*

travel, *v.i.* reizen; zich verplaatsen; zich voortplanten (*waves*). ¶ *v.t.* afreizen, doortrekken *str.* ¶ *n.* reizen *n.n.* ~*s,* reis *n.* **traveller,** *n.* reiziger *n. commercial* ~, handelsreiziger *n.* **travelling,** *a.* reizend; reis . . .

traverse, *v.t.* oversteken *str.*; overtrekken *str.*; doorkruisen. ¶ *n.* dwarsbalk *n.*; traverse *n.* (*military*).

travesty, *n.* travestie *n.*, bespotting *n.* ¶ *v.t.* travesteeren.

trawl, *n.* sleepnet *n.n.*, treil *n.* ¶ *v.i.* treilen. **trawler,** *n.* treiler *n.*

tray, *n.* presenteerblad *n.n.*; bakje *n.n.*

treacherous, *a.*, ~**ly,** *adv.* verraderlijk, bedrieglijk. **treachery,** *n.* verraad *n.n.*

treacle, *n.* stroop *n.* **treacly,** *a.* stroperig.

tread, *v.i.* treden *str. to* ~ *on a person's toes,* iemand op de tenen trappen. ¶ *v.t.* betreden *str.*; trappen. ¶ *n.* tred *n.*, schrede *n.*; hanetred *n.*

treadle, *n.* pedaal *n.*, trapper *n.*

treadmill, *n.* tredmolen *n.*

treason, *n.* verraad *n.n.* **treasonable,** *a.*, ~**bly,** *adv.* verraderlijk.

treasure, *n.* schat *n.* ~ *trove,* gevonden schat

n. ¶ *v.t.* (als een schat) bewaren, in ere houden *irr.* **treasurer,** *n.* penningmeester *n.* **treasurership,** *n.* penningmeesterschap *n.n.* **treasury,** *n.* schatkist *n.* ~ *bill,* schatkistwissel *n.*

treat, *v.t.* behandelen; trakteeren. *to* ~ *oneself to,* zich onthalen op. ¶ *v.i.* onderhandelen. ¶ *n.* onthaal *n.n.*, tractatie *n.*

treatise, *n.* verhandeling *n.* ~ *on,* verhandeling over.

treatment, *n.* behandeling *n.*

treaty, *n.* verdrag *n.n.*, traktaat *n.n.* ~ *port,* verdraghaven *n.*

treble, *a.* drievoudig. ~ *clef,* solsleutel *n.* ¶ *n.* drievoudige *n.*; bovenstem *n.*, sopraan *n.* ¶ *v.t.* verdrievoudigen.

tree, *n.* boom *n.*

trefoil, *n.* klaverblad *n.n.*

trellis, *n.* latwerk *n.n.*, traliewerk *n.n.*

tremble, *v.i.* beven; sidderen. *to* ~ *at,* beven voor, beven bij. **trembling,** *n.* gebeef *n.n.*, rilling *n.*

tremendous, *a.*, ~**ly,** *adv.* geweldig, ontzettend, vreselijk.

tremor, *n.* beving *n.*, trilling *n.* **tremulous,** *a.* beverig; schroomvallig.

trench, *n.* loopgraaf *n.*; sloot *n.*, greppel *n.* ¶ *v.t.* graven *str. to* ~ *down,* inkuilen.

trenchant, *a.* snijdend, scherp.

trencher, *n.* houten schotel *n.* **trencherman,** *n. a good* ~, een duchtig eter *n.*

trend, *n.* richting *n.*, neiging *n.*; stroming *n.*

trepan, *v.t.* trepaneeren. ¶ *n.* schedelboor *n.*

trepidation, *n.* beving *n.*, trilling *n.*; beverigheid *n.*, huiverigheid *n.*

trespass, *v.i.* zich op verboden terrein *n.n.* begeven *str. to* ~ *against,* zondigen tegen; *to* ~ *on,* misbruik *n.n.* maken van; beslag *n.n.* leggen *irr.* op. ¶ *n.* wederrechtelijk betreden *n.n.*; overtreding *n.*; zonde *n.* **trespasser,** *n.* overtreder *n.* ~*s will be prosecuted,* verboden toegang *n.*

tress, *n.* vlecht *n.*

trestle, *n.* schraag *n.*, bok *n.* **trestle-bed,** *n.* veldbed *n.*

trial, *n.* proef *n.*, proefneming *n.*; proeftocht *n.*; gerechtelijk onderzoek *n.n.*, verhoor *n.n.*, proces *n.n. to come up for* ~, terecht staan *irr.* (*person*); vóórkomen *irr.* (*case*). **trial-flight,** *n.* proefvlucht *n.* **trial-trip,** *n.* proefrit *n.* (*car*); proefstomen *n.n.* (*ship*).

triangle, *n.* driehoek *n.* **triangular,** *a.* driehoekig. **triangulate,** *v.t.* trianguleeren.

tribal, *a.* stam . . . **tribe,** *n.* stam *n.*, volksstam *n.*

tribulation, *n.* wederwaardigheid *n.*, beproeving *n.*

tribunal, *n.* tribunaal *n.n.*, rechtbank *n.*, gerechtshof *n.n.* **tribune,** *n.* tribune *n.*; volkstribuun *n.* (*Roman*).

tributary, *a.* schatplichtig. ¶ *n.* schatplichtige *n.*; zijrivier *n.*

tribute, *n.* schatting *n.*; huldebetuiging *n.*

to pay ~ *to*, (*fig.*) hulde *n.* brengen *irr.* aan.

trice, *n. in a* ~, in een ommezien *n.n.* ¶ *v.t.* trijsen.

trick, *n.* kunstje *n.n.*; kunstgreep *n.*, truc *n.*; hebbelijkheid *n.*; slag *n.* (*cards*). ¶ *v.t.* bedriegen *str. to* ~ *a person into*, iemand bedotten tot; *to* ~ *a person out of something*, iemand iets afhandig maken. **trickery**, *n.* bedriegerij *n.*

trickle, *v.i.* druppelen; biggelen (*tears*).

trickster, *n.* bedrieger *n.* **tricky**, *a.* listig; lastig.

tricolour, *a.* driekleurig. ¶ *n.* driekleur *n.*

tricycle, *n.* driewieler *n.*

trident, *n.* drietand *n.*

tried, *a.* beproefd; trouw.

triennial, *a.* driejaarlijks.

trifle, *n.* kleinigheid *n.*; beuzeling *n.*; soort vlapudding *n.* ¶ *v.i.* beuzelen; spotten. ¶ *v.t. to* ~ *away*, verbeuzelen. **trifler**, *n.* beuzelaar *n.* **trifling**, *a.* onbeduidend, onbetekenend.

trig, *n.* remschoen *n.*

trigger, *n.* trekker *n.* **trigger-guard**, *n.* beugel *n.*

trigonometry, *n.* driehoeksmeting *n.*, trigonometrie *n.*

trilateral, *a.* driezijdig.

trilby, *n.* deukhoed *n.*

trilogy, *n.* trilogie *n.*

trim, *a.*, ~ly, *adv.* net, keurig; goed onderhouden. ¶ *v.t.* in orde *n.* maken; garneren (*garment*); tremmen (*ccal*); bijknippen (*hair*); snoeien (*hedge*); bij de wind zetten (*sails*). ¶ *n.* gesteldheid *n.*; zeilvaardigheid *n. in good* ~, in goede staat *n.* **trimmer**, *n.* tremmer *n.* **trimming**, *n.* garneersel *n.n.* **trimness**, *n.* netheid *n.*, keurigheid *n.*

trinity, *n.* drieëenheid *n. T*~, Drievuldigheid *N.*; *T*~ *Sunday*, Drievuldigheidsdag *N.*, Zondag *N.* na Pinksteren *N.*

trinket, *n.* sieraad *n.n.*

trio, *n.* trio *n.n.*

trip, *v.i.* trippelen, huppelen. *to* ~ *up*, struikelen. ¶ *v.t.* doen *irr.* struikelen. ¶ *n.* uitstapje *n.n.*; tochtje *n.n.*

tripartite, *a.* driedelig; drievoudig.

tripe, *n.* pens *n.*; ingewanden *pl.n.n.*; (*fig.*) nonsens.

triple, *a.* driedubbel; drievoudig. **triplet**, *n.* drieling *n.*; triool *n.*

tripod, *n.* drievoet *n.*

tripos, *n.* zeker academisch examen *n.n.* in Cambridge (*B.A.*).

tripper, *n.* plezierreiziger *n.* ~*s*, dagjesmensen *pl.n.n.*

trisyllabic, *a.* driclettergrepig.

trite, *a.*, ~ly, *adv.* afgezaagd, **alledaags**. **triteness**, *n.* afgezaagdheid *n.*

triton, *n.* watersalamander *n.*

triturate, *v.t.* fijnstampen, vermalen.

triumph, *n.* triomf *n.*; zegepraal *n.* ¶ *v.i.* triomferen, zegevieren; zegcpralen.

triumphal, *a.* triomferend, zegevierend. ~ *arch*, triomfboog *n.*, erepoort *n.* **triumphant**, *a.*, ~ly, *adv.* triomfantelijk; zegevierend.

trivial, *a.* triviaal, onbeduidend. **triviality**, *n.* onbeduidendheid *n.*; beuzelarij *n.*

trochaic, *a.* trochaeisch. **trochee**, *n.* trochee *n.*

Trojan, *a.* trojaans. ¶ *N.* Trojaan *N. to work like a* ~, werken als een paard *n.n.*

troll, *n.* aardmannetje *n.n.*; wieltje *n.n.* (*on rod*). ¶ *v.i.* vrolijk zingen *str.*; vissen (met bewegend aas *n.n.*).

trolley, *n.* rolwagentje *n.n.*; contactrol *n.* ~ *car*, trolleytram *n.*

trollop, *n.* slet *n.*, slons *n.*

trombone, *n.* schuiftrompet *n.*

troop, *n.* troep *n.*; hoop *n.*, menigte *n.* ¶ *v.i. to* ~ *in*, binnenstromen; *to* ~ *together*, zich verzamelen, samenscholen. **trooper**, *n.* cavalerist *n. to swear like a* ~, vloeken als een dragonder *n.* **troop-sergeant**, *n.* wachtmeester *n.* **troop-ship**, *n.* transportschip *n.n.*

trope, *n.* trope *n.*, redefiguur *n.*

trophy, *n.* trofee *n.*

tropic, *a.* tropisch. ¶ *n.* keerkring *n. the* ~*s*, de tropen *pl.n.*; *T*~ *of Cancer*, Kreeftskeerkring *N.*; *T*~ *of Capricorn*, Steenbokskeerkring *N.* **tropical**, *a.*, ~ly, *adv.* tropisch.

trot, *v.i.* draven. *to* ~ *along*, komen *irr.* aandraven. ¶ *v.t.* laten *str.* draven. *to* ~ *out*, komen *irr.* aanzetten met. ¶ *n.* draf *n. at a* ~, in draf, op een drafje *n.n.* **trotter**, *n.* draver *n.*, harddraver *n.*; varkenspoot *n.* **trotting-race**, *n.* harddraverij *n.*

trouble, *v.t.* lastig vallen *str.*; storen; verontrusten. *to* ~ *one's head*, zich het hoofd breken *str.* ¶ *v.i.* de moeite nemen *str.* ¶ *v.t. to* ~ *oneself*, zich moeite *n.* geven *str.*; de moeite nemen *str.* ¶ *n.* moeite *n.*; last *n.*; ongemak *n.n.*; verdriet *n.n.* **troubled**, *a.* verontrust; gestoord; onrustig; veelbewogen, **troublesome**, *a.* lastig, hinderlijk.

trough, *n.* trog *n.* ~ *of the sea*, golfdal *n.n.*

trounce, *v.t.* afrossen.

troupe, *n.* troep *n.*

trouser-leg, *n.* broekspijp *n.* **trousers**, *pl.n.* broek *n.*, pantalon *n. pair of* ~, broek *n.*

trousseau, *n.* uitzet *n.*

trout, *n.* forel *n.*

trowel, *n.* troffel *n. to lay it on with a* ~, het er dik opleggen *irr.*

Troy, *N.* Troje *n.N.*

troy-weight, *n.* karaatgewicht *n.n.*

truant, *n.* spijbelaar *n. to play* ~, spijbelen. ¶ *a.* spijbelend, dwalend.

truce, *n.* wapenstilstand *n.*; bestand *n.n.*

truck, *n.* lorrie *n.*, vrachtauto *n.*; wagon *n.*; ruilhandel *n.* (*barter*). *cattle* ~, veewagen *n.*; *to have no* ~ *with*, niets te maken hebben met. ¶ *v.i.* ruilhandel *n.* drijven *str.*

truckle, *v.t.* kruipen *str.* ¶ *n.* wieltje *n.n.*

truckle-bed, *n.* bed *n.n.* op rolletjes *pl.n.n.*

truck-system, *n.* stelsel *n.n.* van gedwongen winkelnering *n.*

truculence, *n.* heftigheid *n.*; branie *n.* truculent, *a.* heftig, braniachtig.

trudge, *v.i.* voortsjokken.

true, *a.* waar; juist; echt; trouw; oprecht. ~ *to nature,* natuurgetrouw. true-blue, *a.* onvervalst. true love, *n.* zoete lief *n.*

truffle, *n.* truffel *n.*

truism, *n.* gemeenplaats *n.*

truly, *adv.* echt; waarlijk, werkelijk; terecht.

trump, *n.* troef *n.* (*cards*); bazuingeschal *n.n. a regular ~,* een beste kerel *n.*; *to turn up ~s,* goed uitvallen *str.*; *the ~ of doom,* de bazuin des oordeels. ¶ *v.t.* troeven. *to ~ up,* opdissen.

trumpery, *n.* prullenboel *n.*, goedkope opschik *n.*

trumpet, *n.* trompet *n.* ¶ *v.t.* trompetten. trumpet-call, *n.* trompetsignaal *n.n.* trumpeter, *n.* trompetter *n.*

truncate, *v.t.* afknotten. ¶ *a.* afgeknot.

truncheon, *n.* gummistok *n.*

trundle, *v.t.* voortrollen. *to ~ a hoop,* hoepelen.

trunk, *n.* stam *n.* (*tree*); romp *n.* (*body*); koffer *n.* (*case*); kaar *n.* (*fish*); slurf *n.* (*elephant*). ~*s,* korte broek *n.* trunk-call, *n.* intercommunaal gesprek *n.n.* trunk-fish, *n.* koffervis *n.* trunk-line, *n.* hoofdlijn *n.*

truss, *n.* bundel *n.*, bos *n.* (*hay*); breukband *n.* ¶ *v.t.* opbinden *str.*

trust, *v.t.* vertrouwen. *to ~ to,* toevertrouwen aan; *to ~ a person with something,* iets toevertrouwen aan. ¶ *v.i. to ~ in,* vertrouwen op. ¶ *n.* vertrouwen *n.n.*; trust *n.* (*business*). *to put one's ~ in,* vertrouwen stellen in; *on ~,* op goed geloof *n.n.* trustee, *n.* beheerder *n.*; curator *n.* trusteeship, *n.* curatorschap *n.n.*, voogdij *n.* trustful, *a.* vertrouwend, vol vertrouwen *n.n.* trustworthy, *a.* betrouwbaar. trusty, *a.* getrouw, beproefd.

truth, *n.* waarheid *n.*; echtheid *n.*; oprechtheid *n.* truthful, *a.* waarheidslievend; waar.

try, *v.t.* proberen, trachten; beproeven; verhoren, onderzoeken *irr.*; op de proef stellen. *to ~ on,* aanpassen, *to ~ it on,* het eens proberen. ¶ *n.* poging *n.* trying, *a.* vermoeiend; lastig. trysail, *n.* gaffelzeil *n.n.*

tub, *n.* tobbe *n.*; kuip *n.*; vat *n.n.*; (*fig.*) schuit *n.*

tuba, *n.* tuba *n.*

tubby, *a.* zo rond als een ton *n.*

tube, *n.* buis *n.*, pijp *n.*; (gummi)slang *n.*; binnenband *n.*; ondergrondse spoorweg *n.* ~ *valve,* ventiel *n.n.*

tuber, *n.* knol *n.*

tubercle, *n.* knolletje *n.n.*, tuberkel *n.*

tubercular, *a.* met tuberkels *pl.n.*; tuberculeus. tuberculosis, *n.* tuberculose *n.* tuberculous, *a.* tuberculeus.

tubing, *n.* buis *n.*; buizen *pl.n.* tubular, *a.* buisvormig. ~ *boiler,* vlampijpketel *n.*

tuck, *v.t.* omslaan *irr. to ~ away,* wegstoppen; *to ~ in,* instoppen (*in bed*), innemen (*material*), flink eten *str.* (*food*). ¶ *n.* plooi *n.*; snoepgoed *n.n.* (*sweets*). tucker, *n.* jabot *n.*, kanten kraag *n.*

Tuesday, *N.* dinsdag *N.*

tufa, *n.*, tuff, *n.* tuf *n.n.*, tufsteen *n.*

tuft, *n.* kuif *n.*; bosje *n.n.*; kwast *n.* tufted, *a.* gekuifd; in bosjes *pl.n.n.*

tug, *v.t.* trekken *str.*, rukken; slepen. *to ~ at,* rukken aan. ¶ *n.* ruk *n.*, haal *n.*; sleepboot *n.* tug-boat, *n.* sleepboot *n.* tug-of-war, *n.* touwtrekken *n.n.*

tuition, *n.* onderwijs *n.n.*; leiding *n.*, toezicht *n.n.*

tulip, *n.* tulp *n.* tulip-tree, *n.* tulpeboom *n.*

tumble, *v.i.* buitelen, duikelen, tuimelen; rollen; halsoverkop gaan *irr. to ~ down,* ineenstorten, neervallen *str.* ¶ *v.t.* gooien. ¶ *n.* buiteling *n.*, tuimeling *n.* tumbledown, *a.* bouwvallig. tumbler, *n.* buitelaar *n.*; glas *n.n.* (zonder voet *n.*).

tumbril, *n.* stortkar *n.*, vuilniswagen *n.*

tumefaction, *n.* opzwelling *n.*; gezwel *n.n.* tumefy, *v.i.* (op)zwellen *str.* ¶ *v.t.* doen *irr.* zwellen. tumescence, *n.* (op)zwelling *n.*; gezwollenheid *n.* tumescent, *a.* gezwollen.

tummy, *n.* buik *n.*, maag *n.*

tumour, *n.* gezwel *n.n.*, zweer *n.*

tumult, *n.* beroering *n.*, opschudding *n.*; geraas *n.n.* tumultuous, *a.*, ~ly, *adv.* onstuimig; woest.

tumulus, *n.* terp *n.n.*; grafheuvel *n.*

tun, *n.* vat *n.n.*, ton *n.*

tuna, *n.* tonijn *n.*

tune, *n.* wijs *n.*; deuntje *n.n. in ~,* zuiver gestemd; *out of ~,* vals; *to the ~ of,* op de wijs van; (*fig.*) ten bedrage van; *to change one's ~,* een toontje *n.n.* lager zingen *str.* ¶ *v.t.* stemmen; afstemmen (*radio*). ¶ *v.i.* harmoniëren. tuneful, *a.* melodieus. tuneless, *a.* onwelluidend. tuner, *n.* stemmer *n.*

tunic, *n.* tuniek *n.*; uniformjas *n.*

tuning-fork, *n.* stemvork *n.*

tunnel, *n.* tunnel *n.*; gang *n.* ¶ *v.t.* een tunnel graven *str.*; boren.

tunny, *n.* tonijn *n.*

turban, *n.* tulband *n.*

turbid, *a.* troebel, drabbig. turbidity, *n.* troebelheid *n.*

turbine, *n.* turbine *n.*

turbot, *n.* tarbot *n.*

turbulence, *n.* woeligheid *n.*, onstuimigheid *n.* turbulent, *a.* woelig, onstuimig, wild.

tureen, *n.* (soep)terrine *n.*

turf, *n.* gras *n.n.*; graszode *n.*; renpaardensport *n.* ¶ *v.t.* met zoden *pl.n.* bedekken.

turfy, *a.* grazig, begraasd.

turgid, *a.* gezwollen; opgeblazen. turgidity, *n.* gezwollenheid *n.*

Turin, *N.* Turijn *n.N.*

Turk, *N.* Turk *N.* Turkey, *N.* Turkije *n.N.* ¶ *a.* Turks.

turkey, *n.* kalkoen *n.* turkey-cock, *n.* kalkoense haan *n.* turkey-hen, *n.* kalkoense hen *n.*

Turkish, *a.* Turks. ~ delight, soort Turks suikergoed *n.n.*

turmoil, *n.* beroering *n.*, verwarring *n.*

turn, *v.t.* draaien, omdraaien; omtrekken *str.*; verzuren. to ~ a corner, een hoek *n.* omslaan *irr.*; not to ~ a hair, geen spier *n.* vertrekken *str.*; ~ed 50, over de 50; to ~ down, omvouwen, (*fig.*) weigeren; to ~ out, buitenzetten; produceren; to ~ over, omdraaien; omzetten. ¶ *v.i.* zich omdraaien; zuur worden *str.*; to ~ against, zich keren tegen; to ~ away, zich afwenden; to ~ off, afslaan *irr.*; to ~ out, blijken *str.*; to ~ round, zich omdraaien; to ~ up, verschijnen *str.*, komen *irr.* opdagen. ¶ *n.* draai *n.*; wending *n.*; keerpunt *n.n.*; beurt *n.*; nummer *n.n.* (*in show*). to do a person a good ~, iemand een goede dienst *n.* bewijzen *str.*; to take ~s, elkaar afwisselen; in ~, om de beurt; in his ~, op zijn beurt; on the ~, op 't punt staan *irr.* zuur te worden (*milk*); done to a ~, juist goed.

turncoat, *n.* overloper *n.*, renegaat *n.*

turncock, *n.* opzichter *n.* (van de waterleiding). turn-down, *a.* omgeslagen.

turning, *n.* draai *n.*; bocht *n.* turning-lathe, *n.* draaibank *n.* turning-point, *n.* keerpunt *n.n.*

turnip, *n.* raap *n.* turnip-tops, *pl.n.* raapstelen *pl.n.*

turnkey, *n.* cipier *n.* turn-out, *n.* opkomst *n.* (*public*). turn-over, *n.* omzet *n.* apple ~, appelflap *n.* turnpike, *n.* tolhek *n.n.* turnstile, *n.* draaiboom *n.* turntable, *n.* draaischijf *n.*

turpentine, *n.* terpentijn *n.*

turpitude, *n.* schandelijkheid *n.*

turps, *pl.n.* See turpentine.

turquoise, *n.* turkoois *n.*

turret, *n.* torentje *n.n.*; geschuttoren *n.* turreted, *a.* met torentjes *pl.n.n.*

turtle, *n.* waterschildpad *n.* to turn ~, kapseizen.

turtle-dove, *n.* tortelduif *n.*

Tuscan, *a.* Toskaans.

tusk, *n.* slagtand *n.*

tussle, *v.i.* worstelen. ¶ *n.* worsteling *n.*

tussock, *n.* bosje *n.n.* gras.

tutelage, *n.* voogdij *n.*; voogdijschap *n.n.*; onmondigheid *n.* tutelary, *a.* bescherm . . .

tutor, *n.* leermeester *n.*; repetitor *n.*; goeverneur *n.* tutorial, *a.* repetitors . . . tutorship, *n.* repetitorswerk *n.n.*; goeverneurschap *n.n.*

tut-tut, *excl.* kom, kom!

twaddle, *n.* gebazel *n.n.*

twain, *n.* twee.

twang, *v.t.* tokkelen. ¶ *n.* nasaal geluid *n.n.*

tweak, *v.t.* plukken.

tweed, *n.* gekeperde wollen stof *n.*

tweezers, *pl.n.* pincet *n.n.*, tangetje *n.n.* pair of ~, tangetje *n.n.*

twelfth, *a.* twaalfde. Twelfth Night, *N.* Driekoningenavond *N.* twelve, *num.* twaalf. twelvemonth, *n.* jaar *n.n.* to-day ~, vandaag over een jaar.

twentieth, *a.* twintigste. twenty, *num.* twintig.

twice, *adv.* tweemaal.

twiddle, *v.t.* ronddraaien. to ~ one's thumbs (*fig.*), zitten *str.* niets doen.

twig, *n.* twijg *n.*, takje *n.n.* ¶ *v.t.* snappen.

twilight, *n.* schemering *n.*, schemeravond *n.*, schemerlicht *n.n.* in the ~, met schemerdonker *n.n.*, tussen licht *n.n.* en donker *n.n.*; ~ of the gods, godenschemering *n.* ¶ *a.* schemer . . . ~ sleep, pijnloze bevalling *n.*

twill, *n.* keper *n.* ¶ *v.t.* keperen.

twin, *a.* twee . . .; tweeling(s) . . .; dubbel. ~ bed, lits jumeaux *n.* ¶ *n.* één van een tweeling *n.* ~s, een tweeling *n.*

twine, *v.t.* strengelen; vlechten *str.* ¶ *v.i.* zich kronkelen. to ~ round . . ., . . . omstrengelen. ¶ *n.* zeilgaren *n.n.*, dun touw *n.n.*

twinge, *v.t.* pijn *n.* doen *irr.*, steken *str.* ¶ *n.* steek *n.*, scheut *n.*; knaging *n.* (*of conscience*).

twinkle, *v.i.* fonkelen, flikkeren. ¶ *n.* fonkeling *n.*, flikkering *n.* twinkling, *n.* in the ~ of an eye, in een oogwenk *n.*

twirl, *v.t.* ronddraaien. twirly, *a.* vol krullen *pl.n.*

twist, *v.t.* draaien, wringen *str.*; strengelen. ¶ *v.i.* zich winden *str.*, kronkelen. ¶ *n.* draai *n.*; strengel *n.*; rolletje *n.n.* (*tobacco*); pluksel *n.n.*, poetskatoen *n.n.* twister, *n.* draaier *n.*

twit, *v.t.* plagen.

twitch, *v.i.* trekken *str.* ¶ *n.* zenuwtrekking *n.* twitchy, *a.* zenuwachtig.

twitter, *v.i.* kwetteren, tjilpen. ¶ *n.* gekwetter *n.n.*, getjilp *n.n.*

two, *num.* twee. ¶ *n.* twee *n.*, tweetal *n.n.* to cut in ~, in tweeën snijden *str.* two-edged, *a.* tweesnijdend. two-faced, *a.* dubbelhartig, onoprecht. twofold, *a.* tweevoudig, dubbel. ¶ *n.* tweevoud *n.n.* two-foot, *a.* van twee voet *n.* twopenny, *a.* van twee stuivers, goedkoop. two-year-old, *a.* tweejarig.

tympanist, *n.* paukenist *n.*

tympanum, *n.* trommel *n.*

type, *n.* type *n.n.*; lettertype *n.n.*, drukletter *n.* movable ~, losse letters *pl.n.*; in ~, in druk *n.*, gezet; to put into ~, zetten. ¶ *v.t.* & *v.i.* typen, tikken. type-case, *n.* letterkast *n.* type-founder, *n.* lettergieter *n.* type-foundry, *n.* lettergieterij *n.* type-script, *n.* in ~, getikt. typesetter, *n.* zetter *n.* typewriter, *n.* schrijfmachine *n.* typewritten, *a.* getikt.

typhoid, *a.* typheus. ~ fever, buiktyphus *n.*

typhoon, *n.* wervelstorm *n.*

typhus, *n.* vlektyphus *n.*

typical, *a.*, ~ly, *adv.* typisch. typify, *v.t.* typeren.

typist, *n.* typiste *n.*

typographer, *n.* typograaf *n.* typographic, *a.* typografisch. typography, *n.* typografie *n.*

tyrannical, *a.* tiranniek. tyrannize, *v.t.* tiranniseren. tyrannous, *a.* tiranniek. tyranny, *n.* tirannie *n.*; dwingelandij *n.* tyrant, *n.* tiran *n.*; dwingeland *n.*; gewelde-naar *n.*

tyre, *n.* band *n.* ~ lever, bandenlichter *n.*

tyro, *n.* beginneling *n.*

U

ubiquitous, *a.* alomtegenwoordig. ubiquity, *n.* alomtegenwoordigheid *n.*

U-boat, *n.* Duitse duikboot *n.*

udder, *n.* uier *n.*

ugliness, *n.* lelijkheid *n.* ugly, *a.* lelijk.

ulcer, *n.* zweer *n.* ulcerate, *v.i.* zweren *str.* ulceration, *n.* verzwering *n.* ulcerous, *a.* vol zweren *pl.n.*

ullage, *n.* wan *n.n.*; doorgesijpelde vloeistof *n.*

ulster, *n.* lange overjas *n.*

ulterior, *a.* verder; later; verborgen. ~ motive, bijbedoeling *n.*

ultimate, *a.* uiterste, allerlaatste. ultimately, *adv.* eindelijk, ten laatste. ultimatum, *n.* ultimatum *n.n.*

ultimo, *adv.* ultimo.

ultra, *a.* ultra, uiterst.

ultramarine, *a.* ultramarijn. ¶ *n.* ultra-marijn *n.n.*

ultraviolet *a.* ultraviolet.

ululate, *v.i.* huilen. ululation, *n.* gehuil *n.n.*

umbel, *n.* scherm *n.n.*

umber, *n.* omber *n.n.*

umbilical, *a.* navel . . .

umbra, *n.* slagschaduw *n.*

umbrage, *n.* aanstoot *n.*, ergernis *n.* to give ~ to, ergeren.

umbrageous, *a.* lichtgeraakt.

umbrella, *n.* paraplu *n.*; parasol *n.*

umpire, *n.* scheidsrechter *n.* ¶ *v.i.* als scheidsrechter optreden *str.*

un-, *prefix.* on . . .; ont . . .; los . . .; niet; zonder.

unabashed, *a.* onbeschaamd; niet verlegen.

unabated, *a.* onverminderd, onverflauwd.

unable, *a.* onbekwaam. to be ~ to, niet in staat zijn te . . ., niet kunnen . . .

unabridged, *a.* onverkort.

unaccented, *a.* zonder klemtoon *n.*

unacceptable, *a.* onaannemelijk, niet aan-vaardbaar.

unaccommodating, *a.* niet inschikkelijk.

unaccompanied, *a.* onvergezeld; zonder begeleiding *n.*

unaccomplished, *a.* onvoltooid, onvervuld.

unaccountable, *a.*, ~bly, *adv.* onverklaar-baar.

unaccustomed, *a.* ongewoon, ongebruikelijk.

unacknowledged, *a.* niet erkend.

unacquainted, *a.* onbekend; niet met elkaar bekend.

unadorned, *a.* onversierd.

unadulterated, *a.* onvervalst, zuiver.

unadvised, *a.*, ~ly, *adv.* onverstandig, onvoorzichtig.

unaffected, *a.*, ~ly, *adv.* ongedwongen, niet geaffecteerd.

unaided, *a.* zonder hulp *n.*; bloot (*eye*).

unaffiliated, *a.* niet aangesloten.

unalloyed, *a.* onvermengd.

unalterable, *a.* onveranderlijk; onwrikbaar. unaltered, *a.* onveranderd.

unambitious, *a.* niet eerzuchtig.

unanimity, *n.* eenstemmigheid *n.*; eensgezind-heid *n.* unanimous, *a.* eenstemmig; eensgezind.

unanswerable, *a.* onweerlegbaar; niet te beantwoorden. unanswered, *a.* onbeant-woord.

unappreciated, *a.* niet gewaardeerd. un-appreciative, *a.* niet waarderend.

unapproachable, *a.* ongenaakbaar.

unarmed, *a.* ongewapend.

unasked, *a.* ongevraagd; ongenood.

unaspiring, *a.* oneerzuchtig.

unassailable, *a.* onaantastbaar. unassailed, *a.* onbetwist.

unassertive, *a.* bescheiden.

unassisted, *a.* zonder hulp *n.*

unassuming, *a.* bescheiden, niet aanmatigend.

unattached, *a.* niet verbonden; niet verloofd.

unattainable, *a.* onbereikbaar.

unattempted, *a.* onbeproefd.

unattended, *a.* niet begeleid; onbewaakt; onbeheerd; verwaarloosd.

unattested, *a.* niet bevestigd.

unattractive, *a.* onaantrekkelijk.

unauthentic, *a.* niet authentiek. unauthenti-cated, *a.* niet bekrachtigd; niet bevestigd; niet gewaarmerkt.

unauthorized, *a.* onbevoegd.

unavailable, *a.* onverkrijgbaar; nutteloos. unavailing, *a.* vergeefs.

unavenged, *a.* ongewroken.

unavoidable, *a.*, ~bly, *adv.* onvermijdelijk.

unaware, *a.* to be ~ of, zich niet bewust zijn van. unawares, *adv.* onbewust; plotseling, onverwacht. to take ~, overvallen *str.*

unawed, *a.* onbeschroomd.

unbacked, *a.* ongesteund.

unbalanced, *a.* onevenwichtig.

unbaptised, *a.* ongedoopt.

unbearable, *a.* ondragelijk.

unbecoming, *a.,* ~**ly,** *adv.* ongepast. *it is* ~, het staat niet goed (*clothes*).
unbefitting, *a.* ongepast.
unbefriended, *a.* zonder vrienden *pl.n.*
unbeknown(st), *a.* onbekend. ~ *to me,* buiten mijn voorkennis *n.*
unbelief, *n.* ongeloof *n.n.;* ongelovigheid *n.* **unbeliever,** *n.* ongelovige *n.* **unbelieving,** *a.* ongelovig.
unbend, *v.t.* ontspannen *irr.* ¶ *v.i.* uit de plooi komen *irr.* **unbending,** *a.* onbuigzaam; ontoegeeflijk.
unbiassed, *a.* onpartijdig.
unbidden, *a.* ongenood.
unbind, *v.t.* losbinden *str.;* bevrijden.
unbleached, *a.* ongebleekt.
unblemished, *a.* onbevlekt, smetteloos.
unblest, *a.* ongezegend.
unblushing, *a.* schaamteloos, zonder blikken *n.n.* of blozen *n.n.*
unbolt, *v.t.* ontgrendelen. **unbolted,** *a.* ongebuideld.
unborn, *a.* ongeboren.
unbosom, *v.r. to* ~ *oneself,* zich ontboezemen.
unbound, *a.* ongebonden, vrij.
unbounded, *a.* onbegrensd.
unbridle, *v.t.* aftomen. **unbridled,** *a.* tomeloos; losbandig.
unbroken, *a.* ongebroken; onafgebroken.
unbuckle, *v.t.* losgespen.
unburden, *v.t.* verlichten. ¶ *v.r. to* ~ *oneself,* zich ontboezemen, zijn hart *n.n.* uitstorten.
unburied, *a.* onbegraven.
unbusinesslike, *a.* onpractisch.
unbutton, *v.t.* losknopen.
uncalled, *a.* ongeroepen. ~ *for,* ongemotiveerd; ongevraagd.
uncancelled, *a.* niet ingetrokken.
uncanny, *a.* geheimzinnig, angstwekkend, eng.
uncared, *a.* ~ *for,* veronachtzaamd.
unceasing, *a.* onophoudelijk, voortdurend.
unceremonious, *a.* zonder complimenten *pl.n.n.*
uncertain, *a.,* ~**ly,** *adv.* onzeker; onbestendig. **uncertainty,** *n.* onzekerheid *n.*
uncertified, *a.* niet gelegaliseerd.
uncertificated, *a.* niet gediplomeerd.
unchain, *v.t.* ontketenen.
unchangeable, *a.* onveranderlijk. **unchanged,** *a.* onveranderd.
uncharitable, *a.* onbarmhartig.
unchaste, *a.* onkuis.
unchecked, *a.* ongehinderd.
unchristian, *a.* onchristelijk.
uncial, *a.* unciaal.
uncivil, *a.* onbeleefd.
uncivilized, *a.* onbeschaafd.
unclaimed, *a.* niet opgeëist.
unclasp, *v.t.* losmaken.
uncle, *n.* oom *n.*
unclean, *a.* onrein. **uncleanness,** *n.* onreinheid

unclench, *v.t.* ontspannen *irr.*
unclouded, *a.* onbewolkt.
uncoil, *v.t.* losrollen.
uncoloured, *a.* ongekleurd.
uncombed, *a.* ongekamd.
uncomely, *a.* onbevallig.
uncomfortable, *a.,* ~**bly,** *adv.* ongemakkelijk, onbehagelijk.
uncommon, *a.* ongewoon. ¶ *adv.* ongewoon. *not* ~, niet zelden.
uncommunicative, *a.* onmeedeelzaam; terughoudend.
uncomplaining, *a.* berustend.
uncompromising, *a.* onbuigzaam.
unconcern, *n.* onverschilligheid *n.* **unconcerned,** *a.,* ~**ly,** *adv.* onverschillig, onbekommerd.
unconditional, *a.* onvoorwaardelijk.
unconfined, *a.* vrij, los.
unconfirmed, *a.* niet bevestigd, ongestaafd.
uncongenial, *a.* niet sympathiek.
unconnected, *a.* niet verbonden; onsamenhangend.
unconquerable, *a.,* ~**bly,** *adv.* onbedwingbaar; onoverwinnelijk. **unconquered,** *a.* onoverwonnen.
unconscionable, *a.,* ~**bly,** *adv.* onredelijk; buitensporig.
unconscious, *a.* onbewust; bewusteloos. **unconsciousness,** *n.* bewusteloosheid *n.*
unconsecrated, *a.* ongewijd.
unconstitutional, *a.* ongrondwettig, niet constitutioneel.
unconstrained, *a.* ongedwongen.
uncontaminated, *a.* onbesmet.
uncontested, *a.* onbetwist.
uncontrollable, *a.,* ~**bly,** *adv.* niet na te gaan; niet te beheersen, onbedwingbaar. **uncontrolled,** *a.* niet gecontroleerd.
uncontroverted, *a.* onbetwist.
unconventional, *a.* niet conventioneel.
unconverted, *a.* onbekeerd.
unconvinced, *a.* niet overtuigd.
uncooked, *a.* ongekookt; ongaar.
uncorrected, *a.* ongecorrigeerd.
uncorrupted, *a.* onbedorven.
uncouple, *v.t.* loskoppelen.
uncouth, *a.* lomp, onbehouwen.
uncover, *v.t.* blootleggen *irr.,* ontbloten. *to stand* ~*ed,* met ongedekten hoofde staan *irr.*
uncritical, *a.* onkritisch.
uncrowned, *a.* ongekroond.
uncrumpled, *a.* ongekreukt.
unction, *n.* zalving *n. extreme* ~, het Heilig Oliesel. **unctuous,** *a.* zalvend.
uncultivated, *a.* onbebouwd; onontwikkeld.
uncultured, *a.* onbeschaafd.
uncurbed, *a.* tomeloos, ongebreideld.
uncurl, *v.i.* uit de krul gaan *irr.*
uncut, *a.* niet opengesneden.
undamaged, *a.* onbeschadigd.
undated, *a.* ongedateerd.
undaunted, *a.* onversaagd.

undeceive, *v.t.* ontgoochelen, uit de droom helpen *str.*
undecided, *a.* onbeslist; besluiteloos.
undecipherable, *a.* onontcijferbaar.
undefended, *a.* onverdedigd.
undefiled, *a.* onbezoedeld.
undefined, *a.* onbepaald.
undemonstrative, *a.* gereserveerd.
undeniable, *a.*, ~bly, *adv.* ontegenzeggelijk, onloochenbaar.
under, *prep.* onder; beneden; minder dan; volgens, krachtens. ~ *age*, onmondig, minderjarig; ~ *God*, naast God *N.*; ~ *repair*, in reparatie *n.* ¶ *adv.* onder, beneden.
underbid, *v.t.* minder bieden *str.* dan.
underclothing, *n.* ondergoed *n.n.*
undercarriage, *n.* onderstel *n.*
undercurrent, *n.* tegenstroom *n.*; verborgen neiging *n.*
undercut, *v.t.* goedkoper leveren dan, onderkruipen *str.* ¶ *n.* filet *n.n.*
underdone, *a.* niet gaar genoeg.
underestimate, *v.t.* onderschatten, te laag aanslaan *irr.*
underexposure, *n.* te korte belichting *n.*
underfed, *a.* onvoldoende gevoed.
underfoot, *adv.* onder de voet.
undergarment, *n.* stuk *n.n.* ondergoed.
undergo, *v.t.* ondergaan *irr.*, doorstaan *irr.*
undergraduate, *n.* student *n.* (zonder graad *n.*).
underground, *a.* ondergronds, onderaards. ¶ *n.* ondergrondse spoorweg *n.*
undergrowth, *n.* kreupelhout *n.n.*
underhand, *a.* onderhands; heimelijk, achterbaks, slinks. ¶ *adv.* onderhands; ter sluiks.
underlie, *v.t.* ten grondslag *n.* liggen *str.* aan.
underline, *v.t.* onderstrepen; de nadruk leggen *irr.* op.
underling, *n.* ondergeschikte *n.*
underlying, *a.* dieper liggend.
undermine, *v.t.* ondermijnen.
underneath, *prep.* onder, beneden. ¶ *n.* benedenkant *n.*
underpaid, *a.* slecht betaald.
underpin, *v.t.* onderstutten.
underrate, *v.t.* onderschatten.
underrun, *v.i.* te kort duren.
underside, *n.* onderkant *n.*
undersign, *v.t.* ondertekenen. undersigned, *n.* ondergetekende *n.*
undersized, *a.* onder de maat.
understaffed, *a.* met onvoldoende personeel *n.n.*
understand, *v.t.* verstaan *irr.*; vernemen *str.*; begrijpen *str.*; opvatten, nemen *str. to ~ by*, verstaan onder; *to ~ from*, vernemen *str.* van. ¶ *v.i. to ~ about*, verstand *n.n.* hebben van. understandable, *a.* verstaanbaar; begrijpelijk. understanding, *n.* verstand *n.n.*, begrip *n.n.*; schikking *n.*; verstandhouding *n. on the ~ that*, met

dien verstande dat. ¶ *a.* oordeelkundig; veelbegrijpend.
understatement, *n.* verklaring *n.* beneden de waarheid.
understudy, *v.t.* doubleren. ¶ *n.* doublure *n.*
undertake, *v.t.* ondernemen *str.*, op zich nemen *str.*
undertaker, *n.* begrafenisondernemer *n.*, lijkbezorger *n.* ~'s *man*, aanspreker *n.*
undertaking, *n.* onderneming *n.*; begrafenisvak *n.n.*
undertone, *n.* lage toon *n.*, gedempte toon *n.*
underwear, *n.* ondergoed *n.n.*
underwood, *n.* hakhout *n.n.*
underwrite, *v.t.* intekenen op; assureren, verzekeren. ¶ *v.i.* assurantiezaken *pl.n.* doen *irr.* underwriter, *n.* assuradeur *n.* underwriting, *n.* assuradeursbedrijf *n.n.*
undeserved, *a.* onverdiend. undeserving, *a.* zonder verdienste *n.*
undesigned, *a.* onopzettelijk.
undesirable, *a.* ongewenst.
undetected, *a.* onontdekt.
undetermined, *a.* onbeslist; onzeker.
undeveloped, *a.* onontwikkeld.
undeviating, *a.* niet afwijkend; onwankelbaar.
undigested, *a.* onverteerd.
undignified, *a.* zonder waardigheid *n.*
undiminished, *a.* onverminderd.
undiscerned, *a.* onopgemerkt. undiscerning, *a.* zonder onderscheidingsvermogen *n.n.*
undisciplined, *a.* ongedisciplineerd.
undiscovered, *a.* onontdekt.
undisguised, *a.* onvermomd; onverbloemd, onverholen.
undismayed, *a.* onverschrokken.
undisputed, *a.* onbetwist.
undissolved, *a.* niet opgelost.
undistinguished, *a.* zich door niets onderscheidend.
undisturbed, *a.* ongestoord.
undivided, *a.* onverdeeld.
undo, *v.t.* opendoen *irr.*; losmaken; losknopen; ongedaan maken, vernietigen. undoing, *n.* ondergang *n.*, verderf *n.n.*
undoubted, *a.*, ~ly, *adv.* ongetwijfeld; ontwijfelbaar.
undress, *v.t.* uitkleden. ¶ *v.i.* zich uitkleden. ¶ *n.* négligé *n.n.*; klein tenue *n.n.* ¶ *a.* in klein tenue.
undue, *a.* bovenmatig, overdreven.
undulate, *v.i.* golven; onduleren. undulation, *n.* golving *n.* undulatory, *a.* golvend.
unduly, *adv.* bovenmatig, overdreven.
undying, *a.* eeuwig, onvergankelijk.
unearned, *a.* onverdiend.
unearth, *v.t.* opgraven *str.*; te voorschijn brengen *irr.*; opschommelen.
unearthly, *a.* bovennatuurlijk; onmenselijk.
uneasiness, *n.* onbehaaglijkheid *n.*; ongerustheid *n.* uneasy, *a.*, ~ily, *adv.* ongemakkelijk; onbehaaglijk; onrustig. ~ *at, about or for*, ongerust over.
uneatable, *a.* oneetbaar.

unedifying, *a.* onstichtelijk.
uneducated, *a.* onopgevoed.
unemotional, *a.* onaandoenlijk; zonder emotie *n.*
unemployed, *a.* werkloos. ¶ *n.* werkloze *n.*
unemployment, *n.* werkloosheid *n.* ~ *benefit,* werklozenuitkering *n.*
unencumbered, *a.* onbezwaard, onbelast.
unending, *a.* eindeloos.
unendowed, *a.* niet gesubsidieerd.
unenlightened, *a.* achterlijk; oningelicht.
unenterprising, *a.* niet ondernemend.
unentertaining, *a.* niet onderhoudend; niet vermakelijk.
unenviable, *a.* niet benijdbaar, niet benijdenswaardig.
unequal, *a.,* ~ly, *adv.* ongelijk, ongelijkmatig. ~ *to,* niet opgewassen tegen. **unequalled,** *a.* ongeëvenaard.
unequivocal, *a.* ondubbelzinnig.
unerring, *a.* nooit falend, nimmer falend.
uneven, *a.,* ~ly, *adv.* oneven; ongelijk, ongelijkmatig. **unevenness,** *n.* onevenheid *n.*; ongelijkmatigheid *n.*
uneventful, *a.* rustig, kalm verlopend.
unexceptionable, *a.* onberispelijk; onaanvechtbaar.
unexpected, *a.,* ~ly, *adv.* onverwacht.
unexpired, *a.* niet verlopen.
unexplained, *a.* onverklaard.
unexplored, *a.* niet geëxploreerd, niet nagegaan.
unfaded, *a.* onverwelkt.
unfailing, *a.* onfeilbaar; onuitputtelijk.
unfair, *a.* onbillijk; oneerlijk.
unfaithful, *a.,* ~ly, *adv.* ontrouw; trouweloos.
unfaltering, *a.* onwankelbaar.
unfamiliar, *a.* onbekend, vreemd. ~ *with,* niet vertrouwd met.
unfashionable, *a.* niet naar de mode. **unfashioned,** *a.* ongevormd.
unfasten, *v.t.* losmaken.
unfathomable, *a.* onpeilbaar.
unfavourable, *a.* ongunstig.
unfeasible, *a.* ondoenlijk.
unfeeling, *a.* ongevoelig, gevoelloos; hardvochtig.
unfeigned, *a.* ongeveinsd.
unfelt, *a.* ongevoeld.
unfermented, *a.* ongegist.
unfetter, *v.t.* ontketenen.
unfilial, *a.* onkinderlijk.
unfilled, *a.* ongevuld.
unfinished, *a.* ongeëindigd, onvoltooid.
unfit, *a.* ongeschikt; onbekwaam. ~ *to be ...,* niet te ..
unfix, *v.t.* losmaken.
unflagging, *a.* onverflauwd, onverslapt.
unfledged, *a.* kaal, zonder veren *pl.n.*; onervaren.
unflinching, *a.* onwankelbaar; onwrikbaar.
unfold, *v.t.* ontvouwen *irr.,* uitspreiden. *to* ~ *a tale,* een verhaal *n.n.* doen *irr.* horen. ¶ *v.i.* opengaan *irr.*

unforced, *a.* ongedwongen.
unforeseen, *a.* onvoorzien.
unforgettable, *a.* onvergetelijk.
unforgivable, *a.* onvergeeflijk. **unforgiving,** *a.* onverzoenlijk.
unfortified, *a.* onversterkt.
unfortunate, *a.,* ~ly, *adv.* ongelukkig.
unfounded, *a.* ongegrond.
unframed, *a.* niet ingelijst.
unfrequented, *a.* zelden bezocht.
unfriendliness, *n.* onvriendelijkheid *n.* **unfriendly,** *a.* onvriendelijk.
unfrock, *v.t.* uit het priesterlijk ambt onzetten.
unfruitful, *a.* onvruchtbaar; vruchtloos.
unfulfilled, *a.* niet vervuld.
unfurl, *v.t.* ontrollen, ontplooien; uitspreiden.
unfurnished, *a.* ongemeubileerd.
ungainly, *a.* onbevallig, lomp.
ungarnished, *a.* onversierd, onopgesmukt.
ungear, *v.t.* ontkoppelen.
ungenerous, *a.* niet royaal.
ungenteel, *a.* niet deftig.
ungentle, *a.* onzacht.
ungentlemanly, *a.* onwellevend.
ungird, *v.t.* losgorden.
unglazed, *a.* onverglaasd.
ungloved, *a.* zonder handschoenen *pl.n.*
ungodliness, *n.* goddeloosheid *n.* **ungodly,** *a.* goddeloos, godvergeten.
ungovernable, *a.* niet te regeren; niet te besturen.
ungraceful, *a.,* ~ly, *adv.* onbevallig; onvriendelijk.
ungracious, *a.,* ~ly, *adv.* onheus, onhoffelijk.
ungrammatical, *a.* ongrammatikaal, niet grammatisch.
ungrateful, *a.* ondankbaar.
ungratified, *a.* onvoldaan.
ungrounded, *a.* ongegrond.
ungrudging, *a.* gul, van harte gegeven. **ungrudgingly,** *adv.* gul, gaarne gegund; grif, van harte.
unguarded, *a.* onbewaakt.
unguent, *n.* zalf *n.*
unhallowed, *a.* ontheiligd, goddeloos.
unhand, *v.t.* loslaten *str.* **unhandy,** *a.* onhandig, links.
unhappiness, *n.* ongelukkigheid *n.* **unhappy,** *a.,* ~ily, *adv.* ongelukkig.
unharmed, *a.* ongedeerd.
unharness, *v.t.* aftuigen.
unhealthy, *a.* ongezond.
unheard, *a.* ongehoord. ~ *of,* ongehoord.
unheeded, *a.* verwaarloosd, ongeacht. **unheeding,** *a.* achteloos, onachtzaam.
unhesitating, *a.* zonder aarzelen *n.n.*
unhindered, *a.* onbelemmerd.
unhinge, *v.t.* uit de hengsels *pl.n.n.* lichten; ontwrichten; *(fig.)* overstuur maken.
unholy, *a.* onheilig, goddeloos.
unhook, *v.t.* loshaken.
unhoped, *a.* ~ *for,* ongehoopt; overhoopt.
unhorse, *v.t.* uit het zadel werpen *str.*

unhurt, *a.* ongedeerd, onbezeerd.
unicorn, *n.* eenhoorn *n.*
unidentified, *a.* niet geïdentificeerd.
unification, *n.* unificatie *n.*
uniform, *a.,* ~ly, *adv.* uniform, onveranderlijk; gelijkmatig; eenparig, constant. ¶ *n.* uniform *n.n.* or *n.* **uniformity,** *n.* uniformiteit *n.*; gelijkmatigheid *n.*
unify, *v.t.* unificeren; eenheid *n.* brengen *irr.* in.
unilateral, *a.* eenzijdig.
unimaginable, *a.* ondenkbaar; onbegrijpelijk.
unimaginative, *a.* zonder verbeeldingskracht *n.*
unimpaired, *a.* onverzwakt, onaangetast.
unimpeachable, *a.* onaantastbaar; onberispelijk.
unimportant, *a.* onbelangrijk.
uninfluenced, *a.* niet beïnvloed. ~ *by,* niet onder de invloed van, niet beïnvloed door.
uninformed, *a.* slecht onderlegd, onwetend. ~ *on,* niet op de hoogte van.
uninhabitable, *a.* onbewoonbaar. **uninhabited,** *a.* onbewoond.
uninjured, *a.* ongedeerd.
uninspired, *a.* onbezield, zonder inspiratie *n.*
uninstructed, *a.* ononderwezen. **uninstructive,** *a.* onleerzaam.
uninsured, *a.* onverzekerd.
unintelligible, *a.,* ~bly, *adv.* onverstaanbaar; onbegrijpelijk.
unintended, *a.,* **unintentional,** *a.* onopzettelijk, niet bedoeld.
uninterested, *a.* niet geïnteresseerd. **uninteresting,** *a.* oninteressant.
uninterrupted, *a.* ononderbroken.
uninvited, *a.* niet uitgenodigd, ongenood, ongevraagd. **uninviting,** *a.* onaanlokkelijk, onaantrekkelijk.
union, *n.* unie *n.*; bond *n.,* vereniging *n.,* verbond *n.n.*; aaneenvoeging *n.*; eendracht *n.* **union-jack,** *n.* Britse Rijksvlag *n.*
unique, *a.* uniek, énig.
unison, *n.* harmonie *n.*; overeenstemming *n.*
unit, *n.* eenheid *n.*
unitarian, *a.* unitaristisch. ¶ *N.* Unitariër *N.*
unite, *v.t.* verenigen; samenvoegen. ¶ *v.i.* samensmelten *str.*; zich verenigen. **united,** *a.* verenigd; eendrachtig, eengezind. **unity,** *n.* eenheid *n.,* eendrachtigheid *n.*
universal, *a.,* ~ly, *adv.* algemeen, universeel. ~ *heir,* enig erfgenaam *n.* **universality,** *n.* algemeenheid *n.* **universe,** *n.* heelal *n.n.*
university, *n.* universiteit *n.,* hogeschool *n.,* academie *n.* ¶ *a.* universitair, universiteits . . .
unjust, *a.,* ~ly, *adv.* onrechtvaardig, onbillijk. ~ *to,* onrechtvaardig tegen; ten opzichte van.
unjustifiable, *a.,* ~bly, *adv.* onverdedigbaar, niet te rechtvaardigen. **unjustified,** *a.* ongerechtvaardigd.
unkempt, *a.* ongekamd; slordig.
unkept, *a.* niet onderhouden.

unkind, *a.* onvriendelijk. **unkindness,** *n.* onvriendelijkheid *n.*
unknowing, *a.* onwetend. **unknowingly,** *adv.* onbewust, zonder 't zelf te weten.
unknown, *a.* onbekend.
unlace, *v.t.* losrijgen *str.*
unladylike, *a.* niet damesachtig.
unlatch, *v.t.* van de klink doen *irr.*
unlawful, *a.,* ~ly, *adv.* onwettig; onrechtmatig.
unlearn, *v.t.* verleren, afleren. **unlearned,** *a.* ongeleerd, ongeletterd.
unleavened, *a.* ongezuurd.
unless, *c.* tenzij, indien . . . niet.
unlicensed, *a.* zonder vergunning *n.*; zonder verlof *n.n.*; ongeoorloofd.
unlike, *a.* niet gelijkend (op), verschillend (van), anders (dan). *that is so* ~ *him,* daar is hij de man niet naar; dat is niets voor hem. **unlikelihood,** *n.* onwaarschijnlijkheid *n.* **unlikely,** *a. & adv.* onwaarschijnlijk.
unlimited, *a.* onbeperkt, onbepaald, onbegrensd.
unload, *v.t.* lossen; ontladen *irr.*; uitstorten. ¶ *v.i.* lossen.
unlock, *v.t.* openen; van het slot doen *irr.*
unlooked, *a.* ~ *for,* onverwacht.
unloose(n), *v.t.* losmaken.
unloved, *a.* onbemind. **unlovely,** *a.* onbeminnelijk. **unloving,** *a.* liefdeloos.
unluckily, *adv.* ongelukkig, ongelukkigerwijs. **unlucky,** *a.* ongelukkig.
unmade, *a.* nog niet gemaakt; onopgemaakt. **unmake,** *v.t.* te niet doen *irr.*; te gronde richten.
unman, *v.t.* ontmannen; ontmoedigen.
unmanageable, *a.* onbestuurbaar; onhandelbaar.
unmanly, *a.* onmannelijk.
unmannerliness, *n.* ongemanierdheid *n.* **unmannerly,** *a.* ongemanierd, onbeleefd.
unmarked, *a.* ongemerkt, zonder merk *n.n.*
unmarketable, *a.* onverkoopbaar.
unmarred, *a.* onbedorven.
unmarried, *a.* ongetrouwd.
unmask, *v.t.* ontmaskeren. ¶ *v.i.* zich demaskeren.
unmastered, *a.* onvermeesterd.
unmatched, *a.* weergaloos, ongeëvenaard.
unmeaning, *a.* nietszeggend, onbeduidend; onopzettelijk.
unmeasurable, *a.* onmetelijk. **unmeasured,** *a.* ongemeten.
unmentionable, *a.* onnoembaar. **unmentioned,** *a.* onvermeld.
unmerciful, *a.,* ~ly, *adv.* ongenadig; onbarmhartig.
unmerited, *a.* onverdiend.
unmethodical, *a.* niet methodisch.
unmindful, *a.* ~ *of,* zonder acht te slaan *irr.* op; niet indachtig van.
unmingled, *a.* onvermengd, ongemengd.
unmistakable, *a.* onmiskenbaar.

unmodified, a. ongewijzijgd.
unmolested, a. ongestoord.
unmoor, v.t. & v.i. losmaken.
unmortgaged, a. onbezwaard.
unmounted, a. onbereden; niet gemonteerd.
unmoved, a. onbewogen.
unmusical, a. niet muzikaal.
unnamed, a. ongenoemd; naamloos.
unnatural, a., ~ly, adv. onnatuurlijk; tegennatuurlijk.
unnecessary, a., ~ily, adv. onnodig, nodeloos, niet noodzakelijk.
unneighbourly, a. niet zoals 't goede buren pl.n. betaamt.
unnerve, v.t. ontzenuwen; verzwakken.
unnoticeable, a. onmerkbaar. unnoticed, a. ongemerkt.
unnumbered, a. talloos, ongeteld.
unobjectionable, a. onberispelijk. it is ~, er valt niets tegen in te brengen.
unobservant, a. onoplettend, onopmerkzaam.
unobserved, a. onopgemerkt.
unobstructed, a. onbelemmerd.
unobtainable, a. onverkrijgbaar, niet te verkrijgen.
unobtrusive, a. bescheiden; niet opdringerig, niet in 't oog vallend.
unoccupied, a. onbezet, vrij; niet bezig.
unoffending, a. niet aanstotelijk; onschadelijk. it is ~, het doet geen kwaad.
unofficial, a. niet officieel; officieus.
unopposed, a. zonder tegenstand n.; zonder tegencandidaat n.
unorthodox, a. niet orthodox; niet volgens de regels.
unostentatious, a. zonder praal n., zonder vertoon n.n.
unpack, v.t. & v.i. uitpakken.
unpaid, a. onbetaald; onbezoldigd. ~ for, onbetaald.
unpalatable, a. onsmakelijk; onverkwikkelijk.
unparalleled, a. ongeëvenaard.
unpardonable, a., ~bly, adv. onvergeeflijk.
unparliamentary, a. niet parlementair.
unpatriotic, a. onvaderlandslievend.
unpaved, a. ongeplaveid, onbestraat.
unperceived, a. ongemerkt, onopgemerkt.
unperturbed, a. onverstoord.
unpick, v.t. lostornen.
unpin, v.t. losspelden.
unpitied, a. onbetreurd. unpitying, a. meedogenloos.
unplaced, a. ongeplaatst.
unpleasant, a., ~ly, adv. onaangenaam, ongenoeglijk, onplezierig, onprettig. unpleasantness, n. onaangenaamheid n.
unploughed, a. ongeploegd.
unpoetical, a. niet poëtisch.
unpolished, a. ongepolijst; niet gepoetst; onbeschaafd.
unpolluted, a. onbezoedeld; onbesmet.
unpopular, a. onpopulair, niet populair. unpopularity, n. geringe populariteit n.

unpractical, a. onpractisch.
unpractised, a. ongeoefenend, onbedreven.
unprecedented, a. zonder precedent n.n.; ongehoord; weergaloos.
unprejudiced, a. onbevooroordeeld.
unpremeditated, a. onopzettelijk, niet te voren bedacht.
unprepared, a. onvoorbereid.
unprepossessing, a. ongunstig, weinig innemend.
unpresuming, a. niet aanmatigend, bescheiden.
unprincipled, a. beginselloos.
unproductive, a. niet productief, niet renderend.
unprofessional, a. in strijd met de usances pl.n. van het beroep.
unprofitable, a. onvoordelig.
unpromising, a. weinig belovend.
unpropitious, a. ongunstig.
unprotected, a. onbeschermd.
unproved, a. onbewezen.
unprovided, a. onvoorzien. ~ for, onverzorgd.
unprovoked, a. niet uitgelokt.
unpublished, a. onuitgegeven.
unpunctual, a. niet op tijd.
unpunished, a. ongestraft.
unpurified, a. ongezuiverd.
unqualified, a. onbevoegd; onvoorwaardelijk; volmondig.
unquenchable, a. onlesbaar; onuitblusbaar.
unquestionable, a., ~bly, adv. onbetwistbaar, ontwijfelbaar. unquestioned, a. onbetwist.
unquiet, a. onrustig, rusteloos.
unravel, v.t. ontwarren; losrafelen.
unread, a. ongelezen. unreadable, a. onleesbaar.
unreadiness, n. ongereedheid n.; onwilligheid n. unready, a. niet gereed; onwillig.
unreal, a. onwezenlijk.
unreasonable, a., ~bly, adv. onredelijk; onbillijk. unreasoned, a. onberedeneerd.
unreclaimed, a. niet ontgonnen.
unrecognizable, a. onherkenbaar.
unreconciled, a. onverzoend.
unrecorded, a. niet opgeschreven; onvermeld.
unredeemed, a. niet afgelost, niet ingelost.
unreel, v.t. afrollen. ¶ v.i. zich ontrollen.
unredressed, a. niet hersteld.
unrefined, a. niet geraffineerd, ongezuiverd; onbeschaafd.
unreflecting, a. onnadenkend.
unregarded, a. ongeacht.
unregistered, a. niet ingeschreven.
unrelenting, a. onverbiddelijk; meedogenloos.
unreliable, a. onbetrouwbaar.
unrelieved, a. niet verlicht.
unremedied, a. onverholpen.
unremitting, a. aanhoudend; onverflauwd.
unremunerative, a. niet lonend.
unrepentant, a. onboetvaardig, verstokt.
unrequited, a. onbeantwoord.
unresented, a. niet kwalijk genomen.

unreserved, a. niet gereserveerd; openhartig.
unreservedly, adv. zonder voorbehoud n.n.
unresisting, a. geen weerstand n. biedend.
unresolved, a. onopgelost; besluiteloos.
unresponsive, a. onverschillig.
unrest, n. onrust n., onrustigheid n.
unrestored, a. niet hersteld; niet teruggegeven.
unrestrained, a. teugelloos.
unreturned, a. niet teruggegeven.
unrevenged, a. ongewroken.
unreversed, a. niet herroepen.
unrevoked, a. niet ingetrokken.
unrewarded, a. onbeloond; onvergolden.
unrighteous, a. zondig. unrighteousness, n. zondigheid n.
unripe, a. onrijp. unripeness, n. onrijpheid n.
unrivalled, a. ongeëvenaard.
unroll, v.t. ontrollen. ¶ v.i. afrollen.
unruffled, a. ongerimpeld; onverstoord, onverstoorbaar.
unruliness, n. weerbarstigheid n. unruly, a. weerbarstig, onhandelbaar.
unsaddle, v.t. uit het zadel werpen str.
unsafe, a. onveilig; onbetrouwbaar; gewaagd.
unsaid, a. ongesproken.
unsalable, a. onverkoopbaar.
unsalaried, a. onbezoldigd.
unsalted, a. ongezouten.
unsanctified, a. ongeheiligd.
unsanctioned, a. onbekrachtigd.
unsatisfactory, a., ~ily, adv. onbevredigend; onvoldoende.
unsatisfied, a. ontevreden, onvoldaan.
unsavoury, a. onsmakelijk, onverkwikkelijk.
unsay, v.t. herroepen; terugnemen str.
unscathed, a. ongedeerd.
unschooled a. ongeschoold.
unscientific, a. onwetenschappelijk.
unscrew, v.t. losschroeven, losdraaien.
unscriptural, a. onschriftuurlijk, onbijbels.
unscrupulous, a. gewetenloos.
unseal, v.t. ontzegelen.
unseasonable, a. ontijdig; ongepast, misplaatst.
unseasoned, a. ongekruid, ongezouten; onervaren.
unseat, v.t. uit het zadel werpen str.; van zijn zetel n. beroven (parliament).
unseaworthiness, n. onzeewaardigheid n. unseaworthy, a. onzeewaardig.
unseconded, a. niet gesteund.
unseeing, a. niet ziende.
unseemliness, n. onbetamelijkheid n. unseemly, a. onbetamelijk.
unseen, a. ongezien. ¶ n. vertaling n. à vue.
unselfish, a., ~ly, adv. onzelfzuchtig, onbaatzuchtig. unselfishness, n. onzelfzuchtigheid n., onbaatzuchtigheid n.
unsent, a. ~ for, ongenood.
unserviceable, a. ondienstig, onbruikbaar.
unset, a. ongezet.
unsettle, v.t. onzeker maken, doen irr. weifelen; in de war sturen. unsettled, a.

onbestendig; ongedurig, rusteloos; besluiteloos; ongeregeld; onuitgemaakt.
unshaken, a. ongeschokt; onwankelbaar.
unshaven, a. ongeschoren.
unsheathe, v.t. uit de schede trekken str.
unship, v.t. lichten. ¶ v.i. losraken.
unshod, a. ongeschoeid.
unshorn, a. ongeschoren.
unshrinking, a. onversaagd.
unsightly, a. onooglijk, afzichtelijk.
unskilful, a., ~ly, adv. onbedreven, onbekwaam. unskilled, a. onbedreven; ongeschoold.
unslaked, a. ongeblust.
unsociable, a. ongezellig. unsocial, a. ongezellig; onmaatschappelijk.
unsoiled, a. onbevlekt.
unsoldierlike, a. onmilitair.
unsolicited, a. ongevraagd.
unsolved, a. onopgelost.
unsophisticated, a. onbedorven; ongekunsteld; natuurlijk.
unsought, a. ongezocht.
unsound, a. ongezond; ondeugdelijk; onbetrouwbaar.
unsparing, a. kwistig, mild. unsparingly, adv. met kwistige hand n.
unspeakable, a., ~bly, adv. onuitsprekelijk; onbeschrijfelijk; afschuwelijk.
unspecified, a. ongespecificeerd, niet nader beschreven.
unspoiled, a. onbedorven.
unspoken, a. onuitgesproken.
unsportsmanlike, a. niet sportief.
unspotted, a. ongevlekt.
unstable, a. onvast, wankel; onbestendig.
unstained, a. onbevlekt; ongeverfd.
unstamped, a. ongefrankeerd; ongestempeld; ongezegeld.
unsteadfast, a. onstandvastig.
unsteady, a., ~ily, adv. ongestadig; onvast.
unstinted, a. kwistig, gul.
unstressed, a. zonder klemtoon n.
unstrung, a. overstuur (nerves).
unsubdued, a. onbedwongen; niet onderworpen.
unsubstantial, a. niet degelijk; onstoffelijk.
unsuccessful, a., ~ly, adv. niet geslaagd, zonder goed gevolg n.n. to be ~, niet slagen.
unsuitability, n. ongeschiktheid n. unsuitable, a., ~bly, adv. ongeschikt. unsuited, a. ongeschikt. ~ to, niet passend bij.
unsullied, a. onbezoedeld.
unsung, a. niet bezongen.
unsupported, a. niet gesteund; door niets gestaafd.
unsurpassed, a. onovertroffen.
unsuspected, a. onverdacht; onvermoed. unsuspecting, a. argeloos, geen kwaad n.n. vermoedend.
unsuspicious, a. niet achterdochtig; niet wantrouwend.

unsustained, *a.* niet ondersteund; niet volgehouden.
unswerving, *a.* niet afwijkend; onwankelbaar.
unsymmetrical, *a.* onsymmetrisch.
unsympathetic, *a.* niet sympathiek, geen sympathie *n.* betonend.
unsystematic, *a.* onsystematisch.
untack, *v.t.* losmaken.
untainted, *a.* onbesmet.
untamable, *a.* ontembaar.   untamed, *a.* ongetemd.
untarnished, *a.* niet aangeslagen; vlekkeloos.
untasted, *a.* onaangeroerd.
untaught, *a.* onwetend; spontaan, natuurlijk.
untaxed, *a.* vrij van belasting *n.*
unteachable, *a.* hardleers.
untenable, *a.* onhoudbaar.
untenanted, *a.* onbewoond; onverhuurd.
untested, *a.* niet onderzocht; niet op de proef gesteld.
unthanked, *a.* onbedankt.   unthankful, *a.* ondankbaar.
unthinkable, *a.* ondenkbaar. *it is* ~, je kunt het je niet indenken.   unthinking, *a,* onnadenkend.   unthought, *a.* ~ *of,* onverwacht.
untidiness, *n.* slordigheid *n.* untidy, *a.,* ~ily, *adv.* slordig; wanordelijk.
untie, *v.t.* losbinden *str.,* losknopen. ¶ *v.i.* losmaken.
until, *prep.* tot. ~ *then,* tot die tijd; *not* ~ *then,* eerst toen; *not* ~ . . ., niet voor . . .; pas in . . . ¶ *c.* tot, totdat.
untilled, *a.* onbebouwd.
untimely, *a.* ontijdig; ongelegen.
untiring, *a.* onvermoeid.
unto, *prep.* tot, tot aan.
untold, *a.* ongeteld; onnoemelijk.
untouchable, *a.* niet aan te raken; onaantastbaar. ¶ *n.* pariah *n.*   untouched, *a.* onaangeroerd.
untoward, *a.* balsturig, weerspannig; ongunstig, onvoorspoedig.
untrained, *a.* ongeoefenend, ongedrild.
untrammelled, *a.* onbelemmerd.
untransferable, *a.* niet over te dragen.
untranslatable, *a.* onvertaalbaar.
untravelled, *a.* onbereisd.
untried, *a.* onbeproefd; onverhoord (*in law*).
untrimmed, *a.* niet gesnoeid; niet bijgeknipt.
untrodden, *a.* onbetreden.
untroubled, *a.* ongestoord; onbezwaard; onbewogen.
untrue, *a.* onwaar; trouweloos; niet haaks (*angle*).   untruly, *adv.* valselijk.
untrustworthy, *a.* onbetrouwbaar.
untruth, *n.* onwaarheid *n.*
unturned, *a.* ongekeerd.
untutored, *a.* niet onderwezen, ongeschoold.
untwist, *v.t.* losdraaien.
unused, *a.* ongebruikt. ~ *to,* niet gewoon aan, niet gewend aan.
unusual, *a.,* ~ly, *adv.* ongewoon.
unutterable, *a.,* ~bly, *adv.* onuitsprekelijk.

unvaried, *a.* onveranderd; onveranderlijk.
unvarnished, *a.* niet gevernist; (*fig.*) onverbloemd.
unvarying, *a.* onveranderlijk.
unveil, *v.t.* ontsluieren; onthullen.
unventilated, *a.* niet geventileerd.
unversed, *a.* onbedreven, onervaren.
unwanted, *a.* niet verlangd; niet nodig, overtollig.
unwariness, *n.* onbehoedzaamheid *n.*; onvoorzichtigheid *n.*
unwarlike, *a.* onkrijgshaftig.
unwarned, *a.* ongewaarschuwd.
unwarrantable, *a.,* ~bly, *adv.* onverdedigbaar, niet te verantwoorden.   unwarranted, *a.* ongerechtvaardigd, ongemotiveerd.
unwary, *a.* onbehoedzaam; onvoorzichtig.
unwashed, *a.* ongewassen.
unwatered, *a.* niet besproeid; zonder water.
unwavering, *a.* onwrikbaar; standvastig.
unweaned, *a.* ongespeend.
unwearied, *a.* onvermoeid.   unwearying, *a.* onvermoeid, onvermoeibaar.
unwedded, *a.* ongehuwd.
unwelcome, *a.* onwelkom, ongezocht.
unwell, *a.* onwel, niet wel; ongesteld.
unwholesome, *a.* ongezond.
unwieldiness, *n.* logheid *n.*; onhandelbaarheid *n.*   unwieldy, *a.* log; onhandelbaar; omslachtig.
unwilling, *a.,* ~ly, *adv.* onwillig; ongewillig. ~ *to,* ongeneigd (om).
unwind, *v.t.* loswinden *str.,* afwikkelen.
unwise, *a.,* ~ly, *adv.* onverstandig.
unwished, *a.* ~ *for,* ongewenst.
unwitting, *a.,* ~ly, *adv.* onbewust.
unwomanly, *a.* onvrouwelijk.
unwonted, *a.* ongewoon.
unworkable, *a.* niet te bewerken; practisch onmogelijk.
unworn, *a.* ongedragen; onversleten.
unworthy, *a.* onwaardig.
unwrap, *v.t.* openmaken; loswikkelen.
unwritten, *a.* ongeschreven.
unyielding, *a.* onbuigzaam; ontoegevend, onverzettelijk.
unyoke, *v.t.* uitspannen *irr.,* het juk afnemen *str.*
up, *adv.* op, naar boven, de hoogte in, in de hoogte; overeind. ~ *to now,* tot nu toe; ~ *there,* daarginds. ¶ *prep.* op. ~ *a tree,* een boom in. ¶ *a.* naar de stad. ¶ *v.i.* opstaan *irr.* ¶ *n.* ~*s and downs,* voor- en tegenspoed *n.*
upbraid, *v.t.* verwijtingen *pl.n.* doen *irr.* *to* ~ *a person with something,* iemand iets verwijten *str.*
upbringing, *n.* opvoeding *n.*
up-country, *adv.* het binnenland in.
up-end, *v.t.* overeind zetten.
upgrade, *n. on the* ~, toenemend.
upheaval, *n.* omwenteling *n.*
uphill, *a.* (berg)opwaarts; ondankbaar. ¶ *adv.* (berg)opwaarts.

uphold, *v.t.* hooghouden *irr.*, handhaven, verdedigen. upholder, *n.* verdediger *n.*, voorstander *n.*

upholster, *v.t.* stofferen. upholsterer, *n.* stoffeerder n. upholstery, *n.* stoffeerwerk *n.n.*; stoffeerderij *n.*

upkeep, *n.* onderhoud *n.n.*; instandhouding *n.*

upland, *n.* hoogland *n.n.*

uplift, *v.t.* verheffen *str.* ¶ *n.* verheffing *n.*

upon, *prep.* op; bij; aan.

upper, *a.* opper, boven. ~ deck, bovendek *n.n.*; ~ hand, overhand *n.*, bovenhand *n.* uppermost, *adv.* bovenaan. to be ~, de overhand hebben.

uppish, *a.* brutaal; aanmatigend.

upraise, *v.t.* verheffen *str.*

upright, *a.* rechtopstaand; kaarsrecht; oprecht, rechtschapen. ¶ *adv.* overeind, rechtop.

uproar, *n.* misbaar *n.n.*; lawaai *n.n.*, herrie *n.* uproarious, *a.*, ~ly, *adv.* luidruchtig; stormachtig.

uproot, *v.t.* ontwortelen.

upset, *v.t.* omverwerpen *str.*, omgooien; in de war sturen; verijdelen; van streek maken.

upshot, *n.* uitkomst *n.*, slotsom *n.*

upside, n. bovenkant. ~ down, ondersteboven.

upstairs, *adv.* boven; naar boven. ¶ *a.* boven . . .

upstart, *n.* parvenu *n.*

uptake, *n.* *quick on the* ~, vlug van begrip.

up-train, *n.* trein *n.* naar de stad.

upward, *a.* opwaarts. ¶ *adv.* opwaarts, naar boven, omhoog. upwards, *adv.* opwaarts. from . . . ~, van . . . af; ~ of . . ., meer dan . . ., vanaf . . .

uranium, *n.* uranium *n.n.*

urban, *a.* stedelijk, stads . . . .

urbane, *a.* hoffelijk, wellevend, voorkomend. urbanity, *n.* hoffelijkheid *n.*

urbanize, *v.t.* steeds maken.

urchin, *n.* dreumes *n.*, kleuter *n.*; jochie *n.n.*

urge, *v.t.* aansporen; dringend verzoeken *irr.* to ~ on, voortdrijven *str.* ¶ *n.* drang *n.*; aandrang *n.*; drift *n.* urgency, *n.* urgentie *n.*; dringende noodzakelijkheid *n.* urgent, *a.*, ~ly, *adv.* dringend; spoedeisend.

uric, *a.* ~ acid, urinezuur *n.n.* urinal, *a.* urine . . . ¶ *n.* urinoir *n.n.*; urineglas *n.n.* urinate, *v.i.* urineren. urine, *n.* urine *n.*

urn, *n.* urn *n.*, vaas *n.*; ketel *n.*

us, *pron.* ons; aan ons.

usable, *a.* bruikbaar. usage, *n.* gebruik *n.n.*; usance *n.*; behandeling *n.* (*treatment*). usance, *n.* uso *n.n.* use, *v.t.* gebruiken; gebruik *n.n.* maken van; aanwenden; benutten; behandelen. to ~ up, verbruiken; he ~d to say . . ., hij placht te zeggen . . .; he ~d to, dat was hij gewoon; to be ~d to, gewoon zijn (aan); there ~d to be . . ., daar was vroeger . . . ¶ *n.* gebruik *n.n.*; ritueel *n.n.*; nut *n.n.* to be of great ~, zeer nuttig zijn; it is not much ~, het

heeft niet veel nut; *it's no* ~, het geeft niets; het helpt niets; het heeft geen zin; to be in ~, in gebruik zijn; to be of ~, van nut zijn; *for the* ~ *of*, ten gebruike van; *for cne's own* ~, te eigen bate. useful, *a.*, ~ly, *adv.* nuttig; bruikbaar. usefulness, *n.* nuttigheid *n.*; bruikbaarheid *n.* useless, *a.* nutteloos; vruchteloos. uselessness, *n.* nutteloosheid *n.*; vruchteloosheid *n.*

usher, *n.* portier *n.*; deurwaarder *n.* ¶ *v.t.* to ~ in, binnenleiden.

usual, *a.* gewoon, gebruikelijk. usually, *adv.* gewoonlijk; doorgaans.

usufruct, *n.* vruchtgebruik *n.n.*

usurer, *n.* woekeraar *n.* usurious, *a.* woeker . . .

usurp, *v.t.* zich (wederrechtelijk) toeëigenen; overweldigen; zich aanmatigen. usurpation, *n.* (wederrechtelijke) inbezitneming *n.*; overweldiging *n.*; usurper, *n.* usurpator *n.*; overweldiger *n.*

usury, *n.* woeker *n.*

utensil, *n.* werktuig *n.n.*, stuk gereedschap *n.n.*

uterine, *n.* uterus . . . uterus, *n.* baarmoeder *n.*

utilitarian, *a.* utilitaristisch. ¶ *n.* utilitarist *n.* utility, *n.* nut *n.n.*, nuttigheid *n.*; utiliteit *n.* utilization, *n.* gebruikmaking *n.*, benutting *n.* utilize, *v.t.* gebruik *n.n.* maken van, benutten; nuttig aanwenden.

utmost, *a.* uiterste; laatste. ¶ *n.* uiterste best *n.n.*

Utopia, *N.* Utopie *N.* Utopian, *a.* utopisch.

utter, *v.t.* uiten (*words*); in omloop *n.* brengen *irr.* (*coins*). ¶ *a.* uiterste; volslagen. utterance, *n.* uiting *n.*; uitlating *n.* utterly, *adv.* volslagen; volkomen, geheel en al.

uvula, *n.* huig *n.* uvular, *a.* huig . . .

uxorious, *a.* verslaafd aan zijn vrouw *n.*

V

vacancy, *n.* ledigheid *n.*, leegte *n.*; vacature *n.* vacant, *a.*, ~ly, *adv.* onbezet; gedachteloos, wezenloos; vacant. vacate, *v.t.* ontruimen.

vacation, *n.* vacantie *n.*; ontruiming *n.*; vacature *n.*

vaccinate, *v.t.* vaccineren, inenten. vaccination, *n.* vaccinatie *n.*, inenting *n.* vaccine, *n.* vaccine *n.*, entstof *n.*; koepokstof *n.*

vacillate, *v.i.* wankelen; weifelen. vacillation, *n.* wankeling *n.*; weifeling *n.*

vacuity, *n.* ledigheid *n.*, ledige ruimte *n.* vacuous, *a.* leeg; zonder uitdrukking *n.* vacuum, *n.* luchtledige *n.n.*

vagabond, *n.* vagebond *n.*, zwerver *n.* ¶ *a.* rondzwervend.

vagary, *n.* gril *n.*, kuur *n.*

vagina, *n.* vagina *n.*, schede *n.* vaginal, *a.* vaginaal.

vagrancy, *n.* landloperij *n.* **vagrant,** *a.* rondzwervend. ¶ *n.* landloper *n.*

vague, *a.,* ~ly, *adv.* vaag, onbepaald, flauw. vagueness, *n.* vaagheid *n.*

vain, *a.,* ~ly, *adv.* ijdel; nutteloos, vergeefs. *in* ~, te vergeefs. **vainglorious,** *a.* snoeverig.

valance, *n.* val *n.,* kap *n.*

vale, *n.* dal *n.n.*

valediction, *n.* afscheidsgroet *n.;* vaarwel *n.n.* **valedictory,** *a.* afscheids . . .

valentine, *n.* minnedicht *n.n.* op 14 Februari.

valerian, *n.* valeriaan *n.*

valet, *n.* knecht *n.,* kamerdienaar *n.*

valetudinarian, *n.* ziekelijk iemand *n.n.,* sukkelaar *n.*

valiant, *a.,* ~ly, *adv.* dapper, moedig, kloek.

valid, *a.* geldig; van kracht *n.;* deugdelijk. **validate,** *v.t.* geldig maken; legaliseren. **validity,** *n.* geldigheid *n.*.

valley, *n.* dal *n.n.,* vallei *n.*

valorous, *a.* dapper, moedig, koen. **valour,** *n.* dapperheid *n.,* moed *n.*

valuable, *a.* waardevol, kostbaar; van waarde *n.* ¶ *n.* ~s, kostbaarheden *pl.n.,* zaken *pl.n.* van waarde. **valuate,** *v.t.* schatten, taxeren. **valuation,** *n.* schatting *n.* value, *n.* waarde *n. to set* ~ *on,* prijs *n.* stellen op; *to the* ~ *of,* ter waarde van. ¶ *v.t.* schatten; waarderen, op prijs *n.* stellen. **valueless,** *a.* waardeloos. **valuer,** *n.* taxeerder *n.*

valve, *n.* klep *n.;* ventiel *n.n.;* (radio)lamp *n.* **valvular,** *a.* klep . . . ~ *disease of the heart,* aandoening *n.* der hartkleppen *pl.n.*

vamp, *n.* gevaarlijke coquette *n.* ¶ *v.i.* op 't gehoor accompagneren.

vampire, *n.* vampier *n.;* bloedzuiger *n.*

van, *n.* wagen *n.,* goederenwagen *n.,* verhuiswagen *n.;* vrachtauto *n.;* voorhoede *n. (of army). in the* ~, aan de spits.

vandal, *n.* vandaal *n.* **vandalism,** *n.* vandalisme *n.n.*

vane, *n.* vaantje *n.n.,* windvaan *n.;* blad *n.n.,* vleugel *n.*

vanguard, *n.* voorhoede *n.*

vanilla, *n.* vanille *n.,* vanielje *n.*

vanish, *v.i.* verdwijnen *str. to* ~ *from sight,* uit het gezicht verdwijnen *str.* **vanishing-point,** *n.* verdwijnpunt *n.n.*

vanity, *n.* ijdelheid *n.* **vanity-bag,** *n.* (dames)tasje *n.n.*

vanquish, *v.t.* overwinnen *str.;* bedwingen *str.* **vanquisher,** *n.* overwinnaar *n.*

vantage, *n.* voordeel *n.n. point of* ~, ~ *point,* gunstige positie *n.*

vapid, *a.* flauw; geesteloos. **vapidity,** *n.* flauwheid *n.*

vaporization, *n.* verdamping *n.* **vaporize,** *v.t.* (doen *irr.*) verdampen; bestuiven *str.* **vaporizer,** *n.* vaporisateur *n.* **vaporous,** *a.* dampig, wasemig; dampvormig; vluchtig. **vapour,** *n.* damp *n.,* wasem *n.* ¶ *v.i.* dampen, wasemen.

variability, *n.* veranderlijkheid *n.* **variable,** *a.,* ~bly, *adv.* veranderlijk; onbestendig; afwisselend. ¶ *n.* veranderlijke grootheid *n.* **variance,** *n.* afwijking *n.;* tegenstrijdigheid *n.,* tegenspraak *n. to be at* ~, het oneens zijn; *at* ~ *with,* in strijd met. **variant,** *a.* veranderlijk, variabel; afwijkend ¶ *n.* variant *n.* **variation,** *n.* afwijking *n.;* variatie *n.;* varieteit *n.*

varicose, *a.* ~ *vein,* spatader *n.*

varied, *a.* gevarieerd; afwisselend; vol afwisseling *n.*

variegate, *v.i.* (bont) schakeren; verscheidenheid *n.* brengen *irr.* in. **variegated,** *a.* bont, kleurig, geschakeerd.

variety, *n.* verscheidenheid *n.;* afwisseling *n.;* varieteit *n.,* soort *n.;* variété *n. a* ~ *of . . .,* tal van . . ., allerlei . . . **various,** *a.* verschillend, verscheiden.

varlet, *n.* knecht *n.;* schurk *n.*

varnish, *n.* vernis *n.n.* ¶ *v.t.* vernissen.

vary, *v.t.* variëren, afwisseling *n.* brengen *irr.* in. ¶ *v.i.* variëren, afwisselen.

vascular, *a.* vaat . . .

vase, *n.* vaas *n.*

vaseline, *n.* vaseline *n.*

vasomotoric, *a.* vasomotorisch.

vassal, *n.* vazal *n.;* leenman *n.* ¶ *a.* ~ *state,* vazalstaat *n.* **vassalage,** *n.* leenmanschap *n.n.;* dienstbaarheid *n.*

vast, *a.* uitgestrekt; onmetelijk; geweldig, enorm. **vastly,** *adv.* geweldig, enorm. **vastness,** *n.* uitgestrektheid *n.;* onmetelijkheid *n.*

vat, *n.* vat *n.n.,* kuip *n.;* ton *n.*

vatican, *N.* Vatikaan *n.N.*

vaticinate, *v.t.* voorspellen.

vault, *n.* gewelf *n.n.;* kelder *n.;* sprong *n.* ¶ *v.t.* overwelven; springen *str.*

vaunt, *v.i.* pochen, snoeven. ¶ *v.t.* prat gaan *irr.* op, bogen op. ¶ *n.* grootspraak *n.* **vaunter,** *n.* snoever *n.*

veal, *n.* kalfsvlees *n.n.* ¶ *a.* kalfs . . .

veer, *v.i.* draaien; ruimen *(of wind). to* ~ *round,* omlopen *str.;* bijdraaien. ¶ *v.t.* vieren.

vegetable, *a.* plantaardig. ~ *dish,* groenteschaal *n.;* ~ *kingdom,* plantenrijk *n.n.;* ~ *marrow,* engelse kalebas *n.;* ~ *mould,* teelaarde *n.* ¶ *n.* groente *n.;* plant *n.,* gewas *n.n.* **vegetal,** *a.* plantaardig. **vegetarian,** *a.* vegetarisch. ¶ *n.* vegetariër *n.* **vegetate,** *v.i.* vegeteren; groeien, wassen *str.* **vegetation,** *n.* plantengroei *n.;* vegetatie *n.* **vegetative,** *a.* vegetatief, groei . . .

vehemence, *n.* heftigheid *n.,* onstuimigheid *n.,* vuur *n.n.* **vehement,** *a.,* ~ly, *adv.* heftig, onstuimig.

vehicle, *n.* voertuig *n.n.;* voertaal *n.(language)* **vehicular,** *a.* vervoer . . ., verkeers . . .

veil, *n.* sluier *n.;* dekmantel *n. under a* ~ *of,* onder het mom van. ¶ *v.t.* omsluieren. **veiled,** *a.* gesluierd; gevoileerd; bedekt.

vein, *n.* ader *n.*; luim *n.*, stemming *n.*; trant *n.* (*fashion*). *to be in* ~, goed op dreef *n.* zijn; *to be in the* ~ *for* . . ., in de stemming zijn om . . . ¶ *v.t.* marmeren.
velar, *a.* velair.
vellum, *n.* velijn *n.n.*, (kalfs)perkament *n.n.*
velocity, *n.* snelheid *n.*
velum, *n.* zacht gehemelte *n.n.*
velvet, *n.* fluweel *n.n. to be on* ~, er goed aan toe zijn. ¶ *a.* fluwelen. **velveteen,** *n.* katoenfluweel *n.n.* **velvety,** *a.* fluwelig, fluweelachtig.
venal, *a.* veil, omkoopbaar. **venality,** *n.* veilheid *n.*, omkoopbaarheid *n.*
vendetta, *n.* vendetta *n.*, bloedwraak *n.*
vendor, *n.* verkoper *n.*
veneer, *n.* vernisje *n.n.*; fineerhout *n.n.*
venerability, *n.* eerbiedwaardigheid *n.* **venerable,** *a.* eerbiedwaardig, achtbaar; eerwaardig. **venerate,** *v.t.* (diep) vereren. **veneration,** *n.* (diepe) verering *n.*
venereal, *a.* venerisch, geslachts . . .
Venetian, *a.* Venetiaans. ~ *blind,* jaloezie *n.*
vengeance, *n.* wraak *n.* **vengeful,** *a.* wraakgierig.
venial, *a.* vergeeflijk. ~ *sin,* dagelijkse zonde *n.*
venison, *n.* wildbraad *n.n.* ~ *pasty,* wildpastei *n.*
venom, *n.* venijn *n.n.*; (ver)gift *n.n.* **venomous,** *a.* venijnig; (ver)giftig.
venous, *a.* aderlijk.
vent, *n.* luchtgat *n.n.*, opening *n.*; aars *n.n. to give* ~ *to,* uiting *n.* geven *str.* aan. ¶ *v.t.* luchten, ruchtbaar maken. **ventilate,** *v.t.* ventileren; ruchtbaar maken. **ventilation,** *n.* ventilatie *n.*, luchtverversing *n.* **ventilator,** *n.* ventilator *n.*, luchtkoker *n.*
ventral, *a.* buik . . .
ventricle, *n.* (hart)kamer *n.*
ventriloquism, *n.* buikspreken *n.n.* **ventriloquist,** *n.* buikspreker *n.*
venture, *v.t.* wagen. ¶ *v.i.* zich verstouten, zich wagen; zo vrij zijn. ¶ *n.* (gewaagde) onderneming *n. at a* ~, op goed geluk *n.n.* **venturesome,** *a.* ondernemend, vermetel.
venue, *n.* plaats *n.*
veracious, *a.* waarheidlievend; geloofwaardig; waarachtig. **veracity,** *n.* waarheidsliefde *n.*; waarheid *n.*; geloofwaardigheid *n.*
veranda(h), *n.* veranda *n.*, serre *n.*
verb, *n.* werkwoord *n.n.*; woord *n.n.* (*biblical*). **verbal,** *a.*, ~ly, *adv.* woordelijk; verbaal; woord . . ., woorden . . . **verbatim,** *adv.* woordelijk, woord *n.n.* voor woord *n.n.* **verbiage,** *n.* woordenvloed *n.*, omhaal *n.* van woorden *pl.n.* **verbose,** *a.* wijdlopig, breedsprakig. **verbosity,** *n.* wijdlopigheid *n.*, breedsprakigheid *n.*
verdant, *a.* groen.
verdict, *n.* uitspraak *n.*, vonnis *n.n. to give or return a* ~, uitspraak doen *irr.*; *to return a* ~ *of guilty,* schuldig bevinden *str.*
verdigris, *n.* kopergroen *n.n.*

verdure, *n.* groen *n.n.*
verge, *n.* rand *n.*, zoom *n.* ¶ *v.i. to* ~ *on,* grenzen aan.
verger, *n.* koster *n.*, kerkdienaar *n.*
verifiable, *a.* te verifiëren. **verification,** *n.* verificatie *n. in* ~ *of,* ten bewijze van. **verifier,** *n.* verificateur *n.* **verify,** *v.t.* verifiëren; nagaan *irr.*; bevestigen.
verily, *adv.* voorwaar, waarlijk.
verisimilitude, *n.* waarschijnlijkheid *n.*
veritable, *a.* waarachtig; werkelijk; echt.
vermicelli, *n.* vermicelli *n.*
vermicle, *n.* wormpje *n.n.* **vermicular,** *a.*, **vermiform,** *a.* wormvormig. **vermifuge,** *a.* wormafdrijvend.
vermilion, *n.* vermiljoen *n.n.* ¶ *a.* vermiljoen. ¶ *v.t.* rood verven.
vermin, *n.* ongedierte *n.n.* **verminous,** *a.* vol ongedierte *n.n.*
vernacular, *n.* landstaal *n.*
vernal, *a.* lente . . ., voorjaars . . .
veronal, *n.* veronal *n.*
veronica, *n.* ereprijs *n.*
verruca, *n.* wrat *n.*
versatile, *a.* veelzijdig. **versatility,** *n.* veelzijdigheid *n.*
verse, *n.* vers *n.n.*; versregel *n.*; poëzie *n. in* ~, in dichtmaat *n.* **versed,** *a.* ~ *in,* bedreven in. **versicle,** *n.* psalmvers *n.n.* **versification,** *n.* versificatie *n.*, versbouw *n.* **versifier,** *n.* verzenmaker *n.*, rijmelaar *n.* **versify,** *v.i.* verzen *pl.n.n.* maken. ¶ *v.t.* berijmen.
version, *n.* vertaling *n.* (in een vreemde taal); lezing *n.*, voorstelling *n.*
verso, *n.* ommezijde *n.*
verst, *n.* werst *n.*
versus, *prep.* tegen.
vertebra, *n.* wervel *n.* **vertebral,** *a.* wervel . . . **vertebrate,** *a.* gewerveld. ¶ *n.* ~s, gewervelde dieren *pl.n.n.*
vertex, *n.* toppunt *n.n.* **vertical,** *a.*, ~ly, *adv.* verticaal, loodrecht. ~ *angle,* tophoek *n.*
vertiginous, *a.* duizelingwekkend. **vertigo,** *n.* duizeligheid *n.*; duizeling *n.*
vertu, *n. articles of* ~, kunstvoorwerpen *pl.n.n.*
vervain, *n.* ijzerkruid *n.n.*
very, *a.* echt, wezenlijk. *the* ~ *best,* het allerbeste; *the* ~ *day,* diezelfde dag *n.*; *before my* ~ *eyes,* vlak voor m'n ogen *pl.n.n.*; *for that* ~ *reason,* juist daarom; *the* ~ *same,* diezelfde; *the* ~ *word,* hét woord. ¶ *adv.* zeer; heel; erg.
Very-light, *N.* lichtgranaat *n.*
vesical, *a.* blaas . . . **vesicle,** *n.* blaasje *n.n.*
vespers, *pl.n.* vesper *n.*
vessel, *n.* vat *n.n.*; vaartuig *n.n.* ~s (*also*), vaatwerk *n.n.*
vest, *n.* borstrok *n.* ¶ *v.t. to* ~ *with,* bekleden met; *to be* ~*ed in,* belegd zijn in; ~*ed interests,* bestaande belangen *pl.n.n.*, groepsbelangen *pl.n.n.*

vesta, *n.* (was)lucifer *n.*
Vestal, *a.* Vestaals; kuis.   ¶ *N.* Vestaalse maagd *n.*
vestibule, *n.* vestibule *n.*; (*fig.*) voorhof *n.*
vestige, *n.* spoor *n.n.*   *not a ~ of,* geen zweem *n.* van. **vestigial,** *a.* rudimentair.
vestment, *n.* gewaad *n.n.*; (altaar)kleed *n.n.*
vestry, *n.* sacristie *n.*; parochiaal bestuur *n.n.*, kerkeraad *n.* **vestryman,** *n.* lid *n.n.* van de kerkeraad *n.*
vesture, *n.* bekleding *n.*
vet., *n.* *See* veterinary surgeon.
vetch, *n.* wikke *n.*
veteran, *n.* veteraan *n.*, oudgediende *n.*
veterinary, *a.* veeartsenijkundig.   ~ *science,* veeartsenij *n.*; ~ *surgeon,* veearts *n.*
veto, *n.* veto *n.n.*   ¶ *v.t.* zijn veto uitspreken *str.* over.
vex, *v.t.* ergeren; kwellen.   ¶ *v.i. to be ~ed at,* zich ergeren over. **vexation,** *n.* ergernis *n.*; verdrietelijkheid *n.*; kwelling *n.* **vexatious,** *a.* ergerlijk, hinderlijk; vervelend. **vexing,** *a.* vervelend.
via, *prep.* via; over.
viable, *a.* levensvatbaar.
viaduct, *n.* viaduct *n.n.*
vial, *n.* flool *n.*
viands, *pl.n.* spijzen *pl.n.*
viaticum, *n.* viaticum *n.n.*; teerpenning *n.*
vibrant, *a.* ~ *with,* trillend van. **vibrate,** *v.i.* trillen; vibreren. **vibration,** *n.* trilling *n.*
vicar, *n.* predikant *n.*, dominee *n.* (*Protestant*); kapelaan *n.* (*Roman Catholic*).   ~ *apostolic,* apostolisch vicaris *n.*; ~*-general,* vicaris-generaal *n.*; ~ *of Christ,* stedehouder *n.* Christi. **vicarage,** *n.* pastorie *n.*, predikants-woning *n.*; vicariaat *n.n.*
vicarious, *a.* plaatsvervangend; in de plaats van een ander; tweedehands.
vice, *n.* ondeugd *n.*; bankschroef *n.*   ¶ *a.* vice.
vice-consul, *n.* vice-consul *n.*
vice-regal, *a.* van de onderkoning. **vice-reine,** *n.* vrouw *n.* van de onderkoning. **viceroy,** *n.* onderkoning *n.*
vice-versa, *adv.* vice versa, omgekeerd.
vicinity, *n.* buurt *n.*
vicious, *a.,* ~**ly,** *adv.* verdorven; vals, boosaardig.   ~ *circle,* vicieuze kring *n.*
vicissitude, *n.* wisselvalligheid *n.*; weder-waardigheid *n.*
victim, *n.* slachtoffer *n.*; dupe *n.* **victimiza-tion,** *n.* dupering *n.* **victimize,** *v.t.* tot slachtoffer *n.n.* maken.
victor, *n.* overwinnaar *n.*
Victorian, *a.* Victoriaans, uit de tijd van koningin Victoria.
victorious, *a.,* ~**ly,** *adv.* overwinnend. zegevierend. *to be ~ over,* zegevieren over. **victory,** *n.* overwinning *n.*; victorie *n.*
victual, *v.t.* provianderen.   ¶ *n.* ~*s,* proviand *n.n.*; leeftocht *n.*, levensmiddelen *pl.n.n.* **victualler,** *n.* proviandmeester *n.* *licensed* ~, slijter *n.*

videlicet, *adv.* namelijk, dat wil zeggen.
vie, *v.i.* wedijveren.
Vienna, *N.* Wenen *n.N.* **Viennese,** *a.* Weens, Wener.   ¶ *n.* Wener *N.*; Wenerin *N.* (*female*).
view, *n.* zicht *n.n.*, gezicht *n.n.*, uitzicht *n.n.*; blik *n.*, aanblik *n.* *at first ~,* op 't eerste gezicht; *in ~,* in zicht *n.n.*; in het vooruit-zicht; *in ~ of,* met het oog op; *in full ~ of,* ten aanschouwe van; *in my ~,* in mijn opinie *n.*, naar mijn mening *n.*; *to have something in ~,* iets op 't oog hebben; *to be on ~,* te bezichtigen zijn; *with a ~ to,* met de bedoeling, ten einde; ~ *of,* gezicht *n.n.* op, kijkje *n.n.* op; *his ~s on,* z'n denkbeelden *pl.n.n.* over; *to have ~s on,* ergens een besliste mening *n.* over hebben; ergens op belust zijn; *point of ~,* gezichtspunt *n.n.*, standpunt *n.n.*   ¶ *v.t.* zien *irr.*; bezichtigen (*house*); beschouwen (*question*).
vigil, *n.* vigilie *n.*; waken *n.n.* ~*s,* nachtwake *n.*; nachtdienst *n.* **vigilance,** *n.* waak-zaamheid *n.* **vigilant,** *a.* waakzaam.
vignette, *n.* vignet *n.*
vigorous, *a.,* ~**ly,** *adv.* krachtig, fors; energiek. **vigour,** *n.* kracht *n.*; energie *n.*
vile, *a.,* ~**ly,** *adv.* laag, laaghartig; verachte-lijk. **vilification,** *n.* laster *n.*, smaad *n.* **vilify,** *v.t.* belasteren.
villa, *n.* villa *n.*, buitenplaats *n.*
village, *n.* dorp *n.n.* **villager,** *n.* dorpeling *n.*, dorpsbewoner *n.*
villain, *n.* schurk *n.*; horige *n.* (*historical*). **villainous,** *a.,* ~**ly,** *adv.* schurkachtig, gemeen. **villainy,** *n.* schurkerij *n.*
vindicate, *v.t.* rechtvaardigen; verdedigen. **vindication,** *n.* rechtvaardiging *n.*; ver-dediging *n.* *in ~ of,* ter verdediging van. **vindicator,** *n.* verdediger *n.* **vindicatory,** *a.* rechtvaardigend, verdedigend; wrekend, straffend.
vindictive, *a.,* ~**ly,** *adv.* wraakgierig, wraak-zuchtig.
vine, *n.* wijnstok *n.*; wingerd *n.* **vine-branch,** *n.* wingerdrank *n.* **vine-clad,** *a.* met wingerdranken *pl.n.* begroeid. **vine-disease,** *n.* druifluisziekte *n.*
vinegar, *n.* azijn *n.* **vinegary,** *a.* azijnachtig, zuur.
vine-grower, *n.* wijnbouwer *n.* **vineyard,** *n.* wijngaard *n.*, wingerd *n.* **viniculture,** *n.* wijnbouw *n.* **vinous,** *a.* wijnachtig, wijn . . . **vintage,** *n.* wijnoogst *n.*; jaargang *n.*, crû *n.* **vintner,** *n.* wijnhuishouder *n.* **viny,** *a.* wijnrijk.
viol, *n.* (ouderwetse) viool *n.*, vedel *n.* **viola,** *n.* viola *n.*; altviool *n.*; knieviool *n.*
violate, *v.t.* verkrachten; geweld *n.n.* aandoen *irr.*; schenden *str.* **violation,** *n.* verkrachting *n.*; inbreuk *n.*; schending *n.* **violator,** *n.* verkrachter *n.*; schender *n.*
violence, *n.* geweld *n.n.*; hevigheid *n.*; heftigheid *n.* *to do ~ to,* geweld aandoen

irr.; *by* ~, met geweld. **violent**, *a.*, ~ly, *adv.* geweldig, hevig, heftig; gewelddadig. *to lay* ~ *hands on*, geweld *n.n.* aandoen *irr.*

violet, *n.* viooltje *n.n.* ¶ *a.* violet, paars.

violin, *n.* viool *n.* **violin-case**, *n.* vioolkist *n.* **violinist**, *n.* violist *n.*; violiste *n.* (*female*). **violoncellist**, *n.* cellist *n.* **violoncello**, *n.* violoncel *n.*

viper, *n.* adder *n.* ~'*s bugloss*, slangenkruid *n.n.*; ~'*s grass*, schorseneer *n.* **viperine**, *a.* adderachtig.

virago, *n.* helleveeg *n.*; manwijf *n.n.*

virescent, *a.* groenend.

virgin, *n.* maagd *n.* ¶ *a.* maagdelijk. *V* ~ *Birth*, Onbevlekte Ontvangenis *N.*; ~ *gold*, gedegen goud *n.n.*; ~ *honey*, ongepijnde honig *n.*, honigzeem *n.*; ~ *oil*, maagdenolie *n.*; ~ *wax*, maagdenwas *n.* **virginal**, *a.* maagdelijk; rein, ongerept. ¶ *n.* ~*s*, spinet *n.n.*

Virginia, *N.* Virginië *n.N.* ~ *creeper*, wilde wingerd *n.*; ~ *rose*, gele lupine *n.*

virginity, *n.* maagdelijkheid *n.*; reinheid *n.*, kuisheid *n.*

viridity, *n.* groenheid *n.*

virile, *a.* mannelijk. **virility**, *n.* mannelijkheid *n.*

virtual, *a.* virtueel, feitelijk. **virtually**, *adv.* virtueel, practisch, in de praktijk.

virtue, *n.* deugd *n.*; deugdzaamheid *n.* *by* (*or in*) ~ *of*, krachtens; *to make a* ~ *of necessity*, van de nood een deugd maken.

virtuosity, *n.* virtuositeit *n.* **virtuoso**, *n.* virtuoos *a.*

virtuous, *a.*, ~ly, *adv.* deugdzaam.

virulence, *n.* kwaadaardigheid *n.*; giftigheid *n.* **virulent**, *a.*, ~ly, *adv.* kwaadaardig, boosaardig; giftig.

virus, *n.* smetstof *n.*; gif *n.n.*

visa, *n.* visum *n.n.* ¶ *v.t.* viseren, aftekenen.

visage, *n.* gelaat *n.n.*

viscera, *pl.n.* ingewanden *pl.n.n.*

viscid, *a.* kleverig. **viscosity**, *n.* kleverigheid *n.*

viscount, *n.* *untranslated, approx.*: burggraaf *n.* **viscountess**, *n.* *untranslated, approx.*: burggravin *n.* **viscounty**, *n.*, **viscountship**, *n.* *untranslated, approx.*: burggraafschap *n.n.*

viscous, *a.* kleverig.

visibility, *n.* zichtbaarheid *n.* **visible**, *a.*, ~bly, *adv.* zichtbaar; waarneembaar, merkbaar. **vision**, *n.* visioen *n.n.*, droombeeld *n.n.*, verschijning *n.*; gezichtsvermogen *n.n.* **visionary**, *a.* hersenschimmig; ingebeeld; onpractisch. ¶ *n.* dromer *n.*, dweper *n.*

visit, *n.* bezoek *n.n.*; visite *n.* *to pay a* ~, een bezoek brengen *irr.*; *to return a* ~, een tegenbezoek *n.n.* brengen *irr.*; *domiciliary* ~, huiszoeking *n.* ¶ *v.t.* bezoeken *irr.*; teisteren. *to* ~ *with*, bezoeken *irr.* met.

visitation, *n.* bezoeking *n.*; beproeving *n.*

visiting-card, *n.* visitekaartje *n.n.* **visiting-committee**, *n.* commissie *n.* van toezicht *n.n.* **visitor**, *n.* bezoeker *n.* *to have* ~*s*, bezoek *n.n.* hebben; ~*s' book*, vreemdelingenboek *n.n.*; ~'*s room*, logeerkamer *n.*

visor, *n.* vizier *n.n.* **visored**, *a.* met een vizier.

vista, *n.* uitzicht *n.n.*; vergezicht *n.n.*

Vistula, *N.* Weichsel *N.*

visual, *a.* gezichts. ~ *point*, oogpunt *n.n.* **visualization**, *n.* veraanschouwelijking *n.* **visualize**, *v.t.* veraanschouwelijken; zich een beeld *n.n.* vormen van.

vital, *a.*, ~ly, *adv.* vitaal; levens . . . *to be* ~ *to* . . ., een levenskwestie *n.* zijn voor . . .; *of* ~ *importance*, van het allerhoogste belang; ~ *parts*, edele delen *pl.n.n.*; ~ *statistics*, bevolkingsstatistiek *n.* **vitality**, *n.* vitaliteit *n.*, levenskracht *n.*; levensvatbaarheid *n.* **vitalize**, *v.t.* levenskracht *n.* geven *str.*

vitamin, *n.* vitamine *n.*

vitiate, *v.t.* bederven *str.*; krachteloos maken.

viticulture, *n.* wijnbouw *n.*, druiventeelt *n.*

vitreous, *a.* glasachtig, glazig; glas . . . **vitrifaction**, *n.* verglazing *n.* **vitrify**, *v.t.* verglazen. ¶ *v.i.* in glas *n.n.* veranderen.

vitriol, *n.* vitriool *n.n.*, zwavelzuur *n.n.* **vitriolic**, *a.* vitrioolachtig; giftig, venijnig.

vituperate, *v.i.* schelden *str.* ¶ *v.t.* uitschelden *str.* **vituperation**, *n.* scheldwoorden *pl.n.n.*, gescheld *n.n.*

vivacious, *a.*, ~ly, *adv.* levendig, opgewekt. **vivacity**, *n.* levendigheid *n.*, opgewektheid *n.*

viva voce, *n.* mondeling examen *n.n.*

vivid, *a.*, ~ly, *adv.* levendig; helder.

vivification, *n.* verlevendiging *n.* **vivify**, *v.t.* verlevendigen, bezielen.

viviparous, *a.* levend barend.

vivisection, *n.* vivisectie *n.*

vixen, *n.* wijfjesvos *n.*; (*fig.*) feeks *n.*

viz., *adv.* namelijk, nl.

vizier, *n.* vizier *n.* *grand* ~, groot-vizier *n.*

vocabulary, *n.* woordenlijst *n.*; woordenschat *n.*

vocal, *a.* mondeling; luidruchtig; stem . . .; zang . . . ~ *chord*, stemband *n.* **vocalist**, *n.* zanger *n.*; zangeres *n.* (*female*). **vocalize**, *v.t.* stem *n.* geven *str.* aan.

vocation, *n.* roeping *n.*; beroep *n.n.* **vocational** *a.* beroeps . . ., vak . . .

vocative, *n.* vocatief *n.*

vociferate, *v.i.* razen, tieren, schreeuwen. **vociferation**, *n.* geraas *n.n.*, getier *n.n.*, geschreeuw *n.n.* **vociferous**, *a.* luidruchtig.

vogue, *n.* mode *n.*; zwang *n.*, trek *n.* *to be in* ~, in zwang zijn.

voice, *n.* stem *n.*; recht *n.n.* van spreken *n.n.*; vorm *n.* (*grammatical*). *to give* ~ *to*, uitdrukking *n.* geven *str.* aan; *in a loud* ~, met luider stem(me); *with one* ~, éénstemmig. ¶ *v.t.* uitdrukking *n.* geven *str.*

aan, vertolken. **voiced,** *a.* stemhebbend.
voiceless, *a.* stemloos; sprakeloos.
void, *a.* leeg; onbezet; nietig, van nul en
gener waarde *n.* ~ *of,* ontbloot van,
zonder. ¶ *n.* leegte *n.* ¶ *v.t.* ledigen,
ruimen; ontlasten; ongeldig verklaren.
voidable, *a.* opzegbaar.
volatile, *a.* vluchtig, vervliegend. ~ *salt,*
vlugzout *n.n.* **volatility,** *n.* vluchtigheid *n.*
volatilize, *v.t.* vluchtig maken, vervluchtigen. ¶ *v.i.* vervliegen *str.*
volcanic, *a.* vulkanisch. **volcano,** *n.* vulkaan
n., vuurspuwende berg *n.*
vole, *n.* veldmuis *n.* *water-*~, waterrat *n.*
volition, *n.* wil *n.*; wilskracht *n.*; wilsuiting *n.*
volley, *n.* salvo *n.n.* (*fire*); volley *n.* (*sport*).
¶ *v.i.* terugslaan *irr.* (*sport*).
volt, *n.* volt *n.* **voltage,** *n.* spanning *n.*
voltameter, *n.* voltameter *n.,* spannings-
meter *n.*
volubility, *n.* radheid *n.* **voluble,** *a.,* ~bly,
adv. rad (van tong *n.*); spraakzaam.
volume, *n.* (boek)deel *n.n.*; volume *n.n.,*
inhoud *n.*; hoeveelheid *n.*; omvang *n.*;
massa *n.* **voluminous,** *a.,* ~ly, *adv.*
omvangrijk; uitgebreid; lijvig.
voluntarily, *adv.* vrijwillig, uit eigen wil *n.,*
uit vrije wil *n.* **voluntary,** *a.* vrijwillig;
spontaan; willekeurig. ¶ *n.* fantasie *n.,*
voorspel *n.n.,* tussenspel *n.n.,* naspel *n.n.*
volunteer, *n.* vrijwilliger *n.* ¶ *a.* vrij-
willigers ... ¶ *v.t.* vrijwillig dienstnemen
str.; zich aanbieden *str.* (om).
voluptuary, *n.* wellusteling *n.* **voluptuous,**
a., ~ly, *adv.* wellustig; weelderig.
vomit, *v.i.* braken, overgeven *str.* ¶ *v.t.*
braken, uitbraken. ¶ *n.* (uit)braaksel *n.n.*
vomitive, *n.* braakmiddel *n.n.*
voracious, *a.,* ~ly, *adv.* vraatzuchtig; gulzig.
voracity, *n.* vraatzucht *n.*; gulzigheid *n.*
vortex, *n.* werveling *n.*; draaikolk *n.,* warrel-
poel *n.,* maalstroom *n.*
Vosges, *pl.N.* Vogezen *pl.N.*
votary, *n.* aanbidder *n.*; aanhanger *n.,*
volgeling *n.*
vote, *n.* stem *n.*; stemming *n.* *to pass a* ~,
een motie *n.* aannemen *str.*; ~ *of censure,*
motie van afkeuring; ~ *of confidence,*
motie van vertrouwen; ~ *of no-confidence,*
motie van wantrouwen; *to put to the* ~,
in stemming brengen *irr.* ¶ *v.i.* stemmen.
to ~ *for,* stemmen op *or* voor. ¶ *v.t.*
bij stemming *n.* verkiezen *str.*; verklaren.
voter, *n.* kiezer *n.*; stemgerechtigde *n.*
voting, *n.* stemmen *n.n.* ~ *paper,*
stembiljet *n.n.*
votive, *a.* votief.
vouch, *v.i.* *to* ~ *for,* instaan *irr.* voor. ¶ *v.t.*
verklaren, bevestigen. **voucher,** *n.* reçu *n.n.*;
bon *n.,* briefje *n.n.* **vouchsafe,** *v.t.* genadig-
lijk toestaan *irr.*; zich verwaardigen
(*answer*).
vow, *n.* gelofte *n.,* plechtige belofte *n.*
to make a ~, een gelofte afleggen *irr.*

¶ *v.t.* (plechtig) beloven, een gelofte *n.*
afleggen *irr.* (van te).
vowel, *n.* klinker *n.*
voyage, *n.* zeereis *n.* ¶ *v.i.* reizen, varen *ur.*
¶ *v.t.* bereizen, bevaren *irr.* **voyager,** *n.*
zeereiziger *n.*; ontdekkingsreiziger *n.*
vulcanite, *n.* vulkaniet *n.n.* **vulcanize,** *v.t.*
vulkaniseren.
vulgar, *a.,* ~ly, *adv.* gewoon; algemeen; ordinair; grof, plat. ~ *fraction,* gewone breuk
n.; *the* ~ *mass,* de grote hoop; ~ *tongue,*
landstaal *n.,* volkstaal *n.* **vulgarian,** *n.*
proleet *n.* **vulgarism,** *n.* platte uitdrukking
n. **vulgarity,** *n.* vulgariteit *n.*; grofheid *n.,*
platheid *n.* **vulgarization,** *n.* popularisatie
n. **vulgarize,** *v.t.* vulgariseren, populariseren.
vulnerability, *n.* kwetsbaarheid *n.* **vulnerable,**
a., ~bly, *adv.* kwetsbaar.
vulnerary, *a.* helend.
vulpine, *a.* vosachtig; listig.
vulture, *n.* gier *n.* **vulturine,** *a.* gierachtig;
roofgierig.
vying, *a.,* ~ly, *adv.* wedijverend, mededingend.

W

wad, *n.* prop *n.*; bos *n.* ¶ *v.t.* watteren,
opvullen.
wadable, *a.* doorwaadbaar.
wadding, *n.* watteersel *n.n.,* opvulsel *n.n.*
waddle, *v.i.* waggelen. *to* ~ *along,* voortsukkelen.
wade, *v.i.* waden. *to* ~ *through,* waden door,
baggeren door. ¶ *v.t.* doorwaden. **wader,** *n.*
wader *n.*; waadvogel *n.* ~*s,* baggerlaarzen
pl.n. **wading-bird,** *n.* waadvogel *n.*
wafer, *n.* wafeltje *n.n.*; ouwel *n.,* hostie *n.*
waffle, *n.* wafel *n.*
waft, *v.t.* overbrengen *irr.,* voeren; wenken;
toewuiven. ¶ *v.i.* zweven, drijven *str.*
¶ *n.* zuchtje *n.n.*
wag, *v.t.* kwispelen (*tail*); schudden (*finger*).
to ~ *one's tail,* kwispelstaarten. ¶ *v.i.*
roeren. *to set tongues* ~*ging,* de tongen
pl.n. doen *irr.* gaan. ¶ *n.* grappenmaker *n.,*
spotvogel *n.*
wage, *n.* loon *n.n.,* arbeidsloon *n.n.* ~*s,*
loon *n.n.*; *living* ~, behoorlijk loon. ¶ *v.t.*
voeren (*war*); leveren (*battle*). **wage-
earner,** *n.* loontrekker *n.*
wager, *n.* weddenschap *n.* *to make* (or *lay*)
a ~, een weddenschap aangaan *irr.* ¶ *v.t.*
wedden, verwedden. ¶ *v.i.* wedden.
waggish, *a.,* ~ly, *adv.* schalks, guitig.
waggle, *v.t.* wiebelen, wippen.
wag(g)on, *n.* wagen *n.,* vrachtwagen *n.*;
wagon *n.* **waggoner,** *n.* voerman *n.,*
vrachtrijder *n.* *the W*~, de Wagenmenner
N. **waggonette,** *n.* wagentje *n.n.*
wagtail, *n.* kwikstaartje *n.n.*

waif, *n.* onbeheerd goed *n.n.*; weggelopen dier *n.n.* ~*s and strays*, verwaarloosde kinderen *pl.n.n.*

wail, *v.i.* weeklagen, jammeren. ¶ *n.* weeklacht *n.*, jammerklacht *n.*; gekerm *n.n.*

wain, *n.* wagen *n.* *Lesser W* ~, Kleine Beer *N.* (*constellation*).

wainscot, *n.*, **wainscoting**, *n.* lambrizering *n.*, beschot *n.n.*

waist, *n.* middel *n.n.*, leest *n.*, taille *n.*; kuil *n.* (*of ship*); smalste gedeelte *n.n.* **waistband**, *n.* gordel *n.*, ceintuur *n.* **waistcoat**, *n.* vest *n.n.*, vestje *n.n.*

wait, *v.i.* wachten. *to* ~ *for*, wachten op; *to* ~ *on*, bedienen; *to* ~ *up for*, opblijven *str.* voor; *to* ~ *and see*, afwachten. ¶ *v.t.* afwachten. ¶ *n.* wachten *n.n.*; pauze *n.* *to lie in* ~ *for*, loeren op. **waiter**, *n.* kellner *n.*, ober *n.* *dumb* ~, stommeknecht *n.*, dienbak *n.* **waiting**, *a.* afwachtend. ¶ *n.* wachten *n.n.* *in* ~, dienstdoend; *lady-in-*~, hofdame *n.* **waiting-room**, *n.* wachtkamer *n.* **waiting-woman**, *n.* kamenier *n.* **waitress**, *n.* kellnerin *n.*, juffrouw *n.*

waits, *pl.n.* Kerstzangers *pl.N.*

waive, *v.t.* afstand *n.* doen *irr.* van.

wake, *n.* zog *n.n.*, kielwater *n.n.* (*of ship*); nachtwake *n.* (*vigil*). ¶ *v.i.* wakker worden *str.*, ontwaken. *to* ~ *up*, wakker worden *str.* ¶ *v.t.* wakker maken; wakker schudden; wekken. *to* ~ . . *up*, wakker maken. **wakeful**, *a.*, ~ly, *adv.* waakzaam; wakend. **waken**, *v.t.* wakker maken. **wake-robin**, *n.* gevlekte aronskelk *n.*

Wales, *N.* Wales *n.N.*, Wallis *n.N.*

walk, *v.i.* lopen *str.*; wandelen; gaan *irr.*; rondwaren, spoken (*ghost*). *to* ~ *into*, aanlopen *str.* tegen; *to* ~ *up to*, toegaan *irr.* naar. ¶ *v.t.* lopen *str.*; wandelen; doen *irr.* lopen; aflopen *str.* ¶ *n.* wandeling *n.*; gang *n.*; wandelweg *n.* ~ *of life*, stand *n.*, werkkring *n.* **walker**, *n.* wandelaar *n.* **walking-stick**, *n.* wandelstok *n.* **walking-tour**, *n.* wandeltocht *n.* **walkover**, *n.* gemakkelijke overwinning *n.*

wall, *n.* muur *n.*; wand *n.* *to push to the* ~, in 't nauw drijven str., *to go to the* ~, het onderspit delven *str.* ¶ *v.t.* ommuren. *to* ~ *off*, door een muur afscheiden; *to* ~ *up*, dichtmetselen. **wall-creeper**, *n.* muurspecht *n.*

wallet, *n.* knapzak *n.* (*bag*); portefeuille *n.*

wall-eyed, *a.* met glazige blik. **wall-fern**, *n.* eikvaren *n.* **wallflower**, *n.* muurbloem *n.*; (*fig.*) muurbloempje *n.n.*

Walloon, *a.* Waals. ¶ *N.* Waal *N.*; Waalse *N.* (*fema'e*).

wallop, *v.t.* slaan *irr.*, meppen. ¶ *n.* slag *n.* ¶ *excl.* pats! pardoes!

wallow, *v.i.* wentelen, rollen. *to* ~ *in money*, in 't geld zwemmen *str.*

wall-paper, *n.* behangsel *n.n.*, behangselpapier *n.n.*

walnut, *n.* walnoot *n.*, okkernoot *n.* ¶ *a.* noten(houten). **walnut-tree**, *n.* notenboom *n.*, notelaar *n.*

walrus, *n.* walrus *n.*

waltz, *n.* wals *n.* ¶ *v.i.* walsen. **waltzer**, *n.* walser *n.*

wan, *a.*, ~ly, *adv.* bleek, flets; flauw.

wand, *n.* staf *n.*, roede *n.* *magic* ~, toverstaf *n.*

wander, *v.i.* (rond)zwerven *str.*, (rond)dolen; afdwalen. *his mind* ~*s*, hij maalt. **wanderer**, *n.* zwerver *n.* **wandering**, *a.* zwervend; nomadisch. *the W* ~ *Jew*, de Wandelende Jood.

wane, *v.i.* afnemen *str.*; tanen. ¶ *n.* afnemen *n.n.* *on the* ~, aan het tanen.

wangle, *v.t.* het weten *irr.* voor elkaar te krijgen. **wangler**, *n.* slimmerik *n.*, gladakker *n.*

wanness, *n.* bleekheid *n.*

want, *v.t.* nodig hebben; vereisen; verlangen, wensen; willen. *to be* ~*ed*, gezocht worden *str.*; *to be* ~*ing*, mankeren; *to be* ~*ing in*, te kort schieten *str.* in; *to be found* ~*ing*, te licht bevonden worden *str.* ¶ *n.* behoefte *n.*; gebrek *n.n.*, gemis *n.n.*; armoede *n.* *for* ~ *of*, bij gebrek aan; *to be in* ~ *of*, nodig hebben.

wanton, *a.*, ~ly, *adv.* dartel, speels; moedwillig, baldadig; wellustig, wulps. ¶ *v.i.* dartelen. ¶ *n.* lichtekooi *n.* wantonness, *n.* dartelheid *n.*; baldadigheid *n.*; wulpsheid *n.*

war, *n.* oorlog *n.* *civil* ~, burgeroorlog *n.*; *to be at* ~, in oorlog zijn; *to go to* ~ *with*, een oorlog aangaan *irr.* met. ¶ *v.i.* oorlog voeren. ¶ *v.t.* beoorlogen.

warble, *v.i.* kwelen, kwinkeleren; op en neer gaan *irr.* (*siren*). ¶ *n.* gekweel *n.n.* **warble-fly**, *n.* horzel *n.*, brems *n.* **warbler**, *n.* zanger *n.*; tjiftjaf *n.* **warbling**, *a.* op en neer gaand. ¶ *n.* gekweel *n.n.*

war-chest, *n.* krijgskas *n.* **war-cry**, *n.* oorlogskreet *n.*

ward, *n.* pupil *n.*; wijk *n.* (*parish*); zaal *n.* (*institution*); werk *n.n.* (*lock*). *to be in* ~, onder voogdij *n.* staan *irr.* ¶ *v.t.* waken. *to* ~ *off*, afweren; pareren (*fencing*).

war-damage, *n.* herstelbetaling *n.*

warden, *n.* custos *n.*; rector *n.*; vader *n.* (*hostel*); bestuurder *n.*, gouverneur *n.*

warder, *n.* gevangenbewaarder *n.*, cipier *n.*

wardrobe, *n.* kleerkast *n.*; garderobe *n.*; kleren *pl.n.n.*

wardroom, *n.* officierskajuit *n.*

wardship, *n.* voogdijschap *n.*

ware, *n.* waar *n.*, werk *n.n.* ~*s*, koopwaar *n.* ¶ *int.* pas op.

warehouse, *n.* pakhuis *n.n.*, magazijn *n.n.* *bonded* ~, entrepôt *n.n.* ¶ *v.t.* opslaan *irr.* **warehouse company**, *n.* veem *n.n.* **warehouse keeper**, *n.* magazijnmeester *n.* **warehouseman**, *n.* pakhuisknecht *n.*; pakhuiseigenaar *n.* **warehouse-room**, *n.* opslagruimte *n.*

war-establishment, *n.* oorlogssterkte *n.*
warfare, *n.* oorlog *n.*, strijd *n.*, krijg *n.*
war-head, *n.* kop *n.*
warily, *adv.* behoedzaam, omzichtig. **wariness,** *n.* behoedzaamheid *n.*, omzichtigheid *n.*
warlike, *a.* krijgshaftig; oorlogszuchtig.
war-lord, *n.* krijgsheer *n.*
warm, *a.,* ~**ly,** *adv.* warm; verhit; vurig; ijverig. *to make it* ~ *for someone,* iemand het vuur aan de schenen *pl.n.* leggen *irr.; it was* ~ *work,* het ging er heet toe. ¶ *v.t.* warmen, verwarmen. ¶ *v.r. to* ~ *oneself,* zich warmen. ¶ *v.i.* warm worden *str. to* ~ *to one's subject,* door z'n onderwerp *n.n.* worden *str.* meegesleept. ¶ *n.* warmte *n.* **warmblooded,** *a.* warmbloedig. **warm-hearted,** *a.* hartelijk. **warming-pan,** *n.* beddepan *n.* **warmth,** *n.* warmte *n.*; (*fig.*) gloed *n.*, vuur *n.n.*
war-monger, *n.* oorlogzoeker *n.*
warn, *v.t.* waarschuwen; verwittigen. *to* ~ *against,* waarschuwen voor (*or* tegen); *to* ~ *away* or *off,* verzoeken *irr.* weg te gaan, niet toelaten *str.* **warning,** *n.* waarschuwing *n.*; vermaning *n.*; verwittiging *n. take* ~!, wees gewaarschuwd!
war office, *N.* Ministerie *n.N.* van Oorlog *N.*
warp, *v.i.* kromtrekken *str.*; krom worden *str.* ¶ *v.t.* doen *irr.* kromtrekken; verdraaien. ¶ *n.* kromtrekking *n.*; geestesafwijking *n.*; schering *n.* (*weaving*).
war-paint, *n.* oorlogsbeschildering *n.*, krijgsdos *n.* **war-path,** *n.* oorlogspad *n.n.* **war-plant,** *n.* fabriek *n.* van oorlogsmateriaal *n.n.*
warrant, *n.* volmacht *n.*, procuratie *n.*; bevelschrift *n.n.*; bevel *n.n.* tot inhechtenisneming *n.*; waarborg *n.* ¶ *v.t.* machtigen; waarborgen, garanderen, instaan *irr.* voor. **warrantable,** *a.* gerechtvaardigd, gewettigd. **warrantee,** *n.* gevolmachtigde *n.* **warrant-officer,** *n.* adjudant-onderofficier *n.*; dekofficier *n.* **warrantor,** *n.* volmachtgever *n.*; waarborger *n.* **warranty,** *n.* waarborg *n.*; garantiebewijs *n.n.*
warren, *n.* konijnenberg *n.*; (*fig.*) warnet *n.n.*
warrior, *n.* krijgsman *n.*; soldaat *n.*
war-risk, *n.* oorlogsrisico *n.n.*; molest *n.n.*
wart, *n.* wrat *n.* **wart-grass,** *n.* kroontjeskruid *n.n.* **wart-hog,** *n.* wrattenzwijn *n.* **wartwort,** *n.* stinkende gouwe *n.* **warty,** *a.* wrattig.
wary, *a.* behoedzaam, omzichtig. *to be* ~ *of,* op zijn hoede voor; zich wel wachten om te . . .
wash, *v.t.* wassen *irr.*; zich wassen *irr.*; schoonwassen; afwassen; spoelen; bespoelen. *to* ~ *ashore,* aan land *n.n.* spoelen; *to* ~ *down,* afspoelen; *to* ~ *overboard,* overboord spoelen; *to* ~ *out,* uitwassen *irr.*; afgelasten; ~*ed out,* bleek, vermoeid; *to* ~ *up,* afwassen. ¶ *v.i. it doesn't* ~, het is niet wasecht; het houdt geen steek. ¶ *v.r.*

to ~ *oneself,* zich wassen. ¶ *n.* was *n.*; wassen *n.n.*; kielwater *n.n.*; golfslag *n. to have a* ~, zich even wassen *irr.* **washable,** *a.* wasbaar; wasecht. **wash-basin,** *n.* (vaste) waskom *n.* **wash-bear,** *n.* wasbeer *n.* **washbowl,** *n.* waskom *n.* **washer,** *n.* wasmachine *n.*; sluitring *n.* **washerwoman,** *n.* wasvrouw *n.* **washing day,** *n.* wasdag *n.* **washing up,** *n.* afwas *n.* **wash-leather,** *n.* zeemleer *n.n.* **washstand,** *n.* wastafel *n.* **washy,** *a.* waterig, slap.
wasp, *n.* wesp *n.* ~ *waist,* wespentaille *n.*; ~*s's nest,* wespennest *n.n.* **waspish,** *a.* scherp, bits.
wassail, *n.* drinkgelag *n.n.* ¶ *v.i.* een drinkgelag houden *irr.*
wastage, *n.* verspilling *n.*; slijtage *n.*; bederf *n.n.* **waste,** *v.t.* verkwisten, verspillen; laten *str.* voorbijgaan (*opportunity*). ~ *not want not,* die wat spaart die wat heeft. ¶ *v.i.* verloren gaan *irr. to* ~ *away,* wegteren, wegkwijnen. ¶ *n.* verkwisting *n.*, verspilling *n.*; woestenij *n.*, woestijn *n.*, wildernis *n.*; afval *n.*; poetskatoen *n.n. to run to* ~, verloren gaan *irr.*; verwilderen. ¶ *a.* woest; verwoest; onbebouwd, braak; *bar. to lay* ~, verwoesten; *to lie* ~, braak liggen *str.*; ongebruikt zijn; ~ *land,* onontgonnen land *n.n.*, onbebouwd terrein *n.n.*; ~ *products,* afvalproducten *pl.n.n.*; ~ *steam,* afgewerkte stoom *n.*; ~ *water,* vuil water *n.n.* **wasteful,** *a.,* ~**ly,** *adv.* verkwistend, spilziek. ~ *of,* roekeloos met. **wastefulness,** *n.* verkwisting *n.* **wastepaper,** *n.* scheurpapier *n.n.* ~ *basket,* scheurmand *n.*, prullenmand *n.* **waste-pipe,** *n.* loospijp *n.*, afvoerbuis *n.* **waster,** *n.* verkwister *n.* **wastrel,** *n.* mislukkeling *n.*
watch, *v.t.* bewaken; letten op, kijken *str.* naar; beloeren; hoeden (*flock*). ¶ *v.i.* waken. *to* ~ *for,* uitkijken *str.* naar; *to* ~ *out,* (goed) uitkijken *str.*; *to* ~ *over,* bewaken; *to* ~ *with* or *by,* waken bij. ¶ *n.* wacht *n.*; wachten *n.n.*; horloge *n.n. middle* ~, hondenwacht *n.*; *in the* ~*es of the night,* in de slapeloze uren *pl.n.n.*; *to keep* ~, de wacht houden *irr.*; *to be on the* ~, op de uitkijk staan *irr.*; *to be on the* ~ *for,* uitkijken *str.* naar. **watch-case,** *n.* horlogekast *n.* **watchdog,** *n.* waakhond *n.* **watcher,** *n.* waker *n.*; waarnemer *n.* **watchful,** *a.,* ~**ly,** *adv.* waakzaam. *to be* ~ *of,* een waakzaam oog *n.n.* houden *irr.* op. **watchfulness,** *n.* waakzaamheid *n.* **watchglass,** *n.* horlogeglas *n.n.* **watchmaker,** *n.* horlogemaker *n.* **watchman,** *n.* wachter *n.*; nachtwaker *n.* **watchword,** *n.* wachtwoord *n.n.*
water, *n.* water *n.n.*; vaarwater *n.n.*; urine *n. of the first* ~, van het zuiverste water; *fresh* ~, zoet water; *to hold* ~, waterdicht zijn; (*fig.*) *it doesn't hold* ~, het houdt geen steek; *to get in hot* ~, zich moeilijkheden *pl.n.*

op de hals halen; *to make* ~, wateren. ¶ *v.t.* begieten *str.*, besproeien; van water *n.n.* voorzien *irr. to* ~ *down*, aanlengen, verslappen. ¶ *v.i.* tranen (*eyes*); water innemen *str.* (*ship*). *my mouth* ~*s*, ik watertand. **water-borne**, *a.* van over zee, te water vervoerd. **water-closet**, *n.* W.C. *n.* **water-colour**, *n.* waterverf *n.*; aquarel *n.* **water-course**, *n.* stroompje *n.n.* **watercress**, *n.* waterkers *n.* **watered**, *a.* verwaterd, aangelengd; moiré. **waterfall**, *n.* waterval *n.* **waterflag**, *n.* gele lis *n.* **waterfowl**, *n.* watervogel *n.*; watervogels *pl.n.* **waterfront**, *n.* waterkant *n.* **watergauge**, *n.* peilglas *n.n.*, niveaubuis *n.* **water-hen**, *n.* waterhoen *n.n.* **water-hole**, *n.* drinkplaats *n.*, wed *n.n.* **watering-can**, *n.* gieter *n.* **watering-cart**, *n.* sproeiwagen *n.* **watering-place**, *n.* badplaats *n.* **water-jacket**, *n.* koelmantel *n.* **water-level**, *n.* waterspiegel *n.*; waterpas *n.n.* **waterlily**, *n.* waterlelie *n.*, plomp *n.* **waterlogged**, *a.* volgelopen met water *n.n.* **watermain**, *n.* hoofdbuis *n.* (van de waterleiding). **watermark**, *n.* watermerk *n.n.* **waterproof**, *a.* waterdicht, waterproef. ¶ *n.* regenjas *n.* **water-rate**, *n.* leidinghuur *n.* **watershed**, *n.* waterscheiding *n.* **waterspout**, *n.* waterhoos *n.* (*phenomenon*); gootpijp *n.* **water-supply**, *n.* watervoorziening *n.* **watertight**, *a.* waterdicht. ~ *compartment*, waterdicht beschot *n.n.* **water-wagtail**, *n.* grijze kwikstaart *n.* **waterway**, *n.* waterweg *n.*; waterloop *n.* **waterwheel**, *n.* waterrad *n.n.* **waterworks**, *pl.n.* waterleiding *n.* **watery**, *a.* waterig, waterachtig.

watt, *n.* watt *n.*

wattle, *n.* horde *n.*, hordenwerk *n.n.* ¶ *v.t.* met horden afzetten.

wave, *n.* golf *n.*; vloed *n.*; wuivend gebaar *n.n.*, gewuif *n.n.* ¶ *v.i.* golven; wapperen (*flag*); wuiven (*hand*). ¶ *v.t.* (doen *irr.*) golven; onduleren (*hair*); wuiven met, zwaaien. **wavelet**, *n.* golfje *n.n.* **waver**, *v.i.* weifelen, aarzelen; flikkeren (*light*); beven (*voice*). **waverer**, *n.* weifelaar *n.* **wavy**, *a.* golvend, gegolfd.

wax, *n.* was *n.*; lak *n.n.* ¶ *v.t.* wassen, boenen. ¶ *v.i.* wassen *str.* (*grow*); gedijen (*thrive*). **wax-cloth**, *n.* wasdoek *n.n.* **waxen**, *a.* wassen; bleek. **waxwork**, *n.* wassenbeeld *n.n.* ~*s*, wassenbeeldenspel *n.n.* **waxy**, *a.* wasachtig.

way, *n.* weg *n.*; straat *n.*; richting *n.*, kant *n.*; manier *n.*, wijze *n.*; gewoonte *n.* ~ *in*, ingang *n.*; ~ *out*, uitgang *n.*; ~*s and means*, geldmiddelen *pl.n.n.*; *a long* ~, een heel eind *n.n.*; *this* ~, hierheen, deze kant *n.* op; *both* ~*s*, op twee manieren *pl.n.*; *one* ~ *or another*, op de een of andere manier; *one's own* ~, op z'n eigen manier *n.*; *the other* ~ *about*, net andersom; *to clear the* ~, ruimte *n.* maken; *to find a* ~, een uitweg *n.* vinden *str.*; *to gather* ~,

vaart *n.* krijgen *str.*; *to get one's* ~, z'n zin *n.* krijgen *str.*; *to give* ~, wijken *str.*; toegeven *str.*; *to give* ~ *to*, zich overgeven *str.* aan; *to go a long* ~ *towards*, heel wat bijdragen *str.* tot; *to know one's* ~, de weg weten *irr.*; weten *irr.* wat te doen; *by* ~ *of*, bij wijze van; via; *by the* ~, onderweg; à propos, tussen twee haakjes *pl.n.n.*; *by a long* ~, verreweg; *not by a long* ~, lang niet; *in a* ~, in zekere zin; *in no* ~, geenszins; *in a* ~ *of speaking*, bij wijze *n.* van spreken *n.n.*; *in a general* ~, in algemene zin *n.*; *once in a* ~, voor een enkele maal *n.*; *to be in a bad* ~, er slecht aan toe zijn; *out of the* ~, afgelegen; ongewoon, buitensporig; *to go out of one's* ~, zich moeite *n.* getroosten; *over the* ~, aan de overkant; *under* ~, aan de gang; op weg; *to get under* ~, het anker lichten. **way-bill**, *n.* geleibrief *n.* **wayfarer**, *n.* reiziger *n.*; zwerver *n.* **waylay**, *v.t.* belagen, overvallen *str.* **wayside**, *n.* kant *n.* van de weg. ¶ *a.* aan de kant van de weg. **wayward**, *a.*, ~*ly*, *adv.* balsturig, dwars.

we, *pron.* wij; we.

weak, *a.* zwak; slap; flauw. **weaken**, *v.t.* verzwakken; slapper maken. ¶ *v.i.* zwak(ker) worden *str.* **weak-kneed**, *a.* zwak in de knieën *pl.n.* **weakling**, *n.* zwakkeling *n.* **weakly**, *a.* zwak; ziekelijk. ¶ *adv.* zwak; slap; zwakjes. **weakness**, *n.* zwakheid *n.*; zwak *n.n.*; zwak punt *n.n.*, zwakke plaats *n.*

weal, *n.* welzijn *n.n.*; striem *n.* (*mark*). ~ *and woe*, lief *n.n.* en leed *n.n.*

wealth, *n.* rijkdom *n.*; weelde *n.*, overvloed *n.* **wealthy**, *a.* rijk.

wean, *v.t.* spenen. *to* ~ *from*, afwennen.

weapon, *n.*, wapen *n.n.*

wear, *v.t.* dragen *str.*, aanhebben; vertonen. ¶ *v.i.* (ver)slijten *str. to* ~ *away*, afslijten *str.; to* ~ *off*, wegslijten *str.; to* ~ *out*, verslijten *str.* ¶ *n.* kleren *pl.n.*; mode *n.*; dracht *n.*; slijtage *n.* ~ *and tear*, slijtage *n.* **wearable**, *a.* draagbaar. **wearer**, *n.* drager *n.*

weariness, *n.* afgematheid *n.*, vermoeidheid *n.* **wearisome**, *a.* vermoeiend; vervelend. **weary**, *a.*, ~*ily*, *adv.* vermoeid, afgemat; vermoeiend; vervelend. ¶ *v.t.* vermoeien, afmatten; vervelen. ¶ *v.i. to* ~ *of something*, iets moe worden *str.*

weasel, *n.* wezel *n.*

weather, *n.* weer *n.n. under the* ~, niet al te wel. ¶ *v.i.* verweren. ¶ *v.t.* te boven komen *irr.* **weatherbeaten**, *a.* verweerd. **weather-cock**, *n.* weerhaan *n.* **weather-forecast**, *n.* weervoorspelling *n.* **weatherproof**, *a.* tegen het weer bestand.

weave, *v.t. & v.i.* weven *irr.* ¶ *n.* weefsel *n.n.* **weaver**, *n.* wever *n.* **weaving**, *n.* weven *n.n.*

web, *n.* web *n.n.*; weefsel *n.n.* **web-footed**, *a.* met zwemvliezen *pl.n.n.*

wed, *v.t.* huwen, trouwen met. ~*ded to*, innig

verbonden aan; verknocht aan. **wedding,**
n. huwelijk *n.n.*; bruiloft *n.* (*feast*).
wedding-breakfast, *n.* lunch *n.* na 't
huwelijk. **wedding ring,** *n.* trouwring
n.
wedge, *n.* wig *n.*; homp *n.* ¶ *v.t.* wiggen, een
wig slaan *irr.* in. ∼*d,* (*fig.*) vast.
wedlock, *n.* huwelijk *n.n. in* ∼, echt; *out
of* ∼, buitenechtelijk.
Wednesday, *N.* woensdag *N.*
wee, *a.* klein.
weed, *n.* onkruid *n.n. sea* ∼, zeewier *n.n.*;
∼*s* (*also*), weduwendracht *n.* ¶ *v.t.* wieden.
to ∼ *out,* uitdunnen. **weeder,** *n.* wieder *n.*;
wiedster *n.* (*female*). **weeding-hook,** *n.*
wiedijzer *n.n.* **weedy,** *a.* vol onkruid *n.n.*;
mager, spichtig.
week, *n.* week *n. this day* ∼, vandaag over
een week; *to-morrow* ∼, morgen over acht
dagen *pl.n.* **weekday,** *n.* weekdag *n.*
on ∼*s,* door de week. **week-end,** *n.* van
Zaterdag *N.* tot Maandag *N.* **weekly,** *a.*
wekelijks; iedere week; week . . . ¶ *adv.*
wekelijks.
weep, *v.i.* wenen; schreien. *to* ∼ *for,* bewenen. ¶ *v.t.* bewenen, betreuren. *to* ∼
tears of joy, vreugdetranen *pl.n.* storten.
weeping-willow, *n.* treurwilg *n.*
weevil, *n.* korenworm *n.*; kalander *n.*
weft, *n.* inslag *n.*
weigh, *v.t.* wegen *str. to* ∼ *in mind,* overwegen *str.; to* ∼ *anchor,* het anker lichten;
to ∼ *down,* (ter)neerdrukken. ¶ *v.i.*
wegen *str. to* ∼ *in,* komen *irr.* aanzetten.
weigh-bridge, *n.* weegbrug *n.* **weigher,** *n.*
waagmeester *n.* **weighing-machine,** *n.*
weegtoestel *n.n.* **weight,** *n.* gewicht *n.n.,*
druk *n. paper*∼, presse-papier *n.*
weightiness, *n.* zwaarwichtigheid *n.*
weighty, *a.,* ∼*ily, adv.* zwaar; gewichtig
(*important*); zwaarwichtig (*ponderous*).
weir, *n.* stuwdam *n.,* keerdam *n.*
weird, *a.* bovennatuurlijk; zonderling,
vreemdsoortig; angstwekkend.
welcome, *v.t.* verwelkomen, welkom heten;
toejuichen. ¶ *a.* welkom. *to make a
person* ∼, iemand welkom heten; *you
are* ∼ *to it,* het is U gegund. ¶ *n.* welkomst
n.; verwelkoming *n.* ¶ *excl.* welkom!
weld, *v.t.* wellen, lassen. **welder,** *n.* lasser *n.*
weldless, *a.* zonder lasnaad *n.*
welfare, *n.* welzijn *n.n.*; welvaart *n.* ∼ *work,*
maatschappelijk werk *n.n.,* maatschap-
pelijk hulpbetoon *n.n.*
well, *n.* wel *n.,* bron *n.,* put *n.* (*stair*) ∼,
trappenhuis *n.n.* ¶ *v.i. to* ∼ *up,* opwellen.
¶ *a.* gezond, wel. ¶ *adv.* goed, wel. *as* ∼,
even goed; *as* ∼ *as,* evenals; net zo goed
als.
well-being, *n.* welzijn *n.n. a sense of* ∼,
een weldadig gevoel *n.n.*
well-bred, *a.* beschaafd, welopgevoed.
well-founded, *a.* gegrond.
well-mannered, *a.* goedgemanierd.

well-meaning, *a.* wel menend, met goede
bedoelingen *pl.n.*
well-off. welgesteld; er goed aan toe. **well-to-
do,** *a.* welgesteld.
well-wisher, *n.* vriend *n.,* begunstiger *n.*
Welsh, *a.* van Wales *n.N.,* uit Wales *n.N.*
∼ *rabbit,* geroosterde kaas *n.* op toast *n.*
¶ *n.* de taal van Wales. **Welshman,** *N.*
inwoner van Wales, man *n.* uit Wales.
welt, *n.* naad *n.* ¶ *v.t.* omboorden.
welter, *n.* verwarring *n.,* warboel *n.* ¶ *v.i.*
wentelen, rollen.
welter-weight, *n.* bokser *n.* tussen licht en
middelzwaar.
wen, *n.* uitwas *n.*
wench, *n.* meid *n.*; deern *n.*
wend, *v.t.* gaan *irr.,* zich begeven *str.*
west, *a.* westelijk; west . . . ; wester . . .
¶ *adv.* westelijk; naar het westen. ∼ *of,*
ten westen van; *to go* ∼, verloren gaan *irr.*
¶ *n.* westen *n.n.,* Westen *n.N.* **westerly,** *a.*
westelijk; westen . . . **western,** *a.* westelijk;
westers (*occidental*). **westward,** *a. & adv.*
westwaarts.
wet, *a.* nat; vochtig. ∼ *to the skin,* doornat,
kletsnat, drijfnat; *a* ∼ *blanket* (*fig.*) een
spelbederver *n.* ¶ *v.t.* nat maken, bevochtigen. ¶ *n.* nat *n.n.,* nattigheid *n.*
wether, *n.* hamel *n.*
wet-nurse, *n.* min *n.* **wettish,** *a.* nattig.
whack, *v.t.* meppen. ¶ *n.* klap *n.,* mep *n.*;
flinke portie *n.*
whale, *n.* walvis *n.* **whalebone,** *n.* balein *n.n.*
(*substance*), *n.* (*object*). **whaler,** *n.* walvis-
vaarder *n.*
wharf, *n.* kaai *n.,* kade *n.*; losplaats *n.* ¶ *v.t.*
lossen; meren. **wharfage,** *n.* kadegeld *n.n.*
wharfinger, *n.* kaaimeester *n.*
what, *interr. pron.* wat, wat voor; welk(e),
welk een. ∼ *for?,* waarvoor?, waarom?;
∼ *of it?,* wat zou dat? ¶ *rel. pron.* wat,
hetgeen, dat(gene) wat. *not but* ∼, niet
dat . . . niet. ¶ *indef. pron.* wat.
∼ *with* . . ., deels door . . . **whatever,**
pron., **whatsoever,** *pron.* wat, wat . . . ook,
al wat. ¶ *a.* welke . . . ook. **whatnot,** *n.*
étagère *n.*
wheat, *n.* tarwe *n.* **wheaten,** *a.* tarwe . . .
wheedle, *v.t.* flikflooien. *to* ∼ *something out of
someone,* iemand iets aftroggelen.
wheel, *n.* wiel *n.n.*; rad *n.n.*; rolletje *n.n.*;
stuurrad *n.n.*; zwenking *n. to break on
the* ∼, radbraken; ∼*s within* ∼*s,* ingewik-
kelde kwestie *n.* ¶ *v.t.* wentelen; voortrollen; kruien; doen *irr.* zwenken. ¶ *v.i.*
zwenken; cirkelen. *to* ∼ *round,* omdraaien.
wheelbarrow, *n.* kruiwagen *n.* **wheel-chair,**
n. ziekenstoel *n.* **wheel-house,** *n.* stuur-
kast *n.* **wheelwright,** *n.* wagenmaker *n.*
wheeled, *a.* wielig.
wheeze, *v.i.* piepen, hijgen.
whelk, *n.* wulk *n.*
whelp, *n.* welp *n.* ¶ *v.t. & v.i.* werpen *str.*
when, *adv.* wanneer. ¶ *c.* wanneer, als, toen;

terwijl. ¶ *pron.* wanneer. **whence**, *adv.* vanwaar, waarvandaan; waaruit. **whenever**, *adv.* wanneer . . . ook; telkens wanneer, telkens als.

where, *adv.* waar; waarheen; waarin. **whereabouts**, *adv.* waar . . . ongeveer. ¶ *n.* plaats waar iemand zich bevindt. **whereafter**, *adv.* waarna. **whereas**, *adv.* terwijl; aangezien. **whereat**, *adv.* waarbij, waaraan. **whereby**, *adv.* waarbij, waardoor. **wherefore**, *adv.* waarvoor. **wherefrom**, *adv.* van waar, waaruit. **wherein**, *adv.* waarin. **whereof**, *adv.* waarvan. **whereupon**, *adv.* waarop. **wherever**, *adv.* waar . . . ook. **wherewithal**, *n.* middelen *pl.n.n.*

wherry, *n.* praam *n.* **wherryman**, *n.* jolleman *n.*

whet, *v.t.* wetten; aanzetten; scherpen.

whether, *c.* of . . . ~ . . . *or* . . . , of . . . of . . . , hetzij . . . of . . .

whetstone, *n.* wetsteen *n.*; slijpsteen *n.*

whey, *n.* wei *n.*

which, *interr. pron.* welk(e), wie, wat. ¶ *rel. pron.* welk(e), die, dat. **whichever**, *pron.* welk(e) . . . ook, wie . . . ook, wat . . . ook.

whiff, *n.* vleugje *n.n.*; pufje *n.n.*; haal *n.*, trekje *n.n.* ¶ *v.i.* paffen.

Whig, *N.* Oud-liberaal *N.*

while, *c.* terwijl; zolang (als). ¶ *n.* wijl *n.*, poos *n.*, tijdje *n.n.* *all this* ~, al die tijd *n.*; *for a* ~, een poosje *n.n.*; *in a little* ~, binnenkort; *once in a* ~, af en toe, een hoogst enkele keer *n.* ¶ *v.t. to* ~ *away*, verdrijven *str.*, zoek brengen *irr.* **whilst**, *c.* terwijl.

whim, *n.* gril *n.*; kuur *n.*

whimper, *v.i.* grienen; zacht janken. ¶ *n.* gegrien *n.n.*; zacht gejank *n.n.*

whimsical, *a.*, ~**ly**, *adv.* grillig.

whin, *n.* gaspeldoorn *n.* **whin-chat**, *n.* paapje *n.n.*

whine, *v.i.* janken; jammeren.

whinny, *v.i.* hinniken. ¶ *n.* gehinnik *n.n.*

whip, *n.* zweep *n.*; partijsecretaris *n.* (*person*); oproeping *n.* (*message*). ¶ *v.t.* zwepen; geselen; kloppen (*egg, cream*). *to* ~ *out*, plotseling voor den dag brengen *irr.*; *to* ~ *up*, bijeentrommelen. **whip-hand**, *n. to have the* ~ *over someone*, iemand de baas zijn.

whippet, *n.* kleine hazewindhond *n.*

whipping-post, *n.* geselpaal *n.* **whipping-top**, *n.* zweeptol *n.*, drijftol *n.*

whirl, *v.i.* dwarrelen; snel ronddraaien. ¶ *v.t.* snel ronddraaien. ¶ *n.* dwarreling *n.*; (*fig.*) maalstroom *n.* **whirligig**, *n.* draaimolen *n.*; molentje *n.* **whirlpool**, *n.* draaikolk *n.*; maalstroom *n.* **whirlwind** *n.* wervelwind *n.*

whirr, *v.i.* snorren, suizen, ronken. ¶ *n.* gesnor *n.n.*, gesuis *n.n.*, geronk *n.n.*

whisk, *v.t.* kloppen; vegen. *to* ~ *away*, vlug wegnemen *str.* ¶ *n.* klopper *n.*

whiskers, *pl.n.* bakkebaard *n.*

whisk(e)y, *n.* whisky *n.*

whisper, *v.i.* fluisteren. ¶ *v.t.* (toe)fluisteren. ¶ *n.* gefluister *n.n.*; fluistering *n.* **whispering**, *n.* gefluister *n.n.*

whist, *n.* whist *n.*

whistle, *v.t. & v.i.* fluiten *str.*; gieren (*wind*) ¶ *n.* gefluit *n.n.*, fluiten *n.n.*; fluitje *n.n.* (*instrument*).

whit, *n.* zier *n.*, jota *n.*

Whit, *a.* ~ *Sunday*, Pinksterzondag *N.*; ~ *Monday*, Pinkstermaandag *N.*, tweede Pinksterdag *N.*; ~ *week*, Pinksterweek *N.*

white, *a.* wit; blank; grijs (*hair*). ~ *heat*, witte gloeihitte *n.*; ~ *man*, blanke *n.*; *a* ~ *paper*, een witboek *n.n.*; ~ *slave*, blanke slavin *n.* ¶ *n.* wit *n.n.* (*colour*); witte *n.n.* (*object*); blanke *n.* (*human*). **whitebait**, *n.* witvis *n.* **whitecrested**, *a.* witgekuifd. **white-hot**, *a.* witgloeiend. **white lead**, *n.* loodwit *n.n.* **white-livered**, *a.* lafhartig. **whiten**, *v.t.* wit maken. **whiteness**, *n.* witheid *n.*; bleekheid *n.* **whitethroat**, *n.* grasmus *n.* **whitewash**, *n.* witkalk *n.* ¶ *v.t.* witkalken, witten.

whither, *adv.* waarheen.

whiting, *n.* wijting *n.* (*fish*).

whitish, *a.* witachtig.

whitlow, *n.* fijt *n.*

Whitsun, *N.* Pinksteren *N.* **Whitsuntide**, *N.* Pinksteren *N.*

whittle, *v.t.* snipperen, kerven *str.*

whiz(z), *v.i.* snorren, suizen.

who, *pron.* wie; die. ~ *goes there?*, werda!; ~*'s* ~?, wie is wat? **whoever**, *pron.* alwie; wie . . . ook.

whole, *a.* geheel, heel; gaaf, ongeschonden. ~ *meal*, ongebuild meel *n.n.*; ~ *milk*, volle melk *n.*; *to go the* ~ *hog*, niet halverwege ophouden *irr.* ¶ *n.* geheel *n.n.* *as a* ~, in z'n geheel; *on the* ~, over 't geheel (genomen). **wholehearted**, *a.* onvermengd. **wholesale**, *a.* in het groot, en gros. ~ *dealer*, groothandelaar *n.*; *in a* ~ *manner*, op grote schaal *n.* ¶ *adv.* in het groot, op grote schaal. **wholesome**, *a.* gezond; heilzaam. **whole-time**, *a.* in volle betrekking. **wholly**, *adv.* geheel, geheel en al, volkomen; helemaal.

whom, *pron.* wie; die; aan wie.

whoop, *v.i.* roepen *str.*, schreeuwen, juichen. ¶ *n.* schreeuw *n.* **whooping-cough**, *n.* kinkhoest *n.*

whop, *v.t.* afranselen. **whopper**, *n.* kanjer *n.* **whopping**, *a.* kolossaal.

whore, *n.* hoer *n.*; prostituée *n.* ¶ *v.i.* hoereren.

whorl, *n.* haspel *n.*

whortleberry, *n.* blauwbes *n.*, blauwe bosbes *n.*

whose, *pron.* van wie; wiens, wier. **whosoever**, *pron.* wie . . . ook.

why, *adv.* waarom; *that's* ~, daarom; ~ *so?*, waarom? ¶ *int.* wel.

wick, *n.* wiek *n.,* pit *n.*

wicked, *a.,* ~**ly,** *adv.* slecht; zondig; boos.
wickedness, *n.* slechtheid *n.;* zondigheid *n.*

wicker, *n.* teen *n.,* rijs *n.n.;* mandewerk *n.n.,*
vlechtwerk *n.n.* ¶ *a.* tenen.   ~ *chair,*
rieten stoel *n.*

wide, *a.,* ~**ly,** *adv.* breed, wijd; veelomvattend, ruim. ~ *of,* ver van. ¶ *adv.* wijd;
mis, ernaast. *far and* ~, wijd en zijd;
~ *awake,* klaar wakker, (*fig.*) bij de pinken.
widen, *v.t.* verbreden; verruimen. ¶ *v.i.*
breder worden *str.,* wijder worden *str.*
wideness, *n.* breedte *n.,* wijdte *n.;* ruimte
n.

widgeon, *n.* smient *n.*

widow, *n.* weduwe *n.* ~*'s weeds,* weduwen-
rouw *n.* ¶ *v.t.* tot weduwe maken.
widower, *n.* weduwnaar *n.* **widowhood,** *n.*
weduwstaat *n.*

width, *n.* breedte *n.,* wijdte *n.*

wield, *v.t.* hanteren; (*fig.*) uitoefenen.

wife, *n.* vrouw *n.;* echtgenote *n. to take to* ~,
tot vrouw nemen *str.* **wifely,** *a.* vrouwelijk.

wig, *n.* pruik *n.*

wiggle, *v.t.* wiebelen (met).

wight, *n.* schepsel *n.n.*

wigwam, *n.* wigwam *n.*

wild, *a.,* ~**ly,** *adv.* wild; woest; verwilderd;
woest, woedend (*angry*). ~ *with,* woest op;
~ *boar,* everzwijn *n.n.;* ~ *goose chase,*
dolzinnige onderneming *n.;* ~ *horses
could not . . . ,* niets zou hem ertoe bewegen . . . ; ~ *statement,* ongegronde
verklaring *n.* ¶ *adv.* in 't wild. ¶ *n.*
~*s,* wildernis *n.,* woestenij *n.* **wild-cat,** *a.*
~ *scheme,* wilde speculatie *n.*

wildebeest, *n.* gnoe *n.*

wilderness, *n.* wildernis *n.,* woestijn *n.*

wildfire, *n. to spread like* ~, zich als een
lopend vuurtje *n.n.* verspreiden. **wildness,**
n. wildheid *n.;* woestheid *n.*

wile, *n.* list *n.,* laag *n.,* slinkse streek *n.*

wilful, *a.,* ~**ly,** *adv.* opzettelijk, moedwillig.
wiliness, *n.* listigheid *n.*

will, *n.* wil *n.;* wilskracht *n.;* testament *n.n.*
to have one's ~, z'n zin krijgen *str.; at* ~,
naar (eigen) goeddunken *n.n.,* naar willekeur *n.; with a* ~, uit alle macht *n.*
¶ *v.t.* willen; suggereren. *to* ~ *away,*
vermaken. ¶ *aux.v.* zullen *irr.;* plegen *irr.*
boys ~ *be boys,* jongens *pl.n.* zijn nu
eenmaal jongens; *they* ~ *do it,* ze doen het
nu eenmaal; *this* ~ *be:* . . . , dit is zeker: . . .
willing, *a.* gewillig; bereid. **willingly,** *adv.*
gaarne. **willingness,** *n.* bereidwilligheid *n.*
will-o'-the-wisp, *n.* dwaallichtje *n.n.*

willow, *n.* wilg *n.* **willowherb,** *n.* wilgen-
roosje *n.n.,* basterdwederik *n.* **willow-
warbler,** *n.* fitis *n.* **willowy,** *a.* vol wilgen
pl.n.; slank.

willy-nilly, *adv.* goedschiks of kwaadschiks,
tegen wil *n.* en dank *n.*

wily, *a.* geslepen, sluw, listig.

wimple, *n.* kap *n.*

win, *v.t.* winnen *str.;* verkrijgen *str.,* behalen,
verwerven *str. to* ~ *the day,* de overwinning
behalen; *to* ~ *over,* overhalen.   ¶ *v.i.*
winnen *str.;* zegevieren.

wince, *v.i.* ineenkrimpen *str. to* ~ *at, to* ~
from, terugdeinzen voor.

winch, *n.* lier *n.,* windas *n.*

wind, *n.* wind *n.;* adem *n.* ~ *and weather
permitting,* bij gunstig weer *n.n.; to cast to
the* ~*s,* overboord gooien; *to get* ~ *of,* lucht
krijgen *str.* van. ¶ *v.t.* buiten adem *n.*
brengen *irr.;* winden *str.,* opwinden *str.;*
wikkelen. *to* ~ *up,* opwinden *str.;* afwikkelen (*business*). ¶ *v.i.* kronkelen, zich
slingeren. **windbag,** *n.* windzak *n.,* blaas-
kaak *n.* **wind-blown,** *n.* verwaaid. **windfall,** *n.* afval *n.n.* (*fruit*); (*fig.*) bonheurtje
n.n., buitenkansje *n.n.* **windiness,** *n.*
winderigheid *n.* **winding,** *a.* kronkelend.
winding-sheet, *n.* doodskleed *n.n.,* lijkwade
n. **winding-stairs,** *pl.n.* wenteltrap *n.*
winding-tackle, *n.* hijstakel *n.* **winding-up,**
n. likwidatie *n.* **wind-instrument,** *n.*
blaasinstrument *n.n.* **windlass,** *n.* windas
n. **windmill,** *n.* (wind)molen *n.*

window, *n.* raam *n.n.,* venster *n.n. french* ~,
openslaand raam; *in the* ~, voor het raam;
in de étalage. **window-blind,** *n.* zonne-
blind *n.n.;* rolgordijn *n.n.* **windowbox,** *n.*
bloembak *n.* op de vensterbank. **window-
dresser,** *n.* étaleur *n.* **window-dressing,** *n.*
étaleren *n.n.;* misleidend vertoon *n.n.*
window-frame, *n.* vensterkozijn *n.n.*
window-ledge, *n.,* **windowsill,** *n.* vensterbank *n.*

windpipe, *n.* luchtpijp *n.* **windswept,** *a.*
verwaaid; blootgesteld aan de wind.
windward, *a.* naar de wind gekeerd;
bovenwinds. *W* ~ *Isles,* Eilanden *pl.n.N.*
boven de Wind. ¶ *adv.* te loevert. ¶ *n.*
loefzijde *n. to get to* ~ *of,* de loef afsteken
str. **windy,** *a.* winderig.

wine, *n.* wijn *n.* ¶ *v.t.* op wijn onthalen.
wine-grower, *n.* wijnboer *n.* **wine list,** *n.*
wijnkaart *n.* **wine merchant,** *n.* wijn-
koper *n.* **wineskin,** *n.* wijnzak *n.*

wing, *n.* vleugel *n.;* wiek *n.,* vlerk *n.;* coulisse
n. (*stage*); vlucht *n.,* eskader *n.n.* *to
take* ~, de vleugels uitslaan *irr.; on the* ~,
in de vlucht. ¶ *v.t.* vliegen *str.;* wieken,
aanschieten *str.* **wing-beat,** *n.* vleugelslag
n. **wing-commander,** *n.* commandant *n.,*
overste-vlieger *n.* **winged,** *a.* gevleugeld;
aangeschoten.

wink, *v.i.* knipogen. *to* ~ *at,* een knipoogje
n.n. geven *str.* aan; (*fig.*) door de vingers
pl.n. zien *irr.* ¶ *n.* knipoogje *n.n.;* oogwenk
n.

winkle, *n.* alikruik *n.,* kreukel *n.*

winner, *n.* winnaar *n.* **winning,** *a.* winnend;
innemend. ¶ *n.* ~*s,* winst *n.*

winnow, *n.* wan *n.* ¶ *v.t.* wannen. **winnower,**
n. wanner *n.* (*person*); **wanmolen** *n.*
(*machine*)

winsome, a. innemend, bekoorlijk.
winter, n. winter n. in ~, 's winters. ¶ v.i. overwinteren. wintry, a. winters, winterachtig.
winy, a. wijnachtig.
wipe, v.t. vegen, afvegen. to ~ away, afwissen, uitwissen. ¶ n. veeg n. wiper, n. wisser n.
wire, n. draad n. (object), n.n. (substance); ijzerdraad n. or n.n., koperdraad n. or n.n.; telegram n.n. to pull the ~s, achter de schermen pl.n.n. werken. ¶ v.t. met metaaldraad n. or n.n. vastmaken; telegraferen. wire-cage, n. traliekooi n. wirecutter, n. draadtang n. wire-drawer, n. draadtrekker n. wirehaired, a. met borstelig haar n.n. wireless, a. draadloos; radio . . . ~ operator, marconist n.; ~ set, radiotoestel n.n. wirepulling, n. invloed n. wiring, n. draadwerk n.; electrische geleiding n. wiry, a. taai, mager en gespierd.
wisdom, n. wijsheid n. ~ tooth, verstandskies n. wise, a. wijs; verstandig. ¶ n. wijs n., wijze n., manier n. wisely, adv. wijs; verstandig; wijselijk. wiseacre, n. waanwijze n.
wish, n. wens n.; verlangen n.n. according to one's ~es, naar wens. ¶ v.t. wensen, verlangen. I ~ I could, ik wou dat ik kon. ¶ v.i. to ~ for, verlangen naar; if you ~, als U 't wenst. wishbone, n. vorkbeen n.n. wishful, a. verlangend.
wishy-washy, a. kleurloos; onbenullig.
wisp, n. wis n., bosje n.n. wispy, a. piekerig.
wistaria, n. blauwe regen n.
wistful, a., ~ly, adv. weemoedig, droefgeestig.
wit, n. verstand n.n.; geest n., geestigheid n.; geestig man n. ~s, verstand n.n., zinnen pl. n.; to be at one's ~'s end, ten einde raad n. zijn; frightened out of one's ~s, buiten zichzelf van schrik n. ¶ v.t. to ~, te weten.
witch, n. heks n., toverheks n. witchcraft, n. tovenarij n. witch-doctor, n. toverdokter n. witchery, n. toverij n.
with, prep. met; met . . . mee; bij; van, door. withal, adv. bovendien.
withdraw, v.t. terugtrekken str.; intrekken str. ¶ v.i. zich terugtrekken str. withdrawal, n. terugtrekken n.n.; terugtrekking n.
wither, v.i. verwelken; verschrompelen. ¶ v.t. doen irr. verwelken. withering, a. vernietigend.
withers, n. schoft n.
withhold, v.t. terughouden irr.; onthouden irr.
within, prep. binnen. ¶ adv. binnen, van binnen.
without, prep. buiten; zonder. ¶ adv. buiten, van buiten. ¶ c. tenzij, als . . . niet.
withstand, v.t. weerstaan irr.
witless, a. dwaas, onverstandig.
witness, n. getuige n. (person); getuigenis n.

(testimony). ~ for the defence, getuige à décharge; ~ for the prosecution, getuige à charge; in ~ whereof, ten getuige waarvan. ¶ v.t. getuigen; betuigen; bijwonen. witness-box, n. getuigenbank n.
witticism, n. geestigheid n. wittingly, adv. willens en wetens. witty, a., ~ily, adv. geestig.
wizard, n. tovenaar n. wizardry, n. tovenarij n.
wizened, a. verschrompeld.
woad, n. wede n.
wobble, v.i. waggelen, wiebelen. wobbly, a. wiebelig, onvast.
woe, n. wee n.n., leed n.n. ¶ int. wee! woe-begone, a. ongelukkig. woeful, a., ~ly, adv. ellendig; betreurenswaardig.
wold, n. heuvelachtig land n.n.
wolf, n. wolf n. ~'s milk, wolfsmelk n. ¶ v.t. opslokken. wolf-dog, n. wolfshond n. wolfish, a. wolfachtig. wolverine, n. veelvraat n.
woman, n. vrouw n. ¶ a. vrouwelijk. ~ friend, vriendin n. woman-hater, n. vrouwenhater n. womanhood, n. vrouwelijkheid n. womanish, a. vrouwelijk, vrouwachtig. womanly, a. (echt) vrouwelijk.
womb, n. baarmoeder n.; (fig.) schoot n.
womenfolk, n. vrouwvolk n.n.
wonder, n. wonder n.n. small ~, geen wonder dat; to do ~s, wonderen verrichten. ¶ v.i. zich verbazen; zich afvragen str. I shouldn't ~, het zou me niet bevreemden. wonderful, a., ~ly, adv. wonderlijk, wonderbaar; verbazend mooi. wonderment, n. bevreemding n., verwondering n. wonderstruck, a. verbaasd. wondrous, a., ~ly, adv. verwonderlijk.
won't = will not.
wont, a. gewend. ~ to, gewend aan. ¶ n. gewoonte n. wonted, a. gewoon.
woo, v.t. het hof maken (aan).
wood, n. hout n.n.; bos n.n. (forest). wines from the ~, wijn van het fust; out of the ~ (fig.), uit de moeilijkheid. woodbine, n. wilde kamperfoelie n. wood-carver, n. houtsnijder n. wood-carving, n. houtsnijwerk n.n. woodcock, n. houtsnip n. woodcut, n. houtsnede n. woodcutter, n. houthakker n. wooded, a. bebost, bosrijk. wooden, a. houten, van hout; (fig.) houterig, stijf. wood engraving, n. houtgravure n. woodland, n. bosland n.n. woodlark, n. boomleeuwerik n. wood-louse, n. houtluis n. woodpecker, n. specht n. wood-pigeon, n. houtduif n. woodruff, n. lieve-vrouwenbedstro n.n. woodshed, n. houtloods n. woodwind, n. houten blaasinstrumenten pl.n.n. woody, a. houtrijk, bosrijk.
woof, n. inslag n.; weefsel n.n.
wool, n. wol n. to pull the ~ over a person's eyes, iemand zand in de ogen pl.n.n.

strooien. **wool-carder,** *n.* wolkaarder *n.*
wool-clip, *n.* wolopbrengst *n.* **wool-comber,** *n.* wolkammer *n.* **wool-gathering,** *n. to go* ~, verstrooid zijn, zitten *str.* te dromen. **woollen,** *a.* wollen, van wol. ~ *draper,* lakenkoper *n.*; ~ *trade,* wolhandel *n.* **woolly,** *a.* wollen; wollig; (*fig.*) vaag, doezelig. **woolpack,** *n.* baal *n.* wol. **woolsack,** *n.* zitplaats *n.* van de Kanselier.

word, *n.* woord *n.n.*; bericht *n.n.* ~*s,* bewoordingen *pl.n. by* ~ *of mouth,* mondeling; *the* ~ *of God,* het woord Gods; *to put in a good* ~ *for,* een goed woordje *n.n.* doen *irr.* voor; *the last* ~, het nieuwste; *to have a* ~ *with,* even spreken *str.*; *too funny for* ~*s,* vreselijk grappig; *in one* ~, om kort te gaan *irr.*; *in other* ~*s,* met andere woorden. ¶ *v.t.* onder woorden *pl.n.n.* brengen *irr.,* formuleren. **wordiness,** *n.* langdradigheid *n.* **wording,** *n.* bewoording *n.*; redactie *n.* **word-splitting,** *n.* woordenzifterij *n.* **wordy,** *a.* langdradig.

work, *v.i.* werken; arbeiden; uitwerking *n.* hebben; gisten. *to* ~ *loose,* zich loswerken; *to* ~ *round,* draaien; *to* ~ *away,* hard doorwerken; *to* ~ *in with,* samengaan *irr.* met; *to* ~ *out at,* komen *irr.* op. ¶ *v.t.* bewerken; verwerken; bereiden; verrichten, teweegbrengen *irr.,* gedaan krijgen *str.*; exploiteren; borduren. *to* ~ *one's passage,* voor z'n (terug)reis *n.* werken; *to* ~ *one's way,* vooruitkomen *irr.,* zich een weg banen; *to* ~ *up,* aanmoedigen. ¶ *n.* werk *n.n.*; arbeid *n.* ~*s,* fabriek *n.*; *to be in* ~, werk hebben; *to be out of* ~, werkloos zijn; *to put to* ~, aan het werk zetten. ¶ *v.r. to* ~ *oneself into a passion,* zich vreselijk kwaad maken. **workable,** *a.* bewerkbaar, verwerkbaar; practisch mogelijk. **workaday,** *a.* alledaags, gewoon. **worker,** *n.* arbeider *n.* ~ *of miracles,* wonderdoener *n.* **workhouse,** *n.* werkhuis *n.n.,* armenhuis *n.n.* **working,** *a.* werkend. ~ *committee,* dagelijks bestuur *n.n.*; ~ *day,* werkdag *n.* ¶ *n.* werken *irr.* **working capital,** *n.* bedrijfskapitaal *n.n.* **working-class,** *n.* arbeidersklasse *n.* **working-man,** *n.* werkman *n.* **working order,** *n. to be in* ~, in orde zijn, gereed staan *irr.* **working point,** *n.* aangrijpingspunt *n.n.* **workman,** *n.* werkman *n.,* arbeider *n.* **workmanlike,** *a.* degelijk; goed uitgevoerd; knap. **workmanship,** *n.* afwerking *n.,* bewerking *n.* **workshop,** *n.* werkplaats *n.* **works-manager,** *n.* bedrijfsleider *n.*

world, *n.* wereld *n. all the* ~, de hele wereld; *to come into the* ~, ter wereld komen *irr.* **worldliness,** *n.* wereldsheid *n.* **worldly,** *a.* werelds, aards. **world-weary,** *a.* levensmoede. **worldwide,** *a.* wereld . . . , over de hele wereld verspreid.

worm, *n.* worm *n.*; schroefdraad *n.* ¶ *v.i.* kruipen *str.* ¶ *v.t. to* ~ *one's way into*

something, **ergens** binnensluipen *str.*; zich ergens op slinkse wijze *n.* binnenwerken; *to* ~ *something out of someone,* iemand iets ontlokken. **worm-eaten,** *a.* wormstekig. **wormwood,** *n.* alsem *n.* **wormy,** *a.* wormig, vol wormen; aangestoken.

worn, *a. See* **wear. worn-out,** *a.* versleten; afgezaagd.

worry, *n.* zorg *n.,* bezorgdheid *n.*; gepieker *n.n.* ¶ *v.i.* piekeren, tobben; zich zorgen *pl.n.* maken, zich bezorgd maken. ¶ *v.t.* lastig vallen *str.*; geen rust *n.* laten *str.*; plagen; rukken aan, trekken *str.* aan.

worse, *a.* erger; slechter. ~ *and* ~, hoe langer hoe erger; *all the* ~, des te erger; *for better or for* ~, in lief en leed *n.n.* ¶ *adv.* erger, slechter. ~ *off,* er slechter aan toe. **worsen,** *v.i.* erger worden *str.,* slechter worden *str.*

worship, *n.* verering *n.,* aanbidding *n.*; eredienst *n.*; godsdienstoefening *n. Your W*~, Edelachtbare *N.*; *his W*~, Zijn Edelachtbare *N.* ¶ *v.t.* vereren, aanbidden *str.* ¶ *v.i.* ter kerke gaan *irr.* **worshipful,** *a.* edelachtbaar. **worshipper,** *n.* vereerder *n.,* aanbidder *n.*; gelovige *n.*

worst, *a.* ergst(e), slechtst(e). ¶ *adv.* ergst. ¶ *n.* het ergst(e). *to get the* ~ *of it,* aan 't kortste eind trekken *str.* ¶ *v.t.* het onderspit doen *irr.* delven.

worsted, *n.* sajet *n.* or *n.n.* ¶ *a.* sajetten.

wort, *n.* kruid *n.n.*

worth, *n.* waarde *n.*; grootheid *n. to get one's money's* ~, waar *n.* voor z'n geld *n.n.* krijgen *str.* ¶ *a.* waard. *it is* ~ *so much,* het is zoveel waard; ~ *having,* ~ *while,* de moeite waard. **worthiness,** *n.* waardigheid *n.* **worthy,** *a.,* ~*ily, adv.* waardig; achtenswaardig. ¶ *n.* beroemd man *n.*

would, *aux.v. See* **will.**

would-be, *a.* zogenaamd; aspirant.

wound, *n.* wond *n.,* wonde *n.* ¶ *v.t.* wonden; kwetsen.

wraith, *n.* schim *n.,* geestverschijning *n.*

wrangle, *v.i.* kibbelen; redetwisten. ¶ *n.* gekibbel *n.n.*

wrap, *v.t.* wikkelen. *to* ~ *up,* inpakken, inwikkelen; *to be* ~*ped up in,* opgaan *irr.* in. ¶ *n.* omslagdoek *n.* **wrapper,** *n.* omslag *n.,* kaft *n.*; kruisband *n. in* ~*s,* ingenaaid.

wrath, *n.* toorn *n.,* gramschap *n.* **wrathful,** *a.* toornig.

wreak, *v.t. to* ~ *one's vengeance on,* wraak *n.* oefenen aan.

wreath, *n.* krans *n.*; kronkel *n.* (*smoke*). **wreathe,** *v.t.* omkransen. ~*d in smiles,* één en al glimlach *n.*

wreck, *n.* wrak *n.n.*; ruïne *n.*; schipbreuk *n.* (*accident*). ¶ *v.t.* verwoesten; doen *irr.* verongelukken, doen *irr.* schipbreuk *n.* lijden. *to be* ~*ed,* vergaan *irr.* (*ship*); verongelukken. **wreckage,** *n.* wrakhout

n.n., wrakgoed *n.n.* **wrecker**, *n.* strandjutter *n.*; vernieler *n.*; bergingsvaartuig *n.n.*
wren, *n.* winterkoninkje *n.n.*
wrench, *v.t.* rukken, trekken *str.*; verdraaien, verwringen *str.* ¶ *n.* ruk *n.*; draai *n.*; pijnlijk ogenblik *n.n.*; schroefsleutel *n.* (*tool*).
wrest, *v.t.* verwringen *str.* to ~ *from*, ontrukken, ontworstelen. ¶ *n.* stemsleutel *n.*
wrestle, *v.i.* worstelen. **wrestler**, *n.* worstelaar *n.* **wrestling-match**, *n.* worstelwedstrijd *n.*
wretch, *n.* ellendeling *n.* *poor* ~, arme stumper *n.* **wretched**, *a.*, ~**ly**, *adv.* ellendig; ongelukkig; armzalig. **wretchedness**, *n.* ellende *n.*; armzaligheid *n.*
wriggle, *v.i.* wriemelen, kronkelen. to ~ *out of it*, zich eruit draaien. ¶ *n.* gewriemel *n.n.*
wring, *v.t.* wringen *str.*; uitwringen *str.* to ~ *tears from*, tranen *pl.n.* persen uit; to ~ *a person's neck*, iemand de nek omdraaien; to ~ *a person's hand*, iemand flink de hand drukken. **wringer**, *n.* wringmachine *n.*
wrinkle, *n.* rimpel *n.*; kreuk *n.*, plooi *n.* ¶ *v.t.* rimpelen; kreukelen.
wrist, *n.* pols *n.* **wrist(let)-watch**, *n.* polshorloge *n.n.*
writ, *n.* geschrift *n.n.*; bevelschrift *n.n.*; dagvaarding *n.* *Holy W~*, de Heilige Schrift; ~ *of execution*, deurwaardersexploit *n.n.*; to *serve a* ~ *on someone*, iemand een dagvaarding betekenen.
write, *v.i.* schrijven *str.* to ~ *away*, erop los schrijven. ¶ *v.t.* schrijven *str.* *it is written that*, er staat geschreven dat; to ~ *down*, opschrijven *str.*; to ~ *off*, afschrijven *str.*; to ~ *to*, schrijven aan; to ~ *a person down as*, iemand beschouwen als. **writer**, *n.* schrijver *n.*; schrijfster *n.* (*female*).
writhe, *v.i.* zich krommen, ineenkrimpen *str.* to ~ *with shame*, van schaamte *n.* vergaan *irr.*
writing, *n.* schrijven *n.n.*; handschrift *n.n.*; stijl *n.* *to take down in* ~, op schrift *n.n.* brengen *irr.* **writing-book**, *n.* schrift *n.n.* **writing-case**, *n.* map *n.* **writing-desk**, *n.* schrijflessenaar *n.* **writing materials**, *pl.n.* schrijfbehoeften *pl.n.* **writing-pad**, *n.* onderlegger *n.*; schrijfbloc *n.n.* **written**, *a.* geschreven; schriftelijk.
wrong, *a.* verkeerd; onjuist. *to be* ~, het mis hebben, ongelijk hebben; *what's* ~?, wat scheelt eraan? ¶ *adv.* verkeerd; mis. *to do* ~, verkeerd doen *irr.*; slecht handelen; *to go* ~, mislopen *str.*; de verkeerde kant opgaan *irr.* ¶ *n.* onrecht *n.n.*; kwaad *n.n.* ~*s*, grieven *pl.n.*; *to do no* ~, niets verkeerds doen *irr.*; *to put in the* ~, in 't ongelijk stellen. ¶ *v.t.* onrecht *n.n.* aandoen *irr.* **wrongful**, *a.*, ~**ly**, *adv.* onrechtvaardig, onbillijk; onrechtmatig. ~ *dismissal*, ongegrond ontslag *n.n.* **wrong-headed**, *a.*

dwars, eigenzinnig. **wrongly**, *adv.* verkeerd; ten onrechte.
wrought, *a.* bewerkt. ~ *iron*, gesmeed ijzer *n.n.*
wrought-up, *a.* opgewonden.
wry, *a.*, ~**ly**, *adv.* krom. ~ *face*, zuur gezicht *n.n.* **wryneck**, *n.* scheefhals *n.*
wyvern, *n.* gevleugelde draak *n.*

X

X-ray, *N.* X-straal *n.*, Röntgen-straal *n.* ¶ *v.t.* met Röntgenstralen behandelen (*or* fotograferen).
xenophobia, *n.* vreemdelingenhaat *n.*
Xmas, *N.* *See* **Christmas**.
xylophone, *n.* xylophoon *n.*

Y

yacht, *n.* jacht *n.n.* **yachting**, *n.* zeilsport *n.* **yachtsman**, *n.* jachteigenaar *n.*
yak, *n.* yak *n.*
yam, *n.* yam *n.*, broodwortel *n.*
yank, *v.t.* rukken (aan).
yap, *v.i.* keffen.
yard, *n.* engelse el *n.* ($\pm$ 91,44cM); ra *n.* (*of mast*); erf *n.n.* (*of farm*); binnenplaats *n.* (*of home*); werf *n.* (*shipbuilding*). **yardstick**, *n.* ellestok *n.*
yarn, *n.* garen *n.n.*, draad *n.*; verhaal *n.n.* *to have a* ~ *with*, een boom *n.* opzetten met. ¶ *v.i.* bomen, verhalen *pl.n.n.* doen *irr.*
yarrow, *n.* duizendblad *n.n.*
yawl, *n.* jol *n.*
yawn, *n.* geeuw *n.* ¶ *v.i.* geeuwen, gapen.
yaws, *pl.n.* framboesia *n.*
ye, *pron.* gij, U; gijlieden, ulieden. ¶ *art.* = *the*.
yea, *adv.* ja. ¶ *n.* ja *n.n.*
year, *n.* jaar *n.n.*; jaargang *n.* ~ *by* ~, jaar op jaar; *of recent* ~*s*, de laatste jaren *pl.n.n.* **yearling**, *n.* éénjarig dier *n.n.* **yearly**, *a.* jaarlijks.
yearn, *v.i.* verlangen. *to* ~ *after* (or *for*), smachten naar. **yearning**, *n.* smachtend verlangen *n.n.*
year-old, *a.* van één jaar *n.n.*
yeast, *n.* gist *n.* **yeasty**, *a.* gistend; gistachtig.
yell, *n.* gil *n.* ¶ *v.i.* gillen.
yellow, *a.* geel; (*fig.*) laf. ¶ *n.* geel *n.n.* **yellowback**, *n.* oude roman *n.* in gekleurde omslag *n.* **yellowhammer**, *n.* geelgors *n.* **yellowish**, *a.* geelachtig. **yellowy**, *a.* gelig.
yelp, *v.i.* janken. ¶ *n.* gejank *n.n.*
yen, *n.* yen *n.*
yeoman, *n.* eigenerfde *n.*; soldaat *n.* van de lijfwacht *n.* **yeomanry**, *n.* stand *n.* der eigenerfden *pl.n.*; vrijwillige militie *n.*

yeoman service, *n.* *to do* ~, trouw ter zijde *n.* staan *irr.*
yes, *adv.* ja; jawel.
yesterday, *adv.* gister(en). *the day before* ~, eergister(en).
yet, *c.* maar toch, toch; nochthans. ¶ *adv.* nog; tot nog toe; nog altijd; toch; toch nog; al. *as* ~, tot nu toe, (voor)alsnog; *never* ~, nog nooit; *not* ~, nog niet.
yew-tree, *n.* taxis(boom) *n.*
Yiddish, *a.* Jiddisch. ¶ *N.* Jiddisch *n.N.*
yield, *v.t.* opbrengen *irr.*, opleveren, afwerpen *str.*; toegeven *str.* ¶ *v.i.* toegeven *str.*, zwichten. *to* ~ *to*, wijken *str.* voor, onderdoen *irr.* voor. ¶ *n.* opbrengst *n.* **yielding,** *a.* toegevend.
yodel, *v.i.* jodelen.
yoke, *n.* juk *n.n.*; span *n.n.* (*oxen*). ¶ *v.t.* het juk aandoen *irr.*, aanspannen.
yokel, *n.* boerenpummel *n.*
yolk, *n.* dooier *n.*
yonder, *a.* ginds. ¶ *adv.* ginder.
yore, *adv.* *of* ~, voorheen; *in the days of* ~, in vroeger dagen *pl.n.*
you, *pron.* U; jij, je; jullie, jelui; gij, ge; men.
young, *a.* jong; nieuw. ¶ *n.* jong *n.n.* *the* ~, de jeugd. **youngish,** *a.* nog jong, jeugdig. **youngster,** *n.* jongeling *n.*, jonge kerel *n.*
your, *pron.* Uw; je, jouw; jullie, jelui's, **you're,** = you are. **yours,** *pron.* de Uwe, het Uwe, van U; de jouwe, het jouwe. van jou; die van jullie, dat van jullie; van jullie. ~ *truly*, hoogachtend. **yourself,** *pron.* U, U zelf; gij, gij zelf; je, je zelf.
youth, *n.* jeugd *n.* **youthful,** *a.* jeugdig. **youthfulness,** *n.* jeugdigheid *n.*
you've, = you have.

yowl, *v.i.* krollen. ¶ *n.* gekrol *n.n.*, gemiauw *n.n.*
Yule, *N.* Kersttijd *N.* **yule-log,** *n.* houtblok *n.n.* voor het Kerstvuur.

Z

zany, *n.* pias *n.*; duvelstoejager *n.*
zeal, *n.* ijver *n.*; geestdrift *n.*
Zealand, *N.* Zeeland *n.N.* ¶ *a.* Zeeuws. **Zealander,** *N.* Zeeuw *N.*
zealot, *n.* ijveraar *n.*; dweper *n.* **zealotry,** *n.* dweepzucht *n.* **zealous,** *a.*, ~ly, *adv.* ijverig, vurig.
zebra, *n.* zebra *n.*
zenith, *n.* zenith *n.*, toppunt *n.n.*, hoogtepunt *n.n.*
zephyr, *n.* zefier *n.*
zero, *n.* nul *n.*; nulpunt *n.n.*
zest, *n.* genot *n.n.*, lust *n.* *to add* ~ *to*, pikant maken.
zigzag, *n.* zigzag *n.* ¶ *a.* zigzagsgewijze. ¶ *v.i.* zigzagsgewijze gaan *irr.*
zinc, *n.* zink *n.n.* ¶ *v.t.* verzinken; galvaniseren. ¶ *a.* zinken.
zip, *v.i.* fluiten *str.*, vliegen *str.*
zip fastener, *n.* ritssluiting *n.*, treksluiting *n.*
Zodiac, *n.* Dierenriem *N.*
zone, *n.* zone *n.*; luchtstreek *n.* ¶ *v.t.* in zones verdelen.
Zoo(logical Gardens), *N.* Dierentuin *N.* **zoological,** *a.* zoölogisch, dierkundig. **zoologist,** *n.* zoöloog *n.*, dierkundige *n.* **zoology,** *n.* zoölogie *n.*, dierkunde *n.*
zoom, *v.i.* gonzen, zoemen.
Zulu, *N.* Zoeloe *N.*
zymotic, *a.* gistings . . .